W9-AAW-127

Date Due

Congressional Districts in the 1990s

Congressional Districts in the 1990s

A PORTRAIT OF AMERICA

Congressional Quarterly Inc.
1414 22nd Street N.W.
Washington, D.C. 20037

Congressional Quarterly Inc.

Congressional Quarterly Inc., an editorial research service and publishing company, serves clients in the fields of news, education, business, and government. It combines the specific coverage of Congress, government, and politics contained in the *Congressional Quarterly Weekly Report* with the more general subject range of an affiliated service, the *CQ Researcher*.

Congressional Quarterly also publishes a variety of books, including college political science textbooks under the CQ Press imprint and public affairs paperbacks on developing issues and events. CQ Books researches, writes, and publishes information directories and reference books on the federal government, national elections, and politics, including the *Guide to the Presidency*, the *Guide to Congress*, the *Guide to the U.S. Supreme Court*, the *Guide to U.S. Elections*, and *Politics in America*. *CQ's Encyclopedia of American Government* is a three-volume reference work providing essential information about the U.S. government. The *CQ Almanac*, a compendium of legislation for one session of Congress, is published each year. *Congress and the Nation*, a record of government for a presidential term, is published every four years.

CQ publishes the *Congressional Monitor*, a daily report on current and future activities of congressional committees, and several newsletters including *Congressional Insight*, a weekly analysis of congressional action. The CQ FaxReport is a daily update available every afternoon when Congress is in session. An electronic online information system, Washington Alert, provides immediate access to CQ's databases of legislative action, votes, schedules, profiles, and analyses.

Printed in the United States of America

Photo credits: Levittown, New York, 1949—Levittown Public Library; The Pittsburgh Skyline, 1983—Bill Lewis, Pittsburgh Post-Gazette; Farm complex, Stephenson County, Illinois—Tim McCabe, Soil Conservation Services; USDA Gypsum Plant, Rogers City, Michigan—Balthazar Korab.

Library of Congress Cataloging-in-Publication Data

Congressional districts in the 1990s: a portrait of America
     p. cm.
    Includes index.
    ISBN 0-87187-722-8
    1. United States. Congress. House—Election districts.
I. Congressional Quarterly Inc.
JK1341.C64   1993   93-34324
328.73'07345—dc20   CIP

Editors: Jon Preimesberger, David Tarr
Research Assistant: Michelle Sobel
Essays: CQ Political Staff
Maps, Business Data: InContext Inc.,
    Laurence J. DeFranco
Voting Data: Polidata, Clark Bensen
Compositor: Paul Pressau
Cover Design: Anne Masters Design
Interior Design: Kaelin Chappell

Congressional Quarterly Inc.

Andrew Barnes   Chairman
Andrew P. Corty   Vice Chairman
Neil Skene   Editor and Publisher
Robert W. Merry   Executive Editor
John J. Coyle   Associate Publisher
Michael L. Koempel   Director of Information Services
Robert E. Cuthriell   Director of Development

Book Division

Patrick Bernuth   General Manager

Editorial Department

David R. Tarr   Editor-in-Chief
Brenda W. Carter   Acquisitions Editor
Jeanne Ferris   Acquisitions Editor
Shana Wagger   Acquisitions Editor
Martha Hawley-Bertsch   Assistant Editor
Charlene Gargasz   Administrative Assistant

Editorial Design and Production Department

Nancy A. Lammers   Director
Ann Davies   Senior Editor
Carolyn Goldinger   Senior Editor
Jerry A. Orvedahl   Project Editor
Jon Preimesberger   Project Editor
Ann F. O'Malley   Senior Production Editor
Laura Carter   Production Editor
Christopher M. Karlsten   Production Editor
Michelle Sobel   Editorial Assistant

Book Marketing and Customer Service Department

Kathryn C. Suárez   Director
Jacqueline A. Davey   Manager, Library and Professional
    Marketing
Kate Quinlin   College Marketing Manager
Joni Berkley   Marketing Coordinator
Heather Wilkinson   Marketing Administrator
Dianne Clack   Administrative Assistant

Production

Ron Knott   Computers/Production Director
I.D. Fuller   Production Manager
Michael Emanuel   Assistant Production Manager
Jhonnie G. Bailey   Assistant to the Production Manager

Table of Contents

Maps

Major Tables

Editor's Note

Congressional Districts in the 1990s is the third volume produced by Congressional Quarterly over the last three decades that chronicles the distribution—and redistribution—of political power in the U.S. House of Representatives. Each time the task of collecting, analyzing and publishing the data has been both more difficult and more interesting as the ceaseless ingenuity of American politicians, this time wedded to the power of computers, is brought to bear on the process.

We have subtitled this edition A Portrait of America because it is a kind of political hitchhiker's guide to the people, problems and opportunities before the nation. The portrait is seen through the prism of political districts from which representatives in the House are elected. The congressional subjects in this picture, the Democrats and Republicans and occasional independent, are the people who eventually must try to resolve America's most challenging social and economic issues. Understanding those districts and the people who live in them is essential to understanding how Congress and the other parts of the national government respond or do not respond.

In this volume, the editors have brought together text descriptions of the districts written by CQ's political reporters, a variety of 1990 census and other data that help explain the needs and political orientation of the population, and maps of all states and many urban areas. The reader can learn, for example, the age, race, ancestry, education, employment and housing patterns of people in the district. Public information sources, such as newspapers and TV and cable stations, are given along with a listing of major employers and colleges and universities. Editors also have included reconfigured actual voting results from 1986 through 1992 to fit the boundaries of the new districts to show the historic preference of residents for one or another party. Military bases in existence in 1991 are listed by district.

The text that accompanies each district brings these data into focus by describing the economic and political forces that shape the area. The reader will learn, for example, about the expanding high-tech industries in the Phoenix area, the difficulties between loggers and environmentalists in Oregon and other northwestern states, and the makeup of Simi Valley in California's Ventura County where an all-white jury in 1992 acquitted four Los Angeles police officers in the beating of a black motorist, igniting the worst rioting in Los Angeles in three decades. The careful reader also will be treated to many interesting tidbits—such as the New York district in which the legendary Woodstock concert was held (NY 20), the Minnesota district that is said to be the inspiration for Garrison Keillor's mythical Lake Wobegon (MN 6) or the Pennsylvania district (PA 5) that is home to the winter-watching groundhog, Punxsutawney Phil.

The most distinctive feature of redistricting for the last decade of this century was the melding of computer power with requirements of the Voting Rights Act to enhance the prospects of minorities winning more House seats. An important political goal of the process was to create districts that came to be known as majority-minority in which certain minority groups in the population had a majority and thus were likely to elect an individual of the same background. This was made possible—with a vengeance, critics say—by use of computers to locate very small numbers of voters to include or exclude from a new district in order to achieve a certain demographic makeup.

It worked, as a number of new majority-minority districts were created—largely in the South. But the side effect was to create some districts so bizarre in shape as to give new meaning to the term "gerrymander." The shape of some of these districts can be seen in outline on maps on pages 164, 191, 316 and 548. More important, the Supreme Court in 1993 questioned the legitimacy of the bizarrely shaped districts in a case that arose from a particularly egregious example in North Carolina (see map on page 548). The Court did not decide the issue, but it was clear at the end of 1993 that the matter would confound a number of states for several years as almost certain new challenges wind their way through lower courts.

The computer's ability to mico-craft district lines was not limited to issues of minority representation. It was used in many areas to improve on the historic and time-honored effort of politicians to divide up the land in ways that benefited one party or the other and one candidate (often an incumbent) over another (usually a nonincumbent). These efforts, too, produced some rather strange-looking districts.

How to Use the Book

A reader may find information in several ways. The book is organized alphabetically by state. Each state profile begins with a general description of the state followed by profiles of each district in numerical sequence. Maps of each state and of a number of urban areas are provided.

Six separate indexes—for cities, counties, universities, military bases, cable companies and major business employers—help the reader locate specific information. If, for example, a reader needs to know the district in which a certain city or county is located turn to those indexes. All are located at the end of the book. The indexes begin on page 877.

Editors also have included in the appendix a list of postal zip codes by congressional district. These begin on page 842.

National data tables also are included in the appendix. These tables bring together the census data for each state that are spread throughout the book, allowing a reader to make quick comparisons between states. In addition, these tables include national figures to allow a reader to compare a state to the same figure for the nation as a whole. These tables begin on page 827.

Contributors

This work is the result of the dedicated effort of many persons at Congressional Quarterly and elsewhere.

Jon Preimesberger, a project editor in the books publishing division, was the general editor and the person most responsible for bringing the many sources of information together in the right place at the right time. He was assisted at crucial moments by Michelle Sobel, Carolyn Goldinger and Laura Carter. Paul Pressau of CQ's Production Department skillfully manipulated hundreds of electronic files to produce the pages of the book.

The text descriptions were prepared by CQ political staff reporters and other Washington political writers. The state essays were prepared by Ceci Connolly, Bob Benenson, John Diamond, Beth Donovan, Phil Duncan, Ronald D. Elving, Jeffrey L. Katz, Dave Kaplan and Charles Mahtesian. The district profiles were prepared by these writers and by Ines Pinto Alicea, Rhodes Cook, Kitty Cunningham, John Cranford, Colette Gergely, Thomas H. Moore, Claude R. Marx, Susan C. Phillips, Keith Glover, Susan Kellam, Nadine Cohodas, Steve Gettinger, Colleen McGuiness, Elizabeth A. Palmer, Kristine A. Imherr, Jeanne Kislitzin, Phillip Marwill, Paul Nyhan, Jennifer S. Thomas, Ilyse J. Veron and Brad Wong.

The census data was prepared under the general direction of Robert Cuthriell, CQ Director of Development, and Ronald Knott, CQ Director of Computers and Production. They were assisted by Daniel Coapstick and Daniel Malks of the Computer Services staff, and George Codrea and Kevin M. Shanley of CQ Electronic Publishing.

The maps and most of the data sets other than census material were prepared by InContext Inc. and Program Flow Inc. under the supervision of Laurence J. DeFranco. These data include information on universities and colleges, newspapers, television stations, cable television systems and business and other major employers.

Election returns were compiled from the official state election returns by Polidata under the direction of Clark Bensen, with the assistance of Steve Ellis.

David Tarr
November 1993

Sources and Explanations

Congressional Districts in the 1990s presents descriptive and statistical profiles of the 435 congressional districts based on the 1990 census and subsequent reapportionment and redistricting.

State Profiles

The book is organized alphabetically by state. Each state section includes the following information.

- A narrative description of important demographic, economic, social and political changes that occurred during the 1980s leading to the new House districts that were created after the 1990 census. These profiles also describe the political forces at work during the redistricting process.

- A map of each state that shows the congressional district boundaries. The maps include county names and boundaries and many city names. For some states additional maps showing urban areas are included. In a few states with controversial oddly shaped districts, maps show the area of the state over which the district is spread.

- Six tables that show population; voting-age statistics; income and occupation; education; and housing patterns by congressional districts. Data for each district and the state are presented in tabular form to allow easy comparison. All tables were prepared from Bureau of the Census data on the 1990 census. For easy state-to-state comparisons, the reader will find in the appendix (page 827) a table showing the state totals for each data group and national figures when available.

Table 1: Population

This table provides population and age data for each district in the state: the total population; the population under 18 years of age; the voting-age population (all persons 18 and over); and the median age. The voting-age population shows all potential voters, not just those registered to vote. The median age is the age that divides the population into two equal groups, one half older than the median and one half younger. The median age for the entire United States in the 1990 census was 32.9 years.

Table 2: Voting-Age Persons

This table shows the voting-age population of men and women and of different race and ancestry groups identified in the census. The size of each population group, shown as a percentage of the total voting-age population, indicates the potential voting strength of each group in the district. The percentages were calculated by Congressional Quarterly from census data. The same categories of race and ancestry also appear in each district profile under the demographics section but as a percentage of the total district population, not just the voting-age population.

Table 3: Voting-Age Persons by Age Group

Voters by age group are listed in this table to indicate the potential voting strength of the group in the district. The percentages, which were calculated by Congressional Quarterly from census data, are stated as a percent of the voting-age population.

Table 4: Income and Occupation

This table presents the median family income, families that fall below the government's poverty line, white- and blue-collar workers, and service and farm employees.

Median family income is the income level that divides families into two equal groups with half having incomes above the median and half below the median. The median family income for the entire United States in the 1990 census was $35,225.

The figures for families in poverty show the percentage of families with income in 1989 below the poverty level. The figures were prepared by the Census Bureau based on government definitions of poverty.

Percentages of white-collar, blue-collar, service, and farm worker are in terms of employed persons age 16 and older and were calculated by Congressional Quarterly from census data.

The Census Bureau divides employed persons into thirteen major industry groups that Congressional Quarterly lists in four categories in the table:

- White-Collar Workers. Managerial and professional specialty occupations (including executive, administrative and managerial occupations and professional specialty occupations); and technical, sales and administrative support occupations (including technicians and related support occupations, sales occupations and administrative support occupations including clerical).

- Blue-Collar Workers. Precision production, craft and repair occupations; and operators, fabricators and laborers (including machine operators; assemblers and inspectors; transportation and material-moving occupations; and handlers, equipment cleaners, helpers and laborers).

- Service Workers. Service occupations (including private household occupations and protective service occupations, and service occupations except protective and household occupations).

- Farms Workers. Farming, forestry and fishing occupations.

Table 5: School Years Completed

Data on years of school completed refer to the adult population 25 years of age or older. The figures that appear in the four columns of the table are for discrete groups of individuals. Figures for high school graduates refer to persons with *only* a high school diploma or the equivalent. Not shown in the tables for each congressional district is the total percentage of all adults who are high school graduates, including those with some level of post-high school education. These figures are found in National Census Table 5 in the appendix, page 829. For the nation, 76.2 percent of persons 25 or older have a high school or higher educational level. Percentages were calculated by Congressional Quarterly from census data.

Table 6: Housing and Residential Patterns

Housing units are divided between owner-occupied and renter-occupied units. Housing units include both individual houses and individual apartments.

People classified as urban by the Census Bureau were those persons living in urbanized areas and in places of 2,500 or more outside urbanized areas. The Census Bureau defines an urbanized area as one in which at least 50,000 people are concentrated, usually consisting of a central city and the surrounding, closely settled, contiguous territory often referred to as suburbs. People classified as rural were all persons not classified as urban.

District Profiles

Following the summary material and tables for the states is information about each individual congressional district.

- A text overview of the district describing the political and economic highlights and the impact of redistricting on the politics of the area.

- Election returns recalculated to fit the boundaries of the new districts. In California and Florida, party registration for 1993 is also provided.

- The 1990 population of the district and the percentage change from the district that had the same number in the previous decade.

- The land area and the population density of the district.

- Counties or parts of counties, and their 1990 populations, in each district.

- Cities or parts of cities with populations of more than 10,000 in each district and their 1990 populations.

- The race and ancestry of the district's residents.

- Universities, with their fall 1990 enrollment, in the district.

- Newspapers that circulate in the district and the total circulation of the paper in all districts.

- Commercial television stations located in the district. Cable TV companies available in the district.

- Military installations (as of July 1991) in the district.

- Major employers (those employing 500 or more people), their product or service, and the reported number of employees.

CDs: The Political Picture

The text profiles were prepared by Congressional Quarterly political reporters. The reader should note that specific information in the text may disagree in minor ways with the tabular data that follows. For example, the text may round off college enrollment numbers or populations. In addition, the texts often refer to a figure, such as a city population, that encompasses an entire unit (the full city's population) even though that city straddles a district line. In such cases, the data in tables will show only the portion applicable to the district. The text material was prepared to show the overall complexion of a district and its place in the politics and economy of the state, which often required including information that applied to more than a single district. The data in the tables apply only to the district.

Election Returns

The election returns provided for each district were compiled by Polidata under the direction of Clark Bensen, with the assistance of Steve Ellis.

The results for the 1992 presidential and congressional elections are estimates from actual results from the geographic components of the districts—that is, the districts' counties, towns, wards and precincts. These data were collected from state and local officials across the country. Results for elections held previous to 1992 are estimates of the elections reconfigured for the new districts. These results estimate what the results would have been had the district lines for the 103rd Congress been in force for the contest held before 1992.

For the 1992 results, the district totals were based on results for precincts effective for the 1992 election. For earlier years, the process varied by state. In some cases the district totals were available from state sources, generally as a result of the redistricting process that occurred during 1991 and 1992. In most cases, however, the general process was one of assigning each precinct, as it existed for the earlier race, to one of the new congressional districts for 1992.

This process is subject to estimation and judgment and is complicated by the year-to-year change in precinct boundaries. Efforts to obtain zero percent population deviation also turned up many 1992 precincts that were split by a district line. An additional complication occurred when absentee ballots were counted at the county level in counties that have portions of more than one district.

Votes are provided for Democrats and Republicans only. The vote for Ross Perot in 1992 is footnoted at the bottom of each table; independent candidates are not listed otherwise, though any contest in which the combined minor party votes was greater than 5 percent is noted. Partisan percentages may not add to 100 percent because of this exclusion. Due to data availability or limitations, some races may not be available for some states.

The vote reconfiguration for earlier years is provided as a means by which the general political behavior of a district can be reviewed. Because the raw total of votes is a result of this process of estimation, the reader is advised that the percentages may be the better indicator of the general pattern of voting in the district.

Population, Area and Density

The population, land area and population density are shown for the new districts. The percentage change in population is shown to give a rough estimate of demographic changes in the area, but the figure must be used with care. The percentage shows the change for the 1990s district that had the same number in the 1980s. However, the district boundaries may be quite different, making that percentage change an inexact comparison. In districts that changed little, the comparison is a fair measure of population movements. But in districts that were significantly redrawn, as occurred in many populous states, the change is only a rough guide to the changing nature of a congressional district.

Counties

Most states are organized by counties. In Louisiana the equivalent divisions are known as parishes. Alaska has no counties. Maryland, Missouri, Nevada and Virginia have a number of cities that are independent of any county and therefore are considered equivalent divisions. A (pt.) indicates counties that are divided between two or more congressional districts.

Cities

The Census Bureau recognizes two kinds of cities. Those that are incorporated and those that are closely settled but fall outside incorporated areas. Congressional Quarterly lists all incorporated places whose total population exceeded 10,000 in the census.

In addition, widely recognized unincorporated places exceeding 10,000 in population are included for districts and are followed by the abbreviation CDP, which stands for Census Designated Place. In some cases, towns, townships and villages are also included. A (pt.) indicates cities that are only partly within the district.

Race and Ancestry

The Census Bureau established these five main racial categories: white; black; American Indian, Eskimo and Aleut; Asian and Pacific Islander; and Other. All people responding to the 1990 census were asked this question based on self-identification. In reporting the data, the bureau noted the self-identification "does not denote any clear-cut scientific definition of biological stock. The data for race represent self-classification by people according to the race with which they most closely identify."

Census included as "white" those persons who indicated their race as "White" or reported entries such as Canadian, German, Italian, Lebanese, Near Easterner, Arab or Polish. It classified as "black" all persons who indicated their race as "Black or Negro" or reported entries such as African American, Afro-American, Black Puerto Rican, Jamaican, Nigerian, West Indian, or Haitian. Persons in the American Indian, Eskimo and Aleut category were those who said they were a member of one of those specific groups as well as those who reported a specific Indian tribe or such entries as Canadian Indian, French American Indian or Spanish American Indian.

Census classified as Asian or Pacific Islander all persons who identified themselves as Asian (including Chinese, Filipino, Japanese, Asian Indian, Korean, and Vietnamese or provided a write-in identification such as Cambodian, Laotian, or Thai), or Pacific Islander groups (including Hawaiian, Samoan, Guamanian, or provided a write-in response such as Tahitian, Polynesian, or Micronesian).

A category of "Other Race" was used for all persons not in the other groups. Persons reported here include write-in entries such as multiracial, multi-ethnic, mixed, interracial, Wesort or a Spanish/Hispanic group (such as Mexican, Cuban, or Puerto Rican).

Data on ancestry was obtained from a sample of persons in the 1990 census, based on self-identification. The Census Bureau said that ancestry "refers to a person's ethnic origin or descent, 'roots,' or heritage or the place of birth of the person or the person's parents or ancestry before their arrival in the United States." The bureau noted the "ancestry question allowed respondents to report one or more ancestry groups. While a large number of respondents listed a single ancestry, the majority of answers included more than one ethnic entry."

The census accepted "American" as a unique ethnicity if it was listed alone, with an ambiguous response, or with the name of a state. If a respondent listed any other ethnic identify, such as "Italian American," generally the bureau did not include the person under "American."

Universities and Colleges

Schools of post-secondary education were located in congressional districts by their official addresses, although in numerous cases in cities that straddle district lines a portion of the school actually may be in the adjoining district. In all such cases, the school will have an impact on both districts. The schools were located using data from the U.S. Department of Education. Enrollments shown are for the fall 1990. The tables include public and private institutions and well as technical, professional and community schools with 200 or more students.

Newspapers

Newspapers that circulate in a congressional district are listed. The purpose of this listing is to show sources of information available to voters in the district. In many cases, the newspaper's home office is located in another district and in the case of major newspapers, in a district many miles away. For example the *Los Angeles Times* is published in Southern California but circulates in cities and counties throughout the state. In all cases, the circulation figures shown are total numbers for a newspaper, which may be larger than the circulation within the district for which the paper is listed. Circulation figures within a district were unavailable. The lists include only daily newspapers with paid circulation, as reported by the Audit Bureau of Circulation, except for major foreign language publications.

Commercial Television Stations

Commercial television stations, and their network affiliation if any, are listed by the location of their transmitter as provided by the Federal Communications Commission.

The ADI listing refers to the Area of Dominant Influence, a geographic market design that defines each TV market exclusive of another based on measurable viewing patterns. An ADI is an area that consists of all counties in which the home market stations are viewed to any significant extent. Each county in the United States is allocated exclusively to only one ADI; there is no overlap. A district may be entirely within one ADI or it may be divided among several ADIs; if the district is divided, estimated percentages are given to indicate the portion of the district allocated to each ADI.

The impact of political news and advertising in a congressional district can be assessed by knowing the cities that have a dominant influence in the viewing patterns of a locale. However, the actual stations that serve a district must be determined by looking at the city or cities listed as the ADI for the district. In many congressional districts no TV station will be listed even though viewers living there will receive a signal from a transmitter located nearby in a different congressional district. For example, in Maryland's 8th District, the ADI listed is Washington, D.C., where most of the major TV station transmitters for the area are located. To determine the names of those stations and their network affiliations, the reader should turn to the listing for Washington, D.C. (in the appendix). The city index is a helpful way of locating the data on any city.

Cable Television Systems

Cable television systems serving a district are listed. The number of cable subscribers given is for the company in total and may include persons in more than one congressional district. Exact subscriber numbers for a cable company in a district were not available. Only systems with 5,000 or more total subscribers were tabulated; these systems represent about 85 to 90 percent of all subscribers in the nation. The cable franchise boundaries were estimated by A. C. Nielsen and are based on zip codes. These codes were used to place cable systems within congressional districts. The cable companies are listed by the common name by which subscribers usually identify them. In the appendix of this book there is an index of cable systems that includes the name of a system's corporate parent in order to allow a reader to identify multisystem ownership.

Military Installation

Congressional Quarterly lists by congressional district all military installations and facilities with full-time military and civilian personnel in 1991. Many of these facilities were being reviewed for closure in 1992 and 1993 following the end of the Cold War.

Business and Other Major Employers

This section lists major employers (with 500 or more employees) in each congressional district. Included are private profit-making companies, professional groups (such as law firms) nonprofit groups, and government offices. The latter includes federal, state and local offices including school districts. The location of an employer was determined by the official address of a company or organization available in standard government and business directories. For each employer, CQ lists the name and a division name if applicable, the location, the product or service provided and the number of employees.

Although the employer's address placed the organization in a specific district, in many cases—particularly in cities that straddle district lines—a portion of a work force may actually be located in an adjoining district. Even in districts where the employing office is entirely within a district, people who work there may live in an adjoining district. As a result, the information presented must be considered a useful but not exact measurement of economic activity in a specific district. The reader should examine the overall picture of the region by looking at listings for each district in an area. The economic impact of a government agency or a private employer in such cases will spread across more than one district and affect several House representatives. The official location of an employer in such cases is less important than the jobs and economic impact the employer has on the region.

With this information, the reader usually can discern the types of industry and business, government employment, and other sources of economic activity prevalent in a congressional district.

Appendix

An appendix starting on page 827 includes a number of important features that supplement the data in the state and district profiles.

- National Census Tables. These tables provide the state and national figures for each of the data groups used throughout the book. This allows the reader to make quick comparisons between states and between an individual state and the nation as a whole.

- Members of Congress. Representatives who served in the 100th to 103rd Congresses are listed.

- District of Columbia. To round out the view of the United States, census and profile data are provided for Washington, D.C.

- Zip Codes. All postal zip codes in the United States are assigned to the congressional district in which they fall. Many zip code areas fall into more than one district.

Indexes

Six subject-specific index are included to help the reader quickly locate data: counties; cities; universities and colleges; military bases; cable TV companies; and employers of 500 or more persons. The cable TV index also lists the corporate parent of the local company to allow the reader to see multiple ownership in the cable industry.

Redistricting for the 1990s

The round of redistricting following the 1990 census confirmed a trend that had been building for years: The process of drawing congressional district boundaries, once regarded by the judiciary as a "political thicket" best left to elected officials, is now a thoroughly litigious business.

In the 1990 reapportionment, 43 states ended up with at least two House districts, and thus faced redistricting. In nearly half of those states, federal or state courts played a significant role in the redistricting debate; judges actually issued the new lines in 10 states, including several of the nation's most populous—California, Florida, Pennsylvania, Illinois and Michigan.

In an earlier time, redistricting was chiefly about crafty politicians designing lines with incumbent protection or partisan advantage in mind. All that scheming still goes on, but nowadays, no savvy politician sits down to map without backup from a team of legal experts who have experience in maneuvering maps through the process of judicial review.

For the 1990s, the litigation began before a single new line was drawn: A group of plaintiffs preemptively objected that the 1990 census would be fatally flawed because the tally would miss millions of Americans, especially urban minorities. As time passed, there also were court disputes over whether to count federal personnel overseas for purposes of reapportionment, and, more broadly, over which mathematical method should be used to reapportion House seats among the states. (*Method of Equal Proportions, page 8; The 1990 Apportionment, page 8; Whom Should the Census Count?, box, page 15*)

As mapmakers set to work on new district boundaries, the question of race and representation provoked many legal disputes. In numerous states, black and Hispanic litigants struggled against whites reluctant to yield power; in other places, blacks and Hispanics struggled with each other over who would represent predominantly minority areas.

And in North Carolina, a group of white plaintiffs lodged the novel claim that their civil rights had been violated when their state's new map included them in a black-majority district with an unusually contorted shape. The challenge to the North Carolina map went all the way to the U.S. Supreme Court. In June 1993 it issued a 5-to-4 ruling (*Shaw v. Reno*) that raised questions about the propriety of the now-common practice of gerrymandering to enhance the political clout of minority

groups. Critics of this practice say that drawing districts designed to elect minorities is a kind of political apartheid—a separating of the races for voting purposes. But defenders of racial gerrymandering maintain that affirmative action in mapping is needed to compensate for historical and ongoing discrimination against minorities.

Redistricting disputes brought wrangling in the legal arena not only about what lines to draw, but also about which judges should do the drawing. In recent years, federal courts typically have been the chief venue for resolving mapping controversies. But in the early 1990s, state courts played an especially prominent role in new-boundary disputes in California, New York, Pennsylvania, Texas and Minnesota. A tussle in Minnesota over whether state or federal judges should draw congressional districts reached the Supreme Court. In a February 1993 ruling (*Growe v. Emison*), the Court unanimously ruled that federal courts generally cannot decide redistricting cases until any parallel proceedings in state courts have run their course.

High-Tech Hair-Splitting

Lawyers are now integral in the redistricting process, but the 1990s round of remapping confirmed that computer jockeys have become indispensable. Not so long ago, it was common practice for politicians to hunch over paper maps to sketch out new district boundaries. No more. Two factors—advances in computer technology and judicial mandates that districts be almost precisely equal in population—have combined to make redistricting a high-tech science. The hair-splitting precision of computer cartographers means it is now ordinary for all the congressional districts in a state to have virtually the same number of people.

The technology that makes this sort of fine-tuning possible also is employed to other ends: Mapmakers now can and often do give House districts very specific partisan and racial characteristics. In many such constituencies, the type of person who wins election—black, Hispanic or white, Democrat or Republican—is practically preordained. Such districts often are not geographically compact, and their lines disregard jurisdictional boundaries of cities and counties. But that rarely seems to disturb judges, as long as the districts adhere to the one-person,

Rich and Poor Districts

Listed below are the 25 congressional districts with the highest median family income and the 25 districts with the lowest median family income, as measured in the 1990 census. Median family income is the income level that divides families into two equal groups with half having incomes above the median and half below the median. The median family income for the entire United States in the 1990 census was $35,225.

Highest Median Income Districts			Lowest Median Income Districts		
Rank	District	Median family income	Rank	District	Median family income
1	Maryland 8	$64,199	1	New York 16	$16,683
2	New Jersey 11	63,574	2	Kentucky 5	17,798
3	New Jersey 12	62,034	3	Louisiana 4	17,957
4	New York 3	61,611	4	Mississippi 2	19,236
5	California 10	60,079	5	Texas 15	19,554
6	Virginia 11	59,989	6	Michigan 15	19,738
7	New York 14	59,953	7	Alabama 7	20,773
8	California 47	59,936	8	New York 15	21,065
9	New Jersey 5	59,583	9	Georgia 2	21,558
10	California 14	59,492	10	Louisiana 2	21,677
11	Virginia 8	58,582	11	Arkansas 1	21,889
12	Illinois 10	58,407	12	New York 12	21,911
13	New York 5	57,915	13	California 33	22,018
14	New Jersey 7	57,563	14	North Carolina 1	22,065
15	New York 19	57,419	15	Texas 29	22,230
16	California 24	57,375	16	West Virginia 3	22,250
17	California 15	57,300	17	Missouri 8	22,406
18	New York 4	56,588	18	Texas 28	22,425
19	California 36	56,567	19	California 20	22,472
20	Connecticut 4	56,320	20	Arizona 2	22,650
21	Michigan 11	56,234	21	South Carolina 6	22,973
22	Illinois 13	55,481	22	Oklahoma 3	23,106
23	Georgia 6	55,056	23	Florida 3	23,685
24	California 29	55,001	24	Texas 27	24,016
25	New York 18	53,968	25	Texas 23	24,064

one-vote principle that the Supreme Court set out in the 1960s and has enforced rigidly during the past decade.

Even in the *Shaw* case out of North Carolina, the Court merely questioned the map that had many oddly shaped districts, including the black-majority one that wriggled halfway across the state. The justices said such a racial gerrymander might still pass constitutional muster if it is "narrowly tailored to further a compelling constitutional interest." Strengthening the legal credibility of the North Carolina map was its population precision: Six of the districts were drawn with 552,387 people, and the other five districts were within just a few people of that "ideal" size.

Reshuffling Promotes Incumbent Exodus

The decennial undertakings of counting the American population and reapportioning and redistricting House seats helps keep the people's chamber in step with demographic changes in the nation.

Because of regional population shifts that showed up in the 1990 census, reapportionment took 19 House seats away from 13 slow-growing states—mostly in the Northeast and Midwest.

Those seats were shifted to eight states, mainly along the nation's western and southern rims, where population increased sharply in the 1980s.

California alone gained seven seats, giving it 52, more than any other state has ever held in the House. Texas moved up three seats to 30, nearly knocking New York from its perch as the second most-populous state. (The Empire State suffered the biggest loss in reapportionment, dropping three seats to end up with a total of 31.) Florida's phenomenal growth in the 1980s moved it up to fourth in the delegate count; it added four seats for a total of 23, surging past Pennsylvania, Illinois and Ohio, each of which lost two seats.

The population shifts between and within states required line-drawers in many cases to revise substantially the congressional district maps that had been in place for a decade. Arguably the most dramatic change came in Montana, which, much to its dismay, did not have to redistrict at all: The state dropped from two seats to one in reapportionment, and its two House incumbents—one Democrat and one Republican—battled for the sole remaining seat.

Elsewhere, some two dozen other incumbents found themselves

Families in Poverty

The table below lists the 25 congressional districts with the largest percentage of families living below the government's poverty line, as measured by the 1990 census.

Rank	District	Families in poverty
1	New York 16	39.5%
2	Louisiana 4	32.8
3	Michigan 15	32.6
4	Texas 15	31.6
5	Mississippi 2	31.0
6	New York 15	29.8
7	Kentucky 5	29.2
8	New York 12	28.3
9	Louisiana 2	27.3
10	Alabama 7	26.2
11	Illinois 7	25.9
12	California 33	24.9
13-14	New York 10	24.6
	Texas 27	24.6
15	Georgia 2	24.3
16-17	Texas 23	24.2
	Texas 28	24.2
18	Texas 29	23.9
19	Pennsylvania 1	23.6
20	California 20	23.2
21-24	Florida 17	22.6
	Texas 16	22.6
	Arizona 2	22.6
	South Carolina 6	22.6
25	North Carolina 1	22.1

remapped into the same district with another incumbent. And numerous other members saw their re-election prospects complicated by maps that gave them thousands of different constituents.

The prospects of campaigning against a House colleague or facing many unfamiliar faces at the polls contributed to the large number of incumbent retirements in the 1992 campaign cycle: 52 members did not seek another House term. That exodus helped create opportunities for newcomer House candidates, and 1992 ended up producing the biggest crop of House freshmen—110— since the election of 1948. That number included 25 freshmen women, bringing the total number of women House members to an all-time high of 47.

Opportunities for Minorities Expand

The upheaval of redistricting also made the House a more racially and ethnically diverse place: The freshman class of 1992 included 16 blacks and eight Hispanics. They owed their election in large part to legislative, judicial and administrative actions during the 1980s that obligated mapmakers in the 1990 round to make special efforts to draw majority-minority House districts wherever possible.

In amending the Voting Rights Act in 1982, Congress broadened the mandate of the original legislation. Under Section

2 of the act as amended, any state law that had the *effect* of diluting minority voting strength was deemed illegal; previously, minorities had needed to demonstrate that the *intent* of a law was discriminatory. Following this change in the law, the Supreme Court in 1986 issued a ruling in *Thornburg v. Gingles* that was widely interpreted to mean that states must create minority districts wherever possible; previously, it had been sufficient for states simply to meet a "nonretrogression" standard, that is, preserving existing minority districts.

In 1987, the Justice Department, which under Section 5 of the Voting Rights Act must "preclear" election law changes in 14 states with histories of racial discrimination, issued new regulations that tracked with the *Gingles* decision. The department said it would not preclear laws that violated Section 2 of the Voting Rights Act; previously, the Justice Department had only held states accountable for meeting the nonretrogression standard.

The new legal environment had a dramatic impact on 1990s mapmaking in many states, as legislators and courts sought for the first time to create majority-minority districts in rough proportion to a state's minority-group population.

These remap efforts led to some historic breakthroughs in the November 1992 election: For the first time since the Reconstruction era, blacks won House races in Alabama, Florida (three districts), North Carolina (two districts), South Carolina and Virginia. Delegations from Louisiana, Maryland and Texas each moved up from having one black House member to two, and Georgia moved up from having one to three. Illinois and New Jersey elected their first-ever Hispanics to the House, and new Hispanic members joined those already representing districts in California, Florida, New York and Texas.

And, of course, because of the nonretrogression standard, the 1990s round of redistricting preserved all the preexisting districts with majority-minority populations.

Remaps Yield Little Partisan Shift

While redistricting offers legal scholars and demographers abundant material for contemplation, political professionals tend to focus on a single paramount concern: Which party gains an advantage in the line-drawing?

At the outset of the 1990 campaign cycle, national Republican strategists felt that redistricting would enhance their party's prospects of significantly cutting into—perhaps even overturning—the Democratic Party's 38-year grip on the House majority. The GOP figured it would benefit from the shift of House seats away from urban, Democratic-dominated areas of the Frost Belt to fast-growing, conservative-leaning areas of the Sun Belt. Also, Republicans believed that the legal mandate to draw more districts for minorities would harm the 1992 re-election prospects of white Democratic incumbents; their minority constituents (nearly all of them Democratic voters) would be pulled away to help build new minority districts, the GOP thought.

But in the November 1992 election, the GOP managed to gain a net of only 10 seats in the House. That was an improvement on the party's showing after the last redistricting; the party lost House seats in 1982. But Democrats retained a substantial cushion in the 103rd Congress, holding 258 seats to the GOP's 176. (There was one independent.)

In part, Republican gains were small because the redistricting process in a number of states had not yielded maps as favorable to Republican candidates as the party initially hoped. But a big part of the GOP's meager House gain stemmed from a factor unrelated to redistricting: the presidential campaign. George

Hispanic Districts

Listed below are the 25 congressional districts with the highest percentage of Hispanic residents, as measured by the 1990 census. Percentages were calculated by Congressional Quarterly from census data for the entire population of a district.

Rank	District	Hispanic as % of population
1	California 33	83.7%
2	Texas 15	74.5
3	Texas 16	70.4
4	Florida 21	69.6
5	Florida 18	66.7
6	Texas 27	66.2
7	Illinois 4	65.0
8	Texas 23	62.5
9	California 34	62.3
10	California 30	61.5
11	Texas 20	60.7
12	Texas 29	60.6
13	Texas 28	60.4
14	New York 16	60.2
15	California 31	58.5
16	New York 12	57.9
17	California 20	55.4
18	California 26	52.7
19	Arizona 2	50.5
20	California 46	50.0
21	New York 15	46.4
22	California 37	45.2
23	California 35	43.1
24	New Mexico 2	42.1
25	New Jersey 13	41.5

Black Districts

Listed below are the 25 congressional districts with the highest percentage of black residents, as measured by the 1990 census. Percentages were calculated by Congressional Quarterly from census data for the entire population of a district.

Rank	District	Blacks as % of population
1	New York 11	74.0%
2	Maryland 7	71.0
3	Michigan 15	70.0
4	Illinois 1	69.7
5	Michigan 14	69.1
6	Illinois 2	68.5
7	Alabama 7	67.5
8	Louisiana 4	66.4
9	District of Columbia	65.8
10	Illinois 7	65.6
11-12	Virginia 3	64.1
	Georgia 11	64.1
13	Mississippi 2	63.0
14	Georgia 5	62.3
15-16	Pennsylvania 2	62.2
	South Carolina 6	62.2
17	Louisiana 2	61.0
18	New York 10	60.7
19	New Jersey 10	60.2
20	Tennessee 9	59.2
21	Ohio 11	58.6
22	Maryland 4	58.5
23	Florida 17	58.4
24	North Carolina 1	57.3
25	Georgia 2	56.6

Bush proved to be a drag on many Republicans down the ticket, particularly in high-growth western states such as California. In the 1992 presidential race Bill Clinton carried the state with 46 percent of the vote, while Bush took only 33 percent. Republicans had talked boldly of gaining partisan parity in the California delegation in 1992; instead, Democrats retained a 30-to-22 majority, compared to a 26-to-19 ratio before redistricting.

Clever Democratic cartography did play a part in holding down the GOP's gains from redistricting. In Texas, for instance, state Democrats controlling the Legislature and governorship crafted an intricate map that created two new Hispanic-majority districts and one new black-majority seat and still managed to give each of the party's House incumbents districts with a Democratic tilt. The Texas delegation, 19-to-8 Democratic before the election, shifted to 21-to-9 in the voting.

In most other states where new majority-minority districts were created, Democratic candidates won those seats, but the GOP fell short of its expectations for picking off white Democratic incumbents who had been weakened in the process of drawing new minority districts.

Ironically, one of the GOP's biggest redistricting success stories was Georgia. The state gained a House seat in reapportionment, and Democrats drew what they intended as a partisan map. It dismantled the district of House Minority Whip Newt Gingrich, but in the process, it weakened a Democratic incumbent and left another suburban Atlanta district up for grabs. In the end, Gingrich won, the weakened Democratic incumbent lost and the suburban seat went Republican. Before the election, the GOP had only one of Georgia's 10 seats; after the vote, it held four of 11.

Going into the 1990s round of redistricting, Republicans had hoped that such blatant partisan gerrymanders as the Democrats' Texas map might not survive legal scrutiny. In a 1986 ruling (*Davis v. Bandemer*), the Supreme Court declared that partisan gerrymanders are subject to constitutional review. But the Court did not suggest what standards it would use to find a partisan gerrymander illegal, and in drawing maps for the 1990s, both parties continued to engage in the practice of trying to draw lines to achieve partisan advantage.

Phil Duncan

Congressional Districts in the 1990s

Reapportionment and Redistricting

Reapportionment, the redistribution of the 435 House seats among the states to reflect shifts in population, and redistricting, the redrawing of congressional district boundaries within the states, are among the most important processes in the U.S. political system. They help to determine whether the House will be dominated by Democrats or Republicans, liberals or conservatives, and whether racial or ethnic minorities receive fair representation.

Reapportionment and redistricting occur every 10 years on the basis of the decennial population census. States where populations grew quickly during the previous 10 years gain congressional seats, while those that lost population or grew much more slowly than the national average lose seats. The number of House members for the rest of the states remains the same.

The states that gain or lose seats must usually make extensive changes in their congressional maps. Even those states with stable delegations must make modifications that account for population shifts within their boundaries, in accordance with Supreme Court "one-person, one-vote" rulings.

In most states, the state legislatures are responsible for drawing up and enacting the new district map. The majority party in each state legislature is thus often in a position to draw a congressional district map that enhances the fortunes of its incumbents and candidates at the expense of the opposing party. "Some members may find their old district no longer recognizable, or their home located in someone else's district. Others will find the music has stopped and they are, quite literally, without a seat. Or they will find themselves thrown together in a single district with another incumbent—often from the same party," wrote one reporter. "The scramble to prevent or minimize such political problems involves some of the most brutal combat in American politics, for the power to draw district lines is the power not only to end one politician's career but often to enfranchise or disenfranchise a neighborhood, a city, a party, a social or economic group or even a race by concentrating or diluting their votes within a given district." [1]

Among the many unique features to emerge in the remarkable nation-creating endeavor of 1787 was a national legislative body whose membership was to be elected by the people and apportioned on the basis of population. In keeping with the nature of the Constitution, however, only fundamental rules and regulations were provided. The interpretation and implementation of the instructions contained in the document were left to future generations.

Within this flexible framework many questions soon arose. How large was the House of Representatives to be? What mathematical formula was to be used in calculating the distribution of seats among the various states? Were the representatives to be elected at large or by districts? If by districts, what standards should be used in fixing their boundaries? Congress and the courts have been wrestling with these questions for two hundred years.

Until the mid-twentieth century such questions generally remained in the hands of the legislators. But with the population increasingly concentrated in urban areas, variations in populations among rural and urban districts in a single state grew more and more pronounced. Efforts to persuade Congress to address the issue of heavily populated but underrepresented areas proved unsuccessful. Legislators from rural areas were so intent on preventing power from slipping from their hands that they managed to block reapportionment of the House after the 1920 census.

Not long afterward litigants tried, repeatedly and unsuccessfully, to persuade the Supreme Court to order the states to revise congressional district boundaries in line with population shifts. A breakthrough finally occurred in 1964 in the case of *Wesberry v. Sanders*, when the Court declared that the Constitution required that "as nearly as practicable, one man's vote in a congressional election is to be worth as much as another's."

In the years that followed the Court repeatedly reaffirmed its one-person, one-vote requirement. Following the 1980 census several states adopted new maps that had districts of nearly equal population but that disregarded other traditional factors—such as the compactness of the district or the integrity of county and city lines. So long as they were equal in population, these partisan gerrymanders, designed to benefit one party at the expense of the other, seemed unassailable in the courts until 1986, when a slim majority of the Supreme Court held that political gerrymanders were subject to constitutional review by federal courts.

The Court, however, offered no opinion on what might constitute an impermissible political gerrymander. As Congress and the state legislatures prepared for the round of redistricting following the 1990 census, the one certainty appeared to be continued litigation on this and other redistricting issues.

Early History

Modern legislative bodies are descended from the councils of feudal lords and gentry that medieval kings summoned for the purpose of raising revenues and armies. The councils represented only certain groups of people, such as the nobility, the clergy, the landed gentry and town merchants; the notion of equal representation for equal numbers of people or even for all groups of people had not yet begun to develop.

Beginning as little more than administrative and advisory arms of the throne, royal councils in time developed into lawmaking bodies and acquired powers that eventually eclipsed those of the monarchs they served. In England the king's council became Parliament, with the higher nobility and clergy making up the House of Lords and representatives of the gentry and merchants making up the House of Commons. The power struggle between king and council climaxed in the mid-1600s, when the king was executed and a "benevolent" dictatorship was set up under Oliver Cromwell. Although the monarchy was soon restored, by 1800 Parliament was clearly the more powerful branch of government.

The growth of the powers of Parliament, as well as the development of English ideas of representation during the seventeenth and eighteenth centuries, had a profound effect on the colonists in America. Representative assemblies were unifying forces behind the breakaway of the colonies from England and the establishment of the newly independent nation.

Colonists in America generally modeled their legislatures after England's, using both population and land units as bases for apportionment. Patterns of early representation varied. "Nowhere did representation bear any uniform relation to the number of electors. Here and there the factor of size had been crudely recognized," Robert Luce noted in his book *Legislative Principles*.[2]

The Continental Congress, with representation from every colony, proclaimed in the Declaration of Independence in 1776 that governments derive "their just powers from the consent of the governed" and that "the right of representation in the legislature" is an "inestimable right" of the people. The Constitutional Convention of 1787 included representatives from all the states. However, in neither of these bodies were the state delegations or voting powers proportional to population.

In New England the town was usually the basis for representation. In the Middle Atlantic region the county frequently was used. Virginia used the county with additional representation for specified cities. In many areas, towns and counties were fairly equal in population, and territorial representation afforded roughly equal representation for equal numbers of people. Delaware's three counties, for example, were of almost equal population and had the same representation in the legislature. But in Virginia the disparity was enormous (from 951 people in one county to 22,015 in another). Thomas Jefferson criticized the state's constitution on the ground that "among those who share the representation, the shares are unequal."[3]

The Framers' Intentions

What, then, did the Framers of the Constitution have in mind about who would be represented in the House of Representatives and how?

The Constitution declares only that each state is to be allotted a certain number of representatives. It does not state specifically that congressional districts must be equal or nearly equal in population. Nor does it explicitly require that a state create districts at all. However, it seems clear that the first clause of Article I, Section 2, providing that House members should be chosen "by the people of the several states," indicates that the House of Representatives, in contrast to the Senate, was to represent people rather than states. (*Constitution on representation, box, page 3*)

The third clause of Article I, Section 2, provided that congressional apportionment among the states must be according to population. "There is little point in giving the states congressmen 'according to their respective numbers' if the states do not redistribute the members of their delegations on the same principle," Andrew Hacker argued in his book *Congressional Districting*. "For representatives are not the property of the states, as are the senators, but rather belong to the people who happen to reside within the boundaries of those states. Thus, each citizen has a claim to be regarded as a political unit equal in value to his neighbors."[4]

Hacker also examined the Constitutional Convention, *The Federalist* papers (essays written by Alexander Hamilton, John Jay, and James Madison in defense of the Constitution) and the state conventions ratifying the Constitution for evidence of the Framers' intentions with regard to representation. He found that the issue of unequal representation arose only once during debate in the Constitutional Convention. The occasion was Madison's defense of Article I, Section 4, of the proposed Constitution, giving Congress the power to override state regulations on "the times . . . and manner" of holding elections for members of Congress. Madison's argument related to the fact that many state legislatures of the time were badly malapportioned: "The inequality of the representation in the legislatures of particular states would produce a like inequality in their representation in the national legislature, as it was presumable that the counties having the power in the former case would secure it to themselves in the latter."[5]

The implication was that states would create congressional districts and that unequal districting was undesirable and should be prevented.

Madison made this interpretation even more clear in his contributions to *The Federalist* papers. Arguing in favor of the relatively small size of the projected House of Representatives, he wrote in No. 56: "Divide the largest state into ten or twelve districts and it will be found that there will be no peculiar local interests . . . which will not be within the knowledge of the Representative of the district."

In the same paper Madison said, "The Representatives of each state will not only bring with them a considerable knowledge of its laws, and a local knowledge of their respective districts, but will probably in all cases have been members, and may even at the very time be members, of the state legislature, where all the local information and interests of the state are assembled, and from whence they may easily be conveyed by a very few hands into the legislature of the United States." And, finally, in the *Federalist* No. 57 Madison stated that "each Representative of the United States will be elected by five or six thousand citizens." In making these arguments, Madison seems to have assumed that all or most representatives would be elected by districts rather than at large.[6]

In the states' ratifying conventions, the grant to Congress by Article I, Section 4, of ultimate jurisdiction over the "times, places and manner of holding elections" (except the places of choosing senators) held the attention of many delegates. There were differences over the merits of this section, but no justification of unequal districts was prominently used to attack the grant of power. Further evidence that individual districts were the intention of the Founding Fathers was given in the New York ratifying convention, when Alexander Hamilton said, "The natural and proper mode of holding elections will be to divide the state into districts in proportion to the number to be elected. This state will consequently be divided at first into six." [7]

From his study of the sources relating to the question of congressional districting, Hacker concluded,

> There is, then, a good deal of evidence that those who framed and ratified the Constitution intended that the House of Representatives have as its constituency a public in which the votes of all citizens were of equal weight.... The House of Representatives was designed to be a popular chamber, giving the same electoral power to all who had the vote. And the concern of Madison ... that districts be equal in size was an institutional step in the direction of securing this democratic principle.[8]

REAPPORTIONMENT: THE NUMBER OF SEATS

The Constitution made the first apportionment, which was to remain in effect until the first census was taken. No reliable figures on the population were available at the time. The Constitution's apportionment yielded a 65-member House. The seats were allotted among the 13 states as follows: New Hampshire, three; Massachusetts, eight; Rhode Island and Providence Plantations, one; Connecticut, five; New York, six; New Jersey, four; Pennsylvania, eight; Delaware, one; Maryland, six; Virginia, ten; North Carolina, five; South Carolina, five; and Georgia, three. This apportionment remained in effect during the First and Second Congresses (1789-93).

Apparently realizing that apportionment of the House was likely to become a major bone of contention, the First Congress submitted to the states a proposed constitutional amendment containing a formula to be used in future reapportionments. The amendment provided that following the taking of a decennial census one representative would be allotted for every 30,000 people until the House membership reached 100. Once that level was reached, there would be one representative for every 40,000 people until the House membership reached 200, when there would be one representative for every 50,000 people.

First Apportionment by Congress

The states, however, refused to ratify the reapportionment-formula amendment, which forced Congress to enact apportionment legislation after the first census was taken in 1790. The first apportionment bill was sent to the president in March 1792. President George Washington sent the bill back to Congress without his signature—the first presidential veto.

The bill had incorporated the constitutional minimum of 30,000 as the size of each district. But the population of each state was not a simple multiple of 30,000; significant fractions were left over. For example, Vermont was found to be entitled

Constitutional Provisions

Article I, Section 2: The House of Representatives shall be composed of Members chosen every second Year by the People of the several States, and the Electors in each State shall have the Qualifications requisite for Electors of the most numerous Branch of the State Legislature. . . .

Representatives and direct Taxes shall be apportioned among the several States which may be included within this Union, according to their respective Numbers, which shall be determined by adding to the whole Number of free Persons, including those bound to Service for a Term of Years, and excluding Indians not taxed, three fifths of all other Persons. The actual Enumeration shall be made within three Years after the first Meeting of the Congress of the United States, and within every subsequent Term of ten Years, in such Manner as they shall by Law direct. The Number of Representatives shall not exceed one for every thirty thousand, but each State shall have at least one Representative. . . .

Article I, Section 4: The Times, Places and Manner of holding Elections for Senators and Representatives, shall be prescribed in each State by the Legislature thereof; but the Congress may at any time by Law make or alter such Regulations, except as to the Place of Chusing Senators. . . .

Amendment XIV, Section 2 to Article I: Representatives shall be apportioned among the several States according to their respective numbers, counting the whole number of persons in each State, excluding Indians not taxed. But when the right to vote at any election for the choice of electors for President and Vice President of the United States, Representatives in Congress, the Executive and Judicial officers of a State, or the members of the Legislature thereof, is denied to any of the male inhabitants of such State, being twenty-one years of age, and citizens of the United States, or in any way abridged, except for participation in rebellion, or other crime, the basis of representation therein shall be reduced in the proportion which the number of such male citizens shall bear to the whole number of male citizens twenty-one years of age in such State.

to 2.851 representatives, New Jersey to 5.98, and Virginia to 21.018. A formula had to be found that would deal in the fairest possible manner with unavoidable variations from exact equality.

Accordingly, Congress proposed in the first apportionment bill to distribute the members on a fixed ratio of one representative for each 30,000 inhabitants, and give an additional member to each state with a fraction exceeding one-half. Washington's veto was based on the belief that eight states would receive more than one representative for each 30,000 people under this formula.

A motion to override the veto was unsuccessful. A new bill meeting the president's objections, approved in April 1792, provided for a ratio of one member for every 33,000 inhabitants and fixed the exact number of representatives to which each state was entitled. The total membership of the House was to be 105. In dividing the population of the various states by 33,000, all remainders were to be disregarded. Thomas Jefferson devised the solution, known as the method of rejected fractions.

Jefferson's Method

Jefferson's method of reapportionment resulted in great inequalities among districts. A Vermont district would contain 42,766 inhabitants, a New Jersey district 35,911, and a Virginia district only 33,187. Jefferson's method emphasized what was considered to be the ideal size of a congressional district rather than what the size of the House ought to be.

The reapportionment act based on the census of 1800 continued the ratio of 33,000, which provided a House of 141 members. The third apportionment bill, enacted in 1811, fixed the ratio at 35,000, yielding a House of 181 members. Following the 1820 census Congress set the ratio at 40,000 inhabitants per district, which produced a House of 213 members. The act of May 22, 1832, fixed the ratio at 47,700, resulting in a House of 240 members.

Dissatisfaction with inequalities produced by the method of rejected fractions grew. Launching a vigorous attack against it, Daniel Webster urged adoption of a method that would assign an additional representative to each state with a large fraction. Webster outlined his reasoning in a report he submitted to Congress in 1832:

> The Constitution, therefore, must be understood not as enjoining an absolute relative equality—because that would be demanding an impossibility—but as requiring of Congress to make the apportionment of Representatives among the several states according to their respective numbers, *as near as may be.* That which cannot be done perfectly must be done in a manner as near perfection as can be.... In such a case approximation becomes a rule.[9]

Following the 1840 census Congress adopted a reapportionment method similar to that advocated by Webster. The method fixed a ratio of one representative for every 70,680 people. This figure was reached by deciding on a fixed size of the House in advance (223), dividing that figure into the total national "representative population," and using the result (70,680) as the fixed ratio. The population of each state was then divided by this ratio to find the number of its representatives and the states were assigned an additional representative for each fraction over one-half. Under this method the actual size of the House dropped. *(Congressional apportionment, box, page 5)*

The modified reapportionment formula adopted by Congress in 1842 was more satisfactory than the previous method, but another change was made following the census of 1850. Proposed by Rep. Samuel F. Vinton of Ohio, the new system became known as the Vinton method.

Vinton Apportionment Formula

Under the Vinton formula Congress first fixed the size of the House and then distributed the seats. The total qualifying population of the country was divided by the desired number of representatives, and the resulting number became the ratio of population to each representative. The population of each state was divided by this ratio, and each state received the number of representatives equal to the whole number in the quotient for that state. Then, to reach the required size of the House, additional representatives were assigned based on the remaining fractions, beginning with the state having the largest fraction. This procedure differed from the 1842 method only in the last step, which assigned one representative to every state having a fraction larger than one-half.

Proponents of the Vinton method pointed out that it had the distinct advantage of fixing the size of the House in advance and taking into account at least the largest fractions. The concern of the House turned from the ideal size of a congressional district to the ideal size of the House itself.

Under the 1842 reapportionment formula, the exact size of the House could not be fixed in advance. If every state with a fraction over one-half were given an additional representative, the House might wind up with a few more or a few less than the desired number. However, under the Vinton method, only states with the largest fractions were given additional House members and only up to the desired total size of the House.

Vinton Apportionments

Six reapportionments were carried out under the Vinton method. The 1850 census act contained three provisions not included in any previous law. First, it required reapportionment not only after the census of 1850 but also after all the subsequent censuses; second, it purported to fix the size of the House permanently at 233 members; and third, it provided in advance for an automatic apportionment by the secretary of the interior under the method prescribed in the act.

Following the census of 1860 an automatic reapportionment was to be carried out by the Interior Department. However, because the size of the House was to remain at the 1850 level, some states faced loss of representation and others were to gain fewer seats than they expected. To avert that possibility, an act was approved in 1862 increasing the size of the House to 241 and giving an extra representative to eight states—Illinois, Iowa, Kentucky, Minnesota, Ohio, Pennsylvania, Rhode Island, and Vermont.

Apportionment legislation following the 1870 census contained several new provisions. The act fixed the size of the House at 283, with the proviso that the number should be increased if new states were admitted. A supplemental act assigned one additional representative each to Alabama, Florida, Indiana, Louisiana, New Hampshire, New York, Pennsylvania, Tennessee and Vermont.

With the Reconstruction era at its height in the South, the reapportionment legislation of 1872 reflected the desire of Congress to enforce Section 2 of the new Fourteenth Amendment. That section attempted to protect the right of blacks to vote by providing for reduction of representation in the House of a state that interfered with the exercise of that right. The number of representatives of such a state was to be reduced in proportion to the number of inhabitants of voting age whose right to go to the polls was denied or abridged. The reapportionment bill repeated the language of Section 2, but the provision never was put into effect because of the difficulty of determining the exact number of people whose right to vote was being abridged.

The reapportionment act of 1882 provided for a House of 325 members, with additional members for any new states admitted to the Union. No new apportionment provisions were added. The acts of 1891 and 1901 were routine as far as apportionment was concerned. The 1891 measure provided for a House of 356 members, and the 1901 statute increased the number to 386.

Problems with Vinton Method

Despite the apparent advantages of the Vinton method, certain difficulties revealed themselves as the formula was

Congressional Apportionment, 1789-1990

	Constitution[2] (1789)	Year of Census[1]																			
		1790	1800	1810	1820	1830	1840	1850	1860	1870	1880	1890	1900	1910	1930[3]	1940	1950	1960	1970	1980	1990
Ala.				1[4]	3	5	7	7	6	8	8	9	9	10	9	9	9	8	7	7	7
Alaska																	1[4]	1	1	1	1
Ariz.														1[4]	1	2	2	3	4	5	6
Ark.						1[4]	1	2	3	4	5	6	7	7	7	7	6	4	4	4	4
Calif.							2[4]	2	3	4	6	7	8	11	20	23	30	38	43	45	52
Colo.										1[4]	1	2	3	4	4	4	4	4	5	6	6
Conn.	5	7	7	7	6	6	4	4	4	4	4	4	5	5	6	6	6	6	6	6	6
Del.	1	1	1	2	1	1	1	1	1	1	1	1	1	1	1	1	1	1	1	1	1
Fla.							1[4]	1	1	2	2	2	3	4	5	6	8	12	15	19	23
Ga.	3	2	4	6	7	9	8	8	7	9	10	11	11	12	10	10	10	10	10	10	11
Hawaii																	1[4]	2	2	2	2
Idaho											1[4]	1	1	2	2	2	2	2	2	2	2
Ill.				1[4]	1	3	7	9	14	19	20	22	25	27	27	26	25	24	24	22	20
Ind.				1[4]	3	7	10	11	11	13	13	13	13	13	12	11	11	11	11	10	10
Iowa							2[4]	2	6	9	11	11	11	11	9	8	8	7	6	6	5
Kan.									1	3	7	8	8	8	7	6	6	5	5	5	4
Ky.		2	6	10	12	13	10	10	9	10	11	11	11	11	9	9	8	7	7	7	6
La.				1[4]	3	3	4	4	5	6	6	6	7	8	8	8	8	8	8	8	7
Maine				7[4]	7	8	7	6	5	5	4	4	4	4	3	3	3	2	2	2	2
Md.	6	8	9	9	9	8	6	6	5	6	6	6	6	6	6	6	7	8	8	8	8
Mass.	8	14	17	13[5]	13	12	10	11	10	11	12	13	14	16	15	14	14	12	12	11	10
Mich.							1[4]	3	4	6	9	11	12	13	17	17	18	19	19	18	16
Minn.									2[4]	2	3	5	7	9	10	9	9	9	8	8	8
Miss.				1[4]	1	2	4	5	5	6	7	7	8	8	7	7	6	5	5	5	5
Mo.					1	2	5	7	9	13	14	15	16	16	13	13	11	10	10	9	9
Mont.											1[4]	1	1	2	2	2	2	2	2	2	1
Neb.									1[4]	1	3	6	6	6	5	4	4	3	3	3	3
Nev.									1[4]	1	1	1	1	1	1	1	1	1	1	2	2
N.H.	3	4	5	6	6	5	4	3	3	3	2	2	2	2	2	2	2	2	2	2	2
N.J.	4	5	6	6	6	6	5	5	5	7	7	8	10	12	14	14	14	15	15	14	13
N.M.														1[4]	1	2	2	2	2	3	3
N.Y.	6	10	17	27	34	40	34	33	31	33	34	34	37	43	45	45	43	41	39	34	31
N.C.	5	10	12	13	13	13	9	8	7	8	9	9	10	10	11	12	12	11	11	11	12
N.D.											1[4]	1	2	3	2	2	2	2	1	1	1
Ohio			1[4]	6	14	19	21	21	19	20	21	21	21	22	24	23	23	24	23	21	19
Okla.														5[4]	8	9	8	6	6	6	6
Ore.								1[4]	1	1	1	2	2	3	3	4	4	4	4	5	5
Pa.	8	13	18	23	26	28	24	25	24	27	28	30	32	36	34	33	30	27	25	23	21
R.I.	1	2	2	2	2	2	2	2	2	2	2	2	2	3	2	2	2	2	2	2	2
S.C.	5	6	8	9	9	9	7	6	4	5	7	7	7	7	6	6	6	6	6	6	6
S.D.											2[4]	2	2	3	2	2	2	2	2	1	1
Tenn.		1[4]	3	6	9	13	11	10	8	10	10	10	10	10	9	10	9	9	8	9	9
Texas							2[4]	2	4	6	11	13	16	18	21	21	22	23	24	27	30
Utah												1[4]	1	2	2	2	2	2	2	3	3
Vt.		2	4	6	5	5	4	3	3	3	2	2	2	2	1	1	1	1	1	1	1
Va.	10	19	22	23	22	21	15	13	11	9	10	10	10	10	9	9	10	10	10	10	11
Wash.											1[4]	2	3	5	6	6	7	7	7	8	9
W.Va.										3	4	4	5	6	6	6	6	5	4	4	3
Wis.							2[4]	3	6	8	9	10	11	11	10	10	10	10	9	9	9
Wyo.											1[4]	1	1	1	1	1	1	1	1	1	1
Total	65	106	142	186	213	242	232	237	243	293	332	357	391	435	435	435	437[6]	435	435	435	435

1. Apportionment effective with congressional election two years after census.
2. Original apportionment made in Constitution, pending first census.
3. No apportionment was made in 1920.
4. These figures are not based on any census, but indicate the provisional representation accorded newly admitted states by Congress, pending the next census.
5. Twenty members were assigned to Massachusetts, but seven of these were credited to Maine when that area became a state.
6. Normally 435, but temporarily increased two seats by Congress when Alaska and Hawaii became states.

Sources: Biographical Directory of the American Congress and Bureau of the Census.

applied. Zechariah Chafee, Jr., of the Harvard Law School summarized these problems in an article in the *Harvard Law Review* in 1929. The method, he pointed out, suffered from what he called the "Alabama paradox." Under that aberration, an increase in the total size of the House might be accompanied by an actual loss of a seat by some states, even though there had been no corresponding change in population. This phenomenon first appeared in tables prepared for Congress in 1881, which gave Alabama eight members in a House of 299 but only seven members in a House of 300. It could even happen that the state that lost a seat was the one state that had expanded in population, while all the others had fewer people.

Chafee concluded from his study of the Vinton method:

Thus, it is unsatisfactory to fix the ratio of population per Representative before seats are distributed. Either the size of the House comes out haphazard, or, if this be determined in advance, the absurdities of the "Alabama paradox" vitiate the apportionment. Under present conditions, it is essential to determine the size of the House in advance; the problem thereafter is to distribute the required number of seats among the several states as nearly as possible in proportion to their respective populations so that no state is treated unfairly in comparison with any other state.[10]

Maximum Membership of House

In 1911 the membership of the House was fixed at 433. Provision was made for the addition of one representative each from Arizona and New Mexico, which were expected to become states in the near future. Thus, the size of the House reached 435, where it has remained with the exception of a brief period, 1959-63, when the admission of Alaska and Hawaii raised the total temporarily to 437.

Limiting the size of the House amounted to recognition that the body soon would expand to unmanageable proportions if Congress continued the practice of adding new seats every 10 years to match population gains without depriving any state of its existing representation. Agreement on a fixed number made the task of reapportionment all the more difficult when the population not only increased but became much more mobile. Population shifts brought Congress up hard against the politically painful necessity of taking seats away from slow-growing states to give the fast-growing states adequate representation.

A new mathematical calculation was adopted for the reapportionment following the 1910 census. Devised by W. F. Willcox of Cornell University, the new system established a priority list that assigned seats progressively, beginning with the first seat above the constitutional minimum of at least one seat for each state. When there were 48 states, this method was used to assign the forty-ninth member, the fiftieth member, and so on, until the agreed upon size of the House was reached. The method was called major fractions and was used after the censuses of 1910, 1930, and 1940. There was no reapportionment after the 1920 census.

1920s Struggle

The results of the fourteenth decennial census were announced in December 1920, just after the short session of the 66th Congress convened. The 1920 census showed that for the first time in history most Americans were urban residents. This came as a profound shock to people accustomed to emphasizing the nation's rural traditions and the virtues of life on farms and in small towns as Thomas Jefferson had. Jefferson once wrote:

Those who labor in the earth are the chosen people of God, if ever He had a chosen people, whose breasts He had made His peculiar deposit for substantial and genuine virtue. . . . The mobs of great cities add just as much to the support of pure government as sores do to the strength of the human body. . . . I think our governments will remain virtuous for many centuries as long as they are chiefly agricultural: and this shall be as long as there shall be vacant lands in any part of America. When they get piled up upon one another in large cities as in Europe, they will become corrupt as in Europe.[11]

As their power waned throughout the latter part of the nineteenth century and the early part of the twentieth, farmers clung to the Jeffersonian belief that somehow they were more pure and virtuous than the growing number of urban residents. When finally faced with the fact that they were in the minority, these country residents put up a strong rearguard action to prevent the inevitable shift of congressional districts to the cities. They succeeded in postponing reapportionment legislation for almost a decade.

Rural representatives insisted that, because the 1920 census was taken as of January 1, the farm population had been undercounted. In support of this contention, they argued that many farm laborers were seasonally employed in the cities at that time of year. Furthermore, midwinter road conditions probably had prevented enumerators from visiting many farms, they said, and other farmers were said to have been uncounted because they were absent on winter vacation trips. The change of the census date to January 1 in 1920 had been made to conform to recommendations of the U.S. Department of Agriculture, which had asserted that the census should be taken early in the year if an accurate statistical picture of farming conditions was to be obtained.

Another point raised by rural legislators was that large numbers of unnaturalized aliens were congregated in northern cities, with the result that these cities gained at the expense of constituencies made up mostly of citizens of the United States. Rep. Homer Hoch, R-Kan., submitted a table showing that in a House of 435 representatives, exclusion from the census count of people not naturalized would have altered the allocation of seats in 16 states. Southern and western farming states would have retained the number of seats allocated to them in 1911 or would have gained, while northern industrial states and California would have lost or at least would have gained fewer seats.

A constitutional amendment to exclude all aliens from the enumeration for purposes of reapportionment was proposed during the 70th Congress (1927-29) by Hoch, Sen. Arthur Capper, R-Kan., and others. But nothing further came of the proposals.

Reapportionment Bills Opposed

The first bill to reapportion the House according to the 1920 census was drafted by the House Census Committee early in 1921. Proceeding on the principle that no state should have its representation reduced, the committee proposed to increase the total number of representatives from 435 to 483. But the House voted 267-76 to keep its membership at 435. The bill then was blocked by a Senate committee, where it died when the 66th Congress expired March 4, 1921.

State Population Totals, House Seat Changes

	1980 Population[1]	1990 Population[1]	% change	1982 seats	1992 seats	1990 seat change
Ala.	3,983,888	4,040,587	3.8	7	7	0
Alaska	401,851	550,043	36.9	1	1	0
Ariz.	2,718,215	3,665,228	34.8	5	6	+1
Ark.	2,286,435	2,350,725	2.8	4	4	0
Calif.	23,667,902	29,760,021	25.7	45	52	+7
Colo.	2,889,964	3,294,394	14.0	6	6	0
Conn.	3,107,576	3,287,116	5.8	6	6	0
Del.	594,338	666,168	12.1	1	1	0
D.C.[2]	638,333	606,900	−4.9	—	—	—
Fla.	9,746,324	12,937,926	32.7	19	23	+4
Ga.	5,463,105	6,478,216	18.6	10	11	+1
Hawaii	964,691	1,108,229	14.9	2	2	0
Idaho	943,935	1,006,749	6.7	2	2	0
Ill.	11,426,518	11,430,602	—	22	20	−2
Ind.	5,490,224	5,544,159	1.0	10	10	0
Iowa	2,913,808	2,776,755	−4.7	6	5	−1
Kan.	2,363,679	2,477,574	4.8	5	4	−1
Ky.	3,660,777	3,685,296	0.8	7	6	−1
La.	4,205,900	4,219,973	0.3	8	7	−1
Maine	1,124,660	1,227,928	9.2	2	2	0
Md.	4,216,975	4,781,468	13.4	8	8	0
Mass.	5,737,037	6,016,425	4.9	11	10	−1
Mich.	9,262,078	9,295,297	0.4	18	16	−2
Minn.	4,075,970	4,375,099	7.3	8	8	0
Miss.	2,520,638	2,573,216	2.1	5	5	0
Mo.	4,916,686	5,117,073	4.1	9	9	0
Mont.	786,690	799,065	1.6	2	1	−1
Neb.	1,569,825	1,578,385	0.5	3	3	0
Nev.	800,493	1,201,833	50.1	2	2	0
N.H.	920,610	1,109,252	20.5	2	2	0
N.J.	7,364,823	7,730,188	5.0	14	13	−1
N.M.	1,302,894	1,515,069	16.3	3	3	0
N.Y.	17,558,072	17,990,455	2.5	34	31	−3
N.C.	5,881,766	6,628,637	12.7	11	12	+1
N.D.	652,717	638,800	−2.1	1	1	0
Ohio	10,797,630	10,847,115	0.5	21	19	−2
Okla.	3,025,290	3,145,585	4.0	6	6	0
Ore.	2,633,105	2,842,321	7.9	5	5	0
Pa.	11,863,895	11,881,632	0.1	23	21	−2
R.I.	947,154	1,003,464	5.9	2	2	0
S.C.	3,121,820	3,486,703	11.7	6	6	0
S.D.	690,768	696,004	0.8	1	1	0
0enn.	4,591,120	4,877,185	6.2	9	9	0
Texas	14,229,191	16,986,510	19.4	27	30	+3
Utah	1,461,037	1,722,850	17.9	3	3	0
Vt.	511,456	562,758	10.0	1	1	0
Va.	5,346,818	6,187,358	15.7	10	11	+1
Wash.	4,132,156	4,866,692	17.8	8	9	+1
W.Va.	1,949,644	1,793,477	−8.0	4	3	−1
Wis.	4,705,767	4,891,769	4.0	9	9	0
Wyo.	469,557	453,588	−3.4	1	1	0
U.S.[3]	226,545,805	248,709,873	9.8	435	435	19

1. For comparative purposes, the 1980 and 1990 figures do not include citizens living overseas.
2. The District of Columbia, which has one nonvoting delegate to the House, is not included in determination of apportionment.
3. Total population for 1980 and 1990 includes the District of Columbia.

Early in the 67th Congress, the House Census Committee again reported a bill, this time fixing the total membership at 460, an increase of 25. Two states—Maine and Massachusetts—would have lost one representative each and 16 states would have gained. On the House floor an unsuccessful attempt was made to fix the number at the existing 435, and the House sent the bill back to committee.

During the 68th Congress (1923-25), the House Census Committee failed to report any reapportionment bill. In April 1926, midway through the 69th Congress (1925-27), it became apparent that the committee would not produce a reapportionment measure. A motion to discharge a reapportionment bill from the committee failed, however, and the matter once again put aside.

Coolidge Intervention

President Calvin Coolidge, who previously had made no reference to reapportionment in his communications to Congress, announced in January 1927 that he favored passage of a new apportionment bill during the short session of the 69th Congress, which would end in less than two months. The House Census Committee refused to act. Its chairman, Rep. E. Hart Fenn, R-Conn., therefore moved in the House to suspend the rules and pass a bill he had introduced authorizing the secretary of commerce to reapportion the House immediately after the 1930 census. The motion was voted down 183-197.

The Fenn bill was rewritten early in the 70th Congress (1927-29) to give Congress itself a chance to act before the proposed reapportionment by the secretary of commerce should go into effect. The House passed an amended version of the Fenn bill in January 1929, and it was quickly reported by the Senate Commerce Committee. Repeated efforts to bring it up for floor action ahead of other bills failed. Its supporters gave up the fight when it became evident that senators from states slated to lose representation were ready to carry on a filibuster that would have blocked not only reapportionment but all other measures.

Hoover Intervention

President Herbert Hoover listed provision for the 1930 census and reapportionment as "matters of emergency legislation" that should be acted upon in the special session of the 71st Congress, which was convened on April 15, 1929. In response to this urgent request, the Senate June 13 passed, 48-37, a combined census-reapportionment bill that had been approved by voice vote of the House two days earlier.

The 1929 law established a permanent system of reapportioning the 435 House seats following each census. It provided that immediately after the convening of the 71st Congress for its short session in December 1930, the president was to transmit to Congress a statement showing the population of each state together with an apportionment of representatives to each state based on the existing size of the House. Failing enactment of new apportionment legislation, that apportionment would go into effect without further action and would remain in effect for ensuing elections to the House of Representatives until another census had been taken and another reapportionment made.

Because two decades had passed between reapportionments, a greater shift than usual took place following the 1930 census. California's House delegation was almost doubled, rising from 11 to 20. Michigan gained four seats, Texas three, and New

Jersey, New York, and Ohio two each. Twenty-one states lost a total of 27 seats; Missouri lost three, and Georgia, Iowa, Kentucky, and Pennsylvania each lost two.

To test the fairness of two allocation methods—the familiar major fractions and the new equal proportions system—the 1929 act required the president to report the distribution of seats by both methods. But, pending legislation to the contrary, the method of major fractions was to be used.

The two methods gave an identical distribution of seats based on 1930 census figures. However, in 1940 the two methods gave different results: under major fractions, Michigan would gain a seat lost by Arkansas; under equal proportions, no change would occur in either state. The automatic reapportionment provisions of the 1929 act went into effect in January 1941. But the House Census Committee moved to reverse the result, favoring the method of equal proportions and the certain Democratic seat in Arkansas over a possible Republican gain if the seat were shifted to Michigan. The Democratic-controlled Congress went along, adopting equal proportions as the method to be used in reapportionment calculations after the 1950 and subsequent censuses, and making this action retroactive to January 1941 to save Arkansas its seat.

While politics doubtless played a part in the timing of the action taken in 1941, the method of equal proportions had come to be accepted as the best available: It had been worked out by Edward V. Huntington of Harvard in 1921. At the request of the Speaker of the House, all known methods of apportionment were considered in 1929 by the National Academy of Sciences Committee on Apportionment. The committee expressed its preference for equal proportions.

Method of Equal Proportions

The method of equal proportions involves complicated mathematical calculations. In brief, each of the 50 states is initially assigned the one seat to which it is entitled by the Constitution. Then "priority numbers" for states to receive second seats, third seats, and so on are calculated by dividing the state's population by the square root of $n(n-1)$, where "n" is the number of seats for that state. The priority numbers are then lined up in order and the seats given to the states with priority numbers until 435 are awarded.

The method is designed to make the proportional difference in the average district size in any two states as small as possible. After the 1981 reapportionment, for example, South Dakota's single district was the most populous, with 690,768 residents, while Montana's two districts, each with slightly fewer than 400,000 people, were the least populous. Under the 1990 apportionment, Montana lost a seat; its remaining district is the most populous, with 803,655 residents. With 455,975 people, Wyoming's single district is the least populous. The mean population per district nationwide is about 572,500.

The 1990 Apportionment

Concern about the accuracy of the 1990 census, which is the basis for reapportionment and redistricting, led to calls for a statistical adjustment of the census count to compensate for a population undercount. An undercount was not a new problem. In 1980 the Census Bureau estimated that it counted about 99 percent of the white population but only about 94 percent of the blacks. In addition to determining the number of House seats each state has, the census is also the basis for distributing

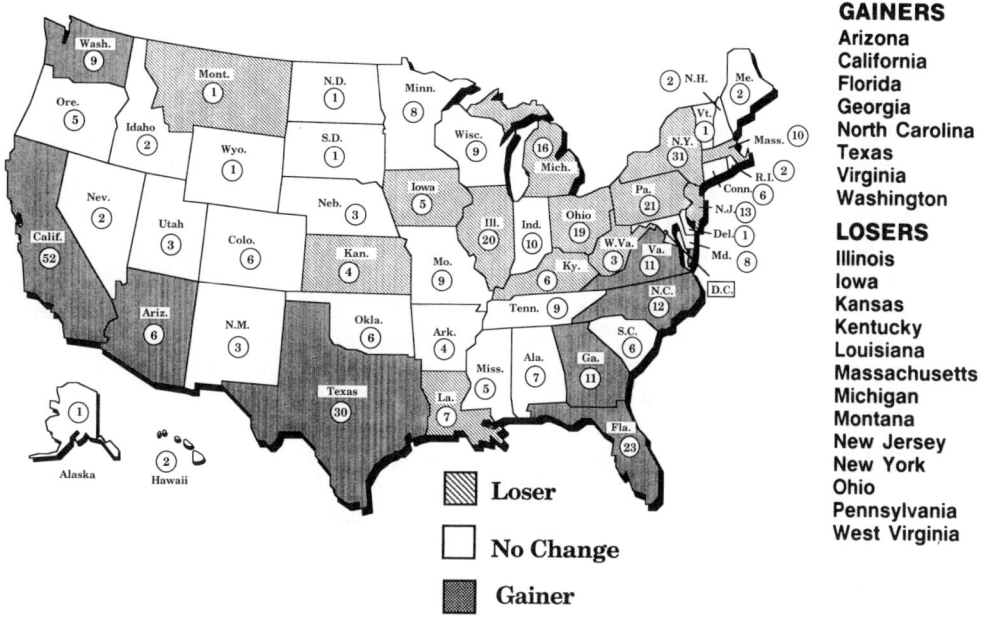

GAINERS
Arizona
California
Florida
Georgia
North Carolina
Texas
Virginia
Washington

LOSERS
Illinois
Iowa
Kansas
Kentucky
Louisiana
Massachusetts
Michigan
Montana
New Jersey
New York
Ohio
Pennsylvania
West Virginia

Loser

No Change

Gainer

Note: Circled number indicates state's House seats under 1990 reapportionment.

funding for many federal aid programs. Democrats, especially those representing inner-city districts where the undercount is comparatively high, have long argued for a statistical adjustment to compensate for undercounting. Several cities with large minority populations sought but failed to win adjustment of the 1980 census count.

Given the disappointing response to the census questionnaire and other problems encountered in conducting the 1990 census, many observers estimated that the undercount would be higher than the 1980 undercount. But the controversy over the 1990 count began even before the census was taken, when the Commerce Department, the parent agency to the Census Bureau, announced in 1987 that it would not statistically adjust the 1990 data. That fueled charges that the Republican administration was undercounting a Democratic constituency. New York City, along with other cities, states, and civil rights organizations, quickly brought a lawsuit to force the Census Bureau to make a statistical adjustment to account for people who were missed. But in April 1993 a federal judge in New York upheld the Commerce Department's decision not to adjust the head count. *(Census count, box, page 15)*

REDISTRICTING: DRAWING THE LINES

Although the Constitution contained provisions for the apportionment of U.S. House seats among the states, it was silent about how the members should be elected. From the beginning

most states divided their territory into geographic districts, permitting only one member of Congress to be elected from each district.

But some states allowed would-be House members to run at large, with voters able to cast as many votes as there were seats to be filled. Still other states created what were known as multimember districts, in which a single geographic unit would elect two or more members of the House. At various times, some states used combinations of these methods. For example, a state might elect 10 representatives from 10 individual districts and two at large.

In the first few elections to the House, New Hampshire, Pennsylvania, New Jersey and Georgia elected their representatives at large, as did Rhode Island and Delaware, the two states with only a single representative. Districts were used in Massachusetts, New York, Maryland, Virginia and South Carolina. In Connecticut a preliminary election was held to nominate three times as many people as the number of representatives to be chosen at large in the subsequent election. In 1840 22 of the 31 states elected their representatives by districts. New Hampshire, New Jersey, Georgia, Alabama, Mississippi, and Missouri, with a combined representation of 33 House seats, elected their representatives at large. Three states, Arkansas, Delaware, and Florida, had only one representative each.

Those states that used congressional districts quickly developed what came to be known as the gerrymander. The term refers to the practice of drawing district lines so as to maximize the advantage of a political party or interest group. The name originated from a salamander-shaped congressional district created by the Massachusetts Legislature in 1812 when Elbridge Gerry was governor. *(Box, page 11)*

Constant efforts were made during the early 1800s to lay down national rules, by means of a constitutional amendment, for congressional districting. The first resolution proposing a mandatory division of each state into districts was introduced in Congress in 1800. In 1802 the legislatures of Vermont and North Carolina adopted resolutions in support of such action. From 1816 to 1826 22 states adopted resolutions proposing the election of representatives by districts.

In Congress Sen. Mahlon Dickerson, R-N.J., proposed such an amendment regularly almost every year from 1817 to 1826. It was adopted by the Senate three times, in 1819, 1820 and 1822, but each time it failed to reach a vote in the House. Although the constitutional amendment was unsuccessful, a law passed in 1842 required contiguous single-member congressional districts. That law required representatives to be "elected by districts composed of contiguous territory equal in number to the representatives to which said state may be entitled, no one district electing more than one Representative."

The districting provisions of the 1842 act were not repeated in the legislation that followed the 1850 census. But in 1862 an act separate from the reapportionment act revived the provisions of the act of 1842 requiring districts to be composed of contiguous territory.

The 1872 reapportionment act again repeated the districting provisions and went even further by adding that districts should contain "as nearly as practicable an equal number of inhabitants." Similar provisions were included in the acts of 1881 and 1891. In the act of 1901, the words "compact territory" were added, and the clause then read "contiguous and compact territory and containing as nearly as practicable an equal number of inhabitants." This requirement appeared also in the legislation of 1911. The "contiguous and compact" provisions of the act subsequently lapsed, and Congress has never replaced them.

Several unsuccessful attempts were made to enforce redistricting provisions. Despite the districting requirements enacted in 1842, New Hampshire, Georgia, Mississippi and Missouri elected their representatives at large that autumn. When the new House convened for its first session, on December 4, 1843, objection was made to seating the representatives of the four states.

The House debated the matter in February 1844. With the Democratic party holding a majority of more than 60, and with 18 of the 21 challenged members being Democrats, the House decided to seat the members. However, by 1848 all four states had come around to electing their representatives by districts.

The next challenge a representative encountered over federal districting laws occurred in 1901. A charge was leveled that the existing Kentucky redistricting law did not comply with the reapportionment law of 1901; the charge aimed at preventing the seating of Rep. George G. Gilbert, D, of Kentucky's Eighth District. The committee assigned to investigate the matter turned aside the challenge, asserting that the federal act was not binding on the states. The reasons given were practical and political:

Your committee are therefore of opinion that a proper construction of the Constitution does not warrant the conclusion that by that instrument Congress is clothed with power to determine the boundaries of Congressional districts, or to revise the acts of a State Legislature in fixing such boundaries; and your committee is further of opinion that even if such power is to be implied from the language of the Constitution, it would be in the last degree unwise and intolerable that it should exercise it. To do so would be to put into the hands of Congress the ability to disfranchise, in effect, a large body of the electors. It would give

Congress the power to apply to all the States, in favor of one party, a general system of gerrymandering. It is true that the same method is to a large degree resorted to by the several states, but the division of political power is so general and diverse that notwithstanding the inherent vice of the system of gerrymandering, some kind of equality of distribution results.[12]

In 1908 the Virginia Legislature transferred Floyd County from the Fifth District to the Sixth District. As a result, the population of the Fifth was reduced from 175,579 to 160,191 and that of the Sixth was increased from 181,571 to 196,959. The average for the state was 185,418. The newly elected representative from the Fifth District, Edward W. Saunders, D, was challenged by his opponent in the election on the ground that the Virginia law of 1908 was null and void because it did not conform with the federal reapportionment law of 1901, or with the constitution of Virginia. Had the district included the counties that were a part of it before enactment of the 1908 state legislation, Saunders's opponent would have had a majority of the votes.

The majority of the congressional investigating committee upheld the challenge and recommended that Saunders's opponent be seated. For the first time, it appeared that the districting legislation would be enforced, but the House did not take action on the committee's report and Saunders was seated.

Court Action on Redistricting

After the long and desultory battle over reapportionment in the 1920s, those who were unhappy over the inaction of Congress and the state legislatures began taking their cases to court. At first, the protestors had no luck. But as the population disparities grew in both federal and state legislative districts and the Supreme Court began to show a tendency to intervene, the objectors were more successful.

Finally, in a series of decisions beginning in 1962 with *Baker v. Carr* (369 U.S. 186) the Court exerted great influence over the redistricting process, ordering that congressional districts as well as state and local legislative districts be drawn so that their populations would be as nearly equal as possible.[13]

Supreme Court's 1932 Decision

Baker v. Carr essentially reversed the direction the Court had taken in 1932. *Wood v. Broom* (287 U.S. 1) was a case challenging the constitutionality of a Mississippi redistricting law because it violated the standards of the 1911 federal redistricting act. The question was whether the federal act was still in effect. That law, which required that districts be separate, compact, contiguous and equally populated, had been neither specifically repealed nor reaffirmed in the 1929 reapportionment act.

Speaking for the Court, Chief Justice Charles Evans Hughes ruled that the 1911 act, in effect, had expired with the approval of the 1929 apportionment act and that the standards of the 1911 act therefore were no longer applicable. The Court reversed the decision of a lower federal court, which had permanently enjoined elections under the new Mississippi redistricting act.

That the Supreme Court upheld a state law that failed to provide for districts of equal population was almost less important than the minority opinion that the Court should not have heard the case. Justices Louis D. Brandeis, Harlan F. Stone, Owen J. Roberts and Benjamin N. Cardozo, while concurring in the majority opinion, said they would have dismissed the Wood suit for "want of equity." The "want-of-equity" phrase in this context suggested a policy of judicial self-limitation with respect to the entire question of judicial involvement in essentially "political" questions.

"Political Thicket"

Not until 1946, in *Colegrove v. Green* (328 U.S. 549), did the Court again rule in a significant case dealing with congressional redistricting. The case was brought by Kenneth Colegrove, a political science professor at Northwestern University, who alleged that congressional districts in Illinois, which varied between 112,116 and 914,053 in population, were so unequal that they violated the Fourteenth Amendment's guarantee of equal protection of the laws. A seven-member Supreme Court divided 4-3 in dismissing the suit.

Justice Felix Frankfurter gave the opinion of the Court, speaking for himself and Justices Stanley F. Reed and Harold H. Burton. Frankfurter's opinion cited *Wood v. Broom* to indicate that Congress had deliberately removed the standard set by the 1911 act. He also said that he, Reed, and Burton agreed with the minority that the Court should have dismissed the case. The issue, Frankfurter said, was

> of a peculiarly political nature and therefore not meant for judicial interpretation. . . . The short of it is that the Constitution has conferred upon Congress exclusive authority to secure fair representation by the states in the popular House and has left to that House determination whether states have fulfilled their responsibility. If Congress failed in exercising its powers, whereby standards of fairness are offended, the remedy lies ultimately with the people. . . . To sustain this action would cut very deep into the very being of Congress. Courts ought not to enter this political thicket. The remedy for unfairness in districting is to secure state legislatures that will apportion properly, or to invoke the ample powers of Congress.

Frankfurter also said that the Court could not affirmatively remap congressional districts and that elections at large would be politically undesirable.

In a dissenting opinion Justice Hugo L. Black, joined by Justices William O. Douglas and Frank Murphy, maintained that the district court did have jurisdiction over congressional redistricting. The three justices cited as evidence a section of the U.S. Code that allowed district courts to redress deprivations of constitutional rights occurring through action of the states. Black's opinion also rested on an earlier case in which the Court had indicated that federal constitutional questions, unless "frivolous," fall under the jurisdiction of the federal courts. Black asserted that the appellants had standing to sue and that the population disparities violated the equal protection clause of the Fourteenth Amendment.

With the Court split 3-3 on whether the judiciary had or should exercise jurisdiction, Justice Wiley B. Rutledge cast the deciding vote in *Colegrove v. Green*. On the question of justiciability, Rutledge agreed with Black, Douglas and Murphy that the issue could be considered by the federal courts. Thus a majority of the Court participating in the *Colegrove* case felt that congressional redistricting cases were justiciable.

Yet on the question of granting relief in this specific instance, Rutledge agreed with Frankfurter, Reed and Burton that the case should be dismissed. He pointed out that four of the nine justices in *Wood v. Broom* had felt that dismissal should be for want of equity. Rutledge saw a "want-of-equity" situation in *Colegrove v. Green* as well. "I think the gravity of the constitutional questions raised [are] so great, together with the possibility

Origins of the Gerrymander

The practice of "gerrymandering"—the excessive manipulation of the shape of a legislative district to benefit a certain incumbent or party—is probably as old as the Republic, but the name originated in 1812.

In that year the Massachusetts Legislature carved out of Essex County a district which historian John Fiske said had a "dragonlike contour." When the painter Gilbert Stuart saw the misshapen district, he penciled in a head, wings, and claws and exclaimed: "That will do for a salamander!"—to which editor Benjamin Russell replied: "Better say a Gerrymander"—after Elbridge Gerry, then governor of Massachusetts.

The Bettmann Archive

of collision [with the political departments of the government], that the admonition [against avoidable constitutional decision] is appropriate to be followed here," Rutledge said. Jurisdiction, he thought, should be exercised "only in the most compelling circumstances." He thought that "the shortness of time remaining [before the forthcoming election] makes it doubtful whether action could or would be taken in time to secure for petitioners the effective relief they seek." Rutledge warned that congressional elections at large would deprive citizens of representation by districts, "which the prevailing policy of Congress demands." In the case of at-large elections, he said, "the cure sought may be worse than the disease." For all these reasons he concluded that the case was "one in which the Court may properly, and should, decline to exercise its jurisdiction."

Changing Views

In the ensuing years, law professors, political scientists and other commentators increasingly criticized the *Colegrove* doctrine and grew impatient with the Supreme Court's reluctance to intervene in redistricting disputes. At the same time, the membership of the Court was changing, and the new members were more inclined toward judicial action on redistricting.

In the 1950s the Court decided two cases that laid some groundwork for its subsequent reapportionment decisions. The first was *Brown v. Board of Education* (347 U.S. 483, 1954), the historic school desegregation case, in which the Court decided that an individual citizen could assert a right to equal protection of the laws under the Fourteenth Amendment, contrary to the "separate but equal" doctrine of public facilities for white and black citizens. Six years later, in *Gomillion v. Lightfoot* (364 U.S. 339, 1960), the Court held that the Alabama Legislature could not draw the city limits of Tuskegee so as to exclude nearly every black vote. In his opinion Justice Frankfurter drew a clear line between redistricting challenges based on the Fourteenth Amendment, such as *Colegrove*, and challenges to discriminatory redistricting based on the Fifteenth Amendment's voting rights protections, as in *Gomillion*. But Justice Charles E. Whittaker said that the equal protection clause was the proper constitutional basis for the decision. One commentator later remarked that *Gomillion* amounted to a "dragon" in the "political thicket" of *Colegrove*.

By 1962 only three members of the *Colegrove* Court remained: Justices Black and Douglas, dissenters in that case, and Justice Frankfurter, aging spokesman for restraint in the exercise of judicial power.

By then it was clear that malapportionment within the states no longer could be ignored. By 1960 not a single state legislative body existed in which there was not at least a 2-to-1 population disparity between the most and the least heavily populated districts. For example, the disparity was 242-1 in the Connecticut House, 223-1 in the Nevada Senate 141-1 in the Rhode Island Senate and 9-1 in the Georgia Senate. Studies of the effective vote of large and small counties in state legislatures between 1910 and 1960 showed that the effective vote of the most populous counties had slipped while their percentage of the national population had more than doubled. The most lightly populated counties, on the other hand, advanced from a position of slight overrepresentation to one of extreme overrepresentation, holding almost twice as many seats as they would be entitled to by population size alone. Predictably, the rural-dominated state legislatures resisted every move toward reapportioning state legislative districts to reflect new population patterns.

Population imbalance among congressional districts was substantially lopsided but by no means so gross. In Texas the 1960 census showed the most heavily populated district had four times as many inhabitants as the most lightly populated. Arizona, Maryland and Ohio each had at least one district with three times as many inhabitants as the least populated. In most cases rural areas benefited from the population imbalance in congressional districts. As a result of the postwar population movement out of central cities to the surrounding areas, the suburbs were the most underrepresented.

Baker v. Carr

Against this background a group of Tennessee city dwellers successfully broke the longstanding precedent against federal court involvement in legislative apportionment problems. For more than half a century, since 1901, the Tennessee Legislature had refused to reapportion itself, even though a decennial reapportionment based on population was specifically required

by the state's constitution. In the meantime, Tennessee's population had grown and shifted dramatically to urban areas. By 1960 the House legislative districts ranged from 3,454 to 36,031 in population, while the Senate districts ranged from 39,727 to 108,094. Appeals by urban residents to the rural-controlled Tennessee Legislature proved fruitless. A suit brought in the state courts to force reapportionment was rejected on grounds that the courts should stay out of legislative matters.

City dwellers then appealed to the federal courts, stating that they had no redress: the legislature had refused to act for more than half a century, the state courts had refused to intervene and Tennessee had no referendum or initiative laws. They charged that there was "a debasement of their votes by virtue of the incorrect, obsolete and unconstitutional apportionment" to such an extent that they were being deprived of their right to equal protection of the laws under the Fourteenth Amendment.

The Supreme Court on March 26, 1962, handed down its historic decision in *Baker v. Carr*, ruling in favor of the Tennessee city dwellers by a 6-2 margin. In the majority opinion, Justice William J. Brennan, Jr., emphasized that the federal judiciary had the power to review the apportionment of state legislatures under the Fourteenth Amendment's equal protection clause. "The mere fact that a suit seeks protection as a political right," Brennan wrote, "does not mean that it presents a political question" that the courts should avoid.

In a vigorous dissent, Justice Frankfurter said the majority decision constituted "a massive repudiation of the experience of our whole past" and was an assertion of "destructively novel judicial power." He contended that the lack of any clear basis for relief "catapults the lower courts" into a "mathematical quagmire." Frankfurter insisted that "there is not under our Constitution a judicial remedy for every political mischief." Appeal for relief, Frankfurter maintained, should not be made in the courts, but "to an informed civically militant electorate."

The Court had abandoned the view that malapportionment questions were outside its competence. But it stopped there and in *Baker v. Carr* did not address the merits of the challenge to the legislative districts.

Gray v. Sanders

The one-person, one-vote rule was set out by the Court almost exactly one year after its decision in *Baker v. Carr*. But the case in which the announcement came did not involve congressional districts.

In *Gray v. Sanders* (372 U.S. 368, 1963) the Court found that Georgia's county-unit primary system for electing state officials—a system that weighted votes to give advantage to rural districts in statewide primary elections—denied voters equal protection of the laws. All votes in a statewide election must have equal weight, the Court held:

> How then can one person be given twice or 10 times the voting power of another person in a statewide election merely because he lives in a rural area or because he lives in the smallest rural county? Once the geographical unit for which a representative is to be chosen is designated, all who participate in the election are to have an equal vote—whatever their race, whatever their sex, whatever their occupation, whatever their income, and wherever their home may be in that geographical unit. This is required by the Equal Protection Clause of the Fourteenth Amendment. The concept of "we the people" under the Constitution visualizes no preferred class of voters but equality among those who meet the

basic qualification. The idea that every voter is equal to every other voter in his State, when he casts his ballot in favor of one of several competing candidates, underlies many of our decisions. . . . The conception of political equality from the Declaration of Independence to Lincoln's Gettysburg Address, to the Fifteenth, Seventeenth, and Nineteenth Amendments can mean only one thing—one person, one vote.

The Rule Applied

The Court's rulings in *Baker* and *Gray* concerned the equal weighting and counting of votes cast in state elections. In 1964, deciding the case of *Wesberry v. Sanders*, the Court applied the one-person, one-vote principle to congressional districts and set equality as the standard for congressional redistricting.

Shortly after the *Baker* decision was handed down, James P. Wesberry, Jr., an Atlanta resident and a member of the Georgia Senate, filed suit in federal court in Atlanta claiming that gross disparity in the population of Georgia's congressional districts violated Fourteenth Amendment rights of equal protection of the laws. At the time, Georgia districts ranged in population from 272,154 in the rural Ninth District in the northeastern part of the state to 823,860 in the Fifth District in Atlanta and its suburbs. District lines had not been changed since 1931. The state's number of House seats remained the same in the interim, but Atlanta's district population—already high in 1931 compared with the others—had more than doubled in 30 years, making a Fifth District vote worth about one-third that of a vote in the Ninth. *(State population totals, House seat changes, page 7)*

In June 1962 the three-judge federal court divided 2-1 in dismissing Wesberry's suit. The majority reasoned that the precedent of *Colegrove* still controlled in congressional district cases. The judges cautioned against federal judicial interference with Congress and against "depriving others of the right to vote" if the suit should result in at-large elections. They suggested that the Georgia Legislature (under court order to reapportion itself) or the U.S. Congress might better provide relief. Wesberry then appealed to the Supreme Court.

On February 17, 1964, the Supreme Court ruled in *Wesberry v. Sanders* (376 U.S. 1) that congressional districts must be substantially equal in population. The Court, which upheld Wesberry's challenge by a 6-3 decision, based its ruling on the history and wording of Article I, Section 2, of the Constitution, which states that representatives shall be apportioned among the states according to their respective numbers and be chosen by the people of the several states. This language, the Court stated, meant that "as nearly as is practicable, one man's vote in a congressional election is to be worth as much as another's."

The majority opinion, written by Justice Black and supported by Chief Justice Earl Warren and Justices Brennan, Douglas, Arthur J. Goldberg, and Byron R. White, said: "While it may not be possible to draw congressional districts with mathematical precision, that is no excuse for ignoring our Constitution's plain objective of making equal representation for equal numbers of people the fundamental goal for the House of Representatives."

In a strongly worded dissent, Justice John M. Harlan asserted that the Constitution did not establish population as the only criterion of congressional districting but left the subject to the discretion of the states, subject only to the supervisory power of Congress. "The constitutional right which the Court creates is manufactured out of whole cloth," Harlan concluded.

The *Wesberry* opinion established no precise standards for

Gerrymandering: The Shape of the House

Traditionally, there are two types of gerrymanders. One is the partisan gerrymander, where a single party draws the lines to its advantage. The other is the proincumbent (sometimes called the "bipartisan" or "sweetheart") gerrymander, where the lines are drawn to protect incumbents, with any gains or losses in the number of seats shared between the two parties. In states where control of the state government is divided, proincumbent gerrymanders are common.

In the eyes of some Republicans, either species of gerrymander was likely to ensure their continued minority status in the House. Democrats, who have controlled the House since 1955, countered that the GOP suffered from unattractive candidates, not gerrymandered districts. The 1990 reapportionment saw widespread examples of a third type of gerrymander: drawing lines to preserve or create minority districts. *(Redistricting in the 1990s, page xv)*

Indeed, some academics maintain that the extent of gerrymandering and its impact on the composition of the House are exaggerated. "To a large extent," said Everett Carll Ladd, the director of the Roper Center for Public Opinion at the University of Connecticut, "the population is voting without regard to party. So the precise location of the congressional district lines is not so important as it was in an earlier era."

Partisan gerrymanders do not always achieve their goals. Indiana Republicans redrew their map in 1981 with the hope that it would turn the Democrats' congressional majority into a 7-3 GOP edge. Instead, by the end of the decade Democrats held a 7-3 advantage.

Given the extremely high incumbent reelection rates that have prevailed since the end of World War II, redistricting does increase the possibility of turnover, because most states must redraw their districts to accommodate population shifts within the state as well as the gain or loss of any seats. Typically, some House members choose to retire rather than stand for election in redesigned districts. But with rare exceptions a proincumbent spin in much of the line drawing diminishes the prospects for dramatic partisan turnover.

Sweetheart gerrymandering rarely attracts much attention. But this method of mapping has a powerful effect on the House. "Districts get more Democratic for Democrats and more Republican for Republicans. Competition is minimized," said Bernard Grofman, a political scientist at the University of California at Irvine. "Because the majority of House seats are controlled by Democrats, proincumbent line drawing helps perpetuate the Democratic House majority."

Source: Robert Benenson, Peter Bragdon, Rhodes Cook, Phil Duncan, Kenneth E. Jaques, *Jigsaw Politics: Shaping the House after the 1990 Census* (Washington, D.C.: Congressional Quarterly, 1990), 38.

districting beyond declaring that districts must be as nearly equal in population "as is practicable." In his dissent Harlan suggested that a disparity of more than 100,000 between a state's largest and smallest districts would "presumably" violate the equality standard enunciated by the majority. On that basis, Harlan estimated, the districts of 37 states with 398 representatives would be unconstitutional, "leaving a constitutional House of 37 members now sitting."

Neither did the Court's decision make any reference to gerrymandering, since it discussed only the population, not the shape of districts. In a separate opinion handed down the same day as *Wesberry,* the Court dismissed a challenge to congressional districts in New York City, which had been brought by voters who charged that Manhattan's "silk-stocking" Seventeenth District had been gerrymandered to exclude blacks and Puerto Ricans.

Strict Equality

Five years elapsed between *Wesberry v. Sanders* and the Court's next application of constitutional standards to congressional districting. In 1967 the Court hinted at the strict stance it would adopt two years later. With two unsigned opinions, the Court sent back to Indiana and Missouri for revision those two states' congressional redistricting plans because they allowed variations of as much as 20 percent from the average district population.

Two years later Missouri's revised plan returned to the Court for full review. By a 6-3 vote, the Court rejected the plan. It was unacceptable, the Court held in *Kirkpatrick v. Preisler* (385 U.S. 450, 1969), because it allowed a variation of as much as 3.1 percent from perfectly equal population districts. Thus the Court made clear its stringent application of the one-person, one-vote rule to congressional districts.

There was no "fixed numerical or percentage population variance small enough to be considered *de minimis* and to satisfy without question the 'as nearly as practicable' standard," Justice Brennan wrote for the Court. "Equal representation for equal numbers of people is a principle designed to prevent debasement of voting power and diminution of access to elected Representatives. Toleration of even small deviations detracts from these purposes."

The only permissible variances in population, the Court ruled, were those that were unavoidable despite the effort to achieve absolute equality or those that could be legally justified. The variances in Missouri could have been avoided, the Court said.

None of Missouri's arguments for the plan qualified as "legally acceptable" justifications. The Court rejected the argument that population variance was necessary to allow representation of distinct interest groups. It said that acceptance of such variances to produce districts with specific interests was "antithetical" to the basic purpose of equal representation.

Justice White dissented from the majority opinion, which he characterized as "an unduly rigid and unwarranted application of the Equal Protection Clause which will unnecessarily involve the courts in the abrasive task of drawing district lines." White added that some "acceptably small" population variance could be established. He indicated that considerations of existing political boundaries and geographical compactness could justify to him some variation from "absolute equality" of population.

Justice Harlan, joined by Justice Potter Stewart, dissented, saying that "whatever room remained under this Court's prior decisions for the free play of the political process in matters of reapportionment is now all but eliminated by today's Draconian judgments."

Practical Results

As a result of the Court's decisions of the 1960s, nearly every state was forced to redraw its congressional district lines— sometimes more than once. By the end of the decade, 39 of the 45 states with more than one representative had made the necessary adjustments.

However, the effect of the one-person, one-vote standard on congressional districts did not bring about immediate population equality in districts. Most of the new districts were far from equal in population, because the only official population figures came from the 1960 census. Massive population shifts during the decade rendered most post-*Wesberry* efforts to achieve equality useless.

But redistricting based on the 1970 census resulted in districts that differed only slightly in population from the state average. Among House members elected in 1972, 385 of 435 represented districts that varied by less than 1 percent from the state average district population.

By contrast, only nine of the districts in the 88th Congress (elected in 1962) deviated less than 1 percent from the state average; 81 were between 1 and 5 percent; 87 from 5 to 10 percent; and in 236 districts the deviation was 10 percent or greater. Twenty-two House members were elected at large.

The Supreme Court made only one major ruling concerning congressional districts during the 1970s. In 1973 the Court declared the Texas congressional districts, as redrawn in 1971, unconstitutional because of excessive population variance among districts. The variance between the largest and smallest districts was 4.9872 percent. The Court returned the case to a three-judge federal panel, which adopted a new congressional district plan.

Precise Equality

Following the 1980 census, several federal courts accepted or imposed redistricting maps that achieved population equality but were drawn for blatant partisan purposes. In Missouri a federal court accepted the Democrats' remap proposal over the Republican plan because its districts were more nearly equal in population. The Democratic map obtained population equality by dismantling a district in a part of the state where population was growing and preserving a district in inner-city St. Louis that had been losing population. The plan cost one Republican incumbent his seat.

In the 1990s most states came very close to precise population equality. For example, all 30 districts of Texas have exactly the same population: 566,217. To achieve such equality, however, the line for many districts in some states may cut through many small cities and towns, dividing their residents between two or three different districts.

Although maps such as these raised the question whether partisan gerrymandering was also a violation of an individual's voting rights, the Supreme Court in 1983 appeared to make it even more difficult to challenge a redistricting map on grounds other than population deviation. In a 5-4 decision, the Court ruled in *Karcher v. Daggett* (462 U.S. 725) that states must adhere as closely as possible to the one-person, one-vote standard and bear the burden of proving that deviations from precise population equality were made in pursuit of a legitimate goal. The decision overturned New Jersey's congressional map because the

Whom Should the Census Count?

Counting the number of people in the United States has never been as easy as one, two, three, and that is not just because of logistical problems. When it comes to the decennial census, the political stakes are high, and so is the interest in how the count is conducted. The constitutionally mandated census not only provides crucial information for reapportioning U.S. House seats among the states, but it also supplies the data for drawing district boundaries for state and local public officials and for distributing certain federal funds.

"It goes straight to the heart of what we are about," said Rep. Tom Ridge, R-Pa., "and that is who votes, how we distribute power . . . who should be included in the political community." This view led Ridge and others into a debate over the Census Bureau's approach to the 1990 count, because the bureau's stated goal has little to do with defining the "political community." Its mission, simply put, is to count everyone.

Some complain that the bureau's effort to count all people living in the United States has unfair political ramifications. In particular, members of Congress and other public officials have taken a strong interest in the traditional inclusion of illegal aliens in the census, and in a historical undercounting of certain groups, especially blacks.

Illegal Aliens

The inclusion of illegal aliens in the population figures used in reapportionment usually stirs heated debate in Congress. The Fourteenth Amendment states that "representatives shall be apportioned among the several states according to their respective numbers, counting the whole number of persons in each state, excluding Indians not taxed." The Census Bureau has never attempted to exclude illegal aliens from the census—a policy very troubling to states that fear losing House seats and clout to states with large numbers of illegal aliens. "At the national, state, and local level, the inclusion of illegal aliens . . . in the population base for reapportionment . . . dilutes the votes of citizens," Ridge said.

According to Rep. Thomas C. Sawyer, D-Ohio, the question of counting illegal aliens has been addressed "in many forms, on many different occasions," and "the conclusion at every turn seems to have been that it was the intent to count everybody."

The Census Bureau does not have a method for excluding illegal aliens, although it has studied some alternatives. Some supporters of the current policy say that any questions used to separate out illegal aliens could discourage others from responding, thus undermining the accuracy of the census.

Missing Persons

The expected undercount of minority groups is another problem with political implications. The Census Bureau estimated that it did not count 1.4 percent of the total population in 1980; the undercount was most significant in minority communities. The bureau estimates that it missed roughly 5.9 percent of the nation's blacks. Many of the "missing" lived in inner-city areas, so the undercount issue was a particular concern for major cities and for the Democrats who tend to represent them.

Making an accurate population count in a crowded and perhaps crime-ridden inner-city neighborhood can be difficult. Government census takers and those they are trying to count may view one another with suspicion or fear. Consequently, some urban politicians have urged the Census Bureau to use a statistical method to adjust the census figure for the undercount.

In 1987 the Commerce Department, of which the Census Bureau is a part, announced that it would not make such an adjustment. But faced with a lawsuit filed by New York City, other state and local governments and civil rights groups, the department in 1989 announced that it would defer a judgment on the adjustment question; the department promised to announce its decision by mid-1991.

On July 15, 1991, Commerce Secretary Robert A. Mosbacher said that he would not adjust the 1990 census despite what appeared to be a 2.1 percent undercount of the population. A post-census survey found that more than 9 million people living in the United States had not been counted, while several million had been counted erroneously, for an estimated undercount of about 5.3 million people. According to the survey, blacks were undercounted by 4.8 percent, American Indians by 5 percent and Hispanics by 5.2 percent. Mosbacher said he was "deeply troubled" by the disproportionate undercount of racial minorities but decided that sticking with the head count would be "fairest for all Americans."

Mosbacher's decision not to adjust the census count was expected to be challenged on several fronts. In a suit brought by New York and others, a federal judge ruled in 1993 in support of the Commerce Department's decision not to make any adjustments. Some states and communities with large numbers of uncounted people are still expected to try to increase their share of federal funds by altering the formulas by which funds are currently distributed.

Overseas Personnel

For the 1990 census the Commerce Department reversed a long-standing policy and counted military personnel and dependents stationed overseas. "Historically we have not included them because the census is based on the concept of usual residence," said Charles Jones, associate director of the Census Bureau. "People overseas have a 'usual residence' overseas." An exception was made once in 1970 during the Vietnam War. For the purposes of reapportionment, overseas personnel, who in 1990 numbered 923,000, were assigned to the state each individual considered home.

---

variation between the most populated and the least populated districts was 0.69 percent.

Brennan, who wrote the Court's opinion in *Baker* and

Kirkpatrick, also wrote the opinion in *Karcher,* contending that population differences between districts "could have been avoided or significantly reduced with a good-faith effort to achieve population equality."

"Adopting any standard other than population equality, using the best census data available, would subtly erode the Constitution's ideal of equal representation," Brennan wrote. "In this case, appellants argue that a maximum deviation of approximately 0.7 percent should be considered *de minimis*. If we accept that argument, how are we to regard deviations of 0.8 percent, 0.95 percent, 1.0 percent or 1.1 percent? . . . To accept the legitimacy of unjustified, though small population deviations in this case would mean to reject the basic premise of *Kirkpatrick* and *Wesberry*."

Brennan said that "any number of consistently applied legislative policies might justify" some population variation. These included "making districts compact, respecting municipal boundaries, preserving the cores of prior districts, and avoiding contests between incumbent Representatives." However, he cautioned, the state must show "with some specificity that a particular objective required the specific deviations in its plan, rather than simply relying on general assertions."

In his dissent Justice White criticized the majority for its "unreasonable insistence on an unattainable perfection in the equalizing of congressional districts." He warned that the decision would invite "further litigation of virtually every congressional redistricting plan in the nation."

Partisan Gerrymandering

In *Karcher* the Court did not address the underlying political issue in the New Jersey case, which was that its map had been drawn to serve Democratic interests. As a partisan gerrymander, the map had few peers, boasting some of the most oddly shaped districts in the country. One constituency, known as the "fishhook" by its detractors, twisted through central New Jersey's industrial landscape, picking up Democratic voters along the way. Another stretched from the suburbs of New York to the fringes of Trenton.

In separate dissents Justices Lewis F. Powell, Jr., and John Paul Stevens broadly hinted that they were willing to hear constitutional challenges to instances of partisan gerrymandering. "A legislator cannot represent his constituents properly—nor can voters from a fragmented district exercise the ballot intelligently—when a voting district is nothing more than an artificial unit divorced from, and indeed often in conflict with, the various communities established in the State," wrote Powell.

The Court's opportunity to address that issue came in *Davis v. Bandemer* (478 U.S. 109). On June 30, 1986, the Court ruled that political gerrymanders are subject to constitutional review by federal courts, even if the disputed districts meet the one-person, one-vote test. The case arose from a challenge by Indiana Democrats who argued that the Republican-drawn map so heavily favored the Republican party that Democrats were denied appropriate representation. But the Court rejected the Democrats' challenge to the alleged gerrymander, saying that one election was insufficient to prove unconstitutional discrimination. Left unclear were what standards the Court would use to find a partisan gerrymander legally unacceptable.

National Republicans expressed delight with the *Bandemer* decision. The GOP had long held that Democratic control over most state legislatures had allowed them to draw congressional and legislative districts to their partisan advantage. In particular, Republicans expressed confidence that the *Bandemer* decision lay the groundwork for overturning California's congressional district map, created by Democratic Rep. Phillip Burton in the early 1980s.

Widely recognized as a classic example of a partisan gerrymander, the map featured a number of oddly shaped districts, drawn neither compactly nor with respect to community boundaries, but all with nearly equal populations. As one commentator described it, "Burton carefully stretched districts from one Democratic enclave to another—sometimes joining them with nothing but a bridge, a stretch of harbor, or a spit of land . . . — avoiding Republicans block for block and household for household." [14] Before the 1982 elections, Democrats held 22 congressional districts, Republicans 21. With the Burton map in place for the 1982 elections, Democrats held 28 seats, Republicans only 17.

Republican Rep. Robert E. Badham filed a lawsuit against the Burton plan in federal district court in 1983. In the wake of the *Bandemer* decision, that court held a hearing on *Badham v. Eu* but dismissed the Republican complaint by a 2-1 vote. The court in essence ruled that a party seeking to overturn a gerrymandered map must show a general pattern of exclusion from the political process, which the California Republican party, in control of the governorship, a Senate seat, and 40 percent of the House seats, could not do. The Republicans appealed to the Supreme Court, but the Court refused to become involved, voting 6-3 in 1989 to reaffirm the lower court's decision without comment.

Minority Representation

One form of gerrymandering is expressly forbidden by law: redistricting for the purpose of racial discrimination. The Voting Rights Act of 1965, extended in 1970, 1975 and 1982, banned redistricting that diluted the voting strength of black communities. Other minorities, including Hispanics, Asian-Americans, American Indians and native Alaskans, subsequently were brought under the protection of the law.

In 1980 the Supreme Court for the first time narrowed the reach of the Voting Rights Act in the case of *Mobile v. Bolden*, a challenge to the at-large system of electing city commissioners used in Mobile, Alabama.[15] By a vote of 6-3, the Court ruled that proof of discriminatory intent by the commissioners was necessary before a violation could be found; the fact that no black had ever been elected under the challenged system was not proof enough.

The *Mobile* decision set off an immediate reaction on Capitol Hill. In extending the Voting Rights Act in 1982, Congress amended it to outlaw any practice that has the effect of discriminating against blacks or other minorities—regardless of the lawmakers' intent.

The Justice Department later adopted a similar "results test" for another part of the act (Section 5), which requires certain states and localities with a history of discrimination to have their electoral plans "precleared" by the department. In 1986 the Supreme Court applied this test in *Thornburg v. Gingles* (478 U.S. 30), ruling that six of North Carolina's multimember legislative districts impermissibly diluted black voting strength. Sharply departing from *Mobile*, the Court held that since very few blacks had been elected from these districts, the system must be in violation of the law.

The Court also used the *Thornburg* decision to develop three criteria that, if met, should lead to the creation of a minority legislative district: The minority group must be large and geographically compact enough to constitute a majority in a single-member electoral district, the group must be politically cohesive and the white majority must vote as a bloc to the degree that it usually can defeat candidates preferred by the minority. Thus, within a period of 10 years the burden of proof was shifted from minorities, who had been required to show that lines were being drawn to dilute their voting strength, to lawmakers, who had to show that they had done all they could to maximize minority voting strength.

In a strange twist on the issue of minority representation and redistricting, the Supreme Court ruled in the 1993 case *Shaw vs. Reno* that "bizarre" and racially gerrymandered districts may be challenged in court. (See the discussion on North Carolina on page 547.)

Congress and Redistricting

Congress considered several proposals in the post-World War II period to enact new legislation on redistricting. Only one of these efforts was successful—enactment of a measure barring at-large elections in states with more than one House seat.

In January 1951 President Harry S. Truman asked for a ban on gerrymandering, an end to at-large seats in states having more than one representative, and a sharp reduction in the huge differences in size among congressional districts within most states. On behalf of the administration, Emanuel Celler, D-N.Y., chairman of the House Judiciary Committee, introduced a bill reflecting these requests, but the committee took no action.

Celler regularly introduced his bill throughout the 1950s and early 1960s, but it made no headway until the Supreme Court handed down the *Wesberry* decision in 1964. The House passed a version of the Celler bill in 1965, largely to discourage the Supreme Court from imposing even more rigid criteria. The Senate, however, took no action and the measure died.

In 1967, after defeating a conference report that would have prevented the courts from ordering a state to redistrict or to hold at-large elections until after the 1970 census, Congress approved a measure to ban at-large elections in all states entitled to more than one representative. Exceptions were made for New Mexico and Hawaii, which had a tradition of electing their represen-

tatives at large. Both states, however, soon passed districting laws, New Mexico for the 1968 elections and Hawaii for 1970.

Bills to increase the size of the House to prevent states from losing seats as a result of population shifts have been introduced after most recent censuses, but Congress has given little consideration to any of them.

Notes

1. Ronald D. Elving, "Redistricting: Drawing Power with a Map," *Editorial Research Reports*, February 15, 1991, 99.
2. Robert Luce, *Legislative Principles* (New York: Houghton Mifflin, 1930; New York: DaCapo Press, 1971), 342.
3. Thomas Jefferson, *The Portable Thomas Jefferson*, ed. Merrill D. Peterson, part 3, *Notes on the State of Virginia* (New York: Viking, 1965), 163.
4. Andrew Hacker, *Congressional Districting: The Issue of Equal Representation*, rev. ed. (Washington, D.C.: Brookings Institution, 1964), 6-7.
5. Max Farrand, ed., *The Records of the Federal Convention of 1787* (New Haven, Conn.: Yale University Press, 1911, 1966), vol. 2, 241.
6. *The Federalist Papers*, with an introduction by Clinton Rossiter (New York: New American Library, 1961), 347-348, 354.
7. Quoted in Laurence F. Schmeckebier, *Congressional Apportionment* (Washington, D.C.: Brookings Institution, 1941), 131.
8. Hacker, *Congressional Districting*, 14.
9. Quoted in Schmeckebier, *Congressional Apportionment*, 113.
10. Zechariah Chafee, "Congressional Reapportionment," *Harvard Law Review* (1929): 1015-1047.
11. Jefferson, *Notes on the State of Virginia*, 217.
12. Schmeckebier, *Congressional Reapportionment*, 137.
13. The following summary is based on *Congressional Quarterly's Guide to the U.S. Supreme Court*, 2nd ed. (Washington, D.C.: Congressional Quarterly, 1990), 483-493.
14. Elving, "Redistricting," 107.
15. The discussion of minority representation is based on Rhodes Cook, "Map-Drawers Must Toe the Line in Upcoming Redistricting," *Congressional Quarterly Weekly Report*, September 1, 1990, 2786-2793.

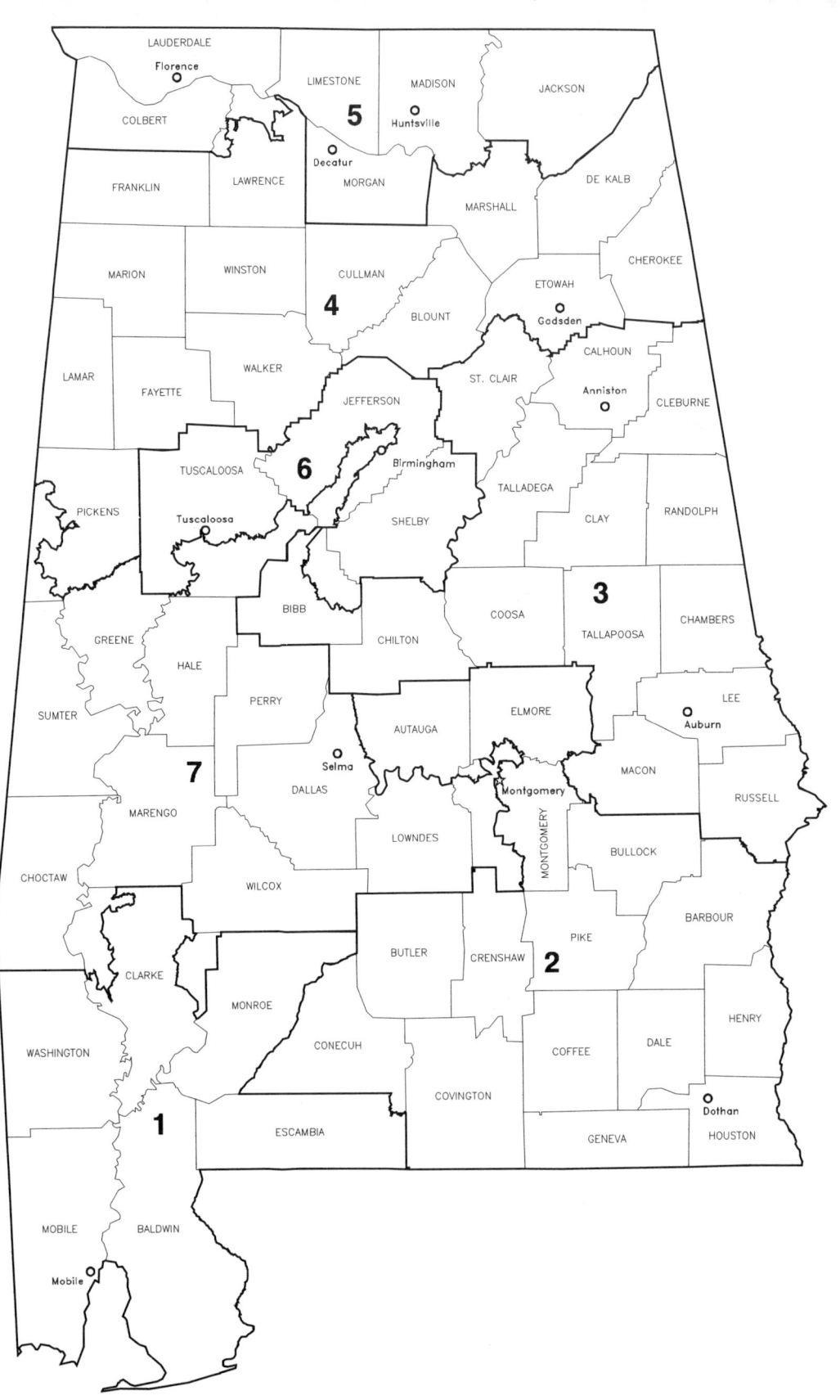

Alabama

The 1980s did not visit significant changes on Alabama's languid southern character. The population rose by just under 4 percent, enough for Alabama to retain its seven congressional districts. The southern part of the state remained dependent on agriculture and textiles. In the north, defense- and space-related industry spurred growth. Birmingham, the state's most-populous city, moved beyond its steel-town image and made itself a financial center. Poverty continued to plague the counties of central Alabama, as it had for a century.

Alabama Republicans emerged elated from 1992 redistricting and for good reason: They trounced the Democrats in congressional redistricting. The map adopted by a federal three-judge panel in Mobile was a slightly modified version of a plan drawn by a Republican state senator.

While creating the black-majority 7th District that in 1992 made Democrat Earl F. Hilliard the first African American to be elected to Congress from Alabama since Reconstruction, the map also fortified both of Alabama's Republican-held districts. And in moving blacks from Birmingham and Tuscaloosa into the 7th to help boost its black population to 67.5 percent, the map created one of the most heavily Republican districts in the country: the 6th, with a population that was 90 percent white. The 6th's Democratic incumbent lost to the Republican challenger in 1992, while a white Democratic incumbent, whose Tuscaloosa base became part of the 7th, chose to retire.

Such a clear Republican victory was unexpected in a state where power had traditionally rested with the Democratic Party. But Republican Gov. Guy Hunt played relentless defense, refusing to call a special session of the state Legislature—where Democrats maintained overwhelming majorities—while he awaited the judgment of a GOP-filed lawsuit in federal district court before three Republican-appointed judges. The judges issued the map on Jan. 27, before the Legislature convened for its 1992 regular session on Feb. 4.

Democrats still had an opportunity to pass a plan of their own. Under the judges' ruling, the court-adopted plan would take effect unless the Legislature passed a plan that became law and was "precleared" by the U.S. Justice Department in time to meet the April 3 filing deadline. But consensus in the Legislature was slow in forming. A last-minute breakthrough in late February propelled passage of a new Democratic map that rescinded the GOP's all-but-sure gain in the 6th, while also creating a black-majority district. The Legislature promptly sent the map to Hunt, who, on March 5, vetoed it. The Legislature overrode his veto the same day and sent it to the Justice Department for preclearance.

But the Justice Department rejected the Legislature's proposal, arguing that the new map unnecessarily fragmented the black population outside the majority-black district, and that the Legislature could have created two black-majority districts. Justice's rejection of the Legislature's map allowed the court-drawn map to go into effect.

In 1993, however, the Alabama Democratic Conference, one of the state's two major black political organizations, filed suit to force the creation of a second black-majority district.

Table 1   Population

District	Population	Population under 18	Voting-age population	Median age
1	577,226	162,750	414,476	32.5
2	577,227	153,903	423,324	33.0
3	577,227	147,716	429,511	32.3
4	577,227	145,078	432,149	35.2
5	577,227	143,917	433,310	33.1
6	577,226	135,564	441,662	33.6
7	577,227	169,860	407,367	31.6
State	4,040,587	1,058,788	2,981,799	33.0

Table 2   Voting-Age Persons

District	White*	Black*	American Indian, Eskimo, or Aleut*	Asian or Pacific Islander*	Other*	Hispanic*	Male*	Female*
1	73.0%	25.5%	0.8%	0.6%	0.1%	0.8%	46.5%	53.5%
2	77.6	21.4	0.3	0.6	0.2	0.7	47.1	52.9
3	75.5	23.6	0.2	0.5	0.2	0.6	47.5	52.5
4	93.4	5.9	0.5	0.2	0.1	0.3	47.1	52.9
5	84.9	13.7	0.5	0.8	0.2	0.7	48.0	52.0
6	90.6	8.4	0.2	0.7	0.1	0.5	47.1	52.9
7	36.1	63.5	0.1	0.2	0.1	0.3	44.0	56.0
State	76.3	22.7	0.4	0.5	0.1	0.6	46.8	53.2

*As percent of voting-age population.

19

Table 3　Voting-Age Persons by Age Groups

District	18-24*	25-44*	45-54*	55-64*	65 and over*
1	13.9%	42.0%	14.3%	12.2%	17.5%
2	14.3	41.9	14.0	11.9	17.9
3	18.1	38.9	13.6	12.1	17.3
4	13.1	38.8	15.1	13.4	19.6
5	14.3	43.3	15.1	12.3	15.0
6	14.9	44.1	13.7	11.5	15.8
7	15.5	40.1	12.5	12.2	19.8
State	14.9	41.3	14.1	12.2	17.5

*As percent of voting-age population.

Table 4　Income and Occupation

District	Median family income	Families in poverty	White collar*	Blue collar*	Service*	Farm*
1	$27,360	16.7%	53.1%	31.6%	13.0%	2.3%
2	29,492	13.0	53.7	31.8	11.3	3.2
3	26,800	14.2	44.8	41.4	11.7	2.2
4	25,401	14.2	39.5	46.9	10.1	3.5
5	33,189	10.0	55.8	31.5	10.9	1.8
6	38,768	6.5	68.9	21.4	8.7	0.9
7	20,773	26.2	44.7	33.8	19.1	2.5
State	28,688	14.3	52.0	33.7	11.9	2.3

*As percent of employed persons age 16 and over.

Table 5　Education: School Years Completed

District	Less than grade 9*	Grades 9-12 no diploma*	High school diploma*	College bachelor's degree or higher*
1	11.8%	19.2%	32.5%	14.7%
2	13.8	18.0	28.2	16.7
3	16.3	22.3	29.8	12.3
4	19.0	23.3	31.3	8.1
5	12.0	16.4	27.9	20.4
6	7.3	13.8	27.5	26.3
7	16.0	23.4	28.8	10.6
State	13.7	19.4	29.4	15.7

*As percent of persons age 25 and over.

Table 6　Housing and Residential Patterns

District	Owner occupied	Renter occupied	Urban	Rural
1	70.9%	29.1%	65.9%	34.1%
2	70.5	29.5	58.1	41.9
3	71.9	28.1	53.0	47.0
4	77.0	23.0	34.3	65.7
5	70.4	29.6	61.1	38.9
6	69.7	30.3	77.5	22.5
7	62.4	37.6	72.7	27.3
State	70.5	29.5	60.4	39.6

1st District

Southwest — Mobile

The proud, history-steeped city of Mobile dominates the 1st. Since Mobile was founded in 1702, the French, British, Spanish and Confederate flags have flown over the city, lending it a cosmopolitan heritage distinct from other Alabama cities. Mobile compares itself with New Orleans; indeed, it claims to celebrate the oldest Mardi Gras festival in the United States.

The 1st backs Republicans for most statewide and federal races, but it is no GOP monolith. Democratic strength lies in the rural counties in the northern part of the district, which have sizable black populations, and in Prichard, a suburb of Mobile with a 79 percent black population. George Bush carried the 1st with 63 percent in 1988. Four years later, he easily won it again. However, the 1st District in 1990 gave Democratic Sen. Howell Heflin 55 percent of the vote and backed the Democratic nominee for lieutenant governor.

The city of Mobile, with just under 200,000 people, lost population during the 1980s. But Mobile County as a whole grew by a modest 4 percent, while Baldwin County, to the east across Mobile Bay, grew by 25 percent, second-fastest in the state. The small Baldwin County city of Daphne, for example, more than tripled in size, growing from 3,400 to 11,300.

Mobile is Alabama's only port city. While the commercial shipbuilding industry has been stagnant for several years, the ship repair business has thrived, keeping Mobile's shipyards busy. The 1985 completion of the Tennessee-Tombigbee Waterway, which connects Mobile Bay and the Tennessee River, was promoted as a tool to allow Mobile's port to compete someday with New Orleans in trade volume.

Continued federal involvement in port development was ensured with the 1988 groundbreaking for Mobile's Navy homeport. But future plans were called into question when the Mobile Naval Station made the 1993 base-closing list.

Timber and textiles also fuel the 1st's economy. Paper companies dot the district, cutting down trees from the forests in the district's rural counties. Alabama River Pulp's new $1.1 billion pulp mill near Claiborne (Monroe County) is the largest single industrial expansion in the history of Alabama. The racial climate in Monroeville, the county seat, inspired the 1960 novel *To Kill a Mockingbird*, but tensions have eased since then. Now, two of the six city council members are black.

Wedged between Mississippi and Florida, the 1st contains all of Alabama's tiny coastline. Along the Gulf of Mexico, fishermen trawl for shrimp. Each October, the National Shrimp Festival at Gulf Shores draws more than 200,000 visitors.

Election Returns

	1st District	Democrat	Republican
1992	President*	84,202 (36.7%)	118,421 (51.6%)
	House	78,742 (36.8%)	128,874 (60.2%)
1990	Senate	75,799 (55.5%)	60,824 (44.5%)
	Governor	68,307 (48.5%)	72,447 (51.5%)
1988	President	60,937 (36.8%)	104,842 (63.2%)

*Vote for Perot was 26,797 (11.7%).

Demographics

Population　577,226

Percent change from 1980　2.4%

Land area　6,785 square miles

Population per square mile 85

Counties, 1990 population

Baldwin 98,280	Mobile 378,643
Clarke (pt.) 24,123	Monroe 23,968
Escambia 35,518	Washington 16,694

Cities, 1990 population (10,000 or more)

Daphne 11,290	Saraland 11,751
Mobile 196,278	Tillmans Corner CDP
Prichard 34,311	17,988

Race and Hispanic origin

White 69.9%

Black 28.5%

American Indian, Eskimo, or Aleut 0.9%

Asian or Pacific Islander 0.7%

Other 0.2%

Hispanic origin 0.8%

Ancestry

American 13.3%	Irish 14.7%
Dutch 1.7%	Italian 1.5%
English 11.5%	Scotch Irish 3.9%
French 4.1%	Scottish 2.2%
German 11.9%	

Universities/colleges, 1990-1991 enrollment

Bishop State Community College, Mobile 2,057

Carver State Tech College, Mobile 535

Faulkner State Junior College, Bay Minette 3,109

Hobson State Tech College, Thomasville 593

Jefferson Davis Community College, Atmore 606

Jefferson Davis State Junior College, Brewton 1,055

Mobile College, Mobile 1,325

Patrick Henry State Junior College, Monroeville 1,160

Southwest State Tech College, Mobile 1,027

Spring Hill College, Mobile 1,305

United States Sports Academy, Daphne 240

University of South Alabama, Mobile 11,584

Newspapers, total circulation (in all districts)

Mobile Press-Register 101,978

Pensacola News Journal 59,139

Commercial television stations, affiliations

ADI: Mobile-Pensacola (100%)

WALA-TV, Mobile (NBC)

WKRG-TV, Mobile (CBS)

WMPV-TV, Mobile (None)

WPMI, Mobile (Fox)

WHBR, Pensacola (None)

WJTC, Pensacola (ABC)

Cable television systems, total subscribers

Comcast Cablevision of Mobile; Mobile 53,729

Storer Cable Communications; Daphne 6,490

US Cable; Mobile 6,472

Military installations, 1991

Mobile Naval Station, Mobile 385

Businesses and other major employers

University of South Alabama; Mobile 3,975

Scott Paper Co.; Mobile; paper mills 3,700

Infirmary Health Systems Inc.; Mobile 3,000

Vanity Fair Mills Inc.; Monroeville; undergarments 2,000

University of South Alabama Medical Center/USA Doctors Hospital; Mobile 1,750

International Paper Co.; Mobile; paper products 1,700

Ciba-Geigy Corp.; McIntosh; agricultural chemicals 1,250

County of Mobile; Mobile 1,000

Providence Hospital Inc.; Mobile 1,000

Vanity Fair Mills Inc.; Atmore; undergarments 875

QMS Inc.; Mobile; computer/office equipment 850

State of Alabama/Mental Health Dept.; Mount Vernon 800

Degussa Corp.; Theodore; industrial organic chemicals 750

Rohr Industries Inc.; Foley; aircraft/parts 700

First Alabama Bank; Mobile; commercial banks 700

Sears Roebuck & Co.; Mobile; department stores 700

Vanity Fair Mills Inc.; Robertsdale; undergarments 685

U.S. Transportation Dept./USCG Aviation; Mobile 650

Teledyne Industries Inc.; Mobile; aircraft/parts 638

Courtaulds Fibers Inc.; Mobile; rayon/synthetics 612

Bender Shipbuilding Co.; Mobile; shipbuilding/repairing 600

Vanity Fair Mills Inc.; Jackson; undergarments 600

C. J. Gayfer Co. Inc.; Mobile; department stores 600

Marriotts Grand Hotel Resort; Point Clear; hotel 600

Container Corp. America/Brewton Pulp & Paper Mill; Brewton; paperboard products 570

Standard Furniture Mfg. Co.; Bay Minette; furniture 550

Judy Bond Inc./Brewton Fashions Div.; Brewton; women's clothing stores 550

Boise Cascade Corp.; Jackson; paper mills 530

Masland Carpets Inc.; Saraland; carpets/rugs 523

2nd District

Southeast — Part of Montgomery; Dothan

Defense and agriculture fuel the economy of the 2nd. The substantial defense presence stands as testament to the influence of Bill Dickinson, who represented the 2nd from 1965 to 1993 and rose to become ranking Republican on the House Armed Services Committee.

Maxwell and Gunter Air Force bases, on the edge of Montgomery, contribute $754 million annually to the 2nd's economy; Gunter was annexed by Maxwell in the early 1990s. Fort Rucker, northwest of Dothan, is where many Army and Air Force helicopter pilots and crews train. More than 13,000 military and civilian personnel work at Fort Rucker, whose annual economic impact is $969 million. Martin Marietta has a new missile factory in Troy (Pike County).

Southeastern Alabama is known as the Wiregrass region for the wiry roots of its native grass. The soil was first tilled for cotton, but in the early part of the century, the boll weevil wiped out more than two-thirds of the cotton crop. Now the sparsely populated area grows more peanuts than almost any other part of the country. The Coffee County town of Enterprise erected a monument to the boll weevil as a tribute to the insect whose destruction of the cotton crop prompted the switch to peanuts.

Although redistricting for the 1990s split the city of Montgomery between the 2nd and the new black-majority 7th District, it is still the 2nd's largest city. Montgomery has long been a national GOP stronghold, voting for Republican presidential candidates as far back as 1956. The other sizable city in the 2nd is Dothan (population 54,000) in Houston County, near the southeastern border with Florida and Georgia.

George Bush carried Houston County with 74 percent in 1988 and 58 percent in 1992. The huge margins the GOP House candidate ran up in Montgomery (19 percentage points) and Houston (20 points) enabled him to withstand losses in 10 of the district's 13 other counties to win in 1992.

Originally a cotton and peanut market town, Dothan has grown and diversified by attracting new industries, including large plants run by Michelin and Sony. Sony manufactures and exports audio and video tapes and computer disks here. Largely nonunion, Dothan's plants represent most of the 2nd's large industry, although Elmore County has some textile plants.

Rural Barbour and Bullock counties were the original home base for former governor and presidential candidate George C. Wallace. They have large black populations (Bullock is majority-black) and are loyally Democratic. Bill Clinton received two-thirds of Bullock's vote in 1992.

Elmore and Autauga counties grew during the 1980s as people who work in Montgomery moved out of the city. Elmore grew by 13 percent, Autauga by 6 percent; they vote Republican. Bush easily carried both counties in 1988 and 1992.

Election Returns

	2nd District	Democrat	Republican
1992	President*	82,550 (35.2%)	124,272 (53.1%)
	House	109,335 (47.9%)	112,906 (49.5%)
1990	Senate	83,406 (55.4%)	67,075 (44.6%)
	Governor	66,136 (42.3%)	90,147 (57.7%)
1988	President	52,058 (32.5%)	108,208 (67.5%)

*Vote for Perot was 27,377 (11.7%).

Demographics

Population 577,227

Percent change from 1980 5.0%

Land area 10,132 square miles

Population per square mile 57

Counties, 1990 population
Autauga 34,222	Dale 49,633
Barbour 25,417	Elmore 49,210
Bullock 11,042	Geneva 23,647
Butler 21,892	Henry 15,374
Coffee 40,240	Houston 81,331
Conecuh 14,054	Montgomery (pt.) 133,457
Covington 36,478	Pike 27,595
Crenshaw 13,635	

Cities, 1990 population (10,000 or more)
Dothan 53,589	Ozark 12,922
Enterprise 20,123	Prattville 19,587
Eufaula 13,220	Troy 13,051
Montgomery (pt.) 120,099	

Race and Hispanic origin
White 74.8%
Black 24.1%
American Indian, Eskimo, or Aleut. 0.3%
Asian or Pacific Islander 0.6%
Other 0.2%
Hispanic origin 0.8%

Ancestry
American 18.2%	Irish 14.1%
Dutch 1.7%	Italian 1.1%
English 12.2%	Scotch Irish 3.8%
French 2.2%	Scottish 2.0%
German 10.1%	

Universities/colleges, 1990-1991 enrollment
Alabama Aviation & Tech College, Ozark 539
Auburn University at Montgomery, Montgomery 6,261
C. Sparks State Tech College, Eufaula 506
Community College of the Air Force, Montgomery 29,567
Douglas MacArthur State Tech College, Opp 560
Enterprise State Junior College, Enterprise 2,108
Faulkner University, Montgomery 276
George C. Wallace Community College, Dothan 3,755
Huntingdon College, Montgomery 791
J. M. Patterson State Tech College, Montgomery 681
Lurleen B. Wallace State Junior College, Andalusia 1,256
Reid State Technical College, Evergreen 364
Southern Technical College, Montgomery 348
Troy State University, Troy 5,024
Troy State University-Dothan, Dothan 1,933

Newspapers, total circulation (in all districts)
Birmingham Post-Herald News 225,490
Columbus Ledger-Enquirer 53,120
Dothan Eagle 25,704
Montgomery Advertiser-Journal 64,576

Commercial television stations, affiliations
ADI: Montgomery-Selma (54%), Dothan (29%), Columbus, GA (9%) and Mobile-Pensacola (8%)
WDHN, Dothan (ABC)
WCOV-TV, Montgomery (Fox)
WMCF-TV, Montgomery (None)
WSFA, Montgomery (NBC)
WDAU, Ozark (Fox)

Cable television systems, total subscribers
Alabama Newchannels; Wetumpka 9,469
Cable TV of Dothan; Dothan 6,000
Comcast Cablevision of Dothan; Dothan 12,000
CVI; Newton 5,548
Storer Cable TV Inc.; Montgomery 52,000
Storer Cable TV Inc.; Prattville 6,500

Military installations, 1991
Fort Rucker (Army), Daleville 10,357
Maxwell Air Force Base, Montgomery 4,425
Hall Air Force Guard Station, Dothan 47
Abston Air Force Guard Station, Abston 16

Businesses and other major employers
Augat Inc./National Industries; Montgomery; electrical equipment/supplies 1,700
U.S. Postal Service; Montgomery; 1,700
Southeast Alabama Medical Center; Dothan 1,600
Showell Farms Inc.; Dothan; poultry 1,500
Auburn University at Montgomery; Montgomery 1,331
Flowers Hospital Inc./Home Care Service; Dothan 1,275
Sony Inc. America; Dothan; electrical equipment/supplies 1,225

West Point-Pepperell Inc.; Abbeville; textile products 1,200
Bidermann Industries Corp./Cluett Peabody & Co.; Andalusia; apparel/piece goods/notions 1,100
Baptist Health Services Corp.; Montgomery 1,100
Amoco Fabrics & Fibers Co.; Andalusia; yarn/thread mills 1,050
ConAgra Inc.; Enterprise; poultry 1,020
Crown Health Care; Montgomery; nursing 1,000
Alabama Power Co.; Columbia; electric services 900
Opp & Micolas Mills Inc.; Opp; cotton mills 840
Kleinerts Inc. of Alabama; Elba; undergarments 825
Goody Products Inc.; Dothan; misc. manufacturers 775
Union Camp Corp.; Prattville; paperboard mills 750
Fieldcrest Apartments; Dothan; real estate operators 750
Covington Industries Inc.; Opp 750
Pemco Aeroplex Inc.; Dothan; aircraft/parts 739
Dales Sportswear Inc.; Hartford; outerwear 700
Ansell Inc.; Dothan; rubber products 700
Dow-United Technologies; Tallassee; aircraft/parts 680
Rheem Mfg. Co.; Montgomery; plumbing/heating 655
ALFA Corp.; Montgomery; holding offices 650
Caffcos Floral Factory; Montgomery; retail stores 650
Dorsey Trailers Inc.; Elba; motor vehicles/equipment 600
Continental Grain Co.; Union Springs; poultry 600
State of Alabama/Highway Dept.; Montgomery; road construction 600
Homemakers of Montgomery Inc.; Montgomery; home health services 600
Troy State University; Troy 525
Montgomery Winn-Dixie Inc.; Montgomery; grocery stores 515
Michelin Tire Corp.; Dothan; tires 510
Bidermann Industries Corp./Cluett Peabody & Co.; Enterprise; apparel/piece goods/notions 506

3rd District

East — Anniston; Auburn

A 14-county amalgam of defense facilities, high-tech businesses, universities, textile mills and poor rural communities, the 3rd lacks a single defining characteristic. Politically, it is conservative Democratic territory that is prone to support Republicans for governor and president.

Anniston, the Calhoun County seat and one of the largest cities in the district with a population of 26,600, is home to two huge military facilities: Fort McClellan and the Anniston Army Depot. Fort McClellan, which houses the Chemical Decontamination Training Facility, was on the 1991 list of defense bases recommended for closure, but it received a reprieve when its champions convinced the base-closing commission of its unique status as the only place where the United States and its allies can train soldiers using active but nonlethal chemical weapons.

Fort McClellan was again targeted for closure in 1993, threatening some 7,800 military and civilian jobs. It was the only large base the Army proposed to close.

Calhoun County has not staked its future on the perpetual presence of Fort McClellan. Area business and civic leaders in 1982 joined to form Forward Calhoun County, an economic development program aimed at promoting diversification by attracting new industry to help the area survive if Fort McClellan closes.

More than half the 3rd's population is contained in its four most-populous counties: Calhoun, Lee, Talladega and St. Clair. George Bush carried all four easily in 1988 and 1992. Auburn (Lee County) is home to Auburn University, the state's largest, with 21,500 students. The first Sunday in May, racing fans flock to the Talladega Superspeedway for the Winston 500.

St. Clair grew by 21 percent during the 1980s, swelled by people who work in Birmingham as well as Calhoun County. St. Clair is Republican terrain; the unsuccessful GOP House candidate carried it in 1992.

The 3rd still contains a thriving textile industry. The Russell Corp., with headquarters in Alexander City (Tallapoosa County), makes uniforms for professional football teams. The cotton and dairy industries have waned as farmers have turned to growing pine trees on their farmland and supplementing their income by raising poultry and catfish.

Macon, the only county in the 3rd with a black majority (86 percent), has had a long history of racial and economic troubles. The county seat, Tuskegee, was at the center of a 1960 landmark Supreme Court ruling striking down a racial gerrymander (*Gomillion v. Lightfoot*). Tuskegee University, founded in 1881 through the efforts of Booker T. Washington, was one of the nation's first black colleges. Today, it has 3,500 students and is a leader in research, science and engineering. Macon traditionally ranks among the most Democratic counties in the country. In the 1992 presidential race, Bill Clinton won 83 percent of the county vote.

Election Returns

	3rd District	Democrat	Republican
1992	President*	92,142 (41.7%)	105,034 (47.5%)
	House	119,175 (60.3%)	73,800 (37.4%)
1990	Senate	78,188 (63.4%)	45,150 (36.6%)
	Governor	62,900 (49.0%)	65,501 (51.0%)
1988	President	54,173 (37.5%)	90,368 (62.5%)

Vote for Perot was 23,772 (10.8%).

Demographics

Population 577,227

Percent change from 1980 3.9%

Land area 8,719 square miles

Population per square mile 66

Counties, 1990 population

Bibb (pt.) 13,057	Lee 87,146
Calhoun 116,034	Macon 24,928
Chambers 36,876	Randolph 19,881
Chilton 32,458	Russell 46,860
Clay 13,252	St. Clair 50,009
Cleburne 12,730	Talladega 74,107
Coosa 11,063	Tallapoosa 38,826

Cities, 1990 population (10,000 or more)

Alexander City 14,917	Phenix City 25,312
Anniston 26,623	Saks CDP 11,138
Auburn 33,830	Sylacauga 12,520
Jacksonville 10,283	Talladega 18,175
Opelika 22,122	Tuskegee 12,257

Race and Hispanic origin

White 73.1%
Black 26.0%
American Indian, Eskimo, or Aleut. 0.2%
Asian or Pacific Islander 0.5%
Other 0.2%
Hispanic origin 0.6%

Ancestry

American 18.9%
Dutch 1.9%
English 10.9%
French 1.6%
German 9.1%

Irish 14.8%
Italian 1.0%
Scotch Irish 2.3%
Scottish 1.5%

Universities/colleges, 1990-1991 enrollment

Auburn University, Auburn 21,537
Cattahoochee Valley Community, Phenix City 1,685
Central Alabama Community College, Alexander City 2,097
Harry M. Ayers State Tech College, Anniston 529
Jacksonville State University, Jacksonville 8,448
Southern Union State Junior College, Wadley 2,896
Talladega College, Talladega 667
Tuskegee University, Tuskegee 3,510

Newspapers, total circulation (in all districts)

Birmingham Post-Herald News 225,490
Columbus Ledger-Enquirer 53,120
Montgomery Advertiser-Journal 64,576
Opelika-Auburn News 11,323
Star Anniston 29,327
St. Clair News-Aegis 3,720
Tuscaloosa News 39,180

Commercial television stations, affiliations

ADI: Birmingham (43%), Columbus, GA (21%), Montgomery-Selma (16%), Atlanta (13%) and Anniston (7%)
WJSU-TV, Anniston (CBS)
WNAL-TV, Gadsden (Fox)
WTJP, Gadsden (None)
WSWS, Opelika (None)

Cable television systems, total subscribers

Anniston Newchannels; Anniston 32,000
Phenix City CATV; Phenix City 12,550
Sammons Communications Inc.; Lanett 10,500
Storer Cable TV Inc.; Sylacauga 5,192

Military installations, 1991

Fort McClellan (Army), Anniston 7,800
Anniston Army Depot Activity, Anniston 4,340

Businesses and other major employers

Russell Corp.; Alexander; sportswear 7,500
Auburn University; Auburn 4,061
Diversified Products Corp.; Opelika; toys/sporting goods 2,300
U.S. Veteran Affairs Dept.; Tuskegee 1,400
Uniroyal Goodrich Tire Co.; Opelika; tires 1,350
Ampex Recording Media Corp.; Opelika; electrical equipment/supplies 1,350
East Alabama Medical Center; Opelika 1,200
Regional Health Services Inc.; Anniston 1,100
Calhoun County Board of Education; Anniston 1,100
Tuskegee University; Tuskegee 1,045
West Point-Pepperell Inc.; Valley; cotton mills 1,000

Tyson Foods Inc.; Ashland; poultry 1,000
Temporary Resources Inc.; Anniston; temp services 999
Alabama Institute for Deaf & Blind; Talladega; 993
General Electric Co.; Rome; electric distribution equipment 950
Amoco Fabrics Fibers Co.; Roanoke; plastics products 790
Jacksonville State University; Jacksonville 702
Redmond Regional Medical Center; Rome 680
West Point-Pepperell Inc.; Opelika; cotton mills 650
Chilton County Board of Education; Clanton 650
Fieldcrest Cannon Inc.; Phenix City; textile products 635
City of Rome; Rome 617
Lee County Board of Education; Opelika 615
Opelika Industries Inc.; Opelika; cotton mills 600
Mount Vernon Mills Inc.; Tallassee; cotton mills 600
Chalk-Line Inc./Sports Wearhouse; Anniston; apparel 600
Springs Industries Inc.; Piedmont; textile products 600
Lee Brass Co.; Anniston; nonferrous foundries (castings) 592
FMC Corp.; Anniston; iron/steel foundries 583
West Point-Pepperell Inc.; Lanett; cotton mills 580
SCT Yarns Inc.; Piedmont; yarn/thread mills 575
Health-Tex Inc.; Centreville; outerwear 520
Montgomery Winn-Dixie Inc.; Opelika; grocery stores 515

4th District

North Central — Gadsden

With fewer blacks and more unionized workers, the 4th has a different character from districts farther south. The 14-county stripe across northern Alabama has mine workers in the west, light and heavy industry in the east and poultry farms throughout.

The 4th has a long populist Democratic heritage; the only district with a more reliably Democratic vote is the black-majority 7th. The "common man" rhetoric of former Gov. James E. Folsom (who grew up in the 4th's Cullman County) always played well in this region.

There is a GOP presence in the 4th dating back to the Civil War. Winston County actually seceded briefly from Alabama when the state seceded from the Union and became the "free state of Winston." George Bush received 55 percent in Winston in 1992; in 1988, he got 68 percent.

The district's only sizable city is Gadsden, an industrial center of 42,500 people in Etowah County. Gadsden's once-thriving textile and heavy industries have suffered setbacks in recent years. Gulf State Steel's smokestacks still belch fumes over the city and Goodyear Tire and Rubber Co. still manufactures tires, but both companies have had significant layoffs. Gadsden's other major industrial employers, Mid-South Industries and its subsidiary, Emco, turn out a diverse range of products, including toasters, fryers and handguns as well as components for mines, bombs and torpedoes.

In and around Gadsden is the largest concentration of Democrats in the district. Bill Clinton carried Etowah with 48 percent of the vote in 1992. Bush won it by only 66 votes in 1988. Gadsden has a 28 percent black population. In the early 1990s, the factory outlet Boaz, about 20 miles northeast of Gadsden, became the top tourist attraction in the state.

The textile and apparel industries have been in decline for several years throughout the South, afflicted by cheap imports and financially weak companies. The effect has been felt across the 4th as companies such as Health-tex and Munsingwear have closed their plants. Counties dependent on textile jobs, such as Marion in the western part of the district, saw their unemployment levels hit double digits in the late 1980s and early 1990s.

The 4th has one of the biggest concentrations of poultry farms and processors in the country. Cullman County is second in the nation in sales of broilers. De Kalb, Marshall and Blount counties are also major chicken-producing counties.

De Kalb also has a large textile presence. The county seat, Fort Payne, calls itself the "Sock Capital of the World." It says that its nearly three dozen hosiery mills make 65 percent of the world's socks.

Coal has been mined in the western part of the 4th for generations, and the United Mine Workers exerts a strong influence for Democratic candidates. In 1992, Clinton carried six of the district's eight westernmost counties.

Election Returns

	4th District	Democrat	Republican
1992	President*	104,557 (43.5%)	107,087 (44.6%)
	House	157,907 (68.5%)	66,934 (29.0%)
1990	Senate	92,913 (64.3%)	51,536 (35.7%)
	Governor	77,982 (50.0%)	78,097 (50.0%)
1988	President	71,397 (43.7%)	91,811 (56.3%)

*Vote for Perot was 28,565 (11.9%).

Demographics

Population 577,227

Percent change from 1980 2.7%

Land area 9,139 square miles

Population per square mile 63

Counties, 1990 population

Blount 39,248	Lamar 15,715
Cherokee 19,543	Lawrence (pt.) 26,499
Cullman 67,613	Marion 29,830
DeKalb 54,651	Marshall 70,832
Etowah 99,840	Pickens (pt.) 17,957
Fayette 17,962	Walker 67,670
Franklin 27,814	Winston 22,053

Cities, 1990 population (10,000 or more)

Albertville 14,507	Gadsden 42,523
Cullman 13,367	Jasper 13,553
Fort Payne 11,838	

Race and Hispanic origin
White 92.5%
Black 6.6%
American Indian, Eskimo, or Aleut 0.6%
Asian or Pacific Islander 0.2%
Other 0.1%
Hispanic origin 0.4%

Ancestry

American 26.6%	German 10.8%
Dutch 2.4%	Irish 20.0%
English 11.2%	Scotch Irish 2.1%
French 1.6%	Scottish 1.4%

Universities/colleges, 1990-1991 enrollment
Brewer State Junior College, Fayette 1,114
Gadsden State Community College, Gadsden 5,478
George C. Wallace Community College, Hanceville 4,043
Northwest Alabama State Junior College, Phil Campbell 1,940
Northeast Alabama State Junior College, Rainsville 1,546
Snead State Junior College, Boaz 1,691
Walker College, Jasper 909
Walker State Tech College, Sumiton 969

Newspapers, total circulation (in all districts)
Birmingham Post-Herald News 225,490
Cullman Times 9,077
Decatur Daily 26,984
Florence Times Daily 33,836
Gadsden Times 29,237
Huntsville Times News 57,589
Jasper Daily Mountain Eagle 13,477
Tuscaloosa News 39,180

Commercial television stations, affiliations
ADI: Birmingham (65%), Huntsville-Decatur-Florence (28%) and Columbus-Tupelo (6%)

Cable television systems, total subscribers
Cablesouth Inc.; Albertville 9,879
Century Cable; Cullman 9,000
Comcast Cablevision of Gadsden; Gadsden 19,100

Businesses and other major employers
Gulf States Steel Inc. Alabama; Gadsden; steel products 2,000
Champion Intl. Corp./Champion Paper Co.; Courtland; paper products 1,580
Goodyear Tire & Rubber Co.; Gadsden; tires 1,500
Gadsden Board of Education; Gadsden 1,348
Tyson Foods Inc.; Gadsden; poultry 1,300
Baptist Memorial Hospital; Gadsden 1,050
Tyson Foods Inc.; Blountsville; poultry 1,000
Lee Apparel Co. Inc.; Boaz; jeans 900
Oneita Industries Inc.; Cullman; sportswear 850
Cavalier Homes of Alabama; Addison; mobile homes 832
Vanity Fair Inc.; Oneonta; outerwear 800
Merico Inc./Earth Grains; Fort Payne; bakery products 800
SCI Systems Inc.; Arab; communications equipment 766
Walker Regional Medical Center; Jasper 753
Health-Tex Inc.; Gadsden; outerwear 750
White Consolidated Industries/WCR Components Div.; Cullman; refrigeration 700
Centre Mfg. Co. Inc.; Centre; apparel 650
Gold Kist Inc.; Guntersville; grain mill products 650
NTN-Bower Corp.; Hamilton; roller bearings/parts 650
McCoy Mfg. Co. Inc.; Sulligent; outerwear 610
Lee Apparel Co. Inc.; Russellville; jeans 606
Hudson Foods Inc./McElrath Farm Div.; Albertville; poultry 600
Continental Grain Co.; Albertville; poultry 600
Golden Poultry Co. Inc.; Russellville; poultry 600
Gold Kist Inc.; Boaz; poultry 580
Bidermann Industries Corp./Clueet Peabody & Co.; Jasper; apparel 560
Comptronix Corp.; Guntersville; electronic components 530
Alabama Power Co.; Parrish; electric services 530
V. I. Prewett & Son Inc.; Fort Payne; hosiery 530

5th District

North — Huntsville

Space- and defense-related growth radiating from Huntsville has spurred the boom that made the 5th the fastest-growing district in the state during the 1980s, with a nearly 10 percent population gain. The Defense Department, the National Aeronautics and Space Administration (NASA) and the Tennessee Valley Authority (TVA) have helped cushion the 5th's economy from recession. The federal government is the district's largest employer.

With just under 160,000 people, Huntsville, the seat of Madison County, is the state's fourth-largest city. It went from cotton town to boom town during World War II when the Army built the Redstone Arsenal to produce chemical-warfare materiel. After the Soviet Union launched Sputnik in October 1957, Wernher von Braun headed the Marshall Space Flight Center in Huntsville to perform the principal research for the fledgling NASA.

Companies that built plants in Huntsville—Boeing and General Electric among them—stayed and diversified when the high-tech government contracts dwindled; other industries moved in. Computer giant Intergraph Corp. has its headquarters here. Chrysler employs about 3,000 at an assembly plant.

As Huntsville has grown, businesses and people have moved out of the city and into surrounding Madison County; Intergraph has built a facility in Madison. The city of Madison's population more than tripled during the 1980s, spurting to 14,800. Madison County grew by 21 percent, the fourth fastest in the state.

Huntsville's federal installations and active labor unions in the metals, automobile and chemical plants along the Tennessee River lend the 5th a solid Democratic presence. In 1992, Bill Clinton carried three of the six counties entirely within the district. But the GOP has picked up strength as Madison County has grown. Madison voted for George Bush by wide margins in 1988 and 1992.

Downstream from Huntsville along the Tennessee, blue-collar jobs predominate. Towns such as Decatur, a chemical manufacturing center, and the Quad Cities of Florence, Sheffield, Tuscumbia and Muscle Shoals came into being as a result of the TVA. Blues pioneer W. C. Handy was born in Florence, which hosts an annual jazz and blues festival in his name. Logging dominates in the rural eastern part of the district.

The TVA has two huge nuclear complexes in the 5th—Browns Ferry at Athens and Bellefonte at Scottsboro. Before Three Mile Island, a 1975 fire at Browns Ferry had been considered the nation's worst nuclear accident. The plant was closed from 1975 to 1977, and again in 1985. After a six-year shutdown, one of Browns Ferry's three reactors began operation again in 1991. Bellefonte's construction has been delayed indefinitely.

Election Returns

	5th District	Democrat	Republican
1992	President*	102,124 (41.0%)	110,256 (44.2%)
	House	160,060 (65.6%)	77,951 (31.9%)
1990	Senate	102,731 (64.1%)	57,479 (35.9%)
	Governor	71,985 (43.7%)	92,686 (56.3%)
1988	President	71,768 (40.9%)	103,866 (59.1%)

*Vote for Perot was 36,918 (14.8%).

Demographics

Population 577,227

Percent change from 1980 5.0%

Land area 4,409 square miles

Population per square mile 131

Counties, 1990 population

Colbert 51,666	Limestone 54,135
Jackson 47,796	Madison 238,912
Lauderdale 79,661	Morgan 100,043
Lawrence (pt.) 5,014	

Cities, 1990 population (10,000 or more)

Athens 16,901	Huntsville 159,789
Decatur 48,761	Madison 14,904
Florence 36,426	Scottsboro 13,786
Hartselle 10,795	Sheffield 10,380

Race and Hispanic origin
White 83.4%
Black 14.9%
American Indian, Eskimo, or Aleut. 0.6%
Asian or Pacific Islander 0.9%
Other 0.2%
Hispanic origin 0.8%

Ancestry

American 19.3%	Irish 18.6%
Dutch 2.1%	Italian 1.4%
English 14.4%	Scotch Irish 3.4%
French 2.4%	Scottish 2.0%
German 14.0%	

Universities/colleges, 1990-1991 enrollment
Alabama A&M University, Normal 4,886
Athens State College, Athens 2,770
J. F. Drake State Tech College, Huntsville 852
J. C. Calhoun State Community College, Decatur 7,833
Oakwood College, Huntsville 1,266
Phillips Junior College, Huntsville 413
Shoals Community College, Muscle Shoals 2,185
University of Alabama, Huntsville 8,139
University of North Alabama, Florence 5,622

Newspapers, total circulation (in all districts)
Athens News Courier 6,755
Birmingham Post-Herald News 225,490
Decatur Daily 26,984
Florence Times Daily 33,836
Huntsville News 16,644
Huntsville Times News 57,589

Commercial television stations, affiliations
ADI: Huntsville-Decatur-Florence (100%)
WOWL-TV, Florence (NBC)
WTRT, Florence (None)
WHNT-TV, Huntsville (CBS)
WZDX, Huntsville (None)
WAAY-TV, Huntsville (ABC)
WAFF, Huntsville (NBC)

Cable television systems, total subscribers
Cable Alabama Corp.; Madison 21,132
Comcast Cablevision of Huntsville; Huntsville 43,000

Comcast Cablevision of The Shoals; Florence 23,764
Decatur Telecable Corp.; Decatur 16,857
Falcon Cable TV; Athens 7,700
Falcon Cable TV; Scottsboro 5,562
Premiere Cable Communications; Hartselle 6,500

Military installations, 1991

Redstone Arsenal (Army), Huntsville 21,218

Businesses and other major employers

Intergraph Corp.; Huntsville; computer services 3,900
Chrysler; Huntsville; automobile assembly plant 3,500
Acustar Inc.; Huntsville; electrical equipment/supplies 3,200
General Motors Corp.; Athens; motor vehicles/equipment 3,500
NASA; Huntsville; federal space research/technology 3,500
Ona Corp.; Huntsville; engines/turbines 3,300
Teledyne Industries Inc.; Huntsville; research services 3,000
Tennessee Valley Authority/Browns Ferry Nuclear Plant; Athens; electric services 2,500
Tennessee Valley Authority; Decatur; electric services 2,500
Huntsville Hospital; Huntsville 2,390
Reynolds Metals Co.; Sheffield; aluminum 2,220
Boeing Co.; Huntsville; computer services 2,000
Eliza Coffee Memorial Hospital; Florence 1,589
General Electric Co.; Decatur; household appliances 1,500
Monsanto Chemical Co.; Decatur; plastics/synthetics 1,250
Tee Jays Mfg. Co.; Florence; knitting mills 1,250
Dunlop Tire Corp.; Huntsville; tires 1,200
University of Alabama; Huntsville 1,200
Avex Electronics Inc.; Huntsville; electrical equipment/supplies 1,050
Humana Hospital Inc.; Huntsville 1,020
Continental Grain Co.; Decatur; poultry products 1,000
Minnesota Mining & Mfg. Co.; Decatur; plastics products 975
Thiokol Corp.; Huntsville; guided missiles/parts 942
Universal Data Systems Inc./Uds; Huntsville; communications equipment 920
Morgan Cnty/Decatur General Hospital; Decatur 902
McDonnell Douglas Corp./McDonnell Douglas; Huntsville; guided missiles/parts 900
Alabama A&M University; Huntsville 900
Wolverine Tube Inc.; Decatur; copper/copper alloy 873
Morgan County Board of Education; Decatur 850
USBI Co. Inc.; Huntsville; guided missiles/parts 800
Steelcase Inc.; Athens; office furniture 770
County of Madison; Huntsville 765
SCI Technology Inc.; Huntsville; electronic components 750
Andover Togs Inc.; Pisgah; knitting mills 747
Amoco Chemical Co.; Decatur; petroleum refining 700
Nichols Research Corp./NRES; Huntsville; computer services 675
ConAgra Inc.; Athens; poultry 670
Andover Togs Inc.; Scottsboro; outerwear 600
Tennessee Valley Authority; Stevenson; electric services 600
PPG Industries Inc.; Huntsville; aircraft/parts 600
Tennessee River Inc.; Florence; outerwear 600
Unisys Corp.; Huntsville; engineering/architectural services 600
Lurleen B. Wallace Development Center; Decatur 590
Goodyear Tire & Rubber Co.; Decatur; textile goods 575
J. C. Calhoun State Community College, Decatur 550
City of Florence/Water Board; Florence 550

City of Huntsville/Utilities Dept.; Huntsville; electric services 545
Sonoco Products Co./Baker Industries Div.; Hartselle; steel products 518
BellSouth; Decatur; telephone communications 504

6th District

Part of Birmingham and Suburbs

Republicans controlled the 1990 redistricting in Alabama, and they claimed the 6th as their trophy. After placing most of the black voters of Birmingham in the new, majority-black 7th, they designed a district that distilled GOP voting strength to near purity. The resulting 6th is 90 percent white and one of the most Republican districts in the country. The makeup enabled a Republican challenger to unseat a 10-year Democratic incumbent in 1992.

The intensity of the district's GOP vote is striking. In 1988, George Bush won the areas that make up the 6th with 76 percent—a mark topped by only one other district in the country: Bush's home in Houston.

The largest portion of the 6th's population is in Jefferson County (Birmingham). Birmingham is moving away from its image as a declining steel town toward one as a financial center. AmSouth, Central Bank of the South and Southtrust are among the large banks with headquarters in Birmingham. Most of the city of Birmingham was placed in the 7th, although the city's symbol, the cast-iron statue of Vulcan, the Roman god of fire and metalworking, is in the 6th, on the summit of Red Mountain. The 55-foot-tall statue, one of the world's largest iron figures, is a monument to the city's iron industry.

Jefferson County's well-to-do, almost exclusively white bedroom communities such as Homewood, Mountain Brook and Hoover are home to people who work in Birmingham's business district.

According to the 1990 census, Mountain Brook, a city of 19,810, had 38 blacks. Nearly all of the Jefferson County suburbs in the 6th have white populations of 90 percent or more. Hoover (95 percent white) and Trussville (99 percent) were the fastest-growing cities in the Birmingham metropolitan area during the 1980s; both more than doubled their population.

South of Jefferson County is Shelby County, the most Republican county in the state—and the fastest-growing. Shelby's population spurted by 50 percent in the 1980s as Birmingham commuters moved into cities such as Alabaster (which grew by 108 percent during the 1980s) and Pelham (39 percent growth). Shelby was Bush's best Alabama county in 1988 (79 percent) and 1992 (68 percent).

Democratic votes can be tilled from the portion of Tuscaloosa County in the 6th. The city of Tuscaloosa (population 77,800) is split between the 6th and 7th districts. It has an industrial base that includes manufacturers of chemicals, fertilizer and rubber products, but it is more often identified as the home of the University of Alabama (19,800 students).

Election Returns

	6th District	Democrat	Republican
1992	President*	77,506 (27.2%)	180,798 (63.5%)
	House	126,062 (45.0%)	146,599 (52.4%)

	6th District	Democrat	Republican
1990	Senate	64,467 (41.9%)	89,352 (58.1%)
	Governor	46,353 (29.5%)	110,949 (70.5%)
1988	President	41,955 (24.1%)	132,282 (75.9%)

Vote for Perot was 26,235 (9.3%).

Demographics

Population 577,226

Percent change from 1980 4.2%

Land area 2,846 square miles

Population per square mile 203

Counties, 1990 population

Bibb (pt.) 3,519	Shelby 99,358
Jefferson (pt.) 393,010	Tuscaloosa (pt.) 81,339

Cities, 1990 population (10,000 or more)

Alabaster 14,732	Hueytown (pt.) 14,705
Birmingham (pt.) 82,554	Mountain Brook 19,810
Center Point CDP 22,658	Northport (pt.) 15,230
Forestdale CDP 10,395	Pinson-Clay-Chalkville CDP 10,987
Homewood 22,922	
Hoover 39,788	Tuscaloosa (pt.) 36,622
	Vestavia Hills 19,749

Race and Hispanic origin

White 89.7%
Black 9.2%
American Indian, Eskimo, or Aleut. 0.2%
Asian or Pacific Islander 0.8%
Other 0.1%
Hispanic origin 0.6%

Ancestry

American 15.8%	Irish 18.4%
Dutch 2.4%	Italian 2.8%
English 18.0%	Scotch Irish 5.2%
French 3.3%	Scottish 3.4%
German 14.4%	

Universities/colleges, 1990-1991 enrollment

Jefferson State Community College, Birmingham 6,639
Phillips Junior College, Mountain Brook 512
Samford University, Birmingham 4,164
University of Alabama, Birmingham 15,356
University of Montevallo, Montevallo 3,250

Newspapers, total circulation (in all districts)

Birmingham Post-Herald News 225,490
Tuscaloosa News 39,180

Commercial television stations, affiliations

ADI: Birmingham (66%) and Tuscaloosa (34%)
WABM, Birmingham (None)
WBMG, Birmingham (CBS)
WBRC-TV, Birmingham (ABC)
WVTM-TV, Birmingham (NBC)
WDBB, Tuscaloosa (Fox)

Cable television systems, total subscribers

Bessemer Cable Communications; Bessemer 12,350
Comcast Cablevision of Tuscaloosa; Tuscaloosa 21,000
Crown Cable; Gardendale 5,520
Crown Cable; Forestdale 6,627
Crown Cable; Pelham 10,798
Crown Cable; Trussville 8,918
Mountain Brook Cablevision Inc; Mountain Brook 13,900
Shelby Cable; North Shelby County 5,600
TCI of Alabama; Fairfield 9,942
TCI of Alabama; Hoover 24,997
Time Warner Cable; Birmingham 61,500

Businesses and other major employers

Baptist Medical Centers Inc.; Birmingham 3,800
Jim Walter Resources Inc.; Brookwood; coal mining 2,700
DCH Regional Medical Center; Tuscaloosa 2,545
Blue Cross/Blue Shield of Alabama; Birmingham; medical service/health insurance 2,273
Harbert Corp.; Birmingham; heavy construction 2,000
State of Alabama/Mental Health Dept.; Tuscaloosa 1,780
Children's Hospital of Alabama; Birmingham 1,650
Shelby County Board of Education; Columbiana 1,623
BellSouth; Birmingham; data processing 1,250
U.S. Veterans Affairs Dept.; Birmingham; hospital 1,250
Rust International Corp.; Birmingham; business services 1,100
St. Vincent's Hospital; Birmingham 1,076
U.S. Veterans Affairs Dept.; Tuscaloosa; hospital 1,050
Medical Center East; Birmingham 915
Bruno's Inc.; Birmingham; warehousing 900
Gold Kist Inc.; Trussville; poultry 875
Hoover City Board of Education; Birmingham 800
STS Co. Inc.; Birmingham; security services 800
Valley View Baptist Church; Leeds; religious organization 750
Samford University; Birmingham 737
Protective Life Corp.; Birmingham; life insurance 700
BE&K Engineering Co.; Birmingham; engineering services 700
Southern Research Institute; Birmingham; engineering/architectural services 694
County of Jefferson/Health Dept.; Birmingham 650
Southern Progress Corp.; Birmingham; periodicals 640
Jim Walter Resources Inc.; Adger; coal mining 619
EBSCO Industries Inc.; Birmingham; periodicals 600
Pepsi Cola Bottling Co.; Birmingham; beverages 600
West Alabama General Hospital; Northport 600
Second Alarm Inc.; Birmingham; real estate operators 575
Pinkerton's Inc.; Birmingham; security services 560
Square D Co./Anderson Electric Co. Div.; Leeds; electric lighting 501

7th District

West Central — Parts of Birmingham, Montgomery and Tuscaloosa

The majority-black 7th is the product of the Voting Rights Act's mandate to increase minority-group representation in the House. Rep. Earl Hilliard, winning 69 percent of the vote in 1992, became Alabama's first black member of Congress since Reconstruction.

The district sprawls over all or part of 14 counties, but it is anchored by two population centers: Birmingham and Montgomery. In between are the rural counties of the Black Belt, one of the most economically deprived regions in the nation. While the term Black Belt is said to refer not to the racial composition but to the rich, cotton-growing soil in rural, west-central Alabama, all but one of the rural counties in the Black Belt portion of the district have black-majority populations. This area is in a perpetual state of poverty; it has not known prosperity since before the Civil War, when cotton plantation owners made fortunes from slave labor. Seven of the eight counties with the highest poverty rates in Alabama are in the Black Belt portion of the 7th. The poverty rate in Greene, Wilcox and Perry counties was more than 40 percent, according to the 1990 census; the others had rates above 30 percent.

The 7th extends a finger into southwestern Jefferson County (Birmingham), scooping out downtown Birmingham and the majority-black cities of Bessemer and Fairfield. Half the district's black population—and 45 percent of its total population—is in Jefferson County.

Reminders of the civil rights struggle that led to the 7th's creation dot the district; it is chronicled at Birmingham's Civil Rights Institute, which opened in November 1992. Four black girls died on Sept. 15, 1963, when the Sixteenth Street Baptist Church in downtown Birmingham was bombed. In March 1965, Selma (Dallas County) was the site of a bloody confrontation between civil rights demonstrators and police when the Rev. Dr. Martin Luther King, Jr., led marchers across the Edmund Pettus Bridge. The Civil Rights Memorial in Montgomery, designed by Vietnam Veterans Memorial architect Maya Lin, commemorates the 40 Americans who died while fighting for civil rights in the 1950s and 1960s.

There are ironies within the confines of the majority-black 7th. The portion of Montgomery within the district contains the state Capitol, which doubled as the Confederate Capitol from February 1861 to July 1861.

Politically, the 7th is every bit as Democratic as the 6th is Republican. Michael S. Dukakis won 69 percent in his 1988 presidential race. In 1990, losing Democratic gubernatorial nominee Paul Hubbert carried the 7th with 72 percent of the vote, 20 percentage points above his statewide tally.

Election Returns

	7th District	Democrat	Republican
1992	President*	137,518 (71.5%)	46,205 (24.0%)
	House †	144,320 (69.5%)	36,086 (17.4%)
1990	Senate	123,442 (79.6%)	31,657 (20.4%)
	Governor	116,515 (72.0%)	45,381 (28.0%)
1988	President	128,173 (68.9%)	57,972 (31.1%)

*Vote for Perot was 8,691 (4.5%).   †Independent/other is greater than 5%.

Demographics

Population 577,227

Percent change from 1980 3.2%

Land area 8,719 square miles

Population per square mile 66

Counties, 1990 population
Choctaw 16,018	Dallas 48,130
Clarke (pt.) 3,117	Greene 10,153
Hale 15,498	Perry 12,759
Jefferson (pt.) 258,515	Pickens (pt.) 2,742
Lowndes 12,658	Sumter 16,174
Marengo 23,084	Tuscaloosa (pt.) 69,183
Montgomery (pt.) 75,628	Wilcox 13,568

Cities, 1990 population (10,000 or more)
Bessemer (pt.) 31,075	Montgomery (pt.) 67,007
Birmingham (pt.) 183,414	Selma 23,755
Fairfield 12,200	Tuscaloosa (pt.) 41,137

Race and Hispanic origin
White 32.1%
Black 67.5%
American Indian, Eskimo, or Aleut. 0.1%
Asian or Pacific Islander 0.2%
Other 0.1%
Hispanic origin 0.3%

Ancestry
American 10.3%	Irish 6.3%
English 5.0%	Scotch Irish 1.5%
German 4.2%	

Universities/colleges, 1990-1991 enrollment
Alabama State University, Montgomery 4,587
Bessemer State Tech College, Bessemer 1,730
Birmingham Southern College, Birmingham 1,902
C. A. Fredd State Tech College, Tuscaloosa 279
Concordia College, Selma 380
George C. Wallace Community College, Selma 1,678
Judson College, Marion 312
Lawson State Community College, Birmingham 1,711
Livingston University, Livingston 1,921
Marion Military Institute, Marion 246
Miles College, Birmingham 584
Selma University, Selma 316
Shelton State Community College, Tuscaloosa 5,113
Stillman College, Tuscaloosa 770
University of Alabama, Tuscaloosa 19,794
Trenholm State Tech College, Montgomery 783
Troy State University, Montgomery 2,736

Newspapers, total circulation (in all districts)
Birmingham Post-Herald News 225,490
Mobile Press-Register 101,978
Montgomery Advertiser-Journal 64,576
Tuscaloosa News 39,180

Commercial television stations, affiliations
ADI: Montgomery-Selma (52%), Meridian (21%), Birmingham (19%), Tuscaloosa (4%) and Mobile-Pensacola (4%)
WHOA-TV, Montgomery (ABC)
WAKA, Selma (CBS)
WCFT-TV, Tuscaloosa (CBS)

Cable television systems, total subscribers
Selma Telecable Corp.; Selma 9,113
Storer Cable TV Inc.; Montgomery 52,000
Time Warner Cable; Birmingham 61,500

Military installations, 1991
Birmingham Municipal Airport Air Force Guard Station, Birmingham 341
Dannelly Field Air Force Base, Montgomery 319

Businesses and other major employers

University of Alabama; Tuscaloosa 6,763

Southtrust Corp.; Birmingham; commercial banks 2,600

American Cast Iron Pipe Co.; Birmingham; iron/steel foundries 2,500

Uniroyal Goodrich Tire Co.; Tuscaloosa; tires 2,400

USX Corp.; Birmingham; steel products 2,200

Torchmark Corp.; Birmingham; medical service/health insurance 2,036

James River Corp./Naheola Mill; Pennington; paper products 2,000

Alabama Power Co.; Birmingham; electric services 1,825

Pemco Aeroplex Inc.; Birmingham; aircraft/parts 1,700

U.S. Postal Service; Birmingham 1,500

Jefferson County School District; Birmingham 1,500

Stockham Valves & Fittings; Birmingham; valves/pipe fittings 1,450

Rite Way Service Inc.; Birmingham; janitorial services 1,300

MacMillan Bloedel Inc.; Pine Hill; paperboard mills 1,200

First Alabama Bancshares Inc.; Montgomery; bank holding 1,200

Partlow State School & Hospital; Tuscaloosa 1,150

Jackson Hospital & Clinic; Montgomery 1,100

County of Jefferson; Birmingham 1,100

Montgomery Winn-Dixie Inc.; Montgomery; grocery stores 1,000

Amsouth Bank; Birmingham; commercial banks 1,000

State of Alabama/Public Health Dept.; Montgomery 932

Jefferson County Works Dept.; Birmingham; engineering/architectural services 900

State of Alabama/Education Dept.; Montgomery 900

Phifer Wire Products Inc.; Tuscaloosa; wire products 850

Humana Hospital-Montgomery; Montgomery 850

First Alabama Bancshares Inc.; Birmingham; bank holding 800

Alabama Gas Corp.; Birmingham; natural gas distribution 752

BellSouth; Montgomery; telephone communications 750

Lloyd Noland Hospital; Fairfield 747

Allied Products Corp.; Selma; farm/garden machinery 723

International Paper Co./Hammermill Paper Co.; Selma; paper mills 700

Golden Flake Snack Foods Inc.; Birmingham; food products 700

Trinity Industries Inc.; Bessemer; railroad equipment 700

Public Schools of Selma; Selma 690

Alabama State University; Montgomery 685

Birmingham News Co. Inc.; Birmingham; newspapers 673

Sonat Inc.; Birmingham; natural gas distribution 600

Palmer Md; Birmingham; medical doctors 600

Wells Fargo Guard Services; Birmingham; security services 600

Oneal Steel Inc.; Birmingham; metals/minerals 580

Birmingham Coca-Cola Bottling; Birmingham; beverages 550

Deaton Inc.; Birmingham; trucking services 550

Parisian Inc.; Birmingham; family clothing stores 550

City of Montgomery/Police Dept.; Montgomery 550

Norwood Clinic Inc.; Birmingham; health services 550

Bessemer Carraway Medical Center; Bessemer 550

JVC America Inc.; Tuscaloosa; blank video tape 525

State of Alabama/Forestry Commission; Montgomery; 520

Vanity Fair Mills Inc.; Demopolis; undergarments 510

State of Alabama/Highway Dept.; Birmingham; road construction 504

Alaska

The March 1989 crash of the *Exxon Valdez* supertanker was a trauma for all of Alaska. The spilling of 10 million gallons of Alaskan crude into the waters of the Prince William Sound focused attention on the environmental risks of oil development. Oil revenues have done a lot for Alaska, but after the spill, more residents wondered what oil might do *to* the state.

The pro-oil majority that controlled the state Legislature during the 1980s—associated with the GOP majority—saw its influence threatened; within months of the wreck, the Legislature passed a spate of environmental protection measures.

And in Congress, environmental activists used publicity about the spill to dampen interest in what was already a controversial Alaskan oil exploration proposal: to allow drilling for oil on the coastal plain of the Arctic National Wildlife Refuge (ANWR), on Alaska's North Slope. When the 102nd Congress passed an energy policy bill, it declined to allow drilling in ANWR. The Clinton administration in 1993 likewise opposed drilling in ANWR.

But in Alaska, as time has passed since the *Valdez* spill, attention has come to focus more and more on this reality: The state is heavily dependent on the oil industry to provide jobs, and 85 percent of state revenues come from the industry. Due to declining production at Alaska's main oil fields at Prudhoe Bay, there are concerns that unless new sources are tapped, a budget crisis looms.

Pro-development forces enjoyed a resurgence in 1992 state legislative elections. And the potential for state revenue shortfalls and other economic trouble is rekindling the resentment many Alaskans harbor toward the federal government—which controls about 60 percent of the state's land—and toward "outsiders" who seek to restrain development.

From this longstanding sentiment springs the state's maverick political tradition, characterized by iconoclasm with a decidedly conservative bent. In 1992, independent presidential candidate Ross Perot won 29 percent of the vote in Alaska, his second-best showing among the states and almost enough to pull him into second place ahead of Bill Clinton, who got 31 percent. Walter J. Hickel, elected governor in 1990, belongs to the Alaskan Independence Party, a group that advocates secession from the United States, though Hickel does not.

George Bush, who took 62 percent of Alaska's presidential vote in 1988, dropped 22 points in 1992 but still carried the state;

Alaska has voted Democratic for president only once since statehood, in 1964. From 1981 to 1993, the GOP held all three of the state's seats in Congress.

The nation's largest state in land area, Alaska ranks 49th in population, with just over 550,000 residents. Despite Alaska's permafrost reputation, residents enjoy the state's breathtaking natural beauty and warm summers. Still, it takes a hardy type to live this far north in the winter.

The state's population nexus is Anchorage, with slightly more than 226,000 residents. Its international airport is a key trade crossroads. Thanks to its equidistance from Tokyo, Frankfurt and New York, Anchorage International leads the country in terms of landed cargo weight. Three of Anchorage's top five nongovernment employers are oil-related; the top private employer is a huge grocery store chain with more than 3,000 employees statewide.

In the wake of Pentagon plans to scale back defense spending, Anchorage was bracing for cuts in 1993. But neither Elmendorf Air Force Base nor the Army's Fort Richardson appeared on that year's base-closure list.

With revenues from the oil industry uncertain, efforts have intensified to diversify the economy. A promising alternative is tourism, which has been growing rapidly. Fishing is already big business. Alaska fishing accounted for more than 50 percent of U.S. production in 1990 and employs about a quarter of the state's work force. Bristol Bay, off the southwest coast, is the world's largest producer of red salmon.

About 350 miles north of Anchorage is Fairbanks (population 31,000), the traditional trading center for the villages of inland Alaska. The city grew as the supply center for the Alaska oil pipeline (which runs north from here to Prudhoe Bay).

Southeast Alaska is separated from the rest of the state by the St. Elias Mountains and the Gulf of Alaska. Juneau, the state capital, is inaccessible by land. Alaska's vast "bush" region is dotted with mostly tiny towns. Native Americans and Eskimos predominate in remote Alaska.

Table 1   Population

District	Population	Population under 18	Voting-age population	Median age
AL	550,043	172,344	377,699	29.4

31

ALASKA

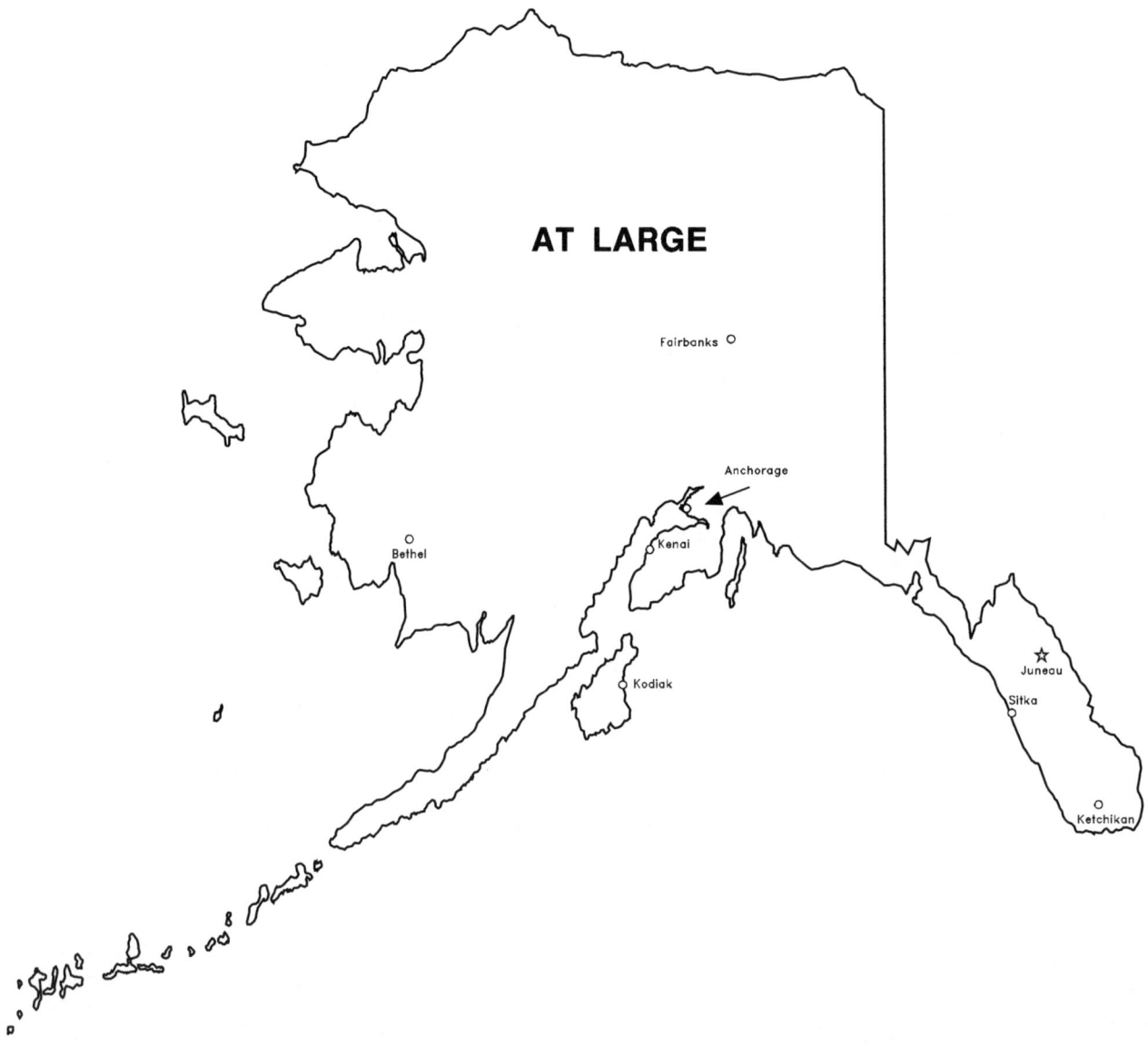

AT LARGE

Fairbanks ○

Anchorage

○ Kenai

○ Bethel

☆ Juneau

Sitka ○

○ Kodiak

Ketchikan ○

Table 2   Voting-Age Persons

District	White*	Black*	American Indian, Eskimo, or Aleut*	Asian or Pacific Islander*	Other*	Hispanic*	Male*	Female*
AL	77.9%	3.9%	13.5%	3.6%	1.2%	2.9%	53.2%	46.8%

*As percent of voting-age population.

Table 3   Voting-Age Persons by Age Groups

District	18-24*	25-44*	45-54*	55-64*	65 and over*
AL	14.8%	57.2%	14.3%	7.8%	5.9%

*As percent of voting-age population.

Table 4   Income and Occupation

District	Median family income	Families in poverty	White collar*	Blue collar*	Service*	Farm*
AL	$46,581	6.8%	60.7%	22.2%	14.4%	2.7%

*As percent of employed persons age 16 and over.

Table 5   Education: School Years Completed

District	Less than grade 9*	Grades 9-12 no diploma*	High school diploma*	College bachelor's degree or higher*
AL	5.1%	8.2%	28.7%	23.0%

*As percent of persons age 25 and over.

Table 6   Housing and Residential Patterns

District	Owner occupied	Renter occupied	Urban	Rural
AL	56.1%	43.9%	67.5%	32.5%

Election Returns

	At Large	Democrat	Republican
1992	President*	78,294 (30.9%)	102,000 (40.2%)
	Senate†	92,065 (38.5%)	127,163 (53.2%)
	House†	102,378 (42.9%)	111,849 (46.8%)
1990	Senate	61,152 (32.7%)	125,806 (67.3%)
	Governor†	60,201 (32.2%)	50,991 (27.3%)
1988	President	72,105 (36.7%)	118,817 (60.4%)
1986	Senate	79,727 (44.9%)	97,674 (55.1%)
	Governor†	84,943 (49.5%)	76,515 (44.6%)

*Vote for Perot was 73,481 (29.0%).   †Independent/other is greater than 5%.

Demographics

Population   550,043

Percent change from 1980   36.9%

Land area   570,374 square miles

Population per square mile   1

Boroughs and census areas, 1990 population*
Aleutians East Borough   2,464
Aleutians West Census Area   9,478
Anchorage Borough   226,338
Bethel Census Area   13,656
Bristol Bay Borough   1,410
Dillingham Census Area   4,012
Fairbanks North Star Borough   77,720
Haines Borough   2,117
Juneau Borough   26,751
Kenai Peninsula Borough   40,802
Ketchikan Gateway Borough   13,828
Kodiak Island Borough   13,309
Lake and Peninsula Borough   1,668
Matanuska-Susitna Borough   39,683
Nome Census Area   8,288
North Slope Borough   5,979
Northwest Arctic Borough   6,113
Prince of Wales-Outer Ketchikan Census Area   6,278
Sitka Borough   8,588
Skagway-Yakutat-Angoon Census Area   4,385
Southeast Fairbanks Census Area   5,913
Valdez-Cordova Census Area   9,952
Wade Hampton Census Area   5,791
Wrangell-Petersburg Census Area   7,042
Yukon-Koyukuk Census Area   8,478

*Alaska has no counties.

Cities, 1990 population (10,000 or more)
Anchorage   226,338   Fairbanks   30,843
College CDP   11,249   Juneau   26,751

Race and Hispanic origin
White   75.5%
Black   4.1%
American Indian, Eskimo, or Aleut.   15.6%
Asian or Pacific Islander   3.6%
Other   1.2%
Hispanic origin   3.2%

Ancestry

American 4.2%	Italian 2.7%
Danish 1.1%	Norwegian 4.2%
Dutch 2.6%	Polish 2.2%
English 13.9%	Russian 1.1%
French 4.3%	Scotch Irish 2.3%
French Canadian 1.1%	Scottish 3.1%
German 23.1%	Swedish 3.2%
Irish 13.5%	Welsh 1.1%

Universities/colleges, 1990-1991 enrollment
Alaska Junior College, Anchorage   393
Alaska Pacific University, Anchorage   1,267
Sheldon Jackson College, Sitka   275
University of Alaska, Fairbanks   7,595
University of Alaska Southeast, Juneau   2,711
University of Alaska, Anchorage   17,498

Newspapers, total circulation
Anchorage Daily News   60,086
Daily Sitka Sentinel   2,554
Fairbank Daily News-Miner   16,844
Juneau Empire   6,348
Kenai Peninsula Clarian   3,874
Ketchikan Daily News   4,549
Kodiak Daily Mirror   3,188

Commercial television stations, affiliations
ADI: Alaska has none.
  KIMO, Anchorage (ABC)
  KTBY, Anchorage (Fox)
  KTUU-TV, Anchorage (NBC)
  KTVA, Anchorage (CBS)
  KYES, Anchorage (None)
  KATN, Fairbanks (ABC)
  KTVF, Fairbanks (CBS)
  KJUD, Juneau (ABC)
  KJNP-TV, North Pole (None)
  KTNL, Sitka (CBS)

Cable television systems, total subscribers
  Prime Cable; Anchorage 47,600
  Cooke Cablevision; Fairbanks; 5,000
  Cooke Cablevision; Juneau; 6,900

Military installations, 1991
  Elmendorf Air Force Base, Anchorage 9,190
  Fort Wainwright (Army), Fairbanks 6,640
  Fort Richardson (Army), Anchorage 5,476
  Eielson Air Force Base, Fairbanks 4,371
  Adak Naval Air Station, Adak 2,259
  Fort Greely (Army), Delta Junction 760
  Shemya Air Force Base, Shemya 733
  Kulis Air National Guard Base, Anchorage 428
  Clear Air Force Station, Anderson 392
  Galena Airport Air Force Station, Galena 375
  King Salmon Airport, Naknek 346

Businesses and other major employers
  University of Alaska; Fairbanks 2,200
  State of Alaska; Juneau 1,660
  State of Alaska/Fish & Game Dept.; Juneau 1,500
  Kenai Peninsula Boro School District; Soldotna 1,100
  State of Alaska/Transportation Dept.; Fairbanks 800
  State of Alaska/Marine System Dept.; Juneau; water transportation 750
  North Slope Borough Law Office; Barrow 743
  State of Alaska/Labor Dept.; Juneau 700
  Veco Inc.; Prudhoe Bay; oil/gas services 625
  Ketchikan Pulp Co.; Ketchikan; pulp mills 600
  Lutheran/Fairbanks Memorial Hospital; Fairbanks 593

Arizona

rizona stands as testament to the population torrent that flowed to the South, West and Southwest in the 1980s. During that decade, Arizona's population swelled by 35 percent, rising by nearly 1 million people.

Some of the fastest-growing areas of the country in the 1980s were found in Arizona. Two of the nation's top 20 congressional districts to register the most population gain in the 1980s were Arizona's 1st (which ranked eighth) and 3rd (ranked 20th). Much of the state's expansion came in the corridor anchored by Phoenix and Tucson and encompassing booming suburban cities such as Mesa, Glendale and Tempe. All five cities registered 20 percent-plus increases in population. Mesa's population rose by nearly 90 percent; at 288,000, it stands as the third most populous city in the state.

As its population has risen, Arizona has grown more Republican. Democrats lost their edge on statewide party registration in the mid-1980s, and the GOP has shown no sign of relinquishing its grip since. The affluent retirees who have migrated to the state tend to support Republicans.

Arizona's Hispanic population also experienced a boom, growing from about 440,000 in 1980 to nearly 700,000 in 1990—according to the Census Bureau's official count, that is. A later statistical survey conducted by the bureau showed that even that rapid growth may have been understated. Although Hispanics are more Democratic, their effect on Arizona's voting patterns is mitigated because they tend to vote in fewer numbers than non-Hispanics.

Arizona's population surge won it an additional House seat in reapportionment. It now has six House seats, more than at any time in state history.

With partisan control of the government split—Democrats held a narrow majority in the state Senate, while Republicans controlled the House and governor's office—legislators failed to reach accord on a redistricting plan, despite months of negotiations. As a result, a panel of three federal judges took over Arizona's redistricting.

The state Senate and state House submitted competing plans to the panel. The judges, however, rejected both approaches. Instead, they relied heavily on a plan submitted by several Indian tribes in the state. The map appeared to favor the state's five incumbents—four Republicans and one Democrat—while making the new, open 6th District a competitive seat. But in 1992, the 1st

District's three-term GOP incumbent was upset by his Democratic foe. And a Democrat won the open 6th, giving Democrats three of the state's six House seats for the 103rd Congress.

The reliably Democratic 2nd, which in 1991 had elected Ed Pastor to be Arizona's first Hispanic member of Congress (to replace longtime Democratic Rep. Morris K. Udall, who resigned due to ill health), became a majority-Hispanic district, as the Hispanic population was boosted from 36 percent to slightly more than 50 percent of the total population.

Table 1 Population

District	Population	Population under 18	Voting-age population	Median age
1	610,872	152,897	457,975	30.3
2	610,871	196,590	414,281	28.2
3	610,871	153,578	457,293	36.3
4	610,871	146,492	464,379	33.9
5	610,871	145,501	465,370	34.2
6	610,872	186,061	424,811	31.3
State	3,665,228	981,119	2,684,109	32.2

Table 2 Voting-Age Persons

District	White*	Black*	American Indian, Eskimo, or Aleut*	Asian or Pacific Islander*	Other*	Hispanic*	Male*	Female*
1	88.5%	2.8%	1.4%	2.3%	4.9%	11.1%	49.2%	50.8%
2	64.4	6.5	3.9	1.4	23.7	44.8	50.0	50.0
3	89.9	1.6	2.6	1.0	4.8	9.4	48.4	51.6
4	93.1	1.6	1.0	1.7	2.5	6.6	47.9	52.1
5	89.5	2.6	0.8	1.8	5.3	14.0	48.4	51.6
6	75.2	1.3	17.6	0.7	5.3	11.3	48.8	51.2
State	83.9	2.7	4.4	1.5	7.5	15.8	48.8	51.2

*As percent of voting-age population.

Table 3 Voting-Age Persons by Age Groups

District	18-24*	25-44*	45-54*	55-64*	65 and over*
1	17.6%	49.4%	12.1%	8.7%	12.2%
2	17.9	44.8	12.3	10.6	14.4

ARIZONA

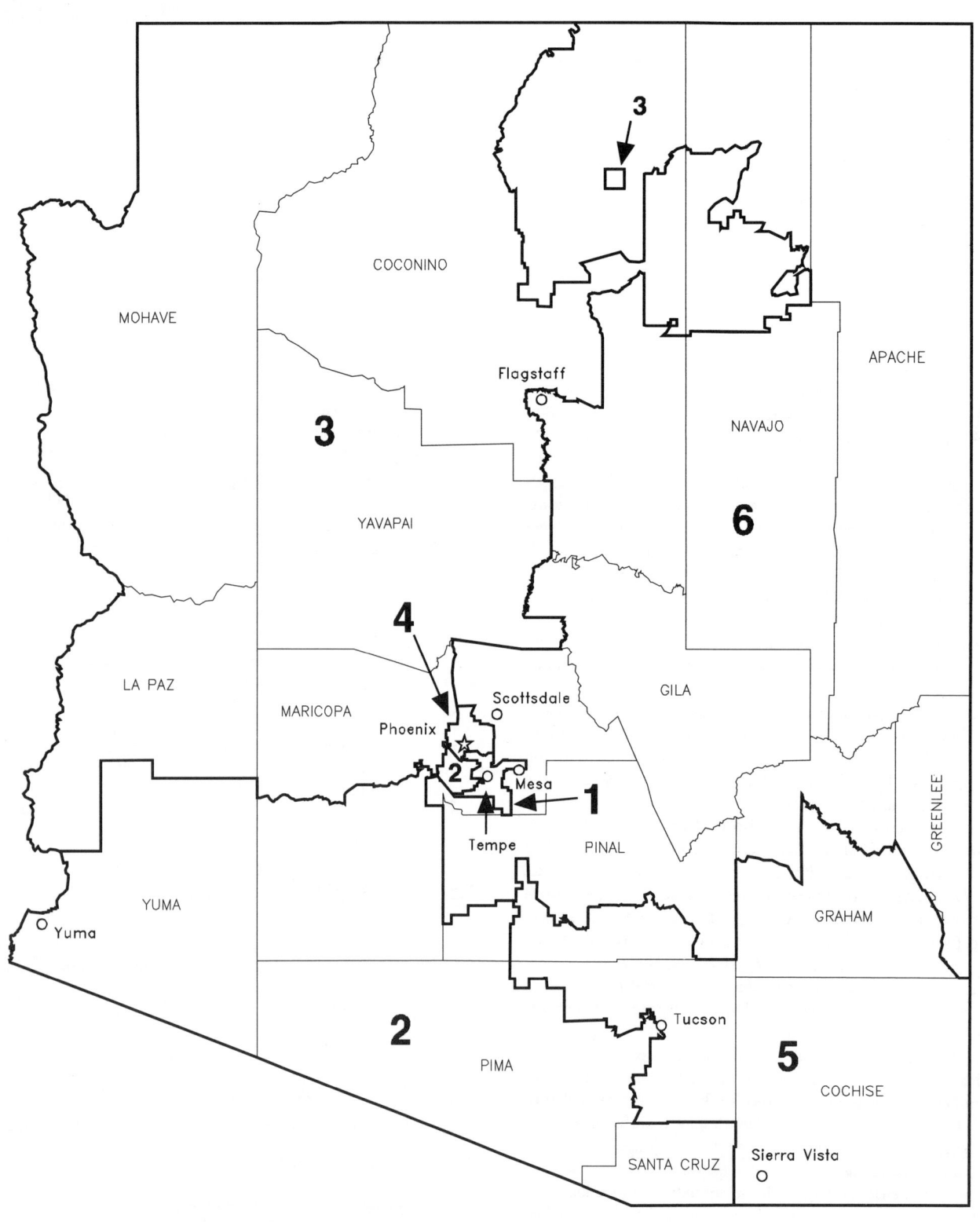

MOHAVE

COCONINO

3

Flagstaff

APACHE

NAVAJO

3

YAVAPAI

6

LA PAZ

4

MARICOPA

Scottsdale

GILA

Phoenix

2

Mesa

1

GREENLEE

Tempe

PINAL

YUMA

Yuma

GRAHAM

2

Tucson

PIMA

5

COCHISE

SANTA CRUZ

Sierra Vista

District	18-24*	25-44*	45-54*	55-64*	65 and over*
3	10.5%	38.3%	12.3%	12.5%	26.4%
4	13.4	45.0	15.4	11.4	14.8
5	14.5	41.2	12.9	11.8	19.5
6	14.2	41.4	12.9	12.0	19.5
State	14.6	43.4	13.0	11.2	17.8

*As percent of voting-age population.

Table 4 Income and Occupation

District	Median family income	Families in poverty	White collar*	Blue collar*	Service*	Farm*
1	$38,232	7.6%	66.3%	19.5%	12.9%	1.3%
2	22,650	22.6	44.5	32.6	18.1	4.7
3	31,663	8.6	54.8	26.5	16.0	2.7
4	40,563	6.2	68.5	18.2	12.1	1.1
5	32,829	9.0	64.2	18.5	15.4	1.9
6	29,273	16.1	55.2	26.4	15.5	2.9
State	32,178	11.4	60.0	22.9	14.7	2.3

*As percent of employed persons age 16 and over.

Table 5 Education: School Years Completed

District	Less than grade 9*	Grades 9-12 no diploma*	High school diploma*	College bachelor's degree or higher*
1	5.0%	8.9%	22.5%	27.6%
2	22.2	18.7	25.7	9.2
3	7.1	13.9	30.3	16.2
4	4.1	9.2	24.6	26.3
5	6.1	9.5	25.2	25.0
6	11.6	14.6	28.4	15.9
State	9.0	12.3	26.1	20.3

*As percent of persons age 25 and over.

Table 6 Housing and Residential Patterns

District	Owner occupied	Renter occupied	Urban	Rural
1	55.1%	44.9%	99.6%	0.4%
2	57.9	42.1	90.3	9.7
3	74.4	25.6	81.5	18.5
4	62.8	37.2	99.9	0.1
5	63.1	36.9	86.5	13.5
6	72.2	27.8	67.2	32.8
State	64.2	35.8	87.5	12.5

1st District

Southeastern Phoenix — Tempe; Mesa

Democrat Sam Coppersmith's unexpected House victory in 1992 was in part an outgrowth of a redistricting plan that shifted some of the Phoenix area's most conservative Republicans into the newly created 6th District.

Mapmakers put East Mesa in the 6th, a step that gives the 1st a more centrist electorate. Remaining in the district are more moderate Republican voters in West Mesa, Tempe, Chandler and parts of Phoenix. Under certain circumstances these cities will consider voting for a Democratic candidate, and the business-oriented Coppersmith added enough of them to the district's Democratic minority to win with 51 percent of the vote.

Still, on paper this looks like it should be a Republican district. Nearly 53 percent of its voters are registered Republicans. The 1992 remap removed some Democratic areas from the 1st: Hispanic neighborhoods surrounding Sky Harbor Airport and the Gila River Indian reservation just south of Phoenix. Voters in those areas are now located in districts with larger minority populations.

In the 1992 presidential contest, George Bush came out on top in the 1st with 40 percent of the vote. Bill Clinton got 34 percent, and the independent streak that runs through many of the voters here showed up in a 26 percent tally for Ross Perot.

The 1st encompasses most of Mesa, where population exploded by almost 90 percent during the 1980s, exceeding 288,000. The district's other suburban pillars are Tempe and Chandler.

Electronics and high-tech companies have thrived here in recent years, spawning a sizable class of well-to-do managers and technicians. They generally have conservative political instincts, as do the thousands of retirees who have settled in the area.

Mesa was founded by Mormons in 1878; it still has a politically active Mormon community and is the site of Arizona's Mormon temple. Mesa is home to eight manufacturing companies on the *Fortune* 500 list, and it is the spring-training base for two professional baseball teams, the Chicago Cubs and California Angels.

Tempe, just to the west, was developed around a flour mill in 1871; today it is primarily a manufacturing city, with more than 200 businesses producing a range of goods, from clothing to electronics. The city usually votes Republican in state and local elections, but Arizona State University's 43,000 students and 1,800 faculty provide Tempe with a significant Democratic presence.

The district also takes in a politically diverse portion of southeastern Phoenix, a tabletop-flat area of the "Valley of the Sun" that includes some upper-middle-class neighborhoods with a distinctly Republican bent. Another change to the 1st in redistricting—a greater portion of Scottsdale—also could add to Republican strength in the district.

Election Returns

	1st District	Democrat	Republican
1992	President*	88,247 (33.7%)	105,784 (40.3%)
	House	130,715 (51.3%)	113,613 (44.6%)
1990	Governor	83,970 (48.6%)	88,849 (51.4%)
1988	President	69,912 (34.7%)	129,027 (64.1%)
	Senate	104,973 (52.8%)	89,880 (45.2%)
1986	Senate	45,446 (32.4%)	94,632 (67.6%)
	Governor†	41,043 (29.3%)	57,184 (40.8%)

*Vote for Perot was 68,143 (26.0%).   †Independent/other is greater than 5%.

Demographics

Population 610,872

Percent change from 1980 12.3%

Land area 211 square miles

Population per square mile 2,900

Counties, 1990 population
Maricopa (pt.)   610,872

Cities, 1990 population (10,000 or more)
Chandler (pt.) 89,245	Scottsdale (pt.) 52,361
Mesa (pt.) 169,237	Tempe (pt.) 141,865
Phoenix (pt.) 152,054	

Race and Hispanic origin
White 86.9%
Black 3.2%
American Indian, Eskimo, or Aleut.   1.7%
Asian or Pacific Islander 2.3%
Other 5.9%
Hispanic origin 13.2%

Ancestry
American 2.3%	Italian 5.4%
Danish 1.4%	Norwegian 2.5%
Dutch 2.8%	Polish 3.4%
English 17.5%	Scotch Irish 2.1%
French 4.7%	Scottish 2.9%
German 28.5%	Swedish 3.2%
Irish 16.6%	Welsh 1.2%

Universities/colleges, 1990-1991 enrollment
Al Collins Graphic Design School, Tempe 475
Arizona State University, Tempe 42,952
ITT Tech Institute, Phoenix 312
Mesa Community College, Mesa 19,818

Newspapers, total circulation (in all districts)
Arizona Republic/Phoenix Gazette 445,214
Chandler Arizonan-Tribune 8,511
Gilbert Tribune 4,545
Mesa Tribune 45,831
Scottsdale Progress 18,139
Sun City Daily News-Sun 18,591
Tempe Daily News-Tribune 11,693

Commercial television stations, affiliations
ADI: Phoenix (100%)

Cable television systems, total subscribers
Times Mirror Cable TV of Arizona; Mesa 41,400
Times Mirror Cable TV of Arizona; Phoenix 310,000

Businesses and other major employers
Motorola Inc.; Mesa; electronic components 5,000
McDonnell Douglas Helicopter Co.; Mesa; helicopters/parts 4,350
Intel Corp.; Chandler; electronic components 3,200
St. Joseph's Hospital & Medical Center; Phoenix 3,000
Allied-Signal Inc./Garrett Fluid Systems Co.; Tempe; machinery/equipment/supplies 2,700
Scottsdale Memorial Hospital; Scottsdale 2,300
Motorola Inc.; Scottsdale; business services 2,100
Security Pacific Bancorp./Arizona Bank; Tempe; commercial banks 2,000
Motorola Inc.; Tempe; electronic components 1,650
Salt River Project; Tempe; electric services 1,500
U.S. Veterans Affairs Dept.; Phoenix; hospital 1,500
Mesa Community College; Mesa 1,434
Bankamerica Corp./Merabank Federal Savings Bank; Phoenix; commercial banks 1,400
Mesa Lutheran Hospital; Mesa; health services 1,400

Desert Samaritan Health Hospital; Mesa 1,366
First Interstate Bank; Tempe; computer services 1,200
Newtree Service Corp.; Phoenix; management services 1,200
U-Haul Intl. Inc.; Phoenix; truck rentals 1,080
City of Scottsdale; Scottsdale 1,067
U.S. West Communications; Phoenix; electrical repair 1,000
Motorola Inc.; Chandler; electronic components 998
Humana Inc./Humana Hospital-Phoenix; Phoenix 957
Continental Circuits Corp.; Phoenix; electronic components 863
Medtronic Inc.; Tempe; electronic components 843
State Farm Life Insurance Co.; Tempe; life insurance 800
KFC National Management Co.; Tempe; management 800
Pedus Service Inc.; Scottsdale; business services 800
Digital Equipment Corp.; Tempe; computer/office equipment 780
Rogers Corp.; Chandler; nonferrous rolling and drawing 700
Apollo Group Inc./Apollo Press Div.; Phoenix 670
Ryobi Outdoor Products Inc.; Chandler; farm/garden machinery 650
Litton Systems Inc.; Tempe; electronic components 650
Arizona State University/Physical Plant; Tempe; building services 650
City of Chandler; Chandler 615
Idea Courier Inc.; Tempe; computer/office equipment 600
Tanner Companies; Phoenix; road construction 600
Salt River Project; Phoenix; engineering/architectural services 600
Avnet Inc./Hamilton Avnet; Chandler; electrical goods 550
Carson Pirie Scott & Co./Ambassador Leather Goods; Phoenix; department stores 550
Rolm Co./IBM Corp.; Phoenix; retail stores 550
Rural/Metro Corp.; Scottsdale; business services 548
Mesa Public School District; Mesa 525
F. H. P. Inc.; Tempe; medical doctors 525

2nd District

Southwest — Southwestern Tucson; Southern Phoenix; Yuma

The 2nd is Arizona's most Hispanic and most Democratic district. Redistricting in 1992 gave the 2nd a bare Hispanic-majority population: 50 percent, up from 36 percent in the 1980s. Hispanics make up 45 percent of the voting-age population.

Some Hispanic activists lobbied mapmakers for a heavier minority concentration, but Rep. Ed Pastor, Arizona's first Hispanic Representative, had no trouble winning his first re-election in 1992, taking two-thirds of the vote as Bill Clinton won a majority in presidential balloting. Clinton's 51 percent tally in the 2nd was easily his best showing in any Arizona district.

The Maricopa County (Phoenix) portion of the 2nd casts the district's largest share of votes, nearly 40 percent. Most of the Maricopa vote comes out of Hispanic areas. The south side of Phoenix, included in the 2nd, traditionally has been the city's poorest economically and most faithfully Democratic. Remapping strengthened the Democratic slant by including the minority neighborhoods near Sky Harbor Airport, which had been in the 1st District.

To the southeast, Pima County (Tucson) accounts for 35 percent of the district vote. Here also Democrats are strong in Hispanic neighborhoods, and in the community surrounding the

University of Arizona. With 35,000 students and 12,000 workers, it is the biggest single factor in Tucson's economy. (The university's campus is partially shared with the 5th District.) Just south of Tucson, the copper-mining town of Ajo and the San Xavier and Papago Indian reservations also favor Democrats.

Tucson has begun to see the same influx of retirees and people attracted by the high-tech industry that has transformed politics in other parts of Arizona. But Tucson's long Democratic tradition is still strong; in 1992 Clinton won 59 percent in the Pima County part of the 2nd, well above his district average.

Though the bulk of Pima County's land area lies within the boundaries of the 2nd, most of the county's residents live in eastern Tucson in the 5th District.

The most Republican part of the 2nd is on the district's western edge, in Yuma County. It casts about one-fifth of the total district vote, and in 1992 not only gave George Bush a first-place finish with 42 percent, but also backed the GOP House candidate, who was crushed districtwide.

Incorporated as Arizona City in 1871 and renamed two years later, Yuma, the county seat, lies south of California on the Colorado River; it continues in its traditional role as a regional commercial crossroads. Interstate 8 running through the city heads west to San Diego, Calif. Yuma County's economic base is agricultural, but two military bases—the Marine Corps Air Station and Yuma Proving Grounds—contribute significantly to the economy.

Rounding out the 2nd is Santa Cruz County, where the heavily Hispanic border town of Nogales and its Mexican sister city of the same name are a major crossing point between the two countries. Clinton won Santa Cruz in 1992, but ran several points below his district average.

Election Returns

	2nd District	Democrat	Republican
1992	President*	74,588 (51.4%)	41,757 (28.8%)
	House	90,693 (66.0%)	41,257 (30.0%)
1990	Governor	66,706 (65.9%)	34,554 (34.1%)
1988	President	68,279 (57.1%)	49,918 (41.8%)
	Senate	84,760 (71.3%)	31,976 (26.9%)
1986	Senate	51,984 (57.4%)	38,570 (42.6%)
	Governor†	46,569 (50.8%)	25,512 (27.8%)

*Vote for Perot was 20,767 (19.8%).   †Independent/other is greater than 5%.

Demographics

Population 610,871

Percent change from 1980 12.5%

Land area 17,710 square miles

Population per square mile 34

Counties, 1990 population

Maricopa (pt.) 276,352	Santa Cruz 29,676
Pima (pt.) 197,212	Yuma 106,895
Pinal (pt.) 736	

Cities, 1990 population (10,000 or more)

Avondale (pt.) 13,110	Phoenix (pt.) 226,721
Glendale (pt.) 14,684	Tucson (pt.) 140,910
Nogales 19,489	Yuma 54,923

Race and Hispanic origin
White 60.1%
Black 6.8%
American Indian, Eskimo, or Aleut. 4.5%
Asian or Pacific Islander 1.3%
Other 27.3%
Hispanic origin 50.5%

Ancestry

American 2.2%	Irish 8.4%
Dutch 1.4%	Italian 1.9%
English 7.4%	Polish 1.1%
French 2.4%	Scotch Irish 1.3%
German 12.2%	Scottish 1.1%

Universities/colleges, 1990-1991 enrollment
Arizona Western College, Yuma 4,913
Gateway Community College, Phoenix 6,821
ITT Tech Institute, Tucson 258
Rio Salado Community College, Phoenix 10,480
South Mountain Community College, Phoenix 3,288
University of Arizona, Tucson 35,735
University of Phoenix, Phoenix 4,149

Newspapers, total circulation (in all districts)
Arizona Daily Star Citizen 141,661
Arizona Republic/Phoenix Gazette 445,214
Casa Grande Dispatch 8,604
Chandler Arizonan-Tribune 8,511
Gilbert Tribune 4,545
Mesa Tribune 45,831
Scottsdale Progress 18,139
Sun City Daily News-Sun 18,591
Tempe Daily News-Tribune 11,693
Yuma Sun-Arizona Sentinel 20,720

Commercial television stations, affiliations
ADI: Tucson (45%), El Centro-Yuma (31%), and Phoenix (24%)
KNXV-TV, Phoenix (Fox)
KPAZ-TV, Phoenix (None)
KPHO-TV, Phoenix (None)
KTSP-TV, Phoenix (CBS)
KTVK, Phoenix (ABC)
KUTP, Phoenix (None)
KPNX-TV, Mesa (NBC)
KMSB-TV, Tucson (Fox)

Cable television systems, total subscribers
Saguaro Cable TV; Nogales 6,100
Times Mirror Cable TV of Arizona; Phoenix 310,000
Tucson Cable; Tucson 74,027

Military installations, 1991
Luke Air Force Base, Litchfield Park 5,652
Yuma Marine Corps Air Station, Yuma 5,612
Yuma Proving Ground (Army), Yuma 2,090
Tucson Intl. Airport Air Force Guard Station, Tucson 879
Phoenix Sky Harbor Intl. Airport Air Force Guard Station, Phoenix 342
Gila Bend Air Force Station, Gila Bend 328

Businesses and other major employers
University of Arizona; Tucson 12,600
State of Arizona/Economic Security Dept.; Phoenix 7,000

Allied-Signal Inc./Garrett Engine Div.; Phoenix; guided missiles/parts 4,500

State of Arizona/Transportation Dept.; Phoenix 4,100

Good Samaritan Hospital; Phoenix 4,000

Revlon Inc.; Phoenix; cosmetics/soaps 3,000

Allied-Signal Inc./Garrett Auxiliary Power Div.; Phoenix; aircraft/parts 2,500

AT&T Network Cable Systems; Phoenix; communications equipment 2,356

Phoenix Newspapers Inc./Arizona Republic; Phoenix; newspapers 2,300

Allied-Signal Inc./Garrett General Aviation Services; Phoenix; search/navigation equipment 2,000

United Parcel Service Inc.; Phoenix; mail services 2,000

Maricopa Medical Center; Phoenix 2,000

State of Arizona/Motor Vehicles Dept.; Phoenix 2,000

U.S. Postal Service; Tucson 1,745

County of Maricopa/Sheriffs Office; Phoenix 1,700

Valley National Corp.; Phoenix; commercial banks 1,500

Phoenix Elementary School District; Phoenix 1,500

County of Maricopa; Phoenix 1,361

Carondelet Health/St. Josephs Hospital; Tucson 1,359

City of Phoenix; Phoenix 1,231

Fleming Companies Inc.; Phoenix; grocery products 1,090

Southern Pacific Co.; Tucson; railroads 1,084

U.S. Veterans Affairs Dept.; Tucson 1,033

Cartwright School District; Phoenix 1,000

Gateway Community College; Phoenix 981

Phoenix Memorial Hospital; Phoenix 981

St. Luke's Medical Center; Phoenix 920

Arizona State Hospital; Phoenix 910

Allied-Signal Inc./Garrett Airline Services Div.; Phoenix; aircraft/parts 900

City of Phoenix/Public Works Dept.; Phoenix 900

Yuma Regional Medical Center; Yuma 850

Swift Transportation Co.; Phoenix; trucking services 800

Pima County/Kino Community Hospital; Tucson 800

State of Arizona/Revenue Dept.; Phoenix 800

Adobeair Inc.; Phoenix; refrigeration 750

National Semiconductor Corp.; Tucson; electronic components 725

General Electric Co.; Nogales; metal products 700

TNI Partners; Tucson; newspapers 700

Capin Mercantile Corp.; Nogales; apparel/piece goods 625

Arizona Public Service Co.; Phoenix; electric services 600

Kingdom Hall of Jehovahs; Yuma; religious organization 600

Asarco Inc./Mission Mine; Sahuarita; copper ores 578

Emco Harvesting Co.; Yuma; farm management services 562

Security Pacific Bank Arizona; Phoenix; commercial banks 556

3rd District

North and West — Glendale; Part of Phoenix; Hopi Reservation

The most eye-catching feature of the 3rd is the oddly shaped northeastern appendage that stems from a decision by federal judges who drew Arizona's House lines to put the reservations of the Hopi and Navajo Indians—two tribes whose land disputes reach back generations—into separate congressional districts.

Redistricting, however, did little to change the fundamental political personality of the 3rd. Once dominated by "pinto Democrats"—ranchers and other conservative rural landowners—the 3rd has become prime GOP turf over the years. And remapping in 1992 only hastened the Republican shift by moving Flagstaff and its Democratic loyalties into the 6th. Voter registration in the 3rd is now 53 percent Republican. George Bush ran first here in 1992, taking 41 percent of the vote.

More than 55 percent of the district's vote is cast in the Maricopa County suburbs west of Phoenix. In Glendale, which produces wide GOP margins, population grew by more than 50 percent in the 1980s. Glendale's economy, once grounded in agriculture, has diversified to include manufacturing jobs in the aerospace, electronics, communications and chemical industries.

In nearby Sun City, an affluent and largely GOP retirement community, the politically active residents typically turn out for elections at an 80 percent or better rate.

The district moves west out of Phoenix, following I-10 into La Paz County, which was created in 1982 by a ballot initiative that split Yuma County, to La Paz's south. The La Paz community of Quartzsite swells during the winter, as travelers flock to take advantage of its warm climate and see its rock and mineral shows.

Mohave County, in Arizona's northwest corner, is home to three groups in constant political tension: Indians, pinto Democrats in Kingman and Republican retirees in Lake Havasu City. Mohave's 1992 presidential verdict shows how easy it is to get a political argument going in the county: Bush got 35 percent, Bill Clinton 33 percent and Ross Perot 32 percent.

Coconino County, where partisan sentiments are mixed, is now split between the 3rd and 6th districts. Most of "the Arizona strip," which includes a heavily Mormon region with strong GOP ties, remains in the 3rd. Sedona, a Republican bastion in the southern part of the county, also remains in the 3rd.

Just north of Flagstaff, the 3rd includes a narrow arm that reaches east to pick up the Hopi reservation, which lies in Coconino and Navajo counties. The court went to great lengths to separate the Navajo from the Hopi, who bitterly complain that the Navajo have long been encroaching on land designated by the federal government as Hopi. The mapmakers even went so far as to include in the 3rd the tiny Hopi village of Moenkopi, which is completely surrounded by Navajo lands that are in the 6th. Moenkopi is connected to the 3rd by an uninhabited stretch of state Route 264.

Election Returns

	3rd District	Democrat	Republican
1992	President*	86,060 (32.0%)	109,840 (40.8%)
	House	88,830 (34.4%)	158,906 (61.5%)
1990	Governor	73,802 (44.0%)	94,011 (56.0%)
1988	President	63,453 (32.8%)	127,805 (66.1%)
	Senate	92,706 (48.3%)	95,804 (50.0%)
1986	Senate	49,625 (34.7%)	93,443 (65.3%)
	Governor†	42,873 (29.8%)	69,428 (48.2%)

*Vote for Perot was 73,356 (27.2%). †Independent/other is greater than 5%.

Demographics

Population 610,871

Percent change from 1980 12.1%

Land area 41,615 square miles

Population per square mile 15

Counties, 1990 population

Coconino (pt.) 28,933	Mohave 93,497
La Paz 13,844	Navajo (pt.) 6,276
Maricopa (pt.) 360,607	Yavapai 107,714

Cities, 1990 population (10,000 or more)

Bullhead City 21,951	Peoria 50,618
Glendale (pt.) 85,088	Phoenix (pt.) 99,033
Kingman 12,722	Prescott 26,455
Lake Havasu City 24,363	Sun City CDP 38,126
New Kingman-Butler CDP 11,627	Sun City West CDP 15,997

Race and Hispanic origin

White 87.6%
Black 1.9%
American Indian, Eskimo, or Aleut. 3.3%
Asian or Pacific Islander 1.1%
Other 6.1%
Hispanic origin 11.8%

Ancestry

American 3.4%	Italian 4.5%
Danish 1.1%	Norwegian 2.2%
Dutch 3.3%	Polish 3.0%
English 18.4%	Scotch Irish 2.7%
French 5.0%	Scottish 2.9%
German 26.6%	Swedish 2.9%
Irish 16.2%	Welsh 1.2%

Universities/colleges, 1990-1991 enrollment

Glendale Community College, Glendale 18,512
Mohave Community College, Kingman 4,947
Prescott College, Prescott 593
Yavapai College, Prescott 6,003

Newspapers, total circulation (in all districts)

Arizona Republic/Phoenix Gazette 445,214
Chandler Arizonan-Tribune 8,511
Flagstaff Arizona Daily Sun 12,681
Gallup Independent 14,901
Gilbert Tribune 4,545
Mesa Tribune 45,831
Prescott Courier 12,488
Scottsdale Progress 18,139
Sun City Daily News-Sun 18,591
Tempe Daily News-Tribune 11,693

Commercial television stations, affiliations

ADI: Phoenix (74%) and Flagstaff (26%)
KMOH-TV, Kingman (None)
KUSK, Prescott (None)
KSWT-TV, Yuma (ABC)

Cable television systems, total subscribers

Dimension Cable Services; Bullhead City 11,960
Dimension Cable Services; Glendale 26,000
Dimension Cable Services; Peoria 16,000
Paragon Cable; Prescott 17,579
Times Mirror Cable TV of Arizona; Phoenix 310,000
Warner Cable Flagstaff; Flagstaff 11,650
Warner Cable Communications Inc.; Kingman 6,000

Businesses and other major employers

Palo Verde Nuclear Power Plant; Palo Verde; electric services 2,500
Honeywell Inc./Honeywell Sperry; Glendale; search/navigation equipment 1,500
AMFAC Resorts Inc.; Grand Canyon; hotels 1,500
Sun Health Corp.; Sun City 1,000
Honeywell Inc./Satellite Systems Operation; Glendale; space vehicles/technology 800
Cyprus Mines Corp./Cyprus Bagdad Copper Corp.; Bagdad; copper ores 750
Salt River Project/Navajo Generating Station; Page; electric services 742
Times Mirror Cable TV Inc./Dimension Cable Services; Phoenix; cable TV services 700
State of Arizona/Corrections Dept.; Goodyear 700
County of Yavapai; Prescott 600
Yavapai College/Prescott Campus; Prescott 600
Better-Bilt Aluminum Co.; Prescott; aluminum doors/windows 550
Yavapai Regional Medical Center; Prescott 543
Mohave Community College; Kingman 539

4th District

Northern Phoenix; Scottsdale

Thanks to rapid growth in northern Phoenix and its suburbs during the 1980s, the 4th today is only a fraction of its former self in territory. The sparsely populated northeastern part of the state that made up most of the old 4th was shifted to the 6th in 1992 redistricting. But the electorate of the 4th remains virtually unchanged. This is Arizona's least minority-influenced district—92 percent of its residents are white—and arguably its most conservative.

Previously in the 4th, most of the vote was cast in the comfortable confines of northern Phoenix and its Maricopa County suburbs. Now, the district is entirely within Maricopa, making it one of Arizona's two all-urban districts.

The 4th is one of four Arizona districts centered in Phoenix, incorporated in 1881 and currently the ninth-largest city in the nation. As both the state capital and Maricopa County seat, Phoenix is understandably the hub of activity in the state, although it is constantly battling Tucson to retain its preeminence in the eyes of employers relocating to Arizona. More than 3,200 manufacturing companies, employing more than 127,000 people, are in the Phoenix metropolitan area.

Northern Phoenix's white-collar population provides generous support for Republican candidates, as do similarly upscale residents in Scottsdale and other Maricopa County suburbs. In the 1992 presidential contest, the 4th was George Bush's best district in Arizona, giving him 43 percent of the vote to Bill Clinton's 31 percent and Ross Perot's 26 percent.

In remapping, the district extended farther west into Maricopa County, picking up several bedroom communities that add to Republican strength in the 4th.

Several high-tech firms have made their home in the area. Honeywell has plants in the district, and a number of residents work in Motorola's Government Tactical Electronics and Communications Division (nearby in the 1st District).

The tourism industry adds to the economic base in the district. Scottsdale is an affluent resort community that attracts visitors with its warm, sunny climate, myriad golf courses and fashionable shops. Scottsdale grew by more than 46 percent in the past decade and is now home to about 130,000 people. Many here are retirees; others commute to work at the management level in Phoenix corporations. In addition to Motorola Inc. and Honeywell, aerospace manufacturer Allied-Signal Co., American Express Travel Related Services Co. and U.S. West Communications are among the largest employers in Phoenix (some of these are located just across district lines in the 1st and 2nd districts). Community names such as Paradise Valley and Carefree bespeak the lifestyle ideal.

Democrats have a base of support in the southern part of the 4th, where the district stretches into downtown Phoenix. But only about one-third of the voters in the 4th are registered Democratic, compared with about 52 percent who call themselves Republicans.

Election Returns

	4th District	Democrat	Republican
1992	President*	86,922 (31.4%)	118,927 (43.0%)
	House †	70,572 (26.7%)	156,330 (59.2%)
1990	Governor	87,649 (43.9%)	111,976 (56.1%)
1988	President	71,605 (31.6%)	152,427 (67.3%)
	Senate	110,473 (49.4%)	108,927 (48.8%)
1986	Senate	57,088 (33.1%)	115,424 (66.9%)
	Governor †	46,163 (26.7%)	70,962 (41.1%)

*Vote for Perot was 70,682 (25.6%).   †Independent/other is greater than 5%.

Demographics

Population 610,871

Percent change from 1980 12.4%

Land area 193 square miles

Population per square mile 3,160

Counties, 1990 population
Maricopa (pt.) 610,871

Cities, 1990 population (10,000 or more)

Glendale (pt.) 48,362	Phoenix (pt.) 501,883
Paradise Valley 11,671	Scottsdale (pt.) 48,022

Race and Hispanic origin
White 92.1%
Black 1.9%
American Indian, Eskimo, or Aleut. 1.2%
Asian or Pacific Islander 1.8%
Other 3.0%
Hispanic origin 7.8%

Ancestry

American 3.2%	Norwegian 2.4%
Danish 1.1%	Polish 4.1%
Dutch 2.8%	Russian 1.9%
English 18.2%	Scotch Irish 2.5%
French 5.0%	Scottish 3.2%
German 29.8%	Swedish 3.0%
Irish 17.5%	Welsh 1.2%
Italian 6.5%	

Universities/colleges, 1990-1991 enrollment
Devry Institute of Technology, Phoenix 2,647
Grand Canyon College, Phoenix 1,813
National Education Center, Glendale 910
Ottawa University, Phoenix 1,577
Paradise Valley Community College, Phoenix 5,557
Phoenix Community College, Phoenix 12,837
Scottsdale Community College, Scottsdale 9,612
Western International University, Phoenix 1,247

Newspapers, total circulation (in all districts)
Arizona Republic/Phoenix Gazette 445,214
Chandler Arizonan-Tribune 8,511
Gilbert Tribune 4,545
Mesa Tribune 45,831
Scottsdale Progress 18,139
Sun City Daily News-Sun 18,591
Tempe Daily News-Tribune 11,693

Commercial television stations, affiliations
ADI: Phoenix (100%)

Cable television systems, total subscribers
TCI of Arizona; Scottsdale 40,690
Times Mirror Cable TV of Arizona; Phoenix 310,000

Businesses and other major employers
Honeywell Inc./Commercial Air Systems Div.; Phoenix; transportation services 5,000
Honeywell Inc./Commercial Flight Systems Group; Phoenix; search/navigation equipment 4,500
American Express Travel Related Services; Phoenix; credit institution 4,500
Honeywell Inc./Industrial Atmtn. Control Div.; Phoenix; measuring/controlling devices 2,500
American Express Co.; Phoenix; business services 2,500
H. N. Bull Information Systems; Phoenix; computer/office equipment 1,500
Karsten Mfg. Corp.; Phoenix; toys/sporting goods 1,200
Thunderbird Samaritan Hospital/Services; Glendale 1,200
Corporate Personnel Services; Phoenix; personnel supply services 1,200
John C. Lincoln Hospital; Phoenix 1,125
Phoenix Resort Corp./The Phoenician; Scottsdale; hotel 1,100
Arizona Biltmore Hotel; Phoenix; hotel 950
U.S. Interior Dept./Bureau of Reclamation; Phoenix 900
F. M. Services Corp.; Phoenix; collection agency 800
Hyatt Corp.; Scottsdale; hotel 750
AG Communication Systems Corp.; Phoenix; communications equipment 748
Scottsdale Insurance Co.; Scottsdale; fire/marine/casualty insurance 704
Marriott Corp./Camelback Inn; Scottsdale; hotel 700
Pointe Resorts Inc./The Pointe at Squaw Peake; Phoenix; hotel 700
National Processing Co.; Phoenix; computer services 700
Blue Cross & Blue Shield of Arizona Inc.; Phoenix; medical service/health insurance 690
Best Western Motels; Phoenix; hotels/business services 660
State of Arizona/Coliseum & State Fair; Phoenix; amusement/recreation services 600
Marriott Corp./Mountain Shadows; Scottsdale; hotel 700
Scottsdale Conference Resort; Scottsdale; hotels 521

5th District

Southeast — Tucson

Registered Democrats outnumber Republicans in the 5th, but the numerical advantage—less than 2 percentage points—is insignificant, especially considering that many of those who call themselves Democrats are of the rural, conservative, "pinto" variety. Thirteen percent of the district's voters are registered as independents.

At election time, this mix of swing voters and independents typically yields an advantage for Republican candidates in elections for higher office. The areas within the district have regularly backed Republican nominees in past presidential elections. But in the 1992 three-way race for the White House, Democrat Bill Clinton finished first in the 5th, taking 42 percent of the vote. The 5th takes in the northeastern corner of Pima County, which includes most of Tucson. The only part of the city that is not in the 5th—its Hispanic neighborhoods—is strongly Democratic. Redistricting by federal judges in 1992 put that southern part of the city into the 2nd District to help ensure the election of a Hispanic there.

Tucson, once Arizona's territorial capital, was the state's most populous city until it was surpassed by Phoenix in 1920. Largely a college town and resort center in the 1950s, Tucson today hosts an impressive number of high-tech companies. Hughes Aircraft is the largest private-sector employer in Tucson, and an IBM plant is on Tucson's southern outskirts. White-collar professional communities with firm Republican ties dominate the city's burgeoning east side.

Wealthy residents of the Santa Catalina foothills and retirees who worked at Davis-Monthan Air Force Base add to the Republican strength in the district. Green Valley, an outlying Pima County town that rivals Sun City among Arizona's largest retirement communities, also has become a major Republican stronghold.

Democratic candidates get some help in the Tucson part of the 5th from voters in the residential area around the University of Arizona. (The campus itself is in the 2nd.) Although the university's student body of 35,000 leans conservative, the faculty and staff retain a Democratic allegiance, and they are more likely to vote than are students.

Outside Pima County, the 5th is largely desert. The Old West county of Cochise, anchoring southeastern Arizona, is the home of Tombstone, "the town too tough to die." Notorious for its boom town lawlessness in the late 1800s, Tombstone still mines some silver, but now its economy relies mainly on the tourist trade.

Election Returns

	5th District	Democrat	Republican
1992	President*	115,986 (41.9%)	104,301 (37.7%)
	House	77,256 (29.7%)	172,867 (66.5%)
1990	Governor	92,167 (52.6%)	83,029 (47.4%)
1988	President	90,035 (43.9%)	112,783 (55.0%)
	Senate	137,510 (67.8%)	62,143 (30.6%)
1986	Senate	69,242 (45.4%)	83,290 (54.6%)
	Governor†	58,808 (38.4%)	55,991 (36.6%)

Vote for Perot was 56,425 (20.4%).   †Independent/other is greater than 5%.

Demographics

Population 610,871

Percent change from 1980 12.5%

Land area 12,691 square miles

Population per square mile 48

Counties, 1990 population
Cochise 97,624	Pima (pt.) 469,668
Graham (pt.) 22,876	Pinal (pt.) 20,703

Cities, 1990 population (10,000 or more)
Casa Grande (pt.) 11,688	Green Valley CDP 13,231
Douglas 12,822	Sierra Vista 32,983
Flowing Wells CDP 14,013	Tucson (pt.) 264,480

Race and Hispanic origin
White 88.0%
Black 3.0%
American Indian, Eskimo, or Aleut. 0.9%
Asian or Pacific Islander 1.9%
Other 6.3%
Hispanic origin 16.5%

Ancestry
American 2.6%	Norwegian 1.9%
Dutch 2.8%	Polish 3.0%
English 18.4%	Russian 1.3%
French 4.8%	Scotch Irish 2.9%
German 26.5%	Scottish 3.1%
Irish 16.0%	Swedish 2.7%
Italian 4.7%	Welsh 1.2%

Universities/colleges, 1990-1991 enrollment
Cochise College, Douglas 4,548
Eastern Arizona College, Thatcher 4,569
Pima Community College, Tucson 28,766

Newspapers, total circulation (in all districts)
Arizona Daily Star Citizen 141,661
Arizona Republic/Phoenix Gazette 445,214
Casa Grande Dispatch 8,604
Mesa Tribune 45,831

Commercial television stations, affiliations
ADI: Tucson (68%), and Phoenix (32%)
KGUN, Tucson (ABC)
KOLD-TV, Tucson (CBS)
KHRR, Tucson (None)
KTTU-TV, Tucson (None)
KVOA-TV, Tucson (NBC)

Cable television systems, total subscribers
Desert Cable; Sierra Vista 22,000
Jones Intercable Inc.; Tucson 42,500
Post-Newsweek Cable; Safford 5,100
Tucson Cable; Tucson 74,027

Military installations, 1991
Fort Huachuca (Army), Sierra Vista 12,312
Davis Monthan Air Force Base, Tucson 6,219

Businesses and other major employers

Hughes Aircraft Co./Missile Systems Group; Tucson; electronic components 5,600

IBM Corp.; Tucson; computer/office equipment 3,000

University Medical Center Corp.; Tucson 2,250

Tucson Medical Center; Tucson 2,200

Allied-Signal Inc./Airsearch Electronics; Tucson; engines/turbines 1,535

Burr-Brown Corp.; Tucson; electronic components 1,170

Tomkins Industries Inc./Krueger Div.; Tucson; metal products 1,000

Arizona State Prison; Tucson 1,000

Westin Hotel Co.; Tucson; hotels 900

Cyprus Sierrita Corp.; Green Valley; copper ores 830

State of Arizona/Corrections Dept.; Douglas 750

Sabino Health Fitness Resort Inc./Canyon Ranch; Tucson; hotel 650

Wats Marketing America Inc./Teleservices; Tucson; telemarketing services 600

Summit Health Ltd./Tuson General Hospital; Tucson 600

Flowing Wells High School; Tucson 600

Hospital Corp. of Northwest/Northwest Hospital; Tucson 600

Southwest Gas Corp.; Tucson; gas production and distribution 530

El Dorado Hospital & Medical Center; Tucson 522

Sheraton El Conquistador; Tucson; hotel 515

6th District

Northeast — Flagstaff; Navajo Reservation

The newly created 6th rivals the western 3rd in size, and American Indian reservations occupy much of its territory. Nearly 22 percent of the district's population—and about 18 percent of its voting age population—is Native American.

From the expansive Navajo reservation, which occupies all of the northeastern corner of the state except for the Hopi reservation, the district runs southward through the San Carlos and Fort Apache reservations, then takes in Greenlee County and parts of Graham and Pinal counties. The eastern border of the 6th is the Arizona-New Mexico line; the western side of the district includes the cities of Gilbert and part of Mesa, in the Phoenix suburbs, as well as the Gila reservation south of Phoenix and the Salt River and Fort McDowell reservations north of the city.

By design, rural voters have a substantial voice in this district. The federal court that drew the new congressional boundaries excluded most of the Phoenix area (Maricopa County) from the 6th. The judges included the city of Flagstaff "to balance out the interests of Maricopa County."

With about 46,000 people, Flagstaff, the seat of Coconino County, is the district's largest city. Two interstate highways—I-40 and I-17—intersect in Flagstaff, making it the commercial center of northern Arizona. Thanks to its proximity to the Grand Canyon, Flagstaff sees a lot of tourist traffic; other leading industries in the city are lumbering and mining. Flagstaff also is home to the Lowell Observatory, where astronomers in 1930 discovered the planet Pluto.

Voters in East Mesa and Gilbert add a conservative flavor to the centrist 6th. Many of the residents there work in the numerous manufacturing companies in Mesa. Maricopa County

is losing one of its longtime economic pillars with the closure of Williams Air Force Base. The base, more than 50 years old, was the training ground for more Air Force pilots than any other U.S. base since World War II.

The 6th District has the potential to be a politically competitive district. Democrats have a registration advantage of about 4 percentage points over Republicans, but nearly 9 percent of the district's registered voters claim no major-party affiliation. Democrats are strongest in Flagstaff, where more than 15 percent of the residents are Hispanic, and in the northern part of the 6th, where the population is concentrated in mining towns and reservations.

The Navajos show a particular affinity for the Democratic Party. In Apache County, where the Navajo influence is most pronounced, Democrats outnumber Republicans by almost 4-1; the Democrats' unsuccessful gubernatorial nominee won many precincts by margins of 10-1 in 1990.

Districtwide in 1992, George Bush squeaked out a narrow 230-vote victory over Bill Clinton, with Ross Perot finishing a distant third.

Election Returns

	6th District	Democrat	Republican
1992	President*	91,247 (38.2%)	91,477 (38.3%)
	House †	124,251 (53.0%)	97,074 (41.4%)
1990	Governor	78,480 (50.3%)	77,642 (49.7%)
1988	President	67,849 (39.3%)	102,604 (59.5%)
	Senate	96,178 (56.2%)	71,864 (42.0%)
1986	Senate	50,391 (40.1%)	75,314 (59.9%)
	Governor †	48,033 (38.0%)	51,370 (40.6%)

*Vote for Perot was 56,368 (23.5%).   †Independent/other is greater than 5%.

Demographics

Population 610,872

Percent change from 1980 (new district in the 1990s)

Land area 41,222 square miles

Population per square mile 15

Counties, 1990 population

Apache 61,591	Greenlee 8,008
Coconino (pt.) 67,658	Maricopa (pt.) 263,399
Gila 40,216	Navajo (pt.) 71,382
Graham (pt.) 3,678	Pinal (pt.) 94,940

Cities, 1990 population (10,000 or more)

Apache Junction 18,100	Gilbert (pt.) 28,244
Flagstaff (pt.) 45,745	Mesa (pt.) 118,854
Fountain Hills 10,030	Scottsdale (pt.) 29,686

Race and Hispanic origin

White 70.3%
Black 1.3%
American Indian, Eskimo, or Aleut. 21.7%
Asian or Pacific Islander 0.7%
Other 5.9%
Hispanic origin 13.0%

Ancestry

American 2.9%	Dutch 2.4%
Danish 1.1%	English 16.0%

French 3.7%
German 20.1%
Irish 12.1%
Italian 3.2%
Norwegian 1.8%

Polish 2.1%
Scotch Irish 2.0%
Scottish 2.3%
Swedish 2.4%

Universities/colleges, 1990-1991 enrollment
Central Arizona College, Coolidge 5,196
Chandler/Gilbert Community College, Chandler 2,885
Navajo Community College, Tsaile 1,631
Northern Arizona University, Flagstaff 16,994
Northland Pioneer College, Holbrook 5,657

Newspapers, total circulation (in all districts)
Arizona Daily Star Citizen 141,661
Arizona Republic/Phoenix Gazette 445,214
Casa Grande Dispatch 8,604
Chandler Arizonan-Tribune 8,511
Flagstaff Arizona Daily Sun 12,681
Gallup Independent 14,901
Gilbert Tribune 4,545
Mesa Tribune 45,831
Scottsdale Progress 18,139
Sun City Daily News-Sun 18,591
Tempe Daily News-Tribune 11,693

Commercial television stations, affiliations
ADI: Phoenix (64%), Flagstaff (18%) and Albuquerque (17%)
    KNAZ-TV, Flagstaff (NBC)
    KKTM, Flagstaff (None)

Cable television systems, total subscribers
Cable America Corp.; Mesa 6,615

Post Newsweek Cable; Show Low 7,641
TCI of Arizona; Scottsdale 40,690
Times Mirror Cable TV of Arizona; Mesa 41,400
Times Mirror Cable TV of Arizona; Phoenix 310,000

Military installations, 1991
Williams Air Force Base, Chandler 2,627

Businesses and other major employers
Magma Copper Co.; San Manuel; copper ores 3,500
Phelps Dodge Corp.; Morenci; copper ores 1,900
Arizona State Prison; Florence 1,100
TRW Inc./TRW Safety Systems; Mesa; motor vehicle equipment 900
W. L. Gore & Assoc. Inc./Medical Products Div.; Flagstaff; nonferrous rolling and drawing 900
Valley Lutheran Hospital; Mesa 833
Asarco Inc.; Hayden; copper ores 800
Asarco Inc.; Kearny; copper ores 800
Flagstaff School District; Flagstaff 800
Mayo Clinic Scottsdale; Scottsdale 785
Pharmaceutical Card System; Scottsdale; computer services 780
Flagstaff Medical Center Inc.; Flagstaff 766
Navajo Tribal Council/Head Start; Window Rock; family services 747
Magma Copper Co.; Miami; copper ores 600
State of Arizona/Economic Security Dept.; Coolidge 600
Space Data Corp.; Chandler; guided missiles/parts 538
Stone Southwest Corp.; Snowflake; paperboard mills 525
Mesa Public School District; Apache Junction 520

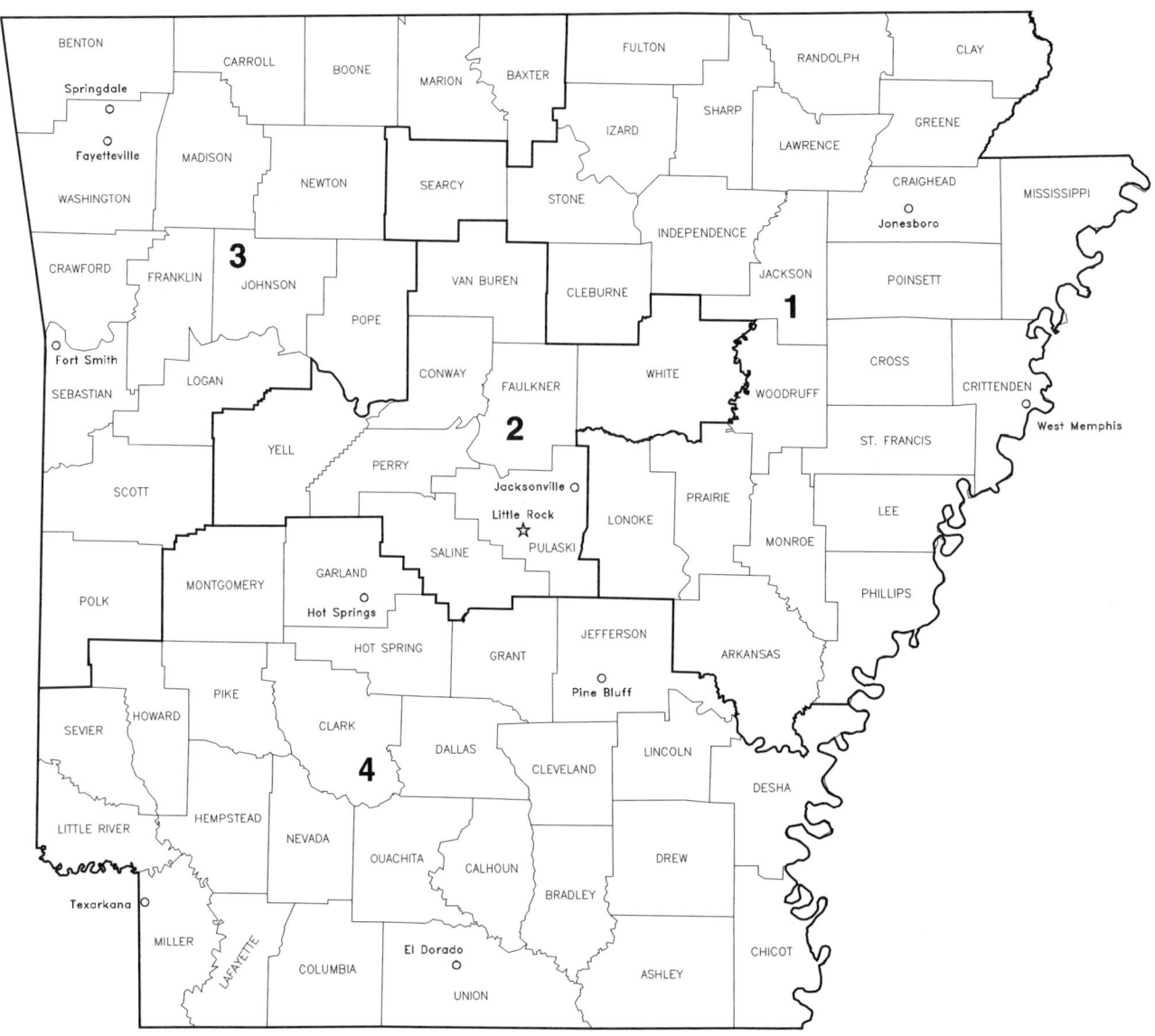

Arkansas

The Republican Party that scored gains across the South during the 1980s found Arkansas rugged terrain. Several factors combined to keep Arkansas Democratic throughout the decade. First, the 1980s economic boom that helped the GOP build support in several southern states bypassed Arkansas. Second, the Arkansas GOP never got in step with the national party approach of targeting disaffected white Democrats and largely conceding black voters. And finally, Arkansas Democrats, such as former Gov. Bill Clinton and Sens. Dale Bumpers and David Pryor, had a knack for holding on to white, working-class voters—people the national Democratic Party was losing.

Moreover, Arkansas saw less friction between blacks and the traditional white Democratics—factions whose feuding in some other southern states weakened local Democratic parties. In Arkansas, the black population was relatively small (16 percent of the total), and voting laws were not subjected to advance Justice Department scrutiny under the Voting Rights Act. As a result, the pace of black political advancement was slow, and conservative whites were able to retain their dominance within the state Democratic Party.

"Democrats have a larger base of white voters in Arkansas than in any other southern state," said Earl Black, a political scientist at the University of South Carolina, "and it's essential to their strength."

Friction may be heating up between white and black Democrats. In 1991, black leaders filed suit against the new congressional remap, demanding the court create a 40 percent black, "minority-influence" district. Under the redistricting plan signed by Clinton on April 10, 1991, blacks were originally divided among three districts: the 4th District was 27 percent black, and the 1st and 2nd districts were 18 percent black. In November 1991, a federal panel in Little Rock ruled for the state, which argued that blacks had more political influence by being distributed through three districts than they would if concentrated into one district. On June 1, 1992, the Supreme Court 7-2 affirmed the ruling, letting stand the redistricting map approved in April 1991.

Despite the outcome of the challenge, the stronger voice of black politicians is changing Democratic politics. "With the redistricting lawsuits and the creation of black major-

ity districts," said Doug Wallace, editor of the political newsletter the *Arkansas Report,* "white politicians are coming to recognize that they have to take blacks more seriously than in the past." In the 1990s, Democratic House members will face more of a challenge in preserving their biracial coalitions.

Redistricting resulted in a map that closely resembled the previous one. In the 1980s, Arkansas' population grew only 2.8 percent; the new map shifted only six counties. Four of the six were taken out of the 3rd, which grew in the 1980s as retirees moved into Ozark Mountain communities. Pockets of growth in this northwestern corner of the state and in the counties surrounding Little Rock are turning noticeably toward the Republican Party. At the same time, some of the most Democratic counties—along the Mississippi River and the southern border—are losing population.

After the 1992 elections, Arkansas Democrats still maintained their dominance at the national level, especially with an Arkansan in the White House. But in the state Legislature, a surprising sea change occurred to sweep out many entrenched Democrats. In 1991, Democrats controlled 123 of 135 state Legislature seats; in 1993, Democrats were reduced to 40 seats.

Table 1 Population

District	Population	Population under 18	Voting-age population	Median age
1	588,588	163,219	425,369	33.8
2	587,412	153,228	434,184	32.7
3	589,523	149,120	440,403	34.5
4	585,202	155,564	429,638	34.6
State	2,350,725	621,131	1,729,594	33.8

Table 2 Voting-Age Persons

District	White*	Black*	American Indian, Eskimo, or Aleut*	Asian or Pacific Islander*	Other*	Hispanic*	Male*	Female*
1	84.4%	14.8%	0.3%	0.3%	0.2%	0.5%	46.5%	53.5%
2	83.7	15.2	0.4	0.6	0.2	0.7	46.9	53.1

District	White*	Black*	American Indian, Eskimo, or Aleut*	Asian or Pacific Islander*	Other*	Hispanic*	Male*	Female*
3	96.4	1.5	1.0	0.9	0.3	1.0	47.8	52.2
4	75.3	23.7	0.4	0.2	0.3	0.7	46.9	53.1
State	85.0	13.7	0.5	0.5	0.2	0.7	47.1	52.9

As percent of voting-age population.

Table 3   Voting-Age Persons by Age Groups

District	18-24*	25-44*	45-54*	55-64*	65 and over*
1	13.2%	38.5%	14.4%	12.8%	21.0%
2	14.6	43.5	13.9	11.3	16.7
3	13.8	38.8	14.0	12.5	21.0
4	13.2	37.8	13.9	12.8	22.3
State	13.7	39.6	14.1	12.3	20.2

As percent of voting-age population.

Table 4   Income and Occupation

District	Median family income	Families in poverty	White collar*	Blue collar*	Service*	Farm*
1	$21,889	19.4%	43.2%	37.1%	12.8%	7.0%
2	30,011	10.8	58.3	27.1	12.7	2.0
3	25,935	11.3	47.1	36.1	12.2	4.6
4	24,217	17.6	45.1	35.4	14.4	5.0
State	25,395	14.8	48.8	33.7	13.0	4.5

As percent of employed persons age 16 and over.

Table 5   Education: School Years Completed

District	Less than grade 9*	Grades 9-12 no diploma*	High school diploma*	College bachelor's degree or higher*
1	21.9%	19.9%	32.1%	9.5%
2	10.0	15.6	31.4	19.0
3	13.7	17.5	33.1	13.3
4	15.3	20.8	34.2	11.4
State	15.2	18.4	32.7	13.3

As percent of persons age 25 and over.

Table 6   Housing and Residential Patterns

District	Owner occupied	Renter occupied	Urban	Rural
1	68.0%	32.0%	47.2%	52.8%
2	66.3	33.7	68.5	31.5
3	71.2	28.8	50.6	49.4
4	72.7	27.3	47.8	52.2
State	69.6	30.4	53.5	46.5

1st District

Northeast — Jonesboro; West Memphis

Covering most of the eastern third of the state, the 1st divides into three geographic regions: the hilly northwest, the Mississippi River Delta, and, between them, the alluvial plain. Though soybeans flourish on the fertile bottomland along the river, and rice thrives on the plain, the 1st is the state's poorest district; and the one with the strongest Old South flavor. In keeping with a tradition that goes back to the Civil War, most of the white voters here still support Democratic candidates.

The large corporate farms in this area, like the cotton plantations that preceded them, sprawl over tens of thousands of acres and coexist with poor, largely black communities. Farm employment has declined annually since the 1940s. Until the 1980s, there was some work in small mills along the river, but many of those jobs went overseas, exacerbating generations-old poverty. In late 1992, about half of the district's 25 counties had double-digit unemployment.

The Delta counties along the Mississippi River have large black populations and are solidly Democratic. Though all the counties lost population during the 1980s, the Delta still accounts for about one-quarter of the district vote.

The largest city in the Delta is West Memphis (Crittenden County), with just over 28,000 people; it is a trucking center and bedroom community for Memphis, Tenn. North of there is the somewhat smaller city of Blytheville (Mississippi County). In 1988, Blytheville attracted hundreds of new jobs with the opening of Nucor-Yamato Steel Co., a U.S.-Japan venture, and in 1992 Nucor opened another plant on its own. But the city suffered a blow in 1992 when Blytheville Air Force Base closed, eliminating 3,000 military and 600 civilian jobs.

The Ozark Mountain counties in the northwestern part of the 1st are culturally distant from the Delta. Home to annual fiddle contests and outhouse races, most of these counties grew during the 1980s with an influx of retirees, many of them from the North. These newcomers diluted the area's traditional Democratic vote and helped put the 1st in the Republican column for president in 1984 and 1988. Searcy County, at the western edge of the 1st, did not even support Bill Clinton for president in 1992; it was the only county in the district he failed to carry.

The other pocket of growth in the 1st, Lonoke County, is also becoming more Republican. The growth is concentrated in suburban Cabot, a suburban town on the highway headed to Little Rock. Outside Cabot, Lonoke County is much like the rest of the alluvial plain, with its conservative Democratic tradition and huge rice farms. The lakes and rivers in and around Arkansas County lure fishermen and duck hunters.

Jonesboro is the district's largest city, with 46,500 people. It has a fairly stable economy built around Arkansas State University (9,300 students) and industrial enterprises engaged in die casting, toolmaking, printing and conveyor-belt production. Jonesboro and outlying communities in Craighead County cast nearly 10 percent of the vote in the 1st; the area is reliably, though not hugely, Democratic.

Election Returns

	1st District	Democrat		Republican	
1992	President*	131,585	(59.0%)	71,160	(31.9%)
	House	149,558	(69.8%)	64,618	(30.2%)
1990	Senate	116,525	(100.0%)	—	
	Governor	101,790	(60.2%)	67,164	(39.8%)
1988	President	93,331	(47.8%)	101,784	(52.2%)
1986	Senate	119,761	(68.1%)	56,020	(31.9%)
	Governor	114,352	(65.9%)	59,257	(34.1%)

Vote for Perot was 20,116 (9.0%).

Demographics

Population 588,588

Percent change from 1980 2.6%

Land area 16,598 square miles

Population per square mile 35

Counties, 1990 population

Arkansas 21,653	Lonoke 39,268
Clay 18,107	Mississippi 57,525
Cleburne 19,411	Monroe 11,333
Craighead 68,956	Phillips 28,838
Crittenden 49,939	Poinsett 24,664
Cross 19,225	Prairie 9,518
Fulton 10,037	Randolph 16,558
Greene 31,804	Searcy 7,841
Independence 31,192	Sharp 14,109
Izard 11,364	St. Francis 28,497
Jackson 18,944	Stone 9,775
Lawrence 17,457	Woodruff 9,520
Lee 13,053	

Cities, 1990 population (10,000 or more)

Blytheville 22,906	Paragould 18,540
Forrest City 13,364	Stuttgart 10,420
Jonesboro 46,535	West Memphis 28,259

Race and Hispanic origin

White 81.3%
Black 17.9%
American Indian, Eskimo, or Aleut. 0.3%
Asian or Pacific Islander 0.3%
Other 0.2%
Hispanic origin 0.6%

Ancestry

American 15.4%	German 15.7%
Dutch 3.2%	Irish 20.4%
English 10.1%	Scotch Irish 2.2%
French 2.5%	Scottish 1.1%

Universities/colleges, 1990-1991 enrollment

Arkansas College, Batesville 833
Arkansas State University, State University 9,264
East Arkansas Community College, Forest City 1,467
Mississippi County Community College, Blytheville 1,878
Phillips Community College, Helena 1,467
Williams Baptist College, Walnut Ridge 690

Newspapers, total circulation (in all districts)

Jonesboro Sun 25,553
Little Rock Arkansas Democrat-Gazette 190,235
Memphis Commercial Appeal 193,211
West Memphis Evening Times 8,975

Commercial television stations, affiliations

ADI: Little Rock (34%), Jonesboro (30%), Memphis (29%) and Springfield (8%)
  KAIT-TV, Jonesboro (ABC)

Cable television systems, total subscribers

American Cablevision/West Memphis; West Memphis 9,300
Batesville Cable TV; Batesville 5,965
Blytheville TV Cable College; Blytheville 7,342
Paragould Cablevision Inc.; Paragould 5,500
Storer Cable TV Inc.; Sherwood 27,421
Twin City Cable TV; Helena 7,000
United Artists Cablevision; Jonesboro 16,911

Military installations, 1991

Eaker Air Force Base, Blytheville 1,557

Businesses and other major employers

Arkansas State University; State University 1,700
American Greetings Corp.; Osceola; greeting cards 1,500
ConAgra Inc.; Batesville; poultry/eggs 1,400
Emerson Electric Co.; Paragould; electrical equipment 1,200
Emerson Electric Co./White-Rodgers; Batesville; measuring/controlling devices 1,170
St. Bernard's Hospital; Jonesboro 1,100
Townsends Inc.; Batesville; poultry/eggs 1,045
Remington Arms Co. Inc.; Lonoke; ammunition 1,000
L. A. Darling Co./Darling Store Fixtures Div.; Paragould; partitions/fixtures 900
Tenneco Corp./Monroe Auto Equipment Co.; Paragould; motor vehicles/equipment 900
Halstead Industries Inc./Metal Products Div.; Wynne; copper tubing 700
Eastman Kodak Co.; Batesville; photographic equipment/supplies 600
Gencorp Inc.; Batesville; rubber products 600
Skil Corp.; Walnut Ridge; metalworking machinery 600
Ringier America Inc.; Jonesboro; books 575
Hytrol Conveyor Co. Inc.; Jonesboro; construction/related machinery 560
Munro & Co. Inc./Addison Shoe Div.; Wynne; footwear 525
L. A. Darling Co./Darling Store Fixtures Co.; Corning; partitions/fixtures 525
Jonesboro School District; Jonesboro 525

2nd District

Central — Little Rock

The political and commercial capital of Arkansas, Little Rock dominates the 2nd. The city and surrounding Pulaski County have a combined population of almost 350,000—nearly 60 percent of the district's total—and their political weight is usually enough to determine the outcome of the 2nd's elections.

With a population one-third black and a well-organized labor community, Little Rock is a Democratic stronghold. The suburbs along the Arkansas River bluffs are home to a large managerial and professional community that prefers to vote Republican, but it will support moderate, business-minded Democrats. In 1992 Bill Clinton got 58 percent of Pulaski County's presidential vote, several points above his statewide average. (Four years earlier, Pulaski went comfortably for George Bush.)

Little Rock did not experience anything like the boom felt by other Sun Belt cities during the 1980s, but the city's 10 percent growth was more than triple that of the state as a whole. Together with North Little Rock—a much smaller, separately incorporated city just across the Arkansas River—Little Rock is more insulated from economic downturns than other parts of Arkansas because of the state government presence, as well as the legal and service industries that support it. Little Rock is also home to a large branch of the

University of Arkansas (11,200 students) and to five major hospitals that serve the metropolitan area and outlying rural communities. There is also a military component in the economy: Little Rock Air Force Base, in northeastern Pulaski County near the town of Jacksonville, has more than 6,000 active-duty personnel.

Once a symbol of the resistance to desegregating public schools in the South, Little Rock today has shed much of its racial tension, and in 1990 the city electorate approved a local tax increase to boost funding for the school system. Downtown Little Rock has a spruced-up business corridor and convention center, but the retail trade has moved to the western suburbs, home to the more affluent residents. Poor and working-class blacks live in east Little Rock.

Many whites have left the city for the once-rural counties that surround Pulaski. While the 20 percent growth in Saline and Faulkner counties during the 1980s weakened their Democratic traditions, the GOP lacks organization here. And Democrats still find a hospitable union movement in the aluminum industry in Saline, the nation's prime domestic source of bauxite.

Republicans have a longer tradition in rural White County, to the east. The GOP has perhaps its strongest organization in the state here, bolstered by the firmly conservative intellectual direction from the academic community at Harding University (3,200 students), an institution affiliated with the Church of Christ. Rural Conway, Yell and Perry counties are more confirmed in their Democratic habits.

Election Returns

	2nd District	Democrat	Republican
1992	President*	130,435 (55.6%)	84,922 (36.2%)
	House	154,946 (74.2%)	53,978 (25.8%)
1990	Senate	132,079 (100.0%)	—
	Governor	103,523 (58.5%)	73,511 (41.5%)
1988	President	89,526 (43.2%)	117,477 (56.8%)
1986	Senate	108,552 (63.6%)	62,048 (36.4%)
	Governor	117,279 (69.4%)	51,608 (30.6%)

*Vote for Perot was 19,348 (8.2%).

Demographics

Population 587,412

Percent change from 1980 3.2%

Land area 5,924 square miles

Population per square mile 99

Counties, 1990 population

Conway 19,151	Saline 64,183
Faulkner 60,006	Van Buren 14,008
Perry 7,969	White 54,676
Pulaski 349,660	Yell 17,759

Cities, 1990 population (10,000 or more)

Benton 18,177	North Little Rock 61,741
Conway 26,481	Searcy 15,180
Jacksonville 29,101	Sherwood 18,893
Little Rock 175,795	

Race and Hispanic origin
White 81.2%
Black 17.6%
American Indian, Eskimo, or Aleut. 0.4%
Asian or Pacific Islander 0.6%
Other 0.2%
Hispanic origin 0.8%

Ancestry

American 11.0%	Irish 19.0%
Dutch 2.8%	Italian 1.6%
English 13.4%	Polish 1.0%
French 3.5%	Scotch Irish 3.4%
German 18.1%	Scottish 1.9%

Universities/colleges, 1990-1991 enrollment
Arkansas Baptist College, Little Rock 291
Arkansas State University, Beebe 1,520
Capital City Junior College, Little Rock 236
Central Baptist College, Conway 201
Harding University, Searcy 3,231
Hendrix College, Conway 1,006
National Education Center, Little Rock 838
Philander Smith College, Little Rock 594
Southern Tech College, Little Rock 628
University of Arkansas for Medicine, Little Rock 1,408
University of Arkansas, Little Rock 11,232
University of Central Arkansas, Conway 8,396

Newspapers, total circulation (in all districts)
Benton Courier 9,561
Little Rock Arkansas Democrat-Gazette 190,235

Commercial television stations, affiliations
ADI: Little Rock (100%)
KARK-TV, Little Rock (NBC)
KLRT, Little Rock (Fox)
KTHV, Little Rock (CBS)
KVTN, Pine Bluff (None)

Cable television systems, total subscribers
Conway Corp.; Conway 9,858
Falcon Cable TV; Shannon Hills 10,677
Storer Cable TV Inc.; Little Rock 49,007
Storer Cable TV Inc.; Sherwood 27,421
White County Video; Searcy 5,005

Military installations, 1991
Little Rock Air Force Base, Jacksonville 6,960

Businesses and other major employers
University of Arkansas/University Arkansas for Medicine; Little Rock 3,600
U.S. Veterans Affairs Dept.; Little Rock; hospital 3,200
Arkansas Children's Hospital; Little Rock 2,300
Baptist Medical System/Arkansas Rehabilitation Institute; Little Rock 2,000
City of Little Rock; Little Rock 1,590
Tyson Foods Inc.; Dardanelle; poultry 1,400
Harding University/Harding Press; Searcy 1,345
Virco Mfg. Corp.; Conway; furniture 1,300
North Little Rock School District; North Little Rock 1,251
State of Arkansas/Human Services Dept.; Conway 1,250
University of Central Arkansas; Conway 1,238
Continental Grain Co./Wayne Farms; Danville; grocery products 1,012

Aluminum Co. of America; Bauxite; aluminum 1,000

Maybelline Products Co.; North Little Rock; cosmetics & toiletries 1,000

Arkansas Blue Cross/Blue Shield; Little Rock; medical service/health insurance 1,000

U.S. Labor Dept.; Little Rock 1,000

State of Arkansas/Children & Family Services; Little Rock 1,000

Southwestern Bell Telephone Co.; Little Rock; accounting 972

AT&T; Little Rock; communications equipment 950

Land O'Frost Inc.; Searcy; meat products 900

State of Arkansas/Health Dept.; Little Rock 848

United Parcel Service Inc.; Little Rock; mail services 800

Little Rock Newspapers Inc./Arkansas Democrat-Gazette; Little Rock; newspapers 800

Gannett River States Publishing Co./Arkansas Gazette; Little Rock; newspapers 800

Heritage Publishing Co./Heritage Co.; North Little Rock; business services 800

H. C. A. Health Services of Midwest/Doctors Hospital; Little Rock 800

Systematics Information Services; Little Rock; computer services 800

Acxiom Corp./CCX Network; Conway; computer services 800

Baptist Medical System/Baptist Memorial Center; North Little Rock 750

Union Pacific Railroad Co.; North Little Rock; railroads 720

University of Central Arkansas; Conway 720

North American Philips Corp.; Little Rock; electric lighting 700

Arkansas Power & Light Co.; Little Rock; electric services 700

American Transportation Corp./Amtran; Conway; bus bodies 700

Wal-Mart Stores Inc.; Searcy; department stores 700

State of Arkansas/Employment Service Dept.; Little Rock 700

State of Arkansas/State Hospital; Little Rock 655

Falcon Jet Corp.; Little Rock; aircraft/parts 650

Kimberly-Clark Corp./Conway Mills; Conway; paper products 650

County of Pulaski; Little Rock 650

ABF Freight System Inc.; Little Rock; trucking services 640

J. B. Hunt Transport Inc.; North Little Rock; trucking services 627

Levi Strauss & Co.; Morrilton; jeans 625

State of Arkansas/Police Dept.; Little Rock 614

Dayton Hudson Corp./Target; Little Rock; warehousing 600

Dayton Hudson Corp./Target; North Little Rock; warehousing 600

State of Arkansas/Highway Commission; Little Rock 600

Dillard Department Stores Inc.; Little Rock; department stores 575

First Commercial Bank; Little Rock; commercial banks 570

Vickers Inc.; Searcy; metal products 525

Affiliated Food Stores Southwest; Little Rock; grocery products 525

3rd District

Northwest — Fort Smith; Fayetteville

The hilly 3rd, Arkansas' most reliably Republican constituency, has roots of GOP allegiance dating back to the Civil War. That conflict struck many of the small-scale farmers here as one fought mostly in behalf of the wealthy slaveholding plantations in the flatter parts of Arkansas. In 1988, George Bush won two-thirds of the district's presidential vote; even in 1992, Arkansan Bill Clinton lost four of the district's 16 counties. And in the counties Clinton won, he typically got less than 50 percent.

Back in 1974, this is where Clinton cut his teeth in electoral politics. As a 28-year-old law professor at the University of Arkansas in Fayetteville, Clinton challenged GOP Rep. John Paul Hammerschmidt and held him to 52 percent; it was the only time Hammerschmidt ever won re-election with less than two-thirds of the vote.

Carroll County (once home to Prohibitionist Carry Nation) conveys the conservative, Bible Belt character of the nearly all-white 3rd in the tourist attractions it offers: The area hosts year-round performances of The Great Passion Play, depicting Christ's last days on Earth. It also has the Bible Museum; the huge Christ of the Ozarks statue; and the Inspirational Wood Carvings Gallery. The warm baths at Eureka Springs are a more earthly attraction.

For generations, the rough terrain here made for a struggling economy dependent on relatively unproductive farmland. Vast pine forests in the Ouachita Mountains provide jobs in sawmills scattered through the rural counties. The large livestock business in the western portion of the 3rd gives a distinctly western feel to the area around Fort Smith, on the Oklahoma border.

In recent years, the economy has been boosted by retirees and two home-grown national corporations, Tyson Foods Inc. and Wal-Mart. Arkansas is the nation's leading broiler producer, and Tyson is the state's poultry industry leader. The company also has moved into hogs, a growth industry along Arkansas' western border. In the 1980s, Tyson's headquarters city, Springdale (Washington County), grew about 20 percent, to almost 30,000.

Bentonville (Benton County) hosts the headquarters of Wal-Mart, as well as a distribution center for the discount chain. Concentrating on small-town markets, founder Sam Walton built Wal-Mart into a retailing behemoth; he died in 1992 as one of the nation's wealthiest men.

The Ozark economy also has benefited from an influx of retirees. The area's mild climate and natural assets—Beaver Lake and Bull Shoals Lake, the Buffalo River and two national forests—have drawn people to newly developed planned communities.

The 3rd's population centers are the manufacturing and livestock city of Fort Smith (Sebastian County), the state's second-largest city with 72,800 residents, and the university city of Fayetteville (Washington County), with just over 42,000 residents. Both cities typically support GOP candidates. In 1992, Clinton won Washington County narrowly, but Bush took Sebastian.

Election Returns

	3rd District	Democrat	Republican
1992	President*	109,111 (43.2%)	107,351 (42.5%)
	House	117,775 (47.2%)	125,295 (50.2%)

3rd District		Democrat	Republican
1990	Senate	118,272 (100.0%)	—
	Governor	89,275 (51.3%)	84,907 (48.7%)
1988	President	67,856 (33.1%)	137,239 (66.9%)
1986	Senate	89,801 (51.6%)	84,103 (48.4%)
	Governor	92,014 (53.9%)	78,709 (46.1%)

*Vote for Perot was 35,991 (14.3%).

Demographics

Population 589,523

Percent change from 1980 2.9%

Land area 11,510 square miles

Population per square mile 51

Counties, 1990 population

Baxter	31,186	Madison	11,618
Benton	97,499	Marion	12,001
Boone	28,297	Newton	7,666
Carroll	18,654	Polk	17,347
Crawford	42,493	Pope	45,883
Franklin	14,897	Scott	10,205
Johnson	18,221	Sebastian	99,590
Logan	20,557	Washington	113,409

Cities, 1990 population (10,000 or more)

Bentonville	11,257	Russellville	21,260
Fayetteville	42,099	Springdale	29,941
Fort Smith	72,798	Van Buren	14,979
Rogers	24,692		

Race and Hispanic origin

White 95.9%
Black 1.6%
American Indian, Eskimo, or Aleut. 1.1%
Asian or Pacific Islander 1.0%
Other 0.4%
Hispanic origin 1.1%

Ancestry

American	12.5%	Italian	1.7%
Dutch	4.3%	Polish	1.0%
English	15.8%	Scotch Irish	3.2%
French	4.1%	Scottish	2.0%
German	22.8%	Swedish	1.2%
Irish	22.3%		

Universities/colleges, 1990-1991 enrollment

Arkansas Tech University, Russellville 4,062
John Brown University, Siloam Springs 912
North Arkansas Community College, Harrison 1,725
Rich Mountain Community College, Mena 417
University of Arkansas-Fayetteville, Fayetteville 14,732
University of the Ozarks, Clarksville 731
Westark Community College, Fort Smith 5,166

Newspapers, total circulation (in all districts)

Baxter Bulletin 8,445
Benton County Daily Record 7,950
Fayetteville Northwest Arkansas Times 12,577
Ft. Smith Southwest Times Record 41,089
Little Rock Arkansas Democrat-Gazette 190,235
Northwest Arkansas Morning News 14,798
Springdale Morning News 17,027
Tulsa World 192,748

Commercial television stations, affiliations

ADI: Ft. Smith (52%), Springfield (28%) and Little Rock (20%)
KHOG-TV, Fayetteville (ABC)
KFSM-TV, Fort Smith (CBS)
KPOM-TV, Fort Smith (NBC)
KFAA, Rogers (NBC)

Cable television systems, total subscribers

Donrey Cablevision/Rogers; Rogers 8,904
TCA Cable TV; Harrison 5,343
TCA Cable TV; Springdale 10,355
TCI of Arkansas; Fort Smith 27,700
Van Buren TV Cable College Inc; Van Buren 5,800
Warner Amex; Russellville 8,125
Warner Cable Communications; Fayetteville 16,517

Military installations, 1991

Fort Chaffee (Army), Fort Smith 1,110
Fort Smith Municipal Airport Air Force Guard Station, Fort Smith 292

Businesses and other major employers

Whirlpool Corp.; Fort Smith; household appliances 4,150
University of Arkansas; Fayetteville 3,600
Rheem Mfg. Co./Rheem & Ruud & Weatherking; Fort Smith; heating/cooling equipment 2,000
Wal-Mart Stores Inc./Sam's Clubs; Bentonville; department stores 2,000
Sparks Regional Medical Center; Fort Smith 1,708
O. K. Foods Inc.; Fort Smith; grain mill products 1,615
Tyson Foods Inc.; Clarksville; poultry 1,500
Tyson Foods Inc.; Green Forest; poultry 1,500
Baxter Healthcare Corp.; Mountain Home; medical instruments/supplies 1,400
Peterson Industries Inc.; Decatur; poultry/eggs 1,400
Tyson Foods Inc.; Waldron; grocery products 1,300
ConAgra Inc.; Russellville; preserved fruits/vegetables 1,250
Campbell Soup Co.; Fayetteville; grocery products 1,150
Baldor Electric Co.; Fort Smith; electrical industrial apparatus 1,100
Rymer Meat Inc.; Van Buren; poultry products 1,100
McKesson Service Co.; Harrison; drugs/proprietaries/sundries 1,000
J. B. Hunt Transport Inc.; Lowell; trucking services 1,000
Springdale Memorial Hospital; Springdale 1,000
Capital-Mercury Shirt Corp./Mar-Bax Shirt Div.; Gassville; outerwear 960
Tyson Foods Inc.; Berryville; meat products 950
McKee Baking Co.; Gentry; bakery products 950
Arkansas Power & Light Co./Arkansas Nuclear One; Russellville; electric services 948
Washington Regional Medical Center; Fayetteville 939
Tyson Foods Inc.; Fayetteville; food products 900
P. A. M. Transportation Services; Tontitown; holding offices 890

Emerson Electric Co.; Rogers; electric motors/generators 800
Wal-Mart Stores Inc.; Bentonville; warehousing 800
St. Edward's Mercy Medical Center; Fort Smith 790
Tyson Foods Inc.; Van Buren; meat products 750
Pace Industries Inc.; Harrison; nonferrous foundries (castings) 740
James River Corp. Virginia; Fort Smith; paper products 700
Cargill Inc.; Springdale; meat products 700
Tyson Foods Inc.; Rogers; meat products 700
Baxter County Regional Hospital; Mountain Home 626
Tyson Foods Inc.; Springdale; poultry/eggs 600
Danaher Corp./Danaher Tool Group; Springdale; cutlery/handtools/hardware 600
Rogers Tool Works Inc.; Rogers; metalworking machinery 600
Superior Industries Intl.; Rogers; nonferrous foundries (castings) 600
Franklin Electric Co. Inc.; Siloam Springs; electric motors 600
City of Fort Smith; Fort Smith 600
Willis Shaw Frozen Express; Elm Springs; trucking services 595
M&M Trucking; Tontitown; personnel supply services 575
Gerber Products Co.; Fort Smith; preserved fruits/vegetables 560
Swift-Eckrich Inc.; Huntsville; meat products 540
Gates Rubber Co.; Siloam Springs; hose/belting/gaskets/packing 530

4th District

South — Pine Bluff, Hot Springs

The 4th traditionally has been staunchly Democratic; in the three decades before 1992, the GOP offered a House candidate here only six times. In 1992 the Republican nominee prevailed narrowly, capitalizing on a bruising Democratic primary, and relying on every possible vote in the parts of the 4th where Republicans have some presence: around the urban centers of Pine Bluff and Hot Springs and along southern Arkansas' "El Dorado fringe."

The 4th stretches from the Texas border on the west to the Mississippi River on the east; it has the most blacks (27 percent of the population) of any Arkansas district, and most of its white voters retain a Civil War-era allegiance to the Democratic Party in elections for local office. In presidential voting, Jimmy Carter carried the district in 1992, and Bill Clinton with 58 percent of the vote defeated George Bush (32 percent) and Ross Perot (10 percent) in 1992.

The 4th's economy depends on agriculture. Scores of paper and plywood mills, most owned by Georgia Pacific and International Paper, dot the district. Rice and soybeans are grown in the Delta counties, and hogs have become an important industry on the western fringe.

With 57,000 people, Pine Bluff (Jefferson County) is the district's largest city. It has a 53 percent black population and casts the highest minority vote of any city in Arkansas. Like the rest of the 4th, Pine Bluff is heavily dependent on the timber industry. International Paper employs about 1,400 people here. The Pine Bluff Arsenal, which once produced the nation's entire

supply of biological weapons, no longer manufactures them. Instead, the arsenal, with 1,700 military and civilian personnel, tests and refurbishes gas masks, including many used in Operation Desert Storm in early 1991.

The district's second-largest city, with 32,000 people, is Hot Springs (Garland County), a popular resort for more than a century. This is where Clinton grew up, after leaving his birthplace in the southwestern Arkansas town of Hope (Hempstead County). The bathhouses and spas of Hot Springs National Park are the center of a tourist economy and a haven for retirees. Garland County's population grew by 5 percent in the 1980s, helping make Hot Springs more Republican.

Farther south is the "El Dorado fringe," Arkansas' narrow "oil band" running along the bottom of the state from Texarkana, on the Texas border, through El Dorado. El Dorado and surrounding Union County are the site of several oil refineries and chemical plants; politically active, conservative oil operators make the area a pocket of Republican strength.

Election Returns

	4th District	Democrat	Republican
1992	President*	134,692 (58.0%)	73,891 (31.8%)
	House	102,918 (47.7%)	113,009 (52.3%)
1990	Senate	127,034 (100.0%)	—
	Governor	105,798 (60.1%)	70,343 (39.9%)
1988	President	98,524 (47.2%)	110,078 (52.8%)
1986	Senate	115,008 (65.7%)	60,142 (34.3%)
	Governor	116,206 (66.4%)	58,841 (33.6%)

Vote for Perot was 23,677 (10.2%).

Demographics

Population 585,202

Percent change from 1980 2.5%

Land area 18,044 square miles

Population per square mile 32

Counties, 1990 population

Ashley	24,319	Hot Spring	26,115
Bradley	11,793	Howard	13,569
Calhoun	5,826	Jefferson	85,487
Chicot	15,713	Lafayette	9,643
Clark	21,437	Lincoln	13,690
Cleveland	7,781	Little River	13,966
Columbia	25,691	Miller	38,467
Dallas	9,614	Montgomery	7,841
Desha	16,798	Nevada	10,101
Drew	17,369	Ouachita	30,574
Garland	73,397	Pike	10,086
Grant	13,948	Sevier	13,637
Hempstead	21,621	Union	46,719

Cities, 1990 population (10,000 or more)

Arkadelphia	10,014	Magnolia	11,151
Camden	14,380	Pine Bluff	57,140
El Dorado	23,146	Texarkana	22,631
Hot Springs	32,462		

Race and Hispanic origin
White 72.4%
Black 26.6%
American Indian, Eskimo, or Aleut. 0.4%
Asian or Pacific Islander 0.3%
Other 0.4%
Hispanic origin 0.8%

Ancestry
American 14.5%   Irish 17.4%
Dutch 2.1%   Italian 1.1%
English 10.1%   Scotch Irish 2.6%
French 2.6%   Scottish 1.1%
German 11.5%

Universities/colleges, 1990-1991 enrollment
Garland Community College, Hot Springs 1,886
Henderson State University, Arkadelphia 4,042
Ouachita Baptist University, Arkadelphia 1,313
Southern Arkansas University El Dorado, El Dorado 791
Southern Arkansas University Magnolia, Magnolia 2,492
Southern Arkansas University Tech, Camden 920
University of Arkansas, Pine Bluff, Pine Bluff 3,672
University of Arkansas, Monticello, Monticello 2,108

Newspapers, total circulation (in all districts)
El Dorado News-Times 10,874
Hot Springs Sentinel-Record 17,530
Little Rock Arkansas Democrat-Gazette 190,235
Pine Bluff Commercial 20,946
Texarkana Gazette 31,922

Commercial television stations, affiliations
ADI: Little Rock (61%), Shreveport-Texarkana (24%), Monroe-
El Dorado (11%) and Greenwood-Greenville (4%)
KTVE, El Dorado (NBC)
KRZB-TV, Hot Springs (None)
KATV, Little Rock (ABC)
KASN, Pine Bluff (None)

Cable television systems, total subscribers
Cam-Tel College; Camden 5,600
Dimension Cable Services: Texarkana 25,000
El Dorado Cablevision; El Dorado 9,300
Pine Bluff Cable TV Inc.; Pine Bluff 13,455
Resort TV Cable College Inc.; Hot Springs 19,635

Military installations, 1991
Pine Bluff Arsenal (Army), Pine Bluff 1,673

Businesses and other major employers
Georgia-Pacific Corp./Mid-Continent Wood Mfg.; Crossett; millwork 3,000
Georgia-Pacific Corp./Southern Pulp & Paper Div.; Crossett; paper mills 1,800
Cooper Tire & Rubber Co.; Texarkana; tires 1,500
Tyson Foods Inc.; Nashville; poultry 1,500
Jefferson Regional Medical Center; Pine Bluff 1,425
ConAgra Inc.; El Dorado; poultry 1,400
International Paper Co.; Pine Bluff; paper mills 1,400
Potlatch Corp.; Warren; sawmills 1,200
St. Joseph's Regional Health Center; Hot Springs Natural Park 1,050
General Dynamics Corp.; Camden; guided missiles/parts 1,000
White Consolidated Industries; Nashville; metalworking machinery 1,000
Pilgrims Pride Corp.; De Queen; poultry/eggs 1,000
State of Arkansas/Corrections Dept.; Pine Bluff 1,000
St. Michael's Hospital; Texarkana 1,000
LTV Aerospace & Defense Co.; Camden; guided missiles/parts 950
Hudson Foods Inc.; Hope; poultry/eggs 950
International Paper Co.; Camden; paperboard mills 900
Burlington Industries Inc.; Monticello; carpets/rugs 900
St. Louis Southwestern Railway Co.; Pine Bluff; railroads 900
Tyson Foods Inc.; Pine Bluff; poultry 900
University of Arkansas; Pine Bluff 650
Alumax Inc.; Magnolia; nonferrous rolling and drawing 600
Weyerhaeuser Co.; Dierks; sawmills 600
White Consolidated Industries; De Queen; farm/garden machinery 600
Munro & Co. Inc./Lake Catherine Footwear Co.; Hot Springs National Park; footwear 600
Human Health Services/NCTR; Jefferson; research services 600
U.S. Health & Human Services Dept./National Center for Toxicological Research; Jefferson 600
Great Lakes Chemical Corp.; El Dorado; industrial inorganic chemicals 550
Champion Parts Inc.; Hope; engine repair/rebuilding 550

California

A state so vast and populous as California all but begs to be subdivided, especially given its range of geographic and demographic diversity. First in the nation by population and third by size, California theoretically could disperse its 30.4 million inhabitants (1993 population) just 195 to the square mile. As it happens, however, mountainous Modoc County averages three people per square mile while San Francisco averages about 15,000. Even with the lopsided distribution, the 58 California counties and 52 California seats in the House might readily be split into half a dozen states—the equivalent in population of a Pennsylvania, a Georgia and four Iowas.

The state's far northern and northeastern counties could form one coherent, Pacific northwestern state as populous as Oregon. After the 1992 redistricting, this region had three Democrats in the House and two Republicans (both Mormons, equaling the total from the Utah delegation).

Another state, formed from California's yawning Central Valley, might well be the nation's most productive farm state. After 1992, the Valley had three Democrats and two Republicans in the House.

A third, central-coastal state could run south from Sonoma County to Monterey County, with the San Francisco Bay Area at its center. With but one Republican among its 11 House members after 1992, this region alone accounted for the Democratic tilt of the statewide delegation.

A fourth state would be based in the Los Angeles Basin, with San Luis Obispo, Santa Barbara and Ventura counties clustered on the north, mammoth Los Angeles at the center and Orange County clinging on the south. After 1992, this megalopolis sent 21 members to Congress—split between 11 Democrats and 10 Republicans.

A fifth California state could be formed from the Inland Empire region of Riverside and San Bernardino counties, which grew by 76 percent and 58 percent, respectively, in the 1980s. After 1992, this region sent five members to Congress, all but one of them Republicans.

A sixth new state could be carved from the five southernmost districts on the existing congressional map, comprising the greater San Diego area and the stretch of Imperial County that runs east to Arizona. Here, Republicans held three of the five seats after 1992.

After slowing in the 1970s, population expansion in California took off again in the 1980s. Overall, the state grew by 25 percent in the decade, adding 6 million people. Twenty counties grew by 33 percent or more. Eight counties now have more than one million residents, and Southern California now has three of the nation's five most populous counties.

The most spectacular increases were recorded among Hispanics and Asians. Although the Census Bureau acknowledged undercounting minorities, it still reported 69 percent growth among Hispanics and 127 percent growth among Asians. In Orange County, the number of Hispanics nearly doubled and the number of Asians nearly tripled.

These demographic shifts have only begun to reshape electoral politics. In November 1992, 81 percent of California's vote was cast by non-Hispanic whites, a group that now constitutes only 57 percent of the population.

Immigration, long a concern among Californians, is an increasingly salient issue in state politics. Local and state officials chafe under federally mandated services for the families of immigrants, legal and illegal. The Los Angeles riots in 1992 highlighted tensions intensified by population growth and by the state's deepest and longest economic downturn since the Great Depression.

The recession seemed worse because California had been booming for so long. Its prosperity, weather and lifestyle had worldwide allure. Its factories furnished high-tech hardware for the Cold War and the space race. But after 1985, Pentagon purchasing declined by nearly one-half (in constant dollars). In 1993, 16 bases and other military facilities in California were listed for possible closure (one-fifth the national total), threatening the loss of 43,000 military personnel and 47,000 civilian jobs.

Even as the economy soured, the previous decade's population growth was driving up California's share of House apportionment from 45 seats to an unprecedented 52 for the 1990s. Republicans were eager to redraw the old map of districts, an artful gerrymander devised by then-Rep. Phillip Burton in 1982. So favorable was that map that, in 1984, Democrats won most of the state's seats even though Republicans got more votes overall.

Still, in 1991, some conservative Republicans wanted to deal with Democratic leaders in the state Legislature. They liked plans assuring them of additional seats and creating GOP safe havens

Districts 7–10, 12–16
San Francisco Bay Area

SAN FRANCISCO

SANTA CRUZ

Districts 24, 26–39
41, 45–47
Los Angeles Area

where ideological conservatives could thrive. But GOP Gov. Pete Wilson vetoed those plans, forcing the issue into the California Supreme Court. Wilson was gambling that a neutral map, while less secure for incumbents, would create more opportunity for Republican gains in districts competitive for both parties.

The court appointed a panel of retired judges who produced a plan stressing compactness and community of interest. They made mainly geographic changes in the northern districts, most of which are competitive for both parties. But in the Bay Area, the new map combined the suburban communities east of Oakland and Berkeley into one predominantly Republican district (the 10th), while making the three other districts more Democratic.

In the Central Valley, one district was fortified for each party while three remained competitive. In the Los Angeles Basin, a fourth majority-Hispanic district was added and the three existing black districts were preserved. Two Democratic districts were weakened, while two brand new Republican districts were created.

In the Inland Empire, two new districts were created with Republican pluralities, two older districts were confirmed as GOP-leaning and one competitive district was left that way.

In San Diego and the most southern part of the state, the new map concentrated minority voters in inner San Diego, surrounding it with four GOP districts (although one, the 49th, proceeded to elect a Democrat in 1992).

The architects of the new map succeeded, at least in the short run, in distributing the party vote more evenly among districts. In 1992, Republicans received 41 percent of the congressional vote in California and won 42 percent of the seats (22 of 52).

Table 1 Population

District	Population	Population under 18	Voting-age population	Median age
1	573,082	149,664	423,418	33.7
2	573,322	148,347	424,975	35.0
3	571,374	154,038	417,336	31.4
4	571,033	144,310	426,723	35.0
5	573,684	151,897	421,787	31.6
6	571,227	127,271	443,956	36.2
7	572,773	151,651	421,122	32.3
8	573,247	92,087	481,160	35.3
9	573,458	126,547	446,911	32.8
10	572,008	140,603	431,405	35.0
11	571,772	167,099	404,673	31.0
12	571,535	116,081	455,454	35.7
13	572,441	146,125	426,316	32.2
14	571,131	114,905	456,226	34.1
15	572,485	128,039	444,446	33.8
16	571,551	162,497	409,054	29.3
17	570,981	151,029	419,952	30.5
18	571,393	180,217	391,176	29.7
19	573,043	168,401	404,642	31.2
20	573,282	199,722	373,560	26.8
21	571,300	173,052	398,248	30.9
22	572,891	130,022	442,869	32.2
23	571,483	158,846	412,637	31.2
24	572,563	121,714	450,849	34.8
25	573,105	158,152	414,953	31.0
26	571,523	161,411	410,112	28.7
27	572,594	127,334	445,260	34.2
28	572,927	149,017	423,910	32.9
29	571,566	75,030	496,536	36.9
30	572,538	157,075	415,463	28.8
31	572,643	168,954	403,689	28.3
32	572,595	137,557	435,038	31.7
33	570,943	186,785	384,158	25.5
34	573,047	170,781	402,266	29.1
35	570,882	181,412	389,470	27.4
36	573,663	111,641	462,022	34.6
37	572,049	196,833	375,216	26.3
38	572,657	137,608	435,049	31.4
39	573,574	143,485	430,089	32.2
40	573,625	166,389	407,236	31.2
41	572,663	172,593	400,070	29.2
42	571,844	190,671	381,173	27.9
43	571,231	170,211	401,020	29.8
44	571,583	154,172	417,411	33.7
45	570,874	120,816	450,058	32.7
46	571,380	165,778	405,602	27.3
47	571,518	129,838	441,680	33.5
48	572,928	146,649	426,279	31.0
49	573,362	93,219	480,143	31.8
50	573,463	174,759	398,704	28.1
51	572,982	141,054	431,928	33.0
52	573,203	157,337	415,866	31.4
State	29,760,021	7,750,725	22,009,296	31.5

Table 2 Voting-Age Persons

District	White*	Black*	American Indian, Eskimo, or Aleut*	Asian or Pacific Islander*	Other*	Hispanic*	Male*	Female*
1	86.5%	3.8%	2.2%	3.3%	4.1%	9.8%	50.3%	49.7%
2	92.9	1.5	2.1	1.8	1.7	5.1	49.0	51.0
3	83.9	2.9	1.3	5.4	6.5	12.1	48.3	51.7
4	92.8	2.0	1.2	2.0	2.0	6.8	50.7	49.3
5	69.8	11.2	1.1	11.8	6.1	12.7	47.4	52.6
6	90.8	2.2	0.7	3.2	3.1	7.9	48.4	51.6
7	65.7	15.2	0.8	13.4	4.9	11.8	48.3	51.7
8	55.8	11.4	0.5	26.2	6.0	14.1	50.7	49.3
9	49.5	29.2	0.6	15.0	5.6	10.7	48.4	51.6
10	88.7	2.2	0.6	5.9	2.5	7.8	48.7	51.3
11	77.9	5.3	1.1	9.7	6.1	19.0	49.7	50.3
12	67.6	3.9	0.4	24.1	4.0	12.8	47.8	52.2
13	66.6	6.8	0.7	18.5	7.3	16.6	49.0	51.0
14	79.8	4.5	0.4	11.5	3.8	11.7	50.3	49.7
15	83.6	2.0	0.5	10.6	3.2	9.7	49.4	50.6
16	57.9	5.1	0.7	20.7	15.6	33.4	51.6	48.4
17	72.8	4.3	0.8	6.3	15.7	26.8	50.9	49.1
18	79.3	2.7	1.0	4.7	12.2	22.4	49.3	50.7
19	77.8	2.9	1.2	5.7	12.4	20.5	47.8	52.2
20	52.5	6.7	1.0	5.1	34.8	50.7	52.3	47.7
21	80.7	3.7	1.4	2.8	11.5	17.1	49.1	50.9
22	83.6	2.7	0.9	3.9	8.9	18.2	50.4	49.6
23	79.0	2.4	0.8	5.1	12.7	26.5	50.4	49.6
24	86.0	1.9	0.4	6.0	5.7	12.0	48.9	51.1
25	81.0	4.3	0.7	6.3	7.7	14.9	50.7	49.4
26	57.5	6.0	0.6	7.6	28.3	46.9	51.1	48.9
27	73.5	7.6	0.4	10.0	8.5	18.4	47.8	52.2
28	73.5	5.1	0.5	12.3	8.6	21.3	47.8	52.2
29	84.7	3.4	0.3	7.5	4.1	11.7	49.0	51.0
30	44.7	3.8	0.5	22.3	28.7	57.1	50.8	49.2
31	49.3	1.7	0.5	24.3	24.3	53.8	49.1	50.9
32	34.9	39.9	0.4	8.5	16.3	26.4	47.0	53.0
33	37.0	5.4	0.6	5.2	51.8	79.5	53.3	46.7
34	59.5	1.8	0.6	9.6	28.6	58.1	49.1	50.9
35	22.8	44.0	0.4	6.7	26.1	38.5	48.3	51.7
36	79.8	2.9	0.5	11.5	5.3	13.1	49.8	50.2

District	White*	Black*	American Indian, Eskimo, or Aleut*	Asian or Pacific Islander*	Other*	Hispanic*	Male*	Female*
37	28.3	34.2	0.5	11.2	25.8	40.8	48.9	51.1
38	73.3	6.8	0.7	8.2	11.0	21.9	49.8	50.2
39	75.2	2.4	0.5	13.0	8.9	20.3	49.2	50.8
40	83.9	4.9	1.4	3.4	6.4	13.6	49.8	50.2
41	69.8	6.7	0.5	9.8	13.1	28.5	50.6	49.4
42	69.0	10.2	0.9	3.9	16.0	30.6	48.7	51.3
43	77.5	5.8	0.8	4.2	11.6	22.0	50.2	49.8
44	80.2	4.5	1.0	2.6	11.8	23.3	48.8	51.2
45	83.9	1.1	0.5	10.0	4.4	13.1	49.9	50.1
46	68.5	2.5	0.6	11.9	16.5	45.3	52.8	47.2
47	84.9	1.7	0.4	9.0	4.1	11.7	48.3	51.7
48	84.8	3.7	1.0	4.3	6.2	15.0	51.7	48.3
49	83.9	4.9	0.7	5.9	4.6	11.2	53.2	46.8
50	50.4	13.8	0.6	14.4	20.7	36.4	49.7	50.3
51	85.8	1.7	0.5	7.6	4.3	12.1	49.8	50.2
52	85.3	2.8	1.0	2.9	7.8	19.4	48.6	51.4
State	71.7	7.0	0.8	9.2	11.3	22.5	49.6	50.4

*As percent of voting-age population.

Table 3 Voting-Age Persons by Age Groups

District	18-24*	25-44*	45-54*	55-64*	65 and over*
1	12.8%	45.1%	13.8%	11.1%	17.3%
2	13.0	40.4	13.4	12.3	20.8
3	15.8	44.8	13.3	11.1	15.0
4	10.7	46.5	14.9	11.8	16.1
5	14.5	47.6	12.2	10.1	15.6
6	10.9	46.6	15.2	10.4	16.8
7	13.4	48.8	13.8	10.0	14.0
8	12.6	48.8	12.3	10.1	16.3
9	16.7	47.0	12.4	8.8	15.2
10	11.3	46.8	17.2	10.9	13.8
11	14.7	45.8	13.5	10.7	15.2
12	12.1	44.8	14.1	11.7	17.4
13	13.3	49.7	13.9	10.4	12.7
14	13.6	47.1	14.4	10.6	14.3
15	12.9	48.2	15.9	10.8	12.2
16	17.2	51.6	12.8	8.5	9.9
17	17.8	46.9	11.7	9.4	14.3
18	14.9	46.5	13.2	10.5	15.0
19	14.7	45.0	13.5	10.9	15.9
20	18.3	46.5	11.9	9.7	13.5
21	13.7	46.4	13.6	10.8	15.4
22	18.9	42.3	11.8	10.1	16.9
23	15.0	47.9	13.9	10.0	13.3
24	13.1	45.7	15.6	11.6	14.0
25	14.6	50.9	14.2	10.0	10.3
26	18.7	50.4	11.4	8.4	11.1
27	12.9	45.7	14.1	10.6	16.7
28	14.6	44.6	14.7	11.2	14.9
29	13.1	45.7	12.6	10.2	18.4
30	19.5	49.3	11.6	8.5	11.1
31	19.3	46.7	11.7	9.6	12.7
32	16.1	46.7	12.3	9.9	15.1
33	24.2	48.9	10.2	7.1	9.7
34	18.0	45.0	13.0	11.2	12.8
35	19.3	48.9	12.2	8.9	10.8
36	12.4	48.1	15.0	11.6	12.9
37	19.9	47.7	12.4	9.4	10.6
38	16.4	46.8	11.7	9.5	15.6
39	16.2	43.7	15.4	12.2	12.5
40	14.5	45.2	12.7	10.9	16.6
41	17.0	52.1	14.0	8.4	8.5
42	16.2	52.2	12.1	8.6	10.9
43	15.7	49.7	12.9	9.5	12.1
44	11.9	40.0	11.3	11.9	25.0
45	15.7	46.3	14.5	10.6	12.9
46	21.7	49.5	10.7	8.4	9.8
47	14.7	46.2	15.2	9.9	14.0
48	17.2	47.5	12.0	9.3	14.0
49	21.1	44.6	10.3	9.1	14.9
50	19.2	47.6	11.6	9.4	12.2
51	13.4	48.9	13.4	9.2	15.1
52	15.1	46.3	13.0	10.6	15.0
State	15.5	46.9	13.2	10.1	14.2

*As percent of voting-age population.

Table 4 Income and Occupation

District	Median family income	Families in poverty	White collar*	Blue collar*	Service*	Farm*
1	$35,909	8.6%	53.6%	26.4%	15.2%	4.9%
2	29,646	11.1	54.5	25.3	15.2	5.0
3	35,293	9.3	58.0	23.8	12.6	5.7
4	40,604	5.7	60.8	23.3	13.9	2.0
5	35,336	12.4	66.0	19.3	13.1	1.6
6	47,395	4.2	66.7	19.1	11.8	2.5
7	43,274	7.5	62.8	23.0	12.7	1.4
8	36,960	11.5	67.2	15.7	16.5	0.5
9	36,561	13.4	69.5	16.6	12.8	1.1
10	60,079	3.2	72.7	17.2	9.0	1.1
11	35,700	11.3	53.7	28.1	12.6	5.6
12	51,727	4.0	69.1	18.1	12.0	0.9
13	48,651	4.7	62.6	26.9	9.6	0.9
14	59,492	3.6	74.8	14.4	9.3	1.6
15	57,300	3.2	72.5	17.8	8.8	0.8
16	45,688	8.4	54.5	30.4	12.8	2.3
17	37,401	8.0	54.5	21.6	14.0	9.8
18	31,574	12.7	47.8	30.8	12.2	9.2
19	33,041	12.6	61.2	21.9	11.6	5.3
20	22,472	23.2	34.6	27.0	13.7	24.7
21	33,174	12.1	55.4	26.1	13.3	5.3
22	39,631	7.3	58.3	21.1	14.9	5.7
23	47,019	5.5	58.1	24.9	11.3	5.7
24	57,375	4.0	73.6	15.7	9.6	1.1
25	51,207	5.1	65.8	22.7	10.4	1.1
26	34,273	12.1	50.0	34.7	13.3	2.1
27	45,016	8.8	71.1	17.7	10.0	1.2
28	49,369	4.9	67.7	21.4	9.9	1.0
29	55,001	7.3	79.9	9.3	10.2	0.6
30	24,390	20.7	46.9	32.5	19.5	1.1
31	31,858	14.7	49.4	35.9	12.9	1.8
32	31,990	15.8	61.1	22.2	15.3	1.4
33	22,018	24.9	31.5	51.6	15.5	1.4
34	38,395	9.1	52.3	35.3	11.2	1.2
35	26,853	21.4	47.4	34.6	16.3	1.7
36	56,567	4.5	74.2	15.8	9.1	0.9
37	28,583	20.6	43.7	40.1	14.4	1.9
38	39,810	9.5	62.3	25.1	11.7	0.8
39	50,777	4.6	65.9	23.3	9.6	1.1
40	34,048	10.2	56.0	28.1	14.0	1.8
41	48,401	7.2	61.7	25.6	10.7	1.9
42	36,818	11.8	53.6	32.0	12.9	1.5
43	41,812	7.2	55.6	30.9	11.2	2.4
44	33,293	9.7	51.6	26.0	16.0	6.3
45	51,028	4.8	68.0	20.5	10.5	1.1
46	36,344	10.7	44.5	36.8	15.4	3.3
47	59,936	3.0	75.3	14.7	9.2	0.8
48	46,683	5.0	65.5	19.8	11.3	3.3

District	Median family income	Families in poverty	White collar*	Blue collar*	Service*	Farm*
49	40,466	6.6	70.9	15.2	12.6	1.2
50	30,213	16.2	51.9	27.4	18.7	2.0
51	50,405	4.1	69.5	17.6	10.7	2.2
52	37,396	9.1	59.3	24.6	12.8	3.2
State	40,559	9.3	61.0	23.9	12.4	2.7

*As percent of employed persons age 16 and over.

District	Less than grade 9*	Grades 9-12 no diploma*	High school diploma*	College bachelor's degree or higher*
52	9.2	12.9	25.8	17.1
State	11.2	12.6	22.3	23.4

*As percent of persons age 25 and over.

Table 5 Education: School Years Completed

District	Less than grade 9*	Grades 9-12 no diploma*	High school diploma*	College bachelor's degree or higher*
1	7.1%	13.3%	27.4%	18.2%
2	6.7	15.0	27.7	16.4
3	8.2	12.8	26.1	19.9
4	4.1	10.8	27.6	21.1
5	8.5	11.9	22.5	24.0
6	4.5	7.7	20.8	33.0
7	6.5	11.4	25.2	23.2
8	12.5	11.3	17.9	33.8
9	8.9	10.9	18.4	35.4
10	3.1	6.8	21.6	35.8
11	13.6	14.9	25.7	14.7
12	6.6	9.0	22.1	31.6
13	7.3	12.2	26.1	22.4
14	5.2	6.7	15.4	44.2
15	3.7	8.0	19.9	34.8
16	15.4	14.9	20.9	19.4
17	14.5	11.0	20.8	23.0
18	16.9	16.7	25.2	12.5
19	11.8	13.7	22.9	20.2
20	32.4	19.7	21.9	6.4
21	11.1	16.2	26.0	15.0
22	8.0	10.6	22.4	25.3
23	11.2	11.7	22.7	20.5
24	5.2	8.6	20.1	33.4
25	5.4	11.8	24.2	22.9
26	22.1	17.2	20.5	15.4
27	9.2	10.6	19.0	31.4
28	6.4	11.1	23.5	25.6
29	6.3	7.3	15.8	43.5
30	30.0	17.2	17.6	16.1
31	24.6	19.0	20.9	13.3
32	14.9	15.2	19.9	23.3
33	44.6	21.8	16.3	5.3
34	18.5	19.8	25.0	12.0
35	23.1	19.8	21.8	10.1
36	5.1	8.2	19.5	36.8
37	23.7	21.5	22.4	9.2
38	9.8	13.7	23.9	21.0
39	7.5	11.0	23.2	25.4
40	6.6	15.1	29.2	16.1
41	10.2	13.0	21.9	21.4
42	10.6	17.2	26.5	12.7
43	8.5	15.0	26.4	15.7
44	12.0	16.6	26.5	13.2
45	6.0	9.5	21.3	27.7
46	24.0	16.2	21.5	12.5
47	3.9	6.5	17.7	37.1
48	5.5	8.1	21.3	27.7
49	4.6	7.6	20.4	33.9
50	15.8	16.3	24.3	13.9
51	5.2	7.2	19.4	34.5

Table 6 Housing and Residential Patterns

District	Owner occupied	Renter occupied	Urban	Rural
1	63.2%	36.8%	66.7%	33.3%
2	64.5	35.6	59.5	40.5
3	59.1	40.9	81.7	18.3
4	69.3	30.7	61.6	38.4
5	53.0	47.0	99.5	0.5
6	62.0	38.0	81.4	18.6
7	62.0	38.0	99.7	0.3
8	29.0	71.0	100.0	0.0
9	43.0	57.0	100.0	0.0
10	71.5	28.5	97.0	3.0
11	58.1	41.9	85.0	15.0
12	59.4	40.6	100.0	0.0
13	62.0	38.0	99.9	0.1
14	54.7	45.3	98.4	1.6
15	63.2	36.8	96.0	4.0
16	60.9	39.1	96.0	4.0
17	52.8	47.2	84.6	15.4
18	58.7	41.3	80.8	19.2
19	58.9	41.1	79.7	20.3
20	51.3	48.7	72.8	27.3
21	61.3	38.7	81.4	18.6
22	56.7	43.3	88.4	11.6
23	63.3	36.7	94.6	5.5
24	62.5	37.5	97.2	2.8
25	71.5	28.5	89.7	10.3
26	44.5	55.5	100.0	0.0
27	49.3	50.7	99.9	0.1
28	67.4	32.6	99.9	0.1
29	35.3	64.7	100.0	0.0
30	24.4	75.6	100.0	0.0
31	48.2	51.8	100.0	0.0
32	36.4	63.6	100.0	0.0
33	24.7	75.3	100.0	0.0
34	62.8	37.2	100.0	0.0
35	36.4	63.6	100.0	0.0
36	52.8	47.2	99.9	0.1
37	50.4	49.6	100.0	0.0
38	45.7	54.3	100.0	0.0
39	64.6	35.4	100.0	0.0
40	64.1	35.9	82.3	17.7
41	67.8	32.2	98.8	1.2
42	62.1	37.9	99.6	0.4
43	66.5	33.5	86.0	14.0
44	68.3	31.7	86.3	13.7
45	56.4	43.6	100.0	0.0
46	48.2	51.8	100.0	0.0
47	65.6	34.4	99.5	0.5
48	63.9	36.1	89.1	10.9
49	42.2	57.8	100.0	0.0
50	47.9	52.1	99.2	0.8
51	65.0	35.0	96.8	3.2
52	59.5	40.5	89.0	11.0
State	55.6	44.4	92.6	7.4

1st District

Northern Coast — Eureka

With all the changes overtaking California's political landscape in 1992, relatively little notice was paid to the reshaping of the 1st. As in the past, it stretches along the Pacific Coast from the Oregon line almost to metropolitan San Francisco. It still includes the big coastal counties of Mendocino, Humboldt and Del Norte, with their breathtaking forests and ocean waves crashing on boulders and beaches. But while these counties dominate the 1st's image, they have less than one-third of the people. Practically their only population center is the port city of Eureka in Humboldt County, the lone port for hundreds of miles, which earns its feast-or-famine living by shipping the region's world-class logs.

Just east of Mendocino, Lake County's mix of ranch, farm and tourism economy remains in the 1st. But south of Mendocino, redistricting altered the 1st. Most of Sonoma County was transferred to the 6th, which shed its city section to become wholly suburban. Included in the shift was Santa Rosa, which grew by 37 percent in the 1980s to become the largest city in the old 1st. Sonoma as a whole cast about half the total district vote in 1990. In 1992, after redistricting, the part of the county remaining in the 1st accounted for less than 10 percent of the district vote.

The new 1st still includes much of Sonoma County's prime wine-producing country. And it has added even more distinction in this arena by annexing all of neighboring Napa County. Wineries, large and small, line Highway 29 throughout the scenic Napa Valley, the source for much of the most prestigious wine in the Western Hemisphere.

Farther east, the 1st also expanded what had been a toehold in the southwestern corner of Solano County, where its holdings now spread north and east to enfold the cities of Fairfield and Vacaville. In the 1980s, the combined population of these two communities rose by roughly 50 percent to more than 150,000. In the 1992 elections, about 40 percent of the 1st's total vote came from Napa and Solano counties.

The politics of coastal Northern California have long required balancing the union sentiments of lumberjacks and other laborers with the Republican stands of timber owners, ranchers and retirees. Travis Air Force Base, at the district's southeastern extreme, has been a counterweight to the waves of "ecotopian" immigrants arriving in search of lifestyle nirvana in the coastal highlands to the north. But Travis' future is uncertain.

In partisan terms, losing Sonoma County was expected to hurt the Democrats—especially because the compensating territory in Napa and Solano counties had been relatively more Republican. But 1992 was an unusually ripe year for Democrats in California. Bill Clinton and Democratic Senate nominees Dianne Feinstein and Barbara Boxer almost achieved a triple sweep of all seven counties in the 1st (Boxer lost one: Del Norte). The Democrats' little-known House candidate also held on to win, carrying Humboldt, Mendocino and Solano with just enough margin to survive losing the other four counties.

Election Returns and Party Registration

	1st District	Democrat	Republican
1992	President*	119,491 (46.8%)	74,597 (29.2%)
	Senate †	120,728 (49.8%)	95,499 (39.4%)
	Senate †‡	142,489 (57.9%)	83,137 (33.8%)
	House †	119,676 (47.6%)	113,266 (45.1%)
1990	Governor †	90,254 (47.2%)	86,868 (45.4%)
1988	President	129,029 (50.8%)	120,636 (47.4%)
	Senate	103,806 (49.5%)	97,629 (46.5%)
1986	Senate	58,856 (49.2%)	57,936 (48.5%)
	Governor	41,386 (34.3%)	76,879 (63.7%)
1993	Party registration †	165,300 (52.1%)	106,218 (33.4%)

*Vote for Perot was 61,160 (24.0%).   †Independent/other is greater than 5%.
‡Special election for the remaining two years of the term of Pete Wilson who was elected governor in 1990. Appointee John Seymour held the seat 1991-1992.

Demographics

Population 573,082

Percent change from 1980 8.9%

Land area 10,804 square miles

Population per square mile 53

Counties, 1990 population

Del Norte 23,460	Napa 110,765
Humboldt 119,118	Solano (pt.) 141,672
Lake 50,631	Sonoma (pt.) 47,091
Mendocino 80,345	

Cities, 1990 population (10,000 or more)

Arcata 15,197	Napa 61,842
Clearlake 11,804	Suisun City (pt.) 17,647
Eureka 27,025	Ukiah 14,599
Fairfield (pt.) 73,787	Vacaville (pt.) 39,926
McKinleyville CDP 10,749	Windsor CDP (pt.) 12,383

Race and Hispanic origin
White 85.0%
Black 3.9%
American Indian, Eskimo, or Aleut. 2.7%
Asian or Pacific Islander 3.6%
Other 4.7%
Hispanic origin 11.2%

Ancestry

American 3.3%	Norwegian 2.3%
Danish 1.5%	Polish 1.8%
Dutch 2.8%	Portuguese 2.3%
English 17.5%	Scotch Irish 2.7%
French 5.2%	Scottish 3.1%
German 22.9%	Swedish 3.0%
Irish 16.6%	Welsh 1.1%
Italian 6.7%	

Universities/colleges, 1990-1991 enrollment
College of the Redwoods, Eureka 6,147
Humboldt State University, Arcata 6,135
Mendocino College, Ukiah 3,455
Napa Valley College, Napa 5,715

Pacific Union College, Angwin 1,770
Solano Community College, Suisun City 9,643

Newspapers, total circulation (in all districts)
Eureka Times-Standard 21,736
Fairfield Daily Republic 19,911
Napa Valley Register 20,016
Oakland Tribune 113,419
Petaluma Argus-Courier 8,573
Sacramento Bee 269,383
San Francisco Chronicle Examiner 692,424
Santa Rosa Press Democrat 95,106
Ukiah Daily Journal 8,422
Vacaville Reporter 19,217
Vallejo Times Herald 22,647

Commercial television stations, affiliations
ADI: San Francisco (57%), Eureka (42%) and Sacramento-
Stockton (1%)
KAEF, Arcata (Fox)
KIEM-TV, Eureka (NBC)
KVIQ-TV, Eureka (CBS)
KFTY, Santa Rosa (None)
KFWU, Fort Bragg (ABC)

Cable television systems, total subscribers
Century Cable; Fort Bragg 5,576
Century Cable; Ukiah 7,332
Cox Cable Humboldt; Eureka 30,500
Donrey Cablevision/Vallejo; Vallejo 23,000
Jones Intercable Inc.; Cobb Mountain 14,192
Multivision Cable TV; Fairfield 25,000
Multivision Cable TV; Sonoma Mountain 44,420
Post Newsweek Cable TV; Santa Rosa 44,955
UA Cablesystem of California; Vacaville 20,400
Viacom Cablevision; Big Rock Ridge 61,632
Viacom Cablevision; Geyser Peak 15,563
Viacom Cablevision; Napa 18,884

Military installations, 1991
Travis Air Force Base, Fairfield 10,800

Businesses and other major employers
Louisiana-Pacific Corp.; Samoa; millwork 2,650
State of California/Napa State Hospital; Napa 2,500
County of Solano; Fairfield 2,200
State of California/Corrections Dept.; Vacaville 2,200
State of California/County of Solano; Fairfield; legal services
2,000
Humboldt State University; Arcata 2,000
Pelican Bay State Prison; Crescent City 1,200
Napa Valley Unified School District; Napa 1,060
Pacific Lumber Co. Inc.; Scotia; sawmills 1,000
Veterans Home of California; Yountville; civic/social associa-
tion 1,000
Napa Valley Medical Center; Napa 943
Solano Community College; Suisun City 896
Napa Valley College; Napa 716
St. Helena Hospital & Health Center; Deer Park 715
County of Lake; Lakeport 650
Georgia-Pacific Corp.; Fort Bragg; sawmills 620
Anheuser-Busch Inc.; Fairfield; brewery 600
AMFAC Resorts Inc./Silverado; Napa; management services
521

2nd District
North and East — Chico; Redding

Redistricting can end a politician's career by shifting a single
square mile of political turf. It can also switch broad swatches of
territory and leave an incumbent unscathed. The new 2nd
demonstrates the latter. The 1992 map tore away enough of the
2nd to encompass several New England states, while adding
enough new real estate to make the district even bigger than
before. It became California's least densely populated district,
and its least racially diverse. The 2nd combines the northern
portions of the old 2nd and the old 14th, consolidating much of
the state's northern, rural Mormon population in the process.

The territorial changes, however, scarcely alter the 2nd's
political coloration. Although GOP registration was slightly
lower (down from 44 percent in the 1980s to 42 percent in 1992),
the Republican incumbent re-election tally in 1992 inched up to
65 percent.

In the 1980s, the 2nd was a north-central inland district
extending hundreds of miles south from the Oregon line to the
outskirts of the Sacramento area. Its asphalt spine was Interstate
5 (which runs from Canada to Mexico), and its central feature
was the mighty Mount Shasta.

The population was widely dispersed through the mountainous forests and rangelands, except for population centers in
Redding (a 120-year-old mining and timber town on I-5) and
Chico (home to a campus of California State University with
15,000 students).

Remapping cut deep into the 2nd's southern portion while
pushing the district's eastern boundary all the way to the Nevada
line. The northern timber counties of Siskiyou, Trinity and
Shasta remain, but moving south toward the Central Valley, the
agricultural counties of Tehama, Glenn, Colusa and Sutter were
removed (along with the southwestern tip of Butte County).

The 2nd added new lands by expanding eastward to Nevada,
embracing the three vast and remote counties of California's far
northeastern corner (Modoc, Lassen and Plumas). These three
lean to the GOP in most statewide elections, but with a
combined registration of about 31,000 voters, they have little
effect.

The 2nd also picked up all of Sierra and Nevada counties,
named for the mountain range that marches through them. Sierra
County is sparsely populated, but just north and west of I-80 lie
Nevada City and Grass Valley, which help make Nevada County
the third-richest cache of votes in the 2nd (and the most
decidedly Republican by registration). A few miles over the
Yuba County line are Beale Air Force Base and Marysville, the
latter at the confluence of the Feather and Yuba rivers.

But most of the 2nd's vote still comes from Butte (Chico) and
Shasta (Redding) counties. Butte cast about one-third of the total
vote in 1992 and gave the GOP House nominee a 2-to-1 victory.
Shasta cast more than one-fourth the district vote, favoring
Republicans for virtually all offices.

Election Returns and Party Registration

	2nd District	Democrat	Republican
1992	President*	93,823 (35.7%)	101,505 (38.7%)
	Senate †	92,538 (35.6%)	136,897 (52.7%)
	Senate †‡	111,154 (42.7%)	122,239 (47.0%)
	House †	71,780 (28.0%)	167,247 (65.2%)

	2nd District	Democrat	Republican
1990	Governor†	77,226 (37.7%)	113,097 (55.2%)
1988	President	90,692 (40.9%)	126,648 (57.2%)
	Senate	84,441 (38.6%)	125,469 (57.3%)
1986	Senate	59,328 (46.8%)	63,607 (50.2%)
	Governor	40,413 (31.5%)	85,786 (66.9%)
1993	Party registration†	145,777 (43.9%)	138,624 (41.7%)

*Vote for Perot was 67,298 (25.6%).   †Independent/other is greater than 5%.
‡Special election for the remaining two years of the term of Pete Wilson who was elected governor in 1990. Appointee John Seymour held the seat 1991-1992.

Demographics

Population 573,322

Percent change from 1980 9.0%

Land area 28,415 square miles

Population per square mile 20

Counties, 1990 population

Butte (pt.) 172,621		Shasta 147,036
Lassen 27,598		Sierra 3,318
Modoc 9,678		Siskiyou 43,531
Nevada 78,510		Trinity 13,063
Plumas 19,739		Yuba 58,228

Cities, 1990 population (10,000 or more)

Chico 40,079	Oroville 11,960
Linda CDP 13,033	Paradise 25,408
Marysville 12,324	Redding 66,462

Race and Hispanic origin
White 91.6%
Black 1.5%
American Indian, Eskimo, or Aleut. 2.4%
Asian or Pacific Islander 2.4%
Other 2.0%
Hispanic origin 6.0%

Ancestry

American 4.2%	Norwegian 2.4%
Danish 1.4%	Polish 1.5%
Dutch 3.7%	Portuguese 1.7%
English 21.3%	Scotch Irish 3.2%
French 5.6%	Scottish 3.4%
German 25.6%	Swedish 3.2%
Irish 18.3%	Welsh 1.3%
Italian 5.3%	

Universities/colleges, 1990-1991 enrollment
Butte College, Oroville 7,928
California State University, Chico 14,979
College of the Siskiyous, Weed 1,851
Feather River College, Quincy 1,245
Lassen College, Susanville 2,563
Shasta College, Redding 8,454
Simpson College, Redding 429
Yuba College, Marysville 7,909

Newspapers, total circulation (in all districts)
Chico Enterprise-Record 29,376
Grass Valley Union 15,267
Oroville Mercury-Register 8,358
Redding Record Searchlight 39,516

Sacramento Bee 269,383
San Francisco Chronicle Examiner 692,424
Yuba-Sutter Appeal Democrat 24,931

Commercial television stations, affiliations
ADI: Medford (36%), Chico-Redding (30%), Sacramento-Stockton (18%) and Reno (16%)
KHSL-TV, Chico (CBS)
KRCR-TV, Redding (ABC)
KCVU, Paradise (None)

Cable television systems, total subscribers
Chambers Cable; Butte County 31,501
Continental Cablevision of California; Marysville 30,350
King Videocable College; Soda Ridge 5,205
TCI of California; Grass Valley 8,000
Viacom Cablevision/North California; Oroville 24,000
Viacom Cablevision/Redding; Redding 31,070

Military installations, 1991
Beale Air Force Base, Marysville 4,152
Sierra Army Depot Activity, Herlong 1,070

Businesses and other major employers
California State University; Chico 1,800
N. T. Enloe Memorial Hospital; Chico 1,600
Mercy Hospital of Redding Inc.; Redding 1,200
Marysville Joint Unfied School District; Marysville 1,100
Shasta College; Redding 1,031
County of Butte; Oroville 1,000
Grass Valley Group Inc.; Grass Valley; broadcasting/communications equipment 973
National Medical Enterprises/Redding Medical Center; Redding 902
Simpson Paper Co.; Anderson; paper mills 879
State of California/Caltrans Dept.; Redding 800
Oroville Hospital; Oroville 750
U.S. Forest Service; Redding 700
Sierra Nevada Memorial Hospital; Grass Valley 650
City of Redding/Information System; Redding 650
Yuba College; Marysville 600
Rideout Memorial Hospital; Marysville 600
California State University/Associated Students; Chico 600
City of Redding; Redding 568
County of Siskiyou/Road Dept.; Yreka 550

3rd District

North Central Valley

The 3rd bears little resemblance to the district so designated before 1992. The old 3rd included much of Sacramento and some of its suburbs to the east, but now the 3rd scalps only the northwestern corner of Sacramento County before running far to the north, west and south to incorporate tracts from the old 2nd and 4th districts.

The 3rd includes all of Yolo County and the eastern portion (10 percent) of Solano County, which were in the old 4th. Remapping gave the 3rd the spacious northern county of Tehama, which serves as a bridge between the flat agricultural lands of the upper Sacramento River Valley and the timber-rich highlands of the Trinity-Shasta region to the north. The 3rd also picked up the farm-oriented counties of Glenn, Colusa and

Sutter, the northern terminus of the state's richly productive Central Valley region.

Despite its vast new lands, however, the 3rd's most populous county is still Sacramento. Even though only the northwestern corner of the county remains, it accounted for about 40 percent of the total district vote in 1992. This corner includes McClellan Air Force Base (just outside the city limits of Sacramento) and a chunk of well-populated suburbs south of Interstate 80 and north of the American River. Residents here work in aerospace and other high-tech industry as well as in Sacramento's main business—state government.

In this vote-rich part of Sacramento county, George Bush prevailed narrowly over Bill Clinton in 1992; but Democratic House incumbent Vic Fazio came up a winner by more than 7,000 votes. Fazio was able to carry two other counties in the 3rd that went for Bush, Colusa and Glenn, and he also won in Tehama County, which went for Clinton by just 89 votes. Glenn, Colusa and Tehama all went strongly for the Republican Senate nominee, who lost badly statewide to Dianne Feinstein.

Yolo County is one of five California counties that voted for Walter F. Mondale for president in 1984, and it includes the college community of Davis, home of a sprawling University of California campus, which has a student population of 23,900. Sutter County is more solidly Republican (the only one of California's 58 counties to give Bush an outright majority in 1992).

Election Returns and Party Registration

	3rd District	Democrat	Republican
1992	President*	99,781 (40.9%)	90,799 (37.2%)
	Senate†	104,130 (44.2%)	106,640 (45.2%)
	Senate†‡	116,482 (49.3%)	98,657 (41.7%)
	House†	122,149 (51.2%)	96,092 (40.3%)
1990	Governor†	77,626 (40.0%)	103,447 (53.3%)
1988	President	95,889 (44.3%)	117,433 (54.3%)
	Senate	87,991 (41.4%)	116,639 (54.8%)
1986	Senate	61,776 (41.7%)	81,977 (55.4%)
	Governor	40,738 (27.3%)	106,167 (71.1%)
1993	Party registration†	152,828 (48.5%)	121,371 (38.6%)

*Vote for Perot was 53,323 (21.9%).   †Independent/other is greater than 5%.
‡Special election for the remaining two years of the term of Pete Wilson who was elected governor in 1990. Appointee John Seymour held the seat 1991-1992.

Demographics

Population   571,374

Percent change from 1980   8.7%

Land area   7,655 square miles

Population per square mile   75

Counties, 1990 population

Butte (pt.) 9,499	Solano (pt.) 53,303
Colusa 16,275	Sutter 64,415
Glenn 24,798	Tehama 49,625
Sacramento (pt.) 212,367	Yolo 141,092

Cities, 1990 population (10,000 or more)
Arden-Arcade CDP (pt.)   24,603

Carmichael CDP (pt.)   39,139
Citrus Heights CDP (pt.)   45,036
Davis   46,209
Dixon   10,401
Foothill Farms CDP   17,135
North Highlands CDP   42,105
Red Bluff   12,363
Vacaville (pt.)   31,553
West Sacramento   28,898
Woodland   39,802
Yuba City   27,437

Race and Hispanic origin
White   82.2%
Black   3.2%
American Indian, Eskimo, or Aleut.   1.4%
Asian or Pacific Islander   5.5%
Other   7.7%
Hispanic origin   14.2%

Ancestry

American 3.7%	Norwegian 2.0%
Danish 1.3%	Polish 1.7%
Dutch 2.9%	Portuguese 2.1%
English 16.7%	Scotch Irish 2.4%
French 4.9%	Scottish 2.9%
German 24.8%	Swedish 2.7%
Irish 16.1%	Welsh 1.1%
Italian 5.1%	

Universities/colleges, 1990-1991 enrollment
U.S. American River College, Sacramento   18,716
University of California, Davis   23,897

Newspapers, total circulation (in all districts)
Chico Enterprise-Record   29,376
Contra Costa Times   88,568
Davis Enterprise   10,863
Fairfield Daily Republic   19,911
Lodi News-Sentinel   17,380
Los Angeles Times   1,169,066
Oakland Tribune   113,419
Oroville Mercury-Register   8,358
Red Bluff Daily News   8,535
Redding Record Searchlight   39,516
Sacramento Bee   269,383
Sacramento Union   46,682
San Francisco Chronicle Examiner   692,424
Vacaville Reporter   19,217
Vallejo Times Herald   22,647
Woodland Daily Democrat   11,151
Yuba-Sutter Appeal Democrat   24,931

Commercial television stations, affiliations
ADI: Chico-Redding (57%) and Sacramento-Stockton (43%)
KCPM, Chico (NBC)

Cable television systems, total subscribers
Chambers Cable; Butte County   31,501
Continental Cablevision of California; Marysville   30,350
Sacramento Cable TV; Sacramento   190,000
Sonic Cable TV; Davis   15,700
UA Cablesystems of California; Vacaville   20,400
United Artist Cable; Davis   8,100
Viacom Cablevision of Red Bluff; Red Bluff   5,035

Military installations, 1991
McClellan Air Force Base, Sacramento 15,918

Businesses and other major employers
University of California; Davis 13,000

Hunt-Wesson Inc./Hunt Tomato; Davis; preserved fruits/vegetables 1,200

Mercy Healthcare Sacramento; Carmichael; medical services/insurance 1,200

Yolo County Schools; Woodland 1,001

Rio Linda Union School District; Rio Linda 1,000

U.S. Internal Revenue Service; North Highlands 900

Dayton Hudson Corp.; Woodland; department stores 765

Lucky Stores Inc.; Vacaville; grocery products 750

Fremont Hospital & Medical Center; Yuba City 700

Woodland Memorial Hospital; Woodland 670

M. T. S. Inc./Tower Records; Sacramento; music/computer stores 600

Davis Joint Unified School District; Davis 576

U.S. American River College; Sacramento 530

4th District

Northeast Central

The number is new, and six of its counties were removed in 1992 redistricting, but the 4th is still at heart the same district that was designated the 14th. The 4th is one of just two districts in Northern California that voted for George Bush in 1992, and one of just two with a Republican registration plurality (45 percent). The 4th is also one of just three districts in all of California where racial minorities constitute less than 15 percent of the population.

This is not to say the district has not changed with redistricting. Gone are the Republican-leaning northern counties of Modoc, Lassen, Plumas and Sierra. Republicans may also miss Nevada County, where nearly 55,000 voters registered in 1992 and a plurality identified themselves with the GOP. Democrats in the district were sorry to see San Joaquin County become part of the 11th District. San Joaquin included Democratic-voting Lodi and a portion of Stockton.

Left intact at the center of the district were the old core counties of Placer, El Dorado, Amador and tiny Alpine (733 registered voters). Placer and El Dorado were the second- and third-largest contributors to the old 14th District vote (after San Joaquin). Now they rank first and third, respectively. Together, they cast 54 percent of the district vote in 1992, giving pluralities to Bush. Alpine and Amador were closer contests, with independent candidate Ross Perot running a close third behind Bill Clinton.

Amador and El Dorado counties triggered the great California gold rush of the mid-19th century (Placerville, the El Dorado county seat, was once among the state's largest cities). Far more recently, the natural beauty of the area (which includes Lake Tahoe) has spawned a more sustainable boom: Amador, Placer and El Dorado were among the eight fastest-growing counties in the state in the 1980s.

Immediately to the south, redistricting brought in three highland counties (Calaveras, Tuolumne and Mono) that, taken as one, provided about 14 percent of the 4th's votes in 1992 and offer a rough balance between the parties. Tuolumne County, which includes most of Yosemite National Park, was carried by Clinton in 1992; Calaveras and Mono went for Bush.

Remapping also gave the 4th the northeastern corner of Sacramento County, where the immediate suburbs of the state capital have grown out to meet the town of Folsom. Once known only for its prison, Folsom is now home to Aerojet, the source of space shuttle technology. (Aerojet facilities are also located nearby in the 5th and 11th districts.) Folsom grew by a stunning 171 percent in the 1980s but has since been hit hard by layoffs at Aerojet.

Sacramento County as a whole votes Democratic, but the portions bordering Placer and El Dorado counties behave more like their upland neighbors.

Election Returns and Party Registration

	4th District	Democrat	Republican
1992	President*	97,501 (33.9%)	117,155 (40.7%)
	Senate †	111,766 (39.7%)	140,902 (50.0%)
	Senate †‡	130,117 (46.0%)	128,046 (45.2%)
	House	129,489 (45.7%)	141,155 (49.8%)
1990	Governor †	75,377 (37.8%)	110,921 (55.6%)
1988	President	88,533 (39.0%)	133,091 (58.6%)
	Senate	80,670 (35.7%)	136,756 (60.5%)
1986	Senate	67,733 (46.2%)	74,867 (51.0%)
	Governor	44,457 (30.2%)	100,239 (68.1%)
1993	Party registration †	150,025 (42.2%)	160,093 (45.1%)

*Vote for Perot was 73,060 (25.4%).   †Independent/other is greater than 5%.
‡Special election for the remaining two years of the term of Pete Wilson who was elected governor in 1990. Appointee John Seymour held the seat 1991-1992.

Demographics

Population 571,033

Percent change from 1980 8.6%

Land area 10,807 square miles

Population per square mile 53

Counties, 1990 population

Alpine 1,113	Mono 9,956
Amador 30,039	Placer 172,796
Calaveras 31,998	Sacramento (pt.) 150,680
El Dorado 125,995	Tuolumne 48,456

Cities, 1990 population (10,000 or more)

Auburn 10,592	North Auburn CDP 10,301
Cameron Park CDP 11,897	Orangevale CDP 26,266
Citrus Heights CDP (pt.) 62,403	Rocklin 19,033
Fair Oaks CDP 26,867	Roseville 44,685
Folsom 29,802	South Lake Tahoe 21,586

Race and Hispanic origin
White 92.7%
Black 1.8%
American Indian, Eskimo, or Aleut. 1.3%
Asian or Pacific Islander 2.1%
Other 2.1%
Hispanic origin 7.4%

Ancestry

American 3.6%	Dutch 3.1%
Danish 1.5%	English 21.4%

French	5.5%	Portuguese	1.9%
German	26.3%	Scotch Irish	3.1%
Irish	17.8%	Scottish	3.3%
Italian	7.0%	Swedish	3.5%
Norwegian	2.4%	Welsh	1.2%
Polish	2.0%		

Universities/colleges, 1990-1991 enrollment
Columbia College, Columbia 2,012
Lake Tahoe Community College, South Lake Tahoe 1,083
Sierra Community College, Rocklin 11,637

Newspapers, total circulation (in all districts)
Auburn Journal 12,838
Lodi News-Sentinel 17,380
Los Angeles Times 1,169,066
Modesto Bee 83,177
Mountain Democrat 13,271
Roseville Press Tribune 13,315
Sacramento Bee 269,383
Sacramento Union 46,682
San Francisco Chronicle Examiner 692,424
Stockton Record 54,568

Commercial television stations, affiliations
ADI: Sacramento-Stockton (59%) and Reno (41%)
   KCMY, Sacramento (None)

Cable television systems, total subscribers
Jones Intercable Inc.; Roseville 11,545
King Videocable College; Placerville 14,512
King Videocable College; San Andreas 7,538
King Videocable College; Mammoth Lakes 6,700
Sacramento Cable TV; Sacramento 190,000
Starstream Communications; Penryn 10,713
TCI of California; South Lake Tahoe 11,972
TCI of Nevada; Crystal Bay 12,300
United Artists Cable; Sonora 5,879
United Artists Cable; Twain Harte 5,384

Businesses and other major employers
Hewlett-Packard Co.; Roseville; computer/office equipment 4,450
Horizon West Inc.; Rocklin; nursing 2,450
Folsom State Prison; Folsom 2,200
Roseville Community Hospital; Roseville 1,200
NEC Electronics Inc.; Roseville; electronic components 1,100
State of California/Corrections Dept.; Jamestown 850
U.S. Computer Services/Cabledata; Folsom; accounting 800
City of Roseville; Roseville 750
Marshall Hospital; Placerville 721
Mule Creek State Prison; Ione 711
Avantek Inc.; Folsom; electrical goods 700
Sierra Community College; Rocklin 600
Auburn Faith Community Hospital; Auburn 600

5th District

Sacramento

No incumbent likes to see his or her district renumbered, a happenstance that confuses constituents, supporters and journalists alike. But for Rep. Robert Matsui, the Democratic incumbent from Sacramento whose 3rd District was redesignated the 5th in the 1992 redistricting, there was little else to regret in the new map.

As the Sacramento metropolitan population grew 34 percent during the 1980s, to 369,000, Matsui's geographical base shrank. On the 1992 map, Matsui got a smaller, concentrated district, but one that was more Democratic. The 5th has a Democratic registration of 59 percent, up 4 percentage points from 1990.

Despite the big Democratic numbers, the old 3rd had been a swing district in statewide elections. Republicans George Bush and Ronald Reagan carried it in the presidential elections of the 1980s, and GOP Sen. Pete Wilson won it in the 1990 gubernatorial contest. But in 1992, with some of its more affluent suburban territory pared away, the district went for Democrat Bill Clinton, giving him an outright majority of 51 percent. The 5th also gave generous victory margins to the campaigns of Democratic Senate nominees Dianne Feinstein and Barbara Boxer.

On paper, the city of Sacramento has several reasons to be reliably Democratic. Labor is better organized here than in all but a few other counties in California. The dominant newspaper is *The Sacramento Bee*, the flagship of the McClatchy chain and a decidedly liberal voice. The city also has a strong mixture of blacks and Hispanics, who constitute more than one-fourth of the district population. There are more than 72,000 Asian Americans in the 5th (although three-fourths of those old enough to vote were not registered in 1992).

But the bedrock of Sacramento politics is the presence of the state government, the source of about 50,000 jobs and a natural pro-government attitude. Years of recession have drained the state treasury and successive Republican governors have sought to limit government spending, but the wellspring of well-being in Sacramento is unlikely to change anytime soon.

There is another Sacramento, of course, that reads the conservative *Sacramento Union* and makes its living in financial services, agribusiness or in the high-tech industries that have sprung up in Sacramento County in recent years. But this sector of the local economy is no longer as robust as in the early 1980s, either. Cutbacks in defense spending have clouded the future, just as base-closing plans have cast shadows over the Sacramento Army Depot (slated to close in 1997) and, east of the city in Rancho Cordova, Mather Air Force Base (scheduled to close late in 1993).

In any event, most of the political impact of this other Sacramento is felt in the county's suburbs and exurban areas, most of which have now been apportioned among three adjoining districts.

Election Returns and Party Registration

	5th District	Democrat	Republican
1992	President*	120,577 (50.9%)	73,562 (31.1%)
	Senate †	127,525 (55.2%)	81,534 (35.3%)
	Senate †‡	139,298 (59.8%)	75,856 (32.6%)
	House †	158,250 (68.6%)	58,698 (25.5%)
1990	Governor †	88,065 (50.3%)	77,737 (44.4%)
1988	President	119,817 (54.4%)	97,662 (44.4%)
	Senate	109,502 (50.6%)	99,009 (45.7%)
1986	Senate	72,266 (48.4%)	73,184 (49.0%)
	Governor	47,446 (31.6%)	100,404 (66.9%)
1993	Party registration †	194,113 (59.1%)	98,191 (29.9%)

*Vote for Perot was 42,566 (18.0%).   †Independent/other is greater than 5%.
‡Special election for the remaining two years of the term of Pete Wilson who was elected governor in 1990. Appointee John Seymour held the seat 1991-1992.

Demographics

Population 573,684

Percent change from 1980 9.1%

Land area 151 square miles

Population per square mile 3,801

Counties, 1990 population
Sacramento (pt.) 573,684

Cities, 1990 population (10,000 or more)
Arden-Arcade CDP (pt.) 67,437
Parkway-South Sacramento CDP 31,903
Elk Grove CDP 17,483
Rosemont CDP 22,851
Florin CDP 24,330
Sacramento (pt.) 368,909
La Riviera CDP 10,986

Race and Hispanic origin
White 65.6%
Black 12.8%
American Indian, Eskimo, or Aleut. 1.2%
Asian or Pacific Islander 13.2%
Other 7.2%
Hispanic origin 14.7%

Ancestry
American 2.2%
Danish 1.1%
Dutch 1.8%
English 13.3%
French 3.6%
German 18.0%
Irish 12.5%
Italian 4.7%
Norwegian 1.4%
Polish 1.5%
Portuguese 1.9%
Scotch Irish 2.0%
Scottish 2.2%
Swedish 2.1%

Universities/colleges, 1990-1991 enrollment
California State University, Sacramento 23,478
Cosumnes River College, Sacramento 8,235
Sacramento City College, Sacramento 14,474

Newspapers, total circulation (in all districts)
Lodi News-Sentinel 17,380
Los Angeles La Opinion 98,557
Los Angeles Times 1,169,066
Sacramento Bee 269,383
Sacramento Union 46,682
San Francisco Chronicle Examiner 692,424

Commercial television stations, affiliations
ADI: Sacramento-Stockton (100%)

Cable television systems, total subscribers
Sacramento Cable TV; Sacramento 190,000

Military installations, 1991
Sacramento Army Depot Activity, Sacramento 3,487
North Highlands Air Force Guard Station, North Highlands 42

Businesses and other major employers
State of California/Transportation Dept.; Sacramento 16,000
University of California, Davis/Medical Center; Sacramento; medical/dental labs 4,218
State of California/General Services; Sacramento 4,000
State of California/Water Resources; Sacramento 3,000
California State University; Sacramento 3,000

State of California/Employment Development Dept.; Sacramento 3,000
Aerojet-General Corp.; Sacramento; space vehicles/research 2,500
Kaiser Permanente Medical Center; Sacramento; medical service/health insurance 2,500
Elk Grove Unified School District; Elk Grove 2,500
State of California/Franchise Tax Board; Sacramento 2,100
Sutter Memorial Hospital; Sacramento 2,100
McClatchy Newspapers Inc./Sacramento Bee; Sacramento; newspapers 2,000
State of California/Motor Vehicle Dept.; Sacramento 2,000
Electronic Data Systems Corp.; Sacramento; computer systems/management 2,000
California Almond Growers/Blue Diamond Growers; Sacramento; almonds 1,867
State of California/Community Colleges; Sacramento 1,600
IDA Courier Inc.; Sacramento; computer/office equipment 1,500
State of California/Education Dept.; Sacramento 1,500
Campbell Soup Co.; Sacramento; canned food 1,300
State of California/Buildings & Grounds Dept.; Sacramento 1,261
County of Sacramento; Sacramento 1,100
United Services Auto Association; Sacramento; life insurance 1,000
BPS Guard Services Inc./Burns Intl.; Sacramento; business services 1,000
Lachman Resource Group; Sacramento; management services 800
State of California/Air Resources Board; Sacramento 780
Methodist Hospital of Sacramento; Sacramento 770
Sacramento Municipal Utility District; Sacramento; electric services 733
Ogden Allied Services Corp./Ogden Food Services Corp.; Sacramento; nonstore retailers 700
Kaiser Foundation Hospitals; Sacramento 700
Hornet Foundation Inc.; Sacramento; research 700
U.S. Interior Dept./Bureau of Reclamation; Sacramento 700
State of California/Toxic Substance Control Dept.; Sacramento 700
State of California/Housing & Community Development Dept.; Sacramento 700
Transco Group Inc.; Sacramento; management consulting services 694
Sacramento City College; Sacramento 670
California Vision Service Inc.; Sacramento; medical service/health insurance 650
County of Sacramento/Sheriffs Dept.; Sacramento 650
Sacramento Regional Transit District; Sacramento 623
Teichert Inc.; Sacramento; road construction 600
City of Sacramento/General Services; Sacramento 600
Nepenthe Homeowners Assn.; Sacramento: 590
Macy's of California Inc.; Sacramento; department stores 570
Hyatt Regency Sacramento; Sacramento; hotel 520

6th District

Northern Bay Area; Sonoma and Marin Counties

Once a seriocomic example of partisan gerrymandering, the 6th is now a model of compactness and community of interest.

It includes all of high-profile Marin County; but instead of reaching in multiple directions for additional votes as it once did, the 6th now weds Marin to the most populous portions of neighboring Sonoma County.

The Marin identity notwithstanding, most of the district's votes are now cast in Sonoma County, where the 6th hugs the Pacific Coast from scenic Bodega Bay north to the Mendocino County line and reaches inland for the county's fast-growing population centers such as Santa Rosa. Once a service town for farmers, Santa Rosa has attracted corporate as well as individual refugees from the congestion of metropolitan San Francisco. It grew by more than one-third in the 1980s, and it is the largest city in the 6th. A few miles down state Highway 12 is Sonoma, a rustic town enlivened by a campus of the California State University system. Fifteen miles to the west on the Sonoma-Marin county line sits the unpretentious city of Petaluma, which once proclaimed itself the "chicken-plucking capital of the world."

To the south, Marin County is home to the city of San Rafael, the famed prison at San Quentin and a small host of commuter suburbs such as Kentfield, Ross, San Anselmo and Fairfax. It has marvelous scenery: Mount Tamalpais, Stinson Beach and the Point Reyes National Seashore. But it is best known for its one-time artist colonies and more affluent suburbs that cling to San Francisco Bay (Sausalito, Tiburon) or nestle deep in the hills between the ocean and the bay (Larkspur, Mill Valley). To mention some of these names is to evoke wistful sighs from former residents, visitors and "California dreamers" who know the area only through song lyrics and other myths of the counterculture. In the past decade, the politics of this social and cultural matrix have supplanted Marin's older GOP pattern. Marin had voted for Republican Gerald R. Ford for president in 1976 and for Ronald Reagan in 1980.

But the county's partisan preferences changed during the 1980s. In 1984, Marin was one of just five California counties voting for Walter F. Mondale. By 1992, GOP registration in the county (as well as in the 6th generally) was down to 30 percent. That figure is remarkably low, considering the 6th is overwhelmingly white (only two of the state's 52 congressional districts have fewer minorities). In 1992, Bill Clinton carried Marin by a more than 2-to-1 margin over George Bush.

Marin's liberal activists in 1992 also elevated one of their own, five-term Rep. Barbara Boxer, into the Senate and delivered her House seat to another Democratic woman, Lynn Woolsey.

Election Returns and Party Registration

	6th District	Democrat	Republican
1992	President*	169,301 (56.1%)	71,564 (23.7%)
	Senate †	177,823 (60.0%)	91,177 (30.8%)
	Senate †‡	199,967 (66.8%)	80,754 (27.0%)
	House	190,322 (66.0%)	98,171 (34.0%)
1990	Governor †	123,499 (58.0%)	77,611 (36.5%)
1988	President	144,054 (58.8%)	97,249 (39.7%)
	Senate	129,891 (53.7%)	103,886 (43.0%)
1986	Senate	105,829 (56.5%)	77,231 (41.2%)
	Governor	75,681 (40.0%)	107,874 (57.0%)
1993	Party registration †	197,474 (55.0%)	109,329 (30.4%)

*Vote for Perot was 60,920 (20.2%).   †Independent/other is greater than 5%.
‡Special election for the remaining two years of the term of Pete Wilson who was elected governor in 1990. Appointee John Seymour held the seat 1991-1992.

Demographics

Population 571,227

Percent change from 1980 8.7%

Land area 1,591 square miles

Population per square mile 359

Counties, 1990 population
Marin 230,096   Sonoma (pt.) 341,131

Cities, 1990 population (10,000 or more)
Larkspur 11,070	Rohnert Park 36,326
Mill Valley 13,038	San Anselmo 11,743
Novato 47,585	San Rafael 48,404
Petaluma 43,184	Santa Rosa (pt.) 109,826

Race and Hispanic origin
White 90.0%
Black 2.4%
American Indian, Eskimo, or Aleut. 0.8%
Asian or Pacific Islander 3.4%
Other 3.4%
Hispanic origin 8.9%

Ancestry
American 2.3%	Polish 2.5%
Danish 1.7%	Portuguese 1.8%
Dutch 2.5%	Russian 2.7%
English 18.8%	Scotch Irish 3.1%
French 5.2%	Scottish 3.9%
German 23.2%	Swedish 3.3%
Irish 18.4%	Swiss 1.2%
Italian 10.2%	Welsh 1.4%
Norwegian 2.4%	

Universities/colleges, 1990-1991 enrollment
College of Marin, Kentfield 9,817
Dominican College of San Rafael, San Rafael 712
Golden Gate Baptist Seminary, Mill Valley 545
Heald Business College, Rohnert Park 200
San Francisco Theological Seminary, San Anselmo 615
Santa Rosa Junior College, Santa Rosa 20,479
California State University, Rohnert Park 6,129

Newspapers, total circulation (in all districts)
Marin Independent Journal 41,031
Petaluma Argus-Courier 8,573
San Francisco Chronicle Examiner 692,424
Santa Rosa Press Democrat 95,106

Commercial television stations, affiliations
ADI: San Francisco (100%)

Cable television systems, total subscribers
Chambers Cable of Novato; Novato 17,200
Multivision Cable TV; Sonoma Mt. 44,420
Post Newsweek Cable TV; Santa Rosa 44,955
Viacom Cablevision; Big Rock Ridge 61,632
Viacom Cablevision; Petaluma 15,046

Businesses and other major employers
City of San Rafael; San Rafael 2,000
State of California/Sonoma Dev. Center; Eldridge 2,000
Hewlett-Packard Co./Signal Analysis Div.; Cotati; measuring devices 1,488

Santa Rosa Junior College; Santa Rosa 1,417

Marin General Hospital; San Rafael 1,350

Santa Rosa High School District; Santa Rosa 1,300

Hewlett-Packard Co./Network Measurements Div.; Santa Rosa; computer/office equipment 1,225

Kaiser Foundation Hospitals; San Rafael 1,200

State Farm; Cotati; fire/marine/casualty insurance 1,099

Santa Rosa Memorial Hospital; Santa Rosa 1,000

Kaiser Foundation Hospitals; Santa Rosa 1,000

Optical Coating Laboratory; Santa Rosa; metal services 978

Sonoma County Community Hospital; Santa Rosa 950

San Quentin State Prison; San Rafael 925

IMCO Realty Services; Santa Rosa; mortgage bankers 900

Pilkington Visioncare Inc./Sola Optical USA; Petaluma; ophthalmic goods 890

American Insurance Co. Inc; Novato; fire/marine/casualty insurance 795

Medical Personnel Pool; Santa Rosa; temp services 750

County of Sonoma; Santa Rosa 675

Amex Life Assurance Co.; San Rafael; medical service/health insurance 650

Hewlett-Packard Co./Microwave Technology Div.; Santa Rosa; measuring/controlling devices 600

Fireman's Fund Insurance Co.; San Rafael; insurance services 600

Marin Community College District; San Rafael 600

Golden Gate Bridge/Golden Gate Transit; San Rafael; transportation 535

Petaluma Valley Hospital; Petaluma 525

7th District

Northeastern Bay Area

California Republicans were generally pleased with the court-fashioned redistricting plan, which seemed to level the state's political playing field for 1992. But there were exceptions. Some in the GOP had hoped that the new map would enable them to go after 18-year House veteran George Miller, the chairman of the House Natural Resources Committee and the scourge of western Republicans on water and environmental issues. But the new map raised Democratic registration in the 7th to 62 percent, making Miller safer than ever.

The 7th has long been based in Contra Costa County, which begins at San Pablo Bay, heads south over the San Pablo Mountains and spreads inland well to the east of Berkeley and Oakland (see map on page 69). Since World War II, the county has seen its population swell from 100,000 to 800,000. In response, the map for the 1990s confines the 7th to those northernmost portions of the county where the growth is oldest.

The new 7th still includes the shore of San Pablo Bay, studded with industrial cities such as Richmond, San Pablo, Pinole and Martinez. Here, oil terminals, factories and warehouses stretch for miles, belying the region's reputation for natural beauty. In 1988, sensitive wetlands in Martinez were soiled by an oil spill. Less than two years later, an explosion at the Shell Oil refinery rattled windows seven miles away. In this part of the 7th, residents are multiracial (Richmond is nearly one-half black), predominantly blue collar and heavily Democratic.

Historically, this Democratic vote was diluted by Republi-can influence in the suburbs to the south and east—on the sunny side of the San Pablo ridge. Concord, currently a terminus for rapid transit trains, became the county's biggest city and passed the 100,000 mark in the 1970s. The unrelenting suburban expansion began altering the political balance. Jimmy Carter carried the 7th easily in 1976, but it went for Ronald Reagan in 1980 and 1984. Slowly, Miller too felt the center of gravity shift. His 61 percent vote share in 1990 was his lowest since 1974.

But the trend was reversed in 1992. The court-appointed "special masters" decided that the bayside residents of the 7th had more in common with their neighbors to the west (in El Cerrito, on the Alameda County line) and to the north (across San Pablo Bay and Suisun Bay in Solano County). So they drew into the 7th the cities of Vallejo, Benicia, Cordelia and Suisun City. These communities, home to farm-support services and industry, are traditionally Democratic. Although new to Miller in 1992, they gave him roughly a 2-to-1 edge over a Republican challenger from Solano County.

At its new southern limit, the 7th still includes Concord. But nearly all the other suburban territory has been removed and added to the 10th District, dropping the Republican share of registered voters in the 7th from 34 percent in 1990 to 24 percent in 1992.

Election Returns and Party Registration

	7th District	Democrat	Republican
1992	President*	140,159 (60.8%)	51,356 (22.3%)
	Senate †	136,483 (63.2%)	59,077 (27.4%)
	Senate †‡	149,484 (70.0%)	50,675 (23.7%)
	House	153,320 (70.3%)	54,822 (25.1%)
1990	Governor	98,484 (62.2%)	52,997 (33.5%)
1988	President	125,807 (62.1%)	74,594 (36.8%)
	Senate	113,105 (57.4%)	78,407 (39.8%)
1986	Senate	90,755 (61.5%)	53,815 (36.5%)
	Governor	66,077 (44.4%)	79,007 (53.1%)
1993	Party registration †	193,439 (62.3%)	75,266 (24.3%)

Vote for Perot was 39,038 (16.9%). †*Independent/other is greater than 5%.* ‡*Special election for the remaining two years of the term of Pete Wilson who was elected governor in 1990. Appointee John Seymour held the seat 1991-1992.*

Demographics

Population 572,773

Percent change from 1980 9.0%

Land area 349 square miles

Population per square mile 1,642

Counties, 1990 population
Contra Costa (pt.) 427,327   Solano (pt.) 145,446

Cities, 1990 population (10,000 or more)

Benicia 24,437	Pittsburg (pt.) 47,559
Concord (pt.) 98,608	Richmond (pt.) 86,780
El Cerrito 22,869	San Pablo 25,158
Hercules (pt.) 16,326	Vallejo 109,199
Martinez (pt.) 31,247	West Pittsburg CDP
Pinole (pt.) 17,307	17,453

SAN FRANCISCO BAY AREA

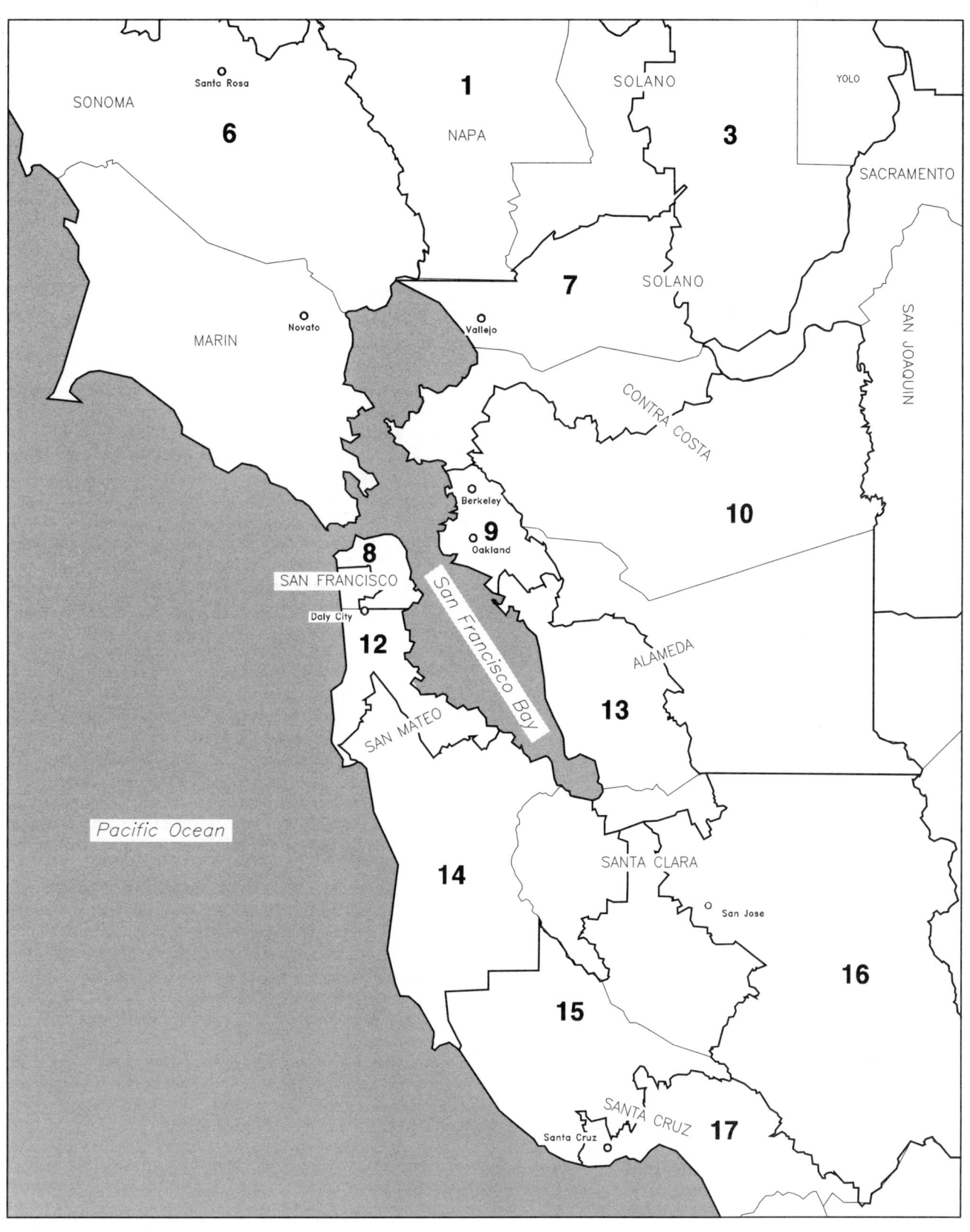

SONOMA

Santa Rosa

6

1

NAPA

SOLANO

YOLO

3

SACRAMENTO

7

SOLANO

MARIN

Novato

Vallejo

CONTRA COSTA

SAN JOAQUIN

Berkeley

9

Oakland

10

8

SAN FRANCISCO

San Francisco Bay

Daly City

12

ALAMEDA

13

SAN MATEO

Pacific Ocean

14

SANTA CLARA

San Jose

16

15

SANTA CRUZ

17

Santa Cruz

Race and Hispanic origin
White 62.7%
Black 16.6%
American Indian, Eskimo, or Aleut. 0.8%
Asian or Pacific Islander 14.4%
Other 5.6%
Hispanic origin 13.3%

Ancestry
American 1.9%	Norwegian 1.5%
Dutch 1.8%	Polish 1.8%
English 11.7%	Portuguese 2.0%
French 3.4%	Scotch Irish 1.9%
German 16.6%	Scottish 2.2%
Irish 12.5%	Swedish 2.1%
Italian 6.2%	

Universities/colleges, 1990-1991 enrollment
California Maritime Academy, Vallejo 376
Contra Costa College, San Pablo 6,634
Los Medanos College, Pittsburg 6,367

Newspapers, total circulation (in all districts)
Antioch Daily Ledger-Post Dispatch 21,371
Contra Costa Times 88,568
Fairfield Daily Republic 19,911
Oakland Tribune 113,419
Pleasanton Valley Herald 34,853
Pleasanton Valley Times 34,065
Richmond West County Times 31,129
Sacramento Bee 269,383
San Francisco Chronicle Examiner 692,424
Vacaville Reporter 19,217
Vallejo Times Herald 22,647

Commercial television stations, affiliations
ADI: San Francisco (99%) and Sacramento-Stockton (1%)

Cable television systems, total subscribers
Bay Cablevision; Hercules 5,130
Concord TV Cable; Concord 41,700
Century Cable of Northern California; San Pablo 8,100
Donrey Cablevision/Vallejo; Vallejo 23,000
Multivision Cable TV; Fairfield 25,000
TCI Cablevision; Pleasant Hill 82,388
Viacom Cablevision; Pittsburg 36,500
Viacom Cablevision; Pinole 5,816

Military installations, 1991
Mare Island Naval Shipyard, Vallejo 10,964
Mare Island Naval Station, Vallejo 4,505
Concord Naval Weapons Station, Concord 4,173

Businesses and other major employers
Chevron Corp.; Concord; petroleum/natural gas 8,000
Chevron Corp.; Richmond; petroleum refining 3,500
U.S. Veterans Affairs Dept.; Martinez; health services 1,137
USS-POSCO Industries; Pittsburg; steel products 1,050
Mt. Diablo Hospital/Medical Center; Concord 1,040
Kaiser Foundation Hospitals; Vallejo 1,020
Tosco Corp./Tosco Refining Co.; Concord; accounting 1,000
Kaiser Foundation Hospitals; Martinez 1,000
C&H Sugar Co.; Crockett; sugar 900
Brookside Hospital; Richmond 900
City of Richmond; Richmond 889
Shell Oil Co.; Martinez; petroleum refining 875
Dow Chemical Co.; Pittsburg; inorganic chemicals 800
County of Contra Costa/Merrithew Memorial Hospital; Martinez 700
County of Contra Costa/Juvenile Dept.; Martinez 700
Tosco Corp./Avon Refinery; Martinez; petroleum refining 670
Pacific Gas & Electric Co.; Concord; electric services 640
Safeway Inc.; Richmond; warehousing 600
City of Concord; Concord 600
Union Oil Co. of California/San Francisco Refinery; Rodeo; petroleum refining 570
Bio-Rad Laboratories Inc.; Rodeo; measuring/controlling devices 550
Staff Network Plus; Martinez; supply services 550
Foodmaker Inc./Jack-in-the-Box; Vallejo; fast-food chain 520

8th District

San Francisco

San Francisco (natives call it "The City") has been romanticized for generations by writers, artists, visitors and residents. Overrun with adventurers during the gold rush era, it kept its reputation as a rough-and-tumble port city long thereafter. More recently, it has hosted successive waves of counterculturalism, notably the beats of the 1950s and the hippies of the 1960s.

Racially, San Francisco is the second most diverse county in the nation, after Queens, N.Y. In the past two decades, the city's well-established homosexual community has grown larger and more visible, wielding greater influence over the city's politics (the gay vote is estimated at one-fifth of the electorate). There has been some backlash in recent years, particularly among working-class families and white ethnic minorities.

But whatever their local disagreements, San Franciscans have little trouble choosing sides in federal elections. In 1992, San Francisco County (which is coterminous with the city) gave 76 percent of its vote to Bill Clinton, who turned out to be the weakling of the ticket. Senate nominees Barbara Boxer and Dianne Feinstein got 76 percent and 81 percent, respectively. Seeing both Feinstein and Boxer elected was a point of special satisfaction: Feinstein is a former mayor of San Francisco, and Boxer represented part of the city throughout her decade in the House.

The 8th resembles the old 5th, except that it comes even closer to encompassing all of San Francisco within a single congressional district (see map on page 69). The old 5th did not include the city's far northwest (including the bridgehead of the Golden Gate Bridge), which was in the 6th (centered in Marin County at the other end of the bridge).

But the map adopted in 1992 reclaimed these sections of the city (including Seacliff, Presidio Park and environs north of Golden Gate Park). Sacrificed instead (this time to the 12th District that adjoins to the south) were the neighborhoods south of Golden Gate Park and west of Twin Peaks (including the Sunset, Parkside and Forest Hill districts).

The shift added nearly 50,000 more city residents to the newly renumbered San Francisco district, reducing the previous Democratic share of registered voters by just 1 percentage point, to 64 percent. The removal of the southwestern neighborhoods affected the district's racial mix. Whites accounted for 59 percent of the old 5th; they constituted 52 percent of the 8th in 1992. In some future Democratic primary, the nomination may well be contested by a candidate from one of the minority communities—the largest of which, Asian Americans, is nearing 30 percent as the Chinese and Japanese are joined by increasing numbers of Koreans, Filipinos and Southeast Asians.

Election Returns and Party Registration

	8th District	Democrat	Republican
1992	President*	187,201 (75.6%)	39,396 (15.9%)
	Senate	186,859 (79.1%)	38,469 (16.3%)
	Senate ‡	198,752 (82.4%)	33,829 (14.0%)
	House †	191,906 (82.5%)	25,693 (11.0%)
1990	Governor	149,501 (72.7%)	47,404 (23.1%)
1988	President	139,831 (78.5%)	36,432 (20.5%)
	Senate	112,058 (74.6%)	34,142 (22.7%)
1986	Senate	103,580 (67.1%)	46,983 (30.4%)
	Governor	83,631 (54.3%)	65,590 (42.6%)
1993	Party registration †	237,121 (64.3%)	58,097 (15.8%)

*Vote for Perot was 21,180 (8.5%).   †Independent/other is greater than 5%.
‡Special election for the remaining two years of the term of Pete Wilson who was elected governor in 1990. Appointee John Seymour held the seat 1991-1992.

Demographics

Population 573,247

Percent change from 1980 9.0%

Land area 34 square miles

Population per square mile 16,659

Counties, 1990 population
San Francisco (pt.) 573,247

Cities, 1990 population (10,000 or more)
San Francisco (pt.) 573,247

Race and Hispanic origin
White 52.0%
Black 12.8%
American Indian, Eskimo, or Aleut. 0.5%
Asian or Pacific Islander 27.8%
Other 6.9%
Hispanic origin 15.7%

Ancestry
American 1.1%   Polish 2.0%
English 8.0%   Russian 3.0%
French 2.7%   Scotch Irish 1.2%
German 10.3%   Scottish 1.9%
Irish 9.3%   Swedish 1.2%
Italian 5.5%

Universities/colleges, 1990-1991 enrollment
California Institute of Integral Studies, San Francisco 525
California College of Podiatric Medicine, San Francisco 348
Fashion Institute of Design, San Francisco 619
Golden Gate University, San Francisco 7,572
Lincoln University, San Francisco 370
New College of California, San Francisco 738
San Francisco Art Institute, San Francisco 715
Hastings College of Law, San Francisco 1,367
University of San Francisco, San Francisco 6,713

Newspapers, total circulation (in all districts)
Los Angeles Times 1,169,066
Oakland Tribune 113,419
San Francisco Chronicle Examiner 692,424
San Jose Mercury News 275,325

Commercial television stations, affiliations
ADI: San Francisco (100%)

Cable television systems, total subscribers
Viacom Cablevision of San Francisco; San Francisco 153,058

Military installations, 1991
Presidio of San Francisco (Army), San Francisco 4,476
Treasure Island Naval Station, San Francisco 3,426

Businesses and other major employers
United Air Lines Inc.; San Francisco; airline 12,000
Bank of America National Trust Savings Assn.; San Francisco; commercial banks 9,000
Pacific Gas & Electric Co.; San Francisco; electric services 7,600
Wells Fargo Bank; San Francisco; commercial banks 6,000
State of California/Caltrans Dept.; San Francisco 5,000
Bechtel Group Inc.; San Francisco; heavy construction 4,400
San Francisco Municipal Railway; San Francisco; railroad 3,784
Southern Pacific Transportaton Co.; San Francisco; railroads 3,000
San Francisco General Hospital; San Francisco 3,000
Russell Personnel Services; San Francisco; personnel supply services 3,000
BankAmerica Corp.; San Francisco; commercial banks 2,500
San Francisco City & County; San Francisco 2,400
United Parcel Service Inc.; San Francisco; mail services 2,000
San Francisco Newspaper Printing Co.; San Francisco; newspapers 2,000
Pacific Telesis Group; San Francisco; telephone communications 2,000
Kaiser Foundation Hospitals/Kaiser Permanente; San Francisco 2,000
State of California/Caltrans Dept.; San Francisco 2,000
American Airlines Inc.; San Francisco; airline 1,600
California Pacific Health Center; San Francisco 1,525
Levi Strauss Assoc. Inc.; San Francisco; outerwear 1,515
Marriott Corp./San Francisco Marriott; San Francisco; bars/restaurants 1,500
State of California; San Francisco 1,500
California State Auto Assn. Inter-Insurance Bureau; San Francisco; casualty insurance 1,457
Chevron Transport Corp.; San Francisco; freight shipping 1,400
St. Mary's Hospital & Medical Center; San Francisco 1,377
U.S. Federal Reserve; San Francisco 1,312
Charles Schwab & Co. Inc.; San Francisco; security brokers 1,300
State Compensation Insurance Fund; San Francisco; fire/marine/casualty insurance 1,250
Yellow Cab Cooperative Inc.; San Francisco; taxicabs 1,200
BanCal Tri-State Corp.; San Francisco; commercial banks 1,200

San Francisco City & County/Recreation & Park Dept.; San Francisco 1,200

Westin Hotels Ltd./St. Francis Hotel; San Francisco; hotels/motels 1,200

Pillsbury Madison & Sutro Inc.; San Francisco; legal services 1,100

San Francisco City & County/San Francisco Intl. Airport; San Francisco 1,012

Americold Corp.; San Francisco; warehousing 1,000

Macy's of California Inc.; San Francisco; department stores 1,000

U.S. Internal Revenue Service; San Francisco 1,000

St. Luke's Hospital; San Francisco 1,000

Kaiser Permanente Group; San Francisco; medical doctors 1,000

University of San Francisco; San Francisco 1,000

Hilton Hotels Corp./San Francisco Hilton; San Francisco; hotel 1,000

San Francisco City & County/Airport Commission; San Francisco 920

Chevron Corp.; San Francisco; petroleum refining 900

Arthur Andersen & Co.; San Francisco; accounting/auditing 850

St. Francis Medical Center; San Francisco 835

Esprit Holdings Inc.; San Francisco; apparel/piece goods 800

Delta Dental Plan of California; San Francisco; medical service/health insurance 800

U.S. Environmental Protection Agency; San Francisco 800

State of California/Public Utilities; San Francisco 800

Davies Medical Center; San Francisco 800

Morrison & Foerster; San Francisco; legal services 800

Hyatt Regency San Francisco; San Francisco; hotel 800

Industrial Indemnity Co.; San Francisco; fire/marine/casualty insurance 775

Continental Baking Co./Hostess Baking Co.; San Francisco; grocery products 700

Del Monte Corp.; San Francisco; preserved fruits/vegetables 700

Marriott Corp./Marriott Host; San Francisco; bars/restaurants 700

Brobeck Phleger & Harrison; San Francisco; legal services 700

University of the Pacific/School of Dentistry; San Francisco 700

McKesson Corp. Maryland; San Francisco; beer/wine/liquor 650

Drug & Health Care Group; San Francisco; drugs and medical services 650

Pacific Bell Directory Inc.; San Francisco; publishing 600

Chevron USA Inc.; San Francisco; petroleum/natural gas 600

U.S. Leasing Intl.; San Francisco; credit institutions 600

Renaissance Hotel Associates/Parc Fifty Five Hotel; San Francisco; hotel 600

U.S. Health & Human Services Dept.; San Francisco 600

Coopers & Lybrand; San Francisco; accounting/auditing 600

KPMG Peat Marwick; San Francisco; accounting/auditing 580

AT&T Communications Inc.; San Francisco; telephone communications 575

BPS Guard Services Inc./Burns Intl. Security Services; San Francisco; business/security services 550

California Hyatt Corp.; San Francisco; hotel 550

Heller Ehrman White McAuliffe; San Francisco; legal services 525

Placer Dome U.S. Inc.; San Francisco; gold/silver ores 520

9th District

Alameda County — Oakland; Berkeley

The 1992 court-ordered district map in California made the old 8th District far more compact, compressing it into Alameda County and renumbering it the 9th (see map on page 69). Gone are the old district lines reaching clear across Contra Costa County and the eastern reaches of Alameda County to the Central Valley.

The 9th consists of Oakland and Berkeley, and a few subsidiaries: the bayside industrial sites of Emeryville and Alameda and the bedroom suburbs of Albany (north of Berkeley) and Piedmont (an independent enclave in the Oakland hills).

The removal of the old district's inland suburbs left longtime Democrat incumbent Ronald Dellums safer than ever in an Oakland-Berkeley-based constituency. In 1992, in the new 9th, he walked off with 72 percent. The politics of the 9th are more complex than these numbers suggest, but Dellums has long since mastered the complexities. A liberal and a dove, he also knew how important the Alameda Naval Air Station was to the district—and how vital the Navy in general was to the Bay Area.

However, three of the district's Navy facilities showed up on the 1993 recommendations for base closures: the Alameda air station, the Naval Aviation Depot in Alameda and the Oakland Naval Supply Center.

Dellums is a native of Oakland, which dominates the district, and a product of the deep-rooted African American community that dominates Oakland. Nearly 45 percent of the city is black, and Oakland's historic tensions between blacks and police gave birth in the 1960s to the Black Panther Party. Overall, the 9th is about one-third black; Asians and Hispanics together account for more than one-fourth of the people.

More recently, Oakland has been better known nationally for hosting three consecutive World Series (1988-1990), one of which was interrupted by a deadly earthquake. The city also has always had wealthy, mostly white neighborhoods in the hills overlooking the Bay (made famous in 1991 by wildfires that obliterated scores of homes).

Berkeley, Oakland's northern neighbor, was founded at about the same time in the mid-1800s. But while Oakland has always been a port, Berkeley (population 103,000) has always been a college town. As the home of the first and foremost campus of the world-renowned University of California, Berkeley is one of those places everyone thinks they know about whether they have been there or not.

Berkeley symbolizes radicalism. But the reality of life here is more removed from the passions of political and social liberation. The recession and the state's budget crises of the early 1990s has hurt the university, and interest in activism has waned somewhat.

This is not likely to matter much in federal elections, in which the 9th is a reliable cache of support for Democrats. In 1992 Bill Clinton's 78.7 percent vote share here was his best in any California district.

Election Returns and Party Registration

	9th District	Democrat	Republican
1992	President*	186,714 (78.7%)	29,394 (12.4%)
	Senate †	187,344 (80.5%)	33,782 (14.5%)
	Senate ‡	194,657 (82.9%)	30,614 (13.0%)
	House	164,265 (71.9%)	53,707 (23.5%)
1990	Governor	139,484 (75.5%)	37,075 (20.1%)
1988	President	182,184 (79.3%)	45,102 (19.6%)
	Senate	168,423 (74.5%)	52,081 (23.0%)
1986	Senate	131,238 (71.9%)	48,656 (26.6%)
	Governor	111,201 (60.3%)	67,680 (36.7%)
1993	Party registration †	224,852 (69.3%)	45,264 (14.0%)

*Vote for Perot was 21,207 (8.9%).   †Independent/other is greater than 5%.
‡Special election for the remaining two years of the term of Pete Wilson who was elected governor in 1990. Appointee John Seymour held the seat 1991-1992.

Demographics

Population 573,458

Percent change from 1980 9.3%

Land area 73 square miles

Population per square mile 7,866

Counties, 1990 population
Alameda (pt.) 573,458

Cities, 1990 population (10,000 or more)

Alameda (pt.) 76,457	Oakland (pt.) 361,584
Albany 16,327	Piedmont 10,602
Berkeley 102,724	

Race and Hispanic origin
White 45.4%
Black 31.8%
American Indian, Eskimo, or Aleut. 0.6%
Asian or Pacific Islander 15.7%
Other 6.6%
Hispanic origin 12.0%

Ancestry

American 1.3%	Norwegian 1.1%
Dutch 1.2%	Polish 2.0%
English 9.0%	Russian 2.5%
French 2.4%	Scotch Irish 1.4%
German 10.6%	Scottish 2.0%
Irish 7.9%	Swedish 1.7%
Italian 3.4%	

Universities/colleges, 1990-1991 enrollment
California School of Professional Psychology at Berkeley, Alameda 517
California College of Arts, Oakland 1,114
College of Alameda, Alameda 4,690
Graduate Theological Union, Berkeley 396
Holy Names College, Oakland 896
Laney College, Oakland 8,571
Merritt College, Oakland 4,810
Mills College, Oakland 1,042
National Hispanic University, Oakland 242
Patten College, Oakland 492
University of California, Berkeley 30,638
Vista College, Berkeley 3,489

Newspapers, total circulation (in all districts)
Alameda Times-Star 7,305
Fremont Argus 32,880
Hayward Daily Review 43,594
Oakland Tribune 113,419
Pleasanton Valley Herald 34,853
Pleasanton Valley Times 34,065
San Francisco Chronicle Examiner 692,424
San Jose Mercury News 275,325

Commercial television stations, affiliations
ADI: San Francisco (100%)

Cable television systems, total subscribers
Cable Oakland; Oakland 66,446
TCI Cablevision of Alameda; Alameda 15,067

Military installations, 1991
Naval Air Station, Alameda 22,813
Oakland Naval Supply Center, Oakland 6,793
Alameda Naval Aviation Depot Activity, Alameda 3,911
Oakland Naval Hospital, Oakland 2,683
Oakland Army Base, Oakland 2,545

Businesses and other major employers
University of California; Berkeley 17,315
Lawrence Livermore Laboratory; Oakland; research services 3,240
Lawrence Berkeley Laboratory; Berkeley; research services 3,000
Blue Cross of California; Oakland; medical service/health insurance 2,500
Pacific Gas & Electric Co.; Oakland; utility services 2,500
Kaiser Foundation Hospitals; Oakland 2,200
Alameda Contra Costa Transit District; Oakland 1,800
Children's Hospital of Northern California; Oakland 1,800
Southern Pacific Co./Western Div.; Oakland; railroads 1,600
AT&T Co.; Oakland; telephone communications 1,500
Highland General Hospital; Oakland 1,500
Samuel Merritt Hospital Inc.; Oakland 1,200
City of Oakland/Police Dept.; Oakland 1,095
TW Services Inc./Volume Services; Oakland; bars/restaurants 1,000
Alta Bates-Herrick Hospital; Berkeley 1,000
Providence Hospital of Oakland; Oakland 900
City of Oakland/Parks & Recreation Dept.; Oakland 858
Owens-Illinois Inc.; Oakland; glass products 820
United Air Lines Inc.; Oakland; airline 800
Clorox Co.; Oakland; soaps/cleaners 775
San Francisco Bay Rapid Transit District; Oakland 770
Safeway Inc.; Oakland; management/grocery stores 750
American President Co. Ltd; Oakland; freight shipping 700
Carter Hawley Hale Stores Inc./Emporium; Oakland; department stores 700
Cetus Corp.; Oakland; research services 650
Pacific Gas & Electric Co.; Oakland; engineering/utility services 640
Oakland Unified School District; Oakland 632
Safeway Inc.; Oakland; grocery stores 630
Mothers Cake & Cookie Co.; Oakland; bakery products 600
Oakland Tribune Inc.; Oakland; newspapers 600

State of California/Health Services Dept.; Berkeley 600
Pacific Racing Assn./Golden Gate Fields; Berkeley; commercial sports 600
East Bay Municipal Water District; Oakland 580
Oakland Scavenger Co./Bay Cities Disposal Co.; Oakland; sanitary services 550
Ingres Corp.; Alameda; computer services 550
Port of Oakland/Oakland Intl. Airport; Oakland 550
University of California/Facilities Management Div.; Berkeley 550
World Savings & Loan; Oakland; savings institution 533
Citibank; Oakland; savings institution 529
Alameda Hospital Inc.; Alameda 520

10th District

Eastern Contra Costa and Alameda Counties

The 10th stands as a monument to the objectives and methods of California's redistricting in 1992. The end product is a district that straddles two counties but unites the affected portions of both in a community of interest. For the residents of the 10th are primarily suburbanites living on the sunrise (and sunny) side of the inland ridge east of San Francisco Bay (see map on page 69). The landscape here features hills and hidden valleys, and the long dry months of the year leave the slopes golden brown.

More than two-thirds of the district's people live in Contra Costa County, the rest in Alameda County. For decades, in election after election, scores of thousands of GOP votes from the Bay ridges and eastward have been swamped in the tide of Democratic ballots cast in the cities that hug the East Bay shoreline: Oakland and Berkeley in Alameda County, Richmond and Martinez and others in Contra Costa.

But since the Bay Area Rapid Transit (BART) system took hold in the 1970s, the growth in once-sleepy towns such as Orinda, Pleasant Hill, Walnut Creek and Antioch has been so great that its political ramifications could no longer be denied when new district lines were drawn.

Most of this growth has been in Contra Costa County, but Alameda communities such as Castro Valley, Dublin, Pleasanton and Livermore have been on the move as well. Livermore is the site of the Lawrence Livermore Laboratory, one of the nation's leading facilities for experimental physics. But high-tech growth has been generalized through the area: Pleasanton's population grew by 44 percent in the 1980s.

By cutting a new and separate district for these voters, the court-appointed cartographers created something that suggests a harp in shape and looks like a solid Republican district in demographics. The proportion of racial minorities in the 10th (less than 18 percent) is the fourth lowest in the state. But in the process of creating this community of interest, the mappers also confirmed the partisan character of surrounding districts. Six districts border or adjoin the 10th, and five of them elected Democrats to the House in 1992.

At the same time, it would be a mistake to view the 10th as a Northern California version of Orange County. Some of the residents here represent white flight from Oakland that is now generations old. But many of the newer commuters are younger and may still identify with San Francisco or Berkeley. While concerned with taxes, crime, schools and drugs, many hold more liberal views on other social and economic questions.

Bill Clinton carried both the Alameda and Contra Costa portions of the 10th in 1992, in both cases receiving about 42 percent of the vote (or about the same as he got nationwide).

Election Returns and Party Registration

	10th District	Democrat	Republican
1992	President*	127,450 (42.4%)	107,191 (35.6%)
	Senate †	139,884 (48.0%)	123,686 (42.5%)
	Senate †‡	165,254 (56.9%)	109,452 (37.7%)
	House	134,635 (48.0%)	145,702 (52.0%)
1990	Governor	84,226 (45.0%)	95,619 (51.1%)
1988	President	90,115 (40.9%)	127,631 (57.9%)
	Senate	79,238 (36.2%)	134,511 (61.4%)
1986	Senate	85,308 (41.0%)	118,558 (56.9%)
	Governor	53,132 (25.3%)	151,886 (72.4%)
1993	Party registration †	159,476 (42.5%)	164,310 (43.8%)

*Vote for Perot was 66,180 (22.0%). †Independent/other is greater than 5%.
‡Special election for the remaining two years of the term of Pete Wilson who was elected governor in 1990. Appointee John Seymour held the seat 1991-1992.

Demographics

Population 572,008

Percent change from 1980 8.5%

Land area 1,024 square miles

Population per square mile 559

Counties, 1990 population
Alameda (pt.) 195,603   Contra Costa (pt.) 376,405

Cities, 1990 population (10,000 or more)
Alamo CDP 12,277   Livermore 56,741
Antioch (pt.) 62,195   Moraga Town 15,852
Ashland CDP 16,590   Oakley CDP 18,374
Castro Valley CDP (pt.)   Orinda 16,642
  41,985   Pleasant Hill (pt.) 26,144
Concord (pt.) 12,740   Pleasanton 50,553
Danville 31,306   San Ramon 35,303
Dublin 23,229   Walnut Creek 60,569
Lafayette 23,501

Race and Hispanic origin
White 87.9%
Black 2.3%
American Indian, Eskimo, or Aleut. 0.6%
Asian or Pacific Islander 6.4%
Other 2.9%
Hispanic origin 8.7%

Ancestry
American 2.4%   Norwegian 2.4%
Danish 1.7%   Polish 2.3%
Dutch 2.6%   Portuguese 3.5%
English 19.6%   Russian 1.7%
French 5.0%   Scotch Irish 2.7%
German 24.1%   Scottish 3.7%
Irish 17.7%   Swedish 3.5%
Italian 8.5%   Welsh 1.3%

Universities/colleges, 1990-1991 enrollment

Diablo Valley College, Pleasant Hill   20,255

John F. Kennedy University, Orinda   1,477

St. Mary's College of California, Moraga   3,940

Newspapers, total circulation (in all districts)

Alameda Times-Star   7,305

Antioch Daily Ledger-Post Dispatch   21,371

Contra Costa Times   88,568

Fremont Argus   32,880

Hayward Daily Review   43,594

Oakland Tribune   113,419

Pleasanton Valley Herald   34,853

Pleasanton Valley Times   34,065

San Francisco Chronicle Examiner   692,424

San Jose Mercury News   275,325

West County Times Richmond   31,129

Commercial television stations, affiliations

ADI: San Francisco (100%)

KFCB, Concord (None)

KICU-TV, San Jose (None)

KFTL, Stockton (None)

Cable television systems, total subscribers

Concord TV Cable; Concord   41,700

TCI Cablevision; Hayward   69,849

TCI Cablevision; Pleasant Hill   82,388

TCI Cablevision of Walnut Creek; Clayton   21,273

Televents of East County Inc.; Knightsen   9,739

Viacom Cablevision; Castro Valley   12,900

Viacom Cablevision; Pittsburg   36,500

Viacom Cablevision; Dublin   47,100

Businesses and other major employers

Lawrence Livermore National Laboratory; Livermore; research services   8,000

Pacific Bell/Corporate Information Center; San Ramon; real estate operators   7,000

Chevron Corp./Chevron Research & Technology; San Ramon; research services   3,000

John Muir Medical Center; Walnut Creek   1,600

County of Alameda; Pleasanton   1,500

Kaiser Foundation Hospitals; Walnut Creek   1,200

County of Alameda/Juvenile Dept.; San Leandro   1,200

Acalanes Union High School District; Lafayette   1,150

Sandia Corp.; Livermore; research services   1,100

Eden Hospital Medical Center; Hayward   1,000

Lesher Communications Inc./Contra Costa Times; Walnut Creek; newspapers   900

Fairmont Hospital; San Leandro   900

St. Mary's College of California; Moraga   825

Castro Valley School District; Hayward   800

Kaiser Foundation Health Plan/Data Center; Walnut Creek; computer services   700

Triad Systems Corp.; Livermore; computer/office equipment   650

Valley Memorial Hospital; Livermore   562

Nordstrom Inc./Place Two; Walnut Creek; clothing stores   550

11th District

Parts of San Joaquin and Sacramento Counties; Stockton; Lodi

In 1992 redistricting, Sacramento County was divided among four congressional districts so different from each other that their meeting point at the outskirts of the state capital is all that unites them. Most of the voters in the county live in the 5th District. But most of the county's square mileage is in the 11th, which incorporates the eastern and southern two-thirds of Sacramento County and aggregates them with nearly all of San Joaquin County to the south.

Many of the 11th District's residents still look to the state capital for their income, activities and media. But the city of Sacramento itself is entirely outside the district, which wraps itself around the city to the east and south. Even the sizable suburb of Elk Grove (population 17,500) sits on the district line but votes in the 5th.

The biggest single source of votes in the 11th is the city of Stockton, 45 miles to the south on Interstate 5. Fifteen minutes north of Stockton on the same road is Lodi (population 51,900). The farms, orchards and ranches in this part of the vast Central Valley grow asparagus, avocados, walnuts, artichokes, peaches and apricots—much of which is processed through Lodi.

The 11th has regular borders on the west and east, following the county lines for Sacramento and San Joaquin counties in both cases. On the south end, the district takes in the towns of Tracy, Lathrop and Manteca and extends at some points to the Stanislaus County line (excepting the town of Ripon). The district's southern limit is defined west of Lathrop by the tracks of the old Union Pacific Railroad—a reminder of that entity's historic role throughout the state.

Stockton, however, is the district's center, not just because it is the county seat of San Joaquin (where three-fourths of the district vote is cast) but because it has stood on its own economically for more than a century. The inland waterways that snake into the Central Valley from San Francisco Bay have their southern terminus here, making Stockton an important port. In the 1980s, the city grew by more than one-third and now approaches 211,000 residents.

On paper, the farmworkers of the valley and the laborers of Lodi and Stockton make the 11th a Democratic district. But there are enough suburban voters in Sacramento County—and enough conservative Democrats in both counties—to make almost every race a tussle. Registration favors the Democrats (52 percent), but in 1992 Bill Clinton carried the 11th by just 2 percentage points over George Bush—and he lost to Bush in the Sacramento County part of the district.

Election Returns and Party Registration

	11th District	Democrat	Republican
1992	President*	79,432 (40.6%)	75,319 (38.5%)
	Senate †	84,209 (42.3%)	94,241 (47.3%)
	Senate †‡	96,565 (48.7%)	85,684 (43.2%)
	House †	90,539 (45.6%)	94,453 (47.6%)
1990	Governor	61,998 (38.8%)	89,960 (56.4%)
1988	President	76,205 (43.6%)	96,574 (55.3%)
	Senate	69,515 (40.3%)	97,077 (56.2%)
1986	Senate	56,904 (45.3%)	65,499 (52.2%)
	Governor	38,236 (30.3%)	86,465 (68.5%)

1993	Party registration †	147,218 (51.4%)	109,678 (38.3%)

Vote for Perot was 41,006 (20.9%). †*Independent/other is greater than 5%.* ‡*Special election for the remaining two years of the term of Pete Wilson who was elected governor in 1990. Appointee John Seymour held the seat 1991-1992.*

Demographics

Population 571,772

Percent change from 1980 8.9%

Land area 1,827 square miles

Population per square mile 313

Counties, 1990 population

Sacramento (pt.) 104,488	San Joaquin (pt.) 467,284

Cities, 1990 population (10,000 or more)

Lodi 51,874	Stockton 210,943
Manteca 40,773	Tracy (pt.) 33,555
Rancho Cordova CDP 48,731	

Race and Hispanic origin
White 74.9%
Black 5.8%
American Indian, Eskimo, or Aleut. 1.1%
Asian or Pacific Islander 11.5%
Other 6.7%
Hispanic origin 21.1%

Ancestry

American 2.3%	Norwegian 1.4%
Dutch 2.6%	Polish 1.1%
English 12.2%	Portuguese 3.0%
French 3.5%	Scotch Irish 1.8%
German 20.2%	Scottish 1.9%
Irish 12.6%	Swedish 1.9%
Italian 5.9%	

Universities/colleges, 1990-1991 enrollment
Humphreys College, Stockton 521
ITT Technical Institute, Sacramento 323
San Joaquin Delta College, Stockton 14,792
University of the Pacific, Stockton 5,497

Newspapers, total circulation (in all districts)
Lodi News-Sentinel 17,380
Los Angeles La Opinion 98,557
Los Angeles Times 1,169,066
Modesto Bee 83,177
Pleasanton Valley Herald 34,853
Sacramento Bee 269,383
Sacramento Union 46,682
San Francisco Chronicle Examiner 692,424
Stockton Record 54,568
Tracy Press 9,015

Commercial television stations, affiliations
ADI: Sacramento-Stockton (100%)
KCRA-TV, Sacramento (NBC)
KRBK-TV, Sacramento (None)
KTXL, Sacramento (Fox)
KXTV, Sacramento (CBS)
KOVR, Stockton (ABC)
KSCH-TV, Stockton (None)

Cable television systems, total subscribers
Continental Cablevision of California; Stockton 50,835
Continental Cablevision of California; Manteca 11,352
King Videocable College; Lodi 14,000
Sacramento Cable TV; Sacramento 190,000

Military installations, 1991
Mather Air Force Base, Rancho Cordova 3,243
Tracy Army Defense Depot Activity, Tracy 2,833
Sharpe Army Depot Activity, Stockton 1,456
Stockton Naval Communications Station, Stockton 1,073

Businesses and other major employers
Aerojet-General Corp.; Rancho Cordova; space vehicles/research 4,000
City of Stockton/Municipal; Stockton 1,788
St. Joseph's Medical Center; Stockton 1,450
San Joaquin General Hospital; French Camp 1,400
City of Stockton/Police Dept.; Stockton 1,300
State of California/Northern California Youth Center; Stockton 1,200
U.S. Computer Services/Cable Data; Rancho Cordova; accounting 1,200
Pacific Bell; Stockton; telephone communications 1,005
Del Monte Corp.; Stockton; preserved fruits/vegetables 1,000
State of California/Vocational Institution; Manteca 1,000
University of the Pacific/McGeorge School of Law; Stockton 1,000
Dameron Hospital; Stockton 995
Stockton State Hospital; Stockton 950
American Savings Bank; Stockton; savings institutions 912
H. J. Heinz Co.; Tracy; preserved fruits/vegetables 900
General Mills Inc.; Lodi; grain mill products 900
San Joaquin Delta College; Stockton 900
Tri-Valley Growers; Stockton; preserved fruits/vegetables 883
Lodi Memorial Hospital; Lodi 800
Tri-Valley Growers; Thornton; preserved fruits/vegetables 796
California Cedar Products; Stockton; wood products 680
J. C. Penney Co. Inc.; Carmichael; nonstore retailers 600
County of San Joaquin; Stockton 600
Owens-Illinois Inc.; Tracy; glass/glassware 547

12th District

Most of San Mateo County; Southwest San Francisco

Not too long ago, San Francisco supplied the vote for two congressional districts that were often split between the city's eastern and western halves. But as it now takes more than 570,000 inhabitants to make a district in California, San Francisco musters just one whole district and about one-fourth of another. The whole one is now the 8th, while the remaining city population is in the 12th (see map on page 69).

The city portion of the 12th consists of the Twin Peaks area and the Sunset District south of Golden Gate Park. The nearby presence of the Pacific is palpable here, as clouds and fog often enshroud the area. The district's city portion also includes Lake Merced, the city zoo and a California State University campus (locally still called San Francisco State).

The city portion of the district is Democratic (64 percent for Bill Clinton in 1992). The Sunset District is increasingly Chinese, and the 12th is 26 percent Asian.

More than 70 percent of the 12th District residents live south of the San Francisco city limit in San Mateo County, and many of them live just over the city limit. The first suburb is Daly City, where spines of close-set, box-like homes appeared on the rocky hillsides after World War II. Hard by the sea itself is Pacifica, harder to reach and blessed in good weather with magnificent views. Across the peninsula on the bay side lies South San Francisco, proclaimed "The Industrial City" by a Hollywood-style sign inscribed in a hillside. "South City," as locals call it, lies between the San Francisco International Airport and Candlestick Park, home of football's 49ers and baseball's Giants.

The center portion of the northern peninsula is occupied by a huge state fish and game refuge. To the west are steep coastal mountains, to the east are heavily populated suburbs. Two freeways carry city commuters south along the eastern portion of the peninsula at night: the Junipero Serra Freeway (I-280) glides along the sparsely populated western route, while the Bayshore Freeway (U.S. 101) plows through the often smoggy, always crowded bayside suburbs. Halfway between the two freeways is another north-south arterial, El Camino Real. This one-time route of Spanish soldiers and priests is now an endless procession of overnight lodgings, restaurants and video stores.

Principal among the Bayshore communities are Brisbane, San Bruno, Millbrae and Burlingame (which pass by before the southbound commuter reaches the county seat of San Mateo) and Foster City to the east. Farther into the peninsula's highlands lies Hillsborough, one of the most exclusive estate communities on the West Coast.

San Mateo County has been somewhat less reliably Democratic than others around the bay. The entire 12th District voted for Ronald Reagan in 1980 and 1984 before switching to support Michael S. Dukakis in 1988. San Mateo portions of the new 12th gave 55 percent to Clinton in 1992.

Election Returns and Party Registration

	12th District	Democrat	Republican
1992	President*	139,244 (57.5%)	64,967 (26.8%)
	Senate †	144,230 (61.7%)	72,917 (31.2%)
	Senate ‡	166,038 (69.8%)	60,987 (25.6%)
	House †	157,205 (68.8%)	53,278 (23.3%)
1990	Governor	106,632 (58.1%)	68,719 (37.4%)
1988	President	121,221 (60.2%)	77,902 (38.7%)
	Senate	106,587 (56.5%)	76,208 (40.4%)
1986	Senate	87,160 (58.5%)	60,025 (40.3%)
	Governor	60,209 (40.0%)	87,959 (58.4%)
1993	Party registration †	173,377 (55.7%)	86,681 (27.8%)

*Vote for Perot was 38,125 (15.7%).   †Independent/other is greater than 5%.
‡Special election for the remaining two years of the term of Pete Wilson who was elected governor in 1990. Appointee John Seymour held the seat 1991-1992.

Demographics

Population 571,535

Percent change from 1980 8.8%

Land area 107 square miles

Population per square mile 5,336

Counties, 1990 population
San Francisco (pt.) 150,712   San Mateo (pt.) 420,823

Cities, 1990 population (10,000 or more)
Burlingame 26,801   San Bruno 38,961
Daly City 92,311   San Francisco (pt.) 150,712
Foster City 28,176   San Mateo 85,486
Hillsborough 10,667   South San Francisco
Millbrae (pt.) 20,408   54,312
Pacifica 37,670

Race and Hispanic origin
White 65.2%
Black 4.1%
American Indian, Eskimo, or Aleut. 0.4%
Asian or Pacific Islander 25.7%
Other 4.5%
Hispanic origin 14.3%

Ancestry
American 1.1%   Italian 8.7%
Arabic 1.2%   Norwegian 1.2%
Dutch 1.1%   Polish 2.0%
English 9.7%   Portuguese 1.0%
French 3.2%   Russian 2.5%
German 13.6%   Scotch Irish 1.5%
Greek 1.1%   Scottish 2.1%
Irish 13.0%   Swedish 1.8%

Universities/colleges, 1990-1991 enrollment
City College of San Francisco, San Francisco 24,408
College of San Mateo, San Mateo 14,150
Menlo College, Atherton 495
San Francisco Conservatory of Music, San Francisco 255
San Francisco State University, San Francisco 24,138
Skyline College, San Bruno 7,798
University of California, San Francisco 3,812

Newspapers, total circulation (in all districts)
Los Angeles Times 1,169,066
Oakland Tribune 113,419
Peninsula Times Tribune 38,442
San Francisco Chronicle Examiner 692,424
San Jose Mercury News 275,325
San Mateo Times 41,088

Commercial television stations, affiliations
ADI: San Francisco (100%)
KTVU, Oakland (Fox)
KBHK-TV, San Francisco (None)
KGO-TV, San Francisco (ABC)
KOFY-TV, San Francisco (None)
KPIX, San Francisco (CBS)
KRON-TV, San Francisco (NBC)
KTSF, San Francisco (None)
KCNS, San Francisco (None)

Cable television systems, total subscribers
Pacific Cable Television; Burlingame 6,950
San Bruno Municipal Cable TV; San Bruno 11,170
TCI Cablevision of California; Hayward 69,849
TCI of California; San Bruno Mountain 14,100
TCI of California; San Mateo 11,933
TCI of California; Pacifica 15,400
Viacom Cablevision; San Francisco 153,058
Western TV Cable; South San Francisco 14,859

Businesses and other major employers

San Francisco State University; San Francisco 3,000

University of California Medical Center; San Francisco 2,863

Oracle Systems Corp.; Redwood City; computer services 2,300

Franklin Resources Inc.; San Mateo; investment offices 1,650

San Francisco City & County/Laguna Hospital Rehabilitation; San Francisco 1,625

Genentech Inc.; San Francisco; pharmaceuticals 1,500

Mills-Peninsula Health Systems; Burlingame; health services 1,447

Seton Medical Center & Hospital; Daly City 1,350

Permanente Medical Group Inc.; San Francisco; medical doctors 1,200

University of California; San Francisco 1,090

Gap Inc./Gapkids; San Bruno; family clothing stores 1,000

City of San Mateo; San Mateo 760

California Casualty Management Co.; San Mateo; fire/marine/casualty insurance 700

California Jockey Club/Race Track; San Mateo; commercial sports 700

Applied Biosystems Inc.; San Mateo; measuring/controlling devices 655

Entenmann's Inc./Oroweat Foods; San Francisco; bakery products 600

Visa USA Inc.; San Mateo; business services 600

Hyatt Corp./Hyatt Regency San Francisco Airport; Burlingame; hotel 600

ISS Intl. Service Systems; San Mateo; building services 550

University of California/Langley Porter Psychiatric Institute; San Francisco 550

13th District

East Bay — Oakland; Hayward; Santa Clara

The 13th (see map on page 69) is a renumbered version of the old 9th, which had been sending Pete Stark to the House for 20 years. Although somewhat altered in 1992 redistricting, the constituency is 58 percent Democratic by registration, exactly the same as the old 9th.

The old 9th began at Hayward, a city of 111,000 on the shore of San Francisco Bay. It then ran inland over the San Leandro Hills to take in the agricultural southeastern portions of Alameda County. The 1980s transformed these environs, as high-tech industry accelerated population growth. So great was the growth that remapping moved eastern Alameda County en masse into another district (the 10th) with suburban Contra Costa County.

Now the district begins in Oakland, on the bay side of the Bay Area Rapid Transit (BART) tracks just south of San Leandro Bay. Here the 13th takes in the Oakland Coliseum, home of the baseball Athletics, and Oakland International Airport. Despite the landmarks, there is relatively little of Oakland's residential population here. The bayshore is dominated by the freeway, miles of warehouses and older factories—many of which no longer function.

The first suburb south of Oakland proper is San Leandro, an old Portuguese enclave with a strong blue-collar vote. Once attracted to Ronald Reagan, the area has returned to the Democratic fold—one of many such venues that account for the turnaround in California's presidential preferences.

Hayward has a large campus of the California State University

system and mixes business and professionals' office complexes with the usual East Bay commerce. Farther south along the multilane traffic crunch of I-880 is Newark, followed by Fremont—the East Bay southern terminus for BART and site of the last operating auto plant in California, a joint venture of General Motors and Toyota. The district line coincides with the eastern limits of these cities, as it does with those of San Leandro and Hayward. In each case, the limit is reached in the highlands. The district no longer reaches into the suburb-dotted interior beyond the ridges.

At its southern extreme, the 13th crosses the county line into Santa Clara County and takes in the alluvial mud flats at the southern end of San Francisco Bay. This is home to a little less than 10 percent of the 13th's residents. At the southwestern extreme, the district takes in a slice of the old Moffett Field Air Station, once home to government-operated dirigibles (the hangars are still visible from the Bayshore Freeway). The southeastern extreme reaches through the industrial city of Milpitas and appropriates a section of San Jose.

By shedding the eastern reaches of Alameda County, the 13th lowered the non-Latino white share of population from 64 percent in 1990 to 55 percent in 1992. The black community remains small and mostly concentrated in Oakland. But in 1992, nearly two residents in five were either Latino or Asian-American.

Election Returns and Party Registration

	13th District	Democrat	Republican
1992	President*	116,829 (54.4%)	55,100 (25.6%)
	Senate †	121,207 (58.0%)	65,709 (31.4%)
	Senate †‡	139,472 (66.1%)	56,658 (26.9%)
	House †	123,795 (60.2%)	64,953 (31.6%)
1990	Governor †	73,909 (56.5%)	49,666 (38.0%)
1988	President	90,714 (54.6%)	73,334 (44.2%)
	Senate	83,317 (51.0%)	74,273 (45.5%)
1986	Senate	72,071 (55.8%)	53,537 (41.4%)
	Governor	49,449 (38.0%)	76,536 (58.8%)
1993	Party registration †	166,046 (58.3%)	76,980 (27.0%)

*Vote for Perot was 43,026 (20.0%).   †Independent/other is greater than 5%.
‡Special election for the remaining two years of the term of Pete Wilson who was elected governor in 1990. Appointee John Seymour held the seat 1991-1992.*

Demographics

Population 572,441

Percent change from 1980 8.7%

Land area 239 square miles

Population per square mile 2,395

Counties, 1990 population

| Alameda (pt.) 510,121 | Santa Clara (pt.) 62,320 |

Cities, 1990 population (10,000 or more)

Cherryland CDP 11,088	Oakland (pt.) 10,658
Fremont (pt.) 173,339	San Jose (pt.) 18,937
Hayward (pt.) 111,495	San Leandro (pt.) 68,108
Milpitas (pt.) 43,124	San Lorenzo CDP 19,987
Newark 37,861	Union City 53,762

Race and Hispanic origin

White 64.2%
Black 7.4%
American Indian, Eskimo, or Aleut. 0.8%
Asian or Pacific Islander 19.4%
Other 8.3%
Hispanic origin 18.4%

Ancestry

American 2.0%	Italian 5.5%
Danish 1.1%	Norwegian 1.3%
Dutch 1.7%	Polish 1.6%
English 10.7%	Portuguese 5.9%
French 3.4%	Scotch Irish 1.6%
German 15.8%	Scottish 2.0%
Irish 11.2%	Swedish 1.9%

Universities/colleges, 1990-1991 enrollment

California State University, Hayward 11,757
Chabot College, Hayward 19,705
Heald Business College, Hayward 201
Life Chiropractic College, San Lorenzo 383
Ohlone College, Fremont 8,130
Queen of Holy Rosary College, Fremont 271

Newspapers, total circulation (in all districts)

Alameda Times-Star 7,305
Fremont Argus 32,880
Gilroy Dispatch 6,177
Hayward Daily Review 43,594
Oakland Tribune 113,419
Pleasanton Valley Herald 34,853
Pleasanton Valley Times 34,065
San Francisco Chronicle Examiner 692,424
San Jose Mercury News 275,325

Commercial television stations, affiliations

ADI: San Francisco (100%)

Cable television systems, total subscribers

Cable Oakland; Oakland 66,446
Pacific Cable Television; Union City 8,400
South Bay Cablevision; Newark 8,030
TCI Cablevision of California; Hayward 69,849
TCI of California; Fremont 34,645
TCI of California; Sunnyvale 20,943

Businesses and other major employers

Lockheed Co.; Sunnyvale; guided missiles/parts 20,713
Mervyn's; Hayward; department stores 5,000
New United Motor Mfg.; Fremont; motor vehicles 3,493
ESL Inc.; Sunnyvale; search/navigation equipment 2,000
Kaiser Foundation Hospitals; Hayward 1,750
California State University; Hayward 1,500
Washington Township Hospital; Fremont 1,400
Lucky Stores Inc.; San Leandro; grocery stores 1,300
Sun Microsystems Inc.; Milpitas; computer services 1,000
Delta America Ltd.; Fremont; electrical goods 935
Loral Aerospace Corp./Space Missions Div.; Sunnyvale; research services 900
LAM Research Corp.; Fremont; electronic components 850
City of Hayward; Hayward 850
Baxter Healthcare Corp.; Hayward; pharmaceuticals 800
Diasonics Inc./Ultrasound Div.; Milpitas; medical instruments 750
Cooper Industries Inc./Delaval Engine; Oakland; electrical industrial apparatus 750
Sister Hayward Hospital/St. Rose Hospital; Hayward 697
Ohlone College; Fremont 680
Hunt-Wesson Inc./United Can Co.; Hayward; metal cans 600
Ross Stores Inc./Dress for Less; Newark; clothing stores 600
Safeway Inc./Safeway Employees Assn.; Fremont; labor organization 600
Acme Building Maintenance Co.; Alviso; building services 600
FME Corp./Friden Alcatel; Hayward; computer/office equipment 550
World Savings & Loan Assn.; San Leandro; savings institutions 550

14th District

Southern San Mateo and Northern Santa Clara Counties

Sustained population growth in the San Francisco peninsula enabled mapmakers in 1992 to fashion a full district from suburbs south of the San Mateo Bridge and north of San Jose. In the main, the 14th (see map on page 69) resembles the old 12th District. But on the north it has annexed more of San Mateo County, including Belmont, San Carlos and Redwood City, whose 60,000 residents make it the district's second-largest city. About 40 percent of the district population is now in San Mateo County, the rest in Santa Clara County.

At its southern end, the district has lost the long tail that had dangled all the way to rural Gilroy and taken in some remote Santa Cruz County turf along the way. The 14th is more compact, with its center in the affluent suburbs on either side of the San Mateo and Santa Clara county line. Some of these communities have existed for more than a century, preserving their individual character despite waves of population growth. Working hardest to do so are the exclusive enclaves of Atherton, Woodside and Portola Valley. But Palo Alto, too, has stabilized its growth and sustained much of its leafy, small-town charm. Its population of 56,000 does not include the students, faculty and staff who live on the sprawling, adjacent campus of Stanford University.

Farther south, change has been more overwhelming in Mountain View, Sunnyvale, Los Altos and Cupertino. Miles of fruit groves have given way to high-tech factories: Hewlett-Packard, Apple Computer and Ford Aerospace are all in the area; Lockheed is nearby. With the rise of microprocessing, this corridor has come to be known as Silicon Valley. Sunnyvale, its informal capital, grew slowly in the 1980s; but with more than 100,000 residents it is easily the most populous city in the 14th.

The lure of comfy suburbs so close to jobs has kept peninsula land values climbing for decades. Million-dollar homes are commonplace, and even ramshackle units come with high price tags in East Palo Alto and other low-income communities along the Bayshore Freeway. The old 12th had the highest median real estate values of any California district in the 1980s.

With its wealth, old and new, this was the Bay Area's one Republican district in past years, favoring GOP presidential candidates back to Gerald Ford in 1976. It also sent a succession of Republicans to Congress, although it preferred the more moderate-to-liberal variety. But the 14th is different enough, and 1992 was lopsided enough, that no one is likely to call this district Republican again soon.

Population shifts and redistricting lowered the percentage of whites from 86 percent to 78 percent. GOP registration dipped accordingly, from 42 percent to 35 percent. Bill Clinton won the 14th by a 2-to-1 margin in 1992, receiving nearly identical percentages in both counties.

Election Returns and Party Registration

	14th District	Democrat	Republican
1992	President*	143,727 (53.5%)	71,736 (26.7%)
	Senate †	155,888 (59.5%)	84,325 (32.2%)
	Senate ‡	174,805 (65.9%)	77,315 (29.1%)
	House	146,873 (56.7%)	101,202 (39.0%)
1990	Governor	111,654 (54.1%)	84,418 (40.9%)
1988	President	139,632 (54.5%)	112,301 (43.9%)
	Senate	121,277 (48.4%)	119,952 (47.9%)
1986	Senate	93,404 (50.4%)	89,029 (48.0%)
	Governor	69,586 (37.2%)	113,323 (60.6%)
1993	Party registration †	161,453 (47.8%)	119,272 (35.3%)

*Vote for Perot was 53,042 (19.8%). †Independent/other is greater than 5%.
‡Special election for the remaining two years of the term of Pete Wilson who was elected governor in 1990. Appointee John Seymour held the seat 1991-1992.

Demographics

Population 571,131

Percent change from 1980 8.6%

Land area 477 square miles

Population per square mile 1,197

Counties, 1990 population
San Mateo (pt.) 228,800   Santa Clara (pt.) 342,331

Cities, 1990 population (10,000 or more)

Belmont 24,127	North Fair Oaks CDP 13,912
Cupertino (pt.) 40,263	Palo Alto 55,900
East Palo Alto 23,451	Redwood City (pt.) 59,707
Los Altos 26,303	San Carlos (pt.) 26,167
Menlo Park 28,040	Stanford CDP 18,097
Mountain View 67,460	Sunnyvale (pt.) 105,736

Race and Hispanic origin
White 78.1%
Black 4.9%
American Indian, Eskimo, or Aleut. 0.4%
Asian or Pacific Islander 12.2%
Other 4.4%
Hispanic origin 13.5%

Ancestry

American 1.6%	Norwegian 1.9%
Danish 1.2%	Polish 2.6%
Dutch 1.9%	Portuguese 1.5%
English 16.1%	Russian 2.3%
French 4.1%	Scotch Irish 2.1%
German 19.4%	Scottish 3.4%
Irish 13.1%	Swedish 2.7%
Italian 6.9%	Welsh 1.1%

Universities/colleges, 1990-1991 enrollment
Canada College, Redwood City 7,586
Cogswell Polytech College, Cupertino 280
College of Notre Dame, Belmont 1,171
De Anza College, Cupertino 21,948
Foothill College, Los Altos 12,811
Foothill-De Anza Community College, Los Altos 21,800
Pacific Graduate School of Psychiatry, Palo Alto 316
Palmer College of Chiropractic, Sunnyvale 585
Stanford University, Stanford 14,725

Newspapers, total circulation (in all districts)
Gilroy Dispatch 6,177
Oakland Tribune 113,419
Peninsula Times Tribune 38,442
San Francisco Chronicle Examiner 692,424
San Jose Mercury News 275,325
San Mateo Times 41,088

Commercial television stations, affiliations
ADI: San Francisco (100%)

Cable television systems, total subscribers
Cable Co-Op; Palo Alto 20,025
South Bay Cablevision; Mountain View 14,370
TCI Cablevision of Cupertino; Cupertino 12,426
TCI of California; San Carlos 49,000
TCI of California; Sunnyvale 20,943
Weststar Communications; El Granada 6,400

Military installations, 1991
Moffett Field Naval Air Station, Moffett Field 5,618
Onizuka Air Force Base, Sunnyvale 1,500

Businesses and other major employers
Stanford University; Palo Alto 9,500
National Semiconductor Corp.; Santa Clara; electronic components 9,000
Hewlett-Packard Co.; Cupertino; computer/office equipment 5,500
Amdahl Corp.; Sunnyvale; computer/office equipment 4,800
Raychem Corp.; Menlo Park; electronic components 4,295
Advanced Micro Devices Inc.; Sunnyvale; electronic components 4,200
North American Philips Corp./Signetics; Sunnyvale; electronic components 4,000
Syntex USA Inc.; Palo Alto; pharmaceuticals 4,000
Varian Assoc. Inc.; Palo Alto; electronic components 4,000
Stanford University Hospital; Palo Alto 4,000
Hewlett-Packard Co.; Palo Alto; computer/office equipment 3,700
Sun Microsystems Inc.; Mountain View; computers 3,500
U.S. Veterans Affairs Dept.; Palo Alto; hospital 3,500
GTE Products Corp./Government Systems; Mountain View; communications equipment 2,500
SRI International; Menlo Park; research services 2,250
Tandem Computers Inc.; Cupertino; computers 2,200
Space Sytems/Loral Inc.; Palo Alto; communications equipment 2,176
Apple Computer Inc.; Cupertino; computers 2,000
City of Sunnyvale; Sunnyvale 1,872
El Camino Hospital District; Mountain View 1,800
Silicon Graphics Computer Systems; Mountain View; computers 1,600
Sequoia Hospital; Redwood City 1,600
National Semiconductor Corp.; Sunnyvale; electronic components 1,500

Ampex Corp.; Redwood City; photographic equipment/
supplies   1,500

U.S. Interior Dept./Geological Survey; Menlo Park   1,500

Watkins-Johnson Co.; Palo Alto; electronic components
1,300

Stanford University/SLAC; Menlo Park; research services
1,250

Hewlett-Packard Co./Personal Office Computer Div.; Sunnyvale; measuring/controlling devices   1,200

Lucile Salter Packard Children's Hospital; Palo Alto   1,200

Lockheed Co.; Palo Alto; guided missiles/parts   1,100

Raytheon Co./Raytheon Semiconductor Div.; Mountain
View; electronic components   1,000

Kaiser Foundation Hospitals; Redwood City   940

Argosystems Inc.; Sunnyvale; measuring/controlling devices
900

Acuson Corp.; Mountain View; medical instruments/supplies
900

CAE-Link Corp./Link Flight Simulation Div.; Sunnyvale;
flight simulators   850

De Anza College; Cupertino   825

Network Equipment Tech. Inc.; Redwood City; communications equipment   800

Measurex Corp.; Cupertino; measuring/controlling devices
735

Nordstrom Inc.; Palo Alto; department stores   700

Macy's of California Inc.; Palo Alto; department stores   700

Palo Alto Medical Foundation; Palo Alto; medical doctors
700

Electric Power Research Inst.; Palo Alto; research services
700

Abbott Laboratories; Mountain View; drugs   650

Litton Industries Inc.; San Carlos; electronic components   620

Spectra-Physics Optics Inc.; Mountain View;
measuring/controlling devices   600

Varian Assoc. Inc./Varian Radiation Div.; Palo Alto; medical
instruments/supplies   600

Varian Assoc. Inc.; San Carlos; electronic components   600

Wilson S. G. R.; Palo Alto; legal services   600

Trimble Navigation Ltd.; Sunnyvale; search/navigation equipment   580

Beckman Instruments Inc./Spinco Div.; Palo Alto; medical
instruments/supplies   580

Diocese of San Jose School Office; Los Altos; religious
organization/education   532

Pinkerton's Inc.; Sunnyvale; business/security services   530

15th District

Santa Clara County — San Jose

San Jose by 1992 was not only the state's third largest city,
but, more surprisingly, had surpassed nearby San Francisco. The
15th District, which encapsulates San Jose, includes half of
seaside Santa Cruz County and has the heavily trafficked state
Highway 17 as its spinal column (see map on page 69).

The 15th has its northern extreme at the Great America
theme park between the Bayshore Freeway (Highway 101) and
the southern tip of the San Francisco Bay. The park is in the city
of Santa Clara, which lies at the south end of Silicon Valley but

retains some of the character of an old college town in the midst
of high-tech plants and proliferating subdivisions. (The University of Santa Clara was founded here by Jesuits in 1851.)

With 94,000 people, Santa Clara is the largest city within the
15th. It has usually been Democratic—although not as decidedly
so as San Jose—and it helps keep Democratic registration in the
15th close to half (46 percent).

At the southeastern end of Santa Clara is an imposing
interchange where Interstates 880 and 280 cross. Southeast of this
landmark, the 15th has San Jose's western neighborhoods,
including recent developments that spread out on either side of
the Almaden Expressway (which shares its name with a giant
nearby winery). Also proceeding south from the intersection of
the interstates is Highway 17, which then runs to the Pacific
Ocean—with the district following it nearly all the way.

Some of the exit ramps from 17 lead to growing middle-class
suburbs such as Campbell and Monte Sereno.

Other off-ramps lead to more affluent communities in the
hills—Los Gatos and Saratoga—where some of the better-paid
professionals of Silicon Valley live. All of these Santa Clara
County suburbs can be good ground for Republican candidates,
making the 15th competitive in statewide elections.

Continuing south on Highway 17 carries the traveler past the
epicenter of the 1989 Loma Prieta earthquake, the area's worst
since 1906. Not far away, the road and the district cross into
Santa Cruz County, a demarcation surrounded by hillsides heavy
with redwoods. Heading down the slope, the 15th takes in Scotts
Valley and Felton.

Racing toward the sea, the district even reaches into the city
of Santa Cruz. All told, Santa Cruz County contributes only
about 10 percent of the district population. But it should help
Democrats: Bill Clinton carried the 15th in 1992, but he received
an outright majority only in its Santa Cruz County portions.

Election Returns and Party Registration

	15th District	Democrat	Republican
1992	President*	127,060 (46.3%)	83,301 (30.3%)
	Senate †	137,240 (51.1%)	102,789 (38.3%)
	Senate †‡	160,569 (59.3%)	90,589 (33.4%)
	House	168,617 (63.7%)	82,875 (31.3%)
1990	Governor †	100,618 (48.9%)	92,749 (45.1%)
1988	President	121,559 (47.5%)	130,157 (50.9%)
	Senate	114,583 (45.4%)	128,394 (50.9%)
1986	Senate	85,426 (48.5%)	85,105 (48.3%)
	Governor	60,360 (34.2%)	111,771 (63.4%)
1993	Party registration †	163,034 (46.5%)	133,286 (38.0%)

Vote for Perot was 64,192 (23.4%).   †Independent/other is greater than 5%.
‡Special election for the remaining two years of the term of Pete Wilson who was
elected governor in 1990. Appointee John Seymour held the seat 1991-1992.

Demographics

Population   572,485

Percent change from 1980   8.9%

Land area   452 square miles

Population per square mile   1,265

Counties, 1990 population
Santa Clara (pt.)   521,375   Santa Cruz (pt.)   51,110

Cities, 1990 population (10,000 or more)

Campbell 36,048	Santa Clara (pt.) 87,319
Los Gatos 27,357	Saratoga (pt.) 27,995
San Jose (pt.) 307,791	Sunnyvale (pt.) 11,493

Race and Hispanic origin

White 82.2%
Black 2.3%
American Indian, Eskimo, or Aleut. 0.6%
Asian or Pacific Islander 11.3%
Other 3.6%
Hispanic origin 10.8%

Ancestry

American 2.2%	Norwegian 1.9%
Danish 1.3%	Polish 2.6%
Dutch 2.2%	Portuguese 2.7%
English 17.1%	Russian 1.4%
French 4.5%	Scotch Irish 2.4%
German 21.7%	Scottish 3.0%
Irish 15.1%	Swedish 2.7%
Italian 9.4%	Welsh 1.1%

Universities/colleges, 1990-1991 enrollment

Bethany College, Scotts Valley 470
Mission College, Santa Clara 10,170
Phillips Junior College, Campbell 1,476
San Jose City College, San Jose 8,767
University of Santa Clara, Santa Clara 7,710
West Valley College, Saratoga 12,595

Newspapers, total circulation (in all districts)

Gilroy Dispatch 6,177
Peninsula Times Tribune 38,442
San Francisco Chronicle Examiner 692,424
San Jose Mercury News 275,325
Santa Cruz Sentinel 28,102
Watsonville Register-Pajaronian 12,396

Commercial television stations, affiliations

ADI: Salinas-Monterey (59%) and San Francisco (41%)
KLXV-TV, San Jose (None)
KNTV, San Jose (ABC)

Cable television systems, total subscribers

South Bay Cablevision; Los Gatos 9,650
South Bay Cablevision; Santa Clara 20,790
TCI of California; San Jose 167,007
United Artist Cable; Scotts Valley 53,000

Businesses and other major employers

IBM Corp.; San Jose; management/computers/services 9,000
Intel Corp.; Santa Clara; electronic components 5,700
FMC Corp./Ground Systems Div.; Santa Clara; motor vehicles/equipment 4,800
Kaiser Foundation Hospitals; Santa Clara 2,500
Kaiser Foundation Hospitals; San Jose 2,000
Avantek Inc.; Santa Clara; electronic components 1,750
Digital Equipment Corp.; Santa Clara; computer equipment 1,700
Hewlett-Packard Co./Santa Clara Div.; Santa Clara; measuring/controlling devices 1,550
Seagate Technology Inc.; Santa Cruz; computer equipment 1,400
Anacomp Inc./Xidex; Santa Clara; computer/office equipment 1,400

Northern Telecom Inc./Private Networks; Santa Clara; communications equipment 1,200
Zycon Corp.; Santa Clara; electronic components 1,180
Airborne Freight Corp.; Santa Clara; insurance services 1,100
LSI Logic Corp.; Santa Clara; electronic components 1,000
Integrated Device Technology; Santa Clara; electronic components 1,000
University of Santa Clara; Santa Clara 1,000
Ungermann-Bass Inc.; Santa Clara; electronic computer equipment 850
Dastek Inc.; San Jose; electronic components 800
Siliconix Inc.; Santa Clara; electronic components 800
Applied Materials Inc.; Santa Clara; industry machinery 800
Underwriters Laboratories Inc.; Santa Clara; research services 755
Permanente Medical Group Inc.; San Jose; medical doctors 750
Pacific Gas & Electric Co.; San Jose; utility services 745
Xerox Engineering Systems; Santa Clara; computer/office equipment 700
Macy's of California Inc.; Santa Clara; department stores 700
Watkins-Johnson Co./Stewart Div.; Santa Cruz; electrical equipment/supplies 650
Analog Devices Inc./Precision Monolithics Div.; Santa Clara; electronic components 650
National Medical Enterprises/Community Hospital; Los Gatos 650
Health Services Inc.; San Jose; nursing 620
ICL Inc.; Santa Clara; motorcycle dealers 600
Borland Intl. Inc.; Santa Cruz; computer services 600
Mission College; Santa Clara 600
American Protective Services; Santa Clara; business/security services 600
Garden City Inc.; San Jose; recreation services 580
Stanford Telecommunications; Santa Clara; guided missiles/parts 550
West Valley Community College; Saratoga 530

16th District

Santa Clara County

Fast-growing Santa Clara County, at the southern end of San Francisco Bay, added another 200,000 residents in the 1980s and now sprawls across four congressional districts. The 16th, however, contains about two-thirds of the county's land and more than one-third of its 1.5 million residents. Most of the district (see map on page 69) consists of more than half of San Jose, whose 782,000 residents in 1990 ranked it the 11th-largest city in the nation. In California, only Los Angeles and San Diego are larger.

The 16th takes in the heart of San Jose, including the recently renovated civic center and a large urban campus of the California State University that is still known locally as San Jose State.

San Jose dates to 1777, when the Spanish founded it as a way station between the missions of San Francisco and Monterey. It also served briefly as the capital in the early days after California's annexation by the United States. Thereafter, however, it languished in the shadow of San Francisco and Oakland. But the migration of industry southward from Oakland (45 miles to the north) and from the San Francisco peninsula has gradually reoriented San Jose to the north and away from the agricultural valleys to the south, east and west.

Now, even as other parts of the Bay Area have reached a steady state, San Jose has continued to grow, expanding by nearly one-fourth just in the 1980s. Some of the new residents were drawn by jobs in the high-tech sector. Per capita income in the city itself nearly doubled in the 1980s and was about $4,000 higher than the statewide average in 1991.

But with the growth has come strain and some resistance. In 1992, local voters were asked to approve a bond issue for a baseball stadium that was supposed to lure the baseball Giants down from San Francisco. But residents raised questions about how the stadium would affect their everyday lives, and the bond issue failed.

Passing out of the city to the south, Highway 101 winds through the scenic countryside, vineyards and wineries of the Santa Clara Valley—with tasting rooms lining the road around Morgan Hill and San Martin. At the district's southern edge lies Gilroy, a farm town famous for its annual garlic festival.

The 16th is Northern California's most Hispanic district, at 37 percent. Twenty-one percent of its residents are Asian. The recent-immigrant presence in the population is reflected in the low number of votes cast relative to the population. Only 165,000 votes were cast for president in the 16th in 1992. This was the lowest number for any House district in Northern California (in the adjacent 10th, more than 300,000 votes were cast for president).

The Democrat House incumbent won the 16th term in 1992 with fewer than 97,000 votes. His GOP opponent had under 50,000. The 16th gave Bill Clinton an absolute majority and held George Bush 2 percentage points below GOP registration for the district.

Election Returns and Party Registration

	16th District	Democrat	Republican
1992	President*	86,418 (52.4%)	44,693 (27.1%)
	Senate †	87,531 (54.4%)	54,681 (34.0%)
	Senate †‡	103,304 (63.8%)	45,908 (28.4%)
	House †	96,661 (62.0%)	49,843 (32.0%)
1990	Governor †	62,757 (54.8%)	44,029 (38.4%)
1988	President	82,930 (55.9%)	63,083 (42.5%)
	Senate	79,336 (54.4%)	59,184 (40.6%)
1986	Senate	56,723 (54.6%)	43,902 (42.3%)
	Governor	43,626 (41.8%)	57,916 (55.5%)
1993	Party registration †	135,561 (55.6%)	70,600 (28.9%)

*Vote for Perot was 33,882 (20.5%). †Independent/other is greater than 5%. ‡Special election for the remaining two years of the term of Pete Wilson who was elected governor in 1990. Appointee John Seymour held the seat 1991-1992.

Demographics

Population 571,551

Percent change from 1980 8.7%

Land area 947 square miles

Population per square mile 604

Counties, 1990 population
Santa Clara (pt.) 571,551

Cities, 1990 population (10,000 or more)

East Foothills CDP 14,898	Morgan Hill 23,928
Gilroy 31,487	San Jose (pt.) 454,705

Race and Hispanic origin
White 55.1%
Black 5.2%
American Indian, Eskimo, or Aleut. 0.8%
Asian or Pacific Islander 21.1%
Other 17.8%
Hispanic origin 36.8%

Ancestry

American 1.7%	Italian 5.1%
Dutch 1.1%	Polish 1.1%
English 7.3%	Portuguese 2.9%
French 2.3%	Scottish 1.3%
German 10.6%	Swedish 1.2%
Irish 7.3%	

Universities/colleges, 1990-1991 enrollment
California State University, San Jose 26,456
Evergreen Valley College, San Jose 7,430
Gavilan College, Gilroy 3,778
Heald Institute of Technology, San Jose 397
San Jose Christian College, San Jose 235

Newspapers, total circulation (in all districts)
Gilroy Dispatch 6,177
Oakland Tribune 113,419
Peninsula Times Tribune 38,442
San Francisco Chronicle Examiner 692,424
San Jose Mercury News 275,325

Commercial television stations, affiliations
ADI: San Francisco (100%)
KSBW, Salinas (NBC)

Cable television systems, total subscribers
Falcon Cable TV; Gilroy 30,835
TCI of California; San Jose 167,007

Businesses and other major employers
County of Santa Clara; San Jose 15,000
FMC Corp.; San Jose; misc. durable goods 3,900
California State University; San Jose 2,500
County of Santa Clara/Transit Dept.; San Jose; bus services 2,423
LSI Logic Corp.; Milpitas; electronic components 2,400
United Technologies Corp.; San Jose; aircraft/parts 2,000
Loral Aerospace Corp.; San Jose; communications equipment 2,000
General Electric Co.; San Jose; engineering services 2,000
County of Santa Clara/Social Services; San Jose 2,000
State of California/Agnews Dev. Center; San Jose 1,800
San Jose Mercury News Inc.; San Jose; newspapers 1,600
O'Connor Hospital Inc.; San Jose 1,550
Conner Peripherals Inc.; San Jose; computer equipment 1,500
Quantum Corp.; Milpitas; computer equipment 1,450
VLSI Technology Inc.; San Jose; electronic components 1,250
City of San Jose/Police Dept.; San Jose 1,003
American Airlines Inc.; San Jose; airline 1,000
Hewlett-Packard Co./Microwave Semiconductor Div.; San Jose; electronic components 1,000
Maxtor Corp.; San Jose; computer equipment 1,000

Xicor Inc.; Milpitas; electronic components   1,000

Alexian Bros. Hospital; San Jose   950

Cypress Semiconductor Corp.; San Jose; electronic components   930

Litton Industries Inc.; San Jose; electronic components   900

Cadence Design Systems Inc.; San Jose; computer services   900

Komag Inc.; Milpitas; computer equipment   800

BT North America Inc.; San Jose; communication services   800

Kaiser Aerospace & Electronics Corp.; San Jose; missile/space vehicle parts   800

Avantek Inc./Telecommunication Group; Milpitas; electrical goods   800

County of Santa Clara/Probation Dept.; San Jose; family services   800

Solectron Corp.; San Jose; electronic components   750

Viking Freight System Inc.; San Jose; trucking services   750

Wyse Technology Inc.; San Jose; computer/office equipment   750

Evergreen School District/Evergreen Transportation; San Jose   750

Fujitsu America Inc.; San Jose; computer terminals & equipment   725

City of San Jose/Fire Dept.; San Jose   720

Read-Rite Corp.; Milpitas; computer equipment   700

KLA Instruments; San Jose; medical instruments/supplies   650

Becton Dickinson & Co.; San Jose; medical instruments/supplies   650

Central County Occupational Center; San Jose   650

McClaskey/Red Lion Inn; San Jose; hotel   650

Wiltron Co.; Morgan Hill; electric measuring devices   600

Del Monte Corp.; San Jose; preserved fruits/vegetables   600

Pacific Bell; San Jose; telephone communications   600

Lifescan Inc.; Milpitas; drugs   600

Racal Data Com. Inc.; Milpitas; communications equipment   600

Flea Market Inc.; San Jose; real estate operators   600

Gilroy Unified School District; Gilroy   600

Exar Corp.; San Jose; electronic components   540

Diocese of San Jose; San Jose; religious organization   535

17th District

Monterey and San Benito Counties

The 17th was for 16 years the political base of Leon E. Panetta, who became director of President Clinton's Office of Management and Budget in 1993. Just before his appointment, Panetta had been re-elected in the redrawn and renumbered district in 1992, running 20 points ahead of Democratic registration.

The district had changed little with the new map, which removed the less-populated half of Santa Cruz County at one end and snipped off the district's old appendix (a coastal section of San Luis Obispo County) at the other. In Santa Cruz County, the 17th keeps all the significant population centers, including the namesake city, the University of California at Santa Cruz and several sizable seaside communities such as Soquel, Aptos and Capitola.

Also intact within the new district are Monterey and San Benito counties. San Benito, with about 37,000 people, is ranching country and swings little weight in district elections. Santa Cruz

and Monterey counties had cast about 80 percent of the vote in the old 16th; they cast nearly 95 percent in the 17th in 1992.

The district includes Monterey peninsula with its fabulous 17-mile drive, legendary golf courses and chic colonies such as Carmel (where Clint Eastwood was mayor for a time). The city of Monterey itself (population 32,000) remains a charming village with a fishing fleet and a small canning industry. Another dominant element on the map is the vast military preserve at Fort Ord, which is slated to close in 1994. Farther down coastal Highway 1 is Big Sur, yet another retreat for artists and the affluent.

Despite these magnets for tourists and retirees, the central enterprise in the 17th remains the agriculture that has sustained the area for centuries. The inland area's capital is Salinas (population 109,000), the county seat of Monterey County and a marketing center for the avocados, artichokes and other trademark truck-farm crops. This is also the focal point for the Hispanics who constitute nearly one-third of the district population. Other farming centers in the district include Watsonville, Hollister and King City.

Despite a 52 percent Democratic registration, the district has been a question mark in statewide voting. In 1992, Democratic Senate nominee Barbara Boxer lost in San Benito County and had only a plurality in Monterey County; but she carried the 17th by piling up a big vote in Santa Cruz County. Clinton managed a majority districtwide, but he too did it by trouncing George Bush in Santa Cruz County (where he won 3-to-1). Clinton managed a plurality in the other two counties.

Election Returns and Party Registration

	17th District	Democrat	Republican
1992	President*	111,937 (52.7%)	57,990 (27.3%)
	Senate †	112,153 (54.3%)	73,942 (35.8%)
	Senate †‡	131,786 (63.2%)	63,611 (30.5%)
	House	151,565 (72.0%)	49,947 (23.7%)
1990	Governor †	48,937 (55.8%)	32,323 (36.9%)
1988	President	98,864 (53.2%)	84,267 (45.4%)
	Senate	93,175 (50.1%)	85,266 (45.8%)
1986	Senate	71,386 (52.4%)	61,166 (44.9%)
	Governor	54,108 (39.5%)	80,099 (58.5%)
1993	Party registration †	144,770 (52.5%)	84,886 (30.8%)

*Vote for Perot was 42,317 (19.9%).   †Independent/other is greater than 5%.
‡Special election for the remaining two years of the term of Pete Wilson who was elected governor in 1990. Appointee John Seymour held the seat 1991-1992.

Demographics

Population   570,981

Percent change from 1980   8.8%

Land area   4,887 square miles

Population per square mile   117

Counties, 1990 population

Monterey 355,660	Santa Cruz (pt.) 178,624
San Benito 36,697	

Cities, 1990 population (10,000 or more)

Capitola 10,171	Live Oak CDP 15,212
Hollister 19,212	Marina 26,436

Monterey 31,954
Pacific Grove 16,117
Salinas 108,777

Santa Cruz (pt.) 47,905
Seaside 38,901
Watsonville 31,099

Race and Hispanic origin
White 69.5%
Black 4.4%
American Indian, Eskimo, or Aleut. 0.9%
Asian or Pacific Islander 6.3%
Other 18.9%
Hispanic origin 31.6%

Ancestry
American 2.5%
Danish 1.2%
Dutch 1.7%
English 12.8%
French 3.7%
German 16.8%
Irish 11.6%
Italian 5.6%

Norwegian 1.2%
Polish 1.6%
Portuguese 2.2%
Scotch Irish 2.0%
Scottish 2.4%
Swedish 1.9%
Swiss 1.0%

Universities/colleges, 1990-1991 enrollment
Cabrillo College, Aptos 12,075
Hartnell College, Salinas 6,762
Monterey Institute of International Studies, Monterey 698
Monterey Peninsula College, Monterey 6,505
Naval Postgraduate School, Monterey 1,749
University of California, Santa Cruz 10,052

Newspapers, total circulation (in all districts)
Hollister Free Lance 3,797
The Monterey County Herald 35,804
Salinas Californian 23,650
San Francisco Chronicle Examiner 692,424
San Jose Mercury News 275,325
Santa Cruz Sentinel 28,102
Watsonville Register-Pajaronian 12,396

Commercial television stations, affiliations
ADI: Salinas-Monterey (100%)
KMST, Monterey (CBS)
KCBA, Salinas (Fox)

Cable television systems, total subscribers
Falcon Cable TV; Gilroy 30,835
Monterey Peninsula TV Cable; Monterey 80,029
Sonic Cable TV; Watsonville 10,900
United Artist Cable; Scotts Valley 53,000
Weststar Communications; Monterey 6,400

Military installations, 1991
Fort Ord (Army), Seaside 17,170
Presidio of Monterey (Army), Monterey 4,867
Naval Postgraduate School, Monterey 3,820
Fort Hunter Liggett (Army), Jolon 880

Businesses and other major employers
Dole Fresh Vegetables Inc.; Salinas; crop services 3,500
University of California; Santa Cruz 3,280
State of California/Correctional Facilities; Soledad 1,500
County of Monterey; Salinas 1,500
Community Hospital; Monterey 1,289
Dominican Santa Cruz Hospital; Santa Cruz 1,200
Salinas Valley Memorial Hospital; Salinas 1,120
Household International Inc.; Salinas; credit institutions 1,000

Roman Catholic Bishop Monterey; Monterey; religious organization 1,000
County of Santa Cruz; Santa Cruz 976
Darrigo Bros. Co. of Cal; Salinas; vegetables/melons 900
Santa Cruz Operation Inc.; Santa Cruz; computer services 900
Tri-Valley Growers; Hollister; preserved fruits/vegetables 816
Basic Vegetable Products; King City; preserved fruits/vegetables 800
TT Miyasaka Inc.; Watsonville; fruit/nuts 800
The Lodge at Pebble Beach; Pebble Beach; hotel 800
Macmillan/McGraw Hill; Monterey; publishing 750
Watsonville Community Hospital; Watsonville 675
Integrated Device Technology; Salinas; electronic components 625
California Hyatt Corp./Hyatt Regency the; Monterey; hotel 600
Natividad Medical Center; Salinas 560
Monterey Mushrooms Inc.; Watsonville; mushrooms 501

18th District

Central Valley — Modesto; Merced

Founded in 1870, Modesto took nine decades to reach a population of about 37,000. In the decade that followed, its population nearly doubled. In the 1970s, its population rose by more than one-half to exceed 100,000. By 1990, it had risen by more than one-half again, nearing 165,000—a total growth of more than 300 percent in 30 years.

Part of this expansion was spurred by businesses fleeing the congestion and land prices of California's coastal cities. Modesto, the Stanislaus County seat, lies near the midpoint of the state on the north bank of the Tuolumne River. Highway 99 passes through, and Interstate 5, the only other major artery through the Central Valley, passes a few miles to the west.

But most of the growth came from growing things—the Valley's phenomenally successful agricultural industry. Modesto bottles, cans, packs and processes the extraordinary variety of fruits, vegetables, grains, fibers and wines produced in the Valley. The Gallo winery here is responsible for about one-third of all the wine bottled in California.

Booming Modesto helped drive the Stanislaus County population from 266,000 to 370,000 in the 1980s, more than the population of better-known counties such as Monterey and Santa Barbara. In essence, the 18th consists of Stanislaus and Merced County, where the city of Merced (56,000) has attracted large numbers of Southeast Asian immigrants and grew by 20,000 in the 1980s. Stanislaus and Merced counties cast 72 percent and 24 percent of the 18th District vote, respectively, in the 1992 House election.

The 18th also takes in the southwest corners of San Joaquin County (the city of Ripon) and Madera County (stopping short of Chowchilla). It also slices off the northeastern tip of Fresno County. But these are sparsely populated areas; all three together cast less than 5 percent of the district vote for president in 1992.

Farmers prosper or fail on the weather, the cost of water and the market price—and government is responsible for two out of three. So farm districts need a member's attention, and this one has been accustomed to getting it from savvy insider Democrats.

In statewide and national elections, the 18th is highly competitive. It voted Republican for president throughout the 1980s. Bill Clinton struggled here, as elsewhere in the Central

Valley. Though many Valley residents are Hispanic and growing numbers are Asian (26 and 6 percent, respectively, in the 18th), they have yet to exercise commensurate influence in the voting booths. Clinton's association with environmental activism and other liberal causes kept his vote share far below the Democratic registration in the district (which slipped by 2 percentage points with redistricting, to 53 percent).

Election Returns and Party Registration

	18th District	Democrat	Republican
1992	President*	74,357 (40.9%)	67,898 (37.3%)
	Senate †	75,260 (43.1%)	81,524 (46.6%)
	Senate †‡	86,189 (49.0%)	74,805 (42.6%)
	House †	139,704 (84.7%)	—
1990	Governor †	42,586 (40.6%)	56,375 (53.7%)
1988	President	59,590 (46.2%)	67,798 (52.6%)
	Senate	54,668 (43.4%)	66,590 (52.9%)
1986	Senate	56,951 (45.6%)	65,147 (52.1%)
	Governor	40,150 (31.9%)	84,317 (66.9%)
1993	Party registration †	135,302 (53.1%)	91,766 (36.0%)

*Vote for Perot was 39,645 (21.8%).   †Independent/other is greater than 5%.
‡Special election for the remaining two years of the term of Pete Wilson who was elected governor in 1990. Appointee John Seymour held the seat 1991-1992.

Demographics

Population   571,393

Percent change from 1980   8.4%

Land area   4,139 square miles

Population per square mile   138

Counties, 1990 population

Fresno (pt.) 7,473	San Joaquin (pt.) 13,344
Madera (pt.) 1,651	Stanislaus 370,522
Merced 178,403	

Cities, 1990 population (10,000 or more)

Atwater 22,282	Modesto 164,730
Ceres 26,314	Oakdale 11,961
Los Banos 14,519	Turlock 42,198
Merced 56,216	

Race and Hispanic origin

White   75.7%
Black   2.8%
American Indian, Eskimo, or Aleut.   1.0%
Asian or Pacific Islander   6.0%
Other   14.4%
Hispanic origin   26.0%

Ancestry

American 3.7%	Italian 4.4%
Dutch 3.6%	Norwegian 1.2%
English 11.4%	Portuguese 6.1%
French 3.2%	Scotch Irish 1.8%
German 17.3%	Scottish 1.7%
Irish 12.9%	Swedish 2.3%

Universities/colleges, 1990-1991 enrollment
California State University-Stanislaus, Turlock   4,822

Merced College, Merced   6,854
Modesto Junior College, Modesto   11,300

Newspapers, total circulation (in all districts)
Fresno Bee   149,933
Lodi News-Sentinel   17,380
Madera Tribune   8,485
Merced Sun Star   24,115
Modesto Bee   83,177
Pleasanton Valley Herald   34,853
Sacramento Bee   269,383
San Francisco Chronicle Examiner   692,424
Stockton Record   54,568
Tracy Press   9,015
Turlock Daily Journal   9,744

Commercial television stations, affiliations
ADI: Fresno-Visalia (59%) and Sacramento-Stockton (41%)

Cable television systems, total subscribers
Post Newsweek Cable TV; Modesto   49,496
Sammons Communications Inc.; Turlock   16,320
Sonic Cable TV; Riverbank   9,100
TCI Cablevision of California; Merced   26,000
TCI of California; Tracy   10,524

Military installations, 1991
Castle Air Force Base, Merced   5,237

Businesses and other major employers
Foster Poultry Farms; Livingston; poultry/eggs   2,500
E. & J. Gallo Winery; Modesto; wine production   1,800
National Medical Enterprises; Modesto   1,800
Foster Poultry Farms; Turlock; poultry   1,500
Hunt-Wesson Inc./Beatrice; Oakdale; preserved fruits/vegetables   1,300
Foster Poultry Farms; Delhi; poultry/eggs   1,000
Gallo Glass Co.; Modesto; glass/glassware   1,000
Farmers Group Inc./Farmers Insurance Group; Merced; life/casualty/fire insurance   900
Emanuel Medical Center; Turlock   900
Memorial Hospitals Assn./Memorial Hospital; Modesto   850
County of Merced; Merced   800
ConAgra Inc.; Turlock; turkey products   775
Kraft; Modesto; preserved fruits/vegetables   700
Procter & Gamble; Modesto; paper mills   700
Campbell Soup Co.; Modesto; canned food products   700
Merced Community Medical Center; Merced   700
Modesto Junior College; Modesto   650
Tri-Valley Growers; Turlock; preserved fruits/vegetables   645
Keller Industries Inc./Keller Extrusions Div.; Merced; nonferrous rolling and drawing   600
World Color Press Inc.; Merced; commercial printing   600
ConAgra Inc.; Turlock; preserved food products   600
Hershey Foods Corp.; Oakdale; candies   600
California State University-Stanislaus; Turlock   600
Valley Fresh Inc.; Turlock   poultry products   550

19th District
Central Valley — Fresno; Madera

At its core, the 19th resembles the old 18th. They have in common all of Madera County (including the cities of Madera and Chowchilla) and most of the city of Fresno. The 19th also has inherited Rep. Richard Lehman, the old 18th's incumbent. At the same time, the 19th has so many new constituents that it is easy to see why Lehman barely survived his first test on his new turf. After running unopposed in 1990, Lehman got just 47 percent of the vote in his 19th District debut.

Gone are the three high-elevation counties (Calaveras, Tuolumne and Mono) that usually voted Republican. But gone too is that populous portion of Stockton (in San Joaquin County) that helped Lehman win his first five House elections. New in the district are Mariposa County, the eastern half of rural Fresno County and the northern third of Tulare County. Losing Tuolumne County means Lehman no longer represents the wild northern half of Yosemite National Park; but the addition of Mariposa County (population 14,000) gives the new district more of the park's most visited areas.

The old 18th did not occupy much more of Fresno County than the city itself, which forms the knot in what resembles a bow tie. The rest of the county unfurls in either direction, approaching San Benito Mountain on the west and embracing Kings Canyon National Park on the east. In between lie thousands of square miles of San Joaquin Valley desert, crisscrossed by irrigation canals and patterned with farms, groves, vineyards and ranches. Fresno County produces about $2.9 billion in agricultural products a year, more than any other county in the United States.

The 19th enfolds the eastern half of this county. It misses downtown Fresno, but includes all of the city north of Belmont Avenue and all parts east of Chestnut Avenue. It includes the California State University campus and its 17,000 students.

The city is an older agribusiness center, saddled with fearsome summer heat and a workaday image. Despite its civic center, symphony orchestra and 10-block downtown mall, one mid-1980s survey called Fresno the least desirable place to live in America (and a satirical TV miniseries named for the city added insult to injury).

Yet Fresno continues to grow impressively. Its population (354,000) increased by 63 percent in the 1980s. Many of the newest arrivals are Central Americans and Southeast Asians who have enlivened and diversified the culture.

But 1992 redistricting gave the district a more rural tilt and dropped Democratic registration from 59 percent to 47 percent. In that year's elections, Lehman would not have survived, except that Fresno County still casts 74 percent of the vote for the House (and most of that came from the city). Lehman had to run far ahead of Bill Clinton to win, as the 19th gave George Bush one of his best showings in the state (43 percent of the districtwide vote). Bush carried every county but Mariposa and even enjoyed an outright majority in Tulare.

Election Returns and Party Registration

	19th District	Democrat	Republican
1992	President*	85,049 (38.1%)	97,124 (43.5%)
	Senate †	73,489 (33.6%)	129,119 (59.1%)
	Senate †‡	90,516 (41.7%)	111,847 (51.5%)
	House †	101,619 (47.1%)	100,590 (46.7%)
1990	Governor †	59,728 (38.6%)	86,150 (55.7%)
1988	President	82,148 (44.1%)	101,053 (54.3%)
	Senate	72,060 (39.3%)	105,198 (57.3%)
1986	Senate	61,887 (45.1%)	71,408 (52.0%)
	Governor	43,293 (31.4%)	93,164 (67.6%)
1993	Party registration †	140,120 (47.3%)	124,460 (42.0%)

*Vote for Perot was 41,052 (18.4%).   †Independent/other is greater than 5%.
‡Special election for the remaining two years of the term of Pete Wilson who was elected governor in 1990. Appointee John Seymour held the seat 1991-1992.

Demographics

Population 573,043

Percent change from 1980 8.9%

Land area 7,642 square miles

Population per square mile 75

Counties, 1990 population
Fresno (pt.) 419,567   Mariposa 14,302
Madera (pt.) 86,439   Tulare (pt.) 52,735

Cities, 1990 population (10,000 or more)
Clovis 50,323   Madera 29,281
Fresno (pt.) 273,792   Visalia (pt.) 18,005

Race and Hispanic origin
White 73.5%
Black 3.3%
American Indian, Eskimo, or Aleut. 1.3%
Asian or Pacific Islander 7.4%
Other 14.6%
Hispanic origin 23.6%

Ancestry
American 2.7%   Italian 4.7%
Danish 1.2%   Norwegian 1.2%
Dutch 2.8%   Polish 1.1%
English 14.1%   Portuguese 1.6%
French 3.6%   Scotch Irish 2.1%
German 20.8%   Scottish 2.2%
Irish 13.3%   Swedish 2.2%

Universities/colleges, 1990-1991 enrollment
California State University, Fresno 17,467
Fresno City College, Fresno 14,710
Fresno Pacific College, Fresno 1,317

Newspapers, total circulation (in all districts)
Fresno Bee 149,933
Madera Tribune 8,485
Porterville Recorder 13,222
San Francisco Chronicle Examiner 692,424
Tulare Advance Register 9,292
Visalia Times-Delta 23,229

Commercial television stations, affiliations
ADI: Fresno-Visalia (100%)
KAIL, Fresno (None)
KFSN-TV, Fresno (ABC)
KJEO, Fresno (CBS)
KSEE, Fresno (NBC)
KMSG-TV, Sanger-Fresno (None)
KMPH, Visalia-Fresno (None)

Cable television systems, total subscribers
Continental Cablevision of California; Fresno 99,700

Military installations, 1991
  Fresno Air Terminal Air Force Guard Station, Fresno 389

Businesses and other major employers
  U.S. Internal Revenue Service; Fresno 6,000
  California State University; Fresno 2,354
  Saint Agnes Medical Center; Fresno 1,900
  Valley Children's Hospital; Fresno 1,250
  Westair Holding Inc./United Express; Fresno; air transportation 1,200
  Diocese of Fresno Educational Corp./KNXT-TV; Fresno; religious organizations 1,030
  Yosemite Park & Curry Co.; Yosemite National Park; hotels/motels 1,025
  Consolidated Citrus Growers/Allied Farming Co.; Exeter; farm management services 1,000
  Fresno City College; Fresno 900
  U.S. Veterans Affairs Dept.; Fresno; hospital 800
  Sanden of America Inc.; Pinedale; refrigeration 700
  State of California/Transportation Dept.; Fresno; road construction 680
  County of Madera; Madera 600

20th District

Parts of Kern, Kings and Fresno Counties

Many Democrats were complaining after the California Supreme Court handed down the 1992 congressional district map, but not Rep. Cal Dooley, who got a good deal in the redraw. This district is descended from the old 17th, which Dooley seized from a troubled Republican incumbent in 1990. But while that district was, for all practical purposes, a Republican one, the 1992 map trimmed away much of the GOP vote.

The 20th reaches from Fresno to Bakersfield (in Kern County). But it has far less of the latter than the old 17th had; moreover, its share of Fresno comes from that city's southeastern neighborhoods, which are home to many blacks and Hispanics who reliably support Democratic candidates.

More generally, the new district represents a dramatic shift to the west, away from the upland portions of Fresno and Tulare counties and toward the portions of Fresno, Kings and Kern counties known as the Westlands. Here, federal water projects have spawned vast farms with battalions of workers. Motorists on Interstate 5 see nary a town while they pass fields filled with virtually every fruit, nut, vegetable, fiber and livestock animal known in the Temperate Zone. Fresno County's annual $2.9 billion agricultural output ranks first in the nation.

Democratic registration in the old 17th had been barely reached 48 percent (with the GOP at 43 percent). But in the 20th, Democratic registration stands at 61 percent, more than twice the GOP's 29 percent. The district also bears much of the burden of the Valley's urban and rural poor. The rates of unemployment, crime, teen pregnancy and disease far outstrip statewide averages.

East of the city of Fresno, the 20th takes in the towns of Sanger, Reedley, Parlier, Dinuba, Orange Cove and Kingsburg— each with its own ethnic flavor and history.

Kingsburg, where Sun Maid raisins and Del Monte peaches are processed, still adorns its main street with Swedish Dala horses. The Scandinavians who came here a century ago have largely turned Republican, as have waves of Armenians, Japanese and migrants from the Dust Bowl, who first were farmworkers.

But where crops must be picked by hand, there will always be new immigrants. In recent generations, the new arrivals have been from Mexico and Central America. Delano, site of the famous farmworkers strike in the 1960s, is in the Kern County portion of the 20th.

Hispanics constitute a 55 percent majority in the 20th; blacks and Asians together are 12 percent. But these groups, restrained by low rates of voter registration and turnout, have yet to play a significant role in primaries or general elections.

Dooley, a relatively conservative, farm-oriented Democrat, got huge margins in all four counties of the 20th in 1992. But "national Democrats" are viewed with suspicion. The same year Bill Clinton managed to carry the district despite winning only its Fresno portion.

Election Returns and Party Registration

	20th District	Democrat	Republican
1992	President*	55,942 (46.9%)	44,674 (37.5%)
	Senate †	46,353 (40.1%)	58,001 (50.2%)
	Senate †‡	53,995 (47.4%)	51,065 (44.9%)
	House	72,679 (64.9%)	39,388 (35.1%)
1990	Governor †	35,644 (41.4%)	44,901 (52.1%)
1988	President	56,498 (51.3%)	51,819 (47.1%)
	Senate †	51,545 (47.2%)	51,919 (47.5%)
1986	Senate	55,417 (48.6%)	56,349 (49.4%)
	Governor	41,255 (35.9%)	72,778 (63.3%)
1993	Party registration †	115,189 (60.8%)	54,778 (28.9%)

*Vote for Perot was 18,568 (15.6%).   †Independent/other is greater than 5%.
‡Special election for the remaining two years of the term of Pete Wilson who was elected governor in 1990. Appointee John Seymour held the seat 1991-1992.

Demographics

Population 573,282

Percent change from 1980 9.0%

Land area 6,857 square miles

Population per square mile 84

Counties, 1990 population
  Fresno (pt.) 240,450   Kings 101,469
  Kern (pt.) 152,060   Tulare (pt.) 79,303

Cities, 1990 population (10,000 or more)
  Bakersfield (pt.) 19,904   Lamont CDP 11,517
  Corcoran 13,364   Lemoore 13,622
  Delano 22,762   Reedley (pt.) 15,561
  Dinuba 12,743   Sanger 16,839
  Fresno (pt.) 80,410   Selma 14,757
  Hanford 30,897   Wasco 12,412

Race and Hispanic origin
  White 48.7%
  Black 6.4%
  American Indian, Eskimo, or Aleut. 1.0%
  Asian or Pacific Islander 5.5%
  Other 38.4%
  Hispanic origin 55.4%

Ancestry
  American 2.8%   English 5.3%
  Dutch 1.7%   French 1.5%

German 8.8%   Portuguese 2.5%
Irish 6.7%   Swedish 1.0%
Italian 1.4%

Universities/colleges, 1990-1991 enrollment
California School of Professional Psychology, Fresno 338
Kings River Community College, Reedley 3,078
West Hills Community College, Coalinga 2,486

Newspapers, total circulation (in all districts)
Bakersfield Californian 81,049
Fresno Bee 149,933
Hanford Sentinel 13,691
Los Angeles Times 1,169,066
Porterville Recorder 13,222
San Francisco Chronicle Examiner 692,424
Tulare Advance Register 9,292
Visalia Times-Delta 23,229

Commercial television stations, affiliations
ADI: Fresno-Visalia (72%) and Bakersfield (27%)

Cable television systems, total subscribers
Continental Cablevision of California; Hanford 13,040
Continental Cablevision of California; Fresno 99,700
Continental Cablevision of California; Tulare 21,500
Cox Cable of Bakersfield; Bakersfield 22,632
Falcon Cable TV; Porterville 16,111
Warner Cable Communications Inc.; Bakersfield 67,500
Weststar Communications; Ward Peak 9,000

Military installations, 1991
Lemoore Naval Air Station, Lemoore 6,796

Businesses and other major employers
Marko Zaninovich Inc./Sunview Marketing Intl.; Delano;
    fruit/nuts 2,000
Zacky Farms Inc.; Fresno; meat products 2,000
Clovis Community Hospital; Fresno 2,000
County of Fresno/Library; Fresno 1,750
Valley Medical Center of Fresno; Fresno 1,720
County of Fresno/Sheriffs Dept.; Fresno 1,500
Mike Yurosek & Son Inc.; Lamont; crop services 1,400
Oscar Mayer Foods Corp./Louis Rich Co.; Tulare; meat
    products 1,400
U.S. Postal Service; Fresno 1,400
Kern County Medical Center; Bakersfield 1,400
State of California/Corrections Dept.; Avenal 1,100
County of Kings; Hanford 1,077
County of Fresno/Social Services Dept.; Fresno; family ser-
    vices 1,000
County of Kern/Human Services Dept.; Bakersfield; social
    services 900
Ruiz Food Products Inc.; Dinuba; preserved fruits/vegetables
    850
McClatchy Newspapers Inc./Fresno Bee; Fresno; newspapers
    800
Wasco State Prison; Wasco 800
Grimmway Farms; Lamont; crop services/food products 700
Pirelli Armstrong Tire Corp.; Hanford; tires 650
City of Fresno/Police Dept.; Fresno 650
W. M. Bolthouse Farms Inc.; Bakersfield; crop services 600
Jostens Inc.; Visalia; publishing 600
Gottschalks Inc./Village East; Fresno; department stores 600
Sun-Maid Growers; Kingsburg; raisins/dried fruits 585
Harris Farms Inc.; Selma; beef products 530

21st District
Kern and Tulare Counties — Bakersfield

One aim of the court-ordered California redistricting of 1992 was to create more districts in which both parties could be competitive. But where that goal conflicted with other priorities, such as compactness and community of interest, it was shelved.

A case in point is the 21st, which is a model of compactness and community of interest, especially alongside the old, Bakersfield-based 20th District, which shared a border with Nevada and still offered beachfront on the Pacific. Beginning high in the Sierras, it took in all of Inyo County, most of Kern County, a swath of Los Angeles County and most of San Luis Obispo County on the coast.

By comparison, the 21st looks sensible enough to be an Iowa district. About three-fourths of its vote is in Kern County (overall population 543,000). The rest comes from new territory pulled in from Tulare County to the north (overall population 312,000).

Tulare County brings into the district the magnificence of the Sequoia National Forest and the western slope of Mount Whitney, which at 14,495 feet is the tallest peak in the Lower 48. It also brings a flock of small towns. The county seat is Visalia, a farming city on Highway 99, straddling the line with the 20th. Running south through Tulare County just east of Highway 99, the district's lines are drawn to include the towns of Tulare, Farmersville, Porterville and Lindsay. This was one of the fastest-growing metropolitan areas in the 1980s; population expanded 27 percent.

South of Shafter, the southern appendage of the 20th District cuts into the Bakersfield metro area along Interstate 5. Farther west, the 21st resumes and picks up the towns of Maricopa and Taft.

But the district's heart beats in Bakersfield, which has a population of 175,000. Bakersfield was brought to life by a gold rush in 1885 and again by an oil strike in 1899. Farmers from the Southwest came in force during the 1930s Dust Bowl years, and the city boomed yet again in the 1980s—when its growth rate of nearly 66 percent ranked ninth among U.S. cities.

The predominance of cotton, other crops and oil hereabouts can still make a Texan feel at home, even if the Texan came to work in the defense-related industries tied to nearby China Lake Naval Air Weapons Station or Edwards Air Force Base (in Kern's southeast corner). Edwards is a frequent landing site for space shuttles because of its seven-mile landing strip in Rogers Dry Lake.

The 21st is actually slightly less white and less Republican than the old 20th (GOP registration is down 3 percentage points to 46 percent). But the Democratic registration has not risen commensurately, and when Republicans have a registration plurality they almost always win big at the polls. George Bush carried both the Tulare and Kern sections of the 21st in 1992.

Election Returns and Party Registration

	21st District	Democrat	Republican
1992	President*	66,284 (32.5%)	94,727 (46.4%)
	Senate †	56,925 (28.4%)	126,675 (63.1%)
	Senate †‡	69,327 (34.5%)	113,532 (56.5%)
	House	68,058 (34.8%)	127,758 (65.2%)
1990	Governor †	47,660 (31.8%)	93,553 (62.4%)

	21st District	Democrat	Republican
1988	President	60,865 (35.1%)	110,082 (63.4%)
	Senate	57,651 (32.9%)	111,565 (63.7%)
1986	Senate	57,845 (43.0%)	73,452 (54.6%)
	Governor	41,870 (30.9%)	92,204 (68.1%)
1993	Party registration †	115,296 (41.8%)	127,561 (46.3%)

*Vote for Perot was 43,016 (21.1%).   †Independent/other is greater than 5%.
‡Special election for the remaining two years of the term of Pete Wilson who was elected governor in 1990. Appointee John Seymour held the seat 1991-1992.

Demographics

Population 571,300

Percent change from 1980 8.8%

Land area 8,916 square miles

Population per square mile 64

Counties, 1990 population
Kern (pt.) 391,417   Tulare (pt.) 179,883

Cities, 1990 population (10,000 or more)
Bakersfield (pt.) 154,916   Ridgecrest 27,725
Oildale CDP 26,553   Tulare (pt.) 32,935
Porterville 29,563   Visalia (pt.) 49,090

Race and Hispanic origin
White 77.7%
Black 4.0%
American Indian, Eskimo, or Aleut. 1.5%
Asian or Pacific Islander 3.2%
Other 13.6%
Hispanic origin 20.3%

Ancestry
American 4.6%   Norwegian 1.2%
Dutch 3.0%   Polish 1.1%
English 15.3%   Portuguese 1.7%
French 4.0%   Scotch Irish 2.2%
German 20.3%   Scottish 2.1%
Irish 15.1%   Swedish 1.8%
Italian 3.2%

Universities/colleges, 1990-1991 enrollment
Bakersfield College, Bakersfield 10,776
California State College, Bakersfield 4,650
Cerro Coso Community College, Ridgecrest 3,673
College of the Sequoias, Visalia 7,839
Porterville College, Porterville 2,334
Taft College, Taft 797

Newspapers, total circulation (in all districts)
Bakersfield Californian 81,049
Fresno Bee 149,933
Los Angeles Times 1,169,066
Porterville Recorder 13,222
San Francisco Chronicle Examiner 692,424
Tulare Advance Register 9,292
Visalia Times-Delta 23,229

Commercial television stations, affiliations
ADI: Los Angeles (37%) Bakersfield (33%) and Fresno-Visalia (30%)

KBAK-TV, Bakersfield (ABC)
KUZZ, Bakersfield (None)
KERO-TV, Bakersfield (CBS)
KGET, Bakersfield (NBC)

Cable television systems, total subscribers
Continental Cablevision of California; Tulare 21,500
Cox Cable of Bakersfield; Bakersfield 22,632
Falcon Cable TV; Porterville 16,111
Kern Valley Cable TV; Wofford Heights 6,665
Warner Cable Communications; Bakersfield 67,500

Military installations, 1991
China Lake Naval Weapons Center, China Lake 9,455
Edwards Air Force Base, Rosamond 8,842

Businesses and other major employers
State of California/Dev. Center; Porterville 1,800
Kaweah Delta Hospital District; Visalia 1,468
Mercy Hospital; Bakersfield 1,443
Sun World Inc./Superior Farms; Bakersfield; garden stores 1,324
City of Bakersfield; Bakersfield 1,091
Dole Bakersfield Inc.; Bakersfield; fruit/nuts 1,000
Computer Sciences Corp.; Edwards; computer services 1,000
NASA/Aims Dryden Flight Research Facility; Edwards; space research/technology 1,000
Bakersfield Memorial Hospital; Bakersfield 955
Visalia Adult School; Visalia 930
Bakersfield College; Bakersfield 900
U.S. Postal Service; Bakersfield 857
United States Borax Chemical Corp.; Boron; inorganic chemicals 850
Pride Petroleum Services Inc.; Bakersfield; oil services 700
Comarco Inc./Weapons Support Div.; Ridgecrest; engineering services 660
San Joaquin Community Hospital; Bakersfield 655
Connecticut General Life Insurance Co.; Visalia; insurance services 580
Dairyman's Cooperative Creamery; Tulare; dairy products 570
County of Kern/Fire Dept.; Bakersfield 565
Sierra View Local Hospital District; Porterville 530

22nd District
Santa Barbara; Santa Maria; San Luis Obispo

Santa Barbara County, with about 370,000 residents, was the mainstay of the old 19th District. It was connected to the Los Angeles area to the south by Ventura County, which had most of its land (though not most of its people) in the 19th. The two neighboring counties shared the calm waters of the Santa Barbara Channel and the rugged grandeur of Los Padres National Forest, a 1.7 million-acre preserve spread over several small mountain ranges running parallel to the coast.

The 1992 redistricting separated these two counties, combining Santa Barbara with San Luis Obispo, its coastline neighbor to the north. The two counties are topographically similar, separated only by the Cuyama River that runs down from the Sierra Madre Mountains to the Pacific.

The 22nd takes in all of both counties, except for the coastal town of Carpinteria just south of Santa Barbara and adjacent acreage on the Ventura County line. Thrown in for good measure are four islands offshore in the Santa Barbara Channel: San Miguel, Santa Rosa, Santa Cruz and Santa Barbara (but not Anacapa Islands).

San Luis Obispo includes its namesake city (home to California Polytechnic State University and about one-fifth of the county's 217,000 residents) and the northern end of the Los Padres forest. North of the city, Highway 101 angles inland to Atascadero, Paso Robles and San Miguel. Alternatively, the tourist can take the breathtaking Highway 1, which continues to hug the coast on its way to memorable Morro Bay and then to San Simeon—the fabled mansion of media magnate William Randolph Hearst.

About 60 percent of the district's vote is still cast in Santa Barbara County, the population centers of which include Vandenberg Air Force Base and the small cities of Lompoc and Santa Maria. The city of Santa Barbara was founded 200 years ago by the Spanish on a natural harbor discovered 250 years before that by the Portuguese.

More than most of contemporary California, Santa Barbara has striven to maintain some of its Iberian charm—in part with a measured pace of life. A major campus (18,400 students) of the University of California is just outside of town. Many of the city's nearly 86,000 residents are retirees; others have settled here less to make money than to make the most of the money they have.

The old 19th had a slight Democratic tilt in registration (45 percent to the GOP's 41 percent) but it generally voted Republican. In the 22nd the two parties are about even in registration. Both counties preferred Democrats Bill Clinton for president and Dianne Feinstein for the Senate in 1992.

Election Returns and Party Registration

	22nd District	Democrat	Republican
1992	President*	106,815 (41.1%)	92,045 (35.4%)
	Senate †	110,137 (43.5%)	120,471 (47.6%)
	Senate †‡	123,312 (48.7%)	109,661 (43.3%)
	House †	87,328 (35.0%)	131,242 (52.5%)
1990	Governor †	73,123 (42.3%)	90,408 (52.3%)
1988	President	101,851 (43.4%)	129,418 (55.2%)
	Senate	91,770 (38.8%)	136,871 (57.8%)
1986	Senate	69,358 (45.3%)	78,900 (51.6%)
	Governor	50,944 (33.1%)	99,815 (64.9%)
1993	Party registration †	133,216 (41.1%)	135,792 (41.9%)

*Vote for Perot was 61,030 (23.5%).   †Independent/other is greater than 5%.
‡Special election for the remaining two years of the term of Pete Wilson who was elected governor in 1990. Appointee John Seymour held the seat 1991-1992.

Demographics

Population 572,891

Percent change from 1980 8.8%

Land area 6,038 square miles

Population per square mile 95

Counties, 1990 population
San Luis Obispo 217,162   Santa Barbara (pt.) 355,729

Cities, 1990 population (10,000 or more)
Arroyo Grande 14,378
Atascadero 23,138
Baywood-Los Osos CDP 14,377
El Paso de Robles (Paso Robles) 18,583
Grover City 11,656
Isla Vista CDP 20,395
Lompoc 37,649
San Luis Obispo 41,958
Santa Barbara 85,571
Santa Maria 61,284

Race and Hispanic origin
White 81.7%
Black 2.8%
American Indian, Eskimo, or Aleut. 1.0%
Asian or Pacific Islander 3.9%
Other 10.7%
Hispanic origin 21.3%

Ancestry
American 2.4%
Danish 1.6%
Dutch 2.7%
English 17.6%
French 4.6%
German 22.2%
Irish 14.6%
Italian 5.2%
Norwegian 1.9%
Polish 2.1%
Portuguese 1.7%
Russian 1.2%
Scotch Irish 2.5%
Scottish 3.4%
Swedish 2.7%
Welsh 1.2%

Universities/colleges, 1990-1991 enrollment
Allan Hancock College, Santa Maria 7,975
Antioch University, Santa Barbara 213
California Polytechnic State University, San Luis Obispo 15,912
Cuesta College, San Luis Obispo 7,127
Fielding Institute, Santa Barbara 751
Santa Barbara City College, Santa Barbara 11,031
University of California, Santa Barbara 18,391
Westmont College, Santa Barbara 1,268

Newspapers, total circulation (in all districts)
Lompoc Record 8,847
Los Angeles Times 1,169,066
San Francisco Chronicle Examiner 692,424
San Luis Obispo Telegram 31,357
Santa Barbara News Press 53,429
Santa Maria Times 21,156

Commercial television stations, affiliations
ADI: Santa Barbara-Santa Maria-San Luis Obispo (100%)
KSBY-TV, San Luis Obispo (NBC)
KEYT-TV, Santa Barbara (ABC)
KCOY-TV, Santa Maria (CBS)

Cable television systems, total subscribers
Comcast Cablevision; Lompoc 14,820
Comcast Cablevision; Mt. Solomon 26,340
Cox Cable Santa Barbara; Santa Barbara 60,480
Falcon Cable TV; San Luis Obispo 14,544
Sonic Cable TV; San Luis Obispo 44,700

Military installations, 1991
Vandenberg Air Force Base, Lompoc 7,732

Businesses and other major employers
University of California; Santa Barbara 7,462
County of Santa Barbara; Santa Barbara 2,620
County of San Luis Obispo; San Luis Obispo 2,483
California Polytechnic University; San Luis Obispo 2,100

Raytheon Co./Electromagnetic Systems Div.; Santa Barbara;
electrical equipment/supplies 1,800
Santa Barbara Research Center; Santa Barbara; research services 1,700
Santa Barbara Cottage Hospital; Santa Barbara 1,699
State of California/Mental Health Dept.; Atascadero 1,600
Applied Magnetics Corp.; Santa Barbara; computer/office
equipment 1,500
Pacific Gas & Electric Co./Diablo Canyon Power Plant; Avila
Beach; gas production/distribution 1,500
General Motors Hughes Electronics Corp./Delco Systems;
Santa Barbara; electronic components 1,430
ITT Federal Services Corp.; Lompoc; communications 1,250
United Foods Inc./Pictsweet Frozen Foods; Santa Maria;
preserved fruits/vegetables 1,200
City of Santa Barbara/Fire Dept.; Santa Barbara 1,016
Santa Barbara City College; Santa Barbara 1,000
Martin Marietta Corp.; Lompoc; business services 800
Marian Medical Center Inc.; Santa Maria 685
Dole Fresh Vegetables Inc./Bud of California; Guadalupe;
vegetables/melons 600
Santa Barbara Four Seasons; Santa Barbara; hotel 600
County of Santa Barbara/Health Care Service; Santa Barbara
600
State of California/Caltrans Dept.; San Luis Obispo 600
Celite Corp./Celite; Lompoc; mineral services 550
Sierra Vista Hospital; San Luis Obispo 525

23rd District

Most of Ventura County; Oxnard; Ventura; Simi Valley

Simi Valley, a burgeoning Ventura County suburb of about
100,000 residents, had been usually associated with its large
winery. But in the spring of 1992, a jury with no blacks here
acquitted four white L.A. police officers in the beating of a black
motorist, igniting the worst rioting in Los Angeles in nearly 30
years.

Simi Valley accounts for little more than one-sixth of the
23rd District, but it is not atypical of the district (blacks
constitute only 3 percent of the 23rd's population). Some call it a
haven for families and middle-class values, others call it flight
from the Los Angeles Basin's cauldron of racial distrust. Either
way, Simi Valley and Ventura County have lost their anonymity
and become a touchstone for racial tension in the region.

Ventura County as a whole came into its own with the
redistricting of 1992. Another decade of rapid growth (26 percent
in the 1980s) had lifted its population to 669,000—more than
enough for a full district. The lines of the 23rd District are nearly
identical to those of Ventura County.

There are two small exceptions, at the southwest and
northeast corners, and one large exception in the southeast near
the Los Angeles County line. Here, the city of Thousand Oaks
(with 104,000 people the second-largest in the county) was drawn
into the Los Angeles-based 24th District.

The 23rd still comprises more than 80 percent of Ventura
County, including the cities of Ventura, Oxnard, Simi Valley,
Camarillo and Santa Paula. About 97 percent of the district vote
was cast by county residents in 1992 (the rest was cast in
Carpinteria and neighboring precincts just across the Santa
Barbara County line).

Republican registration in the 23rd is 42 percent, roughly

equal to Democratic registration. In most years in most districts,
that margin would be enough for Republicans to win with ease.
But 1992 was not a Republican year in California, especially in
recent-vintage suburbs where high-wage jobs in aerospace and
other defense industries were disappearing.

George Bush got just a fraction over 35 percent of the vote in
Ventura County, which was carried by Bill Clinton with 37
percent. The news was better for the Republican candidates for
the Senate, both of whom carried the county.

Election Returns and Party Registration

	23rd District	Democrat	Republican
1992	President*	82,613 (38.4%)	74,106 (34.5%)
	Senate †	86,473 (40.6%)	105,175 (49.4%)
	Senate †‡	98,345 (46.2%)	96,569 (45.3%)
	House	88,225 (41.5%)	115,504 (54.3%)
1990	Governor †	57,302 (38.1%)	83,381 (55.5%)
1988	President	76,635 (38.9%)	117,999 (59.9%)
	Senate	70,663 (35.7%)	120,598 (60.9%)
1986	Senate	58,794 (43.7%)	71,709 (53.2%)
	Governor	42,976 (31.8%)	90,115 (66.7%)
1993	Party registration †	127,152 (43.3%)	122,116 (41.6%)

*Vote for Perot was 58,177 (27.1%).   †Independent/other is greater than 5%.
‡Special election for the remaining two years of the term of Pete Wilson who was
elected governor in 1990. Appointee John Seymour held the seat 1991-1992.

Demographics

Population 571,483

Percent change from 1980 8.6%

Land area 1,782 square miles

Population per square mile 321

Counties, 1990 population
Santa Barbara (pt.) 13,879   Ventura (pt.) 557,604

Cities, 1990 population (10,000 or more)
Camarillo 52,303	Port Hueneme 20,319
Carpinteria (pt.) 13,283	San Buenaventura
Fillmore 11,992	(Ventura) 92,575
Moorpark 25,494	Santa Paula 25,062
Oxnard 142,216	Simi Valley (pt.) 100,213

Race and Hispanic origin
White 76.9%
Black 2.5%
American Indian, Eskimo, or Aleut. 0.8%
Asian or Pacific Islander 5.2%
Other 14.6%
Hispanic origin 30.0%

Ancestry
American 2.3%	Norwegian 1.6%
Dutch 2.3%	Polish 2.4%
English 14.8%	Russian 1.4%
French 4.2%	Scotch Irish 2.1%
German 19.6%	Scottish 2.6%
Irish 13.3%	Swedish 2.2%
Italian 5.2%	Welsh 1.0%

Universities/colleges, 1990-1991 enrollment

Moorpark College, Moorpark   10,471
Oxnard College, Oxnard   5,542
Sawyer College at Ventura, Ventura   258
Ventura College, Ventura   11,200

Newspapers, total circulation (in all districts)

Camarillo Daily News   9,772
Los Angeles Daily News   208,005
Los Angeles La Opinion   98,557
Los Angeles Times   1,169,066
Oxnard Press-Courier   17,420
Simi Enterprise   15,716
Thousand Oaks News Chronicle   21,388
Ventura Star Free Press   50,398

Commercial television stations, affiliations

ADI: Los Angeles (100%)
KADY-TV, Oxnard (None)

Cable television systems, total subscribers

Avenue TV Cable Service Inc.; Ventura   10,890
Century Cable; East Ventura   15,000
Comcast Cablevision; Simi   20,000
Jones Intercable Inc.; Oxnard   35,154
Ventura County Cable; Ojai   6,530
Ventura County Cable; Thousand Oaks   65,302
Ventura County Cable; Camarillo   9,795

Military installations, 1991

Pacific Missile Test Center (Navy), Point Mugu   11,142
Port Hueneme Naval Construction Battalion Center, Port Hueneme   9,225
Channel Island Air Force Guard Station, Oxnard   368

Businesses and other major employers

Camarillo State Hospital; Camarillo   2,000
Ventura County Medical Center; Ventura   1,500
County of Ventura/Health Care Agency; Ventura   1,500
City of Oxnard; Oxnard   1,104
St. John's Regional Medical Center; Oxnard   1,100
Community Memorial Hospital; Ventura   1,050
Everest & Jennings Inc.; Camarillo; medical instruments/supplies   900
First Interstate Bank of California/Bancard Center; Simi Valley; credit institutions   900
Pneumo Abex Corp.; Oxnard; aircraft parts   890
Minnesota Mining & Mfg. Co.; Camarillo; electrical equipment/supplies   800
Simi Valley Adventist Hospital; Simi Valley   750
Kavlico Corp.; Moorpark; electronic components   700
Humana Inc./Humana Hospital West Hills; Ojai   700
Nabisco Brands Inc./Del Monte Foods; Oxnard; preserved fruits/vegetables   600
Unisys Corp.; Camarillo; computer services   600
Moorpark College; Moorpark   600
Personnel Pool Ventura County; Oxnard; temp services   600
Moorpark Unified School District; Moorpark   576
Litton Systems Inc.; Moorpark; research services   570
Spectramed Inc./Viggro Spectramed; Oxnard; medical instruments/supplies   560
City of San Buenaventura; Ventura   556
Wambold Marker; Simi Valley; furniture   540
Pleasant Valley Hospital; Camarillo   520

24th District
Northwest Los Angeles County Suburbs

Redistricting in 1992 seemed to toss Rep. Anthony Beilenson a hard bone to chew when it put Ventura County's conservative Thousand Oaks into his constituency. The city has three registered Republicans for every Democrat. But the dynamics of that election year that produced unusually lopsided Democratic successes in California gave Beilenson a break. While Beilenson took only 39 percent in Thousand Oaks—not bad considering that he was running against a Thousand Oaks-based Republican—he received 60 percent in the Los Angeles County portion of the 24th. This gave him a comfortable 17-point margin of victory and made him the first Democrat to represent any part of Ventura County in the House since 1948.

The eastern end of the 24th District (see map on page 97) begins in the San Fernando Valley, in Van Nuys and Encino. Its main artery, the Ventura Freeway, splits the valley and heads west. This area is thoroughly suburban. Its industries tend to be service-oriented; traditional heavy industry is limited to a few struggling aerospace contractors.

A few miles west of Encino is Tarzana, envisioned by *Tarzan* author Edgar Rice Burroughs as 550 acres of sanctuary from civilization. But just six years after he bought the land in 1919, Burroughs divided it up into tracts; the resulting community is just another subdivision along the Ventura Freeway.

The 24th's commercial districts are found about a mile south of Route 101 along Ventura Boulevard. There are miles of suburban fast-food outlets and strip-mall stores, and while there are some high-rise office towers, they tend to house branch offices of banks, not their headquarters. Transportation issues dominate in the valley; concerns about further development are centered on how growth will affect the already-strangling traffic congestion.

As Highway 101 heads west toward Thousand Oaks, development thins. The valley narrows, with the Santa Monica Mountains National Recreation Area to the south and the Santa Susana Mountains to the north. Any industry out here is likely to be of the "clean" variety, such as the biotechnology company Amgen Inc. Beyond the recreation area lie Malibu and the Santa Monica Bay.

Malibu is reached most easily by the Pacific Coast Highway, with canyon roads wandering off to connect smaller communities in the hills. Malibu tends to be less Democratic than other towns this side of the mountains; many of its wealthy residents live inside gated developments.

Development is sparse by design; Malibu has seen the fate of its built-up southeastern neighbor, Santa Monica, and opted instead for controlled residential construction on its beaches and hillsides. While many in the San Fernando Valley are concerned about traffic, many in Malibu are free to focus instead on the environment.

Election Returns and Party Registration

	24th District	Democrat	Republican
1992	President*	128,572 (48.3%)	79,728 (30.0%)
	Senate †	130,902 (50.0%)	111,847 (42.7%)
	Senate †‡	147,202 (56.5%)	96,453 (37.0%)
	House †	141,742 (55.5%)	99,835 (39.1%)
1990	Governor	87,109 (45.3%)	96,681 (50.3%)

	24th District	Democrat	Republican
1988	President	116,146 (45.4%)	137,034 (53.6%)
	Senate	103,088 (40.8%)	143,425 (56.8%)
1986	Senate	96,152 (50.3%)	91,073 (47.6%)
	Governor	71,625 (37.3%)	117,219 (61.1%)
1993	Party registration †	150,508 (46.2%)	131,131 (40.3%)

Vote for Perot was 57,625 (21.7%). †Independent/other is greater than 5%. ‡Special election for the remaining two years of the term of Pete Wilson who was elected governor in 1990. Appointee John Seymour held the seat 1991-1992.

Demographics

Population 572,563

Percent change from 1980 8.9%

Land area 304 square miles

Population per square mile 1,886

Counties, 1990 population
Los Angeles (pt.) 461,151   Ventura (pt.) 111,412

Cities, 1990 population (10,000 or more)
Agoura Hills 20,390   Thousand Oaks (pt.)
Los Angeles (pt.) 386,333   96,339

Race and Hispanic origin
White 84.6%
Black 2.1%
American Indian, Eskimo, or Aleut 0.4%
Asian or Pacific Islander 6.4%
Other 6.5%
Hispanic origin 13.5%

Ancestry
American 3.0%	Irish 12.2%
Arabic 1.2%	Italian 6.6%
Austrian 1.2%	Norwegian 1.6%
Dutch 1.7%	Polish 5.4%
English 13.8%	Russian 8.0%
French 3.8%	Scotch Irish 1.8%
German 17.8%	Scottish 2.5%
Hungarian 1.7%	Swedish 2.2%

Universities/colleges, 1990-1991 enrollment
California Lutheran University, Thousand Oaks 2,970
Los Angeles Pierce College, Woodland Hills 16,970
Pepperdine University, Malibu 7,199

Newspapers, total circulation (in all districts)
Camarillo Daily News 9,772
Los Angeles Daily News 208,005
Los Angeles Times 1,169,066
Oxnard Press-Courier 17,420
Santa Monica Outlook 26,324
Simi Enterprise 15,716
Thousand Oaks News Chronicle 21,388
Ventura Star Free Press 50,398

Commercial television stations, affiliations
ADI: Los Angeles (100%)

Cable television systems, total subscribers
Century Cable; Sherman Oaks 36,635
Falcon Cable TV; Corral Canyon 9,157
Ventura County Cable; Thousands Oaks 65,302
West Valley Cablevision; Chatsworth 71,669

Businesses and other major employers
Rockwell Intl. Corp./Rocketdyne Div.; Canoga Park; aerospace/research services 8,481
Litton Industries Inc.; Woodland Hills; communications equipment 3,000
GTE California Inc.; Thousand Oaks; telephone communications 2,400
Blue Cross of California; Woodland Hills; medical service/health insurance 2,060
Contel of California Inc.; Thousand Oaks; telephone communications 1,800
Northridge Hospital/Medical Center; Northridge 1,596
State Farm Mutual Auto Insurance Co.; Thousand Oaks; life insurance 1,568
Cooke Media Group Inc./Daily News of Los Angeles; Woodland Hills; newspapers 1,200
Los Angeles Pierce College; Woodland Hills 1,200
Dataproducts Corp.; Woodland Hills; computer equipment 1,100
Pepperdine University; Malibu 1,100
20th Century Industries; Woodland Hills; fire/marine/casualty insurance 1,000
Butler Service Group Inc.; Encino; supply services 1,000
Transamerica Insurance Group; Woodland Hills; fire/marine/casualty insurance 950
C. &. F Inc./17th Street Cantinas; Malibu; bars/restaurants 912
Packard Bell Electronics Inc.; Chatsworth; computer/office equipment 900
Northrop Corp.; Thousand Oaks; aircraft/parts 800
Los Robles Regional Medical Center; Thousand Oaks 800
AMI Medical Center; North Hollywood 775
AMI Medical Center; Tarzana 750
Unilab Corp.; Tarzana; medical/dental labs 750
Judge Productions Ltd.; Agoura Hills; entertainers 700
Humana West Hills Hospital; Canoga Park 700
Damon Clinical Labs; Thousand Oaks; medical/dental labs 700
Teradyne Inc.; Agoura Hills; measuring/controlling devices 650
Motion Picture & TV Fund; Woodland Hills 650
Payco General American Credits; Thousand Oaks; credit reporting 630
Pleasant Travel Service; Thousand Oaks; travel services 600
Amgen Inc.; Thousand Oaks; pharmaceuticals 600
Bullock's; Van Nuys; department stores 600
Nordstrom Inc.; Canoga Park; department stores 600
SRB Inc./Top Service; North Hollywood; supply services 600
Davis Market Research Services; Calabasas; research services 600
Marriott Corp.; Woodland Hills; hotel 516

25th District

Northern Los Angeles County; Lancaster; Palmdale

The 25th encompasses northern Los Angeles County, running to the borders of Ventura County to the west, Kern County to the north and San Bernardino County to the east. Much of the land area of this district is consumed by the San Gabriel Mountains in the Angeles National Forest and other lands controlled by the federal Bureau of Land Management. The district's southwest end reaches down into the city of Los Angeles.

This district is a mix of rural and suburban areas, with three roughly equally sized pockets of population separated by the federal lands: the Antelope Valley in the northeast, the Santa Clarita Valley in the west and L.A.'s upper San Fernando Valley in the far southwest.

The northwest part of the San Fernando Valley in the 25th is primarily residential, as is most of the valley, with electronics and aerospace manufacturing to the west side.

The Santa Clarita Valley, just north of the San Fernando Valley, is also primarily composed of Los Angeles suburbs, but along with its vast tracts of new homes it is attracting a lot of new manufacturing that cannot afford to locate in Los Angeles proper. Santa Clarita, a city of 111,000 created in 1987 when the communities of Valencia, Canyon Country, Saugus and Newhall merged, features one large industrial park with another in the works.

Up in the high desert past the national forest is the Antelope Valley, the fastest-growing area of the three. It consists of a lot of desert, a part of Edwards Air Force Base and two cities, Lancaster (population 97,000) and Palmdale (population 69,000). This rapidly growing area's economy revolves around aerospace; it is home to about 80 percent of Edwards' 15,000 workers.

Palmdale is the home of Plant 42, also known as the Flight Test Center, which runs a whole range of aircraft through their paces, including the space shuttle and the SR-71.

The Antelope Valley is not nearly as dependent on Los Angeles as are the Santa Clarita and San Fernando valleys, but over the past decade it has been attracting some residents who are willing to commute the 50 or so miles it takes to get to jobs in Los Angeles.

Republicans enjoy an advantage in the 25th, with 49 percent of the registered voters to the Democrats' 39 percent. All three of the population centers are considered quite conservative, with the residents of the Antelope Valley the most conservative, followed by those in the San Fernando and Santa Clarita valleys. In Santa Clarita heightened concern over environmental issues tips the political balance of the area toward the center.

Sixteen percent of the district's residents are Hispanic, 6 percent are Asian and 4 percent are black. George Bush won the 25th in 1992, taking 39 percent of the vote to Bill Clinton's 36 percent and Ross Perot's 25 percent.

Election Returns and Party Registration

	25th District	Democrat	Republican
1992	President*	83,305 (36.1%)	89,987 (39.0%)
	Senate †	83,153 (36.6%)	122,412 (53.9%)
	Senate †‡	96,121 (43.1%)	106,796 (47.9%)
	House †	72,233 (33.0%)	113,611 (51.9%)
1990	Governor †	53,011 (33.7%)	95,283 (60.6%)
1988	President	66,940 (32.8%)	134,961 (66.1%)
	Senate	61,856 (30.8%)	134,389 (66.9%)
1986	Senate	53,643 (37.1%)	88,670 (61.3%)
	Governor	38,720 (26.4%)	104,607 (71.4%)
1993	Party registration †	111,528 (38.6%)	140,421 (48.6%)

*Vote for Perot was 57,398 (24.9%).   †Independent/other is greater than 5%.
‡Special election for the remaining two years of the term of Pete Wilson who was elected governor in 1990. Appointee John Seymour held the seat 1991-1992.

Demographics

Population 573,105

Percent change from 1980 9.1%

Land area 2,058 square miles

Population per square mile 279

Counties, 1990 population
Los Angeles (pt.) 573,105

Cities, 1990 population (10,000 or more)
Lancaster 97,291	Palmdale 68,842
Los Angeles (pt.) 180,546	Santa Clarita (pt.) 110,642

Race and Hispanic origin
White 80.0%
Black 4.5%
American Indian, Eskimo, or Aleut. 0.7%
Asian or Pacific Islander 6.5%
Other 8.4%
Hispanic origin 16.4%

Ancestry
American 3.2%	Norwegian 1.8%
Dutch 2.3%	Polish 3.6%
English 14.5%	Russian 3.2%
French 4.3%	Scotch Irish 2.2%
German 21.5%	Scottish 2.5%
Irish 14.0%	Swedish 2.5%
Italian 6.5%	

Universities/colleges, 1990-1991 enrollment
Antelope Valley College, Lancaster 8,077
California State University, Northridge 29,401
California Institute of Arts, Valencia 1,020
College of the Canyons, Santa Clarita 4,815
Master's College, Newhall 1,004

Newspapers, total circulation (in all districts)
Antelope Valley Press 58,250
Los Angeles Daily News 208,005
Los Angeles Times 1,169,066
Thousand Oaks News Chronicle 21,388

Commercial television stations, affiliations
ADI: Los Angeles (100%)

Cable television systems, total subscribers
ATC Cablevision; Canyon Country 20,200
Jones Intercable Inc.; Palmdale 62,996
King Videocable College; Newhall 26,340
United Artist Cable; San Fernando 84,500
West Valley Cablevision: Chatsworth 71,669

Businesses and other major employers
County of Los Angeles/Sheriffs Dept.; Lancaster 2,000
Teledyne Inc.; Northridge; navigation equipment 1,806
Great Western Financial Corp.; Chatsworth; savings institutions 1,800
Rockwell Intl. Corp.; Palmdale; aircraft/parts 1,523
U.S. Veterans Affairs Dept.; San Fernando 1,400
County of Los Angeles/Peter Pitches Honor Ranch; Santa Clarita 1,400
Antelope Valley Hospital; Lancaster 1,173

JBL Inc./Harman Speaker Mfg.; Northridge; audio equipment 1,090

Lockheed Corp.; Palmdale; aircraft/parts 900

Boeing Co.; Lancaster; aircraft/parts 800

Coast Federal Bank; San Fernando; banks 800

Borden Inc./Serv-Portion-Inc.; Chatsworth; preserved fruits/vegetables 700

Micropolis Corp.; Chatsworth; computer equipment 600

Times Mirror Co./Los Angeles Times; Chatsworth; newspapers 600

Baxter Healthcare Corp.; Santa Clarita; medical instruments/supplies 600

Great Western Bank; Northridge; savings institutions 600

PS National Inc.; San Fernando; temp services 600

Mayo Henry Newhall Memorial Hospital; Santa Clarita 600

Granada Hills Community Hospital; San Fernando 575

26th District

San Fernando Valley

The 26th is the heart of the San Fernando Valley (see map on page 97). The district begins at the Angeles National Forest and drops south through the valley down to the Ventura Freeway. This part of the valley has undergone striking demographic changes. Areas such as Pacoima and Van Nuys that had only a small minority presence 20 years ago are now heavily Hispanic.

Also new are the small clusters of black families that have appeared throughout this district. While the number of blacks in downtown Los Angeles has dropped over the past 10 years, it has risen in the county overall—and areas like this are where they are going: middle-class suburbs where blacks did not live 10 years ago.

A variety of manufacturing facilities are spread throughout the 26th, but the heaviest concentration of the heaviest industry is toward the north, in Pacoima and Sylmar. The area is desperately searching for a replacement for its lucrative but dying aerospace industry. Defense conversion issues are a primary concern, with an eye toward getting the area's aerospace contractors into advanced transportation, such as magnetic-levitation trains, instead. General Motors, which had been the district's largest employer, stopped making cars in Van Nuys in August 1992, putting a squeeze on a city already reeling from the loss of the Lockheed plant in neighboring Burbank in the 27th District.

Van Nuys is trying to avoid having the GM plant site cut up into shopping malls and is struggling to attract another large manufacturer to the area. The city has tried to sell it as a site to build electric cars; California's stringent clean air rules will soon be heavily favoring them and other alternatively fueled vehicles.

The open spaces of Sylmar, rare for the Los Angeles area, have made this community at the district's northern edge one of the fastest-growing areas in the city.

Just south of Sylmar is San Fernando, an independent city embedded within Los Angeles; 83 percent of its 22,600 middle-class residents classify themselves as Hispanic.

On the 26th's eastern edge is Sun Valley, distinctive within the district in that it is made up primarily of a white working class with relatively few Hispanics. North Hollywood, along the Ventura Freeway, is a mix, its eastside heavily Hispanic and its westside much less so. Much of the district's Jewish population lives toward the west.

Bill Clinton took 57 percent of the district vote in 1992;

George Bush received 24 percent of the vote. The incumbent House Democrat drew support fairly evenly across the 26th in 1992, and received 61 percent of the vote, the same as in 1990.

Election Returns and Party Registration

	26th District	Democrat	Republican
1992	President*	72,673 (56.8%)	31,013 (24.3%)
	Senate †	69,640 (55.4%)	44,806 (35.6%)
	Senate †‡	75,982 (61.5%)	37,214 (30.1%)
	House †	73,807 (61.0%)	36,453 (30.1%)
1990	Governor †	47,088 (51.3%)	39,367 (42.9%)
1988	President	77,111 (55.7%)	59,572 (43.0%)
	Senate	69,803 (51.3%)	61,452 (45.2%)
1986	Senate	69,972 (56.6%)	49,810 (40.3%)
	Governor	56,867 (45.8%)	64,110 (51.6%)
1993	Party registration †	103,653 (60.0%)	47,636 (27.6%)

*Vote for Perot was 24,167 (18.9%).   †Independent/other is greater than 5%.
‡Special election for the remaining two years of the term of Pete Wilson who was elected governor in 1990. Appointee John Seymour held the seat 1991-1992.

Demographics

Population 571,523

Percent change from 1980 8.6%

Land area 70 square miles

Population per square mile 8,181

Counties, 1990 population
Los Angeles (pt.) 571,523

Cities, 1990 population (10,000 or more)
Los Angeles (pt.) 548,419   San Fernando 22,580

Race and Hispanic origin
White 53.5%
Black 6.2%
American Indian, Eskimo, or Aleut. 0.6%
Asian or Pacific Islander 7.3%
Other 32.4%
Hispanic origin 52.7%

Ancestry

American 2.0%	Italian 3.1%
English 5.7%	Polish 1.8%
French 1.9%	Russian 2.0%
German 8.1%	Scottish 1.0%
Irish 5.7%	

Universities/colleges, 1990-1991 enrollment
California Family Study Center, Valley Village 282
ITT Technical Institute, Van Nuys 355
Los Angeles Mission College, San Fernando 4,628
Los Angeles Valley College, Van Nuys 16,457

Newspapers, total circulation (in all districts)
Daily Variety 21,274
Los Angeles Daily News 208,005
Los Angeles La Opinion 98,557
Los Angeles Times 1,169,066
Thousand Oaks News Chronicle 21,388

LOS ANGELES COUNTY AREA

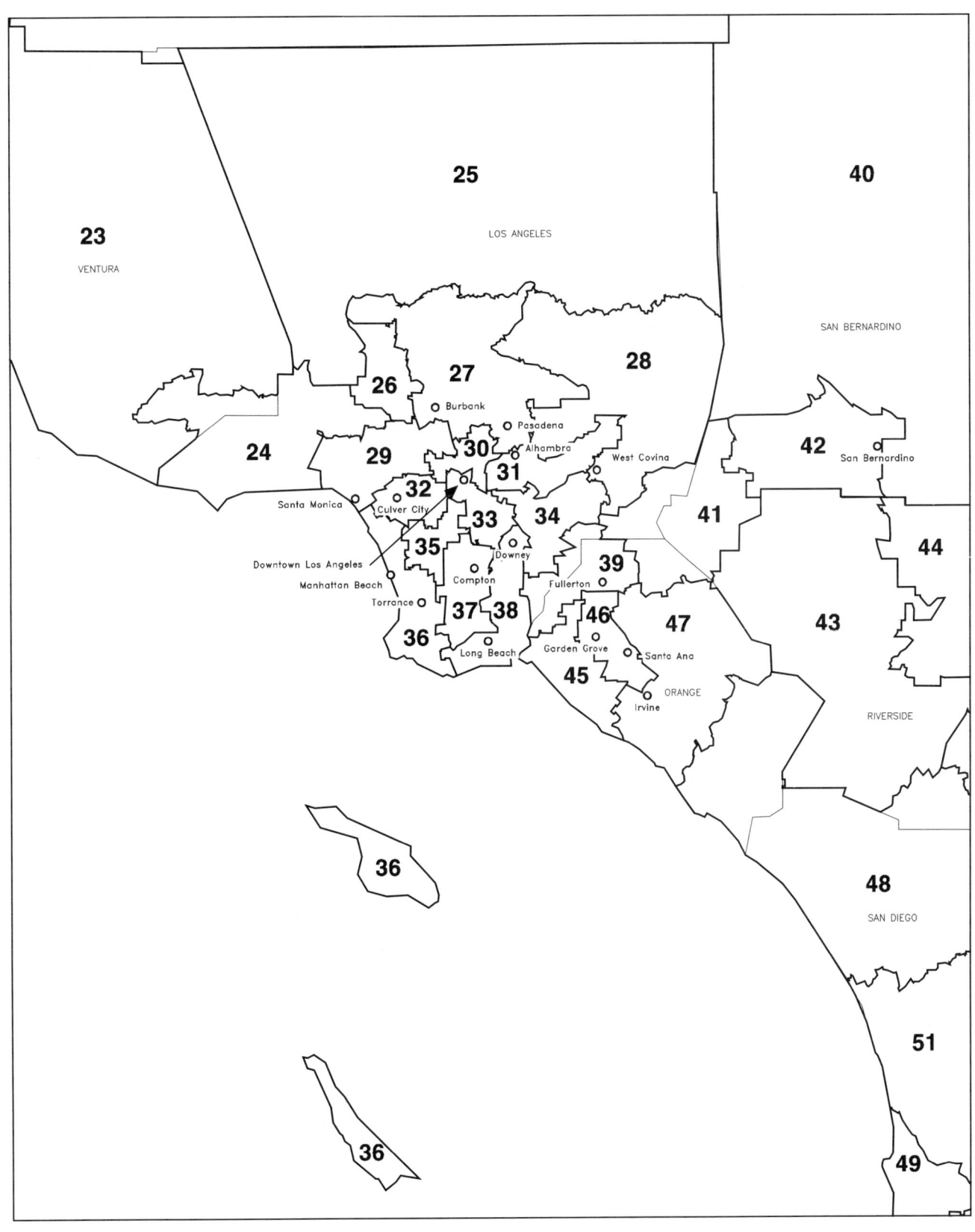

23 VENTURA

25 LOS ANGELES

40

28

SAN BERNARDINO

42 San Bernardino

26

27

○ Burbank

○ Pasadena
Alhambra

West Covina

24

29

30

31

41

44

32

Santa Monica ○

○ Culver City

33

34

43

Downtown Los Angeles

35

○ Downey

39

Fullerton

47

Manhattan Beach ○

Torrance ○

37 38

○ Compton

46

RIVERSIDE

○ Garden Grove

○ Santa Ana

36

○ Long Beach

45

ORANGE

Irvine

48
SAN DIEGO

36

51

36

49

Commercial television stations, affiliations
ADI: Los Angeles (100%)

Cable television systems, total subscribers
King Videocable College; Tujunga 29,800
United Artist Cable; San Fernando 84,500
West Valley Cablevision: Chatsworth 71,669

Businesses and other major employers
Kaiser Foundation Hospitals; Van Nuys 3,000
Litton Industries Inc./Data Systems; Van Nuys; aircraft navigational systems 3,000
Olive View Medical Center; San Fernando 2,500
Southern California Permanente Medical Group; Van Nuys; medical service/health insurance 2,200
Price Pfister Inc.; Pacoima; plumbing/heating 1,800
Anheuser-Busch Inc.; Van Nuys; brewery 1,700
Health Dynamics Inc.; Van Nuys 1,590
U.S. Postal Service; Van Nuys 1,500
Valley Presbyterian Hospital; Van Nuys 1,400
ITT Corp./ITT Gilfillan; Van Nuys; search/navigation equipment 1,200
Smith Kline Beecham Clinical Labs; Van Nuys; medical/dental labs 1,200
May Department Stores Co.; Van Nuys; clothing stores 1,020
Superior Industries Intl.; Van Nuys; motor vehicle parts/equipment 1,000
Allied-Signal Inc./Ocean Defense Corp.; San Fernando; search/navigation equipment 1,000
Holy Cross Medical Center; San Fernando 885
Warnaco Group Inc./Olga Co.; Van Nuys; undergarments 800
GKN Automotive Inc.; San Fernando; motor vehicle parts/equipment 650
Valley Hospital; Van Nuys 650
Familian Corp.; Van Nuys; hardware/plumbing/heating 600
Allied-Signal Inc./Electrodynamics Div.; North Hollywood; search/navigation equipment 550

27th District

Northeastern Los Angeles County; Pasadena; Burbank

Set in the rolling San Gabriel Mountains, the 27th (see map on page 97) is dominated on the north by the Angeles National Forest and spread evenly with suburbs through the south.

The district is a mirror of the demographic changes that California has seen in the past decade. Immigration has transformed formerly white areas into rainbows of ethnicity. This development, along with new areas the 27th gained in redistricting, makes the once reliably Republican seat much more competitive.

Burbank, a city of 94,000 with a sizable share of conservative-minded Democrats, took a big hit in 1990 when Lockheed began closing its 64-year-old plant and moving or laying off the 12,000 workers there. The area is still heavily blue collar, but it now relies more on its entertainment industry, including the NBC and Disney studios. Burbank's City Council has been active in trying to fill the void left by Lockheed. Economic pain has served to moderate the city's traditional bias against growth: One idea floated has been to build an arena on the Lockheed site to lure the L.A. Clippers basketball team.

Glendale, with 180,000 residents, is the largest city in the

district and the third largest in Los Angeles County after L.A. proper and Long Beach. A decade or so ago, it was a sleepy, bedroom community, but no more. There has been an influx of about 35,000 Soviet Armenians since 1985, and large numbers of Filipinos, Koreans and Hispanics have settled here; now, less than half of Glendale's public school students speak English as a first language. The Soviet Armenians are joining a small, much wealthier, Iranian Armenian community that has lived in Glendale since the shah lost his grip on power in the late 1970s.

These changes have taken their toll on the city's onetime habit of supporting the GOP: In 1992, Bill Clinton won the city by about 100 votes—unthinkable just a few years before.

While Burbank and Glendale are less than 2 percent black, 19 percent of Pasadena's 132,000 residents are black; it is the heavily black and Hispanic half of Pasadena that the district gained in 1992 redistricting. The only part of Pasadena outside the 27th is a heavily Republican sliver to the east in the 28th District. The city includes many engineering firms that have flocked to CalTech and its Jet Propulsion Laboratory, which is a bit to the northwest in La Cañada.

Pasadena is flanked by the working-class suburbs of Altadena on the north and South Pasadena to the southwest, and by the very wealthy community of San Marino to the southeast. Altadena is 39 percent black and overwhelmingly Democratic, while South Pasadena is only 3 percent black and has always tended toward Republicans. Old-money San Marino, home to the Huntington Library and gardens, is a GOP mainstay.

Election Returns and Party Registration

	27th District	Democrat	Republican
1992	President*	98,057 (44.3%)	80,986 (36.6%)
	Senate †	97,685 (44.9%)	103,295 (47.5%)
	Senate †‡	108,198 (50.7%)	89,951 (42.1%)
	House †	83,805 (39.4%)	105,521 (49.7%)
1990	Governor	65,313 (38.7%)	95,585 (56.6%)
1988	President	95,699 (42.5%)	126,644 (56.3%)
	Senate	85,248 (38.3%)	131,379 (59.1%)
1986	Senate	78,792 (42.2%)	103,401 (55.4%)
	Governor	63,980 (34.1%)	120,996 (64.5%)
1993	Party registration †	119,543 (42.9%)	122,005 (43.8%)

*Vote for Perot was 42,071 (19.0%).   †Independent/other is greater than 5%.
‡Special election for the remaining two years of the term of Pete Wilson who was elected governor in 1990. Appointee John Seymour held the seat 1991-1992.

Demographics

Population 572,594

Percent change from 1980 8.9%

Land area 305 square miles

Population per square mile 1,879

Counties, 1990 population
Los Angeles (pt.) 572,594

Cities, 1990 population (10,000 or more)
Altadena CDP 42,658
Burbank (pt.) 93,643
Glendale (pt.) 180,038
La Cañada Flintridge 19,378

La Crescenta-Montrose CDP   16,968
Los Angeles (pt.)   53,494
Pasadena (pt.)   126,228
San Marino   12,959
South Pasadena   23,936

Race and Hispanic origin
White   70.9%
Black   8.3%
American Indian, Eskimo, or Aleut.   0.4%
Asian or Pacific Islander   10.5%
Other   9.8%
Hispanic origin   20.6%

Ancestry

American 1.8%	Italian 5.1%
Arabic 1.2%	Norwegian 1.4%
Dutch 1.7%	Polish 1.9%
English 12.9%	Russian 1.3%
French 3.1%	Scotch Irish 2.0%
German 14.9%	Scottish 2.6%
Irish 9.9%	Swedish 2.0%

Universities/colleges, 1990-1991 enrollment
Art Center College of Design, Pasadena   1,266
California Institute of Technology, Pasadena   1,861
Fuller Theological Seminary, Pasadena   2,159
Glendale Community College, Glendale   12,072
Pacific Oaks College, Pasadena   470
Pasadena City College, Pasadena   19,581
Woodbury University, Burbank   1,024

Newspapers, total circulation (in all districts)
Daily Variety   21,274
Los Angeles Daily News   208,005
Los Angeles La Opinion   98,557
Los Angeles Times   1,169,066
Pasadena Star News   39,771

Commercial television stations, affiliations
ADI: Los Angeles (100%)
   KABC-TV, Los Angeles (ABC)
   KCAL, Los Angeles (None)
   KCBS-TV, Los Angeles (CBS)
   KCOP, Los Angeles (None)
   KNBC-TV, Los Angeles (NBC)
   KTLA, Los Angeles (None)
   KTTV, Los Angeles (Fox)
   KWHY-TV, Los Angeles (None)
   KHSC, Ontario (None)
   KTBN-TV, Santa Ana (None)

Cable television systems, total subscribers
American Cablevision; South Pasadena   6,580
Cencom Cable TV; Pasadena   17,400
Cencom Cable TV; Altadena   9,500
King Videocable College; Tujunga   29,800
Sammons Communications Inc.; Glendale   65,000
United Artists Cable; San Fernando   84,500

Businesses and other major employers
California Institute of Technology/Jet Propulsion Laboratory;
   Pasadena; research services   5,000
Walt Disney Co. Inc.; Burbank; movie production/amusement
   parks   4,500
U.S. Postal Service; Pasadena   3,100

Parsons Corp.; Pasadena; heavy construction   3,000
NBC Inc.; Burbank; movie & television production   3,000
California Institute of Technology; Pasadena   2,600
Glendale Unified School District; Glendale   2,600
Huntington Memorial Hospital; Pasadena   2,500
Warner Bros. Inc.; Burbank; movie production   2,200
Pasadena Unified School District; Pasadena   2,100
Security Pacific Automation Co.; Glendale; computer ser-
   vices   2,000
City of Glendale; Glendale   1,935
Kaiser Foundation Health Plan; Pasadena; medical doctors
   1,700
Pasadena City College; Pasadena   1,607
Walt Disney Imagineering; Glendale; design/architectural ser-
   vices   1,500
Glendale Community College District; Glendale   1,400
Glendale Adventist Medical Center; Glendale   1,219
Nestle USA Inc.; Glendale; food products   1,200
Morrison Inc.; Glendale; bars/restaurants   1,000
City of Burbank/Water & Power Dept.; Burbank   1,000
Columbia Tri-Star Films; Burbank; movie production   1,000
Mel Bernie & Co. Inc.; Burbank; costume jewelry   950
Countrywide Funding Corp.; Pasadena; mortgage bankers
   900
Glendale Memorial Hospital; Glendale   900
Worldwide Church of God; Pasadena; religious organization
   875
GlenFed Inc.; Glendale; savings institutions   850
Citadel Holding Corp.; Glendale; savings institutions   827
Pasadena Financial Center Engr.; Pasadena; security and
   commodity services   800
Cigna Healthplan Inc.; Glendale; medical doctors   800
Datatape Inc.; Pasadena; audio/video equipment   750
Baxter Healthcare Corp.; Los Angeles; pharmaceuticals   700
Columbia Pictures Industries; Burbank; movie production
   700
Verdugo Hills Hospital; Glendale   675
Fuller Theological Seminary; Pasadena   670
Librascope Corp.; Glendale; search/navigation equipment
   650
Ritz-Carlton Huntington Hotel; Pasadena; hotel   650
Bendix Field Engineering Corp.; Pasadena; research services
   650
Coltec Industries Inc./Menasco Calif-Aerosystems Div.; Bur-
   bank; aircraft/parts   600
Crane Co./Hydro-Aire Div.; Burbank; aircraft/parts   600
Avon Products Inc.; Pasadena; nonstore retailers   600
James M. Montgomery; Pasadena; engineering/architectural
   services   550
Cadam Inc.; Burbank; computer services   550
Jacobs Engineering Group Inc.; Pasadena; heavy construc-
   tion   534
St. Luke's Medical Center; Pasadena   520
Aviall Inc.; Burbank; repair shops   510

28th District
Northeastern Los Angeles Suburbs

The Angeles National Forest and its mountains run through
the northern half of the 28th District (see map on page 97). The
210 Freeway, also known as the Foothill Freeway, runs through

the lower half, an area spread evenly with Los Angeles bedroom communities.

From west to east along the 210, the district takes in a sliver of eastern Pasadena and the cities of Sierra Madre, Arcadia, Monrovia, Covina and San Dimas. La Verne and Claremont lie farther east. Temple City is south of Arcadia, and West Covina and Walnut are to the south of Covina. These are comfortable suburbia neighborhoods typical of Southern California.

Much of the development here arrived right after World War II, and many of the people who arrived then are still here. In large part, these are people whose parents grew up nearby and whose children are now populating Orange County and San Bernardino.

Arcadia, a city of 48,000 with a 1989 per capita income of more than $25,000, boasts of its "beautiful homes, tree-lined streets, magnificent gardens and its more than 3,489 private swimming pools."

Driving through the district, it is hard to tell when one city has been left behind and another entered. The district just misses some much less wealthy areas, such as El Monte, southeast of Temple City. The industry that does exist here is confined to small defense subcontractors and service industries.

The city of Duarte, south of Monrovia, is known for its City of Hope National Medical Center, a nonprofit treatment and research hospital specializing in rare medical problems that treats its patients for free. Bradbury, a town of about 800 residents set in the hills just north of Duarte, had a per capita income of $46,361 in 1989.

While the residents of the 28th primarily identify themselves as citizens of the separate towns in which they live, they also identify as residents of the San Gabriel Valley. Although many of them commute to downtown Los Angeles for work, they do not consider themselves part of that city—so much so that residents have agitated unsuccessfully for years to declare the San Gabriel Valley a county of its own. The cities within the valley work closely together on such issues as transportation and water. A light rail line stops in Covina and continues west into Los Angeles.

Politically, the district is spread as evenly as its buildings. The seven-term GOP House incumbent won in 1992 by a steady margin across the district. That same year George Bush won the district with 41 percent of the vote to Bill Clinton's 38 percent. As in many of Los Angeles' suburbs, residents here tend to be socially moderate and economically conservative.

Election Returns and Party Registration

	28th District	Democrat	Republican
1992	President*	82,958 (37.8%)	90,644 (41.3%)
	Senate †	79,584 (36.9%)	118,217 (54.8%)
	Senate †‡	95,128 (44.8%)	99,638 (46.9%)
	House †	76,525 (36.5%)	122,353 (58.4%)
1990	Governor †	58,254 (34.2%)	102,725 (60.3%)
1988	President	83,297 (36.4%)	142,437 (62.3%)
	Senate	76,053 (33.6%)	145,088 (64.0%)
1986	Senate	74,354 (41.3%)	99,367 (55.2%)
	Governor	60,077 (33.2%)	117,184 (64.8%)
1993	Party registration †	114,203 (41.4%)	127,834 (46.3%)

*Vote for Perot was 45,623 (20.8%).   †Independent/other is greater than 5%.
‡Special election for the remaining two years of the term of Pete Wilson who was elected governor in 1990. Appointee John Seymour held the seat 1991-1992.

Demographics

Population 572,927

Percent change from 1980 9.0%

Land area 464 square miles

Population per square mile 1,234

Counties, 1990 population
Los Angeles (pt.) 572,927

Cities, 1990 population (10,000 or more)

Arcadia (pt.) 48,283	Monrovia 35,761
Claremont 32,503	Pomona (pt.) 25,076
Covina 43,207	San Dimas 32,397
Duarte (pt.) 20,688	Sierra Madre 10,762
East San Gabriel CDP (pt.) 10,649	Temple City (pt.) 30,549
	Vincent CDP (pt.) 11,096
Glendora (pt.) 47,295	Walnut 29,105
La Verne 30,897	West Covina (pt.) 92,126

Race and Hispanic origin
White 70.9%
Black 5.7%
American Indian, Eskimo, or Aleut. 0.5%
Asian or Pacific Islander 13.0%
Other 9.8%
Hispanic origin 24.1%

Ancestry

American 1.9%	Italian 5.5%
Dutch 2.1%	Norwegian 1.4%
English 13.9%	Polish 1.9%
French 3.5%	Scotch Irish 2.2%
German 17.7%	Scottish 2.5%
Irish 11.9%	Swedish 2.2%

Universities/colleges, 1990-1991 enrollment
Azusa Pacific University, Azusa 3,159
Citrus College, Glendora 8,786
Claremont Graduate School, Claremont 1,678
Claremont McKenna College, Claremont 849
Harvey Mudd College, Claremont 583
ITT Technical Institute, West Covina 687
Life Bible College, San Dimas 341
Mount San Antonio College, Walnut 20,563
Pacific Coast Bible College, San Dimas 220
Pitzer College, Claremont 828
Pomona College, Claremont 1,384
School of Theology at Claremont, Claremont 249
Scripps College, Claremont 635
University of La Verne, La Verne 6,130

Newspapers, total circulation (in all districts)
Daily Variety 21,274
Inland Valley Daily Bulletin 73,003
Los Angeles Daily News 208,005
Los Angeles La Opinion 98,557
Los Angeles Times 1,169,066
Pasadena Star News 39,771
San Gabriel Valley Tribune 63,573
Whittier Daily News 16,802

Commercial television stations, affiliations
ADI: Los Angeles (100%)

KDOC-TV, Anaheim (None)
KRCA, Riverside (None)
KAGL, San Bernardino (None)
KSCI, San Bernardino (None)

Cable television systems, total subscribers
Continental Cablevision of California, Covina 9,500
Cencom Cable TV; Monterey Park 54,000
Cencom Cable TV; West Covina 18,000
Jones Intercable Inc.; Walnut Valley 16,653
Southwestern Cable; Black Mountain 157,000

Businesses and other major employers
Claremont Graduate School; Claremont; building services 3,167
Mount San Antonio College, Walnut 2,500
Pomona Valley Hospital & Medical Center; Pomona 2,226
Inter-Community Health Services; Covina 1,400
Queen of the Valley Hospital; West Covina 1,250
Methodist Hospital; Arcadia 1,200
McDonnell Douglas Corp.; Monrovia; search/navigation equipment 1,000
Vons Co. Inc.; Arcadia; grocery stores 900
Fedco Inc.; Pasadena; department stores 820
Monrovia Unified School District; Monrovia 820
Arcadia Unified School District; Arcadia 760
Citrus Community College District; Glendora 615
Peterson Industries; Arcadia; laundry services 608
Miles Inc./Cutter Labs; Covina; pharmaceuticals 600
Automatic Data Proc.; San Dimas; computer services 550
World Vision Inc.; Monrovia; religious organization 532
Loral Electro-Optical Systems; Pomona; communications equipment 525
Ormco Corp.; Glendora; medical instruments/supplies 524
National Service Industries/Lithonia West; La Puente; electric lighting 512

29th District

West Los Angeles County; Santa Monica; West Hollywood

The 29th begins at the coast in Santa Monica and curves northeast to take in some of California's best-known areas: West Los Angeles, Beverly Hills, West Hollywood, most of Hollywood, the Hollywood Hills and just a bit of the San Fernando Valley (see map on page 97). This affluent, predominantly white district is heavily Democratic.

The city of Santa Monica is strikingly more liberal than its coastal counterparts south of Los Angeles. The city gave 55 percent of its vote to Walter F. Mondale in 1984, 65 percent to Michael S. Dukakis in 1988 and 63 percent to Bill Clinton in 1992. George Bush took 21 percent in 1992.

Santa Monica voters in 1988 supported a proposition—which was soundly defeated statewide—to use fines paid by violators of housing and restaurant codes to increase funding for the hungry and the homeless.

Although Santa Monica's 87,000 residents are mostly affluent, the city has a large renter population; 75 percent of the city's housing units are occupied by renters, who have brought about very strict rent-control laws over the years. It boasts substantially more commercial activity than Malibu, its northern neighbor, with several very successful commercial-industrial parks, shopping malls and regular street fairs.

The city and its environs grew steadily in the 1980s; Pacific Palisades, just north of Santa Monica right on the coast, has some large new developments, but because so much of the area is already fully developed, much of the new construction consists of knocking down existing structures and replacing them.

Heading out of the city on Santa Monica Boulevard, the flat land turns to the rolling foothills of the Santa Monica Mountains. Set onto the hills' southern slopes are Westwood, home to the University of California-Los Angeles (with 36,400 students), and Bel Air, the retirement home of the Reagans.

Just past Westwood is Beverly Hills, with its fabulously elaborate homes north of Sunset Boulevard and low-rise (but high-rent) apartment buildings south of it.

The residents of the heavily Jewish area of Fairfax, just east of Beverly Hills, have supported Democratic Rep. Henry Waxman, both financially and with high voter registration and turnout, devotedly since his first win in 1974.

Farther east along the boulevard is West Hollywood, a city of 36,000 residents that was incorporated in 1984. It has a large, politically well-organized homosexual population and a high concentration of senior citizens.

Districtwide, Waxman ran well in 1992, racking up 57 percent of the vote in Santa Monica, 65 percent in Beverly Hills and 68 percent in West Hollywood.

Before reapportionment, many of the motion-picture industry's heavyweights were packed into one district. Now they are split between two: the 29th retains the bulk of the Hollywood area and all of Universal City to the north, but the 30th District pokes up just enough to take in the Paramount Studios lot and the southeastern side of Hollywood—including the eastern half of the intersection of Hollywood Boulevard and Vine Street, the symbolic center of the movie industry.

Election Returns and Party Registration

	29th District	Democrat	Republican
1992	President*	183,233 (66.3%)	55,924 (20.2%)
	Senate	183,811 (67.7%)	74,572 (27.4%)
	Senate ‡	195,266 (72.5%)	63,449 (23.6%)
	House †	160,312 (61.3%)	67,141 (25.7%)
1990	Governor	126,163 (62.2%)	70,103 (34.5%)
1988	President	171,064 (63.5%)	95,908 (35.6%)
	Senate	154,612 (58.1%)	105,451 (39.7%)
1986	Senate	140,270 (64.6%)	73,795 (34.0%)
	Governor	111,814 (51.3%)	101,280 (46.5%)
1993	Party registration †	194,815 (57.8%)	90,187 (26.8%)

*Vote for Perot was 37,217 (13.5%). †Independent/other is greater than 5%.
‡Special election for the remaining two years of the term of Pete Wilson who was elected governor in 1990. Appointee John Seymour held the seat 1991-1992.

Demographics

Population 571,566

Percent change from 1980 8.7%

Land area 118 square miles

Population per square mile 4,847

Counties, 1990 population
Los Angeles (pt.) 571,566

Cities, 1990 population (10,000 or more)

Beverly Hills (pt.) 31,971	Santa Monica 86,905
Los Angeles (pt.) 415,442	West Hollywood 36,118

Race and Hispanic origin

White 83.8%
Black 3.5%
American Indian, Eskimo, or Aleut. 0.3%
Asian or Pacific Islander 7.7%
Other 4.7%
Hispanic origin 13.2%

Ancestry

American 2.6%	Irish 9.1%
Arabic 1.2%	Italian 4.8%
Austrian 1.5%	Norwegian 1.1%
Dutch 1.2%	Polish 5.6%
English 11.5%	Russian 10.6%
French 3.6%	Scotch Irish 1.6%
German 13.4%	Scottish 2.3%
Hungarian 2.0%	Swedish 1.7%

Universities/colleges, 1990-1991 enrollment

Mount St. Mary's College, Los Angeles 1,179
Southern California Institute of Architecture, Santa Monica 376
Santa Monica College, Santa Monica 18,108
University of California, Los Angeles 36,427

Newspapers, total circulation (in all districts)

Daily Variety 21,274
Los Angeles Daily News 208,005
Los Angeles La Opinion 98,557
Los Angeles Times 1,169,066
Santa Monica Outlook 26,324

Commercial television stations, affiliations

ADI: Los Angeles (100%)

Cable television systems, total subscribers

Century Cable; Eagle Rock 40,107
Century Cable; Pacific Palisades 7,729
Century Cable; Santa Monica 44,829
Century Cable; Sherman Oaks 36,635

Businesses and other major employers

University of California; Los Angeles 20,000
Universal City Studios Inc.; North Hollywood; movie production 7,000
Cedars-Sinai Medical Center; Los Angeles 6,000
Capital Cities/ABC Inc.; Los Angeles; radio/TV broadcasting 5,000
MCA Inc./MCA TV; North Hollywood; movie production 5,000
Kaiser Foundation Hospitals; Los Angeles 4,396
UCLA Medical Center; Los Angeles 4,119
U.S. Veterans Affairs Dept.; Los Angeles; hospital 4,000
Caesars New Jersey Inc./Circus Maximus; Los Angeles; hotels/motels 3,500
Medical Management Consultants; Los Angeles; management/public relations 3,125
UCLA Associated Students; Los Angeles; retail stores 2,500
State of California/Neurological Psychiatric Institute; Los Angeles 2,000
Farmers Group Inc.; Los Angeles; fire/marine/casualty insurance 1,767

Continental Graphics Corp.; Los Angeles; commercial printing 1,500
Twentieth Century-Fox TV Intl.; Los Angeles; radio/TV broadcasting 1,400
CBS Inc.; Los Angeles; radio/TV broadcasting 1,200
Century Plaza Hotel Co.; Los Angeles; hotel 1,200
Unihealth America/Santa Monica Hospital & Medical Center; Santa Monica 1,175
Santa Monica Comunity College; Santa Monica 1,140
Rand Corp.; Santa Monica; research services 1,100
World Book Inc.; North Hollywood; nonstore retailers 1,000
Associated Hosts Inc.; Beverly Hills; restaurants & hotels 1,000
Gillette Co./Papermate Div.; Santa Monica; office supplies 900
CBS Inc./CBS Television Network; Los Angeles; radio/TV broadcasting 894
First Executive Corp.; Los Angeles; life insurance 825
Griffin Group Inc./Beverly Hilton; Beverly Hills; hotel 825
Lear Astronics Corp.; Santa Monica; aircraft/parts 800
National Medical Enterprises/Hospital Group; Santa Monica; building construction 800
Pinkerton's Inc.; Santa Monica; business/security services 800
Regent Beverly Wilshire; Beverly Hills; hotel 800
Teledyne Industries Inc./Teledyne Controls Div.; Los Angeles; electronic components 750
Princess Cruises Inc.; Los Angeles; cruise line 700
Church of Scientology Intl./Golden Era Productions; Los Angeles; religious organization/movie production 700
U.S. Justice Dept./FBI; Los Angeles 700
City of Beverly Hills: Beverly Hills 650
National Medical Enterprises/Century City Hospital; Los Angeles 650
Petersen Publishing Co.; Los Angeles; periodical publishing 600
Sajahtera Inc./Beverly Hills Hotel; Beverly Hills; hotel 600
Candle Corp.; Los Angeles; computer services 540
Marriott Corp.; Los Angeles; hotels/motels 515
Johnson & Higgins California; Los Angeles; insurance services 509
Transaction Technology Inc.; Santa Monica; computer services 504

30th District

Central, East and Southeast Los Angeles

This very densely populated district starts just west of downtown Los Angeles, swings up and around, and comes down on downtown's eastern side (see map on page 97). The western side of the 30th—East Hollywood, the mid-Wilshire area and especially Koreatown—was hit hard by the May 1992 riots.

Koreatown is in an extremely compact corner in the 30th's southwest region. More than 100,000 Koreans live here. The area sustained some of the worst damage in the city. Rioters torched more than 300 businesses, and damage was estimated at $200 million, according to local media reports.

Voter registration is low in the 30th, and even lower in Koreatown, described as a "transitional area," with many recent arrivals who are either illegal or applying for residency. The community itself is in transition; Koreans are just now beginning to flex their political muscle. Koreatown tends to look inward and does not rely on tourism as heavily as do Chinatown and Little Tokyo.

Just north of Koreatown is the mid-Wilshire area, with high-rise office buildings along Wilshire Boulevard and apartment buildings everywhere else. Farther north is East Hollywood, less dense and less affluent than the mid-Wilshire area. It is a lower-middle-class community; the homes get bigger and more expensive to the west, in the 29th District. These areas also suffered in the riots, but not nearly as much as Koreatown.

Dodger Stadium, north of downtown in Elysian Park, serves as the 30th's centerpiece. Elysian Park is a blue-collar neighborhood, with a moderate number of Hispanics. Directly west of Elysian Park are the communities of Silver Lake (half of which is in the 29th, half in the 30th) and Echo Park, which have strong reputations for community activism and liberal voting patterns. The areas are troubled by some gang activity and "tagging"—the local term for graffiti. An estimated one-fourth of their residents are homosexual.

On the northeastern end of the district is the bedroom community of Eagle Rock, a hilly, middle-class pocket of relative affluence that votes Democratic, but whose leanings are more toward the center than other parts of the 30th. Dropping down the eastern side leads to Highland Park, a heavily Hispanic, blue-collar area with a significant Mexican immigrant presence.

Across the Pasadena Freeway from Highland Park is Lincoln Heights, and on the district's southeastern tip, Boyle Heights. Both are more than 80 percent Hispanic, according to some estimates.

Between Boyle Heights and Lincoln Heights is tiny Mount Washington, the 30th's most affluent section, with great views of the city and a reputation for social activism.

The district is overwhelmingly Democratic, although it showed some of the strongest support in California for third-party candidates in 1992 House voting. Green Party and Peace and Freedom Party candidates scored 8 percent and 7 percent, respectively. Bill Clinton drew 63 percent in the 30th, far ahead of George Bush's 24 percent and Ross Perot's 13 percent.

Election Returns and Party Registration

	30th District	Democrat	Republican
1992	President*	56,378 (62.7%)	21,750 (24.2%)
	Senate †	53,945 (61.2%)	26,741 (30.3%)
	Senate †‡	57,614 (66.7%)	22,472 (26.0%)
	House †	48,800 (58.4%)	20,034 (24.0%)
1990	Governor †	33,861 (56.8%)	22,330 (37.5%)
1988	President	57,191 (62.8%)	32,511 (35.7%)
	Senate	51,599 (57.8%)	33,607 (37.7%)
1986	Senate	48,686 (63.2%)	26,712 (34.7%)
	Governor	42,430 (54.4%)	33,571 (43.0%)
1993	Party registration †	78,834 (61.2%)	29,945 (23.3%)

*Vote for Perot was 11,842 (13.2%). †Independent/other is greater than 5%. ‡Special election for the remaining two years of the term of Pete Wilson who was elected governor in 1990. Appointee John Seymour held the seat 1991-1992.

Demographics

Population 572,538

Percent change from 1980 9.1%

Land area 37 square miles

Population per square mile 15,372

Counties, 1990 population
Los Angeles (pt.) 572,538

Cities, 1990 population (10,000 or more)
Los Angeles (pt.) 572,403

Race and Hispanic origin
White 43.6%
Black 3.5%
American Indian, Eskimo, or Aleut. 0.5%
Asian or Pacific Islander 21.3%
Other 31.1%
Hispanic origin 61.5%

Ancestry
American 1.2%   Irish 2.5%
English 2.8%   Italian 1.4%
German 3.4%

Universities/colleges, 1990-1991 enrollment
Cleveland Chiropractic College, Los Angeles 376
Los Angeles City College, Los Angeles 14,479
Occidental College, Los Angeles 1,672
Southwestern University School, Los Angeles 1,103
West Coast University, Los Angeles 1,205

Newspapers, total circulation (in all districts)
Daily Variety 21,274
Los Angeles Daily News 208,005
Los Angeles La Opinion 98,557
Los Angeles Times 1,169,066
Pasadena Star News 39,771

Commercial television stations, affiliations
ADI: Los Angeles (100%)

Cable television systems, total subscribers
Continental Cablevision of California; Culver City 43,000
Century Cable; Eagle Rock 40,107

Businesses and other major employers
County of Los Angeles/USC Medical Center; Los Angeles 9,000
Children's Hospital of Los Angeles; Los Angeles 3,176
Carter Hawley Hale Stores Inc./Broadway; Los Angeles; department stores 2,500
WCS Ltd.; Los Angeles; building services 2,300
White Memorial Medical Center; Los Angeles 1,431
Pedus Building Services Inc.; Los Angeles; building services 1,400
Hollywood Presbyterian Hospital; Los Angeles 1,200
Paramount Pictures Corp.; Los Angeles; movie production 1,150
Evans Community Adult School; Los Angeles 1,064
County of Los Angeles/Engineer Facilities Dept.; Los Angeles; 1,000
County of Los Angeles/Parks & Recreation Dept.; Los Angeles 1,000
Shield Security Inc.; Los Angeles; business/security services 1,000
Thrifty Corp.; Los Angeles; drug stores 763
Metropolitan Water District; Los Angeles; 700
Ralphs Grocery Co.; Los Angeles; grocery stores 700

CBS Inc./KNX-AM; Los Angeles; radio/TV broadcasting
650

Goodwill Industries of Southern California; Los Angeles;
thrift stores 650

Daniel Mann Johnson Mendenhall; Los Angeles;
engineering/architectural services 600

McKesson Corp. Maryland; Los Angeles; grocery products
540

31st District

Eastern Los Angeles County; El Monte; Alhambra; Azusa

The middle-income, blue-collar 31st takes in the southern San Gabriel Valley heading west from its section of East Los Angeles to Azusa, including along the way a handful of good-size, independent cities (see map on page 97). The influx of Hispanics to the area is turning even the district's Republican areas Democratic.

Hispanics make up 59 percent of the district's population but just 42 percent of its voters; Asians are 23 percent of the 31st but just 10 percent of its voters. This pattern of low minority registration is seen throughout Los Angeles.

Like many members of newly arrived immigrant groups, the district's Hispanics and Asians identify strongly with the Democratic Party despite cultural patterns that might otherwise tag them as conservatives. In the 31st, 59 percent of the residents register Democratic and 28 percent register Republican.

A number of engineers live here and work for small employers in the district or head south toward Long Beach. Many Los Angeles municipal and county employees call the 31st home as well.

The East Los Angeles section of the 31st is the residential section of that lower-income community; its business neighborhoods are south, in the 34th.

Monterey Park and San Gabriel are the relatively wealthy areas of the district. Almost 60 percent of Monterey Park's 61,000 residents are Asian, and more than 30 percent are Hispanic. San Gabriel is now about one-third Asian and one-third Hispanic. Less than 1 percent of each city's residents are black. Republicans used to be able to count on San Gabriel's residents, but the Democratic House nominee won the city in 1992.

In the middle of the district are Rosemead, South El Monte and El Monte. Half of Rosemead's 52,000 residents are Hispanic, 85 percent of South El Monte's population of 21,000 is and nearly three-fourths of El Monte's 106,000 inhabitants are.

Baldwin Park resembles the East Los Angeles part of the 31st; its residents' incomes range from the middle of the spectrum to the poverty level.

Most of the business in the district is small and midsize. Irwindale has a few exceptions, such as a Miller Brewing Co. facility, one of the district's largest employers. Many of the city's rock quarries have been converted into industrial parks. Heavy industry exists only outside the district, in such nearby areas as Vernon.

Farthest to the east, Azusa is another former Republican stronghold that now leans Democratic. The city has been able to attract a concentration of high-tech companies.

The San Gabriel Valley is said to be more moderate than L.A.'s east side, and less likely than other parts of Los Angeles County to stick to partisan lines, but the 31st stuck pretty close

to those lines in 1992. Bill Clinton won the 31st with 52 percent of the vote, above his statewide average.

Election Returns and Party Registration

		31st District	Democrat	Republican
1992	President*		59,616 (51.7%)	37,250 (32.3%)
	Senate †		54,776 (48.9%)	45,981 (41.1%)
	Senate †‡		63,156 (57.7%)	36,905 (33.7%)
	House		68,324 (62.6%)	40,873 (37.4%)
1990	Governor †		39,444 (48.4%)	36,805 (45.1%)
1988	President		65,313 (53.5%)	55,610 (45.6%)
	Senate		60,849 (50.6%)	54,158 (45.0%)
1986	Senate		60,193 (56.9%)	42,807 (40.5%)
	Governor		48,184 (45.0%)	55,343 (51.7%)
1993	Party registration †		96,676 (58.5%)	46,238 (28.0%)

*Vote for Perot was 18,449 (16.0%).   †Independent/other is greater than 5%.
‡Special election for the remaining two years of the term of Pete Wilson who was elected governor in 1990. Appointee John Seymour held the seat 1991-1992.*

Demographics

Population 572,643

Percent change from 1980 8.8%

Land area 75 square miles

Population per square mile 7,593

Counties, 1990 population
Los Angeles (pt.) 572,643

Cities, 1990 population (10,000 or more)

Alhambra 82,106	Los Angeles (pt.) 29,468
Azusa (pt.) 39,583	Monterey Park (pt.) 60,738
Baldwin Park (pt.) 68,300	Rosemead (pt.) 51,153
East Los Angeles CDP	San Gabriel (pt.) 36,987
(pt.) 49,060	South El Monte 20,850
El Monte (pt.) 105,444	

Race and Hispanic origin
White 48.3%
Black 1.7%
American Indian, Eskimo, or Aleut. 0.5%
Asian or Pacific Islander 22.8%
Other 26.7%
Hispanic origin 58.5%

Ancestry

American 1.2%	German 4.7%
English 3.5%	Irish 3.5%
French 1.2%	Italian 2.1%

Universities/colleges, 1990-1991 enrollment
California School of Professional Psychology, Alhambra 503
California State University, Los Angeles 17,960
Don Bosco Technical Institute, Rosemead 276
East Los Angeles College, Monterey Park 12,447

Newspapers, total circulation (in all districts)
Daily Variety 21,274
Los Angeles La Opinion 98,557
Los Angeles Times 1,169,066
Pasadena Star News 39,771

Commercial television stations, affiliations
ADI: Los Angeles (100%)

Cable television systems, total subscribers
Cencom Cable TV; Azusa 6,400
Cencom Cable TV; Monterey Park 54,000
Liberty Cable; El Monte 6,450
Buenavision Cable TV; East Los Angeles 5,960

Businesses and other major employers
County of Los Angeles; Los Angeles; building services 5,000
Southern California Edison Co.; Rosemead; electric services 3,800
Aerojet-General Corp.; Azusa; research services 2,500
Wells Fargo Bank/Data Processing Center; El Monte; computer services 2,500
California Federal Bank; Rosemead; savings institutions 2,000
Inter-Con Security Systems; Alhambra; security services 1,500
County of Los Angeles/Public Works Dept.; Alhambra 1,500
C. F. Braun Inc.; Alhambra; engineering/architectural services 1,400
Home Savings of America; Baldwin Park; savings institutions 1,200
Miller Brewing Co.; Baldwin Park; brewery 1,036
Alpha Therapeutic Corp.; Los Angeles; drugs 1,000
County of Los Angeles; Baldwin Park 1,000
Garfield Medical Center; Monterey Park 900
City of El Monte; El Monte 740
Monrovia Nursery Co.; Azusa; horticultural specialties 723
Optical Radiation Corp.; Azusa; ophthalmic goods 720
Baxter Healthcare Corp./Baxter Pharmaseal Division; Baldwin Park; medical instruments/supplies 700
Southern California Rapid Transit District; El Monte; bus facilities 700
Ticor of California; Rosemead; title insurance 700
South Coast Air Quality Mgt. District; El Monte 700
San Gabriel Valley Medical Center; San Gabriel 596
A. J. Industries Inc./Sargent-Fletcher Co.; El Monte; aircraft/parts 550
Jewelry Dept. Inc.; Alhambra; costume jewelry 548

32nd District

West Los Angeles; Culver City

This compact, diverse district begins about a mile inland from Venice Beach, runs east through Culver City and ends up in south-central Los Angeles (see map on page 97). Sandwiched between these areas are dozens of distinct ethnic neighborhoods.

Economically, the 32nd runs the gamut, taking in very wealthy neighborhoods such as Rancho Park in the north, middle- and upper-middle-income suburbs in the west and very poor sections of south-central Los Angeles in the east.

This area is undergoing its second demographic sea change in 30 years. A generation ago, its Jewish population migrated toward the district's northwest end, and the center of the district became predominantly black.

Now there is a new wave of immigrants: Hispanics. Blacks are still the district's largest racial group, but their dominance is slipping as more blacks migrate toward Los Angeles' suburbs. Of the district's residents, 40 percent are black, 30 percent are Hispanic and 8 percent are Asian.

Despite vast differences between the district's neighborhoods—the Baldwin Hills area actually features operating oil wells—a huge majority of the people in the 32nd vote Democratic: Three-fourths of the district's registered voters are Democrats; only 13 percent are Republicans. In 1992, Bill Clinton won his highest level of support in Southern California here, taking 78 percent of the vote. George Bush got only 13 percent.

The eastern end of the 32nd is a black working-class area; moving north, the concentration of Hispanics increases. The northeast, near Pico Union, has considerable multifamily housing; to the southeast there are more single-family homes and higher levels of home ownership.

While south-central Los Angeles could be described as "blighted," it is not the type of blight typically found in the very poor areas of Chicago or New York. South-central's blight shows itself in its commercial districts rather than in its residential areas; its residents actually live in fairly well-maintained, older single-family homes.

South-central's commercial areas suffered some of the worst violence during the city's 1992 riots. Many of the stores targeted were owned by Koreans who had been attracted to the area's low property costs. The epicenters of the riot were elsewhere, but substantial violence traveled up Crenshaw Boulevard from Inglewood and down Western Avenue from Koreatown.

Curiously, none of this area used to be known as south-central Los Angeles. South-central traditionally has been thought of as being farther east, but post-riot media coverage has widened the term's scope. "Apparently, anywhere blacks live is now south-central," says an observer.

On the issues, people living on the 32nd's eastern side tend to have crime and economic concerns uppermost in mind, while residents on the western side of the district tend to mirror the coast's high level of environmental concern.

Election Returns and Party Registration

	32nd District	Democrat	Republican
1992	President*	147,623 (78.0%)	23,956 (12.7%)
	Senate †	141,380 (76.5%)	33,451 (18.1%)
	Senate ‡	146,764 (80.5%)	27,613 (15.1%)
	House †	150,644 (87.2%)	—
1990	Governor	101,573 (74.7%)	29,698 (21.9%)
1988	President	155,876 (78.4%)	40,460 (20.4%)
	Senate	146,919 (75.2%)	44,610 (22.8%)
1986	Senate	130,438 (80.9%)	28,723 (17.8%)
	Governor	123,774 (75.2%)	39,225 (23.8%)
1993	Party registration †	196,761 (76.1%)	33,949 (13.1%)

*Vote for Perot was 17,561 (9.3%). †Independent/other is greater than 5%.
‡Special election for the remaining two years of the term of Pete Wilson who was elected governor in 1990. Appointee John Seymour held the seat 1991-1992.*

Demographics

Population 572,595

Percent change from 1980 8.5%

Land area 47 square miles

Population per square mile 12,161

Counties, 1990 population
Los Angeles (pt.) 572,595

Cities, 1990 population (10,000 or more)

Culver City 38,793
Los Angeles (pt.) 514,832

View Park-Windsor Hills
CDP 11,769

Race and Hispanic origin

White 32.2%
Black 40.3%
American Indian, Eskimo, or Aleut. 0.4%
Asian or Pacific Islander 7.9%
Other 19.2%
Hispanic origin 30.2%

Ancestry

American 1.7%
English 3.7%
French 1.4%
German 5.0%
Irish 3.4%

Italian 1.6%
Polish 1.8%
Russian 2.7%
West Indian 1.6%

Universities/colleges, 1990-1991 enrollment

Los Angeles Trade Tech College, Los Angeles 12,030
University of Southern California, Los Angeles 29,657
University of West Los Angeles, Los Angeles 704
West Los Angeles College, Culver City 8,282

Newspapers, total circulation (in all districts)

Daily Variety 21,274
Los Angeles Daily News 208,005
Los Angeles La Opinion 98,557
Los Angeles Times 1,169,066
Santa Monica Outlook 26,324

Commercial television stations, affiliations

ADI: Los Angeles (100%)

Cable television systems, total subscribers

Continental Cablevision of California; Culver City 43,000
Continental Cablevision of California; Westchester 19,698

Businesses and other major employers

University of Southern California; Los Angeles 14,000
Avnet Inc./Hamilton; Culver City; electrical goods 6,500
UCLA Medical Centerr/Los Angeles County Hospital; Los Angeles 6,000
Los Angeles Memorial Coliseum; Los Angeles; commercial sports 2,045
Kaiser Foundation Hospitals; Los Angeles 2,000
Baker Industries Inc.; Culver City; security services 1,700
McDonnell Douglas Corp.; Culver City; helicopters 1,600
ISS Intl. Services; Los Angeles; building services 1,500
Los Angeles Trade Tech College; Los Angeles 1,500
Los Angeles County Flood Control District; Los Angeles 1,136
Brotman Medical Center; Culver City 1,100
La Gear California Inc.; Los Angeles; apparel/shoes 1,008
Enslow Health Professionals/Nursing Care Professionals; Los Angeles; personnel supply services 1,000
American Airlines Inc.; Los Angeles; airline 1,000
California Federal Bank; Los Angeles: commercial banks; 1,000
Continental Baking Co./Hostess; Los Angeles; bakery products 900
University of Southern California/Dentistry; Los Angeles 900
Goffman Services Inc.; Culver City; building maintenance 900
Los Angeles Community Adult School; Los Angeles 808
TW Services Inc.; Los Angeles; bars/restaurants 800
Midway Hospital & Medical Center; Los Angeles 700
West Los Angeles College; Culver City 700
MGM-Pathe Communications Co.; Culver City; movie production 700
City of Culver City; Culver City 650
Upjohn Co.; Los Angeles; home health services 600

33rd District

East-Central Los Angeles

The 33rd (see map on page 97) is a poor, densely populated and heavily Hispanic area that avoided further economic trouble by being just east of Los Angeles' worst May 1992 rioting.

The section of south-central in the 33rd is mostly residential and was hit less by the riots than south-central's business districts.

The northwest corner of the 33rd, the downtown area, is composed primarily of office buildings. It is laced with Los Angeles' legendary crowded expressways. Some residents live in single-room-occupancy hotels and shelters for homeless families and women, but the bulk of this area's people live just north and south of downtown in Pico Union and Chinatown. Stores in Pico Union's downtown area were looted in the riots, but the wholesale destruction seen in most of south-central did not occur.

Two cities in the district's midsection, Commerce and Vernon, house much of the 33rd's industry, with facilities including food processing plants and metal-plating operations. The district depends less on military contractors than much of the rest of Los Angeles, so neither the defense industry's 1980s boom nor its early 1990s problems played much of a role in the economy here.

Economic development is a perennial issue in the economically struggling 33rd. Bright spots include "green" industries, such as recycling companies, that are opening.

The southeast areas of the district, including Cudahy, Maywood, Bell and Bell Gardens, are very poor, very densely populated and primarily residential, tending to have more single-family homes than apartment buildings.

The development in the district's southern region is very even; it is difficult to distinguish one community from another without a map. Most of the housing stock here was built in the 1960s and 1970s. It is different from the development found on the east side and downtown, where the bulk of the housing is 30 to 40 years older.

South Gate lies just south of Cudahy. This city has successfully converted itself over the past several years from heavy industries to small businesses and light manufacturing. It is not as Democratic as the rest of the district; it voted Republican for president throughout the 1980s.

Los Angeles' new Red Line subway, opened in January 1993 inside the 33rd, holds the promise of creating economic development, as does the Blue Line commuter train that runs from Long Beach to downtown through much of the district.

The 33rd tops the state in two areas: It is 84 percent Hispanic, and 92 percent of its residents are members of minority groups. But fewer voters are registered in this district than in any other in the state—just 86,991. No other district has fewer than 100,000 registered voters.

In 1992, turnout here was so low that Bill Clinton's 63 percent of the vote translated to only 33,642 votes—the smallest number cast for Clinton in any California district.

Election Returns and Party Registration

	33rd District	Democrat	Republican
1992	President*	33,642 (63.0%)	12,607 (23.6%)
	Senate †	30,880 (59.3%)	15,587 (29.9%)
	Senate †‡	33,596 (65.8%)	13,206 (25.9%)
	House †	32,010 (63.0%)	15,428 (30.4%)
1990	Governor †	20,095 (56.6%)	13,517 (38.1%)
1988	President	36,490 (63.2%)	20,673 (35.8%)
	Senate †	33,674 (59.1%)	20,440 (35.8%)
1986	Senate	28,945 (64.9%)	14,507 (32.5%)
	Governor	25,353 (56.2%)	18,786 (41.6%)
1993	Party registration †	59,718 (66.6%)	18,298 (20.4%)

*Vote for Perot was 7,149 (13.4%).   †Independent/other is greater than 5%.
‡Special election for the remaining two years of the term of Pete Wilson who was elected governor in 1990. Appointee John Seymour held the seat 1991-1992.

Demographics

Population   570,943

Percent change from 1980   8.5%

Land area   48 square miles

Population per square mile   11,940

Counties, 1990 population
Los Angeles (pt.)   570,943

Cities, 1990 population (10,000 or more)

Bell Gardens (pt.) 42,355	Huntington Park 56,065
Bell 34,365	Los Angeles (pt.) 214,359
Commerce (pt.) 12,083	Maywood 27,850
Cudahy 22,817	South Gate 86,284
East Los Angeles CDP (pt.) 25,216	Walnut Park CDP 14,722
Florence-Graham CDP (pt.) 34,672	

Race and Hispanic origin
White   35.7%
Black   4.5%
American Indian, Eskimo, or Aleut.   0.6%
Asian or Pacific Islander   4.3%
Other   55.0%
Hispanic origin   83.7%

Ancestry
American   1.5%   German   1.9%
English   1.3%   Irish   1.5%

Universities/colleges, 1990-1991 enrollment
Biola University, La Mirada   2,576
Fashion Institute of Design & Merchandising, Los Angeles   1,583
Otis Art Institute of Parsons School of Design, Los Angeles   783

Newspapers, total circulation (in all districts)
Daily Variety   21,274
Los Angeles La Opinion   98,557
Los Angeles Times   1,169,066

Commercial television stations, affiliations
ADI: Los Angeles (100%)

Cable television systems, total subscribers
Cencom Cable TV; Monterey Park   54,000
Continental Cablevision of California; Downey   42,543

Businesses and other major employers
State of California/Caltrans Dept.; Los Angeles   15,000
Times Mirror Co./Los Angeles Times; Los Angeles; newspapers   12,000
City of Los Angeles; Los Angeles   11,200
Southern California Gas Co.; Los Angeles; gas distribution   3,100
Transamerica Occidental Life; Los Angeles; life insurance   3,021
IBM Corp.; Los Angeles; professional/commercial computers/equipment   3,000
Associated Dry Goods Corp./J. W. Robinson; Los Angeles; department stores   2,500
County of Los Angeles; Los Angeles   2,500
Bank of America/Data Center; Los Angeles; banking/computer services   2,500
First Interstate Bank of California/Operations Center; Los Angeles; commercial banks   2,400
Atlantic Richfield Co.; Los Angeles; petroleum   2,200
Bradford Building Services Inc.; Los Angeles; building services   2,000
Bell Gardens Bicycle Club; Bell; card casino   1,950
Sears Roebuck & Co.; Los Angeles; catalog retailers   1,800
Hospital of the Good Samaritan; Los Angeles   1,719
California Commerce Club Inc.; Los Angeles; card casino   1,700
Masco Building Products Corp./Norris Industries; Los Angeles; ordnance/accessories   1,600
Certified Grocers of California Ltd.; Los Angeles; warehousing   1,500
Pacific West Advertising; Los Angeles; advertising   1,500
Arthur Andersen & Co.; Los Angeles; accounting/auditing   1,500
U.S. Internal Revenue Service; Los Angeles   1,440
Guess Inc.; Los Angeles; outerwear   1,400
St. Vincent Medical Center; Los Angeles   1,350
Unihealth America/California Hospital Medical Center; Los Angeles; health management   1,300
Belmont Community Adult School; Los Angeles   1,216
Ernst & Young; Los Angeles; accounting/auditing   1,200
Automobile Club of Southern California; Los Angeles; auto insurance/membership service   1,200
Unocal Corp.; Los Angeles; petroleum refining   1,149
Southern California Rapid Transit District; Los Angeles   1,100
U.S. Postal Service; Bell   1,000
Aluminum Co. of America; Los Angeles; aluminum tubing   1,000
Clougherty Packing Co./Farmer John Brand Co.; Los Angeles; meat products   1,000
Rykoff-Sexton Inc.; Los Angeles; grocery products   1,000
National Railroad Pass Corp./Amtrak; Los Angeles; railroads   1,000
County of Los Angeles/Treasurer & Tax Collector; Los Angeles   1,000
Los Angeles Unified School District; Los Angeles   1,000
City of Los Angeles/Municipal Court; Los Angeles   1,000
Deloitte & Touche; Los Angeles; accounting/auditing   900
Coopers & Lybrand; Los Angeles; accounting/auditing   825
Insilco Corp./Sinclair Paint; Los Angeles; paints   800
State of California; Los Angeles; building services   800
Wior Corp./Gerry of California; Los Angeles; apparel   800

Anchor Glass Corp.; Huntington Park; glass/glassware 800
Mead Corp./Zellerbach; Los Angeles; paper products 800
Coca-Cola; Los Angeles; bottling 800
Cigna Hospital; Los Angeles 800
Omelveny & Myers; Los Angeles; legal services 769
Huntington Park Community Adult School; Huntington Park 757
County of Los Angeles/Health Dept.; Los Angeles 750
Latham & Watkins; Los Angeles; legal services 730
E. & J. Gallo Winery/Wine Co.; Los Angeles; wine production/distribution 700
U.S. Army Corps of Engineers; Los Angeles; construction/engineering services 700
United Presort Services Inc.; Los Angeles; mailing/repro services 700
Nestle Food Co./Dairies; Los Angeles; food products 700
American Red Cross; Los Angeles; social services 691
United Auto Workers; Maywood; labor organization 690
KPMG Peat Marwick; Los Angeles; accounting/auditing 670
M&B Mini Blind Corp.; Los Angeles; fixtures 650
TAT Los Angeles Co. Ltd./Biltmore Hotel; Los Angeles; hotel 650
Los Angeles Hilton; Los Angeles; hotel 650
U.S. Federal Reserve; Los Angeles 640
Owens-Illinois Inc.; Los Angeles; glass/glassware 616
Barth & Dreyfuss/Royal Terry; Los Angeles; textile products 600
Bullock's; Los Angeles; department stores 600
Unilever United States Inc./Lawry's Wine & Gourmet Shop; Los Angeles; food stores 600
Fremont Insurance Co.; Los Angeles; life insurance 600
R. G. Canning Enterprises; Maywood; business services 600
Hotel Grande Assoc./Sheraton Grande Hotel; Los Angeles; hotel 600
Gibson Dunn & Crutcher; Los Angeles; legal services 583
American Protective Services; Los Angeles; business/security services 575
Minnesota Mining & Mfg. Co.; Los Angeles; medical instruments/supplies 550
Young's Market Co.; Los Angeles; beer/wine/liquor 550
County of Los Angeles/Medical Services Div.; Los Angeles 544
JB Hunt Transport Inc.; South Gate; trucking services 523
Nina Ricci; Los Angeles; outerwear 510
Paul Hastings Janofsky Walker; Los Angeles; legal services 501

34th District

East Los Angeles County Suburbs; West Covina

The 34th (see map on page 97) is emerging as a middle-class Hispanic district that likes to vote Democratic. It begins with more than a third of East Los Angeles, goes east through Montebello and Pico Rivera, goes up north a bit for La Puente, and drops down to pick up most of Whittier and all of Santa Fe Springs and Norwalk.

The section of East Los Angeles contained in the 34th is the heart of East L.A.'s business district. The stores are well-kept, and owned or operated by Hispanics. The area just to the north, around the 60 Freeway, is populated by what some call "Muppies," or Mexican yuppies, who have come in and fixed up many of the area's old homes.

Montebello is an upper-middle-class Hispanic area, with a lot of home-grown residents who have never lived anywhere else. The area has many white-collar workers; it is bordered by four freeways, making it a convenient area for commuters. Montebello is heavily Democratic.

Pico Rivera has been described as pure middle America, Hispanic-style. "The values that people have, the outlook on life, what they want for their kids—it is Peoria, Ill.," says a resident. The biggest employer in the city is Northrop, which builds part of the B-2 bomber here. This area was also very supportive of Democrats.

Up in the district's northeastern corner past Rose Hills Memorial Park (one of the country's largest cemeteries) is La Puente, a working-class, heavily Hispanic city with 37,000 residents and a Democratic registration of 67 percent.

Down south a bit, the district includes most of Whittier, the 34th's most Republican area (a 2-point GOP voter registration advantage). The city is still recovering from being the epicenter of an October 1987 earthquake. Some houses damaged in the quake have been repaired, but vacant lots are not uncommon. Multifamily homes are mixed closely with single-family homes in some areas, but not in the part of Whittier just outside the district, where half-million-dollar houses (and the GOP) dominate.

Farther south is Santa Fe Springs, a healthy industrial area featuring light manufacturing and oil wells. Two-thirds of the city's 15,500 residents are Hispanic, but they have not flexed their political muscles here as they have elsewhere.

At the southern end of the 34th is Norwalk, the district's largest city with 94,000 residents. It has close to a majority of Hispanics and a majority of Democrats; they tend to be conservative-minded in presidential voting, though Norwalk went heavily for Bill Clinton in 1992. The city is bounded by four freeways. Los Angeles' Green Line light rail is scheduled to open in 1994, which will give the area a further economic boost.

In 1992, Bill Clinton carried 51 percent of the 34th's vote to George Bush's 31 percent.

Election Returns and Party Registration

	34th District	Democrat	Republican
1992	President*	78,889 (50.9%)	48,181 (31.1%)
	Senate †	71,692 (47.0%)	64,110 (42.1%)
	Senate †‡	83,783 (56.1%)	51,089 (34.2%)
	House †	91,738 (61.3%)	50,907 (34.0%)
1990	Governor †	51,539 (46.9%)	51,151 (46.5%)
1988	President	82,904 (52.0%)	75,030 (47.1%)
	Senate	78,285 (49.8%)	72,066 (45.8%)
1986	Senate	65,517 (55.4%)	48,486 (41.0%)
	Governor	53,316 (44.9%)	62,347 (52.5%)
1993	Party registration †	132,900 (61.6%)	60,383 (28.0%)

*Vote for Perot was 27,944 (18.0%).   †Independent/other is greater than 5%.
‡Special election for the remaining two years of the term of Pete Wilson who was elected governor in 1990. Appointee John Seymour held the seat 1991-1992.

Demographics

Population 573,047

Percent change from 1980 8.9%

Land area 90 square miles

Population per square mile 6,342

Counties, 1990 population
Los Angeles (pt.) 573,047

Cities, 1990 population (10,000 or more)

Avocado Heights CDP 14,232	Santa Fe Springs (pt.) 15,520
East Los Angeles CDP (pt.) 52,103	South Whittier CDP 49,514
Hacienda Heights CDP (pt.) 51,816	Valinda CDP (pt.) 15,377
La Puente 36,955	West Puente Valley CDP 20,254
Montebello (pt.) 59,564	West Whittier-Los Nietos CDP 24,164
Norwalk (pt.) 94,279	
Pico Rivera (pt.) 59,177	Whittier (pt.) 56,997

Race and Hispanic origin
White 56.7%
Black 1.9%
American Indian, Eskimo, or Aleut. 0.6%
Asian or Pacific Islander 9.3%
Other 31.4%
Hispanic origin 62.3%

Ancestry

American 1.5%	German 7.9%
Dutch 1.1%	Irish 5.8%
English 5.7%	Italian 2.5%
French 1.8%	

Universities/colleges, 1990-1991 enrollment
Rio Hondo College, Whittier 12,048
Whittier College, Whittier 1,840

Newspapers, total circulation (in all districts)
Los Angeles La Opinion 98,557
Los Angeles Times 1,169,066
San Gabriel Valley Tribune 63,573
Whittier Daily News 16,802

Commercial television stations, affiliations
ADI: Los Angeles (100%)

Cable television systems, total subscribers
Cencom Cable TV; Monterey Park 54,000
Continental Cablevision of California; Downey 42,543
Sammons Communications Inc.; Whittier 12,000
United Artists Cable TV; City of Industry 37,443
United Artists Cable TV; South Whittier 15,978

Businesses and other major employers
U.S. Postal Service; La Puente 3,600
United Parcel Service Inc.; Montebello; mail services 3,500
Northrop Corp.; Pico Rivera; research services 2,000
County of Los Angeles; Whittier; sanitary services 1,500
Presbyterian Intercommunity Hospital; Whittier 1,500
State of California/Mental Health Dept.; Norwalk 1,500
Western Fire Chief Assn.; Whittier; professional organizations 1,500
Illuminators Inc.; Santa Fe Springs; business services 1,100
Rio Hondo College; Whittier 1,100
Beverly Community Hospital; Montebello 1,100
Whittier Union High School District; Whittier 1,007
Public Health Foundation Los Angeles; La Puente 983
Standard Precision Inc./Accuride; Santa Fe Springs; handtools/hardware 900
Entenmann's Inc./Oroweat Baking Co.; Montebello; bakery products 850
Vons Companies Inc.; Santa Fe Springs; warehousing 800
Bechtel Power Corp.; Norwalk; building construction 700
Eastman Kodak Co.; Whittier; professional/commercial equipment 700
Associated Dry Goods Corp./J. W. Robinson Co.; La Puente; department stores 700
Lucas Industries Inc./Lucas Western Inc.; La Puente; aircraft/parts 600
Peerless Pump Co.; Montebello; industry machinery 600
Schurr Adult School; Montebello 600
City of Industry/Industry Hills-Sheriton Resort; La Puente; retail stores 550
IBM Corp.; Norwalk; professional/commercial computers/equipment 530
ITT Corp.; La Puente; measuring/controlling devices 530
Rose Hills Memorial Park; Whittier; subdividers/developers 525

35th District
South-Central Los Angeles

The 35th (see map on page 97) is a very poor, very heavily minority district that is home to what many consider the flash point of the 1992 riot, the intersection of Normandie and Florence avenues—the scene of brutal attacks on passers-by. Other areas in the 35th—part of south-central Los Angeles and the three independent cities of Inglewood, Hawthorne and Gardena—were also scarred by the rioting.

The eastern edge of the district is the most desperately poor. As one heads west toward Inglewood, relative affluence increases. The commercial districts in this area along Vermont and Manchester (and to a lesser extent Western) avenues were devastated by looting and burning.

To the west of south-central is Inglewood, whose police force was able to keep much of the rioting there under control. Inglewood suffered some damage but was spared the wholesale destruction found in south-central. Inglewood is a historically white city that has changed dramatically; now, more than half its 110,000 residents are black. The city is home to the Hollywood Park racetrack and the L.A. Lakers, who play in the Great Western Forum. Several shipping companies have set up shop here to take advantage of its location due east of Los Angeles International Airport.

Hawthorne, with 71,000 residents, is about 10 percent Asian with the rest split almost equally among Hispanics, whites and blacks. Its political power, however, is largely concentrated among its whites because they tend to register to vote at higher levels than the other groups. Hawthorne was the birthplace of Northrop Corp., a major defense contractor that still has its manufacturing headquarters here. The city is alone in the district in having allowed large apartment buildings to be built.

For years, Gardena (population 50,000) received a strong revenue stream from being the only city in Los Angeles County that allowed poker parlors; their contributions made up about 15 percent of the city's budget. The extra money allowed the city to save a substantial sum, part of which it used to start a municipal insurance company to keep its costs down. The southern part of the city is heavily Japanese; they are about a quarter of the city's total population. The community has been influential for some time; the city elected California's first Japanese mayor in 1972. Honda has its U.S. headquarters here.

Overall, the district is 43 percent black (the highest proportion of blacks in the state), 43 percent Hispanic and 6 percent Asian—a full 90 percent minority. Politically the 35th is overwhelmingly Democratic, the most Democratic district in California: 80 percent of its voters are registered Democrats. Bill Clinton won 78 percent here in 1992.

Election Returns and Party Registration

	35th District	Democrat	Republican
1992	President*	100,432 (77.8%)	16,685 (12.9%)
	Senate †	94,567 (75.3%)	23,180 (18.5%)
	Senate †‡	98,026 (79.2%)	19,356 (15.6%)
	House	102,941 (82.5%)	17,417 (14.0%)
1990	Governor	63,902 (72.6%)	20,381 (23.2%)
1988	President	107,935 (77.1%)	30,068 (21.5%)
	Senate	103,661 (75.3%)	30,584 (22.2%)
1986	Senate	87,050 (78.7%)	21,799 (19.7%)
	Governor	84,152 (74.2%)	28,288 (25.0%)
1993	Party registration †	156,166 (79.6%)	22,049 (11.2%)

*Vote for Perot was 11,950 (9.3%).   †Independent/other is greater than 5%.
‡Special election for the remaining two years of the term of Pete Wilson who was elected governor in 1990. Appointee John Seymour held the seat 1991-1992.

Demographics

Population 570,882

Percent change from 1980 8.5%

Land area 44 square miles

Population per square mile 13,109

Counties, 1990 population
Los Angeles (pt.) 570,882

Cities, 1990 population (10,000 or more)

Florence-Graham CDP (pt.) 15,301	Inglewood (pt.) 109,229
Gardena 49,847	Lennox CDP 22,757
Hawthorne (pt.) 71,330	Los Angeles (pt.) 244,712
	Westmont CDP 31,044

Race and Hispanic origin
White 21.3%
Black 42.7%
American Indian, Eskimo, or Aleut. 0.4%
Asian or Pacific Islander 6.0%
Other 29.7%
Hispanic origin 43.1%

Ancestry

American 1.4%	German 2.9%
English 2.0%	Irish 2.2%

Universities/colleges, 1990-1991 enrollment
Los Angeles Southwest College, Los Angeles 5,296
Northrop University, Inglewood 1,277

Newspapers, total circulation (in all districts)
Daily Variety 21,274
Los Angeles La Opinion 98,557
Los Angeles Times 1,169,066
Torrance Daily Breeze 85,367

Commercial television stations, affiliations
ADI: Los Angeles (100%)

Cable television systems, total subscribers
Continental Cablevision of California; Inglewood 12,300
Continental Cablevision of California; Westchester 19,698
Paragon Cable; Gardena 62,304

Businesses and other major employers
Northrop Corp.; Hawthorne; aircraft/parts 17,568
Centinela Hospital/Medical Center; Inglewood 1,490
Daniel Freeman Memorial Hospital; Inglewood 1,200
Marriott Corp.; Los Angeles; hotel 1,000
BP Chemicals Inc.; Gardena; guided missiles/parts 850
LA Aiport Hilton & Towers; Los Angeles; hotel 850
Teledyne Industries Inc./Teledyne Relays Div.; Hawthorne; electrical industrial apparatus 700
Robert F. Kennedy Medical Center; Hawthorne 700
Normandie Casino; Gardena; card casino 650
U.S. Federal Aviation Administration; Lawndale 600
Virco Mfg. Corp.; Los Angeles; furniture 550
Neutrogena Corp.; Los Angeles; soaps/cosmetics 520

36th District

West Los Angeles County; Manhattan Beach; Torrance

The 36th hugs the Pacific coast, running south from Venice Beach to San Pedro and the port of Los Angeles (see map on page 97). Along the way, it takes in some of California's most Democratic and Republican areas.

The 36th's economic core is along the ocean and the Pacific Coast Highway. Its main industry—aerospace—is found in the upper third of the district in El Segundo, home of Hughes Aircraft, Lockheed and TRW plants. Shrinking spending in both the military and civilian sectors of the aerospace business has been devastating; it is not unusual to see people with doctorates collecting unemployment compensation.

The northern end of the district is anchored by Venice, a "very, very crunchy, nuts-and-berries kind of place," as one local observer put it; Venice is widely regarded as the most liberal place in California outside Berkeley. Designed by Abbot Kinney to duplicate the Italian city, Venice opened in 1904 complete with canals and gondolas. Its heyday was short; by 1958 the city had fallen into such disrepair that Orson Welles used it as the location for the seedy town in the film *Touch of Evil*. The area has been revitalized by wealthy full-time residents and weekenders drawn to the town's beautiful location and funky reputation.

Just south of Venice and Marina Del Rey lies the Los Angeles International Airport, which stretches all the way to the 405 Freeway, the eastern border of the district. The airport's expansion during the 1980s is expected to meet air traffic demands until another terminal is built at the end of the 1990s. The airport is not expected to receive much public works money in the meantime, although plans are proceeding to bring a light-rail extension of Los Angeles' new rapid-transit system here in this decade.

The land is fairly flat continuing down the coast, past El Segundo and through some of the wealthiest ocean suburbs in the region, including Manhattan, Hermosa and Redondo beaches—whose 110,000 residents collectively had per capita incomes of over $31,000 in 1989.

The land and the incomes take a steep rise at the Palos Verdes Peninsula, where the bulk of the district's Republicans live. Nearly three-fourths of the peninsula's 90,000 residents are white. The area is almost uniformly upscale, and some communities qualify as havens of the truly wealthy: For instance, the per capita income of the 1,900 residents in Rolling Hills is $85,000.

In the 1992 House race, the area's brand of social moderation and fiscal conservatism did not embrace the GOP nominee as warmly as it had Republican candidates in the past. A voter-registration surge in the months before the 1992 elections turned a 15,000-vote GOP margin into a slight Democratic plurality; that shift helped produce the Democrats' 16,000-vote victory.

The surge helped Bill Clinton, who also won this district in 1992 by about 15,000 votes; he took 41 percent to George Bush's 36 percent and Ross Perot's 23 percent.

Election Returns and Party Registration

	36th District	Democrat	Republican
1992	President*	111,014 (41.3%)	95,646 (35.5%)
	Senate †	117,397 (44.4%)	126,516 (47.9%)
	Senate †‡	131,093 (50.3%)	110,425 (42.3%)
	House †	125,751 (48.4%)	109,684 (42.2%)
1990	Governor †	76,325 (38.0%)	114,290 (56.8%)
1988	President	106,360 (39.7%)	158,090 (59.0%)
	Senate	95,261 (36.2%)	160,909 (61.1%)
1986	Senate	85,810 (42.2%)	112,814 (55.5%)
	Governor	64,689 (31.6%)	136,893 (66.9%)
1993	Party registration †	140,331 (42.5%)	140,817 (42.6%)

*Vote for Perot was 62,458 (23.2%).   †Independent/other is greater than 5%.
‡Special election for the remaining two years of the term of Pete Wilson who was elected governor in 1990. Appointee John Seymour held the seat 1991-1992.

Demographics

Population 573,663

Percent change from 1980 8.6%

Land area 232 square miles

Population per square mile 2,477

Counties, 1990 population
Los Angeles (pt.) 573,663

Cities, 1990 population (10,000 or more)
El Segundo 15,223
Hermosa Beach 18,219
Lawndale (pt.) 27,331
Lomita 19,382
Los Angeles (pt.) 163,650
Manhattan Beach 32,063
Palos Verdes Estates 13,512
Rancho Palos Verdes 41,659
Redondo Beach 60,167
Torrance 133,107
West Carson CDP 20,143

Race and Hispanic origin
White 77.7%
Black 3.2%
American Indian, Eskimo, or Aleut. 0.5%
Asian or Pacific Islander 12.5%
Other 6.1%
Hispanic origin 14.9%

Ancestry
American 2.0%
Danish 1.1%
Dutch 2.0%
English 15.3%
French 4.0%
German 19.7%
Irish 14.0%
Italian 6.6%
Norwegian 1.8%
Polish 3.1%
Russian 2.6%
Scotch Irish 2.1%
Scottish 2.9%
Swedish 2.5%

Universities/colleges, 1990-1991 enrollment
Antioch University, Los Angeles 451
El Camino College, Torrance 25,789
Loyola Marymount University, Los Angeles 6,430
Marymount College, Rancho Palos Verdes 1,077

Newspapers, total circulation (in all districts)
Daily Variety 21,274
Los Angeles Daily News 208,005
Los Angeles La Opinion 98,557
Los Angeles Times 1,169,066
Santa Monica Outlook 26,324
Torrance Daily Breeze 85,367

Commercial television stations, affiliations
ADI: Los Angeles (100%)

Cable television systems, total subscribers
Century Cable of Santa Monica 44,829
Century Cable of Southern California Inc.; Redondo Beach 15,500
Continental Cable of California; Westchester 19,698
Multivision Cable TV; Manhattan Beach 18,000
Paragon Cable; Gardena 62,304
TM/Palos Verdes Peninsula; Rancho Palos Verdes 24,800

Military installations, 1991
Los Angeles Air Force Base, El Segundo 3,770

Businesses and other major employers
Hughes Aircraft Co./Radar Systems Group; El Segundo; radar communications 9,500
Allied-Signal Inc./Air Research Div.; Torrance; nonferrous foundries (castings) 6,700
Xerox Corp.; El Segundo; computer/office equipment 4,000
Aerospace Corp.; El Segundo; research services 3,700
Harbor-UCLA Medical Center; Torrance 3,000
Trans World Airlines Inc.; Los Angeles; airline 2,800
TRW Inc.; Redondo Beach; guided missiles/parts 2,400
Rockwell Intl. Corp.; El Segundo; aircraft/parts 2,000
Torrance Memorial Medical Center; Torrance 1,700
City of Los Angeles/Hyperion Treatment Plant; Venice 1,600
City of Torrance; Torrance 1,597
Mattel Toys USA; El Segundo; toys/sporting goods 1,500
City of Los Angeles/Airports Dept.; Los Angeles 1,450
Chevron Corp.; El Segundo; petroleum refining 1,300
Magnavox; Torrance; research services 1,300
Teledyne Industries Inc./Teledyne Microelectronics; Los Angeles; electronic components 1,165
American Honda Motor Co. Inc.; Torrance; motor vehicles 1,150
International Rectifier Corp.; El Segundo; electronic components 1,050
Little Company of Mary Hospital; Torrance 1,025

Quotron Systems Inc.; Los Angeles; security and commodity services 1,000

Computer Sciences Corp./Info Technology Serv.; El Segundo; computer services 1,000

North American Philips Corp.; Torrance; industry machinery 985

Hughes Aircraft Co./Electron Dynamics Div.; Torrance; search/navigation equipment 950

Mobil Petroleum Co. Inc.; Torrance; petroleum refining 950

Hi-Shear Corp.; Torrance; screw machine products 900

Hughes Aircraft Co./Electro-Optical & Data Systems; Los Angeles; measuring/controlling devices 900

El Camino Community College; Torrance 864

San Pedro Peninsula Hospital; San Pedro 850

Research & Education Institute; Torrance; professional organizations 850

Jaguar Intl. Ltd.; Los Angeles; building construction 817

Supershuttle Intl.; Los Angeles; airport transportation 800

Standard Brands Paint Co.; Torrance; paint stores 800

CCH Computax Inc.; Torrance; computer services 800

Loyola Marymount University; Los Angeles 800

Stouffer Concourse Hotel; Los Angeles; hotel 750

Sky Chefs Inc.; Los Angeles; bars/restaurants 725

Sheraton Plaza La Reina Hotel; Los Angeles; hotel 710

Fairchild Industries Inc.; Torrance; screw machine products 700

Kingsbacher-Murphy Co.; Torrance; bookbinding 700

Copley Press Inc./Daily Breeze; Torrance; newspapers 700

United Air Lines Inc.; El Segundo; airline 700

County of Los Angeles; Venice; beach/lifeguard services 700

Teradata Corp.; El Segundo; computers 680

Caterair Intl. Corp./Marriott Inflite Services; Los Angeles; bars/restaurants 650

Fairchild Industries Inc./Specialty Fasteners Div.; Redondo Beach; screw machine products 650

Matrix Science Corp.; Torrance; electric lighting 600

Republic Airlines Inc.; Los Angeles; airline 600

City of Los Angeles; Los Angeles; airports/services 600

Unocal Corp.; Wilmington; petroleum refining 575

First American Tax Service; Los Angeles; business services 550

Harper's; Torrance; office furniture 530

South Bay Community Hospital; Redondo Beach 525

37th District

Southern Los Angeles County; Compton; Carson

The 37th includes some of Los Angeles' poorest and most overwhelmingly Democratic communities, taking in the Carson, Compton and Lynwood areas of the city (see map on page 97).

Residents of the 37th have quite a stake in efforts aimed at post-Cold War adjustments to the nation's defense industries. The scheduled closings of the Long Beach shipyard and naval station just south of the district are likely to squeeze the area anew. Long Beach's port area draws many of its blue-collar workers from the district (the naval station alone employs more than 10,000 civilian and military personnel), and many others in the 37th work in small businesses that support the port. Military contractors concentrated in the district's southern end also are suffering.

Carson, just north of the port, is a blue-collar city of 84,000,

with its population split almost evenly among Hispanics, blacks, whites and Asians. This area was largely spared in the rioting of May 1992, even though it is sandwiched between Long Beach and Compton, which both suffered fairly heavy damage.

Scores of Compton's businesses went up in the smoke of 135 separate fires. California's recession had been hurting the already-poor area, and many of the surviving jobs were lost as businesses damaged in the riot closed. The lots with burned buildings and debris were cleared, leaving them vacant—and hard to distinguish from the many vacant lots the city had before the riots.

Compton's Hispanic community has grown tremendously in the past decade. Forty-four percent of the city's 90,000 residents are Hispanic and 53 percent are black.

At the north end of the district is Lynwood, 70 percent of whose 62,000 residents are Hispanic and 21 percent of whom are black. The area sustained some damage during the riots, with more than 60 fires reported and 138 arrests.

One ray of light for the district is the Alameda Corridor project, an attempt to create a smooth conduit for goods to enter California through Long Beach without the traffic hassles of the Long Beach Freeway. The project runs the length of the district up Alameda Street and includes rail and road transportation improvements.

Another addition to the district is the 105 Freeway, known for years as the Century Freeway, which gave rise to a local joke that the road, planned since the middle part of this century, would not be completed until the next. But it bears a new name— retired Democratic Rep. Glenn Anderson's—and new hope for completion. The very eastern end near Norwalk is slated to open in late 1993, and the freeway's last legs are expected to be finished in about three years, finally fully connecting the area to the metropolitan area's freeway grid.

The 37th's Democratic House member was one of only three representatives in the state who did not draw major-party opposition in 1992. Bill Clinton received 74 percent of the district's presidential vote that year.

Election Returns and Party Registration

	37th District	Democrat	Republican
1992	President*	90,523 (73.8%)	19,299 (15.7%)
	Senate †	85,100 (70.9%)	25,670 (21.4%)
	Senate †‡	89,147 (75.7%)	20,826 (17.7%)
	House †	97,159 (85.7%)	—
1990	Governor	57,790 (69.9%)	20,823 (25.2%)
1988	President	98,562 (75.5%)	30,315 (23.2%)
	Senate	94,425 (73.4%)	30,692 (23.8%)
1986	Senate	80,122 (78.0%)	20,399 (19.9%)
	Governor	76,944 (73.7%)	26,568 (25.5%)
1993	Party registration †	150,787 (76.8%)	26,130 (13.3%)

*Vote for Perot was 12,905 (10.5%).   †Independent/other is greater than 5%.
‡Special election for the remaining two years of the term of Pete Wilson who was elected governor in 1990. Appointee John Seymour held the seat 1991-1992.

Demographics

Population   572,049

Percent change from 1980   9.0%

Land area   72 square miles

Population per square mile 7,925

Counties, 1990 population
Los Angeles (pt.) 572,049

Cities, 1990 population (10,000 or more)

Carson 83,995	Los Angeles (pt.) 146,111
Compton 90,454	Lynwood 61,945
Long Beach (pt.) 127,044	Willowbrook CDP 32,772

Race and Hispanic origin
White 26.2%
Black 33.6%
American Indian, Eskimo, or Aleut. 0.5%
Asian or Pacific Islander 10.8%
Other 28.9%
Hispanic origin 45.2%

Ancestry

American 1.4%	German 3.3%
English 2.3%	Irish 2.6%

Universities/colleges, 1990-1991 enrollment
California State University-Dominguez Hills, Carson 7,460
Compton Community College, Compton 3,972
Los Angeles Harbor College, Wilmington 8,319

Newspapers, total circulation (in all districts)
Daily Variety 21,274
Long Beach Press-Telegram 126,076
Los Angeles La Opinion 98,557
Los Angeles Times 1,169,066
San Pedro News Pilot 15,747
Torrance Daily Breeze 85,367

Commercial television stations, affiliations
ADI: Los Angeles (100%)

Cable television systems, total subscribers
Continental Cablevision of California; Carson 12,042
Continental Cablevision of California; Compton 19,162
Copley/Colony Cablevision; Wilmington 20,780
CVI; Long Beach 67,000
Paragon Cable; Gardena 62,304

Businesses and other major employers
Compton Unified School District; Compton 3,800
Martin Luther King Jr. General Hospital & Medical Center; Los Angeles 3,800
Long Beach Memorial Medical Center; Long Beach 3,700
Inchon Iron & Steel Co.; Gardena; durable goods 3,000
Lynwood Unified School District; Lynwood 1,557
TRW Inc.; Carson; management/public relations 1,400
St. Francis Medical Center; Lynwood 1,350
American Racing Equipment; Compton; racing equipment 1,200
Atlantic Richfield Co.; Carson; petroleum refining 1,100
Robertshaw Holdings Corp./Grayson Controls Div.; Long Beach; thermostatic controls 1,100
Martin Marietta Corp.; Torrance; metal products 1,100
Media Advertising Packagers; Gardena; advertising 1,015
Nissan Motor Corp.; Gardena; motor vehicles 1,000
Toyota Motor Distributors Inc.; Torrance; motor vehicles/parts/supplies 1,000
Los Angeles Harbor College; Wilmington 1,000
California State University-Dominguez Hills, Carson 1,000
R. R. Donnelley & Sons Co.; Torrance; commercial printing 850
Ralphs Grocery Co.; Compton; grocery stores 800
Bekins Co./Business Relocation Group; Compton; moving/relocation services 704
Shell Oil Co.; Long Beach; petroleum refining 700
Kraco Enterprises Inc.; Compton; motor vehicle parts/supplies 700
Charles R. Drew University; Los Angeles 675
Corryhiebert Corp.; Long Beach; office furniture 650
Shell Oil Co.; Carson; petroleum refining 650
Coastcast Corp.; Compton; iron/steel foundries 650
Pepsi-Cola Bottling Co.; Carson; beverages 600
Texaco; Wilmington; petroleum refining 568
Long Beach Public Transportaton Co.; Long Beach; transportation 550
Cal-Style Furniture Mfg. Co.; Compton; furniture 550
Ashton-Tate; Torrance; computer/office equipment 541
Pacific Hospital of Long Beach; Long Beach 540
Jordon Locke Community Adult School; Los Angeles 504

38th District

Long Beach; Downey; Lakewood

Though there is a working-class Democratic tradition in the 38th (and a twelve-point Democratic registration advantage), blue-collar conservatism often will shift the area toward Republican candidates. In the open seat in 1992, the Republican nominee beat his Democratic opponent 49 percent to 43 percent. But Bill Clinton managed to beat George Bush here 45 percent to 33 percent.

Long Beach, along the coast, is the world's second-largest port and by far the largest city in the district with 429,000 residents. All but the western end is contained within the 38th (see map on page 97). About a quarter of the city's residents are Hispanic, and more than half are white non-Hispanics. The remaining quarter are a rainbow of ethnicities: 49 languages are spoken in the Long Beach Unified School District's schools. Overall, the district is about 25 percent Hispanic, 9 percent Asian and 8 percent black.

The southwestern side of Long Beach was hard hit by the April 1992 riots that ripped through the Los Angeles area. More than 400 fires were reported, more than 300 people were injured and at least one person was killed. Much of the damage was along the Pacific Coast Highway and the city's Cambodian area along Anaheim Street.

The beautiful *Queen Mary* is docked here, but the fight to keep the Long Beach Naval Shipyard open has diverted the eyes of most residents. The shipyard employs thousands across Southern California; any move to close it is serious trouble for the area. (The shipyard made the mid-1993 list of military facilities targeted for closure.) While important, the shipyard is just part of the 38th's industrial landscape. Aerospace plants extend along the flat, brown land, sharing space with fuel tanks and oil wells. In the older homes of Long Beach are the descendants of the fishermen and sailors of many European nationalities who settled here.

Downey, a middle- to upper-middle-income city of 91,000 at the district's northern tip, has a Republican lean. The city houses Rockwell's huge aerospace plant (where the space shuttle is manufactured) on its south end, as well as many of the high-tech workers who are employed there. While Rockwell is still a major employer, levels have dropped off dramatically from their peaks of yesteryear.

Just south of Downey is Paramount, a very blue-collar city of 48,000. About 60 percent of Paramount's residents are Hispanic, far higher levels than are found elsewhere in the 38th. The city has high unemployment and high crime rates.

Directly east of Paramount is Bellflower, a quiet bedroom city of 62,000 that is similar to Downey. It has no industry that compares with Rockwell.

More than half of Lakewood's 74,000 residents are in the 38th. This community, just south of Bellflower, was built all at once after World War II to house veterans and other workers who came to the area to work in the aerospace industry and decided to stay. One of the city's claims to fame is the Lakewood Center Mall, one of America's first shopping malls.

Election Returns and Party Registration

	38th District	Democrat	Republican
1992	President*	88,728 (44.6%)	66,647 (33.5%)
	Senate †	88,629 (45.1%)	90,949 (46.3%)
	Senate †‡	98,521 (50.9%)	76,445 (39.5%)
	House †	82,108 (43.4%)	92,038 (48.6%)
1990	Governor †	60,192 (39.6%)	82,854 (54.5%)
1988	President	90,677 (43.5%)	115,595 (55.5%)
	Senate	83,265 (40.5%)	116,686 (56.8%)
1986	Senate	74,341 (44.9%)	84,113 (50.8%)
	Governor	52,505 (31.8%)	109,934 (66.6%)
1993	Party registration †	128,290 (49.7%)	97,651 (37.8%)

*Vote for Perot was 43,596 (21.9%). †Independent/other is greater than 5%. ‡Special election for the remaining two years of the term of Pete Wilson who was elected governor in 1990. Appointee John Seymour held the seat 1991-1992.

Demographics

Population 572,657

Percent change from 1980 9.0%

Land area 74 square miles

Population per square mile 7,712

Counties, 1990 population
Los Angeles (pt.) 572,657

Cities, 1990 population (10,000 or more)

Bellflower 61,815	Long Beach (pt.) 296,670
Downey (pt.) 91,444	Los Angeles (pt.) 15,629
Lakewood (pt.) 49,714	Paramount (pt.) 47,666

Race and Hispanic origin
White 69.2%
Black 7.7%
American Indian, Eskimo, or Aleut. 0.7%
Asian or Pacific Islander 9.1%
Other 13.2%
Hispanic origin 25.7%

Ancestry

American 2.2%	French 3.6%
Dutch 2.7%	German 17.0%
English 12.6%	Irish 12.0%
Italian 4.3%	Scotch Irish 2.1%
Norwegian 1.6%	Scottish 2.1%
Polish 1.9%	Swedish 2.0%
Russian 1.1%	

Universities/colleges, 1990-1991 enrollment
Brooks College, Long Beach 534
California State University, Long Beach 33,179
Long Beach City College, Long Beach 18,378

Newspapers, total circulation (in all districts)
Daily Variety 21,274
Long Beach Press-Telegram 126,076
Los Angeles La Opinion 98,557
Los Angeles Times 1,169,066
Orange County Register 341,875
San Pedro News Pilot 15,747

Commercial television stations, affiliations
ADI: Los Angeles (100%)

Cable television systems, total subscribers
CVI; Long Beach 67,000
Colony Communication; Lakewood 14,000
Comcast Cablevision; Seal Beach 9,090
Continental Cablevision of California; Downey 42,543

Military installations, 1991
Long Beach Naval Station, Long Beach 15,680
Long Beach Naval Shipyard, Long Beach 6,625

Businesses and other major employers
McDonnell Douglas Corp.; Long Beach; aircraft/parts 41,000
Rockwell Intl. Corp./Space Systems Div.; Downey; space vehicles 8,000
County of Los Angeles/Internal Services Dept.; Downey 4,000
U.S. Veterans Affairs Dept.; Long Beach; hospital 3,500
California State University; Long Beach 3,500
County of Los Angeles/Education Dept.; Downey 3,500
Rancho Los Amigos Hospital; Downey 2,600
Southern California Permanente Medical Group/Kaiser Medical; Bellflower; insurance services 2,000
Downey Unified School District; Downey 2,000
St. Mary Medical Center; Long Beach 1,600
U.S. Postal Service; Long Beach 1,500
County of Los Angeles; Downey 1,500
Long Beach Community College District; Long Beach 1,400
City of Long Beach; Long Beach 1,200
Downey Community Hospital; Downey 1,100
Long Beach Community Hospital; Long Beach 1,050
Hanjin Shipping Co. Ltd.; Long Beach; freight shipping 1,000
May Dept. Stores Co.; Lakewood; department stores 1,000
Rockwell Intl. Corp.; Lakewood; engineering services 800
Star-Kist Foods Inc./Heinz Pet Products; Long Beach; grain mill products 700
City of Los Angeles/Port of Los Angeles; San Pedro 670
Twin Coast Newspapers Inc./Press-Telegram; Long Beach; newspapers 650
Eastman Inc.; Long Beach; paper products 640
National Medical Enterprises/Doctors Hospital; Lakewood 590
Bragg Investment Co. Inc.; Long Beach; business services 575

American Protective Services; Long Beach; business/security services 575

City of Lakewood; Lakewood 526

39th District

Parts of Orange and Los Angeles Counties — Fullerton

This district straddles the line between Orange and Los Angeles counties (see map on page 97). It is where the more-affluent parts of Los Angeles County's suburbs meet the less-affluent sections of Orange County; it is a seamless fit.

From all appearances, and spiritually speaking, this is an Orange County district. Its L.A. County portion looks like what many think of when they envision Orange County: bedroom communities, small commercial areas and regional malls. Its residents tend to vote Republican, hold conservative economic views and not identify themselves as Los Angelenos. Residents throughout the 39th typically work at jobs inside the district's borders. About three-fifths of the people are non-Hispanic whites, but there is a sizable presence of Hispanics (almost 23 percent) and Asians (14 percent).

The job situation is the top concern here, as it is throughout Southern California, but next on the list is crime. There is not a lot of violent crime or gang activity within the borders of the 39th, but this problem exists just across the line in Anaheim and in Santa Ana, and it is creeping this way.

Most of the terrain here is flat, with some hills in Fullerton and La Habra Heights. Though the cities in the district are largely residential, many have an industrial area: Machine shops, plastic injection-molding facilities, aerospace subcontractors and food manufacturers are among the installations.

Fullerton, the 39th's largest city, is upper-middle class, a label that applies to much of the district. Fullerton is home to a variety of industries and the district's largest employers, including Hughes Aircraft's ground systems division, which employs 7,000 workers who design and manufacture such things as radar, communications equipment and air traffic control equipment. Other major employers are Beckman Instruments, where 2,500 workers manufacture scientific equipment, and Hunt-Wesson, which employs 2,000 in its food plants making ketchup and other foodstuffs.

There is little variation among the communities inside the 39th. One of the only interruptions in the thoroughly developed area is Knott's Berry Farm, a major amusement park in Buena Park toward the south. Especially affluent areas include La Habra Heights, and the eastern, more Republican half of Whittier, both of which are in the 39th's northern region in L.A. County.

On the flip side, Hawaiian Gardens in L.A. County is more working-class and more Democratic than is the norm in the 39th. The district also picks up an industrial portion of Anaheim to the east.

Though this is a district landlocked in freeways, its southwestern corner reaches down to within four miles of the Pacific Ocean.

Republicans hold a 49 percent to 40 percent edge in the 39th, and local Republican candidates did correspondingly well in 1992. In the presidential race that year, George Bush received 44 percent; Bill Clinton, 34 percent; and Ross Perot, 22 percent.

Election Returns and Party Registration

	39th District	Democrat	Republican
1992	President*	78,305 (34.1%)	100,669 (43.8%)
	Senate †	76,129 (33.8%)	130,248 (57.7%)
	Senate †‡	90,804 (40.6%)	112,544 (50.3%)
	House	81,728 (38.2%)	122,472 (57.3%)
1990	Governor †	54,894 (31.5%)	109,442 (62.8%)
1988	President	75,898 (32.8%)	153,726 (66.4%)
	Senate	72,098 (31.0%)	154,478 (66.4%)
1986	Senate	66,298 (38.2%)	100,239 (57.7%)
	Governor	49,950 (28.8%)	120,952 (69.6%)
1993	Party registration †	111,142 (39.6%)	136,166 (48.5%)

*Vote for Perot was 50,834 (22.1%).   †Independent/other is greater than 5%.
‡Special election for the remaining two years of the term of Pete Wilson who was elected governor in 1990. Appointee John Seymour held the seat 1991-1992.

Demographics

Population 573,574

Percent change from 1980 9.0%

Land area 105 square miles

Population per square mile 5,472

Counties, 1990 population
Los Angeles (pt.) 188,098   Orange (pt.) 385,476

Cities, 1990 population (10,000 or more)
Artesia 15,464	La Habra 51,266
Brea (pt.) 32,047	La Mirada (pt.) 40,452
Buena Park (pt.) 62,674	La Palma 15,392
Cerritos 53,240	Lakewood (pt.) 23,843
Cypress (pt.) 38,354	Los Alamitos 11,676
Fullerton (pt.) 113,983	Placentia (pt.) 35,610
Hawaiian Gardens 13,639	Whittier (pt.) 20,674

Race and Hispanic origin
White 72.8%
Black 2.6%
American Indian, Eskimo, or Aleut. 0.5%
Asian or Pacific Islander 13.8%
Other 10.2%
Hispanic origin 22.8%

Ancestry
American 2.0%	Norwegian 1.7%
Dutch 2.8%	Polish 2.2%
English 14.2%	Russian 1.1%
French 3.8%	Scotch Irish 2.2%
German 19.3%	Scottish 2.3%
Irish 12.9%	Swedish 2.3%
Italian 5.0%	

Universities/colleges, 1990-1991 enrollment
Biola University/Talbot School of Theology; La Mirada 3,500
California State University, Fullerton 23,376
Cerritos Community College, Norwalk 15,886
Cypress College, Cypress 11,917
Fullerton College, Fullerton 17,548
ITT Technical Institute, Buena Park 854
Los Angeles College of Chiropractic Medicine, Whittier 947

Pacific Christian College, Fullerton 483
Southern California College of Optometry, Fullerton 383
Western State University College of Law, Fullerton 1,538

Newspapers, total circulation (in all districts)
Inland Valley Daily Bulletin 73,003
Long Beach Press-Telegram 126,076
Los Angeles La Opinion 98,557
Los Angeles Times 1,169,066
Orange County Register 341,875
San Gabriel Valley Tribune 63,573
Whittier Daily News 16,802

Commercial television stations, affiliations
ADI: Los Angeles (100%)

Cable television systems, total subscribers
Apollo Cablevision; Cerritos 7,400
Century Cable of Southern California Inc.; Brea 16,000
Comcast Cablevision; Fullerton 15,295
Comcast Cablevision; Buena Park 11,187
Copley/Colony Cablevision; Cypress 8,158
Paragon Cable; Garden Grove 21,921

Businesses and other major employers
General Motors Corp./Hughes Aircraft Co. Ground Systems
  Group; Fullerton; computer services 9,000
Knott's Berry Farm; Buena Park; amusement park 2,600
Beckman Instruments Inc./Altex Div.; Fullerton;
  measuring/controlling devices 2,500
Northrop Corp./Electro-Mechanical Div.; Anaheim; commu-
  nications equipment 2,000
Hunt-Wesson Inc./Beatrice; Fullerton; preserved
  fruits/vegetables 2,000
Beatrice Co./United Can Co.; Fullerton; metal cans 2,000
Alpha Beta Co.; La Habra; grocery stores 2,000
Lucky Stores Inc.; Buena Park; grocery stores 1,500
Beckman Instruments Inc./Diagnostic Systems Group; Brea;
  medical instruments 1,200
Pacificare Health Systems; Cypress; medical service/health
  insurance 1,100
Friendly Hills Regional Medical Center; La Habra 1,037
St. Jude Hospital & Medical Center; Fullerton 1,035
Cerritos Community College; Norwalk 1,004
Chevron Corp.; La Habra; petroleum/natural gas 1,000
Union Oil Co. of Cal.; Fullerton; research services 1,000
Unocal Corp.; Brea; research services 1,000
J. C. Penney Co. Inc.; Buena Park; management/public
  relations 943
Allstate Insurance Co.; Brea; insurance services 900
Fullerton Elementary School District; Fullerton 900
Automatic Data Processing; Buena Park; computer services
  800
Tuftex Carpet Mills Inc./Designweave; Santa Fe Springs;
  carpets/rugs 750
Kirkhill Rubber Co.; Brea; rubber products 730
Whittier Hospital & Medical Center; Whittier 710
Weber Aircraft Inc.; Fullerton; aircraft/parts 700
Masco Corp./Weiser Lock Div.; Seal Beach; door locks 700
Travelers Insurance Co.; Brea; insurance services 700
Kimberly-Clark Corp.; Fullerton; paper products 650
Albertsons Inc.; Brea; warehousing 630
Los Alamitos Medical Center; Los Alamitos 625
Western Wheel Corp.; La Mirada; auto parts 620

James Gile & Co. Inc./Golden State Picture Frame; Fullerton;
  wood products 600
GTE Directories Corp.; Los Alamitos; publishing 600
Brea Development Co. Ltd./Brea Community Hospital; Brea
  600
Mullikin Medical Center; Artesia; medical doctors 600
Biola University/Talbot School of Theology; La Mirada 600
GI Trucking Co.; La Mirada; trucking services 591
Sasco Electric; Artesia; electrical work 550
Mercury Casualty Co.; Brea; fire/marine/casualty insurance
  550
Fedco; Artesia; department stores 550
Mitsubishi Electronics America; Cypress; electrical goods 530

40th District
San Bernardino County — Redlands

The 40th is a desert district of massive proportions. It takes in
most of San Bernardino County's 20,000 square miles and all of
Inyo County's 10,000. San Bernardino County is the largest in the
nation; between it and Inyo, the 40th covers almost one-fifth of
California.

Most of the district's residents are packed into the far
southwest corner in three areas: the Inland Empire, the Victor
Valley region and the Morongo Basin.

The Inland Empire section of the district's south includes just
a few eastern areas in the city of San Bernardino and such cities
as Highland and Redlands, largely bedroom communities with
many retirees from Norton Air Force Base. Yucaipa, a bit farther
east, has an especially high number of retirees. Loma Linda, just
west of Redlands, is a Seventh-day Adventist community and
home to the Loma Linda University Medical Center, best known
for its infant heart transplant program (including the 1984 "Baby
Fay" case, in which an infant was given a baboon's heart).

Victor Valley, north of San Bernardino, has grown by leaps
and bounds. It includes the cities of Victorville, Hesperia, Apple
Valley and Adelanto. It is an area that used to look to the
military for support, but that presence is diminishing—George
Air Force Base has closed in 1992 and Norton Air Force Base in
San Bernardino is slated to do so in 1994.

Victor Valley's growth over the past 10 years has been fueled
by Los Angeles workers looking for affordable housing. From
the Victor Valley, they head south on the 15 Freeway through
the San Bernardino Mountains' Cajon Pass—"down the hill," as
they put it—and two hours later they are in downtown Los
Angeles.

The Morongo Basin, east of the Inland Empire along the
southern border with Riverside County, is the smallest of the
three population centers, taking in cities such as Yucca Valley,
Joshua Tree and Twentynine Palms. These are just north of the
Joshua Tree National Monument and depend heavily on the
nearby military presence, which includes the massive Twentynine
Palms Marine Corps base.

The district also includes Fort Irwin, where the Army trained
Desert Storm's troops for desert maneuvers, and the China Lake
Naval Weapons Center. About 60,000 troops a year train at Fort
Irwin.

The rest of the 40th is barren. It includes most of the Death
Valley National Monument (some of which is in Nevada), whose
tourists drive the economy of many of the area's small, scattered
towns, such as Lone Pine, Independence and Bishop.

The Republican House incumbent drew strong support across the district in 1992, beating his opponent by more than 2-to-1. Victorville gave him almost 60 percent of its vote, Redlands, 63 percent and Yucca Valley, 70 percent. This is traditionally Reagan Democrat country that went for George Bush in 1988. Bush won here again in 1992, though less impressively.

Election Returns and Party Registration

	40th District	Democrat	Republican
1992	President*	76,363 (35.2%)	86,453 (39.9%)
	Senate†	67,604 (32.8%)	114,836 (55.7%)
	Senate†‡	83,163 (39.6%)	104,046 (49.5%)
	House†	63,881 (31.1%)	129,563 (63.1%)
1990	Governor†	49,990 (33.6%)	87,993 (59.1%)
1988	President	64,592 (34.8%)	117,997 (63.5%)
	Senate	62,215 (33.8%)	115,950 (63.0%)
1986	Senate	52,743 (39.0%)	78,215 (57.9%)
	Governor	39,881 (29.5%)	93,518 (69.1%)
1993	Party registration†	119,420 (39.7%)	140,102 (46.6%)

*Vote for Perot was 53,955 (24.9%). †Independent/other is greater than 5%. ‡Special election for the remaining two years of the term of Pete Wilson who was elected governor in 1990. Appointee John Seymour held the seat 1991-1992.

Demographics

Population 573,625

Percent change from 1980 9.2%

Land area 29,912 square miles

Population per square mile 19

Counties, 1990 population
Inyo 18,281
San Bernardino (pt.) 555,344

Cities, 1990 population (10,000 or more)

Apple Valley 46,079	Twentynine Palms Base
Barstow 21,472	CDP 10,606
Hesperia 50,418	Twentynine Palms 11,821
Highland (pt.) 30,651	Victorville 40,674
Loma Linda 17,400	Yucaipa 32,824
Redlands 60,394	Yucca Valley CDP 13,701
San Bernardino (pt.) 36,489	

Race and Hispanic origin
White 82.1%
Black 5.4%
American Indian, Eskimo, or Aleut. 1.5%
Asian or Pacific Islander 3.5%
Other 7.5%
Hispanic origin 16.1%

Ancestry

American 3.5%	Norwegian 1.8%
Dutch 3.4%	Polish 2.0%
English 16.5%	Scotch Irish 2.5%
French 4.9%	Scottish 2.6%
German 23.5%	Swedish 2.5%
Irish 15.4%	Welsh 1.1%
Italian 4.8%	

Universities/colleges, 1990-1991 enrollment
Barstow College, Barstow 2,233
California State University, San Bernardino 9,154
Crafton Hills College, Yucaipa 3,990
Loma Linda University, Loma Linda 2,481
University of Redlands, Redlands 3,043
Victor Valley College, Victorville 4,858

Newspapers, total circulation (in all districts)
Los Angeles Times 1,169,066
Palm Springs Desert Sun 46,871
Press-Enterprise Riverside 158,521
Redlands Daily Facts 9,169
San Bernardino County Sun 91,810
Victorville Daily Press 26,577

Commercial television stations, affiliations
ADI: Los Angeles (100%)
KHIZ, Barstow (None)

Cable television systems, total subscribers
Benchmark Communications; Ridgecrest 10,271
Century Cable; Twentynine Palms 5,100
Century Cable; Yucca Valley 8,360
Chambers Cable/Southern California Inc.; San Bernardino 14,300
Comcast Cable; Fontana 17,700
Falcon Cable TV; Big Bear Lake 12,475
Falcon Cable TV; Lake Arrowhead 15,668
Falcon Cable TV; Hesperia 11,678
Hi Desert Cablevision; Victorville 34,800
Warner Cable of Barstow; Barstow 10,675

Military installations, 1991
Marine Corps Air Force Combat Center, Twentynine Palms 13,071
Norton Air Force Base, San Bernardino 7,345
Fort Irwin (Army), Barstow 6,254
George Air Force Base, Adelanto 3,184
Marine Corps Logistics Base, Barstow 2,794

Businesses and other major employers
Loma Linda University Medical Center; Loma Linda 4,976
Dyncorp; Barstow; electrical work 2,800
County of San Bernardino/Public Safety Dept.; San Bernardino 2,000
Draper Charles Stark Lab Inc.; San Bernardino; aircraft/parts 1,600
State of California/Mental Health Dept.; Patton 1,300
U.S. Postal Service; San Bernardino 1,200
Kerr-McGee Chemical Corp.; Trona; inorganic chemicals 1,000
Medical Personnel Services; Loma Linda; management/public relations 1,000
Morongo Unified School District; Twentynine Palms 900
St. Mary Desert Valley Hospital; Apple Valley 900
Contel of California Inc.; Victorville; telephone communications 790
Redlands Community Hospital; Redlands 700
Rockwell Intl. Corp./Command & Control Systems Center; San Bernardino; space research/technology 700
Victor Valley Community Hospital; Victorville 630
U.S. Veterans Affairs Dept.; Loma Linda 600
Environmental Systems; Redlands; professional/commercial equipment 520

41st District

Parts of Orange, Los Angeles and San Bernardino Counties

One goal of California's court-ordered reapportionment was to create as many districts as possible that follow county and city borders. The suburban 41st was not one of the successes: It splits three counties and runs up against a fourth (see map on page 97). Its center is the intersection of Orange, Los Angeles and San Bernardino counties, and it reaches east to the northwestern border of Riverside County.

Primarily, this district consists of bedrooms for Los Angeles and the rest of Orange County. Some people in the eastern end of the district head farther east to work in the factories in Fontana.

About half the district's voters are in San Bernardino County, 20 percent in Orange County and 30 percent in Los Angeles County. In Orange County, the 41st includes Yorba Linda, part of Anaheim Hills and bits of Brea and Placentia. In Los Angeles County, it takes in Diamond Bar, a little bit of Walnut and a big bit of Pomona. In San Bernardino County, it includes Chino, Chino Hills, Montclair, Upland and Ontario.

The Orange County section of the 41st is a representative slice of the county: It is white-collar, conservative and affluent. Republicans outnumber Democrats 2 to 1 here.

The section of San Bernardino County in the 41st is called the Inland Empire's west end. Real estate prices are relatively low, and many of its residents head south down the Carbon Canyon to work in Orange County.

Chino Hills' 28,000 residents are among the 41st's most conservative and affluent. Just north is Chino, a middle-income area whose 60,000 residents are almost evenly registered in both the parties.

North of Chino is the largest city in the district, Ontario, with 133,000 residents split between the 41st and the 42nd, which has the Democratic eastern side. The city's burgeoning airport—increasingly a passenger and cargo gateway into Los Angeles—is one of the area's primary growth engines. The airport's ability to bring passengers in and send goods out has spawned hotels, restaurants and distribution facilities nearby.

Upland, in the northern corner of the district, resembles its eastern neighbor, Rancho Cucamonga, in the 42nd. It is another conservative, wealthy area.

The economics begin to shift downward moving southwest to Montclair and into Los Angeles County, with the 41st's piece of Pomona. Montclair lacks the retailing and manufacturing activity that supports Ontario. Just south of Pomona is Diamond Bar, a more affluent suburb.

George Bush won the 41st in 1992, taking 43 percent of the vote in the three-way race. It was one of Bush's relatively few California bright spots in what turned out to be a tough year for him statewide.

Election Returns and Party Registration

	41st District	Democrat	Republican
1992	President*	64,666 (35.0%)	78,902 (42.7%)
	Senate†	61,999 (34.8%)	99,383 (55.7%)
	Senate †‡	76,284 (42.8%)	86,511 (48.5%)
	House†	58,777 (34.4%)	101,753 (59.6%)
1990	Governor†	42,001 (32.8%)	77,600 (60.7%)
1988	President	58,092 (33.3%)	114,516 (65.6%)
	Senate	53,971 (31.2%)	113,861 (65.8%)
1986	Senate	50,390 (40.0%)	70,723 (56.1%)
	Governor	38,607 (30.2%)	83,922 (65.7%)
1993	Party registration†	97,930 (39.8%)	119,411 (48.5%)

*Vote for Perot was 41,112 (22.3%).   †Independent/other is greater than 5%.
‡Special election for the remaining two years of the term of Pete Wilson who was elected governor in 1990. Appointee John Seymour held the seat 1991-1992.

Demographics

Population   572,663

Percent change from 1980   8.9%

Land area   230 square miles

Population per square mile   2,494

Counties, 1990 population
Los Angeles (pt.)   201,183   San Bernardino (pt.)
Orange (pt.)   80,288   291,192

Cities, 1990 population (10,000 or more)
Anaheim (pt.)   18,703   Ontario (pt.)   81,708
Chino Hills CDP   27,608   Pomona (pt.)   106,647
Chino   59,682   Rowland Heights CDP
Diamond Bar   53,672   (pt.)   37,416
Montclair   28,434   Upland   63,374
                                              Yorba Linda (pt.)   51,532

Race and Hispanic origin
White   68.0%
Black   6.8%
American Indian, Eskimo, or Aleut.   0.5%
Asian or Pacific Islander   10.1%
Other   14.6%
Hispanic origin   31.5%

Ancestry
American   2.2%   Italian   4.7%
Dutch   2.5%   Norwegian   1.1%
English   11.0%   Polish   2.2%
French   3.3%   Scotch Irish   1.6%
German   16.7%   Scottish   1.8%
Irish   10.5%   Swedish   1.8%

Universities/colleges, 1990-1991 enrollment
California State Polytechnic University, Pomona   17,905
College of Osteopathic Medicine of the Pacific, Pomona   485

Newspapers, total circulation (in all districts)
Inland Valley Daily Bulletin   73,003
Los Angeles Times   1,169,066
Orange County Register   341,875
Press-Enterprise Riverside   158,521
Redlands Daily Facts   9,169
San Bernardino County Sun   91,810
San Gabriel Valley Tribune   63,573
Whittier Daily News   16,802

Commercial television stations, affiliations
ADI: Los Angeles (100%)

Cable television systems, total subscribers
Chino Valley Cable TV College; Chino   16,391

Comcast Cable; Ontario 19,000
Continental Cablevision of California; Pomona 14,187
DCA Cablevision; Rancho Cucamonga 8,053
Dimension Cable; Rancho Santa Margarita 5,885
Jones Intercable Inc.; Walnut Valley 16,653
Yorba Linda Cable TV; Yorba Linda 14,160

Military installations, 1991
Ontario International Airport Air Force Guard Station, Ontario (shared with the 42nd District) 26

Businesses and other major employers
Lockheed Corp.; Ontario; guided missiles/parts 2,500
California State Polytechnic University, Pomona 2,000
California Institution for Medicine; Chino 1,800
San Antonio Community Hospital; Upland 1,746
State of California/Lanterman Dev. Center; Pomona 1,600
Walnut Valley Unified School District; Walnut 1,100
Kaiser Foundation Hospitals; Anaheim 1,000
Sysco Corp./Continental; Walnut; grocery products 900
State of California/Youth Training School; Chino; residential care 850
General Electric Co./GE Aircraft Engine; Ontario; repair shops 850
City of Pomona; Pomona; family services 800
Upland Unified School District; Upland 776
California Acrylic Industries; Pomona; spas 700
Pacific Bell; Anaheim; telephone communications 600
Sunkist Growers Inc.; Ontario; crop services 562
Doctors Hospital of Montclair; Montclair 529

42nd District

San Bernardino County — San Bernardino

This is the heart of the Inland Empire, composed of blue-collar bedrooms for Orange County and Los Angeles employers and a small manufacturing base.

San Bernardino (most of whose 164,000 people are in the 42nd) is an older community that grew about 40 percent during the 1980s; as brisk as that growth rate sounds, it was far outpaced by the population explosion in cities west of San Bernardino, such as Rancho Cucamonga and Ontario. Each of these now has upward of 100,000 residents.

San Bernardino is one of the last havens of affordably priced housing within tolerable commuting reach of Los Angeles; many who live here drive the 90 minutes it takes to get to jobs in L.A. Local leaders are trying to attract more industry to the area to spare residents from the treadmill of daily long-distance driving.

The San Bernardino area was a fruit-packing center in the 1930s. Today, its citrus industry shares space with electronics and aerospace firms. But the city is bracing for the 1994 closing of Norton Air Force Base. Studies are under way to determine what new use the base should be put to; options include an airport. One complicating factor is the need to clean up hazardous wastes at the facility.

Colton, a town of about 40,000 just southwest of San Bernardino, is about half Hispanic, 37 percent white, 8 percent black and 4 percent Asian. Many of its residents head a few miles west to work in Fontana's factories.

Fontana (population 88,000) is the area's factory town. It has a bit of a tough reputation: The Ku Klux Klan has been active here, and it is home to one of the world's largest Hell's Angels chapters.

The city's industry has been suffering. Kaiser Steel's Fontana works employed 9,000 in its heyday, but the company began slipping in the late 1970s, declared bankruptcy in 1983 and closed and sold the Fontana plant. The buyer, California Steel Industries, has 850 employees producing coiled steel, but the raw steel for that work has to come from elsewhere; the old Fontana blast furnace is being dismantled and shipped to China.

The western part of the 42nd rejects the Inland Empire label. Many of Rancho Cucamonga's 100,000 residents instead identify with Los Angeles, a half-hour to the west, and they cover their relatively high cost of living by commuting on the 10 Freeway to jobs in the city. Rancho Cucamonga is almost 70 percent white and 20 percent Hispanic.

The city of San Bernardino, pulled by its large minority population, consistently votes Democratic in presidential elections. Much of the rest of the district, led by such areas as Rancho Cucamonga, votes Republican. Overall, voter registration in the 42nd is 53 percent Democratic to 37 percent Republican. In 1992 presidential voting, this mix yielded a solid showing for Bill Clinton: He won 46 percent of the district's vote.

Election Returns and Party Registration

	42nd District	Democrat	Republican
1992	President*	76,964 (45.9%)	54,978 (32.8%)
	Senate †	68,803 (43.2%)	72,335 (45.4%)
	Senate †‡	82,083 (50.8%)	64,331 (39.8%)
	House †	79,780 (50.7%)	69,251 (44.0%)
1990	Governor †	50,148 (43.8%)	57,016 (49.8%)
1988	President	70,736 (44.8%)	85,197 (54.0%)
	Senate	67,374 (43.2%)	82,787 (53.0%)
1986	Senate	59,428 (47.6%)	60,798 (48.7%)
	Governor	44,556 (35.6%)	78,317 (62.6%)
1993	Party registration †	139,706 (53.2%)	97,454 (37.1%)

Vote for Perot was 35,828 (21.4%).   †*Independent/other is greater than 5%.*
‡*Special election for the remaining two years of the term of Pete Wilson who was elected governor in 1990. Appointee John Seymour held the seat 1991-1992.*

Demographics

Population 571,844

Percent change from 1980 9.1%

Land area 210 square miles

Population per square mile 2,726

Counties, 1990 population
San Bernardino (pt.) 571,844

Cities, 1990 population (10,000 or more)
Bloomington CDP 15,116
Colton (pt.) 40,050
Fontana (pt.) 87,535
Grand Terrace 10,946
Ontario (pt.) 51,471
Rancho Cucamonga (pt.) 101,409
Rialto 72,388
San Bernardino (pt.) 127,675

Race and Hispanic origin
White 66.0%
Black 11.1%
American Indian, Eskimo, or Aleut 0.9%
Asian or Pacific Islander 4.0%

Other 18.1%
Hispanic origin 34.3%

Ancestry

American 2.9%	Italian 4.2%
Dutch 2.0%	Norwegian 1.0%
English 10.1%	Polish 1.5%
French 3.4%	Scotch Irish 1.7%
German 16.3%	Scottish 1.5%
Irish 11.3%	Swedish 1.4%

Universities/colleges, 1990-1991 enrollment
Chaffey Community College, Alta Loma 10,985
San Bernardino Valley College, San Bernardino 10,157

Newspapers, total circulation (in all districts)
Los Angeles Times 1,169,066
Orange County Register 341,875
Press-Enterprise Riverside 158,521
San Bernardino County Sun 91,810

Commercial television stations, affiliations
ADI: Los Angeles (100%)

Cable television systems, total subscribers
Comcast Cablevision; Fontana 17,700
Comcast Cablevision; Ontario 19,000
Falcon Cable TV; Lake Arrowhead 15,668
Simmons Communications Inc.; Alta Loma 11,003

Military installations, 1991
Ontario Intl. Airport Air Force Guard Station, Ontario (shared with 41st District) 26

Businesses and other major employers
General Dynamics Corp.; Cucamonga; guided missiles/parts 3,450
Kaiser Foundation Hospitals; Fontana 2,700
St. Bernardine Medical Center; San Bernardino 1,800
Arrowhead Health Care System; San Bernardino 1,500
Chaffey Community College; Alta Loma 1,400
Stater Bros. Inc.; Colton; grocery stores 1,000
State of California; San Bernardino 900
California Steel Industries; Fontana; steel products 850
State of California/Caltrans Dept.; San Bernardino 800
Campus Crusade for Christ; San Bernardino; religious organizations 700
Southland Corp.; San Bernardino; warehousing 650
Sun Co.; San Bernardino; newspapers 508

43rd District

Riverside County — Western Suburbs

California gained seven House seats in the 1990 reapportionment, and this district is part of that bounty.

The old 37th District grew so much during the 1980s that by the time redistricting rolled around, there were enough people in it to fill up two complete districts: the 43rd, which takes in Riverside County's western edge, and the 44th, the county's eastern expanse.

To a great extent the 43rd serves as a bedroom district for three California regions. Its southern edge is just close enough to San Diego to house people who work in that city; immediately

west of the 43rd lies Orange County and its aerospace industries and scattered small businesses; and beyond that—a full two-or-three-hour drive for marathon commuters in the 43rd—are the office towers of downtown Los Angeles.

But in addition to its bedrooms, the district contains some of the largest avocado and citrus producers in the state, dairy ranchers to the west and March Air Force Base to the southeast of Riverside.

The largest city in the 43rd is Riverside, the county's seat, which was established as a silkworm-breeding center around 1870 and soon after jumped into the business of growing navel oranges. After decades of steady growth, the city's population began to take off in the 1950s.

Since this period of explosive growth started, Riverside city has been shifted in and out of the Riverside County district. In the 1960s, it was completely included; in the 1970s, it was completely removed; in the 1980s, it was split, but in a manner beneficial to the already-dominant GOP.

Now the city, with a population of 227,000, can anchor a district by itself. The 43rd has all of Riverside, including the city's more Democratic northern neighborhoods, its blue-collar communities and the area around the University of California at Riverside (8,700 students).

Despite the addition of Riverside's Democratic areas, Republicans retain a slight voter registration advantage over Democrats in the 43rd—46 percent to 42 percent. The GOP's edge is bolstered by such fast-growing Riverside suburbs as Corona and Norco (populations 76,000 and 23,000, respectively). About 80,000 live in unincorporated county territory. The district is about one-quarter Hispanic, 6 percent black and 4 percent Asian.

The 1992 House race was tight all over the district. The Republican's razor-thin victory turned on the count of about 34,000 absentee ballots. That number of absentee ballots, which would be extraordinary in other places, is more common in California's bedroom community districts: "If you leave for work at 5 in the morning and don't get home until 8 at night, you've got to vote absentee; the polls are closed," one local observer notes.

The district's 1992 presidential race was similarly close. George Bush beat Bill Clinton by only 797 votes out of about 200,000 cast.

Election Returns and Party Registration

	43rd District	Democrat	Republican
1992	President*	76,040 (37.8%)	76,837 (38.2%)
	Senate †	73,645 (37.1%)	104,488 (52.6%)
	Senate †‡	85,563 (43.2%)	91,449 (46.2%)
	House †	88,468 (46.9%)	88,987 (47.2%)
1990	Governor	44,829 (36.8%)	68,549 (56.3%)
1988	President	64,837 (39.1%)	98,996 (59.7%)
	Senate	62,821 (38.2%)	96,312 (58.5%)
1986	Senate	45,389 (45.0%)	51,757 (51.4%)
	Governor	35,788 (35.4%)	63,555 (62.9%)
1993	Party registration †	118,332 (42.4%)	126,986 (45.5%)

*Vote for Perot was 48,197 (24.0%). †Independent/other is greater than 5%.
‡Special election for the remaining two years of the term of Pete Wilson who was elected governor in 1990. Appointee John Seymour held the seat 1991-1992.

Demographics

Population 571,231

Percent change from 1980 8.2%

Land area 747 square miles

Population per square mile 764

Counties, 1990 population
Riverside (pt.) 571,231

Cities, 1990 population (10,000 or more)
Corona 76,095
Glen Avon CDP 12,663
Lake Elsinore 18,285
Mira Loma CDP 15,786
Norco 23,302
Riverside (pt.) 226,505
Rubidoux CDP 24,367
Wildomar CDP 10,411

Race and Hispanic origin
White 75.7%
Black 5.9%
American Indian, Eskimo, or Aleut. 0.8%
Asian or Pacific Islander 4.3%
Other 13.2%
Hispanic origin 25.0%

Ancestry
American 3.4%
Dutch 2.9%
English 13.6%
French 4.3%
German 20.6%
Irish 14.0%
Italian 4.5%
Norwegian 1.7%
Polish 2.1%
Scotch Irish 2.0%
Scottish 2.3%
Swedish 2.1%

Universities/colleges, 1990-1991 enrollment
California Baptist College, Riverside 667
Riverside Community College, Riverside 15,683
University of California, Riverside 8,715

Newspapers, total circulation (in all districts)
Hemet News 18,535
Los Angeles Times 1,169,066
Orange County Register 341,875
Press-Enterprise Riverside 158,521
San Bernardino County Sun 91,810
San Diego Union-Tribune 385,197
Temecula Californian 10,251

Commercial television stations, affiliations
ADI: Los Angeles (100%)

Cable television systems, total subscribers
Cencom Cable TV; Riverside 54,000
Continental Cablevision of California; Corona 9,800
King Videocable College; Lake Elsinore 20,756

Military installations, 1991
March Air Force Base, Sunnymead 4,924

Businesses and other major employers
Rohr Industries Inc.; Riverside; aircraft/parts 2,900
City of Riverside/Sheriffs Dept.; Riverside 1,600
International Multifoods; Riverside; preserved
   fruits/vegetables 1,500
Riverside General Hospital; Riverside 1,500
Kaiser Foundation Hospitals; Riverside 1,500
Williams Construction; Riverside; carpentry 1,200
Riverside Community Hospital; Riverside 1,195
Riverside Community College; Riverside 1,165
Press Enterprise Co./Press Enterprise; Riverside; newspapers
   1,110
University of California; Riverside 1,000

General Conference Seventh-Day Adventists; Riverside; reli-
   gious organizations 1,000
Parkview Community Hospital & Medical Center; Riverside
   948
City of Riverside; Riverside 850
Toro Co./Irrigation Div.; Riverside; irrigation systems 800
Consolidated Freightways Corp.; Mira Loma; trucking facili-
   ties 700
County of Riverside; Riverside 700
Starcrest Products of California/T-Michael Intl.; Perris;
   nonstore retailers 650
County of Riverside/Probation Dept.; Riverside; family ser-
   vices 625
Corona Community Hospital; Corona 620
State of California/Rehabilitation Center; Norco; residential
   care 610
Dyncorp; Norco Div.; computer services 600
Fleetwood Enterprises Inc.; Riverside; mobile homes 595
E. R. Carpenter Co. Inc.; Riverside; plastics products 550

44th District

Eastern Riverside County

The 44th looks similar to the old 37th district, but remapping lopped off more than 500,000 people who had been on its western side. The old 37th saw more population growth during the past decade than any other district in the country. Census-takers in 1990 found that the old 37th had enough constituents to fill two districts.

Population in Moreno Valley, which is just east of Riverside and has 119,000 residents, is exploding. Before growth restric-tions and the recession put on the brakes, it was picking up an additional 10,000 families a year. The city anchors the western side of the 44th, with cities such as Beaumont and Perris nearby.

The eastern portion of the district's population lives in the Coachella Valley, through which runs the 10 Freeway on its way out to Blythe and the Arizona border. Out here, the leisure class of the oasis resorts of Rancho Mirage and Palm Springs contribute their ample wealth to the local economies. Although former President Gerald R. Ford has made his home in the area, it is better known for its Hollywood set.

Although one-quarter of Palm Springs' residents are 65 or older, the city is a bit younger than it used to be; the median age of its residents dropped 3 years during the 1980s. The city expanded from 32,000 residents in 1980 to 40,000 in 1990—a 25 percent growth rate (which is positively sluggish by the high standards of this booming area).

A few miles southeast of Palm Springs is Palm Desert, where the population almost doubled in the 1980s, to 23,000. Here the older set became more dominant: The 65-and-over population went up almost 150 percent.

While this area is famed as a retirement destination, and while the number of older residents did grow rapidly, overall in Riverside County their influx was overshadowed by a larger immigration of younger people. The percentage of all residents 65 and older in the county dropped from 15 percent to 13 percent during the 1980s.

Despite the growth of the district's suburbs and resorts, farmers continue to play a major role in the economy and politics of the 44th. Irrigation ditches knife across Riverside County, and cotton, date and livestock producers battle to keep their scarce water resources from being diverted to the urbanized areas. Riverside was originally a trade center for the citrus ranches of the Santa Ana River basin; the first domestic navel orange was grown here in the 1870s. Now the farming centers around Blythe, a burg of 8,000 reached by taking the 10 Freeway 80 miles east through the desert.

This is traditionally a very Republican district—the GOP's 1-point registration advantage understates the point—but Bill Clinton did very well here in 1992, taking 41 percent of the vote, 5 points more than George Bush.

Election Returns and Party Registration

	44th District	Democrat	Republican
1992	President*	87,180 (40.6%)	76,772 (35.7%)
	Senate †	83,747 (39.6%)	106,699 (50.4%)
	Senate †‡	98,090 (46.5%)	93,095 (44.1%)
	House †	81,693 (40.1%)	110,333 (54.2%)
1990	Governor †	49,271 (38.8%)	70,843 (55.8%)
1988	President	65,751 (40.2%)	95,875 (58.6%)
	Senate	63,561 (39.1%)	93,681 (57.7%)
1986	Senate	46,385 (41.6%)	62,512 (56.1%)
	Governor	35,866 (32.0%)	74,976 (66.8%)
1993	Party registration †	129,994 (44.6%)	127,205 (43.6%)

*Vote for Perot was 50,867 (23.7%).   †Independent/other is greater than 5%.
‡Special election for the remaining two years of the term of Pete Wilson who was elected governor in 1990. Appointee John Seymour held the seat 1991-1992.

Demographics

Population   571,583

Percent change from 1980   8.7%

Land area   6,359 square miles

Population per square mile   90

Counties, 1990 population
Riverside (pt.)   571,583

Cities, 1990 population (10,000 or more)

Banning 20,570	La Quinta 11,215
Cathedral City 30,085	Moreno Valley (pt.)
Coachella 16,896	111,488
Desert Hot Springs 11,668	Palm Desert 23,252
East Hemet CDP 17,611	Palm Springs 40,181
Hemet 36,094	Perris (pt.) 16,348
Indio 36,793	San Jacinto 16,210
	Sun City CDP 14,930

Race and Hispanic origin
White   76.5%
Black   5.1%
American Indian, Eskimo, or Aleut.   1.1%
Asian or Pacific Islander   2.9%
Other   14.4%
Hispanic origin   28.1%

Ancestry

American 3.5%	Irish 13.1%
Dutch 2.5%	Italian 4.0%
English 14.6%	Norwegian 1.6%
French 4.3%	Polish 1.9%
German 18.6%	Russian 1.0%

Scotch Irish 2.3%	Swedish 2.0%
Scottish 2.3%	

Universities/colleges, 1990-1991 enrollment
College of the Desert, Palm Desert   7,231
Mount San Jacinto College, San Jacinto   3,978
Palo Verde College, Blythe   768

Newspapers, total circulation (in all districts)
Hemet News   18,535
Los Angeles Times   1,169,066
Palm Spring Desert Sun   46,871
Press-Enterprise Riverside   158,521
San Bernardino County Sun   91,810
San Diego Union-Tribune   385,197

Commercial television stations, affiliations
ADI: Phoenix (48%), Palm Springs (31%) and Los Angeles (21%)
    KMIR-TV, Palm Springs (NBC)
    KESQ-TV, Palm Springs (ABC)

Cable television systems, total subscribers
Colony Communications; Banning   6,666
Colony Communications; Palm Desert   63,100
Desert Hot Springs Cablevision; Desert Hot Springs   8,000
Inland Valley Cablevision; Idyllwild   30,930
Warner Cable/Palm Springs; Palm Springs   29,477

Businesses and other major employers
Marriott Desert Springs Resort; Palm Desert; hotel   1,800
Eisenhower Medical Center; Rancho Mirage   1,800
Desert Hospital; Palm Springs   1,500
Hemet Valley Hospital District; Hemet   1,350
Landmark Land Co. Inc.; La Quinta; subdividers/developers   1,200
Sun World Inc./Coachella Packing & Handling; Coachella; crop services   1,192
Deutsch Engineered Connecting Devices; Banning; electronic components   1,000
La Quinta Hotel; La Quinta; hotel   950
Advanced Cardiovascular Systems; Temecula; medical instruments   900
Chuckawalla Valley State Prison; Blythe   800
Mount San Jacinto College, San Jacinto   680
Stouffer Esmeralda Resort; Palm Springs; hotel   600
Westin Mission Hills Resort; Rancho Mirage; hotel   550

45th District
Coastal Orange County

In the 45th District (see map on page 97), there are two distinct flavors of communities—coastal and interior—but they both taste Republican. Seal Beach anchors the coastal section. A quarter of its 25,000 residents live in a seniors-only community, which makes for quite a gray city: 37 percent of Seal Beach's residents are over 65, 22 percent are over 75 and 7 percent are over 85. Ninety percent of its residents are non-Hispanic whites.

Heading southeast down the coast is Huntington Beach, whose permanent population of 182,000—mostly young aerospace and other high-tech workers and their families—is supplemented in the summer by those eager to "shred" some waves in surfing competitions, hence its nickname "Surf City." Huntington Harbor is an affluent section of the city, with such accouterments as backyard boat slips. The rest of the city consists of huge housing tracts with a few small business districts sprinkled in.

Huntington Beach also has a McDonnell Douglas plant that is the prime design and manufacturing facility for the space station *Freedom*. It employs 6,000 people, which so far has cushioned the 45th from the worst of Southern California's recession, but the district obviously has a lot of eggs in the space station basket. If the program is cut back, this area could be pinched.

Newport Beach resembles the other coastal communities—more bedrooms for aerospace white-collar workers—but looks a little different: Its terrain lifts into some rolling hills and Newport Bay runs right up its middle.

Compared with the coast, the 45th's interior areas tend to be more blue-collar and less affluent, and they have a higher Democratic registration. But they are conservative and they vote Republican: "If there's a place where there are Reagan Democrats, it's Westminster, Garden Grove [in the 46th] and Stanton," a local GOP observer says reverently.

The blue collar of the interior is sky blue, with many working for aerospace companies within the district or commuting to those in Anaheim, Torrance or Long Beach.

Westminster, just inland from Huntington Beach, is heavily Republican, but with a high Democratic registration for this district. Costa Mesa, between Huntington and Newport Beach, has a mix of white- and blue-collar workers and boasts a huge shopping mall—South Coast Plaza, which is placed on maps of the region.

The district reaches north between Cypress and Garden Grove to take in Stanton. Democrats here have a 7-point registration advantage, a figure much higher than elsewhere in the district. The city is not as wealthy as others in the 45th; 15 percent of its housing units are either mobile homes or trailers. To the north, the district takes in a small residential slice of Anaheim.

George Bush won this district in 1992 with 42 percent of its vote, compared with 32 percent for Bill Clinton and 25 percent for Ross Perot.

Election Returns and Party Registration

	45th District	Democrat	Republican
1992	President*	80,646 (32.2%)	105,893 (42.3%)
	Senate†	83,729 (34.0%)	139,418 (56.6%)
	Senate †‡	98,940 (40.4%)	121,445 (49.5%)
	House†	88,508 (39.0%)	123,731 (54.5%)
1990	Governor†	58,317 (31.5%)	116,265 (62.8%)
1988	President	77,667 (31.6%)	165,391 (67.3%)
	Senate	73,307 (29.6%)	167,077 (67.5%)
1986	Senate	62,429 (35.4%)	105,011 (59.6%)
	Governor	47,273 (27.0%)	124,880 (71.2%)
1993	Party registration†	105,684 (34.8%)	155,668 (51.3%)

*Vote for Perot was 63,609 (25.4%).   †Independent/other is greater than 5%.
‡Special election for the remaining two years of the term of Pete Wilson who was elected governor in 1990. Appointee John Seymour held the seat 1991-1992.

Demographics

Population 570,874

Percent change from 1980 8.6%

Land area 91 square miles

Population per square mile 6,247

Counties, 1990 population
Orange (pt.) 570,874

Cities, 1990 population (10,000 or more)
Anaheim (pt.) 35,599
Costa Mesa (pt.) 95,126
Fountain Valley (pt.) 52,491
Garden Grove (pt.) 18,868
Huntington Beach 181,519
Newport Beach (pt.) 35,031
Seal Beach (pt.) 23,573
Stanton (pt.) 28,587
Westminster (pt.) 77,694

Race and Hispanic origin
White 82.1%
Black 1.2%
American Indian, Eskimo, or Aleut. 0.6%
Asian or Pacific Islander 11.0%
Other 5.1%
Hispanic origin 14.8%

Ancestry
American 2.5%
Danish 1.1%
Dutch 2.6%
English 16.3%
French 4.7%
German 21.7%
Irish 14.7%
Italian 5.8%
Norwegian 1.8%
Polish 2.6%
Russian 1.6%
Scotch Irish 2.3%
Scottish 2.9%
Swedish 2.6%
Welsh 1.1%

Universities/colleges, 1990-1991 enrollment
Coastline Community College, Fountain Valley 10,950
Golden West College, Huntington Beach 13,137
Orange Coast College, Costa Mesa 22,365
Southern California College, Costa Mesa 919

Newspapers, total circulation (in all districts)
Long Beach Press-Telegram 126,076
Los Angeles La Opinion 98,557
Los Angeles Times 1,169,066
Orange County Register 341,875

Commercial television stations, affiliations
ADI: Los Angeles (100%)

Cable television systems, total subscribers
Comcast Cablevision; Newport Beach 26,832
Copley/Colony Cablevision; Costa Mesa 22,815
Paragon Cable; Garden Grove 21,921
Paragon Cable; Huntington Beach 90,640

Military installations, 1991
Seal Beach Naval Weapons Station, Seal Beach 5,989

Businesses and other major employers
McDonnell Douglas Corp./Space Systems; Huntington Beach; space vehicles/guided missiles 6,000
Rockwell Intl. Corp./Satellite & Space Elec. Div.; Seal Beach; communications equipment 3,000
Hoag Memorial Hospital; Newport Beach 2,058
Times Mirror Co./Los Angeles Times; Costa Mesa; newspapers 2,000
Orange County Special Olympics; Anaheim; recreation services 2,000
Coast Community College District; Huntington Beach 1,806

Fairview State Hospital; Costa Mesa 1,700

Hughes Aircraft Co./Microelectronic Circuits Div.; Newport Beach; electronic components 1,500

State Farm Co.; Costa Mesa; insurance services 1,500

Fountain Valley Regional Hospital; Santa Ana 1,300

Automobile Club of Southern California Inc.; Costa Mesa; auto insurance/membership services 1,100

City of Huntington Beach; Huntington Beech 1,100

C&D Plastics Inc.; Huntington Beach; aircraft/parts 1,000

Nordstrom Inc.; Costa Mesa; department stores 1,000

Security Pacific National Bank; Costa Mesa; commercial banks 1,000

Coast Telecourses; Costa Mesa 1,000

Coast Telecourses; Santa Ana 1,000

FHP Inc./FHP Hospital; Santa Ana 830

Filenet Corp.; Costa Mesa; computer/office equipment 741

AST Research Inc.; Santa Ana; computer/office equipment 700

Home Fashions Inc./Louver Drape; Westminster; fixtures 700

Rockwell Intl. Corp.; Seal Beach; information systems 700

Fedco; Costa Mesa; department stores 660

IBM Corp.; Costa Mesa; computer/office equipment 650

Pilkington Aerospace Inc.; Garden Grove; plastics products 635

Emulex Corp.; Costa Mesa; computer/office equipment 600

Bullock's; Costa Mesa; department stores 600

Fountain Valley School District; Santa Ana 600

Employee Benefits America Administration Corp.; Santa Ana; insurance services 575

County of Orange/Sanitation District; Santa Ana 550

Air Industries Corp.; Garden Grove; screw machine products 550

Safeco Insurance Co.; Santa Ana; insurance services 524

Red Lion Inn; Costa Mesa; hotel 510

46th District

Part of Orange County; Santa Ana; Garden Grove

The 46th (see map on page 97) is a blue-collar district, full of older suburban homes and younger families. Its defense subcontractors are the backbone of the region's large defense and aerospace companies. But with the defense and aerospace industries flat on their backs, the 46th is hurting. Most of the district's population is contained within two cities, Santa Ana in the south and Garden Grove in the north.

Santa Ana, with 294,000 residents in total, is the area's hub and the seat of Orange County. It has the crime and gang problems typical of many California cities, and these problems are spilling into Garden Grove and adjacent districts. (Garden Grove is struggling with Asian gangs that have cropped up in recent years.)

Garden Grove is a more residential area than Santa Ana. It divides roughly into three sections: the western, more affluent part; the center, which is a mix of Vietnamese, Koreans and Hispanics; and the eastern, very heavily Hispanic part. Little Saigon sits just south of the district in Westminster. Garden Grove is probably best known for the "positive thinking" television ministry of Robert Schuller and his Crystal Cathedral.

In recent years, there has been an influx of Indochinese refugees into Garden Grove, spurring a conservative backlash

from some of its white, blue-collar workers. Garden Grove is now 20 percent Asian, 23 percent Hispanic and 1 percent black. On the whole, the district is half Hispanic, 12 percent Asian and 2 percent black.

The northern part of the 46th includes the southern part of Anaheim, a chunk that has the look and feel of Garden Grove, which it borders.

The 46th does not include the wealthier area of Anaheim off to the east known as Anaheim Hills, which is split between the 41st and 47th districts. The part of Anaheim that is in the 46th does include Disneyland, many of whose employees come from the district. The park employs about 9,000 in the winter and 12,000 in the summer. Thousands of jobs at a variety of hotels and other supporting businesses depend on the park.

Other than Disneyland, there is no one employer within the 46th that drives its economy; the district is dotted with defense subcontractors and small businesses. Some residents head an hour west to the shipyard in Long Beach, but most scatter to companies all over Orange County.

The Democratic Party has a registration advantage over the GOP here, 48 to 41 percent, but most of the Democrats are conservative and the district votes Republican.

In 1992, the GOP House incumbent won by 9 points; in the presidential race George Bush took 40 percent of the vote, compared with 37 percent for Bill Clinton and 23 percent for Ross Perot.

Election Returns and Party Registration

	46th District	Democrat	Republican
1992	President*	44,352 (37.1%)	47,689 (39.9%)
	Senate †	42,753 (36.2%)	62,601 (53.1%)
	Senate †‡	49,825 (42.6%)	53,411 (45.7%)
	House †	45,435 (41.0%)	55,659 (50.2%)
1990	Governor †	30,501 (34.5%)	51,449 (58.1%)
1988	President	47,838 (36.7%)	80,834 (61.9%)
	Senate	44,733 (34.2%)	80,553 (61.6%)
1986	Senate †	37,851 (39.7%)	51,494 (54.0%)
	Governor	31,353 (33.2%)	61,061 (64.6%)
1993	Party registration †	77,298 (47.5%)	67,159 (41.3%)

*Vote for Perot was 27,542 (23.0%).   †Independent/other is greater than 5%.
‡Special election for the remaining two years of the term of Pete Wilson who was elected governor in 1990. Appointee John Seymour held the seat 1991-1992.

Demographics

Population 571,380

Percent change from 1980 (new district in the 1990s)

Land area 63 square miles

Population per square mile 9,091

Counties, 1990 population
Orange (pt.) 571,380

Cities, 1990 population (10,000 or more)
Anaheim (pt.) 151,589
Garden Grove (pt.) 124,182
Santa Ana (pt.) 271,662

Race and Hispanic origin
White 66.5%

Black 2.5%
American Indian, Eskimo, or Aleut. 0.6%
Asian or Pacific Islander 12.3%
Other 18.2%
Hispanic origin 50.0%

Ancestry

American 1.9%		Italian 2.7%
Dutch 1.4%		Polish 1.3%
English 7.3%		Scotch Irish 1.1%
French 2.3%		Scottish 1.2%
German 11.1%		Swedish 1.0%
Irish 7.3%		

Universities/colleges, 1990-1991 enrollment

Rancho Santiago College, Santa Ana 20,532

Newspapers, total circulation (in all districts)

Los Angeles La Opinion 98,557
Los Angeles Times 1,169,066
Orange County Register 341,875

Commercial television stations, affiliations

ADI: Los Angeles (100%)

Cable television systems, total subscribers

Comcast Cablevision, Newport Beach 26,832
Multivision Cable TV; Anaheim 38,500
Paragon Cable; Garden Grove 21,921

Businesses and other major employers

County of Orange; Santa Ana 18,500
Walt Disney Co. Inc./Disneyland; Anaheim; amusement park 10,000
Parker Hannifin Corp./Product Support Div.; Irvine; aircraft fluid/machinery/equipment/supplies 5,000
University of California/UCI Medical Center; Orange 2,700
ITT Corp.; Santa Ana; management/public relations 2,000
McGaw Inc.; Irvine; pharmaceuticals 2,000
City of Anaheim; Anaheim 1,950
TRW Inc.; Orange; credit reporting 1,900
County of Orange/Sheriffs Dept.; Santa Ana 1,800
Orange County Transportation Authority; Garden Grove 1,750
Baxter Healthcare Corp.; Irvine; professional/commercial equipment 1,700
WCO Hotels Inc./Disneyland Hotel; Anaheim; hotels/motels 1,500
Kwikset Corp.; Anaheim; cutlery/handtools/hardware 1,240
Steelcase Inc.; Tustin; office furniture 1,200
Rancho Santiago College; Santa Ana 1,200
Anaheim Hilton & Towers; Anaheim; hotels 1,200
Shiley Inc.; Irvine; medical instruments/supplies 1,150
St. John Knits Inc./S. J. Accessories; Irvine; durable goods 1,100
Textron Inc./Cherry Fasteners Div. Textron; Santa Ana; costume jewelry 1,100
Anaheim Memorial Hospital; Anaheim 1,022
Tokos Medical Corp.; Santa Ana 972
Freedom Newspapers Inc./Register; Santa Ana; newspapers 900
City of Garden Grove; Garden Grove 850
Taco Bell Corp.; Irvine; fast-food chain 800
Vicki Heston Personnel Serv.; Irvine; supply services 790

Martin Luther Hospital; Anaheim 770
Pacific Telesis Group/PacTel Cellular; Irvine; cellular telephones 700
Mitsubishi Consumer Electronics America; Santa Ana; audio/video equipment 700
McDonnell Douglas Corp.; Santa Ana; computer services 700
Calcomp Inc.; Anaheim; computer/office equipment 700
Anaheim Marriott Hotel; Anaheim; hotel 700
Ingram Micro Inc.; Santa Ana; professional/commercial equipment 650
City of Santa Ana/Transportation Dept.; Santa Ana 650
Printronix Inc.; Irvine; computer/office equipment 614
Bergen Brunswig Corp.; Orange; drugs/proprietaries 600
U.S. Federal Deposit Insurance Corp.; Irvine 600
Carl Karcher Enterprises/Carl's Jr.; Anaheim; fast-food chain 600
Garden Grove Hospital & Medical Center; Garden Grove 580
SPS Technologies Inc.; Santa Ana; costume jewelry 550
Odetics Inc./GYYR Products Div.; Anaheim; measuring/controlling devices 545
Service Mortgage Co.; Irvine; management consulting services 510

47th District

Coastal — Central Orange County; Irvine

The 47th (see map on page 97) is very, very safe GOP territory. It boasts the highest proportion of registered Republicans in the state, with 57 percent to the Democrats' 30 percent. It gave George Bush the strongest support he got in California in 1992, 46 percent of the vote, compared with Bill Clinton's 31 percent.

It is difficult for candidates to be too conservative for the voters here. John Schmitz, who represented part of this region for a term in the early 1970s, was later removed from the executive council of the John Birch Society for extremism.

The 47th sports several different kinds of coast. To the north is part of Newport Beach, a wealthy enclave noted for its beautiful sandy beaches and luxurious housing. To the south, rocky Laguna Beach attracts more scuba divers than swimmers. Between them is the Crystal Cove State Park, which covers about half of the district's coastline.

Laguna Beach's 23,000 residents are considered more liberal than those in Newport Beach, and the city is renowned as "the arts community." At the city's annual summer festival well-known paintings are recreated by live models on stage.

While much of Southern California can be characterized by random suburban sprawl, Irvine's 110,000 residents live in a city whose main streets meet at right angles and whose corporate and residential areas are meticulously planned.

The University of California at Irvine is building housing for some of its 16,900 students and faculty to try to shed its image as a commuter school. The campus concentrates on engineering and other technical fields and has drawn a number of technology companies to the area, including the computer manufacturer AST Research Inc., a division of Rockwell International and Rogerson Aircraft Corp.

Just north of Irvine on the 5 Freeway is Tustin, a city of 51,000 divided into two areas: The south has this city's business district and its lower- to middle-income residents; the north, into the hills a bit, is its high-income area.

Farther north on the freeway is Orange, one of the county's oldest cities. There are 111,000 residents here, Victorian-style homes in the downtown area, affluent suburbs to the west near Anaheim and lower-income areas off to the east. The east also includes some farms.

Villa Park is Orange County's smallest city and is likely to remain that way: It is completely surrounded by Anaheim and Orange and has nowhere to go to grow. The city forbids more than two houses per acre within much of its borders, which has kept crowding down (only 6,300 people live here), the skyline low and the house prices high.

The 47th also has a lot of unincorporated county land out to the east. Silverado Canyon was a bustling silver mining area in the early 1920s and is now a secluded farming area. Much of the district's eastern end is grassy, hilly land that large development companies, with an eye on potential future growth, have snatched up.

Election Returns and Party Registration

	47th District	Democrat	Republican
1992	President*	86,279 (31.0%)	127,700 (45.9%)
	Senate †	92,349 (33.7%)	160,805 (58.7%)
	Senate †‡	108,930 (39.9%)	142,799 (52.3%)
	House	76,924 (30.3%)	165,004 (64.9%)
1990	Governor	56,966 (30.0%)	123,216 (65.0%)
1988	President	69,964 (28.5%)	172,489 (70.3%)
	Senate	64,213 (26.0%)	176,958 (71.6%)
1986	Senate	56,373 (31.6%)	114,580 (64.3%)
	Governor	42,744 (24.0%)	132,130 (74.3%)
1993	Party registration †	99,615 (30.3%)	185,433 (56.5%)

*Vote for Perot was 64,227 (23.1%).   †Independent/other is greater than 5%.
‡Special election for the remaining two years of the term of Pete Wilson who was elected governor in 1990. Appointee John Seymour held the seat 1991-1992.

Demographics

Population 571,518

Percent change from 1980 (new district in the 1990s)

Land area 304 square miles

Population per square mile 1,878

Counties, 1990 population
Orange (pt.) 571,518

Cities, 1990 population (10,000 or more)
Anaheim (pt.) 51,668
El Toro CDP (pt.) 61,604
Irvine (pt.) 109,774
Laguna Beach (pt.) 20,093
Laguna Hills CDP (pt.) 42,062
Mission Viejo (pt.) 16,528
Newport Beach (pt.) 31,612
Orange (pt.) 105,200
Santa Ana (pt.) 22,062
Tustin Foothills CDP 24,358
Tustin (pt.) 46,029

Race and Hispanic origin
White 83.6%
Black 1.8%
American Indian, Eskimo, or Aleut. 0.4%
Asian or Pacific Islander 9.6%
Other 4.6%
Hispanic origin 13.1%

Ancestry
American 2.4%
Danish 1.2%
Dutch 2.3%
English 17.5%
French 4.8%
German 23.3%
Hungarian 1.0%
Irish 15.0%
Italian 5.9%
Norwegian 2.0%
Polish 3.2%
Russian 2.2%
Scotch Irish 2.4%
Scottish 3.3%
Swedish 3.0%
Welsh 1.1%

Universities/colleges, 1990-1991 enrollment
Chapman College-Academic Center Orange 5,815
Chapman University, Orange 2,256
Christ College Irvine, Irvine 592
Irvine Valley College, Irvine 4,678
University of California, Irvine 16,817

Newspapers, total circulation (in all districts)
Long Beach Press-Telegram 126,076
Los Angeles La Opinion 98,557
Los Angeles Times 1,169,066
Orange County Register 341,875

Commercial television stations, affiliations
ADI: Los Angeles (100%)

Cable television systems, total subscribers
Cablevision of Orange; Orange 23,100
Comcast Cablevision; Santa Ana 24,996
Comcast Cablevision; Newport Beach 26,832
Continental Cablevision of California; Tustin 9,441
Dimension Cable Services; Irivne 41,324
Dimension Cable Services; Mission Viejo 122,000
Multivision Cable TV; Anaheim 38,499
Paragon Cable; Huntington Beach 90,640

Military installations, 1991
El Toro Marine Corps Air Station, Irvine 7,514
Tustin Marine Corps Air Station, Tustin 4,760

Businesses and other major employers
University of California; Irvine 5,000
Rockwell Intl. Corp./Autonetics Strategic Systems Div.; Anaheim; communications equipment 4,310
Fluor Corp.; Irvine; building construction 3,500
Parker Hannifin Corp.; Irvine; aircraft/parts 2,800
St. Joseph Hospital of Orange; Orange 2,000
Pacific Mutual Life Insurance Co.; Newport Beach; life insurance 1,593
Western Digital Corp.; Irvine; electronic components 1,500
Allergan Inc.; Irvine; ophthalmic goods 1,500
Rockwell Intl. Corp./Digital Communications Div.; Newport Beach; communications equipment 1,500
Vans Inc.; Orange; footwear 1,500
United Parcel Service Inc.; Anaheim; mail services 1,500
Sun World Inc./Treasure Farms; Irvine; crop services 1,349
Saddleback Memorial Medical Center; Laguna Beach 1,300
Toshiba America Info Systems; Irvine; computer/office equipment 1,275
Unisys Corp.; San Juan Capistrano; computer equipment 1,200
AST Research Inc.; Irvine; computer equipment 1,200
Silicon Systems Inc.; Tustin; electronic components 1,200

Interstate Electronics Corp.; Anaheim; measuring/controlling devices 1,200

Western Medical Center; Santa Ana 1,200

Professional Community Mgt./Leisure World; Laguna Beach; real estate agents 1,100

County of Orange/Fire Dept.; Orange 1,080

Children's Hospital of Orange; Orange 1,065

Chapman University/Chapman College; Orange 1,050

Lucky Stores Inc.; Irvine; grocery warehousing 1,000

Aliso Viejo Co.; San Juan Capistrano; subdividers/developers 1,000

Volvo North America Corp.; Irvine; used car dealers 1,000

Ogden Allied Services Corp.; Anaheim; grocery stores 1,000

MAI Systems Corp.; Tustin; computer services 1,000

Avco Financial Services Inc.; Irvine; credit institutions 975

Amcil Equities Inc.; Irvine; millwork 700

United Intl. Investigative Services; Anaheim; business/security services 700

Catholic Diocese of Orange/School Office; Orange: religious organization 692

3 Day Blinds Inc.; Anaheim; fixtures 680

Denny's Holdings Inc.; Irvine; restaurants 650

Marriott Hotel; Irvine; hotel 640

Alcon Laboratories Inc.; Irvine; surgical instruments/supplies 628

Symbol Technologies Inc.; Costa Mesa; electrical goods 600

Nordstrom Inc.; Santa Ana; clothing stores 600

Wickes Companies Inc.; Irvine; management/public relations 600

Service Employee Intl. Union; Anaheim; labor organization 600

Computer Inventory Services; Laguna Beach; business services 595

Amisub Irvine Medical Center; Irvine 590

Hines Nurseries Inc.; Irvine; horticultural specialties 550

Canon Business Machines Inc.; Costa Mesa; photographic equipment/supplies 550

E. L. Yeager Construction Co.; Santa Ana; heavy construction 550

Xerox Corp.; Santa Ana; management/public relations 550

Newport Beach Marriott Hotel; Newport Beach; hotel 535

Berryman Health Inc.; Orange; nursing 511

48th District

Part of Orange, San Diego and Riverside Counties

Like many of Southern California's coastal districts, the 48th is firmly in the Republican column. The party has a 55 percent to 30 percent registration advantage over the Democrats, a level surpassed in California only by the 47th District just up the coast.

As one observer put it, residents are "conservative, upper-middle class, well-educated, [and have] 2.5 kids [and] two cars."

Each of the 48th's three counties gave George Bush strong support in 1992. Overall, he won 44 percent of the 48th's vote in 1992, compared with 29 percent for Bill Clinton and 27 percent for Ross Perot. Forty-nine percent of the district's vote is cast in Orange County, 45 percent is from San Diego County and 4 percent is cast in Riverside County.

Heading down the Pacific Coast Highway, the 48th takes in some of Laguna Beach and all of Dana Point and San Clemente

in Orange County, and Camp Pendleton Marine Corps Base and Oceanside in San Diego County.

The coastal area relies heavily on tourism dollars. The economies of Oceanside, and to a lesser extent San Clemente, also depend on the Marine base. Camp Pendleton supplied many of the personnel for Desert Shield/Desert Storm in 1990-1991. Oceanside is the district's largest city with 128,000 residents in total.

The district breaks into Riverside County to the north only to pick up Temecula, a newer, pro-business, pro-growth community whose 27,000 residents live in the wine-producing Temecula Valley. Other new cities such as Dana Point and Laguna Niguel have incorporated in the past several years. Laguna Niguel is a centrally planned community due east from Laguna Beach.

San Marcos, in San Diego County, has burgeoned; its population more than tripled in the 1970s and grew by 123 percent in the 1980s to 39,000. It is the site of one of the newest universities in the country—California State University, San Marcos, which opened in 1991.

Even the town of San Juan Capistrano, famous for the swallows that flock to its ancient Spanish mission each spring, is being transformed. But the town's historic nature remains unscathed; artifacts of California's mission period were unearthed here recently.

The 48th has escaped some of the economic suffering felt throughout the rest of Southern California. Its economy relies more on service industries and on tourism, and not as much on aerospace and military contracts as does the neighboring 47th's. A steady stream of visitors to the 48th District's beach communities provides a cushion for the economy.

While this area may have been considered "lily white" in the late 1970s, there has been steady, though slow, growth in its minority populations. Now, 17 percent of its residents are Hispanic, 5 percent are Asian and 4 percent are black. The area also has a growing number of military retirees.

Election Returns and Party Registration

	48th District	Democrat	Republican
1992	President*	71,621 (29.1%)	108,581 (44.1%)
	Senate †	77,172 (32.1%)	140,131 (58.2%)
	Senate †‡	91,834 (38.4%)	123,986 (51.9%)
	House †	67,415 (29.2%)	140,935 (61.1%)
1990	Governor †	42,579 (29.1%)	94,066 (64.4%)
1988	President	50,688 (29.6%)	118,525 (69.3%)
	Senate	45,687 (26.8%)	120,501 (70.6%)
1986	Senate	37,569 (32.4%)	72,820 (62.9%)
	Governor	27,976 (24.0%)	83,376 (71.4%)
1993	Party registration †	91,362 (29.6%)	168,983 (54.8%)

*Vote for Perot was 65,980 (26.8%).   †Independent/other is greater than 5%.
‡Special election for the remaining two years of the term of Pete Wilson who was elected governor in 1990. Appointee John Seymour held the seat 1991-1992.

Demographics

Population 572,928

Percent change from 1980 (new district in the 1990s)

Land area 1,518 square miles

Population per square mile 378

Counties, 1990 population

Orange (pt.)   231,020   San Diego (pt.)   314,309
Riverside (pt.)   27,599

Cities, 1990 population (10,000 or more)

Camp Pendleton North   Oceanside (pt.)   118,192
  CDP   10,373   Rancho Santa Margarita
Camp Pendleton South   CDP   11,390
  CDP   11,299   San Clemente   41,100
Carlsbad (pt.)   14,293   San Juan Capistrano   26,183
Dana Point   31,896   Temecula (pt.)   25,506
Fallbrook CDP   22,095   Vista (pt.)   66,944
Laguna Niguel (pt.)   44,400
Mission Viejo (pt.)   56,292

Race and Hispanic origin

White   83.3%
Black   4.0%
American Indian, Eskimo, or Aleut.   1.1%
Asian or Pacific Islander   4.5%
Other   7.1%
Hispanic origin   17.2%

Ancestry

American   2.5%   Norwegian   2.0%
Danish   1.1%   Polish   2.7%
Dutch   2.6%   Russian   1.4%
English   17.0%   Scotch Irish   2.4%
French   4.5%   Scottish   3.0%
German   23.1%   Swedish   2.9%
Irish   15.5%   Welsh   1.1%
Italian   6.1%

Universities/colleges, 1990-1991 enrollment

Mira Costa College, Oceanside   7,517
Saddleback College, Mission Viejo   14,527

Newspapers, total circulation (in all districts)

Enterprise Fallbrook, weekly   7,237
Escondido Times-Advocate   40,558
Los Angeles La Opinion   98,557
Los Angeles Times   1,169,066
North County Blade-Citizen   40,199
Orange County Register   341,875
San Clemente Sun-Post   7,987
San Diego Daily Transcript   9,638
San Diego Union-Tribune   385,197
Temecula Californian   10,251

Commercial television stations, affiliations

ADI: San Diego (79%) and Los Angeles (21%)

Cable television systems, total subscribers

Daniels Cablevision Inc.; Carlsbad   48,000
Dimension Cable Services; Mission Viejo   122,000
Dimension Cable Services; Oceanside   37,023
Dimension Cable Services; Vista   85,977
Inland Valley Cablevision; Temecula   12,040

Military installations, 1991

Camp Pendleton Marine Corps Base, Oceanside   44,482
Camp Pendleton Marine Corps Air Station, Oceanside   3,364
Camp Pendleton Naval Hospital, Camp Pendleton   1,372

Businesses and other major employers

Saddleback Community College District/Irvine Valley College; San Juan Capistrano   2,025

Tri-City Medical Center; Oceanside   2,000
U.S. Internal Revenue Service; Laguna Beach   2,000
Southern California Edison Co./San Onofre Nuclear Generating Station; San Clemente; electric services   1,800
Nichols Institute; San Juan Capistrano; medical/dental labs   1,100
Mission Hospital Regional Medical Center; San Juan Capistrano   1,000
Ritz-Carlton Hotel Co.; Laguna Beach; hotel   800
Ritz-Carlton Laguna Niguel; Dana Point; hotel   750
Astec America Inc./ACDC Electronics; Oceanside; electronic components   700
Hughes Aircraft Co.; San Juan Capistrano; aircraft/parts   640
Birtcher Real Estate; Laguna Beach; subdividers/developers   600
South Coast Medical Center; Laguna Beach   600

49th District

North San Diego; Coronado; Imperial Beach

The coastal 49th is the engine that drives the surrounding districts. It includes San Diego's downtown, most of its military bases, most of its other large employers and most of its coast. The 51st and the 50th districts to the north and south of the 49th, respectively, are packed with the area's bedrooms.

The district begins just south of Del Mar and runs down the coast to La Jolla, Pacific Beach, Point Loma and northern and downtown San Diego. It then skips through the San Diego Bay to Imperial Beach, and swings north up the slender Silver Strand Boulevard to take in Coronado, a peninsula that reaches up to the mouth of the bay. The northern and southern parts of the district are not connected by any land. Though this is an urban district, traffic is manageable here; it is possible to hop on the 5 Freeway in La Jolla and arrive in Imperial Beach, 30 miles south, in just 30 minutes.

Compared with the south side of the city, the 49th is relatively homogeneous. Only 13 percent of its residents are Hispanic, compared with 41 percent in the 50th District; only 7 percent of the 49th's residents are Asian, and 5 percent are black, compared with 15 and 14 percent, respectively, in the 50th.

The 49th is also a lot more Republican than southern San Diego: The GOP has a 3-point registration edge here, compared with a 16-point deficit in the 50th District. Despite the registration numbers, Bill Clinton won the 49th in 1992 with 43 percent of the vote; George Bush got 32 percent and Ross Perot 25 percent.

In 1992, the successful Democratic House candidate was able to win support in many of San Diego's moderate, middle-income neighborhoods, including Clairemont, downtown, Mission Hills and the largely gay area of Hillcrest. She also ran well on the 49th's southern end, in the lower-income area of Imperial Beach. She narrowly won La Jolla, one of the city's wealthier areas. She did not fare so well in Coronado and Point Loma, among the district's most Republican and conservative areas.

The beautiful community of Coronado is home to 27,000 residents, many of them retired Navy officers. Thirteen percent of its population is 65 or older. Also in Coronado is the North Island Naval Air Station, which has maintenance depots for F/A-18 Hornets and other Navy aircraft. It employs thousands of military personnel and civilians and was added to the 1993 list of military facilities that may be closed. Just across the bridge from

Coronado on the mainland is the National Steel and Shipbuilding Company (known as NASSCO), which employs 3,000 to 8,000 people, depending on the nature of the projects going on at the facility. It is the only shipyard in the western United States that still builds large oceangoing ships. It has been owned by its employees since 1989.

Though the area is heavily dependent on the military—one-sixth of San Diego's gross product depends directly on military procurement, retirement benefits and salaries—the economy is diversifying a bit. A number of biotechnology, biomedical and high-tech engineering firms have set up shop in Sorrento Valley just north of La Jolla. These firms benefit from the nearby presence of the supercomputer facilities at the University of California, San Diego.

Election Returns and Party Registration

	49th District	Democrat	Republican
1992	President*	114,081 (43.4%)	82,834 (31.5%)
	Senate †	125,319 (49.3%)	105,626 (41.5%)
	Senate †‡	136,686 (53.9%)	98,153 (38.7%)
	House †	127,280 (51.1%)	106,170 (42.7%)
1990	Governor †	72,731 (42.4%)	87,413 (51.0%)
1988	President	96,893 (43.8%)	121,115 (54.8%)
	Senate	80,911 (37.1%)	130,978 (60.0%)
1986	Senate	75,686 (44.8%)	87,542 (51.8%)
	Governor	54,175 (31.9%)	110,707 (65.1%)
1993	Party registration †	143,972 (39.4%)	156,157 (42.7%)

*Vote for Perot was 65,856 (25.1%).   †Independent/other is greater than 5%. ‡Special election for the remaining two years of the term of Pete Wilson who was elected governor in 1990. Appointee John Seymour held the seat 1991-1992.

Demographics

Population 573,362

Percent change from 1980 8.6%

Land area 118 square miles

Population per square mile (new district in the 1990s)

Counties, 1990 population
San Diego (pt.) 573,362

Cities, 1990 population (10,000 or more)
Coronado (pt.) 26,540   San Diego (pt.) 520,257
Imperial Beach (pt.) 26,512

Race and Hispanic origin
White 82.1%
Black 5.3%
American Indian, Eskimo, or Aleut. 0.7%
Asian or Pacific Islander 6.6%
Other 5.3%
Hispanic origin 12.8%

Ancestry
American 2.3%   Irish 15.4%
Dutch 2.1%   Italian 6.0%
English 15.7%   Norwegian 2.0%
French 4.6%   Polish 3.0%
French Canadian 1.1% Portuguese 1.1%
German 22.6%   Russian 2.1%

Scotch Irish 2.7%   Swedish 2.6%
Scottish 3.1%   Welsh 1.2%

Universities/colleges, 1990-1991 enrollment
Fashion Institute of Design, San Diego 233
Kelsey-Jenney Business College, San Diego 594
National University, San Diego 8,836
Point Loma Nazarene College, San Diego 2,256
San Diego City College, San Diego 13,737
San Diego Mesa College, San Diego 23,410
San Diego State University, San Diego 34,155
University of California-San Diego, La Jolla 17,797
University of San Diego, San Diego 6,027
Western State University College of Law, San Diego 590

Newspapers, total circulation (in all districts)
El Cajon Daily Californian 22,478
Los Angeles La Opinion 98,557
Los Angeles Times 1,169,066
San Diego Daily Transcript 9,638
San Diego Union-Tribune 385,197

Commercial television stations, affiliations
ADI: San Diego (100%)
KFMB-TV, San Diego (CBS)
KGTV, San Diego (ABC)

Cable television systems, total subscribers
American Cablevision of Coronado; Coronado 5,059
Americable Intl.; Coronado 5,600
Cox Cable San Diego; San Diego 323,246
Southwestern Cable; Black Mountain 157,000

Military installations, 1991
Miramar Naval Air Station, San Diego 28,906
San Diego Naval Training Center, San Diego 11,240
San Diego Marine Corps Recruitment Depot Activity, San Diego 7,711
San Diego Naval Submarine Base, San Diego 6,777
Coronado Naval Amphibious Base, San Diego 5,525
San Diego Naval Hospital, San Diego 5,307
Naval Ocean Systems Center, San Diego 4,795
North Island Naval Aviation Depot Activity, North Island 4,365
Pacific Fleet Training Center (Navy), San Diego 2,285
San Diego Naval Supply Center, San Diego 1,962
Pacific Fleet Combat Training Center, San Diego 1,280
Naval Electronic Systems Engineering Center, San Diego 873
San Diego Naval Communications Station, San Diego 574

Businesses and other major employers
General Dynamics Corp./Convair Div.; San Diego; aircraft/parts 8,800
City of San Diego; San Diego 6,400
National Steel & Shipbuilding Co.; San Diego; shipbuilding/repairing 4,000
SAIC; San Diego; defense systems/scientific research 3,500
Solar Turbines Inc.; San Diego; engines/turbines 3,300
Sharp Memorial Hospital; San Diego 3,000
General Dynamics Corp.; San Diego; space vehicles/guided missiles 3,000
University of California/University Hospital; San Diego 2,350
San Diego City College; San Diego 2,114
Copley Press Inc./Union-Tribune Publishing Co.; San Diego; newspapers 1,700

Busch Entertainment Corp./Wave Inc.; San Diego; amusement park 1,700

Kaiser Foundation Hospitals; San Diego 1,600

General Atomics; San Diego; research services 1,575

Scripps Memorial Hospitals; La Jolla 1,550

Teledyne Industries Inc./Teledyne Ryan; San Diego; aircraft/parts 1,500

University of California-San Diego; La Jolla 1,500

Children's Hospital San Diego; San Diego 1,480

County of San Diego; San Diego 1,390

Hotel Del Coronado; San Diego; hotel 1,350

State of California/Transportation Dept.; San Diego 1,300

University of California/Scripps Institute of Oceanography; La Jolla 1,300

San Diego Zoo; San Diego; zoo 1,200

American Airlines Inc.; San Diego; airline 1,022

Kyocera Intl. Inc.; San Diego; electronic components 1,000

Pilkington Visioncare Inc./Sola/Barnes-Hind; San Diego; measuring/controlling devices 1,000

Home Federal Corp.; San Diego; savings institutions 1,000

University of San Diego; San Diego 1,000

Computer Sciences Corp.; San Diego; management/computer services 1,000

San Diego Transit Corp.; San Diego; transportation 997

San Diego Gas & Electric Co.; San Diego; electric services 960

San Diego Unified School District; San Diego 949

Conic Corp./Loral Conic; San Diego; communications equipment 925

Cubic Corp.; San Diego; electrical equipment/supplies 900

Ivac Corp.; San Diego; medical instruments/supplies 900

Ace Parking Inc.; San Diego; parking services 859

Service America Corp.; San Diego; bars/restaurants 800

Sheraton Harbor Island East; San Diego; hotel 800

Atlas Hotels Inc.; San Diego; hotels 730

Sundstrand Corp.; San Diego; engines/turbines 728

County of San Diego/Education Dept.; San Diego 697

Maxwell Laboratories Inc.; San Diego; electronic components 680

National University; San Diego 680

Qualcomm Inc.; San Diego; communications equipment 660

Hybritech Inc.; San Diego; pharmaceuticals 650

Pinkerton's Inc.; San Diego; business/security services 650

Merck & Co. Inc./Kelco Div.; San Diego; drugs 600

Titan Corp./Titan-Linkabit Corp.; San Diego; professional/commercial equipment 600

Atlas Hotels Inc./Hanalei Hotel; San Diego; bars/restaurants 600

National Medical Transportation Network/Medtrans; San Diego; transportation 560

Nordstrom Inc.; San Diego; clothing stores 550

Coronado Hospital; San Diego 550

American Building Maint. Co.; San Diego; building services 550

Salk Institute for Biological Studies; La Jolla; biological research 530

San Diego Marriott & Marina; San Diego; hotel 526

Aventine Partners; San Diego; hotels 525

San Diego Financial Corp.; San Diego; commercial banks 510

50th District

Central and South San Diego; Chula Vista; National City

This ethnic, blue-collar urban-suburban district is a world apart from the districts that surround it. It is far more diverse: 41 percent of its residents are Hispanic, 15 percent are Asian and 14 percent are black. It is also as Democratic as the others are Republican. Fifty-one percent of its registered voters are Democrats and only 34 percent are Republicans.

The northern part of the district, just south of San Diego's downtown, houses the worst of San Diego's urban problems: its highest crime rates, its most serious gang activity and so on. It is built up with rows of two-story apartment complexes, and, while certain parts are being gentrified by "urban pioneers," much of the area is downtrodden.

Farther south, the booming suburb of Chula Vista splits the city of San Diego in two; even more southern areas of San Diego such as San Ysidro and Otay Mesa are contiguous only by a legal line that extends through the bay. Residents of the southern region, cut off geographically from the rest of San Diego, sometimes feel cut off politically as well.

Chula Vista has a large number of military personnel and tends to be more Republican than the rest of the 50th. On Chula Vista's east end is East Lake, one of the largest developments in the county. Any new housing growth the 50th experiences is likely to be here; much of the rest of the district is either stagnant or built out.

Otay Mesa is an industrial area south of Chula Vista that represents the last opportunity for expansion of San Diego's large-scale manufacturing. The area is heavily developed between the 5 and 805 freeways, but farther east is mostly empty land zoned for industry. Much of the existing industry is in the form of *maquiladoras*, factories that finish and ship goods that were partially manufactured in sibling factories in Mexico. It is unclear how the North American Free Trade Agreement might affect this area's economic potential.

The San Diego-Tijuana border crossing at San Ysidro is the world's busiest. The area's problems stem not so much from the number of immigrants, but from criminals who prey on them. One controversial border-hopper is the Tijuana River, which enters the United States here and brings with it 13 million gallons a day of raw sewage from Mexico.

The area is reeling from the deconstruction of General Dynamics over the past several years. The aerospace firm had been the district's (and the county's) largest private-sector employer for years, but it is down to a fraction of its former size. In spring 1992, the company sold its Tomahawk missile manufacturing operations to Hughes, which closed the San Diego plant and moved manufacturing to Arizona.

Bill Clinton won 49 percent of the 50th District's vote in 1992 to 30 percent for George Bush and 21 percent for Ross Perot. Clinton's big margin in the district—26,716 votes—was pivotal in helping swing San Diego County into his column.

Election Returns and Party Registration

	50th District	Democrat	Republican
1992	President*	69,546 (48.8%)	42,830 (30.0%)
	Senate †	68,587 (49.8%)	53,719 (39.0%)
	Senate †‡	74,914 (54.5%)	48,877 (35.6%)
	House	77,293 (56.6%)	39,531 (28.9%)

	50th District	Democrat	Republican
1990	Governor †	41,370 (44.3%)	44,616 (47.7%)
1988	President	64,676 (51.5%)	59,351 (47.3%)
	Senate	56,021 (45.1%)	63,816 (51.4%)
1986	Senate	55,075 (48.0%)	54,974 (47.9%)
	Governor	41,322 (36.0%)	70,202 (61.2%)
1993	Party registration †	117,436 (50.6%)	79,779 (34.4%)

*Vote for Perot was 30,267 (21.2%). †Independent/other is greater than 5%.
‡Special election for the remaining two years of the term of Pete Wilson who was elected governor in 1990. Appointee John Seymour held the seat 1991-1992.

Demographics

Population 573,463

Percent change from 1980 (new district in the 1990s)

Land area 135 square miles

Population per square mile 4,245

Counties, 1990 population
San Diego (pt.) 573,463

Cities, 1990 population (10,000 or more)

Bonita CDP 12,542	National City 54,249
Chula Vista 135,163	San Diego (pt.) 360,331

Race and Hispanic origin
White 46.5%
Black 14.4%
American Indian, Eskimo, or Aleut. 0.6%
Asian or Pacific Islander 14.8%
Other 23.6%
Hispanic origin 40.6%

Ancestry

American 2.1%	Italian 2.3%
English 6.4%	Polish 1.1%
French 2.2%	Scotch Irish 1.2%
German 10.1%	Scottish 1.1%
Irish 6.9%	Swedish 1.0%

Universities/colleges, 1990-1991 enrollment
Educational Cultural Complex, San Diego 632
Pacific Coast College, Chula Vista 205
Southwestern Community College, Chula Vista 13,010

Newspapers, total circulation (in all districts)
Los Angeles La Opinion 98,557
Los Angeles Times 1,169,066
San Diego Daily Transcript 9,638
San Diego Union-Tribune 385,197

Commercial television stations, affiliations
ADI: San Diego (100%)

Cable television systems, total subscribers
Cox Cable San Diego; San Diego 323,246

Military installations, 1991
San Diego Naval Station, San Diego 35,378

Businesses and other major employers
Southwest Marine Inc.; San Diego; shipbuilding/repairing 1,500
State of California/Corrections Dept.; San Ysidro 1,200

Cox Cable San Diego Inc.; San Diego; cable TV services 853
Chula Vista Community Hospital; Chula Vista 740
Paradise Valley Hospital Inc.; National City 690
Southwestern Community College; Chula Vista 658
Coca-Cola Bottling of Los Angeles; San Diego; beverage bottling 600
City of Chula Vista; Chula Vista 513

51st District

San Diego Area — Northern County Suburbs

The 51st reverses the pattern found throughout much of Southern California: As one moves inland from the coast, the political mood becomes more conservative, in part because of many coastal residents' emphasis on environmental issues. This group of San Diego suburbs constitutes a very Republican district: Registered Republicans outnumber Democrats 51 percent to 30 percent.

The 15 Freeway runs north through the 51st's conservative areas like a spine, passing the Miramar Naval Air Station, Poway, Rancho Bernardo and Escondido. To the west, the 5 Freeway heads north along the district's coastal communities: Del Mar, Solana Beach, Encinitas and Carlsbad.

Del Mar is a small beach community, an overwhelming proportion of whose 5,000 residents are white non-Hispanics—93 percent. Carlsbad, a city of 63,000 residents, grows and distributes most of the West Coast's fresh-cut flowers.

The 51st's beach communities have more permanent residents than others in the area. San Diego's primary tourist beaches are to the south, in the 49th District.

Moving inland, the Miramar Naval Air Station anchors the district's southern border. Home to the Navy Fighter Weapons School—popularly known as the "Top Gun" pilot school, it employs 13,000 civilians and military personnel. Miramar was added in May 1993 to the list of military facilities that may close. Many of those who have long eyed the base's demise want the site to serve as an alternative to San Diego's crowded downtown Lindbergh Field airport.

Up the 15 is Poway, an independent city of 44,000 surrounded by the city of San Diego. It has more of a rural, horsy feel to it than the surrounding suburban sprawl. Just north of Poway is an expanse of evenly developed suburbs that includes Rancho Bernardo, an area within San Diego's city limits that has attracted many retirees.

San Diego's relentless spread across the county has caught up to the old city of Escondido, farther north. With 109,000 residents, it is larger than some of the bedroom communities closer to San Diego, but its age gave it a head start on growth.

East and north of Escondido are avocado and citrus orchards and a lot of land that speculators have bought with the idea of settling San Diego's next population spasm here.

In 1992, George Bush took 40 percent of the district's presidential vote to Bill Clinton's 32 percent and Ross Perot's 27 percent. The 51st was Bush's largest pocket of support in the county: He beat Clinton by 21,600 votes here. Overall, however, Bush lost San Diego County by slightly more than 15,000 votes, making him the first Republican presidential candidate in four decades to lose the county. Bush won San Diego County by nearly 200,000 votes in 1988.

Election Returns and Party Registration

	51st District	Democrat	Republican
1992	President*	86,870 (32.3%)	108,470 (40.3%)
	Senate †	99,274 (38.2%)	135,415 (52.1%)
	Senate †‡	112,271 (43.3%)	124,327 (48.0%)
	House †	85,148 (33.7%)	141,890 (56.1%)
1990	Governor †	54,204 (31.7%)	105,851 (61.8%)
1988	President	62,972 (32.4%)	129,086 (66.4%)
	Senate	52,316 (27.2%)	134,932 (70.3%)
1986	Senate	51,678 (37.1%)	82,043 (59.0%)
	Governor	37,142 (26.6%)	98,279 (70.4%)
1993	Party registration †	105,716 (30.4%)	178,828 (51.4%)

*Vote for Perot was 73,580 (27.4%). †Independent/other is greater than 5%. ‡Special election for the remaining two years of the term of Pete Wilson who was elected governor in 1990. Appointee John Seymour held the seat 1991-1992.

Demographics

Population 572,982

Percent change from 1980 8.6%

Land area 496 square miles

Population per square mile 1,155

Counties, 1990 population
San Diego (pt.) 572,982

Cities, 1990 population (10,000 or more)

Carlsbad (pt.) 48,833	Poway 43,516
Encinitas 55,386	San Diego (pt.) 204,554
Escondido 108,635	San Marcos (pt.) 38,918
Oceanside (pt.) 10,206	Solana Beach 12,962

Race and Hispanic origin
White 84.6%
Black 1.8%
American Indian, Eskimo, or Aleut. 0.6%
Asian or Pacific Islander 8.2%
Other 4.9%
Hispanic origin 13.6%

Ancestry

American 2.5%	Norwegian 2.1%
Danish 1.2%	Polish 3.2%
Dutch 2.7%	Russian 1.9%
English 18.1%	Scotch Irish 2.4%
French 4.6%	Scottish 3.3%
German 24.4%	Swedish 3.0%
Irish 15.2%	Welsh 1.2%
Italian 5.8%	

Universities/colleges, 1990-1991 enrollment
California School of Professional Psychology, San Diego 528
California Western School of Law, San Diego 831
Palomar Community College, San Marcos 16,707
San Diego Miramar College, San Diego 5,378
United States International University, San Diego 2,254

Newspapers, total circulation (in all districts)
Escondido Times-Advocate 40,558
Los Angeles La Opinion 98,557
Los Angeles Times 1,169,066
North County Blade-Citizen 40,199
San Diego Daily Transcript 9,638
San Diego Union-Tribune 385,197

Commercial television stations, affiliations
ADI: San Diego (100%)

Cable television systems, total subscribers
Cox Cable; San Diego 323,246
Daniels Cablevision; Carlsbad 48,000
Dimension Cable Services; Vista 85,977
Southwestern Cable; Black Mountain 157,000

Military installations, 1991
Miramar Naval Air Station, San Diego 13,279

Businesses and other major employers
Palomar Community College; San Marcos 3,300
Motorola; San Diego; electrical goods 2,000
Hewlett-Packard Co.; San Diego; electrical equipment/supplies 2,000
Fisher Scientific Co.; San Diego; medical instruments/supplies 1,200
Palomar Pomerado Medical Center; Escondido 1,200
La Costa Resort & Spa; Carlsbad; hotel 1,200
State of California/Agricultural District; Del Mar 1,000
Signet Armorlite Inc.; San Marcos; ophthalmic goods 911
Unisys Corp.; San Diego; computer equipment 850
NCR Corp.; San Diego; computer equipment 800
TRW Inc.; San Diego; military research services 780
State of California/Southern California Exposition; Del Mar 758
Home Federal Bank; San Diego; savings institutions 742
Pedus Building Services Inc.; San Diego; business services 700
Hughes Aircraft Co.; Carlsbad; electronic components 675
City of Escondido; Escondido 656
IMED Corp.; San Diego; medical instruments/supplies 640
Geico; San Diego; insurance services 600
Brodart Co.; San Diego; management services 600
Golden Eagle Insurance Co.; San Diego; fire/marine/casualty insurance 550

52nd District

Inland San Diego and Imperial Counties

The 52nd is California's far southeastern corner, including the whole of Imperial County and about half of San Diego County's land area. A vast barren area in the middle of the district divides its two main population concentrations—a suburban west and an agricultural east.

The bulk of the district's San Diego County residents are in three suburban cities on the western edge of the 52nd: El Cajon is the largest of the three with 89,000 residents, La Mesa's population is 53,000 and Spring Valley's is 55,000. Economically, La Mesa is a bit better off than the other two, and votes a bit more Democratic, but otherwise the three cities are very similar.

These suburbs have a mix of blue and white collars, with many defense workers and a lot of military personnel; the important role of the military-industrial complex in San Diego's economy contributes significantly to the conservative tenor of the area.

East along the 8 Freeway out of El Cajon are mountains,

followed by a different type of mountains that consist mostly of boulders piled on boulders. This area is the Anza-Borrego Desert State Park, which looks to the casual observer less like a nature refuge than a rock refuge.

The huge Salton Sea just east of the park used to be a terrific fishing and recreational area, but agricultural runoff has increased the sea's salinity level above that of the Pacific Ocean, and that has killed most of the fish.

Beyond the park, the land flattens into desert. The district's agricultural sector begins a few miles before El Centro, Imperial County's largest city with 31,000 residents. Everything east is agriculture.

This is the Imperial Valley—known as the "salad bowl of the country"—and it lives and dies on farming. Lately, it has been dying: It has the nation's highest unemployment rate—26 percent in December 1992, down from a high of 33 percent.

The area has had more than its share of tough luck lately: A plague of white flies devastated crops in the early 1990s, then there were floods, followed by more flies.

The region depends on the Colorado River for its lifeblood: water. The river defines the California-Arizona border on the district's eastern edge, and water issues dominate the farmers' political attention. The importance of irrigation is vividly evident here; along some roads, stark desert lies on one side while plush alfalfa fields flank the other.

The 52nd is heavily Republican: 46 percent of its registered voters are Republicans; 39 percent are Democrats. The district is over one-fifth Hispanic, and about 3 percent each black and Asian.

George Bush won the 52nd in 1992 with 37 percent of the vote to Bill Clinton's 34 percent and Ross Perot's 29 percent. Clinton actually won Imperial County with 44 percent of the vote, to Bush's 39 percent and Perot's 17 percent, but the effect was muted; San Diego County casts almost 90 percent of the district's ballots.

Election Returns and Party Registration

	52nd District	Democrat	Republican
1992	President*	74,913 (34.1%)	81,421 (37.1%)
	Senate †	82,973 (38.8%)	105,142 (49.2%)
	Senate †‡	91,276 (43.0%)	97,283 (45.9%)
	House †	88,076 (41.2%)	112,995 (52.9%)
1990	Governor †	49,449 (33.3%)	86,582 (58.2%)
1988	President	61,314 (34.9%)	111,872 (63.6%)
	Senate	54,151 (31.0%)	114,961 (65.8%)
1986	Senate	55,100 (42.0%)	70,579 (53.8%)
	Governor	40,430 (30.5%)	86,402 (65.1%)
1993	Party registration †	118,244 (38.6%)	139,381 (45.5%)

*Vote for Perot was 63,176 (28.8%).   †Independent/other is greater than 5%.
‡Special election for the remaining two years of the term of Pete Wilson who was elected governor in 1990. Appointee John Seymour held the seat 1991-1992.

Demographics

Population 573,203

Percent change from 1980 (new district in the 1990s)

Land area 6,434 square miles

Population per square mile 89

Counties, 1990 population
Imperial 109,303	San Diego (pt.) 463,900

Cities, 1990 population (10,000 or more)
Bostonia CDP 13,670	Lakeside CDP 39,412
Brawley 18,923	Lemon Grove (pt.) 23,585
Calexico 18,633	Ramona CDP (pt.) 12,982
Casa de Oro-Mount Helix CDP 30,727	San Diego (pt.) 25,407
	Santee (pt.) 52,902
El Cajon 88,693	Spring Valley CDP (pt.) 51,197
El Centro 31,384	
La Mesa (pt.) 52,893	

Race and Hispanic origin
White 83.6%
Black 3.1%
American Indian, Eskimo, or Aleut. 1.1%
Asian or Pacific Islander 3.0%
Other 9.2%
Hispanic origin 22.6%

Ancestry
American 3.6%	Norwegian 1.8%
Dutch 2.7%	Polish 2.4%
English 15.8%	Scotch Irish 2.5%
French 4.8%	Scottish 2.5%
German 23.1%	Swedish 2.7%
Irish 15.0%	Welsh 1.1%
Italian 4.8%	

Universities/colleges, 1990-1991 enrollment
Christian Heritage College, El Cajon 327
Coleman College, La Mesa 893
Cuyamaca College, El Cajon 3,614
Grossmont College, El Cajon 15,357
Grossmont-Cuyamaca Community College, El Cajon 17,241
ITT Technical Institute, La Mesa 546
Imperial Valley College, Imperial 3,761

Newspapers, total circulation (in all districts)
El Cajon Daily Californian 22,478
Escondido Times-Advocate 40,558
Imperial Valley Press 11,576
Los Angeles Times 1,169,066
San Diego Union-Tribune 385,197

Commercial television stations, affiliations
ADI: El Centro-Yuma (66%) and San Diego (34%)
KYMA, Yuma (ABC)
KECY-TV, El Centro-Yuma (CBS)
KNSD, San Diego (NBC)
KTTY, San Diego (None)
KUSI-TV, San Diego (None)

Cable television systems, total subscribers
Century Cable; Yuma 26,000
Century Cable; El Centro 17,800
Colony Communications; Palm Desert 63,100
Cox Cable San Diego; San Diego 323,246
Jones Intercable Inc.; Spring Valley 6,660

Military installations, 1991
El Centro Naval Air Facility, El Centro 717

Businesses and other major employers
Grossmont Hospital; La Mesa 2,683
Grossmont-Cuyamaca Community College, El Cajon 1,500

Alvarado Hospital & Medical Center; San Diego 1,200
Noblesse Oblige Inc./Eight Star Equipment; El Centro; crop
  services 907
Calipatria State Prison; Calipatria 900
Schlage Lock Co.; Tecate; locks 800
Imperial County/Fire Dept.; El Centro 800

Imperial Irrigation District; Imperial; utility services 600
Chem-Tronics Inc.; El Cajon; aircraft/parts 600
Sycuan Gaming Center; El Cajon; casino 570
El Centro Community Hospital; El Centro 550
Ketema Inc.; El Cajon; aerospace electronics 539
Ramona Unified School District; Ramona 525

Colorado

Colorado conjures images of dude ranches, fields of Aspen trees, gold mines, ski resorts and the rushing waters of its namesake river. Indeed, Colorado has these things. But in terms of its population, the state is as urban as any along the East Coast. According to the Census Bureau, 82 percent of the state's 3.3 million residents are urban or suburban dwellers. For that reason, most of the changes in the state's congressional district map took place in and around the state capital and largest city, Denver.

Following the pattern established by East Coast cities, Denver lost population to its suburbs during the 1980s, forcing enlargement of the 1st District. The territory the district gained to the northwest and south did little to change the liberal-Democratic voting profile of the district. Statewide, a 14 percent increase in population was not enough to add to Colorado's six-member House delegation.

Expansion of the 1st District, encompassing Denver, cut territory out of the suburban 6th District to the south without changing its largely Republican character. The 5th District, centered south of Denver around Colorado Springs, was the state's fastest growing region, gaining nearly 100,000 residents during the 1980s. This overwhelmingly Republican district with its defense-dependent economy was expected to remain in the GOP column in the 1990s despite losing chunks of territory to the mountainous 3rd District.

Colorado is one of those states with a decidedly split political personality. Voters supported term limits for federal and state officeholders but show unbending loyalty to certain politicians. Republican Hank Brown had an unbroken string of electoral successes beginning in the state Senate in 1972 and stretching to the U.S. Senate in the 1990s. And Democratic House member Patricia Schroeder began serving her 11th term in 1993 with no opponent able to come within 30 points of her in nearly a decade. In White House races Ronald Reagan swept the state in 1984, George Bush won with 53 percent of the vote in 1988, but Bill Clinton was victorious with 40 percent in 1992.

The "granola belt," a swatch of territory taking in the ski resorts of Vail, Aspen, Steamboat Springs and Crested Butte, is about as liberal a region as any in the country. Just to the east, the 5th District is home to the Air Force Academy, the nation's underground nuclear war command center, and a solidly Repub-

lican voting base. The split came to the fore in 1992 when 53 percent of the state's voters approved an amendment banning state and local gay rights laws that had been established in Denver, Boulder and Aspen. A subsequent court ruling overturned the amendment.

Colorado was founded just before the Civil War by gold prospectors, and today the state is using its old mining towns to tap a new financial vein: gambling. The strategy is designed to expand the vital tourism revenue that flows into the state and to keep up with other states that are opening the doors to casinos.

Through more than a century of development, Colorado rode the waves of boom and bust cycles, first in gold, then in cattle, and most recently in shale oil. Coloradoans were hoping the ups and downs would even out in the 1990s by diversifying the economy to the point where no one product controls their fate. Communities such as Boulder may be having too much success, with longtime residents complaining that yuppies are taking over the pleasant college town.

Denver and the region to the south are seeking ways to cope with the bust-cycle in defense spending that is threatening military bases in the region as well as weapons contractors such as Martin Marietta. The city is banking on major public works projects to return dividends through the 1990s and beyond. These projects include construction of a huge new airport, a convention center and a baseball stadium for the Colorado Rockies, a major league baseball expansion team. For tourists, the rivers, slopes and forests still beckon--now joined by one-armed bandits.

Table 1 Population

District	Population	Population under 18	Voting-age population	Median age
1	549,068	124,935	424,133	33.5
2	549,072	141,670	407,402	31.8
3	549,062	145,129	403,933	33.9
4	549,070	152,164	396,906	31.7
5	549,066	155,027	394,039	31.1
6	549,056	142,341	406,715	32.9
State	3,294,394	861,266	2,433,128	32.5

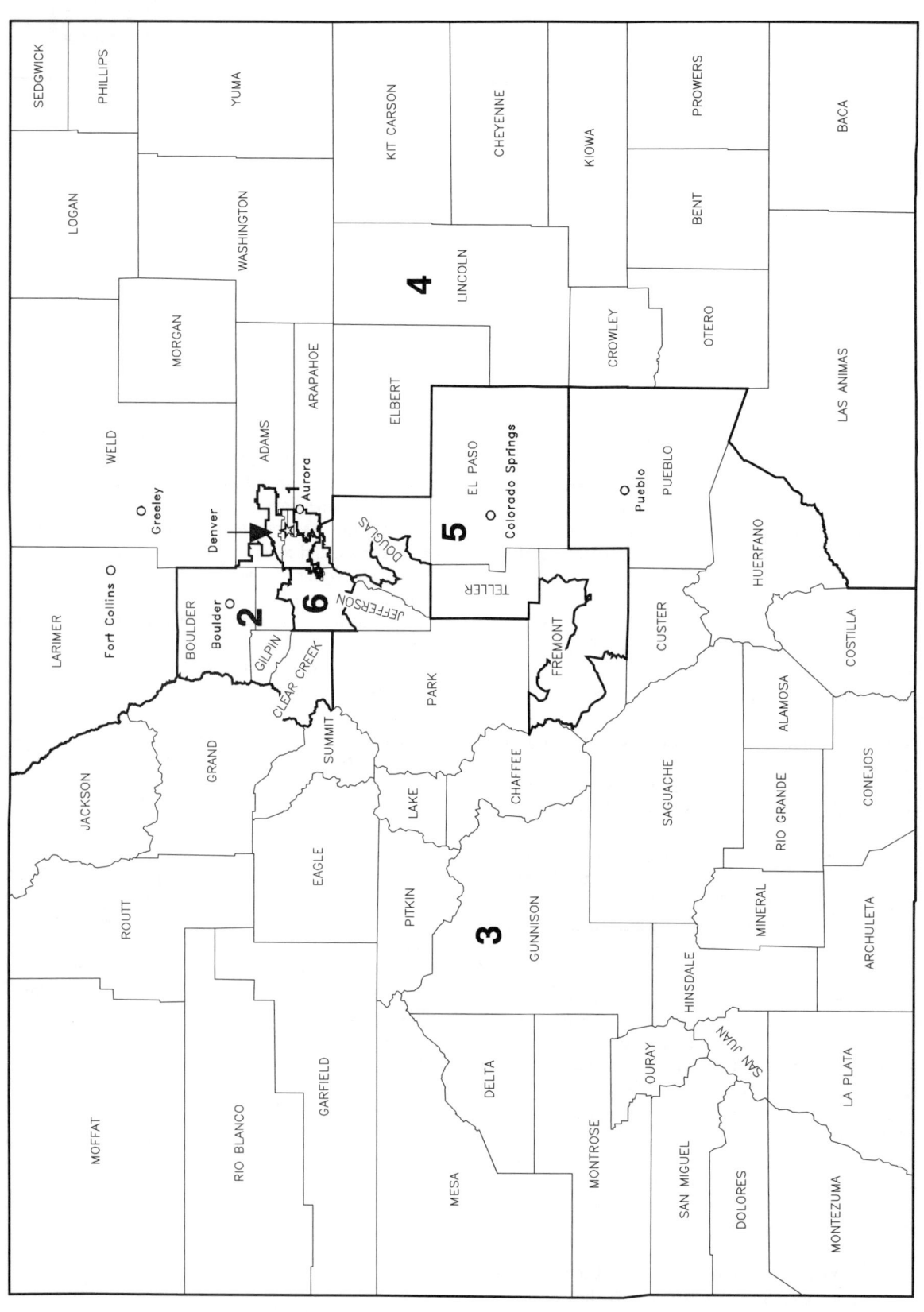

Table 2 Voting-Age Persons

District	White*	Black*	American Indian, Eskimo, or Aleut*	Asian or Pacific Islander*	Other*	Hispanic*	Male*	Female*
1	76.7%	11.5%	1.0%	2.3%	8.5%	18.3%	48.0%	52.0%
2	93.5	0.8	0.6	2.2	3.0	8.1	49.0	51.0
3	92.7	0.6	1.2	0.5	5.0	15.4	49.3	50.7
4	92.4	0.7	0.6	1.0	5.3	12.5	48.8	51.2
5	89.6	5.2	0.7	2.1	2.5	6.6	50.0	50.0
6	92.4	3.2	0.5	2.1	1.7	5.7	48.3	51.7
State	89.4	3.7	0.8	1.7	4.4	11.2	48.9	51.1

*As percent of voting-age population.

Table 3 Voting-Age Persons by Age Groups

District	18-24*	25-44*	45-54*	55-64*	65 and over*
1	12.9%	47.4%	11.7%	10.7%	17.3%
2	15.2	50.5	14.2	9.5	10.5
3	12.5	44.8	13.7	11.8	17.2
4	15.6	45.3	13.4	10.4	15.3
5	14.6	51.1	14.5	9.6	10.2
6	12.0	51.8	15.4	10.1	10.7
State	13.8	48.5	13.8	10.3	13.5

*As percent of voting-age population.

Table 4 Income and Occupation

District	Median family income	Families in poverty	White collar*	Blue collar*	Service*	Farm*
1	$31,355	13.3%	63.1%	20.0%	15.8%	1.1%
2	41,332	5.6	66.0	21.8	11.3	0.9
3	28,350	12.3	53.5	24.4	17.4	4.7
4	31,903	9.7	54.2	25.5	13.8	6.5
5	38,651	6.9	67.9	17.8	13.1	1.2
6	43,922	4.0	71.9	16.7	10.8	0.7
State	35,930	8.6	63.1	20.9	13.6	2.4

*As percent of employed persons age 16 and over.

Table 5 Education: School Years Completed

District	Less than grade 9*	Grades 9-12 no diploma*	High school diploma*	College bachelor's degree or higher*
1	7.6%	13.5%	25.0%	26.8%
2	3.6	8.7	26.4	29.5
3	8.2	12.0	30.7	20.5
4	8.9	11.4	29.8	21.5
5	3.1	7.4	24.0	30.1
6	2.2	6.6	23.2	33.4
State	5.6	10.0	26.5	27.0

*As percent of persons age 25 and over.

Table 6 Housing and Residential Patterns

District	Owner occupied	Renter occupied	Urban	Rural
1	49.7%	50.3%	100.0%	0.0%
2	65.4	34.6	92.1	7.9
3	66.0	34.0	54.0	46.0
4	65.4	34.6	64.6	35.4
5	64.0	36.0	88.7	11.3
6	65.0	35.0	95.2	4.8
State	62.2	37.8	82.4	17.6

1st District

Denver

With nearly 468,000 people, Colorado's capital city of Denver anchors the 1st and is the starting point for Democratic victories in the state.

In 1992, Bill Clinton swept the city of Denver by nearly 67,000 votes; he won the rest of Colorado by just 288 votes. At the same time, Colorado's controversial gay rights ban, approved statewide by more than 100,000 votes, was defeated in Denver by a margin of nearly 40,000 votes.

Denver's liberal cast is due in no small part to its large minority population—nearly one-quarter Hispanic and 13 percent black. Two of Denver's recent mayors have been from the minority community—Federico F. Peña (who left to become Clinton's Transportation secretary) and Wellington Webb, Denver's first black mayor.

Peña put so much emphasis on major building projects—including a new airport, a new convention center and a 40,000-seat baseball stadium—that one critic accused him of having an "edifice complex."

Yet Peña's building spree was the latest example of Denver's ability to roll with the punches. It was founded on the eve of the Civil War in response to rumors of gold in Cherry Creek (a stream that flows near downtown). By 1908, when Democrats assembled in Denver to nominate William Jennings Bryan a third time for president, it was a thriving cow town. By the 1970s, Denver had established itself as headquarters for large-scale energy operations in the Rockies.

Now, a boom-and-bust cycle later, the economy of Colorado's largest city is more diversified. And Denver is expecting millions of dollars in revenue from its new major league baseball franchise, the Colorado Rockies, fielding its first team in 1993.

But Denver's economic future is far from secure. Much of its recent recovery has been due to fixed-life construction projects. The largest, the new $2.7-billion Denver International Airport, is to open in late 1993. The facility, about 25 miles northeast of the city, covers 53 square miles and is billed as the world's largest airport site.

Redistricting did little to change the 1st's political complexion. Denver lost 5 percent of its population during the 1980s, so the district has moved north and east into Adams and Arapahoe counties to pick up much of Commerce City and the northern chunk of the city of Aurora. The 1st also regained several neighborhoods in the southwest corner of the city that had been in the 6th District and picked up one household in Jefferson County.

Yet 85 percent of the district's population still live in Denver, and the additions are largely blue-collar neighborhoods that swell Democratic majorities.

Much of the new land the 1st takes in is part of the vast Rocky Mountain Arsenal near Commerce City, formerly a chemical weapons storage site that is being converted into a wildlife preserve. The large vacant slice of real estate is home to myriad eagles, foxes, deer and prairie dogs, but no voters.

Election Returns

	1st District	Democrat	Republican
1992	President*	135,372 (56.0%)	63,207 (26.1%)
	House	156,629 (68.8%)	70,902 (31.2%)
1990	Governor	103,724 (73.1%)	38,119 (26.9%)
1988	President	138,416 (60.9%)	89,043 (39.1%)
1986	Senate	114,619 (64.8%)	62,186 (35.2%)
	Governor	126,910 (71.3%)	50,960 (28.7%)

*Vote for Perot was 43,243 (17.9%).

Demographics

Population 549,068

Percent change from 1980 14.0%

Land area 218 square miles

Population per square mile 2,515

Counties, 1990 population
Adams (pt.) 48,195   Denver 467,610
Arapahoe (pt.) 33,260   Jefferson (pt.) 3

Cities, 1990 population (10,000 or more)
Aurora (pt.) 55,504   Denver 467,610
Commerce City (pt.) 15,424

Race and Hispanic origin
White 73.0%
Black 12.9%
American Indian, Eskimo, or Aleut. 1.1%
Asian or Pacific Islander 2.4%
Other 10.5%
Hispanic origin 21.9%

Ancestry
American 2.0%   Norwegian 1.7%
Dutch 2.3%   Polish 2.4%
English 13.0%   Russian 1.6%
French 3.7%   Scotch Irish 2.3%
German 23.2%   Scottish 2.4%
Irish 13.5%   Swedish 2.9%
Italian 3.8%

Universities/colleges, 1990-1991 enrollment
Colorado Institute of Art, Denver 1,328
Community College of Denver, Denver 5,714
Denver Baptist Seminary, Denver 536
Denver Technical College, Denver 639
Iliff School of Theology, Denver 320
Metropolitan State College, Denver 17,403
Regis University, Denver 5,495
Rocky Mountain College of Art, Denver 217
University of Colorado Health Science Center, Denver 1,806
University of Colorado, Denver 11,521
University of Denver, Denver 7,544

Newspapers, total circulation (in all districts)
Denver Post 263,720
Denver Rocky Mountain News 359,148

Commercial television stations, affiliations
ADI: Denver (100%)

Cable television systems, total subscribers
Mile Hi Cablevision; Denver 91,556
TCI of Colorado; Mt. Morrison 171,834

Military installations, 1991
Lowry Air Force Base, Denver 5,070
Fitzsimons Army Medical Center, Aurora 3,714

Businesses and other major employers
Continental Airlines Inc.; Denver; airline 7,000
University of Colorado; Denver 5,500
Provenant Health Partners; Denver 4,500
U.S. Veterans Affairs Dept./Denver; hospital 2,700
Denver General Hospital; Denver 2,600
St. Joseph Hospital Inc.; Denver 2,260
U.S. Interior Dept./Bureau of Reclamation; Denver; heavy construction 2,000
U.S. West Communications; Denver; telephone communications 2,000
Children's Hospital Assn.; Denver 1,800
Porter Memorial Hospital; Denver 1,600
N. W. Transport Services Inc.; Commerce City; trucking services 1,530
United Bank of Denver; Denver; commercial banks 1,511
Gates Corp.; Denver; hose/belting 1,500
Colorado Seminary/University of Denver; Denver 1,382
Colorado National Bank of Denver; Denver; commercial banks 1,287
Metropolitan State College; Denver 1,250
Samsonite Corp.; Denver; luggage 1,200
Denver Post Corp.; Denver; newspapers 1,200
Public Service Co. of Colorado; Denver; electric services 1,200
State of Colorado/Accounting Dept.; Denver 1,200
Rocky Mountain Health Care Corp.; Denver; management/public relations 1,200
U.S. Internal Revenue Service; Denver 1,200
Rose Medical Center; Denver 1,140
National Jewish Hospital; Denver 1,070
General Health Corp. Inc.; Denver; holding offices 1,023
Denver Publishing Co./Rocky Mountain News; Denver; newspapers 1,000
Keebler Co.; Denver; bakery products 1,000
First Bank System Inc./Center Bank of Denver; Denver; commercial banks 1,000
Texaco Exploration & Production; Denver; management/public relations 1,000
First Interstate Bank; Denver; commercial banks 990
Presbyterian Denver Hospital; Denver 978
General Services Administration; Denver 929
Amoco Production Co.; Denver; petroleum/natural gas 900
MCI Telecommunications Corp.; Denver; telephone communications 900
Manville Sales Corp.; Denver; mineral products 900
Personnel Systems Inc./Lang Management; Denver; supply services 850
Adams County School District; Commerce City 800
County of Denver/Central Food Stamp Office; Denver 780
Oppenheimer Management Corp.; Denver; security and commodity services 750
Denver Water Board; Denver; water supply 725
State of Colorado/Transportation Dept.; Denver 700
Mobil Oil Corp.; Denver; oil/gas services 700

Miltope Corp.; Denver; computer/office equipment 695

Rocky Mountain Bankcard Systems; Denver; business services 690

Alliant Techsystems Inc./Metrum Information Storage; Denver; computer/office equipment 650

Nobel Sysco. Food Services; Denver; grocery products 650

U.S. Postal Service; Denver 647

Safeway Inc.; Denver; grocery products 600

Security Life of Denver Insurance Co.; Denver; life insurance 600

Central Bancorporation Inc./Central Banks of Colorado; Denver; commercial banks 600

American Patrol & Guard Co.; Denver; security services 600

Preferred Temporaries Inc. Co.; Denver; temp services 600

Mercy Medical Center; Denver 600

State of Colorado; Denver 600

U.S. Housing & Urban Development Dept.; Denver 600

Harbridge Merchant Services; Denver; business services 600

Hospital Shared Service of Colorado; Denver; business assn. 580

State of Colorado/Motor Vehicles Dept.; Denver 557

State of Colorado/Youth Services Dept.; Denver 545

2nd District

Northwest Denver Suburbs; Boulder

The 2nd is almost equally suburbs and mountains, but it is probably defined most in the national mind by the college town of Boulder, the largest community in the 2nd, with slightly more than 83,000 people.

Lying at the base of the Front Range of the Rockies, Boulder is a sort of Berkeley East. It is the headquarters of Celestial Seasonings, the herbal tea producer. The large academic community at the University of Colorado (28,600 students), augmented by many young professionals drawn to the area's scenery and outdoorsy lifestyle, give Boulder's politics a decidedly liberal hue.

The rest of Boulder County is less so, with the old farming center of Longmont anchoring the northern end of the county and suburbs such as Lafayette, Louisville and Broomfield clustered in the south. Boulder County pulsates with government research facilities such as the National Oceanic and Atmospheric Administration and related scientific and high-tech companies.

For years, the county was comfortable voting GOP for president. When it went for Michael S. Dukakis in 1988, it was the first time since 1964 that Boulder County had backed a Democrat for president. Since then, it has veered left with a vengeance. In 1992, former California Gov. Edmund G. "Jerry" Brown, Jr., easily swept the county in the Democratic presidential primary, taking 43 percent of the vote.

In November 1992, Bill Clinton swamped George Bush in Boulder County by 2-to-1. At the same time, the successful statewide ballot measure to gut local gay rights ordinances in cities such as Boulder was rejected by nearly 60 percent of the county's voters.

Slightly more than 40 percent of the district's population live in Boulder County. Most of the rest live closer to Denver in portions of two suburban counties, Adams and Jefferson; each has nearly 30 percent of the people in the 2nd. Adams has a more blue-collar flavor; Jefferson is historically Republican. Redistricting in 1992 shifted some of Adams out of the 2nd and added turf in Jefferson. Bush carried Jefferson County by less than 2,000

votes in 1992, while Democratic Senate candidate Ben Nighthorse Campbell won it by more than 10,000 votes.

Nearly half the district's land area (but only 2 percent of its voters) is a short drive west in the mountain counties of Clear Creek and Gilpin. To help lure tourist dollars, Gilpin County's 19th-century mining towns of Central City and Black Hawk have legalized gambling.

Less of a tourist draw but more vital to the district economy is the controversial Rocky Flats plutonium plant near the Boulder-Jefferson county line. An erstwhile manufacturer of triggers for nuclear weapons, the plant is in the environmental cleanup phase.

Election Returns

	2nd District	Democrat	Republican
1992	President*	123,341 (45.2%)	82,991 (30.4%)
	House †	164,790 (60.7%)	88,470 (32.6%)
1990	Governor	113,909 (69.7%)	49,555 (30.3%)
1988	President	112,358 (51.4%)	106,418 (48.6%)
1986	Senate	97,911 (57.7%)	71,894 (42.3%)
	Governor	106,966 (62.4%)	64,576 (37.6%)

*Vote for Perot was 66,550 (24.4%).   †Independent/other is greater than 5%.

Demographics

Population 549,072

Percent change from 1980 14.0%

Land area 1,530 square miles

Population per square mile 359

Counties, 1990 population

Adams (pt.) 152,542	Gilpin 3,070
Boulder 225,339	Jefferson (pt.) 160,502
Clear Creek 7,619	

Cities, 1990 population (10,000 or more)

Arvada (pt.) 89,229	Northglenn (pt.) 27,195
Boulder 83,312	Sherrelwood CDP 16,636
Broomfield (pt.) 24,607	Thornton (pt.) 32,577
Lafayette 14,548	Westminster (pt.) 73,342
Longmont 51,555	Wheat Ridge 29,419
Louisville 12,361	

Race and Hispanic origin

White 92.7%

Black 0.8%

American Indian, Eskimo, or Aleut. 0.6%

Asian or Pacific Islander 2.4%

Other 3.4%

Hispanic origin 9.5%

Ancestry

American 2.5%	Italian 6.1%
Czechoslovakian 1.0%	Norwegian 2.7%
Danish 1.5%	Polish 3.3%
Dutch 3.0%	Russian 1.2%
English 18.9%	Scotch Irish 2.9%
French 5.1%	Scottish 3.4%
German 36.0%	Swedish 4.5%
Irish 18.1%	Welsh 1.4%

Universities/colleges, 1990-1991 enrollment

Denver Institute of Technology, Denver 766

Front Range Community College, Westminster 9,706

Naropa Institute, Boulder 241

University of Colorado, Boulder 28,605

Newspapers, total circulation (in all districts)

Boulder Daily Camera 33,107

Denver Post 263,720

Denver Rocky Mountain News 359,148

Longmont Daily Times-Call 19,227

Commercial television stations, affiliations

ADI: Denver (100%)

Cable television systems, total subscribers

American Cablevision; Wheat Ridge 9,879

Jones Intercable Inc.; Boulder 5,783

Mile Hi Cablevision; Denver 91,556

Scripps Howard Cable Co.; Longmont 9,401

TCI of Colorado; Boulder 16,000

TCI of Colorado; Mt Morrison 171,834

Businesses and other major employers

IBM Corp.; Boulder; engineering services 6,000

Storage Technology Corp./Storagetek; Louisville; computer/office equipment 4,800

AT&T Co.; Denver; communications equipment 3,000

Ball Corp.; Westminster; metal containers 2,950

Ball Corp.; Broomfield; communications equipment 2,400

Ball Corp./Ball Aerospace; Boulder; electronic communications equipment 2,200

Lutheran Medical Center; Wheat Ridge 2,005

Boulder Community Hospital; Boulder 1,400

AT&T Co.; Denver; research services 1,200

ConAgra Poultry Co./Longmont Foods Co.; Longmont; meat products 1,100

Cobe Laboratories Inc./Cobe Arvada; Arvada; medical instruments/supplies 1,000

St. Anthony Hospital Systems/St. Anthony's North; Westminster 1,000

Valleylab Inc.; Boulder; medical instruments/supplies 850

Official Airline Guides Inc.; Boulder; publishing 800

Front Range Community College; Westminster 800

National Center for Atmospheric Research; Boulder 800

Miller Intl. Inc./Prior Co.; Denver; outerwear 750

Exabyte Corp.; Boulder; computer/office equipment 750

State of Colorado/Wheat Ridge Regional Center; Wheat Ridge 730

Longmont United Hospital Assn./United Medical Center; Longmont 690

U.S. Commerce Dept./National Oceanic Atmospheric Administraton; Boulder 600

City of Longmont; Longmont 600

Sundstrand Corp.; Denver; aircraft/parts 586

City of Arvada; Arvada 550

Climax Molybdenum Co./Amax-Henderson Mine; Empire; ferroalloy ores 525

Boulder Publishing Inc./Daily Camera; Boulder; newspapers 520

U.S. West Advanced Technologies; Boulder; research services 520

3rd District

Western Slope; Pueblo

This expansive district captures much of the vast spectrum of Colorado: the rural poor, the resort rich, the old steel-mill town of Pueblo and the isolated Hispanic counties of southern Colorado. Taken together, the 3rd is probably the most politically competitive district in the state.

Most of its voters live on the western slope of the Rockies—an area that features two different lifestyles, two different sets of voting habits.

Upscale ski resorts anchor the "granola belt," a swath of terrain that extends west and south from Boulder to include the communities of Aspen (Pitkin County), Vail (Eagle), Breckinridge (Summit), Steamboat Springs (Routt), Crested Butte (Gunnison), Telluride (San Miguel) and Durango (La Plata).

The granola belt is about as liberal as any stretch of real estate in the country. It was integral to former California Gov. Edmund G. "Jerry" Brown Jr.'s victory in the first-ever Colorado Democratic presidential primary in March 1992 (13 of 21 counties he carried were entirely in the 3rd). It also was a cornerstone of opposition to the antigay rights ballot measure in November 1992. In addition, the granola belt was firmly in Bill Clinton's corner that year.

Juxtaposed to it are rural counties as conservative in their politics and social attitudes as other parts of the ranching West. In 1992, they tended to support both George Bush and the antigay rights measure.

What united the two different sectors politically in 1992 was strong support for the Senate bid of the district's three-term representative, Democrat Ben Nighthorse Campbell, and significant interest in the independent presidential candidacy of Ross Perot. The two Colorado counties that Perot carried were both in the 3rd (Moffat and San Juan), as well as 14 of the 19 counties in which he ran second.

Although much of the district is federally owned national forest, it is one of the most energy-rich corners of America. The western slope is a prime source of oil shale, uranium, zinc and a number of other minerals, as well as the source of the Colorado River, which provides water for much of the Front Range and Southern California.

Yet the boom-and-bust cycles of the extractive industries have led many towns in the 3rd to look for more stable employment from smaller businesses. This is the case in Pueblo, the district's largest city with almost 100,000 people, where the decline of the local steel industry has led many members of the heavily unionized work force to accept nonunion jobs from an array of smaller employers.

During the 1980s the most dramatic population growth in the 3rd was concentrated in the resort counties that lie along Interstate 70. Eagle County grew by 65 percent; Summit County by 46 percent. Yet nearby in the old mining center of Lake County (Leadville), the population declined by nearly one-third, the biggest population falloff in the state. And four other counties on the Western Slope suffered population losses of at least 10 percent.

That, in part, forced the district to expand eastward to pick up three small mountain counties (Chaffee, Lake and Park) and rural portions of two counties in the Denver suburbs, Douglas and Jefferson.

Election Returns

	3rd District	Democrat	Republican
1992	President*	107,330 (40.2%)	92,314 (34.6%)
	House	114,480 (43.7%)	143,293 (54.7%)
1990	Governor	96,759 (64.6%)	52,965 (35.4%)
1988	President	100,459 (47.4%)	111,355 (52.6%)
1986	Senate	88,177 (49.7%)	89,399 (50.3%)
	Governor	104,044 (58.0%)	75,406 (42.0%)

*Vote for Perot was 67,201 (25.2%).

Demographics

Population 549,062

Percent change from 1980 13.9%

Land area 57,044 square miles

Population per square mile 10

Counties, 1990 population

Alamosa 13,617	La Plata 32,284
Archuleta 5,345	Lake 6,007
Chaffee 12,684	Mesa 93,145
Conejos 7,453	Mineral 558
Costilla 3,190	Moffat 11,357
Custer 1,926	Montezuma 18,672
Delta 20,980	Montrose 24,423
Dolores 1,504	Ouray 2,295
Douglas (pt.) 3,042	Park 7,174
Eagle 21,928	Pitkin 12,661
Fremont (pt.) 13,640	Pueblo 123,051
Garfield 29,974	Rio Blanco 5,972
Grand 7,966	Rio Grande 10,770
Gunnison 10,273	Routt 14,088
Hinsdale 467	Saguache 4,619
Huerfano 6,009	San Juan 745
Jackson 1,605	San Miguel 3,653
Jefferson (pt.) 3,104	Summit 12,881

Cities, 1990 population (10,000 or more)

Clifton CDP 12,671	Grand Junction 29,034
Durango 12,430	Pueblo 98,640

Race and Hispanic origin

White 91.7%
Black 0.7%
American Indian, Eskimo, or Aleut. 1.4%
Asian or Pacific Islander 0.5%
Other 5.7%
Hispanic origin 17.4%

Ancestry

American 4.2%	Italian 5.0%
Danish 1.2%	Norwegian 1.7%
Dutch 3.1%	Polish 1.6%
English 18.5%	Scotch Irish 3.0%
French 4.2%	Scottish 3.0%
German 26.8%	Swedish 3.3%
Irish 15.3%	Welsh 1.2%

Universities/colleges, 1990-1991 enrollment

Adams State College, Alamosa 5,236
Colorado Mountain College, Glenwood Springs 9,697
Colorado Northwestern Community College, Rangely 1,440
Fort Lewis College, Durango 3,939
Mesa State College, Grand Junction 4,613
Pueblo Community College, Pueblo 2,863
University of Southern Colorado, Pueblo 4,366
Western State College Colorado, Gunnison 2,407

Newspapers, total circulation (in all districts)

Canon City Daily Record 8,201
Colorado Springs Gazette-Telegraph 100,903
Denver Post 263,720
Denver Rocky Mountain News 359,148
Durango Herald 6,654
Grand Junction Daily Sentinel 30,362
Pueblo Chieftain 50,009

Commercial television stations, affiliations

ADI: Denver (58%), Albuquerque (19%), Grand Junction-Durango (12%), Colorado Springs-Pueblo (9%) and Salt Lake City (2%)

KREZ-TV, Durango (CBS)
KREG-TV, Glenwood Springs (CBS)
KJCT-TV, Grand Junction (ABC)
KREX-TV, Grand Junction (CBS)
KREY-TV, Montrose (CBS)
KOAA-TV, Pueblo (NBC)
KSBS-TV, Steamboat Springs (None)

Cable television systems, total subscribers

Cablevision Co. Springs; Colorado Springs 60,000
TCI Cablevision Western Co.; Grand Junction 23,650
TCI of Colorado; Avon 7,700
TCI of Colorado; Dillon 8,000
TCI of Colorado; Pueblo 22,063

Military installations, 1991

Pueblo Army Depot Activity, Pueblo 718

Businesses and other major employers

Keystone Resort; Dillon; hotels 1,800
CF&I Steel Corp.; Pueblo; steel products 1,600
Mesa County Valley School District; Grand Junction 1,589
Colorado State Hospital; Pueblo 1,300
St. Mary-Corwin Hospital; Pueblo 1,200
West Central Colorado Uniservice; Grand Junction; professional organization 1,200
Parkview Health System Inc.; Pueblo 1,100
Keystone Resort Property Management Co.; Dillon; real estate agents 1,000
St. Mary's Hospital & Medical Center; Grand Junction 975
State of Colorado/Corrections Dept.; Canon City 900
Breckenridge Ski Corp.; Breckenridge; hotel/restaurants 850
Unisys Corp.; Pueblo; computer equipment 600
State of Colorado; Grand Junction 600
Chem-Nuclear Geotech Inc.; Grand Junction; sanitary services 570

4th District

North and East — Fort Collins; Greeley

Cows, colleges and conservatives abound in the 4th, which covers the agricultural breadbasket of Colorado, the eastern third of the state.

Although the district usually votes Republican, it is not a knee-jerk reaction; the most populous county in the 4th (Larimer) is comparatively liberal and is growing quickly, by a 25 percent rate in the 1980s.

Politics in Larimer County have been leavened in recent years by some of the same forces that have made neighboring Boulder one of the Rockies' most liberal counties. The largest of several colleges in the district (Colorado State University) is in the county seat of Fort Collins (population 87,800), and there has been a steady influx of newcomers to the area drawn by jobs in high-tech companies such as Hewlett-Packard.

In 1992, Bill Clinton became the first Democratic presidential candidate to carry Larimer County since 1964.

Yet it is hard to see Fort Collins and its environs ever becoming another Boulder. Colorado State (28,600 students) is a land-grant college focused on agricultural research. Ranching is still a major income producer in much of the county and across the 4th.

One-third of the district's residents live in Larimer County; one-fourth live in neighboring Weld, where the economy is more dependent on agriculture. For years Greeley (with almost 61,000 people) has been known as the home of Montfort of Colorado, one of the largest feed lots and packing plants in the country. The facility is now operated by Omaha-based ConAgra.

Remapping in 1992 altered district boundaries slightly around the Denver suburbs, although the city's far northern and eastern suburbs in Adams and Arapahoe counties still make up roughly 15 percent of the 4th's population. The rest of the voters live on the eastern plains, a vast agricultural region of cattle, corn and wheat covering the terrain between Denver and the Kansas border.

Some of the most Republican counties in Colorado are on the eastern plains. Elbert County, which was added to the 4th by redistricting, is the only Colorado county that voted for Alfred M. Landon in 1936, Barry Goldwater in 1964 and George Bush in 1992. The county is close enough to Denver to be home for many "weekend cowboys," white-collar workers who own ranches they visit on weekends.

While Elbert County grew 41 percent in the 1980s, most counties on the plains have been losing population for decades. One of them, Baca County in southeast Colorado, has been a center of agrarian ferment; the American Agricultural Movement was born there in the mid-1970s.

South toward the New Mexico border the Hispanic population tends to increase, along with the residents' willingness to vote Democratic. Las Animas County, which includes the old coal-mining town of Trinidad, was the only county entirely within the 4th to vote Democratic for president, Senate and House in 1992.

Election Returns

	4th District	Democrat	Republican
1992	President*	93,922 (36.9%)	97,062 (38.2%)
	House	101,957 (42.2%)	139,884 (57.8%)
1990	Governor	103,173 (66.4%)	52,102 (33.6%)
1988	President	94,418 (45.3%)	114,206 (54.7%)
1986	Senate	82,236 (49.6%)	83,622 (50.4%)
	Governor	94,898 (56.7%)	72,596 (43.3%)

*Vote for Perot was 63,402 (24.9%).

Demographics

Population 549,070

Percent change from 1980 14.0%

Land area 40,285 square miles

Population per square mile 14

Counties, 1990 population

Adams (pt.) 64,301	Lincoln 4,529
Arapahoe (pt.) 20,414	Logan 17,567
Baca 4,556	Morgan 21,939
Bent 5,048	Otero 20,185
Cheyenne 2,397	Phillips 4,189
Crowley 3,946	Prowers 13,347
Elbert 9,646	Sedgwick 2,690
Kiowa 1,688	Washington 4,812
Kit Carson 7,140	Weld 131,821
Larimer 186,136	Yuma 8,954
Las Animas 13,765	

Cities, 1990 population (10,000 or more)

Brighton 14,203	Loveland 37,352
Fort Collins 87,758	Sterling 10,362
Greeley 60,536	Thornton (pt.) 22,454

Race and Hispanic origin
White 91.3%
Black 0.7%
American Indian, Eskimo, or Aleut. 0.6%
Asian or Pacific Islander 1.1%
Other 6.3%
Hispanic origin 14.7%

Ancestry

American 3.3%	Italian 3.7%
Czechoslovakian 1.0%	Norwegian 2.2%
Danish 1.5%	Polish 1.9%
Dutch 3.3%	Scotch Irish 2.8%
English 16.7%	Scottish 2.7%
French 4.1%	Swedish 4.4%
German 37.9%	Welsh 1.1%
Irish 15.3%	

Universities/colleges, 1990-1991 enrollment
Aims Community College, Greeley 8,835
Colorado State University, Fort Collins 26,837
Lamar Community College, Lamar 969
Morgan Community College, Fort Morgan 908
National Technological University, Fort Collins 1,443
Northeastern Junior College, Sterling 3,686
Otero Junior College, La Junta 838
Parks Junior College, Denver 968
Trinidad State Junior College, Trinidad 1,550
University of Northern Colorado, Greeley 12,423

Newspapers, total circulation (in all districts)
Denver Post 263,720
Denver Rocky Mountain News 359,148
Fort Collins Coloradoan 24,866
Greeley Daily Tribune 23,577
Longmont Daily Times-Call 19,227
Loveland Reporter-Herald 16,117

Pueblo Chieftain 50,009
Trinidad Chronicle-News 2,695

Commercial television stations, affiliations
ADI: Denver (54%) and Colorado Springs-Pueblo (46%)
KTVS, Sterling (CBS)
KWHD, Castle Rock (None)

Cable television systems, total subscribers
American Cablevision; Thornton 16,761
Cablevision Co. Springs; Colorado Springs 60,000
Columbine Cablevision; Fort Collins 22,506
Mile Hi Cablevision; Denver 91,556
Scripps Howard Cable Co.; Loveland 7,602
TCI of Colorado; Greeley 15,143
TCI of Colorado; Mt Morrison 171,834

Businesses and other major employers
Colorado State University; Fort Collins 7,700
Hewlett-Packard Co.; Fort Collins; computer/office equipment 3,000
ConAgra Inc.; Greeley; meat products 2,700
Eastman Kodak Co.; Windsor; photographic equipment 2,550
Hewlett-Packard Co./Instrument Div.; Loveland; measuring/controlling devices 1,800
Poudre Valley Hospital District; Fort Collins 1,700
University of Northern Colorado; Greeley 1,400
County of Adams/Riverdale Golf Course; Brighton 1,350
Vipont Royalty Income Fund; Fort Collins; business services 1,300
Excel Corp.; Fort Morgan; beef products 1,200
Woodward Governor Co.; Fort Collins; aircraft/engine parts 1,000
County of Weld; Greeley 850
Hewlett-Packard Co.; Greeley; computer/office equipment 738
State Farm Life Insurance Co.; Greeley; life insurance services 700
Aims Community College; Greeley 700
Teledyne Inc./Teledyne Water Pik; Fort Collins; commercial equipment 656
NCR Corp./Microelectronics Div.; Fort Collins; electronic components 610
Lutheran/McKee Medical Center; Loveland 600
Hach Co.; Loveland; measuring/controlling devices 550
Anheuser-Busch Inc.; Fort Collins; brewery 550
Adams County School District; Denver 550
City of Greeley; Greeley 515

5th District

South Central — Colorado Springs

As Colorado's fastest-growing district in the 1980s, the 5th had to jettison nearly 100,000 residents in remapping to reach population parity with the state's five other districts. Pared away were three counties on the mountainous western side of the 5th, its large slice of suburban Jefferson County, a sliver of neighboring Douglas County on the north and all of rural Elbert County on the east. District lines also were redrawn in suburban Arapahoe and mountainous Fremont counties.

While substantial, the changes did not alter the essence of the 5th. It is an overwhelmingly Republican district that revolves around Colorado Springs. With more than 281,000 people, the city is the second largest in the state and the southern anchor of the rapidly growing Front Range. Population in El Paso County, which Colorado Springs dominates, grew 28 percent in the 1980s, double the statewide growth rate.

With its sunny climate, nearby springs and Pikes Peak looming in the distance, Colorado Springs began as a resort. Tourism remains an economic mainstay. But since World War II, Colorado Springs has become one of the nation's premier military centers. North of the city is the Air Force Academy; east is Peterson Air Force Base (headquarters of the U.S. Space Command); south is Fort Carson; and deep in a mountain to the west is NORAD (the North American Air Defense Command), maintaining a round-the-clock alert for an enemy attack, even in this post-Cold War era.

Colorado Springs is nervous about its future but so far has not been significantly affected by defense cutbacks. The economy has diversified beyond defense-related companies; employers now range from the U.S. Olympic Committee (with its training complex) to more than two dozen evangelical organizations, including Focus on the Family, which brought nearly 1,000 jobs to the area when it moved from California.

One aspect of Colorado Springs, though, has remained constant: its conservative politics. Only in the worst of GOP years does El Paso County stray into the Democratic column. Although George Bush lost statewide in 1992, he swept El Paso County. Districtwide, Bush won nearly half the vote, by far his best showing in the state.

The Democrats have no reliable source of votes elsewhere in the 5th to act as a counterweight. The portions of suburban Arapahoe and Douglas counties in the 5th are firmly Republican, as are the mountain precincts in Teller County and the portion of Fremont County in the 5th.

Douglas County, which provides moderately priced exurban housing for Denver commuters, had the highest growth rate of any county in Colorado in the 1980s, more than doubling its population. Teller County, which includes the old gold mining town of Cripple Creek (which has legal gambling), grew by 55 percent. Bill Clinton ran third in both counties in 1992, trailing Bush and independent Ross Perot.

Election Returns

	5th District	Democrat	Republican
1992	President*	70,671 (27.8%)	125,664 (49.5%)
	House	62,550 (25.7%)	173,096 (71.1%)
1990	Governor	63,952 (43.3%)	83,642 (56.7%)
1988	President	58,834 (30.7%)	133,076 (69.3%)
1986	Senate	47,601 (33.8%)	93,186 (66.2%)
	Governor	64,043 (45.5%)	76,852 (54.5%)

Vote for Perot was 57,450 (22.6%).

Demographics

Population 549,066

Percent change from 1980 14.0%

Land area 4,232 square miles

Population per square mile 130

Counties, 1990 population

Arapahoe (pt.) 63,602   Fremont (pt.) 18,633
Douglas (pt.) 57,349   Teller 12,468
El Paso 397,014

Cities, 1990 population (10,000 or more)

Castlewood CDP 24,392
Cimarron Hills CDP 11,160
Colorado Springs 281,140
Fort Carson CDP 11,309
Highlands Ranch CDP 10,181
Security-Widefield CDP 23,822
Southglenn CDP (pt.) 24,147

Race and Hispanic origin

White 88.8%
Black 5.6%
American Indian, Eskimo, or Aleut. 0.7%
Asian or Pacific Islander 2.2%
Other 2.8%
Hispanic origin 7.4%

Ancestry

American 3.2%   Italian 4.9%
Danish 1.2%   Norwegian 2.8%
Dutch 3.2%   Polish 2.8%
English 18.7%   Scotch Irish 3.1%
French 5.0%   Scottish 3.3%
French Canadian 1.0% Swedish 3.5%
German 33.7%   Welsh 1.4%
Irish 17.6%

Universities/colleges, 1990-1991 enrollment

Beth El College of Nursing, Colorado Springs 245
Blair Junior College, Colorado Springs 693
Colorado College, Colorado Springs 1,955
Colorado Technical College, Colorado Springs 1,250
Nazarene Bible College, Colorado Springs 424
Pikes Peak Community College, Colorado Springs 7,791
U.S. Air Force Academy, Colorado Spring 4,416
University of Colorado, Colorado Springs 6,650

Newspapers, total circulation (in all districts)

Canon City Daily Record 8,201
Colorado Springs Gazette-Telegraph 100,903
Denver Post 263,720
Denver Rocky Mountain News 359,148
Pueblo Chieftain 50,009

Commercial television stations, affiliations

ADI: Colorado Springs-Pueblo (73%) and Denver (27%)
KXRM-TV, Colorado Springs (Fox)
KKTV, Colorado Springs (CBS)
KRDO-TV, Colorado Springs (ABC)

Cable television systems, total subscribers

Cablevision Co. Springs; Colorado Springs 60,000
TCI of Colorado; Mt. Morrison 171,834

Military installations, 1991

Fort Carson (Army), Colorado Springs 18,608
Peterson Air Force Base, Colorado Springs 6,726
U.S. Air Force Academy, Colorado Springs 4,996
Falcon Air Force Base, Ellicott 2,539
Cheyenne Mountain Air Force Base (NORAD), Colorado Springs 1,346

Businesses and other major employers

Jones Intercable Investors Lp.; Englewood; cable TV services 3,500
General Electric Co./Computer Service Div.; Englewood; computer services 2,500
Digital Equipment Corp.; Colorado Springs; computer equipment 1,965
Current Inc.; Colorado Springs; greeting cards 1,950
Penrose-St. Francis Healthcare Service; Colorado Springs 1,910
Hewlett-Packard Co.; Colorado Springs; computers/measuring devices 1,761
Memorial Hospital; Colorado Springs 1,728
Citicorp/Diners Club Intl.; Englewood; credit institutions 1,500
Martin Marietta Corp./Information & Communication Systems; Littleton; computer services 1,300
Broadmoor Hotel Inc.; Colorado Springs; hotel 1,200
Add Staff Inc.; Colorado Springs; temp services 1,020
Martin Marietta Corp.; Englewood; computer services 903
Loral Aerospace Corp.; Colorado Springs; research services 850
American Express; Englewood; information services 850
Schlage Lock Co.; Colorado Springs; locks 800
U.S. West Communications Inc.; Colorado Springs; telephone communications 800
Texas Instruments Inc.; Colorado Springs; electronic components 800
Western Forge Corp.; Colorado Springs; handtools 800
Information Handling Services; Englewood; publishing 800
Focus on the Family/Family Research Council; Colorado Springs; family services 733
Atmel Corp.; Colorado Springs; electronic components 700
Marquest Medical Products; Englewood; medical instruments/supplies 700
Freedom Newspapers Inc./Gazette-Telegraph; Colorado Springs; newspapers 600
Lincoln National Life Insurance; Colorado Springs; life insurance 600
Pikes Peak Community College; Colorado Springs 600
Kaman Sciences Corp.; Colorado Springs; research services 600
SCI Systems Inc.; Colorado Springs; electronic components 550
Jeppesen Sanderson Inc.; Englewood; publishing 550
American Postal Workers Union; Colorado Springs; labor organization 550
Colorado Interstate Gas Co.; Colorado Springs; gas production/distribution 540
Colorado College; Colorado Springs 525
United Services Auto Assn.; Colorado Springs; insurance services: 516

6th District

Denver Suburbs — Aurora; Lakewood

The 6th connects the eastern, southern and western suburbs of Denver. Generally white-collar and Republican-oriented, they have an added link in the early 1990s—a concern about their economic future.

Like others across the country whose prosperity has been

closely tied to military and aerospace spending, many residents of the 6th are not sure how they will fare during the nation's economic transition.

Denver's Lowry Air Force Base, which employs a number of workers in the Arapahoe County suburbs on the 6th's eastern side, is slated for closure, as is Denver's nearby Stapleton Airport, which is to be replaced in December 1993 by a more distant facility. Martin Marietta, the aerospace company, which has a large plant near Littleton in the southern suburbs (5th District), laid off workers through the early 1990s.

The 6th has enough economic diversity to provide a safety net of sorts. Many of the federal government's regional facilities have headquarters in the Denver Federal Center in Lakewood, just west of Denver. The Coors brewery and the National Renewable Energy Lab are in nearby Golden.

Golden is in a portion of western Jefferson County added by redistricting. Jefferson also includes the affluent communities of Evergreen and Conifer and mountain homes hidden in the foothills of the Rockies.

But with a 20 percent population growth in the 1980s, the 6th had to lose more people than it gained. Pared away were a few neighborhoods in southwest Denver as well as the northern portion of the city of Aurora on the eastern side of the district. The 6th, which in the 1980s included portions of Adams, Arapahoe, Denver and Jefferson counties, now is limited to portions of only Arapahoe and Jefferson. The district population is almost evenly divided between the two.

The portion of Aurora that was lost includes the "Colfax Corridor," a strip of small businesses on the main boulevard extending east from Denver, and the Fitzsimons Army Medical Center.

But the district retains other pieces of Americana. Near the affluent community of Cherry Hills Village just south of Denver is the Cherry Hills Country Club, site of a number of professional golf tournaments including the 1960 U.S. Open, won by a young Arnold Palmer. Near Golden is the grave of the legendary frontiersman and showman, William F. "Buffalo Bill" Cody. Not far from Evergreen is the notorious Troublesome Gulch, where the media staked out Gary Hart's home in the dying days of his campaign for the Democratic presidential nomination in May 1987.

In general, GOP candidates enjoy a long head start in the 6th, thanks to the moderate to affluent bedroom communities. But the large number of registered independents will occasionally look at other options. In 1992, with Ross Perot drawing 25.4 percent of the three-way vote (his best showing in any Colorado district), George Bush carried the 6th by fewer than 3,000 votes.

Election Returns

	6th District	Democrat	Republican
1992	President*	99,045 (36.8%)	101,613 (37.8%)
	House	91,073 (39.1%)	142,021 (60.9%)
1990	Governor	105,907 (65.6%)	55,469 (34.4%)
1988	President	90,948 (41.2%)	129,595 (58.8%)
1986	Senate	74,406 (46.5%)	85,521 (53.5%)
	Governor	90,988 (56.3%)	70,617 (43.7%)

*Vote for Perot was 68,165 (25.4%).

Demographics

Population 549,056

Percent change from 1980 14.0%

Land area 420 square miles

Population per square mile 1,308

Counties, 1990 population
Arapahoe (pt.) 274,235   Jefferson (pt.) 274,821

Cities, 1990 population (10,000 or more)
Applewood CDP (pt.)   Ken Caryl CDP 24,391
11,069   Lakewood (pt.) 126,481
Aurora (pt.) 166,137   Littleton (pt.) 28,577
Columbine CDP 23,969   Southglenn CDP (pt.)
Englewood 29,387   18,940
Golden 13,116

Race and Hispanic origin
White 91.7%
Black 3.5%
American Indian, Eskimo, or Aleut. 0.5%
Asian or Pacific Islander 2.3%
Other 1.9%
Hispanic origin 6.4%

Ancestry
American 2.3%   Italian 5.1%
Czechoslovakian 1.2%   Norwegian 2.8%
Danish 1.4%   Polish 3.0%
Dutch 3.2%   Russian 1.3%
English 20.2%   Scotch Irish 3.2%
French 5.1%   Scottish 3.5%
German 36.2%   Swedish 4.2%
Irish 18.3%   Welsh 1.4%

Universities/colleges, 1990-1991 enrollment
Arapahoe Community College, Littleton 7,478
Bel-Rea Institute of Animal Technology, Denver 224
Colorado Christian College, Lakewood 852
Colorado School of Mines, Golden 2,870
Community College of Aurora, Aurora 4,098
ITT Technical Institute, Aurora 287
Red Rocks Community College, Golden 6,477

Newspapers, total circulation (in all districts)
Denver Post 263,720
Denver Rocky Mountain News 359,148

Commercial television stations, affiliations
ADI: Denver (100%)
KCNC-TV, Denver (NBC)
KDVR, Denver (Fox)
KMGH-TV, Denver (CBS)
KTVD, Denver (None)
KUSA-TV, Denver (ABC)
KWGN-TV, Denver (None)

Cable television systems, total subscribers
American Cablevision; Littleton 10,360
Jones Tri-City Intercable Inc.; Littleton 16,678
Mile Hi Cablevision; Denver 91,556
TCI of Colorado; Mt. Morrison 171,834

Military installations, 1991

Buckley Air National Guard Base, Aurora   1,357

Businesses and other major employers

Adolph Coors Co.; Golden; brewery   8,000

Swedish Medical Center; Englewood   2,000

Cobe Laboratories Inc.; Denver; medical instruments/ supplies   1,800

Coors Porcelain Co.; Golden; ceramics   1,500

Arapahoe Community College; Littleton   1,500

U.S. Interior Dept./Bureau of Reclamation; Denver   1,500

United Artists Holdings Inc.; Englewood; cable TV services   1,400

United Engineers & Constrs.; Englewood; building construction   1,326

United Steelworkers Union; Golden; labor organization   1,050

American Building Maint. Inds.; Golden; building services   1,000

EG&G Rocky Flats Inc.; Golden; research services   1,000

American Express; Englewood; banking services   925

Covia Partnership; Englewood; computer services   840

U.S. West Marketing Resources Group/U.S. West Direct; Aurora; publishing   800

Norgren Co.; Littleton; metal products   700

Humana of Aurora/Humana Hospital; Aurora   700

Red Rocks Community College; Golden   625

Hughes Aircraft Co.; Aurora; electronic components   600

Unipac Service Corp.; Aurora; credit institutions   600

City of Lakewood; Denver   600

CUC Travel Services Inc.; Aurora; passenger transportation   575

Pace Membership Warehouse; Englewood; general merchandise stores   575

Colorado School of Mines; Golden   575

Metropolitan Life Insurance Co.; Englewood; health insurance   570

State of Colorado; Denver   570

City of Aurora/Police Dept.; Aurora   540

County of Jefferson; Golden   525

City of Englewood; Englewood   513

Connecticut

Since 1960, Connecticut has established a record of doing better in even-numbered decades. The 1990s began true to form with the state in the depths of a prolonged economic slump after the boom years of the 1980s. Just as the OPEC oil crisis and the end of Vietnam-era defense spending spelled trouble for Connecticut in the 1970s, so the end of the Reagan arms buildup and the collapse of the region's real estate market hurt the economy in the early 1990s.

Connecticut's population grew by 5.8 percent during the 1980s, lower than the national average but just enough to enable the state to keep its six House seats with little tinkering to the district borders. The economic trouble gave the state congressional delegation members some scares in the 1992 election. But despite 25 percent turnover in Congress that year, all six House members and the state's senior Democratic senator won re-election. By 1993, the last delegation member voted out of office was Lowell Weicker, who lost his Senate seat in 1988. Weicker, of course, came back by dropping his Republican Party affiliation and winning the governor's race as an independent candidate in 1990.

The tendency away from the machine politics typified by Democratic boss John Bailey in the 1950s and 1960s and toward independent voting is likely to continue. Ross Perot got nearly a quarter of the vote in the 1992 presidential race, and unaffiliated voters are rivaling registered Democrats as the single biggest voting block in the state.

The volatility of Connecticut politics is likely to increase in the 1990s as the state faces wrenching economic changes. The Electric Boat Division of General Dynamics Corp. in Groton has planned to cut its work force of 21,000 in half by 1998 because of the sharp drop-off of Navy submarine orders. And the state's largest private employer, United Technologies Corp., has actually considered moving jet engine giant Pratt & Whitney out of Connecticut because of the rising cost of doing business in the state.

Connecticut's active military force dodged a bullet when the Defense Base Closure and Realignment Commission in 1993 opposed a move to close the Navy submarine base in Groton and approved a plan that would boost total employment there to nearly 15,000. The move means the base will remain intact until at least the year 2000.

Economically, the main emphasis by state planners, public officials and some business leaders is on converting weapons industries into civilian ventures. But whether such efforts will save most of the jobs once dependent on Pentagon spending remains in doubt.

A recovering banking industry, a stable insurance industry and a solid core of wealthy professionals commuting to New York City kept Connecticut in first place as the wealthiest state in the nation. In 1992 per capita income in Connecticut was $27,000—a 4 percent increase over the previous year. The flight of manufacturing employment that began in the 1970s continued. By 1991 the state had lost 17 percent of its manufacturing employment, the seventh largest percentage decline in the country.

Connecticut remains divided racially and economically with black and Hispanic populations concentrated in Bridgeport, Hartford and New Haven, the state's three largest cities. The greatest population growth during the 1980s occurred in smaller cities and suburbs along the Interstate 84 corridor where the cost of living was favorable compared to tony Fairfield County.

In the early 1990s, the Weicker administration initiated a statewide income tax designed to correct economic inequities of the sales tax system. The state government also launched what promised to be a decade-long effort to equalize the quality of public education between the poor cities and the better-off suburbs. Faced with these social and economic pressures, the mechanically inclined state that brought the world Colt handguns, vulcanized rubber, Stanley tools, top-notch cigar wrappers and Trident submarines is going to have to reinvent itself again.

Table 1   Population

District	Population	Population under 18	Voting-age population	Median age
1	548,016	124,699	423,317	34.6
2	548,041	126,997	421,044	32.5
3	547,765	121,208	426,557	34.6
4	547,765	121,625	426,140	35.2
5	547,764	131,121	416,643	34.4
6	547,765	123,931	423,834	35.2
State	3,287,116	749,581	2,537,535	34.4

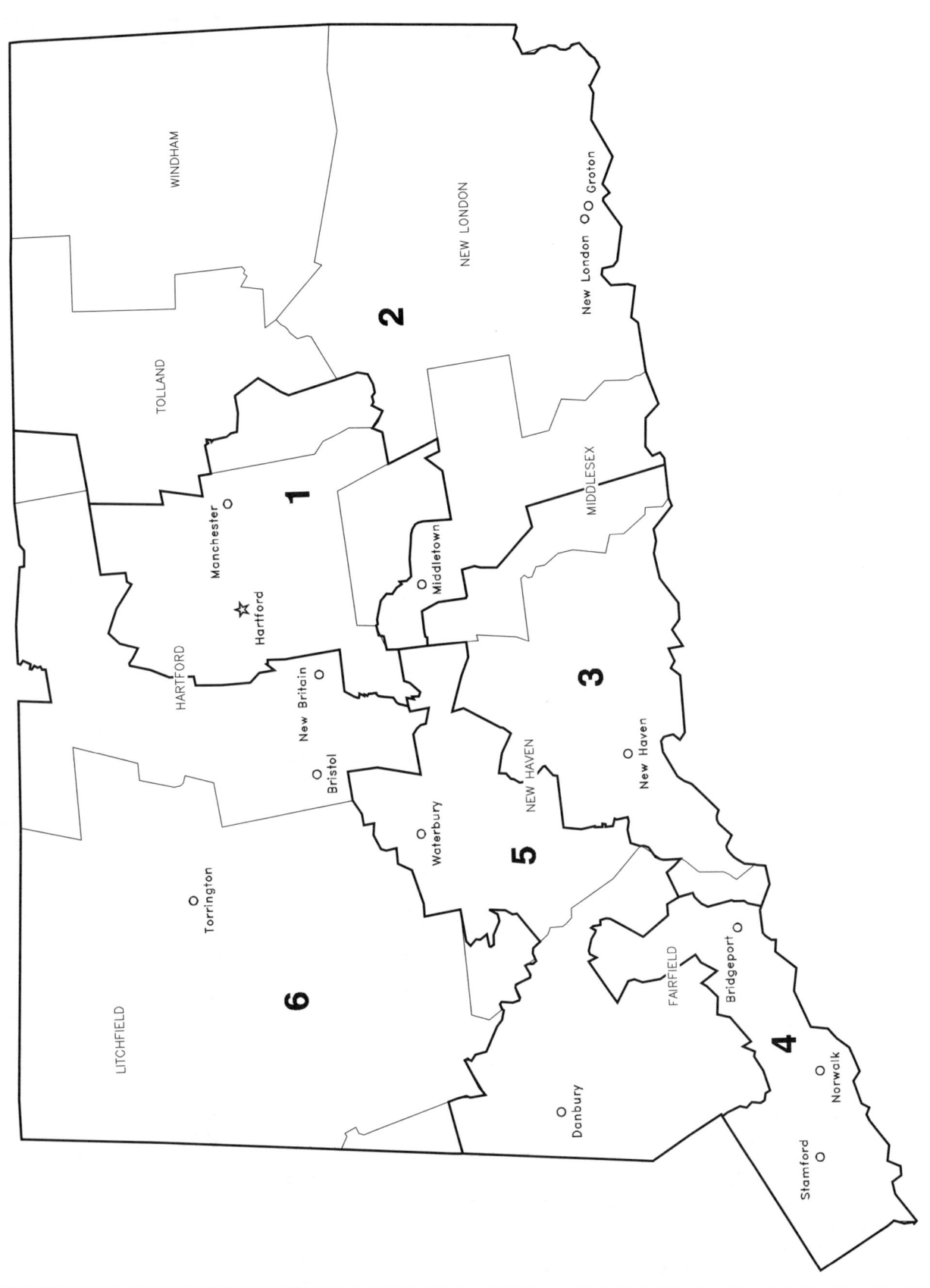

WINDHAM

NEW LONDON

New London ○ ○ Groton

TOLLAND

2

MIDDLESEX

Manchester ○

1

Middletown ○

HARTFORD

☆
Hartford

New Britain ○

3

New Haven ○

Bristol ○

NEW HAVEN

New Haven

Waterbury ○

5

Torrington ○

FAIRFIELD

Bridgeport ○

6

LITCHFIELD

4

Danbury ○

Norwalk ○

Stamford ○

Table 2 Voting-Age Persons

District	White*	Black*	American Indian, Eskimo, or Aleut*	Asian or Pacific Islander*	Other*	Hispanic*	Male*	Female*
1	81.3%	12.7%	0.2%	1.6%	4.2%	7.9%	46.9%	53.1%
2	94.0	3.3	0.3	1.3	1.0	2.5	49.2	50.8
3	86.3	10.3	0.2	1.5	1.7	4.1	46.9	53.1
4	82.6	11.6	0.1	2.0	3.7	9.5	46.8	53.3
5	92.3	4.4	0.2	1.2	2.0	5.3	48.0	52.0
6	95.6	2.2	0.1	0.9	1.2	2.9	48.2	51.8
State	88.7	7.4	0.2	1.4	2.3	5.4	47.6	52.4

*As percent of voting-age population.

Table 3 Voting-Age Persons by Age Groups

District	18-24*	25-44*	45-54*	55-64*	65 and over*
1	13.4%	42.8%	13.6%	11.6%	18.6%
2	16.7	44.1	13.2	10.5	15.4
3	14.1	42.2	13.3	11.6	18.7
4	12.6	41.8	14.8	12.8	17.9
5	12.5	44.3	14.8	11.4	16.9
6	12.2	43.7	14.3	11.9	17.9
State	13.6	43.1	14.0	11.6	17.6

*As percent of voting-age population.

Table 4 Income and Occupation

District	Median family income	Families in poverty	White collar*	Blue collar*	Service*	Farm*
1	$47,493	7.3%	67.5%	20.1%	11.6%	0.8%
2	44,314	4.4	59.7	25.5	13.2	1.5
3	47,357	5.5	65.3	22.4	11.6	0.7
4	56,320	5.6	69.0	18.7	11.1	1.2
5	51,420	4.5	63.8	24.5	10.8	1.0
6	49,864	3.1	62.9	25.3	10.6	1.2
State	49,199	5.0	64.7	22.8	11.5	1.1

*As percent of employed persons age 16 and over.

Table 5 Education: School Years Completed

District	Less than grade 9*	Grades 9-12 no diploma*	High school diploma*	College bachelor's degree or higher*
1	9.1%	13.0%	29.3%	26.6%
2	8.4	11.9	31.9	23.2
3	7.7	12.6	31.2	26.8
4	8.7	11.9	25.2	34.0
5	8.6	12.3	29.3	26.9
6	8.1	12.5	30.3	25.3
State	8.4	12.4	29.5	27.2

*As percent of persons age 25 and over.

Table 6 Housing and Residential Patterns

District	Owner occupied	Renter occupied	Urban	Rural
1	61.0%	39.0%	89.2%	10.8%
2	65.8	34.2	54.8	45.2
3	64.7	35.3	87.8	12.2
4	63.5	36.5	95.4	4.6
5	68.7	31.3	79.2	20.8
6	70.1	29.9	68.3	31.7
State	65.6	34.4	79.1	20.9

1st District

Central — Hartford

With Hartford as the hub and 19 surrounding communities as its spokes, the 1st is a classic example of a core urban center with interdependent suburbs. Many of the 1st's 548,000 residents work in Hartford.

Situated 100 miles southwest of Boston and 110 miles northeast of New York, Hartford is well-positioned to remain a regional commerce center. Companies such as Aetna, The Travelers and CIGNA helped earn Hartford the moniker "insurance capital of the world." But the city is also the state capital and a major financial center.

During the 1980s, banks, insurance companies and related businesses flourished, creating pockets of extreme wealth in the bedroom communities outside Hartford. But when the stock market plummeted, real estate sagged and defense contracts began to dwindle; Hartford caught the brunt of it all.

The situation appeared to stabilize in 1992 as unemployment leveled off and the aerospace industry targeted commercial customers to replace lost military contracts. Like much of Connecticut, the 1st is watching anxiously to see how defense-related companies weather the post-Cold War downsizing.

United Technologies, the state's largest private employer with headquarters in Hartford, plans more than 5,300 layoffs in the district by 1995. The state government, Hartford's largest employer, has been in a similar belt-tightening mode under independent Gov. Lowell P. Weicker Jr. And the city remains the nation's eighth-poorest.

Once the domain of the Democratic political czar John Bailey, the 1st was passed on to his daughter, Rep. Barbara Kennelly, in 1982. From 1986 to 1992 Kennelly garnered an average of 72 percent of the vote; political security has given her latitude to become an inside player on Capitol Hill. She became chief deputy majority whip in 1991.

Minorities, which make up slightly more than a quarter of the 1st, play an increasingly powerful role. In 1981, Hartford became the first New England city to elect a black mayor, and it has had one ever since. Hispanics were involved in shaping state legislative and congressional districts in 1992 and have put up candidates for several local offices.

Registered Democrats far outnumber Republicans in the 1st—144,000 to 69,000. In 1988, Democrat Michael S. Dukakis won the old 1st District, thanks primarily to Hartford's large black community, and four years later Bill Clinton carried every community in the 1st. The 81,000 unaffiliated voters are expected to be a key swing group in future national and statewide elections.

The district has a rich literary history. Mark Twain and Harriet Beecher Stowe both hailed from Hartford. And *The Hartford Courant,* founded in 1764, is the nation's oldest newspaper in continuous circulation.

Election Returns

	1st District	Democrat	Republican
1992	President*	133,686 (49.9%)	82,086 (30.6%)
	House	164,735 (67.1%)	75,113 (30.6%)
1990	Governor†	42,459 (21.8%)	48,989 (25.1%)
1988	President	135,377 (55.5%)	108,730 (44.5%)
	Senate	124,184 (52.5%)	112,389 (47.5%)
1986	Senate	121,611 (68.9%)	54,177 (30.7%)
	Governor	113,657 (63.5%)	63,757 (35.6%)

*Vote for Perot was 52,154 (19.5%).   †Independent/other is greater than 5%.

Demographics

Population 548,016

Percent change from 1980 6.2%

Land area 472 square miles

Population per square mile 1,160

Counties, 1990 population

Hartford (pt.) 503,026	Tolland (pt.) 13,858
Middlesex (pt.) 31,132	

Cities, 1990 population (10,000 or more)

Berlin 16,787	Newington 29,208
Bloomfield 19,483	Rocky Hill 16,554
Cromwell 12,286	West Hartford 60,110
East Hartford 50,452	South Windsor 22,090
Hartford 139,739	Wethersfield 25,651
Glastonbury 27,901	Windsor 27,817
Manchester 51,618	

Race and Hispanic origin

White 78.3%
Black 14.2%
American Indian, Eskimo, or Aleut. 0.2%
Asian or Pacific Islander 1.7%
Other 5.6%
Hispanic origin 10.1%

Ancestry

American 2.3%	Polish 9.3%
English 11.9%	Portuguese 1.7%
French 7.8%	Russian 2.6%
French Canadian 3.5%	Scotch Irish 1.1%
German 10.4%	Scottish 2.1%
Irish 16.9%	Swedish 2.6%
Italian 15.2%	West Indian 2.4%
Lithuanian 1.5%	

Universities/colleges, 1990-1991 enrollment

Greater Hartford Community College, Hartford 3,068
Hartford Graduate Center, Hartford 2,385
Hartford State Tech College, Hartford 872
Holy Apostles College, Cromwell 221
Manchester Community College, Manchester 6,493
St. Joseph College, West Hartford 1,871
Trinity College, Hartford 2,137
University of Hartford, West Hartford 7,887

Newspapers, total circulation (in all districts)

Hartford Courant 230,425
Manchester Journal Inquirer 47,296
New Britain Herald 33,936
New Haven Register 100,545
New York Daily News 757,053
New York Post 551,443
Springfield Union-News/Republic 111,178

Commercial television stations, affiliations

ADI: Hartford-New Haven (100%)

Cable television systems, total subscribers

Comcast Cablevision/Middletown; East Hampton 20,301
Cox Cable/Greater Hartford; Manchester 54,637
TCI Cablevision of Central Connecticut; Bolton 19,724
TCI Cablevision of Central Connecticut; Farmington 146,960

Businesses and other major employers

United Technologies Corp./Pratt Whitney; Hartford; aircraft/parts 27,000
Aetna Life & Casualty Co.; Hartford; life insurance 17,650
Travelers Corp.; Hartford; fire/marine/casualty insurance 12,000
Connecticut General Life Insurance Co.; Bloomfield; life insurance 6,476
Hartford Accident Indemnity Co.; Hartford; health insurance 5,000
Nutmeg Insurance Co.; Hartford; insurance services 5,000
Hartford Hospital/Jefferson House; Hartford 4,700
State of Connecticut/Health Dept.; Hartford 3,811
Combustion Engineering Inc./ABB Combustion Engineering; Windsor; engines/turbines 3,500
State of Connecticut/Transportation Dept.; Hartford 3,500
St. Francis Hospital & Medical Center; Hartford 3,000
Connecticut Light & Power Co.; Kensington; electric services 2,850
Aetna Life & Casualty Co.; Windsor; life insurance 2,500
City of Hartford; Hartford 2,119
U.S. Postal Service; Hartford 2,100
City of Hartford/Board of Education; Hartford 2,000
Connecticut Mutual Life Insurance Co./Square Management; Hartford; life insurance 1,930
Town of West Hartford; Hartford 1,752
Building Maintenance Corp.; Hartford; building services 1,600
State of Connecticut/Welfare Dept.; Hartford 1,600
Shawmut National Corp.; Hartford; commercial banks 1,556
Phoenix Mutual Life Insurance Co.; Hartford; insurance services 1,500
J. C. Penney Co. Inc.; Manchester; catalog retailers 1,500
MMH Corp./Manchester Memorial Hospital; Manchester 1,500
Mount Sinai Hospital Corp.; Hartford 1,400
West Hartford Public Schools; Hartford 1,250
Connecticut National Bank; Hartford; commercial banks 1,200
Hartford National Corp.; Hartford; commercial banks 1,200
Town of Manchester; Manchester 1,200
American Airlines Inc.; Hartford; airline 1,000
Hartford Courant Co.; Hartford; newspapers 1,000
Coltec Industries Inc./Chandler-Evans Div.; Hartford; aircraft/parts 1,000
Kaman Aerospace Corp.; Windsor; machinery/equipment/supplies 1,000

Culbro Corp.; Windsor; tobacco products 1,000
Ames Dept. Stores Inc./Crafts & More; Rocky Hill; department stores 1,000
Cigna Corp.; Hartford; life insurance 1,000
Twin City Fire Insurance Co./Hartford Insurance Group; Windsor; fire/marine/casualty insurance 1,000
University of Hartford; West Hartford 974
State of Connecticut/Motor Vehicles Dept.; Hartford 950
Stanadyne Automotive Corp./Diesel Systems; Windsor; auto equipment 925
Plaza Corp.; Hartford; insurance services 850
Newington Children's Hospital; Hartford 831
Black & Decker Corp.; Kensington; handtools/hardware 800
Kaman Aerospace Corp.; Bloomfield; aircraft/parts 800
State of Connecticut/Revenue Services Dept.; Hartford 800
H. N. S. Management Co. Inc./Connecticut Transit; Hartford; management/public relations 800
Connecticut National Bank; Hartford; commercial banks 796
Wiremold Co.; Hartford; electric lighting 750
Northeast Utilities Service Co.; Rocky Hill; accounting/auditing 740
Metropolitan District; Hartford; water supply 718
Colts Manufacturing Co. Inc.; Hartford; small arms & accessories 700
IBM Corp.; Hartford; computer services 700
U.S. Veterans Affairs Dept.; Hartford; hospital 700
State of Connecticut/Connecticut Legislature; Hartford 687
City of Hartford/Police Dept.; Hartford 678
Town of Windsor; Windsor 652
Institute of Living; Hartford 650
Town of Newington; Hartford 650
United Technologies Corp./Hamilton Standard Div.; East Windsor; medical instruments/supplies 600
State of Connecticut/Labor Dept.; Hartford 600
Town of Berlin/Board of Education; Kensington 560
Wethersfield Board of Education; Hartford 550
Arthur Andersen & Co.; Hartford; accounting/auditing 550
Bloomfield Town Schools; Bloomfield 550
Connecticut Natural Gas Corp.; Hartford; gas production and distribution 538
State of Connecticut/Veterans Home & Hospital; Rocky Hill 525

2nd District

East — New London

The fate of the nuclear attack submarine *Seawolf* may shape the economic and political future of the 2nd more than any other factor. A region once devastated by the death of a single industry (the wool mills) is again faced with the prospect of seeing its economic lifeblood drain away.

In the 1980s, more than half the jobs in the district—particularly those along the seacoast—were provided by defense-related companies. But with the Pentagon budget shrinking in the post-Cold War era, the 2nd is virtually guaranteed ongoing job losses.

Entering the 1990s, about 15,000 people worked at the region's largest employer, Groton-based Electric Boat Co. (EB). A division of General Dynamics, EB expects to deliver its last submarine on order in 1997. High hopes for building dozens of

Seawolf subs were sunk in 1992 when President Bush recommended scrapping the program.

After lobbying by the state's bipartisan delegation, Congress and the administration agreed to spend $1.5 billion on one *Seawolf* and set aside an additional $376 million for possible future subs. The decision saved jobs in the short run, but by the end of the decade, it seems likely that EB's current work force will be cut in half.

Voters in the 2nd demonstrated a predilection for voting Republican in presidential contests of the 1980s, but in 1992 they embraced Democrat Bill Clinton. Still, the balloting appeared to be more of a vote against the status quo than an endorsement of the Democratic Party.

The largest district in the state geographically and considered rural by East Coast standards, the 2nd includes some of Connecticut's poorest villages and towns. Unemployment hovered around 12 percent in the early 1990s, compared with a state average of about 7.5 percent.

Unlike Lowell, in neighboring Massachusetts, the communities along the Quinnebaug and Shetucket rivers never really recovered from the wool mills' departures in the 1960s. After several decades of economic stagnation, an effort is now under way to designate the former mill towns as a National Heritage Corridor, complete with museums and recreational opportunities.

The corridor plan fits in well with southeastern Connecticut's strategy to rejuvenate the economy with tourism. In 1989, tourism was credited with generating $435 million in revenue and $50 million in taxes in New London County. Mystic, with its historic seaport, museums, aquarium and other attractions, is the biggest success story, bringing in more than $165 million in tourist revenue annually.

Another lure for visitors is the Foxwoods casino in Ledyard. Run by the Mashantucket Pequot tribe, the casino was drawing about 8,000 people a day just a few months after its winter 1992 opening. The numbers are expected to swell as the tribe builds hotels, a golf course and convention center.

Election Returns

		Democrat	Republican
1992	President*	113,553 (42.8%)	79,110 (29.8%)
	House	123,291 (50.8%)	119,416 (49.2%)
1990	Governor†	37,739 (20.9%)	54,743 (30.3%)
1988	President	111,913 (49.2%)	115,427 (50.8%)
	Senate	106,283 (48.7%)	111,869 (51.3%)
1986	Senate	106,017 (68.5%)	48,252 (31.2%)
	Governor	95,994 (60.9%)	60,252 (38.2%)

*Vote for Perot was 72,782 (27.4%).   †Independent/other is greater than 5%.

Demographics

Population 548,041

Percent change from 1980 5.8%

Land area 1,704 square miles

Population per square mile 322

Counties, 1990 population
Middlesex (pt.) 84,826   Tolland (pt.) 105,733
New London 254,957   Windham 102,525

Cities, 1990 population (10,000 or more)

Colchester 10,980	Montville 16,673
Conning Towers-Nautilus Park CDP 10,013	New London 28,540
	Norwich 37,391
Coventry 10,063	Plainfield 14,363
East Lyme 15,340	Stanford 11,091
Ellington 11,197	Stonington 16,919
Griswold 10,384	Storrs CDP 12,198
Groton 45,144	Tolland 11,001
Killingly 15,889	Vernon 29,841
Ledyard 14,913	Waterford 17,930
Mansfield 21,103	Willimantic CDP 14,746
Middletown (pt.) 42,762	Windham 22,039

Race and Hispanic origin

White 93.3%
Black 3.7%
American Indian, Eskimo, or Aleut. 0.4%
Asian or Pacific Islander 1.4%
Other 1.3%
Hispanic origin 3.0%

Ancestry

American 2.6%	Italian 13.7%
Dutch 1.4%	Polish 10.6%
English 18.5%	Portuguese 1.4%
French 13.9%	Russian 1.7%
French Canadian 6.3%	Scotch Irish 1.8%
German 15.8%	Scottish 3.2%
Irish 19.8%	Swedish 2.9%

Universities/colleges, 1990-1991 enrollment

Connecticut College, New London 1,978
Eastern Connecticut State University, Willimantic 4,475
Middlesex Community College, Middletown 3,230
Mitchell College, New London 942
Mohegan Community College, Norwich 3,194
Quinebaug Valley Community College, Danielson 1,270
Thames Valley State Tech College, Norwich 947
U.S. Coast Guard Academy, New London 950
University of Connecticut, Storrs 25,497
Wesleyan University, Middletown 3,417

Newspapers, total circulation (in all districts)

Hartford Courant 230,425
Manchester Journal Inquirer 47,296
Middletown Press 17,872
New London Day 38,745
New York Daily News 757,053
New York Post 551,443
Norwich Bulletin 33,745
Westerly Sun 12,210
Willimantic Chronicle 11,054

Commercial television stations, affiliations

ADI: Hartford-New Haven (100%)
WTWS, New London (None)

Cable television systems, total subscribers

Century Norwich Cable; Norwich 11,293
Comcast Cablevision/Middletown; East Hampton 20,301
Continental Cablevision of Connecticut; Stafford 31,000
Crown-Media Co.; Ashford 27,223
Eastern Connecticut Cable TV Inc.; Montville 27,145
Eastern Connecticut Television Inc.; Plainfield 14,914
Storer Cable TV Inc.; Killingworth 20,481
Storer Cable TV Inc.; North Stonington 27,550
TCI Cablevision of Central Connecticut; Bolton 19,724

Military installations, 1991

New London Naval Submarine Base, Groton 12,644

Businesses and other major employers

General Dynamics Corp./Electric Boat Div.; Groton; ship building/repairing 18,000
Aetna Life & Casualty Co.; Middletown; medical service/health insurance 5,500
United Technologies Corp.; Middletown; aircraft/parts 3,500
Northeast Utilities Service Co./Millstone Nuclear Power; Waterford; electric services 1,700
Lawrence Memorial Hospital; New London 1,600
Pfizer Inc.; Groton; medicinal chemicals 1,500
City of Middletown; Middletown 1,343
Middlesex Memorial Hospital; Middletown 1,320
William Backus Hospital; Norwich 1,200
State of Connecticut/Norwich Hospital; Norwich 1,100
Town of Groton; Groton 957
Connecticut Valley Hospital; Middletown 953
Wesleyan University; Middletown 902
State of Connecticut/Seaside Center; Waterford 900
Windham Community Memorial Hospital; Willimantic 819
Northeast Utilities Vol. Assoc./Northeast Nuclear Energy Co.; Waterford 800
City of New London; New London 800
Town of Windham; Willimantic 800
Wyman-Gordon Inv. Castings; Groton; castings 700
Rockville General Hospital; Vernon 650
Waterford School District; Waterford 600
Middletown Public Schools; Middletown 600
Kimball Day Hospital; Putnam 590
Raymond Engineering Inc.; Middletown; computer equipment 574
Anchor Glass Container Corp.; Dayville; glass/glassware 524
Kaman Aerospace Corp.; Moosup; metalworking machinery 520
Johnson Memorial Hospital; Stafford Spgs 520
Lee Co.; Westbrook; measuring/controlling devices 510
Franklin Mushroom Farms Inc.; North Franklin; mushrooms 505

3rd District

South — New Haven

To the outside world, New Haven is synonymous with Yale University. The prestigious Ivy League school with its famous theater, renowned academics and rich history is a symbol of top-rank higher education. But while Yale has been a fixture in New Haven since the 18th century, the prosperous academic community has little in common with the poorer white ethnic groups and minorities who dominate the city.

New Haven is a busy port along Long Island Sound with a substantial population of blue-collar workers; one-third of its 130,000 residents are black. But sizable swaths of the community are economically impoverished; one-fifth of New Haven's population has income below the poverty level. Most of the national headlines the city has garnered in recent years have been about racial tensions, violent crime and the infant mortality rate, which is the highest among small American cities.

There has long been tension between the upscale and intellectual Yalies and the townfolk around them. Many residents believe that their tax burden is unduly heavy because the university—the city's largest landowner—is not required to pay taxes on property it uses for academic purposes. Yale often is pilloried as an enclave for the elite that cares little about the city as a whole.

The university has tried to mend fences, promising $50 million for city projects over a 10-year period. School officials are widely credited with helping persuade Macy's department store not to abandon downtown New Haven. The store is symbolically important; in the 1950s, it was a key component in helping New Haven earn a reputation as a national leader in urban renewal. Yale also continues to be the largest employer in the city.

One thing the Yalies and the townies agree on: They like Democrats. In 1992, Democrats on every level amassed huge margins in New Haven.

Districtwide, defense manufacturers and hundreds of related subcontractors employ the most people, particularly in suburbs such as West Haven, Hamden and Wallingford. They seem likely to face continued uncertainty in the years ahead as military budgets are trimmed.

Italian-Americans dominated House elections in the 3rd from 1952 through 1980, and they re-emerged as a force in 1990 with the election of Rep. Rosa DeLauro, daughter of an Italian immigrant. The 3rd went Republican in 1980 but reverted to the Democrats two years later. The Democratic bent of New Haven's blacks and its white ethnics makes the 3rd tough turf for the GOP in House elections; DeLauro won two-thirds of the vote in 1992.

Still, migration from the city to the suburbs has diminished the city's clout in the 3rd and made it possible for the GOP to carry the district in contests for higher office. The 3rd supported Hubert H. Humphrey for president in 1968 but then did not back another Democrat for the White House until 1992, when Bill Clinton won the district.

Election Returns

	3rd District	Democrat	Republican
1992	President*	121,163 (44.6%)	96,085 (35.4%)
	House	162,568 (65.7%)	84,952 (34.3%)
1990	Governor†	60,269 (30.9%)	68,418 (35.1%)
1988	President	119,432 (49.6%)	121,488 (50.4%)
	Senate	125,658 (54.5%)	105,042 (45.5%)
1986	Senate	112,696 (67.3%)	54,027 (32.3%)
	Governor	100,192 (59.0%)	68,452 (40.3%)

*Vote for Perot was 54,147 (20.0%).   †Independent/other is greater than 5%.

Demographics

Population 547,765

Percent change from 1980 5.6%

Land area 425 square miles

Population per square mile 1,288

Counties, 1990 population
Fairfield (pt.) 49,389   New Haven (pt.) 471,138
Middlesex (pt.) 27,238

Cities, 1990 population (10,000 or more)

Branford 27,603	New Haven 130,474
Clinton 12,767	New Branford 12,996
East Haven 26,144	North Haven 22,249
Guilford 19,848	Orange 12,830
Hamden 52,434	Stratford 49,389
Madison 15,485	Wallingford 40,822
Milford 49,938	West Haven 54,021

Race and Hispanic origin
White 84.1%
Black 11.9%
American Indian, Eskimo, or Aleut. 0.2%
Asian or Pacific Islander 1.5%
Other 2.2%
Hispanic origin 4.9%

Ancestry

American 2.1%	Lithuanian 1.0%
English 12.9%	Polish 8.1%
French 4.5%	Russian 2.7%
French Canadian 2.0%	Scotch Irish 1.3%
German 13.2%	Scottish 2.2%
Hungarian 1.8%	Slovakian 2.0%
Irish 19.1%	Swedish 2.2%
Italian 25.7%	

Universities/colleges, 1990-1991 enrollment
Albertus Magnus College, New Haven 734
Greater New Haven Tech College, North Haven 715
Paier College of Art, Hamden 309
Quinnipiac College, Hamden 3,405
South Central Community College, New Haven 4,017
Southern Connecticut State University, New Haven 13,618
University of New Haven, West Haven 6,065
Yale University, New Haven 10,998

Newspapers, total circulation (in all districts)
Connecticut Post 67,190
Hartford Courant 230,425
Middletown Press 17,872
Milford Citizen 6,894
New Haven Register 100,545
New York Daily News 757,053
New York Post 551,443
New York Times 746,924

Commercial television stations, affiliations
ADI: Hartford-New Haven (96%) and New York (4%)
    WTNH-TV, New Haven (ABC)

Cable television systems, total subscribers
Cablevision of Southern Connecticut; Bridgeport 79,000
Storer Cable TV Inc.; Killingworth 20,481
Storer Cable TV Inc.; West Haven 69,122
TCI Cablevision; North Branford 57,168

Military installations, 1991
Orange Air National Guard Station, New Haven 46

Businesses and other major employers
United Technologies Corp./Sikorsky Aircraft Div.; Stratford; aircraft/parts 12,000

Yale University & New Haven Hospital; New Haven 6,600

Avco Corp./Textron Lycoming Div.; Stratford; aircraft/parts 4,500

City of New Haven; New Haven 3,725

Hospital of St. Raphael Inc.; New Haven 3,300

United Technologies Corp./Pratt & Whitney Div.; North Haven; aircraft 3,200

Blue Cross/Blue Shield of Connecticut; North Haven; medical service/health insurance 2,200

City of Milford; Milford 1,615

U.S. Veterans Affairs Dept.; New Haven; hospital 1,500

Sanitary Maintenance Service; New Haven; building services 1,500

Town of Stratford; Stratford 1,334

Yale University; New Haven 1,200

U.S. Postal Service; New Haven 1,000

Service America Corp.; New Haven; nonstore retailers 1,000

Bic Corp.; Milford; pens/office supplies 900

IBM Corp.; Milford; professional/commercial equipment 900

Bristol-Myers Squibb Co.; Wallingford; pharmaceutical research services 850

Sargent Mfg. Co.; New Haven; cutlery/handtools/hardware 825

Automotive Controls Corp./Autotune; Branford; electrical equipment/supplies 800

State of Connecticut/Mental Retardation Dept.; New Haven 727

American Cyanamid Co./AC Moulding Compounds; Wallingford; pharmaceuticals 700

Warner-Lambert Co./Schick; Milford; warehousing 700

Town of Guilford; Guilford 694

United Illuminating Co. Inc.; New Haven; electric services 660

Town of Hamden/Town of Hampton; New Haven 660

New Haven Register Inc.; New Haven; newspapers 650

Town of East Haven; New Haven 650

Town of North Haven; North Haven 650

Dunhill Personnel of New Haven; New Haven; personnel supply services 650

Caldor Inc.; Bridgeport; department stores 630

Quinnipiac College Inc.; New Haven 625

University of New Haven; New Haven 603

Conopco Inc.; Clinton; soaps/cleaners 600

National Railroad Pass Corp./Amtrak; New Haven; railroads 600

Corometrics Medical Systems; Wallingford; medical instruments/supplies 600

Madison Board of Education; Madison 600

Southern New England Telecommunications Corp; New Haven; telephone communications 594

Ogden Allied Security Services; New Haven; security services 575

Faith Mount Gideon; New Haven; religious organization 571

U.S. Surgical Corp.; North Haven; medical instruments 560

U.S. Repeating Arms Co./Winchester; New Haven; ordnance/accessories 540

Milford Hospital Inc.; Milford 540

Town of Branford; Branford 516

City of Milford; Milford 502

4th District

Southwest — Stamford; Bridgeport

Bridgeport is a decaying former whaling community that earned notoriety in 1991 when its mayor tried to have the city declared bankrupt. Nearby Greenwich is an enclave where some of the wealthiest people in America reside. The contrast highlights the split personality of the 4th. The district includes the affluent white-collar communities of Connecticut's "Gold Coast," along Long Island Sound, but it also has Bridgeport, a city plagued by poverty, where one neighborhood was dubbed Mount Trashmore because of its three-story garbage pile. (The eyesore was finally removed in late 1992 after dominating the area for two decades.)

Taking in Bridgeport as well as better-off Stamford and Norwalk, the 4th has the largest urban population of any Connecticut district. Bridgeport produced one-quarter of all munitions used by the Allied forces in World War II; its strategic importance made it one of two Connecticut cities to be protected by Nike missile bases in the 1950s and early 1960s.

But as the missiles shielded Bridgeport from external enemies, the city deteriorated from within; population shrank in the 1970s and remained static in the 1980s. The 142,000 people who live in Bridgeport now are among the neediest in Connecticut; 15 percent of the city's residents fall below the poverty line.

The city's economy could get a boost with the resuscitation of the University of Bridgeport. Its enrollment dropped from about 8,000 to 2,000 in the 1980s, but then the institution was bought by the Unification Church, headed by the Rev. Sun Myung Moon. While grateful for the bailout, some locals are wary of what the church has in mind for its new acquisition.

Voting and unemployment data reflect the contrasts in the 4th. Bridgeport voted overwhelmingly for Democrat Bill Clinton in the 1992 presidential contest, although George Bush carried most of the other communities in the 4th. Jobless rates in Stamford and Norwalk have frequently fallen below the state average, while Bridgeport's unemployment (near double digits through much of 1992) has routinely led Connecticut.

The dominant political force in the district is the Republican-minded upper-crust towns along the coast, which are a short drive or train-ride from New York City. Most of the towns have GOP mayors, and together they host dozens of corporate headquarters and their officers. Stamford has the third-largest concentration of corporate headquarters in the nation, including well-known names such as Pitney Bowes, GTE, Champion International and Xerox.

Election Returns

	4th District	Democrat	Republican
1992	President*	109,122 (42.0%)	110,072 (42.3%)
	House	58,666 (26.7%)	147,816 (67.3%)
1990	Governor †	27,127 (16.2%)	81,931 (49.0%)
1988	President	101,217 (42.3%)	138,301 (57.7%)
	Senate	101,549 (45.3%)	122,632 (54.7%)
1986	Senate	90,119 (59.5%)	60,834 (40.2%)
	Governor	81,158 (52.2%)	73,604 (47.3%)

Vote for Perot was 40,802 (15.7%).   †Independent/other is greater than 5%.

Demographics

Population 547,765

Percent change from 1980 5.6%

Land area 254 square miles

Population per square mile 2,160

Counties, 1990 population
Fairfield (pt.) 547,765

Cities, 1990 population (10,000 or more)

Bridgeport 141,686	New Canaan 17,864
Darien 18,196	Norwalk 78,331
Fairfield 53,418	Stamford 108,056
Greenwich 58,441	Trumbull 32,016
Monroe (pt.) 15,347	Westport 24,410

Race and Hispanic origin
White 80.0%
Black 13.1%
American Indian, Eskimo, or Aleut. 0.2%
Asian or Pacific Islander 2.2%
Other 4.5%
Hispanic origin 11.1%

Ancestry

American 2.3%	Italian 17.9%
Dutch 1.2%	Polish 6.3%
English 11.8%	Portuguese 1.3%
French 2.9%	Russian 3.4%
French Canadian 1.0%	Scotch Irish 1.3%
German 12.1%	Scottish 2.4%
Greek 1.3%	Slovakian 2.2%
Hungarian 3.0%	Swedish 1.7%
Irish 15.9%	West Indian 2.0%

Universities/colleges, 1990-1991 enrollment
Bridgeport Engineering Institute, Fairfield 417
Fairfield University, Fairfield 4,821
Housatonic Community College, Bridgeport 2,403
Norwalk Community College, Norwalk 3,698
Norwalk State Tech College, Norwalk 978
Sacred Heart University, Fairfield 4,266
University of Bridgeport, Bridgeport 4,278

Newspapers, total circulation (in all districts)
Connecticut Post 67,190
Greenwich Time 13,194
Hartford Courant 230,425
New York Daily News 757,053
New York Post 551,443
New York Times 746,924
Norwalk Hour 21,402
Stamford Advocate 30,970

Commercial television stations, affiliations
ADI: New York (100%)

Cable television systems, total subscribers
Cablevision of Connecticut; Norwalk 83,000
Cablevision of Southern Connecticut; Bridgeport 79,000
Crown Cable of Newtown; Monroe 25,077

Businesses and other major employers

City of Bridgeport; Bridgeport 4,153
Pitney Bowes Inc.; Stamford; computer/office equipment 4,000
Thomas Tilling Inc.; Stamford; road construction 3,635
Bridgeport Hospital Inc.; Bridgeport 2,400
Employees Assistance Program; Norwalk; supply services 2,400
Norwalk Hospital; Norwalk 2,200
Saks & Co./Saks Fifth Ave; Stamford; department stores 2,100
St. Vincent's Medical Center; Bridgeport 2,000
Town of Greenwich/Board of Education; Greenwich 1,967
Norden Systems Inc.; Norwalk; search/navigation equipment 1,900
United Technologies Corp./Sikorsky Aircraft Div.; Bridgeport; aircraft/parts 1,750
City of Stamford; Stamford 1,550
Clairol Inc.; Stamford; hair preparations 1,500
Cadbury Schweppes Holdings; Stamford; food products 1,500
Service Management Group Inc.; Bridgeport; janitorial services 1,500
Peoples Bank; Bridgeport; savings institutions 1,435
GTE Service Corp.; Stamford; public relations 1,200
Greenwich Hospital Assn. Inc.; Greenwich 1,200
Stamford Hospital; Stamford 1,160
Brynwood Partners; Greenwich; investment offices 1,150
Conopco Inc./Ragu Foods Co.; Bridgeport; preserved fruits/vegetables 1,100
Remington Products Inc.; Bridgeport; household appliances 1,000
General Electric Co.; Bridgeport; appliances 1,000
U.S. Surgical Corp./Auto Suture Co. Div.; Norwalk; medical instruments 1,000
Perkin-Elmer Corp.; Norwalk; measuring/controlling devices 1,000
General Electric Capital Corp.; Stamford; credit institutions 1,000
General RE Corp.; Stamford; fire/marine/casualty insurance 945
Pepperidge Farm Inc.; Norwalk; bakery products 900
James River Corp. Virginia; Norwalk; paper products 800
Town of Westport; Westport 800
Emson Foreign Sales Corp.; Bridgeport; machinery/equipment/supplies 750
Caldor Inc.; Norwalk; department stores 750
Fairfield University Inc.; Fairfield 750
Saint Joseph's Medical Center; Stamford 717
Macmillan Inc.; Greenwich; book publishing 700
Walden Book Co. Inc.; Stamford; bookstores 700
Olin Corp./Olin Chemical Group; Stamford; inorganic chemicals 690
Stew Leonard's; Norwalk; grocery products 650
University of Bridgeport; Bridgeport 629
Hubbell Inc./Hubbell Wiring Device Div.; Bridgeport; metal-working machinery 600
Chase Manhattan Bank; Bridgeport; commercial banks 600
John Brown Inc.; Stamford; business services 600
General Electric Company; Fairfield; aircraft/parts 550
Raytheon Co./Raytheon Medical Systems; Stamford; medical instruments/supplies 550
Citytrust Bancorp Inc.; Bridgeport; commercial banks 550

CPC Intl. Inc./Arnold Bakeries; Greenwich; retail bakeries 550
Bridgeport Health Care Center; Bridgeport; nursing 550
IBM Credit Corp.; Stamford; credit institutions 530
Jewish Home Elderly Fairfield County; Fairfield; nursing 525
Vitramon Inc.; Monroe; electronic components 517

5th District

West — Waterbury; Danbury

Three of Connecticut's 10 largest cities are in the 5th—Waterbury, Danbury and Meriden—but any Democratic tendencies in those urban areas are counterbalanced by two dozen smaller towns where Republican candidates usually run well among middle-class voters, and by a number of *Fortune* 500 companies whose headquarters employ a substantial white-collar work force.

Registered Democrats outnumber Republicans almost 3-to-2 in the 5th. But many of the nominal Democrats—especially those in the working-class Naugatuck Valley—feel the national party has become too liberal. That helps explain why a Democratic presidential candidate has not carried the 5th since 1968.

In Connecticut's heated three-way 1990 gubernatorial election, Waterbury and Danbury voted for Republican John G. Rowland (who had represented the 5th since 1985); Meriden split between Rowland and Lowell P. Weicker Jr., who won election as the state's first independent governor.

In Waterbury, the 5th District's largest city with 109,000 people, Democrats have had some trouble retaining a dominant position even in local politics. Waterbury had a Republican mayor from 1985 to 1991. Rep. Gary Franks, born in Waterbury, made enough of a dent in Waterbury's usual Democratic margin to win two House elections. In both of those contests Franks also benefited from campaign visits by high-level Republicans, who were eager to help one of their party's few high-level black politicians. (Blacks make up only 5 percent of the district's population.)

Franks gets his strongest electoral support from a number of smaller, wealthier towns in the district, places filled with white-collar business people who commute to corporate jobs in Danbury and other venues closer to New York City.

Danbury, in Fairfield County, is home to some of the 5th's most affluent residents. The median family income in Danbury tops $51,000, and its public school system is among the nation's finest. Located in the media and cultural orbit of New York, Danbury boasts several corporate headquarters, including Union Carbide and Hughes Optical, the district's two largest employers. The city also draws visitors to the Danbury Fair Mall, New England's largest shopping center.

But the wealth of Danbury and its surrounding suburbs has not spread to the district's two other cities.

Downtown Waterbury was sprucing up in the mid-1980s, but when New England fell into recession in the late 1980s, renewal stalled as unemployment soared. Waterbury once was hailed as the "brass capital of the world" and known for the watches it made. But those industries are no more, and the city is searching for ways to fill the void. Two hospitals are the city's major employers. Just to the east is Meriden. Once the region's silversmithing capital, Meriden remains a mostly blue-collar community, with many residents working for defense contractors located outside the district.

Election Returns

	5th District	Democrat	Republican
1992	President*	93,966 (35.3%)	111,327 (41.8%)
	House†	74,791 (31.1%)	104,891 (43.7%)
1990	Governor†	31,397 (16.6%)	101,868 (54.0%)
1988	President	95,189 (40.8%)	138,037 (59.2%)
	Senate	111,118 (49.8%)	112,097 (50.2%)
1986	Senate	97,678 (61.5%)	60,421 (38.0%)
	Governor	89,170 (55.3%)	70,333 (43.6%)

*Vote for Perot was 60,891 (22.9%).   †Independent/other is greater than 5%.

Demographics

Population 547,764

Percent change from 1980 5.6%

Land area 586 square miles

Population per square mile 934

Counties, 1990 population
Fairfield (pt.) 227,682   New Haven (pt.) 320,082

Cities, 1990 population (10,000 or more)

Ansonia 18,403	New Fairfield 12,911
Bethel 17,541	Newtown 20,779
Brookfield 14,113	Ridgefield 20,919
Cheshire 25,684	Seymour 14,288
Danbury 65,585	Shelton 35,418
Derby 12,199	Waterbury 108,961
Meriden 59,479	Wilton 15,989
Naugatuck 30,625	Wolcott 13,700

Race and Hispanic origin
White 91.2%
Black 4.8%
American Indian, Eskimo, or Aleut. 0.2%
Asian or Pacific Islander 1.4%
Other 2.4%
Hispanic origin 6.2%

Ancestry

American 2.2%	Lithuanian 1.8%
Dutch 1.2%	Polish 9.2%
English 13.3%	Portuguese 2.1%
French 6.7%	Russian 2.5%
French Canadian 2.8%	Scotch Irish 1.3%
German 15.2%	Scottish 2.2%
Hungarian 1.8%	Slovakian 2.1%
Irish 21.1%	Swedish 2.2%
Italian 23.3%	

Universities/colleges, 1990-1991 enrollment
Mattatuck Community College, Waterbury 4,270
Teikyo Post College, Waterbury 2,082
Waterbury State Tech College, Waterbury 1,502
Western Connecticut State University, Danbury 6,245

Newspapers, total circulation (in all districts)
Ansonia Sentinel 15,891
Connecticut Post 67,190
Danbury News-Times 38,126
Hartford Courant 230,425

Meriden Record-Journal 30,702
Naugatuck News 4,650
New Haven Register 100,545
New York Daily News 757,053
New York Post 551,443
New York Times 746,924
Waterbury Republican-American 60,007

Commercial television stations, affiliations
ADI: New York (57%) and Hartford-New Haven (43%)
WHAI-TV, Bridgeport (None)
WTXX, Waterbury (None)

Cable television systems, total subscribers
Cablevision of Connecticut; Norwalk 83,000
Comcast Cablevision; Danbury 29,000
Crown Cable of Newtown; Monroe 25,077
Dimension Cable Services; Meriden 38,483
Sammons Communications; Waterbury 43,800
TCI Cablevision; North Branford 57,168
Tele-Media Co.; Seymour 40,663

Businesses and other major employers
City of Waterbury; Waterbury 3,200
Union Carbide Corp.; Danbury; organic chemicals 2,000
The Danbury Hospital; Danbury 1,900
Boehrnger Inglheim; Ridgefield; pharmaceuticals 1,800
General Datacomm Industries; Middlebury; communications equipment 1,800
City of Danbury; Danbury 1,800
St. Mary's Hospital Corp.; Waterbury 1,700
City of Meriden; Meriden 1,690
The Waterbury Hospital; Waterbury 1,474
Veterans' Memorial Medical Center/Meriden-Wallingford Hospital; Meriden 1,375
Griffin Hospital Inc.; Derby 1,100
State Voc. Fed. Tach. Local 4200 A; Meriden; labor organizations 1,050
Perkin-Elmer Corp.; Wilton; measuring/controlling devices 1,000
North American Philips Corp./Airpax Co.; Cheshire; electric distribution equipment 1,000
Barden Corp.; Danbury; precision ball bearings 1,000
City of Meriden/Board of Education; Meriden 918
Dresser Industries Inc.; Newtown; measuring/controlling devices 900
Grolier Inc.; Danbury; books 900
Hughes Danbury Optical Systems; Danbury; measuring/controlling devices 850
Fairfield Hills Hospital; Newtown 850
SVG Lithography Systems Inc.; Wilton; industrial machinery 800
Eaton Corp./Pressure Sensors Div.; Bethel; electronic components 800
Cuno Inc.; Meriden; refrigeration 700
General Datacomm Industries; Naugatuck; communications equipment 700
Allied-Signal Inc./Bendix Cheshire; Cheshire; search/navigation equipment 650
American Cyanamid Co./Davis-Geck; Danbury; drugs 650
Centerbank; Waterbury; savings institutions 650
Richardson-Vicks Inc./Vicks Research Div.; Shelton; pharmaceutical research 650
Town of Newtown; Newtown 650

Deloitte & Touche; Wilton; accounting/auditing 625
Flagg C. N. Power Inc.; Meriden; building construction 600
The Napier Co.; Meriden; costume jewelry 600
Federal Prison Industries/Unicor; Danbury; steel products 600
Town of Cheshire; Cheshire 600
Pitney Bowes Inc.; Danbury; photographic equipment/supplies 563
Uniroyal Chemical Co.; Middlebury; agricultural chemicals 550
Bank of Boston Connecticut; Waterbury; commercial banks 508

6th District
Northwest — New Britain

The 6th blends the pastoral and peaceful—villages and small towns, dairy farms and nurseries—with more modern influences: hundreds of defense subcontractors. The Litchfield Hills, at the foot of the Berkshires, have attracted escapees from New York.

But for many other residents of the 6th, downsizing in the defense industry may mean hard times ahead.

United Technologies Corp. plans to reduce its Connecticut work force by more than 6,000 by 1995, and thousands of those layoffs will occur at divisions spread throughout the 6th, including Hamilton Standard in Windsor Locks, Pratt & Whitney in Southington, and Otis elevators and Carrier air conditioning, both in Farmington. When Pratt & Whitney announced it was scaling back, the Shop Rite grocery store in Southington said it too would shut down. Similar stories of retrenchment are often heard at the 300 defense subcontractors in the 6th.

Nowhere are economic problems more evident than in New Britain, the largest city in the 6th and one hit particularly hard by industrial decline. Since the Fafnir ball-bearing plant closed in the late 1980s, the city of 75,500 people has seen a number of its businesses fold or move.

Take a walk down one of New Britain's two main thoroughfares, Arch or Broad streets, and the struggle is obvious. The sidewalks and roads are crumbling; much of the housing is archaic. A city once filled with Polish immigrants is now a melting pot of blacks, Asians, Hispanics, Italians and Poles straining to get along.

The city's largest employer, tool manufacturer Stanley Works, has enabled New Britain to retain its longtime moniker "Hardware City."

Smaller communities in the district are not immune from bigger-city problems. Many retail stores have abandoned Main Street locales in favor of shopping malls. A 4.5 percent state income tax imposed in 1991 is putting an extra pinch on middle-income families struggling to get through recessionary times.

In a state where most people have been accustomed to comfortable lifestyles, unemployment is bringing difficulties normally associated with inner cities, such as drug abuse and homelessness. Officials are wrestling with questions about where to build homeless shelters, how to set up community health clinics and finding money for drug treatment centers.

Residents of the 6th supported Republican presidential candidates in the good-times 1980s, but the dramatically different economic climate of 1992 helped Bill Clinton score a comfortable victory in the district.

The House seat switched from Democratic to Republican

control with Nancy Johnson's narrow open-seat victory in 1982. Into the early 1990s, her moderate-to-liberal House voting record well satisfied the voters; even in 1992, Johnson won overwhelmingly.

Election Returns

	6th District	Democrat	Republican
1992	President*	110,828 (39.8%)	99,633 (35.8%)
	House †	60,373 (25.2%)	166,967 (69.7%)
1990	Governor †	37,650 (19.0%)	71,891 (36.3%)
1988	President	113,456 (46.9%)	128,258 (53.1%)
	Senate	119,708 (51.1%)	114,425 (48.9%)
1986	Senate	104,575 (62.2%)	62,728 (37.3%)
	Governor	95,467 (56.1%)	72,092 (42.4%)

*Vote for Perot was 67,995 (24.4%).   †Independent/other is greater than 5%.

Demographics

Population 547,765

Percent change from 1980 5.9%

Land area 1,404 square miles

Population per square mile 390

Counties, 1990 population
Fairfield (pt.) 2,809	New Haven (pt.) 12,999
Hartford (pt.) 348,757	Tolland (pt.) 9,108
Litchfield 174,092	

Cities, 1990 population (10,000 or more)
Avon 13,937	Simsbury 22,023
Bristol 60,640	Southbury (pt.) 12,999
Enfield 45,532	Southington 38,518
Farmington 20,608	Suffield 11,427
New Britain 75,491	Torrington 33,687
New Milford 23,629	Watertown 20,456
Plainville 17,392	Winchester 11,524
Plymouth 11,822	Windsor Locks 12,358

Race and Hispanic origin
White 95.0%
Black 2.3%
American Indian, Eskimo, or Aleut. 0.1%
Asian or Pacific Islander 1.1%
Other 1.5%
Hispanic origin 3.5%

Ancestry
American 2.4%	Lithuanian 1.7%
Dutch 1.3%	Polish 13.5%
English 16.2%	Russian 1.7%
French 11.8%	Scotch Irish 1.5%
French Canadian 4.7%	Scottish 2.8%
German 15.5%	Slovakian 1.4%
Irish 19.4%	Swedish 2.9%
Italian 19.1%	

Universities/colleges, 1990-1991 enrollment
Asnuntuck Community College, Enfield 1,838
Briarwood College, Southington 393
Central Connecticut State University, New Britain 13,809
Charter Oak College, Farmington 810
Northwest Connecticut Community College, Winsted 2,204
Tunxis Community College, Farmington 3,882
University of Connecticut Health Center, Farmington 483

Newspapers, total circulation (in all districts)
Bristol Press 19,154
Connecticut Post 67,190
Hartford Courant 230,425
Milford Citizen 6,894
New Britain Herald 33,936
New Haven Register 100,545
New York Daily News 757,053
New York Post 551,443
New York Times 746,924
Springfield Union-News/Republic 111,178
Torrington Register Citizen 16,683

Commercial television stations, affiliations
ADI: Hartford-New Haven (98%) and New York (2%)
  WFSB, Hartford (CBS)
  WHCT-TV, Hartford (None)
  WTIC-TV, Hartford (Fox)
  WVIT, New Britain (NBC)

Cable television systems, total subscribers
Continental Cablevision of Connecticut; Stafford 31,000
Crown Media Inc.; New Milford 14,500
Dimension Cable Services; Meriden 38,483
Laurel Cablevision Inc.; Torrington 24,200
Pegasus Cable; Winsted 6,558
Sammons Communications; Waterbury 43,800
TCI Cablevision; Farmington 146,960

Military installations, 1991
Bradley International Airport Air Force Guard Station, Windsor Locks 299

Businesses and other major employers
FNS Holding Co. Inc.; Windsor Locks; grocery stores 10,000
United Technologies Corp./Hamilton Standard Div.; Windsor Locks; search/navigation equipment 8,500
Torrington Co.; Torrington; industry machinery 3,000
United Technologies Corp.; Southington; repair shops 3,000
IBM Corp.; Southbury; computer services 2,500
New Britain General Hospital; New Britain 2,000
State of Connecticut/Southbury Training School; Southbury; residential care 2,000
United Technologies Corp./Pratt & Whitney Aircraft Div.; Southington; aircraft/parts 1,600
City of Bristol; Bristol 1,600
The Fire Casualty Insurance of Connecticut; Farmington; fire/marine/casualty insurance 1,550
Twin City Fire Insurance Co./Hartford Insurance Group; Southington; insurance services 1,500
City of New Britain; New Britain 1,500
Hartford Life Insurance Co.; Simsbury; life insurance 1,350
General Electric Co.; Plainville; electric distribution equipment 1,300
Kimberly-Clark Corp.; New Milford; textile goods 1,250
Springfield Sugar Co.; Suffield; warehousing 1,200
Bristol Hospital Inc.; Bristol 1,100
General Motors Corp./Delco Moraine; Bristol; industry machinery 1,000
Pitney Bowes; New Hartford; photographic equipment/supplies 1,000

Allstate Insurance Co.; Farmington; fire/marine/casualty insurance 1,000

Nynex Meridian Systems; Farmington; management/public relations 1,000

John N. Dempsey Hospital; Farmington 1,000

State of Connecticut/Corrections Dept.; Somers 1,000

Springfield Sugar & Products Co.; Suffield; grocery wholesaling 1,000

Otis Elevator Co.; Farmington; construction/related machinery 995

Cigna Corp.; Plainville; fire/marine/casualty insurance 900

Central Connecticut State University; New Britain 900

Town of Southington; Southington 850

The Charlotte Hungerford Hospital; Torrington 840

Lego Systems Inc.; Enfield; toys/sporting goods 810

International/Auto Workers Union; Bristol; pension/health/welfare funds 750

Dexter Corp./Nonwovers Div.; Windsor Locks; paper mills 700

Tilcon Inc.; New Britain; road construction 700

Litton Systems Inc./Winchester Electronics; Watertown; electronic components 700

U.S. Shoe Corp./Women's Specialty Retailing; Enfield; women's clothing stores 700

City of Torrington; Torrington 684

Town of Simsbury; Simsbury 659

New Britain Memorial Hospital; New Britain 650

Dexter Corp.; Windsor Locks; chemical products 600

Ensign-Bickford Industries; Simsbury; chemical products 600

Becton Dickinson & Co.; Canaan; medical instruments 600

Community Services of Connecticut Inc.; Oakville; social services 600

Critikon Inc.; Southington; medical instruments/supplies 550

Hallmark Cards Inc.; Enfield; greeting cards 550

Bristol Babcock Inc./Helicoid Div.; Watertown; measuring/controlling devices 530

DELAWARE

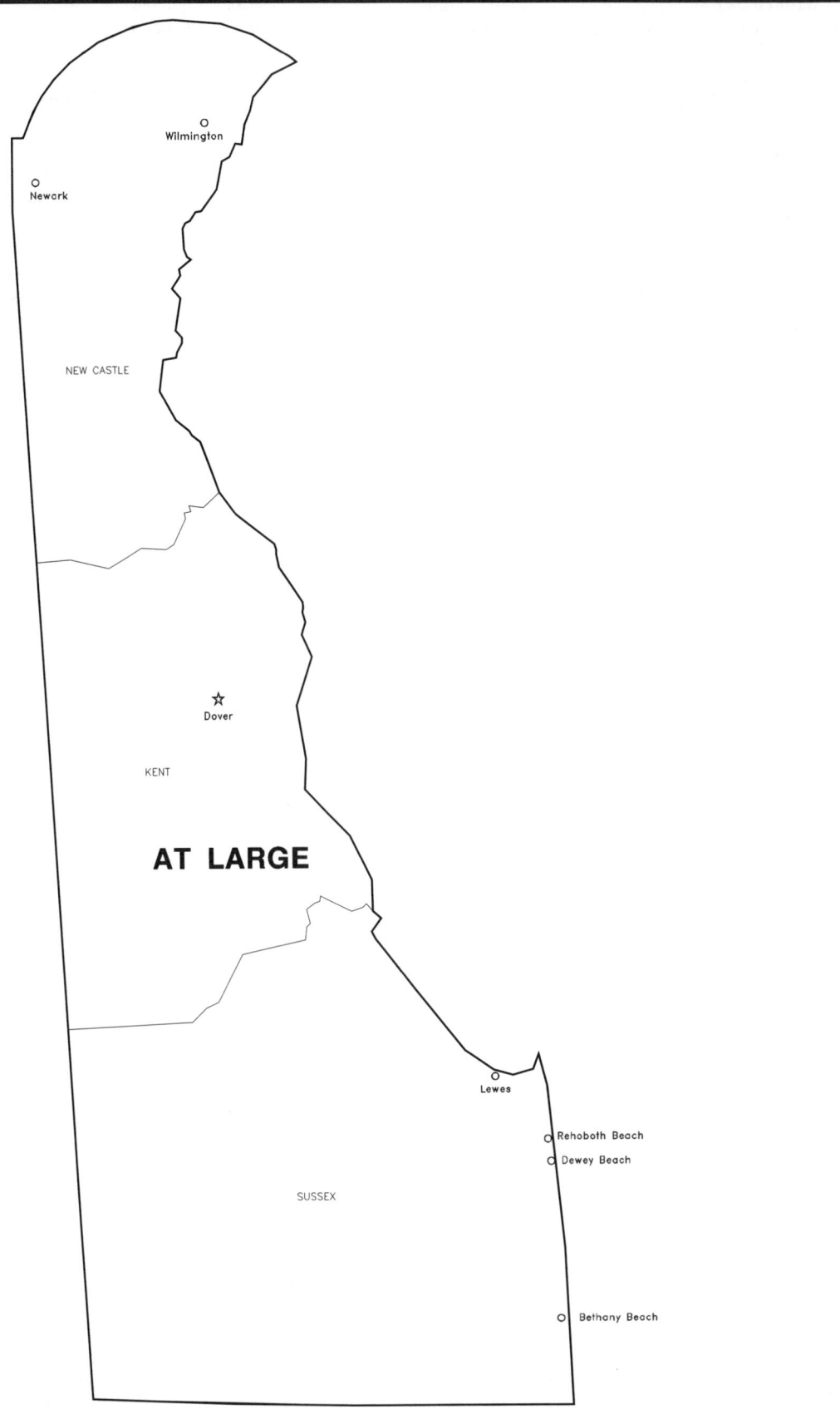

Wilmington

Newark

NEW CASTLE

☆
Dover

KENT

AT LARGE

Lewes

Rehoboth Beach

Dewey Beach

SUSSEX

Bethany Beach

Delaware

Delaware is a bellwether in national elections—it has supported the winning presidential ticket 11 times in a row—and pursues ticket-splitting with relish in the elections within its borders.

The state's four major statewide officeholders—its governor, two senators and House representative—are evenly split between the parties. Delaware voted in 1992 to send a Democrat to the White House, its former Republican governor to the U.S. House and its Democratic House member to the governor's mansion.

Delaware's inclination for split-tickets is sometimes attributed to the compactness of the state. Personal campaigning is more important than party identification. Voters expect to see their candidates, and over the course of a campaign, candidates are able to meet a large part of the electorate. The absence of a commercial statewide television station accentuates the importance of grassroots campaigning.

Despite its track record of voting for presidential winners, Delaware has had trouble producing any of its own. No president has ever been elected from Delaware, and neither of the two candidates emerging from the state in 1988, former Republican Gov. Pierre S. "Pete" du Pont IV and Democratic Sen. Joseph R. Biden Jr., traveled far on the road to the White House.

Up in the small but relatively dense area north of the Chesapeake and Delaware Canal, Democrats are strong in Wilmington, the state's largest city. Fifty years ago, almost half the state's people resided in Wilmington, but the city's 72,000 residents now cast only about 11 percent of Delaware's vote. As the city has shrunk, its suburbs have grown; New Castle County, which encompasses them both, casts a full 68 percent of the state's total vote.

The GOP's strength lies in Wilmington's suburbs and down south of the canal, in the poultry farms and coastal marshes of the Delmarva peninsula, whose name is an amalgam of its ingredients: Delaware and the eastern ends of Maryland and Virginia.

Thanks to its liberal business incorporation rules, Delaware is the on-paper home to about half the *Fortune* 500 and over 200,000 smaller corporations. Wilmington is the very real home to the Du Pont Co., which is Delaware's largest employer. It employs 125,000 worldwide. The recession has hit even Du Pont; it shed 3,500 workers in 1991 and braced for another wave of reductions in mid-1993.

Dover, Delaware's capital, is set in the state's midsection, in Kent County. It, too, has a strong Democratic constituency. A few miles south of the city is Dover Air Force Base, the East Coast's largest. The base employs nearly 9,000 military and civilian personnel who played a critical role in transporting cargo to the Middle East during the Persian Gulf War. But it has also brought something of a grim image to the city; its huge mortuary has received thousands of dead servicemen over the past three decades, including Persian Gulf casualties. Other major Dover employers include General Foods, Playtex, Scott Paper and a variety of chemical corporations.

Down at the southern end of the state is Sussex County, Delaware at its most rural. Sussex produces more poultry than any other county in the country, along with sorghum, corn and soybeans.

Tourism also has its place in this county, at its far southeast end. A string of beach resorts from the mouth of the Delaware Bay down the peninsula to Fenwick Island draw thousands of oceangoers each year. A series of storms that have battered the coast have washed away a series of beach rebuilding projects.

Rehoboth Beach is a popular summer resort whose sizable gay population has lately become a permanent fixture, raising tensions with the community's more-traditional visitors and older residents.

The increasing number of retirees residing in the beach communities have made Sussex the fastest-growing county in the state; they add to the county's already conservative tenor.

Ronald Reagan and George Bush won consistently in Sussex throughout the 1980s. But in 1992, Bush managed just 39 percent, 1,300 votes more than Bill Clinton.

A new bypass that leads to the beach may forever change the character of the southern counties. Relief Route 1 promises to cut the travel time between northern and southern Delaware and is expected to boost the local economies. But it is expected to do so by attracting city and suburban folks from New Castle County as new residents, a prospect that concerns the area's farmers.

Table 1 Population

District	Population	Population under 18	Voting-age population	Median age
AL	666,168	163,341	502,827	32.9

Table 2 Voting-Age Persons

District	White*	Black*	American Indian, Eskimo, or Aleut*	Asian or Pacific Islander*	Other*	Hispanic*	Male*	Female*
AL	82.2%	15.3%	0.3%	1.3%	0.9%	2.0%	47.6%	52.4%

*As percent of voting-age population.

Table 3 Voting-Age Persons by Age Groups

District	18-24*	25-44*	45-54*	55-64*	65 and over*
AL	15.2%	43.4%	13.5%	11.9%	16.1%

*As percent of voting-age population.

Table 4 Income and Occupation

District	Median family income	Families in poverty	White collar*	Blue collar*	Service*	Farm*
AL	$40,252	6.1%	60.6%	25.0%	12.6%	1.8%

*As percent of employed persons age 16 and over.

Table 5 Education: School Years Completed

District	Less than grade 9*	Grades 9-12 no diploma*	High school diploma*	College bachelor's degree or higher*
AL	7.2%	15.3%	32.7%	21.4%

*As percent of persons age 25 and over.

Table 6 Housing and Residential Patterns

District	Owner occupied	Renter occupied	Urban	Rural
AL	70.2%	29.8%	73.0%	27.0%

Election Returns

	At Large	Democrat	Republican
1992	President*	126,054 (43.8%)	102,313 (35.6%)
	House	117,426 (42.5%)	153,037 (55.4%)
	Governor	179,365 (64.7%)	90,725 (32.7%)
1990	Senate	112,918 (62.7%)	64,554 (35.8%)
1988	President	108,647 (43.8%)	139,639 (56.2%)
	Senate	92,378 (37.9%)	151,115 (62.1%)
	Governor	70,236 (29.3%)	169,733 (70.7%)

*Vote for Perot was 59,213 (20.6%).

Demographics

Population 666,168

Percent change from 1980 12.1%

Land area 1,955 square miles

Population per square mile 341

Counties, 1990 population
Kent 110,993 Sussex 113,229
New Castle 441,946

Cities, 1990 population (10,000 or more)
Brookside CDP 15,307 Pike Creek CDP 10,163
Dover 27,630 Wilmington 71,529
Newark 25,098

Race and Hispanic origin
White 80.3%
Black 16.9%
American Indian, Eskimo, or Aleut. 0.3%
Asian or Pacific Islander 1.4%
Other 1.1%
Hispanic origin 2.4%

Ancestry
American 4.4% Polish 5.7%
Dutch 2.2% Russian 1.0%
English 18.4% Scotch Irish 2.1%
French 2.9% Scottish 2.5%
German 20.7% Swedish 1.2%
Irish 20.9% Welsh 1.5%
Italian 9.5%

Universities/colleges, 1990-1991 enrollment
Delaware Technical & Community College, Newark 5,983
Delaware Technical & Community College, Georgetown 2,989
Delaware Technical & Community College, Dover 1,856
Delaware State College, Dover 2,606
Goldey Beacom College, Wilmington 1,886
University of Delaware, Newark 20,818
Wesley College, Dover 1,168
Widener University, Wilmington 1,032
Widener University School of Law, Wilmington 1,873
Wilmington College, New Castle 1,796

Newspapers, total circulation (in all districts)
Philadelphia Daily News 196,141
Philadelphia Inquirer 500,733
Salisbury Daily & Sunday Times 26,139
Washington Post 810,904
Wilmington News Journal 120,121

Commercial television stations, affiliations
ADI: Philadelphia (52%) and Salisbury (48%)
WBOC-TV, Salisbury (CBS)

Cable television systems, total subscribers
American Cable TV; Omar 19,301
Marcus Cable; Harrington 13,218
Storer Cable TV Inc.; Dover 18,493
Storer Cable TV Inc.; Lewes 13,000
Storer Cable TV Inc.; Seaford 5,907
TCI of New Castle County; New Castle 124,000
United Cable TV Eastern Shore; Ocean City 31,415

Military installations, 1991
Dover Air Force Base, Dover 5,735
New Castle Airport Air Force Guard Station, Newport 260

Businesses and other major employers

Du Pont E. I. De Nemours & Co.; Wilmington; petroleum refining 6,400

ICI Americas Inc.; Wilmington; pharmaceuticals 6,000

Du Pont E. I. De Nemours & Co./Imaging Systems Div.; Wilmington; professional/commercial equipment 5,000

Medical Center of Delaware/Christiana Hospital; Newark 5,200

MBNA America Bank National Assn.; Newark; commercial banks 4,500

Du Pont E. I. De Nemours & Co.; Wilmington; research services 4,500

Chrysler Corp.; Newark; motor vehicles 4,210

General Motors Corp.; Wilmington; motor vehicles 3,700

Du Pont E. I. De Nemours & Co./Defense Specialties; Wilmington; chemical products 3,500

University of Delaware; Newark 3,030

Du Pont E. I. De Nemours & Co./Engineering Dept.; Newark; research services 2,800

Du Pont E. I. De Nemours & Co./Du Pont Louviers; Newark; engineering/architectural services 2,640

Du Pont E. I. De Nemours & Co.; Seaford; yarn/thread mills 2,500

Du Pont E. I. De Nemours & Co./Medical Products Dept.; Newark; medical instruments/supplies 2,000

Du Pont E. I. De Nemours & Co./Medical Products Dept.; Bear; drugs 1,800

Wilmington Security Trust; Wilmington; investing sevices 1,800

St. Francis Hospital Inc.; Wilmington 1,650

Townsends Inc.; Millsboro; poultry/eggs 1,600

Medical Center of Delaware/Christiana Hospital; Newark 1,500

Du Pont-Merck Co.; Wilmington; pharmaceutical research 1,500

Chase Manhattan Bank; Wilmington; commercial banks 1,400

Brandywine School District; Claymont 1,322

Hercules Inc.; Wilmington; organic chemicals 1,300

Kraft General Foods Inc.; Dover; food products 1,200

American Meter Holdings Corp.; Wilmington; measuring/controlling devices 1,200

Wilmington Trust Co.; Wilmington; commercial banks 1,200

Kent General Hospital Inc.; Dover 1,091

NVF Co.; Yorklyn; steel products 1,000

County of New Castle; Wilmington 1,000

Medical Center of Delaware/Christiana Hospital; Wilmington 1,000

Cigna Corp.; Wilmington; fire/marine/casualty insurance 950

Avon Products Inc.; Newark; proprietaries/sundries 903

Greenwood Trust Co.; New Castle; commercial banks 900

Delmarva Power & Light Co.; Newark; telephone communications 850

Beebe Medical Center Inc.; Lewes 850

Allen Family Foods Inc./Cargill Inc.; Harbeson; meat products 800

Perdue Farms Inc.; Georgetown; poultry/eggs 800

Du Pont E. I. De Nemours & Co./Eagle Run Imaging Systems Div.; Newark; petroleum/natural gas 800

Du Pont E. I. De Nemours & Co./C&P Dept.; Wilmington; organic chemicals 800

State of Delaware/Stockley Center; Georgetown; nursing 800

State of Delaware/Williams Service Center; Dover 800

Bank of New York Delaware Inc.; Newark; commercial banks 798

PNC National Bank; Wilmington; commercial banks 759

U.S. Veterans Affairs Dept.; Wilmington; hospital 753

Delaware Hospital; Smyrna 750

State of Delaware/Family Services Dept.; Wilmington 750

Werner Holding Co.; Wilmington; metal products 700

Morgan Guaranty Trust Co. of New York/Morgan Christiana Corp.; Newark; savings institutions 700

American Life Insurance Co.; Wilmington; life insurance 686

Draper Canning Co. Inc.; Milton; preserved fruits/vegetables 650

ILC Industries; Frederica; medical instruments/supplies 650

Star Enterprise/Texaco Oil Co.; Delaware City; gasoline stations 650

Nemours Foundation/Alfred I. Du Pont Institute; Wilmington 640

County of New Castle/Public Safety Dept.; New Castle 616

Gannett Co. Inc./News Journal Co.; New Castle; newspapers 600

Du Pont Optical Storage Holding/Philips & Du Pont Optical Inc; Wilmington; glass/glassware 600

Sears Roebuck & Co.; Wilmington; department stores 600

Rodney Czeser School District; Camden 600

State of Delaware/Corrections Center; Smyrna 600

State of Delaware/Public Instruction Dept.; Wilmington 600

Nanticoke Homes Inc.; Greenwood; wood buildings/mobile homes 585

Servicelink Holding Corp.; New Castle; business services 560

J. P. Morgan Services/Morgan Christiana Corp.; Wilmington; computer services 560

Milford Memorial Hospital Inc.; Milford 553

Playtex Family Products Corp.; Dover; apparel 550

National Railroad Pass Corp.; Wilmington; warehousing 550

Brandywine Building Services; Wilmington; building services 550

Delaware State College; Dover 541

Star States Corp.; Wilmington; holding offices 530

Delaware Trust Co.; Wilmington; commercial banks 516

Strawbridge & Clothier; Newark; department stores 515

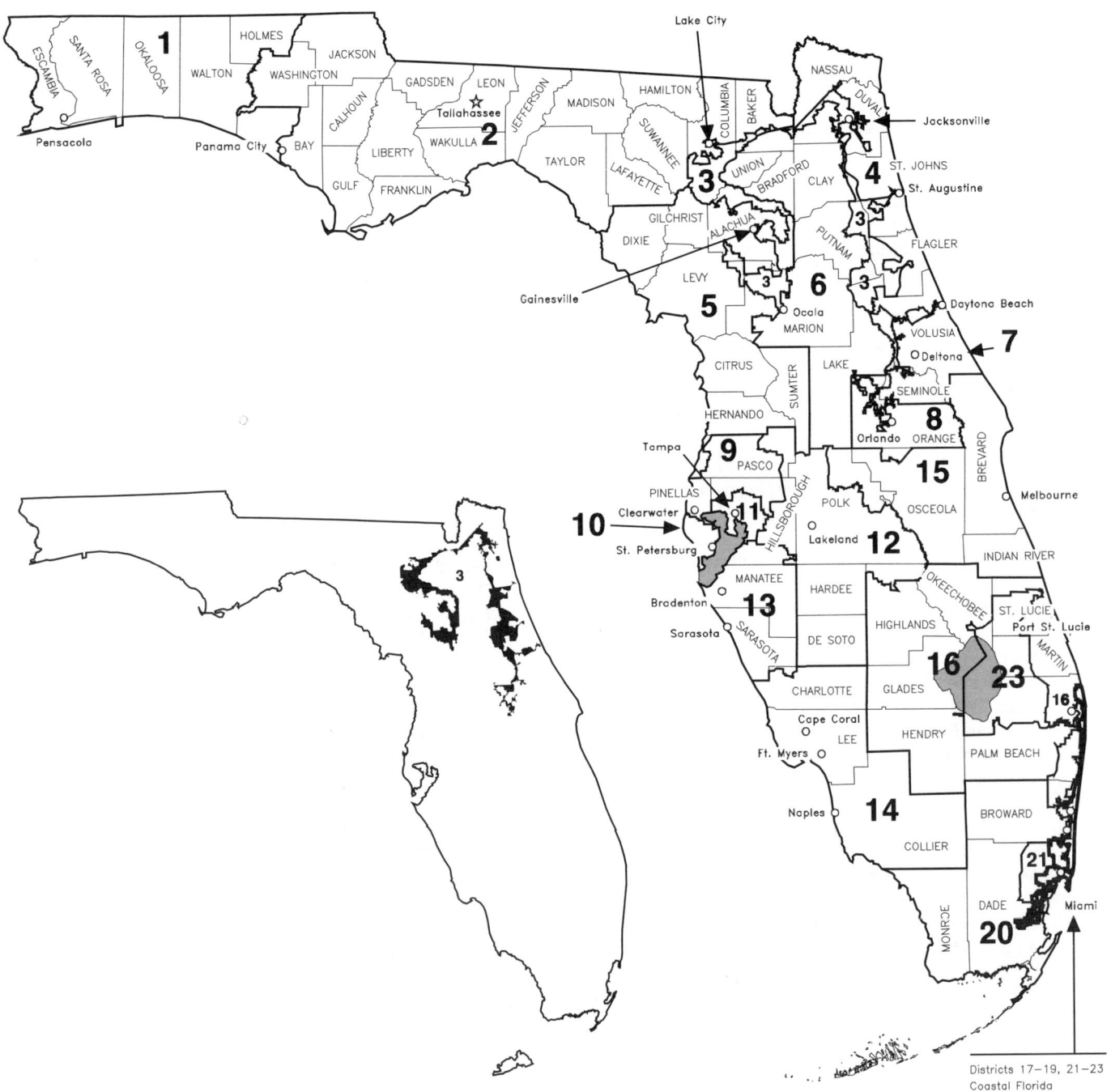

Districts 17-19, 21-23
Coastal Florida

Florida

Florida, one of the fastest-growing states in the nation, nearly doubled in population over the past 20 years to reach 12.9 million in 1990. The growth spurt enabled it to gain four seats in the 1990 reapportionment—an increase second only to California's—and become the fourth largest House delegation with 23 seats.

Florida's lures as a vacation and retirement mecca are now legion. The beaches, warm weather, entertainment attractions and low taxes have melded with an economy built on real estate development, services, health care (partly to serve all those retirees) and defense.

But decades of unchecked development have taken their toll. Floridians can hardly miss what low taxes and rampant population growth have wrought in overburdened schools, roads and sewer systems, as well as environmental threats.

And yet a slowdown in population growth was also wrenching to the state in the recessionary early 1990s. The strong influx of newcomers had become the main engine of the state's economy. The economic downturn nearly tipped Florida to Bill Clinton in 1992. That would have been a stunning development considering that George Bush won the state with 61 percent of the votes there in 1988—his fifth highest percentage in the country. From 1968 to 1992 Florida went Democratic only once for president and that was for Jimmy Carter in 1976.

Presidential contests illustrate just how fractured the Florida electorate has become. So many cities with widely different influences are dispersed across the state that it has been difficult for a statewide identity to take hold. "It's a geographic place. It's not a cultural place," said Richard K. Scher, an associate professor in political science at the University of Florida, and author of *Politics in the New South*. With so many media markets, so many newcomers and so little sense of place, running for statewide office in Florida is an expensive proposition.

A quick overview of Florida might logically begin with the most prominent feature in the north, the panhandle reaching across the top of the Gulf of Mexico. Defense installations and white sand beaches have attracted plenty of military personnel, tourists and retirees (many of whom are veterans). This gives the area a decidedly conservative, Old South Democratic cast. Straight east, along the state's north Atlantic shore, lies Jacksonville, which is influenced by some of the same southern

conservative Democrat politics. North Florida's population growth has been steady but modest by state standards.

Central Florida, spreading out from Orlando—the state's only major interior city—has been booming. The citrus industry came first. Then Walt Disney World spawned a wave of tourist attractions. Next came a more diversified economy based partly on a burgeoning airport and high-tech jobs. Because Orlando is, in a sense, the state's newest city, area residents are among the state's most rootless. Political affiliations are weak. The ticket-splitters who live in central Florida—from the space center-based Brevard County to the rapidly growing communities along the Interstate 4 corridor—can strongly influence statewide elections.

At the western terminus of I-4 lies Tampa Bay. St. Petersburg traditionally has been a retirement and winter resort; Tampa the state's most blue-collar and industrial city. Consequently, Midwestern retirees helped St. Petersburg give birth to the state's Republican Party while Tampa remained reliably Democratic. But the lines have blurred. The splintered GOP vote helped Clinton draw barely enough in both cities in 1992 to carry the St. Petersburg-based 10th District and the Tampa-based 11th.

The area along the gulf from Pasco County south to Naples is heavily influenced by retirees, many of them from the Midwest. Fast-growing Sarasota and Lee counties are GOP strongholds.

The state's most populous region is still its southeast, along the Gold Coast from Dade County north into Palm Beach County. This is also Florida's most ethnically diverse region. Cubans, blacks and Jews from the Northeast dominate communities throughout this area. Overcrowding and concerns about crime have helped fuel migration further north, pushing into St. Lucie County. Growth management is now a major issue all along the coast. Politically, Dade and Broward counties are Democratic strongholds, although some individual communities veer to the GOP.

Florida's balkanization has made it difficult for urban or suburban coalitions to form in the state legislature and break down regional differences.

The GOP, which held a 10-9 edge in U.S. House seats in 1992, looked for big gains after redistricting. Republicans had made strong registration strides in the 1980s, thanks largely to Florida's suburban-like growth. But Democrats seemed to hold a trump card—they controlled both chambers of the Legislature as well as the governor's office.

The Democrats' upper hand quickly faded amidst the overlapping interests of African Americans, Hispanics and whites. Congressional incumbents had their own agendas for self-preservation, and several key Democratic legislators plotted none-too-secretly to create a winnable congressional seat for themselves. Further complicating the legislators' task was the difficulty of drawing districts of common interests in a state with so many large and often narrow population centers, separated by sparsely populated areas. The state House and Senate passed different maps during the regular legislative session and were unable to resolve their differences in conference. Then, in a special session, the Senate was unable to pass a plan of its own.

The Republican Party, eager to protect its interests, didn't even wait until the first legislative vote on redistricting before filing a lawsuit in federal court. A three-judge federal panel announced March 27 that it would draw new district lines, without preempting the legislature from doing the same. When the legislature abandoned the task, all eyes focused on the court.

The final plan adopted by the panel May 29 followed the recommendations of a court-appointed expert who said he drew the map without knowing where the incumbents lived. That was apparent by how the map jumbled congressional districts.

Three districts drawn to enhance the electoral candidacies of blacks were drawn with particular cartographic aplomb. The new 3rd district looked like a wishbone or horseshoe, wandering across parts of 14 north Florida counties to find a black majority. Two other districts, the 17th and 23rd, looked like kites as they sought black voters in south Florida (see maps on pages 164 and 191).

Upheaval caused by redistricting and restlessness among voters contributed to an unusually large turnover in the state's congressional delegation even before the first votes were cast in 1992. Six of 19 House incumbents retired, including some of the state's most senior and powerful members, diminishing Florida's congressional clout.

Most prominent among the retirees were three Democrats— Dante B. Fascell, chairman of the Foreign Affairs Committee; William Lehman, chairman of the Appropriations Subcommittee on Transportation; and Charles E. Bennett, the second-ranking Democrat on the Armed Services Committee.

But the most surprising aspect of Florida's redistricting in 1992 was not in the twists and turns of its new congressional districts or that Republicans ended up winning 13 of the 23 seats in the elections that year. It was that after a decade of population growth, a year of voter anger and a recession, all 13 House incumbents who sought re-election did so successfully.

Table 1 Population

District	Population	Population under 18	Voting-age population	Median age
1	562,518	143,028	419,490	32.6
2	562,519	142,816	419,703	31.7
3	562,519	161,760	400,759	31.0
4	562,518	126,460	436,058	34.5
5	562,518	102,395	460,123	41.3
6	562,518	135,129	427,389	36.5
7	562,519	126,533	435,985	35.6
8	562,518	126,308	436,210	31.9
9	562,518	114,675	447,843	39.4
10	562,518	99,982	462,536	42.1
11	562,519	131,753	430,766	32.5

District	Population	Population under 18	Voting-age population	Median age
12	562,519	142,683	419,836	35.4
13	562,518	97,379	465,139	46.8
14	562,518	106,541	455,977	43.1
15	562,519	121,892	440,627	37.4
16	562,519	114,754	447,765	40.1
17	562,519	171,504	391,015	30.1
18	562,519	112,471	450,048	37.8
19	562,519	101,071	461,448	42.2
20	562,518	122,051	440,467	36.9
21	562,519	138,164	424,355	32.6
22	562,519	71,687	490,832	47.6
23	562,519	155,201	407,318	31.7
State	12,937,926	2,866,237	10,071,689	36.4

Table 2 Voting-Age Persons

District	White*	Black*	American Indian, Eskimo, or Aleut*	Asian or Pacific Islander*	Other*	Hispanic*	Male*	Female*
1	85.9%	11.2%	0.9%	1.7%	0.5%	1.9%	48.8%	51.2%
2	77.1	21.0	0.5	0.9	0.5	2.0	48.2	51.8
3	47.6	50.6	0.3	0.8	0.8	2.7	46.8	53.2
4	92.4	5.1	0.2	1.5	0.9	2.8	48.7	51.3
5	93.6	4.7	0.2	1.1	0.5	2.6	47.6	52.5
6	91.6	6.4	0.3	1.0	0.7	2.6	48.8	51.3
7	94.1	3.5	0.3	1.2	1.0	5.0	48.0	52.0
8	90.1	4.6	0.3	2.1	2.9	10.2	49.4	50.6
9	95.5	2.8	0.2	0.8	0.6	3.7	46.9	53.1
10	90.7	7.6	0.2	1.1	0.4	2.1	45.7	54.3
11	81.7	14.5	0.3	1.4	2.1	13.7	47.6	52.4
12	86.7	10.6	0.3	0.6	1.8	5.1	47.7	52.3
13	94.4	4.2	0.2	0.5	0.8	3.5	46.2	53.8
14	93.7	4.3	0.2	0.5	1.3	5.4	48.1	51.9
15	91.7	6.3	0.3	1.0	0.6	3.0	48.8	51.2
16	94.4	3.2	0.3	0.7	1.4	5.4	47.7	52.3
17	40.9	54.0	0.2	1.3	3.6	24.1	46.8	53.2
18	89.6	3.7	0.1	1.2	5.4	67.5	47.1	52.9
19	95.6	2.2	0.1	1.2	0.8	8.5	46.5	53.5
20	93.0	3.9	0.3	1.4	1.4	11.5	48.2	51.8
21	87.8	4.0	0.1	1.5	6.5	70.6	47.2	52.8
22	95.1	2.4	0.1	0.9	1.4	11.7	46.2	53.8
23	50.9	45.7	0.2	0.9	2.2	9.1	48.2	51.8
State	85.6	11.4	0.3	1.1	1.6	11.7	47.6	52.4

*As percent of voting-age population.

Table 3 Voting-Age Persons by Age Groups

District	18-24*	25-44*	45-54*	55-64*	65 and over*
1	14.7%	43.2%	14.4%	12.6%	15.2%
2	18.0	41.8	13.4	11.1	15.6
3	15.4	42.9	13.0	11.6	17.0
4	13.3	43.6	13.1	11.8	18.2
5	13.7	30.1	10.7	14.1	31.4
6	11.1	38.4	13.4	13.7	23.4
7	11.9	42.4	13.2	12.1	20.4
8	16.9	45.9	12.3	10.5	14.4
9	9.5	38.0	12.6	12.6	27.4
10	9.2	34.5	11.7	12.8	31.8
11	15.2	44.8	13.3	11.1	15.6
12	12.4	38.0	13.5	13.1	23.0
13	8.1	29.3	10.9	14.3	37.4
14	8.9	32.1	11.8	15.6	31.6
15	10.7	38.1	13.2	14.3	23.7
16	8.9	35.8	11.8	13.5	30.0

District	18-24*	25-44*	45-54*	55-64*	65 and over*
17	15.5	45.3	13.9	11.0	14.2
18	12.5	37.0	14.7	14.1	21.7
19	8.4	35.1	10.7	11.3	34.4
20	10.3	42.6	14.3	11.9	20.8
21	13.8	45.8	15.2	12.0	13.2
22	7.6	31.9	11.7	13.3	35.5
23	14.1	44.9	12.7	10.2	18.1
State	12.1	39.0	12.8	12.6	23.5

As percent of voting-age population.

District	Less than grade 9*	Grades 9-12 no diploma*	High school diploma*	College bachelor's degree or higher*
19	5.0	12.3	32.4	22.8
20	6.0	13.1	30.3	21.9
21	17.3	15.0	22.5	19.4
22	7.0	13.4	28.7	24.1
23	15.4	23.2	29.6	11.0
State	9.5	16.1	30.1	18.3

As percent of persons age 25 and over.

Table 4   Income and Occupation

District	Median family income	Families in poverty	White collar*	Blue collar*	Service*	Farm*
1	$29,821	11.6%	57.3%	24.9%	15.7%	2.0%
2	28,560	13.6	59.5	22.2	14.6	3.7
3	23,685	20.5	47.1	28.7	21.1	3.1
4	37,168	5.2	66.0	20.3	11.6	2.2
5	25,824	9.5	58.9	22.7	15.0	3.4
6	29,825	7.8	55.0	28.2	13.4	3.3
7	35,395	5.2	63.8	21.5	13.0	1.8
8	36,110	5.7	61.8	20.6	15.9	1.7
9	34,585	5.6	65.4	19.9	12.8	2.0
10	31,582	6.8	60.9	22.7	14.9	1.5
11	31,197	11.2	61.8	22.6	13.9	1.7
12	29,239	10.2	51.2	29.5	14.0	5.3
13	32,512	5.7	56.3	23.7	15.9	4.1
14	33,291	6.0	56.4	23.9	15.6	4.1
15	34,313	6.3	59.0	23.6	14.8	2.6
16	35,025	5.6	59.6	22.6	13.4	4.4
17	24,636	22.6	47.7	28.1	21.6	2.6
18	30,814	13.5	60.1	23.9	14.2	1.7
19	40,691	3.5	68.8	17.0	12.4	1.9
20	41,369	4.7	66.2	19.2	12.6	2.0
21	34,528	9.9	63.0	25.4	10.8	0.8
22	39,419	6.4	67.4	16.7	14.6	1.3
23	26,238	17.3	45.8	27.5	21.6	5.1
State	32,212	9.0	59.4	23.2	14.8	2.6

As percent of employed persons age 16 and over.

Table 6   Housing and Residential Patterns

District	Owner occupied	Renter occupied	Urban	Rural
1	67.0%	33.0%	74.0%	26.0%
2	68.0	32.0	53.7	46.3
3	57.5	42.5	83.8	16.2
4	66.8	33.2	87.1	12.9
5	74.6	25.4	58.3	41.7
6	77.1	22.9	52.0	48.0
7	71.3	28.7	88.5	11.5
8	60.0	40.0	91.4	8.6
9	74.4	25.6	81.0	19.0
10	68.6	31.4	100.0	0.0
11	56.7	43.3	98.8	1.2
12	71.6	28.4	66.1	33.9
13	74.9	25.1	89.2	10.8
14	72.8	27.2	82.2	17.8
15	71.1	28.9	82.1	17.9
16	75.7	24.3	78.2	21.8
17	50.4	49.6	100.0	0.0
18	50.3	49.7	99.8	0.2
19	76.4	23.6	97.8	2.2
20	74.8	25.2	91.1	8.9
21	59.3	40.7	99.2	0.8
22	62.9	37.1	100.0	0.0
23	54.9	45.1	95.3	4.7
State	67.2	32.8	84.8	15.2

1st District

Panhandle — Pensacola; Fort Walton Beach

Two enterprises dominate the westernmost part of Florida's Panhandle—military bases and tourism. Tourists are attracted to the soft, white-sand beaches along the Gulf Coast. The huge Eglin Air Force Base primarily develops and tests weapons systems and hosts combat-ready fighter wings. Pensacola's Naval Air Station features a naval education and training center. Among the district's other bases are those involved in naval research and development, the Air Force Special Operations Command and a Navy helicopter training center. But one facility, the Naval Aviation Depot, showed up on the 1993 base-closure list.

The strong military presence helps give the 1st a right-of-center political complexion. Its Democrats tend to be conservative, and in statewide elections, GOP candidates usually fare well.

In Pensacola, the district's largest city, the military's contribution to the economy is complemented by manufacturing of chemicals, plastics, textiles and paper. Despite its large natural harbor, Pensacola's potential as a trading port is restricted

Table 5   Education: School Years Completed

District	Less than grade 9*	Grades 9-12 no diploma*	High school diploma*	College bachelor's degree or higher*
1	8.0%	14.5%	29.0%	18.4%
2	11.9	16.5	29.3	19.5
3	13.5	23.3	30.9	9.9
4	5.3	12.2	29.8	23.4
5	9.4	19.2	33.2	15.4
6	8.8	18.4	35.5	12.4
7	5.5	13.2	30.0	20.5
8	5.9	12.7	29.5	22.7
9	6.0	14.1	31.7	19.8
10	7.2	16.8	31.9	17.3
11	9.1	16.4	28.7	19.4
12	12.8	20.2	32.2	13.0
13	7.3	14.9	33.1	18.5
14	7.4	15.2	33.4	17.7
15	6.1	14.1	31.1	18.9
16	6.9	15.2	33.1	18.4
17	18.9	23.4	25.8	11.0
18	21.9	15.8	20.1	21.2

somewhat because nearby Mobile and New Orleans have much of the gulf trade.

The 100-mile stretch of beach from Pensacola to Panama City, dubbed the "Miracle Strip" by boosters, also has been called the "Redneck Riviera" because it attracts visitors from Georgia, Alabama and other southeastern states. Along the coastal strip, military retirees have settled in Fort Walton Beach and Destin, both in Okaloosa County, just a few miles from Eglin Air Force Base.

Inland, the sparsely settled rural area is occupied mostly by soybeans, corn, tomatoes, cantaloupes, cattle and pine trees.

The district was not particularly hard hit by the 1990-1991 recession. Many of its tourists arrive by car for relatively low-cost vacations. And the local military bases did not suffer major job reductions in 1991.

Local politics are shaped largely by the bases' influence. They provide numerous civilian jobs, and many enlisted personnel remain in the area after leaving the service.

Although Democrats retain a clear registration edge in the 1st, voters districtwide feel little kinship with the national party. In 1988, George Bush drew 72 percent of the presidential vote and Republican Connie Mack 63 percent in the Senate race, their best showings in the state. Bush swept the district again in 1992.

Escambia County (Pensacola), which accounts for nearly half the district's population, has voted Republican in the past six presidential elections. The GOP trend is strong in Okaloosa County, which is less diversified than Escambia and more reliant on the military.

Election Returns and Party Registration

	1st District	Democrat	Republican
1992	President*	59,247 (25.7%)	117,712 (51.1%)
	House	118,941 (52.0%)	100,349 (43.9%)
1990	Governor	63,882 (45.7%)	75,895 (54.3%)
1988	President	47,607 (28.4%)	120,028 (71.6%)
	Senate	60,186 (36.6%)	104,394 (63.4%)
1986	Governor	50,917 (39.4%)	78,465 (60.6%)
1990	Party registration	168,917 (62.2%)	91,848 (33.8%)

*Vote for Perot was 53,286 (23.1%).

Demographics

Population 562,518

Percent change from 1980 9.7%

Land area 4,477 square miles

Population per square mile 126

Counties, 1990 population

Bay (pt.) 30,798	Okaloosa 143,776
Escambia 262,798	Santa Rosa 81,608
Holmes 15,778	Walton 27,760

Cities, 1990 population (10,000 or more)

Bellview CDP 19,386	Niceville 10,507
Brent CDP 21,624	Pensacola 58,165
Ensley CDP 16,362	Warrington CDP 16,040
Ferry Pass CDP 26,301	West Pensacola CDP
Fort Walton Beach 21,471	22,107
Myrtle Grove CDP 17,402	Wright CDP 18,945

Race and Hispanic origin
White 84.0%
Black 12.8%
American Indian, Eskimo, or Aleut. 0.9%
Asian or Pacific Islander 1.8%
Other 0.5%
Hispanic origin 2.1%

Ancestry

American 9.3%	Irish 18.3%
Dutch 2.4%	Italian 3.4%
English 15.6%	Polish 1.6%
French 4.1%	Scotch Irish 4.2%
French Canadian 1.1%	Scottish 2.8%
German 18.5%	Swedish 1.3%

Universities/colleges, 1990-1991 enrollment
Gulf Coast Community College, Panama City 5,149
Okaloosa-Walton Community College, Niceville 5,270
Pensacola Junior College, Pensacola 10,866
University of West Florida, Pensacola 7,877

Newspapers, total circulation (in all districts)
Northwest Florida Daily News 34,751
Panama City News-Herald 34,919
Pensacola News Journal 59,139

Commercial television stations, affiliations
ADI: Mobile-Pensacola (59%), Panama City (31%) and Dothan (10%)
  WTVY, Dothan (CBS)
  WFGX, Fort Walton Beach (None)
  WPAN, Fort Walton Beach (None)

Cable television systems, total subscribers
Cox Cable Pensacola; Pensacola 66,500
Emerald Coast Cable; Niceville 8,019
Emerald Coast Cable TV; Crestview 5,936
Emerald Coast Cable TV; Destin 7,555
Emerald Coast Cable TV; Fort Walton Beach 32,421
Jones Spacelink; Panama City Beach 6,700
U.S. Cable; Gulf Breeze 9,862
U.S. Cable; Milton 7,732

Military installations, 1991
Eglin Air Force Base, Valpariso 14,135
Pensacola Naval Air Station, Pensacola 12,824
Eglin Auxiliary Air Field 9 (Hurlburt Field), Mary Esther 9,196
Pensacola Naval Aviation Depot, Pensacola 3,798
Corry Station Naval Technical Training Center, Pensacola 3,192
Whiting Field Naval Air Station, Milton 2,391
Naval Coastal Systems Center, Panama City 2,103
Saufley Naval Outlying Landing Field, Pensacola 1,660
Naval Education and Training Program Management Support, Pensacola 1,230
Eglin Auxiliary Air Field 3 (Duke Field), Crestview 617

Businesses and other major employers
Monsanto Chemical Co.; Pensacola; plastics/synthetics 2,500
State of Florida; Pensacola 2,000
Sacred Heart Hospital of Pensacola; Pensacola 1,685
Baptist Hospital; Pensacola 1,670
West Florida Regional Medical Center; Pensacola 1,445

Vitro Services Corp.; Ft. Walton Beach; research services 1,350

University of West Florida; Pensacola 1,325

Champion Intl. Corp.; Cantonment; paper mill 1,000

Pensacola Junior College; Pensacola 1,000

Vitro Services Corp.; Valpariso; computer services 900

City of Pensacola/Port of Pensacola; Pensacola 871

Showell Farms Inc. of Florida/Cookin Good; De Funiak Springs; meat products 850

Hodnette Medical Center/Clinic; Pensacola; medical doctors 825

Humana Inc./Humana Hospital; Ft. Walton Beach 750

Vanity Fair Mills Inc.; Milton; undergarments 700

Southern Bell Telephone & Telegraph Co.; Pensacola; telephone communications 600

Westinghouse Electric Corp.; Pensacola; engines/turbines 555

2nd District

Panhandle — Tallahassee; Part of Panama City

A Florida adage has it that the farther north you go from Miami, the farther South you get. Natives consider North Florida to be the "real Florida," but some city dwellers outside the district regard the 2nd as a land of "rednecks" and "crackers."

1992 remapping made the sprawling 2nd more compact. The district shed some counties to the south and east while adding much of Bay County (Panama City) to the west. About 34 percent of the district's residents live in Leon County (Tallahassee). The rest are scattered in 17 other counties; except for Panama City, none of them has a town with even 15,000 residents. The boundary shifts did little to alter the district's conservative Democratic nature.

Two major interstates—I-75 and I-10—intersect in Columbia County (Lake City). But this is just a passing-through point for most motorists headed for state beaches and tourist attractions elsewhere. The bulk of the 2nd has just begun to see hints of the kind of development that has transformed much of Florida.

Tallahassee, the capital, is economically sustained by state government and two universities, Florida State and Florida A&M, with a combined total of about 37,000 students. These institutions, along with health care, high technology and publishing industries, help make Leon County more politically diverse than the rural areas surrounding it. But Tallahassee's elegant antebellum homes and flower gardens symbolize a Deep South strain in its personality that persists in the face of development and rapid population growth. Tallahassee—the only Confederate state capital east of the Mississippi River that was not captured during the Civil War—remains a Democratic stronghold.

The addition of Panama City to the 2nd gives it a major military installation—Tyndall Air Force Base, an air defense training facility. Panama City also has some industry and burgeoning retirement communities that attract military veterans and others who value the proximity to beaches.

The "Big Bend" Gulf Coast is mostly undeveloped. Pine trees stretch for miles, sustaining companies making paper, tobacco, pulp and chemicals. Prime agricultural products include peanuts, cotton, corn and honey. There is a local seafood industry, but its future is clouded by concerns about overfishing and environmental degradation.

Gadsden County is making a transition from tobacco crops to vegetables, especially tomatoes. The change has been tough; Gadsden was one of only two Florida counties to lose population in the 1980s. Gadsden, which is majority black, is the only Florida county to vote Democratic in the last three presidential elections. It helps give the district the state's fourth-highest percentage of black residents.

The district's Democratic presidential vote slid from 53 percent in 1980 to 40 percent in 1988 before rebounding slightly in 1992. GOP registration has increased, and conservative church groups have gotten active in anti-abortion politics. But Democratic loyalties that were forged a century ago are still strong locally. By recapturing the 2nd District seat in 1990, Democrats showed that the Republican incumbent had overestimated the district's drift toward the GOP when he switched to that party in 1989.

Election Returns and Party Registration

	2nd District	Democrat	Republican
1992	President*	101,623 (42.3%)	91,760 (38.2%)
	House	167,215 (73.5%)	60,425 (26.5%)
1990	Governor	95,240 (61.1%)	60,739 (38.9%)
1988	President	71,164 (40.5%)	104,543 (59.5%)
	Senate	95,845 (56.3%)	74,393 (43.7%)
1986	Governor	69,051 (49.6%)	70,111 (50.4%)
1990	Party registration	216,487 (78.6%)	48,686 (17.7%)

Vote for Perot was 46,808 (19.5%).

Demographics

Population 562,519

Percent change from 1980 9.6%

Land area 11,191 square miles

Population per square mile 50

Counties, 1990 population

Baker (pt.) 8,844	Jefferson 11,296
Bay (pt.) 96,196	Lafayette 5,578
Calhoun 11,011	Leon 192,493
Columbia (pt.) 26,070	Liberty 5,569
Franklin 8,967	Madison 16,569
Gadsden 41,105	Suwannee 26,780
Gulf 11,504	Taylor 17,111
Hamilton 10,930	Wakulla 14,202
Jackson 41,375	Washington 16,919

Cities, 1990 population (10,000 or more)

Callaway 12,253	Tallahassee 124,773
Panama City (pt.) 29,250	

Race and Hispanic origin

White 74.9%

Black 23.2%

American Indian, Eskimo, or Aleut. 0.5%

Asian or Pacific Islander 1.0%

Other 0.5%

Hispanic origin 2.0%

Ancestry

American 11.9%	Irish 15.4%
Dutch 2.1%	Italian 2.4%
English 14.2%	Polish 1.2%
French 3.1%	Scotch Irish 3.7%
German 14.2%	Scottish 2.5%

Universities/colleges, 1990-1991 enrollment

Chipola Junior College, Marianna 1,922
Florida A&M University, Tallahassee 8,344
Florida Baptist Theology College, Graceville 443
Florida State University, Tallahassee 28,170
Fort Lauderdale College, Tallahassee 351
Lake City Community College, Lake City 1,893
North Florida Junior College, Madison 1,220
Tallahassee Community College, Tallahassee 7,264

Newspapers, total circulation (in all districts)

Florida Times-Union 179,796
Gainesville Sun 54,352
Lake City Reporter 8,993
Panama City News-Herald 34,919
Tallahassee Democrat 57,658

Commercial television stations, affiliations

ADI: Tallahassee-Thomasville (52%), Panama City (40%) and
    Jacksonville (8%)
    WJHG-TV, Panama City (NBC)
    WMBB, Panama City (ABC)
    WPGX, Panama City (Fox)
    WTWC, Tallahassee (NBC)
    WTXL-TV, Tallahassee (ABC)

Cable television systems, total subscribers

Comcast Cablevision; Tallahassee 51,200
Comcast Cablevision/Panama City; Lynn Haven 24,708
Warner Cable Communications Inc.; Lake City 7,147

Military installations, 1991

Tyndall Air Force Base, Panama City 6,001

Businesses and other major employers

Florida State University; Tallahassee 7,014
State of Florida/Highway Safety Dept.; Tallahassee 4,200
Florida State Hospital; Chattahoochee 3,000
Tallahassee Memorial Regional Medical Center; Tallahassee
    2,500
State of Florida/Natural Resources Dept.; Tallahassee 2,445
State of Florida/Revenue Dept.; Tallahassee 2,411
Occidental Chemical Corp.; White Springs; inorganic chemi-
    cals 1,850
State of Florida/Education Dept.; Tallahassee 1,600
State of Florida/Environmental Regulation Dept.; Tallahas-
    see 1,500
Bay Medical Center; Panama City 1,400
Procter & Gamble Cellulose Co.; Perry; pulp mills 1,100
Florida A&M University; Tallahassee 1,100
St. Joe Paper Co.; Port St. Joe; pulp mills 1,000
State of Florida/CLE Dept.; Tallahassee 1,000
Watkins Engineers & Constrs.; Tallahassee; building construc-
    tion 997
State of Florida/Office of Controller; Tallahassee; building
    construction 900
Central Telephone Co. of Florida; Tallahassee; telephone
    communications 888

State of Florida/Law Enforcement Dept.; Tallahassee 874
State of Florida/Sunland Center of Marianna; Marianna 850
State of Florida/Banking & Finance Dept.; Tallahassee 825
U.S. Veterans Affairs Dept.; Lake City; hospital 806
State of Florida/Lottery of Florida; Tallahassee 750
West Point-Pepperell Inc.; Chipley; cotton mills 647
Stone Southwest Corp.; Panama City; wood products 630
Gold Kist Inc./Gold Kist Poultry; Live Oak; poultry/eggs
    600
U.S. Postal Service; Tallahassee 600
County of Suwannee/School Board; Live Oak 600
Tallahassee Community Hospital; Tallahassee 587
Apalachee Correctional Institution; Sneads 535
Dixie Packers Inc.; Madison; meat products 511

3rd District

North — Parts of Jacksonville, Orlando, Daytona Beach, Gainesville

Nothing is more remarkable about the 3rd than its shape. On a map, the district looks something like a jagged horseshoe or gnawed wishbone. Florida gained four House seats in 1990 reapportionment, and mapmakers seeking to increase minority representation drew three new majority-minority districts in south Florida and this one in the north. The 3rd meanders about 250 miles through 14 counties, taking in nearly every black neighborhood from Orlando north to the Georgia state line, linking them with white working-class areas.

Starting at its southeastern point in Orlando, the district (see map on page 164) heads north to Jacksonville, jutting toward the Atlantic to grab black neighborhoods in Daytona Beach and St. Augustine. After reaching Jacksonville, the district turns west to Lake City before dropping south to Gainesville and Ocala. The result of all these twists and turns is a district in which blacks make up 55 percent of the total population. Three of four registered voters are Democrats.

Jacksonville is the district's cartographic and demographic apex; about 45 percent of the 3rd's population lives here, and in 1992, both parties' House primaries were dominated by candidates from Jacksonville. Orange County (Orlando) is home to one-fifth of the people in the 3rd.

Unlike Florida cities farther south that are oriented toward leisure activities and have many northern-state transplants, Jacksonville is a workaday city with a southern feel. Some neighborhoods are integrated, but basically the city's black and white populations live apart, even though the military, long a vital component of Jacksonville's economy, has provided middle-class means to many blacks as well as whites in the area.

The retiree population of the 3rd is significant, if not as large as that seen in many other Florida districts. The seniors in the Jacksonville area tend to be middle-income types—former teachers, former military personnel and the like—who have lived locally for much of their lives. In that respect the typical retiree-filled high-rise here is different from those farther south in Florida, whose residents are often later-in-life arrivals to the Sunshine State.

Tourism accounts for more than 40 percent of the jobs in metropolitan Orlando (Orange County), home of Disney World and other attractions. There is a large blue-collar work force in service-oriented businesses.

In Gainesville (Alachua County), the University of Florida,

though not in the 3rd District, is the largest employer.

Statistics reveal the tough economic plight of many in the 3rd. It is the second-poorest district in the state, and both its poverty rate (over 25 percent) and its incidence of single-woman households are nearly double the state average.

The district has some splinters of white conservatism, in such areas as suburban Clay County, the wealthiest area in the 3rd, and Palatka in Putnam County. But GOP votes from these areas are outweighed by big Democratic margins elsewhere.

Election Returns and Party Registration

3rd District		Democrat	Republican
1992	President*	93,384 (57.3%)	49,288 (30.3%)
	House	91,918 (59.3%)	63,115 (40.7%)
1990	Governor	73,612 (67.2%)	35,932 (32.8%)
1988	President	79,807 (59.1%)	55,335 (40.9%)
	Senate	86,503 (64.8%)	47,026 (35.2%)
1986	Governor	76,932 (66.4%)	38,873 (33.6%)
1990	Party registration	179,099 (78.1%)	39,891 (17.4%)

*Vote for Perot was 20,255 (12.4%).

Demographics

Population 562,519

Percent change from 1980 9.7%

Land area 1,757 square miles

Population per square mile 320

Counties, 1990 population

Alachua (pt.) 39,977	Levy (pt.) 1,994
Baker (pt.) 3,860	Marion (pt.) 25,809
Clay (pt.) 8,443	Orange (pt.) 118,161
Columbia (pt.) 16,543	Putnam (pt.) 27,383
Duval (pt.) 250,032	Seminole (pt.) 22,668
Flagler (pt.) 2,002	St. Johns (pt.) 7,623
Lake (pt.) 2,203	Volusia (pt.) 35,821

Cities, 1990 population (10,000 or more)

Daytona Beach (pt.) 21,225	Orlando (pt.) 42,756
Gainesville (pt.) 16,472	Pine Hills CDP (pt.) 15,605
Jacksonville (pt.) 248,582	Sanford (pt.) 11,073
Ocala (pt.) 10,298	

Race and Hispanic origin

White 43.1%
Black 55.0%
American Indian, Eskimo, or Aleut. 0.3%
Asian or Pacific Islander 0.8%
Other 0.9%
Hispanic origin 2.8%

Ancestry

American 5.8%	Irish 9.2%
Dutch 1.2%	Italian 1.8%
English 8.1%	Scotch Irish 1.7%
French 2.1%	Scottish 1.2%
German 9.1%	West Indian 1.4%

Universities/colleges, 1990-1991 enrollment

Bethune Cookman College, Daytona Beach 2,342
Central Florida Community College, Ocala 3,995
Daytona Beach Community College, Daytona Beach 9,365
Edward Waters College, Jacksonville 597
Jacksonville University, Jacksonville 2,517
Jones College Jacksonville, Jacksonville 1,573

Newspapers, total circulation (in all districts)

Daytona Beach News-Journal 95,461
Florida Times-Union 179,796
Gainesville Sun 54,352
Lake City Reporter 8,993
Ocala Star Banner 45,134
Orlando Sentinel 284,136
Palatka Daily News 12,947
St. Augustine Record 15,217
St. Petersburg Times 351,635
Tampa Tribune 285,163

Commercial television stations, affiliations

ADI: Jacksonville (42%), Orlando-Daytona Beach-Melbourne (38%) and Gainesville (20%)
WAYQ, Daytona Beach (None)
WAWS-TV, Jacksonville (None)
WJKS, Jacksonville (ABC)
WOGX, Ocala (Fox)

Cable television systems, total subscribers

Cablevision Industries; Deland 21,000
Continental Cablevision of Florida; Jacksonville 181,150
Cox Cable University City; Gainesville 41,414
CV of Central Florida; Winter Park 186,531
Storer Cable TV Inc.; Altamonte Springs 16,100
TCI of Florida; Port Orange 38,500

Military installations, 1991

Jacksonville Naval Air Station, Jacksonville 17,181
Cecil Field Naval Air Station, Cecil Field 9,549
Jacksonville Naval Aviation Depot, Jacksonville 3,628

Businesses and other major employers

Walt Disney World Co./Epcot Center; Orlando; amusement park/recreational services 32,000
Universal Studios Florida; Orlando; amusement park 3,500
CSX Transportation Inc./Seaboard System Railroad; Jacksonville; railroads 3,000
State of Florida/Health Services Dept.; Orlando 3,000
University Hospital Jacksonville; Jacksonville 2,800
U.S. Internal Revenue Service; Jacksonville 1,800
First Union Corp. of Florida; Jacksonville; commercial banks 1,704
District School Board of Putnam County; Palatka 1,650
W. B. Johnson Properties Inc./North Lake Foods; Orlando; bars/restaurants 1,600
Memorial Medical Center of Jacksonville; Jacksonville 1,549
Georgia-Pacific Corp.; Palatka; paper mills 1,500
Martin Marietta Corp./Ordnance Systems; Orlando; guided missiles/parts 1,500
American Express Co.; Jacksonville; business services 1,500
Florida Power & Light Co.; Daytona Beach; electric services 1,281
Independent Insurance Group; Jacksonville; life insurance 1,158
Florida Community College; Jacksonville 1,100
Bellsouth Corp./Southern Bell; Jacksonville; telephone communications 1,000

Winn-Dixie Stores Inc./Marketplace; Jacksonville; grocery stores 1,000

Tamar Inns Inc./Quality Inn Intl.; Orlando; hotel 1,000

Olsten Corp.; Jacksonville; supply services 1,000

State of Florida/Human Resources Dept.; Jacksonville 1,000

Alachua General Hospital Inc.; Gainesville 991

Methodist Hospital Inc.; Jacksonville 881

Cincinnati Bell Info Systems/Auxton Computer Enterprises; Maitland; computer services 850

North Florida Regional Medical Center; Gainesville 840

U.S. Postal Service; Jacksonville 802

Bocep Ventures/Peabody Hotel; Orlando; hotel 800

Florida Publishing Co./Florida Times-Union; Jacksonville; newspapers 750

AT&T Co.; Orlando; microelectronic components 733

United Telephone Co. of Florida; Apopka; telephone communications 677

Navy Resale Services; Jacksonville; general stores 640

AT&T Co.; Maitland; telephone communications 600

Scholastic Book Fair Inc.; Maitland; books 600

Prescott Group of Florida Inc.; Maitland; supply services 600

Cybernetics & Services Inc.; Jacksonville; computer services 600

County of Alachua; Gainesville 600

Royal Services Inc./Watchman Marketing; Jacksonville; building services 590

City of Jacksonville; Jacksonville 560

Continental Cablevision of Florida; Jacksonville; cable TV services 550

4th District

Northeast — Part of Jacksonville; Northern Volusia County

The 4th includes much of eastern Jacksonville and the Atlantic coastal communities from the Georgia state line to part of Daytona Beach. Democrats retain a voter-registration edge here, but it seems attributable to habit and a desire to have a say in local Democratic primaries.

These conservative Democrats—combined with a GOP trend and the transfer of black neighborhoods from the 4th to the 3rd in redistricting—should make the 4th reliably Republican at the top of the ticket. George Bush received 70 percent of the presidential vote in 1988. The 4th also gave Republican Sen. Connie Mack his second highest percentage vote here in 1988.

Jacksonville, which accounts for about half the district's population, is the state's most populous city and the nation's largest in land mass, thanks to its consolidation in 1969 with surrounding Duval County. The city's business and political leaders have generally preferred steady if unspectacular economic expansion based on the city's traditional economic foundations of shipping, insurance, banking and defense.

The strategy has paid dividends at the port along the St. Johns River, one of the world's few northerly flowing rivers. By touting its fine harbor and ready access to rail lines and roads that lead to dealers in the lucrative Southeastern market, Jacksonville has become the leading East Coast port of entry for foreign vehicles.

Workers who handle cargo and build and repair ships form much of Jacksonville's blue-collar community. Prudential, Independent Life and American Heritage insurance companies are

among the largest white-collar employers in the city, as are AT&T/Universal Card, Winn-Dixie supermarkets, Blue Cross & Blue Shield and Barnett Banks.

Military installations include the Naval Aviation Depot, which repairs and maintains naval aeronautic equipment, and Mayport Naval Air Station, home base of the *Saratoga* aircraft carrier. Because several other ships based at Mayport have either been decommissioned or moved, civic leaders are seeking to have the base designated as capable of handling nuclear-powered ships.

The city's increasingly important medical industry includes a Mayo Clinic branch in southeast Jacksonville, a growing area that affords easy access to nearby beaches.

Northeast Florida markets itself as "Florida's First Coast," a reference to Ponce de Leon being the first European to set foot on Florida soil in the 16th century. He landed near what is now Ponte Vedra, current home of the Professional Golfers Association and the Association of Tennis Professionals.

Continuing south, Flagler County was the state's fastest growing county during the 1980s, with a population increase of 163 percent. Much of the boom was fed by an influx of retirees to the Palm Coast area.

The district extends into northern Volusia and Daytona Beach. This southernmost part of the district may be the 4th's most reliably Democratic region.

Election Returns and Party Registration

	4th District	Democrat	Republican
1992	President*	75,323 (30.3%)	131,930 (53.1%)
	House	103,534 (43.2%)	135,887 (56.8%)
1990	Governor	65,404 (42.4%)	88,947 (57.6%)
1988	President	55,227 (30.0%)	129,156 (70.0%)
	Senate	69,240 (38.9%)	108,975 (61.1%)
1986	Governor	56,208 (41.7%)	78,652 (58.3%)
1990	Party registration†	145,951 (54.5%)	107,274 (40.0%)

*Vote for Perot was 41,115 (16.6%).   †Independent/other is greater than 5%.

Demographics

Population 562,518

Percent change from 1980 9.7%

Land area 2,154 square miles

Population per square mile 261

Counties, 1990 population
Duval (pt.) 324,505
Flagler (pt.) 26,699
Nassau 43,941
St. Johns (pt.) 76,206
Volusia (pt.) 91,167

Cities, 1990 population (10,000 or more)
Atlantic Beach 11,636
Daytona Beach (pt.) 19,620
Holly Hill 11,141
Jacksonville Beach 17,839
Jacksonville (pt.) 288,214
Ormond Beach 29,721
Palm Coast CDP 14,287

Race and Hispanic origin
White 91.3%
Black 5.8%
American Indian, Eskimo, or Aleut 0.2%

Asian or Pacific Islander 1.6%
Other 1.1%
Hispanic origin 3.1%

Ancestry

American 6.5%	Italian 5.6%
Dutch 2.3%	Polish 2.8%
English 19.8%	Scotch Irish 3.6%
French 4.8%	Scottish 3.7%
French Canadian 1.1%	Swedish 1.5%
German 22.0%	Welsh 1.0%
Irish 19.3%	

Universities/colleges, 1990-1991 enrollment

Flagler Career Institute, Jacksonville 257
Flagler College, St. Augustine 1,228
Florida Community College, Jacksonville 16,778
University of North Florida, Jacksonville 8,021

Newspapers, total circulation (in all districts)

Daytona Beach News-Journal 95,461
Florida Times-Union 179,796
Orlando Sentinel 284,136
St. Augustine Record 15,217

Commercial television stations, affiliations

ADI: Jacksonville (75%) and Orlando-Daytona Beach-Melbourne (25%)
WJXT, Jacksonville (CBS)
WNFT, Jacksonville (None)
WTLV, Jacksonville (NBC)

Cable television systems, total subscribers

CVI; St. Augustine 15,500
Cablevision of Central Florida; Ormond Beach 18,000
Continental Cablevision of Florida; Jacksonville 181,150
Continental Cablevision of Florida; Ponte Vedra 7,200
Fernandina Cablevision; Fernandina Beach 6,300
Palm Cable Inc.; Palm Coast 6,608
TCI of Florida; Port Orange 38,500

Military installations, 1991

Mayport Naval Station, Mayport 17,110
Jacksonville Intl. Airport Air Force Guard Station, Callahan 395

Businesses and other major employers

St. Johns River Hospital; Jacksonville 4,000
AT&T Co./Directory Sales Center; Jacksonville; telephone communications 3,500
Blue Cross/Blue Shield of Florida; Jacksonville; medical service/health insurance 3,500
Prudential Insurance of America Inc.; Jacksonville; life insurance 2,800
Barnett Technologies Inc.; Jacksonville; computer services 2,600
St. Vincent's Medical Center; Jacksonville 2,336
Baptist Medical Center; Jacksonville 2,300
Florida Community College; Jacksonville 2,000
U.S. Postal Service; Jacksonville 1,341
Trailer Marine Transport Corp./Crowley Maritime; Jacksonville; freight shipping 1,300
Grumman St. Augustine Corp.; St. Augustine; aircraft/parts 1,250
American Transtech Inc.; Jacksonville; security/commodity services 1,140

Nassau County School District; Fernandina Beach 1,040
Independent Life; Jacksonville; insurance services 1,000
Terminal Freight Handling Co./Sears Logistics Services; Jacksonville; nonstore retailers 1,000
St. Luke's Hospital; Jacksonville 1,000
Mayo Clinic Jacksonville Inc.; Jacksonville; medical doctors 900
Anheuser-Busch Inc.; Jacksonville; brewery 850
Trans World Airlines Inc.; Jacksonville; airline 800
Amelia Island Plantation; Fernandina Beach; hotel 800
Excel Industries of Florida; Jacksonville; glass products 700
State Farm Mutual Auto Insurance Co.; Jacksonville; fire/marine/casualty insurance 700
U.S. Federal Aviation Agency; Hilliard 700
County of St. Johns; St Augustine 680
Memorial Hospital-Ormond Beach; Ormond Beach 642
Florida School for Deaf & Blind; St. Augustine 600
County of Duval/Public School Systems; Jacksonville 600
University of North Florida; Jacksonville 567
News-Journal Corp./News-Journal; Daytona Beach; newspapers 550
Ritz-Carlton Hotel Co.; Fernandina Beach; hotel 550
St. Johns River Power Park; Jacksonville; electric services 531
Florida Windstorm Underwriting Assn.; Jacksonville; insurance services 527
Humana Inc.; Jacksonville; insurance services 515

5th District

Northern West Coast — Parts of Alachua and Pasco Counties; Hernando County

The 5th collects all or parts of nine counties as it comes around the "Big Bend" Gulf Coast from Dixie to Pasco counties. It includes several distinct regions.

About 57 percent of district residents live in Hernando, Citrus and western Pasco counties north of Tampa-St. Petersburg, where retirees have spurred rapid growth along the coast. About 25 percent live in parts of Alachua County, which is noted mainly for the presence of the University of Florida (35,000 students). Most of the remaining district residents live in lightly populated rural counties.

Democrats have wide registration leads in Alachua County and most of the rural areas, while Republicans are more competitive in the retirement areas. But except for Alachua, most of the Democrats are conservative and can be swayed to vote for Republicans at the top of the ticket. Democrat Bill Clinton won most of the counties in the 5th in 1992, but with the exception of Alachua County, his margins were quite small.

Western Pasco County, which was carved from the GOP-held 9th District in 1992 redistricting, has retirees and military veterans, as do Citrus and Hernando counties, which were transferred from the 6th District. These retirees from the Midwest and Northeast generally have modest incomes. They include former blue-collar workers who retain allegiance to the United Auto Workers, which has a presence here, and to such civic groups as Italian-American and Polish-American clubs.

The area has an abundance of recreational opportunities, including gulf beaches, the Withlacoochee State Forest and Weeki Wachee Spring. Manatees, which are endangered mammals, frequent the Crystal River. The health-care industry is a leading local employer, and there are two nuclear power plants.

The district includes most of Alachua County and Gainesville. Although minority neighborhoods are part of the adjacent 3rd, the presence of the University of Florida puts this area to the left of conservative Democrats who predominate in most of north Florida. Gainesville is a medical center for the northern interior of the state, and the university attracts high-tech companies. Agriculture—including peanuts, watermelon and dairy products—dominates elsewhere in the county.

The other counties in the 5th are quite rural. The parts of Marion County in the district include Rainbow Springs; some thoroughbred horses are raised here. Sumter County is at the confluence of Florida's Turnpike and Interstate 75. Dixie, Gilchrist and Levy counties have large forested areas and commercial fishing entities. The Cedar Key archipelago, off the coast of Levy County, once boasted a prosperous port and pencil-making industry, but fishing and tourism now dominate. Cedar Key resists development and resembles Key West circa 1930.

Election Returns and Party Registration

		Democrat	Republican
	5th District		
1992	President*	110,058 (41.6%)	90,598 (34.2%)
	House †	129,718 (49.2%)	114,356 (43.4%)
1990	Governor	112,598 (60.2%)	74,513 (39.8%)
1988	President	84,771 (43.5%)	109,886 (56.5%)
	Senate	122,744 (59.4%)	84,058 (40.6%)
1986	Governor	80,257 (48.1%)	86,694 (51.9%)
1990	Party registration †	174,007 (55.3%)	119,230 (37.9%)

*Vote for Perot was 64,144 (24.2%).   †Independent/other is greater than 5%.

Demographics

Population 562,518

Percent change from 1980 9.7%

Land area 4,689 square miles

Population per square mile 120

Counties, 1990 population
Alachua (pt.) 141,619	Levy (pt.) 23,929
Citrus 93,515	Marion (pt.) 28,620
Dixie 10,585	Pasco (pt.) 121,891
Gilchrist 9,667	Sumter 31,577
Hernando 101,115	

Cities, 1990 population (10,000 or more)
Bayonet Point CDP (pt.) 14,548	Jasmine Estates CDP 17,136
Gainesville (pt.) 68,298	New Port Richey 14,044
Holiday CDP 19,360	Spring Hill CDP 31,117

Race and Hispanic origin
White 92.5%
Black 5.6%
American Indian, Eskimo, or Aleut. 0.3%
Asian or Pacific Islander 1.1%
Other 0.5%
Hispanic origin 2.8%

Ancestry
American 6.2%	Italian 8.2%
Dutch 3.0%	Polish 4.0%
English 18.0%	Scotch Irish 3.0%
French 5.0%	Scottish 3.1%
French Canadian 1.2%	Swedish 1.8%
German 24.0%	Welsh 1.0%
Irish 18.6%	

Universities/colleges, 1990-1991 enrollment
Santa Fe Community College, Gainesville 9,633
University of Florida, Gainesville 35,477

Newspapers, total circulation (in all districts)
Citrus County Chronicle 18,295
Florida Times-Union 179,796
Gainesville Sun 54,352
Leesburg Daily Commercial 28,623
Ocala Star Banner 45,134
Orlando Sentinel 284,136
St. Petersburg Times 351,635
Tampa Tribune 285,163

Commercial television stations, affiliations
ADI: Gainesville (57%), Tampa-St. Petersburg (25%) and Orlando-Daytona Beach-Melbourne (18%)
WCLF, Clearwater (None)
WCJB, Gainesville (ABC)
WTSP-TV, St. Petersburg (ABC)

Cable television systems, total subscribers
Cablevision of Central Florida; Lecanto 20,966
Cablevision of Central Florida; Spring Hill 15,247
Cox Cable Greater Ocala; Ocala 27,000
Cox Cable University City; Gainesville 41,414
TCI of Florida; New Port Richey 60,000
Telesat Cablevision; Inverness 8,000

Businesses and other major employers
University of Florida; Gainesville 8,000
Shands Teaching Hospital & Clinic; Gainesville 4,059
State of Florida/Sunland Center; Gainesville 1,570
U.S. Veterans Affairs; Gainesville; hospital 1,520
Gates Energy Products Inc.; Gainesville; electrical equipment/supplies 1,400
Emergency One Inc.; Ocala; motor vehicles/equipment 1,100
Hospital Corp. America/New Port Richey Community Hospital; New Port Richey 1,000
Mark III Industries Inc.; Ocala; automotive repair 970
Nationwide Mutual Insurance Co.; Gainesville; insurance services 800
Golf Host Resorts Inc./Innisbrook; Tarpon Springs; hotel 800
Hospital Corp. America/Oak Hill Hospital; Brooksville 740
Gainesville Regional Utilities; Gainesville; utility services 738
Hernando County School Board; Brooksville 700
Citrus Memorial Hospital; Inverness 635
County of Hernando/Jail; Brooksville 600
University of Florida/Florida Cooperative Ext. Service; Gainesville 600
Sante Fe Community College; Gainesville 570
University of Florida/Institute of Food & Agricultural Sciences; Gainesville 555
County of Marion; Ocala 536

6th District

*North Central — Lake and Marion Counties;
Part of Jacksonville*

The 6th spans the interior of northeast and central Florida. Democrats could once consider this friendly territory, but 1992 remapping has sharpened the district's focus more on conservative rural areas that are increasingly receptive to the GOP. The 6th shed Gainesville and the Gulf Coast retirement meccas of Citrus and Hernando, nudging the district north and east into part of Jacksonville.

Democrats vying for state offices can still run competitively in the district's southernmost counties, Lake and Marion, which together account for about half of the 6th's population.

Lake County features citrus groves and about 1,400 lakes along its rolling landscape. Watermelons and berries are grown around Leesburg. Besides the citrus industry, leading employers include metal fabrication, concrete and mobile home construction.

Some of central Florida's high-technology companies have expanded operations into Ocala (Marion County), including Martin Marietta and Microdine Corp., which makes telemetry and satellite receivers. Other major employers include Emergency One, makers of fire engine equipment, and Mark III van conversions. Among the area's tourist attractions are Silver Springs and the Ocala National Forest. The county's limestone-based soil also has made it a good place to breed and raise racehorses.

Both Lake and Marion counties attract retirees from the Northeast and Midwest. Marion grew by 59 percent in the 1980s, while Lake County grew by 45 percent. Although the newcomers to Marion County tend to vote Republican, most of its rural residents are traditional southern Democrats. Those groups were closely matched in 1976, when Jimmy Carter barely carried the county, but Republicans have carried the county in subsequent presidential elections.

Southeast of Union is Putnam County, adjacent to the St. Johns River. Bass fishing is popular there, and cabbages and watermelon are common crops.

This is also the district's most Democratic area. In GOP Rep. Stearns' easy 1992 re-election bid, he barely carried Putnam County. He also barely won Bradford County in the district's northwest reaches, and he lost Union County, the state's smallest county in land area.

Clay County nearly doubled in population in the 1980s, attributable partly to the proximity of Duval County (Jacksonville) to the north and the popularity of beach recreation in adjacent St. Johns County.

The 6th also extends into southwest Jacksonville. North of Interstate 10, many of the residents are middle-class, blue-collar workers. South of the interstate, the residents are predominantly professionals. Many in the community work in nearby Cecil Field, a naval air base providing strategic defense.

The Jacksonville portion of the district, along with Clay County, provides Republicans with some of their best percentages in the 6th.

Election Returns and Party Registration

	6th District	Democrat	Republican
1992	President*	74,349 (31.2%)	113,029 (47.4%)
	House	76,419 (34.6%)	144,195 (65.4%)
1990	Governor	65,543 (45.6%)	78,102 (54.4%)
1988	President	48,313 (29.7%)	114,552 (70.3%)
	Senate	73,709 (45.0%)	90,035 (55.0%)
1986	Governor	47,496 (37.9%)	77,969 (62.1%)
1990	Party registration †	131,628 (53.2%)	101,390 (41.0%)

*Vote for Perot was 51,266 (21.5%).   †Independent/other is greater than 5%.

Demographics

Population 562,518

Percent change from 1980 9.7%

Land area 4,076 square miles

Population per square mile 138

Counties, 1990 population

Baker (pt.) 5,782	Lake (pt.) 149,901
Bradford 22,515	Marion (pt.) 140,404
Clay (pt.) 97,543	Putnam (pt.) 37,687
Duval (pt.) 98,434	Union 10,252

Cities, 1990 population (10,000 or more)

Bellair-Meadowbrook Terrace CDP (pt.) 15,600	Lakeside CDP 29,137
	Leesburg 14,903
Eustis 12,967	Ocala (pt.) 28,473
Jacksonville (pt.) 98,434	

Race and Hispanic origin

White 90.4%
Black 7.4%
American Indian, Eskimo, or Aleut. 0.3%
Asian or Pacific Islander 1.2%
Other 0.8%
Hispanic origin 2.9%

Ancestry

American 8.2%	Irish 18.9%
Dutch 3.2%	Italian 4.3%
English 18.4%	Polish 2.3%
French 5.0%	Scotch Irish 3.3%
French Canadian 1.1%	Scottish 2.9%
German 22.4%	Swedish 1.3%

Universities/colleges, 1990-1991 enrollment

Lake-Sumter Community College, Leesburg 2,078
St. Johns River Community College, Palatka 2,453

Newspapers, total circulation (in all districts)

Florida Times-Union 179,796
Gainesville Sun 54,352
Leesburg Daily Commercial 28,623
Ocala Star Banner 45,134
Orlando Sentinel 284,136
Palatka Daily News 12,947
St. Petersburg Times 351,635
Tampa Tribune 285,163

Commercial television stations, affiliations

ADI: Orlando-Daytona Beach-Melbourne (52%) and Jacksonville (48%)

Cable television systems, total subscribers
Cablevision Industries Inc.; Palatka 8,800
Clay Video Inc.; Orange Park 19,121
Continental Cablevision of Florida; Jacksonville 181,150
Cox Cable Greater Ocala; Ocala 27,000
Lake County Cablevision; Fruitland Park 16,000
Lake County Cablevision; Mount Dora 13,150

Businesses and other major employers
Martin Marietta Corp./Ocala Operations; Ocala; communication services 1,500
Auto Workers AFL-CIO; Ocala; labor organization 1,500
North East Florida State Hospital; MacClenny 1,150
Big Sun Healthcare Systems/Monroe Regional Medical Center; Ocala 1,090
State of Florida/North Florida Reception; Lake Butler 1,028
Waterman Medical Center Inc.; Eustis 900
Marion Community Hospital; Ocala 801
Certified Grocers of Florida; Ocala; grocery products 800
United Parcel Service Inc.; Jacksonville; mail services 800
Humana Inc./Humana Hospital; Orange Park 725
United Telephone Co. of Florida; Leesburg; telephone communications 700
Leesburg Regional Medical Center; Leesburg 656
State of Florida/Union Correctional Institute; Raiford 650
Lake County/Mosquito Control Dept.; Tavares 567
State of Florida/Corrections Dept.; Starke 550
Clairson Intl. Corp./Cabinet Maid; Ocala; metal products 507

7th District

Central — Southern Seminole and Volusia Counties; Deltona; Port Orange

The 7th is an overwhelmingly suburban district created in 1992 redistricting as a result of robust growth in the Orlando area.

Although the district likely will be reliably Republican in presidential and congressional elections, GOP support is not uniform across the 7th. Republicans seem firmly entrenched in Seminole County, which accounts for nearly half the district's population, and in the piece of Orange County that makes up about 10 percent of the district. But Democrats at the top of the ticket are competitive in Volusia County.

Interstate 4 transverses the district from Daytona Beach to Orlando; it is a familiar roadway to residents of Seminole County, which grew by 60 percent during the 1980s, mainly because of its convenient location directly north of Orlando. Many county residents hop onto I-4 to commute south to such Orlando institutions as Disney World, Martin Marietta, the University of Central Florida and Orlando International Airport. So many residents clog the interstate that freshman Rep. John Mica secured a seat on the Public Works and Transportation Committee in 1993 to try to get funding for more alternate routes into the city.

Altamonte Springs and Casselberry, just north of the Orange County line, are Republican, upper-middle-class bedroom communities predominated by professionals. North along the interstate is affluent Heathrow. Sanford is the southern terminus of Amtrak's Virginia-to-Florida auto train.

Heading into Volusia County, unincorporated Deltona is the district's largest community, with 51,000 residents. It has a mixture of retirees and young working couples, as well as a growing Hispanic contingent. The district's next largest area, Port Orange, directly south of Daytona Beach, also has some light industry and business, and some blue-collar retirees who help give it a Democratic cast.

The 7th includes about one-third of Daytona Beach. As Florida's population began to boom in the 1950s, Daytona became the most popular resort on the state's east coast for vacationers who do not want to make a longer trip down the peninsula. The city woos winter visitors from Canada, and the Daytona International Speedway schedules its Daytona 500 auto race in February to lure tourists.

However, the boardwalk and some of the city's motels are reaching middle age, and competition from neighboring beaches and inland attractions has increased. Daytona's success at attracting new jobs has been modest compared with neighboring Orlando and Jacksonville. Leading private employers include those involved in medical supplies, electronics and transportation.

Although both Seminole and Volusia counties went for George Bush in 1988, the 7th revealed its split personality in 1992. Seminole County went strongly for Bush and the GOP House nominee, while Volusia County gave a slight edge to Democrats in the presidential and House contests.

Election Returns

	7th District	Democrat	Republican
1992	President*	81,312 (34.4%)	105,263 (44.6%)
	House	96,950 (43.5%)	125,830 (56.5%)
1990	Governor	72,645 (52.4%)	66,005 (47.6%)
1988	President	54,186 (33.2%)	109,192 (66.8%)
	Senate	68,961 (43.0%)	91,468 (57.0%)
1986	Governor	49,502 (41.5%)	69,774 (58.5%)
1990	Party registration†	106,209 (42.6%)	125,013 (50.1%)

*Vote for Perot was 49,582 (21.0%).   †Independent/other is greater than 5%.

Demographics

Population 562,518

Percent change from 1980 9.7%

Land area 969 square miles

Population per square mile 580

Counties, 1990 population
Orange (pt.) 53,933   Volusia (pt.) 243,724
Seminole (pt.) 264,861

Cities, 1990 population (10,000 or more)
Altamonte Springs (pt.) 33,287
Casselberry (pt.) 18,911
Daytona Beach (pt.) 21,076
De Land (pt.) 11,558
Deltona CDP 50,828
Edgewater 15,337
Forest City CDP 10,638
Lockhart CDP (pt.) 10,851
Longwood 13,316
New Smyrna Beach 16,543
Oviedo 11,114
Pine Hills CDP (pt.) 15,123
Port Orange 35,317
Sanford (pt.) 21,314
South Daytona 12,482
Wekiva Springs CDP (pt.) 22,525
Winter Springs 22,151

Race and Hispanic origin

White 93.2%

Black 4.0%

American Indian, Eskimo, or Aleut. 0.3%

Asian or Pacific Islander 1.3%

Other 1.2%

Hispanic origin 5.5%

Ancestry

American 5.2%	Italian 7.7%
Dutch 2.8%	Polish 3.7%
English 19.4%	Russian 1.1%
French 5.2%	Scotch Irish 2.9%
French Canadian 1.4%	Scottish 3.4%
German 25.5%	Swedish 1.7%
Irish 19.1%	Welsh 1.1%

Universities/colleges, 1990-1991 enrollment

Embry-Riddle Aeronautical University, Daytona Beach
    10,821

Seminole Community College, Sanford 6,996

Stetson University, De Land 3,003

Newspapers, total circulation (in all districts)

Daytona Beach News-Journal 95,461

Orlando Sentinel 284,136

Commercial television stations, affiliations

ADI: Orlando-Daytona Beach-Melbourne (100%)

WESH, Daytona Beach (NBC)

WACX, Leesburg (None)

Cable television systems, total subscribers

Cablevision Industries; De Land 21,000

Cablevision Industries; New Smyrna Beach 14,000

Cablevision Industries Inc.; Union Park 24,021

CV of Central Florida; Winter Park 186,531

Storer Cable TV Inc.; Altamonte Springs 16,100

TCI of Florida; Port Orange 38,500

Businesses and other major employers

Siemens Stromberg Carlson; Lake Mary; telecommunications
    equipment 1,400

Seminole Community College; Sanford 1,250

General Electric Co.; Daytona Beach 1,100

Florida Hospital Altamonte; Altamonte Springs 1,070

American Automobile Assn.; Lake Mary; auto
    service/membership organization 934

Sherwood Medical Co./Monoject; De Land; medical
    instruments/supplies 900

United Telephone Co. of Florida; Altamonte Springs; tele-
    phone communications 800

Tri City Electrical; Altamonte Springs; electrical work 750

Embry-Riddle Aeronautical University; Daytona Beach 750

Central Florida Regional Hospital; Sanford 608

West Volusia Memorial Hospital; De Land 601

ABB Power Distribution Inc.; Sanford; electric distribution
    equipment 540

8th District

Central — Orange County; Part of Orlando

In a state famous for its coastline, Orlando is the only one of
Florida's four large metropolitan areas without one. But that has
not been a hindrance to economic development or population
growth in and around the city. In fact, metropolitan Orlando has
a more diversified economic base than many of Florida's beach
meccas, where the economy is skewed toward tourism, construction and real estate speculation.

This is not to underestimate the impact of tourism. Walt
Disney is still Orange County's leading private employer; Disney
World and Epcot are joined by other attractions such as Sea
World and Universal Studios, which is just across the 3rd
District line. Orlando boasts that its hotel-room supply rivals that
in many bigger cities.

Disney has been a major catalyst for growth in metropolitan
Orlando. The tourists it helps attract provide a strong and steady
flow of traffic through Orlando's airport, which has taken on
international flights and become a hub for adjacent warehousing
and distribution facilities. Thanks to Disney and Universal, there
is work in the movie- and television-production business.

Also in Orlando is the world headquarters of Westinghouse's
power generation unit, and Minute Maid has a processing plant
for oranges. The University of Central Florida (21,500 students) is
growing on the city's east side. Its emphasis on high-tech fields
such as lasers fits in well with the area's numerous aerospace and
defense contractors working on missiles and aircraft-control
systems. Orlando's Naval Training Center, which showed up on
the 1993 base-closure list, provides simulators and training for
the military.

In 1980, the district stretched from the gulf almost to the
Atlantic. Population growth has led the district to be whittled
down in successive redistricting rounds. It now includes only
parts of Orange County plus the Kissimmee area in Osceola
County.

Growth has brought its share of problems to the Orlando
area. Demand for water has increased dramatically, and sinkholes
occasionally open up as the water table drops. More frequent
problems occur with congested highways and overcrowded
schools.

The parts of Orlando in the 8th contain a mixture of
residents, many of them retirees and young families. North and
east of the city are the affluent Orange County communities of
Winter Park and Maitland. Home to Orlando's older, established
elite, they strongly support the GOP. To the west, near Lake
Apopka, lie Ocoee and Winter Garden. Fresh vegetables grow
along the lake, while the foliage industry (growing houseplants,
shrubbery and the like) has a presence in the city of Apopka.

Hispanics, especially Puerto Ricans, account for a significant
minority of residents in Buena Ventura Lakes, near Kissimmee,
and in Kissimmee itself. Kissimmee, which promotes itself as a
centrally situated base for tourists visiting local attractions, is
competitive territory politically.

Election Returns and Party Registration

	8th District	Democrat	Republican
1992	President*	67,724 (31.7%)	102,514 (48.0%)
	House	65,145 (31.5%)	141,977 (68.5%)
1990	Governor	64,526 (53.2%)	56,730 (46.8%)
1988	President	40,573 (28.6%)	101,190 (71.4%)
	Senate	60,420 (41.6%)	84,773 (58.4%)
1986	Governor	44,095 (39.2%)	68,484 (60.8%)
1990	Party registration†	85,911 (41.5%)	105,527 (51.0%)

*Vote for Perot was 43,472 (20.3%).   †Independent/other is greater than 5%.

Demographics

Population 562,518

Percent change from 1980 9.7%

Land area 843 square miles

Population per square mile 667

Counties, 1990 population
Orange (pt.) 505,397   Osceola (pt.) 57,121

Cities, 1990 population (10,000 or more)
Buena Ventura Lakes   Oak Ridge CDP (pt.)
   CDP 14,148   15,051
Conway CDP 13,159   Ocoee 12,778
Fairview Shores CDP (pt.)   Orlando (pt.) 113,498
   10,768   Winter Park (pt.) 18,671
Kissimmee (pt.) 29,897

Race and Hispanic origin
White 88.8%
Black 5.2%
American Indian, Eskimo, or Aleut. 0.3%
Asian or Pacific Islander 2.3%
Other 3.3%
Hispanic origin 11.4%

Ancestry
American 5.5%   Italian 6.4%
Dutch 2.6%   Polish 3.1%
English 16.7%   Scotch Irish 2.9%
French 4.8%   Scottish 2.8%
French Canadian 1.2%   Swedish 1.6%
German 22.9%   Welsh 1.0%
Irish 17.2%

Universities/colleges, 1990-1991 enrollment
Orlando College, Orlando 2,127
Rollins College, Winter Park 3,589
Southeastern Academy, Kissimmee 720
University of Central Florida, Orlando 21,541
Valencia Community College, Orlando 14,840

Newspapers, total circulation (in all districts)
Orlando Sentinel 284,136
Tampa Tribune 285,163

Commercial television stations, affiliations
ADI: Orlando-Daytona Beach-Melbourne (100%)
   WKCF, Clermont (None)
   WCPX-TV, Orlando (CBS)
   WOFL, Orlando (Fox)
   WFTV, Orlando (ABC)

Cable television systems, total subscribers
Cablevision Industries Inc.; Union Park 24,021
CV of Central Florida; Winter Park 186,531
Kissimmee Cablevision; Osceola County 15,253

Military installations, 1991
Naval Training Center, Orlando 15,425

Businesses and other major employers
Walt Disney Co. Inc./Walt Disney World; Orlando; amusement park/recreation services 24,000

Martin Marietta Corp.; Orlando; communication services 5,220
Florida Hospital Medical Center; Orlando 4,000
University of Central Florida; Orlando 3,700
Florida EG&G Inc.; Orlando; research services & product testing 3,000
Orlando Regional Medical Center; Orlando; medical doctors 2,800
McDonnell Douglas Corp./McDonald Douglas Space Systems; Orlando; business services 2,100
NASA/John F. Kennedy Space Center; Orlando; space research/technology 2,100
Sun Bank/Suntrust Bank; Orlando; commercial banks 1,925
Busch Entertainment Corp./Sea World of Florida; Orlando; amusement park 1,800
Southern Bell Telephone & Telegraph Co.; Orlando; telephone communications 1,689
Dolphin Hotel Associates/Walt Disney World Dolphin; Orlando; hotel 1,500
Harcourt General Inc./Harcourt Brace; Orlando; book publishing 1,400
Winter Park Memorial Hospital; Winter Park 1,389
Rockwell Intl. Corp./Space Systems Div.; Orlando; search/navigation equipment 1,345
Sentinel Communications Co./Orlando Sentinel; Orlando; newspapers 1,250
Westinghouse Electric Corp./Power Generation Div.; Orlando; engines/turbines 1,200
Martin Marietta Corp.; Orlando; computer services 1,200
County of Orange/Correctional Institute; Orlando 1,157
Hyatt Corp./Grand Cypress Resort Inc.; Orlando; hotel 1,100
Walt Disney Co. Inc./Grand Floridian Hotel; Orlando; hotel 1,100
U.S. Postal Service; Orlando 1,000
AT&T Communications Inc.; Orlando; accounting/auditing 1,000
Orlando Regional Medical Center; Orlando; medical doctors 1,000
Buena Vista Investment Fund/Buena Vista Palace; Orlando; hotel 1,000
ECC Intl. Corp.; Orlando; computer peripherals 950
Sears Roebuck & Co.; Winter Park; electrical repair 950
Valencia Community College; Orlando 950
General Mills Inc.; Orlando; bars/restaurants 900
Humana Inc./Humana Hospital Lucerne; Orlando 825
Super Food Services Inc.; Orlando; grocery products 800
USBI Co. Inc.; Orlando; space vehicles/guided missiles 780
GDC-VRDI Inc./Vistana Resort Dev.; Orlando; subdividers/developers 742
County of Orange/Public Utility Dept.; Orlando 725
Cox Enterprises Inc./Florida Auto Auction of Orlando; Ocoee; motor vehicle auction 704
Pepsicola Beverages of Tampa; Orlando; beverages 700
Hubbard Construction Co./Mid-Florida Materials Div.; Winter Park; road construction 700
Walt Disney World Co.; Orlando; retail stores 700
Stouffer Corp./Stouffer Orlando Resort; Orlando; hotel 700
CPI Church Street Inc./Church Street Station; Orlando; restaurants/personal services 700
Hilton Hotels Corp./American Vineyards; Orlando; hotel 700
Page Avjet Corp.; Orlando; airport services 650
Travelers Corp.; Orlando; fire/marine/casualty insurance 640

Dart Industries Inc.; Kissimmee; furniture 600

Southland Corp.; Orlando; warehousing 600

Williams Telecom; Orlando; communication services 600

Sears Roebuck & Co.; Orlando; department stores 600

Anne O'Briant Agency Inc.; Orlando; advertising/promotional services 600

City of Orlando; Orlando 600

FMC Corp./Airline Equipment Fire Apparatus Div.; Orlando; misc. industrial equipment 575

Centex-Great Southwest Corp.; Orlando; building construction 550

Regal Marine Industries Inc./Regal Boats; Orlando; ship building/repairing 550

Vista-United Telecom; Orlando; telephone communications 520

Humana Inc./Humana Hospital; Kissimmee 501

9th District

West — Northern Pinellas and Hillsborough Counties; Central Pasco County; Clearwater

The 9th sits above Tampa and St. Petersburg, patching together pieces of three counties. North Pinellas County accounts for about half the district's population; the rest is split between north Hillsborough and central Pasco counties.

Although the 9th looks like a Republican district, Democrats can be competitive here. Democrat Lawton Chiles carried the areas within the 9th in the 1990 gubernatorial race. GOP Rep. Michael Bilirakis received less than 60 percent of the vote in 1990 and 1992.

The parts of Pinellas County in the district are solidly Republican. Democrats running for state and federal office are lucky to win 45 percent of the Pinellas vote.

Clearwater, historically a beach resort, has benefited from the arrival of high-tech industry to metropolitan St. Petersburg. Honeywell, much of which is just south of the district in the 10th, is a significant employer in the area, as is Unisys.

Light industry, services and a tourism trade, some of it associated with the gulf beaches, all have a role in the county's economy.

Real estate development is also important; the area has attracted middle- to upper-middle-class retirees.

North of Clearwater is Palm Harbor, the district's second-largest city, which features more boat docks than beaches. Many residents here still commute into Tampa-St. Petersburg.

Continuing north, a substantial Greek community lives in Tarpon Springs, a century after their ancestors first came to harvest the offshore sponge beds.

Democrats are more competitive in Pasco County. Many of the retirees who have settled in the county in recent years come from working-class backgrounds in the Northeast and Midwest and cling to Democratic voting habits, particularly in contests for local office.

Even so, Bilirakis was dismayed that 1992 redistricting stripped the 9th of western Pasco County, an area filled with retirees and military veterans whose interests he worked hard to promote.

The 9th still includes some residents in areas of west Pasco. Many of the retirees also recently relocated to the area in communities such as Zephyrhills. Some are former union members who carry their conservative Democratic orientation with them.

The growth of development in Pasco County has generally been from west to east, moving into rolling hills containing dairy farms and some citrus crops. Redistricting also cost the 9th the easternmost part of Pasco County, near Dade City.

Hillsborough County accounts for about one-fifth of the district's population. One development of note is Carrollwood Village, a bedroom community for Tampa. Democrats can also be competitive here, though liberal candidates do not fare well.

Election Returns and Party Registration

	9th District	Democrat	Republican
1992	President*	93,626 (34.2%)	112,832 (41.2%)
	House	110,135 (41.1%)	158,028 (58.9%)
1990	Governor	106,225 (60.5%)	69,326 (39.5%)
1988	President	77,216 (38.2%)	125,044 (61.8%)
	Senate	98,952 (51.6%)	92,795 (48.4%)
1986	Governor	70,004 (42.9%)	93,272 (57.1%)
1990	Party registration †	124,086 (41.4%)	145,284 (48.5%)

*Vote for Perot was 67,379 (24.6%).   †Independent/other is greater than 5%.

Demographics

Population 562,518

Percent change from 1980 9.6%

Land area 896 square miles

Population per square mile 628

Counties, 1990 population
Hillsborough (pt.) 138,990   Pinellas (pt.) 289,141
Pasco (pt.) 134,387

Cities, 1990 population (10,000 or more)
Carrollwood Village CDP   Lutz CDP 10,552
    15,051   Palm Harbor CDP 50,256
Clearwater (pt.) 96,886   Safety Harbor 15,124
Dunedin 34,012   Tarpon Springs 17,906
Greater Northdale CDP
    16,318

Race and Hispanic origin
White 94.6%
Black 3.4%
American Indian, Eskimo, or Aleut. 0.3%
Asian or Pacific Islander 1.0%
Other 0.7%
Hispanic origin 4.1%

Ancestry
American 4.9%   Italian 8.9%
Dutch 2.9%   Norwegian 1.0%
English 18.6%   Polish 4.5%
French 5.3%   Russian 1.0%
French Canadian 1.2%   Scotch Irish 2.8%
German 25.9%   Scottish 3.4%
Greek 1.7%   Swedish 2.1%
Irish 18.9%   Welsh 1.2%

Universities/colleges, 1990-1991 enrollment
Clearwater Christian College, Clearwater 419
Saint Leo College, Saint Leo 5,311

Newspapers, total circulation (in all districts)
Lakeland Ledger 77,413
St. Petersburg Times 351,635
Tampa Tribune 285,163

Commercial television stations, affiliations
ADI: Tampa-St. Petersburg (100%)

Cable television systems, total subscribers
Jones Intercable Inc.; Tampa 56,269
Paragon Cable; Largo 47,596
Paragon Cable; Temple Terrace 8,136
TCI of Florida; Dunedin 16,000
TCI of Florida; New Port Richey 60,000
Vision Cable of Pinellas Inc.; Clearwater 39,000
Vision Cable of Pinellas Inc.; Palm Harbor 18,700

Businesses and other major employers
GTE Data Services Inc.; Tampa; computer services 2,204
Morton Plant Hospital Assn.; Clearwater 2,000
City of Clearwater; Clearwater 1,681
Golf Hosts Inc.; Palm Harbor; hotel 1,200
Mease Hospital/Mease Health Care; Dunedin 1,200
County of Pasco; Land O'Lakes 1,155
Pasco County Board of Commissioners; New Port Richey 1,032
Nutmeg Industries Inc.; Tampa; outerwear 1,000
Nesco Design Group Inc.; Tampa; engineering/architectural services 975
Saddlebrook Resorts Inc.; Zephyrhills; hotels 850
Raymond James Financial Inc.; St. Petersburg; security brokers 800
Allstate Insurance Co.; St. Petersburg; insurance services 800
Diversicare Corp. America; Clearwater; nursing 800
GTE Florida Inc.; Clearwater; telephone communications 750
County of Pasco/Sheriffs Dept.; New Port Richey 750
Hospital Corp. America/Bayonet Point Regional Medical Center; Port Richey 700
Unisys Corp.; Oldsmar; computer equipment 615
Johnson & Johnson; Tampa; medical supplies 600
National Business Solutions Inc.; Clearwater; supply services 600
East Pasco Medical Center Inc.; Zephyrhills 516

10th District

West — Southern Pinellas County; St. Petersburg

The modern era of Florida politics began in this St. Petersburg-based district four decades ago. In 1954, the district made William C. Cramer the state's first Republican House member in the 20th century. Cramer owed his election to the influence of conservative retirees. Other GOP candidates prospered later as the retirees' influence expanded elsewhere in Florida.

Today, the retirees are still crucial in the politics of the 10th, but no candidate can afford to ignore the growing numbers of young people drawn by its steadily diversifying economy. The young newcomers, like their peers moving into other parts of Florida, also tend to identify with the GOP.

Not too long ago, St. Petersburg was known almost exclusively as a retirement haven. The retirees who settled there—many of them storekeepers, office workers and civil servants

from small towns in the Midwest—brought their Republican preferences with them. The economy was mostly service-oriented, geared to the needs of tourists and elderly residents. The morning rush hour saw many younger workers from St. Petersburg driving to jobs in Tampa, which provided employment in a greater variety of fields and offered a faster pace of life.

But St. Petersburg has broadened its economic base by stressing that it offers a good climate for business investment. Where the Shuffleboard Hall of Fame was once the big attraction, visitors are drawn to the Salvador Dali Museum and Sunken Gardens. The Women's Tennis Association is here. The search for a major league baseball team prompted the construction of the Florida Suncoast Dome.

St. Petersburg and Pinellas County companies such as Honeywell, Paradyne, E-Systems and Martin Marietta are busy with research, development, production and marketing of computers, communications equipment and other high-tech items.

A number of the major employers and subcontractors are engaged in defense-related work. Defense cuts and nervousness about the economy throughout the area undercut George Bush's support in 1992. After Bush won the district with 55 percent in 1988, defections to Ross Perot four years later enabled Bill Clinton to carry the 10th. But statewide GOP candidates are still more likely to campaign here than in the Tampa-based 11th. Republicans outnumber Democrats and most local officials identify with the GOP.

Although the median age of Pinellas County has dropped over the years, as younger residents have replaced retirees, the southern part of the county is already so crowded that it is growing much more slowly than the state as a whole.

Elsewhere, Pinellas Park is generally a blue-collar, lower-middle-class community, with some residents living in mobile home parks. Largo includes a large concentration of retirees. Residents of the adjacent gulf beaches are generally less affluent than those who live along the Sarasota or Miami-Fort Lauderdale coasts.

Election Returns and Party Registration

	10th District	Democrat	Republican
1992	President*	107,685 (40.0%)	97,492 (36.2%)
	House	114,809 (43.4%)	149,606 (56.6%)
1990	Governor	120,775 (65.5%)	63,654 (34.5%)
1988	President	98,842 (44.8%)	121,719 (55.2%)
	Senate	122,166 (55.0%)	99,788 (45.0%)
1986	Governor	95,347 (48.5%)	101,234 (51.5%)
1990	Party registration†	143,992 (44.5%)	148,795 (46.0%)

Vote for Perot was 64,280 (23.9%).   †Independent/other is greater than 5%.

Demographics

Population 562,518

Percent change from 1980 9.7%

Land area 151 square miles

Population per square mile 3,730

Counties, 1990 population
Pinellas (pt.) 562,518

Cities, 1990 population (10,000 or more)

Gulfport 11,727	Pinellas Park 43,426
Largo (pt.) 65,110	St. Petersburg (pt.) 236,203
Lealman CDP 21,748	

Race and Hispanic origin

White 88.6%
Black 9.4%
American Indian, Eskimo, or Aleut. 0.2%
Asian or Pacific Islander 1.3%
Other 0.4%
Hispanic origin 2.3%

Ancestry

American 4.1%	Italian 7.3%
Dutch 2.7%	Polish 4.0%
English 18.7%	Scotch Irish 3.0%
French 5.5%	Scottish 3.3%
French Canadian 1.4%	Swedish 2.1%
German 26.0%	Welsh 1.1%
Irish 17.8%	

Universities/colleges, 1990-1991 enrollment

Eckerd College, St. Petersburg 1,344
St. Petersburg Junior College, St. Petersburg 18,870

Newspapers, total circulation (in all districts)

St. Petersburg Times 351,635
Tampa Tribune 285,163

Commercial television stations, affiliations

ADI: Tampa-St. Petersburg (100%)

Cable television systems, total subscribers

Paragon Cable; Largo 47,596
Paragon Cable; St. Petersburg 65,729
Vision Cable of Pinellas Inc.; Clearwater 39,000
Vision Cable of Pinellas Inc.; Pinellas Park 53,950

Businesses and other major employers

Home Shopping Network Inc.; St. Petersburg; TV network retailers 3,377
U.S. Energy Dept./Pinellas Plant; Largo; electrical industrial apparatus 1,600
General Electric Co./Neutron Devices Dept.; Largo; electrical equipment/supplies 1,600
Bayfront Medical Center; St. Petersburg 1,544
AT&T Paradyne Corp.; Largo; communications equipment 1,500
U.S. Postal Service; St. Petersburg 1,400
All Children's Hospital Inc.; St. Petersburg 1,300
St. Anthony's Health Care Center; St. Petersburg 1,245
Florida Power Corp.; St. Petersburg; electric services 1,100
Jack Eckerd Corp./Eckerd Drug Stores; Largo; drug/proprietary stores 1,100
Essilor of America Inc.; St. Petersburg; glass/glassware 1,000
Honeywell Inc./Florida Operations; St. Petersburg; electrical equipment/supplies 900
Largo Medical Center Hospital; Largo 800
City of Largo; Largo 760
Hercules Defense Electronic Systems; Clearwater; electronic components 750
National Medical Enterprises/Palms of Pasadena Hospital; St. Petersburg 750
E-Systems Inc.; St. Petersburg; communications equipment 700

Linvatec Corp.; Largo; medical instruments/supplies 700
Florida Federal Savings; St. Petersburg; savings institutions 700
Times Publishing Co./St. Petersburg Times; St. Petersburg; newspapers 675
State Auto Mutual Insurance Co.; Largo; insurance services 650
Sun Coast Hospital Inc.; Largo 650
Humana Hosco Inc./Humana Hospital-Northside; St. Petersburg 590
Val-Pak Direct Marketing Systems; Largo; mailing/repro services 562
U.S. Veterans Affairs Dept.; St. Petersburg; social services 550

11th District

West — Southern Hillsborough County; Tampa

Ever since a Key West cigar factory moved to Tampa in 1886, this has been a city with a blue-collar orientation. Cubans came to work in the cigar business, and they were joined later by southerners looking for jobs in factories around the harbor.

Tampa's cigar industry is greatly diminished. But other traditional industries are still strong, among them brewing, commercial fishing, steel-making and ship construction. The city is also a major port; much of the phosphate mined from adjacent Polk County is shipped from here. That gives it an interest in international markets and free-trade politics.

The large working-class community makes Tampa the Florida city that most closely approximates Northern industrial cities. But the Democratic tendency this Tampa-based district historically has shown in state and national elections has been waning. There were not enough Democratic votes in the city to prevent George Bush from carrying surrounding Hillsborough County in 1992 with suburban GOP support.

Unlike many Northern industrial cities, however, Tampa has diversified to compete for the lucrative tourist trade. Busch Gardens, which started as a brewery tour, has been expanded into a 300-acre amusement park that is a leading Florida tourist attraction.

Tampa has a growing financial sector; Salomon Brothers and Citicorp recently moved some operations here. Tampa International Airport, on the city's western edge, is a major employer, as is GTE Florida. The University of South Florida, one of the state's largest with about 33,000 students, is on the city's northern end.

The university's presence, combined with MacDill Air Force Base, has helped attract some high-technology industries. There have been some questions about MacDill's future, however. The base is scheduled to lose its F-16 training facility, and the continued operation of its runway is in doubt. Local officials hope that the recent relocation of the National Oceanic and Atmospheric Administration at the base will stabilize matters. The base also continues to serve as Special Operations Command and Central Command.

The district is 14 percent Hispanic. The influence of Cuban and Spanish culture is most pronounced in Ybor City, a long-established community in southeast Tampa named after the man who brought the cigar factory here from Key West. Although relatively few people still live in Ybor City—Hispanics are more prevalent in West Tampa and the community of Town and Country—the area is undergoing a commercial resurgence.

Blacks, who account for 17 percent of the district's population, live mostly in inner-city Tampa. Racial incidents occasionally occur. In early 1993, three white men were convicted in what authorities called the racially motivated burning of a black New York tourist whom the men kidnapped in Valrico, east of Tampa.

Election Returns and Party Registration

		11th District	Democrat	Republican
1992	President*		82,898 (41.1%)	79,126 (39.2%)
	House †		100,984 (52.8%)	77,640 (40.6%)
1990	Governor		87,703 (66.3%)	44,596 (33.7%)
1988	President		70,867 (44.4%)	88,734 (55.6%)
	Senate		70,305 (59.1%)	48,715 (40.9%)
1986	Governor		70,489 (51.9%)	65,376 (48.1%)
1990	Party registration †		142,935 (60.2%)	77,308 (32.5%)

*Vote for Perot was 39,796 (19.7%). †Independent/other is greater than 5%.

Demographics

Population 562,519

Percent change from 1980 9.7%

Land area 253 square miles

Population per square mile 2,225

Counties, 1990 population
Hillsborough (pt.) 562,519

Cities, 1990 population (10,000 or more)
Brandon CDP (pt.) 43,864
Egypt Lake CDP 14,580
Lake Magdalene CDP (pt.) 15,083
Palm River-Clair Mel CDP 13,691
Tampa (pt.) 275,508
Temple Terrace 16,444
Town 'n' Country CDP 60,946
University West CDP 23,760
West Park CDP 10,347

Race and Hispanic origin
White 78.7%
Black 17.2%
American Indian, Eskimo, or Aleut. 0.3%
Asian or Pacific Islander 1.4%
Other 2.3%
Hispanic origin 13.9%

Ancestry
American 5.1%
Dutch 2.1%
English 13.9%
French 3.7%
German 18.3%
Irish 14.6%
Italian 6.4%
Polish 2.4%
Scotch Irish 2.7%
Scottish 2.2%
Swedish 1.1%

Universities/colleges, 1990-1991 enrollment
Florida College, Temple Terrace 373
Hillsborough Community College, Tampa 15,573
ITT Technical Institute, Tampa 559
National Educational Center, Tampa 1,115
Tampa College, Tampa 910
United Electronics Institute of Florida, Tampa 620
University of South Florida, Tampa 32,326
University of Tampa, Tampa 2,503

Newspapers, total circulation (in all districts)
Lakeland Ledger 77,413
St. Petersburg Times 351,635
Tampa Tribune 285,163

Commercial television stations, affiliations
ADI: Tampa-St. Petersburg (100%)

Cable television systems, total subscribers
Jones Intercable Inc.; Tampa 56,269
Paragon Cable; Brandon 39,889

Military installations, 1991
MacDill Air Force Base, Tampa 7,066

Businesses and other major employers
GTE Florida Inc.; Tampa; telephone communications 9,000
University of South Florida; Tampa 4,500
Tampa General Hospital; Tampa 3,093
U.S. Postal Service; Tampa 3,000
CSX Transportation Inc.; Tampa; railroads 2,500
St. Joseph's Hospital Inc.; Tampa 2,500
U.S. Veterans Affairs Dept.; Tampa; hospital 2,500
GTE South Inc.; Tampa; telephone communications 2,463
Staffing Concepts Intl.; Tampa; personnel supply services 2,300
Southeastern Staffing Inc.; Tampa; personnel supply services 2,300
County of Hillsborough/Sheriffs Office; Tampa 2,000
U.S. Veterans Affairs Dept.; Tampa; hospital 2,000
Rolm Co./IBM; Tampa; computer services 2,000
A. G. Edwards & Sons Inc.; Tampa; mortgage bankers 1,700
GTE Communication Systems Corp.; Tampa; electrical goods 1,500
Busch Entertainment Corp./Busch Gardens; Tampa; amusement park 1,400
United Services Auto Assn.; Tampa; fire/marine/casualty insurance 1,300
Tribune Co. Inc./Tampa Tribune; Tampa; newspapers 1,200
North American Philips Corp./Philips Circuit Assemblies; Tampa; audio/video equipment 1,200
Time Warner/Time Customer Service Inc.; Tampa; management services 1,200
University Community Hospital; Tampa 1,100
City of Tampa/Police Dept.; Tampa 1,050
Metropolitan Life Insurance Co.; Tampa; life insurance 1,000
Humana Hospital; Brandon 1,000
First Florida Bank; Tampa; commercial banks 1,000
Maas Inc.; Tampa; computer services 1,000
National Bank of Florida; Tampa; commercial banks 1,000
ConAgra Inc./Singleton Seafood; Tampa; grocery products 900
Moffitt H. Lee Cancer Center; Tampa 890
Tampa Electric Co.; Tampa; electric services 880
Group Technologies Corp.; Tampa; communications equipment/repair services 750
County of Hillsborough; Tampa 750
Marriott Corp./Tampa Marriott Westshore; Tampa; hotel 750
Budd Services Inc./Vickers Security Service; Tampa; business/security services 750

Progressive American Insurance Co.; Tampa;
   fire/marine/casualty insurance 740
Aetna Life & Casualty Co.; Tampa; insurance services 700
IBM Corp.; Tampa; computer services 700
Humana Inc./Humana Women's Hospital; Tampa 675
Hillsborough Community College; Tampa 623
Pepsico Inc.; Tampa; beverages 600
Citicorp Services Inc.; Tampa; banking services 600
Kash N Karry Food Stores Inc.; Tampa; grocery stores 600
Pharmacy Management Services; Tampa; pharmaceuticals/
   proprietaries/sundries 575
Pepsicola Beverages of Tampa/Pepsi-Cola Bottling Co.
   Tampa; Tampa; bottling 575
Sears Roebuck & Co.; Tampa; department stores 550
County of Hillsborough/School Board; Tampa 550
City of Tampa/Fire Dept.; Tampa 550
County of Hillsborough/Sheriffs Office; Tampa 550

12th District

Central — Polk County; Lakeland; Parts of Hillsborough County

Across much of Florida, land once devoted to agriculture is being eaten away by shopping centers, motels and condominiums. But in Polk County, centerpiece of the 12th District, citrus is still a major force.

Thousands of jobs are connected with the growing, picking, packing, processing and loading of oranges, orange concentrate and grapefruit. Besides Minute Maid, there are many smaller growers whose efforts combine to make the 12th among the nation's foremost citrus-producing districts.

However, Polk County's citrus industry has hit bumpy times in recent years, and periodic freezes have prompted some growers to move farther south. Also moving south are elements of the county's other leading industry, phosphate mining. The removal and processing of phosphate, the raw material of fertilizer, has fluctuated in recent years because of uneven demand for the product and the county's dwindling supply. IMC Fertilizer remains a leading private employer, however.

Food processing is also important in Polk County; Pepperidge Farms and BG Shrimp are leading employers. Lakeland, the county seat, is also headquarters for Publix supermarkets, the largest private employer in the state. But the county lost another leading employer in the 1980s when Piper Aircraft closed.

Tourists are drawn to Cypress Gardens, a botanical and water-show attraction in Winter Haven, just east of Lakeland.

The county grew by 26 percent in the 1980s, partly due to an influx of retirees. In the main, these retirees are less affluent than others who settle to the west along the Gulf Coast; some of them settle into mobile home parks. Large fundamentalist churches are commonplace in the district, and their parishioners contribute to the area's conservative leanings, especially on social issues.

The Dixie roots of the new arrivals are also apparent in the Democratic Party's decided registration edge in the district, 61 percent to 36 percent. But here as elsewhere, southern Democrats often vote across party lines, and Republicans are making inroads in county offices. Ronald Reagan and George Bush carried the district by a 2-to-1 margin in the 1980s, while Democrat Buddy MacKay held a slim edge in the close 1988 Senate race.

The shaky economy held down Bush's margin in the district in 1992. It also made for the state's most competitive open-seat House race, with the GOP candidate squeezing by.

The part of eastern Hillsborough County within the district includes Plant City, noted for its annual strawberry festival. Agriculture is a key here, with citrus and winter vegetables of some importance. The 12th also has part of Brandon, a Tampa suburb. Also in the district are De Soto and Hardee counties and part of Polk County.

Election Returns and Party Registration

	12th District	Democrat	Republican
1992	President*	67,802 (34.5%)	89,585 (45.6%)
	House	92,346 (47.9%)	100,484 (52.1%)
1990	Governor	75,895 (57.0%)	57,177 (43.0%)
1988	President	49,047 (33.7%)	96,503 (66.3%)
	Senate	74,168 (51.3%)	70,431 (48.7%)
1986	Governor	53,342 (42.4%)	72,517 (57.6%)
1990	Party registration	131,249 (61.0%)	76,583 (35.6%)

Vote for Perot was 39,229 (20.0%).

Demographics

Population 562,519

Percent change from 1980 9.6%

Land area 3,503 square miles

Population per square mile 161

Counties, 1990 population
De Soto 23,865
Hardee 19,499
Highlands (pt.) 16,467
Hillsborough (pt.) 95,179
Pasco (pt.) 24,853
Polk (pt.) 382,656

Cities, 1990 population (10,000 or more)
Bartow 14,716
Bloomingdale CDP (pt.) 12,398
Haines City (pt.) 11,558
Lakeland 70,576
Plant City (pt.) 22,368
Winter Haven 24,725

Race and Hispanic origin
White 84.1%
Black 12.6%
American Indian, Eskimo, or Aleut. 0.3%
Asian or Pacific Islander 0.6%
Other 2.3%
Hispanic origin 6.1%

Ancestry
American 9.9%
Dutch 2.8%
English 16.4%
French 3.7%
German 19.0%
Irish 16.8%
Italian 3.3%
Polish 1.7%
Scotch Irish 3.0%
Scottish 2.4%
Swedish 1.2%

Universities/colleges, 1990-1991 enrollment
Florida Southern College, Lakeland 2,684
Pasco Hernando Community College, Dade City 3,973
Polk Community College, Winter Haven 5,879

Southeastern College of the Assemblies of God, Lakeland
1,192
South Florida Community College, Avon Park 1,308
Warner Southern College, Lake Wales 470
Webber College, Babson Park 224

Newspapers, total circulation (in all districts)
Lakeland Ledger 77,413
Orlando Sentinel 284,136
Sarasota Herald Tribune 115,577
St. Petersburg Times 351,635
Tampa Tribune 285,163

Commercial television stations, affiliations
ADI: Tampa-St. Petersburg (100%)
WTMV, Lakeland (None)
WTOG, St. Petersburg (None)
WTTA, St. Petersburg (None)
WBHS, Tampa (None)
WFLA-TV, Tampa-St. Petersburg (NBC)
WFTS, Tampa-St. Petersburg (Fox)
WTVT, Tampa-St. Petersburg (CBS)

Cable television systems, total subscribers
Cablevision of Central Florida; Lakeland North 5,900
Cablevision of Central Florida; Lakeland South 14,600
CV of Central Florida; Winter Haven 27,000
Paragon Cable; Brandon 39,889
Paragon Cable; Lakeland 17,105
Storer Cable TV Inc.; Sebring 11,526
Storer Cable TV of Florida Inc.; Bartow 7,201

Military installations, 1991
Avon Park Air Force Station, Avon Park 144

Businesses and other major employers
County of Polk; Bartow 2,272
Lakeland Regional Medical Center; Lakeland 2,230
Publix Super Markets Inc./Food World; Lakeland; grocery stores 2,000
IMC Fertilizer Group Inc./Noralyn Mine; Bartow; chemicals/fertilizers 1,375
IMC Fertilizer Group Inc./New Wales Operations; Mulberry; chemicals/fertilizers 1,170
G. Pierce Wood Memorial Hospital; Arcadia 1,100
State Farm Mutual Auto Insurance Co.; Winter Haven; insurance services 1,000
Lykes Bros Inc.; Plant City; meat products 835
Scottys Inc./Scottys; Winter Haven; lumber/building materials 800
Walker Memorial Medical Center; Avon Park 795
Seminole Fertilizer Corp.; Bartow; chemicals/fertilizers 770
Watson Clinic; Lakeland; medical doctors 758
City of Lakeland/Electric & Water Dept.; Lakeland 754
Coca-Cola Co. Inc./Minute Maid; Auburndale; fruit juices 700
Florida Cypress Gardens Inc./Cypress Gardens; Winter Haven; amusement park 700
GTE Florida Inc.; Lakeland; telephone communications 550
Polk General Hospital; Bartow 550

13th District

Southwest — Sarasota and Manatee Counties; Sarasota; Bradenton

When redistricting and retirements created 10 open seats in Florida in 1992, Republicans knew they had little to worry about in the newly designed 13th. The district's 56 percent GOP registration is the second highest in the state, barely below that of the adjacent 14th.

Sarasota County accounts for slightly less than half the 13th's population, and Manatee County represents just under 40 percent. The remainder live in parts of Charlotte and Hillsborough counties. More populous Sarasota was expected to have the upper hand in district politics, but in 1993 the GOP House member was from Manatee County.

George Bush ran stronger in Sarasota and Manatee than he did in the state as a whole in 1992, but the 43 percent he garnered in both counties was not overwhelming.

The political personality of the 13th is most influenced by retirees from the suburbs and small towns of the Midwest. These people changed their addresses but not their party registration, and they contribute to the burgeoning strength of the GOP in Florida.

Although they closely identify with the GOP, residents of the 13th are not necessarily conservative on social issues. The 1992 House race, for example, was dominated by candidates who supported abortion rights. The proximity to gulf beaches, barrier islands and a large state park also makes the environment a bipartisan concern, with residents attuned to the problems of beach erosion and the effects of rapid population growth.

Sarasota County cultivates a refined image with its art museums, theaters and symphony performances. It generally draws a more highly educated and wealthier class of retirees than most other west coast communities in Florida. Leading private employers include tourism, retailing, health care and banking. The city of Sarasota includes some minorities and retirees who are not quite as affluent as those on the barrier islands of Longboat Key, Siesta Key and Casey Key.

Sarasota County grew by 37 percent in the 1980s. The area poised for the next growth spurt is immediately south of the city, down the coast along Route 41 to Venice. The residents of Venice itself tend to be a little older and of more modest means than residents of the county's northern end.

Manatee, which grew by 43 percent in the 1980s, has some residents who commute to work over the Sunshine Skyway Bridge to Tampa Bay. Leading employers in the county include Tropicana, which grows, picks and packs citrus, and Wellcraft Marine, which builds pleasure boats.

Bradenton, the county seat and retail center, has a somewhat diverse population both by income and ethnicity. It is also not quite as midwestern-oriented as Sarasota.

The 13th also stretches south into Charlotte County to pick up parts of Port Charlotte and Murdock. Residents there are generally older, less affluent and more Democratic. It also extends north into Hillsborough County to pick up Sun City Center and Ruskin, where Republicans fare well.

Election Returns and Party Registration

	13th District	Democrat	Republican
1992	President*	100,950 (34.7%)	124,271 (42.8%)
	House	115,767 (42.2%)	158,881 (57.8%)

13th District		Democrat	Republican
1990	Governor	103,189 (53.2%)	90,725 (46.8%)
1988	President	72,236 (34.3%)	138,489 (65.7%)
	Senate	97,242 (49.3%)	100,137 (50.7%)
1986	Governor	62,328 (34.6%)	117,602 (65.4%)
1990	Party registration †	122,206 (36.5%)	188,581 (56.3%)

*Vote for Perot was 65,297 (22.5%).   †Independent/other is greater than 5%.

Demographics

Population 562,518

Percent change from 1980 9.6%

Land area 1,540 square miles

Population per square mile 365

Counties, 1990 population
Charlotte (pt.) 35,669	Manatee 211,707
Hillsborough (pt.) 37,366	Sarasota 277,776

Cities, 1990 population (10,000 or more)
Bayshore Gardens CDP 17,062	Sarasota Springs CDP 16,088
Bradenton 43,779	Sarasota 50,961
Englewood CDP (pt.) 10,079	South Bradenton CDP 20,398
Gulf Gate Estates CDP 11,622	South Venice CDP 11,951
North Port 11,973	Venice 16,922
Port Charlotte CDP (pt.) 30,731	

Race and Hispanic origin
White 92.8%
Black 5.4%
American Indian, Eskimo, or Aleut. 0.2%
Asian or Pacific Islander 0.5%
Other 1.0%
Hispanic origin 4.3%

Ancestry
American 4.5%	Norwegian 1.1%
Dutch 3.4%	Polish 3.4%
English 20.5%	Russian 1.2%
French 5.5%	Scotch Irish 3.0%
French Canadian 1.2%	Scottish 3.5%
German 27.4%	Swedish 2.1%
Irish 17.1%	Welsh 1.3%
Italian 6.3%	

Universities/colleges, 1990-1991 enrollment
Manatee Community College, Bradenton 7,874
Ringling School of Art & Design, Sarasota 576
Sarasota Vocational-Tech Center, Sarasota 13,000

Newspapers, total circulation (in all districts)
Bradenton Herald 40,934
Charlotte Sun Herald 20,135
Fort Myers News-Press 92,118
Lakeland Ledger 77,413
Sarasota Herald Tribune 115,577

St. Petersburg Times 351,635
Tampa Tribune 285,163

Commercial television stations, affiliations
ADI: Tampa-St. Petersburg (61%), Sarasota (37%) and Ft. Myers-Naples (2%)
WWSB, Sarasota (ABC)
WBSV, Venice (None)

Cable television systems, total subscribers
Cablevision Industries Inc.; Wimauma 9,347
Cablevision Industries of Florida Inc.; Palmetto 5,969
Paragon Cable; Anna Maria 7,433
Paragon Cable; Bradenton 48,034
Paragon Cable; Brandon 39,889
Storer Cable TV Inc.; Venice 21,007
Storer Cable TV of Florida Inc.; Cape Haze 16,745
Storer Cable TV of Florida Inc.; Sarasota 74,006

Businesses and other major employers
Sarasota Memorial Hospital; Sarasota 2,600
Tropicana Products Inc.; Bradenton; fruit juices 2,000
County of Sarasota; Sarasota 1,751
County of Manatee; Bradenton 1,600
County of Charlotte; Punta Gorda 1,315
Manatee Memorial Hospital; Bradenton 1,260
Florida Power & Light Co.; Sarasota; electric services 1,254
Hospital Corp. America/Blake Memorial Hospital; Bradenton 1,100
Venice Hospital Inc.; Venice 1,027
City of Sarasota; Sarasota 1,002
Genmar Industries Inc./Wellcraft Marine Div.; Sarasota; ship building/repairing 1,000
Loral Fairchild Corp.; Sarasota; search/navigation equipment 825
Trans World Airlines Inc.; Sarasota; airline 800
Doctors Hospital of Sarasota; Sarasota 800
Barnett Banks Inc.; Sarasota; commercial banks 700
St. Joseph Hospital of Port Charlotte; Punta Gorda 607
Arvida Co./JMB Partners; Longboat Key; real estate agents 600
Charlotte Community Hospital/Fawcett Memorial Hospital; Punta Gorda 600
Manatee Community College; Bradenton 550

14th District

Southwest — Lee and Collier Counties; Cape Coral; Fort Myers; Naples

The 14th is an area of steadfast Republicanism and robust population growth. Fully 57 percent of district residents are registered Republicans, the highest percentage in the state. And the three counties that make up the district grew by more than 50 percent during the 1980s.

Lee County, which accounts for more than half the district's population, grew most slowly—at a 63 percent clip. The increase was pushed by Cape Coral, which grew by 134 percent and is now the district's largest city. Originally a retirement community, Cape Coral has been attracting young professionals, service industries and those involved in land development. Located near the gulf and along the Caloosahatchee River, the city features canals, easy access to the gulf and reasonable land costs.

To the west lie the barrier islands of Captiva and Sanibel, which have tried to restrict development to protect their natural beauty and preserve their images as upscale resort getaways. Across the river east of Cape Coral is Fort Myers, an older city once known for raising gladiolas. Acreage once devoted to gladiolas has since given way to land development. Health care is also an important employer here. Small pockets of blacks and blue-collar Democrats give Fort Myers a slightly less Republican cast than Cape Coral.

George Bush captured 68 percent of the Lee County vote in 1988, and his 44 percent in 1992 was still above his state average.

The region's growth spurred approval of a new state college, tentatively named Florida Gulf University, to be built in Lee County. The area also received boosts from the completion of Florida International Airport and the expansion of Interstate 75. The highway follows the gulf from Tampa, swinging east near Naples (Collier County) to cross the Everglades at Alligator Alley.

Naples, situated on the gulf, has some exclusive high-rise condominiums and large homes in its midst. The upper-income retirees, many from New England and the Midwest, support wide-ranging cultural activities, including the Naples Philharmonic center. Marco Island is a planned community noted for its wealthy residents and strong GOP inclination. Elsewhere in Collier County, citrus growers are increasingly attracted to the availability of open land and low risk of freezes. Immokalee, in the county's northern interior, has a large farm area and is home to many migrants and seasonal workers.

Collier, which grew 77 percent in the 1980s, is a solid Republican base; Bush captured 75 percent of the votes in 1988 and 53 percent in 1992.

Democrats often find their best chance in the district in Charlotte County, where Bush edged Democrat Bill Clinton in 1992, 39 percent to 37 percent.

Charlotte, known formerly as a retirement haven, has drawn a somewhat younger crowd recently, spurring a 90 percent population growth in the 1980s. Most of Charlotte County is in the 14th District except for some areas around Port Charlotte.

Election Returns and Party Registration

	14th District	Democrat	Republican
1992	President*	87,856 (31.3%)	129,605 (46.2%)
	House †	—	220,351 (82.1%)
1990	Governor	77,012 (44.8%)	95,043 (55.2%)
1988	President	59,131 (31.1%)	131,028 (68.9%)
	Senate	79,023 (40.7%)	115,076 (59.3%)
1986	Governor	55,686 (37.5%)	92,901 (62.5%)
1990	Party registration †	97,883 (35.7%)	156,812 (57.2%)

*Vote for Perot was 63,149 (22.5%).   †Independent/other is greater than 5%.

Demographics

Population 562,518

Percent change from 1980 9.7%

Land area 3,494 square miles

Population per square mile 161

Counties, 1990 population

Charlotte (pt.) 75,306   Lee 335,113
Collier 152,099

Cities, 1990 population (10,000 or more)

Bonita Springs CDP   Naples 19,505
    13,600   North Fort Myers CDP
Cape Coral 74,991   30,027
Cypress Lake CDP 10,491   North Naples CDP 13,422
East Naples CDP 22,951   Port Charlotte CDP (pt.)
Fort Myers 45,206   10,804
Golden Gate CDP 14,148   Punta Gorda 10,747
Immokalee CDP 14,120   San Carlos Park CDP
Lehigh Acres CDP 13,611   11,785

Race and Hispanic origin

White 91.9%
Black 5.7%
American Indian, Eskimo, or Aleut. 0.2%
Asian or Pacific Islander 0.5%
Other 1.7%
Hispanic origin 6.6%

Ancestry

American 4.3%	Italian 7.2%
Dutch 3.1%	Norwegian 1.2%
English 18.7%	Polish 3.7%
French 5.3%	Scotch Irish 2.9%
French Canadian 1.1%	Scottish 3.3%
German 26.8%	Swedish 2.1%
Irish 17.9%	Welsh 1.1%

Universities/colleges, 1990-1991 enrollment

Edison Community College, Fort Myers 7,249

Newspapers, total circulation (in all districts)

Charlotte Sun Herald 20,135
Fort Myers News-Press 92,118
Miami Herald 400,336
Naples Daily News 40,726
Sarasota Herald Tribune 115,577

Commercial television stations, affiliations

ADI: Ft. Myers-Naples (100%)
    WFTX, Cape Coral (Fox)
    WBBH-TV, Fort Myers (NBC)
    WINK-TV, Fort Myers (CBS)
    WEVU, Naples (ABC)
    WNPL, Naples (None)

Cable television systems, total subscribers

CVI; Cape Coral 15,000
Cablevision of Golden Gate; Golden Gate 5,943
Colony Cablevision; Bonita Springs 23,043
Colony Cablevision; North Fort Myers 10,639
Colony Cablevision; Naples 30,885
Jones Intercable Inc.; Fort Myers 31,839
Storer Cable TV Inc.; Lehigh Acres 5,092
Storer Cable TV Inc.; Port Charlotte 24,852
Storer Cable TV of Florida Inc.; Cape Haze 16,745

Businesses and other major employers

Lee Memorial Hospital; Fort Myers 2,300
Naples Community Hospital Inc.; Naples 1,800
County of Lee; Fort Myers 1,729
County of Collier; Naples 1,100

U.S. Postal Service; Fort Myers 1,000

Cape Coral Hospital; Fort Myers 1,000

W. B. Johnson Properties Inc./Ritz-Carlton Hotel; Naples; hotel 900

Collier County School District; Naples 864

Marriott Corp./Marco Island Resort; Marco Island; hotel 843

Yoder Bros. Inc.; Alva; horticultural specialties 730

Mariner Group Inc./South Seas Plantation Co.; Captiva; hotel 720

State of Florida/Gulf Coast Center; Fort Myers; residential care 700

County of Lee/Sheriffs Dept.; Fort Myers 600

News-Press Publishing Co./News Press; Fort Myers; newspapers 590

Lehigh Corp.; subdividers/developers 585

Citizens Southern National Bank Florida; Fort Myers; commercial banks 580

Edison Community College; Fort Myers 550

Boran Craig Barber Construction Co.; Naples; building construction 535

15th District

Central — Brevard, Osceola and Indian River Counties; Palm Bay; Melbourne

Brevard County is 72 miles long on the Atlantic Coast and only 20 miles wide. But it is less famous for its beaches than for what is launched from them. This is the self-proclaimed "Space Coast," home of NASA's Kennedy Space Center.

The county boomed during the era of Mercury, Gemini and Apollo space flights in the 1960s, then stalled when space exploration slipped as a national priority. The high-tech industries that had been lured to the area trimmed jobs, but a core of engineers and other skilled workers remained.

In the 1980s, the shuttle program and increased military spending brought new opportunities for aerospace and defense-related work, spurring another round of population growth. The 1986 explosion of the shuttle *Challenger* cast an economic and psychological pall over Brevard that began to lift when shuttle flights resumed in late 1988.

The space program still has an enormous economic impact on the county, and some of the companies it contracts with have taken on defense contracts as well. This reliance on government spending, either through space or defense funding, has forced several companies to adjust to a peacetime economy. Among the leading private employers are the Harris Corp., Grumman and Lockheed.

Tourists are drawn to the space enterprises and to the beaches. The county still has some citrus, and cattle graze in southwest Brevard. Patrick Air Force Base provides support for the space program.

The county's population grew by 46 percent during the 1980s. Most residents live along the Indian River. Titusville, the county seat, is just north of the space center. Many of its residents are in working-class trades related to the space industry and are more prone to vote Democratic than the district as a whole. The Cocoa and Rockledge area, near the space center's entrance, tends to draw tourists. It is politically competitive. Farther south, Melbourne has more defense-related industries, and Palm Bay's largest employer is the Harris Corp., producing electronic systems and other high-tech equipment.

The 15th usually votes Republican at the top of the ticket, although in the 1992 presidential race Ross Perot captured about one-fourth of the votes in Brevard and in the district overall, holding down George Bush's winning margin.

The retirees who have settled into Vero Beach and other coastal communities in Indian River County are fairly affluent and accustomed to voting Republican. Democrats have made few inroads there.

The parts of Osceola County in the 15th are mostly agricultural, and the small part of Polk County is largely populated by cows, though Disney has plans to launch Celebration City, a mixed commercial and residential project there.

Election Returns and Party Registration

	15th District	Democrat	Republican
1992	President*	83,679 (30.9%)	117,685 (43.4%)
	House	132,412 (50.7%)	128,873 (49.3%)
1990	Governor	81,483 (48.1%)	88,049 (51.9%)
1988	President	55,785 (29.7%)	131,787 (70.3%)
	Senate	82,220 (41.8%)	114,592 (58.2%)
1986	Governor	62,076 (41.3%)	88,352 (58.7%)
1990	Party registration †	126,387 (44.0%)	141,141 (49.1%)

*Vote for Perot was 69,749 (25.7%).   †Independent/other is greater than 5%.

Demographics

Population 562,519

Percent change from 1980 9.7%

Land area 3,133 square miles

Population per square mile 180

Counties, 1990 population

Brevard 398,978	Osceola (pt.) 50,607
Indian River 90,208	Polk (pt.) 22,726

Cities, 1990 population (10,000 or more)

Cocoa Beach 12,123	South Patrick Shores CDP 10,249
Cocoa 17,722	
Florida Ridge CDP 12,218	St. Cloud 12,453
Melbourne 59,646	Titusville 39,394
Merritt Island CDP 32,886	Vero Beach South CDP 16,973
Palm Bay 62,632	
Rockledge 16,023	Vero Beach 17,350
Sebastian 10,205	

Race and Hispanic origin

White 90.2%

Black 7.6%

American Indian, Eskimo, or Aleut. 0.3%

Asian or Pacific Islander 1.1%

Other 0.7%

Hispanic origin 3.4%

Ancestry

American 6.4%	German 25.1%
Dutch 2.9%	Irish 18.8%
English 19.0%	Italian 7.1%
French 5.2%	Polish 3.3%
French Canadian 1.3%	Scotch Irish 3.3%

Scottish 3.2%   Welsh 1.1%
Swedish 1.8%

Universities/colleges, 1990-1991 enrollment
Brevard Community College, Cocoa 12,375
Florida Institute of Technology, Melbourne 5,929
Phillips Junior College, Melbourne 855

Newspapers, total circulation (in all districts)
Florida Today 82,494
Lakeland Ledger 77,413
Miami Herald 400,336
Orlando Sentinel 284,136
Tampa Tribune 285,163
Vero Beach Press Journal 30,475

Commercial television stations, affiliations
ADI: Orlando-Daytona Beach-Melbourne (75%), West Palm
    Beach-Ft. Pierce-Vero Beach (15%) and Tampa-St. Pe-
    tersburg (10%)
WTGL-TV, Cocoa (None)
WIRB, Melbourne (None)
WBSF, Melbourne (None)

Cable television systems, total subscribers
Cablevision of Central Florida; Cocoa Beach 13,600
Cablevision of Central Florida; Melbourne 109,200
Cablevision of Central Florida; Winter Haven 27,000
Falcon Cable TV; Sebastian 7,484
Kissimmee Cablevision; Osceola County 15,253
TCI of Florida; Titusville 13,225
United Artists/TCI; Vero Beach 27,199

Military installations, 1991
Patrick Air Force Base, Cocoa Beach 6,621
Cape Canaveral Air Force Station, Port Canaveral 3,487

Businesses and other major employers
Harris Corp.; Melbourne; electronic components 9,000
Johnson Controls World Services; Cape Canaveral; airport
    services 6,900
Lockheed Space Operations Co.; Titusville; transportation
    services 6,500
Florida EG&G Inc.; Cocoa; engineering services 2,300
McDonnell Douglas Corp.; Titusville; missile systems 2,098
Holmes Regional Medical Center; Melbourne 2,020
Computer Sciences Corp.; Cocoa Beach; computer services
    2,000
Brevard County School District; Melbourne 1,953
Grumman Technical Services; Titusville; airport services
    1,800
Harris Corp./Government Aerospace; Melbourne;
    search/navigation equipment 1,500
Harris Corp./Government Info Systems Div.; Melbourne;
    communications equipment 1,500
County of Brevard/School Board; Melbourne 1,500
Premier Cruise Lines Ltd.; Cape Canaveral; cruise line 1,400
Rockwell Intl. Corp./Space Systems Div.; Cape Canaveral;
    space research/technology 1,400
Grumman Corp./Grumman Melbourne Systems Div.; Mel-
    bourne; search/navigation equipment 1,300
Indian River Memorial Hospital; Vero Beach 1,150
Wuesthoff Memorial Hospital; Rockledge 1,060
McDonnell Douglas Corp.; Titusville; space
    research/technology 1,000

Harris Corp./Electronic Systems Div.; Melbourne; electrical
    repair 1,000
Parrish Medical Center; Titusville 800
Rockwell Intl. Corp.; Melbourne; communications equip-
    ment 750
Brevard Community College; Cocoa Beach 750
Piper Aircraft Corp.; Vero Beach; aircraft 650
Dictaphone Corp./Pitney Bowes; Melbourne; office
    equipment/answering machines 650
Florida Institute of Technology; Melbourne 650
County of Brevard/Sheriffs Dept.; Titusville 633
Cape Canaveral Hospital; Cocoa 620
Martin Marietta Corp./Aerospace Div.; Cocoa Beach; com-
    munications equipment 600
Hyatt Corp./Hyatt-Orlando; Kissimmee; hotel 600
Cape Publications Inc./Florida Today; Melbourne; newspa-
    pers 590
City of Vero Beach; Vero Beach 567
Storage Technology Corp./Storageter Printer Operations;
    Melbourne; computer/office equipment 525

16th District

Central — Coastal Martin, Palm Beach and
St. Lucie Counties

The large 16th is something of a link between central Florida and the southeast's Gold Coast. Although most of its land mass is in four lightly populated counties along the western edge of Lake Okeechobee, most of its population lives in three Atlantic coast counties.

Republicans hold a bare registration edge in the 16th, which means GOP candidates typically run better than their statewide average in top-of-the-ticket races.

The area has attracted large numbers of newcomers from more congested areas farther south along the coast. Palm Beach County, which accounts for nearly half of the district's population, grew at an overall rate of 50 percent during the 1980s. St. Lucie County grew by 72 percent and Martin County grew by 58 percent. Growth management has become the most important local concern.

The 16th includes parts of north Palm Beach County. Controversies over the pace of development and its impact on the environment have been present in the community of Jupiter, which tripled in size in the 1970s and more than doubled in the 1980s. Many of the newcomers are young, middle-income families who commute south to work in an area from West Palm Beach to Boca Raton. Transportation is a concern here, deciding where to build access roads and how to move travelers through the county. Some bedroom communities are no longer interested in attracting more residents. Jupiter, a mix of conservative Democrats and Republicans, is enticing to boaters because of its access to the Atlantic as well as the Intracoastal Waterway.

Palm Beach Gardens is headquarters for the Professional Golfers Association and features a golf resort. Wellington is a GOP stronghold. Other areas attractive to retirees are Fountains of Lake Worth, where many residents live on a fixed income and lean Democratic, and Golden Lakes Village.

Farming is important in less-developed areas of the county, especially sugar, cattle, vegetables and citrus. Pratt & Whitney builds jet engines at a plant northwest of Palm Beach Gardens, while golf courses and beaches draw tourists to the coast.

Martin County faces some of the same issues of growth management. It has quite a few moderate- to high-income retirees and remains a GOP bastion.

Citrus is an important industry in St. Lucie County, where Indian River Citrus is known for its sweet grapefruit. Port St. Lucie quadrupled in population in the 1980s, with Republicans cutting into the county's traditional Democratic bent. Fort Pierce, which grew by a relatively modest 9 percent during the 1980s, has a wider spread of incomes than the rest of the coastal communities.

The other four counties in the district—Glades, Hendry, Highlands and Okeechobee—are largely agricultural, with some predominantly fixed-income retirees. Lake Okeechobee, which is adjacent, offers plenty of recreational opportunities for fishing and boating. In the 1992 presidential election, Ross Perot cut into George Bush's margin enough for Bill Clinton to carry Glades and Okeechobee counties.

Election Returns and Party Registration

	16th District	Democrat	Republican
1992	President*	97,621 (35.6%)	108,426 (39.5%)
	House	101,237 (39.2%)	157,322 (60.8%)
1990	Governor	86,008 (52.1%)	79,190 (47.9%)
1988	President	68,885 (35.9%)	123,220 (64.1%)
	Senate	78,873 (46.2%)	91,886 (53.8%)
1986	Governor	60,666 (40.6%)	88,584 (59.4%)
1990	Party registration†	133,538 (45.3%)	135,791 (46.0%)

*Vote for Perot was 68,452 (24.9%).   †Independent/other is greater than 5%.

Demographics

Population 562,519

Percent change from 1980 9.6%

Land area 5,273 square miles

Population per square mile 107

Counties, 1990 population
Glades 7,591	Okeechobee (pt.) 18,267
Hendry (pt.) 22,233	Palm Beach (pt.) 251,434
Highlands (pt.) 51,965	St. Lucie (pt.) 117,993
Martin (pt.) 93,036	

Cities, 1990 population (10,000 or more)
Fort Pierce (pt.) 16,132	Port St. Lucie 55,866
Greenacres City (pt.) 13,905	Royal Palm Beach (pt.) 11,753
Hobe Sound CDP 11,507	Stuart 11,936
Jupiter (pt.) 24,986	Wellington CDP (pt.) 15,958
Palm Beach Gardens (pt.) 14,963	

Race and Hispanic origin
White 93.0%
Black 4.0%
American Indian, Eskimo, or Aleut. 0.4%
Asian or Pacific Islander 0.8%
Other 1.8%
Hispanic origin 6.3%

Ancestry
American 5.2%	Italian 8.9%
Dutch 2.7%	Polish 4.2%
English 17.6%	Russian 2.4%
French 4.8%	Scotch Irish 2.7%
French Canadian 1.3%	Scottish 2.9%
German 22.8%	Swedish 1.7%
Irish 17.5%	Welsh 1.0%

Universities/colleges, 1990-1991 enrollment
Indian River Community College, Ft. Pierce 9,483

Newspapers, total circulation (in all districts)
Ft. Lauderdale Sun-Sentinel 255,270
Ft. Pierce/Port St. Lucie Tribune 24,895
Ft. Myers News-Press 92,118
Miami Herald 400,336
Stuart News 30,351
Tampa Tribune 285,163
Vero Beach Press Journal 30,475
West Palm Beach Post 178,030

Commercial television stations, affiliations
ADI: West Palm Beach-Ft. Pierce-Vero Beach (46%), Ft. Myers-Naples (37%) and Tampa-St. Petersburg (17%)
WTVX, Ft. Pierce (None)
WFLX, West Palm Beach (Fox)
WPEC, West Palm Beach (CBS)
WPTV, West Palm Beach (NBC)
WPBF, Tequesta (ABC)

Cable television systems, total subscribers
Adelphia Cable; Lake Park 81,389
Adelphia Cable; Stuart 72,859
CVI; Okeechobee 8,427
Comcast Cablevision; West Palm Beach 32,764
National Cable; Wellington 7,271
Storer Cable TV Inc.; Sebring 11,526
United Artists/TCI; Ft. Pierce 23,241

Businesses and other major employers
United Technologies Corp./Pratt & Whitney; West Palm Beach; aircraft engines/parts 6,800
Harmon Fruit Contractors Inc.; Ft. Pierce; personnel supply services 4,000
U.S. Sugar Corp.; Clewiston; field crops 2,550
Coastal Health Corp.; Stuart; accounting/auditing 1,884
Martin Memorial Hospital Assn.; Stuart 1,200
Hospital Corp. America/Lawnwood Medical Center; Ft. Pierce 1,169
A. Duda & Sons Inc.; Belle Glade; vegetables/melons 1,100
Grumman Aerospace Corp./Grumman Aircraft Systems; Stuart; aircraft 1,030
Indian River Community College; Ft. Pierce 975
Florida Power & Light Co.; Jensen Beach; electric services 723
Evans Properties Inc.; Okeechobee; farm management services 600
Jupiter Hospital Inc.; Jupiter 600
United Technologies Corp./Sikorsky Aircraft; Jupiter; aircraft 550

17th District

Southeast — Parts of North Dade County; Parts of Miami, Carol City

The 17th (see map on page 191) has the state's highest percentage of black residents and is Florida's most staunchly Democratic district. Democrats account for more than 75 percent of the registered voters, and they routinely deliver the highest percentage of votes for Democrats running statewide.

All three 1992 House aspirants were black Democrats. They were vying to represent a district that has seen widespread devastation. Starting at the Broward County line, the district runs through such northern Miami suburbs as Carol City and Opa-Locka, then picks up the impoverished Miami neighborhoods of Liberty City and Overtown. It follows U.S. 1 heading southwest to include predominantly black neighborhoods in Richmond Heights, Perrine, Homestead and Florida City. Some of these areas were leveled by Hurricane Andrew on Aug. 24, 1992.

Unincorporated Carol City is predominantly black and Hispanic. (Hispanics overall account for about one-quarter of the district's population.) Most residents are blue-collar workers who commute south to Miami. The area has a mix of single-family homes, apartments and housing projects. Opa-Locka, which suffers from high unemployment and high crime rates, is overwhelmingly black. As in the rest of the district, local political organizations usually center around churches. Opa-Locka is also noted for its Arabian theme and its large private airport.

Unincorporated Rolling Oaks is an affluent black neighborhood near Joe Robbie Stadium (home of football's Dolphins and baseball's Marlins). North Miami Beach contains some of the largest numbers of whites in the district, many of whom are Jewish retirees on fixed incomes. They are well-organized, Democratic and interested in health care and crime. The west side of North Miami, which is in the district, is a mix of blacks, whites and Hispanics, and somewhat less Democratic.

The Miami neighborhoods in the 17th include Little Haiti, which has a growing core of recent immigrants from the Caribbean. They tend to be Democrats but are not yet a political force. The black neighborhoods of Liberty City and Overtown have been plagued by economic despair and violence. A 1980 riot left 18 dead after an all-white jury acquitted four white Miami police officers in the beating death of a black insurance executive. Riots erupted again in 1989 after a Latino officer shot a black motorcyclist. Some improvements have been made— there are new apartment complexes and stores in Liberty City and the Miami Arena (home of pro basketball's Miami Heat) is reinvigorating part of Overtown—but progress is slow.

The district takes in the ethnically mixed areas of South Miami, then delves into the more rural communities near U.S. 1 that Andrew hit hard. Perrine, Richmond Heights and Florida City are heavily black; Homestead is mixed. Some residents were homeless or living in trailers for months after the hurricane struck, while others moved into northern Dade County. Homestead Air Force Base, which was hit hard by Andrew, was on the 1993 base-closure list.

Election Returns and Party Registration

	17th District	Democrat	Republican
1992	President*	99,539 (74.4%)	24,721 (18.5%)
	House	102,784 (100.0%)	—
1990	Governor	81,943 (83.0%)	16,836 (17.0%)
1988	President	83,380 (70.7%)	34,495 (29.3%)
	Senate	76,775 (73.6%)	27,566 (26.4%)
1986	Governor	74,865 (72.0%)	29,154 (28.0%)
1990	Party registration†	155,960 (78.3%)	32,552 (16.4%)

*Vote for Perot was 9,474 (7.1%).   †Independent/other is greater than 5%.

Demographics

Population 562,519

Percent change from 1980 9.6%

Land area 105 square miles

Population per square mile 5,361

Counties, 1990 population
Dade (pt.) 562,519

Cities, 1990 population (10,000 or more)

Brownsville CDP (pt.) 15,068	North Miami (pt.) 39,540
Carol City CDP (pt.) 43,858	Opa-Locka 15,283
Gladeview CDP 15,637	Palmetto Estates CDP 12,293
Golden Glades CDP 25,474	Perrine CDP (pt.) 11,574
Homestead (pt.) 13,514	Pinewood CDP 15,518
Miami (pt.) 127,376	Scott Lake CDP 14,588
North Miami Beach (pt.) 24,803	South Miami Heights CDP (pt.) 12,361
	West Little River CDP 33,575

Race and Hispanic origin
White 36.6%
Black 58.4%
American Indian, Eskimo, or Aleut. 0.2%
Asian or Pacific Islander 1.3%
Other 3.6%
Hispanic origin 23.0%

Ancestry

American 3.6%	Italian 1.9%
English 3.3%	Polish 1.2%
French 1.1%	Russian 1.0%
German 4.1%	West Indian 14.9%
Irish 3.5%	

Universities/colleges, 1990-1991 enrollment
Barry University, Miami 5,903
Flagler Career Institute, Miami 987
Florida Memorial College, Opa-Locka 1,402
St. Thomas University, Opa-Locka 2,662
Southeastern University of Health, Miami 403

Newspapers, total circulation (in all districts)
Ft. Lauderdale Sun-Sentinel 255,270
Miami Diario Las Americas (Spanish) 66,174
Miami Herald 400,336

Commercial television stations, affiliations
ADI: Miami (100%)

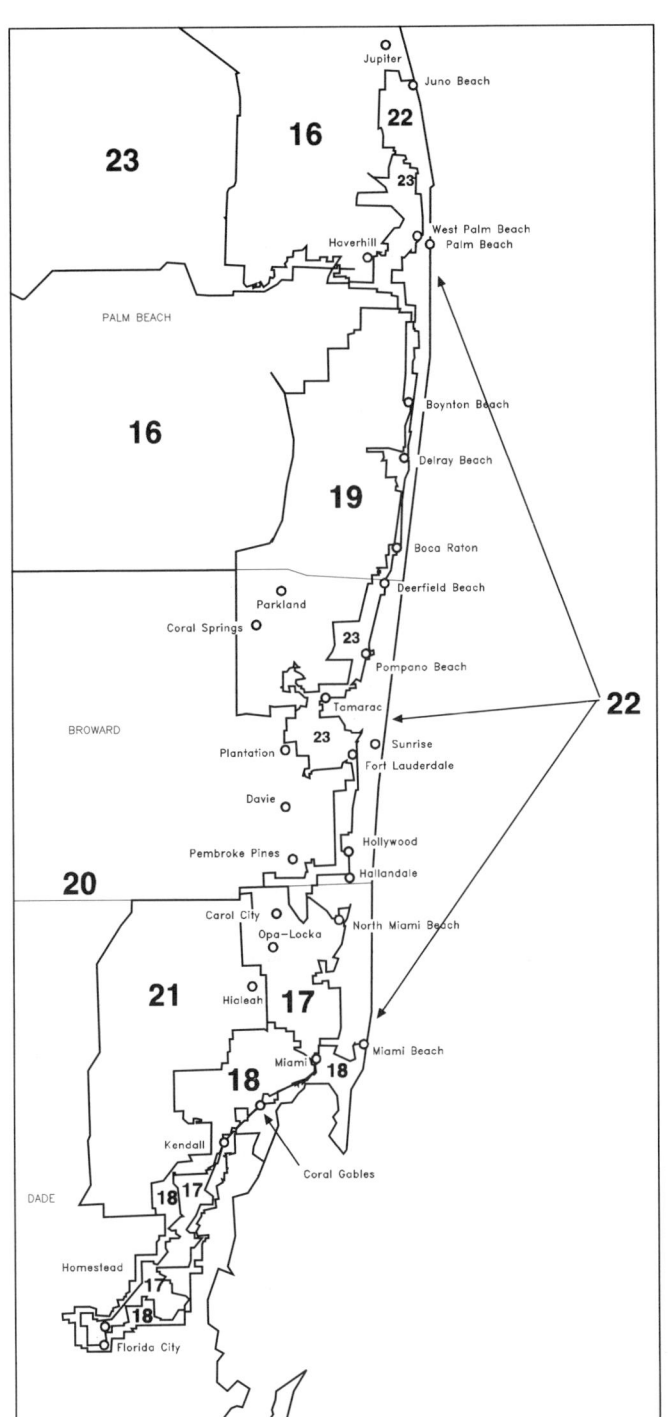

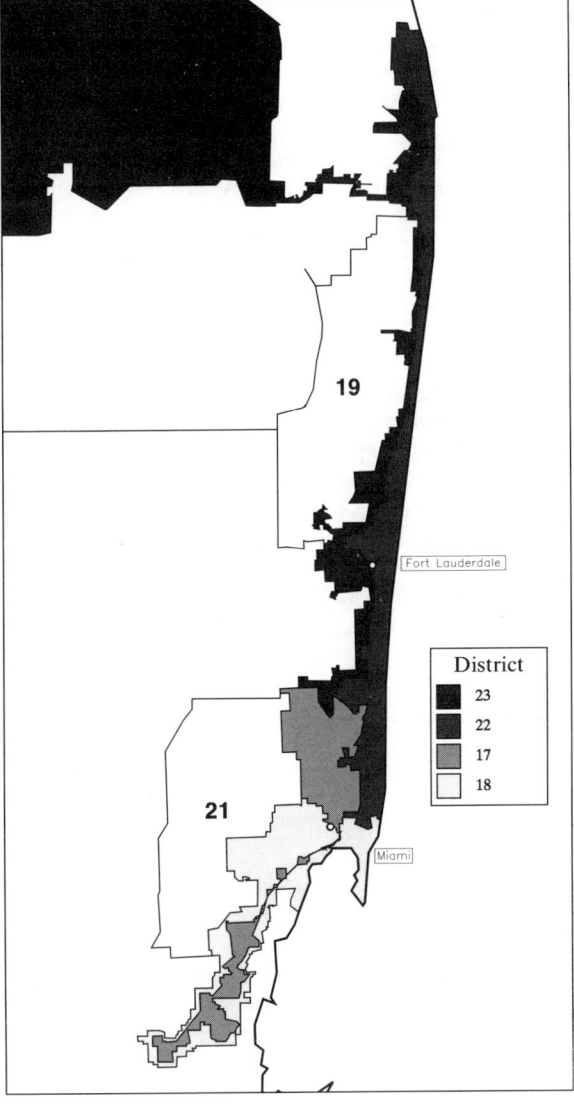

Cable television systems, total subscribers
  Adelphia Cable; Miami 56,000
  Storer Cable TV of Florida Inc.; North Dade County 89,868
  TCI of Florida; Miami 39,960

Military installations, 1991
  Homestead Air Force Base, Homestead 5,671
  Homestead Naval Security, Homestead 412

Businesses and other major employers
  State of Florida/Health Services Dept.; Miami 5,000
  University of Miami Medical School; Miami 2,000
  County of Dade/Parks & Recreation Dept.; Miami 1,900
  Cedars Medical Center Inc.; Miami 1,700
  County of Dade/Public Schools; Miami 1,600
  State of Florida/Education Dept.; Miami 1,454
  North Shore Medical Center; Miami 1,200
  American Bankers Insurance Group; Miami;
    fire/marine/casualty insurance 1,100
  Publix Super Markets Inc./Southeast Coast Div.; Miami;
    warehousing 1,000
  Paradise Island Ltd.; Miami; subdividers/developers 1,000
  Republic Health Corp./Parkway Regional Medical Center;
    Miami 1,000
  Burdines Inc./Store 1; Miami; department store 900
  Burdines Inc./Store 7; Miami; department store 900
  Sheffield Industries Inc.; Miami; knitting mills 850
  Miami Jewish Home/Hosptal for Aged/Douglas Gardens;
    Miami; nursing 850
  School Board of Dade County/North County Elementary;
    Opa-Locka 810
  Barry University; Miami 800
  Injection Footwear Corp.; Miami; footwear 750
  Entenmann's Inc.; Miami; bakery products 700
  Greenwich Air Services Inc./Batch Air Universal; Miami;
    airports/services 700
  Republic Health Corp./Coral Gables Hospital; Miami 650
  World Radio Missionary Fellowship/HCJB World Radio;
    Opa-Locka; religious organizations 650
  South Dade Healthcare Group/Deering Hospital; Miami 625
  State of Florida; Miami 600
  Bloomingdale's Inc.; Miami; department stores 550
  Sysco Food Services of South Florida; Miami; grocery
    products 550

18th District

Southeast — Parts of Dade County; Part of Miami

The 18th (see map on page 191) is one of two Hispanic-majority Florida districts. Although it includes much of downtown Miami, its spiritual heart is the inner-city neighborhood known as Little Havana.

Many of Miami's Cubans came to this country in the 1960s, fleeing Castro's takeover. Many were well-educated professionals and business people in Cuba, and they have achieved positions of status here. The Cubans, Puerto Ricans, Haitians, Nicaraguans and Colombians who have arrived more recently tend to be unskilled workers, and integrating them into society is more difficult.

The Cuban-American community for a time was consumed with discussing and plotting to overthrow Castro; U.S. elections were not a focus. They are now, and that is good news for the

GOP. The party's hawkish anticommunist stance helped persuade most Cuban voters to register Republican. That makes this a safe GOP district.

The 18th is hardly homogenous, however. South Miami Beach, traditionally home to Jewish retirees, is attracting young professionals and some Hispanics. It features the Art Deco district of colorful hotels. Downtown Miami, hit by the bankruptcies of Eastern and Pan Am airlines, focuses on international trade. Brickell Avenue contains high-rise offices, and residences for Hispanics and the upper-middle class; it is a swing area politically.

Across a causeway is Key Biscayne, an upper-middle-class suburb and one of the city's first areas to turn Republican. Richard M. Nixon used to vacation here. Back on the mainland and heading south from downtown along the coast is Coconut Grove, a trendy neighborhood that attracts young liberals. Next comes Coral Gables, home of the University of Miami (14,000 students). The southern end of Coral Gables is more white and has expensive houses and yacht clubs.

The 18th includes the east side of Kendall, an upper-middle-class suburban area that leans Republican. The district extends farther south, to include small parts of Cutler Ridge and Perrine, then loops around endangered Homestead Air Force Base into South Miami Heights. This area includes blue-collar, conservative Democrats and Cubans and was hit by Hurricane Andrew in 1992.

The west side of Kendall is somewhat more Democratic than the east side and is home to young professionals, white-collar workers, some Cubans and a Jewish community. Olympia Heights and Westchester attract middle-class Cuban-Americans from Miami who want greener spaces. Florida International University (22,500 students) is in Westchester.

Most of Miami in the 18th is south of the Miami River except for Allapattah, an older section of the city that has become more Hispanic. While many of the Cubans who arrived in Little Havana have moved elsewhere, those who remain tend to be older and less affluent. Crime tends to be more of a problem with recent refugees. The west side of the city is also predominantly Hispanic but more middle class. The Orange Bowl is in the district, as is most of Miami International Airport.

Election Returns and Party Registration

	18th District	Democrat	Republican
1992	President*	54,252 (32.6%)	94,963 (57.0%)
	House	52,142 (33.2%)	104,755 (66.8%)
1990	Governor	54,727 (49.5%)	55,919 (50.5%)
1988	President	43,805 (30.3%)	100,691 (69.7%)
	Senate	50,631 (40.3%)	74,903 (59.7%)
1986	Governor	43,591 (34.7%)	81,924 (65.3%)
1990	Party registration †	78,765 (40.2%)	99,797 (50.9%)

*Vote for Perot was 17,281 (10.4%).   †Independent/other is greater than 5%.

Demographics

Population 562,519

Percent change from 1980 9.6%

Land area 115 square miles

Population per square mile 4,889

Counties, 1990 population
Dade (pt.) 562,519

Cities, 1990 population (10,000 or more)
Coral Gables (pt.) 38,052
Coral Terrace CDP 23,255
Glenvar Heights CDP (pt.) 14,823
Kendall CDP (pt.) 28,571
Miami Beach (pt.) 33,721
Miami (pt.) 228,969
Olympia Heights CDP (pt.) 37,792
South Miami Heights CDP (pt.) 16,577
Westchester CDP (pt.) 29,883
Westwood Lakes CDP 11,522

Race and Hispanic origin
White 88.7%
Black 4.2%
American Indian, Eskimo, or Aleut. 0.1%
Asian or Pacific Islander 1.2%
Other 5.8%
Hispanic origin 66.7%

Ancestry
American 2.4%　　Italian 2.6%
English 5.2%　　Polish 1.7%
French 1.7%　　Russian 2.0%
German 6.2%　　West Indian 1.0%
Irish 4.5%

Universities/colleges, 1990-1991 enrollment
Florida International University, Miami 22,466
Miami Christian College, Miami 225
Miami-Dade Community College, Miami 43,880
University of Miami, Coral Gables 13,845

Newspapers, total circulation (in all districts)
Ft. Lauderdale Sun-Sentinel 255,270
Miami Herald 400,336
Miami Diario Las Americas (Spanish) 66,174

Commercial television stations, affiliations
ADI: Miami (100%)

Cable television systems, total subscribers
Adelphia Cable; Miami 56,000
Americable International; South Miami 8,000
Storer Cable TV of Florida Inc.; North Dade County 89,868
Storer South Dade; Miami 44,056
TCI of Florida; Miami 39,960

Businesses and other major employers
County of Dade/Public Health Trust; Miami 7,000
University of Miami; Coral Gables 4,418
U.S. Veterans Affairs Dept.; Miami; hospital 2,800
County of Dade/Metro Transit Agency; Miami 2,500
County of Dade/MDTA Mayor Overhaul; Miami 2,200
Florida Power & Light Co.; Miami; electric services 2,043
South Miami Hospital Inc.; Miami 2,000
County of Dade/Water-Sewer Authority; Miami; water supply 1,744
Miami Children's Hospital; Miami 1,650
Florida International University; Miami 1,551
Burdines Inc./Burdines; Miami; department stores 1,500
Dade County Clerk Courts; Miami 1,175

Kloster Cruise Limited/Norwegian Cruise Line; Miami; cruise line 1,000
Miami Dade Community College; Miami 1,100
U.S. Transportation Dept.; Miami 1,000
Citizens; Miami; savings institutions 889
State of Florida/Landmark Learning Center; Miami 850
Doctors Hospital; Miami 815
Ramsay-HMO Inc.; Miami; medical doctor group 800
Caterair Intl. Corp.; Miami; bars/restaurants 700
Republic National Bank of Miami; Miami; commercial banks 700
Pan American Hospital Corp.; Miami 685
Baxter Healthcare Corp.; Miami; medical instruments & pharmaceuticals 650
County of Dade/Housing & Urban Development Dept.; Miami 650
Victoria Hospital; Miami 625
TW Services Inc./Volume Services; Miami; bars/restaurants 600
Miami Dade Community College/Dade Medical Jr. College; Miami 600
Price Waterhouse; Miami; professional organizations 590
Sky Chefs Inc./Sky Chefs Div.; Miami; bars/restaurants 562
Marriott Corp./Miami Marriott Airport Hotel; Miami; hotel 550
Island Developers Ltd./The Fisher Island Club; Miami; subdividers/developers 527
Bertram-Trojan Inc.; Miami; shipbuilding 520

19th District

Southeast — Parts of Palm Beach and Northern Broward Counties; Boca Raton

The 19th (see map on page 191) is one of Florida'a most compact and most Democratic districts. It lies generally west of Interstate 95, running north-south from Lake Worth in Palm Beach County to Tamarac in Broward County. The district's population is nearly evenly split between the two counties.

The large registration edge that Democrats enjoy among voters in some other Florida districts is illusory in state and federal elections because conservative Democrats often vote Republican at the top of the ticket.

But the 19th is filled with devoted and lifelong Democrats who retired here from the Northeast. It routinely rolls up some of the state's most impressive margins for Democratic candidates. And it does so with the smallest percentage of black residents of any district in Florida. The 19th is the "whitest" of the four Florida districts that Michael S. Dukakis carried in the 1988 presidential race.

The district's retirees, many of whom are Jewish and from New York, give the area a northeastern orientation. Delicatessens and bagel bakeries are popular, and residents strongly support cultural offerings in nearby West Palm Beach and Fort Lauderdale. Health care and Social Security are vital concerns.

Although safely Democratic, the 19th has pockets of strong Republican support, and those areas are growing rapidly. Republicans are slightly more competitive in the district's Palm Beach County communities.

Lake Worth, Boynton Beach and Delray Beach are all less Democratic than the district as a whole. That is partly because they are somewhat less retirement-oriented and have a mix of young professionals and families living in single-family homes.

Boca Raton, which has some single-family homes as well as exclusive condominium subdivisions, is among the district's most Republican communities.

Also in the area are large private employers, including IBM and Siemens Stromberg Carlson (which produces telephone switching systems), both in Boca Raton, and Motorola in Boynton Beach.

Just south of the Palm Beach-Broward line lies Deerfield Beach. Many residents here are retired New Yorkers who live in middle-income condominium complexes; they vote Democratic in huge numbers.

To the west is fast-growing Coral Springs, the district's largest city, which grew by 113 percent in the 1980s. Coral Springs is also friendly territory for the Republican Party. It features upper-middle-class houses that attract professionals, some of whom commute to Fort Lauderdale.

Continuing east and south, the district picks up more Democratic strongholds. They include Margate, which has some blue-collar workers, Tamarac and Coconut Creek, which grew by two-thirds in the 1980s. Democrats can turn out impressive numbers in these areas because they are so well organized.

Election Returns and Party Registration

	19th District	Democrat	Republican
1992	President*	158,752 (53.9%)	88,829 (30.2%)
	House	177,423 (63.1%)	103,867 (36.9%)
1990	Governor	112,674 (66.0%)	58,009 (34.0%)
1988	President	105,941 (51.1%)	101,241 (48.9%)
	Senate	106,142 (58.9%)	73,935 (41.1%)
1986	Governor	86,206 (54.1%)	73,200 (45.9%)
1990	Party registration †	164,175 (51.9%)	119,181 (37.7%)

*Vote for Perot was 46,859 (15.9%).   †Independent/other is greater than 5%.

Demographics

Population 562,519

Percent change from 1980 9.7%

Land area 263 square miles

Population per square mile 2,138

Counties, 1990 population
Broward (pt.) 276,571   Palm Beach (pt.) 285,948

Cities, 1990 population (10,000 or more)
Boca Del Mar CDP 17,754   Kings Point CDP 12,422
Boca Raton (pt.) 36,076   Margate (pt.) 42,058
Boynton Beach (pt.) 24,723   North Lauderdale (pt.)
Coconut Creek (pt.) 27,483   13,344
Coral Springs 79,443   Pompano Beach (pt.)
Deerfield Beach (pt.)   10,657
  22,087   Sandalfoot Cove CDP
Delray Beach (pt.) 18,113   14,214
Hamptons at Boca Raton   Sunrise (pt.) 15,927
  CDP 11,686   Tamarac (pt.) 36,292

Race and Hispanic origin
White 94.8%
Black 2.7%
American Indian, Eskimo, or Aleut. 0.1%
Asian or Pacific Islander 1.4%
Other 0.9%
Hispanic origin 6.2%

Ancestry
American 4.3%   Italian 12.8%
Austrian 2.1%   Polish 8.0%
Dutch 1.6%   Romanian 1.1%
English 10.9%   Russian 10.1%
French 3.3%   Scotch Irish 1.5%
German 18.0%   Scottish 2.0%
Hungarian 2.1%   Swedish 1.4%
Irish 13.9%   West Indian 1.4%

Universities/colleges, 1990-1991 enrollment
Florida Atlantic University, Boca Raton 12,767
Lynn University, Boca Raton 957
Palm Beach Community College, Lake Worth 13,121

Newspapers, total circulation (in all districts)
Ft. Lauderdale Sun-Sentinel 255,270
Miami Diario Las Americas (Spanish) 66,174
Miami Herald 400,336
West Palm Beach Post 178,030

Commercial television stations, affiliations
ADI: West Palm Beach-Ft. Pierce-Vero Beach (65%) and
  Miami (35%)

Cable television systems, total subscribers
Adelphia Cable; Lake Park 81,389
Cable TV of Coral Springs; Coral Springs 23,436
Comcast Cablevision; Boynton Beach 15,444
Comcast Cablevision/Boca Raton; Boca Raton 17,000
Continental Cablevision of Florida; Pompano Beach 148,929
Leadership Cablevision; Delray Beach 35,000
Tele-Media Co.; Boca Raton 5,712
Tele-Media Co.; Deerfield Beach 8,508
Telecable of Broward County; Margate 29,427
West Boca Cable; Boca Raton 27,111

Businesses and other major employers
Florida Atlantic University; Boca Raton 2,056
Motorola Inc.; Boynton Beach; communications equipment
  2,000
Boca Raton Community Hospital; Boca Raton 1,680
Bethesda Memorial Hospital; Boynton Beach 1,555
JFK Medical Center Inc.; Lake Worth 1,350
Siemens Stromberg Carlson; Boca Raton;
  engineering/architectural services 1,100
Palm Beach Community College; Lake Worth 1,049
J. M. Family Enterprises Inc.; Deerfield Beach; motor
  vehicles/parts/supplies 1,000
City of Sunrise; Ft. Lauderdale 900
National Medical Enterprises/Delray Community Hospital;
  Delray Beach 850
Nationl Council on Compensation Insurance Inc.; Boca
  Raton; workers' compensation insurance 700
Coral Springs Medical Center; Pompano Beach 700
National Medical Enterprises/West Boca Medical Center;
  Boca Raton 700
Sensormatic Electronics Corp.; Deerfield Beach;
  search/navigation equipment 647

City of Coral Springs; Pompano Beach   625
University Hospital Ltd.; Ft. Lauderdale   550

20th District

South — Southern and Western Broward County;
Hollywood; the Keys

While the two cultures that coexist in the 20th are as different as the music of Lawrence Welk and Jimmy Buffett, the retirees and suburbanites of Broward County hold the key to political success in the 20th.

The portion of Broward County in the 20th holds 75 percent of the district's residents. Though Republicans can be competitive here, voters typically support Democrats in statewide elections.

Democrats derive their pivotal backing in Broward from planned retirement villages with heavily Jewish populations, such as Sunrise Lakes. Many of the middle-income retirees who dwell in these sprawling developments hail from areas of New York where (generally speaking) everyone voted, and everyone voted Democratic. The city of Hollywood, part of which is in the district, also reflects that tradition.

But another important and growing voting bloc in the 20th is the young people who are moving into Broward bedroom communities such as Pembroke Pines (population 65,000), the largest city wholly within the district, and Cooper City (population 21,000). Pembroke Pines grew more than 80 percent in the 1980s, and Cooper City's population almost doubled.

With virtually no industry in the district, the mainly white professionals and midlevel managers commute to jobs in Miami and Fort Lauderdale. In the mid-1980s, I-595 was built largely to accommodate them.

The Dade County portion of the district is the least significant politically, with only 29,000 registered voters. Hurricane Andrew hammered the largely agricultural community of Homestead in 1992; community leaders hope that the planned closing of Homestead Air Force Base, part of which is in the 20th, will not cause a mass exodus of the active duty and retired military personnel who live in the area alongside a significant Hispanic population.

Much of the district's land area, particularly in western Dade and mainland Monroe counties, has practically no people, but it teems with life: The Florida Everglades is here; it is the largest subtropical wilderness in the United States. Currently, there is great concern that development and other examples of human influence may have irrevocably altered the fragile environment.

Virtually all of Monroe County's 78,000 residents live on the Florida Keys, which stretch 135 miles from the mainland to Key West, the largest city on the Keys, in the Gulf of Mexico. With its traditions of tolerance, independence and even lawlessness, Key West has a unique political culture. The significant homosexual community routinely forms alliances with Republican environmentalists who battle an entrenched Democratic power structure. Many of these Republicans will not hesitate to vote for a Democrat for statewide office, if he or she has strong environmentalist credentials.

Election Returns and Party Registration

	20th District	Democrat	Republican
1992	President*	116,547 (46.8%)	83,626 (33.6%)
	House †	130,959 (55.1%)	91,589 (38.5%)
1990	Governor	94,980 (65.6%)	49,769 (34.4%)
1988	President	85,726 (46.7%)	97,774 (53.3%)
	Senate	101,039 (58.4%)	71,954 (41.6%)
1986	Governor	77,260 (52.1%)	71,154 (47.9%)
1990	Party registration †	158,361 (55.0%)	106,550 (37.0%)

Vote for Perot was 48,845 (19.6%).   †Independent/other is greater than 5%.

Demographics

Population   562,518

Percent change from 1980   (new district in the 1990s)

Land area   3,460 square miles

Population per square mile   163

Counties, 1990 population
Broward (pt.)   421,015   Monroe   78,024
Dade (pt.)   63,479

Cities, 1990 population   (10,000 or more)
Cooper City 20,791	Key Largo CDP 11,336
Cutler Ridge CDP (pt.) 13,639	Key West 24,832
	Lauderhill (pt.) 10,694
Davie 47,217	Miramar (pt.) 27,422
Fort Lauderdale (pt.) 17,595	Pembroke Pines 65,452
	Plantation (pt.) 61,296
Hollywood (pt.) 71,510	Sunrise (pt.) 43,400

Race and Hispanic origin
White   92.1%
Black   4.4%
American Indian, Eskimo, or Aleut.   0.3%
Asian or Pacific Islander   1.6%
Other   1.6%
Hispanic origin   12.3%

Ancestry
American 4.7%	Italian 11.1%
Austrian 1.2%	Polish 5.8%
Dutch 1.6%	Russian 5.6%
English 12.7%	Scotch Irish 1.8%
French 3.8%	Scottish 2.1%
German 18.9%	Swedish 1.4%
Hungarian 1.4%	West Indian 2.0%
Irish 15.5%	

Universities/colleges, 1990-1991 enrollment
Broward Community College, Fort Lauderdale   21,682
Florida Keys Community College, Key West   1,840
Nova University, Fort Lauderdale   9,562

Newspapers, total circulation (in all districts)
Ft. Lauderdale Sun-Sentinel   255,270
Key West Citizen   7,833
Miami Diario Las Americas (Spanish)   66,174
Miami Herald   400,336

Commercial television stations, affiliations
ADI: Miami (100%)
WCIX, Miami (CBS)

Cable television systems, total subscribers
  Adelphia Cable; Miami 56,000
  Jones Intercable Inc.; Davie 45,000
  Selkirk Communications Inc.; Ft. Lauderdale 68,000
  Storer Cable; Hollywood 29,396
  Storer Cable TV of Florida Inc.; North Dade County 89,868
  TCI of Florida; Key Largo 9,194
  TCI of Florida; Key West 10,471

Military installations, 1991
  Key West Naval Air Station, Key West 4,234

Businesses and other major employers
  American Express Travel Related Services; Ft. Lauderdale; credit institutions 4,000
  Broward Community College; Hollywood 3,095
  Motorola Inc./Radio Products Group; Ft. Lauderdale; communications equipment 3,000
  Memorial Hospital; Hollywood 2,561
  Racal Data Communications Inc.; Ft. Lauderdale; communications equipment 1,300
  Nova University; Ft. Lauderdale 1,150
  Medical Personnel Pool; Hollywood; personnel supply services 1,030
  City of Pembroke Pines; Hollywood 896
  Florida Power & Light Co./Turkey Point Fossil Plants; Homestead; electric services 823
  County of Monroe/Public Works Dept.; Key West 800
  Humana Medical Plan Inc.; Hollywood; medical doctors 800
  Humana Inc./Humana Hospital; Ft. Lauderdale 755
  Encore Computer Corp.; Ft. Lauderdale; computers 700
  Burger King Corp.; Miami; fast-food chain 700
  Hollywood Medical Center Inc.; Hollywood 700
  National Bancard Corp./Nabanco; Ft. Lauderdale; business services 700
  Humana Inc./Humana Hospital Pembroke; Hollywood 664
  City of Plantation; Ft. Lauderdale 650
  Macy's South Inc.; Ft. Lauderdale; department stores 600

21st District

Southeast — Part of Dade County; Hialeah

Of South Florida's two Hispanic-majority districts, the 21st is the newest both politically and in its history as a Hispanic stronghold.

The 21st (see map on page 191) is immediately west of the black-majority 17th District and Hispanic-majority 18th. While the focus of the 18th is Little Havana, where 1960s Cuban exiles settled, the 21st centers on Hialeah, where many of those exiles later relocated. The 21st has the state's highest percentage of Hispanics—70 percent. Republicans make impressive showings here. George Bush captured 71 percent in 1988 and 58 percent in 1992.

Much of the district's fierce Republicanism can be traced to Hialeah, which accounts for about one-third of district residents. Hialeah began growing rapidly after World War II, when many soldiers who trained in south Florida moved to the area. In the 1960s and 1970s, it became increasingly popular with middle- to low-income Cuban-Americans looking for more space than they could find in Miami. Its location near the airport made it accessible to jobs there, and it offered a mix of midsize single-family homes and apartment complexes.

Hialeah also has a large industrial area. Much of the apparel industry there has been struggling recently with competition from imports, especially from Caribbean countries that have cheaper labor costs. UPS has its main south Florida facility near here. Also present is the Hialeah racetrack. State and national politicians make a point of stopping by Chico's to eat black beans and rice, drink Cuban coffee and shake hands.

Farther south is Miami Springs, a largely Republican and white bedroom suburb of Miami. An unincorporated area west of the airport, known as Doral, is growing fast thanks to industry and corporate relocations. Ryder Systems, with its truck and airplane rentals, has its world headquarters here. Carnival Cruise Lines, a district office of the Federal Reserve and IVAX, a biotechnology company, also are in the area. There is also some light industry, primarily distribution centers with economic ties to the airport.

Sweetwater, another predominantly Hispanic municipality, attracts Cubans and Nicaraguans and has a high concentration of elderly residents.

The fast-growing area of Kendall in the district is generally white, but it also has some second-generation Cuban-Americans. It is considerably more Democratic than the district as a whole. Kendall Lakes is more compact, conservative and older, with smaller lots than Kendall and less rapid growth.

Tamiami is a generally Hispanic area, with young professionals in single-family homes. Its strong Republican orientation rivals that of Hialeah.

Election Returns and Party Registration

	21st District	Democrat	Republican
1992	President*	45,561 (31.1%)	85,342 (58.3%)
	House†	—	—
1990	Governor	40,369 (48.9%)	42,148 (51.1%)
1988	President	32,989 (28.6%)	82,212 (71.4%)
	Senate	39,142 (39.2%)	60,731 (60.8%)
1986	Governor	30,460 (34.7%)	57,308 (65.3%)
1990	Party registration‡	59,585 (36.8%)	87,422 (54.0%)

Vote for Perot was 15,501 (10.6%). †No votes tabulated; Republican candidate ran unopposed. ‡Independent/other is greater than 5%.

Demographics

Population 562,519

Percent change from 1980 (new district in the 1990s)

Land area 238 square miles

Population per square mile 2,367

Counties, 1990 population
  Dade (pt.) 562,519

Cities, 1990 population (10,000 or more)
  Hammocks CDP 10,897
  Hialeah (pt.) 183,233
  Kendale Lakes CDP 48,524
  Kendall CDP (pt.) 43,393
  Lindgren Acres CDP 22,290
  Miami Lakes CDP 12,750
  Miami Springs (pt.) 13,268
  Sweetwater 13,909
  Tamiami CDP (pt.) 33,845

Race and Hispanic origin

White 87.6%
Black 4.1%
American Indian, Eskimo, or Aleut. 0.1%
Asian or Pacific Islander 1.5%
Other 6.7%
Hispanic origin 69.6%

Ancestry

American 2.4%	Italian 3.1%
English 3.8%	Polish 1.4%
French 1.4%	Russian 1.4%
German 5.5%	West Indian 1.7%
Irish 4.0%	

Universities/colleges, 1990-1991 enrollment

Caribbean Center for Advanced Study, Miami 243

Newspapers, total circulation (in all districts)

Ft. Lauderdale Sun-Sentinel 255,270
Miami Diario Las Americas (Spanish) 66,174
Miami Herald 400,336

Commercial television stations, affiliations

ADI: Miami (100%)

Cable television systems, total subscribers

Adelphia Cable; Miami 56,000
Storer Cable TV of Florida Inc.; North Dade County 89,868
Storer South Dade; Miami 44,056

Businesses and other major employers

Baptist Hospital of Miami; Miami 3,000
Coulter Corp.; Hialeah; lab apparatus/analyzers 2,500
System One Holding Inc./System One Corp.; Miami; tranportation/computer services 2,000
Southern Bell Telephone & Telegraph Co.; Miami; telephone communications 1,520
Hialeah Hospital; Hialeah 1,400
Ryder System Inc.; Miami; truck rentals 1,322
Suave Shoe Corp.; Hialeah; footwear 1,200
Palmetto General; Hialeah 1,200
Cordis Corp.; Hialeah; medical instruments/supplies 1,150
Trailer Marine Transport Corp.; Miami; freight shipping 1,000
John Alden Financial Corp.; Miami; life insurance 1,000
County of Dade/Solid Waste Mgt. Dept.; Miami 1,000
Carol Management Corp./Doral Resort & Country Club; Miami; hotels/retail stores 900
Gator Industries Inc.; Hialeah; footwear 896
J. I. Kislak Inc.; Hialeah; mortgage bankers 803
Baxter Healthcare Corp.; Miami; medical instruments/supplies 800
State of Florida/Retardation Health Dept.; Opa-Locka 791
Rinker Materials Corp.; Hialeah; concrete/gypsum/plaster products 700
Prestressed Systems Industries/Basch Products; Miami; concrete/building products 700
State of Florida/Transportation Dept.; Miami 700
Kendall Regional Medical Center; Miami 700
Fleming Companies Inc.; Miami; grocery products 600
Amerifirst Federal Savings Bank; Miami; savings institutions 600
Citibank Federal Savings Bank/Citicorp Savings of Florida; Miami; commercial banks 600

Barnett Bank of Jacksonville; Hialeah; commercial banks 600
County of Dade/High School District; Miami 550
TPL Cordis Inc.; Hialeah; medical instruments/supplies 514
Palm Springs General Hospital; Hialeah 510

22nd District

Southeast — Coastal Broward, Dade and Palm Beach Counties; Fort Lauderdale

The 22nd is a long shoestring of a district, hugging the south Atlantic coast from Juno Beach south to Miami Beach (see map on page 191). It is roughly 90 miles long and in some places just a few blocks wide. Its width never extends beyond 3 miles.

The strange shape, which enables the 22nd to pick up fragments of about 50 different municipalities, was dictated largely by the desire to place minority-oriented neighborhoods in districts to the west, notably the 23rd. Four House incumbents lived within its borders when the 22nd was drawn in 1992.

Most residents of the coastal neighborhoods are white, and their economic status ranges from comfortable to wealthy. Corporate executives abound. There are also quite a few retirees in oceanfront condominiums.

The district is less Republican than the state overall, and thus competitive politically. Although George Bush captured 57 percent of the presidential vote here in 1988, he lost the district in 1992.

Democrats start with a solid base in the Dade County portions of the district; Republicans have a clear edge in the Palm Beach part.

Within the borders of the 22nd are the ports of Palm Beach and Fort Lauderdale, as well as the mouth of the port of Miami. The district also contains the Miami Beach and Fort Lauderdale convention centers, the performing arts center in Miami Beach, the famous Breakers hotel in Palm Beach and Fountainbleau in Miami Beach, fashionable shopping areas such as Worth Avenue in Palm Beach and Las Olas Boulevard in Fort Lauderdale, and miles upon miles of beaches.

The city of Palm Beach is affluent and staunchly Republican. Democrats fare slightly better in the areas of West Palm Beach in the district.

Partisan orientations vary considerably among the municipalities within Broward County. Hallandale is strongly Democratic, while Hollywood is more competitive.

Republicans hold the upper hand in Pompano Beach and Fort Lauderdale, which has the largest concentration of district residents. Fort Lauderdale is dominated by conservative Democrats and Republicans, an outgrowth of the conservative retirees who settled there from the Midwest three decades ago. Fort Lauderdale is still less influenced by the liberal attitudes of northeastern Jewish émigrés than are most other major south Florida cities. Even the Jewish voters who do live in the city tend not to vote as a bloc.

The Dade County portions of the district have more of the northeastern influence. These southernmost stretches of the 22nd are heavily Jewish and Hispanic.

Election Returns and Party Registration

	22nd District	Democrat	Republican
1992	President*	114,938 (44.5%)	98,148 (38.0%)
	House†	91,625 (37.1%)	128,400 (52.0%)

22nd District		Democrat	Republican
1990	Governor	97,618 (58.4%)	69,510 (41.6%)
1988	President	91,764 (42.7%)	123,148 (57.3%)
	Senate	98,100 (51.9%)	90,903 (48.1%)
1986	Governor	87,188 (45.4%)	104,927 (54.6%)
1990	Party registration†	150,189 (47.2%)	138,528 (43.5%)

*Vote for Perot was 45,134 (17.5%).   †Independent/other is greater than 5%.

Demographics

Population 562,519

Percent change from 1980 (new district in the 1990s)

Land area 128 square miles

Population per square mile 4,405

Counties, 1990 population
Broward (pt.) 267,489	Palm Beach (pt.) 129,688
Dade (pt.) 165,342	

Cities, 1990 population (10,000 or more)
Aventura CDP (pt.) 14,914	North Miami Beach (pt.)
Boca Raton (pt.) 13,908	10,556
Deerfield Beach (pt.)	North Miami (pt.) 10,458
13,209	North Palm Beach 11,343
Fort Lauderdale (pt.)	Oakland Park (pt.) 24,474
70,157	Ojus CDP (pt.) 14,671
Hallandale (pt.) 26,979	Pompano Beach (pt.)
Hollywood (pt.) 32,712	33,485
Ives Estates CDP 13,531	Sunny Isles CDP 11,772
Lake Worth (pt.) 11,641	West Palm Beach (pt.)
Lighthouse Point 10,378	22,851
Miami Beach (pt.) 58,918	Wilton Manors 11,804

Race and Hispanic origin
White 94.2%
Black 3.0%
American Indian, Eskimo, or Aleut. 0.1%
Asian or Pacific Islander 1.1%
Other 1.7%
Hispanic origin 12.8%

Ancestry
American 4.2%	Irish 13.4%
Austrian 1.5%	Italian 9.0%
Dutch 1.6%	Polish 6.0%
English 12.6%	Russian 6.7%
French 4.0%	Scotch Irish 1.8%
French Canadian 1.2%	Scottish 2.3%
German 17.2%	Swedish 1.4%
Hungarian 1.7%	West Indian 1.3%

Universities/colleges, 1990-1991 enrollment
Art Institute of Ft. Lauderdale, Ft. Lauderdale 1,893
Ft. Lauderdale College, Ft. Lauderdale 444
International Fine Arts College, Miami 446
National Educational Center-Bauder College, Ft. Lauderdale 723
Prospect Hall College, Hollywood 260

Newspapers, total circulation (in all districts)
Ft. Lauderdale Sun-Sentinel 255,270
Miami Diario Las Americas (Spanish) 66,174
Miami Herald 400,336
West Palm Beach Post 178,030

Commercial television stations, affiliations
ADI: Miami (63%) and West Palm Beach-Ft. Pierce-Vero Beach (37%)

Cable television systems, total subscribers
Continental Cablevision of Florida; Pompano Beach 148,929
Selkirk Communications Inc.; Fort Lauderdale 68,000
Selkirk Communications Inc.; Hallandale 11,500
Storer Cable; Hollywood 29,396
Storer Cable TV of Florida Inc.; North Dade County 89,868

Businesses and other major employers
Mount Sinai Medical Center; Miami 2,750
Southern Bell Telephone & Telegraph Co.; Ft. Lauderdale; telephone communications 1,700
Boca Raton Hotel & Club; Boca Raton; hotel 1,400
Holy Cross Hospital Inc.; Ft. Lauderdale 1,300
Hotelerama Associates Ltd./Fontainebleau Hilton Resort; Miami; hotel 1,200
Good Samaritan Medical Center; West Palm Beach 1,150
Palm Beach Newspapers Inc.; West Palm Beach; newspapers 1,000
Miami Heart Institute; Miami 950
Marriott Corp./Harbor Beach Resort; Ft. Lauderdale; hotel 900
Florida Power & Light Co.; West Palm Beach; electric services 850
Palm Beach Gardens Medical Center; West Palm Beach 850
Advanced Telecom Corp./ATC Long Distance; Boca Raton; telephone communications 800
American Medical Intl.; Ft. Lauderdale 800
St. Francis Hospital; Miami 750
Breakers Palm Beach Inc./Breakers Hotel; Palm Beach; hotel 750
Humana Inc./Humana Hospital Biscayne; Miami 700
Select Export Corp./Trident of North America; Ft. Lauderdale; office/art supplies 650
FDR Washington Inc./Monte Carlo; Ft. Lauderdale; bars/restaurants 635
Marriott Corp./Ft. Lauderdale Marriot Hotel; Ft. Lauderdale; hotel 607
Turnbrry Isle Yacht Country Club; Miami; recreation services 600
Imperial Point Hospital; Ft. Lauderdale 600
County of Palm Beach; West Palm Beach 600
School Board Palm Beach County; West Palm Beach 600
ITT Sheraton Corp./Sheraton; Miami; hotel 575
United Tech Opt. Systems; West Palm Beach; measuring/controlling devices 550
Omni International Hotel; Miami; hotel 520

23rd District

Southeast — Parts of St. Lucie, Martin, Broward and Palm Beach Counties

One of the most unusual characteristics of Florida's congressional map for the 1990s is the kite-like 23rd. The district extends over seven counties. Most of its land mass is in western St. Lucie,

Martin and Palm Beach counties, near Lake Okeechobee. But most of the people in the 23rd live inland from the Atlantic, along a narrow strip that follows Interstate 95. Half the district residents live in Broward County; one-third live in Palm Beach County.

The district is heavily Democratic and designed to help black House candidates, but the election of a black is not assured. Blacks account for only a bare majority of the district's total population and about 44 percent of its voting-age population. The black Democratic nominee for the House won in 1992 with 58 percent.

Agriculture dominates the western part of the district. Western St. Lucie and Martin counties as well as southeast Okeechobee County is citrus territory, with vegetable and lettuce crops also attracting some migrant workers. The sugar industry has a strong presence near Belle Glade in western Palm Beach County. Although Okeechobee is mostly white, the rest of this part of the district includes a high percentage of blacks and some Hispanics. The northeastern part of the district also extends into Fort Pierce to include most of its black neighborhoods.

The long strip of the district that runs adjacent to I-95 includes many public-sector workers, especially for county government and public schools. Public employee unions are strong political organizing forces, as are neighborhood associations.

The residents of Riviera Beach, an overwhelmingly black city, cast an extraordinarily high percentage of their votes for Democrats. Most residents are middle class, and some work at the nearby Pratt & Whitney plant. The portions of West Palm Beach in the district, which are also majority-black, include some neighborhoods that attract professionals. The portions that are in the 23rd from Delray Beach and Boynton Beach are about one-half black, Lake Worth is a little less so, and the part of Boca Raton included is overwhelmingly white and a GOP enclave.

Heading into Broward, the parts of Deerfield Beach and especially Pompano Beach in the 23rd are majority black. Deerfield Beach is mainly lower-middle class, with some farm workers commuting west, while Pompano is more middle-class oriented.

The district broadens somewhat in Broward County to include mainly black neighborhoods in Fort Lauderdale and, to the west, Lauderhill and Lauderdale Lakes. But it also includes predominantly white areas of Lauderdale Lakes that are middle class and, in some cases, retirement-oriented. Norland, a predominantly black community, accounts for most of the district's residents in Dade County.

Election Returns and Party Registration

	23rd District	Democrat	Republican
1992	President*	96,629 (63.1%)	34,659 (22.6%)
	House †	84,249 (58.5%)	44,807 (31.1%)
1990	Governor	70,870 (72.2%)	27,253 (27.8%)
1988	President	78,122 (60.7%)	50,556 (39.3%)
	Senate	79,059 (66.7%)	39,432 (33.3%)
1986	Governor	71,421 (62.3%)	43,234 (37.7%)
1990	Party registration †	151,285 (69.2%)	53,762 (24.6%)

*Vote for Perot was 21,967 (14.3%).   †Independent/other is greater than 5%.

Demographics

Population 562,519

Percent change from 1980 (new district in the 1990s)

Land area 1,230 square miles

Population per square mile 457

Counties, 1990 population

Broward (pt.) 290,413
Dade (pt.) 20,716
Hendry (pt.) 3,540
Martin (pt.) 7,864
Okeechobee (pt.) 11,360
Palm Beach (pt.) 196,448
St. Lucie (pt.) 32,178

Cities, 1990 population (10,000 or more)

Belle Glade (pt.) 10,902
Boca Raton (pt.) 11,508
Boynton Beach (pt.) 16,200
Deerfield Beach (pt.) 11,029
Delray Beach (pt.) 21,539
Fort Lauderdale (pt.) 59,553
Fort Pierce (pt.) 20,698
Hollywood (pt.) 17,475
Lake Worth (pt.) 12,146
Lauderdale Lakes (pt.) 26,176
Lauderhill (pt.) 29,098
Miramar (pt.) 13,241
Norland CDP (pt.) 15,341
North Lauderdale (pt.) 13,162
Pompano Beach Highlands CDP (pt.) 11,809
Pompano Beach (pt.) 28,269
Riviera Beach (pt.) 21,056
West Palm Beach (pt.) 35,608

Race and Hispanic origin

White 44.8%
Black 51.6%
American Indian, Eskimo, or Aleut. 0.2%
Asian or Pacific Islander 0.9%
Other 2.4%
Hispanic origin 9.4%

Ancestry

American 4.3%
Dutch 1.1%
English 6.1%
French 2.1%
German 9.0%
Irish 7.5%
Italian 4.6%
Polish 2.2%
Russian 1.4%
Scottish 1.1%
West Indian 11.1%

Universities/colleges, 1990-1991 enrollment

New England Institute Tech, West Palm Beach 649
Palm Beach Atlantic College, West Palm Beach 1,535

Newspapers, total circulation (in all districts)

Ft. Lauderdale Sun-Sentinel 255,270
Ft. Pierce/Port St. Lucie Tribune 24,895
Le Journal De Montreal 2,261
Miami Herald 400,336
Vero Beach Press Journal 30,475
West Palm Beach Post 178,030

Commercial television stations, affiliations

ADI: West Palm Beach-Ft. Pierce-Vero Beach (95%) and Miami (5%)
WSCV, Ft. Lauderdale (None)
WYHS, Hollywood (None)
WBFS-TV, Miami (None)
WHFT, Miami (None)
WPLG, Miami (ABC)
WDZL, Miami (None)
WSVN, Miami (Fox)
WTVJ, Miami (NBC)

Cable television systems, total subscribers

Adelphia Cable; Lake Park 81,389

Adelphia Cable; Stuart 72,859
Continental Cablevision of Florida; Pompano Beach 148,929
Jones Intercable Inc.; Davie 45,000
Leadership Cablevision; Delray Beach 35,000
Selkirk Communications Inc.; Fort Lauderdale 68,000
United Artists/TCI; Fort Pierce 23,241

Businesses and other major employers

American Airlines Inc.; Miami; airline 3,168
State of Florida/Health & Rehab Services Dept.; Ft. Lauderdale 3,000
St. Marys Hospital Inc.; West Palm Beach 2,500
County of Palm Beach/Sheriffs Office; West Palm Beach 2,037
U.S. Postal Service; Ft. Lauderdale 2,000
County of Broward/Sheriffs Office; Ft. Lauderdale 2,000
City of Hollywood; Hollywood 1,600
Southern Bell Telephone & Telegraph Co.; West Palm Beach; telephone communications 1,500
Florida Medical Center Ltd.; Ft. Lauderdale 1,500
Glendale Federal Bank; Ft. Lauderdale; savings institutions 1,300
Allied-Signal Inc./Bendix King Air Transport; Ft. Lauderdale; search/navigation equipment 1,060

News & Sun Sentinel Co.; Deerfield Beach; newspapers 1,000
County of Broward; Ft. Lauderdale 1,000
North Broward Medical Center; Pompano Beach 983
City of Boca Raton; Boca Raton 964
Hospital Development Service/Plantation General Hospital; Ft. Lauderdale 950
Broward County Jail; Ft. Lauderdale 900
North American Philips Corp.; West Palm Beach; electrical industrial apparatus 820
County of Palm Beach/Health Dept; West Palm Beach 800
Martin Marietta Corp./Perry Technologies; West Palm Beach; electronic components 650
Community Hospital Palm Beach/Humana Hospital Palm Beach; West Palm Beach 630
News & Sun Sentinel Co./Sun Sentinel; Ft. Lauderdale; newspapers 600
County of Broward/Environmental Service Office; Pompano Beach 600
South Florida Water Mgt. District; West Palm Beach 600
Solitron Devices Inc.; West Palm Beach; electronic components 557
Publix Super Markets Inc./Distribution Center; Deerfield Beach; warehousing 520

Georgia

Republican House candidates in Georgia enjoyed a breakthrough year in 1992. Long consigned to one House seat in what had been a 10-member delegation, the GOP picked up four of the state's 11 seats in 1992. (Thanks to healthy population growth during the 1980s, Georgia had gained a House seat in 1990 reapportionment.)

The GOP upswing occurred even though the Democratic Party controlled all the levers of the redistricting process in Georgia, with Gov. Zell Miller and the overwhelmingly Democratic state Legislature in charge. However, Republican officials played a part in undercutting that Democratic dominance by supporting the efforts of minority-group activists to increase black representation in the Georgia House delegation—a strategy that was not without political irony.

Although minority voters had for years overwhelmingly favored Democratic candidates in most places, the GOP supported more majority-minority districts in Georgia in the hope that their outreach effort might at least ease the antipathy many black and Hispanic voters held for the conservative-oriented Republican Party.

But Republican strategists made no effort to disguise their short-term goal, which was hardly unselfish if not a little Machiavellian. The Republicans anticipated that in order to create more minority districts, the mainly black and Hispanic constituencies would have to be drawn from the districts of incumbent white Democratic House members who had strongly relied on the Democratic habits of the minority-group voters. These members would then be left with districts that would be more white, conservative and potentially accommodating to Republican candidates.

Under the previous district map, Georgia had one black-majority district, the Atlanta-based 5th. With the 1990 census showing that blacks made up 27 percent of the state's residents, minority-rights activists argued that black candidates should have at least a solid shot of winning in three of the 11 districts.

State Democrats initially attempted to finesse the issue. In January 1992, the Legislature passed and Miller signed a redistricting plan that maintained the Atlanta black-majority seat and created a second black-majority district, the 11th, stretching from the Atlanta outskirts east to the city of Augusta and south to Savannah, picking up some largely black rural territory in between.

However, Georgia is one of those states that must have its redistricting plans approved by the U.S. Justice Department under the Voting Rights Act. And Justice rejected the remap on the grounds that it diluted black voting strength by maintaining a 2nd District in rural southwest Georgia that had a slim majority.

The Justice Department also rejected a second map produced by the Legislature, which created a 2nd District with a 49 percent black population. Finally, the Legislature gave in, redrawing the 2nd so that it would have a 57 percent black population. Although it remained heavily Democratic, the demographic change was politically fatal for the 2nd's white Democratic incumbent, who was defeated by black state Sen. Sanford D. Bishop in the 1992 Democratic primary.

In Georgia, party protection during the redistricting was superseded by an overriding goal: an effort to unseat Republican Rep. Newt Gingrich, the House minority whip and an outspoken conservative antagonist of Democrats both nationally and locally. The Democratic remap dismembered Gingrich's existing district, which had stretched from the southern Atlanta suburbs west through rural areas to the Alabama border. The new 6th District, in the north and west suburbs of Atlanta, included none of Gingrich's former constituency. However, Gingrich thwarted the Democratic scheme to unseat him. He moved to the new 6th, eked out a narrow primary win, then scored an easier win in the heavily Republican district.

Meanwhile, the redistricting machinations contributed directly to the defeat of one Democratic House incumbent, whose 3rd District absorbed much of Gingrich's former south suburban GOP territory.

Other Republican seat gains were in the newly created 4th District in Atlanta's fast-growing eastern suburbs and in the conservative-leaning southeast Georgia 1st District that had been vacated by a retiring Democrat.

Like most southern states, Georgia has frequently suspended its Democratic voting traditions in presidential contests, backing Republicans Barry M. Goldwater in 1964, Richard M. Nixon in 1972, Ronald Reagan in 1984 and George Bush in 1988. (Native Georgian Jimmy Carter carried the state easily during his victorious 1976 campaign and held on to it during his landslide loss to Reagan in 1980.)

However, Republican voting for lower offices has hardly become a habit. As of 1993, Georgia had not had a Republican

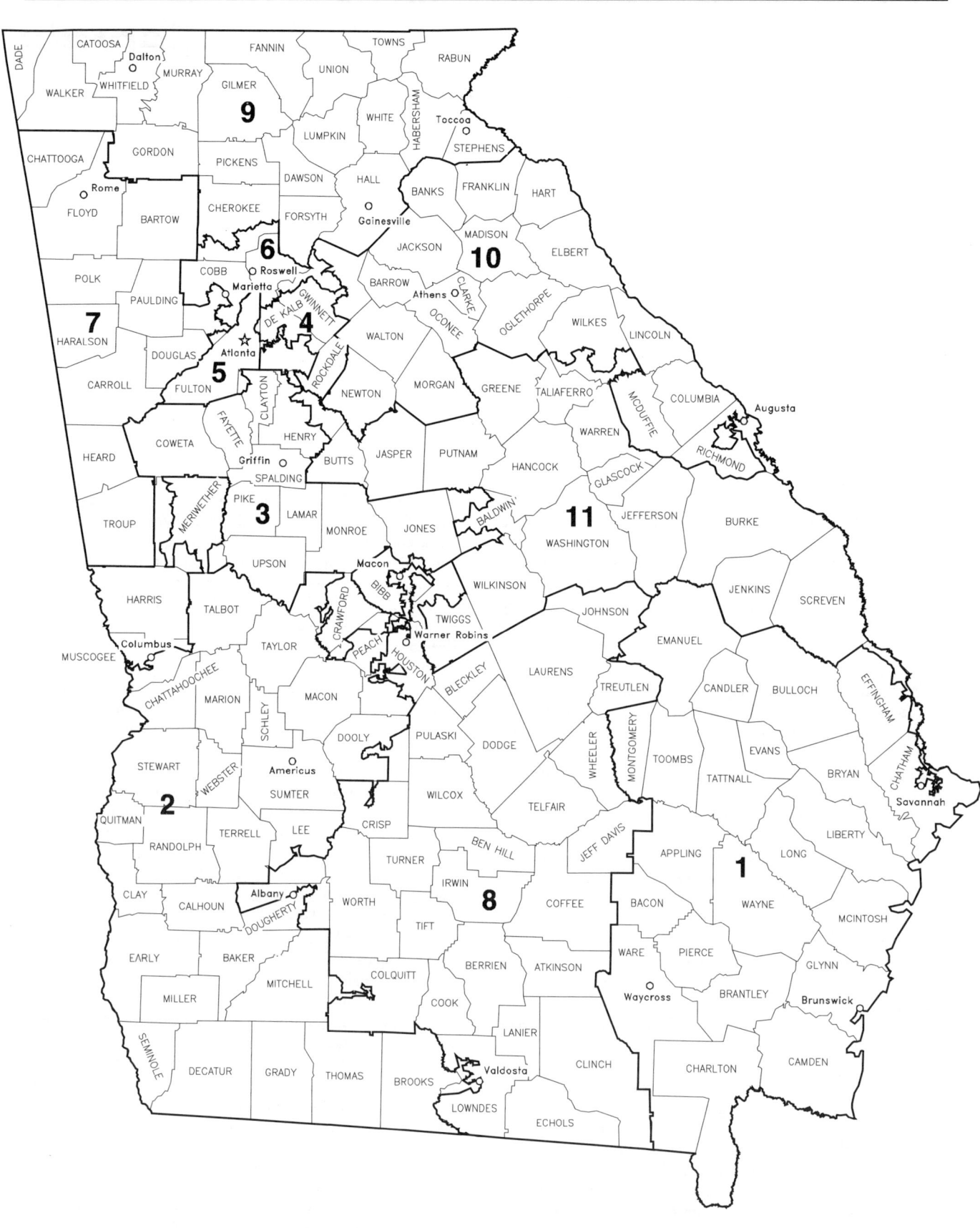

governor since the post-Civil War Reconstruction; Republican Paul Coverdell's narrow 1992 runoff victory over Democratic incumbent Wyche Fowler, Jr., made him only the second GOP senator from Georgia in the 20th century, joining Mack Mattingly, who won a seat in 1980 but was unseated by Fowler six years later.

The watershed wins by Coverdell and the three Republican House newcomers in 1992 came despite a Republican failure at the top of the ticket. Democrat Bill Clinton carried Georgia, but his 43.5 percent of the state vote was just four percentage points higher than that achieved by landslide loser Michael S. Dukakis in 1988. However, Republican incumbent Bush collapsed from the 60 percent he received in 1988 to 43 percent in 1992.

Despite some setbacks in the early 1990s, Georgia Democrats have hardly surrendered their edge in state politics. In fact, Georgia's dominant political figure during the period was a Democrat: Sen. Sam Nunn, chairman of the Senate Armed Services Committee. In each of three Senate elections beginning in 1978, Nunn carried at least 80 percent of the general election vote; he ran without opposition in 1990.

Table 1   Population

District	Population	Population under 18	Voting-age population	Median age
1	589,546	160,467	429,079	30.7
2	591,699	175,922	415,777	29.7
3	591,328	161,985	429,343	32.3
4	588,293	140,114	448,179	31.8
5	586,485	145,575	440,910	31.2
6	587,118	148,271	438,847	32.1
7	588,071	156,132	431,939	32.0
8	591,615	164,168	427,447	32.3
9	586,222	149,497	436,725	33.3
10	591,644	152,390	439,254	31.1
11	586,195	172,782	413,413	30.4
State	6,478,216	1,727,303	4,750,913	31.6

Table 2   Voting-Age Persons

District	White*	Black*	American Indian, Eskimo, or Aleut*	Asian or Pacific Islander*	Other*	Hispanic*	Male*	Female*
1	77.9%	20.3%	0.2%	0.8%	0.7%	1.6%	49.0%	51.0%
2	46.3	52.3	0.3	0.5	0.6	1.6	46.3	53.7
3	82.0	16.3	0.2	1.1	0.4	1.3	47.4	52.6
4	84.4	10.8	0.2	3.4	1.2	3.3	48.2	51.8
5	40.5	57.5	0.2	1.1	0.8	1.8	46.3	53.7
6	91.6	5.8	0.2	1.8	0.5	1.9	48.6	51.4
7	87.2	11.7	0.2	0.5	0.4	1.0	47.5	52.5
8	80.4	18.4	0.2	0.5	0.5	1.4	47.3	52.7
9	95.0	3.5	0.3	0.4	0.9	1.1	48.1	51.9
10	81.9	16.5	0.2	1.1	0.3	1.1	48.4	51.6
11	38.2	60.4	0.2	0.9	0.4	1.0	46.0	54.0
State	73.5	24.6	0.2	1.1	0.6	1.6	47.6	52.4

As percent of voting-age population.

Table 3   Voting-Age Persons by Age Groups

District	18-24*	25-44*	45-54*	55-64*	65 and over*
1	17.4%	43.5%	13.1%	10.7%	15.2%
2	18.0	41.2	12.6	11.2	17.1
3	13.8	46.1	15.5	11.2	13.5
4	14.3	52.7	13.6	8.9	10.4
5	17.0	47.0	13.0	9.4	13.7
6	12.9	55.6	15.9	8.4	7.2
7	15.1	44.6	14.3	11.2	14.9
8	14.4	42.9	14.6	11.8	16.3
9	14.4	42.4	15.2	12.2	15.8
10	18.2	43.5	13.7	10.5	14.1
11	15.6	47.2	13.4	10.1	13.7
State	15.5	46.1	14.1	10.5	13.8

As percent of voting-age population.

Table 4   Income and Occupation

District	Median family income	Families in poverty	White collar*	Blue collar*	Service*	Farm*
1	$29,277	12.9%	51.5%	31.5%	13.8%	3.2%
2	21,558	24.3	41.7	36.2	17.0	5.0
3	36,742	7.7	55.8	31.8	11.0	1.4
4	46,435	4.0	72.7	17.5	8.9	0.9
5	30,269	18.9	61.6	21.4	16.0	1.0
6	55,056	2.5	77.3	13.7	8.2	0.8
7	33,046	8.9	49.7	37.6	11.3	1.5
8	30,397	13.0	51.5	33.0	10.9	4.5
9	30,691	9.2	45.3	41.8	10.2	2.7
10	32,582	10.4	52.5	33.7	11.1	2.6
11	28,499	16.5	49.9	31.4	16.6	2.1
State	33,529	11.5	56.5	29.3	12.0	2.2

As percent of employed persons age 16 and over.

Table 5   Education: School Years Completed

District	Less than grade 9*	Grades 9-12 no diploma*	High school diploma*	College bachelor's degree or higher*
1	12.0%	17.9%	34.1%	14.9%
2	19.1	23.2	31.1	9.7
3	10.7	17.6	33.5	15.5
4	4.1	8.8	23.2	34.6
5	9.4	17.0	24.9	25.9
6	3.2	6.3	20.5	40.0
7	15.1	20.4	33.5	12.4
8	13.8	18.4	33.3	14.5
9	18.3	20.8	31.3	11.4
10	13.6	18.7	30.5	17.9
11	14.1	19.8	31.2	13.2
State	12.0	17.1	29.7	19.3

As percent of persons age 25 and over.

Table 6   Housing and Residential Patterns

District	Owner occupied	Renter occupied	Urban	Rural
1	66.3%	33.7%	54.8%	45.2%
2	57.3	42.7	62.8	37.2
3	71.3	28.7	56.5	43.5
4	61.4	38.6	92.1	7.9
5	45.4	54.6	97.2	2.8
6	66.9	33.1	88.9	11.1
7	70.5	29.5	53.9	46.1
8	70.2	29.8	48.7	51.3
9	75.4	24.6	22.1	77.9
10	68.5	31.5	47.4	52.6
11	62.1	37.9	71.5	28.5
State	64.9	35.1	63.2	36.8

1st District

Southeast — Savannah Suburbs; Brunswick; Statesboro

The 1st reaches from Georgia's Atlantic coast 100 miles inland to the state's timber and agricultural centers. There is a solid Republican vote in the district's more-populous areas—around Savannah, Brunswick and Statesboro—while most of the rural areas are fairly reliably Democratic. All across the district, voters have a common preference for conservative candidates. In the 1992 House race, Jack Kingston's success at portraying his Democratic opponent as a liberal helped him become the first Republican to represent the 1st since the Reconstruction era.

Farming provides a substantial part of the district's economic base—crops include Vidalia onions, corn, soybeans, wheat, peanuts and tobacco—but the tourism industry, federal government, frozen seafood companies and timber-related businesses are also large employers.

Chatham County (Savannah) casts more than one-fourth of the district vote. Coastal southern cities typically have a richer ethnic mix than areas inland, and Savannah fits that mold, with Irish Catholics, French Huguenots, Greeks and a substantial Jewish community. The bulk of the city's black population is included in the black-majority 11th District.

Historic Savannah attracts thousands of tourists each year, and industry includes Union Camp (timber processing) and Gulfstream Aerospace (jet manufacturing), each employing more than 3,400 people. The largest government employers in this northern end of the district are Hunter Army Airfield in Savannah and Fort Stewart, in nearby Liberty County.

In Glynn County, the southern anchor of GOP strength in the district, the city of Brunswick is a large port for shipping agricultural products. Along the county's coast there are a number of upscale beach resort communities, such as St. Simon's Island and Jekyll Island. Wealthy retirees help give Glynn its GOP tilt, as do employees of the Federal Law Enforcement Training Center, which is located at a former naval air station that was converted in the 1970s.

During the 1980s, growth in the 1st was fastest in the district's southeastern corner, where population in coastal Camden County exploded by 126 percent. Much of the influx stemmed from the opening of the Kings Bay Nuclear Submarine Base, the East Coast homeport for Trident nuclear submarines. Also, the Cumberland Island National Seashore draws visitors. Camden County is more Democratic than neighboring Glynn; while George Bush carried both in 1992, Camden did not join Glynn in supporting Kingston for the House.

Inland, there are pockets of Republican strength in Bulloch County (Statesboro) and in Ware County (Waycross), but surrounding rural counties have provided a strong vote for most Democrats running statewide in recent years. In presidential elections, however, many rural voters side with the GOP. Bush carried the district comfortably over Bill Clinton in 1992.

Election Returns

	1st District	Democrat		Republican	
1992	President*	75,066	(38.8%)	89,692	(46.4%)
	House	75,808	(42.2%)	103,932	(57.8%)
1990	Senate	67,648	(100.0%)	—	
	Governor	58,722	(58.1%)	42,307	(41.9%)
1988	President	51,380	(35.6%)	93,105	(64.4%)
1986	Senate	29,330	(44.4%)	36,688	(55.6%)
	Governor	47,098	(76.8%)	14,244	(23.2%)

Vote for Perot was 28,517 (14.8%).

Demographics

Population 589,546

Percent change from 1980 8.9%

Land area 10,471 square miles

Population per square mile 56

Counties, 1990 population

Appling	15,744	Evans	8,724
Bacon	9,566	Glynn	62,496
Brantley	11,077	Liberty	52,745
Bryan	15,438	Long	6,202
Bulloch	43,125	McIntosh	8,634
Camden	30,167	Montgomery	7,163
Candler	7,744	Pierce	13,328
Charlton	8,496	Tattnall	17,722
Chatham (pt.)	144,430	Toombs	24,072
Effingham (pt.)	24,300	Ware	35,471
Emanuel	20,546	Wayne	22,356

Cities, 1990 population (10,000 or more)

Brunswick	16,433	Statesboro	15,854
Fort Stewart CDP	13,774	Vidalia	11,078
Hinesville	21,603	Waycross	16,410
Savannah (pt.)	73,034	Wilmington Island CDP	
St. Simons CDP	12,026		11,230

Race and Hispanic origin
White 75.4%
Black 22.7%
American Indian, Eskimo, or Aleut. 0.2%
Asian or Pacific Islander 0.8%
Other 0.8%
Hispanic origin 1.8%

Ancestry

American	15.2%	Irish	15.5%
Dutch	1.6%	Italian	1.7%
English	13.1%	Scotch Irish	2.8%
French	2.7%	Scottish	2.2%
German	13.5%		

Universities/colleges, 1990-1991 enrollment
Armstrong State College, Savannah 4,170
Brewton-Parker College, Mount Vernon 1,870
Brunswick College, Brunswick 1,441
East Georgia College, Swainsboro 617
Georgia Southern College, Statesboro 12,249
Okefenoke Tech Institute, Waycross 329
Savannah College of Art & Design, Savannah 1,979
Savannah Technical Institute, Savannah 2,156
South College, Savannah 465
Swainsboro Technical Institute, Swainsboro 554
Waycross College, Waycross 669

Newspapers, total circulation (in all districts)
Atlanta Journal-Constitution 494,556

Florida Times-Union 179,796
Savannah Morning News Evening Press 73,752

Commercial television stations, affiliations
ADI: Savannah (63%), Jacksonville (31%) and Augusta (6%)
WJCL, Savannah (ABC)
WSAV-TV, Savannah (NBC)
WTOC-TV, Savannah (CBS)
WTGS, Hardeeville (Fox)
WBSG, Brunswick (None)

Cable television systems, total subscribers
Cablevision of Savannah; Pooler 8,930
Cablevision of Savannah; Savannah 32,000
Coastal Cablevision; Hinesville 10,776
Rentavision; Brunswick 18,534
Statesboro CATV Inc.; Statesboro 7,339
Waycross Cable Co. Inc.; Waycross 10,864

Military installations, 1991
Fort Stewart (Army), Hinesville 18,620
Kings Bay Naval Submarine Base, Kings Bay 9,355
Hunter Army Airfield, Savannah 4,613
Savannah Intl. Airport Air Force Guard Station, Savannah
267

Businesses and other major employers
Savannah-Chatham Board of Education; Savannah 4,200
Union Camp Corp./Kraft Paper & Board Div.; Savannah;
paper mills 3,500
Gulfstream Aerospace Corp.; Savannah; aircraft/parts 3,500
City of Savannah; Savannah 1,830
Georgia Southern College; Statesboro 1,750
Candler General Hospital; Savannah 1,600
CSX Transportation Inc.; Waycross; railroads 1,500
B. E. & K. Construction Co.; Savannah; building construc-
tion 1,400
Gilman Paper Co.; Saint Mary's; pulp mills 1,300
St. Joseph's Hospital; Savannah 1,221
ITT Rayonier Inc.; Jesup; pulp mills 1,200
Southeast Georgia Regional Medical Center; Brunswick
1,200
Fort Howard Corp.; Rincon; paper mills 1,015
Johnson Controls World Service/Pan Am World Services Inc.;
Saint Mary's 1,000
Sea Island Co./The Cloister; Sea Island; hotel 1,000
U.S. Army Corps of Engineers; Savannah; engineering ser-
vices 1,000
County of Chatham/Finance Dept.; Savannah 1,000
Oxford Industries Inc./Oxford of Vidalia; Vidalia; outerwear
950
Norman W. Fries Inc./Claxton Poultry Co.; Claxton;
poultry/eggs 800
Reidsville State Prison; Reidsville 727
State of Georgia; Jesup 722
Grinnell Corp.; Statesboro; iron/steel foundries 706
PWS Holding Corp.; Vidalia; grocery stores 700
County of Glynn/St. Simons Island Water & Sewage; Bruns-
wick 700
Lockheed Corp.; Saint Mary's; search/navigation equipment
689
Rich-Seapak Processing Corp.; Brunswick; food products
654

Savannah Foods & Industries/Savannah Sugar Refinery; Sa-
vannah; sugar/confectionery products 650
Satilla Health Services Inc./Memorial Hospital; Waycross
650
Georgia Ports Authority; Savannah 612
Hercules Inc.; Brunswick; organic chemicals 580
Brunswick Pulp & Paper Co.; Brunswick; pulp mills 550
Bulloch Memorial Hospital; Statesboro 550
King & Prince Seafood Corp.; Brunswick; seafood 548

2nd District
Southwest — Parts of Macon, Columbus, Albany and Valdosta

This is one of the three black-majority constituencies included in Georgia's redistricting plan for the 1990s, but it was by
no means certain that the 2nd would elect a black to Congress in
1992. For while blacks make up 57 percent of the district's total
population, they are only 52 percent of its voting-age population.

The district consists of parts of four urban areas—predominantly
black sections of Macon (Bibb County), Columbus (Muscogee
County), Albany (Dougherty County) and Valdosta (Lowndes
County), connected by mostly rural counties that are dependent on
agriculture for economic sustenance. Peanuts and tobacco are big
here, but soybeans, pecans and cotton are also important.

In partisan terms, the 2nd is solidly Democratic. In 1992 Bill
Clinton far outpaced George Bush here, and the black Democratic candidate glided to victory in the House with 64 percent.

Located on the Alabama border in the 2nd's northwestern
corner is Columbus. It benefits from the Army's Fort Benning,
the state's largest military base and its site for basic training.
About 30,000 military and civilian personnel are employed at the
base. Columbus also is home to several small colleges.

To the east is the old textile and railroad town of Macon, long
a trading and processing center for the agricultural lands of middle
Georgia that surround it. To the south, in the central part of the
2nd, is Albany, whose industrial activities include shelling and
packing locally produced pecans and peanuts. Albany is also
home to the Marine Corps Logistics Base, which is responsible for
maintaining supplies for the Marines and employs about 7,300.

In the middle part of the district is Sumter County, where in
the late 1970s the little town of Plains gained international fame
as the home of President Jimmy Carter. Sumter backed Clinton
in 1992, but it was one of just a handful of district counties that
went for the GOP nominee in the House race that year.

In the southeastern corner of the 2nd is Valdosta, which is
surrounded by the vast reaches of southern Georgia's piney
woods. Paper mills, sawmills and other wood-products manufacturers anchor the local economy, and Levi Strauss has a plant
here. The Interstate 75 exits for Valdosta are a stopping-off point
for many highway travelers heading to or just leaving Florida.

In the 2nd in 1992, the district's urbanized areas went
Democratic by huge margins: The combined November vote
from Bibb, Muscogee, Dougherty and Lowndes counties was
better than 3-to-1 Democratic in the House race.

The rural counties of the 2nd generally add to Democratic
strength, particularly in state and local elections, but there are
some GOP pockets, notably at the southern end of the district.
Thomas County, which lies on the border with Florida, has a
good share of Republican-minded retirees and supported Bush
for president in 1992.

Election Returns

	2nd District	Democrat	Republican
1992	President*	97,077 (60.1%)	47,171 (29.2%)
	House	95,789 (63.7%)	54,593 (36.3%)
1990	Senate	65,223 (100.0%)	—
	Governor	56,524 (63.8%)	32,048 (36.2%)
1988	President	71,152 (55.5%)	57,162 (44.5%)
1986	Senate	54,552 (64.8%)	29,573 (35.2%)
	Governor	64,933 (83.8%)	12,508 (16.2%)

*Vote for Perot was 17,368 (10.7%).

Demographics

Population 591,699

Percent change from 1980 7.6%

Land area 10,134 square miles

Population per square mile 58

Counties, 1990 population

Baker 3,615	Marion 5,590
Bibb (pt.) 74,401	Meriwether (pt.) 14,744
Brooks 15,398	Miller 6,280
Calhoun 5,013	Mitchell 20,275
Chattahoochee 16,934	Muscogee (pt.) 89,814
Clay 3,364	Peach (pt.) 10,573
Colquitt (pt.) 8,490	Quitman 2,209
Crawford (pt.) 2,291	Randolph 8,023
Crisp (pt.) 7,191	Schley 3,588
Decatur 25,511	Seminole 9,010
Dooly (pt.) 8,922	Stewart 5,654
Dougherty (pt.) 52,574	Sumter 30,228
Early 11,854	Talbot 6,524
Grady 20,279	Taylor 7,642
Houston (pt.) 22,537	Terrell 10,653
Lee (pt.) 4,117	Thomas 38,986
Lowndes (pt.) 24,038	Webster 2,263
Macon 13,114	

Cities, 1990 population (10,000 or more)

Albany (pt.) 46,553	Macon (pt.) 69,303
Americus 16,512	Thomasville 17,457
Bainbridge 10,712	Valdosta (pt.) 19,645
Columbus (pt.) 89,814	Warner Robins (pt.) 11,618
Fort Benning South CDP 14,617	

Race and Hispanic origin

White 42.0%
Black 56.6%
American Indian, Eskimo, or Aleut. 0.2%
Asian or Pacific Islander 0.5%
Other 0.7%
Hispanic origin 1.7%

Ancestry

American 11.2%	German 6.0%
English 6.7%	Irish 8.3%
French 1.2%	Scotch Irish 1.6%

Universities/colleges, 1990-1991 enrollment

Albany State College, Albany 2,405
Andrew College, Cuthbert 306
Bainbridge College, Bainbridge 898
Fort Valley State College, Fort Valley 2,158
Georgia Southwestern College, Americus 2,225
Macon College, Macon 4,210
Macon Technical Institute, Macon 1,013
Meadows Junior College, Columbus 358
Mercer University, Macon 5,872
Moultrie Technical Institute, Moultrie 812
South Georgia Technical Institute, Americus 501
Thomas College, Thomasville 360
Thomas Technical Institute, Thomasville 446
Valdosta State College, Valdosta 7,144
Valdosta Technical Institute, Valdosta 857

Newspapers, total circulation (in all districts)

Albany Herald 36,686
Atlanta Journal-Constitution 494,556
Columbus Ledger-Enquirer 53,120
Macon Telegraph 72,390
Thomasville Times-Enterprise 10,657
Warner Robins Daily Sun 8,938

Commercial television stations, affiliations

ADI: Columbus (39%), Tallahassee-Thomasville (26%), Albany (19%), Macon (7%), Dothan (5%) and Atlanta (3%)
WCTV, Thomasville, (CBS)
WTLH, Bainbridge (None)
WLTZ, Columbus (NBC)
WRBL, Columbus (CBS)
WTVM, Columbus (ABC)
WXTX, Columbus (Fox)

Cable television systems, total subscribers

Storer Cable TV Inc.; Albany 27,812
Storer Cable TV Inc.; Americus 5,943
TCI of Georgia; Columbus 14,250
TCI of Georgia; Pine Park 8,800
Telecable of Columbus Inc.; Columbus 28,648

Military installations, 1991

Fort Benning (Army), Columbus 31,362
Robins Air Force Base, Warner Robins 25,191
Moody Air Force Base, Valdosta 3,549

Businesses and other major employers

Macon-Bibb County Hospital Authority; Macon 3,022
City of Columbus; Columbus 1,980
Amoco Fabrics Fibers Co./Bainbridge Mills; Bainbridge; man-made fabric mills 1,815
Phoebe Putney Memorial Hospital; Albany 1,700
Procter & Gamble; Albany; paper products 1,525
John D. Archbold Memorial Hospital/Brooks County Hospital; Thomasville 1,400
Medical Center Inc.; Columbus 1,330
Bird Blue Body Co./Blue Bird Wanderlodge; Fort Valley; bus bodies/trailers 1,300
Swift Textiles Inc.; Columbus; cotton mills 1,207
Boeing of Georgia; Macon; aircraft/parts 1,200
St. Francis Hospital; Columbus 1,138
Textron Inc./Davidson Exterior Trim; Americus; plastics products 1,000

United Technologies Corp./Pratt & Whitney; Columbus; aircraft 973

Levi Strauss & Co.; Valdosta; jeans 900

Goody Products Inc.; Manchester; misc. manufacturers 851

Coliseum Park Hospital; Macon 842

Georgia-Pacific Corp./Great Southern Paper Co.; Cedar Springs; paperboard mills 830

Curtice Burns Foods Inc./Southern Frozen Foods Div.; Montezuma; frozen food products 800

Southern Bell Telephone & Telegraph Co.; Macon; telephone communications 740

Dougherty County School District; Albany 738

Southwestern State Hospital; Thomasville 727

Valdosta State College; Valdosta 679

Sunshine Biscuits Inc.; Columbus; bakery products 675

Bibb Co. Inc.; Fort Valley; man-made fabric mills 650

Healthtrust Inc./Northern Virginia Doctors Hospital; Columbus 650

Lummus Industries Inc.; Columbus; industry machinery 600

Tom's Foods Inc.; Columbus; candies/confectionery products 600

Bibb Co. Inc.; Columbus; furniture stores 600

Interstate Brands Corp./Dolly Madison Bakery; Columbus; bakery products 597

Salant Corp./Manhattan Shirt; Americus; outerwear 575

Langdale Co. Inc.; Valdosta; sawmills 550

Horticultural Farms Inc.; Cairo; horticultural specialties 550

Cagles Inc.; Macon; meat products 550

Engelhard Corp.; Attapulgus; nonferrous metals 535

Knight-Ridder Inc./Ledger Enquirer Newspapers; Columbus; newspapers 525

Macon Kraft Inc.; Macon; paperboard mills 512

3rd District

West Central — Griffin; Atlanta and Columbus Suburbs

The 3rd is a mix of old-time southern Democrats and Republican-leaning retirees and young professionals. Roughly (very roughly) triangular in shape, it starts at the peach orchards in aptly named Peach County, runs north to the Hartsfield Atlanta International Airport in Clayton County, then heads south and west to the suburbs of Columbus, in Muscogee County.

The booming population growth of the suburbs and exurbs to the south and west of Atlanta, along with increasing acceptance of the GOP among rural, traditionally Democratic conservatives, have made the 3rd fertile ground for Republican candidates.

The counties that contain these suburbs—Clayton (Jonesboro), Coweta (Newnan), Fayette (Fayetteville), Henry (McDonough) and Spalding (Griffin)—cast about 60 percent of the vote in the 3rd. All five went decisively for the GOP House candidate in 1992. George Bush won all but Clayton on his way to victory over Bill Clinton.

The biggest growth occurred in the suburbs abutting Atlanta to the south. Clayton County grew 21 percent during the 1980s, and with more than 150,000 residents it is the most populous county in the 3rd, casting one-fifth of the district vote. The sprawling and ever-bustling international airport (which is split between the 3rd and 5th districts) is a prime driver of the district's economy. Ford also makes its hugely popular Taurus automobiles in Clayton and adjoining Fulton County.

Next door in Fayette County, population grew 115 percent in the past decade.

In Spalding County, textiles are still important to the Griffin economy. Dundee Mills, a towel manufacturer, is one of the largest employers here. The county is also home to the Atlanta Motor Speedway.

Moving into Coweta County, the atmosphere changes, although GOP voting habits do not. Newnan's wealth is tied less to Atlanta's recent growth than to the more distant past; spared during the Civil War, Newnan is known as the "the City of Homes" for its stately antebellum mansions.

In addition to the many district residents who depend on airport activity for their paychecks, thousands of others look to the military for employment. Fort Gillem in Clayton County has the second largest payroll in Atlanta, after Delta Airlines, which has its headquarters nearby in the 5th District. Others in the northern end of the district commute to the Army's Fort McPherson in the southern Atlanta suburbs in the neighboring 5th District. To the south (in the adjoining 2nd District) is Robins Air Force Base in Warner Robins. And a number who live in the Columbus area commute there to the Army's Fort Benning, the state's largest military base (also located in the 2nd District).

The most loyal support for Democratic candidates comes from a swath of mainly rural counties in the southern part of the 3rd—Peach, Monroe, Jones, Baldwin and Crawford. All went Democratic in the 1992 House race.

Election Returns

	3rd District	Democrat	Republican
1992	President*	80,954 (37.1%)	105,426 (48.3%)
	House	94,271 (45.2%)	114,107 (54.8%)
1990	Senate	70,521 (100.0%)	—
	Governor	52,629 (52.1%)	48,435 (47.9%)
1988	President	49,639 (31.9%)	105,919 (68.1%)
1986	Senate	40,789 (44.4%)	51,106 (55.6%)
	Governor	60,095 (66.9%)	29,742 (33.1%)

Vote for Perot was 32,112 (14.7%).

Demographics

Population 591,328

Percent change from 1980 9.3%

Land area 3,829 square miles

Population per square mile 154

Counties, 1990 population

Baldwin (pt.) 8,744	Lamar 13,038
Clayton (pt.) 150,642	Meriwether (pt.) 7,667
Coweta 53,853	Monroe 17,113
Crawford (pt.) 6,700	Muscogee (pt.) 89,464
Fayette 62,415	Peach (pt.) 10,616
Harris 17,788	Pike 10,224
Henry (pt.) 47,291	Spalding 54,457
Jones (pt.) 15,016	Upson 26,300

Cities, 1990 population (10,000 or more)

Columbus (pt.) 88,867	Newnan 12,497
Forest Park 16,925	Peachtree City 19,027
Griffin 21,347	

Race and Hispanic origin

White 80.3%
Black 17.8%
American Indian, Eskimo, or Aleut. 0.2%
Asian or Pacific Islander 1.2%
Other 0.4%
Hispanic origin 1.4%

Ancestry

American 15.2% Irish 18.0%
Dutch 2.1% Italian 1.8%
English 15.4% Polish 1.0%
French 2.6% Scotch Irish 3.5%
German 13.7% Scottish 2.3%

Universities/colleges, 1990-1991 enrollment

Clayton State College, Morrow 4,140
Columbus College, Columbus 4,154
Columbus Technical Institute, Columbus 856
Gordon College, Barnesville 1,480
Phillips Junior College, Columbus 574
Upson Technical Institute, Thomaston 287

Newspapers, total circulation (in all districts)

Atlanta Journal-Constitution 494,556
Columbus Ledger-Enquirer 53,120
Macon Telegraph 72,390
Griffin Daily News 12,292

Commercial television stations, affiliations

ADI: Atlanta (55%), Macon (30%) and Columbus (15%)

Cable television systems, total subscribers

Chattahoochee Cablevision; Newnan 5,200
Cox Cable Middle Georgia; Macon 42,816
Insight Cablevision; Griffin 7,200
Premiere Cable Communications; McDonough 9,270
TCI of Georgia; Columbus 14,250
Telecable of Columbus Inc.; Columbus 28,648
Thomaston Cablevision; Thomaston 5,200
Wometco Cable TV/Clayton County; Jonesboro 37,659
Wometco Cable TV/Fayette County; Fayetteville 7,406

Military installations, 1991

Fort Gillem (Army), Forest Park 3,810

Businesses and other major employers

Fieldcrest Cannon Inc.; Columbus; textile products 2,500
J. C. Penney Co. Inc.; Forest Park; catalog retailers 2,100
Southern Regional Medical Center; Riverdale 1,600
Georgia Power Co.; Juliette; electric services 1,300
Dominion Textile Inc./Martha Mills; Thomaston; textile goods 1,300
American Family Life; Columbus; medical service/health insurance 1,150
Forstmann & Co. Inc.; Milledgeville; yarn/thread mills 1,000
Georgia Power Co.; Forest Park; electric services 950
Rheem Mfg. Co.; Milledgeville; refrigeration 928
Callaway Gardens Resort; Pine Mountain; hotel 825
Fuqua Industries Inc./Snapper Power Equipment; McDonough; farm/garden machinery 800
William L. Bonnell Co.; Newnan; aluminum doors/products 800
U.S. Federal Aviation Administration; Hampton 800
Blue Cross/Blue Shield of Georgia; Columbus; medical service/health insurance 781

Matsushita Communication/MCC-Panasonic; Fayetteville; communications equipment 681
NEC Technologies Inc.; McDonough; audio/video equipment 650
NCR Corp.; Peachtree City; professional/commercial equipment 650
J. B. Hunt Transport Inc.; Forest Park; trucking services 627
Columbus Foundries Inc.; Columbus; iron/steel foundries 600
Cagles Inc.; Pine Mountain Valley; meat products 600
K-Mart Corp.; Newnan; warehousing 600
Grumman Aerospace Corp.; Milledgeville; aircraft/parts 550
Amisub/Spalding Regional Hospital; Griffin 550
Columbus Mills Inc./Carpet Mill Stores; Columbus; carpets/rugs 525
Reed Group Inc./R. R. Bowker Co.; Midland; management/public relations 525
Clayton State College; Morrow 525

4th District

Atlanta Suburbs — Parts of De Kalb and Gwinnett Counties

As Atlanta blossomed into the South's financial capital during the 1960s and 1970s, De Kalb County (just east of the city) was the pacesetter of suburban growth. With more than a half-million people, De Kalb is now Georgia's second most populous county. But growth here has slowed as development has spread into outlying jurisdictions; lately, the hot spots have been farther east, in Gwinnett and Rockdale counties. Because of the expansion of suburbia there, the 4th tilts Republican. George Bush won the district in 1992, taking 46 percent of the vote.

Historically, this district has shifted between the parties. The 4th was represented in the House by Republicans from 1972-1974 and 1984-1988 and was recaptured by the GOP in 1992.

De Kalb and Gwinnett counties cast 47 percent and 41 percent of the district's vote in 1992. The 4th includes the north-central part of De Kalb and all but the northern section of Gwinnett. The two counties are quite different in their electoral behavior.

Democratic candidates get a warm reception in the central and western parts of De Kalb. Decatur, the county seat, was a 19th-century commercial center until it lost out as a railroad center to Atlanta; it still has some industry and a Democratic complexion. As one of the district's largest employers, 9,400-student Emory University and the communities around it—many of them with substantial Jewish or black populations—give local politics a liberal slant. Chamblee, a blue-collar community in northern De Kalb, has a large immigrant community of both Asians and Hispanics, and they bolster the Democratic vote. Republicans' best showings in De Kalb generally come in the suburban neighborhoods around Stone Mountain. The mountain itself, with a gigantic carving of Robert E. Lee and other heroes of the Confederacy, is a big tourist draw.

Gwinnett County delivers a hefty Republican vote. In 1992, the margins that Bush piled up in Gwinnett offset his defeat in the De Kalb part of the 4th. Population in Gwinnett expanded nearly 50 percent during the 1980s; the county has newly established neighborhoods filled with recent arrivals who have no connection with the area's Democratic past.

To the south is Rockdale County. Long a rural and conservative Democratic area, Rockdale has been transformed by suburban growth. Dotted now with subdivisions, its vote has shifted dramatically to the GOP. In 1992, Bush won a majority in Rockdale, and the GOP House candidate topped 60 percent. The county casts just under 10 percent of the vote in the 4th.

The district also has a small slice of Fulton County, on Atlanta's eastern edge, composed largely of white-collar suburbs. Prominent district employers include the Centers for Disease Control and Prevention, Scientific Atlanta, General Motors, AT&T, Frito Lay Corp. and UPS, which has a distribution center in the 4th.

Election Returns

	4th District	Democrat		Republican	
1992	President*	101,990	(40.5%)	116,418	(46.3%)
	House	123,819	(49.5%)	126,495	(50.5%)
1990	Senate	60,683	(100.0%)	—	
	Governor	38,791	(49.1%)	40,291	(50.9%)
1988	President	47,951	(41.8%)	66,830	(58.2%)
1986	Senate	35,278	(49.1%)	36,584	(50.9%)
	Governor	40,532	(57.7%)	29,731	(42.3%)

*Vote for Perot was 33,226 (13.2%).

Demographics

Population 588,293

Percent change from 1980 8.5%

Land area 443 square miles

Population per square mile 1,327

Counties, 1990 population
De Kalb (pt.) 269,375   Gwinnett (pt.) 251,752
Fulton (pt.) 13,075   Rockdale 54,091

Cities, 1990 population (10,000 or more)
Atlanta (pt.) 21,767   North Decatur CDP
Decatur 17,336   13,936
Druid Hills CDP 12,174   North Druid Hills CDP
Lawrenceville (pt.) 13,481   14,170
Mountain Park CDP   Snellville (pt.) 12,084
  11,025   Tucker CDP 25,781
North Atlanta CDP 27,812

Race and Hispanic origin
White 83.3%
Black 11.6%
American Indian, Eskimo, or Aleut. 0.2%
Asian or Pacific Islander 3.7%
Other 1.3%
Hispanic origin 3.4%

Ancestry
American 8.3%   Polish 2.2%
Dutch 2.1%   Russian 1.3%
English 19.7%   Scotch Irish 4.7%
French 3.9%   Scottish 4.0%
German 19.1%   Swedish 1.1%
Irish 17.8%   Welsh 1.1%
Italian 3.1%

Universities/colleges, 1990-1991 enrollment
Agnes Scott College, Decatur 593
Columbia Theological Seminary, Decatur 619
De Kalb Technical Institute, Clarkston 3,675
Devry Institute of Technology, Decatur 3,121
Emory University, Atlanta 9,390
Gwinnett Technical Institute, Lawrenceville 2,575
Oglethorpe University, Atlanta 1,095

Newspapers, total circulation (in all districts)
Atlanta Journal-Constitution 494,556
Rockdale Citizen 10,005

Commercial television stations, affiliations
ADI: Atlanta (100%)
  WAGA-TV, Atlanta (CBS)
  WATL, Atlanta (Fox)
  WGNX, Atlanta (None)
  WHSG, Monroe (None)

Cable television systems, total subscribers
Georgia Cable TV/Comm; Atlanta 92,544
Georgia Cable TV/Comm; Decatur 99,456
Gwinnett Cable TV; Lilburn 60,464
North De Kalb Cable; Chamblee 24,051

Businesses and other major employers
Emory University & Emory University Hospital; Atlanta 10,000
United Parcel Service Inc.; Atlanta; mail services 5,000
U.S. Internal Revenue Service; Atlanta 5,000
General Motors Corp./CPC Div.; Atlanta; motor vehicles 2,500
County of Gwinnett; Lawrenceville 2,025
National Service Industries/Lithonia Lighting Div.; Conyers; electric lighting 2,000
De Kalb Hospital Authority; Decatur 1,976
Primerica Financial Services; Duluth; life insurance 1,800
St. Joseph's Hospital of Atlanta; Atlanta 1,800
General Electric Co.; Norcross; computer services 1,700
Emory Clinic; Atlanta; medical doctors 1,500
U.S. Veterans Affairs Dept.; Decatur 1,460
Northern Telecom Inc./Atlanta Transmission Div.; Stone Mountain; communications equipment 1,400
Wachovia Corp./First of Atlanta; Atlanta; commercial banks 1,400
Metropolitan Atlanta Transit; Decatur; transportation 1,300
Buford Hospital; Lawrenceville 1,300
Massachusetts Indemnity Life; Duluth; medical service/health insurance 1,200
H. A. Simons Ltd.; Decatur; engineering/architectural services 1,100
Henrietta Egleston Hospital; Atlanta 1,095
AT&T Co.; Conyers; telephone communications 1,000
National Service Industries/Reloc Wiring Systems; Conyers; electric lighting 1,000
De Kalb County/Service Center; Tucker; automotive repair 1,000
Decatur Federal Savings & Loan Assn.; Decatur; savings institutions 840
Sears Roebuck & Co.; Atlanta; catalog retailers 800
Simons-Eastern Consultants; Decatur; engineering/architectural services 800
National Data Corp.; Atlanta; computer services 800

Foote & Davies Inc./American Signature; Atlanta; commercial printing 750

C&S/Sovran Corp./C&S National Bank; Tucker; credit institutions 750

Days Inn of America Franchising; Atlanta; misc. investing 735

American Building Maint. Co.; Atlanta; building services 710

General Motors Corp.; Atlanta; warehousing 700

Orkin Exterminating Co./Rollins Protective Service; Atlanta; business services 700

Payroll Inc.; Atlanta; personnel supply services 669

Rich's Inc.; Stone Mountain; department stores 650

Kraft General Foods Inc.; Decatur; dairy products 600

Rockwell Intl. Corp./Tactical Systems Div.; Duluth; search/navigation equipment 600

Metropolitan Atlanta Transit; Atlanta; transportation 600

Indal Inc.; Norcross; metal products 600

Macy's South Inc.; Atlanta; department stores 600

U.S. Center for Disease Control; Atlanta 600

Kysor Industrial Corp./Warren-Sherer Div.; Conyers; refrigeration 564

Hospital Corp. America/Northlake Regional Medical Center; Tucker; health services 550

Scientific-Atlanta Inc./Broadband Communications Div.; Norcross; communications equipment 525

Rockdale Hospital; Conyers 525

5th District

Parts of Atlanta

The obvious symbol of the 5th is Atlanta's alluring skyline, with the state Capitol, the steel-and-glass office skyscrapers and the towering hotels that make the city the commercial center of the Southeast and the symbolic capital of the New South.

However, in the shadows of those buildings is another Atlanta, a mostly black city struggling with typical urban social problems—unemployment, crime and drugs. While Atlanta's business boom spurred continued suburban sprawl through the 1980s, the city's population dropped slightly, to just over 394,000.

But as host city for the 1996 Summer Olympics, Atlanta is on the cusp of another building boom: Construction of Olympic venues could total $500 million. One of the largest Olympic construction projects is a new stadium that will be home to the Atlanta Falcons.

The 5th takes in most of Atlanta and surrounding Fulton County, as well as some suburban territory in neighboring counties, including the southern half of De Kalb County and fragments of northwest Clayton and southern Cobb counties. Blacks account for 62 percent of the district's population and 54 percent of its registered voters, and they help make the 5th a Democratic bastion. In the 1992 presidential contest, Bill Clinton took just over two-thirds of the vote in the 5th, his best showing in all of Georgia's 11 districts. Democrat Rep. John Lewis topped 70 percent in winning re-election in 1992.

Fulton is reliable Democratic territory, though there are pockets of GOP strength in its northern suburbs. One of those communities is Sandy Springs, a booming area of white-collar, middle-level managers.

The heart of the district is Atlanta itself. Its downtown has enjoyed new attention with the recent opening of Underground Atlanta, a tourist shopping complex, and the nearby Coca-Cola museum. Tourists also can pay homage to late civil rights leader the Rev. Dr. Martin Luther King, Jr.; his birthplace, the church where he preached and his Center for Non-Violent Change are all here.

South of Atlanta, the district takes in East Point, a lower-middle-class community. Many of its residents work at Hartsfield Atlanta International Airport, which is divided between the 5th and 3rd districts. The 1991 closure of Eastern Airlines took a bite out of aviation employment, costing 10,000 people their jobs. But TWA recently made Atlanta a mini-hub, and other job opportunities in the metropolitan area should mitigate the loss of Eastern.

Among the 5th's largest employers are Delta Airlines, the Fort McPherson Army Forces Command, Coca-Cola, Cable News Network, Bell South and timber giant Georgia Pacific.

More than 90 percent of the district's vote comes out of Fulton County. Of the rest, the biggest share (about 4 percent) comes from northwest Clayton County, home to many blue-collar, white middle-class airport workers and a growing Asian population.

Election Returns

	5th District	Democrat		Republican	
1992	President*	140,270	(67.6%)	52,087	(25.1%)
	House	147,445	(72.1%)	56,960	(27.9%)
1990	Senate	95,000	(100.0%)	—	
	Governor	76,436	(66.6%)	38,390	(33.4%)
1988	President	116,731	(64.8%)	63,406	(35.2%)
1986	Senate	99,729	(71.1%)	40,569	(28.9%)
	Governor	97,200	(72.2%)	37,463	(27.8%)

*Vote for Perot was 15,214 (7.3%).

Demographics

Population 586,485

Percent change from 1980 6.6%

Land area 406 square miles

Population per square mile 1,445

Counties, 1990 population
Clayton (pt.) 31,410	De Kalb (pt.) 24,847
Cobb (pt.) 11,104	Fulton (pt.) 519,124

Cities, 1990 population (10,000 or more)
Atlanta (pt.) 372,250	Sandy Springs CDP (pt.)
College Park 20,457	51,957
East Point 34,402	

Race and Hispanic origin
White 35.6%
Black 62.3%
American Indian, Eskimo, or Aleut. 0.2%
Asian or Pacific Islander 1.1%
Other 0.8%
Hispanic origin 1.8%

Ancestry
American 5.2%	French 1.5%
English 8.7%	German 6.9%

Irish 6.8%   Scotch Irish 2.1%
Italian 1.1%   Scottish 1.7%

Universities/colleges, 1990-1991 enrollment
American College of Applied Arts, Atlanta 705
Art Institute of Atlanta, Atlanta 1,288
Atlanta College of Art, Atlanta 374
Atlanta Metropolitan College, Atlanta 1,620
Bauder Fashion College, Atlanta 693
Clark Atlanta University, Atlanta 3,507
Georgia Institute of Technology, Atlanta 12,241
Georgia State University, Atlanta 23,336
Interdenominational Theological Center, Atlanta 294
Massey Business College, Atlanta 465
Morehouse College, Atlanta 2,720
Morris Brown College, Atlanta 1,354
Spelman College, Atlanta 1,710

Newspapers, total circulation (in all districts)
Atlanta Journal-Constitution 494,556
Marietta Daily Journal Sunday Record 26,330

Commercial television stations, affiliations
ADI: Atlanta (100%)
WSB-TV, Atlanta (ABC)
WTBS, Atlanta (None)
WVEU, Atlanta (None)
WXIA-TV, Atlanta (NBC)

Cable television systems, total subscribers
Georgia Cable TV/Comm; Atlanta 92,544
Georgia Cable TV/Comm; Decatur 99,456
Wometco Cable TV/Clayton County; Jonesboro 37,659

Military installations, 1991
Fort McPherson (Army), Atlanta 4,128

Businesses and other major employers
Delta Air Lines Inc.; Atlanta; airline 24,199
NationsBank; Atlanta; commercial banks 15,000
Georgia Institute of Technology; Atlanta 6,478
State of Georgia/Corrections Dept.; Atlanta 6,000
Grady Memorial Hospital; Atlanta 4,950
City of Atlanta; Atlanta 4,000
Suntrust Banks Inc.; Atlanta; commercial banks 3,923
Coca-Cola Co. Inc.; Atlanta; beverages 3,500
Ford Motor Co./Ford Mercury; Atlanta; motor vehicles 2,630
Turner Broadcasting System; Atlanta; radio/TV broadcasting 2,407
Piedmont Hospital Inc.; Atlanta 2,385
Georgia Baptist Hospital; Atlanta 2,300
Northside Hospital; Atlanta 2,280
Georgia Power Co.; Atlanta; electric services 2,250
Georgia-Pacific Corp./Wood Products Div.; Atlanta; sawmills 2,000
AT&T Co.; Atlanta; personnel supply services 2,000
Marriott Corp./Atlanta Marriott Marquis; Atlanta; hotel 1,800
Law Intl. Inc.; Atlanta; engineering/architectural services 1,600
Georgia Technical Research Institute; Atlanta; research services 1,500
Northwest Airlines Inc.; Atlanta; airline 1,400

Bellsouth Telecommunications/Southern Bell Telephone; Atlanta; telephone communications 1,388
ICS-Southern Services Inc.; Atlanta; building services 1,305
Bank South Corp.; Atlanta; holding offices 1,300
State of Georgia/Natural Resources Dept.; Atlanta 1,300
Cable News Network Inc./CNN; Atlanta; cable TV services 1,275
Equifax Inc.; Atlanta; insurance services 1,200
State of Georgia/Transportation Dept.; Atlanta 1,200
State of Georgia/Revenue Dept.; Atlanta 1,200
County of Fulton/Sheriffs Dept.; Atlanta 1,200
U.S. Environmental Protection Agency; Atlanta 1,200
Atlanta Gas Light Co.; Atlanta; petroleum products 1,123
Macy's South Inc.; Atlanta; department stores 1,100
Life Insurance Co. of Georgia; Atlanta; life insurance 1,100
State of Georgia/Administrative Services Dept.; Atlanta 1,100
Georgia Tech Research Corp.; Atlanta; research services 1,100
Hospital Corp. America/HCA West Paces Ferry Hospital; Atlanta 1,100
Tri-City Hospital Authority/South Fulton Medical Center; Atlanta 1,091
Wachovia Bank of Georgia; Atlanta; commercial banks 1,070
Georgia Power Co.; Atlanta; electric services 1,000
Rich's Inc./Rich's at Lenox; Atlanta; department stores 1,000
State of Georgia/Building Authority; Atlanta 1,000
Dobbs Intl. Services; Atlanta; bars/restaurants 1,000
Chatham Land & Dev. Co.; Atlanta; real estate agents 1,000
James Pair Inc.; Atlanta; personnel supply services 1,000
NationsBank; Atlanta; business services 1,000
Peachtree Hotel Co./Westin Peachtree Plaza Hotel; Atlanta; hotel 1,000
U.S. Internal Revenue Service; Atlanta 1,000
Bellsouth Corp.; Atlanta; telephone communications 982
Federal Reserve Bank Atlanta; Atlanta 980
Owens-Illinois Inc./Owens Brockway Div; Atlanta; glass/glassware 920
IBM Corp.; Atlanta; management/public relations 900
Scottish Rite Hospital; Atlanta 900
Clark Atlanta University; Atlanta 900
Hyatt Hotels Corp./Hyatt Regency Atlanta; Atlanta; hotel 850
Atlanta Housing Authority; Atlanta 833
U.S. Postal Service; Atlanta 800
U.S. Federal Aviation Administration; Atlanta 800
State of Georgia; Atlanta; labor organizations 800
AT&T Co./AT&T Technologies; Atlanta; electrical repair 800
Transus Inc.; Atlanta; trucking services 750
AT&T Co.; Atlanta; telephone communications 750
Ernst & Young; Atlanta; accounting/auditing 750
Nabisco Brands Inc.; Atlanta; bakery products 700
Georgia Assoc. Marriage; Atlanta; family services 700
U.S. Commerce Dept.; Atlanta 700
Blue Cross/Blue Shield of Georgia; Atlanta; medical service/health insurance 675
Union Security Life Insurance Co.; Atlanta; life insurance 660
Printpack Inc.; Atlanta; paper products 650
Knowledgeware Inc.; Atlanta; computer services 650
Atlantic Steel Co.; Atlanta; steel products 623
King & Spalding; Atlanta; legal services 620

Bellsouth Mobility Inc.; Atlanta; telephone communications 610

Owens-Corning Fiberglas Corp.; Fairburn; mineral products 600

Treasure Chest Advertising Co.; Atlanta; commercial printing 600

Flowers Industries Inc./Flowers Baking Co. Chattooga; Atlanta; horticultural specialties 600

Mead Corp./Mead Packaging Div.; Atlanta; paperboard mills 600

AT&T Co.; Atlanta; accounting services 600

Atlanta Center Ltd./Atlanta Hilton & Towers; Atlanta; hotel 600

Omni Hotels Management Corp./Omni Hotel at CNN Center; Atlanta; hotel 570

U.S. Penitentiary; Atlanta 550

Weight Watchers of Greater Atlanta; Atlanta; diet services 550

American Software Inc.; Atlanta; computer services 550

Goode Brothers Poultry Inc.; Atlanta; grocery products 525

6th District

Atlanta Suburbs — Roswell; Part of Marietta

Anchored in Atlanta's burgeoning northern suburbs, the 6th covers parts of five counties that are laden with Republican voters who work in high-technology and other white-collar occupations. This area is commonly referred to as the Golden Crescent; it is sandwiched between three of the state's major interstate highways—I-75, I-85 and the I-285 perimeter highway.

Cobb County, which lies northwest of Atlanta, accounts for more than 50 percent of the district's vote. About three-fourths of Cobb's residents are in the 6th; most of the rest of the county is in the 7th. Voters in the 6th District part of Cobb gave George Bush a decisive 55 percent in the 1992 presidential contest. That year the entire district went handily for GOP candidates Paul Coverdell for the Senate and Newt Gingrich for the House.

Though it is well within Atlanta's orbit, Marietta (which is divided between the 6th and 7th districts) provides Cobb County with its own population and commercial center. Marietta has a thriving base of service-oriented small businesses (the city won notice from *The Wall Street Journal* in 1989 as the nation's small-business development capital), and Cobb County is headquarters for a number of well-known larger concerns, including Sprint, Home Depot and The Weather Channel. Many workers in the district commute to jobs at the nearby Dobbins Air Reserve Base and an adjoining Lockheed facility (which are both located in the part of Marietta in the 7th District).

Marietta has three colleges—Kennesaw State College, Southern College of Technology and Life College (one of the largest chiropractic schools in the nation). An important local tourist attraction is the Kennesaw Mountain National Battlefield.

In the central part of the 6th are more GOP-leaning suburbs in northern Fulton County. Two major towns here are Alpharetta and Roswell. Alpharetta was once home to a number of large farms that have since been converted into suburban developments. Roswell used to be a cotton-milling center, but now is a booming bedroom community with the sort of white-collar, managerial types that seem ubiquitous in the Atlanta area. About one-fifth of the district's vote is cast in Fulton County, and this is where Bush ran strongest in the 6th in 1992, taking 58 percent of the vote.

The remaining share of the vote in the district—about 25 percent—comes from northern De Kalb County, northern Gwinnett County and southern Cherokee County. Again, all are solidly Republican.

In northern De Kalb County, affluent Dunwoody is a haven for the professional class, with well-manicured lawns and country clubs. Many of these suburbanites came to Atlanta from other areas of the country. Holiday Inn and United Parcel Service have their headquarters in Dunwoody.

Gwinnett and Cherokee counties were among the state's fastest-growing in the 1980s, also attracting newcomers with no connections to the region's traditional Democratic ties.

Election Returns

	6th District	Democrat		Republican	
1992	President*	82,355	(29.4%)	155,760	(55.6%)
	House	116,196	(42.3%)	158,761	(57.7%)
1990	Senate	25,225	(100.0%)	—	
	Governor	32,452	(32.6%)	67,181	(67.4%)
1988	President	42,318	(24.9%)	127,643	(75.1%)
1986	Senate	31,472	(33.9%)	61,463	(66.1%)
	Governor	48,699	(53.1%)	43,028	(46.9%)

Vote for Perot was 41,876 (15.0%).

Demographics

Population 587,118

Percent change from 1980 7.0%

Land area 586 square miles

Population per square mile 1,002

Counties, 1990 population

Cherokee (pt.) 53,198	Fulton (pt.) 116,752
Cobb (pt.) 312,072	Gwinnett (pt.) 60,593
De Kalb (pt.) 44,503	

Cities, 1990 population (10,000 or more)

Alpharetta 13,002	Sandy Springs CDP (pt.)
Dunwoody CDP 26,302	15,885
Marietta (pt.) 16,761	Smyrna (pt.) 30,981
Roswell 47,923	

Race and Hispanic origin
White 91.2%
Black 6.0%
American Indian, Eskimo, or Aleut. 0.2%
Asian or Pacific Islander 2.0%
Other 0.6%
Hispanic origin 2.1%

Ancestry

American 6.8%	Polish 2.8%
Dutch 2.5%	Russian 1.5%
English 22.7%	Scotch Irish 4.8%
French 4.4%	Scottish 4.1%
German 23.3%	Swedish 1.6%
Irish 20.2%	Welsh 1.2%
Italian 4.5%	

Universities/colleges, 1990-1991 enrollment
Kennesaw State College, Marietta 10,018

Newspapers, total circulation (in all districts)
Atlanta Journal-Constitution 494,556
Marietta Daily Journal Sunday Record 26,330

Commercial television stations, affiliations
ADI: Atlanta (100%)

Cable television systems, total subscribers
Acworth Cable TV; Kennesaw 16,125
Georgia Cable TV/Comm; Atlanta 92,544
Georgia Cable TV/Comm; Decatur 99,456
Gwinnett Cable TV; Lilburn 60,464
North De Kalb Cable; Chamblee 24,051
Roswell Cablevision; Roswell 11,000
Smyrna Cable TV; Smyrna 20,000
Summit Cable Service Georgia Inc.; Marietta 50,000
Wometco Cable TV; Marietta 23,487

Military installations, 1991
McCollum Air Guard Station, Kennesaw 48

Businesses and other major employers
AT&T Co./AT&T Network Systems; Norcross; research
  services 3,450
Trust Co. of Georgia; Atlanta; holding offices 2,911
Southern Bell Telephone & Telegraph Co.; Atlanta;
  telegraph/other communications 2,000
Venture Restaurant Management; Atlanta;
  management/public relations 1,987
Ciba Vision Corp.; Atlanta; ophthalmic goods 1,900
Riverwood Intl. Corp.; Atlanta; paper mills 1,700
Kimberly-Clark Corp.; Roswell; paper mills 1,500
Equifax Inc.; Alpharetta; insurance services 1,300
AT&T Communications Inc.; Alpharetta; communications
  equipment 1,200
Georgia Air National Guard; Marietta 1,200
Kennesaw State College; Marietta 1,018
Cox Enterprises Inc./Atlanta Journal; Atlanta; newspapers
  1,000
Nimslo Corp.; Duluth; heavy construction 1,000
Progressive Corp.; Marietta; insurance services 1,000
Great Southeastern Restaurants/Great American Group;
  Norcross; restaurants/management 1,000
United Parcel Service Inc.; Atlanta; mail services 900
Barge-Wagener Inc.; Atlanta; building construction 900
State of Georgia/Brook Run; Atlanta; residential care 900
HBO & Co.; Atlanta; cable TV services 800
Fulton North Regional Hospital; Roswell 790
Unisys Corp./Southern Regional Office; Atlanta;
  professional/commercial equipment 700
OKI America Inc./OKI Telecom; Suwanee; communications
  equipment 700
Confederation Life Insurance Co.; Atlanta; insurance services
  690
Avon Products Inc.; Atlanta; cosmetics 600
Federated Dept. Stores/Sabre Group; Norcross; department
  stores 600
Richs Inc./Richs; Atlanta; department stores 600
Stouffer Corp./Stouffer Waverly Hotel; Atlanta; hotel 600
Siemens Energy & Automation; Alpharetta; electrical goods
  566
Nu Skin Intl.; Marietta; cosmetics/vitamins 550

7th District
Northwest — Rome; Part of Marietta

Starting in suburbs north and west of Atlanta, the 7th runs
west to the Alabama border, taking in 10 full counties and part of
another. But in terms of population concentration, it is bottom-
heavy. Nearly half the district's voters live in just three counties
that adjoin Atlanta's Fulton County—Cobb, Douglas and Carroll.

The 7th delivered a split verdict in the 1992 election. For
president, the district preferred George Bush, who won 47
percent of the vote; Bill Clinton managed to carry only four
largely rural counties on the Alabama border. But in voting for
the House, Democratic Rep. George Darden polled 57 percent,
carrying all but one of the counties in the district.

The 7th takes in the southwestern part of Cobb County,
including part of the city of Marietta. This is Darden's home
base; he took 56 percent of the Cobb vote in 1992, even as those
same voters backed Bush for president. The county is a
collection of largely white-collar, middle-income suburbs.

The Marietta area has a diverse economic base, with numerous small businesses, several corporate headquarters and military-
and aerospace-related employment at Lockheed and the Dobbins
Air Reserve Base. The Lockheed facility laid off several thousand
workers in the late 1980s, but a new contract to manufacture the
F-22 advanced tactical fighter is expected to provide about 1,500
jobs in coming years.

Cobb's neighbor to the south is Douglas County, the only
county in the 7th that gave a majority to Darden's Republican
challenger in 1992. Bush carried Douglas with 50 percent. Thanks
to the expansion of west-of-Atlanta bedroom communities,
Douglas saw its population grow by 25 percent during the 1980s.

Moving beyond the metropolitan Atlanta orbit, the land is
given over to agricultural pursuits, and there are a number of
small towns traditionally reliant on textile trades. A number of
the counties on the western edge of the 7th endured economic
difficulties in the 1980s and are searching for new sources of
income. Chattooga County now has a state prison; an Anheuser
Busch brewery is coming into Bartow County. The biggest city
in this part of 7th is Rome, the seat of Floyd County. Rome is a
mill town that was once the district's largest city. Though
eclipsed now by Marietta, it is a regional health-care center.

In 1992, Floyd County went narrowly for Bush but decisively
for Darden; traditional Democratic voting patterns remain fairly
strong in the district's more rural counties. Clinton carried
Chattooga County, north of Floyd, and he also won three of the
four counties directly to the south (Polk, Haralson and Heard).
Jobs in these counties are found in the beef and timber industries
and with a few manufacturers.

At the southwestern extreme of the district, Troup County
may be poised for industrial expansion and population growth. It
lies midway between Atlanta and Columbus, with I-85 slicing
across its middle.

Election Returns

	7th District	Democrat		Republican	
1992	President*	77,103	(38.5%)	93,175	(46.5%)
	House	111,374	(57.3%)	82,915	(42.7%)
1990	Senate	70,071	(100.0%)	—	
	Governor	61,386	(54.0%)	52,254	(46.0%)
1988	President	49,017	(32.5%)	101,901	(67.5%)

	7th District	Democrat	Republican
1986	Senate	39,717 (48.3%)	42,554 (51.7%)
	Governor	55,626 (69.2%)	24,753 (30.8%)

Vote for Perot was 30,097 (15.0%).

Demographics

Population 588,071

Percent change from 1980 7.7%

Land area 3,703 square miles

Population per square mile 159

Counties, 1990 population

Bartow 55,911	Haralson 21,966
Carroll 71,422	Heard 8,628
Chattooga 22,242	Paulding 41,611
Cobb (pt.) 124,569	Polk 33,815
Douglas 71,120	Troup 55,536
Floyd 81,251	

Cities, 1990 population (10,000 or more)

Carrollton 16,029	Lithia Springs CDP 11,403
Cartersville 12,035	Mableton CDP (pt.) 22,174
Douglasville 11,635	Marietta (pt.) 27,368
La Grange 25,597	Rome 30,326

Race and Hispanic origin

White 85.9%
Black 12.9%
American Indian, Eskimo, or Aleut. 0.2%
Asian or Pacific Islander 0.6%
Other 0.4%
Hispanic origin 1.1%

Ancestry

American 18.3%	Irish 19.1%
Dutch 2.4%	Italian 1.6%
English 13.8%	Scotch Irish 2.8%
French 2.3%	Scottish 1.9%
German 12.3%	

Universities/colleges, 1990-1991 enrollment

Berry College, Rome 1,805
Chattahoochee Technical Institute, Marietta 1,401
Coosa Valley Tech Institute, Rome 927
Floyd College, Rome 2,017
La Grange College, La Grange 993
Life College, Marietta 1,867
Shorter College, Rome 858
Southern College of Technology, Marietta 4,007
West Georgia College, Carrollton 7,068
West Georgia Tech Institute, La Grange 517

Newspapers, total circulation (in all districts)

Atlanta Journal-Constitution 494,556
Chattanooga News-Free Press 89,205
Marietta Daily Journal Sunday Record 26,330

Commercial television stations, affiliations

ADI: Atlanta (100%)

Cable television systems, total subscribers

Acworth Cable TV; Kennesaw 16,125
Cartersville Cable TV; Cartersville 5,981
Cobb County Cable TV; Mableton 19,531
Falcon Cable TV; Cedartown 7,835
La Grange Cablevision; La Grange 13,000
Scripps-Howard Cable; Dallas 6,000
Scripps-Howard Cable; Rome 22,438
Smyrna Cable TV; Smyrna 20,000
Summit Cable Service Georgia Inc.; Marietta 50,000
Wometco Cable TV; Marietta 23,487
Wometco Cable TV/Douglas County; Douglasville 13,485

Military installations, 1991

Dobbins Air Force Base, Marietta 1,714
Atlanta Naval Air Station, Marietta 1,099

Businesses and other major employers

Lockheed Corp./Lockheed Aeronautical Systems; Marietta; aircraft/parts 10,200
Southwire Co./Senator Wire & Cable Co.; Carrollton; metal wire 2,800
Kennestone Hospital; Marietta 2,500
Mount Vernon Mills Inc.; Trion; apparel/fabrics 1,528
Cobb Hospital Inc./Cobb Hospital & Medical Center; Austell 1,451
Galey & Lord Inc./Brighton Plant; Shannon; man-made fabric mills 1,263
Sony Music Entertainment Inc.; Carrollton; audio/video equipment 1,200
Bremen-Bowdon Investment Co.; Bowdon; men's suits/coats 1,000
Bartow County School District; Cartersville 1,000
Floyd County Medical Center; Rome 940
Greenwood Mills Inc./Lindale Mfg. Co.; Lindale; cotton mills 900
West Georgia Medical Center/Florence Hand Nursing Home; La Grange 862
Fieldcrest Cannon Inc./Bigelow Sanford; Summerville; carpets/rugs 850
Yellow Freight System Inc.; Marietta; trucking services 800
La Mar Mfg. Co.; Bowdon; men's suits/coats 800
Fieldcrest Cannon Inc./Bigelow Sanford; Lyerly; carpets/rugs 800
State of Georgia/Human Resources Dept.; Rome 800
Interface Inc./Heuga USA Inc.; La Grange; carpets/rugs 720
West Georgia College; Carrollton 720
Inland Container Corp./Inland Rome Inc.; Rome; paper mills 700
Tillotson Corp./Best Manufacturing Corp.; Menlo; apparel 665
First Brands Corp.; Cartersville; paper products 650
Southern College of Technology; Marietta 650
Engineered Fabrics Corp.; Rockmart; aircraft/parts 600
Goodyear Tire & Rubber Co.; Cartersville; textile goods 600
Bekaert Corp.; Rome; steel wire 600
West Point-Pepperell Inc./Dunson Mill; La Grange; cotton mills 550
Bidermann Industries Corp./Cluet Peabody & Co.; Cedartown; apparel/piece goods/notions 550
Medical Center West Inc./HCA Parkway Medical Center; Lithia Springs 540
Georgia Hughes Inc.; La Grange; guided missiles 530
Freudenberg-NOK; La Grange; gaskets/packing/sealing devices 506

8th District

South Central — Warner Robins; Parts of Albany, Valdosta and Macon

Covering a 32-county swath of south-central Georgia, the 8th is largely rural. In 1992, a majority of those 32 counties cast fewer than 5,000 votes apiece in the presidential contest.

But on the edges of the district, the 8th includes parts of four urbanized areas—Macon (Bibb County), Warner Robins (Houston County), Albany (Dougherty County) and Valdosta (Lowndes County).

Those four counties account for more than 40 percent of the total district vote. In 1992 all four supported George Bush's re-election, and three of the four went against Democrat Roy Rowland in his successful House election.

Redistricting in 1992 made the 8th more politically competitive. In his old district, Rowland had never gotten less than 69 percent of the vote. But remapping deprived him of many reliably Democratic black voters in the 8th's urban areas. Blacks now are 21 percent of the district's population, down from 35 percent in the 1980s.

Basically, what remains in those urban areas are whites—many of them conservative religious activists—who tend to vote Republican. On the strength of their support, Bush carried the 8th over Bill Clinton, even though Clinton won nearly all the 8th's less-populous counties.

Contributing to the 8th's conservative tenor are three large military bases—Robins Air Force Base (in Warner Robins), Moody Air Force Base (in Valdosta) and the Marine Corps Logistics Center (in Albany). The bases are the 8th's largest employers, but the district's economy also depends heavily on agriculture, particularly pecans and peanuts.

In the northwestern corner of the district is Macon, an old textile and railroad town that has long been a trading and processing center for the agricultural lands of middle Georgia that surround it. From here, Atlanta is just a little more than an hour up Interstate 75, but the boom in the capital region has not had a great impact in Macon. The city's population dropped almost 9 percent during the 1980s, to 107,000. Macon has a cherry blossom festival that draws thousands of visitors each spring, and there are redevelopment and preservation efforts, including renovation of some small pre-Civil War houses into low-cost housing.

The second-largest city in the 8th is Albany, on the district's western side. Albany's economy was set back by the closing of a Firestone Tire & Rubber plant, but Miller Brewing (beer), Procter & Gamble (paper products) and Coats and Clark (thread) remain as major employers.

Just a few miles short of Florida is Valdosta (Lowndes County). Surrounded by the vast reaches of south Georgia's Piney Woods, it makes much of its living from the forests, with planing and paper mills and sawmills providing many paychecks.

Although the 8th's more urbanized areas were a struggle for Rowland in 1992, he typically amassed sizable margins elsewhere in the district, where Democratic traditions are strong. He won Laurens County, his home base, with 72 percent.

Election Returns

	8th District	Democrat	Republican
1992	President*	83,332 (39.8%)	94,018 (44.9%)
	House	108,472 (55.7%)	86,220 (44.3%)
1990	Senate	82,841 (100.0%)	—
	Governor	64,642 (52.0%)	59,744 (48.0%)
1988	President	59,542 (36.8%)	102,454 (63.2%)
1986	Senate	36,133 (46.7%)	41,286 (53.3%)
	Governor	55,934 (76.1%)	17,586 (23.9%)

Vote for Perot was 32,090 (15.3%).

Demographics

Population 591,615

Percent change from 1980 9.2%

Land area 10,644 square miles

Population per square mile 56

Counties, 1990 population

Atkinson	6,213	Jeff Davis	12,032
Ben Hill	16,245	Johnson	8,329
Berrien	14,153	Jones (pt.)	5,723
Bibb (pt.)	75,566	Lanier	5,531
Bleckley	10,430	Laurens	39,988
Clinch	6,160	Lee (pt.)	12,133
Coffee	29,592	Lowndes (pt.)	51,943
Colquitt (pt.)	28,155	Pulaski	8,108
Cook	13,456	Telfair	11,000
Crisp (pt.)	12,820	Tift	34,998
Dodge	17,607	Treutlen	5,994
Dooly (pt.)	979	Turner	8,703
Dougherty (pt.)	43,737	Twiggs (pt.)	2,710
Echols	2,334	Wheeler	4,903
Houston (pt.)	66,671	Wilcox	7,008
Irwin	8,649	Worth	19,745

Cities, 1990 population (10,000 or more)

Albany (pt.)	31,569	Tifton	14,215
Douglas	10,464	Valdosta (pt.)	20,161
Dublin	16,312	Warner Robins (pt.)	32,108
Macon (pt.)	37,309		

Race and Hispanic origin

White 77.7%
Black 21.0%
American Indian, Eskimo, or Aleut. 0.2%
Asian or Pacific Islander 0.5%
Other 0.5%
Hispanic origin 1.4%

Ancestry

American	19.4%	Irish	16.0%
Dutch	1.5%	Italian	1.1%
English	13.7%	Scotch Irish	3.0%
French	2.0%	Scottish	1.9%
German	10.2%		

Universities/colleges, 1990-1991 enrollment

Abraham Baldwin Agricultural College, Tifton 2,497
Ben Hill-Irwin Tech Institute, Fitzgerald 528
Crandall Junior College, Macon 544
Darton College, Albany 2,123
Heart of Georgia Tech Institute, Dublin 293
Middle Georgia College, Cochran 1,505

South Georgia College, Douglas 1,107
Wesleyan College, Macon 511

Newspapers, total circulation (in all districts)
Albany Herald 36,686
Atlanta Journal-Constitution 494,556
Dublin Courier Herald 11,011
Florida Times-Union 179,796
Macon Telegraph 72,390
Valdosta Daily Times 19,590
Warner Robins Daily Sun 8,938

Commercial television stations, affiliations
ADI: Albany (43%), Macon (33%), Tallahassee-Thomasville
   (8%), Jacksonville (8%), Savannah (5%) and Augusta (3%)
   WALB-TV, Albany (NBC)
   WFXL, Albany (Fox)
   WSST-TV, Cordele (None)
   WGXA, Macon (ABC)
   WMAZ-TV, Macon (CBS)
   WMGT, Macon (NBC)
   WVGA, Valdosta (ABC)
   WGNM, Macon (None)

Cable television systems, total subscribers
Cablevision; Douglas 7,000
Cox Cable Middle Georgia; Macon 42,816
Cox Cable Middle Georgia; Warner Robins 21,184
Peachtree Cable TV Inc.; Dublin 7,252
Storer Cable TV Inc.; Albany 27,812
Storer Cable TV Inc.; Tifton 6,573
TCI of Georgia; Valdosta 15,877

Military installations, 1991
Marine Corps Logistics Base, Albany 3,842

Businesses and other major employers
Brown & Williamson Tobacco; Macon; tobacco products:
   2,500
Forstmann & Co. Inc.; Dublin; wool mills 1,600
Geico; Macon; insurance services 1,300
South Georgia Medical Center; Valdosta 1,300
Amoco Fabrics & Fibers Co./Patchogue Plymouth Div.;
   Hazlehurst; accounting/auditing 1,280
Amoco Fabrics & Fibers Co./Nashville Mills Div.; Nashville;
   rubber products 1,200
National Service Industries/Lithonia Lighting; Cochran; elec-
   tric lighting 1,150
Miller Brewing Co.; Albany; brewery 1,000
Houston Medical Center; Warner Robins 950
Boeing Georgia Inc.; Macon; aircraft/parts 936
Associated Materials Inc./Amer. Cord Inc.; Lumber City;
   textile goods 850
U.S. A YKK Inc./Macon Div.; Macon; costume jewelry 800
U.S. Veterans Affairs Dept.; Dublin 770
Golden Poultry Co. Inc.; Douglas; meat products 715
Keebler Co. Inc.; Macon; bakery products 700
Tift General Hospital; Tifton 660
Joseph Campbell Co.; Douglas; meat products 650
Burlen Corp./Fitzgerald Underwear; Tifton; undergarments:
   650
Roydon Wear Inc.; McRae; outerwear 650
PCC Airfoils Inc./Douglas Div.; Douglas; aircraft/parts 600
Queen Carpet Corp.; Tifton; yarn/thread mills 600

Tifton Aluminum Co. Inc.; Tifton; aluminum rolling and
   drawing 600
Insurance Co. of North America/Cigna Property Casualty
   Companies; Macon; insurance services 600
Flint River Textiles Inc.; Albany; cotton mills 575
State of Georgia/Transportation Dept.; Tifton; road construc-
   tion 560
HCA Palmyra Medical Center; Albany 534
City of Warner Robins; Warner Robins 530
Shaw Industries Inc.; Fitzgerald; yarn/thread mills 526
House of Ronnie Delaware/Nashville Textile Corp.; Nashville;
   outerwear 515

9th District

North — Dalton; Gainesville; Toccoa

The 9th, anchored in north Georgia's mountains, runs across the state, from Alabama on the west to South Carolina on the east. At the local level, Democrats have long been dominant in most parts of the district, and when the 9th was open in 1992, the Democrat nominee easily held it for his party. The GOP, however, is gaining here.

The 9th has longstanding Republican pockets, particularly in the north-central counties of Union, Fannin, Gilmer and Towns counties; their allegiance to the GOP dates to the Civil War. And now, Republicans are becoming more prevalent in the southern part of the district, where Cherokee and Forsyth counties are filling up with Atlanta suburbanites.

Cherokee and Forsyth both gave a majority of their 1992 presidential votes to George Bush. In fact, despite his struggles nationally, Bush ran reasonably well all across the 9th, losing only two counties to Bill Clinton. The district also was strong for successful GOP Senate candidate Paul Coverdell.

In economic terms, the 9th is a blend of new and old. Many of those living in the metropolitan Atlanta orbit have white-collar and service-oriented occupations. Elsewhere, apparel manufacturing, poultry processing and carpet-making are major providers, and tourism and recreation are increasingly important.

The raising and processing of chickens is big business in Hall County (Gainesville) and Whitfield County (Dalton), the district's two most populous. Gainesville calls itself the "poultry capital of the world," and in the center of town is the Georgia Poultry Federation's monument to the industry: an obelisk with a chicken statue on top. Hall went easily for Bush in 1992, but in the House race it voted by better than 2-to-1 for the Democratic candidate.

Dalton, in the northwestern part of the district, is one of the country's top carpet-making centers. Despite its substantial blue-collar employment base, Whitfield County generally favors Republicans in competitive elections for state or federal office. Bush got 54 percent in Whitfield, and Coverdell also carried it.

In the district's extreme northwestern corner are Walker, Catoosa and Dade counties, conservative pillars whose economic fortunes are linked to Chattanooga, just over the border in Tennessee.

Millions who have never set foot in Georgia have seen its rugged northeastern corner on film. *Deliverance* was set in Rabun County, and *Smokey and the Bandit* was made in the area.

Tourist dollars play a crucial role in the district's economy. Dotting the mountains are an array of attractions, including Cloudland Canyon (Walker County), the manmade Lake Lanier

(Hall County), the wineries of Habersham County, and, in White County, the hamlet of Helen, a Swiss village replica, and the Cabbage Patch Hospital, a shop decorated like a hospital where visitors can buy Cabbage Patch dolls.

Election Returns

	9th District	Democrat	Republican
1992	President*	70,969 (35.1%)	98,184 (48.6%)
	House	113,024 (59.2%)	77,919 (40.8%)
1990	Senate	82,583 (100.0%)	—
	Governor	67,481 (55.9%)	52,700 (43.7%)
1988	President	46,194 (29.5%)	110,357 (70.5%)
1986	Senate	34,934 (46.5%)	40,202 (53.5%)
	Governor	50,926 (71.0%)	20,789 (29.0%)

*Vote for Perot was 32,806 (16.2%).

Demographics

Population 586,222

Percent change from 1980 6.2%

Land area 5,804 square miles

Population per square mile 101

Counties, 1990 population

Catoosa 42,464	Lumpkin 14,573
Cherokee (pt.) 37,006	Murray 26,147
Dade 13,147	Pickens 14,432
Dawson 9,429	Rabun 11,648
Fannin 15,992	Stephens 23,257
Forsyth 44,083	Towns 6,754
Gilmer 13,368	Union 11,993
Gordon 35,072	Walker 58,340
Habersham 27,621	White 13,006
Hall 95,428	Whitfield 72,462

Cities, 1990 population (10,000 or more)
Dalton 21,761   Gainesville 17,885

Race and Hispanic origin
White 94.7%
Black 3.7%
American Indian, Eskimo, or Aleut. 0.3%
Asian or Pacific Islander 0.4%
Other 1.0%
Hispanic origin 1.7%

Ancestry

American 18.4%	Irish 19.6%
Dutch 2.8%	Italian 1.1%
English 15.7%	Scotch Irish 2.8%
French 2.1%	Scottish 2.0%
German 13.5%	

Universities/colleges, 1990-1991 enrollment
Brenau College, Gainesville 1,839
Covenant College, Lookout Mountain 606
Dalton College, Dalton 2,500
Gainesville College, Gainesville 2,482
Lanier Technical Institute, Oakwood 455
North Georgia College, Dahlonega 2,518
North Georgia Tech Institute, Clarkesville 577
Pickens Technical Institute, Jasper 629
Piedmont College, Demorest 495
Reinhardt College, Waleska 768
Toccoa Falls College, Toccoa Falls 790
Truett McConnell College, Cleveland 1,631
Walker Technical Institute, Rock Spring 524
Young Harris College, Young Harris 435

Newspapers, total circulation (in all districts)
Anderson Independent-Mail 40,941
Atlanta Journal-Constitution 494,556
Chattanooga News-Free Press 89,205
Dalton Daily Citizen News 11,558
Gainesville Times 21,636

Commercial television stations, affiliations
ADI: Atlanta (66%), Chattanooga (31%) and Greenville-Spartanburg-Asheville (3%)
WNEG-TV, Toccoa (None)
WFLI-TV, Cleveland (None)
WTLK, Rome (None)

Cable television systems, total subscribers
Battlefield Cable TV; Rossville 13,057
C-4 Media Cable Southeast; Chatsworth 5,015
Falcon Cable TV; Dalton 21,972
Gainesville Cable TV; Gainesville 19,000
Gainesville Cable TV; Oakwood 7,306
Scripps-Howard Cable; Calhoun 6,545

Businesses and other major employers
Horizon Industries Inc./Horizon Carpets; Calhoun; carpets/rugs 2,100
Roper Corp./GE Appliance Div.; La Fayette; household appliances 2,100
World Carpets Inc./Customweave Carpets; Dalton; carpets/rugs 1,800
Fieldale Farms Corp.; Cornelia; meat products 1,500
Queen Carpet Corp.; Dalton; carpets/rugs 1,500
Northeast Georgia Medical Center; Gainesville 1,275
Shaw Industries Inc.; Dalton; carpets/rugs 1,258
ConAgra Poultry Co.; Gainesville; poultry/eggs 1,200
Coats & Clark Inc./Coats American; Toccoa; yarn/thread mills 1,200
Aladdin Mills Inc./Town House Mills; Dalton; carpets/rugs 1,200
Coronet Industries Inc.; Dalton; carpets/rugs 1,200
Synthetic Industries Inc./Fibermesh; Chickamauga; man-made fabric mills 1,150
Hutcheson Medical Center; Rossville 1,150
Whitfield County School District; Dalton 1,100
Tyson Foods Inc.; Cumming; meat products 1,000
Galaxy Carpet Mills Inc.; Chatsworth; carpets/rugs 1,000
Coronet Industries Inc./B. J. Bandy Plant; Dalton; carpets/rugs 1,000
Diamond Rug & Carpet Mills; Eton; carpets/rugs 900
Mannington Carpets Inc./Wellco Business Carpet Div.; Calhoun; carpets/rugs 822
White Consolidated Industries/Tappan; Dalton; industry machinery 750
County of Hall; Gainesville 750
Salem Carpet Mills Inc.; Ringgold; carpets/rugs 701
Burlington Industries Inc.; Rabun Gap; carpets/rugs 700

Mount Vernon Mills Inc.; Alto; apparel/piece goods/notions 686

J&J Industries Inc.; Dalton; carpets/rugs 675

Seaboard Corp./Seaboard Farms; Canton; poultry 660

Peachtree Doors Inc.; Gainesville; metal doors 650

Carriage Industries Inc./Carriage Transport Ltd.; Calhoun; carpets/rugs 650

State of Georgia/Transportation Dept.; Gainesville 650

Shaw Industries Inc./Plant 4; Dalton; carpets/rugs 619

Shaw Industries Inc./Plant 81; Dalton; carpets/rugs 619

Torrington Co.; Calhoun; ball bearings/parts 615

Shaw Industries Inc./Plant 6; Dalton; yarn/thread mills 603

Dittler Brothers Inc./Moreno Press; Oakwood; commercial printing 600

Liberty Mutual Insurance Co.; Gainesville; life insurance 600

Shaw Industries Inc./Armstrong-E & B Carpet Mills; Dalton; yarn/thread mills 580

Dittler Brothers Inc./Moreno Press Div.; Gainesville; commercial printing 550

ConAgra Inc.; Dalton; meat products 550

Stephens County School District; Toccoa 550

10th District

Northeast — Athens; Augusta Suburbs

This 19-county chunk of eastern Georgia has clumps of population at both ends and in the middle, and its voters are a mix of staunchly conservative Republicans, steadfast liberal Democrats and middle-of-the-roaders. In 1992, the contest for the open 10th District seat was one of Georgia's most competitive; the Democratic candidate won with 54 percent of the vote.

The district has two Republican bulwarks. The biggest is on the east, in the Augusta suburbs and exurbs of Richmond and Columbia counties. On the western edge of the 10th, the GOP is strong in Gwinnett County (which is split between the 10th, 4th and 6th districts).

Taken together, those two population concentrations cast almost 40 percent of the district vote, and they helped George Bush carry the 10th in 1992 presidential voting.

Between them is a stretch of counties that remains largely rural. Many of their voters are traditionally Democratic; Bill Clinton carried a half-dozen of the lightly settled counties in 1992.

But he found his strongest support at the center of the district, in Clarke County, home to the University of Georgia. Its 28,400 students and nearly 2,000 faculty members have moved Clarke well to the left of the district mainstream; Clinton carried the county with 53 percent of the vote. Tempering the liberal influence of the university community are military and civilian employees at the Navy Supply Corps School. It adds about $3 million yearly to the local economy.

In the Augusta area, conservative-minded white-collar suburbanites mingle with a substantial population of active-duty and retired military personnel associated with Fort Gordon, home of the Army Signal Corps. Though the city of Augusta itself is mostly in the 11th District, the 10th has the bulk of surrounding Richmond County. Bush won 52 percent here in 1992, and to the north in neighboring Columbia County, he soared to a 59 percent tally.

Other large employers in this part of the 10th are the Medical College of Georgia and the federal government's Savannah River

nuclear facility, located just downriver in South Carolina's Aiken and Barnwell counties. The plant, which processed tritium for use in nuclear weapons, has been stymied by safety and environmental problems in recent years.

At the district's northeastern corner, bordering Hart County, is Hartwell Lake, one of the largest man-made lakes in the country. To the west, there is a Mitsubishi plant in Jackson County, and the little town of Braselton there made headlines recently when actress Kim Basinger purchased it for $20 million. Heading south, the 10th meanders through cotton, soybean, tobacco and corn country.

At its western edge, the 10th's portion of Gwinnett County is less densely settled than the areas of the county in the 4th and 6th districts, but Republican preferences are almost as strong. In 1992 Bush won 52 percent in the 10th District part of Gwinnett.

Election Returns

	10th District	Democrat		Republican	
1992	President*	81,014	(39.4%)	95,164	(46.3%)
	House	108,426	(53.8%)	93,059	(46.2%)
1990	Senate	83,888	(100.0%)	—	
	Governor	59,493	(52.3%)	54,196	(47.7%)
1988	President	51,316	(35.2%)	94,599	(64.8%)
1986	Senate	38,735	(46.1%)	45,271	(53.9%)
	Governor	60,563	(74.2%)	21,038	(25.8%)

*Vote for Perot was 29,452 (14.3%).

Demographics

Population 591,644

Percent change from 1980 7.5%

Land area 5,114 square miles

Population per square mile 116

Counties, 1990 population

Banks 10,308	Madison 21,050
Barrow 29,721	McDuffie 20,119
Clarke 87,594	Morgan 12,883
Columbia 66,031	Newton 41,808
Elbert 18,949	Oconee 17,618
Franklin 16,650	Oglethorpe 9,763
Gwinnett (pt.) 40,565	Richmond (pt.) 96,715
Hart 19,712	Walton 38,586
Jackson 30,005	Wilkes (pt.) 6,125
Lincoln 7,442	

Cities, 1990 population (10,000 or more)

Athens 45,734	Martinez CDP 33,731
Augusta (pt.) 19,704	South Augusta CDP (pt.)
Covington 10,026	16,721
Evans CDP 13,713	West Augusta CDP (pt.)
Gaines School CDP 11,354	24,870

Race and Hispanic origin

White 80.3%

Black 18.1%

American Indian, Eskimo, or Aleut 0.2%

Asian or Pacific Islander 1.1%

Other 0.4%

Hispanic origin 1.2%

Ancestry

American	15.1%	
Dutch	1.6%	
English	15.0%	
French	2.6%	
German	13.6%	
Irish	16.6%	
Italian	1.6%	
Polish	1.0%	
Scotch Irish	3.2%	
Scottish	2.2%	

Universities/colleges, 1990-1991 enrollment

Athens Technical Institute, Athens 1,182
Augusta College, Augusta 5,185
Emmanuel College, Franklin Springs 395
Medical College of Georgia, Augusta 2,426
Phillips Junior College, Augusta 586
University of Georgia, Athens 28,395

Newspapers, total circulation (in all districts)

Anderson Independent-Mail 40,941
Augusta Chronicle Augusta Herald 82,491
Athens News/Banner-Herald 27,902
Atlanta Journal-Constitution 494,556

Commercial television stations, affiliations

ADI: Atlanta (56%), Augusta (27%) and Greenville-Spartan-burg-Asheville (17%)
WNGM-TV, Athens (None)

Cable television systems, total subscribers

Covington Cable TV; Covington 6,023
Gwinnett Cable TV; Lilburn 60,464
Jones Intercable Inc.; Augusta 61,080
Northeast Gwinnett Cablevision; Lawrenceville 17,000
TCI of Georgia; Athens 23,500
Wometco Cable TV/Rockdale County; Conyers 11,600

Military installations, 1991

Fort Gordon (Army), Augusta 14,287
Navy Supply Corps School, Athens 326

Businesses and other major employers

Seaboard Farms of Athens Inc.; Athens; poultry products 15,000
University of Georgia; Athens 10,102
Medical College of Georgia & Hospital; Augusta 6,326
Richmond County School District; Augusta 4,500
U.S. Veterans Affairs Dept.; Augusta; hospital 2,340
Athens Regional Medical Center; Athens 1,790
Humana Hospital of Augusta; Augusta 1,500
City of Athens; Athens 1,400
Saint Mary's Hospital of Athens; Athens 1,350
Continental Grain Co./Wayne Poultry Div.; Pendergrass; poultry products 1,200
Columbia County School District; Appling 1,006
Gold Kist Inc./Poultry & Pork Processing Div.; Athens; meat products 1,000
ABB Power T&D Co. Inc.; Athens; electric distribution equipment 1,000
St. Joseph Hospital of Augusta; Augusta 1,000
Hercules Inc.; Covington; plastics/synthetics 950
Mobil Oil Corp./Mobil Chemical Co.; Covington; paper products 900
Johnson Controls World Services Inc./Base Support Div./Fort; Augusta; airport services 894
General Time Corp./Westclox Div.; Athens; watches/clocks 840
Reliance Electric Co.; Athens; electrical industrial apparatus 800
Monroe Auto Equipment Co.; Hartwell; motor vehicles/equipment 800
Salant Corp./Thomson Co.; Thomson; outerwear 750
Seaboard Farms/Seaboard Foods; Elberton; grocery products 700
Carole Fabrics Corp.; Augusta; man-made fabric mills 625
Spartan Mills/John P. King Mfg. Div.; Augusta; cotton mills 600
Mitsubishi Electronics America; Braselton; audio/video equipment 600
Kendall Co.; Augusta; cotton mills 550
Du Pont E. I. De Nemours and Co.; Athens; yarn/thread mills 520
Georgia Regional Hospital; Augusta 508

11th District

East Central — Atlanta Suburbs; Parts of Augusta and Savannah

The black-majority 11th begins in Atlanta's southeastern suburbs and then sweeps east and south across two-thirds of Georgia, ending 250 miles distant in the Atlantic coast city of Savannah. It includes all or part of 22 counties, but more than 60 percent of the vote comes out of just three urbanized counties— De Kalb (east of Atlanta), Richmond (Augusta) and Chatham (Savannah).

The 11th is one of two new majority-minority districts created by Georgia mapmakers in 1992 to comply with Voting Rights Act mandates to increase minority representation. Of the state's three minority districts, the 11th has the heaviest concentration of black residents: 64 percent. Blacks make up 60 percent of the district's registered voters.

Democrats dominate all across the district. With the exceptions of Henry and Glascock counties, Bill Clinton swept the 11th in 1992 presidential voting.

His victories were landslides in De Kalb (78 percent) and Chatham (79 percent). Richmond County gave him a more modest 60 percent. The Democratic nominee took even bigger margins in winning election to the open House seat.

The southern part of De Kalb County is an unassuming area of modest residences, but economic activity here is likely to step up over the next few years as preparations are made for the 1996 Summer Olympics. With events scheduled for Atlanta as well as Savannah and Augusta, the 11th will have more sites of Olympic competition than any other district.

On the district's eastern edge, most of the conservative voters of Richmond County (Augusta) were placed by mapmakers in the 10th District, leaving a Democratic core in the 11th.

From Augusta, the district drops south along the South Carolina line and snakes into Savannah, taking in the city's heavily Democratic areas, including parts of historic Savannah, the port and its waterfront. The city's economy has gotten a boost from the success of River Street, a string of restaurants, nightclubs, shops and hotels along the waterfront that tourists frequent.

Between the urban pockets of the 11th are mile after mile of agricultural acreage. This area once was known as Georgia's cotton belt, but today many of the people here depend more on other crops, including corn, soybean and peanuts.

Also prominent in this part of the 11th is the kaolin mining industry, which provides the white clay for use in white paint, china and stationery.

The district is home to three of the four cities that have served as Georgia's capital. The first was Savannah, founded in 1736 by James Oglethorpe. Milledgeville (Baldwin County) was later designated the capital because of its central location, but during the Civil War, it was seen as vulnerable and Augusta became the capital. Later, Atlanta was given the honor.

Many of those who live in the district's rural areas have a hard time keeping their head above water financially. Hancock County, for instance, is said to be the poorest in Georgia; About 40 percent of the families earn less than $10,000 per year.

Election Returns

	11th District	Democrat		Republican	
1992	President*	118,708	(64.6%)	48,026	(26.2%)
	House	120,168	(73.1%)	44,221	(26.9%)
1990	Senate	77,819	(100.0%)		—
	Governor	68,899	(67.1%)	33,814	(32.9%)
1988	President	93,156	(60.5%)	60,817	(39.5%)
1986	Senate	58,098	(65.9%)	30,114	(34.1%)
	Governor	68,574	(81.1%)	16,019	(18.9%)

*Vote for Perot was 16,883 (9.2%).

Demographics

Population 586,195

Percent change from 1980 (new district in the 1990s)

Land area 6,784 square miles

Population per square mile 86

Counties, 1990 population

Baldwin (pt.) 30,786	Jefferson 17,408
Burke 20,579	Jenkins 8,247
Butts 15,326	Putnam 14,137
Chatham (pt.) 72,505	Richmond (pt.) 93,004
De Kalb (pt.) 207,112	Screven 13,842
Effingham (pt.) 1,387	Taliaferro 1,915
Glascock 2,357	Twiggs (pt.) 7,096
Greene 11,793	Warren 6,078
Hancock 8,908	Washington 19,112
Henry (pt.) 11,450	Wilkes (pt.) 4,472
Jasper 8,453	Wilkinson 10,228

Cities, 1990 population (10,000 or more)

Augusta (pt.) 24,935	Milledgeville (pt.) 17,038
Belvedere Park CDP 18,089	Redan CDP 24,376
Candler-McAfee CDP 29,491	Savannah (pt.) 64,526
	South Augusta CDP (pt.) 39,277

Race and Hispanic origin

White 34.5%
Black 64.1%
American Indian, Eskimo, or Aleut. 0.2%
Asian or Pacific Islander 0.9%
Other 0.4%
Hispanic origin 1.1%

Ancestry

American 9.1%	German 5.5%
English 6.4%	Irish 6.9%
French 1.1%	Scotch Irish 1.5%

Universities/colleges, 1990-1991 enrollment

Augusta Technical School, Augusta 2,108
De Kalb Community College, Decatur 13,944
Georgia College, Milledgeville 4,948
Georgia Military College, Milledgeville 1,892
Paine College, Augusta 606
Savannah State College, Savannah 2,319

Newspapers, total circulation (in all districts)

Atlanta Journal-Constitution 494,556
Augusta Chronicle Augusta Herald 82,491
Macon Telegraph 72,390
Savannah Morning News Evening Press 73,752

Commercial television stations, affiliations

ADI: Augusta (44%), Atlanta (22%), Macon (22%) and Savannah (11%)

Cable television systems, total subscribers

Georgia Cable TV/Comm; Decatur 99,456
Jones Intercable Inc.; Augusta 61,080

Businesses and other major employers

Central State Hospital; Milledgeville; psychiatric hospital 3,583
University Hospital; Augusta 3,300
County of De Kalb/Public Safety Dept.; Decatur 1,600
County of De Kalb; Decatur 1,499
Gracewood State School & Hospital; Gracewood; psychiatric hospital 1,450
County of De Kalb/Board of Education; Clarkston 1,400
Textron Inc.; Augusta; toys/sporting goods 1,176
Middle Georgia Correctional Complex; Hardwick 1,100
City of Augusta/Transit Dept.; Augusta 1,000
Engelhard Corp./Engelhard Minerals & Chemicals Div.; McIntyre; clay/ceramics 928
Federal Paper Board Co./Continental Research & Dev; Augusta; paper mills 925
Kemira Holdings Inc.; Savannah; inorganic chemicals 780
Macy's South Inc.; Decatur; warehousing 650
De Kalb Community College; Decatur 650
Engelhard Corp./Englehard Kaolin Co.; Gordon; clay/ceramics 635
Horton Industries Inc.; Eatonton; wood buildings/mobile homes 600
Georgia Regional Hospital; Decatur 600
BASF Corp.; Sylvania; yarn/thread mills 557
ECC America Inc.; Sandersville; clay/ceramics 556
AN Speedy Temporary Employment; Augusta; personnel supply services 525
Thermal Ceramics Inc.; Augusta; clay products 524
Health-Tex Inc.; Warrenton; outerwear 508

Hawaii

From its days as a U.S. territory through the attainment of statehood in 1959, Hawaii was run by a mostly white Republican business elite, including descendants of the sugar and pineapple planters who settled modern Hawaii. The Democratic Party, meanwhile, became a magnet for Hawaii's many other racial and ethnic groups. Energized by Japanese-Americans who fought for the United States in World War II, and backed by a powerful union movement, the Democrats became an overwhelming majority. Now run by Japanese-Americans, the state Democratic Party, over the years, has seen the increased influence of other ethnic groups—especially native Hawaiians and Filipinos.

Republicans chipped away during the 1980s at the near-monolithic Democratic control of Hawaii politics. In 1984, Ronald Reagan became the second GOP presidential candidate to carry the state (Richard M. Nixon in 1972 was the first). In 1986 longtime state senator Patricia Saiki, an American of Japanese ancestry (or "AJA," in Hawaii's parlance), became the first Republican elected to the House from Hawaii. She won re-election to her 1st District seat in 1988 but unsuccessfully ran for the Senate in 1990.

But the Democrats resurged toward the end of the 1980s and their dominance was once again overwhelming—a fact unlikely to be affected by minor boundary changes made in July 1991 by a bipartisan redistricting commission. After the 1992 elections, all major statewide offices were held by Democrats, including the governorship and both Senate and both House seats. In the state legislature, 89 percent of the seats were held by Democrats.

Republican optimism for partisan growth in the 1980s was predicated in part on an economic boom in Hawaii. During the decade, population grew by 15 percent, and tourism soared past agriculture as the state's leading industry. Hawaii welcomed nearly 7 million visitors in 1990, compared with about 4 million in 1980. Unemployment was below 3 percent at the beginning of the 1990s.

The state's economic security was bolstered by growth in its large state and federal government sectors. The federal government employed nearly 34,000 Hawaiians, many of whom worked on military bases—including the Pearl Harbor Naval Reservation—that formed the nexus of the U.S. Pacific Command. These facilities gained from the defense spending increases during the Reagan years. Even in the early-1990s era of fiscal restraint and military cutbacks, Hawaiian officials hoped for some benefits from the rupture of U.S. military compacts with the Philippines, which had been a key Pacific outpost.

Republicans looked to find new voters within two major constituencies: white emigrants from the mainland, who settled in affluent enclaves in east Honolulu, in suburban Kailua and on the west sides of the islands of Hawaii and Maui; and younger members of other groups, including Japanese-Americans, who were more likely than their elders to work in Hawaii's major businesses.

But to the GOP's dismay, the wave of white emigrants turned out to be much less substantial than expected. In 1990, whites made up about one-third of Hawaii's population, and Asians and Pacific Islanders more than 65 percent—about the same as in 1980.

Also, Republican efforts to recruit among the upwardly mobile of all races is hindered by worries about a declining standard of living, brought on by the state's high cost of living. Especially troublesome are housing prices, forced up by a lack of land and by an infusion of investment during the 1980s from Japan. The median price in 1990 for an owner-occupied unit in Hawaii was $245,300, more than double the national figure. Many young adults have to remain in their parents' homes. Homelessness among the poor is a critical problem.

The boom did not reach many of those near the bottom of the economic ladder—including large numbers within the growing Filipino community—who work as laborers or in low-paid service jobs. Most aggrieved are native Hawaiians, roughly 5 percent of the population. They have higher poverty and disease rates and lower life expectancies than the general population.

Table 1 Population

District	Population	Population under 18	Voting-age population	Median age
1	554,119	122,634	431,485	34.1
2	554,110	157,492	396,618	31.1
State	1,108,229	280,126	828,103	32.6

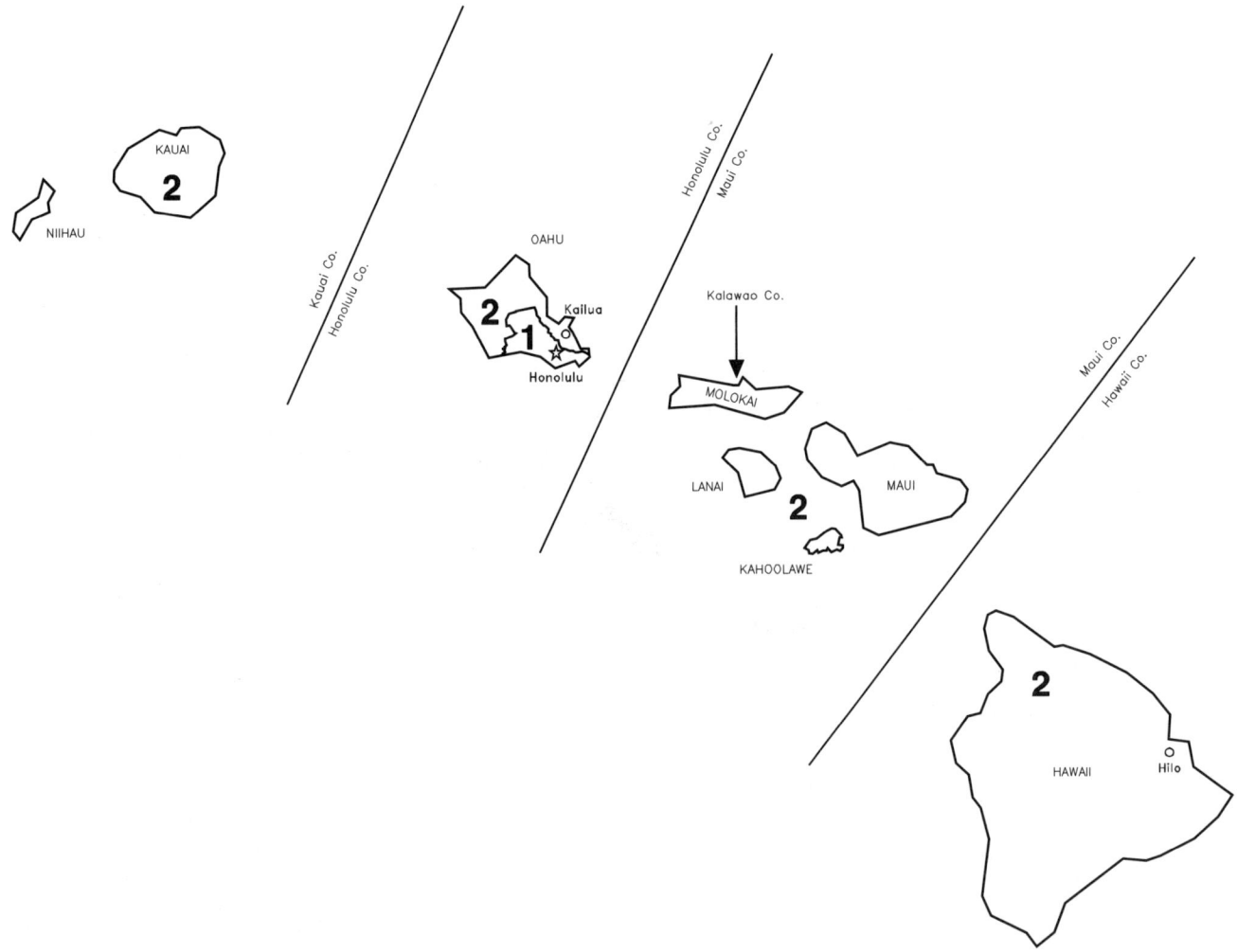

Table 2   Voting-Age Persons

District	White*	Black*	American Indian, Eskimo, or Aleut*	Asian or Pacific Islander*	Other*	Hispanic*	Male*	Female*
1	29.7%	2.3%	0.3%	66.4%	1.3%	4.7%	50.0%	50.0%
2	39.4	2.3	0.5	55.7	2.1	7.6	51.4	48.6
State	34.4	2.3	0.4	61.3	1.7	6.1	50.7	49.3

*As percent of voting-age population.

Table 3   Voting-Age Persons by Age Groups

District	18-24*	25-44*	45-54*	55-64*	65 and over*
1	14.1%	44.8%	13.3%	11.8%	16.1%
2	15.3	46.8	13.0	10.9	14.0
State	14.6	45.8	13.1	11.4	15.1

*As percent of voting-age population.

Table 4   Income and Occupation

District	Median family income	Families in poverty	White collar*	Blue collar*	Service*	Farm*
1	$46,389	4.7%	64.5%	17.7%	16.8%	1.0%
2	40,385	7.4	53.0	23.6	18.4	4.9
State	43,176	6.0	59.0	20.5	17.6	2.9

*As percent of employed persons age 16 and over.

Table 5   Education: School Years Completed

District	Less than grade 9*	Grades 9-12 no diploma*	High school diploma*	College bachelor's degree or higher*
1	9.6%	9.0%	27.1%	26.6%
2	10.7	10.7	30.6	18.8
State	10.1	9.8	28.7	22.9

*As percent of persons age 25 and over.

Table 6   Housing and Residential Patterns

District	Owner occupied	Renter occupied	Urban	Rural
1	50.4%	49.6%	99.8%	0.2%
2	57.8	42.2	78.2	21.8
State	53.9	46.1	89.0	11.0

1st District

Honolulu — Pearl City

The compact 1st takes in the narrow plain between the Koolau mountain range and the western coast of the island of Oahu. But this small area includes the city of Honolulu, the engine that drives all of Hawaii.

Honolulu is Hawaii's capital, home to most of its businesses and about one-third of its people. In its western end are the Pearl Harbor Naval Reservation and Hickam Air Force Base, major parts of a military sector that is vital to Hawaii's economy.

East of downtown Honolulu is Waikiki, heart of the tourist trade that is Hawaii's leading industry. Waikiki, with its numer-

ous high-rise hotels, is one of the most densely populated places anywhere during tourist season. Those who come with dreams of "grass-shack" Hawaii are disappointed. But others who visit find it the perfect mix of stunning scenery, sandy beaches and urban amenities.

Farther east are Honolulu's most affluent neighborhoods, which include a large population of whites, known as *haoles* in the Hawaiian language.

The middle-class neighborhoods of central Honolulu are dominated by Americans of Japanese ancestry; for many in that ethnic group, employment in state government has been the route to economic security.

Kalihi, in northwest Honolulu, is a working-class community heavily populated by Filipinos and native Hawaiians. Scattered throughout are Chinese, Koreans, Vietnamese, Samoans, Portuguese, Puerto Ricans and other ethnic groups.

To the west are such towns as Pearl City, Aiea, Mililani Town and part of Kapolei, which is planned to become Oahu's "second city" by the 21st century.

Ewa Beach is connected to the district by a band rimming Pearl Harbor; Japan's attack on the naval base in December 1941 was the catalyst for the United States' entry into World War II. Inland is Camp H. M. Smith Marine Corps Base, the headquarters for the unified military command for the Pacific.

The 1st contributes to Hawaii's strong Democratic tilt. Japanese-Americans have long dominated the state Democratic Party; they are joined in their partisan tendencies by many other "minority group" constituents who make up the majority of 1st District residents.

The large military-oriented community, a growing number of Japanese-Americans gaining corporate advancement and the Republican leanings of many white residents occasionally allow a GOP candidate to carry the district. Republican Patricia Saiki made history by winning the House seat in 1986 and 1988. Overall, though, the 1st retains a Democratic tilt; high turnout among the still largely Democratic Japanese-American electorate contributes.

In 1992 Bill Clinton carried the district by more than 8 percentage points, though his 48 percent plurality was below the Democratic norm. That same year the Democratic House nominee took 73 percent of the district.

Election Returns

	1st District	Democrat	Republican
1992	President*	87,632 (47.8%)	72,156 (39.4%)
	House	129,332 (72.9%)	41,575 (23.4%)
1990	Senate †	92,430 (51.5%)	87,132 (48.5%)
	Governor	103,598 (59.4%)	70,734 (40.6%)
1988	President	101,028 (54.3%)	84,926 (45.7%)
	Senate	127,702 (79.7%)	32,540 (20.3%)
1986	Senate	132,191 (73.6%)	47,371 (26.4%)
	Governor	94,723 (52.0%)	87,530 (48.0%)

*Vote for Perot was 23,438 (12.8%).   †Special election for the remaining four years of the term of Spark M. Matsunaga who died in April 1990.

Demographics

Population 554,119

Percent change from 1980 14.9%

Land area 182 square miles

Population per square mile 3,052

Counties, 1990 population
Honolulu (pt.) 554,119

Cities, 1990 population (10,000 or more)
Ewa Beach CDP 14,315
Halawa CDP 13,408
Honolulu CDP 377,059
Mililani Town CDP 29,359
Pearl City CDP 30,993
Waimalu CDP 29,967
Waipio CDP 11,812

Race and Hispanic origin
White 29.1%
Black 2.5%
American Indian, Eskimo, or Aleut. 0.3%
Asian or Pacific Islander 66.6%
Other 1.5%
Hispanic origin 5.5%

Ancestry
English 5.9%
French 1.7%
German 8.5%
Irish 5.5%
Italian 1.7%
Polish 1.0%
Portuguese 3.2%
Scottish 1.1%

Universities/colleges, 1990-1991 enrollment
Chaminade University of Honolulu, Honolulu 2,408
Hawaii Pacific College, Honolulu 5,557
Honolulu Community College, Honolulu 4,292
Kapiolani Community College, Honolulu 5,467
Leeward Community College, Pearl City 5,439
University of Hawaii at Manoa, Honolulu 18,810
University of Hawaii-West Oahu, Pearl City 652

Newspapers, total circulation (in all districts)
Honolulu Advertiser-Star Bulletin 188,384

Commercial television stations, affiliations
ADI: Hawaii has none.
KBFD, Honolulu (None)
KGMB, Honolulu (CBS)
KHON-TV, Honolulu (NBC)
KITV, Honolulu (ABC)
KOBN, Honolulu (None)
KWHE, Honolulu (None)

Cable television systems, total subscribers
Chronicle Cablevision; Hawaii Kai 7,145
Oceanic Cablevision; Honolulu 205,000

Military installations, 1991
Pearl Harbor Naval Station, Pearl Harbor 15,971
Hickam Air Force Base, Honolulu 6,457
Pearl Harbor Naval Shipyard, Pearl Harbor 5,908
Pearl Harbor Naval Submarine Base, Pearl Harbor 5,192
Fort Shafter (Army), Honolulu 3,994
Tripler Army Medical Center, Honolulu 2,485
Camp H. M. Smith (Marine Corps), Honolulu 1,970
Fort Derussy (Army), Honolulu 738

Businesses and other major employers
City & County of Honolulu; Honolulu 7,700
University of Hawaii; Honolulu 4,538
Kyo-Ya Co. Ltd.; Honolulu; hotel 3,400
Bank of Hawaii; Honolulu; commercial banks 3,293
State of Hawaii/Honolulu Police Dept.; Honolulu 3,000
The Queens Medical Center; Honolulu 2,595

First Hawaiian Bank; Honolulu; commercial banks 2,204
Hilton Hotels Corp./Hilton Hawaiian Village Hotel; Honolulu; hotel 2,150
Kaiser Foundation Hospital; Honolulu 2,000
Hawaiian Electric Industries; Honolulu; electric services 1,925
Straub Clinic & Hospital Inc.; Honolulu 1,800
Continental Airlines Inc.; Honolulu; airline 1,700
U.S. Coast Guard/14th Coast Guard District; Honolulu 1,700
St. Francis Hospital & Medical Center; Honolulu 1,612
Liberty House Inc.; Honolulu; department stores 1,500
Kuakini Medical Center; Honolulu 1,395
Kapiolani Medical Center; Honolulu 1,390
Sheraton Corp./Sheraton Hotels in Hawaii; Honolulu; hotel 1,300
Hyatt Corp./Hyatt Regency Waikiki; Honolulu; hotel 1,230
Sears Roebuck & Co.; Honolulu; department stores 1,200
KM Hawaii Inc./Hyatt Regency Maui Hotel; Honolulu; hotel 1,200
Hawaii Medical Service Assn.; Honolulu; medical service/health insurance 1,050
Kaukani Corp./Westin Maui; Honolulu; hotel 850
Halekulani Hotel; Honolulu; hotel 750
Bernice P. Bishop Estate Trust; Honolulu; real estate operators 715
Gannett Pacific Corp./Honolulu Star-Bulletin; Honolulu; newspapers 700
MTL Inc.; Honolulu; transportation 700
Safeway Inc.; Honolulu; grocery stores 700
Kaiser Foundation Hospitals; Honolulu 700
Board of Water Supply; Honolulu 640
HonFed Bank; Honolulu; savings institutions 637
Oahu Community Correctional Center; Honolulu 610
Dole Food Co. Inc./Castle & Cooke Properties; Honolulu; subdividers/developers 600
ITT Sheraton Corp./Sheraton Moana Surfrider Hotel; Honolulu; hotel 600
Azabu USA Corp./Ala Moana Hotel; Honolulu; hotel 600
Na Kahu Malama Nurses Inc.; Honolulu; personnel supply services 600
Hawaiian Building Maintenance Co. Ltd.; Honolulu; building services/maintenance 590
WKH Corp./Kahala Hilton Hotel; Honolulu; hotel 575
Jowa Hawaii Co. Ltd./Ilikai Hotel; Honolulu; hotel 550
Personnel Pool of Hawaii Inc./Medical Personnel Pool; Honolulu; personnel supply services 550
Sheraton Management Corp./Royal Hawaiian Hotel; Honolulu; hotel 530
Security Pacific Financial System Inc.; Honolulu; credit institutions 514

2nd District

Suburban and Outer Oahu — "Neighbor Islands"

The heavily Democratic 2nd takes in seven major "neighbor islands," plus hundreds of reefs and atolls. But more than half the people in the 2nd live on Oahu. Although it has a racial and ethnic patchwork similar to that in the 1st District, the 2nd has a somewhat higher proportion of white residents (more than one-third of the population is white). There are some predominantly white, conservative-leaning communities, mostly on Oahu and Maui, that regularly vote Republican.

But these areas barely dent Democrats' dominance of the 2nd. In 1992 the Democrats won the House seat with better than a 3-to-1 margin; Bill Clinton took 49 percent and bested George Bush by more than 14 percentage points.

Hilo, on the "Big Island" of Hawaii, is the district's largest city with nearly 38,000 people; but the Oahu cities of Kailua and Kaneohe are very close behind. Kailua, on Oahu's eastern side, is one of the few majority-white cities in Hawaii. The Asian and Pacific Islander majority of neighboring Kaneohe is more typical of Hawaii's ethnic mix. Across the island at the edge of Pearl Harbor, working-class Waipahu is more than 80 percent Asian or Pacific Islander.

Oahu's numerous military installations are central to the life and economy of the 2nd. However, one facility, the Barber's Point Naval Air Station, showed up on the 1993 base closure list.

Away from Honolulu, population on Oahu thins, and tourist outposts are more dispersed. Laie is a Mormon enclave that includes a campus of Brigham Young University. Oahu's north coast is famous for its surfing. The side of the island has many native Hawaiians.

The spacious island of Hawaii saw its population expand by nearly a third during the 1980s. Much of the growth was on the scenic Kona coast. The city of Hilo is a commercial center on the rainy eastern part of the Big Island; its attraction to tourists is its proximity to the active Mauna Loa and Kilauea volcanoes and extinct Mauna Kea. Agricultural products—including sugar, macadamia nuts, flowers, cattle and coffee—make up a major segment of the island's economy.

After Oahu, the island of Maui has the state's most developed tourism industry. Maui County has three other islands, including Lanai, a longtime pineapple plantation, much of which is being converted into a tourist resort; relatively undeveloped Molokai; and deserted Kahoolawe, used from the late 1930s until 1990 as a military bombing range.

Although Kauai has a large sugar industry, the island makes much of its living from tourism. The coastal resorts and Kauai's populace were staggered in September 1992, when Hurricane Iniki scored a direct hit on the island. Kauai County includes the island of Niihau, set aside by its patrician owners as a place where native Hawaiians can maintain their traditional lifestyles; access by outsiders is limited.

Election Returns

	2nd District	Democrat	Republican
1992	President*	91,630 (49.3%)	64,635 (34.8%)
	House †	131,454 (72.6%)	40,070 (22.1%)
1990	Senate ‡	96,471 (58.4%)	68,846 (41.6%)
	Governor	99,894 (62.3%)	60,576 (37.7%)
1988	President	91,336 (55.3%)	73,699 (44.7%)
	Senate	120,239 (77.7%)	34,447 (22.3%)
1986	Senate	109,681 (73.5%)	39,525 (26.5%)
	Governor	78,932 (52.0%)	72,930 (48.0%)

*Vote for Perot was 29,558 (15.9%).   †Independent/other is greater than 5%.
‡Special election for the remaining four years of the term of Spark M. Matsunaga who died in April 1990.

Demographics

Population 554,110

Percent change from 1980 14.9%

Land area 6,242 square miles

Population per square mile 89

Counties, 1990 population

Hawaii 120,317	Kauai 51,177
Honolulu (pt.) 282,112	Maui 100,374
Kalawao 130	

Cities, 1990 population (10,000 or more)

Hilo CDP 37,808	Kihei CDP 11,107
Kahului CDP 16,889	Schofield Barracks CDP 19,597
Kailua CDP 36,818	Wahiawa CDP 17,386
Kaneohe CDP 35,448	Wailuku CDP 10,688
Kaneohe Station CDP 11,662	Waipahu CDP (pt.) 25,057

Race and Hispanic origin

White 37.6%
Black 2.4%
American Indian, Eskimo, or Aleut 0.6%
Asian or Pacific Islander 57.1%
Other 2.3%
Hispanic origin 9.2%

Ancestry

English 7.0%	Polish 1.1%
French 2.2%	Portuguese 7.2%
German 10.1%	Scottish 1.4%
Irish 6.3%	Swedish 1.0%
Italian 2.2%	

Universities/colleges, 1990-1991 enrollment

Brigham Young University Hawaii, Laie 2,119
Hawaii Loa College, Kaneohe 556
Kauai Community College, Lihue 1,231
Maui Community College, Kahului 1,995
University of Hawaii at Hilo, Hilo 3,634
Windward Community College, Kaneohe 1,555

Newspapers, total circulation (in all districts)

Hilo Tribune Herald 20,065
Honolulu Advertiser-Star Bulletin 188,384
Lihue Garden Island 7,205
Maui News 17,551
West Hawaii Today 11,234

Commercial television stations, affiliations

ADI: Hawaii has none.
  KGMD-TV, Hilo (CBS)
  KHAW-TV, Hilo (NBC)
  KHBC-TV, Hilo (None)
  KHVO, Hilo (ABC)
  KFVE, Honolulu (None)
  KHAI-TV, Honolulu (None)
  KLEI, Kailua-Kona (None)
  KAII-TV, Wailuku (NBC)
  KGMV, Wailuku (CBS)
  KMAU, Wailuku (ABC)
  KOGG, Wailuku (None)

Cable television systems, total subscribers

Chronicle Cablevision; Mt. Haleaka 15,418
Garden Isle Cablevision; Kalaheo 5,900
Jones Spacelink; Hilo: 15,000
Kauai Cablevision; Kukuiolono 8,930

Oceanic Cablevision; Honolulu 205,000
Sun Cablevision; Kailua Kona 12,800

Military installations, 1991
Schofield Barracks Military Reserve (Army), Wahiawa 15,517
Kaneohe Bay Marine Corps Air Station, Kailua 10,254
Barbers Point Naval Air Station, Barbers Point 4,906
Lualualei Naval Magazine, Lualualei 1,235
EPAC Naval Communications Master Station, Wahiawa 1,090
Kokee Air Force Station, Kekaha 37

Businesses and other major employers
Hyatt Corp./Hyatt Regency Waikoloa; Kamuela; hotel 2,200
Leeward School District; Waipahu 2,000
KM Hawaii Inc./Hyatt Regency Maui Hotel; Lahaina; hotel 1,200
Polynesian Cultural Center; Laie; cultural/amusement park 1,000
Azabu USA Corp./Maui Marriott Hotel; Lahaina; hotel 850
Castle Medical Center; Kailua 800
Seibu Railroad Co. Inc./Mauna Kea Beach Hotel; Kailua; hotel 800

Hamakua Sugar Co. Inc./Big Island Meat-Div.; Paauilo; field crops 740
Nabisco Brands Inc./Del Monte Corp.; Kunia; fruit/nuts 700
Lani Mauna Bay Hotel Inc.; Kamuela; hotel 685
State of Hawaii/Education Dept.; Lihue 654
State of Hawaii/Palm Tree; Hilo 650
C. Brewer & Co. Ltd.; Pepeekeo; field crops 600
East Kauai Water Co.; Lihue; water supply 600
Wailea Beach Palace Co./Four Seasons Resort; Kihei; hotel 600
University of Hawaii; Hilo 570
Stouffer Corp./Waiohai Beach Resort; Koloa; hotel 554
Hilton Hotels Corp./Turtle Bay Hilton & Country Club; Kahuku; hotel 551
Dole Food Co. Inc./Waialua Sugar Co.; Waialua; field crops 550
Lanai Resort Partners/Manele Bay Resort; Lanai City; hotel 550
Kau Agribusiness Co. Inc.; Pahala; fruit/nuts 545
Pleasant Travel Service/Royal Lahaina Resort; Lahaina; hotel 520

Idaho

In several states, divided partisan control of congressional redistricting resulted in stalemates that had to be resolved in court. But in Idaho—with Democratic Gov. Cecil D. Andrus, a Republican-controlled state House and an evenly divided state Senate—the remap was accomplished quickly and without rancor.

Idaho's redistricting effort was unusually routine for three reasons.

First, since a 1967 remap, Idaho had been divided into an eastern and a western district, with only one county—Ada (Boise), the state's largest—split between the districts. The state legislators who considered the new district map showed no inclination to tamper with the basic design.

Second, population trends in the state did not justify a major map overhaul. The 1990 census reported modest population growth rates in both districts. The western 1st District grew slightly faster and had 12,561 more residents than the 2nd prior to redistricting. Thus, a minor net shift of a little more than 6,000 people between the districts was needed to balance the populations.

Third, the legislators were willing to let congressional redistricting pass quickly to get to a political issue closer to their hearts: the redrawing of districts for the state House and Senate. (While the congressional map sailed through to passage in January 1992, the state legislative remap was tied up until March and for a time threatened to delay Idaho's 1992 political calendar.)

The new congressional map was designed by a bipartisan Legislature committee in August 1991, during the part-time Legislature's long recess. The map adjusted the dividing line as it passed through the state capital of Boise, transferring a handful of voting precincts between the districts. The changes had no detectable partisan impact. Under both the old and new maps, George Bush took 60 percent of the 1988 presidential vote in the 1st District and 66 percent in the 2nd District. In 1992, Bush won the state with 42 percent to Bill Clinton's 31 percent.

Table 1   Population

District	Population	Population under 18	Voting-age population	Median age
1	503,357	144,820	358,537	33.2
2	503,392	163,585	339,807	29.9
State	1,006,749	308,405	698,344	31.5

Table 2   Voting-Age Persons

District	White*	Black*	American Indian, Eskimo, or Aleut*	Asian or Pacific Islander*	Other*	Hispanic*	Male*	Female*
1	95.6%	0.2%	1.2%	0.9%	2.1%	3.7%	49.0%	51.0%
2	94.5	0.4	1.3	0.9	2.9	5.1	49.1	50.9
State	95.1	0.3	1.2	0.9	2.5	4.4	49.0	51.0

*As percent of voting-age population.

Table 3   Voting-Age Persons by Age Groups

District	18-24*	25-44*	45-54*	55-64*	65 and over*
1	12.8%	42.8%	14.7%	11.5%	18.1%
2	15.4	43.7	13.6	10.8	16.6
State	14.1	43.2	14.2	11.2	17.4

*As percent of voting-age population.

Table 4   Income and Occupation

District	Median family income	Families in poverty	White collar*	Blue collar*	Service*	Farm*
1	$29,226	9.4%	52.4%	27.3%	13.8%	6.5%
2	29,736	10.0	51.5	26.2	13.3	9.1
State	29,472	9.7	52.0	26.8	13.5	7.8

*As percent of employed persons age 16 and over.

Table 5   Education: School Years Completed

District	Less than grade 9*	Grades 9-12 no diploma*	High school diploma*	College bachelor's degree or higher*
1	7.8%	13.4%	31.5%	16.7%
2	6.9	12.4	29.3	18.7
State	7.4	12.9	30.4	17.7

*As percent of persons age 25 and over.

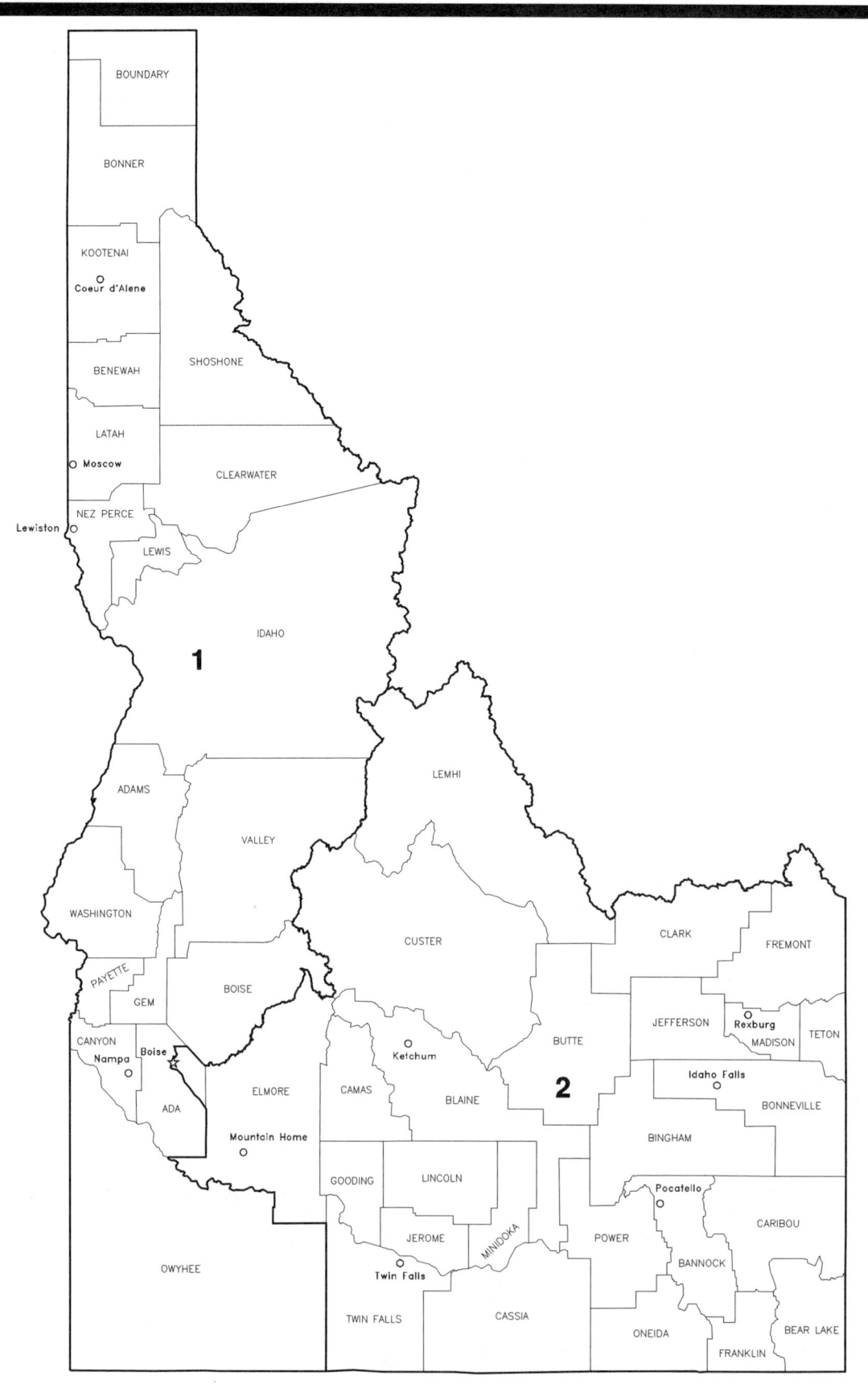

1

2

BOUNDARY

BONNER

KOOTENAI
○ Coeur d'Alene

SHOSHONE

BENEWAH

LATAH
○ Moscow

CLEARWATER

NEZ PERCE
Lewiston ○

LEWIS

IDAHO

ADAMS

LEMHI

VALLEY

WASHINGTON

CUSTER

CLARK

FREMONT

PAYETTE

GEM

BOISE

JEFFERSON

Rexburg ○
MADISON

TETON

CANYON
Nampa ○

Boise

ADA

ELMORE

CAMAS

BLAINE

Ketchum ○

BUTTE

Idaho Falls ○

BONNEVILLE

Mountain Home ○

BINGHAM

GOODING

LINCOLN

Pocatello ○

CARIBOU

OWYHEE

JEROME

MINIDOKA

POWER

BANNOCK

Twin Falls ○

TWIN FALLS

CASSIA

ONEIDA

BEAR LAKE

FRANKLIN

Table 6 Housing and Residential Patterns

District	Owner occupied	Renter occupied	Urban	Rural
1	71.3%	28.7%	54.2%	45.8%
2	68.7	31.3	60.7	39.3
State	70.1	29.9	57.4	42.6

1st District

West — Boise; Tampa; Panhandle

The 1st District ranges nearly 500 miles from British Columbia to Nevada. This mainly conservative district usually shows a strong Republican lean. Democratic Rep. Larry LaRocco's sweeping win in 1992 (he carried every county) went against partisan form.

Ada County (Boise) has about 20 percent of Idaho's population. It is the only county split between the 1st and 2nd districts; the line bisects Boise, the state's capital and largest city. The 1st skips Boise's downtown and takes in its mainly residential western portion. The 1st has most of Ada County's territory and about two-thirds of its population. Boise's white-collar constituency combines with voters in agricultural communities to provide Republicans with a solid base. Voters here and in the suburbs helped Bush win Ada County with 63 percent of the vote in 1988 and hang on with 45 percent in 1992.

The Republican grip is stronger in Canyon County (Nampa), on Ada's western border. Idaho's second-largest county gave Bush 51 percent in 1992, his best showing in the 1st; LaRocco's win in Canyon that year (also with 51 percent) broke sharply with partisan habit. The county is the state's top producer of cattle and corn and a leader in sugar beets.

In 1992 George Bush finished first in all counties from Idaho County south, and victorious Republican Senate candidate (and former Boise Mayor) Dirk Kempthorne defeated his Democratic opponent by a whopping margin in the southern part of the 1st.

To the north is a spread of mainly rural areas, including vast Idaho County. This Republican turf gives way to the panhandle, where Democratic habits were implanted by a long period of labor activism in the timberlands, ore-mining areas and the industrial city of Lewiston. The most solid Democratic bloc is in blue-collar areas of the northern panhandle. Bill Clinton led the field in seven of the nine northernmost counties.

Some Democratic-leaning areas have relatively stable economies. Lewiston, in Nez Perce County, has a grain-shipping port and the Potlatch pulp and paper factory; Latah County has the University of Idaho in Moscow (10,500 students). But the collapse of silver prices in the early 1980s crushed mining-dependent Shoshone County, which still has a jobless rate of more than 20 percent. Clinton took 49 percent in Shoshone, easily his best county showing in Idaho.

In some parts of this mountain and lake country, an expansion of the tourist industry and the arrival of many retirees have boosted the population and weakened the Democrats' position. Bush finished first in Kootenai County (Coeur d'Alene)—the panhandle's most populous jurisdiction—and Kempthorne pulled down 57 percent.

The 1st district also showed a strain of Sagebrush independence, giving Ross Perot more than a quarter of its presidential vote.

Election Returns

	1st District	Democrat	Republican
1992	President*	75,499 (30.8%)	101,787 (41.6%)
	House	140,985 (58.1%)	90,983 (37.5%)
1990	Senate	61,967 (38.8%)	97,873 (61.2%)
	Governor	111,910 (69.5%)	49,099 (30.5%)
1988	President	79,011 (39.9%)	119,142 (60.1%)
1986	Senate	93,753 (50.8%)	90,684 (49.2%)
	Governor	98,290 (53.2%)	86,406 (46.8%)

Vote for Perot was 67,677 (27.6%).

Demographics

Population 503,357

Percent change from 1980 6.6%

Land area 39,553 square miles

Population per square mile 13

Counties, 1990 population

Ada (pt.) 138,397	Kootenai 69,795
Adams 3,254	Latah 30,617
Benewah 7,937	Lewis 3,516
Boise 3,509	Nez Perce 33,754
Bonner 26,622	Owyhee 8,392
Boundary 8,332	Payette 16,434
Canyon 90,076	Shoshone 13,931
Clearwater 8,505	Valley 6,109
Gem 11,844	Washington 8,550
Idaho 13,783	

Cities, 1990 population (10,000 or more)

Boise City (pt.) 61,564	Lewiston 28,082
Caldwell 18,400	Moscow 18,519
Coeur d'Alene 24,563	Nampa 28,365

Race and Hispanic origin
White 94.9%
Black 0.2%
American Indian, Eskimo, or Aleut. 1.3%
Asian or Pacific Islander 1.0%
Other 2.5%
Hispanic origin 4.6%

Ancestry

American 4.5%	Italian 2.6%
Danish 2.4%	Norwegian 4.0%
Dutch 4.1%	Polish 1.3%
English 23.3%	Scotch Irish 3.2%
French 5.3%	Scottish 3.7%
German 31.3%	Swedish 4.9%
Irish 16.4%	Welsh 1.6%

Universities/colleges, 1990-1991 enrollment
Albertson College of Idaho, Caldwell 1,176
Lewis-Clark State College, Lewiston 2,667
North Idaho College, Coeur d'Alene 2,820
Northwest Nazarene College, Nampa 1,086
University of Idaho, Moscow 10,544

Newspapers, total circulation (in all districts)
Boise Idaho Statesman 60,678
Spokane Spokesman-Review 119,439

Commercial television stations, affiliations
ADI: Spokane (53%) and Boise (47%)
KBCI-TV, Boise (CBS)
KTVB, Boise (NBC)
KIVI, Nampa (ABC)
KTRV, Nampa (Fox)

Cable television systems, total subscribers
Kootenai Cablevision Inc.; Coeur d'Alene 14,075
Pullman/Moscow TV Cable Cos.; Moscow 12,665
TCI Cablevision of Treasure Valley; Boise 50,000
TCI Cablevision of Treasure Valley; Caldwell 7,500
TCI of Idaho; Whitman County, WA 13,000
Weststar Communications; Silverton 5,186

Businesses and other major employers
J. R. Simplot Co.; Caldwell; potatoes 5,000
Hewlett-Packard Co.; Boise; computer equipment 3,700
Micron Technology Inc.; Boise; electronic components 3,500
Potlatch Corp.; Lewiston; paper products 3,500
University of Idaho; Moscow 3,200
St. Alphonsus Regional Medical Center; Boise 1,578
Meridian School District; Meridian 1,200
Morrison Knudsen Corp.; Boise; heavy construction 1,100
GTE Northwest Inc.; Coeur d'Alene; telephone communications 1,100
Boise Cascade Corp.; Boise; paper mills 974
Hagadone Hospitality/Coeur d'Alene Resort; Coeur d'Alene; hotel 900
Kootenai Medical Center; Coeur d'Alene 900
Nampa School District; Nampa 750
State of Idaho/Transportation Dept.; Boise 700
Idaho State School & Hospital; Nampa; residential care 680
Boise Cascade Corp./Timber Wood Products Div.; Emmett; sawmills 650
St. Joseph Regional Medical Center; Lewiston 630
Mercy Medical Center; Nampa 600
Bonner School District; Sandpoint 600
Blount Inc./Sporting Equipment Div.; Lewiston; ordnance 550
Morrison-Knudsen Co. Inc./Boise Locomotive Div.; Boise; railroad equipment 520

2nd District

East — Pocatello; Idaho Falls; Twin Falls

The Republican win of the 2nd District in 1992 ended the four-term Democratic hold, established by Richard Stallings (who ran unsuccessfully for the Senate). The Stallings era was a rare break in the Republicans' domination of this conservative region.

Although George Bush in 1992 ran far behind his 1988 vote in the 2nd, he carried all but one county. He won Madison County (Rexburg) with 59 percent; Bill Clinton hit bottom here with less than 10 percent. Ross Perot bested Clinton in all but six of the district's counties.

By far, most district residents are of northern European heritage. Members of the Church of Jesus Christ of Latter-day Saints make up the largest religious group; like Mormons everywhere, most have strongly conservative views.

Much of the district is farmland irrigated by the Snake River. At the district's western edge is the part of Boise that includes the state Capitol, major business offices and some affluent communities.

To the east, near Idaho Falls, is the Idaho National Engineering Laboratory (INEL), a federal research complex that is the state's largest single employment site (Westinghouse, the Department of Energy and Argonne all have workers here).

Boise is one of the nation's most economically vibrant small cities. Many of its businesses reflect the region's links to the land: The J. R. Simplot Co. raises potatoes and cattle, and Ore-Ida makes frozen french fries. Boise Cascade is a diversified forest products company. But some are industrial (the Morrison Knudsen heavy construction company) or cutting-edge (Micron Technology). Boise State University, with more than 13,400 students, is also in the district.

To the east is Elmore County, site of the Mountain Home Air Force Base. In the south-central part of the district is Twin Falls, hub of the Magic Valley region where potatoes, sugar beets, grain, livestock and trout are raised, and GOP votes are cast.

Farther east, in Bannock County, is Pocatello, where the largest employers are Idaho State University (9,100 students) and the Union Pacific Railroad. There are Democratic votes in the academic and blue-collar communities; Bush edged Clinton in Bannock by 3 percentage points in 1992.

After irrigating the potato and wheat fields of Bingham County, the Snake runs through Idaho Falls; the city's economy is highly dependent on contractors employed by the nearby INEL complex. In the Upper Snake River Valley is Rexburg, home of Mormon-run Ricks College (a two-year school with about 7,800 students).

In the mountainous center of the district is Blaine County and the bucolic Ketchum-Sun Valley area. Urban exiles, artists and outdoor enthusiasts boosted Blaine's population by 38 percent in the 1980s and gave it an un-Idaholike liberal tinge. It was the only county in the 2nd that Clinton carried in 1992 (albeit with 36 percent).

Election Returns

	2nd District	Democrat	Republican
1992	President*	61,514 (27.3%)	100,858 (44.8%)
	House	81,450 (35.4%)	139,783 (60.8%)
1990	Senate	60,328 (38.6%)	95,768 (61.4%)
	Governor	106,763 (66.9%)	52,838 (33.1%)
1988	President	68,253 (33.6%)	134,733 (66.4%)
1986	Senate	88,322 (46.0%)	103,592 (54.0%)
	Governor	91,961 (47.7%)	100,872 (52.3%)

*Vote for Perot was 62,718 (27.9%).

Demographics

Population 503,392

Percent change from 1980 6.8%

Land area 43,198 square miles

Population per square mile 12

Counties, 1990 population

Ada (pt.) 67,378	Franklin 9,232
Bannock 66,026	Fremont 10,937
Bear Lake 6,084	Gooding 11,633
Bingham 37,583	Jefferson 16,543
Blaine 13,552	Jerome 15,138
Bonneville 72,207	Lemhi 6,899
Butte 2,918	Lincoln 3,308
Camas 727	Madison 23,674
Caribou 6,963	Minidoka 19,361
Cassia 19,532	Oneida 3,492
Clark 762	Power 7,086
Custer 4,133	Teton 3,439
Elmore 21,205	Twin Falls 53,580

Cities, 1990 population (10,000 or more)

Boise City (pt.) 64,174	Rexburg 14,302
Idaho Falls 43,929	Twin Falls 27,591
Pocatello 46,080	

Race and Hispanic origin

White 93.9%
Black 0.4%
American Indian, Eskimo, or Aleut. 1.4%
Asian or Pacific Islander 0.9%
Other 3.4%
Hispanic origin 5.9%

Ancestry

American 4.1%	Norwegian 2.5%
Danish 5.7%	Polish 1.0%
Dutch 3.0%	Scotch Irish 2.1%
English 34.5%	Scottish 4.2%
French 3.8%	Swedish 5.6%
German 24.1%	Swiss 1.6%
Irish 11.8%	Welsh 2.5%
Italian 2.2%	

Universities/colleges, 1990-1991 enrollment

Boise State University, Boise 13,378
College of Southern Idaho, Twin Falls 2,787
Idaho State University, Pocatello 9,139
ITT Technical Institute, Boise 434
Ricks College, Rexburg 7,795

Newspapers, total circulation (in all districts)

Twin Falls Times-News 20,480
Boise Idaho Statesman 60,678
Idaho Falls Post Register 28,561
Pocatello Idaho State Journal 18,536
Logan Herald Journal 13,932

Commercial television stations, affiliations

ADI: Idaho Falls-Pocatello (67%), Boise (16%), Twin Falls (10%) and Salt Lake City (7%)
  KIDK, Idaho Falls (CBS)
  KIFI-TV, Idaho Falls (NBC)
  KPVI, Pocatello (ABC)
  KKVI, Twin Falls (ABC)
  KMVT, Twin Falls (CBS)

Cable television systems, total subscribers

King Videocable; Buhl 10,249
TCI Cablevision of Treasure Valley; Boise 50,000
TCI of Idaho; Burley 5,200
TCI of Idaho; Iona 22,500
TCI of Idaho; Pocatello 14,200

Military installations, 1991

Mountain Home Air Force Base, Mountain Home 2,513
Boise Air Terminal Air Guard Station, Boise 526

Businesses and other major employers

EG&G Idaho Inc.; Idaho Falls; research services 5,299
Boise State University; Boise 2,623
Idaho State University; Pocatello 1,880
St. Luke's Regional Medical Center; Boise 1,800
Universal Foods Corp./Idaho Frozen Foods; Twin Falls; preserved fruits/vegetables 1,700
Ore-Ida Foods Inc.; Burley; frozen potatoes 1,200
Westinghouse Idaho Nuclear Co./Winco; Idaho Falls; nuclear power services 1,200
U.S. West Communications Inc./Mountain Bell; Boise; telephone communications 1,130
J. R. Simplot Co.; Heyburn; preserved fruits/vegetables 1,000
Eastern Idaho Regional Medical Center; Idaho Falls 1,000
Idaho Falls School District; Idaho Falls 1,000
Sinclair Oil Corp./Sun Valley Co.; Sun Valley; hotel 1,000
Gould Inc./Semiconductor Div.; Pocatello; electrical equipment 1,000
Albertsons Inc./Grocery Warehouse; Boise; grocery stores 950
Basic American Inc.; Blackfoot; crop services 900
West One Bancorp; Boise; commercial banks 900
Idaho Power Co.; Boise; electric services 897
University of Chicago/Argonne National Laboratory; Idaho Falls; research services 850
Ricks College; Rexburg 830
Universal Frozen Foods Co./Tater-Boy; Twin Falls; frozen potatoes 800
Pillsbury Co.; Shelley; preserved vegetables 800
Magic Valley Regional Medical Center; Twin Falls 686
Idaho Falls School District; Idaho Falls 660
J. R. Simplot Co./Mineral & Chemical Div.; Pocatello; agricultural chemicals 630
Bannock Regional Medical Center; Pocatello 610
FMC Corp./Phosphorus Chemicals Div.; Pocatello; inorganic chemicals 600
Amalgamated Sugar Co./White Satin Inc.; Paul; sugar/confectionery products 600
Burley School District; Burley 586
Lamb-Weston Inc.; American Falls; preserved vegetables 560
Taylor Corp./Artco; Rexburg; commercial printing 550

ILLINOIS

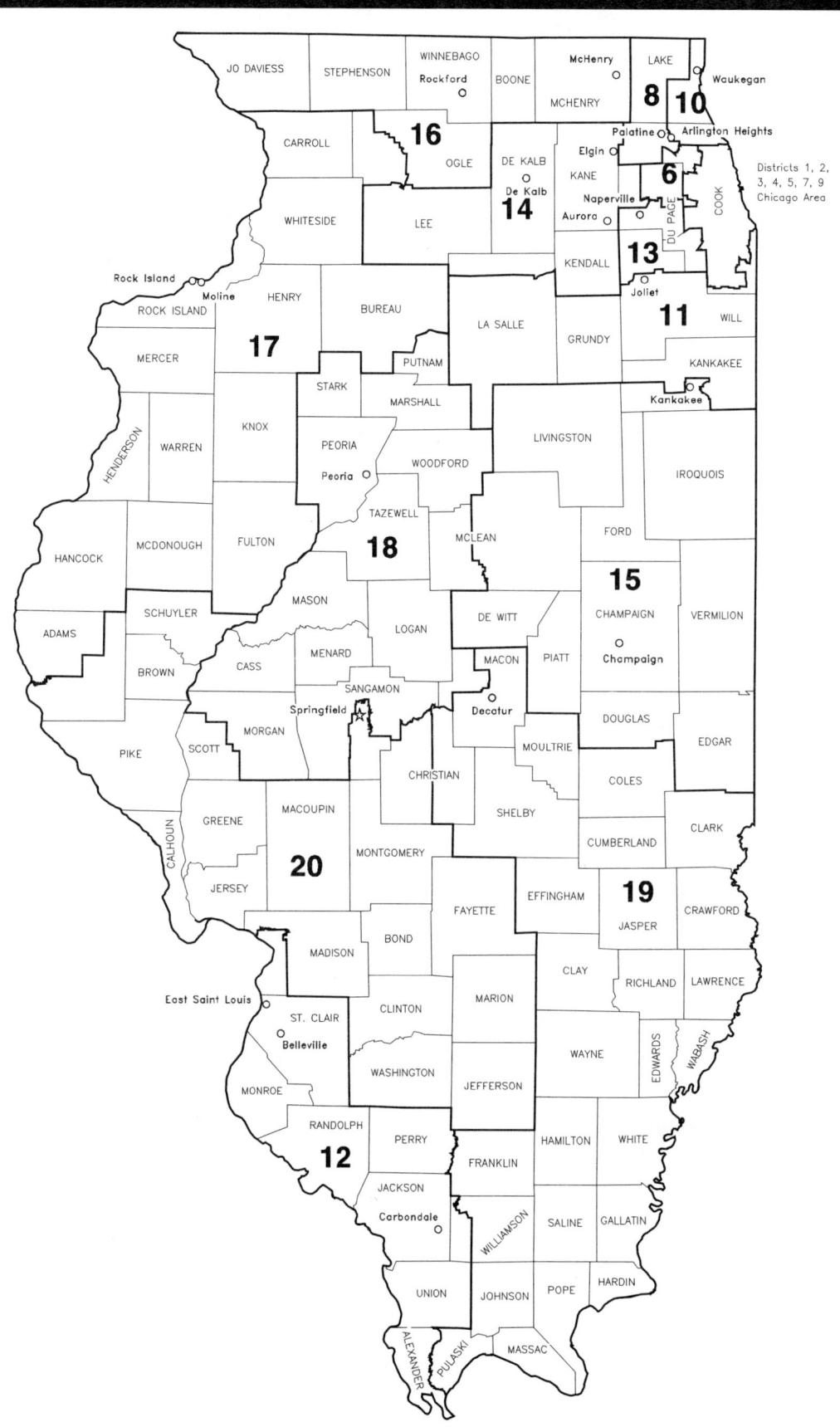

JO DAVIESS
STEPHENSON
WINNEBAGO
Rockford
BOONE
McHenry
LAKE
Waukegan

MCHENRY
8
10

CARROLL
16
OGLE
DE KALB
KANE
Palatine
Arlington Heights

Elgin
6

De Kalb
Districts 1, 2, 3, 4, 5, 7, 9
Chicago Area

WHITESIDE
LEE
14
Naperville
Aurora
COOK

DU PAGE

KENDALL
13

Rock Island
Moline
ROCK ISLAND
HENRY
BUREAU
LA SALLE
GRUNDY
Joliet
11
WILL

MERCER
17
PUTNAM
KANKAKEE
Kankakee

STARK
MARSHALL

KNOX
PEORIA
WOODFORD
LIVINGSTON
IROQUOIS

HENDERSON
WARREN
Peoria

TAZEWELL
FORD

HANCOCK
MCDONOUGH
FULTON
18
MCLEAN

SCHUYLER
MASON
DE WITT
15
CHAMPAIGN
VERMILION

ADAMS
LOGAN
PIATT
Champaign

BROWN
CASS
MENARD
MACON
Decatur

PIKE
SCOTT
MORGAN
SANGAMON
Springfield
DOUGLAS
EDGAR

CHRISTIAN
MOULTRIE
COLES

GREENE
MACOUPIN
SHELBY
CUMBERLAND
CLARK

CALHOUN
JERSEY
20
MONTGOMERY
FAYETTE
EFFINGHAM
19
CRAWFORD

JASPER

MADISON
BOND
CLAY
RICHLAND
LAWRENCE

East Saint Louis
CLINTON
MARION
WAYNE
EDWARDS
WABASH

ST. CLAIR
Belleville

WASHINGTON
JEFFERSON

MONROE

RANDOLPH
PERRY
HAMILTON
WHITE

12
FRANKLIN

JACKSON
Carbondale
WILLIAMSON
SALINE
GALLATIN

UNION
JOHNSON
POPE
HARDIN

ALEXANDER
PULASKI
MASSAC

Illinois

By the time the 1990 census was over, the demand for political change in Illinois was more than a slogan. It was a brutal fact played out in striking changes to the congressional district map that allowed new faces to emerge following the 1992 elections. Illinois lost two House seats in 1990 reapportionment. Under a Republican-drawn redistricting map, six Democratic House incumbents were merged into three House districts: two ended their careers in primary defeats and the third chose to retire after twenty-eight years in Congress.

This dramatic shakeup that began the 1990s also could be viewed as part of an evolution in Illinois politics. Illinois was adjusting to a long period of economic and demographic change that complicated its image as one of nation's premier partisan "swing" states. Throughout the post-World War II era, Illinois—with its mix of urban, suburban, and rural areas with white-collar, blue-collar, and farm workers—was a politically competitive state.

In the 1940s, Illinois' political balance could be defined simply as Chicago versus "downstate." At the time, Chicago—Illinois' behemoth and for years the nation's second-largest city—maintained its historical role as a manufacturing giant. Its multi-ethnic, largely blue-collar constituency trooped loyally to the polls to support the dominant Democratic political machine that came to be personified by Mayor Richard J. Daley, who towered over Chicago politics from 1955 to 1976.

The downstate vote, combined with that in the wealthy, Republican-populated Chicago suburbs, effectively balanced the Democratic margins in Chicago. Republican sentiments in farm country and small towns typically outweighed the labor vote in Illinois' smaller industrial cities and the "border-state" Democratic tendencies in the coal and timber lands in the south. But over time the bipolar definition ceased to fit. Illinois' political fabric became much more of a patchwork.

While Chicago (2.8 million residents) remained a heavily Democratic city, the bulwarks of the Democratic majorities were its large populations of blacks (1.1 million)—the result of a historic migration from the South between 1940 and 1970—and Hispanics (more than half a million, mainly Puerto Ricans and Mexicans) who arrived in large numbers beginning in the early 1970s. The growing minority clout produced the mayoral victories of black Democrat Harold Washington in 1983 and 1987. And of the six congressional districts that were mainly in

Chicago after the 1992 elections, three were held by African Americans and one by a Hispanic.

But Democratic majorities in Chicago were not as overwhelming as in past days. The Democratic machine withered following Daley's death in 1976. Many "ethnic" Chicagoans—including residents of the cozy brick bungalows of the city's northwest and southwest sides—subsequently broke from their partisan moorings.

Conservative on social and foreign policy issues and alienated by the national Democratic Party's liberal image, many became staunch "Reagan Democrats." Their antagonism to rising black political power in Chicago, as shown in their rejection of Harold Washington, exposed the city's deeply rooted racial divisions and further weakened the Democratic affiliation of many whites (although ethnic voters provided crucial backing to Democratic Mayor Richard M. Daley, son of the legendary machine boss, in his 1989 and 1991 campaigns). Only two ethnic Chicago Democratic incumbents were left to run for re-election to the House in November 1992.

Epic changes to the local economy also had an impact on Chicago-area politics. Manufacturing concerns still existed in Chicago, but much of its industrial base met a "Rust Belt" demise. The famed stockyards and many of its huge steel mills were long gone. The city, however, ascended in its other economic roles, as the Midwest's center of finance, commerce, and tourism.

One result of this shift from a blue-collar to a white-collar and service base was the explosive population growth in Chicago's suburbs and exurbs (including several cities, such as Schaumburg, Oak Brook, and Naperville, that became employment centers in their own rights). Affluent and overwhelmingly Republican, the "collar counties" surrounding Chicago—suburban Cook, DuPage, Lake, McHenry, Kane, and Will—became populous enough to act as a countervailing force to urban Chicago. Republican candidates for statewide office would thus win easily if they could maintain traditional GOP margins downstate. That, however, was less a certainty.

The industrial decline and downsizing seen in Chicago was repeated in many smaller industrial cities—Peoria and Decatur, Joliet and Danville, Rock Island and Kankakee—that lacked the big city's cushioning economic diversity. The recession of the early 1980s was an economic hemorrhage for these cities. The remainder of the decade, a boom time for much of America, was a period of slow and uneven recovery. Southern Illinois, downstate's poorest region, suffered most as coal operators mechanized and laid off thousands of miners.

The political result was a Democratic swing in parts of downstate Illinois. Of the eight House districts that were mainly downstate, five were held by Democrats in 1993. Clinton carried seven of these districts in 1992.

Underlying these outcomes, though, was an Illinois redistricting map that aggressively reshaped many of Democratic-held House districts. The remap was considered one of the biggest Republican redistricting victories of the 1990s—moreover because Illinois Democrats handed it to them on a silver platter.

National Democratic strategists expected their party to have a strong voice in the Illinois redistricting process. Although Gov. Jim Edgar, a Republican, would have veto power over a redistricting plan, both houses of the Legislature in 1991 were controlled by Democrats. But redistricting required the termination of three House incumbents' careers, two because of reapportionment and one because of the perceived need, under the federal Voting Rights Act, to create a Hispanic-majority district in Chicago. The Democratic leaders in the Legislature did not want to take on this politically dangerous task alone, and the members of the Democratic congressional delegation failed to come up with volunteers for the sacrifice. Lacking any consensus, the Legislature failed to act before a state constitutional deadline of June 30, 1991.

Redistricting then moved to federal district court, where Republicans had an upper hand: The three judges on the federal panel were appointees of President Ronald Reagan. In November 1991, the judges approved a plan submitted by Republican members of the Illinois House delegation that gave the GOP a good shot at reducing the Democrats' advantage in the delegation.

The most direct impact was on incumbents whose districts were merged. The remaining House Democrats had new districts that were not much different from those they carried in 1990. The map protected the interests of all seven Republican incumbents. One verity of the Illinois delegation was that minority-group representation would increase from three to four.

Table 1 Population

District	Population	Population under 18	Voting-age population	Median age
1	571,530	152,730	418,800	32.5
2	571,530	169,314	402,216	30.8
3	571,531	129,307	442,224	35.6
4	571,530	188,033	383,497	26.8
5	571,530	103,946	467,584	34.9
6	571,530	134,335	437,195	33.9
7	571,530	164,559	406,971	30.0
8	571,530	151,172	420,358	31.8
9	571,530	104,391	467,139	35.2
10	571,530	146,287	425,243	33.5
11	571,528	153,611	417,917	33.3
12	571,530	150,088	421,442	32.4
13	571,531	158,798	412,733	32.2
14	571,530	163,789	407,741	30.7
15	571,532	138,108	433,424	31.3
16	571,530	156,050	415,480	33.2
17	571,530	143,653	427,877	35.3
18	571,580	149,550	422,030	34.6
19	571,530	141,941	429,589	35.6
20	571,480	146,704	424,776	34.6
State	11,430,602	2,946,366	8,484,236	32.8

Table 2 Voting-Age Persons

District	White*	Black*	American Indian, Eskimo, or Aleut*	Asian or Pacific Islander*	Other*	Hispanic*	Male*	Female*
1	29.3%	67.8%	0.1%	1.2%	1.6%	3.1%	44.1%	55.9%
2	30.1	66.0	0.1	0.5	3.2	5.9	45.4	54.6
3	94.3	1.7	0.1	1.3	2.6	6.1	47.1	52.9
4	52.9	6.0	0.4	2.8	38.0	59.2	51.3	48.7
5	88.5	1.3	0.2	5.3	4.6	11.0	47.4	52.6
6	92.8	1.3	0.1	4.4	1.4	4.6	48.1	51.9
7	34.7	59.8	0.1	3.6	1.8	4.1	45.5	54.5
8	93.0	1.5	0.2	3.7	1.7	4.9	49.2	50.8
9	76.1	10.7	0.3	9.2	3.7	8.4	47.4	52.6
10	87.9	5.6	0.2	3.6	2.7	6.3	49.4	50.6
11	89.1	7.5	0.2	0.6	2.6	5.4	47.9	52.1
12	83.7	14.8	0.2	0.9	0.3	1.2	47.6	52.4
13	92.3	3.0	0.1	3.8	0.8	2.7	48.8	51.2
14	90.1	3.7	0.2	1.7	4.3	8.3	49.0	51.0
15	90.7	6.5	0.2	2.0	0.7	1.5	48.2	51.8
16	93.9	4.0	0.2	0.8	1.2	2.6	48.2	51.8
17	95.3	2.9	0.2	0.5	1.1	2.5	47.4	52.6
18	94.7	4.3	0.2	0.6	0.3	0.8	47.3	52.7
19	96.2	3.3	0.2	0.3	0.1	0.4	46.9	53.1
20	95.5	3.7	0.2	0.4	0.2	0.6	47.4	52.6
State	80.5	13.5	0.2	2.4	3.5	6.8	47.7	52.3

*As percent of voting-age population.

Table 3 Voting-Age Persons by Age Groups

District	18-24*	25-44*	45-54*	55-64*	65 and over*
1	14.6%	40.9%	12.9%	12.5%	19.0%
2	15.7	42.9	15.4	12.4	13.7
3	12.1	40.5	13.4	13.0	21.0
4	20.0	48.2	11.5	8.7	11.5
5	12.6	45.2	12.4	11.3	18.6
6	12.9	44.7	14.5	12.3	15.6
7	16.2	46.1	12.9	10.7	14.1
8	13.2	51.4	15.5	9.9	10.1
9	13.8	43.1	12.0	11.1	20.1
10	14.0	44.3	15.5	12.2	14.0
11	13.1	42.7	14.3	12.0	18.0
12	15.8	41.2	12.7	12.0	18.4
13	12.8	51.1	15.9	9.6	10.8
14	16.1	47.6	13.8	9.7	12.9
15	20.3	40.0	12.1	10.6	16.9
16	12.3	45.0	14.8	11.3	16.5
17	13.4	37.9	13.8	12.8	22.1
18	12.6	41.2	14.6	12.4	19.2
19	13.0	37.4	13.8	12.7	23.1
20	12.3	40.4	13.6	12.5	21.3
State	14.3	43.5	13.8	11.5	16.9

*As percent of voting-age population.

Table 4 Income and Occupation

District	Median family income	Families in poverty	White collar*	Blue collar*	Service*	Farm*
1	$30,644	19.8%	62.3%	21.4%	16.0%	0.3%
2	33,794	15.1	57.3	26.7	15.7	0.4
3	42,405	3.9	59.0	28.9	11.6	0.5
4	25,285	21.5	38.1	45.4	15.2	1.2
5	40,112	5.3	63.0	24.4	12.3	0.3
6	50,729	2.0	69.3	21.6	8.6	0.5
7	28,513	25.9	63.4	21.9	14.4	0.3

District	Median family income	Families in poverty	White collar*	Blue collar*	Service*	Farm*
8	53,105	2.3	69.2	21.3	8.7	0.8
9	42,697	8.3	71.3	16.0	12.3	0.4
10	58,407	3.0	74.2	16.1	8.9	0.8
11	39,073	6.3	52.9	32.0	13.5	1.7
12	31,003	13.1	53.5	28.3	16.2	2.0
13	55,481	1.8	73.0	18.2	8.3	0.5
14	45,377	4.5	57.9	29.0	11.1	2.0
15	33,972	8.6	56.2	25.3	14.8	3.7
16	40,060	5.7	53.9	32.2	11.2	2.7
17	30,838	9.7	48.2	31.1	15.5	5.2
18	36,423	8.0	57.1	25.6	13.9	3.5
19	28,741	11.7	45.7	33.6	15.6	5.0
20	31,846	9.3	52.3	28.4	14.5	4.8
State	38,664	9.0	59.6	26.0	12.6	1.8

*As percent of employed persons age 16 and over.

Table 5 Education: School Years Completed

District	Less than grade 9*	Grades 9-12 no diploma*	High school diploma*	College bachelor's degree or higher*
1	10.2%	19.1%	25.7%	18.4%
2	10.4	19.5	28.4	13.1
3	10.1	15.4	34.2	15.7
4	32.0	21.5	23.0	8.4
5	12.4	14.0	26.3	26.1
6	5.8	9.1	27.8	28.6
7	11.7	21.7	23.5	21.0
8	4.5	8.4	26.3	30.2
9	9.1	9.8	20.9	36.6
10	5.3	7.1	21.1	40.4
11	9.7	14.5	36.5	13.4
12	12.9	15.2	32.4	13.9
13	3.6	7.3	24.5	35.0
14	8.0	11.6	30.1	22.7
15	8.8	11.6	34.8	21.1
16	7.8	13.4	35.4	17.1
17	9.6	14.1	38.5	13.3
18	9.0	12.0	35.8	17.5
19	14.9	14.5	36.3	11.1
20	13.3	12.8	37.6	13.2
State	10.3	13.5	30.0	21.0

*As percent of persons age 25 and over.

Table 6 Housing and Residential Patterns

District	Owner occupied	Renter occupied	Urban	Rural
1	44.7%	55.3%	100.0%	0.0%
2	62.9	37.1	99.8	0.2
3	73.8	26.2	99.9	0.1
4	36.0	64.0	100.0	0.0
5	48.8	51.2	100.0	0.0
6	73.7	26.3	100.0	0.0
7	36.9	63.1	100.0	0.0
8	74.2	25.8	94.4	5.6
9	45.8	54.2	100.0	0.0
10	74.4	25.6	99.4	0.6
11	73.7	26.3	79.7	20.3
12	66.6	33.4	77.6	22.4
13	77.4	22.6	95.8	4.2
14	71.1	28.9	78.9	21.1
15	64.0	36.0	66.4	33.6
16	72.5	27.5	74.0	26.0
17	70.0	30.0	61.7	38.3
18	70.3	29.7	63.1	36.9
19	74.6	25.4	49.3	50.7
20	73.1	26.9	51.7	48.3
State	64.2	35.8	84.6	15.4

1st District

Chicago — South and Southwest Sides

As early as the 1920s, Chicago's near South Side was the center of a booming black population and the core of the nation's first urban black-majority House district, numbered the 1st. Even as the great migration from the South between 1940 and 1970 expanded the boundaries of Chicago's black neighborhoods, the 1st retained a rather compact form in the southeast section of Chicago.

In recent years, the territory covered by the 1st has grown, largely to compensate for the deterioration and depopulation of the 1st's low-income portions. During the 1980s, the district lost one-fifth of its population.

The 1st (see map on page 236) begins on the east side at 26th Street in the historic black hub, then moves south through mainly residential neighborhoods to 103rd Street, at the edge of a once-thriving industrial belt. At its midsection, the district swings west through inner-city communities. However, it also reaches an arm into Chicago's southwest side and close-in suburbs, home to most of the 1st's white residents and much of its sparse Republican vote.

The changing geography has had little impact on the district's demographics or politics. The 1st remains a majority-black Democratic stronghold. In some recent years, low voter turnout in the 1st undercut the chances of statewide Democratic candidates. But 1992 efforts by successful House candidate Bobby Rush—who headed Bill Clinton's national minority voter outreach program—and by Carol Moseley-Braun—who became the first black woman senator—spurred a turnout that was above the average for Illinois' House districts.

The 1st has had just eight House members since 1929, all of them black. Rush, a 1960s Black Panther-leader-turned-liberal-pragmatist, has his base in the near South Side. Much of this area is fighting to stem urban blight.

Just east of the Dan Ryan Expressway is the crime-plagued Stateway Gardens housing project; the 1st crosses the highway to take in the new Comiskey Park, home of baseball's White Sox. To the southeast is Hyde Park, site of the University of Chicago (10,800 students) and its mainly white, largely liberal community. Then come Woodlawn and South Shore, black areas with alternating pockets of poverty and stability. In the southeast end of the 1st are solid middle-class black communities such as Chatham and Avalon Park.

The district crosses town through mainly low-income black areas such as Englewood, then banks south and crosses Western Avenue, the unofficial but widely recognized boundary between white and black Chicago. This area includes such communities as Lithuanian Village and Beverly, an enclave of affluent Irish Americans, and suburban Evergreen Park. The 1st also takes in parts of Oak Lawn, Alsip and Blue Island.

CHICAGO AREA (Cook and Du Page Counties)

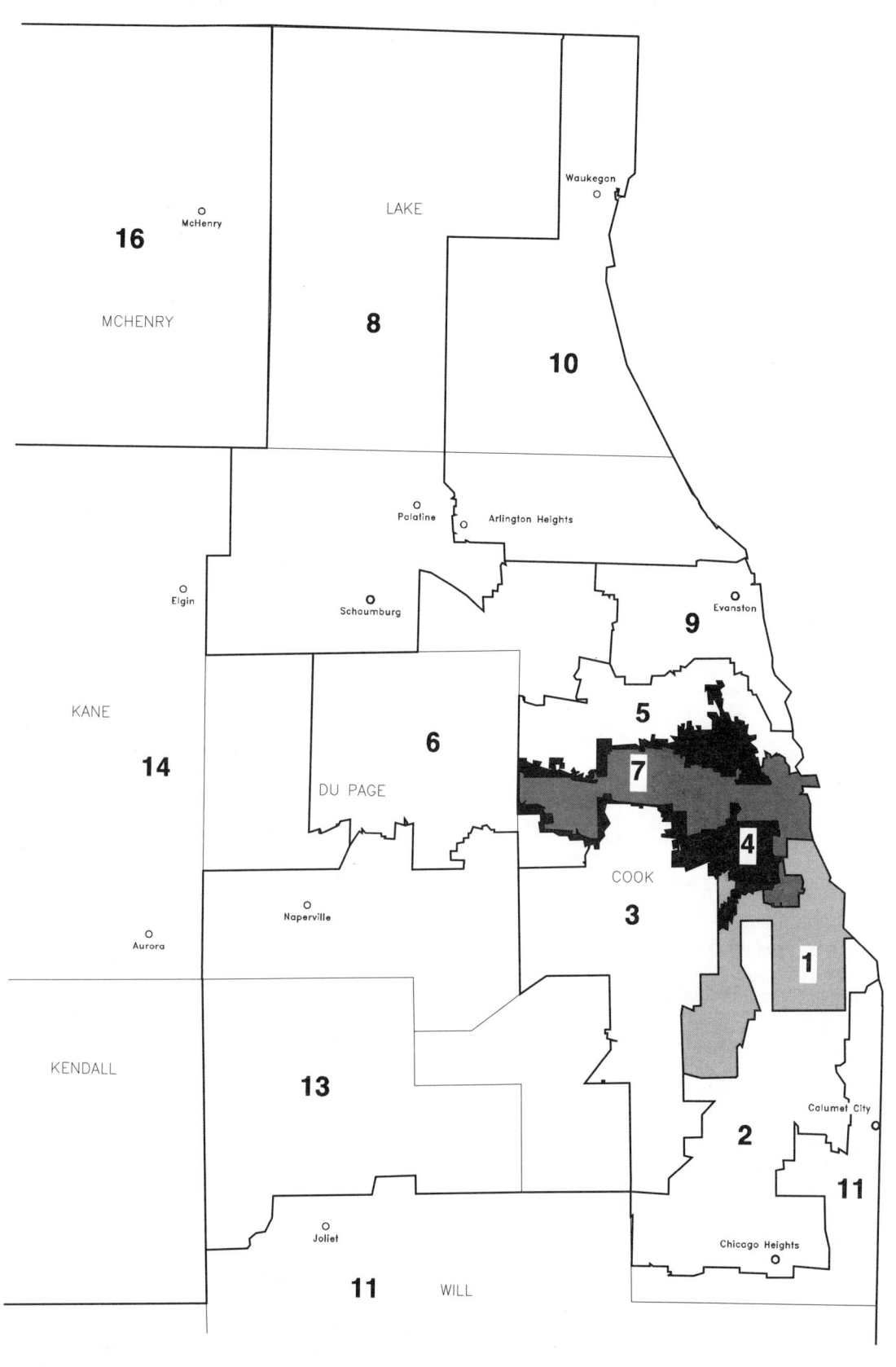

Election Returns

	1st District	Democrat	Republican
1992	President*	214,045 (81.1%)	32,628 (12.4%)
	House	209,258 (82.8%)	43,453 (17.2%)
1990	Senate	138,235 (85.2%)	23,963 (14.8%)
	Governor	110,209 (70.2%)	46,761 (29.8%)
1988	President	202,507 (80.3%)	49,665 (19.7%)
1986	Senate	162,882 (89.3%)	19,514 (10.7%)
	Governor†	20,800 (11.2%)	42,989 (23.2%)

*Vote for Perot was 17,195 (6.5%). †Independent/other is greater than 5%.

Demographics

Population 571,530

Percent change from 1980 10.1%

Land area 56 square miles

Population per square mile 10,298

Counties, 1990 population
Cook (pt.) 571,530

Cities, 1990 population (10,000 or more)
Alsip (pt.) 13,485   Evergreen Park 20,874
Chicago (pt.) 516,419

Race and Hispanic origin
White 27.3%
Black 69.7%
American Indian, Eskimo, or Aleut. 0.1%
Asian or Pacific Islander 1.0%
Other 1.9%
Hispanic origin 3.6%

Ancestry
American 1.1%   Italian 2.3%
English 2.0%   Lithuanian 1.4%
German 7.2%   Polish 4.5%
Irish 9.2%

Universities/colleges, 1990-1991 enrollment
Catholic Theological Union, Chicago 325
Chicago City College (Kennedy-King), Chicago 9,508
Chicago City College (Olive-Harvey), Chicago 8,763
Chicago State University, Chicago 7,152
Illinois College of Optometry, Chicago 547
Illinois Institute of Technology, Chicago 6,504
International Academy of Merchandising & Design, Chicago 546
Lutheran School of Theology, Chicago 385
McCormick Theology Seminary, Chicago 592
Prairie State College, Chicago Heights 5,127
Saint Xavier College, Chicago 2,641
University of Chicago, Chicago 10,867

Newspapers, total circulation (in all districts)
Chicago Defender 23,377
Chicago Sun-Times 529,632
Chicago Tribune 721,559
Daily Southtown Economist Chicago 52,223
Munster Times 64,780

Commercial television stations, affiliations
ADI: Chicago (100%)

Cable television systems, total subscribers
Multimedia Cablevision Inc.; Oak Lawn 25,376
TCI of Illinois; Chicago-Northside 83,021
TCI of Illinois; Chicago-Southside 66,685
TCI of Illinois; Chicago-Southwest 54,208

Businesses and other major employers
University of Chicago; Chicago 6,750
University of Chicago Hospital/Bernard Mitchell Hospital; Chicago 4,575
Mercy Hospital & Medical Center; Chicago 2,000
Little Company of Mary Hospital; Chicago 1,800
Holy Cross Hospital; Chicago 1,650
Central Steel & Wire Co.; Chicago; metals/minerals 1,250
South Chicago Community Hospital; Chicago 1,102
R. R. Donnelley & Sons Co.; Chicago; commercial printing 1,000
Park Jackson Hospital Foundation; Chicago 738
World Book Inc.; Chicago; nonstore retailers 722
Catholic Charities; Chicago; religious organization 700
Illinois Institute of Technology; Chicago 700
St. Bernard Hospital; Chicago 642
Kraft General Foods Inc.; Chicago; grain mill products 600
American National Can Co.; Chicago; metal containers 600
Sears Roebuck & Co.; Chicago; department stores 600
Allied Products Corp./Verson Allsteel Press Div.; Chicago; metalworking machinery 581
Museum of Science & Industry; Chicago; musuems 577
South Shore Hospital Corp.; Chicago 560
University of Chicago Library; Chicago 550
Norfolk & Western Railway Co./Norfolk Southern Railroad; Chicago; railroads 519

2nd District

Chicago — Far South Side; South Suburbs; Chicago Heights

More than two-thirds of the people in the 2nd are black, and Democrats dominate in contests from president right down the ballot. But after redistricting, which added suburban turf to the 2nd, only slightly more than half the district's residents are within the Chicago city limits.

In 1992, the only question in the 2nd was who the Democratic House nominee was going to be. Democrat Mel Reynolds ousted the incumbent in the primary and, with strong appeals to suburban voters, including Jews, conservative white ethnics and blacks with more moderate views, steamrolled his GOP opponent by gaining 78 percent of the vote.

Within the city, the 2nd is roughly U-shaped (see map on page 236). Much of the western arm, which runs north to 63rd Street, is low-income. There are middle-class pockets, though, in such far South Side sections as Morgan Park and Pullman. The eastern arm begins at 71st Street in the South Shore area. In neighboring South Chicago, belching factories once employed thousands. The USX Corp.'s April 1992 closure of its already downsized South Works plant symbolized the decline of Chicago's industrial base.

For several years, Chicago Mayor Richard M. Daley pushed a pet project, a massive new airport in the Lake Calumet area, another former industrial hub. Backed by claims that the project would be a catalyst for cleaning up industrial pollution and would offer new employment opportunities, Daley in early 1992 gained Republican Gov. Jim Edgar's support for the airport. But the state Legislature refused to go along, pleasing locals who complained about the displacement and noise a new airport would bring.

South of the city are working-class suburbs: Several, including Harvey, Markham and Robbins, are nearly all black. Some, including Ford Heights and parts of urbanized Chicago Heights, are poor, while others, such as Country Club Hills, are more affluent.

The district's southernmost reaches have most of its white population. Jewish residents are numerous in such well-to-do suburbs as Homewood, Flossmoor, and Olympia Fields. Bloom Township has a longstanding Italian-American community; this is the most Republican area in the 2nd.

Election Returns

	2nd District	Democrat	Republican
1992	President*	194,796 (80.0%)	31,730 (13.0%)
	House †	182,614 (78.1%)	31,957 (13.7%)
1990	Senate	108,366 (81.5%)	24,631 (18.5%)
	Governor	84,267 (65.4%)	44,592 (34.6%)
1988	President	165,992 (77.6%)	47,826 (22.4%)
1986	Senate	121,383 (83.7%)	23,586 (16.3%)
	Governor †	17,885 (12.2%)	40,854 (27.9%)

*Vote for Perot was 16,968 (7.0%).   †Independent/other is greater than 5%.

Demographics

Population 571,530

Percent change from 1980 10.1%

Land area 124 square miles

Population per square mile 4,592

Counties, 1990 population
Cook (pt.) 571,530

Cities, 1990 population (10,000 or more)

Blue Island (pt.) 13,288	Dolton 23,930
Calumet City (pt.) 14,859	Harvey 29,771
Chicago Heights (pt.) 33,048	Hazel Crest 13,334
Chicago (pt.) 295,554	Homewood (pt.) 19,278
Country Club Hills (pt.) 15,422	Markham 13,136
	Matteson (pt.) 10,362
	Riverdale 13,671

Race and Hispanic origin
White 27.1%
Black 68.5%
American Indian, Eskimo, or Aleut. 0.1%
Asian or Pacific Islander 0.6%
Other 3.7%
Hispanic origin 6.6%

Ancestry

American 1.3%	French 1.0%
Dutch 1.1%	German 8.0%
English 2.7%	Irish 6.0%

Italian 3.6%	Swedish 1.3%
Polish 4.8%	

Universities/colleges, 1990-1991 enrollment
South Suburban College, South Holland 8,581

Newspapers, total circulation (in all districts)
Chicago Defender 23,377
Chicago Sun-Times 529,632
Chicago Tribune 721,559
Daily Southtown Economist Chicago 52,223
Munster Times 64,780

Commercial television stations, affiliations
ADI: Chicago (100%)
WJYS, Hammond (None)

Cable television systems, total subscribers
Cablevision of Homewood; Homewood 17,199
Continental Cablevision of Illinois; Dolton 17,325
Multimedia Cablevision Inc.; Oak Forest 7,500
TCI of Illinois; Chicago-Southside 66,685

Businesses and other major employers
Ford Motor Co.; Chicago; motor vehicles 2,900
Ford Motor Co.; Chicago Heights; metal forgings/stampings 2,600
Ingalls Memorial Hospital; Harvey 2,000
Acme Steel Co.; Chicago; steel products 1,900
St. James Hospital/Medical Center; Chicago Heights 1,500
South Suburban Hospital; Hazel Crest 1,265
Roadway Express Inc.; Chicago Heights; trucking facilities 1,200
Atcor Inc.; Harvey; electric lighting 1,200
St. Francis Hospital & Health Center; Blue Island 1,175
Thrall Car Mfg. Co. Inc.; Chicago Heights; railroad equipment 1,100
Discovery South Group Ltd.; Tinley Park; real estate operators 1,000
Sherwin-Williams Co.; Chicago; paints 800
South Suburban College; South Holland 800
Roseland Community Hospital; Chicago 634
Prudential Insurance of America Inc.; Matteson; medical service/health insurance 530

3rd District

Chicago — Southwest Side; South and West Suburbs

The working- and middle-class constituency on Chicago's southwest side provides a solid Democratic political base. This is part of the city's "bungalow belt," with block after block of small, neatly kept brick homes mainly occupied by people with ethnic roots in Poland and other Eastern European nations, Italy and Ireland.

During the 1980s, most of the 3rd was within the city limits. But in 1991 redistricting, the district was shunted west, as a new Hispanic-majority district was created to go with the city's three black-majority districts. The 3rd (see map on page 236) now roughly follows the pattern of white migration to the southwest suburbs. Only a quarter of its residents live within Chicago's borders.

Still, there is a strong similarity between the southwest side and the 3rd's close-in suburbs, including Berwyn, Burbank,

Hometown and parts of Cicero and Oak Lawn. Residents in both areas tend to think of themselves as Democrats, but on social issues they are more conservative than the national Democratic Party's line.

There is a Republican vote in the more affluent suburbs in western Cook County and in some of the newer subdivisions at the southern end of the district. While the Democratic base seems secure, the 3rd's conservative tilt makes it something of a swing district. George Bush in 1988 won 61 percent of the vote in the areas that make up the 3rd.

But in 1992, opposition to Bush's economic policies sent many of the district's "Reagan Democrats" back to their traditional party or to the populist campaign of Ross Perot. Bill Clinton carried the 3rd, though with his smallest plurality of any Chicago-based district.

Midway Airport, located within the city and surrounded by southwest side residential communities, has been the district's largest employer. But the airport was dealt a blow in late 1991, when Midway Airlines shut down, and the facility could be threatened if a proposed new airport for the south Chicago area ever gets beyond the talking stage.

The 3rd is bisected by an industrial belt adjacent to Interstate 55 (the main route to the mostly residential suburban area) and the Chicago Sanitary and Ship Canal. Although close to downtown and surrounded by suburbia, this area has few residences among its factories and railroad yards. Bedford Park, home to a Corn Products Corp. factory and one of the district's largest communities in land area, had only 566 residents in 1990.

Election Returns

	3rd District	Democrat	Republican
1992	President*	108,211 (41.0%)	102,626 (38.9%)
	House	162,165 (63.5%)	93,128 (36.5%)
1990	Senate	115,357 (64.2%)	64,377 (35.8%)
	Governor	87,977 (49.3%)	90,621 (50.7%)
1988	President	99,247 (38.9%)	156,118 (61.1%)
1986	Senate	121,830 (65.8%)	63,214 (34.2%)
	Governor †	9,204 (4.9%)	109,816 (58.6%)

*Vote for Perot was 52,892 (20.1%).   †Independent/other is greater than 5%.

Demographics

Population 571,531

Percent change from 1980 10.1%

Land area 127 square miles

Population per square mile 4,518

Counties, 1990 population
  Cook (pt.) 571,531

Cities, 1990 population (10,000 or more)

Berwyn 45,426	La Grange 15,362
Bridgeview 14,402	Oak Forest (pt.) 24,269
Brookfield (pt.) 11,045	Oak Lawn (pt.) 46,540
Burbank 27,600	Palos Heights 11,478
Chicago Ridge 13,643	Tinley Park (pt.) 14,211
Chicago (pt.) 147,861	Western Springs (pt.)
Cicero (pt.) 39,480	11,513
Justice 11,137	Worth 11,208

Race and Hispanic origin
  White 93.3%
  Black 1.9%
  American Indian, Eskimo, or Aleut. 0.1%
  Asian or Pacific Islander 1.4%
  Other 3.2%
  Hispanic origin 7.4%

Ancestry

American 1.3%	Italian 11.7%
Czechoslovakian 5.8%	Lithuanian 3.3%
Dutch 2.6%	Polish 22.8%
English 5.8%	Scotch Irish 1.2%
French 2.4%	Scottish 1.1%
German 24.3%	Slovakian 3.0%
Greek 1.6%	Swedish 2.9%
Irish 23.5%	

Universities/colleges, 1990-1991 enrollment
  Chicago City College (Richard J. Daley), Chicago 8,338
  Morton College, Cicero 4,195
  Trinity Christian College, Palos Heights 546

Newspapers, total circulation (in all districts)
  Chicago Defender 23,377
  Chicago Sun-Times 529,632
  Chicago Tribune 721,559
  Daily Southtown Economist Chicago 52,223

Commercial television stations, affiliations
  ADI: Chicago (100%)

Cable television systems, total subscribers
  Cablevision of Chicago; Oak Park 10,486
  Continental Cablevision of Illinois; North Lake 68,319
  Jones Intercable Inc.; Countryside 8,054
  Metrovision; Hickory Hills 23,136
  Multimedia Cablevision Inc.; Oak Lawn 25,376
  TCI of Illinois; Chicago-Southside 66,685
  TCI of Illinois; Chicago-Southwest 54,208

Businesses and other major employers
  Christ Hospital & Medical Center; Oak Lawn 4,000
  General Motors Corp./Electro-Motive Div.; La Grange; engines 3,707
  R. J. R. Nabisco; Chicago; bakery products 3,000
  Oak Forest Hospital; Oak Forest 2,225
  Metro Water District of Chicago; Berwyn 2,000
  Palos Community Hospital; Palos Heights 1,950
  Reynolds Metals Co.; La Grange; metal products 1,800
  Yellow Freight System Inc.; Chicago Ridge; trucking services 1,574
  MacNeal Memorial Hospital; Berwyn 1,400
  U.S. Postal Service; Forest Park 1,300
  Sweetheart Cup Co. Inc.; Chicago; paper products 1,200
  La Grange Memorial Hospital; La Grange 1,078
  Minnesota Mining & Mfg. Co.; Summit; paper products 1,000
  Commonwealth Edison Co.; Chicago; utility services 935
  Panduit Corp.; Tinley Park; electric lighting 900
  Chicago Public School District; Chicago 900
  Viskase Corp.; Chicago; plastics products 853
  Certified Grocers Midwest; La Grange; warehousing 710
  Tootsie Roll Industries Inc.; Chicago; candies 700

Pulitzer Community Newspapers/Southtown Economist; Chicago; newspapers 651

CPC Intl. Inc.; Summit; furniture 625

Bagcraft Corp. of America; Chicago; paper products 600

Talman Home Federal Savings & Loan; Chicago; savings institutions 600

Guardsmark Inc.; Worth; security/business services 570

Sears Roebuck & Co.; Chicago Ridge; department stores 550

Bremen School District; Midlothian 550

Tinley Park Mental Health Center; Tinley Park 535

Ames Dept. Stores Inc.; Worth; department store warehousing 530

Lyons High School District; La Grange 510

4th District

Chicago — Parts of North Side, Southwest Side

The 1990 census reported that Chicago had 545,852 Hispanic residents, more than twice as many as in 1970. A result of this boom has been a rise in political clout, as symbolized by the creation of the Hispanic-majority 4th.

Hispanics account for 65 percent of the district's population. But many of its Puerto Ricans are poor and have yet to establish community roots; many Mexicans are recent arrivals who are not citizens.

Because of these factors, the 4th lags in voter participation—its 1992 turnout was less than half the average for Illinois House districts—and provides opportunities for non-Hispanic whites, including many of Polish heritage, to influence local elections.

Democratic primaries should be decisive in the 4th. The combination of minority-group and working-class ethnic voters makes the district a Democratic stronghold; Luis Gutierrez won the 1992 House election by better than 3-to-1.

Drawing the 4th required a creative touch (see map on page 236). Most Chicago Hispanics live in two blocs, one northwest of downtown and the other nearby to the southwest. However, a direct linkup would have cut through the black-majority 7th District. To avoid this, the 4th takes in a mostly Hispanic section of the North Side, follows a narrow, 10-mile band along the northern border of the 7th to the Cook County line, then moves south and east along the 7th to hook up with the other Hispanic concentration. Despite its reach, 92 percent of the 4th's population is within Chicago; 5 percent is in adjacent Cicero. Most of the suburban territory is composed of railroad tracks, forest preserves, cemeteries and interstates.

Puerto Ricans hold sway in much of the northern part of the 4th. The former "Polish downtown" along lower Milwaukee Avenue is now mainly Hispanic. Parts of the West Town community are "gentrifying," but nearby Humboldt Park is mainly low-income, and has one of the city's worst gang problems. To the north is Logan Square, which still has a substantial Polish community; there is industry there, in or adjacent to the narrow stretch to the west.

The southern part of the 4th is largely composed of two Mexican-American sections: Little Village, with a thriving business district and many single-family homes, and Pilsen, a poorer area that is upholding its heritage as a point of entry for immigrants.

In the 4th's southern reaches are ethnically mixed sections, including parts of Bridgeport and Back of the Yards. The latter area declined when the famed stockyards closed in the early 1970s, but community organizers have helped attract light industry and revive the retail trade.

Election Returns

	4th District	Democrat	Republican
1992	President*	82,497 (65.0%)	29,091 (22.9%)
	House	90,452 (77.6%)	26,154 (22.4%)
1990	Senate	63,637 (80.2%)	15,692 (19.8%)
	Governor	53,472 (68.1%)	25,042 (31.9%)
1988	President	78,122 (63.1%)	45,680 (36.9%)
1986	Senate	73,813 (80.6%)	17,711 (19.4%)
	Governor†	11,337 (12.1%)	36,841 (39.4%)

*Vote for Perot was 15,392 (12.1%).   †Independent/other is greater than 5%.

Demographics

Population 571,530

Percent change from 1980 10.1%

Land area 39 square miles

Population per square mile 14,470

Counties, 1990 population
Cook (pt.) 571,530

Cities, 1990 population (10,000 or more)
Chicago (pt.) 527,492   Cicero (pt.) 27,956

Race and Hispanic origin
White 48.6%
Black 6.3%
American Indian, Eskimo, or Aleut. 0.4%
Asian or Pacific Islander 2.6%
Other 42.1%
Hispanic origin 65.0%

Ancestry
American 1.1%   Irish 5.8%
English 1.3%   Italian 3.5%
German 6.8%   Polish 8.9%

Universities/colleges, 1990-1991 enrollment
Devry Institute of Technology, Chicago 3,303

Newspapers, total circulation (in all districts)
Chicago Defender 23,377
Chicago Sun-Times 529,632
Chicago Tribune 721,559
Daily Southtown Economist Chicago 52,223

Commercial television stations, affiliations
ADI: Chicago (100%)

Cable television systems, total subscribers
Prime Cable of Chicago; Chicago 115,000
TCI of Illinois; Chicago-Northside 83,021
TCI of Illinois; Chicago-Southwest 54,208

Businesses and other major employers
National Fire Insurance Co.; Chicago; fire/marine/casualty insurance 17,200
American Airlines Inc.; Chicago; airline 10,000

First National Bank of Chicago; Chicago; commercial banks 8,500

CNA Financial Corp.; Chicago; fire/marine/casualty insurance 6,000

Montgomery Ward & Co. Inc.; Chicago; department stores 2,600

County of Cook/Corrections Dept.; Chicago 2,400

Spiegel Inc.; Chicago; catalog retailers 2,250

Joseph T. Ryerson & Son; Chicago; metals/minerals 1,500

General Electric Co.; Chicago; household appliances 1,500

County of Cook; Chicago 1,500

Illinois Air National Guard; Chicago 1,446

Stewart-Warner Corp.; Chicago; measuring/controlling devices 1,400

City of Chicago/Board of Education; Chicago 1,400

Commonwealth Edison Co.; Chicago; utility services 1,321

Sky Chefs Inc.; Chicago; bars/restaurants 1,150

W. M. Wrigley Jr. Co.; Chicago; gum/candies 1,100

Cotter & Co./True Value Hardware Stores; Chicago; hardware 1,000

Williams Electronic Games/Midway Mfg.; Chicago; misc. manufacturers 1,000

Kimco Corp.; Chicago; building services 1,000

Sidley & Austin; Chicago; legal services 991

United Air Lines Inc.; Chicago; airline 900

Marshall Field & Co.; Chicago; warehousing 800

Ekco Group Inc.; Chicago; nonferrous foundries (castings) 775

St. Elizabeth's Hospital of Chicago; Chicago 754

U.S. Postal Service; Chicago 750

Edsal Mfg. Co.; Chicago; partitions/fixtures 700

Joslyn Corp./Joslyn Mfg. Co.; Chicago; switchgears/electric fuses/industrial controls 700

County of Cook/Adult Probation Dept.; Chicago 700

Norwegian-American Hospital; Chicago 690

Litton Systems Inc.; Chicago; aircraft/parts 670

Farley Candy Co.; Chicago; candies 650

Harris Marcus Group Inc.; Chicago; electric lighting 600

Mars Inc./M&M Mars; Chicago; candies 600

Finley M. Maxson; Chicago; legal services 570

Ball Corp.; Chicago; metal services 550

Commonwealth Edison Co.; Chicago; electric services 550

5th District

Chicago — North Side

The 5th, which spans the North Side of Chicago (see map on page 236), can be thought of as two districts in one. On the city's east side is a mainly liberal, partly upscale area. Across town, the northwest side is part of Chicago's "bungalow belt," where middle- and working-class residents from a variety of southern and eastern European backgrounds hold more conservative views.

Both groups have Democratic traditions, but their voting behavior can vary widely. East Side liberals may balk at the local Democratic organization during primary campaigns, but they regularly vote Democratic in November. Democratic voters on the northwest side usually take cues from the party's organization in primaries, but the area can swing to GOP candidates in general elections for major office.

The result of this mix is a district that votes regularly though

not certainly Democratic. After going strongly for Ronald Reagan in 1984 and narrowly for George Bush in 1988, the 5th went for Bill Clinton by a scant majority in 1992.

It is not inconceivable that Republicans could compete for this seat in a post-Dan Rostenkowski future, but neither is it likely. Dealing in 1992 with a series of ethics allegations, Democrat Rostenkowski won an 18th House term by a margin that, while subpar for him, was still comfortable.

The district ranges to Lake Michigan just north of downtown, taking in some of the upscale high-rises along Lake Shore Drive's "Gold Coast." Nearby is the Lincoln Park community, home to numerous political activists, young professionals and DePaul University students.

Opponents of the city's Democratic Party machine had their heyday here in the 1970s, during the waning days of Richard J. Daley's reign as mayor. Somewhat dormant in recent years, the "lakefront liberals" emerged again when one of their number, activist Dick Simpson, challenged Rostenkowski in the 1992 primary.

The district follows Lincoln Avenue northwest past well-to-do Ravenswood and multi-ethnic Lincoln Square. To the west along Lawrence Avenue is a Korean-American community. The 5th then drops south to Jackowo, still a first stop for immigrants from Poland.

Much of the district's western end is a grid of small brick houses where families of city workers, commuters and O'Hare Airport employees live. Few blacks live here: In her 1992 bid to become the first black woman senator, Democrat Carol Moseley-Braun had trouble in parts of the northwest side. Harold Washington was anathema to many northwest voters during his tenure as Chicago's first black mayor in the mid-1980s.

The 5th also takes in two independent towns, Norridge and Harwood Heights, that are within Chicago's city limits, and such suburban Cook County communities as Franklin Park, Northlake and Melrose Park. Matsushita, the Japanese appliance maker, is expanding an existing Franklin Park facility into the world's largest microwave oven factory.

Election Returns

	5th District	Democrat	Republican
1992	President*	124,437 (51.1%)	80,139 (32.9%)
	House	132,889 (57.3%)	90,738 (39.1%)
1990	Senate	112,784 (70.2%)	47,894 (29.8%)
	Governor	83,747 (52.4%)	76,023 (47.6%)
1988	President	115,595 (48.5%)	122,755 (51.5%)
1986	Senate	120,692 (72.0%)	46,985 (28.0%)
	Governor †	9,769 (5.7%)	92,629 (54.1%)

*Vote for Perot was 39,153 (16.1%).   †Independent/other is greater than 5%.

Demographics

Population 571,530

Percent change from 1980 10.1%

Land area 53 square miles

Population per square mile 10,830

Counties, 1990 population
Cook (pt.) 571,530

Cities, 1990 population (10,000 or more)

Chicago (pt.) 460,009	Melrose Park (pt.) 15,680
Elmwood Park (pt.) 17,144	Norridge 14,459
Franklin Park 18,485	Northlake (pt.) 11,463

Race and Hispanic origin

White   86.8%
Black   1.5%
American Indian, Eskimo, or Aleut.   0.3%
Asian or Pacific Islander   5.9%
Other   5.6%
Hispanic origin   13.3%

Ancestry

American 1.2%	Irish 15.4%
Czechoslovakian 1.1%	Italian 12.9%
English 5.1%	Norwegian 1.5%
French 2.1%	Polish 19.8%
German 22.1%	Russian 2.3%
Greek 2.4%	Scottish 1.1%
Hungarian 1.0%	Swedish 2.7%

Universities/colleges, 1990-1991 enrollment

Chicago City College (Wilbur Wright), Chicago   8,297
Dr. Scholl College of Podiatric Medicine, Chicago   378
North Park College & Theological Seminary, Chicago   1,034
Northeastern Illinois University, Chicago   10,453
Triton College, River Grove   16,759

Newspapers, total circulation (in all districts)

Chicago Sun-Times   529,632
Chicago Tribune   721,559
Chicago Defender   23,377
Daily Southtown Economist Chicago   52,223

Commercial television stations, affiliations

ADI: Chicago (100%)

Cable television systems, total subscribers

Continental Cablevision of Illinois; North Lake   68,319
Prime Cable of Chicago; Chicago   115,000
TCI of Illinois; Chicago-Northside   83,021

Businesses and other major employers

U.S. Postal Service; River Grove   3,500
Zenith Electronics Corp./Rauland Div.; Melrose Park; electronic components   3,200
Jewel Food Stores Inc.; Melrose Park; warehousing   3,000
Illinois Masonic Medical Center; Chicago   2,700
Children's Memorial Hospital; Chicago   1,790
Bankers Life & Casualty Co.; Chicago; life insurance   1,630
Marquette National Life Insurance Co.; Chicago; life insurance   1,600
Carlyle Ltd.; Chicago; real estate operators   1,500
Matsushita Electric Corp. America; Franklin Park; microwave ovens/televisions/electronic products   1,400
Chicago City College (Wilbur Wright), Chicago   1,356
Navistar Intl.; Melrose Park; engines/turbines   1,200
Grant Hospital of Chicago; Chicago   1,200
Ravenswood Hospital Medical Center; Chicago   1,200
Gottlieb Memorial Hospital; Melrose Park   1,200
Duo-Fast Corp.; Franklin Park; metal products   1,100
Columbus-Cuneo-Cabrini Medical Center; Chicago   1,100
Our Lady of the Resurrection Hospital; Chicago   1,100
Nabisco Brands Inc.; Franklin Park; confectionery products   1,000

American National Can Co.; Chicago; metal cans   900
Westlake Community Hospital; Melrose Park   870
Alberto-Culver Co.; Melrose Park; toiletries   800
Bloomingdale's Inc.; Chicago; department stores   800
City of Chicago/Police Dept.; Chicago   800
Triton College; River Grove   800
Chicago Read Mental Health Center; Chicago   780
Binks Mfg. Co.; Franklin Park; industry machinery   750
Vista Intl. Illinois Inc./Drake Hotel; Chicago; hotel   711
Entenmann's Inc.; Melrose Park; bakery products   700
Dominick's Finer Foods Inc./Ludwig Dairy; Melrose Park; grocery stores   700
Saranow Co. Inc.; Chicago; security brokers   700
Automatic Data Processing; Chicago; computer services   700
Laidlaw Transit Inc./Willett Motor Coach Co.; Chicago; school buses   675
Bodine Electric Co./Piedmont Motor & Control Div.; Chicago; electrical industrial apparatus   670
Continental Baking Co./Hostess Cake; Schiller Park; bakery products   650
Centel Corp.; Chicago; telephone communications   639
AG Communication Systems Corp./GTE Auto Electric Labs; Melrose Park; electric lighting   625
Sloan Valve Co./Railroad Products Div.; Franklin Park; plumbing/heating   620
Washington Health Corp.; Chicago   618
Sears Roebuck & Co.; Chicago; department stores   600
Advance Presort Service Inc.; Chicago; business services   550
Fearn Intl. Inc./Le Gout Foods Div.; Franklin Park; preserved fruits/vegetables   525
John O. Butler Co.; Chicago; misc. manufacturers   505

6th District

Northwest and West Chicago Suburbs

All the growth stages of Chicago's western suburbs are represented in the 6th (see map on page 236). To the south are such long-established suburbs as Elmhurst, Villa Park, Lombard, Glen Ellyn and Wheaton, which grew up along an early commuter rail line. To the north are suburbs that boomed in the 1960s, as nearby O'Hare established itself as one of the world's busiest airports. In between are newer suburbs that have seen much of the area's recent population growth.

The 6th is mainly white collar and overwhelmingly Republican. Two-thirds of its population is in Du Page County, often cited by political analysts as a symbol of GOP affluence; the remainder of the district is in equally Republican parts of suburban Cook County.

Failure by a statewide Republican candidate to clean up in the 6th, and in Du Page County as a whole, means certain defeat. In 1992, George Bush carried Du Page with 48 percent. This was his best county total in Illinois, but his 63,707-vote victory margin over Bill Clinton here was barely half what Bush amassed in 1988 against Michael S. Dukakis. Ross Perot took 21 percent of the county vote in 1992.

O'Hare (an extension of the city of Chicago) is a major employer of district residents and the economic engine for much of the 6th. Rosemont, a Cook County suburb just east of the airport, has few residents, but it has business offices and thousands of hotel rooms. The Horizon arena is in Rosemont.

Des Plaines, the largest city within the 6th, is pretty much built out, as is neighboring Park Ridge, a mainly Republican suburb whose best-known native is a Democrat: Hillary Rodham Clinton. On the airport's west side are newer subdivisions in Elk Grove Village (where United Airlines has headquarters) and Bensenville, which had double-digit growth rates during the 1980s.

The Du Page suburbs at the southern end of the 6th are mainly bedroom communities whose residents commute to downtown Chicago or to such burgeoning suburban employment centers as nearby Oak Brook and Naperville.

During the 1980s, residential subdivisions, some of them quite pricey, sprung from farmland and open space in northern Du Page; this growth was fueled by the development boom that turned Schaumburg (just over the line in the 8th) into a semi-urban center. The city of Carol Stream, at the western edge of the 6th, more than doubled in population during the 1980s. Such towns as Roselle, Bloomingdale and Glendale Heights also grew at healthy, albeit more modest, rates.

Years ago, Du Page's farms drew a number of migrant workers, including some Hispanics. Today, Hispanics make up 5 percent of the 6th's population, which is overwhelmingly white; blacks account for slightly more than 1 percent.

The 6th also butts back into western Cook County to take in La Grange Park and parts of Westchester and Brookfield.

Election Returns

		Democrat	Republican
	6th District	Democrat	Republican
1992	President*	86,444 (33.1%)	121,863 (46.7%)
	House	86,891 (34.5%)	165,009 (65.5%)
1990	Senate	85,277 (52.5%)	77,020 (47.5%)
	Governor	53,173 (32.9%)	108,300 (67.1%)
1988	President	75,552 (32.2%)	159,025 (67.8%)
1986	Senate	74,515 (50.2%)	73,955 (49.8%)
	Governor †	4,432 (3.0%)	106,826 (71.4%)

*Vote for Perot was 52,734 (20.2%).   †Independent/other is greater than 5%.

Demographics

Population 571,530

Percent change from 1980 10.1%

Land area 184 square miles

Population per square mile 3,105

Counties, 1990 population
Cook (pt.) 197,305   DuPage (pt.) 374,225

Cities, 1990 population (10,000 or more)

Addison 32,058	La Grange Park 12,861
Bensenville (pt.) 17,767	Lombard (pt.) 38,032
Bloomingdale 16,614	Mount Prospect (pt.)
Carol Stream (pt.) 19,030	10,890
Des Plaines (pt.) 52,639	Park Ridge (pt.) 36,175
Elk Grove Village (pt.)	Roselle (pt.) 17,499
21,375	Villa Park 22,253
Elmhurst 42,029	Wheaton (pt.) 38,464
Glen Ellyn (pt.) 24,887	Wood Dale 12,425
Glendale Heights 27,973	

Race and Hispanic origin
White 91.8%
Black 1.5%
American Indian, Eskimo, or Aleut. 0.1%
Asian or Pacific Islander 4.9%
Other 1.6%
Hispanic origin 5.3%

Ancestry

American 1.1%	Italian 14.6%
Czechoslovakian 3.2%	Lithuanian 1.1%
Danish 1.0%	Norwegian 2.5%
Dutch 2.1%	Polish 14.9%
English 9.5%	Russian 1.4%
French 3.2%	Scotch Irish 1.5%
German 32.7%	Scottish 1.8%
Greek 2.0%	Slovakian 1.5%
Irish 19.2%	Swedish 4.5%

Universities/colleges, 1990-1991 enrollment
Chicago College of Osteopathic Medicine, Downers Grove 471
College of Du Page, Glen Ellyn 29,187
Elmhurst College, Elmhurst 3,006
National College of Chiropractic, Lombard 797
Northern Baptist Theological Seminary, Lombard 218
Wheaton College; Wheaton 2,533

Newspapers, total circulation (in all districts)
Chicago Defender 23,377
Chicago Sun-Times 529,632
Chicago Tribune 721,559
Daily Southtown Economist Chicago 52,223

Commercial television stations, affiliations
ADI: Chicago (100%)

Cable television systems, total subscribers
Continental Cablevision of Illinois; North Lake 68,319
Jones Spacelink; West Chicago 37,000
Metrovision/Du Page; Addison 28,200
TCI of Illinois; Mount Prospect 45,179

Military installations, 1991
O'Hare Intl. Airport Air Reserve Station, Chicago 812

Businesses and other major employers
Lutheran General Hospital Inc.; Park Ridge 4,000
United Air Lines Inc.; Mount Prospect; airline 3,625
E. J. Brach & Sons Inc.; Villa Park; candies 3,200
Ameritech Services Inc.; Schaumburg; business services 2,500
IRCA (North America) Inc.; Wheaton; electrical goods 2,400
Dominick's Finer Foods Inc./Omni Super Stores; Glen Ellyn; grocery stores 2,300
College of Du Page; Glen Ellyn 2,100
Wallace Computer Services Inc.; Melrose Park; business forms 2,000
Elmhurst Memorial Hospital; Elmhurst 2,000
TW Services Inc./Canteen Corp.; Elmhurst; management/public relations 2,000
Alexian Brothers Medical Center; Elk Grove Village 2,000
Littelfuse Inc.; Des Plaines; circuit control devices 1,685
Allied-Signal Inc./Norplex/Oak; Des Plaines; machinery/equipment/supplies 1,600
McDonald's Corp.; Hinsdale; fast-food chain 1,500
Good Samaritan Hospital; Downers Grove 1,337
Household Intl. Inc.; Wood Dale; credit institutions 1,200
AT&T Co.; ELk Grove Village; engineering services 1,200

Waste Management Inc.; Hinsdale; waste removal 1,000

McGraw-Edison Co./Cooper Lighting; Elk Grove Village; electric lighting 1,000

Spraying Systems Co.; Wheaton; metal products 1,000

Wheaton Community United School District; Wheaton 1,000

Central Telephone Co. of Illinois; Des Plaines; telephone communications 980

Covia Partnership/Apollo Travel Services; Des Plaines; travel services 900

Inland Property Mgt. Group; Hinsdale; holding offices 900

General Signal Corp./Sola Electric; Elk Grove Village; electronic components 879

Wheaton Park District; Wheaton; recreation services 855

Midcon Corp.; Lombard; gas production and distribution 805

Boise Cascade Office Products; Itasca; paper products 800

Holy Family Hospital; Des Plaines 800

Hyatt Corp./Hyatt Regency O'Hare; Des Plaines; hotel 790

Official Airline Guides Inc.; Hinsdale; publishing 750

Wisconsin Central Transportation Corp.; Des Plaines; railroads 750

Gary-Wheaton Corp.; Wheaton; commercial banks 750

Comdisco Inc.; Des Plaines; computer services 750

Field Container Corp./Southfield Carton Div.; Elk Grove Village; paperboard mills 700

Bake-Line Products Inc.; Des Plaines; bakery products 700

Digital Equipment Corp.; Elk Grove Village; professional/commercial equipment 700

Wackenhut Corp.; Downers Grove; business services 700

Unisys Corp.; Lombard; computers 700

Central States Se. & Sw. Pen.; Des Plaines; pension/health/welfare funds 668

Marianjoy Inc.; Wheaton; rehabilitation sevices 650

Terminal Freight Handling Co./Sears Logistics Services; Itasca; freight shipping 600

Enesco Corp.; Elk Grove Village; novelty gifts 600

Household Intl. Inc./Household Finance; Elmhurst; credit institutions 600

Weight Watchers Chicago Inc.; Hinsdale; diet services 600

George S. May Intl. Co.; Park Ridge; management/public relations 600

County of Du Page; Wheaton 600

Policy Management Systems Corp.; Bloomingdale; computer services 600

Joint Commission; Villa Park; professional organizations 590

Keebler Co.; Elmhurst; bakery products 579

Healthcare Compare Corp.; Downers Grove; management/public relations 550

Ramada Hotel O'Hare; Des Plaines; hotel 550

American Service Bureau Inc./Bodimetric Health Service; Des Plaines; home health services 537

Westin Hotel O'Hare; Des Plaines; hotel 529

Wheaton College; Wheaton 516

7th District

Chicago — Downtown; West Side

The black-majority 7th (see map on page 236) links Chicago's bustling downtown business district with the city's poorest minority neighborhoods. These economic extremes are symbol-ized by two stretches of apartment buildings. One lines Lake Shore Drive running north from downtown: These are the plush high-rises of the "Gold Coast." The other is in the 7th's southern end, on a barren stretch overlooking the Dan Ryan Expressway: a huge housing project, the Robert Taylor Homes. Abject poverty, crime, drugs, teenage pregnancy and other urban ills are rife here.

Poverty is also persistent on the city's West Side, home to most of the district's blacks. Parts of this area are moonscapes of abandoned factories and rubble-strewn lots.

Although the 7th fills up daily with white commuters, the permanent population is nearly two-thirds black. The district is reliably Democratic across the ballot.

Democratic Rep. Cardiss Collins was elected to a tenth term in 1992. Generally safe from general-election competition, she faced tough primaries in 1984 and 1986. And there is cause for concern. In 1992, Democratic voters in the city's other majority-black districts (the 1st and 2nd) ousted veteran incumbents in favor of younger primary challengers.

At the eastern end of the district is downtown Chicago and the corporate headquarters, financial institutions and professional organizations that make it the Midwest's leading business center. Sears Tower, the world's tallest building, is here.

Across the Chicago River is the upscale "Magnificent Mile" shopping area, the skyscraping John Hancock Building and the Gold Coast. But even on the North Side there is anguish, in the troubled Cabrini-Green housing project. South of downtown, the 7th picks up Soldier Field (home of football's Bears), Chinatown and white, ethnic Bridgeport, the political base of the Daley family. The district then edges through black areas including the Robert Taylor Homes, whose buildings were once seen as exemplars of progressive social policy, but today are denounced as vertical ghettos.

The near West Side is bisected by the Eisenhower Expressway. To the north is a mainly black and poor area; Chicago Stadium, where basketball's Bulls and hockey's Black Hawks play, is here. To the south of the highway is the University of Illinois at Chicago (24,900 students) and the hospitals that make up the West Side Medical Center.

The West Side neighborhoods of Garfield Park and Lawndale define Chicago ghetto life. As late as the 1950s, Lawndale was a largely Jewish area. But an influx of blacks spurred a "white flight" exacerbated by block-busting real estate agents. Parts of Lawndale have never recovered from riots in the 1960s and a siege of "arson for profit" blazes in the 1970s.

Austin, at Chicago's western edge, has some better-off areas that border the largely prosperous suburbs of Oak Park and River Forest. Oak Park is the most settled of Chicago's western suburbs; 70 percent of its housing stock was built before 1940. Farther west are middle- and working-class suburbs, several of which are largely black.

Election Returns

	7th District	Democrat	Republican
1992	President*	184,383 (78.2%)	35,437 (15.0%)
	House	182,811 (81.1%)	35,346 (15.7%)
1990	Senate	107,836 (82.1%)	23,531 (17.9%)
	Governor	87,492 (68.2%)	40,751 (31.8%)
1988	President	165,619 (76.2%)	51,784 (23.8%)
1986	Senate	124,790 (85.3%)	21,544 (14.7%)
	Governor †	19,527 (13.2%)	38,873 (26.2%)

*Vote for Perot was 15,952 (6.8%).   †Independent/other is greater than 5%.

Demographics

Population 571,530

Percent change from 1980 10.1%

Land area 51 square miles

Population per square mile 11,254

Counties, 1990 population
Cook (pt.) 571,530

Cities, 1990 population (10,000 or more)

Bellwood 20,241	Oak Park (pt.) 45,049
Chicago (pt.) 424,013	River Forest (pt.) 11,669
Maywood (pt.) 25,141	

Race and Hispanic origin
White 29.0%
Black 65.6%
American Indian, Eskimo, or Aleut. 0.1%
Asian or Pacific Islander 3.2%
Other 2.0%
Hispanic origin 4.3%

Ancestry

American 1.2%	Irish 6.5%
English 3.0%	Italian 4.7%
German 7.8%	Polish 3.3%

Universities/colleges, 1990-1991 enrollment
American Academy of Art, Chicago 739
Chicago City College (Chicago-Washington), Chicago 8,313
Chicago City College (City-Wide), Chicago 9,604
Chicago City College (Malcom X), Chicago 9,602
Columbia College, Chicago 6,795
Concordia University, River Forest 1,310
DePaul University, Chicago 15,718
East-West University, Chicago 331
Harrington Institute of Interior Design, Chicago 404
Illinois Medical Training Centers, Chicago 371
Illinois School of Professional Psychology, Chicago 468
John Marshall Law School, Chicago 1,280
Keller Graduate School of Management, Chicago 1,786
MacCormac College, Chicago 464
Moody Bible Institute, Chicago 1,480
Ray College of Design, Chicago 659
Robert Morris College, Chicago 1,894
Roosevelt University, Chicago 6,374
Rosary College, River Forest 1,848
Rush University, Chicago 1,144
School of Art Institute of Chicago, Chicago 2,129
Spertus College Judaica, Chicago 209
Taylor Business Institute, Chicago 211
University of Illinois, Chicago 24,961

Newspapers, total circulation (in all districts)
Chicago Defender 23,377
Chicago Sun-Times 529,632
Chicago Tribune 721,559
Daily Southtown Economist Chicago 52,223

Commercial television stations, affiliations
ADI: Chicago (100%)
WEHS, Aurora-Chicago (None)
WBBM-TV, Chicago (CBS)
WCFC-TV, Chicago (None)
WFLD, Chicago (Fox)
WGN-TV, Chicago (None)
WLS-TV, Chicago (ABC)
WMAQ-TV, Chicago (NBC)
WPWR-TV, Chicago-Gary, Indiana (None)
WGBO-TV, Joliet (None)

Cable television systems, total subscribers
Continental Cablevision of Illinois; North Lake 68,319
Prime Cable of Chicago; Chicago 115,000
TCI of Illinois; Chicago-Northside 83,021

Businesses and other major employers
Continental Assurance Co.; Chicago; medical service/health insurance 17,200
U.S. Postal Service; Chicago 16,000
University of Illinois; Chicago 15,000
Sears Roebuck & Co.; Chicago; department stores 7,400
Johnston R. Bowman Center; Chicago 7,000
Arthur Andersen & Co.; Chicago; accounting/auditing 6,630
Cook County Hospital; Chicago 6,343
Northern Trust Corp.; Chicago; commercial banks 5,784
Continental Bank Corp.; Chicago; commercial banks 5,700
Tribune Co.; Chicago; newspapers 4,000
U.S. Veterans Affairs Dept.; Hines 4,000
Heatherton Staff Leasing Ltd.; Chicago; personnel supply services 4,000
Harris Trust & Savings Bank; Chicago; commercial banks 3,827
Amoco Corp.; Chicago; petroleum refining 3,800
Commonwealth Edison Co.; Chicago; management/public relations 3,580
General Dynamics Corp./Material Service Co.; Chicago; cement 3,500
National Cleaning Contractors; Chicago; building services 3,500
Illinois Bell Telephone Co.; Chicago; telephone communications 3,000
State of Illinois/Employment Security Dept.; Chicago 3,000
Aims Corp.; Chicago; marketing/management consulting services 3,000
County of Cook; Chicago; health services 3,000
Marshall Field & Co.; Chicago; department stores 2,500
Health Care Service Corp./Blue Cross/Blue Shield of Illinois; Chicago; medical service/health insurance 2,500
City of Chicago/Health Dept.; Chicago 2,500
City of Chicago; Chicago 2,500
La Salle National Corp.; Chicago; commercial banks 2,497
City of Chicago/Water System; Chicago 2,329
Montgomery Ward & Co. Inc./Pit Stop; Chicago; business services 2,300
Northern Trust Co.; Chicago; banking services 2,200
Leo Burnett Co.; Chicago; advertising 2,200
University of Illinois Hospital & Clinic; Chicago 2,200
County of Cook; Chicago 2,161
Y. K. Equities & Co.; Chicago; mortgage bankers 2,006
IBM Corp.; Chicago; paper products 2,000
Sargent & Lundy Engineers; Chicago; engineering/architectural services 2,000
U.S. Veterans Affairs Dept; Chicago; hospital 2,000
Federal Reserve Bank of Chicago; Chicago 1,845

Sun-Times Co.; Chicago; newspapers 1,700
Citibank; Chicago; savings institutions 1,600
Hyatt Hotels Corp.; Chicago; hotels 1,600
American National Corp.; Chicago; commercial banks 1,562
Hart Schaffner & Marx Inc.; Chicago; men's suits/coats 1,500
AT&T Co.; Chicago; communication services 1,500
State of Illinois/Employment Dept.; Chicago 1,500
U.S. Environmental Protection Agency; Chicago 1,500
Mount Sinai Hospital Medical Center; Chicago 1,500
Reuters Info Services Corp.; Chicago; advertising 1,448
City of Chicago/Police Dept.; Chicago 1,300
West Suburban Hospital Medical Center; Oak Park 1,240
U.S. Veterans Affairs Dept; Chicago; hospital 1,235
Quaker Oats Co.; Chicago; grain mill products 1,200
Columbia College; Chicago 1,200
Palmer House Hotel; Chicago; hotel 1,200
U.S. Railroad Retirement Board; Chicago 1,200
St. Mary of Nazareth Hospital; Chicago 1,140
Peoples Energy Corp.; Chicago; gas production/distribution 1,100
MCI Telecommunications Corp./Midwest Div.; Chicago; telephone communications 1,100
Rehabilitation Institute of Chicago; Chicago 1,100
Chicago Title & Trust Co.; Chicago; title insurance 1,050
Kemper Financial Services; Chicago; security brokers 1,045
Interstate Brands Corp./Butternut Baking Co.; Chicago; breads & bakery products 1,025
American Medical Assn.; Chicago; profess. organization 1,025
Mayer Brown & Platt; Chicago; legal services 1,010
Leaf Inc.; Chicago; candies/gum 1,005
United Parcel Service Inc.; Chicago; mail services 1,000
USG Corp.; Chicago; concrete/gypsum/plaster 1,000
World Medical Assn./American Medical Assn.; Chicago; periodicals 1,000
Chicago Transit Authority; Chicago 1,000
Schering-Plough Corp./Wesley-Jessen Div.; Chicago; ophthalmic goods 1,000
Borg-Warner Automotive Inc.; Bellwood; motor vehicle parts 1,000
Old Republic Title Insurance; Chicago; title insurance 1,000
Chicago Hilton & Towers; Chicago; hotel 1,000
U.S. Health & Human Services; Chicago 1,000
American Building Maintenance Industries; Chicago; building services 1,000
Art Institute of Chicago Inc.; Chicago; musuem 1,000
Marriott Corp./Chicago Marriott Hotel; Chicago; hotel 1,000
Northwestern University; Evanston 1,000
State of Illinois/Supreme Court; Chicago 1,000
Town Parking Stations; Chicago; automobile parking 1,000
Myerscough Healthcare Ltd.; Chicago; health personnel supply services 999
Encyclopaedia Britannica Inc.; Chicago; encyclopedias/book publishing 975
Financial Protection Services; Chicago; insurance services 925
Chicago Board Options Exchange; Chicago; security &commodity exchanges 920
Continental White Cap Inc.; Chicago; metal forgings/stampings 900

Wright Marketing Inc./National Homecare Systems; Chicago; home health services 900
Ernst & Young; Chicago; accounting/auditing 900
La Salle National Bank; Chicago; commercial banks 898
Chicago Mercantile Exchange/International Monetary Market; Chicago; security & commodity exchanges 882
JWP Midwest Inc.; Maywood; electrical work 850
AON Corp.; Chicago; life insurance 850
Fairmont Hotel Management Co./Fairmont Hotel; Chicago; hotel 850
Kirkland & Ellis; Chicago; legal services 850
Globe Glass & Mirror Co.; Chicago; automotive repair 850
Coopers & Lybrand; Chicago; accounting/auditing 850
City of Chicago/General Service Dept.; Chicago 841
American Hospital Assn.; Chicago; profess. organization 834
McDermott Will & Emery; Chicago; legal services 820
Oscar Mayer Foods Corp.; Chicago; meat products 800
Chicago & Northwestern Transportation Co.; Chicago; railroads 800
Continental Bank National Assn.; Chicago; commercial banks 800
Hilton Hotels Corp.; Chicago; hotels 800
Rollins Burdick Hunter Group; Chicago; management/public relations 800
Information Resources; Chicago; research services 800
Combined Insurance Co. of America; Chicago; medical service/health insurance 750
Jenner & Block; Chicago; legal services 750
DePaul University; Chicago 738
Roosevelt University; Chicago 737
Chicago State University; Chicago 725
Fluor Daniel Inc.; Chicago; professional organization 720
Metro Water Reclaim District of Chicago; Chicago 720
Midwest Stock Exchange Inc./Kray & Co.; Chicago; security and commodity exchanges 700
U.S. Postal Service; Chicago 700
Spencer H. Raymond Ltd.; Chicago; legal services 700
Foote Cone Building Communications; Chicago; advertising 700
Winston & Strawn; Chicago; legal services 700
Loretto Hospital; Chicago 700
Heller Financial Inc.; Chicago; credit institutions 659
U.S. Justice Dept./FBI; Chicago 650
Keck Mahin & Cate; Chicago; legal services 650
Katten Muchin & Zavis; Chicago; legal services 650
Bethany Hospital; Chicago 633
Baker & McKenzie; Chicago; legal services 632
Chapman & Cutler; Chicago; legal services 622
National Railroad Pass Corp./Amtrak; Chicago; transportation services 620
Morton Intl. Inc.; Chicago; chemical products 600
Pyle National Inc.; Chicago; electronic connectors/lighting 600
Robert Bosch Corp.; Maywood; motor vehicle parts 600
Board of Trade of the City of Chicago; Chicago; security and commodity exchanges 600
Continental Insurance Co.; Chicago; insurance services 600
Hartmarx Corp.; Chicago; men's clothing stores 600
DDB Needham Worldwide Inc.; Chicago; advertising 600
American Bar Assn.; Chicago; profess. organization 600
Ritz-Carlton Water Tower/Hotel; Chicago; hotel 600
Follett Corp./Follett Service Co. Div.; Chicago; computer services 600

Chicago Corp.; Chicago; security brokers 593

Blue Cross/Blue Shield Association; Chicago; business assn. 560

Inland Steel Industries Inc.; Chicago; steel products 558

St. Anthony Hospital; Chicago 556

CBS Inc.; Chicago; radio/TV broadcasting 550

Trans Union Corp.; Chicago; credit reporting 550

Deloitte & Touche; Chicago; accounting/auditing 550

U.S. Health & Human Services Dept.; Chicago 550

Zenith Electronics Corp.; Chicago; business services 550

Lord Bissell & Brook; Chicago; legal services 548

Rudnick & Wolfe; Chicago; legal services 530

Nestle USA Inc./Stouffer Rivier Hotel; Chicago; hotel 525

St. Frances X. Cabrini Hospital; Chicago 525

Illinois Central Railroad Co.; Chicago; railroads 520

Helene Curtis Industries Inc.; Chicago; hair preparations/lotions 512

8th District

Northwest Cook County — Schaumburg; Palatine

There are House districts in the Chicago area where the major concerns are economic development and jobs. Then there are districts, such as the suburban and affluent 8th, where the main worries are overdevelopment and traffic.

The 8th is made up of the suburbs of northwest Cook County (which provide more than 60 percent of the district's votes); the developing exurbia of southwestern Lake County; and the more remote (but also growing) lake-country towns near Wisconsin. These areas combine to make the 8th the most Republican district in Illinois.

Although Democratic Sen. Paul Simon won every Illinois district in 1990, he took just 52 percent in the 8th. In 1992, the district returned to form, supporting Republican Senate candidate Rich Williamson over Democratic winner Carol Moseley-Braun.

Yet there are signs that recent suburban growth may have tempered the staunch conservatism that long made Rep. Philip Crane virtually untouchable. In 1992, he struggled to fend off a more moderate GOP primary foe, then defeated his Democratic challenger with a subpar 56 percent. George Bush carried the 8th but with far less than the 71 percent he rang up in 1988.

The district has some well-established suburbs in its southeast corner, the nearest part to Chicago, including Mount Prospect and the southern part of Arlington Heights (the rest is in the 10th District). The biggest boom has been farther west; development has been abetted by access to Interstates 90 and 290 and proximity to O'Hare Airport (in the 6th District). Just 30 years ago, Schaumburg was still mainly rural. Today, it is a satellite city of 68,000 and the largest community within the 8th. The Motorola electronics company is in Schaumburg, as is Zurich American Life Insurance. Hoffman Estates has expanded nearly as fast; and retailer Sears has moved its merchandising group to the city.

Rolling Meadows, with some high-tech industry, and mainly residential Palatine lie to the north. At the west end of Cook County is a portion of Elgin that has experienced residential growth.

Some exclusive communities have sought to remain exclusive. Barrington Hills, which sprawls among Cook, Lake, McHenry and Kane counties, has slightly more than 4,000 residents.

But growth is unbridled in other Lake County communities: Lake Zurich grew by 81 percent in the 1980s to 15,000 residents. The Kemper insurance company is based in nearby Long Grove.

The northern part of the district, with its "chain o' lakes," has a number of vacation homes but is far less densely populated. Residents who rely on seasonal employment are also less well-off than the district norm.

At the northeast edge of the 8th is Gurnee, across the 10th District line from Waukegan. Spurred by its location on Interstate 94, Gurnee nearly doubled in population in the 1980s, to just under 14,000.

Election Returns

	8th District	Democrat	Republican
1992	President*	76,327 (30.6%)	118,714 (47.6%)
	House	96,419 (40.4%)	132,887 (55.7%)
1990	Senate	67,428 (51.5%)	63,423 (48.5%)
	Governor	42,785 (33.1%)	86,632 (66.9%)
1988	President	58,748 (29.3%)	141,985 (70.7%)
1986	Senate	51,082 (49.5%)	52,165 (50.5%)
	Governor	2,338 (2.2%)	76,513 (73.4%)

*Vote for Perot was 54,269 (21.8%).   †Independent/other is greater than 5%.

Demographics

Population 571,530

Percent change from 1980 10.1%

Land area 432 square miles

Population per square mile 1,324

Counties, 1990 population

Cook (pt.) 370,272   Lake (pt.) 201,258

Cities, 1990 population (10,000 or more)

Arlington Heights (pt.) 34,340

Elgin (pt.) 15,400

Elk Grove Village (pt.) 12,054

Gurnee (pt.) 13,690

Hanover Park (pt.) 18,662

Hoffman Estates (pt.) 46,561

Lake Zurich 14,947

Mount Prospect (pt.) 23,315

Palatine 39,253

Rolling Meadows (pt.) 22,591

Round Lake Beach 16,434

Schaumburg (pt.) 68,586

Streamwood 30,987

Race and Hispanic origin

White 92.2%

Black 1.7%

American Indian, Eskimo, or Aleut. 0.2%

Asian or Pacific Islander 4.0%

Other 1.9%

Hispanic origin 5.5%

Ancestry

American 1.5%

Czechoslovakian 1.8%

Danish 1.2%

Dutch 1.9%

English 10.6%

French 3.5%

German 37.0%

Greek 1.2%

Irish 19.6%

Italian 11.0%

Norwegian 2.8%

Polish 14.5%

Russian 1.3%

Scotch Irish 1.5%

Scottish 2.1%   Swedish 5.3%
Slovakian 1.4%

Universities/colleges, 1990-1991 enrollment
College of Lake County, Grayslake 13,526
ITT Technical Institute, Hoffman Estates 377
Oakton Community College, Des Plaines 12,395
University of St. Mary of the Lake Seminary, Mundelein 290
William Rainey Harper College, Palatine 16,509

Newspapers, total circulation (in all districts)
Arlington Heights Herald 114,266
Chicago Defender 23,377
Chicago Sun-Times 529,632
Chicago Tribune 721,559
Daily Southtown Economist Chicago 52,223
Elgin Courier News 30,863
Waukegan News-Sun 39,157

Commercial television stations, affiliations
ADI: Chicago (100%)

Cable television systems, total subscribers
Continental Cablevision of Illinois; Rolling Meadows 46,107
Jones Intercable Inc.; Lake Zurich 14,200
Jones Intercable Inc.; Libertyville 13,362
TCI of Illinois; McHenry 19,500
TCI of Illinois; Mount Prospect 45,179
TCI of Illinois; Schaumburg 13,775
US Cable of Lake County; North Chicago 45,460

Businesses and other major employers
Northrop Corp./Defense Systems Div.; Arlington Heights; communications equipment 5,000
Motorola Communications & Elec.; Schaumburg; electrical goods 3,500
Baxter Healthcare Corp.; Round Lake; professional/commercial equipment 3,500
Logan Graphic Products Inc.; Wauconda; metalworking machinery 3,040
Zurich American Life Insurance Co.; Schaumburg; fire/marine/casualty insurance 2,600
Kemper Corp.; Lake Zurich; security brokers 2,500
American Motorists Insurance Co.; Lake Zurich; fire/marine/casualty insurance 2,500
Northwest Community Hospital; Arlington Heights 2,300
American Manufacturers Mutual Insurance Co.; Lake Zurich; fire/marine/casualty insurance 1,900
Lumbermen's Mutual Casualty Co.; Lake Zurich; fire/marine/casualty insurance 1,800
Oakton Community College; Des Plaines 1,250
Signature Financial Marketing; Schaumburg; membership organization 1,230
William Rainey Harper College; Palatine 1,100
Suburban Medical Center/Humana Hospital; Schaumburg 1,000
Siemens Gammasonics Inc.; Schaumburg; medical instruments/supplies 900
Sears Technology Services Inc.; Schaumburg; management/public relations 900
Cherry Corp.; Waukegan; computer equipment 895
Union Oil Co. of California; Schaumburg; oil co. management 850

Sears Roebuck & Co.; Schaumburg; department stores 800
Baxter Healthcare Corp.; Waukegan; computer services 800
Ameritech MBL Communications; Schaumburg; telephone communications 750
Sears Roebuck & Co.; Mundelein; department stores 700
Good Shepherd Hospital; Barrington 700
Recon/Optical Inc.; Barrington; photographic equipment/supplies 550
J. C. Penney Co. Inc.; Schaumburg; department stores 550
CFM Franchising Co.; Schaumburg; misc. investing 550
U.S. Can Co.; Elgin; metal containers 525

9th District

Chicago — North Side Lakefront and Suburbs; Evanston

The political core of the 9th is a wedge that takes in the northeast corner of Chicago and the near-in suburbs of Evanston and Skokie (see map on page 236). This district, the most ethnically and racially diverse in the Chicago area, is also one of the most liberal-voting areas in Illinois. It provides a secure base for Democrats and offsets more conservative turf in the district's western end.

A bit more than two-thirds of the district's residents are non-Hispanic whites; the remaining constituency is divided nearly evenly among blacks, Hispanics and people of Asian heritage. Although the sizable minority population has an influence on its partisan direction, the 9th stands out as the most Democratic white-majority district in the state.

In 1992, Bill Clinton won comfortably here (as had Michael S. Dukakis in 1988) with 61 percent of the vote, and the 9th backed Democratic Senate nominee Carol Moseley-Braun, giving her 62 percent.

About two-thirds of the district's residents live within Chicago's boundaries. The 9th reaches a point at Diversey Street and Lake Michigan. A series of high-rises along Lake Shore Drive, many of them upscale, overlook Lincoln Park and the Lakeview community. This part of the 9th was home to some of the "lakefront liberals" who rose up to challenge the Democratic machine during the 1970s. The community of New Town is a center for the Chicago gay population.

To the north, at Addison and Clark, is venerable Wrigley Field, home to baseball's Cubs. The surrounding neighborhood had grown a bit seedy over the years, but an influx of young professionals has made "Wrigleyville" a hot real estate market.

The community of Uptown is mainly working-class, with some low-income areas. Much of the district's Hispanic population lives here; there is a settlement of Vietnamese immigrants as well. The largest black concentration in the Chicago part of the district is nearby.

Bordering the lake just to the north is the campus of Loyola University (14,800 students). Rogers Park, tucked in the city's northeast corner, is polyglot and mainly middle-class. Much of the district's Jewish population lives in the Chicago community of West Ridge and in Skokie, an adjacent suburb.

Evanston, with a population of more than 70,000, is the district's lakeside suburb. Blacks make up a fifth of the city's population and live mainly in the urbanized south part of the city. Northwestern University and its 17,000 students dominate northern Evanston; the surrounding residential areas anchor suburban Chicago's affluent North Shore region.

In the district's western reaches, its ethnicity and political attitudes change. Many of the residents are of Irish, Italian and eastern European heritage and have moved from the city's "bungalow belt" to single-family homes in comfortable Norwood Park and Niles or upscale Forest Glen.

Election Returns

	9th District	Democrat	Republican
1992	President*	155,503 (61.4%)	68,485 (27.0%)
	House	162,942 (68.0%)	64,760 (27.0%)
1990	Senate	121,935 (73.1%)	44,878 (26.9%)
	Governor	89,272 (54.2%)	75,504 (45.8%)
1988	President	144,128 (58.2%)	103,679 (41.8%)
1986	Senate	125,441 (74.4%)	43,081 (25.6%)
	Governor†	6,941 (4.0%)	85,608 (49.7%)

*Vote for Perot was 29,314 (11.6%). †Independent/other is greater than 5%.

Demographics

Population 571,530

Percent change from 1980 10.1%

Land area 54 square miles

Population per square mile 10,636

Counties, 1990 population
Cook (pt.) 571,530

Cities, 1990 population (10,000 or more)

Chicago (pt.) 377,262	Morton Grove 22,408
Evanston 73,233	Niles (pt.) 19,165
Lincolnwood 11,365	Skokie 59,432

Race and Hispanic origin
White 73.1%
Black 12.1%
American Indian, Eskimo, or Aleut. 0.3%
Asian or Pacific Islander 10.0%
Other 4.5%
Hispanic origin 9.7%

Ancestry

American 1.8%	Lithuanian 1.1%
English 6.0%	Norwegian 1.3%
French 2.0%	Polish 10.8%
German 17.7%	Russian 6.7%
Greek 1.9%	Scottish 1.3%
Hungarian 1.1%	Swedish 2.6%
Irish 12.5%	West Indian 1.0%
Italian 5.5%	

Universities/colleges, 1990-1991 enrollment
Chicago City College (Chicago-Truman), Chicago 16,467
Garrett-Evangelical Theological Seminary, Evanston 478
Hebrew Theological College, Skokie 235
Kendall College, Evanston 371
Loyola University of Chicago, Chicago 14,780
Montay College, Chicago 468
National Louis University, Evanston 6,721
Northwestern University, Evanston 17,041
St. Augustine College, Chicago 1,455

Newspapers, total circulation (in all districts)
Chicago Defender 23,377
Chicago Sun-Times 529,632
Chicago Tribune 721,559
Daily Southtown Economist Chicago 52,223

Commercial television stations, affiliations
ADI: Chicago (100%)

Cable television systems, total subscribers
Prime Cable of Chicago; Chicago 115,000
TCI of Illinois; Chicago-Northside 83,021
TCI of Illinois; Skokie 9,200

Businesses and other major employers
G. D. Searle & Co.; Skokie; research services 9,000
Loyola University of Chicago; Chicago 5,000
Northwestern University; Evanston 4,000
Northwestern Memorial Hospital; Chicago 3,665
Kraft General Foods Inc.; Glenview; meat products 2,100
Fel-Pro Inc.; Skokie; hose/belting/gaskets/packing 2,000
G. D. Searle & Co.; Skokie; pharmaceuticals 2,000
Admiral Maintenance Service Co.; Chicago; building services 2,000
Resurrection Hospital Assn.; Chicago 2,000
St. Francis Hospital; Evanston 1,900
Millard Maintenance Service Co.; Chicago; building services 1,900
John Crane Inc./Crane Packing Co.; Morton Grove; hose/belting/gaskets/packing 1,600
St. Joseph Hospital & Health Care; Chicago 1,600
S&C Electric Co.; Chicago; electric distribution equipment 1,550
Cablevision Systems Corp.; Chicago; cable TV services 1,500
Avon Products Inc.; Morton Grove; cosmetics 1,500
Washington National Corp.; Evanston; medical service/health insurance 1,358
Lincolnwood Associates; Chicago; real estate operators 1,200
D-A Lubricant Co./Newark Electronics Div.; Chicago; electrical goods 1,000
A. B. Dick Co.; Chicago; computer/office equipment 1,000
BPS Guard Services Inc.; Chicago; security services 1,000
Evanston School District; Evanston 987
Rush North Shore Medical Center; Skokie 980
Northern Telecom Inc./Cook Electric Div.; Morton Grove; communications equipment 950
Louis A. Weiss Memorial Hospital; Chicago 925
Sears Roebuck & Co.; Skokie; catalog retailers 830
Tempel Steel Co.; Chicago; metal products 800
Switchcraft Inc./Sorensen Co.; Chicago; electric lighting 800
Klein Tools Inc.; Chicago; handtools/hardware 800
ITT Corp./Bell & Gossett Div.; Morton Grove; industry machinery 780
Rand McNally & Co.; Skokie; publishing 700
Edgewater Medical Center; Chicago 570
Bell Howell Document Mgt.; Chicago; professional/commercial equipment 550
Ring Response Ltd.; Skokie; business services 550
Jas Intl. Group; Morton Grove; security & commodity services 540
Pittway Corp./Barr Co. Div.; Chicago; business services 530
W. W. Grainger Inc.; Skokie; electrical goods 522
Evanston Township High School District; Evanston 501

10th District

North and Northwest Chicago Suburbs — Waukegan

Drivers following lake-hugging Sheridan Road north from Evanston reach some of Chicago's oldest and wealthiest suburbs. Affluent North Shore communities here such as Wilmette, Kenilworth, Winnetka and Glencoe have long set a Republican tone in Illinois' northeastern section.

GOP candidates rarely sweat the outcome in the 10th, which includes northern Cook County suburbia and a swath of Lake County that reaches to Wisconsin. George Bush's struggles here in 1992 were not typical; he took 61 percent of the district vote in 1988. Sen. Paul Simon staged a rare Democratic win in 1990, but the 10th went against Democratic Senate nominee Carol Moseley-Braun in 1992.

Most of the residences in the wealthy near-in suburbs were built before 1940; although these communities are hardly in decline, their growth days may be past. Highland Park, site of the summertime Ravinia music festival, won a national award for downtown revitalization.

Nearby is the Army's Fort Sheridan, which is being phased out under the 1989 base-closing law and Glenview Naval Air Station, which is on the 1993 base-closure list. However, the Great Lakes Naval Training Center a few miles north remains by far the 10th's largest single employer. In between are two affluent suburbs, Lake Forest and Lake Bluff, that have been gaining residents. The district's boom has been in newer subdivisions near its western border. Arlington Heights (partially in the 8th District) and surrounding communities expanded rapidly in the 1980s. Buffalo Grove's population grew by 64 percent; Wheeling and Prospect Heights were up by 29 percent. At the outer edge of the Chicago commuting zone, Lake County communities such as Mundelein, Vernon Hills and Libertyville also attracted numerous new residents.

Although most of the 10th's communities are known as bedroom suburbs, several major employers are scattered around the district. The Walgreen drug store chain (Deerfield), Zenith Electronics Corp. (Glenview) and Underwriters Laboratories (Northbrook) have headquarters here.

The Cook County portion of the 10th provided slightly more of the votes in 1992 than the Lake County part. The Cook vote is solidly Republican; the GOP House incumbent got 67 percent here in 1992.

Lake County has the 10th's largest blocs of Democratic voters in the industrial cities of Waukegan and North Chicago. Just over half of Waukegan's residents are white, and the city has slightly more than half the entire district's minority-group residents. The Outboard Marine Corp., which makes boat motors, is based in Waukegan; Abbott Laboratories' home is in North Chicago.

Election Returns

	10th District	Democrat	Republican
1992	President*	108,149 (41.4%)	112,401 (43.0%)
	House	85,400 (35.5%)	155,230 (64.5%)
1990	Senate	92,472 (57.5%)	68,235 (42.5%)
	Governor	57,618 (36.2%)	101,345 (63.8%)
1988	President	90,306 (38.6%)	143,671 (61.4%)
1986	Senate	79,642 (58.2%)	57,260 (41.8%)
	Governor†	3,157 (2.3%)	90,419 (65.3%)

*Vote for Perot was 40,719 (15.6%).   †Independent/other is greater than 5%.

Demographics

Population 571,530

Percent change from 1980 10.0%

Land area 244 square miles

Population per square mile 2,339

Counties, 1990 population
Cook (pt.) 256,370   Lake (pt.) 315,160

Cities, 1990 population (10,000 or more)
Arlington Heights (pt.) 41,120
Buffalo Grove 36,427
Deerfield 17,327
Glenview (pt.) 31,668
Highland Park 30,575
Lake Forest 17,836
Libertyville (pt.) 19,163
Mount Prospect (pt.) 18,965
Mundelein (pt.) 11,842
North Chicago 34,978
Northbrook 32,308
Prospect Heights 15,239
Vernon Hills 15,319
Waukegan (pt.) 66,179
Wheeling 29,911
Wilmette 26,690
Winnetka 12,174
Zion 19,775

Race and Hispanic origin
White 86.5%
Black 6.2%
American Indian, Eskimo, or Aleut. 0.2%
Asian or Pacific Islander 4.1%
Other 3.1%
Hispanic origin 7.1%

Ancestry
American 2.4%   Irish 16.0%
Czechoslovakian 1.2%   Italian 7.2%
Danish 1.0%   Lithuanian 1.2%
Dutch 1.7%   Norwegian 2.1%
English 10.9%   Polish 10.6%
French 3.0%   Russian 6.8%
German 28.0%   Scotch Irish 1.5%
Greek 1.3%   Scottish 2.3%
Hungarian 1.2%   Swedish 4.2%

Universities/colleges, 1990-1991 enrollment
Barat College, Lake Forest 678
Forest Institute of Professional Psychology, Wheeling 253
Lake Forest College, Lake Forest 1,103
Lake Forest Graduate School/Management, Lake Forest 627
Trinity College, Deerfield 898
Trinity Evangelical Divinity School, Deerfield 1,457
University of Health Science-Chicago Medical School, North Chicago 906

Newspapers, total circulation (in all districts)
Arlington Heights Herald 114,266
Chicago Defender 23,377
Chicago Sun-Times 529,632
Chicago Tribune 721,559
Daily Southtown Economist Chicago 52,223
Waukegan News-Sun 39,157

Commercial television stations, affiliations
ADI: Chicago (100%)

Cable television systems, total subscribers

Continental Cablevision of Illinois; Morton Grove 15,984

Continental Cablevision of Illinois; Rolling Meadows 46,107

Jones Intercable Inc.; Libertyville 13,362

Post Newsweek Cable TV; Highland Park 16,486

TCI of Illinois; Mount Prospect 61,031

US Cable of Lake County; North Chicago 45,460

Military installations, 1991

Great Lakes Naval Training Center, Great Lakes 41,103

Glenview Naval Air Station, Glenview 2,611

Fort Sheridan (Army), Highland Park 2,587

Businesses and other major employers

Abbott Laboratories/Ross Laboratories Div.; North Chicago; pharmaceuticals 10,300

Abbott Laboratories/Waukegan Flight Operations; Waukegan; freight shipping 9,000

Allstate Insurance Co.; Northbrook; fire/marine/casualty insurance 5,000

Motorola Inc.; Arlington Heights; cellular phones 3,000

Waukegan School District; Waukegan 2,100

Sara Lee Corp.; Deerfield; frozen bakery products 2,000

U.S. Veterans Affairs Dept.; Great Lakes; hospital 2,000

County of Lake/Winchester House; Waukegan 1,776

Underwriters Laboratories Inc.; Northbrook; commercial testing lab 1,690

Baxter Healthcare Corp.; Deerfield; pharmaceuticals 1,500

Outboard Marine Corp.; Waukegan; engines/turbines 1,500

Hewitt Associates; Lincolnshire; management consulting 1,500

Lake Forest Hospital; Lake Forest 1,318

Sears Consumer Financial Corp.; Deerfield; credit institutions 1,306

Premark FEG Corp.; Deerfield; refrigeration 1,200

Highland Park Hospital; Highland Park 1,200

Trustmark Life Insurance Co.; Lake Forest; medical service/health insurance 1,160

Walgreen Co.; Deerfield; drugstores 1,130

St. Therese Medical Center; Waukegan 1,080

Zenith Electronics Corp.; Glenview; audio/video equipment 1,000

Motorola Inc.; Arlington Heights; communications equipment 1,000

Household Intl. Inc.; Prospect Heights; credit institutions 1,000

Quill Corp.; Lincolnshire; nonstore retailers 925

Marriott Corp./Marriotts Lincolnshire Resort; Highland Park; hotel 900

Rank Video Services America; Deerfield; movie production 900

Victory Memorial Hospital Assn.; Waukegan 826

HarperCollins Publishers Inc./Scott Foresman; Glenview; book publishing 820

Commonwealth Edison Co./Zion Station; Zion; electric services 800

State of Illinois/Waukegan Developmental Center; Waukegan; residential care 731

Landis & Gyr Powers Inc.; Wheeling; electric controlling devices 725

Solar Corp./Solar Plastics Div.; Libertyville; textile products 700

Medline Industries Inc.; Mundelein; professional/commercial equipment 700

Household Finance Corp.; Northbrook; credit institution 700

Honeywell Inc./Commercial Div.; Arlington Heights; engineering/architectural services 700

ABB Impell Corp.; Lincolnshire; engineering/architectural services 700

Culligan Intl. Co.; Northbrook; refrigeration 650

Marriott's Lincolnshire Resort; Lincolnshire; hotel 650

General Binding Corp.; Northbrook; binding/collating 600

Paddock Publications Inc.; Arlington Heights; newspapers 600

Allstate Life Insurance Co.; Deerfield; life insurance 600

Baxter Healthcare Corp./Clintec Nutrition Div.; Deerfield; surgical/medical instruments 600

Lake Forest College; Lake Forest 577

Solo Cup Co.; Highland Park; paperboard products 575

Catholic Bishop of Chicago/Maryville Academy; Des Plaines; residential care 575

Kraft General Foods Inc.; Glenview; food research services 560

Commerce Clearing House Inc.; Deerfield; statistical reports & publishing/printing 550

Motorola Inc.; Wheeling; communications equipment 550

11th District

South Chicago Suburbs and Exurbs — Joliet

The 11th may be contiguous, but it is not exactly coherent. It reaches from the working-class neighborhoods of far southeast Chicago past suburbs and exurbs to industrial Joliet, then through the farmland and small cities of Will, Kankakee, Grundy and La Salle counties.

With its mix of constituencies, the 11th shapes up as a classic swing district. George Bush carried the district in 1988 with 57 percent; in 1992, the 11th swung to Bill Clinton, even though he won Will, the district's largest county, by just 39 percent to 38 percent over Bush (Ross Perot pulled down 22 percent there).

Three of the district's counties, including Will, went against Democrat Carol Moseley-Braun in the 1992 Senate race. The Democratic House nominee won thanks to big margins in Will County and in the areas of Cook County; he narrowly lost the other three counties.

At the northeast corner of the 11th is a small chunk of Chicago that would have been largely depopulated had Chicago Mayor Richard M. Daley's plan for a third Chicago-area airport gone through. In 1992, he announced plans for an airport in the Lake Calumet area; he said the project would create jobs and clean up the polluted industrial site. But the thousands of residents who would be displaced—the blue-collar, ethnic community of Hegewisch would have been wiped out—protested; the state Legislature, citing cost, blocked the plan; and Daley drew back. In 1993, airport proponents were looking at other sites, including rural Will and Kankakee counties in the southern part of the 11th.

The district also rims the south suburban area of Cook County. There are mainly middle- and working-class communities in Calumet City, Lansing and South Holland, to the east; in the southern part is comfortable Park Forest. Just south of the Will County line is University Park, a mainly black, middle-class suburb that is the site of Governors State University.

The southern portion of Will County in the 11th has more than a third of the district's population. The loss of much of its industry sent Joliet into a downturn that hit bottom in the early 1980s; it has stabilized now, with regional malls and the Rialto Square performing arts center (an elaborate former movie theater) drawing people to town. There are still a number of factories, including a Caterpillar plant; the Statesville prison north of town is a major employer.

The towns of Mokena and Frankfort are being absorbed into Chicago's south suburbia. Some rural communities to the east, along Interstate 57, are also growing. Farther south, the 11th takes in mainly rural northern Kankakee County, reaching to the edge but not into the city of Kankakee.

To the west, in Grundy County, is Morris, site of a nuclear power plant; Bush won this GOP-leaning county in 1992. However, Democrats compete in La Salle County, which has light industry in La Salle, Ottawa and Streator; Clinton beat Bush there by 14 percentage points.

Election Returns

	11th District	Democrat	Republican
1992	President*	108,447 (43.6%)	90,085 (36.2%)
	House	135,387 (55.7%)	107,860 (44.3%)
1990	Senate	103,087 (62.8%)	61,049 (37.2%)
	Governor	78,893 (48.3%)	84,334 (51.7%)
1988	President	95,785 (43.3%)	125,175 (56.7%)
1986	Senate	98,875 (63.6%)	56,538 (36.4%)
	Governor †	8,867 (5.7%)	91,242 (58.3%)

*Vote for Perot was 50,200 (20.2%).   †Independent/other is greater than 5%.

Demographics

Population   571,528

Percent change from 1980   10.1%

Land area   2,598 square miles

Population per square mile   220

Counties, 1990 population
Cook (pt.)   168,550
Grundy   32,337
Kankakee (pt.)   60,968
La Salle (pt.)   91,307
Will (pt.)   218,366

Cities, 1990 population (10,000 or more)
Bourbonnais   13,934
Bradley   10,792
Calumet City (pt.)   22,981
Chicago (pt.)   34,829
Joliet (pt.)   76,291
Lansing   28,086
Morris   10,270
Ottawa   17,451
Park Forest (pt.)   21,259
Richton Park (pt.)   10,523
South Holland (pt.)   17,404
Streator (pt.)   14,028

Race and Hispanic origin
White   87.4%
Black   8.6%
American Indian, Eskimo, or Aleut.   0.2%
Asian or Pacific Islander   0.7%
Other   3.2%
Hispanic origin   6.5%

Ancestry
American   2.2%
Czechoslovakian   1.0%
Dutch   4.3%
English   10.5%
French   5.0%
German   31.6%
Irish   19.3%
Italian   9.2%
Lithuanian   1.0%
Norwegian   2.2%
Polish   11.6%
Scotch Irish   1.6%
Scottish   1.6%
Slovakian   3.1%
Swedish   3.5%
Yugoslavian   1.5%

Universities/colleges, 1990-1991 enrollment
College of St. Francis, Joliet   3,998
Governors State University, University Park   5,595
Illinois Valley Community College, Oglesby   4,207
Joliet Junior College, Joliet   9,645
Olivet Nazarene University, Kankakee   1,670

Newspapers, total circulation (in all districts)
Arlington Heights Herald   114,266
Chicago Sun-Times   529,632
Chicago Tribune   721,559
Daily Southtown Economist Chicago   52,223
Joliet Herald News   48,344
Kankakee Daily Journal   29,671
La Salle News Tribune   19,052
Munster Times   64,780
Ottawa Times   12,004
Streator Times Press   8,722

Commercial television stations, affiliations
ADI: Chicago (100%)
  WWTO-TV, La Salle (None)

Cable television systems, total subscribers
Cablevision of Homewood; Homewood   17,199
Continental Cablevision of Illinois; Romeoville   54,868
Jones Intercable Inc.; Lansing   18,100
Jones Intercable Inc.; Park Forest   5,367
Sammons Communications of Illinois Inc.; Ottawa   10,237
TCI Cablevision of Illinois Valley; Peru   11,337
TCI of Illinois; Chicago-Southside   66,685
TCI of Illinois; Kankakee   20,000

Businesses and other major employers
St. Joseph Medical Center; Joliet; health services   1,670
Silver Cross Hospital; Joliet   1,480
State of Illinois/Stateville Penitentiary; Joliet   1,000
C. F. Braun & Co. Inc.; Morris; heavy construction   900
Commonwealth Edison Co./Dresden Station; Morris; electric services   812
State of Illinois/Elizabeth Ludeman Developmental Center; Park Forest; residential care   800
Commonwealth Edison Co./La Salle County Station; Marseilles; electric services   792
Commonwealth Edison Co./Braidwood Station; Braceville; heavy construction   750
Owens-Illinois Inc./Owens-Broakway Glass; Streator; glass/glassware   707
Armour Pharmaceuticals; Bradley; warehousing   700
Quantum Chemical Corp.; Morris; inorganic chemicals   670
Commonwealth Edison Co.; Joliet; electric services   650
Mobil Oil Corp.; Elwood; petroleum refining   630
V. J. Mattson Co. Inc.; Mokena; masonry/plastering   600
Consolidated Freightways Corp.; Peru; trucking facilities   600
Johnson & Johnson; Wilmington; paper products   588

W. R. Grace & Co./Baker & Taylor; Momence; nondurable goods 550

State of Illinois/Transportation Dept.; Ottawa; engineering/architectural services 550

Federal Signal Corp.; Park Forest; communications equipment 526

Mobil Oil Corp.; Frankfort; plastics products 505

12th District

Southwest — Carbondale; East St. Louis

The numbering system is one of the peculiarities of Illinois' House district map for the 1990s. Districts 1 through 13 are all in the Chicago metropolitan area—except the 12th, which is hundreds of miles away in the state's southwest corner.

The 12th also stands out for economic and demographic reasons. This is the most industrial district in southern Illinois, with a belt of factories and refineries on the Mississippi River near St. Louis and a coal-mining region south and east. Blacks are more numerous in the 12th than in any other district outside Chicago. The district contains some of the most economically depressed areas in Illinois.

Those factors combine to make this solidly Democratic turf. In 1992, Bill Clinton carried every county in the 12th, taking a majority in all but one. Democratic Senate candidate Carol Moseley-Braun also won big.

St. Clair County, with more than two-fifths of the 12th's residents, is its hub. The district's most troubled community, East St. Louis, is here. As late as the 1960s, the city was an industrial center. But the closure of its stockyards set off an economic collapse. In the 1980s, East St. Louis lost a quarter of its population, and now has about 41,000 residents. Most who remain are black and poor; more than half of the city's children live below the poverty level.

Belleville, the St. Clair County seat and now its largest city with 43,000 people, is mainly white. It has a mix of poor, working-class and well-off residents, some of whom commute to St. Louis. Nearby is Scott Air Force Base, which is headquarters for the Air Mobility Command and is the district's largest employer. To the north, the district takes in the industrial western section of Madison County. Employers include the Laclede Steel plant in Alton and a Shell Oil refinery in Wood River. Alton was the first Illinois city to revive riverboat gambling. Although Alton is home to conservative activist Phyllis Schlafly, it is mainly Democratic.

South of St. Clair are Perry and Randolph counties, among Illinois' leading coal producers. Although demand for Illinois coal has remained steady, rapid mechanization during the past decade left thousands of miners looking for work. Coal is also mined in Jackson County; the county's economy is bolstered by Southern Illinois University in Carbondale, which has 24,000 students and more than 6,000 employees.

At the southern tip of the district is Alexander County and the weary Mississippi River town of Cairo. The scene of racial conflict in the 1960s, the city of about 4,800 residents is something of a micro-version of East St. Louis. Alexander County gave nearly 60 percent to Clinton in 1992.

There is farm territory in the western part of the district; wheat is a major crop. This is one area where the Democrats' hold is weak. Monroe was the only county in the 12th in 1992 to go for the GOP Senate nominee over Moseley-Braun; Clinton won there by a narrow plurality.

Election Returns

	12th District	Democrat	Republican
1992	President*	132,556 (54.2%)	69,850 (28.6%)
	House	168,762 (71.2%)	68,115 (28.8%)
1990	Senate	111,520 (71.1%)	45,404 (28.9%)
	Governor	93,357 (59.3%)	64,060 (40.7%)
1988	President	123,541 (56.5%)	95,276 (43.5%)
1986	Senate	107,656 (73.2%)	39,506 (26.8%)
	Governor†	16,954 (11.4%)	74,829 (50.5%)

*Vote for Perot was 42,191 (17.2%).   †Independent/other is greater than 5%.

Demographics

Population 571,530

Percent change from 1980 10.1%

Land area 3,506 square miles

Population per square mile 163

Counties, 1990 population

Alexander 10,626	Randolph 34,583
Jackson 61,067	St. Clair 262,852
Madison (pt.) 130,214	Union 17,619
Monroe 22,422	Williamson (pt.) 10,735
Perry 21,412	

Cities, 1990 population (10,000 or more)

Alton 32,905	Fairview Heights 14,351
Belleville 42,785	Granite City 32,862
Cahokia 17,550	O'Fallon 16,073
Carbondale 27,033	Wood River 11,490
East St. Louis 40,944	

Race and Hispanic origin

White 81.5%
Black 17.0%
American Indian, Eskimo, or Aleut 0.2%
Asian or Pacific Islander 0.9%
Other 0.4%
Hispanic origin 1.3%

Ancestry

American 4.7%	Irish 17.9%
Dutch 2.5%	Italian 2.9%
English 12.2%	Polish 2.8%
French 5.8%	Scotch Irish 2.1%
German 38.9%	Scottish 1.4%

Universities/colleges, 1990-1991 enrollment

Belleville Area College, Belleville 14,180
John A. Logan College, Carterville 5,216
McKendree College, Lebanon 1,229
Parks College of St. Louis University, Cahokia 1,120
State Community College, East St. Louis 1,236
University of Southern Illinois, Carbondale 24,084

Newspapers, total circulation (in all districts)

Alton Telegraph 33,926
Belleville News Democrat 50,303

Carbondale Southern Illinoisan 29,212
Edwardsville Intelligencer 6,580
St. Louis Post-Dispatch 369,005

Commercial television stations, affiliations
ADI: Paducah-Cape Girardeau-Harrisburg-Marion (50%) and
St. Louis (50%)

Cable television systems, total subscribers
Cencom Cable TV; Maryville 31,346
Continental Cablevision St. Louis; Belleville 29,134
Continental Cablevision of Illinois: St. Clair County 7,981
TCI of Illinois; Alton 18,134
TCI of Illinois; Carbondale 6,426

Military installations, 1991
Scott Air Force Base, Belleville 16,541
Chas M. Price Support Center (Army), Granite City 521

Businesses and other major employers
University of Southern Illinois; Carbondale 10,512
Olin Corp./Winchester Div.; East Alton; inorganic chemicals
4,000
National Steel Corp./Granite City Steel Div.; Granite City;
steel products 3,500
Belleville Area College, Belleville 2,000
Protestant Memorial Medical Center; Belleville 1,872
Laclede Steel Co.; Alton; steel products 1,750
Shell Oil Co.; Roxana; petroleum refining 1,600
St. Elizabeth's Hospital; Belleville 1,470
East St. Louis School District; East St. Louis 1,462
World Color Press Inc./Spartan Printing Co.; Sparta; commer-
cial printing 1,200
St. Elizabeth Medical Center; Granite City 1,113
Cerro Copper Products Co.; East St. Louis; copper tubing
940
Alton Memorial Hospital; Alton 850
Arch of Illinois Inc.; Percy; coal mining 800
Monsanto Co./W. G. Krummrich Plant; East St. Louis;
organic chemicals 800
St. Anthony's Hospital; Alton 700
Choate Mental Center; Anna 660
Amsted Industries Inc./American Steel Foundries Div.; Gran-
ite City; iron/steel forgings 600
Memorial Hospital; Carbondale 560

13th District

Southwest Chicago Suburbs — Naperville

The 13th District, which covers southern Du Page County
and parts of exurban Cook and Will counties, is a place of wide
lawns and spacious houses where business executives live. It is
one of the most inevitably Republican districts in the country.

George Bush's failure in 1992 to make the most of this
advantage contributed to his crushing defeat by Bill Clinton in
Illinois. In 1988, Bush took 69 percent of the 13th's vote; in 1992,
he slipped all the way to 47 percent. Clinton did not get much
more than the Democratic base vote, but even in this seat of
suburban comfort, populist Ross Perot pulled down a fifth of
the vote.

The major demographic changes in late 20th-century America
have included the emergence of suburban centers as satellite
"downtowns" and population explosion in outlying exurbs. The

13th has prime examples of each, in the communities of Oak
Brook and Naperville.

Oak Brook, just west of the Cook-Du Page County line, is
not especially populous. But its location near the nexus of
Interstates 88, 294 and 290 has abetted its development into a
leading business center. Its corporate roster includes the headquarters of the McDonald's chain, the Ace Hardware Corp.,
Federal Signal Corp. and the Spiegel mail-order company.

South of Oak Brook along I-88 is a string of suburbs that
grew up along the Burlington Northern commuter tracks and
long served as the hub of southern Du Page County. (Overall,
the county provides about three-fifths of the 13th's population.)
With room to spread out, these cities—the largest of which is
Downers Grove—gained population; the growth has given Lisle,
one of the rare traditional working-class towns in the 13th, a
more suburban veneer.

But the spectacular growth has been in Naperville. In 1970,
Naperville was a small city amid Du Page and northern Will
County farmland; by 1980, it caught up with Downers Grove in
population. Then, over the next 10 years, Naperville doubled its
population to more than 85,000, making it Illinois' sixth-largest
city. It has also become an employment center: Allied Van Lines,
Burlington Northern Railroad and Nalco Chemical have headquarters there.

Scientific research is a major source of jobs. Argonne
National Laboratory is in southeast Du Page; district residents
also work at the Fermi National Accelerator Laboratory, across
the line in the 14th District.

Southern Du Page's fast growth has spilled over to the
northern Will County city of Bolingbrook. The remainder of the
13th's section of Will County is mainly rural, dotted with
towns—Lockport, Romeoville, Plainfield—whose links are
mainly with the 11th District city of Joliet.

The 13th also takes in the mainly residential southwest corner
of Cook County that includes the fast-growing exurbs of Orland
Park and Tinley Park.

Election Returns

	13th District	Democrat	Republican
1992	President*	88,324 (32.1%)	128,627 (46.8%)
	House	82,985 (31.6%)	179,257 (68.4%)
1990	Senate	80,964 (52.1%)	74,356 (47.9%)
	Governor	52,655 (34.2%)	101,317 (65.8%)
1988	President	70,072 (31.3%)	153,956 (68.7%)
1986	Senate	64,222 (52.2%)	58,819 (47.8%)
	Governor†	3,622 (2.9%)	88,513 (71.4%)

*Vote for Perot was 58,125 (21.1%).   †Independent/other is greater than 5%.

Demographics

Population 571,531

Percent change from 1980 10.0%

Land area 404 square miles

Population per square mile 1,415

Counties, 1990 population
Cook (pt.) 111,859   Will (pt.) 138,947
Du Page (pt.) 320,725

Cities, 1990 population (10,000 or more)

Aurora (pt.) 14,038	Lisle 19,512
Bolingbrook 40,843	Naperville (pt.) 85,351
Darien 18,341	Orland Park (pt.) 34,936
Downers Grove (pt.) 43,365	Palos Hills (pt.) 14,196
	Romeoville 14,074
Goodings Grove CDP 14,054	Tinley Park (pt.) 22,808
	Westmont (pt.) 20,036
Hinsdale (pt.) 13,956	Woodridge 26,256

Race and Hispanic origin

White 91.6%
Black 3.2%
American Indian, Eskimo, or Aleut. 0.1%
Asian or Pacific Islander 4.2%
Other 0.9%
Hispanic origin 3.0%

Ancestry

American 1.4%	Italian 10.9%
Czechoslovakian 4.1%	Lithuanian 2.3%
Dutch 2.7%	Norwegian 1.9%
English 10.9%	Polish 15.5%
French 3.2%	Scotch Irish 1.7%
German 32.8%	Scottish 2.0%
Greek 1.5%	Slovakian 2.7%
Irish 22.4%	Swedish 4.1%

Universities/colleges, 1990-1991 enrollment

DeVry Institute of Technology, Lombard 2,512
Illinois Benedictine College, Lisle 2,627
Lewis University, Romeoville 3,708
Moraine Valley Community College, Palos Hills 13,601
North Central College, Naperville 2,577

Newspapers, total circulation (in all districts)

Aurora Beacon News 38,686
Chicago Defender 23,377
Chicago Sun-Times 529,632
Chicago Tribune 721,559
Daily Southtown Economist Chicago 52,223
Joliet Herald News 48,344
Kankakee Daily Journal 29,671

Commercial television stations, affiliations

ADI: Chicago (100%)

Cable television systems, total subscribers

Continental Cablevision of Illinois; North Lake 68,319
Continental Cablevision of Illinois; Romeoville 54,868
Jones Intercable Inc.; Naperville 19,300
Jones Intercable Inc.; Orland Park 9,383
Metrovision; Hickory Hills 23,136
Multimedia Cablevision of Lisle; Lisle 6,995

Businesses and other major employers

AT&T Co./Bell Laboratories; Naperville; research services 5,000
U.S. Veterans Affairs Dept.; Hinsdale 3,000
Stanley Smith Security Inc.; Naperville; business/security services 2,500
Hinsdale Hospital; Hinsdale 2,460
Caterpillar Inc.; Joliet; construction machinery 2,000
Amoco Corp.; Naperville; research services 2,000
Illinois State Toll Highway Authority; Hinsdale 1,800

Metropolitan Life Insurance Co.; Aurora; insurance services 1,600
Tellabs Inc.; Lisle; communications equipment 1,292
Edward Hospital Assn.; Naperville 1,200
Nalco Chemical Co.; Naperville; chemical products 985
Sears Roebuck & Co.; Aurora; department stores 970
Allied Van Lines Inc.; Naperville; trucking services 818
Andrew Corp.; Orland Park; communications equipment 800
Rockwell Graphic Systems; Westmont; industry machinery 800
Nordstrom Inc.; Hinsdale; clothing stores 800
Travelers Corp.; Naperville; insurance services 800
Case Corp.; Hinsdale; engineering/architectural services 800
Rockwell Intl. Corp./Switching Systems Div.; Downers Grove; communications equipment 750
Sears Roebuck & Co.; Hinsdale; department stores 750
Zale Corp./Marshall Fields; Hinsdale; retail stores 750
Uno-Ven Co.; Lemont; petroleum refining 700
Ace Hardware Corp.; Hinsdale; hardware/plumbing/heating 700
Northern Illinois Gas Co.; Naperville; gas production &distribution 700
Molex Inc.; Lisle; electronic components 650
U.S. Energy Dept.; Lemont 650
Spiegel Inc.; Hinsdale; catalog retailers 600

14th District

North Central — Aurora; Elgin; De Kalb

A decade ago, the historically industrial cities of Aurora and Elgin in eastern Kane County were in a prolonged state of Rust Belt decline. However, the cities' location at the edge of metropolitan Chicago, their proximity to such booming satellite cities as Schaumburg and Naperville, and their reasonable land values gave them a new life and boosted their populations during the 1980s.

The growth here and in other Fox River Valley communities reinforced Kane County's dominance in the 14th; it contributes more than half the district's population. The rest of the people are distributed among a section of exurban Du Page County to the east and a mainly rural stretch south and west that includes Kendall, De Kalb, Lee and the northern part of La Salle counties. Exurban and rural Republican tendencies dominate the 14th's politics, offsetting the Democratic habits of some blue-collar whites and minority-group voters.

This GOP lean made the 14th one of George Bush's best Illinois districts in 1992, but that is faint praise. Although Bush won in five of the six full or partial counties in the 14th, he fell short of his 65 percent total in 1988. Ross Perot's populism struck a nerve here; he took 20 percent or better in every county.

Aurora, with nearly 100,000 residents, is the district's largest city. It maintains an industrial heritage, with Caterpillar Tractor Co. and the All-Steel office furniture company as major employers. But the growth sector is in white-collar operations, including Toyota's Midwest headquarters.

The economic mix is similar in Elgin, which has about 77,000 total residents. Factory workers here still make a variety of products, including Elgin street sweepers. But the largest private employer is First Chicago Corp.'s credit card processing center.

Much of the residential and retail growth has been in new subdivisions on the cities' east sides, leaving aging downtowns behind. Yet urban Kane County has attracted a growing number of Hispanic residents.

Between Elgin and Aurora are St. Charles, Geneva and Batavia, site of the Fermi National Accelerator Laboratory that extends into Du Page County. The 14th's section of Du Page includes West Chicago and part of Bartlett. To the south is lightly populated, conservative-voting Kendall County.

Just west of the Fox River Valley, the 14th leaves the metropolis and enters rural downstate Illinois. The only large break in the farmscape is De Kalb, site of Northern Illinois University (24,500 students): Clinton carried De Kalb County with 40 percent. In Lee County is Dixon, former President Ronald Reagan's boyhood hometown.

Election Returns

	14th District	Democrat	Republican
1992	President*	83,107 (34.4%)	105,698 (43.7%)
	House	75,294 (32.7%)	155,271 (67.3%)
1990	Senate	76,453 (54.2%)	64,497 (45.8%)
	Governor	53,213 (38.1%)	86,498 (61.9%)
1988	President	66,308 (34.6%)	125,072 (65.4%)
1986	Senate	63,365 (52.1%)	58,357 (47.9%)
	Governor†	4,522 (3.7%)	84,019 (69.0%)

*Vote for Perot was 52,914 (21.9%).   †Independent/other is greater than 5%.

Demographics

Population 571,530

Percent change from 1980 9.5%

Land area 2,452 square miles

Population per square mile 233

Counties, 1990 population

De Kalb 77,932	Kendall 39,413
Du Page (pt.) 86,716	La Salle (pt.) 15,606
Kane 317,471	Lee 34,392

Cities, 1990 population (10,000 or more)

Aurora (pt.) 85,543	Dixon 15,144
Bartlett (pt.) 12,097	Elgin (pt.) 61,610
Batavia 17,076	Geneva 12,617
Carol Stream (pt.) 12,686	St. Charles 22,501
Carpentersville 23,049	Warrenville (pt.) 10,905
De Kalb 34,925	West Chicago 14,796

Race and Hispanic origin

White 88.8%
Black 4.2%
American Indian, Eskimo, or Aleut. 0.2%
Asian or Pacific Islander 1.7%
Other 5.1%
Hispanic origin 9.8%

Ancestry

American 2.4%	Irish 17.8%
Czechoslovakian 1.6%	Italian 6.0%
Danish 1.1%	Norwegian 3.8%
Dutch 2.3%	Polish 7.2%
English 12.6%	Scotch Irish 1.6%
French 3.7%	Scottish 1.9%
German 39.4%	Swedish 5.8%

Universities/colleges, 1990-1991 enrollment

Aurora University, Aurora 2,116
Elgin Community College, Elgin 7,066
Judson College, Elgin 576
Kishwaukee College, Malta 3,035
Northern Illinois University, De Kalb 24,509
Sauk Valley Community College, Dixon 3,109
Waubonsee Community College, Sugar Grove 6,089

Newspapers, total circulation (in all districts)

Arlington Heights Herald 114,266
Aurora Beacon News 38,686
Chicago Sun-Times 529,632
Chicago Tribune 721,559
De Kalb Daily Chronicle 10,096
Dixon Telegraph 9,796
Elgin Courier News 30,863
La Salle News Tribune 19,052
Rockford Register Star 75,020

Commercial television stations, affiliations

ADI: Chicago (70%) and Rockford (30%)

Cable television systems, total subscribers

Jones Intercable Inc.; Elgin 17,086
Jones Intercable Inc.; Oswego 28,429
Jones Spacelink; West Chicago 37,000
TCI Cablevision; Algonquin 26,178
TCI of Illinois; Dixon 5,800
Warner Amex; Sycamore 10,704

Businesses and other major employers

Caterpillar Inc.; Aurora; construction machinery 4,000
Caterpillar Inc.; Montgomery; construction machinery 3,000
Universities Research Assn./Fermi National Accelerator Laboratory; Batavia; atomic research 2,400
FCC National Bank/First Card; Elgin; business services 1,700
Sherman Hospital Assn.; Elgin 1,500
State of Illinois/Elgin Mental Health Center; Elgin 1,250
AT&T Co.; West Chicago; telephone communications 1,100
Allsteel Inc.; Aurora; office furniture 1,071
Mercy Center for Health Care Service; Aurora 1,015
St. Joseph Hospital; Elgin 900
Copley Memorial Hospital Inc.; Aurora 894
Waubonsee Community College; Sugar Grove 850
Burlington Northern Railroad Co.; Aurora; railroads 800
U.S. Federal Aviation Administration; Aurora 800
County of Kane; Geneva 800
General Mills Inc.; West Chicago; grain mill products 700
St. Charles Community United Schools; St. Charles 700
City of Elgin; Elgin 700
Dukane Corp.; St. Charles; audio/visual equipment 654
Furnas Electric Co.; Batavia; industrial controls 650
Safety-Kleen Corp.; Elgin; industry machinery 642
Pittway Corp./BRK Electronics Div.; Aurora; communications equipment 620
Arthur Andersen & Co.; St. Charles; accounting 620
Lyon Metal Products Inc.; Aurora; partitions/fixtures 600
Dial Corp.; Montgomery; soaps 600
Chicago Rawhide Mfg. Co.; Elgin; gaskets 600
Farmers Group Inc.; North Aurora; insurance services 600
Delnor Community Hospital; Geneva 600
Delnor Community Health System; St. Charles 600
State of Illinois/Transportation Dept.; Dixon 540

15th District

East Central — Champaign; Kankakee

Most counties of downstate Illinois struggled with double-digit unemployment at the height of the recent recession. But two adjacent 15th District counties were islands of economic stability: McLean, which has an unusually thriving business sector, and Champaign, home of the University of Illinois.

This relative prosperity, combined with a traditional Republican base in surrounding farm country, makes the 15th a quintessential midwestern Republican district. Though there are faded industrial areas and liberal academic communities that provide some Democratic votes, they are rarely enough to swing the partisan balance.

Thus, George Bush's weak 1992 district showing stands out. Bush—who in 1988 carried 10 of the 11 counties in the 15th—won just five in 1992, none with a majority.

Bloomington and Normal, in McLean County at the west end of the district, form its largest urban center. The cities have more than 90,000 residents between them. State Farm Insurance, the world's largest auto insurer, has its headquarters in Bloomington; Country Companies, another insurance firm, is based here. Normal has Illinois State University, with 22,000 students and nearly 4,000 employees; and Diamond-Star Motors, a joint venture of Mitsubishi and Chrysler, builds cars.

The rest of McLean County as well as De Witt County to the south and Livingston, Ford and Iroquois counties north and east contain some of the state's most prolific corn and soybean farms. These five counties make up the 15th's Republican core; these are the five Bush carried in the 1992 presidential campaign.

But a mix of academia, industry and farming makes Champaign County a swing-voting area. The Republican House nominee and the Democrat Senate nominee won majorities in the county in 1992; Bill Clinton won a plurality. The University of Illinois dominates the economic landscape in the twin cities of Champaign and Urbana. Its payroll of 13,000 people supports a student enrollment of slightly more than 38,000. A Kraft food oils plant is the city's largest industrial facility.

Other urban areas of the district are not as economically healthy. Even in Champaign County, Rantoul is coping with the shutdown of Chanute Air Force Base under the 1989 base-closing law. Vermilion County has been hurt by factory layoffs in Danville and the demise of the tapped-out coal industry nearby. It was the only county to favor the Democratic House challenger in 1992; Clinton beat Bush there by 17 percentage points.

Kankakee, at the district's northern edge, has been seeking an economic formula since the departure of two large industrial employers in the early 1980s. The city is one-third black, giving it the largest minority population in the 15th.

Election Returns

	15th District	Democrat	Republican
1992	President*	107,962 (42.6%)	98,372 (38.8%)
	House	97,190 (40.6%)	142,167 (59.4%)
1990	Senate	102,079 (59.9%)	68,349 (40.1%)
	Governor	67,123 (39.7%)	102,138 (60.3%)
1988	President	95,127 (42.8%)	127,279 (57.2%)
1986	Senate	90,503 (59.5%)	61,723 (40.5%)
	Governor†	8,232 (5.3%)	93,165 (60.3%)

Vote for Perot was 47,259 (18.6%).   †Independent/other is greater than 5%.

Demographics

Population 571,532

Percent change from 1980 10.1%

Land area 7,492 square miles

Population per square mile 76

Counties, 1990 population

Champaign 173,025	Kankakee (pt.) 35,287
De Witt 16,516	Livingston 39,301
Douglas 19,464	McLean (pt.) 119,477
Edgar 19,595	Piatt 15,548
Ford 14,275	Vermilion 88,257
Iroquois 30,787	

Cities, 1990 population (10,000 or more)

Bloomington 51,972	Normal (pt.) 40,018
Champaign 63,502	Pontiac 11,428
Danville 33,828	Rantoul 17,212
Kankakee (pt.) 27,498	Urbana 36,344

Race and Hispanic origin
White 89.7%
Black 7.4%
American Indian, Eskimo, or Aleut. 0.2%
Asian or Pacific Islander 1.9%
Other 0.8%
Hispanic origin 1.6%

Ancestry

American 5.1%	Italian 3.1%
Dutch 3.4%	Norwegian 1.2%
English 16.1%	Polish 2.6%
French 5.0%	Scotch Irish 2.5%
German 39.0%	Scottish 2.1%
Irish 18.4%	Swedish 2.9%

Universities/colleges, 1990-1991 enrollment
Danville Community College, Danville 3,534
Illinois State University, Normal 22,661
Illinois Wesleyan University, Bloomington 1,750
Kankakee Community College, Kankakee 3,789
Parkland College, Champaign 8,570
University of Illinois, Urbana-Champaign 38,163

Newspapers, total circulation (in all districts)
Bloomington Pantagraph 50,507
Champaign News Gazette 43,896
Chicago Tribune 721,559
Danville Commercial-News 23,645
Decatur Herald & Review 42,406
Kankakee Daily Journal 29,671

Commercial television stations, affiliations
ADI: Springfield-Decatur-Champaign (64%), Peoria (26%), Terre Haute (8%) and Chicago (2%)
WCIA, Champaign (CBS)
WICD, Champaign (NBC)
WCCU, Urbana (Fox)

Cable television systems, total subscribers
Champaign-Urbana Cablevision; Urbana 36,000
See-More TV Corp.; Westville 6,200
TCI of Illinois; Kankakee 20,000

Telecable-Bloomington-Normal; Bloomington/Normal
30,538

Warner Cable Communications Corp.; Danville   14,276

Military installations, 1991

Chanute Air Force Base, Rantoul   3,439

Businesses and other major employers

University of Illinois; Urbana-Champaign   12,830

State Farm Mutual Auto Insurance Co.; Bloomington;
fire/marine/casualty insurance   5,355

Diamond-Star Motors Corp.; Normal; motor vehicle parts
3,000

Illinois State University; Normal   3,000

Kraft General Foods Inc.; Champaign; dairy products   1,800

Carle Clinic Assn.; Urbana; medical doctors   1,600

Brokaw Hospital Employee Credit Union; Normal; credit
unions   1,500

U.S. Veterans Affairs Dept.; Danville: hospital   1,400

Bromenn Healthcare/Brokaw Hospital; Normal   1,400

Riverside Medical Center; Kankakee   1,389

State of Illinois/Shapiro Development Center; Kankakee
1,350

General Motors Corp./Powertrain Div.; Danville; iron/steel
foundries   1,200

White Consolidated Industries/Eureka Co. Div.; Bloomington; household appliances   1,200

GTE North Inc.; Bloomington; telephone communications
1,200

Carle Foundation Hospital; Urbana   1,200

Illinois Power Co./Clinton Power Station; Clinton; utility
services   1,150

United Samaritan Medical Center; Danville   1,080

Caterpillar Inc.; Pontiac; engines/turbines   1,026

Super Valu Stores Inc.; Urbana; grocery stores   1,000

Covenant Medical Center; Urbana   1,000

University of Illinois/College of Agriculture; Urbana   942

St. Mary's Hospital; Kankakee   906

.State of Illinois/Pontiac Correctional Center; Pontiac   902

Hyster Co./North America Industries Trucking Div.; Danville;
warehousing   900

St. Joseph's Medical Center; Bloomington   850

Teepak Inc.; Danville; meat products   833

Parkland College; Champaign   800

R. R. Donnelley & Sons Co.; Dwight; commercial printing
750

Country Mutual Insurance Co.; Bloomington;
fire/marine/casualty insurance   725

American Medical Software Inc.; Champaign; computer services   700

U.S. Army Corps of Engineers; Champaign; engineering
services   700

Quantum Chemical Corp.; Tuscola; petroleum refining   656

Stolle Corp./Caradco; Rantoul; millwork   640

Bloomington Public School District; Bloomington   632

County of Champaign; Urbana   609

Valmont Electric Inc.; Danville; electric distribution equipment   600

Heatcraft Inc.; Danville; electrical industrial apparatus   600

Revere Ware Corp./Crown Corning Revere; Clinton; pottery
600

General Electric Co.; Bloomington; generators   600

Champion Federal Savings & Loan Assn.; Bloomington;
savings institutions   600

State of Illinois/Transportation Dept.; Paris   580

Kankakee School District; Kankakee   571

Quaker Oats Co.; Danville; food products   550

Rantoul Products Inc.; Rantoul; plastics products   550

County of McLean; Bloomington   525

Country Life Insurance Co.; Bloomington; life insurance   504

16th District

Northwest — Rockford; McHenry

After an uncharacteristic fling at Democratic voting,
the 16th returned to its Republican form in 1992. The
GOP House challenger unseated the one-term Democratic
incumbent, and George Bush carried the district, though by
less than a Republican presidential candidate typically wins
here.

The Yankees and Scandinavian farmers who settled the
northern tier of Illinois gave it a lasting Republican tenor.
Republicans held the region's House seat throughout the 20th
century—until 1990.

There is a core Democratic vote in the 16th, much of it
centered in industrial Rockford (Winnebago County). But even
within Winnebago County (which provides more than 40
percent of the 16th's votes), the Democratic edge is tempered
by a Republican suburban and rural vote. And the overall
Republican advantage in the 16th is cemented by McHenry
County, a GOP bastion in exurban Chicago at the district's
eastern end.

Rockford, with nearly 140,000 residents, is Illinois' second-
largest city. Democrats rely on the city's blue-collar work force.
Rockford has about 21,000 black residents, more than three-
quarters of the district's black population.

A Chrysler plant and Sundstrand Corp. (a defense contractor
based here) are the largest employers of Rockford's residents.
Unemployment soared to 20 percent at one point during the
early 1980s recession, but the city's extensive park system and
other amenities made it harder to leave than some other
industrial cities: Rockford had a net loss of fewer than 300
people between 1980 and 1990.

This relative stability pales, though, compared with McHenry
County's boom during that period. Located at the northwest
edge of Chicago's exurbia, McHenry increased its population by
24 percent during the 1980s.

This growth brought dramatic change to McHenry's larger
towns: McHenry, Crystal Lake, Cary, Algonquin, Woodstock.
But much of the county remains devoted to the traditional
farming pursuits that emboldened the town of Harvard to call
itself "the milk capital of the world." McHenry may be Illinois'
most Republican county: Bush beat Bill Clinton here by 19
points, even though Ross Perot pulled down a quarter of the
county's vote.

The other counties of this Wisconsin-border district
are among Illinois' leading dairy producers. Jo Daviess County,
in Illinois' northwest corner, leads the state in raising beef
cattle. The city of Galena, in rolling hills near the Mississippi
River, has a tourist-based economy: It features the home of
President Ulysses S. Grant and numerous bed-and-breakfast
establishments.

Election Returns

	16th District	Democrat	Republican
1992	President*	95,102 (36.5%)	108,949 (41.9%)
	House	113,555 (44.4%)	142,388 (55.6%)
1990	Senate	88,597 (54.8%)	72,990 (45.2%)
	Governor	63,138 (39.7%)	95,994 (60.3%)
1988	President	84,100 (38.7%)	133,476 (61.3%)
1986	Senate	76,605 (53.9%)	65,415 (46.1%)
	Governor†	6,644 (4.6%)	92,716 (64.7%)

*Vote for Perot was 56,169 (21.6%).   †Independent/other is greater than 5%.

Demographics

Population 571,530

Percent change from 1980 10.1%

Land area 3,094 square miles

Population per square mile 185

Counties, 1990 population

Boone 30,806	Ogle (pt.) 34,697
Jo Daviess 21,821	Stephenson 48,052
McHenry 183,241	Winnebago 252,913

Cities, 1990 population (10,000 or more)

Algonquin (pt.) 10,194	Loves Park 15,462
Belvidere 15,958	Machesney Park 19,033
Cary 10,043	McHenry 16,177
Crystal Lake 24,512	Rockford 139,426
Freeport 25,840	Woodstock 14,353

Race and Hispanic origin

White 92.9%

Black 4.7%

American Indian, Eskimo, or Aleut. 0.2%

Asian or Pacific Islander 0.9%

Other 1.4%

Hispanic origin 3.1%

Ancestry

American 2.6%	Italian 6.5%
Czechoslovakian 1.4%	Norwegian 4.2%
Danish 1.2%	Polish 6.3%
Dutch 2.9%	Scotch Irish 1.6%
English 13.1%	Scottish 2.1%
French 3.8%	Swedish 9.0%
German 43.5%	Swiss 1.1%
Irish 18.5%	

Universities/colleges, 1990-1991 enrollment

Highland Community College, Freeport 3,258

McHenry County College, Crystal Lake 3,768

Rock Valley College, Rockford 8,730

Rockford College, Rockford 1,512

Newspapers, total circulation (in all districts)

Chicago Sun-Times 529,632

Chicago Tribune 721,559

Dixon Telegraph 9,796

Dubuque Telegraph Herald 33,791

Freeport Journal-Standard 16,955

Northwest Herald Crystal Lake 27,977

Rockford Register Star 75,020

Commercial television stations, affiliations

ADI: Rockford (62%), Davenport-Rock Island-Moline (20%) and Chicago (20%)

WIFR-TV, Freeport (CBS)

WQRF-TV, Rockford (Fox)

WREX-TV, Rockford (ABC)

WTVO, Rockford (NBC)

Cable television systems, total subscribers

Beloit Cablevision; Beloit 18,100

Cablevision Rockford/Park; Loves Park 55,500

Continental Cablevision of Illinois; Freeport 9,200

TCI Cablevision; Algonquin 26,178

TCI of Illinois; McHenry 19,500

Businesses and other major employers

Sundstrand Corp./Sundstrand Aviation; Rockford; guided missiles 4,046

Chrysler Corp./Belvidere Assembly Plant; Belvidere; motor vehicles 4,000

Rockford Memorial Hospital; Rockford 2,000

Ingersoll Milling Machine Co.; Rockford; metal-cutting machinery 1,800

Gaffney Employment Services; Rockford; personnel supply services 1,600

Swedish American Hospital; Rockford 1,500

Amerock Corp.; Rockford; metal cabinet hardware 1,450

Kelly-Springfield Tire Co.; Freeport; tires 1,400

St. Anthony Medical Center; Rockford 1,200

Rock Valley College; Rockford 1,200

Woodward Governor Co.; Rockford; aircraft engines/parts 1,150

Warner-Lambert Co./American Chicle Co. Div.; Rockford; candies/gum 1,119

Intermatic Inc.; Spring Grove; watches/clocks 1,080

Elco Industries Inc.; Rockford; bolts/screws/rivets 1,000

Rockford Products Corp.; Rockford; bolts/screws/rivets 875

Union Special Corp.; Huntley; industry machinery 800

Precision Twist Drill Co.; Crystal Lake; metalworking machinery 800

Economy Fire & Casualty Co.; Freeport; fire/marine/casualty insurance 800

Northern Illinois Medical Center; McHenry 800

U.S. Postal Service; Rockford 750

Commonwealth Edison Co./Byron Station; Byron; electric services 739

Freeport Memorial Hospital; Freeport 730

Caron Intl. Inc.; Rochelle; yarn mills 721

Hydraulics Inc.; McHenry; motor vehicles/equipment 700

Dana Corp./Warner Electric Div.; South Beloit; motor vehicles/equipment 700

Textron Inc./Greenlee Div.; Rockford; metalworking machinery 650

Rockford Clinic Ltd.; Rockford; medical doctors 620

Anchor Hocking Corp./Newell Window Furnishings Co.; Freeport; household furnishings 613

Sun Electric Corp.; Crystal Lake; measuring/controlling devices 600

FDL Foods Inc.; Rochelle; meat products 600

Arnold Engineering Co. Inc.; Marengo; metal products 600

Pioneer Life Insurance Co.; Rockford; life insurance 600

Branigar Organization Inc.; Galena; subdividers/developers 600

Specialty Equipment Co./Taylor Co.; Rockton; industry machinery 583

Rockford Powertrain Inc.; Rockford; motor vehicle parts 575

Memorial Hospital; Woodstock 542

17th District

West — Rock Island; Moline

For western Illinois' 17th, the recession of the early 1990s was mild compared with the economic devastation that occurred in the previous decade. Then, the industrial regions centered on the neighboring cities of Rock Island and Moline (at the 17th's western end) and Peoria (across its eastern border in the 18th District) hit the skids.

Layoffs and factory closures in the district's essential industry—farm equipment manufacturing—caused severe hardship. Job-seekers left the area. Although economic stability has slowly and shakily returned, the earlier near-depression conditions had a lasting political impact: The 17th, a former GOP bastion, now leans to the Democrats.

Democratic Rep. Lane Evans blazed the partisan trail by narrowly capturing this House seat in 1982. He has since dominated the 17th, winning two-thirds of the vote in 1990 before settling down to 60 percent in 1992 in a somewhat redrawn district.

The 17th remains more competitive in major-office contests; for example, Republican Jim Edgar took 53 percent for governor here in 1990. But in 1992, Bill Clinton carried the 17th, finishing first in 11 of the 14 counties that are all or part in the district. George Bush won just 29 percent in Fulton County, near Peoria.

Farm machinery is still king in the Quad Cities: Rock Island and Moline in Illinois, Davenport and Bettendorf in Iowa across the Mississippi River. Deere & Co., makers of John Deere tractors, has its headquarters in Moline as well as production and distribution facilities around the region. There is other farm-related industry, including meat packing; the federal arsenal at Rock Island is also a major employer.

Moline, with about 43,000 residents, is the district's largest city; Rock Island (Evans' base) is next with just over 40,000. Blacks and Hispanics make up more than 10 percent of Rock Island County, the largest minority-group concentration in the district. Clinton beat Bush by nearly 20 percentage points in the county.

Galesburg (Knox County)—the hometown of Illinois' late poet laureate, Carl Sandburg—is also broad-shouldered: Its largest employer is an Admiral refrigerator plant. At its southern end, the 17th takes in Quincy (Adams County), a river town that relies on agribusiness for jobs. Some coal is mined in McDonough and Fulton counties at the southeast end of the 17th.

The rest of the district is mainly rich farmland, with corn, hogs and soybeans abundant. Before the rise of Evans and the onset of economic difficulties, the large rural Republican vote usually offset the Democratic urban vote in the 17th.

At the district's north end, Carroll County and the part of Ogle County in the 17th were the only two to go against Evans in 1992. Bush also won these, though Clinton took most of the rural counties by pluralities.

Election Returns

	17th District	Democrat	Republican
1992	President*	124,173 (46.8%)	95,553 (36.0%)
	House	156,233 (60.1%)	103,719 (39.9%)
1990	Senate	125,080 (65.6%)	65,617 (34.4%)
	Governor	89,181 (47.0%)	100,677 (53.0%)
1988	President	126,887 (51.5%)	119,662 (48.5%)
1986	Senate	112,242 (61.8%)	69,526 (38.2%)
	Governor†	14,769 (8.1%)	93,180 (51.2%)

*Vote for Perot was 45,566 (17.2%).   †Independent/other is greater than 5%.

Demographics

Population 571,530

Percent change from 1980 10.1%

Land area 8,328 square miles

Population per square mile 69

Counties, 1990 population

Adams (pt.) 52,052	Knox 56,393
Bureau 35,688	McDonough 35,244
Carroll 16,805	Mercer 17,290
Fulton 38,080	Ogle (pt.) 11,260
Hancock 21,373	Rock Island 148,723
Henderson 8,096	Warren 19,181
Henry 51,159	Whiteside 60,186

Cities, 1990 population (10,000 or more)

Canton 13,922	Moline 43,202
East Moline 20,147	Quincy 39,681
Galesburg 33,530	Rock Island 40,552
Kewanee 12,969	Sterling 15,132
Macomb 19,952	

Race and Hispanic origin

White 94.7%
Black 3.3%
American Indian, Eskimo, or Aleut. 0.2%
Asian or Pacific Islander 0.6%
Other 1.4%
Hispanic origin 3.0%

Ancestry

American 4.7%	Italian 2.7%
Belgian 3.3%	Norwegian 1.2%
Dutch 5.0%	Polish 2.0%
English 15.8%	Scotch Irish 2.6%
French 3.6%	Scottish 2.0%
German 39.9%	Swedish 8.8%
Irish 18.6%	

Universities/colleges, 1990-1991 enrollment

Augustana College, Rock Island 2,253
Black Hawk College East, Kewanee 768
Black Hawk College Quad-City, Moline 5,811
Carl Sandburg College, Galesburg 2,639
John Wood Community College, Quincy 2,743
Knox College, Galesburg 945
Monmouth College, Monmouth 656
Morrison Institute of Technology, Morrison 211
Quincy College, Quincy 1,270

Spoon River College, Canton 1,970
Western Illinois University, Macomb 13,754

Newspapers, total circulation (in all districts)
Burlington Hawk-Eye 17,394
Chicago Tribune 721,559
Clinton Herald 17,710
Daily Gazette Sauk Valley 14,711
Dixon Telegraph 9,796
Freeport Journal-Standard 16,955
Galesburg Register-Mail 17,881
Kewanee Star Courier 7,076
Moline Dispatch 28,403
Peoria Journal Star 86,859
Quad-City Times 54,414
Quincy Herald Whig 24,797
Rockford Register Star 75,020
Rock Island Argus 13,813

Commercial television stations, affiliations
ADI: Davenport-Rock Island-Moline (66%), Quincy-Hannibal (21%), Peoria (10%) and Rockford (3%)
KLJB-TV, Davenport (Fox)
WQAD-TV, Moline (ABC)
WTJR, Quincy (None)
WGEM-TV, Quincy (NBC)
KHQA-TV, Hannibal (CBS)

Cable television systems, total subscribers
Continental Cablevision of Illinois; Quincy 14,266
Cox Cable Quad Cities; Moline 56,208
Heritage Cablevision; Clinton 18,850
TCI of Illinois; Macomb 5,219
TCI of Illinois; Rock Island 12,571
TCI of Illinois; Sterling 9,864

Military installations, 1991
Rock Island Arsenal (Army), Rock Island 7,897
Savannah Army Depot Activity, Savannah 606

Businesses and other major employers
Northwestern Steel & Wire Co.; Sterling; steel products 2,725
Deere & Co.; East Moline; farm/garden machinery 2,600
Maytag Corp./Admiral Div.; Galesburg; refrigeration 2,500
Deere & Co.; Moline; freight shipping 1,918
Western Illinois University; Macomb 1,700
Case Corp.; East Moline; farm/garden machinery 1,600
Case Corp.; Moline; farm/garden machinery 1,600
United Medical Center Inc.; Moline 1,350
IBP Inc.; Hillsdale; meat products 1,300
Franciscan Medical Center; Rock Island 1,165
Blessing Hospital; Quincy 1,027
Burlington Northern Railroad Co.; Galesburg; railroads 1,000
Munson Transportation Inc.; Monmouth; trucking services 950
Eagle Food Centers Inc.; Milan; grocery stores 850
Deere & Co.; Moline; farm/garden machinery 840
General Electric Co.; Morrison; electrical industrial apparatus 800
City of Quincy; Quincy 800
Commonwealth Edison Co./Quad Cities Station; Cordova; electric services 710
Harper Wyman Co.; Princeton; metal products 700
Quebecor Printing Mt. Morris; Mt. Morris; commercial printing 700

Black Hawk College Quad City; Moline 700
CGH Medical Center; Sterling 690
Titan Wheel Intl./Can-Am Industries; Quincy; motor vehicle parts 650
National Mfg. Co.; Sterling; hardware 650
Plumbers Pipefitters Union; Rock Island; labor organization 640
Deere & Co.; East Moline; iron/steel foundries 626
Butler Mfg. Co.; Galesburg; metal products 600
Galesburg Board of Education; Galesburg 600
Coltec Industries Inc./Quincy Compressor Div.; Quincy; industry machinery 580
NTN-Bower Corp.; Macomb; industry machinery 577
Methode Electronics Inc.; Carthage; electronic components 575
Illini Hospital; Silvis 574
St. Mary Hospital Inc.; Quincy 570
Purina Mills Inc.; Monmouth; meat products 550
Montgomery Elevator Co.; Moline; elevators 550
McDonough County Hospital District; Macomb 550
Augustana College; Rock Island 550
St. Mary's Medical Center; Galesburg 530
Galesburg Cottage Hospital; Galesburg 525

18th District
Central — Peoria; Part of Springfield

With its modest-sized industrial cities, small towns and farms, the 18th is in some ways a model of middle-class, middle American conservatism.

In various permutations through a series of redistrictings, this central Illinois district from 1956 to 1992 elected Republican Robert Michel, who became the House minority leader in 1981. In 1993, Michel announced he would retire at the end of the 103rd Congress.

Yet the 18th also has some concerns that make it less than a Republican bastion—including a Peoria-based industrial sector that has lost thousands of jobs in recent years and an economically worried working-class constituency.

Bill Clinton won by pluralities over George Bush in 1992 in Peoria and Tazewell, the 18th's most populous counties; he won four other counties in the Illinois River Valley and even won in the heavily Republican northern part of Sangamon County (Springfield) that is in the 18th. Bush finished first in just six mainly rural counties. Michel won comfortably, but even he was held to 55 percent in Peoria County and lost two other counties.

At some points during their House careers, several veteran House members have been forced by redistricting to move their residences in order to keep up with their constituencies. Michel is an opposite case; he has stayed in one place—his hometown of Peoria—while his district has been peripatetic.

In the 1960s, Peoria (Peoria County) anchored the southern end of the district held by Michel; in the 1970s, the city was at the district's center. In the 1980s, Peoria was near the northeast corner of a district that ran west to the Mississippi River; in the 1990s, it is in the northwest portion of a mainly north-south district.

The 18th's economic health is largely dependent on Caterpillar Inc. The manufacturer of earth-moving equipment and other heavy machinery is based in Peoria and employs nearly 18,000 people at its headquarters and plants, the largest of which is in

East Peoria (Tazewell County, which also includes the cities of Pekin and Morton).

Caterpillar's slump in the early 1980s contributed to a migration from the region: Peoria, still Illinois' third-largest city with about 113,000 residents, lost about a tenth of its population during the 1980s. The company has rebounded somewhat in recent years, though a labor dispute closed Caterpillar's factories for six months beginning in November 1991 and caused regional hardship.

Any Democratic leanings in the industrial area are usually canceled out by the solid GOP rural vote: Michel in 1992 took 65 percent or better in three counties in the eastern part of the 18th. In the district's southern end, the 18th covers much of Sangamon County, reaching past soybean and corn farms to take in the northern, mainly white-collar portion of Springfield, the state capital.

Election Returns

	18th District	Democrat	Republican
1992	President*	116,864 (42.1%)	113,656 (41.0%)
	House	114,413 (42.2%)	156,533 (57.8%)
1990	Senate	120,578 (61.5%)	75,542 (38.5%)
	Governor	82,520 (42.1%)	113,624 (57.9%)
1988	President	107,976 (43.4%)	140,873 (56.6%)
1986	Senate	91,091 (51.4%)	86,072 (48.6%)
	Governor †	8,073 (4.6%)	96,907 (55.1%)

*Vote for Perot was 46,990 (16.9%).   †Independent/other is greater than 5%.

Demographics

Population 571,580

Percent change from 1980 10.1%

Land area 6,173 square miles

Population per square mile 93

Counties, 1990 population

Cass 13,437	Morgan 36,397
Logan 30,798	Peoria 182,827
Macon (pt.) 8,949	Putnam 5,730
Marshall 12,846	Sangamon (pt.) 80,581
Mason 16,269	Stark 6,534
McLean (pt.) 9,703	Tazewell 123,692
Menard 11,164	Woodford 32,653

Cities, 1990 population (10,000 or more)

East Peoria 21,378	Pekin 32,254
Jacksonville 19,324	Peoria 113,504
Lincoln 15,418	Springfield (pt.) 35,294
Morton 13,799	Washington 10,099

Race and Hispanic origin

White 93.7%
Black 5.1%
American Indian, Eskimo, or Aleut. 0.2%
Asian or Pacific Islander 0.7%
Other 0.3%
Hispanic origin 0.9%

Ancestry

American 4.5%	Italian 3.6%
Dutch 3.4%	Polish 1.9%
English 17.8%	Scotch Irish 2.5%
French 4.3%	Scottish 2.3%
German 44.6%	Swedish 2.8%
Irish 19.3%	

Universities/colleges, 1990-1991 enrollment

Bradley University, Peoria 6,068
Eureka College, Eureka 441
Illinois Central College, East Peoria 12,724
Illinois College, Jacksonville 888
Lincoln Christian College, Lincoln 616
Lincoln College, Lincoln 1,489
MacMurray College, Jacksonville 1,117
Midstate College, Peoria 417

Newspapers, total circulation (in all districts)

Bloomington Pantagraph 50,507
Chicago Tribune 721,559
Decatur Herald & Review 42,406
Jacksonville Journal Courier 14,634
La Salle News Tribune 19,052
Lincoln Courier 6,624
Pekin Daily Times 15,354
Peoria Journal Star 86,859
Springfield State Journal-Register 68,004

Commercial television stations, affiliations

ADI: Peoria (56%) and Springfield-Decatur-Champaign (43%)
WYZZ-TV, Bloomington (Fox)
WEEK-TV, Peoria (NBC)
WHOI, Peoria (ABC)
WMBD-TV, Peoria (CBS)
WCFN, Springfield (CBS)
WICS, Springfield (NBC)
WRSP-TV, Springfield (None)

Cable television systems, total subscribers

Continental Cablevision of Illinois; Pekin 13,264
Dimension Cable Services; Springfield 49,100
Sammons Communications of Illinois Inc.; Jacksonville 8,237
Telecable; Bloomington/Normal 30,538
UA Cablesystems of Illinois; Peoria 55,300

Military installations, 1991

Greater Peoria Airport Air Force Guard Station, Bartonville 261

Businesses and other major employers

Caterpillar Inc.; Peoria; engines/turbines 5,700
Caterpillar Inc./Engine Div.; Mossville; construction machinery 4,200
St. Francis Medical Center; Peoria 3,500
Methodist Medical Center of Illinois; Peoria 2,400
Caterpillar Inc.; Peoria; construction machinery 2,000
Illinois Central College; East Peoria 1,775
Caterpillar Inc.; Morton; construction machinery 1,680
Keystone Consolidated Industries; Peoria; steel products 1,500
Excel Corp.; Beardstown; grocery products 1,500
Mobil Oil Corp.; Jacksonville; chemical products 1,200
Central Illinois; Peoria; medical service/health insurance 1,200

Proctor Community Hospital; Peoria 1,150

Bradley University; Peoria 1,094

State of Illinois/Air National Guard; Peoria 1,006

Foster & Gallagher Inc.; Peoria; catalog retailers 1,000

Caterpillar Inc.; Mapleton; iron/steel foundries 950

Komatsu Dresser Co./Haulpak Div.; Peoria; construction/related machinery 900

Capitol-EMI Music Inc.; Jacksonville; audio/video equipment 850

State of Illinois/Land Pollution Control; Springfield 805

State of Illinois; Heyworth 800

Greater Peoria Riverboat Corp./Par-A-Dice Riverboat Casino; Peoria; riverboat casino 800

LTV Steel Co. Inc.; Hennepin; steel products 750

State of Illinois/Lincoln Developmental Center; Lincoln 739

Passavant Memorial Area Hospital; Jacksonville 681

U.S. Postal Service; Peoria 650

Eaton Corp./Eaton Cutler Hammer; Lincoln; electric distribution equipment 600

Hertzberg-New Method Inc./Perma-Bound Div.; Jacksonville; nondurable goods 600

State of Illinois/Jacksonville Developmental Center; Jacksonville 600

Bosch Robut Corp.; Elkhart; motor vehicle parts/supplies 550

Pekin Memorial Hospital; Pekin 550

ABF Freight System Inc.; Springfield; trucking facilities 512

19th District

Rural — Southern Counties; Decatur

The northern part of the 19th is a familiar landscape of downstate Illinois. At the edge of the district is its only large city, Decatur, where heavy industry and grain processing plants employ a large blue-collar work force. For miles south, flat land produces corn and soybeans.

The southern part of the district, though, is different. The hilly territory produces coal and timber. Portions of this "border state" area are Appalachian-like. Of the 11 southernmost counties in the 19th, six have poverty rates above 20 percent.

This region was settled from the south and has a strong southern Democratic tradition that tends to predominate in the 19th. The Democratic House nominee carried every district county in the 1992 election; he won four counties in the southern part of the district with better than 80 percent of the vote.

Bill Clinton also carried the 11 southern counties in 1992. Although there is a Republican base in the heavily farmed northern part (which enabled George Bush to narrowly carry the 19th in 1988), Clinton won most counties there by pluralities.

Bush won just four of the district's 27 counties, three of them in a band across the 19th's midsection. One of these counties, Edwards, was one of two won by Republican Lynn Martin in her ill-fated 1990 challenge to Democratic Sen. Paul Simon. Although there are few blacks in the 19th, Democrat Carol Moseley-Braun carried 18 counties in her 1992 Senate bid.

Four of Illinois' 10 leading coal-producing counties are in the southern part of the 19th. Steady demand for coal has been offset in recent years by job losses caused by mechanization; unemployment is an endemic problem in much of the region.

Pope, Illinois' least populous county, is almost entirely within the Shawnee National Forest. At the southern tip of the 19th are

Massac and Pulaski counties, whose river towns near the confluence of the Ohio and Mississippi have seen better days. Williamson County (Marion), at the western edge, benefits from its proximity to Southern Illinois University (in the 12th).

At the top of the district is Decatur (Macon County); with about 80,500 residents, the city is more populous than any of the 19th's other counties. Corn and soybean processors Archer Daniels Midland and A. E. Staley are economic mainstays, although a Caterpillar plant is the city's largest single employer. Industrial downsizing has taken a toll on Decatur. The city usually reinforces the southern Democratic vote.

In between is mainly farming country, dotted with such small cities as Mattoon and Effingham. Charleston is the site of Eastern Illinois University (11,100 students).

Election Returns

	19th District	Democrat	Republican
1992	President*	131,483 (47.3%)	95,672 (34.4%)
	House	187,156 (69.1%)	83,526 (30.9%)
1990	Senate	140,861 (66.5%)	71,000 (33.5%)
	Governor	112,793 (53.2%)	99,223 (46.8%)
1988	President	118,972 (47.6%)	130,868 (52.4%)
1986	Senate	136,292 (66.8%)	67,636 (33.2%)
	Governor†	16,459 (8.0%)	107,069 (51.8%)

*Vote for Perot was 50,665 (18.2%).   †Independent/other is greater than 5%.

Demographics

Population 571,530

Percent change from 1980 10.3%

Land area 10,733 square miles

Population per square mile 53

Counties, 1990 population

Christian (pt.) 13,319	Lawrence 15,972
Clark 15,921	Macon (pt.) 108,257
Clay 14,460	Massac 14,752
Coles 51,644	Moultrie 13,930
Crawford 19,464	Pope 4,373
Cumberland 10,670	Pulaski 7,523
Edwards 7,440	Richland 16,545
Effingham 31,704	Saline 26,551
Franklin 40,319	Shelby 22,261
Gallatin 6,909	Wabash 13,111
Hamilton 8,499	Wayne 17,241
Hardin 5,189	White 16,522
Jasper 10,609	Williamson (pt.) 46,998
Johnson 11,347	

Cities, 1990 population (10,000 or more)

Charleston 20,398	Herrin (pt.) 10,857
Decatur (pt.) 80,458	Marion 14,545
Effingham 11,851	Mattoon 18,441

Race and Hispanic origin

White 95.5%

Black 3.9%

American Indian, Eskimo, or Aleut. 0.2%

Asian or Pacific Islander 0.3%

Other 0.1%
Hispanic origin 0.5%

Ancestry

American 8.6%		Italian 2.1%
Dutch 3.8%		Polish 1.5%
English 17.8%		Scotch Irish 2.8%
French 3.9%		Scottish 1.9%
German 36.0%		Swedish 1.1%
Irish 20.2%		

Universities/colleges, 1990-1991 enrollment

Eastern Illinois University, Charleston 11,116
Illinois Eastern Community College, Olney 8,556
Lake Land College, Mattoon 4,437
Millikin University, Decatur 1,859
Richland Community College, Decatur 3,801
Shawnee Community College, Ullin 1,575
Southeastern Illinois College, Harrisburg 3,032

Newspapers, total circulation (in all districts)

Carbondale Southern Illinoisan 29,212
Charleston Times-Courier 7,187
Chicago Tribune 721,559
Decatur Herald & Review 42,406
Effingham Daily News 12,667
Evansville Courier/Press 95,655
Mattoon Journal Gazette 11,729
Paducah Sun 29,509
Springfield State Journal-Register 68,004
Taylorville Breeze-Courier 6,584
Terre Haute Tribune Star 35,169
Vincennes Sun-Commercial 13,507

Commercial television stations, affiliations

ADI: Paducah-Cape Girardeau-Harrisburg-Marion (30%),
Terre Haute (28%), Springfield-Decatur-Champaign
(27%) and Evansville (15%)
WAND, Decatur (ABC)
WFHL, Decatur (None)
WSIL-TV, Harrisburg (ABC)
WTCT, Marion (None)
WEVV, Evansville (Fox)

Cable television systems, total subscribers

TCI of Illinois; Charleston 6,017
TCI of Illinois; Decatur 33,500
TCI of Illinois; Herrin 6,858

Businesses and other major employers

Caterpillar Inc.; Decatur; construction machinery 3,300
Bridgestone/Firestone Inc.; Decatur; tires 2,000
Decatur Memorial Hospital; Decatur 1,696
Decatur Public Schools; Decatur 1,690
United Parcel Service Inc.; Decatur; mail
services/management 1,600
A. E. Staley Mfg. Co.; Decatur; grain mill products 1,580
Eastern Illinois University; Charleston 1,500
World Color Press Inc.; Effingham; commercial printing
1,400
St. Mary's Hospital; Decatur 1,300
R. R. Donnelley & Sons Co.; Mattoon; commercial printing
1,175
Illinois Power Co.; Decatur; electric services 1,078
Lake Land College; Mattoon 1,000

Maytag Corp./Magic Chef Div.; Herrin; household appli-
ances 962
Roadmaster Corp.; Olney; toys/sporting goods 900
Trailmobile Inc.; Charleston; truck trailers/motor vehicle
parts 900
Imperial Bondware Corp.; Shelbyville; paperboard mills 900
Amax Inc.; Keensburg; coal mining 881
Wagner Castings Co.; Decatur; iron/steel foundries 850
Sarah Bush Lincoln Health Center; Mattoon 825
United Industrial Syndicate Inc./Airtex Products Co. Div.;
Fairfield; motor vehicle parts 750
General Electric Co.; Mattoon; electric lighting 750
Snap-On Tools Corp.; Mount Carmel; handtools 714
Norfolk & Western Railway Co.; Decatur; railroads 700
Mueller Co.; Decatur; measuring/controlling devices 700
Champion Labs. Inc.; West Salem; motor vehicle parts 676
Peabody Coal Co.; Shawneetown; coal mining 655
Marathon Oil Co.; Robinson; petroleum refining 640
Champion Labs. Inc.; Albion; motor vehicle parts 600
United Technologies Automotive; Newton; automotive hard-
ware 600
White Consolidated Industries; Arthur; millwork 600
Carmi Community United School District; Carmi 600
PPG Industries Inc.; Mount Zion; flat glass 590
St. Anthony Memorial Hospital; Effingham 575
Consolidation Coal Co./Mt. Vernon Coal Co.; Sesser; coal
mining 550

20th District

West Central — Part of Springfield; Collinsville

The 20th takes in a border-state portion of Illinois; its western
edge lies along the Mississippi River, across from Missouri. Its
southern Democratic traditions are maintained by blue-collar
voters near the Mississippi, many of the state employees in
Springfield and coal industry workers in the southern part of the
20th.

This is a Democratic district, but the prevailing political tone
is moderate-to-conservative, which means the 20th is not completely out of reach for the GOP; George Bush narrowly won
here in 1988. The district has a portion of Springfield (the rest is
in the 18th District), but otherwise there are no large cities, and
there are few minority-group residents. Typically the farm-
country constituency is Republican.

Still, in 1992, the 20th returned to Democratic form. Bill
Clinton defeated Bush by a wide margin in 16 of the 19 counties,
winning majorities in four. Democratic Senate winner Carol
Moseley-Braun also ran well; Rep. Richard Durbin, who became
a politically dominant figure in the region during the 1980s, won
by more than 35,000 votes, overcoming a tough challenger and a
new, sharply changed district map.

Population is diffuse in the 20th. The section of Madison
County in the district has about 20 percent of the total; the part
of Sangamon County (Springfield) in the 20th is close behind.
But the remaining residents are spread across 15 counties and
parts of two others.

About half of Madison County's residents are in the 20th.
Although most of the county's industry is located in the 12th
District, the factories provide jobs for many residents in such
20th District communities as Edwardsville, Collinsville and Glen
Carbon. Edwardsville is the site of a Southern Illinois University

campus (11,700 students). Agriculture-based Collinsville calls itself the "horseradish capital" of the United States.

The southern part of Springfield, the state capital, is the 20th's largest single urban area; about two-thirds of the city's 105,000 residents are in the 20th. Nearly a fifth of these constituents are black, by far the largest minority concentration in the district.

The state government payroll provides economic stability, as do the city's academic institutions, Sangamon State University and Southern Illinois University's medical school. The county also has some industry.

The economy is not nearly as generous in some of the district's less populous areas, which have had bouts of double-digit unemployment in recent years. The jobless rate in sparsely populated Calhoun County, on the Mississippi, is among the highest in Illinois.

Farming is widespread through the district's more rural counties. Adams and Pike counties, in the northwest corner, are major livestock producers; nearby Scott County, also rural, stayed with Bush in 1992. Near the southern end is Illinois' wheat belt.

In Clinton and Washington counties, farms give way to coal mines. A rural Republican vote prevails in Washington. But neighboring Jefferson, a leading coal-producing county, is a Democratic stronghold.

Election Returns

	20th District	Democrat	Republican
1992	President*	130,383 (46.4%)	94,532 (33.7%)
	House	154,869 (56.5%)	119,219 (43.5%)
1990	Senate	137,640 (64.5%)	75,826 (35.5%)
	Governor	114,333 (53.5%)	99,313 (46.5%)
1988	President	122,901 (49.0%)	128,089 (51.0%)
1986	Senate	128,599 (65.5%)	67,617 (34.5%)
	Governor	14,122 (7.1%)	111,613 (56.1%)

*Vote for Perot was 55,824 (19.9%). †Independent/other is greater than 5%.

Demographics

Population 571,480

Percent change from 1980 10.1%

Land area 9,449 square miles

Population per square mile 60

Counties, 1990 population

Adams (pt.) 14,038	Macoupin 47,679
Bond 14,991	Madison (pt.) 119,024
Brown 5,836	Marion 41,561
Calhoun 5,322	Montgomery 30,728
Christian (pt.) 21,099	Pike 17,577
Clinton 33,944	Sangamon (pt.) 97,805
Fayette 20,893	Schuyler 7,498
Greene 15,317	Scott 5,644
Jefferson 37,020	Washington 14,965
Jersey 20,539	

Cities, 1990 population (10,000 or more)

Centralia 14,274	Mount Vernon 16,988
Collinsville (pt.) 20,086	Springfield (pt.) 69,933
Edwardsville 14,579	Taylorville (pt.) 10,985

Race and Hispanic origin

White 95.0%
Black 4.2%
American Indian, Eskimo, or Aleut. 0.2%
Asian or Pacific Islander 0.4%
Other 0.2%
Hispanic origin 0.7%

Ancestry

American 5.5%	Italian 4.1%
Dutch 3.2%	Polish 2.3%
English 15.9%	Scotch Irish 2.4%
French 4.5%	Scottish 1.9%
German 44.8%	Swedish 1.0%
Irish 19.8%	

Universities/colleges, 1990-1991 enrollment

Blackburn College, Carlinville 438
Greenville College, Greenville 837
Kaskaskia College, Centralia 3,269
Lewis & Clark Community College, Godfrey 5,886
Lincoln Land Community College, Springfield 7,717
Principia College, Elsah 634
Rend Lake College, Ina 3,766
Sangamon State University, Springfield 4,347
Southern Illinois University, Edwardsville 11,686
Springfield College in Illinois, Springfield 332

Newspapers, total circulation (in all districts)

Alton Telegraph 33,926
Belleville News Democrat 50,303
Centralia Sentinel 14,839
Chicago Tribune 721,559
Edwardsville Intelligencer 6,580
Jacksonville Journal Courier 14,634
Mt. Vernon Register News 10,966
Quincy Herald Whig 24,797
Springfield State Journal-Register 68,004
St. Louis Post-Dispatch 369,005
Taylorville Breeze-Courier 6,584

Commercial television stations, affiliations

ADI: St. Louis (63%), Quincy-Hannibal (24%) and Springfield-Decatur-Champaign (13%)
WCEE, Mount Vernon (None)

Cable television systems, total subscribers

Cable Equities of Co. Ltd.; Mount Vernon 6,320
Cablevision; Centralia 5,354
Cencom Cable TV; Maryville 31,346
Continental Cablevision of Illinois; Quincy 14,266
Dimension Cable Services; Springfield 49,100
TCI of Illinois; Alton 18,134

Military installations, 1991

Capital Municipal Airport Air Force Guard Station, Springfield 330

Businesses and other major employers

State of Illinois/Mental Health Dept.; Springfield 13,500
State of Illinois/Public Aid Dept.; Springfield 10,000
St. Johns Hospital; Springfield 3,300
State of Illinois/Child & Family Services Dept.; Springfield 3,000
Memorial Medical Center; Springfield 2,400
State of Illinois/Revenue Dept.; Springfield 2,000

General Tire Inc.; Mount Vernon; tires   1,800
Southern Illinois University; Edwardsville   1,800
Franklin Life Insurance Co.; Springfield; life insurance   1,500
Horace Mann Educators Corp.; Springfield;
   fire/marine/casualty insurance   1,415
Illinois Central Railroad Co.; Centralia; railroads   1,200
County of Madison/Detention Home; Edwardsville   1,091
World Color Press Inc./Salem Gravure; Salem; periodicals
   1,066
Illinois Bell Telephone Co./Ameritech Corp.; Springfield;
   telephone communications   1,000
Southern Illinois University/School of Medicine; Springfield
   1,000
Rockwell Intl. Corp./Plastics Products Div.; Centralia; motor
   vehicles/equipment   900
City of Springfield/Public Aid Dept.; Springfield; legal ser-
   vices   900
St. Mary's Hospital; Centralia   774
U.S. Postal Service; Springfield   740
City of Springfield/Water Light & Power; Springfield; electric
   services   726
State of Illinois/Transportation Dept.; Collinsville   700

State of Illinois/Public Health Dept.; Springfield   700
State of Illinois/Agriculture Dept.; Springfield   700
State of Illinois/Board of Education; Springfield   700
Basler Electric Co.; Highland; electric distribution equipment
   690
Exxon Corp./Monterey Coal Co.; Albers; coal mining   660
State of Illinois/Energy-Natural Resources Dept.; Springfield
   650
State of Illinois/Murray Warren G. Developmental Center;
   Centralia; residential care   637
Rend Lake College; Ina   600
Good Samaritan Hospital; Mount Vernon   595
United Stationers Inc.; Greenville; paper products   590
Nascote Industries Inc.; Nashville; motor vehicles/equipment
   553
Automotive Brake Co. Inc.; Litchfield; motor vehicle parts
   550
Collinsville Community School District; Collinsville   550
State of Illinois/Community Affairs Dept.; Springfield   550
State of Illinois/Health Dept.; Springfield   550
Edwardsville Community School District; Edwardsville   515

Indiana

In Indiana, some things don't change: Each March, Hoosiers go crazy over their state high school basketball tournament; in May, their attention turns to the Indianapolis 500 auto race; and every fourth November, Indiana voters pull the lever for the Republican presidential ticket. In 1984, when many local economies still were struggling, President Ronald Reagan carried the state with 62 percent of the vote. Four years later, with second-term Indiana Sen. Dan Quayle as his running mate, George Bush nearly matched Reagan's tally. Bush and Quayle won the state again in 1992 with 43 percent. In the presidential elections since 1940, only Lyndon B. Johnson in 1964 carried Indiana for the Democrats.

But politics in Indiana in the early 1990s was not what it was in the early 1980s, when Quayle broke onto the national scene with an upset Senate victory. By 1993, the GOP hold on Indiana, while still strong at the top of the ticket, was shaken lower on the ballot. While Quayle had risen to prominence as George Bush's running mate, Indiana Democrats surged.

The young phenomenon of Indiana politics was not the vice president but Democratic Gov. Evan Bayh. In 1988, while the Bush-Quayle ticket swept Indiana, Bayh ended a 20-year GOP hold on the state's highest office. Two years later, Democrats narrowly gained control of the state House and threatened the Republicans' majority in the state Senate. And since the early 1980s, a new generation of Democrats grabbed House districts that otherwise voted solidly Republican in most presidential and U.S. Senate elections. By 1993, Democrats had seven out of the ten House seats. All of those Democrats represented areas that backed Bush-Quayle in 1988.

Economic conditions played a role in the political shakeup. Employment in Indiana's industrial, agricultural and resource sectors took a hit in the 1980s, particularly during the 1982-1983 recession, when Anderson, Gary and other cities endured unemployment rates unseen since the Great Depression. A number of factories closed down for good, while others significantly trimmed their payrolls. Thousands of family farmers left the land.

Yet by 1992, the economy was no longer the drag on Republican candidates that it was in the mid-1980s. Indiana modernized in several sectors. While major steel companies closed shop in many cities, they put money into new facilities in

northwest Indiana. In South Bend, Studebaker was dead and long gone, but the military's multipurpose "Humvee" vehicles were being built there. Increasing mechanization cut coal mining jobs in southwestern Indiana, but more tonnage was mined than in the early 1980s. Numerous Indiana communities that once relied on heavy manufacturing or farming had sizable payrolls in education, health care, insurance and even tourism.

Throughout the 1980s, Indiana's traditional Republicanism was shored up by the economic health of the state's hub and capital, Indianapolis. It enjoyed a boom in its white-collar, service and recreational sectors, and population exploded in the affluent Republican suburbs that rung the city. Indianapolis had stronger Republican tendencies than most major U.S. cities. Although Indiana had been part of the midwestern manufacturing belt since the 19th century, it was more white and less ethnic than most industrial states. Many blue-collar workers maintained the conservative attitudes of their origins in rural Indiana and in the South.

Under Indiana law, a commission—composed of an appointee of the governor and two leaders of each house of the Legislature—would be designated to draw a map for the 1990s if the Legislature failed to act on redistricting by its May 1991 adjournment.

Democrats, guaranteed a majority on the commission because they held the governorship and the state House, had little incentive to debate a new map. The Legislature adjourned without action on redistricting, and the commission was impaneled May 29. The next day, it approved a map designed by the Legislature's Democratic leadership.

The call of a special session of the Indiana Legislature in June to deal with the state budget gave Republicans a chance to reopen redistricting. However, most Republicans showed little interest. A couple of amendments that slightly shifted GOP territory among Republican-held districts were attached to the redistricting measure, which with the budget bill was passed by both houses of the Legislature June 13, 1991. Bayh signed it into law June 14.

As Indiana retained all of its ten seats after redistricting, Democratic mappers were somewhat limited in their ambitions. Their main mission was to protect two of the newer and more vulnerable Democrats in the northern part of the state and were only halfway successful.

INDIANA

Districts Established June 13, 1991

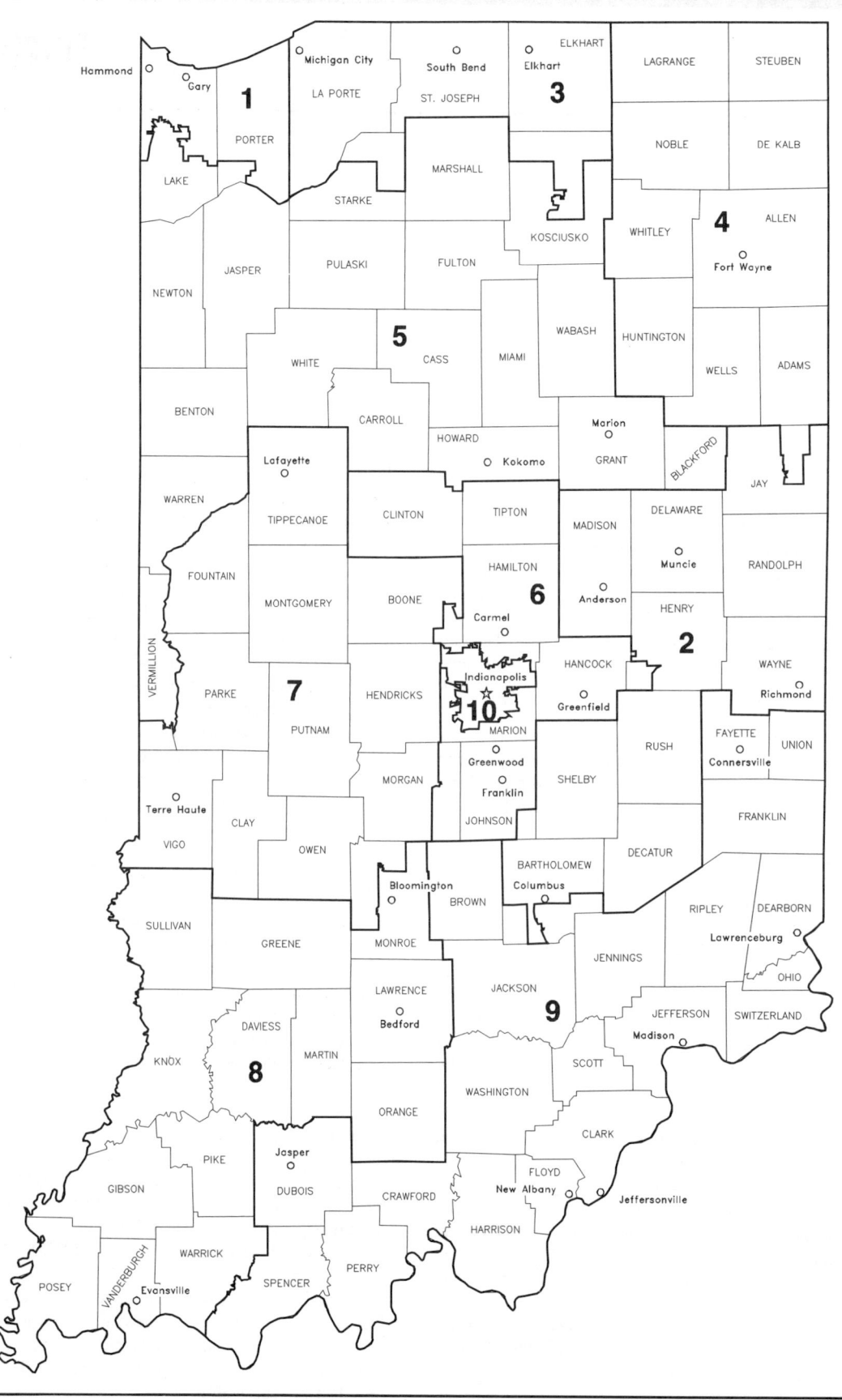

The benefactor in the plan was 1st District Democratic Rep. Peter J. Visclosky, whose Gary-based district had the most Democrats to spare. His 1st District surrendered blue-collar, Democratic-leaning Michigan City to the 3rd District, held uneasily by a freshman Democrat. The 1st also picked up GOP portions of the Lake and Porter County suburbs (taken from the 5th). This strategy worked as both Democrats won re-election in 1992.

But by giving up some unfavorable turf to the 1st, the Democratic-held 5th had to, in turn, absorbed some rural territory in Starke, Marshall and Kosciusko counties that had been in the 3rd. This turf was Republican-oriented and might have been the cause of the three-term Democratic incumbent's undoing as the GOP challenger won in 1992 by 2 percentage points.

Table 1   Population

District	Population	Population under 18	Voting-age population	Median age
1	554,416	154,219	400,197	33.0
2	554,416	138,016	416,400	33.9
3	554,416	146,648	407,768	32.7
4	554,416	158,192	396,224	32.0
5	554,415	150,572	403,843	33.8
6	554,416	146,359	408,057	33.6
7	554,416	135,893	418,523	31.9
8	554,416	132,651	421,765	33.0
9	554,416	149,603	404,813	33.6
10	554,416	143,811	410,605	30.9
State	5,544,159	1,455,964	4,088,195	32.8

Table 2   Voting-Age Persons

District	White*	Black*	American Indian, Eskimo, or Aleut*	Asian or Pacific Islander*	Other*	Hispanic*	Male*	Female*
1	76.6%	19.2%	0.2%	0.6%	3.4%	7.4%	46.9%	53.1%
2	95.5	3.8	0.2	0.4	0.2	0.5	47.2	52.8
3	91.8	6.5	0.3	0.7	0.7	1.6	48.1	51.9
4	93.9	4.7	0.2	0.6	0.6	1.3	47.8	52.2
5	97.0	2.0	0.4	0.3	0.4	1.1	47.7	52.3
6	97.9	1.0	0.2	0.8	0.2	0.7	47.2	52.8
7	96.2	2.0	0.2	1.3	0.3	0.8	48.9	51.1
8	96.1	2.8	0.2	0.8	0.1	0.6	47.1	52.9
9	97.9	1.6	0.2	0.2	0.1	0.4	47.9	52.1
10	71.3	27.2	0.2	0.9	0.4	1.0	46.1	53.9
State	91.5	7.1	0.2	0.7	0.6	1.5	47.5	52.5

*As percent of voting-age population.

Table 3   Voting-Age Persons by Age Groups

District	18-24*	25-44*	45-54*	55-64*	65 and over*
1	13.6%	42.6%	14.6%	12.7%	16.5%
2	15.6	39.0	14.7	12.4	18.2
3	15.0	42.4	13.3	11.7	17.6
4	13.7	44.4	13.7	11.4	16.7
5	12.8	41.1	15.0	12.8	18.3
6	11.6	46.8	15.2	11.4	15.1
7	19.2	40.0	13.4	11.0	16.4
8	17.8	39.3	13.0	11.5	18.3
9	12.8	42.7	14.8	12.2	17.5
10	15.4	46.2	11.9	10.9	15.5
State	14.8	42.4	14.0	11.8	17.0

*As percent of voting-age population.

Table 4   Income and Occupation

District	Median family income	Families in poverty	White collar*	Blue collar*	Service*	Farm*
1	$36,640	10.7%	53.6%	32.3%	13.5%	0.6%
2	31,533	9.3	47.4	35.3	14.5	2.8
3	34,458	6.5	51.6	34.5	12.3	1.6
4	35,821	5.5	50.1	35.3	12.1	2.4
5	32,210	7.6	42.5	39.8	13.5	4.2
6	44,668	3.1	66.2	22.4	9.8	1.5
7	33,877	6.9	52.9	30.4	14.2	2.6
8	31,375	9.2	51.7	31.3	14.3	2.7
9	31,425	8.3	43.9	39.5	13.2	3.3
10	29,818	12.6	57.1	26.5	15.6	0.7
State	34,082	7.9	51.9	32.6	13.3	2.2

*As percent of employed persons age 16 and over.

Table 5   Education: School Years Completed

District	Less than grade 9*	Grades 9-12 no diploma*	High school diploma*	College bachelor's degree or higher*
1	8.7%	16.3%	38.1%	14.2%
2	9.4	17.4	41.1	12.3
3	8.3	16.9	37.4	16.1
4	7.8	14.0	38.3	15.0
5	8.3	16.6	44.0	10.9
6	4.4	10.3	33.3	26.7
7	6.6	14.6	39.9	17.4
8	10.0	15.5	37.7	15.7
9	13.1	17.0	40.8	10.2
10	8.6	19.8	31.5	16.9
State	8.5	15.8	38.2	15.6

*As percent of persons age 25 and over.

Table 6   Housing and Residential Patterns

District	Owner occupied	Renter occupied	Urban	Rural
1	68.6%	31.4%	91.1%	8.9%
2	71.2	28.8	57.1	42.9
3	72.5	27.5	71.5	28.5
4	74.3	25.7	59.6	40.4
5	75.1	24.9	42.4	57.6
6	72.8	27.2	76.3	23.7
7	71.4	28.6	52.1	47.9
8	70.1	29.9	58.3	41.7
9	76.0	24.0	40.7	59.3
10	52.0	48.0	100.0	0.0
State	70.2	29.8	64.9	35.1

1st District

Northwest — Gary; Hammond

With its large blue-collar work force and 21 percent black population, the 1st is a Democratic bastion. Industrial decline and urban decay in Gary and other cities along Lake Michigan cost the 1st nearly 10 percent of its population in the 1980s; Gary itself lost 23 percent of its population, a steeper rate of decline than in any U.S. city during the 1980s. To compensate, 1991 redistricting added a substantial suburban swath in Lake and Porter counties.

Though Porter County, with its pockets of GOP voters, slightly dilutes the 1st's Democratic vote, it is still solidly Democratic. In 1992, Bill Clinton won a majority of the vote here, and the Democratic nominee took 69 percent in the House race.

Gary and urban Lake County are Democratic pillars. Minorities have a major impact: Once packed with factory workers of Slavic extraction, Gary is now more than 80 percent black. The Hispanic presence has increased in Hammond and East Chicago.

Gary, named for turn-of-the-century steel baron Elbert H. Gary, has become the heart of U.S. steelmaking. While factories were abandoned in other Rust Belt regions, companies such as USX, Inland Steel and Bethlehem Steel modernized plants here. The 1st produces more steel than any other district in the country.

But the steelmakers' revival came after recessions and the effects of foreign competition had whittled payrolls. And the streamlined, automated factories require fewer workers. Socio-economic problems are endemic.

Hammond, on the Illinois border and the 1st's other urban anchor, has a more varied economy, including a longstanding Lever Brothers bar soap plant. A marina has recently been built as part of an economic development effort. An Amoco oil refinery takes up most of the land area in neighboring Whiting.

As the 1st moves south of the Indiana Toll Road into such communities as Merrillville and Crown Point, the population becomes more white and the employment more white collar. Many residents of these suburbs are eastern European ethnics who have maintained their Democratic loyalties. In recent decades, rivalry between white ethnics and blacks has been a feature of the 1st's Democratic politics. But of late, tension between the two camps has diminished, thanks in part to the governing style of Gary's black Mayor Thomas V. Barnes, who is a more consensus-oriented politician than his predecessor.

Porter County's demographics and politics sharply contrast with Lake's. It is racially homogenous (less than 1 percent black) and growing. Chesterton, Valparaiso and other exurban communities are home to a number of former residents of Lake County and to Chicago commuters, who came here seeking cheaper housing. Although there is a Democratic vote in Portage and Burns Harbor, Porter is friendly to GOP candidates. In 1992, George Bush won Porter County with 40 percent of the vote, edging past Clinton, who got 37 percent.

Election Returns

	1st District	Democrat	Republican
1992	President*	117,126 (52.6%)	68,403 (30.7%)
	House	147,054 (69.4%)	64,770 (30.6%)
1990	Senate †	71,274 (58.5%)	50,504 (41.5%)
1988	President	119,755 (54.3%)	100,781 (45.7%)
	Senate	99,475 (48.1%)	107,534 (51.9%)
	Governor	141,388 (66.3%)	71,981 (33.7%)
1986	Senate	73,130 (55.5%)	58,602 (44.5%)

*Vote for Perot was 37,136 (16.7%). †Special election for the remaining two years of the term of Dan Quayle who was elected vice president in 1988. Appointee Daniel Coats held the seat 1988-1990 before winning the 1990 election.

Demographics

Population 554,416

Percent change from 1980 1.3%

Land area 650 square miles

Population per square mile 853

Counties, 1990 population

Lake (pt.) 430,393	Porter (pt.) 124,023

Cities, 1990 population (10,000 or more)

Dyer 10,923	Lake Station 13,899
East Chicago 33,892	Merrillville 27,257
Gary 116,646	Munster 19,949
Griffith 17,916	Portage 29,060
Hammond 84,236	Schererville 19,926
Highland 23,696	Valparaiso 24,414
Hobart 21,822	

Race and Hispanic origin

White 74.2%
Black 21.1%
American Indian, Eskimo, or Aleut 0.2%
Asian or Pacific Islander 0.6%
Other 3.9%
Hispanic origin 8.5%

Ancestry

American 2.8%		Italian 4.0%
Dutch 3.1%		Polish 10.6%
English 9.3%		Scotch Irish 1.6%
French 2.7%		Scottish 1.3%
German 24.3%		Slovakian 4.3%
Greek 1.2%		Swedish 2.5%
Hungarian 2.1%		Yugoslavian 1.4%
Irish 14.8%		

Universities/colleges, 1990-1991 enrollment

Calumet College of St. Joseph, Whiting 976
Commonwealth Business College, Merrillville 287
Davenport College, Merrillville 476
Indiana University Northwest, Gary 5,074
Indiana Vocational Tech College-Northwest, Gary 2,818
Purdue University-Calumet, Hammond 8,506
Valparaiso University, Valparaiso 3,864

Newspapers, total circulation (in all districts)

Chicago Sun-Times 529,632
Chicago Tribune 721,559
Gary Post-Tribune 72,842
Munster Times 64,780
Vidette Messenger 15,523

Commercial television stations, affiliations

ADI: Chicago (100%)

Cable television systems, total subscribers

Metrovision of Indiana; Portage 8,254
Multimedia Cablevision, Inc.; Valparaiso 15,794
TCI of Indiana; Gary 13,000
US Cable of North Indiana; Griffith 50,369
United Cable of North Indiana; Hammond 21,355

Businesses and other major employers

Inland Steel Co.; East Chicago; steel mill 13,500
USX Corp./Gary Works Div.; Gary; steel foundries 7,500
Bethlehem Steel Corp./Burns Harbor Plant; Chesterton; steel mill 5,846
LTV Steel Co. Inc./Indiana Harbor Works; East Chicago; steel products 4,600

St. Margaret's Hospital; Hammond 1,800

National Steel Corp./Midwest Steel Div.; Portage; galvanized steel products 1,700

City of Gary; Gary 1,667

Amoco Oil Co.; Whiting; petroleum refining 1,600

Quality Labor Service Inc./Payroll Data; Crown Point; personnel supply services 1,512

Methodist Southlake Hospital; Gary 1,380

Porter Memorial Hospital; Valparaiso 1,270

Munster Community Hospital; Hammond 1,200

Methodist Hospitals Inc.; Gary 1,100

Union Tank Car Co.; East Chicago; railroad tank cars 1,000

Northern Indiana Public Service Co.; Gary; engineering services 1,000

Our Lady of Mercy Hospital; Dyer 900

White Lodging Services Corp.; Gary; hotels 800

St. Mary Medical Center Inc.; Gary 800

Elgin Joliet & Eastern Railway Co.; Gary; railroads 750

Indiana University Northwest; Gary 738

McGill Mfg. Co. Inc.; Valparaiso; industry machinery 735

Lakeshore Health System Inc.; East Chicago 721

Valparaiso University; Valparaiso 720

Koppers Co. Inc.; Chesterton; building construction 700

Conopco Inc./Lever Brothers Div.; Hammond; soaps/cleaners 650

City of Hammond/Water Dept.; Hammond 640

Metrovision of Indiana; Portage; cable TV services 600

American Maize-Products Co.; Hammond; grain mill products 600

Labor Resources Inc.; Hammond; personnel supply services 600

State of Indiana/Public Welfare Dept.; Gary 586

Purdue University-Calumet; Hammond 540

Whiteco Industries Inc./Radisson Hotel at Star Plaza; Gary; hotel 530

2nd District

East Central — Muncie; Anderson; Columbus

Although manufacturing is a major factor in the medium-size cities across east-central Indiana, the 2nd's Democratic vote is outweighed by a GOP tradition in presidential elections. George Bush won easily here in 1988, and in 1992 he outdistanced Bill Clinton by almost 20,000 votes districtwide.

Yet a series of industrial recessions and the financial uncertainties of family farmers have made the district's mainly conservative electorate more receptive to Democrats at other levels. Democratic Gov. Evan Bayh swept the district in his 1992 re-election victory. The incumbent House Democrat, first elected in 1974, won comfortably in 1992.

Unemployment throughout the 2nd is well below the near-depression levels of the early 1980s, when local auto-related industries laid off thousands. However, the long-term downscaling of the blue-collar work force has taken its toll: 1990 population in Delaware County (Muncie) was down more than 7 percent from 1980, and Madison County (Anderson) was down nearly that much. Rural areas such as Randolph and Henry counties also saw their economies and populations slip.

In the 1920s, Muncie was the model for *Middletown,* a study of small-town American life. Today, with about 71,000 residents, it is the largest city in the 2nd. Muncie's biggest private employer

is Borg-Warner Automotive, which makes transmissions. The city's economy also benefits from Ball State University, which has 20,300 students and employs more than 6,100 people, and from the Ball Corp. It was founded and has its headquarters in Muncie, although most of its glass canning jars are made elsewhere.

Anderson's economy is heavily reliant on auto components manufacturing; the city is still trying to recover from layoffs and downsizing in that sector during the 1980s. Its largest employers are affiliates of General Motors: The Delco Remy division makes car ignition systems and electrical components; Inland Fisher Guide makes lighting equipment and bumpers. Officials in both Anderson and Muncie are working to use their locations on the White River for economic development and recreational purposes.

Although Columbus (Bartholomew County) has a strong industrial base—it is home to the Cummins Engine Co. and Arvin Industries—many of the voters are conservative: Bush took Bartholomew with 48 percent of the vote in 1992. Columbus boasts an array of modern buildings designed by leading architects; a local foundation helped fund the designs. Richmond (Wayne County), which Quakers founded in the 19th century, has an opera company.

The land outside the cities is rural and heavily farmed. Soybeans, oats and wheat are major crops in the northern part of the 2nd.

Election Returns

		Democrat	Republican
	2nd District		
1992	President*	81,915 (35.1%)	101,341 (43.4%)
	House	130,881 (57.1%)	90,593 (39.5%)
1990	Senate †	74,530 (44.5%)	93,117 (55.5%)
1988	President	88,329 (39.4%)	135,738 (60.6%)
	Senate	67,181 (30.4%)	153,577 (69.6%)
	Governor	119,002 (53.0%)	105,410 (47.0%)
1986	Senate	66,524 (37.9%)	108,860 (62.1%)

*Vote for Perot was 50,424 (21.6%). †Special election for the remaining two years of the term of Dan Quayle who was elected vice president in 1988. Appointee Daniel Coats held the seat 1988-1990 before winning the 1990 election.

Demographics

Population 554,416

Percent change from 1980 0.2%

Land area 3,888 square miles

Population per square mile 143

Counties, 1990 population

Bartholomew (pt.) 55,490	Madison 130,669
Decatur 23,645	Randolph 27,148
Delaware 119,659	Rush 18,129
Henry (pt.) 44,126	Shelby 40,307
Jay (pt.) 18,177	Wayne 71,951
Johnson (pt.) 5,115	

Cities, 1990 population (10,000 or more)

Anderson 59,459	New Castle 17,753
Columbus (pt.) 31,635	Richmond 38,705
Muncie 71,035	Shelbyville 15,336

Race and Hispanic origin

White 95.0%
Black 4.1%
American Indian, Eskimo, or Aleut. 0.2%
Asian or Pacific Islander 0.4%
Other 0.2%
Hispanic origin 0.6%

Ancestry

American 10.9%	Irish 17.8%
Dutch 3.7%	Italian 1.6%
English 15.0%	Scotch Irish 2.1%
French 3.1%	Scottish 2.0%
German 34.9%	

Universities/colleges, 1990-1991 enrollment

Anderson University, Anderson 2,124
Ball State University, Muncie 20,343
Earlham College, Richmond 1,221
Indiana University East, Richmond 2,053
Indiana Vocational Tech College, Richmond 854
Indiana Vocational Tech College, Columbus 2,255
Indiana Vocational Tech College, Muncie 1,646

Newspapers, total circulation (in all districts)

Anderson Herald-Bulletin 32,736
Columbus Republic 21,658
Franklin Daily Journal 16,173
Indianapolis News 328,936
Muncie Star/Evening Press 43,039
Richmond Palladium-Item 19,821
Shelbyville News 10,933

Commercial television stations, affiliations

ADI: Indianapolis (70%), Louisville (12%), Dayton (10%) and Ft. Wayne (8%)

Cable television systems, total subscribers

Cardinal Communications Inc.; Columbus 14,038
Century Cable; Muncie 30,369
SBC Cable; Shelbyville 5,779
TCI Cable; Anderson 26,600
TCI of Indiana; New Castle 7,400
TCI of Indiana; Richmond 12,904

Businesses and other major employers

Cummins Engine Co. Inc.; Columbus; engines/turbines 8,700
Ball State University; Muncie 6,096
General Motors Corp./Delco Remy Div.; Anderson; motor vehicle parts/electrical components 5,275
General Motors Corp./Inland Fisher-Guide Div.; Anderson; motor vehicle parts 5,000
Borg-Warner Automotive; Muncie; transmissions 2,500
Ball Memorial Hospital Inc.; Muncie 2,100
Saint John's Medical Center; Anderson 1,450
New Venture Gear; Muncie; motor vehicle parts/equipment 1,400
Bartholomew County Consolidated Schools; Columbus 1,400
Bartholomew County Hospital; Columbus 1,236
Cooper Industries Inc./Belden Electronic Wire & Cable; Richmond; nonferrous rolling and drawing 1,200
Knauf Fiberglass; Shelbyville; fiberglass 1,200
Acustar Inc.; New Castle; motor vehicle parts 1,200
Asea Brown Boveri Inc.; Muncie; electric distribution equipment 1,100

Cosco Inc.; Columbus; toys/sporting goods 1,000
Reid Memorial Hospital; Richmond 993
Masco Corp. of Indiana/Delta Faucet Co.; Greensburg; plumbing/heating 900
Richmond State Hospital; Richmond 690
Community Hospital-Anderson/Madison; Anderson 650
James River Corp. Virginia/Film Products Div.; Greensburg; plastics products 645
Libbey-Owens-Ford Co.; Shelbyville; flat glass 600
Owens-Illinois Inc./Owens-Brockway Glass; Lapel; glass/glassware 600
Ball Corp.; Muncie; glass jars/containers 600
State of Indiana/State Reformatory; Pendleton 600
Interstate Brands Corp./Dolly Madison; Columbus; bakery products 550
New Castle State Hospital; New Castle 550
Anchor Glass Container Corp.; Winchester; glass/glassware 540
Gecom Corp.; Greensburg; motor vehicles/equipment 525
Golden Casting Corp.; Columbus; iron/steel foundries 510

3rd District

Northern Tier — South Bend; Elkhart

The 3rd, dominated by industrial cities that line the Indiana Toll Road near the state's northern border, has been something of a barometer of national political trends. At the peak of the Reagan Revolution, in 1980, Republicans took this district from the Democrats, as 27-year-old John Hiler ousted House Majority Whip John Brademas. Ten years later, the 3rd offered evidence that the Reagan-Bush era was drawing to a close, as Democrat Tim Roemer ousted Hiler.

The 3rd has long been politically competitive. It has voters across the political spectrum, from staunchly conservative and Republican Elkhart (Elkhart County) to swing-voting La Porte city and more Democratic South Bend (St. Joseph County) and Michigan City (La Porte County).

La Porte County has two urban areas—La Porte and Michigan City. The latter is a blue-collar city with most of the county's minorities. Employers include Anco Inc., which makes automotive accessories, and the Jaymar-Ruby clothing company. Officials in Michigan City have oriented their economic growth efforts toward exploiting the tourist potential of its Lake Michigan location. Much of the development has been in shopping centers and vacation-home communities near the Indiana Dunes National Seashore.

To the southeast is the city of La Porte, which also has an industrial base. Employers include a Howmet Corp. plant that makes aerospace castings and a Whirlpool Corp. appliance distribution center.

With just over 105,000 residents, South Bend is the district's population nexus; neighboring Mishawaka adds 42,000 people. Although best known nationally for the University of Notre Dame, South Bend is also a center for tool-and-die manufacturing and the production of plastics. AM General Division, based in South Bend, makes military vehicles, including the "Humvee" transport. The manufacturing facility is in Mishawaka.

Like many industrial midwestern locales, St. Joseph County has had its share of shocks. The collapse of the Studebaker Co. in the 1960s was a harbinger of the decline of the U.S. auto industry. The home-grown Bendix Corp. is now part of Allied-Signal Inc., which has headquarters elsewhere.

But the region has shown resilience. While foreign competition has hurt some local manufacturers, St. Joseph County has benefited from the location in New Carlisle of the supermodern I/N Tek steel plant, a joint venture of Inland Steel Co. and Japan's Nippon Steel Corp.

Elkhart is a center for manufactured housing and recreational vehicle construction, and it has long been known as the band instrument capital of the United States. One of the largest in that business is the Selmer Co., which gave Bill Clinton two saxophones just before his inauguration in 1993. Locally, the band instruments are far more likely to be played at GOP than Democratic rallies.

Outside the cities, the landscape shifts to farmland. Elkhart County, with a large Amish population, is the state's largest milk-producer

Election Returns

	3rd District	Democrat	Republican
1992	President*	82,483 (38.3%)	91,708 (42.5%)
	House	121,269 (57.4%)	89,834 (42.6%)
1990	Senate †	64,087 (44.9%)	78,659 (55.1%)
1988	President	83,781 (41.9%)	115,936 (58.1%)
	Senate	59,633 (30.6%)	135,484 (69.4%)
	Governor	109,216 (55.1%)	88,966 (44.9%)
1986	Senate	54,188 (39.8%)	82,099 (60.2%)

*Vote for Perot was 41,358 (19.2%).   †Special election for the remaining two years of the term of Dan Quayle who was elected vice president in 1988. Appointee Daniel Coats held the seat 1988-1990 before winning the 1990 election.

Demographics

Population 554,416

Percent change from 1980 −0.7%

Land area 1,816 square miles

Population per square mile 305

Counties, 1990 population

Elkhart 156,198	St. Joseph 247,052
Kosciusko (pt.) 37,542	Starke (pt.) 6,558
La Porte 107,066	

Cities, 1990 population (10,000 or more)

Elkhart 43,627	Michigan City 33,822
Goshen 23,797	Mishawaka 42,608
Granger CDP 20,241	South Bend 105,511
La Porte 21,507	

Race and Hispanic origin

White 90.7%
Black 7.4%
American Indian, Eskimo, or Aleut. 0.3%
Asian or Pacific Islander 0.8%
Other 0.8%
Hispanic origin 1.9%

Ancestry

American 4.4%	Dutch 4.5%
Belgian 1.6%	English 10.8%
French 3.8%	Polish 9.5%
German 40.4%	Scotch Irish 1.7%
Hungarian 2.6%	Scottish 1.7%
Irish 16.8%	Swedish 2.2%
Italian 3.2%	Swiss 1.7%

Universities/colleges, 1990-1991 enrollment

Bethel College, Mishawaka 699
Davenport College, South Bend, Granger 334
Goshen College, Goshen 1,107
Grace College, Winona Lake 643
Holy Cross College, Notre Dame 437
Indiana University, South Bend 7,215
Indiana Vocational Tech College-North Central, South Bend 2,445
Purdue University-North Central, Westville 3,446
St. Mary's College, Notre Dame 1,718
University of Notre Dame, Notre Dame 9,335

Newspapers, total circulation (in all districts)

Chicago Tribune 721,559
Elkhart Truth 27,208
Ft. Wayne Journal-Gazette 117,410
Goshen News 15,370
La Porte Herald Argus 13,002
South Bend Tribune 85,870

Commercial television stations, affiliations

ADI: South Bend-Elkhart (67%) and Chicago (33%)
WSJV, Elkhart (ABC)
WHME-TV, South Bend (None)
WNDU-TV, South Bend (NBC)
WSBT-TV, South Bend (CBS)

Cable television systems, total subscribers

Heritage Cablevision; Elkhart 22,934
Heritage Cablevision; South Bend 53,512
Multimedia Cablevision Inc.; La Porte 10,825
US Cable; Michigan City 12,332

Businesses and other major employers

University of Notre Dame; Notre Dame 3,300
Memorial Hospital of South Bend; South Bend 2,217
Allied-Signal Inc./Bendix Energy Controls; South Bend; search/navigation equipment 2,000
Fairmont Homes Inc.; Nappanee; mobile homes 1,550
St. Joseph's Medical Center; South Bend 1,376
Anco Inc.; Michigan City; motor vehicle parts/equipment 1,119
Elkhart General Hospital; Elkhart 1,115
Miles Laboratories Inc.; Elkhart; pharmaceuticals 1,000
Sisters of the Holy Cross Inc./St. Mary's Convent; Notre Dame; religious organizations 1,000
State of Indiana/Westville Correctional Center; Westville 950
Uniroyal Plastics Co. Inc.; Mishawaka; plastics products 925
American Home Products Corp./Whitehall Laboratories Div.; Elkhart; pharmaceuticals 900
AM General Corp.; Mishawaka; military vehicles/equipment 900
Communication Workers of America; La Porte; labor organization 900
La Porte Hospital Inc.; La Porte 850
Goshen Rubber Co. Inc.; Goshen; rubber products 800
Howmet Corp./La Porte Casting Div.; La Porte; aerospace castings 775

State of Indiana/Transportation Dept.; La Porte 750

Coachmen Industries Inc.; Middlebury; recreational vehicles 725

Sealed Power Tech; Mishawaka; nonferrous foundries (castings) 700

Associates Commercial Corp.; South Bend; credit institutions 700

CTB Inc./Chore-Time Equipment; Milford; metal products 650

Sullair Corp./Maco-Sullair; Michigan City; industry machinery 650

Goshen General Hospital; Goshen 650

Whirlpool Corp.; La Porte; distribution center 625

Home-Crest Corp.; Goshen; millwork 600

Jayco Inc.; Middlebury; transportation equipment 600

Johnson Controls Inc./Penn Div.; Goshen; measuring/controlling devices 600

Miles Laboratories Inc.; Mishawaka; medical supplies 600

Jaymar-Ruby Inc.; Michigan City; apparel/outerwear 600

Marley Co./Weil-McLain Div.; Michigan City; plumbing/heating 600

Starcraft Automotive Corp.; Goshen; automotive repair 600

St. Anthony's Hospital; Michigan City 600

Reliance Electric Co./Dodge Mfg. Div.; Mishawaka; industry machinery 550

CTS Corp.; Elkhart; electronic components 541

Crown Intl. Inc.; Elkhart; audio/video equipment 530

Boehringer Mannheim Corp./De Puy Div.; Warsaw; medical instruments/supplies 525

4th District

Northeast — Fort Wayne

Fort Wayne, which dominates the ten-county 4th, avoided the economic upheaval and population exodus that plagued many large midwestern cities in the 1980s. The population of Indiana's second-largest city is nearly the same now as it was a decade ago, just over 173,000.

But if the 4th's economy has stayed fairly steady, its representation in the House has changed noticeably. In 1980, the 4th was held by a young conservative Republican named Dan Quayle, who successfully ran for the Senate that year. In 1989, a Democratic woman won the seat.

Quayle aide Daniel R. Coats succeeded his boss in the 4th in 1981, and Coats took Quayle's Senate seat when he became vice president in 1989. In the special House election to pick a replacement for Coats, Democrat Jill Long prevailed, and she won the next two full terms, scoring an impressive 62 percent in 1992.

As the 4th evolved from a Republican stronghold to a district held by a Democrat, the GOP presidential vote here also slumped. In 1988, the Bush-Quayle ticket won two-thirds of the 4th District vote. In 1992, fewer than half the voters in the 4th cast a Republican ballot for president. At the same time, Democratic Gov. Evan Bayh carried every county in the district.

But Coats also swept the 4th in his 1992 Senate election, and this remains a conservative-minded area. Representative Long's success is attributable more to her personal appeal and her agrarian background—she owns a farm in the Whitley County community of Larwill—than to her party label.

Fort Wayne and its Allen County environs have several large industrial facilities: General Electric has a factory and General Motors builds trucks and buses at a plant just outside town. But Fort Wayne's economy is buffered from industrial downturns by its large white-collar sector. Much of the area's manufacturing is technology-oriented: Magnavox's Government and Industrial Electronics Co. (which makes military radios) and ITT Corp.'s aerospace and communications division (producing meteorological instruments) are here. Another large employer is the Lincoln National Life Insurance Co.

German Americans, a rather conservative constituency, remain Allen County's largest ethnic group: Fort Wayne's Germanfest is an annual social highlight.

Fort Wayne's cityscape gives way to some of Indiana's most fertile farms. Allen County leads the state in production of wheat, is second in oats and is near the top in soybeans. Lagrange County trails only Elkhart County (in the 3rd) in milk production. Like Elkhart, Lagrange has one of the nation's largest Amish populations.

Small cities dot the 4th's fields: Huntington is Quayle's hometown. The town has a walking tour called The Quayle Trail, and in 1993 the Dan Quayle Commemorative Museum opened. Huntington County gave the GOP presidential ticket 57 percent in 1992.

Election Returns

		Democrat	Republican
	4th District		
1992	President*	69,292 (31.3%)	102,779 (46.4%)
	House	134,907 (62.1%)	82,468 (37.9%)
1990	Senate †	61,813 (39.5%)	94,850 (60.5%)
1988	President	68,495 (33.0%)	139,064 (67.0%)
	Senate	51,787 (25.5%)	151,648 (74.5%)
	Governor	102,436 (49.5%)	104,492 (50.5%)
1986	Senate	46,330 (33.8%)	90,849 (66.2%)

Vote for Perot was 49,565 (22.4%).   †Special election for the remaining two years of the term of Dan Quayle who was elected vice president in 1988. Appointee Daniel Coats held the seat 1988-1990 before winning the 1990 election.

Demographics

Population 554,416

Percent change from 1980 0.1%

Land area 3,607 square miles

Population per square mile 154

Counties, 1990 population

Adams	31,095	Lagrange	29,477
Allen	300,836	Noble	37,877
De Kalb	35,324	Steuben	27,446
Huntington	35,427	Wells	25,948
Jay (pt.)	3,335	Whitley	27,651

Cities, 1990 population (10,000 or more)

Fort Wayne 173,072   Huntington 16,389

Race and Hispanic origin

White 92.9%

Black 5.5%

American Indian, Eskimo, or Aleut. 0.3%

Asian or Pacific Islander 0.6%

Other 0.7%
Hispanic origin 1.6%

Ancestry

American	5.3%	Italian	1.9%
Dutch	3.3%	Polish	2.0%
English	12.6%	Scotch Irish	1.5%
French	5.4%	Scottish	2.0%
German	51.2%	Swedish	1.1%
Irish	14.9%	Swiss	3.0%

Universities/colleges, 1990-1991 enrollment

Concordia Theologial Seminary, Fort Wayne 389
Huntington College, Huntington 601
Indiana Institute of Technology, Fort Wayne 1,108
Indiana University-Purdue University, Fort Wayne 11,889
Indiana Vocational Tech College-Northeast, Fort Wayne 2,895
International Business College, Fort Wayne 504
ITT Technical Institute, Fort Wayne 1,067
Lutheran College, Fort Wayne 408
St. Francis College, Fort Wayne 879
Summit Christian College, Fort Wayne 376
Tri-State University, Angola 1,193

Newspapers, total circulation (in all districts)

Auburn Evening Star 7,097
Ft. Wayne Journal-Gazette 117,410
Kendallville News-Sun 6,946
Muncie Star/Evening Press 43,039

Commercial television stations, affiliations

ADI: Ft. Wayne (89%) and South Bend-Elkhart (11%)
WANE-TV, Fort Wayne (CBS)
WFFT-TV, Fort Wayne (Fox)
WKJG-TV, Fort Wayne (NBC)
WPTA, Fort Wayne (ABC)

Cable television systems, total subscribers

Comcast Cablevision of Indiana; New Haven 47,891

Military installations, 1991

Fort Wayne Municipal Airport Air Force Guard Station, Fort Wayne 350

Businesses and other major employers

Magnavox Electronic Systems Co.; Fort Wayne; communications/electronic equipment 4,600
Lincoln National Life Insurance Corp.; Fort Wayne; fire/marine/casualty insurance 4,500
General Motors Corp.; Roanoke; trucks/buses 3,000
North American Van Lines Inc.; Fort Wayne; trucking services 2,969
GTE North Inc.; Fort Wayne; telephone communications 2,500
Parkview Memorial Hospital; Fort Wayne 2,488
General Electric Co./GE Motors; Fort Wayne; electrical motors 2,000
Lutheran Hospital of Indiana; Fort Wayne 1,939
Dana Corp./Spicer Axle Div.; Fort Wayne; axles 1,800
ITT Corp./ITT Airspace/Communications Div.; Fort Wayne; search/navigation equipment 1,800
Uniroyal Goodrich Tire Co.; Woodburn; tires 1,675
Sears Roebuck & Co.; Fort Wayne; catalog retailers 1,600
Dana Corp./Weatherhead Div.; Fort Wayne; steel products 1,500

City of Fort Wayne; Fort Wayne 1,500
St. Joseph's Medical Center; Fort Wayne 1,200
East Allen County Schools; New Haven 1,100
State of Indiana/Developmental Center; Fort Wayne 1,000
Indiana University-Purdue University, Fort Wayne 1,000
Zollner Co.; Fort Wayne; pistons 898
Super Valu Stores Inc.; Fort Wayne; grocery products 850
Summit Bank; Fort Wayne; commercial banks 800
Magnetek Inc./Triad; Huntington; electric distribution equipment 800
Navistar Intl. Transportation; Fort Wayne; engineering services 761
Slater Steels Corp.; Fort Wayne; stainless steel 760
Franklin Electric Co. Inc.; Bluffton; electrical industrial apparatus 750
Essex Group Inc.; Fort Wayne; nonferrous rolling and drawing 700
Time Services Inc.; Fort Wayne; personnel supply services 620
American Electric Power/Indiana Michigan Power Co.; Fort Wayne; electric services 600
General Electric Co.; Fort Wayne; small motors 600
Cooper Tire & Rubber Co.; Auburn; rubber products 600
Carrier Corp./Hamilton Standard Controls; Huntington; business services 600
Metropolitan School District; Fort Wayne 600
Fort Wayne Newspapers Inc./News-Sentinel; Fort Wayne; newspapers 590
Fleetwood Enterprises Inc.; Decatur; mobile homes 550
Kraft General Foods Inc.; Kendallville; candies 550
Caylor-Nickel Hospital Inc.; Bluffton 540

5th District

Northern Rural — Kokomo

The 5th stretches across a mainly rural area that calls itself the "Hoosier Heartland." One would expect such a place to have a Republican tilt, and it does: George Bush carried 17 of the district's 20 counties in 1992. Redistricting in 1991 enhanced GOP strength in the 5th, and that helped the GOP challenger to defeat a three-term Democratic incumbent.

With economies heavily reliant on auto parts manufacturing, many of the district's small cities have struggled. Like many areas across the Midwest, several 5th District counties declined in population during the 1980s. Industrial Grant County (Marion) lost 8 percent of its population, while Howard County (Kokomo) fell by 7 percent. Warren, a farm county on Indiana's western border, was down by 9 percent.

Kokomo, with about 45,000 people, is the district's largest city. It was long a center for industrial innovation: Kokomo resident Elwood Haynes produced the first successful gasoline-powered car and later invented stainless steel (Haynes International Inc., a producer of metal alloys, is one of Kokomo's major employers). The biggest job-provider in the city is Delco Electronics Corp., known for its automobile sound systems. Much of Kokomo's hopes for economic growth are based on Delco's development of electronic pollution-control systems and safety devices such as air bags. Employment at Chrysler's transmission plant has been steady.

Economic recovery has been difficult in Marion and nearby

Gas City. A General Motors auto body stamping plant is the largest employer in Marion.

To the north are a string of smaller working-class cities: Wabash, Peru and Logansport. Their distance from major highways is a hindrance to growth; locals are pushing for a "Hoosier Heartland Highway," which would modernize routes 24 and 25 that connect these cities with Fort Wayne and Lafayette.

Peru has a colorful past—it was the hometown of songwriter Cole Porter and the base for a number of traveling circuses—but a tenuous present; nearby Grissom Air Force Base is on the Pentagon's base-closing list and is set to close in 1994.

At its northwest corner, the 5th reaches into the smaller suburbs of central Lake County. In Porter County, only the town of Hebron is in the 5th.

Most of the remaining land in the 5th is farmed. In the district's northeast corner is part of Kosciusko County, which calls itself Indiana's leading agricultural county. This is strong Republican country: Bush beat Bill Clinton here by more than 2-to-1 in 1992, and the GOP candidate took the county in the House race that year.

To the west, the 5th contains counties that are prolific producers of corn, soybeans and hogs. At its southwest extreme, the 5th's terrain and politics change quickly. Vermillion County, where Indiana's coal-mining territory begins, is heavily Democratic. In 1992 Clinton won in Vermillion; Democratic Gov. Evan Bayh took three-fourths of its vote.

Election Returns

	5th District	Democrat	Republican
1992	President*	70,893 (31.3%)	103,118 (45.6%)
	House	107,973 (49.0%)	112,492 (51.0%)
1990	Senate †	67,142 (42.1%)	92,514 (57.9%)
1988	President	76,144 (35.8%)	136,522 (64.2%)
	Senate	58,798 (28.6%)	146,514 (71.4%)
	Governor	108,865 (51.4%)	103,009 (48.6%)
1986	Senate	58,382 (35.1%)	107,939 (64.9%)

*Vote for Perot was 52,354 (23.1%).   †Special election for the remaining two years of the term of Dan Quayle who was elected vice president in 1988. Appointee Daniel Coats held the seat 1988-1990 before winning the 1990 election.

Demographics

Population 554,415

Percent change from 1980 1.1%

Land area 6,962 square miles

Population per square mile 80

Counties, 1990 population

Benton 9,441	Marshall 42,182
Blackford 14,067	Miami 36,897
Carroll 18,809	Newton 13,551
Cass 38,413	Porter (pt.) 4,909
Fulton 18,840	Pulaski 12,643
Grant 74,169	Starke (pt.) 16,189
Howard 80,827	Vermillion (pt.) 9,055
Jasper 24,960	Wabash 35,069
Kosciusko (pt.) 27,752	Warren 8,176
Lake (pt.) 45,201	White 23,265

Cities, 1990 population (10,000 or more)

Crown Point (pt.) 10,948	Marion 32,618
Kokomo 44,962	Peru 12,843
Logansport 16,812	Wabash 12,127

Race and Hispanic origin
White 96.7%
Black 2.2%
American Indian, Eskimo, or Aleut. 0.4%
Asian or Pacific Islander 0.3%
Other 0.4%
Hispanic origin 1.3%

Ancestry

American 8.4%	Italian 2.1%
Dutch 5.3%	Polish 2.9%
English 14.0%	Scotch Irish 2.1%
French 3.8%	Scottish 1.9%
German 40.5%	Swedish 1.7%
Irish 18.1%	

Universities/colleges, 1990-1991 enrollment
Ancilla Domini College, Donaldson 618
Indiana University, Kokomo 3,332
Indiana Vocational Tech College, Kokomo 2,197
Indiana Wesleyan College, Marion 2,719
Manchester College, North Manchester 1,097
St. Joseph's College, Rensselaer 1,033
Taylor University, Upland 1,718

Newspapers, total circulation (in all districts)
Chicago Sun-Times 529,632
Chicago Tribune 721,559
Ft. Wayne Journal-Gazette 117,410
Gary Post-Tribune 72,842
Indianapolis News 328,936
Kokomo Tribune 26,636
Lafayette Journal and Courier 37,929
Logansport Pharos-Tribune 14,272
Marion Chronicle-Tribune 20,517
Muncie Star/Evening Press 43,039
Munster Times 64,780
South Bend Tribune 85,870
Terre Haute Tribune Star 35,169
Vidette Messenger 15,523

Commercial television stations, affiliations
ADI: Indianapolis (47%), South Bend-Elkhart (26%), Chicago (18%), Ft. Wayne (6%) and Terre Haute (3%)

Cable television systems, total subscribers
Cardinal Communications Inc.; Monticello 5,800
Cardinal Communications Inc.; Peru 8,330
Cardinal Communications Inc.; Wabash 5,100
Heritage Cablevision; South Bend 53,512
Marion Cable Television Inc.; Marion 15,900
Sammons Communications Inc.; Logansport 8,400
Telecable of Kokomo Inc.; Kokomo 26,004
US Cable of North Indiana; Griffith 50,369

Military installations, 1991
Grissom Air Force Base, Bunker Hill 3,227

Businesses and other major employers
Delco Electronics Corp.; Kokomo; audio equipment/motor vehicle parts 10,500

Chrysler Corp.; Kokomo; transmissions 4,000

General Motors Corp.; Marion; auto body stamping 3,300

Thomson Consumer Electronics; Marion; electronic components 2,100

County of Lake; Crown Point 2,000

Zimmer Inc.; Warsaw; medical instruments/supplies 1,995

R. R. Donnelley & Sons Co.; Warsaw; commercial printing 1,800

Wilson Foods Corp.; Logansport; meat products 1,400

St. Anthony Medical Center Inc.; Crown Point 1,400

Haynes Intl. Inc.; Kokomo; steel alloy products 1,200

Gencorp Inc./Engineered Elastomers Div.; Wabash; hard rubber products 1,000

U.S. Veterans Affairs Dept.; Marion; hospital 1,000

St. Joseph Hospital & Health Center; Kokomo 990

Marion General Hospital Inc.; Marion 897

Rosby Corp.; Monon; motor vehicles/equipment 850

Logansport State Hospital; Logansport 807

Biomet Inc.; Warsaw; medical instruments/supplies 750

Howard County Community Hospital; Kokomo 705

American National Can Co./Foster Forbes Glass Div.; Marion; glass containers 630

Dalton Foundries Inc.; Warsaw; iron/steel foundries 610

Gencorp Inc./Reinforced Plastics Div.; Marion; hoses/belting/gaskets/packing 600

Indiana Packers Co.; Delphi; animal services 600

Electronic Data Systems Corp./Delco Electronics Corp.; Kokomo; computer services 600

Emerson Electric Co./White Rogers Div.; Logansport; electric distribution equipment 525

6th District

Central — Suburban Indianapolis

Over the past couple of decades, the farms and undeveloped tracts of Hamilton, Johnson and outer Marion counties have been overtaken by Indianapolis subdivisions. Growth in some areas outside the city's widely looping beltway (Interstate 465) has been explosive. The population of once-pastoral Hamilton County has doubled since 1970, and it increased 33 percent in the 1980s, reaching about 109,000 in 1990.

The boom has changed the look, but not the politics, of the outlying areas that make up the core of the 6th. The wealthy and near-wealthy who have moved there are nearly as conservative as the farmers who live nearby. Republican vote totals are consistently high—George Bush won 62 percent of the Hamilton County vote in 1992. In neighboring Hancock County, Bush took 54 percent.

The Democrats in the state House who controlled redistricting in 1991 packed even more Republicans into the 6th than it contained in the 1980s: Increasingly suburban sections of Morgan and Boone counties, as well as mainly rural Clinton, Tipton, Hancock and a slice of Henry counties were transferred to the 6th. As a result, the district is not only the most Republican in Indiana, but also is one of the most GOP-oriented House districts in the nation. There is almost no minority-group constituency: Hamilton's black population in 1990 was less than 1 percent.

The 6th takes in the loyally Republican sections of northern and southern Marion County; the rest of Marion is in the Democratic-held 10th. Leaders in the GOP parade are the

established suburbs of Washington Township, and the growth area to the northeast around Geist Reservoir. Castleton and part of the city of Lawrence are also in the district.

The northern sections of Marion County blend with the white-collar suburbs of Hamilton County. Although it is just 15 miles from downtown Indianapolis, Carmel in 1970 was a town of about 7,000 people; now, more than 25,000 live there. Noblesville and the nearby Morse Reservoir area also have grown significantly. Zionsville, in the southeast corner of Boone County, continues to advertise its quaint appearance even as it is further absorbed into the Indianapolis sphere.

There is suburban wealth in the district's southern reaches, but a number of residents of more modest means also live there. Some working-class Marion County suburbanites work at the Amtrak repair shops in Beech Grove and at Indianapolis Metropolitan Airport; the 6th takes in the city of Speedway, host of the Indianapolis 500 auto race. Johnson County, which grew by 14 percent in the 1980s, combines suburban sprawl with an industrial presence: Arvin Industries makes auto parts in Greenwood and Franklin.

The suburbs have encroached somewhat on Hancock County (Greenfield). However, the northernmost counties, Clinton and Tipton, are still primarily farmland.

Election Returns

	6th District	Democrat	Republican
1992	President*	61,171 (22.7%)	153,280 (56.9%)
	House	71,952 (27.8%)	186,499 (72.2%)
1990	Senate †	53,682 (34.4%)	102,377 (65.6%)
1988	President	62,106 (25.2%)	183,956 (74.8%)
	Senate	44,390 (18.5%)	195,308 (81.5%)
	Governor	88,614 (36.2%)	155,942 (63.8%)
1986	Senate	39,647 (26.1%)	112,062 (73.9%)

Vote for Perot was 54,718 (20.3%).   †Special election for the remaining two years of the term of Dan Quayle who was elected vice president in 1988. Appointee Daniel Coats held the seat 1988-1990 before winning the 1990 election.

Demographics

Population 554,416

Percent change from 1980 2.5%

Land area 2,038 square miles

Population per square mile 272

Counties, 1990 population

Boone (pt.) 10,688	Johnson (pt.) 82,994
Clinton 30,974	Marion (pt.) 242,743
Hamilton 108,936	Morgan (pt.) 12,422
Hancock 45,527	Tipton 16,119
Henry (pt.) 4,013	

Cities, 1990 population (10,000 or more)

Carmel 25,380	Greenwood 26,265
Frankfort 14,754	Indianapolis (pt.) 213,375
Franklin 12,907	Noblesville 17,655
Greenfield 11,657	

Race and Hispanic origin
White 97.7%
Black 1.1%

American Indian, Eskimo, or Aleut. 0.2%
Asian or Pacific Islander 0.9%
Other 0.2%
Hispanic origin 0.8%

Ancestry

American 7.4%		Italian 2.7%
Dutch 3.7%		Polish 1.8%
English 19.2%		Scotch Irish 2.8%
French 4.2%		Scottish 3.1%
German 40.0%		Swedish 1.2%
Irish 20.2%		Welsh 1.1%

Universities/colleges, 1990-1991 enrollment

Franklin College Indiana, Franklin 880
International Business College, Indianapolis 228
ITT Technical Institute, Indianapolis 1,050

Newspapers, total circulation (in all districts)

Anderson Herald-Bulletin 32,736
Franklin Daily Journal 16,173
Greenfield Daily Reporter 7,389
Indianapolis News 328,936
Kokomo Tribune 26,636
Lafayette Journal and Courier 37,929
Muncie Star/Evening Press 43,039

Commercial television stations, affiliations

ADI: Indianapolis (100%)
   WIIB, Bloomington (None)
   WCLJ, Bloomington (None)
   WTTV, Bloomington (None)
   WISH-TV, Indianapolis (CBS)
   WTHR, Indianapolis (NBC)
   WTTK, Kokomo (None)
   WLFI-TV, Lafayette (CBS)
   WMCC, Marion (None)

Cable television systems, total subscribers

American Cablevision-Indianapolis; Indianapolis 69,916
Comcast Cablevision; Castleton 108,050
Insight Cablevision; Noblesville 8,322
Insight Cablevision; Tipton 10,678
Jones Intercable Inc.; Carmel 11,103
Post Newsweek Cable TV; Greenwood 9,900
Telecable of Kokomo Inc.; Kokomo 26,004

Military installations, 1991

Naval Avionics Center, Indianapolis 3,491

Businesses and other major employers

Boehringer Mannheim Corp.; Indianapolis; measuring/controlling devices 1,500
Little Caesar Enterprises Inc.; Indianapolis; bars/restaurants 1,500
American Trans Air Inc.; Indianapolis; air transportation 1,300
Resort Condominiums Intl.; Indianapolis; business services 1,112
United Student Aid Funds Inc./USA Funds; Fishers; federal credit 1,105
Carrier Corp.; Indianapolis; air conditioning/heating equipment 1,000
Eli Lilly & Co.; Greenfield; research services 917
Best Universal Lock Co. Inc.; Indianapolis; locks 900

Yellow Freight System Inc.; Indianapolis; trucking services 900
Mayflower Transit Inc.; Carmel; trucking services 857
GTE North Inc./GTE Midwestern Operations; Westfield; telephone communications 800
State of Indiana/Highway Dept.; Greenfield 800
Bankers National Life Insurance Co.; Carmel; life insurance 753
State of Indiana/Transportation Dept.; Greenfield 700
Bridgestone/Firestone Inc.; Carmel; rubber products 700
Community Hospital of Indiana; Indianapolis 700
Riverview Hospital; Noblesville 700
Dayton Hudson Corp./Target; Indianapolis; apparel 650
Dowelanco; Indianapolis; research services 650
Arvin Industries Inc.; Franklin; motor vehicle parts 600
Federal-Mogul Corp.; Frankfort; motor vehicle parts 600
Federated Dept. Stores/Lazarus; Indianapolis; department stores 600
Indiana Precision Technology; Greenfield; motor vehicle equipment 590
Conseco Inc.; Carmel; life insurance 550
Johnson Memorial Hospital; Franklin 550
AT&T Co./Consumer Products-Lab; Indianapolis; research services 535
Hancock Memorial Hospital; Greenfield 520
Stewart-Warner Corp./South Wind Div.; Indianapolis; metal products 510

7th District

West — Terre Haute; Lafayette

The Wabash River recalls to Hoosier nostalgists the days when western Indiana was settled by newcomers who arrived on flatboats and steamers. The 7th, which ranges across this region, has long been identified with cities that sprang up along the river: Lafayette and Terre Haute.

However, rapid growth in the suburban counties west of Indianapolis has given the 7th a third population center. Adding to this new suburban clout is the northwest section of Monroe County, which contains expanding communities near Bloomington.

In the Indianapolis orbit is Hendricks County, the largest of the district's suburban counties; its population increased nearly 9 percent in the 1980s to 76,000. Growth was also flush to the south in Morgan County and to the north in Boone County, most of which are in the 7th.

Each of these counties is relatively affluent and has a minuscule minority population: just nine blacks were counted among Morgan County's 56,000 residents in 1990. The conservative tone of these counties has strongly reinforced the district's long-held Republican tendencies.

Lafayette and Terre Haute remain the 7th's major urban centers. The tale of these cities is a study in contrasts.

The Lafayette area (Tippecanoe County) has enjoyed economic growth. Some is attributed to Purdue University—which helps attract technology-oriented businesses—in West Lafayette. With more than 37,000 students, Purdue employs more than 16,000 full-time workers, the most in the area. With its specialties in engineering, science and agricultural research, Purdue has attracted a number of technology-oriented businesses to greater Lafayette.

Industry also has expanded around Lafayette: One of the most touted Japanese investments in Indiana, a Subaru-Isuzu plant that employs about 2,000 people, is here. Other facilities include an Eli Lilly chemical plant, an Alcoa aluminum plant and a Fairfield plant that makes gear shafts.

While its blue-collar sector provides some Democratic votes, Tippecanoe has held fast to its GOP traditions.

But Terre Haute (Vigo County) has a Democratic bent that economic hard times reinforced. Once a hotbed of radicalism—Terre Haute was the hometown of socialist Eugene V. Debs—Vigo supported Bill Clinton in 1992 with 43 percent of the vote. George Bush won here narrowly in 1988.

Terre Haute is coping with long-term industrial decline. At the northern end of Indiana's coal country, the city suffered from the national coal industry's ailments. Today, the largest area employer is Columbia House, the mail-order distributor of tapes and records. Several factories produce plastics and films; Pfizer has a pharmaceutical plant nearby. Local officials tout the city's colleges: Indiana State University (12,000 students) and the Rose-Hulman Institute.

The rest of the 7th is mainly GOP farmland, dotted with small cities such as Crawfordsville (Montgomery County), which has a large R. R. Donnelly printing plant. Greencastle (Putnam County) is home to DePauw University (2,400 students).

Election Returns

	7th District	Democrat	Republican
1992	President*	70,699 (31.6%)	103,700 (46.4%)
	House	88,005 (40.5%)	129,189 (59.5%)
1990	Senate †	63,252 (42.8%)	84,611 (57.2%)
1988	President	74,321 (35.6%)	134,669 (64.4%)
	Senate	56,312 (27.3%)	150,058 (72.7%)
	Governor	105,650 (50.4%)	103,946 (49.6%)
1986	Senate	50,231 (33.5%)	99,771 (66.5%)

*Vote for Perot was 49,103 (22.0%). †Special election for the remaining two years of the term of Dan Quayle who was elected vice president in 1988. Appointee Daniel Coats held the seat 1988-1990 before winning the 1990 election.

Demographics

Population 554,416

Percent change from 1980 −0.1%

Land area 4,752 square miles

Population per square mile 117

Counties, 1990 population

Boone (pt.) 27,459	Owen 17,281
Clay 24,705	Parke 15,410
Fountain 17,808	Putnam 30,315
Hendricks 75,717	Tippecanoe 130,598
Monroe (pt.) 23,364	Vermillion (pt.) 7,718
Montgomery 34,436	Vigo 106,107
Morgan (pt.) 43,498	

Cities, 1990 population (10,000 or more)

Crawfordsville 13,584	Plainfield 10,433
Lafayette 43,764	Terre Haute 57,483
Lebanon 12,059	West Lafayette 25,907
Martinsville 11,677	

Race and Hispanic origin

White 96.3%
Black 2.0%
American Indian, Eskimo, or Aleut. 0.2%
Asian or Pacific Islander 1.2%
Other 0.3%
Hispanic origin 0.8%

Ancestry

American 8.3%	Italian 2.2%
Dutch 4.8%	Polish 1.6%
English 17.1%	Scotch Irish 2.7%
French 4.0%	Scottish 2.7%
German 36.0%	Swedish 1.2%
Irish 18.7%	Welsh 1.1%

Universities/colleges, 1990-1991 enrollment

DePauw University, Greencastle 2,347
Indiana State University, Terre Haute 11,783
Indiana Vocational Tech College-Wabash Valley, Terre Haute 1,935
Indiana Vocational Tech College, Lafayette 1,783
Purdue University, West Lafayette 37,588
Rose-Hulman Institute of Technology, Terre Haute 1,419
St. Mary-of-the-Woods College, St. Mary-of-the-Woods 1,040
Wabash College, Crawfordsville 854

Newspapers, total circulation (in all districts)

Bloomington Herald-Times 28,626
Chicago Tribune 721,559
Crawfordsville Journal & Review 10,596
Danville Commercial-News 23,645
Indianapolis News 328,936
Lafayette Journal and Courier 37,929
Terre Haute Tribune Star 35,169

Commercial television stations, affiliations

ADI: Indianapolis (63%), Terre Haute (26%) and Lafayette (11%)

Cable television systems, total subscribers

American Cablevision; Terre Haute 29,000
American Cablevision-Indianapolis; Avon 8,023
Cable Brazil Inc.; Brazil 5,000
Cardinal Communications Inc.; Crawfordsville 6,700
TCI of Indiana; Bloomington 18,046
TM Cable of Greater Lafayette; Lafayette 38,000

Military installations, 1991

Hulman Regional Airport Air Force Guard Station, Terre Haute 304

Businesses and other major employers

Purdue University; West Lafayette 16,650
R. R. Donnelley & Sons Co.; Crawfordsville; book publishing 2,500
General Electric Co.; Bloomington; household appliances 2,200
State of Indiana; Terre Haute 2,000
Subaru-Isuzu Automotive Inc.; Lafayette; motor vehicles 1,910
Indiana State University; Terre Haute 1,850
Eli Lilly & Co./Tippecanoe Laboratories; Lafayette; pharmaceuticals 1,450

Aluminum Co. of America; Lafayette; elevators/escalators 1,400

Union Hospital Inc.; Terre Haute 1,400

Eli Lilly & Co.; Clinton; grain mill products 1,300

PSI Resources Inc.; Plainfield; electric services 1,200

Sony Music Entertainment Inc./Columbia House; Terre Haute; music merchandising 1,200

Lafayette Home Hospital Inc.; Lafayette 1,200

St. Elizabeth Hospital & Medical Center; Lafayette 1,100

Wabash National Corp.; Lafayette; motor vehicle parts 1,058

Fairfield Mfg. Co.; Lafayette; auto gears 1,031

Landis & Gyr Metering Inc.; Lafayette; measuring devices 1,000

Lafayette School Corp.; Lafayette 1,000

Digital Audio Disc Corp.; Terre Haute; audio equipment 880

SMS Schloemann Siemag; Crawfordsville; metalworking machinery 800

Healthtrust Inc./Terre Haute Regional Hospital; Terre Haute 800

Harrison Steel Castings Co.; Attica; iron/steel foundries 728

Bemis Co. Inc.; Terre Haute; plastics products 725

Otis Elevator Co./United Technologies Corp.; Bloomington; elevators/escalators 700

TRW Inc./Ross Gear Div.; Lafayette; motor vehicle parts 655

DePauw University; Greencastle 650

City of Terre Haute; Terre Haute 650

National Service Industries/Hi-Tek Lighting Div.; Crawfordsville; electric lighting 640

State of Indiana/Veterans Home; Lafayette; residential care 620

Harman-Motive Inc.; Martinsville; audio/video equipment 606

Asea Brown Boveri Inc.; Bloomington; electrical industrial apparatus 600

Pfizer Inc.; Terre Haute; pharmaceuticals 600

State Farm Mutual Auto Insurance Co.; Lafayette; insurance services 600

Hendricks County Hospital; Danville 600

Raybestos Co.; Crawfordsville; mineral products 585

8th District

Southwest — Evansville; Bloomington

Heading toward the Ohio River, Indiana leaves the Corn Belt and enters the hilly border South. The political tradition in much of the 8th is of the southern Democratic variety, and there is a significant GOP base vote.

Although the Democratic House member won six consecutive elections from 1982-1992, he only once has topped 55 percent. His electoral troubles came in a handful of conservative, mostly rural counties—Knox, Daviess, Lawrence and Orange. Yet Democrat Evan Bayh carried every county in the district in his 1992 gubernatorial re-election bid. And Bill Clinton won in the district's presidential voting that year, breaking a long dry spell: The 8th had not voted for a Democratic presidential candidate since 1964, when it contributed to Lyndon B. Johnson's landslide.

Three groupings provide much of the Democratic vote: industrial workers in Evansville and Bloomington; the university

communities in those cities; and the miners who work the coal lodes in seven of the district's 13 counties.

Evansville (Vanderburgh County), an Ohio River port, is southern Indiana's industrial center. With just over 126,000 residents, it is Indiana's third-largest city. A Bristol-Myers pharmaceutical plant and a Whirlpool refrigerator factory are two of the leading employers; residents also commute east to an Alcoa aluminum plant in Newburgh (Warrick County) and west to a General Electric plastics plant in Mount Vernon (Posey County). Although Evansville has access to Interstate 64, it is the only large city in Indiana without a direct highway link to Indianapolis.

While the city hosts two small colleges, the University of Southern Indiana and the University of Evansville, it is Bloomington—home of Indiana University—that is the district's college town. "IU" has 35,000 students and employs 6,000 people. Although the campus and blue-collar crowds rarely mix—tensions between students and working-class Bloomington youths were the background of the film *Breaking Away*—they combine politically to give Democrats an edge. A General Electrics refrigerator factory, a French-owned Thomson electronics plant and an Otis Elevator factory are the city's largest industrial companies.

Past the limestone quarries of Monroe and Lawrence counties is the Naval Surface Warfare Center in Crane (Martin County), one of the district's largest employers, which develops naval systems and produces ammunition.

Then come the counties where coal is strip-mined. Indiana coal tonnage was 2.3 percent higher in 1991 than in 1982, but increasing mechanization came at the expense of jobs. Coal employment fell dramatically during the 1980s. Sullivan County was hit hard, losing 10 percent of its population in the 1980s. Most coal counties lean Democratic; in 1992, all but one of them backed Clinton for president.

Several of the district's small towns have unique attractions for tourists. Vincennes (Knox County), on the Wabash River, was the site of a key Revolutionary War battle. New Harmony (Posey County) was the scene of 19th-century experiments in communal life led by Father George Rapp and Robert Owen. French Lick (Orange County) has many ornate but aging hotels that denote its past as a resort town.

Election Returns

	8th District	Democrat	Republican
1992	President*	103,697 (42.5%)	97,070 (39.8%)
	House	125,244 (52.5%)	108,054 (45.3%)
1990	Senate †	91,211 (53.2%)	80,340 (46.8%)
1988	President	98,444 (43.3%)	129,146 (56.7%)
	Senate	73,711 (33.0%)	149,883 (67.0%)
	Governor	130,805 (57.6%)	96,228 (42.4%)
1986	Senate	74,636 (39.4%)	114,659 (60.6%)

Vote for Perot was 43,181 (17.7%). †Special election for the remaining two years of the term of Dan Quayle who was elected vice president in 1988. Appointee Daniel Coats held the seat 1988-1990 before winning the 1990 election.

Demographics

Population 554,416

Percent change from 1980 1.4%

Land area 5,227 square miles

Population per square mile 106

Counties, 1990 population

Daviess 27,533	Orange 18,409
Gibson 31,913	Pike 12,509
Greene 30,410	Posey 25,968
Knox 39,884	Sullivan 18,993
Lawrence 42,836	Vanderburgh 165,058
Martin 10,369	Warrick 44,920
Monroe (pt.) 85,614	

Cities, 1990 population (10,000 or more)

Bedford 13,817	Vincennes 19,859
Bloomington (pt.) 58,116	Washington 10,838
Evansville 126,272	

Race and Hispanic origin

White 95.8%
Black 3.1%
American Indian, Eskimo, or Aleut. 0.2%
Asian or Pacific Islander 0.8%
Other 0.2%
Hispanic origin 0.6%

Ancestry

American 7.8%		Irish 19.2%
Dutch 2.7%		Italian 1.6%
English 16.2%		Polish 1.2%
French 4.2%		Scotch Irish 2.3%
German 40.3%		Scottish 2.0%

Universities/colleges, 1990-1991 enrollment

Indiana University, Bloomington 35,453
Indiana Vocational Tech College-Southwest, Evansville 2,011
ITT Technical Institute, Evansville 488
Oakland City College, Oakland City 732
University of Evansville, Evansville 2,933
University of Southern Indiana, Evansville 6,480
Vincennes University, Vincennes 9,162

Newspapers, total circulation (in all districts)

Bedford Times Mail 14,188
Bloomington Herald-Times 28,626
Chicago Tribune 721,559
Evansville Courier/Press 95,655
Indianapolis News 328,936
Terre Haute Tribune Star 35,169
Vincennes Sun-Commercial 13,507
Washington Times-Herald 9,769

Commercial television stations, affiliations

ADI: Terre Haute (43%), Evansville (35%), Indianapolis (14%) and Louisville (8%)
  WTVW, Evansville (ABC)
  WBAK-TV, Terre Haute (ABC)
  WTHI-TV, Terre Haute (CBS)
  WTWO, Terre Haute (NBC)

Cable television systems, total subscribers

Heritage Cablevision; Bedford 5,689
TCI of Indiana; Bloomington 18,046
UA Cablesystems of Indiana; Evansville 43,107
Wabash Cablevision; Vincennes 7,800
Warrick Cablevision; Newburgh 6,000

Military installations, 1991

Naval Weapons Support Center, Crane 5,447
Crane Army Ammunition Activity, Crane 708

Businesses and other major employers

Indiana University; Bloomington 6,000
Aluminum Co. of America/Alcoa Warrick Operations; Newburgh; rigid containers 3,500
Whirlpool Corp.; Evansville; refrigerators 3,000
Bristol-Myers Squibb Co.; Evansville; pharmaceuticals 3,000
Thomson Consumer Electronics; Bloomington; communications equipment 2,000
St. Mary's Medical Center; Evansville 1,794
Deaconess Hospital Inc.; Evansville 1,790
General Electric Co.; Mount Vernon; plastics/synthetics 1,700
Bloomington Hospital Inc.; Bloomington 1,700
General Motors Corp./Central Foundry; Bedford; aluminum foundries 1,500
TJX Operating Cos. Inc./TJ Maxx; Evansville; family clothing stores 1,400
Welborn Memorial Baptist Hospital Inc.; Evansville 1,300
Good Samaritan Hospital; Vincennes 1,260
Traylor Bros. Inc.; Evansville; heavy construction 1,200
Vincennes University; Vincennes 1,106
Ford Motor Co.; Bedford; motor vehicles/equipment 941
Perdue Farms Inc.; Washington; meat products 900
County of Vanderburgh; Evansville 810
Industrial Contractors Inc.; Evansville; building construction 700
Lawrence North Community Schools; Bedford 639
State of Indiana/Highway Dept.; Vincennes 600
Evansville State Hospital; Evansville 570
PSI Energy Inc./Gibson Generating Station; Owensville; electric services 568

9th District

Southeast Hill Country — New Albany

Much of the 9th has more in common with Kentucky to the south than with the flatlands of Indiana to the north. The district's population centers—New Albany (Floyd County) and Jeffersonville (Clark County)—are just across the Ohio River from Louisville. The inland areas are scenic but remote and dependent on resource industries, such as timber and coal; rural poverty is present in the 9th.

The voting tendencies are those seen in many districts with southern Democratic roots. First elected in 1965, Rep. Lee Hamilton won comfortably in every county in 1992, and he took about three-quarters of the vote in Floyd and Clark counties. In presidential balloting, though, Republicans have fared well in the 9th. The Bush-Quayle ticket carried the district in 1988, but lost it in 1992 by fewer than 1,000 votes.

The more Democratic part of the 9th is its hilly southern region: Bill Clinton won 10 southern counties in 1992. To the north, where the land levels out, patterns are similar to those in the rest of Indiana's farmland: Bush beat Clinton by a slight margin.

The towns in Louisville's sphere grew up as shipbuilding centers: The *Robert E. Lee* and other famed riverboats were built in New Albany. Although the largest area employer—a U.S.

Census Bureau data preparation center—is white collar, this remains an industrial region. New Albany's factories include a Pillsbury plant that makes refrigerated dough products. To the east, Clarksville has a Colgate-Palmolive plant topped by a clock 40 feet in diameter that is said to be the second largest in the world.

Jeffersonville still builds boats, including barges. Since 1974, it also has been home to the Hillerich and Bradsby sporting goods factory. Tourist interest in seeing its famous baseball bats has led the company to plan a new complex back across the river in the original home of the "Louisville Slugger."

Northeast along the Ohio is Madison; its industrial base includes producers of automotive equipment and women's shoes. The local economy is adjusting to the phaseout, under the 1989 base-closing law, of the Army's Jefferson Proving Ground, which sprawled across Jefferson and Ripley counties. Upriver is Lawrenceburg (Dearborn County), site of a Joseph E. Seagram whiskey distillery. Although Dearborn's economy has taken some blows—a Schenley distillery closed in 1988—the county has grown, thanks to its proximity to Cincinnati: Population was up 13 percent in the 1980s.

At the district's extremes are two small industrial cities: In the northeast part of the 9th, Connersville is the site of a Ford auto air conditioning plant and a Frigidaire appliance factory. At the western end of the 9th is Jasper (Dubois County), a city dominated by German Americans that bills itself as the nation's "wood office furniture capital." Some coal is mined in Dubois and in Spencer County to the south. In between are forests that attract recreationists to southern Indiana. But unemployment runs well above the state norm in most of the rural counties.

Election Returns

	9th District	Democrat	Republican
1992	President*	98,063 (40.8%)	97,441 (40.5%)
	House	160,980 (69.7%)	70,057 (30.3%)
1990	Senate †	77,088 (52.4%)	70,014 (47.6%)
1988	President	90,520 (41.8%)	125,842 (58.2%)
	Senate	74,402 (36.0%)	132,300 (64.0%)
	Governor	124,201 (58.4%)	88,509 (41.6%)
1986	Senate	72,587 (42.8%)	97,202 (57.2%)

*Vote for Perot was 44,873 (18.7%).   †Special election for the remaining two years of the term of Dan Quayle who was elected vice president in 1988. Appointee Daniel Coats held the seat 1988-1990 before winning the 1990 election.

Demographics

Population 554,416

Percent change from 1980 1.8%

Land area 6,733 square miles

Population per square mile 82

Counties, 1990 population

Bartholomew (pt.) 8,167	Floyd 64,404
Brown 14,080	Franklin 19,580
Clark 87,777	Harrison 29,890
Crawford 9,914	Jackson 37,730
Dearborn 38,835	Jefferson 29,797
Dubois 36,616	Jennings 23,661
Fayette 26,015	Ohio 5,315
Perry 19,107	Switzerland 7,738
Ripley 24,616	Union 6,976
Scott 20,991	Washington 23,717
Spencer 19,490	

Cities, 1990 population (10,000 or more)

Clarksville 19,833	Madison 12,006
Connersville 15,550	New Albany 36,322
Jasper 10,030	Seymour 15,576
Jeffersonville 21,841	

Race and Hispanic origin

White 97.7%
Black 1.7%
American Indian, Eskimo, or Aleut. 0.2%
Asian or Pacific Islander 0.3%
Other 0.1%
Hispanic origin 0.4%

Ancestry

American 9.1%	Irish 19.6%
Dutch 2.6%	Italian 1.3%
English 13.8%	Scotch Irish 2.0%
French 4.0%	Scottish 1.8%
German 44.5%	

Universities/colleges, 1990-1991 enrollment

Hanover College, Hanover 1,075
Indiana University-Southeast, New Albany 5,642
Indiana Vocational Tech College-Southeast, Madison 750
Indiana Vocational Tech College-South Central, Sellersburg 1,455

Newspapers, total circulation (in all districts)

Cincinnati Enquirer 162,669
Columbus Republic 21,658
Evansville Courier/Press 95,655
Indianapolis News 328,936
Louisville Courier Journal 235,144
New Albany Tribune 11,292
Seymour Daily Tribune 9,150

Commercial television stations, affiliations

ADI: Louisville (43%), Cincinnati (24%), Evansville (18%) and Indianapolis (15%)
 WDRB-TV, Louisville (Fox)
 WHAS-TV, Louisville (ABC)
 WLKY-TV, Louisville (CBS)

Cable television systems, total subscribers

Cardinal Communications Inc.; Connersville 6,474
Cardinal Communications Inc.; New Albany 13,973
Cardinal Communications Inc.; Seymour 6,135
Insight Cablevision; Jeffersonville 15,800
Simmons Communications Inc.; Madison 5,401
TCI of Indiana; Jasper 5,380
Warner Cable Communications Inc.; Cincinnati/Blue Ash 181,000

Military installations, 1991

Jefferson Proving Ground (Army), Madison 425

Businesses and other major employers

Hillenbrand Industries Inc.; Batesville; caskets/hospital equipment 2,700
Ford Eletronic & Refrigeraton Corp.; Connersville; auto air conditioning 3,300

Hill-Rom Co. Inc.; Batesville; furniture/fixtures 1,700

U.S. Census Bureau; Jeffersonville 1,563

State of Indiana/Muscatatuck Developmental Center; Butlerville 1,300

Kimball Electronics Inc.; Jasper; electronic components 1,200

Clark County Memorial Hospital; Jeffersonville 1,150

ICI Americas Inc./Indiana Army Ammunition Plant; Charlestown; ordnance/accessories 1,100

Batesville Co.; Batesville; caskets 1,100

Floyd Memorial Hospital; New Albany 1,062

Joseph E. Seagram & Sons Inc.; Lawrenceburg; distillery 1,000

White Consolidated Industries/Frigidaire Co.; Connersville; household appliances 1,000

Madison State Hospital; Madison 1,000

Colgate-Palmolive Co.; Jeffersonville; soaps/toiletries 950

Smith Cabinet Mfg. Co. Inc.; Salem; cabinets 900

Aristokraft Inc./Decora; Jasper; millwork 900

GTE Products Corp.; Seymour; electric lighting 750

State of Indiana/Transportation Dept.; Seymour 700

Pillsbury Co.; New Albany; flour products 675

U.S. Shoe Corp.; Crothersville; footwear 675

U.S. Shoe Corp.; Madison; footwear 600

Cummins Engine Co. Inc./Cummins Industrial Center; Seymour; freight shipping 600

Holm Industries Inc.; Scottsburg; hose/belting/gaskets/packing 590

Farbest Foods Inc.; Huntingburg; meat products 575

Dresser Industries Inc./Roots Div.; Connersville; oil field machinery 560

King's Daughters Hospital; Madison 552

General Electric Co.; Tell City; electrical motors 550

Aisin USA Mfg. Inc.; Seymour; motor vehicles/equipment 550

Aurora Casket Co. Inc.; Aurora; caskets 544

10th District

Central — Indianapolis

Geographically and figuratively, Indianapolis is at the center of Indiana life. With just over 730,000 residents in 1990, the state capital had more than four times the population of Fort Wayne, Indiana's second-largest city. Indianapolis is the state's banking and commercial hub, and it retains its traditional role as an industrial city.

Under a unitary city-county government instituted in 1970 (it collects all taxes and handles most services except schools and public safety), Indianapolis takes in all of Marion County except for the small cities of Lawrence, Beech Grove, Speedway and Southport. Consolidation brought large blocks of affluent suburbia into the city limits, reinforcing its standing as one of the most conservative large cities in the country. Its largely nonethnic white population leans Republican.

However, the 10th is crafted to take in the city's most Democratic areas. In 1992, Bill Clinton won the 10th, taking 47 percent of the vote. The district includes most of Indianapolis' black population, which makes up 23 percent of the city's total.

A downtown building boom in the 1980s and a relatively low unemployment rate have made Indianapolis a success story among midwestern cities. Federal, state and city-county governments employ tens of thousands; the Indiana University-Purdue University campus, Butler University and numerous large health-care complexes are also major employers. Banks, insurance companies and the headquarters for the Eli Lilly pharmaceutical company add to the white-collar base.

Long known for its "500" auto race each Memorial Day weekend, Indianapolis has become a major-league sports city and convention site. Construction of the Hoosier Dome, just across the commons from the state Capitol, lured football's Colts from Baltimore in 1984. The Indiana Pacers basketball team plays in nearby Market Square Arena. Indianapolis is also headquarters for the Amateur Athletic Union.

Heavy industry continues to play a role in the city's economy, with blue-collar workers turning out products such as turbine engines and transmissions. General Motors, Ford and Chrysler all maintain automotive components plants in the city. But Indy's economic picture has not been cloudless. Chrysler and Western Electric closed plants on the east side; the warehousing and light-manufacturing companies that filled the space are less labor-intensive. In general, the city's economic growth has been in white-collar and service industries that are inaccessible or unappealing to many former industrial workers. Indianapolis is also bracing for the phaseout of the Army's Fort Benjamin Harrison, scheduled to close by the summer of 1997. The base includes the Defense Finance and Accounting Center, which may be relocated before the base closes. Some of the district's workers commute to the Naval Air Warfare Center in the neighboring 6th.

Election Returns

	10th District	Democrat	Republican
1992	President*	92,514 (47.2%)	70,458 (35.9%)
	House	117,604 (64.0%)	64,378 (35.0%)
1990	Senate †	64,523 (56.6%)	49,563 (43.4%)
1988	President	98,974 (50.6%)	96,457 (49.4%)
	Senate	83,404 (43.5%)	108,271 (56.5%)
	Governor	110,408 (56.8%)	84,054 (43.2%)
1986	Senate	59,372 (48.3%)	63,659 (51.7%)

Vote for Perot was 33,229 (16.9%).   †*Special election for the remaining two years of the term of Dan Quayle who was elected vice president in 1988. Appointee Daniel Coats held the seat 1988-1990 before winning the 1990 election.*

Demographics

Population 554,416

Percent change from 1980 2.3%

Land area 197 square miles

Population per square mile 2,820

Counties, 1990 population
Marion (pt.) 554,416

Cities, 1990 population (10,000 or more)
Beech Grove (pt.) 10,434   Lawrence (pt.) 20,008
Indianapolis (pt.) 517,952

Race and Hispanic origin
White 68.6%
Black 29.8%
American Indian, Eskimo, or Aleut. 0.2%
Asian or Pacific Islander 0.9%

Other 0.5%
Hispanic origin 1.2%

Ancestry

American 6.9%	Irish 14.1%
Dutch 2.2%	Italian 2.0%
English 10.4%	Polish 1.2%
French 2.6%	Scotch Irish 1.7%
German 24.3%	Scottish 1.8%

Universities/colleges, 1990-1991 enrollment

Butler University, Indianapolis 3,908
Christian Theologial Seminary, Indianapolis 279
Indiana University-Purdue University, Indianapolis 27,518
Indiana Vocational Tech College-Central Indiana, Indianapolis 4,408
Marian College, Indianapolis 1,242
Martin Center College, Indianapolis 328
University of Indianapolis, Indianapolis 3,391

Newspapers, total circulation (in all districts)

Indianapolis News 328,936

Commercial television stations, affiliations

ADI: Indianapolis (100%)
WHMB-TV, Indianapolis (None)
WRTV, Indianapolis (ABC)
WXIN, Indianapolis (Fox)

Cable television systems, total subscribers

American Cablevision-Indianapolis; Indianapolis 69,916
Comcast Cablevision; Castleton 108,050

Military installations, 1991

Fort Benjamin Harrison (Army), Indianapolis 10,960

Businesses and other major employers

Eli Lilly and Co.; Indianapolis; pharmaceuticals 8,500
General Motors Corp./Allison Gas Turbine Div.; Indianapolis; aircraft/parts 7,500
Methodist Hospital of Indiana; Indianapolis 5,900
General Motors Corp./Allison Transmission Div.; Indianapolis; transmissions 5,600
St. Vincent Hospital; Indianapolis 4,200
Indiana Bell Telephone Co. Inc; Indianapolis; telephone communications 4,000
Associated Insurance Cos./Blue Cross-Blue Shield Indiana; Indianapolis; medical service/insurance 3,291
Ford Motor Co./Transmission & Chassis Div.; Indianapolis; motor vehicles/equipment 3,000
General Motors Corp./Truck & Bus Group; Indianapolis; auto stampings 3,000
William N. Wishard Memorial Hospital; Indianapolis 3,000
Community Hospital of Indiana; Indianapolis 2,800
May Dept. Stores Co.; Indianapolis; department stores 2,021
Thomson Consumer Electronics; Indianapolis; audio/video equipment 1,919
Bank One Indianapolis; Indianapolis; commercial banks 1,793

Indianapolis Newspapers Inc.; Indianapolis; newspapers 1,650
U.S. Veterans Affairs Dept.; Indianapolis; hospital 1,500
National Railroad Pass Corp./Amtrack; Beech Grove; railroads 1,200
INB National Bank; Indianapolis; commercial banks 1,200
Brylane Inc.; Indianapolis; computer services 1,200
State of Indiana/Transportation Dept.; Indianapolis; road construction 1,200
American States Insurance Co.; Indianapolis; fire/marine/casualty insurance 1,200
Merchants National Bank & Trust Co.; Indianapolis; commercial banks 1,000
Hook-Superx Inc./Hooks Drugs; Indianapolis; warehousing 1,000
Bertelsmann Music Group; Indianapolis; music merchandise 1,000
State of Indiana/Board of Health; Indianapolis 950
Celadon Trucking Services of Indiana; Indianapolis; trucking services 900
Intl. Casting Corp.; Indianapolis; iron/steel foundries 900
American United Life Insurance Co.; Indianapolis; pension/health/welfare funds 895
Chrysler Corp./Indianapolis Chrysler Foundry; Indianapolis; engine foundry 844
United Farm Bur. Mutual Insurance Co.; Indianapolis; fire/casualty insurance 829
County of Marion/Sheriffs Dept.; Indianapolis 807
Midwest Medical Center; Indianapolis 800
BPS Guard Services Inc.; Indianapolis; business/security services 800
Maytag Corp./Jenn Air Co.; Indianapolis; household appliances 767
Bridgeport Brass Corp./Olin Indianapolis; Indianapolis; castings 750
State of Indiana/Environmental Dept.; Indianapolis 730
Golden Rule Financial Corp.; Indianapolis; medical service/health insurance 700
GSF Safeway Inc.; Indianapolis; building/security services 700
Central State Hospital; Indianapolis 700
AT&T Co.; Indianapolis; telephone communications 657
White Castle System Inc.; Indianapolis; management/public relations 633
Roadway Express Inc.; Indianapolis; trucking facilities 600
Continental Baking Co./Wonder Bread; Indianapolis; bakery products 600
Indopco Inc./National Starch and Chemical Corp; Indianapolis; plastics/synthetics 600
Indiana Insurance Co.; Indianapolis; life/casualty insurance 600
Pinkertons Inc.; Indianapolis; security services 600
Amsted Industries Inc./Diamond Chain Co.; Indianapolis; power transmissions 550
Indianapolis Power & Light Co.; Indianapolis; electric services 501

Iowa

If Ronald Reagan were asked about Iowa, he would be apt to answer with warm memories about his days in the 1930s as a radio sportscaster in Davenport and Des Moines. If Iowans were asked about Ronald Reagan, they likely would grumble about the harsh economic realities of the 1980s—family farms on the auction block and unemployment as high as 20 percent. Therein lies the political portrait of Iowa in the 1990s.

In the decade defined by the Reagan presidency, nearly 140,000 people abandoned Iowa in search of better economic opportunities. In the process, the Republican firm hold on the Hawkeye State eroded. Reagan electorally conquered the nation, but he barely carried Iowa in his 1984 landslide. George Bush lost the state in 1988 and 1992. While Iowans have stayed loyal to their Republican governor and Sen. Charles E. Grassley, Democrats made significant gains. They seized control of the General Assembly in 1982 (although they gave up control of the House in 1992), and in 1990, for the first time, re-elected a Democratic senator for a second full term.

In 1984, Iowa's Democratic Party counted about 62,000 more voters in its ranks than the GOP. By 1990 the Democratic advantage was nearly 99,000—an all-time high. That helped Democrats win county offices even in some of the state's most conservative places.

For all this, nothing could be taken for granted in Iowa politics. The state's voters took pride in their independent, contrarian streak. Fully 30 percent of Iowa's 1.5 million voters declined to affiliate with either party. In the 1992 presidential contest, independent Ross Perot took 19 percent of the vote.

But the exodus of young Iowans produced the most dramatic political emblem of the state's economic difficulties. As a result, Iowa's congressional representation following the 1990 census dropped from six to five seats, the state's smallest delegation since the 1850s.

In Iowa, redistricting was done through a process that aimed to eliminate partisan gerrymandering. State law dictated that the nonpartisan Legislative Service Bureau draw a new map. The law's mandate in line-drawing was to follow "objective" criteria, such as population equality among districts, and to ignore the partisan concerns of the incumbents. In addition, the state constitution stipulated that districts be drawn using only whole counties, and a statute required that districts be convenient and contiguous.

By 39-10, the plan passed the state Senate May 10, 1991; the House approved it 93-7 on May 11. Gov. Terry Branstad signed the new map into law May 30.

Republicans held four of the five seats by 1993. The 1st District, although picking up Johnson County (Iowa City)—home to the University of Iowa and the most Democratic county in the state—re-elected its GOP incumbent to a ninth term in 1992.

In reducing the state's districts to five, the new map threw a three-term Democrat against a freshman Republican in the 2nd. With redistricting taking some support away from both of them, an expensive, hard-fought campaign resulted in a razor-thin victory to the GOP candidate in 1992.

The new 3rd District became less Republican than its former manifestation, picking up 17 counties, many with Democratic leanings, such as Story County (Ames), Des Moines County (Burlington) and Wappello County (Ottumwa). Also, a strong Republican base in Pottawattamie County (Council Bluffs) was taken out and placed in the new 4th District. But in 1992 the GOP House incumbent scored a stunning, come-from-behind victory, winning by a 5,000 vote margin.

With nearly two-thirds of the vote in the new 4th cast in the two urbanized, and Democratic, Polk (Des Moines) and neighboring Warren counties, even the addition of GOP-leaning Council Bluffs did not outweigh the Democratic advantage; Rep. Neal Smith took 62 percent of the vote in 1992 to win his 18th term.

The new 5th offered its Republican incumbent the strongest partisan base in the state. While the rural counties in northwestern district were not as staunchly Republican as they once were, the Democrats did not even field an opponent in 1992.

Table 1 Population

District	Population	Population under 18	Voting-age population	Median age
1	555,229	141,508	413,721	32.1
2	555,494	147,025	408,469	34.6
3	555,299	137,556	417,743	34.7
4	555,276	143,105	412,171	33.6
5	555,457	149,686	405,771	35.6
State	2,776,755	718,880	2,057,875	34.0

IOWA

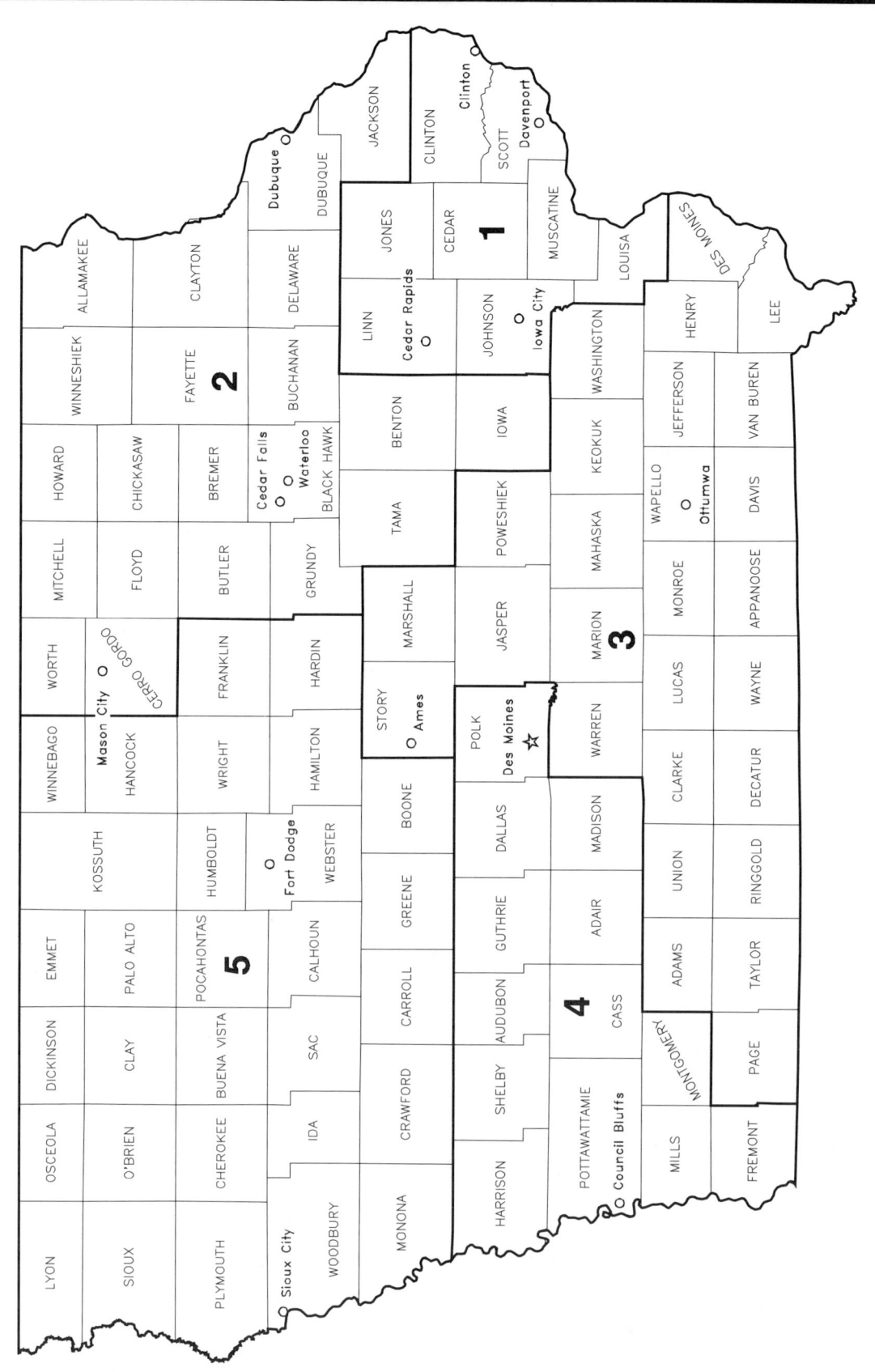

Table 2 Voting-Age Persons

District	White*	Black*	American Indian, Eskimo, or Aleut*	Asian or Pacific Islander*	Other*	Hispanic*	Male*	Female*
1	95.7%	2.2%	0.2%	1.2%	0.6%	1.6%	48.0%	52.0%
2	97.9	1.4	0.2	0.4	0.2	0.5	47.3	52.7
3	97.7	0.9	0.2	1.0	0.3	0.7	48.1	51.9
4	95.9	2.5	0.2	1.0	0.4	1.2	46.7	53.3
5	98.5	0.5	0.3	0.4	0.3	0.7	47.2	52.8
State	97.1	1.5	0.2	0.8	0.4	1.0	47.5	52.5

*As percent of voting-age population.

Table 3 Voting-Age Persons by Age Groups

District	18-24*	25-44*	45-54*	55-64*	65 and over*
1	16.7%	43.3%	13.3%	10.7%	16.0%
2	13.4	38.1	13.6	12.6	22.2
3	15.0	37.9	13.1	12.1	22.0
4	12.9	43.2	13.6	11.8	18.5
5	11.0	37.7	12.9	13.5	24.9
State	13.8	40.0	13.3	12.1	20.7

*As percent of voting-age population.

Table 4 Income and Occupation

District	Median family income	Families in poverty	White collar*	Blue collar*	Service*	Farm*
1	$35,846	7.8%	56.9%	25.7%	14.2%	3.2%
2	30,470	9.4	45.8	28.7	15.6	9.9
3	30,286	9.1	48.8	29.1	14.8	7.3
4	34,018	7.4	59.9	22.7	13.4	4.0
5	28,989	8.3	45.9	27.9	14.9	11.2
State	31,659	8.4	51.7	26.7	14.6	7.0

*As percent of employed persons age 16 and over.

Table 5 Education: School Years Completed

District	Less than grade 9*	Grades 9-12 no diploma*	High school diploma*	College bachelor's degree or higher*
1	6.8%	10.4%	33.7%	22.7%
2	11.5	10.7	42.0	13.8
3	9.8	10.9	40.3	15.7
4	6.4	11.1	36.8	18.9
5	11.4	10.5	39.7	13.4
State	9.2	10.7	38.5	16.9

*As percent of persons age 25 and over.

Table 6 Housing and Residential Patterns

District	Owner occupied	Renter occupied	Urban	Rural
1	66.7%	33.3%	76.4%	23.6%
2	72.2	27.8	51.1	48.9
3	71.2	28.8	53.7	46.3
4	68.3	31.7	74.4	25.6
5	71.7	28.3	47.5	52.5
State	70.0	30.0	60.6	39.4

1st District

East — Cedar Rapids; Davenport; Iowa City

The 1st is Iowa's most urbanized district, with three of the state's six most-populous cities. Cedar Rapids (Linn County) and Davenport (Scott County) grew up around heavy industry, and Iowa City (Johnson County) is home to the University of Iowa.

These urban centers give the 1st a Democratic tilt. In 1992 presidential voting, Bill Clinton prevailed by comfortable margins in all three counties. In the House, the GOP incumbent, adroit at mixing fiscal conservatism with more liberal social views, was re-elected to a ninth term in 1992.

Cedar Rapids emerged as Iowa's second-largest city in the late 1980s; nearly a third of the district's residents live in or around it. Long a prominent center for the grain-processing business, Cedar Rapids has weathered hard economic times of late with help from high-technology work, such as production of electronic and telecommunications equipment. Rockwell International, which makes avionics equipment, eclipsed Quaker Oats as the city's largest employer during the decade. In 1991, Eastman Kodak and Cultur Limited teamed up to build an $85 million biotechnology complex in Cedar Rapids.

Nearly 30 percent of the people in the 1st live in Scott County. Davenport and neighboring Bettendorf, along with the Illinois cities of Rock Island and Moline, make up the Quad Cities urban concentration. These are old, industrial Mississippi River cities whose economies suffered badly during the 1980s, as did the nearby manufacturing cities of Clinton and Muscatine.

Emblematic of the difficulties is a Caterpillar plant outside Davenport that once employed 4,000 people; briefly abandoned in the 1980s, it has recently found new life, but as a storage warehouse for several local businesses. Davenport and the other river cities are trying to rebound by capitalizing on tourist dollars drawn to riverboat gambling, permitted under a 1990 law. Scott County voted Democratic for president in 1988 and 1992.

Iowa City, the next-largest population center, grew by nearly 18 percent in the 1980s. The city and Johnson County cast just under one-fifth of the district's vote. Once labeled "Berkeley of the Midwest," Johnson County remains a Democratic bastion, although suburban and high-tech influences have moderated its politics. In the past, the 1,900 University of Iowa faculty members were predominantly liberal, while the 29,000-member student body was more conservative. Students' attitudes—particularly on social issues—recently have shifted leftward, and they have become more concerned about whether the economy will afford them the opportunity of gainful employment after graduation.

Export sales by companies such as Stanley Engineering and Hon Industries give the district's economy an international dimension. But the traditional lifeblood, agriculture, is still important: By one estimate, there are four hogs to every person in the district, and its range of crops includes corn, tomatoes, soybean and watermelons.

Election Returns

	1st District	Democrat	Republican
1992	President*	128,655 (46.4%)	95,660 (34.5%)
	House	81,600 (31.4%)	178,042 (68.6%)
1990	Senate	102,479 (54.3%)	86,079 (45.7%)
	Governor	74,343 (40.3%)	110,016 (59.7%)

	1st District	Democrat	Republican
1988	President	136,716 (56.4%)	105,683 (43.6%)
1986	Senate	52,127 (33.0%)	105,816 (67.0%)
	Governor	80,704 (50.0%)	80,795 (50.0%)

Vote for Perot was 52,983 (19.1%).

Demographics

Population 555,229

Percent change from 1980 14.3%

Land area 4,481 square miles

Population per square mile 124

Counties, 1990 population

Cedar 17,381	Linn 168,767
Clinton 51,040	Louisa 11,592
Johnson 96,119	Muscatine 39,907
Jones 19,444	Scott 150,979

Cities, 1990 population (10,000 or more)

Bettendorf 28,132	Davenport 95,333
Cedar Rapids 108,751	Iowa City 59,738
Clinton 29,201	Marion 20,403
Coralville 10,347	Muscatine 22,881

Race and Hispanic origin
White 95.0%
Black 2.6%
American Indian, Eskimo, or Aleut. 0.2%
Asian or Pacific Islander 1.3%
Other 0.8%
Hispanic origin 2.0%

Ancestry

American 2.9%	Italian 1.8%
Czechoslovakian 4.7%	Norwegian 3.3%
Danish 1.9%	Polish 1.7%
Dutch 4.1%	Scotch Irish 2.3%
English 13.7%	Scottish 1.9%
French 3.6%	Swedish 3.7%
German 50.6%	Welsh 1.1%
Irish 20.8%	

Universities/colleges, 1990-1991 enrollment
Coe College, Cedar Rapids 1,250
Cornell College, Mount Vernon 1,140
Eastern Iowa Community College, Davenport 5,747
Hamilton Technical College, Davenport 414
Kirkwood Community College, Cedar Rapids 8,625
Mount Mercy College, Cedar Rapids 1,528
Mount St. Clare College, Clinton 311
Palmer Chiropractic College, Davenport 1,663
St. Ambrose University, Davenport 2,323
Teikyo Marycrest College, Davenport 1,799
University of Iowa, Iowa City 28,785

Newspapers, total circulation (in all districts)
Cedar Rapids Gazette 69,469
Clinton Herald 17,710
Des Moines Register 193,358
Iowa City Press Citizen 15,667
Muscatine Journal 10,279
Quad-City Times 54,414

Commercial television stations, affiliations
ADI: Davenport-Rock Island-Moline (58%) and Cedar Rapids-Waterloo-Dubuque (42%)
KWQC-TV, Davenport (NBC)
WHBF-TV, Rock Island (CBS)
KOCR, Cedar Rapids (Fox)
KQCT, Davenport (None)

Cable television systems, total subscribers
Cox Cable Cedar Rapids Inc.; Cedar Rapids 40,456
Cox Cable Quad Cities; Moline 56,208
Heritage Cablevision; Clinton 18,850
TCI Cable; Iowa City 22,000

Businesses and other major employers
University of Iowa; Iowa City 22,253
Rockwell Intl. Corp./Avionics Div.; Cedar Rapids; avionics equipment 4,196
Aluminum Co. of America; Bettendorf; aluminum products 2,825
St. Luke's Methodist Hospital; Cedar Rapids 2,300
Rockwell Intl. Corp./Air Transport Div.; Cedar Rapids; electronic communications equipment 1,800
Oscar Mayer Foods Corp.; Davenport; meat products 1,500
Quaker Oats Co.; Cedar Rapids; grain mill products 1,400
U.S. Veterans Affairs Dept.; Iowa City; hospital 1,306
IBP Inc.; Columbus Junction; meat products 1,200
St. Luke's Hospital; Davenport 1,132
Oscar Mayer Foods Corp./Louis Rich Co.; West Liberty; meat products 1,100
Iowa City Community School District; Iowa City 1,100
Rockwell Intl. Corp./Graphic Systems Div.; Cedar Rapids; industry machinery 1,040
United Tech Auto Systems; Iowa City; plastics products 972
Deere & Co.; Davenport; construction machinery 950
Mercy Hospital; Davenport 900
Aegon USA Inc.; Cedar Rapids; life insurance 898
Inter Innovation Le Febure Mfg.; Cedar Rapids; computer/office equipment 895
City of Davenport/Housing Commission; Davenport 853
H. J. Heinz Co.; Muscatine; preserved fruits/vegetables 850
International Paper Co.; Clinton; paperboard products 850
State of Iowa/National Guard; Cedar Rapids; commercial banks 800
Grain Processing Corp./Horizon Products; Muscatine; organic chemicals 795
American College Testing Program; Iowa City; educational testing 750
Square D Co.; Cedar Rapids; electric distribution equipment 726
Mercy Hospital; Iowa City 700
National Computer Systems; Iowa City; computer services 660
City of Iowa City; Iowa City 640
Procter & Gamble Mfg. Co.; Iowa City; soaps/cleaners 630
General Mills Inc.; Cedar Rapids; grain mill products 600
Cedar Rapids Gazette Inc.; Cedar Rapids; newspapers 600
MCI Telecommunications Corp.; Cedar Rapids; nonstore retailers 600
Kirkwood Community College; Cedar Rapids 600
Hon Industries Inc.; Muscatine; office furniture 550

Rockwell Intl. Corp./Coraville Oper.; Iowa City; electronic components 550

Norand Corp.; Cedar Rapids; computer/office equipment 520

2nd District

Northeast — Waterloo; Dubuque

The 2nd is dominated by two midsize industrial cities, Waterloo and Dubuque, and a university town, Cedar Falls. But nearly two-thirds of the vote comes from their rural surroundings.

Black Hawk County, with Waterloo and Cedar Falls, is Iowa's fourth-largest metropolitan area and traditionally a strong Democratic base. The county casts more than one-fifth of the 2nd's vote. Waterloo had the first gasoline-tractor manufacturer, and it now has a large John Deere facility. The city grew up around the farm-implement and meatpacking industries. Hogs are still slaughtered here at the world's largest pork plant. (Neighboring Delaware County leads the nation in hog production.)

Until 1986, the GOP prevailed in House voting in Black Hawk County, despite the industrial and union influences in Waterloo and an academic community at the University of Northern Iowa in Cedar Falls. The majority in Black Hawk seemed politically more akin to those in the surrounding Republican-voting farmlands. In the mid- to late 1980s, Black Hawk County voters occasionally split their tickets, going for Michael S. Dukakis in 1988 and Bill Clinton in 1992.

Dubuque is the district's other population center. Together with Dubuque County, the area contributes more than 15 percent of the 2nd's vote.

Built on and against the bluffs facing the Mississippi River, Dubuque is Iowa's oldest city. Its economic base shifted from lead mines and lumbering to manufacturing and meatpacking, which suffered in the 1980s. The city is now seeking to lure tourists with a new industry, riverboat gambling. Dubuque also has gotten a lift from people trekking to nearby Dyersville to see the site featured in the movie *Field of Dreams*.

Dubuque is predominantly Democratic by registration, but elections reveal the conservative outlook of this ethnic and heavily Catholic city. Republican Rep. Tom Tauke carried the county throughout the 1980s and in his unsuccessful 1990 Senate bid. In 1992 Clinton won in Dubuque, although half the votes in the county went to GOP House nominee.

Almost 10 percent of the district's vote comes out of Mason City (Cerro Gordo County), on the northwestern edge of the 2nd. The can-do spirit that inspired native son Meredith Willson to compose *The Music Man* helped the city weather the farm crisis; the city has emerged as a health-care hub. Residents here demonstrate their independence at the polls; in 1990 Democrat Tom Harkin narrowly carried Cerro Gordo County in his Senate contest, but in 1992 the Republican Senate nominee and the Democratic House nominee won the county.

While pork, grain and dairy remain integral industries in the 2nd, much of the district is rural, with dairying and a bucolic northern European flavor. The German-influenced Amana Colonies are in Iowa County and Decorah in Winneshiek County has a fine Norwegian museum.

Election Returns

	2nd District	Democrat	Republican
1992	President*	120,228 (44.4%)	95,005 (35.1%)
	House	131,570 (49.1%)	134,536 (50.2%)
1990	Senate	98,543 (48.5%)	104,628 (51.5%)
	Governor	75,421 (37.2%)	127,090 (62.8%)
1988	President	137,842 (55.9%)	108,563 (44.1%)
1986	Senate	61,646 (32.5%)	128,043 (67.5%)
	Governor	95,008 (49.3%)	97,759 (50.7%)

*Vote for Perot was 55,279 (20.4%).

Demographics

Population 555,494

Percent change from 1980 14.4%

Land area 12,261 square miles

Population per square mile 45

Counties, 1990 population

Allamakee 13,855	Fayette 21,843
Benton 22,429	Floyd 17,058
Black Hawk 123,798	Grundy 12,029
Bremer 22,813	Howard 9,809
Buchanan 20,844	Iowa 14,630
Butler 15,731	Jackson 19,950
Cerro Gordo 46,733	Mitchell 10,928
Chickasaw 13,295	Tama 17,419
Clayton 19,054	Winneshiek 20,847
Delaware 18,035	Worth 7,991
Dubuque 86,403	

Cities, 1990 population (10,000 or more)

Cedar Falls 34,298	Mason City 29,040
Dubuque 57,546	Waterloo 66,467

Race and Hispanic origin

White 97.3%
Black 1.7%
American Indian, Eskimo, or Aleut. 0.2%
Asian or Pacific Islander 0.5%
Other 0.2%
Hispanic origin 0.7%

Ancestry

American 2.4%	Irish 18.4%
Czechoslovakian 3.2%	Italian 1.0%
Danish 2.4%	Norwegian 7.9%
Dutch 3.2%	Scotch Irish 1.4%
English 11.2%	Scottish 1.5%
French 3.2%	Swedish 2.1%
German 61.9%	

Universities/colleges, 1990-1991 enrollment

Clarke College, Dubuque 876
Hawkeye Institute of Technology, Waterloo 1,820
Loras College, Dubuque 1,905
Luther College, Decorah 2,216
North Iowa Area Community College, Mason City 2,771
Northeast Iowa Community College, Calmar 1,829
University of Dubuque, Dubuque 1,121
University of Northern Iowa, Cedar Falls 13,435

Upper Iowa University, Fayette   2,215
Wartburg College, Waverly   1,440
Wartburg Theological Seminary, Dubuque   229

Newspapers, total circulation (in all districts)

Cedar Rapids Gazette   69,469
Clinton Herald   17,710
Des Moines Register   193,358
Dubuque Telegraph Herald   33,791
Marshalltown Times-Republican   11,920
Mason City Globe Gazette   19,520
Oelwein Daily Register   5,567
Waterloo Courier   47,139

Commercial television stations, affiliations

ADI: Cedar Rapids-Waterloo-Dubuque (75%), Rochester-Mason City-Austin (20%) and Davenport-Rock Island-Moline (5%)

KCRG-TV, Cedar Rapids (ABC)
KGAN, Cedar Rapids (CBS)
KIMT, Mason City (CBS)
KWWL, Waterloo (NBC)

Cable television systems, total subscribers

Heritage Cablevision; Mason City   11,806
TCI of Iowa; Dubuque   27,392
Westmarc Cable; Waterloo   16,554

Businesses and other major employers

Deere & Co.; Dubuque; farm/garden machinery   3,300
Amana Refrigeration Inc.; Amana; refrigerators   2,600
FDL Foods Inc.; Dubuque; meat products   1,850
Dubuque Community School District; Dubuque   1,440
Mercy Health Center; Dubuque   1,400
St. Joseph Mercy Hospital; Mason City   1,400
Hawkeye Institute of Technology; Waterloo   1,390
Deere & Co.; Waterloo; farm/garden machinery   1,225
Allen Memorial Hospital; Waterloo   1,030
Brown Publishers; Dubuque; book publishing   803
Covenant Medical Center.; Waterloo   780
Deere & Co./Product Engineering Center; Cedar Falls; engineering services   730
Flexsteel Industries Inc.; Dubuque; furniture   700
Hanson Industries; Dyersville; toys/sporting goods   700
Viking Pump Inc.; Cedar Falls; industry machinery   700
Allied Products Corp./White-New Idea; Charles City; farm/garden machinery   700
City of Waterloo; Waterloo   648
Sara Lee Corp.; New Hampton; bakery products   627
Waterloo Industries Inc.; Waterloo; metal tools   600
Finley Hospital; Dubuque   600
Deere & Co./Engine Works; Waterloo; engineering services   575
Medical Assoc. Realty Corp.; Dubuque; real estate operators   560
Curries Co.; Mason City; metal products   556
Chamberlain Mfg. Corp.; Waterloo; ordnance/accessories   550
Century Life of America; Waverly; life insurance   550
Mason City Community School District; Mason City   512

3rd District

South Central — Ames; Burlington

Taking in 27 counties, nearly 14,000 square miles and six media markets, the 3rd gives a fair picture of Iowa. Within its borders are relatively well-off urban and suburban areas, depressed rural counties and industrial cities, and scattered towns with high hopes for economic development. Although this area trended Democratic during the 1980s, district voters frequently split their tickets.

The largest city is Ames (Story County), home to Iowa State University (25,700 students). Coupled with the state Department of Transportation office, the university ensures stability for Ames in hard times. The city, just 25 miles north of Des Moines, is positioned for future growth.

Story County makes up nearly 15 percent of the 3rd's population and is essentially Democratic. Story voted narrowly for Republican Gov. Terry E. Branstad in 1990, but it went Democratic in the 1992 presidential and House elections.

Roughly one-quarter of the district's people live in the other four counties near Des Moines. Many of the voters here are independents; they backed all but one statewide Democratic candidate in 1990 but were divided in the 1992 presidential race.

Some of Iowa's most productive farms are in this area, but the number of Des Moines bedroom communities is growing, and some towns have developed independent economic bases. Newton, in Jasper County, is Maytag Corp.'s headquarters—where F. L. Maytag built the first mechanized washer in 1909. Pella, in Marion County, is home to the windowmaker Rolscreen. Tourists visit the Dutch-influenced town's restored Victorian center, known for its tulips and glockenspiel.

The 3rd's other population concentration is to the southeast, along the Mississippi River in Des Moines County (Burlington) and Lee County (Fort Madison). They account for 15 percent of the district's residents. These two old manufacturing cities, set in rolling hills and forests, have turned to tourism and riverboat gambling to spur the economy. Des Moines, Lee and Wapello counties all voted Democratic for president in 1992, though by narrower margins than in 1988.

The rest of the district's population is spread across Iowa's southern tier, bordering Missouri. Once forest and rough grazing land, much of this area was put into production during the 1970s.

Although hard times helped Democratic candidates here in the 1980s, voters moved back toward their traditional Republican roots in 1992. On the western side of the 3rd, several smaller, rural counties—including Page, Taylor, Union, Adams and Ringgold—helped the GOP House incumbent stave off a tough re-election challenge.

Only two southern counties show much potential for growth: Jefferson (Fairfield) and Henry (Mount Pleasant). Maharishi International University, which moved to Fairfield in 1972, helped lure several small software companies. Mount Pleasant got a boost when Wal-Mart Stores Inc. opened a regional distribution center there.

Election Returns

	3rd District	Democrat	Republican
1992	President*	120,495 (45.6%)	96,515 (36.6%)
	House	121,063 (47.1%)	125,931 (49.0%)

	3rd District	Democrat	Republican
1990	Senate	117,713 (58.9%)	81,994 (41.1%)
	Governor	83,821 (42.0%)	115,883 (58.0%)
1988	President	138,616 (56.5%)	106,573 (43.5%)
1986	Senate	66,513 (36.4%)	116,412 (63.6%)
	Governor	93,966 (50.2%)	93,249 (49.8%)

Vote for Perot was 47,028 (17.8%).

Demographics

Population 555,299

Percent change from 1980 14.4%

Land area 13,833 square miles

Population per square mile 40

Counties, 1990 population

Adams 4,866	Marshall 38,276
Appanoose 13,743	Monroe 8,114
Clarke 8,287	Page 16,870
Davis 8,312	Poweshiek 19,033
Decatur 8,338	Ringgold 5,420
Des Moines 42,614	Story 74,252
Henry 19,226	Taylor 7,114
Jasper 34,795	Union 12,750
Jefferson 16,310	Van Buren 7,676
Keokuk 11,624	Wapello 35,687
Lee 38,687	Warren 36,033
Lucas 9,070	Washington 19,612
Mahaska 21,522	Wayne 7,067
Marion 30,001	

Cities, 1990 population (10,000 or more)

Ames 47,198	Marshalltown 25,178
Burlington 27,208	Newton 14,789
Fort Madison 11,618	Oskaloosa 10,632
Indianola 11,340	Ottumwa 24,488
Keokuk 12,451	

Race and Hispanic origin

White 97.5%
Black 0.9%
American Indian, Eskimo, or Aleut. 0.2%
Asian or Pacific Islander 1.1%
Other 0.3%
Hispanic origin 0.8%

Ancestry

American 4.4%	Italian 1.5%
Czechoslovakian 1.2%	Norwegian 3.8%
Danish 1.5%	Polish 1.0%
Dutch 9.3%	Scotch Irish 3.1%
English 16.6%	Scottish 2.3%
French 4.0%	Swedish 4.5%
German 41.9%	Welsh 1.4%
Irish 19.2%	

Universities/colleges, 1990-1991 enrollment

Central University of Iowa, Pella 1,503
Graceland College, Lamoni 2,370
Grinnell College, Grinnell 1,278
Indian Hills Community College, Ottumwa 3,015

Iowa State University, Ames 25,738
Iowa Valley Community College, Marshalltown 2,344
Iowa Wesleyan College, Mount Pleasant 914
Maharishi International University, Fairfield 2,533
Simpson College, Indianola 1,735
Southeastern Community College, West Burlington 2,683
Southwestern Community College, Creston 1,150
William Penn College, Oskaloosa 737

Newspapers, total circulation (in all districts)

Burlington Hawk-Eye 17,394
Des Moines Register 193,358
Marshalltown Times-Republican 11,920
Omaha World Herald 221,762
Ottumwa Courier 18,012

Commercial television stations, affiliations

ADI: Des Moines (61%), Omaha (11%), Ottumwa-Kirksville (10%), Cedar Rapids-Waterloo-Dubuque (8%), Davenport-Rock Island-Moline (6%) and Quincy-Hannibal (4%)

KJMH, Burlington (Fox)
KYOU-TV, Ottumwa (None)

Cable television systems, total subscribers

Heritage Cablevision; Ames 10,700
Heritage Cablevision; Marshalltown 7,907
TCI Cablevision; Des Moines 80,450
Westmarc Cable; Burlington 10,128
Westmarc Cablevision; Ottumwa 9,354

Businesses and other major employers

Iowa State University; Ames 11,623
Maytag Corp./Hardwick Stove Co. Div.; Newton; washing machines 3,633
Rolscreen Co.; Pella; millwork 2,360
Monfort Inc.; Marshalltown; meat products 2,000
Fisher Controls Intl.; Marshalltown; metal products 2,000
Case Corp.; Burlington; construction machinery 1,300
Chemidyne Corp./Packers Sanitation Services; Mt. Pleasant; building services 1,300
Deere & Co.; Ottumwa; farm/garden machinery 1,276
Mary Greeley Medical Center; Ames 1,240
Vermeer Mfg. Co.; Pella; construction machinery 1,150
Mason Hanger-Silas Mason Co.; Middletown; ammunition 1,050
Excel Corp.; Ottumwa; meat products 1,050
City of Ames/Electric Utility; Ames 1,000
Burlington Medical Center; Burlington 980
State of Iowa/Transportation Dept.; Ames 950
Hy-Vee Food Stores Inc./Save U More Foods; Chariton; grocery stores 922
U.S. Veterans Affairs Dept.; Knoxville; psychiatric hospital 900
Wal-Mart Stores Inc.; Mt. Pleasant; warehousing 850
State of Iowa/Veterans Home; Marshalltown; nursing 815
Ottumwa Regional Health Center; Ottumwa 770
General Electric Co.; West Burlington; aircraft engines 750
Grinnell Mutual Reinsurance Co.; Grinnell; fire/marine/casualty insurance 685
Eaton Sheaffer Inc.; Fort Madison; office/art supplies 650
General Electric Co.; Burlington; switchgears 650
Marshalltown Medical Surgical Center; Marshalltown 640
United Technologies Corp.; Keokuk; rubber products 600

Burlington Northern Railroad Co.; West Burlington; railroads 600

Burlington Community School District; Burlington 600

Motorola Inc.; Mt. Pleasant; communications equipment 550

Eaton Corp./Transmission Div.; Shenandoah; motor vehicle parts 546

Grinnell College; Grinnell 530

McFarland Clinic; Ames; medical doctors 502

4th District

Southwest — Des Moines; Council Bluffs

Though the new 4th sprawls from central Iowa all the way west to the Missouri River, its anchor is Des Moines (Polk County), the region's commercial, financial and governmental center and home to Iowa's influential statewide newspaper, the *Des Moines Register*. Nearly 60 percent of the 4th's voters live in Polk County, a dominance that is apt to increase if current population trends continue through the 1990s. Polk grew nearly 8 percent in the 1980s, though the state lost residents.

Des Moines emerged fairly unscathed from the farm and manufacturing recessions that racked Iowa in the 1980s. The relative prosperity helped spawn the phrase "Golden Circle" to describe the towns and suburbs within a 50-mile radius of the city. The web of skywalks in downtown Des Moines, built during a $1 billion development spree during the 1980s, gives it a gleam of success.

Des Moines managed to flourish in part because of its white-collar employment base and its independence from agriculture. It is home to the state government and also is the nation's second-largest insurance center. About 60 insurance companies have headquarters or major offices in the city, led by Principal Financial Group. And Des Moines' role in the state's commerce grew as economies crumbled in the small towns that once offered medical care and other basic services.

Des Moines always has been more like Minneapolis than Chicago or Milwaukee: It is predominantly white, Protestant and middle class. Polk County's Democratic tradition has strengthened in recent years. Des Moines' prosperity has created a comfortable middle class that is largely missing disaffected white ethnics and go-go entrepreneurs—two groups that voted Republican in other parts of the country during the 1980s.

Polk has been more reliably Democratic than most parts of the country, supporting Walter F. Mondale in 1984, Michael S. Dukakis in 1988 and Bill Clinton in 1992. The Democratic House incumbent as usual trounced his opponent here in 1992.

This voting pattern and the city's size minimize the influence in the 4th of the western city of Council Bluffs (Pottawattamie County), a GOP stronghold. Built against bluffs, the city was once a bustling crossroads for three westward trails in the early 1800s and five railroads later met here. Today, many workers cross the Missouri River to work in Omaha in businesses lured by Nebraska's lower tax rates.

The 1980s farm crisis failed to shake the GOP grip on Pottawattamie and the rural counties surrounding it. In 1992, the incumbent House Democrat managed to capture just a slight edge in Pottawattamie, and it was also one of the few Iowa counties to give George Bush a solid victory in the 1992 presidential voting.

The farmers in Harrison and Shelby counties have been relatively prosperous, thanks to fertile soil. To the south and east, the land is rough and relatively dry, more suitable for grazing than farming.

Election Returns

	4th District	Democrat	Republican
1992	President*	117,863 (43.1%)	107,745 (39.4%)
	House	158,610 (61.6%)	94,045 (36.5%)
1990	Senate	113,724 (58.1%)	81,849 (41.9%)
	Governor	78,112 (41.3%)	111,089 (58.7%)
1988	President	131,550 (55.4%)	106,044 (44.6%)
1986	Senate	60,888 (36.5%)	105,722 (63.5%)
	Governor	80,908 (47.8%)	88,528 (52.2%)

Vote for Perot was 47,835 (17.5%).

Demographics

Population 555,276

Percent change from 1980 14.4%

Land area 7,499 square miles

Population per square mile 74

Counties, 1990 population

Adair 8,409	Madison 12,483
Audubon 7,334	Mills 13,202
Cass 15,128	Montgomery 12,076
Dallas 29,755	Polk 327,140
Fremont 8,226	Pottawattamie 82,628
Guthrie 10,935	Shelby 13,230
Harrison 14,730	

Cities, 1990 population (10,000 or more)

Ankeny 18,482	Urbandale 23,500
Council Bluffs 54,315	West Des Moines 31,702
Des Moines 193,187	

Race and Hispanic origin
White 95.3%
Black 2.8%
American Indian, Eskimo, or Aleut. 0.2%
Asian or Pacific Islander 1.2%
Other 0.5%
Hispanic origin 1.5%

Ancestry

American 3.7%	Italian 3.0%
Czechoslovakian 1.3%	Norwegian 3.9%
Danish 5.1%	Polish 1.3%
Dutch 5.4%	Scotch Irish 3.0%
English 17.1%	Scottish 2.3%
French 4.0%	Swedish 5.2%
German 42.4%	Welsh 1.4%
Irish 20.5%	

Universities/colleges, 1990-1991 enrollment
American Institute of Business, Des Moines 1,054
Des Moines Community College, Ankeny 10,553
Drake University, Des Moines 8,029
Faith Baptist Bible College, Ankeny 295
Grand View College, Des Moines 1,420
Iowa Methodist School of Nursing, Des Moines 205
Iowa Western Community College, Council Bluffs 3,288

National Education Center, West Des Moines 309
University of Osteopathic Medicine, Des Moines 1,180

Newspapers, total circulation (in all districts)
Council Bluffs Nonpareil 17,361
Des Moines Register 193,358
Omaha World Herald 221,762

Commercial television stations, affiliations
ADI: Omaha (56%) and Des Moines (44%)
    WOI-TV, Ames (ABC)
    KCCI-TV, Des Moines (CBS)
    KDSM-TV, Des Moines (Fox)
    WHO-TV, Des Moines (NBC)

Cable television systems, total subscribers
American Heritage Cablevision; Council Bluffs 15,000
TCI Cablevision; Des Moines 80,450

Military installations, 1991
Des Moines Intl. Airport Air Force Guard Station, Des Moines 333

Businesses and other major employers
State of Iowa/Human Services Dept.; Des Moines 7,000
Principal Mutual Life Insurance Co./Principal Financial Group; Des Moines; life insurance 5,200
Iowa Methodist Medical Center; Des Moines 3,300
Mercy Hospital & Medical Center; Des Moines 2,700
U.S. West Inc.; Des Moines; telephone communications 2,600
City of Des Moines; Des Moines 2,170
Meredith Corp.; Des Moines; publishing/periodicals 2,100
Monfort Inc.; Des Moines; meat products 2,000
Amco Insurance Co.; Des Moines; insurance services 1,750
Deere & Co.; Ankeny; farm/garden machinery 1,500
Amoco Oil Co.; Waukee; pipelines 1,300
Amoco Oil Co./Customer Service Center; West Des Moines; business services 1,300
Iowa Lutheran Hospital; Des Moines 1,250
Communications Data Services; Des Moines; advertising 1,200
Glenwood State Hospital & School; Glenwood; nursing 1,200
Pirelli Armstrong Tire Corp.; Des Moines; tires 1,100
Bridgestone/Firestone Inc.; Des Moines; tires 1,100
County of Polk; Des Moines 1,100
IASD Health Services Corp./Blue Cross of Iowa; Des Moines; medical service/health insurance 1,090
Woodward State Hospital-School; Woodward; nursing 1,069
Des Moines Register; Des Moines; newspapers 970
United Parcel Service Inc.; Des Moines; mail services 925
R. R. Donnelley & Sons Co.; Des Moines; commercial printing 900
Communications Data Services; Des Moines; advertising 900
Norwest Bank Iowa; Des Moines; commercial banks 892
Iowa Power Inc.; Des Moines; electric services 871
Broadlawns Medical Center; West Des Moines 860
Drake University; West Des Moines 845
State of Iowa/Public Safety Dept.; Des Moines 800
IBP Inc.; Council Bluffs; meat products 750
Employers Mutual Casualty Co.; Des Moines; fire/marine/casualty insurance 702
City of Des Moines/Intl. Airport; Des Moines; airport/services 700

IBP Inc.; Perry; meat products 700
U.S. Veterans Affairs Dept.; Des Moines; hospital 700
Oscar Mayer & Co. Inc.; Perry; meat products 685
Mercy Hospital; Council Bluffs 680
Pitt-Des Moines Inc.; Des Moines; special contractors 650
Kirke Van Orsdel Inc.; Des Moines; insurance services 650
Jennie Edmundson Memorial Hospital; Council Bluffs 650
T. L. Grantham & Assoc.; Des Moines; management/public relations 602
Sears Roebuck & Co.; Des Moines; warehousing 600
Super Valu Stores Inc.; Des Moines; grocery products 600
Douglas & Lomason Co.; Red Oak; farm/garden machinery 600
ConAgra Inc.; Council Bluffs; frozen food products 600
Des Moines General Hospital; Des Moines 594
Norwest Financial Services; Des Moines; credit institutions 575
Greyhound Lines Inc.; West Des Moines; bus service/management 549
State of Iowa/Agriculture Dept.; Des Moines 535
American Republic Insurance Co.; Des Moines; medical service/health insurance 501

5th District

Northwest — Sioux City; Fort Dodge

The 5th takes in nearly 18,000 square miles of fertile soil and gently undulating hills. The farms here are some of the nation's most productive, turning out impressive yields of corn, soybeans and hogs.

The bountiful land has allowed the region to remain more like the Iowa of old than any other part of the state. Virtually every town has a working grain elevator, and nearly every adult is involved in the farm-to-market agricultural network. Politically, Iowa's GOP tradition holds sway. The 5th is the only district in which registered Republicans outnumber Democrats; to win statewide, GOP candidates need lopsided margins here.

Yet even here, demographic and political change is evident. The area suffered dramatic population losses during the 1980s as many small-scale farmers sold their land to agribusiness operations. Each of the district's 30 counties lost population, and 18 lost more than 10 percent. In 1992, George Bush took 42 percent of the vote while Bill Clinton took 38 percent.

The smallest population loss was in Woodbury County (Sioux City), which is the district's largest, accounting for about 20 percent of the 5th's population. Once a meatpacking town, Sioux City has evolved into a more service-oriented center for a region that includes part of South Dakota and Nebraska. Some Sioux City businesses have moved across the river to take advantage of more favorable tax laws in South Dakota and Nebraska, but Woodbury County has sprouted numerous bedroom communities to house their employees—who prefer Iowa's schools and government services.

Politically, Sioux City has long leaned Republican. This pattern held during the 1980s, as the shift of voters to the Democrats on economic and peace issues was offset by the declining influence of labor. In 1992, Bush and GOP Sen. Charles E. Grassley both won Woodbury County, although Grassley's 3-to-1 margin was considerably larger than Bush's.

The district's only other significant population center is Fort Dodge (Webster County). The county is home to less than 10 percent of the 5th's voters—a figure that underscores the region's rural character. An industrial center near large gypsum mines, Fort Dodge emerged as a leader in veterinary pharmaceuticals in the 1980s. The city is in the heart of a region first settled by Irish Catholics. Webster and its heavily Catholic neighbor, Greene County, typically vote Democratic.

Iowa's playground of Spirit Lake and East and West Okoboji lakes (Dickinson County) attracts tourists, making it the rare Iowa county debating how fast and how much it should grow.

Elsewhere, county fairs are the annual highlight: Clay County's is the nation's second-largest. The September Tulipfest in conservative, Dutch-settled Orange City (Sioux County) is a must-attend event for GOP candidates.

Election Returns

	5th District	Democrat	Republican
1992	President*	99,112 (38.2%)	109,966 (42.4%)
	House	—	196,942 (100.0%)
1990	Senate	103,516 (52.9%)	92,319 (47.1%)
	Governor	67,675 (34.6%)	127,774 (65.4%)
1988	President	125,833 (51.5%)	118,492 (48.5%)
1986	Senate	58,232 (30.5%)	132,887 (69.5%)
	Governor	86,401 (43.5%)	112,381 (56.5%)

*Vote for Perot was 50,343 (19.4%).

Demographics

Population 555,457

Percent change from 1980 14.4%

Land area 17,801 square miles

Population per square mile 31

Counties, 1990 population

Boone 25,186	Ida 8,365
Buena Vista 19,965	Kossuth 18,591
Calhoun 11,508	Lyon 11,952
Carroll 21,423	Monona 10,034
Cherokee 14,098	O'Brien 15,444
Clay 17,585	Osceola 7,267
Crawford 16,775	Palo Alto 10,669
Dickinson 14,909	Plymouth 23,388
Emmet 11,569	Pocahontas 9,525
Franklin 11,364	Sac 12,324
Greene 10,045	Sioux 29,903
Hamilton 16,071	Webster 40,342
Hancock 12,638	Winnebago 12,122
Hardin 19,094	Woodbury 98,276
Humboldt 10,756	Wright 14,269

Cities, 1990 population (10,000 or more)

Boone 12,392	Sioux City 80,505
Fort Dodge 25,894	Spencer 11,066

Race and Hispanic origin

White 98.0%

Black 0.6%

American Indian, Eskimo, or Aleut. 0.4%

Asian or Pacific Islander 0.6%

Other 0.4%

Hispanic origin 0.9%

Ancestry

American 2.3%	German 54.3%
Czechoslovakian 1.4%	Irish 16.0%
Danish 4.3%	Norwegian 8.5%
Dutch 9.6%	Scotch Irish 1.9%
English 11.5%	Scottish 1.7%
French 3.7%	Swedish 6.3%

Universities/colleges, 1990-1991 enrollment

Briar Cliff College, Sioux City 1,122

Buena Vista College, Storm Lake 2,332

Dordt College, Sioux Center 1,054

Iowa Central Community College, Fort Dodge 2,224

Iowa Lakes Community College, Estherville 1,634

Morningside College, Sioux City 1,356

Northwest Iowa Tech College, Sheldon 521

Northwestern College, Orange City 1,064

Teikyo Westmar College, Le Mars 653

Waldorf College, Forest City 654

Western Iowa Tech College, Sioux City 1,678

Newspapers, total circulation (in all districts)

Des Moines Register 193,358

Fort Dodge Messenger 20,243

Mason City Globe Gazette 19,520

Omaha World Herald 221,762

Sioux City Journal 48,301

Sioux Falls Argus Leader 48,044

Webster City Freeman Journal 3,427

Worthington Daily Globe 13,758

Commercial television stations, affiliations

ADI: Sioux City (42%), Des Moines (35%), Rochester-Mason City-Austin (11%), Sioux Falls-Mitchell (6%), Omaha (4%) and Mankato (2%)

KCAU-TV, Sioux City (ABC)

KMEG, Sioux City (CBS)

KTIV, Sioux City (NBC)

Cable television systems, total subscribers

Sooland Cablecom Corp.; Sioux City 20,197

TCI of Heartlands; Fort Dodge 8,724

Military installations, 1991

Sioux City Municipal Airport Air Force Guard Station, Sergeant Bluff 283

Businesses and other major employers

Marian Health Center; Sioux City 1,536

White Consolidated Industries; Webster City; laundry equipment 1,500

Sioux City Community School District; Sioux City 1,400

St. Luke's Regional Medical Center; Sioux City 1,360

Long Lines Ltd./Pioneer Hardware; Sergeant Bluff; business services 1,200

John Morrell & Co. Inc.; Sioux City; meat products 1,100

Farmland Foods Inc.; Denison; meatpacking 1,000

Tyson Iowa Corp./Tyson Beef; Le Mars; beef products 950

Trinity Regional Hospital; Fort Dodge 823

Style Craft Inc.; Milford; furniture 800

Wilson Foods Corp.; Cherokee; meat products 623

Fleetguard Inc.; Lake Mills; industry machinery 550

K-Products Inc.; Orange City; hats/caps 550

Snap-On Tools Corp.; Algona; tool chests 540

Kansas

The farm remains the predominant symbol of Kansas. In its wide-open rural spaces are the fields that make Kansas the nation's top wheat-producing state and the ranges where millions of cattle graze.

But the Kansas of the 1990s is not the same place to which the storybook Dorothy returned after her trip to Oz. The small landholdings worked by numerous farmhands have been replaced, because of mechanization and the economies of scale in modern agriculture, by large farms—many owned by corporations instead of families—requiring fewer laborers.

Demographic changes have had a dramatic effect. All but a handful of rural counties in Kansas lost population between 1980 and 1990. Most endured net declines of 10 percent or more. As many of those who left the land before them, a number of rural migrants headed for Kansas' centers of industry, commerce, government and education—Wichita, Topeka, Lawrence—or for Johnson County's booming suburbs of Kansas City, Missouri. Of the state's leading population centers, only Kansas City, Kansas, an aging industrial hub, saw its population decrease during the 1980s.

As a result, the Kansas constituency is much more urban and suburban and less rural than ever. The five largest of Kansas' 105 counties—Sedgwick (Wichita), Johnson (Overland Park), Wyandotte (Kansas City), Shawnee (Topeka) and Douglas (Lawrence)—make up nearly half the state's population.

Many of those who left the land, however, also left the state. This cost Kansas not only in human capital, but also in political clout.

At the height of its farm labor days in the late 19th and early 20th centuries, Kansas had eight members in the House. As late as 1962, there were six. But that year, Kansas lost a seat. The result was the merger of two western Kansas constituencies into the sprawling 1st District. As rural population continued to decline, the "Big 1st" grew to absorb about two-thirds of the state's land area.

The state held at five members for three decades. But Kansas' 5 percent population increase in the 1980s—roughly half the national growth rate—cost it another seat in 1990 reapportionment. The state Legislature thus needed to redraw the state's House district map for four members. The decision by the 5th District Republican member not to run for re-election in 1990 made the outcome of redistricting practically inevitable. With other Kansas incumbents—two Republicans and two Democrats—planning to run in 1992, the odd-man-out was the one-term Republican successor to the 5th District.

Although quibbling over the political destinies of just three counties delayed passage of a redistricting map until May 1992, the plan stuck to the basic script. The 5th District, mainly in southeast Kansas, was divided three ways. Most of the district's constituents were placed either in the 2nd District or in the 4th, with a small portion going to the 1st. The GOP incumbent from the 5th ran and lost his party's primary for the 4th District in 1992.

In 1992, the two GOP and two Democrat House incumbents all won re-election by easy margins. George Bush won the state with 39 percent of the vote to Bill Clinton's 34 percent and Ross Perot's 27 percent. Republican Bob Dole won a fifth-term in the Senate, securing his position as Minority Leader.

Table 1 Population

District	Population	Population under 18	Voting-age population	Median age
1	619,370	166,641	452,729	34.6
2	619,391	161,234	458,157	32.5
3	619,439	163,606	455,833	31.7
4	619,374	170,133	449,241	32.9
State	2,477,574	661,614	1,815,960	32.9

Table 2 Voting-Age Persons

District	White*	Black*	American Indian, Eskimo, or Aleut*	Asian or Pacific Islander*	Other*	Hispanic*	Male*	Female*
1	95.1%	1.3%	0.4%	0.7%	2.6%	4.1%	48.1%	51.9%
2	90.9	5.8	1.0	1.1	1.2	2.6	49.3	50.7
3	88.5	7.9	0.7	1.6	1.2	2.9	47.4	52.6
4	90.2	5.8	1.1	1.4	1.5	3.0	47.9	52.1
State	91.2	5.2	0.8	1.2	1.6	3.1	48.2	51.8

*As percent of voting-age population.

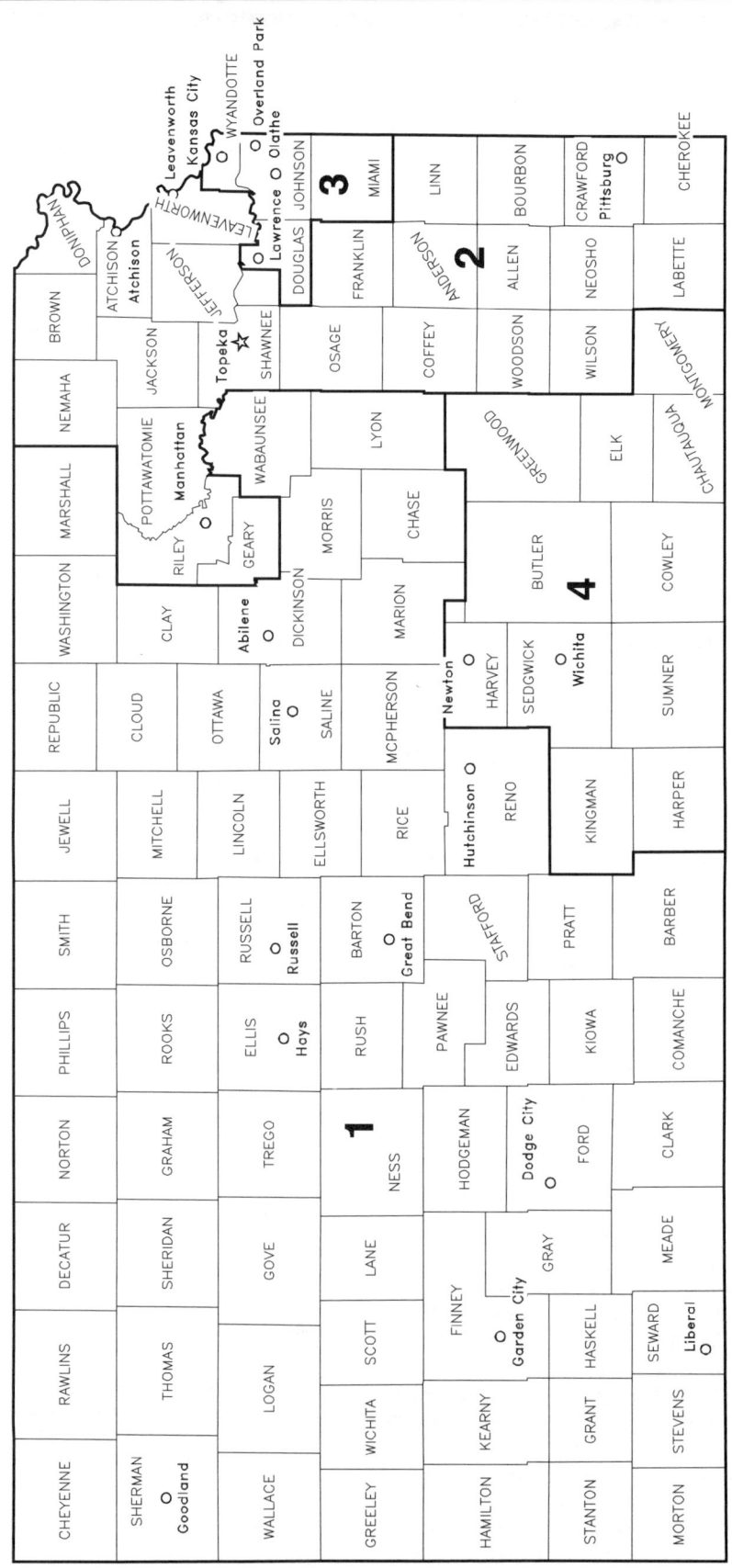

Table 3   Voting-Age Persons by Age Groups

District	18-24*	25-44*	45-54*	55-64*	65 and over*
1	12.0%	38.9%	12.9%	12.7%	23.6%
2	16.0	41.1	12.5	11.1	19.3
3	15.4	46.8	13.4	10.3	14.0
4	12.6	43.8	13.1	11.9	18.6
State	14.0	42.7	13.0	11.5	18.9

*As percent of voting-age population.

Table 4   Income and Occupation

District	Median family income	Families in poverty	White collar*	Blue collar*	Service*	Farm*
1	$28,624	9.0%	45.8%	28.5%	15.1%	10.6%
2	30,340	9.8	53.7	26.4	15.4	4.5
3	41,605	6.4	68.0	19.7	11.2	1.1
4	34,210	8.2	56.3	28.6	12.5	2.6
State	32,966	8.3	56.3	25.7	13.5	4.6

*As percent of employed persons age 16 and over.

Table 5   Education: School Years Completed

District	Less than grade 9*	Grades 9-12 no diploma*	High school diploma*	College bachelor's degree or higher*
1	10.7%	11.4%	35.2%	15.2%
2	8.3	11.0	36.7	18.4
3	4.9	9.2	26.4	31.5
4	7.0	12.4	33.0	19.6
State	7.7	11.0	32.8	21.1

*As percent of persons age 25 and over.

Table 6   Housing and Residential Patterns

District	Owner occupied	Renter occupied	Urban	Rural
1	71.2%	28.8%	48.7%	51.3%
2	67.7	32.3	59.2	40.8
3	65.7	34.3	92.8	7.2
4	67.0	33.0	75.8	24.2
State	67.9	32.1	69.1	30.9

1st District

Rural West — Salina; Hutchinson; Dodge City

Sprawling across 66 counties and more than two-thirds of Kansas' land area, the "Big 1st" is larger than many eastern states. This is wheat-growing and cattle-raising country, dotted with small cities (none with more than 42,300 residents) and otherwise sparsely populated.

While much of the nation was enjoying an economic boom during the 1980s, western Kansas endured a period of "farm crisis" along with the typical vagaries of drought and freeze. These factors, along with continuing farm mechanization and concentration of land ownership, exacerbated population decline: Most counties in the 1st lost people in the 1980s.

But those who want to work in western Kansas can. Unemployment is extraordinarily low: In December 1992, several western counties had jobless rates below 2 percent.

1992, a year of GOP trial nationwide, proved the strength of the 1st's rural Republican voting traditions. George Bush finished first in all but one 1st District county. Bill Clinton finished third behind Bush and Ross Perot in 47 of the 66 counties. (Perot carried Wabaunsee and Morris counties in the eastern end of the 1st.) Republicans Sen. Bob Dole, a native of the 1st, and Rep. Pat Roberts swept the district.

The two largest population centers are in the 1st's eastern reaches. Salina (Saline County) is a traditional farm-market town, but it has an industrial element. Beech Aircraft has a factory here; food products, car batteries and light bulbs are also produced. Not far east is Abilene (Dickinson County), site of Dwight D. Eisenhower's burial place and his presidential library.

Industry in Hutchinson (Reno County) is largely farm- and food-related. Located 54 miles northwest of Wichita, Hutchinson is the site of the annual Kansas State Fair. The city of McPherson is nearby to the north; Emporia is at the district's eastern edge.

In recent years, the nation's meatpacking industry has dispersed from big-city stockyards to smaller towns closer to the Midwest's cattle ranches. Such southwest Kansas locales as Garden City and Dodge City have benefited from the trend and bucked Kansas' population slump. Finney County (Garden City) had the state's largest population increase (32 percent) during the 1980s, a boost fueled by Mexican and Asian immigrants who came to work in the huge IBP and Monfort beef-processing plants.

An Excel beef plant is the heart of Dodge City's economy. But the town also relies on a tourist trade based on its "Wild West" history. At the district's western edge is a sparsely populated rural region that was one of the strongest areas in the nation for Bush in 1992; he pulled down 64 percent in Wallace County, along the Colorado border.

At the district's center is Russell, Dole's hometown. But just west is Ellis County: Populated largely by farmers of German and Russian extraction, Ellis developed a Democratic habit that is abetted by Fort Hays State University's academic community. It was the only 1st District county that Clinton carried—with just 37 percent.

Election Returns

	1st District	Democrat	Republican
1992	President*	81,526 (28.1%)	123,019 (42.4%)
	House	83,620 (29.3%)	194,912 (68.3%)
1990	Senate	52,352 (22.9%)	176,205 (77.1%)
	Governor	97,769 (47.0%)	110,066 (53.0%)
1988	President	105,303 (39.4%)	161,817 (60.6%)
1986	Senate	77,901 (30.5%)	177,320 (69.5%)
	Governor	102,780 (39.8%)	155,224 (60.2%)

*Vote for Perot was 85,550 (29.5%).

Demographics

Population 619,370

Percent change from 1980 31.2%

Land area 56,245 square miles

Population per square mile 11

Counties, 1990 population

Barber 5,874	Meade 4,247
Barton 29,382	Mitchell 7,203
Chase 3,021	Morris 6,198
Cheyenne 3,243	Morton 3,480
Clark 2,418	Ness 4,033
Clay 9,158	Norton 5,947
Cloud 11,023	Osborne 4,867
Comanche 2,313	Ottawa 5,634
Decatur 4,021	Pawnee 7,555
Dickinson 18,958	Phillips 6,590
Edwards 3,787	Pratt 9,702
Ellis 26,004	Rawlins 3,404
Ellsworth 6,586	Reno 62,389
Finney 33,070	Republic 6,482
Ford 27,463	Rice 10,610
Gove 3,231	Rooks 6,039
Graham 3,543	Rush 3,842
Grant 7,159	Russell 7,835
Gray 5,396	Saline 49,301
Greeley 1,774	Scott 5,289
Hamilton 2,388	Seward 18,743
Haskell 3,886	Sheridan 3,043
Hodgeman 2,177	Sherman 6,926
Jewell 4,251	Smith 5,078
Kearny 4,027	Stafford 5,365
Kiowa 3,660	Stanton 2,333
Lane 2,375	Stevens 5,048
Lincoln 3,653	Thomas 8,258
Logan 3,081	Trego 3,694
Lyon 34,732	Wabaunsee 6,603
Marion (pt.) 11,353	Wallace 1,821
Marshall 11,705	Washington 7,073
McPherson 27,268	Wichita 2,758

Cities, 1990 population (10,000 or more)

Dodge City 21,129	Hutchinson 39,308
Emporia 25,512	Liberal 16,573
Garden City 24,097	McPherson 12,422
Great Bend 15,427	Salina 42,303
Hays 17,767	

Race and Hispanic origin

White 94.2%
Black 1.3%
American Indian, Eskimo, or Aleut. 0.4%
Asian or Pacific Islander 0.8%
Other 3.2%
Hispanic origin 5.2%

Ancestry

American 4.7%	German 45.2%
Czechoslovakian 2.0%	Irish 14.4%
Dutch 4.4%	Scotch Irish 2.7%
English 15.3%	Scottish 2.0%
French 4.5%	Swedish 4.2%

Universities/colleges, 1990-1991 enrollment

Barton City Community College, Great Bend 3,224
Bethany College, Lindsborg 653
Central College, McPherson 238
Cloud City Community College, Concordia 2,337
Colby Community College, Colby 2,163
Dodge City Community College, Dodge City 2,428
Emporia State University, Emporia 6,077
Fort Hays State University, Hays 5,500
Garden City Community College, Garden City 2,198
Hutchinson Community College, Hutchinson 3,888
Kansas Wesleyan University, Salina 801
McPherson College, McPherson 464
Pratt Community College, Pratt 1,218
St. Mary of the Plains College, Dodge City 1,071
Seward County Community College, Liberal 1,490
Sterling College, Sterling 495
Tabor College, Hillsboro 432

Newspapers, total circulation (in all districts)

Emporia Gazette 9,971
Hutchinson News 37,846
Salina Journal 29,288
Topeka Capital Journal 65,944
Wichita Eagle 117,878

Commercial television stations, affiliations

ADI: Wichita-Hutchinson (84%), Lincoln-Hastings-Kearney (9%) and Topeka (7%)
KLBY, Colby (ABC)
KBSD-TV, Ensign (CBS)
KSNG, Garden City (NBC)
KUPK-TV, Garden City (ABC)
KBSL-TV, Goodland (CBS)
KSNC, Great Bend (NBC)
KBSH-TV, Hays (CBS)
KAAS-TV, Salina (None)
WIBW-TV, Topeka (CBS)
KWCH-TV, Wichita (CBS)
KSNK, McCook (NBC)

Cable television systems, total subscribers

Cablevision of Emporia; Emporia 9,100
Century Cable; Liberal 5,270
Hays Cable TV Co.; Hays 6,767
Multimedia Cablevision Inc.; Great Bend 5,713
TCI of Kansas; Dodge City 5,700
TCI of Kansas; Garden City 7,500
TCI of Kansas; Hutchinson 12,000
TCI of Kansas; Salina 15,000

Businesses and other major employers

IBP Inc.; Holcomb; beef products 3,500
Idle Wild Foods Inc./Supreme Feeders; Liberal; meat products 1,975
IBP Inc./Iowa Beef Packers; Emporia; beef products 1,800
Excel Corp.; Dodge City; beef/grocery products 1,800
Schwans Sales Enterprises Inc.; Salina; frozen foods 1,200
Monfort Inc.; Garden City; beef products 1,200
Eaton Corp./Hydraulics Div.; Hutchinson; industrial machinery 1,130
Eaton Corp./Cessna Fluid Power Div.; Hutchinson; aircraft/parts 1,100
Larned State Hospital; Larned 909
Emporia State University; Emporia 900
Hutchinson Hospital Corp.; Hutchinson 809
Asbury-Salina Regional Medical Center; Salina 709
Interstate Brands Corp./Dolly Madison; Emporia; bakery products 700
Dillon Companies Inc.; Hutchinson; supermarkets/milk processing 700

North American Philips Corp.; Salina; electric lighting 660
Unified School District; Garden City 600
Exide Corp.; Salina; batteries 570
Fort Hays State University; Hays 531
Hutchinson Community College; Hutchinson 525

2nd District

East — Topeka; Leavenworth; Pittsburg

The 25-county 2nd sweeps from Kansas' eastern corners, touching Nebraska to the north and Oklahoma to the south and making up most of Kansas' border with Missouri in between. Two-thirds of the residents live in or north of Shawnee County. Topeka (the state capital and the third-biggest city in Kansas, with nearly 120,000 residents), Leavenworth and Manhattan are here. The small city of Pittsburg, with 17,800 residents, is the biggest town in the 2nd's southern reaches.

The 2nd has a conservative bent, but Democrat Rep. Jim Slattery won solidly in 1992 even though redistricting gave him much new turf in the district's southern end. George Bush, who won the 2nd with 53 percent of the vote in 1988, finished first in 1992, but just barely. He did best in 1992 in the district's more rural northern and south-central regions; even there, he topped 40 percent in just four counties. Bill Clinton ran first in the urbanized north-central area influenced by Topeka and Kansas City, Mo., and in the blue-collar, southeast corner of Kansas. The 2nd showed an independent streak: Ross Perot topped 30 percent in 13 district counties and won two.

The 11 northern counties that make up Slattery's longtime base include numerous state employees and a scattering of minority-group concentrations. The coal mines and oil fields of southeastern Kansas long ago drew southern Democrats and eastern European immigrants (because of whom this hilly area was nicknamed "the Balkans"). Although these resource industries faded, there is enough remaining manufacturing to sustain a blue-collar Democratic vote.

State government is Topeka's largest employer. Medical centers, including the Menninger Foundation's psychiatric facilities, employ thousands. The economy includes an industrial component. A Goodyear tire factory and the Atchison, Topeka & Santa Fe Railway are leading employers.

To the west is Manhattan with Kansas State University (21,000 students); this agriculture-oriented school gives Riley County a conservative tone that is reinforced by the military community at Fort Riley, which sprawls into Geary County and is home to the Army's 1st Infantry Division.

Geary has a substantial minority population—nearly a quarter is black, but the county, like neighboring Riley, votes consistently Republican for higher offices.

At the district's eastern edge is Leavenworth, home to the well-known federal penitentiary and the fort that hosts the Army's Command and General Staff College. Leavenworth County has been drawn into the suburban sphere of Kansas City, Mo.; its population grew 17 percent in the 1980s.

To the north and south of Topeka is mainly farmland where soybeans are grown, hogs are raised and mostly Republican votes are cast. The two counties Slattery lost in 1992—Coffey and Linn—are in the south-central region. Most of the rural counties have suffered the kind of population slump seen in the western 1st District.

Election Returns

	2nd District	Democrat	Republican
1992	President*	98,527 (36.1%)	98,999 (36.2%)
	House	151,019 (56.2%)	109,801 (40.8%)
1990	Senate	51,702 (26.9%)	140,810 (73.1%)
	Governor	99,432 (56.7%)	75,904 (43.3%)
1988	President	103,512 (45.9%)	121,910 (54.1%)
1986	Senate	62,529 (31.8%)	134,103 (68.2%)
	Governor	98,606 (49.5%)	100,555 (50.5%)

Vote for Perot was 75,600 (27.7%).

Demographics

Population 619,391

Percent change from 1980 31.0%

Land area 13,975 square miles

Population per square mile 44

Counties, 1990 population

Allen 14,638	Jefferson 15,905
Anderson 7,803	Labette 23,693
Atchison 16,932	Leavenworth 64,371
Bourbon 14,966	Linn 8,254
Brown 11,128	Nemaha 10,446
Cherokee 21,374	Neosho 17,035
Coffey 8,404	Osage 15,248
Crawford 35,568	Pottawatomie 16,128
Doniphan 8,134	Riley 67,139
Douglas (pt.) 2,872	Shawnee 160,976
Franklin 21,994	Wilson 10,289
Geary 30,453	Woodson 4,116
Jackson 11,525	

Cities, 1990 population (10,000 or more)

Atchison 10,656	Manhattan 37,712
Fort Riley North CDP 12,848	Ottawa 10,667
	Parsons 11,924
Junction City 20,604	Pittsburg 17,775
Leavenworth 38,495	Topeka 119,883

Race and Hispanic origin

White 90.1%
Black 6.3%
American Indian, Eskimo, or Aleut. 1.2%
Asian or Pacific Islander 1.1%
Other 1.3%
Hispanic origin 3.0%

Ancestry

American 5.3%	Italian 2.1%
Dutch 3.9%	Polish 1.4%
English 15.9%	Scotch Irish 3.0%
French 4.5%	Scottish 2.2%
German 38.6%	Swedish 3.2%
Irish 18.0%	Welsh 1.1%

Universities/colleges, 1990-1991 enrollment

Allen County Community College, Iola 1,458
Benedictine College, Atchison 795
Fort Scott Community College, Fort Scott 1,766
Highland Community College, Highland 1,744

Kansas State University, Manhattan 21,137
Labette Community College, Parsons 2,465
Manhattan Christian College, Manhattan 205
Neosho County Community College, Chanute 1,215
Ottawa University, Ottawa 536
Pittsburg State University, Pittsburg 5,918
St. Mary College, Leavenworth 990
Washburn University of Topeka, Topeka 6,492

Newspapers, total circulation (in all districts)
Joplin Globe 36,407
Junction City Daily Union 6,973
Kansas City Star/Times 283,061
Lawrence Journal World 18,061
Leavenworth Times 9,160
Manhattan Mercury 11,918
St. Joseph News-Press Gazette 41,417
Topeka Capital Journal 65,944

Commercial television stations, affiliations
ADI: Topeka (45%), Joplin-Pittsburg (33%) and Kansas City (23%)
   KOAM-TV, Pittsburg (CBS)
   KSNT, Topeka (NBC)
   KTKA-TV, Topeka (ABC)

Cable television systems, total subscribers
American Cablevision; Leavenworth 12,090
Douglas Cable Communications; Topeka 6,343
Pittsburg Cable TV; Pittsburg 6,463
TCI of Kansas; Junction City 7,658
TCI of Kansas; Manhattan 14,232
TCI of Kansas; Topeka 37,000

Military installations, 1991
Fort Riley (Army), Junction City 18,611
Fort Leavenworth (Army), Leavenworth 7,522
Forbes Field Air Force Guard Station, Pauline 382

Businesses and other major employers
Kansas State University; Manhattan 5,000
Goodyear Tire & Rubber Co.; Topeka; tires 2,000
Blue Cross/Blue Shield of Kansas; Topeka; medical
  service/insurance 1,600
Day & Zimmermann Inc./Kansas Army Ammunition Plant;
  Parsons; ordnance/accessories 1,500
State of Kansas/Revenue Dept.; Topeka 1,500
St. Francis Hospital & Medical Center; Topeka 1,363
Southwestern Bell Telephone Co.; Topeka; telephone commu-
  nications 1,300
U.S. Veterans Affairs Dept.; Topeka; hospital 1,300
Stormont-Vail Regional Medical Center; Topeka 1,300
Menninger Foundation Inc.; Topeka; psychiatric hospital
  1,269
American Yearbook Co. Inc./Jostens; Topeka; book
  publishing/printing 1,200
Washburn University of Topeka; Topeka 1,166
Wolf Creek Nuclear Operation Corp.; Burlington; electric
  services 1,088
Hallmark Cards Inc.; Topeka; greeting cards 1,000
U.S. Veterans Affairs Dept.; Leavenworth; supply service
  1,000
Kansas Air National Guard; Topeka 956
State of Kansas/Admin. Dept.; Topeka 930
State of Kansas/Human Resources Dept.; Topeka; job train-
ing 900
Kansas Neurological Institute; Topeka; residential care 848
Superior Industries Intl./Pittsburg Plant; Pittsburg; foundry
  800
Hallmark Cards Inc.; Leavenworth; paper products 700
Payless Shoesource Inc.; Topeka; shoe stores 700
Pittsburg State University; Pittsburg 644
Atchison Casting Corp.; Atchison; foundry 643
National Mills; Pittsburg; textile finishing 600
Security Benefit Life Insurance Co; Topeka; life insurance
  600
McBiz Ltd.; Topeka; misc. investing 600
Frito-Lay Inc.; Topeka; food products 580
Parsons State Hospital; Parsons; nursing 563
Mt. Carmel Medical Center Inc.; Pittsburg 548
Kansas Power & Light Co. Inc.; Topeka; utility services 525
State of Kansas/Lansing Correctional Facility; Lansing 520
Stauffer Communications Inc.; Topeka; newspapers 509

3rd District
Kansas City Region — Overland Park; Lawrence

The 3rd, bordering Missouri in eastern Kansas, is not like the state's other districts. Geographically compact, it is almost entirely within the metropolitan sphere of Kansas City, Mo. Its population is mainly in the graceful suburbs of Johnson County, in the grittier urban environs of Kansas City, Kan., and in Lawrence (home to the University of Kansas and its 29,000 students).

There are sharp contrasts within the 3rd. Non-Hispanic whites make up more than 90 percent of Johnson County's population. But more than a third of the residents in Kansas City (in neighboring Wyandotte County) are black or Hispanic. The 1990 census reported a poverty rate in Johnson County of 3.6 percent; Wyandotte's rate was nearly five times higher.

Johnson County, with more than 350,000 people, dominates the 3rd; its strong Republican lean usually tips the district to GOP candidates. But Wyandotte County sometimes provides a counterbalance that gives Democrats a fighting chance. The 1992 campaign, in which Bill Clinton scored a rare Democratic win over George Bush in the 3rd, was illustrative. Bush won Johnson (though with 44 percent, nearly 20 percentage points below his 1988 figure). Clinton took Wyandotte with 55 percent, by far his best showing in Kansas; Bush's 20 percent put him in third, behind Ross Perot, who won nearly a quarter of the 3rd's vote overall.

Johnson County has been booming since the 1960s. The growth has turned Overland Park into a satellite city with more than 110,000 residents. Numerous companies are based in Johnson, which bills itself as "Executive Country." Westwood is home to U.S. Sprint. Residential growth has spread to exurban areas west of Overland Park: Olathe, the county seat, has more than 63,000 residents. Lenexa, a farm town of 2,400 in 1960, is now a city of 34,000.

Bordering to the north is Wyandotte County and Kansas City. Overshadowed by its namesake across the Missouri River, Kansas City, Kan., is an industrial town that has had its share of Rust Belt blues due to factory closures and the long-term decline of urban stockyards. But Kansas City maintains a large industrial base and has attracted some growth in its biotechnology sector. Successful efforts by Kansans in Congress to place a new federal courthouse here and to transfer a regional Housing and Urban Development office from Kansas City, Mo., have provided a boost.

To the west, the 3rd takes in Lawrence and most of Douglas County. The county's eastern portions along state Route 10 are becoming increasingly suburban. University-centered Lawrence has some liberal activists, but the outlying farm areas lean Republican. Bush in 1988 carried Douglas, but with just 50 percent; the county swung to Clinton in 1992 by 46 percent to 31 percent. Meyers carried Douglas narrowly.

At the district's southern end is Miami County, which is lightly populated and has a Republican tilt, though that has been tempered by some recent economic troubles. Clinton narrowly won it in 1992.

Election Returns

	3rd District	Democrat	Republican
1992	President*	116,729 (38.1%)	114,220 (37.3%)
	House	110,071 (37.6%)	169,929 (58.0%)
1990	Senate	52,207 (30.7%)	117,685 (69.3%)
	Governor	85,070 (55.6%)	67,811 (44.4%)
1988	President	113,409 (45.7%)	134,998 (54.3%)
1986	Senate	45,231 (27.1%)	121,747 (72.9%)
	Governor	98,164 (55.9%)	77,598 (44.1%)

*Vote for Perot was 75,608 (24.7%).

Demographics

Population 619,439

Percent change from 1980 31.1%

Land area 1,551 square miles

Population per square mile 399

Counties, 1990 population

Douglas (pt.) 78,926	Miami 23,466
Johnson 355,054	Wyandotte 161,993

Cities, 1990 population (10,000 or more)

Kansas City 149,767	Olathe 63,352
Lawrence 65,608	Overland Park 111,790
Leawood 19,693	Prairie Village 23,186
Lenexa 34,034	Shawnee 37,993
Merriam 11,821	

Race and Hispanic origin

White 87.2%
Black 8.9%
American Indian, Eskimo, or Aleut. 0.7%
Asian or Pacific Islander 1.7%
Other 1.5%
Hispanic origin 3.3%

Ancestry

American 3.8%	Norwegian 1.2%
Dutch 3.3%	Polish 2.5%
English 17.3%	Russian 1.1%
French 4.3%	Scotch Irish 3.1%
German 35.2%	Scottish 2.7%
Irish 19.7%	Swedish 3.1%
Italian 2.8%	Welsh 1.3%

Universities/colleges, 1990-1991 enrollment

Baker University, Baldwin City   1,367
Donnelly College, Kansas City   394
Haskell Indian Junior College, Lawrence   831
Johnson County Community College, Overland Park   13,744
Kansas City Community College, Kansas City   4,990
Mid-America Nazarene College, Olathe   1,243
Ottawa University-Kansas City, Overland Park   334
University of Kansas, Lawrence   26,436
University of Kansas Medical Center, Kansas City   2,473

Newspapers, total circulation (in all districts)

Kansas City Star/Times   283,061
Lawrence Journal World   18,061
Olathe Daily News   7,915
Topeka Capital Journal   65,944

Commercial television stations, affiliations

ADI: Kansas City (100%)
   KMCI, Lawrence (None)

Cable television systems, total subscribers

American Cablevision; Kansas City   27,359
American Cablevision; Kansas City (north)   20,050
Jones Intercable Inc.; Olathe   14,591
Sunflower Cablevision; Lawrence   21,584
Telecable of Overland Park; Overland Park   73,808

Businesses and other major employers

University of Kansas; Lawrence   8,000
University of Kansas Medical Center; Kansas City   5,300
General Motors Corp.; Kansas City; motor vehicles   2,500
County of Johnson; Olathe   2,100
Cargill Inc./Nutrena Feed Div.; Kansas City; grain mill products   2,000
King Radio Corp./Bendix; Olathe; search/navigation equipment   1,500
Shawnee Mission Medical Center; Shawnee Mission   1,443
J. C. Penney Co. Inc.; Shawnee Mission; warehousing   1,200
Yellow Freight System Inc.; Shawnee Mission; trucking services   1,100
Bethany Medical Center; Kansas City   1,043
Atchison, Topeka & Santa Fe; Kansas City; railroad/trucking facilities   1,000
Hallmark Cards Inc.; Lawrence; greeting cards   1,000
Johnson County Community College; Shawnee Mission   1,000
Board of Public Utilities; Kansas City; utility services   900
Associated Wholesale Grocers; Kansas City; grocery products   900
United Telephone Co. of Kansas; Shawnee Mission; telephone communications   896
Kansas City Community College; Kansas City   850
Owens-Corning Fiberglas Corp.; Kansas City; building materials   800
Olathe Medical Center Inc.; Olathe   800
Humana Inc./Humana Hospital-Overland Park; Shawnee Mission   800
City of Kansas City; Kansas City   800
Sunflower Racing Inc./The Woodlands; Kansas City; commercial sports   800
Pritchard Corp.; Shawnee Mission; engineering services   750
Hercules Inc./Sunflower Army Ammunition Plant; De Soto; ordnance/chemical products   704

United Telecommunications; Shawnee Mission; telephone communications 700

Certainteed Corp.; Kansas City; mineral products 700

Colgate-Palmolive Co.; Kansas City; soaps/cleaners 675

Osawatomie State Hospital; Osawatomie 639

United Telephone Co. of Kansas; Gardner; telephone communications 600

Sunshine Biscuits Inc.; Kansas City; bakery products 600

King Radio Corp./Bendix; Lawrence; communications equipment 600

Lawrence Memorial Hospital; Lawrence 569

Student Loan Marketing Assn.; Lawrence; federal credit 550

Home Office Reference Lab Inc.; Shawnee Mission; medical/dental labs 550

Metmor Financial Inc.; Shawnee Mission; mortgage bankers 540

Employers Reinsurance Corp.; Shawnee Mission; fire/marine/casualty insurance 535

Lee Apparel Co. Inc.; Shawnee Mission; jeans/outerwear 526

Black & Veatch; Shawnee Mission; engineering/architectural services 525

4th District

South Central — Wichita

The 4th takes in 11 whole counties (and a corner of Marion County) in south-central Kansas. But the district is dominated by Kansas' largest city, Wichita (Sedgwick County). Sedgwick provides about two-thirds of the district's population; Wichita alone, with more than 300,000 residents, makes up nearly half.

A center for military, commercial and general aviation aircraft production, Wichita has a large number of blue-collar whites with roots in Oklahoma, Texas and elsewhere in the South. Blacks and Hispanics make up about 16 percent of Wichita's population, a modest proportion by big-city standards but huge compared with the rest of the 4th.

The Democratic traditions of the district's southern whites and the strong partisan affiliation of minority voters has boosted centrist Democratic candidates for statewide office. But with its overall conservative tone, the 4th is not a "Democratic" district.

George Bush took 40 percent of the 4th's vote in 1992, yet easily defeated Bill Clinton, carrying all 11 counties. Clinton was second in Sedgwick, but ran third behind Ross Perot in all but three other counties.

Democrat Dan Glickman's close 1992 re-election exposed a divide in the 4th. He carried the seven western counties (including Sedgwick), most of which he had long represented. But he lost the four easternmost counties in a mainly rural region that was added to the 4th in 1992 redistricting.

While many industrial cities struggled during the 1980s, Wichita rode the wings of its aviation industry. The decade's big growth in defense spending boosted Boeing's military aircraft lines in Wichita; the national business boom aided Learjet, Cessna and Beech, civilian plane-builders affiliated with larger companies but based in Wichita.

The decline in defense spending is creating local concerns not only about the aviation industry but also the future of McConnell Air Force Base, site of a B-1 bomber fleet. The early 1990s recession and the downward spiral of the nation's passenger airlines have already rocked aviation's commercial side. Once

rock-solid, Boeing announced in February 1993 that it planned to cut its Wichita work force by about 30 percent.

The city is hardly a one-industry town. The Coleman recreation equipment company and the Pizza Hut restaurant chain are headquartered here, as is Koch Industries, a leader in development of southern Kansas' oil and gas resources. Wichita State University (16,100 students) is also a major employer.

Wichita has developed a growing suburbia. Derby, a few miles south on Kansas 15, has nearly 15,000 residents, almost double its population 20 years ago. There has been some spillover into Butler County (El Dorado).

Much of the rest of the 4th (including rural parts of Sedgwick) is farmland. Sumner County, on the Oklahoma border, is Kansas' leading wheat-growing county; that crop is also important to Harper and Kingman counties to the west. Cattle graze in sparsely populated Greenwood, Elk and Chautauqua counties to the east.

Election Returns

		Democrat	Republican
	4th District		
1992	President*	93,652 (33.1%)	113,713 (40.2%)
	House †	143,671 (51.7%)	117,070 (42.1%)
1990	Senate	51,228 (26.3%)	143,903 (73.7%)
	Governor	98,316 (55.2%)	79,806 (44.8%)
1988	President	100,400 (42.6%)	135,322 (57.4%)
1986	Senate	61,001 (29.8%)	143,730 (70.2%)
	Governor	104,786 (50.5%)	102,888 (49.5%)

Vote for Perot was 75,600 (26.7%).   †*Independent/other is greater than 5%.*

Demographics

Population 619,374

Percent change from 1980 30.9%

Land area 10,052 square miles

Population per square mile 62

Counties, 1990 population

Butler 50,580	Harvey 31,028
Chautauqua 4,407	Kingman 8,292
Cowley 36,915	Marion (pt.) 1,535
Elk 3,327	Montgomery 38,816
Greenwood 7,847	Sedgwick 403,662
Harper 7,124	Sumner 25,841

Cities, 1990 population (10,000 or more)

Arkansas City 12,762	Newton 16,700
Coffeyville 12,917	Wichita 304,011
Derby 14,699	Winfield 11,931
El Dorado 11,504	

Race and Hispanic origin

White 88.8%

Black 6.6%

American Indian, Eskimo, or Aleut. 1.2%

Asian or Pacific Islander 1.6%

Other 1.9%

Hispanic origin 3.7%

Ancestry

American	5.4%	Italian	1.4%
Dutch	4.5%	Scotch Irish	3.2%
English	17.0%	Scottish	2.4%
French	4.5%	Swedish	2.3%
German	37.3%	Welsh	1.0%
Irish	18.3%		

Universities/colleges, 1990-1991 enrollment

Bethel College, North Newton 559
Butler County Community College, El Dorado 4,688
Coffeyville Community College, Coffeyville 2,015
Cowley County Community College, Arkansas City 2,503
Friends University, Wichita 1,182
Hesston College, Hesston 486
Independence Community College, Independence 1,928
Kansas Newman College, Wichita 956
Southwestern College, Winfield 702
Wichita State University, Wichita 16,151

Newspapers, total circulation (in all districts)

Hutchinson News 37,846
Independence Reporter 6,237
Wichita Eagle 117,878
Winfield Daily Courier 5,335

Commercial television stations, affiliations

ADI: Wichita-Hutchinson (87%) and Tulsa (13%)
  KAKE-TV, Wichita (ABC)
  KSAS-TV, Wichita (Fox)
  KSNW, Wichita (NBC)

Cable television systems, total subscribers

Multimedia Cablevision Inc.; Wichita 94,061
TCI of Kansas; Arkansas City 6,091
TCI of Kansas; Derby 6,200

Military installations, 1991

McConnell Air Force Base, Wichita 4,425

Businesses and other major employers

Boeing Co.; Wichita; military aircraft 18,300
Beech Aircraft Corp.; Wichita; aircraft/parts 7,000
Wichita State University; Wichita 3,400
HCA Wesley Medical Center; Wichita 3,080
St. Francis Regional Medical Center; Wichita 2,900
Learjet Inc.; Wichita; aircraft/parts 2,500
City of Wichita; Wichita 2,200
St. Joseph Medical Center; Wichita 2,022
Koch Industries Inc.; Wichita; gas & petroleum refining 1,600
Cessna Aircraft Co.; Wichita; aircraft 1,537
Coleman Co. Inc.; Wichita; toys/sporting goods 1,500
Southwestern Bell Telephone Co.; Wichita; telephone communications 1,438
State of Kansas/Social Rehabilitation Dept.; Winfield; nursing 1,200
County of Sedgwick; Wichita 1,200
Fourth Financial Corp.; Wichita; commercial banks 1,095
Hay & Forage Industries; Hesston; farm/garden machinery 1,000
World Book Inc./World Book; Wichita; book publishing 1,000
Boeing Co./Boeing Computer Services; Wichita; computer services 1,000
U.S. Postal Service; Wichita 876
Automotive Controls Corp.; Independence; industry machinery 850
General Electric Co.; Arkansas City; airport services 850
Winfield Rubbermaid Inc.; Winfield; plastic products 850
U.S. Veterans Affairs Dept.; Wichita 830
Dunhill Temporary; Wichita; temp services 804
Ruffin Co.; Wichita; real estate operators 800
Emerson Electric Co.; Independence; electrical industrial apparatus 750
Vulcan Materials Co.; Wichita; industrial inorganic chemicals 750
Pizza Hut of America Inc.; Wichita; fast-food restaurants 738
IFR Systems Inc.; Wichita; measuring/controlling devices 640
Wichita Eagle & Beacon Publishing; Wichita; newspapers 600
Evcon Industries Inc./Red T Coil Co.; Wichita; refrigeration 535
Funk Mfg. Co.; Coffeyville; motor vehicle equipment 510

KENTUCKY

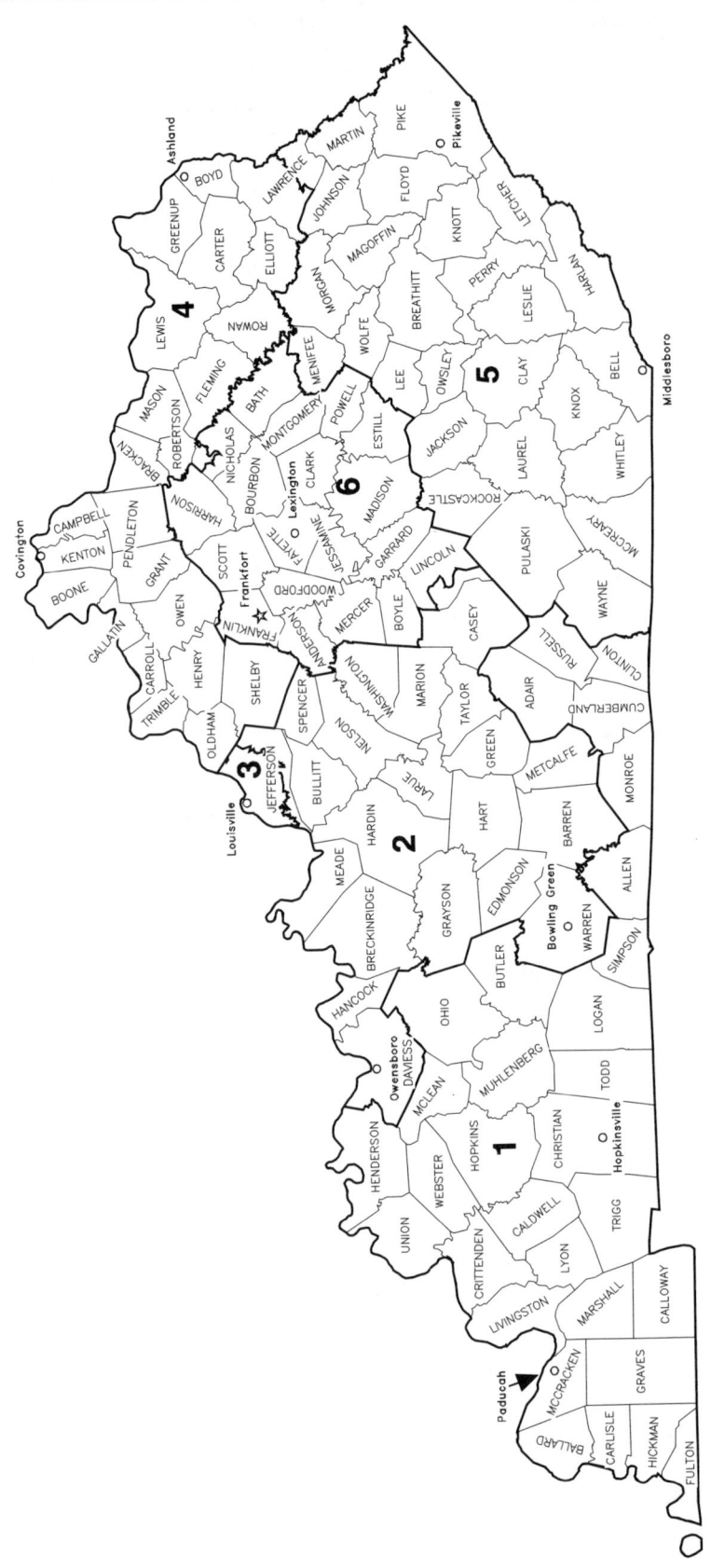

Kentucky

Kentucky Republicans entered the 1990s with a whimper. For all the talk of growing two-party competitiveness in this traditionally Democratic state, the GOP suffered an ignominious defeat in the 1991 gubernatorial race. One year later, in the post-redistricting elections of 1992, they failed to pick up either of two open seats. And redistricting merged Kentucky's only solidly Republican district, the 5th, with the staunchly Democratic 7th.

But given the Democratic control of both legislative chambers (as well as the governorship), the GOP fared reasonably well in the redistricting process. The levels of competitiveness vary widely between districts, but for the next decade, the GOP is within striking distance in all six districts.

In heavily Democratic western Kentucky, the addition of a handful of Republican counties chipped away at the 1st District's considerable Democratic advantage, though hardly enough to worry local Democrats. Mustering a credible Republican candidate is a particularly strenuous task in the 1st, since traditional political sentiments closely mirror those of the Deep South. Western Kentucky was the birthplace of Jefferson Davis, and a place where slaves were once an essential part of the agrarian economy. Even to this day, the county courthouse structure is dominated by the Democratic Party.

Perhaps more troubling to the GOP was the loss of the competitive 3rd and 6th districts. Both featured Republican-friendly demographics, with significant numbers of white-collar voters and independent or GOP-leaning suburbanites, but both remained in the Democratic column in 1992.

Over the last two redistricting sessions, Louisville's gradual population decline has stretched the city-based 3rd District farther into the burgeoning suburbs of Jefferson County. Sparked by a court-ordered busing plan of the 1970s, this primarily white out-migration has altered politics in the metropolitan Louisville area. The whites who fled the city often jettisoned their traditional Democratic ties, resulting in increased GOP strength in surrounding Jefferson, Oldham and Bullitt counties.

Within Louisville, though, the Democratic Party still holds sway. Industrial decline and the emergence of Louisville's new service-oriented economy has sapped Democratic strength, but a coalition of blacks and organized labor keeps the city comfortably in the Democratic column.

Despite the population erosion, the Louisville metropolitan region remains the largest source of votes in the state. But rural and small-town antagonism toward the state's largest city usually spells trouble for Louisville-based candidates in statewide elections. Frequently, the rest of the state will vote in unison against a Louisville candidate.

The state's other open seat in 1992, the Lexington-based 6th, has the markings of a GOP-friendly district, but it delivered a runaway victory for the Democratic nominee. Redistricting did little, if anything, to affect the political balance of the district. Still, white-collar job growth and the development of Bluegrass region farm and pastureland keeps the 6th competitive for GOP candidates.

The 1970s and 1980s were a time of sustained population growth in the northern Kentucky suburbs of Cincinnati. The counties here are more closely associated with Cincinnati than with Louisville or Lexington—a sensitive issue for locals, who claim their interests are not looked after in Frankfort, the state capital, because of their ties to Ohio. The 4th District covers these northern-tier counties, along with some newly added eastern counties that stretch all the way to the city of Ashland.

West of Louisville, the small towns of the Pennyrile favor Democrats at the local levels, but at the presidential level, Republican hegemony has not been threatened seriously since 1976. Democrats here are a socially conservative lot, with political affiliation more likely to be passed down from generation to generation than out of any allegiance to the Democratic platform.

Redistricting grafted on some GOP votes from the Jefferson County suburbs and from a few newly added rural counties in the southeastern corner, but Democrats still hold a hefty voter registration advantage. Along the Ohio River, Owensboro, the largest city in the district, is western Kentucky's leading trade center. Kentucky's congressional delegation keeps a close eye on the tobacco, oil and coal interests that are mainstays of the local economy.

A far deeper vein of Democratic votes exists in mountainous eastern Kentucky, among the unionized coal miners along the West Virginia border. Since the New Deal they have turned out huge Democratic majorities, even in the lean years of liberal nominees like Walter Mondale and Michael S. Dukakis.

Democrats still have an edge in registered voters, but far less so than in its previous incarnation as the 7th District. Under the current map, the 5th covers virtually all of economically disadvantaged Appalachian Kentucky, ranging from the rock-ribbed mountain Republicans of the old 5th to the equally partisan Democrats of coal country.

Table 1 Population

District	Population	Population under 18	Voting-age population	Median age
1	614,226	153,327	460,899	34.4
2	614,833	166,599	448,234	32.0
3	613,603	148,232	465,371	34.3
4	614,245	164,481	449,764	32.9
5	614,119	172,375	441,744	32.3
6	614,270	149,080	465,190	32.3
State	3,685,296	954,094	2,731,202	33.0

Table 2 Voting-Age Persons

District	White*	Black*	American Indian, Eskimo, or Aleut*	Asian or Pacific Islander*	Other*	Hispanic*	Male*	Female*
1	92.2%	7.1%	0.2%	0.3%	0.2%	0.6%	48.0%	52.0%
2	93.9	5.1	0.2	0.6	0.3	0.7	48.4	51.6
3	82.7	16.3	0.2	0.7	0.1	0.6	45.7	54.3
4	97.4	2.1	0.1	0.3	0.1	0.4	47.6	52.4
5	98.7	0.9	0.1	0.1	0.0	0.2	47.7	52.3
6	91.3	7.6	0.1	0.8	0.1	0.6	47.1	52.9
State	92.6	6.6	0.2	0.5	0.2	0.5	47.4	52.6

*As percent of voting-age population.

Table 3 Voting-Age Persons by Age Groups

District	18-24*	25-44*	45-54*	55-64*	65 and over*
1	14.1%	39.1%	14.1%	12.3%	20.3%
2	15.4	43.1	14.3	11.6	15.6
3	12.8	43.0	13.3	12.6	18.3
4	14.0	43.3	14.4	11.9	16.5
5	14.5	42.6	14.4	11.9	16.6
6	17.0	43.5	13.6	10.8	15.2
State	14.6	42.4	14.0	11.8	17.1

*As percent of voting-age population.

Table 4 Income and Occupation

District	Median family income	Families in poverty	White collar*	Blue collar*	Service*	Farm*
1	$24,800	15.4%	41.9%	39.2%	13.7%	5.2%
2	27,031	14.0	44.9	37.1	12.8	5.2
3	32,863	11.4	60.2	25.5	13.5	0.8
4	31,257	12.5	52.7	31.5	12.4	3.4
5	17,798	29.2	42.9	41.2	13.1	2.8
6	30,482	12.8	55.8	26.4	13.1	4.8
State	27,028	16.0	50.4	32.8	13.1	3.7

*As percent of employed persons age 16 and over.

Table 5 Education: School Years Completed

District	Less than grade 9*	Grades 9-12 no diploma*	High school diploma*	College bachelor's degree or higher*
1	20.8%	17.2%	34.3%	9.5%
2	19.2	15.7	35.2	11.2
3	9.7	16.2	29.7	19.7
4	16.1	16.3	33.8	13.4
5	33.5	18.4	28.3	7.6
6	15.3	14.7	29.2	19.9
State	19.0	16.4	31.8	13.6

*As percent of persons age 25 and over.

Table 6 Housing and Residential Patterns

District	Owner occupied	Renter occupied	Urban	Rural
1	73.4%	26.6%	38.6%	61.4%
2	72.8	27.2	44.1	55.9
3	63.3	36.7	98.2	1.8
4	71.9	28.2	54.0	46.0
5	74.5	25.5	13.1	86.9
6	62.7	37.3	63.0	37.0
State	69.6	30.4	51.8	48.2

1st District

West — Paducah

Western Kentucky's 1st District is the state's version of the Deep South. In the Civil War era, regional sentiment here strongly favored the Confederacy—Jefferson Davis was born here in 1808—and slaves helped cultivate the tobacco and cotton crops. Kentucky's eight westernmost counties even plotted to secede and form their own state along with some renegade Tennessee counties.

The Confederate legacy translates into Democratic votes. When the birth of quintuplets caused a sensation in Mayfield (Graves County) in 1896, the local paper ran a picture with the caption "Five New Democrats." Today, politics is much the same: 95 percent of registered voters in Graves County are Democrats.

That is the story in the rest of western Kentucky as well. Most counties are, at the very least, 80 percent Democratic. In the 1980s, the region began drifting toward supporting Republican candidates for president, but Bill Clinton brought them home in 1992.

Five television markets reach western Kentucky, but no city in the 1st has more than 30,000 people. Many of the district's people are employed in agriculture, from soybeans and tobacco to chicken processing in Mayfield.

Hopkins, Muhlenberg, Ohio and Union counties have a coal-country tradition, but jobs in the mining industry have waned in recent years. In 1980, mining jobs accounted for about a quarter of all jobs in Muhlenberg and Ohio counties, but by 1990 that share had dropped to under 10 percent. Hopkins County has better weathered the post-World War II coal industry decline by evolving into a regional industrial and medical center.

Tourism and recreation also play a role in the regional economy, especially in the area around the Land Between the Lakes Recreation Area. Nearby Murray has become a preferred retirement destination.

The Ohio River port of Paducah (McCracken County) has traditionally been the political and population center of western Kentucky, but its population has been surpassed by Hopkinsville (Christian County), an agricultural market center with a dependence on nearby Fort Campbell military base.

The Atomic Energy Commission plant steered to Paducah by native son Alben W. Barkley—the longtime Democratic senator and then vice president under Harry S. Truman—is a major employer, though new uranium-generation technology has cast doubts on its future.

The main source of Republican votes in the 1st comes from the economically disadvantaged mountain counties on the far eastern edge of the district. Bordering Tennessee to the south and the 5th District to the east, counties such as Adair, Clinton, Cumberland, Monroe and Russell have been turning in GOP majorities since the Civil War.

Election Returns

	1st District	Democrat	Republican
1992	President*	116,637 (47.8%)	96,602 (39.6%)
	House	128,524 (60.5%)	83,088 (39.1%)
1990	Senate	71,348 (47.6%)	78,445 (52.4%)
1988	President	101,965 (45.8%)	120,551 (54.2%)
1987	Governor	89,905 (75.1%)	29,872 (24.9%)
1986	Senate	75,294 (78.4%)	20,761 (21.6%)

*Vote for Perot was 30,869 (12.6%).

Demographics

Population 614,226

Percent change from 1980 16.8%

Land area 11,230 square miles

Population per square mile 55

Counties, 1990 population

Adair (pt.) 15,321	Livingston 9,062
Allen 14,628	Logan 24,416
Ballard 7,902	Lyon 6,624
Butler 11,245	Marshall 27,205
Caldwell 13,232	McCracken 62,879
Calloway 30,735	McLean 9,628
Carlisle 5,238	Monroe 11,401
Christian 68,941	Muhlenberg 31,318
Clinton 9,135	Ohio 21,105
Crittenden 9,196	Russell 14,716
Cumberland 6,784	Simpson 15,145
Fulton 8,271	Todd 10,940
Graves 33,550	Trigg 10,361
Henderson 43,044	Union 16,557
Hickman 5,566	Webster 13,955
Hopkins 46,126	

Cities, 1990 population (10,000 or more)

Fort Campbell North CDP 18,861	Madisonville 16,200
	Murray 14,439
Henderson 25,945	Paducah 27,256
Hopkinsville 29,809	

Race and Hispanic origin
White 91.4%
Black 7.8%
American Indian, Eskimo, or Aleut. 0.2%
Asian or Pacific Islander 0.3%
Other 0.3%
Hispanic origin 0.7%

Ancestry

American 18.3%	Irish 18.8%
Dutch 2.2%	Italian 1.0%
English 14.4%	Scotch Irish 2.7%
French 2.4%	Scottish 1.6%
German 16.0%	

Universities/colleges, 1990-1991 enrollment
Henderson Community College, Henderson 1,363
Hopkinsville Community College, Hopkinsville 1,823
Institute of Electronic Technology, Paducah 224
Lindsey Wilson College, Columbia 1,327
Madisonville Community College, Madisonville 2,134
Murray State University, Murray 8,079
Paducah Community College, Paducah 2,788

Newspapers, total circulation (in all districts)
Bowling Green Daily News 21,386
Evansville Courier/Press 95,655
Henderson Gleaner 11,175
Hopkinsville Kentucky New Era 13,593
Madisonville Messenger 10,836
Owensboro Messenger Inquirer 32,470
Paducah Sun 29,509

Commercial television stations, affiliations
ADI: Paducah-Cape Girardeau-Harrisburg-Marion (33%), Nashville (31%), Evansville (26%), Bowling Green (7%) and Lexington (2%)
WEHT, Evansville (CBS)
WFIE-TV, Evansville (NBC)
WGRB, Campbellsville (None)
WLCN, Madisonville (None)
WPSD-TV, Paducah (NBC)

Cable television systems, total subscribers
Cencom Cable TV; Hopkinsville 9,548
Comcast Cablevision/Paducah; Paducah 17,991
Madisonville Cablevision; Madisonville 9,900
Murray Cablevision Inc.; Murray 5,300
TCI of Kentucky; Henderson 6,900
Telescripps Cable Co.; Powderly 5,565

Military installations, 1991
Fort Campbell (Army), Clarksville 26,137

Businesses and other major employers
Union Underwear Co. Inc.; Jamestown; underwear 3,250
Martin Marietta Energy Systems; Paducah; inorganic chemicals 1,750
General Tire Inc.; Mayfield; tires 1,600
Lourdes Hospital Inc.; Paducah 1,545
Western Baptist Hospital; Paducah 1,400
Hopkins County Hospital; Madisonville 1,250
Fisher-Price Inc.; Murray; toys/sporting goods 1,200
Murray State University; Murray 1,186
Sumitomo Electric Wiring Systems; Morgantown; motor vehicle parts 1,000

General Electric Co.; Scottsville; electrical industrial apparatus 875

Kendall Co./Polyken Technologies; Franklin; medical instruments/supplies 800

Emerson Electric Co./Motor Div.; Russellville; electrical motors 800

General Electric Co./Aircraft Engine Group; Madisonville; aircraft engines/parts 800

Minact Inc./Earl C. Clements Job Center; Morganfield; job training 800

Alcan Aluminum Corp.; Henderson; aluminum smelting 780

Dolgencorp Inc.; Scottsville; warehousing 760

Logan Inc.; Russellville; aluminum rolling/drawing 757

Gibbs Die Casting Aluminum Corp.; Henderson; aluminum castings 721

Accuride Corp.; Henderson; motor vehicles/equipment 693

Briggs & Stratton Corp.; Murray; engines/turbines 654

Community United Methodist Hospital; Henderson 634

Western State Hospital; Hopkinsville 620

Tennessee Valley Authority/Paradise Steam Plant; Drakesboro; electric services 602

Stuart Jennie Medical Center; Hopkinsville 600

Murray-Calloway County Hospital; Murray 596

Oshkosh B'gosh Inc.; Columbia; outerwear 590

Sutton Shirt Corp.; Albany; outerwear 565

E. R. Carpenter Co. Inc.; Russellville; plastics products 550

Westvaco Corp./Fine Papers Div.; Wickliffe; pulp mills 550

Red Kap Industries Inc.; Russellville; outerwear 525

2nd District

West Central — Owensboro

The wide Democratic registration advantage in the 2nd is misleading. This is a competitive district in state and national elections. The 2nd includes three distinct areas of the state: the outer Bluegrass region in the east, suburban Louisville to the north and the rolling hill country of the Pennyrile in the southwest.

More than two-thirds of the district's voters are registered as Democrats. But they have an independent streak and a penchant for backing Republicans at the federal level. In good GOP years, statewide candidates have a shot at the 2nd's three major population centers: Daviess County (Owensboro), Hardin County (the Fort Knox area) and Warren County (Bowling Green).

GOP Sen. Mitch McConnell won Hardin and Warren counties in his 1990 re-election effort; George Bush won the district in 1992, but failed to prevail in Daviess County.

There are some smaller counties that Republicans can always count on. Casey County gave Bush a better than 2-to-1 margin in 1992. Grayson and Edmonson, centers of Union support during the Civil War, also voted for Bush in 1992. And Edmonson was one of just 13 counties—out of 120—that GOP Rep. Larry J. Hopkins carried in his failed 1991 gubernatorial bid.

Owensboro, along the Ohio River in the far northwestern edge of the district, is the largest city in the 2nd. Tobacco, oil and coal are mainstays of the local economy, making it Western Kentucky's leading trade center.

At the other end of the Green River Parkway lies Bowling Green (Warren County), the district's second-largest city. Metals and machinery are some of Bowling Green's industrial output, but the GM Corvette assembly plant there draws more attention.

Western Kentucky University, the largest college in the state west of Louisville, overlooks the city.

Hardin County, home to Fort Knox, is between Owensboro and Louisville. Adjacent to the military reservation is the Treasury Department's Gold Depository, where bars of almost pure gold are locked in a vault behind a door weighing more than 20 tons. Active-duty military families and retired military help fuel the economies of nearby Radcliff and Elizabethtown.

Closer to Louisville, the 2nd includes some Republican-leaning Jefferson County suburbs and Bullitt County, an extension of Louisville's suburbs. White flight from Louisville fueled a 66 percent population increase in Bullitt in the 1970s, though growth tapered off considerably in the 1980s. The county's sizable blue-collar element frequently bolts the Democratic ticket, but Bullitt went narrowly for Bill Clinton in 1992.

Bardstown (Nelson County) claims to be "The Bourbon Capital of the World," and several distilleries are in the vicinity, including Maker's Mark in Loretto. As if to balance the worldly pleasure that bourbon brings, the names of several area towns connote ethereality, including Holy Cross, Calvary, St. Mary, St. Francis, Saint Catharine and Gethsemane.

Election Returns

		Democrat	Republican
	2nd District	**Democrat**	**Republican**
1992	President*	98,955 (41.3%)	107,339 (44.8%)
	House	126,894 (61.4%)	79,684 (38.6%)
1990	Senate	71,490 (46.7%)	81,496 (53.3%)
1988	President	83,411 (40.2%)	123,833 (59.8%)
1987	Governor	79,786 (66.4%)	40,374 (33.6%)
1986	Senate	78,018 (74.9%)	26,115 (25.1%)

Vote for Perot was 33,192 (13.9%).

Demographics

Population 614,833

Percent change from 1980 18.1%

Land area 7,762 square miles

Population per square mile 79

Counties, 1990 population

Adair (pt.) 39	Jefferson (pt.) 51,334
Barren 34,001	Larue 11,679
Breckinridge 16,312	Lincoln (pt.) 4,326
Bullitt 47,567	Marion 16,499
Casey 14,211	Meade 24,170
Daviess 87,189	Metcalfe 8,963
Edmonson 10,357	Nelson 29,710
Grayson 21,050	Spencer 6,801
Green 10,371	Taylor 21,146
Hancock 7,864	Warren 76,673
Hardin 89,240	Washington 10,441
Hart 14,890	

Cities, 1990 population (10,000 or more)

Bowling Green 40,641	Glasgow 12,351
Elizabethtown 18,167	Owensboro 53,549
Fort Knox CDP 21,495	Radcliff 19,772

Race and Hispanic origin

White 93.4%
Black 5.5%
American Indian, Eskimo, or Aleut. 0.2%
Asian or Pacific Islander 0.6%
Other 0.3%
Hispanic origin 0.8%

Ancestry

American 18.8% Irish 19.5%
Dutch 1.9% Italian 1.4%
English 15.3% Scotch Irish 2.3%
French 2.7% Scottish 1.9%
German 20.2%

Universities/colleges, 1990-1991 enrollment

Brescia College, Owensboro 731
Campbellsville College, Campbellsville 853
Elizabethtown Community College, Elizabethtown 3,356
Kentucky Wesleyan College, Owensboro 707
Owensboro Community College, Owensboro 2,415
Owensboro Junior College, Owensboro 318
St. Catharine College, St. Catharine 233
Western Kentucky University, Bowling Green 15,170

Newspapers, total circulation (in all districts)

Bowling Green Daily News 21,386
Danville Advocate-Messenger 11,344
Elizabethtown News-Enterprise 15,487
Louisville Courier Journal 235,144
Owensboro Messenger Inquirer 32,470

Commercial television stations, affiliations

ADI: Louisville (64%), Bowling Green (15%), Evansville (9%),
    Lexington (7%) and Nashville (6%)
    WBKO, Bowling Green (ABC)
    WKGB-TV, Bowling Green (Fox)
    WBNA, Louisville (None)

Cable television systems, total subscribers

Century Cable; Owensboro 20,750
Storer Cable TV Inc.; Louisville 172,000
Storer Cable of Southern Kentucky; Bowling Green 17,958
TCI of Kentucky; Shepherdsville 6,766
Telecable of Radcliff; Radcliff 10,736
Telescripps Cable Co.; Campbellsville 5,400
Telescripps Cable Co.; Elizabethtown 12,117
Telescripps Cable Co.; Glasgow 5,000

Military installations, 1991

Fort Knox (Army), Louisville 19,201

Businesses and other major employers

Union Underwear Co. Inc./Fruit of the Loom; Campbellsville;
    underwear 4,200
Western Kentucky University; Bowling Green 1,739
Owensboro-Daviess County Hospital; Owensboro 1,424
R. R. Donnelley & Sons Co.; Glasgow; periodicals 1,400
Wax Works Inc./Disc Jockey; Owensboro; durable goods
    1,400
Union Underwear Co. Inc./Fruit of the Loom; Bowling
    Green; underwear 1,300
Hardin Memorial Hospital; Elizabethtown 1,225
General Motors Corp.; Bowling Green; motor vehicles 1,100
Publishers Press Inc.; Shepherdsville; management/public rela-
    tions 1,100

Commonwealth Aluminum Corp./Lewisport Rolling Mill;
    Lewisport; rolling mill 1,000
Bowling Green Community Hospital; Bowling Green 925
Sumitomo Electric Wiring Systems; Edmonton; electrical
    work 920
Oshkosh B'gosh Inc.; Liberty; children's clothing stores 900
American Greetings Corp.; Bardstown; greeting cards 763
T. J. Samson Community Hospital; Glasgow 720
Eaton Corp./Axle Div.; Glasgow; motor vehicle parts 700
Mercy Hospital of Owensboro; Owensboro 648
Gates Rubber Co.; Elizabethtown; rubber auto parts 625
S. K. F. USA Inc.; Glasgow; tapered roller bearings 600
Crucible Materials Corp./Crucible Magnetics Div.;
    Elizabethtown; magnets 600
Texas Gas Transmission Corp.; Owensboro; gas distribution
    592
AP Technoglass Corp.; Elizabethtown; glass products 590
Coltec Industries Inc.; Bowling Green; industrial machinery
    561
Eaton Corp.; Bowling Green; electrical industrial apparatus
    560
General Electric Co.; Owensboro; electric motors 550
MPD Inc.; Owensboro; electronic components 520
Louisville Gas & Electric Co./Mill Creek Station; Louisville;
    utility services 506
Hardin County School District; Elizabethtown 501

3rd District

Louisville and Suburbs

Rural and small-town Kentuckians have always considered themselves different from Louisville, the state's largest city. In a state where blacks make up just 7 percent of the population, Louisville is 30 percent black. The city also has an exceptionally large Catholic population, a legacy of a massive German immigration in the mid-19th century. And Louisville's *Courier-Journal* newspaper is a leading liberal voice in a state that generally prefers moderate-to-conservative politicians.

That suspicion of Louisville is usually reflected at the ballot box in statewide elections, when the rest of the state bands together to vote against the Louisville-based candidate. GOP Sen. Mitch McConnell, re-elected to a second term in 1990, has been an exception.

Every first Saturday in May, though, the rest of the state turns to Louisville, to be serenaded with the state's official song, "My Old Kentucky Home," and to witness one of horse-racing's biggest spectacles, the Kentucky Derby.

In a state known for its contentious politics, Louisville is no exception. Court-ordered busing of students in the 1970s inflamed passions throughout Jefferson County, leading to riots and violent demonstrations. And in the 1980s, Louisville became known as "Strike City" for its fractious labor-management relations.

Despite some job losses from industrial decline, labor strength runs deep among the blue-collar, white residents of the South End; it translates into Democratic votes. Blacks who live near downtown in the West End turn in even larger Democratic majorities. Republicans live in the affluent East End by the Ohio River.

Louisville's newer jobs are more service-oriented, with employers such as United Parcel Service, which operates a hub out of Standiford Airport, and Galen (formerly Humana), which runs for-profit hospitals.

In the 1970s, the city of Louisville—with the addition of a few suburbs—held enough population for its own congressional district. But massive white flight to the suburbs forced mapmakers in the two subsequent rounds of redistricting to expand the 3rd District's lines even farther into the Jefferson County suburbs. Louisville now accounts for less than half the district vote.

That has meant a shift in the 3rd District balance of power. Before the black Democratic vote became a force in the mid- to late 1960s, Jefferson County was fertile ground for Republicans. And in the 3rd, the pendulum is swinging back in that direction, as the suburbs increasingly flex their muscles.

This version of the 3rd is considerably more receptive to Republicans, particularly in the higher-income areas (such as the Brownsboro Road-Interchange 71 corridor) outside the city and in areas closer to the Oldham County border. The turf between St. Matthews and Middletown—on the 2nd District border—is Republican, well-educated and affluent. The new suburban majority made the 1992 congressional election the closest in more than 20 years, with the Democratic incumbent winning with 53 percent of the vote.

Election Returns

	3rd District	Democrat	Republican
1992	President*	143,824 (50.4%)	105,520 (37.0%)
	House	148,066 (52.7%)	132,689 (47.3%)
1990	Senate	97,631 (53.6%)	84,606 (46.4%)
1988	President	113,948 (48.8%)	119,355 (51.2%)
1987	Governor	69,348 (55.1%)	56,575 (44.9%)
1986	Senate	97,784 (70.9%)	40,122 (29.1%)

*Vote for Perot was 35,902 (12.6%).

Demographics

Population 613,603

Percent change from 1980 17.5%

Land area 239 square miles

Population per square mile 2,572

Counties, 1990 population
Jefferson (pt.) 613,603

Cities, 1990 population (10,000 or more)
Fern Creek CDP (pt.) 16,130
Highview CDP (pt.) 11,052
Jeffersontown (pt.) 23,193
Louisville 269,063
Newburg CDP 21,647
Okolona CDP 18,902
Pleasure Ridge Park CDP 25,131
Shively 15,535
St. Dennis CDP 10,326
St. Matthews 15,800
Valley Station CDP (pt.) 15,278

Race and Hispanic origin
White 80.6%
Black 18.3%
American Indian, Eskimo, or Aleut. 0.2%
Asian or Pacific Islander 0.7%
Other 0.2%
Hispanic origin 0.7%

Ancestry
American 10.0%
Dutch 2.2%
English 14.6%
French 3.4%
German 29.4%
Irish 20.4%
Italian 2.2%
Polish 1.1%
Scotch Irish 2.5%
Scottish 2.0%

Universities/colleges, 1990-1991 enrollment
Bellarmine College, Louisville 3,907
Jefferson Community College, Louisville 10,234
Louisville Tech Institute, Louisville 500
National Education Center, Louisville 339
R. E. T. S. Electronic Institute, Louisville 338
Southern Baptist Seminary, Louisville 2,245
Spalding University, Louisville 1,059
Sullivan College, Louisville 1,713
University of Louisville, Louisville 22,979

Newspapers, total circulation (in all districts)
Louisville Courier Journal 235,144

Commercial television stations, affiliations
ADI: Louisville (100%)

Cable television systems, total subscribers
Storer Cable TV Inc.; Louisville 172,000

Military installations, 1991
Louisville Naval Ordnance Station, Louisville 2,782
Standiford Field Air Force Guard Station, Louisville 314

Businesses and other major employers
General Electric Co.; Louisville; household appliances 10,800
Humana Inc.; Louisville; hospital management 4,100
University of Louisville; Louisville 4,039
Ford Motor Co./Louisville Assembly Plant; Louisville; motor vehicles 3,300
N. K. C. Hospitals Inc./Norton Hospital; Louisville 3,200
Philip Morris Inc.; Louisville; cigarettes 2,800
Ford Motor Co./Kentucky Truck Plant; Louisville; trucks 2,600
Jewish Hospital Inc.; Louisville 2,054
PNC Financial Corp./Citizens Fidelity Bank; Louisville; commercial banks 2,036
Humana Inc./Humana Hospital-Audubon; Louisville 2,000
National Processing Co.; Louisville; computer services 1,710
First National Bank of Louisville; Louisville; commercial banks 1,670
Blue Cross & Blue Shield of Kentucky; Louisville; medical service/health insurance 1,500
County of Jefferson; Louisville 1,500
Humana Inc./Humana Hospital-University; Louisville 1,500
Henry Vogt Machine Co.; Louisville; metal valves 1,400
Humana Inc./Humana Hospital-Suburban; Louisville 1,300
Gannett Satellite Info Network/Louisville Courier Journal; Louisville; newspapers 1,241
Brown-Forman Corp.; Louisville; distillery 1,100
Bellsouth Telecommunications; Louisville; telephone communications 1,000
U.S. Veterans Affairs Dept.; Louisville; hospital 1,000
St. Anthony's Medical Center; Louisville 985
Alliant Health System Inc.; Louisville 950
U.S. Army Corp. of Engineers; Louisville; engineering services 950
Brown & Williamson Tobacco; Louisville; cigarettes 879

KFC Corp./Procurement Dept.; Louisville; fast-food chain 850

Rohm & Haas Kentucky Inc.; Louisville; plastics/synthetics 800

Saints Mary & Elizabeth Hospital; Louisville 800

KFC National Management Co.; Louisville; accounting/auditing 785

Apparel Group Ltd./Damon Creations Inc.; Louisville; outerwear 750

Southern Baptist/Boyce Bible School; Louisville 750

Du Pont E. I. De Nemours & Co./Du Pont Polymers; Louisville; plastics/synthetics 700

Presbyterian Church USA; Louisville; religious organizations 700

Home Supply Co./Galt House East; Louisville; hotel 700

Prudential Service Bureau; Louisville; medical service/health insurance 675

Monfort Inc.; Louisville; meat products 600

White Castle System Inc.; Louisville; bars/restaurants 600

American Building Maintenance Co.; Louisville; building services 600

United Parcel Service Inc.; Louisville; mail services 550

United Catalysts Inc.; Louisville; inorganic chemicals 550

State of Kentucky/Transportation Dept.; Louisville 535

State of Kentucky/Cabinet for Human Resources; Louisville; social services 535

Liberty National Bank & Trust; Louisville; commercial banks 521

4th District

North and East — Covington; Ashland

Of the state's six congressional districts, the 4th is the least distinctly Kentuckian. Almost half the district's population is located in the Cincinnati suburbs; Ashland, the 4th's second-largest city, is on the far eastern fringe, near where the Ohio River forms a border with Ohio and West Virginia.

Boone, Campbell (Newport) and Kenton (Covington) counties are associated much more closely with Cincinnati—where much of the area's population commutes to work—than with Lexington or Louisville. The Greater Cincinnati International Airport is actually in Kentucky, a few miles west of Covington.

Newport has battled its reputation as a "sin city"—for its go-go bars and nightclubs—where some of Cincinnati's residents go to blow off steam. Ohioans also escape their state-run liquor stores by buying less expensive alcohol in Covington.

A frequently voiced complaint in Covington is that the state ignores them because of their close ties to Ohio. But the federal government certainly has not: A regional center of the Internal Revenue Service is the city's largest employer. The peak of tax season adds even more jobs to the district's largest city.

Boone County attracted population spillover from Campbell and Kenton counties in the 1970s and 1980s, growing more than 75 percent over the past two decades.

The politics of these three counties is nominally Democratic, but increasingly Republican-friendly. George Bush won all three easily in 1992, as did the GOP nominee for the House. For a Democrat to win the 4th, the candidate must remain competitive in these counties and then run up sizable margins in the eight rural-suburban counties closer to Louisville.

Most of these rural counties are Democratic, but suburban

Oldham County (at the 4th's western edge, closest to Louisville) is leaning Republican. In the 1970s, Oldham's population swelled by 91 percent, thanks to white-collar out-migration from Louisville and an influx of out-of-state business executives. Population growth tapered off considerably in the 1980s, but Oldham has an unmistakable GOP stamp.

Any Democratic strategy for the 4th also has to factor in the industrial city of Ashland (Boyd County), home to Ashland Oil and Armco Steel. Strong unions kept the oil refinery workers and steelworkers of Boyd and neighboring Greenup counties in the Democratic column for decades, but their grip has weakened. Still, in 1992 Bill Clinton and the Democratic House challenger carried Boyd and Greenup counties.

Before redistricting, these counties clustered by the West Virginia border were part of eastern Kentucky's heavily Democratic, coal-producing Appalachian district. That voting tradition lives on in sparsely populated and 98 percent Democratic Elliott County. Lewis County marches to its own GOP beat, dating to the time when it was a stop on the Underground Railroad.

Election Returns

	4th District	Democrat	Republican
1992	President*	94,335 (39.1%)	106,695 (44.2%)
	House	86,890 (38.4%)	139,634 (61.6%)
1990	Senate	62,478 (42.6%)	84,325 (57.4%)
1988	President	85,699 (40.5%)	125,957 (59.5%)
1987	Governor	83,146 (66.6%)	41,720 (33.4%)
1986	Senate	85,301 (74.2%)	29,636 (25.8%)

*Vote for Perot was 40,438 (16.7%).

Demographics

Population 614,245

Percent change from 1980 17.4%

Land area 5,843 square miles

Population per square mile 105

Counties, 1990 population

Boone 57,589	Kenton 142,031
Boyd 51,150	Lawrence (pt.) 10,718
Bracken 7,766	Lewis 13,029
Campbell 83,866	Mason 16,666
Carroll 9,292	Nicholas (pt.) 631
Carter 24,340	Oldham 33,263
Elliott 6,455	Owen 9,035
Fleming 12,292	Pendleton 12,036
Gallatin 5,393	Robertson 2,124
Grant 15,737	Rowan 20,353
Greenup 36,742	Shelby 24,824
Henry 12,823	Trimble 6,090

Cities, 1990 population (10,000 or more)

Ashland 23,622	Fort Thomas 16,032
Covington 43,264	Independence 10,444
Erlanger 15,979	Newport 18,871
Florence 18,624	

Race and Hispanic origin
White 97.3%
Black 2.1%

American Indian, Eskimo, or Aleut. 0.1%
Asian or Pacific Islander 0.3%
Other 0.1%
Hispanic origin 0.4%

Ancestry
American 11.1%		Irish 22.0%
Dutch 2.8%		Italian 2.0%
English 15.9%		Scotch Irish 2.4%
French 2.9%		Scottish 1.8%
German 34.7%		

Universities/colleges, 1990-1991 enrollment
Ashland Community College, Ashland 3,057
Kentucky Christian College, Grayson 566
Maysville Community College, Maysville 1,024
Morehead State University, Morehead 8,605
Northern Kentucky University, Highland Heights 11,254
Thomas More College, Crestview Hills 1,297

Newspapers, total circulation (in all districts)
Ashland Daily Independent 22,256
Cincinnati Enquirer 162,669
Cincinnati Post 92,070
Huntington Herald-Dispatch 42,242
Lexington Herald-Leader 121,674
Louisville Courier Journal 235,144

Commercial television stations, affiliations
ADI: Cincinnati (34%), Charleston-Huntington (33%), Louisville (20%) and Lexington (13%)
WAVE, Louisville (NBC)

Cable television systems, total subscribers
Dimension Cable Services; Ashland 17,400
Storer Cable TV Inc.; Edgewood 49,661
Storer Cable TV Inc.; Louisville 172,000

Businesses and other major employers
Armco Inc./Armco Steel; Ashland; iron & steel products 3,200
U.S. Internal Revenue Service; Covington 3,000
Corporate Cleaning Systems; Covington; building/janitorial services 1,500
Emerson Electric Co./Browning Mfg. Div.; Maysville; power equipment 1,300
St. Luke Hospital Inc.; Newport 1,200
Ashland Hospital Corp./King's Daughters Medical Center; Ashland 1,095
Morehead State University; Morehead 1,000
Northern Kentucky University; Highland Heights 1,000
St. Elizabeth Medical Center; Covington 1,000
County of Oldham/Board of Education; Buckner 900
DHL Airways Inc./DHL Worldwide Express; Covington; air courier services 840
Gap Inc./Hemisphere; Covington; apparel 800
Our Lady of Bellefonte Hospital; Russell 708
Motor Inn Inc./Drawbridge/Oldenberg; Covington; hotels 660
St. Luke Hospital Inc.; Florence 650
Equitable Bag Co. Inc.; Florence; plastic/shopping bags 630
Addington Inc.; Ashland; coal mining 600
Sabatasso Foods Inc./Sabatassos Pizza; Florence; food products 600
Covington Landing Ltd.; Covington; real estate operators 600

St. Claire Medical Center/Bath County Health Service; Morehead 600
R. A. Jones & Co. Inc.; Covington; industrial packaging machinery 510

5th District
Southeast — Middlesboro; Pikeville

Appalachian eastern Kentucky has long been one of the state's most downtrodden areas. Lexington and Louisville are culturally, economically and geographically distant from the 5th District, the state's poorest, sickest and least-educated. With no city that has more than 12,000 residents, the 5th spans 26 counties and part of Lawrence County. Most of Democratic eastern Kentucky is within its confines, along with the Republican southeastern region along the Tennessee border.

One tie that binds the district is the staggering poverty that differentiates it from the rest of the state. About one in five households lacks a telephone or makes less than $5,000 per year.

The 1970s coal boom brought many former residents from the urban Midwest back to the hills and hollows of Appalachia. But the revival died out as coal production began to shift from the East to the West, where, typically, it is cheaper and easier to mine coal.

The decline of the once-mighty coal industry—the state lost 20,000 mining jobs in the 1980s—has brought even harder times to the region's mountain people, who never had it easy to begin with.

Besides the abandoned mines and scarred hillsides, King Coal is leaving behind a legion of crippled miners, whether they suffer from black lung disease or are disabled by some other mine-related injury. Fourteen percent of the people in the district have a work-related disability that prevents them from working.

The United Mine Workers union (UMW) speaks loudly for these residents and carries a big stick in the coal counties in the eastern half of the district. These counties bordering Virginia and West Virginia have turned in huge Democratic majorities since the New Deal.

Pitted against the coal counties is a firewall of mountain counties that have been voting Republican since the 1860s; they used to form the backbone of the old GOP 5th District before it was merged with the Democratic 7th in 1992 redistricting. Taken as a whole, the district has a slight Democratic voter registration advantage.

Counting Leslie County and moving west, the old 5th went overwhelmingly for George Bush in 1988 and remained loyal in 1992. Likewise, the Democratic eastern half strongly backed Bill Clinton. In Pike (Pikeville) and Floyd (Prestonsburg) counties—the district's first and third most populous—Clinton won by better than 2-to-1 margins.

Bell County (Middlesborough), on the Tennessee border, is one of the few competitive counties. In 1992, voters backed Clinton while crossing over for the Republican incumbent for the House seat.

Population in the western section is concentrated in Pulaski (Somerset) and Laurel (London) counties. Like the rest of the west, Somerset—the 5th's second-largest city after Middlesboro—relies heavily on tourism and recreation. Lake Cumberland is nearby, as is the Big South Fork National River and Recreation area.

Election Returns

	5th District	Democrat	Republican
1992	President*	109,591 (47.8%)	95,831 (41.8%)
	House	95,760 (45.4%)	115,255 (54.6%)
1990	Senate	62,862 (46.2%)	73,341 (53.8%)
1988	President	97,898 (46.7%)	111,780 (53.3%)
1987	Governor	79,638 (67.5%)	38,411 (32.5%)
1986	Senate	74,485 (72.8%)	27,803 (27.2%)

Vote for Perot was 23,888 (10.4%).

Demographics

Population 614,119

Percent change from 1980 17.3%

Land area 10,018 square miles

Population per square mile 61

Counties, 1990 population

Bell 31,506	Magoffin 13,077
Breathitt 15,703	Martin 12,526
Clay 21,746	McCreary 15,603
Floyd 43,586	Menifee 5,092
Harlan 36,574	Morgan 11,648
Jackson 11,955	Owsley 5,036
Johnson 23,248	Perry 30,283
Knott 17,906	Pike 72,583
Knox 29,676	Pulaski 49,489
Laurel 43,438	Rockcastle 14,803
Lawrence (pt.) 3,280	Wayne 17,468
Lee 7,422	Whitley 33,326
Leslie 13,642	Wolfe 6,503
Letcher 27,000	

Cities, 1990 population (10,000 or more)

Middlesborough 11,328	Somerset 10,733

Race and Hispanic origin
White 98.7%
Black 1.0%
American Indian, Eskimo, or Aleut. 0.1%
Asian or Pacific Islander 0.2%
Other 0.0%
Hispanic origin 0.3%

Ancestry

American 26.3%	German 10.5%
Dutch 1.7%	Irish 14.7%
English 12.6%	Scotch Irish 1.5%
French 1.2%	

Universities/colleges, 1990-1991 enrollment
Alice Lloyd College, Pippa Passes 548
Cumberland College, Williamsburg 1,812
Hazard Community College, Hazard 1,314
Lees College, Jackson 352
Pikeville College, Pikeville 972
Prestonsburg Community College, Prestonsburg 2,438
Somerset Community College, Somerset 2,085
Southeast Community College, Cumberland 2,063
Sue Bennett College, London 517
Union College, Barbourville 1,022

Newspapers, total circulation (in all districts)
Harlan Daily Enterprise 6,365
Lexington Herald-Leader 121,674
Williamson Daily News 10,791

Commercial television stations, affiliations
ADI: Lexington (51%), Charleston-Huntington (25%), Knoxville (17%) and Bristol-Kingsport-Johnson City (7%)
WLJC-TV, Beattyville (None)
WYMT-TV, Hazard (CBS)

Cable television systems, total subscribers
Falcon Cable TV; Corbin 7,105
Falcon Cable TV; Somerset 7,488
Simmons Communications Inc.; London 7,200
TV Service Inc.; Hindman 6,500
Tel-Com Inc.; Martin 17,112

Businesses and other major employers
CSX Transportation Inc.; Corbin; railroads 2,000
U.S. Interior Dept./U.S. Geological Survey; Williamsburg; engineering services 2,000
Palm Beach Co.; Somerset; suits/coats 1,050
Tecumseh Products Co./Somerset Div.; Somerset; refrigeration 1,000
American Greetings Corp.; Corbin; greeting cards 900
Appalachian Computer Services; London; computer services 800
Methodist Hospital of Kentucky; Pikeville 750
County of Perry/Board of Education; Hazard 750
South-East Coal Co.; Isom; coal mining 700
State of Kentucky/Oakwood Training Center; Somerset; nursing 650
Cyprus Mountain Coals Corp.; Hazard; coal mining 608
Cyprus Minerals Co./Lost Mountain Mining; Bulan; coal mining 567
County of Clay/Board of Education; Manchester 550

6th District

East Central — Lexington; Frankfort

The 6th embodies the culture and the economic pursuits that most outsiders associate with the state of Kentucky. This district is the heart of the Bluegrass region, which regularly spawns Kentucky Derby champions and is host to considerable tobacco and liquor interests.

Lexington, the district's largest city, is known best as the hub of the country's horse-breeding industry. Hundreds of horse farms—ranging in size from just a few acres to more than 6,000—cover the rich bluegrass pastureland within a 35-mile radius of the city.

Consolidated with Fayette County in 1974, Lexington experienced moderate growth in the 1970s and 1980s, spurred by the arrival of some clean, high-tech industry. By the early 1990s, the growth flattened out, in part because of some job losses associated with IBM's sale of its printer division to Lexmark. But, as the market center of the state's burley tobacco industry and home to the University of Kentucky, the city has been able to avoid an economic freefall.

The areas outside Fayette County experienced more rapid

population growth and industrial development in the 1980s, raising concerns about overdevelopment. Bourbon distilleries, tobacco and horse farms used to dominate the landscape, but they are being joined by new residential divisions and light industrial sprawl.

In Georgetown (Scott County), a Toyota Camry assembly plant that opened in 1988 was already expanding in 1993. Neighboring Woodford County is reaping some of the economic rewards of the plant; it ranks as the state's second-highest in per capita income.

Within commuting distance of Lexington, the northern portion of Madison County—the district's second-most populous—includes bedroom communities for Lexington workers. Eastern Kentucky University (15,300 students) is in the southern portion of the district in the tobacco market town of Richmond.

The influx of white-collar executives and engineers to Lexington, and the changing landscape in the farming counties to the south and west, have increased Republican competitiveness across the district.

The region's partisan roots are reflected in voter registration figures that favor the Democratic Party, but Republicans regularly carry Fayette County. In 1992 George Bush carried almost all the counties south and west of Fayette. At the congressional level, though, every county in the 6th voted for the longtime Democratic mayor of Lexington in the open-seat House race.

In 1992 Bill Clinton was able to carry Franklin County on the strength of state government workers in Frankfort. Chosen as the state capital in a compromise between Lexington and Louisville, this Kentucky River Valley city has stayed modest-sized and content to do the business of government.

East of Lexington, Democratic strength is found in the farming counties that remain largely untouched by Lexington sprawl.

Election Returns

	6th District	Democrat	Republican
1992	President*	101,762 (41.3%)	105,191 (42.7%)
	House	135,613 (60.7%)	87,816 (39.3%)
1990	Senate	69,240 (48.8%)	72,734 (51.2%)
1988	President	89,837 (42.0%)	124,021 (58.0%)
1987	Governor	74,630 (58.9%)	51,999 (41.1%)
1986	Senate	84,880 (76.5%)	26,026 (23.5%)

*Vote for Perot was 39,655 (16.1%).

Demographics

Population 614,270

Percent change from 1980 18.4%

Land area 4,642 square miles

Population per square mile 132

Counties, 1990 population

Anderson	14,571	Fayette	225,366
Bath	9,692	Franklin	43,781
Bourbon	19,236	Garrard	11,579
Boyle	25,641	Harrison	16,248
Clark	29,496	Jessamine	30,508
Estill	14,614	Lincoln (pt.)	15,719
Madison	57,508	Powell	11,686
Mercer	19,148	Scott	23,867
Montgomery	19,561	Woodford	19,955
Nicholas (pt.)	6,094		

Cities, 1990 population (10,000 or more)

Danville	12,420	Nicholasville	13,603
Frankfort	25,968	Richmond	21,155
Georgetown	11,414	Winchester	15,799
Lexington-Fayette	225,366		

Race and Hispanic origin
White 90.7%
Black 8.1%
American Indian, Eskimo, or Aleut. 0.1%
Asian or Pacific Islander 0.8%
Other 0.2%
Hispanic origin 0.7%

Ancestry

American	14.8%	Irish	18.0%
Dutch	2.2%	Italian	1.5%
English	17.2%	Scotch Irish	3.2%
French	2.5%	Scottish	2.4%
German	19.1%		

Universities/colleges, 1990-1991 enrollment
Asbury College, Wilmore 1,042
Asbury Theological Seminary, Wilmore 671
Berea College, Berea 1,535
Centre College, Danville 858
Eastern Kentucky University, Richmond 15,290
Georgetown College, Georgetown 1,595
Kentucky College of Business, Lexington 712
Kentucky State University, Frankfort 2,506
Lexington Community College, Lexington 4,580
Midway College, Midway 556
Transylvania University, Lexington 1,091
University of Kentucky, Lexington 22,542

Newspapers, total circulation (in all districts)
Danville Advocate-Messenger 11,344
Lexington Herald-Leader 121,674
Louisville Courier Journal 235,144

Commercial television stations, affiliations
ADI: Lexington (100%)
WDKY-TV, Danville-Lexington (Fox)
WKYT-TV, Lexington (CBS)
WLEX-TV, Lexington (NBC)
WTVQ-TV, Lexington (ABC)

Cable television systems, total subscribers
Community Cable SVC Div.; Frankfort 11,800
Simmons Communications Inc.; Richmond 9,700
Simmons Communications Inc.; Winchester 5,908
TCI of North Central Kentucky; Danville 5,729
Telecable of Lexington Inc.; Lexington 71,418

Military installations, 1991
Lexington Bluegrass Army Depot Activity, Lexington 2,214

Businesses and other major employers
State of Kentucky/Cabinet of Human Resources; Frankfort 11,021
University of Kentucky & Medical Center; Lexington 8,900
Toyota Motor Mfg. USA; Georgetown; motor vehicles 4,000

Lexmark Intl.; Lexington; computer/office equipment 3,000
State of Kentucky/Social Services Dept.; Frankfort 3,000
State of Kentucky/Parks Dept.; Frankfort 2,500
State of Kentucky; Frankfort 1,900
Eastern Kentucky University; Richmond 1,700
St. Joe's Hospital; Lexington 1,700
Union Underwear Co. Inc.; Frankfort; underwear knitting mills 1,200
Square D Co.; Lexington; electric distribution equipment 1,089
American Standard Inc./Trane Co.; Lexington; refrigeration 1,075
Central Baptist Hospital; Lexington 1,020
Mid-Central Investment Co.; Lexington; credit institutions 1,000
State of Kentucky/Police Academy; Frankfort 1,000
Rand McNally & Co.; Versailles; publishing 900
Kentucky Central Life Insurance Co.; Lexington; life insurance 845
Link-Belt Construction Equipment Co.; Lexington; construction machinery 820
American Greetings Corp.; Danville; greeting cards 800
County of Madison/Board of Education; Richmond 780
ATR Wire & Cable Co.; Danville; textile goods 700

Jockey Intl. Inc./Jockey; Cynthiana; underwear 700
GTE Products Corp./Sylvania Lighting; Versailles; electric lighting 700
Texas Instruments Inc.; Versailles; measuring devices 700
McAlpin Co.; Lexington; department stores 700
Good Samaritan Hospital; Lexington 700
State of Kentucky/Education Dept.; Frankfort 700
Kentucky State University; Frankfort 700
R. R. Donnelley & Sons Co.; Danville; commercial printing 670
Matsushita Floor Care Co.; Danville; household appliances 670
County of Jessamine/Board of Education; Nicholasville 650
State of Kentucky/Transportation Dept.; Frankfort 617
Humana Inc./Humana Hospital Lexington; Lexington 600
Jockey Intl. Inc.; Carlisle; underwear 600
House of Laird; Lexington; catalog retailers 600
Serv-Air Inc.; Lexington; airport services 564
Berea College; Berea 552
Whirlpool Corp./Kitchen Aide; Mt. Sterling; household appliances 550
Herald Lexington Leader Co.; Lexington; newspapers 549
Minnesota Mining & Mfg. Co.; Cynthiana; paper mills 520

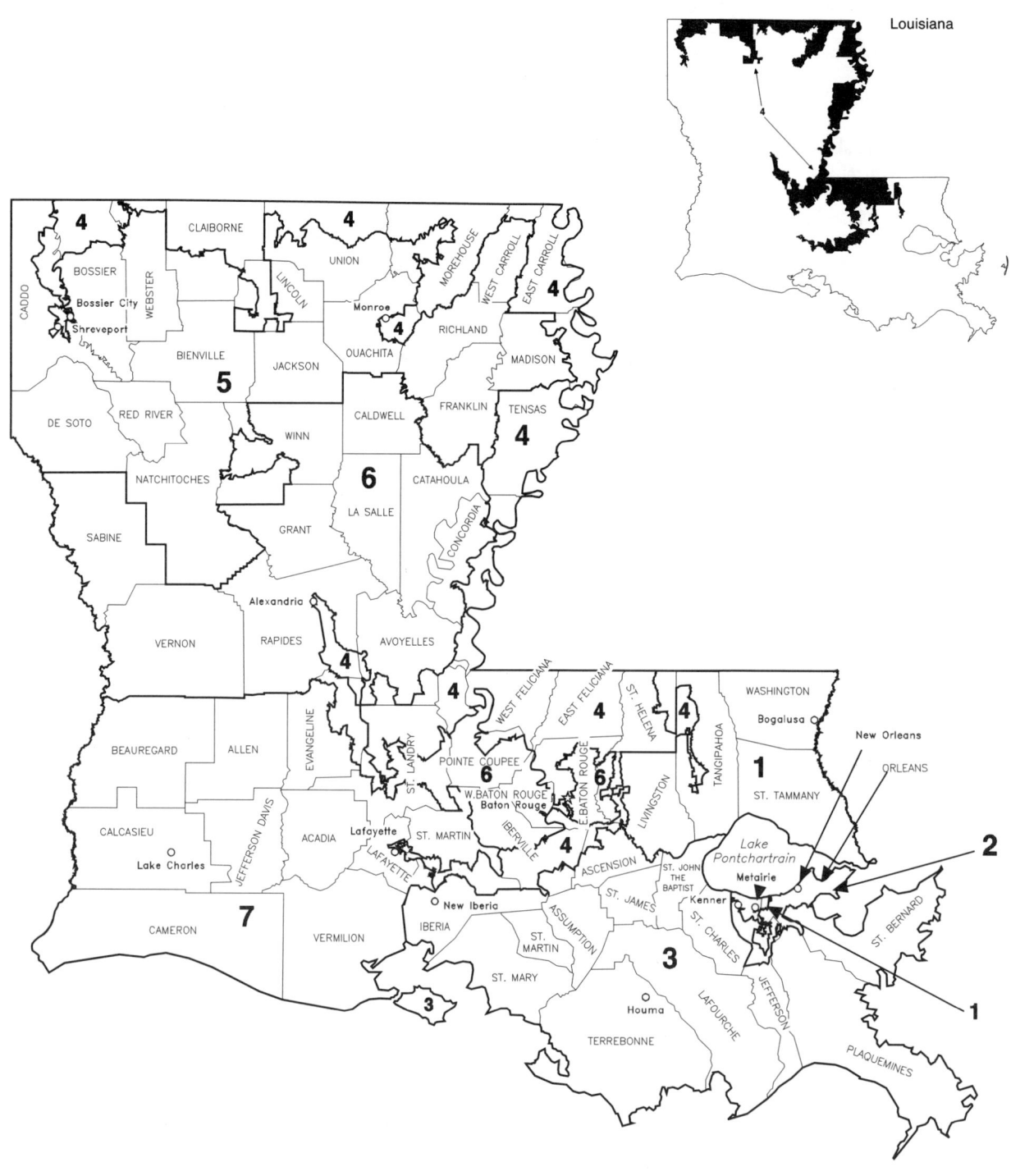

Louisiana

Louisiana

Louisiana entered 1992 redistricting compelled to create a second majority-black district. The mapmakers' task was complicated, however, by the loss of one of its House seats in reapportionment, dropping its total to seven. (During the 1980s, Louisiana's population grew by fewer than 15,000 people.) That meant that to draw a new, open black seat, incumbents would have to be paired in two other districts.

As the 1990s began, Louisiana continued to weather a nearly decade-long recession stemming from a decline in its oil and gas industries. The state's economic malaise contributed to Democratic Gov. Edwin W. Edwards' 1987 defeat for re-election at the hands of then-Democrat Buddy Roemer.

The 1991 gubernatorial election, in which Edwards ousted Roemer, who had become a Republican, had a profound effect on redistricting. Not only did the party label switch in the governor's mansion, but the legislative leadership was realigned. Edwards, whose political career thrived on support among Louisiana's blacks, was propelled to a landslide victory over former Ku Klux Klan leader and former Nazi sympathizer David Duke, fueled in large measure by a vigorous voter-registration and get-out-the-vote effort waged on his behalf by the African American community.

With Edwards in the governor's mansion, legislators resistant to drawing a second black-majority district had no chance of prevailing.

Louisiana's first black-majority district was created after a federal court in 1983 upheld a voting-rights challenge to the map in place for the 1982 elections. Although the new 2nd District had a 58 percent black population, it continued to re-elect its white incumbent until she retired in 1991. In 1990, Democrat William J. Jefferson became Louisiana's first black elected to Congress since Reconstruction.

Drawing another black district, however, would not be as simple as creating the 2nd. Based in New Orleans, the 2nd is the state's most compact district. But with the 2nd needing to gain people to attain the required population level, legislators could not rely on New Orleans' population for the new district, ensuring that it would have to twist around the state across several rural parishes (Louisiana's equivalent of counties) with substantial black populations.

The map that the Legislature passed in May 1992 contained one of the strangest-looking congressional districts in the country—and perhaps in U.S. history. The open 4th District, with a 66 percent black population, starts in Shreveport, in northwest Louisiana. Moving east, it narrowly paints the state's northern border with Arkansas. It turns south to follow the Mississippi River along the eastern border with Mississippi, and then juts west into central Louisiana, east to gather part of the Florida parishes and south into the state capital, Baton Rouge. Patricia Lowrey of the nonpartisan House Reapportionment Project dubbed it "the 'Z' with drips," and so it is: an enormous, Z-shaped creature collecting all or part of 28 parishes. Democrat Cleo Fields of Baton Rouge, who chaired the state Senate committee charged with drawing the new map, was elected in 1992.

The new map paired four white incumbents in two districts. In the 5th, which cut a swath across most of northern Louisiana, Republican Jim McCrery bested an eight-term Democrat. And in the 6th, which sprawled across central Louisiana but also reached into Baton Rouge, Republican Richard H. Baker edged past a fellow Republican, whose 8th District had been disintegrated.

A 1993 court challenge based on the racial composition of the state's seven districts put the future of Louisiana's map in doubt. Most likely the outcome will be decided by the U.S. Supreme Court, which in 1993 in a separate redistricting case (*Shaw v. Reno*) called into question bizarre-looking racial gerrymanders similar to Louisiana's.

Table 1 Population

District	Population	Population under 18	Voting-age population	Median age
1	602,859	158,715	444,144	33.4
2	602,689	176,414	426,275	30.4
3	602,950	187,955	414,995	29.9
4	602,884	189,384	413,500	29.2
5	602,816	165,795	437,021	32.4
6	602,854	168,176	434,678	30.8
7	602,921	180,830	422,091	30.8
State	4,219,973	1,227,269	2,992,704	31.0

317

Table 2 Voting-Age Persons

District	White*	Black*	American Indian, Eskimo, or Aleut*	Asian or Pacific Islander*	Other*	Hispanic*	Male*	Female*
1	89.1%	8.7%	0.3%	1.0%	0.9%	4.0%	47.1%	52.9%
2	40.5	56.2	0.2	1.9	1.1	3.8	45.5	54.5
3	78.1	19.5	1.3	0.7	0.4	2.4	47.8	52.2
4	36.7	62.6	0.1	0.3	0.2	0.9	46.1	53.9
5	79.5	19.5	0.3	0.5	0.3	1.1	46.6	53.4
6	85.1	12.9	0.4	1.1	0.4	1.9	48.4	51.6
7	81.2	17.7	0.2	0.6	0.3	1.3	47.5	52.5
State	70.3	27.9	0.4	0.9	0.5	2.2	47.0	53.0

*As percent of voting-age population.

Table 3 Voting-Age Persons by Age Groups

District	18-24*	25-44*	45-54*	55-64*	65 and over*
1	12.8%	44.9%	14.3%	11.8%	16.1%
2	16.3	44.5	12.8	10.8	15.6
3	15.2	46.0	14.2	11.3	13.2
4	17.8	41.8	12.6	11.2	16.6
5	15.2	40.8	13.9	12.2	17.9
6	16.7	44.1	13.5	10.9	14.8
7	14.8	44.3	13.7	12.0	15.3
State	15.5	43.8	13.6	11.5	15.7

*As percent of voting-age population.

Table 4 Income and Occupation

District	Median family income	Families in poverty	White collar*	Blue collar*	Service*	Farm*
1	$33,061	11.2%	65.2%	21.7%	11.4%	1.7%
2	21,677	27.3	57.3	22.3	19.3	1.1
3	27,116	17.8	49.2	35.9	12.2	2.7
4	17,957	32.8	44.8	29.4	22.3	3.5
5	27,817	15.9	57.0	27.7	12.4	3.0
6	29,808	14.0	61.7	24.5	11.4	2.4
7	25,609	19.2	52.8	31.4	12.8	3.0
State	26,313	19.4	55.9	27.4	14.2	2.5

*As percent of employed persons age 16 and over.

Table 5 Education: School Years Completed

District	Less than grade 9*	Grades 9-12 no diploma*	High school diploma*	College bachelor's degree or higher*
1	10.1%	13.6%	30.7%	22.0%
2	14.3	19.9	26.1	17.5
3	19.5	17.7	36.0	9.8
4	19.4	22.6	30.3	11.1
5	11.0	16.1	32.3	17.5
6	11.1	13.7	33.2	19.9
7	18.3	16.0	33.1	14.1
State	14.7	17.0	31.7	16.1

*As percent of persons age 25 and over.

Table 6 Housing and Residential Patterns

District	Owner occupied	Renter occupied	Urban	Rural
1	68.9%	31.1%	71.8%	28.2%
2	45.8	54.2	99.7	0.3
3	75.0	25.0	66.5	33.5
4	61.9	38.1	69.7	30.3
5	70.5	29.5	56.4	43.6
6	69.1	30.9	54.7	45.3
7	70.4	29.6	57.7	42.3
State	65.9	34.1	68.1	31.9

1st District

Southeast — Metairie; Kenner

The 1st District is conservative territory dominated by the mostly white suburban communities that ring New Orleans. The district starts in New Orleans' upper-class northwest corner, takes in the city's southwestern suburbs in east Jefferson Parish and then runs north to include the northeastern corner of southern Louisiana.

The east bank of Jefferson Parish anchors the district. The area is made up of affluent New Orleans suburbs such as Metairie, the base of the state legislative seat held until 1992 by David Duke, the former Ku Klux Klansman-turned-GOP-conservative. Nearly half the district resides in east Jefferson; the area is packed with white-collar conservatives, many of whom sleep in the affluent suburbs dotting the shore of Lake Pontchartrain and work in New Orleans.

Historically, conservative candidates have done well in the 1st. District voters gave Duke 56 percent of the vote in his 1990 Senate primary and George Bush received 56 percent in 1992. Redistricting for the 1990s pushed the 1st further to the right, as cartographers struggled to carve a second black-majority district. The mapmakers' effort left the 1st with the smallest black population in any district in the state, 10 percent. Blacks constitute 31 percent of the statewide populace.

From east Jefferson the 1st skips across Lake Pontchartrain to take in most or all of four parishes north of New Orleans: St. Tammany, Washington, Tangipahoa and Livingston. The richest parish in the state, St. Tammany is home to nearly a quarter of the 1st's voters. Once an isolated vacation area for residents escaping the heat and humidity of New Orleans, St. Tammany has been the fastest-growing parish in the state in the last two decades. In the 1970s its population grew nearly 70 percent; in the 1980s it grew more than 30 percent. Many of the newcomers are transplants from the East and Midwest who have maintained GOP voting habits. St. Tammany gave George Bush 56 percent of the vote in 1992 to 31 percent for Bill Clinton.

To the west of St. Tammany lies the former strawberry capital of the world, Tangipahoa Parish. It is now home to many New Orleans and Baton Rouge commuters, but Tangipahoa farms still produce great amounts of strawberries and bell peppers. The parish economy has diversified and is sustained by Southeastern Louisiana University (10,300 students) and distribution centers for Winn-Dixie and Superfine supermarkets. A General Dynamics plant chosen to build magnets for the federal superconducting super collider project was to bring more than 1,000 new jobs to the parish, by Congress' 1993 decision to kill the project left the job prospects in doubt.

Redistricting bolstered the conservative nature of the 1st by adding rural Washington Parish to the district's northeastern corner. Voters there in 1968 gave George Wallace more than 70 percent of the presidential vote, and they supported Duke in his 1990 and 1991 campaigns. Predominantly a farming community that grows watermelons and breeds chickens, Washington Parish resembles the Mississippi counties it borders.

Election Returns

	1st District	Democrat	Republican
1992	President*	86,886 (31.4%)	155,422 (56.1%)
	House †	—	83,685 (72.7%)
1988	President	94,981 (33.3%)	190,589 (66.7%)

*Vote for Perot was 34,494 (12.5%).   †Data from open primary.

Demographics

Population 602,859

Percent change from 1980 14.8%

Land area 2,881 square miles

Population per square mile 209

Parishes, 1990 population*
Jefferson Parish (pt.) 276,800
Livingston Parish (pt.) 29,453
Orleans Parish (pt.) 40,975
St. Helena Parish (pt.) 2,481
St. Tammany Parish 144,508
Tangipahoa Parish (pt.) 65,457
Washington Parish 43,185

Parishes are Louisiana's equivalent of counties.

Cities, 1990 population (10,000 or more)
Bogalusa 14,280
Estelle CDP 14,091
Jefferson CDP (pt.) 12,607
Kenner (pt.) 51,573
Marrero CDP (pt.) 16,639
Metairie CDP (pt.) 146,321
New Orleans (pt.) 40,975
River Ridge CDP (pt.) 13,533
Slidell 24,124

Race and Hispanic origin
White 87.6%
Black 10.1%
American Indian, Eskimo, or Aleut. 0.3%
Asian or Pacific Islander 1.1%
Other 0.9%
Hispanic origin 4.1%

Ancestry
American 5.7%
Dutch 1.2%
English 10.9%
French 21.6%
French Canadian 5.4%
German 22.5%
Irish 18.2%
Italian 11.8%
Scotch Irish 2.3%
Scottish 1.4%

Universities/colleges, 1990-1991 enrollment
Delgado Community College, New Orleans 11,614
Southeastern Louisiana University, Hammond 10,262
Tulane University, New Orleans 10,791

Newspapers, total circulation (in all districts)
Baton Rouge Advocate 100,187
Hammond Daily Star 11,303
New Orleans Times-Picayune 266,592

Commercial television stations, affiliations
ADI: New Orleans (79%) and Baton Rouge (21%)

Cable television systems, total subscribers
Cablevision Ind. of St. Tammany; Mandeville 6,539
Cablevision Ind. of St. Tammany; Slidell 17,250
Cox Cable New Orleans; New Orleans 88,911
Cox Cable/Jefferson Parish Inc.; Jefferson Parish 114,700
Parish Cablevision; Hammond 19,000

Military installations, 1991
Hammond Air National Guard Communications Station, Hammond 28

Businesses and other major employers
Tulane University; New Orleans 4,318
Ochsner Alton Medical Foundation Hospital; New Orleans 2,800
East Jefferson General Hospital; Metairie 1,900
Livingston Parish School Board; Livingston 1,625
AT&T Co.; Metairie; telephone communication services 1,500
National Tea Co./Superfine; Metairie; grocery stores 1,500
Medforce Intl. Inc.; Metairie; health services 1,500
Southeastern Louisiana University; Hammond 1,247
Ochsner Clinic Health Services Corp.; New Orleans; medical doctors 1,200
Advantage Nursing Services; Metairie; personnel supply services 1,200
Boeing Co./Boeing Petroleum Services Inc.; New Orleans; petroleum products 1,110
Winn-Dixie Louisiana Inc.; New Orleans; grocery stores 1,000
Slidell Memorial Hospital & Medical Center; Slidell 880
Hammond Developmental Center; Hammond 845
Children's Hospital; New Orleans 800
Seventh Ward General Hospital; Hammond 753
Washington Parish School District; Franklinton 700
Southeastern Louisiana Hospital; Mandeville 650
Gaylord Container Corp./Milling Plant; Bogalusa; paper mills 635
Audubon Institute/Park Zootique; New Orleans; zoo 600
St. Tammany Parish Hospital; Covington 559
American Nursing Service Inc.; Metairie; personnel supply services 550

2nd District

East — New Orleans

New Orleans' melange of temptations, sensations and attractions gives it a unique mystique in America and lures a steady stream of visitors. But the city of just under a half-million residents has more on its mind than granting hedonists their fancies.

In recent years the city has endured population decline, budget crunches, teacher strikes, drug problems and racial hostility. Mardi Gras itself—a $500 million golden goose for the local economy every year—has been caught up in controversy. Since the 1992 passage of a city ordinance outlawing many social clubs' exclusive practices, there has been considerable debate over whether the krewes (carnival organizations) that are the backbone of the Mardi Gras parade should be punished for discriminatory practices.

New Orleans' economy is rooted in service industries. A few energy, mining and construction firms have headquarters here, including McDermott International Inc., but retail and hospitality services such as hotels, restaurants and bars employ a majority of the city's workers. The French Quarter is famous for its art galleries and fine dining. Nearby, sports fans descend on the 75,000-seat Louisiana Superdome to root for pro football's Saints.

New Orleans is an ethnic potpourri, with blacks, Italians, Irish, Cubans and the largest Honduran population outside Central America. The city also has more than 50,000 college students; schools include the University of New Orleans, Tulane University (1st District), Loyola University and Xavier University, the nation's only Catholic college with a predominantly black student population.

The Algiers section, which sits on the west bank of the Mississippi River, is a blend of high- and low-income residents, new condominiums and well-tended historic buildings. On the east bank between the Mississippi and Lake Pontchartrain is a fascinating variety of neighborhoods: comfortable Carrolton, an area of middle-class whites on the west side of the city; the wealthy Uptown section, with its professionals and academics; the predominantly black Lower 9th Ward; and fast-growing New Orleans East, reaching into the city's marshland and home to middle-class black and white families.

Created by court order in 1983, the 2nd was Louisiana's first black-majority House district. Despite its demographics, the 2nd continued to elect its white Democrat incumbent until she retired in 1991. In 1990, William Jefferson was elected to become the state's first black Representative since Reconstruction.

As it emerged from 1992 redistricting, the 2nd includes 85 percent of New Orleans and has a black population of 61 percent. It takes in southern parts of Kenner, a growing suburb west of New Orleans that includes the international airport. A quarter of the district's people live in northern Jefferson Parish.

The electorate is overwhelmingly Democratic. Bill Clinton won nearly 70 percent here in 1992.

Election Returns

	2nd District	Democrat	Republican
1992	President*	153,342 (69.2%)	54,555 (24.6%)
	House †	67,030 (73.5%)	—
1988	President	109,297 (70.1%)	46,567 (29.9%)

*Vote for Perot was 13,813 (6.2%).   †Data from open primary.

Demographics

Population 602,689

Percent change from 1980 14.4%

Land area 258 square miles

Population per square mile 2,335

Parishes, 1990 population*
Jefferson Parish (pt.) 146,726   Orleans Parish (pt.) 455,963
Parishes are Louisiana's equivalent of counties.

Cities, 1990 population (10,000 or more)
Gretna 17,208   Kenner (pt.) 20,460
Harvey CDP (pt.) 17,737   Marrero CDP (pt.) 20,032
New Orleans (pt.) 455,963
Terrytown CDP (pt.) 14,136
Westwego 11,218

Race and Hispanic origin
White 35.5%
Black 61.0%
American Indian, Eskimo, or Aleut. 0.2%
Asian or Pacific Islander 2.2%
Other 1.1%
Hispanic origin 3.7%

Ancestry
American 2.9%   German 9.1%
English 4.3%   Irish 6.4%
French 9.0%   Italian 4.3%
French Canadian 3.0%

Universities/colleges, 1990-1991 enrollment
Dillard University, New Orleans 1,998
Louisiana State University Medical Center, New Orleans 2,539
Loyola University, New Orleans 5,400
New Orleans Baptist Theological Seminary, New Orleans 1,461
Our Lady of Holy Cross College, New Orleans 1,049
Southern University, New Orleans 4,064
Xavier University, New Orleans 2,944
University of New Orleans 15,322

Newspapers, total circulation (in all districts)
New Orleans Times-Picayune 266,592

Commercial television stations, affiliations
ADI: New Orleans (100%)
WCCL, New Orleans (None)
WGNO, New Orleans (None)
WWL-TV, New Orleans (CBS)

Cable television systems, total subscribers
Cox Cable New Orleans; New Orleans 88,911
Cox Cable/Jefferson Parish Inc.; Jefferson Parish 114,700

Businesses and other major employers
Avondale Industries Inc.; Westwego; shipbuilding/repairing 7,500
Louisiana State University Medical Center; New Orleans 5,000
NASA/Michoud Assembly Facility; New Orleans; space research services 5,000
Martin Marietta Corp./Manned Space Systems; New Orleans; space vehicles/parts 3,800
Charity Hospital of New Orleans; New Orleans 3,339
Tulane University Medical Center; New Orleans; medical doctors 3,000
U.S. Postal Service; New Orleans 2,887
U.S. Transportation Dept.; New Orleans 2,520
Odeco Oil & Gas Co./Contract Drilling Div.; New Orleans; oil/gas services 2,101
Touro Infirmary; New Orleans 1,850
First Commerce Corp.; New Orleans; commercial banks 1,706
Hibernia Corp.; New Orleans; commercial banks 1,630
Touro Community Mental Health Center; New Orleans 1,600
U.S. Veterans Affairs Dept.; New Orleans 1,600

City of New Orleans/Sewage & Water Board; New Orleans 1,562

Hilton Hotels Corp./New Orleans Hilton Riverside Tower; New Orleans; hotel 1,500

West Jefferson Medical Center; Marrero 1,470

U.S. Army Corp. of Engineers; New Orleans 1,400

U.S. Agriculture Dept./National Finance Center; New Orleans 1,400

Southern Baptist Hospital; New Orleans 1,380

Regional Transit Authority; New Orleans; transportation 1,321

Whitney Holding Corp.; New Orleans; commercial banks 1,305

City of New Orleans; New Orleans 1,300

Entergy Corp.; New Orleans; electric services 1,200

U.S. Coast Guard; New Orleans 1,200

New Orleans Public Service; New Orleans; utility services 1,108

Mercy Hospital of New Orleans; New Orleans 1,100

Pendleton Memorial Methodist Hospital; New Orleans 1,031

Texaco Exploration & Production; New Orleans; petroleum management 1,000

Chevron USA Inc.; New Orleans; petroleum management 1,000

Times Picayune Publishing Corp.; New Orleans; newspapers 990

Exxon Corp.; New Orleans; petroleum/natural gas 900

Hotel Dieu Hospital; New Orleans 900

Delta Air Lines Inc.; New Orleans; airline 880

Hyatt Corp./Hyatt Regency; New Orleans; hotel 830

Freeport-McMoran Inc.; New Orleans; chemicals/fertilizers 800

Pellerin Milnor Corp.; Kenner; commercial laundry equipment 800

CS&M Assoc./Sheraton New Orleans Hotel; New Orleans; hotel 800

Marriott Corp./New Orleans Marriott; New Orleans; hotel 800

New Orleans Roosevelt Venture/Fairmont Hotel of New Orleans; New Orleans; hotel 800

Archdiocese of New Orleans/Archdiocese Food Service Dept.; New Orleans; religious organizations 700

City of Kenner; Kenner 698

American Cyanamid Co./Chemical Products Div.; Westwego; pharmaceuticals 658

Pan American Life Insurance; New Orleans; life insurance 650

Mobil Exploration Producing Service; New Orleans; oil/gas services 645

U.S. Customs Services; New Orleans 630

Xavier University; New Orleans 618

Textron Inc./Textron Marine Systems; New Orleans; shipbuilding/repairing 600

Louisiana Coca Cola Bottling Co.; New Orleans; beverages 600

Trinity Industries Inc./Equitable Shipyard Div.; New Orleans; shipbuilding/repairing 600

Vinson Guard Service Inc.; New Orleans; business/security services 600

Loyola University; New Orleans 600

State of Louisiana/Transportation Dept.; Westwego; road construction 587

National Building Service & Maintenance; New Orleans; building services 582

Tidex Intl. Inc.; New Orleans; boat charters 575

National Medical Enterprises/Joellen Smith Medical Center; New Orleans; medical doctors 550

Wemco Inc.; New Orleans; outerwear 530

Louisiana Land Exploration; New Orleans; petroleum/natural gas 525

3rd District

South Central — Houma; New Iberia

The 3rd begins below Lafayette, in the Cajun heartland of Louisiana, and sweeps east. New Iberia, whose nearby Avery Island produces Tabasco hot sauce, marks a western boundary. The Gulf of Mexico lies to the east and south.

Bayous, grassy marshes and hardwood swamps finger into the gulf for hundreds of miles here, making this a major wetlands area where ecosystems and the economy often intertwine. Alligators, game fish and water birds abound, but so do offshore oil and gas rigs and shrimp boats.

Intertwining is not always easy. Commercial fishermen required to attach turtle-excluder devices to their nets complain that the trapdoor releases free not only turtles but also their catch. Environmentalists contend that channels dredged so that rigs can be hauled offshore accelerate coastal erosion. Local residents have begun recycling Christmas trees as reef-builders in the gulf.

Economically, though, the 3rd has been hard hit for a long time. The lushness of the land has belied a Dust Bowl economy during much of the last decade. And Hurricane Andrew added to the malaise late in August 1992.

After devastating Homestead, Fla., the storm tore through the district, on a path roughly parallel to U.S. 90, causing more than $500 million in damage. Everyone feared the worst for the sugar cane, the agricultural mainstay here, but farmers turned in a record crop, up 10 percent in harvested acres from a year earlier.

In the oil and gas industry, no such storybook recovery has been forthcoming. The district, a dominant player in the oil extraction business, has been retrenching ever since Louisiana crude oil prices fell from a 1981 high of $37 a barrel to $10.50 a barrel in 1986. Prices have climbed back to about $20 a barrel, but after a modest rally, drilling activity in the 3rd has gone sluggish.

Louisiana produces nearly 30 percent of the nation's natural gas, which is abundant in the 3rd. Drilling for gas took up some economic slack here, but lower demand led to a glut and tumbling prices in the early 1990s, and the district economy wobbled again.

Chemical manufacturing has made a major comeback from its 1980s hard times. Many chemical plants operate along the Mississippi River between Baton Rouge and New Orleans. Most of this stretch lies in territory the 3rd picked up in 1992 redistricting: one precinct in Iberville, nearly all of Ascension and all of St. James and St. John, the Baptist parishes.

Large black populations in St. James and St. John parishes and the presence of labor unions in the chemical plants produce a more liberal tilt here than in the rest of the 3rd. St. James, which is 50 percent black, cast 60 percent of its 1992 presidential vote for Bill Clinton. Redistricting otherwise left the 3rd largely unchanged. White-dominated, Catholic and strongly Democratic at the local levels, the district remains inclined to vote Republican (or at least not Democratic) for president. The combined George Bush-Ross Perot tally in 1992 was 55 percent.

Election Returns

	3rd District	Democrat	Republican
1992	President*	115,406 (44.8%)	105,989 (41.1%)
	House †	82,047 (81.7%)	—
1988	President	101,357 (45.9%)	119,656 (54.1%)

*Vote for Perot was 36,200 (14.1%).   †Data from open primary.

Demographics

Population 602,950

Percent change from 1980 14.6%

Land area 6,566 square miles

Population per square mile 92

Parishes, 1990 population*

Ascension Parish (pt.) 48,214	St. Charles Parish 42,437
Assumption Parish 22,753	St. James Parish 20,879
Iberia Parish 68,297	St. John the Baptist Parish 39,996
Iberville Parish (pt.) 1,068	St. Martin Parish (pt.) 1,392
Jefferson Parish (pt.) 24,780	
Lafourche Parish 85,860	St. Mary Parish 58,086
Plaquemines Parish 25,575	Terrebonne Parish 96,982
St. Bernard Parish 66,631	

Parishes are Louisiana's equivalent of counties.

Cities, 1990 population (10,000 or more)

Bayou Cane CDP 15,876	Morgan City 14,531
Chalmette CDP 31,860	New Iberia 31,828
Houma 30,495	Thibodaux 14,035
La Place CDP 24,194	

Race and Hispanic origin
- White 75.3%
- Black 21.8%
- American Indian, Eskimo, or Aleut. 1.5%
- Asian or Pacific Islander 0.9%
- Other 0.4%
- Hispanic origin 2.4%

Ancestry

American 4.8%	German 12.1%
English 4.6%	Irish 8.0%
French 20.5%	Italian 6.5%
French Canadian 25.1%	

Universities/colleges, 1990-1991 enrollment
Nicholls State University, Thibodaux 7,356
St. Bernard Parish Community College, Chalmette 1,021

Newspapers, total circulation (in all districts)
Baton Rouge Advocate 100,187
Houma Courier 19,974
Lafayette Advertiser 34,089
New Orleans Times-Picayune 266,592
Thibodaux Daily Comet 11,970

Commercial television stations, affiliations
ADI: New Orleans (74%), Baton Rouge (16%) and Lafayette (10%)
WDSU-TV, New Orleans (NBC)
WNOL-TV, New Orleans (Fox)
WVUE, New Orleans (ABC)

Cable television systems, total subscribers
Allen's TV Cable Service Inc.; Morgan City 6,350
CVI; Lafourche Parish 10,579
Callais Cablevision Inc.; Golden Meadow 9,887
Cox Cable/Jefferson Parish Inc.; Jefferson Parish 114,700
New Iberia Cable TV; New Iberia 13,900
Riverlands Cablevision; La Place 7,927
St. Charles Cable Co.; Luling 10,000
TCI; Violet 15,480
TCI of Louisiana; Gonzales 11,275
Terrebonne Cablevision; Bourg 7,920
Vision Cable of Houma; Houma 19,000

Military installations, 1991
New Orleans Naval Air Station, New Orleans 1,965

Businesses and other major employers
McDermott Inc.; Morgan City; industrial machinery 3,000
McDermott Intl. Inc.; Amelia; construction machinery 2,000
Martin Mills Inc./Jeanerette Mills; Jeanerette; knitting mills 1,800
Iberia Parish School Board; New Iberia 1,759
Shell Oil Co.; Norco; gasoline 1,700
BASF Corp.; Geismar; industrial inorganic chemicals 1,200
Union Carbide Chemicals & Plastics Co.; Hahnville; petroleum refining 1,100
Boeing Petroleum Services Inc.; St. James; business services 1,085
St. Bernard Parish School Board; Chalmette 1,070
St. Charles Parish School Board; Luling 1,069
Iberia Parish Airport Authority/Acadian Regional Airport; New Iberia; airport 1,000
Terrebonne General Medical Center; Houma 950
Louisiana Power & Light Co.; Hahnville; electric services 919
Entergy Operations Inc./LP&L Inc.; Killona; metal forgings/stampings 900
Parish of Plaquemines; Braithwaite 775
State of Louisiana/Health & Human Resources Dept.; Houma 742
State of Louisiana/Metropolitan Development Center; Belle Chasse 674
Mobil Oil Corp.; Chalmette; petroleum refining 665
Parish of St. Bernard; Chalmette 650
Bollinger Machine Shop & Shipyard; Lockport; shipbuilding/repairing 620
National Medical Enterprises/Meadowcrest Hospital; Gretna 602
Kaiser Aluminum & Chemical Corp.; Gramercy; aluminum/mineral products 600
Nicholls State University; Thibodaux 600
Du Pont E. I. De Nemours & Co.; La Place; inorganic chemicals/synthetic rubber 590
Gulf Island Fabrication Inc.; Houma; boat sections/metal products 560
Offshore Food Service Inc.; Houma; bars/restaurants 550
Shell Oil Co./Shell Chemical Co. Div.; Geismar; organic chemicals/pesticides 542

4th District

North and East — Parts of Monroe, Shreveport and Baton Rouge

A Z-shaped creature, the far-flung 4th zigzags through all or part of 28 parishes and five of Louisiana's largest cities, digesting black communities to create the state's second black-majority district (see district map on page 316).

From industrial Shreveport, the district snakes east along the Arkansas border, then follows the Mississippi River southward. At Pointe Coupee Parish it splits: One finger plunges west, deep into central Louisiana, and the other continues east and south to the Cajun city of Lafayette. The bizarre shape of the 4th represents what the Louisiana Legislature had to do to create a new district with a black majority (the 4th is 66 percent black). Until 1992 redistricting, Louisiana had only one black-majority district (New Orleans' 2nd), although blacks make up 31 percent of the state's population.

Poverty permeates many of the nooks and crannies of this overwhelmingly Democratic district. Registered Democrats outnumber registered Republicans by more than 8-to-1. In 1988, when Michael S. Dukakis lost Louisiana decisively, he still got 55 percent of votes cast in areas that now make up the 4th.

While the 4th includes rural farming areas, it is dominated by the black communities of five Louisiana cities. As chairman of the 1992 state redistricting committee, then-state Sen. Cleo Fields ensured that Baton Rouge, his home base, anchored the 4th; he went on to win the House seat in 1992. The Baton Rouge metropolitan area is home to 28 percent of the district's people. The district's part of the city also includes Louisiana State University (26,100 students) and predominantly black Southern University, both of which were key Fields support bases in 1992.

Splitting the city with the 6th District, the 4th captures all of northern and parts of southern Baton Rouge, which includes lower- and middle-income black and racially mixed neighborhoods. Many residents work in nearby chemical plants, including the Exxon Corp. Manufacturing Complex, one of the city's largest private employers.

The 4th winds through the rich cotton and soybean farmlands of northern Louisiana, taking in much of the city of Monroe, longtime trading hub of northeast Louisiana. The district ends in Shreveport in the northwest corner of the state. The 4th gobbles up almost every black resident in the city, including those in populous Cooper Road, among Louisiana's oldest black communities. Once a booming oil and gas town, Shreveport now counts AT&T Consumer Products and a General Motors plant in its economic mix.

Outside Baton Rouge in central and northeastern Louisiana the amoeba-like district is anchored by the black sections in blue-collar Alexandria and Lafayette, the center of the state's Cajun culture. Along the Mississippi border, the 4th picks up most or all of the timber and potato producing parishes of St. Helena and West and East Feliciana.

Election Returns

	4th District	Democrat	Republican
1992	President*	150,000 (68.0%)	54,230 (24.6%)
	House †	143,980 (73.9%)	—
1988	President	117,278 (54.5%)	97,966 (45.5%)

Vote for Perot was 16,475 (7.5%).   †*Other candidate was Democrat.*

Demographics

Population 602,884

Percent change from 1980 14.8%

Land area 6,731 square miles

Population per square mile 90

Parishes, 1990 population*
Ascension Parish (pt.) 10,000
Avoyelles Parish (pt.) 4,768
Bossier Parish (pt.) 7,866
Caddo Parish (pt.) 82,473
Claiborne Parish (pt.) 12,276
Concordia Parish (pt.) 13,212
East Baton Rouge Parish (pt.) 167,843
East Carroll Parish 9,709
East Feliciana Parish 19,211
Iberville Parish (pt.) 17,653
Lafayette Parish (pt.) 24,174
Lincoln Parish (pt.) 19,973
Livingston Parish (pt.) 13,597
Madison Parish (pt.) 8,139
Morehouse Parish (pt.) 14,456
Ouachita Parish (pt.) 44,222
Pointe Coupee Parish (pt.) 8,065
Rapides Parish (pt.) 23,204
St. Helena Parish (pt.) 7,393
St. Landry Parish (pt.) 25,336
St. Martin Parish (pt.) 7,853
Tangipahoa Parish (pt.) 20,252
Tensas Parish 7,103
Union Parish (pt.) 6,387
Webster Parish (pt.) 7,791
West Baton Rouge Parish (pt.) 5,293
West Carroll Parish (pt.) 1,720
West Feliciana Parish 12,915

Parishes are Louisiana's equivalent of counties.

Cities, 1990 population (10,000 or more)
Alexandria (pt.) 18,780	Monroe (pt.) 32,050
Baton Rouge (pt.) 115,717	Opelousas (pt.) 12,962
Lafayette (pt.) 22,299	Shreveport (pt.) 80,552
Merrydale CDP 10,395	

Race and Hispanic origin
White 32.9%
Black 66.4%
American Indian, Eskimo, or Aleut. 0.1%
Asian or Pacific Islander 0.3%
Other 0.2%
Hispanic origin 0.9%

Ancestry
American 5.9%	German 4.5%
English 4.2%	Irish 7.2%
French 4.7%	Italian 1.7%
French Canadian 4.5%	Scotch Irish 1.2%

Universities/colleges, 1990-1991 enrollment
Grambling State University, Grambling 6,485
Louisiana State University, Baton Rouge 26,116
Louisiana Tech University, Ruston 10,011
Southern University, Baton Rouge 8,941

Newspapers, total circulation (in all districts)

Alexandria Daily Town Talk 40,152
Baton Rouge Advocate 100,187
Hammond Daily Star 11,303
Lafayette Advertiser 34,089
Monroe News-Star 37,671
New Orleans Times-Picayune 266,592
Opelousas Daily World 12,924
Shreveport Times 82,292

Commercial television stations, affiliations

ADI: Monroe-El Dorado (42%), Baton Rouge (29%), Shreveport-Texarkana (14%), Lafayette (8%), Alexandria (4%) and New Orleans (2%)
WAFB, Baton Rouge (CBS)
KMSS-TV, Shreveport (Fox)

Cable television systems, total subscribers

Cablevision; West Monroe 33,000
Cablevision of Baton Rouge Ltd.; Baton Rouge 93,000
Cablevision of Shreveport; Shreveport 60,000
TCI Inc.; Baker 8,536
United Cable TV; Bossier City 19,500

Businesses and other major employers

State of Louisiana/Transportation Dept.; Baton Rouge 5,337
University Hospital; Shreveport 5,000
City of Baton Rouge; Baton Rouge 3,761
State of Louisiana/Public Safety Service; Baton Rouge 2,500
Dow Chemical Co.; Baton Rouge; accounting/auditing 2,400
Our Lady of the Lake Regional Medical Center; Baton Rouge 2,250
Exxon Corp./Exxon Chemical Co.; Baton Rouge; petroleum refining 1,900
Exxon Corp./Exxon USA-Baton Rouge Refinery; Baton Rouge; petroleum refining 1,700
St. Francis Medical Center; Monroe 1,687
Rapides General Hospital; Alexandria 1,642
Louisiana State Penitentiary; Angola 1,607
Southern University; Baton Rouge 1,492
General Health Inc./Baton Rouge General Medical Center; Baton Rouge 1,400
Willis-Knighton Medical Center/South Hospital; Shreveport 1,270
Louisiana Tech University; Ruston 1,220
Jacobs Engineering Group Inc./Union Construction Div.; Baton Rouge; engineering/architectural services 1,113
Premier Bancorp Inc.; Baton Rouge; holding offices 1,000
City of Baton Rouge/Public Works Dept.; Baton Rouge 1,000
Gulf States Utilities Co.; St. Francisville; electric services 906
Georgia-Pacific Corp./Communication Papers Div.; Zachary; paper mills 900
Libbey Glass Inc.; Shreveport; glass/glassware 900
Maison Blanche Inc./Goudchaux; Baton Rouge; department stores 900
U.S. Veterans Affairs Dept.; Shreveport 900
Arkla Inc./Arkansas Louisiana Gas Co.; Shreveport; gas production/ distribution 850
Earl K. Long Memorial Hospital; Baton Rouge 845
State Time Morning Advocate; Baton Rouge; newspapers 800
Grambling State University; Grambling 800
E. A. Conway Memorial Hospital; Monroe 750
Ditto Apparel of California; Bastrop; jeans 700
State Farm Mutual Auto Insurance Co.; Monroe; insurance services 700
National Maintenance Corp.; Baton Rouge; building services 700
City of Shreveport/Police Dept.; Shreveport 700
State of Louisiana/Hunt Correctional Center; Saint Gabriel 643
Georgia Gulf Corp.; Plaquemine; plastics/synthetics 610
Copolymer Rubber & Chemical Corp.; Baton Rouge; plastics/synthetics 600
State of Louisiana/Environmental Quality Dept.; Baton Rouge 600
Lane Memorial Hospital; Zachary 600
Villa Feliciana Hospital; Jackson 600
Concordia Parish School District; Vidalia 576
Ciba-Geigy Corp.; St. Gabriel; herbicides 550
Lincoln General Hospital; Ruston 547

5th District

North — Bossier City; Parts of Shreveport and Monroe

While the 5th is anchored in the northwestern Louisiana city of Shreveport, it runs for miles to the east, taking in expanses of both hilly and flat agricultural land and reaching nearly to the Mississippi River along the state's eastern border.

Shreveport (Caddo Parish), Louisiana's third-largest city, has been a bastion of conservatism since the 1930s when it voted against Gov. Huey P. Long. Redistricting in 1992 reinforced Republican dominance of the district by carving all of Shreveport's black communities out of the district and placing them in the new majority-minority 4th District. In the part of Caddo Parish that falls within the 5th, 82 percent of the population is white. Overall, almost 30 percent of people in the 5th live in Caddo Parrish.

In the beginning of the 20th century, oil was discovered near Shreveport, providing the region with prominence and wealth. The city has never fully recovered from the fading of the oil boom; in the 1980s, its population growth was quite slow. Today the city's largest employers include AT&T Consumer Products, General Motors and Thiokol Corp. Shreveport is also the home of the Frymaster Corp. and the site of the annual Poulan Weedeater Independence Bowl.

Just across the Red River from Shreveport is the district's third-largest city, Bossier City (population 52,700). The largest single employer for both cities is Barksdale Air Force Base, headquarters for a unit of the Air Combat Command and home to most of the Air Force's fleet of B-52s. The base employs 1,200 civilians and 5,900 military personnel.

The central part of the district, made up of Union, Lincoln, Jackson and a portion of Winn parishes, is the hilly timber region where Louisiana's softwood pine is harvested. These parishes are dotted with small lumber and paper mills. The rural voters here have leaned Republican in presidential voting; in 1988, George Bush carried all four of these parishes. Bush did not fare as well in 1992, though, carrying only Lincoln and Union.

Monroe (Ouachita Parish) is the district's second-largest city (population 54,900) and an agricultural trading hub, and falls squarely between the forest section and the fertile Delta region. International Paper Co. is the city's largest single employer.

Ouachita gave Bush 69 percent of the vote in 1988; in 1992, he got 67 percent.

West Carroll, Madison, Franklin and Morehouse parishes are part of Louisiana's Northern Delta Region. The alluvial soil and the flat land of the Delta lend it naturally to the cultivation of such row crops as cotton, rice and soybeans. These crops take up nearly 900,000 acres in the eastern reach of the 5th.

Despite Bush's recent falling fortunes in the 5th, it appears that the district has not developed any special affection for Democratic presidential candidates. In 1992, George Bush took 49 percent to Bill Clinton's 37 percent.

Election Returns

	5th District	Democrat	Republican
1992	President*	95,048 (36.7%)	127,134 (49.1%)
	House	90,079 (37.0%)	153,501 (63.0%)
1988	President	93,215 (37.8%)	153,307 (62.2%)

*Vote for Perot was 36,537 (14.1%).

Demographics

Population 602,816

Percent change from 1980 14.3%

Land area 9,715 square miles

Population per square mile 62

Parishes, 1990 population*

Bienville Parish 15,979	Natchitoches Parish 36,689
Bossier Parish (pt.) 78,222	Ouachita Parish (pt.)
Caddo Parish (pt.) 165,780	97,969
Claiborne Parish (pt.) 5,129	Red River Parish 9,387
De Soto Parish 25,346	Richland Parish 20,629
Franklin Parish 22,387	Union Parish (pt.) 14,303
Jackson Parish 15,705	Webster Parish (pt.) 34,198
Lincoln Parish (pt.) 21,772	West Carroll Parish (pt.)
Madison Parish (pt.) 4,324	10,373
Morehouse Parish (pt.) 17,482	Winn Parish (pt.) 7,142

*Parishes are Louisiana's equivalent of counties.

Cities, 1990 population (10,000 or more)

Bossier City (pt.) 49,974	Ruston (pt.) 10,587
Minden 13,661	Shreveport (pt.) 117,973
Monroe (pt.) 22,859	West Monroe 14,096
Natchitoches 16,609	

Race and Hispanic origin

White 76.8%
Black 22.1%
American Indian, Eskimo, or Aleut. 0.3%
Asian or Pacific Islander 0.5%
Other 0.3%
Hispanic origin 1.1%

Ancestry

American 11.8%	German 12.8%
Dutch 2.1%	Irish 20.7%
English 13.3%	Italian 2.2%
French 7.1%	Scotch Irish 3.7%
French Canadian 2.3%	Scottish 1.6%

Universities/colleges, 1990-1991 enrollment

Bossier Community College, Bossier City 3,335
Centenary College of Louisiana, Shreveport 998
Louisiana State University, Shreveport 4,107
Northeast Louisiana University, Monroe 10,686
Northwestern State University, Natchitoches 7,334
Southern Technical College, Shreveport 258
Southern Technical College, Monroe 379
Southern University, Shreveport 1,020

Newspapers, total circulation (in all districts)

Alexandria Daily Town Talk 40,152
Monroe News-Star 37,671
Shreveport Times 82,292

Commercial television stations, affiliations

ADI: Shreveport-Texarkana (56%) and Monroe-El Dorado (44%)
  KSLA-TV, Shreveport (CBS)
  KTBS-TV, Shreveport (ABC)
  KTAL-TV, Texarkana (NBC)
  KMCT-TV, West Monroe (None)

Cable television systems, total subscribers

Cablevision; West Monroe 33,000
Cablevision of Shreveport; Shreveport 60,000
Teleservice Corp. of America; Natchitoches 7,400
United Cable TV; Bossier City 19,500

Military installations, 1991

Barksdale Air Force Base, Bossier City 7,081

Businesses and other major employers

General Motors Corp.; Shreveport; trucks/bus assembly 2,700
Sisters of Charity/Schumpert Medical Center; Shreveport 2,021
AT&T Co.; Shreveport; communications equipment 1,850
Thiokol Corp./Louisiana Army Ammunition Plant Div.; Minden; ordnance/accessories 1,800
Thiokol Corp./Louisiana Div.; Shreveport; chemical products 1,700
Thiokol Corp./Ordnance Operations; Doyline; guided missiles/parts 1,500
Northeast Louisiana University; Monroe 1,200
International Paper Co./Louisiana Mill; Bastrop; paper products 1,100
Cherry Ridge Nursing Home Inc.; Shreveport; nursing 1,001
City of Monroe; Monroe 975
Webster Parish School Board; Minden 929
General Motors Corp./Inland Fisher Guide Div.; Monroe; electric lighting systems 875
ConAgra Inc.; Natchitoches; meat products 824
Glenwood Regional Medical Center; West Monroe 812
Stone Hodge Inc./Stone Container Corp.; Hodge; paperboard mills 760
Riverwood Intl. Corp.; West Monroe; paperboard products 700
Beaird Industries Inc.; Shreveport; metal products 697
Bossier General Hospital; Bossier City 620
ConAgra Inc.; Arcadia; poultry products 600
General Electric Co./Industrial & Power System; Shreveport; electronic components 600
Winnsboro School District; Winnsboro 600
Louisiana State University; Shreveport 600

Northwestern State University, Natchitoches 550
HCA North Monroe Community Hospital; Monroe 512

6th District

Central — Parts of Alexandria, Baton Rouge and Lafayette

The kite-shaped 6th is an economic microcosm of Louisiana, taking in both an urban center and rural agricultural country. But politically speaking, the 6th is lopsidedly conservative; it is the only Louisiana district where a majority of voters supported former Ku Klux Klan leader David Duke in his 1990 Senate race and 1991 gubernatorial bid.

Thanks to 1992 redistricting, the 6th is no longer compact. It now sprawls across 17 parishes. It begins in Sabine Parish along the Texas border, cuts a wide swath across the state nearly to the Mississippi River, and then meanders south to the state capital, Baton Rouge. The district includes former Gov. Huey P. Long's birthplace in rural Winn Parish as well as his grave on the grounds of the state Capitol.

Within its boundaries, the 6th contains a variety of business pursuits linked to the land. In Caldwell Parish in the northeastern reach of the district, 72 percent of the acreage is devoted to commercial forestry. Farther south, in Avoyelles Parish, rice is the primary cash crop. Sugar cane fields dot Point Coupee Parish and soybeans are grown in southernmost Iberville Parish.

In electoral terms, Baton Rouge is the single biggest influence in the 6th. Remappers splintered the capital city, ceding all of the predominantly black neighborhoods to the majority-minority 4th District. However, East Baton Rouge Parish is still home to more than one-third of the 6th's population.

Downtown Baton Rouge, like so many other center cities, has been strapped economically by suburban flight; there has been relatively little major construction here in the past 20 years. Many state agencies, requiring more space than is available near the Capitol, lease space in other parts of the city. Recently, though, in an attempt to lure businesses and agencies back to the capital area, the state began buying up downtown parcels in the hope of building more than 500,000 square feet of office space. (A budget shortfall could cause some problems, however.) City officials also are hopeful that Catfish Town, a city-assisted retail development on the Mississippi River that is a potential site for riverboat gambling, along with the nearby Naval War Museum, will help attract tourists and conventions to the city.

Baton Rouge remains the center of the South's petrochemical industry. The Exxon Corp. Manufacturing Complex in Baton Rouge (4th District) has the nation's second-largest chemical manufacturing facility. The petrochemical industry employs more than 14,000 in the Baton Rouge area.

Voter registration in the 6th belies its decidedly GOP tilt, with registered Democrats outnumbering Republicans nearly 3-to-1. In the 1988 presidential election, 60 percent of the vote in the old 6th went to George Bush. La Salle Parish in the northern part of the 6th gave him nearly 75 percent of the vote. But in 1992, Bush's tally in La Salle fell off precipitously, to 48 percent, and districtwide he took just 52 percent to Bill Clinton's 35 percent.

Election Returns

	6th District	Democrat	Republican
1992	President*	92,040 (34.9%)	135,915 (51.6%)
	House†	—	123,953 (50.6%)
1988	President	72,236 (33.4%)	143,847 (66.6%)

*Vote for Perot was 35,673 (13.5%).   †Other candidate was Republican.

Demographics

Population 602,854

Percent change from 1980 14.9%

Land area 9,220 square miles

Population per square mile 65

Parishes, 1990 population*
Avoyelles Parish (pt.)
  34,391
Caldwell Parish 9,810
Catahoula Parish 11,065
Concordia Parish (pt.)
  7,616
East Baton Rouge Parish
  (pt.) 212,262
Evangeline Parish (pt.)
  5,760
Grant Parish 17,526
Iberville Parish (pt.) 12,328
La Salle Parish 13,662

Livingston Parish (pt.)
  27,476
Pointe Coupee Parish (pt.)
  14,475
Rapides Parish (pt.)
  108,352
Sabine Parish 22,646
St. Landry Parish (pt.)
  20,271
Vernon Parish 61,961
West Baton Rouge Parish
  (pt.) 14,126
Winn Parish (pt.) 9,127

Parishes are Louisiana's equivalent of counties.

Cities, 1990 population (10,000 or more)
Alexandria (pt.) 30,408
Baker (pt.) 11,032
Baton Rouge (pt.) 103,814

Fort Polk South CDP
  10,911
Pineville 12,251
Shenandoah CDP 13,429

Race and Hispanic origin
White 83.4%
Black 14.6%
American Indian, Eskimo, or Aleut. 0.4%
Asian or Pacific Islander 1.1%
Other 0.5%
Hispanic origin 2.0%

Ancestry
American 9.5%
Dutch 1.4%
English 11.4%
French 14.8%
French Canadian 10.6%

German 13.4%
Irish 16.8%
Italian 4.3%
Scotch Irish 2.9%
Scottish 1.4%

Universities/colleges, 1990-1991 enrollment
Louisiana College, Pineville 1,075
Louisiana State University, Alexandria 2,404

Newspapers, total circulation (in all districts)
Alexandria Daily Town Talk 40,152
Baton Rouge Advocate 100,187
New Orleans Times-Picayune 266,592
Opelousas Daily World 12,924
Shreveport Times 82,292

Commercial television stations, affiliations
ADI: Alexandria (41%), Monroe-El Dorado (31%), Baton Rouge (12%), Shreveport-Texarkana (11%) and Lafayette (5%)
KALB-TV, Alexandria (NBC)
KLAX-TV, Alexandria (ABC)
WBRZ, Baton Rouge (ABC)
WGMB, Baton Rouge (Fox)
WVLA, Baton Rouge (NBC)
KNOE-TV, Monroe (CBS)
KARD, West Monroe (ABC)

Cable television systems, total subscribers
Cablevision of Baton Rouge Ltd.; Baton Rouge 93,000
Vision Cable of Alpine; Pineville 28,133
Vista Communications; Leesville 6,250

Military installations, 1991
Fort Polk (Army), Leesville 19,729
England Air Force Base, Alexandria 1,488

Businesses and other major employers
Dow Chemical Co.; Plaquemine; chemical products 2,200
State of Louisiana/Pinecrest State School; Pineville 1,800
Rayford Enterprises; Alexandria; nursing 1,500
U.S. Veterans Affairs Dept.; Alexandria; hospital 1,015
Boise Cascade Corp./Timber & Wood Products Div.; Florien; wood products 900
St. Frances Cabrini Hospital; Alexandria 896
State of Louisiana/Wildlife & Fisheries Dept.; Baton Rouge 800
Woman's Hospital Foundation; Baton Rouge 800
Avoyelles Parish School Board; Marksville 800
Dresser Industries Inc./Industrial Valve Operations; Alexandria; industrial valves/equipment 659
Blue Cross/Blue Shield of Louisana; Baton Rouge; medical service/health insurance 625
Performance Contractors Inc.; Baton Rouge; heavy construction 600
Allen Canning Co./Pillsbury Co.; Hessmer; canned fruits/vegetables 600
Sears Roebuck & Co.; Baton Rouge; department stores 600
State of Louisiana/Central Louisiana State Hospital; Pineville 550
Ditto Apparel of California; Colfax; jeans 525
Healthtrust Inc./Medical Center of Baton Rouge; Baton Rouge 525

7th District

Southwest — Lake Charles; Part of Lafayette

Literally, the Cajun expression "Lache pas la patate" means "Don't drop the potato." Figuratively, it comes closer to "Hang in there," and that is what the 7th District has been doing with increasing success since the oil bust of the mid-1980s. The district, which begins in the Cajun core of south-central Louisiana, runs to Texas on the west and borders the Gulf of Mexico on the south.

Dotted with waterfowl and wildlife refuges, the 7th's gulf edge also serves sports and commercial fishermen. Menhaden, which is ground into feed and industrial oil, accounts for a large

share of the commercial catch. Back on land, some of the farms north and west of Crowley that grow rice now alternately raise crawfish in fallow rice fields.

Lake Charles, a refining and chemical-producing hub in the southwest corner of the district, offers a sharp industrial contrast to the 7th's rural areas. A union and Democratic stronghold, the city has seen a rebound in chemical sales abroad, and many refineries have been able to offer hundreds of construction jobs because of environmentally oriented projects undertaken to meet looming deadlines set in the 1990 Clean Air Act.

The closing of a Boeing aircraft repair facility cost Lake Charles 2,000 jobs early in the decade. But Grumman, which builds JSTARS radar planes, moved in and expects to employ 1,500 by 1997.

Defense downsizing worries De Ridder, the largest town in the 7th's northwest corner, which depends on Fort Polk as an economic mainstay. In 1991 Fort Polk employed nearly 20,000 military and civilian personnel. The army base, about 20 miles to the north in the 6th District, is due for realignments and cutbacks.

Oakdale, east of De Ridder, hosts a federal detention center and a federal correctional institution, which together employ about 575 people.

The timber industry is also an important employer in this area. Boise Cascade Corp. employs almost 900 in Beauregard and Allen parishes.

Southwest of Oakdale on U.S. Highway 165 lies the little town of Kinder, which hopes to gain a big name for itself with a gambling casino run by the Coushatta Indians. The tribe is planning a 100,000-square-foot gaming facility, to open early in 1994, employing as many as 1,200—Native Americans and non-Native Americans alike. If they tire of the tables, visitors might head east to sample Cajun fare and the Acadian lifestyle in nearby communities.

The largest city in the 7th is Lafayette and is as close to a political opposite of Lake Charles as the district offers. George Bush, who lost the 7th by 9 percentage points in 1992, made his strongest showing in Lafayette Parish. He took 51 percent of the vote, compared with Bill Clinton's 35 percent and Ross Perot's 14 percent.

A center for both on- and offshore oil and gas extraction activity, Lafayette survived the 1980s downturn through diversification. In 1992, the National Wetlands Research Center, a U.S. Fish and Wildlife Service migratory bird and ecology laboratory, opened there. Lafayette also welcomed expansion of Fruit of the Loom garment assembly factories in nearby communities including Crowley and Abbeville. Total employment at the plants in the area is about 6,500, and more growth is planned.

Redistricting in 1992 only slightly realigned the 7th. The main loss was of sections of Lafayette Parish, moved into the black-majority 4th District. The 7th remains overwhelmingly Democratic, with 75 percent of registered voters aligning themselves with the party.

Election Returns

	7th District	Democrat	Republican
1992	President*	123,248 (47.1%)	100,140 (38.3%)
	House †	84,149 (73.0%)	—
1988	President	115,440 (51.4%)	109,302 (48.6%)

Vote for Perot was 38,285 (14.6%).   †Data from open primary.

Demographics

Population 602,921

Percent change from 1980 14.8%

Land area 8,194 square miles

Population per square mile 74

Parishes, 1990 population*

Acadia Parish 55,882
Allen Parish 21,226
Beauregard Parish 30,083
Calcasieu Parish 168,134
Cameron Parish 9,260
Evangeline Parish (pt.)
27,514
Jefferson Davis Parish
30,722
Lafayette Parish (pt.)
140,588
St. Landry Parish (pt.)
34,724
St. Martin Parish (pt.)
34,733
Vermilion Parish 50,055

Parishes are Louisiana's equivalent of counties.

Cities, 1990 population (10,000 or more)

Abbeville 11,187
Crowley 13,983
Eunice 11,162
Jennings 11,305
Lafayette (pt.) 72,141
Lake Charles 70,580
Sulphur 20,125

Race and Hispanic origin

White 79.4%
Black 19.5%
American Indian, Eskimo, or Aleut. 0.2%
Asian or Pacific Islander 0.6%
Other 0.3%
Hispanic origin 1.3%

Ancestry

American 5.8%
English 6.9%
French 13.6%
French Canadian 35.3%
German 9.8%
Irish 8.7%
Italian 2.0%
Scotch Irish 1.5%

Universities/colleges, 1990-1991 enrollment

Louisiana State University, Eunice 2,261
McNeese State University, Lake Charles 7,671
Southern Technical College, Lafayette 642
University of Southwestern Louisiana, Lafayette 15,769

Newspapers, total circulation (in all districts)

Alexandria Daily Town Talk 40,152
Baton Rouge Advocate 100,187
Lafayette Advertiser 34,089
Lake Charles American Press 37,468
Opelousas Daily World 12,924

Commercial television stations, affiliations

ADI: Lake Charles (53%) and Lafayette (47%)
KADN, Lafayette (None)
KATC, Lafayette (ABC)
KLFY-TV, Lafayette (CBS)
KPLC-TV, Lake Charles (NBC)
KVHP, Lake Charles (Fox)

Cable television systems, total subscribers

Abbeville Cable TV; Abbeville 6,811
Cox Cable/Jefferson Parish Inc.; Jefferson Parish 114,700
Lafayette Cable TV Service; Lafayette 45,000
TCI of Louisiana; Lake Charles 25,119
TCI of Louisiana; Sulphur 6,846
Video Design; Westlake 7,664

Businesses and other major employers

Martin Mills Inc./Fruit of the Loom; St. Martinville; underwear 2,700
Boeing Co.; Lake Charles; aircraft/parts 2,100
Petroleum Helicopters Inc.; Lafayette; helicopter transportation 1,850
Citgo Petroleum Corp.; Lake Charles; petroleum refining 1,700
PPG Industries Inc./Pittsburgh Plate; Westlake; inorganic chemicals 1,700
PPG Industries Inc./Chemicals; Lake Charles; inorganic chemicals 1,580
University of Southwestern Louisiana; Lafayette 1,500
Our Lady of Lourdes Regional Hospital; Lafayette 1,200
Lafayette General Hospital; Lafayette 1,092
Lake Charles Memorial Hospital; Lake Charles 1,000
International Maintenance; Sulphur; building services 1,000
St. Patrick Hospital Inc.; Lake Charles 950
Olin Corp./Chemicals Group; Lake Charles; organic chemicals 862
Boise Cascade Corp./Southern Paper Mill; De Ridder; pulp mills 850
University Medical Center; Lafayette 800
Jefferson Parish School Board; Jennings 800
Conoco Inc.; Westlake; petroleum refining 750
McNeese State University; Lake Charles 706
McKellar & Assoc. Inc./Minute-Man Temporary Service; Scott; temp services 700
City of Lake Charles; Lake Charles 692
Himont USA Inc.; Lake Charles; plastics/synthetics 600
Stuller Settings Inc.; Lafayette; jewelry/silverware/plated ware 525

Maine

Maine was the last state to engage in congressional redistricting for the 1990s; its new House map was not complete until the state supreme court issued a ruling on June 29, 1993. While all other multidistrict states had redrawn their new district maps in time for the 1992 House elections, Maine officials operated under a state law that defers redistricting until after a decade's first elections.

The congressional map required only minor changes. The population difference between Maine's two districts, as counted by the 1990 census, was slight: The 1st District had 45,044 more residents than the 2nd District, requiring the shift of about half that many people to restore a balance.

This was easily achieved with the accord of Maine's incumbent House members. The 1st District's Democratic House incumbent was happy to divest rural, Republican-leaning portions of Waldo and Kennebec counties to the Republican-held 2nd District.

Although this land swap marginally strengthened the districts' partisan standing, neither appears to be a "safe" district in perpetuity. The Portland-based 1st is the more urbanized district and has a strong Democratic base; but as recently as 1984, its voters elected a Republican to the House. The 2nd is mainly rural and has a long Yankee Republican heritage; yet the GOP incumbent struggled through tough re-election contests in 1990 and 1992.

Underpinning this partisan flexibility is an element of political independence within the Maine electorate. This was evident in the 1992 presidential vote. Democrat Bill Clinton carried Maine, but with just 39 percent of the vote; independent candidate Ross Perot finished second with 30 percent (his best showing across the country), edging Republican incumbent (and part-year Maine resident) George Bush by 316 votes.

This type of partisan iconoclasm has a history in Maine. In 1974, independent candidate James B. Longley was elected governor over Democratic and Republican contenders. In 1986, the strong showing of two independent candidates allowed GOP gubernatorial nominee John R. McKerran to win with only a 40 percent plurality.

Table 1 Population

District	Population	Population under 18	Voting-age population	Median age
1	636,486	157,939	478,547	34.1
2	591,442	151,063	440,379	33.7
State	1,227,928	309,002	918,926	33.9

Table 2 Voting-Age Persons

District	White*	Black*	American Indian, Eskimo, or Aleut*	Asian or Pacific Islander*	Other*	Hispanic*	Male*	Female*
1	98.7%	0.4%	0.2%	0.6%	0.1%	0.5%	47.5%	52.5%
2	98.5	0.3	0.6	0.4	0.1	0.4	48.1	51.9
State	98.6	0.4	0.4	0.5	0.1	0.5	47.8	52.2

*As percent of voting-age population.

Table 3 Voting-Age Persons by Age Groups

District	18-24*	25-44*	45-54*	55-64*	65 and over*
1	12.9%	44.6%	13.5%	11.4%	17.7%
2	14.1	42.1	13.7	12.2	17.9
State	13.5	43.4	13.6	11.8	17.8

*As percent of voting-age population.

Table 4 Income and Occupation

District	Median family income	Families in poverty	White collar*	Blue collar*	Service*	Farm*
1	$36,067	6.0%	57.2%	27.3%	13.3%	2.1%
2	29,273	10.0	48.3	33.3	14.9	3.5
State	32,422	8.0	53.2	30.0	14.0	2.8

*As percent of employed persons age 16 and over.

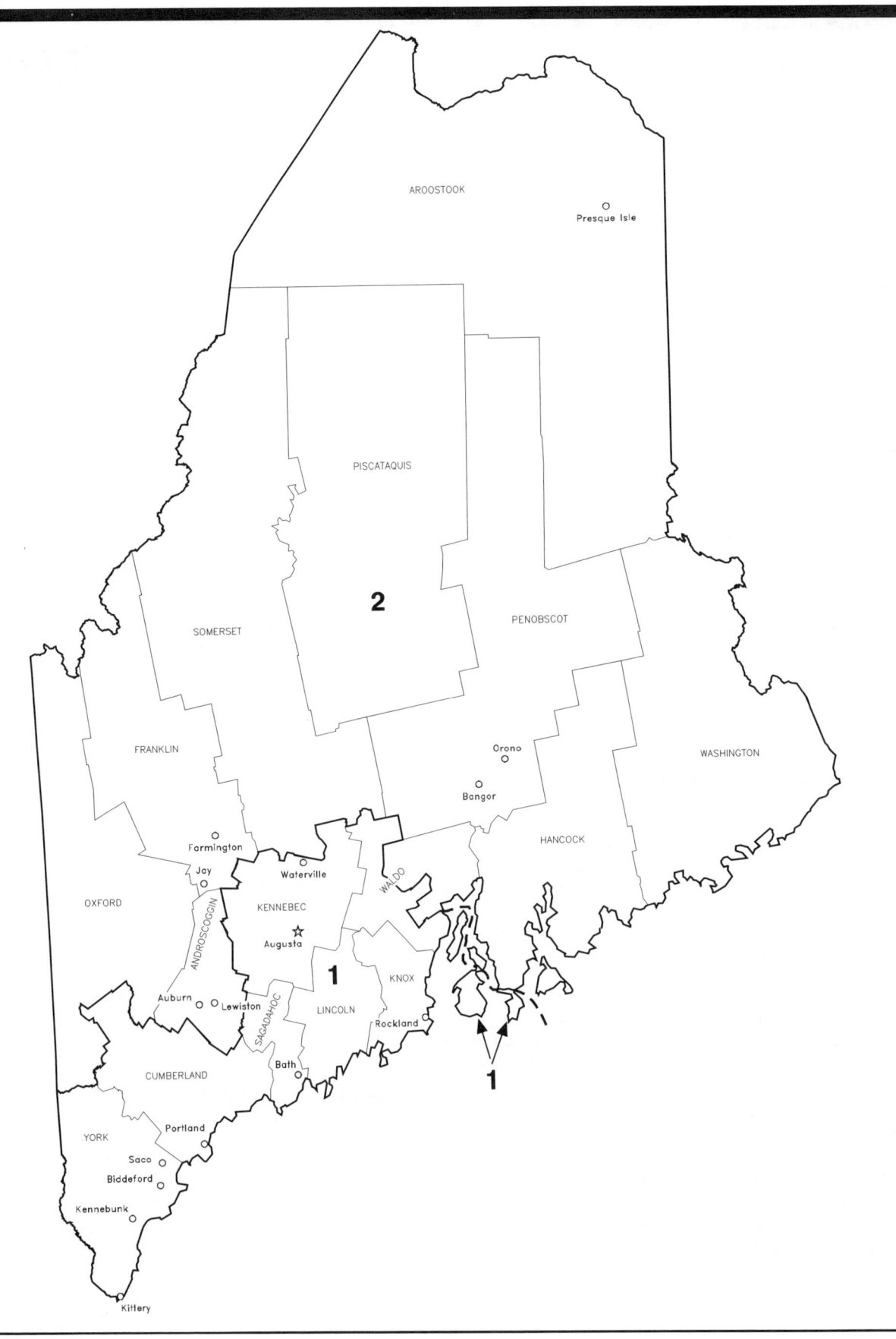

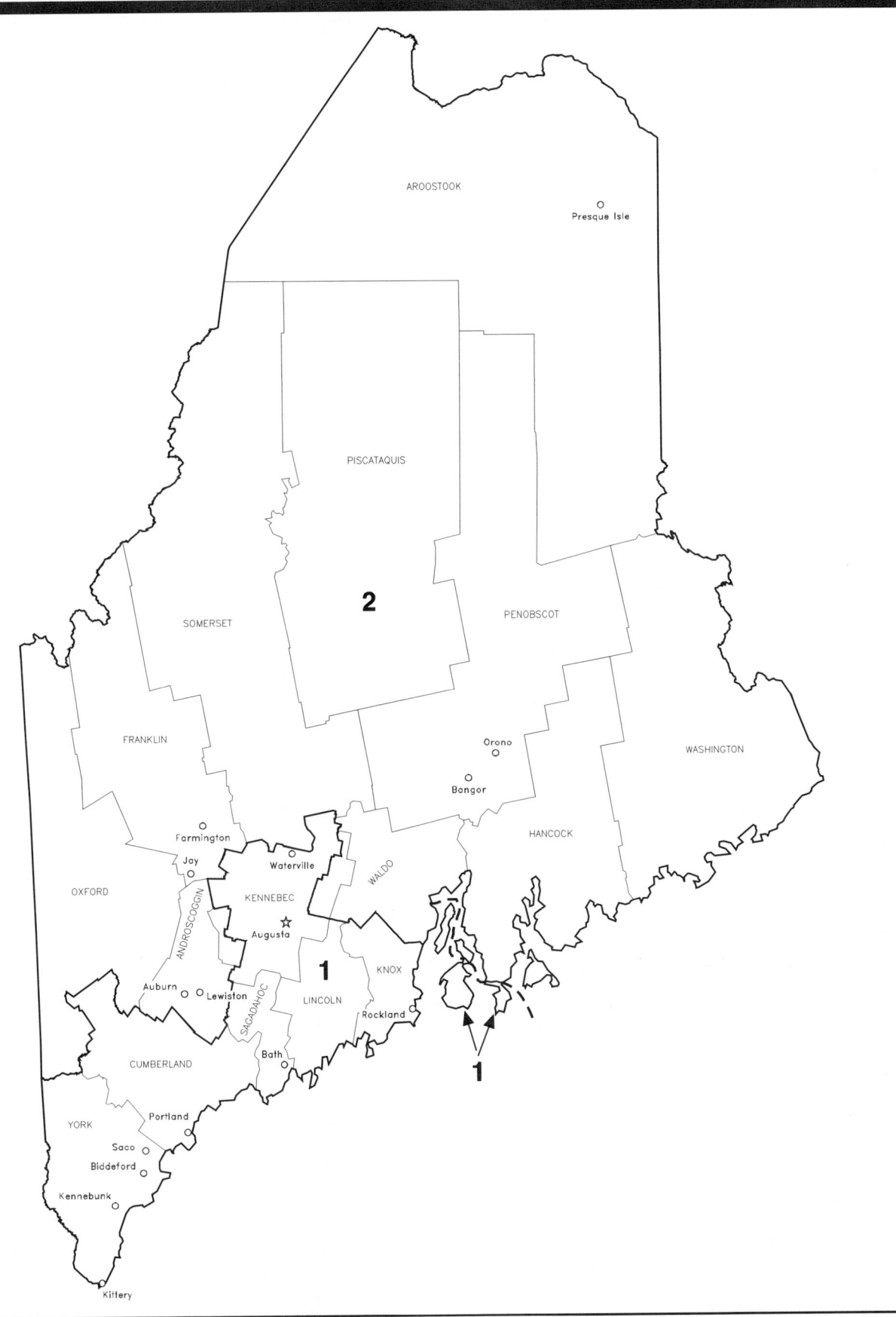

Table 5   Education: School Years Completed

District	Less than grade 9*	Grades 9-12 no diploma*	High school diploma*	College bachelor's degree or higher*
1	7.0%	11.2%	34.8%	22.4%
2	10.8	13.6	39.6	14.7
State	8.8	12.4	37.1	18.8

As percent of persons age 25 and over.

Table 6   Housing and Residential Patterns

District	Owner occupied	Renter occupied	Urban	Rural
1	69.6%	30.4%	48.9%	51.1%
2	71.5	28.5	40.0	60.0
State	70.5	29.5	44.6	55.4

1st District

South — Portland; Augusta

Maine's Democratic core follows Interstate 95 through the heart of the 1st, from industrial Biddeford and Saco in the south through urban Portland and on to blue-collar Waterville in the north.

But the 1st is hardly a sure thing for Democratic candidates; Maine's Yankee Republican heritage is still respected in many suburbs of Portland, inland rural areas and small coastal towns (including Kennebunkport, the vacation hometown of George Bush).

In 1988, Bush carried the 1st by more than 38,000 votes. But his fortunes faded here, and he lost to Bill Clinton in 1992 by nearly 30,000 votes. The 1st's status as a swing district is cemented by a large bloc of independent voters; Ross Perot carried more than a quarter of the 1st's votes in 1992.

Powered by the waters of Maine's rivers, industries here have made shoes, textiles, lumber, paper and ships throughout the 20th century.

Portland is Maine's largest city with about 64,000 people. Working-class communities combine with an environmentalist white-collar vote to provide Democrats with a base that often enables them to carry Cumberland County.

The spread of high-tech industry from Boston brought a modest boom to Portland in the 1980s; high-rise office buildings sprouted, and downtown streets welcomed trendy boutiques and restaurants. But recent hard times have heightened some urban problems, including an upswing in homelessness. Impending post-Cold War defense cuts cause concerns in communities that depend on the 1st's military-related employers, such as Brunswick Naval Air Station in Cumberland County and Bath Iron Works, a Navy shipbuilder in Sagadohoc County. In 1993, the Portsmouth Naval Shipyard was targeted for possible closure, and the district was nicked in the 1991 round by the closing of Pease Air Force Base (just across the New Hampshire border) and by cutbacks in the naval shipyard at Kittery.

Kittery is at the tip of York, Maine's southernmost county; Biddeford and Saco, with their Democratic leanings, are in northern York. While Bush managed to win with 48 percent in Kennebunkport, he narrowly lost the county to Clinton.

In the northern part of the 1st is Augusta, the state capital, which is split rather evenly between white-collar government workers and factory workers. Augusta and the textile city of Waterville usually give Democrats an edge in Kennebec County.

After the 1993 remap, most of Kennebec remained in the 1st, but the county became the only one in Maine split between the two House districts. Three rural communities at the eastern edge of the county and two on its western border were placed in the 2nd District. Waldo County, which had been split between the two districts, was placed wholly in the 2nd (see 1993 map on page 331).

The GOP heartland lies along the northern coast. Lincoln, Knox and Waldo counties consist mainly of coastal towns that help make Maine first in the nation in lobster catch.

Election Returns[1]

	1st District (1983 map)	Democrat	Republican
1992	President*	145,191 (39.9%)	115,697 (31.8%)
	House	232,696 (65.0%)	125,236 (35.0%)
1990	Governor	127,433 (49.2%)	131,747 (50.8%)
1988	President	131,078 (43.6%)	169,292 (56.4%)
	Senate	246,280 (81.3%)	56,718 (18.7%)
1986	Governor †	67,791 (29.3%)	89,394 (38.6%)

Vote for Perot was 102,828 (28.3%).   †Independent/other is greater than 5%.

Demographics[1]

Population   636,486

Percent change from 1980   9.5%

Land area   4,162 square miles

Population per square mile   153

Counties, 1990 population

Cumberland 243,135	Sagadahoc 33,535
Kennebec 115,904	Waldo (pt.) 12,658
Knox 36,310	York 164,587
Lincoln 30,357	

Cities, 1990 population (10,000 or more)

Augusta 21,325	Sanford 20,463
Biddeford 20,710	Scarborough 12,518
Brunswick 20,906	South Portland 23,163
Gorham 11,856	Waterville 17,173
Portland 64,358	Westbrook 16,121
Saco 15,181	Windham 13,020

Race and Hispanic origin

White 98.5%
Black 0.4%
American Indian, Eskimo, or Aleut. 0.3%
Asian or Pacific Islander 0.7%
Other 0.1%
Hispanic origin 0.6%

Ancestry

American 6.3%	French Canadian 9.3%
Canadian 1.1%	German 10.3%
Dutch 1.4%	Irish 19.1%
English 30.0%	Italian 5.4%
French 16.5%	

[1]The election returns and demographics data presented here are based on the 1983 district map. The 1993 district map will go in effect for the 1994 elections.

Polish 2.4%   Scottish 6.5%
Scotch Irish 3.2%   Swedish 2.1%

Universities/colleges, 1990-1991 enrollment
Andover College, Portland   435
Bowdoin College, Brunswick   1,399
Casco Bay College, Portland   272
Colby College, Waterville   1,767
Portland School of Art, Portland   305
Southern Maine Tech College, South Portland   2,102
St. Joseph's College, Windham   3,757
Thomas College, Waterville   1,026
University of Maine, Augusta   4,773
University of New England, Biddeford   1,259
University of Southern Maine, Portland   10,487
Westbrook College, Portland   565

Newspapers, total circulation (in all districts)
Augusta Kennebec Journal   18,838
Biddeford Journal Tribune   13,004
Boston Globe   503,578
Boston Herald   339,813
Brunswick Times-Record   13,305
Central Maine Morning Sentinel   24,233
Foster's Daily Democrat   30,189
Portland Press Herald Telegram   73,391
Portsmouth Herald   14,211

Commercial television stations, affiliations
ADI: Portland-Poland Springs (91%) and Bangor (9%)
WCSH-TV, Portland (NBC)
WGME-TV, Portland (CBS)
WPXT, Portland (Fox)

Cable television systems, total subscribers
Better Cable TV; Fairfield   13,216
Cable TV of Kennebunk; Kennebunk   6,279
Casco Cable TV Inc.; Topsham   11,963
Continental Cablevision of Maine; Saco   8,615
Continental Cablevision of New Hampshire; Dover   16,500
Continental Cablevision of New Hampshire; Portsmouth   22,700
New England Cablevision; Moody   8,427
New England Cablevision; Saco   5,856
New England Cablevision; Sanford   6,645
Public Cable Co.; South Portland   37,970
State Cable TV Corp.; Hallowell   19,140
United Video Cablevision; Rockland   5,511
United Video Cablevision; Bar Mills   5,104

Military installations, 1991
Portsmouth Naval Shipyard; Kittery   8,000
Brunswick Naval Air Station, Brunswick   3,662
South Portland Air Force Guard Station, South Portland   41

Businesses and other major employers
Bath Iron Works Corp.; Bath; shipbuilding/repairing   8,500
Maine Medical Center; Portland   3,700
Unum Corp.; Portland; life insurance   3,296
Scott Paper Co.; Westbrook; paper mills   2,500
State of Maine/Human Services Dept.; Augusta   2,400
State of Maine/Transportation Dept.; Augusta   2,200
United Technologies Corp./Pratt & Whitney Aircraft Group; North Berwick; aircraft   1,900
City of Portland; Portland   1,811

National Semiconductor Corp./Digital Logic Unit; Portland; electronic components   1,800
Boise Cascade Corp./Coated Paper Div.; Portland; paper products   1,679
L. L. Bean Inc.; Freeport; catalog retailers   1,500
U.S. Postal Service; Portland   1,200
Mid-Maine Medical Center/Thayer Div.; Waterville   1,200
University of Southern Maine; Portland   1,128
Bath Iron Works Corp.; Portland; shipbuilding/repairing   1,100
Sprague Electric Co.; Sanford; electrical industrial apparatus   1,050
Warnaco Inc./Hathaway Co. Div.; Waterville; suits/coats   1,000
Keyes Fibre Co.; Waterville; paper products   1,000
University of Southern Maine; Gorham   1,000
U.S. Veterans Affairs; Augusta; hospital   1,000
Mercy Hospital; Portland   972
Portland City Airport; Portland; airport   850
Shape Inc.; Biddeford; electrical equipment/supplies   850
Town of Gorham; Gorham   829
Hannaford Bros. Co./Wellby Super Drug; Scarborough; grocery stores   800
Kennebec Valley Medical Center; Augusta   775
Southern Maine Medical Center; Biddeford   765
Scott Paper Co./Scott Worldwide Div.; Waterville; pulp mills   750
State of Maine/Pineland Center; Pownal; nursing   720
City of Biddeford; Biddeford   720
Central Maine Power Co.; Augusta; electric services   715
Digital Equipment Corp.; Augusta; electronic components   700
Town of Scarborough; Scarborough   700
Brighton Medical Center; Portland   625
Town of Sanford; Sanford   625
School Administrative District; Bar Mills   620
Prime Tanning Co. Inc.; Berwick; leather production   600
Saco Defense Inc.; Saco; ordnance/accessories   600
Statler Industries Inc./Statler Tissue Co. Div.; Augusta; paper products   600
City of Westbrook; Westbrook   600
Bowdoin College; Brunswick   599
Colby College; Waterville   594
Penobscot Bay Medical Center; Rockland   581
Carleton Woolen Mills Inc.; Winthrop; wool mills   543
U.S. Postal Service; Augusta   525

2nd District

North — Lewiston; Auburn; Bangor

America's largest congressional district east of the Mississippi, the 2nd accounts for the vast bulk of Maine's territory. Its northern reaches are heavily forested; its people are clustered at the southern end, closer to the state's industrial core.

Heavily dependent on factories, farms and fishing, the 2nd is the less affluent of Maine's House districts. Pockets of poverty are found in coastal Washington County, which is less accessible to tourists than the seaside regions in the 1st District, and in remote Aroostook County, where economic problems are being deepened by the 1991 decision to close Loring Air Force Base.

Until recently, rural Republican traditions remained sturdy in the 2nd. GOP Rep. Olympia Snowe coasted through the 1980s; in 1988 George Bush carried the district by 10 percentage points. But the recession of the early 1990s soured many voters on Republicans and created opportunities for Democrats and independent candidates. Snowe struggled to hold her seat in the 1990 and 1992 campaigns. In 1992 presidential voting, Bill Clinton won the 2nd with a plurality, while Ross Perot captured fully a third of the vote; Bush collapsed to third place with 29 percent.

The 2nd's Democratic base is in Androscoggin County, a part of Maine's industrial belt. The Democratic vote is anchored in blue-collar Lewiston (Maine's second-largest city with nearly 40,000 people); Snowe's Democratic challenger took 58 percent here in 1992. But Snowe held on narrowly in her hometown of Auburn, which claims to be the birthplace of Maine's shoe industry.

The only other city of significant size in the 2nd is Bangor, which has slightly more than 33,000 people. Bangor's heyday as a shipmaking center is over. But its wood-products industry and modest port remain in operation, and its international airport is a refueling station for many transoceanic flights.

Democrats are competitive in local elections, but GOP Sen. William S. Cohen's hometown is usually more dependable for Republicans seeking higher office. The University of Maine (13,300 students) is nearby in Orono.

The rest of the district is rural, much of it covered with the forests that supply trees to Maine's lumber and paper mills. The district also produces potatoes (mainly in Aroostook County), apples, corn and chickens.

The redistricting plan enacted on June 29, 1993, reunited coastal Waldo County in the 2nd; it had been shared with the 1st District under the previous map. But the 2nd also took in five rural communities in Kennebec County, making it the only county in Maine that is now split between the two districts (see 1993 map on page 331).

Election Returns[1]

	2nd District (1983 map)	Democrat	Republican
1992	President*	118,229 (37.8%)	90,807 (29.0%)
	House †	130,824 (42.0%)	153,022 (49.1%)
1990	Governor	102,044 (47.8%)	111,622 (52.2%)
1988	President	112,819 (45.0%)	137,772 (55.0%)
	Senate	206,592 (81.3%)	47,370 (18.7%)
1986	Governor †	61,128 (31.3%)	80,948 (41.4%)

*Vote for Perot was 103,992 (33.2%).   †Independent/other is greater than 5%.

Demographics[1]

Population 591,442

Percent change from 1980 8.8%

Land area 26,702 square miles

Population per square mile 22

Counties, 1990 population

Androscoggin	105,259	Franklin	29,008
Aroostook	86,936	Hancock	46,948

[1]The election returns and demographics data presented here are based on the 1983 district map. The 1993 district map will go in effect for the 1994 elections.

Oxford	52,602	Somerset	49,767
Penobscot	146,601	Waldo (pt.)	20,360
Piscataquis	18,653	Washington	35,308

Cities, 1990 population (10,000 or more)

Auburn	24,309	Orono	10,573
Bangor	33,181	Presque Isle	10,550
Lewiston	39,757		

Race and Hispanic origin

White 98.3%
Black 0.4%
American Indian, Eskimo, or Aleut. 0.7%
Asian or Pacific Islander 0.4%
Other 0.2%
Hispanic origin 0.5%

Ancestry

American	7.9%	Irish	16.2%
Canadian	1.1%	Italian	2.9%
Dutch	1.1%	Polish	1.5%
English	30.7%	Scotch Irish	3.6%
French	20.0%	Scottish	5.2%
French Canadian	9.1%	Swedish	1.8%
German	7.3%		

Universities/colleges, 1990-1991 enrollment

Bates College, Lewiston 1,577
Beal College, Bangor 353
Central Maine Technical College, Auburn 783
Eastern Maine Technical College, Bangor 1,328
Husson College, Bangor 1,850
Kennebec Valley Vocational-Technical School, Fairfield 1,136
Maine Maritime Academy, Castine 603
Mid-State College, Auburn 278
Northern Maine Technical College, Presque Isle 1,217
University of Maine, Farmington 2,438
University of Maine, Fort Kent 571
University of Maine, Machias 1,008
University of Maine, Orono 13,278
University of Maine, Presque Isle 1,458
Washington City Tech College, Calais 320

Newspapers, total circulation (in all districts)

Bangor Daily News 74,689
Central Maine Morning Sentinel 24,233
Lewiston Sun-Journal 40,687
Portland Press Herald Telegram 73,391

Commercial television stations, affiliations

ADI: Bangor (61%), Presque Isle (24%) and Portland-Poland Springs (15%)
WABI-TV, Bangor (CBS)
WLBZ-TV, Bangor (NBC)
WVII-TV, Bangor (ABC)
WAGM-TV, Presque Isle (CBS)

Cable television systems, total subscribers

Adams Russell Cable Services Maine; Orono 15,163
Bee Line Cable TV; Wilton 5,500
Cablevision; Lewiston 18,400
Paragon Cable; Caribou 9,000
State Cable TV Corp.; Rumford 5,800

Military installations, 1991

Loring Air Force Base, Limestone   3,512

Winter Harbor Naval Security Group Activity, Winter Harbor   406

Bangor Air Force Guard Station, Bangor   375

Businesses and other major employers

University of Maine; Orono   3,000

Eastern Maine Medical Center; Bangor   2,000

Bowater Inc./Great Northern Paper Co.; Millinocket; paper mills   1,800

Boise Cascade Corp./White Paper Div.; Rumford; paper mills   1,600

Champion Intl. Corp.; Bucksport; paper mills   1,300

International Paper Co./White Papers Group; Jay; paper mills   1,100

Fraser Paper Ltd.; Madawaska; paper mills   1,100

Scott Paper Co.; Skowhegan; paper mills   1,060

Dexter Shoe Co.; Dexter; footwear   1,000

City of Lewiston; Lewiston   950

Central Maine Medical Center; Lewiston   914

McCain Foods Inc.; Easton; preserved fruits/vegetables   900

St. Mary's General Hospital; Lewiston   850

James River Corp. Virginia; Old Town; pulp mills   800

Great Northern Nekoosa Corp./Georgia Pacific; East Millinocket; paper mills   800

G. H. Bass & Co.; Wilton; footwear   750

Guilford of Maine Inc.; Guilford; man-made fabric mills   750

Eastland Woolen Mill Inc.; Corinna; wool mills   600

Jackson Laboratory; Bar Harbor; medical/dental labs   600

State of Maine/Bangor Mental Health Institute; Bangor   600

City of Bangor; Bangor   600

Bangor Mental Health; Bangor   600

Bates College; Lewiston   600

Washburn Regional Health Center; Presque Isle   600

F. R. Le Page Bakery Inc.; Lewiston; bakery products   525

MARYLAND

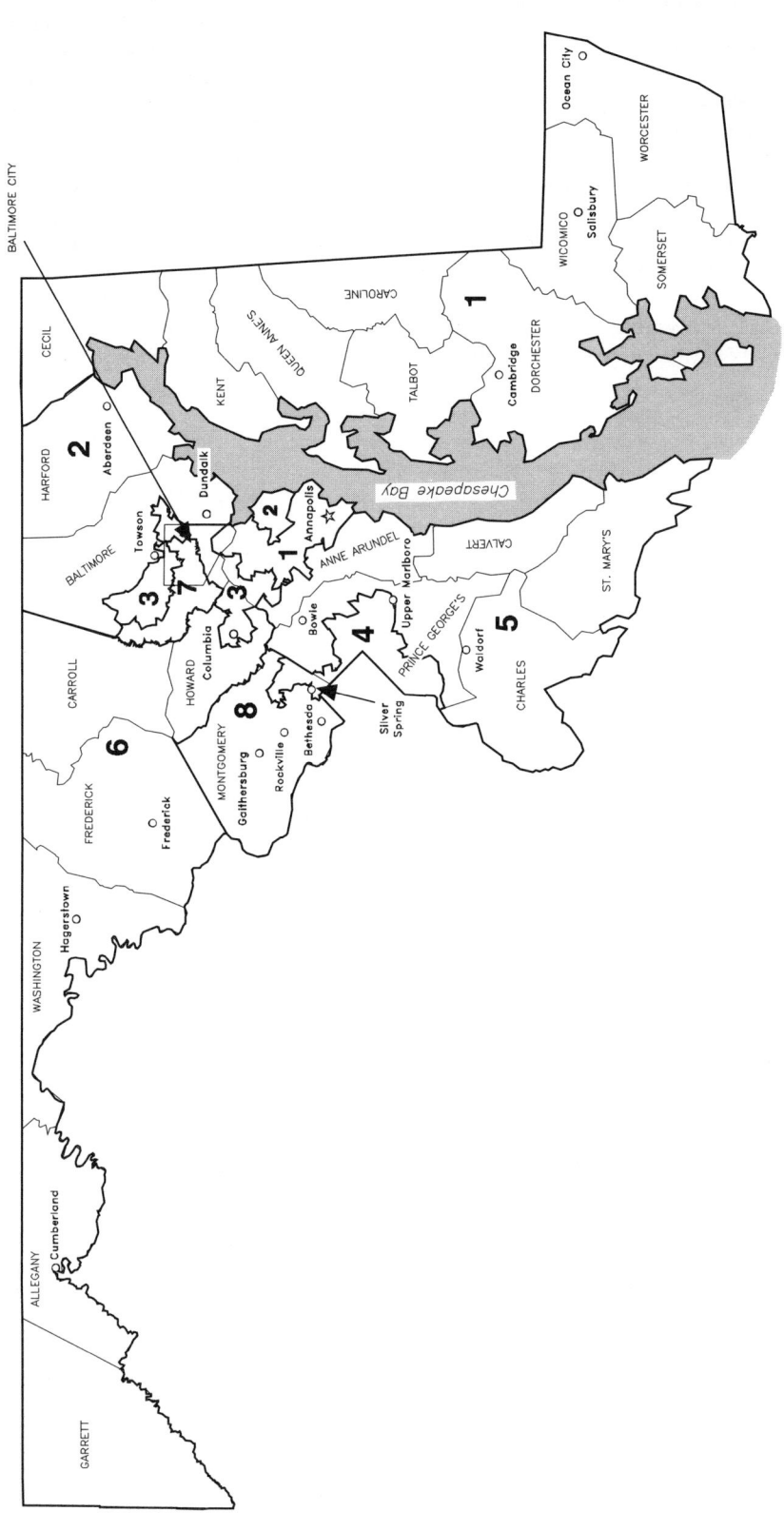

Maryland

Maryland boosters liked to describe the state as "America in Miniature." Despite its small size, Maryland reflected the vast sweep of American demographics. From the rustic, Old South-flavored Eastern Shore region, through the megalopolitan Baltimore-Washington corridor, to the hill country of the western panhandle, Maryland took in just about every variety of urban, suburban, exurban and rural community found in the nation. That description appeared on target for the last decade of the century.

Maryland held steady with eight congressional districts following the 1990 census and, after the first political test in 1992, a House delegation alignment pretty much like the one that prevailed in the 1980s. Republicans picked up one seat in 1992, to increase to four statewide, but that addition in the western and central 6th District reflected voters' basically Republican outlook after a conservative Democratic incumbent was unexpectedly defeated in the primary. Only at the other end of the state, in the 1st District that encompassed the Eastern Shore and the state capital Annapolis, was the race competitive, with the Republican winning with 52 percent.

This lineup was seen as a likely portrait of the 1990s. Although the number of Maryland seats did not change, population shifts required redrawn district lines, which were built around a new, open, black-majority 4th District largely made up of the inner part of Prince George's County, on the border of Washington, D.C. Prince George's County was in many ways a success story of black upward mobility. Middle-class blacks moved from the District of Columbia to the county's near-in suburbs, following a trail blazed by middle-class whites. More than 58 percent of the 4th's population was black, most living in Prince George's. The district's 37,962 Hispanics raised the nonwhite percentage to 67 percent, a margin that led to the election of a black in 1992 and appeared to assure a black seat for the rest of the decade.

The creation of the black-majority 4th District required the redrawing of the 5th District that gave that area a different makeup and outlook from the primarily suburban complexion that characterized it during the 1980s. The new 4th siphoned off blacks and made the 5th more dependent on less urbanized areas of Prince George's County, southern Anne Arundel County, and an area known as southern Maryland, made up of Charles, St.

Mary's, and Calvert counties. The southern counties had a rural heritage, with tobacco as a major crop. The political tradition was Democratic but conservative, which had translated into success for Republican presidential candidates. Nevertheless, a Democrat held the district seat in 1992.

Baltimore and its surrounds made up the 2nd, 3rd and 7th districts, with quite different complexions. Baltimore's population peaked at 939,000 in the mid-1960s, but the subsequent spread of urban problems sparked an out-migration to the suburbs. By 1990, the city's population was 736,000, and an increasing number of middle-class blacks were joining whites in moving to the suburbs.

The 2nd District, to the north, had more than enough Republican territory in Hartford and Baltimore counties to keep it as a base for a Republican seat.

The 3rd District included downtown and ethnic Baltimore. The city of Baltimore long had had an ethnically diverse, Democrat-dominated House district. But by the 1990s that district ranged far and wide to take in thousands of city natives who moved to the suburbs. The city still had the largest share (251,647 residents) of the 3rd's population. Although the House seat is securely in the Democrat camp, the district's large suburban constituency makes the 3rd competitive in other elections.

The 7th District included inner-city Baltimore and western Baltimore County with low-income black neighborhoods of west Baltimore and residential areas north and east of the city center. The areas' endemic ills—crime, drugs, teenage pregnancy, school dropouts—were a stark contrast to the vitality and glitter of a resurgent downtown area dominated by a rebuilt retail and entertainment area along the harbor. As a result, the new 7th District—which was wholly within the city when created as a black-majority seat in the 1970s—swung out across a swath of western Baltimore County. However, by following black suburban migration, the 7th maintained a 71 percent black population.

The 8th District, the other GOP seat in 1992, was Montgomery County, which—like Prince George's—bordered on Washington, D.C. A huge federal government presence and a burgeoning private sector spurred a boom in Montgomery County during the 1980s, increasing the population 31 percent to 757,027 and putting the county ahead of the city of Baltimore as

Maryland's largest jurisdiction. The seat had been held throughout much of the 1970s and 1980s by moderate to liberal Republicans, a trend likely to be continued by the county's large population of educated and affluent professionals.

Table 1 Population

District	Population	Population under 18	Voting-age population	Median age
1	597,684	142,778	454,906	34.0
2	597,683	140,482	457,201	34.4
3	597,680	138,567	459,113	33.7
4	597,690	150,567	447,123	31.3
5	597,681	147,483	450,198	31.3
6	597,688	149,900	447,788	33.6
7	597,680	149,503	448,177	32.1
8	597,682	142,961	454,721	34.3
State	4,781,468	1,162,241	3,619,227	33.0

Table 2 Voting-Age Persons

District	White*	Black*	American Indian, Eskimo, or Aleut*	Asian or Pacific Islander*	Other*	Hispanic*	Male*	Female*
1	84.4%	14.1%	0.2%	1.0%	0.3%	1.0%	48.6%	51.4%
2	92.5	5.3	0.2	1.7	0.3	1.1	48.0	52.0
3	81.6	15.7	0.3	2.1	0.4	1.6	46.6	53.4
4	36.4	55.8	0.3	4.5	3.0	6.1	46.5	53.5
5	78.1	17.8	0.4	3.0	0.7	2.3	49.7	50.3
6	94.0	4.5	0.2	1.1	0.2	0.8	48.6	51.4
7	30.3	67.8	0.3	1.4	0.2	0.9	45.7	54.3
8	82.8	7.5	0.2	7.6	1.9	6.0	47.5	52.5
State	72.6	23.5	0.3	2.8	0.9	2.5	47.7	52.3

*As percent of voting-age population.

Table 3 Voting-Age Persons by Age Groups

District	18-24*	25-44*	45-54*	55-64*	65 and over*
1	14.0%	42.9%	14.6%	12.2%	16.3%
2	13.0	44.2	14.7	12.4	15.7
3	12.8	46.1	13.1	10.7	17.3
4	15.2	51.4	14.4	9.1	9.8
5	16.7	48.3	15.1	9.8	10.1
6	13.4	45.1	15.0	11.2	15.3
7	15.4	44.8	12.5	11.2	16.1
8	11.3	47.9	16.0	11.2	13.7
State	14.0	46.3	14.4	11.0	14.3

*As percent of voting-age population.

Table 4 Income and Occupation

District	Median family income	Families in poverty	White collar*	Blue collar*	Service*	Farm*
1	$40,440	6.1%	57.7%	26.8%	12.4%	3.1%
2	45,303	3.9	64.4	24.1	10.4	1.2
3	41,804	6.5	68.8	19.5	11.1	0.6
4	46,396	4.8	68.9	17.4	13.0	0.6
5	51,367	2.9	66.9	21.1	10.6	1.4
6	42,229	5.3	59.7	26.1	11.7	2.4
7	30,115	17.4	57.2	23.2	18.9	0.8
8	64,199	2.3	80.0	10.4	8.7	0.9
State	45,034	6.0	65.9	20.8	11.9	1.4

*As percent of employed persons age 16 and over.

Table 5 Education: School Years Completed

District	Less than grade 9*	Grades 9-12 no diploma*	High school diploma*	College bachelor's degree or higher*
1	9.4%	15.9%	33.0%	19.9%
2	8.0	14.0	30.8	22.3
3	9.7	15.2	26.0	27.2
4	5.5	11.6	27.5	27.7
5	5.4	11.4	30.7	25.4
6	9.0	13.5	33.7	20.9
7	12.7	23.2	27.4	16.1
8	3.5	5.2	16.5	51.1
State	7.9	13.7	28.1	26.5

*As percent of persons age 25 and over.

Table 6 Housing and Residential Patterns

District	Owner occupied	Renter occupied	Urban	Rural
1	70.3%	29.7%	54.1%	45.9%
2	70.5	29.5	82.4	17.6
3	63.3	36.7	98.1	1.9
4	52.8	47.2	99.4	0.6
5	71.9	28.1	70.1	29.9
6	71.9	28.1	53.1	46.9
7	46.9	53.1	99.2	0.8
8	72.8	27.2	94.3	5.7
State	65.0	35.0	81.3	18.7

1st District

Cross Bay — Eastern Shore; Annapolis; Glen Burnie

The 4.3-mile-long Chesapeake Bay Bridge links the mainly rural counties of the Bay's Eastern Shore and the fast-growing suburbia of Anne Arundel County. These regions are different in many ways, but they share a conservative tilt that often benefits Republican candidates. George Bush swept the 1st in 1988 and bettered Bill Clinton here by 7 percentage points in 1992.

Yet the 1st is no lock for a Republican House candidate, as illustrated by Rep. Wayne Gilchrest's close 1992 contest against his Democrat opponent. Much of the Eastern Shore has a Democratic tradition (albeit of the conservative southern brand). Annapolis, the state capital, has many government employees. Blacks make up 15 percent of the 1st's population; Annapolis, as well as Salisbury and Cambridge on the Eastern Shore, have large minority communities.

About three-fifths of the district's population is spread across the nine counties of the Eastern Shore. Isolated until the Bay Bridge was completed in the 1950s, most of the region remains rural. The Perdue poultry company has a large work force at its Salisbury headquarters and plants.

But the shore's rusticity is disrupted on summer weekends by vacationers from the Washington and Baltimore areas heading for Ocean City on the Atlantic or such villages as St. Michael's and Crisfield on the bay. The shore's larger communities have some manufacturing. An upswing in cross-bay commuting has boosted the populations of such central areas as Queen Anne's and Talbot counties.

Gilchrest in 1992 benefited from the regionalism of Eastern Shore residents and their Republican tilt in federal contests. The small town and farm country in the central part of the district is the GOP heartland: Gilchrest ran up better than 70 percent in Talbot and Kent counties. But he slipped below 55 percent in the southernmost part, with its larger working-class and black constituencies. He won narrowly in Cecil County, at the edges of the Baltimore and Philadelphia metropolitan areas in Maryland's northeast corner.

Most of the 1st's remaining residents are in Anne Arundel County. Annapolis is by far the district's largest urban center; with the Capitol, the U.S. Naval Academy, a thriving waterfront area and a stock of well-preserved colonial-era buildings, the city has a large tourist industry.

With a population that is one-third black, Annapolis leans Democratic. But there is a GOP tilt in the affluent suburban areas to the north and west whose residents commute to Baltimore, Washington and Annapolis. At the county's north end are Glen Burnie and other working-class suburbs that lean Democratic but are rather conservative. Gilchrest only tallied 42 percent of the vote, but Bush edged Clinton, 43 percent to 38 percent, in the Anne Arundel part of the 1st.

The 1st also covers a small, blue-collar part of Baltimore city that is heavily Democratic but has few voters.

Election Returns

	1st District	Democrat	Republican
1992	President*	93,165 (37.4%)	109,039 (43.7%)
	House	112,771 (48.4%)	120,084 (51.6%)
1990	Governor	67,244 (43.9%)	85,827 (56.1%)
1988	President	73,930 (37.1%)	125,335 (62.9%)
	Senate	99,078 (54.6%)	82,477 (45.4%)
1986	Senate	70,699 (50.5%)	69,301 (49.5%)
	Governor	113,602 (82.1%)	24,759 (17.9%)

*Vote for Perot was 47,188 (18.9%).

Demographics

Population 597,684

Percent change from 1980 13.6%

Land area 3,476 square miles

Population per square mile 172

Counties, 1990 population
Anne Arundel (pt.) 239,623	Queen Anne's 33,953
Baltimore city (pt.) 14,292	Somerset 23,440
Caroline 27,035	Talbot 30,549
Cecil 71,347	Wicomico 74,339
Dorchester 30,236	Worcester 35,028
Kent 17,842	

Cities, 1990 population (10,000 or more)
Annapolis 33,187	Parole CDP 10,054
Arnold CDP 20,261	Salisbury 20,592
Baltimore (pt.) 14,292	Severna Park CDP (pt.)
Cambridge 11,514	19,389
Glen Burnie CDP 37,305	South Gate CDP 27,564

Race and Hispanic origin
White 83.4%
Black 15.0%
American Indian, Eskimo, or Aleut. 0.2%
Asian or Pacific Islander 1.0%
Other 0.3%
Hispanic origin 1.1%

Ancestry
American 5.9%	Italian 4.7%
Dutch 2.1%	Polish 3.7%
English 20.8%	Scotch Irish 2.2%
French 3.0%	Scottish 2.8%
German 25.9%	Swedish 1.0%
Irish 19.4%	Welsh 1.2%

Universities/colleges, 1990-1991 enrollment
Anne Arundel Community College, Arnold 12,152
Cecil Community College, North East 1,525
Chesapeake College, Wye Mills 2,064
Salisbury State College, Salisbury 5,734
St. John's College, Annapolis 442
University of Maryland-Eastern Shore, Princess Anne 2,067
U.S. Naval Academy, Annapolis 4,368
Washington College, Chestertown 1,046
Wor-Wic Technical Community College, Salisbury 1,385

Newspapers, total circulation (in all districts)
Annapolis Capital 44,232
Baltimore Sun 391,415
Salisbury Daily & Sunday Times 26,139
Washington Post 810,904
Washington Times 91,509
Wilmington News Journal 120,121

Commercial television stations, affiliations
ADI: Baltimore (65%) and Salisbury (34%)
WMDT, Salisbury (ABC)

Cable television systems, total subscribers
Falcon Cable TV; Wye Mills 7,130
Jones Intercable Inc.; Gambrills 46,425
North Arundel Cable; Millersville 40,469
Storer Cable TV Inc.; Salisbury 20,415
TCI of Maryland; Elkton 7,996
UA Cable of Baltimore; Baltimore 100,023
United Cable TV; Annapolis 21,500
United Cable TV Eastern Shore; Ocean City 31,415

Military installations, 1991
U.S. Naval Academy, Annapolis 9,223

Businesses and other major employers
State of Maryland/Transportation Dept.; Glen Burnie 1,940
ConAgra Inc.; Hurlock; poultry products 1,900
Peninsula Regional Medical Center; Salisbury 1,900
Anne Arundel Medical Center; Annapolis 1,700
State of Maryland/Fisheries, Forests & Wildlife; Wye Mills 1,500
Gould Inc./Ocean Systems Div.; Glen Burnie; research services 1,440
North Arundel Hospital Assn.; Glen Burnie 1,400
State of Maryland/Comptroller's Office; Annapolis 1,300
Anne Arundel Community College; Arnold 1,200
Memorial Hospital of Easton; Easton 1,100
Campbell Soup Co.; Salisbury; frozen foods 1,000
North American Philips Corp./Cambridge Div.; Cambridge; electric distribution equipment 1,000
Martin Marietta Corp./Aero Naval Systems Div.; Glen Burnie; search/navigation equipment 1,000
Arinc Inc.; Annapolis; telephone communications 1,000

Black & Decker Corp.; Easton; metalworking machinery 866
Showell Farms Inc.; Showell; poultry products 800
Dresser Industries Inc./Wayne Div.; Salisbury; refrigeration 800
Nevamar Corp.; Odenton; plastics products 800
Westinghouse Electric Corp./Oceanic Div.; Annapolis; engineering/architectural services 800
W. R. Grace & Co./Davison Chemical Div.; Baltimore; inorganic chemicals 750
Union Hospital of Cecil County; Elkton 715
IIT Research Institute; Annapolis; scientific research 700
Thiokol Corp./Elkton Div.; Elkton; ordnance/accessories 650
Westinghouse Electric Corp./Manufacturing & Operations; Glen Burnie; business services 600
Perdue Farms Inc.; Salisbury; poultry/grains 555
GB Glenmark Ltd. Co./Leedmark; Glen Burnie; grocery stores 550
State of Maryland/Automobile Insurance Fund; Annapolis 537
City of Annapolis; Annapolis 535
State of Maryland/Agriculture Dept.; Annapolis 501

2nd District

Baltimore and Harford Counties

The 2nd has more than enough Republican territory to provide a firm base for GOP candidates. In Baltimore County—home to slightly more than 60 percent of the 2nd's residents—the district takes in middle-class areas of Towson and such upper-income communities as Lutherville, Cockeysville and Hunt Valley, then sweeps north into horse country. The district also includes conservative-minded Harford County, which has experienced a burst of exurban growth.

Successful GOP candidates can also find support from blue-collar workers in the grimy southeastern part of Baltimore County. To the traditionally Democratic voters there, the GOP party label is less important than support for the port of Baltimore and strong views against unfair foreign competition.

Bethlehem Steel's complex at Sparrows Point is still Baltimore County's largest employer, but its 6,200 jobs are a fraction of the number during the steel industry's heyday. Many of the workers live across the Baltimore Beltway in Dundalk, at the Baltimore city line. Essex and nearby Middle River are largely blue-collar.

To the north, the 2nd moves into more suburban environs, including the county's most affluent communities and its burgeoning employment centers. Diversification has helped keep Baltimore County moving forward even as its heavy-industry sector has declined. The McCormick food company's headquarters are in Hunt Valley; tool manufacturer Black & Decker is based in Towson.

However, several county employers (Martin Marietta, AAI, Allied-Signal and Westinghouse, for example) rely on defense contracts, a cause for concern in an era of Pentagon cuts. Westinghouse has laid off about 4,500 workers in the past two years. But AAI is trying to diversify and recently won a contract to build weather monitoring systems for airports.

Job and other economic concerns dampened the GOP advantage here in 1992. Although the GOP House candidate again dominated in her home base, George Bush carried the part

of Baltimore County that is in the 2nd by just 44 percent to 38 percent over Bill Clinton. His subpar performance here—combined with the typically strong Democratic vote in the parts of the county that are in the 3rd and 7th districts—allowed Clinton to become the first Democratic presidential candidate to win Baltimore County since 1964.

Republican loyalties are stronger to the east in Harford County. Bush beat Clinton by 11 percentage points. Harford grew by 25 percent in the 1980s, as commuters poured into subdivisions in such towns as Bel Air and Joppatowne. Much of Harford's economic base is defense-related: With more than 16,600 employees, the Aberdeen weapons proving ground is by far the region's largest employer.

At its southern end, the 2nd leaps across the Patapsco River into an upscale, strongly Republican corner of Anne Arundel County, including parts of suburban Pasadena and Severna Park.

Election Returns

	2nd District	Democrat	Republican
1992	President*	98,267 (36.1%)	121,087 (44.5%)
	House	88,658 (34.9%)	165,443 (65.1%)
1990	Governor	79,507 (49.1%)	82,474 (50.9%)
1988	President	80,630 (36.5%)	140,530 (63.5%)
	Senate	115,896 (54.4%)	96,969 (45.6%)
1986	Senate	91,193 (56.9%)	68,989 (43.1%)
	Governor	134,846 (83.9%)	25,935 (16.1%)

Vote for Perot was 52,668 (19.4%).

Demographics

Population 597,683

Percent change from 1980 13.6%

Land area 904 square miles

Population per square mile 661

Counties, 1990 population
Anne Arundel (pt.) 45,283   Harford 182,132
Baltimore (pt.) 370,268

Cities, 1990 population (10,000 or more)
Aberdeen 13,087   Lutherville-Timonium
Bel Air North CDP 14,880   CDP 16,442
Bel Air South CDP 26,421   Mays Chapel CDP (pt.)
Carney CDP 25,578   10,106
Cockeysville CDP 18,668   Middle River CDP 24,616
Dundalk CDP 65,800   Perry Hall CDP (pt.)
Edgewood CDP 23,903   15,176
Essex CDP 40,872   Rosedale CDP (pt.) 13,325
Joppatowne CDP 11,084   Towson CDP (pt.) 37,864
Lake Shore CDP 13,269

Race and Hispanic origin
White 91.7%
Black 5.9%
American Indian, Eskimo, or Aleut 0.3%
Asian or Pacific Islander 1.8%
Other 0.3%
Hispanic origin 1.2%

Ancestry

American	3.8%	Irish	22.7%
Czechoslovakian	1.1%	Italian	8.8%
Dutch	2.2%	Polish	8.0%
English	16.7%	Scotch Irish	2.1%
French	3.2%	Scottish	2.6%
German	39.3%	Slovakian	1.1%
Greek	1.1%	Welsh	1.4%

Universities/colleges, 1990-1991 enrollment

Essex Community College, Baltimore 11,022
Goucher College, Towson 891
Harford Community College, Bel Air 5,105
Towson State University, Towson 15,034

Newspapers, total circulation (in all districts)

Annapolis Capital 44,232
Baltimore Sun 391,415
Washington Post 810,904
Washington Times 91,509

Commercial television stations, affiliations

ADI: Baltimore (100%)

Cable television systems, total subscribers

Comcast Cablevision; Essex 158,000
Comcast/Hartford County; Churchville 35,000
Jones Intercable Inc.; Gambrills 46,425
North Arundel Cable; Millersville 40,469
UA Cable of Baltimore; Baltimore 100,023

Military installations, 1991

Aberdeen Proving Ground (Army), Aberdeen 16,623
Martin State Air Force Guard Station, Baltimore 490

Businesses and other major employers

Bethlehem Steel Corp./Sparrows Point Steel Plant; Baltimore; steel production 6,153
Westinghouse Electric Corp./Integrated Logistics Support Div.; Hunt Valley; electric distribution/testing equipment 4,500
Martin Marietta Corp./Aero Naval Systems Div.; Baltimore; aircraft/parts 3,700
Greater Baltimore Medical Center; Baltimore 2,500
Allied-Signal Inc./Allied-Bendix Div.; Baltimore; communications equipment 2,300
St. Joseph Hospital Inc.; Baltimore 2,151
AAI Corp.; Cockeysville; search/navigation equipment 2,100
Franklin Square Hospital Center; Baltimore 2,100
Black & Decker U.S. Inc./Professional Products Div.; Cockeysville; power tools 1,850
AT&T Co.; Hunt Valley; telephone communications 1,700
Noxell Corp.; Cockeysville; cosmetics/soaps 1,400
Becton Dickinson & Co.; Hunt Valley; pharmaceuticals 1,000
Sheppard & Enoch Pratt Hospital; Baltimore 990
PHH FleetAmerica; Cockeysville; auto sales 961
General Instrument Corp./Amtote Div.; Hunt Valley; electric repair 900
McCormick & Co. Inc./McCormick Schilling Div.; Hunt Valley; tea/spices 900
Citibank Maryland; Baltimore; commercial banks 900
Chesapeake Potomac Telephone of Maryland; Cockeysville; telephone services 900
County of Baltimore; Baltimore 800

PHH Corp.; Hunt Valley; management/financing services 800
SCM Chemicals Inc./White Marsh Office; Baltimore; industrial chemicals 785
Harford Community College; Bel Air 775
Stella Maris Operating Corp.; Baltimore; residential care 750
Pinkerton's Inc.; Baltimore; business/security services 700
Fallston General Hospital; Fallston 700
Macy's Northeast Inc.; Hunt Valley; department stores 682
Essex Community College; Baltimore 668
Eastern Stainless Corp.; Baltimore; steel products 650
Becton Dickinson & Co.; Sparks Glencoe; medical diagnostic instruments 600
Harford Memorial Hospital; Havre De Grace 600
County of Harford; Bel Air 600
Texas Instruments Inc./Industrial Systems; Hunt Valley; electronic components 550
U.S. Health Inc.; Baltimore; recreation services 530
Stevens Painton Corp.; Baltimore; building construction 525

3rd District

Downtown and Ethnic Baltimore; Columbia

The city of Baltimore has long had an ethnically diverse, Democrat-dominated district. But today that district ranges far and wide to take in thousands of city natives who moved to the suburbs.

The 3rd, a reverse-C shape, wends in and out of Baltimore to pick up the Democratic voters. Democrats Rep. Benjamin Cardin and Sen. Barbara A. Mikulski ran very well here in 1992. With its large suburban constituency, the 3rd can be somewhat more competitive in presidential contests; but Bill Clinton easily bested George Bush in 1992.

The city still has the largest share (about two-fifths) of the 3rd's residents. At the heart of the district is Baltimore's rejuvenated downtown. Spurred by the success of Harborplace, a retail-and-entertainment complex along the once-forsaken waterfront, Baltimore's downtown has sprouted hotels and office buildings: The USF&G insurance company, Maryland National Bank and Crown Central Petroleum have headquarters here.

In 1992, baseball's Orioles moved into a new stadium just west of downtown. To the south, the 3rd moves through gentrifying Federal Hill, takes in a blue-collar stretch around the harbor leading to Fort McHenry, then jumps across the Patapsco River's Middle Branch to mainly black Cherry Hill.

East of downtown is the city's ethnic heartland: Little Italy and Highlandtown (whose Polish and German voters gave Mikulski her political start). There is a working-class accent here: The city is "Bawlamer" and its ball team is the "Eryals." General Motors has a factory in east Baltimore. The 3rd moves north through working-class sections on the city's east edge, then west to pick up some of Baltimore's wealthier communities. The mainly Jewish areas of northwest Baltimore make up Cardin's base.

In its part of Baltimore County (about a third of the total population), the 3rd follows the path of Jewish migration north from wealthy Pikesville to middle-class Reisterstown and west to Randallstown (which has a significant black population). Skimming the city's northern border, the 3rd takes in affluent, less Democratic areas in Ruxton and Towson, growing Perry Hall and modest suburbs such as Parkville.

On the other side of the city, the 3rd includes middle-class suburbs in south Baltimore County and northwest Anne Arundel County near Baltimore-Washington International Airport: Linthicum—site of a Westinghouse facility pinched by defense cuts—and the part of Fort Meade that houses the National Security Agency are here.

The 3rd also includes the eastern portion of Howard County and Columbia, with its planned racial mix and liberal-leaning electorate. The city has become an economic engine in the middle of the newly combined Washington-Baltimore metropolitan area. The Rouse development company, which built Columbia and Harborplace, and several high-tech companies are here.

Election Returns

	3rd District	Democrat	Republican
1992	President*	136,829 (53.8%)	82,494 (32.4%)
	House	163,354 (73.5%)	58,869 (26.5%)
1990	Governor	85,846 (61.9%)	52,906 (38.1%)
1988	President	110,269 (51.3%)	104,530 (48.7%)
	Senate	135,613 (66.3%)	68,877 (33.7%)
1986	Senate	105,812 (69.5%)	46,404 (30.5%)
	Governor	133,987 (88.2%)	17,890 (11.8%)

*Vote for Perot was 34,973 (13.8%).

Demographics

Population 597,680

Percent change from 1980 13.3%

Land area 213 square miles

Population per square mile 2,802

Counties, 1990 population

Anne Arundel (pt.) 64,075	Baltimore city (pt.) 251,647
Baltimore (pt.) 194,261	Howard (pt.) 87,697

Cities, 1990 population (10,000 or more)

Arbutus CDP 19,750	Overlea CDP 12,137
Baltimore (pt.) 251,647	Parkville CDP (pt.) 26,285
Columbia CDP (pt.) 68,184	Pikesville CDP 24,815
Elkridge CDP 12,953	Randallstown CDP (pt.)
Ferndale CDP (pt.) 10,254	15,505
Fort Meade CDP (pt.)	Reisterstown CDP (pt.)
12,473	15,177
Lansdowne-Baltimore	Severn CDP (pt.) 21,866
Highlands CDP 15,509	Towson CDP (pt.) 11,581

Race and Hispanic origin

White 79.5%
Black 17.5%
American Indian, Eskimo, or Aleut. 0.3%
Asian or Pacific Islander 2.2%
Other 0.5%
Hispanic origin 1.7%

Ancestry

American 3.5%	French 2.4%
Dutch 1.6%	German 29.3%
English 11.8%	Greek 1.0%

Irish 17.8%	Russian 4.7%
Italian 6.9%	Scotch Irish 1.6%
Polish 7.6%	Scottish 1.9%

Universities/colleges, 1990-1991 enrollment

Baltimore Hebrew University, Baltimore 263
College of Notre Dame of Maryland, Baltimore 2,618
Dundalk Community College, Baltimore 3,410
Howard Community College, Columbia 4,447
Loyola College, Baltimore 6,358
Ner Israel Rabbinical College, Baltimore 370
Saint Mary's Seminary and University, Baltimore 304
University of Maryland, Baltimore 4,727
Villa Julie College, Stevenson 1,596

Newspapers, total circulation (in all districts)

Annapolis Capital 44,232
Baltimore Sun 391,415
Washington Post 810,904
Washington Times 91,509

Commercial television stations, affiliations

ADI: Baltimore (100%)
  WBAL-TV, Baltimore (CBS)
  WBFF, Baltimore (Fox)
  WJZ-TV, Baltimore (ABC)
  WMAR-TV, Baltimore (NBC)

Cable television systems, total subscribers

Comcast Cablevision; Essex 158,000
Howard Cable Television; Ellicott City 41,600
North Arundel Cable; Millersville 40,469
UA Cable of Baltimore; Baltimore 100,023

Military installations, 1991

Fort George G. Meade (Army), Odenton 32,906
Fort Holabird (Army), Baltimore 628

Businesses and other major employers

Westinghouse Electric Corp./Westinghouse Defense; Linthicum; electrical equipment/supplies 17,000
General Motors Corp.; Baltimore; truck/bus assembly 3,500
St. Agnes Hospital; Baltimore 2,800
USF&G Co.; Baltimore; fire/marine/casualty insurance 2,300
USAir Inc.; Baltimore; airline 2,000
Francis Scott Key Medical Center; Baltimore 2,000
First Maryland Bancorp; Baltimore; commercial banks 1,628
Abacus Corp./Abacus Security Service; Baltimore; building services 1,405
Baltimore Gas & Electric Co.; Baltimore; electric services 1,400
State of Maryland/Vocational Rehabilitation; Owings Mills; nursing 1,350
Mercy Medical Center; Baltimore 1,300
Blue Cross/Blue Shield of Maryland; Owings Mills; medical doctors 1,300
Chesapeake Potomac Telephone of Maryland; Baltimore; telephone communications 1,270
Howard County General Hospital; Columbia 1,225
Harbor Hospital Center Inc.; Baltimore 1,200
U.S. Army Corps of Engineers; Baltimore 1,200
Hall Perry Corp./Farm Fresh Supermarkets; Baltimore; grocery stores 1,000
National Data Corp.; Hanover; computer services 1,000
County of Baltimore/Board of Education; Baltimore 1,000

Unilever U.S. Inc.; Baltimore; soaps/cleaners 975
General Electric Co.; Columbia; household appliances 950
State of Maryland/Environment Dept.; Baltimore 900
Broadway Services Inc.; Baltimore; building services 900
Patuxent Medical Group; Columbia; medical doctors 850
T. Rowe Price Assoc. Inc.; Baltimore; security/commodity services 840
Baltimore Specialty Steels Corp.; Baltimore; steel products 805
Browning-Ferris Inc.; Linthicum; sanitary services 800
Loral Aerospace Corp.; Hanover; research services 800
State of Maryland/Education Dept.; Baltimore 750
Maryland Medical Laboratory; Baltimore; medical/dental labs 720
Alex Brown & Sons Inc.; Baltimore; security brokers 702
W. R. Grace & Co. Inc./Research Div.; Columbia; research services 655
F&D Holding Corp.; Baltimore; surety insurance 600
State of Maryland/Attorney General's Office; Baltimore 600
BPS Guard Services Inc./Burns Intl. Security Services; Baltimore; business services 600
Fidelity & Deposit Co. of Maryland; Baltimore; surety insurance 570
Harrison's at Pier Five Inc.; Baltimore; bars/restaurants 550
CSX Transportation Inc./Chessie Computer Service; Baltimore; computer services 550
Maryland National Bank; Baltimore; commercial banks 522
Duratek Corp.; Columbia; industry machinery 513

4th District

Inner Prince George's County; Silver Spring

The emergence of Prince George's as one of the nation's few suburban counties with a black majority sparked the creation of the 4th. Blacks are about three-fifths of the district's population; most of them live in Prince George's, which makes up the major part of the 4th. Adding Hispanics, whose numbers have steadily grown in recent years, more than two-thirds of the 4th's residents are of minority groups.

Still, there is a substantial white population, particularly in the southeast section of Montgomery County that contributes slightly more than a quarter of the district's residents. When the first House primary was held in the new black-majority 4th in 1992, black Democratic activists worried that a white candidate might maneuver through a large crowd of black contenders. But Albert Wynn used a biracial appeal in both counties to take the nomination.

The primary was the hard part in this sure Democratic district. In the general election, Wynn piled up 84 percent of the vote in Prince George's County and took 59 percent in Montgomery. Bill Clinton ran just slightly behind Wynn in Prince George's but ahead of him in the Montgomery section.

Prince George's is in many ways a success story of black upward mobility. For blacks, it is among the nation's leading jurisdictions in business formation, home ownership and education. Many residents work in Washington, D.C., and at a complex in Suitland (which includes the Census Bureau and the National Weather Service) and at Andrews Air Force Base. There are large private employers in Landover (such as the Giant supermarket chain that dominates the area) and in the New Carrollton business center. The USAir Arena is in Largo.

For some residents, however, there has been no escape from the drugs and guns that many hoped to leave behind when they moved from the District of Columbia. Drug trafficking and attendant violence plague a number of the 4th's low-income communities, which are mostly inside the Capital Beltway that rings Washington.

The largest concentrations of Hispanics are in working-class and low-income communities in western Prince George's County and in the Silver Spring area of eastern Montgomery County. Takoma Park, which straddles the county line, has a bohemian image: Liberal activists declared it a "nuclear free zone" in the 1980s.

Silver Spring, one of Washington's first suburbs, saw its once-bustling downtown grow seedy as the retail trade moved to regional malls. Local officials have finally resolved a years-long battle between developers and residents over how to rejuvenate the city; developers now plan a new mall and office buildings, while residents will enjoy a civic plaza and the restoration of the downtown's Art Deco elements.

North of Silver Spring the 4th follows the Route 29 business corridor. The middle- and upper-middle-income communities in this area are whiter and more conservative than communities in the rest of the district.

Election Returns

	4th District	Democrat	Republican
1992	President*	149,262 (74.2%)	37,716 (18.8%)
	House	136,902 (75.2%)	45,166 (24.8%)
1990	Governor	85,098 (82.7%)	17,830 (17.3%)
1988	President	118,517 (69.3%)	52,439 (30.7%)
	Senate	121,433 (74.5%)	41,515 (25.5%)
1986	Senate	74,898 (72.4%)	28,530 (27.6%)
	Governor	84,925 (83.5%)	16,812 (16.5%)

Vote for Perot was 14,160 (7.0%).

Demographics

Population 597,690

Percent change from 1980 13.7%

Land area 193 square miles

Population per square mile 3,098

Counties, 1990 population
Montgomery (pt.) 159,345
Prince George's (pt.) 438,345

Cities, 1990 population (10,000 or more)
Andrews AFB CDP (pt.) 10,034
Aspen Hill CDP (pt.) 17,700
Camp Springs CDP (pt.) 13,346
Chillum CDP 31,309
Colesville CDP (pt.) 18,819
Coral Hills CDP 11,032
Fairland CDP (pt.) 16,920
Forestville CDP 16,731
Fort Washington CDP 24,032
Hillcrest Heights CDP 17,136
Langley Park CDP (pt.) 15,773
Mitchellville CDP 12,593

Oxon Hill-Glassmanor CDP   35,794
Silver Spring CDP (pt.)   52,068
Suitland-Silver Hill CDP   35,111
Takoma Park   16,700
Walker Mill CDP   10,920
White Oak CDP (pt.)   18,671

Race and Hispanic origin
White   33.5%
Black   58.5%
American Indian, Eskimo, or Aleut.   0.3%
Asian or Pacific Islander   4.6%
Other   3.2%
Hispanic origin   6.4%

Ancestry
American 2.4%		Polish 1.5%	
English 6.7%		Russian 1.3%	
French 1.3%		Scotch Irish 1.1%	
German 9.1%		Scottish 1.1%	
Irish 7.1%		Subsaharan African 2.4%	
Italian 2.8%		West Indian 2.5%	

Universities/colleges, 1990-1991 enrollment
Columbia Union College, Takoma Park   1,344
Montgomery College, Takoma Park   4,810
Prince George's Community College, Upper Marlboro
   13,087
Washington Theological Union, Silver Spring   229

Newspapers, total circulation (in all districts)
Baltimore Sun   391,415
Frederick Post & News   41,654
Montgomery Journal   38,135
Prince George's Journal   38,745
Washington Post   810,904
Washington Times   91,509

Commercial television stations, affiliations
ADI: Washington, D.C. (100%)

Cable television systems, total subscribers
Cable TV Montgomery; Rockville   149,614
Metrovision/Prince George's; Capitol Heights   58,266
Multivision Cable TV; Lanham   71,700

Military installations, 1991
Andrews Air Force Base, Camp Springs   13,223
D.W. Taylor Naval Ship Research & Development Center,
   Bethesda   2,950
Defense Mapping Agency Hydro/Topographic Center
   (Army), Brookmont   2,611
Naval Surface Weapons Center, Silver Spring   1,950
Harry Diamond Laboratories (Army), Adelphi   1,661

Businesses and other major employers
U.S. Census Bureau; Suitland   4,500
U.S. Postal Service; Capitol Heights   4,000
Digital Equipment Corp.; Hyattsville; computer equipment
   2,500
Giant Food Inc.; Landover; grocery stores   2,000
Washington Adventist Hospital; Silver Spring   1,750
Prince George's Community College; Upper Marlboro   1,700
Chesapeake & Potomac Telephone Co.; Silver Spring; tele-
   phone communications   1,500
County of Prince George's/Police Dept.; Forestville   1,100

Gannett Satellite Info Network/U.S.A Today; Silver Spring;
   computer services   1,000
County of Prince George's; Upper Marlboro   905
AT&T Co.; Silver Spring; telephone communications   850
Centennial One Inc.; Lanham-Seabrook; building services   800
Hills Capitol Security Inc.; Silver Spring; security services   735
Driggs Corp.; Capitol Heights; special contractors   700
Hughes STX Corp.; Lanham-Seabrook; computer services
   700
U.S. National Weather Service; Suitland   700
State of Maryland/Great Oaks Center; Silver Spring   650
E. M. S. Inc.; Silver Spring; building services   650
Potomac Electric Power Co.; Forestville; electric services   600
Sting Security Inc.; Temple Hills; security services   600
Potomac Rose Society Inc.; Silver Spring; social services   600
Manor Care Inc.; Silver Spring; nursing   600
Gotham Building Maintenance; Silver Spring; building ser-
   vices   600
Banctec Systems Inc.; Silver Spring; office equipment   591

5th District
Outer Prince George's; Southern Maryland

The 5th has a different makeup and outlook from the primarily suburban district of the 1980s. The creation of the black-majority 4th in 1991 redistricting siphoned off many black Democrats, while pushing the 5th into less urbanized areas of Prince George's County, southern Anne Arundel County and southern Maryland (Charles, St. Mary's and Calvert counties).

The southern counties have a rural heritage, with tobacco as a major crop. The political tradition is Democratic but conservative, a tendency augmented by an influx of commuters and exurbanites. Winning candidates for major office here are usually conservatives and are often Republicans.

The reshaping of the 5th to include this territory was expected to cause Democratic Rep. Steny Hoyer trouble in 1992, and it did. After years of easy victories, Hoyer had to campaign vigorously to defeat the GOP challenger by 9 percentage points. Hoyer was saved by a solid Democratic vote in his remaining portion of Prince George's County, where he took 60 percent; he trailed elsewhere in the 5th. Similarly, in the presidential race that year, Bill Clinton failed to crack 38 percent in any of the southern Maryland counties, but won a plurality in the 5th thanks to his 53 percent in Prince George's County.

P.G. County (as some locals call it) accounts for nearly half the 5th's population. In the northern part of the county, the 5th ducks inside the Capital Beltway to pick up such heavily black communities as Hyattsville. Also in Prince George's County is the University of Maryland's flagship campus at College Park, with 35,000 students. The university is among the public employers that bolster the district's job base. Up the I-95/Baltimore-Washington Parkway corridor toward Greenbelt and Laurel are NASA's Goddard Space Flight Center and the National Agricultural Research Center. Next door in the 3rd District, Fort Meade, despite downsizing in 1989, still assists numerous government organizations.

The 5th sweeps east through Bowie, whose location between Washington and Annapolis brought a growth spurt in the 1980s, then around Andrews Air Force Base into southern Prince George's. Upper Marlboro, the county seat, is here. The 5th also takes in a portion of southern Anne Arundel County that contributes about 15 percent of the district's residents; upscale communities such as Crofton and Davidsonville are here, but much of the area retains a rural feel.

The southern counties all grew rapidly in the 1980s. Charles County's population grew 39 percent to more than 100,000, as commuters poured into subdivisions along Route 301 and Indian Head Highway. Population in St. Mary's County increased 27 percent. There is much defense-related work in the southern counties: Charles County has the Naval Ordnance Station at Indian Head, and St. Mary's City has the Patuxent River Naval Air Test Center and the Naval Electronics Systems Engineering center, which appeared on the 1993 base-closure list. Calvert County's population grew 48 percent, but it remains the state's second-least-populous county west of the Chesapeake Bay.

Election Returns

	5th District	Democrat	Republican
1992	President*	107,618 (44.8%)	95,356 (39.7%)
	House	118,312 (53.0%)	97,982 (43.9%)
1990	Governor	82,085 (65.5%)	43,298 (34.5%)
1988	President	82,121 (42.4%)	111,658 (57.6%)
	Senate	104,195 (58.6%)	73,558 (41.4%)
1986	Senate	62,913 (54.6%)	52,283 (45.4%)
	Governor	88,972 (78.5%)	24,371 (21.5%)

Vote for Perot was 37,441 (15.6%).

Demographics

Population 597,681

Percent change from 1980 13.3%

Land area 1,567 square miles

Population per square mile 381

Counties, 1990 population
Anne Arundel (pt.) 78,258	Prince George's (pt.)
Calvert 51,372	290,923
Charles 101,154	St. Mary's 75,974

Cities, 1990 population (10,000 or more)
Beltsville CDP 14,476	Hyattsville (pt.) 12,085
Bowie 37,589	Laurel 19,438
Clinton CDP 19,987	South Laurel CDP 18,591
College Park 21,927	St. Charles CDP 28,717
Crofton CDP (pt.) 11,433	Waldorf CDP 15,058
Greenbelt 21,096	

Race and Hispanic origin
White 77.2%
Black 18.6%
American Indian, Eskimo, or Aleut. 0.4%
Asian or Pacific Islander 3.0%
Other 0.8%
Hispanic origin 2.4%

Ancestry
American 4.2%	Irish 19.7%
Dutch 2.0%	Italian 5.9%
English 18.5%	Polish 3.0%
French 3.6%	Russian 1.1%
German 24.4%	Scotch Irish 2.6%
Scottish 2.7%	Welsh 1.1%
Swedish 1.1%	

Universities/colleges, 1990-1991 enrollment
Bowie State College, Bowie 4,189
Capitol College, Laurel 737
Charles County Community College, La Plata 5,282
St. Mary's College of Maryland, St. Mary's City 1,568
University of Maryland, College Park 34,837
University of Maryland-University College, College Park 14,477
Washington Bible College, Lanham 457

Newspapers, total circulation (in all districts)
Annapolis Capital 44,232
Baltimore Sun 391,415
Prince George's Journal 38,745
Washington Post 810,904
Washington Times 91,509

Commercial television stations, affiliations
ADI: Washington, D.C. (87%) and Baltimore (13%)

Cable television systems, total subscribers
American Cable TV; Leonardtown 13,774
Cable TV Montgomery; Rockville 149,614
Jones Intercable Inc.; Gambrills 46,425
Jones Intercable Inc.; Prince Frederick 11,496
Jones Intercable Inc.; Waldorf 16,099
Metrovision/Prince Georges; Capitol Heights 58,266
Multivision Cable TV; Lanham 71,700
United Cable TV; Annapolis 21,500

Military installations, 1991
Patuxent River Naval Air Test Center, Patuxent River 9,373
Indian Head Naval Ordnance Station (Navy), Indian Head 4,189
Naval Electronic Systems Engineering, St. Mary's City 1,127

Businesses and other major employers
NASA/Goddard Space Flight Center; Greenbelt; space research/technology 13,000
University of Maryland & University of Maryland-University College, College Park 10,200
Baltimore Gas & Electric Co./Calvert Cliffs Nuclear Center; Lusby; electric services 2,000
State of Maryland/Sanitary Commission; Hyattsville 2,000
District of Columbia/Human Resources Dept.; Laurel; residential care 1,500
U.S. National Agricultural Research Center; Beltsville 1,500
Southern Maryland Hospital; Clinton 1,353
Litton Systems Inc./Amecom Div.; College Park; special contractors 1,200
Alfred H. Smith Jr./Smith's Sand & Gravel Co.; College Park; road construction 950
District Photo Inc./Clark Color Labs; Beltsville; photo developing 900
Doctors Community Hospital; Lanham-Seabrook 850
Bendix Field Engineering Corp.; La Plata; satellite communication services 800
Tracor Inc./Tracor Applied Sciences; California; research services 800
Computer Sciences Corp./Health Administrative Services Div.; Lanham-Seabrook; computer systems 750
County of Charles; La Plata 740

Dimensions Health Corp./Greater Laurel-Beltsville Hospital;
   Laurel   700
Arbitron Co.; Laurel; survey service   675
State of Maryland/Correctional Facility; Jessup   649
Dyncorp; Lexington Park; airport services   610
American Pool Service Inc.; Lanham-Seabrook; pool mainte-
   nance   600
Computer Sciences Corp.; Beltsville; computer services   600
Arbitron Co.; Beltsville; research services   600
Citizens Bank of Maryland; Laurel; savings institutions   575
Computer Sciences Corp./System Sciences Div.; Laurel; com-
   puter services   550
Crownsville Hospital Center; Crownsville   530

6th District

Central and West — Frederick; Hagerstown

During the 14 years (1978-1992) that Democrat Beverly B. Byron dominated the 6th, local Republicans insisted that it was only her record as one of the most conservative House Democrats that kept the GOP-leaning district from falling into their hands. The events of 1992 justified their contention. Byron was upset by a more liberal Democrat in the primary. But in the general election, the 6th stuck to its conservative form, electing the Republican candidate by a margin of nearly 20,000 votes.

The 6th takes in the five westernmost counties along Maryland's northern border—Garrett, Allegany, Washington, Frederick and Carroll—and more than half the population of Howard County. These places include some of the state's most reliably Republican territory. George Bush swept all the counties in 1992; his 48 percent here was by far his best in any state district. Garrett—one of Maryland's least populous counties and one with a "mountain Republican" tradition—was the only county to go against Democratic Sen. Barbara A. Mikulski's landslide, giving her Republican opponent 59 percent of its vote.

Most of the 6th's people live in the rapidly growing exurban areas of central Maryland. At its southern end, the 6th takes in the recently built subdivisions of western Howard County, then skirts south past the city of Columbia. The growth in the southern part of the 6th drew in a less conservative sort of Democrat who turned against Byron in 1992. But the district's conservative majority, including a number of traditional Democratic voters, rebelled against that result, and the GOP captured the district.

Frederick County's population also blossomed over the past decade; many residents commute on I-270 to Washington or on I-70 to Baltimore, or to high-tech businesses along those highways. The National Cancer Institute and the Defense Department's Medical Research Center are in the city of Frederick. The Camp David retreat is in Thurmont, in northern Frederick County.

To the east is Carroll County, parts of which have turned into bedroom suburbs of Baltimore. Both Frederick and Carroll counties still have a good deal of farmland and are Republican strongholds.

While development is an issue in central Maryland, slow growth is the problem in the hilly western panhandle. Though the largest private employer in Hagerstown (Washington County) is a Mack Truck factory, the manufacturing sector has diminished; a Citicorp credit card service center has taken up some of the employment slack.

In Cumberland (Allegany County), officials are laboring to replace jobs lost in the late 1980s, when Kelly-Springfield (which has headquarters here) closed its tire plant. Hard times give Democrats a chance, but conservatism usually prevails. Bush won the area with 45 percent.

With few economic options, Garrett County is trying to make the most of its remote location. Its tourism industry draws visitors to man-made Deep Creek Lake and winter-sport players to its mountain towns.

Election Returns

	6th District	Democrat	Republican
1992	President*	88,196 (33.9%)	125,494 (48.3%)
	House	106,224 (45.8%)	125,564 (54.2%)
1990	Governor	69,399 (48.2%)	74,542 (51.8%)
1988	President	68,919 (34.1%)	133,163 (65.9%)
	Senate	94,599 (50.3%)	93,362 (49.7%)
1986	Senate	57,562 (44.7%)	71,215 (55.3%)
	Governor	95,795 (76.7%)	29,040 (23.3%)

Vote for Perot was 46,376 (17.8%).

Demographics

Population   597,688

Percent change from 1980   13.2%

Land area   2,853 square miles

Population per square mile   210

Counties, 1990 population

Allegany 74,946	Garrett 28,138
Carroll 123,372	Howard (pt.) 99,631
Frederick 150,208	Washington 121,393

Cities, 1990 population (10,000 or more)

Cumberland 23,706	Hagerstown 35,445
Ellicott City CDP (pt.) 41,233	North Laurel CDP (pt.) 15,006
Frederick 40,148	Westminster 13,068

Race and Hispanic origin

White   93.8%
Black   4.5%
American Indian, Eskimo, or Aleut.   0.2%
Asian or Pacific Islander   1.3%
Other   0.2%
Hispanic origin   0.9%

Ancestry

American 5.3%	Italian 5.2%
Dutch 2.6%	Polish 2.8%
English 16.3%	Scotch Irish 2.3%
French 3.1%	Scottish 3.0%
German 44.2%	Welsh 1.4%
Irish 18.9%	

Universities/colleges, 1990-1991 enrollment

Allegany Community College, Cumberland   2,650
Frederick Community College, Frederick   3,976
Frostburg State University, Frostburg   5,019
Garrett Community College, McHenry   652
Hagerstown Business College, Hagerstown   360

Hagerstown Junior College, Hagerstown 3,353
Hood College, Frederick 1,988
Mount St. Mary's College, Emmitsburg 1,807
Western Maryland College, Westminster 2,223

Newspapers, total circulation (in all districts)
Baltimore Sun 391,415
Carroll County Times 20,935
Cumberland News 31,511
Frederick Post & News 41,654
Hagerstown Herald-Mail 40,013
Hanover Evening Sun 20,379
Washington Post 810,904

Commercial television stations, affiliations
ADI: Washington, D.C. (38%), Pittsburgh (23%), Baltimore (23%) and Hagerstown (16%)
WHAG-TV, Hagerstown (NBC)

Cable television systems, total subscribers
Antietam Cable TV Inc.; Hagerstown 28,000
Cable TV Montgomery; Rockville 149,614
Carroll County Cable TV; Westminster 20,622
Frederick Cablevision Inc.; Frederick 19,967
Frederick Cablevision Inc.; Jefferson 6,010
Howard Cable Television; Ellicott City 41,600
TCI of Maryland; Cumberland 23,786

Military installations, 1991
Fort Detrick (Army), Frederick 4,210
Fort Ritchie (Army), Cascade 2,282

Businesses and other major employers
Johns Hopkins University/Applied Physics Lab; Laurel; research services 2,800
Westvaco Corp./Fine Papers Div.; Westernport; paper mills 1,880
Citicorp Credit Services of Maryland; Hagerstown; credit services 1,663
State Farm Mutual Auto Insurance Co.; Frederick; fire/marine/casualty insurance 1,651
Washington County Hospital Assn.; Hagerstown 1,650
Springfield Hospital Center; Sykesville 1,600
Mack Trucks Inc./Powertrain Div.; Hagerstown; trucks 1,500
County of Howard; Ellicott City 1,400
Frederick Memorial Hospital; Frederick 1,400
Program Resources Inc.; Frederick; management services 1,200
W. D. Byron & Sons Inc.; Williamsport; leather production 1,100
Sacred Heart Hospital; Cumberland 1,050
Random House Inc.; Westminster; book publishing 1,000
CSX Transportation Inc.; Cumberland; railroad equipment 1,000
Bendix Field Engineering Corp.; Columbia; communication services 950
Carroll County General Hospital; Westminster 850
Eastalco Aluminum Co.; Frederick; aluminum 844
Mount St. Mary's College; Emmitsburg 828
Memorial Hospital & Medical Center; Cumberland 828
Bausch & Lomb Inc.; Oakland; optical devices 765
Prudential Home Mortgage Co.; Frederick; mortgage bankers 750
County of Washington/School District; Hagerstown 705

Londontown Corp./London Fog; Sykesville; coats/apparel 700
C. M. Offray & Son Inc./Maryland Ribbon; Hagerstown; fabric mills 700
County of Carroll; Westminster 696
County of Garrett/School District; Oakland 655
Rohr Industries Inc./Composites/Bonding Center; Hagerstown; lumber/building materials 637
State of Maryland/Correctional Institution; Hagerstown 611
Black & Decker U.S. Inc.; Hampstead; power tools 600
Kelly-Springfield Tire Co.; Cumberland; tires/management 572
Telemecanique North America; Westminster; electrical industrial apparatus 510

7th District

Inner-City Baltimore; Western Baltimore County

Downtown Baltimore's resurgence looks like a mirage to residents of the low-income black neighborhoods of west Baltimore and to those living north and east of the city center. The areas' ills—crime, drugs, teen pregnancies, school dropouts, lack of job opportunities—starkly contrast the vitality of the Inner Harbor.

Baltimore's population reached 939,000 in the 1960s, but the subsequent spread of urban problems sparked an exodus. By 1990, the city's population was 736,000, and an increasing number of middle-class blacks were joining whites in the suburbs.

As a result, the 7th—once wholly within the city—now swings out across western Baltimore County. But by following the black migration west on Liberty Heights toward Randallstown and down the Baltimore National Pike to Catonsville, the 7th maintains a 71 percent black population.

Recent trends have begun to channel development money back into the district, specifically to low-income communities in the flats east of downtown, to row houses along Broadway and to tenements in west Baltimore. But major improvements have been slow.

The picture within the city (which contributes nearly 80 percent of the 7th's population) is not all bleak. Just north of the downtown business district is the gentrified Mount Vernon area, home of the Walters Art Gallery and the Peabody music academy. Farther north are Johns Hopkins University and the Baltimore Museum of Art.

To the west is Druid Hill Park and the Baltimore Zoo. To the east is integrated Waverly and Memorial Stadium, home of the baseball Orioles for 37 years; the team left for a new downtown park in 1992. To the northeast is Morgan State University.

Though overshadowed by Harborplace, the old retail section west of the downtown hub survives; the Lexington food market and Baltimore Arena are here. There are middle-class black communities along Liberty Heights Road in west Baltimore. The national headquarters of the NAACP is near the city's western border. Over the line in Baltimore County are mainly black suburban settlements in Woodlawn and Lochearn. The Social Security Administration complex and Security Square Mall in Woodlawn are important sources of jobs.

To the south is Catonsville, site of the University of Maryland at Baltimore County. To the north, the 7th reaches to Randallstown, then leaps through a mostly undeveloped area to Reisterstown (both suburbs are shared with the 3rd). Although black residents have a strong presence in many of the 7th's suburban areas, the Baltimore County portion of the 7th is three-fifths white.

Democrats are assured of victories in the 7th. Bill Clinton piled up 87 percent of the vote in the city in 1992. But getting the vote out can be a problem for Democrats; only 67 percent of the registered voters in the city part of the 7th turned out in November 1992, well below the 81 percent rate for the state.

Election Returns

	7th District	Democrat	Republican
1992	President*	159,191 (77.8%)	32,431 (15.8%)
	House	152,689 (85.3%)	26,304 (14.7%)
1990	Governor	65,558 (70.6%)	27,354 (29.4%)
1988	President	139,443 (76.8%)	42,095 (23.2%)
	Senate	137,429 (79.4%)	35,617 (20.6%)
1986	Senate	105,659 (82.9%)	21,821 (17.1%)
	Governor	115,768 (91.6%)	10,667 (8.4%)

*Vote for Perot was 13,009 (6.4%).

Demographics

Population 597,680

Percent change from 1980 13.3%

Land area 109 square miles

Population per square mile 5,490

Counties, 1990 population
Baltimore (pt.) 127,605   Baltimore city (pt.) 470,075

Cities, 1990 population (10,000 or more)
Baltimore (pt.) 470,075
Catonsville CDP (pt.) 35,233
Lochearn CDP (pt.) 19,775
Milford Mill CDP (pt.) 19,520
Randallstown CDP (pt.) 10,772
Woodlawn CDP 32,907

Race and Hispanic origin
White 27.2%
Black 71.0%
American Indian, Eskimo, or Aleut. 0.3%
Asian or Pacific Islander 1.3%
Other 0.2%
Hispanic origin 0.9%

Ancestry
American 2.2%   Irish 6.7%
English 5.0%   Italian 2.2%
German 10.3%   Polish 1.7%

Universities/colleges, 1990-1991 enrollment
Catonsville Community College, Catonsville 12,770
Coppin State College, Baltimore 2,578
Johns Hopkins University, Baltimore 13,363
Maryland Institute College of Art, Baltimore 1,382
Morgan State University, Baltimore 4,693
New Community College of Baltimore, Baltimore 4,745
Peabody Institute of Johns Hopkins, Baltimore 492

Sojourner-Douglas College, Baltimore 253
University of Baltimore, Baltimore 5,772
University of Maryland, Baltimore 10,150

Newspapers, total circulation (in all districts)
Baltimore Sun 391,415
Carroll County Times 20,935
Hanover Evening Sun 20,379
Washington Post 810,904

Commercial television stations, affiliations
ADI: Baltimore (100%)
 WHSW, Baltimore (None)
 WNUV-TV, Baltimore (None)

Cable television systems, total subscribers
Comcast Cablevision; Essex 158,000
UA Cable of Baltimore; Baltimore 100,023

Businesses and other major employers
U.S. Social Security Administration; Baltimore 17,735
State of Maryland/Health Dept.; Baltimore 13,500
State of Maryland/New Directions Inc.; Baltimore; family services 7,500
U.S. Postal Service; Baltimore 5,000
Johns Hopkins Hospital Inc.; Baltimore 4,890
State of Maryland/Transportation Dept.; Baltimore 4,200
University of Maryland; Baltimore 3,985
University of Maryland Medical System Corp.; Baltimore 3,132
Johns Hopkins University/Applied Physics Laboratory; Baltimore 3,000
State of Maryland/Human Resources Dept.; Baltimore 2,500
Sinai Hospital of Baltimore; Baltimore 2,500
Union Memorial Hospital Inc.; Baltimore 2,081
Times Mirror Co./Baltimore Sun; Baltimore; newspapers 2,000
Church Home & Hospital; Baltimore 1,400
Spring Grove Hospital Center; Baltimore 1,300
Good Samaritan Hospital of Maryland; Baltimore 1,300
Baltimore County General Hospital; Randallstown 1,206
Maryland Casualty Co.; Baltimore; fire/marine/casualty insurance 1,200
New Community College of Baltimore; Baltimore 1,135
Liberty Medical Center Inc.; Baltimore 1,100
All Star Personnel Services; Baltimore; personnel supply services 1,010
Maryland General Hospital; Baltimore 970
Bon Secours Hospital; Baltimore 900
U.S. Veterans Affairs Dept.; Baltimore; hospital 875
State of Maryland/Licensing Regulation; Baltimore 800
State of Maryland; Baltimore 800
Kennedy Institute Inc.; Baltimore 750
Premier Management Group Inc./Action Janitorial Services; Baltimore; building services 750
Morgan State University; Baltimore 704
City of Baltimore/Baltimore City Schools; Baltimore 700
Homewood Hospital Center; Baltimore 660
Life of Maryland Inc.; Baltimore; life insurance 655
Catonsville Community College; Baltimore 650
Maryland National Bank; Baltimore; commercial banks 600
Waverly Inc./Waverly Press; Baltimore; periodicals 600
Barre-National Inc.; Baltimore; pharmaceuticals 505

8th District

Montgomery County

A huge federal government presence and a burgeoning private sector spurred a boom in Montgomery County during the 1980s, increasing population by nearly a third to more than 750,000. That put Montgomery ahead of the city of Baltimore as Maryland's largest jurisdiction.

With its steady employment base and large population of educated professionals, Montgomery County is one of the nation's most affluent places. In Potomac, million-dollar homes are interspersed with horse farms. Upscale stores in Chevy Chase and Bethesda anchor a bustling retail trade along Route 355.

Still, the recession of the early 1990s slowed the real estate development and retail sales that keyed Montgomery County's growth. And the county is not entirely dominated by upper-income residents. Most of the county's recent growth has been in middle-income communities in outer suburbs such as Gaithersburg, Germantown and Olney.

Older parts of Rockville, Gaithersburg and the Kensington-Wheaton area have working-class and some low-income areas, home to many of the county's black residents. There are also growing numbers of Hispanic and Asian immigrants.

Public employment—there are about 60,000 federal employees and more than 20,000 county workers—underpins Montgomery's economy and sets its political tone. Although Democrats have long dominated local politics here, GOP Rep. Constance Morella, with her reputation as one of the most liberal House Republicans, won her fourth term easily in 1992. And the county is suburban enough to make it a challenge for Democratic presidential candidates. Bill Clinton mastered Montgomery, beating George Bush in the 8th by 53 percent to 35 percent (and taking the whole county, part of which is in the 4th District, with 55 percent). But the 1984 and 1988 Democratic tickets won Montgomery narrowly.

Despite Clinton's 1992 surge, there are Republicans who view Montgomery County as a potential partisan growth area. They point to the increased importance of such private-sector employers as IBM, which provides thousands of jobs in the county, and the Marriott Corp., based in Bethesda.

Still, many of the county's private employers are research and development companies that rely on federal contracts or assistance. A number of these companies are along the I-270 "technology corridor." Nearby are such federal installations as the National Institutes of Health (Bethesda), the National Institute of Standards and Technology (Gaithersburg) and Department of Energy labs (Germantown). Montgomery County is a national center for biotechnology research.

County officials have tried to preserve the remnants of Montgomery's farming heritage in the northern and western areas of the county. Attitudes in these areas are more conservative and Republican habits stronger than elsewhere in the county.

Election Returns

	8th District	Democrat	Republican
1992	President*	156,043 (52.9%)	103,477 (35.1%)
	House	77,042 (27.5%)	203,377 (72.5%)
1990	Governor	115,882 (68.6%)	53,053 (31.4%)
1988	President	127,562 (49.6%)	129,839 (50.4%)
	Senate	156,054 (61.0%)	99,697 (39.0%)

	8th District	Democrat	Republican
1986	Senate	91,210 (57.5%)	67,357 (42.5%)
	Governor	117,095 (74.4%)	40,237 (25.6%)

Vote for Perot was 35,599 (12.1%).

Demographics

Population 597,682

Percent change from 1980 13.2%

Land area 459 square miles

Population per square mile 1,302

Counties, 1990 population
Montgomery (pt.) 597,682

Cities, 1990 population (10,000 or more)
Aspen Hill CDP (pt.) 27,794
Bethesda CDP 62,936
Gaithersburg 39,542
Germantown CDP 41,145
Montgomery Village CDP 32,315
North Bethesda CDP 29,656
North Potomac CDP 18,456
Olney CDP 23,019
Potomac CDP 45,634
Redland CDP 16,145
Rockville 44,835
Silver Spring CDP (pt.) 23,978
Wheaton-Glenmont CDP (pt.) 53,720

Race and Hispanic origin
White 81.5%
Black 8.2%
American Indian, Eskimo, or Aleut. 0.2%
Asian or Pacific Islander 8.0%
Other 2.0%
Hispanic origin 6.3%

Ancestry
American 2.8%
Dutch 1.7%
English 16.4%
French 3.4%
German 21.6%
Greek 1.4%
Hungarian 1.2%
Irish 16.4%
Italian 5.9%
Polish 5.2%
Russian 5.9%
Scotch Irish 2.4%
Scottish 3.1%
Swedish 1.4%
Welsh 1.2%

Universities/colleges, 1990-1991 enrollment
Montgomery College, Germantown 3,183
Montgomery College, Rockville 14,365
Uniformed Services University of Health Sciences, Bethesda 794

Newspapers, total circulation (in all districts)
Baltimore Sun 391,415
Frederick Post & News 41,654
Montgomery Journal 38,135
Washington Post 810,904
Washington Times 91,509

Commercial television stations, affiliations
ADI: Washington, DC (100%)
WDCA-TV, Washington (None)

Cable television systems, total subscribers
Cable TV Montgomery; Rockville 149,614

Military installations, 1991
Naval Medical Command, Bethesda 6,047

Businesses and other major employers
U.S. National Institutes of Health; Bethesda 15,000
U.S. National Oceanic & Atmospheric Administration; Rockville 15,000
Vitro Corp.; Silver Spring; computer systems 3,400
U.S. National Institute of Standards & Technology; Gaithersburg 3,200
Bechtel Power Corp./Gaithersburg Power Div.; Gaithersburg; heavy construction 2,500
U.S. Energy Dept.; Germantown; energy research 2,500
Oxford Realty Services Corp.; Bethesda; real estate agents 1,800
Fairchild Space & Defense Corp.; Germantown; guided missiles/parts 1,500
Suburban Hospital; Bethesda 1,450
Claims Administration Corp.; Rockville; insurance services 1,430
Holy Cross Hospital; Silver Spring 1,403
IBM Corp./Federal Systems Div.; Gaithersburg; research services 1,300
Montgomery General Hospital; Olney 1,247
County of Montgomery/Police Dept.; Rockville 1,154
National Geographic Society; Gaithersburg; periodicals 1,100
Shady Grove Adventist Hospital; Rockville 1,057
General Electric Co./Info Services; Rockville; computer services 1,000
County of Montgomery; Rockville 900
Hughes Network Systems Inc.; Germantown; communications equipment 850
NationsBank/Maryland; Bethesda; commercial banks 802
John J. Kirlin Inc.; Rockville; plumbing/heating/air-conditioning 800
Montgomery Community College; Rockville 800
Westat Inc.; Rockville; research services 763
Hebrew Home of Greater Washington; Rockville; residential care 750
County of Montgomery/Public Schools; Rockville 750
U.S. National Library of Medicine; Bethesda 700
Computer Data Systems Inc./Energy Systems Div.; Germantown; computer services 652
Watkins-Johnson Co.; Gaithersburg; communications equipment 650
Halliburton Nus Environmental Corp.; Gaithersburg; engineering services 650
Edgewood Mangement Corp.; Bethesda; real estate operators 600
Pritchard Industries; Bethesda; building services 600
Human Health Services; Rockville; research services 600
Tracor Inc./Systems Technolgy Operations; Rockville; commercial physical research 600
Computer Data Systems Inc.; Rockville; computer services 550
Swiss Properties Inc.; Bethesda; subdividers/developers 549
H. G. N. Inc./Harlequin Dinner Theater; Rockville; entertainers 533
Consumer Product Safety Commission; Bethesda 529
Asbury Methodist Home Inc./Asbury Methodist Village; Gaithersburg; nursing 510

Massachusetts

The 1980s were Massachusetts' version of the Roaring 20's. Intoxicated with the "Massachusetts Miracle," everyone from real estate developers to military contractors to bankers reaped the rewards of a period of astronomical growth. The successes were so great that the state's Democratic governor, Michael Dukakis, was catapulted onto the national stage in 1988 as the party's presidential nominee.

But like most financial booms, this one went bust—producing a terrible statewide hangover of record unemployment, national political humiliation and enormous anxiety over the future. The headache still lingered into the 1990s, prompting some residents and businesses to flee and others to retrench.

A study by Northeastern University found that the state lost 112,000 jobs in a 14-month period between 1974 and 1975 and lost four times that amount in a similar period beginning in early 1989. The construction and manufacturing industries were hit particularly hard. Some of the state's largest employers—Wang Laboratories, Digital Equipment Corp., General Motors—filed for bankruptcy protection, left the state or scaled back its work force. Cuts in defense spending rippled down to Massachusetts' researchers. And even the prosperous health-care industry began discussing staff and program reductions.

Blue-collar workers pinned much of their hope for the future on several public works projects that should last into the 21st century, including construction of a third tunnel under the Boston Harbor, a new sports arena in the capital city and a new downtown highway called the Central Artery.

But most state leaders believe the state's future lies with small- to medium-sized high-tech and biotechnology firms. More than 100 institutions of higher education—including Harvard and the Massachusetts Institute of Technology—provide much of the creative innovation for the start-up companies. The question in the early 1990s was whether the businesses would take their inventions to other states where the cost of living is significantly lower.

The lengthy economic recession took a toll politically as well.

Angered by Dukakis' embarassing finish in the presidential race and feeling the financial pinch, voters rebuffed the Democrats in 1990, choosing a Republican governor and state treasurer. Several incumbent state legislators were also ousted in what was widely interpreted as an anti-government movement.

By 1992, when the nation tackled congressional redistricting in earnest, Massachusetts was faced with another political crisis: Because the state did not grow as quickly as others in the 1980s, the Bay State lost a seat, reducing its delegation from 11 to 10.

The retirement of one Democratic incumbent helped ease the crunch, and GOP Gov. William Weld and the Democrats controlling the state Legislature formed an odd alliance guaranteeing each of the 10 remaining incumbents a district from which to run. Weld protected some Democratic incumbents because he valued their clout and seniority in Washington. He also won concessions from the Democrats to redraw a handful of districts better suited to GOP candidates.

Ironically, the districts redrawn to suit Weld's allies did not produce winners for the GOP. In the end, the redistricting had little impact on the 1992 races. Anti-incumbent fever and citizen disgust with the House bank scandal in Washington did more to oust three incumbents than the new lines. The two seats the GOP picked up—the 6th on Boston's North Shore and the 3rd in central and southeastern Massachusetts—will be up for grabs throughout the 1990s.

Redistricting also created a minority-influence district in the Boston-based 8th. But African Americans have a way to go before they will represent even half the district's voters and it is unclear when that group will exert true political influence.

Long considered a bastion of liberalism, Massachusetts still lives up to its reputation in many respects. Although voters have demonstrated an increasing willingness to elect Republicans, the winners from the GOP remain some of the most left-leaning in their party. Weld, for instance, is a staunch advocate of abortion rights and won his first campaign in 1990 with strong backing from women's groups and gay rights organizations. As of 1993, both of Congress' openly gay members were from Massachusetts—Gerry Studds and Barney Frank.

In several polls in the early 1990s, Massachusetts residents said they would be willing to pay higher taxes for a wide range of services—from education to medical care to highways—if the money were earmarked. The state gave Bill Clinton a 48 percent win in the three-way 1992 presidential campaign, even though Republican George Bush boasted he was born in Milton, Mass.

Ever since the *Mayflower* landed at Plymouth Rock in 1620, Massachusetts has produced a crop of historical figures includ-

MASSACHUSETTS

Districts Established July 9, 1992

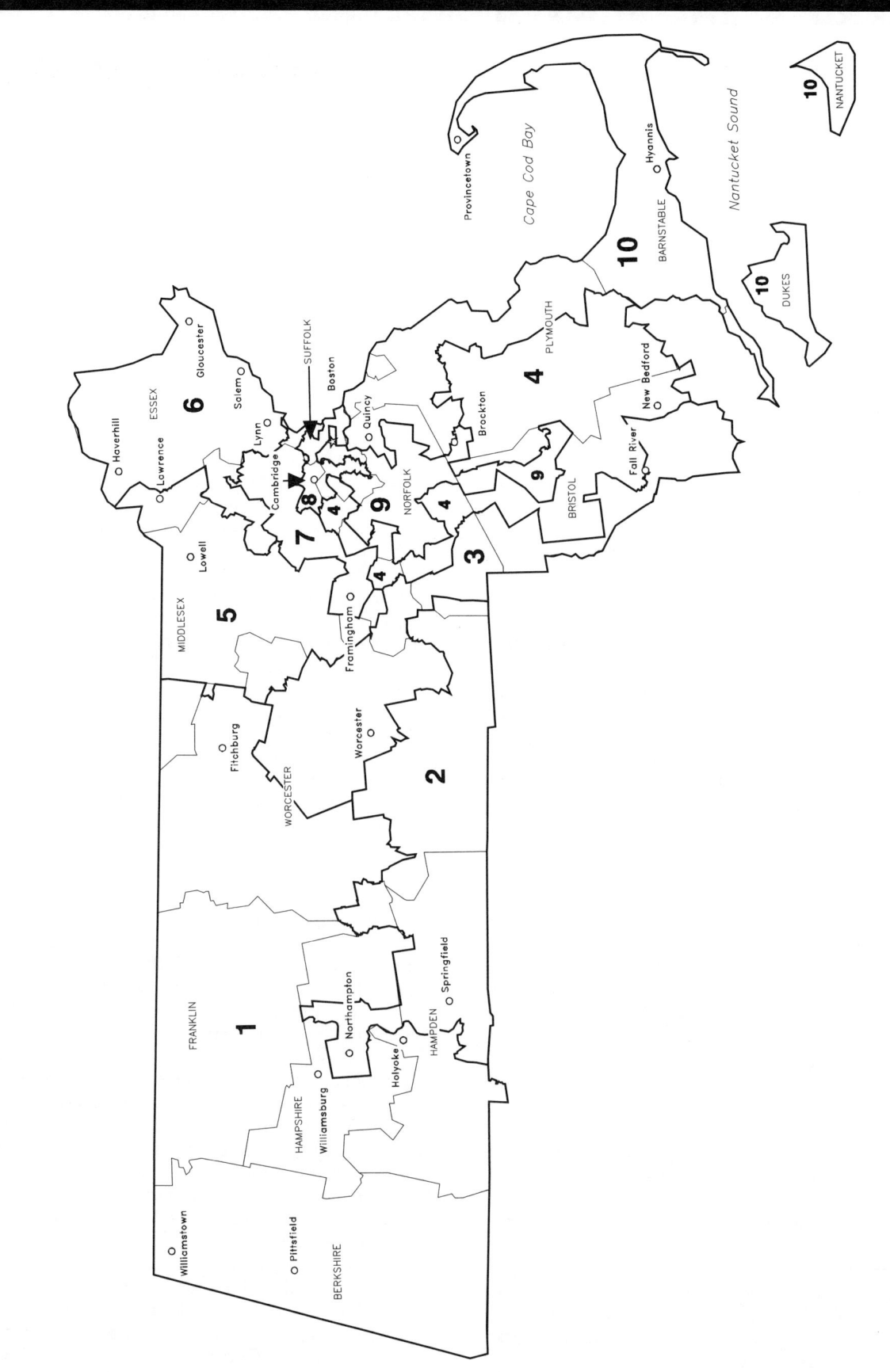

ing four presidents—John Adams, John Quincy Adams, Calvin Coolidge and John F. Kennedy. Edward J. Brooke was the first black U.S. senator elected since Reconstruction. Presidential aspirations are common in Massachusetts politicians. In 1980 Sen. Edward Kennedy and in 1992 Sen. Paul Tsongas ran for the top office. Some of the nation's most colorful politicians hail from the Bay State, including former House Speaker Thomas P. "Tip" O'Neill.

Massachusetts remains a predominantly white, young, well-educated, middle-class state with pockets of minorities in several large cities. The state has seen an influx of Asian refugees, particularly in such cities as Quincy, Lowell and Lawrence. But like much of America, the state's power centers have shifted from big cities to the suburbs. The communities along two highway loops—Route 128 and Interstate 495—have been the fastest growing. Planned communities and shopping malls dot the landscape just beyond these beltways.

With its Atlantic beaches, Berkshire Mountains, rich history, cultural activities and sports teams, Massachusetts is a popular tourist destination. In the summer, the shores of Cape Cod, scenic Walden Pond and Plimoth Plantation draw big crowds. In the winter, the Boston Celtics, art museums and ski slopes provide entertainment.

Table 1   Population

District	Population	Population under 18	Voting-age population	Median age
1	601,643	143,780	457,863	33.1
2	601,642	147,238	454,404	33.4
3	601,642	143,455	458,187	33.5
4	601,642	140,569	461,073	34.1
5	601,643	154,887	446,756	32.3
6	601,643	135,660	465,983	35.0
7	601,642	115,938	485,704	35.0
8	601,643	107,308	494,335	29.8
9	601,643	128,756	472,887	34.4
10	601,642	135,484	466,158	35.7
State	6,016,425	1,353,075	4,663,350	33.6

Table 2   Voting-Age Persons

District	White*	Black*	American Indian, Eskimo, or Aleut*	Asian or Pacific Islander*	Other*	Hispanic*	Male*	Female*
1	95.2%	1.5%	0.2%	1.2%	1.9%	3.6%	47.4%	52.6%
2	91.4	4.9	0.2	0.9	2.6	4.5	46.5	53.5
3	95.4	1.6	0.1	1.5	1.4	2.9	47.4	52.6
4	94.0	2.1	0.2	2.0	1.8	2.2	46.4	53.6
5	91.3	2.1	0.2	3.0	3.4	6.4	48.6	51.4
6	96.2	1.6	0.1	1.2	0.9	2.3	47.0	53.0
7	94.5	2.1	0.1	2.5	0.8	2.6	46.4	53.6
8	70.0	20.0	0.3	5.5	4.2	9.0	47.6	52.4
9	89.4	5.7	0.2	2.6	2.2	3.8	46.8	53.2
10	95.8	1.8	0.3	1.3	0.8	1.2	46.7	53.3
State	91.2	4.4	0.2	2.2	2.0	3.9	47.1	52.9

*As percent of voting-age population.

Table 3   Voting-Age Persons by Age Groups

District	18-24*	25-44*	45-54*	55-64*	65 and over*
1	16.8%	41.6%	12.3%	10.8%	18.4%
2	14.7	42.6	12.8	11.2	18.7
3	14.9	42.8	13.1	11.1	17.9
4	14.9	42.9	13.6	10.7	17.8
5	14.6	46.3	14.4	10.6	14.1
6	12.8	43.4	14.0	12.0	17.8
7	14.1	42.4	12.7	12.0	18.8
8	23.5	45.5	9.8	8.2	13.1
9	13.4	43.5	12.8	11.7	18.6
10	12.0	42.0	13.4	12.0	20.5
State	15.2	43.3	12.9	11.0	17.6

*As percent of voting-age population.

Table 4   Income and Occupation

District	Median family income	Families in poverty	White collar*	Blue collar*	Service*	Farm*
1	$38,762	7.7%	58.0%	26.3%	14.3%	1.4%
2	39,812	7.9	58.1	27.1	13.8	1.0
3	43,812	5.9	62.3	24.3	12.5	0.9
4	45,875	5.8	65.5	21.6	11.6	1.3
5	49,832	7.0	66.1	22.2	11.0	0.7
6	48,728	5.2	66.2	21.0	11.8	1.0
7	50,284	4.2	71.0	17.1	11.3	0.6
8	35,764	13.5	69.0	14.9	15.7	0.4
9	46,736	6.7	67.2	19.2	13.0	0.6
10	45,134	4.9	63.9	21.2	13.3	1.5
State	44,367	6.7	64.9	21.4	12.8	0.9

*As percent of employed persons age 16 and over.

Table 5   Education: School Years Completed

District	Less than grade 9*	Grades 9-12 no diploma*	High school diploma*	College bachelor's degree or higher*
1	8.5%	13.5%	33.0%	21.4%
2	9.6	15.7	32.7	18.8
3	10.3	13.0	28.7	24.2
4	11.3	11.2	26.0	30.9
5	8.3	11.8	28.2	28.8
6	5.9	10.8	29.7	27.4
7	5.6	10.4	31.3	30.6
8	10.2	13.0	23.4	36.0
9	7.5	11.0	31.3	27.8
10	3.6	9.7	32.7	26.4
State	8.0	12.0	29.7	27.2

*As percent of persons age 25 and over.

Table 6   Housing and Residential Patterns

District	Owner occupied	Renter occupied	Urban	Rural
1	62.8%	37.2%	64.0%	36.0%
2	63.9	36.1	79.3	20.7
3	61.7	38.3	81.8	18.2
4	63.8	36.2	73.1	26.9
5	64.4	35.6	83.9	16.1
6	65.5	34.5	89.9	10.1
7	57.4	42.6	99.1	0.9
8	29.1	70.9	100.0	0.0
9	57.4	42.6	98.5	1.5
10	68.7	31.3	73.0	27.0
State	59.3	40.7	84.3	15.7

1st District

West — Berkshire Hills; Fitchburg; Amherst

The enormous 1st, which is framed by Connecticut on the south, New York on the west and Vermont and New Hampshire on the north, seems more like three districts than one.

Residents of the bucolic Berkshire Hills identify most naturally with New Yorkers; they get their news from Albany and many of their visitors from Manhattan. In the central part of the 1st lies the Connecticut River Valley, a rural region known for its maple syrup and a scenic 63-mile stretch of state Route 2 (the Mohawk Trail), which runs from Greenfield to Williamstown. On the eastern side of the 1st are a handful of medium-sized industrial cities more closely linked to Worcester in the 3rd District than to the rest of the 1st.

A theme repeats itself across the district: Major textile industries have died, workers have left, and a handful of educational institutions and small businesses are struggling to revive the region. Shoe factories have closed, Gardner is no longer a furniture capital, and in Pittsfield, General Electric's work force has plummeted from 15,000 in the 1950s to 3,000 in the 1990s. (Martin Marietta purchased GE's aerospace division in 1992, creating even more uncertainty for the Pittsfield workers.) Paper mills still thrive in the district and plastic production is lively in Pittsfield and Leominster.

The residents of western Massachusetts see themselves as a hardy, self-reliant lot. For years this was the only state district sending a Republican to Congress, although ironically, a major contributor to the long tenure of GOP Rep. Silvio O. Conte (1959-1991) in the 1st was his success at using his Appropriations Committee seat to produce federal dollars and jobs. After Conte's death, the GOP lost the 1st in a 1991 special election, and it stayed Democratic in 1992.

The liberal enclaves of Amherst, Belchertown, Williamstown and Pelham help support Democratic candidates. Heavily Catholic communities such as Holyoke, Westfield and Pittsfield have many people who like to vote an anti-abortion line, but they will often support Democrats if both parties nominate abortion-rights supporters (as was the case in the 1992 House race). Bill Clinton with 48 percent of the vote carried the 1st in 1992.

The district's numerous colleges provide an injection of youth and growth potential to the otherwise aging region. The largest school is the University of Massachusetts at Amherst, with 26,000 students. Its world-class Polymer Research Center has spawned several small businesses in the area. At other area universities, work in the fields of astronomy, computer science and agribusiness has the potential to spur local economic development.

By the standards of overwhelmingly white western Massachusetts, a few towns in the 1st have minority populations of some significance. One-third of Holyoke is Hispanic, and there are small African American and Asian communities in Fitchburg and Leominster. But the district's predominant non-Yankee groups are Poles, French Canadians and Italians.

Election Returns

	1st District	Democrat	Republican
1992	President*	130,311 (48.1%)	72,246 (26.6%)
	House	135,049 (51.5%)	113,828 (43.4%)
1990	Senate	121,601 (52.8%)	108,549 (47.2%)
	Governor	103,852 (47.2%)	108,314 (49.2%)
1988	President	139,002 (55.5%)	111,249 (44.5%)
	Senate	167,165 (67.8%)	79,411 (32.2%)
1986	Governor	115,817 (72.4%)	44,077 (27.6%)

Vote for Perot was 68,541 (25.3%).

Demographics

Population 601,643

Percent change from 1980 15.1%

Land area 3,032 square miles

Population per square mile 198

Counties, 1990 population

Berkshire 139,352	Hampshire (pt.) 86,555
Franklin 70,092	Middlesex (pt.) 11,213
Hampden (pt.) 123,792	Worcester (pt.) 170,639

Cities, 1990 population (10,000 or more)

Amherst 35,228	Holyoke 43,704
Athol 11,451	Leominster 38,145
Belchertown 10,579	North Adams 16,797
Easthampton 15,537	Pittsfield 48,622
Fitchburg 41,194	Westfield 38,372
Gardner 20,125	West Springfield 27,537
Greenfield 18,666	

Race and Hispanic origin

White 94.2%
Black 1.7%
American Indian, Eskimo, or Aleut. 0.2%
Asian or Pacific Islander 1.3%
Other 2.6%
Hispanic origin 4.8%

Ancestry

American 3.1%	Italian 11.6%
Dutch 1.3%	Lithuanian 1.2%
English 17.1%	Polish 10.8%
Finnish 1.5%	Russian 1.3%
French 18.8%	Scotch Irish 1.7%
French Canadian 8.7%	Scottish 3.5%
German 11.3%	Swedish 2.2%
Irish 21.8%	

Universities/colleges, 1990-1991 enrollment

Amherst College, Amherst 1,602
Berkshire Community College, Pittsfield 2,621
Fitchburg State College, Fitchburg 6,224
Greenfield Community College, Greenfield 2,354
Hampshire College, Amherst 1,316
Holyoke Community College, Holyoke 5,321
Mt. Wachusett Community College, Gardner 3,682
North Adams State College, North Adams 2,421
Simons Rock of Bard College, Great Barrington 281
University of Massachusetts, Amherst 26,032
Westfield State College, Westfield 5,292
Williams College, Williamstown 2,056

Newspapers, total circulation (in all districts)

Boston Globe 503,578
Boston Herald 339,813

Daily Hampshire Gazette 20,326
Fitchburg Sentinel & Enterprise 20,058
Gardner News 8,090
Greenfield Recorder 14,697
Holyoke Transcript-Telegram 16,531
Middlesex News 35,996
New York Daily News 757,053
New York Post 551,443
Pittsfield Berkshire Eagle 29,936
Springfield Union-News/Republic 111,178

Commercial television stations, affiliations

ADI: Springfield (47%), Albany-Schenectady-Troy (30%) and
  Boston (22%)
  WCDC, Adams (ABC)
  WGGB-TV, Springfield-Holyoke (ABC)

Cable television systems, total subscribers

Adams Russell Cable Services Massachusetts; Fitchburg
  16,442
Adams Russell Cable Services Massachusetts; Gardner 5,658
Adelphia Cable; North Adams 13,545
Century Cable; Great Barrington 7,400
Continental Cablevision of Massachusetts; Northampton
  9,725
Continental Cablevision of Massachusetts; West Springfield
  34,000
Greater Easthampton Cable; Easthampton 6,000
Pioneer Valley Cablevision Inc.; Amherst 6,200
TM Cable TV/Pioneer Valley; Montague 10,800
Warner Cable; Athol 6,400
Warner Cable Communications Inc.; Pittsfield 20,000

Military installations, 1991

Barnes Municipal Airport Air Force Guard Station, Westfield 304

Businesses and other major employers

General Electric/Defense Systems; Pittsfield;
  ordnance/accessories 3,500
City of Holyoke; Holyoke 1,600
City of Pittsfield; Pittsfield 1,539
Commonwealth of Massachusetts/Belchertown State School;
  Belchertown 1,500
Berkshire Medical Center Inc.; Pittsfield 1,325
Digital Equipment Corp.; Westminster; semiconductors 1,200
Simplex Time Recorder Co.; Gardner; time recorders 1,200
L. S. Starrett Co./Webber Gage Div.; Athol; precision tools
  1,200
General Electric Co./Industrial & Power System; Fitchburg;
  engines/turbines 1,000
Digital Equipment Corp.; Westfield; computers 1,000
Ampad Corp.; Holyoke; paper products 1,000
City of Westfield; Westfield 1,000
University of Massachusetts; Amherst 1,000
Franklin Medical Center; Greenfield 977
City of Fitchburg; Fitchburg 900
Williams College; Williamstown 850
Holyoke Hospital Inc.; Holyoke 840
City of Leominster; Leominster 800
Burbank Hospital Inc.; Fitchburg 800
Town of Easthampton; Easthampton 800
Town of West Springfield; West Springfield 775
Leominster Public School District; Leominster 750

Crane & Co. Inc./Byron Weston Co.; Dalton; paper mills 725
General Electric Co.; Pittsfield; plastics products 700
Amherst College; Amherst 618
Western Massachusetts Electric Co.; West Springfield; electric
  services 600
Phoenix Mutual Life Insurance Co./Phoenix American Life
  Insurance Co.; Greenfield; life insurance 600
Town of Southwick; Southwick 600
International Paper Co./Old Colony Envelope; Westfield;
  paper products 575
Providence Hospital Inc.; Holyoke 561
North Adams Regional Hospital; North Adams 550
Henry Heywood Memorial Hospital; Gardner 512

2nd District

West Central — Northampton; Springfield

The city of Springfield dwarfs all other communities in the
2nd in size, population and economic importance. Located on
the banks of the Connecticut River, Springfield was named in
1636 by fur trader William Pynchon after his hometown in
England.

Since then, Springfield has laid claim to a string of "firsts,"
including the first federal armory (approved by Congress in
1794), the first gasoline-powered car, the first Pullman railcar and
the first basketball game.

Many of the city's successes of the 1990s are tied to that rich
history. Companies such as Spalding Sports Worldwide and
Smith & Wesson guns have kept the economy going as heavy
manufacturing has fallen off. And attractions such as the
Basketball Hall of Fame and the Springfield Armory National
Historic Site have helped lure tourists.

Ultimately, the region's future rests with the insurance and
financial services industries. Despite staff reductions in late 1992,
Massachusetts Mutual Life Insurance Co. remains a major
employer. Some small manufacturers remain, although others
(such as the R. E. Phelon machine parts company) are moving to
southern locales where the cost of doing business is lower.

Residents in the district also worry about defense spending
cutbacks, specifically those affecting United Technologies, the
largest private employer in neighboring Connecticut and an
important source of jobs for the 2nd as well.

A sizable Hispanic population moved into the 2nd in the
1950s to work in tobacco fields. Although the business has
dwindled, West Springfield and Hadley still have many laborers
picking leaves that form cigar wrappers. The minority population
in the 2nd now tops 10 percent.

Springfield and Chicopee, the second-largest city in the
district, together offer a reliable base of votes for any Democratic candidate. Democratic voter registration in the 2nd is four
times that of the GOP. Bill Clinton surpassed 60 percent here in
1992 presidential voting. Anti-abortion stances sit well with this
heavily Catholic area.

A drive through the rest of the 2nd is a glimpse of New
England at its quaintest. In towns such as Longmeadow, Hadley,
Palmer and Ware, village life is still focused on a town green.
Two of the "Seven Sisters" schools—Mount Holyoke College
and Smith College—add to the traditional New England look.

Although not as well known as the nearby Berkshire Hills or
Cape Cod along the coast, the 2nd is a popular recreational area.
Boating and cross-country skiing are popular, and the brilliant

fall foliage always draws a crowd. Virtually every town capitalizes on the scenery with a variety of special events, from Chicopee's World Kielbasa Festival to cider-making at Sturbridge Village.

Election Returns

	2nd District	Democrat	Republican
1992	President*	121,750 (46.1%)	76,244 (28.9%)
	House†	131,215 (53.1%)	76,795 (31.1%)
1990	Senate	107,462 (52.6%)	96,766 (47.4%)
	Governor	102,229 (50.0%)	95,867 (46.9%)
1988	President	132,244 (54.9%)	108,456 (45.1%)
	Senate	158,463 (67.0%)	78,152 (33.0%)
1986	Governor	108,494 (71.2%)	43,813 (28.8%)

*Vote for Perot was 65,924 (25.0%).   †Independent/other is greater than 5%.

Demographics

Population 601,642

Percent change from 1980 15.3%

Land area 886 square miles

Population per square mile 679

Counties, 1990 population
Hampden (pt.) 332,518   Norfolk (pt.) 14,877
Hampshire (pt.) 60,013   Worcester (pt.) 194,234

Cities, 1990 population (10,000 or more)
Agawam 27,323   Oxford 12,588
Bellingham 14,877   Palmer 12,054
Chicopee 56,632   Southbridge 17,816
East Longmeadow 13,367   South Hadley 16,685
Leicester 10,191   Spencer 11,645
Longmeadow 15,467   Springfield 156,983
Ludlow 18,820   Uxbridge 10,415
Milford 25,355   Webster 16,196
Millbury 12,228   Wilbraham 12,635
Northampton 29,289

Race and Hispanic origin
White 89.6%
Black 5.6%
American Indian, Eskimo, or Aleut. 0.2%
Asian or Pacific Islander 1.0%
Other 3.6%
Hispanic origin 6.0%

Ancestry
American 2.4%   Lithuanian 1.1%
English 13.0%   Polish 13.1%
French 19.2%   Portuguese 2.2%
French Canadian 8.9%   Russian 1.3%
German 8.1%   Scotch Irish 1.3%
Greek 1.1%   Scottish 2.8%
Irish 20.9%   Swedish 2.6%
Italian 12.0%

Universities/colleges, 1990-1991 enrollment
American International College, Springfield 1,831
Bay Path College, Longmeadow 577
Becker College Leicester, Leicester 474
College of Our Lady of Elms, Chicopee 1,116
Mount Holyoke College, South Hadley 1,931
Nichols College, Dudley 1,945
Smith College, Northampton 3,058
Springfield College, Springfield 3,577
Springfield Technical Community College, Springfield 5,865
Western New England College, Springfield 5,404

Newspapers, total circulation (in all districts)
Boston Globe 503,578
Boston Herald 339,813
Daily Hampshire Gazette 20,326
Holyoke Transcript-Telegram 16,531
Milford Daily News 13,133
New York Daily News 757,053
New York Post 551,443
Springfield Union-News/Republic 111,178
Worcester Telegram-Gazette 116,392

Commercial television stations, affiliations
ADI: Boston (53%) and Springfield (47%)
WWLP, Springfield (NBC)

Cable television systems, total subscribers
Continental Cablevision of Massachusetts; Milford 6,235
Continental Cablevision of Massachusetts; Springfield 46,000
Greater Media; Ludlow 14,800
Greater Media Cablevision; Leicester 19,700
Greater Media Cablevision; North Oxford 6,489
Greater Media Cablevision; Webster 16,300
Greater Chicopee Cablevision Inc.; Chicopee 18,300
TM Cable TV/Pioneer Valley; Palmer 11,100
United Video Cablevision; Uxbridge 6,020

Military installations, 1991
Westover Air Force Base, Chicopee 1,009

Businesses and other major employers
Massachusetts Mutual Life Insurance Co.; Springfield; life insurance 4,235
U.S. Postal Service; Springfield 3,500
Baystate Medical Center Inc.; Springfield 2,600
Mercy Hospital; Springfield 1,690
Commonwealth of Massachusetts/Monson Developmental Center; Palmer 1,600
Mount Holyoke College; South Hadley 1,500
Smith & Wesson Corp.; Springfield; small arms/accessories 1,470
Smith College; Northampton 1,300
Millipore Corp./Water Chromatograph; Milford; measuring devices 1,200
Spalding & Evenflo Co./Spalding Sports Worldwide; Chicopee; sporting goods 1,100
Citation Insurance Co.; Webster; insurance services 1,050
Monsanto Co./Monsanto Chemical Co.; Springfield; resins/plastics 1,000
Massachusetts Turnpike Authority; Millbury 1,000
U.S. Veterans Affairs Dept.; Northampton; hospital 1,000
Graphics Technology Intl.; South Hadley; plastics products 950
Roman Catholic Bishop of Springfield; Springfield; religious organizations 900
City of Springfield; Springfield 900
Republican Co. Inc./Springfield Newspapers; Springfield; newspapers 850
Cooley Dickinson Hospital; Northampton 850

Friendly Ice Cream Corp.; Wilbraham; bars/restaurants 800
Town of Oxford; Oxford 750
Town of Millbury; Millbury 750
Western New England College; Springfield 718
Flexcon Co. Inc.; Spencer; plastics products 700
Harrington Memorial Hospital; Southbridge 700
Town of Agawam; Agawam 675
American Saw & Mfg. Co./Lenox; East Longmeadow; saw blades 635
Westvaco Corp.; Springfield; envelopes 600
Dow Jones & Co. Inc.; Chicopee; newspapers 600
Milford-Whitinsville Regional Hospital; Milford 590
Tambrands Inc.; Palmer; personal hygiene products 560
Town of Webster; Webster 550
Town of East Longmeadow; East Longmeadow 550
Springfield Municipal Hospital; Springfield 550
Titeflex Corp.; Springfield; plastic hoses 530

3rd District

Central and Southeast — Worcester; Coastal Towns

Political wags dubbed the snakelike 3rd the "Ivy League" district because it stretches from the town of Princeton in central Massachusetts to Dartmouth on the southeastern coast. (The schools by those names are located elsewhere.)

The nickname is ironic because the 3rd is anchored by two of the state's grittier cities, Fall River and Worcester. In the 1992 House election, the GOP candidate lost in those two cities, but he won the seat by taking solid margins in the suburban areas of the 3rd, such as Westboro, Attleboro and Shrewsbury.

Fall River, at the southern end of the 3rd, is a fishing community that routinely has the highest unemployment of any city in Massachusetts. Split between the 3rd and 4th districts, Fall River long has been a bastion of blue-collar, white ethnic Democrats.

To the north of Fall River is another working-class city and the population hub of the 3rd: Worcester, with 170,000 people. It was once a thriving industrial center but did not benefit much from the "Massachusetts Miracle" of the 1980s that saw a boom in high-technology employment elsewhere in the state. Missing out on the "miracle," however, spared Worcester severe pain when the statewide economy nosedived in the late 1980s. As other communities were reeling, Worcester was plotting for the future.

Building on a foundation of respected hospitals in the region, Worcester is working to expand its role in the medical services field. New laboratories, research institutes and drug-manufacturing plants dot the city; the Biotechnology Research Park is growing. On the drawing board are plans for Medical City, a downtown complex that would include a hospital, medical labs, offices, restaurants and shops. Several banks, insurance companies and colleges are also located in Worcester.

Federal, state and city officials have committed money to a $27 million expansion of the Worcester Centrum, a popular arena that draws sporting events and big concerts. And by the mid- to late 1990s, the city may have commuter rail stations on a line to Boston.

Suburban communities to the north and south of Worcester already have as many votes as the urban areas of the district, and they are likely to have increasing influence on elections in the 3rd. A number of these suburbanites commute to jobs outside the district in Boston or Providence, R.I.

Democratic candidates traditionally have had an overall edge in the areas that make up the 3rd, but "unenrolled voters" are more numerous than Republicans or Democrats, and a number of them are conservative-leaning. Anti-abortion sentiment is widespread in the 3rd, and the National Rifle Association claims that the largest share of its Massachusetts members live here.

Election Returns

	3rd District	Democrat	Republican
1992	President*	122,900 (45.3%)	84,711 (31.2%)
	House †	115,587 (44.3%)	131,473 (50.4%)
1990	Senate	116,048 (53.7%)	99,871 (46.3%)
	Governor	112,803 (49.8%)	108,217 (47.7%)
1988	President	126,694 (50.7%)	123,361 (49.3%)
	Senate	161,096 (65.0%)	86,591 (35.0%)
1986	Governor	109,740 (68.1%)	51,308 (31.9%)

*Vote for Perot was 63,596 (23.4%).   †Independent/other is greater than 5%.

Demographics

Population 601,642

Percent change from 1980 15.4%

Land area 721 square miles

Population per square mile 834

Counties, 1990 population
Bristol (pt.) 204,791   Norfolk (pt.) 55,289
Middlesex (pt.) 22,117   Worcester (pt.) 319,445

Cities, 1990 population (10,000 or more)
Attleboro 38,383   Northborough 11,929
Clinton 13,222   Northbridge 13,371
Dartmouth 27,244   Seekonk 13,046
Fall River (pt.) 45,024   Shrewsbury 24,146
Franklin 22,095   Somerset 17,655
Grafton 13,035   Swansea 15,411
Holden 14,628   Westborough 14,133
Holliston 12,926   Westport 13,852
North Attleborough   Worcester 169,759
  25,038

Race and Hispanic origin
White 94.4%
Black 1.8%
American Indian, Eskimo, or Aleut. 0.2%
Asian or Pacific Islander 1.8%
Other 1.9%
Hispanic origin 3.7%

Ancestry
American 2.5%
Arabic 1.0%
English 15.9%
French 14.9%
French Canadian 6.4%
German 7.6%
Irish 24.9%
Italian 12.4%

Universities/colleges, 1990-1991 enrollment

Anna Maria College, Paxton 1,412
Assumption College, Worcester 2,974
Atlantic Union College, South Lancaster 795
Becker Junior College, Worcester 1,196
Clark University, Worcester 3,292
College of The Holy Cross, Worcester 2,693
Dean Junior College, Franklin 2,535
Quinsigamond Community College, Worcester 4,707
University of Massachusetts, North Dartmouth 7,343
University of Massachusetts Medical School, Worcester 557
Worcester Polytechnic Institute, Worcester 3,911
Worcester State College, Worcester 6,451

Newspapers, total circulation (in all districts)

Attleboro Sun Chronicle 23,647
Boston Globe 503,578
Boston Herald 339,813
Fall River Herald News 34,812
Fitchburg Sentinel & Enterprise 20,058
New Bedford Standard-Times 43,355
Pawtucket Times 22,336
Providence Journal-Bulletin 196,118
Woonsocket Call & Reporter 26,543
Worcester Telegram-Gazette 116,392

Commercial television stations, affiliations

ADI: Boston (68%) and Providence-New Bedford (32%)
WHLL, Worcester (None)

Cable television systems, total subscribers

CVI; Foxborough 48,403
Continental Cablevision of Massachusetts; Sterling 8,427
Greater Media Cablevision; Westborough 13,000
Greater Media Cablevision; Worcester 46,000
Greater Fall River Cable TV Inc.; Fall River 25,641
Inland Cable Communications; Attleborough 12,000
Shrewsbury Cablevision; Shrewsbury 7,781
UA Columbia Cablevision of Massachusetts; North Attleborough 6,623
United Video Cablevision; Westport 6,629
Whaling City Cable TV; New Bedford 36,560

Military installations, 1991

Worchester Air Force Guard Station, Worchester 65

Businesses and other major employers

CDK Holding Corp.; Mansfield; surgical instruments/supplies 10,000
City of Worcester; Worcester 5,500
Data General Corp.; Westborough; computer equipment 4,500
University of Massachusetts Hospital; Worcester 4,500
Foxboro Co.; Foxborough; industrial measuring devices 3,000
Norton Co.; Worcester; mineral products 2,700
Digital Equipment Corp.; Shrewsbury; computers 2,200
Commonwealth of Massachusetts/Wrentham State School; Wrentham 2,200
St. Vincent Hospital Inc.; Worcester 2,015
State Mutual Life Insurance Co. of America; Worcester; life insurance 2,000
Medical Center of Central Massachusetts; Worcester 1,980
New England Power Service Co.; Westborough; heavy construction 1,765

Paul Revere Life Insurance Co.; Worcester; medical service/health insurance 1,615
Wyman-Gordon Co.; North Grafton; nonferrous forgings 1,500
Lechmere Inc.; Seekonk; department stores 1,250
Codex Corp.; Mansfield; industrial testing equipment 1,200
City of Attleboro; Attleboro 1,150
Quaker Fabric Corp.; Fall River; man-made fabric mills 1,100
Town of Dartmouth; North Dartmouth 1,100
U.S. Postal Service; Worcester 1,100
Duro Industries Inc.; Fall River; textile finishing 1,000
L. G. Balfour Co. Inc.; Attleboro; precious metals 1,000
New England Telephone & Telegraph Co.; Worcester; telephone communications 1,000
Suburban Temporaries Inc.; Westborough; temp services 1,000
Neles-Jamesbury Inc.; Worcester; industrial valves 900
TJX Operating Companies Inc./TJ Maxx; Worcester; family clothing stores 900
Sturdy Memorial Hospital Inc.; Attleboro 900
Astra Pharmaceutical Products; Westborough; pharmaceuticals 861
College of The Holy Cross; Worcester 842
Commonwealth of Massachusetts/State Hospital; Westborough 810
Ames Dept. Stores Inc.; Mansfield; warehousing 800
University of Massachusetts; North Dartmouth 800
Town of Somerset; Fall River 775
Swank Inc.; Attleboro; leather goods 700
Allegro Microsystems Inc.; Worcester; electronic components 700
Town of Foxborough; Foxborough 700
Worcester City Hospital; Worcester 700
Town of North Attleborough; North Attleborough 674
St. Anne's Health Care Systems; Fall River 659
GTE Corp./Strategic Systems Div.; Westborough; engineering services 650
Town of Shrewsbury; Shrewsbury 650
Raytheon Co./Special Microwave Devices; Northborough; electronic components 600
Chronicle Publishing Co. Inc./Worcester Telegram & Gazette; Worcester; newspapers 600
Cincinnati Milacron-Heald; Worcester; metalworking machinery 600
Nypro Inc.; Clinton; plastics products 600
Digital Equipment Corp.; Northborough; computer services 600
Garelick Farms Inc.; Franklin; dairy products 590
Hanover Insurance Co. Inc.; Worcester; fire/marine/casualty insurance 565
Town of Mansfield; Mansfield 560
Clark University; Worcester 535

4th District

Boston Suburbs — Newton; New Bedford; Part of Fall River

The contorted shape of the 4th is proof positive that the state where the term gerrymander was coined remains true to its tradition of politically motivated mapmaking.

The 4th District begins just over the Boston line in Brookline, juts out west to Sherborn, descends to Fall River and New Bedford on the southern coast and then reaches back north to Pembroke.

Democrats Bill Clinton in the presidential race and Barney Frank in the House race both won the 4th easily in 1992, in part a reflection of the hard economic times plaguing many people here. Fall River, a fishing port where the median income is less than $15,000, struggles with a declining business base that has resulted in double-digit unemployment. Anderson Little shut down its Fall River clothing plant in 1992; soon thereafter, shoemaker Stride Rite moved out of New Bedford to Louisville, Ky.

New Bedford boasts the largest dollar-volume catch in the nation, thanks primarily to its lucrative scallop industry. But with the American waters being fished out of other seafood, local fishermen are traveling over the line to fish in Canadian waters, which is illegal. The city lost at least 1,300 jobs in the early 1990s, and no new companies have expressed a desire to relocate to the area.

The early textile mills drew large groups of Portuguese and Cape Verdeans to the coastal communities. Today, Portuguese own most of New Bedford's fleet.

To the northeast, in an area known as the South Shore, cranberry bogs in Carver and Lakeville compete with bogs in Wisconsin.

Even some of the wealthiest communities in the 4th suffered tough economic times in the late 1980s and early 1990s, as computer companies such as Wang Laboratories laid off thousands and the credit crunch crippled smaller entrepreneurial firms.

A sign of the times in 1992: lines down the block to get into the food pantry at the Unitarian Church in West Newton. Waiting their turn in this well-to-do suburb were teachers, computer programmers and other professionals trying to feed their families and hang on to their expensive homes.

Brookline, another comfortable suburb just over the line from Boston, became famous in 1988 when native Michael S. Dukakis ran for president. As governor, he commuted to work on the trolley line that connects Brookline to downtown. There are now more students and other transient types mixed in with Brookline's homeowners, but the town still boasts one of the best public school systems in the state.

Despite the dramatic socioeconomic differences between the district's southern cities and its Boston suburbs, the communities share a strong loyalty to the Democratic Party. Republicans are numerous only in a handful of upper-crust towns such as Dover, Sherborn and Wellesley.

Election Returns

	4th District	Democrat	Republican
1992	President*	144,352 (51.1%)	75,080 (26.6%)
	House †	182,633 (67.7%)	70,665 (26.2%)
1990	Senate	142,231 (59.4%)	97,226 (40.6%)
	Governor	112,654 (46.8%)	121,615 (50.6%)
1988	President	148,186 (56.4%)	114,408 (43.6%)
	Senate	178,175 (68.3%)	82,695 (31.7%)
1986	Governor	125,804 (72.1%)	48,705 (27.9%)

*Vote for Perot was 63,040 (22.3%).   †Independent/other is greater than 5%.

Demographics

Population 601,642

Percent change from 1980 15.3%

Land area 762 square miles

Population per square mile 789

Counties, 1990 population
Bristol (pt.) 242,031   Norfolk (pt.) 125,899
Middlesex (pt.) 86,574   Plymouth (pt.) 147,138

Cities, 1990 population (10,000 or more)
Bridgewater 21,249   New Bedford 99,922
Brookline 54,718   Newton 82,585
Carver 10,590   Norton 14,265
East Bridgewater 11,104   Pembroke 14,544
Easton 10,136   Sharon 15,517
Fairhaven 16,132   Wareham 19,232
Fall River (pt.) 47,679   Wellesley 26,615
Middleborough 17,867

Race and Hispanic origin
White 93.5%
Black 2.2%
American Indian, Eskimo, or Aleut. 0.2%
Asian or Pacific Islander 2.1%
Other 2.0%
Hispanic origin 2.5%

Ancestry
American 2.8%   Lithuanian 1.1%
Canadian 1.0%   Polish 5.0%
English 16.9%   Portuguese 16.4%
French 9.5%   Russian 4.7%
French Canadian 4.7%   Scotch Irish 1.7%
German 8.0%   Scottish 3.1%
Irish 21.9%   Subsaharan African 2.0%
Italian 9.7%   Swedish 2.2%

Universities/colleges, 1990-1991 enrollment
Aquinas College at Milton, Newton 290
Babson College, Wellesley 3,091
Bridgewater State College, Bridgewater 8,827
Bristol Community College, Fall River 5,001
Lasell College, Newton 447
Massachusetts Bay Community College, Wellesley Hills 4,664
Mount Ida Junior College, Newton 1,537
Newbury College, Brookline 4,282
Pine Manor College, Chestnut Hill 549
Wellesley College, Wellesley 2,279
Wheaton College, Norton 1,263

Newspapers, total circulation (in all districts)
Boston Globe 503,578
Boston Herald 339,813
Brockton Enterprise 54,632
Fall River Herald News 34,812
New Bedford Standard-Times 43,355
Taunton Daily Gazette 14,047

Commercial television stations, affiliations
ADI: Boston (65%) and Providence-New Bedford (35%)
WHDH-TV, Boston (CBS)

WJAR, Providence (NBC)
WNAC-TV, Providence (Fox)
WPRI-TV, Providence (ABC)

Cable television systems, total subscribers
Cablevision Fairhaven-Acushnet; Fairhaven 8,081
Cablevision of Boston; Brookline 13,600
Continental Cablevision; Brockton 32,200
Continental Cablevision of Massachusetts; Marion 11,120
Continental Cablevision of Massachusetts; Middleborough 11,046
Continental Cablevision of Massachusetts; Newton 32,420
Greater Fall River Cable TV Inc.; Fall River 25,641
Harron Cablevision of Massachusetts; Pembroke 6,083
Whaling City Cable TV; New Bedford 36,560

Military installations, 1991
Wellesley Air Force Guard Station, Wellesley 44

Businesses and other major employers
Harcourt General/General Cinema Corp. Theaters Inc.; Brookline; movie theaters/department stores management 8,000
City of New Bedford; New Bedford 3,415
Wellesley Newton Hospital; Newton Lower Falls 2,200
Acushnet Co./Titleist & Foot-Joy Worldwide; New Bedford; sporting goods 2,100
Roman Catholic Diocese of Fall River; Fall River; religious organizations 2,000
St. Luke's Hospital; New Bedford 1,874
Acushnet Co./Titleist & Footjoy Worldwide; Acushnet; sporting goods 1,500
City of New Bedford/School District; New Bedford 1,200
Charlton Memorial Hospital; Fall River 1,160
Commonwealth Electric Co.; Wareham; business services 1,110
Aetna Life & Casualty Co.; Fall River; life insurance 1,000
Homecare PRN Inc.; Newton Center; home health services 1,000
Wellesley College; Wellesley 1,000
Sysco Corp./Hallsmith-Sysco Food Services; Norton; grocery products 900
Foxboro Co.; East Bridgewater; industrial measuring devices 800
Talbot's Inc.; Middleborough; women's clothing stores 800
Southeastern Massachusetts Correctional Center; Bridgewater 800
Massasoit Greyhound Assn./Raynham Dog Track; Raynham; commercial sports 800
Harvard Community Health Plan; Brookline; medical doctors 800
Town of Wellesley; Wellesley 800
Foxboro Co.; Foxboro; industrial measuring devices 750
Palm Beach Co.; New Bedford; men's suits/coats 740
Town of Westport; Westport 736
Bridgewater State College; Bridgewater 675
Reed Publishing USA Inc./Cahners Publishing Co.; Newton; periodicals 650
Town of Easton; North Easton 630
Shaws Supermarkets Inc./Super Shaws; East Bridgewater; grocery stores 600
Globe Mfg. Co./R. E. Smith & Co.; Fall River; rubber products 550
Northeast Security Inc.; Brookline; security services 525

Shipley Co. Inc.; Newton Lower Falls; industrial organic chemicals 510
Richman Brothers Co./Anderson Little Div.; Fall River; outerwear 500

5th District

North Central — Lawrence; Lowell

Although located on the northeastern edges of the 5th, the gritty cities of Lawrence and Lowell dominate this otherwise suburban district. An intense rivalry between the two mill cities dates back to the 1800s: Lowell, the model "company town," was watched over by paternalistic Yankee Protestants, while immigrant workers in Lawrence labored in unsafe factories and lived in substandard quarters. Ever since, it seems Lawrence has trailed the city to the south.

With the help of some federal dollars and arm-twisting in Congress, downtown Lowell was designated a national historic park in 1978. Earning that status was a boost to tourism, and it helped draw business.

But Lowell and its 103,400 people have not been able to escape the recessionary times of the 1990s. Wang Laboratories, the lifeblood of the city's resurgence and a onetime employer of 10,000, filed for bankruptcy protection and announced massive layoffs.

There are similar troubles elsewhere in the district. Digital Equipment moved a plant from Maynard to New Hampshire. The Fort Devens Army Base in Ayer is to close by 1995, taking with it thousands of military and civilian jobs. By one estimate, the 5th lost 30,000 jobs from 1988 through 1991.

Lawrence, a city of 70,000, has problems on a scale normally reserved for only the largest of metropolitan areas: arson, drug trafficking, car thefts, teen pregnancy and double-digit unemployment. Police set up barricades in one neighborhood and checked the license of every person entering to try to curtail the drug trade. Minorities are about 45 percent of the city's population: The largest single group, Hispanics, have begun to flex political muscle, electing the first Hispanic to the school board.

Despite the tough times, some of the district's smaller nontraditional businesses are finding profitable niches. Marlborough, situated on Interstate 495, is home to snack maker Smartfoods and Stratus Computer.

Businesses in the northern tier of the 5th are competing more successfully with no-sales-tax New Hampshire, thanks to a relaxation of Massachusetts' blue laws that allows merchants within 10 miles of the border to open on Sundays. Sprinkled through the Merrimack Valley are some of the country's most well-known preparatory schools, including Phillips Academy in Andover and the Groton School and Lawrence Academy, both in Groton. The 5th is also home to Walden Pond in Concord, where 19th-century authors Henry David Thoreau and Ralph Waldo Emerson derived inspiration.

Lawrence and Lowell continue to give Democrats a strong anchor in the 5th. In 1992, they were the key to the district going for Bill Clinton and the Democratic House nominee. But independents, or "unenrolled" voters, outnumber those registered in either major party, which makes the district competitive. Republican William F. Weld won here in his successful 1990 gubernatorial bid against Democrat John Silber.

Election Returns

	5th District	Democrat	Republican
1992	President*	112,959 (42.1%)	85,260 (31.7%)
	House†	133,844 (52.2%)	96,206 (37.5%)
1990	Senate	119,893 (52.4%)	108,831 (47.6%)
	Governor	97,801 (42.2%)	127,937 (55.2%)
1988	President	117,082 (47.1%)	131,270 (52.9%)
	Senate	152,725 (61.4%)	95,872 (38.6%)
1986	Governor	97,474 (63.4%)	56,173 (36.6%)

*Vote for Perot was 70,391 (26.2%). †Independent/other is greater than 5%.

Demographics

Population 601,643

Percent change from 1980 16.1%

Land area 586 square miles

Population per square mile 1,026

Counties, 1990 population
Essex (pt.) 139,348 Worcester (pt.) 25,387
Middlesex (pt.) 436,908

Cities, 1990 population (10,000 or more)
Acton 17,872	Lowell 103,439
Andover 29,151	Marlborough 31,813
Ashland 12,066	Maynard 10,325
Billerica 37,609	Methuen 39,990
Chelmsford 32,383	Pepperell 10,098
Concord 17,076	Sudbury 14,358
Dracut 25,594	Tewksbury 27,266
Harvard 12,329	Wayland 11,874
Hudson 17,233	Westford 16,392
Lawrence 70,207	

Race and Hispanic origin
White 89.4%
Black 2.3%
American Indian, Eskimo, or Aleut. 0.2%
Asian or Pacific Islander 3.6%
Other 4.5%
Hispanic origin 8.1%

Ancestry
American 2.9%	Italian 13.0%
Canadian 1.3%	Lithuanian 1.0%
English 16.4%	Polish 4.6%
French 11.5%	Portuguese 3.2%
French Canadian 7.1%	Russian 1.6%
German 8.9%	Scotch Irish 2.0%
Greek 1.9%	Scottish 3.5%
Irish 26.0%	Swedish 2.0%

Universities/colleges, 1990-1991 enrollment
University of Massachusetts, Lowell 14,265

Newspapers, total circulation (in all districts)
Boston Globe 503,578
Boston Herald 339,813
Hudson Daily Sun 2,649
Lawrence Eagle-Tribune 55,007
Lowell Sun 55,194
Marlborough Enterprise 3,971
Middlesex News 35,996

Commercial television stations, affiliations
ADI: Boston (100%)
WHSH, Marlborough (None)

Cable television systems, total subscribers
Adams Russell Cable Services Massachusetts; Maynard 13,500
Continental Cablevision of Massachusetts; Marlborough 9,276
Heritage Cablevision; Andover 19,628
Lowell Cable TV Inc.; Lowell 41,199
Nashoba Communications; Westford 25,893

Military installations, 1991
Fort Devens (Army), Ayer 6,978

Businesses and other major employers
Raytheon Co.; Andover; search/navigation equipment 6,000
Digital Equipment Corp.; Maynard; computers 5,000
Wang Laboratories Inc./Professional Services Group; Lowell; computer/office equipment 5,000
U.S. Internal Revenue Service; Andover 4,084
Raytheon Co.; Tewksbury; guided missiles/parts 3,500
H. N. Bull Information Systems; Billerica; computers 3,200
Raytheon Co.; Lowell; guided missiles/parts 2,700
Raytheon Co./Raytheon Equipment Div.; Sudbury; research services 2,500
Raytheon Co.; Wayland; communications equipment 2,025
Digital Equipment Corp.; Hudson; computers 2,000
City of Lowell; Lowell 1,993
Hewlett-Packard Co.; Chelmsford; computer/office equipment 1,500
Malden Mills Industries Inc.; Lawrence; knitting mills 1,500
Town of Billerica; Billerica 1,478
Emerson Hospital Inc.; Concord 1,224
Du Pont E. I. De Nemours & Co.; North Billerica; industry machinery 1,200
Data General Corp.; Southborough; computer services 1,200
Lawrence General Hospital; Lawrence 1,200
Holy Family Hospital Inc.; Methuen 1,160
City of Lawrence/School District; Lawrence 1,150
City of Marlborough; Marlborough 1,100
St. John's Hospital Inc.; Lowell 1,100
University of Massachusetts; Lowell 1,100
Tewksbury Hospital; Tewksbury 1,030
C. R. Bard Inc./Vascular Systems; Billerica; medical instruments 1,000
Lowell General Hospital; Lowell 1,000
Digital Equipment Corp.; Stow; computer services 950
Town of Chelmsford; Chelmsford 940
Genrad Inc.; Concord; electric testing devices 900
Digital Equipment Corp.; Acton; computer services 850
New England Business Service; Groton; business forms 800
St. Joseph's Hospital Inc.; Lowell 745
Town of Concord; Concord 719
Digital Equipment Corp.; Marlborough; computers 700
Joan Fabrics Corp.; Lowell; cotton mills 700
Marlborough Hospital; Marlborough 690
Stratus Computer Inc.; Marlborough; computers 650
NEC Technologies Inc.; Acton; computer equipment 650

Gillette Co./Andover Mfg. Center; Andover; personal care products 650

H. N. Bull Information Systems; Lawrence; computers 620

General Signal Technology Corp./Systems Group; Andover; industry machinery 600

Purity Supreme Inc.; North Billerica; grocery stores 600

Dynamics Research Corp./Systems Div.; Andover; data processing 600

Grieco Bros. Inc.; Lawrence; men's suits/coats 598

Courier-Citizen Co.; Lowell; real estate operators 550

Town of Wayland; Wayland 550

Yankee Atomic Electric Co.; Bolton; electric services 537

Nuclear Metals Inc.; Acton; nonferrous foundries; metal powder 529

6th District

North Shore — Lynn; Peabody

The North Shore area is more open to Republican entreaties than most communities in Massachusetts, a state with a strong affinity for Democrats. In 1992 Republican Peter Torkildsen captured the House seat with the aid of Democrat Rep. Nicholas Mavroules' pending criminal indictment.

Registered Democrats outnumber Republicans in much of Massachusetts, but the 6th is dominated by independent voters. GOP candidates can succeed by targeting them, holding the votes of wealthy Republican suburbanites who support abortion rights, and picking off some conservative lunch-bucket Democrats who are angry about high taxes and expensive social programs.

The more than 35 cities and towns that constitute the 6th are a melange of scruffy fishing ports, aristocratic suburbs, unspoiled coastland and well-worn factory towns.

Lynn, with 81,000 people, is by far the largest community in the 6th. Lynn's major employer is the General Electric Co., which makes aircraft engines for the F/A-18 Hornet, helicopters and some commercial planes. Employment at the GE plant has dropped from 13,000 workers in 1981 to 6,500 as of early 1993. Torkildsen will be under pressure to duplicate the success Mavroules had at funneling federal contracts into the district; he was a senior member of the Armed Services Committee. In 1992, Mavroules helped the GE plant secure a $754 million contract for work on engines for the next generation of F-18 fighter planes.

Despite the relative proximity of Lynn to Boston, the city's officials often feel isolated from the state capital. In early 1993 state leaders began debating the prospects of extending one of Boston's subway lines to Lynn. If approved, the project would create jobs and provide a smoother trip from Lynn to Boston's airport, financial district and tourist attractions.

The coast north of Lynn includes some of the most beautiful landscapes in the state. Each town has its own personality and attitudes. Tourists and fishermen share the coastal communities of Gloucester, Rockport and Marblehead. Among the three, Gloucester, home to General Mills' Gorton's seafood company and other processing plants, has the largest population and fishing catch and the most visitors.

Most of the beaches on the North Shore are pristine, protected and open to the public. Manchester-by-the-Sea is something of an exception; a tony town of 5,000 that voted to change its name from just plain Manchester, it discourages outsiders from using its beaches by enforcing a residents-only parking rule. The area has a number of antique shops that draw visitors.

In 1992, Salem marked the tricentennial of the city's 1692 witch trials with a series of re-enactments, lectures and museum exhibits.

Redistricting in 1992 added Bedford, home of the Hanscom Air Force Base, to the 6th.

Election Returns

	6th District	Democrat	Republican
1992	President*	134,424 (43.8%)	96,857 (31.5%)
	House	130,248 (45.0%)	159,165 (55.0%)
1990	Senate	143,929 (55.3%)	116,240 (44.7%)
	Governor	117,793 (44.5%)	140,689 (53.2%)
1988	President	145,106 (50.9%)	140,249 (49.1%)
	Senate	182,321 (63.8%)	103,419 (36.2%)
1986	Governor	121,709 (66.5%)	61,307 (33.5%)

Vote for Perot was 75,893 (24.7%).

Demographics

Population 601,643

Percent change from 1980 16.0%

Land area 498 square miles

Population per square mile 1,209

Counties, 1990 population
Essex (pt.) 530,732   Middlesex (pt.) 70,911

Cities, 1990 population (10,000 or more)
Amesbury 14,997	Marblehead 19,971
Bedford 12,996	Newburyport 16,317
Beverly 38,195	North Andover 22,792
Burlington 23,302	North Reading 12,002
Danvers 24,174	Peabody 47,039
Gloucester 28,716	Salem 38,091
Haverhill 51,418	Saugus 25,549
Ipswich 11,873	Swampscott 13,650
Lynn 81,245	Wilmington (pt.) 17,651
Lynnfield 11,274	

Race and Hispanic origin
White 95.3%
Black 1.9%
American Indian, Eskimo, or Aleut. 0.1%
Asian or Pacific Islander 1.5%
Other 1.2%
Hispanic origin 2.9%

Ancestry
American 2.8%	Italian 16.7%
Canadian 1.4%	Polish 5.4%
English 19.9%	Portuguese 2.6%
French 10.6%	Russian 2.3%
French Canadian 5.3%	Scotch Irish 2.2%
German 8.0%	Scottish 4.1%
Greek 2.8%	Swedish 2.5%
Irish 28.2%	

Universities/colleges, 1990-1991 enrollment

Bradford College, Bradford 439
Endicott College, Beverly 868
Gordon College, Wenham 1,146
Gordon-Conwell Theological Seminary, South Hamilton 855
Merrimack College, North Andover 3,510
Middlesex Community College, Bedford 6,469
Montserrat College of Art, Beverly 227
Northern Essex Community College, Haverhill 6,651
North Shore Community College, Danvers 5,782
Salem State College, Salem 9,815

Newspapers, total circulation (in all districts)

Boston Globe 503,578
Boston Herald 339,813
Beverly Times 9,207
Gloucester Daily Times 11,632
Haverhill Gazette 13,945
Lynn Daily Evening Item 25,893
Middlesex News 35,996
Newburyport Daily News 12,692
Peabody Times 3,122
Salem Evening News 29,847

Commercial television stations, affiliations

ADI: Boston (100%)
WMFP, Lawrence (None)

Cable television systems, total subscribers

Adams Russell Cable Services Massachusetts; Haverhill 16,000
Adams Russell Cable Services Massachusetts; Peabody 13,903
Continental Cablevision of Massachusetts; Beverly 22,171
Continental Cablevision of Massachusetts; Newburyport 12,200
Continental Cablevision of Massachusetts; North Andover 31,930
Continental Cablevision of Massachusetts; Saugus 8,617
Nashoba Communications; Danvers 6,762
New England Cablevision; Amesbury 8,218
New England Cablevision; Gloucester 12,700
Warner Cable Communications Inc.; Lynn 21,292
Warner Cable Communications Inc.; Salem 11,016

Military installations, 1991

Hanscom Air Force Base, Bedford 5,782

Businesses and other major employers

General Electric Co.; Lynn; aircraft engines 6,500
American Telephone & Telgraph Co.; North Andover; communications equipment 6,500
Mitre Corp./Bedford Park Group; Bedford; research services 3,800
ARA Services Inc.; Wilmington; business services 2,500
Lahey Clinic Hospital Inc.; Burlington 2,291
Textron Inc./Textron Defense Systems; Wilmington; aircraft parts 2,200
Prime Computer Inc.; Bedford; computer services 2,000
City of Haverhill; Haverhill 1,841
Salem Hospital Inc.; Salem 1,500
Nynex Info Resources Co.; Middleton; publishing 1,400
Beverly Hospital Corp.; Beverly 1,400
Town of Danvers; Danvers 1,400
U.S. Veterans Affairs Dept.; Bedford; hospital 1,400

Analog Devices Inc.; Wilmington; semiconductors 1,300
Raytheon Service Co.; Burlington; defense systems 1,300
City of Beverly & Beverly Airport; Beverly 1,200
Commonwealth of Massachusetts/Charles V. Hogan Regional Center; Danvers 1,200
Analogic Corp./Medical Imaging Products Div.; Peabody; medical instruments/supplies 1,186
General Electric Co./Defense Systems; Burlington; search/navigation equipment 1,100
BASF Corp./Information System; Bedford; plastics products 1,100
Millipore Corp.; Bedford; measuring devices 1,038
Ametek Aerospace Products; Wilmington; aircraft parts 1,000
Coopers & Lybrand; Burlington; accounting/auditing 1,000
AGFA Corp./Compugraphic Div.; Wilmington; business services 1,000
Town of Burlington; Burlington 1,000
Northern Essex Community College, Haverhill 1,000
General Mills Inc./Gorton Div.; Gloucester; seafood products 900
City of Peabody; Peabody 845
Modicon Inc.; North Andover; measuring/controlling devices 800
Sweetheart Cup Co. Inc.; Wilmington; paperboard products 774
GTE Corp./Sylvania Lighting Service; Danvers; lamps/fixtures 700
M/A-Com Inc./Microwave Circuits; Burlington; communications equipment 700
Town of Saugus; Lynn 695
Altron Inc.; Wilmington; electronic components 688
Anna Jaques Hospital Inc.; Newburyport 659
Amesbury Hospital; Amesbury 625
Varian Assoc. Inc./Varian Ion Implant Systems; Gloucester; measuring devices 620
West Lynn Creamery Inc.; Lynn; dairy products 600
Gould Inc.; Newburyport; electric distribution equipment 600
Hilltop Steak House Inc.; Lynn; restaurants 600
Jordan Marsh Stores Corp.; Burlington; department stores 600
Salem State College; Salem 600
Aldworth Co. Inc.; Lynnfield; personnel supply services 600
J. C. J. Transportation Inc.; Lynnfield; trucking personnel services 600
Digital Equipment Corp.; Bedford; computer services 600
Town of North Andover; North Andover 590
Gilbert Addison Hospital; Gloucester 565
Digital Equipment Corp.; Burlington; computers 508

7th District

Northwest Suburbs — Woburn; Framingham; Revere

Although the 7th lies outside Boston, the city is the occupational and cultural focal point for most residents of this district. It is a collection of medium-sized cities and towns that almost completely rings Boston, giving the 7th a strong commuter orientation.

The well-educated, liberal-minded suburbanites are reliably Democratic. In his competitive 1990 re-election bid, Democratic

Sen. John Kerry took the 7th with 62 percent of the vote. Bill Clinton ran 21 points ahead of George Bush here in 1992 (although Ross Perot got a solid 21 percent), and Democrat Rep. Edward Markey carried every community except Weston. Malden, Framingham and Woburn provide a solid start for building large Democratic margins.

Redistricting in 1992 added Framingham and Natick to the western end of the district, boosting the presence of high technology in the 7th. Route 128, often compared with California's Silicon Valley, has a variety of large and small computer, telecommunications and engineering companies. The 7th's largest employer is Lexington-based Raytheon, maker of the Patriot missile system. The company has weathered defense cuts in part by diversifying into commercial products such as refrigerators and stoves.

Waltham, a working-class city once known for its watch factories, has experienced a technological surge in recent years. Smaller new companies—such as Kendall Square Research, a supercomputer manufacturer, and IDG, a computer magazine publishing house—are off Route 128 in Waltham. The Charles River Museum of Industry pays tribute to the city's grand industrial past.

Nearby universities, such as Harvard and the Massachusetts Institute of Technology, have helped fuel the local electronics industry. Boston Technologies in Wakefield began in 1986 with just five people. By 1993 the "voice mail" firm employed 200 and had signed a contract to provide voice mail services to a Japanese phone company.

The cities of Medford and Malden are often seen as one metropolitan area, with some shared city services and a rivalry in football. Although many of the residents commute to blue-collar jobs in Boston, the New England processing center for Fleet Bank is a major employer in Malden. Houses in Medford, Malden, Everett and Melrose have been passed on through several generations of Irish and Italian families.

Irish immigrants originally settled in Revere, too, but Southeast Asian immigrants began moving into that coastal city in the 1980s. Revere offers the growing Asian community affordable housing and easy access to service-sector jobs in downtown Boston.

Weston, Lincoln and Lexington are the most affluent communities in the 7th, home to professional athletes and media celebrities such as *Boston Globe* columnist Mike Barnacle. Lexington, site of the first Revolutionary War conflict, is popular with out-of-state visitors and Massachusetts students. Re-enactments of the Battle of Lexington are held every April.

Election Returns

	7th District	Democrat	Republican
1992	President*	150,102 (50.1%)	87,432 (29.2%)
	House †	174,837 (62.1%)	78,262 (27.8%)
1990	Senate	160,374 (61.0%)	102,340 (39.0%)
	Governor	124,300 (46.6%)	135,770 (50.8%)
1988	President	161,335 (55.4%)	129,719 (44.6%)
	Senate	188,841 (65.2%)	100,689 (34.8%)
1986	Governor	131,913 (67.6%)	63,275 (32.4%)

Vote for Perot was 61,965 (20.7%).   †Independent/other is greater than 5%.

Demographics

Population 601,642

Percent change from 1980 14.8%

Land area 173 square miles

Population per square mile 3,484

Counties, 1990 population
Middlesex (pt.) 540,729	Suffolk (pt.) 60,913

Cities, 1990 population (10,000 or more)
Arlington 44,630	Revere 42,786
Everett 35,701	Stoneham 22,203
Framingham 64,989	Wakefield 24,825
Lexington 28,974	Waltham 57,878
Malden 53,884	Weston 10,200
Medford 57,407	Winchester 20,267
Melrose 28,150	Winthrop 18,127
Natick 30,510	Woburn 35,943
Reading (pt.) 17,579	

Race and Hispanic origin
White 93.8%
Black 2.3%
American Indian, Eskimo, or Aleut. 0.1%
Asian or Pacific Islander 2.8%
Other 1.0%
Hispanic origin 3.0%

Ancestry
American 2.8%	Italian 25.3%
Canadian 1.6%	Polish 3.8%
English 13.7%	Portuguese 1.9%
French 5.7%	Russian 3.0%
French Canadian 3.5%	Scotch Irish 2.0%
German 7.8%	Scottish 3.3%
Greek 1.5%	Swedish 2.0%
Irish 29.9%	

Universities/colleges, 1990-1991 enrollment
Bentley College, Waltham 7,440
Brandeis University, Waltham 3,793
Framingham State College, Framingham 6,683
Regis College, Weston 1,145
Tufts University, Medford 7,899

Newspapers, total circulation (in all districts)
Boston Globe 503,578
Boston Herald 339,813
Middlesex News 35,996
Waltham News Tribune 9,228

Commercial television stations, affiliations
ADI: Boston (100%)

Cable television systems, total subscribers
Continental Cablevision of Massachusetts; Arlington 11,363
Continental Cablevision of Massachusetts; Revere 14,238
Framingham Cablevision; Framingham 15,700
Waltham Cable; Waltham 11,756
Warner Amex; Wakefield 6,373
Warner Cable Communications Inc.; Malden 76,208

Military installations, 1991

Natick Research & Development Laboratories (Army), Natick 1,243

Material & Mechanical Research Center (Army), Watertown 566

Businesses and other major employers

Raytheon Co./Missile Systems Div.; Lexington; missiles 4,500

Raytheon Co.; Waltham; communications equipment 3,516

Dennison Mfg. Co.; Framingham; paper products 3,000

Commonwealth of Massachusetts/Walter E. Fernald State School; Waltham; residential care 2,250

Massachusetts Institute of Technology/Lincoln Laboratory; Lexington; research services 2,200

Tufts University; Medford 1,988

Polaroid Corp.; Waltham; cameras/photo supplies 1,800

Brandeis University; Waltham 1,580

Metrowest Medical Center; Natick 1,400

City of Woburn; Woburn 1,300

New England Memorial Hospital; Stoneham 1,200

Hewlett-Packard Co.; Waltham; medical instruments 1,150

Malden Hospital Inc.; Malden 1,100

TJX Companies Inc./TJ Maxx; Framingham; family clothing stores 1,000

Melrose Wakefield Hospital; Melrose 1,000

Winchester Hospital; Winchester 1,000

Town of Natick; Natick 1,000

Computervision Corp.; Natick; computer services 1,000

City of Revere; Revere 958

Bentley College; Waltham 950

IBM Corp.; Waltham; computer/support services 900

Town of Framingham/School District; Framingham 900

Pinpoint Inc.; Waltham; furniture 831

Baybanks Systems Inc.; Waltham; accounting 824

New England Rehabilitation Hospital; Woburn; health services 805

Town of Wakefield; Wakefield 805

Raytheon Co./Microwave & Power Tube Div.; Waltham; electronic components 800

Lechmere Inc.; Woburn; computer stores 800

Everett Cottage Hospital/Whidden Memorial Hospital; Everett 800

Lawrence Memorial Hospital; Medford 800

Waltham Weston Hospital & Medical Center; Waltham 789

Continental Baking Co.; Natick; bakery products 780

Raytheon Co./D. C. Heath & Co.; Lexington; search/navigation equipment 750

Loral Infrared Imaging Systems; Lexington; search/navigation equipment 750

Litton Systems Inc./Itek Optical Systems Div.; Lexington; measuring/controlling devices 750

Instrumentation Lab. Inc.; Lexington; medical instruments 750

GTE Service Corp./GTE Laboratories; Waltham; research services 750

Baybank Harvard Trust Co.; Arlington; commercial banks 710

Symmes Hospital Inc.; Arlington 700

Lutheran Service Assn. of New England; Framingham; nursing 700

Jordan Marsh Stores Corp./Jordan Marsh; Arlington; department stores 650

City of Malden; Malden 650

U.S. Army Corps of Engineers; Waltham 640

Addison-Wesley Publishing Co.; Reading; book publishing 600

Alpha Industries Inc.; Woburn; electronic components 600

Bose Corp.; Framingham; audio/video equipment 600

Automatic Data Processing; Waltham; nursing 600

City of Medford/Public Schools; Medford 600

Town of Weston; Weston 600

Metcalf & Eddy Inc.; Wakefield; engineering services 588

8th District

Parts of Boston and Suburbs — Cambridge; Somerville

The 8th, with a population almost 40 percent minority, is an outgrowth of mapmakers' attempt in 1992 to create a district where minorities would have substantial political influence. It links Hispanics in Chelsea, Haitians in Somerville and blacks in the Boston neighborhoods of Dorchester, Roxbury and Mattapan. Blacks are 23 percent of the district's population, Hispanics 11 percent and Asians 6 percent.

The large minority population helps fuel the service economy that dominates the 8th. Many work as custodians, clerical staff, orderlies and cooks at the local hospitals, universities, hotels and government offices. There is a degree of tension in the 8th between these laborers and white-collar professionals who work at the same institutions, but they coexist in reasonable peace partly because of their shared liberalism.

Two of the world's most renowned universities—Harvard and the Massachusetts Institute of Technology—lie along the banks of the Charles River in Cambridge. Jokingly known as the Kremlin on the Charles, the exceedingly liberal city of 96,000 votes staunchly Democratic. It helped Bill Clinton carry the 8th with 68 percent in 1992, by far his best showing in any Massachusetts district.

The two universities employ about 24,000 and educate nearly 35,000. Their research activities helped spawn a bevy of highly specialized computer and biotechnology firms in the area.

One of the few cities that still enforces rent-control laws, Cambridge has grown increasingly crowded, and that has sent students and young workers looking for quarters in neighboring Somerville.

Despite the influx of yuppies and a handful of upscale restaurants and boutiques in the 1980s, Somerville remains a working-class, tight-knit community of triple-decker houses, neighborhood pubs and home-style eateries.

More than half the district's residents live in Boston, a city with a metropolitan air but small-town charm, thanks to its many and varied neighborhoods. At least 10 distinct Boston sections are within the 8th. They include: Fenway, home to the Red Sox baseball stadium (Fenway Park) and a large gay population; Mattapan, where black professionals have refurbished single family homes; Jamaica Plain, a thriving liberal enclave with popular ethnic restaurants and retail shops; Beacon Hill, the historic district of stately brick townhouses behind the Massachusetts Statehouse; and Roxbury, an overwhelmingly poor black neighborhood rife with vacant lots.

The 8th also has Chelsea, a destitute city polluted by toxic waste discharged by oil ships traveling up Chelsea Creek. Things got so dire here in the early 1990s that the city government was put into state receivership and the schools were handed over to

Boston University to manage.

Belmont, with its bankers, lawyers and other professionals, is the 8th's only suburban turf. One of the nation's largest concentrations of Armenians lives in neighboring Watertown.

Election Returns

	8th District	Democrat	Republican
1992	President*	136,582 (67.8%)	39,284 (19.5%)
	House †	149,903 (83.1%)	—
1990	Senate	122,014 (72.1%)	47,155 (27.9%)
	Governor	85,730 (50.6%)	79,226 (46.8%)
1988	President	139,745 (68.4%)	64,616 (31.6%)
	Senate	149,346 (74.2%)	51,878 (25.8%)
1986	Governor	108,898 (77.1%)	32,377 (22.9%)

*Vote for Perot was 25,503 (12.7%).   †Independent/other is greater than 5%.

Demographics

Population 601,643

Percent change from 1980 15.4%

Land area 44 square miles

Population per square mile 13,520

Counties, 1990 population
Middlesex (pt.) 230,016   Suffolk (pt.) 371,627

Cities, 1990 population (10,000 or more)
Belmont 24,720   Chelsea 28,710
Boston (pt.) 342,917   Somerville 76,210
Cambridge 95,802   Watertown 33,284

Race and Hispanic origin
White 65.5%
Black 23.3%
American Indian, Eskimo, or Aleut. 0.3%
Asian or Pacific Islander 5.6%
Other 5.3%
Hispanic origin 10.6%

Ancestry
American 1.8%   Polish 3.0%
English 8.2%   Portuguese 2.6%
French 3.1%   Russian 3.1%
French Canadian 1.8%   Scotch Irish 1.2%
German 7.0%   Scottish 2.1%
Greek 1.1%   Subsaharan African 1.4%
Irish 17.6%   Swedish 1.1%
Italian 12.0%   West Indian 5.0%

Universities/colleges, 1990-1991 enrollment
Bay State College, Boston 566
Berklee College of Music, Boston 2,734
Boston Architectural Center, Boston 945
Boston College, Chestnut Hill 14,515
Boston Conservatory, Boston 363
Boston University, Boston 28,001
Bunker Hill Community College, Boston 5,609
Cambridge College, Cambridge 824
Emerson College, Boston 2,692
Emmanuel College, Boston 1,079
Fisher College, Boston 2,084
Franklin Institute of Boston, Boston 413
Harvard University, Cambridge 22,855
Katherine Gibbs School, Boston 500
Lesley College, Cambridge 5,500
Massachusetts College of Arts, Boston 1,848
Massachusetts College of Pharmacy & Allied Health Sciences, Boston 1,139
Massachusetts Institute of Technology, Cambridge 9,628
New England College of Optometry, Boston 382
New England Conservatory of Music, Boston 741
New England School of Law, Boston 1,186
Northeastern University, Boston 30,515
Roxbury Community College, Roxbury 1,887
School of the Museum of Fine Arts, Boston 1,371
Simmons College, Boston 2,819
Wentworth Institute of Technology, Boston 3,904
Wheelock College, Boston 1,648

Newspapers, total circulation (in all districts)
Boston Globe 503,578
Boston Herald 339,813
New York Post 551,443

Commercial television stations, affiliations
ADI: Boston (100%)
WQTV, Boston (None)

Cable television systems, total subscribers
Cablevision of Boston; Boston 84,000
Cablevision of Boston; Brookline 13,600
Continental Cablevision of Massachusetts; Cambridge 18,237
Continental Cablevision of Massachusetts; Watertown 8,300

Businesses and other major employers
Harvard University; Cambridge 9,400
John Hancock Mutual; Boston; insurance services 8,359
Massachusetts Institute of Technology; Cambridge; research services 8,029
Brigham & Women's Hospital; Boston 7,200
Massachusetts Commonwealth/Public Health Dept.; Boston 4,200
Children's Hospital; Boston 3,300
New England Mutual Life Insurance Co.; Boston; pension/health/welfare funds 3,000
Boston University; Boston 2,900
Polaroid Corp.; Cambridge; cameras/photo supplies 2,700
St. Elizabeth's Hospital of Boston; Boston 2,500
Liberty Mutual Insurance Co.; Boston; fire/marine/casualty insurance 2,413
New England Deaconess Hospital; Boston 2,248
Delta Air Lines Inc.; Boston; airline/airport services 2,100
Northeastern University; Boston 2,100
Boston College; Newton 2,000
Browning-Ferris Industries; Boston; sanitary services 1,920
U.S. Veterans Affairs Dept.; Boston; hospital 1,800
Mount Auburn Hospital; Cambridge 1,800
Bolt Beranek & Newman Inc.; Cambridge; computer equipment 1,700
McLean Hospital Corp.; Belmont 1,600
Draper Charles Stark Lab Inc.; Cambridge; research services 1,550
American Airlines Inc.; Boston; airline 1,500
Carney Hospital Inc.; Boston 1,500

ISS Intl. Service System; Somerville; building services 1,500

Boston Edison Co.; Boston; electric services 1,450

Lotus Development Corp.; Cambridge; computer services 1,300

Arthur D. Little Inc.; Cambridge; consulting services 1,300

Harvard Student Agencies Inc.; Cambridge; personnel supply services 1,250

First Church of Christ; Boston; religious organizations 1,210

New England Baptist Hospital; Boston 1,200

Marriott Corp./Boston Marriott; Boston; hotel 1,100

IBM Corp.; Boston; computer equipment 1,000

Harvard Medical School; Boston 1,000

Massachusetts Port Authority/Massport; Boston; airport services 900

News Group Boston Inc./Boston Herald; Boston; newspapers 850

Town of Belmont; Belmont 850

Prudential Insurance of America Inc./Sheraton Boston Hotel & Tower; Boston; hotel 825

Massachusetts Electric Construction Co.; Boston; electrical work 800

Dana-Farber Cancer Institute; Boston; medical research 800

Westin Hotel Co.; Boston; hotel 800

Badger Co. Inc.; Cambridge; engineering services 800

City of Cambridge/Cambridge Hospital; Cambridge 800

Youville Rehabilitation & Hospital; Cambridge 800

Boston Scientific Corp.; Watertown; medical instruments/supplies 750

Boston Park Plaza Hotel Operating Co./Boston Park Plaza Hotel & Towers; Boston; hotel 750

American Cleaning Co. Inc.; Cambridge; building services 750

WGBH Educational Foundation/Channel 2; Boston; movie production 750

Christian Science Publishing Society/World Monitor News; Boston; newspapers 740

Moran Research Labs Inc./Bioran Medical Labs; Cambridge; medical/dental labs 725

H. N. Bull Information Systems; Boston; electronic components 700

First Congregational Church Stoneham; Belmont; religious organization 700

H. P. Hood Inc.; Boston; dairy products 650

U.S. Defense Dept./Army Materials Technology Lab.; Watertown 650

Francisca Children's Hospital; Boston 620

Security Systems Inc./Sentry Protective Systems; Boston; security services 600

Bunker Hill Community College; Boston 600

Massachusetts Bay Transportation Authority; Boston 600

Bain & Co.; Boston; consulting services 600

Bay State Health Care Inc.; Cambridge; medical doctors 600

First Security Services Corp.; Boston; business/security services 600

Camp Dresser & McKee Inc.; Cambridge; engineering/architectural services 600

Symmes Hospital Inc.; Somerville 600

Somerville Hospital; Somerville 600

U.S. Transportation Dept.; Cambridge 550

Perkins School for the Blind/Howe Memorial Press; Watertown 550

Gillette Co./Liquid Paper Corp.; Boston; correction fluid 550

9th District

Part of Boston, Southern Suburbs — Taunton; Braintree; Part of Brockton

Three major federally funded projects will be under way in Boston through the 1990s: construction of a third tunnel under Boston Harbor connecting downtown to Logan International Airport; the depression and reconstruction of a north-south highway called the Central Artery; and cleanup of the polluted Boston Harbor. Some estimates say that the three projects will employ 20,000 once they are in full swing. And with construction under way for a new arena to house basketball's Celtics and hockey's Bruins, even more jobs will be created.

The projects are especially important to the 9th, where many working-class residents have not had a steady paycheck since the bottom fell out of the commercial real estate market in the late 1980s, halting new construction work. These blue-collar Democrats live primarily in Boston's ethnic neighborhoods. Italians reside in the North End, a compact section near the waterfront where suburbanites trek for some of the region's best food. South Boston, still overwhelmingly white and Irish, was the center of bitter opposition to school busing in the 1970s. Most of the residents of middle-class West Roxbury and Roslindale work downtown at banks, insurance companies, law offices and government agencies.

The 9th takes in nearly all the white sections of Boston. Redistricting in 1992 put most of the city's black, Hispanic and Asian neighborhoods into the 8th to create a minority-influence district.

South of Boston, the 9th includes half the city of Brockton. This former shoemaking capital has struggled since those factories departed in the 1960s. Brockton's population slipped slightly in the 1980s to just under 93,000. Brockton went Republican in the three presidential elections of the 1980s, but Bill Clinton carried it in 1992.

Despite the presence of Boston, Brockton and (farther south) the city of Taunton, the 9th is evenly divided between urban and suburban communities. Many Boston executives live in and give a conservative flavor to the towns of Milton, Randolph, Medfield and Braintree. These communities (south and west of Boston) are known for their neatly manicured lawns, good schools and predominantly white populations. The state's burgeoning anti-abortion movement is centered in Braintree.

In a state where many areas saw significant population decline in the 1980s, Milton held steady and Randolph grew. Adding to Milton's appeal is the nearby Blue Hills Reservation, a 6,500-acre preserve with hiking trails, tennis courts, a golf course and small ski slope. Although Milton is George Bush's birthplace, it went narrowly for Clinton in 1992; Bush won Medfield.

Many of the 9th's suburban residents work outside the district, traveling the Route 128 beltway to companies such as Raytheon and Digital Equipment Corp.

Election Returns

	9th District	Democrat	Republican
1992	President*	131,539 (48.0%)	85,981 (31.4%)
	House †	175,550 (69.2%)	54,291 (21.4%)
1990	Senate	143,489 (61.1%)	91,428 (38.9%)
	Governor	120,086 (50.0%)	114,170 (47.6%)

9th District		Democrat	Republican
1988	President	147,127 (55.0%)	120,399 (45.0%)
	Senate	173,023 (65.4%)	91,609 (34.6%)
1986	Governor	119,747 (68.3%)	55,562 (31.7%)

*Vote for Perot was 56,609 (20.7%).   †Independent/other is greater than 5%.

Demographics

Population 601,643

Percent change from 1980 15.9%

Land area 254 square miles

Population per square mile 2,367

Counties, 1990 population

Bristol (pt.) 59,503	Plymouth (pt.) 52,474
Norfolk (pt.) 258,300	Suffolk (pt.) 231,366

Cities, 1990 population (10,000 or more)

Boston (pt.) 231,366	Needham 27,557
Braintree 33,836	Norwood (pt.) 28,700
Brockton (pt.) 52,474	Randolph 30,093
Canton 18,530	Stoughton 26,777
Dedham 23,782	Taunton 49,832
Medfield 10,531	Walpole 21,212
Milton 25,725	Westwood 12,557

Race and Hispanic origin

White 87.6%
Black 6.7%
American Indian, Eskimo, or Aleut. 0.2%
Asian or Pacific Islander 2.8%
Other 2.7%
Hispanic origin 4.6%

Ancestry

American 2.6%	Lithuanian 1.5%
Arabic 1.3%	Polish 4.3%
Canadian 1.5%	Portuguese 4.3%
English 11.5%	Russian 2.6%
French 5.0%	Scotch Irish 1.8%
French Canadian 2.5%	Scottish 2.8%
German 6.9%	Subsaharan African 1.4%
Greek 1.5%	Swedish 2.0%
Irish 34.5%	West Indian 1.3%
Italian 14.0%	

Universities/colleges, 1990-1991 enrollment

Andover Newton Theological School, Newton 458
Aquinas College, Milton 341
Catherine Laboure College, Boston 444
Curry College, Milton 1,218
Massasoit Community College, Brockton 6,675
Suffolk University, Boston 5,277
University of Massachusetts, Boston 13,722

Newspapers, total circulation (in all districts)

Boston Globe 503,578
Boston Herald 339,813
Brockton Enterprise 54,632
Dedham Daily Transcript 8,588
New Bedford Standard-Times 43,355
New York Post 551,443

Quincy Patriot Ledger 86,987
Taunton Daily Gazette 14,047

Commercial television stations, affiliations
ADI: Boston (75%) and Providence-New Bedford (25%)
WBZ-TV, Boston (NBC)
WCVB-TV, Boston (ABC)
WFXT, Boston (Fox)
WSBK-TV, Boston (None)
WLVI-TV, Cambridge (None)

Cable television systems, total subscribers
Adams Russell Cable Serivces Massachusetts; Braintree 8,200
Adams Russell Cable Services Massachusetts; Norwood 10,340
Cablevision of Boston; Boston 84,000
Cablevision of Boston; West Roxbury 16,300
Continental Cablevision of Massachusetts; Dedham 5,827
Continental Cablevision of Massachusetts; Stoughton 14,500
UA Columbia Cablevision of Massachusetts; Taunton 13,632

Businesses and other major employers
General Hospital Corp./Massachusetts General Hospital; Boston 9,900
U.S. Postal Service; Boston 8,500
Bank of Boston Corp.; Boston; commercial banks 7,000
New England Medical Center Hospital; Boston 4,848
F. M. R. Corp.; Boston; investment services 4,325
Commonwealth of Massachusetts; Boston 4,000
Blue Cross/Blue Shield of Massachusetts; Boston; medical service/health insurance 3,500
Stone & Webster Engineering Corp.; Boston; engineering/architectural services 3,400
GTE Government Systems Corp.; Needham Heights; communications equipment 3,000
Boston Safe Deposit & Trust Co.; Boston; commercial banks 2,600
Globe Newspaper Co./Boston Globe; Boston; newspapers 2,500
Boston Public Schools District; Boston 2,363
Commonwealth of Massachusetts/Employment & Training Dept.; Boston 2,210
City of Brockton/School Dept.; Brockton 2,000
Melrose Management Inc.; Boston; movie theaters 2,000
University Hospital Inc.; Boston 2,000
Shawmut Corp.; Boston; holding offices 1,808
New England Telephone & Telegraph Co.; Boston; telephone communications 1,800
Boston Co. Inc.; Milton; commercial banks 1,800
City of Boston; Boston 2,750
Jordan Marsh Stores Corp.; Boston; department stores 1,500
Fleet Bank Massachusetts; Boston; commercial banks 1,500
Norwood Hospital; Norwood 1,486
Bradlee's New Jersey Inc./Bradlee's; Braintree; department stores 1,400
Commonwealth of Massachusetts/Paul A. Dever State School; Taunton; nursing 1,400
U.S. Veterans Affairs Dept.; Brockton; hospital 1,400
Federal Reserve Bank of Boston; Boston 1,350
State Street Boston Corp.; Boston; commercial banks 1,350
Northrop Corp./Electronic Systems Group; Norwood; search/navigation equipment 1,300
Coopers & Lybrand; Boston; accounting/auditing 1,250
City of Taunton; Taunton 1,200

City of Boston/Housing Authority; Boston 1,200
Commercial Union Corp.; Boston; life insurance 2,000
Cardinal Cushing Hospital Inc.; Brockton 1,130
Faulkner Hospital Inc.; Boston 1,100
Massachusetts Eye & Ear Infirmary; Boston 1,100
GTE Government Systems Corp.; Taunton; communications equipment 1,000
Analog Devices Inc.; Norwood; electronic components 1,000
Putnam Companies Inc.; Boston; investment offices 1,000
May Dept. Stores Co./Filene's; Boston; department stores 1,000
Town of Stoughton; Stoughton 950
Spaulding Rehabilitation Hospital; Boston 890
St. Margaret's Hospital for Women; Boston 831
City of Brockton; Brockton 810
U.S. Postal Service; Brockton 800
Teradyne Inc.; Boston; measuring/controlling devices 800
City of Taunton/School Dept.; Taunton 800
Town of Braintree; Braintree 800
Hebrew Rehabilitation Center for Aged; Boston 800
Everett Industries Inc.; Westwood; personnel supply services 800
Children's Medical Center Corp./Martha Eliot Medical Center; Boston 800
Morton Hospital; Taunton 795
Ropes & Gray; Boston; legal services 790
Commonwealth of Massachusetts/Environmental Protection Agency; Boston 776
County of Suffolk/Sheriffs Dept.; Boston 770
Town of Norwood; Norwood 770
United Parcel Service; Norwood; mail services 750
Town of Randolph; Randolph 750
Kelton Corp./Braintree Hospital; Braintree; residential care 750
Teradyne Inc.; Boston; communications equipment 700
Morse Shoe Inc.; Canton; shoe stores 700
Town of Walpole/School District; Walpole 700
Arthur Andersen & Co.; Boston; accounting/auditing 700
Town of Westwood; Westwood 700
Hale & Dorr; Boston; legal services 694
Houghton Mifflin Co.; Boston; book publishing 691
National Financial Services Corp.; Boston; security brokers 680
Goodwin Procter & Hoar; Boston; legal services 675
Taunton State Hospital; Taunton 670
LTX Corp.; Westwood; computer testing/repair 650
Medfield State Hospital; Medfield 650
New England Sinai Hospital; Stoughton 620
Boston Water & Sewer Commission; Boston; water supply 600
Beacon O'Connell Joint Venture; Boston; building construction 600
Hill's Stores Co.; Canton; department stores 600
Scudder Stevens & Clark Inc.; Boston; security/commodity services 600
Goddard Medical Assoc.; Brockton; medical doctors 600
Suffolk University; Boston 600
Town of Dedham; Dedham 600
Emery Air Freight Corp./Emery Worldwide; Boston; freight shipping 587
Boston Consulting Group Inc.; Boston; management/public relations 585
Baybank; Dedham; commercial banks 558

Milton Hospital Inc.; Milton 550
Armstrong World Industries; Braintree; wood products 525
Faxon Co. Inc.; Westwood; periodicals 525
Trans Ubiquity Corp./Minute Man Delivery Systems; Dedham; trucking/courier services 525
Multibank Financial Corp.; Dedham; computer services 520

10th District

South Shore — Cape Cod; Islands

A researcher at Woods Hole Oceanographic Institution starts his own business to produce a new medicine he developed from squid blood. The Maritime Administration moors the *Southern Cross*, a 450-foot ship, at the all but abandoned Fore River Shipyard in Quincy. The boat becomes the first floating classroom in the nation.

These are the kind of small but notable developments that are helping the coastal communities of the 10th shift gears into the 1990s. Just as whaling gave way to textiles after the Civil War, and textiles were replaced with fishing and shipbuilding in the 1920s, now newly emerging technologies offer economic promise for the residents of Cape Cod, the islands and Massachusetts' South Shore.

Since the 10th has never relied on the defense industry and did not partake in the high-tech boom of the 1980s, its economy has stayed more constant than much of the state's.

The coastal towns, particularly on Cape Cod, rely on tourists to help them survive the long, arduous winters. Though the Cape is referred to as a single locale, it is an eclectic mix of communities, some of them ritzy summer vacation spots, some of them middle-class communities with year-round residents; one—Provincetown, at the tip of the cape—is a liberal, predominantly gay artists' colony. Martha's Vineyard and Nantucket are summer retreats for the rich (and often, famous).

The mainland coastal towns of the 10th are commonly referred to as the South Shore communities. With the exception of a handful of thriving cranberry bogs, most of the South Shore towns consist of bedroom developments for Boston's professionals or Quincy's blue-collar workers. Commuter boats shuttle lawyers and doctors from Hingham and Hull across Boston Harbor to downtown.

Cape Cod, Hingham, Duxbury and Cohasset can offer a trove of votes to the right Republican. Although Rep. Gerry Studds handily defeated his two opponents in those communities in 1992, the presidential contest was closer; George Bush won several towns in the south, including Duxbury, Chatham, Hingham and Hanover.

Quincy, popularized in the mid-1970s by white Bostonians fleeing the city's forced busing policies to integrate the schools, continues its tradition as an ethnic melting pot. Irish and Italian immigrants led the way south; now Asian Americans are becoming a visible presence in Quincy.

The city of Brockton dominates the inland communities of the 10th. Split between the 9th and 10th districts, it has been suffering since the decline of its shoemaking industry in the 1960s.

The 10th overall is one of the Democrats' weaker districts in Massachusetts. In 1992, President Bush did better here than in any other district (though he still got only 32 percent), and the 10th was independent candidate Ross Perot's second-best district, giving him almost 26 percent.

Election Returns

	10th District	Democrat	Republican
1992	President*	133,776 (42.3%)	101,936 (32.2%)
	House†	189,342 (60.8%)	75,887 (24.4%)
1990	Senate	144,671 (53.7%)	124,511 (46.3%)
	Governor	122,628 (44.8%)	144,012 (52.6%)
1988	President	144,894 (49.0%)	150,908 (51.0%)
	Senate	182,189 (61.5%)	113,951 (38.5%)
1986	Governor	118,191 (63.2%)	68,767 (36.8%)

*Vote for Perot was 80,791 (25.5%).   †Independent/other is greater than 5%.

Demographics

Population 601,642

Percent change from 1980 15.2%

Land area 881 square miles

Population per square mile 683

Counties, 1990 population

Barnstable 186,605	Norfolk (pt.) 161,722
Dukes 11,639	Plymouth (pt.) 235,664
Nantucket 6,012	

Cities, 1990 population (10,000 or more)

Abington 13,817	Hyannis CDP 14,120
Barnstable 40,949	Marshfield 21,531
Bourne 16,064	Plymouth 45,608
Brockton (pt.) 40,314	Quincy 84,985
Denis 13,864	Sandwich 15,489
Duxbury 13,895	Scituate 16,789
Falmouth 27,960	South Yarmouth CDP
Hanover 11,912	10,358
Harwich 10,275	Weymouth 54,063
Hingham 19,821	Whitman 13,240
Holbrook 11,041	Yarmouth 21,174
Hull 10,466	

Race and Hispanic origin

White 95.1%
Black 2.1%
American Indian, Eskimo, or Aleut. 0.4%
Asian or Pacific Islander 1.5%
Other 0.9%
Hispanic origin 1.4%

Ancestry

American 3.2%	Italian 13.8%
Canadian 1.5%	Lithuanian 1.3%
Dutch 1.1%	Polish 3.4%
English 20.4%	Portuguese 3.6%
French 7.2%	Russian 1.1%
French Canadian 2.9%	Scotch Irish 2.7%
German 9.3%	Scottish 5.0%
Greek 1.0%	Swedish 3.3%
Irish 35.6%	

Universities/colleges, 1990-1991 enrollment

Cape Cod Community College, West Barnstable 4,328
Eastern Nazarene College, Wollaston 919
Mass Maritime Academy, Buzzards Bay 598
Quincy College, Quincy 2,644
Stonehill College, North Easton 3,025

Newspapers, total circulation (in all districts)

Boston Globe 503,578
Boston Herald 339,813
Brockton Enterprise 54,632
Cape Cod Times 45,867
New Bedford Standard-Times 43,355
Quincy Patriot Ledger 86,987

Commercial television stations, affiliations

ADI: Boston (88%) and Providence-New Bedford (12%)
WHRC, Norwell (None)
WCVX, Vineyard Haven (None)

Cable television systems, total subscribers

Adelphia Cable; Falmouth 9,759
Adelphia Cable; Plymouth 18,714
Adelphia Cable Marshfield; Marshfield 6,873
Continental Cablevision; Quincy 49,565
Continental Cablevision; Brockton 32,200
Continental Cablevision of Massachusetts; Orleans 12,953
Continental Cablevision of Massachusetts; Scituate 21,000
Dimension Cable Services; Weymouth 15,000
Harron Cablevision of Cape Cod; Bourne 9,228
Harron Cablevision of Massachusetts; Rockland 7,647

Military installations, 1991

South Weymouth Naval Air Station, South Weymouth 1,111
Otis Air Force Guard Base, Falmouth 737
Cape Cod Air Force Station, Bourne 202

Businesses and other major employers

U.S. Interior Dept./Cape Cod National Seashore; South Wellfleet 2,000
South Shore Hospital Inc.; South Weymouth 1,775
City of Boston/Long Island Hospital; Quincy 1,500
Boston Financial Data Services; Quincy; security brokers 1,300
Brockton Hospital Inc.; Brockton 1,300
Cape Cod Hospital; Hyannis 1,100
Quincy City Hospital; Quincy 975
Woods Hole Ocanographic Institution; Falmouth; research services 950
Town of Plymouth; Plymouth 950
Town of Marshfield; Marshfield 850
Haemonetics Corp.; Braintree; medical instruments 800
Putnam Investor Services Inc.; Quincy; investment services 800
Town of Hingham; Hingham 800
Talbot's Inc.; Hingham; women's clothing stores 750
Raytheon Co./Microwave & Power Tube Div.; Quincy; household appliances 725
Boston Edison Co./Pilgrim Station; Plymouth; electric services 700
Wear-Guard Corp.; Norwell; catalog uniform retailers 700
Falmouth Hospital Assn.; Falmouth 700
Jordan Hospital Inc.; Plymouth 700
Town of Whitman; Whitman 655
Commonwealth of Massachusetts/Education Dept.; Quincy 600
George W. Prescott Publishing Co./Patriot Ledger; Quincy; newspapers 585
Town of Sandwich; Sandwich 570
Town of Bourne; Buzzards Bay 525
Stonehill College; North Easton 502

Michigan

Going into the 1992 redistricting process, it was no secret that Michigan's congressional delegation had to shrink from 18 to 16 seats. The state's population declined again in the 1980s, most noticeably in Detroit, where almost 15 percent of all residents left the city.

The depopulation of Detroit was merely a continuation of a pattern of flight to the suburbs that began in the 1950s. In 1960, the city contained 1.8 million inhabitants. Many held jobs in the auto industry, which had transformed Detroit into an industrial colossus. But by the 1990 census, the city barely exceeded 1 million in population. A walk through the city would turn up block after neighborhood block of burned down or bombed out houses, or abandoned factory hulks that littered the downtown landscape.

It took a corrosive racial dynamic to transform the Motor City into the embodiment of urban America's woes. In 30 years of white flight, from 1960 to 1990, the city went from two-thirds white to three-quarters black. Relations between Detroit and the emerging, self-sustaining edge cities were bitter. Race relations also affected voting patterns at the federal and local levels, where white ethnics shed their traditional Democratic and union sympathies in favor of a Republican Party perceived as tougher on law-and-order issues.

The decline of the domestic automobile industry exacerbated the situation. The auto industry kept Detroit working and prosperous for decades after the opening of Henry Ford's Highland Park factory in 1909, but as jobs left for Mexico and other nonunion locales, the city's economic fortunes withered.

Though Detroit has hemorrhaged voters at a breakneck pace, it still holds firm to its position as Michigan's most populous city. No Democratic candidate for statewide office can expect to win without its rich vein of Democratic votes. The 1990 gubernatorial election served to re-emphasize the city's importance to the Democratic coalition. Without a large Democratic turnout in the city to offset GOP margins turned in by the rest of the state, Democratic Gov. James J. Blanchard's re-election effort went down in defeat to GOP challenger John Engler.

During redistricting machinations, Republicans contended that population trends indicated Democrats should bear the two-seat loss. After all, they argued, Democratic southeastern Michigan was hemorrhaging voters, not the GOP-controlled regions

of central and western Michigan. Democrats drew up their own plan, one that dealt a one-seat loss to each party. But instead of selecting one of the parties' plans, a panel of federal judges handed down their own map, which radically redrew the lines. The judges also renumbered all but one district (the 16th).

Most of Detroit's population loss in the 1980s occurred in the two black-majority, city-based districts. One of the two, the old 13th, lost 23 percent of its population. But the Voting Rights Act mandates black-majority districts be preserved, so instead, the federal panel expanded the two city-based districts (the 14th and 15th) into the immediate suburbs, imperiling the white Democrats whose districts bordered the city. Other incumbents throughout the state were similarly distressed, having witnessed their districts dismembered or altered to such an extent that they chose to retire. By the end of the 1992 elections, primarily because of the new map, seven incumbents either lost races or retired.

The northernmost district was numbered the 1st, containing the upper peninsula (UP) and northern lower Michigan. The western reaches of the UP, the former mining counties known as "Copper Country," are Democratic strongholds, where union ties have persevered through the decline of traditional mining and logging industries. Below the Straits of Mackinac, the dividing line between the UP and lower Michigan, the territory is more Republican-friendly. Affluent and Republican Traverse City, the population center of northern lower Michigan, was added to balance out the district's population.

Farther south, covering the geographic heart of Michigan, is the 4th. The city of Midland is the population nexus, with conservative small towns and farming communities filling in the rest. After the 1st, in terms of land mass, it is the state's largest district.

Western Michigan is a motherlode of GOP votes. With a rich conservative Dutch heritage that still permeates local culture, the region is solid Republican territory. Labor strength pales in comparison to heavily unionized southeastern Michigan.

The cities of Grand Rapids, Holland and Kalamazoo form what is known as the "Dutch Triangle," a region settled by immigrants from the Netherlands in the mid-19th century. In the 2nd District, which borders Lake Michigan to the west, Holland is surpassed in population only by industrial Muskegon. Outside the cities, agriculture and tourism revenues are staples of the

MICHIGAN

Isle Royale

KEWEENAW

Lake Superior

KEWEENAW

HOUGHTON

Lake Superior

Marquette

ONTONAGON

BARAGA

GOGEBIC

IRON

MARQUETTE

1

ALGER

LUCE

SCHOOLCRAFT

CHIPPEWA

DICKINSON

DELTA

MACKINAC

MENOMINEE

Lake Michigan

Lake Huron

EMMET

CHEBOYGAN

1

PRESQUE ISLE

CHARLEVOIX

ANTRIM

OTSEGO

MONTMORENCY

ALPENA

LEELANAU

Traverse City

KALKASKA

CRAWFORD

OSCODA

ALCONA

BENZIE

GRAND
TRAVERSE

MANISTEE

WEXFORD

MISSAUKEE

ROSCOMMON

OGEMAW

IOSCO

MASON

LAKE

OSCEOLA

CLARE

GLADWIN

ARENAC

Saginaw Bay

HURON

2

4

OCEANA

NEWAYGO

MECOSTA

ISABELLA

MIDLAND

Midland

BAY

Bay City

5

MONTCALM

GRATIOT

SAGINAW

Saginaw

TUSCOLA

SANILAC

MUSKEGON

Muskegon

KENT

IONIA

CLINTON

Grand
Rapids

3

SHIAWASSEE

GENESEE

Flint

LAPEER

ST. CLAIR

Port Huron

OTTAWA

Holland

9

OAKLAND

Pontiac

MACOMB

10

BARRY

EATON

☆ Lansing

8

LIVINGSTON

11

12

ALLEGAN

7

INGHAM

WASHTENAW

WAYNE

VAN BUREN

Kalamazoo

Battle Creek

Jackson

13

Districts 13, 14,
15 and 16
Wayne County,
including city
of Detroit

Benton Harbor

6

KALAMAZOO

CALHOUN

JACKSON

Ypsilanti

St. Joseph

BERRIEN

CASS

ST. JOSEPH

BRANCH

HILLSDALE

LENAWEE

MONROE

16

Ann Arbor

local economy. The 6th, which covers the southern portion of the Lake Michigan shoreline to the Indiana border, is also agriculture-oriented, with the cities of Benton Harbor and St. Joseph more geared toward industry. Redistricting added the city of Kalamazoo to the 6th, after the old 3rd District was dissolved and pieced into several different districts.

Farther inland, Grand Rapids, the state's second largest city after Detroit, anchors the 3rd. It boasts a relatively diversified economic base, making it one of the few cities outside the Sun Belt to emerge relatively unscathed from the recession of the early 1990s.

The recession looked less favorably on the other side of the state. Deep cuts, layoffs and downsizing in the auto industry wreaked economic havoc across southeastern Michigan. Heavily Democratic Flint (9th), the birthplace of General Motors—and the United Auto Workers (UAW) three decades later—has been economically devastated by GM downsizing and layoffs.

Any auto industry tremor also reverberates through the other districts of southeast Michigan. The gritty and industrial Bay City-Saginaw 5th District is densely populated with UAW members, as are the seats nearer to Detroit, such as the 10th, 12th (formed from the merger of the old 14th and 17th), 13th and 16th.

Table 1 Population

District	Population	Population under 18	Voting-age population	Median age
1	580,956	149,313	431,643	34.8
2	580,956	165,988	414,968	32.3
3	580,956	164,328	416,628	30.8
4	580,956	155,301	425,655	32.3
5	580,956	161,994	418,962	33.2
6	580,956	154,054	426,902	32.5
7	580,957	156,656	424,301	33.3
8	580,956	149,421	431,535	31.0
9	580,956	160,070	420,886	31.4
10	580,956	146,863	434,093	33.4
11	580,956	136,711	444,245	35.4
12	580,956	138,093	442,863	34.1
13	580,956	138,511	442,445	30.5
14	580,956	171,993	408,963	30.8
15	580,956	162,732	418,224	31.9
16	580,956	146,737	434,219	33.9
State	9,295,297	2,458,765	6,836,532	32.6

Table 2 Voting-Age Persons

District	White*	Black*	American Indian, Eskimo, or Aleut*	Asian or Pacific Islander*	Other*	Hispanic*	Male*	Female*
1	96.5%	1.0%	2.0%	0.4%	0.1%	0.5%	49.3%	50.7%
2	93.8	4.0	0.6	0.5	1.2	2.5	48.4	51.6
3	90.9	6.7	0.5	0.8	1.2	2.2	48.1	51.9
4	97.4	1.1	0.6	0.4	0.6	1.4	48.6	51.4
5	90.5	7.2	0.5	0.4	1.4	2.7	47.3	52.7
6	89.9	8.1	0.5	0.9	0.7	1.4	47.3	52.7
7	92.7	5.5	0.4	0.5	0.9	2.0	48.7	51.3
8	91.4	5.3	0.6	1.6	1.2	2.4	48.0	52.0
9	81.8	15.7	0.5	0.9	1.0	2.4	47.5	52.5
10	96.9	1.8	0.4	0.6	0.3	1.1	47.7	52.3
11	93.6	3.9	0.2	2.0	0.2	1.1	47.9	52.1
12	93.9	3.5	0.3	2.1	0.2	1.1	47.3	52.7
13	86.3	10.0	0.4	2.9	0.5	1.6	48.1	51.9
14	33.3	65.3	0.3	0.9	0.3	1.0	44.2	55.8
15	28.7	68.2	0.4	0.7	2.1	3.7	45.4	54.6
16	97.0	1.3	0.4	0.8	0.5	2.1	47.7	52.3
State	84.9	12.8	0.5	1.0	0.8	1.8	47.6	52.4

*As percent of voting-age population.

Table 3 Voting-Age Persons by Age Groups

District	18-24*	25-44*	45-54*	55-64*	65 and over*
1	13.0%	40.0%	13.3%	12.6%	21.1%
2	13.5	43.5	14.0	11.7	17.3
3	15.3	46.5	12.7	10.4	15.1
4	16.8	39.9	14.3	12.2	16.7
5	13.0	41.8	14.6	12.6	18.0
6	15.8	42.1	13.9	11.6	16.6
7	13.4	43.5	14.6	11.9	16.6
8	19.0	44.9	14.2	9.8	12.1
9	15.0	47.1	14.7	10.6	12.6
10	13.2	44.3	14.1	12.2	16.1
11	10.8	44.7	15.3	13.0	16.2
12	12.7	44.0	14.6	12.0	16.7
13	19.9	46.2	13.0	9.7	11.3
14	15.7	44.2	12.8	11.0	16.3
15	15.1	41.6	11.9	11.9	19.5
16	12.9	43.0	14.0	12.7	17.4
State	14.7	43.6	13.9	11.6	16.2

*As percent of voting-age population.

Table 4 Income and Occupation

District	Median family income	Families in poverty	White collar*	Blue collar*	Service*	Farm*
1	$27,482	9.9%	49.3%	30.0%	17.9%	2.8%
2	33,251	8.8	47.8	35.7	13.6	3.0
3	37,093	7.2	54.5	31.2	12.9	1.4
4	30,754	11.3	49.5	32.3	15.0	3.2
5	31,422	12.5	48.0	34.5	14.7	2.9
6	33,578	10.2	52.8	31.1	13.5	2.6
7	34,694	8.8	50.4	33.0	14.2	2.4
8	42,821	7.2	59.9	25.2	13.4	1.5
9	40,647	11.8	55.4	30.3	13.3	1.0
10	42,003	5.2	55.4	31.6	12.1	1.0
11	56,234	2.2	73.3	17.8	8.3	0.6
12	45,143	4.5	63.2	25.3	11.1	0.4
13	44,509	6.5	61.6	24.5	13.2	0.8
14	28,875	21.9	53.5	27.9	18.1	0.5
15	19,738	32.6	50.7	28.5	20.2	0.6
16	40,922	6.8	53.2	32.7	13.2	0.8
State	36,652	10.2	55.5	29.3	13.7	1.6

*As percent of employed persons age 16 and over.

Table 5 Education: School Years Completed

District	Less than grade 9*	Grades 9-12 no diploma*	High school diploma*	College bachelor's degree or higher*
1	9.2%	13.8%	38.1%	14.5%
2	9.2	14.9	36.5	13.6
3	6.6	13.6	32.6	19.1
4	8.6	15.2	37.9	13.5

District	Less than grade 9*	Grades 9-12 no diploma*	High school diploma*	College bachelor's degree or higher*
5	10.0	16.3	37.8	10.7
6	8.1	14.7	32.0	18.6
7	7.0	14.8	35.7	13.9
8	4.8	11.2	28.4	24.1
9	6.2	15.8	30.9	17.7
10	7.0	15.7	35.1	12.8
11	3.5	8.8	24.5	34.4
12	6.9	14.5	30.5	19.9
13	5.4	13.0	27.0	27.3
14	8.9	21.9	29.0	12.5
15	14.2	27.2	25.9	11.1
16	8.8	17.2	34.7	12.9
State	7.8	15.5	32.3	17.4

As percent of persons age 25 and over.

Table 6 Housing and Residential Patterns

District	Owner occupied	Renter occupied	Urban	Rural
1	75.8%	24.2%	30.7%	69.3%
2	78.7	21.3	47.9	52.1
3	70.8	29.2	75.5	24.5
4	78.1	21.9	28.1	71.9
5	75.7	24.3	49.5	50.5
6	70.0	30.0	50.0	50.0
7	74.0	26.0	48.1	51.9
8	70.1	29.9	60.3	39.7
9	67.9	32.1	79.8	20.2
10	76.8	23.2	83.3	16.7
11	77.9	22.1	95.1	4.9
12	73.9	26.1	100.0	0.0
13	61.6	38.4	93.4	6.6
14	64.9	35.1	100.0	0.0
15	45.2	54.8	100.0	0.0
16	75.4	24.6	86.8	13.2
State	71.0	29.0	70.5	29.5

1st District

Upper Peninsula; Northern Lower Michigan

Built in 1957, the Mackinac Bridge connects the 1st's two regions—Michigan's upper peninsula (UP) and northern lower Michigan.

Above the Straits of Mackinac, the UP covers 315 miles of woodland, bordering Wisconsin and Canada. Three of the Great Lakes form its boundaries—Huron to the southeast, Michigan to the south and Superior to the north.

The UP's rugged terrain breeds a special brand of independence, qualities ascribed to the "Yoopers" that live here. They must contend with prevailing northwesterly winds that dump several hundred inches of snow every year in the northern reaches of the area. And economic opportunity has been in short supply since the mining industries began to fade at the turn of the century.

The western UP has been hit the hardest. The extraction of copper, iron and timber long supported the area, but mining is almost nonexistent and timber jobs have dwindled. Tourism and recreation are the only growth industries.

Known as "Copper Country," these western counties once produced about 90 percent of the copper mined in the United States. Back then, the mines—and forests—attracted Irish, German, Scandinavian and eastern European immigrants. But by 1890, most of the purest copper had been mined and prices began to fall.

Calumet, located in the northwestern arm of the UP, was once a booming copper-mining town of 50,000. Now it is a village of 4,000. On Lake Superior, Marquette tells the same story. Some shipping still departs from the city, but many of the ore docks are abandoned. Still, Marquette County is the UP's most populous.

Marquette's economy was hit hard again when K. I. Sawyer Air Force Base showed up on the 1993 base-closure list. The base's payroll for more than 3,600 military and civilian employees is responsible for about 20 percent of the local economy.

The descendants of the miners, loggers, mill workers and longshoremen retain a union-oriented tradition, thus making the western UP a Democratic stronghold. In the open 1992 House race, the Democratic candidate won every county north of the Straits of Mackinac—the dividing line between the UP and lower Michigan.

The UP's eastern section votes more like the counties south of the bridge. Chippewa and Mackinac counties lean Republican and are more dependent on tourism and farming. The only major city in this area is Sault Ste. Marie (Chippewa), a port city on the Canadian border. In 1992, Chippewa was the only UP county to vote for George Bush.

About half the district vote is cast on the Republican turf south of the bridge. The population center of northern lower Michigan is Traverse City (Grand Traverse County), a GOP stronghold. Tourists and vacationers come for the resorts, golf courses and sandy beaches of Grand Traverse Bay.

Outside the Traverse City area, the communities are a conservative lot, though newly arrived retired autoworkers have boosted the Democratic vote in Cheboygan, Emmet and Presque Isle counties.

Election Returns

	1st District	Democrat	Republican
1992	President*	118,879 (41.7%)	100,997 (35.4%)
	House	144,857 (53.9%)	117,056 (43.6%)
1990	Senate	106,751 (61.8%)	65,997 (38.2%)
	Governor	85,326 (48.8%)	89,424 (51.2%)
1988	President	115,027 (45.6%)	137,198 (54.4%)
	Senate	146,585 (63.8%)	83,073 (36.2%)
1986	Governor	114,949 (70.8%)	47,317 (29.2%)

Vote for Perot was 65,339 (22.9%).

Demographics

Population 580,956

Percent change from 1980 12.9%

Land area 22,766 square miles

Population per square mile 26

Counties, 1990 population

Alger	8,972	Baraga	7,954
Alpena	30,605	Benzie	12,200
Antrim	18,185	Charlevoix	21,468

Cheboygan 21,398	Keweenaw 1,701
Chippewa 34,604	Leelanau 16,527
Crawford (pt.) 3,212	Luce 5,763
Delta 37,780	Mackinac 10,674
Dickinson 26,831	Marquette 70,887
Emmet 25,040	Menominee 24,920
Gogebic 18,052	Montmorency 8,936
Grand Traverse 64,273	Ontonagon 8,854
Houghton 35,446	Otsego 17,957
Iron 13,175	Presque Isle 13,743
Kalkaska 13,497	Schoolcraft 8,302

Cities, 1990 population (10,000 or more)

Alpena 11,354	Sault Ste. Marie 14,689
Escanaba 13,659	Traverse City 15,155
Marquette 21,977	

Race and Hispanic origin
White 96.2%
Black 0.8%
American Indian, Eskimo, or Aleut. 2.4%
Asian or Pacific Islander 0.4%
Other 0.2%
Hispanic origin 0.6%

Ancestry

American 4.3%	German 28.5%
Belgian 1.1%	Irish 12.3%
Czechoslovakian 1.2%	Italian 4.5%
Dutch 3.5%	Norwegian 2.2%
English 15.3%	Polish 9.0%
Finnish 9.2%	Scotch Irish 1.7%
French 14.4%	Scottish 2.8%
French Canadian 2.5%	Swedish 7.0%

Universities/colleges, 1990-1991 enrollment
Alpena Community College, Alpena 2,309
Bay de Noc Community College, Escanaba 2,166
Gogebic Community College, Ironwood 1,340
Lake Superior State University, Sault Ste. Marie 3,407
Michigan Technological University, Houghton 6,497
North Central Michigan College, Petoskey 1,932
Northern Michigan University, Marquette 8,505
Northwestern Michigan College, Traverse City 4,391
Suomi College, Hancock 530

Newspapers, total circulation (in all districts)
Alpena News 12,035
Detroit News & Free Press 1,014,197
Escanaba Daily Press 10,862
Houghton Daily Mining Gazette 11,828
Iron Mountain Daily News 10,459
Marquette Mining Journal 18,304
Petoskey News-Review 10,818
Traverse City Record-Eagle 25,380

Commercial television stations, affiliations
ADI: Traverse City-Cadillac (42%), Marquette (33%), Green Bay-Appleton (18%), Duluth-Superior (5%) and Alpena (3%)
WTOM-TV, Cheboygan (NBC)
WJMN-TV, Escanaba (ABC)
WLUC-TV, Marquette (ABC)
WGTQ, Sault Ste. Marie (ABC)
WWUP-TV, Sault Ste. Marie (CBS)
WGTU, Traverse City (ABC)

Cable television systems, total subscribers
Bresnan Communications Inc.; Houghton 10,223
Bresnan Communications Inc.; Negaunee 16,000
C-Tec; Traverse City 16,397
Westmarc Cable; Alpena 8,097
Westmarc Cable; Petoskey 6,508

Military installations, 1991
K. I. Sawyer Air Force Base, Gwinn 3,672

Businesses and other major employers
Munson Medical Center; Traverse City 1,900
Cleveland-Cliffs Inc./Empire Mine; Palmer; copper ores 1,600
Escanaba Land Co.; Escanaba; paper mills 1,500
Marquette General Hospital; Marquette 1,500
Northern Michigan Hospitals/Little Traverse Div.; Petoskey 1,200
Michigan Technological University; Houghton 1,170
Empire Iron Mining Partnership/Empire Mine; Ishpeming; iron ores 1,100
Copper Range Co. Inc.; White Pine; copper ores 1,089
Northern Michigan University; Marquette 1,010
Tilden Magnetite Partnership/Tilden Mine; Ishpeming; iron ores 970
United Technologies Corp.; Traverse City; electrical equipment/supplies 750
State of Michigan/Corrections Dept.; Marquette 600
Grand Traverse Resort Village; Acme; hotel 585
Champion Intl. Corp./Quinnesec Mill; Quinnesec; building construction 550
Dickinson County Community Schools; Iron Mountain 550
Burns Clinic Medical Center; Petoskey 515
Marquette Area Public Schools; Marquette 515

2nd District

West — Holland; Muskegon

In terms of GOP hegemony, the 2nd is rivaled only by the 3rd District as the state's staunchest Republican district. From the fruit and vegetable farmers to the conservative Dutch communities on the 2nd's southern border, Democrats find little sympathy.

The district covers nearly 100 miles of Lake Michigan shoreline, from Manistee County south to Allegan County, but population is concentrated in three counties—Allegan, Muskegon and Ottawa.

The city of Holland, on the border between Allegan and Ottawa counties, is a GOP bastion with a strong Dutch influence. The westernmost point of the "Dutch Triangle" (formed by Holland, Grand Rapids and Kalamazoo), Holland and its environs were settled by immigrants from the Netherlands in the mid-19th century.

That heritage is highlighted at an entertainment complex—Dutch Village—where life in the Old Country is replicated, or at the city's two wooden shoe factories. In May, the city hosts a Tulip Festival.

Ottawa County has voted Republican in every presidential election since 1928. In 1988, it voted for George Bush by better than 3-to-1, and gave 68 percent to the GOP's ill-fated Senate nominee. Four years later, Bush took 59 percent, 22 points higher than his statewide average.

Three of the nation's four top office furniture makers are based in western Michigan, and the fourth has a major plant in the region. Two of the companies—Herman Miller and Haworth Inc.—have headquarters here.

The 2nd's limited Democratic strength is found north of Ottawa and Allegan counties in and around the industrial city of Muskegon. The city has one of western Michigan's heaviest manufacturing bases, including a number of primary metal industries (such as foundries), fabricated metal producers and machinery operations, all of which have been struggling.

The black inland precincts and the city's ethnic neighborhoods turn out a strong Democratic vote, though the surrounding suburbs often offset their votes. Heavily forested Lake and Manistee counties are also sources of Democratic votes, as is the small industrial city of Cadillac (Wexford County).

Tourism, farming and food-processing are the economic mainstays for the rest of the district. Towns along the Lake Michigan shoreline, such as Manistee, are heavily reliant on retirees, Chicago tourists and boaters who sail across the lake into their municipal marinas.

Cherries and asparagus are among the products grown by local farms and processed within the district. Fremont, in Newaygo County, is home to the international headquarters of Gerber baby foods. Much of the fresh produce used by Gerber is grown within a 100-mile radius of Fremont.

Election Returns

	2nd District	Democrat	Republican
1992	President*	95,342 (34.0%)	127,008 (45.3%)
	House	86,265 (35.0%)	155,577 (63.1%)
1990	Senate	82,500 (46.3%)	95,587 (53.7%)
	Governor	67,851 (37.8%)	111,682 (62.2%)
1988	President	87,792 (35.5%)	159,710 (64.5%)
	Senate	111,502 (47.8%)	121,619 (52.2%)
1986	Governor	90,700 (60.0%)	60,489 (40.0%)

*Vote for Perot was 58,258 (20.8%).

Demographics

Population 580,956

Percent change from 1980 12.9%

Land area 5,469 square miles

Population per square mile 106

Counties, 1990 population

Allegan (pt.) 72,792	Muskegon 158,983
Barry (pt.) 19,012	Newaygo 38,202
Lake 8,583	Oceana 22,454
Manistee 21,265	Ottawa 187,768
Mason 25,537	Wexford 26,360

Cities, 1990 population (10,000 or more)

Cadillac 10,104	Muskegon Heights 13,176
Grand Haven 11,951	Muskegon 40,283
Holland 30,745	Norton Shores 21,755
Jenison CDP 17,882	

Race and Hispanic origin
White 92.9%
Black 4.4%
American Indian, Eskimo, or Aleut. 0.6%
Asian or Pacific Islander 0.7%
Other 1.5%
Hispanic origin 3.0%

Ancestry

American 3.8%	Irish 12.6%
Danish 1.2%	Italian 1.9%
Dutch 25.5%	Norwegian 1.2%
English 14.2%	Polish 6.4%
French 6.1%	Scotch Irish 1.5%
French Canadian 1.5%	Scottish 1.9%
German 29.2%	Swedish 4.6%

Universities/colleges, 1990-1991 enrollment
Baker College of Muskegon, Muskegon 1,877
Grand Valley State University, Allendale 11,726
Hope College, Holland 2,813
Muskegon Community College, Muskegon 5,121
West Shore Community College, Scottville 1,305

Newspapers, total circulation (in all districts)
Battle Creek Enquirer 28,206
Detroit News & Free Press 1,014,197
Grand Haven Tribune 10,103
Grand Rapids Press 148,659
Holland Sentinel 19,278
Kalamazoo Gazette 64,709
Ludington News 7,251
Muskegon Chronicle 46,639

Commercial television stations, affiliations
ADI: Grand Rapids-Kalamazoo-Battle Creek (60%) and
        Traverse City-Cadillac (40%)
    WOOD, Grand Rapids (NBC)
    WXMI, Grand Rapids (Fox)
    WZZM-TV, Grand Rapids (ABC)
    WOTV, Battle Creek (ABC)
    WLLA, Kalamazoo (None)
    WWMT, Kalamazoo (CBS)
    WTLJ, Muskegon (None)
    WPBN-TV, Traverse City (NBC)

Cable television systems, total subscribers
C-Tec; Grand Haven 11,189
Continental Cablevision of Michigan; Holland 7,700
TCI Cablevision of West Michigan; Grand Rapids 117,385
Westmarc Cable; Muskegon 33,946

Businesses and other major employers
Herman Miller Inc.; Zeeland; office furniture 2,800
Haworth Inc.; Holland; office furniture 1,900
L. Perrigo Co.; Allegan; pharmaceuticals 1,500
Howmet Corp./Whitehall Casting Div.; Whitehall; iron/steel foundries 1,500
Gerber Products Co.; Fremont; baby food 1,200
Planters Life Savers Co.; Holland; candies 1,120
Sara Lee Corp./Bill Mar Foods; Zeeland; meat products 1,100
S. D. Warren Co./Scott Paper Co.; Muskegon; paper mills 1,070
Hackley Hospital & Medical Center; Muskegon 1,000

Holland Community Hospital; Holland 940

General Motors Corp./Rochester Div.; Coopersville; motor vehicles 925

Brunswick Bowling & Billiards Corp.; Muskegon; sporting equipment 900

Mercy Hospital; Muskegon 875

GTE North Inc.; Muskegon; telephone communications 860

Sealed Power Tech Ltd.; Muskegon; industrial machinery 830

Muskegon Public Schools; Muskegon 800

Grand Haven Public Schools; Grand Haven 750

Bradford-White Corp.; Middleville; household appliances 700

Knoll North America Inc.; Muskegon; office furniture 700

Albert Trostel & Sons Co./Eagle-Ottawa Leather Div.; Grand Haven; leather production 675

Prince Corp.; Holland; textile products 650

Grand Valley State University; Allendale 642

Murco Inc.; Plainwell; meat products 600

Donnelly Corp.; Holland; glass products 600

Hart & Cooley Inc.; Holland; metal products 600

Venturedyne Ltd./Thermotron Industries; Holland; industry machinery 600

Muskegon General Hospital; Muskegon 573

Kaydon Corp.; Muskegon; industry machinery 550

Four Winns Inc.; Cadillac; shipbuilding/repairing 550

Henry House Inc.; Holland; smoked meat products 530

3rd District

West Central — Grand Rapids

Politically, the Grand Rapids-based 3rd looks a lot like it did when Gerald R. Ford represented the area. Both the middle-class residents of the city and the farmers and small-town denizens of the surrounding counties make it a GOP stronghold.

Kent County is home to more than 85 percent of the population, most of whom live in Grand Rapids, Michigan's second-largest city. With its diversified economic base, the city was one of the few outside the Sunbelt to emerge relatively unscathed from the 1990-1991 recession.

Part of the reason can be attributed to the variety of products made in Kent County. The 10 largest employers count nine different industries, including footwear and leather products, fabricated metal products, office furniture, avionics systems, automotive stampings and children's apparel.

The furniture-making industry is one of Kent County's largest employers. Unlike the furniture industry of North Carolina, western Michigan's furniture makers mostly produce office furniture, much of it the metal variety.

Beginning with the 1970s invention of systems furniture, local companies prospered and experienced record growth. That slowed, however, by the the early 1990s as growth in office space stagnated and companies nationwide began to cut their white-collar work forces.

General Motors has a significant presence in Grand Rapids, but the city has not felt the same pain that southeastern Michigan has. Another major employer is the Amway Corp., a home- and personal-care products company whose Amway Grand Hotel dominates the newly emerging skyline. The DeVos family, which runs the company, is a leading financial supporter of the state Republican Party.

Grand Rapids has a sizable blue-collar work force—and a high number of black and Hispanic residents for western Michigan—many of whom have moved to townships north and south of the city. Still, it is not nearly enough to offset the GOP wave from the rest of the city and county.

The local GOP has two wings. The "Dutch Wing" is more conservative, made up of white-collar executives and the small Christian college communities. The "Ford Wing" is a more moderate brand of Republicanism, found mostly in the northeast, East Grand Rapids and Kentwood.

George Bush breezed in Kent County in 1992. Across the district, Bush won easily, carrying the 3rd with 47 percent.

Outside Kent, in Ionia County and part of Barry County, the 3rd is Republican and agriculture-oriented, though not fruit-producing like coastal western Michigan. Ionia County has no town or village even close to having 10,000 residents.

Flat, rural and Republican Barry County is home to Hastings, which boasts the distinction of being listed in a 1993 book as one of America's 100 best small towns.

Election Returns

	3rd District	Democrat	Republican
1992	President*	94,721 (34.3%)	128,677 (46.6%)
	House	95,927 (36.2%)	162,451 (61.3%)
1990	Senate	79,820 (47.7%)	87,380 (52.3%)
	Governor	59,342 (35.5%)	108,041 (64.5%)
1988	President	85,727 (36.3%)	150,037 (63.7%)
	Senate	109,067 (48.2%)	117,000 (51.8%)
1986	Governor	82,888 (58.2%)	59,560 (41.8%)

*Vote for Perot was 52,779 (19.1%).

Demographics

Population 580,956

Percent change from 1980 12.9%

Land area 1,665 square miles

Population per square mile 349

Counties, 1990 population

Barry (pt.) 23,301	Kent 500,631
Ionia 57,024	

Cities, 1990 population (10,000 or more)

Cutlerville CDP 11,228	Kentwood 37,826
East Grand Rapids 10,807	Northview CDP 13,712
Forest Hills CDP 16,690	Walker 17,279
Grand Rapids 189,126	Wyoming 63,891
Grandville 15,624	

Race and Hispanic origin
White 89.6%
Black 7.5%
American Indian, Eskimo, or Aleut. 0.5%
Asian or Pacific Islander 1.0%
Other 1.5%
Hispanic origin 2.8%

Ancestry

American 3.1%	Dutch 22.8%
Danish 1.0%	English 15.1%

French 5.4%
French Canadian 1.3%
German 29.3%
Irish 14.6%
Italian 2.6%
Polish 8.2%
Scotch Irish 1.5%
Scottish 2.1%
Swedish 2.8%

Universities/colleges, 1990-1991 enrollment

Aquinas College, Grand Rapids 2,633
Calvin College, Grand Rapids 4,260
Calvin Theological Seminary, Grand Rapids 228
Davenport College, Grand Rapids 3,827
Grand Rapids Baptist College, Grand Rapids 894
Grand Rapids Community College, Grand Rapids 12,054
Jordan College, Cedar Springs 2,322
Kendall College of Art & Design, Grand Rapids 701

Newspapers, total circulation (in all districts)

Battle Creek Enquirer 28,206
Detroit News & Free Press 1,014,197
Grand Rapids Press 148,659
Kalamazoo Gazette 64,709
Lansing State Journal 71,128

Commercial television stations, affiliations

ADI: Grand Rapids-Kalamazoo-Battle Creek (100%)

Cable television systems, total subscribers

TCI Cablevision of West Michigan; Grand Rapids 117,385

Businesses and other major employers

Steelcase Inc.; Grand Rapids; steel/padded office furniture 9,893
Amway Corp.; Ada; soaps/cleaners 5,300
Butterworth Hospital; Grand Rapids 2,732
General Motors Corp./CPC Div.; Grand Rapids; motor vehicles 2,700
Blodgett Memorial Medical Center; Grand Rapids 2,000
St. Mary's Health Services; Grand Rapids 2,000
Meijer Companies Ltd.; Grand Rapids; department stores 1,800
General Motors Corp./Inland Fisher Guide Div.; Grand Rapids; metal forgings/stampings 1,500
Spartan Stores Inc.; Grand Rapids; grocery products 1,400
General Motors Corp./Rochester Div.; Grand Rapids; engines 1,200
Knoll North America Inc.; Grand Rapids; office furniture 1,000
Foremost Corp. America; Caledonia; fire/marine/casualty insurance 1,000
City of Grand Rapids/Public Schools; Grand Rapids 1,000
Keeler Brass Co.; Grand Rapids; motor vehicle equipment 950
Metropolitan Hospital; Grand Rapids 900
Herald Co. Inc./Grand Rapids Press; Grand Rapids; newspapers 850
Amway Grand Plaza Hotel; Grand Rapids; hotel 850
Bissell Inc.; Grand Rapids; vacuum cleaners/household appliances 825
American Seating Co.; Grand Rapids; office furniture 800
Pine Rest Christian Hospital; Grand Rapids 790
Rapistan De Mag Corp.; Grand Rapids; construction machinery 733
Knape & Vogt Mfg. Co.; Grand Rapids; hardware 700
H. H. Cutler Co.; Grand Rapids; outerwear 700
Sears Roebuck & Co.; Grand Rapids; department stores 700

Foremost Insurance Co.; Grand Rapids; computer services 700
Calvin College & Theological Seminary; Grand Rapids 670
American Bumper & Mfg. Co.; Ionia; bumpers 665
Grand Rapids Community College; Grand Rapids 650
Diesel Technology Corp.; Grand Rapids; motor vehicle equipment 629
Steelcase Inc.; Caledonia; office furniture 625
Gordon Food Service Inc.; Grand Rapids; grocery products 600
Benteler Industries Inc./Tubular Products Div.; Grand Rapids; motor vehicle parts 600
Autodie Corp.; Grand Rapids; metalworking machinery 600
Rogers Dept. Store; Grand Rapids; family clothing stores 600
Gencorp Inc./Gencorp Automotive; Ionia; business services 600
Old Kent Bank & Trust Co.; Grand Rapids; commercial banks 587
Kent Community Hospital; Grand Rapids 574

4th District

North Central — Midland

While the 4th is Michigan's second-largest district in terms of land mass (after the massive 1st), most of the district's residents live in the southern half. North of Midland, much of the terrain is forested and sparsely populated. With few cities of size, most of the vote is cast in the small towns and farming communities that traditionally favor the GOP. Bill Clinton ran competitively in the 4th in 1992, but he is an exception to recent Democratic presidential nominees. In 1992, the GOP incumbent House member won every county.

Midland, the site of one of the largest single chemical complexes in the United States, is the 4th's population and industrial center. There, on 1,900 acres, the Dow Chemical Co. keeps its international headquarters and produces more than 500 products. Between Dow Chemical and the Dow Corning Corp., there are more than 13,000 employees in the Midland area. Dow Corning is the world's largest producer of silicone.

Accordingly, the Dow name is firmly stamped on Midland. Residents can browse at the Grace A. Dow Memorial Library or learn about the man who started it all at the Herbert H. Dow Historical Museum. Their son, Alden, designed many of the city's churches, homes, schools and business complexes. For botanists, there is Dow Gardens.

The company also sets the tone for Midland County's Republican politics, with GOP candidates running well. In 1992, George Bush carried Midland County rather easily.

South of Midland, the district is primarily agricultural. The second-leading source of votes in the 4th is Saginaw County, although the city of Saginaw belongs to the 5th. The city is heavily Democratic and unionized, but the farmers to the south and west generally favor Republicans.

Clinton County sports a fair number of Lansing commuters, but they, along with farmers and small-town voters, favor Republican candidates.

Owosso (Shiawassee County) and Alma (Gratiot County) are more traditional, small manufacturing cities. Gratiot tilts Republican, but both produce some Democratic votes.

Tourism and recreation fuel the economy north of these

areas. Local residents are more likely to travel farther north toward the upper peninsula for vacations, but many autoworkers from Michigan's industrial southeast favor the lakes and woodland of Montcalm and Mecosta counties.

Retirees from the southeastern cities have also made their mark in the far northern portion of the 4th. Counties such as Clare, Gladwin, Ogemaw and Roscommon are no longer routinely Republican; Blanchard carried three of the four in 1990 and Clinton carried all four in 1992.

Election Returns

	4th District	Democrat	Republican
1992	President*	104,709 (37.9%)	103,464 (37.5%)
	House	87,573 (34.8%)	157,337 (62.6%)
1990	Senate	87,836 (50.8%)	85,067 (49.2%)
	Governor	81,121 (47.1%)	91,129 (52.9%)
1988	President	97,495 (42.1%)	134,127 (57.9%)
	Senate	128,787 (58.4%)	91,865 (41.6%)
1986	Governor	109,853 (68.5%)	50,417 (31.5%)

*Vote for Perot was 67,873 (24.6%).

Demographics

Population 580,956

Percent change from 1980 12.9%

Land area 8,675 square miles

Population per square mile 67

Counties, 1990 population

Clare 24,952	Missaukee 12,147
Clinton 57,883	Montcalm 53,059
Crawford (pt.) 9,048	Ogemaw 18,681
Gladwin 21,896	Osceola 20,146
Gratiot 38,982	Oscoda 7,842
Isabella 54,624	Roscommon 19,776
Mecosta 37,308	Saginaw (pt.) 76,206
Midland 75,651	Shiawassee (pt.) 52,755

Cities, 1990 population (10,000 or more)

Big Rapids 12,603	Mount Pleasant 23,285
Midland (pt.) 37,819	Owosso 16,322

Race and Hispanic origin
White 97.1%
Black 1.1%
American Indian, Eskimo, or Aleut. 0.7%
Asian or Pacific Islander 0.4%
Other 0.7%
Hispanic origin 1.8%

Ancestry

American 5.2%	Irish 15.1%
Czechoslovakian 1.2%	Italian 2.1%
Danish 1.3%	Polish 5.8%
Dutch 5.7%	Scotch Irish 1.8%
English 18.7%	Scottish 3.0%
French 8.4%	Slovakian 1.4%
French Canadian 2.1%	Swedish 2.1%
German 39.1%	

Universities/colleges, 1990-1991 enrollment
Alma College, Alma 1,229
Baker College, Owosso 954
Central Michigan University, Mt. Pleasant 18,286
Ferris State University, Big Rapids 12,037
Kirtland Community College, Roscommon 1,271
Mid-Michigan Community College, Harrison 1,925
Montcalm Community College, Sidney 2,040
Northwood Institute, Midland 1,601

Newspapers, total circulation (in all districts)
Bay City Times 39,645
Detroit News & Free Press 1,014,197
Flint Journal 104,430
Grand Rapids Press 148,659
Greenville Daily News 7,910
Lansing State Journal 71,128
Midland Daily News 16,309
Mt. Pleasant Morning Sun 10,191
Saginaw News 57,255

Commercial television stations, affiliations
ADI: Flint-Saginaw-Bay City (50%), Traverse City-Cadillac (36%), Grand Rapids-Kalamazoo-Battle Creek (8%) and Lansing (7%)
WGKI, Cadillac (Fox)
WWTV, Cadillac (CBS)
WSMH, Flint (Fox)
WJRT-TV, Flint (ABC)
WAQP, Saginaw (None)

Cable television systems, total subscribers
Bresnan Communications Inc.; Midland 13,298
Cablevision Inc.; Mount Pleasant 5,000
Continental Cablevision of Michigan; Holt 56,500
Cox Cable Saginaw; Saginaw 30,700
Westmarc Cable; Owosso 6,191

Businesses and other major employers
Dow Chemical Co./Michigan Div.; Midland; organic chemicals 9,000
Dow Chemical Co./Dow Chemical U.S.A; Midland; plastics/synthetics 3,000
Central Michigan University; Mt. Pleasant 2,072
Dow Corning Corp.; Midland; plastics/synthetics 1,800
White Consolidated Industries/Westinghouse Inc.; Greenville; household appliances 1,700
Ferris State University; Big Rapids 1,537
Mid-Michigan Regional Medical Center; Midland 1,375
Acustar Inc./Evart Products Co.; Evart; plastics products 800
Meijer Inc.; Mt. Pleasant; department stores 800
Owosso Memorial Hospital; Owosso 700
Federal-Mogul Corp.; Greenville; motor vehicles/equipment 600
Meijer Inc.; Saginaw; grocery stores 600
Mt. Pleasant Regional Center; Mt. Pleasant 585
Federal-Mogul Corp./Powertrain Products Operation; St. Johns; machine tools 567
State of Michigan/Correctional Facility; Carson City 550
Gratiot Community Hospital; Alma 545
Delfield Co.; Mt. Pleasant; refrigeration 527

5th District

East — Saginaw; Bay City

The 5th covers more than 200 miles of Lake Huron shoreline, but population is centered along the Bay City-Saginaw corridor. There, the heavy Democratic vote is usually enough to offset the Republican-voting areas that outline the district.

Saginaw, the largest city in the 5th, has a manufacturing sector that includes a heavy General Motors presence. Accordingly, the United Auto Workers (UAW) union carries a big stick.

Outside the city, Saginaw County's rich agricultural land produces sugar beets, dry beans, corn and soybeans. The importance of such commodities—along with the auto industry's presence—make the North American Free Trade Agreement of great interest. Many sugar beet growers, for example, fear cheap sugar imports from Mexico.

UAW strength and a significant blue-collar base make the city a Democratic stronghold. Democrat Michael S. Dukakis carried Saginaw County by 3,215 votes in 1988, and Bill Clinton had a much easier time winning it in 1992.

The second-largest city in the 5th is Bay City (Bay County). Once situated in the midst of a vast pine forest, Bay City was weaned on the lumber industry. Inhabitants used to refer to their home as the "Lumber Capital of the World," in deference to the more than 50 mills that once operated here.

The economy now, like Saginaw's, is more reliant on heavy manufacturing. Its blue-collar workers make boats, auto parts, jet engine components and tubing. The city is also one of the Great Lakes' top-ranked ports in terms of waterborne tonnage.

Bay County voters are even more reliably Democratic than their neighbors in Saginaw County. In the 1992 open seat House race, the Democratic nominee won 75 percent of the county vote.

Forested Arenac County, north of Bay County, is a popular vacation spot and home to retired autoworkers. Their UAW loyalties are reflected at the ballot box, where Democrats usually prevail. In 1990, all four Democrats running for statewide office won in Arenac. Clinton captured the county in 1992.

North of Arenac, Alcona and Iosco counties are preferred weekend destinations for Detroit suburbanites. Military retirees from Wurtsmith Air Force Base help keep Iosco County competitive for the GOP, but in 1992, voters expressed their dissatisfaction over the scheduled shutdown of Wurtsmith by voting for Bill Clinton. Alcona County backed George Bush in 1992, along with the Republican candidate for the House.

The other source of GOP votes is in Michigan's Thumb. Once heavily forested, the vast flat reaches of the region produce sugar beets, dry beans, corn, wheat and dairy products; Sanilac and Huron are top dairy counties. Just as Saginaw and Bay City experienced population losses in the 1980s, the counties of the Thumb declined also, though not as dramatically. Along the Lake Huron coastline, small fishing villages and lakeside resorts dot the landscape.

Election Returns

	5th District	Democrat	Republican
1992	President*	118,699 (44.9%)	84,525 (32.0%)
	House	147,618 (60.3%)	93,098 (38.0%)
1990	Senate	99,460 (60.0%)	66,417 (40.0%)
	Governor	87,427 (52.5%)	79,102 (47.5%)
1988	President	120,462 (50.7%)	117,242 (49.3%)
	Senate	153,347 (67.6%)	73,510 (32.4%)
1986	Governor	117,000 (74.3%)	40,429 (25.7%)

*Vote for Perot was 60,990 (23.1%).

Demographics

Population 580,956

Percent change from 1980 12.9%

Land area 5,454 square miles

Population per square mile 107

Counties, 1990 population
Alcona 10,145	Iosco 30,209
Arenac 14,931	Lapeer (pt.) 33,584
Bay 111,723	Saginaw (pt.) 135,740
Genesee (pt.) 114,247	Sanilac 39,928
Huron 34,951	Tuscola 55,498

Cities, 1990 population (10,000 or more)
Bay City 38,936	Saginaw South CDP
Beecher CDP 14,465	13,987
Saginaw North CDP	Saginaw 69,512
23,018	

Race and Hispanic origin
White 88.9%
Black 8.4%
American Indian, Eskimo, or Aleut. 0.6%
Asian or Pacific Islander 0.5%
Other 1.7%
Hispanic origin 3.4%

Ancestry
American 3.7%	Irish 13.8%
Dutch 3.0%	Italian 2.1%
English 14.8%	Polish 12.0%
French 10.9%	Scotch Irish 1.7%
French Canadian 2.8%	Scottish 3.0%
German 36.8%	Swedish 1.2%
Hungarian 1.4%	

Universities/colleges, 1990-1991 enrollment
Delta College, University Center 11,118
Great Lakes Business College, Saginaw 2,082
Saginaw Valley State University, University Center 6,185

Newspapers, total circulation (in all districts)
Bay City Times 39,645
Detroit News & Free Press 1,014,197
Flint Journal 104,430
Huron Daily Tribune 8,343
Port Huron Times Herald 30,214
Saginaw News 57,255

Commercial television stations, affiliations
ADI: Flint-Saginaw-Bay City (81%), Alpena (13%) and Detroit (7%)
WBKB-TV, Alpena (CBS)
WNEM-TV, Bay City-Saginaw-Flint (NBC)
WEYI-TV, Saginaw (CBS)

Cable television systems, total subscribers
Bresnan Communications Inc.; Essexville   22,655
Comcast Cablevision; Burton   77,224
Cox Cable Saginaw; Saginaw   30,700
Tele-Media Co.; Oscoda   10,947

Military installations, 1991
Wurtsmith Air Force Base, Oscoda   3,276

Businesses and other major employers
General Motors Corp./Saginaw Div.; Saginaw; motor vehicles   10,000
General Motors Corp./Saginaw Grey Iron Plant; Saginaw; iron/steel foundries   3,000
General Motors Corp./CPC Headquarters; Bay City; metal forgings/stampings   1,800
St. Mary's Medical Center of Saginaw; Saginaw   1,756
General Motors Corp./Delco Chassis Div.; Saginaw; motor vehicles/equipment   1,600
Bay Medical Center; Bay City   1,600
General Motors Corp./Inland Fisher Guide Div.; Flint; hardware   1,500
General Motors Corp./Central Foundry Div.; Saginaw; nonferrous foundries (castings)   1,350
St. Luke's Hospital; Saginaw   1,350
Saginaw General Hospital; Saginaw   1,300
Delta College; University Center   1,200
Active Tool & Mfg. Co.; Elkton; metal forgings/stampings   845
County of Saginaw; Saginaw   790
Caro Regional Mental Health Center; Caro; nursing   700
Meijer Inc.; Bay City; grocery stores   650
Saginaw Valley State University, University Center   600
Saginaw Township Community Schools; Saginaw   600
Guardian Industries Corp.; Carrollton; flat glass   550

6th District

Southwest — Kalamazoo; Benton Harbor; St. Joseph

Nestled in the southwestern corner of Michigan, bordered to the west by Lake Michigan and to the south by Indiana, the 6th is prime agricultural and Republican turf.

With 80,000 residents, Kalamazoo is the largest city in the 6th by far. A significant manufacturing sector provides the base for a strong union presence and blue-collar vote, despite the scheduled closure of Kalamazoo County's second-largest employer, a General Motors body-stamping plant. Other employers make printing and packaging paper, aircraft components, automotive parts and medical equipment.

The Upjohn Co., maker of pharmaceuticals, medical equipment and chemicals, has its worldwide headquarters in Portage, just outside the city of Kalamazoo.

Education and health-care services also have emerged as major employers. The city has a large academic community that includes the students of Western Michigan University and Kalamazoo College (28,200 combined).

The area's Dutch heritage, when combined with corporate managers and the agriculture-oriented townships on the outskirts of Kalamazoo County, helps turn out a moderate-to-conservative vote. GOP Rep. Fred Upton easily carried the county in 1992, but Bill Clinton also won here. Split tickets were also the rule in 1990, when Kalamazoo County, voted for Republican John

Engler for governor while sticking with Democratic Carl Levin in the Senate race.

The twin cities of Benton Harbor and St. Joseph make Berrien County the second-most populous in the district. Outside these cities, fruits and berries are grown; there is some food-processing industry. The area along the wooded Lake Michigan shoreline, where many affluent Chicagoans maintain second homes and vacation cottages, is known as "Harbor Country."

The cities are more geared toward industry. Separated by the St. Joseph River, more populous Benton Harbor and St. Joseph eye each other warily. Benton Harbor—once a stop along the Underground Railroad—is more than 90 percent black; St. Joseph is more than 90 percent white.

St. Joseph used to be a bedroom community for Benton Harbor, but a migration of Southern blacks to nearby fruit farms sparked a wave of white flight to St. Joseph. Today, St. Joseph is noticeably more prosperous and less gripped by urban decline.

Democrats run well in this area, but votes for them usually are negated by the rural voters and retirees of the outlying Republican towns. Both Engler and the GOP candidate for the Senate won Berrien County in 1990; in 1992, the county stuck with George Bush.

The flat croplands of Republican Cass and St. Joseph counties form the northeastern edge of the Corn Belt. Dowagiac (Cass) and Three Rivers (St. Joseph) have some industry, but the workers are conservative Democrats at best.

Election Returns

	6th District	Democrat	Republican
1992	President*	100,683 (39.7%)	97,200 (38.3%)
	House	89,020 (38.2%)	144,083 (61.8%)
1990	Senate	65,229 (47.3%)	72,567 (52.7%)
	Governor	60,220 (42.9%)	80,190 (57.1%)
1988	President	87,493 (40.7%)	127,330 (59.3%)
	Senate	100,637 (49.8%)	101,278 (50.2%)
1986	Governor	84,351 (64.7%)	45,961 (35.3%)

Vote for Perot was 55,667 (22.0%).

Demographics

Population   580,956

Percent change from 1980   12.9%

Land area   2,907 square miles

Population per square mile   200

Counties, 1990 population
Allegan (pt.)   17,717   Kalamazoo   223,411
Berrien   161,378   St. Joseph   58,913
Cass   49,477   Van Buren   70,060

Cities, 1990 population (10,000 or more)
Benton Harbor   12,818   Portage   41,042
Kalamazoo   80,277   Sturgis   10,130
Niles   12,458

Race and Hispanic origin
White   88.1%
Black   9.5%
American Indian, Eskimo, or Aleut.   0.5%

Asian or Pacific Islander 0.9%
Other 0.8%
Hispanic origin 1.8%

Ancestry

American 4.3%	Irish 15.8%
Dutch 10.7%	Italian 2.9%
English 16.1%	Polish 5.1%
French 4.8%	Scotch Irish 1.8%
French Canadian 1.1%	Scottish 2.4%
German 34.9%	Swedish 2.5%

Universities/colleges, 1990-1991 enrollment

Andrews University, Berrien Springs 2,877
Davenport College, Kalamazoo 1,443
Glen Oaks Community College, Centreville 1,428
Kalamazoo College, Kalamazoo 1,263
Kalamazoo Valley Community College, Kalamazoo 10,495
Lake Michigan College, Benton Harbor 3,422
Nazareth College, Kalamazoo 638
Southwestern Michigan College, Dowagiac 2,551
Western Michigan University, Kalamazoo 26,995

Newspapers, total circulation (in all districts)

Benton Harbor Herald-Palladium 33,142
Chicago Tribune 721,559
Detroit News & Free Press 1,014,197
Kalamazoo Gazette 64,709
South Bend Tribune 85,870

Commercial television stations, affiliations

ADI: Grand Rapids-Kalamazoo-Battle Creek (63%) and South Bend-Elkhart (37%)

Cable television systems, total subscribers

Cablevision of Michigan; Kalamazoo 39,000
Consolidated Cable; St. Joseph 8,467
Westmarc Cable; Niles 8,704
Westmarc Cable; St. Joseph 8,059

Businesses and other major employers

General Motors Corp./Buick-Oldsmobile-Cadillac Div.; Kalamazoo; motor vehicle stampings 3,400
Indiana Michigan Power Co./Cook Nuclear Power Plant; Bridgman; electric services 3,000
Western Michigan University; Kalamazoo 3,000
Andrews University; Berrien Springs 1,900
Borgess Medical Center Inc.; Kalamazoo 1,839
Bronson Methodist Hospital; Kalamazoo 1,784
Whirlpool Corp.; Benton Harbor; household appliances 1,600
Meijer Inc.; Kalamazoo; grocery stores 1,550
Heath Co. Delaware/Zenith Educational Systems; St. Joseph; computer/office equipment 1,500
Zenith Electronics Corp./Zenith Data Support Group; St. Joseph; professional/commercial equipment 1,400
James River Corp. Virginia; Kalamazoo; plastics products 1,250
Pneumo Abex Corp./NWL Control Systems; Kalamazoo; aircraft/parts 1,200
Allied-Signal Inc./Bendix Auto Systems Group; St. Joseph; motor vehicle equipment 1,100
Mercy-Memorial Medical Center; St. Joseph 1,042
Grumman Allied Industries Inc./Grumman-Olson Div.; Sturgis; motor vehicle parts/equipment 1,000
City of Kalamazoo; Kalamazoo 950

Cooper Industries Inc./Kirsch Co. Div.; Sturgis; furniture/fixtures 900
Kalamazoo Regional Psychiatric Hospital; Kalamazoo 900
Checker Motors Co.; Kalamazoo; metal stampings 750
Leco Corp./Tem-Press Div.; Saint Joseph; lab apparatus 750
National-Standard Co.; Niles; steel products 730
Michigan National Bank; Cassopolis; commercial banks 700
Eaton Corp./Medium Duty Transmission Div.; Galesburg; motor vehicle parts 650
Long Corn Detasseling; White Pigeon; grains 600
General Motors Corp./Saginaw Div.; Three Rivers; motor vehicles 600
Upjohn Co.; Kalamazoo; pharmaceuticals 600
U.S. Postal Service; Kalamazoo 600
Mercy-Memorial Medical Center; Benton Harbor 536
United Tech Auto Holdings; Niles; motor vehicle parts 525
Sealed Power Tech Ltd./Contech Div.; Dowagiac; nonferrous foundries (castings) 515

7th District

South Central — Battle Creek; Jackson

When Bill Clinton carried the Republican 7th by 600 votes in 1992, it was less an indication of his popularity than a protest vote against George Bush. This is a district of conservative small towns and agricultural communities, with a few midsize cities thrown in for good measure. In 1990, GOP challenger John Engler won every county in the 7th against Democratic incumbent Gov. James J. Blanchard. In 1992's open-seat House race, Democrats did not even bother to put up a candidate.

Battle Creek, or "Cereal City," is the largest city in the 7th. It is the home of "Tony the Tiger" of Frosted Flakes fame and to the breakfast cereal plants that employ many of the city's residents.

The Kellogg Co., headquartered in Battle Creek, is the top individual employer and a prominent force in the city. The federal government also has a heavy local presence; almost half the federal employees work at a Veterans Administration medical center.

Besides the money that Kellogg has poured into civic improvements, the company also left its imprint on local government. In the early 1980s, Kellogg told Battle Creek in no uncertain terms to merge the city and Battle Creek Township governments. Fearful that the company would move its headquarters, the city annexed the township, adding 21,000 residents to its population.

With a fair amount of blue-collar Democrats, Battle Creek often makes Calhoun County competitive for Democrats. Outside the city, the vote of corporate executives and outlying small towns tilts Republican. In 1992, Clinton posted 44 percent in Calhoun County, his best showing in the district.

About an hour's drive away on I-94, the industrial city of Jackson is another source of Democratic votes. The city is smaller in population than Battle Creek, but as a whole, Jackson is the most populous county wholly within the 7th.

Layoffs at the tool-and-die and auto parts shops have caused some pain in the city, but Bush was able to carry Jackson County in 1992 on the strength of the outlying towns and farming areas.

In 1992 Bush drew some support from city-based Democrats—a socially conservative lot, with a tendency to pull the lever for the GOP at the presidential level. Unlike Detroit's autoworkers, many of those living here have roots in the surrounding Republican countryside.

Bush also carried Eaton County. Small-town conservatives and Republican white-collar executives who work in Lansing (which is in the neighboring 8th District) boosted Bush to 39 percent.

Next door to Eaton County, Barry County is divided among the 2nd, 3rd and 7th districts. The southwestern 7th portion provides fewer than 5,000 votes.

The agricultural flatland of Branch, Hillsdale, Jackson and Lenawee counties long has been fertile ground for the GOP. Until Bush lost in Lenawee County in 1992, all four counties on the northern edge of the Corn Belt had voted Republican in presidential contests since 1964.

Election Returns

	7th District	Democrat	Republican
1992	President*	96,940 (37.9%)	96,336 (37.6%)
	House †	—	133,972 (87.7%)
1990	Senate	82,238 (52.5%)	74,473 (47.5%)
	Governor	69,511 (44.0%)	88,357 (56.0%)
1988	President	87,603 (40.0%)	131,207 (60.0%)
	Senate	111,542 (54.1%)	94,616 (45.9%)
1986	Governor	96,694 (66.9%)	47,766 (33.1%)

*Vote for Perot was 62,673 (24.5%).   †Independent/other is greater than 5%.

Demographics

Population 580,957

Percent change from 1980 12.9%

Land area 4,137 square miles

Population per square mile 140

Counties, 1990 population

Barry (pt.) 7,744	Hillsdale 43,431
Branch 41,502	Jackson 149,756
Calhoun 135,982	Lenawee 91,476
Eaton 92,879	Washtenaw (pt.) 18,187

Cities, 1990 population (10,000 or more)

Adrian 22,097	Jackson 37,446
Albion 10,066	Waverly CDP 15,614
Battle Creek 53,540	

Race and Hispanic origin

White 92.3%
Black 5.6%
American Indian, Eskimo, or Aleut. 0.4%
Asian or Pacific Islander 0.5%
Other 1.1%
Hispanic origin 2.4%

Ancestry

American 5.2%	Irish 16.7%
Dutch 5.7%	Italian 2.3%
English 20.2%	Polish 5.2%
French 5.8%	Scotch Irish 1.7%
French Canadian 1.4%	Scottish 2.6%
German 36.8%	Swedish 1.6%

Universities/colleges, 1990-1991 enrollment

Adrian College, Adrian 1,180
Albion College, Albion 1,569
Hillsdale College, Hillsdale 1,110
Jackson Community College, Jackson 6,493
Kellogg Community College, Battle Creek 5,816
Olivet College, Olivet 754
Siena Heights College, Adrian 1,837
Spring Arbor College, Spring Arbor 1,645

Newspapers, total circulation (in all districts)

Adrian Telegram 16,256
Ann Arbor News 51,727
Battle Creek Enquirer 28,206
Detroit News & Free Press 1,014,197
Jackson Citizen Patriot 37,170
Lansing State Journal 71,128
Toledo Blade 150,637
Ypsilanti Press 14,840

Commercial television stations, affiliations

ADI: Lansing (45%), Grand Rapids-Kalamazoo-Battle Creek (33%), Toledo (18%) and Detroit (4%)
WSYM-TV, Lansing (Fox)
WLAJ, Lansing (ABC)

Cable television systems, total subscribers

Continental Cablevision of Michigan; Holt 56,500
Continental Cablevision of Michigan; Jackson 15,350
Mercom Inc.; Coldwater 7,915
Summit-Leoni Cable TV; Summit Township 12,464
TCI Cablevision of Michigan; Battle Creek 23,494
Westmarc Cable; Adrian 9,325

Military installations, 1991

W. K. Kellogg Regional Airport Air Force Guard Station, Battle Creek 250

Businesses and other major employers

Kellogg Co.; Battle Creek; grain mill products 3,000
Consumers Power Co.; Jackson; electric services 2,500
State of Michigan/Resident Store; Jackson 2,000
Battle Creek Health System; Battle Creek 1,600
U.S. Veterans Affairs Dept.; Battle Creek; hospital 1,500
W. A. Foote Memorial Hospital; Jackson 1,469
Tecumseh Products Co.; Tecumseh; refrigeration 1,400
State Farm Fire Casualty Co.; Marshall; fire/marine/casualty insurance 1,355
Kraft General Foods Inc./Post Div.; Battle Creek; grain mill products 1,300
Battle Creek Public Schools; Battle Creek 1,200
Meijer Inc.; Lansing; grocery products 1,100
Nippondenso Mfg. USA; Battle Creek; motor vehicles 1,082
General Motors Corp./Warehousing & Distributing Div.; Lansing; motor vehicles 1,024
General Motors Corp./Inland Div.; Adrian; motor vehicles 1,000
David J. Stanton & Assoc./Wendy's Restaurants; Jackson; fast-food chain 1,000
Aeroquip Corp./Aerospace Div.; Jackson; aircraft/parts 850
Auto Owners Insurance Co.; Lansing; life insurance 810
Emma L. Bixby Hospital; Adrian 800
Ypsilanti Regional Psychatric Hospital; Ypsilanti 750
Eaton Corp./Fluid Power Div.; Marshall; motor vehicle equipment 700

Meijer Inc.; Jackson; grocery stores 700
Jackson Community College; Jackson 669
Jacobson Stores Inc.; Jackson; department stores 650
Michigan Farm Bureau; Lansing; membership organizations 650
Community Health Center; Coldwater 620
County of Jackson; Jackson 605
Harvard Industries Inc./Albion Div.; Albion; iron/steel foundries 600
Meijer Inc.; Battle Creek; department stores 600
State of Michigan/Charles L. Egeler Facility; Jackson 600
Libbey-Owens-Ford Co./Modular Products; Clinton; flat glass 520

8th District

Central — Part of Lansing

The 8th reaches from the state capital of Lansing to the outskirts of Flint and Ann Arbor, but the majority of voters live in just two counties, Ingham (Lansing) and Livingston. Between them, they hold almost 70 percent of the district population. While Bill Clinton and the Democratic House candidate won here in 1992, the district has a Republican character.

Residents of Lansing, the largest city in the 8th, live by the area's three Cs: cars, campus and the Capitol. General Motors is the city's largest employer, employing more than 20,000 workers who build Pontiacs, Buicks and Oldsmobiles. Ransom Eli Olds founded his Olds Motor Vehicle Co. here in 1897, at first turning out horseless carriages.

The state Capitol complex is the next largest employer, followed by Michigan State University in East Lansing. The 44,000 students are a source of Democratic votes, which, when combined with autoworkers, state employees and the university faculty who live in places such as Okemos Township, tilts Ingham County toward Democrats.

Livingston County retains much of its agricultural character, despite a population influx over the past two decades. In the 1970s, Livingston was the state's second-fastest-growing county, though growth slowed in the 1980s. Many of these new residents were whites fleeing Detroit, Flint, Lansing and Pontiac.

Much of the vote comes from small towns and farming communities such as Fowlerville and Howell, which celebrates the muskmelon harvest with its annual Melon Festival.

The county's traditional conservatism has not been affected by the newcomers. Settled by German Protestant farmers, it was a center of German American Bund activism in the 1930s. In 1990, GOP challenger John Engler won 62 percent against Democratic Gov. James J. Blanchard; the Republican nominee for the Senate also carried the county that year, though he won just 41 percent statewide. In 1992, Clinton garnered just 29 percent in Livingston.

The rest of the district includes parts of Genesee, Oakland, Shiawassee and Washtenaw counties. The Genesee portion takes in the southwestern part of the county, reaching to the Flint city limits. The strongly Democratic heritage of Flint spills over into these areas, and they turn out a Democratic vote.

The northwestern Washtenaw County portion, starting from the edge of Ann Arbor, is mostly small townships and part of the city of Saline. Unlike the Democratic university community in Ann Arbor, these areas prefer Republican candidates. Bush carried the county in 1992.

The small segment of Oakland County in the district adds a small number of voters, most of whom vote the same way the rest of the county does—Republican.

Election Returns

	8th District	Democrat	Republican
1992	President*	117,654 (40.7%)	103,725 (35.8%)
	House †	135,517 (47.6%)	131,906 (46.3%)
1990	Senate	126,849 (61.0%)	81,133 (39.0%)
	Governor	111,977 (54.1%)	95,090 (45.9%)
1988	President	150,282 (49.8%)	151,276 (50.2%)
	Senate	190,834 (64.8%)	103,507 (35.2%)
1986	Governor	138,694 (72.2%)	53,445 (27.8%)

*Vote for Perot was 67,983 (23.5%).   †Independent/other is greater than 5%.

Demographics

Population 580,956

Percent change from 1980 12.9%

Land area 1,942 square miles

Population per square mile 299

Counties, 1990 population
Genesee (pt.) 101,381   Oakland (pt.) 13,778
Ingham 281,912   Shiawassee (pt.) 17,015
Livingston 115,645   Washtenaw (pt.) 51,225

Cities, 1990 population (10,000 or more)
East Lansing 50,677   Lansing (pt.) 122,700
Haslett CDP 10,230   Okemos CDP 20,216
Holt CDP 11,744

Race and Hispanic origin
White 90.4%
Black 5.8%
American Indian, Eskimo, or Aleut. 0.6%
Asian or Pacific Islander 1.7%
Other 1.4%
Hispanic origin 2.9%

Ancestry
American 3.7%   Irish 16.7%
Dutch 4.2%   Italian 3.5%
English 19.6%   Polish 7.0%
Finnish 1.0%   Scotch Irish 2.1%
French 6.9%   Scottish 3.7%
French Canadian 2.3%   Slovakian 1.0%
German 34.0%   Swedish 2.1%
Hungarian 1.2%

Universities/colleges, 1990-1991 enrollment
Baker College, Flint 3,506
Davenport College Lansing, Lansing 1,446
Lansing Community College, Lansing 22,349
Michigan State University, East Lansing 44,317
Thomas M. Cooley Law School, Lansing 1,542
Washtenaw Community College, Ann Arbor 10,977

Newspapers, total circulation (in all districts)
Ann Arbor News 51,727
Detroit News & Free Press 1,014,197
Flint Journal 104,430

Lansing State Journal 71,128
Oakland Press 73,533
Ypsilanti Press 14,840

Commercial television stations, affiliations

ADI: Detroit (53%), Lansing (28%) and Flint-Saginaw-Bay City (19%)

WBSX, Ann Arbor (None)

WLNS-TV, Lansing (CBS)

WILX-TV, Lansing-Onondaga (NBC)

Cable television systems, total subscribers

Columbia Cable; Ann Arbor 49,500

Columbia Cable; Brighton 9,600

Comcast Cablevision; Burton 77,224

Continental Cablevision of Michigan; Holt 56,500

DF Cablevision; Fenton 6,900

United Cable TV; East Lansing 18,400

Businesses and other major employers

Michigan State University; East Lansing 11,000

State of Michigan/Transportation Dept.; Lansing 4,000

General Motors Corp./Fisher Body Co. Div.; Lansing; metal forgings/stampings 3,000

State of Michigan/Police Dept.; East Lansing 3,000

Edward W. Sparrow Hospital Assn.; Lansing 3,000

Ford Motor Co./Plastics Paint & Vinyl Div.; Saline; motor vehicles/equipment 2,400

General Motors Corp./Parts Div.; Flint; motor vehicle parts/supplies 2,337

St. Joseph Mercy Hospital; Ann Arbor 2,050

Lansing Community College; Lansing 2,050

State of Michigan/Social Serivce Dept.; Lansing 2,000

Ingham Medical Center Corp.; Lansing 1,800

State of Michigan/Public Health Dept.; Lansing 1,500

State of Michigan/Treasury Dept.; Lansing 1,450

State of Michigan/Management & Budget Dept.; Lansing 1,300

County of Ingham; Mason 1,200

Alberici/Clark; Lansing; heavy construction 1,160

Citizens Insurance Co. of America; Howell; fire/marine/casualty insurance 1,012

State of Michigan/Natural Resources Dept.; Lansing 1,000

State of Michigan/Labor Dept.; Lansing 1,000

Lansing General Hospital Inc.; Lansing 950

City of Lansing/Water & Light Board; Lansing; water supply 900

Combined Insurance Co. of America; Okemos; life insurance 875

Chelsea Community Hospital; Chelsea 800

University Microfilms Inc.; Ann Arbor; microfilms & publishing 759

Meijer Inc./Thrifty Acres; Lansing; department stores 750

City of East Lansing/Board of Education; East Lansing 700

Electronic Data Systems Corp.; Lansing; computer services 700

City of Lansing; Lansing 700

McPherson Hospital; Howell 695

Creative Industries Group Inc./Cars & Concepts; Brighton; motor vehicles/equipment 675

Vemco Inc.; Grand Blanc; plastics products 600

Michigan Bell Telephone Co.; Lansing; telephone communications 600

Sears Roebuck & Co.; Flint; department stores 600

Gelman Sciences Inc.; Ann Arbor; measuring/controlling devices 560

Chrysler Corp./Chrysler Proving Grounds; Chelsea; research services 550

Consumers Power Co.; Lansing; utility services 540

9th District

East Central — Flint; Pontiac

Nearly any conversation about the city of Flint nowadays invariably includes mention of the 1989 documentary *Roger and Me*. Produced by a local filmmaker, it painted a scathing portrait of General Motors (GM) and the effects of its massive layoffs on this company town.

This was the birthplace of GM in 1908, and later, the United Auto Workers (UAW). Thirty years after the first plant opening, the modern labor movement sprouted forth from UAW sit-down strikes that paralyzed two GM factories.

At its employment peak, 80,000 people worked at Flint's GM plants. Today, that number is close to 40,000, with little hope of recovery. No longer do residents enjoy the benefits of what used to be GM's "womb to tomb" paternalism. However, when Chrysler begins operations here in 1995, the 9th will have nearly 100,000 autoworkers—more than in any district.

Abandoned neighborhoods and shuttered businesses reflect the city's population decline. The city has tried valiantly to retain its residents and draw in visitors through numerous civic projects, but unemployment remains high and tourism revenues low.

The UAW is still potent, although it has suffered as members have moved in search of jobs. The city continues to be a Democratic bastion, but the outlying Genesee County vote is less partisan.

In 1984, Ronald Reagan managed to win Genesee, but in 1988 and 1992, the county voted for a Democrat for president. Flint's high unemployment rates spurred a backlash against George Bush in 1992, when he won 24 percent in Genesee, barely enough to squeak by Ross Perot.

Michigan's 1992 redistricting radically redrew the district, so that Genesee is divided among the 5th, 8th and 9th districts. Only Flint, Grand Blanc and the southeastern portion of the county remain in the 9th. Flint is still the largest city in the district, but the bulk of the vote now comes from Republican Oakland County.

Pontiac, Oakland's largest city in the 9th, is made up of low-income blacks, Hispanics and socially conservative whites, whose families migrated from the South to work in the auto industry. They lean Democratic but are more independent than their counterparts in Flint.

Outside Pontiac, the townships in the northeastern corner of the county are less developed and more Republican. The GOP vote from areas such as Auburn Hills and Rochester, along with Addison, Orion and Oakland townships, counters the Flint vote and keeps the district competitive for Republicans. In 1992, Democratic Rep. Dale Kildee faced the closest race of his career, in part because his GOP opponent racked up 57 percent in Oakland County.

Lapeer County, whose southern half is in the district, is also less-than-receptive to Democratic candidates. Eastern Lapeer has a more Democratic cast, a vestige of Flint-UAW spillover, but the county as a whole is more rural than the rest of the district.

The rural Republican vote is often enough to tilt the county toward the GOP side as it did in 1992, when Bush and the GOP House challenger won here.

Election Returns

	9th District	Democrat	Republican
1992	President*	117,872 (44.4%)	92,262 (34.8%)
	House	133,956 (53.7%)	111,798 (44.8%)
1990	Senate	59,927 (54.0%)	51,061 (46.0%)
	Governor	46,704 (42.1%)	64,253 (57.9%)
1988	President	61,768 (40.0%)	92,533 (60.0%)
	Senate	84,882 (57.3%)	63,280 (42.7%)
1986	Governor	62,875 (64.9%)	33,971 (35.1%)

*Vote for Perot was 55,077 (20.8%).

Demographics

Population 580,956

Percent change from 1980 12.9%

Land area 816 square miles

Population per square mile 712

Counties, 1990 population
Genesee (pt.) 214,831   Oakland (pt.) 324,941
Lapeer (pt.) 41,184

Cities, 1990 population (10,000 or more)
Auburn Hills 17,076   Rochester Hills 61,766
Burton 27,617   Waterford CDP (pt.)
Flint (pt.) 140,761   66,692
Pontiac 71,166

Race and Hispanic origin
White 79.4%
Black 17.8%
American Indian, Eskimo, or Aleut. 0.6%
Asian or Pacific Islander 1.0%
Other 1.2%
Hispanic origin 2.8%

Ancestry
American 4.5%   Irish 15.5%
Dutch 2.8%   Italian 3.9%
English 15.8%   Polish 7.2%
French 6.9%   Scotch Irish 1.9%
French Canadian 2.5%   Scottish 3.4%
German 26.9%   Slovakian 1.0%
Hungarian 1.2%   Swedish 1.6%

Universities/colleges, 1990-1991 enrollment
Charles Mott Community College, Flint 9,965
Detroit College of Business, Flint 902
General Motors Institute, Flint 3,204
Michigan Christian College, Rochester Hills 268
Oakland University, Rochester Hills 12,400
University of Michigan, Flint 6,593

Newspapers, total circulation (in all districts)
Detroit News & Free Press 1,014,197
Flint Journal 104,430
Oakland Press 73,533

Commercial television stations, affiliations
ADI: Detroit (83%) and Flint-Saginaw-Bay Cty (17%)

Cable television systems, total subscribers
Comcast Cablevision; Burton 77,224
Comcast Cablevision; Pontiac 10,615
Comcast Cablevision; Waterford 14,170
Concord Cablevision; Oxford 6,600
TCI Cable; Royal Oak 66,507
United Cable of Oakland County; Clarkston 13,656

Businesses and other major employers
General Motors Corp./Rochester Div.; Flint; motor vehicles 6,500
General Motors Corp./Assembly Div.; Lake Orion; motor vehicle assembly 6,000
General Motors Corp./Assembly Div.; Pontiac; motor vehicle assembly 5,500
General Motors Corp./General Motors Engine Div.; Flint; motor vehicle parts 5,000
General Motors Corp.; Flint; motor vehicle sales 4,700
General Motors Corp.; Flint; motor vehicles 4,500
General Motors Corp./Metal Fabricating Plant; Flint; motor vehicles 3,800
General Motors Corp./Truck & Bus Group Div.; Pontiac; trucks/buses 3,300
General Motors Corp./Cadillac Div.; Grand Blanc; motor vehicle parts 3,200
Hurley Medical Center; Flint 2,950
County of Oakland; Pontiac 2,200
St. Joseph Hospital Corp.; Flint 2,080
General Motors Corp./Pontiac West Assembly; Pontiac; motor vehicle assembly 2,000
Comerica Bank; Pontiac; commercial banks 2,000
St. Joseph Mercy Hospital; Pontiac 2,000
Oakland University; Rochester 1,871
McClaren Regional Medical Center; Flint 1,800
ITT Corp./ITT Higbie Baylock Mfg.; Pontiac; rubber hoses/belts 1,700
Flint Osteopathic Hospital; Flint 1,200
Pontiac General Hospital; Pontiac 1,020
Crittenton Hospital; Rochester 986
Pontiac Osteopathic Hospital; Pontiac 925
Voplex Corp./Lapeer Fabricators Div.; Lapeer; molded plastic 900
U.S. Postal Service; Flint 900
Volkswagen of America Inc./U.S. Div.; Pontiac; motor vehicles 850
Lapeer Regional Hospital; Lapeer 850
General Motors Corp.; Drayton Plains; motor vehicles 750
Citizens Banking Corp.; Flint; holding offices 700
Chrysler Corp./Featherstone Road Engineering Center; Pontiac; engineering services 700
State of Michigan/Social Services Dept.; Flint; family services 700
Lectron Products Inc.; Rochester; motor vehicle eletrical equipment 650
State of Michigan/Clinton Valley Center; Pontiac 600
City of Clarkston/Board of Education; Clarkston 600
Warner-Lambert Co./Park-Davis; Rochester; pharmaceuticals 550
ITT Corp./Parts Supply Div.; Pontiac; motor vehicle parts/supplies 550

10th District

Southeast — Macomb County; Port Huron

This is the home of the famed voters of Macomb County. Every four years, national reporters lug their laptops and cameras to the county to get an earful of what working-class America has to say. Political consultants probe their sentiments in focus groups. For presidential candidates, it is a must-stop.

Some of its renown stems from its reputation as an electoral bellwether. In 15 of the past 17 elections for president, governor or U.S. senator, the winner in Macomb has also been the statewide winner. But in 1992, George Bush became one of the exceptions.

Back in 1960, Macomb was solidly Democratic, suburban territory and proved it by delivering an almost 2-to-1 margin for John F. Kennedy. Voters stayed true to the party through most of the decade, backing Lyndon B. Johnson in 1964 and Hubert H. Humphrey in 1968.

But the late 1960s were a time of political transition for local residents, as they became increasingly disenchanted with the counterculture movement and frightened by the Detroit riots. By 1972, Richard M. Nixon had claimed the county.

As busing and civil rights emerged as prominent local issues, voters associated the national Democratic Party with the policies of the far left; by 1984, Ronald Reagan won by a 2-to-1 margin.

Strong union loyalties have not been enough to override the social conservatism of the Catholic Italians and eastern European working-class voters. Democrats are still stigmatized as the party of permissiveness, one that is soft on crime and intent on raising taxes.

Bush won here on those issues in 1988 and in 1992 despite deep discontent among local voters. Japanese trade practices and layoffs weighed heavily on residents' minds. In statewide and local races, Democrats are more competitive. In 1990, Macomb showed its ticket-splitting tendency by backing GOP challenger John Engler against Democratic Gov. James J. Blanchard, while choosing Democratic Sen. Carl Levin. In 1992, rising Democratic star David Bonior was re-elected here while presidential candidate Bill Clinton lost.

Not all of Macomb County is in the 10th: The district includes the newer subdivisions north of Mount Clemens and Clinton Township, and extends to the grittier neighborhoods, such as East Pointe (formerly called East Detroit), which is shared with the 12th. Fraser and Roseville are in the 10th, but Warren and Sterling Heights are on the 12th District side.

The rest of the vote comes from St. Clair County. More rural in composition, it leans Republican. Port Huron, a source of blue-collar voters, is beginning to feel the effects of residential and commercial spillover from the Detroit metro area. Retailers and developers are moving into the city because it is less developed than areas closer to Detroit and for the potential market of Canadian consumers from nearby Ontario.

Election Returns

	10th District	Democrat	Republican
1992	President*	100,587 (36.3%)	115,849 (41.8%)
	House	138,193 (53.1%)	114,918 (44.2%)
1990	Senate	92,533 (57.2%)	69,190 (42.8%)
	Governor	71,917 (44.4%)	90,079 (55.6%)
1988	President	86,722 (38.6%)	138,126 (61.4%)
	Senate	126,833 (59.1%)	87,913 (40.9%)
1986	Governor	96,545 (66.8%)	47,990 (33.2%)

Vote for Perot was 60,927 (22.0%).

Demographics

Population 580,956

Percent change from 1980 12.9%

Land area 1,130 square miles

Population per square mile 514

Counties, 1990 population
Macomb (pt.) 435,349   St. Clair 145,607

Cities, 1990 population (10,000 or more)
Clinton CDP 85,866   Port Huron 33,694
East Pointe (pt.) 30,013   Roseville 51,412
Fraser 13,899   Shelby CDP 48,655
Harrison CDP 24,685   St. Clair Shores 68,107
Mount Clemens 18,405

Race and Hispanic origin
White 96.5%
Black 2.0%
American Indian, Eskimo, or Aleut. 0.4%
Asian or Pacific Islander 0.7%
Other 0.4%
Hispanic origin 1.3%

Ancestry
American 2.6%   Hungarian 1.2%
Arabic 1.3%   Irish 16.4%
Belgian 3.0%   Italian 11.9%
Dutch 2.0%   Polish 17.0%
English 13.1%   Scotch Irish 2.1%
French 9.5%   Scottish 3.2%
French Canadian 2.9% Slovakian 1.4%
German 36.1%   Swedish 1.2%

Universities/colleges, 1990-1991 enrollment
St. Clair Community College, Port Huron 4,467

Newspapers, total circulation (in all districts)
Detroit News & Free Press 1,014,197
Macomb Daily 45,743
Port Huron Times Herald 30,214

Commercial television stations, affiliations
ADI: Detroit (100%)
    WADL, Mount Clemens (None)

Cable television systems, total subscribers
Comcast Cablevision; Mount Clemens 15,588
Comcast Cablevision; St. Clair Shores 19,824
Comcast Cablevision; Utica 13,974
Continental Cablevision of Michigan; Roseville
    12,550
Harron Cable TV; New Haven 28,674
Harron Cable TV; Port Huron 21,708
Maclean Hunter Cable TV; East Pointe 10,002

Military installations, 1991
  Selfridge Air Force Guard Base, Mt. Clemens 1,465
  Selfridge U.S. Army Garrison, Selfridge 1,241

Businesses and other major employers
  Ford Motor Co./Utica Trim Plant; Utica; motor vehicles
    4,200
  St. Joe Hospital; Mt. Clemens 1,700
  Ford Motor Co./T&C Div.; Livonia; motor vehicles 1,600
  Port Huron Area School District; Port Huron 1,314
  Ford Motor Co./Chesterfield Trim Plant; Mt. Clemens; textile
    products 1,300
  Mt. Clemens General Hospital; Mt. Clemens 1,300
  Port Huron Hospital; Port Huron 934
  TRW Inc./Vehicle Safety Systems Div.; Washington; textile
    products 800
  Lake Shore Public Schools; St. Clair Shores 619
  Mercy Hospital; Port Huron 600
  Detroit Edison Co.; St. Clair; electric services 550

11th District

Southeast — Part of Oakland County

The 11th is the lone Republican stronghold in metropolitan Detroit. Unlike the other suburban districts, which sometimes flirt with local GOP candidates and flock to Republican presidential candidates, the 11th is GOP turf in good times and bad. In 1992, George Bush won quite easily here, as did the Republican nominee in the open seat House race.

A mixture of white, upper- and middle-class residents, the 11th covers the southwestern portion of Oakland County and the city of Livonia in Wayne County. Much of the vote is cast in the populous eastern section, which is better educated and more affluent than the western half of the county.

Birmingham and Bloomfield hold the mansions and homes of auto executives and professionals. Birmingham's tony downtown shopping district used to be considered Michigan's version of Rodeo Drive, while Bloomfield Hills was George Romney's hometown in his days as an auto executive (before he was governor and a presidential candidate). More than half the housing units in Bloomfield and Bloomfield Hills have four bedrooms or more.

Farmington Hills, Southfield and West Bloomfield are population centers whose recent growth has qualified them for "edge city" status. Located north of 8 Mile Road—Detroit's northern boundary—these municipalities sit in the corridor between Grand River Avenue and the Northwestern Freeway that has served as one of the primary routes for white flight from the city.

While the rest of Oakland County is hostile to Detroit and unreceptive to blacks moving out of the city, Southfield has a relatively large and growing black population. Nearly 30 percent of the city's residents are black; many are middle-class families trying to escape Detroit's high crime rates. As Detroit has declined, businesses have flocked to surrounding suburbs such as Southfield. Southfield now has more multipurpose office space than Detroit.

The rest of the 11th is overwhelmingly white. Lathrup Village is slightly more than 20 percent black, but outside of it and Southfield, there is little racial diversity.

The northwestern part of the 11th is covered with lakes and recreation areas. Places such as Novi, South Lyon and Wixom in the southwest have newer subdivisions and are populated with a fair number of socially conservative blue-collar workers.

Wayne County's portion of the 11th consists of Redford Township and part of Livonia. Professionals and middle-level managers from the area's auto plants give a GOP tilt to Livonia, which is shared with the 13th District. Those sentiments may change, however, once General Motors completes the scheduled closure of its Livonia plant.

Election Returns

	11th District	Democrat	Republican
1992	President*	117,274 (37.0%)	149,109 (47.0%)
	House	117,725 (40.2%)	168,940 (57.6%)
1990	Senate	110,896 (55.5%)	88,743 (44.5%)
	Governor	92,722 (46.5%)	106,866 (53.5%)
1988	President	97,372 (35.0%)	180,993 (65.0%)
	Senate	141,662 (52.9%)	126,221 (47.1%)
1986	Governor	103,632 (59.5%)	70,422 (40.5%)

Vote for Perot was 50,675 (16.0%).

Demographics

Population 580,956

Percent change from 1980 12.9%

Land area 380 square miles

Population per square mile 1,528

Counties, 1990 population
  Oakland (pt.) 445,968   Wayne (pt.) 134,988

Cities, 1990 population (10,000 or more)
  Beverly Hills 10,610   Novi 32,998
  Birmingham 19,997   Redford CDP 54,387
  Bloomfield CDP 42,137   Southfield (pt.) 67,949
  Farmington Hills 74,652   West Bloomfield CDP
  Farmington 10,132   (pt.) 54,843
  Livonia (pt.) 80,601

Race and Hispanic origin
  White 93.0%
  Black 4.1%
  American Indian, Eskimo, or Aleut. 0.3%
  Asian or Pacific Islander 2.4%
  Other 0.2%
  Hispanic origin 1.3%

Ancestry
  American 3.0%   Irish 16.7%
  Arabic 1.7%   Italian 6.4%
  Dutch 2.1%   Polish 12.9%
  English 16.1%   Russian 4.3%
  Finnish 1.5%   Scotch Irish 2.3%
  French 6.5%   Scottish 4.2%
  French Canadian 1.9%   Slovakian 1.1%
  German 27.2%   Swedish 2.0%
  Hungarian 1.9%

Universities/colleges, 1990-1991 enrollment
  Lawrence Institute of Technology, Southfield 5,469
  Oakland Community College, Bloomfield Hills 28,068

St. Mary's College, Orchard Lake   433
William Tyndale College, Farmington Hills   382

Newspapers, total circulation (in all districts)
Detroit News & Free Press   1,014,197
Monroe Evening News   22,676
Oakland Press   73,533
Royal Oak Daily Tribune   28,145

Commercial television stations, affiliations
ADI: Detroit (100%)
   WDIV, Detroit (NBC)
   WKBD-TV, Detroit (Fox)
   WXON, Detroit (None)
   WXYZ-TV, Detroit (ABC)

Cable television systems, total subscribers
Barden Cablevision; Detroit   115,252
Booth Communications Inc.; Birmingham   21,099
Continental Cablevision of Southfield; Southfield   30,491
Metrovision of Livonia; Livonia   25,000
Metrovision of Oakland; Farmington Hills   30,948
Metrovision of Redford; Redford   12,400
TCI Cablevision; Walled Lake   20,100

Businesses and other major employers
Ford Motor Co./Wixom Assembly Plant; Wixom; motor vehicles   3,700
General Motors Corp./GM Proving Grounds; Milford; research services   3,500
Ford Motor Co./Ford Parts & Services Div.; Detroit; accounting services   2,000
IBM Corp.; Southfield; computer services   2,000
Botsford General Hospital; Farmington   1,650
General Motors Corp./Powertrain Div.; Livonia; engines/turbines   1,500
Nation Wide Security Inc.; Southfield; security/business services   1,500
City of Farmington/Public School District; Farmington   1,500
General Motors Corp./Inland Fisher Guide Div.; Livonia; metal stampings   1,300
Huron Valley Board of Education; Milford   1,200
City of Birmingham/Public School District; Birmingham   1,110
United Parcel Service Inc.; Livonia; mail services   1,000
Foodland Distributors; Livonia; grocery products   1,000
Dayton Hudson Corp.; Novi; department stores   1,000
Northwest Airlines Inc.; Livonia; airline   900
Blue Cross/Blue Shield of Michigan; Southfield; medical service/health insurance   900
Source One Mortgage Services Corp.; Farmington; mortgage bankers   900
Williams Intl. Corp.; Walled Lake; aircraft parts   850
City of Southfield; Southfield   785
Allnet Communication Services; Birmingham; telephone communications   700
Meijer Inc.; Orchard Lake; department stores   700
Michigan National Bank; Farmington; commercial banks   679
Fourmidable Group Inc.; Farmington; real estate agents   640
Royal MacCabees Life Insurance Co.; Southfield; life insurance   625
Jervis B. Webb Co./Unibilt Overhead Div.; Farmington; construction machinery   600
Sears Roebuck & Co.; Livonia; department stores   600

Alexander Hamilton Life; Farmington; life insurance   586
Huron Valley Hospital Inc.; Milford   568
Federal-Mogul Corp.; Southfield; motor vehicle parts   550
Thomson Publishing Corp.; Novi; book publishing   550
Lawrence Institute of Technology; Southfield   550
American Community Mutual Insurance Co.; Livonia; medical service/health insurance   520

12th District
Suburban Detroit — Warren; Sterling Heights

Think of the suburban 12th (see map on page 390) as a square. The top half contains fast-growing Troy and Sterling Heights. The southwest corner includes some older, racially mixed areas, while the city of Warren anchors the southeastern corner.

The auto industry is the thread that binds the 12th and with the industry comes the United Auto Workers (UAW) as a force. But unlike in the other heavily unionized districts of southeastern Michigan, that does not automatically translate into Democratic votes.

In Troy, a burgeoning high-tech sector revolves around auto industry consulting work that has been farmed out to smaller companies. EDS—one of the largest of these firms—is a major employer; it does computer consulting for General Motors. Another economic presence is Kmart, which keeps its world headquarters in Troy.

On the western side of the district, along what is known as the Golden Corridor, more traditional methods of car-making are evident. From 8 Mile Road—the northern border of Detroit—to Utica in the northern extreme of the 12th, this stretch includes a number of auto plants that make virtually every aspect of the car.

Close by the industrial corridor, in Warren, stands the GM Tech Center, a design and engineering center. Not far from there is a General Dynamics tank assembly plant, where in 1988 Democratic presidential nominee Michael S. Dukakis took his ill-advised tank ride.

Across the district, Democrats have an edge, but at the presidential level, a large contingent of Reagan Democrats boosts the GOP. In 1992, George Bush lost the 12th by fewer than 4,000 votes.

With a large number of blue-collar workers, the 12th is fertile ground for Democratic candidates.

Warren, the district's largest city, is a traditional Democratic stronghold, yet socially conservative. Within the city, Republicans have run well in the north, where voters are better off.

A solid Democratic vote is also cast in majority-black Royal Oak Township and in Oak Park, where more than a third of the population is black. A sizable Jewish population in affluent Huntington Woods, Oak Park and Southfield, which is shared with the 11th District, favors Democratic candidates.

Voters in Troy are more likely to be transplants to the area and less likely to be strongly affiliated with a political party than those in the southern half of the 12th. They lean toward the GOP. Sterling Heights is less transient; a large number of its residents are upwardly mobile, former Warren residents.

Republican strength in Troy—supplemented by the white-collar influx—and the swing voters of Sterling Heights kept the district competitive. In 1992 Bush managed to carry the Macomb County portion of the 12th, which includes Warren and Sterling Heights.

DETROIT AREA

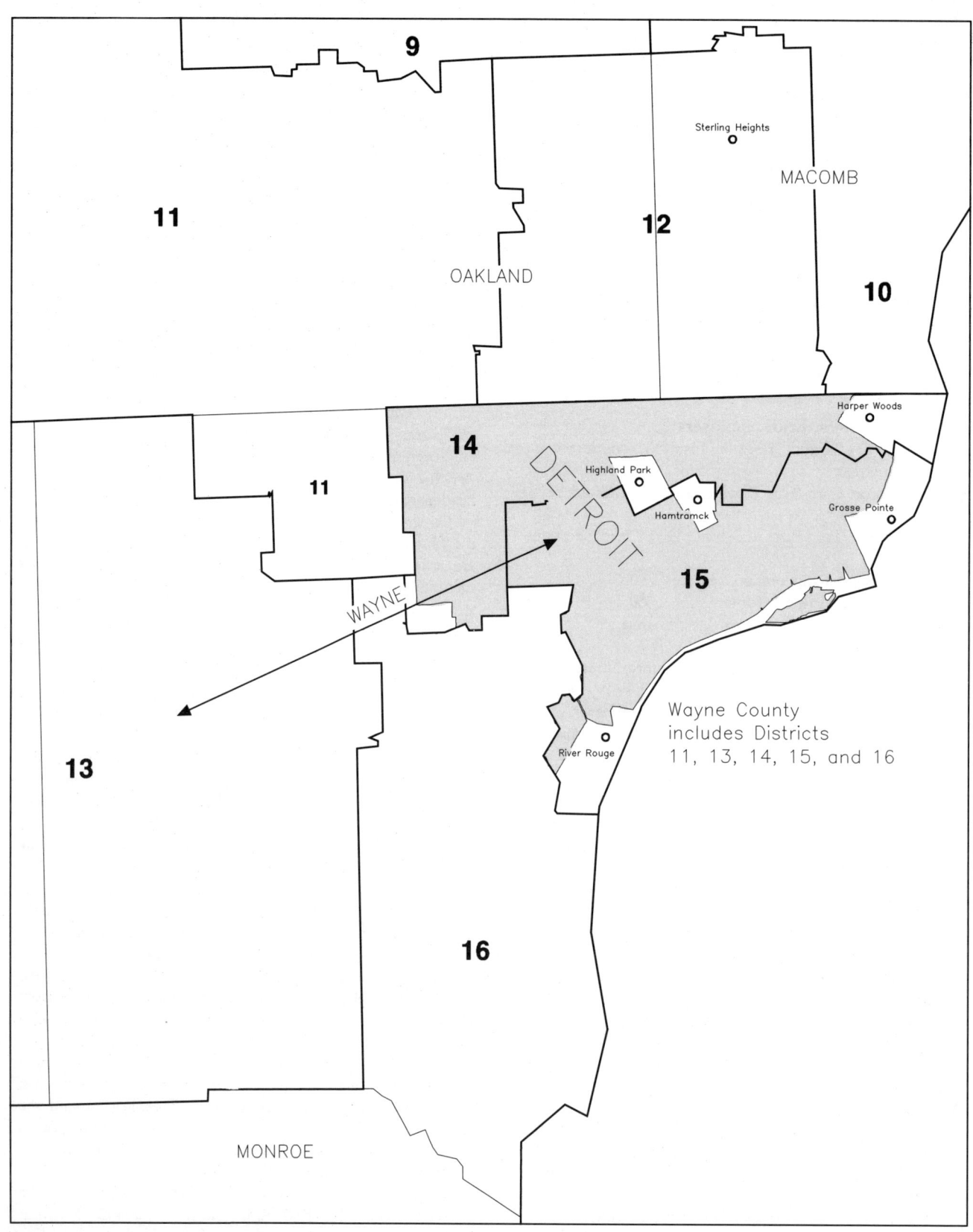

9

11

OAKLAND

Sterling Heights ○

MACOMB

12

10

Harper Woods ○

14

DETROIT

Highland Park ○

Hamtramck ○

Grosse Pointe ○

11

15

WAYNE

Wayne County
includes Districts
11, 13, 14, 15, and 16

River Rouge ○

13

16

MONROE

Election Returns

	12th District	Democrat	Republican
1992	President*	119,055 (42.0%)	115,065 (40.6%)
	House	137,514 (52.6%)	119,357 (45.7%)
1990	Senate	103,219 (60.9%)	66,164 (39.1%)
	Governor	86,321 (50.8%)	83,592 (49.2%)
1988	President	100,895 (41.7%)	140,952 (58.3%)
	Senate	139,933 (61.1%)	88,987 (38.9%)
1986	Governor	110,578 (69.1%)	49,361 (30.9%)

*Vote for Perot was 49,519 (17.5%).

Demographics

Population 580,956

Percent change from 1980 12.9%

Land area 149 square miles

Population per square mile 3,899

Counties, 1990 population

Macomb (pt.) 282,051	Oakland (pt.) 298,905

Cities, 1990 population (10,000 or more)

Berkley 16,960	Oak Park 30,462
Clawson 13,874	Royal Oak 65,410
Ferndale 25,084	Sterling Heights 117,810
Hazel Park 20,051	Troy 72,884
Madison Heights 32,196	Warren 144,864

Race and Hispanic origin

White 93.3%
Black 3.7%
American Indian, Eskimo, or Aleut. 0.4%
Asian or Pacific Islander 2.4%
Other 0.2%
Hispanic origin 1.2%

Ancestry

American 2.7%	Irish 16.1%
Arabic 2.0%	Italian 10.0%
Belgian 1.3%	Polish 18.9%
Dutch 2.0%	Russian 1.9%
English 13.2%	Scotch Irish 2.1%
Finnish 1.0%	Scottish 3.2%
French 6.6%	Slovakian 1.6%
French Canadian 2.3%	Swedish 1.3%
German 27.8%	Ukrainian 1.3%
Hungarian 1.3%	

Universities/colleges, 1990-1991 enrollment

Detroit College of Business, Warren 1,036
Macomb Community College, Warren 31,542
Walsh College of Accounting & Business, Troy 3,326

Newspapers, total circulation (in all districts)

Detroit News & Free Press 1,014,197
Macomb Daily 45,743
Oakland Press 73,533
Royal Oak Daily Tribune 28,145

Commercial television stations, affiliations

ADI: Detroit (100%)

WGPR-TV, Detroit (None)
WJBK-TV, Detroit (CBS)

Cable television systems, total subscribers

Comcast Cable of Warren; Warren 28,000
Comcast Cablevision; Sterling Heights 24,016
Continental Cablevision of Michigan; Madison Heights 7,800
TCI Cable; Royal Oak 66,507

Military installations, 1991

Detroit Arsenal (Army), Warren 5,861

Businesses and other major employers

General Dynamics Corp.; Sterling Heights; tanks 8,500
William Beaumont Hospital; Royal Oak 6,620
General Motors Corp.; Warren; automobile engineering 5,508
Chrysler Corp.; Sterling Heights; metal stampings 3,900
Chrysler Corp./Warren Truck & Assembly Plant; Warren; trucks 3,500
Kmart Corp.; Troy; department stores 3,500
Ford Motor Co.; Sterling Heights; motor vehicles 3,400
Providence Hospital; Southfield 3,200
Ford Motor Co./Van Dyke Transmission Chassis Div.; Sterling Heights; motor vehicle parts 1,800
Macomb Hospital Center; Warren 1,500
Electronic Data Systems Corp.; Troy; computer services 1,500
General Dynamics Corp./Land Systems Div.; Warren; tank assembly 1,400
Macomb Community College; Warren 1,250
General Motors Corp./Advanced Products Engineering Group; Warren; engineering services 1,200
Consumers Power Co.; Royal Oak; utility services 1,100
Chrysler Corp./Service & Parts Div.; Center Line; motor vehicle parts/supplies 1,000
Sears Roebuck & Co.; Troy; department stores 1,000
General Motors Corp./Chevrolet Motor Div.; Warren; motors 1,000
General Motors Corp./Research Laboratories; Warren; research services 975
Guardian Protective Service; Southfield; business services 970
Saturn Corp.; Troy; motor vehicles 950
William Beaumont Hospital; Troy 947
Standard Federal Bank; Troy; savings institutions 921
Rockwell Intl. Corp./Automotive Operations; Troy; motor vehicles/equipment 900
Detroit Osteopathic Hospital; Warren 839
Detroit News Inc.; Sterling Heights; newspapers 800
Kelly Services Inc.; Troy; personnel supply services 800
General Oakland Hospital; Royal Oak 768
Electronic Data Systems Corp.; Troy; computer services 750
General Motors Corp./Inland Fisher Guide Div.; Warren; management/public relations 700
Lintas Campbell-Ewald Co.; Warren; advertising 650
TRW Inc./Suspension Div; Sterling Heights; motor vehicle parts 627
Henkel Corp./Parker Amchem; Royal Oak; chemical products 600
Meijer Inc.; Sterling Heights; grocery stores 600
Dayton-Hudson Corp.; Sterling Heights; department stores 600
City of Sterling Heights; Sterling Heights 600
Du Pont E. I. De Nemours & Co.; Troy; research services 600

13th District

Southeast — Ann Arbor; Westland; Ypsilanti

One of the first things Rep. William Ford did upon his election as House Education and Labor chairman in 1990 was to inform staff members that all staff parking spaces would be reserved for American cars only.

There was good reason behind his edict: Back then, as now, his district had about two dozen auto plants scattered across eastern Washtenaw and western Wayne counties. That number may soon diminish, as General Motors continues its employment cutbacks and completes the scheduled closing of the Willow Run assembly plant in Ypsilanti Township.

For the new 13th District (see map on page 390), Western Wayne County provides more than 60 percent of the vote, much of it coming from the cities east of I-275, on the eastern edge of the district. Many of these cities, such as Garden City, Inkster, Romulus and Westland, are primarily blue-collar, with a heavy dependence on auto industry jobs. These residents turn out a reliably Democratic vote, as do the mostly black voters of Inkster.

In recent presidential elections, many have crossed over to vote for GOP nominees, but auto industry cutbacks and the recession brought them back to Bill Clinton in 1992.

Farther west, closer to Washtenaw County, the townships are less industrialized and more Republican. Canton, Northville and Plymouth generally have higher incomes than their county neighbors who live closer to Detroit; they are receptive to GOP candidates. Recognizing the area as one of the few sources of GOP votes in southeastern Michigan, George Bush made several campaign stops here in 1992.

Democratic Ann Arbor, the state's seventh-largest city, casts the bulk of Washtenaw County's ballots. Before 1992 redistricting, back when the city was part of the old 2nd District, the liberal community of the University of Michigan was a sure-fire source of Democratic votes against then-GOP Rep. Carl D. Pursell. A large number of blacks in Ypsilanti and Ypsilanti Township also boosts local and statewide Democrats.

Traditionally, Washtenaw County as a whole has swung back and forth at the presidential level, as a result of the GOP small towns and farmers who populate the rest of the county. It was the only county in the nation to support George McGovern in 1972, then back Gerald R. Ford in 1976.

Fortunately for 13th District Democrats, most of the Republicans in Washtenaw County now live in the 7th and 8th districts. While the auto industry remains a vital source of jobs, an emerging high-tech corridor has taken shape in the Ann Arbor-Detroit corridor, between I-94 and I-96. Known as "automation alley," this stretch draws on the engineering skills and brainpower of the University of Michigan, and to a lesser extent, Eastern Michigan University in Ypsilanti. Robotics companies have clustered in the area, making factory automation equipment that, eventually, will lead to even more job losses in the auto industry.

Election Returns

	13th District	Democrat	Republican
1992	President*	125,913 (49.3%)	86,769 (34.0%)
	House †	127,642 (51.9%)	105,169 (42.8%)
1990	Senate	82,108 (60.5%)	53,545 (39.5%)
	Governor	74,249 (52.8%)	66,328 (47.2%)

	13th District	Democrat	Republican
1988	President	109,986 (50.2%)	108,929 (49.8%)
	Senate	126,215 (64.5%)	69,601 (35.5%)
1986	Governor	93,131 (64.1%)	52,131 (35.9%)

*Vote for Perot was 42,875 (16.8%).   †Independent/other is greater than 5%.

Demographics

Population 580,956

Percent change from 1980 12.9%

Land area 455 square miles

Population per square mile 1,276

Counties, 1990 population
Washtenaw (pt.) 213,525   Wayne (pt.) 367,431

Cities, 1990 population (10,000 or more)
Ann Arbor 109,592	Plymouth CDP 23,646
Canton CDP 57,047	Romulus 22,897
Garden City 31,846	Wayne 19,899
Inkster 30,772	Westland 84,724
Livonia (pt.) 20,249	Ypsilanti 24,846

Race and Hispanic origin
White 85.2%
Black 11.0%
American Indian, Eskimo, or Aleut. 0.4%
Asian or Pacific Islander 2.9%
Other 0.5%
Hispanic origin 1.7%

Ancestry
American 3.5%	Irish 17.2%
Dutch 2.8%	Italian 5.0%
English 15.2%	Polish 11.3%
Finnish 1.1%	Russian 1.2%
French 6.4%	Scotch Irish 2.2%
French Canadian 2.1%	Scottish 3.4%
German 28.5%	Slovakian 1.1%
Hungarian 1.6%	Swedish 1.7%

Universities/colleges, 1990-1991 enrollment
Cleary College, Ypsilanti 977
Concordia College, Ann Arbor 611
Eastern Michigan University, Ypsilanti 25,024
Madonna College, Livonia 4,392
Schoolcraft College, Livonia 9,177
University of Michigan, Ann Arbor 36,394
Washtenaw Community College; Ann Arbor 9,400

Newspapers, total circulation (in all districts)
Ann Arbor News 51,727
Detroit News & Free Press 1,014,197
Ypsilanti Press 14,840

Commercial television stations, affiliations
ADI: Detroit (100%)

Cable television systems, total subscribers
Columbia Cable; Ann Arbor 49,500
Continental Cablevision; Dearborn Heights 37,651
Maclean Hunter Cable TV; Garden City 7,810
Maclean Hunter Cable TV; Taylor 49,908

Metrovision of Livonia; Livonia 25,000
Metrovision of Oakland; Farmington Hills 30,948
Omnicom Cablevision; Westland 27,695
Omnicom of Michigan; Romulus 7,003

Businesses and other major employers
General Motors Corp./Powertrain Div.; Ypsilanti; motor vehicle parts 9,000
University of Michigan & Hospital; Ann Arbor 8,000
Northwest Airlines Inc./Northwest Orient; Romulus; airlines 7,200
General Motors Corp./Willow Run Assembly; Ypsilanti; motor vehicle assembly 5,000
Ford Motor Co./Livonia Transmission Plant; Livonia; motor vehicle parts 4,200
Ford Motor Co./Wayne Body & Stamping; Wayne; motor vehicle parts 4,000
Mazda Motor Mfg. USA Corp.; Flat Rock; motor vehicles 3,500
Catherine McAley Health Center; Ypsilanti 3,000
General Motors Corp./Delco Product Div.; Livonia; motor vehicle parts 2,500
County of Wayne/Sheriffs Dept.; Livonia 2,000
Eastern Michigan University; Ypsilanti 2,000
Ford Motor Co./Sheldon Road Plant; Plymouth; motor vehicles 1,800
Ford Motor Co./Electrical & Electronic Div.; Ypsilanti; motor vehicles/equipment 1,350
Ford Motor Co./Transmissions & Chassis; Livonia; motor vehicle parts 1,300
Northville Psychiatric Hospital; Northville 1,300
Warner-Lambert Co./Parke Davis; Ann Arbor; research services 1,300
City of Ann Arbor; Ann Arbor 1,200
County of Washtenaw; Ann Arbor 1,150
City of Ypsilanti/Public School District; Ypsilanti 1,100
Washtenaw Community College; Ann Arbor 1,100
Kelsey-Hayes Co.; Romulus; motor vehicle parts 1,000
Unisys Corp./Mfg. Engineering Div.; Plymouth; computer/office equipment 1,000
Meijer Inc.; Northville; department stores 1,000
City of Garden City/Public School District; Garden City 996
Schoolcraft College; Livonia 950
Zantop Intl. Airlines; Ypsilanti; airline 900
Oakwood United Hospitals Inc./Annapolis Hospital; Wayne 884
Environmental Research Institute of Michigan; Ann Arbor; research services 766
Valassis Inserts Inc.; Livonia; commercial printing 675
Meijer Inc.; Ypsilanti; department stores 650
Meijer Inc.; Westland; grocery stores 600
Highland Superstores Inc./Highland Appliance Co.; Plymouth; computer stores 600
Willow Run Community Schools; Ypsilanti 600
Edwards Brothers Inc.; Ann Arbor; books 550

14th District

Parts of Detroit; Harper Woods; Highland Park

Henry Ford built his first large factory in Highland Park in 1909, followed by Buick, R. E. Olds and the Fisher brothers.

Soon afterward the nascent automobile industry attracted rural Michiganders, residents of Appalachia, southern blacks and eastern Europeans, many of whom sought housing in the sea of single and two-family homes on Detroit's north side.

The industry kept Detroit working and prosperous for much of the century, but over the past few decades, the city has been losing jobs and people rapidly. The auto industry jobs have moved to Mexico and other nonunionized areas. The residents have moved to the mainly white suburbs that ring the city.

In 1960, the city contained about 1.7 million inhabitants, two-thirds of whom were white. By 1990, the city barely exceeded 1 million residents, three-quarters of whom were black. Highland Park exemplifies this demographic change. Completely enveloped by Detroit, Highland Park was once a white-ethnic bastion and home to the Chrysler Corp. headquarters. Now it is primarily black, with a significant contingent of retired autoworkers. Rising unemployment and tough economic times have gradually chipped away at the city's middle-class character. Conditions may worsen now that Chrysler has decided to move its headquarters to suburban Auburn Hills.

The rest of the district is centered on the north side of Detroit (see map on page 390), taking in Harper Woods, Grosse Pointe Woods and Grosse Pointe Shores on the eastern edge and a handful of precincts from Dearborn Heights (the rest are in the 16th District) on the southwestern fringe. It is generally more residential and better off than the city's other congressional district, the 15th.

Rosedale is home to larger residences that were built for General Motors executives in the 1930s. North of 7 Mile Road, there are racially mixed communities with a relatively high percentage of professionals and white-collar city employees. Toward the west side are some of the city's largest and most politically active black churches.

Politically, this is a Democratic stronghold where Republicans have virtually no presence. In presidential elections, Democratic nominees regularly rack up the state's highest percentages here and in the 15th District. In statewide politics, Democratic candidates must run up huge margins in Detroit to offset their losses outside of southeastern Michigan. Democratic then-Gov. James J. Blanchard's 1990 upset loss to Republican John Engler was partly attributed to Blanchard's inability to win big in the Motor City.

The only places where Republicans find quarter are outside the city. The blue-collar and middle-class denizens of Harper Woods lean Republican at the statewide and national levels, but they are swing voters who often split tickets. The doctors, lawyers, auto executives and other white-collar workers of affluent Grosse Pointe Woods and Grosse Pointe Shores are even more receptive to GOP candidates.

Election Returns

	14th District	Democrat	Republican
1992	President*	180,007 (81.3%)	28,937 (13.1%)
	House	165,496 (82.4%)	32,036 (15.9%)
1990	Senate	117,245 (86.7%)	17,947 (13.3%)
	Governor	106,023 (82.7%)	22,232 (17.3%)
1988	President	157,052 (81.1%)	36,511 (18.9%)
	Senate	180,226 (88.5%)	23,329 (11.5%)
1986	Governor	132,984 (88.4%)	17,473 (11.6%)

*Vote for Perot was 12,600 (5.7%).

Demographics

Population 580,956

Percent change from 1980 12.9%

Land area 80 square miles

Population per square mile 7,276

Counties, 1990 population
Wayne (pt.) 580,956

Cities, 1990 population (10,000 or more)
Detroit (pt.) 517,514   Harper Woods 14,903
Grosse Pointe Woods   Highland Park 20,121
  17,715

Race and Hispanic origin
White 29.2%
Black 69.1%
American Indian, Eskimo, or Aleut. 0.3%
Asian or Pacific Islander 1.0%
Other 0.4%
Hispanic origin 1.1%

Ancestry
American 1.6%   Irish 4.8%
English 3.2%   Italian 2.9%
French 2.0%   Polish 7.0%
German 7.6%

Universities/colleges, 1990-1991 enrollment
Highland Park Community College, Highland Park
  2,343
Lewis College of Business, Detroit 233
Marygrove College, Detroit 1,238
Sacred Heart Major Seminary, Detroit 258
University of Detroit, Detroit 5,702

Newspapers, total circulation (in all districts)
Detroit News & Free Press 1,014,197

Commercial television stations, affiliations
ADI: Detroit (100%)

Cable television systems, total subscribers
Barden Cablevision; Detroit 115,252
Grosse Pointe Cable Inc.; Grosse Pointe Woods 14,500

Businesses and other major employers
Chrysler Corp.; Detroit; motor vehicles 4,300
Chrysler Corp./Industrial Engineering; Detroit; computer services 4,000
Detroit Diesel Corp.; Detroit; engines/turbines 2,700
Sinai Hospital; Detroit 2,485
Grace Hospital; Detroit 2,300
Chrysler Corp./Detroit Axle; Detroit; motor vehicle parts 1,500
Dayton Hudson Corp./Hudson's Eastland; Detroit; department stores 1,500
Chrysler Corp./Outer Drive Mfg. Technical Center; Detroit; research services 1,050
Chrysler Corp./Car & Truck Assembly; Detroit; motor vehicle assembly 1,000
Detroit Osteopathic Hospital; Detroit 901
Holy Cross Hospital; Detroit 765
University of Detroit; Detroit 695

Carboloy Inc.; Warren; metalworking machinery 600
Lear Seating Corp./General Seating Div.; Detroit; furniture 535
Chrysler Transport Inc./Lynch Road Terminal; Detroit; trucking services 505

15th District

Parts of Detroit; Grosse Pointe; Hamtramck; River Rouge

The depopulation of Detroit has been under way for decades, leading the city to be called the Beirut of America, a desolate, burned-out hulk showing few signs of life. By 1992, a local editorial columnist asked, "Has the city of Detroit ceased to exist?"

If it has, a variety of factors contributed over the past four decades. In 1960, Detroit was a metropolis of 1.7 million people. Thirty years later, local officials fretted when a preliminary census count showed fewer than 1 million residents. The final 1990 census numbers confirmed that Detroit had just over 1 million inhabitants.

The domestic automobile industry's woes economically devastated southeastern Michigan and Detroit, but some of the population decline can be linked to the 1967 riots, the worst in terms of property damage and deaths this century.

Particularly hard hit was the area that now makes up the 15th District. Taking in the older parts of the city, the 15th contains the skeletal remains of an era when Detroit was a manufacturing powerhouse. Even though the 15th (see map on page 390) contains the city's downtown and waterfront areas, it also houses many of the city's most downtrodden residents, who live in bombed-out, boarded-up neighborhoods largely clustered south of the Ford Freeway.

The city's downtown and riverfront areas have been the focus of numerous redevelopment projects over the years, aimed at luring residents back. The 73-story Renaissance Center was opened in 1977 to try to revitalize the city's commercial core. Those efforts have met with some success, but the emergence of the outlying suburban cities as commercial centers has made the task even more daunting.

In sharp contrast to the city's mostly poor and working-class blacks are the wealthy white communities of Grosse Pointe Park, Grosse Pointe and Grosse Pointe Farms, nestled in the northeast corner of the district. Like the rest of the white suburban communities that surround Detroit, residents here are usually hostile toward city politics.

Hamtramck is another white enclave, surrounded on all sides by Detroit. Once home to 50,000 people, many of whom worked at the huge and now closed Dodge plant at the southern end of town, the city's population has dwindled to below 20,000. Still, a tight-knit Polish community exists, leavened by newly arrived Yugoslavs, Albanians and some immigrants from the Middle East. Other Arab communities of Syrians, Palestinians and Chaldeans exist in southeast Detroit.

River Rouge and Ecorse are grafted on to the 15th's southern extreme; they are populated with autoworkers and steelworkers, many of whom are black.

Election Returns

	15th District	Democrat	Republican
1992	President*	144,092 (80.6%)	26,421 (14.8%)
	House	148,908 (80.5%)	31,849 (17.2%)

15th District		Democrat	Republican
1990	Senate	93,944 (85.2%)	16,316 (14.8%)
	Governor	84,952 (80.8%)	20,211 (19.2%)
1988	President	125,840 (79.1%)	33,192 (20.9%)
	Senate	144,408 (87.2%)	21,208 (12.8%)
1986	Governor	106,555 (87.0%)	15,885 (13.0%)

Vote for Perot was 8,278 (4.6%).

Demographics

Population 580,956

Percent change from 1980 12.9%

Land area 84 square miles

Population per square mile 6,880

Counties, 1990 population
Wayne (pt.) 580,956

Cities, 1990 population (10,000 or more)
Detroit (pt.) 510,460   Grosse Pointe Park 12,857
Ecorse 12,180   Hamtramck 18,372
Grosse Pointe Farms   River Rouge 11,314
  10,092

Race and Hispanic origin
White 26.4%
Black 70.0%
American Indian, Eskimo, or Aleut. 0.4%
Asian or Pacific Islander 0.7%
Other 2.4%
Hispanic origin 4.3%

Ancestry
American 2.1%   Irish 4.9%
English 3.0%   Italian 1.5%
French 1.9%   Polish 5.0%
German 5.9%

Universities/colleges, 1990-1991 enrollment
Center for Creative Studies, Detroit 1,002
Detroit College of Law, Detroit 659
Wayne County Community College, Detroit 11,986
Wayne State University, Detroit 33,872

Newspapers, total circulation (in all districts)
Detroit News & Free Press 1,014,197

Commercial television stations, affiliations
ADI: Detroit (100%)

Cable television systems, total subscribers
Barden Cablevision/Detroit; Detroit 115,252
Grosse Pointe Cable Inc.; Grosse Pointe Woods
  14,500

Businesses and other major employers
NBO Bancorporation/NBD Bank; Detroit; commercial
  banks 10,392
Chrysler Corp./Chrysler Motors; Detroit; motor vehicles
  6,000
County of Wayne; Detroit 5,945
Chrysler Corp./Jefferson Assembly Plant; Detroit; motor vehi-
  cle assembly 5,000

City of Detroit/Police Dept.; Detroit 4,700
National Steel Corp./Great Lakes Steel Div.; Detroit; steel
  products 4,600
Blue Cross/Blue Shield of Michigan; Detroit; medical
  service/health insurance 3,700
Detroit Newspaper Agency; Detroit; newspapers 3,500
Comerica Inc.; Detroit; commercial banks 3,500
St. John Hospital & Medical Center; Detroit 3,158
General Motors Corp./Saginaw-Detroit Plants; Detroit; motor
  vehicle forgings 3,065
City of Detroit/Water & Sewerage Dept.; Detroit; water
  supply 3,000
General Motors Corp./BOC Div.; Detroit; motor
  vehicles/equipment 3,000
General Motors Corp.; Detroit; motor vehicles 2,800
National Cleaning Contractors/ISS Prudential Maintenance;
  Detroit; building services 2,500
State of Michigan/Employment Security Commission; De-
  troit 2,500
Detroit Edison Co.; Detroit; electric services 2,300
Michigan Bell Telephone Co.; Detroit; telephone communica-
  tions 2,200
Hutzel Hospital; Detroit 2,020
City of Detroit; Detroit 2,000
Children's Hospital of Michigan; Detroit 1,654
Detroit Medical Center; Detroit 1,550
Ford Motor Co./Ford Glass Div.; Detroit; flat glass 1,500
Budd Co./Stamping & Framing Div.; Detroit; metal
  stampings 1,500
Mercy Hospital; Detroit 1,500
County of Wayne/Public Services Dept.; Detroit 1,500
City of Detroit/Board of Education; Detroit 1,500
Sisters of Bon Secours Hospital; Detroit 1,400
American Natural Resources Co.; Detroit; gas distribution
  1,300
Unisys Corp./Worldwide Marketing; Detroit;
  management/public relations 1,300
Wayne State University; Detroit 1,259
MCN Corp.; Detroit; gas distribution 1,225
County of Wayne/Sheriffs Dept.; Detroit 1,100
ANR Pipeline Co.; Detroit; gas distribution 1,000
Acustar Inc./McGraw Glass Plant; Detroit; glass products
  1,000
Ford Motor Co./Sales Operation Div.; Detroit; auto sales
  1,000
City of Detroit/Recreation Dept.; Detroit 1,000
City of Detroit/Health Dept.; Detroit 910
General Motors Corp./Saginaw Detroit Forge; Detroit; metal
  forgings 900
State of Michigan/Thirty-Sixth District; Detroit 900
General Motors Corp./Regional Personnel Div.; Detroit;
  personnel supply services 856
Deloitte & Touche; Detroit; accounting/auditing 800
General Motors Corp./Photographic Div.; Detroit;
  management/public relations 700
Metro Detroit Professional Services; Detroit; personnel supply
  services 700
Cottage Hospital Corp./Cottage Hospital Grosse Pointe;
  Detroit 656
General Motors Corp./Detroit Assembly Plant; Detroit; mo-
  tor vehicle assembly 600
Coopers & Lybrand; Detroit; accounting/auditing 580
Thorn Apple Valley Inc.; Detroit; smoked meat products 550

Honigman Miller Schwartz Cohn; Detroit; legal services 525
North Detroit General Hospital; Detroit 525
Grand Trunk Corp.; Detroit; railroads 510

16th District

Southeast Wayne County; Monroe County

A gray stretch of gritty communities along the Detroit River, the 16th is one of the most industrialized districts in the country. In a previous incarnation, two rounds of redistricting ago, the *Detroit News* called it "the most polluted congressional district in the nation." The borders are somewhat different now, but the character is quite similar.

Dearborn, its largest city, is home to the Ford Motor Co. and the factory that was once the largest on Earth. Known simply as "the Rouge," spread over 1,200 acres, its assembly line employed nearly 100,000 workers during its heyday. Now the automotive facilities employ fewer than 10,000.

The tool-and-die shops, foundries, assembly lines and chemical plants of the 16th served as a powerful magnet for U.S. and international job-seekers in the early and mid-20th century. Residents of Appalachia, Germans, Poles, Czechs, Italians and southern blacks all migrated here in search of jobs, filling communities such as Melvindale, Wyandotte and Allen Park.

Another wave of migration brought large numbers of Arabs to the Dearborn area. Some Shiite Moslems came during World War I, after Henry Ford opened the massive plant in the southern end of the city. For decades afterwards, Egyptians, Iraqis, Lebanese, Syrians, Palestinians, Jordanians, Saudis and Yemenis would come into the city in spurts. Today, the Arab business district along Warren Avenue supports the nation's largest Arab-American community.

The migration to the state's ninth largest city has not included blacks. Whites make up 98 percent of Dearborn; relations with majority-black Detroit are strained.

Nearby Dearborn Heights is shared with the Detroit-based 14th District; most of the city is in the 16th. Farther south, just inside the Wayne County limits on the southern edge, is the Flat Rock automotive plant, a joint U.S.-Japanese venture and one of the district's larger employers. The plant produces the Mazda MX-6 and Ford Probe.

The Wayne County portion of the district is the most populous. Thoroughly unionized and mostly blue collar, this area regularly turns in Democratic margins. There are some pockets of Republican affluence, mainly in Riverview and Grosse Ile.

Monroe County, south of Wayne, is more politically competitive. Local factories have a union presence, but farther west, the turf is less industrialized and more conservative. Some retirees from the Detroit and Toledo areas have moved to communities on the county's Lake Erie shoreline.

Bill Clinton won Monroe in 1992, but two years before, voters displayed their independence by splitting their tickets in statewide races. Democratic Sen. Carl Levin carried the county in his 1990 re-election bid, but successful GOP gubernatorial challenger John Engler captured 53 percent against Democratic Gov. James J. Blanchard.

Election Returns

	16th District	Democrat	Republican
1992	President*	118,079 (43.9%)	97,968 (36.4%)
	House	156,964 (65.1%)	75,694 (31.4%)
1990	Senate	76,930 (56.0%)	60,517 (44.0%)
	Governor	69,567 (48.1%)	74,963 (51.9%)
1988	President	103,050 (45.6%)	123,110 (54.4%)
	Senate	118,255 (60.1%)	78,663 (39.9%)
1986	Governor	87,258 (59.7%)	58,918 (40.3%)

*Vote for Perot was 52,963 (19.7%).

Demographics

Population 580,956

Percent change from 1980 12.9%

Land area 699 square miles

Population per square mile 831

Counties, 1990 population
Monroe 133,600   Wayne (pt.) 447,356

Cities, 1990 population (10,000 or more)
Allen Park 31,092	Riverview 13,894
Dearborn Heights (pt.) 51,979	Southgate 30,771
Dearborn 89,286	Taylor 70,811
Lincoln Park 41,832	Trenton 20,586
Melvindale 11,216	Woodhaven 11,631
Monroe 22,902	Wyandotte 30,938

Race and Hispanic origin
White 96.6%
Black 1.4%
American Indian, Eskimo, or Aleut. 0.4%
Asian or Pacific Islander 1.0%
Other 0.6%
Hispanic origin 2.4%

Ancestry
American 3.8%	Irish 18.1%
Arabic 2.9%	Italian 7.5%
Dutch 2.4%	Polish 15.3%
English 12.8%	Scotch Irish 2.0%
French 10.1%	Scottish 2.8%
French Canadian 2.5%	Slovakian 1.5%
German 30.5%	Swedish 1.1%
Hungarian 3.9%	

Universities/colleges, 1990-1991 enrollment
Detroit College of Business, Dearborn 2,712
Henry Ford Community College, Dearborn 16,150
Monroe County Community College, Monroe 3,313
University of Michigan, Dearborn 7,684

Newspapers, total circulation (in all districts)
Detroit News & Free Press 1,014,197
Monroe Evening News 22,676
Toledo Blade 150,637

Commercial television stations, affiliations
ADI: Detroit (100%)

Cable television systems, total subscribers
CVI; Dearborn 21,500
Contintental Cablevision; Dearborn Heights 37,651
Maclean Hunter Cable TV; Taylor 49,908

Mercom Inc.; Monroe 9,848
TCI; Woodhaven 25,562
Cable System; Monroe 8,460
Wyandotte Cable TV; Wyandotte 9,464

Businesses and other major employers
Rouge Steel Co.; Dearborn; steel products 3,350
Ford Motor Co./Woodhaven Stamping Plant; Trenton; metal stampings 2,650
Chrysler Corp./Trenton Engine Plant; Trenton; engines 2,600
Ford Motor Co./Dearborn Assembly Plant; Dearborn; motor vehicle assembly 2,300
Oakwood Hospital Corp.; Dearborn 2,300
Ford Motor Co./Mfg. Staff; Dearborn; management/public relations 2,000
Ford Motor Co./Body Assembly; Monroe; motor vehicles/equipment 1,700
Ford Motor Co./Dearborn Stamping Plant; Dearborn; metal stampings 1,600
Wyandotte Hospital and Medical Center; Wyandotte 1,386
Detroit Edison Co./Fermi 2 Power Plant; Monroe; electric services 1,250
Ford Motor Co./Ford Parts & Service Div.; Dearborn; motor vehicles/parts/supplies 1,200
Henry Ford Community College; Dearborn 1,030
Ford Motor Co./Ford Parts Redistribution; Romulus; warehousing 1,000
Meijer Inc.; Taylor; department stores 1,000

United Technologies Corp./United Technologies Automotive; Dearborn; electrical equipment/supplies 1,000
Ford Motor Credit Co.; Dearborn; credit institutions 1,000
University of Michigan/Child Development Center; Dearborn; child day care 954
BASF Corp.; Wyandotte; shipbuilding/repairing 800
Oakwood United Hospitals Inc./United Care Inc.; Taylor 800
Mercy-Memorial Hospital Corp.; Monroe 763
U.S. Postal Service; Allen Park 750
Holophane Co. Inc.; Dearborn; electric lighting 700
Dayton Hudson Corp.; Dearborn; warehousing 700
Detroit Osteopathic Hospital/Riverside Osteopathic Hospital; Trenton 700
Hyatt Corp./Hyatt Regency Dearborn; Dearborn; hotel 700
Edison Institute/Henry Ford Museum; Dearborn; musuems 700
Detroit Edison Co./Monroe Power Plant; Monroe; electric services 680
United Air Lines Inc.; Dearborn; airline 600
Sears Roebuck & Co.; Lincoln Park; department stores 600
Henry Ford Medical Center; Dearborn; medical doctors 600
Security Bank & Trust Co.; Dearborn; commercial banks 587
National Steel Corp./Technical Research Center; Trenton; research services 550
North Star Steel Co.; Monroe; steel products 543
Bedford Public Schools; Temperance 515

MINNESOTA

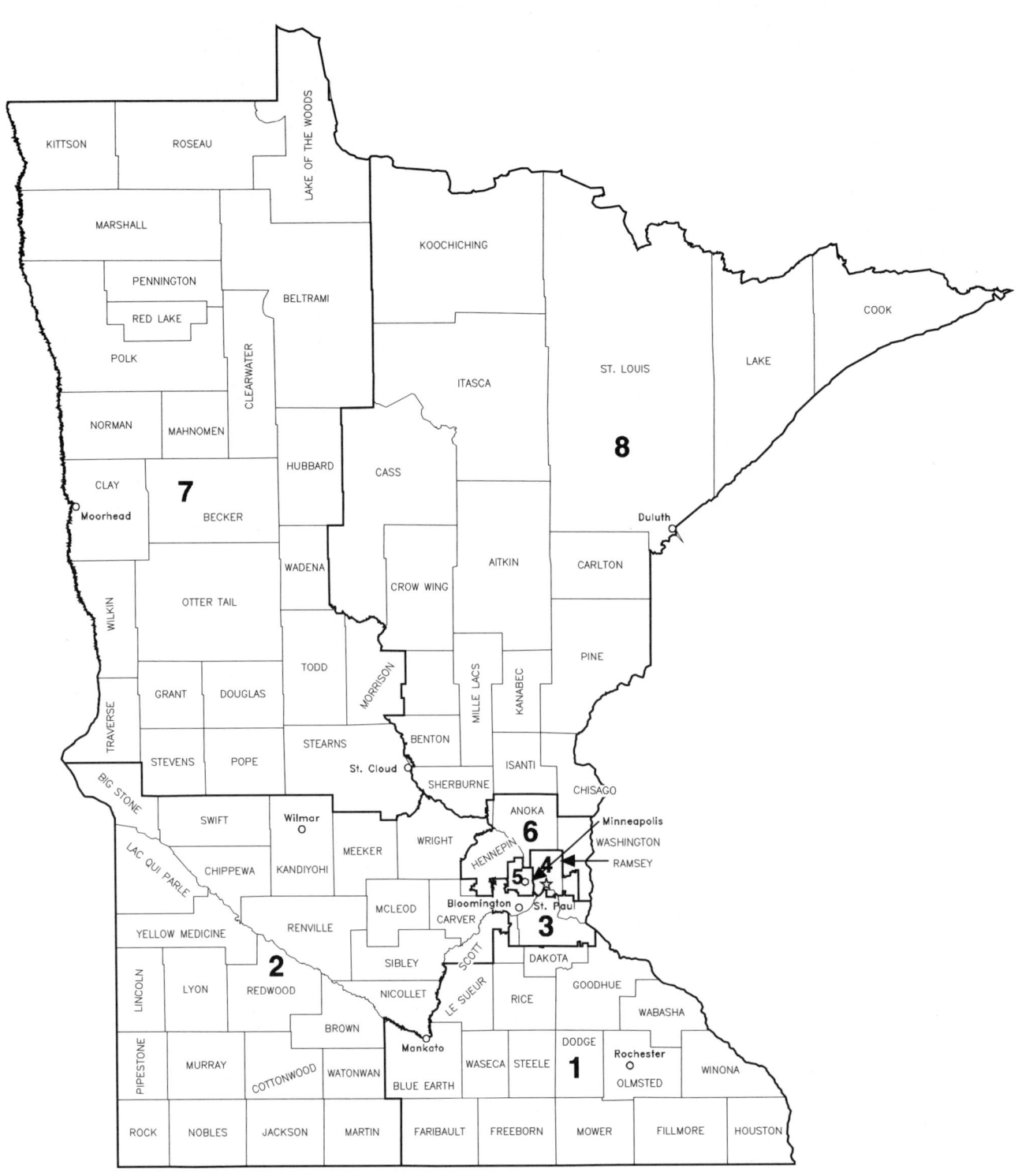

KITTSON
ROSEAU
LAKE OF THE WOODS
MARSHALL
PENNINGTON
RED LAKE
POLK
KOOCHICHING
BELTRAMI
CLEARWATER
COOK
NORMAN
MAHNOMEN
ST. LOUIS
LAKE
CLAY
Moorhead
7
BECKER
HUBBARD
CASS
8
WADENA
AITKIN
CARLTON
Duluth
ITASCA
WILKIN
OTTER TAIL
CROW WING
PINE
TRAVERSE
TODD
MORRISON
MILLE LACS
KANABEC
GRANT
DOUGLAS
STEVENS
POPE
STEARNS
BENTON
ISANTI
St. Cloud
SHERBURNE
CHISAGO
BIG STONE
SWIFT
Wilmar
WRIGHT
ANOKA
6
Minneapolis
WASHINGTON
RAMSEY
LAC QUI PARLE
CHIPPEWA
KANDIYOHI
MEEKER
HENNEPIN
4
5
St. Paul
Bloomington
3
YELLOW MEDICINE
RENVILLE
MCLEOD
CARVER
SCOTT
DAKOTA
LINCOLN
LYON
REDWOOD
2
SIBLEY
NICOLLET
LE SUEUR
RICE
GOODHUE
WABASHA
BROWN
Mankato
DODGE
Rochester
WINONA
PIPESTONE
MURRAY
COTTONWOOD
WATONWAN
BLUE EARTH
WASECA
STEELE
1
OLMSTED
ROCK
NOBLES
JACKSON
MARTIN
FARIBAULT
FREEBORN
MOWER
FILLMORE
HOUSTON

Minnesota

Minnesota's hold on the nation's political psyche was set for 20 years as the standard bearer of Democratic presidential tickets.

A Minnesota Democrat claimed a spot on the party ticket in five of the six campaigns from 1964 to 1984. Hubert H. Humphrey and Walter F. Mondale knew good times and bad—each succeeding once as vice-presidential candidates, losing as presidential candidates. But they could always count on carrying their home state. In fact, they helped Minnesota become one of the most reliably Democratic states in the country, enabling the party to carry it in eight of the nine presidential elections from 1960 to 1992.

Humphrey's leadership built Minnesota's Democratic Party in the late 1940s and the 1950s, moving it to dominance. It is known as the Democratic-Farm-Labor party in the state, a merger of Scandinavian wheat farmers who ran the socialist-minded Non-Partisan League and urban ethnic Catholics from the Democratic Party.

Some semblance of political balance was restored in 1978, the year of Humphrey's death, when Republicans took over the governorship and both U.S. Senate seats after more than a decade without any of them.

Democrats retained control over the Legislature and governor's office throughout much of the 1980s, though Minnesotans in the 1990s resist a strong party orientation. Independent presidential candidate Ross Perot captured 24 percent of their votes in 1992.

One issue that has kept politicians in both parties on edge is abortion. Anti-abortion activists have been especially prevalent in the Republican Party. But they have also made their presence felt among Democrats, leading to pitched battles in party primaries and splits in delegations to national conventions. Throughout the state, a large concentration of socially conservative Catholics and Lutherans sees some appeal in government intervention, whether it be regulating the economy or abortions.

The Minneapolis-St. Paul area continued to be the population and economic center of the state—though as in so many other places of the country, more of the growth in the 1980s was felt in the suburbs and exurbs than in the cities themselves. The immediate metropolitan area accounted for little more than one-half of the state's population, while an oblong-shaped area encompassing the region from St. Cloud to Rochester accounted

for about two-thirds of the state's population.

Democrats are most entrenched in the Minneapolis-based 5th District. They are also ensconced in the St. Paul-based 4th District and in the labor stronghold of the 8th District, which includes the Iron Range and the vast expanse of the state's northeast quadrant.

Republicans seem most secure in the two suburban districts outside of the Twin Cities. The 3rd District, which extends south and west from the cities, is a wealthy GOP stronghold. The horseshoe-shaped 6th District to the north is more competitive.

The mostly rural 1st and 2nd districts in the south are Republican but independent-minded. Perot ran strongest there in 1992, while conservative Democrats prevailed in House elections. The sprawling 7th District in the northwest is the state's most fiercely competitive.

Redistricting after the 1990 census looked to be perfunctory, considering that Minnesota had exhibited no major population changes in the previous decade and had retained its eight congressional districts. But drawing new district lines became a contentious and litigious affair.

The initial disagreement had a partisan cast. On Jan. 10, 1992, GOP Gov. Arne Carlson vetoed a map that the Democratic-controlled Legislature had passed the day before, a map closely resembling the one Minnesota had used for a decade.

A federal court stepped in Feb. 19, breaking the logjam with its own plan for congressional and legislative districts. It seemed to lessen Democratic support in the competitive 6th and 7th districts.

State officials appealed, saying the federal court exceeded its authority in cutting off the efforts of a state court, which was at work on its own congressional and legislative maps. On March 11, Associate Supreme Court Justice Harry A. Blackmun ordered that Minnesota's 1992 U.S. House elections be run under the map issued by the federal panel.

But state officials finally had their way on Feb. 23, 1993, when the Supreme Court ruled that federal courts generally cannot decide redistricting cases until parallel proceedings in state courts have run their course. Writing for the 9-0 majority in *Growe v. Emison*, Justice Antonin Scalia said the federal courts must defer so long as the state court moves in a timely manner.

The Supreme Court's decision meant that while the state's eight representatives could remain in office through the 103rd

Congress, there would be slightly different district lines for the 1994 election. Following the map drawn by the state court, the 6th District became a little more Democratic, while the 3rd District became more Republican.

Note: Tables and district data are based on the 1992 district lines.

Table 1   Population

District	Population	Population under 18	Voting-age population	Median age
1	546,887	147,824	399,063	32.6
2	546,887	156,407	390,480	33.5
3	546,888	148,075	398,813	32.0
4	546,887	136,432	410,455	32.1
5	546,887	112,624	434,263	32.6
6	546,888	164,583	382,305	30.6
7	546,888	151,962	394,926	32.5
8	546,887	148,876	398,011	34.7
State	4,375,099	1,166,783	3,208,316	32.5

Table 2   Voting-Age Persons

District	White*	Black*	American Indian, Eskimo, or Aleut*	Asian or Pacific Islander*	Other*	Hispanic*	Male*	Female*
1	98.2%	0.3%	0.2%	0.9%	0.3%	0.8%	48.2%	51.8%
2	98.9	0.1	0.3	0.4	0.3	0.7	48.6	51.4
3	96.7	1.1	0.3	1.6	0.3	0.8	48.1	51.9
4	91.8	3.4	0.7	3.1	1.0	2.2	46.7	53.3
5	87.7	7.3	1.8	2.7	0.6	1.5	47.3	52.7
6	97.1	1.0	0.5	1.1	0.2	0.7	49.6	50.4
7	97.5	0.2	1.7	0.4	0.2	0.6	48.7	51.3
8	97.5	0.4	1.7	0.3	0.1	0.4	48.8	51.2
State	95.6	1.8	0.9	1.3	0.4	1.0	48.2	51.8

*As percent of voting-age population.

Table 3   Voting-Age Persons by Age Groups

District	18-24*	25-44*	45-54*	55-64*	65 and over*
1	15.3%	41.0%	13.2%	11.1%	19.4%
2	11.6	41.3	13.5	11.8	21.7
3	12.1	51.4	15.1	10.3	11.1
4	14.9	46.2	12.4	10.3	16.1
5	15.4	47.4	10.7	9.3	17.3
6	13.1	54.3	15.7	8.8	8.1
7	15.9	38.3	12.6	11.9	21.3
8	11.9	40.5	13.9	12.5	21.2
State	13.8	45.1	13.4	10.7	17.0

*As percent of voting-age population.

Table 4   Income and Occupation

District	Median family income	Families in poverty	White collar*	Blue collar*	Service*	Farm*
1	$34,403	6.4%	51.2%	26.5%	15.4%	6.8%
2	32,084	7.4	46.2	29.6	14.0	10.1
3	49,714	2.7	71.0	17.8	10.5	0.7
4	40,605	7.5	66.6	19.6	13.2	0.6
5	36,817	10.2	66.9	18.4	14.2	0.5
6	46,461	3.8	62.1	25.9	11.2	0.8
7	28,104	11.1	48.4	26.0	16.5	9.1

District	Median family income	Families in poverty	White collar*	Blue collar*	Service*	Farm*
8	30,259	9.8	49.3	30.5	16.4	3.8
State	36,916	7.3	58.5	24.0	13.7	3.8

*As percent of employed persons age 16 and over.

Table 5   Education: School Years Completed

District	Less than grade 9*	Grades 9-12 no diploma*	High school diploma*	College bachelor's degree or higher*
1	10.8%	9.5%	36.0%	18.3%
2	14.9	9.3	38.4	13.5
3	2.6	5.1	26.7	33.2
4	6.1	8.6	30.2	28.3
5	5.6	9.9	27.0	29.3
6	3.4	7.3	33.5	22.7
7	15.9	9.8	34.7	14.4
8	10.1	12.5	37.8	13.9
State	8.6	9.0	33.0	21.8

*As percent of persons age 25 and over.

Table 6   Housing and Residential Patterns

District	Owner occupied	Renter occupied	Urban	Rural
1	75.3%	24.7%	52.1%	47.9%
2	77.2	22.8	42.4	57.6
3	74.5	25.5	97.6	2.4
4	63.3	36.7	99.8	0.2
5	54.8	45.2	100.0	0.0
6	79.9	20.1	89.6	10.4
7	74.8	25.2	37.7	62.3
8	78.8	21.2	39.6	60.4
State	71.8	28.2	69.9	30.1

1st District

Southeast — Rochester; Part of Mankato

When he talks to audiences unfamiliar with the 1st, Rep. Timothy Penny describes it this way: "It's Redwing Shoes, the Mayo Clinic, Hormel and the valley of the Jolly Green Giant."

The "valley" is still mostly rural, and agriculture—corn, grains, dairy and hog farming—is the major focus. The rolling hills that extend from the Mississippi River to the great bend in the Minnesota River offer farmers some of the state's most productive land. Except for Rochester and some Mississippi River towns, the population centers in the 1st are devoted to serving the surrounding farms, or in the case of Austin, processing the main local product—hogs.

Austin's economy is fed by the meat- and food-processing plants in the area, and the name Hormel says it all. George A. Hormel founded the company in 1891. At the Mower County Historical Center, visitors can see the original Hormel building, along with steam locomotives and horse-drawn carriages.

And while there are pockets of Democratic strength (Mower County is the most consistently Democratic in the 1st), the district as a whole is overwhelmingly Republican with a keen independent streak.

The state's redistricting odyssey has not changed that configuration. A 1993 Supreme Court decision upheld a state-drawn redistricting map and invalidated a plan crafted by the federal courts. The federally drawn plan was used in the 1992 election. However, the new state-drafted districts will be in effect for the 1994 congressional election. Although the 1st will change little, it gained North Mankato. Now the whole metropolitan area of Mankato, the district's second largest city, will be in the same congressional district.

In 1992, the district gave Ross Perot about 27 percent of the vote—more than in any state district except the 2nd. The state overall was one of Perot's biggest successes. In 1988, George Bush won the old 1st with only 51 percent of the vote; Bill Clinton narrowly carried the 1st in 1992.

Still a fixture in the 1st is Redwing Shoes. Located in Red Wing, the company employs more than 1,000 people. The district is also known for the world-famous Mayo Clinic, located in Rochester. The facility now employs about 1,000 physicians in the 19-story facility. And IBM's largest domestic facility, which employs about 7,600 people, is in Rochester.

Rochester (Olmsted County) has a more white-collar orientation than the rest of the district. Its voters are more reliably Republican than many of the 1st's farmers, who often stray from GOP traditions.

Another of the 1st's claims to fame is as the scene of one of the last chapters of Old West history. It was in Northfield (Rice County) that Jesse James and his gang were finally stopped in 1876 when they attempted to rob the Northfield Bank and were ambushed by townfolk. Each Labor Day weekend, thousands attend the "Defeat of Jesse James Days" celebration.

Election Returns

	1st District	Democrat	Republican
1992	President*	109,829 (38.7%)	98,384 (34.7%)
	House	206,369 (74.0%)	72,367 (26.0%)
1990	Senate	97,808 (43.8%)	125,614 (56.2%)
	Governor	99,936 (45.4%)	120,383 (54.6%)
1988	President	128,761 (48.4%)	137,036 (51.6%)
	Senate	101,727 (38.6%)	162,088 (61.4%)
1986	Governor	100,513 (53.0%)	89,201 (47.0%)

*Vote for Perot was 75,227 (26.5%).

Demographics

Population 546,887

Percent change from 1980 7.3%

Land area 9,425 square miles

Population per square mile 58

Counties, 1990 population

Blue Earth	54,044	Mower	37,385
Dakota (pt.)	7,495	Olmsted	106,470
Dodge	15,731	Rice	49,183
Faribault	16,937	Scott (pt.)	6,999
Fillmore	20,777	Steele	30,729
Freeborn	33,060	Wabasha	19,744
Goodhue	40,690	Waseca	18,079
Houston	18,497	Winona	47,828
Le Sueur	23,239		

Cities, 1990 population (10,000 or more)

Albert Lea	18,310	Owatonna	19,386
Austin	21,907	Red Wing	15,134
Faribault	17,085	Rochester	70,745
Mankato (pt.)	31,468	Winona	25,399
Northfield	14,684		

Race and Hispanic origin

White 97.8%
Black 0.3%
American Indian, Eskimo, or Aleut. 0.3%
Asian or Pacific Islander 1.2%
Other 0.4%
Hispanic origin 1.0%

Ancestry

American	1.5%	Irish	14.0%
Czechoslovakian	3.8%	Italian	1.0%
Danish	3.2%	Norwegian	21.3%
Dutch	2.8%	Polish	4.0%
English	8.6%	Scotch Irish	1.2%
French	3.9%	Scottish	1.4%
German	55.3%	Swedish	6.1%

Universities/colleges, 1990-1991 enrollment

Austin Community College, Austin 1,244
Bethany Lutheran College, Mankato 311
Carleton College, Northfield 1,857
Mankato State University; Mankato 16,575
Mayo Grad School of Medicine, Rochester 1,083
Mayo School of Health-Related Sciences, Rochester 214
Pillsbury Baptist Bible College, Owatonna 367
Rochester Community College, Rochester 4,156
St. Mary's College, Winona 2,167
St. Olaf College, Northfield 3,097
University of Minnesota Technical College, Waseca 1,042
Winona State University, Winona 7,713
Winona Technical College, Winona 631

Newspapers, total circulation (in all districts)

Albert Lea Tribune 8,925
Austin Daily Herald 8,020
Fairmont Sentinel 9,608
La Crosse Tribune 35,788
Mankato Free Press 25,156
Minneapolis Star Tribune 408,869
Owatonna People's Press 7,060
Red Wing Republican Eagle 7,875
Rochester Post-Bulletin 39,117
St. Paul Pioneer Press 205,116
Winona Daily News 13,774

Commercial television stations, affiliations

ADI: Minneapolis-St. Paul (37%), Rochester-Mason City-Austin (35%), Mankato (15%) and La Crosse-Eau Claire (13%)
KAAL, Austin (ABC)
KTTC, Rochester (NBC)
WLAX, La Crosse (Fox)
WXOW-TV, La Crosse (ABC)

Cable television systems, total subscribers

Jones Intercable Inc.; Owatonna 6,013
Mankato Cablevision; Mankato 16,000
TCI of Southern Minnesota; Rochester 31,085
TCI of Southern Minnesota; Winona 9,610

Westmarc Cable; Albert Lea 5,200
Westmarc Cable; Austin 5,600
Westmarc Cable; La Crosse 14,955

Businesses and other major employers

Mayo Foundation; Rochester; medical doctors 15,800
IBM Corp.; Rochester; computers 7,600
Guy F. Atkinson Co.; Winona; metal forgings/stampings 1,500
George A. Hormel & Co.; Austin; meatpacking 1,300
Gruner & Jahr USA Printing & Publishing Co./Brown Printing Co. Div.; Waseca; periodicals 1,300
Mankato State University; Mankato 1,100
Redwing Shoe Co., Red Wing 1,100
State of Minnesota/Faribault Regional Center; Faribault 1,100
Smead Mfg. Co.; Hastings; paper products 1,000
Federated Mutual Insurance Co.; Owatonna; fire/marine/casualty insurance 1,000
E. F. Johnson Co.; Waseca; radios/transmitters 900
Sheldahl Inc.; Northfield; electronic components 828
Crenlo Inc./Emcor Products; Rochester; cabinets/fixtures 810
SPX Corp.; Owatonna; cutlery/handtools/hardware 800
Winona State University; Winona 800
Kahler Corp.; Rochester; hotel operations 800
City of Faribault/Public Schools; Faribault 750
Farmstead Foods Inc.; Albert Lea; meatpacking 725
St. Olaf College; Northfield 675
City of Rochester/Utilities Dept.; Rochester 666
Streater Inc.; Albert Lea; store partitions/fixtures 665
Swift-Eckrich Inc.; Wells; meat products 600
Winona Health Services Inc.; Winona 591
ICI Composites Inc./ICI Fiberite Corp.; Winona; plastics/molds 560
Treasure Island Bingo & Casino; Welch; casino 525

2nd District

Southwest — Willmar

Much of the landscape of the 2nd District is dotted for mile upon mile with silos and grain elevators, broken up occasionally by small crossroads market centers. The 2nd's largest town, Willmar, has only about 18,000 people.

The 2nd supports a small industrial economy, which includes three Minnesota Mining and Manufacturing Co. facilities—one in New Ulm and two in Hutchinson. (Hutchinson is the site of the company's largest facility, which employs about 2,000 people.) Turkey growing and processing is big business in Worthington (Nobles County).

But the economy is still driven by farming. Bisected by the broad Minnesota River, the sprawling 27-county district includes some of the best farmland in the state. The well-to-do farmers in the south along the Iowa border enjoy bountiful harvests of corn and soybeans. Moving north along the Minnesota River, dairy farms become more common.

The political flavor of the 2nd tends to be Republican with an independent streak. In 1992, Democrat Bill Clinton carried the 2nd with 37 percent of the vote; George Bush took 35 percent, Ross Perot 28 percent.

In the prairie counties north of the Minnesota River, the land

is sandy and rocky and the politics more unpredictable. Farmers here have to work harder to scratch out a living, and they display a frequent dissatisfaction with any party that is in power.

Many voters in the southern tier of counties are of German ethnic stock. Like those in the adjoining 1st District, they share a strong Republican tradition and an allegiance to the Farm Bureau, the most conservative of the state's major farm organizations.

At the turn of the century, the Scandinavian settlers here battled constantly with railroads, bankers and grain merchants. Disillusioned by Republicans and Democrats, they were ripe for third-party alternatives.

The Farmer-Labor Party found early support in this region, as did presidential candidate Robert La Follette in 1924, when his Progressive Party carried many of the counties in this area. Today, with strong support from the National Farmers Union, Democrats often run well in this part of the district.

The economies of some small towns—Morton, Redwood Falls and Granite Falls in the southern part of the district—have benefited from casinos that are owned and operated by the Sioux Indians. The casinos have produced an influx of visitors and jobs to the towns; Redwood Falls has been building new lodging facilities to accommodate the added traffic.

In 1993, the Supreme Court rejected the federally drawn redistricting map that had been used in the 1992 election. Candidates will run under a state-drawn plan in 1994. Changes for the 2nd were minimal: North Mankato moved to the 1st.

Election Returns

	2nd District	Democrat	Republican
1992	President*	103,447 (36.8%)	98,015 (34.9%)
	House	132,156 (47.9%)	131,587 (47.7%)
1990	Senate	92,160 (44.4%)	115,357 (55.6%)
	Governor	94,827 (47.1%)	106,380 (52.9%)
1988	President	114,451 (48.1%)	123,445 (51.9%)
	Senate	98,103 (41.1%)	140,493 (58.9%)
1986	Governor	89,947 (47.9%)	97,681 (52.1%)

Vote for Perot was 79,610 (28.3%).

Demographics

Population 546,887

Percent change from 1980 7.3%

Land area 16,121 square miles

Population per square mile 34

Counties, 1990 population

Big Stone 6,285	McLeod 32,030
Brown 26,984	Meeker 20,846
Carver 47,915	Murray 9,660
Chippewa 13,228	Nicollet 28,076
Cottonwood 12,694	Nobles 20,098
Hennepin (pt.) 5,157	Pipestone 10,491
Jackson 11,677	Redwood 17,254
Kandiyohi 38,761	Renville 17,673
Lac qui Parle 8,924	Rock 9,806
Lincoln 6,890	Scott (pt.) 38,087
Lyon 24,789	Sibley 14,366
Martin 22,914	Swift 10,724

Watonwan 11,682   Yellow Medicine 11,684
Wright (pt.) 68,192

Cities, 1990 population (10,000 or more)
Chanhassen (pt.) 11,732   North Mankato (pt.)
Chaska 11,339   10,164
Fairmont 11,265   Prior Lake 11,482
Hutchinson 11,523   Shakopee 11,739
Marshall 12,023   Willmar 17,531
New Ulm 13,132

Race and Hispanic origin
White 98.5%
Black 0.2%
American Indian, Eskimo, or Aleut. 0.4%
Asian or Pacific Islander 0.5%
Other 0.5%
Hispanic origin 1.0%

Ancestry
American 1.5%   French 3.8%
Belgian 1.2%   German 60.7%
Czechoslovakian 2.4%   Irish 10.0%
Danish 2.8%   Norwegian 17.3%
Dutch 4.5%   Polish 3.5%
English 5.9%   Swedish 10.9%
Finnish 1.2%

Universities/colleges, 1990-1991 enrollment
Dr. Martin Luther College, New Ulm 442
Gustavus Adolphus College, St. Peter 2,371
Southwest State University, Marshall 3,060
Willmar Community College, Willmar 1,380
Willmar Technical College, Willmar 1,411
Worthington Community College, Worthington 851

Newspapers, total circulation (in all districts)
Fairmont Sentinel 9,608
Mankato Free Press 25,156
Marshall Independent 8,233
Minneapolis Star Tribune 408,869
New Ulm Journal 9,673
Worthington Daily Globe 13,758

Commercial television stations, affiliations
ADI: Minneapolis-St. Paul (82%) and Sioux Falls-Mitchell (18%)
KEYC-TV, Mankato (CBS)
KRWF, Redwood Falls (ABC)

Cable television systems, total subscribers
American Cablevision; Marshall 5,000
Heritage Cablevision; Willmar 7,200
Triax Cablevision USA; Lake Minnetonka 11,656

Businesses and other major employers
IDS Financial Corp.; Olivia; investment offices 3,000
Hutchinson Technology Inc.; Hutchinson; computer equipment 2,140
Taylor Corp./Carlson Craft Div.; Mankato; commercial printing 2,100
Minnesota Mining & Mfg. Co./Magnetic Audio-Video Product Div.; Hutchinson; electronic components 2,000
Schwans Sales Enterprises Inc./Plum Creek Finer Foods; Marshall; frozen foods 1,500
Jennie-O Foods Inc.; Willmar; turkey products 1,500

Monfort Inc.; Worthington; meat products 1,200
Rosemount Inc.; Chanhassen; measuring/controlling devices 1,000
Jackpot Junction Bingo & Casino; Morton; casino 920
State of Minnesota/St. Peter Regional Treatment Center; Saint Peter 900
Minnesota Mining & Mfg. Co./Electric Products Div.; New Ulm; photographic equipment/supplies 775
State of Minnesota/Willmar Regional Treatment Center; Willmar 750
Nordictrack Inc.; Chaska; exercise equipment 700
Suttle Apparatus Corp.; Hector; communications equipment 650
Rice Memorial Hospital; Willmar 650
City of Willmar/Municipal Utilities Commission; Willmar 650
Kraft General Foods Inc.; New Ulm; dairy products 600
Sathers Inc./Powells Div.; Round Lake; grocery products 600
Waconia Ridgeview Hospital Foundation; Waconia 600
Gustavus Adolphus College; St. Peter 550
Reliance Electric Co./Kato Engineering Co.; Mankato; electrical industrial apparatus 515
Lake Region Mfg. Co.; Chaska; medical instruments 506

3rd District

Southern Twin Cities Suburbs — Bloomington; Minnetonka

With its abundance of high-tech industries, white-collar workers, golf courses and middle-class homes, the 3rd is for the most part the very picture of suburban living.

The last round of the state's redistricting pingpong was good news for Rep. Jim Ramstad. The 3rd, already a Republican safe haven, became slightly more so when the Supreme Court rejected the federally drawn map that had been used in the 1992 elections. In 1993, the high court ruled that federal courts must stand aside until challenges to redistricting plans run their course in state courts. In 1994, candidates will run in districts drawn by the state court in 1992.

In 1992, the district included parts of Dakota, Hennepin, Scott and Washington counties. Under the state plan upheld by the Supreme Court, the 3rd will include more Wright County than Washington County, will pick up Republican Plymouth and western Hennepin County communities, and will gain the largely Democratic cities of Brooklyn Park and Brooklyn Center.

The 3rd extends beyond the western and southern extremities of the metropolitan area. Suburbanization has touched most of the 3rd except the very farthest reaches, which remain rural.

The district is a popular home for Fortune 500 companies. Several, including Cargill Inc., the world's largest privately owned corporation, are here. Cargill, which is based in Minnetonka and employs about 2,500 people there, is a diversified company that handles everything from wheat and corn processing to financial trading. Other Fortune 500 companies with headquarters in the 3rd include lawnmower maker Toro; food giant General Mills; high-tech Control Data; Cray Research, which makes supercomputers; and grocery chain Super Valu.

But perhaps most crucial to many local businesses is the fate of one of the area's largest employers, the financially troubled Northwest Airlines, which employs about 15,000 people. The airline headquarters is located just across district lines in the 4th District.

The 3rd also has another claim to fame—the nation's largest shopping mall. The Mall of America in Bloomington (Hennepin County) measures 4.2 million square feet. Nearly a third of the 30 million people who visited the mall during the first two months after it opened in 1992 were tourists, some coming from as far as Japan, England and Germany.

A few Democrats can be found in Dakota County, but its comparatively small number of voters will not be enough to loosen the hold the GOP typically enjoys in the 3rd. Republican influence is so strong here that in 1984, home-state Democratic presidential nominee Walter F. Mondale drew less than one-third of the vote in a number of precincts.

In 1988, George Bush won the old 3rd with 54 percent of the vote. However, voters were not as enthusiastic in 1992, giving Bush 36 percent to Bill Clinton's 40 percent and Ross Perot's 24 percent.

Election Returns

	3rd District	Democrat	Republican
1992	President*	129,171 (39.5%)	117,975 (36.1%)
	House	104,606 (33.3%)	200,240 (63.8%)
1990	Senate	111,401 (46.5%)	128,209 (53.5%)
	Governor	88,644 (38.3%)	142,905 (61.7%)
1988	President	125,616 (46.1%)	146,650 (53.9%)
	Senate	87,434 (32.7%)	179,887 (67.3%)
1986	Governor	71,364 (49.1%)	74,096 (50.9%)

*Vote for Perot was 79,877 (24.4%).

Demographics

Population 546,888

Percent change from 1980 7.3%

Land area 595 square miles

Population per square mile 920

Counties, 1990 population
Dakota (pt.) 238,083	Scott (pt.) 12,760
Hennepin (pt.) 259,236	Washington (pt.) 36,809

Cities, 1990 population (10,000 or more)
Apple Valley 34,598	Hastings 15,445
Bloomington 86,335	Inver Grove Heights
Burnsville 51,288	22,477
Cottage Grove 22,935	Lakeville 24,854
Eagan 47,409	Minnetonka (pt.) 48,370
Eden Prairie 39,311	Richfield 35,710
Edina (pt.) 43,060	

Race and Hispanic origin
White 96.0%
Black 1.3%
American Indian, Eskimo, or Aleut. 0.3%
Asian or Pacific Islander 2.0%
Other 0.4%
Hispanic origin 1.1%

Ancestry
American 1.3%	Irish 16.5%
Czechoslovakian 2.3%	Italian 2.6%
Danish 2.4%	Norwegian 16.8%
Dutch 2.2%	Polish 4.9%
English 11.0%	Russian 1.1%
Finnish 1.3%	Scotch Irish 1.4%
French 5.6%	Scottish 2.0%
French Canadian 1.1%	Swedish 13.1%
German 46.3%	

Universities/colleges, 1990-1991 enrollment
Dakota County Tech Institute, Rosemount 1,782
Inver Hills Community College, Inver Grove Heights 5,136
Normandale Community College, Bloomington 8,851
Northwestern Chiropractic College, Bloomington 522
Rasmussen Business College, Hopkins 326

Newspapers, total circulation (in all districts)
Minneapolis Star Tribune 408,869
St. Paul Pioneer Press 205,116

Commercial television stations, affiliations
ADI: Minneapolis-St. Paul (100%)

Cable television systems, total subscribers
Cable TV North Central; Eagan/Burnsville 22,407
Continental Cablevision of Minnesota; St. Paul 60,000
King Videocable Co.; Newport 9,287
Nortel Cable TV; Bloomington 18,344
Paragon Cable; Eden Prairie 43,800
Paragon Cable; Minneapolis 66,400
Star Cablevision; Rosemount 15,198

Businesses and other major employers
Paramax Inc.; St. Paul; computer equipment 7,500
Unisys Corp./Electronic Info Systems Group; St. Paul; computer services 5,000
Rosemount Inc./Analytical Div.; Hopkins; industrial controls 2,900
Cargill Inc.; Wayzata; farm-product raw materials 2,500
Blue Cross/Blue Shield of Minnesota; St. Paul; medical service/health insurance 2,400
Seagate Technology Inc.; Minneapolis; computer services 2,000
Super Valu Stores Inc.; Hopkins; grocery products 1,965
Control Data Corp./Computer Products Group; Minneapolis; professional/commercial equipment 1,800
Control Data Corp./Government Systems Div.; Minneapolis; computer equipment 1,500
Rosemount Inc./Aero Space Div.; Savage; measuring/controlling devices 1,200
Johnston Coca-Cola Bottling Group/Midwest Coca-Cola Bottling; St. Paul; beverages 1,200
National Car Rental System; Minneapolis; auto rentals 1,200
United Healthcare Corp.; Hopkins; medical doctors 1,200
Cray Research Inc.; St. Paul; supercomputers 1,000
County of Dakota; Hastings 1,000
Minnesota Mining & Mfg. Co.; Cottage Grove; chemical products 980
MTS Systems Corp.; Hopkins; measuring/controlling devices 950
City of Savage/Independent School District; Savage 950
Fingerhut Corp.; Hopkins; catalog retailers 900

Thermo King Corp.; Minneapolis; refrigeration 850

Partners National Health Plans; Minneapolis; medical service/health insurance 800

Guy Schoenecker Inc.; Minneapolis; furniture 750

Eaton Corp./Hydraulics Div.; Hopkins; motor vehicles/equipment 750

Gelco Corp.; Hopkins; credit institutions 750

City of Wayzata/Independent School District; Wayzata 740

Starkey Laboratories Inc.; Hopkins; medical instruments/supplies 670

Farmers Union Central Exchange Inc.; St. Paul; petroleum/natural gas 650

Donaldson Co. Inc.; Minneapolis; industrial machinery 640

Toro Co.; Minneapolis; lawn mowers 625

Northgate Computer Systems; Hopkins; computer equipment 610

Worldwide Cryogenics Holdings; Minneapolis; cryogenic tanks 600

American Medical Systems Inc.; Hopkins; medical instruments/supplies 600

Datacard Corp.; Hopkins; office equipment 600

American Family Mutual Insurance Co./American Family Insurance Co.; Hopkins; insurance services 600

U.S. Postal Service; St. Paul 592

Control Data Corp./Government Systems Operation; Hopkins; computer services 564

Dayton Hudson Corp.; Savage; department stores 550

City of Lakeville/Independent School District; Lakeville 550

Dataserv Inc.; Hopkins; computer services 550

City of Bloomington; Minneapolis 514

4th District

St. Paul and Suburbs

The 4th, with its deep roots in the labor movement and its liberal academic communities, is in many ways a Democratic candidate's dream.

The economy of the 4th is fueled by the government, education and industry. St. Paul, the capital, is the hub of state government, whose agencies employ thousands of unionized workers. The headquarters for the Minnesota Mining and Manufacturing Co., better known as 3M Co., is in a suburb of St. Paul and employs about 19,000 people, many of whom also are union members. West Publishing Co., the nation's largest publisher of legal books, employs 2,000.

The district, which includes Ramsey County and parts of Dakota and Washington counties, also has numerous college campuses. The influence of the University of Minnesota (which is located mostly in the 5th District) and its 57,000 students can also be felt.

St. Paul (population 272,000), located in Ramsey County, is a traditionally Democratic city with a large German and Irish-Catholic population. The city developed as a major port and railroading center and still has a strong labor tradition. Many portions of the district are middle- or high-income areas.

The city became more diverse during the 1970s and 1980s, when there was an influx of Hmong refugees from southeast Asia. In some neighborhoods in mostly northern and eastern sections of the city, some business signs are written in Hmong. The first Hmong elected to public office in the nation was elected to St. Paul's school board in 1991.

The city's Hispanic population has also increased. On the west side of the city (and in the city of West St. Paul) is a well-organized, solidly Democratic Hispanic community.

The working-class neighborhoods on St. Paul's East Side are drab and solidly Democratic. The precincts here have routinely supported virtually every major statewide Democratic candidate of recent years.

More than 30 years ago, when Eugene J. McCarthy represented St. Paul in the House, nearly 90 percent of the district vote came from the city. But with the growth of the suburbs and a decline in St. Paul's population (from its 1960 peak of 313,000), St. Paul now accounts for just half the district vote.

Most of the suburban vote lies north of the city in Ramsey County, which leans to the GOP. Farther north are the more-affluent suburbs of Shoreview, North Oak and White Bear Lake, which vote Republican more often.

A 1993 Supreme Court decision upheld a state-drawn redistricting map, rejecting a plan crafted by the federal courts and used in the 1992 election. The state plan will be used in the 1994 election.

Under the state plan approved by the high court, Mendota Heights, which votes Republican, was returned to the 4th. Redistricting also added Sunfish Lake, a small conservative suburb.

Election Returns

	4th District	Democrat	Republican
1992	President*	148,046 (51.6%)	79,690 (27.8%)
	House †	159,796 (57.6%)	101,744 (36.7%)
1990	Senate	132,518 (59.2%)	91,438 (40.8%)
	Governor	92,362 (43.6%)	119,655 (56.4%)
1988	President	160,662 (61.2%)	101,706 (38.8%)
	Senate	115,355 (45.8%)	136,475 (54.2%)
1986	Governor	94,660 (59.4%)	64,645 (40.6%)

Vote for Perot was 59,361 (20.7%).   †*Independent/other is greater than 5%.*

Demographics

Population 546,887

Percent change from 1980 7.3%

Land area 211 square miles

Population per square mile 2,596

Counties, 1990 population

| Dakota (pt.) 29,649 | Washington (pt.) 31,473 |
| Ramsey 485,765 | |

Cities, 1990 population (10,000 or more)

Maplewood 30,954	South St. Paul (pt.) 10,401
Mounds View 12,541	St. Paul 272,235
New Brighton 22,207	Vadnais Heights 11,041
North St. Paul 12,376	West St. Paul 19,248
Oakdale (pt.) 10,879	White Bear Lake (pt.) 24,288
Roseville 33,485	
Shoreview 24,587	Woodbury (pt.) 16,477

Race and Hispanic origin

White 88.9%

Black 4.2%

American Indian, Eskimo, or Aleut. 0.9%

Asian or Pacific Islander 4.7%
Other 1.2%
Hispanic origin 2.9%

Ancestry

American 1.0%	German 43.0%
Czechoslovakian 2.2%	Irish 16.7%
Danish 2.0%	Italian 3.6%
Dutch 1.7%	Norwegian 11.2%
English 8.2%	Polish 6.2%
Finnish 1.1%	Scotch Irish 1.2%
French 6.4%	Scottish 1.6%
French Canadian 1.5%	Swedish 11.5%

Universities/colleges, 1990-1991 enrollment

Bethel College, St. Paul 1,791
Bethel Theological Seminary, St. Paul 495
College of St. Catherine, St. Paul 2,523
College of St. Thomas, St. Paul 9,805
Concordia College, St. Paul 1,235
Hamline University, St. Paul 2,514
Lakewood Community College, St. Paul 6,217
Luther Northwestern Theological Seminary, St. Paul 746
Macalester College, St. Paul 1,853
Metropolitan State University, St. Paul 5,228
National College-St. Paul, St. Paul 211
Northwestern College, St. Paul 950
St. Paul Technical College, St. Paul 2,369
United Theological Seminary, New Brighton 210
William Mitchell College of Law, St. Paul 1,152

Newspapers, total circulation (in all districts)

Minneapolis Star Tribune 408,869
St. Paul Pioneer Press 205,116

Commercial television stations, affiliations

ADI: Minneapolis-St. Paul (100%)
    KARE, Minneapolis (NBC)
    KITN, Minneapolis (Fox)
    KMSP-TV, Minneapolis (None)
    KLGT, Minneapolis (None)
    WCCO-TV, Minneapolis (CBS)
    KSTP-TV, St. Paul (ABC)

Cable television systems, total subscribers

Cable TV North Central; Roseville 22,921
Cable TV North Central; White Bear Lake 22,277
Continental Cablevision of Minnesota; St. Paul 60,000

Businesses and other major employers

Minnesota Mining & Mfg. Co.; St. Paul; paper products/mineral products/cleaners 19,000
Northwest Airlines Inc.; St. Paul; airline 15,000
U.S. Veterans Affairs Dept.; St. Paul; hosptial 3,000
U.S. Postal Service; St. Paul 2,673
State of Minnesota/Community College Dept.; St. Paul 2,500
St. Paul Companies Inc.; St. Paul; fire/marine/casualty insurance 2,496
Marsden Building Maintenance Co.; St. Paul; building services 2,400
United Hospital Inc.; St. Paul 2,300
Ford Motor Co./Twin Cities Assembly Plant; St. Paul; motor vehicle assembly: St. Paul 2,200

Fair Oakes Lake Apartments/Anoka Maple Manor; St. Paul; nursing 2,200
West Publishing Co.; St. Paul; legal book publishing 2,000
Alliant Techsystems Inc.; St. Paul; ordnance/accessories 2,000
State of Minnesota/Jobs & Training Dept.; St. Paul 1,950
St. Paul Ramsey Medical Center; St. Paul 1,800
Minnesota Mutual Life Insurance Co.; St. Paul; life insurance 1,700
Quebecor Printing USA Inc.; St. Paul; commercial printing 1,250
Burlington Northern Railroad Co.; St. Paul; railroads 1,200
Ryder Truck Rental Inc./Ryder Student Transportation; St. Paul; bus charter service 1,200
State of Minnesota/Revenue Dept.; St. Paul 1,200
Bethesda Lutheran Medical Center; St. Paul 1,185
St. Joseph's Hospital; St. Paul 1,150
State of Minnesota/Metro Waste Control Commission; St. Paul 1,100
University of St. Thomas; St. Paul 1,005
Northwest Publications Inc./Pioneer Press Dispatch; St. Paul; newspapers 1,000
Ecolab Inc.; St. Paul; soaps/cleaners 1,000
Waldorf Corp.; St. Paul; paperboard mills 1,000
U.S. Internal Revenue Service; St. Paul 1,000
First Bank National Assn.; St. Paul; commercial banks 996
Higher Education Assistance Foundation; St. Paul 950
Best Inc.; St. Paul; bars/restaurants 900
Hamline University; St. Paul 900
Land O'Lakes Inc.; St. Paul; butter/dairy products 800
Control Data Corp.; St. Paul; measuring/controlling devices 800
American Security Corp.; St. Paul; business services 800
Baker Industries Inc./Sims Security; St. Paul; security/business services 800
State Farm Life Insurance Co.; St. Paul; management/public relations 800
County of Ramsey; St. Paul 750
Metropolitan State University; St. Paul 750
Gillette Co.; St. Paul; toiletries 700
Koch Refining Co. Inc.; St. Paul; petroleum refining 700
U.S. Army Corps of Engineers; St. Paul; engineering services 700
Western Life Insurance Co. Inc.; St. Paul; life insurance 685
Dayton Hudson Corp./Target Stores; St. Paul; department stores 675
State of Minnesota/Pollution Control Agency; St. Paul 650
Deluxe Corp.; St. Paul; bookbinding 600
University of Minnesota/College of Veterinary Medicine; St. Paul 600
State of Minnesota/Natural Resources Dept.; St. Paul 600
Mutual Service Casualty Insurance Co.; St. Paul; fire/casualty insurance 590
U.S. Postal Service; St. Paul 550
Prom Management Group Inc./Prom Catering Co.; St. Paul; bars/restaurants 550
William Mitchell College of Law; St. Paul 550
Children's Hospital Inc.; St. Paul 534
Brown & Bigelow Inc./Hoyle Products Div.; St. Paul; commercial printing 525

5th District

Minneapolis and Suburbs

In 1992, when many a voter was rediscovering his or her more liberal roots, most residents of the 5th could honestly say they never left the Democratic fold. The district is home to former Vice President Walter F. Mondale. Voters here gave him 63 percent of the vote against Ronald Reagan in 1984. Michael S. Dukakis and Bill Clinton also won the 5th in 1988 and 1992 with about 60 percent of the vote.

Minneapolis residents account for nearly three-fourths of the 5th's voters, and except for those on the city's southwest side, they predictably choose liberal candidates over conservatives.

Scandinavians remain the most conspicuous ethnic group; it is no coincidence that Rep. Martin Sabo includes his middle name, Olav, on all his official papers to eliminate any doubt that he is of Norwegian heritage.

Although many of the flour mills that once lined the Mississippi River at St. Anthony's Falls have moved, the major companies that settled in Minneapolis—Pillsbury and General Mills—have remained and diversified. They are among the major employers in the Twin Cities, along with the new "brain power" companies that find Minneapolis ideally suited for their needs. Honeywell has its worldwide headquarters here. The white-collar professionals who have been attracted by these "clean" industries help to give the city an image that is reflected in the glistening towers of its downtown area.

However, even the presence of Fortune 500 companies could not halt a late 1980s downturn in the regional economy. In 1993, the Supreme Court rejected the federally drawn redistricting map that had been used in the 1992 election. Candidates will now run under a state-drawn plan. The state redistricting barely changed the boundaries of the 5th, and made little change in the political landscape.

Past redistricting efforts have added considerable suburban territory to the 5th. A number of suburban areas—including Golden Valley and New Hope—were added under the federal plan and will remain here in 1994.

When the federal plan was upheld in 1992, Republicans had hoped that these suburbs would mean more Republican votes and a chance to beat Sabo, but the effect was negligible.

While the power of organized labor has waned over the years, it is still a factor. In addition, the district has the state's highest number of minorities, who tend to vote Democratic. Hennepin County has the state's largest number of Hispanic and black voters at 60,114 and 13,978, respectively.

Minneapolis is not only parks, lakes, glass and chrome. Northwest of the downtown office towers are some poor neighborhoods, home to blacks and some of the city's Chippewa Indian population. East of the Mississippi are older, more traditional blue-collar areas adjoining the main campus of the University of Minnesota (57,000 students).

Election Returns

	5th District	Democrat	Republican
1992	President*	167,941 (58.2%)	68,072 (23.6%)
	House †	174,139 (63.0%)	77,093 (27.9%)
1990	Senate	143,798 (63.4%)	83,069 (36.6%)
	Governor	108,972 (49.5%)	111,345 (50.5%)
1988	President	182,523 (65.0%)	98,140 (35.0%)
	Senate	126,378 (48.1%)	136,229 (51.9%)

	5th District	Democrat	Republican
1986	Governor	110,256 (65.1%)	59,187 (34.9%)

Vote for Perot was 52,374 (18.2%).   †*Independent/other is greater than 5%.*

Demographics

Population 546,887

Percent change from 1980 7.3%

Land area 104 square miles

Population per square mile 5,264

Counties, 1990 population
Hennepin (pt.) 546,887

Cities, 1990 population (10,000 or more)

Brooklyn Center (pt.) 28,887	Minneapolis 368,383
Crystal 23,788	New Hope 21,853
Golden Valley 20,971	Robbinsdale 14,396
Hopkins 16,534	St. Louis Park 43,787

Race and Hispanic origin
White 83.7%
Black 9.6%
American Indian, Eskimo, or Aleut. 2.4%
Asian or Pacific Islander 3.5%
Other 0.7%
Hispanic origin 1.8%

Ancestry

American 1.3%	Irish 13.6%
Czechoslovakian 1.7%	Italian 2.0%
Danish 1.9%	Norwegian 14.3%
Dutch 1.6%	Polish 5.5%
English 9.0%	Russian 1.9%
Finnish 1.8%	Scotch Irish 1.3%
French 5.2%	Scottish 1.8%
French Canadian 1.1%	Swedish 12.5%
German 33.1%	

Universities/colleges, 1990-1991 enrollment
Augsburg College, Minneapolis 2,505
College of St. Catherine-St. Mark, Minneapolis 843
Medical Institute of Minnesota, Minneapolis 540
Minneapolis College Art & Design, Minneapolis 712
Minneapolis Community College, Minneapolis 4,064
National Education Center, Minneapolis 1,409
North Central Bible College, Minneapolis 1,182
University of Minnesota, Minneapolis 57,175
Walden University, Minneapolis 420

Newspapers, total circulation (in all districts)
Minneapolis Star Tribune 408,869
St. Paul Pioneer Press 205,116

Commercial television stations, affiliations
ADI: Minneapolis-St. Paul (100%)

Cable television systems, total subscribers
King Videocable Co.; Brooklyn Park 47,415
Nortel Cable TV; St. Louis Park 9,351
Paragon Cable; Eden Prairie 43,800
Paragon Cable; Minneapolis 66,400

Military installations, 1991

Minneapolis/St. Paul Intl. Airport Air Force Reserve Station, Minneapolis 661

Businesses and other major employers

University of Minnesota; Minneapolis 30,015

University of Minnesota/Hospital & Clinic; Minneapolis 5,100

Honeywell Inc./Space & Aviation Systems; Minneapolis; aircraft parts 5,000

City of Minneapolis; Minneapolis 5,000

Fairview Hospital Healthcare; Minneapolis 4,751

Dayton Hudson Corp.; Minneapolis; department stores 4,000

Riverside Medical Center Inc./St. Mary's Hospital; Minneapolis 3,751

IDS Financial Corp.; Minneapolis; management/public relations 3,304

Hennepin County Medical Center; Minneapolis 3,300

Honeywell Inc./Residential Div.; Minneapolis; measuring/controlling devices 3,000

North Memorial Medical Center; Minneapolis 2,950

U.S. Postal Service; Minneapolis 2,800

Methodist Hospital; Minneapolis 2,500

Honeywell Inc./Protective Services Div.; Minneapolis; business/security services 2,400

Northwestern National Life Insurance Co.; Minneapolis; life insurance 2,200

Pillsbury Co./Ford Service Div.; Minneapolis; food products 2,000

Media Cowles Co./Star Tribune; Minneapolis; newspapers 2,000

Honeywell Inc./Military Avionics Div.; Minneapolis; electrical industrial apparatus 2,000

County of Hennepin; Minneapolis 2,000

Dayton Hudson Corp.; Minneapolis; management/public relations 2,000

Northern States Power Co.; Minneapolis; electric services 1,975

General Mills Inc.; Minneapolis; bars/restaurants 1,900

Alliant Techsystems Inc./Underseas Systems Div.; Hopkins; ordnance/accessories 1,800

First Bank National Assn.; Minneapolis; commercial banks 1,700

Robbinsdale Independent School District; Minneapolis 1,581

Prudential Insurance of America Inc.; Minneapolis; life insurance 1,500

Norwest Bank Minnesota; Minneapolis; commercial banks 1,500

Honeywell Inc.; Minneapolis; measuring/controlling devices 1,300

Minneapolis Children's Medical Center; Minneapolis 1,200

Federal Reserve Bank of Minneapolis; Minneapolis 1,050

Lutheran Brotherhood Inc.; Minneapolis; life insurance 1,014

American Building Maintenance Co.; Minneapolis; building services 1,000

Retail Grocers Insurance Trust; Minneapolis; insurance services 900

Park Nicollet Medical Center; Minneapolis; medical doctors 900

TW Services Inc./Volume Services; Minneapolis; bars/restaurants 856

Tennant Co.; Minneapolis; refrigeration 800

Piper Jaffray Inc.; Minneapolis; security brokers 800

Honeywell Inc.; Minneapolis; business services 800

Becklund Home Health Care; Minneapolis; home health services 800

State of Minnesota/Transportation Dept.; Minneapolis 800

TCF Bank Savings; Minneapolis; savings institutions 775

Norwest Technical Services; Minneapolis; management/public relations 773

Augsburg College; Minneapolis 714

ITT Financial Corp./ITT Consumer Services; Minneapolis; credit institutions 700

Policy Management Systems Corp.; Hopkins; insurance services 700

Dorsey & Whitney; Minneapolis; legal services 700

Defense Manufacturers Suppliers Assn. Corp.; Minneapolis; management/public relations 680

Walker Methodist Health Center; Minneapolis; nursing 675

Musicland Stores Corp./Musicland; Minneapolis; music stores 650

Health One Corp./Metropolitan-Mt. Sinai Medical Center; Minneapolis 650

United Parcel Service Inc.; Minneapolis; mail services 600

International Multifoods Corp.; Minneapolis; grocery products 600

Gateway Foods Inc.; Minneapolis; warehousing 600

Inter-Regional Financial Group; Minneapolis; security brokers 600

State of Minnesota/Health Dept.; Minneapolis 600

Group Health Plan Inc.; Minneapolis; medical doctors 587

Dahlberg Inc./Dahlberg Hearing Systems; Minneapolis; medical instruments 555

Sandoz Nutrition Corp./Precision Foods Co. Div.; Minneapolis; food products 550

St. Therese Home Inc.; Minneapolis; nursing 550

Faegre & Benson; Minneapolis; legal services 541

Ellerbe Becket Co.; Minneapolis; engineering/architectural services 525

6th District

Northern Twin Cities Suburbs

The horseshoe-shaped 6th District wraps around the Twin Cities, taking in surrounding suburbs, plus a bit of farmland farther out. The district includes marginally Democratic areas, some Democratic strongholds and GOP-leaning suburbs. Redistricting made the area slightly more Democratic.

In the latest round of the state's redistricting pingpong, the Supreme Court in 1993 rejected the federally drawn map that had been used in the 1992 election. The high court ruled that federal courts must stand aside until challenges to redistricting plans run their course in state courts. In 1994, candidates will run under a state-drawn plan.

Most of the areas lost by the 6th under the state plan, including the northern and western Hennepin County suburbs, were represented by Republicans in the state Legislature.

The district gained east and central Dakota County and southern Washington County. These areas are developed or emerging suburbs with white-collar voters. However, these voters tend to favor abortion rights and increased funding of education; the Republican Party cannot count on them for reliable support.

The state court also added Farmington, Hastings and Inver Grove Heights, which tend to be more Democratic than their neighbors. (Apple Valley, Eagan and Rosemount in Dakota County were also added for the 1994 elections.)

Anoka County, which casts nearly 45 percent of the vote, is the strongest Democratic area in the 6th. It remained loyal to Walter F. Mondale in 1984, Michael S. Dukakis in 1988 and Bill Clinton in 1992. In 1992, the county chose the GOP challenger at least in part because of the Democratic incumbent's 697 overdrafts at the House bank.

Anoka is a mix of new suburbs, farms and small towns. Lake Wobegon, the mythical town in Garrison Keillor's one-time weekly radio program "A Prairie Home Companion," is modeled after Keillor's boyhood home in Anoka County.

But the Lake Wobegons of this part of Minnesota are quickly disappearing as the Twin Cities metropolitan area continues to expand farther into the surrounding counties.

The district, which included one of the youngest average populations in the country, picked up more young educated workers. Nearly 80 percent of the homes in the district are owner occupied, compared with about 72 percent statewide. Many of those homeowners are young professionals who work at large companies in the 6th that turn out products from computers to defense equipment.

The major employer in the area is Northwest Airlines, which is actually next door in the 4th District. The airline's headquarters employs about 15,000 people, and its survival is crucial to the local economy.

Another large employer is FMC Corp., a defense contractor located in Fridley, a Minneapolis suburb. The Fridley operation is home to the company's Naval Systems Division, and employs about 2,500 people. The division makes gun and missile launching systems for Navy ships. Medtronic, which produces heart pacemakers and other medical instruments, employs more than 2,000.

Election Returns

	6th District	Democrat	Republican
1992	President*	119,847 (39.5%)	101,495 (33.5%)
	House †	100,016 (33.3%)	133,564 (44.4%)
1990	Senate	106,303 (49.4%)	108,892 (50.6%)
	Governor	91,031 (44.0%)	115,850 (56.0%)
1988	President	122,527 (50.2%)	121,744 (49.8%)
	Senate	94,290 (39.0%)	147,270 (61.0%)
1986	Governor	76,050 (54.9%)	62,441 (45.1%)

*Vote for Perot was 81,908 (27.0%).   †Independent/other is greater than 5%.

Demographics

Population 546,888

Percent change from 1980 7.4%

Land area 1,009 square miles

Population per square mile 542

Counties, 1990 population

Anoka 243,641   Washington (pt.) 77,614
Hennepin (pt.) 221,151 Wright (pt.) 518
Sherburne (pt.) 3,964

Cities, 1990 population (10,000 or more)

Andover 15,216   Coon Rapids 52,978
Anoka 17,192   Fridley 28,335
Blaine (pt.) 38,975   Maple Grove 38,736
Brooklyn Park 56,381   Plymouth 50,889
Champlin 16,849   Ramsey 12,408
Columbia Heights 18,910 Stillwater 13,882

Race and Hispanic origin

White 96.6%
Black 1.2%
American Indian, Eskimo, or Aleut. 0.6%
Asian or Pacific Islander 1.4%
Other 0.3%
Hispanic origin 0.9%

Ancestry

American 1.2%   German 47.0%
Czechoslovakian 1.8%   Irish 15.1%
Danish 2.2%   Italian 2.4%
Dutch 2.1%   Norwegian 16.9%
English 9.3%   Polish 7.0%
Finnish 2.5%   Scotch Irish 1.3%
French 7.1%   Scottish 1.5%
French Canadian 1.6%   Swedish 15.8%

Universities/colleges, 1990-1991 enrollment

Anoka-Ramsey Community College, Coon Rapids
    6,688
North Hennepin Community College, Brooklyn Park
    6,163
Northwestern Electronics Institute, Columbia Heights 543
St. Paul Bible College, St. Bonifacius 517

Newspapers, total circulation (in all districts)

Minneapolis Star Tribune 408,869
St. Cloud Times 27,865
St. Paul Pioneer Press 205,116

Commercial television stations, affiliations

ADI: Minneapolis-St. Paul (100%)

Cable television systems, total subscribers

Cable TV North Central; Anoka 8,161
Cable TV North Central; Blaine 20,980
Cable TV North Central; White Bear Lake 22,277
King Videocable Co.; Brooklyn Park 47,415
Paragon Cable; Eden Prairie 43,800
Triax Cablevision USA; Lake Minnetonka 11,656

Businesses and other major employers

Andersen Corp./Andersen Windows; Bayport; millwork
    3,900
Prudential Insurance of America Inc.; Minneapolis; insurance
    services 3,000
FMC Corp./Naval Systems Div.; Minneapolis;
    ordnance/accessories 2,500
Federal-Hoffman Inc./Federal Cartridge Co.; Anoka;
    ordnance/accessories 2,100
Medtronic Inc.; Minneapolis; medical instruments/supplies
    2,080
Onan Corp./Power Electronics Div.; Minneapolis; electrical
    industrial apparatus 1,975
Carlson Marketing Group Inc.; Minneapolis; passenger trans-
    portation 1,500
Health One Corp./Unity Medical Center; Minneapolis 1,300

Health One Corp./Mercy Hospital Div.; Minneapolis 1,200

Carlson Holdings Inc.; Minneapolis; management/public relations 1,200

Honeywell Inc./Commercial Aviation Div.; Minneapolis; computer/office equipment 1,000

Scimed Life Systems Inc.; Osseo; medical instruments/supplies 800

Wayzata Independent School District; Minneapolis 800

Advance Machine Co.; Minneapolis; floor washing/polishing machines 750

State of Minnesota; Stillwater 735

Dayton Hudson Corp./Target; Minneapolis; department stores 700

Schneider USA Inc.; Minneapolis; medical instruments/supplies 687

Honeywell Inc./Solid State Electronics Center; Minneapolis; electronic components 650

Cornelius IMI Inc.; Anoka; refrigeration 650

State of Minnesota/Transportation Dept.; St. Paul 650

County of Washington; Stillwater 630

Control Data Corp./Empros System Intl.; Minneapolis; management/public relations 585

Honeywell Inc./Honeywell Residential Div.; Minneapolis; measuring/controlling devices 550

7th District

Northwest — Moorhead; Part of St. Cloud

From the prairie wheat fields along the Red River at the western border of the state to the hills, forests and lakes in the middle of the state, this vast district is Minnesota's most marginal—economically as well as politically.

While some district counties, including Kittson, Mahnomen and Beltrami, continue to struggle economically, many of the lake regions are either stable or growing. The area's economy is fueled by farming—dairy, grains and row crops—light manufacturing, tourism and education (the 7th has many community colleges). Many farmers struggle each year to meet high operating costs on land that does not match the quality of the soil farther south. The region's lumber business, once in decline, has revived. And the snowmobile industry has recovered from a spell of dry winters and the 1980s recession.

Politically, the district has been in the marginal category since popular Democrat Bob Bergland left it in 1977 to become Jimmy Carter's secretary of Agriculture. Republican Arlan Stangeland, who represented the 7th from 1977 until 1991, won five of six re-elections with less than 55 percent of the vote.

The district's map changed little under recent redistricting, and neither did the political landscape. In 1993, the Supreme Court rejected the federally drawn map that had been used in the 1992 election. The decision upheld a state redistricting plan.

St. Cloud, which was placed in the 8th District in the federal plan, is included in the 7th under the state map. The seat of Stearns County, St. Cloud, with 49,000 residents, is the district's largest city and one of the fastest growing in the state. For years, it was a major center for granite quarrying. Today the descendants of the old stonecutters share their ancestors' support of the Democratic Party on economic issues, but they often stray to the GOP when social issues, especially abortion, become paramount.

The state plan also returned a major employer. St. Cloud is home to Fingerhut, a mail-order house that sells gadgets and novelty items. Employing more than 4,000 people, Fingerhut is the district's largest employer.

Apart from St. Cloud and Moorhead, a sister city to Fargo, N.D., there are few population centers. But there is a significant Catholic influence in the small towns near St. Cloud, where large churches loom above the surrounding farmland—giving the area some of the feel of rural France or Germany.

But many of the district's towns are vintage Americana. Sauk Centre—about 40 miles northwest of St. Cloud—was the birthplace of novelist Sinclair Lewis, who used his hometown as the model for his novel *Main Street*. Signs along the prime thoroughfare, in fact, call it the "Original Main Street."

The wheat-growing central sections of the district are slightly more populous than the rest and also more Republican.

Sugar beets are grown around Moorhead in the Red River Valley, which possesses some of the 7th's most fertile farmland. In the rolling countryside just to the east, hunters, fishermen and summer tourists are drawn to hundreds of lakes.

Election Returns

	7th District	Democrat	Republican
1992	President*	104,359 (38.4%)	103,624 (38.2%)
	House	133,886 (50.7%)	130,396 (49.3%)
1990	Senate	97,315 (45.1%)	118,258 (54.9%)
	Governor	111,832 (54.2%)	94,345 (45.8%)
1988	President	119,866 (48.0%)	129,977 (52.0%)
	Senate	100,647 (40.3%)	149,126 (59.7%)
1986	Governor	107,319 (52.7%)	96,240 (47.3%)

Vote for Perot was 63,610 (23.4%).

Demographics

Population 546,888

Percent change from 1980 7.3%

Land area 26,282 square miles

Population per square mile 21

Counties, 1990 population

Becker	27,881	Norman	7,975
Beltrami	34,384	Otter Tail	50,714
Benton (pt.)	14,722	Pennington	13,306
Clay	50,422	Polk	32,498
Clearwater	8,309	Pope	10,745
Douglas	28,674	Red Lake	4,525
Grant	6,246	Roseau	15,026
Hubbard	14,939	Stearns	118,791
Kittson	5,767	Stevens	10,634
Lake of the Woods	4,076	Todd	23,363
Mahnomen	5,044	Traverse	4,463
Marshall	10,993	Wadena	13,154
Morrison (pt.)	22,721	Wilkin	7,516

Cities, 1990 population (10,000 or more)

Bemidji	11,245	Moorhead	32,295
Fergus Falls	12,362	St. Cloud (pt.)	43,566

Race and Hispanic origin

White 96.8%
Black 0.2%
American Indian, Eskimo, or Aleut. 2.2%

Asian or Pacific Islander 0.5%
Other 0.3%
Hispanic origin 0.8%

Ancestry

American 1.8%	French 4.8%
Czechoslovakian 2.2%	German 48.5%
Danish 1.7%	Irish 8.3%
Dutch 1.8%	Norwegian 25.5%
English 5.5%	Polish 6.1%
Finnish 1.9%	Swedish 10.3%

Universities/colleges, 1990-1991 enrollment

Alexandria Technical College, Alexandria 1,585
Bemidji State University, Bemidji 5,428
College of Saint Benedict, Saint Joseph 1,916
Concordia College, Moorhead 2,948
Fergus Falls Community College, Fergus Falls 1,228
Moorhead State University, Moorhead 8,900
Northland Community College, Thief River Falls 905
St. Cloud State University, Saint Cloud 17,076
St. John's University, Collegeville 2,035
Thief River Falls Tech College, Thief River Falls 560
University of Minnesota, Morris 2,167
University of Minnesota Tech College, Crookston 1,221

Newspapers, total circulation (in all districts)

Fargo Forum 53,270
Fergus Falls Daily Journal 10,603
Grand Forks Herald 38,953
Minneapolis Star Tribune 408,869
St. Cloud Times 27,865
St. Paul Pioneer Press 205,116

Commercial television stations, affiliations

ADI: Fargo (62%) and Minneapolis-St. Paul (38%)
KCCO-TV, Alexandria (CBS)
KSAX, Alexandria (ABC)
KBRR, Thief River Falls (Fox)
KVRR, Fargo (Fox)

Cable television systems, total subscribers

Midwest Cable Communications Inc.; Bemidji 5,000
TCI Cable; Sauk Rapids 18,000
TCI of Minnesota; Moorhead 6,200

Businesses and other major employers

Fingerhut Corp./COMB; St. Cloud; catalog retailers 4,500
St. Cloud State University; St. Cloud 1,300
Cold Spring Granite Co.; Cold Spring; stone products 1,000
Jennie-O Foods Inc.; Melrose; turkey products 780
Golden Plump Poultry Inc.; Cold Spring; poultry products 750
Moorhead State University; Moorhead 750
Champion Intl. Corp.; Sartell; paper mills 670
St. John's University; Collegeville 635
City of Bemidji/Independent School District; Bemidji 630
Concordia College; Moorhead 629
Bankers Systems Inc.; St. Cloud; commercial printing 610
Genmar Industries Inc./Lund American Div.; Little Falls; shipbuilding/repairing 600
Polaris Industries Partners; Roseau; transportation equipment 600
Bemidji State University; Bemidji 600

West Central Turkeys Inc.; Pelican Rapids; turkey products 550
Lake Region Hospital & Nursing; Fergus Falls 535

8th District
Northeast — Iron Range; Duluth

If the 8th were dropped onto a map of the East Coast, it would reach from Washington to Connecticut. The district measures about 26,000 square miles and is generally Democratic territory. The mostly rural area encompasses a vast stretch of land that includes flat farmland, steep bluffs and lakes. The district's largest city, Duluth (population 85,500), is also the state's fourth largest. From here much of the grain from the Plains states is shipped east.

Singer Bob Dylan grew up in Hibbing, which calls itself the "Iron Ore Capital of the World." A local bus line that started in Hibbing in 1914 with one open touring car became the Greyhound Bus Lines. And the nation's only gas station designed by Frank Lloyd Wright is in Cloquet.

Based in the barren and remote northern reaches of Minnesota, the district has a long Democratic tradition.

Immigrants from Sweden, Finland and eastern Europe settled here after the turn of the century to work in the iron mines scattered throughout the Mesabi and Vermillion iron ranges. Strongly allied with unions, the workers on the Iron Range today are unswerving in their allegiance to the Democrats.

The economy is fueled by a variety of industries. Tourism is crucial and the timber industry is also a major employer, both in timber harvesting and in the production of paper and wood products.

In the southern counties farmers grow corn and small grain. Dairy farming slowed in the south during the mid-1980s when many farmers here sold their herds. The federal government paid milk producers to send their herds to slaughter in order to cut milk production and reduce the government's purchases of dairy surpluses.

The economy has taken its share of knocks. The discovery of new taconite mining technology helped boost the local economy after the high-quality iron ore mines were largely depleted in the mid-1940s. But taconite mining is heavily mechanized and employs fewer people than the old underground mining operations.

The prolonged slump of the steel industry and the ups and downs of the automobile industry have created additional job shortages. And domestic steel production has faced intense foreign competition.

Casinos on Indian reservations have been one economic bright spot. The gambling enterprises have brought jobs and spurred sales and construction in many nearby towns.

The district changed only slightly in the last act of the state's redistricting odyssey. In 1993, the Supreme Court rejected the federally drawn map that had been used in the 1992 election. In 1994, candidates will run under a state-drawn plan. The 8th lost portions of Benton and Sherburne counties to the 7th.

Election Returns

	8th District	Democrat	Republican
1992	President*	138,357 (47.8%)	80,586 (27.8%)
	House †	167,104 (59.2%)	83,823 (29.7%)

	8th District	Democrat	Republican
1990	Senate	130,925 (58.3%)	93,803 (41.7%)
	Governor	142,771 (65.1%)	76,612 (34.9%)
1988	President	154,795 (59.9%)	103,621 (40.1%)
	Senate	132,744 (51.6%)	124,625 (48.4%)
1986	Governor	138,608 (68.7%)	63,151 (31.3%)

Vote for Perot was 70,539 (24.4%).   †*Independent/other is greater than 5%.*

Demographics

Population 546,887

Percent change from 1980 7.3%

Land area 25,870 square miles

Population per square mile 21

Counties, 1990 population

Aitkin 12,425	Kanabec 12,802
Benton (pt.) 15,463	Koochiching 16,299
Carlton 29,259	Lake 10,415
Cass 21,791	Mille Lacs 18,670
Chisago 30,521	Morrison (pt.) 6,883
Cook 3,868	Pine 21,264
Crow Wing 44,249	Sherburne (pt.) 37,981
Isanti 25,921	St. Louis 198,213
Itasca 40,863	

Cities, 1990 population (10,000 or more)

Brainerd 12,353	Duluth 85,493
Cloquet 10,885	Hibbing 18,046

Race and Hispanic origin

White 96.9%
Black 0.4%
American Indian, Eskimo, or Aleut. 2.1%
Asian or Pacific Islander 0.4%
Other 0.2%
Hispanic origin 0.5%

Ancestry

American 2.4%	Irish 10.7%
Czechoslovakian 1.7%	Italian 3.3%
Danish 1.8%	Norwegian 15.1%
Dutch 2.1%	Polish 6.4%
English 7.8%	Scotch Irish 1.4%
Finnish 8.5%	Scottish 1.5%
French 6.5%	Swedish 17.8%
French Canadian 1.3%	Yugoslavian 1.7%
German 35.9%	

Universities/colleges, 1990-1991 enrollment

Brainerd Community College, Brainerd 1,837
College of St. Scholastica, Duluth 1,969
Hibbing Community College, Hibbing 2,047
Itasca Community College, Grand Rapids 1,423
Mesabi Community College, Virginia 1,536
Rainy River Community College, International Falls 626
University of Minnesota, Duluth 10,339
Vermilion Community College, Ely 634

Newspapers, total circulation (in all districts)

Duluth News-Tribune 58,551
Minneapolis Star Tribune 408,869
St. Cloud Times 27,865
St. Paul Pioneer Press 205,116

Commercial television stations, affiliations

ADI: Duluth-Superior (70%) and Minneapolis-St. Paul (30%)
  WDIO-TV, Duluth (ABC)
  KBJR-TV, Superior (NBC)
  KDLH-TV, Duluth (CBS)
  WIRT, Hibbing (ABC)
  KCCW-TV, Walker (CBS)

Cable television systems, total subscribers

Bresnan Communications Inc.; Brainerd 5,700
Bresnan Communications Inc.; Duluth 23,964
Northland Cablevision; Eveleth 6,660
Range TV Cable Co. Inc.; Hibbing 5,583
TCI Cable; Sauk Rapids 18,000

Military installations, 1991

Duluth Intl. Airport Air Force Guard Station, Duluth 407

Businesses and other major employers

St. Mary's Medical Center; Duluth 1,969
Potlatch Corp./Northwest Paper Div.; Cloquet; pulp mills 1,800
LTV Corp./LTV Steel Mining Corp.; Hoyt Lakes; iron ores 1,500
University of Minnesota; Duluth 1,450
St. Luke's Hospital of Duluth; Duluth 1,200
Blandin Paper Co.; Grand Rapids; paper mills 1,050
Pamida Inc.; Elk River; apparel/accessory stores 1,000
Minnesota Power & Light Co.; Duluth; electric services 950
Corporate/Grand Casino Mille Lacs; Onamia; hotel 800
Miller-Dwan Medical Center; Duluth 733
State of Minnesota/Human Services Center; Cambridge 710
Potlatch Corp./Northwest Paper Div.; Brainerd; paper mills 700
City of Brainerd/Independent School District; Brainerd 700
State of Minnesota/Human Services Center; Brainerd 650
Edgell Communications Inc.; Duluth; school supplies 600
Duluth Clinic Ltd. Inc.; Duluth; medical doctors 600
St. Joseph's Medical Center; Brainerd; religious organizations 600
Hibbing Taconite; Hibbing; iron ores 575
United Steelworkers; Iron; labor organization 570
State of Minnesota/Moose Lake Regional Treatment Center; Moose Lake 545
Chisago Health Services; Chisago 524

Mississippi

While most of the Sunbelt sets a fast pace for economic development, progress in Mississippi can be measured at the pace of one of its sluggish, muddy rivers. Mississippi has long stood out for the depth of its problems, including the nation's lowest per capita income ($13,343) and highest adult illiteracy rate (33 percent). But no longer can Mississippi take solace in being the slowest economic performer in a slow region. While population grew and the job market expanded in other southern states during the 1980s, Mississippi's population grew by only 2 percent and opportunities for the poor beyond cotton and soybean picking and low-wage catfish farming remained scant.

The slow population growth—in the South only Louisiana and Kentucky recorded slower growth—left Mississippi's five-member House delegation intact. The remap process mainly corrected for population inequities, but not before a federal judge in 1991 rejected Mississippi's redistricting plan for discriminating against blacks. Despite decades of migration up the Mississippi Valley to northern cities, 36 percent of the state's population is black, the largest proportion in the country. And while blacks have made painfully slow progress improving their economic situation, their political clout is increasing. The 2nd District, stretching eastward from the Mississippi delta region, gained 13 precincts in Jackson, the state capital. This added poor black precincts to the 2nd while leaving more affluent black neighborhoods in the Republican-leaning 4th District. The Gulf Coast 5th District gained half of Jones County from the 3rd, and there were slight district line adjustments between the 1st and 2nd Districts in the northwest corner of the state.

None of this was expected to change the overall voting patterns of the state through the 1990s. Mississippi hews to a pattern established by many southern states: the more local the elected official, the more likely he or she will be black and Democratic. In 1993, the governor and the state's two senators were white Republicans; one of the five Democratic House members was black as were 24 percent of the 174 state legislators; and both legislative branches had a Democratic majority. At the national level, Mississippi was staunch in its support of the GOP. In 1992, half of Mississippi voters supported President Bush, his biggest proportion of any state.

Through the 1990s Mississippi's dependence on agriculture shows no signs of abating. The 1990 census showed that 53 percent of state residents are rural dwellers; only Vermont, West Virginia and Maine had a higher percentage. Cotton and soybeans are the leading crops. Timber and chicken farming are major pursuits. And one district, the 2nd, encompassing the delta region, produces three-fourths of the nation's catfish. The reality in Mississippi is not so much an overabundance of farms as an absence of urban areas. Jackson, the largest city in the state, has a population under 200,000, and no other city in the state reported more than 50,000 residents in 1990. In fact, the state's only other quasi-urban areas are in the extreme north and southwest corners outside of Memphis, Tenn., and New Orleans.

In terms of industry, Mississippi remains dangerously dependent on defense and aerospace spending. The major defense-related employers include Keesler Air Force Base—the nation's fourth largest—along the Gulf Coast in Biloxi, Ingalls Shipyard and Naval station in Pascagoula, Meridian Naval Air Station near the Alabama border and Lockheed Corp. plants in Meridian and Iuka. Economists estimate that as many as half the 5th District's residents in the southeastern corner of Mississippi work in defense-related industries, rivaling southeastern Connecticut and Southern California as the nation's most defense-dependent regions.

The state also shows two other telltale signs of economic vulnerability: a dependence on tourist dollars from visitors to the hundreds of antebellum mansions in the Mississippi Valley; and development of a new casino. It is a sign of the depth of economic despair that the $200,000 a month generated by the Splash Casino in Tunica County, poorest county in the state and one of the poorest in the nation, was enough to cut county unemployment in half in the early 1990s.

Mississippi also must survive the 1990s without the aid of one of its great benefactors, Rep. Jamie Whitten. The 1st District House member came into the decade as the senior-most member of Congress—he voted to declare war on Japan after Pearl Harbor. But in 1992, in ailing health, he lost his chairmanship of the House Appropriations Committee. The days when Whitten could bring a gigantic water project like the Tennessee-Tombigbee Waterway to his home state with the wave of a pen are over.

And although Mississippi is light-years ahead of where it was

MISSISSIPPI

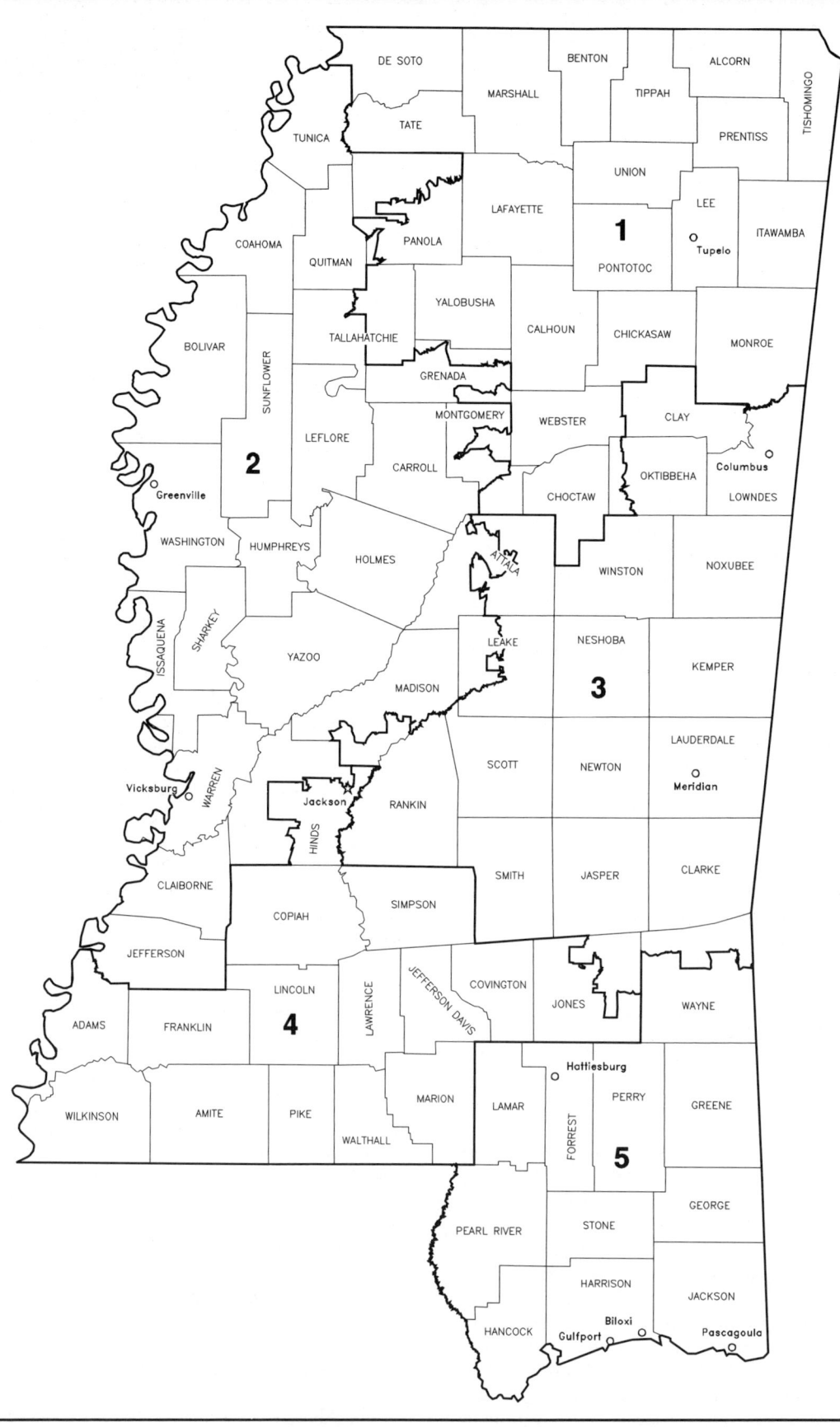

in race relations in the 1950s and 1960s, problems persist. There was the federal court rejection of the state's initial redistricting plan in 1991. Two years later the U.S. Attorney General's office launched an investigation into suspicious jailhouse deaths of blacks. And well into the decade blacks continued to press a case in the federal courts that predominantly black colleges in the state get proportionately less money than the predominantly white schools.

Table 1   Population

District	Population	Population under 18	Voting-age population	Median age
1	514,548	140,620	373,928	32.3
2	514,845	168,902	345,943	29.3
3	515,314	145,024	370,290	31.4
4	513,853	146,100	367,753	31.9
5	514,656	146,115	368,541	31.0
State	2,573,216	746,761	1,826,455	31.2

Table 2   Voting-Age Persons

District	White*	Black*	American Indian, Eskimo, or Aleut*	Asian or Pacific Islander*	Other*	Hispanic*	Male*	Female*
1	79.6%	20.0%	0.1%	0.3%	0.1%	0.4%	46.9%	53.1%
2	41.5	58.1	0.1	0.3	0.1	0.5	44.9	55.1
3	70.7	27.9	0.9	0.5	0.1	0.5	46.8	53.2
4	63.0	36.5	0.1	0.3	0.1	0.4	45.8	54.2
5	81.0	17.5	0.2	1.1	0.2	1.1	48.1	51.9
State	67.5	31.6	0.3	0.5	0.1	0.6	46.5	53.5

*As percent of voting-age population.

Table 3   Voting-Age Persons by Age Groups

District	18-24*	25-44*	45-54*	55-64*	65 and over*
1	15.8%	39.7%	14.4%	11.9%	18.2%
2	16.7	39.9	12.9	11.4	19.2
3	16.3	41.8	13.4	11.6	17.0
4	15.2	41.3	13.1	12.1	18.4
5	16.4	42.5	14.0	11.8	15.3
State	16.1	41.0	13.6	11.7	17.6

*As percent of voting-age population.

Table 4   Income and Occupation

District	Median family income	Families in poverty	White collar*	Blue collar*	Service*	Farm*
1	$25,412	15.8%	43.3%	44.3%	9.7%	2.7%
2	19,236	31.0	46.6	32.3	14.5	6.5
3	26,396	17.6	51.7	33.9	11.3	3.1
4	24,491	20.4	54.5	29.7	12.9	2.9
5	25,736	17.1	52.9	31.4	13.5	2.2
State	24,448	20.2	49.8	34.6	12.3	3.4

*As percent of employed persons age 16 and over.

Table 5   Education: School Years Completed

District	Less than grade 9*	Grades 9-12 no diploma*	High school diploma*	College bachelor's degree or higher*
1	18.1%	22.3%	29.6%	10.8%
2	22.0	22.6	22.8	13.5
3	13.7	19.7	28.1	16.1
4	13.6	18.7	26.2	18.1
5	11.1	17.3	30.7	15.1
State	15.6	20.1	27.5	14.7

*As percent of persons age 25 and over.

Table 6   Housing and Residential Patterns

District	Owner occupied	Renter occupied	Urban	Rural
1	77.2%	22.8%	32.9%	67.1%
2	64.4	35.6	45.3	54.7
3	74.0	26.0	39.4	60.6
4	71.3	28.7	52.7	47.3
5	70.0	30.0	65.0	35.0
State	71.5	28.5	47.1	52.9

1st District

North — Tupelo

Change has slowly crept into this overwhelmingly rural area, awakening the sluggish economy and bringing some jobs and industries that might have been unthinkable to residents 20 years ago. While much of the district remains loyally Democratic, the economic evolution has brought an increase in Republican white-collar voters.

One recent sign of the shift came with groundbreaking for a Lockheed Corp. manufacturing plant in Iuka in Tishomingo County that will produce Advanced Solid Rocket Motors for NASA. By 1993, the construction of the plant employed about 1,000 workers. The project has spurred construction of a hospital and a high school in the county.

In addition, northeastern Mississippi has become a hub for furniture manufacturing, particularly lower-priced pieces such as recliners. A national furniture market is held twice a year in the Lee County city of Tupelo, which is the district's biggest, with 31,000 people. However, Tupelo is still best known as the birthplace of Elvis Presley. The shotgun house where Presley was born is now a tourist attraction.

Another boost to local economic development came with the 1985 opening of the Tennessee-Tombigbee Waterway, which cuts through a handful of counties in the northeastern corner of the 1st, connecting the Tennessee and Tombigbee rivers to create an unbroken link to the Gulf of Mexico.

On the western side of the district in Lafayette County is Oxford, site of the University of Mississippi (11,300 students). Popularly known as "Ole Miss," the university is the home of the Center for the Study of Southern Culture. Square Books, on the town square, attracts area literati, including local authors such as Willie Morris and John Grisham. Oxford was the home base for William Faulkner, whose stately home, Rowan Oak, is host to thousands of Faulkner enthusiasts each year.

Beyond a handful of built-up areas, the district remains largely rural. It takes in the flat, rich farmland on the edge of the Delta region in northwestern Mississippi and the less fertile plots of the northeastern Hill Country. Although cotton was once the dominant crop in this region, 1st District farmers now also produce soybeans, rice, corn, wheat, livestock and poultry.

Over the past two decades, the steadiest population growth in the 1st has come in the Memphis, Tenn., suburbs of De Soto County. Population has nearly doubled there since 1970, and De Soto now casts more votes than any other county in the 1st—about 13 percent of the total. In a district where many retain their traditional allegiance to the Democratic Party, white-collar De Soto is unmistakably Republican. Since 1976, the county has supported GOP presidential candidates (George Bush won 59 percent here in 1992), and it also voted against Democrat Rep. Jamie Whitten in the 1992 election, giving his GOP challenger 61 percent.

Election Returns

	1st District	Democrat	Republican
1992	President*	84,648 (41.5%)	101,265 (49.7%)
	House	121,664 (59.5%)	82,952 (40.5%)
1991	Governor	65,056 (51.5%)	61,163 (48.5%)
1988	President	54,460 (39.2%)	84,355 (60.8%)
	Senate	82,091 (53.6%)	71,144 (46.4%)
1987	Governor	68,758 (52.5%)	62,247 (47.5%)

*Vote for Perot was 17,979 (8.8%).

Demographics

Population 514,548

Percent change from 1980 1.9%

Land area 10,396 square miles

Population per square mile 49

Counties, 1990 population

Alcorn 31,722	Montgomery (pt.) 3,481
Benton 8,046	Oktibbeha (pt.) 2,164
Calhoun 14,908	Panola (pt.) 17,270
Chickasaw 18,085	Pontotoc 22,237
Choctaw 9,071	Prentiss 23,278
De Soto 67,910	Tallahatchie (pt.) 7,767
Grenada (pt.) 1,264	Tate 21,432
Itawamba 20,017	Tippah 19,523
Lafayette 31,826	Tishomingo 17,683
Lee 65,581	Union 22,085
Marshall 30,361	Webster 10,222
Monroe 36,582	Yalobusha 12,033

Cities, 1990 population (10,000 or more)

Corinth 11,820	Tupelo 30,685
Southaven 17,949	

Race and Hispanic origin

White 76.8%
Black 22.8%
American Indian, Eskimo, or Aleut. 0.1%
Asian or Pacific Islander 0.3%
Other 0.1%
Hispanic origin 0.5%

Ancestry

American 16.4%	Irish 20.0%
Dutch 1.7%	Italian 1.1%
English 11.3%	Scotch Irish 3.0%
French 1.8%	Scottish 1.2%
German 9.0%	

Universities/colleges, 1990-1991 enrollment

Blue Mountain College, Blue Mountain 347
Itawamba Community College, Fulton 3,281
Northeast Mississippi Community College, Booneville 2,955
Northwest Mississippi Community College, Senatobia 3,893
Rust College, Holly Springs 1,021
University of Mississippi, University 11,288
Wood Junior College, Mathiston 519

Newspapers, total circulation (in all districts)

Corinth Daily Corinthian 8,943
Jackson Clarion-Ledger 106,717
Memphis Commercial Appeal 193,211
Northeast Mississippi Daily Journal 38,548

Commercial television stations, affiliations

ADI: Columbus-Tupelo (60%), Memphis (37%) and Greenwood-Greenville (3%)
WTVA, Tupelo (NBC)
WLOV-TV, West Point (ABC)

Cable television systems, total subscribers

Comcast Cablevision; Corinth 7,439
Comcast Cablevision; Tupelo 11,000
Heritage Cablevision; Oxford 5,632
Memphis Cablevision; Memphis 148,135

Businesses and other major employers

North Mississippi Medical Center; Tupelo 2,530
University of Mississippi; University 1,800
Panola Mills Inc.; Batesville; underwear 1,250
Universal Furniture Industries/Bench Craft; Ripley; furniture 1,200
Cortelco USA Inc.; Corinth; telephone/telegraph equipment 1,185
Cooper Tire & Rubber Co.; Tupelo; tires 1,000
Malone & Hyde Inc.; Southaven; grocery products 1,000
Super Sagless Corp.; Tupelo; metal furniture parts 950
Washington Furniture Mfg. Co.; Houlka; furniture 920
Dover Elevator Intl.; Horn Lake; elevators 850
Universal Furniture Industries/Benchcraft Div.; Blue Mountain; furniture 800
Ringier America Inc.; Corinth; periodicals/textbooks 749
Mohasco Upholstered Furniture/Stratford Co.; Okolona; furniture 700
Day-Brite Lighting Inc.; Tupelo; electric lighting 700
Action Industries Inc./Comfort Craft Chairs; Tupelo; furniture 700
Amory Garment Co.; Amory; outerwear 699
Magnolia Hospital; Corinth 615
Coltec Industries Inc./Holley Automotive Div.; Water Valley; motor vehicle parts 600
Denton Mills Inc./Obion-Denton Mills Inc.; New Albany; undergarments 600
County of Alcorn; Corinth 584
Townhouse-Penthouse Industries; Amory; furniture 580
Lucky Star Industries Inc.; Baldwyn; work pants 550
Franklin Corp.; Houston; furniture 550

Tecumseh Products Co.; Verona; refrigeration 550

Sunbeam Corp./Oster; Holly Springs; household appliances 550

ASG Acquisition Corp./American Signature; Olive Branch; commercial printing 550

Piper Impact Inc.; New Albany; nonferrous rolling/drawing 524

2nd District

West Central — Mississippi Delta

The 2nd is known both for the rich culture and extreme poverty of its people. The latter has produced an atmosphere that is kinder to Democratic candidates than elsewhere in the state. Bill Clinton took 58 percent here in 1992.

"The Birthplace of the Blues," the Delta was home to many musicians. Muddy Waters was born in Rolling Fork, near Greenville, and grew up on a Clarksdale plantation in Coahoma County. Ike Turner and John Lee Hooker are also from Clarksdale, which boasts a blues museum.

Ever since swamp-draining technology and cheap black labor transformed the Delta into an agricultural gold mine in the years after the Civil War, the region has had a far larger population of poor rural blacks than affluent white cotton growers.

In the past generation, thousands of Delta blacks, pushed out of work by farm mechanization, moved to Chicago, St. Louis and closer Sun Belt cities such as Little Rock and Memphis.

While a black middle class has always existed in the 2nd, many blacks here live in abject poverty. With 50 percent of majority-black Tunica County living below the poverty line, the county is the poorest in the state and one of the poorest in the nation. However, those figures are expected to change with the advent of casino gambling. Long lines of patrons from across the region wait for a chance to play at the Splash Casino, which has generated nearly $200,000 a month since it opened in October 1992. The state gaming commission says the casino has cut the county's unemployment figures in half.

Some residents of the 2nd still make a living off the land. While soybeans have replaced cotton as the largest cash crop, more acreage is devoted to cotton.

More recently the Delta has become synonymous with "aquaculture" because it produces about 75 percent of the nation's catfish. While the catfish processing industry has provided jobs, it has been criticized for the low wages it pays. Striking workers have gained some concessions from the plant owners. The Catfish Institute, an industry trade group, is based in Belzoni.

The largest city in the 2nd is Greenville, an old river port and cotton market and the historical "capital" of the Mississippi Delta. The city, which has slightly more than 45,000 people and is the seat of Washington County, is one of the few areas that has grown in recent years.

In the southern part of the district, in Warren County, is the city of Vicksburg. It is still best known for the Battle of Vicksburg, a 47-day siege in 1863 that resulted in the city's surrender to Union Gen. Ulysses S. Grant. Two regional medical centers are here. And the U.S. Army Corps of Engineers employs about 3,800 people in environmental and water resources projects.

Redistricting added 13 precincts in Jackson, the state capital, to the 2nd. (One more was added just outside the city.) Many of those residents added were poor blacks, leaving more affluent blacks in the more conservative 4th.

Election Returns

	2nd District	Democrat	Republican
1992	President*	105,052 (58.0%)	66,350 (36.6%)
	House	133,361 (76.4%)	41,248 (23.6%)
1991	Governor	76,128 (59.5%)	51,871 (40.5%)
1988	President	97,424 (55.4%)	78,556 (44.6%)
	Senate	102,922 (58.8%)	72,261 (41.2%)
1987	Governor	82,450 (62.9%)	48,729 (37.1%)

*Vote for Perot was 9,805 (5.4%).

Demographics

Population 514,845

Percent change from 1980 2.0%

Land area 12,251 square miles

Population per square mile 42

Counties, 1990 population

Attala (pt.) 6,678	Leflore 37,341
Bolivar 41,875	Madison (pt.) 27,538
Carroll 9,237	Montgomery (pt.) 8,907
Claiborne 11,370	Panola (pt.) 12,726
Coahoma 31,665	Quitman 10,490
Grenada (pt.) 20,291	Sharkey 7,066
Hinds (pt.) 51,123	Sunflower 32,867
Holmes 21,604	Tallahatchie (pt.) 7,443
Humphreys 12,134	Tunica 8,164
Issaquena 1,909	Warren 47,880
Jefferson 8,653	Washington 67,935
Leake (pt.) 4,443	Yazoo 25,506

Cities, 1990 population (10,000 or more)

Canton 10,062	Grenada 10,864
Clarksdale 19,717	Indianola 11,809
Cleveland 15,384	Jackson (pt.) 34,454
Greenville 45,226	Vicksburg 20,908
Greenwood 18,906	Yazoo City 12,427

Race and Hispanic origin

White 36.6%
Black 63.0%
American Indian, Eskimo, or Aleut 0.1%
Asian or Pacific Islander 0.3%
Other 0.1%
Hispanic origin 0.5%

Ancestry

American 8.0%	Irish 9.3%
English 5.7%	Italian 1.3%
French 1.3%	Scotch Irish 2.3%
German 4.6%	

Universities/colleges, 1990-1991 enrollment

Alcorn State University, Lorman 2,863
Coahoma Community College, Clarksdale 1,351
Delta State University, Cleveland 3,995
Holmes Community College, Goodman 2,073

Mississippi Delta Junior College, Moorhead 2,123
Mississippi Valley State University, Itta Bena 1,873

Newspapers, total circulation (in all districts)

Clarksdale Press Register 7,016
Bolivar Commercial 7,104
Greenville Delta Democrat-Times 12,366
Greenwood Commonwealth 8,612
Jackson Clarion-Ledger 106,717
Memphis Commercial Appeal 193,211
Vicksburg Post 14,392

Commercial television stations, affiliations

ADI: Jackson (50%), Greenwood-Greenville (31%), Memphis
(14%) and Columbus-Tupelo (4%)
WXVT, Greenville (CBS)
WABG-TV, Greenwood (ABC)

Cable television systems, total subscribers

Cablecom of Clarksdale; Clarksdale 6,939
Capitol Cablevision Inc.; Jackson 62,800
Century Mississippi Cable; Greenwood 8,779
Delta Cablevision; Greenville 14,500
Vicksburg Video Inc.; Vicksburg 7,000
Warner Amex; Cleveland 6,500

Businesses and other major employers

U.S. Army Corp. of Engineers; Vicksburg 2,000
U.S. Army Corp. of Engineers/Waterways Experiment; Vicks-
burg 1,800
Mississippi State Penitentiary; Drew 1,500
Heatcraft Inc.; Grenada; electrical motor parts 1,400
Baxter Healthcare Corp./Baxter Intl.; Cleveland; pharmaceuti-
cals 1,400
City of Vicksburg/Public School District; Vicksburg 1,300
Sunburst Bank; Grenada; commercial banks 1,115
Delta Pride Catfish Inc.; Indianola; fish processing 1,100
Entergy Operations Inc./Grand Gulf Nuclear Station; Port
Gibson; electric services 971
Esmark Apparel Inc./Pennaco Hosiery Div.; Grenada; knitting
mills 950
Country Skillet Catfish Co.; Isola; fish processing 900
Bechtel Construction Co.; Port Gibson; heavy construction 800
MTD Products Inc.; Indianola; farm/garden machinery 800
Super Valu Stores Inc./Lewis Grocer; Indianola; grocery
products 800
Anderson-Tully Co.; Vicksburg; sawmills 700
Alcorn State University; Lorman 600
Delta Medical Center; Greenville 600
Northwest Mississippi Regional Meducak Center; Clarksdale
600
McGraw-Edison Co./Cooper Lighting; Vicksburg; electric
lighting 575
Frito-Lay Inc.; Jackson; grocery products 570
Commonwealth National Life Insurance Co.; Cleveland; life
insurance 550
Greenwood Leflore Hospital; Greenwood 550

3rd District

East Central — Meridian

The 3rd combines east Mississippi Hill Country with suburbs
of the city of Jackson in Rankin County. Although Democrat

Rep. G. V. Montgomery wins re-election with ease, all the
building blocks of this district—the rural areas, the small cities
and especially the Jackson suburbs—are fertile ground for
Republican candidates.

In the 1992 presidential contest, Bill Clinton managed only
about one-third of the vote in the 3rd. Texas billionaire Ross
Perot also fared poorly here, finishing in single digits, well below
his national average. By contrast, George Bush soared toward 60
percent in the district.

Nearly one-fifth of the total district vote is cast in
Rankin County, one of the fastest-growing areas of the
state during the 1980s. The white-collar professionals
here, most of whom have jobs in and around the state capital
of Jackson, are among the most faithful GOP voters in the
South.

Rankin went solidly Republican in the 1987 gubernatorial
contest, helping the GOP nominee to an unexpectedly strong
statewide showing, and in 1991 Rankin was instrumental in
making Kirk Fordice the first Republican governor of Mississippi since Reconstruction. Rankin gave Bush nearly 80 percent
of its presidential vote in 1988. Four years later, as Bush was
falling below 40 percent nationally, he still took 68 percent of
the vote in Rankin.

Due east of Rankin on the Alabama border is Lauderdale
County (Meridian), the district's second most populous. Merid-
ian is an industrial city with a General Motors facility. The
Meridian Naval Air Station trains naval pilots. Lauderdale
County was just a step behind Rankin in loyalty to Bush in 1992,
giving him 63 percent of the vote.

In the center of the 3rd is one of Mississippi's most
infamous locales: the Neshoba County seat of Philadelphia.
Near here in 1964, three civil rights workers were murdered.
The annual Neshoba County fair is a must stop for any
Mississippi politician. In presidential election years, even White
House aspirants have been known to include the fair on their
itinerary.

In the northeastern corner of the district, Oktibbeha County
(Starkville) hosts Mississippi State University and its 14,400
students. Neighboring Lowndes County is the district's third
biggest. The county seat of Columbus is the birthplace of
playwright Tennessee Williams, and it has more than 100
antebellum homes, some of which are open for viewing each
April.

Columbus also has a major Air Force base that provides basic
training for prospective pilots, and the military-related population
helps boost the GOP in Lowndes County. In 1992, Bush won 56
percent of the county's presidential vote.

The rest of the district is mostly rural and agricultural
territory. There are a significant number of poultry and poultry-
processing businesses, as well as employers in the timber and oil
and gas industries.

Election Returns

	3rd District	Democrat	Republican
1992	President*	67,552 (33.6%)	117,313 (58.4%)
	House	162,864 (81.2%)	37,710 (18.8%)
1991	Governor	54,138 (38.0%)	88,317 (62.0%)
1988	President	56,910 (33.5%)	113,005 (66.5%)
	Senate	69,421 (40.1%)	103,853 (59.9%)
1987	Governor	63,038 (47.6%)	69,526 (52.4%)

Vote for Perot was 16,158 (8.0%).

Demographics

Population 515,314

Percent change from 1980 2.3%

Land area 10,004 square miles

Population per square mile 52

Counties, 1990 population

Attala (pt.) 11,803	Neshoba 24,800
Clarke 17,313	Newton 20,291
Clay 21,120	Noxubee 12,604
Jasper 17,114	Oktibbeha (pt.) 36,211
Jones (pt.) 19,872	Rankin 87,161
Kemper 10,356	Scott 24,137
Lauderdale 75,555	Smith 14,798
Leake (pt.) 13,993	Wayne (pt.) 3,189
Lowndes 59,308	Winston 19,433
Madison (pt.) 26,256	

Cities, 1990 population (10,000 or more)

Brandon 11,077	Pearl 19,588
Columbus 23,799	Ridgeland 11,714
Meridian 41,036	Starkville 18,458

Race and Hispanic origin

White 67.0%
Black 31.3%
American Indian, Eskimo, or Aleut. 1.1%
Asian or Pacific Islander 0.5%
Other 0.1%
Hispanic origin 0.6%

Ancestry

American 13.8%	German 8.7%
Dutch 1.3%	Irish 16.2%
English 10.4%	Scotch Irish 3.9%
French 2.2%	Scottish 1.5%

Universities/colleges, 1990-1991 enrollment

East Central Community College, Decatur 1,303
East Mississippi Community College, Scooba 1,085
Hinds Community College, Raymond 8,750
Mary Holmes College, West Point 742
Meridian Community College, Meridian 2,952
Mississippi State University, Starkville 14,391
Mississippi University for Women, Columbus 2,407

Newspapers, total circulation (in all districts)

Jackson Clarion-Ledger 106,717
Laurel Leader Call 8,822
Meridian Star 21,355

Commercial television stations, affiliations

ADI: Meridian (33%), Jackson (30%), Columbus-Tupelo (26%)
and Laurel-Hattiesburg (11%)
WCBI-TV, Columbus (CBS)
WGBC-TV, Meridian (NBC)
WTOK-TV, Meridian (ABC)
WTZH, Meridian (CBS)

Cable television systems, total subscribers

Capitol Cablevision Inc.; Jackson 62,800
Columbus TV Cable Corp.; Columbus 13,500
Comcast Cablevision; Meridian 16,000
Northland Cable TV; Starkville 5,187
Rankin County Cablevision; Pearl 9,485

Military installations, 1991

Meridian Naval Air Station, Meridian 3,480
Columbus Air Force Base, Columbus 2,306
Pascagula Naval Station, Pascagula 460
Key Field (Air Force), Meridian 368

Businesses and other major employers

Mississippi State University; Starkville 2,785
Bryan Foods Inc./Sweet Sue Kitchens Div.; West Point;
meatpacking 2,406
United Technologies Motor Systems; Columbus; motors 1,700
Peavey Electronics Corp.; Meridian; audio electronic systems 1,500
Babcock & Wilcox Co.; West Point; metal products 1,000
La-Z-Boy Chair Co.; Newton; chairs/couches 917
East Mississippi State Hospital; Meridian 900
Nazareth/Century Mills Inc.; Quitman; outerwear 800
Nemanco Inc.; Philadelphia; jeans 800
Golden Triangle Regional Medical Center; Columbus 800
Blue Cross/Blue Shield of Mississippi; Jackson; medical
service/health insurance 780
Jeff Anderson Regional Medical Center; Meridian 760
Green Acre Farms Inc.; Sebastopol; poultry products 750
Gulf South Detective Inc.; West Point; security services 750
Howard Industries Inc.; Laurel; electric transformers 740
Job Mate Inc.; Ridgeland; personnel supply services 714
Sanderson Plumbing Products; Columbus; wood products 713
Burlington Industries Inc.; Stonewall; cotton mills 700
Weyerhaeuser Co./Pulp & Paper; Columbus; sawmills 700
Gencorp Inc./Polymer Products; Columbus;
plastics/synthetics 695
Riley Memorial Hospital; Meridian 672
B. C. Rogers Processors Inc.; Morton; poultry products 663
TRW Inc./Vehicle Safety Systems; Louisville; motor vehicle
products 662
General Motors Corp./Delco Remy Div.; Meridian; electrical
equipment/systems 650
Hughes Aircraft Mississippi; Forest; aircraft measuring de-
vices 650
Johnston-Tombigbee Furniture Mfg. Co.; Columbus; wooden
furniture 600
Rush Medical Foundation; Meridian 600
Taylor Machine Works Inc.; Louisville; construction machin-
ery 595
State of Mississippi/Hudspeth Retardation Center; Whitfield;
nursing 560
Siemens Energy & Automation; Jackson; switchgears 550
City of Meridian; Meridian 515

4th District

Southwest — Jackson

The 4th holds a mixture of old southern charm and New South savvy. Natchez, with a population of just over 19,000, sits on the banks of the Mississippi River in Adams County and is the embodiment of the Old South. Dripping with Spanish moss, it is home to 500 antebellum mansions ever-popular with tourists.

In the recession of the late 1980s and early 1990s, the southwestern counties of the 4th were hit hard. While its oil and gas industry suffered, Natchez's economy stayed afloat with other enterprises, with tourism topping the list. The small river city and its antebellum homes attract 150,000 people a year. Other residents find work in the timber industry in such businesses as wood processing and paper production. One such facility in Brookhaven in Lincoln County converts logs into wood chips.

North of Natchez is Jackson, the state capital, in Hinds County. Burned during the Civil War, Jackson has refashioned itself into an urban center and the state's largest city, with a population of nearly 200,000. About 56 percent of the city's population is black, up from 47 percent in 1980.

Jackson and surrounding Hinds County give Republicans a strong political base to build on. Jackson is home to many of the state GOP's financial kingpins, and Hinds County has not voted Democratic in a presidential election since 1956. But the part of Hinds County that is in the neighboring 2nd is Democratic territory, which helped keep George Bush's 1992 margin to about 2,000 votes over Democrat Bill Clinton.

Redistricting may have made that GOP base even more formidable. The 4th picked up most of Republican-leaning Jones County, including the industrial city of Laurel, population 19,000, and its timber-related industry fueled by its proximity to Mississippi's Piney Woods. Redistricting also moved less-affluent black sections of Jackson into the 2nd District, leaving the more well-to-do black sections of the city in the much more conservative 4th.

Black voters, however, have shown political strength in the 4th, making it winnable for any Democrats who could link black voters with rural white voters. In the 1970s, independent black candidates were a force: In 1972, 1978 and 1980, independent black challengers siphoned enough votes from Democratic House nominees to elect Republican candidates for the House and Senate.

Along with the Gulf Coast 5th, the Jackson-based 4th is the backbone of the GOP resurgence in Mississippi. Yet Democratic House candidates built a winning coalition of rural white and black votes to keep the 4th in the Democratic column from 1981-1993.

Election Returns

	4th District	Democrat	Republican
1992	President*	84,089 (41.3%)	102,666 (50.5%)
	House †	130,927 (67.3%)	43,705 (22.5%)
1991	Governor	66,649 (43.5%)	86,736 (56.5%)
1988	President	77,734 (38.9%)	122,157 (61.1%)
	Senate	93,192 (45.5%)	111,628 (54.5%)
1987	Governor	76,917 (50.5%)	75,428 (49.5%)

*Vote for Perot was 16,744 (8.2%).   †Independent/other is greater than 5%.

Demographics

Population 513,853

Percent change from 1980 2.0%

Land area 7,835 square miles

Population per square mile 66

Counties, 1990 population

Adams 35,356	Lawrence 12,458
Amite 13,328	Lincoln 30,278
Copiah 27,592	Marion 25,544
Covington 16,527	Pike 36,882
Franklin 8,377	Simpson 23,953
Hinds (pt.) 203,318	Walthall 14,352
Jefferson Davis 14,051	Wilkinson 9,678
Jones (pt.) 42,159	

Cities, 1990 population (10,000 or more)

Brookhaven 10,243	Laurel (pt.) 18,581
Clinton (pt.) 20,252	McComb 11,591
Jackson (pt.) 161,452	Natchez 19,460

Race and Hispanic origin

White 58.8%
Black 40.7%
American Indian, Eskimo, or Aleut. 0.1%
Asian or Pacific Islander 0.3%
Other 0.1%
Hispanic origin 0.4%

Ancestry

American 11.9%	German 7.8%
Dutch 1.0%	Irish 13.7%
English 9.9%	Scotch Irish 4.0%
French 2.4%	Scottish 1.5%

Universities/colleges, 1990-1991 enrollment

Belhaven College, Jackson 868
Copiah-Lincoln Junior College, Natchez 472
Copiah-Lincoln Junior College, Wesson 1,494
Jackson State University, Jackson 6,838
Jones County Junior College, Ellisville 4,122
Millsaps College, Jackson 1,410
Mississippi College, Clinton 3,620
Phillips Junior College, Jackson 639
Reformed Theological Seminary, Jackson 617
Southwest Mississippi Community College, Summit 1,520
Tougaloo College, Tougaloo 956
University of Mississippi Medical Center, Jackson 1,637

Newspapers, total circulation (in all districts)

Brookhaven Daily Leader 7,608
Hattiesburg American 25,014
Jackson Clarion-Ledger 106,717
Laurel Leader Call 8,822
McComb Enterprise-Journal 10,959

Commercial television stations, affiliations

ADI: Jackson (64%), Laurel-Hattiesburg (18%) and Baton Rouge (18%)
WAPT, Jackson (ABC)
WDBD, Jackson (Fox)
WJTV, Jackson (CBS)
WLBT-TV, Jackson (NBC)
WDAM-TV, Laurel (NBC)

Cable television systems, total subscribers

Capitol Cablevision Inc.; Jackson 62,800
Comcast Cablevision of Laurel; Laurel 9,000
Sammons Communications Inc.; McComb 6,700

Military installations, 1991

Allen C. Thompson Field (Air Force), Flowood 309

Businesses and other major employers

State of Mississippi/Social Services; Jackson 4,900
State of Mississippi/Mississippi; Jackson 3,448
University of Mississippi Medical Center; Jackson 3,000
City of Jackson; Jackson 2,300
General Motors Corp./Packard Electric Div.; Clinton; motor vehicle equipment 1,700
Jackson State University; Jackson 1,500
McCarty Processors Inc.; Jackson; poultry products 1,449
Magnetek Inc.; Mendenhall; transformers 1,440
Croft Metals Inc., McComb; aluminum doors 1,400
U.S. Veterans Affairs Dept.; Jackson; hospital 1,400
Jackson State University; Jackson 1,300
State of Mississippi/Ellisville State School; Ellisville 1,200
St. Dominic Memorial Hospital; Jackson 1,200
Methodist Medical Center; Jackson 1,200
Trustmark National Bank; Jackson; commercial banks 1,061
State of Mississippi/Wild Life Dept.; Jackson 1,050
Croft Metals Inc.; Magnolia; metal products 1,000
Vickers Inc./Aireal Space Marine Defense; Jackson; aircraft parts 1,000
South Central Regional Medical Center; Laurel 913
International Paper Co.; Natchez; pulp mills 903
Dr. Robert Hanvey; Hazlehurst; religious organization 900
State of Mississippi/Tax Commission; Jackson 900
City of Jackson/Municipal Airport; Jackson; airport 800
City of Natchz-Adams County/Public School System; Natchez 720
McCarty Foods Inc.; Jackson; poultry products 715
City of Jackson/Public School Systems; Jackson 701
McRaes Inc.; Jackson; warehousing 700
Deposit Guaranty Corp.; Jackson; commercial banks 685
Sanderson Farms Processing Div.; Collins; poultry products 650
Challenger Electrical Equipment; Jackson; warehousing 640
Southern Farm Bureau Life Insurance Co.; Jackson; life insurance 621
Georgia-Pacific Corp./St. Regis Paper Div.; Monticello; pulp mills 610
Rex J. H. Rutter Mfg. Co.; Columbia; outerwear 600
State of Mississippi/Health Dept.; Jackson 600
Medical Enterprises Ltd./Professional Building Service; Jackson; building services 600
County of Hinds; Jackson 580
Southwest Mississippi Regional Medical Center; McComb 564
Royal Maid Assn. for the Blind; Hazlehurst; plastics products 558
Masonite Corp./Central Hardboard Div.; Laurel; wood products 516

5th District

Southeast — Gulf Coast; Hattiesburg

At the core of the 5th's economy is defense-related industry, so much so that it would be hard to imagine the district without it.

Some observers estimate that at least half the district's residents have some connection to one of these enterprises. The 5th is home to the state's biggest private employer, Ingalls Shipbuilding, a division of Litton Industries, located in Pascagoula (Jackson County). It employs about 16,000 people.

In 1992, the city of 26,000 saw the opening of Naval Station Pascagoula at Singing River Island. The facility employs about 1,100 military personnel and will eventually employ about 150 civilians.

The Gulf Coast counties, with their white sand beaches and resort cities, bear little resemblance to the rest of the state. The Harrison County cities of Gulfport and Biloxi attract thousands of tourists each year. The area is also home to gulf shrimpers and seafood-processing plants. Gulfport is the site of the annual four-day Mississippi Deep Sea Fishing Rodeo held during the week of July 4.

Biloxi is also home of Keesler Air Force Base, the premier training center for the Air Force and one of the four largest bases in the country. Keesler employs about 8,000 military personnel and civilians, and specializes in communications, electronics and medical training. Beauvoir, the last home of Jefferson Davis, the president of the Confederacy, is also in Biloxi.

In neighboring Hancock County is the Stennis Space Center, named for the late Sen. John C. Stennis, who represented the state from 1947 to 1989. A small division of NASA, the center tests rocket engines.

Hattiesburg, the seat of Forrest County, is the sole population center in the northern part of the 5th. The leading employer in the predominantly white-collar town is the University of Southern Mississippi, with 13,500 students. The tier of counties above the coast—George, Stone, Pearl River, Greene, Perry, Forrest and Lamar—are part of the poorer Piney Woods region, where the economy is driven by the production of wood products, poultry and dairy farming.

In addition, the textile industry has also been a significant employer in the district with several manufacturing plants.

Mississippi's long-dormant Republican Party made its initial inroads in the 5th, a solidly conservative region where Democrats are no longer competitive in national elections. Ronald Reagan carried Mississippi in 1980 only because of a 30,000-vote edge in the 5th. As George Bush carried the state easily in 1988, the 5th was his strongest district. In 1992, Bush carried every county in the district.

Yet while the district has been a GOP beachhead, it is not impregnable, evidenced by the Democratic House nominee's comfortable victory in 1992 with 63 percent of the vote.

Redistricting pushed northern Wayne County into the 3rd and western Jones County into the 4th, while adding portions of Jones to the south. It is expected to have no affect on politics in the 5th.

Election Returns

	5th District	Democrat	Republican
1992	President*	58,905 (32.0%)	100,128 (54.4%)
	House	120,766 (63.2%)	67,619 (35.4%)
1991	Governor	56,229 (49.2%)	58,026 (50.8%)
1988	President	43,267 (29.2%)	104,742 (70.8%)
	Senate	43,900 (31.1%)	97,329 (68.9%)
1987	Governor	60,252 (51.6%)	56,564 (48.4%)

Vote for Perot was 24,941 (13.6%).

Demographics

Population 514,656

Percent change from 1980 2.2%

Land area 6,427 square miles

Population per square mile 80

Counties, 1990 population

Forrest 68,314

George 16,673

Greene 10,220

Hancock 31,760

Harrison 165,365

Jackson 115,243

Lamar 30,424

Pearl River 38,714

Perry 10,865

Stone 10,750

Wayne (pt.) 16,328

Cities, 1990 population (10,000 or more)

Biloxi 46,319

Gautier 10,088

Gulfport 40,775

Hattiesburg 41,882

Long Beach 15,804

Moss Point 17,837

Ocean Springs 14,658

Orange Grove CDP 15,676

Pascagoula 25,899

Picayune 10,633

Race and Hispanic origin

White 78.3%

Black 20.0%

American Indian, Eskimo, or Aleut. 0.2%

Asian or Pacific Islander 1.2%

Other 0.2%

Hispanic origin 1.1%

Ancestry

American 13.8%

Dutch 1.4%

English 12.1%

French 8.9%

French Canadian 1.7%

German 13.5%

Irish 17.1%

Italian 2.8%

Scotch Irish 3.9%

Scottish 2.0%

Universities/colleges, 1990-1991 enrollment

Mississippi Gulf Coast Community College, Perkinston 9,526

Pearl River Community College, Poplarville 3,363

Phillips Junior College, Gulfport 1,172

University of Southern Mississippi, Hattiesburg 13,490

William Carey College, Hattiesburg 1,574

Newspapers, total circulation (in all districts)

Biloxi Sun Herald 49,607

Hattiesburg American 25,014

Jackson Clarion-Ledger 106,717

Mississippi Press 22,839

New Orleans Times-Picayune 266,592

Commercial television stations, affiliations

ADI: Biloxi-Gulfport-Pascagoula (39%), Laurel-Hattiesburg (34%), New Orleans (20%) and Mobile-Pensacola (7%)

WLOX-TV, Biloxi (ABC)

WXXV-TV, Gulfport (Fox)

WHLT, Hattiesburg (CBS)

Cable television systems, total subscribers

Coast TV Cable Inc.; Long Beach 8,479

Pinebelt Cable; Hattiesburg 19,235

Post Newsweek Cable TV; Gulfport 20,538

Sammons Communications; Escatawpa 17,500

TCI; Biloxi 15,228

TCI; Ocean Springs 10,112

Military installations, 1991

Keesler Air Force Base, Biloxi 7,994

Gulfport Naval Construction Center, Gulfport 4,480

Naval Oceanographic Office, Bay St. Louis 1,876

Gulfport/Biloxi Municipal Airport Air Force Guard Station, Gulfport 114

Businesses and other major employers

Ingalls Shipbuilding Inc.; Pascagoula; shipbuilding/repairing 16,000

Forrest County General Hospital; Hattiesburg 2,000

Memorial Hospital at Gulfport; Gulfport 1,300

Singing River Memorial Hospital; Pascagoula 1,150

Chevron USA Inc.; Pascagoula; petroleum refining 1,100

International Paper Co.; Moss Point; paper mills 1,050

County of Jackson/Board of Education; Pascagoula 763

City of Moss Point/Public School District; Moss Point 700

Methodist Hospital of Hattiesburg; Hattiesburg 651

City of Hattiesburg; Hattiesburg 650

Du Pont E. I. De Nemours & Co.; Pass Christian; inorganic chemicals 600

Murray Envelope Corp./Frank Lloyd Co.; Hattiesburg; paper products 550

County of Jackson; Pascagoula 550

Johnson Controls World Services Inc./Foss Project; Bay St. Louis; building services 523

Sverdrup Technology Inc.; Bay St. Louis; engineering/architectural services 520

Missouri

In the early 1990s Missouri reflected where the country stood demographically, economically and politically. It had booming suburbs and decaying urban areas, dying farm communities in the north and bountiful agricultural areas farther south. Its population mix was transforming. While young people were leaving the farms, retirees were flocking to the state's resort areas.

Missouri's economy and politics have maintained an equilibrium that rarely produces upheaval. According to the 1990 census, Missouri grew by a modest 4 percent during the 1980s. That was enough for it to retain all nine of its congressional seats, even though its two leading cities, Kansas City and St. Louis, lost population. Unemployment in the state was close to the national average.

The diversity of Missouri's economy helped it avoid the severe economic and fiscal troubles that plagued many other states hit hard by recession. The resort areas of west-central and southwest Missouri—the Lake of the Ozarks and Table Rock Lake—long have been popular vacation spots, but population ballooned during the 1980s as retirees from elsewhere in the state and from across the Midwest arrived. Population grew by more than 10 percent in both the 4th District (Lake of the Ozarks) and the 7th District (Table Rock Lake and Branson).

But for those who argued that the Reagan era brought the country a "Swiss cheese" economy, Missouri offered evidence. In the rural northern part of the state, the 1980s were anything but prosperous. The farm depression in the first half of the decade devastated many communities, particularly those along the Iowa border. Thirty of the 44 counties north of the Missouri River lost population during the decade. From Atchison County in the northwest corner to Clark County in the northeast, all but one county on the northern frontier lost more than 10 percent of their population. Across north Missouri, towns withered as young people evacuated their families' farms to search for a more stable living.

Poverty and crime turned sections of St. Louis into the starkest manifestation of urban decay, while the city's population fell by 12 percent in the 1980s, its fourth consecutive decade of double-digit decline. With 397,000 people, it lost its status as Missouri's largest city, even though Kansas City, the leader with 435,000 people, lost about 3 percent of its population during the 1980s. Downtown Kansas City experienced some of the ravages that scarred downtown and north St. Louis, but the suburbs of Kansas City—like those of St. Louis—bulged.

It often is said that wherever the country is going, California is already there; it could be said that Missouri is where the country is today. Its voters may not be trendsetters, but they can accurately reflect national trends.

Anti-tax fervor hit Missouri about the same time it reached the rest of the nation. In 1980, voters approved a ballot initiative on state spending that led to an amendment to the state constitution that limited spending and taxes. It was dubbed the "Hancock amendment," for anti-tax activist and later 7th District Republican Rep. Mel Hancock.

In the 1990 elections, Missouri was part of another national mood swing—a reaction against congressional incumbency. One House member was ousted from office, and five others—including House Majority Leader Richard A. Gephardt—were held under 60 percent of the vote.

Missouri once was part of the Democratic Party's Solid South, but its voters, like many elsewhere in the country, were shedding partisan identities and switching sides from election to election—even from office to office on the same ballot. But in the 1992 elections, Democrats showed they maintained enduring support in the state by sweeping every statewide contest from governor on down except one—Republican Christopher S. Bond's Senate race. Democrats also controlled both houses of the state Legislature. In contests for the White House, the state remained competitive: Democrat Michael S. Dukakis got 48 percent of its presidential vote in 1988, while Bill Clinton won in 1992 with 44 percent.

Redistricting went smoothly by Missouri standards. For the first time in at least 40 years, the state's redistricting plan did not find itself embroiled in a court challenge. Because the population within the state did not shift significantly, mapmakers were not required to change drastically the shape of the districts. After a plan was drawn to satisfy Republican Gov. John Ashcroft's demand that no rural counties be split between districts, both houses of the Legislature approved the map by wide margins.

Without question, the member expected to feel the pinch of the new map the most was the freshman Democrat from the suburban St. Louis 2nd District, Joan Kelly Horn. In 1990, Horn upset the Republican incumbent by 54 votes. Until then, the two other St.

MISSOURI

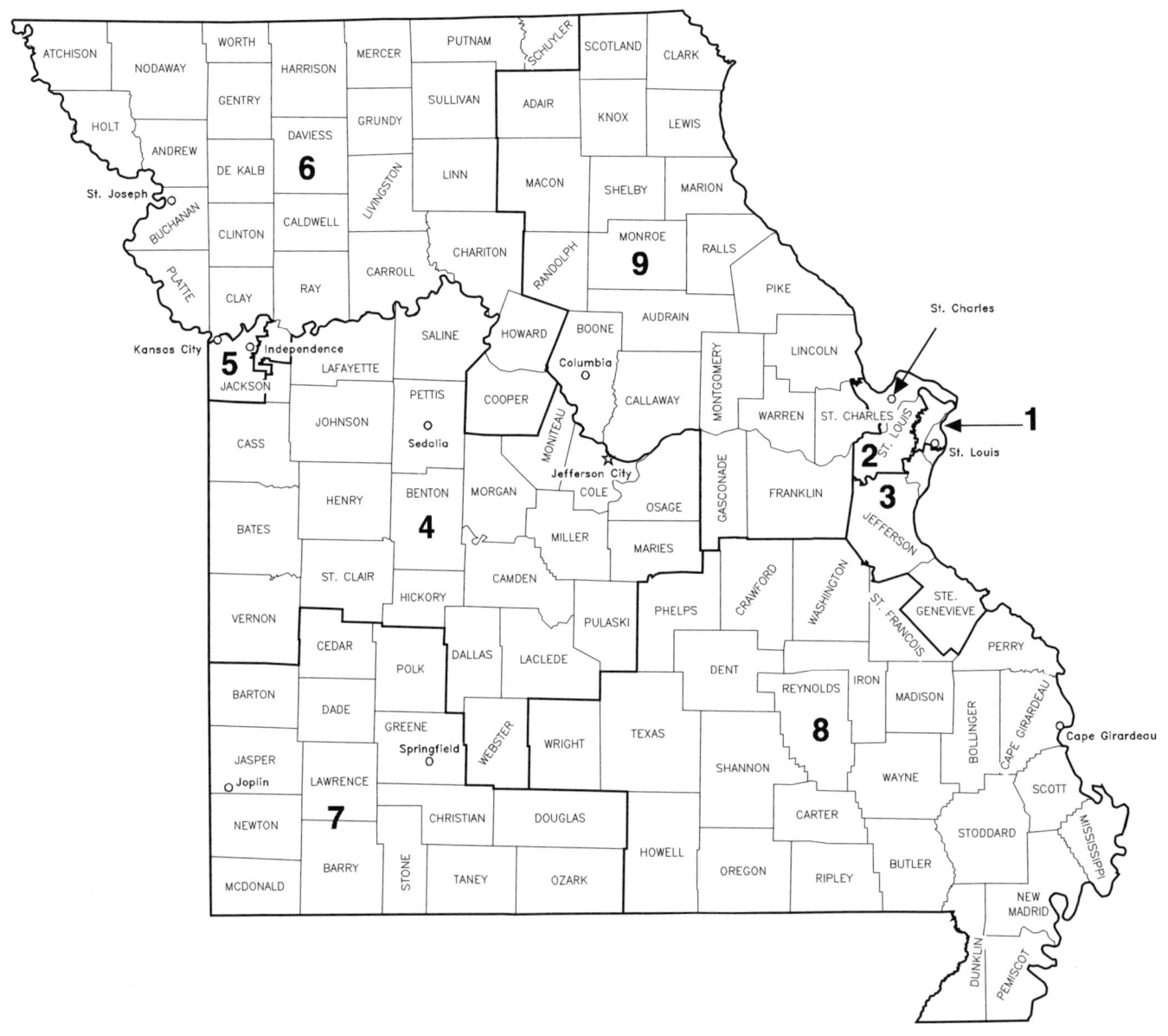

Louis-area members, 1st District Democrat William L. Clay and 3rd District Democrat Gephardt, figured that in redistricting they would bequeath Republican votes to the 2nd, making it solidly Republican while making their districts more comfortable Democratic territory. But Horn's victory scuttled those plans, as she beseeched assistance to make the 2nd less precarious.

Horn met with limited success. While she was able to retain two-thirds of the Democratic city of Florissant, Clay and Gephardt rebuffed her request for part of the city of St. Louis, which remained split between the 1st and the 3rd. And the 2nd District doubled its stake in politically marginal St. Charles County.

Women in the state Legislature blasted Clay and Gephardt for not accommodating Horn's political needs. Clay feathered his district by picking up a third of Florissant, the predominantly black St. Louis County municipalities of Berkeley and Kinloch and pockets of the middle-class black population in other municipalities and townships. Gephardt, who was held to 57 percent in 1990, added rural Democratic Ste. Genevieve County.

In 1992, both Clay and Gephardt markedly improved over their 1990 results. Horn, however, could not overcome the strong GOP tide in the 2nd; she lost to Republican James M. Talent by nearly 9,000 votes.

Table 1 Population

District	Population	Population under 18	Voting-age population	Median age
1	568,285	149,554	418,731	32.4
2	568,306	147,655	420,651	33.8
3	568,326	139,547	428,779	34.2
4	569,146	148,799	420,347	33.6
5	569,130	140,904	428,226	33.3
6	569,131	148,085	421,046	34.0
7	568,017	139,190	428,827	34.5
8	568,385	150,046	418,339	34.7
9	568,347	151,046	417,301	31.8
State	5,117,073	1,314,826	3,802,247	33.5

Table 2 Voting-Age Persons

District	White*	Black*	American Indian, Eskimo, or Aleut*	Asian or Pacific Islander*	Other*	Hispanic*	Male*	Female*
1	50.6%	48.0%	0.2%	1.0%	0.2%	0.9%	44.5%	55.5%
2	94.7	3.5	0.2	1.5	0.2	0.9	47.8	52.2
3	96.9	1.9	0.2	0.8	0.2	1.0	46.6	53.4
4	95.4	3.2	0.4	0.5	0.4	0.9	48.9	51.1
5	76.1	21.1	0.5	1.0	1.4	2.8	46.2	53.8
6	96.7	2.0	0.4	0.5	0.4	1.3	47.6	52.4
7	97.6	0.9	0.9	0.5	0.2	0.6	47.1	52.9
8	95.6	3.6	0.3	0.4	0.1	0.4	47.2	52.8
9	95.3	3.5	0.3	0.8	0.2	0.7	47.9	52.1
State	88.8	9.7	0.4	0.8	0.4	1.1	47.1	52.9

*As percent of voting-age population.

Table 3 Voting-Age Persons by Age Groups

District	18-24*	25-44*	45-54*	55-64*	65 and over*
1	14.6%	42.5%	12.2%	11.8%	18.9%
2	11.6	46.6	16.0	11.7	14.0
3	11.7	43.5	13.1	12.1	19.6
4	14.0	39.9	13.8	12.5	19.7
5	13.0	43.7	13.1	12.0	18.2
6	12.9	41.5	14.3	11.8	19.4
7	14.8	38.3	13.7	12.5	20.7
8	13.1	37.6	14.2	13.1	22.0
9	16.5	42.0	13.3	10.8	17.4
State	13.6	41.7	13.8	12.0	18.9

*As percent of voting-age population.

Table 4 Income and Occupation

District	Median family income	Families in poverty	White collar*	Blue collar*	Service*	Farm*
1	$30,858	15.1%	60.0%	22.2%	17.2%	0.6%
2	50,632	2.5	72.6	17.0	9.8	0.6
3	36,896	6.0	59.0	27.1	13.0	0.9
4	27,440	10.3	47.6	31.9	14.6	5.9
5	33,443	10.4	61.2	23.8	14.3	0.7
6	32,516	8.7	53.6	28.3	13.0	5.0
7	26,368	11.1	49.6	31.7	14.1	4.6
8	22,406	18.1	42.4	37.4	14.2	6.1
9	31,682	9.2	50.9	30.6	13.8	4.6
State	31,838	10.1	55.8	27.4	13.7	3.1

*As percent of employed persons age 16 and over.

Table 5 Education: School Years Completed

District	Less than grade 9*	Grades 9-12 no diploma*	High school diploma*	College bachelor's degree or higher*
1	11.8%	17.7%	27.1%	19.5%
2	5.4	8.2	25.0	33.6
3	12.2	14.7	32.3	17.2
4	13.0	14.9	38.4	12.7
5	6.9	14.3	32.4	20.0
6	9.3	12.3	38.3	16.0
7	11.2	15.8	35.4	14.6
8	22.2	18.8	34.1	9.5
9	12.4	14.1	35.6	16.6
State	11.6	14.5	33.1	17.8

*As percent of persons age 25 and over.

Table 6 Housing and Residential Patterns

District	Owner occupied	Renter occupied	Urban	Rural
1	56.6%	43.4%	99.2%	0.8%
2	75.5	24.5	96.9	3.1
3	70.0	30.0	84.1	15.9
4	72.8	27.2	39.0	61.0
5	60.0	40.0	98.8	1.2
6	70.8	29.2	62.6	37.4
7	70.7	29.3	51.9	48.1
8	71.3	28.7	37.3	62.7
9	72.3	27.7	48.6	51.4
State	68.8	31.2	68.7	31.3

1st District

North St. Louis; Northeast St. Louis County

Almost everything that outsiders identify with the city of St. Louis is in the 1st. The Gateway Arch, Laclede's Landing, Busch

Stadium and Forest Park all lie north of the line that divides the two city-dominated districts.

The other, equally familiar St. Louis is also here: the crime-ridden streets, the rundown neighborhoods, the closed factories and businesses. Parts of the downtown area have declined so far that they shock even visitors accustomed to inner-city blight.

Blacks and whites have fled the city. The well-off have gone to distant suburbia and the less affluent to neighborhoods just outside the city limits. Blacks have also begun to move to the predominantly white neighborhoods of south St. Louis, and, as a consequence, many south St. Louis whites have headed for the suburbs. Once the nation's third-largest city, St. Louis' population has shrunk to less than half its 1950 total. It fell by 12 percent during the 1980s; with about 400,000 residents in the 1990 census, St. Louis has fallen behind Kansas City as Missouri's most-populous city. Politically, the 1st is Missouri's most reliably Democratic district.

The St. Louis area has been rocked in recent years by plant closings and layoffs. In 1991, Chrysler closed one of its two St. Louis County assembly plants. McDonnell Douglas has cut thousands of workers through attrition and layoffs; cancellation of McDonnell Douglas' A-12 attack plane in January 1991 prompted another wave of layoffs. Trans World Airlines, whose domestic hub is at St. Louis' Lambert International Airport, filed for bankruptcy in July 1991. General Dynamics Corp. moved its corporate headquarters to Northern Virginia in January 1992.

North St. Louis is not uniformly dilapidated. There remain pockets of stable older residential areas, such as the central west end and adjacent neighborhoods north and east of Forest Park, as well as the Mark Twain and Walnut Park neighborhoods near the northern city limits.

But most of north St. Louis is in decay. Some of the worst areas lie just north and west of downtown. Much of the central city has become a battle zone of drive-by shootings and drug deals.

The city has waged an ambitious program to renovate its historic buildings. Monumental Union Station, for example, has been rehabilitated into an upscale marketplace with shops, restaurants, nightclubs and a hotel. But these efforts offer scant solace to the poor residents of crime-ravaged north St. Louis.

The 1st also takes in many of the blacks who have left the city for nearby St. Louis County suburbs. Affluent black professionals live in University City, Clayton and Florissant. Clayton was once the prototypical prosperous suburb, but its profile has been changing of late, as upscale shops relocate west to more-affluent locales.

The rest of the 1st is composed largely of white working-class conservatives who work in the auto assembly and aerospace manufacturing facilities ringing the city.

Election Returns

	1st District	Democrat	Republican
1992	President*	161,794 (68.5%)	44,980 (19.0%)
	House	158,693 (68.1%)	74,482 (31.9%)
1988	President	141,977 (72.4%)	54,017 (27.6%)
	Senate	109,835 (56.8%)	83,621 (43.2%)
	Governor	111,878 (58.6%)	78,981 (41.4%)
1986	Senate	97,043 (69.8%)	41,903 (30.2%)

*Vote for Perot was 29,586 (12.5%).

Demographics

Population　568,285

Percent change from 1980　4.0%

Land area　146 square miles

Population per square mile　3,901

Counties, 1990 population
St. Louis (pt.)　346,759　　　St. Louis city (pt.)　221,526

Cities, 1990 population (10,000 or more)
Bellefontaine Neighbors 10,922　　　Jennings　15,905
Berkeley (pt.)　11,511　　　Richmond Heights　10,448
Clayton　13,874　　　Spanish Lake CDP　20,322
Ferguson　22,286　　　St. Louis (pt.)　221,526
Florissant (pt.)　14,247　　　University City (pt.)　40,058

Race and Hispanic origin
White　46.3%
Black　52.3%
American Indian, Eskimo, or Aleut.　0.2%
Asian or Pacific Islander　1.0%
Other　0.3%
Hispanic origin　0.9%

Ancestry
American　2.7%　　　Irish　12.1%
Dutch　1.1%　　　Italian　3.2%
English　6.9%　　　Polish　2.2%
French　3.2%　　　Russian　1.0%
German　21.8%　　　Scotch Irish　1.1%

Universities/colleges, 1990-1991 enrollment
Barnes Hospital School of Nursing, St. Louis　297
Concordia Seminary, St. Louis　489
Fontbonne College, St. Louis　1,139
Harris-Stowe State College, St. Louis　1,973
Ranken Technical Institute, St. Louis　1,414
St. Louis College of Pharmacy, St. Louis　752
St. Louis Community College, St. Louis　32,349
St. Louis University, St. Louis　12,896
University of Missouri, St. Louis　15,397
Washington University, St. Louis　11,498

Newspapers, total circulation (in all districts)
St. Louis Post-Dispatch　369,005

Commercial television stations, affiliations
ADI: St. Louis (100%)

Cable television systems, total subscribers
American Cablevision-St. Louis; Ferguson　11,800
Cencom III of Missouri; Florissant　30,350
Continental Cablevision-St. Louis; Jennings　9,480
Continental Cablevision-St. Louis; Overland　35,000
TCI of Missouri; St. Louis　52,000

Military installations, 1991
Defense Mapping Agency Aerospace Center, St. Louis　3,338
St. Louis Army Ammunition Plant, St. Louis　529
Jefferson Barracks Air Force Guard Station, St. Louis　62

Businesses and other major employers

Southwestern Bell Telephone Co.; St. Louis; telephone communications 7,000

McDonnell Douglas Corp./Missile System Co.; St. Louis; guided missiles 5,538

Barnes Hospital; St. Louis 3,900

Boatmen's National Bank of St. Louis; St. Louis; commercial banks 3,000

Jewish Hospital of St. Louis; St. Louis 2,700

Washington University; St. Louis 2,643

Ralston Purina Co.; St. Louis; animal feeds 2,500

Emerson Electric Co.; St. Louis; measuring/controlling devices 2,500

City of St. Louis/Police Dept.; St. Louis 2,200

Edison Brothers Stores Inc.; St. Louis; men's clothing stores 2,100

Sportservice Corp.; St. Louis; bars/restaurants 2,025

McDonnell Douglas Corp./McDonnell Douglas Electronic; St. Louis; search/navigation equipment 2,000

Electronics & Space Corp.; St. Louis; defense systems 2,000

Mercantile Bank; St. Louis; commercial banks 2,000

Boatmen's Bancshares Inc.; St. Louis; commercial banks 2,000

St. Louis University; St. Louis 2,000

Catholic Archdiocese of St. Louis/Catholic Center; St. Louis; religious organizations 2,000

McDonnell Douglas Corp./Systems Integration Div.; Hazelwood; computer services 2,000

Christian Hospital Northeast-Northwest; St. Louis 1,989

A. G. Edwards Inc.; St. Louis; security brokers 1,900

Brown Group Inc.; St. Louis; shoe stores 1,800

St. Mary's Health Center; St. Louis 1,800

St. Louis Children's Hospital; St. Louis 1,768

St. Louis University Hospital; St. Louis 1,700

University of Missouri; St. Louis 1,700

Union Electric Co.; St. Louis; electric services 1,575

Blue Cross/Blue Shield of Missouri; St. Louis; medical service/health insurance 1,500

Sigma Chemical Co.; St. Louis; chemical products 1,400

Cardinal Glennon Children's Hospital; St. Louis 1,400

Pulitzer Publishing Co./St. Louis Post-Dispatch; St. Louis; newspapers 1,300

St. Louis Regional Medical Center; St. Louis 1,239

Spann Building Maintenance Co./Twenty-First Street Supply; St. Louis; building services 1,200

Missouri Pacific Railroad Co.; St. Louis; railroads 1,000

Mallinckrodt Inc.; St. Louis; inorganic chemicals 1,000

City of St. Louis; St. Louis 1,000

Mitch Murch's Maintenance Management; St. Louis; janitorial/building services 1,000

State of Missouri/Family Services; St. Louis 1,000

Continental Baking Co.; St. Louis; bakery products 900

Consumer Programs Inc./Sears Portrait Studio; St. Louis; photographic studios 900

Clean Tech Co.; St. Louis; building services 900

State of Missouri/Mental Health Dept.; St. Louis 900

Federal Reserve Bank of St. Louis; St. Louis 816

J. S. Alberici Construction Co.; St. Louis; building construction 800

Emerson Electric Co.; St. Louis; electrical motors 800

U.S. Farmer Homes Administration; St. Louis; federal credit 800

National Cleaning Contractors/ISS Intl. Service System; St. Louis; building services 800

Incarnate Word Hospital; St. Louis 794

Moog Automotive Inc.; St. Louis; motor vehicle parts 700

National Super Markets Inc.; Hazelwood; grocery stores 700

HBE Corp./Adams Mark Hotel; St. Louis; hotel 700

Sverdrup Corp.; St. Louis; engineering/architectural services 690

Sunnen Products Co.; St. Louis; metalworking machinery 665

Alcan Aluminum Corp.; St. Louis; electrical goods 640

Cardinal Ritter Institute; St. Louis; residential care 605

Mallinckrodt Inc.; Hazelwood; pharmaceuticals 600

Gateway Hotel Holdings Inc./Clarion Hotel; St. Louis; hotel 600

Pet Inc./Frozen Foods Div.; St. Louis; dairy products 550

Calgon Corp.; St. Louis; chemical products 550

American Red Cross; St. Louis; health services 550

2nd District

Western St. Louis County; Eastern St. Charles County

The suburban 2nd has some of Missouri's most affluent suburbs and some of the fastest-growing communities in the country. Republicans dominate much of the terrain, but enough independent voters and blue-collar households remain for a Democratic candidate to compete.

Separate from the city of St. Louis since 1876, St. Louis County, the largest in Missouri, makes up about 80 percent of the 2nd's population. The county has steadily filled with former St. Louis residents fleeing the declining urban center.

The heaviest concentration of Republicans is along the U.S. 40 corridor, across the heart of the 2nd. Communities such as Ladue and Frontenac have some of the area's wealthiest residents; the GOP vote is unshakable.

The affluent suburban vote has been spreading as the St. Louis suburbs have expanded west and northwest. Municipalities such as Chesterfield, Town and Country and Ballwin are attracting the suburbanites who used to settle in Webster Groves, Kirkwood and other suburbs closer to the city. In the western part of the county, where subdivisions give way to unincorporated areas and farmland, affluent new arrivals mix with longtime residents of less lofty incomes and less predictable voting habits.

The southwestern part of the 2nd is home to the ghost town of Times Beach, site of one of the worst U.S. environmental disasters. Residents were threatened by health problems associated with dioxin-tainted soil.

The auto industry is a major employer in the district. At the southeastern corner, the district takes in the Chrysler assembly plant at Fenton. Two plants operated at the Fenton site until mid-1991, when Chrysler closed one, laying off about 4,000 workers. The second plant continues to turn out minivans. Ford's Hazelwood plant is here. General Motors' Wentzville facility, in the 9th District, provides jobs for many residents of the 2nd.

McDonnell Douglas Corp. has its headquarters in the 2nd and a plant adjacent to St. Louis' Lambert International Airport, which is one of the area's largest employers. These workers lend a blue-collar tinge to the "North County." Traditional working-class communities such as St. Ann, Overland, Bridgeton and Olivette are Democratic strongholds. A proposed airport expansion, which would eliminate almost 1,000 homes in predominantly white Bridgeton, has added a volatile element to local politics. The 2nd also takes in two-thirds of reliably Democratic Florissant.

About 20 percent of the district lies over the Missouri River in St. Charles County, which in each of the past two decades has grown about 50 percent.

Settled by a French Canadian fur trader in 1769, the city of St. Charles served as Missouri's first capital from 1821 to 1826. The historic buildings on South Main Street have been restored, including the original Capitol. McDonnell Douglas manufactures the Harpoon missile at its St. Charles plant.

The rest of the 2nd in St. Charles County is rural. Soybeans and corn grow in the rich soil of the northern flood plain.

Election Returns

	2nd District	Democrat	Republican
1992	President*	114,792 (36.5%)	126,788 (40.3%)
	House	148,729 (47.6%)	157,594 (50.4%)
1988	President	110,788 (39.1%)	172,567 (60.9%)
	Senate	66,073 (23.5%)	215,364 (76.5%)
	Governor	71,074 (25.4%)	209,062 (74.6%)
1986	Senate	77,298 (39.5%)	118,354 (60.5%)

*Vote for Perot was 73,048 (23.2%).

Demographics

Population 568,306

Percent change from 1980 4.1%

Land area 537 square miles

Population per square mile 1,058

Counties, 1990 population
St. Charles (pt.) 127,286   St. Louis (pt.) 441,020

Cities, 1990 population (10,000 or more)
Ballwin 21,816	Kirkwood (pt.) 25,728
Bridgeton 17,779	Maryland Heights 25,407
Chesterfield 37,991	St. Ann 14,489
Creve Coeur 12,304	St. Charles 54,555
Florissant (pt.) 36,959	St. Peters (pt.) 34,743
Hazelwood (pt.) 12,856	

Race and Hispanic origin
White 94.3%
Black 3.7%
American Indian, Eskimo, or Aleut 0.2%
Asian or Pacific Islander 1.6%
Other 0.2%
Hispanic origin 1.0%

Ancestry
American 3.1%	Italian 5.7%
Dutch 2.2%	Polish 3.9%
English 16.6%	Russian 2.2%
French 6.5%	Scotch Irish 2.3%
German 46.6%	Scottish 2.4%
Irish 23.2%	Swedish 1.6%

Universities/colleges, 1990-1991 enrollment
Covenant Theological Seminary, St. Louis 316
ITT Technical Institute, Earth City 544
Lindenwood College, St. Charles 2,431
Logan College of Chiropractic, Chesterfield 679
Maryville University, St. Louis 3,274
Missouri Baptist College, St. Louis 1,059
St. Charles Community College, St. Peters 3,505

Newspapers, total circulation (in all districts)
St. Louis Post-Dispatch 369,005

Commercial television stations, affiliations
ADI: St. Louis (100%)

Cable television systems, total subscribers
Cencom I of Missouri; Olivette 55,538
Cencom II of Missouri; Olivette 25,558
Cencom III of Missouri; Florissant 30,350
Continental Cablevision St. Louis; Overland 35,000
TCI of Missouri; St. Peters 29,000
United Video Cablevision/Missouri Inc.; Chesterfield 13,618

Military installations, 1991
Lambert/St. Louis Intl. Airport Air Force Guard Station, St. Ann 451

Businesses and other major employers
McDonnell Douglas Corp./Information Systems Co.; Hazelwood; professional/commercial equipment 12,000
Chrysler Corp.; Fenton; motor vehicle assembly 5,000
St. John's Mercy Medical Center; St. Louis 3,500
Maritz Inc./Maritz Motivation; Fenton; business services 3,100
Monsanto Co.; St. Louis; plastics/synthetics 3,000
Ford Motor Co.; Hazelwood; motor vehicle assembly 2,400
Fru-Con Construction Corp.; Ballwin; building construction 2,202
St. Luke's Episcopal Presbyterian Hospital; Chesterfield 2,142
De Paul Health Center Inc.; Hazelwood 2,100
Hussmann Corp.; Hazelwood; refrigeration/heating equipment 2,000
McDonnell Douglas Corp./Electronic Systems; St. Charles; search/navigation equipment 2,000
Citicorp Mortgage Inc.; St. Louis; mortgage bankers 2,000
Missouri Baptist Medical Center; St. Louis 1,560
Unidynamics Corp./National Vendors; Hazelwood; refrigeration 1,500
AT&T Co.; Ballwin; research services 1,500
Six Flags Over Mid America; Eureka; amusement park 1,299
Monsanto Co.; St. Louis; research services 1,250
Citicorp Mortgage Inc.; Ballwin; mortgage bankers 1,200
St. Joseph Health Center/St. Joseph Hospital West; St. Charles 1,200
Jones Financial Companies; Hazelwood; security brokers 1,153
St. Joseph Hospital; St. Louis 1,100
Christian Hospital Northeast-Northwest; Florissant 1,000
Sverdrup Corp.; Hazelwood; engineering/architectural services 875
Group One Capital Inc.; St. Louis; investing services 850
State of Missouri/Highway & Transportation Dept.; St. Louis 820
State of Missouri/St. Louis Disability Treatment Center; St. Louis; residential care 800
Interstate Cleaning Corp.; St. Louis; building services 800
Unigroup Inc.; Fenton; trucking services 780

Trans World Airlines Inc.; St. Ann; airline 750

Crane Co.; Hazelwood; refrigeration 700

Executive Security Service; Chesterfield; business services 700

U.S. Postal Service; Hazelwood 686

Worldwide Underwriters Insurance Co.; St. Louis; fire/marine/casualty insurance 680

Smithkline Beecham Corp./Smith Kline Clinical Labs Div.; St. Louis; research services 650

Storz Instrument Co.; St. Louis; medical instruments 600

Western Union Financial Services; Hazelwood; telegraph/other communications 600

Stoehner Security Service; St. Louis; business/security services 600

Contico Intl. Inc./Continental Mfg.; Hazelwood; plastics products 575

IBM Corp.; St. Louis; computer services 550

3rd District

South St. Louis; Southeast St. Louis County; Jefferson and Ste. Genevieve Counties

For years, south St. Louis has been a collection of white working-class neighborhoods that reflect the European heritage of their residents. While the city's high-crime and low-income areas are primarily associated with north St. Louis (the 1st District), the south has not been immune. Crime has risen in south St. Louis and spilled over the city limits into St. Louis County.

With its declining population, the city accounts for less than a third of the vote in the new 3rd. Much of that vestige still has a heavily ethnic cast. Italians are clustered in The Hill, where family-owned businesses have survived for generations. Bevo Mill and Carondelet are old-line German communities. Mounting threats of crime have energized the growth of powerful neighborhood associations to arrest the decline of housing values in south St. Louis. In some neighborhoods, these groups rival the Democratic ward machines for power and organization.

McDonnell Douglas Corp., Anheuser-Busch, Monsanto and the area automobile assembly plants are major employers of the blue-collar workers who live in the 3rd. Many have been affected by recent shutdowns and layoffs. In 1991, Chrysler closed one of its two assembly plants in Fenton in south St. Louis County, just across the line in the 2nd District. McDonnell Douglas, with operations in the 1st and 2nd districts, has reduced its work force by thousands through attrition and layoffs.

The wards along the Mississippi, near the Anheuser-Busch brewery, are home to the poorest whites. Affluent whites live in the St. Louis Hills neighborhood, in the southwest part of the city. It is the only Republican area in the city. For the most part, south St. Louis is residential and middle class.

Monsanto and Mallinckrodt chemical facilities and barge operations along the Mississippi are important to the 3rd's economy. But the most prominent enterprise in this part of the city is Anheuser-Busch, which employs 5,900 people.

Looking to escape from typical urban ills in many north St. Louis neighborhoods, blacks have been moving into the south wards. Whites, in turn, have sought the St. Louis County suburbs, in communities such as Lemay, Affton and Concord. Some kept on going until they reached Jefferson County, where the population ballooned from about 146,000 to more than 171,000 during the 1980s. The southern part of Jefferson remains predominantly rural. Farmers in the Hillsboro area regularly truck their produce to markets in downtown St. Louis. Jefferson, which cast nearly as many 3rd District votes in 1992 as the city of St. Louis, is a swing area. George Bush carried Jefferson in 1988, but in 1992, Bill Clinton won it by 16 percentage points.

Ste. Genevieve County has escaped the rapid residential expansion of its neighbors. Founded by French lead miners in the 1720s, the city of Ste. Genevieve was the first permanent settlement in Missouri. Its roots are evident in restored French homes downtown. The Mississippi Lime Co. tops the list of city employers, but much of the county's land is devoted to corn, soybeans and hogs.

Election Returns

		3rd District	Democrat	Republican
1992	President*	120,866 (44.3%)	87,406 (32.0%)
	House	174,000 (64.0%)	90,006 (33.1%)
1988	President	110,509 (47.0%)	124,690 (53.0%)
	Senate	77,356 (33.0%)	157,099 (67.0%)
	Governor	77,848 (33.4%)	155,469 (66.6%)
1986	Senate	76,493 (45.4%)	92,035 (54.6%)

Vote for Perot was 64,511 (23.6%).

Demographics

Population 568,326

Percent change from 1980 4.1%

Land area 1,260 square miles

Population per square mile 451

Counties, 1990 population

Jefferson 171,380	St. Louis city (pt.) 175,159
St. Louis (pt.) 205,750	Ste. Genevieve 16,037

Cities, 1990 population (10,000 or more)

Affton CDP 21,106	Oakville CDP 31,750
Arnold 18,828	Sappington CDP (pt.) 10,345
Concord CDP 19,859	
Crestwood 11,234	St. Louis (pt.) 175,159
Lemay CDP 18,005	Webster Groves (pt.)
Mehlville CDP 27,557	20,910

Race and Hispanic origin

White 96.3%

Black 2.3%

American Indian, Eskimo, or Aleut. 0.2%

Asian or Pacific Islander 0.8%

Other 0.3%

Hispanic origin 1.1%

Ancestry

American 4.0%	Irish 23.5%
Czechoslovakian 1.6%	Italian 6.6%
Dutch 2.2%	Polish 3.2%
English 12.0%	Scotch Irish 1.7%
French 9.0%	Scottish 1.5%
German 50.0%	

Universities/colleges, 1990-1991 enrollment

Jefferson College, Hillsboro 3,937

Webster University, St. Louis 8,745

Newspapers, total circulation (in all districts)
St. Louis Post-Dispatch 369,005

Commercial television stations, affiliations
ADI: St. Louis (100%)
KDNL-TV, St. Louis (Fox)
KMOV, St. Louis (CBS)
KNLC, St. Louis (None)
KPLR-TV, St. Louis (None)
KSDK, St. Louis (NBC)
KTVI, St. Louis (ABC)
WHSL, East St. Louis (None)

Cable television systems, total subscribers
Cencom I of Missouri; Olivette 55,538
TCI of Missouri; Hillsboro 11,500
TCI of Missouri; St Louis 52,000

Military installations
Defense Mapping Agency Aerospace Center, St. Louis 3,500

Businesses and other major employers
Anheuser-Busch Companies Inc.; St. Louis; brewery 5,900
St. Anthony's Medical Center; St. Louis 2,900
Deaconess Hospital; St. Louis 2,495
U.S. Veterans Affairs Dept.; St. Louis; hospital 2,200
Luken's Steel Co.; St. Louis; steel products 2,000
General American Life Insurance Co.; St. Louis; life insurance 1,700
Pasta House Co.; St. Louis; bars/restaurants 1,000
Mehlville School District; St. Louis 1,000
St. Louis State Hospital; St. Louis 1,000
Alexian Brothers Hospital; St. Louis 825
Jefferson Memorial Hospital; Crystal City 819
Emerson Electric Co./White Rodgers Div.; St. Louis; measuring/controlling devices 800
Yellow Freight System Inc.; St. Louis; freight shipping 780
National Medical Enterprises/Lutheran Medical Center; St. Louis 775
Mississippi Lime Co.; Ste. Genevieve; crushed/broken stone 750
Guarantee Electrical Co.; St. Louis; electrical work 750
Jefferson County School District; Arnold 750
Nooter Corp.; St. Louis; metal products 600
Reorganized School District 1; House Springs 568
State of Missouri/Malcolm Bliss Mental Health Center; St. Louis 564
Sears Roebuck & Co.; St. Louis; department stores 507

4th District

West Central — Kansas City Suburbs; Jefferson City

The 4th is splayed two-thirds of the way across the state, stretching south and east from suburban bedroom communities in Jackson County (Kansas City) to encompass rural farmland, resort areas and small cities—including the state capital of Jefferson City. The easternmost point of the 4th in Osage County is just 75 miles from St. Louis.

Voters in the 4th are conservative, and outside Jackson County the GOP presidential nominee usually fares well: George Bush in 1988 carried every county wholly within the 4th except Saline. But the district is more conservative Democratic than staunchly Republican, and the right kind of Democrat can do

quite well. In 1992 Bill Clinton carried 13 whole counties plus the 4th's share of Jackson; he came within 1,801 votes of winning the 4th.

Democrats running for statewide office can find support in the western portion of the 4th. In 1992, successful Democratic gubernatorial nominee Mel Carnahan won every county west of Laclede. Toward the east, however, voter tendencies take a Republican turn. Democrats in competitive contests rarely top one-third of the vote in Cole, Miller and Osage counties.

Much of the 4th is devoted to small farming. While the farm economy has brightened considerably since the mid-1980s, it remains unsettled. Here, as elsewhere in the state, young people are leaving the farms to find steadier employment.

Corn, wheat and soybeans are grown in the rich soil along the Missouri River, on the 4th's northern frontier, as well as in the west. Livestock and dairy production dominate the southern part of the district, where the terrain turns hilly and rocky.

The greatest growth in the 1980s within the 4th was registered in the Lake of the Ozarks resort area and in the suburbs outside Kansas City (especially the burgeoning Cass County suburbs to the south). Retirees have been drawn to the Lake of the Ozarks area, in the center of the district.

State government has been a fairly reliable source of jobs in Cole County, just slightly less populous than Cass. But budget constraints have introduced some uncertainty in the area's economy, threatening state workers with layoffs. Jefferson City also has some light industry. Chesebrough Ponds makes Q-Tips at its Jefferson City plant.

Military installations have been a major factor in the economy. Whiteman Air Force Base in Johnson County is to house the first wing of B-2 stealth bombers, which are expected to begin arriving late in 1993. The Pentagon's 1991 base-closing plan ordered the closure of Richards-Gebaur Air Force Base in Cass County, but the Army's Fort Leonard Wood in Pulaski County escaped shutdown.

Sedalia (Pettis County) once was a railhead of the Missouri Pacific Railroad and an entertainment mecca for railworkers. Ragtime composer Scott Joplin got his start in a Sedalia club. Every June, Sedalia holds the Scott Joplin Ragtime Festival, attracting artists from across the country.

Election Returns

	4th District	Democrat	Republican
1992	President*	94,951 (37.0%)	96,752 (37.7%)
	House	176,977 (70.4%)	74,475 (29.6%)
1988	President	91,572 (40.7%)	133,544 (59.3%)
	Senate	59,341 (26.5%)	164,703 (73.5%)
	Governor	69,403 (31.0%)	154,316 (69.0%)
1986	Senate	67,789 (41.7%)	94,870 (58.3%)

Vote for Perot was 65,231 (25.4%).

Demographics

Population 569,146

Percent change from 1980 4.1%

Land area 14,102 square miles

Population per square mile 40

Counties, 1990 population

Bates 15,025	Maries 7,976
Benton 13,859	Miller 20,700
Camden 27,495	Moniteau 12,298
Cass 63,808	Morgan 15,574
Cole 63,579	Osage 12,018
Dallas 12,646	Pettis 35,437
Henry 20,044	Pulaski 41,307
Hickory 7,335	Saline 23,523
Jackson (pt.) 24,492	St. Clair 8,457
Johnson 42,514	Vernon 19,041
Laclede 27,158	Webster 23,753
Lafayette 31,107	

Cities, 1990 population (10,000 or more)

Belton 18,150	Jefferson City (pt.) 35,175
Blue Springs (pt.) 10,469	Marshall 12,711
Fort Leonard Wood CDP 15,863	Sedalia 19,800
	Warrensburg 15,244

Race and Hispanic origin

White 95.4%
Black 3.2%
American Indian, Eskimo, or Aleut. 0.5%
Asian or Pacific Islander 0.6%
Other 0.4%
Hispanic origin 1.1%

Ancestry

American 8.4%	Italian 1.7%
Dutch 3.6%	Polish 1.2%
English 15.6%	Scotch Irish 2.9%
French 4.4%	Scottish 1.9%
German 39.0%	Swedish 1.5%
Irish 19.9%	

Universities/colleges, 1990-1991 enrollment

Calvary Bible College, Kansas City 273
Central Missouri State University, Warrensburg 11,429
Cottey College, Nevada 348
Lincoln University, Jefferson City 3,619
Missouri Valley College, Marshall 1,054
State Fair Community College, Sedalia 2,369
Wentworth Military Academy, Lexington 331

Newspapers, total circulation (in all districts)

Kansas City Star/Times 283,061
Post-Tribune/Capital News 21,221
Sedalia Democrat 13,635
Springfield News-Leader 58,298
St. Louis Post-Dispatch 369,005
Warrensburg Daily Star Journal 4,439

Commercial television stations, affiliations

ADI: Kansas City (37%), Springfield (35%), Columbia-Jefferson City (22%) and Joplin-Pittsburg (6%)
KMIZ, Columbia (ABC)
KDEB-TV, Springfield (Fox)
KOLR, Springfield (CBS)
KSPR, Springfield (ABC)
KYTV, Springfield (NBC)

Cable television systems, total subscribers

Cable America Corp.; St. Robert 7,000
Falcon Cable TV; Osage Beach 8,945
Falcon Cable TV; Sedalia 8,080
Jones Intercable Inc.; Raymore 53,201
TCI of Missouri; Jefferson City 13,647

Military installations, 1991

Fort Leonard Wood (Army), Jefferson City 20,696
Whiteman Air Force Base, Knob Noster 4,005

Businesses and other major employers

Werley Enterprises Inc.; Warrensburg; nonstore retailers 5,000
State of Missouri/Labor-Industrial Relations Dept.; Jefferson City 2,500
Central Missouri State University; Warrensburg 2,170
State of Missouri/Revenue Dept.; Jefferson City 2,016
State of Missouri/Education Dept.; Jefferson City 2,000
Lee Apparel Co. Inc.; Lebanon; jeans 1,200
State of Missouri/Health Dept.; Jefferson City 1,200
State of Missouri/Economic Development Dept.; Jefferson City 1,080
ABB Power T&D Co. Inc.; Jefferson City; electric distribution equipment 1,000
State of Missouri/Habilitation Center; Marshall 1,000
State of Missouri/Habilitation Center; Nevada 900
ConAgra Inc.; Marshall; preserved fruits/vegetables 850
State of Missouri/Highway & Transportation Dept.; Jefferson City 850
Fasco Industries Inc.; Eldon; electrical industrial apparatus 800
Marriott Corp./Marriott's Tan-Tar-A Resort; Osage Beach; hotel 800
Wilson Foods Corp.; Marshall; meat products 750
SSM Health Care System/St. Mary's Health Center; Jefferson City 750
Bothwell Regional Health Center; Sedalia 698
State of Missouri/Correctional Facility; Jefferson City 688
Missouri Osteopathic Foundation/Still Regional Medical Center; Jefferson City 672
Scholastic Book Clubs Inc.; Jefferson City; magazines/books 670
Four Seasons Group Inc.; Lake Ozark; hotel 650
Tracker Marine Corp.; Lebanon; shipbuilding/repairing 600
State of Missouri/Aging Div.; Jefferson City 577
State of Missouri/Habilitation Center; Higginsville 560
Detroit Tool Group Inc.; Lebanon; custom industrial machinery 550
State of Missouri/Natural Resources Dept.; Jefferson City 550

5th District

Kansas City and Eastern Suburbs; Independence

From its fountains and skyscrapers to its barbecue joints and sports complex, one-time cowtown Kansas City is now a modern, front-line U.S. city. In the 1990 census, it passed St. Louis as Missouri's most populous city.

While it remains a nationally prominent feeder cattle and hard winter wheat market, the city's economy is far more diverse than its longtime image implies. The stockyards' heyday ended decades ago. Diversity enabled Kansas City to weather economic doldrums better than many urban areas.

The district is solidly Democratic: Presidential nominees Michael S. Dukakis and Bill Clinton both carried the 5th by wide margins in 1988 and 1992. Democratic Rep. Alan Wheat, with steady biracial support, was elected to a sixth term in 1992.

Long a center for automobile production, metropolitan Kansas City is the nation's sixth-largest auto producer. Ford has a plant north of the city in Claycomo (in the 6th District); General Motors' Fairfax assembly plant is just across the Missouri River in Kansas. Many autoworkers live in blue-collar neighborhoods in Kansas City and in the nearby city of Independence.

Other blue-collar workers who live in the district work at Kansas City International Airport (KCI), north of the city. Trans World Airlines, which filed for bankruptcy in July 1991, has a large base where it overhauls its aircraft. KCI is a contender in the bidding war for the production facility for McDonnell Douglas' new passenger airplane.

With many regional offices in the city and across the Kansas border, the federal government is one of the area's largest employers. The steel, transportation and communications industries are significant as well. Hallmark Cards is a hometown corporation and has spent millions on commercial redevelopment within the city. Hallmark built Crown Center, which includes an array of restaurants, shops, pricey apartments and a luxury hotel. Hallmark and other major corporations received some unflattering attention in 1991 with their "screening committee" to dub an acceptable mayoral candidate. Ultimately, City Council member Emanuel Cleaver, who had been snubbed by the corporate elite, won the election, becoming Kansas City's first black mayor.

Though Kansas City has not suffered the flight of people and businesses that has drained St. Louis, its population has declined to about 435,000—fewer people than were living in the city 30 years ago. For a generation there has been steady out-migration to Jackson County suburbs and into Johnson County, Kan.

But Kansas City has not capitulated. Yuppies have been lured back to the central city by projects such as the restoration of the Quality Hill section, one of Kansas City's oldest areas, and of City Market, an outdoor market in use since the 1800s. And the city boasts an outstanding housing stock around the University of Missouri-Kansas City.

To the east, the 5th includes Independence (population 112,300), the fourth most populous city in Missouri and hometown of Harry S. Truman.

Election Returns

	5th District	Democrat	Republican
1992	President*	134,932 (52.3%)	67,503 (26.1%)
	House	151,014 (59.1%)	93,562 (36.6%)
1988	President	124,234 (61.2%)	78,726 (38.8%)
	Senate	84,394 (42.0%)	116,778 (58.0%)
	Governor	91,986 (45.9%)	108,422 (54.1%)
1986	Senate	80,916 (58.8%)	56,713 (41.2%)

*Vote for Perot was 55,763 (21.6%).

Demographics

Population   569,130

Percent change from 1980   4.1%

Land area   374 square miles

Population per square mile   1,523

Counties, 1990 population
Jackson (pt.)   569,130

Cities, 1990 population (10,000 or more)

Grandview 24,967	Lee's Summit (pt.) 45,985
Independence (pt.) 111,215	Raytown 30,601
Kansas City (pt.) 341,179	

Race and Hispanic origin
White   73.2%
Black   23.7%
American Indian, Eskimo, or Aleut.   0.5%
Asian or Pacific Islander   1.0%
Other   1.6%
Hispanic origin   3.2%

Ancestry

American 4.3%	Italian 3.2%
Dutch 2.8%	Polish 1.3%
English 14.3%	Scotch Irish 2.9%
French 3.7%	Scottish 2.0%
German 26.1%	Swedish 1.8%
Irish 17.5%	Welsh 1.0%

Universities/colleges, 1990-1991 enrollment
Avila College, Kansas City   1,368
Cleveland Chiropractic College, Kansas City   297
Devry Institute of Technology, Kansas City   1,747
Kansas City Art Institute, Kansas City   575
Longview Community College, Lee's Summit   9,625
Nazarene Theological Center, Kansas City   339
Penn Valley Community College, Kansas City   5,778
Rockhurst College, Kansas City   2,806
St. Paul School of Theology, Kansas City   269
University of Health Sciences, Kansas City   553
University of Missouri, Kansas City   11,271

Newspapers, total circulation (in all districts)
Kansas City Star/Times   283,061

Commercial television stations, affiliations
ADI: Kansas City (100%)
KCTV, Kansas City (CBS)
KMBC-TV, Kansas City (ABC)
KSHB-TV, Kansas City (Fox)
KSMO, Kansas City (None)
KYFC, Kansas City (None)
WDAF-TV, Kansas City (NBC)

Cable television systems, total subscribers
American Cablevision; Kansas City   27,359
American Cablevision; Kansas City   107,902
Jones Intercable Inc.; Raymore   53,201

Military installations, 1991
Marine Corps Support Activity, Kansas City   1,073
Richards-Gebaur Air Force Reserve Station, Belton   655

Businesses and other major employers
Hallmark Cards Inc.; Kansas City; greeting cards   7,000
Allied-Signal Inc.; Kansas City; navigation equipment   6,230
U.S. Sprint Communications Ltd.; Kansas City; telephone communications   3,500
U.S. Postal Service; Kansas City   3,200
Black & Veatch; Kansas City; engineering & construction services   3,100
St. Luke's Hospital of Kansas City; Kansas City   2,700
AT&T Communications Inc.; Kansas City; telephone communications   2,600

Trans World Airlines Inc.; Kansas City; airline 2,500

Olin Corp./Olin Defense Systems Group; Independence; ordnance/accessories 2,300

United Missouri Bank; Kansas City; commercial banks 2,014

U.S. General Services Administration; Kansas City 2,000

Research Medical Center/Research Belton Hospital; Kansas City 2,000

TW Services Inc.; Kansas City; bars/restaurants 1,900

AT&T Co.; Lee's Summit; telecommunications equipment 1,800

BGM Industries Inc.; Kansas City; building services 1,775

Kansas City Power & Light Co.; Kansas City; electric services 1,750

Kansas City Star Co.; Kansas City; newspapers 1,650

Commerce Property & Casualty; Kansas City; fire/marine/casualty insurance 1,500

City of Kansas City; Kansas City 1,500

House of Lloyd Inc.; Grandview; nonstore retailers 1,450

DST Systems Inc.; Kansas City; accounting/auditing 1,400

Truman Medical Center West; Kansas City 1,300

St. Joseph Health Center; Kansas City 1,220

Commerce Bancshares; Kansas City; holding offices 1,200

U.S. Census Bureau; Kansas City 1,200

U.S. Veterans Affairs Dept.; Kansas City; hospital 1,200

Independence Regional Health Center; Independence 1,192

Mercy Children's Hospital; Kansas City 1,185

Menorah Medical Center; Kansas City 1,050

Armco Inc.; Kansas City; steel products 1,000

Boatmen's First National Bank of Kansas City; Kansas City; commercial banks 1,000

City of Kansas City/Police Dept.; Kansas City 1,000

Trinity Lutheran Hospital; Kansas City 995

U.S. Agriculture Dept.; Kansas City 980

Baptist Medical Center/Physicians' Home Care Services; Kansas City 950

Penn Valley Community College; Kansas City 906

Yellow Freight System Inc.; Kansas City; trucking facilities 900

Federal Reserve Bank of Kansas City; Kansas City 900

Burns & McDonnell Engineering; Kansas City; engineering services 900

Utilicorp United Inc./Missouri Public Service; Kansas City; utility services 889

City of Kansas City/Water Dept.; Kansas City 850

U.S. Army Corps of Engineers; Kansas City 850

Business Men's Assurance Co. of America; Kansas City; medical service/health insurance 825

Western Missouri Mental Health Center; Kansas City 822

State of Missouri/Highway & Transportation Dept.; Kansas City 800

Twentieth Century Services; Kansas City; computer services 800

Kansas City Area Transportation Authority; Kansas City 775

Marion Merrell Dow Inc.; Kansas City; pharmaceuticals 750

Payless Cashways Inc./Furrow; Kansas City; lumber/building materials 750

City of Kansas City/Fire Dept.; Kansas City 750

John Knox Village; Lees Summit; real estate operators 700

Government Employees Hospital; Kansas City; insurance services 700

IBM Corp.; Kansas City; computer stores 700

Truman Medical Center Inc.; Kansas City 700

County of Jackson/Family Services; Kansas City 700

Western Auto Supply Co.; Kansas City; auto supply stores 650

Blue Cross/Blue Shield; Kansas City; medical service/health insurance 625

Hyatt Corp./Hyatt Regency Crown Center; Kansas City; hotel 620

Tension Envelope Corp.; Kansas City; envelopes 600

Deutz-Allis Corp.; Independence; credit institutions 600

BPS Guard Services Inc./Danguard; Kansas City; business services 600

Pinkerton's Inc.; Kansas City; business services 587

Unity School of Christianity; Lee's Summit; periodicals 550

Kemper Financial Companies/Kemper Service Co.; Kansas City; security brokers 550

Westin Crown Plaza Hotel Co.; Kansas City; hotel 550

6th District

Northwest — St. Joseph

The 6th encompasses prosperous suburbs east and north of Kansas City and struggling farms along the Iowa border. The economic disparities are mirrored in its political diversity: It is the state's most marginal district. George Bush carried what was then the 6th in 1988, but just barely. In 1992, Democrat Bill Clinton carried all but two of the 28 counties wholly or partly within the 6th. Clinton took 40 percent of the vote districtwide, while Bush finished second with 33 percent and Ross Perot a close third with 27 percent. That year, Democratic gubernatorial nominee Mel Carnahan carried all but four counties, while GOP Sen. Christopher S. Bond won all but three district counties.

The substantial population losses in the 1980s in the district's northern tier reflect the devastation of the farm economy. Northwest Missouri is still recovering from the mid-1980s farm crisis; erosion, drought and flooding have taken their toll. Some soybean and corn farmers and their families have turned up on welfare rolls. In towns such as Princeton (Mercer County), businesses that sold farm equipment are boarding up. Being far from the state's four-lane highways perpetuates the sense of isolation.

Farther west in the district, farming is becoming more of a part-time occupation, as many farmers take second jobs. Small to medium-size companies dot the region. Agricultural research critical to the local farming economy is conducted at Northwest Missouri State University (6,100 students) in Maryville (Nodaway County).

The river city of St. Joseph (Buchanan County) gained a place in history as the eastern end of the Pony Express. A booming supply depot for gold prospectors heading to California in the 1800s, St. Joseph had more than 100,000 people in 1900. But the city shrank steadily thereafter as the stockyards declined, and people looked to jobs and metropolitan life in Kansas City, 35 miles to the south. Things seemed to hit bottom in the 1960s with the exodus of meatpacking companies, and St. Joseph's 1990 population (about 71,900) was its lowest in 100 years.

Attempting to right itself, the city's business sector has diversified. Recent location decisions by new and existing businesses have offered some hope of improvement.

Times have not been as hard in the southwestern part of the 6th, where Kansas City-area workers opting for a more bucolic exurb moved into surrounding counties. Platte and Clay counties registered double-digit percentage gains in population in the

1980s. The portion of Jackson County in the 6th contains affluent, Republican-leaning suburban voters.

Kansas City International Airport (KCI) is another vital organ of the regional economy. Cutbacks at KCI, particularly by Trans World Airlines, have upset the economy. The airport is now considered a focus of agricultural exports. An export facility there ships cattle by air to Asia.

Other areas have turned to some innovative economic development ideas. Cameron (Clinton County), for example, has a private minimum-security prison and is eager to host another.

Election Returns

	6th District	Democrat	Republican
1992	President*	110,064 (40.1%)	89,005 (32.5%)
	House	148,887 (55.4%)	119,637 (44.6%)
1988	President	110,960 (49.7%)	112,133 (50.3%)
	Senate	67,761 (31.2%)	149,468 (68.8%)
	Governor	75,542 (34.6%)	142,742 (65.4%)
1986	Senate	81,398 (49.5%)	83,185 (50.5%)

*Vote for Perot was 75,185 (27.4%).

Demographics

Population 569,131

Percent change from 1980 4.1%

Land area 13,571 square miles

Population per square mile 42

Counties, 1990 population

Andrew 14,632	Holt 6,034
Atchison 7,457	Howard 9,631
Buchanan 83,083	Jackson (pt.) 39,610
Caldwell 8,380	Linn 13,885
Carroll 10,748	Livingston 14,592
Chariton 9,202	Mercer 3,723
Clay 153,411	Nodaway 21,709
Clinton 16,595	Platte 57,867
Cooper 14,835	Putnam 5,079
Daviess 7,865	Ray 21,971
DeKalb 9,967	Schuyler 4,236
Gentry 6,848	Sullivan 6,326
Grundy 10,536	Worth 2,440
Harrison 8,469	

Cities, 1990 population (10,000 or more)

Blue Springs (pt.) 29,294	Liberty 20,459
Excelsior Springs 10,354	Maryville 10,663
Gladstone 26,243	St. Joseph 71,852
Kansas City (pt.) 93,925	

Race and Hispanic origin
White 96.5%
Black 2.1%
American Indian, Eskimo, or Aleut. 0.4%
Asian or Pacific Islander 0.5%
Other 0.5%
Hispanic origin 1.5%

Ancestry

American 9.2%	English 17.7%
Dutch 3.9%	French 4.5%

German 36.7%	Scotch Irish 3.5%
Irish 21.8%	Scottish 2.3%
Italian 2.5%	Swedish 2.1%
Polish 1.4%	Welsh 1.2%

Universities/colleges, 1990-1991 enrollment
Central Methodist College, Fayette 887
Maple Woods Community College, Kansas City 4,753
Midwestern Baptist Theological Seminary, Kansas City 428
Missouri Western State College, St. Joseph 4,555
North Central Missouri College, Trenton 903
Northwest Missouri Community College, St. Joseph 202
Northwest Missouri State University, Maryville 6,093
Park College, Parkville 4,793
William Jewell College, Liberty 2,056

Newspapers, total circulation (in all districts)
Kansas City Star/Times 283,061
St. Joseph News-Press Gazette 41,417

Commercial television stations, affiliations
ADI: Kansas City (50%), St. Joseph (18%), Columbia-Jefferson City (13%), Ottumwa-Kirksville (11%), Omaha (4%) and Des Moines (3%)
KQTV, St. Joseph (ABC)
KTAJ, St. Joseph (None)

Cable television systems, total subscribers
American Cablevision; Kansas City 107,902
American Cablevision; Leavenworth 12,090
Jones Intercable Inc.; Raymore 53,201
St. Joseph Cablevision; St Joseph 26,434

Military installations, 1991
Rosecrans Memorial Airport Air Force Guard Station, Elwood 279

Businesses and other major employers
Ford Motor Co.; Kansas City; motor vehicle assembly 4,500
Marion Merrell Dow Inc.; Kansas City; pharmaceuticals 3,000
Hallmark Cards Inc.; Liberty; warehousing 1,200
Walsworth Publishing Co. Inc.; Marceline; publishing 1,000
North Kansas City Memorial Hospital; Kansas City 1,000
Pars Service Partnership; Kansas City; reservation services 1,000
Farmland Industries Inc.; Kansas City; petroleum refining 915
Lindsey & Lindsey Inc.; Blue Springs; nonstore retailers 900
Heartland Hospital West; St. Joseph 850
Mead Corp.; St. Joseph; paper mills 800
Wilcox Electric Inc.; Kansas City; search/navigation equipment 758
ConAgra Inc. ConAgra Frozen Foods Div.; Milan; frozen meat products 750
Liberty Hospital; Liberty 750
Quaker Oats Co.; St. Joseph; grain mill products 700
St. Joseph State Hospital; St. Joseph 700
Eveready Battery Co. Inc.; Maryville; batteries 650
Citicorp/Credit Services; Kansas City; credit institutions 650
American Family Mutual Insurance Co.; St. Joseph; insurance services 650
Northwest Missouri State University; Maryville 608
Wire Rope Corp./Wireco; St. Joseph; metal wires 600
Johnson Controls Inc.; St. Joseph; batteries 525

7th District

Southwest — *Springfield; Joplin*

Two decades of rapid growth have helped lift southwestern Missouri from poor hillbilly hideaway to burgeoning resort region with a growing industrial base. Since the 1970s, this part of Missouri has outpaced the rest of the state in population growth. It is solidly Republican territory.

The 7th boomed during the 1980s as a stream of retirees and other newcomers settled in the resort area around Table Rock Lake. Branson (Taney County) has become a magnet for country music fans, attracting 4 million visitors a year to its many theaters and studios.

The recreational trade nourishes local services and industries. Bass Pro Shops, which manufactures and sells fishing boats and other sporting goods, is based in Springfield (Greene County), the district's industrial and commercial center. Nationwide customers of Bass Pro's mail-order catalog are lured to the Springfield store much as devotees of L. L. Bean descend on its site in Maine.

Springfield also counts Zenith, Litton and Kraft among its major employers, and it is home to Southwest Missouri State University (19,500 students). More than 40 percent of the 7th's residents live in Greene and neighboring Christian County.

Joplin is the district's other population center. An old lead- and zinc-mining town, Joplin is now a center for manufacturing and trucking operations. Nearby Carthage, the Jasper County seat, competes for attention with its larger neighbor. Leggett & Platt, which makes box springs and other bedding and furniture components, has its headquarters and three manufacturing plants in Carthage, employing about 1,300 throughout the city.

Wheat, soybeans and corn are grown in the 7th's western counties. The hillier Ozark counties raise beef and dairy cattle. Poultry farming and production also contribute to the district's economy.

The rural and agricultural character of the Ozarks has not entirely yielded to development and modernization. There remain many small, isolated communities, legacies of the region's settlers—Scotch-Irish mountaineers from eastern Tennessee, western Virginia and Kentucky. Many of these rural counties struggle economically.

Southwestern Missouri is a breeding ground for statewide GOP politicians. The last Republican governor, secretary of state, attorney general and state treasurer all had roots in the southwest. George Bush carried every county in the 7th in 1992 even as he lost by 10 points statewide.

The area's Republican lineage dates from the Civil War. Though there was some slave trading on Springfield's town square, most of the Ozark settlers had no use for slavery on their small, hilly farms; pro-Union sentiment was strong. The GOP preference in the Joplin area was cemented when President Woodrow Wilson lowered tariffs on lead and zinc and crippled the mining industry.

The 7th's conservatism is also reflected in its politically active religious organizations. The national headquarters of the Assemblies of God, the nation's largest Pentecostal church, is in Springfield, and the Pentecostal Church of God's international headquarters is in Joplin. Southwest Baptist University in Bolivar (Polk County) has about 3,000 students.

Election Returns

	7th District	Democrat	Republican
1992	President*	96,621 (36.6%)	118,817 (45.0%)
	House	99,762 (38.4%)	160,303 (61.6%)
1988	President	90,969 (38.6%)	144,758 (61.4%)
	Senate	51,832 (22.2%)	181,871 (77.8%)
	Governor	56,605 (24.2%)	177,577 (75.8%)
1986	Senate	65,328 (39.1%)	101,750 (60.9%)

Vote for Perot was 48,824 (18.5%).

Demographics

Population 568,017

Percent change from 1980 4.0%

Land area 9,291 square miles

Population per square mile 61

Counties, 1990 population

Barry 27,547	Lawrence 30,236
Barton 11,312	McDonald 16,938
Cedar 12,093	Newton 44,445
Christian 32,644	Ozark 8,598
Dade 7,449	Polk 21,826
Douglas 11,876	Stone 19,078
Greene 207,949	Taney 25,561
Jasper 90,465	

Cities, 1990 population (10,000 or more)

Carthage 10,747	Springfield 140,494
Joplin 40,961	

Race and Hispanic origin

White 97.3%
Black 0.9%
American Indian, Eskimo, or Aleut. 1.0%
Asian or Pacific Islander 0.5%
Other 0.2%
Hispanic origin 0.8%

Ancestry

American 7.3%	Italian 1.7%
Dutch 4.6%	Polish 1.2%
English 19.1%	Scotch Irish 3.5%
French 4.7%	Scottish 2.2%
German 30.7%	Swedish 1.8%
Irish 22.1%	

Universities/colleges, 1990-1991 enrollment

Assemblies of God Theological Seminary, Springfield 216
Baptist Bible College, Springfield 825
Central Bible College, Springfield 1,091
College of the Ozarks, Point Lookout 1,512
Crowder College, Neosho 1,608
Drury College, Springfield 3,501
Evangel College, Springfield 1,540
Missouri Southern State College, Joplin 6,016
Ozark Christian College, Joplin 634
Phillips Junior College, Springfield 300
Southwest Baptist University, Bolivar 2,954
Southwest Missouri State University, Springfield 19,480

Newspapers, total circulation (in all districts)
Joplin Globe 36,407
Springfield News-Leader 58,298

Commercial television stations, affiliations
ADI: Springfield (75%) and Joplin-Pittsburg (25%)
    KODE-TV, Joplin (ABC)
    KSNF, Joplin (NBC)

Cable television systems, total subscribers
Cablecom of Joplin; Joplin 13,021
Telecable of Springfield; Springfield 43,200

Businesses and other major employers
St. John's Regional Health Center; Springfield 4,000
Lester E. Cox Medical Center; Springfield 2,400
Zenith Electronics Corp.; Springfield; audio/video equipment 1,900
Bass Pro Shops Inc.; Springfield; sporting goods 1,600
St. John's Regional Medical Center; Joplin 1,335
Southwest Missouri State University; Springfield 1,325
Tyson Foods Inc.; Monett; meat products 1,200
Sweetheart Cup Co. Inc.; Springfield; paperboard products 1,100
O'Sullivan Industries Inc.; Lamar; furniture 1,100
La-Z-Boy Chair Co.; Neosho; furniture 1,010
Kraft General Foods Inc./Kraft USA; Springfield; dairy products 1,000
Hudson Foods Inc.; Noel; poultry products 1,000
Contract Freighters Inc.; Joplin; trucking services 1,000
Eagle-Picher Industries Inc.; Joplin; electrical equipment/supplies 1,000
General Council/Assemblies of God; Springfield; 985
Leggett & Platt Inc./Cyclo-Index; Carthage; furniture 950
O'Reilly Automotive Inc.; Springfield; auto parts 947
Litton Systems Inc./Litton Industries; Springfield; electronic components 900
Tyson Foods Inc./Honeybear Foods; Neosho; poultry products 900
EFCO Corp.; Monett; metal tanks; food products machinery 850
Paul Mueller Co.; Springfield; metal products 830
General Electric Co.; Springfield; electrical industrial apparatus 800
Freeman Hospital; Joplin 800
Fasco Industries Inc.; Ozark; electrical motors 700
Emerson Electric Co.; Ava; electrical motors 600
Associated Wholesale Grocers; Springfield; warehousing 600
State of Missouri/Highway & Transportation Dept.; Springfield 600
Hudson Foods Inc.; Springfield; poultry products 600
Schreiber Foods Inc.; Carthage; dairy products 600
Healthcare Services of the Ozarks/Oxford Healthcare; Springfield; personnel supply services 600
U.S. Justice Dept./Bureau of Prisons; Springfield 600
George's Inc./George's Processing Inc.; Cassville; poultry products 550
Sunbeam Corp./Sunbeam Outdoor Products; Neosho; household appliances 550
ConAgra Poultry Co./ConAgra Turkey Co.; Carthage; poultry/eggs 540

8th District
Southeast — Cape Girardeau

Within the borders of the 8th is some of the state's most bountiful farmland, and the district's agricultural diversity is matched by its political breadth. The 8th spans the spectrum from solidly Republican counties in the west and northeast along the Mississippi River to "yellow dog" Democratic territory in the southeastern bootheel.

The 8th's growth during the 1980s came primarily in its northernmost counties, not far from metropolitan St. Louis. Washington and St. Francois counties both had double-digit growth as commuters settled into bedroom communities. Both counties solidly backed Bill Clinton in 1992.

In the southeastern corner is the bootheel, a cluster of counties that look and vote like the Old South. Predominantly a wheat-growing region until the mid-1920s, the bootheel was transformed when cotton growers and black sharecroppers from Mississippi, Alabama and Tennessee, driven north by the boll weevil, discovered the area's rich delta land and settled. The seven counties in the southeastern corner—Mississippi, New Madrid, Pemiscot, Dunklin, Butler, Stoddard and Scott—grow 35 percent of the state's cash crops. Clinton carried all seven in 1992.

The bootheel is the northernmost area in the country where cotton and rice grow. Dunklin ranks 14th among the nation's cotton-harvesting counties; Butler is in the top 25 for rice. The port at New Madrid has Missouri's only rice mill; it opened in 1988. Dunklin is the nation's third largest watermelon-harvesting county and is also a major peach producer.

Soybeans and corn have supplanted cotton as the bootheel's leading crops, but the Southern Democratic habits forged during cotton's heyday have persisted. A search of the bootheel counties' courthouses would reveal only the occasional Republican. But in statewide contests, these Democratic strongholds are largely offset by Republican votes from Cape Girardeau and Perry counties. The cluster of Cape Girardeau, Perry and Bollinger counties makes up three of the four district counties George Bush won in 1992.

Above the bootheel, along the Mississippi River, dairy production and beef cattle fuel the economy. Livestock, timber and fruit production flourish in other parts of the 8th. Wright is Missouri's foremost dairy county. Oregon County breeds feeder pigs for Iowa slaughterhouses. Apples are grown in the Mark Twain National Forest. Other "specialty" crops such as blueberries, strawberries and cantaloupe are also cultivated in the district.

Even the ground beneath the 8th yields riches. The vast majority of the nation's lead—and most of the world's—is mined in southeast Missouri. The discovery of a "New Lead Belt" called the Viburnum Trend during the late 1950s revitalized an industry that dates back to the early 1700s, when French explorers mined in Mine La Motte (Madison County). Most of today's lead mining is centered in the New Lead Belt of western Iron County and Reynolds County.

The forests of the Ozarks once provided the timber that built St. Louis. Small lumber mills in the area still produce pallets and other wood products. The Ozarks also attract recreation-seekers who fish and canoe in the Eleven Point and Current rivers and in the Ozark National Scenic Riverways.

Election Returns

	8th District	Democrat	Republican
1992	President*	109,858 (45.6%)	89,238 (37.1%)
	House	86,730 (37.0%)	147,398 (63.0%)
1988	President	86,900 (44.9%)	106,446 (55.1%)
	Senate	58,806 (31.0%)	131,103 (69.0%)
	Governor	72,618 (37.8%)	119,392 (62.2%)
1986	Senate	65,411 (45.3%)	79,004 (54.7%)

*Vote for Perot was 41,558 (17.3%).

Demographics

Population 568,385

Percent change from 1980 4.1%

Land area 17,470 square miles

Population per square mile 33

Counties, 1990 population

Bollinger	10,619	Pemiscot	21,921
Butler	38,765	Perry	16,648
Cape Girardeau	61,633	Phelps	35,248
Carter	5,515	Reynolds	6,661
Crawford	19,173	Ripley	12,303
Dent	13,702	Scott	39,376
Dunklin	33,112	Shannon	7,613
Howell	31,447	St. Francois	48,904
Iron	10,726	Stoddard	28,895
Madison	11,127	Texas	21,476
Mississippi	14,442	Washington	20,380
New Madrid	20,928	Wayne	11,543
Oregon	9,470	Wright	16,758

Cities, 1990 population (10,000 or more)

Cape Girardeau	34,438	Poplar Bluff	16,996
Farmington	11,598	Rolla	14,090
Kennett	10,941	Sikeston	17,641

Race and Hispanic origin

White 94.8%
Black 4.4%
American Indian, Eskimo, or Aleut. 0.3%
Asian or Pacific Islander 0.4%
Other 0.1%
Hispanic origin 0.5%

Ancestry

American	11.1%	Irish	22.5%
Dutch	3.6%	Italian	1.3%
English	13.3%	Scotch Irish	2.2%
French	6.3%	Scottish	1.2%
German	28.9%		

Universities/colleges, 1990-1991 enrollment

Mineral Area College, Flat River 2,649
Southeast Missouri State University, Cape Girardeau 8,801
Southwest Missouri State University, West Plains 855
Three Rivers Community College, Poplar Bluff 2,062
University of Missouri, Rolla 5,443

Newspapers, total circulation (in all districts)

Flat River Daily Journal 9,089
Sikeston Standard & Democrat 9,618
Springfield News-Leader 58,298
St. Louis Post-Dispatch 369,005

Commercial television stations, affiliations

ADI: Paducah-Cape Girardeau-Harrisburg-Marion (39%), Springfield (34%), St. Louis (20%), Jonesboro (4%) and Memphis (3%)
  KBSI, Cape Girardeau (Fox)
  KFVS-TV, Cape Girardeau (CBS)
  KPOB-TV, Poplar Bluff (ABC)

Cable television systems, total subscribers

Enstar Cable TV; Poplar Bluff 7,121
Falcon Cable TV; Sikeston 6,215
Fidelity Cablevision; Rolla 5,500
TCI of Missouri; Jackson 12,308

Businesses and other major employers

Southeast Missouri Hospital; Cape Girardeau 1,387
Procter & Gamble; Cape Girardeau; paper products 1,300
Noranda Aluminum Inc.; New Madrid; aluminum production 1,200
St. Francis Medical Center; Cape Girardeau 1,115
University of Missouri; Rolla 992
Siegel-Robert Inc./Plastene Supply Co.; Portageville; plastics products 800
Arvin Industries Inc.; Dexter; motor vehicle parts 750
Lee-Rowan Co.; Jackson; steel products 730
Ozarks Medical Center Inc.; West Plains 730
Hart Schaffner & Marx/Thorngate Ltd.; Cape Girardeau; suits/coats 690
State of Missouri/Southeast Missouri Mental Health Center; Farmington 670
Missouri Delta Medical Center; Sikeston 651
American Medical Intl./Lucy Lee Hospital; Poplar Bluff 625
Emerson Electric Co.; Kennett; electrical motors 600
Wheaton Industries Inc./Flat River Glass Co. Div.; Flat River; glass bottles 600
Wal-Mart Stores Inc.; Poplar Bluff; department stores 600
Southeast Missouri State University; Cape Girardeau 600
Southwest Mobile Systems Corp.; West Plains; semitrailers 550
State of Missouri/Correctional Center; Farmington 520
Brown Group Inc.; Bernie; footwear 506

9th District

Northeast — Columbia

Stark contrasts of prosperity and penury define the 9th. Population in the southeastern part of the district skyrocketed in the 1980s as the St. Louis suburbs expanded into adjacent counties: St. Charles County grew by 48 percent; the populations of Lincoln and Warren counties increased by about 30 percent.

Many of the new arrivals commute to St. Louis to work at McDonnell Douglas Corp. in St. Charles and St. Louis counties; others work at the General Motors assembly plant in Wentzville. Local concerns revolve around bridges and roads to support the population crunch.

But the blossoming at this end of the district is countered by bleak conditions in the northern counties, where farm families find it increasingly difficult to survive. The agricultural depression of the 1980s has abated elsewhere but lingers in many parts of the 9th. Young people, leaving their hometowns for more reliable employment, often cross the border to work in Iowa or Illinois.

Agriculture remains the mainstay of the 9th's economy. Winter wheat, corn and soybeans are grown throughout the district. St. Charles County still has some wheat and cornfields. Cattle and hogs are raised across the district. Vineyards in Gasconade and Warren counties grow grapes for area wineries that date back more than 150 years. Among Missouri's first settlers were Virginians and Kentuckians who found the rich soil to their liking. Those settlers had pro-southern sympathies during the Civil War, but they could not pull Missouri into the Confederacy; their descendants still vote Democratic.

Their allegiance toward the national party faded in the early 1980s. Of the core Little Dixie counties in the 9th—Ralls, Pike, Monroe, Audrain, Callaway, Randolph and Boone—Ronald Reagan won four in 1980. Four years later, he carried them all. But by 1988, farmers hurt by the farm crisis returned to the Democratic Party. Michael S. Dukakis carried all but Callaway. In 1992, Bill Clinton won everywhere but Gasconade and St. Charles.

The economy in Boone County is steadied by the University of Missouri in Columbia (25,100 students), the oldest state university west of the Mississippi River. The moderate-to-liberal university community lends uncertainty to Boone elections. In 1988, Boone County voted Democratic for president and Republican for governor. In 1992, Boone went Democratic for president and governor but Republican for Senate.

East of Boone is Callaway County, whose residents declared it a kingdom unto itself in defiance of the Union during the Civil War. Many state government employees who work in Jefferson City live here.

On the banks of the Mississippi lies Hannibal, where a once-thriving cement industry provided jobs for Italians, Hungarians, Czechs and other European immigrants in the 19th century. Hannibal is best known as Mark Twain's birthplace, and it attracts more than 250,000 visitors a year to view his boyhood home and "Tom Sawyer's fence."

Election Returns

	9th District	Democrat	Republican
1992	President*	109,995 (41.4%)	90,669 (34.1%)
	House†	124,694 (47.7%)	118,811 (45.5%)
1988	President	107,808 (45.5%)	128,999 (54.5%)
	Senate	66,355 (28.2%)	169,015 (71.8%)
	Governor	77,361 (32.9%)	157,464 (67.1%)
1986	Senate	70,984 (43.5%)	92,322 (56.5%)

*Vote for Perot was 65,032 (24.5%).   †Independent/other is greater than 5%.

Demographics

Population 568,347

Percent change from 1980 4.1%

Land area 12,147 square miles

Population per square mile 47

Counties, 1990 population

Adair 24,577		Boone 112,379	
Audrain 23,599		Callaway 32,809	
Clark 7,547		Montgomery 11,355	
Franklin 80,603		Pike 15,969	
Gasconade 14,006		Ralls 8,476	
Knox 4,482		Randolph 24,370	
Lewis 10,233		Scotland 4,822	
Lincoln 28,892		Shelby 6,942	
Macon 15,345		St. Charles (pt.) 85,621	
Marion 27,682		Warren 19,534	
Monroe 9,104			

Cities, 1990 population (10,000 or more)

Columbia 69,101	Moberly 12,839
Fulton 10,033	O'Fallon (pt.) 18,653
Hannibal 18,004	St. Peters (pt.) 11,036
Kirksville 17,152	Washington 10,704
Mexico 11,290	

Race and Hispanic origin

White 95.0%

Black 3.7%

American Indian, Eskimo, or Aleut. 0.3%

Asian or Pacific Islander 0.8%

Other 0.2%

Hispanic origin 0.7%

Ancestry

American 7.9%	Italian 2.6%
Dutch 3.0%	Polish 1.6%
English 15.1%	Scotch Irish 2.6%
French 4.9%	Scottish 2.0%
German 44.4%	Swedish 1.4%
Irish 20.0%	

Universities/colleges, 1990-1991 enrollment

Columbia College, Columbia 4,220

Culver-Stockton College, Canton 1,129

East Central College, Union 2,915

Hannibal-LaGrange College, Hannibal 1,010

Kirksville College of Osteopathic Medicine, Kirksville 542

Moberly Community College, Moberly 1,518

Northeast Missouri State University, Kirksville 6,151

Stephens College, Columbia 1,191

University of Missouri, Columbia 25,063

Westminster College, Fulton 784

William Woods College, Fulton 767

Newspapers, total circulation (in all districts)

Columbia Daily Tribune 16,738

Mexico Ledger 9,742

Post-Tribune/Capital News 21,221

Quincy Herald Whig 24,797

St. Louis Post-Dispatch 369,005

Commercial television stations, affiliations

ADI: St. Louis (33%), Quincy-Hannibal (33%), Columbia-Jefferson City (22%) and Ottumwa-Kirksville (11%)

KTVO, Kirksville (ABC)

KOMU-TV, Columbia (NBC)

KNLJ, Jefferson City (None)

KRCG, Jefferson City (CBS)

Cable television systems, total subscribers

Cablecom of Kirksville; Kirksville 5,427

TCI of Missouri; Columbia 18,800

TCI of Missouri; Hannibal 5,826

TCI of Missouri; St. Peters 29,000

Businesses and other major employers

University of Missouri; Columbia 11,146

General Motors Corp.; Wentzville; motor vehicle assembly 5,000

MEMC Electronic Materials; O'Fallon; electronic components 1,600

Union Electric Co./Callaway Nuclear Power Plant; Fulton; electric services 1,500

Boone County Hospital; Columbia 1,500

Fulton State Hospital; Fulton 1,298

A. B. Chance Co.; Centralia; electric distribution equipment 1,200

Union Electric Co.; Portland; utility services 1,000

Venture Stores Inc.; O'Fallon; variety stores 1,000

Shelter Insurance Co.; Columbia; fire/marine/casualty insurance 1,000

U.S. Veterans Affairs Dept.; Columbia; hospital 1,000

Contel Corp.; Wentzville; telephone communications 900

Lifemark Hospital of Missouri/Columbia Regional Hospital; Columbia 837

Audrain Health Care Inc./Audrain Medical Center; Mexico 750

Northeast Missouri State University; Kirksville 750

State Farm Life Insurance Co.; Columbia; fire/marine/casualty insurance 740

City of Columbia/Water & Light Co.; Columbia 685

American Trading & Production Corp.; Washington; office products 617

National Refractories & Minerals Corp.; Mexico; clay products 600

A. P. Green Industries Inc.; Mexico; clay products 600

Toastmaster Inc.; Macon; household appliances 600

Saint John's Mercy Hospital; Washington 578

MONTANA

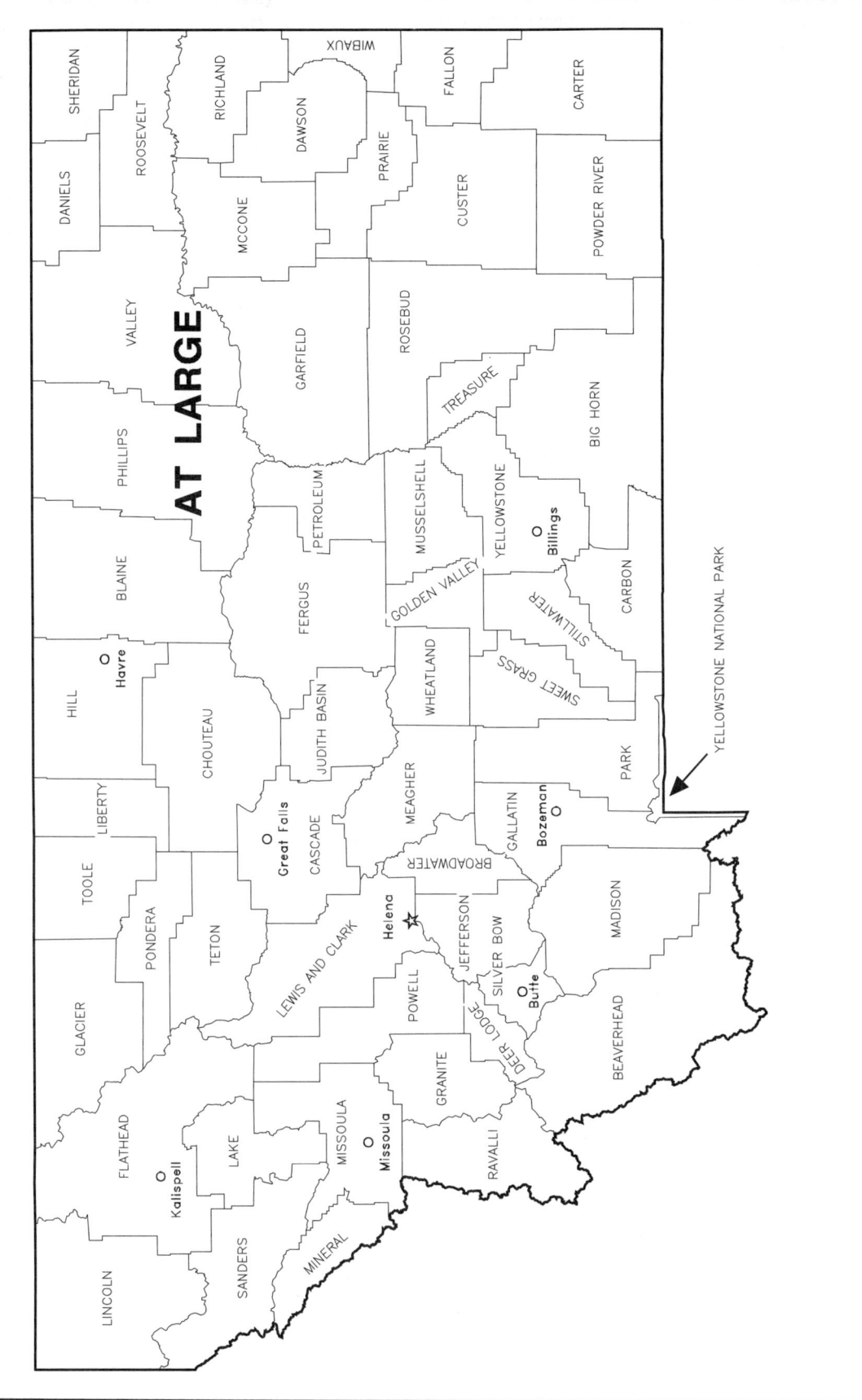

AT LARGE

YELLOWSTONE NATIONAL PARK

SHERIDAN
RICHLAND
WIBAUX
FALLON
CARTER
DANIELS
ROOSEVELT
MCCONE
DAWSON
PRAIRIE
CUSTER
POWDER RIVER
VALLEY
GARFIELD
ROSEBUD
LINCOLN
PHILLIPS
TREASURE
BIG HORN
BLAINE
PETROLEUM
MUSSELSHELL
YELLOWSTONE
○ Billings
HILL
○ Havre
FERGUS
GOLDEN VALLEY
STILLWATER
CARBON
CHOUTEAU
JUDITH BASIN
WHEATLAND
SWEET GRASS
LIBERTY
CASCADE
○ Great Falls
MEAGHER
GALLATIN
○ Bozeman
PARK
TOOLE
TETON
PONDERA
LEWIS AND CLARK
Helena ☆
BROADWATER
JEFFERSON
SILVER BOW
MADISON
GLACIER
POWELL
DEER LODGE
○ Butte
BEAVERHEAD
FLATHEAD
LAKE
MISSOULA
○ Missoula
GRANITE
RAVALLI
○ Kalispell
SANDERS
MINERAL

Montana

A sprawling expanse on the nation's northern border, Montana lost one of its two House seats in the 1990 reapportionment—relegating it to the unenvied group of states that have but one at-large House member. Montana ended up this way because of weak population growth during the 1980s; the state had a net gain of about 2 percent, well below the 10 percent rate for the United States as a whole.

State officials did not give up the second House seat without a fight, though. They argued all the way to the U.S. Supreme Court that the federal government's method for apportioning House seats was unfair.

How to divvy up a fixed number of House seats has been a quandary since the nation's beginnings. The only way to create districts of exactly equal populations would be to divide the number of House seats into the total U.S. population. But that is impossible, because the Constitution requires that House districts be contained within states and guarantees at least one House seat to each state, even those with populations that are less than the "ideal" average.

Nonetheless, Montana officials sued to overturn the complicated mathematical formula, in use since 1941, by which House seats are apportioned. They based their suit on the fact that the population of Montana's district would be nearly 800,000 people—the most populous district in U.S. history and 100,000 more than the next largest current district, the at-large seat in neighboring South Dakota.

But lawyers for the U.S. Department of Commerce (which conducts the decennial reapportionment) countered that such population inequities are inevitable and have existed under every apportioning formula ever proposed or tried. Had the Court gone along with Montana's suggested formula, the state would have retained two House seats; but each would have had about 400,000 residents, far fewer than the national average for congressional districts.

The justices decided this would be no more fair than the formula that the Montanans were protesting. The Court ruled unanimously in April 1992 against the complaint, ensuring that Montana would have one House seat during the 1990s.

Prior to 1990, a line roughly following the Continental Divide had split the state between a Democratic-leaning western district and a Republican-dominated eastern district. The merging of these sectors underscored Montana's status as one of the more politically competitive states, particularly in the conservative West.

In 1992, Montana's House incumbents, Democrat Pat Williams and Republican Ron Marlenee, faced off for the new at-large seat. Williams won, but his 50.5 percent to 47.0 percent tally indicated that this was unlikely to be a "safe" seat. Republican Marc Racicot won narrowly for governor on the same ballot, but Democrats won easily for two other major statewide offices that year.

The 1992 presidential results also highlighted an independent strain among Montana's voters. Democrat Bill Clinton became the first Democratic nominee to carry the state since 1964, but he defeated Republican incumbent George Bush by just 38 percent to 35 percent; independent candidate Ross Perot pulled down 26 percent of the vote.

The core of the Democratic vote in Montana is located in the hilly West. Mining, lumbering and some manufacturing were established by the late 19th century; union activism followed, giving the region an enduring Democratic tilt.

Although mining of copper and other ores in and around Butte (Silver Bow County) has declined—leaving the city with burdensome waste sites—its Democratic traditions are sturdy. Williams in 1992 won more than 70 percent in Silver Bow and neighboring Deer Lodge counties. Democrats also have an advantage in Missoula: The University of Montana there has the most liberal academic community in the state.

The state government bureaucracy and a mining heritage give Democrats a smaller edge in the capital of Helena (Lewis and Clark County). An industrial presence gives Democrats a base in Great Falls (Cascade County); but this city at the edge of the plains often goes Republican.

Republicans have some outposts in the west: in Bozeman (Gallatin County), site of agriculture-oriented Montana State University; in farm areas; and in locations near Glacier and Yellowstone national parks, where the economy is tourist- and recreation-oriented.

But the GOP heartland is in the farm and ranch lands of eastern Montana, where cattle and wheat are the main moneymakers. Billings (Yellowstone County), a longtime farm market town grown into the commercial center for the region, is Montana's largest city. Billings usually helps set the Republican tone in the east (though strong Democratic candidates can carry the city).

The big Republican edge elsewhere in eastern Montana is diminished by the fact that few people live in its wide open spaces. In 1992, Marlenee took 83 percent in Garfield County; but just 815 county residents voted.

Democrats have a few pockets of strength in eastern Montana, mainly in counties such as Big Horn, Rosebud and Roosevelt that have large Native American populations.

Table 1   Population

District	Population	Population under 18	Voting-age population	Median age
AL	799,065	222,104	576,961	33.8

Table 2   Voting-Age Persons

District	White*	Black*	American Indian, Eskimo, or Aleut*	Asian or Pacific Islander*	Other*	Hispanic*	Male*	Female*
AL	94.0%	0.3%	4.8%	0.5%	0.4%	1.2%	48.8%	51.2%

*As percent of voting-age population.

Table 3   Voting-Age Persons by Age Groups

District	18-24*	25-44*	45-54*	55-64*	65 and over*
AL	12.1%	43.3%	14.3%	11.8%	18.5%

*As percent of voting-age population.

Table 4   Income and Occupation

District	Median family income	Families in poverty	White collar*	Blue collar*	Service*	Farm*
AL	$28,044	12.0%	52.5%	22.9%	16.4%	8.2%

*As percent of employed persons age 16 and over.

Table 5   Education: School Years Completed

District	Less than grade 9*	Grades 9-12 no diploma*	High school diploma*	College bachelor's degree or higher*
AL	8.1%	10.9%	33.5%	19.8%

*As percent of persons age 25 and over.

Table 6   Housing and Residential Patterns

District	Owner occupied	Renter occupied	Urban	Rural
AL	67.3%	32.7%	52.5%	47.5%

Election Returns

	At Large	Democrat	Republican
1992	President*	154,507 (38.1%)	144,207 (35.5%)
	House	203,711 (50.5%)	189,570 (47.0%)
1990	Senate	217,563 (68.1%)	93,836 (29.4%)
1988	President	168,936 (46.2%)	190,412 (52.1%)
	Senate	175,809 (48.1%)	189,445 (51.9%)
	Governor	169,313 (46.1%)	190,604 (51.9%)

*Vote for Perot was 107,225 (26.4%).

Demographics

Population 799,065

Percent change from 1980 1.6%

Land area 145,556 square miles

Population per square mile 5

Counties, 1990 population

Beaverhead 8,424	Meagher 1,819
Big Horn 11,337	Mineral 3,315
Blaine 6,728	Missoula 78,687
Broadwater 3,318	Musselshell 4,106
Carbon 8,080	Park 14,562
Carter 1,503	Petroleum 519
Cascade 77,691	Phillips 5,163
Chouteau 5,452	Pondera 6,433
Custer 11,697	Powder River 2,090
Daniels 2,266	Powell 6,620
Dawson 9,505	Prairie 1,383
Deer Lodge 10,278	Ravalli 25,010
Fallon 3,103	Richland 10,716
Fergus 12,083	Roosevelt 10,999
Flathead 59,218	Rosebud 10,505
Gallatin 50,463	Sanders 8,669
Garfield 1,589	Sheridan 4,732
Glacier 12,121	Silver Bow 33,941
Golden Valley 912	Stillwater 6,536
Granite 2,548	Sweet Grass 3,154
Hill 17,654	Teton 6,271
Jefferson 7,939	Toole 5,046
Judith Basin 2,282	Treasure 874
Lake 21,041	Valley 8,239
Lewis and Clark 47,495	Wheatland 2,246
Liberty 2,295	Wibaux 1,191
Lincoln 17,481	Yellowstone 113,419
Madison 5,989	Yellowstone National
McCone 2,276	Park 52

Cities, 1990 population

Anaconda-Deer Lodge County 10,278	Havre 10,201
Billings 81,151	Helena 24,569
Bozeman 22,660	Kalispell 11,917
Butte-Silver Bow 33,336	Missoula 42,918
Great Falls 55,097	Orchard Homes CDP 10,317

Race and Hispanic origin
White 92.7%
Black 0.3%
American Indian, Eskimo, or Aleut. 6.0%
Asian or Pacific Islander 0.5%
Other 0.5%
Hispanic origin 1.5%

Ancestry

American 3.0%	Irish 17.4%
Czechoslovakian 1.2%	Italian 2.7%
Danish 2.1%	Norwegian 10.8%
Dutch 3.4%	Polish 2.0%
English 17.2%	Scotch Irish 3.2%
French 5.4%	Scottish 3.5%
French Canadian 1.0%	Swedish 4.6%
German 35.7%	Welsh 1.2%

Universities/colleges, 1990-1991 enrollment

Blackfeet Community College, Browning 264
Carroll College, Helena 1,209
College of Great Falls, Great Falls 1,081
Dawson Community College, Glendive 648
Dull Knife Memorial College, Lame Deer 281
Eastern Montana College, Billings 3,953
Flathead Valley Community College, Kalispell 1,824
Fort Peck Community College, Poplar 246
Miles Community College, Miles City 585
Montana College of Mineral Science & Technology, Butte 1,929
Montana State University, Bozeman 10,392
Northern Montana College, Havre 1,765
Rocky Mountain College, Billings 758
Salish Kootenai Community College, Pablo 684
University of Montana, Missoula 8,879
Western Montana College, Dillon 1,101

Newspapers, total circulation (in all districts)

Billings Gazette 54,262
Bozeman Daily Chronicle 11,916
Great Falls Tribune 33,306
Helena Independent Record 13,283
Missoulian 28,579

Commercial television stations, affiliations

ADI: Great Falls (30%), Billings-Hardin (27%), Butte (12%), Minot-Bismarck-Dickinson (10%), Missoula (10%), Rapid City (5%), Spokane (4%) and Helena (2%)
KTVQ, Billings (CBS)
KULR-TV, Billings (NBC)
KCTZ, Bozeman (ABC)
KTVM, Butte (NBC)
KXLF-TV, Butte (CBS)
KXGN-TV, Glendive (CBS)
KFBB-TV, Great Falls (ABC)
KRTV, Great Falls (CBS)
KTGF, Great Falls (NBC)
KOUS-TV, Hardin (ABC)
KTVH, Helena (NBC)
KCFW-TV, Kalispell (NBC)
KYUS-TV, Miles City (ABC)
KECI-TV, Missoula (NBC)
KPAX-TV, Missoula (CBS)
KTMF, Missoula (ABC)

Cable television systems, total subscribers

TCI of Montana; Billings 24,000
TCI of Montana; Bozeman 6,430
TCI of Montana; Butte 9,100
TCI of Montana; Great Falls 16,258
TCI of Montana; Helena 11,964
TCI of Montana; Kalispell 14,000
TCI of Montana; Missoula 14,500

Military installations, 1991

Malmstrom Air Force Base, Great Falls 5,032
Great Falls Intl. Airport Air Force Guard Station 379

Businesses and other major employers

Montana State University; Bozeman 4,400
University of Montana; Missoula 1,900
St. Vincent Hospital & Health Center; Billings 1,500
Montana Deaconess Medical Center; Great Falls 1,200
West-Montana Home Health Services; Helena; nursing 1,200
Deaconess Medical Center of Billings; Billings 1,095
State of Montana/Air National Guard; Great Falls 1,058
City of Great Falls/Public Schools; Great Falls 800
Community Medical Center Inc.; Missoula 800
Blackfeet Nation/Blackfeet Property Management; Browning; social assn. 800
Columbia Falls Aluminum Co.; Columbia Falls; aluminum production 740
Stone Mill Operating Corp.; Missoula; paperboard mills 712
Champion Intl. Corp./Champion Building Products; Bonner; millwork 700
Columbus Hospital; Missoula 700
Montana Power Co. Inc.; Colstrip; electric services 697
State of Montana/Dept. Institutions Div.; Warm Springs 665
City of Billings/Logan Intl. Airport; Billings 650
State of Montana/Employment Services; Helena 650
Bechtel Group Inc.; Billings; operative builders 600
Champion Intl. Corp.; Libby; sawmills 600
St. James Community Hospital; Butte 600
City of Missoula/School District; Missoula 600
Montana College of Mineral Science & Technology, Butte 550

NEBRASKA

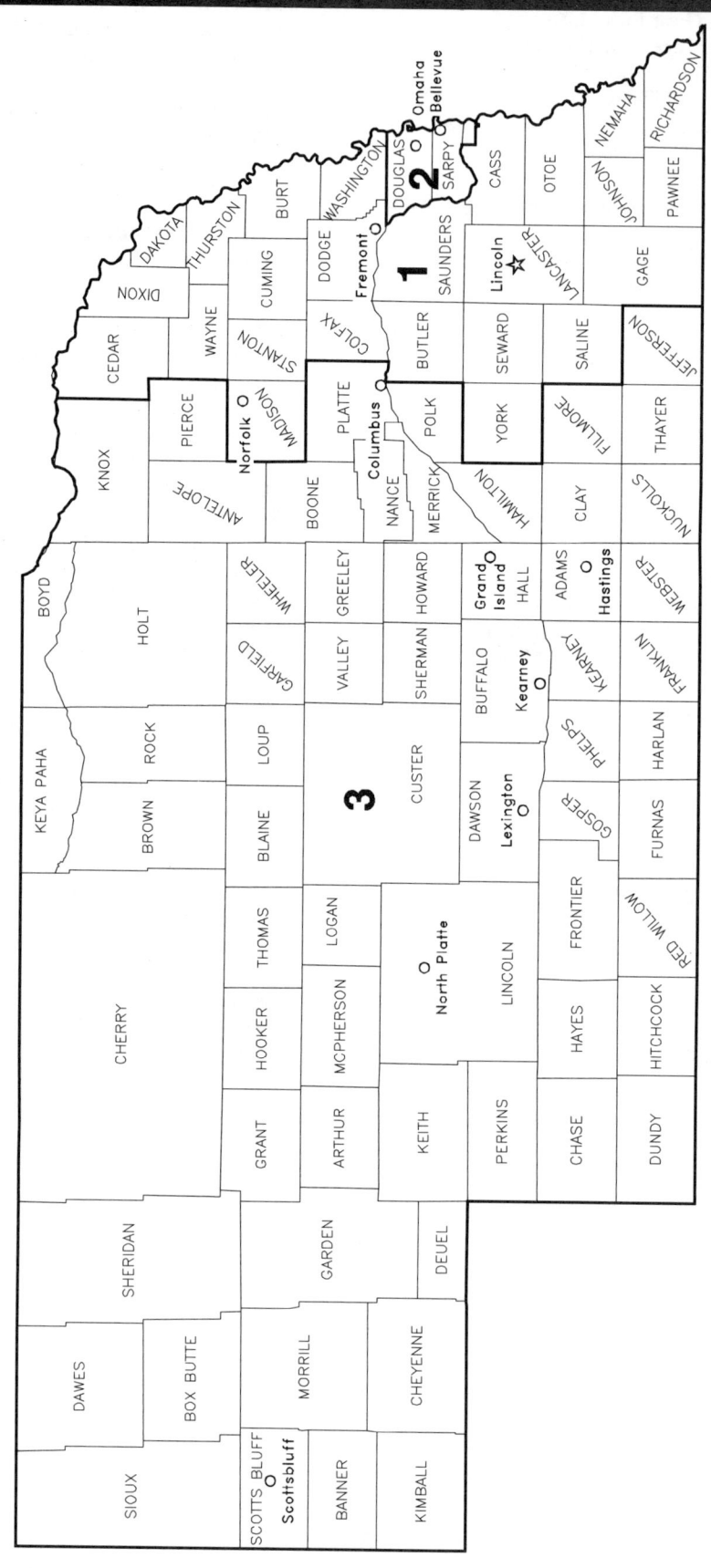

Nebraska

The homesteading farmers who settled Nebraska in the 1860s and turned it into one of the nation's premier "bread-baskets" would be surprised to see where the state stood as it headed into the 21st century. Although an overwhelming 96 percent of its land was farmed, Nebraska's population was becoming much more urban and less rural.

The boom in Omaha's Sarpy County suburbs had been spectacular. Long the industrial center of the rural Midwest, Omaha underwent an economic metamorphosis. Although it retained a large blue-collar sector, Omaha primarily was a white-collar city. Its ailing downtown was revived by the construction of office buildings that housed national and regional headquarters for major corporations. Omaha also became a center for the telemarketing industry, which chose the city because of its location in the Central Time Zone, an abundance of telephone capacity (created as a result of the proximity of the Strategic Air Command headquarters, just south of Omaha) and a pool of part-time employees.

Lincoln, Nebraska's capital and second largest city, also grew steadily due to expansion of its professional and service sectors. Never a major industrial city, Lincoln's economy was centered on government and education (it is home to the University of Nebraska). Its populace was more affluent and better educated than the state norm.

To the north and west of Nebraska's major urban centers, the vast rural lands were dotted with cities and towns that grew up as farm market centers. Several of these places had diversified economies and joined in the state's urban upswing.

In the meantime, many rural areas were losing population, some at a rapid pace. During the 1980s, 83 counties lost population, with three dropping by 20 percent or more. Six counties grew by 5 percent or less. The exodus from the farmland was the result of fundamental structural changes in the economy and society—the ongoing mechanization of agriculture, the consolidation of farmland holdings, the rise of agribusiness and the "brain drain" of young, college-trained Nebraskans uninterested in carrying on family-farming traditions. The number of farms in the state declined from 65,000 in 1980 to an estimated 57,000 in 1990.

These changes shifted political clout from rural to urban areas, but they did not affect Nebraska's Republican tilt. The party had more registered voters, and GOP presidential candidates won by landslide margins. George Bush carried the state with 60 percent in 1988 and 47 percent in 1992.

But Democratic candidates for federal and state offices could and did win in Nebraska. Those with moderate demeanors and populist messages tapped into the concerns of blue-collar workers (in Omaha and elsewhere) about the downsizing of the state's industrial base, and they addressed rural voters' concerns about the future of family farms and Nebraska's small towns. Both of those traditional institutions saw tough times during the mid-1980s downturn in the agricultural economy.

In 1993, the state's governor, Ben Nelson, and its two senators, Jim Exon and Bob Kerrey, were Democrats. In 1988, Peter Hoagland recaptured for the Democrats the Omaha-based 2nd District House seat that had been held by Republicans for four previous terms.

Congressional redistricting in 1991 was not much of a distraction for Nebraska politicos. Modest population differences among the three districts required the unicameral (single-house) Legislature to make few changes in the boundary lines.

The 2nd District, which had 7 percent population growth during the 1980s, had to lose some territory. Mainly rural and heavily Republican Burt and Washington counties and part of Cass County were shifted to the 1st District. The 2nd became more focused than ever on Omaha, which contained a sizable Democratic base of blue-collar and minority-group voters.

The 1st District, which had flat growth over the decade, in turn had to donate turf to the rural 3rd District, which lost 6 percent of its population. Four rural counties—Knox and Pierce in the north and Fillmore and Jefferson in the south—were moved to the 3rd. This shift of Republican counties had no effect on either district as they had both been firmly GOP to start.

Table 1 Population

District	Population	Population under 18	Voting-age population	Median age
1	526,297	136,445	389,852	33.0
2	526,567	147,236	379,331	31.1
3	525,521	145,331	380,190	35.3
State	1,578,385	429,012	1,149,373	33.0

Table 2 Voting-Age Persons

District	White*	Black*	American Indian, Eskimo, or Aleut*	Asian or Pacific Islander*	Other*	Hispanic*	Male*	Female*
1	96.9%	1.0%	0.8%	0.8%	0.5%	1.1%	48.1%	51.9%
2	89.0	8.5	0.5	1.1	1.0	2.5	47.6	52.4
3	98.0	0.2	0.6	0.3	1.0	2.2	47.7	52.3
State	94.7	3.2	0.6	0.7	0.8	1.9	47.8	52.2

As percent of voting-age population.

Table 3 Voting-Age Persons by Age Groups

District	18-24*	25-44*	45-54*	55-64*	65 and over*
1	15.4%	40.7%	12.5%	11.5%	19.9%
2	14.4	47.8	13.3	10.5	14.0
3	10.8	38.4	13.2	13.2	24.3
State	13.6	42.3	13.0	11.7	19.4

As percent of voting-age population.

Table 4 Income and Occupation

District	Median family income	Families in poverty	White collar*	Blue collar*	Service*	Farm*
1	$31,546	7.3%	51.5%	26.6%	14.9%	7.1%
2	37,128	7.2	65.4	20.3	13.3	1.0
3	27,357	9.5	43.6	26.3	15.2	14.8
State	31,634	8.0	53.7	24.4	14.5	7.5

As percent of employed persons age 16 and over.

Table 5 Education: School Years Completed

District	Less than grade 9*	Grades 9-12 no diploma*	High school diploma*	College bachelor's degree or higher*
1	8.7%	9.9%	35.6%	18.5%
2	4.7	9.7	30.0	24.8
3	10.6	10.9	38.4	13.8
State	8.0	10.2	34.7	18.9

As percent of persons age 25 and over.

Table 6 Housing and Residential Patterns

District	Owner occupied	Renter occupied	Urban	Rural
1	66.9%	33.1%	60.7%	39.3%
2	62.8	37.2	93.7	6.3
3	69.6	30.4	44.0	56.0
State	66.5	33.5	66.1	33.9

1st District

East — Lincoln; Norfolk

Not long ago, Lincoln was a sleepy town that came to life only during the Legislature's sessions and on autumn Saturdays when the University of Nebraska played football. Back then, Cornhusker crowds nearly matched the city's population. Today, however, Lincoln is thriving: Its population has nearly doubled over the past 40 years to 192,000. A diversified employment base makes Lincoln (Lancaster County) a picture of economic health.

The city's boom has been led by the expanding state and city governments and by the university, which has 24,500 students. Lincoln has three major hospital complexes, and the white-collar base features banks and insurance companies. In addition, Lincoln (like Omaha) is fast becoming a telecommunications hub. Gallup Organization Inc., the polling company, is in Lincoln. Lincoln does have industrial employers, including a Goodyear factory that makes rubber belts and hoses. There are also a number of food-processing companies.

The 1st has pockets of population growth elsewhere. Norfolk (Madison County) is known for pursuing industry; beef products, electronic components and steel products are made here. The district includes Omaha exurbs to the north (Washington County) and south (most of Cass County), as well as Dakota County suburbs of Sioux City, Iowa (where IBP, the nation's largest beef processor, is headquartered), and Dodge County.

In the more sparsely populated rural sections of the 1st is some of the nation's most productive farmland. Counties in the northern part of the 1st are among Nebraska's leaders in hog and milk production; York County, to the west, is a leading corn producer. Farming in the rural parts of Lancaster County outside Lincoln makes the county the biggest sorghum producer.

The rural Republican vote gives the GOP an advantage in the 1st. In 1992, Madison County gave 57 percent to George Bush, although that was well below his 1988 tally of 76 percent. GOP Rep. Doug Bereuter won re-election in 1992 with 60 percent of the vote, carrying all but one county in the 1st.

But Lancaster, which casts more than 40 percent of the district's total vote, tends to be a swing county, tipping Republican for president, but it has backed such Democrats as Sens. Jim Exon and Bob Kerrey, who hail from Lincoln.

In 1992, Bush won Lancaster over Bill Clinton by just 193 votes, out of more than 104,000 cast. Four years earlier, Bush won the county by 345 votes.

The strongest Democratic counties are at opposite corners of the district. In the northeast are Dakota County, with a large blue-collar contingent and some Hispanic and Asian residents, and Thurston County, made up almost entirely of Winnebago and Omaha Indian reservations. In the southwest is rural Saline County, dominated by people of Czech heritage with a long-standing Democratic tradition.

Election Returns

	1st District	Democrat	Republican
1992	President*	80,700 (32.6%)	107,092 (43.2%)
	House	96,309 (40.3%)	142,713 (59.7%)
1990	Senate	132,298 (65.2%)	70,695 (34.8%)
	Governor	107,604 (54.4%)	90,180 (45.6%)
1988	President	96,096 (43.8%)	123,083 (56.2%)
	Senate	135,366 (61.8%)	83,774 (38.2%)
1986	Governor	96,742 (50.4%)	95,323 (49.6%)

Vote for Perot was 59,979 (24.2%).

Demographics

Population 526,297

Percent change from 1980 0.6%

Land area 13,400 square miles

Population per square mile 39

Counties, 1990 population

Burt 7,868	Nemaha 7,980
Butler 8,601	Otoe 14,252
Cass (pt.) 13,778	Pawnee 3,317
Cedar 10,131	Richardson 9,937
Colfax 9,139	Saline 12,715
Cuming 10,117	Saunders 18,285
Dakota 16,742	Seward 15,450
Dixon 6,143	Stanton 6,244
Dodge 34,500	Thurston 6,936
Gage 22,794	Washington 16,607
Johnson 4,673	Wayne 9,364
Lancaster 213,641	York 14,428
Madison 32,655	

Cities, 1990 population (10,000 or more)

Beatrice 12,354	Lincoln 191,972
Fremont 23,680	Norfolk 21,476

Race and Hispanic origin

White 96.4%
Black 1.1%
American Indian, Eskimo, or Aleut. 1.1%
Asian or Pacific Islander 0.9%
Other 0.6%
Hispanic origin 1.4%

Ancestry

American 1.8%	Irish 15.3%
Czechoslovakian 8.5%	Italian 1.1%
Danish 3.9%	Norwegian 1.9%
Dutch 3.3%	Polish 2.1%
English 12.4%	Scotch Irish 2.1%
French 3.4%	Scottish 1.6%
German 56.3%	Swedish 6.2%

Universities/colleges, 1990-1991 enrollment

Concordia Teachers College, Seward 818
Dana College, Blair 507
Doane College, Crete 1,229
Midland Lutheran College, Fremont 960
Nebraska Indian Community College, Winnebago 329
Nebraska Wesleyan University, Lincoln 1,691
Northeast Technical Community College, Norfolk 2,815
Peru State College, Peru 1,526
Southeast Community College, Beatrice 710
Southeast Community College, Lincoln 4,689
Southeast Community College, Milford 972
Union College, Lincoln 617
University of Nebraska, Lincoln 24,453
Wayne State College, Wayne 3,512
York College, York 337

Newspapers, total circulation (in all districts)

Fremont Tribune 10,548
Lincoln Journal-Lincoln Star 78,565
Norfolk News 20,966
Omaha World Herald 221,762
Sioux City Journal 48,301

Commercial television stations, affiliations
ADI: Omaha (51%), Sioux City (25%) and Lincoln-Hastings-Kearney (24%)
KOLN, Lincoln (CBS)

Cable television systems, total subscribers
Cablecom of Norfolk; Norfolk 7,090
Cablevision of Lincoln; Lincoln 69,902
Fremont Cablevision; Fremont 5,897

Military installations, 1991
Lincoln Municipal Airport Air Force Guard Station, Lincoln 331

Businesses and other major employers
IBP Inc.; Dakota City; meat products 6,000
University of Nebraska, Lincoln 5,000
Burlington Northern Railroad Co.; Lincoln; freight shipping 2,500
Bryan Memorial Hospital Inc.; Lincoln 2,002
Goodyear Tire & Rubber Co.; Lincoln; hose/belting 1,500
Lincoln Telecommunications Co.; Lincoln; telephone communications 1,302
Excel Corp.; Schuyler; meat products 1,250
St. Elizabeth Community Health Center; Lincoln 1,200
George A. Hormel & Co.; Fremont; meatpacking 1,031
Farmland Foods Inc.; Crete; pork products 1,000
Mid-America Webpress Inc./American Signature; Lincoln; commercial printing 1,000
State of Nebraska/Beatrice State Home; Beatrice; residential care 875
Smithkline Beecham Corp.; Lincoln; pharmaceuticals 820
Omaha Public Power District; Fort Calhoun; electric services 800
Concord Hospitality Inc./Village Inn; Lincoln; bars/restaurants 800
Metromail Corp.; Lincoln; mailing/repro services 800
Ameritas Life Insurance Corp.; Lincoln; life insurance 750
Madonna Centers Inc.; Lincoln; nursing 750
State of Nebraska/Roads Dept.; Lincoln 750
Cushman Inc./Ryan Turf Equipment; Lincoln; grounds equipment 700
Square D Co.; Lincoln; circuit breakers 677
Vishay Intertechnology Inc.; Norfolk; electronic components 650
Memorial Hospital of Dodge County; Fremont 605
State Farm & Fire Casualty Insurance Co.; Lincoln; insurance services 600
Selection Research Inc.; Lincoln; business consulting 580
County of Lancaster; Lincoln 568
Sherwood Medical Co./Monoject Div.; Norfolk; medical instruments/supplies 550
M. G. Waldbaum Co./Crystal Foods; Wakefield; egg processing 550
Tabitha Home; Lincoln; residential care 525

2nd District

East — Omaha; Sarpy County Suburbs

Omaha grew up as a blue-collar city: a railroad center, a Missouri River port and a place where cattle became steaks. To outsiders, this broad-shouldered, gritty image remains. But

Omaha (Douglas County) has become mainly a place of white-collar jobs and new downtown office buildings. Douglas County is also reliably in the Republican camp, voting for the GOP White House candidate every time but once in the post-Roosevelt era. In 1992, George Bush won the county with 50 percent of the vote.

Omaha's economic health is reflected in its continued growth: The city's 1990 population topped 335,000, up by 7 percent since 1980. Once-rural Sarpy County, which borders Douglas County to the south, continues to blossom: Now with more than 102,000 people, it is the state's third most-populous county.

As its core has filled with people through the years, the Omaha-based 2nd has become more compact. It now covers just Douglas and Sarpy counties and a tiny slice of Cass County including the city of Plattsmouth.

Metropolitan Omaha's economy is a mix of new and old. The largest employer is the Strategic Air Command at Offutt Air Force Base in Sarpy County, another Republican stronghold. A large telemarketing and credit-processing industry has been established in Omaha. Yet the Mutual of Omaha insurance company, long a community pillar, remains its largest private employer. Downtown includes the corporate headquarters for ConAgra—the agricultural products giant that ranks 25th among the *Fortune* 500—and the Union Pacific Railroad. While most of Omaha's stockyards are now obsolete, more than 20 food processing companies are here.

Blue-collar jobs historically drew an ethnic population—including large numbers of Irish, Italians, Germans and eastern Europeans—to Omaha's south side. Mainly Roman Catholics, they set the political tone for the 2nd. It has a Democratic tradition, and victory here is essential for Democrats who hope to win statewide.

However, the longtime partisan leanings are tempered by a strong conservative streak, especially on social issues. Many working-class residents vote with more affluent residents, which has enabled recent GOP presidential candidates to carry the 2nd. Bush won the county by 13 points over Bill Clinton in 1992. The city is 13 percent black, a large proportion by Nebraska standards; more than three-fourths of the state's entire black population live in Omaha.

Long known mainly for the Boys Town orphanage, western Omaha is now heavily residential, with some new, affluent subdivisions. Nearby, onetime crossroads communities are now burgeoning cities. Bellevue, with nearly 31,000 people, is Nebraska's fourth-largest city.

The area benefits from Omaha's status as Nebraska's cultural and sports capital. It is home to the Ak-Sar-Ben (Nebraska spelled backward) racetrack and hosts the World Series of college baseball each spring.

Election Returns

	2nd District	Democrat	Republican
1992	President*	78,697 (32.4%)	115,244 (47.5%)
	House	119,512 (51.2%)	113,828 (48.8%)
1990	Senate	105,954 (58.5%)	75,237 (41.5%)
	Governor	89,765 (49.9%)	90,276 (50.1%)
1988	President	88,449 (42.2%)	121,254 (57.8%)
	Senate	130,661 (63.4%)	75,402 (36.6%)
1986	Governor	77,844 (49.0%)	81,042 (51.0%)

*Vote for Perot was 48,652 (20.1%).

Demographics

Population 526,567

Percent change from 1980 0.7%

Land area 599 square miles

Population per square mile 879

Counties, 1990 population
Cass (pt.) 7,540	Sarpy 102,583
Douglas 416,444	

Cities, 1990 population (10,000 or more)
Bellevue 30,982	Omaha 335,795
Offutt AFB West CDP 10,883	Papillion 10,372

Race and Hispanic origin
White 87.5%
Black 9.7%
American Indian, Eskimo, or Aleut. 0.6%
Asian or Pacific Islander 1.2%
Other 1.2%
Hispanic origin 2.8%

Ancestry
American 1.6%	Irish 21.0%
Czechoslovakian 5.4%	Italian 4.7%
Danish 3.6%	Norwegian 2.3%
Dutch 2.4%	Polish 5.8%
English 12.7%	Scotch Irish 2.2%
French 3.7%	Scottish 1.7%
German 40.5%	Swedish 5.3%

Universities/colleges, 1990-1991 enrollment
Bellevue College, Bellevue 2,048
Bishop Clarkson College, Omaha 511
College of St. Mary, Omaha 1,280
Creighton University, Omaha 6,168
Gateway Electronics Institute, Omaha 332
Grace College of the Bible, Omaha 257
Methodist Hospital College of Nursing, Omaha 364
Metropolitan Technical Community College, Omaha 8,520
University of Nebraska, Omaha 15,811
University of Nebraska Medical Center, Omaha 2,444

Newspapers, total circulation (in all districts)
Lincoln Journal-Lincoln Star 78,565
Omaha World Herald 221,762

Commercial television stations, affiliations
ADI: Omaha (100%)
KETV, Omaha (ABC)
KMTV, Omaha (CBS)
KPTM, Omaha (Fox)
WOWT, Omaha (NBC)

Cable television systems, total subscribers
Cox Cable Omaha; Omaha 83,585
Douglas County Cablevision; Elkhorn 15,469
TCI Cable of the Midlands; Bellevue 15,643
TCI Cable of the Midlands; La Vista 16,428

Military installations, 1991
Offutt Air Force Base, Bellevue 14,478

Businesses and other major employers

Mutual of Omaha Insurance Co.; Omaha; life insurance 7,315
University of Nebraska & Medical Center; Omaha 5,000
Union Pacific Railroad Co.; Omaha; railroads 4,500
First Data Resources Inc.; Omaha; computer services 4,000
Drivers Management Inc.; Omaha; auto services 2,840
City of Omaha; Omaha 2,769
Creighton University; Omaha 2,000
Wats Marketing America Inc.; Omaha; telemarketing 2,000
Immanuel Healthcare Systems Inc.; Omaha 1,886
Nebraska Methodist Hospital; Omaha 1,748
United Parcel Service Inc.; Omaha; mail services 1,500
Bishop Clarkson Memorial Hospital; Omaha 1,400
West Telemarketing Corp.; Omaha; telemarketing 1,400
Bergan Medical Center; Omaha 1,323
First National Bank of Omaha; Omaha; commercial banks 1,227
Valmont Industries Inc.; Valley; metal products 1,200
Vickers Inc.; Omaha; industry machinery 1,100
Utilicorp United Inc./Peoples Natural Gas Div.; Omaha; gas distribution 1,022
Lozier Corp.; Omaha; store partitions/fixtures 1,000
City of Bellevue/Public Schools; Bellevue 1,000
Father Flanagan's Boys Home; Boys Town; residential care 1,000
Marriott Corp./Worldwide Reservation Center; Omaha; hotel services 1,000
Omaha World Herald Co.; Omaha; newspapers 980
Campbell Soup Co.; Omaha; soup/grocery products 950
Sitel Corp./Sitel Interactive; Omaha; telemarketing 950
Omaha Public Power District; Omaha; electric services 900
City of Omaha/Police Dept.; Omaha 900
Kellogg Co.; Omaha; grain mill products 850
U.S. West Communications Inc.; Omaha; telephone communications 800
Kwik Kafe Co. Inc.; Omaha; bars/restaurants 800
Lutheran Medical Center; Omaha 800
Metropolitan Utilities District; Omaha; utility services 777
Children's Memorial Hospital; Omaha 700
Firstier Bank of Omaha; Omaha; commercial banks 670
Nebraska Furniture Mart Inc.; Omaha; furniture stores 637
State of Nebraska/Social Services Dept.; Omaha 600
Douglas County Hospital; Omaha 600
Neodata Telemedia Services; Omaha; telemarketing 600
Blue Cross/Blue Shield of Nebraska; Omaha; medical service/health insurance 550
Central States Health Life of Omaha; Omaha; medical service/health insurance 545
Midlands Community Hospital; Omaha 535
Physicians Mutual Insurance Co.; Omaha; health insurance 100

3rd District

Rural West — Grand Island; North Platte

As ever, agriculture is king in the 3rd. To the east are the state's most productive corn-growing regions and several leading hog-raising counties; the west has the biggest wheat farms. Western Nebraska is also a national leader in production of sugar beets and dry beans.

On the plains in the northern and central parts of the 3rd, the old saw that there are more cows than people is a gross understatement. Vast Cherry County, with fewer than 7,000 people, had more than 300,000 head of cattle in 1992.

In this part of Nebraska, one can drive for hours along straight, flat roads without passing any community larger than a village. Between 1980 and 1990, 63 of the 66 counties in the 3rd lost population.

The 3rd is traditionally the most Republican district in the state—its 1980s incarnation gave more than 70 percent of its vote to Ronald Reagan in 1980 and 1984, and 67 percent to George Bush in 1988. In 1992, Bush carried the district with 50 percent. Bush's decline was no help to Bill Clinton, though; he finished third in the district with 24 percent, behind Ross Perot's 27 percent.

The only city in the 3rd with more than 30,000 people is Grand Island (Hall County), a retail center for the surrounding farmlands. Grand Island's major industries are farm implements and meatpacking.

North of Grand Island are the only counties in the district with a significant Democratic registration lead (Sherman, Greeley and Howard). Another, Nance, has a slimmer Democratic registration edge. Their residents tend to vote almost as Democratic as their Polish and Irish ancestors did generations ago.

The smaller population centers of Kearney, North Platte and Scottsbluff are strung along the Platte River west of Grand Island. Much of Kearney's growth has come from its campus of the University of Nebraska.

West of Kearney along the Platte is Lexington, a town of 6,600. It struggled in the mid-1980s farm crisis, but was revitalized in 1990 with the opening of a huge IBP meatpacking plant.

North Platte, located in the valley where the North and South Platte rivers meet, was the home of William F. "Buffalo Bill" Cody; it tries to coax Omaha-to-Denver travelers into staying awhile by putting on Buffalo Bill shows and rodeos. The Union Pacific runs through North Platte and is its biggest employer. Corn and livestock are raised in the valley, with wheat fields to the west and huge cattle ranches to the north.

The Oregon and Mormon trails run through Scottsbluff, which has the only sizable Hispanic population in western Nebraska, a legacy of the migrant labor used to harvest sugar beets over a period of several decades. Great northern beans are a major crop in the farm areas surrounding Scottsbluff. The major employer is the Regional West Medical Center, a hospital and health-management organization.

Election Returns

	3rd District	Democrat	Republican
1992	President*	57,467 (23.5%)	121,342 (49.7%)
	House	67,457 (28.3%)	170,857 (71.7%)
1990	Senate	98,055 (54.1%)	83,078 (45.9%)
	Governor	83,271 (47.2%)	92,996 (52.8%)
1988	President	70,299 (32.8%)	144,093 (67.2%)
	Senate	105,986 (48.7%)	111,595 (51.3%)
1986	Governor	83,405 (43.0%)	110,779 (57.0%)

*Vote for Perot was 65,473 (26.8%).

Demographics

Population 525,521

Percent change from 1980 0.3%

Land area   62,879 square miles

Population per square mile   8

Counties, 1990 population

Adams 29,625	Holt 12,599
Antelope 7,965	Hooker 793
Arthur 462	Howard 6,055
Banner 852	Jefferson 8,759
Blaine 675	Kearney 6,629
Boone 6,667	Keith 8,584
Box Butte 13,130	Keya Paha 1,029
Boyd 2,835	Kimball 4,108
Brown 3,657	Knox 9,534
Buffalo 37,447	Lincoln 32,508
Chase 4,381	Logan 878
Cherry 6,307	Loup 683
Cheyenne 9,494	McPherson 546
Clay 7,123	Merrick 8,042
Custer 12,270	Morrill 5,423
Dawes 9,021	Nance 4,275
Dawson 19,940	Nuckolls 5,786
Deuel 2,237	Perkins 3,367
Dundy 2,582	Phelps 9,715
Fillmore 7,103	Pierce 7,827
Franklin 3,938	Platte 29,820
Frontier 3,101	Polk 5,675
Furnas 5,553	Red Willow 11,705
Garden 2,460	Rock 2,019
Garfield 2,141	Scotts Bluff 36,025
Gosper 1,928	Sheridan 6,750
Grant 769	Sherman 3,718
Greeley 3,006	Sioux 1,549
Hall 48,925	Thayer 6,635
Hamilton 8,862	Thomas 851
Harlan 3,810	Valley 5,169
Hayes 1,222	Webster 4,279
Hitchcock 3,750	Wheeler 948

Cities, 1990 population (10,000 or more)

Columbus 19,480	Kearney 24,396
Grand Island 39,386	North Platte 22,605
Hastings 22,837	Scottsbluff 13,711

Race and Hispanic origin
White 97.6%
Black 0.2%
American Indian, Eskimo, or Aleut. 0.7%
Asian or Pacific Islander 0.3%
Other 1.2%
Hispanic origin 2.9%

Ancestry

American 2.7%	Irish 15.4%
Czechoslovakian 4.7%	Norwegian 1.5%
Danish 3.9%	Polish 3.8%
Dutch 3.2%	Scotch Irish 2.3%
English 14.5%	Scottish 1.7%
French 3.3%	Swedish 7.3%
German 54.4%	

Universities/colleges, 1990-1991 enrollment
Central Community College, Grand Island 10,915
Chadron State College, Chadron 3,061
Hastings College, Hastings 965
Kearney State College, Kearney 9,899
McCook Community College, North Platte 864
Mid Plains Community College, North Platte 2,027
Western Nebraska Community College, Scottsbluff 1,940

Newspapers, total circulation (in all districts)
Alliance Times-Herald 3,206
Columbus Telegram 10,380
Grand Island Independent 24,363
Hastings Tribune 14,355
Holdrege Daily Citizen 3,143
Kearney Hub 12,390
Lincoln Journal-Lincoln Star 78,565
Norfolk News 20,966
North Platte Telegraph 13,533
Omaha World Herald 221,762
Scottsbluff Star-Herald 14,689

Commercial television stations, affiliations
ADI: Lincoln-Hastings-Kearney (43%), Rapid City (14%), North Platte (13%), Sioux Falls-Mitchell (10%), Denver (9%), Sioux City (6%), Wichita-Hutchinson (3%), Cheyenne-Scottsbluff-Sterling (1%) and Omaha (1%)
KCAN, Albion (ABC)
KGIN, Grand Island (CBS)
KHAS-TV, Hastings (NBC)
KWNB-TV, Hayes Center (ABC)
KHGI-TV, Kearney (ABC)
KNOP-TV, North Platte (NBC)
KDUH-TV, Scottsbluff (ABC)
KSTF, Scottsbluff (CBS)
KSNB-TV, Superior (ABC)

Cable television systems, total subscribers
Columbus Cable TV; Columbus 6,520
TCI of Nebraska; Grand Island 7,000
TCI of Nebraska; Hastings 5,950
TCI of Nebraska; North Platte 6,522
TCI of Nebraska; Scottsbluff 7,500

Businesses and other major employers
Monfort Inc.; Grand Island; meatpacking 1,700
Burlington Northern Railroad Co.; Alliance; railroads 1,500
IBP Inc.; Lexington; meatpacking 1,000
Dale Electronics Inc.; Columbus; electronic components 946
New Holland Ford Inc.; Grand Island; farm machinery 900
St. Francis Medical Center; Grand Island 900
Regional West Medical Center; Scottsbluff 864
Douglas & Lomason Co.; Columbus; furniture 800
Eaton Corp.; Kearney; industrial machinery 800
Baldwin Filters Inc.; Kearney; motor vehicle filters 775
Nebraska Public Power District; Columbus; electric services 700
Good Samaritan Hospital; Kearney 695
Mary Lanning Memorial Hospital; Hastings 684
Emerson Electric Co.; Columbus; electrical motors 630
Behlen Mfg. Co.; Columbus; farm machinery 600
Monroe Auto Equipment Co.; Cozad; motor vehicle equipment 600
Union Pacific Railroad Co.; North Platte; railroads 600
Chief Industries Inc./Bonnavilla Div.; Grand Island; mobile homes 575
Becton Dickinson & Co.; Holdrege; medical instruments/supplies 525
State of Nebraska/Hastings Regional Center; Hastings 525

Nevada

In the late 1940s, this harsh desert and mountain state was the least populous in the nation. But Nevada grew exponentially, with its population expanding by 650 percent since 1950. This phenomenal growth, said University of Las Vegas-Reno political scientist John Marini, "has exacerbated the split in Nevada politics between the north and the south"—between older, more conservative Reno and glitzier Las Vegas. The sparsely populated rural areas, known as the "cow counties," shared a taste for conservatism with the north. "Everybody recognizes that power and influence is moving to the south," Marini said.

Las Vegas, which had fewer than 8,500 residents in 1940, tripled in size by 1950 and was home to 258,000 people by 1990. The 1990 census showed Clark County with a population of 741,000, roughly 60 percent of Nevada's 1.2 million residents. Washoe County (Reno), which was Nevada's most populous county in 1950, ran a distant second, with 255,000 residents.

The rampant growth produced fissures within the Clark County community. For the first time in Las Vegas' history, antigrowth voices were heard above the din of development. Traffic congestion was a worry, and air quality problems surfaced in step. The effort to ensure an adequate water supply for the south pitted Clark County against several rural counties with water reserves.

Quandaries of growth and development faced the rest of Nevada just as squarely. Reno, with 134,000 residents the state's second-largest city, tried to pursue a more measured development plan than Las Vegas but did not escape nettlesome problems such as smog. Nearby Lake Tahoe's health was under stress from residents and businesses drawn to its shores.

Some of the long-ignored rural counties were riding the crest of a modern-day gold rush—one that outpaced the profits of the 19th-century discovery of the Comstock Lode, but also strained the resources of small towns ill-prepared to accommodate the hordes of fortune seekers.

Redistricting was not a controversial matter. Nevada, which gained a second House seat in 1981 reapportionment, held at two for the 1990s. Democratic Rep. James Bilbray and GOP Rep. Barbara F. Vucanovich agreed on a plan that gave each a secure

seat. The new 1st District was an odd-shaped island within Clark County. It was smaller in land area than the former 1st District and more Democratic. Democratic votes were picked up in heavily black North Las Vegas, while Republican territory to the south was discarded. The expanded 2nd now took in 99 percent of the state's land area. With Reno, Carson City and the Cow Counties, the 2nd also picked up conservative, politically active Mormon communities in Boulder City and Overton in southern and northeastern Clark County.

Table 1   Population

District	Population	Population under 18	Voting-age population	Median age
1	600,957	144,820	456,137	33.5
2	600,876	152,128	448,748	33.2
State	1,201,833	296,948	904,885	33.3

Table 2   Voting-Age Persons

District	White*	Black*	American Indian, Eskimo, or Aleut*	Asian or Pacific Islander*	Other*	Hispanic*	Male*	Female*
1	81.9%	9.0%	0.8%	3.7%	4.6%	10.8%	50.4%	49.6%
2	89.9	2.5	2.2	2.5	2.9	7.4	51.2	48.8
State	85.8	5.8	1.5	3.1	3.8	9.1	50.8	49.2

*As percent of voting-age population.

Table 3   Voting-Age Persons by Age Groups

District	18-24*	25-44*	45-54*	55-64*	65 and over*
1	13.6%	44.4%	15.2%	12.3%	14.5%
2	12.7	47.2	14.9	11.5	13.7
State	13.1	45.8	15.0	11.9	14.1

*As percent of voting-age population.

NEVADA

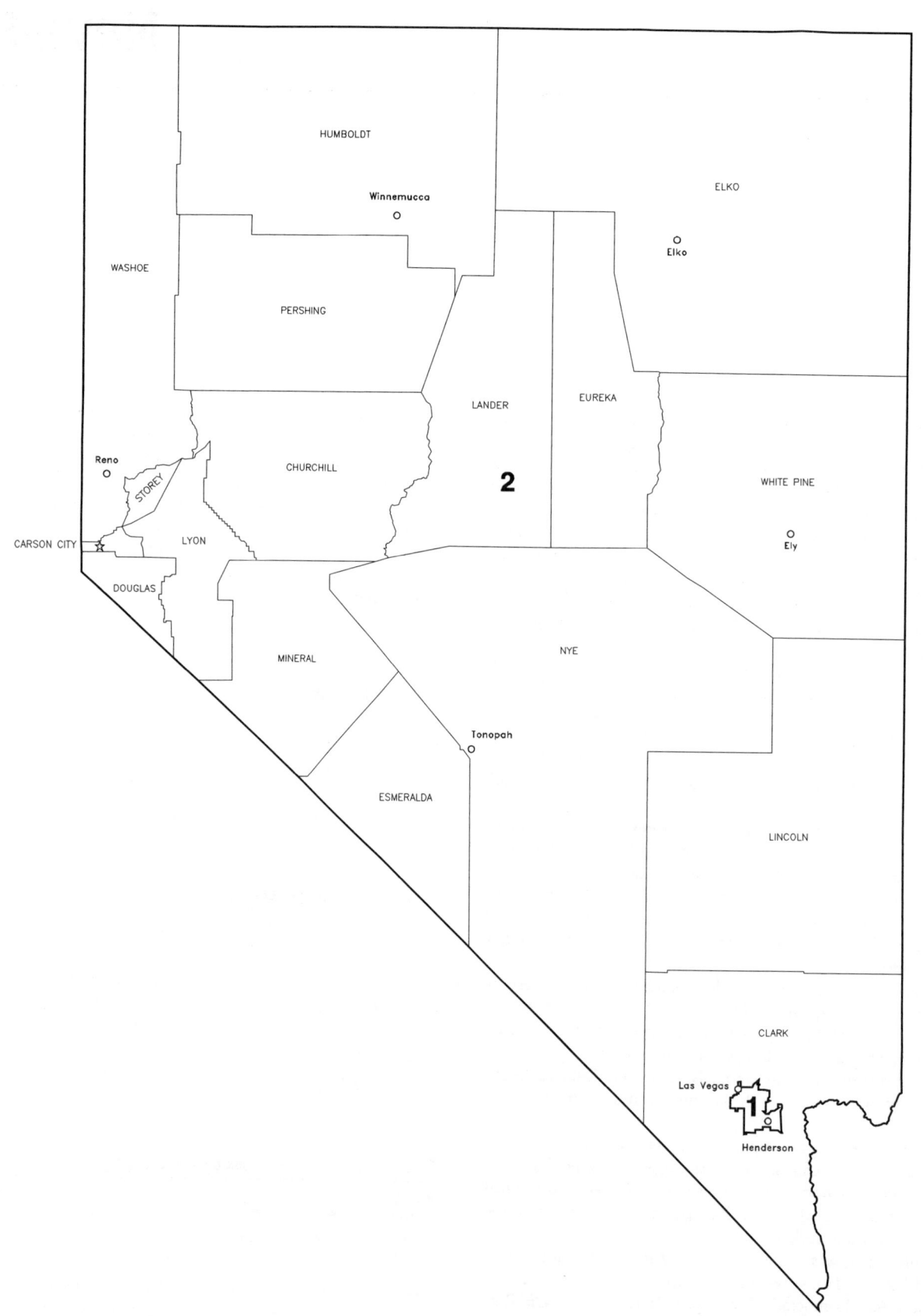

HUMBOLDT

Winnemucca

ELKO

Elko

WASHOE

PERSHING

LANDER

EUREKA

WHITE PINE

Reno

STOREY

CHURCHILL

2

Ely

CARSON CITY

LYON

DOUGLAS

MINERAL

NYE

Tonopah

ESMERALDA

LINCOLN

CLARK

Las Vegas

1

Henderson

Table 4 Income and Occupation

District	Median family income	Families in poverty	White collar*	Blue collar*	Service*	Farm*
1	$34,114	8.2%	50.4%	20.9%	27.6%	1.1%
2	37,251	6.4	53.9	24.1	20.0	2.0
State	35,837	7.3	52.2	22.5	23.8	1.6

*As percent of employed persons age 16 and over.

Table 5 Education: School Years Completed

District	Less than grade 9*	Grades 9-12 no diploma*	High school diploma*	College bachelor's degree or higher*
1	7.1%	17.0%	32.2%	13.3%
2	5.0	13.3	30.8	17.3
State	6.1	15.2	31.5	15.3

*As percent of persons age 25 and over.

Table 6 Housing and Residential Patterns

District	Owner occupied	Renter occupied	Urban	Rural
1	50.1%	49.9%	99.8%	0.2%
2	59.6	40.4	76.8	23.2
State	54.8	45.2	88.3	11.7

1st District

South — Las Vegas

For the second time this century, Las Vegas is undergoing a transformation. Once a dusty railroad stop on the Union Pacific Line, the town evolved after World War II into Sin City, a garish neon pleasure palace where gambling flourished and visiting businessmen could hop a private plane to a rural bordello.

The gaming industry is still king—it is the building block of the local economy—but albino tigers, flaming man-made volcanoes and Wayne Newton are no longer the only stories in Vegas.

Economic diversification is the city's new buzzword, and it is coming none too soon. Some of the older casinos, such as The Dunes, have gone under. Meanwhile, high-tech companies have joined such well-known gambling establishments as Bally's, Caesar's Palace and the Mirage on the local business roster.

Attracted by low taxes and a pro-business environment, nearly 100 companies relocated to the Las Vegas area during the past decade. The jobs they offered were a magnet for newcomers: 275,000 people moved to the Las Vegas valley in the 1980s. Local authorities claim that the population influx is continuing at the rate of about 3,500 per month, many from neighboring California.

While Chamber of Commerce officials drool, many longtime residents are clamoring for a development slowdown. The valley is experiencing air quality problems, traffic congestion worsens daily, and schools are bursting at the seams. Water resources are severely strained.

Mormon conservatism flavors Clark County politics, but within the city limits of Las Vegas, Democrats have the edge. The 1st encompasses the downtown areas and the city of Henderson, to the southeast, which despite recent development maintains its blue-collar image.

Unionized service workers, many of whom work in the glittery resort hotels along "The Strip" just south of Las Vegas, include a number of blacks who live on the city's west side. Democrats also can tap the city of North Las Vegas (which is 37 percent black) for votes. Under the 1980s map, North Las Vegas was divided between the 1st and 2nd districts. Now, virtually all of it is in the 1st.

During World War II, Henderson produced magnesium; it still supports itself with chemical manufacturing. Green Valley, home to professionals, young families and California transplants, is a GOP oasis. Workers at Nellis Air Force Base (just northeast of Las Vegas) and at the Energy Department's Nevada Test Site also tend to favor GOP candidates.

Rural portions of Clark County were pared from the 1st in 1991 redistricting, creating a constituency that is almost exclusively urban. Yet as in the 1980s, it contains more than 80 percent of the county's population.

Overall, Clark County casts more than half the vote in Nevada, so winning it has become crucial to statewide victory. In 1992 Bill Clinton carried only two of Nevada's 17 counties; Democratic Sen. Harry Reid carried just six. But each won statewide with the help of a substantial lead in Clark County. George Bush carried the 1st in 1988, primarily by running strongly outside the city. But GOP presidential candidates may have a tougher time in the new 1st, now that it has jettisoned conservative areas in southern and northeastern Clark County.

Election Returns

	1st District	Democrat	Republican
1992	President*	98,801 (43.8%)	70,586 (31.3%)
	House	128,278 (57.9%)	84,217 (38.0%)
1990	Governor	90,937 (70.4%)	38,308 (29.6%)
1988	President	66,024 (43.7%)	85,158 (56.3%)
	Senate	86,283 (57.4%)	64,106 (42.6%)
1986	Senate	67,772 (63.4%)	39,108 (36.6%)
	Governor	82,863 (77.0%)	24,710 (23.0%)

*Vote for Perot was 56,058 (24.9%).

Demographics

Population 600,957

Percent change from 1980 50.0%

Land area 231 square miles

Population per square mile 2,602

Counties, 1990 population
Clark (pt.) 600,957

Cities, 1990 population (10,000 or more)
East Las Vegas CDP 11,087
Henderson 64,942
Las Vegas (pt.) 189,641
North Las Vegas (pt.) 45,240
Paradise CDP (pt.) 124,656
Spring Valley CDP (pt.) 46,880
Sunrise Manor CDP (pt.) 83,566
Winchester CDP 23,365

Race and Hispanic origin
White 79.5%
Black 10.5%
American Indian, Eskimo, or Aleut. 0.8%

Asian or Pacific Islander 3.8%
Other 5.4%
Hispanic origin 12.2%

Ancestry

American 3.1%	Norwegian 1.6%
Danish 1.3%	Polish 3.4%
Dutch 2.3%	Russian 1.4%
English 14.9%	Scotch Irish 2.1%
French 4.7%	Scottish 2.3%
German 21.2%	Swedish 2.2%
Irish 15.4%	Welsh 1.0%
Italian 7.6%	

Universities/colleges, 1990-1991 enrollment
Community College of Southern Nevada, North Las Vegas 14,164
University of Nevada, Las Vegas 17,938

Newspapers, total circulation (in all districts)
Las Vegas Review-Journal 168,896
Los Angeles Times 1,169,066

Commercial television stations, affiliations
ADI: Las Vegas (100%)
   KVVU-TV, Henderson (Fox)
   KRLR, Las Vegas (None)
   KVBC, Las Vegas (NBC)
   KBLR, Paradise (None)

Cable television systems, total subscribers
Prime Cable; Las Vegas 164,183

Military installations, 1991
Nellis Air Force Base, Las Vegas 8,333

Businesses and other major employers
Mirage Casino-Hotal; Las Vegas; casino/hotel 7,100
Boyd Group; Las Vegas; casino/hotel 7,000
Circus Circus Enterprises/Excalibur Hotel; Las Vegas; casino/hotel 5,000
Hilton Hotels Corp./Flamingo Hilton; Las Vegas; casino/hotel 4,100
Bally's Grand Inc.; Las Vegas; casino/hotel 4,000
Desert Palace Inc./Caesar's Palace; Las Vegas; casino/hotel 3,805
Circus Circus Enterprises/Circus Circus Hotel; Las Vegas; casino/hotel 3,500
Las Vegas Hilton Corp.; Las Vegas; casino/hotel 3,000
Holiday Casino Inc./Holiday Inn Hotel; Las Vegas; casino/hotel 2,900
Mare-Bear Inc./Stardust Hotel; Las Vegas; casino/hotel 2,800
Horseshoe Club Operating Co./Horseshoe Club; Las Vegas; casino/hotel 2,600
Hotel Ramada of Nevada/Tropicana; Las Vegas; casino/hotel 2,500
Humana Hospital Sunrise; Las Vegas 2,500
Imperial Palace Inc.; Las Vegas; casino/hotel 2,500
Gold Coast Ltd.; Las Vegas; casino/hotel 2,300
Riviera Inc.; Las Vegas; casino/hotel 2,200
University Medical Center-Southern Nevada; Las Vegas 2,175
City of Las Vegas; Las Vegas 2,010
MGM Desert Inn Inc.; Las Vegas; casino/hotel 2,000
City of Las Vegas/Police Dept.; Las Vegas 2,000

Minami Inc./Dunes Hotel & Casino; Las Vegas; casino/hotel 1,800
Palace Station Inc.; Las Vegas; casino/hotel 1,800
Central Telephone Co.; Las Vegas; telephone communications 1,700
EG&G Inc.; North Las Vegas; research services 1,650
County of Clark/Extension Agency; Las Vegas 1,632
Sahara Casino Partners; Las Vegas; casino/hotel 1,600
Union Plaza Hotel & Casino; Las Vegas; casino/hotel 1,600
Raytheon Co.; Las Vegas; search/navigation equipment 1,500
Unbelievable Inc./Frontier Hotel; Las Vegas; casino/hotel 1,500
Showboat Inc./Lamp Lighter Motel; Las Vegas; casino/hotel 1,500
Showboat Operating Co./Showboat Casino; Las Vegas; casino 1,500
Ginji Corp./Aladdin Hotel & Casino; Las Vegas; casino/hotel 1,400
Las Vegas Sands Inc./Sands Las Vegas; Las Vegas; casino/hotel 1,400
Citibank of Las Vegas; Las Vegas; commercial banks 1,300
Four Queens Inc./Four Queens; Las Vegas; casino/hotel 1,300
Vegas World; Las Vegas; casino/hotel 1,200
Exber Inc./El Cortez Hotel; Las Vegas; casino/hotel 1,150
Marcor Resort Properties Inc.; Las Vegas; casino/hotel 1,100
California Hotel & Casino/Sam's Town; Las Vegas; casino/hotel 1,100
Church Street Station Ltd.; Las Vegas; casino/hotel 1,100
Baby Grand Corp./Maxim; Las Vegas; casino/hotel 1,050
Fitzgerald Las Vegas Ltd./Fitzgerald Hotel & Casino; Las Vegas; casino/hotel 1,000
America West Airlines Inc.; Las Vegas; airline 995
Yellow Cab Co. of Nevada; Las Vegas; taxicabs 975
Universal Health Services/Valley Hospital; Las Vegas 930
Westward Ho Casino; Las Vegas; casino/hotel 925
Pepper Mill Resort Hotel & Casino; Mesquite; gas stations & casino/hotel 920
Barbary Coast; Las Vegas; casino/hotel 900
Arizona Charlie's Hotel & Casino; Las Vegas; casino/hotel 900
Charter Medical Corp./Desert Springs Hospital; Las Vegas 805
Reynolds Electric & Engineering Co.; Las Vegas; building services 800
Gemini Inc./Lady Luck; Las Vegas; casino/hotel 800
Eastern-Western Hotel Corp./Ramada Hotel San Remo; Las Vegas; casino/hotel 650
Titanium Metals Corp./Tremont; Henderson; titanium 615
Donrey Inc./Las Vegas Review-Journal; Las Vegas; newspapers 600
University of Nevada; Las Vegas 600
Hotel Continental Inc.; Las Vegas; casino/hotel 580
Nevada Power Co.; Las Vegas; electric services 575
BRT Inc./El Rancho Hotel & Casino; Las Vegas; casino/hotel 560
Las Vegas Valley Water District; Las Vegas; water supply 550
City of North Las Vegas; North Las Vegas 535

2nd District

Reno, the Cow Counties and Part of Clark County

Campaigning in the 2nd is an awesome task. It contains 99.8 percent of the land area (nearly 110,000 square miles) of the nation's seventh-largest state.

While redistricting enlarged the 2nd so it now encompasses all but the heart of Las Vegas and its immediate environs, the district's population nexus is in the north, in the Reno (Washoe County) area. Reno is older, more conservative and less reliant on the gaming industry than Las Vegas. Proximity to California and the Pacific Northwest make warehousing an important part of the local economy. Bender Warehousing Co. is one of the state's largest.

Formerly a GOP stronghold, Reno's politics have been moderated by an influx of environmentally conscious newcomers (its population grew 33 percent in the 1980s). Catholics make up a significant portion of the electorate, but they tend not to be as politically active as the Mormons in Clark County.

The state capital of Carson City is in the 2nd, as is Lake Tahoe, a year-round resort area astride the California-Nevada line that attracts visitors to its golf courses, casinos and chalets.

The rural "cow" counties cover most of the state but hold few of its residents: Several of these enormous counties are home to fewer than 10,000 people. Agriculture and ranching are the main pursuits, and huge expanses of uninhabited mountain and desert land are used as military test ranges.

Yucca Mountain looms ominously over Nye County as the site Congress has proposed for a federal nuclear waste dump. Nevadans share a bipartisan resentment of what they call the "Screw Nevada" dump bill, which Congress passed in 1987.

Resentment of the federal government—which owns nearly 90 percent of the district's land—is most adamant in the conservative-voting cow counties. Federal water and grazing regulations generate animosity, as do airspace restrictions that local pilots face near the bombing ranges.

Retired military personnel are numerous in Hawthorne (Mineral County), site of the Hawthorne Army Ammunition Plant. State politicians rarely miss the small town's annual armed forces parade.

A modern-day mining boom has spurred growth in a number of rural communities to the north, particularly in Elko (Elko County), Lovelock (Pershing County) and Battle Mountain (Lander County).

The location of Ely (White Pine County) on the eastern end of U.S. 50 makes it a regional center for commerce and business. The highway, snaking across central Nevada past Carson City, became known as "the loneliest road in America" after a *Life* magazine article claimed travelers needed survival skills to cross this stretch of empty and desolate desert.

In 1992, all but two of the counties in the 2nd voted for George Bush. Storey County, which includes the famous 19th-century mining center of Virginia City, backed Ross Perot. White Pine County, where a unionized work force once mined copper and other minerals from huge pits, voted for Bill Clinton.

Agriculture is the main business in Churchill, Humboldt, Lyon and Pershing counties. Yerington (Lyon) grows most of the state's alfalfa and much of its garlic. Large concentrations of Hispanics work the farms of Humboldt and Pershing. Basques are also numerous in the region, descendants of shepherds who flocked to northwestern Nevada in the early 1940s.

Election Returns

	2nd District	Democrat	Republican
1992	President*	90,347 (33.2%)	105,242 (38.7%)
	House†	117,199 (43.3%)	129,575 (47.9%)
1990	Governor	115,344 (67.0%)	56,745 (33.0%)
1988	President	62,932 (35.4%)	114,766 (64.6%)
	Senate	84,170 (47.6%)	92,485 (52.4%)
1986	Senate	62,874 (44.8%)	77,482 (55.2%)
	Governor	104,112 (72.1%)	40,353 (27.9%)

Vote for Perot was 76,522 (28.1%).   †*Independent/other is greater than 5%.*

Demographics

Population 600,876

Percent change from 1980 50.3%

Land area 109,575 square miles

Population per square mile 5

Counties, 1990 population

Carson City 40,443	Lincoln 3,775
Churchill 17,938	Lyon 20,001
Clark (pt.) 140,502	Mineral 6,475
Douglas 27,637	Nye 17,781
Elko 33,530	Pershing 4,336
Esmeralda 1,344	Storey 2,526
Eureka 1,547	Washoe 254,667
Humboldt 12,844	White Pine 9,264
Lander 6,266	

Cities, 1990 population (10,000 or more)

Boulder City 12,567	Sparks 53,367
Carson City 40,443	Sun Valley CDP 11,391
Elko 14,736	Sunrise Manor CDP (pt.)
Las Vegas (pt.) 68,654	11,796
Reno 133,850	

Race and Hispanic origin

White 89.0%
Black 2.7%
American Indian, Eskimo, or Aleut. 2.4%
Asian or Pacific Islander 2.6%
Other 3.4%
Hispanic origin 8.5%

Ancestry

American 3.7%	Italian 7.0%
Danish 1.9%	Norwegian 2.3%
Dutch 2.8%	Polish 2.2%
English 19.6%	Scotch Irish 2.6%
French 5.3%	Scottish 3.1%
German 25.4%	Swedish 3.0%
Irish 17.8%	Welsh 1.3%

Universities/colleges, 1990-1991 enrollment

Northern Nevada Community College, Elko 2,604
Sierra Nevada College, Incline Village 313
Truckee Meadows Community College, Reno 9,741
University of Nevada, Reno 11,487
Western Nevada Community College, Carson City 5,320

Newspapers, total circulation (in all districts)
Carson City Nevada Appeal 10,464
Las Vegas Review-Journal 168,896
Los Angeles Times 1,169,066
Reno Gazette/Journal 66,379
San Francisco Chronicle-Examiner 692,424

Commercial television stations, affiliations
ADI: Reno (53%), Salt Lake City (24%) and Las Vegas (23%)
KFBT, Las Vegas (None)
KLAS-TV, Las Vegas (CBS)
KTNV, Las Vegas (ABC)
KAME-TV, Reno (Fox)
KOLO-TV, Reno (ABC)
KRNV, Reno (NBC)
KTVN, Reno (CBS)

Cable television systems, total subscribers
Columbia Cable; Gardnerville 6,788
Continental Cablevision of Nevada; Washoe County 7,987
Prime Cable; Las Vegas 164,183
TCI of Nevada; Carson City 12,090
TCI of Nevada; Crystal Bay 12,300
TCI of Nevada; Elko 5,082
TCI of Nevada; Reno 35,968

Military installations, 1991
Fallon Naval Air Station, Fallon 2,006
Hawthorne Army Ammunition Plant; Hawthorne 700
Reno Cannon Intl. Airport Air Force Guard Station, Reno 326

Businesses and other major employers
State of California/Industrial Relations; Carson City 3,540
Harrah's; Stateline; casino/hotel 3,200
Bally's Grand Inc./Bally's Reno; Reno; casino/hotel 2,800
Harrah's Club; Reno; casino/hotel 2,500
Circus Circus Enterprises/Circus Circus; Reno; casino/hotel 2,400
Sparks Nugget Inc.; Sparks; casino/hotel 2,400
Newmont Gold Co.; Carlin; gold/silver ores 2,300
Hilton Hotels Corp./Flamingo Hilton; Laughlin; casino/hotel 2,000
Harvey's Wagon Wheel Inc.; Stateline; casino/hotel 2,000
Desert Palace Inc./Caesar's Tahoe; Stateline; casino/hotel 2,000
El Dorado Hotel Associates; Reno; casino/hotel 2,000
Colorado Belle Corp.; Laughlin; casino/hotel 1,550
Washoe Medical Center Inc.; Reno 1,533
Neary Marshall & Associates/Travel Lodge Tropicana; Las Vegas; hotel 1,500
Nevada Properties/Peppermill; Reno; casino/hotel 1,500

St. Mary's Regional Medical Center; Reno 1,430
State of Nevada/Transportation Dept.; Carson City 1,400
Hilton Hotels Corp./Flamingo Hilton; Reno; casino/hotel 1,350
California Hotel & Casino/Gold River Hotel; Laughlin: casino/hotel 1,300
Sam's Town Gold River; Laughlin; casino/hotel 1,300
Riverside Resort; Laughlin; casino/hotel 1,300
Citibank Nevada; Las Vegas; banking services 1,300
Wimar Tahoe Corp.; Stateline; casino/hotel 1,300
Sierra Development Co.; Reno; casino 1,300
City of Reno; Reno 1,218
Zante Inc.; Reno; casino/hotel 1,044
J. C. Penney Co. Inc.; Reno; department stores 1,000
Harrah's/Harrah's Del Rio; Laughlin; casino/hotel 1,000
Jean Development Co./Gold Strike; Jean; casino/hotel 1,000
State of Nevada/Correctional Center; Carson City 950
Hyatt Corp./Hyatt Lake Tahoe; casino/hotel 950
Bently Nevada Corp.; Minden; measuring/controlling devices 920
James Hardie Industries USA; Carson City; metal products 900
Ramada Express Inc.; Searchlight; casino/hotel 900
Sierra Pacific Power Co./Westpac Utilities Div.; Reno; electric services 875
American Barrick Resources/Barrick Goldstrike Mines; Elko; gold mining 870
State of Nevada/Motor Vehicles Dept.; Carson City 825
International Game Technology; Reno; amusement/gambling machines 800
Pioneer Hotel & Gambling Hall; Searchlight; casino/hotel 800
Cactus Pete Inc./Cactus Pete's; Jackpot; casino/hotel 800
Boomtown Inc.; Verdi; casino/hotel 800
Day & Zimmermann Inc.; Hawthorne; ordnance/accessories 700
County of Washoe; Reno 700
Western Village Associates; Sparks; casino/hotel 640
U.S. Veterans Affairs Dept.; Reno 633
Comstock Hotel & Casino; Reno; casino/hotel 625
Independence Mining Co. Inc.; Elko; gold/silver ores 600
U.S. Postal Service; Reno 600
Mirage Resorts Inc./Golden Nugget; Laughlin; casino/hotel 600
Carson Nugget Inc./Carson Nugget; Carson City; casino 600
Sundowner Hotel-Casino; Reno; casino/hotel 600
Carson-Tahoe Hospital; Carson City 571
Holmes & Narver Inc.; Mercury; engineering/architectural services 569
Loftin Associates Inc./Ormsby House; Carson City; hotel 530
County of Washoe/Sheriffs Office; Reno 503

New Hampshire

Both the politics and the economy of the Granite State have been showing some erosion in recent years and the 1990s could determine whether the change is a trend or a bubble.

New Hampshire, long known for its solid Republicanism, set two milestones in the 1992 presidential election: It went for a Democrat for the first time since the 1964 election; and Bill Clinton's victory in the national campaign marked the first time since 1952 that a candidate captured the presidency without winning New Hampshire's first-in-the-nation primary. A severe economic recession during the tenure of President George Bush, a man who owed much of his political success to New Hampshire voters, led directly to the political turnaround in 1992. And it appeared that the duration of that slump would have much to do with the direction of state politics for the rest of the decade.

Although New Hampshire's population grew by a robust 20 percent during the 1980s, the state was sufficiently small to begin with that the House delegation remained at two members. The 1st District, occupying the southeastern corner of the state and a few northern counties, lost a half dozen towns on its western fringe near the state capital of Concord, stretching from San-bornton in the north to Chichester in the south. The change reflected the sharp population growth in the lower reaches of the district. There, high-technology industries and proximity to Boston and its suburban high-tech centers drew residents seeking the low-tax lifestyle New Hampshire offers.

The principle that what goes up comes down hit home with a vengeance in the early 1990s. By 1992, New Hampshire had lost 70,000 jobs and its unemployment had tripled from the peak four years earlier. That neighboring Massachusetts, with its more liberal government and higher taxes, suffered a similarly deep recession indicated that recession did not stop at ideological borders. In New Hampshire, the trouble was that four pillars of the state economy—paper products, tourism, high technology and defense spending—went into a slump simultaneously. The state's past support for President Bush could not save Pease Air Force Base from closure in 1991. And the state barely dodged a bullet two years later when the government decided to keep open the Portsmouth Naval Shipyard in Kittery, Maine.

Politically, the recession backlash took hold at the national level. While throwing its support to Clinton, New Hampshire voters replaced retiring moderate Sen. War-ren Rudman with GOP fiscal conservative Judd Gregg.

The 2nd District, encompassing the northern paper mill country, the White Mountains and lake region and a stretch of suburbs along the Massachusetts border, re-elected Democratic Dick Swett in 1992. His election in 1990 marked only the second time in the century that the district sent a Democrat to Washington. A strong independent streak has always been a key ingredient for success in flinty New Hampshire. It was hardly surprising that many voters disillusioned with Bush in 1992 cast their ballots (23 percent) for independent Ross Perot.

Despite its small size, New Hampshire has long been accustomed to playing a key role in American history. It was the first colony to establish an independent government; anti-British activity there predated the Battle of Lexington and Concord in Massachusetts; it cast the deciding vote in ratifying the Constitution; and in the 19th century it was one of the first states to take part in the Industrial Revolution.

But there is a limit to New Hampshire's openness to change. Its presidential votes may well have reflected, rather than determined, the national mood. And despite the population growth, the state remains 98 percent white, second only to Vermont in the nation in that category. New Hampshire voters are capable of venting resentment; but no wholesale political changeover is in the offing.

Table 1 Population

District	Population	Population under 18	Voting-age population	Median age
1	554,360	138,476	415,884	32.4
2	554,892	140,279	414,613	33.2
State	1,109,252	278,755	830,497	32.8

Table 2 Voting-Age Persons

District	White*	Black*	American Indian, Eskimo, or Aleut*	Asian or Pacific Islander*	Other*	Hispanic*	Male*	Female*
1	98.2%	0.7%	0.2%	0.8%	0.2%	0.9%	48.2%	51.8%
2	98.2	0.5	0.2	0.8	0.2	0.9	48.4	51.6
State	98.2	0.6	0.2	0.8	0.2	0.9	48.3	51.7

*As percent of voting-age population.

NEW HAMPSHIRE

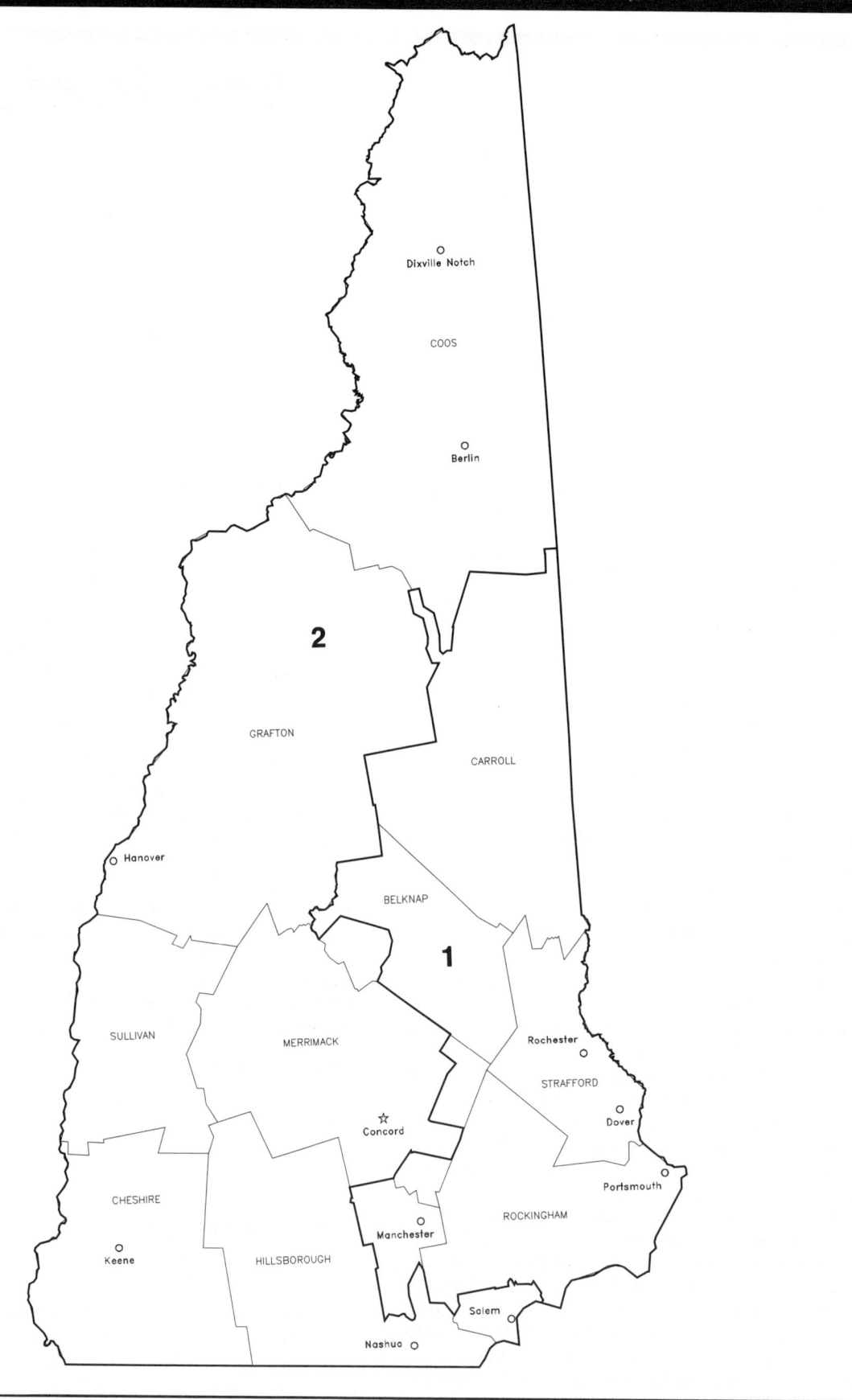

Dixville Notch ○

COOS

Berlin ○

2

GRAFTON

CARROLL

Hanover ○

BELKNAP

1

SULLIVAN

MERRIMACK

Rochester ○

STRAFFORD

Dover ○

☆
Concord

CHESHIRE

Portsmouth ○

Manchester ○

ROCKINGHAM

Keene ○

HILLSBOROUGH

Salem ○

Nashua ○

Table 3 Voting-Age Persons by Age Groups

District	18-24*	25-44*	45-54*	55-64*	65 and over*
1	14.4%	47.5%	13.1%	10.3%	14.7%
2	13.9	45.8	13.9	10.9	15.4
State	14.2	46.7	13.5	10.6	15.1

*As percent of voting-age population.

Table 4 Income and Occupation

District	Median family income	Families in poverty	White collar*	Blue collar*	Service*	Farm*
1	$41,959	4.3%	61.1%	25.6%	12.1%	1.2%
2	41,291	4.4	59.6	26.9	11.9	1.6
State	41,628	4.4	60.4	26.2	12.0	1.4

*As percent of employed persons age 16 and over.

Table 5 Education: School Years Completed

District	Less than grade 9*	Grades 9-12 no diploma*	High school diploma*	College bachelor's degree or higher*
1	6.7%	10.9%	31.3%	23.8%
2	6.7	11.4	32.1	24.9
State	6.7	11.2	31.7	24.4

*As percent of persons age 25 and over.

Table 6 Housing and Residential Patterns

District	Owner occupied	Renter occupied	Urban	Rural
1	66.3%	33.7%	55.0%	45.0%
2	70.1	29.9	47.0	53.0
State	68.2	31.8	51.0	49.0

1st District

East — Manchester

The 1st qualifies as New Hampshire's urban district. It covers barely one-quarter of the state's land area yet contains seven of the 11 largest communities in New Hampshire, including the largest, Manchester, which has nearly 100,000 people.

As in the neighboring 2nd, most of the district's population lives in the southern tier within 30 miles of the Massachusetts border, with the largest concentration of voters in the Golden Triangle—an area extending roughly from Nashua and Salem on the south to Manchester on the north that straddles the line between the two most populous counties in the state, Hillsborough and Rockingham.

Within the Triangle are many of the high-tech companies and bedroom communities (all within easy commuting range of Boston) that have helped New Hampshire nearly double its population since 1960.

The southern half of the triangle along the Massachusetts line is in the 2nd District. But the 1st includes many of the faster-growing towns that stretch to the north along Interstate 93 and Route 3. During the 1980s, Derry grew by 57 percent, London-

derry by 45 percent, Merrimack by 44 percent. Each town currently boasts a population in excess of 19,000.

The growth has been stymied in the 1990s by the slump in New Hampshire's economy. But the biggest hit in the 1st was suffered along the Atlantic seacoast with the 1991 closure of Pease Air Force Base in Newington. Commuter airlines have begun to use the facility, but that has not offset the thousands of jobs that were lost. The region avoided a double whammy when the government decided in early 1993 to keep open the Portsmouth Naval Shipyard in nearby Kittery, Maine.

The economic uncertainties helped the Democrats in 1992 carry more than their usual beachheads in Durham (Strafford County), the home of the University of New Hampshire, and the gentrified seaport of Portsmouth (Rockingham County).

In the 1992 presidential race, Bill Clinton not only swept old mill towns such as Rochester and Somersworth, but also carried the historic Yankee town of Exeter, site of the Phillips Exeter Academy. And he carried Manchester, where the huge Franco-American vote is nominally Democratic but subject to blandishments from the city's conservative newspaper, the Manchester Union Leader.

But George Bush narrowly won the 1st in 1992 by combining the votes of high-tech workers and tax-conscious commuters in the Golden Triangle with rural voters in the picturesque land of lakes and mountains to the north. Carroll County, which anchors the northern end of the district, has voted for a Democratic presidential candidate in only one election this century, 1912. Still, independent Ross Perot carved deeply enough into the GOP vote, especially in the Golden Triangle, to enable Clinton to carry the state.

In 1992 redistricting, the 1st shed a half-dozen towns on its western fringe near Concord, from Sanborntown on the north to Chichester on the south.

Election Returns

	1st District	Democrat	Republican
1992	President*	101,415 (37.9%)	104,653 (39.1%)
	House	108,578 (42.5%)	135,936 (53.2%)
1990	Senate	42,819 (30.3%)	98,348 (69.7%)
	Governor	46,774 (33.6%)	92,425 (66.4%)
1988	President	78,235 (35.5%)	141,952 (64.5%)
	Governor	87,378 (40.1%)	130,259 (59.9%)
1986	Senate	38,358 (31.3%)	78,191 (63.8%)
	Governor	56,374 (44.6%)	69,945 (55.4%)

*Vote for Perot was 61,571 (23.0%).

Demographics

Population 554,360

Percent change from 1980 20.3%

Land area 2,507 square miles

Population per square mile 221

Counties, 1990 population

Belknap (pt.) 43,840	Merrimack (pt.) 16,059
Carroll 35,410	Rockingham (pt.) 205,911
Hillsborough (pt.) 148,907	Strafford 104,233

Cities, 1990 population (10,000 or more)

Bedford 12,563	Laconia 15,743
Derry 29,603	Londonderry 19,781
Dover 25,042	Manchester 99,567
Durham 11,818	Merrimack 22,156
Exeter 12,481	Portsmouth 25,925
Goffstown 14,621	Rochester 26,630
Hampton 12,278	Somersworth 11,249

Race and Hispanic origin

White 98.0%
Black 0.7%
American Indian, Eskimo, or Aleut. 0.2%
Asian or Pacific Islander 0.8%
Other 0.3%
Hispanic origin 1.0%

Ancestry

American 4.0%	Greek 1.7%
Canadian 1.3%	Irish 22.2%
Dutch 1.3%	Italian 7.6%
English 23.6%	Polish 4.8%
French 18.1%	Scotch Irish 2.6%
French Canadian 11.6%	Scottish 5.1%
German 10.7%	Swedish 2.3%

Universities/colleges, 1990-1991 enrollment

Hesser College, Manchester 2,000
McIntosh College, Dover 454
New Hampshire College, Manchester 6,403
New Hampshire Vocational Tech College, Manchester 1,844
New Hampshire Vocational Tech College, Nashua 950
New Hampshire Vocational Tech College, Stratham 971
New Hampshire Vocational Tech College, Laconia 1,068
Notre Dame College, Manchester 1,153
School for Lifelong Learning, Durham 1,405
St. Anselm's College, Manchester 1,987
University of New Hampshire, Durham 13,262
University of New Hampshire, Manchester 424

Newspapers, total circulation (in all districts)

Boston Globe 503,578
Boston Herald 339,813
Concord Monitor 21,312
Foster's Daily Democrat 30,189
Laconia Evening Citizen 10,981
Manchester Union Leader-News 70,806
Portsmouth Herald 14,211

Commercial television stations, affiliations

ADI: Boston (63%) and Portland-Poland Springs (37%)
WMUR-TV, Manchester (ABC)
WGOT, Merrimack (None)

Cable television systems, total subscribers

Continental Cablevision of New Hampshire; Derry 21,325
Continental Cablevision of New Hampshire; Dover 16,500
Continental Cablevision of New Hampshire; Exeter 15,219
Continental Cablevision of New Hampshire; Portsmouth 22,700
New England Cablevision; Rochester 12,500
State Cable TV Corp.; Conway 7,459
United Cable Co. of New Hampshire; Goffstown 40,000

Military installations, 1991

Portsmouth Naval Shipyard, Portsmouth 8,267
Pease Air Force Guard Station, Newington 362

Businesses and other major employers

Staffing Network Inc.; Manchester; personnel supply services 3,500
University of New Hampshire; Durham 3,400
New England Telephone & Telegraph Co.; Manchester; telephone communications 2,670
General Electric Co.; Somersworth; electric distribution equipment 2,000
Digital Equipment Corp.; Merrimack; computers 2,000
Liberty Mutual Insurance Co.; Portsmouth; medical service/health insurance 1,700
Sequa Corp./Kollsman; Merrimack; search/navigation equipment 1,500
Textron Inc./Davidson Interior Trim; Dover; metal stampings 1,300
American Fidelity Co.; Manchester; insurance services 1,300
U.S. Postal Service; Manchester 1,200
Elliot Hospital; Manchester 1,200
City of Manchester; Manchester 1,200
Harris Heidelberg Inc.; Dover; industry machinery 977
Public Service Co. of New Hampshire/Seabrook Nuclear Power; Seabrook; electric services 901
General Electric Co./Aircraft Engine; Manchester; aircraft engines/parts 900
Wentworth-Douglass Hospital; Dover 850
Textron Inc./Davidson Instrument Panel Div.; Farmington; motor vehicle equipment 750
City of Rochester; Rochester 731
Kingston-Warren Corp.; Newfields; rubber products 710
Exeter Health Resources Inc.; Exeter 700
Raytheon Co./Manchester Operations Div.; Manchester; missile guidance systems 664
Velcro USA Inc.; Manchester; fabric tapes 650
Portsmouth Regional Hospital; Portsmouth 650
U.S. Veterans Affairs Dept.; Manchester; hospital 610
Simplex Wire & Cable Co.; Portsmouth; wire products 600
Hadco Corp.; Derry; printed circuit boards 600
GTE Products Corp.; Manchester; electric lighting 600
School Administrative Unit; Merrimack 600
Anheuser-Busch Inc.; Merrimack; brewery 592
Public Service Co. of New Hampshire/Yankee Div.; Manchester; electric services 550
Phillips Exeter Academy; Exeter 543
Exeter School District; Exeter 540
Lakes Region General Hospital Assn.; Laconia 540
Frisbie Memorial Hospital; Rochester 520

2nd District

West — Concord; Nashua

Through most of the century, the 2nd has been regarded as one of the most rock-ribbed Republican districts in the country. Only once before 1990 did the district elect a Democrat to Congress—that in 1912 during the GOP-Bull Moose bloodletting and then for only two years.

But in 1990, western New Hampshire voters elected Democrat Dick Swett to the House, and two years later they not only re-elected him overwhelmingly but also gave Bill Clinton a 10,000-vote plurality. That helped Clinton become the first Democratic presidential candidate since Lyndon B. Johnson in 1964 to carry the Granite State. Clinton received 41 percent of the vote in the 2nd District in 1992; George Bush took 37 percent, and Ross Perot finished third with 22 percent.

It is too early to tell whether the Democratic inroads are an aberration or an indicator of a basic overhaul in the district's politics. But New Hampshire's sharp economic downturn in the early 1990s has affected normal voting patterns—shaking loose a number of Republican-oriented rural voters while bringing back to the Democratic fold blue-collar voters in old mill towns such as Berlin (Coos County) and Claremont (Sullivan County).

The only reliable source of Democratic votes in the 2nd had been the liberal college town of Hanover (Grafton County), home of Dartmouth College. It is arguably the only recession-proof community in the district.

The economy of the heavily forested "North Country" is closely tied to paper manufacturing and wood products. The populous southern tier along the Massachusetts border has gone boom and bust with high-tech industries deeply involved in computers and defense electronics. In between, many of western New Hampshire's picturesque small towns depend on tourist dollars—from summer vacationers at the myriad lakes to winter-time skiers in the White Mountains. Each area has suffered during New Hampshire's downturn.

Loaded with well-educated, upwardly mobile refugees from "Taxachusetts," many of the towns along the southern tier have remained reliably Republican despite the recession. The largest city in the 2nd, Nashua (with almost 80,000 residents) voted for Clinton in 1992. But the nearby bedroom communities of Hudson, Milford and Salem all backed George Bush.

That was not the case in major communities of the 2nd outside the southern tier. Newcomers there are apt to be more attuned to environmental concerns than taxes. The state capital of Concord (Merrimack County) and the college town of Keene (Cheshire County) both backed Clinton.

Altogether, five of the six New Hampshire counties that Clinton won were totally or primarily within the 2nd. So were four of the five counties that went Democratic for Senate in 1992, and both of the counties that voted Democratic for governor. (Statewide, Republicans won both contests.)

Yet it is hard to see the 2nd becoming a nest of Yankee bolshevism. Conservative commentator Patrick J. Buchanan made his best showing in the 1992 New Hampshire GOP primary in Sullivan and Coos, cracking 40 percent of the vote in both.

Election Returns

	2nd District	Democrat	Republican
1992	President*	107,625 (40.6%)	97,831 (36.9%)
	House	157,328 (61.7%)	91,126 (35.7%)
1990	Senate	48,443 (34.7%)	91,282 (65.3%)
	Governor	55,112 (39.3%)	85,186 (60.7%)
1988	President	85,461 (38.0%)	139,585 (62.0%)
	Governor	85,165 (38.4%)	136,805 (61.6%)
1986	Senate	40,867 (33.5%)	75,899 (62.1%)
	Governor	59,768 (47.9%)	64,879 (52.1%)

* Vote for Perot was 59,766 (22.5%).

Demographics

Population 554,892

Percent change from 1980 20.7%

Land area 6,462 square miles

Population per square mile 86

Counties, 1990 population

Belknap (pt.) 5,376	Hillsborough (pt.) 187,166
Cheshire 70,121	Merrimack (pt.) 103,946
Coos 34,828	Rockingham (pt.) 39,934
Grafton 74,929	Sullivan 38,592

Cities, 1990 population (10,000 or more)

Berlin 11,824	Lebanon 12,183
Claremont 13,902	Milford 11,795
Concord 36,006	Nashua (pt.) 79,662
Hudson 19,530	Salem 25,746
Keene 22,430	

Race and Hispanic origin

White 98.1%
Black 0.6%
American Indian, Eskimo, or Aleut. 0.2%
Asian or Pacific Islander 0.9%
Other 0.3%
Hispanic origin 1.0%

Ancestry

American 5.2%	Greek 1.1%
Canadian 1.1%	Irish 19.7%
Dutch 1.3%	Italian 7.1%
English 24.3%	Polish 4.0%
Finnish 1.2%	Russian 1.0%
French 19.0%	Scotch Irish 2.4%
French Canadian 9.9%	Scottish 5.1%
German 10.6%	Swedish 2.3%

Universities/colleges, 1990-1991 enrollment

Antioch New England Graduate School, Keene 750
Castle College, Windham 290
Colby-Sawyer College, New London 515
Daniel Webster College, Nashua 996
Dartmouth College, Hanover 4,862
Franklin Pierce College, Rindge 3,587
Franklin Pierce Law Center, Concord 406
Keene State College, Keene 4,349
New England College, Henniker 1,146
New Hampshire Technical Institute, Concord 2,488
New Hampshire Vocational Tech College, Berlin 494
New Hampshire Vocational Tech College, Claremont 557
Plymouth State College, Plymouth 4,365
Rivier College, Nashua 2,689

Newspapers, total circulation (in all districts)

Boston Globe 503,578
Boston Herald 339,813
Claremont Eagle Times 9,165
Concord Monitor 21,312
Keene Sentinel 15,688
Lebanon-Hanover Valley News 18,114
Manchester Union Leader-News 70,806
Nashua Telegraph 28,671

Commercial television stations, affiliations
ADI: Boston (46%), Portland-Poland Springs (28%) and Burlington-Plattsburgh (27%)
WMTW-TV, Portland-Poland Spring (ABC)
WQNH, Derry (None)

Cable television systems, total subscribers
Americable; Merrimack 17,000
Continental Cablevision of New Hampshire; Concord 18,704
Continental Cablevision of New Hampshire; Deering 5,963
Continental Cablevision of New Hampshire; Derry 21,325
Paragon Cable; Keene 10,106
Twin State Cable TV Inc.; Lebanon 12,000
Warner Cable Communications Inc.; Berlin 6,156
Warner Cable of Nashua; Nashua 23,020

Military installations, 1991
New Boston Air Force Guard Station, Mt. Vernon 204

Businesses and other major employers
Mary Hitchcock Memorial Hospital/Dartmouth Medical Center; Lebanon 2,834
Digital Equipment Corp./Software Engineering; Nashua; computer services 2,500
State of New Hampshire; Concord 2,000
James River Corp. Virginia; Berlin; pulp mills 1,650
Nashua Corp./Coated Products; Nashua; paper products 1,600
Lowell Shoe Inc.; Hudson; footwear 1,200
Lockheed Sanders Inc.; Nashua; defense systems 1,200
Concord Hospital Inc.; Concord 1,076

Sturm Ruger & Co. Inc.; Newport; firearms/accessories 1,021
Nashua Memorial Hospital; Nashua 1,000
St. Joseph Hospital; Nashua 980
M. P. B. Corp.; Keene; ball bearings 975
Freudenberg-NOK; Bristol; motor vehicle parts 857
M. P. B. Corp.; Lebanon; split ball bearings 835
Blue Cross/Blue Shield of New Hampshire; Concord; medical service/health insurance 820
GTE Products Corp.; Hillsboro; electric lighting 800
State of New Hampshire/Health & Human Services Dept.; Concord 800
Union School District; Concord 800
Chubb Life Insurance Co. of America; Concord; life insurance 797
Cheshire Medical Center; Keene 780
Markem Corp.; Keene; labeling machinery 748
Hitchiner Mfg. Co.; Milford; iron/steel foundries 700
State of New Hampshire/State Prison; Concord 700
Lockheed Corp./Sanders-Calcomp; Hudson; defense systems/equipment 600
Watts Regulator Co.; Franklin; metal valves 600
New Hampshire National Guard; Concord 600
State of New Hampshire/Liquor Commission; Concord 568
New Hampshire Ball Bearings; Peterborough; ball bearings 550
Sims Inc./Concord/Portex; Keene; plastics products 540
Kingsbury Corp.; Keene; metalworking machinery 525
Ingersoll-Rand Co.; Nashua; industrial machinery 506

New Jersey

After months of negotiations in 1991, New Jersey state legislators agreed that they could not agree on what the state's congressional districts should look like for the next decade. So the chore was handed off to a bipartisan commission, one similar to a panel that drew state legislative districts in 1991.

The commission was a further manifestation of the havoc wreaked on Democrats in legislative elections in 1991, when, in a massive repudiation of the fiscal policies of Democratic Gov. James J. Florio, voters swept Republicans into control of both legislative chambers. To add insult to injury, Republicans were given veto-proof majorities. Better known as the "Florio factor," this roiling anti-tax sentiment first surfaced in the 1990 elections, when several congressional incumbents—including Democratic Sen. Bill Bradley—were almost dragged down to defeat. Gov. Florio later lost his re-election bid in 1993.

With the state due to lose one seat to reapportionment, delegation members jockeyed behind the scenes to help the commission craft a map to their advantage. In the end, the commission adopted a GOP-drafted version, which pitted two Democratic incumbents against each other in the new central Jersey-based 6th. Rather than battle a Democratic colleague in the 1992 primary, one incumbent chose to retire.

Political exigencies led to the merger of districts in the middle of the state, not demographic changes. In fact, the only counties to lose population in the 1980s (Bergen, Essex, Hudson and Union) were clustered to the north, in the New York metropolitan orbit. Theoretically, a district should have been excised from the depopulating older, industrial cities of that region.

Farther south, population growth ranged from steady to strong: All three south Jersey districts posted gains in the 1980s. Still, the population increases failed to fundamentally alter the fact that the southern counties are culturally, demographically and economically different from the northern part of the state. Excluding fast-growing Ocean County, the seven counties south of Trenton have a lower per capita income and lower median home value than in the north, which, despite pockets of urban poverty, is fairly affluent. The middle-class flavor of south Jersey made voters particularly sensitive to property taxes, and many reacted with great hostility to Florio's tax increase package. Even the state's athletic allegiances reflect a certain schizophrenia:

Philadelphia teams are the choice of south Jersey residents while north Jersey fans prefer New York teams.

The final map left the three southern districts relatively unscathed. The largest city in south Jersey—Camden—remained the anchor for the 1st District, although declining population has diluted the city's influence in Camden County politics. The 2nd covers the agricultural regions south of Camden as well as Atlantic City and more placid shore communities like Cape May. In the suburban and Republican-leaning 3rd, which includes Cherry Hill, unchecked growth is a concern in Burlington and Ocean counties. (In refiguring the districts, the commission renumbered the old 13th as the 3rd.)

The shore communities in the center of the state fought hard to remain together in one district, but were parceled out of the old 3rd and into several other districts. Arguing that they were communities of common interest, local officials banded together to save the "Shore" district, but the commission failed to grant their wish. Instead, the 3rd, 4th and 12th districts now stretch west to east, from the Delaware River (which forms the Pennsylvania border) to the Atlantic coastline. The Trenton-based 4th covers the state's midsection, an area where the Garden State begins to make the transition from south Jersey to north Jersey, while the 12th is based in Hunterdon County and takes in Princeton as it winds its way east, stopping just short of the Atlantic Ocean. The 3rd is the southernmost of these three east-west districts.

Part of the old "Shore" district was also added to the 6th, which is now rooted in Monmouth and Middlesex counties. Bordering the Raritan Bay, the 6th sweeps south to hug the Monmouth County shoreline. Here middle-class and independent-minded voters make the 3rd a swing district and an important component of any successful statewide electoral strategy.

The most cartographically creative district is the 13th. Drawn as the state's second minority-majority district, its strange shape covers parts of Jersey City, Newark and Elizabeth. Hispanics comprise 42 percent of the population, but they are not a homogenous community: Their ranks are bolstered by immigrants from more than 20 Latin American countries. Most of these Hispanic voters prefer Democrats, but the Cuban community leans Republican. In November 1992, the 13th became the

NEW JERSEY

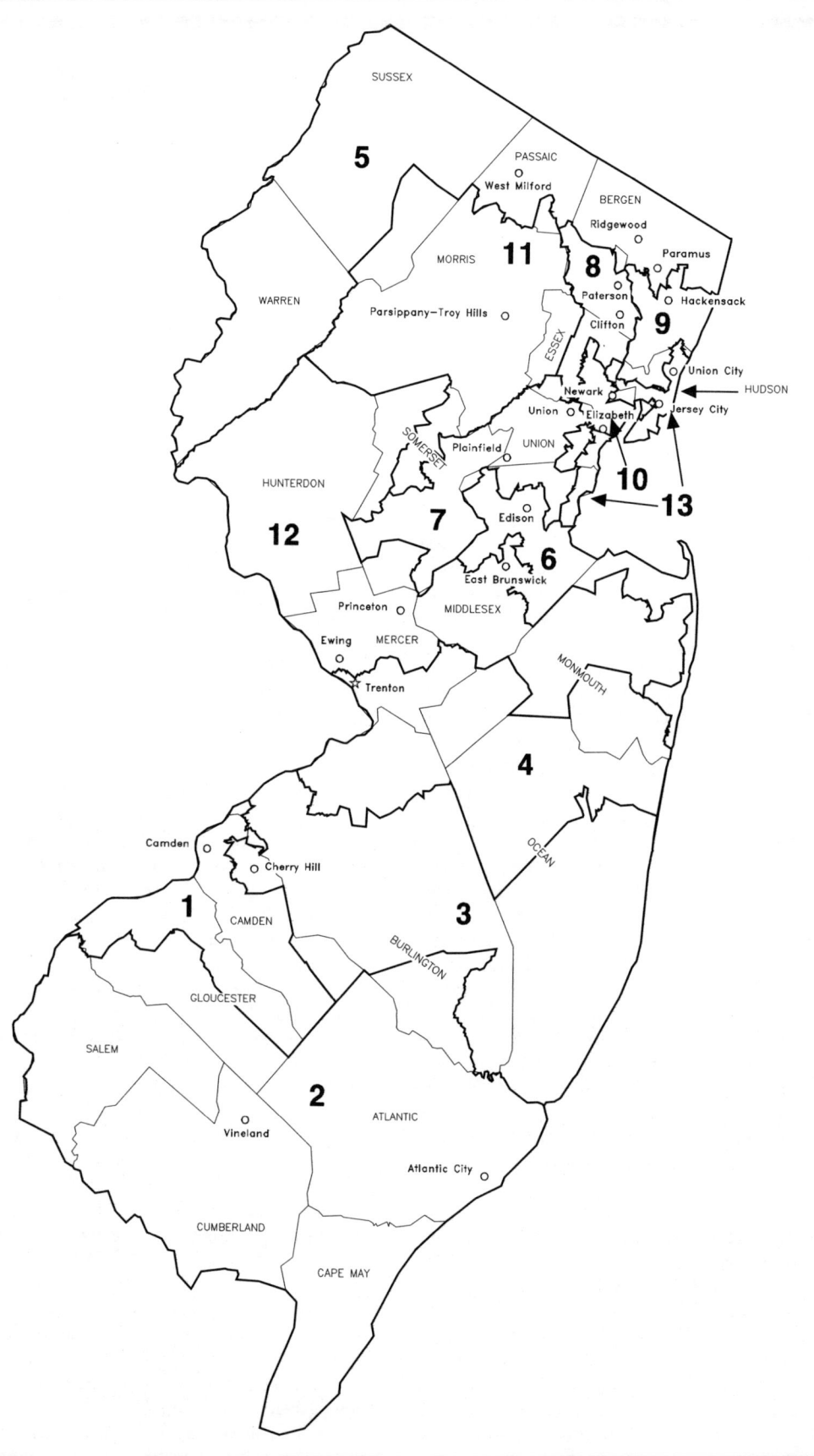

first congressional district in New Jersey to elect a Hispanic representative. The state's other minority-majority district, the Newark-based 10th, has hemorrhaged residents—particularly whites—for decades, but it was relatively unaffected by redistricting because it was protected by the Voting Rights Act that mandates black-majority districts must be preserved.

The 7th (parts of Essex, Middlesex, Somerset and Union counties) and 8th (Paterson) districts are essentially suburban swing districts that added or subtracted a few towns and suburbs. The 7th leans Republican, but both are competitive.

The Bergen County-based 9th also has a suburban identity, though it is wealthier than its neighbors. Farther west, the land is less densely populated in the 5th and 11th districts and per capita income rises sharply. Both are home to large numbers of Republicans and white-collar employees, many of whom were hit hard by cutbacks and downsizing in the 1990s after a decade of booming white-collar service industry growth in New Jersey.

The 5th stretches from Warren County north to the New York border, then all the way across the northern tier to the Hudson River. No municipality has more than 30,000 residents. It includes some of the state's most scenic, wealthiest and Republican areas. The 11th is anchored by suburban and Republican Morris County.

Table 1   Population

District	Population	Population under 18	Voting-age population	Median age
1	594,630	158,773	435,857	32.2
2	594,630	144,246	450,384	34.2
3	594,630	142,809	451,821	35.8
4	594,630	142,703	451,927	34.9
5	594,630	142,043	452,587	36.2
6	594,630	128,931	465,699	33.2
7	594,629	127,236	467,393	36.1
8	594,629	133,172	461,457	34.8
9	594,630	113,953	480,677	36.7
10	594,630	150,543	444,087	32.0
11	594,630	135,973	458,657	35.4
12	594,630	138,806	455,824	35.2
13	594,630	140,274	454,356	32.3
State	7,730,188	1,799,462	5,930,726	34.5

Table 2   Voting-Age Persons

District	White*	Black*	American Indian, Eskimo, or Aleut*	Asian or Pacific Islander*	Other*	Hispanic*	Male*	Female*
1	80.8%	14.5%	0.2%	1.5%	3.0%	5.1%	47.1%	52.9%
2	82.6	12.9	0.4	1.2	2.9	5.6	47.4	52.6
3	89.9	7.3	0.2	1.9	0.7	2.3	47.8	52.2
4	85.3	11.3	0.2	1.4	1.8	4.6	47.0	53.0
5	94.2	1.3	0.2	3.9	0.4	2.7	47.8	52.2
6	83.3	10.3	0.2	4.5	1.8	5.5	47.8	52.2
7	85.0	9.5	0.1	4.1	1.3	4.6	47.7	52.3
8	77.6	11.6	0.2	3.3	7.3	15.6	46.7	53.3
9	85.2	6.1	0.1	5.9	2.7	10.5	47.1	52.9
10	36.0	57.3	0.3	2.4	4.0	11.5	45.6	54.4
11	92.8	2.7	0.1	3.5	0.9	3.9	48.3	51.7
12	90.2	5.2	0.1	3.9	0.6	2.5	48.5	51.5
13	70.2	12.4	0.3	4.5	12.6	38.9	48.1	51.9
State	81.1	12.4	0.2	3.2	3.1	8.7	47.5	52.5

*As percent of voting-age population.

Table 3   Voting-Age Persons by Age Groups

District	18-24*	25-44*	45-54*	55-64*	65 and over*
1	13.6%	46.1%	13.2%	11.2%	16.0%
2	13.4	41.7	13.2	12.2	19.5
3	12.3	40.6	14.4	12.8	19.9
4	11.8	42.5	12.6	11.1	21.9
5	11.5	42.1	16.6	13.3	16.5
6	15.9	44.0	13.2	11.4	15.5
7	11.3	43.2	14.6	13.3	17.6
8	13.6	41.5	13.6	12.4	18.9
9	11.6	41.9	13.4	13.1	20.0
10	15.5	44.3	13.5	11.1	15.6
11	12.3	44.0	17.2	12.5	14.0
12	13.1	44.1	16.2	11.6	14.9
13	15.0	44.7	13.0	11.5	15.9
State	13.1	43.1	14.2	12.1	17.4

*As percent of voting-age population.

Table 4   Income and Occupation

District	Median family income	Families in poverty	White collar*	Blue collar*	Service*	Farm*
1	$40,674	7.8%	61.2%	25.9%	12.2%	0.8%
2	38,172	7.3	52.5	25.6	20.1	1.9
3	46,870	3.1	66.8	20.5	11.7	1.0
4	43,707	5.0	61.9	23.8	12.9	1.4
5	59,583	2.2	70.9	19.3	8.6	1.2
6	49,729	4.3	65.0	22.9	11.5	0.7
7	57,563	2.2	71.5	19.1	8.8	0.6
8	46,731	6.4	63.7	25.3	10.4	0.6
9	48,584	4.4	67.7	21.9	9.9	0.5
10	34,679	14.1	55.1	28.3	16.1	0.5
11	63,574	1.7	73.8	17.0	8.3	0.9
12	62,034	1.7	75.8	14.9	8.0	1.3
13	32,311	14.4	52.3	34.1	13.1	0.5
State	47,589	5.6	64.9	22.7	11.5	0.9

*As percent of employed persons age 16 and over.

Table 5   Education: School Years Completed

District	Less than grade 9*	Grades 9-12 no diploma*	High school diploma*	College bachelor's degree or higher*
1	8.7%	17.0%	36.3%	16.9%
2	11.0	17.7	35.5	14.9
3	6.2	13.2	33.1	24.1
4	8.8	15.3	34.5	18.7
5	5.6	9.0	30.4	32.6
6	7.5	13.0	32.2	24.9
7	7.1	10.2	30.0	32.4
8	12.7	14.9	30.4	24.5
9	11.1	14.0	31.2	24.7
10	12.6	21.7	31.4	14.6
11	4.9	7.8	27.0	37.4
12	4.6	7.8	25.4	39.7
13	21.8	20.2	27.4	15.9
State	9.4	13.9	31.1	24.9

*As percent of persons age 25 and over.

Table 6   Housing and Residential Patterns

District	Owner occupied	Renter occupied	Urban	Rural
1	69.1%	30.9%	96.1%	3.9%
2	69.0	31.0	70.3	29.7
3	82.3	17.7	81.6	18.4
4	73.6	26.4	84.1	15.9
5	80.8	19.2	81.4	18.6
6	63.1	36.9	99.7	0.3
7	74.6	25.4	95.9	4.1
8	57.2	42.8	100.0	0.0
9	54.6	45.4	100.0	0.0
10	35.7	64.3	100.0	0.0
11	76.4	23.6	87.1	12.9
12	78.3	21.7	65.9	34.1
13	31.0	69.0	100.0	0.0
State	64.9	35.1	89.4	10.6

1st District

Southwest — Camden

More than two-thirds of the 1st District hails from Camden County, an amalgam of older suburbs, developing countryside and the city of Camden.

Once a major industrial center and Delaware River port, Camden now is one of the nation's most distressed cities. More than 70 percent of its children live below the poverty line. Businesses and middle-class residents have fled in droves to the suburbs, decimating the tax base.

City officials have pinned their hopes for economic revival on a new $52 million aquarium, the anchor for an ambitious waterfront redevelopment that is designed to draw suburban residents back into the city and provide a tourism lure for the neighbors across the river in Philadelphia.

Camden was once the hub of Camden County's powerful Democratic machine. Democratic Gov. James J. Florio was a product of its farm system. But as population decreased precipitously over the past three decades, suburban GOP strength has made the county more competitive.

The city now holds less than 20 percent of county residents. Most of the county is in the 1st, with the exception of Cherry Hill and several smaller municipalities that are in the 3rd District.

Along the Delaware River, the cities are gritty and industry-oriented. The factories and oil storage yards of mostly working-class and poor Pennsauken, on the northern tip of the 1st, give it a Democratic character. Democrats can also find refuge in the older blue-collar towns farther south along the Black Horse Pike. East of Camden, the district becomes more suburban and Republican.

Florio won 62 percent in the 1st in his gubernatorial bid in 1989, but after passing a $2.8 billion tax package in his first year in office, some of the most virulent opposition in the state came from the county's suburban voters. During the 1990 elections, Democrats lost control of the freeholder board for the first time in nearly two decades.

Republicans have experienced gains in the growing southern portion of Camden County and in suburban Gloucester County, which is shared with the 2nd. Roughly a quarter of the district's population hails from Gloucester County.

Commercial growth in and around Cherry Hill has spurred runaway population growth in Camden County locales such as

Washington, middle-class Gloucester and white-collar Voorhees townships, though the growth is beginning to stabilize. Many residents moved to escape the older suburbs closer to Camden, but others sought the relatively easy access to Center City Philadelphia or Cherry Hill.

Not so long ago, Voorhees was a farming hamlet. But between 1970 and 1980, population more than doubled. From 1980 to 1990, it doubled again.

Election Returns

	1st District	Democrat	Republican
1992	President*	118,060 (48.3%)	78,095 (32.0%)
	House	153,525 (67.3%)	65,123 (28.6%)
1990	Senate	86,094 (59.7%)	58,138 (40.3%)
1989	Governor	123,866 (73.3%)	45,181 (26.7%)
1988	President	102,338 (47.0%)	115,449 (53.0%)
	Senate	125,375 (59.1%)	86,909 (40.9%)

*Vote for Perot was 48,157 (19.7%).

Demographics

Population   594,630

Percent change from 1980   13.0%

Land area   321 square miles

Population per square mile   1,851

Counties, 1990 population
Burlington (pt.)   29,042   Gloucester (pt.)   159,020
Camden (pt.)   406,568

Cities, 1990 population (10,000 or more)
Bellmawr   12,603   Maple Shade CDP   19,211
Camden   87,492   Pennsauken CDP   34,733
Collingswood   15,289   Williamstown CDP   10,891
Gloucester City   12,649   Woodbury   10,904
Lindenwold   18,734

Race and Hispanic origin
White   78.4%
Black   15.8%
American Indian, Eskimo, or Aleut.   0.2%
Asian or Pacific Islander   1.7%
Other   4.0%
Hispanic origin   6.3%

Ancestry
American   1.8%   Italian   19.5%
Dutch   1.5%   Polish   6.9%
English   12.4%   Russian   1.4%
French   2.3%   Scotch Irish   1.5%
German   24.8%   Scottish   1.6%
Irish   25.8%

Universities/colleges, 1990-1991 enrollment
Camden County College, Blackwood   12,014
Rutgers University, Camden   5,337

Newspapers, total circulation (in all districts)
Burlington County Times   42,638
Camden Courier Post   98,658

Gloucester County Times 29,572
Philadelphia Daily News 196,141
Philadelphia Inquirer 500,733
Trentonian 72,634
Trenton Times 82,521

Commercial television stations, affiliations
ADI: Philadelphia (100%)

Cable television systems, total subscribers
Garden State Cable; Audubon 144,261
Jones Intercable Inc.; Turnersville 29,399
Storer Cable/Gloucester County; Woodbury 30,585
TKR Cable Co. of Gloucester; Gloucester City 5,179
TKR Cable of Maple Shade; Maple Shade 6,199

Businesses and other major employers
General Electric Co.; Camden; iron/steel foundries 2,400
Cooper Hospital; Camden 2,250
Our Lady of Lourdes Medical Center; Camden 1,900
Consolidated Newspapers Inc.; Woodbury; newspapers 1,733
Campbell Soup Co.; Camden; grocery products 1,500
Underwood Memorial Hospital; Woodbury 1,400
West Jersey Health System; Camden 1,394
West Jersey Health System; Voorhees 1,311
City of Camden; Camden 1,281
Camden County College; Blackwood 1,000
Cigna Corp./Cigna Systems; Voorhees; computer services
1,000
County of Camden; Barrington 1,000
Mobil Oil Corp.; Paulsboro; petroleum refining 850
County of Camden/Social Services; Camden 833
Aluminum Shapes Inc.; Camden; aluminum rolling/drawing
700
Kennedy Memorial Hospital; Stratford 700
Holt Cargo Systems Inc.; Gloucester City; trucking services
686
Delaware River; Camden; freight services 650
Macy's Northeast Inc.; Woodbury; department stores 600
Rutgers University; Camden 600
County of Camden/Health Services; Blackwood 550
U.S. Postal Service; Gloucester City 540
Township of Pennsauken; Camden 515

2nd District

South — Atlantic City; Vineland

The Mason-Dixon Line does not cross the Delaware River, but if it did, the 2nd would fit right in with the South. Like the rest of the southern parts of the state (Burlington and all counties south of it), the 2nd is generally less affluent than the northern half of the state; median home values are lower and the area is less densely populated.

Though New Jersey is known better as an urban and suburban state, agriculture is a leading industry in the 2nd. The district is also known for its dislike of gun control measures.

Taking in all of Atlantic, Cape May, Cumberland and Salem counties—along with part of Gloucester County and one township from Burlington—the 2nd covers the bottom portion of New Jersey.

The towns along the Delaware River are more industrialized, and many residents work in the chemical plants across the river from Wilmington and in refineries on the Jersey side, just south of Philadelphia.

Farther inland, in Salem and Cumberland counties, there are pockets of rural poverty in an agricultural area that is one of the nation's leading egg producers. Agriculture is not the only business of Cumberland County; there is glass-making in Vineland and Millville.

The 2nd's best-known city is Atlantic City (Atlantic County). Once known as "Sodom by the Sea" for its seedy nightlife, this resort town fell on hard times before gambling was legalized in the mid-1970s.

But while glitzy casinos and hotels have sprouted up on the Boardwalk and property values have soared, the prosperity has been slow to trickle down to the mainly black and poor residents of the city.

The shore communities south of Atlantic City, in Cape May County, have fared much better. From north to south, the county takes in family-oriented Ocean City, wealthy Avalon and Stone Harbor, then rowdier Wildwood.

On the southern tip, the city of Cape May has prospered as GOP-voting retirees have flocked to this old seaside resort of Victorian homes and small cottages.

The coastal character—and vast pinelands west of the shoreline—places environmental issues at the forefront of political discourse. In Cape May County, wetlands preservation is a volatile issue. Federal flood insurance and ocean dumping are also weighty concerns to residents of the hurricane-sensitive shore communities.

Politically, the 2nd has a Republican tilt. Ronald Reagan and George Bush easily carried it in 1984 and 1988, but in statewide elections, Democrats have fared well. Sen. Bill Bradley won every county in the district in his tight 1990 victory; then-Democratic Rep. James J. Florio also carried all the counties in his successful 1989 gubernatorial bid. In the 1992 presidential race, Bush managed to hold only two counties that are wholly within the district—agricultural Salem and Cape May. In the more industrial towns such as Bridgeton, Millville and Vineland—which has a significant number of Hispanic and black voters—and in Atlantic City, Democrats have an advantage.

Election Returns

	2nd District	Democrat	Republican
1992	President*	101,718 (40.6%)	97,696 (39.0%)
	House	132,465 (55.9%)	98,315 (41.5%)
1990	Senate	82,192 (57.2%)	61,589 (42.8%)
1989	Governor	108,085 (62.9%)	63,840 (37.1%)
1988	President	90,180 (41.2%)	128,488 (58.8%)
	Senate	110,546 (52.9%)	98,506 (47.1%)

Vote for Perot was 50,870 (20.3%).

Demographics

Population 594,630

Percent change from 1980 13.0%

Land area 1,912 square miles

Population per square mile 311

Counties, 1990 population

Atlantic 224,327	Cumberland 138,053
Burlington (pt.) 805	Gloucester (pt.) 71,062
Cape May 95,089	Salem 65,294

Cities, 1990 population (10,000 or more)

Atlantic City 37,986	Ocean City 15,512
Bridgeton 18,942	Pennsville CDP 12,218
Brigantine 11,354	Pleasantville 16,027
Glassboro 15,614	Somers Point 11,216
Hammonton 12,208	Ventnor City 11,005
Millville 25,992	Vineland 54,780

Race and Hispanic origin

White 80.7%
Black 14.1%
American Indian, Eskimo, or Aleut. 0.4%
Asian or Pacific Islander 1.2%
Other 3.5%
Hispanic origin 6.6%

Ancestry

American 3.2%	Italian 18.0%
Dutch 2.1%	Polish 4.5%
English 14.2%	Russian 1.8%
French 2.7%	Scotch Irish 1.4%
German 24.2%	Scottish 1.7%
Irish 20.8%	Swedish 1.3%

Universities/colleges, 1990-1991 enrollment

Atlantic Community College, Mays Landing 5,004
Cumberland County College, Vineland 2,476
Glassboro State College, Glassboro 9,670
Gloucester County College, Sewell 4,373
Salem Community College, Carneys Point 1,356
Stockton State College, Pomona 5,639

Newspapers, total circulation (in all districts)

Bridgeton Evening News 10,293
Burlington County Times 42,638
Camden Courier Post 98,658
Gloucester County Times 29,572
New York Daily News 757,053
Philadelphia Daily News 196,141
Philadelphia Inquirer 500,733
Press of Atlantic City 78,439
Salem Today's Sunbeam 10,642
Vineland Daily Journal 20,546
Wilmington News Journal 120,121

Commercial television stations, affiliations

ADI: Philadelphia (100%)
WWAC-TV, Atlantic City (None)
WMGM-TV, Wildwood (NBC)

Cable television systems, total subscribers

Harron Cable/New Jersey; Mays Landing 6,495
Jones Intercable Inc.; Turnersville 29,399
Sammons Communications Inc.; Atlantic City 19,750
Sammons Communications Inc.; Bridgeton 7,482
Sammons Communications Inc.; Cardiff 35,000
Sammons Communications Inc.; Palermo 16,650
Sammons Communications Inc.; Ventnor City 23,600
Sammons Communications Inc.; Vineland 21,325
South Jersey Cable; Swedesboro 10,000
TKR Cable Co./Rio Grande; Rio Grande 41,117
Tri-County Cable TV Co.; Salem 6,200
Warner Cable Communications; Swainton 9,700

Military installations, 1991

Atlantic City Municipal Airport Air Force Guard Station, Pleasantville 371

Businesses and other major employers

Trump Taj Mahal Associates; Atlantic City; casino/hotel 5,000
Promus Companies Inc./Holiday Inns Inc.; Atlantic City; casino/hotel 3,900
Adamar of New Jersey Inc./Trop World Casino; Atlantic City; casino/hotel 3,700
Resorts Intl. Hotel; Atlantic City; casino/hotel 3,600
Ocean Showboat Inc.; Atlantic City; casino/hotel 3,600
Du Pont E. I. De Nemours & Co.; Deepwater; organic chemicals 3,500
Boardwalk Regency Corp./Caesar's; Atlantic City; casino/hotel 3,500
Trump Plaza Associates; Atlantic City; casino/hotel 3,500
Bally's Park Place Inc.; Atlantic City; casino/hotel 3,400
Trump's Castle Associates Ltd.; Atlantic City; casino/hotel 3,084
Wheaton Industries Inc.; Millville; glass/glassware 3,000
GNOC Corp./Bally's Grand; Atlantic City; casino/hotel 3,000
Great Bay Hotel/Sands Hotel; Atlantic City; casino/hotel 2,800
Claridge at Park Place Inc.; Atlantic City; casino/hotels 2,130
State of New Jersey/Vineland Developmental Center; Vineland 2,000
U.S. Federal Aviation Administration; Atlantic City; space research/technology 1,500
Shore Memorial Hospital; Somers Point 1,300
County of Cape May; Cape May 1,200
State of New Jersey/Human Resources Dept.; Woodbine 1,200
Ancora Psychiatric Hospital; Hammonton 1,200
Atlantic City Medical Center; Atlantic City 1,125
Lenox China Inc.; Pomona; china 1,000
Prudential Property Casualty Insurance; Linwood; fire/marine/casualty insurance 1,000
Burdette Tomlin Memorial Hospital; Cape May 1,000
American Home Products Corp./Whitehall Laboratories; Hammonton; pharmaceuticals 950
Prudential Insurance of America Inc.; Millville; insurance services 950
Newcomb Medical Center; Vineland 950
Atlantic City Medical Center; Pomona 900
Sony Music Entertainment Inc./CBS Records Inc.; Pitman; music recordings 800
New Jersey Air National Guard; Pomona 800
Glassboro State College; Glassboro 800
Memorial Hospital of Salem; Salem 775
Atlantic City Electric Co.; Pleasantville; electric services 750
Mannington Mills Inc.; Salem; floor coverings 650
State of New Jersey/Correctional Facility; Delmont 650
American National Can Co./Foster-Forbes; Millville; glass/glassware 600
State of New Jersey/Bayside State Prison; Leesburg 596
New Jersey National Guard; Bridgeton 551
Durand Glass Mfg. Co.; Millville; glass/glassware 550

Stockton State College; Pomona   550
South Jersey Hospital System; Bridgeton   550
County of Salem; Salem   550
Public Service Electric & Gas Co.; Hancocks Bridge; electrical
    work   500

3rd District

South Central — Cherry Hill

On the surface, the Camden and Burlington County suburbs would seem to have little in common with the shore communities of Ocean County. But both share an affinity for Republican candidates and concerns about the spiraling growth that is affecting their quality of life. The new housing developments, office parks and shopping malls have changed the complexion of this once-rural hamlet, but at a price: traffic congestion.

Only four Camden County municipalities are included in the 3rd, but they include Cherry Hill, a city that has experienced uninterrupted growth over the past three decades as a result of out-migration from Philadelphia and Camden. The young, mostly white suburbanites who live here lean Republican, but they are an independent lot.

During the political tax revolt spurred by Democratic Gov. James J. Florio's 1990 tax increase—while Democrats across the state were being swept out of the Legislature—Republicans actually lost a local state Senate seat. In 1992, voters split their tickets for Democrat Bill Clinton and the Republican House nominee.

A much larger share of the 3rd District vote is cast in the suburbs of Burlington County. Democrats run well in the industrial towns along the Delaware River, and in Willingboro, a Levittown-style community that is more than 50 percent black. Cinnaminson and Delran are more affluent, though not as upscale as Moorestown.

West of these towns, suburban sprawl takes over. Population has exploded in places such as Mount Laurel and Evesham, which are situated by highways that facilitate white-collar employees who commute to Trenton, Philadelphia and corporate facilities in the north.

Away from the riverfront, the vote is more Republican. Though Clinton carried the county by more than 5,000 votes, the Republican incumbent won the House seat in a breeze in 1992.

After Burlington County, the second-largest population cluster is in rapidly growing Ocean County (which is split between the 3rd and 4th districts). Many live in the Toms River area, and the rest are scattered in smaller, seaside communities. Retirees are an important constituency; there are age-restricted housing developments in Berkeley township.

Retirees have not been the only ones moving to Ocean County. The 1950s extension of the Garden State Parkway to the shore area made the area attractive for commuters and spawned Parkway bedroom communities. Closer to the fragile Atlantic coastline, barrier beach development has pitted builders against environmentalists.

The newcomers have helped keep Ocean County in the GOP column. Florio carried the county in his successful 1989 gubernatorial bid, but a year later, the GOP Senate challenger bested Democratic Sen. Bill Bradley. Of the three counties that make up the 3rd, Ocean was the only one to back George Bush in 1992.

Election Returns

	3rd District	Democrat	Republican
1992	President*	114,503 (40.4%)	113,583 (40.1%)
	House	94,012 (36.8%)	151,368 (59.2%)
1990	Senate	75,773 (46.5%)	87,047 (53.5%)
1989	Governor	110,826 (60.8%)	71,344 (39.2%)
1988	President	94,849 (38.1%)	154,415 (61.9%)
	Senate	120,906 (49.9%)	121,232 (50.1%)

Vote for Perot was 54,989 (19.4%).

Demographics

Population   594,630

Percent change from 1980   13.3%

Land area   966 square miles

Population per square mile   615

Counties, 1990 population
Burlington (pt.)   284,522   Ocean (pt.)   213,852
Camden (pt.)   96,256

Cities, 1990 population (10,000 or more)
Brown Mills CDP   11,429   Marlton CDP   10,228
Cherry Hill CDP   69,319   Moorestown-Lenola CDP
Cinnaminson CDP   14,583   13,242
Fort Dix CDP (pt.)   10,082   Mount Holly CDP   10,639
Haddonfield   11,628   Willingboro CDP   36,291
Holiday City-Berkeley
    CDP   14,293

Race and Hispanic origin
White   88.9%
Black   8.0%
American Indian, Eskimo, or Aleut.   0.2%
Asian or Pacific Islander   2.1%
Other   0.9%
Hispanic origin   2.6%

Ancestry
American   2.4%   Italian   19.5%
Dutch   1.9%   Polish   8.6%
English   13.9%   Russian   3.2%
French   2.7%   Scotch Irish   1.7%
German   25.1%   Scottish   2.4%
Hungarian   1.6%   Slovakian   1.3%
Irish   24.3%   Swedish   1.2%

Universities/colleges, 1990-1991 enrollment
Burlington County College, Pemberton   6,711
Georgian Court College, Lakewood   2,316
Ocean County College, Toms River   7,424

Newspapers, total circulation (in all districts)
Asbury Park Press   162,357
Burlington County Times   42,638
Camden Courier Post   98,658
New York Daily News   757,053
New York Post   551,443
New York Times   746,924
Ocean County Observer   17,648

Philadelphia Daily News 196,141
Philadelphia Inquirer 500,733
Press of Atlantic City 78,439
Trentonian 72,634
Trenton Times 82,521

Commercial television stations, affiliations
ADI: Philadelphia (58%) and New York (42%)
WHSP, Vineland (None)

Cable television systems, total subscribers
Adelphia Cable; Toms River 87,000
Garden State Cable; Arney's Mount 41,951
Garden State Cable; Audubon 144,261
Monmouth Cablevision; Seaside Heights 8,031
TKR Cable Co. of Long Beach Island; Spray Beach 17,342

Military installations, 1991
McGuire Air Force Base, Wrightstown 6,768
Fort Dix (Army), Trenton (shared with the 4th District) 4,916

Businesses and other major employers
General Electric Co.; Moorestown; search/navigation equipment 5,000
City of Toms River/Board of Education; Toms River 2,000
J&J Temporaries; Cherry Hill; temp services 2,000
County of Burlington; Mount Holly 1,800
Community Medical Center; Toms River 1,790
City of Cherry Hill/Board of Education; Cherry Hill 1,425
Computer Sciences Corp.; Moorestown; computer services 1,350
State of New Jersey/New Lisbon Developmental Center; New Lisbon 1,334
Memorial Hospital/Larchmont Medical Center; Mount Holly 1,200
City of Willingboro/Board of Education; Willingboro 1,200
Stewall Corp./Leader Nursing Rehabilitation Center; Cherry Hill; nursing 1,200
Deborah Heart & Lung Center/Deborah Hospital; Browns Mills 1,100
Subaru America Operations Corp.; Cherry Hill; motor vehicles 1,000
General Electric Co.; Moorestown; electrical industrial apparatus 1,000
Macmillan Inc.; Riverside; book warehousing 1,000
Associated Building Maintenance Co. Inc.; Medford; building services 1,000
Zurbrugg Memorial Hospital; Willingboro 1,000
Township of Pemberton/School District; Browns Mills 910
Jersey Central Power & Light Co.; Forked River; electric services 900
World Baptists Evangelical Assn.; Cherry Hill; religious organizations 690
Elkins-Sinn Inc.; Cherry Hill; pharmaceuticals 654
Ciba-Geigy Corp.; Toms River; plastics/synthetics 650
Computer Sciences Corp./Automobile Insurance Div.; Mount Laurel; fire/marine/casualty insurance 600
Sears Roebuck & Co.; Moorestown; department stores 600
Kennedy Memorial Hospital; Cherry Hill 600
County of Ocean; Toms River 584
Ocean County College; Toms River 561
Automatic Data Processing; Mount Laurel; computer services 550
OKI America Inc./OKI Data; Mount Laurel; computer equipment 528
Visiting Homemaker; Toms River; home health services 525
PHH U.S. Mortgage Corp.; Cherry Hill; mortgage bankers 520
PMG Services Inc.; Pemberton; management/public relations 511

4th District

Central — Trenton

Stretching from Trenton to the Atlantic Ocean, the 4th covers the state's midsection, an area where the Garden State begins to make the transition from south Jersey to north Jersey. The motto of the state capital—and the district's largest city—is "Trenton Makes, the World Takes." That catchy phrase refers to the city's industrial heritage, but nowadays, the city makes less and takes a lot more federal aid.

Minorities make up more than half the city's population, though there are a few remaining white ethnic enclaves such as the Italian section of Chambersburg. Hispanics and blacks, when combined with the contingent of state employees, help Trenton turn out a fairly sizable Democratic vote. It is usually enough to put Mercer County into the Democratic column in statewide elections. In 1988, Michael S. Dukakis edged out George Bush there, and Democratic Sen. Frank R. Lautenberg carried the county by more than 30,000 votes in his competitive re-election bid. In 1992, Mercer backed Bill Clinton, though he lost the district. At the same time, Mercer gave GOP Rep. Christopher Smith a relatively easy victory.

Countering Trenton is a burgeoning suburban voice, made up mostly of Trenton expatriates. These white suburbanites are more independent voters who, at the federal level, tend to prefer GOP candidates. Many blue-collar Irish and Italians settled in Hamilton township after leaving Trenton. Its population has boomed as Trenton's declined; now it is only slightly smaller.

Ocean County is the site of the top concentration of voters in the district. If a Democratic candidate comes out ahead in Mercer, that lead is likely to be blunted by the Republican advantage in Ocean County. Retirement communities have sprouted up in Lakewood, and in Brick and Manchester townships, sparking creation of new service industries geared to the elderly. Ocean County—which the 4th shares with the 3rd District—houses one of the largest concentrations of retirees in the Northeast.

These retirees come out in large numbers on Election Day, enough so that in 1992, Ocean County easily bested Mercer County in voter turnout percentage in the 4th.

Parts of Monmouth and Burlington counties round out the district. The Monmouth County portion includes some fast-growing inland communities such as Howell, where white-collar employees commute to Trenton or New York City. In 1992 Monmouth voters backed the GOP House incumbent by a better than 2-to-1 margin; Bush outdistanced Clinton by more than 7,000 ballots.

The Burlington County portion is slightly smaller than Monmouth's but more Democratic. The industrial areas closer to the Delaware River favor Democrats, but farther east, Republicans fare better because of places such as Mansfield, a community where posh housing developments are growing in number, facilitated by access to Princeton, Philadelphia and Trenton.

Election Returns

Vote for Perot was 50,768 (19.1%).

Demographics

Population 594,630

Percent change from 1980 12.7%

Land area 699 square miles

Population per square mile 851

Counties, 1990 population
Burlington (pt.) 80,697
Mercer (pt.) 208,522
Monmouth (pt.) 86,060
Ocean (pt.) 219,351

Cities, 1990 population (10,000 or more)
Brick CDP 66,473
Lakewood CDP 26,095
Leisure Village West-Pine
    Lake Park CDP 10,139
Mercerville-Hamilton
    Square CDP 26,873
Point Pleasant 18,177
Trenton 88,675

Race and Hispanic origin
White 83.7%
Black 12.5%
American Indian, Eskimo, or Aleut. 0.2%
Asian or Pacific Islander 1.5%
Other 2.1%
Hispanic origin 5.2%

Ancestry
American 2.5%
Dutch 2.1%
English 11.3%
French 2.5%
German 21.6%
Hungarian 2.9%
Irish 21.2%
Italian 19.3%
Polish 9.5%
Russian 2.2%
Scotch Irish 1.2%
Scottish 2.1%
Slovakian 2.3%
Swedish 1.0%

Universities/colleges, 1990-1991 enrollment
Beth Medrash Govoha, Lakewood 1,393
Thomas A. Edison State College, Trenton 7,811
Trenton State College, Trenton 7,410

Newspapers, total circulation (in all districts)
Asbury Park Press 162,357
Burlington County Times 42,638
Camden Courier Post 98,658
New York Daily News 757,053
New York Post 551,443
New York Times 746,924
Ocean County Observer 17,648
Philadelphia Daily News 196,141
Philadelphia Inquirer 500,733
Trentonian 72,634
Trenton Times 82,521

Commercial television stations, affiliations
ADI: New York (67%) and Philadelphia (33%)

Cable television systems, total subscribers
Adelphia Cable; Toms River 87,000
Comcast Cablevision; Trenton 34,000
Garden State Cable; Arney's Mount 41,951
Monmouth Cablevision; Jackson 8,872
Monmouth Cablevision; Lakewood 20,065
Monmouth Cablevision East; Wall 30,043
Storer Cable TV Inc.; Brick 33,828
Storer Cable TV Inc.; East Windsor 27,381
TKR Cable Co./Hamilton; Hamilton Square 28,400

Military installations, 1991
Fort Dix (Army), Trenton (shared with the 3rd District) 4,916
Lakehurst Naval Air Engineering Center, Lakehurst 3,297

Businesses and other major employers
State of New Jersey/Corrections Dept.; Trenton 9,000
General Electric Co./Astro Space Div.; Hightstown; guided missiles/parts 5,000
State of New Jersey/Labor Dept.; Trenton 4,044
State of New Jersey/Motor Vehicle Dept.; Trenton; personal services 2,700
State of New Jersey/Labor & Industry Building; Trenton 2,000
McGraw-Hill Inc.; Hightstown; book distributing 1,800
City of Trenton; Trenton 1,611
Ocean Health Systems Inc.; Brielle 1,500
Medical Center of Ocean County; Brick 1,500
St. Francis Medical Center; Trenton 1,500
Kimball Medical Center; Lakewood 1,444
State of New Jersey/Education Dept.; Trenton 1,400
Mercer Medical Center; Trenton 1,280
Medical Center of Ocean County; Point Pleasant Beach 1,200
Helene Fuld Medical Center; Trenton 1,200
Township of Brick/Board of Education; Brick 1,140
Falcon Mfg. Inc.; Trenton; refrigeration 1,000
State of New Jersey/Health Dept.; Trenton 1,000
Trenton State College; Trenton 946
Paco Pharmaceutical Services; Lakewood; pharmaceuticals 900
American Standard Inc./Trane Co. Div.; Trenton; plumbing/heating 900
Township of Hamilton; Trenton 825
Fluid Packaging Co. Inc.; Lakewood; packaging services 800
Building Maintenance Systems; Trenton; building services 800
State of New Jersey; Trenton 670
IMO Industries Inc./Delavel Turbine Div.; Trenton; engines/turbines 650
Hamilton Hospital Inc.; Trenton 615
New Jersey Transit Corp.; Point Pleasant Beach; railroads 600
Township of Jackson/Board of Education; Jackson 600
State of New Jersey/Federation Tax Administration; Trenton 600
Township of Howell/Board of Education; Howell 563
Frequency Engineering Labs Corp.; Farmingdale; glass products 560

County of Mercer/Social Services; Trenton 550

State of New Jersey/Youth Reception Correction Center; Trenton 525

State of New Jersey/Environmental Protection Dept.; Trenton 500

5th District

North and West — Ridgewood

The 5th has little in common with the stereotype of New Jersey as a state within a turnpike. In fact, the New Jersey Turnpike actually stops short of entering the district in Bergen County.

This is one of the state's least densely packed districts, stretching from Warren County north to the New York border, then all the way across the northern tier to the Hudson River. No municipality has more than 30,000 residents. It includes some of the state's most scenic, wealthy and Republican areas.

Northern Bergen County provides the bulk of the vote. These affluent voters are so heavily Republican that Democrats often have a hard time finding sacrificial candidates to run in legislative races. Ronald Reagan captured 70 percent here in 1984; four years later, George Bush racked up 66 percent. Bush had a tougher time in 1992 but managed to win with 50 percent.

Property values and income levels are among the highest in the state. Alpine is home to sports stars and celebrities; Saddle River is where Richard M. Nixon resides. Less famous denizens include the corporate executives and white-collar New York commuters who live in places such as Ridgewood and Oradell. It is only fitting that the company that makes the car of choice for many upscale buyers—BMW—keeps its U.S. headquarters in Woodcliff Lake. Park Ridge also serves as a corporate headquarters site.

In his too-close-for-comfort 1990 re-election bid, Democratic Sen. Bill Bradley ran poorly in these areas. He lost Bergen County—as well as the rest of the district. Voters were equally hostile to Bill Clinton in 1992: George Bush won 50 percent in the 5th District portion of Bergen.

The rest of the population lives in Warren County and in parts of Passaic and Sussex counties. The mountains of Warren and affluent Sussex counties are dotted with sparsely populated small towns. Phillipsburg, situated across the Delaware River from Easton, Pa., has some industry and is Warren County's only town with as many as 15,000 residents.

The scenic backcountry of western Sussex attracts some tourists, especially around the Delaware Water Gap region. Much of the county remains rural, despite experiencing a 13 percent jump in population in the 1980s as affluent, young professionals stretched the New York metropolitan orbit even farther west.

The small towns and boroughs of Sussex are much like those in Warren, but even more Republican. In 1992, GOP Rep. Marge Roukema won 72 percent in Sussex County and went on to win the district by as much. Bush won here by more than 2-to-1. The less-populous portion of upper Passaic County contributes four municipalities to the 5th. It is more Republican and less industrialized than its southern section, which is mostly in the 8th District. It includes West Milford township, which, at about 25,000 in population, barely beats out suburban Paramus (Bergen County) as the 5th's most populous.

Election Returns

	5th District	Democrat	Republican
1992	President*	99,733 (33.9%)	146,004 (49.6%)
	House	67,579 (24.6%)	196,198 (71.5%)
1990	Senate	73,670 (42.7%)	98,682 (57.3%)
1989	Governor	95,887 (50.9%)	92,340 (49.1%)
1988	President	90,966 (33.8%)	178,466 (66.2%)
	Senate	119,426 (45.7%)	142,023 (54.3%)

Vote for Perot was 48,666 (16.5%).

Demographics

Population 594,630

Percent change from 1980 13.0%

Land area 1,076 square miles

Population per square mile 553

Counties, 1990 population
Bergen (pt.) 351,588	Sussex (pt.) 86,037
Passaic (pt.) 65,398	Warren 91,607

Cities, 1990 population (10,000 or more)
Bergenfield 24,458	Ramsey 13,228
Dumont 17,187	Ridgewood 24,152
Glen Rock 10,883	Ringwood 12,623
Hawthorne 17,084	Tenafly 13,326
Oakland 11,997	West Milford CDP 25,430
Paramus 25,067	Westwood 10,446
Phillipsburg 15,757	Wyckoff CDP 15,372

Race and Hispanic origin
White 93.5%
Black 1.3%
American Indian, Eskimo, or Aleut. 0.2%
Asian or Pacific Islander 4.5%
Other 0.5%
Hispanic origin 2.8%

Ancestry
American 2.6%	Italian 22.1%
Austrian 1.1%	Norwegian 1.1%
Dutch 5.5%	Polish 7.6%
English 11.2%	Russian 3.8%
French 2.7%	Scotch Irish 1.3%
German 24.6%	Scottish 2.3%
Greek 1.2%	Slovakian 1.5%
Hungarian 2.3%	Swedish 1.4%
Irish 22.8%	

Universities/colleges, 1990-1991 enrollment
Bergen Community College, Paramus 12,119
Centenary College, Hackettstown 846
Ramapo College of New Jersey, Mahwah 4,525
Sussex Community College, Newton 1,946
Warren Community College, Washington 1,232

Newspapers, total circulation (in all districts)
Easton Express-Times 41,761
Hackensack Record 164,181
Jersey City Journal 66,241

Newark Star Ledger 473,730
New Jersey Herald 17,480
New York Daily News 757,053
New York Post 551,443
New York Times 746,924
North Jersey Herald & News 68,167

Commercial television stations, affiliations
ADI: New York (100%)

Cable television systems, total subscribers
Cablevision of New Jersey; Bergenfield 40,800
Sammons Communications Inc.; Mine Hill 55,530
Sammons Communications of Pennsylvania Inc.; Easton 27,115
Service Electric Cable TV/New Jersey; Sussex 33,000
Storer Cable TV Inc.; Port Murray 20,817
TKR Cable of Warwick; Warwick 17,100
UA Cablesystems of New Jersey; Wayne 192,000

Businesses and other major employers
Bergen Pines County Hospital; Paramus 2,153
Valley Hospital; Ridgewood 2,000
Macy's Northeast Inc.; Paramus; department stores 1,500
City of Ridgewood/Board of Education; Ridgewood 1,500
United Parcel Service Corp.; Mahwah; mail services 1,300
IBM Corp.; Montvale; computer services 1,300
Nordstrom Inc.; Paramus; family clothing stores 1,200
Pascack Valley Hospital Assn.; Westwood 1,200
Butler Telecom Group; Montvale; engineering services 1,018
Ingersoll-Rand Co.; Phillipsburg; pumps/equipment 1,000
Selective Insurance Group Inc.; Branchville; fire/marine/casualty insurance 1,000
IMB Corp./National Service Div.; Franklin Lakes; business services 1,000
Federated Dept. Stores/Abraham & Strauss; Paramus; department stores 950
Sony Corp. of America; Park Ridge; electrical goods 900
Sharp Electronics Corp.; Mahwah; office/commercial equipment 900
Burns & Roe Holdings Inc.; Oradell; engineering/architectural services 900
County of Bergen; Paramus 850
Hoffmann-La Roche Inc.; Belvidere; pharmaceuticals 800
Becton Dickinson & Co.; Franklin Lakes; medical instruments/supplies 800
New Valley Corp.; Saddle River; telegraph/other communications 750
Great Atlantic & Pacific Tea Co. Inc.; Montvale; grocery stores 750
Simon & Schuster Inc./Prentice-Hall; Westwood; book publishing 750
Newton Memorial Hospital; Newton 715
Eagle Industries Inc./Elastimold Div.; Hackettstown; electric lighting 700
Mars Inc./M&M Mars Div.; Hackettstown; candies 700
Gogo Tours Inc.; Ramsey; travel agencies 700
Warren Hospital; Phillipsburg 700
National Medical Care Inc./Medical Products Div.; Northvale; professional/commercial equipment 675
Volvo North America Corp.; Northvale; auto sales 650
Bergen Nursing Team Inc.; Westwood; home health services 650
City of Westwood/Board of Education; Westwood 650

KPMG Peat Marwick; Montvale; accounting/auditing 650
Hertz Corp.; Park Ridge; automotive rentals 620
MEM Co. Inc.; Northvale; toiletries/cosmetics 600
Loving Hands Healthcare Agency; Oradell; personnel supply services 600
Ramapo College of New Jersey; Mahwah 600
Melville Corp./Meldisco Div.; Mahwah; management offices 600
Bergen Community College; Paramus 580
Toys R Us Inc./Kids R Us; Paramus; retail stores 560
United Air Lines Inc.; Northvale; airlines 550

6th District

Central — Part of Edison; New Brunswick; Long Branch

From industrial Middlesex County to the shore communities of Monmouth County, the 6th is one of the most competitive districts in the state. This mostly middle-class and independent-voting slice of New Jersey is a crucial component of any successful statewide effort.

The 1992 presidential campaign emphasized the district's competitive nature. Both Bill Clinton and George Bush made concerted efforts here, but in the Monmouth County portion, neither could gain a decisive advantage: Bush won by about 1,100 votes. In 1984 and 1988, Ronald Reagan and George Bush won the 6th, respectively, but in 1989, Democrat James J. Florio carried the district with 56 percent in his successful gubernatorial bid.

Jobs and the economy are pressing issues in Middlesex County, where almost 60 percent of the district population comes from 13 towns. Democrats traditionally run well in the county, though more recently, residents have shown few qualms about splitting tickets.

Edison—a part of which is in the 7th District—is the largest city in the district, and home to some manufacturing concerns and corporate headquarters. Some of Edison's white-collar employees live nearby in Metuchen.

Black voters and the Rutgers University community boost Democrats in New Brunswick. Across the Raritan River, Republicans are competitive in more affluent Piscataway and Highland Park. Suburban ticket-splitting and independent voting is more prevalent in populous Old Bridge and Sayreville.

The inland portion of Monmouth County is suburban, and less affluent and Republican than the rest of the county, which is divided into the 4th, 6th and 12th districts. In the 4th and 12th parts, Republicans carried the House and presidential races relatively easily. But in the 6th's, Bush barely squeaked by, while the Democratic House candidate won by more than 7,000 votes.

Most of the suburban, Republican turf of Middletown—the largest town in Monmouth County—is in the 6th, but a part of it is in the 12th District. Working-class Red Bank is fertile ground for Democrats.

In coastal Monmouth County, the environment weighs heavily in political debates. Ocean dumping, beach erosion and hurricane protection are matters of import to locals. The coastal region begins with the Sandy Hook part of the Gateway National Recreation Area, which extends like a thin finger from the top of Monmouth County.

Farther south, the shore communities used to attract the 19th-century elite. President James A. Garfield was brought to his summer cottage in Long Branch in 1881 after he was shot; he died there a few weeks later. The aging seaside resort of Asbury Park—glorified by singer and local hero Bruce Springsteen—has faded in prominence. The black community in Asbury Park helps keep it in the Democratic column. Deal is a wealthier, residential community.

Election Returns

	6th District	Democrat	Republican
1992	President*	110,821 (44.2%)	98,397 (39.2%)
	House	118,266 (52.3%)	100,949 (44.6%)
1990	Senate	74,525 (51.6%)	69,784 (48.4%)
1989	Governor	107,304 (63.0%)	63,049 (37.0%)
1988	President	103,801 (44.0%)	131,930 (56.0%)
	Senate	124,603 (55.0%)	101,971 (45.0%)

*Vote for Perot was 41,646 (16.6%).

Demographics

Population 594,630

Percent change from 1980 13.5%

Land area 202 square miles

Population per square mile 2,947

Counties, 1990 population
Middlesex (pt.) 344,661   Monmouth (pt.) 249,969

Cities, 1990 population (10,000 or more)

Asbury Park 16,799	North Brunswick CDP
Edison CDP (pt.) 63,996	31,287
Highland Park 13,279	Old Bridge CDP 22,151
Keansburg 11,069	Red Bank 10,636
Long Branch 28,658	Sayreville 34,986
Metuchen 12,804	South River 13,692
New Brunswick 41,711	

Race and Hispanic origin
White 81.8%
Black 11.2%
American Indian, Eskimo, or Aleut. 0.2%
Asian or Pacific Islander 4.8%
Other 2.0%
Hispanic origin 6.1%

Ancestry

American 2.0%	Italian 19.3%
Dutch 1.6%	Polish 10.6%
English 7.6%	Russian 3.4%
French 2.2%	Scotch Irish 1.1%
German 17.8%	Scottish 1.6%
Hungarian 3.4%	Slovakian 2.0%
Irish 22.4%	Ukrainian 1.0%

Universities/colleges, 1990-1991 enrollment
Middlesex County College, Edison 11,019
Rutgers University, New Brunswick 33,023

Newspapers, total circulation (in all districts)
Asbury Park Press 162,357
Bridgewater Courier News 51,108

Newark Star Ledger 473,730
New Brunswick Home News 51,098
New York Daily News 757,053
New York Post 551,443
New York Times 746,924
Trentonian 72,634
Trenton Times 82,521
Woodbridge News Tribune 53,185

Commercial television stations, affiliations
ADI: New York (100%)

Cable television systems, total subscribers
Monmouth Cablevision East; Wall 30,043
Storer Cable TV Inc.; East Keansburg 24,676
Storer Cable TV Inc.; Eatontown 36,710
TKR Cable; Warren 71,632
TKR Cable; Metuchen 46,770
TKR Cable; Parlin 11,904

Military installations, 1991
Fort Monmouth (Army), Red Bank (shared with the 12th District) 10,558
Earle Naval Weapons Station, Colts Neck (shared with the 12th District) 3,825

Businesses and other major employers
Rutgers University; New Brunswick 8,000
University of Medicine; New Brunswick 5,000
Revlon Inc.; Edison; cosmetics 4,000
E. R. Squibb & Sons Inc./Bristol-Myers Squibb Co.; New Brunswick; pharmaceuticals 3,000
University of Medicine; Piscataway; research services 2,500
Robert Wood Johnson University Hospital; New Brunswick 2,410
United Parcel Service; Edison; mail services 2,400
AT&T Co.; Piscataway; telephone communications 2,400
Community Hospital Group Inc./J. F. K. Medical Center; Edison 2,400
Riverview Medical Center; Red Bank 1,990
Monmouth Medical Center; Long Branch 1,975
Jersey Shore Medical Center; Neptune 1,875
White Consolidated Industries/Frigidaire Co.; Edison; air conditioners 1,800
St. Peter's Medical Center; New Brunswick 1,784
Noxell Corp./Max Factor & Co.; Edison; toiletries/cosmetics 1,500
Bell Communications Research/Bellcore; Piscataway; computer services 1,385
Ford Motor Co.; Edison; motor vehicle assembly 1,200
Township of Middletown/Board of Education; Middletown 1,200
Township of Edison/Board of Education; Edison 1,200
Staff Builders Healthcare; New Brunswick; home health services 1,200
County of Middlesex; New Brunswick 1,100
Township of Piscataway/Board of Education; Piscataway 1,100
Twin County Grocers Inc./Alpine Distributors Div.; Edison; grocery products 1,050
Du Pont E. I. De Nemours & Co./Imaging Systems; Parlin; professional/commercial equipment 1,000
Johnson & Johnson; New Brunswick; toiletries 1,000
Macy's Northeast Inc.; Edison; department stores 1,000

First Fidelity Bank of New Jersey; New Brunswick; commercial banks 1,000

Roosevelt Hospital; Edison 1,000

Home Life Insurance Co.; Piscataway; security brokers 941

Asbury Park Press/Addresses Unlimited; Neptune; newspapers 900

Sunshine Biscuits Inc.; Sayreville; bakery products 900

Union Carbide Chemical & Plastic Co.; Piscataway; chemical products 890

Continental Insurance Co.; Neptune; computer services 865

Hercules Inc.; Parlin; chemical products 750

IBM Corp.; Edison; computer equipment 700

City of New Brunswick/Board of Education; New Brunswick 700

City of New Brunswick/Fire Dept.; New Brunswick 680

MCI Intl. Inc.; Piscataway; telephone communications 675

Middlesex County College; Edison 660

Aqualon Co.; Parlin; organic chemicals 650

Phillips-Van Heusen Corp.; Piscataway; apparel 635

Sea-Land Service Inc.; Edison; freight shipping 600

City of Long Branch/Board of Education; Long Branch 600

Township of Old Bridge; Old Bridge 600

Kimberly-Clark Corp.; Spotswood; paper mills 590

U.S. Life; Neptune; life insurance 575

ISS Intl. Service System; New Brunswick; building services 562

Inn America Hospitality; Edison; real estate operators 550

Prudential Insurance of America Inc.; Edison; investment offices 525

Township of Neptune/Board of Education; Neptune 510

South Amboy Hospital Assn.; South Amboy 508

7th District

North and Central — Parts of Woodbridge and Union

Before GOP Rep. Matthew J. Rinaldo unexpectedly announced his post-primary retirement in 1992, it was assumed that he would easily win re-election to the Republican 7th. Redistricting removed urban, industrial and Democratic Elizabeth, though it had hardly been a problem for Rinaldo in the past since the Republican suburbs usually drowned out Elizabeth's vote.

After Rinaldo dropped out, Democrats harbored illusions that they might pull an upset here in the open race, only to be doused with a splash of reality: The Democratic nominee managed only 43 percent. Republican Bob Franks carried all the parts of four counties that make up the 7th—Essex, Middlesex, Somerset and Union.

Franks' open-seat victory was presaged by previous election results in the 7th: In 1984, Ronald Reagan won 64 percent and four years later, George Bush captured 60 percent. In the open 1989 gubernatorial race, the Republican nominee carried the district with 51 percent, though he won just 37 percent statewide.

Roughly half the vote is cast in Union County. Predominantly black and Democratic Plainfield is the most-populous place in the Union County portion, followed closely by Union township (a small part of Union township is in the 10th District). Plainfield was one of the first of New Jersey's cities to explode in the riots of 1967.

North of Plainfield, the towns are mostly suburban, white and Republican. Summit, Westfield and Cranford are bedroom communities for New York City and Newark.

About a quarter of the population comes from each of Middlesex and Somerset counties. Middlesex only contributes two whole municipalities and parts of two others, but they constitute a significant voting bloc. It includes most of New Jersey's largest suburb, middle-class Woodbridge, along with part of Edison. (Most of Edison is in the neighboring 6th District.) Woodbridge experienced explosive growth between 1950 and 1970; it is now larger than Camden.

Farther west, in southern Somerset County, corporate and industrial growth along Interstate 287 and U.S. 22 has led to growth in Bridgewater and Hillsborough.

Somerset generally backs Republican candidates. In 1990, the GOP Senate challenger carried the county over Democratic Sen. Bill Bradley. But Democratic votes can be found in the industrial boroughs, such as Manville and Bound Brook, to the south.

The Johns-Manville plant that gave Manville its name attracted large numbers of Poles and other Slavic immigrants in the 1930s and 1940s. By 1982, though, the company was forced to file for bankruptcy after being slapped with tens of thousands of asbestos-related lawsuits. In 1985, the factory shut down.

A small section of western Essex County is also grafted onto the 7th. It adds parts of two towns, Maplewood and affluent Millburn.

Election Returns

		Democrat	Republican
	7th District		
1992	President*	115,846 (41.1%)	125,592 (44.5%)
	House	105,761 (42.6%)	132,174 (53.3%)
1990	Senate	78,569 (47.8%)	85,775 (52.2%)
1989	Governor	110,568 (58.5%)	78,577 (41.5%)
1988	President	108,389 (40.5%)	159,199 (59.5%)
	Senate	137,307 (52.4%)	124,903 (47.6%)

*Vote for Perot was 40,708 (14.4%).

Demographics

Population 594,629

Percent change from 1980 13.1%

Land area 273 square miles

Population per square mile 2,175

Counties, 1990 population

Essex (pt.) 21,742	Somerset (pt.) 148,090
Middlesex (pt.) 144,768	Union (pt.) 280,029

Cities, 1990 population (10,000 or more)

Avenel CDP 15,504	North Plainfield 18,820
Berkeley Heights CDP 11,980	Plainfield 46,567
	Roselle Park 12,805
Clark CDP 14,629	Scotch Plains CDP 21,160
Colonia CDP 18,238	Somerset CDP 22,070
Cranford CDP 22,624	South Plainfield 20,489
Edison CDP (pt.) 24,684	Springfield CDP 13,420
Fords CDP 14,392	Summit 19,757
Iselin CDP 16,141	Union CDP (pt.) 45,371
Manville 10,567	Westfield 28,870
Middlesex 13,055	Woodbridge CDP (pt.) 17,309
Millburn CDP (pt.) 18,221	
New Providence 11,439	

Race and Hispanic origin

White 83.6%
Black 10.2%
American Indian, Eskimo, or Aleut. 0.1%
Asian or Pacific Islander 4.6%
Other 1.5%
Hispanic origin 5.0%

Ancestry

American 2.0%	Italian 20.2%
Austrian 1.1%	Polish 11.4%
Dutch 1.5%	Russian 4.2%
English 8.4%	Scotch Irish 1.1%
French 2.0%	Scottish 1.8%
German 18.7%	Slovakian 2.6%
Hungarian 3.1%	Ukrainian 1.7%
Irish 17.4%	

Universities/colleges, 1990-1991 enrollment

DeVry Technical Institute, Woodbridge 1,990
Kean College of New Jersey, Union 13,307
Union County College, Cranford 9,981

Newspapers, total circulation (in all districts)

Asbury Park Press 162,357
Bridgewater Courier News 51,108
Newark Star Ledger 473,730
New Brunswick Home News 51,098
New York Daily News 757,053
New York Post 551,443
New York Times 746,924
North Jersey Herald & News 68,167
Trentonian 72,634
Trenton Times 82,521
Woodbridge News Tribune 53,185

Commercial television stations, affiliations

ADI: New York (100%)

Cable television systems, total subscribers

C-Tec; Belle Mead 23,484
Storer Cable TV Inc.; Plainfield 17,900
Suburban Cablevision; Verona 134,660
Suburban Cablevision; Woodbridge 91,280
TKR Cable; Warren 71,632
TKR Cable; Metuchen 46,770

Businesses and other major employers

Wong Seechung; Summit; pharmaceuticals 2,500
Ethicon Inc.; Somerville; medical instruments/supplies 2,500
Overlook Hospital Assn.; Summit 2,449
Schering-Plough Corp.; Kenilworth; industry machinery 2,300
Federal Insurance Co.; Plainfield; fire/marine/casualty insurance 2,100
Ciba-Geigy Corp.; Summit; pharmaceuticals 2,000
Merrill Lynch & Co. Inc.; Somerset; security brokers 2,000
Amerada Hess Corp./Hess Oil Virgin Islands Corp.; Woodbridge; petroleum refining 1,750
Muhlenberg Regional Medical Center; Plainfield 1,740
Township of Woodbridge/Board of Education; Woodbridge 1,500
Spartus Holdings Inc.; Iselin; watches/clocks 1,450
Schering Corp.; Union; pharmaceuticals 1,400
Kean College of New Jersey; Union 1,280

State of New Jersey/Human Services Dept.; Woodbridge 1,200
County of Somerset; Somerville 1,200
AT&T Co.; Plainfield; telephone communications 1,200
BOC Group Inc./Airco Industrial Gases Div.; New Providence; inorganic chemicals 1,000
Union Hospital; Union 950
Prudential Insurance of America Inc.; Iselin; insurance services 935
Engelhard Corp.; Iselin; inorganic chemicals 900
Siemens Medical Systems Inc.; Iselin; medical equipment 900
Cosmair Inc.; Rahway; hair preparations 900
Indopco Inc./National Starch & Chemical Co.; Somerville; chemical products 900
Supermarkets General Corp./Pathmark; Woodbridge; grocery stores 900
Carrier Foundation Inc.; Belle Mead 872
Reed Publishing Inc./R. R. Bowker Div.; New Providence; book publishing 800
Prudential Insurance of America Inc.; South Plainfield; insurance services 800
Federated/Abraham & Straus; Woodbridge; department stores 800
Sears Roebuck & Co.; Plainfield; department stores 800
World Book Inc.; Middlesex; book publishing 750
Wackenhut Services Inc.; Somerset; business/security services 650
City of Scotch Plains/Board of Education; Scotch Plains 650
Harvard Industries Inc.; Union; hardware 600
Penn-Del Inc.; Somerset; advertising 600
Fair Oaks Hospital; Summit 600
City of Westfield/Board of Education; Westfield 573
Fleming Food East Inc./Royal Food Distributors; Woodbridge; grocery products 550
United Parcel Service Inc.; Bound Brook; mail services 550
City of Plainfield; Plainfield 550
Tuscan Dairy Farms Inc.; Union; dairy products 540
Emerson Quiet Kool Corp.; Woodbridge; refrigeration 520
Union County College; Cranford 520

8th District

North — Paterson

After surveying the Great Falls of the Passaic River in the late 18th century, Treasury Secretary Alexander Hamilton figured it would be an ideal place to develop some homegrown industry, independent of England. So he created the Society for Establishing Useful Manufactures to build facilities to harness the water power in Paterson.

The industrial complex was slow to develop, but by the mid-19th century, Paterson had attracted a wave of English, Irish and Dutch immigrants to staff its silk mills. A second wave would bring Italians, Poles and Slavs to work the looms.

Hamilton's vision thrived, and "Silk City" (as Paterson became known) developed into one of the world's leading textile producers. But the introduction of rayon and other 20th-century synthetic fabrics triggered an economic freefall from which the city has never fully recovered. Today, Paterson suffers from chronic unemployment and the side effects of industrial decline.

Though the jobs left, Paterson's (Passaic County) minority population increased: Blacks and Hispanics currently make up 74 percent. Combined with the city's strong labor tradition, Paterson turns out a reliable Democratic vote.

The city of Passaic is a smaller but equally troubled version of Paterson. For a Democrat to win the district, the candidate must carry both cities handily. That is no small task, especially in Paterson, where voter turnout and registration is low.

The white ethnics who left these cities moved to Passaic County suburbs such as Wayne and Clifton, one of New Jersey's largest and oldest suburban communities.

Along with suburban Essex County voters, these suburbanites keep GOP candidates competitive. The Essex County portion—about a third of the 8th's population—is mainly suburban turf, from the more affluent areas such as Montclair and South Orange to the blue-collar and middle-class towns of Nutley and Belleville. Italian Catholics make up a notable segment; there are also pockets of Jewish voters.

Democrats hold the edge in districtwide registration, but they usually run best at the local and statewide levels. In 1989, Democrat James J. Florio won the district in his successful gubernatorial bid. At the presidential level, the GOP often flexes its muscle: In 1984, Ronald Reagan racked up 59 percent and in 1988, George Bush won 55 percent.

Essex is one of New Jersey's traditional Democratic strongholds, and its party politics are rife with the usual internecine battles. The 8th District portion does not include the Democratic stronghold of Newark, but the county's Democratic machine still casts a long shadow.

Bloomfield, Essex County's largest city in the 8th, even managed to play a role in the 1988 presidential election. It was at a local flag factory that Bush met with the local makers of Old Glory, in order to publicize the controversy surrounding Democratic nominee Michael S. Dukakis and the Pledge of Allegiance.

Election Returns

	8th District	Democrat	Republican
1992	President*	107,304 (45.6%)	99,974 (42.5%)
	House†	96,742 (47.0%)	84,674 (41.1%)
1990	Senate	65,408 (51.4%)	61,881 (48.6%)
1989	Governor	101,859 (62.7%)	60,656 (37.3%)
1988	President	102,035 (45.5%)	122,073 (54.5%)
	Senate	121,369 (57.2%)	90,828 (42.8%)

*Vote for Perot was 27,797 (11.8%).   †Independent/other is greater than 5%.

Demographics

Population 594,629

Percent change from 1980 13.0%

Land area 104 square miles

Population per square mile 5,691

Counties, 1990 population
Essex (pt.) 214,497   Passaic (pt.) 380,132

Cities, 1990 population (10,000 or more)

Belleville CDP 34,213	Little Falls CDP 11,294
Bloomfield CDP 45,061	Maplewood CDP (pt.)
Cedar Grove CDP 12,053	14,067
Clifton 71,742	Montclair CDP (pt.) 21,011

Nutley CDP 27,099	Totowa 10,177
Passaic 58,041	Verona CDP 13,597
Paterson 140,891	Wayne CDP 47,025
Pompton Lakes 10,539	West Orange CDP (pt.)
South Orange CDP (pt.)	28,183
12,137	West Paterson 10,982

Race and Hispanic origin
White 74.7%
Black 13.0%
American Indian, Eskimo, or Aleut. 0.2%
Asian or Pacific Islander 3.6%
Other 8.6%
Hispanic origin 17.8%

Ancestry

American 2.2%	Italian 23.1%
Arabic 1.5%	Polish 7.4%
Dutch 2.9%	Russian 3.3%
English 5.5%	Scottish 1.3%
French 1.4%	Slovakian 1.4%
German 11.8%	Ukrainian 1.1%
Hungarian 1.5%	West Indian 1.0%
Irish 12.7%	

Universities/colleges, 1990-1991 enrollment
Berkeley College of Business, West Paterson 1,447
Bloomfield College, Bloomfield 1,649
Montclair State College, Montclair 13,074
Passaic County Community College, Paterson 3,273
William Paterson College of New Jersey, Wayne 10,041
Seton Hall University, South Orange 9,929

Newspapers, total circulation (in all districts)
Hackensack Record 164,181
Newark Star Ledger 473,730
New York Daily News 757,053
New York Post 551,443
New York Times 746,924
North Jersey Herald & News 68,167

Commercial television stations, affiliations
ADI: New York (100%)

Cable television systems, total subscribers
Cablevision of Newark; Newark 41,902
Suburban Cablevision; Verona 134,660
UA Cablesystems of New Jersey; Wayne 192,000
US Cable of Paterson; Paterson 21,802

Businesses and other major employers
Hoffmann-La Roche Inc.; Newark; pharmaceuticals 6,500
St. Joseph's Hospital & Medical Center; Paterson 3,155
City of Paterson/Board of Education; Paterson 3,055
ITT Corp./Avionics Div.; Clifton; search/navigation equipment 3,000
County of Passaic; Paterson 3,000
Kearfott Guidance Navigation Corp; Wayne; guided missiles 2,679
ITT Corp./Avionics Div.; Newark; communications equipment 2,500
American Cyanamid Co.; Wayne; pharmaceuticals 2,500
M. Fortunoff of Westbury Corp.; Wayne; department stores 2,500
City of Paterson; Paterson 1,701
General Hospital Center; Passaic 1,600

CEC Marconi Electronic Systems Corp.; Wayne; navigation
equipment 1,500
Clara Maass Medical Center; Newark 1,500
Professional Security Bureau Ltd.; Newark; security services
1,200
Montclair State College; Montclair 1,200
State of New Jersey/Developmental Center; Paterson; nurs-
ing 1,100
Township of Wayne/Board of Education; Wayne 1,046
Essex County Hospital Center; Cedar Grove 1,016
Astronautics Corp. of America/Kearfott Guidance Navigation
Div.; Little Falls; aircraft parts 1,000
State Farm Mutual Auto Insurance Co.; Wayne; fire/marine/
casualty insurance 1,000
Automatic Data Processing; Clifton; computer services 1,000
William Paterson College of New Jersey; Wayne 1,000
Schering Corp.; Bloomfield; organic chemicals 870
U.S. Postal Service; Paterson 850
Seton Hall University; South Orange 825
Barnert Memorial Hospital Center; Paterson 820
City of Clifton/Board of Education; Clifton 800
Payrolling Partners Inc.; Clifton; management services 800
Wayne General Hospital Corp.; Wayne 800
CPC Intl. Inc./Best Foods; Paterson; bakery products 750
GAF Corp.; Wayne; organic chemicals 750
Beth Israel Hospital Assn.; Passaic 750
St. Mary's Hospital; Passaic 737
New Jersey Transit Bus Operations; Maplewood; bus ser-
vices 705
Wallace & Tiernan Inc.; Newark; industry machinery 700
Drake Bakeries; Wayne; sugar 700
Macy's Northeast Inc.; Wayne; department stores 700
Givaudan Corp.; Clifton; toiletries 650
Board of Education of South Orange; Maplewood 625
Public Service Electric & Gas Co.; Clifton; utility services 600
Grand Union Co.; Wayne; grocery stores 600
Town & Campus Inc.; Orange; bars/restaurants 580
City of Clifton; Clifton 575
City of Passaic; Passaic 512

9th District

North — Fort Lee; Hackensack

Sports fans and concertgoers are familiar with the Meadowlands stadium complex in East Rutherford, but otherwise, there
is little to distinguish the 9th from other suburban New Jersey
districts.

By one measure—money—the 9th stands out. With more
than half the population of Bergen County, one of the country's
wealthiest counties, the district is more affluent than its suburban
and urbanized north Jersey counterparts.

It covers southeastern Bergen County and part of Hudson
County, with prestigious Bergen addresses clustered in Englewood and the northern reaches of the 9th. The blue-collar areas
are in the south.

The George Washington Bridge, connecting Manhattan's 181st
Street and the New Jersey Palisades, is a fitting symbol for the 9th.
Opened in 1931, the span spurred the growth of Bergen County.

South of posh Englewood, Fort Lee is home to affluent Asian
Americans, including a thriving Japanese community. Farther
west from the Hudson River, the Jewish voters of Teaneck and

Fair Lawn—part of which is in the 5th District—help turn out a
Democratic vote, despite the towns' relative affluence. Hackensack has some affluent sections, but is more blue-collar, with a
large black population.

Beginning south of the city of Hackensack, the Hackensack
Meadowlands area is a 30-mile commercial and residential
engine, experiencing increasing development amid the swamps
of the region.

The southern reaches of the 9th contain working-class towns
with large numbers of white ethnics, in places such as North
Arlington, Lyndhurst and Kearny (Hudson County). Most of
Kearny is in the 9th, with the exception of about 300 residents
who live in the 13th.

Hudson County contributes about a fifth of the district
population and contains a mix of Hispanics and white ethnics,
drawn from parts of Jersey City, Kearny, North Bergen and all of
Secaucus.

The Jersey City segment is carved from the northern part of
the city; it includes many Hispanics. The 9th is one of three
districts that splice into Jersey City, the other two being the
majority-minority 10th and 13th districts.

The 9th has no single dominant industry. Englewood Cliffs
houses some corporate headquarters; Secaucus has attracted new
restaurants, offices, hotels and shopping outlets. It is also a
warehousing and distribution center.

The politics of the 9th are firmly Democratic, but the 9th
District portion does not include the rock-ribbed Republican
communities on the northern tier.

In 1992, Bill Clinton won 48 percent in this part of Bergen.
The successful Democratic House candidate carried Bergen by
almost 42,000 votes at the same time, against a highly touted
GOP challenger.

Election Returns

	9th District	Democrat	Republican
1992	President*	122,676 (47.8%)	102,578 (39.9%)
	House	139,188 (58.3%)	88,179 (36.9%)
1990	Senate	88,262 (57.1%)	66,300 (42.9%)
1989	Governor	121,907 (66.8%)	60,524 (33.2%)
1988	President	128,988 (48.2%)	138,345 (51.8%)
	Senate	152,427 (59.9%)	102,140 (40.1%)

Vote for Perot was 31,527 (12.3%).

Demographics

Population 594,630

Percent change from 1980 12.8%

Land area 93 square miles

Population per square mile 6,426

Counties, 1990 population
Bergen (pt.) 473,792   Hudson (pt.) 120,838

Cities, 1990 population (10,000 or more)
Cliffside Park 20,393   Fairview 10,733
Elmwood Park 17,623   Fort Lee 31,997
Englewood 24,850   Garfield 26,727
Fair Lawn (pt.) 23,058   Hackensack 37,049

Hasbrouck Heights 11,488
Jersey City (pt.) 52,668
Kearny (pt.) 34,603
Lodi 22,355
Lyndhurst CDP 18,262
New Milford 15,990
North Arlington 13,790
North Bergen CDP (pt.) 19,506
Palisades Park 14,536
Ridgefield Park 12,454
River Edge 10,603
Rutherford 17,790
Saddle Brook CDP 13,296
Secaucus 14,061
Teaneck CDP 37,825
Wallington 10,828

Race and Hispanic origin
White 83.7%
Black 6.5%
American Indian, Eskimo, or Aleut 0.1%
Asian or Pacific Islander 6.6%
Other 3.1%
Hispanic origin 11.4%

Ancestry
American 2.0%
Arabic 1.1%
Austrian 1.1%
Dutch 1.4%
English 4.5%
French 1.6%
German 13.9%
Greek 1.5%
Hungarian 1.4%
Irish 15.4%
Italian 24.8%
Polish 9.6%
Russian 3.8%
Scottish 1.4%
Slovakian 1.4%
West Indian 1.0%

Universities/colleges, 1990-1991 enrollment
Fairleigh Dickinson University, Teaneck 11,790
Felician College, Lodi 730

Newspapers, total circulation (in all districts)
El Diario La Prensa (Spanish) 53,841
Hackensack Record 164,181
Jersey City Journal 66,241
Newark Star Ledger 473,730
New York Daily News 757,053
New York Post 551,443
New York Times 746,924
North Jersey Herald & News 68,167

Commercial television stations, affiliations
ADI: New York (100%)

Cable television systems, total subscribers
Cable TV of Jersey City; Jersey City 29,486
Comcast Cablevision; Lyndhurst 32,500
Suburban Cablevision; Verona 134,660
UA Cablesystems of New Jersey; Wayne 192,000
Vision Cable TV Co.; Palisades Park 45,000

Businesses and other major employers
Allied-Signal Inc./Test Systems Div.; Hackensack; motor vehicles/equipment 5,000
U.S. Postal Service; Jersey City 3,800
New Jersey Sports & Expo Authority; Rutherford; commercial sports 3,000
Hackensack Medical Center; Hackensack 2,700
United Parcel Service Inc.; Secaucus; mail services 2,200
Englewood Hospital; Englewood 2,200
Fairleigh Dickinson University; Teaneck 2,000
Metpath Inc.; Hackensack; medical/dental labs 1,800
Matsushita Electric Corp. America/Panasonic Co.; Secaucus; electrical goods 1,600
Macromedia Inc.; Hackensack; newspapers 1,533

Nabisco Brands Inc./Fair Lawn Bakery; Fair Lawn; bakery products 1,500
Holy Name Hospital Inc.; Teaneck 1,500
County of Bergen; Hackensack 1,500
United Parcel Service Inc.; Rochelle Park; mail services 1,400
Donaldson Lufkin Jenrette/Pershing; Jersey City; security brokers 1,400
Pfizer Hospital Products Group; Rutherford; medical instruments/supplies 1,300
Christ Hospital; Jersey City 1,200
Leaseway Customized Transport; Rutherford; trucking services 1,000
Marcal Paper Mills Inc.; Elmwood Park; paper products 1,000
Jamesway Corp.; Secaucus; department stores 1,000
Salomon Inc.; Rutherford; security brokers 1,000
MT&T Marine Services; Hackensack; personnel supply services 1,000
Colin Service Systems Inc.; Hackensack; building services 1,000
Conopco Inc./Thomas J. Lipton Div.; Englewood; food products 839
Keystone Freight Corp.; Secaucus; trucking services 800
Schiavone Construction Co.; Secaucus; heavy construction 800
Macmillan Inc./Maxwell Macmillan; Englewood; book publishing 800
UJB Financial Corp.; Ridgefield; holding offices 800
Bloomingdale's Inc.; Hackensack; department stores 800
United Jersey Bank; Hackensack; commercial banks 800
Popular Club Plan Inc.; Garfield; catalog retailers 800
Marine Personnel Provisioning; Secaucus; personnel supply services 800
Monarch Building Maintenance; Elmwood Park; building services 800
Meadowlands Hospital & Medical Center; Secaucus 777
West Hudson Hospital Assn.; Kearny 772
CPC Intl. Inc.; Englewood; grain mill products 750
Arrow Fastener Co. Inc.; Rochelle Park; office equipment 700
Hudson County Meadowview Hospital; Secaucus 625
City of Fair Lawn/Board of Education; Fair Lawn 625
City of Teaneck/Board of Education; Teaneck 620
Becton Dickinson & Co.; Rutherford; medical instruments/supplies 600
Petrie Stores Corp.; Secaucus; women's clothing stores 600
Palisades Medical Center; North Bergen 600
New York Times Co. Inc.; Rutherford; newspaper advertising 600
Public Service Electric & Gas Co./Pallisades Electric; Secaucus; electric services 534
Unilever U.S. Inc./Unilever Research; Edgewater; research services 520

10th District
Parts of Newark and Jersey City

At midcentury, Newark was a city of a nearly half-million people. Nine percent of the state's population lived here; it was a commercial center with about 15 percent of all New Jersey jobs.

Now, as the century winds down, Newark tells a different story. Population has declined to about 275,000. The city is still the most populous in the state—and the largest employment center—but its share of New Jersey's jobs is only about 4 percent.

The decade after the riots of the late 1960s saw a steep decline in the number of jobs and an increase in the number of whites moving out of the city. As the Irish and Italians who used to vie for political power fled to the suburbs, blacks became a majority, and accordingly, grabbed the reins of power at City Hall; an African American has held the mayoralty since 1970. Districtwide, blacks make up about 60 percent of the population.

Blacks and whites have lived an uneasy coexistence in Newark, but both communities are as one in their inurement to the political intrigue and ethical improprieties of local politics.

In political circles, Essex County Democrats have been stabbing each other in the back since the late 1970s, when the county switched to a county executive form of government, thus diminishing the influence of local party bosses.

Redistricting split the city between the 10th and 13th districts, but more than half the residents of Newark live in the 10th. The 10th District portion is made up of the primarily black central and south wards, with some Hispanics and Portuguese from the east ward.

The central ward was decimated in the riots of 1967 and has never fully recovered. There have been efforts to revitalize the area, but the desperate living conditions and deep poverty have changed little.

From Newark, the district extends into the Essex County suburbs that combine with the city to make up almost two-thirds of the district's population. Outside the city are some racially mixed, working-class suburbs such as Irvington and Montclair (which is shared with the 8th District).

Orange and populous East Orange are majority black. More affluent are South and liberal West Orange, although most of both places are in the 8th.

Union County adds a little more than a quarter of the vote. Democratic and blue-collar Elizabeth is a hefty chunk of this portion, even though it is divided between the 13th and the 10th. Republicans can find votes in Rahway and Roselle.

Parts of two Democratic Hudson County municipalities—Jersey City and Bayonne—round out the 10th. This section of Jersey City includes about one-fourth of New Jersey's second-largest city; the Bayonne segment consists of about 5,000 residents. Like virtually everywhere else in the district—which is far and away the most Democratic in the state—they churn out healthy Democratic margins.

Election Returns

	10th District	Democrat	Republican
1992	President*	125,922 (71.3%)	35,930 (20.3%)
	House	117,287 (78.4%)	30,160 (20.2%)
1990	Senate	63,588 (72.7%)	23,903 (27.3%)
1989	Governor	91,503 (78.9%)	24,516 (21.1%)
1988	President	159,645 (69.4%)	70,527 (30.6%)
	Senate	158,171 (73.9%)	55,843 (26.1%)

*Vote for Perot was 14,854 (8.4%).

Demographics

Population 594,630

Percent change from 1980 13.1%

Land area 55 square miles

Population per square mile 10,825

Counties, 1990 population
Essex (pt.) 369,818	Union (pt.) 166,198
Hudson (pt.) 58,614	

Cities, 1990 population (10,000 or more)
East Orange 73,552	Newark (pt.) 169,368
Elizabeth (pt.) 67,038	Orange CDP 29,925
Hillside CDP 21,044	Rahway 25,325
Irvington CDP (pt.) 59,774	Roselle 20,314
Jersey City (pt.) 53,495	West Orange CDP (pt.) 10,920
Linden (pt.) 27,824	
Montclair CDP (pt.) 16,718	

Race and Hispanic origin
White 32.6%
Black 60.2%
American Indian, Eskimo, or Aleut 0.3%
Asian or Pacific Islander 2.4%
Other 4.5%
Hispanic origin 12.3%

Ancestry
American 1.4%	Polish 4.1%
English 1.7%	Portuguese 1.6%
German 4.6%	Subsaharan African 1.1%
Irish 5.6%	West Indian 4.2%
Italian 6.6%	

Universities/colleges, 1990-1991 enrollment
Essex County College, Newark 6,710
Jersey City State College, Jersey City 7,691
Katherine Gibbs School, Montclair 240
New Jersey Institute of Technology, Newark 7,670
Rutgers University, Newark 9,343
University of Medicine and Dentistry of New Jersey, Newark 3,215
Upsala College, East Orange 1,139

Newspapers, total circulation (in all districts)
Bridgewater Courier News 51,108
El Diario La Prensa (Spanish) 53,841
Hackensack Record 164,181
Jersey City Journal 66,241
Newark Star Ledger 473,730
New York Daily News 757,053
New York Post 551,443
New York Times 746,924
North Jersey Herald & News 68,167
Woodbridge News Tribune 53,185

Commercial television stations, affiliations
ADI: New York (100%)

Cable television systems, total subscribers
Cablevision of Newark; Newark 41,902
Suburban Cablevision; Verona 134,660
Suburban Cablevision; Woodbridge 91,280

Businesses and other major employers

Prudential Insurance of America Inc.; Newark; life insurance 6,000

University of Medicine/University Hospital; Newark 5,592

Merck & Co. Inc.; Rahway; pharmaceuticals 4,000

City of Jersey City/Board of Education; Jersey City 3,940

City of Newark; Newark 3,800

Public Service Electric & Gas Co.; Newark; electric services 3,000

Newark Beth Israel Medical Center; Newark 2,700

County of Essex; Newark 2,500

U.S. Veterans Affairs Dept.; East Orange 2,000

St. Michael's Medical Center; Newark 1,800

City of Newark/Fire Dept.; Newark 1,800

Continental Airlines Inc.; Newark; airline 1,500

Mountainside Hospital Inc.; Montclair 1,500

Anheuser-Busch Inc.; Newark; brewery 1,400

Orange Memorial Hospital; Orange 1,300

United Hospitals Medical Center; Newark 1,250

Tri-Maintenance & Contracts Inc.; Maplewood; building services 1,200

U.S. Maintenance Corp.; Linden; building services 1,116

Economic Chemical Dist. Inc.; Jersey City; industrial inorganic chemicals 1,000

Sea-Land Service Inc.; Elizabeth; freight shipping 1,000

AT&T Co.; Newark; telephone communications 1,000

New Jersey Institute of Technology; Newark 1,000

Rahway Hospital; Rahway 980

Hayward Industries Inc.; Elizabeth; refrigeration 900

Exxon Corp.; Linden; research services 900

City of Newark/Housing Authority; Newark 900

East Orange General Hospital; East Orange 900

American Intl. Group; East Orange; life insurance 800

Jersey City State College; Jersey City 800

Patient Care Inc.; Orange; home health services 800

Township of West Orange/Board of Education; Orange 700

New Community Corp.; Newark; social services 600

U.S. Customs Service; Newark 600

Pinkerton's Inc.; Maplewood; security services 600

City of Orange/Board of Education; Orange 600

11th District

North — Morris County

The 11th covers all of Morris County and parts of four others, but it can be described best by one word: Republican. By all standards, this is the most rock-ribbed Republican district in the state. In 1984, Ronald Reagan captured 71 percent of the vote, when its boundaries were similarly drawn. Four years later, his vice president, George Bush, racked up 68 percent.

If that is not enough evidence of the 11th's voting habits, witness the 1989 gubernatorial election results: Democrat James J. Florio, who won 61 percent statewide, posted an anemic 35 percent here, his worst showing of all the state's 13 congressional districts.

The Republican dominance continued in the 1992 campaign, despite tough times for north Jersey white-collar employees. Bush won 52 percent, his best showing in New Jersey. GOP Rep. Dean Gallo won by about 120,000 votes.

More than two-thirds of the vote comes from Morris County. The middle-class Parsippany-Troy Hills community is the largest

in the district; it is occasionally receptive to Democratic candidates. After years of rapid growth, population stabilized by the late 1980s.

Central and northern Morris County is mostly white and affluent, populated by well-educated white-collar professionals, bankers, lawyers and stockbrokers who live in upscale places such as Chatham, Kinnelon and Mendham. Harding is especially well-off, even by Morris County standards.

Minorities make up a tiny portion of the 11th's population. Morristown has a relatively large black community; Hispanics live in blue-collar Dover and Victory Gardens.

Toward the west, the county has lost some of its pastoral landscape to newer tract developments that are rapidly altering the character of the area.

Eastern Morris is home to a number of *Fortune* 500 companies that keep headquarters in local corporate office complexes.

During the 1980s, a number of corporate complexes sprouted up across the county, but the recession and white-collar downsizing have left the area with a glut of vacant office space.

After Morris County, Essex County is the most-populous portion with about 66,000 residents. This handful of western municipalities is wealthier than the county as a whole. Livingston, hometown of former GOP Gov. Thomas H. Kean, is Republican but contains a large Jewish community that leans Democratic.

A grab bag of towns from Somerset and Sussex counties are also grafted onto the 11th, along with Bloomingdale, the lone town from Passaic County. Somerset adds Bernards township, Raritan borough, Somerville and Bridgewater—which is shared with the 7th District. Hopatcong and Sparta are the largest towns from Sussex County. Their voting tendencies fit right in with Morris County Republicans.

Election Returns

	11th District	Democrat	Republican
1992	President*	97,697 (32.8%)	153,731 (51.6%)
	House	68,871 (25.7%)	188,165 (70.1%)
1990	Senate	69,800 (41.9%)	96,733 (58.1%)
1989	Governor	90,099 (48.5%)	95,643 (51.5%)
1988	President	86,140 (32.1%)	181,819 (67.9%)
	Senate	116,255 (44.2%)	146,568 (55.8%)

Vote for Perot was 46,418 (15.6%).

Demographics

Population 594,630

Percent change from 1980 13.2%

Land area 638 square miles

Population per square mile 933

Counties, 1990 population

Essex (pt.) 66,296   Somerset (pt.) 54,545

Morris 421,353   Sussex (pt.) 44,906

Passaic (pt.) 7,530

Cities, 1990 population (10,000 or more)

Dover 15,115
Hanover CDP 11,538
Hopatcong 15,586
Lincoln Park 10,978
Livingston CDP (pt.) 26,609
Madison 15,850
Morristown 16,189
Parsippany-Troy Hills CDP 48,478
Pequannock CDP 12,844
Somerville 11,632
Succasunna-Kenvil CDP 11,781
West Caldwell CDP 10,422

Race and Hispanic origin

White 92.3%
Black 2.7%
American Indian, Eskimo, or Aleut. 0.1%
Asian or Pacific Islander 3.9%
Other 1.0%
Hispanic origin 4.1%

Ancestry

American 2.3%
Austrian 1.2%
Dutch 3.1%
English 12.6%
French 2.7%
German 22.8%
Hungarian 2.0%
Irish 21.8%
Italian 22.7%
Norwegian 1.1%
Polish 8.6%
Russian 3.9%
Scotch Irish 1.6%
Scottish 2.9%
Slovakian 2.1%
Swedish 1.6%
Ukrainian 1.2%

Universities/colleges, 1990-1991 enrollment

Caldwell College, Caldwell 1,187
College of St. Elizabeth, Morristown 1,155
County College of Morris, Randolph 9,424
Drew University, Madison 2,276
Rabbinical College of America, Morristown 235
Raritan Valley Community College, Somerville 5,387

Newspapers, total circulation (in all districts)

Morristown Daily Record 54,663
Newark Star Ledger 473,730
New Jersey Herald 17,480
New York Daily News 757,053
New York Post 551,443
New York Times 746,924
North Jersey Herald & News 68,167

Commercial television stations, affiliations

ADI: New York (100%)

Cable television systems, total subscribers

Sammons Communications Inc.; Mine Hill 55,530
Sammons Communications of New Jersey Inc.; Morristown 34,470
Suburban Cablevision; Verona 134,660
TKR Cable; Warren 71,632
UA Cablesystems of New Jersey; Wayne 192,000

Military installations, 1991

Picatinny Arsenal (Army), Dover 5,321

Businesses and other major employers

AT&T Communications of New Jersey; Basking Ridge; telephone communications 4,000
Warner-Lambert Co./American Chicle Co; Morris Plains; gum/candies 3,000
Nabisco Brands Inc.; East Hanover; bakery products 2,500

Blue Cross & Blue Shield of New Jersey; Florham Park; medical service/health insurance 2,500
St. Barnabas Medical Center; Livingston 2,500
Morristown Memorial Hospital; Morristown 2,400
Security Operations Systems; Parsippany; business/security services 1,800
Sandoz Pharmaceuticals Corp.; East Hanover; pharmaceuticals 1,700
Ortho Pharmaceutical Corp.; Raritan; pharmaceuticals 1,600
Allied-Signal Inc.; Morristown; research services 1,500
Allied-Signal Inc.; Morristown; aircraft/parts 1,400
AT&T Co.; Parsippany; computer services 1,400
BASF Corp./Engineering Polymers & Resins Group; Parsippany; chemical products 1,300
Prudential Insurance of America Inc.; Roseland; insurance services 1,300
St. Clare's-Riverside Medical Center; Denville 1,300
Forrest S. Chilton Memorial Hospital; Pompton Plains 1,276
Somerset Medical Center; Somerville 1,257
Dover General Hospital & Medical Center; Dover 1,255
Automatic Switch Co.; Florham Park; switchgears 1,200
AT&T Co./Bell Laboratories; Short Hills; research services 1,200
Tarkett Stora Inc.; Parsippany; sawmills 1,100
Howmet Corp./Dover Casting Div.; Dover; nonferrous foundries (castings) 1,040
Bell Communications Research/Bellcore; Livingston; computer services 1,017
Nynex Meridian Systems; Parsippany; electrical work 1,000
Mennen Co.; Morristown; toiletries/soaps 1,000
Johnson & Johnson; Raritan; pharmaceuticals 1,000
Automatic Data Processing; Roseland; computer services 1,000
City of Morristown; Morristown 1,000
Prudential Insurance of America Inc.; Florham Park; insurance services 950
Township of Parsippany-Troy; Parsippany 950
R. W. Maintenance Inc./Aetna Maintenance Co.; Caldwell; building services 900
AT&T Capital Corp.; Morristown; credit institutions 887
General Public Utilities Corp.; Parsippany; electric services 800
Macy's Northeast Inc.; Livingston; department stores 800
Crum & Forster Inc.; Morristown; fire/marine/casualty insurance 800
AT&T Co.; Parsippany; electrical repair 800
Roche Biomedical Laboratories; Raritan; medical/dental labs 800
U.S. Fire Insurance Co.; Basking Ridge; fire/marine/casualty insurance 770
New Jersey Office Supply Inc.; Whippany; paper products 700
Exxon Corp./Central Services Div.; Florham Park; computer services 700
Fireman's Fund Insurance Co.; Parsippany; insurance services 650
Jersey Central Power & Light Co.; Morristown; electric services 610
Travelers Insurance Co.; Morris Plains; life insurance 606
BASF Corp./Knoll Pharmaceuticals; Whippany; pharmaceuticals 600
CIT Group Inc.; Livingston; credit institutions 600
Macy's Northeast Inc.; Rockaway; department stores 600

Sears Roebuck & Co.; Rockaway; department stores 600
Arthur Andersen & Co.; Roseland; accounting/auditing 600
County of Morris/Road Dept.; Morristown 600
Rowe Intl. Inc.; Whippany; refrigeration 575
County of Morris/Nursing Home; Morris Plains; nursing 570
Raritan Valley Community College; Somerville 560
Drew University; Madison 550
Hackettstown Community Hospital; Hackettstown 550

12th District

North and Central — Flemington; Princeton

Reaching from the Delaware River, on its western border, almost to the Atlantic Ocean, the 12th meanders across New Jersey's midsection. Parts of four counties—and all of Hunterdon County—make up the district, all with one common trait: an affinity for Republican candidates.

More than a third of the population lives in Republican-leaning Monmouth County. Mostly middle-class or affluent, this portion includes rapidly growing towns such as Manalaplan and Marlboro. Voters favor Republican candidates down to the local level, particularly so in wealthy Rumson and Shrewsbury. The district border stops just short of the fragile strip of Atlantic coastline, which belongs to the neighboring 6th District.

Hunterdon, Mercer and Middlesex counties each contribute about one-fifth of the district's population. The Mercer portion includes the affluent, white-collar Trenton suburbs and middle-class, blue-collar Ewing. Colonial Princeton—home to the Ivy League institution of the same name and its 6,500 students—is a source of Democratic votes cast by the liberal academic community.

Commercial and residential spillover from the Princeton and Route 1 corridor has translated into new growth in southern Middlesex County, especially in Plainsboro and South Brunswick.

Upscale East Brunswick—the district's largest city—is as far north as the 12th's border stretches in Middlesex.

Hunterdon is the lone county wholly contained in the 12th. Here the green pastureland and riverside hamlets breed a brand of Republicanism that permeates every level of governance.

The river towns, such as Frenchtown and Lambertville, are filled with quaint antique shops and bed-and-breakfasts. Flemington, the county seat, is a shopping outlet center. The 1980s rousted this sleepy county to the reality of soaring land values and development as it became a popular East Coast weekend getaway destination and second-home community.

These changes did little to alter the county's traditional Republican character. In the 1992 presidential race, George Bush easily carried Hunterdon. The successful GOP House candidate ran even better, winning here by a more than 4-to-1 margin.

Northern Somerset County adds a handful of lightly populated, wealthy communities, including Far Hills and Peapack, from the hunt country.

Taken as a whole, the old-money towns and affluent suburbs of the 12th give Republicans a near lock. Ronald Reagan won 64 percent in 1984, followed by Bush's 61 percent in 1988. Even in the 1989 gubernatorial election, when Democrat James J. Florio carried the state with 61 percent, the GOP nominee took 53 percent here. And in 1992, another breezy year for Republicans, Bush defeated Democrat Bill Clinton.

Election Returns

	12th District	Democrat	Republican
1992	President*	121,447 (40.1%)	130,651 (43.2%)
	House †	83,035 (30.4%)	174,216 (63.9%)
1990	Senate	80,291 (46.6%)	91,863 (53.4%)
1989	Governor	105,704 (56.5%)	81,529 (43.5%)
1988	President	103,703 (39.3%)	159,965 (60.7%)
	Senate	131,610 (51.5%)	123,958 (48.5%)

*Vote for Perot was 50,477 (16.7%).   †Independent/other is greater than 5%.

Demographics

Population 594,630

Percent change from 1980 12.9%

Land area 1,022 square miles

Population per square mile 582

Counties, 1990 population

Hunterdon 107,776   Monmouth (pt.) 217,095
Mercer (pt.) 117,302   Somerset (pt.) 37,644
Middlesex (pt.) 114,813

Cities, 1990 population (10,000 or more)

East Brunswick CDP   Princeton 12,016
  43,548   Tinton Falls 12,361
Eatontown 13,800   West Freehold CDP
Ewing CDP 34,185   11,166
Freehold 10,742

Race and Hispanic origin

White 89.6%
Black 5.2%
American Indian, Eskimo, or Aleut. 0.1%
Asian or Pacific Islander 4.4%
Other 0.7%
Hispanic origin 2.7%

Ancestry

American 2.7%   Italian 18.5%
Austrian 1.3%   Polish 10.2%
Dutch 2.5%   Russian 5.7%
English 12.9%   Scotch Irish 1.5%
French 2.5%   Scottish 2.5%
German 21.4%   Slovakian 1.7%
Hungarian 2.7%   Swedish 1.4%
Irish 19.2%   Ukrainian 1.1%

Universities/colleges, 1990-1991 enrollment

Brookdale Community College, Lincroft 11,888
Mercer County Community College, Trenton 8,779
Monmouth College, West Long Branch 4,275
Princeton Theological Seminary, Princeton 792
Princeton University, Princeton 6,483
Rider College, Lawrenceville 5,734
Westminster Choir College, Princeton 345

Newspapers, total circulation (in all districts)

Easton Express-Times 41,761
New Brunswick Home News 51,098
New York Daily News 757,053
New York Post 551,443

New York Times 746,924
Trentonian 72,634
Trenton Times 82,521

Commercial television stations, affiliations
ADI: New York (86%) and Philadelphia (14%)

Cable television systems, total subscribers
C-Tec; Belle Mead 23,484
C-Tec; Flemington 14,107
Comcast Cablevision; Trenton 34,000
Monmouth Cablevision; Lakewood 20,065
Monmouth Cablevision East; Wall 30,043
Monmouth Cablevision West; Freehold 22,752
Sammons Communications of Pennsylvania Inc.; Easton 27,115
Storer Cable TV Inc.; East Brunswick 17,100
Storer Cable TV Inc.; East Keansburg 24,676
Storer Cable TV Inc.; East Windsor 27,381
Storer Cable TV Inc.; Eatontown 36,710
Storer Cable TV Inc.; Port Murray 20,817
TKR Cable; Warren 71,632

Military installations, 1991
Fort Monmouth (Army), Red Bank (shared with the 6th District) 10,558
Earle Naval Weapons Station, Colts Neck (shared with the 6th District) 3,825
Naval Air Propulsion Center, Trenton 742

Businesses and other major employers
State of New Jersey/Transportation Dept.; Trenton 5,500
Princeton University; Princeton 4,000
General Motors Corp./Fisher Guide Div.; Trenton; motor vehicle parts 3,400
AT&T Co.; Bedminster; telephone communications 2,900
General Electric Co./Aerospace; Princeton; communications equipment 2,700
State of New Jersey/Law & Public Safety Dept.; Trenton 2,700
Bell Communications Research/Bellcore; Red Bank; research services 2,500
Educational Testing Service; Princeton; testing services 2,400
Mid Atlantic Health Group Inc.; Rumson 2,200
Carter-Wallace Inc.; Cranbury; grain mill products 2,000
Firemen's Insurance Co. of Newark; Cranbury; medical service/health insurance 2,000
State of New Jersey/Turnpike Authority; East Brunswick 1,929
Merrill Lynch & Co. Inc.; Plainsboro; security brokers 1,700
Squibb Corp.; Princeton; pharmaceuticals 1,700
Treibacher USA Corp.; Princeton; metals/minerals 1,500
Centrastate Medical Center; Freehold 1,500
Mercer County Community College; Trenton 1,500
IBM Corp.; Princeton; computer services 1,400
Prudential Property Casualty Insurance; Holmdel; fire/marine/casualty insurance 1,395
Marlboro Psychiatric Hospital; Marlboro 1,335
Princeton Medical Center; Princeton 1,220
AT&T Co.; Lincroft; research services 1,200
State of New Jersey/Developmental Center; Skillman 1,200
State of New Jersey/Developmental Center; Clinton 1,200
Varo Inc.; Trenton; optical instruments 1,150
IBM Corp.; Dayton; electrical goods 1,000

Hunterdon Medical Center; Flemington 1,000
New Jersey Manufacturers Insurance Co.; Trenton; fire/marine/casualty insurance 977
Johnson & Johnson; Skillman; medical supplies 900
Shop Rite of Malverne Inc.; Freehold; grocery stores 900
Bayshore Community Hospital; Holmdel 900
Foster Wheeler Corp.; Clinton; industrial engineering 900
Dow Jones & Co. Inc./News Service; Princeton; periodicals 800
Hoechst Celanese Corp.; Somerville; printing services 800
H. C. Copeland & Assoc.; East Brunswick; insurance services 800
Princeton University/Plasma Physics Laboratory; Princeton; research services 800
David Sarnoff Research Center; Princeton; research services 800
Trenton Psychiatric Hospital; Trenton 800
American Cyanamid Co.; Princeton; pharmaceuticals 750
Macy's Northeast Inc.; Eatontown; department stores 750
Monmouth College; West Long Branch 732
American Re-Insurance Co.; Princeton; fire/marine/casualty insurance 725
Continental Baking Co./Wonder Bread; East Brunswick; bakery products 700
New Jersey National Corp.; Pennington; commercial banks 700
FMC Corp.; Princeton; research services 700
Unisys Corp.; Flemington; computer equipment 675
Conopco Inc./Lipton Co.; Flemington; grocery products 660
New Jersey National Bank; Trenton; commercial banks 658
Brookdale Community College; Lincroft 650
Rider College, Lawrenceville 650
Owens-Brockway Glass; Freehold; glass containers 600
Koh-I-Noor Rapidograph Inc.; Bloomsbury; office/art supplies 600
Mobil Oil Corp.; Pennington; research services 600
Township of Ewing/Board of Education; Trenton 600
County of Monmouth; Freehold 580
County of Hunterdon; Flemington 550
Beneficial Management Corp.; Peapack; credit institutions 540

13th District

Parts of Jersey City and Newark

Not far from the place that welcomed the tired, the poor and the huddled masses yearning to be free rests Jersey City, a modern-day melting pot. Ellis Island, the onetime processing point for countless numbers of immigrants, and the Statue of Liberty are appropriately situated a short ferry ride away from the city's Liberty State Park. Although the subject is of some dispute, city boosters say the statue is within city limits.

Legendary political boss Frank "I Am the Law" Hague's machine controlled Hudson County politics from 1917 to the late 1940s, oiled by the votes of those white, working-class European immigrants. But now more than half the votes in Jersey City come from minorities, many of whom came in a second wave of immigration, primarily from Spanish-speaking countries.

About half of Jersey City—the state's second-largest city—is in the 13th, with the rest shared between the 9th and 10th districts. This portion consists mainly of the eastern parts of the city, including the downtown area, which has experienced some gentrification as young professionals have been forced across the Hudson River by New York City's housing prices.

There are Russian immigrants living downtown, and scattered pockets of Indian, Korean and Filipino immigrants, but blacks and Hispanics together make up more than half the city's population.

The local Hispanic community is far from monolithic; it consists of immigrants from more than 20 countries. The 13th as a whole has a Hispanic population of 42 percent, so it was not surprising that the district sent the state's first Hispanic representative to Washington.

The Hispanic communities are scattered across the district, as far south as Elizabeth (Union County) and Perth Amboy (Middlesex County). Union City, North Bergen, Guttenberg and especially West New York have politically active Cuban communities that tend to vote Republican at the presidential level and Democratic in local elections.

Outside of those Republican votes, the GOP presence is muted. The various Hispanic communities and large numbers of blue-collar whites favor Democratic candidates. Though Hispanics make up a significant chunk of population, they are not registered to vote in proportion. In terms of voter registration, Hispanics comprise just under 20 percent. Yet Democrat Robert Menendez won the 13th seat in 1992 with 64 percent of the vote to become New Jersey's first Hispanic House member.

Another Hudson County locale that has been gentrified is Hoboken, where yuppies have taken over the city's eastern section. The city may be better known, though, as Frank Sinatra's birthplace and the setting for the 1954 film *On the Waterfront*.

From Hudson County, the 13th extends to Newark (Essex County) to siphon Puerto Rican and Italian voters from the city's north and east wards.

Middlesex and Union counties also contribute voters, but on a smaller scale. All of Perth Amboy and Carteret along with a small portion of suburban Woodbridge together make up about 10 percent of the district. Parts of Elizabeth and Linden round out the Union County contingent.

Election Returns

	13th District	Democrat	Republican
1992	President*	95,144 (54.4%)	64,727 (37.0%)
	House†	93,670 (64.3%)	44,529 (30.6%)
1990	Senate	60,170 (67.4%)	29,154 (32.6%)
1989	Governor	91,146 (75.3%)	29,884 (24.7%)
1988	President	136,024 (59.4%)	93,058 (40.6%)
	Senate	142,574 (66.2%)	72,762 (33.8%)

Vote for Perot was 14,911 (8.5%).   †Independent/other is greater than 5%.

Demographics

Population   594,630

Percent change from 1980   13.0%

Land area   57 square miles

Population per square mile   10,410

Counties, 1990 population
Essex (pt.) 105,853	Middlesex (pt.) 67,538
Hudson (pt.) 373,647	Union (pt.) 47,592

Cities, 1990 population (10,000 or more)
Bayonne (pt.) 56,325	North Bergen CDP (pt.)
Carteret 19,025	28,908
Elizabeth (pt.) 42,964	Perth Amboy 41,967
Harrison 13,425	Union City 58,012
Hoboken 33,397	Weehawken CDP 12,385
Jersey City (pt.) 122,374	West New York 38,125
Newark (pt.) 105,853	

Race and Hispanic origin
White 67.4%
Black 13.7%
American Indian, Eskimo, or Aleut. 0.3%
Asian or Pacific Islander 4.6%
Other 14.1%
Hispanic origin 41.5%

Ancestry
American 1.5%	Italian 11.9%
English 2.0%	Polish 6.3%
German 5.7%	Portuguese 4.3%
Hungarian 1.0%	Russian 1.1%
Irish 8.8%	Slovakian 1.4%

Universities/colleges, 1990-1991 enrollment
Hudson County Community College, Jersey City 2,832
Stevens Institute of Technology, Hoboken 2,859
St. Peter's College, Jersey City 3,356

Newspapers, total circulation (in all districts)
El Diario La Prensa (Spanish) 53,841
Jersey City Journal 66,241
Newark Star Ledger 473,730
New York Daily News 757,053
New York Post 551,443
New York Times 746,924
North Jersey Herald & News 68,167
Woodbridge News Tribune 53,185

Commercial television stations, affiliations
ADI: New York (100%)

Cable television systems, total subscribers
Cable TV of Jersey City; Jersey City 29,486
Cablevision of Newark; Newark 41,902
Riverview Cablevision; North Bergen 42,000
Suburban Cablevision; Woodbridge 91,280

Military installations, 1991
Bayonne Military Ocean Terminal, Bayonne 2,236

Businesses and other major employers
General Motors Corp.; Linden; motor vehicle assembly 2,300
Jersey City Medical Center; Jersey City 2,000
State of New Jersey; Newark 2,000
Liz Claiborne Inc.; North Bergen; outerwear 1,800
Raritan Bay Medical Center/Perth Amboy General Hospital; Perth Amboy 1,700
U.S. Postal Service; Newark 1,500
First Fidelity Bank of New Jersey; Newark; commercial banks 1,500
Elizabeth General Medical Center; Elizabeth 1,500
County of Union; Elizabeth 1,500

Mutual Benefit Life Insurance Co.; Newark; life insurance 1,499

New Jersey Bell Telephone Co.; Newark; telephone communications 1,400

Bankers Trust Co.; Jersey City; commercial banks 1,400

Margaretten & Co. Inc.; Perth Amboy; mortgage bankers 1,200

Paine Webber Group Inc.; Union City; security brokers 1,200

St. Elizabeth Hospital Inc.; Elizabeth 1,169

City of Jersey/City School District; Jersey City 1,100

Port Authority Trans-Hudson; Jersey City 1,100

ADP Brokerage Services Group; Jersey City; security brokers 1,000

Hartz Group Inc.; Harrison; real estate operators 1,000

City of Bayonne/Board of Education; Bayonne 1,000

City of Union City/School District; Union City 1,000

County of Essex/Welfare Board; Newark; family services 1,000

Herman's Sporting Goods Inc.; Carteret; sporting goods stores 920

St. Mary Hospital Inc.; Hoboken 900

Bayonne Hospital; Bayonne 900

County of Hudson; Jersey City 900

Elizabeth School District; Elizabeth 900

Kraft General Foods Inc./Maxwell House Coffee Co.; Hoboken; coffee 800

City of Bayonne; Bayonne 783

Universal Maritime Service; Jersey City; water transportation 750

Block Drug Co. Inc.; Jersey City; toiletries 750

St. Francis Hospital Inc.; Jersey City 750

A-P-A Transport Corp.; North Bergen; trucking services 700

Blue Cross & Blue Shield of New Jersey; Newark; medical service/health insurance 700

Columbus Hospital Inc.; Newark 643

St. Peter's College; Jersey City 625

National Retail Systems Inc.; North Bergen; trucking services 600

Unimark Inc./Macy's; Bayonne; business services 600

Pollak Hospital; Jersey City 600

Telerate Systems Inc.; Jersey City; computer services 600

U.S. Co.-Steel Ltd.; Perth Amboy; steel products 555

City of Perth Amboy; Perth Amboy 550

St. James Hospital; Newark 550

Township of North Bergen; North Bergen 515

Passaic Valley Sewerage Commission; Newark 504

New Mexico

On the last page of New Mexico's monthly culture and travel magazine, a feature entitled "One of Our Fifty is Missing" lampoons the geographic illiteracy exhibited by out-of-state residents who are under the mistaken impression that New Mexico is a foreign country.

But demographically compared to most states, it is. Only 50 percent classify themselves as white, non-Hispanics—referred to as Anglos—and almost half the state's population is either Native American or of Hispanic origin. The next census may report New Mexico as the nation's first minority-majority state.

Unlike other states where significant minority populations are underrepresented in the political equation, New Mexico's roster of public officials is as likely to list Hispanic surnames like Baca or Vigil as Smith or Johnson. Even at the executive level, Hispanics have been enfranchised; two of the past four governors have been Hispanic. Native Americans, who comprise 9 percent of the population, are represented by six state legislators, the highest number of any state. Though the sometimes clashing interests of these distinct communities have created tension at times, the politics of color does not have the same appeal here that it retains elsewhere.

The latest round of redistricting left the political scene relatively undisturbed, though in the future, some of the minor cartographic alterations could sap GOP strength in the 1st and 2nd districts. Several counties were shifted between districts, but the new map retained the basic configuration of having a northern, central and southern seat.

The 1st District covers the Albuquerque (Bernalillo County) metropolitan area. A moderate brand of Republicanism plays well with the primarily Anglo voters, because unlike the city's Sunbelt contemporaries, Albuquerque has never been noted for a militant brand of conservatism, even though the area is considered a wellspring of Republican votes in a predominantly Democratic state.

While a moderate political philosophy is more in line with the thinking of the state's post-World War II Anglo migrants, a brand of western conservatism suits the constituency of rural Anglo ranchers in the 2nd. Descendants of 19th-century Texas settlers, these rugged men and women of the land have little in common with city-dwelling newcomers. Living in the oil- and gas-producing southeastern region known as "Little Texas," this group registers as Democrats, but has little use for liberal ideology.

Hispanics and Indians make up a majority in the 3rd District, giving it a distinctly Democratic tilt. Colfax, Mora, Rio Arriba, Santa Fe, San Miguel and Taos counties, located in the mountainous north-central section of the state, are heavily Hispanic and monolithically Democratic.

Indians have far less access to the political gears than Hispanics or Anglos. Low turnout and voter registration levels have hampered political empowerment efforts, though in recent years both have been on the upswing.

Democratic candidates often neglect the various tribes, which, among others include Navajos, Jicarilla and Mescalero Apaches and Pueblos, because they are already presumed to vote as a Democratic bloc. While Indian voters—particularly the populous Navajo tribe—tend to identify strongly with the Democratic party, they are willing to cross party lines. In 1980, four years after Jimmy Carter had solicited and won the support of tribal leaders, Native Americans rejected him because they felt he had not followed through on issues of importance to the Indian community.

Table 1 Population

District	Population	Population under 18	Voting-age population	Median age
1	505,491	133,616	371,875	32.2
2	504,659	154,102	350,557	30.7
3	504,919	159,023	345,896	30.8
State	1,515,069	446,741	1,068,328	31.3

Table 2 Voting-Age Persons

District	White*	Black*	American Indian, Eskimo, or Aleut*	Asian or Pacific Islander*	Other*	Hispanic*	Male*	Female*
1	79.8%	2.4%	2.4%	1.4%	14.0%	34.7%	48.1%	51.9%
2	85.6	2.0	3.3	0.7	8.4	37.6	48.9	51.1
3	69.3	1.1	17.1	0.6	11.9	33.2	48.3	51.7
State	78.3	1.9	7.5	0.9	11.5	35.2	48.4	51.6

As percent of voting-age population.

NEW MEXICO

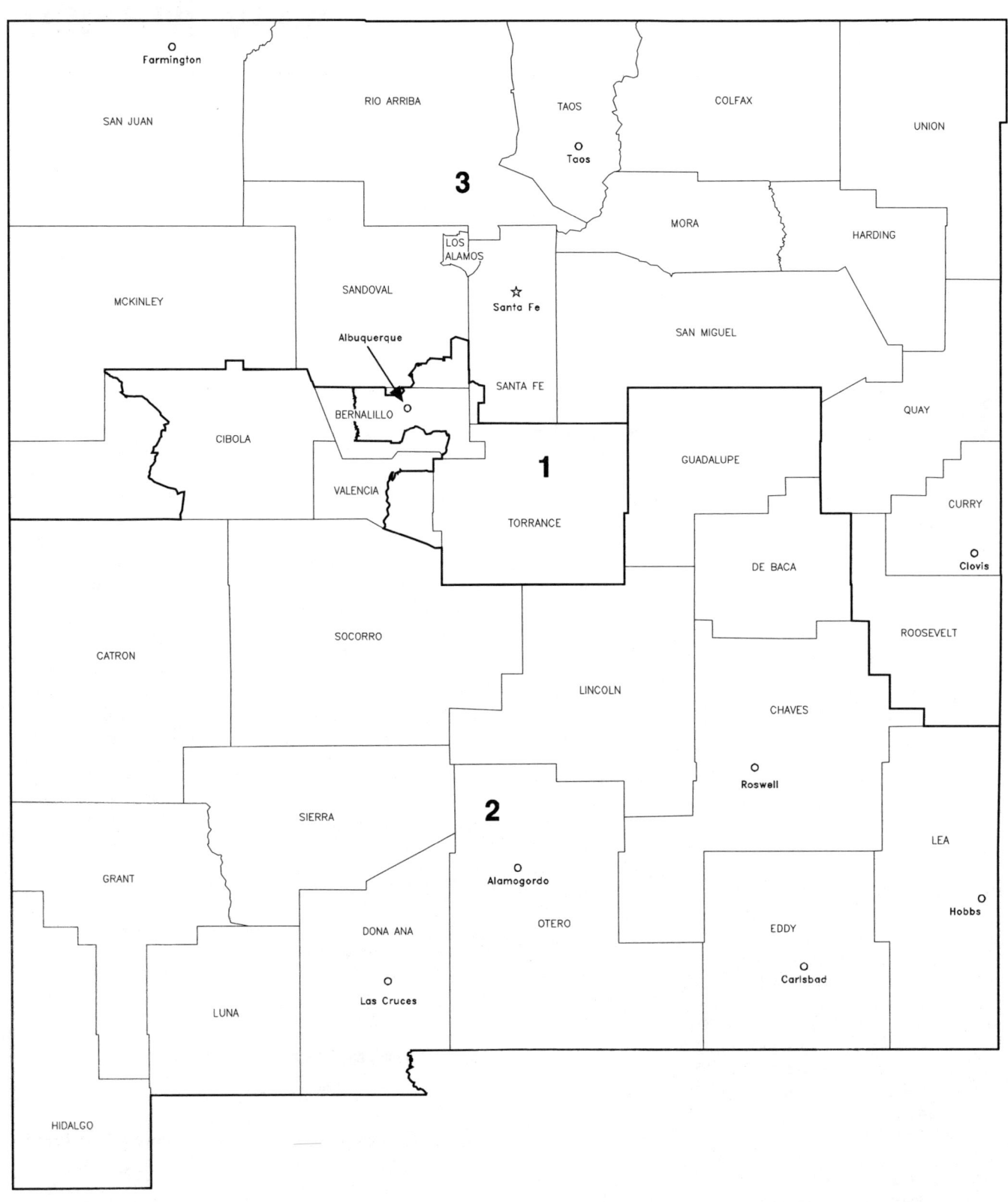

Farmington

RIO ARRIBA   TAOS   COLFAX   UNION

SAN JUAN

3

Taos

MORA   HARDING

LOS ALAMOS

MCKINLEY   SANDOVAL   ☆ Santa Fe   SAN MIGUEL

Albuquerque   SANTA FE   QUAY

CIBOLA   BERNALILLO   GUADALUPE

1

VALENCIA   CURRY

TORRANCE   Clovis

DE BACA

CATRON   SOCORRO   ROOSEVELT

LINCOLN   CHAVES

SIERRA   **2**   Roswell   LEA

GRANT   Alamogordo

OTERO   Hobbs

DONA ANA   EDDY

Las Cruces   Carlsbad

LUNA

HIDALGO

Table 3   Voting-Age Persons by Age Groups

District	18-24*	25-44*	45-54*	55-64*	65 and over*
1	14.0%	47.3%	13.7%	10.7%	14.3%
2	15.1	42.2	13.3	12.4	17.0
3	13.5	46.4	14.4	11.1	14.5
State	14.2	45.3	13.8	11.4	15.3

*As percent of voting-age population.

Table 4   Income and Occupation

District	Median family income	Families in poverty	White collar*	Blue collar*	Service*	Farm*
1	$32,051	11.2%	64.8%	20.4%	13.6%	1.2%
2	24,588	18.9	50.9	28.3	15.9	5.0
3	26,681	19.3	58.2	24.2	14.6	3.0
State	27,623	16.5	58.5	24.0	14.6	2.9

*As percent of employed persons age 16 and over.

Table 5   Education: School Years Completed

District	Less than grade 9*	Grades 9-12 no diploma*	High school diploma*	College bachelor's degree or higher*
1	7.1%	11.3%	28.0%	26.0%
2	15.5	15.1	29.7	15.0
3	12.0	14.3	28.6	19.7
State	11.4	13.5	28.7	20.4

*As percent of persons age 25 and over.

Table 6   Housing and Residential Patterns

District	Owner occupied	Renter occupied	Urban	Rural
1	61.9%	38.1%	92.4%	7.6%
2	69.4	30.6	66.9	33.1
3	71.7	28.3	59.6	40.4
State	67.4	32.6	73.0	27.0

1st District

Central — Albuquerque

Albuquerque's postwar emergence as New Mexico's commercial hub and a GOP stronghold was fueled by the development of a prosperous military-aerospace industry. Despite a Democratic edge in registration (55 percent to 38 percent), the GOP has maintained its hold on the seat by offering fiscally conservative, defense-oriented moderate candidates.

However, the existence of a large state and local government work force and a big minority population gives Democrats a foothold in Bernalillo County, alongside Republican-voting white-collar professionals employed in the area's defense and aerospace industries. About 38 percent of the 1st District's population is Hispanic. The city and the county together cast about one-third of the state vote.

Before World War II, Albuquerque was a lightly populated regional trade center, better known as a health resort where tubercular patients could alleviate their suffering by taking advantage of the dry climate.

Since the A-bomb was developed in 1945 (less than 100 miles north at Los Alamos), Albuquerque has seen its population multiply from 35,000 people in 1940 to about 385,000 today. The district has a high concentration of scientists and engineers who work in the military-aerospace industry. A large employer is Sandia National Laboratories, which specializes in nuclear and solar research and testing. Kirtland Air Force Base is also in the district. Defense and aviation technology companies such as Honeywell and General Electric are here as are scores of newer electronics, computer and communications companies. (Honeywell and GE have suffered a few layoffs in the post-Cold War era.)

Teachers also form an important bloc; the University of New Mexico and the Albuquerque public school system account for 23,000 jobs.

Much of the GOP vote is cast in the city's heavily non-Hispanic, upper-middle-class and residential Northeast Heights section. The Hispanic-majority South Valley, on the south and west sides of the Rio Grande, boosts Democratic totals.

Until 1992, Bernalillo County had supported the GOP presidential nominee in all but one election since 1952. Bill Clinton took 46 percent of the county's vote, making him the first Democrat to win here since Lyndon B. Johnson in 1964. Despite its GOP tendencies, strong Democratic candidates can win here. In 1990, Bernalillo backed Democrats for Senate and for governor.

Bernalillo serves as the population center of the district, but rural Torrance County has most of the land area with 3,300 square miles. Torrance accounts for only about 1 percent of the district vote.

Portions of three other counties make up the balance of the 1st. About 13,000 voters—mainly professionals—live in Albuquerque bedroom communities in eastern Valencia County, and about 11,000 voters hail from a primarily rural section of Sandoval County, just north of Bernalillo County.

Election Returns

	1st District	Democrat	Republican
1992	President*	95,677 (45.6%)	81,046 (38.6%)
	House	76,600 (37.4%)	128,426 (62.6%)
1990	Senate	31,300 (22.5%)	107,591 (77.5%)
	Governor	72,999 (52.4%)	66,393 (47.6%)
1988	President	82,132 (46.0%)	96,279 (54.0%)
	Senate	111,759 (63.0%)	65,741 (37.0%)
1986	Governor	58,421 (48.0%)	63,369 (52.0%)

*Vote for Perot was 33,032 (15.7%).

Demographics

Population 505,491

Percent change from 1980 16.4%

Land area 4,711 square miles

Population per square mile 107

Counties, 1990 population

Bernalillo (pt.) 469,775	Torrance 10,285
Sandoval (pt.) 10,828	Valencia (pt.) 12,868
Santa Fe (pt.) 1,735	

Cities, 1990 population (10,000 or more)

Albuquerque (pt.) 382,725   South Valley CDP (pt.)
North Valley CDP 12,507   35,701

Race and Hispanic origin

White 77.6%
Black 2.7%
American Indian, Eskimo, or Aleut. 2.7%
Asian or Pacific Islander 1.5%
Other 15.6%
Hispanic origin 38.1%

Ancestry

American 2.7%	Italian 3.4%
Dutch 1.9%	Norwegian 1.4%
English 13.8%	Polish 1.9%
French 3.5%	Scotch Irish 2.6%
German 19.1%	Scottish 2.4%
Irish 12.1%	Swedish 1.7%

Universities/colleges, 1990-1991 enrollment

Almontes Academy of Cosmetology, Albuquerque 9,741
University of New Mexico, Albuquerque 23,955
University of New Mexico, Los Lunas 1,135

Newspapers, total circulation (in all districts)

Albuquerque Journal Tribune 157,965
Santa Fe New Mexican 21,919

Commercial television stations, affiliations

ADI: Albuquerque (100%)
KGSW-TV, Albuquerque (Fox)
KNAT, Albuquerque (None)
KOAT-TV, Albuquerque (ABC)
KOB-TV, Albuquerque (NBC)
KRQE-TV, Albuquerque (CBS)

Cable television systems, total subscribers

Jones Intercable Inc.; Albuquerque 91,043

Military installations, 1991

Kirtland Air Force Base, Albuquerque 8,350

Businesses and other major employers

Sandia Corp./Sandia National Laboratories; Albuquerque; research services 7,400
University of New Mexico; Albuquerque 5,500
City of Albuquerque; Albuquerque 5,215
Honeywell Inc./Defense Avionics Systems Div.; Albuquerque; aircraft/parts 2,500
University of New Mexico Medical Center; Albuquerque 2,300
Lovelace Medical Center; Albuquerque 2,200
Public Service Co. of New Mexico/Gas Co. of New Mexico; Albuquerque; electric services 2,190
Presbyterian Healthcare Services; Albuquerque 2,000
General Electric Co./Aircraft Engines; Albuquerque; aircraft engines/parts 1,550
City of Albuquerque/Public Works Dept.; Albuquerque 1,500
St. Joseph Health Care System; Albuquerque 1,500
Execu-Staff Inc.; Albuquerque; personnel supply services 1,500
U.S. Veterans Affairs Dept.; Albuquerque; hospital 1,400
County of Bernalillo; Albuquerque 954
U.S. Postal Service; Albuquerque 900
U.S. West Communications Inc.; Albuquerque; telephone communications 900
North American Philips Corp./Signetics Div.; Albuquerque; measuring/controlling devices 900
State of New Mexico/Labor Dept.; Albuquerque 835
Albuquerque Publishing Co.; Albuquerque; newspapers 805
Digital Equipment Corp.; Albuquerque; computer equipment 700
Ethicon Inc.; Albuquerque; medical supplies 680
U.S. Fish & Wildlife Service; Albuquerque 650
Kirk-Mayer Inc.; Albuquerque; engineering services 630
Levi Strauss & Co.; Albuquerque; jeans 575
New Mexico Blue Cross; Albuquerque; medical service/health insurance 550

2nd District

South — Little Texas; Las Cruces; Roswell

Southern New Mexico was once firmly Democratic, but traditional party ties have eroded here. During the 1970s, the area developed a strong habit of voting Republican in statewide contests, as ranchers and other southern-style Democrats came to resent their party's national program.

In 1991, redistricting wrought more changes. To try to make the district more competitive for Democrats, the state's Democratic Legislature drew district lines to include more liberal voters. The population of Hispanics jumped from 34 percent to 42 percent.

In addition, the 2nd District lost Curry, Quay and Roosevelt counties, all Democratic but conservative. The district picked up De Baca and Guadalupe, where ranching is the mainstay.

In what was once resolutely GOP country, George Bush in 1992 lost the district to Bill Clinton by 1 percentage point.

Other Democratic strongholds are in the Mexican Highlands, along the Arizona border, where copper and lead mines have attracted union labor. But they have provided less than 10 percent of the vote.

"Little Texas," the southeastern corner of New Mexico, remains an important focus, making up about 50 percent of the 2nd. This region, settled by Texans early in the 20th century, is more culturally and economically attuned to conservative, Baptist West Texas than to the more liberal capital city of Santa Fe. Most of the land here is devoted to grazing cattle or sheep. But oil and military projects have reshaped voting habits in a Republican direction.

The oil- and gas-producing centers of Chaves and Lea counties are bastions of conservatism.

Near Carlsbad in Eddy County are the nation's most productive salt mines. Democratic miners occasionally influence county elections. The subterranean salt beds will be the site of the nation's first nuclear waste dump, the controversial Waste Isolation Pilot Plant, which is scheduled to begin operations in late 1993 or early 1994. Many in the Carlsbad area support the project, expected to inject millions of dollars into the stagnant local economy; meanwhile, the safety of the Carlsbad nuclear repository has ignited a firestorm of criticism statewide.

To the west are Otero and Doña Ana counties, which account for more than one-third of the 2nd's population. Otero County favors the GOP. Doña Ana, which includes Las Cruces, has a Hispanic majority, giving the Democrats a substantial base, but Republicans generally carry it. Parts of Doña Ana, Otero and

Sierra counties hold the sprawling White Sands Missile Range.

Holloman Air Force Base in Otero County also provides GOP strength. Just north of Otero, in the southeastern corner of Socorro County, the world's first atomic bomb was exploded in 1945.

The tiny village of Mesilla, in Las Cruces, also served briefly as the Confederate capital of the Arizona Territory.

Election Returns

	2nd District	Democrat	Republican
1992	President*	70,646 (41.3%)	68,754 (40.2%)
	House	73,157 (43.5%)	94,838 (56.5%)
1990	Senate	36,996 (28.0%)	95,195 (72.0%)
	Governor	68,663 (51.1%)	65,732 (48.9%)
1988	President	72,871 (43.4%)	94,894 (56.6%)
	Senate	99,861 (60.4%)	65,429 (39.6%)
1986	Governor	58,769 (47.5%)	64,851 (52.5%)

*Vote for Perot was 31,782 (18.6%).

Demographics

Population 504,659

Percent change from 1980 15.7%

Land area 67,345 square miles

Population per square mile 7

Counties, 1990 population

Bernalillo (pt.) 3,278	Hidalgo 5,958
Catron 2,563	Lea 55,765
Chaves 57,849	Lincoln 12,219
Cibola (pt.) 21,747	Luna 18,110
De Baca 2,252	Otero 51,928
Dona Ana 135,510	Sierra 9,912
Eddy 48,605	Socorro 14,764
Grant 27,676	Valencia (pt.) 32,367
Guadalupe 4,156	

Cities, 1990 population (10,000 or more)

Alamogordo 27,596	Hobbs 29,115
Artesia 10,610	Las Cruces 62,126
Carlsbad 24,952	Roswell 44,654
Deming 10,970	Silver City 10,683

Race and Hispanic origin

White 84.0%
Black 2.1%
American Indian, Eskimo, or Aleut. 3.7%
Asian or Pacific Islander 0.7%
Other 9.5%
Hispanic origin 42.1%

Ancestry

American 4.3%	Irish 11.3%
Dutch 2.2%	Italian 1.5%
English 12.7%	Scotch Irish 2.2%
French 2.7%	Scottish 1.6%
German 14.0%	Swedish 1.0%

Universities/colleges, 1990-1991 enrollment

College of the Southwest, Hobbs 276
Eastern New Mexico University, Roswell 1,859
New Mexico Institute of Mining & Technology, Socorro 1,306
New Mexico Junior College, Hobbs 2,438
New Mexico Military Institute, Roswell 449
New Mexico State University, Alamogordo 1,759
New Mexico State University, Carlsbad 1,077
New Mexico State University, Grants 469
New Mexico State University, Las Cruces 14,812
Western New Mexico University, Silver City 1,881

Newspapers, total circulation (in all districts)

Alamogordo Daily News 7,882
Albuquerque Journal Tribune 157,965
Carlsbad Current-Argus 8,291
El Paso Times 91,177
Hobbs Daily News-Sun 11,780
Las Cruces Sun-News 19,094
Lubbock Avalanche Journal 66,342

Commercial television stations, affiliations

ADI: Albuquerque (92%), El Paso (6%) and Odessa-Midland (2%)
KVIO-TV, Carlsbad (ABC)
KZIA, Las Cruces (None)
KBIM-TV, Roswell (CBS)
KOBR, Roswell (NBC)
KRPV, Roswell (None)
KOVT-TV, Silver City (ABC)

Cable television systems, total subscribers

Jones Intercable Inc.; Albuquerque 91,043
Las Cruces TV Cable; Las Cruces 21,726
Lincoln Cablevision Inc.; Alto 6,563
Paragon Cable; El Paso 86,000
Post Newsweek Cable TV; Roswell 12,600
Simmons Communications Inc.; Alamogordo 9,983
TCI of New Mexico; Carlsbad 9,200
TCI of New Mexico; Hobbs 10,000

Military installations, 1991

White Sands Missile Range (Army), White Sands 6,954
Holloman Air Force Base, Alamogordo 4,793

Businesses and other major employers

New Mexico State University; Las Cruces 7,902
Transportation Mfg. Corp.; Roswell; buses 1,420
Chino Mines Co.; Hurley; copper mining 1,150
Memorial Medical Center; Las Cruces 1,020
Gadsden Independent School District; Anthony 1,000
New Mexico Institute of Mining & Technology, Socorro 925
Sara Lee Corp./L'eggs Products Inc.; Mesilla Park; hosiery 900
Los Lunas Hospital & Training; Los Lunas; nursing 900
City of Las Cruces; Las Cruces 860
Hobbs Municipal School; Hobbs 815
Phelps Dodge Corp.; Tyrone; copper ores 709
City of Alamogordo/Public Schools; Alamogordo 694
Levi Strauss & Co.; Roswell; jeans 640
IMC Fertilizer Group Inc.; Carlsbad; fertilizers 600
Eastern New Mexico Medical Center Hospital; Roswell 600
Lockheed Corp.; Las Cruces; engineering services 600
State of New Mexico/Physical Science Laboratory; Las Cruces; engineering services 600

City of Los Lunas/School District; Los Lunas 560
County of Grants/School District; Grants 536
Phelps Dodge Corp.; Lordsburg; nonferrous smelting 533

3rd District

North and East Central — Farmington; Santa Fe

With more than half its voters either Hispanic or American Indian, the 3rd is more liberal and more Democratic than either of the state's other districts. It contains eight of the 10 New Mexico counties that Michael S. Dukakis carried in 1988. In 1992, Bill Clinton took 51 percent of the 3rd's vote.

However, 1991 redistricting made the district a bit less Democratic, trading a chunk of Hispanic territory for a piece of conservative GOP turf.

In the 1990s the constituency of the 3rd is about 35 percent Hispanic, down from 39 percent in the 1980s. Non-Hispanics make up about 40 percent; the remainder is American Indian. The population is divided between the Hispanic counties of northern New Mexico and some energy-rich Indian lands along the Arizona border.

Areas of the 3rd, particularly Cibola, McKinley and Mora counties, are plagued with high unemployment and poverty. In most of the counties that ring the Santa Fe-Taos area, between one-third and one-half of the residents, many of whom are unskilled minorities, live in poverty. Unemployment levels here routinely run about 10 percent for most of these counties; the Mora County jobless rate hovered above 30 percent for much of the 1980s. And although programs have targeted alcoholism, it remains a problem in poorer pockets of the 3rd.

The scenery in parts of the 3rd is breathtaking, making it a trendy tourist spot. Taos, home of Taos Ski Valley and many art galleries and specialty shops, attracts thousands of tourists.

The 3rd gained some conservative farming and ranching territory when it picked up Curry, Quay and Roosevelt counties in 1991 redistricting. Curry is home to Cannon Air Force Base and a considerable number of military retirees who make this area a conservative bastion.

The centerpiece of the region is Santa Fe, the third-largest city in the state. The city has evolved into a regional arts center, supporting more than 150 art galleries and hundreds of shops that peddle distinctive southwestern and Indian art styles. Artists, state employees, Hispanics, Indians and Anglo liberals combine to make the city a Democratic stronghold; Democrats outnumber Republicans here by about 3-to-1.

The rest of the Hispanic north is primarily mountainous, semi-arid grazing land that supports some subsistence farming.

An economic oasis is the non-Hispanic community of Los Alamos, where the atomic bomb was developed during World War II. One of the most prosperous counties in the country, it has well-educated and largely Republican voters.

In Indian country, voters turn out in small numbers and divide more closely at the polls. However, American Indians, most of them Navajo, usually vote Democratic.

The largest county in the region is San Juan, where a conservative non-Hispanic population settled around Farmington (population 34,000) to tap the vast supply of oil, gas and coal in the Four Corners area. San Juan went solidly for George Bush in 1988 and 1992.

Election Returns

	3rd District	Democrat	Republican
1992	President*	95,294 (51.4%)	63,024 (34.0%)
	House	122,850 (67.4%)	54,569 (29.9%)
1990	Senate	40,342 (30.6%)	91,285 (69.4%)
	Governor	80,325 (60.7%)	52,096 (39.3%)
1988	President	87,094 (53.1%)	76,932 (46.9%)
	Senate	107,352 (66.6%)	53,775 (33.4%)
1986	Governor	68,693 (56.3%)	53,241 (43.7%)

Vote for Perot was 27,081 (14.6%).

Demographics

Population 504,919

Percent change from 1980 16.7%

Land area 49,308 square miles

Population per square mile 10

Counties, 1990 population

Bernalillo (pt.) 7,524	Rio Arriba 34,365
Cibola (pt.) 2,047	Roosevelt 16,702
Colfax 12,925	San Juan 91,605
Curry 42,207	San Miguel 25,743
Harding 987	Sandoval (pt.) 52,491
Los Alamos 18,115	Santa Fe (pt.) 97,193
McKinley 60,686	Taos 23,118
Mora 4,264	Union 4,124
Quay 10,823	

Cities, 1990 population (10,000 or more)

Clovis 30,954	Los Alamos CDP 11,455
Farmington 33,997	Portales 10,690
Gallup 19,154	Rio Rancho (pt.) 30,658
Las Vegas 14,753	Santa Fe 55,859

Race and Hispanic origin

White 65.4%

Black 1.2%

American Indian, Eskimo, or Aleut. 20.1%

Asian or Pacific Islander 0.6%

Other 12.6%

Hispanic origin 34.6%

Ancestry

American 3.0%	Italian 2.4%
Dutch 1.7%	Polish 1.1%
English 11.0%	Scotch Irish 1.9%
French 2.5%	Scottish 1.8%
German 13.3%	Swedish 1.2%
Irish 9.1%	

Universities/colleges, 1990-1991 enrollment

Clovis Community College, Clovis 2,750
College of Santa Fe, Santa Fe 1,052
Eastern New Mexico University, Portales 3,619
Institute of the American Indian, Santa Fe 208
New Mexico Highlands University, Las Vegas 2,445
Northern New Mexico Community, Espanola 1,628
San Juan College, Farmington 3,028
Santa Fe Community College, Santa Fe 2,705
St. John's College, Santa Fe 469

University of New Mexico, Gallup 2,062
University of New Mexico, Los Alamos 897

Newspapers, total circulation (in all districts)
Albuquerque Journal Tribune 157,965
Clovis News Journal 9,322
Farmington Daily Times 15,308
Gallup Independent 14,901
Santa Fe New Mexican 21,919

Commercial television stations, affiliations
ADI: Albuquerque (84%) and Amarillo (16%)
KVIH-TV, Clovis (ABC)
KOBF, Farmington (NBC)
KASA, Santa Fe (None)
KCHF, Santa Fe (None)

Cable television systems, total subscribers
Jones Intercable Inc.; Albuquerque 91,043
Post Newsweek Cable; Rio Rancho 5,993
TCA Cable TV of Clovis; Clovis 12,000
TCI Cablevision of Gallup; Gallup 5,844
TCI Cablevision of Santa Fe; Santa Fe 15,320
TCI of New Mexico; Farmington 14,887

Military installations, 1991
Cannon Air Force Base, Clovis 6,684

Businesses and other major employers
U.S. Energy Dept.; Los Alamos; research services 7,600
University of California/Los Alamos National Laboratory; Los Alamos; research services 7,000
State of New Mexico/Human Services Dept.; Santa Fe 2,100
Intel Corp.; Albuquerque; electronic components 1,500
City of Santa Fe/Board of Education; Santa Fe 1,146
St. Vincent Hospital Inc.; Santa Fe 1,022
State of New Mexico/Tax & Revenue Dept.; Santa Fe 1,000
Las Vegas Medical Center; Las Vegas 911
BHP Utah Intl. Inc.; Fruitland; coal mining 900
State of New Mexico/Consolidated Schools; Kirtland 890
Clovis Municipal Schools; Clovis 800
State of New Mexico/Highway Dept.; Santa Fe 800
Arizona Public Service Co./Four Corners Power Plant; Fruitland; utility services 714
State of New Mexico/Police Dept.; Santa Fe 710
State of New Mexico/Youth Authority; Santa Fe 635
Public Service Co. of New Mexico; Waterflow; electric services 616
San Juan Regional Medical Center; Farmington 613
J. C. Penney Co. Inc.; Albuquerque; department stores 600
State of New Mexico/Espanola Public Schools; Espanola 600
U.S. Bureau of Indian Affairs; Shiprock 600
Gallup Indian Medical Center; Gallup 589

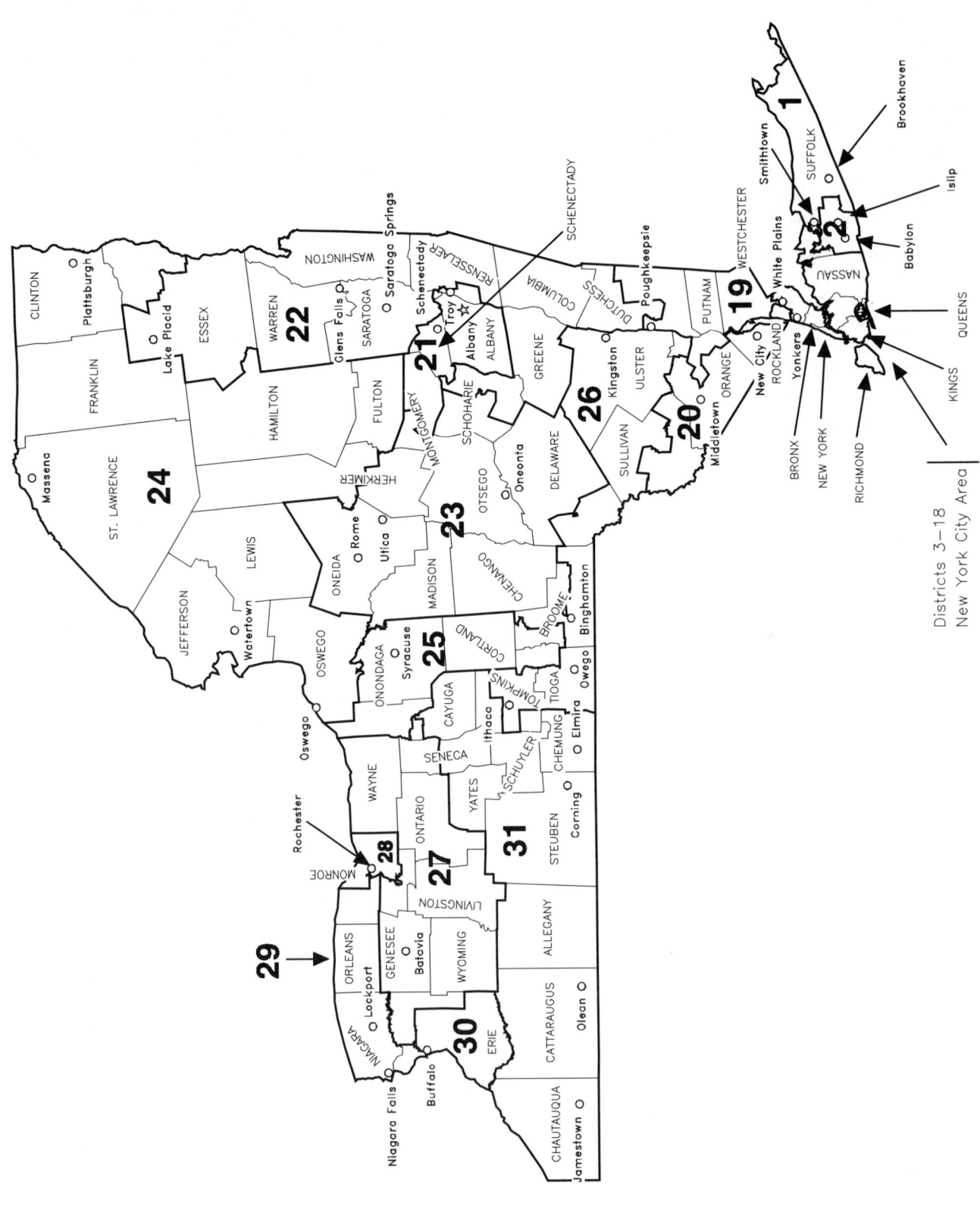

Districts 3–18
New York City Area

New York

No one could argue that New York is without influence in Congress. Its population of nearly 18 million in 1990 qualifies it for 31 House seats, still the second-highest number among the 50 states.

But California, which first exceeded New York in population and House representation with the 1970 census, now has topped it with 52 seats. Texas, challenging New York's runner-up position, has 30 seats.

It is a far cry from New York's position—beginning in the nation's early days right through the mid-20th century—as America's most populous and influential state. Long the national center for the manufacturing industry, trade, finance, transportation, communications and entertainment; the arrival point and adopted home for millions of immigrants; the site of New York City, by far the country's largest and most cosmopolitan locality; New York could justifiably boast of its haughty nickname, "The Empire State."

In recent years, however, New York has been a declining empire. Facing a plethora of urban problems—a large poor population, racial tensions, high taxes, decaying infrastructure, a huge and cumbersome municipal bureaucracy—New York City has seen its census population fall from a peak of nearly 8 million in 1970 to 7.3 million in 1990.

Of those who moved out, many went east to the suburbs of Nassau and Suffolk counties on Long Island and north to Westchester County. But many others left the state altogether, for suburban New Jersey and Connecticut or out of the high-cost-of-living region altogether. In recent years, even some of the densely populated New York suburbs have lost people as the communities age and develop their own sets of social and economic troubles.

New York City has also lost much of its manufacturing base since the end of World War II, as business owners abandoned their aging industrial plants and unionized work forces for lower production costs in the southern United States or overseas. This problem has also affected the economies of upstate New York's major cities, such as Buffalo, Rochester, Yonkers and Syracuse.

New York's flagging dynamism has cost it congressional clout. The state peaked at 45 House seats in the 1930s through the 1940s. The decline was gradual at first, with the state losing two seats each following the census counts of 1950, 1960 and 1970. Its population continued to grow—to a high of 18.2 million in 1970—though, not as fast as in the boom states of the South and West.

However, New York was hit hard by each of the last two congressional reapportionments. After losing a net total of about 700,000 residents during the 1970s (a nearly 4 percent drop), New York in 1980 lost five of its then 39 House seats. The population eased back up by 2 percent during the 1980s, but this pace lagged well behind the national average: New York lost another three seats, setting its current House delegation at 31 members.

The last time a census gave New York as few as 31 House members was in 1860, when there was a total of just 243 House members, as opposed to the 435 today.

This hardly means that gloom pervades all aspects of New York's public life. New York City is still by far the nation's most populous city, with more than twice as many residents as second-place Los Angeles. Wall Street remains the United States' preeminent financial center. Manhattan also retains the headquarters of dozens of leading corporations, the national television networks and much of its print media. The Broadway theatre district continues its legendary role in the nation's cultural life.

Other cities that lost blue-collar jobs are trying to reinvent themselves for the post-industrial era. Buffalo, long one of the nation's leading steelmaking centers and now the site of many rusting factory hulks, is trying to grow its commercial and financial sectors to take advantage of the city's location on the border of the leading U.S. trading partner, Canada.

And despite the state's overall population stagnation, it has in recent years been receiving a renewed influx of foreign immigrants. Immigration from Europe, which made New York a multi-ethnic patchwork, has long since peaked. But the state, and particularly New York City, remains a magnet for many from Latin America, Asia, the West Indies and Africa who are in search of the American dream.

Not all New Yorkers see this new burst of immigration as a positive. Many of the new arrivals are economically disadvantaged, adding to the economic and social problems that already burden the state.

However, like the immigrant groups that came before them, many of New York's burgeoning ethnic communities are forming their own clusters and starting entrepreneurial businesses. Some are even reviving working-class urban neighborhoods that had been in decline.

The most significant growth during the 1980s was in the Hispanic population. For the state as a whole, the Hispanic portion of the state's total population increased from 9 percent in 1980 to 12 percent in 1990. In New York City, Hispanics went from 17 percent in 1980 to 23 percent a decade later.

This rapid jump became a central issue in the redrawing of New York's House districts for the 1990s. Previously, the state had just one Hispanic-majority district. Hispanic activists demanded and state leaders of both major parties agreed to the creation of at least one more in New York City.

But crafting that district would be no easy task. The term "Hispanic" covers a wide range of national origins. From the years after World War II through the 1970s, New York's Hispanic population derived overwhelmingly from Puerto Rico. But during the 1980s, the state absorbed large numbers of immigrants from South America and the Dominican Republic. Thus, while many of the city's Hispanics shared a common native language and low-income economic status, they did not necessarily view themselves as sharing a common ethnic heritage.

Also, New York's Hispanics settled in demographic pockets widely scattered across the city's five boroughs. This contrasted with the city's African American constituencies, which are largely concentrated in inner-city blocs.

The challenge of drawing together disparate Hispanic communities into a viable congressional district, combined with the need to eliminate the three seats New York had lost in reapportionment, stymied a state Legislature whose partisan split (Republicans controlled the state Senate, Democrats held the Assembly) itself had made gridlock likely. The legislators deferred to, and in June 1992 enacted a plan drawn by, a state Supreme Court panel.

In order to carry out its mandate, the judges endorsed some of the most creative redistricting cartography in history. The new Hispanic-majority 12th District meanders along a mainly narrow path from a heavily Hispanic area of Queens through parts of Brooklyn before jumping across the East River to take in a Hispanic area on Manhattan's Lower East Side.

The district's squiggly lines had a ripple effect. Other unusual-looking districts include the 5th, which takes in a chunk of urban Queens before moving far to the east through the suburbs on the northern rim of Long Island; the 8th, which follows the Hudson River along Manhattan's West Side, then crosses New York Bay, rims the Brooklyn waterfront and plunges south to Coney Island's Atlantic Ocean beaches; and the 18th, which covers much of the southern part of suburban Westchester County, rims the east edge of The Bronx and reaches an arm across the East River into the center of Queens.

The remap succeeded in increasing minority representation. New York sent a second Hispanic member to the House in 1992, to go with the four African American incumbents who were re-elected that year. But for some activists, that was not enough. They filed a lawsuit, demanding that a third Hispanic-majority district—based in the heavily Puerto Rican and Dominican sections of northern Manhattan—be created. The suit remained pending in federal district court as of October 1993.

The new map's other major consequence was to rearrange existing constituencies and make a number of districts—temporarily at least—politically competitive. In 14 of the 31 districts in 1992, the House winner received 57 percent of the vote or less; four victors won with just 50 percent. Eight of the close winners were Democrats, while six were Republicans.

Overall, Democrats held 18 of New York's 31 House seats following the 1992 election. Democrat Bill Clinton finished first in 22 of the districts in that year's presidential election.

Table 1 Population

District	Population	Population under 18	Voting-age population	Median age
1	580,338	147,165	433,173	33.4
2	580,337	142,902	437,435	32.8
3	580,337	124,497	455,840	36.7
4	580,338	129,593	450,745	35.8
5	580,337	117,832	462,505	37.9
6	580,337	148,150	432,187	32.4
7	580,337	107,809	472,528	36.7
8	580,337	94,041	486,296	36.6
9	580,338	110,759	469,579	38.5
10	580,335	165,728	414,607	30.3
11	580,337	165,773	414,564	30.7
12	580,340	162,407	417,933	29.8
13	580,337	130,766	449,571	34.7
14	580,337	64,356	515,981	38.8
15	580,337	142,853	437,484	31.9
16	580,338	195,150	385,188	27.1
17	580,337	142,047	438,290	33.2
18	580,337	112,956	467,381	37.7
19	580,337	136,022	444,315	34.2
20	580,338	151,009	429,329	34.0
21	580,337	128,562	451,775	34.1
22	580,337	145,799	434,538	34.1
23	580,337	144,175	436,162	33.6
24	580,338	153,813	426,525	31.0
25	580,337	144,414	435,923	32.6
26	580,338	133,933	446,405	32.9
27	580,337	146,389	433,948	33.9
28	580,337	141,181	439,156	33.1
29	580,337	138,621	441,716	34.1
30	580,337	139,029	441,308	34.3
31	580,337	151,818	428,519	33.8
State	17,990,455	4,259,549	13,730,906	33.9

Table 2 Voting-Age Persons

District	White*	Black*	American Indian, Eskimo, or Aleut*	Asian or Pacific Islander*	Other*	Hispanic*	Male*	Female*
1	93.5%	3.7%	0.3%	1.7%	0.8%	4.3%	48.1%	51.9%
2	86.9	8.9	0.2	1.5	2.5	8.8	48.0	52.0
3	94.8	1.9	0.1	2.2	0.9	4.2	47.9	52.1
4	80.1	15.0	0.2	2.8	2.0	7.0	47.0	53.0
5	85.4	3.2	0.1	9.7	1.6	6.8	47.2	52.8
6	31.8	54.5	0.6	6.2	6.9	16.0	45.6	54.4
7	72.3	9.2	0.2	11.0	7.3	19.6	46.5	53.5
8	82.0	7.7	0.2	6.1	3.9	11.5	48.4	51.6
9	88.6	3.1	0.1	5.9	2.4	7.7	46.2	53.8
10	28.9	59.4	0.4	2.5	8.8	18.5	44.2	55.8
11	20.5	72.4	0.4	3.0	3.8	11.1	43.4	56.6
12	35.9	12.9	0.5	21.2	29.5	54.3	47.9	52.1
13	88.3	4.7	0.2	5.1	1.8	6.6	46.8	53.2
14	86.9	4.4	0.2	5.4	3.1	9.7	45.9	54.1
15	29.7	46.7	0.6	2.7	20.3	43.6	45.9	54.1
16	21.4	42.2	0.6	2.2	33.5	58.7	43.2	56.8
17	44.1	40.1	0.4	3.6	11.8	26.1	43.7	56.3
18	82.6	7.0	0.1	7.5	2.8	9.7	46.2	53.8
19	89.5	7.1	0.2	2.1	1.2	5.1	49.3	50.7
20	87.5	7.8	0.2	3.1	1.4	5.6	48.1	51.9
21	92.3	5.4	0.2	1.5	0.6	1.8	46.7	53.3

District	White*	Black*	American Indian, Eskimo, or Aleut*	Asian or Pacific Islander*	Other*	Hispanic*	Male*	Female*
22	96.6	2.3	0.2	0.6	0.4	1.5	49.1	50.9
23	96.1	2.7	0.2	0.6	0.4	1.4	48.2	51.8
24	95.2	2.8	0.7	0.6	0.7	1.7	49.8	50.2
25	92.4	5.5	0.5	1.2	0.4	1.2	47.0	53.0
26	91.3	5.1	0.2	2.0	1.3	3.8	48.3	51.7
27	95.7	2.5	0.3	1.0	0.4	1.2	48.3	51.7
28	84.6	11.6	0.3	1.8	1.7	3.4	46.7	53.3
29	93.7	4.0	0.7	0.6	1.1	2.2	46.8	53.2
30	83.3	15.1	0.5	0.6	0.5	1.3	46.6	53.4
31	96.1	2.3	0.5	0.5	0.6	1.4	48.0	52.0
State	76.4	14.7	0.3	3.8	4.8	11.2	46.9	53.1

*As percent of voting-age population.

Table 3   Voting-Age Persons by Age Groups

District	18-24*	25-44*	45-54*	55-64*	65 and over*
1	14.3%	44.1%	15.1%	10.6%	15.8%
2	14.7	44.1	15.8	12.6	12.8
3	12.3	40.4	14.9	15.3	17.1
4	13.5	39.6	14.2	13.7	18.9
5	11.2	39.8	15.2	14.3	19.4
6	15.3	42.8	14.9	12.0	15.0
7	12.1	41.4	13.1	12.5	20.9
8	11.5	46.8	12.9	10.6	18.1
9	10.7	39.1	12.5	13.4	24.3
10	16.3	45.2	14.2	10.8	13.6
11	15.5	48.5	14.3	9.9	11.8
12	17.3	46.9	13.7	10.4	11.7
13	13.2	42.7	14.0	12.0	18.1
14	9.7	46.5	14.7	11.7	17.5
15	16.1	44.6	13.2	10.6	15.5
16	18.7	46.4	14.3	10.0	10.6
17	14.5	41.8	13.4	11.4	18.9
18	11.7	39.7	14.1	13.4	21.1
19	13.8	44.7	15.4	11.5	14.5
20	12.8	43.5	16.2	12.5	15.0
21	16.1	40.4	12.2	11.5	19.8
22	13.1	43.5	14.6	11.8	17.1
23	16.0	39.0	13.4	11.8	19.9
24	18.0	42.1	12.8	11.1	16.1
25	16.2	42.3	12.9	11.5	17.2
26	17.6	41.0	13.0	11.3	17.1
27	14.2	42.3	14.3	12.0	17.2
28	14.8	43.8	13.3	10.8	17.3
29	14.0	41.5	12.9	12.4	19.3
30	14.0	40.1	13.3	13.0	19.6
31	14.4	39.9	13.5	12.5	19.7
State	14.2	42.7	13.9	11.9	17.2

*As percent of voting-age population.

Table 4   Income and Occupation

District	Median family income	Families in poverty	White collar*	Blue collar*	Service*	Farm*
1	$50,313	3.7%	62.8%	22.6%	12.9%	1.7%
2	53,215	3.4	60.3	25.8	12.9	1.0
3	61,611	2.0	72.5	16.5	10.3	0.7
4	56,588	3.1	68.6	18.3	12.2	0.9
5	57,915	3.3	74.8	14.7	9.9	0.6
6	40,927	8.9	58.5	22.6	18.6	0.4
7	36,643	9.3	59.9	23.3	16.5	0.3
8	39,777	13.3	79.1	10.8	9.9	0.2
9	43,401	6.9	71.1	17.7	11.0	0.2
10	26,177	24.6	61.7	19.4	18.6	0.3
11	29,141	19.1	59.1	18.7	22.1	0.2
12	21,911	28.3	44.3	33.2	22.1	0.3
13	46,598	7.2	66.4	20.0	13.4	0.3
14	59,953	5.6	82.7	8.5	8.6	0.2
15	21,065	29.8	57.9	20.8	21.0	0.3
16	16,683	39.5	46.9	27.1	25.5	0.5
17	32,400	15.8	60.1	20.2	19.3	0.4
18	53,968	4.2	71.5	15.8	11.9	0.7
19	57,419	3.1	69.1	18.0	11.7	1.2
20	53,782	4.4	66.8	19.8	12.1	1.3
21	39,150	6.5	67.1	19.0	13.0	0.9
22	38,589	5.2	58.6	25.7	13.4	2.4
23	31,352	8.4	53.8	27.3	15.0	3.9
24	30,372	10.0	49.3	29.7	17.1	3.9
25	37,404	7.1	62.9	22.6	13.1	1.5
26	37,323	7.4	60.6	23.0	14.9	1.5
27	40,025	4.6	57.8	26.8	12.7	2.7
28	41,851	9.0	65.0	21.7	12.6	0.6
29	35,193	8.2	56.4	28.3	14.2	1.2
30	32,576	10.7	55.3	27.9	15.9	1.0
31	30,172	9.6	49.7	29.8	16.5	4.0
State	39,741	10.0	63.1	21.4	14.4	1.1

*As percent of employed persons age 16 and over.

Table 5   Education: School Years Completed

District	Less than grade 9*	Grades 9-12 no diploma*	High school diploma*	College bachelor's degree or higher*
1	5.8%	11.9%	32.8%	22.8%
2	6.6	13.2	35.2	18.9
3	4.8	8.9	31.6	29.9
4	7.2	11.5	31.2	26.2
5	6.9	9.2	26.2	34.8
6	11.4	19.6	31.1	14.6
7	15.0	17.2	31.4	18.0
8	10.2	11.2	19.3	42.1
9	10.4	14.5	31.5	24.2
10	14.5	23.6	26.4	16.8
11	11.7	21.3	27.5	17.5
12	29.3	23.3	22.8	10.5
13	10.6	15.1	34.1	19.3
14	7.2	7.9	15.5	51.4
15	20.4	22.8	22.1	17.6
16	24.1	28.8	25.0	6.1
17	14.5	18.9	29.0	17.1
18	8.6	11.0	26.6	33.4
19	6.1	10.5	26.6	32.4
20	6.8	11.5	28.0	29.6
21	7.8	12.9	31.3	24.2
22	7.4	13.6	33.4	20.4
23	8.8	15.8	35.0	15.9
24	9.3	16.9	38.1	13.7
25	6.4	13.6	31.4	22.7
26	8.4	14.2	30.7	22.5
27	6.7	13.0	32.4	22.0
28	7.1	13.5	27.0	27.4
29	8.1	14.7	34.1	17.8
30	9.7	17.5	34.0	14.6

District	Less than grade 9*	Grades 9-12 no diploma*	High school diploma*	College bachelor's degree or higher*
31	8.3	16.2	36.9	15.0
State	10.2	15.0	29.5	23.1

*As percent of persons age 25 and over.

Table 6 Housing and Residential Patterns

District	Owner occupied	Renter occupied	Urban	Rural
1	79.1%	20.9%	92.2%	7.8%
2	79.6	20.5	99.9	0.1
3	83.8	16.2	99.6	0.4
4	78.1	21.9	100.0	0.0
5	66.6	33.4	99.2	0.8
6	54.5	45.5	100.0	0.0
7	32.5	67.5	100.0	0.0
8	22.9	77.1	100.0	0.0
9	42.9	57.1	100.0	0.0
10	23.6	76.4	100.0	0.0
11	18.5	81.5	100.0	0.0
12	15.3	84.7	100.0	0.0
13	52.4	47.6	100.0	0.0
14	25.8	74.2	100.0	0.0
15	6.4	93.6	100.0	0.0
16	8.2	91.8	100.0	0.0
17	21.8	78.2	100.0	0.0
18	53.7	46.3	100.0	0.0
19	71.0	29.0	69.9	30.1
20	71.8	28.2	77.5	22.5
21	59.1	40.9	84.9	15.1
22	73.6	26.4	33.3	66.7
23	70.0	30.0	45.2	54.8
24	68.3	31.7	35.3	64.7
25	64.9	35.1	74.4	25.6
26	63.9	36.1	57.0	43.0
27	75.8	24.2	44.5	55.5
28	62.3	37.7	96.3	3.7
29	64.5	35.5	77.1	22.9
30	63.5	36.5	87.0	13.0
31	70.9	29.1	39.7	60.3
State	52.2	47.8	84.3	15.7

1st District

Eastern Suffolk County — Brookhaven; Smithtown

Located more than 100 miles from downtown Manhattan, Long Island's lightly populated East End presents a tableau of the Suffolk County of 40 years ago. Farms, fishing villages and the vacation homes of the wealthy (in such enclaves as the Hamptons and Shelter Island) remain this region's most prominent features.

Nonetheless, suburban sprawl has thoroughly overtaken the closer-in areas on the western side of the 1st. Brookhaven Town, the 1st's core jurisdiction, increased in population more than ninefold between 1950 and 1990, from 44,500 to 408,000.

Suburbanization has not greatly changed the Republican tilt that dates to the 1st District's rural days. George Bush took 60 percent of the 1st's vote in 1988; although he fell off sharply in 1992, he still managed to eke out a win over Bill Clinton in 1992.

Yet Rep. George Hochbrueckner, who won his fourth term in 1992 with 51 percent of the vote, has proved that a Democrat can win here. There is a small minority population on which to build a Democratic base, and the district has large numbers of Irish- and Italian-Americans, many with blue-collar, urban roots. The 1st has some industrial employment, including a defense-production base that has become tenuous in the post-Cold War era. A reliance on seasonal employment in many of the 1st's exurban and rural areas provides modest incomes for many district residents.

Constituents' environmental concerns have also benefited Hochbrueckner. He was a leader in the successful effort to decommission a nuclear power plant in Shoreham and has pushed to clean up the ocean waters that are vital to the 1st's fishing and tourism industries.

The bulk of the 1st's residents live in a part of Smithtown, at the district's western end, and in Brookhaven, which covers a large swath spanning the width of Suffolk County. The North Shore area along Long Island Sound has several well-off subdivisions, but most of the 1st's suburbs are middle class.

Coram, with just over 30,000 residents, is the largest of Brookhaven's many sizable suburban communities. The mainly residential area includes the state university at Stony Brook (17,600 students), a center for scientific research. In the exurbs to the east is Brookhaven National Laboratory. Nearby, in Riverhead, is Calverton and a Grumman Inc. factory that has been hit hard by cutbacks in Navy aviation programs.

Five less-populous towns—Riverhead, East Hampton, Shelter Island, Southampton and Southold—make up the East End. There are still many potato and duck farms here; a number of small vineyards also have been established on Long Island's North Fork, which has a climate and soil similar to the Burgundy region of France.

The beaches along the 1st's southern edge are summer playgrounds; parts of Fire Island are long-established retreats for New York's gay community. But these coastal areas are vulnerable to damage by storms, such as the fierce nor'easters that hit during the winter of 1992-1993.

Election Returns

	1st District	Democrat	Republican
1992	President*	96,890 (38.3%)	101,160 (40.0%)
	House	117,940 (51.1%)	110,043 (47.7%)
1990	Governor†	64,366 (46.3%)	67,496 (48.6%)
1988	President	87,396 (39.2%)	134,505 (60.4%)
	Senate	116,746 (55.4%)	91,384 (43.3%)
1986	Senate	49,046 (36.3%)	79,720 (58.9%)
	Governor	86,239 (62.7%)	44,894 (32.6%)

*Vote for Perot was 54,128 (21.4%).   †Independent/other is greater than 5%.

Demographics

Population 580,338

Percent change from 1980 12.4%

Land area 637 square miles

Population per square mile 911

Counties, 1990 population
Suffolk (pt.) 580,338

Cities, 1990 population (10,000 or more)

Centereach CDP 26,720	Nesconset CDP 10,712
Coram CDP 30,111	Patchogue 11,060
East Patchogue CDP 20,195	Ridge CDP 11,734
	Selden CDP 20,608
Farmingville CDP 14,842	Setauket-East Setauket
Holtsville CDP (pt.) 12,530	CDP 13,634
Kings Park CDP (pt.) 11,415	Shirley CDP 22,936
	Smithtown CDP (pt.) 15,349
Lake Ronkonkoma CDP 18,997	St. James CDP 12,703
Mastic Beach CDP 10,293	Stony Brook CDP 13,726
Mastic CDP 13,778	Terryville CDP 10,275
Medford CDP 21,274	

Race and Hispanic origin

White 93.0%
Black 4.1%
American Indian, Eskimo, or Aleut. 0.3%
Asian or Pacific Islander 1.7%
Other 0.9%
Hispanic origin 4.7%

Ancestry

American 2.2%	Italian 28.8%
Dutch 1.3%	Norwegian 1.4%
English 9.4%	Polish 8.3%
French 2.5%	Russian 3.2%
German 24.8%	Scotch Irish 1.0%
Greek 1.3%	Scottish 1.6%
Hungarian 1.1%	Swedish 1.5%
Irish 26.3%	

Universities/colleges, 1990-1991 enrollment

Long Island University, Southampton 1,257
State University of New York, Stony Brook 17,623
St. Joseph's College, Patchogue 1,936
Suffolk County Community College, Riverhead 2,440
Suffolk County Community College, Selden 12,395

Newspapers, total circulation (in all districts)

Long Island Newsday 788,998
New York Daily News 757,053
New York Post 551,443
New York Times 746,924

Commercial television stations, affiliations

ADI: New York (100%)
WLIG, Riverhead (None)
WHSI, Smithtown (None)

Cable television systems, total subscribers

Cablevision of East Hampton; East Hampton 9,769
Cablevision of Hauppauge; Hauppauge 139,000
Cablevision of Long Island; Riverhead 41,000
TCI Cable of Brookhaven; Farmingville 64,050

Military installations, 1991

Suffolk County Airport Air Force Guard Station, Westhampton Beach 266

Businesses and other major employers

State University of New York; Stony Brook 7,000
Associated Universities Inc./Brookhaven National Laboratory; Upton; research services 3,300

Grumman Aerospace Corp./Electronics Systems Div.; Great River; aircraft 2,000
Brookhaven Memorial Hospital & Medical Center; Patchogue 1,600
Whitman Packaging Corp.; Yaphank; plastics products 1,200
St. Charles Hospital; Port Jefferson 1,200
John T. Mather Memorial Hospital; Port Jefferson 1,200
St. John's Episcopal Hospital; Smithtown 1,200
County of Suffolk/Public Works Dept.; Yaphank 900
Community Hospital of Western Suffolk County; Smithtown 860
Southampton Hospital Assn.; Southampton 728
County of Suffolk/Sheriffs Dept.; Westhampton 700
Maryhaven Center of Hope; Port Jefferson; family services 700
Clinical Practice Management Plan; Stony Brook; management services 700
Independent Group Home Living; East Moriches; residential care 685
Central Suffolk Hospital; Riverhead 670
Suffolk County Community College; Selden 658
Sears Roebuck & Co.; Lake Grove; department stores 620

2nd District

Western Suffolk County — Islip; Babylon

During an 18-year House career, Democrat Thomas J. Downey withstood the Republican tendencies of western Suffolk County's well-established, middle-class suburbs. But the 2nd's partisan tilt meant that any error would leave Downey vulnerable.

That slip came in 1992, when Downey got entangled in the House bank controversy. The timing was fortuitous for Republican Rick Lazio, his party's strongest House challenger in years. A moderate with some appeal to independents and even Democrats disappointed in Downey, Lazio reinstated the GOP claim on the 2nd District.

The 1992 presidential contest provided an odd counterpoint to the House race: The middle-class dissatisfaction with Washington that toppled Downey also hindered George Bush in the 2nd. He got only 41 percent of the district's vote in 1992 (well below his 1988 tally); Bill Clinton took 40 percent.

Despite the district's overall tendencies, Democratic candidates do have a base that is sizable by suburban Long Island standards. While the district's mainly white-collar work force includes many who commute to New York City, there is a blue-collar constituency, including a number of workers dependent on Long Island's defense-related industries that have been hit hard by funding cutbacks.

The 2nd has more than 56,000 Hispanics—the largest Hispanic population among the Long Island districts—and as many blacks. More than a third of the 45,000 residents of Brentwood (the largest community in Islip town) are Hispanics; blacks make up three-quarters of the nearly 14,000 residents of North Amityville in Babylon town.

Islip and Babylon—the two townships that make up the southwest corner of Suffolk County—took full part in the post-World War II suburban boom, but they hit a plateau in the 1970s. Islip, where population jumped from about 71,500 in 1950 to 279,000 in 1970, gained a net of just 20,000 people over the next 20 years. Babylon (which had 45,000 residents in 1950) topped 200,000 in 1970 but stuck there.

Islip town—which takes in such communities as Brentwood, West Islip, Central Islip and Bay Shore—contains much of the district's employment base. Hauppauge, the seat of Suffolk County's government, is shared with the 1st District; the 2nd has the county office complex and much of the community's commercial real estate.

While Babylon town is made up mainly of residential communities—the largest of which, with just over 42,000 residents, is West Babylon—there is some industry: AIL Systems makes defense electronics in Deer Park. But defense-industry employment has been faltering since a Fairchild Republic aircraft plant in Farmingdale closed in the late 1980s.

The northern part of the 2nd also takes in parts of Huntington town and Smithtown. These areas have large Jewish populations and Democratic leanings.

Election Returns

	2nd District	Democrat	Republican
1992	President*	91,430 (39.8%)	92,762 (40.4%)
	House	96,328 (46.2%)	109,386 (52.5%)
1990	Governor	57,380 (47.9%)	56,513 (47.2%)
1988	President	82,710 (39.0%)	128,366 (60.6%)
	Senate	113,636 (57.0%)	82,904 (41.6%)
1986	Senate	46,074 (36.5%)	73,950 (58.5%)
	Governor†	79,304 (61.7%)	42,628 (33.2%)

*Vote for Perot was 44,603 (19.4%).   †Independent/other is greater than 5%.

Demographics

Population 580,337

Percent change from 1980 12.6%

Land area 190 square miles

Population per square mile 3,061

Counties, 1990 population
Suffolk (pt.) 580,337

Cities, 1990 population (10,000 or more)

Babylon 12,249	Lindenhurst 26,879
Bay Shore CDP 21,279	North Amityville CDP
Brentwood CDP 45,218	13,849
Central Islip CDP 26,028	North Babylon CDP
Copiague CDP 20,769	18,081
Deer Park CDP 28,840	North Bay Shore CDP
Dix Hills CDP (pt.) 23,827	12,799
East Islip CDP 14,325	North Lindenhurst CDP
Hauppauge CDP (pt.)	10,563
12,738	Ronkonkoma CDP 20,391
Holbrook CDP (pt.) 20,210	Sayville CDP 16,550
Huntington Station CDP	West Babylon CDP 42,410
(pt.) 22,606	West Islip CDP 28,419
Islip CDP 18,924	

Race and Hispanic origin
White 85.5%
Black 9.8%
American Indian, Eskimo, or Aleut. 0.2%
Asian or Pacific Islander 1.7%
Other 2.9%
Hispanic origin 9.7%

Ancestry

American 2.1%	Italian 29.5%
Dutch 1.1%	Norwegian 1.1%
English 6.5%	Polish 5.7%
French 1.9%	Russian 2.7%
German 21.0%	Scottish 1.2%
Greek 1.0%	Swedish 1.1%
Hungarian 1.0%	West Indian 1.5%
Irish 23.5%	

Universities/colleges, 1990-1991 enrollment
Dowling College, Oakdale 3,977
Immaculate Conception Seminary, Huntington 202
Long Island University, Brentwood 835
New York Institute of Technology, Central Islip 1,888
Suffolk County Community College, Brentwood 5,055

Newspapers, total circulation (in all districts)
Long Island Newsday 788,998
New York Daily News 757,053
New York Post 551,443
New York Times 746,924

Commercial television stations, affiliations
ADI: New York (100%)

Cable television systems, total subscribers
Cablevision of Hauppauge; Hauppauge 139,000
Cablevision of Islip; Islip 13,785
Cablevision of Long Island; Hicksville 349,000

Businesses and other major employers
State of New York/Long Island Developmental Center; Huntington Station 2,400
Good Samaritan Hospital; West Islip 1,980
Brentwood Union Free School District; Brentwood 1,794
Southside Hospital Inc.; Bay Shore 1,750
Eaton Corp./AIL Systems Div.; Ronkonkoma; electronic components 1,500
Jewish Board of Family & Child Services; Brightwaters; residential care 1,500
County of Suffolk/Social Services; Smithtown 1,500
AIL Systems Inc.; Deer Park; electricity measuring devices 1,400
Brunswick Hospital Center Inc.; Amityville 1,300
Long Island Home Ltd./Broadlawn Manor Nursing Home; Amityville 1,245
Hazeltine Corp./Government Products Div.; Commack; communications equipment 1,200
Half Hollow Hills; Huntington Station 1,200
Genovese Drug Stores Inc.; Bohemia; warehousing 1,110
State of New York/Transportation Dept.; Smithtown 1,100
State of New York/Psychiatric Center; Central Islip 1,056
County of Suffolk; Smithtown 1,000
State of New York/General Services; Smithtown 1,000
North Babylon Union Free School District; Babylon 1,000
Napco Security Systems Inc.; Amityville; security systems 929
Gull Inc./Gull Airborne; Smithtown; freight shipping 900
Alcott Staff Leasing Inc.; Farmingdale; personnel supply services 800
Town of Huntington; Huntington 725
Symbol Technologies Inc.; Bohemia; office equipment 700

ILC Data Device Corp./Electronics Mfg.; Bohemia; data processing equipment 700

U.S. Transportation Dept.; Ronkonkoma 700

Township of Babylon; Lindenhurst 650

DEL Laboratories Inc./Sally Hansen Div.; Farmingdale; cosmetics 630

Di Giorgio Corp./White Rose Food Co. Div.; Farmingdale; grocery products 600

Dale New Co. Inc.; Farmingdale; newspapers 600

Federated Dept. Stores/Abraham & Strauss; Huntington Station; department stores 600

Central Islip Union School District; Central Islip 600

Dowling College; Oakdale 582

Nature's Bounty/Starlen Labs; Bohemia; vitamins & pharmaceuticals 550

Deer Park Union Free School District; Deer Park 550

3rd District

Eastern Nassau County — Oyster Bay

Redistricting changed little in the 3rd District's long tenure as a GOP base. The 3rd's suburban population is more than 90 percent non-Hispanic white; it has more pockets of affluence than of poverty. In addition, a Republican machine has controlled Nassau County politics for decades. Its most prominent alumnus, GOP Sen. Alfonse M. D'Amato, hails from Island Park in the southwest part of the 3rd.

Yet the economic problems of the early 1990s hit home in the 3rd and loosened the GOP grip in 1992. The impact of the national recession on the 3rd's mainly white-collar work force was amplified by the district's dependence on a declining defense industrial base; Grumman, a contractor that has lost several large Navy aircraft projects, has its headquarters and a production facility in Bethpage.

The resulting dissatisfaction with George Bush's economic program in the 3rd was matched by anger toward local GOP officials held largely responsible for a county budget gap and burdensome property tax rates. As a result, Bush—who in 1988 defeated Democrat Michael S. Dukakis by more than 40,000 votes in the 3rd—lost to Bill Clinton in 1992 by 5,000 votes. In the House race that year the Republican candidate won by a narrow plurality the open seat vacated by an 11-term Republican.

The 3rd (see map on page 502) reaches a finger into northwest Nassau County, taking in such well-off communities as Plandome Manor, Manhasset and North Hills. The district then broadens to cover much of eastern Nassau County.

The Long Island Expressway (LIE) roughly bisects this area. To the north is estate country in such communities as Brookville and Old Westbury. The Sagamore Hill estate of President Theodore Roosevelt is near Long Island Sound. The district's campuses of the State University of New York, C.W. Post College and the New York Institute of Technology are in the north part of the 3rd.

The bulk of the 3rd's people are in the portions of Hempstead Town and Oyster Bay south of the LIE. This is mainly white-collar suburbia, with many commuters to the financial and corporate offices of Manhattan. Despite cutbacks, Grumman is the largest employer in the 3rd, which also has the headquarters of the Long Island Lighting Co. in Hicksville.

The 3rd has just over half the residents of Levittown, the development that sparked Long Island's suburban boom in the 1940s. The district has a large number of Italian-American and Jewish residents: Massapequa, in the southeast corner, was once nicknamed "Matzo-Pizza" for its ethnic mix, though it is now mainly Italian.

Election Returns

	3rd District	Democrat	Republican
1992	President*	126,112 (43.6%)	121,176 (41.9%)
	House	116,915 (45.8%)	124,727 (48.9%)
1990	Governor	78,072 (48.0%)	76,427 (47.0%)
1988	President	111,333 (40.2%)	164,473 (59.3%)
	Senate	147,171 (55.3%)	115,397 (43.3%)
1986	Senate†	64,434 (35.6%)	105,342 (58.3%)
	Governor†	100,631 (55.9%)	64,990 (36.1%)

*Vote for Perot was 40,450 (14.0%).   †Independent/other is greater than 5%.

Demographics

Population 580,337

Percent change from 1980 12.0%

Land area 155 square miles

Population per square mile 3,750

Counties, 1990 population
Nassau (pt.) 580,337

Cities, 1990 population (10,000 or more)

Baldwin CDP (pt.) 14,826	Merrick CDP (pt.) 23,042
Bellmore CDP 16,438	North Bellmore CDP (pt.)
Bethpage CDP 15,761	17,315
East Massapequa CDP	North Massapequa CDP
19,550	19,365
East Rockaway 10,152	North Merrick CDP
Freeport (pt.) 20,327	12,113
Glen Cove (pt.) 13,829	Oceanside CDP 32,423
Hicksville CDP 40,174	Plainview CDP (pt.) 18,323
Jericho CDP 13,141	Seaford CDP 15,597
Levittown CDP (pt.)	South Farmingdale CDP
26,868	15,377
Long Beach 33,510	Syosset CDP 18,967
Massapequa CDP 22,018	Wantagh CDP 18,567
Massapequa Park 18,044	

Race and Hispanic origin
White 94.4%
Black 2.0%
American Indian, Eskimo, or Aleut. 0.1%
Asian or Pacific Islander 2.6%
Other 1.0%
Hispanic origin 4.4%

Ancestry

American 3.8%	Irish 22.8%
Austrian 2.2%	Italian 26.8%
English 6.0%	Polish 8.6%
French 1.7%	Russian 8.1%
German 19.0%	Scottish 1.2%
Greek 1.9%	Swedish 1.0%
Hungarian 1.9%	

NEW YORK CITY AREA

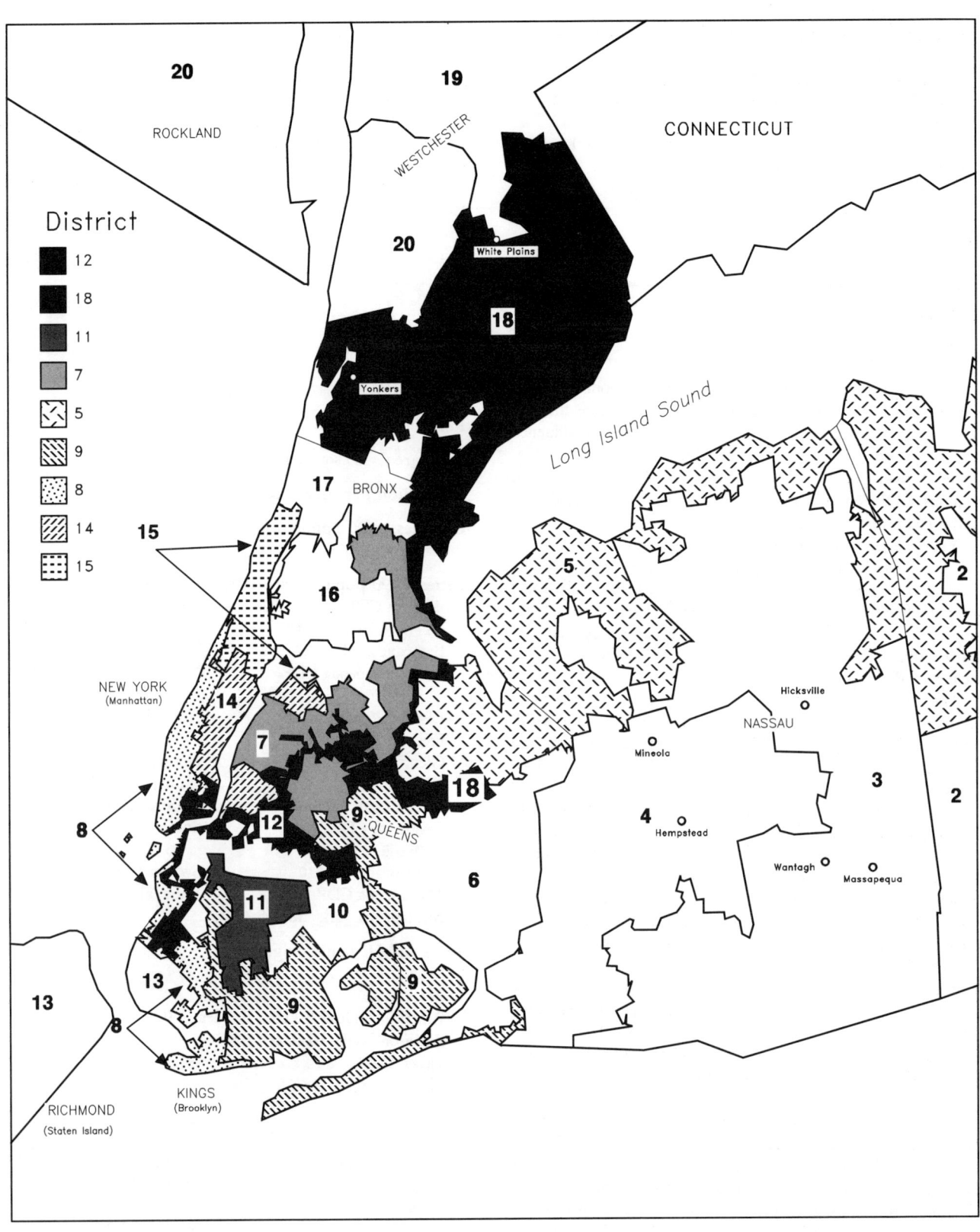

District
- ■ 12
- ■ 18
- ■ 11
- ■ 7
- 5
- 9
- 8
- 14
- 15

20
ROCKLAND

19

WESTCHESTER

CONNECTICUT

20

White Plains

18

Yonkers

Long Island Sound

17 BRONX

15

16

5

2

NEW YORK
(Manhattan)

14

Hicksville

NASSAU

7

Mineola

8

18

3

2

12

9

4

Hempstead

QUEENS

6

Wantagh

Massapequa

11

10

13

9

9

13

9

8

KINGS
(Brooklyn)

RICHMOND
(Staten Island)

Universities/colleges, 1990-1991 enrollment

Briarcliffe School, Hicksville 659
Five Towns College, Seaford 541
Long Island University-C. W. Post College, Greenvale 8,690
New York Institute of Technology, Old Westbury 6,944
State University of New York, Old Westbury 4,262
State University of New York Agricultural & Technical College, Farmingdale 11,106

Newspapers, total circulation (in all districts)

Long Island Newsday 788,998
New York Daily News 757,053
New York Law Journal 13,583
New York Post 551,443
New York Times 746,924

Commercial television stations, affiliations

ADI: New York (100%)

Cable television systems, total subscribers

Cablevision of Long Island; Hicksville 349,000

Businesses and other major employers

Grumman Aerospace Corp.; Bethpage; aircraft/parts 17,000
Long Island Lighting Co.; Hicksville; electric services 2,950
Cablevision Systems Corp.; Woodbury; cable TV services 1,500
Geico Insurance Co.; Woodbury; life insurance 1,400
Pall Corp.; Greenvale; medical instruments/supplies 1,200
South Nassau Communities Hospital; Rockville Centre 1,085
Epicure Products Inc./Concord Auto Sound; Woodbury; audio equipment 1,000
Sears Roebuck & Co.; Hicksville; department stores 1,000
New York Institute of Technology; Old Westbury 1,000
North Shore University Hospital; Glen Cove 1,000
Massapequa Union Free School District; Massapequa 900
Recco Home Care Service Inc.; Massapequa; home health services 850
Loral Fairchild Corp.; Syosset; search/navigation equipment 800
Baldwin Union Free School District; Baldwin 800
Central General Hospital Inc.; Hicksville 759
Mid-Island Hospital Inc.; Bethpage 735
Long Beach Memorial Hospital; Long Beach 721
City of Long Beach/School District; Long Beach 700
Farmingdale Union Free School District; Farmingdale 650
Macy's Northeast Inc.; Massapequa; department stores 600
Health Insurance Plan of Greater New York/Syosset Community Hospital; Syosset 600
National Cleaning Contractors; Hicksville; building services 600
Smithkline Beecham Corp./Mid-Atlantic Div.; Syosset; medical/dental labs 550

4th District

Southwest Nassau County — Hempstead; Mineola

The 4th shares many Republican traits with the neighboring 3rd District. The 4th (see map on page 502) has some of New York City's longest established suburbs: Its middle-to-upper-income residents head to work on the Long Island Railroad and such congested routes as the Southern State Parkway and Long Island Expressway. The 4th, which includes the Nassau County seat of Mineola, is a stronghold for the county's GOP organization.

Yet the 4th does have some elements that can make it potentially competitive for a Democratic candidate. Nearly a quarter of the district's residents are black or Hispanic, the largest minority-group constituency of any Long Island House district.

There are a number of working-class residents who work at John F. Kennedy International Airport (across the district line in Queens), the Belmont Park horse track in Floral Park and such large shopping centers as Roosevelt Field and Green Acres. Even some of the district's wealthiest communities, in its southwestern corner, are mainly Jewish and lean Democratic.

These constituencies provide Democrats with a foothold in the 4th. This base—combined with the national recession, cutbacks in the region's defense and banking industries and fiscal problems in the Republican-controlled county government—enabled Bill Clinton to defeat George Bush here in 1992. Clinton won 47 percent of the districtwide vote to Bush's 41 percent; Ross Perot trailed with 11 percent. That year, GOP House candidate David Levy won with just under half the vote.

More than 80 percent of the district's population is in the sprawling township of Hempstead; the remainder is in North Hempstead. The foundation of GOP success is such middle- and upper-middle-income suburbs as Valley Stream, New Hyde Park, Garden City and Franklin Square; these communities are nearly all white.

The ethnic mix of the district includes many Italian- and Irish-Americans. Rockville Centre is the seat of suburban Long Island's Roman Catholic diocese.

The district's black population, and much of its Democratic vote, is mainly in such east side communities as Roosevelt, Uniondale, Hempstead and New Cassel. While these are largely middle-class areas, their poverty rates are well above the district's average.

The other Democratic bloc is at the other end of the district and income scale, in the largely Jewish "Five Towns" of Inwood, Lawrence, Cedarhurst, Woodmere and Hewlett. Nearby Atlantic Beach makes up the 4th's coastline, the shortest of any suburban Long Island district.

At the district's eastern end is about half of the historic suburban development of Levittown. The largest employment hub is between Garden City and Uniondale. It includes the Roosevelt Field shopping complex and the former site of the Mitchell Field airport, which now supports the Nassau County Veterans' Memorial Coliseum and the campuses of Hofstra University and Nassau Community College. Adelphi University is also in the district.

Election Returns

	4th District	Democrat	Republican
1992	President*	119,947 (46.5%)	106,016 (41.1%)
	House †	100,386 (44.8%)	110,710 (49.4%)
1990	Governor †	74,711 (48.9%)	70,286 (46.0%)
1988	President	106,957 (42.4%)	144,324 (57.1%)
	Senate	133,786 (55.2%)	105,132 (43.4%)
1986	Senate †	61,062 (35.2%)	102,011 (58.9%)
	Governor †	95,235 (55.1%)	63,465 (36.7%)

Vote for Perot was 30,476 (11.8%).   †*Independent/other is greater than 5%.*

Demographics

Population 580,338

Percent change from 1980 12.0%

Land area 84 square miles

Population per square mile 6,889

Counties, 1990 population
Nassau (pt.) 580,338

Cities, 1990 population (10,000 or more)

East Meadow CDP 36,909
Elmont CDP 28,612
Floral Park 15,947
Franklin Square CDP
  28,205
Freeport (pt.) 19,567
Garden City 21,686
Hempstead 49,453
Levittown CDP (pt.)
  26,418
Lynbrook (pt.) 19,205
Mineola 18,994
New Cassel CDP 10,257

North New Hyde Park
  CDP (pt.) 14,359
North Valley Stream CDP
  14,574
Rockville Centre 24,727
Roosevelt CDP 15,030
Salisbury CDP 12,226
Uniondale CDP 20,328
Valley Stream 33,946
West Hempstead CDP
  17,689
Westbury (pt.) 12,948
Woodmere CDP 15,578

Race and Hispanic origin
White 78.3%
Black 16.2%
American Indian, Eskimo, or Aleut. 0.2%
Asian or Pacific Islander 3.2%
Other 2.2%
Hispanic origin 7.5%

Ancestry

American 3.1%
Austrian 1.4%
English 4.3%
French 1.3%
German 15.2%
Greek 1.3%

Hungarian 1.3%
Irish 19.0%
Italian 24.0%
Polish 6.6%
Russian 5.2%
West Indian 3.4%

Universities/colleges, 1990-1991 enrollment
Adelphi University, Garden City 8,755
Hofstra University, Hempstead 12,430
Molloy College, Rockville Centre 1,635
Nassau Community College, Garden City 21,541

Newspapers, total circulation (in all districts)
Long Island Newsday 788,998
New York Daily News 757,053
New York Law Journal 13,583
New York Post 551,443
New York Times 746,924

Commercial television stations, affiliations
ADI: New York (100%)

Cable television systems, total subscribers
Cablevision of Long Island; Hicksville 349,000
Time Warner Cable; Queens 116,000

Military installations, 1991
Garden City (Marine Corps), New York 1,199

Businesses and other major employers

Nassau County Medical Center; Hempstead 3,000
Plaza Employment Agency Inc.; Lynbrook; personnel supply
  services 3,000
Nassau Community College; Garden City 2,965
Winthrop-University Hospital; Mineola 2,550
Hofstra University; Hempstead 2,200
County of Nassau; Hempstead 1,800
Deutsche Lufthansa; Hempstead; airline 1,500
Mercy Medical Center; Rockville Centre 1,500
Adelphi University; Garden City 1,400
County of Nassau/Public Works Dept.; Mineola 1,300
European American Bancorp; Hempstead; commercial banks
  1,200
Avis Inc.; Garden City; automotive rentals 1,200
Franklin Hospital Medical Center; Valley Stream 1,090
Propoco Inc.; Lynbrook; building services 1,000
County of Nassau/Social Services Dept.; Mineola 1,000
Computer Assoc. Intl.; Garden City; computer services 950
M. Fortunoff of Westbury Corp.; Westbury; furniture stores
  900
European American Bank; Hempstead; commercial banks
  800
Hempstead General Hospital & Medical Center; Hempstead
  780
City of Hempstead/Public Schools; Hempstead 760
Robert Plan of New York Corp.; Lynbrook; insurance
  services 730
Depository Trust Co. Inc.; Garden City; security/commodity
  services 700
Westchester Marine Shipping Co; New Hyde Park; personnel
  supply services 600
Metropolitan Suburban Bus Authority; Garden City; transpor-
  tation 570
Central Senior High School; Valley Stream 570
Liberty Mutual Insurance Co.; Lynbrook; insurance services
  550
La Shellda Maintenance Corp.; Lynbrook; building services
  550

5th District

Northeast Queens; Northern Nassau and Suffolk Counties

One of the noted wits in the House, Democratic Rep. Gary Ackerman used humor to express his displeasure with the 1992 redistricting plan that created the elongated, politically competitive 5th.

Congressional districts are supposed to be compact and contiguous. When state legislators showed the proposed remap to Ackerman, he asked how the shore-hugging district—which is connected in three places only by the waters of Long Island Sound—could be contiguous. By that reasoning, Ackerman said, Maine, New Jersey and Florida, connected only by the Atlantic Ocean, are contiguous.

But the 5th remained as drawn, one of New York's several irregularly shaped districts (see map on page 502). And its difficult navigability turned out to be just one of Ackerman's problems in 1992. Almost exactly half the district's population lives in suburban Long Island; even the portion of the New York City borough of Queens (Ackerman's base) that is in the 5th is more suburban than urban. As such, Democrats have no lock on the district.

The 1992 election results indicated that the 5th, while Democratic-leaning, has potential to be a political swing district. Ackerman edged a local Republican official by just 7 percentage points; Bill Clinton's majority win here was strong by suburban Long Island standards but weak compared with his performance in other New York City-based districts.

The portion of Queens that makes up the western end of the 5th is the Democratic base: Ackerman won 61 percent here in 1992. It has many Jewish residents and a large number of Asians (including a Chinese-American constituency centered on the community of Flushing). Flushing, one of Queens' "downtown" centers, is the most urbanized area of the district and has some low-income population.

Among the major employers in the Queens part of the 5th are Queens College of the City University of New York in South Flushing and the Long Island Jewish Medical Center in New Hyde Park.

Just across the Nassau County border are two peninsulas that contain some of the nation's wealthiest communities, including Sands Point, Kings Point and Great Neck. Despite its affluence, this area, which has a large Jewish population, is usually strong for Democrats. Ackerman pulled down nearly 60 percent here in 1992.

The U.S. Merchant Marine Academy is in Kings Point. Unisys, a maker of high-tech defense systems, is in Great Neck; Canon USA is based in Lake Success.

The exurban part of the district on Suffolk County's North Shore provides a sharp political contrast. Taking in most of the town of Huntington before terminating in the western part of Smithtown, the Suffolk County portion of the 5th votes steadily Republican.

Melville, at Suffolk's western border, is a commercial center. The newspaper *Newsday* and the Long Island offices of Chase Manhattan and Chemical Bank are there.

Election Returns

	5th District	Democrat	Republican
1992	President*	131,095 (52.3%)	88,586 (35.3%)
	House	110,476 (51.9%)	94,907 (44.6%)
1990	Governor	80,561 (58.0%)	53,838 (38.8%)
1988	President	117,173 (49.0%)	121,329 (50.7%)
	Senate	154,577 (67.3%)	73,377 (31.9%)
1986	Senate	72,427 (46.5%)	77,974 (50.0%)
	Governor	104,485 (66.4%)	46,856 (29.8%)

Vote for Perot was 30,475 (12.2%).

Demographics

Population 580,337

Percent change from 1980 13.0%

Land area 152 square miles

Population per square mile 3,823

Counties, 1990 population
Nassau (pt.) 126,673   Suffolk (pt.) 161,189
Queens (pt.) 292,475

Cities, 1990 population (10,000 or more)
Commack CDP (pt.) 27,881
East Northport CDP 20,411
Glen Cove (pt.) 10,320
Huntington CDP (pt.) 16,308
Melville CDP (pt.) 10,167
New York (pt.) 292,475
Port Washington CDP (pt.) 14,739
Smithtown CDP (pt.) 10,289

Race and Hispanic origin
White 84.0%
Black 3.5%
American Indian, Eskimo, or Aleut. 0.1%
Asian or Pacific Islander 10.6%
Other 1.7%
Hispanic origin 7.3%

Ancestry
American 3.2%   Hungarian 1.9%
Austrian 2.2%   Irish 15.2%
English 4.8%   Italian 19.7%
French 1.5%   Polish 8.4%
German 13.2%   Russian 8.9%
Greek 2.7%

Universities/colleges, 1990-1991 enrollment
City University of New York-Queens College, Flushing 16,942
City University of New York-School of Law, Flushing 455
City University of New York-York College, Jamaica 4,834
Katherine Gibbs School, Melville 347
Queensborough Community College, Flushing 11,644
U.S. Merchant Marine Academy, Kings Point 851

Newspapers, total circulation (in all districts)
Long Island Newsday 788,998
New York Daily News 757,053
New York Law Journal 13,583
New York Post 551,443
New York Times 746,924

Commercial television stations, affiliations
ADI: New York (100%)

Cable television systems, total subscribers
Cablevision of Hauppauge; Hauppauge 139,000
Cablevision of Long Island; Great Neck 11,000
Cablevision of Long Island; Hicksville 349,000
Time Warner Cable; Queens 116,000

Military installations, 1991
Roslyn Air Force Guard Station, Roslyn 50

Businesses and other major employers
Long Island Jewish Medical Center; New Hyde Park 7,100
State of New York/Psychiatric Center; Kings Park 3,000
City University of New York-Queens College; Flushing 2,300
Booth Memorial Medical Center; Flushing 2,000
Flushing Hospital Medical Center; Flushing 2,000
Gyrongnam Bank Ltd.; Flushing; commercial banks 1,600
National Westminster Bank USA; Huntington Station; commercial banks 1,500
State of New York/Psychiatric Center; Northport 1,500
St. Francis Hospital; Roslyn 1,429
Great Neck Union Free School District; Great Neck 1,400

Photocircuits Corp.; Glen Cove; electronic components 1,300
Huntington Hospital Assn.; Huntington 1,270
Queensborough Community College; Flushing 1,200
Hazeltine Corp.; Greenlawn; search equipment 1,100
Nynex Corp./New York Telephone Co.; Flushing; telephone communications 1,000
Hillside Hospital; Floral Park 1,000
Parker Jewish Geriatric Institute; New Hyde Park; nursing 1,000
North Shore University Hospital; Manhasset 1,000
City of Northport-East Northport; East Northport 900
CMP Publications Inc.; Manhasset; periodicals 840
Norden Systems Inc./Marine Systems; Huntington Station; measuring/controlling devices 800
Underwriters Laboratories Inc.; Huntington Station; research services 800
Long Island Savings Bank; Huntington Station; savings institutions 752
Canon USA Inc.; New Hyde Park; copiers/office equipment 750
Automatic Data Processing; Huntington Station; computer services 700
Huntington Union Free School District; Huntington 700
Green Point Savings Bank; Flushing; savings institutions 693
United Presbyterian Home at Syosset; Woodbury; residential care 680
Anything Sales Inc.; Flushing; misc. manufacturers 659
Henry Schein Inc.; Port Washington; dental/medical equipment 650
Custom Looms Rug Mills Inc.; Roslyn Heights; carpets/rugs 600
Paramax Inc.; Great Neck; computer equipment 600
Publishers Clearing House; Port Washington; mail order periodicals 600
Ozanam Hall of Queens Nursing Home; Flushing; nursing 600
City University of New York-York College; Jamaica 600
Herricks Union Free School District; New Hyde Park 596
Miltope Corp.; Huntington Station; computer equipment 580
Thomson Industries Inc.; Port Washington; industry machinery 525

6th District

Southeast Queens — Jamaica; St. Albans

The southeast portion of Queens first sent an African American to the House in 1986; its black majority (about 56 percent of the population) is one of the most narrow of any district served by a black member. But a challenge to black representation here appears unlikely: Hispanics (about 17 percent) contribute to a minority-group voting bloc, while non-Hispanic whites (less than a quarter of the population) provide little counterweight.

The 6th provides a dependable partisan base for Democrats. In 1992 Rep. Floyd Flake took 80 percent of the general-election vote; Bill Clinton dominated the 6th, winning 75 percent. Any political action here is going to be in the Democratic primaries.

With an eastern border that follows the line between the New York City borough of Queens and suburban Nassau County (see map on page 502), the 6th is one of the most economically sound minority-majority districts. Its poverty rate is less than the

rate for New York state as a whole; the poverty rates for blacks and Hispanics are about half the figures for those groups statewide.

More than a generation ago, such communities as Springfield Gardens and St. Alban's were settled by a burgeoning Roman Catholic middle class. Today, the economic profile of these areas is not much different: Its brick homes house many civil servants, teachers and small-business owners. But the demographics are completely different. Instead of Irish and Italian Americans, most of the residents now are blacks.

John F. Kennedy International Airport and airlines based there provide a steady job base. It is also the district's most prominent geographical feature: Originally named Idlewild for the marshlands on which it was built, "JFK" occupies a huge swath of the 6th along the north shore of Jamaica Bay.

Despite its overall middle-class veneer, the 6th does have some areas that are much less well off. South Jamaica, where such urban problems as low high school graduation rates, welfare dependency, crime and drugs are rife, is the focus of efforts by economic development advocates (including Flake). The 6th's portion of the Rockaway peninsula—across Jamaica Bay from the airport with no direct land link to the rest of the district—has several public housing projects.

Much of the district's mainly middle-class white population is in its northeast end, in such communities as Bellerose and Queens Village, and near its western border, in Ozone Park. These areas are mainly Irish and Italian, with a scattering of Jewish residents. They lean Democratic, though the Republican vote is heavier than in the rest of the 6th. The Aqueduct horse track is in South Ozone Park.

Election Returns

	6th District	Democrat	Republican
1992	President*	115,253 (75.4%)	27,855 (18.2%)
	House	96,972 (80.3%)	22,687 (18.8%)
1990	Governor	58,870 (78.3%)	14,740 (19.6%)
1988	President	103,157 (73.0%)	37,715 (26.7%)
	Senate	107,816 (83.0%)	21,048 (16.2%)
1986	Senate	51,456 (60.4%)	31,007 (36.4%)
	Governor	73,031 (79.3%)	16,837 (18.3%)

Vote for Perot was 9,335 (6.1%).

Demographics

Population 580,337

Percent change from 1980 12.3%

Land area 38 square miles

Population per square mile 15,464

Counties, 1990 population
Queens (pt.) 580,337

Cities, 1990 population (10,000 or more)
New York (pt.) 580,337

Race and Hispanic origin
White 29.3%
Black 56.2%
American Indian, Eskimo, or Aleut 0.6%
Asian or Pacific Islander 6.3%

Other 7.5%
Hispanic origin 16.9%

Ancestry

American 1.8%	Italian 8.6%
English 1.1%	Polish 1.8%
German 4.4%	West Indian 12.2%
Irish 5.0%	

Universities/colleges, 1990-1991 enrollment

Derech Ayson Rabbinical Seminary, Far Rockaway 630
Long Island Seminary for Jewish Studies, Far Rockaway 552

Newspapers, total circulation (in all districts)

El Diario La Prensa (Spanish) 53,841
Long Island Newsday 788,998
New York Daily News 757,053
New York Law Journal 13,583
New York Post 551,443
New York Times 746,924

Commercial television stations, affiliations

ADI: New York (100%)

Cable television systems, total subscribers

Time Warner Cable; Queens 164,000

Businesses and other major employers

American Airlines Inc.; Jamaica; airline 3,300
Trans World Airlines Inc.; Jamaica; airline 3,000
State of New York/Creedmoor Psychiatric Center; Jamaica 2,400
Catholic Medical Center/Mary Immaculate Hospital; Jamaica 1,600
Jamaica Hospital Inc.; Jamaica 1,500
St. John's Episcopal Hospital; Far Rockaway 1,354
Rockaway Home Attendant Services; Far Rockaway; home health services 1,200
Peninsula Hospital Center; Far Rockaway 1,010
Port Authority of New York & New Jersey/Airport Operator; Jamaica; taxicabs 1,000
Marriott Corp./Host Intl.; Jamaica; bars/restaurants 1,000
Federal Express Corp./Flying Tigers; Jamaica; air transportation 960
Port Authority of New York & New Jersey/JFK Intl. Airport; Jamaica 900
U.S. Customs Service; Jamaica 850
Alert Security Inc.; Jamaica; security services 800
New York Racing Assn. Inc./Belmont Race Track; Jamaica; commercial sports 800
Social Concern Community Development; Jamaica; family services 725
Central Civic Assoc. Home/Attendents of Hollis Inc.; Jamaica; home health services 700
U.S. Veterans Affairs Dept./Extended Care Center; Jamaica 650
U.S. Federal Aviation Adminstration; Jamaica 600
County of Queens/Supreme Court; Jamaica 600

7th District

Parts of Queens and the Bronx; Long Island City

Democrats have a strong registration advantage in the 7th, a multi-ethnic, mainly middle-class, urban district that connects northern Queens with the southern Bronx (see map on page 502). There is a substantial minority presence: Over a fifth of the residents are Hispanic, with blacks and Asians (including a Chinese-American concentration in Flushing) each making up about a tenth of the population.

Yet the Democratic vote here is somewhat less dependable than in most of New York City. Non-Hispanic whites make up just under 60 percent of the 7th's population but vote in greater numbers than its minority-group residents, and many of these whites are of working-class backgrounds and of ethnic groups that have conservative tendencies on social issues.

The 7th supported Ronald Reagan in the 1980s, even in 1984 when Geraldine A. Ferraro—who then represented much of the 7th District in the House—was the Democratic vice presidential nominee. The 7th narrowly returned to the Democratic side in the 1988 presidential contest, but Bill Clinton won it by a wide margin in 1992.

Also in 1992, Democratic Rep. Thomas Manton easily defeated his GOP opponent. But nearly all of his 17,000-vote margin came from Queens, where he is county Democratic chairman. Manton won barely more than half the vote in the Bronx portion of the 7th.

The 7th owes its irregular shape in Queens (which has about three-quarters of the district's population) to the Hispanic-majority 12th District, which winds around northern Queens to pick up pockets of Hispanic residents.

At the 7th's western end is Long Island City, which faces Manhattan across the East River. This longtime industrial center still has blue-collar employers, including the Swingline stapler and Pepsi-Cola Bottling companies, but has lost many of its factories in recent years.

A Citicorp skyscraper, the tallest building in Queens, is in Long Island City. The Astoria Film Center, a studio used since the silent-movie days, is nearby, as is much of Astoria's Greek community. Sunnyside has Amtrak and Long Island Rail Road yards.

The 7th picks up a largely Irish section in Jackson Heights, then wraps around the 12th to take in much of its own Hispanic population in such areas as East Elmhurst and Corona. Bordering Flushing Bay are LaGuardia Airport and Flushing Meadow Park, site of Shea Stadium, the National Tennis Center (site of the U.S. Open) and the 1939 and 1964-1965 world's fairs.

To the east, the district covers residential College Point and Whitestone, then moves across the Bronx-Whitestone Bridge. The 7th's portion of the Bronx is shaped roughly like the number seven. Italian Americans make up the predominant ethnic group. The Bronx section has a large hospital complex that includes Yeshiva University's Albert Einstein College of Medicine.

Election Returns

	7th District	Democrat	Republican
1992	President*	91,803 (55.6%)	57,783 (35.0%)
	House	72,280 (56.4%)	54,639 (42.7%)
1990	Governor	52,019 (61.2%)	30,554 (35.9%)
1988	President	84,714 (53.5%)	73,290 (46.3%)
	Senate	104,793 (71.2%)	41,284 (28.0%)
1986	Senate	45,835 (46.0%)	50,349 (50.5%)
	Governor	70,115 (66.7%)	31,924 (30.4%)

Vote for Perot was 15,118 (9.2%).

Demographics

Population 580,337

Percent change from 1980 11.8%

Land area 26 square miles

Population per square mile 22,480

Counties, 1990 population
Bronx (pt.) 133,743   Queens (pt.) 446,594

Cities, 1990 population (10,000 or more)
New York (pt.) 580,337

Race and Hispanic origin
White 70.0%
Black 10.1%
American Indian, Eskimo, or Aleut. 0.3%
Asian or Pacific Islander 11.5%
Other 8.1%
Hispanic origin 21.3%

Ancestry

American 1.5%	Irish 11.7%
English 1.8%	Italian 19.7%
French 1.0%	Polish 4.4%
German 8.2%	Russian 2.3%
Greek 2.6%	West Indian 1.4%
Hungarian 1.0%	Yugoslavian 1.0%

Universities/colleges, 1990-1991 enrollment
Albert Einstein College of Medicine; Bronx 179
College of Aeronautics, Flushing 1,315
La Guardia Community College, Long Island City 8,998
Plaza Business Institute, Flushing 706
State University of New York-Maritime College, Bronx 821

Newspapers, total circulation (in all districts)
El Diario La Prensa (Spanish) 53,841
Long Island Newsday 788,998
New York Daily News 757,053
New York Law Journal 13,583
New York Post 551,443
New York Times 746,924

Commercial television stations, affiliations
ADI: New York (100%)

Cable television systems, total subscribers
Time Warner Cable; Queens 116,000
Time Warner Cable; Woodside 80,000

Businesses and other major employers
Bronx Municipal Hospital Center; Bronx 4,000
Citibank; Long Island City; commercial banks 3,500
Albert Einstein College of Medicine; Bronx 3,000
New York City Health Hospitals Corp./Emergency Medical
    Service; Flushing; medical transportation 2,600
American Airlines Inc.; Flushing; airline 2,120
Macy's Northeast Inc.; Flushing; department stores 2,000
City of New York/Board of Education-School Facilities;
    Long Island City 1,900
Montefiore Medical Center; Bronx 1,700
Home Services Systems Inc.; Long Island City; social services
    1,540

Madison Building Services Group; Long Island City; building
    services 1,500
Ridgewood Bushwick; Flushing; family services 1,400
White Castle System Inc.; Flushing; restaurants 1,150
Sunnyside Home Care Project; Long Island City; nursing
    1,000
Consolidated Edison Co. of New York; Bronx; automotive
    repair 1,000
Swingline Inc.; Long Island City; stapling equipment 900
Pepsi-Cola Bottling Co. Inc.; Long Island City; beverages 900
Anheuser-Busch Companies Inc.; Long Island City; beer 850
Queens Surface Corp.; Flushing; bus services 800
Nastasi-White Inc.; Flushing; carpentry 700
Calvary Hospital Inc.; Bronx 700
State of New York/Bronx Developmental Center; Bronx;
    residential care 700
Standard Motor Products Inc./Champ Service Line Div.;
    Long Island City; motor vehicle parts 675
EDO Corp./Government Systems Div.; Flushing;
    aircraft/parts 600
E-J Electric Installation Co.; Long Island City; electrical work
    550
British Airways; Flushing; airline 510
Astoria General Hospital Inc.; Long Island City 510

8th District
West Side Manhattan; Parts of Southwest Brooklyn

A strong strain of liberalism prevails in the 8th District; the West Side of Manhattan (see map on page 502) has many liberal-voting Jewish residents and one of the nation's largest concentrations of homosexuals. Containing nearly three-fifths of the 8th's population, this area gives Democrats a lock on the district.

The portion of Brooklyn that has the remainder of the 8th's population does not look very different. Like the Manhattan side, this is a thoroughly urban area of apartment dwellers; Jews are a large constituency.

But while most of Manhattan's Jewish residents lead mainly secular lifestyles, the Brooklyn part of the 8th has large communities of Hasidic Jews, whose religion-centered lives and orthodox reading of the Old Testament set a more conservative political tone. Though Democrats have a huge registration advantage, these communities are not averse to supporting socially conservative Republicans who meet a major condition: strong support for Israel. One such figure, Sen. Alfonse M. D'Amato, was backed by key Hasidic leaders during his 1992 campaign against a liberal Jewish Democrat.

Although Democrats still typically dominate the Brooklyn part, their numbers are slightly lower than in Manhattan. The Democratic House nominee in 1992 won 84 percent of the vote in the Manhattan part of the 8th and 73 percent in Brooklyn. Bill Clinton easily carried both sections.

The district's liberal lean belies its status as a world center of finance and commerce. The Wall Street financial district is at the southern tip of Manhattan in the 8th, as are the twin towers of the World Trade Center, second in height only to Chicago's Sears Tower and the site of a terrorist bomb attack in February 1993. The Empire State Building, in midtown, long reigned as the world's tallest skyscraper. The district takes in Manhattan's commercial waterfront along the Hudson River.

The 8th is also a world-famous cultural center. On the Upper

West Side is Lincoln Center; the Broadway theater district and Madison Square Garden are farther downtown. Greenwich Village, a longtime magnet for artists, is also the hub for the gay community. New York University is also here.

Much of the 8th's low-income population, including a number of blacks and Hispanics, lives in its far northern part, near Columbia University (in the 15th District). In midtown near the river is a working-class area, initially populated by Irish Americans, that was long known as one of the city's roughest areas: Officially named Clinton, it was better known as "Hell's Kitchen."

After crossing the Brooklyn-Battery Tunnel and skimming along the Brooklyn waterfront, the 8th takes in mainly residential areas, including the orthodox Jewish center of Borough Park and part of ethnically mixed, racially tense Bensonhurst. At its southern end, the district meets the Atlantic Ocean at Brighton Beach, the setting for Neil Simon's autobiographical plays; Coney Island, whose century-old amusement park is a place of faded glory, has a population mix of minorities and Jews, many of them elderly.

Election Returns

	8th District	Democrat	Republican
1992	President*	169,005 (77.1%)	37,614 (17.2%)
	House	138,296 (80.9%)	25,548 (14.9%)
1990	Governor	80,071 (79.1%)	20,013 (19.8%)
1988	President	141,444 (72.4%)	53,543 (27.4%)
	Senate	159,155 (86.3%)	24,454 (13.3%)
1986	Senate	81,416 (70.3%)	32,841 (28.4%)
	Governor	96,959 (83.3%)	18,209 (15.6%)

*Vote for Perot was 12,216 (5.6%).

Demographics

Population 580,337

Percent change from 1980 13.3%

Land area 16 square miles

Population per square mile 37,165

Counties, 1990 population
Kings (pt.) 240,204   New York (pt.) 340,133

Cities, 1990 population (10,000 or more)
New York (pt.) 580,337

Race and Hispanic origin
White 80.4%
Black 8.6%
American Indian, Eskimo, or Aleut. 0.2%
Asian or Pacific Islander 6.3%
Other 4.6%
Hispanic origin 12.7%

Ancestry

American 2.6%	Irish 8.1%
Arabic 1.0%	Italian 13.1%
Austrian 1.9%	Polish 7.6%
English 6.0%	Romanian 1.2%
French 1.9%	Russian 10.1%
German 8.7%	Scottish 1.4%
Hungarian 2.5%	West Indian 1.0%

Universities/colleges, 1990-1991 enrollment
Bank Street College of Education, New York 755
Beth Hatalmud Rabbinical College, Brooklyn 215
Borough of Manhattan Community College, New York 12,647
College for Human Service, New York 868
College of Insurance, New York 710
Cooper Union, New York 1,036
Fashion Institute of Technology, New York 12,100
Interboro Institute, New York 744
John Jay College of Criminal Justice, New York 7,308
Juilliard School, New York 1,026
Mannes College of Music, New York 582
New School for Social Research, New York 6,321
New York Institute of Tech Met., New York 2,483
New York Law School, New York 1,372
New York University, New York 30,753
Pace University, New York 8,487
Technical Career Institutes, New York 1,897
Touro College, New York 4,901

Newspapers, total circulation (in all districts)
Daily Variety 21,274
El Diario La Prensa (Spanish) 53,841
Long Island Newsday 788,998
New York Daily News 757,053
New York Law Journal 13,583
New York Post 551,443
New York Times 746,924
Washington Post 810,904

Commercial television stations, affiliations
ADI: New York (100%)
WHSE, Newark (None)
WABC-TV, New York (ABC)
WCBS-TV, New York (CBS)
WNBC-TV, New York (NBC)
WNYW, New York (Fox)
WPIX, New York (None)
WNJU, Linden (None)
WWOR-TV, Secaucus (None)

Cable television systems, total subscribers
Cablevision; Brooklyn 51,402
Paragon Cable Manhattan; New York 165,889
Time Warner Cable; Manhattan (lower) 255,000

Businesses and other major employers
J. P. Morgan & Co. Inc.; New York; real estate operators 14,000
City of New York/Sanitation Dept.; New York 13,000
J. P. Morgan & Co. Inc./Morgan Guaranty Trust Co.; New York; commercial banks 9,600
Ogden Allied Maintenance Corp./Comtech; New York; building services 8,000
Prudential Securities Group; New York; security brokers 7,000
New York University; New York 7,000
R. H. Macy & Co. Inc.; New York; department stores 6,000
Beth Israel Medical Center; New York; health services 6,000
City of New York/Telecommunications Dept.; New York; telephone services 5,000
Smith Barney Shearson Inc.; New York; security brokers 5,000

City of New York/Police Dept.; New York 5,000
Chase Manhattan Corp.; New York; commercial banks 4,700
Salomon Brothers Holding Co.; New York; security brokers 4,670
Goldman Sachs & Co.; New York; security brokers 4,600
New York Times Co. Inc.; New York; newspapers 4,200
American Intl. Group; New York; fire/marine/casualty insurance 4,000
Maimonides Medical Center Inc.; Brooklyn 3,600
Port Authority of New York & New Jersey; New York; airports/services 3,500
Federal Reserve Bank of New York; New York 3,100
Capital Cities/ABC Inc.; New York; broadcasting/periodicals 3,000
Prudential-Bache Securities; New York; security brokers 3,000
Bank of New York Co. Inc.; New York; commercial banks 3,000
Dean Witter Reynolds Inc.; New York; security brokers 3,000
Smokefree Educational Services; New York; family services 3,000
City University of New York Inc./CUNY Research Foundation; New York 3,000
Kidder Peabody & Co. Inc.; New York; security brokers 2,900
Morgan Guaranty Trust Co. of New York/Stock Transfer Group; New York; commercial banks 2,500
New York University; New York 2,500
Depository Trust Co. Inc.; New York; security brokers 2,400
Ebasco Services Inc.; New York; engineering/architectural services 2,400
Donaldson Lufkin & Jenrette; New York; security brokers 2,200
Boro Manhattan Community Co.; New York 2,110
Legal Aid Society Inc.; New York; legal services 2,100
St. Vincent's Hospital; New York 2,075
State Insurance Fund/New York State Insurance Fund; New York; fire/marine/casualty insurance 2,049
New York Telephone Co.; New York; telephone communications 2,000
Glens Falls Insurance Co.; New York; fire/marine/casualty insurance 2,000
Fidelity & Casualty Co. of New York; New York; fire/marine/casualty insurance 2,000
U.S. Justice Dept./FBI; New York 2,000
Automatic Data Processing; New York; computer services 2,000
U.S. Customs Service; New York 2,000
Visiting Nurse Service of New York; New York; home health services 2,000
Hearst Corp./Magazines Div.; New York; periodicals 1,700
Viacom Intl. Inc.; New York; movie production 1,700
Woolworth Corp.; New York; variety stores 1,600
JWP Forest Electric Corp.; New York; electrical work 1,500
Sara Lee Corp./Coach Leatherwear; New York; leather goods 1,500
Niagara Fire Insurance Co.; New York; fire/marine/casualty insurance 1,500
Home Insurance Co. Inc.; New York; fire/marine/casualty insurance 1,500

Pace University; New York 1,500
American Express Co.; New York; business services 1,500
Ogilvy & Mathers Worldwide; New York; advertising 1,500
Manufacturers Hanover Trust Co.; New York; security/commodity services 1,400
New York City Health Hospitals Corp.; New York 1,400
Group Health Inc./Health Service Corp.; New York; medical service/health insurance 1,300
Saatchi & Saatchi Advertising; New York; advertising 1,300
Andover Togs Inc./Dover Mills; New York; outerwear 1,200
Gotham Building Maintenance; New York; building services 1,200
Fashion Institute of Technogoly; New York 1,200
ITT Sheraton Corp./Sheraton Hotel & Towers; New York; hotel 1,200
Deloitte & Touche; New York; accounting/auditing 1,200
U.S. Labor Dept.; New York 1,150
New York Stock Exchange Inc.; New York; security & commodity exchange 1,100
First Chicago Trust Co. of New York; New York; commercial banks 1,100
Wackenhut Corp.; New York; business/security services 1,100
Cravath Swaine & Moore; New York; legal services 1,095
Brown Brothers Harriman & Co.; New York; banking services 1,028
Standard & Poor's Corp.; New York; periodicals 1,000
Dow Jones & Co. Inc.; New York; newspapers 1,000
Port Authority Trans-Hudson; New York; transportation 1,000
Capital Cities/ABC Inc./Fairchild Publications; New York; newspapers 1,000
British Airways; New York; airline 1,000
Wundies Enterprises Inc.; New York; undergarments 1,000
American Broadcasting Companies; New York; radio/TV broadcasting 1,000
Hudson-Shatz Painting Co. Inc.; New York; painting services 1,000
Barclays Bank; New York; foreign bank 1,000
Swiss Bank Corp.; New York; commercial banks 1,000
Chemical Bank; New York; commercial banks 1,000
Bank of New York; New York; commercial banks 1,000
Smith Barney Harris Upham Inc.; New York; security brokers 1,000
Milbank Tweed Hadley & McCloy; New York; legal services 1,000
New York Downtown Hospital; New York 1,000
National Assn. Holy Name Society; New York; religious organizations 1,000
State of New York/Management & Budget Office; New York 1,000
State of New York/District Attorney; New York 1,000
City of New York/Law Dept.; New York 1,000
N. W. Ayer Inc.; New York; advertising 1,000
City of New York/Building Dept.; New York 996
Davis Polk & Wardwell; New York; legal services 980
IBM Corp.; New York; computers 950
Mirror Inc./Racing Times; New York; newspapers 950
U.S. Environmental Protection Agency; New York 950
John Jay College of Criminal Justice, New York 950
CBS Inc./News Div.; New York; radio/TV broadcasting 900
Perfect Building Maintenance; New York; building services 900

Ogden Allied Building & Airport Services; New York; maintenance services 900

Juilliard School; New York 900

St. Clare's Hospital & Health Center; New York 900

Cleary Gottlieb Steen Hamilton; New York; legal services 850

Proskuer Rose Goetz & Mendelsohn; New York; legal services 850

American Stock Exchange Inc.; New York; security & commodity exchange 845

Guy Carpenter & Co. Inc.; New York; insurance services 819

Inhilco Inc./Windows on the World; New York; bars/restaurants 800

Guardian Service Industries; New York; building/security services 800

State of New York/Law Dept.; New York 800

Madison Detective Bureau Inc.; New York; security services 800

Building Maintenance Service; New York; building services 800

Frank Harris Fried; New York; legal services 795

National Westminster Bancorp; New York; commercial banks 750

City of New York; New York 750

Amcom Books-Sales; New York; books 750

Metropolitan Opera Assn.; New York; entertainment services 750

City of New York/Housing Authority; New York 750

U.S. Justice Dept./DEA; New York 750

Kinney Shoe Corp.; New York; footwear 750

Reliance National Risk Specialists; New York; insurance services 742

M. J. G. Nursing Home Co. Inc.; Brooklyn; nursing 740

IBJ Schroder Bank & Trust Co.; New York; commercial banks 700

Cahill Gordon & Reindel; New York; legal services 700

City of New York/Juvenile Justice Dept.; New York 700

Hilton Intl./Vista Intl.; New York; hotel 700

Information Builders Inc.; New York; computer services 700

Ogden Allied Services Corp.; New York; building services 700

Darcy Masius Benton & Bowles; New York; advertising 700

Fitzgerald Cantor Securities; New York; security brokers 680

State of New York/Mental Health Dept.; New York; residential care 675

Scholastic Inc./Intl. Div.; New York; book publishing 650

U.S. Postal Service; New York 650

State of New York/Insurance Dept.; New York; insurance services 650

Insurance Services Office Inc.; New York; insurance services 650

Madison Square Garden Center; New York; entertainment services 650

O. C. S. Security Inc.; New York; business/security services 650

Universal Maintenance Corp.; New York; building services 650

Paramount Insurance Co.; New York; insurance services 630

Sfuzzi Inc.; New York; bars/restaurants 620

Empire Insurance Co. Inc.; New York; fire/marine/casualty insurance 617

Andin Intl. Inc.; New York; jewelry 615

Kateri Residence; New York; nursing 612

American Home Assurance Co.; New York; fire/marine/casualty insurance 611

Cadwalader Wickersham & Taft; New York; legal services 610

Kinney Shoe Corp.; New York; footwear 600

Hachette Magazines Inc.; New York; periodicals 600

Cowen & Co.; New York; security brokers 600

Connecticut General Life Insurance Co./Cigna; New York; life insurance 600

Bank of Nova Scotia; New York; foreign bank 600

B. Dalton Bookseller Inc.; New York; bookstores 600

CIT Group Holdings Inc.; New York; credit institutions 600

Winthrop Stimson Putnam & Roberts; New York; legal services 600

Ameriscribe Management Services; New York; management services 600

National Service Corp./Youth Service Corps; New York; social services 600

Stone & Webster Inc.; New York; engineering/architectural services 600

Ascot Associates Ltd./Ramada Hotel; New York; hotel 600

State of New York/Parole Dept.; New York 580

Spear Leeds & Kellogg; New York; security brokers 574

Matthew Bender & Co. Inc.; New York; book publishing 550

Chemical Bank; New York; commercial banks 550

Electra Cleaning Contractors Corp.; New York; building services 550

Lehman Commercial Paper Inc.; New York; investment offices 525

Nomura Securities Intl.; New York; security brokers 520

Fiduciary Trust Co. Intl.; New York; commercial banks 510

Reed Publishing/Cahners Publishing Co.; New York; periodicals 500

9th District

Parts of Brooklyn and Queens — Sheepshead Bay; Forest Hills

Contiguity, a supposed criterion for congressional districts, may be in the eye of the beholder. But it would be hard to find a more geographically disparate district anywhere than the 9th (see map on page 502), which takes in widely separated parts of Brooklyn and Queens.

One of the most interesting of the many abstract designs on the current map, the 9th reaches a point in the Park Slope section of central Brooklyn, then follows a narrow corridor south before broadening out along that borough's waterfront. It jumps across an inlet to the Rockaways, running the length of the narrow peninsula that forms the southern part of Queens. It also heads back across Jamaica Bay (touching several islands that make up a wildlife refuge) to the mainland and follows another narrow band north, before broadening out across a swath of west-central Queens.

The only connections between the three regions are the two auto causeways to and from the Rockaways and the broad waters of Jamaica Bay. At the south side of the mainland, the district's pieces are separated by about a mile across the 10th District. But at the northern extremes, the Queens and Brooklyn branches of the 9th are more than four miles apart, with parts of the 10th, 11th and 12th districts in between.

It is only when the demographics of the 9th are considered that its design begins to make sense. Under the mandates of the Voting Rights Act, remappers drew the 9th around the minority-group concentrations in the intervening districts, two of which are majority-black, the other majority-Hispanic. As a result, the population is about 82 percent non-Hispanic white.

The lack of a large minority base does not keep the 9th from being a regularly Democratic district that has been tailor-made for Rep. Charles Schumer. Like the all-Brooklyn district Schumer represented during the 1980s, the mostly middle-class and residential 9th has large Jewish and ethnic populations (mainly Italian and Irish Americans) that give it a strong Democratic flavor. Schumer had no GOP opponent in 1992; Bill Clinton won the 9th by 26 percentage points.

There are pockets of social conservatism, however, and racial tension is not unknown. The Howard Beach community in Queens is still living down a 1986 incident in which a gang of whites chased a black man onto a highway, where he was struck by a car and killed.

From its Brooklyn tip in Park Slope, an upscale community by sprawling Prospect Park, the 9th takes in the Brooklyn College campus and such middle-class areas as Sheepshead Bay and Canarsie. It then crosses the Marine Parkway Bridge to Queens, running the length of the peninsula from Breezy Point to Far Rockaway (where it abuts the 6th District).

Cross Bay Boulevard carries the district back to the mainland at Howard Beach, then north to Woodhaven. At the northeast corner of the 9th are two of its wealthiest communities, Forest Hills (site of the West Side Tennis Center, the former home of the U.S. Open) and Kew Gardens.

Election Returns

	9th District	Democrat	Republican
1992	President*	121,110 (58.8%)	66,917 (32.5%)
	House †	116,545 (87.7%)	—
1990	Governor	70,531 (63.6%)	37,554 (33.9%)
1988	President	102,222 (52.2%)	93,318 (47.6%)
	Senate	140,404 (75.7%)	43,802 (23.6%)
1986	Senate	64,174 (50.1%)	59,878 (46.8%)
	Governor	92,312 (70.5%)	34,962 (26.7%)

*Vote for Perot was 17,574 (8.5%).   †Independent/other is greater than 5%.

Demographics

Population   580,338

Percent change from 1980   12.4%

Land area   38 square miles

Population per square mile   15,463

Counties, 1990 population
Kings (pt.)   348,591   Queens (pt.)   231,747

Cities, 1990 population (10,000 or more)
New York (pt.)   580,338

Race and Hispanic origin
White   87.6%
Black   3.3%

American Indian, Eskimo, or Aleut.   0.1%
Asian or Pacific Islander   6.2%
Other   2.7%
Hispanic origin   8.5%

Ancestry

American 3.5%		Hungarian 1.9%	
Arabic 1.8%		Irish 13.2%	
Austrian 2.1%		Italian 20.6%	
English 2.5%		Polish 9.0%	
German 9.5%		Romanian 1.1%	
Greek 1.1%		Russian 9.7%	

Universities/colleges, 1990-1991 enrollment
Bnos Jerusalem Seminary, Brooklyn   336
Bramson Ort Tech Institute, Flushing   1,096
Kingsborough Community College, Brooklyn   12,817
Taylor Business, New York   536
Yeshiva & Kollel Harbotzas, Brooklyn   366

Newspapers, total circulation (in all districts)
El Diario La Prensa (Spanish)   53,841
Long Island Newsday   788,998
New York Daily News   757,053
New York Post   551,443
New York Times   746,924

Commercial television stations, affiliations
ADI: New York (100%)

Cable television systems, total subscribers
Cablevision; Brooklyn   51,402
Time Warner Cable; Brooklyn   38,000
Time Warner Cable; Queens   164,000
Time Warner Cable; Woodside   80,000

Businesses and other major employers
Consolidated Edison Co. of New York; Flushing; electric services   2,250
Coney Island Hospital; Brooklyn   2,200
Methodist Hospital of Brooklyn; Brooklyn   2,190
MacClean Service Co. Inc.; Jamaica; building services   1,850
Beth Emeth Home Attendant Services; Brooklyn; home health services   880
City of New York/Board of Education; Jamaica   750
Parkway Hospital Inc.; Flushing   600
Kings Highway Hospital; Brooklyn   600
Dial Car Inc.; Brooklyn; business assn.   550
Americare Inc.; Brooklyn; home health services   516

10th District

Parts of Brooklyn — Bedford-Stuyvesant; Brooklyn Heights

During the 1980s, Democrat Edolphus Towns represented a Brooklyn district in which blacks made up just a plurality of the population; a large Hispanic constituency composed a competing power bloc. But in the 1992 redistricting, many of these Hispanic constituents were drawn off into the new Hispanic-majority 12th District, which forms the western and northern borders of the 10th (see map on page 502).

Now blacks make up more than three-fifths of the 10th's population; non-Hispanic whites and Hispanics are roughly one-fifth each. This breakdown appears enough to ensure the election of a black representative. More than 80 percent of the 10th's registered voters are Democrats. In 1992 Towns had no GOP opponent in the general election; Bill Clinton also cleaned up that year, winning 83 percent.

The district is roughly the shape of an upside-down letter U. It runs from just inside Brooklyn's industrial waterfront along New York Bay to the Queens border and the shores of Jamaica Bay. Connecting the east and west parts of the district is Atlantic Avenue, one of Brooklyn's main east-west thoroughfares and commercial corridors.

In the central part of the district is Bedford-Stuyvesant, a mainly low-income black area. Once a well-off white area, "Bed-Stuy" has long since been a minority ghetto. Though troubles still abound, the community has been a target for economic revival efforts since the 1960s, when Sen. Robert F. Kennedy promoted an urban industrial park regarded as a forerunner of the "enterprise zone" concept.

To the east is the even more devastated part of East New York, which has one of New York City's highest murder rates. The 10th then follows Pennsylvania Avenue south to the Belt Parkway and Jamaica Bay. Nearby is Starrett City, a high-rise apartment complex that is racially integrated. But there are parts of working-class Canarsie, which has a large Italian-American population, where blacks are known to be unwelcome. The 10th also has an appendage that reaches into mostly black East Flatbush.

The predominantly white and affluent parts of the 10th are on its west side. This section includes the landmarked brownstones of Brooklyn Heights, Boerum Hill and part of Park Slope, and middle-class, Italian-American Carroll Gardens. Much of Brooklyn's civic life—including Borough Hall, its court houses, St. Francis College and the Brooklyn campus of Long Island University—is here.

The biggest problem here is the district's aging infrastructure. One of the oldest areas of the city, its water and sewer lines are prone to collapse. Heavy truck traffic is eroding the Brooklyn-Queens Expressway and residential streets leading up to the Brooklyn and Manhattan bridges (located in the 12th District, which hugs the waterfront).

Election Returns

	10th District	Democrat	Republican
1992	President*	125,206 (83.2%)	19,177 (12.7%)
	House	97,509 (95.0%)	—
1990	Governor	63,731 (88.4%)	7,676 (10.7%)
1988	President	110,807 (82.3%)	23,437 (17.4%)
	Senate	107,458 (90.2%)	10,885 (9.1%)
1986	Senate	51,755 (73.1%)	17,327 (24.5%)
	Governor	65,229 (87.3%)	8,739 (11.7%)

*Vote for Perot was 5,711 (3.8%).

Demographics

Population 580,335

Percent change from 1980 13.1%

Land area 17 square miles

Population per square mile 34,359

Counties, 1990 population
Kings (pt.) 580,335

Cities, 1990 population (10,000 or more)
New York (pt.) 580,335

Race and Hispanic origin
White 26.8%
Black 60.7%
American Indian, Eskimo, or Aleut. 0.4%
Asian or Pacific Islander 2.3%
Other 9.7%
Hispanic origin 19.7%

Ancestry
American 2.1%   Polish 1.7%
English 1.5%   Russian 2.0%
German 2.1%   Subsaharan African 1.1%
Irish 2.5%   West Indian 9.4%
Italian 4.1%

Universities/colleges, 1990-1991 enrollment
Brooklyn Law School, Brooklyn 1,426
Long Island University, Brooklyn 5,959
New York City Technical College, Brooklyn 10,329
Polytechnic University of New York, Brooklyn 3,701
Pratt Institute, Brooklyn 3,384
St. Francis College, Brooklyn 1,743
St. Joseph's College, Brooklyn 827
Toldos Yakor Yosef, Brooklyn 307
United Talmudical Academy, Brooklyn 455

Newspapers, total circulation (in all districts)
El Diario La Prensa (Spanish) 53,841
Long Island Newsday 788,998
New York Daily News 757,053
New York Post 551,443
New York Times 746,924

Commercial television stations, affiliations
ADI: New York (100%)

Cable television systems, total subscribers
Cablevision; Brooklyn 51,402
Time Warner Cable; Brooklyn 38,000

Businesses and other major employers
Watchtower Bible & Tract Society of New York; Brooklyn; periodicals 3,000
New York City Transit Authority; Brooklyn 3,000
Long Island College Hospital; Brooklyn 2,800
State of New York/Brooklyn Developmental Center; Brooklyn 1,800
New York City Technical College; Brooklyn 1,560
Consolidated Edison Co. of New York; Brooklyn; utility services 1,500
Long Life Home Care Inc.; Brooklyn; home health services 1,500
Builders for Family & Youth/Alhambra Adult Treatment Center; Brooklyn; residential care 1,351
Brooklyn Union Gas Co. Inc; Brooklyn; gas distribution 1,325
Cumberland Neighborhood Medical Center; Brooklyn 1,300
State of New York/Board of Education; Brooklyn 1,000
BPS Guard Services Inc.; Brooklyn; security services 925

Securities Industry Automation Corp.; Brooklyn; data processing 900

City of New York/Kings County District Attorney; Brooklyn 825

City of New York/City Collector; Brooklyn 800

Long Island University; Brooklyn 800

John C. Mandel Security Bureau; Brooklyn; business services 750

Pfizer Inc.; Brooklyn; pharmaceuticals 600

Stanley Morgan & Co. Inc.; Brooklyn; security brokers 600

Polytechnic University of New York; Brooklyn 588

Cobble Hill Nursing Home Inc.; Brooklyn; nursing 580

Marsel Mirror & Glass Products/Barlow Art Products; Brooklyn; glass products 550

11th District

Central Brooklyn — Flatbush; Crown Heights; Brownsville

The concentration of black residents in the central core of Brooklyn allowed House mapmakers to construct the 11th as a rather compact district (see map on page 502); its minority majority is one of the largest of any of the House districts. More than two-thirds of the 11th's residents are non-Hispanic blacks, with Hispanics topping 10 percent; non-Hispanic whites make up less than a fifth of the population.

The 11th follows the overwhelmingly Democratic pattern of minority-dominated districts nationwide. More than 80 percent of the registered voters are Democrats. In 1992, Democratic Rep. Major Owens ran without Republican opposition (as he had in 1990). In the 1992 presidential race Bill Clinton ran up 87 percent of the vote here; George Bush got 10 percent.

The heart of the 11th is Flatbush. Through the years immediately after World War II, this was a mainly white, working-class area. In the 1990s, Flatbush has a sizable black plurality and a number of Hispanics; much of the white population (about a third of Flatbush's total) is elderly. Though there is some poverty, this remains a working-class area, as does much of adjacent, predominantly black East Flatbush. A large medical complex that includes Kings County Hospital, Kingsbrook Jewish Medical Center and the State University of New York Health Sciences Center is in Flatbush.

To the north, across Eastern Parkway, is Crown Heights, where a black majority and a Hasidic Jewish community have a tense relationship. When the car of an assistant to an orthodox rabbi struck and killed a black child in 1991, rioting broke out, and a Jewish theological student was killed.

Ebbets Field, the home of baseball's Brooklyn Dodgers, was in Crown Heights. The team's departure for Los Angeles after the 1957 season deprived the borough of much of its national identity. The stadium site is now a housing project.

At the eastern extreme of the 11th is Brownsville, its most economically troubled community. More than 40 percent of its residents are on some kind of government income support, nearly a third on public assistance.

However, the rapid depopulation that occurred during the 1970s was reversed in the last decade, in part because of an influx of immigrants from the Caribbean, including many Jamaicans, Haitians and Guyanans. (West Indians have also located in many other black communities in the 11th.)

Much of the district's white population lives on its west side,

in heavily Jewish, middle-class Kensington and Midwood and in well-to-do Park Slope.

Such attractions as the Brooklyn Museum, Botanical Garden and Academy of Music are in this west section, which rims sprawling Prospect Park (mostly in the 9th District).

Election Returns

	11th District	Democrat	Republican
1992	President*	104,678 (86.7%)	11,709 (9.7%)
	House †	80,028 (92.8%)	—
1990	Governor	48,338 (88.1%)	5,915 (10.8%)
1988	President	86,581 (83.0%)	17,302 (16.6%)
	Senate	85,819 (91.3%)	7,483 (8.0%)
1986	Senate	39,486 (74.4%)	12,343 (23.3%)
	Governor	47,881 (87.2%)	6,289 (11.4%)

Vote for Perot was 3,916 (3.2%). †*Independent/other is greater than 5%.*

Demographics

Population 580,337

Percent change from 1980 12.0%

Land area 10 square miles

Population per square mile 57,996

Counties, 1990 population
Kings (pt.) 580,337

Cities, 1990 population (10,000 or more)
New York (pt.) 580,337

Race and Hispanic origin
White 18.7%
Black 74.0%
American Indian, Eskimo, or Aleut. 0.4%
Asian or Pacific Islander 2.8%
Other 4.1%
Hispanic origin 11.5%

Ancestry
American 2.9%   Polish 1.9%
German 1.4%   Russian 2.7%
Irish 1.9%   Subsaharan African 2.2%
Italian 1.6%   West Indian 23.8%

Universities/colleges, 1990-1991 enrollment
Beth Jacob Hebrew Teachers College, Brooklyn 539
Cent Yeshiva Tomchei Tmimim, Brooklyn 427
City University of New York-Brooklyn College, Brooklyn 15,933
City University of New York-Medgar Evers College, Brooklyn 2,431
Mesivta Torah Vodaath Sem, Brooklyn 435
State University of New York Health Science Center, Brooklyn 1,642

Newspapers, total circulation (in all districts)
El Diario La Prensa (Spanish) 53,841
Long Island Newsday 788,998
New York Daily News 757,053
New York Law Journal 13,583
New York Post 551,443
New York Times 746,924

Commercial television stations, affiliations
ADI: New York (100%)

Cable television systems, total subscribers
Cablevision; Brooklyn 51,402

Businesses and other major employers
Kings County Hospital Center; Brooklyn 6,000
Brookdale Hospital & Medical Center; Brooklyn 3,800
Interfaith Medical Center; Brooklyn 2,919
Brooklyn Hospital Center; Brooklyn 2,500
Dime Savings Bank of America; Brooklyn; commercial banks 2,200
Kingsbrook Jewish Medical Center; Brooklyn 2,100
City of New York/Board of Education; Brooklyn 1,986
City University of New York-Brooklyn College, Brooklyn 1,706
St. Mary's Hospital; Brooklyn 989
Alexander's Inc.; Brooklyn; department stores 900
Brooklyn Community School District 23; Brooklyn 750

12th District

Lower East Side of Manhattan; Parts of Brooklyn and Queens

One certainty of New York's most recent redistricting was that a second Hispanic-majority district would be created. As a result of an ongoing influx that began just after World War II, the Hispanic population had grown to nearly a quarter of the city's total. Yet only the South Bronx House district had sent a Hispanic to Congress.

The execution of a new Hispanic-majority district, however, was no easy matter. Unlike blacks—who are mainly in large concentrations—Hispanic immigrants had located in disparate low- and middle-income communities scattered across the city's five boroughs. The mapmakers had to go block-by-block to build a district that could reasonably assure a Hispanic's election. The result was the 12th, one of the most unusually shaped House districts in the nation's history (see map on page 502). It follows a wildly meandering path through parts of three New York City boroughs: Queens, Brooklyn and Manhattan.

Along with its geographic sampling, the 12th also has an ethnic variety that the generic term Hispanic—which applies to nearly three-fifths of the district's residents—fails to capture. Puerto Ricans, by far the largest single group, make up nearly half the Hispanic population. The other groups came from Mexico, the Caribbean, Central America and South America.

The district's design had its desired effect in 1992: Democrat Nydia Velázquez, a Puerto Rican activist, won out over a crowded Democratic primary field. She then easily won the general election in this overwhelmingly Democratic district. But voter participation in the 12th is greatly dampened by such factors as recent immigration status and poverty. While most New York House districts had turnouts of more than 200,000 voters, fewer than 75,000 cast ballots for the 12th District seat.

The district's northeastern terminus is well into Queens (the borough has slightly more than a quarter of the population). The district's parts of Jackson Heights, Corona and Elmhurst are largely Hispanic (many residents are of South American origin).

The district then moves southwest through Woodside and Maspeth and into Brooklyn, which has just over half the 12th's

population. Hispanics share this section with blacks in East New York and Bushwick and Hasidic Jews in Williamsburg; Sunset Park, at the southern end, is racially and ethnically mixed.

From there, the 12th crosses the East River—on the Brooklyn and Manhattan bridges and the Brooklyn-Battery Tunnel—to Manhattan's Lower East Side. There is a mainly low-income Hispanic concentration in "Alphabet City," where the streets have letter names —Avenue A, Avenue B. But the Manhattan portion (about a fifth of the district) is the only one where Hispanics are in the minority. Asians are the largest racial group; the district takes in most of Chinatown. There are also remnants of the Lower East Side's once-teeming Jewish population.

Election Returns

	12th District	Democrat	Republican
1992	President*	67,114 (68.4%)	25,622 (26.1%)
	House	55,926 (75.9%)	14,976 (20.3%)
1990	Governor	34,386 (78.6%)	8,586 (19.6%)
1988	President	64,141 (70.7%)	26,430 (29.1%)
	Senate	60,944 (79.9%)	14,649 (19.2%)
1986	Senate	27,702 (58.7%)	17,967 (38.1%)
	Governor	40,130 (77.2%)	10,823 (20.8%)

Vote for Perot was 5,121 (5.2%).

Demographics

Population 580,340

Percent change from 1980 12.3%

Land area 14 square miles

Population per square mile 42,156

Counties, 1990 population
Kings (pt.) 292,898   Queens (pt.) 162,588
New York (pt.) 124,854

Cities, 1990 population (10,000 or more)
New York (pt.) 580,340

Race and Hispanic origin
White 33.8%
Black 13.7%
American Indian, Eskimo, or Aleut. 0.5%
Asian or Pacific Islander 19.7%
Other 32.3%
Hispanic origin 57.9%

Ancestry
American 1.2%   Italian 4.4%
German 1.8%   Polish 1.2%
Irish 2.6%   West Indian 1.5%

Newspapers, total circulation (in all districts)
Daily Variety 21,274
El Diario La Prensa (Spanish) 53,841
Long Island Newsday 788,998
New York Daily News 757,053
New York Law Journal 13,583
New York Post 551,443
New York Times 746,924

Commercial television stations, affiliations
  ADI: New York (100%)

Cable television systems, total subscribers
  Cablevision; Brooklyn 51,402
  Time Warner Cable; Brooklyn 38,000
  Time Warner Cable; Manhattan (lower) 255,000
  Time Warner Cable; Woodside 80,000

Businesses and other major employers
  City Hospital Center at Elmhurst; Flushing 3,000
  Wood Hull Mental & Health Center; Brooklyn 2,500
  Lutheran Medical Center; Brooklyn 2,400
  City of New York/Sanitation Dept.; Brooklyn 1,500
  United Parcel Service Inc.; mail services; Brooklyn 1,500
  Bulova Corp; Flushing: clocks/watches 1,450
  Ridgewood Bushwick; Brooklyn: home health services 1,400
  Harry M. Stevens; Flushing; bars/restaurants 1,000
  Johnson & Wiggins; New York; insurance services 1,000
  Wyckoff Heights Medical Center; Brooklyn 1,000
  New York Post Corp.; New York: newspapers 985
  Amboy Bus Co. Inc.; Flushing: school buses 750
  Art Leather Mfg. Co.; Flushing: bookbinding 600
  New York Eye & Ear Infirmary Inc.; New York 600
  Mademoiselle Knitwear Inc./Coguillage; Brooklyn; knitting mills 590

13th District

Staten Island; Part of Southwest Brooklyn

With Staten Island—the most suburban of the five boroughs—making up nearly two-thirds of its population, the 13th stands out among New York City's House districts (see map on page 502). Although there are some Democratic pockets in the more working-class ethnic parts of Brooklyn, the 13th is the only consistently Republican district in the otherwise Democratic-dominated city. George Bush carried Staten Island (officially Richmond County) by 9 percentage points over Bill Clinton in 1992; Bush's 48 percent there was exactly double his percentage for New York City as a whole.

The 13th, with a working population of mainly middle- to upper-middle-class commuters, has the lowest poverty rate of any district wholly in New York City. Italian Americans, many of them social conservatives, make up the largest ethnic group in the 13th (which also includes part of Brooklyn across the New York Bay Narrows); Irish Americans are also a large constituency. The non-Hispanic white population is more than 85 percent; there are few minority voters to provide a Democratic base.

If some community activists have their way, the 13th will no longer be the most Republican district in New York City—because Staten Island would no longer be part of New York City. A once-belittled movement to secede from the city has become serious: A November 1993 referendum was approved by borough voters to bring a secession measure before the state Legislature.

Staten Island has always been distant, both physically and psychologically, from the rest of the city. It is the least populous of the boroughs, with about 380,000 residents, and the most remote (its only land link is the Verrazano-Narrows Bridge, opened in 1964, that connects it with Brooklyn; the Staten Island Ferry is still the only direct route to Manhattan).

Residents have become increasingly angry over the use of Staten Island as a literal dumping ground: Its Fresh Kills landfill, one of the world's largest facilities, receives much of the city's garbage.

Secession opponents say Staten Island, which has few major employers, lacks the tax base to go it alone. But supporters argue otherwise, citing such recent business locations as the headquarters of Teleport Communications Group, which provides telecommunications services for large corporations.

Staten Island does have to worry about the fate of its Navy base, which was to have been larger under a Reagan-era plan to greatly expand the U.S. naval force. Not only was the plan for that project scrapped, but the Staten Island base was placed on the preliminary 1993 base-closing list.

The Brooklyn portion of the 13th includes Bay Ridge—setting for the 1977 disco movie *Saturday Night Fever*—and part of Bensonhurst, a mainly Italian community and the site of unrest after the murder of a black youth in 1989.

Election Returns

		Democrat	Republican
1992	President*	82,796 (39.4%)	100,761 (47.9%)
	House †	73,520 (37.9%)	107,903 (55.6%)
1990	Governor	65,970 (56.7%)	45,108 (38.8%)
1988	President	71,999 (38.9%)	112,523 (60.8%)
	Senate	106,087 (62.0%)	63,005 (36.8%)
1986	Senate	36,614 (34.1%)	65,583 (61.1%)
	Governor	70,588 (63.6%)	36,220 (32.6%)

Vote for Perot was 26,317 (12.5%).   †*Independent/other is greater than 5%.*

Demographics

Population 580,337

Percent change from 1980 11.8%

Land area 65 square miles

Population per square mile 8,910

Counties, 1990 population
  Kings (pt.) 201,360   Richmond 378,977

Cities, 1990 population (10,000 or more)
  New York (pt.) 580,337

Race and Hispanic origin
  White 86.7%
  Black 5.6%
  American Indian, Eskimo, or Aleut. 0.2%
  Asian or Pacific Islander 5.5%
  Other 2.1%
  Hispanic origin 7.5%

Ancestry

American 1.7%	Irish 17.5%
Arabic 2.1%	Italian 41.4%
English 3.0%	Norwegian 2.0%
French 1.2%	Polish 4.9%
German 8.2%	Russian 2.8%
Greek 1.9%	

Universities/colleges, 1990-1991 enrollment
  City University of New York-Staten Island, Staten Island
    10,675
  Mirrer Yeshiva Cen Institute, Brooklyn 235
  Wagner College, Staten Island 1,538

Newspapers, total circulation (in all districts)
  Long Island Newsday 788,998
  New York Daily News 757,053
  New York Law Journal 13,583
  New York Post 551,443
  New York Times 746,924
  Staten Island Advance 77,272

Commercial television stations, affiliations
  ADI: New York (100%)

Cable television systems, total subscribers
  Staten Island Cable; Staten Island 70,536
  Time Warner Cable; Brooklyn 38,000

Military installations, 1991
  New York Naval Station, Staten Island-Brooklyn 2,264
  Fort Hamilton (Army), Brooklyn 854

Businesses and other major employers
  Staten Island University Hospital; Staten Island 2,400
  St. Vincent's Medical Center of Richmond; Staten Island
    2,347
  New York City Transit Authority; Brooklyn 2,000
  U.S. Veterans Affairs Dept.; Brooklyn; hospital 2,000
  State of New York/South Beach Pyschiatric Center; Staten
    Island 2,000
  Bayley Seton Hospital; Staten Island 830
  State of New York/Development Center; Staten Island;
    nursing 800
  City University of New York-Staten Island, Staten Island 750
  Sea View Hospital & Home; Staten Island 700
  Eger Health Care Center; Staten Island; nursing 655
  City of New York/Transportation Dept.; Staten Island 600
  Procter & Gamble Co./Port Ivory Plant; Staten Island;
    soaps/cleaners 600
  Victory Memorial Hospital Inc.; Brooklyn 600
  Clove Lake Nursing Home; Staten Island; nursing 580
  Carmel Richmond Nursing Home; Staten Island; nursing
    575

14th District

East Side Manhattan; Parts of Queens and Brooklyn

A bastion of urban liberalism, the House district centered on Manhattan's East Side presented a paradox during the 1980s. Voters strongly supported all Democratic presidential candidates, including landslide losers such as Walter F. Mondale in 1984. Yet during this same period, the district sent a liberal Republican, Bill Green, to the House.

Yet even Green, who had won eight House contests, could not buck the Democratic surge in 1992. The 14th District, which backed Bill Clinton by a wide margin, also chose the Democratic nominee over Green for the House seat.

Green, in fact, was able to narrowly carry his Manhattan base. But he was undone by a redistricting plan that added two working-class areas, in Queens and Brooklyn, where voters had

more regularly Democratic habits in House contests.

The East Side of Manhattan has a Republican heritage. Known as the "Silk Stocking" district, its avenues were once lined with the mansions of Republican industrialists. (Most have long since been replaced by apartment buildings; others, such as the Frick mansion owned by a steel magnate, have been preserved as museums.)

But by the 1960s, young urban liberals, Jewish voters and other Democratic support groups had gained dominance. The social and cultural liberalism of even some wealthy residents gave rise to the term "limousine liberal." Today, the only Republicans who have a shot in the 14th are liberals like Green. Democrats have a 3-to-1 voter registration advantage here.

The East Side district (see map on page 502) has many of the office towers that make up the skyline, including the Citicorp and AT&T buildings. The U.N. building, the Chrysler Building, Grand Central Station and the main New York Public Library touch on 42nd Street. Such landmarks as Rockefeller Center and the Metropolitan Museum of Art are in the 14th, as is all of Central Park (which the 14th crosses to take in a small piece of the West Side).

The district's population is 80 percent non-Hispanic white. The largest minority-group concentrations are at the north end, near Harlem, and south in the Lower East Side, which has a large Hispanic population. The 14th also takes in part of Chinatown, as well as the East Village, a nexus for artists and counterculturalists.

The rest of the 14th is one of those marvels of New York redistricting. It crosses the East River to parts of Astoria in Queens and Greenpoint in Brooklyn, which are three miles apart on either side of the 7th District.

Despite being more conservative than the Manhattan side, these parts were decisive in a Democrat's winning the 1992 House race. The mainly ethnic residents (Greeks and Italians in Astoria, Poles and Italians in Greenpoint) generally stick with their Democratic traditions, but there is a strain of social conservatism.

Election Returns

	14th District	Democrat	Republican
1992	President*	159,750 (69.4%)	53,675 (23.3%)
	House	101,652 (50.1%)	97,215 (47.9%)
1990	Governor	77,582 (71.4%)	29,491 (27.1%)
1988	President	134,698 (65.2%)	71,562 (34.7%)
	Senate	159,276 (80.5%)	37,574 (19.0%)
1986	Senate	71,462 (60.0%)	45,823 (38.5%)
	Governor	89,910 (74.3%)	29,219 (24.2%)

Vote for Perot was 16,419 (7.1%).

Demographics

Population 580,337

Percent change from 1980 12.5%

Land area 13 square miles

Population per square mile 43,399

Counties, 1990 population
  Kings (pt.) 56,939   Queens (pt.) 67,136
  New York (pt.) 456,262

Cities, 1990 population (10,000 or more)
New York (pt.)   580,337

Race and Hispanic origin
White   85.9%
Black   4.6%
American Indian, Eskimo, or Aleut.   0.2%
Asian or Pacific Islander   5.6%
Other   3.8%
Hispanic origin   10.9%

Ancestry

American 2.6%	Irish 11.7%
Arabic 1.1%	Italian 10.8%
Austrian 2.5%	Polish 9.6%
English 8.0%	Romanian 1.1%
French 2.5%	Russian 10.5%
German 11.9%	Scotch Irish 1.0%
Greek 2.8%	Scottish 1.9%
Hungarian 2.6%	Ukrainian 1.0%

Universities/colleges, 1990-1991 enrollment
American Academy of Dramatic Art, New York   212
Berkeley School of New York, New York   834
City University of New York-Bernard Baruch College, New York   16,463
City University of New York-Graduate School and University Center, New York   4,142
City University of New York-Hunter College, New York   20,754
Cornell University Medical Center, New York   572
Katharine Gibbs School, New York   412
Laboratory Institute of Merchandising, New York   204
Marymount Manhattan College, New York   1,332
Mount Sinai School of Medicine, New York   504
New York School of Interior Design, New York   643
New York Theological Seminary, New York   361
School of Visual Arts, New York   4,804
State University of New York College of Optometry, New York   287
Stenotype Academy, New York   738
Wood School, New York   492

Newspapers, total circulation (in all districts)
Daily Variety   21,274
El Diario La Prensa (Spanish)   53,841
Long Island Newsday   788,998
New York Daily News   757,053
New York Law Journal   13,583
New York Post   551,443
New York Times   746,924
Washington Post   810,904

Commercial television stations, affiliations
ADI: New York (100%)

Cable television systems, total subscribers
Paragon Cable Manhattan; New York   165,889
Time Warner Cable; Manhattan (lower)   255,000
Time Warner Cable; Woodside   80,000

Businesses and other major employers
Merrill Lynch & Co. Inc.; New York; security brokers   10,100
New York University/New York University Medical Center; New York   8,000

Rusk Institute for Rehabilitation; New York; health services   8,000
Metropolitan Life Insurance Co.; New York; life insurance   7,000
American Express Co.; New York; security brokers   7,000
Empire Blue Cross Blue Shield; New York; medical service/health insurance   6,500
Bellevue Hospital Center; New York   6,000
Mount Sinai Hospital Inc.; New York   5,900
Metro-North Commuter Railroad Co.; New York; transportation   5,800
Helmsley Enterprises Inc./Harley Hotels; New York; real estate operators   5,000
Equitable Life Assurance Society of the U.S.; New York; life insurance   5,000
United Nations; New York   5,000
Accurate Temporary Services; New York; personnel supply services   5,000
KPMG Peat Marwick; New York; accounting/auditing   5,000
New York Hospital; New York   4,630
New York Life Insurance Co.; New York; life insurance   4,546
CS First Boston Inc.; New York; security brokers   4,319
Lorillard Tobacco Co.; New York; cigarettes   4,092
New York Telephone Co.; New York; telephone communications   4,000
U.S. Postal Service; New York   4,000
Time Inc. Magazine Co.; New York; periodical/book publishing   4,000
Paine Webber Group Inc.; New York; security brokers   4,000
Smith Barney Harris Upham Inc.; New York; security brokers   3,551
Consolidated Edison Co. of New York; New York; electric services   3,500
Shearson Lehman Brothers Inc.; New York; security brokers   3,500
Teachers Insurance & Annuity; New York; life insurance   3,380
Memorial Hospital/Allied; New York   3,100
IBM Corp.; New York; computers   3,000
Bear Stearns & Co. Inc.; New York; security brokers   3,000
May Dept. Stores Co./Lord & Taylor; New York; department stores   3,000
Bankers Trust New York Corp.; New York; commercial banks   3,000
Morgan Stanley Group Inc.; New York; security brokers   3,000
Ernst & Young; New York; accounting/auditing   3,000
Republic New York Corp.; New York; commercial banks   2,953
Initi; New York; laundry services   2,900
Lenox Hill Hospital; New York   2,700
National Broadcasting Co. Inc.; New York; radio/TV broadcasting   2,631
Pfizer Inc.; New York; pharmaceuticals   2,500
Hearst Corp.; New York; periodicals   2,500
Bloomingdale's Inc.; New York; department stores   2,500
Ernst & Young; New York; accounting/auditing   2,500
Arthur Andersen & Co.; New York; accounting/auditing   2,500
McGraw-Hill Inc.; New York; book publishing   2,400
J. Walter Thompson Co.; New York; advertising   2,400

International Seaways Corp.; New York; freight shipping 2,200

Citicorp; New York; commercial banks 2,000

ISS Intl. Service Systems; New York; computer services 2,000

Coopers & Lybrand; New York; accounting/auditing 1,900

CBS Inc./CBS Television Network Div.; New York; radio/TV broadcasting 1,800

Chemical Banking Corp.; New York; commercial banks 1,800

Hilton Hotels Corp./Waldorf-Astoria; New York; hotel 1,800

Skadden Arps Slate Meagher & Flom; New York; legal services 1,750

Cornell University; New York 1,700

Oppenheimer & Co. Inc.; New York; security brokers 1,644

Young & Rubicam Inc.; New York; advertising 1,600

City University of New York-Bernard Baruch College, New York 1,600

Rockefeller University Inc./Rockefeller Archives Center; New York; research services 1,600

Metropolitan Museum of Art Inc; New York; musuems 1,600

Macmillan Capital Corp.; New York; book publishing 1,500

Bristol-Myers Squibb Co.; New York; pharmaceuticals 1,500

AT&T Co.; New York; telephone communications 1,500

Guardian Life Insurance Co. of America; New York; life insurance 1,500

Primerica Corp.; New York; fire/marine/casualty insurance 1,500

Hilton Hotels Corp./New York Hilton; New York; hotel 1,500

Cabrini Medical Center; New York 1,475

Apple Bancorp Inc.; New York; holding offices 1,444

Philip Morris Companies Inc.; New York; cigarettes 1,400

Sony Music Entertainment Inc./CBS Records Inc.; New York; audio recordings/equipment 1,400

Swiss Bank/New York Branch; New York; foreign bank 1,400

Shearman & Sterling; New York; legal services 1,400

Hyatt Corp./Grand Hyatt Hotel; New York; hotel 1,400

Weil Gotshal & Manges; New York; legal services 1,318

Random House Inc.; New York; book publishing 1,300

Grey Advertising Inc.; New York; advertising 1,300

Plaza Operating Partners Ltd./Plaza Hotel; New York; hotel 1,300

Home Health Management Services; New York; home health services 1,247

Leviton Mfg. Co. Inc.; Brooklyn; electric lighting 1,200

Hearst Corp./Popular Mechanics; New York; periodicals 1,200

Bell Security Inc.; New York; security services 1,200

National Kinney Security Inc.; New York; business services 1,200

New York Society for Relief/Hospital for Special Surgery; New York 1,200

MRA Assoc. Inc.; New York; business/security services 1,200

Thacher & Bartlett Simpson; New York; legal services 1,170

Hospital for Jnt. Disabilities.; New York 1,166

Winthrop Sterling Inc.; New York; pharmaceuticals 1,100

Rockefeller Center Management Corp.; New York; real estate operators 1,100

Backer Spielvogel Bates Inc.; New York; advertising 1,100

Montefiore Medical Center; Flushing; medical doctors 1,100

YMCA/92nd St.; New York; civic assn. 1,100

U.S. Trust Co. of New York; New York; commercial banks 1,070

Unilever U.S. Inc.; New York; soaps/cleaners 1,035

John Wiley & Sons Inc.; New York; book publishing 1,000

Effective Security Systems; New York; electrical goods 1,000

Joseph E. Seagram & Sons Inc.; New York; alcohol/beverages 1,000

Volt Information Sciences Inc./Voltelcon Div.; New York; electrical work 1,000

General Cigar Co. Inc.; New York; cigars 1,000

Colgate-Palmolive Co.; New York; soaps/cleaners 1,000

Eastman Kodak Co.; New York; professional/commercial equipment 1,000

Estee Lauder Inc.; New York; cosmetics 1,000

Avon Products Inc.; New York; cosmetics: 1,000

City of New York/Triborough Bridge & Tunnel Authority; New York 1,000

Tiffany & Co.; New York; jewelry stores 1,000

Paul Weiss; New York; legal services 1,000

Palace Co./Helmsley Palace; New York; hotel 950

Charmer Industries Inc.; Long Island City; wine/liquor 900

Salant Corp./Manhattan Industries Div.; New York; outer-wear 900

Temco Service Industries; New York; building services 900

Debevoise & Plimpton; New York; legal services 900

U.S. Environmental Protection Agency; New York 900

Terence Cooke Heal Care Center; New York 900

Bergdorf Goodman Inc.; New York; women's clothing stores 890

School of Visual Arts; New York 885

Shearson Lehman Hutton Inc.; New York; security brokers 855

American Home Products Corp./Wyeth-Ayerst Laboratories Div.; New York; pharmaceuticals 850

Swissre Holding North America; New York; fire/marine/casualty insurance 850

Swiss Reinsurance Co./Northamerican Reinsurance Co.; New York; medical service/health insurance 825

Peerless Importers Inc.; Brooklyn; wine/liquor 813

Manhattan Cable Television; New York; cable TV services 810

Westwind Africa Line Ltd./Southern Star Shipping; New York; freight shipping 800

Home Box Office Inc./HBO; New York; cable TV services 800

McCann-Erickson Inc.; New York; advertising 800

Beth Israel Hospital North; New York 800

City University of New York; New York 794

Associated Press Inc.; New York; business services 780

American Institute of CPA's; New York; periodicals 779

Willkie Farr & Gallagher; New York; legal services 770

Hauser Communications Inc.; New York; cable TV services 750

Mutual of America Life Insurance Co.; New York; life insurance 750

Batten Barton Durstine Osborn; New York; advertising 750

Owners Maintenance Corp.; New York; building services 747

Paramount Communications Inc.; New York; movie production 743

White & Case; New York; legal services 738

Ziff Communications Co./Ziff Davis Publishing Co.; New York; periodicals 700

Newsweek Inc.; New York; periodicals 700

Simon & Schuster Inc.; New York; book publishing 700

Canadian Imperial Bank Commerce; New York; foreign bank 700

Choice Courier Systems; New York; courier services 700

Collins Building Services; New York; building services 700

New York Public Library/Astor Lenox Tilden Foundation; New York 700

Aramis Inc.; New York; toiletries 700

DDB Needham Worldwide Inc.; New York; advertising 700

American Museum of Natural History; New York; musuems 690

Health Insurance Plan of Greater New York; New York; medical service/health insurance 670

Maxwell Group Holdings Inc.; New York; newspapers 650

Bantam Doubleday Dell Publishing Group; New York; book publishing 650

Manhattan Eye Ear Throat Hospital; New York 650

Four Seasons Hotels Inc./Pierre; New York; hotel 650

UN Intl. Corp.; New York 642

Columbia Pictures Industries; New York; movie production 640

Rosenman & Colin; New York; legal services 634

Coopers & Lybrand; New York; accounting/auditing 625

Le Boeuf Lamb Leiby & MacRae; New York; legal services 615

Alitalia Airlines; New York; airline 606

Sotheby's Holdings Inc.; New York; business services 603

Springs Industries Inc.; New York; fabrics/draperies 600

Revlon Finance Corp.; New York; cosmetics 600

HarperCollins Publishers Inc.; New York; book publishing 600

Tishman Construction Corp.; New York; building construction 600

Foster Wheeler Intl.; New York; durable goods 600

Time Warner Inc.; New York; periodicals 600

Dreyfus Fund Inc.; New York; investment offices 600

Katz Communications Inc./Katz Radio Div.; New York; advertising 600

Marriott Corp./East Side Marriott; New York; hotel 600

Ferlin Service Industries Inc.; New York; building services 600

Wilson Elser; New York; legal services 600

Charles Norman Inc./Beneficial Temporaries; New York; personnel supply services 600

Towers Perrin Forster & Crosby; New York; management services 600

Brooks Brothers Inc.; New York; accounting/auditing 600

Goodwill Industries of Greater New York; Long Island City; job training 600

H. R. H. Construction Corp.; New York; building construction 600

Warner Publishers Services; New York; sales promotions/advertising 600

Dewey Ballantine; New York; legal services 600

John M. Lewis; New York; legal services 600

Wells Rich Greene BBDP Inc.; New York; advertising 600

Kaye Scholer Fierman Hays & Handler; New York; legal services 590

Price Waterhouse; New York; accounting/auditing 583

Wertheim Schroder & Co. Inc.; New York; security brokers 576

Varig Brazilian Airlines; New York; airlines 575

De Witt Nursing Home; New York; nursing 574

Read Dillon & Co. Inc.; New York; security brokers 570

Bellevue Hospital; New York 560

Domino Sugar Corp.; Brooklyn; sugar products 550

Cranston Print Works Co.; New York; fabrics 550

Montrose Realty Corp.; New York; real estate agents 550

Young & Rubicam Inc.; New York; advertising 550

Shea & Gould; New York; legal services 550

Meridien Hotels Inc./Parker Meridien Hotel Div.; New York; hotel 550

Omni Hotels Management Corp./Omni Park Central Hotel; New York; hotel 550

Bower & Gardner; New York; legal services 540

Israel Discount Bank of New York; New York; commercial banks 527

Florence Nightingale Nursing Home; New York; nursing 523

Lehrer McGovern Bovis Inc.; New York; consulting services 521

UBS Securities Inc.; New York; security brokers 510

York Building Maintenance; New York; building services 510

Mitsubishi Intl. Corp.; New York; metals/minerals 506

Barclay Operating Corp./Hotel Inter-Continental; New York; hotel 505

15th District

Northern Manhattan — Harlem; Washington Heights

One of the original seats of black political power, the upper Manhattan area centered on Harlem has been transformed in recent decades: There has been a major influx of Hispanics, mainly from Puerto Rico and the Dominican Republic, with a large sampling of other Latin American ethnicities.

Hispanics now make up a large plurality (46 percent) of the population in the 15th, which blankets upper Manhattan from 96th Street to its northern tip (see map on page 502). But in part because of low Hispanic voter participation rates, the non-Hispanic blacks who make up about 37 percent of the population continue to have the political upper hand.

Since first sending an African American to Congress, the Harlem-based district has had just two House members, both Democrats: the flamboyant Adam Clayton Powell Jr., who won a landmark election in 1944, and the low-key Charles Rangel, who unseated the ailing and scandal-plagued Powell in 1970 and who was re-elected to a twelfth term in 1992.

Democrats have a lock on the constituency covered by the 15th. Throughout his career, Rangel has received the endorsement not only of the local Democrats, but of the minuscule GOP organization as well.

At the turn of the 20th century, Harlem, located about 10 miles north of New York City's original hub, was an upscale suburb with a nearly all-white population. But in 1904, blacks—

steered by a black real estate agent named Philip A. Payton Jr.—began to move in. By the 1920s, the height of its cultural "renaissance," Harlem was mainly black and upscale. By the 1940s, the trickle of low-income blacks arriving there became a flood, turning much of Harlem into the economically troubled area it remains.

The largest concentration of blacks in the 15th is in west-central Harlem. Puerto Ricans dominate in East Harlem; West Harlem and Washington Heights farther north have large Dominican communities. Most of the 15th's non-Hispanic whites live in three areas: its south end in the Upper East and West sides; the Inwood section at the north end; and a longtime Italian-American community in East Harlem.

Large parts of the 15th have the array of social problems plaguing low-income minority communities. A third of its residents live in poverty; less than 60 percent of persons 25 and older graduated high school. Harlem has some relatively affluent areas, such as Strivers' Row and Lenox Terrace. There has been some reversal of the outflow of upwardly mobile blacks in such areas as Mount Morris Park, where once-grand brownstones are being restored.

On the west side of the 15th are the campuses of Columbia University and the City College of New York. The district contains such historic sites as the massive Cathedral of St. John the Divine and the tomb of Ulysses S. Grant. The George Washington Bridge crosses the Hudson River to connect upper Manhattan with New Jersey.

An incongruous appendage to the 15th is Rikers Island, located two miles off Manhattan in the East River. A New York City prison complex occupies the island.

Election Returns

	15th District	Democrat	Republican
1992	President*	124,594 (85.8%)	15,589 (10.7%)
	House †	105,011 (94.3%)	—
1990	Governor	64,787 (90.2%)	6,420 (8.9%)
1988	President	118,326 (86.5%)	18,166 (13.3%)
	Senate	105,670 (91.6%)	8,989 (7.8%)
1986	Senate	56,386 (78.6%)	14,168 (19.8%)
	Governor	68,850 (88.2%)	8,401 (10.8%)

*Vote for Perot was 4,726 (3.3%).   †Independent/other is greater than 5%.

Demographics

Population 580,337

Percent change from 1980 12.4%

Land area 11 square miles

Population per square mile 53,272

Counties, 1990 population
Bronx (pt.) 14,050   Queens (pt.) 0
New York (pt.) 566,287

Cities, 1990 population (10,000 or more)
New York (pt.) 580,337

Race and Hispanic origin
White 27.6%
Black 46.9%
American Indian, Eskimo, or Aleut. 0.7%
Asian or Pacific Islander 2.4%
Other 22.4%
Hispanic origin 46.4%

Ancestry
American 1.7%   Italian 1.3%
English 1.4%   Polish 1.2%
German 2.5%   Russian 1.4%
Irish 2.3%   West Indian 3.2%

Universities/colleges, 1990-1991 enrollment
Barnard College, New York 2,173
Boricua College, New York 1,100
City University of New York-City College, New York 12,778
Columbia University, New York 18,242
Helene Fuld School of Nursing, New York 207
Jewish Theological Seminary of America, New York 450
Manhattan School of Music, New York 818
New York College of Podiatric Medicine, New York 415
Rabbi Isaac Elchanan Seminary, New York 319
Teachers College at Columbia University, New York 4,259
Union Theological Seminary, New York 293
Yeshiva University, New York 4,543

Newspapers, total circulation (in all districts)
El Diario La Prensa (Spanish) 53,841
New York Daily News 757,053
New York Law Journal 13,583
New York Post 551,443
New York Times 746,924

Commercial television stations, affiliations
ADI: New York (100%)

Cable television systems, total subscribers
Paragon Cable Manhattan; New York 165,889

Businesses and other major employers
Presbyterian Hospital of New York; New York 6,970
Columbia University; New York 5,500
St. Luke's Roosevelt Hospital; New York 3,400
U.S. Postal Service; New York 2,500
City of New York/Waste Water Treatment; New York 1,800
Manhattan Psychiatric Center; New York 1,700
Triborough Bridge & Tunnel Authority; New York 1,633
City University of New York-City College; New York 1,200
Teachers College at Columbia University; New York 1,026
State of New York/Research Foundation for Mental Health; New York 1,000
North General Hospital; New York 870
Home Savings of America/Bowery Bank; New York; commercial banks 813
North General Home; New York; residential care 760
National Railroad Pass Corp./Amtrak; New York; railroad transportation 700
Isabella Home Nursing Home; New York; nursing 700
State of New York/Housing & Community Renewal Div.; New York 700
Jewish Home & Hospital for Aged/Kittay House; New York; residential care 650
Alexander Karten; New York; laundry services 650
Barnard College; New York 631
Paragon Cable Manhattan; New York; cable TV services 600

16th District

South Bronx

One of the most economically devastated areas in the United States, the mostly Hispanic South Bronx had by the 1970s become a metaphor for the nation's urban ills. Its stretches of refuse-strewn lots and burned-out buildings provide backdrops for visiting politicians of both parties, who prescribe varying solutions to revive the inner cities. Residents have complained bitterly that these photo sessions have resulted in no improvements for the low-income communities of the South Bronx.

But the fragile seedlings of an economic turnaround have begun to take root in parts of the area that form the 16th (see map on page 502). Like frontier settlements, several developments of single-family homes and low-rise apartments have been built on vacated lots by subsidized economic development organizations and occupied by working-class, minority families. These areas, together with more settled, middle-class Hispanic communities in the eastern part of the 16th, provide hope for improvement.

The South Bronx, overtaken by the post-World War II influx of Hispanics to New York City, has since 1970 elected Democrats of Puerto Rican origin to the House. That year, Herman Badillo became the first Puerto Rican to serve in Congress. In 1978, he was succeeded by Robert Garcia. In 1989, Jose Serrano stepped in and was easily re-elected to a second full term in 1992.

Once largely the province of working-class white ethnics, Jews and blacks, the 16th's territory is now 60 percent Hispanic. About a third of the residents are non-Hispanic blacks; fewer than 5 percent are non-Hispanic whites, one of the lowest proportions in any district. Overwhelming Democratic strength here is consistent with other mainly minority districts. Another consistent pattern is low voter turnout, a result of such factors as recent immigration status, political alienation and poverty. A turnout effort in 1992 boosted the number of votes cast in the House contest to more than 90,000 (91 percent went to Serrano). But that was still less than half the average for New York House districts.

A range of inner-city problems affects the residents of the 16th. It has the lowest median family income of the 435 House districts. More than 40 percent of all residents (and nearly half the Hispanic residents) live in poverty. Less than half of the people 25 or older have high school diplomas.

The hardest-pressed communities, such as Mott Haven, Melrose, Morrisania and East Tremont, are in the south and central parts of the district. Some of the new developments are scattered here among the ruins of urban decay. Across the Bronx River, in Soundview and Clason Point, are communities of middle-class Hispanic homeowners.

Once a major factory area, the South Bronx still has a handful of industrial employers, as well as two large wholesale food centers, the Hunts Point and the Bronx terminal markets; Yankee Stadium is near the latter. The 16th comes to a northern point in Bronx Park, site of the Bronx Zoo and the New York Botanical Garden.

Election Returns

	16th District	Democrat	Republican
1992	President*	100,602 (81.3%)	18,834 (15.2%)
	House	85,222 (90.8%)	7,975 (8.5%)
1990	Governor	48,460 (90.6%)	4,465 (8.3%)
1988	President	96,055 (85.0%)	16,665 (14.8%)
	Senate	82,045 (89.7%)	8,686 (9.5%)
1986	Senate	36,084 (73.0%)	11,780 (23.8%)
	Governor	51,027 (87.0%)	6,889 (11.8%)

Vote for Perot was 4,042 (3.3%).

Demographics

Population 580,338

Percent change from 1980 12.4%

Land area 15 square miles

Population per square mile 37,567

Counties, 1990 population
Bronx (pt.) 580,338

Cities, 1990 population (10,000 or more)
New York (pt.) 580,338

Race and Hispanic origin
White 20.0%
Black 42.2%
American Indian, Eskimo, or Aleut. 0.6%
Asian or Pacific Islander 2.1%
Other 35.1%
Hispanic origin 60.2%

Ancestry
American 1.7%   Subsaharan African 1.0%
Italian 1.7%   West Indian 4.2%

Universities/colleges, 1990-1991 enrollment
Bronx Community College, Bronx 5,728

Newspapers, total circulation (in all districts)
El Diario La Prensa (Spanish) 53,841
New York Daily News 757,053
New York Post 551,443
New York Times 746,924

Commercial television stations, affiliations
ADI: New York (100%)

Cable television systems, total subscribers
Cablevision; Bronx 26,598

Businesses and other major employers
Bronx Lebanon Hospital Center/Fulton Div.; Bronx 2,000
St. Barnabas Hospital; Bronx 1,500
Bronx Community College; Bronx 1,000
Bronx Board of Education; Bronx 853
Southeast Bronx Neighborhood Center; Bronx; social services 800
Westchester Square Medical Center; Bronx 700
Daughters of Jacob Nursing Home; Bronx; nursing 610
New York Zoological Society; Bronx; zoos 600
V. N. S. Family Care Services; Bronx; home health services 600
Union Hospital of the Bronx; Bronx 550

17th District

North Bronx; Parts of Southern Westchester

Reflective of the demographic changes the borough of the Bronx has undergone in recent years, the 17th is one of the most ethnically and racially diverse congressional districts. Blacks, with a more than two-fifths plurality, make up the largest racial group in the 17th, which takes in nearly all of the northern part of the Bronx as well as urbanized parts of Yonkers, Mount Vernon and New Rochelle in Westchester County (see map on page 502). But Hispanics and non-Hispanic whites are just behind, almost tied with about a third of the population each.

The non-Hispanic white constituency subdivides among dozens of ethnic groups, with longstanding communities of Italian and Irish Americans, eastern Europeans and Jews.

Many white ethnics are traditionally Democratic but hold conservative views on social issues: They provided the political base for such figures as former Rep. Mario Biaggi, who held the North Bronx district for nearly two decades before running afoul of the law in 1988.

But the 17th, as configured by redistricting in 1992, is a majority-minority district where the liberal views of Democrat Eliot Engel, who was re-elected to a third term in 1992, may be more in keeping. Like Biaggi, Engel has signed onto the various foreign policy causes of his district's European ethnics. But he must maintain a liberal voting record and build multiracial coalitions to forestall future primary challenges by minority-group candidates.

Any serious House contest in the 17th will almost have to be in the primary: Nearly three-quarters of the registered voters are Democrats. Bill Clinton triumphed with 76 percent in the 1992 election. Clinton received 120,286 votes to George Bush's 30,133 and Ross Perot's 7,945.

There are some low-income pockets in the 17th, including some housing projects located in an odd arm that follows the Major Deegan Expressway into an area of the South Bronx adjacent to (but not including) Yankee Stadium. The poverty rate for Hispanic residents in the 17th, about 30 percent, is on par with New York state's rate.

But by and large, this is a middle- to working-class district where the city meets the suburbs. The poverty rate for blacks in the 17th is well below that for the state. A composite of the district can be found in middle-income Co-Op City, a massive complex of high-rise apartments in the eastern part of the 17th. It has a large Jewish population that is Engel's political base, but also many black and Hispanic residents.

At the western border of the Bronx is its most affluent and suburbanlike community, heavily Jewish Riverdale. Just to the north, though, is much of the western part of the city of Yonkers, which is two-thirds minority and mainly low-income. The concentration of minorities in this section has led to a drawn-out federal court battle over housing discrimination in Yonkers.

On its east side, the 17th takes in a part of Mount Vernon that is three-quarters black, a small and racially mixed part of Pelham, and a part of New Rochelle (including its downtown) that is two-thirds black. Fordham University and the Herbert H. Lehman College of the City University of New York are in the Bronx part of the district.

Election Returns

	17th District	Democrat	Republican
1992	President*	120,286 (75.7%)	30,133 (19.0%)
	House †	98,068 (79.3%)	16,511 (13.4%)
1990	Governor	65,105 (77.2%)	17,394 (20.6%)
1988	President	114,792 (73.5%)	41,000 (26.2%)
	Senate	120,248 (83.7%)	22,182 (15.4%)
1986	Senate	61,192 (63.4%)	32,375 (33.5%)
	Governor	78,434 (77.2%)	20,409 (20.1%)

*Vote for Perot was 7,945 (5.0%).   †Independent/other is greater than 5%.

Demographics

Population 580,337

Percent change from 1980 12.4%

Land area 22 square miles

Population per square mile 26,917

Counties, 1990 population
Bronx (pt.) 454,628   Westchester (pt.) 125,709

Cities, 1990 population (10,000 or more)
Mount Vernon (pt.) 45,181   New York (pt.) 454,628
New Rochelle (pt.) 10,695   Yonkers (pt.) 68,968

Race and Hispanic origin
White 40.3%
Black 41.9%
American Indian, Eskimo, or Aleut. 0.4%
Asian or Pacific Islander 3.7%
Other 13.7%
Hispanic origin 29.1%

Ancestry
American 1.8%   Polish 2.6%
English 1.2%   Russian 2.4%
German 3.2%   Subsaharan African 1.1%
Irish 7.7%   West Indian 9.0%
Italian 6.2%

Universities/colleges, 1990-1991 enrollment
City University of New York-Herbert & Lehman College, Bronx 9,496
College of Mount St. Vincent, Bronx 1,022
Fordham University, Bronx 13,158
Hostos Community College, Bronx 4,024
Manhattan College, Bronx 3,794
Monroe College, Bronx 2,407

Newspapers, total circulation (in all districts)
El Diario La Prensa (Spanish) 53,841
Mt. Vernon Argus 7,427
New Rochelle Standard Star 11,054
New York Daily News 757,053
New York Post 551,443
New York Times 746,924
Yonkers Herald Statesman 25,187

Commercial television stations, affiliations
ADI: New York (100%)

Cable television systems, total subscribers
CATV Enterprises Inc.; Riverdale 9,240
Cablevision; Bronx 26,598
Paragon Cable; Mount Vernon 11,828
Paragon Cable Manhattan; New York 165,889

Businesses and other major employers
Montefiore Medical Center/Henry & Lucy Moses Medical Center; Bronx 7,500
Lincoln Hospital; Bronx 4,000
State of New York/Housing & Community Renewal Div.; Bronx 4,000
National Data Services Inc.; Mount Vernon; computer services 3,000
Our Lady of Mercy Medical Center; Bronx 2,400
North Central Bronx Hospital; Bronx 2,200
Fordham University; Bronx 2,028
U.S. Veterans Affairs Dept.; Bronx; hospital 2,000
New York City Transit Authority; Bronx 2,000
W. K. Nursing Home Corp.; Bronx; nursing 1,200
Refined Sugars Inc.; Yonkers; sugar products 1,140
City School; New Rochelle 1,100
City of Yonkers; Yonkers 1,022
Jewish Home & Hospital for the Aged; Bronx; nursing 1,000
City of New Rochelle; New Rochelle 950
TW Services Inc./Canteen Corp.; Bronx; bars/restaurants 900
River Bay Corp./Co-Op City; Bronx; real estate operators 900
Hostos Community College; Bronx 900
Alexander's Inc.; Bronx; department stores 850
Hebrew Home for the Aged; Bronx; nursing 850
St. Joseph's Medical Center; Yonkers 850
Mount Vernon Hospital Inc.; Mount Vernon 823
HM Holdings Inc.; Bronx; household appliances 800
City of New York/Child Welfare Administration; Bronx 800
City University of New York-Herbert & Lehman College, Bronx 800
Beth Abraham Hospital; Bronx 750
Kings Harbor Care Center; Bronx; nursing 700
State of New York/District Attorney; Bronx 650
Hebrew Hospital for the Chronic Sick; Bronx; nursing 650
City of Mount Vernon; Mount Vernon 650
Manhattan College; Bronx 650
Yonkers General Hospital Inc.; Yonkers 650
Leake & Watts Services Inc.; Yonkers; family services 578
Ferdinand Arrigoni Inc./New York Bus Service; Bronx; bus transportation 550
Precision Valve Corp.; Yonkers; metal valves 550
Infirmary for Aged Foundation; Bronx; nursing 550
Alliance Home Service Inc.; Bronx; family services 550
City of Yonkers/Police Dept.; Yonkers 538

18th District

Parts of Westchester, Bronx and Queens Counties

The 18th is one of many jigsaw-puzzle pieces in New York's district map. It stretches from the southern part of Westchester County (which has two-thirds of the district's population), down a ribbon of the East Bronx bordering Long Island Sound, across the mouth of the East River and down a narrow corridor into central Queens (see map on page 502).

Before 1992 redistricting, Democrat Nita Lowey's constitu-

ency was wholly within Westchester. But the drastic reshaping left the political makeup pretty much intact: The 18th is one of New York's most competitive districts, with a slight Democratic lean in recent elections.

The remap removed mainly black, Democratic-voting communities on the urban southern edge of Westchester. But it replaced them with heavily Jewish parts of Queens, where Lowey took 71 percent of the vote in 1992, cinching her victory over the Republican she unseated four years earlier.

The Westchester portion of the district is a toss-up: Lowey won 53 percent there in 1992. This section has some of the most affluent communities in New York state. Most—including such places as Bronxville and Harrison—lean Republican, though Scarsdale, with its large Jewish population, often goes Democratic. The 18th's coastal location along the Long Island Sound also breeds an environmental consciousness that has benefited Lowey.

The most Democratic sections are in the low- to middle-income areas of the large cities, including parts of New Rochelle and White Plains, the county's seat and commercial center. The 18th has the largest portion of Yonkers, Westchester's most populous city (which is split among three districts—the 17th, 18th and 20th).

While Yonkers provides some Democratic votes from its ethnic white, working-class population, it is not a liberal place; it has been tied up for years in a federal court battle over whether there is intentional housing discrimination. The part of the city in the 18th (mainly on the east side) is nearly 90 percent non-Hispanic white, while the southwest part in the 17th District is two-thirds minority.

While there is much commuting to New York City, the portion of Westchester in the 18th has several large employers, including the headquarters of Texaco (White Plains) and Pepsico (Purchase). There is a significant retail trade, much of it in White Plains. Educational institutions include Iona College and the Colege of New Rochelle in New Rochelle and exclusive Sarah Lawrence College in Yonkers.

On its east side, the district takes in an edge of the Bronx, including Pelham Bay Park and City Island. This area's small population, mainly working-class Italian Americans, is heavily Republican.

The 18th then enters Queens via the Throgs Neck Bridge and follows a winding path through urban Flushing, which gives it much of its Asian population. After enveloping the southern part of Flushing Meadow Park, the district spreads west to take in the community of Rego Park and east to Utopia, site of St. John's University.

Election Returns

	18th District	Democrat	Republican
1992	President*	117,937 (50.1%)	94,754 (40.2%)
	House	115,841 (54.9%)	92,687 (44.0%)
1990	Governor	80,307 (56.8%)	56,089 (39.7%)
1988	President	107,577 (46.4%)	123,597 (53.3%)
	Senate	140,851 (64.7%)	74,459 (34.2%)
1986	Senate	66,855 (41.3%)	89,625 (55.4%)
	Governor	100,166 (61.0%)	59,605 (36.3%)

Vote for Perot was 22,019 (9.4%).

Demographics

Population 580,337

Percent change from 1980 12.0%

Land area 94 square miles

Population per square mile 6,175

Counties, 1990 population

Bronx (pt.) 21,030	Westchester (pt.) 388,586
Queens (pt.) 170,721	

Cities, 1990 population (10,000 or more)

Eastchester CDP 18,537	Port Chester 24,728
Harrison 23,308	Rye 14,936
Mamaroneck 17,325	Scarsdale 16,987
Mount Vernon (pt.) 21,972	White Plains (pt.) 30,935
New Rochelle (pt.) 56,570	Yonkers (pt.) 114,743
New York (pt.) 191,751	

Race and Hispanic origin

White 81.1%
Black 7.5%
American Indian, Eskimo, or Aleut. 0.1%
Asian or Pacific Islander 8.2%
Other 3.1%
Hispanic origin 10.4%

Ancestry

American 2.7%	Irish 14.2%
Austrian 1.7%	Italian 24.4%
English 4.5%	Polish 5.9%
French 1.6%	Russian 6.6%
German 9.8%	Scottish 1.2%
Greek 1.3%	West Indian 1.7%
Hungarian 1.5%	

Universities/colleges, 1990-1991 enrollment

Berkeley College of Westchester, White Plains 577
College of New Rochelle, New Rochelle 4,491
Concordia College, Bronxville 576
Iona College, New Rochelle 7,594
Manhattanville College, Purchase 1,583
Sarah Lawrence College, Yonkers 1,193
State University of New York, Purchase 4,619
St. John's University, Utopia 19,105
St. Joseph's Seminary & College, Yonkers 272
Westchester Business Institute, White Plains 1,111

Newspapers, total circulation (in all districts)

El Diario La Prensa (Spanish) 53,841
Mamaroneck Times 5,773
Mt. Vernon Argus 7,427
New Rochelle Standard Star 11,054
New York Daily News 757,053
New York Post 551,443
New York Times 746,924
Port Chester Daily Item 9,496
White Plains Reporter Dispatch 49,425
Yonkers Herald Statesman 25,187

Commercial television stations, affiliations

ADI: New York (100%)

Cable television systems, total subscribers

Cablevision of Westchester; Port Chester 10,511
Cablevision of Westchester; Yonkers 38,500
Time Warner Cable; Queens 116,000
Time Warner Cable; Woodside 80,000
UA Cablesystems/Westchester; Alpine, NJ 81,249

Businesses and other major employers

Long Island Jewish Medical Center; Jamaica 3,900
St. John's University; Jamaica 2,600
Queens High School District; Flushing 2,416
County of Westchester; White Plains 2,000
MCI Telecommunications Corp./Northeast Div.; Port Chester; telephone communications 1,850
Yonkers Contracting Co. Inc.; Yonkers; road construction 1,750
Pepsico Inc.; Purchase; beverages 1,500
Catholic Medical Center/St. John's Hospital; Flushing 1,500
Texaco Inc.; White Plains; petroleum/natural gas 1,300
State University of New York, Purchase 1,500
New Rochelle Hospital & Medical Center; New Rochelle 1,232
Loral Corp./Electronic Systems; Yonkers; communications equipment 1,200
White Plains Hospital & Medical Center; White Plains 1,100
National Cleaning Contractors/Esco Exterminators; White Plains; building services 1,000
St. John's Riverside Hospital; Yonkers 1,000
United Hospital Medical Center; Port Chester 970
Alexander's Inc.; Flushing; department stores 930
La Guardia Hospital; Flushing 920
Lawrence Hospital Inc.; Yonkers 910
Bus Associates Inc.; Yonkers; bus transportation 900
Nestle Chocolate & Confection Co.; Purchase; candies 900
MCI Telecommunications Corp./MCI Intl. Inc.; Rye; telephone communications 800
IBM World Trade Corp./IBM; White Plains; communications equipment 800
New York Power Authority; White Plains; electric services 800
Mutual Life Insurance Co. of New York; Purchase; life insurance 800
Westchester-Rockland Newspapers; White Plains; newspapers 700
Pomonok Home Services Inc.; Flushing; home health services 650
Yonkers Racing Corp.; Yonkers; commercial sports 650
Winifred Burke Rehabilitation Center; White Plains; residential care 630
Liberty Lines Transit Inc.; Yonkers; bus transportation 600
IBM Corp.; Port Chester; computer equipment 600
Catholic Medical Center/St. Joseph's Hospital; Flushing 600
Iona College; New Rochelle 600
IBM Corp.; Rye; computer services 600
Richard L. Aronson Inc.; White Plains; personnel supply services 600
IBM Corp.; Harrison; computer services 550
Dollar Dry Dock Bank; White Plains; savings institutions 510

19th District

Hudson Valley — Poughkeepsie

From its southern edge in Westchester County, the 19th links the densely packed New York City constituencies to the spacious districts of upstate New York. Though it takes in part of White Plains and Poughkeepsie, the 19th is largely exurban and even partially rural.

The 19th provides a comfortable base for the GOP though it is not the state's most Republican district. The New York City-oriented Westchester part of the 19th, which provides just under half the population, can be competitive; while the rest of the district is solidly Republican.

Still, George Bush could not avoid a sharp dropoff in 1992. He lost to Bill Clinton by a plurality in the Westchester County portion of the 19th. He carried the northern part of the district, but he fell from 66 percent in 1988 to 46 percent in Putnam County in 1992.

Much of the 19th's Democratic vote comes from White Plains and working-class communities along the Hudson River. A General Motors plant in North Tarrytown is closing under a corporate restructuring plan. Ossining is the site of the Sing Sing correctional facility; its location on the Hudson gave rise to the warning about being "sent up the river." In Buchanan, near Peekskill, is the Indian Point nuclear power plant. Minority groups make up a higher proportion of the population in these areas than in the rest of the Westchester part of the 19th.

That portion is otherwise made up mainly of white-collar and middle- to upper-middle-class homeowners. During its boom years, IBM—which has its corporate headquarters in Armonk and an international marketing office in White Plains—spurred rapid residential growth in exurban northern Westchester. IBM's recent financial downturn has brought on unprecedented job cuts and economic worries for the 19th.

Among other employers based here is the Reader's Digest Co. in Pleasantville. The Rockefeller family estate, much of it now a state park, is in Pocantico Hills.

Putnam County has experienced some exurban growth, but much of it remains relatively rural. The same can be said about eastern Dutchess County, estate country that has a number of horse farms. Across the Hudson, the 19th takes in a piece of Orange County that includes the U.S. Military Academy at West Point.

The population in the Dutchess County portion is concentrated near its western border with the Hudson. IBM's fallout has also shaken this area. Vassar (in the 22nd District) and Marist colleges are in Poughkeepsie.

Election Returns

	19th District	Democrat	Republican
1992	President*	104,950 (40.2%)	109,965 (42.2%)
	House	92,854 (39.4%)	139,610 (59.3%)
1990	Governor	70,170 (45.3%)	78,040 (50.4%)
1988	President	94,390 (39.6%)	143,005 (60.0%)
	Senate	129,072 (57.5%)	92,166 (41.1%)
1986	Senate	53,084 (35.3%)	91,634 (61.0%)
	Governor	80,247 (52.7%)	67,544 (44.3%)

Vote for Perot was 45,088 (17.3%).

Demographics

Population 580,337

Percent change from 1980 13.4%

Land area 1,080 square miles

Population per square mile 537

Counties, 1990 population
Dutchess (pt.) 172,228	Putnam 83,941
Orange (pt.) 51,784	Westchester (pt.) 272,384

Cities, 1990 population (10,000 or more)
Arlington CDP 11,948	Peekskill 19,536
Jefferson Valley-Yorktown CDP 14,118	Poughkeepsie 28,844
	White Plains (pt.) 17,783
Ossining 22,582	

Race and Hispanic origin
White 89.0%
Black 7.3%
American Indian, Eskimo, or Aleut. 0.2%
Asian or Pacific Islander 2.3%
Other 1.3%
Hispanic origin 5.2%

Ancestry
American 2.3%	Italian 24.3%
Austrian 1.2%	Polish 5.9%
Dutch 2.2%	Russian 3.9%
English 10.8%	Scotch Irish 1.4%
French 3.0%	Scottish 2.3%
German 18.5%	Slovakian 1.2%
Hungarian 1.5%	Swedish 1.4%
Irish 23.6%	

Universities/colleges, 1990-1991 enrollment
Dutchess Community College, Poughkeepsie 7,076
King's College, Briarcliff Manor 495
Marist College, Poughkeepsie 4,980
New York Medical College, Valhalla 1,312
Pace University, Pleasantville 4,145
Pace University, White Plains 4,109
U.S. Military Academy, West Point 4,310
Westchester Community College, Valhalla 10,046

Newspapers, total circulation (in all districts)
New York Daily News 757,053
New York Post 551,443
New York Times 746,924
Ossining Citizen-Register 6,498
Peekskill Evening Star 6,403
Poughkeepsie Journal 43,943
White Plains Reporter Dispatch 49,425

Commercial television stations, affiliations
ADI: New York (100%)

Cable television systems, total subscribers
C-Tec; Carmel 9,845
Cablevision of Westchester; Bedford 5,134
Cablevision of Westchester; Putnam Valley 17,300
Continental Cablevision of New York; Ossining 42,200
Paragon Cable; Newburgh 25,164

TCI of New York; Poughkeepsie 18,300
U.S. Cablevision Corp.; Mt. Beacon 47,933

Military installations, 1991
West Point Military Reservation, West Point 8,620
Stewart Intl. Airport Air Force Guard Station, New Windsor 671

Businesses and other major employers
State of New York/Sing Sing Correctional Facility; Ossining 15,000
IBM Corp.; Hopewell Junction; computer components 11,000
IBM Corp./Data Systems Div.; Poughkeepsie; computer systems 10,000
Westchester County Medical Center; Valhalla 3,500
IBM Corp./Networking Systems; Somers; computer equipment 3,000
IBM Corp./Research Div.; Yorktown Heights; research services 3,000
Reader's Digest Association Inc.; Pleasantville; periodicals 2,760
State of New York; Wassaic 2,300
New York Medical College; Valhalla 2,250
Pepsico Inc./Pepsi Cola Co. Div.; Somers; beverages 2,000
County of Dutchess; Poughkeepsie 1,783
Dutchess Community College; Poughkeepsie 1,700
U.S. Veterans Affairs Dept.; Montrose; hospital 1,474
State of New York/Grow Workshop; Poughkeepsie 1,420
State of New York/Transportation Dept.; Poughkeepsie 1,400
Prodigy Services Co.; White Plains; communication services 1,250
State of New York/Fishkill Correctional Facility; Beacon 1,221
IBM Corp.; Armonk; computers/management 1,200
County of Westchester/Correction Dept.; Valhalla 1,200
Vassar Bros. Hospital; Poughkeepsie 1,200
State of New York/Harlem Valley Psychiatric Center; Wingdale 1,140
Society of New York Hospital Inc.; White Plains; research services 1,100
St. Francis Hospital; Poughkeepsie 1,100
Effective Security Systems; White Plains; security services 1,000
AT&T Co.; White Plains; accounting services 1,000
Lakeland Control School District; Shrub Oak 1,000
State of New York/Greenhaven Correctional Facility; Stormville 1,000
Northern Westchester Hospital; Mount Kisco 975
State of New York/Bedford Hills Correctional Facility; Bedford Hills 800
Phelps Memorial Hospital Assn.; Tarrytown 780
St. Agnes Hospital; White Plains 750
Accent Maintenance Corp.; Ossining; building services 750
U.S. Veterans Affairs Dept.; Beacon; hospital 711
Consolidated Edison Co. of New York; Buchanan; electric services 700
Four Winds Hospital; Katonah 700
Putnam Center Inc.; Carmel 700
IBM Corp./Research Div.; Hawthorne; research services 700
Gene-Ett Maintenance Co. Inc.; Valhalla; building services 675

Macy's Northeast Inc.; White Plains; department stores 673
Texaco Inc./Research Center; Glenham; research services 620
Bloomingdale's Inc.; White Plains; department stores 600
Poughkeepsie School District; Poughkeepsie 600
New York Power Authority/Indian Point #3; Buchanan; electric services 590
Empire Blue Cross Blue Shield; Yorktown Heights; insurance services 550
Peekskill Community Hospital; Peekskill 550
Chappaqua Control School District; Chappaqua 520
Central Hudson Gas & Electric Corp.; Poughkeepsie; electric services 515

20th District

Rockland and Parts of Westchester, Orange and Sullivan Counties

The 20th, near the outer edge of New York City's sphere, has a Republican lean but not a full tilt. Its Rockland and Orange county subdivisions have been populated since World War II largely by relocated New York City residents, many of them Irish and Italian Americans and Jews; a number brought Democratic voting traditions that were tempered by their new exurban lifestyles. A moderate Republican can draw out a solid GOP vote. But in races featuring more conservative GOP candidates, the 20th is somewhat more competitive.

In 1992, Republican Benjamin Gilman took 65 percent of the vote in the 20th, a typical figure for him; Republican Sen. Alfonse D'Amato carried the district by a somewhat lower margin. But Democrat Bill Clinton defeated George Bush here. In Rockland County—which has just less than half the district's population—Clinton got 47 percent and defeated Bush by 6 percentage points.

The 20th actually starts fairly close in to New York City, in the Westchester County suburbs. It takes in the northeast corner of Yonkers (including its affluent Beech Hill section), Greenburgh (a mainly middle-class town that includes part of the Central Avenue retail corridor) and such mainly comfortable riverside communities as Hastings-on-Hudson, Dobbs Ferry and Tarrytown. A 17 percent combined black and Hispanic population contributes to making this the most Democratic part of the 20th; Gilman took just 52 percent of the vote there in 1992.

But Gilman dominated in his home base of Rockland County, winning two-thirds of the vote in 1992. Though Rockland does not have a single urban center—its population is spread among such communities as Spring Valley, Pearl River, Nyack, Congers, New City and Suffern—it is rather thoroughly developed: More than 90 percent of the population is classified by the Census Bureau as urban.

Rockland has a number of employers, the largest of which is a facility of the Lederle Laboratories pharmaceutical company in Pearl River. But many residents drive across the Tappan Zee Bridge to offices in Westchester or make the long commute into New York City.

The county has a large Jewish population that includes several long-established Hasidic communities. The district's parts of Orange and Sullivan counties, which take in some of the Catskill Mountains' "borscht belt" resorts, have unusually large Jewish populations for less urbanized areas.

Orange County contributes about a third of the 20th's population; its largest towns are Warwick and Middletown. On the county's north side, near the 26th District city of Newburgh, is Stewart Airport, a former Air Force base that is now a major cargo terminal. Much of the county is rural, with dairy, stud horse and onion farms.

Sullivan County has less than 5 percent of the 20th's population, but has its most famous latter-day cultural site. The Woodstock music festival was held in a farm field near the town of Bethel in 1969.

Election Returns

	20th District	Democrat	Republican
1992	President*	116,294 (44.5%)	107,107 (41.0%)
	House	66,826 (29.0%)	150,301 (65.2%)
1990	Governor	75,661 (48.8%)	73,133 (47.2%)
1988	President	99,205 (42.1%)	135,484 (57.5%)
	Senate	139,269 (62.6%)	80,128 (36.0%)
1986	Senate	58,973 (39.8%)	83,261 (56.1%)
	Governor	86,560 (57.6%)	58,665 (39.0%)

*Vote for Perot was 37,011 (14.2%).

Demographics

Population 580,338

Percent change from 1980 13.3%

Land area 1,288 square miles

Population per square mile 451

Counties, 1990 population
Orange (pt.) 205,351	Sullivan (pt.) 21,325
Rockland 265,475	Westchester (pt.) 88,187

Cities, 1990 population (10,000 or more)
Middletown 24,160	Spring Valley 21,802
Monsey CDP 13,986	Stony Point CDP 10,587
Nanuet CDP 14,065	Suffern 11,055
New City CDP 33,673	Tarrytown 10,739
Pearl River CDP 15,314	

Race and Hispanic origin
White 86.6%
Black 8.2%
American Indian, Eskimo, or Aleut. 0.2%
Asian or Pacific Islander 3.4%
Other 1.6%
Hispanic origin 6.1%

Ancestry
American 3.7%	Irish 20.8%
Austrian 1.5%	Italian 18.9%
Dutch 2.6%	Polish 7.6%
English 8.0%	Russian 5.9%
French 2.3%	Scottish 1.5%
German 17.1%	Slovakian 1.0%
Hungarian 2.1%	West Indian 2.4%

Universities/colleges, 1990-1991 enrollment
Bais Medrash L'Torah, Monsey 432
Beth Medrash Eeyun Hatalmud, Monsey 573
Beth Rochel Seminary, Monsey 241
Dominican College of Blauvelt, Orangeburg 1,495
Gruss Girls Seminary, Spring Valley 455
Long Island University Rockland, Orangeburg 481
Marymount College, Tarrytown 1,125
Mercy College, Dobbs Ferry 4,801
Nyack College, Nyack 784
Orange County Community College, Middletown 5,427
Rockland Community College, Suffern 8,023
St. Thomas Aquinas College, Sparkill 2,077

Newspapers, total circulation (in all districts)
Middletown Times Herald-Record 84,398
New York Daily News 757,053
New York Post 551,443
New York Times 746,924
Nyack Journal-News 40,698
Tarrytown Daily News 3,874
White Plains Reporter Dispatch 49,425
Yonkers Herald Statesman 25,187

Commercial television stations, affiliations
ADI: New York (100%)

Cable television systems, total subscribers
Cablevision Industries Inc.; Monticello 9,000
Cablevision Industries Inc.; Wurtsboro Mt. 34,652
Continental Cablevision of New York; West Haverstraw 12,000
TKR Cable Co.; Mahwah 10,099
TKR Cable Co.; Monsey 26,875
TKR Cable Co.; Warwick 17,100
UA Cablesystems/Westchester; Alpine, NJ 81,249
US Cablevision Corp.; Monroe 8,969

Businesses and other major employers
American Cyanamid Co./Lederle Laboratories Div.; Pearl River; pharmaceuticals 4,000
County of Rockland Inc.; New City 3,500
State of New York/Letchworth Psychiatric Center; Thiells 2,800
Nyack Hospital Inc.; Nyack 1,575
Miles Inc./Diagnostics Div.; Tarrytown; medical instruments/supplies 1,500
Good Samaritan Hospital; Suffern 1,500
County of Orange; Goshen 1,500
Horton Memorial Hospital; Middletown 1,400
State of New York/Middletown Psychiatric Center; Middletown 1,130
Ciba-Geigy Corp.; Ardsley; pharmaceuticals 1,100
Chromalloy Gas Turbine Corp.; Orangeburg; metal services 1,100
IBM Corp.; Sterling Forest; computer/office equipment 900
Kolmar Laboratories Inc.; Port Jervis; cosmetics 900
Yellow Freight System Inc.; Maybrook; trucking facilities 880
Haverstaw Stony Point Control School District; Garnerville 700
Orange County Community College; Middletown 700
Wakefern Food Corp./Shop Rite; Middletown; grocery products 660
Orange & Rockland Utilities; Pearl River; electric services 655
Arden Hill Hospital Inc.; Goshen 650
Mercy Community Hospital; Port Jervis 650
Children's Village Inc.; Dobbs Ferry; residential care 610

Kraft General Foods Inc.; Tarrytown; food research   610

State of New York/Helen Hayes Hospital; West Haverstraw   610

Agfa Corp.; Orangeburg; medical instruments/supplies   600

Union Carbide Chemical & Plastic Co.; Tarrytown; research services   600

New York Foundling Hospital/St. Agatha Home; Nanuet; residential care   600

State of New York/Mid-Orange Correctional Facility; Warwick   600

Orange Ulster Boces; Goshen   600

State of New York/Westchester Developmental; Tarrytown   592

Orange & Rockland Utilities/Rockland Electric; Spring Valley; electric services   580

Greenburgh Central School District; Hartsdale   536

Town of Greenburgh; Elmsford   528

Insurance Services Office Inc.; Pearl River; computer services   525

21st District

Capital District — Albany; Schenectady; Troy

With government employment and manufacturing as its economic mainstays, New York's capital district has long provided Democrats—including Rep. Michael McNulty and his predecessor, the late Samuel S. Stratton—with a solid political base.

Yet the 21st is no liberal stronghold; its minority population is not large, and its major ethnic groups are Irish and Italian Americans, many of whom are conservative on social issues. McNulty is one of the few New York Democrats who seeks and receives the endorsement of the state's Conservative Party.

Bill Clinton carried the 21st in 1992, but won a majority of the vote only in Albany County (which has just over half the district's residents). Ross Perot took more than 20 percent of the vote in Schenectady, Rensselaer and Montgomery counties.

The 21st covers most of the Albany-Schenectady-Troy metropolitan area. Albany, the capital, is the district's largest city with just over 100,000 residents. It has the 21st's largest minority concentration; more than half the district's blacks live there.

Albany provides the foundations for Democratic wins in the 21st; despite pockets of Republican votes in the suburbs (the largest of which is adjacent Colonie), Albany County usually goes Democratic. It was one of only three upstate counties to favor the Democratic nominee in the 1992 Senate race.

The state bureaucracy and regional federal offices in Albany provide economic stability (even though fiscal problems have forced some public agencies to trim their payrolls). Nearly half of all employment in Albany is in the public sector.

Albany County, on the west bank of the Hudson River, has a longstanding industrial sector that includes the arsenal in Watervliet. But its private-sector growth has been in such fields as health care and insurance. The state university campus in Albany (17,400 students) is the largest higher educational institution in the 21st; others include Rensselaer Polytechnic Institute (6,700 students) in Troy and Union College (2,900 students) in Schenectady.

Industrial employment remains more integral in Troy, across the Hudson in Rensselaer County, and west along the Mohawk River in Schenectady and Amsterdam (Montgomery County).

General Electric makes power-generating equipment and has its research and development center in Schenectady.

Even though it remains the 21st's largest employer, GE cut its work force deeply over the past decade; overall industrial employment in Schenectady County declined by more than a third during the 1980s. The blow was cushioned by an aggressive economic development effort that attracted smaller manufacturers and service providers.

But Montgomery County has been struggling since its major employer, a Mohawk Carpet plant, moved south in the 1960s. It has the lowest median household income among the district's counties.

Election Returns

	21st District	Democrat	Republican
1992	President*	140,251 (48.1%)	99,094 (34.0%)
	House	166,371 (62.2%)	91,184 (34.1%)
1990	Governor	110,111 (53.4%)	88,964 (43.1%)
1988	President	154,309 (55.7%)	121,615 (43.9%)
	Senate	181,445 (69.5%)	77,405 (29.6%)
1986	Senate	98,482 (45.6%)	112,125 (52.0%)
	Governor	137,386 (62.5%)	75,578 (34.4%)

Vote for Perot was 51,086 (17.5%).

Demographics

Population   580,337

Percent change from 1980   12.3%

Land area   1,087 square miles

Population per square mile   534

Counties, 1990 population

Albany 292,594	Saratoga (pt.) 8,695
Montgomery (pt.) 41,824	Schenectady 149,285
Rensselaer (pt.) 87,939	

Cities, 1990 population (10,000 or more)

Albany 101,082	Roessleville CDP 10,753
Amsterdam 20,714	Rotterdam CDP 21,228
Cohoes 16,825	Schenectady 65,566
Latham CDP 10,131	Troy 54,269
Loudonville CDP 10,822	Watervliet 11,061

Race and Hispanic origin

White   91.3%
Black   6.3%
American Indian, Eskimo, or Aleut.   0.2%
Asian or Pacific Islander   1.5%
Other   0.8%
Hispanic origin   2.1%

Ancestry

American 2.0%	Italian 18.6%
Dutch 5.4%	Polish 9.6%
English 13.0%	Russian 2.0%
French 9.1%	Scotch Irish 1.4%
French Canadian 2.7%	Scottish 2.2%
German 21.8%	Swedish 1.0%
Irish 25.7%	Ukrainian 1.1%

Universities/colleges, 1990-1991 enrollment

Albany College of Pharmacy, Albany 672
Albany Law School, Albany 826
Albany Medical College, Albany 610
Bryant & Stratton Business Institute, Albany 422
College of St. Rose, Albany 3,685
Hudson Valley Community College, Troy 9,401
Maria College, Albany 916
Rensselaer Polytechnic Institute, Troy 6,692
Russell Sage College, Troy 4,272
Schenectady County Community College, Schenectady 3,234
Siena College, Loudonville 3,454
State University of New York, Albany 17,405
State University of New York Regents External Degree Program, Albany 16,476
Union College, Schenectady 2,877

Newspapers, total circulation (in all districts)

Albany Times Union 108,960
Amsterdam Recorder 11,681
New York Daily News 757,053
New York Post 551,443
Schenectady Gazette 60,888
Troy Record 38,182

Commercial television stations, affiliations

ADI: Albany-Schenectady-Troy (100%)
WTEN, Albany (ABC)
WXXA-TV, Albany (Fox)
WRGB, Schenectady (CBS)

Cable television systems, total subscribers

Cablevision; Bethlehem 5,263
Capital Cablevision; Loudonville 63,000
Gateway Cablevision; Amsterdam 13,200
TCI of New York; Schenectady 29,825

Military installations, 1991

Watervliet Arsenal (Army), Watervliet 2,408
Schenectady Airport Air Force Guard Station, Schenectady 253

Businesses and other major employers

State of New York/Labor Dept.; Albany 5,500
Albany Medical Center Hospital; Albany 3,500
St. Peter's Hospital; Albany 2,764
State of New York/Controller Dept.; Albany 2,500
State of New York/Tax & Finance Dept.; Albany 2,500
General Electric Co./Knolls Atomic Power Laboratory; Schenectady; research 2,250
State of New York/Health Dept.; Albany 2,000
State of New York/Labor Relations Dept.; Albany 2,000
Rensselaer Polytechnic Institute; Troy 1,992
State of New York/Social Service Dept.; Albany 1,800
New York Federation; Albany; job training 1,800
Empire Blue Cross Blue Shield; Albany; insurance services 1,700
County of Schenectady; Schenectady 1,588
General Electric Co.; Waterford; silicone 1,535
Consolidated Rail Corp.; Selkirk; railroads 1,500
U.S. Veterans Affairs Dept.; Albany; hospital 1,500
Ellis Hospital; Schenectady 1,430

Niagara Mohawk Power Corp.; Albany; electric services 1,300
U.S. Postal Service; Albany 1,300
St. Clare's Hospital of Schenectady; Schenectady 1,250
State of New York/Transportation Dept.; Albany 1,200
Albany Memorial Hospital; Albany 1,110
State of New York/Housing & Building Code; Albany 1,100
State of New York/Civil Service Dept.; Albany 1,100
State of New York/Heck Developmental Center; Schenectady 1,100
Samaritan Hospital; Troy 1,068
City of Albany/School District; Albany 1,050
Allied-Signal Inc./Bendix Friction Materials Div.; Troy; motor vehicle equipment 1,007
State of New York/Unemployment Insurance Div.; Albany 1,000
County of Albany; Albany; nursing 1,000
State of New York/Education Dept.; Albany 1,000
St. Mary's Hospital of Troy; Troy 954
Sears Roebuck & Co.; Albany; department stores 900
Winthrop Sterling Inc.; Rensselaer; research services 900
Golub Corp./Price Chopper Supermarkets; Schenectady; grocery stores 850
LTC Eddy Inc.; Troy; nursing 850
U.S. Justice Dept.; Albany 850
State of New York/Environmental Conservation Dept.; Albany 800
Garden Way Inc./Troy Bilt; Troy; garden equipment 800
LIA Group; Schenectady; new/used car dealers 800
State of New York/Insurance Dept.; Albany 800
State of New York/Criminal Justice Dept.; Albany 800
American Patriot Health Insurance Co.; Albany; medical service/health insurance 750
Hudson Valley Community College; Troy 750
City of Troy/School District; Troy 750
St. Mary's Hospital; Amsterdam 725
Capital Area Community Health Plan/Healthshield; Latham; medical doctors 704
General Electric Co./Industrial & Power System; Schenectady; engines/turbines 700
City of Troy; Troy 670
Leonard Hospital; Troy 650
Siena College; Loudonville 650
Ralston Purina Co./Beech-Nut; Canajoharie; preserved fruits/vegetables 644
State of New York/Central Administration; Albany 640
State of New York/Thruway Authority; Albany; transportation services 627
Union College; Schenectady 620
General Electric Co.; Selkirk; electrical work 600
Matthew Bender & Co. Inc.; Albany; periodicals 600
Albany Intl. Corp.; Albany; paper products 600
Standard Products Co./Campbell Plastics Inc. Div.; Schenectady; plastics/synthetics 600
State of New York/General Services Dept.; Albany 600
State of New York/Equalization & Assessment Div.; Albany 600
Town of East Greenbush/Central School District; East Greenbush 600
County of Rensselaer/Social Services Dept.; Troy 600
Workshop Inc.; Albany; job training 600
Health Research Inc.; Albany; research services 600
State of New York/Management Services Div.; Albany 600

Town of Guilderland/Central School District; Guilderland 600

Amsterdam Memorial Hospital; Amsterdam 600

Hearst Corp./Capital Newspaper Div.; Albany; periodicals 577

Norton Co./Coated Abrasive Div.; Watervliet; mineral products 550

Town of Amsterdam/School District; Amsterdam 525

Niskayuna Central School District; Schenectady 515

Diocese of Albany/School Office; Albany; religious organization 508

22nd District

Rural East — Glens Falls; Saratoga Springs

The 22nd runs nearly 200 miles south to north, from the Dutchess County estate country at the edge of the New York City metropolis, around Albany and on to the Adirondack mountain region not far from Canada. It takes in most of New York's eastern border with the New England states.

This largely rural and conservative district has held more strongly to its Yankee Republican voting traditions than its New England neighbors. The 22nd was carried overwhelmingly in 1992 by Republican Rep. Gerald Solomon, who has been one of the most outspoken conservatives in the House.

In 1992 Solomon carried the four full and five partial counties in the 22nd with no less than 62 percent of the vote (and as much as 69 percent). Republican Sen. Alfonse M. D'Amato topped 55 percent in all 22nd District counties as he narrowly won re-election in 1992.

George Bush, who won nearly 60 percent of the district's vote in 1988, fell off sharply in 1992, but still managed a plurality win over Bill Clinton, who failed to reach 40 percent in any of the district's county portions. Ross Perot topped a fifth of the vote in every county.

The 22nd is 97 percent non-Hispanic white; it has the smallest minority population among New York districts. The population hub of the 22nd is in its center, in the Albany-Schenectady-Troy metropolitan area. This district has none of those cities, but much of their GOP suburbia.

Saratoga County, just north of Albany at the confluence of the Hudson and Mohawk rivers, has by far the district's largest population share (with about 30 percent of the district's residents). The ongoing suburbanization of the southern part of the county, in such communities as Half Moon and Clifton Park, was reflected in Saratoga County's 18 percent population increase during the 1980s.

Across the Hudson, the 22nd takes in much of Rensselaer County. But its largest bloc of Democratic votes, in industrial Troy, is snatched away by the 21st District, leaving the 22nd with its suburbs and dairy lands.

In northern Saratoga County is the resort town of Saratoga Springs. Nearby is a Revolutionary War battlefield, one of many 18th century historical sites in the 22nd.

The district follows Interstate 87 (the Northway) into mountainous, scenic Adirondack Park and the resort areas of Lake George and Lake Champlain. In Essex County at the northwest corner of the district is Lake Placid, site of the 1932 and 1980 Winter Olympics. Though tourism is heavy, this area—dependent on seasonal employment and on factory jobs in the Warren County city of Glens Falls—has its share of economic problems.

The southern end of the 22nd is made up of mainly rural territory in Schoharie, Greene, Columbia and northern Dutchess County. Near the south edge of the district is Hyde Park and the estate of President Franklin D. Roosevelt, the patrician Democrat who in his time was regarded by much of the area's landed gentry as a "traitor to his class."

Election Returns

		Democrat	Republican
	22nd District	Democrat	Republican
1992	President*	99,988 (35.8%)	116,238 (41.6%)
	House	86,896 (34.3%)	164,436 (64.9%)
1990	Governor	67,792 (38.2%)	103,019 (58.1%)
1988	President	98,002 (39.9%)	146,513 (59.7%)
	Senate	123,428 (54.1%)	102,646 (45.0%)
1986	Senate	54,220 (32.3%)	109,234 (65.2%)
	Governor	84,714 (49.7%)	80,934 (47.5%)

*Vote for Perot was 62,533 (22.4%).

Demographics

Population 580,337

Percent change from 1980 12.3%

Land area 6,510 square miles

Population per square mile 89

Counties, 1990 population

Columbia 62,982	Saratoga (pt.) 172,581
Dutchess (pt.) 73,991	Schoharie (pt.) 13,300
Essex (pt.) 27,715	Warren 59,209
Greene 44,739	Washington 59,330
Rensselaer (pt.) 66,490	

Cities, 1990 population (10,000 or more)

Brunswick 10,645	Malta 11,709
Catskill 11,965	Milton 14,658
Clifton Park 30,117	Moreau 13,022
Glens Falls 15,023	Queensbury 22,630
Halfmoon 13,879	Saratoga Springs 25,001
Hyde Park 21,230	Schodack 11,839
Kingsbury 11,851	Wilton 10,623
La Grange (pt.) 13,220	

Race and Hispanic origin

White 96.6%
Black 2.2%
American Indian, Eskimo, or Aleut. 0.2%
Asian or Pacific Islander 0.7%
Other 0.4%
Hispanic origin 1.5%

Ancestry

American 3.9%	Italian 13.4%
Dutch 6.2%	Polish 6.3%
English 18.3%	Russian 1.3%
French 12.6%	Scotch Irish 2.0%
French Canadian 3.0%	Scottish 3.3%
German 23.2%	Swedish 1.4%
Irish 25.3%	Welsh 1.2%

Universities/colleges, 1990-1991 enrollment

Adirondack Community College, Queensbury 3,378
Bard College, Annandale-on-Hudson 1,114

Columbia-Greene Community College, Hudson 1,696
Culinary Institute of America, Hyde Park 1,822
Skidmore College, Saratoga Springs 2,605
State University of New York-Empire State College, Saratoga
  Springs 6,900
Vassar College, Poughkeepsie 2,453

Newspapers, total circulation (in all districts)
Albany Times Union 108,960
Glens Falls Post-Star 34,282
Kingston Daily Freeman 22,329
New York Daily News 757,053
New York Post 551,443
New York Times 746,924
Poughkeepsie Journal 43,943
Saratogian 12,041
Schenectady Gazette 60,888
Troy Record 38,182

Commercial television stations, affiliations
ADI: Albany-Schenectady-Troy (72%), Burlington-Plattsburgh
  (22%) and New York (6%)
WNYT, Albany (NBC)

Cable television systems, total subscribers
Cablevision Industries; Lake George 10,574
Cablevision Industries; Saratoga Springs 17,229
Harron Cable TV; Queensbury 14,423
Mid-Hudson Cablevision Inc.; Catskill 15,343
TCI of New York; Poughkeepsie 18,300
Troy Newchannels; Troy 46,550
US Cablevision Corp.; Mt. Beacon 47,933

Businesses and other major employers
Glens Falls Hospital; Glens Falls 2,000
State of New York/Wilton Developmental Center; Saratoga
  Springs 1,030
Finch Pruyn & Co. Inc.; Glens Falls; paper mills 998
Saratoga Hospital Inc.; Saratoga Springs 996
International Paper Co.; Ticonderoga; paper mills 900
County of Warren; Lake George 900
C. R. Bard Inc.; Glens Falls; catheters 800
Continental Insurance Co.; Glens Falls; insurance services 700
Columbia-Greene Medical Center; Hudson 700
County of Columbia; Hudson 700
County of Saratoga; Ballston Spa 700
Skidmore College; Saratoga Springs 700
State Farm Mutual Auto Insurance Co.; Ballston Spa; insur-
  ance services 678
General Electric Co.; Ft. Edward; electronic components 650
International Paper Co./Hudson River Mill; Corinth; paper
  mills 600
County of Washington; Fort Edward 600
Scott Paper Co.; Fort Edward; paper mills 565
State of New York/Correctional Dept.; West Coxsackie 550
State of New York/Correctional Dept.; Comstock 534
Mallinckrodt Medical Inc.; Argyle; medical supplies 531

23rd District
Central — Utica; Rome

The 23rd, which takes in four full counties and parts of five
others in central New York, is a demographic sampler. It has a
few cities, including Utica and Rome in Oneida County, many
more small towns and rural stretches that make up most of this
large district's land area.

A Republican heritage in this upstate region allows most
GOP candidates to carry the 23rd usually by solid margins.
Republican Sherman Boehlert's record as a moderate has
appealed to the mix of farm, Main Street and urban voters; he
has never been seriously challenged since being first elected in
1982.

However, many of the 23rd's voters showed their disaffection
with George Bush in 1992. He carried the district, but won more
than 40 percent in just four counties. Economic problems in
some blue-collar and rural areas gave Ross Perot an audience; he
topped a fifth of the vote in all district counties.

Oneida County, Boehlert's home base, has more than 40
percent of the district's population. The biggest concentration is
in the short stretch of the Mohawk River Valley that connects
Utica and Rome.

Blue-collar jobs continue to be important in these aging
industrial cities: The largest private-sector employer is the Oneida
silverware company. But the manufacturing sector has declined
over the years. Utica's poverty rate is above 20 percent. Local
officials look to service industry jobs and such high-tech fields as
fiber optics and photonics for growth. Rome's economy has
been cushioned by nearby Griffiss Air Force Base. But that good
fortune may soon run out: A military-base downsizing proposal
submitted in March 1993 by a federal commission targeted
Griffiss for a major realignment.

The remainder of Oneida County is mainly rural. Although
there is some Democratic vote in the cities, the county usually
sets a Republican tone for the district. Boehlert took two-thirds
of the vote and GOP Sen. Alfonse M. D'Amato took 61 percent
here in 1992.

Other areas of the 23rd have concerns about the post-Cold
War defense budget. A Simmonds plant in Chenango County
makes military jet engines. The area of Broome County in the
southern end of the 23rd is affected by cutbacks in nearby
Binghamton's defense-related industries.

There are other industrial facilities, including Remington
Arms and Chicago Pneumatic Tool plants in Herkimer County.
The district's educational institutions include Colgate University
in Hamilton (Madison County; 2,700 students), Hartwick College
in Oneonta (Otsego County; 1,600 students) and the state
university in Oneonta (6,300 students).

At the south end of Otsego Lake (the source of the
Susquehanna River) is Cooperstown, a small village that hosts
the Baseball Hall of Fame. It was here that James Fenimore
Cooper wrote the stories of frontier days that gave central New
York its nickname—the "Leatherstocking Region."

Election Returns

	23rd District	Democrat	Republican
1992	President*	92,549 (37.2%)	99,497 (40.0%)
	House†	61,835 (27.8%)	139,774 (62.8%)
1990	Governor	66,524 (38.3%)	101,027 (58.1%)
1988	President	103,312 (44.5%)	128,279 (55.2%)
	Senate	125,658 (59.0%)	84,471 (39.7%)
1986	Senate	56,832 (33.1%)	110,562 (64.3%)
	Governor	98,949 (56.3%)	72,885 (41.5%)

Vote for Perot was 55,902 (22.5%).   †*Independent/other is greater than 5%.*

Demographics

Population 580,337

Percent change from 1980 12.3%

Land area 5,986 square miles

Population per square mile 97

Counties, 1990 population

Broome (pt.) 19,998	Montgomery (pt.) 10,157
Chenango 51,768	Oneida 250,836
Delaware (pt.) 41,023	Otsego 60,517
Herkimer (pt.) 58,359	Schoharie (pt.) 18,559
Madison 69,120	

Cities, 1990 population (10,000 or more)

German Flatts 14,345	Oneonta 13,954
Herkimer 10,401	Rome 44,350
Kirkland 10,153	Sullivan 14,622
New Hartford 21,640	Utica 68,637
Oneida 10,850	Whitestown 18,985

Race and Hispanic origin

White 95.8%
Black 2.9%
American Indian, Eskimo, or Aleut. 0.2%
Asian or Pacific Islander 0.6%
Other 0.5%
Hispanic origin 1.5%

Ancestry

American 3.8%	Italian 15.5%
Dutch 5.5%	Polish 8.4%
English 19.7%	Scotch Irish 1.5%
French 7.0%	Scottish 2.8%
French Canadian 1.7%	Swedish 1.1%
German 26.3%	Welsh 3.4%
Irish 21.1%	

Universities/colleges, 1990-1991 enrollment

Cazenovia College, Cazenovia 1,072
Colgate University, Hamilton 2,710
Hamilton College, Clinton 1,658
Hartwick College, Oneonta 1,552
Herkimer Community College, Herkimer 2,412
Mohawk Valley Community College, Utica 6,470
State University of New York Agricultural & Tech College; Cobleskill 2,630
State University of New York Agricultural & Tech College; Delhi 2,374
State University of New York Agricultural & Tech College; Utica 2,542
State University of New York, Morrisville 3,289
State University of New York, Oneonta 6,317
Utica College of Syracuse University, Utica 2,553
Utica School of Commerce, Utica 502

Newspapers, total circulation (in all districts)

Binghamton Press & Sun-Bulletin 70,739
Herkimer Evening Telegram 6,604
New York Daily News 757,053
New York Post 551,443
Norwich Evening Sun 5,228
Oneonta Daily Star 19,389
Rome Daily Sentinel 17,967
Utica Observer-Dispatch 56,020

Commercial television stations, affiliations

ADI: Binghamton (37%), Utica (33%), Syracuse (23%) and Albany-Schenectady-Troy (7%)
  WFXV, Utica (Fox)
  WKTV, Utica (NBC)
  WUTR, Utica-Rome (ABC)

Cable television systems, total subscribers

Binghamton Newchannels; Binghamton 61,125
Cablevision Industries Inc.; Oneida 10,707
Harron Cable/New York; Utica 44,921
Oneonta Newchannels; Oneonta 10,071
Paragon Cable; Litchfield 13,500
Rome Newchannels; Rome 17,568
Syracuse Newchannels; North Syracuse 35,000

Military installations, 1991

Griffiss Air Force Base, Rome 6,675

Businesses and other major employers

General Electric Co./Aerospace Systems; Utica; aircraft equipment 2,000
Oneida Ltd./Silversmiths Div.; Oneida; stainless steelware 1,900
Amphenol Corp./Bendix Connectors; Sidney; electrical goods 1,800
General Electric Co.; Utica; engineering services 1,800
Mohawk Valley Psychiatric Center; Utica 1,700
Norwich Eaton Pharmaceuticals; Norwich; pharmaceuticals 1,650
Mary Imogene Bassett Hospital; Cooperstown 1,600
Metropolitan Life Insurance Co.; Oriskany; life insurance 1,300
St. Luke's Memorial Hospital Center; New Hartford 1,200
Fleet/Norstar Services Corp.; Utica; computer services 1,139
Remington Arms Co. Inc.; Ilion; firearms/accessories 1,100
State of New York/Social Services Dept.; Utica 1,100
St. Elizabeth Hospital; Utica 1,020
City of Rome/School District; Rome 1,000
Faxton-Children's Hospital; Utica 900
State University of New York; Oneonta 834
Fox Aurelia Osborn Memorial Hospital; Oneonta 810
Raymond Corp.; Greene; industrial machinery 800
New York Central Mutual Fire Insurance; Edmeston; fire/marine/casualty insurance 800
Colgate University; Hamilton 800
Par Technology Corp.; New Hartford; office equipment 750
Utica Corp.; Whitesboro; aircraft engines 750
Graphic Arts Mutual Insurance Co.; New Hartford; fire/marine/casualty insurance 750
Camden Wire Co. Inc.; Camden; copper wire 725
Chicago Pneumatic Tool Co.; Utica; power handtools 700
Utica Mutual Insurance Co.; New Hartford; fire/marine/casualty insurance 700
Rome Hospital & Murphy Memorial Hospital; Rome 700
CAE-Link Corp.; Binghamton; flight simulations 650
Simmonds Precision Engine Systems; Norwich; aircraft engines 650
State University of New York; Morrisville 625
State of New York/Mohawk Correctional Facility; Rome 572

Cullman Ventures Inc.; Sidney; commercial printing 550
Revere Copper Products Inc.; Rome; copper/brass 550
USAir Group Inc./Piedmont Airlines; Rome; airlines 550
County of Delaware; Delhi 545
County of Madison; Wampsville 534
Masonic Home; Utica; nursing 524
Hamilton College; Clinton 505

24th District

North Country — Plattsburgh; Watertown; Oswego

The 24th, which forms the northern border of New York state, is one of the East's most sprawling congressional districts. It covers all of eight counties and parts of two others. Beginning in the east along Lake Champlain, the 24th tracks north to the Canadian border, west along the St. Lawrence River, then south along Lake Ontario as far as Oswego. Its southern edge reaches east to the outskirts of metropolitan Albany. The Adirondack Mountains make up much of the district's middle.

Although there is blue-collar industry along its waterways, the 24th is a mainly rural district that holds strongly to a Yankee Republican tradition. The importance of defense-related facilities—including the Army's Fort Drum and Plattsburgh Air Force Base—and the lack of a significant minority population reinforce the GOP strength.

The Republican House candidate easily won the open House seat in 1992; GOP Sen. Alfonse M. D'Amato swept the 24th's counties, winning most with 60 percent or more.

The district's GOP tendencies have remained solid despite its rather stagnant economy, a result of its reliance on heavy industry and its remote location. But economic concerns took a toll on George Bush in 1992. Though he carried all but two counties in the 24th, his margins were mainly meager pluralities. He did, however, manage 53 percent in sparsely populated Hamilton, the only county in New York in which he won a majority.

The counties that form the 24th's western border, Oswego, Jefferson and St. Lawrence, are its most populous. Oswego has a number of industrial employers, including an electricity-generating plant, a paper mill, and a brewery. There is a State University of New York campus in the city of Oswego.

Industry in Jefferson County is centered in Watertown, the 24th's largest city. Fort Drum, home of the Army's 10th Mountain Division, is the driving economic force: It has about 13,000 military and civilian employees. The New York Air Brake Co., maker of air brakes for railcars, is a major employer.

Massena, in St. Lawrence County, depends on the factories of the Aluminum Company of America and Reynolds Metals. An organized labor presence makes St. Lawrence and Franklin counties the most Democratic areas in the 24th. Bill Clinton won both in 1992.

Although Fort Drum, which received a heavy investment in new facilities during the 1980s, has not yet felt the post-Cold War fiscal squeeze, Plattsburgh Air Force Base (near the 24th's eastern edge) came close to the brink in 1991; it was on an initial list of the military base-closing commission that year. But it escaped with most of its jobs intact when the commission decided to close Maine's Loring Air Force Base instead.

The interior of the 24th includes some of New York's leading dairy farming areas (including parts of Jefferson and St. Law-rence counties) and the mountain-and-lake country of the Adirondacks, where much of the economy is recreation- and tourist-oriented.

Election Returns

	24th District	Democrat	Republican
1992	President*	85,078 (37.5%)	86,357 (38.1%)
	House †	47,675 (23.4%)	122,257 (60.1%)
1990	Governor	57,206 (38.9%)	83,863 (57.0%)
1988	President	89,381 (43.7%)	114,758 (56.1%)
	Senate	106,953 (57.4%)	76,977 (41.3%)
1986	Senate	43,271 (31.0%)	92,687 (66.5%)
	Governor	83,277 (58.4%)	56,505 (39.7%)

Vote for Perot was 54,537 (24.1%).   †Independent/other is greater than 5%.

Demographics

Population   580,338

Percent change from 1980   12.6%

Land area   12,393 square miles

Population per square mile   47

Counties, 1990 population

Clinton 85,969	Herkimer (pt.) 7,438
Essex (pt.) 9,437	Jefferson 110,943
Franklin 46,540	Lewis 26,796
Fulton 54,191	Oswego 121,771
Hamilton 5,279	St. Lawrence 111,974

Cities, 1990 population (10,000 or more)

Canton 11,120	Massena 13,826
Fort Drum CDP 11,578	Ogdensburg 13,521
Fulton 12,929	Oswego 19,195
Gloversville 16,656	Plattsburgh 21,255
Le Ray 17,973	Potsdam 16,8221
Malone 12,982	Watertown 29,429

Race and Hispanic origin
White 95.4%
Black 2.6%
American Indian, Eskimo, or Aleut. 0.8%
Asian or Pacific Islander 0.6%
Other 0.7%
Hispanic origin 1.6%

Ancestry

American 6.0%	Irish 20.9%
Dutch 4.4%	Italian 7.5%
English 18.9%	Polish 4.1%
French 21.1%	Scotch Irish 1.7%
French Canadian 5.1%	Scottish 3.2%
German 19.2%	Welsh 1.1%

Universities/colleges, 1990-1991 enrollment
Clarkson University, Potsdam 3,386
Clinton Community College, Plattsburgh 2,144
Fulton-Montgomery Community College, Johnstown 2,001
Jefferson Community College, Watertown 2,482
Mater Dei College, Ogdensburg 547
North Country Community College, Saranac Lake 1,483
Paul Smith's College of Arts & Sciences, Paul Smiths 792

State University of New York, Oswego 8,942
State University of New York, Plattsburgh 6,548
State University of New York, Potsdam 4,829
State University of New York Agricultural & Tech College; Canton 2,662
St. Lawrence University, Canton 2,091

Newspapers, total circulation (in all districts)
Gloversville Leader-Herald 12,842
Oswego Palladium-Times 10,118
Plattsburgh Press-Republican 22,898
Syracuse Post Standard/Herald Journal 179,066
Watertown Daily Times 40,441

Commercial television stations, affiliations
ADI: Watertown-Carthage (42%), Burlington-Plattsburgh (25%), Albany-Schenectady-Troy (18%), Syracuse (8%) and Utica (8%)
WOCD, Amsterdam (None)
WWNY-TV, Carthage (CBS)
WPTZ, North Pole (NBC)
WWTI, Watertown (ABC)

Cable television systems, total subscribers
Adelphia Cable; Harrietstown 7,900
Cablesystems of Watertown; Watertown 14,339
Carthage Newchannels; Carthage 6,796
Falcon Cable TV; Plattsburgh 15,191
Fulton Newchannels; Fulton 7,137
Harron Cable/New York; Utica 44,921
Malone Newchannels; Malone 5,861
Massena Newchannels; Massena 7,400
Ogdensburg Newchannels; Ogdensburg 5,780
Paragon Cable; Oswego 8,910
Potsdam Newchannels; Potsdam 9,418
Sammons Communications of New York Inc.; Gloversville 11,140

Military installations, 1991
Fort Drum (Army), Watertown 12,934
Plattsburgh Air Force Base, Plattsburgh 2,577

Businesses and other major employers
Aluminum Co. of America; Massena; aluminum 2,800
Niagara Mohawk Power Corp.; Lycoming; electric services 2,400
Chemipulp Process Inc.; Watertown; special contractors 1,900
Champlain Valley Hospital & Medical Center; Plattsburgh 1,400
State of New York/Clinton Correctional Facility; Dannemora 1,400
House of the Good Samaritan Hospital; Watertown 1,300
State of New York/Developmental Center; Tupper Lake 1,250
State University of New York; Oswego 1,250
Miller Brewing Co.; Fulton; brewery 1,200
Nestle Chocolate & Confection Co.; Fulton; candies 1,200
Wyeth Laboratories Inc.; Rouses Point; pharmaceuticals 1,150
State University of New York; Potsdam 1,000
State of New York/Mental Health Dept.; Ogdensburg 1,000
Clarkson University; Potsdam 989
Alcan Aluminum Corp.; Oswego; aluminum rolling/drawing 900

State University of New York; Plattsburgh 900
Wolverine World Wide Inc./Tru Stitch Footwear Div.; Malone; leather footwear 800
County of St. Lawrence; Canton 800
Reynolds Metals Co.; Massena; aluminum 765
City of Oswego/School District; Oswego 686
Knorr Bremse/New York Air Brake; Watertown; air brakes 660
Collins & Aikman Corp.; Plattsburgh; paper products 650
St. Lawrence University; Canton 630
Georgia-Pacific Corp.; Plattsburgh; paper mills 600
Sealright Co. Inc./Eastern Div.; Fulton; paper mills 600
State of New York/Bare Hill Correctional Facility; Malone 600
State of New York/Franklin Correctional Facility; Malone 580
County of Lewis; Lowville 570
Mercy Hospital of Watertown; Watertown 560
Oswego Hospital Inc./Oswego Hospital; Oswego 550
Nathan Littauer Hospital; Gloversville 544

25th District

Central — Syracuse

Syracuse, the dominant city in the 25th, is in the center of Onondaga County. That county has more than 80 percent of the district's population, and the traditional Republican advantage there gives GOP candidates a jump on carrying the district.

The economic evolution of Syracuse was similar to that of many Northern industrial towns, but its politics were all upstate New York. While the ethnic populations of other blue-collar cities were drafted into Democratic machines, it was a Republican organization that for years held the loyalties of the various Syracuse constituencies, including large Irish, Italian, Polish and Jewish populations. The electorate's GOP leanings were reinforced by the typical upstate antipathy toward Democratic New York City.

The Republican hold on the city itself has weakened; the GOP machine has faded, and the decline of the city's once-thriving industrial sector has helped the Democratic Party gain ground. Aided by minority-group residents who make up more than a quarter of the city's population, Democrats have dominated the mayor's office in recent years.

But the sizable Republican base that remains in the city is coupled with a strong GOP lean in suburban and outlying areas, and that tips the partisan balance in Onondaga County. Facing a grumpy electorate in 1992, the GOP House incumbent held the county with 54 percent of the vote; GOP Sen. Alfonse M. D'Amato took 57 percent. Yet not even Republican tradition could salvage George Bush, who lost the 25th.

Once the nation's leading producer of salt, Syracuse grew into a thriving but grimy center for such industries as glass, steel and chemicals. But the manufacturing sector faded, with service industries picking up some slack.

The city's clearer skies make Syracuse somewhat more livable, though it is harder for some blue-collar workers to make a living. Today, Syracuse University (21,900 students) competes with Carrier Corp. (a division of United Technologies) to be the area's top employer. General Electric is also a major employer.

The largest of Syracuse's suburbs is middle-class Clay; smaller, more affluent towns include Manlius and Pompey.

To the west, the 25th skims the north edge of the Finger Lakes to take in part of Cayuga County. This is a mainly rural Republican area, though there is some working-class Democratic vote in Auburn, which produces auto components, climate-control equipment and recycled steel.

South of Syracuse, the district follows I-81 into Cortland County, a hilly dairy farming area that has some industry. The county will take a big job hit if Smith-Corona carries out plans to move its Cortland factory operations to Mexico; it is the last large-scale producer of typewriters and word processors in the United States.

At the southern end of the 25th are a chunk of Broome County northwest of Binghamton and a lightly populated piece of Tioga County.

Election Returns

	25th District	Democrat	Republican
1992	President*	108,334 (41.2%)	95,476 (36.3%)
	House	107,310 (43.8%)	135,076 (55.1%)
1990	Governor	76,040 (45.4%)	85,997 (51.4%)
1988	President	113,234 (46.7%)	128,647 (53.0%)
	Senate	154,003 (67.7%)	70,948 (31.2%)
1986	Senate	66,654 (37.5%)	106,459 (59.9%)
	Governor	114,594 (63.0%)	63,236 (34.7%)

*Vote for Perot was 58,239 (22.2%).

Demographics

Population 580,337

Percent change from 1980 12.7%

Land area 1,838 square miles

Population per square mile 316

Counties, 1990 population
Broome (pt.) 10,274	Onondaga 468,973
Cayuga (pt.) 45,482	Tioga (pt.) 6,645
Cortland 48,963	

Cities, 1990 population (10,000 or more)
Auburn (pt.) 17,420	Geddes 17,677
Camillus 23,625	Lysander 16,346
Cicero 25,560	Manlius 30,656
Clay 59,749	Onondaga 18,396
Cortland 19,801	Salina 35,145
De Witt 25,148	Syracuse 163,860
Fairmount CDP 12,266	Van Buren 13,367

Race and Hispanic origin
White 91.0%
Black 6.6%
American Indian, Eskimo, or Aleut. 0.6%
Asian or Pacific Islander 1.3%
Other 0.5%
Hispanic origin 1.4%

Ancestry
American 2.2%	French Canadian 2.2%
Dutch 3.7%	German 24.7%
English 19.2%	Irish 23.3%
French 7.2%	Italian 16.3%

Polish 7.9%	Scottish 2.7%
Russian 1.3%	Ukrainian 1.4%
Scotch Irish 1.6%	Welsh 1.3%

Universities/colleges, 1990-1991 enrollment
Bryant & Stratton Business Institute, Syracuse 1,176
Cayuga County Community College, Auburn 2,904
Central City Business Institute, Syracuse 336
Le Moyne College, Syracuse 2,355
Onondaga Community College, Syracuse 8,316
State University of New York, Cortland 7,238
State University of New York College of Environmental Science & Forestry, Syracuse 1,715
State University of New York Health Science Center, Syracuse 1,027
Syracuse University, Syracuse 21,900

Newspapers, total circulation (in all districts)
Auburn Citizen 16,191
Binghamton Press & Sun-Bulletin 70,739
New York Post 551,443
Syracuse Post Standard/Herald Journal 179,066

Commercial television stations, affiliations
ADI: Syracuse (87%) and Binghamton (13%)
WIXT, Syracuse (ABC)
WSTM-TV, Syracuse (NBC)
WSYT, Syracuse (Fox)
WTVH, Syracuse (CBS)

Cable television systems, total subscribers
Adelphia Communications; Syracuse 41,500
Auburn Cablevision; Fleming 13,974
Binghamton Newchannels; Binghamton 61,125
CVI; Baldwinsville 7,977
Sammons Communications of New York Inc.; Cortland 10,100
Syracuse Newchannels; Manlius 48,699
Syracuse Newchannels; North Syracuse 35,000

Military installations, 1991
Hancock Field Air Force Guard Station, Syracuse 372

Businesses and other major employers
Syracuse University; Syracuse 4,700
United Technologies Corp./Carrier Transicold Div.; Syracuse; air conditioning equipment 4,200
General Electric Co.; Syracuse; search/navigation equipment 4,000
New Venture Gear/New Process Div.; East Syracuse; motor vehicle equipment 2,750
Irving Crouse Memorial Hospital; Syracuse 2,700
City of Syracuse/School District; Syracuse 2,600
St. Joseph's Hospital & Health Center; Syracuse 2,450
Niagara Mohawk Power Corp.; Syracuse; electric services 2,100
County of Onondaga/Onondaga Correctional Facility; Syracuse 2,000
New York Telephone Co.; Syracuse; telephone communications 1,600
Crucible Materials Corp.; Syracuse; steel products 1,500
General Motors Corp./Inland Fisher Guide Div.; Syracuse; motor vehicles 1,500
Mutual Life Insurance Co. of New York; Syracuse; insurance services 1,500

Cooper Industries Inc./Crouse-Hinds; Syracuse; electronic parts 1,400

Community General Hospital of Greater Syracuse; Syracuse 1,400

Smith Corona Corp.; Cortland; typewriters/office equipment 1,300

U.S. Veterans Affairs Dept.; Syracuse; hospital 1,300

State of New York/Syracuse Developmental Center; Syracuse 1,300

Auburn Memorial Hospital; Auburn 1,200

Welch Allyn Inc.; Skaneateles Falls; medical instruments 1,100

Agway Inc.; Syracuse; preserved fruits/vegetables 1,000

Bristol-Myers Squibb Co.; Syracuse; pharmaceuticals 1,000

General Electric Co.; Liverpool; search/navigation equipment 1,000

State University of New York; Cortland 1,000

Sage-Dey Inc.; Syracuse; department stores 1,000

Onondaga Community College; Syracuse 990

State of New York/Hutchings Psychiatric Center; Syracuse 900

Anheuser-Busch Inc.; Baldwinsville; brewery 850

Holiday Festival of Trees; Syracuse; retail stores 800

West Genesee Central Hospital; Camillus 800

Research Foundation of University of New York; Syracuse; research services 756

Pall Trinity Micro Corp.; Cortland; filters 750

Fays Inc./Wheels Discount Auto Supply; Liverpool; auto stores 700

Empire Blue Cross/Blue Shield; Syracuse; medical service/health insurance 650

James Square Nursing Home Inc.; Syracuse; nursing 650

Cortland Memorial Hospital; Cortland 650

NCC Industries Inc./Lilyette Brassiere Div.; Cortland; undergarments 600

Herald Co. Inc./Syracuse Herald Journal; Syracuse; newspapers 600

U.S. Postal Service; Syracuse 600

Marine Midland Banks Inc.; Syracuse; commercial banks 600

County of Onondaga/Van Duyn Home & Hospital; Syracuse 600

Staff Leasing of Central New York; Syracuse; personnel supply services 600

Loretto Rest Nursing Home Co.; Syracuse; nursing 600

Pyramid Management Group Inc.; Syracuse; management services 550

Nationwide Mutual Insurance Co.; Syracuse; insurance services 503

26th District

South — Kingston; Binghamton; Ithaca

The elongated 26th reaches from high above Cayuga Lake's waters to the banks of the Hudson River. Most of the population is found in pockets at the district's extremes: the Ithaca and Binghamton areas to the west, and the Hudson Valley region—which includes the cities of Kingston, Newburgh and Beacon—on the eastern edge.

Although the 26th, like most upstate districts, has a Republican heritage, its demographics have made it a political swing district. Although the Democratic Party has had a longtime hold

on the region's House seat, the 26th can still go Republican in contests for major office.

With Cornell University (20,800 students) and Ithaca College (6,400 students) fostering a liberal academic community, Tompkins County is one of the Democrats' strongholds in New York. The part of Broome County in the 26th takes in the "Triple Cities" of Binghamton, Johnson City and Endicott; its mix of high-tech employees and a traditional blue-collar constituency make Broome politically competitive. Ulster County (Kingston) has industry, but much rural territory; Republicans usually win it.

However, the 26th showed its unpredictability in 1992. The Democratic House nominee carried Ulster (his home county) with 58 percent of the vote; his 64 percent in Tompkins cinched his victory. But Broome County, usually essential to Democratic victory, gave 56 percent to the locally based GOP candidate. In the 1992 presidential race Bill Clinton carried the 26th with a plurality; for the Senate seat, Republican Alfonse M. D'Amato won every county but Tompkins.

One thing that binds this diverse district is its reliance on a major employer: International Business Machines (IBM), which was founded in Endicott. IBM's pre-eminence in mainframe computer technology made it a corporate giant; it also led the transition of Broome County's traditional smokestack economy to a high-tech base. But IBM's failure to keep up with rapid changes in the industry has caused huge financial losses and unprecedented job cutbacks.

Layoffs in IBM facilities have stung such cities as Kingston and Owego (Tioga County). And the Binghamton area, whose defense contractors produce such products as aircraft components and flight simulators, has been further battered by post-Cold War budget cuts.

But economic development officials base hopes for future high-tech growth on the region's skilled work force and the presence of such academic institutions as Cornell and the state university campus in Binghamton (12,200 students).

The economy in less-populous areas relies largely on farming (Ulster County's crops include apples and wine grapes) and recreation. The portion of Sullivan County in the district includes much of the Catskill Mountain resort area, a longtime magnet for middle-class Jews and Italians from the New York City area.

Election Returns

	26th District	Democrat	Republican
1992	President*	116,525 (44.5%)	91,625 (35.0%)
	House	119,557 (49.8%)	110,738 (46.1%)
1990	Governor	82,317 (49.3%)	79,265 (47.4%)
1988	President	114,754 (47.6%)	125,476 (52.1%)
	Senate	138,928 (63.0%)	78,465 (35.6%)
1986	Senate	62,699 (38.5%)	95,589 (58.8%)
	Governor	98,275 (59.4%)	63,615 (38.4%)

*Vote for Perot was 52,886 (20.2%).

Demographics

Population 580,338

Percent change from 1980 12.4%

Land area 3,083 square miles

Population per square mile 188

Counties, 1990 population

Broome (pt.)	181,888	Sullivan (pt.)	47,952
Delaware (pt.)	6,202	Tioga (pt.)	45,692
Dutchess (pt.)	13,243	Tompkins (pt.)	69,545
Orange (pt.)	50,512	Ulster	165,304

Cities, 1990 population (10,000 or more)

Beacon	13,243	Newburgh	26,454
Binghamton	53,008	New Paltz	11,388
Chenango (pt.)	10,492	Owego	21,279
Dryden	13,251	Saugerties	18,467
Endicott	13,531	Shawangunk	10,081
Endwell CDP	12,602	Thompson (pt.)	12,646
Fallsburg	11,445	Ulster	12,329
Ithaca	29,541	Union	59,786
Johnson City	16,890	Vestial	26,733
Kingston	23,095	Wawarsing	12,348

Race and Hispanic origin

White 90.6%
Black 5.7%
American Indian, Eskimo, or Aleut. 0.2%
Asian or Pacific Islander 2.0%
Other 1.5%
Hispanic origin 4.3%

Ancestry

American	2.9%	Italian	14.4%
Dutch	5.3%	Polish	6.7%
English	16.2%	Russian	3.1%
French	4.0%	Scotch Irish	1.6%
French Canadian	1.0%	Scottish	2.4%
German	23.6%	Slovakian	3.2%
Hungarian	1.2%	Swedish	1.3%
Irish	20.9%	Welsh	1.6%

Universities/colleges, 1990-1991 enrollment

Broome Community College, Binghamton 6,433
Cornell University, Ithaca 20,839
Ithaca College, Ithaca 6,432
Mount St. Mary College, Newburgh 1,428
State University of New York, Binghamton 12,202
State University of New York, New Paltz 8,612
Sullivan Community College, Loch Sheldrake 2,090
Tompkins-Cortland Community College, Dryden 2,775
Ulster Community College, Stone Ridge 2,927

Newspapers, total circulation (in all districts)

Binghamton Press & Sun-Bulletin 70,739
Ithaca Journal 18,749
Kingston Daily Freeman 22,329
Middletown Times Herald-Record 84,398
New York Post 551,443
Oneonta Daily Star 19,389
Poughkeepsie Journal 43,943
Syracuse Post Standard/Herald Journal 179,066

Commercial television stations, affiliations

ADI: New York (56%), Binghamton (35%) and Syracuse (9%)
WBNG-TV, Binghamton (CBS)
WICZ-TV, Binghamton (NBC)
WMGC-TV, Binghamton (ABC)
WTZA, Kingston (None)
WTBY, Poughkeepsie (None)

Cable television systems, total subscribers

American Community Cablevision; Dryden 25,900
Binghamton Newchannels; Binghamton 61,125
Cablevision Industries Inc.; Wurtsboro Mt. 34,652
Paragon Cable; Newburgh 25,164
TCI of New York; Port Ewen 16,900
U.S. Cablevision Corp.; Mt. Beacon 47,933

Military installations, 1991

Stewart Annex (Army), Newburgh 1,207

Businesses and other major employers

IBM Corp.; Endicott; computers 10,000
Cornell University; Ithaca 9,194
IBM Corp.; Kingston; computer equipment 5,700
IBM Corp.; Owego; computers 4,000
County of Broome; Binghamton 3,000
General Electric Co./Aircraft Control Systems Dept.; Binghamton; navigation equipment 2,000
Endicott Johnson Corp./John A. Frye Co.; Endicott; footwear 2,000
General Electric Co./Aircraft Equipment Div.; Johnson City; navigation equipment 1,950
CAE-Link Corp.; Binghamton; flight simulators 1,900
State University of New York; Binghamton 1,700
County of Ulster; Kingston 1,680
Our Lady of Lourdes Memorial Hospital; Binghamton 1,495
Universal Instruments Corp.; Binghamton; industry machinery 1,350
Ithaca College; Ithaca 6,432
New York State Electric & Gas Corp.; Binghamton; electric services 1,100
City of Newburgh/School District; Newburgh 1,100
State of New York/Binghamton Psychiatric Center; Binghamton 1,030
International Paper Co./Anitec Image Div.; Binghamton; photographic equipment/supplies 1,000
Benedictine Hospital; Kingston 980
United Health Services Hospitals; Binghamton 915
Watchtower Bible & Tract Society of New York; Wallkill; periodicals 900
County of Sullivan; Monticello 900
State of New York/Transportation Dept.; Binghamton 900
City of Binghamton; Binghamton 830
Borg-Warner Automotive Inc.; Ithaca; motor vehicle equipment 800
Metropolitan Life Insurance Co.; Kingston; insurance services 800
State University of New York; New Paltz 800
Research Foundation of University of New York; New Paltz; research services 800
St. Luke's Hospital of Newburgh; Newburgh 782
Emerson Power Transmission; Ithaca; motor vehicle equipment 750
Community General Hospital; Harris 750
Dover Electronics Co.; Binghamton; electronic components 743
Tompkins Community Hospital; Ithaca 735
Maple Press Co.; Kirkwood; book publishing 700
State of New York/Correctional Facility; Napanoch 680

Vail-Ballou Press Inc./Maple Vail Book Mfg. Group; Binghamton; book publishing 650

New York State Electric & Gas Corp.; Ithaca; utility services 600

Board of Cooperative Educational Services; Binghamton 600

Broome Community College; Binghamton 597

Kingston Hospital Inc.; Kingston 550

City of Vestal/Central School District; Vestal 550

Amphenol Interconnect Products; Endicott; electronic components 540

State of New York/Shawangunk Correctional Facility; Wallkill 525

27th District

Suburban Buffalo and Rural West — Amherst

During 1992 redistricting, Rep. Bill Paxon lobbied former colleagues in the state Legislature for a comfortably Republican constituency. His efforts appeared endangered when a Democratic-dominated state court panel took control of the process from the deadlocked legislators. Yet the jurists produced a map that created the suburban-and-rural 27th, which is as solidly a Republican district as Paxon could have designed himself.

The 27th takes in the northeastern suburbs of Buffalo, some suburbia to the south and west of Rochester and a largely farming region stretching 100 miles across northwestern New York. In 1992, Paxon carried the five full and four partial counties in the 27th, most by wide margins. George Bush won the 27th with a solid plurality, topping 45 percent of the vote (a strong showing for him in New York) in four counties.

There was voter dissatisfaction in 1992, but it did not do much to help Bill Clinton, who received less than a third of the vote in most jurisdictions and finished third in rural Wyoming County with 25 percent. Ross Perot ran strongly, especially in Wyoming County, where he took 30 percent.

Amherst, a Buffalo suburb at the western end of the 27th, is the district's anchor; with more than 111,000 residents, it has nearly a fifth of the people in the 27th. The main campus of the State University of New York at Buffalo (27,600 students) is here. Greater Buffalo International Airport, just across the Buffalo city line (in the 30th District), is another jobs producer.

Unlike Buffalo, the Erie County suburbs in the 27th have little blue-collar industry and a small minority population. Republicans usually run well in Amherst (Paxon's hometown) and even better in the towns east and south, where the landscape quickly shifts from suburban to exurban to rural.

The New York Thruway links Erie County to the Rochester suburbs of Monroe County. The largest of these communities in the 27th is Chili, with about 25,000 residents. Republicans usually carry these mainly middle-class suburbs.

Between and to the east are the dairy, vegetable and grain farms of rural western New York. In Genesee County is Batavia, a small city that lost a Sylvania television plant in the mid-1980s and has been fighting further industrial decline since. Batavia's leading employers include companies that make electrical insulation and canned food.

Wyoming County is heavily agricultural, but it has a facility that is distinctly unbucolic: the state penitentiary at Attica, the site in 1971 of one of the worst prison riots in U.S. history.

In Ontario and Seneca counties, the 27th moves into part of the Finger Lakes region, including some of its grape vineyards and the cities of Geneva and Seneca Falls (the site of a convention in 1848 that is regarded as the origin of the women's rights movement). The western end of Wayne County (which borders Lake Ontario) is within Rochester's sphere; in its southern reaches are several towns that grew up along the Erie Canal.

Election Returns

	27th District	Democrat	Republican
1992	President*	90,194 (32.9%)	115,432 (42.1%)
	House	89,906 (36.1%)	156,596 (62.8%)
1990	Governor	65,382 (38.7%)	96,844 (57.3%)
1988	President	100,341 (41.2%)	142,436 (58.5%)
	Senate	136,634 (60.5%)	86,412 (38.2%)
1986	Senate	47,712 (29.2%)	110,776 (67.8%)
	Governor	99,195 (59.5%)	63,125 (37.9%)

*Vote for Perot was 67,721 (24.7%).

Demographics

Population 580,337

Percent change from 1980 12.4%

Land area 3,594 square miles

Population per square mile 161

Counties, 1990 population

Cayuga (pt.) 4,074	Ontario 95,101
Erie (pt.) 157,741	Seneca (pt.) 23,009
Genesee 60,060	Wayne 89,123
Livingston 62,372	Wyoming 42,507
Monroe (pt.) 46,350	

Cities, 1990 population (10,000 or more)

Alden 10,372	Chili 25,178
Amherst 111,711	Clarence 20,041
Arcadia 14,855	Farmington 10,381
Batavia 16,310	Geneva 14,143
Canandaigua 10,725	

Race and Hispanic origin

White 95.5%
Black 2.5%
American Indian, Eskimo, or Aleut. 0.3%
Asian or Pacific Islander 1.1%
Other 0.5%
Hispanic origin 1.3%

Ancestry

American 2.6%	Italian 14.0%
Dutch 6.8%	Polish 8.1%
English 21.2%	Scotch Irish 1.6%
French 5.1%	Scottish 2.8%
French Canadian 1.3%	Swedish 1.2%
German 36.6%	Welsh 1.0%
Irish 20.8%	

Universities/colleges, 1990-1991 enrollment

Community College of the Finger Lakes, Canandaigua 3,866
Daemen College, Amherst 1,946
Erie Community College, Williamsville 6,603
Genesee Community College, Batavia 3,572

Hobart & William Smith Colleges, Geneva 1,848
New York Chiropractic College, Seneca Falls 690
State University of New York, Buffalo 27,643
State University of New York, Geneseo 5,599

Newspapers, total circulation (in all districts)
Auburn Citizen 16,191
Batavia Daily News 16,360
Buffalo News 307,387
Canandaigua Daily Messenger 13,753
Finger Lakes Times 19,339
New York Post 551,443
Rochester Democrat/Chronicle 213,223
Syracuse Post Standard/Herald Journal 179,066

Commercial television stations, affiliations
ADI: Rochester (57%), Buffalo (37%) and Syracuse (6%)
WGRZ-TV, Buffalo (NBC)
WNYB-TV, Buffalo (None)

Cable television systems, total subscribers
Adelphia Cable; Tonawanda 56,354
Cablevision Industries Inc.; Canandaigua 9,439
Cablevision Industries Inc.; Geneva 8,220
Cablevision Industries Inc.; Newark 5,309
Greater Rochester Cablevision; Rochester 195,000
Jones Intercable Inc.; Lancaster 11,997
TCI of New York; Buffalo 84,000
Tri-County Cablevision; Stafford 18,852

Businesses and other major employers
State University of New York; Buffalo 3,200
Goulds Pumps Inc.; Seneca Falls; industry machinery 2,500
County of Ontario; Canandaigua 1,600
State of New York/Newark Developmental Center; Newark 1,500
U.S. Veterans Affairs Dept.; Canandaigua; hospital 1,200
Business Contract Staffing; Geneseo; personnel supply services 1,200
Research Foundation of University of New York/Social Service Training Project; Buffalo 1,200
Genesee Management Inc.; Rochester; real estate agents 1,000
U.S. Census Bureau; Buffalo 1,000
County of Wayne; Lyons 962
Garlock Inc.; Palmyra; gaskets/packing 950
State of New York/Craig Developmental Center; Sonyea 900
Champion Products Inc.; Perry; textile finishing 850
Manufacturers & Traders Trust Co./M&T Bank; Buffalo; commercial banks 850
Champion Products Inc.; Perry; outerwear 800
State University of New York; Geneseo 800
County of Wyoming; Warsaw 800
County of Genesee; Batavia 800
State of New York/Correctional Facility; Attica 800
Thompson Frederick Ferris Hospital; Canandaigua 750
Mobil Oil Corp./Chemical Div.; Canandaigua; plastics/synthetics 700
Millard Fillmore Hospital; Buffalo 700
County of Erie/County Home; Alden; residential care 652
Geneva General Hospital Inc.; Geneva 615
IEC Electronics Corp.; Newark; computers 600
Mobil Oil Corp./Chemical Corp.; Macedon; plastics products 550
Clifton Springs Sanitarium Co.; Clifton Springs 550

Foster Wheeler Energy Corp.; Dansville; metal products 533
Wayne Newark Community Hospital; Newark 515

28th District
Rochester and Most of Suburban Monroe County

Rochester's location on Lake Ontario and the Erie Canal made it an industrial center by the early 19th century. Yet unlike many northern cities with blue-collar bases, Rochester long held to a Republican tradition typical of upstate New York. Only in recent years has the city—which dominates the 28th—developed a lean toward Democratic candidates.

Known early on as the "Flour City" (for its grain mills) and then the "Flower City" (for its commercial nurseries), Rochester grew to be New York's third-largest city with a push from a pair of giant corporations: Eastman Kodak (founded in the 1880s) and the Xerox Corp. (which began producing copying machines in the 1940s).

These companies spawned a large white-collar managerial class that leaned Republican. They also pursued a rather paternalistic management style that rubbed off on Rochester's civic life. Moderate Republicans long dominated local Rochester politics, but in 1986 Democrat Louise Slaughter won the House seat. And the city's tilt away from conservatism benefited Democratic presidential candidates in 1988 and 1992.

Still, to carry the 28th, Democrats must do exceedingly well within the city (which has about two-fifths of the 28th's population). More than half the registered voters in the city are Democrats, but Republicans hold a wide plurality among registrants in suburban Monroe County. While the city has a large blue-collar population, the suburbs are mainly white-collar. Rochester's population is nearly one-third black and nearly a tenth Hispanic, but less than 5 percent of the suburban population is black or Hispanic.

Kodak remains the district's largest employer, but has undergone a serious downsizing in recent years, from 60,000 citywide jobs in 1981 to fewer than 40,000 today. Employment has remained rather constant at Xerox, the Bausch and Lomb optical company, and a pair of General Motors parts plants; among the region's smaller companies are a number of high-tech startups that benefit from their proximity to the major corporations and the area's major academic institutions, Rochester Institute of Technology (12,000 students) and the University of Rochester (9,300 students).

While the jobless rate has remained relatively moderate in recent years, much of the job slack has been picked up by service industries, which generally provide lower salaries than the manufacturing sector. This transition has exacerbated the problems of Rochester's low-income residents: The city's poverty rate tops 20 percent.

The recent recession took an unusually hard toll on white-collar workers, but the Monroe County suburbs in the 28th are relatively affluent compared with the city. The most populous suburbs, Greece and Irondequoit, are north of the city; Pittsford, the wealthiest suburb, is southeast.

Election Returns

	28th District	Democrat	Republican
1992	President*	119,055 (43.8%)	103,544 (38.1%)
	House	140,908 (54.8%)	112,273 (43.6%)

28th District		Democrat	Republican
1990	Governor	91,346 (53.7%)	74,133 (43.6%)
1988	President	128,981 (51.4%)	121,213 (48.3%)
	Senate	163,308 (70.2%)	67,080 (28.8%)
1986	Senate	62,743 (35.4%)	110,048 (62.2%)
	Governor	128,663 (71.1%)	49,167 (27.2%)

Vote for Perot was 48,467 (17.8%).

Demographics

Population 580,337

Percent change from 1980 12.3%

Land area 276 square miles

Population per square mile 2,105

Counties, 1990 population
Monroe (pt.) 580,337

Cities, 1990 population (10,000 or more)

Brighton CDP 34,455	Perinton 43,015
Greece CDP 15,632	Pittsford 24,497
Henrietta (pt.) 35,473	Rochester (pt.) 231,624
Irondequoit CDP 52,322	Webster 31,639
Penfield 30,219	

Race and Hispanic origin
White 81.5%
Black 14.0%
American Indian, Eskimo, or Aleut. 0.3%
Asian or Pacific Islander 2.0%
Other 2.3%
Hispanic origin 4.3%

Ancestry

American 2.0%	Italian 18.5%
Dutch 3.5%	Polish 5.6%
English 14.8%	Russian 1.5%
French 4.2%	Scotch Irish 1.3%
French Canadian 1.2%	Scottish 2.5%
German 27.0%	Swedish 1.1%
Irish 17.8%	Ukrainian 1.4%

Universities/colleges, 1990-1991 enrollment
Bryant & Stratton Business Institute, Rochester 1,177
Colgate Rochester Divinity School/Bexley-Croser Theological Seminary, Rochester 211
Monroe Community College, Rochester 13,548
Nazareth College of Rochester, Rochester 2,822
Rochester Business Institute, Rochester 495
Rochester Institute of Technology, Rochester 12,346
St. John Fisher College, Rochester 2,504
University of Rochester, Rochester 9,291

Newspapers, total circulation (in all districts)
New York Post 551,443
Rochester Democrat/Chronicle 213,223

Commercial television stations, affiliations
ADI: Rochester, NY (100%)
WHEC-TV, Rochester (NBC)
WOKR, Rochester (ABC)
WROC-TV, Rochester (CBS)
WUHF, Rochester (Fox)

Cable television systems, total subscribers
Greater Rochester Cablevision; Rochester 195,000

Businesses and other major employers
Eastman Kodak Co./Kodak Park Site; Rochester; photographic equipment/supplies 10,000
Eastman Kodak Co.; Rochester; photographic equipment/supplies 8,200
Xerox Corp.; Webster; office copiers 8,000
Rochester Institute of Technology; Rochester 5,100
Eastman Kodak Co.; Rochester; camera repair shops 5,000
General Motors Corp.; Rochester; motor vehicle parts 3,500
Bausch & Lomb Inc.; Rochester; ophthalmic goods 3,500
Rochester General Hospital; Rochester 2,540
Gleason Works; Rochester; motor vehicle gears 2,400
Chase Lincoln First Bank; Rochester; commercial banks 2,300
Genesee Hospital Inc./Riverton Medicine Center; Rochester 2,200
Bausch & Lomb Inc./Eyewear Div.; Rochester; glasses/lenses 2,000
Eastman Kodak Co./Clinical Products Div.; Rochester; measuring/controlling devices 2,000
Eastman Kodak Co./Research Lab; Rochester; research services 2,000
Xerox Corp.; Rochester; repair shops 1,800
Xerox Corp./U.S. Marketing Office; Rochester; management services 1,800
Rochester St. Mary's Hospital; Rochester 1,535
Gannett Co. Inc.; Rochester; newspapers 1,500
State of New York/Rochester Psychiatric Center; Rochester 1,345
Board of Cooperative Educational Services; Fairport 1,300
Monroe Community College; Rochester 1,200
State of New York/Monroe Developmental Center; Rochester 1,200
Highland Hospital of Rochester; Rochester 1,150
Harris Corp.; Rochester; communications equipment 1,100
Park Ridge Hospital Inc.; Rochester 1,100
Rochester Hospital Service/Blue Cross; Rochester; medical service/health insurance 1,005
U.S. Postal Service; Rochester 1,000
Asea Brown Boveri Inc.; Rochester; transformers 1,000
First Federal Savings; Rochester; savings institutions 1,000
Allstate Insurance Co.; Fairport; insurance services 1,000
Monroe Community Hospital; Rochester; nursing 1,000
Hickey-Freeman Co. Inc.; Rochester; men's suits/coats 880
Fisons Corp.; Rochester; pharmaceuticals 800
General Railway Signal Corp.; Rochester; communications equipment 800
Eastman Kodak Co./Customer Equipment Services; Rochester; professional/commercial equipment 800
Rochester Gas & Electric Corp.; Rochester; electric services 750
Rochester Telephone Corp.; Rochester; telephone communications 700
Genesee Brewing Co. Inc.; Rochester; brewery 700
ABB Kent-Taylor Inc.; Rochester; industrial measuring devices 700
Commercial Janitor Service; Rochester; building services 700

Doyle Group Inc.; Rochester; business services 675
General Signal Corp.; Rochester; industry machinery 650
City of Rochester; Rochester 610
Du Pont E. I. De Nemours & Co.; Rochester; photographic equipment/supplies 600
McCurdy & Co. Inc.; Rochester; department stores 600
County of Monroe; Rochester 600
Nalge Co.; Rochester; plastics products 587
St. John's Nursing Home Inc.; Rochester; nursing 550
Regional Transit Service Inc.; Rochester; transportation 535
Josten's Inc./Josten's Photography; Webster; photographic studios 509

29th District

Northwest — Part of Buffalo; Niagara Falls

The many industrial workers in the Buffalo-Niagara Falls region provide a political base for Democratic candidates in the 29th. However, the district also has a piece of GOP-leaning Buffalo suburbia and Rochester suburbs at its eastern extreme; in between is some solidly Republican rural turf. Many traditional Democratic voters in the Buffalo area are socially conservative white "ethnics" with roots in Italy, eastern Europe and Ireland.

These factors make the 29th potentially competitive. Democrat John LaFalce (a leading Democratic opponent of abortion) has maintained his party's grasp on the seat, but his once-dominant hold has slipped: He took 55 percent in 1990 and 54 percent in 1992.

In 1992, Bill Clinton beat George Bush in the 29th, but his plurality was one of the smallest of any district that he carried in the state. Working-class unhappiness with the two major parties led to an exceptional turnout for independent Ross Perot: In Niagara County, Clinton won 37 percent to 32 percent for Bush and 31 percent for Perot.

Most of the district's residents live in northwest Erie County and all of Niagara County (each of these jurisdictions provides about 40 percent of the 29th's population).

The 29th takes in the northwest corner of the city of Buffalo. Though it has a small part of downtown and the Peace Bridge that connects the city with Fort Erie, Ontario, this is a mainly residential area, where Italian Americans make up the predominant constituent group.

To the north are such mixed blue- and white-collar suburbs as Tonawanda and Grand Island. Like the rest of Buffalo, this area is adjusting from an economy dependent on heavy industry to one based on service providers and lighter manufacturers. Unemployment is down but so are wages for formerly unionized blue-collar workers.

The natural grandeur of Niagara Falls makes its namesake city one of the world's leading tourist stops. But the Niagara River also made the region a major industrial center. Its chemical industry provides thousands of jobs but has given the area a somewhat sinister ecological reputation. A community had to be abandoned in 1978 because of toxic dumping in the city's Love Canal; part of the area has been cleaned up and reoccupied.

Though there has been some retrenchment, blue-collar industry is still central: Occidental Chemical and Du Pont factories are in Niagara Falls, as is a Nabisco shredded-wheat factory. General Motors' components plant in Lockport has thus far avoided the financially struggling company's downsizing: GM committed

$50 million to the Lockport facility in 1992 for air-conditioning equipment that will not use ozone-depleting refrigerants.

The remainder of Niagara and Orleans County to the east are largely rural, with many dairy and produce farms. Orleans is by far the most Republican part of the 29th: Bush beat Clinton there by 45 percent to 30 percent in 1992.

Election Returns

	29th District	Democrat	Republican
1992	President*	103,528 (39.6%)	86,732 (33.2%)
	House	128,230 (53.8%)	98,031 (41.1%)
1990	Governor	75,445 (48.9%)	72,963 (47.3%)
1988	President	123,634 (51.2%)	117,286 (48.5%)
	Senate	156,684 (70.7%)	61,967 (28.0%)
1986	Senate	59,651 (36.9%)	97,139 (60.1%)
	Governor	113,655 (68.1%)	49,224 (29.5%)

Vote for Perot was 70,231 (26.9%).

Demographics

Population 580,337

Percent change from 1980 12.4%

Land area 1,182 square miles

Population per square mile 491

Counties, 1990 population
Erie (pt.) 230,454
Niagara 220,756
Monroe (pt.) 87,281
Orleans 41,846

Cities, 1990 population (10,000 or more)
Buffalo (pt.) 113,145
Niagara Falls 61,840
Gates-North Gates CDP 14,995
North Tonawanda 34,989
Grand Island 17,561
Ogden 16,912
Kenmore 17,180
Parma 13,873
Lewiston 15,453
Sweden 14,181
Lockport 24,426
Tonawanda CDP 65,284
Wheatfield 11,125

Race and Hispanic origin
White 92.6%
Black 4.5%
American Indian, Eskimo, or Aleut. 0.8%
Asian or Pacific Islander 0.7%
Other 1.4%
Hispanic origin 2.8%

Ancestry
American 1.9%
Hungarian 1.3%
Dutch 2.5%
Irish 19.4%
English 15.5%
Italian 19.7%
French 4.5%
Polish 11.7%
French Canadian 1.2%
Scotch Irish 1.4%
German 34.1%
Scottish 2.8%

Universities/colleges, 1990-1991 enrollment
Bryant & Stratton Business Institute, Buffalo 3,110
D'Youville College, Buffalo 1,482
Niagara Community College, Sanborn 5,272
Niagara University, Niagara Falls 3,065
Roberts Wesleyan College, Rochester 969
State University of New York, Brockport 9,661

Newspapers, total circulation (in all districts)
Buffalo News 307,387
Lockport Union Sun-Journal 17,731
Medina Journal-Register 5,046
New York Post 551,443
Niagara Gazette 25,858
Rochester Democrat/Chronicle 213,223

Commercial television stations, affiliations
ADI: Buffalo (50%) and Rochester (50%)
WUTV, Buffalo (Fox)

Cable television systems, total subscribers
Adelphia Cable; Tonawanda 56,354
Adelphia Cable/Niagara; Niagara Falls 25,861
Greater Rochester Cablevision; Brockport 12,100
Greater Rochester Cablevision; Rochester 195,000
Jones Intercable Inc.; Lockport 25,201
TCI of New York; Buffalo 84,000

Military installations, 1991
Niagara Falls Intl. Airport Air Force Reserve Station, Niagara
Falls 749

Businesses and other major employers
Eastman Kodak Co./Copy Products Div.; Rochester; photo-
graphic equipment/supplies 4,000
General Motors Corp./Powertrain Div.; Tonawanda; motor
vehicle equipment 3,960
Occidental Chemical Corp.; Niagara Falls; inorganic chemi-
cals 2,500
Children's Hospital of Buffalo; Buffalo 2,200
General Motors Corp.; Lockport; motor vehicle parts 1,800
M. Wile & Co. Inc.; Buffalo; men's suits/coats 1,500
Kenmore-Tonwanda Union Free School District; Buffalo
1,500
County of Niagara; Lockport 1,500
City of Niagara Falls/Board of Education; Niagara Falls
1,500
Dunlop Tire Corp.; Tonawanda; tires 1,450
State of New York/Buffalo Psychiatric Center; Buffalo 1,180
Niagara Falls Memorial Medical Center; Niagara Falls 1,176
Union Carbide Chemical & Plastics Co.; Tonawanda;
crypogenic tanks 1,100
Kenmore Mercy Hospital; Buffalo 1,048
Fisher-Price Inc.; Medina; toys 900
Outokumpu American Brass Inc.; Buffalo; copper
rolling/drawing 900
R. O. Staffing Services Corp.; Rochester; personnel supply
services 900
State University of New York; Brockport 9,661
City of Niagara Falls; Niagara Falls 870
De Graff Memorial Hospital Inc.; North Tonawanda 850
Du Pont E. I. De Nemours & Co.; Niagara Falls; industrial
inorganic chemicals 845
Gates Chili Central School District; Rochester 825
Wegman's Food Markets Inc.; Rochester; grocery stores 800
Trico Products Corp.; Buffalo; motor vehicles/equipment
750
Rich Products Corp.; Buffalo; dairy products 750
General Motors Corp./Saginaw Div. Tonawanda; auto
stampings 700
Mount St. Mary's Hospital; Lewiston 637
City of Brockport/School District; Brockport 600

BPS Guard Services Inc.; Buffalo; business/security services
600
Westwod-Squibb Pharmaceuticals; Buffalo; pharmaceuticals
575
City of Lockport/School District; Lockport 573
Town of Tonawanda; Buffalo 554

30th District
West — Buffalo

The 30th, dominated by its part of Buffalo, provided a
paradoxical result in the 1992 election. The district, with its large,
economically worried working-class population, went to Democrat Bill Clinton; George Bush finished behind independent
candidate Ross Perot. Yet even as the district was resoundingly
rejecting Bush, it elected to a first term in the House a
Republican advocating political reform. This was a major upset
for the Democrats who had held the district over the previous 18
years. Dissatisfaction with the political status quo may be the
reason behind both of these results.

Political alienation is one lingering effect of the decline of the
region's traditional heavy industry base. Decades of Rust Belt
decline had a corrosive effect on Buffalo's morale and national
image. Though still one of the nation's 50 largest cities with just
over 328,000 people, Buffalo lost 29 percent of its population in
the 1970s, and 9 percent in the 1980s.

The city is slowly resurrecting its economic prospects. The
U.S.-Canada free-trade agreement enacted in 1989 is paying
business dividends for Buffalo; there was a major upswing in its
financial industry. The unemployment rate, as high as 15 percent
in the early 1980s, was just over 6 percent at the end of 1992.
Pilot Field, a 19,000-seat ballpark widely praised by baseball fans,
has drawn record-breaking crowds to AAA-level minor league
games.

Still, the city's transition has hardly been painless for blue-
collar whites or the large low- to middle-income black constituency. The manufacturing jobs in the Buffalo area declined by
45,000 between 1980 and 1991. The once-dominant steel industry
is now a fragment: Much of the steel-making center in
Lackawanna is a wasteland. Though service industry jobs grew
by even more than manufacturing jobs fell, many of them
provide a fraction of the wages to which unionized factory
workers were accustomed.

About two-thirds of the city of Buffalo, including most of its
downtown, is in the 30th. Black residents make up about 43
percent of the Buffalo section. Polish Americans are the largest
ethnic group in both Buffalo and Cheektowaga. South Buffalo
has a large Irish population.

South of the city along the lake are the industrial parts of
Lackawanna and Hamburg that provide a usually dependable
Democratic vote. But the southern and eastern reaches of the
30th are suburban and exurban areas, some of which provide a
Republican counterweight. Orchard Park is the site of Rich
Stadium, home of football's Buffalo Bills.

Election Returns

	30th District	Democrat	Republican
1992	President*	119,115 (45.5%)	68,172 (26.1%)
	House	111,445 (45.2%)	125,734 (51.0%)
1990	Governor	91,630 (58.2%)	59,442 (37.8%)

30th District		Democrat	Republican
1988	President	149,176 (59.5%)	100,303 (40.0%)
	Senate	173,536 (76.9%)	48,951 (21.7%)
1986	Senate	76,997 (45.0%)	87,995 (51.4%)
	Governor	129,987 (73.0%)	42,693 (24.0%)

Vote for Perot was 73,333 (28.0%).

Demographics

Population 580,337

Percent change from 1980 12.3%

Land area 725 square miles

Population per square mile 801

Counties, 1990 population
Erie (pt.) 580,337

Cities, 1990 population (10,000 or more)

Aurora 13,433	Hamburg 10,442
Buffalo (pt.) 214,978	Lackawanna 20,585
Cheektowaga CDP 84,387	Lancaster 11,940
Depew 17,673	Orchard Park 24,632
Elma 10,355	West Seneca CDP 47,866
Evans 17,478	

Race and Hispanic origin
White 81.5%
Black 16.7%
American Indian, Eskimo, or Aleut. 0.6%
Asian or Pacific Islander 0.6%
Other 0.7%
Hispanic origin 1.5%

Ancestry

American 1.3%	Irish 17.1%
English 7.6%	Italian 12.5%
French 2.8%	Polish 25.1%
German 31.1%	Scottish 1.5%

Universities/colleges, 1990-1991 enrollment
Canisius College, Buffalo 4,693
Erie Community College, Buffalo 3,682
Erie Community College, Orchard Park 3,518
Hilbert College, Hamburg 715
Medaille College, Buffalo 1,105
Trocaire College, Buffalo 970
Villa Maria College of Buffalo, Buffalo 519

Newspapers, total circulation (in all districts)
Buffalo News 307,387

Commercial television stations, affiliations
ADI: Buffalo (100%)
WIVB-TV, Buffalo (CBS)
WKBW-TV, Buffalo (ABC)

Cable television systems, total subscribers
Adelphia Cable; Lackawanna 84,530
Adelphia Cable; Tonawanda 56,354
Jones Intercable Inc.; Lancaster 11,997
Jones Intercable Inc.; Orchard Park 5,712
TCI of New York; Buffalo 84,000

Businesses and other major employers
City of Buffalo; Buffalo 3,804
Buffalo General Hospital; Buffalo 3,325
U.S. Postal Service; Buffalo 3,228
Millard Fillmore Hospital; Buffalo 2,726
New York Telephone Co.; Buffalo; telephone communications 2,500
County of Erie; Buffalo 2,500
Ford Motor Co.; Buffalo; auto stampings 2,400
Marine Midland Banks Inc.; Buffalo; commercial banks 2,400
State of New York/Roswell Park Memorial Institute; Buffalo; research services 2,300
Erie County Medical Center; Buffalo 2,200
Moog Inc.; East Aurora; navigation equipment 2,050
Niagara Mohawk Power Corp.; Buffalo; electric services 2,000
Mercy Hospital; Buffalo 2,000
Sisters Hospital; Buffalo 1,971
General Motors Corp./Saginaw Div.; Buffalo; motor vehicles 1,800
U.S. Veterans Affairs Dept.; Buffalo 1,800
West Seneca Developmental Center; Buffalo 1,600
Arcata Graphics Buffalo Inc.; Depew; books 1,450
Berkshire Hathaway Inc./Buffalo News; Buffalo; newspapers 1,150
Niagara Frontier Transit Metro System; Buffalo; transportation 1,090
Blue Cross of Western New York; Buffalo; medical service/health insurance 1,085
LTV Aerospace & Defense Co.; Buffalo; electronic components 1,000
Our Lady of Victory Hospital; Buffalo 1,000
State of New York/Gowanda Psychiatric Center; Helmuth 950
M. Wile & Co. Inc.; Buffalo; outerwear 900
St. Joseph Hospital; Buffalo 900
Leica Inc./Reichert-Jung; Buffalo; measuring devices 850
Fisher-Price Inc.; East Aurora; toys goods 800
Adam Meldrum & Anderson Inc.; Buffalo; department stores 750
County of Erie/Sheriffs Dept.; Orchard Park 750
Kimberly Quality Care Inc.; Buffalo; personnel supply services 750
Dynamic Enterprises Inc./Quality Inn; Buffalo; real estate operators 700
Graphic Controls Corp.; Buffalo; commercial printing 675
Calspan Corp./SRL Div.; Buffalo; research services 675
Health Research Inc.; Buffalo; consulting services 675
Buffalo Forge Co.; Buffalo; industry machinery 650
National Fuel Gas Distribution Corp.; Buffalo; gas distribution 650
Canisius College; Buffalo 644
General Motors Corp./Harrison Div.; Buffalo; motor vehicles/equipment 630
General Mills Inc.; Buffalo; grain mill products 600
Sorrento Cheese Co. Inc.; Buffalo; dairy products 563
Bethlehem Steel Corp.; Buffalo; steel products 523
Town of Orchard/Central Schools; Orchard Park 520

31st District

Southern Tier — Jamestown; Corning; Elmira

The 31st stretches across the bottom of New York state for more than 100 miles, from Lake Erie on the west to Elmira in the east. This hilly, mainly rural country strongly favors Republicans.

Although the landscape is dotted with small industrial cities, Democrats have never been able to make many inroads here. GOP Rep. Amo Houghton's 70 percent in 1992 was typical of his strong showings since his election in 1986. His Democratic predecessor held the same House seat for a decade, but he was an exception.

The nation's economic problems have been felt in parts of the 31st (most counties in the district had small net population losses during the 1980s), and residents' concerns were reflected in the 1992 presidential results: George Bush, who took about three-fifths of the 31st's vote in 1988, fell to 40 percent.

Still, Bush won a solid plurality here. The district was no friendlier to Bill Clinton than to previous Democratic candidates; he received less than 30 percent in three 31st District counties, including Cattaraugus, where his 29 percent placed him third behind Ross Perot. (The independent Perot took 31 percent there and won more than a quarter of the vote in most other counties.)

Chautauqua County, at the district's western end, is the 31st's most populous; it has about a quarter of the district's residents. Jamestown, which with its population of nearly 35,000 is the 31st's largest city, is a furniture-making center.

The county is the only one in the district where Democrats are often competitive. Clinton carried the county, albeit with just 36 percent (to 34 percent for Bush and 30 percent for Perot). GOP Sen. Alfonse M. D'Amato's Chautauqua tally of 53 percent in 1992 was by far his weakest showing in the 31st.

But Republicans dominate in the counties to the east, including Cattaraugus; its big town is industrial Olean, also home to St. Bonaventure University (2,800 students). Agribusiness plays an important role in neighboring Allegany County. Welch's, a grape-growing cooperative best known for its juice products, is based in Wellsville.

Steuben County contains Corning, one of America's better-known company towns. Houghton's family has long controlled Corning Inc., which produces utilitarian dishes, cookware and medical glass products; its Steuben Glass Works makes more costly decorative crystal pieces.

The Elmira area (Chemung County) is also industrial. Its largest employers are Hardinge Brothers, which makes precision machines, and a Toshiba Display Devices facility.

To the north, the 31st moves into the vineyards and vacation lands of the Finger Lakes region. The large Taylor and Great Western wineries are here, along with numerous small family-run operations. The district also takes in part of Auburn, the commercial center of Cayuga County.

Election Returns

	31st District	Democrat	Republican
1992	President*	82,959 (34.1%)	97,447 (40.0%)
	House †	52,010 (24.1%)	150,696 (69.7%)
1990	Governor	59,917 (39.3%)	86,194 (56.5%)
1988	President	91,438 (40.6%)	132,883 (59.0%)
	Senate	116,808 (56.6%)	87,009 (42.1%)
1986	Senate	51,419 (31.6%)	107,794 (66.2%)
	Governor	99,041 (59.0%)	65,541 (39.1%)

*Vote for Perot was 62,325 (25.6%). †Independent/other is greater than 5%.

Demographics

Population 580,337

Percent change from 1980 12.7%

Land area 6,587 square miles

Population per square mile 88

Counties, 1990 population

Allegany 50,470	Schuyler 18,662
Cattaraugus 84,234	Seneca (pt.) 10,674
Cayuga (pt.) 32,757	Steuben 99,088
Chautauqua 141,895	Tompkins (pt.) 24,552
Chemung 95,195	Yates 22,810

Cities, 1990 population (10,000 or more)

Auburn (pt.) 12,677	Horseheads 19,926
Bath 12,724	Jamestown 34,681
Corning 11,938	Olean 16,946
Dunkirk 13,989	Pomfret 14,224
Elmira 33,724	Southport 11,571
Fredonia 10,436	

Race and Hispanic origin

White 95.9%
Black 2.3%
American Indian, Eskimo, or Aleut. 0.6%
Asian or Pacific Islander 0.6%
Other 0.6%
Hispanic origin 1.5%

Ancestry

American 3.8%	Italian 9.9%
Dutch 5.5%	Polish 7.2%
English 22.7%	Scotch Irish 2.1%
French 4.5%	Scottish 2.7%
German 31.3%	Swedish 5.6%
Irish 20.1%	Welsh 1.4%

Universities/colleges, 1990-1991 enrollment

Alfred University, Alfred 1,736
College of Ceramics at Alfred, Alfred 854
Corning Community College, Corning 3,694
Elmira College, Elmira 1,880
Houghton College, Houghton 1,178
Jamestown Business College, Jamestown 312
Jamestown Community College, Jamestown 4,647
Keuka College, Keuka Park 596
State University of New York, Fredonia 5,041
State University of New York Agricultural & Tech College, Alfred 3,700
St. Bonaventure University, St. Bonventure 2,772
Wells College, Aurora 381

Newspapers, total circulation (in all districts)

Auburn Citizen 16,191
Buffalo News 307,387
Corning Leader 14,743

Dunkirk Observer 14,446
Elmira Star Gazette 34,960
Finger Lakes Times 19,339
Ithaca Journal 18,749
Jamestown Post-Journal 26,100
Olean Times Herald 22,350
Rochester Democrat/Chronicle 213,223
Syracuse Post Standard/Herald Journal 179,066

Commercial television stations, affiliations
ADI: Buffalo (51%), Elmira (27%) and Syracuse (22%)
   WENY-TV, Elmira (ABC)
   WETM-TV, Elmira (NBC)
   WTJA, Jamestown (None)

Cable television systems, total subscribers
American Community Cablevision; Dryden 25,900
Corning Newchannels; Corning 12,500
Harbor-Vue Cable TV Inc.; Dunkirk 5,891
Hornell TV Service Inc.; Hornell 6,100
Paragon Cable; Ellicott 21,729
Paragon Cable of Elmira; Big Flats 26,000
Warner Cable of Olean; Olean 10,608

Military installations, 1991
Seneca Army Depot, Romulus 1,656

Businesses and other major employers
Corning Inc.; Corning; glass/glassware 7,000
Dresser-Rand Co./Engine Process Compressor Div.; Painted Post; industry machinery 1,535
Morrison-Knudsen Co. Inc.; Hornell; railroad equipment 1,400
Bush Industries Inc.; Jamestown; furniture 1,300
Arnot Ogden Medical Center; Elmira 1,300
Toshiba Display Devices Inc.; Horseheads; electronic components 1,200
Corning Inc./Erwin Mfg. Complex; Painted Post; electrical goods 1,200

Dresser-Rand Co./Turbo Products Div.; Olean; gas turbines 1,200
Woman's Christian Assn. Hospital; Jamestown 1,100
State of New York/Developmental Center; Perrysburg; nursing 1,100
St. Joseph's Hospital; Elmira 1,000
State of New York/Developmental Center; Olean; nursing 1,000
TRW Inc.; Union Springs; electrical equipment 920
Olean General Hospital Inc.; Olean 915
Hardinge Brothers Inc.; Horseheads; precision machinery 900
Cummins Engine Co. Inc./Jamestown Engine Plant; Lakewood; engines 900
State of New York/Auburn Correctional Facility; Auburn 820
State of New York/Elmira Correctional Facility; Elmira 800
State of New York/Willard Psychiatric Center; Willard 800
City of Jamestown/School District; Jamestown 800
Mercury Aircraft Inc.; Hammondsport; metal stampings 750
AL Tech Specialty Steel Corp.; Dunkirk; steel tubes 725
Borg-Warner Corp.; Ithaca; motor vehicle parts 711
State of New York/Transportation Dept.; Hornell 700
North American Philips Corp.; Bath; electric lighting 650
St. James Mercy Hospital; Hornell 650
State University of New York; Fredonia 615
McWane Inc./Kennedy Valve Co. Div.; Elmira; valves/hydrants 600
SKF USA Inc.; Falconer; ball/roller bearings 600
State of New York/Mental Hygiene Dept.; Elmira 600
West Valley Nuclear Services Co.; West Valley; hazardous waste collection 600
State of New York/Correctional Services Dept.; Brocton 600
Schweizer Aircraft Corp.; Big Flats; aircraft/helicopters 590
ABB Air Preheater Inc.; Wellsville; metal products 590
County of Chautauqua; Mayville 550
Corning Inc./Fall Brook Plant; Corning; glass/glassware 548
Brooks Memorial Hospital; Dunkirk 520

North Carolina

After almost two years of political infighting, dealmaking and litigation, it was only fitting that North Carolina's redistricting plan ended up in the nation's highest court. Besides, it was in keeping with the highly publicized, circus-like circumstances of the Tar Heel State's mapmaking process. From the first machinations, to the U.S. Supreme Court's 1993 decision to allow white residents of the 12th District to challenge the constitutionality of the new map, the state's redistricting process was arguably the most convoluted of any state. Given the follies that marked some other states' efforts to draw lines for the 1990s, it was an especially dubious achievement.

The Supreme Court case, *Shaw vs. Reno,* was brought by five white voters—two of whom were 12th District residents—who claimed racial separation of voters violated their constitutional rights. State officials defended the map, pointing to Voting Rights Act mandates that require creation and preservation of minority-majority districts whenever possible. In allowing challenges to "bizarre" and racially gerrymandered districts, the high court may have opened a window of opportunity for legal challenges to majority-minority districts across the country.

North Carolina's story began back in July 1991, when the state Legislature approved a map that included a black-majority seat in the rural eastern part of the state. That seat would likely have elected the state's first black to Congress this century, but the Justice Department nullified the plan, ruling that one minority-majority seat was not enough. (Under Voting Rights Act provisions, North Carolina is one of 14 states that must have their congressional maps "precleared" by the Justice Department.)

Legislators responded quickly, revising the map in a January 1992 special session. They created a second black-majority district, this one an urban-based, heavily Democratic district that followed the path of Interstate 85 for over 150 miles from Durham to Charlotte. Republicans were outraged—they believed the one-seat reapportionment gain should be theirs—but the Justice Department approved this new version one month later. In fact, under the first rejected version, Democrats actually conceded the additional seat to the GOP.

At least Republicans could find solace in the fact that the new map gave three of the party's House incumbents comfortable seats, all located in the Piedmont region and west. And in the Asheville-based 11th, voters in 1992 re-elected their first-term GOP incumbent by a wider-than-expected margin. Prior to that year, the fickle voters of western North Carolina tossed out their House incumbent in 1980, 1982, 1984, 1986 and 1990.

The neighboring 10th District qualifies as the state's most rock-ribbed Republican district. It is the epitome of small-town North Carolina, with textiles, furniture and agriculture forming the backbone of the economy. The 9th is also comfortably Republican, but of a more moderate variety, leavened by the old-line GOP establishment in Charlotte and the city's working-class Democrats. Charlotte, the state's most populous city, transformed during the boom times of the 1970s and 1980s into the economic colossus of North Carolina and the Southeast, rivaling only Atlanta in stature.

The third GOP-friendly seat—the Greensboro-based 6th—is reliant on textiles and furniture making; in the city of Greensboro, the economy is a blend of manufacturing and service industry. A close look at the geography of the 6th reveals a fissure across the district, which is where the 12th District cuts through along I-85. The point where the two halves of the 6th connect (congressional districts must be contiguous) is invisible to the naked eye.

In creating the infamous 12th District, legislators had to reach into a handful of Democratic-controlled districts to siphon traditionally Democratic-voting black voters. Black neighborhoods from Charlotte, Durham, Gastonia, Greensboro, High Point and Winston-Salem were extracted from other districts and grafted onto the 12th. Not one whole county is taken in. Piecing together African American communities was an easier task in the 1st District in the eastern part of the state. Here there are larger concentrations of black voters, including a string of majority black counties.

The crafting of two safely Democratic, black-majority districts sent ripples through the other districts, creating a handful of competitive seats stretching from the central Piedmont region to eastern North Carolina. The Raleigh-based 4th has a distinct Democratic advantage, but Republicans find fertile ground in the 2nd, 3rd, 5th, 7th and 8th districts.

The 2nd takes in parts of Durham and Rocky Mount while reaching as far south as the Sandhills resort and retirement

NORTH CAROLINA

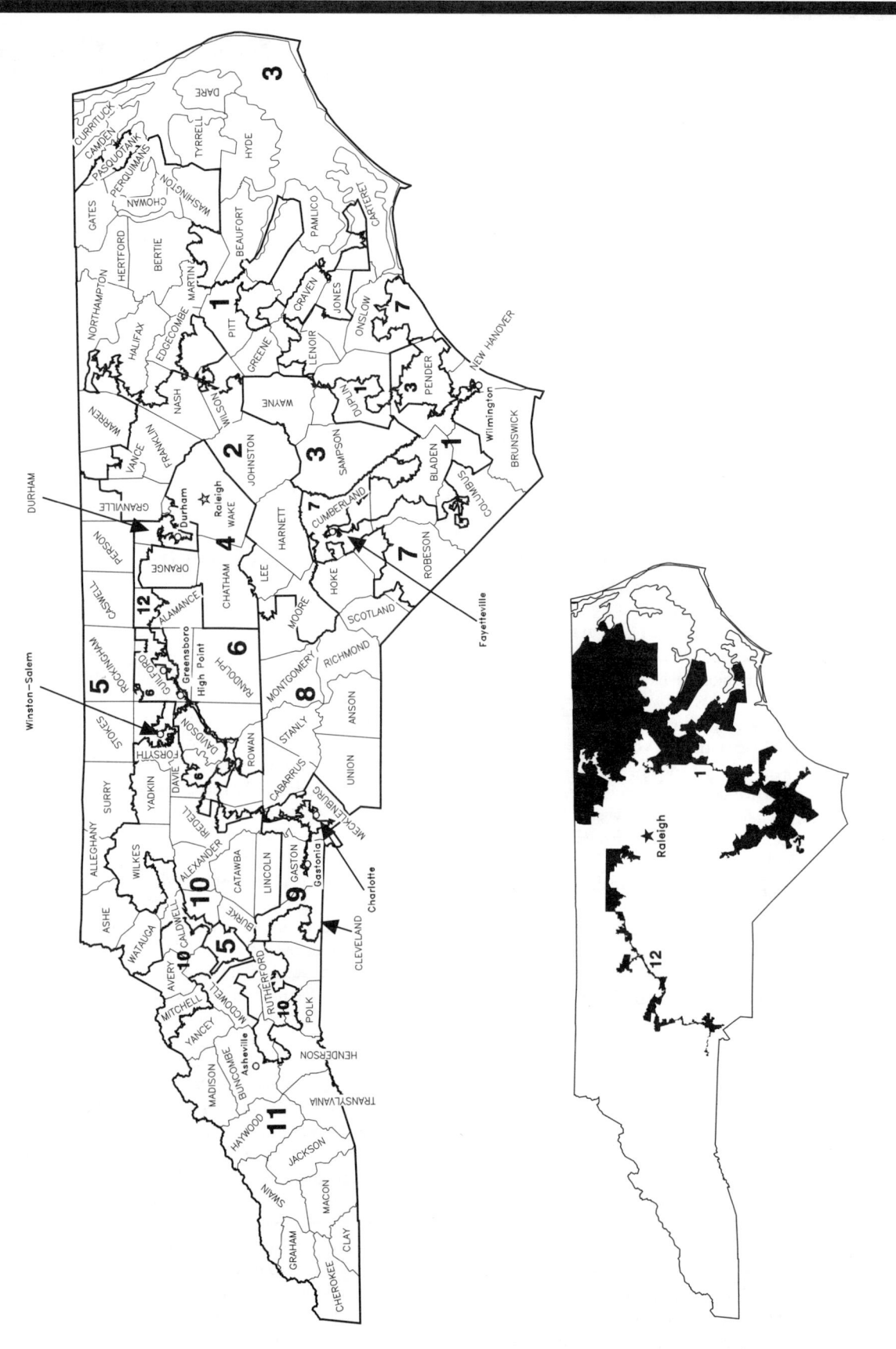

communities on the district's southwestern fringe. The rambling 3rd ranges from the tidewater region to the tobacco-producing areas of the coastal plain. While both districts have significant Democratic voter registration edges, it no longer translates into success in statewide or national races. In recent years, conservative white Democrats have gravitated toward Republican candidates. In the southeastern 7th, which takes in parts of Fayetteville and Wilmington, voters have not strayed quite as far from their Democratic roots.

The 5th and 8th districts cover the north and south central sections of the Piedmont Plateau. Winston-Salem, an old-time tobacco town anchors the 5th, which runs along the state's northwestern tier. Beginning in the 1970s, 5th District voters began abandoning the Democratic Party in droves, particularly in presidential election years. The excision of black voters further damages Democratic prospects, though Democratic Rep. Stephen L. Neal was re-elected to a tenth term in 1992.

The textile-producing 8th has trended Republican as well, with the GOP faring best in the I-85 and I-77 corridors. Charlotte bedroom communities in Union County are also wellsprings of GOP votes. Democrats find quarter in the poorer, rural counties in the eastern portion of the district.

Table 1   Population

District	Population	Population under 18	Voting-age population	Median age
1	552,394	152,516	399,878	32.9
2	552,378	132,200	420,178	33.9
3	552,387	139,124	413,263	32.4
4	552,387	123,403	428,984	31.3
5	552,386	123,604	428,782	34.7
6	552,385	124,289	428,096	34.8
7	552,386	137,973	414,413	28.7
8	552,387	148,709	403,678	32.5
9	552,387	130,771	421,616	33.1
10	552,386	130,930	421,456	35.1
11	552,387	121,930	430,457	37.7
12	552,387	140,700	411,687	31.5
State	6,628,637	1,606,149	5,022,488	33.1

Table 2   Voting-Age Persons

District	White*	Black*	American Indian, Eskimo, or Aleut*	Asian or Pacific Islander*	Other*	Hispanic*	Male*	Female*
1	45.5%	53.4%	0.6%	0.2%	0.3%	0.7%	45.0%	55.0%
2	78.2	20.1	0.5	0.7	0.5	1.1	47.1	52.9
3	78.6	19.6	0.4	0.7	0.6	1.4	48.4	51.6
4	78.5	18.9	0.3	1.8	0.4	1.2	48.0	52.0
5	85.1	14.0	0.2	0.4	0.3	0.7	46.9	53.1
6	91.9	7.1	0.3	0.6	0.2	0.6	47.6	52.4
7	74.0	17.2	6.4	1.0	1.4	2.7	53.5	46.5
8	75.6	20.9	2.2	0.7	0.6	1.2	47.5	52.5
9	90.2	8.0	0.3	1.2	0.3	1.0	47.6	52.4
10	94.3	4.9	0.2	0.3	0.2	0.6	48.2	51.8
11	92.0	6.4	1.2	0.3	0.1	0.6	46.7	53.3
12	45.2	53.3	0.4	0.8	0.3	0.8	45.4	54.6
State	77.7	20.1	1.1	0.7	0.4	1.1	47.7	52.3

*As percent of voting-age population.

Table 3   Voting-Age Persons by Age Groups

District	18-24*	25-44*	45-54*	55-64*	65 and over*
1	14.1%	40.7%	13.3%	12.7%	19.3%
2	14.2	43.0	13.8	11.9	17.1
3	16.0	42.6	13.6	12.3	15.5
4	18.6	48.7	13.0	8.9	10.8
5	15.0	40.6	14.3	12.2	17.8
6	14.2	42.2	15.1	12.4	16.1
7	23.5	42.9	11.8	10.0	11.8
8	14.7	43.1	14.4	11.8	16.1
9	14.0	47.2	14.3	11.0	13.4
10	12.9	42.4	16.0	12.7	16.1
11	12.5	36.7	14.5	13.5	22.7
12	17.1	43.9	12.7	10.8	15.6
State	15.6	42.8	13.9	11.7	16.0

*As percent of voting-age population.

Table 4   Income and Occupation

District	Median family income	Families in poverty	White collar*	Blue collar*	Service*	Farm*
1	$22,065	22.1%	38.2%	41.6%	14.9%	5.3%
2	32,469	9.6	53.5	32.6	10.6	3.4
3	28,625	11.1	49.6	32.4	12.8	5.2
4	42,478	5.7	69.2	18.8	10.5	1.5
5	30,996	9.0	46.8	39.3	11.2	2.7
6	35,953	5.3	53.2	36.3	9.1	1.4
7	28,092	11.4	51.4	33.0	12.7	3.0
8	30,399	9.3	44.0	42.8	10.6	2.5
9	41,441	4.6	63.6	26.6	8.9	0.9
10	32,577	6.5	44.1	44.1	9.3	2.5
11	28,240	10.1	46.0	39.2	12.2	2.6
12	27,977	14.5	46.8	35.7	16.2	1.3
State	31,548	9.9	51.1	34.9	11.4	2.6

*As percent of employed persons age 16 and over.

Table 5   Education: School Years Completed

District	Less than grade 9*	Grades 9-12 no diploma*	High school diploma*	College bachelor's degree or higher*
1	19.0%	23.2%	30.1%	9.3%
2	13.2	16.4	29.7	18.1
3	11.9	16.5	31.1	14.4
4	6.2	9.8	21.5	35.9
5	16.4	18.3	29.4	14.8
6	11.1	16.8	30.2	19.0
7	9.7	15.3	31.6	15.8
8	14.1	20.1	31.5	11.4
9	8.2	13.3	23.5	26.2
10	15.0	19.6	30.2	13.6
11	14.1	17.7	30.6	15.3
12	13.1	21.3	28.5	14.3
State	12.7	17.3	29.0	17.4

*As percent of persons age 25 and over.

Table 6   Housing and Residential Patterns

District	Owner occupied	Renter occupied	Urban	Rural
1	62.2%	37.8%	41.9%	58.1%
2	68.4	31.6	41.8	58.2

District	Owner occupied	Renter occupied	Urban	Rural
3	69.4	30.6	37.8	62.2
4	61.0	39.0	69.3	30.7
5	70.3	29.7	39.6	60.4
6	73.7	26.3	47.2	52.8
7	65.2	34.8	58.8	41.2
8	73.0	27.0	45.1	54.9
9	69.0	31.0	75.7	24.3
10	78.9	21.1	29.4	70.6
11	74.3	25.7	31.3	68.7
12	50.0	50.0	86.4	13.6
State	68.0	32.0	50.4	49.6

1st District

East — Parts of Rocky Mount, Fayetteville and Greenville

When the Justice Department finally approved the radical redrawing of North Carolina's congressional districts in 1992, black voting power was concentrated in two districts, one rural and one urban.

The 1st is primarily rural and agricultural, stretching from the Virginia border almost to South Carolina, winding through 28 counties to patch together the black communities of northeastern North Carolina down to Wilmington and Fayetteville (see district profile map on page 548).

Covering 2,039 miles around its perimeter, the 1st takes in nine whole counties and parts of 19 more. The main body is located on the Virginia border; from there, it snakes south in widely varying directions.

The northern part includes the mostly poor blacks of Bertie, Hertford and Northampton counties. Roanoke Rapids (Halifax County), a textile and wood products center, and populous Rocky Mount (Nash County) are shared with the 2nd District.

Pitt County (Greenville), which is divided between the 1st and the 3rd, has some pharmaceutical and paper products manufacturing, but its main employer is government. About one-tenth of the district's population is located in Pitt County, making it the most populous county in the 1st.

On the western edge of Lenoir County, the district narrows into a thin corridor along the Lenoir and Wayne County borders. From there, it expands into Duplin County, skirting Sampson County without crossing in, and breaks north through Bladen County into Cumberland County.

Once in Cumberland—which is also parceled into the 7th and 8th districts—the 1st takes in some of Fayetteville, which is dominated by Fort Bragg and Pope Air Force Base. The Cumberland County segment is the second-biggest population source. Black neighborhoods from Wilmington (New Hanover County) are also a source of votes in the southern extremity.

The 1st is staunchly Democratic—nearly 90 percent of the district's voters are registered Democrats. It was fertile ground for Senate nominee Terry Sanford in 1986 and Bill Clinton in 1992.

Blacks make up 57 percent of the district's population, but that figure is somewhat deceiving. When it comes to voter registration numbers—a better voting pattern indicator—whites make up about 49 percent of the electorate.

The white voters of the 1st claim the Democratic roots of their forefathers, but often support GOP candidates at the state and national level. A fair number are "Jessecrats," conservative Democratic supporters of GOP Sen. Jesse Helms. Republicans can also find quarter in some of the increasingly affluent coastal turf of Beaufort and Craven counties.

Election Returns

	1st District	Democrat	Republican
1992	President*	111,398 (61.1%)	53,026 (29.1%)
	House	116,078 (67.0%)	54,457 (31.4%)
1990	Senate	95,188 (60.8%)	61,500 (39.3%)
1988	President	95,502 (60.5%)	62,457 (39.5%)
	Governor	104,141 (63.1%)	60,874 (36.9%)

Vote for Perot was 18,040 (9.9%).

Demographics

Population 552,394

Percent change from 1980 3.0%

Land area 8,151 square miles

Population per square mile 68

Counties, 1990 population

Beaufort (pt.) 19,674	Lenoir (pt.) 26,624
Bertie 20,388	Martin (pt.) 17,642
Bladen (pt.) 16,150	Nash (pt.) 15,831
Chowan 13,506	New Hanover (pt.) 22,509
Columbus (pt.) 15,010	Northampton 20,798
Craven (pt.) 24,771	Pasquotank (pt.) 16,011
Cumberland (pt.) 33,711	Pender (pt.) 6,865
Duplin (pt.) 14,135	Perquimans 10,447
Edgecombe (pt.) 31,256	Pitt (pt.) 59,953
Gates 9,305	Vance (pt.) 20,285
Greene 15,384	Warren 17,265
Halifax (pt.) 33,497	Washington 13,997
Hertford 22,523	Wayne (pt.) 131
Jones (pt.) 4,303	Wilson (pt.) 30,423

Cities, 1990 population (10,000 or more)

Fayetteville (pt.) 26,985	New Bern (pt.) 13,921
Greenville (pt.) 19,249	Rocky Mount (pt.) 26,527
Henderson (pt.) 11,796	Wilmington (pt.) 20,168
Kinston (pt.) 14,306	Wilson (pt.) 20,849

Race and Hispanic origin
White 41.6%
Black 57.3%
American Indian, Eskimo, or Aleut. 0.6%
Asian or Pacific Islander 0.2%
Other 0.3%
Hispanic origin 0.7%

Ancestry

American 11.3%	Irish 6.1%
English 10.3%	Scotch Irish 2.1%
French 1.0%	Scottish 1.1%
German 5.0%	

Universities/colleges, 1990-1991 enrollment
Barton College, Wilson 1,718
Beaufort Community College, Washington 1,194
Cape Fear Community College, Wilmington 2,783

Chowan College, Murfreesboro 889
College of the Albemarle, Elizabeth City 1,627
Craven Community College, New Bern 2,193
East Carolina University, Greenville 17,564
Elizabeth City State University, Elizabeth City 1,746
Fayetteville State University, Fayetteville 3,337
Halifax Community College, Weldon 815
James Sprunt Community College, Kenansville 946
Martin Community College, Williamston 677
Roanoke-Chowan Community College, Ahoskie 432
Vance-Granville Community College, Henderson 2,309
Wilson Tech Community College, Wilson 1,308

Newspapers, total circulation (in all districts)
Elizabeth City Daily Advance 13,453
Fayetteville Observer-Times 71,114
Greenville Daily Reflector 18,339
Henderson Daily Dispatch 10,139
Kinston Daily Free Press 13,756
New Bern Sun-Journal 16,287
Norfolk Virginian-Pilot/Ledger-Star 223,461
Raleigh News & Observer 142,433
Roanoke Rapids Herald 12,177
Rocky Mount Evening Telegram 17,097
Washington Daily News 10,305
Wilmington Star 50,382
Wilson Daily Times 18,275

Commercial television stations, affiliations
ADI: Greenville-New Bern-Washington (42%), Raleigh-Durham (29%), Wilmington (15%) and Norfolk-Portsmouth-Newport News-Hampton (14%)
WNCT-TV, Greenville (CBS)
WCTI, New Bern (ABC)
WITN-TV, Washington (NBC)

Cable television systems, total subscribers
CVI; Wilson 12,900
Cablevision of Fayetteville; Fayetteville 65,000
Multimedia Cablevision; Greenville 17,632
Multimedia Cablevision; Rocky Mount 23,697
Multimedia Cablevision; Washington 5,074
Roanoke Rapids Telecable; Roanoke Rapids 10,800

Military installations, 1991
Cherry Point Marine Corps Air Station, Havelock 11,567
Cherry Point Naval Aviation Depot, Cherry Point 4,000

Businesses and other major employers
Pitt County Memorial Hospital; Greenville 3,500
Weyerhaeuser Co.; Plymouth; paper mills 3,000
General Electric Co.; Wilmington; inorganic chemicals 2,400
Perdue Farms Inc.; Lewiston; poultry 2,200
National Spinning Co. Inc.; Washington; yarn/thread mills 1,800
Bridgestone/Firestone Inc.; Wilson; tires 1,700
Harriet & Henderson Yarns Inc.; Henderson; yarn/thread mills 1,700
Consolidated Diesel Co.; Whitakers; engines/turbines 1,640
Federal Paper Board Co./Riegelwood Operations; Riegelwood; paper mills 1,500
Burroughs Wellcome Co.; Greenville; pharmaceuticals 1,500
Rose's Stores Inc.; Henderson; variety stores 1,500
Texasgulf Inc.; Aurora; inorganic chemicals 1,300
Craven Regional Medical Center; New Bern 1,250

Hampton Industries Inc.; Kinston; outerwear 1,200
County of New Hanover/Sheriffs Dept.; Wilmington 1,000
Americal Corp.; Henderson; knitting mills 950
County of Halifax/Public Schools; Halifax 899
Collins & Aikman Corp.; Farmville; knitting mills 820
Yale Materials Handling Corp.; Greenville; construction machinery 800
Sara Lee Corp.; Tarboro; bakery products 800
Louisiana-Pacific Corp.; Lewiston; sawmills 800
Whiteville Apparel Corp.; Whiteville; men's suits/coats 800
U.S. Veterans Affairs Dept.; Fayetteville; hospital 750
Genmar Industries Inc./Hatteras Yachts; New Bern; yachts 742
Halifax Memorial Hospital Inc.; Roanoke Rapids 740
Ithaca Industries Inc.; Chadbourn; undergarments 725
BB&T Financial Corp.; Wilson; commercial banks 700
Procter & Gamble Co.; Greenville; paper products 650
HCA/Highsmith Rainey Memorial Hospital; Fayetteville 642
City of Wilson; Wilson 630
Weyerhaeuser Co.; New Bern; paper mills 610
VF Corp./Wrangler East; Wilson; warehousing 600
Champion Intl. Corp.; Roanoke Rapids; pulp mills 600
Royal Home Fashions Inc./Durham Drapery Co.; Henderson; cotton mills 600
Perdue Farms Inc.; Robersonville; poultry products 580
Bibb Co. Inc.; Roanoke Rapids; cotton mills 551
Kinston Shirt Co. Inc.; Kinston; outerwear 550
Southern Quilters-Carolina Comforters; Henderson; quilts/comforters 525
County of Hertford/School District; Winton 525

2nd District

North Central — Parts of Durham and Rocky Mount

The half-moon shaped 2nd is home to features of North Carolina's past, present and future economies. The northern edge of the crescent holds the high-tech industry of Research Triangle Park; the southern edge contains resorts and retirement communities. They are connected by a rich tobacco-producing region.

In the 1950s, an unusual coalition of academic, political and business leaders decided North Carolina needed to diversify its economic base beyond the traditional furniture, tobacco and textile industries. They came up with the idea of Research Triangle Park, a new industrial area where America's emerging high-tech industries could draw on the brainpower of nearby Duke University, the University of North Carolina-Chapel Hill and North Carolina State University.

Today, in the 2nd District's portion of southern Durham County, that vision is the source of thousands of jobs in biotechnology, supercomputers, microelectronics and pharmaceuticals.

Outside the Triangle, tobacco, the state's traditional cash crop, is a crucial component of the local economy. The tobacco fields of Nash, Edgecombe, Harnett and Wilson counties make it the district's chief agricultural commodity. Tobacco is the major agricultural crop of Johnston County, with sweet potatoes coming in second.

The golfing resorts of Pinehurst and Southern Pines (Moore County) attract vacationers and affluent retirees to the Sandhills area of the district's southwestern fringe.

Unlike the white-collar executives and engineers attracted to

Durham County—many of whom hew to Durham's progressive political traditions—the newcomers to Moore County are more reliably Republican.

With only four counties wholly contained in the 2nd—along with parts of nine others—the district includes partial sections of a number of smaller-sized cities.

Rocky Mount, shared with the 1st, is a food processing and textile center. Also shared with the 1st is tobacco-oriented Wilson and a sliver of Halifax County reaching into Roanoke Rapids.

The politics of the 2nd is as varied as its economic interests. Party registration figures give Democrats an almost 3-to-1 advantage, but many of those small-town voters are Democratic in name only: In the 1990 Senate race, conservative GOP Sen. Jesse Helms won 59 percent in the areas that make up the 2nd.

In 1992, Johnston County, the second most-populous jurisdiction after Durham County, gave 51 percent to the unsuccessful GOP House challenger. Black voters help boost Democratic fortunes, particularly in Franklin and Granville counties, where blacks make up more than a third of the population. District-wide, about 22 percent of the population is black.

Election Returns

	2nd District	Democrat	Republican
1992	President*	85,542 (39.8%)	98,516 (45.9%)
	House	113,693 (53.7%)	93,893 (44.4%)
1990	Senate	69,183 (40.8%)	100,259 (59.2%)
1988	President	67,733 (39.1%)	105,541 (60.9%)
	Governor	72,722 (41.2%)	103,787 (58.8%)

*Vote for Perot was 30,643 (14.3%).

Demographics

Population 552,378

Percent change from 1980 3.0%

Land area 4,135 square miles

Population per square mile 134

Counties, 1990 population

Durham (pt.) 87,343	Lee 41,374
Edgecombe (pt.) 25,302	Moore (pt.) 43,813
Franklin 36,414	Nash (pt.) 60,846
Granville (pt.) 31,127	Vance (pt.) 18,607
Halifax (pt.) 22,019	Wake (pt.) 767
Harnett 67,822	Wilson (pt.) 35,638
Johnston 81,306	

Cities, 1990 population (10,000 or more)

Durham (pt.) 61,564	Rocky Mount (pt.) 22,470
Roanoke Rapids (pt.) 13,973	Sanford 14,475
	Wilson (pt.) 16,081

Race and Hispanic origin

White 76.2%
Black 21.9%
American Indian, Eskimo, or Aleut 0.6%
Asian or Pacific Islander 0.7%
Other 0.5%
Hispanic origin 1.2%

Ancestry

American 14.8%	Irish 11.6%
Dutch 1.2%	Italian 1.5%
English 17.3%	Scotch Irish 5.0%
French 1.9%	Scottish 3.1%
German 11.3%	

Universities/colleges, 1990-1991 enrollment

Campbell University, Buies Creek 5,043
Central Carolina Community College, Sanford 2,804
Edgecombe Community College, Tarboro 1,696
Johnston Community College, Smithfield 2,413
Louisburg College, Louisburg 891
Nash Community College, Rocky Mount 1,549
North Carolina Wesleyan College, Rocky Mount 1,436
Sandhills Community College, Pinehurst 2,145

Newspapers, total circulation (in all districts)

Durham Herald-Sun 50,987
Henderson Daily Dispatch 10,139
Raleigh News & Observer 142,433
Roanoke Rapids Herald 12,177
Rocky Mount Evening Telegram 17,097
Sanford Herald 13,608
Wilson Daily Times 18,275

Commercial television stations, affiliations

ADI: Raleigh-Durham (100%)
WKFT, Fayetteville (None)
WYED, Goldsboro (None)
WRMY, Rocky Mount (None)

Cable television systems, total subscribers

CVI; Wilson 12,900
Cablevision Industries Inc.; Apex 20,585
Cablevision of Fayetteville; Fayetteville 65,000
Cencom Cable TV; Sanford 7,926
Durham Cablevision Inc.; Durham 45,000
Multimedia Cablevision; Rocky Mount 23,697
Sandhills Cablevision; Southern Pines 7,600

Businesses and other major employers

IBM Corp.; Durham; computer equipment 14,000
Northern Telecom Inc./Public Networks Div.; Durham; electrical goods 2,700
Abbott Laboratories; Rocky Mount; pharmaceuticals 2,300
Durham County General Hospital; Durham 2,025
National Institutes of Health; Durham; research services 1,800
State of North Carolina/Murdock Center for Multiple Handicapped; Butner; residential care 1,600
Rhone-Poulenc AG Co.; Clayton; agricultural research 1,512
Burroughs Wellcome Co.; Durham; pharmaceuticals 1,500
U.S. Veterans Affairs Dept.; Durham; hospital 1,400
Moore Regional Hospital; Pinehurst 1,320
Research Triangle Institute; Durham; research services 1,310
John Umstead Hospital; Butner 1,251
County of Nash/Board of Education; Nashville 1,155
Swift Textiles Inc.; Erwin; cotton mills 1,100
CSX Transportation Inc.; Rocky Mount; railroads 1,000
Carolina Telephone & Telegraph Co.; Tarboro; telephone communications 915
Black & Decker Corp.; Tarboro; power hand tools 850
Hardee's Food Systems Inc.; Rocky Mount; fast-food chain 800

City of Rocky Mount; Rocky Mount 770

TEXFI Industries Inc.; Rocky Mount; man-made fabric mills
750

Pfizer Inc./Coty Div.; Sanford; soaps/cleaners 726

Allied-Signal Inc./Energy Control Div.; Rocky Mount;
search/navigation equipment 700

Data General Corp.; Clayton; computer equipment 700

City of Rocky Mount/City Schools; Rocky Mount 700

County of Granville/School District; Oxford 700

JPS Carpet Corp.; Aberdeen; carpets/rugs 650

Carolina Enterprises Inc.; Tarboro; toys 600

ILCO Unican Corp.; Rocky Mount; keys/locks/hardware
600

Miles Inc./Cutter Laboratories Div.; Clayton; pharmaceuticals 600

Almay Inc.; Oxford; cosmetics 600

Burlington Industries Inc.; Oxford; yarn/thread mills 600

Gold Kist Inc.; Sanford; poultry products 600

GKN Automotive Inc.; Sanford; motor vehicle parts 600

Centura Bank Inc.; Rocky Mount; commercial banks 600

BNR Inc.; Durham; research services 600

Campbell University Inc.; Buies Creek 593

County of Johnston/School District; Smithfield 583

Weber USA Inc.; Sanford; motor vehicle parts 575

Avnet Inc./Channel Master; Smithfield; communications
equipment 560

Standard Products Co.; Rocky Mount; rubber products 550

Resorts of Pinehurst Inc.; Pinehurst; hotel 550

Rocky Mount Mills; Rocky Mount; yarn/thread mills 503

Nash General Hospital; Rocky Mount 200

3rd District

East — Goldsboro; Part of Greenville; Outer Banks

In a state full of horribly disfigured congressional districts,
the 3rd ranks as one of the worst. It includes the Tidewater
region as far south as Onslow County, then juts west before
sweeping into the tobacco-producing areas of the Coastal Plain.

The fragile barrier islands of the Outer Banks bring tourism
dollars into the 3rd, particularly during the summer. Development
is a serious concern of the year-round residents of the northern
islands, around Nags Head, but is a less vexing issue farther south
where the islands are less accessible and much of the land is
designated as a protected seashore. Other issues of importance to
the region are hurricane aid and wetlands protection.

On the mainland, tourism is also a prominent economic
feature of Albemarle and Pamlico sounds, as is fishing and the
seafood canning industry.

Onslow County (Jacksonville), the southern edge of the 3rd's
coastline, is economically dependent on Camp Lejeune Marine
Corps training base. The 1991 deployment of troops to the
Persian Gulf War so drained Onslow's economic lifeblood that
then-Gov. James G. Martin declared the county an "economic
emergency area."

Farther inland, the business of the 3rd is agriculture. A finger
reaches into Pitt County (Greenville); turkey-producing Duplin
County is the gateway to the tobacco country of Sampson and
Wayne counties.

All of rural and agricultural Sampson is included in the 3rd
along with most of Wayne County, where the landscape is
dominated by huge tobacco warehouses and fields.

Goldsboro, the Wayne County seat, was another "economic
emergency area" after the pilots of Seymour Johnson Air Force
Base left for the Persian Gulf. Almost one-fifth of the district's
people live in Wayne County, making it the most populous
jurisdiction in the 3rd.

Eastern Carolina has long been a Democratic stronghold, but
in recent years dissatisfaction with state and national Democratic
candidates has translated into Republican gains.

In his 1986 Senate race, Terry Sanford won every county east
of Raleigh, but in his 1992 re-election effort, his only strength in
the east came in the heavily black northeastern counties of the
1st District. In the 3rd, blacks make up slightly more than 20
percent of the population.

GOP Senate nominee Lauch Faircloth carried many of the
state's southeastern counties in his successful 1992 bid against
Sanford, including Onslow and Wayne counties, where voters
remembered Sanford's vote against authorizing force in the
Persian Gulf. And despite the heavy Democratic registration
advantage, conservative GOP Sen. Jesse Helms won 59 percent
in the district in 1990.

Democratic Rep. Martin Lancaster, who voted in favor of
using force, carried all but two counties in 1992. Holdouts for
Lancaster's Republican challenger were Onslow and Craven
counties, where GOP strength has increased with the influx of
affluent, conservative-minded retirees.

Election Returns

	3rd District	Democrat	Republican
1992	President*	74,639 (38.9%)	89,038 (46.4%)
	House	101,739 (54.4%)	80,759 (43.2%)
1990	Senate	64,539 (41.2%)	92,262 (58.8%)
1988	President	63,207 (39.1%)	98,282 (60.9%)
	Governor	73,857 (44.0%)	93,886 (56.0%)

*Vote for Perot was 28,223 (14.7%).

Demographics

Population 552,387

Percent change from 1980 3.1%

Land area 7,533 square miles

Population per square mile 73

Counties, 1990 population

Beaufort (pt.) 22,609	Martin (pt.) 7,436
Camden 5,904	Onslow (pt.) 57,490
Carteret 52,556	Pamlico 11,372
Craven (pt.) 56,842	Pasquotank (pt.) 15,287
Currituck 13,736	Pender (pt.) 15,718
Dare 22,746	Pitt (pt.) 47,971
Duplin (pt.) 25,860	Sampson 47,297
Hyde 5,411	Tyrrell 3,856
Jones (pt.) 5,111	Wayne (pt.) 104,535
Lenoir (pt.) 30,650	

Cities, 1990 population (10,000 or more)

Goldsboro 40,709	Jacksonville (pt.) 21,257
Greenville (pt.) 25,723	Kinston (pt.) 10,989
Havelock (pt.) 20,268	

Race and Hispanic origin
White 76.6%
Black 21.5%
American Indian, Eskimo, or Aleut. 0.4%
Asian or Pacific Islander 0.7%
Other 0.7%
Hispanic origin 1.6%

Ancestry
American 12.9%	Irish 13.3%
Dutch 1.4%	Italian 2.1%
English 18.8%	Polish 1.1%
French 2.7%	Scotch Irish 3.9%
German 13.2%	Scottish 2.2%

Universities/colleges, 1990-1991 enrollment
Carteret Community College, Morehead City 1,444
Coastal Carolina Community College, Jacksonville 3,388
Lenoir Community College, Kinston 2,138
Mount Olive College, Mount Olive 756
Pitt Community College, Greenville 4,211
Sampson Community College, Clinton 948
Wayne Community College, Goldsboro 2,364

Newspapers, total circulation (in all districts)
Elizabeth City Daily Advance 13,453
Fayetteville Observer-Times 71,114
Goldsboro-News Argus 22,043
Greenville Daily Reflector 18,339
Jacksonville Daily News 22,579
Kinston Daily Free Press 13,756
New Bern Sun-Journal 16,287
Raleigh News & Observer 142,433
Sampson Independent 7,455
Washington Daily News 10,305

Commercial television stations, affiliations
ADI: Greenville-New Bern-Washington (60%), Raleigh-Durham (20%), Norfolk-Portsmouth-Newport News-Hampton (15%) and Wilmington (5%)
WFXI, Morehead City (Fox)

Cable television systems, total subscribers
CVI; Goldsboro 19,500
Cablevision of Fayetteville; Fayetteville 65,000
Cox Cable of Hampton Road; Virginia Beach 182,487
Falcon Cable TV; Manteo 14,195
Jacksonville TV Cable Co. Inc.; Jacksonville 16,300
Multimedia Cablevision; New Bern 11,800
Multimedia Cablevision; Greenville 17,632
Multimedia Cablevision; Kinston 9,200
Vision Cable of Morehead City; Newport 26,590

Military installations, 1991
Seymour Johnson Air Force Base, Goldsboro 5,636

Businesses and other major employers
East Carolina University; Greenville 3,438
Du Pont E. I. De Nemours & Co.; Kinston; knitting mills 2,000
State of North Carolina/Caswell Center; Kinston; nursing 1,806
Carolina Turkeys; Mount Olive; turkey products 1,700
Cherry Hospital; Goldsboro 1,200
Morris Brothers Blueberry Farm; New Bern; fruit 1,000

Hamilton Beach/Proctor-Silex; Clinton; household appliances 1,000
Wayne Memorial Hospital Inc.; Goldsboro 951
Lenoir Memorial Hospital Inc.; Kinston 945
Hamilton Beach/Proctor-Silex; Washington; household appliances 800
Atlantic Veneer Corp.; Beaufort; millwork 700
Bosch Robert Power Tool Corp.; New Bern; metalworking machinery 650
AP Parts Mfg. Co.; Goldsboro; motor vehicle parts 650
Delta Woodside Industries Inc.; Wallace; knitting mills 620
City of Greenville; Greenville 600
Carteret General Hospital; Morehead City 591
Albemarle Hospital; Elizabeth City 565
Universal Furniture Industries; Goldsboro; furniture 550

4th District

Central — Raleigh; Chapel Hill

Of the state's 10 majority-white congressional districts, the 4th is the most progressive. Located on the eastern edge of the Piedmont plateau, it was the only white-majority district to back black 1990 Democratic Senate nominee Harvey B. Gantt against GOP Sen. Jesse Helms; Democrats make up about two-thirds of all the voters here.

The Democratic base draws deeply from a well of votes in the Research Triangle area, two corners of which are in the 4th. The University of North Carolina (23,900 students) is in Chapel Hill (Orange County); Raleigh (Wake County) has North Carolina State University (27,200 students).

The large numbers of white-collar and professional jobs in the region make it one of the most affluent districts in the state.

Orange County has a more liberal bent than the rest of the 4th, due primarily to the university community of Chapel Hill. In 1992, the Democrat House candidate won Orange by nearly 3-to-1; Bill Clinton won more than 60 percent.

But the bulk of 4th District residents live outside Orange County. Wake County is the population nexus, casting about three-fourths of the vote. Much of that vote comes from the state government complex in Raleigh, North Carolina's capital. The pool of state employees gives the county a Democratic tilt, but the high-growth suburbs outside Raleigh are gradually redefining local politics.

One town, Cary, grew so fast in the 1980s that it surpassed Chapel Hill in population. Before the opening of Research Triangle Park in the early 1960s, Cary was a sleepy hamlet, surrounded by undeveloped fields and farmland. But its proximity to the Triangle and its location along the Interstate 40 corridor spurred a population boom from 7,600 people to 43,900 between 1970 and 1990—a 471 percent increase.

Like other emerging northern and western Wake County towns, Cary fits the classic suburban demographic profile: Large numbers of double-income, young, mostly white families who are independent or GOP voters. A high percentage of residents are white-collar executives who work at the biotechnology, pharmaceutical, supercomputer and electronics industries of Research Triangle Park (outside the 4th in southern Durham County) or in the office parks of Wake County.

The towns outlying Raleigh exhibited a tendency for split-ticket voting in 1992. Clinton carried the county—though he ran below his districtwide average—and Price cruised with 62 percent. But in the Senate race, Republican nominee Lauch Faircloth edged out the Democratic incumbent.

On the western edge of the 4th, largely rural Chatham County is the least populous county in the 4th, but is reliably Democratic: Democratic candidates swept the presidential, Senate and House races in 1992. Its agrarian landscape includes some textile industry, along with Chapel Hill spillover growth along its northern border with Orange County.

Election Returns

	4th District	Democrat	Republican
1992	President*	126,616 (46.7%)	105,555 (38.9%)
	House	171,299 (64.6%)	89,345 (33.7%)
1990	Senate	118,115 (58.9%)	82,250 (41.1%)
1988	President	89,198 (46.9%)	100,909 (53.1%)
	Governor	88,680 (43.9%)	113,463 (56.1%)

*Vote for Perot was 38,854 (14.3%).

Demographics

Population 552,387

Percent change from 1980 3.5%

Land area 1,836 square miles

Population per square mile 301

Counties, 1990 population
Chatham 38,759   Wake (pt.) 422,613
Orange (pt.) 91,015

Cities, 1990 population (10,000 or more)
Carrboro 11,553   Garner 14,967
Cary 43,858   Raleigh 207,951
Chapel Hill (pt.) 37,604

Race and Hispanic origin
White 77.2%
Black 20.1%
American Indian, Eskimo, or Aleut. 0.3%
Asian or Pacific Islander 1.9%
Other 0.5%
Hispanic origin 1.3%

Ancestry
American 7.6%   Irish 12.9%
Dutch 1.6%   Italian 2.7%
English 20.1%   Polish 1.8%
French 3.0%   Scotch Irish 5.9%
German 17.9%   Scottish 4.0%

Universities/colleges, 1990-1991 enrollment
Meredith College, Raleigh 2,245
North Carolina State University, Raleigh 27,199
Peace College, Raleigh 434
Phillips Junior College, Raleigh 643
Shaw University, Raleigh 1,846
Southeastern Baptist Theological Seminary, Wake Forest 644
St. Augustine's College, Raleigh 1,900
St. Mary's College, Raleigh 344
University of North Carolina, Chapel Hill 23,878
Wake Tech Community College, Raleigh 6,129

Newspapers, total circulation (in all districts)
Durham Herald-Sun 50,987
Raleigh News & Observer 142,433

Commercial television stations, affiliations
ADI: Raleigh-Durham (100%)
WPTF-TV, Durham (NBC)
WTVD, Durham (ABC)
WLFL-TV, Raleigh (Fox)
WRAL-TV, Raleigh (CBS)

Cable television systems, total subscribers
Cablevision Industries Inc.; Apex 20,585
Cablevision Industries Inc.; Garner 10,300
Cablevision of Chapel Hill; Chapel Hill 17,358
Durham Cablevision Inc.; Durham 45,000
Time Warner Cable; Raleigh 66,000

Businesses and other major employers
State of North Carolina/Transportation Dept.; Raleigh 10,848
North Carolina State University; Raleigh 10,500
North Carolina Memorial Hospital; Chapel Hill 3,803
University of North Carolina; Chapel Hill 2,800
Rex Hospital; Raleigh 2,600
County of Wake; Raleigh 2,415
Carolina Power & Light Co.; Raleigh; electric services 2,300
Wake County Medical Center; Raleigh 2,200
American Airlines Inc.; Cary; airline 2,000
SAS Institute Inc./Software Media Consultants; Cary; computer services 1,531
State of North Carolina/Highway Patrol; Raleigh 1,387
Dorothea Dix Hospital; Raleigh 1,300
Alcatel Network Systems; Raleigh; communications equipment 1,250
State of North Carolina/Administration Dept.; Raleigh 1,200
State of North Carolina/Environment Health & Natural Resource Dept.; Raleigh 1,200
Memorex Telex Corp.; Raleigh; computer equipment 1,100
Carolina Power & Light Co.; New Hill; electric services 950
State of North Carolina/Education Dept.; Raleigh 950
Square D Co./Control Products Div.; Knightdale; electric switchgears 871
IBM Corp.; Cary; computer equipment/research 800
Nationwide Mutual Insurance Co.; Raleigh; insurance 800
State of North Carolina/Motor Vehicles Dept.; Raleigh 800
Bahlsen Inc./Austin Quality Snacks; Cary; bakery products 780
Wake Tech Community College; Raleigh 775
Data General Corp.; Apex; computer equipment 750
ABB Power T&D Co. Inc./Westinghouse ABB Power; Raleigh; electric meters 700
Glendale Hosiery Co.; Siler City; knitting mills 700
Collins & Aikman Corp.; Siler City; wool mills 700
General Electric Capital Corp.; Raleigh; surety insurance 700
Raychem Corp.; Fuquay Varina; plastics/synthetics 650
First Citizens Bancshares Inc.; Raleigh; commercial banks 650
County of Chatham/Board of Education; Pittsboro 640
Allied-Signal Inc.; Moncure; man-made fabric mills 625
Siemens Energy & Automation; Wendell; electric services 600
News & Observer Publishing Co.; Raleigh; newspapers 600
Exide Electronics Corp.; Raleigh; power conversion units 600
Asplundh Tree Expert Co.; Raleigh; landscape services 600

Cooper Industries Inc.; Apex; metalworking machinery 600
Showell Farms Inc.; Siler City; meat products 600
Belk-Hudson-Leggett Co.; Raleigh; department stores 600
State of North Carolina/Cultural Resources Dept.; Raleigh 600
State of North Carolina/Central Prison; Raleigh 600
State of North Carolina/Employment Security Commission; Raleigh 600
HCA/Raleigh Community Hospital; Raleigh 570
IBM Corp./Mid-Atlantic Marketing Div.; Raleigh; computer services 550

5th District

Northwest — Part of Winston-Salem

Beginning in the 1970s, voters in the 5th started a march toward the Republican side, creating a quadrennial panic among local Democratic officeholders, who feared being dragged down by their party's national ticket. A recession-induced interruption in 1992 marked the first time Democrats saw a break in that procession.

The heart of the district is Winston-Salem, an old-time tobacco town dominated by the leaf since Richard Joshua Reynolds built his first plug chewing tobacco factory in the 1870s. The city remains a tobacco-producing center, where the R.J. Reynolds conglomerate still keeps its tobacco and Planters Lifesavers headquarters, but it has strayed from its industrial origins.

Textiles are also an important component of the local economy, but nowadays, tobacco and textiles take a back seat to service industries, now the largest employment sector. Health-care services is the largest single industry in Forsyth County.

In the 1980s, downsizing in the tobacco industry and the gradual erosion of the manufacturing base translated into slower growth for Winston-Salem than in North Carolina's other major cities.

The 1992 presidential election was a prime indicator of local economic unrest, as the Democratic presidential ticket remained competitive in Forsyth County and across the district for the first time since 1976.

It was not enough, though, for Democratic Sen. Terry Sanford, who lost populous Forsyth and virtually every other county in the 5th. Two years earlier, GOP Sen. Jesse Helms won 56 percent of the district vote.

One exception in the 1990 and 1992 Senate races was rural Caswell County, a Democratic stronghold in the eastern reaches of the 5th, where blacks make up about 40 percent of the electorate.

The city of Winston-Salem is about 40 percent black also, but most of the black neighborhoods were excised from the 5th during 1992 redistricting and added to the majority-minority 12th District.

Republicans have traditionally run well in the GOP hill country in the western reaches of the 5th, between the Blue Ridge and Appalachian mountains. Early settlers of the area set up small farms with dairy cows, poultry, apple trees and tobacco, and developed strong antagonism toward the flatland tobacco planters who were wealthier, politically powerful and Democratic.

From mountainous Watauga County, the 5th shoots east and south to take in parts of Republican Wilkes County, and parts of furniture- and textile-producing Burke and Caldwell counties.

The mostly rural counties of the northern tier, along the Virginia border, are typified by small textile towns such as Mount Airy. The fictional town of Mayberry, the setting for the long-running "Andy Griffith Show," was loosely based on Griffith's memories of growing up in this Surry County town. Surry and neighboring Stokes County backed George Bush in 1992.

Election Returns

	5th District	Democrat	Republican
1992	President*	97,821 (43.0%)	99,087 (43.6%)
	House	117,835 (52.7%)	102,086 (45.6%)
1990	Senate	78,995 (43.8%)	101,441 (56.2%)
1988	President	81,155 (42.1%)	111,795 (57.9%)
	Governor	89,229 (45.0%)	109,190 (55.0%)

Vote for Perot was 30,560 (13.4%).

Demographics

Population 552,386

Percent change from 1980 3.2%

Land area 4,243 square miles

Population per square mile 130

Counties, 1990 population

Alleghany 9,590	Guilford (pt.) 3,939
Ashe 22,209	Person 30,180
Burke (pt.) 44,584	Rockingham 86,064
Caldwell (pt.) 21,184	Stokes 37,223
Caswell 20,693	Surry 61,704
Forsyth (pt.) 154,656	Watauga 36,952
Granville (pt.) 7,218	Wilkes (pt.) 16,190

Cities, 1990 population (10,000 or more)

Boone 12,915	Morganton 15,085
Eden 15,238	Reidsville 12,183
Kernersville (pt.) 10,836	Winston-Salem (pt.) 97,404
Lenoir (pt.) 10,800	

Race and Hispanic origin
White 83.9%
Black 15.2%
American Indian, Eskimo, or Aleut. 0.2%
Asian or Pacific Islander 0.4%
Other 0.3%
Hispanic origin 0.8%

Ancestry

American 16.5%	Irish 12.7%
Dutch 2.7%	Italian 1.3%
English 15.3%	Scotch Irish 4.2%
French 1.8%	Scottish 2.5%
German 17.5%	

Universities/colleges, 1990-1991 enrollment
Appalachian State University, Boone 11,931
Blue Ridge Community College, Flat Rock 1,449
Forsyth Tech Community College, Winston-Salem 4,896
Piedmont Bible College, Winston-Salem 298
Piedmont Community College, Roxboro 1,081
Rockingham Community College, Wentworth 1,817

Salem College, Winston-Salem 724
Surry Community College, Dobson 2,816
West Piedmont Community College, Morganton 2,709
Wake Forest University, Winston-Salem 5,477
Wilkes Community College, Wilkesboro 2,023
Winston-Salem State University; Winston-Salem 2,500

Newspapers, total circulation (in all districts)

Burlington Times-News 29,480
Durham Herald-Sun 50,987
Greensboro News & Record 112,897
Lenoir News-Topic 12,880
Morganton News Herald 11,442
Winston-Salem Journal 90,650

Commercial television stations, affiliations

ADI: Greensboro-Winston-Salem-High Point (61%), Charlotte (24%) and Raleigh-Durham (15%)
WLXI-TV, Greensboro (None)
WXII, Winston-Salem (NBC)
WNRW, Winston-Salem-Greensboro-High Point (Fox)

Cable television systems, total subscribers

CVI; Reidsville 5,967
High Country Cable TV; Boone 9,206
Roxboro Cablevision; Roxboro 5,600
Summit Cable Services of Forsyth County; Kernersville 13,031
Summit Cable Services of Forsyth County; Winston-Salem 42,541
Summit Cable Services of Forsyth County; Rural Hall 18,428

Businesses and other major employers

North Carolina Baptist Hospital; Winston-Salem 5,000
Sara Lee Corp./Knit Products Div.; Winston-Salem; underwear 4,000
Appalachian State University; Boone 3,866
Forsyth Memorial Hospital Inc.; Winston-Salem 3,220
Tyson Foods Inc./Holly Farms Foods; Wilkesboro; poultry products 2,000
Chatham Mfg. Co.; Elkin; man-made fabric mills 1,985
Broughton Hospital; Morganton 1,600
Henredon Furniture Industries/North Carolina Schoonbeck Co.; Morganton; furniture 1,500
Miller Brewing Co.; Eden; brewery 1,500
Ithaca Industries Inc.; Wilkesboro; knitting mills 1,500
Collins & Aikman Corp.; Roxboro; wool mills 1,400
Sara Lee Corp./Hosiery Div.; Winston-Salem; knitting mills 1,400
Lowe's Companies Inc.; North Wilkesboro; lumber/building materials 1,372
American Tobacco Co. Inc.; Reidsville; cigarettes 1,300
Cross Creek Apparel Inc.; Mount Airy; outerwear 1,300
Wake Forest University; Winston-Salem 1,275
State of North Carolina; Morganton; nursing 1,100
USAir Inc.; Winston-Salem; airline 1,029
Hamilton Beach/Proctor-Silex; Mount Airy; household appliances 1,000
R. J. R. Nabisco Inc.; Winston-Salem; cigarettes 1,000
Crown Crafts Inc.; Roxboro; textile products 950
Spencer's Inc.; Mount Airy; undergarments 950
Sara Lee Corp./L'eggs Products; Winston-Salem; hosiery 915
Unifi Inc.; Reidsville; textile finishing 900
Roadway Express Inc.; Kernersville; trucking services 900

Sara Lee Corp./Hosiery Div.; Winston-Salem; hosiery 864
AT&T Co.; Winston-Salem; communications equipment 777
Thomasville Furniture; Lenoir; furniture 750
Kentucky Derby Hosiery Co. Inc; Mount Airy; knitting mills 750
Leviton Mfg. Co. Inc.; Morganton; electric lighting 700
Fairfield Chair Co.; Lenoir; furniture 700
Ladd Furniture Inc./American Drew; North Wilkesboro; furniture 700
Winston-Salem State University; Winston-Salem 700
Wachovia Corp.; Winston-Salem; computer services 700
City of Winston-Salem/Forsyth County Schools; Winston-Salem 700
Sara Lee Corp./Marketing Div.; Rural Hall; catalog retailers 650
Tultex Corp.; Mayodan; knitting mills 622
City of Wilkesboro; North Wilkesboro 610
Sara Lee Corp./Hanes Printables Inc.; Morganton; underwear 600
Continental Grain Co./Wayne Farms; Dobson; poultry products 600
Sara Lee Corp./Knit Products Div.; Jefferson; knitting mills 600
Grace Hospital; Morganton 600
State of North Carolina/Transportation Dept.; Wilkesboro 600
Wilkes Regional Medical Center; North Wilkesboro 600
Fieldcrest Cannon Inc./Decorative Bedding; Eden; textile products 550
Golden Needles Knitting Inc.; Wilkesboro; knitting mills 525
Caldwell Memorial Hospital; Lenoir 525
Eastern Band of Cherokee Ind./Carolina Mirror Co.; North Wilkesboro; glass products 520

6th District

Central — Part of Greensboro

The 6th is a monument to the folly of North Carolina's 1992 redistricting process. Many of the districts are cartographically imaginative, but the 6th is exceptional. It is split in half by a thin reed that is the 12th District; the point where the two halves of the 6th District connect cannot be seen by the naked eye.

Almost 40 percent of the district's population lives in middle-class Guilford County (Greensboro), home to two corners of the Piedmont Triad. The third-largest city in North Carolina, Greensboro's economy is a blend of manufacturing and service industry.

Textile manufacturers such as Burlington Industries and Guilford Mills employ thousands, as does AT&T Technologies. There is an American Express regional credit card service center, tobacco-processing, insurance services, and six colleges and universities.

Furniture-making High Point is located in the southwestern part of Guilford County. The third corner of the Triad, Winston-Salem, is outside 6th District confines, in the neighboring 5th District.

Guilford County's relatively large managerial class produces a Republican vote, though it is far from monolithic. In 1992, Bill

Clinton carried the county, while the GOP House candidate racked up 73 percent. Democratic Sen. Terry Sanford squeaked by successful Republican challenger Lauch Faircloth in 1992.

Prior to 1992 redistricting, all of Greensboro and surrounding Guilford County was included in the 6th; now the 6th lacks the black neighborhoods of the city, which were added to the majority-minority 12th District. The 12th divides the 6th along the I-85 population corridor.

Textile-oriented Alamance County produces hosiery, upholstery and drapery fabrics, textured yarn and other finished fabrics.

North of the interstate, the Alamance turf belongs to the 12th. Some of the factory outlet town of Burlington is in the 6th, but most of its black residents are in the 12th. Less-developed southern Alamance is in the 6th.

With a union-resistant textile industry, Alamance usually stays in the Republican fold, despite a Democratic registration edge. Ronald Reagan won comfortable margins in both 1980 and 1984, and George Bush carried the county easily in 1988. In 1992, votes were harder to come by, but Bush still managed to win the county.

Randolph County (Asheboro) and Davidson County produce furniture, textiles and Republican votes. In 1992, both Randolph and Davidson backed the unsuccessful GOP candidate for governor; Bush scored better than 50 percent in each that same year in the presidential race.

Parts of Davie and Rowan counties—mostly outside the population centers—are also included in the 6th. Both backed Bush in 1992; Davie gave GOP Sen. Jesse Helms 70 percent in his 1990 re-election.

Election Returns

	6th District	Democrat	Republican
1992	President*	75,652 (32.2%)	120,684 (51.4%)
	House	67,200 (29.2%)	162,822 (70.8%)
1990	Senate	67,064 (36.9%)	114,485 (63.1%)
1988	President	65,497 (33.3%)	131,073 (66.7%)
	Governor	65,649 (34.0%)	127,606 (66.0%)

Vote for Perot was 38,448 (16.4%).

Demographics

Population 552,385

Percent change from 1980 4.3%

Land area 2,459 square miles

Population per square mile 225

Counties, 1990 population
Alamance (pt.) 83,726	Guilford (pt.) 207,721
Davidson (pt.) 103,193	Randolph 106,546
Davie (pt.) 15,579	Rowan (pt.) 35,620

Cities, 1990 population (10,000 or more)
Asheboro 16,362	Greensboro (pt.) 84,734
Burlington (pt.) 32,457	High Point (pt.) 41,990
Graham (pt.) 10,419	

Race and Hispanic origin
White 91.3%
Black 7.5%
American Indian, Eskimo, or Aleut 0.4%
Asian or Pacific Islander 0.6%
Other 0.2%
Hispanic origin 0.7%

Ancestry
American 13.9%	Irish 14.5%
Dutch 3.2%	Italian 1.8%
English 17.0%	Scotch Irish 5.6%
French 2.2%	Scottish 3.1%
German 24.5%	

Universities/colleges, 1990-1991 enrollment
Catawba College, Salisbury 967
ECPI Computer Institute, Greensboro 228
Elon College, Elon College 3,263
Greensboro College, Greensboro 1,116
Guilford College, Greensboro 1,753
Guilford Technical Institute, Jamestown 4,200
Randolph Community College, Asheboro 1,426
University of North Carolina, Greensboro 12,882

Newspapers, total circulation (in all districts)
Asheboro Courier Tribune 17,030
Burlington Times-News 29,480
Greensboro News & Record 112,897
High Point Enterprise 30,592
Kannapolis Daily Independent 10,750
Lexington Dispatch 14,487
Salisbury Post 25,256
Winston-Salem Journal 90,650

Commercial television stations, affiliations
ADI: Greensboro-Winston Salem-High Point (91%) and Charlotte (9%)
WAAP, Burlington (None)
WFMY-TV, Greensboro (CBS)
WGGT, Greensboro (Fox)
WGHP-TV, High Point (ABC)
WEJC, Lexington (None)

Cable television systems, total subscribers
Archdale Cable; Archdale 6,052
Cablevision Industries Inc.; Greensboro 23,509
Cablevision of Alamance; Burlington 20,709
Cablevision of Asheboro; Asheboro 10,200
High Point/Jamestown Cable; High Point 18,100
Summit Cable Services of Forsyth County; Winston-Salem 42,541
Summit Cable Services of Forsyth County; Lexington 16,443
Time Warner; Greensboro 48,000
Vision Cable of Salisbury Inc.; Salisbury 15,368

Businesses and other major employers
AT&T Co.; McLeansville; communications equipment 3,700
AT&T Co.; Greensboro; electrical goods 3,200
Klaussner Corp.; Asheboro; furniture 2,300
American Express Travel Related Services; Greensboro; credit services 2,300
County of Davidson/Board of Education; Lexington 1,738
PPG Industries Inc./Fiber Glass Profit Center; Lexington; man-made fabric mills 1,500
County of Randolph/Board of Education; Asheboro 1,500
Roche Biomedical Lab.; Burlington; medical labs 1,500
Guilford Mills Inc.; Greensboro; knitting mills 1,475

High Point Regional Hospital; High Point   1,430
University of North Carolina; Greensboro   1,400
Gilbarco Inc.; Greensboro; gas pumps   1,300
Food Lion Inc.; Salisbury; grocery stores   1,300
Terminal Freight Handling Co./Sears Logistics Services;
   Greensboro; freight shipping   1,200
Ciba-Geigy Corp./Dyestuff & Chemicals Div.; Greensboro;
   research services   1,200
Burlington Industries Inc.; Greensboro; cotton mills   1,100
Wesley Long Community Hospital; Greensboro   1,100
Thomas Built Buses Inc.; High Point; bus bodies   1,000
USAir Group Inc./Piedmont Airlines; Greensboro; airline
   1,000
Burlington Industries Inc./Pioneer Plant; Burlington; cotton
   mills   900
Jefferson-Pilot Life Insurance Co.; Greensboro; life insurance
   900
West Point-Pepperell Inc.; Burlington; man-made fabric mills
   800
Guilford Technical Institute; Jamestown   785
Ramtex Inc.; Ramseur; cotton mills   753
Copland Fabrics Inc.; Burlington; man-made fabric mills   750
Black & Decker U.S. Inc.; Asheboro; household appliances
   740
Alamance County Hospital Inc.; Burlington   650
GKN Automotive Inc.; Mebane; motor vehicle parts   639
Crown Wood Products Co.; Mocksville; furniture   625
Alamance Memorial Hospital; Burlington   623
Sara Lee Corp./Stedman; Asheboro; knitting mills   600
General Electric Co.; Mebane; industrial controls   600
SCI Systems Inc.; Graham; electronic components   540
Guilford Mills Inc./Oak Ridge Textiles Div.; Greensboro;
   knitting mills   505

7th District

Southeast — Part of Fayetteville

It is no coincidence that Rep. Charlie Rose slipped to a career-low 57 percent in the 1992 election after his 1991 vote against authorizing force in the Persian Gulf. For in the military-dependent southeastern region of North Carolina, that stand was extremely controversial.

Cumberland County is the 7th's most-populous county, and it has a heavy military cast. It is home to more than 40,000 troops stationed at Fort Bragg and Pope Air Force Base, and thousands of military retirees.

When 75 percent of the troops stationed here were deployed in the Gulf war, the county took the equivalent of an economic Scud missile. Local business suffered: Unemployment claims and food stamp applications soared, sales tax revenues plummeted, and mobile home sales were cut in half. GOP Gov. James G. Martin declared Cumberland and three other counties economic emergency areas.

One of the other economic emergency areas was coastal Onslow County (Jacksonville), site of the Camp Lejeune Marine Corps training base. Like Cumberland, the Onslow economy is heavily dependent on the troops who spend their paychecks on the local service industries.

The 7th shares Cumberland County with the 1st and the 8th—and Onslow County with the 3rd—and many voters in these counties showed their dissatisfaction with Rose's Gulf vote at

the ballot box in 1992. Rose won in Cumberland County, but not as easily as he had in past elections. Onslow County, which was added to the 7th in redistricting, backed Rose's GOP challenger.

As a whole, the district has a Democratic tilt—Democrats make up 70 percent of registered voters—that is usually reflected at the local and statewide levels. But in recent years, the vote has drifted toward the GOP at the national level.

New Hanover County, in the Cape Fear region, is the district's second most-populous. Population is centered in Wilmington, a 250-year-old port city nestled between the Cape Fear River and the Atlantic Ocean. The restoration of its waterfront area has brought tourism and some white-collar prosperity into this old fishing center, and the completion of I-40, which connects Wilmington to the Raleigh-Durham area, is expected to further boost the economy.

GOP strength is more pronounced in New Hanover County than in the rest of the 7th; it voted Republican in the 1988 presidential and gubernatorial elections. In 1992, Republicans carried the House, Senate and presidential elections, though former Democratic Gov. James B. Hunt Jr. did win New Hanover in the open gubernatorial race.

Blacks make up a sizable chunk of the region's population, but most are taken in by the fingers of the majority-minority 1st District, which reaches in all directions through the 7th.

Native Americans are the 7th's other significant minority. Of the 80,000 American Indians who live in North Carolina, half of them reside in Robeson County. The county is shared with the 8th District, but most of the Democratic-voting Native Americans live in the 7th.

Election Returns

	7th District	Democrat	Republican
1992	President*	70,664 (43.3%)	70,136 (43.0%)
	House	92,414 (56.7%)	66,536 (40.8%)
1990	Senate	63,833 (49.3%)	65,593 (50.7%)
1988	President	55,522 (43.7%)	71,676 (56.3%)
	Governor	63,260 (48.6%)	66,985 (51.4%)

*Vote for Perot was 22,216 (13.6%).

Demographics

Population   552,386

Percent change from 1980   2.5%

Land area   3,614 square miles

Population per square mile   153

Counties, 1990 population

Bladen (pt.) 12,513	New Hanover (pt.) 97,775
Brunswick 50,985	Onslow (pt.) 92,348
Columbus (pt.) 34,577	Pender (pt.) 6,272
Cumberland (pt.) 176,368	Robeson (pt.) 81,548

Cities, 1990 population (10,000 or more)

Camp Lejeune Central CDP 36,716	Fort Bragg CDP 34,744
	Lumberton 18,601
Fayetteville (pt.) 48,710	Wilmington (pt.) 35,362

Race and Hispanic origin
   White   71.5%
   Black   18.7%

American Indian, Eskimo, or Aleut. 7.3%
Asian or Pacific Islander 1.1%
Other 1.5%
Hispanic origin 2.9%

Ancestry

American 9.3%	Irish 13.5%
Dutch 1.5%	Italian 2.6%
English 13.0%	Polish 1.4%
French 3.0%	Scotch Irish 5.5%
German 15.1%	Scottish 2.8%

Universities/colleges, 1990-1991 enrollment

Bladen Community College, Dublin 591
Brunswick Community College, Supply 712
Fayetteville Technical College, Fayetteville 5,488
Methodist College, Fayetteville 1,254
Pembroke State University, Pembroke 3,133
Phillips Junior College, Fayetteville 310
Robeson Community College, Lumberton 1,470
Southeastern Community College, Whiteville 1,547
University of North Carolina, Wilmington 7,567

Newspapers, total circulation (in all districts)

Fayetteville Observer-Times 71,114
Jacksonville Daily News 22,579
Lumberton Robesonian 13,730
Wilmington Star 50,382

Commercial television stations, affiliations

ADI: Wilmington (77%), Raleigh-Durham (14%) and Green-
ville-New Bern-Washington (9%)
WECT, Wilmington (NBC)
WJKA, Wilmington (CBS)
WWAY, Wilmington (ABC)

Cable television systems, total subscribers

Atlantic Telephone Membership Corp.; Shallotte 7,341
Cablevision of Fayetteville; Fayetteville 65,000
Cablevision of Lumberton; Lumberton 7,700
Jacksonville TV Cable Co. Inc.; Jacksonville 16,300
Vision Cable of North Carolina; Supply 8,640
Vision Cable of North Carolina; Wilmington 32,000

Military installations, 1991

Fort Bragg (Army), Fayetteville 50,157
Camp Lejeune Marine Corps Base, Jacksonville 34,342
New River Marine Corps Air Station, Jacksonville 5,527
Pope Air Force Base, Fayetteville 5,087
Camp Lejeune Naval Hospital, Jacksonville 1,362
Sunny Point Military Ocean Terminal (Army), Southport 314

Businesses and other major employers

County of New Hanover/School District; Wilmington 3,300
Kelly-Springfield Tire Co.; Fayetteville; tires 2,900
New Hanover Memorial Hospital; Wilmington 2,400
Cape Fear Valley Medical Center; Fayetteville 2,000
Du Pont E. I. De Nemours & Co.; Leland;
  plastics/synthetics 1,600
Converse Inc.; Lumberton; footwear 1,400
West Point-Pepperell Inc.; Lumberton; knitting mills 1,300
Black & Decker Corp.; Fayetteville; power tools 1,100
Purolator Products Co.; Fayetteville; motor vehicle equip-
  ment 1,000
Carolina Power & Light Co./Brunswick Nuclear Project;
  Southport; electric services 900

Kayser-Roth Corp.; Lumberton; knitting mills 900
University of North Carolina; Wilmington 879
Southeastern General Hospital; Lumberton 850
Corning Inc.; Wilmington; nonferrous rolling/drawing 800
Campbell Soup Co.; Maxton; grocery products 750
M. J. Soffe Co.; Fayetteville; outerwear 750
International Jensen Inc.; Lumberton; knitting mills 700
Onslow Memorial Hospital Inc.; Jacksonville 700
Columbus County Hospital; Whiteville 650
National Spinning Co. Inc.; Whiteville; yarn/thread mills 600
Cape Fear Memorial Hospital Inc.; Wilmington 600
Thorn Apple Valley Inc./Carolina Div.; Holly Ridge; meat
  products 550

8th District

South Central — Kannapolis; Part of Fayetteville

Geography and jobs determine politics in the 8th. Along the
I-77 and I-85 corridors, the textile-producing counties are
wealthier and vote Republican. The poorer, rural counties that
make up the district's eastern portion are Democratic.

The Republican voters of the 8th can be divided into two
groups. The textile workers of Rowan and Cabarrus counties are
centered in the towns of Concord, Kannapolis and Salisbury.
They. make textiles and textile machinery, and there is some
tobacco processing.

Only part of Salisbury (Rowan County) is in the 8th, but all of
Kannapolis is included. All of Cabarrus County (Concord), on
the southern border of Rowan, is within 8th District confines.

Farther south, the Republican vote is of a suburban variety, in
the Charlotte orbit (Mecklenburg County). Only a tiny part of
Mecklenburg itself is in the 8th; the real lode of GOP votes is
found in the bedroom communities of Union County, which is
the district's second most-populous county after Cabarrus.

The vote here has become increasingly Republican over the
past two decades, as Union County experienced a quadrupling of
GOP registration. Many of these voters live in Charlotte satellites
such as Indian Trail, Stallings and Monroe, the Union County
seat. Concord has also seen some Charlotte spillover.

In 1990, these Republican areas helped boost GOP Sen. Jesse
Helms to a 53 percent showing in the 8th District. In 1992
presidential voting, George Bush carried the district's western
section.

Anson County and the counties east of the Pee Dee River are
more rural and agriculture-oriented; they also have a higher
percentage of black voters than the rest of the 8th. Of North
Carolina's 10 white-majority congressional districts, the 8th has
the highest percentage of blacks—23 percent.

Blacks and American Indians make up a majority in the
Democratic stronghold of Hoke County. A small portion of
Robeson County—home to a significant number of Lumbee
Indians—is grafted onto the district's far southeastern fringe.
Most of the county's Democratic-voting Indians are in the 7th
District.

In the 1992 presidential election, Bill Clinton easily won
Anson, Hoke, Richmond and Robeson counties.

Neighboring Cumberland County is home to Fort Bragg and
a chunk of black voters. The county is parceled among the 1st,
7th and 8th districts, all of which delve into the city of
Fayetteville.

Moore County, in the Sandhills region, was once Democratic,

but it is now an anomaly in the Democratic east. A steady stream of retirees to resorts and golfing communities has made it a Republican bastion. Most of the county—including the resorts of Pinehurst and Southern Pines—is in the 4th.

Election Returns

	8th District	Democrat	Republican
1992	President*	81,697 (42.0%)	85,758 (44.1%)
	House	113,162 (59.3%)	71,842 (37.6%)
1990	Senate	76,022 (47.0%)	85,693 (53.0%)
1988	President	67,736 (42.0%)	93,425 (58.0%)
	Governor	74,794 (46.2%)	87,063 (53.8%)

*Vote for Perot was 27,019 (13.9%).

Demographics

Population   552,387

Percent change from 1980   3.1%

Land area   4,439 square miles

Population per square mile   124

Counties, 1990 population

Anson 23,474	Moore (pt.) 15,200
Cabarrus 98,935	Richmond 44,518
Cumberland (pt.) 64,487	Robeson (pt.) 23,631
Hoke 22,856	Rowan (pt.) 51,961
Iredell (pt.) 11,172	Scotland 33,754
Mecklenburg (pt.) 3,077	Stanly 51,765
Montgomery 23,346	Union 84,211

Cities, 1990 population (10,000 or more)

Albemarle 14,939	Laurinburg 11,643
Concord 27,347	Monroe 16,127
Kannapolis 29,696	Salisbury (pt.) 11,058

Race and Hispanic origin
White 72.8%
Black 23.2%
American Indian, Eskimo, or Aleut. 2.5%
Asian or Pacific Islander 0.8%
Other 0.6%
Hispanic origin 1.4%

Ancestry

American 11.9%	Irish 11.3%
Dutch 2.2%	Italian 1.2%
English 11.0%	Scotch Irish 6.0%
French 1.7%	Scottish 2.7%
German 19.0%	

Universities/colleges, 1990-1991 enrollment
Anson Community College, Polkton 885
Barber-Scotia College, Concord 422
Davidson College, Davidson 1,508
Livingstone College, Salisbury 682
Montgomery Community College, Troy 543
Pfeiffer College, Misenheimer 958
Richmond Community College, Hamlet 1,002
Rowan Cabarrus Community College, Salisbury 2,991
St. Andrews Presbyterian College, Laurinburg 719
Stanly Community College, Albemarle 1,303
Wingate College, Wingate 1,558

Newspapers, total circulation (in all districts)
Charlotte Observer 230,883
Concord Daily Tribune 12,796
Fayetteville Observer-Times 71,114
Kannapolis Daily Independent 10,750
Monroe Enquirer Journal 13,876
Raleigh News & Observer 142,433
Richmond County Daily Journal 8,718
Salisbury Post 25,256

Commercial television stations, affiliations
ADI: Charlotte (60%), Raleigh-Durham (24%), Greensboro-Winston Salem-High Point (11%) and Wilmington (5%)
WFCT, Fayetteville (None)

Cable television systems, total subscribers
Cablevision of Fayetteville; Fayetteville 65,000
Century Cable; Laurinburg 6,282
Monroe Cable TV Inc.; Monroe 12,300
Rockingham-Hamlet Cablevision; Rockingham 10,915
Vision Cable of Albemarle; Albemarle 10,866
Vision Cable of Metrolina; Kannapolis 27,990

Military installations, 1991
Badin Air Force Guard Station, Badin 29

Businesses and other major employers
Fieldcrest Cannon Inc.; Kannapolis; cotton mills 6,500
West Point-Pepperell Inc./Scotland Plant; Wagram; cotton mills 2,000
Union Underwear Co. Inc./Fruit of the Loom; Rockingham; knitting mills 2,000
Philip Morris Inc.; Concord; cigarettes 1,700
Tyson Foods Inc./Holly Farm Foods; Monroe; poultry products 1,601
Cabarrus Memorial Hospital; Concord 1,296
Burlington Industries Inc.; Raeford; wool mills 1,258
House of Raeford Farms Inc.; Raeford; poultry products 1,200
American Marketing Industries/Allison Mfg. Co.; Albemarle; outerwear 1,200
Abbott Laboratories; Laurinburg; pharmaceuticals 1,000
Dawson Consumer Products Inc.; Wadesboro; knitting mills 1,000
Teledyne Industries Inc.; Monroe; nonferrous rolling/drawing 1,000
County of Moore/Board of Education; Carthage 980
Wiscassett Mills Co.; Albemarle; yarn/thread mills 900
Southbury Rowan Headstart; Salisbury; child day care 853
Perdue Farms Inc.; Rockingham; poultry products 850
Fieldcrest Cannon Inc.; Concord; cotton mills 850
Cone Mills Corp.; Salisbury; cotton mills 795
Sara Lee Corp./L'eggs Products; Rockingham; knitting mills 790
Collins & Aikman Corp.; Albemarle; auto carpeting 765
Ithaca Industries Inc.; Robbins; knitting mills 750
Russell Hosiery Mills Inc./Fruit of the Loom; Star; knitting mills 720
Dominion Yarn Corp.; Landis; yarn/thread mills 700
Libbey-Owens-Ford Co.; Laurinburg; flat glass 675
Eaton Corp.; Laurinburg; rubber products 660
Aluminum Co. of America; Badin; aluminum production 660

Union Underwear Co. Inc.; Albemarle; yarn/thread mills 630

Burlington Industries Inc.; Cordova; man-made fabric mills 625

Croft Metals Inc.; Lumber Bridge; metal products 600

Union Memorial Hospital Inc.; Monroe 540

Davidson College; Davidson 515

9th District

West Central — Part of Charlotte

The boom times of the 1970s and 1980s have transformed Charlotte into the economic colossus of North Carolina and a rival to Atlanta in regional economic clout. With a highly diversified economy, Charlotte serves as a supply, service and distribution center for the Piedmont region of North and South Carolina. The city's big banking concerns have expanded their influence beyond the southeast, becoming prominent players in financial affairs all along the eastern seaboard. And if having a professional basketball team is a prerequisite for a city to claim national prominence, then the recent arrival of the Hornets franchise meets that condition.

The Uptown central business district has the headquarters of the Duke Power Co., NationsBank and First Union Bank as well as numerous other banking and insurance operations. Many of the white-collar executives who work in the downtown office towers commute from the affluent southeastern part of the city, where the old-line GOP establishment is based.

The city's Republican leanings are leavened by working-class Democratic allegiances and a black community that accounts for one-third of the population. The city weathered racial tensions over busing in the early 1970s, and in 1983 Charlotte elected its first black mayor, Harvey B. Gantt. He won virtually all the black vote, but also drew significant white support.

Attending Charlotte's economic prosperity has been rampant growth in the city and surrounding Mecklenburg County, leading to problems with traffic congestion and scraps between established neighborhoods and developers. The county once had substantial rural areas, particularly in the north, but the pastoral lands are giving way to suburban sprawl.

Politically, Mecklenburg is a mixed bag. Blacks and working-class whites keep the county competitive for Democrats at the state and local levels. In 1990, Gantt, the Democratic nominee against GOP Sen. Jesse Helms, carried 58 percent of the county's vote. Former Democratic Gov. James B. Hunt Jr. won Mecklenburg with 53 percent in his 1992 bid to recapture the office.

Presidential elections are a different story. From 1980-1992 the county went Republican in the White House contests, albeit narrowly for George Bush in 1992.

The 9th used to contain the county in its entirety, but 1992 redistricting divided it between the 9th and 12th districts (with a small part in the 8th). Most of the county's blacks, who live north and west of the central city, are included in the black-majority 12th.

Mecklenburg County has roughly two-thirds of the 9th's population, and, without Charlotte's black votes, the district is a GOP stronghold.

The 12th cuts a thin line west through the 9th, into Gastonia (Gaston County) to siphon out more black votes. Most of the Republican, textile-oriented county is in the 9th, though, accounting for nearly a third of the district's population.

Election Returns

	9th District	Democrat	Republican
1992	President*	80,953 (32.5%)	131,335 (52.7%)
	House	74,583 (32.7%)	153,650 (67.3%)
1990	Senate	82,603 (45.2%)	100,268 (54.8%)
1988	President	58,054 (30.6%)	131,726 (69.4%)
	Governor	56,252 (29.3%)	135,996 (70.7%)

Vote for Perot was 36,706 (14.7%).

Demographics

Population 552,387

Percent change from 1980 3.0%

Land area 1,042 square miles

Population per square mile 530

Counties, 1990 population
Cleveland (pt.) 42,604   Mecklenburg (pt.) 346,167
Gaston (pt.) 163,616

Cities, 1990 population (10,000 or more)
Charlotte (pt.) 240,568   Matthews 13,651
Gastonia (pt.) 43,686   Mint Hill 11,567

Race and Hispanic origin
White 89.1%
Black 8.9%
American Indian, Eskimo, or Aleut. 0.3%
Asian or Pacific Islander 1.3%
Other 0.3%
Hispanic origin 1.1%

Ancestry
American 9.8%   Irish 16.4%
Dutch 2.9%   Italian 2.7%
English 15.9%   Polish 1.5%
French 2.7%   Scotch Irish 8.8%
German 23.4%   Scottish 3.4%

Universities/colleges, 1990-1991 enrollment
Belmont Abbey College, Belmont 1,022
Gardner-Webb College, Boiling Springs 2,074
Gaston College, Dallas 3,503
Johnson C. Smith University, Charlotte 1,182
Queens College, Charlotte 1,579
University of North Carolina, Charlotte 14,699

Newspapers, total circulation (in all districts)
Charlotte Observer 230,883
Gastonia Gazette 40,821
Shelby Star 18,192

Commercial television stations, affiliations
ADI: Charlotte (100%)
WJZY, Belmont (None)
WBTV, Charlotte (CBS)
WCCB, Charlotte (Fox)
WCNC-TV, Charlotte (NBC)
WSOC-TV, Charlotte (ABC)

Cable television systems, total subscribers
Cablevision of Belmont; Mt. Holly 8,310

Cablevision of Charlotte; Charlotte 93,684
Cablevision of Gastonia; Gastonia 14,082
Jones Intercable Inc.; Cramerton 10,026
Jones Intercable Inc.; Kings Mountain 7,615
Vision Cable of North Carolina; Mint Hill 38,500
Vision Cable of Shelby Inc.; Shelby 14,000

Military installations, 1991

Charlotte/Douglas Intl. Airport Air Force Guard Station, Charlotte 1,362

Businesses and other major employers

IBM Corp.; Charlotte; computer equipment 5,000
Charlotte Mecklenburg Hospital Inc.; Charlotte 4,000
PCA National Inc.; Matthews; photographic studios 3,300
Duke Power Co.; Charlotte; electric services 2,100
AMP Inc.; Lowell; electronic components 2,000
Carolina Freight Corp.; Cherryville; trucking services 2,000
University of North Carolina; Charlotte 1,900
General Tire Inc.; Charlotte; tires 1,800
Duke Power Co./McGuire Nuclear Station; Huntersville; electric services 1,800
USAir Group Inc.; Charlotte; airline/aiport services 1,547
NationsBank; Charlotte; commercial banks 1,500
Wachovia Bank & Trust Co.; Charlotte; commercial banks 1,500
Dana Corp./Wix Div.; Gastonia; motor vehicle parts 1,500
Hoechst Celanese Corp.; Charlotte; textile management 1,500
Gaston Memorial Hospital Inc.; Gastonia 1,486
Freightliner Corp.; Mt. Holly; construction machinery 1,400
First Union Bank of North Carolina; Charlotte; commercial banks 1,300
Royal Group Inc.; Charlotte; insurance services 1,100
Westinghouse Electric Corp.; Charlotte; turbines 1,000
County of Gaston; Gastonia 975
Textron Inc./Homelite Div.; Gastonia; construction machinery 850
Du Pont E. I. De Nemours & Co.; Charlotte; plastics/synthetics 800
Family Dollar Stores Inc.; Matthews; variety stores 800
Union Underwear Co. Inc.; Kings Mountain; outerwear 750
Systems Assoc. Inc.; Charlotte; computer services 750
Ithaca Industries Inc.; Gastonia; knitting mills 725
Philips & Dupont Optical Co.; Grover; glass/glassware 700
Dixie Yarns Inc.; Gastonia; yarn/thread mills 700
Kemet Electronics Corp.; Shelby; electronic components 700
American Red Cross; Charlotte; health services 700
Oak White Manor Inc.; Kings Mountain; nursing 700
Carolina Mills Inc.; Gastonia; yarn/thread mills 650
County of Mecklenburg/Social Services Dept.; Charlotte 650
Charlotte Pipe & Foundry Co./Plastics; Charlotte; plastic products 600
Barclays American Corp.; Charlotte; credit institutions 600
Winn-Dixie Charlotte Inc.; Charlotte; warehousing 600
Eaton Corp.; Kings Mountain; transmissions 600
Chas T. Main Inc.; Charlotte; engineering services 585
Staffamerica Corp.; Charlotte; personnel supply services 580
Radiator Specialty Co.; Charlotte; chemical products 550
Allstate Insurance Co.; Charlotte; insurance services 550

10th District

West — Hickory; Lincolnton

Splashed across the western Piedmont Plateau and the Appalachian and Blue Ridge mountains is the most rock-ribbed Republican district in North Carolina—the 10th.

In 1990, GOP Sen. Jesse Helms posted his best showing in any North Carolina district in what was the 10th, capturing 66 percent of the vote. In 1992 presidential voting, George Bush won the 10th with more than 50 percent, one of his better showings in the country.

The 10th is composed of six whole counties and parts of 11 more. It is small-town North Carolina: No city has more than 30,000 residents. Textiles, furniture and agriculture form the backbone of the economy.

From the main body of the district, three heads sprout forth: one in the north, one reaching northwest to the Tennessee border and one stretching west toward Asheville, but stopping short.

Catawba County, in the main cluster of counties, is the population center. The furniture-making industry—particularly upholstered furniture—employs a large segment of the work force in Hickory (the largest city entirely in the 10th). There is also production of cotton and synthetic yarns.

Neighboring Iredell County—split among the 8th, 10th and 12th districts—is mostly rural and agricultural, with some manufacturing. It is the second-most populous jurisdiction in the 10th.

Northeast of Catawba County, the district takes in parts of Davie and Forsyth counties and all of Yadkin County. The Forsyth portion is west of Winston-Salem.

Textile- and furniture-oriented Davie and textile- and to-bacco-producing Yadkin are die-hard Republican bastions. Yadkin was one of just 13 North Carolina counties to back Barry Goldwater in 1964. In 1980, when the Republican gubernatorial nominee pulled in an anemic 37 percent, Yadkin and Davie counties were in his corner. Helms is especially popular in these counties: In 1990, he won 70 percent in Davie.

West of Yadkin County, the district line makes a loop through Republican Wilkes County. A section of the 5th District slices down into the 10th; beyond it are more Republican votes in mountainous Avery and Mitchell counties, on the Tennessee border.

In 1992, both counties voted a straight Republican ticket: presidential, Senate, gubernatorial and House. Both backed successful GOP Senate challenger Lauch Faircloth over Democratic Sen. Terry Sanford by better than 2-to-1.

A segment of the 10th reaches into the woodlands of Western North Carolina, taking in parts of Buncombe, Henderson, McDowell, Polk and Rutherford counties. Forestry, tourism and recreation are staples of the local economies here. Buncombe is competitive for both parties but does not provide enough votes to make a dent in the 10th. The other counties lean Republican.

Election Returns

	10th District	Democrat	Republican
1992	President*	76,021 (31.9%)	127,067 (53.2%)
	House	79,206 (33.7%)	148,999 (63.4%)
1990	Senate	64,373 (34.5%)	122,486 (65.6%)

10th District	Democrat	Republican
1988 President	60,287 (30.1%)	140,002 (69.9%)
Governor	67,654 (33.2%)	135,878 (66.8%)

*Vote for Perot was 35,546 (14.9%).

Demographics

Population 552,386

Percent change from 1980 3.6%

Land area 4,367 square miles

Population per square mile 127

Counties, 1990 population

Alexander 27,544	Iredell (pt.) 60,613
Avery 14,867	Lincoln 50,319
Buncombe (pt.) 15,597	McDowell (pt.) 8,755
Burke (pt.) 31,160	Mitchell 14,433
Caldwell (pt.) 49,525	Polk (pt.) 1,364
Catawba 118,412	Rutherford (pt.) 9,283
Davie (pt.) 12,280	Wilkes (pt.) 43,203
Forsyth (pt.) 57,730	Yadkin 30,488
Henderson (pt.) 6,813	

Cities, 1990 population (10,000 or more)

Hickory 28,301	Statesville (pt.) 11,861

Race and Hispanic origin

White 93.7%
Black 5.5%
American Indian, Eskimo, or Aleut. 0.2%
Asian or Pacific Islander 0.4%
Other 0.3%
Hispanic origin 0.7%

Ancestry

American 15.3%	Irish 14.7%
Dutch 4.3%	Italian 1.4%
English 14.5%	Scotch Irish 5.1%
French 2.1%	Scottish 2.6%
German 26.9%	

Universities/colleges, 1990-1991 enrollment

Caldwell Community College, Lenoir 2,613
Catawba Valley Community College, Hickory 3,161
Lees-McRae College, Banner Elk 863
Lenoir-Rhyne College, Hickory 1,648
Mayland Community College, Spruce Pine 813
Mitchell Community College, Statesville 1,431

Newspapers, total circulation (in all districts)

Asheville Citizen-Times 64,175
Charlotte Observer 230,883
Greensboro News & Record 112,897
Hendersonville Times-News 20,996
Hickory Daily Record 24,977
Lenoir News-Topic 12,880
Morganton News Herald 11,442
Statesville Record & Landmark 16,844
Winston-Salem Journal 90,650

Commercial television stations, affiliations

ADI: Charlotte (48%), Greensboro-Winston Salem-High Point (28%), Greenville-Spartanburg-Asheville (18%) and Bristol-Kingsport-Johnson City (6%)
WHKY-TV, Hickory (None)

Cable television systems, total subscribers

Catawba Valley Cable TV; Hickory 24,438
Cencom of North Carolina; Lenoir 14,500
Falcon Cable TV; North Wilkesboro 8,280
Falcon Classic Cable; High Peak Mt. 9,600
Prestige Cable TV Inc.; Statesville 9,847
Summit Cable Services of Forsyth County; Rural Hall 18,428
Summit Cable Services of Forsyth County; Winston Salem 42,541
TCI of Asheville; Asheville 26,791
TCI of North Carolina; Morganton 6,600

Businesses and other major employers

Baxter Healthcare Corp.; Marion; pharmaceuticals 2,700
Pilot Research Corp.; Valdese; research services 1,500
County of Catawba/Board of Education; Newton 1,400
County of Caldwell/Board of Education; Lenoir 1,253
Comm/Scope Inc.; Catawba; nonferrous rolling/drawing 1,200
Alcatel National Cable Systems Inc.; Claremont; nonferrous rolling/drawing 1,200
General Electric Co.; Hickory; electric distribution equipment 1,000
Unifi Inc.; Yadkinville; textile finishing 1,000
Frye Regional Medical Center; Hickory 1,000
Fab Industries Inc./Mohican Mills; Lincolnton; knitting mills 975
Kincaid Furniture Co. Inc.; Hudson; furniture 950
Merchants Distributors Inc.; Hickory; grocery products 920
Henredon Furniture Industries; Spruce Pine; furniture 900
Sara Lee Corp./Hanes Hosiery; Yadkinville; knitting mills 900
Catawba Memorial Hospital; Hickory 900
Iredell Memorial Hospital; Statesville 884
Home Curtain Corp.; Mooresville; textile products 800
Joan Fabrics Corp.; Hickory; man-made fabric mills 800
Steelcase Inc.; Fletcher; office furniture 800
Bassett Furniture Industries Inc.; Conover; reupholstery 800
Cochrane Furniture Co.; Lincolnton; furniture 768
Bassett Furniture Industries Inc; Newton; furniture 750
County of Catawba/Industrial Development Commission; Newton 670
Sherrill Furniture Co.; Hickory; furniture 630
Clark Components Intl./Clark Hurth Components; Statesville; motor vehicles/equipment 625
Midway Carpet Distributors; Newton; furniture stores 612
R. R. Donnelley & Sons Co.; Newton; commercial printing 600
Intercraft Industries Corp.; Statesville; wood products 600
Ethan Allen Inc.; Maiden; furniture 600
Lane Co. Inc./Hickory Chair Div.; Hickory; furniture 600
American Thread Co. Inc.; Marion; yarn/thread mills 600
Caldwell Community College; Hudson 575
Thomasville Upholstery Inc.; Statesville; furniture 573

Kewaunee Scientific Corp.; Statesville; laboratory apparatus 565

Timken Co.; Iron Station; steel products 550

Rockwell Intl. Corp./On-Highway Products Div.; Fletcher; motor vehicle equipment 510

11th District

West — Asheville

In the 1980s, the mountains of western North Carolina were the stage for arguably the most competitive congressional district in the nation. In 1980, 1982, 1984, 1986 and 1990, voters tossed out their incumbent. Every contest between 1982 and 1990 was decided by fewer than 5,000 votes.

The current 11th District is slightly more Democratic than the 1980s version, but as voters proved in the 1992 House race, party affiliation counts for little.

Most of the mountainous district is covered by the Cherokee, Nantahala and Pisgah national forests or the Great Smoky Mountains National Park. Accordingly, the local political and economic agenda often revolves around development and natural resource issues. Tourism and recreation revenues also have a disproportionate impact on local economies, especially in the poorer, far western tip of the state.

The heart of Western North Carolina is Asheville (Buncombe County). Known as "The Land of the Sky" for its location high in the Blue Ridge Mountains, the city is the biggest in the 11th.

An expanding health-care industry and some light industry anchor Asheville's economy, and the city is also a hub for the southern Appalachian and Cherokee arts and crafts produced in the region.

Asheville and surrounding communities have found recent years especially prosperous, due to a wave of newcomers who have discovered the region's low property taxes and temperate climate.

Retirees and business executives seeking a second home have fueled a building boom in towns such as Flat Rock and Hendersonville in Henderson County, and in Tryon (Polk County), where upscale condominiums are popping up on mountainsides and in the piney woods. The University of North Carolina-Asheville responded to the influx by setting up the North Carolina Center for Creative Retirement.

The combination of retirees and traditional mountain Republicans keeps the 11th competitive, despite a wide Democratic registration advantage. Two traditional sources of Democratic support—labor unions and black voters—are mostly absent from Asheville, but populous Buncombe County still tends to support Democrats for local and statewide office. Buncombe usually leans Republican in presidential elections, although it did back Bill Clinton in 1992. About 30 percent of the 11th District's people live here.

The second-most populous county in the 11th is Henderson County. Retirees have helped move Henderson and Polk into the GOP column; both supported George Bush in 1988 and 1992. Thousands stood in pouring rain to catch Bush's brief visit to Hendersonville's apple festival in 1992.

Outside Buncombe County, there is some labor strength in the paper and pulp mill towns. The poorer Tennessee-border counties have experienced trying times as several sawmills have shut down; this translated into support for Clinton in 1992.

Election Returns

	11th District	Democrat	Republican
1992	President*	105,064 (43.0%)	104,383 (42.8%)
	House	108,003 (45.3%)	130,158 (54.7%)
1990	Senate	89,942 (47.0%)	101,383 (53.0%)
1988	President	87,066 (42.3%)	118,667 (57.7%)
	Governor	93,856 (44.6%)	116,631 (55.4%)

Vote for Perot was 34,646 (14.2%).

Demographics

Population 552,387

Percent change from 1980 4.0%

Land area 6,071 square miles

Population per square mile 91

Counties, 1990 population

Buncombe (pt.) 159,224	Macon 23,499
Cherokee 20,170	Madison 16,953
Clay 7,155	McDowell (pt.) 26,926
Cleveland (pt.) 42,110	Polk (pt.) 13,052
Graham 7,196	Rutherford (pt.) 47,635
Haywood 46,942	Swain 11,268
Henderson (pt.) 62,472	Transylvania 25,520
Jackson 26,846	Yancey 15,419

Cities, 1990 population (10,000 or more)

Asheville 61,607	Shelby (pt.) 14,659

Race and Hispanic origin
White 90.9%
Black 7.2%
American Indian, Eskimo, or Aleut. 1.4%
Asian or Pacific Islander 0.3%
Other 0.2%
Hispanic origin 0.7%

Ancestry

American 12.2%	Irish 18.2%
Dutch 3.6%	Italian 1.4%
English 18.0%	Scotch Irish 6.8%
French 2.5%	Scottish 3.2%
German 17.6%	

Universities/colleges, 1990-1991 enrollment
Asheville Buncombe Tech College, Asheville 3,467
Brevard College, Brevard 779
Cecils Junior College of Business, Asheville 343
Cleveland Community College, Shelby 1,506
Haywood Community College, Clyde 1,236
Isothermal Community College, Spindale 1,576
Mars Hill College, Mars Hill 1,331
McDowell Tech Community College, Marion 600
Montreat-Anderson College, Montreat 387
Southwestern Community College, Sylva 1,345
Tri-County Community College, Murphy 912
University of North Carolina, Asheville 3,271
Warren Wilson College, Swannanoa 573
Western Carolina University, Cullowhee 6,411

Newspapers, total circulation (in all districts)

Asheville Citizen-Times 64,175
Charlotte Observer 230,883
Gastonia Gazette 40,821
Hendersonville Times-News 20,996
Shelby Star 18,192

Commercial television stations, affiliations

ADI: Greenville-Spartanburg-Asheville (85%), Chattanooga (8%), Atlanta (4%) and Charlotte (3%)
  WHNS, Greenville-Spartanburg-Asheville (Fox)
  WASV-TV, Asheville (None)
  WLOS, Asheville (ABC)
  WEMT, Greenville (Fox)

Cable television systems, total subscribers

Cencom of North Carolina; Asheville 11,509
Sammons Communications Inc.; Waynesville 9,700
Sylvan Valley CATV Co.; Brevard 6,553
TCI of Asheville; Asheville 26,791
US Cable; Hendersonville 13,500
Vision Cable of Shelby Inc.; Shelby 14,000

Businesses and other major employers

Champion Intl. Corp.; Canton; paper mills 1,926
Memorial Mission Hospital Inc.; Asheville 1,875
P. H. Glatfelter Co./Ecusta Div.; Pisgah Forest; paper mills 1,600
PPG Industries Inc.; Shelby; glass/glassware 1,500
Western Carolina University; Cullowhee 1,450
St. Joseph's Hospital; Asheville 1,250
Du Pont E. I. De Nemours & Co.; Brevard; professional/commercial equipment 1,200
Collins & Aikman Corp./Mastercraft Div.; Spindale; furniture 1,200
General Electric Co.; Hendersonville; electrical goods 1,200
Dayco Products Inc.; Waynesville; foam rubber products 1,200
County of Buncombe; Asheville 1,200
BASF Corp.; Enka; yarn/thread mills 1,193
U.S. Veterans Affairs Dept.; Asheville; hospital 1,068
Cone Mills Corp.; Cliffside; cotton mills 1,016
Stonecutter Mills Corp.; Spindale; cotton mills 1,000
County of Haywood/School District; Waynesville 1,000
City of Asheville; Asheville 950
Wilson Tree Co. Inc.; Shelby; landscape services 900
B. E. & K. Construction Co.; Canton; building construction 900
Fasco Industries Inc.; Shelby; electrical industrial controls 840
Beacon Mfg. Co.; Swannanoa; cotton mills 800
Marion Fabrics Inc.; Marion; cotton mills 755
Champion Products Inc.; Asheville; knitting mills 750
Collins & Aikman Corp.; Old Fort; carpets/rugs 730
Astronautics Corp. of America; Black Mountain; aircraft parts 700
Asheville Industries Inc.; Arden; engineering services 680
New Cherokee Corp.; Spindale; man-made fabric mills 655
Square D Co./Control Business Products; Asheville; electric switchgears 651
Tanner Companies Inc.; Rutherfordton; outerwear 650
Margaret R. Pardee Memorial Hospital; Hendersonville 625
Sara Lee Corp./Hanes Printables; Forest City; knitting mills 620
ITT Corp.; Asheville; motor vehicle equipment 600

Asheville Buncombe Tech College, Asheville 586
Doran Textiles Inc.; Shelby; man-made fabric mills 575
Cone Mills Corp./Haynes Plant; Henrietta; cotton mills 574
Drexel Heritage Furnishings; Marion; furniture 550
Broyhill Furniture Industries; Rutherfordton; furniture 544
Kimberly-Clark Corp./Berkley Mills; Balfour; medical instruments/supplies 537
Westinghouse Electric Corp.; Arden; electrical industrial apparatus 525
County of Buncombe/District Courts; Asheville 517
Haywood County Hospital; Clyde 515
Cleveland Mills Co.; Lawndale; knitting mills 506

12th District

The I-85 Corridor — Parts of Charlotte, Greensboro and Durham

The 12th is best described as the mother of all gerrymanders, a congressional district so notorious in its design that it sparked an editorial in *The Wall Street Journal* and drew criticism from 1992 GOP presidential candidate Patrick J. Buchanan during a campaign stop in North Carolina.

The scandal was in the shape. Known as the "I-85 District," the serpentine 12th winds across the Piedmont Plateau mostly along the Interstate 85 corridor, linking small parts of 10 counties while not encompassing a single whole county (see district profile map on page 548).

The district was the Democratic-controlled Legislature's response to the 1992 Justice Department mandate that North Carolina have two majority-minority districts. Rather than significantly weaken white Democratic incumbents, the 12th was stretched to extremes.

Through the marvels of computer technology, mapmakers were able to pick and choose precincts to give the 12th a 57 percent black population and an overwhelming 4-to-1 Democratic registration advantage.

The predominantly black neighborhoods of Durham, Greensboro, Winston-Salem, Charlotte and Gastonia provide much of the vote. The district closely parallels the old Southern Railroad system route, which had a hand in dictating black settlement patterns in a bygone era of the state's history.

Durham is the 12th's eastern frontier. Tobacco processing was once the big game in town here, but nowadays, Duke University is Durham County's largest single employer.

Durham has long been home to a black political and economic elite, whose rise was nurtured by an organization that used to be known as the Durham Committee for Negro Affairs. Now referred to simply as the Durham Committee, the group has been a locus of power in black politics since pre-World War II days.

Besides Duke, the district also takes in several of the state's historically black colleges and universities.

From Durham, the lines travel west, cutting into Burlington (Alamance County) and into the cities of the Piedmont Triad: Greensboro (Guilford County), Winston-Salem (Forsyth County) and High Point (Guilford County).

More than half the district lives in either Guilford (Greensboro) or Mecklenburg (Charlotte) counties. The 12th only covers part of Charlotte, but it is the population anchor of the district; it contains more black voters than any city in the 12th.

Any candidate for the 12th must be careful, though, not to

couch his or her message in Charlotte-oriented terms, for voters in other cities along I-85 have expressed concern about a Charlotte-dominated district that will be less attuned to their local interests.

Economically, the 12th is widely diverse. Since it courses through six of the state's 10 largest cities, it relies on the fortunes of the state's traditional industries—tobacco, textiles and furniture. In Charlotte, banking and financial concerns dominate the local economy.

Election Returns

	12th District	Democrat	Republican
1992	President*	127,941 (66.0%)	49,105 (25.3%)
	House	127,262 (70.4%)	49,402 (27.3%)
1990	Senate	120,900 (71.0%)	49,286 (29.0%)
1988	President	102,503 (62.5%)	61,423 (37.5%)
	Governor	102,371 (61.8%)	63,278 (38.2%)

*Vote for Perot was 16,936 (8.7%).

Demographics

Population 552,387

Percent change from 1980 (new district in the 1990s)

Land area 829 square miles

Population per square mile 666

Counties, 1990 population

Alamance (pt.) 24,487	Guilford (pt.) 135,760
Davidson (pt.) 23,484	Iredell (pt.) 21,146
Durham (pt.) 94,492	Mecklenburg (pt.) 162,189
Forsyth (pt.) 53,492	Orange (pt.) 2,836
Gaston (pt.) 11,477	Rowan (pt.) 23,024

Cities, 1990 population (10,000 or more)

Charlotte (pt.) 155,366	Greensboro (pt.) 98,787
Durham (pt.) 75,030	High Point (pt.) 27,506
Gastonia (pt.) 11,046	Winston-Salem (pt.) 36,830

Race and Hispanic origin

White 41.8%
Black 56.6%
American Indian, Eskimo, or Aleut. 0.4%
Asian or Pacific Islander 0.9%
Other 0.3%
Hispanic origin 0.9%

Ancestry

American 7.3%	German 9.8%
Dutch 1.5%	Irish 7.2%
English 7.4%	Scotch Irish 3.1%
French 1.2%	Scottish 1.3%

Universities/colleges, 1990-1991 enrollment

Alamance Community College, Haw River 3,569
Bennett College, Greensboro 586
Central Piedmont Community College, Charlotte 16,311
Davidson Community College, Lexington 2,313
Duke University, Durham 11,293
Durham Tech Community College, Durham 4,812
Guilford Tech Community College, Jamestown 6,996
High Point University, High Point 2,308
North Carolina Agricultural & Technical State University, Greensboro 6,595
North Carolina Central University, Durham 5,482
North Carolina School of the Arts, Winston-Salem 486

Newspapers, total circulation (in all districts)

Burlington Times-News 29,480
Charlotte Observer 230,883
Durham Herald-Sun 50,987
Gastonia Gazette 40,821
Greensboro News & Record 112,897
High Point Enterprise 30,592
Lexington Dispatch 14,487
Raleigh News & Observer 142,433
Salisbury Post 25,256
Statesville Record & Landmark 16,844
Winston-Salem Journal 90,650

Commercial television stations, affiliations

ADI: Greensboro-Winston Salem-High Point (39%), Charlotte (35%) and Raleigh-Durham (26%)

Cable television systems, total subscribers

Cablevision of Alamance; Burlington 20,709
Cablevision of Charlotte; Charlotte 93,684
Durham Cablevision Inc.; Durham 45,000
Summit Cable Services of Forsyth County; Winston-Salem 42,541
Time Warner; Greensboro 48,000
Vision Cable of North Carolina; Mint Hill 38,500

Businesses and other major employers

Duke University & Duke University Medical Center; Durham 16,350
R. J. R. Nabisco Inc.; Winston-Salem; cigarettes 10,000
City of Charlotte; Charlotte 5,154
County of Mecklenburg; Charlotte 3,753
Wachovia Corp.; Winston-Salem; commercial banks 3,200
Presbyterian Hospital; Charlotte 3,100
Southern Bell Telephone & Telegraph Co.; Charlotte; telephone communications 3,000
Central Piedmont Community College; Charlotte 2,983
Moses H. Cone Memorial Hospital; Greensboro 2,980
Lorillard Inc.; Greensboro; cigarettes 2,500
Hoechst Celanese Corp.; Salisbury; plastics/synthetics 2,100
Cone Mills Corp./Olympic Products Co.; Greensboro; business services 2,080
Hubbell Inc.; Charlotte; electric lighting 2,000
Blue Cross/Blue Shield of North Carolina; Durham; medical service/health insurance 1,895
Lance Inc.; Charlotte; bakery products 1,700
Glaxo Inc.; Durham; pharmaceuticals 1,528
U.S. Postal Service; Charlotte 1,500
U.S. Veterans Affairs Dept.; Salisbury; hospital 1,350
Continental Graphics Corp./Delmar Photographic & Printing Co; Charlotte; publishing 1,300
Winn-Dixie Charlotte Inc.; Gastonia; grocery stores 1,258
North Carolina Agricultural & Technical State University, Greensboro 1,210
CCB Financial Corp.; Durham; commercial banks 1,200
Knight Publishing Co. Inc./Charlotte Observer; Charlotte; newspapers 1,184
City of High Point/Transit Systems; High Point 1,178
County of Durham; Durham 1,175

Integon Corp.; Winston-Salem; fire/marine/casualty insurance 1,144
Belk Stores Services Inc.; Charlotte; department stores 1,100
Liggett Group Inc./Liggett & Myers; Durham; cigarettes 1,000
Burlington Industries Inc.; Mooresville; cotton mills 1,000
Mercy Hospital; Charlotte 1,000
Rowan Memorial Hospital Inc.; Salisbury 965
ISS Intl. Service Systems; Charlotte; building services 950
Biggers Brothers Inc.; Charlotte; grocery products 850
Yellow Freight System Inc.; Charlotte; trucking services 850
U.S. Postal Service; Greensboro 850
North Carolina Central University; Durham 825
Alamance Community College; Haw River 785
County of Davidson; Lexington 744
Mantech Environmental Technology; Durham; research services 700
Great American Knitting Mills; Burlington; knitting mills 650
National Institute of Environmental Health Sciences; Durham 650
Interstate Brands Corp.; Charlotte; bakery products 600
Durham Tech Community College, Durham 600
Piedmont Publishing Co. Inc./Winston-Salem Journal; Winston-Salem; newspapers 598
Stroh Brewery Co.; Winston-Salem; brewery 550
Cone Mills Corp.; Greensboro; cotton mills 550
Burns Aerospace Corp.; Winston-Salem; furniture 550
Edward Weck Inc.; Durham; medical instruments/supplies 525
Cone Mills Corp.; Haw River; cotton mills 523
Pepsi Cola Bottling Co.; Winston-Salem; bottling 503

North Dakota

The decade of the 1980s is one that North Dakotans—and especially the North Dakota Republican Party—probably are glad to have behind them. With weakness in the agricultural economy and a drop in farmland values causing many small farms to disappear from the map, North Dakota became one of only four states in the nation to lose population during the 1980s, dropping 2 percent to just under 639,000. In the 1990s it has the unwelcome distinction of being the only state with fewer people now than it had in 1930.

The GOP too saw its fortunes decline during the 1980s. At the start of the decade, Republicans were riding high; Jimmy Carter had flopped spectacularly in the state's 1980 presidential voting, taking only 26 percent, the lowest for any Democratic nominee since the 1920s. Republicans captured the governorship, and they vastly outnumbered Democrats in the state Legislature.

But Democrats retook the governorship in 1984, and two years later—with economic hard times settling in—they won control of the state Senate for the first time in history. Many struggling farmers had come to view the state Democratic Party as the modern vehicle for an old force in North Dakota politics, the agrarian populist movement. The original organized expression of that populism was the Non-Partisan League (NPL), which early in this century spoke for the "little man" and his suspicions of concentrated business interests— railroads, banks and grain companies.

The legacy of the NPL is visible today in the state-owned bank and grain mill, and in a weak executive-strong legislature governmental system that provides for maximum citizen influence.

As the calendar turned to the 1990s, there were signs that agriculture in North Dakota was getting back on an even keel, albeit with large-scale, highly mechanized operations playing a more dominant role. In the 1992 election, Republican Edward T. Schafer won the governorship, and the state voted Republican for president, as it has in every postwar election except one (1964).

But George Bush in 1992 won with only 44 percent of the vote, barely better than Barry Goldwater's losing 1964 tally. Bill Clinton bombed, taking only 32 percent. Ross Perot captured 23 percent and ran second (ahead of Clinton) in 18 counties in the southern and western parts of the state, where agrarian populist discontent with the Establishment always has been most palpable.

Much of North Dakota's population exodus has occurred from the western portion of the state. As farmland values dropped during the 1980s, small farms began disappearing from the map. Too dry for a good wheat crop, the dry buttes and rolling grasslands attracted cattle ranches. There is also some energy development, although the area oil industry was hard hit by the 1980s slide in oil prices.

The coal industry in the southwestern part of the state also has been through some rough times, although it got a boost from the coal gasification plant in Beulah (Mercer County). The plant is the only such facility in North America. Constructed with grand expectations of transforming huge amounts of coal to natural gas, the plant's financial competitiveness suffered with the downturn in energy prices, but private interests bought it from the federal government in 1988 and turned a profit one year later.

Still, within the state, population migration in recent years has been from west to east. The biggest population centers are both on the Red River, which defines North Dakota's eastern border with Minnesota. Fargo (Cass County) grew 21 percent in the 1980s to a population of 74,000. To the north are the 49,000 residents of Grand Forks (Grand Forks County). With major medical facilities and the two major state universities (the University of North Dakota in Grand Forks and North Dakota State University in Fargo), eastern North Dakota offers most of the white-collar jobs that are available in the state.

The east is also the state's most prosperous agricultural area— the moisture in the soil allowed it to weather even the great dust storms of the 1930s. The Red River flows through a region that produces wheat, sugar beets and potatoes.

The two other population centers are in the central part of the state: Bismarck (Burleigh County) and Minot (Ward County). Bismarck is the state capital, and every fall representatives of the United Tribes (from all over the Americas) gather here for the International Powwow.

One of North Dakota's two major Air Force bases, Grand Forks, was added to the list in May 1993 of military facilities that may close.

NORTH DAKOTA

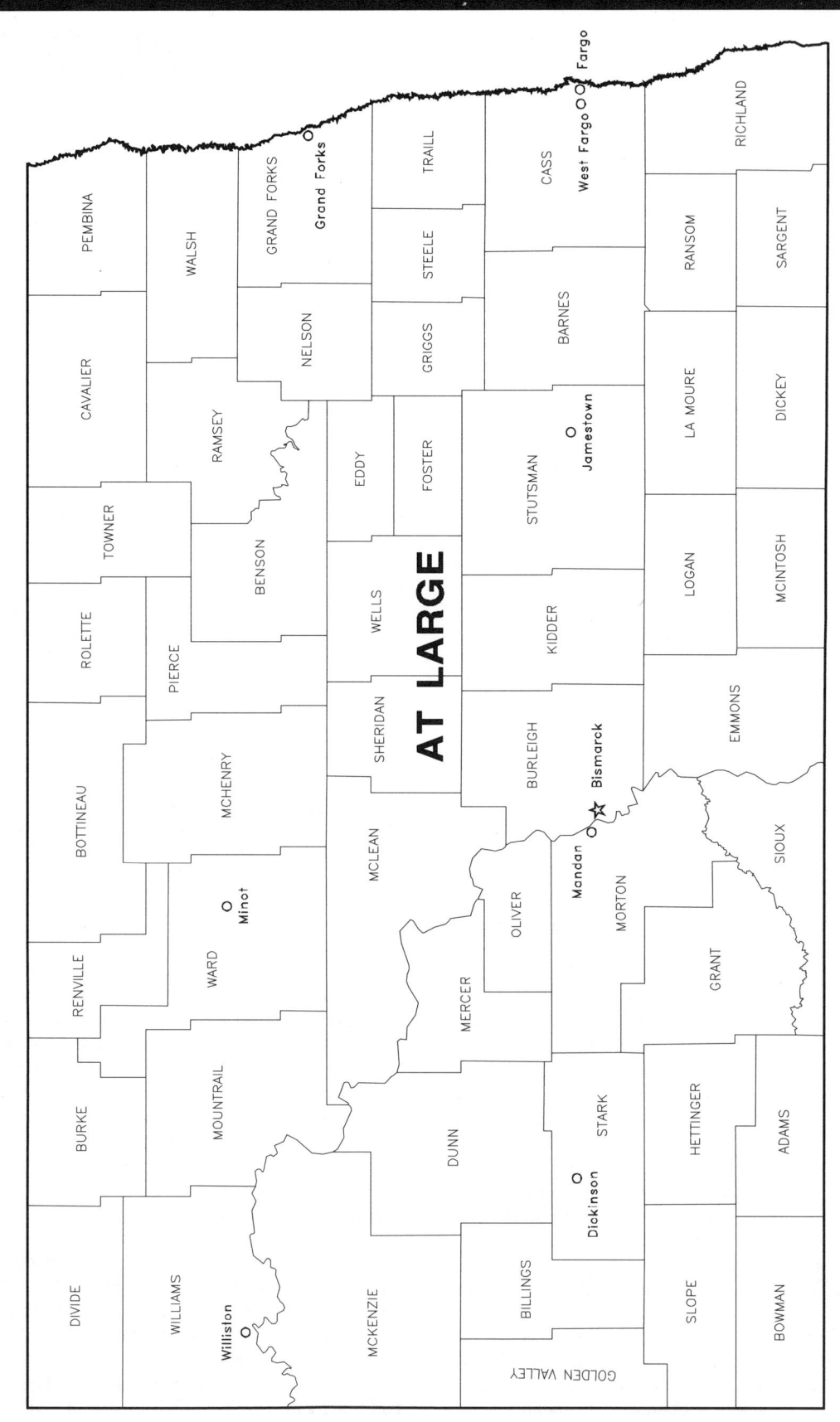

Table 1 Population

District	Population	Population under 18	Voting-age population	Median age
AL	638,800	175,385	463,415	32.4

Table 2 Voting-Age Persons

District	White*	Black*	American Indian, Eskimo, or Aleut*	Asian or Pacific Islander*	Other*	Hispanic*	Male*	Female*
AL	95.7%	0.5%	3.1%	0.5%	0.2%	0.6%	49.2%	50.8%

*As percent of voting-age population.

Table 3 Voting-Age Persons by Age Groups

District	18-24*	25-44*	45-54*	55-64*	65 and over*
AL	14.6%	41.9%	12.3%	11.5%	19.6%

*As percent of voting-age population.

Table 4 Income and Occupation

District	Median family income	Families in poverty	White collar*	Blue collar*	Service*	Farm*
AL	$28,707	10.9%	51.7%	21.6%	16.6%	10.1%

*As percent of employed persons age 16 and over.

Table 5 Education: School Years Completed

District	Less than grade 9*	Grades 9-12 no diploma*	High school diploma*	College bachelor's degree or higher*
AL	15.0%	8.3%	28.0%	18.1%

*As percent of persons age 25 and over.

Table 6 Housing and Residential Patterns

District	Owner occupied	Renter occupied	Urban	Rural
AL	65.6%	34.4%	53.3%	46.7%

Election Returns

	At Large	Democrat	Republican
1992	President*	99,168 (32.4%)	136,244 (44.5%)
	House	169,273 (56.8%)	117,442 (39.4%)
1988	President	127,739 (43.4%)	166,559 (56.6%)
	Senate	171,899 (60.4%)	112,937 (39.6%)
	Governor	179,007 (59.9%)	120,073 (40.1%)
1986	Senate	143,932 (50.4%)	141,812 (49.6%)

* Vote for Perot was 71,084 (23.2%).

Demographics

Population 638,800

Percent change from 1980 -2.1%

Land area 68,994 square miles

Population per square mile 9

Counties, 1990 population

Adams 3,174	McLean 10,457
Barnes 12,545	Mercer 9,808
Benson 7,198	Morton 23,700
Billings 1,108	Mountrail 7,021
Bottineau 8,011	Nelson 4,410
Bowman 3,596	Oliver 2,381
Burke 3,002	Pembina 9,238
Burleigh 60,131	Pierce 5,052
Cass 102,874	Ramsey 12,681
Cavalier 6,064	Ransom 5,921
Dickey 6,107	Renville 3,160
Divide 2,899	Richland 18,148
Dunn 4,005	Rolette 12,772
Eddy 2,951	Sargent 4,549
Emmons 4,830	Sheridan 2,148
Foster 3,983	Sioux 3,761
Golden Valley 2,108	Slope 907
Grand Forks 70,683	Stark 22,832
Grant 3,549	Steele 2,420
Griggs 3,303	Stutsman 22,241
Hettinger 3,445	Towner 3,627
Kidder 3,332	Traill 8,752
LaMoure 5,383	Walsh 13,840
Logan 2,847	Ward 57,921
McHenry 6,528	Wells 5,864
McIntosh 4,021	Williams 21,129
McKenzie 6,383	

Cities, 1990 population (10,000 or more)

Bismarck 49,256	Mandan 15,177
Dickinson 16,097	Minot 34,544
Fargo 74,111	West Fargo 12,287
Grand Forks 49,425	Williston 13,131
Jamestown 15,571	

Race and Hispanic origin

White 94.6%
Black 0.6%
American Indian, Eskimo, or Aleut. 4.1%
Asian or Pacific Islander 0.5%
Other 0.3%
Hispanic origin 0.7%

Ancestry

American 1.6%	Irish 8.4%
Czechoslovakian 2.6%	Norwegian 29.6%
Danish 1.7%	Polish 2.7%
Dutch 1.6%	Russian 2.9%
English 6.1%	Scotch Irish 1.3%
French 4.4%	Scottish 1.3%
German 50.9%	Swedish 5.6%

Universities/colleges, 1990-1991 enrollment

Bismarck State College, Bismarck 2,304
Dickinson State University, Dickinson 1,429
Jamestown College, Jamestown 899
Mayville State University, Mayville 763
Minot State University, Minot 3,637
North Dakota State College of Science, Wahpeton 2,116
North Dakota State University, Fargo 8,707
North Dakota State University, Bottineau 452
Standing Rock Community College, Fort Yates 202
Trinity Bible College, Ellendale 394

Turtle Mountain Community College, Belcourt 309
United Tribes Tech College, Bismarck 208
University of Mary, Bismarck 1,603
University of North Dakota, Grand Forks 11,659
University of North Dakota, Devils Lake 996
University of North Dakota, Williston 714
Valley City State University, Valley City 1,082

Newspapers, total circulation (in all districts)
Bismarck Tribune 30,929
Dickinson Press 6,922
Forum (Fargo) 53,270
Grand Forks Herald 38,953
Minot Daily News 24,553

Commercial television stations, affiliations
ADI: Minot-Bismarck-Dickinson (65%) and Fargo (35%)
  KBMY, Bismarck (ABC)
  KFYR-TV, Bismarck (NBC)
  KXMB-TV, Bismarck (CBS)
  WDAZ-TV, Devils Lake (ABC)
  KQCD-TV, Dickinson (NBC)
  WDAY-TV, Fargo (ABC)
  KXMA-TV, Dickinson (CBS)
  KTHI-TV, Fargo (NBC)
  KJRR, Jamestown (None)
  KMCY, Minot (ABC)
  KMOT, Minot (NBC)
  KXMC-TV, Minot (CBS)
  KNRR, Pembina (None)
  KXJB-TV, Valley City (CBS)
  KUMV-TV, Williston (NBC)
  KXMD-TV, Williston (CBS)

Cable television systems, total subscribers
Cable Services of Jamestown; Jamestown 5,000
Cablecom of Fargo; Fargo 17,500
Meredith Cable; Bismarck 21,000
TCI of North Dakota; East Grand Forks 12,920
TCI of North Dakota; Minot 9,000

Military installations, 1991
Minot Air Force Base, Minot 5,872
Grand Forks Air Force Base, Emerado 5,641
Hector Field Intl. Airport Air Force Guard Station, Fargo 388
Cavalier Air Force Station, Mountain 157

Businesses and other major employers
North Dakota State University; Fargo 3,000
University of North Dakota; Grand Forks 2,600
St. Luke's Hospitals of Fargo; Fargo 2,100
United Hospital; Grand Forks 1,450
St. Alexius Medical Center; Bismarck 1,297
Medcenter One Health Systems; Bismarck 1,073
State of North Dakota/Human Resources Dept.; Bismarck 1,034
State of North Dakota/Transportation Dept.; Bismarck 1,000
Dakota Hospital & Medical Center; Fargo 1,000
State of North Dakota/Developmental Center; Grafton 993
City of Bismarck/Public School District; Bismarck 950
Dakota Clinic Ltd.; Fargo; medical doctors 800
North Dakota State Hospital; Jamestown 758
Basin Electric Power Coop; Beulah; electric power generation/distribution & coal gasification 755
Blue Cross/Blue Shield of North Dakota; Fargo; medical service/health insurance 750
Ecolab Pest Elimination Services; Grand Forks; building services 750
City of Fargo/Park District; Fargo 700
U.S. Veterans Affairs Dept.; Fargo; hospital 700
Fargo Clinic Ltd.; Fargo; medical doctors 700
North American Coal Corp./Western Div.; Bismarck; coal mining 588
Clark Equipment Co./Melroe Co.; Gwinner; farm machinery 582
Trinity Medical Center; Minot 580
St. Joseph's Hospital; Minot 537
Clark Equipment Co./Melroe Co.; Bismarck; farm machinery 517

Ohio

Ohio entered the last decade of the 20th century as a state well engaged in the compulsory transition from its role as a keystone of the nation's industrial base—a role fulfilled throughout much of the past 100 years.

The symbol of the changing Ohio is Columbus, the state capital and home of Ohio State University. Columbus' white- and pink-collar economy, affordable cost of living and reputation as a good place to raise a family helped the city register a 12 percent growth in population in the 1980s. In the 1990 census, Columbus passed Cleveland as the state's most populous city—the first time since 1850 that Columbus has had a greater population than the industrial center on Lake Erie.

Ohio's longstanding identity as a manufacturing center has not disappeared—but it has undergone some remarkable changes.

While Ohio's steel industry is operating at but a specter of its former vitality—the steel furnaces of the depressed Youngstown area and the surrounding Mahoning Valley, now mostly dark, employed thousands more even 10 years ago—the automobile and tire industries remain important engines in the state's economic composition. In the Ohio economy of the 1990s, however, their roles are quite different.

While U.S. automakers' plants have downsized or closed, Honda of America thrived during the 1980s; Honda employs nearly 10,000 people in its central Ohio facilities.

Akron's heritage as the capital of the U.S. tire industry is not in doubt—Goodyear, Goodrich, Firestone and General Tire companies still have their corporate headquarters there. But Akron no longer makes tires. The manufacturing jobs left over the last 25 years, heading to new Sun Belt plants. But the companies' headquarters and laboratories remain, employing engineers and scientists and helping keep the city's unemployment down.

And Cleveland has emerged from the rockiest 20-year period in its history with a steady gaze cast on the future. While its steel, auto and aluminum plants are still operating, the city has emerged as one of the stronger Rust Belt cities, moving toward a diversified, service-based economy as it implements its long-term plan for growth. For the first time in a generation, downtown Cleveland is attracting new businesses and residents. Two projects under construction—the Gateway sports complex (the future home of baseball's Indians and basketball's Cavaliers) and the Rock and Roll Hall of Fame—are drawing national notice to Cleveland.

One Ohio trend remained unchanged, however: the decline of the steel industry and the consequent climb of unemployment in the Youngstown area. Youngstown's population in the 1990 census fell below 100,000, an 80-year low.

Political change was also resonating through the state at the start of the decade. Although Bill Clinton became only the third Democrat since World War II to carry Ohio, the prevailing attitude in the 1992 elections was more restlessness than partisanship. Seven of Ohio's 19 House members—more than one-third of the delegation—began their service in 1993. The changes came without regard to party. Democrat Ted Strickland defeated GOP Rep. Bob McEwen in the southern Ohio 6th, a Republican bastion; in the 10th, Republican Martin Hoke ousted veteran Democratic Rep. Mary Rose Oakar from her Cleveland stronghold. In each case, voters sided with a little-known but untainted outsider against their scandal-plagued, longtime incumbent.

With Ohio's population growing by fewer than 50,000 people in the 1980s, the state lost congressional seats for the fourth consecutive decade. Thirty years ago, Ohio sent 24 members to the House; the state's current 19-member House delegation is its smallest since 1870.

Unlike remapping for the state's legislative districts, a bitterly partisan affair that went all the way to the U.S. Supreme Court, congressional redistricting required bipartisan cooperation, needing the approval of the Democratic-controlled state House, the Republican-controlled Senate and the Republican governor.

Not long after Ohio learned that it would lose two seats in reapportionment, Democratic and Republican leaders reached an informal accord on redistricting: Democrats would lose a seat from northern Ohio, and Republicans would lose a seat from the south.

The task for Democrats grew considerably easier when two northern Ohio Democrats announced that they would retire at the end of the 102nd Congress. But the two retirements did not scuttle the legislative leaders' deal, which meant that Republican Clarence E. Miller remained a marked man, for it was Miller's 10th District that had been consigned to oblivion.

OHIO

Districts Established March 27, 1992

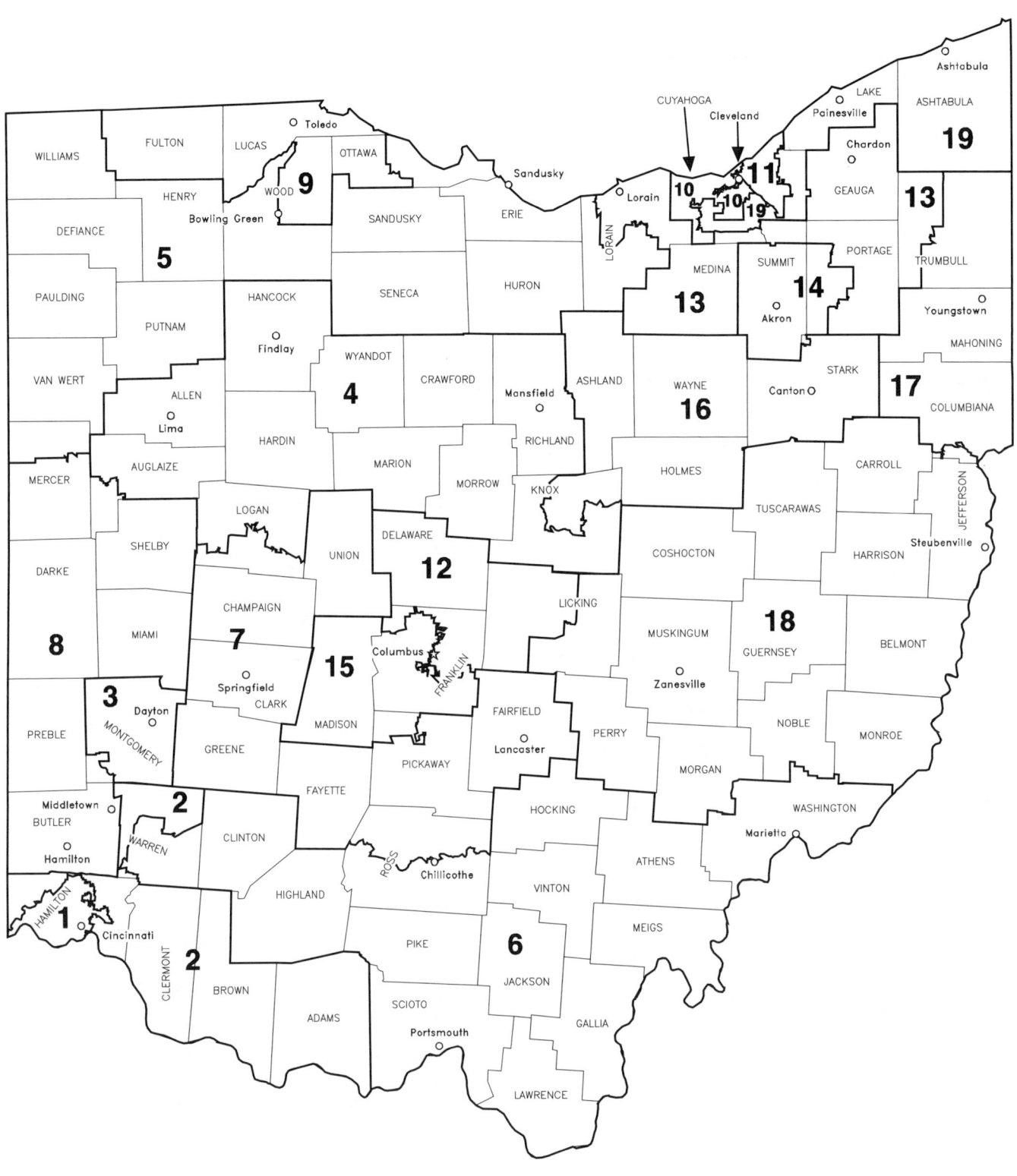

With Miller's fate sealed—even Republicans turned a deaf ear to the 13-term incumbent's entreaties to spare his southeastern Ohio constituency—the remaining battles to be waged were largely over turf. But turf battles—primarily among the three Cleveland-area Democratic incumbents—held up action on the plan for weeks in the spring of 1992. Then, partisan recriminations from the ongoing court fight over the legislative remap spilled over into the congressional debate, freezing bipartisan cooperation. Action on the congressional map came to a standstill with legislators one step away from approving a bipartisan compromise plan.

After nearly a month's deadlock, the map was finally sent to Republican Gov. George Voinovich. But the delay forced the state to move its congressional and presidential primaries from May to June. Aside from Miller, the map left the state's other House incumbents with comfortable districts in which to run.

In Cincinnati, the black population, previously split between the 1st and 2nd districts, was concentrated into the 1st, bolstering the Democratic tilt of the 1st while increasing Republican strength in the 2nd. Similarly, the black population of Columbus, previously split between the 15th and the 12th, was solidified into the 12th.

In partisan terms, the new map created nine seats favoring the GOP and nine seats with a Democratic cast, leaving an open, Cleveland-area 19th as competitive. Except for the reversals in the 6th and the 10th, the results of the 1992 elections followed the established patterns, and Democrat Eric D. Fingerhut edged past his GOP foe in the 19th. Ohio's congressional delegation for the 103rd Congress had 10 Democrats and nine Republicans.

Table 1 Population

District	Population	Population under 18	Voting-age population	Median age
1	570,900	150,432	420,468	31.7
2	570,902	153,118	417,784	33.3
3	570,901	141,828	429,073	33.3
4	570,901	153,760	417,141	33.6
5	570,901	159,895	411,006	33.2
6	570,901	149,842	421,059	33.1
7	570,902	149,446	421,456	33.5
8	570,901	155,225	415,676	32.4
9	570,901	149,560	421,341	31.9
10	570,903	135,436	435,467	34.5
11	570,901	146,183	424,718	33.6
12	570,902	154,849	416,053	31.4
13	570,894	157,808	413,086	33.2
14	570,900	137,477	433,423	33.5
15	570,902	127,738	443,164	31.0
16	570,902	151,160	419,742	33.9
17	570,900	142,495	428,405	35.9
18	570,900	149,157	421,743	35.0
19	570,901	134,335	436,566	36.4
State	10,847,115	2,799,744	8,047,371	33.3

Table 2 Voting-Age Persons

District	White*	Black*	American Indian, Eskimo, or Aleut*	Asian or Pacific Islander*	Other*	Hispanic*	Male*	Female*
1	71.5%	27.2%	0.2%	1.0%	0.1%	0.6%	45.7%	54.3%
2	96.8	2.2	0.1	0.8	0.1	0.5	47.7	52.3
3	82.5	16.2	0.2	1.0	0.2	0.7	46.8	53.2
4	94.8	4.3	0.2	0.4	0.3	0.8	48.2	51.8
5	96.4	1.9	0.2	0.3	1.3	2.5	48.1	51.9
6	97.0	2.2	0.2	0.5	0.1	0.3	47.5	52.5
7	93.6	5.4	0.2	0.6	0.2	0.6	48.2	51.8
8	96.5	2.6	0.1	0.6	0.1	0.4	47.7	52.3
9	86.8	10.7	0.2	1.0	1.3	2.7	46.7	53.3
10	95.1	1.8	0.2	1.3	1.7	3.2	46.8	53.2
11	43.5	54.8	0.2	1.1	0.4	1.0	44.2	55.8
12	76.9	21.4	0.2	1.3	0.2	0.8	46.6	53.4
13	94.4	4.1	0.2	0.5	0.9	2.4	48.0	52.0
14	89.1	9.6	0.2	0.9	0.1	0.5	46.8	53.2
15	92.6	4.8	0.2	2.1	0.3	0.9	49.2	50.8
16	95.1	4.2	0.2	0.4	0.1	0.6	47.0	53.0
17	90.6	8.5	0.2	0.4	0.4	1.1	46.4	53.6
18	97.4	2.2	0.2	0.2	0.1	0.3	46.8	53.2
19	97.1	1.6	0.1	0.9	0.2	0.7	47.0	53.0
State	88.8	9.8	0.2	0.8	0.4	1.1	47.1	52.9

*As percent of voting-age population.

Table 3 Voting-Age Persons by Age Groups

District	18-24*	25-44*	45-54*	55-64*	65 and over*
1	15.9%	42.1%	12.1%	11.8%	18.2%
2	12.2	45.5	14.7	11.9	15.7
3	14.1	43.0	13.9	12.3	16.7
4	13.3	41.5	14.5	12.5	18.1
5	12.9	42.4	14.4	12.4	17.9
6	15.5	40.1	14.2	12.4	17.8
7	14.5	42.2	15.3	11.9	16.1
8	15.3	42.7	14.3	11.9	15.8
9	16.7	42.1	12.8	11.4	17.0
10	12.2	42.6	13.1	12.2	20.0
11	13.5	41.2	12.6	12.6	20.1
12	15.3	47.3	13.9	10.7	12.9
13	13.2	44.3	15.6	12.0	14.9
14	15.9	41.4	12.9	12.1	17.6
15	19.1	46.2	11.9	9.9	12.9
16	13.5	41.2	14.2	12.4	18.7
17	11.9	39.2	13.9	13.8	21.2
18	11.9	39.9	14.3	13.4	20.5
19	11.2	40.5	14.6	13.7	20.1
State	14.1	42.4	13.8	12.2	17.5

*As percent of voting-age population.

Table 4 Income and Occupation

District	Median family income	Families in poverty	White collar*	Blue collar*	Service*	Farm*
1	$32,697	14.0%	61.7%	22.7%	14.9%	0.7%
2	40,261	6.5	61.3	26.1	11.0	1.6
3	36,045	9.8	62.0	24.5	12.7	0.7
4	32,105	8.7	45.6	37.5	14.1	2.8
5	34,855	6.4	43.8	40.1	13.0	3.1
6	26,535	16.3	48.6	33.9	14.6	2.9
7	34,979	8.5	52.7	31.7	13.2	2.5
8	36,254	7.0	52.3	33.2	12.1	2.4
9	35,473	10.7	55.1	29.1	14.6	1.2
10	37,053	8.2	62.0	25.5	12.0	0.5
11	28,710	18.7	59.5	24.0	15.8	0.6
12	37,089	10.6	65.6	20.7	12.7	1.0

District	Median family income	Families in poverty	White collar*	Blue collar*	Service*	Farm*
13	39,210	6.7	54.0	32.3	12.1	1.6
14	34,362	9.7	58.6	26.6	14.0	0.9
15	38,070	6.3	66.6	21.1	11.2	1.1
16	32,131	9.1	50.0	33.2	13.9	3.0
17	30,413	11.7	50.1	34.7	13.8	1.4
18	27,586	12.6	43.6	39.0	14.6	2.8
19	40,093	4.5	61.0	27.1	10.7	1.3
State	34,351	9.7	55.8	29.4	13.1	1.7

*As percent of employed persons age 16 and over.

Table 5   Education: School Years Completed

District	Less than grade 9*	Grades 9-12 no diploma*	High school diploma*	College bachelor's degree or higher*
1	9.2%	18.6%	29.2%	18.7%
2	8.5	14.6	30.5	23.7
3	7.6	14.6	30.8	20.1
4	8.1	16.6	44.0	11.3
5	7.6	15.4	44.6	12.4
6	12.6	19.1	38.8	11.4
7	7.4	16.4	39.2	15.3
8	8.3	16.4	39.3	14.8
9	7.4	15.7	35.1	16.3
10	7.3	17.2	32.8	19.5
11	9.3	22.2	27.9	18.2
12	5.3	14.5	31.2	23.5
13	6.7	14.8	37.4	16.5
14	6.3	15.4	34.4	19.7
15	5.1	13.9	29.8	27.0
16	9.5	16.4	41.0	13.7
17	8.1	17.5	41.9	12.3
18	10.2	18.4	46.0	8.5
19	5.7	14.4	36.4	19.5
State	7.9	16.4	36.3	17.0

*As percent of persons age 25 and over.

Table 6   Housing and Residential Patterns

District	Owner occupied	Renter occupied	Urban	Rural
1	52.2%	47.8%	98.8%	1.2%
2	71.6	28.4	70.8	29.2
3	62.8	37.2	95.5	4.5
4	73.0	27.0	54.3	45.7
5	76.0	24.0	45.9	54.1
6	71.3	28.7	40.4	59.6
7	70.8	29.2	57.3	42.7
8	72.3	27.7	62.0	38.0
9	66.3	33.7	86.4	13.6
10	65.6	34.4	99.7	0.3
11	51.7	48.3	100.0	0.0
12	57.6	42.4	85.4	14.6
13	76.9	23.1	64.0	36.0
14	67.1	32.9	91.8	8.2
15	58.0	42.0	90.4	9.6
16	70.6	29.4	63.3	36.7
17	72.5	27.5	74.3	25.7
18	74.1	25.9	40.2	59.8
19	75.4	24.6	87.8	12.2
State	67.5	32.5	74.1	25.9

1st District

Hamilton County — Western Cincinnati and Suburbs

Nestled snugly in the southwestern corner of the state, the 1st reaches out to take in almost every Democrat in the Cincinnati area, leaving the surrounding 2nd District as solidly Republican as this district is Democratic.

Cincinnati's black population helped former Democratic Rep. Thomas A. Luken build a majority here in the 1980s, and the 1992 round of redistricting has made that majority even more solid. The latest redistricting was aimed at aiding Luken's successor, his son Charles, who took over the seat in 1990 after his father retired. In 1992, the younger Luken decided against running for re-election, and his Democratic successor went on to win the seat that year against two independent candidates after the Republican nominee was disqualified from the ballot.

The new 1st includes about 85 percent of Cincinnati's 364,000 residents. Democrats count on heavy support from the city's black community—blacks make up 44 percent of this part of Cincinnati and only 14 percent of the rest of the district. Only 5 percent of the residents of the 2nd District's eastern slice of the city are black.

Forming another dominant political bloc are the German Catholics who have defined the city's cautious, conservative personality for more than 100 years. Once clustered in the west section of the city known as "Over-the-Rhine," the German Americans gradually moved out to suburbs such as Cheviot and Green Township.

As a fairly conservative Catholic Democrat, Charles Luken was able to retain the support of this crucial bloc in 1990. But in state and national contests, the German Catholics often vote Republican.

At the bottom of Walnut Hill, in the flat Ohio River basin, is downtown Cincinnati, with the Taft Museum and wharves for old stern-wheelers such as the Delta Queen. Construction of Riverfront Stadium and Coliseum (home of baseball's Reds and football's Bengals) in the early 1970s symbolized a downtown renewal project designed to lure suburban dollars back to the city.

A major Ohio River port and a regional center of commerce, the city is headquarters for the giant Procter & Gamble Co. and Cincinnati Milacron, a world leader in the production of machine tools. (Cincinnati Milacron's manufacturing plants are located in the 2nd District.)

Cincinnati's diverse economy prevented it from suffering the degree of hardship that hit other industrial cities in the state in the early 1980s recession.

The 1980s defense buildup boosted the revenues of numerous area defense contractors, the largest being General Electric Co., which provides jobs for blue-collar workers in the western section of the city.

In 1992 presidential voting, both Bill Clinton and George Bush took 43 percent of the vote in the 1st. Clinton was the raw-vote winner, collecting 155 more ballots than Bush.

Election Returns

	1st District	Democrat	Republican
1992	President*	104,494 (42.8%)	104,339 (42.7%)
	House†	120,190 (50.7%)	—
1990	Governor	78,280 (45.3%)	94,363 (54.7%)

	1st District	Democrat	Republican
1988	President	100,591 (44.5%)	125,238 (55.5%)
	Senate	131,534 (58.0%)	95,231 (42.0%)

Vote for Perot was 34,531 (14.1%).   †*Independent/other is greater than 5%.*

Demographics

Population 570,900

Percent change from 1980 10.7%

Land area 177 square miles

Population per square mile 3,229

Counties, 1990 population
Hamilton (pt.) 570,900

Cities, 1990 population (10,000 or more)
Bridgetown North CDP 11,748
Cincinnati (pt.) 311,159
Finneytown CDP 13,096
Forest Park (pt.) 18,609
North College Hill 11,002
Northbrook CDP 11,471
White Oak CDP 12,430

Race and Hispanic origin
White 68.6%
Black 30.1%
American Indian, Eskimo, or Aleut. 0.2%
Asian or Pacific Islander 0.9%
Other 0.2%
Hispanic origin 0.6%

Ancestry
American 3.1%
Dutch 1.5%
English 9.0%
French 2.6%
German 39.9%
Irish 15.9%
Italian 3.8%
Polish 1.1%
Scotch Irish 1.1%
Scottish 1.2%

Universities/colleges, 1990-1991 enrollment
Art Academy of Cincinnati, Cincinnati 247
Cincinnati Bible Seminary, Cincinnati 873
Cincinnati Metropolitan College, Cincinnati 204
Cincinnati Technical College, Cincinnati 4,883
College of Mount St. Joseph on the Ohio, Cincinnati 2,648
Southern Ohio College, Cincinnati 232
Union Institute, Cincinnati 1,087
University of Cincinnati, Cincinnati 31,013
Xavier University, Cincinnati 6,680

Newspapers, total circulation (in all districts)
Cincinnati Enquirer 162,669
Cincinnati Post 92,070

Commercial television stations, affiliations
ADI: Cincinnati (100%)
WCPO-TV, Cincinnati (CBS)
WKRC-TV, Cincinnati (ABC)
WLWT, Cincinnati (NBC)
WSTR, Cincinnati (None)
WXIX-TV, Cincinnati-Newport (Fox)

Cable television systems, total subscribers
Metrovision-Green Township Inc.; Hamilton County 14,298
Warner Cable Communications Inc.; Cincinnati/Blue Ash 181,000

Businesses and other major employers
General Electric Co./Aircraft Engines; Cincinnati; aircraft engines/parts 18,000
University of Cincinnati; Cincinnati 13,000
Procter & Gamble Co.; Cincinnati; soaps/cleaners 4,900
Hamilton County; Cincinnati 3,800
Children's Hospital & Medical Center; Cincinnati 3,460
Good Samaritan Hospital of Cincinnati; Cincinnati 3,000
Christ Hospital Inc.; Cincinnati 2,800
Delta Air Lines Inc.; Cincinnati; airline 2,500
Bethesda Inc.; Cincinnati 2,400
City of Cincinnati/Safety Dept.; Cincinnati 2,200
Jewish Hospitals Inc./Jewish Hospital; Cincinnati 2,200
Cincinnati Gas & Electric Co. Inc.; Cincinnati; electric services 2,100
U.S. Shoe Corp./Casual Corner; Cincinnati; women's clothing stores 1,500
Gibson Greetings Inc.; Cincinnati; greeting cards 1,400
CSX Transportation Inc.; Cincinnati; railroads 1,400
Western Southern Life Insurance; Cincinnati; life insurance 1,300
Westinghouse Environmental Management of Ohio; Cincinnati; sanitary services 1,200
U.S. Veterans Affairs Dept.; Cincinnati; hospital 1,200
Providence Hospital; Cincinnati 1,135
Federated Dept. Stores/Abraham & Straus; Cincinnati; department stores 1,100
Cincinnati Bell Telephone Co.; Cincinnati; telephone communications 900
Community Mutual Insurance Co./Blue Cross/Blue Shield; Cincinnati; medical service/health insurance 1,000
Deaconess Hospital; Cincinnati 1,000
American Building Maintenance Co.; Cincinnati; building services 950
American Airlines Inc.; Cincinnati; airline 925
Southwest Ohio Transit Authority; Cincinnati; transportation 900
Mercantile Stores Co. Inc.; Cincinnati; department stores 825
AT&T Co.; Cincinnati; telephone communications 800
Chemed Corp.; Cincinnati; chemical products 800
Union Central Life Insurance Co.; Cincinnati; life insurance 780
White Castle System Inc.; Cincinnati; fast-food chain 750
Nutone Inc.; Cincinnati; household fans/appliances 700
Great American Holding Corp.; Cincinnati; fire/marine/casualty insurance 700
Professional Maintenance of Cincinnati; Cincinnati; building services 700
U.S. Environmental Protection Agency; Cincinnati 700
Henkel Corp./Emery Group; Cincinnati; chemical products 650
R. L. Polk & Co.; Cincinnati; publishing 625
Sara Lee Corp./Hillshire Farm Div.; Cincinnati; meat products 600
Central Trust Co.; Cincinnati; commercial banks 600
Star Banc Corp.; Cincinnati; commercial banks 600
Xavier University; Cincinnati 600
Drake Center Inc.; Cincinnati; residential care 600
South-Western Publishing Co.; Cincinnati; book publishing 590
State of Ohio/Pauline Warfield Lewis Center; Cincinnati 568
Andrew Jergens Co.; Cincinnati; toiletries/soaps 550
Kroger Co./Grocery Products; Cincinnati; warehousing 549
Cincinnati Enquirer; Cincinnati; newspapers 510

2nd District

Southwest and Eastern Cincinnati and Suburbs

Redistricting in 1992 made the formerly politically mixed 2nd and 1st districts politically distinct seats—the 1st for Democrats and this district for Republicans.

The map shifted most of the Democratic eastern part of Cincinnati out of the 2nd; in exchange, the 2nd added rural western Hamilton County, a reliably Republican area.

The 2nd also picked up all of Adams County and the northern and western parts of Warren County, two more rural Republican counties, from the old 6th District.

The net effect of these changes has been to create a district that is the most solidly Republican in the state, and one with a distinct split between its suburban and rural elements.

Only 53,000 of the 364,000 residents in the city of Cincinnati remain in the 2nd. Only 5 percent of those 53,000 are black; overall, the city is 38 percent black.

Not quite 60 percent of the district's vote is cast in the Hamilton County areas.

Cincinnati's wealthy Republican establishment—including the Taft family—has exercised a great deal of political influence over the years. But that influence is now concentrated more in the suburbs than in the city. Unlike suburban Cleveland, suburban Cincinnati is solidly in Republican hands.

The Cincinnati area has less heavy industry than the urban centers of northeastern Ohio. But manufacturing plants dot the Mill Creek Valley, which extends north from downtown into the suburbs.

More than 150,000 of the 2nd's residents and 23 percent of its voters are in fast-growing Clermont County just east of Hamilton County. It grew 34 percent in the 1970s and 9 percent in the 1980s. As Clermont has moved closer to the Cincinnati metropolitan orbit, it has become more Republican. The outlying counties of the 2nd—Brown, Adams and Warren—have considerably less political pull than Hamilton and Clermont, casting under one-fifth of the district vote. The suburbanization of Clermont County is moving it more into sync with Hamilton, dropping further the influence of the rural counties.

Almost 60 percent of Warren County's residents are in the 2nd, living along the county's western and northern sides. Northern Warren is in Dayton's media market, making it the only portion of the district to be outside Cincinnati's gravitational pull.

Ironically, while mapmakers designed this district with GOP Rep. Bill Gradison's comfort in mind, he left the House before he could fully enjoy the benefits of the new lines. After winning the 2nd with 69 percent of the vote in 1992, Gradison resigned early in 1993. In a special election in 1993, Republican Rob Portman won the seat with 70 percent of the vote.

George Bush ran very strongly here in 1992, pulling down 53 percent of the vote to Bill Clinton's 28 percent and Ross Perot's 19 percent.

Election Returns

	2nd District	Democrat	Republican
1992	President*	78,957 (28.4%)	146,098 (52.6%)
	House	75,898 (29.6%)	177,650 (69.3%)
1990	Governor	61,718 (34.5%)	117,411 (65.5%)

	2nd District	Democrat	Republican
1988	President	67,648 (29.8%)	159,613 (70.2%)
	Senate	103,585 (45.6%)	123,796 (54.4%)

Vote for Perot was 52,006 (18.7%).

Demographics

Population 570,902

Percent change from 1980 11.0%

Land area 1,948 square miles

Population per square mile 293

Counties, 1990 population

Adams 25,371	Hamilton (pt.) 295,328
Brown 34,966	Warren (pt.) 65,050
Clermont 150,187	

Cities, 1990 population (10,000 or more)

Blue Ash 11,860	Reading 12,038
Cincinnati (pt.) 52,881	Sharonville (pt.) 11,312
Franklin 11,026	Springdale 10,621
Norwood (pt.) 23,674	

Race and Hispanic origin

White 96.7%
Black 2.3%
American Indian, Eskimo, or Aleut. 0.1%
Asian or Pacific Islander 0.8%
Other 0.1%
Hispanic origin 0.5%

Ancestry

American 5.9%	Italian 3.8%
Dutch 2.8%	Polish 1.6%
English 17.1%	Scotch Irish 2.2%
French 3.9%	Scottish 2.4%
German 44.8%	Welsh 1.1%
Irish 22.8%	

Universities/colleges, 1990-1991 enrollment

Athenaeum of Ohio, Cincinnati 290
Kenyon College, Gambier 1,523
University of Cincinnati-Clermont General & Technical College, Batavia 1,409
University of Cincinnati-Raymond Walters General & Technical College, Cincinnati 4,078

Newspapers, total circulation (in all districts)

Cincinnati Enquirer 162,669
Cincinnati Post 92,070
Dayton Daily News 174,309
Middletown Journal 5,645

Commercial television stations, affiliations

ADI: Cincinnati (100%)

Cable television systems, total subscribers

Coaxial Communications; Amelia 10,364
Continental Cablevision of Ohio; Kettering 65,000
TCI of Ohio; Middletown 24,663
Warner Cable Communications Inc.; Cincinnati/Blue Ash 181,000

Businesses and other major employers

Marion Merrell Dow Inc.; Cincinnati; research services 2,500

Ford Motor Co./Transmission Div.; Cincinnati; motor vehicle equipment 2,000

Ford Motor Co./Batavia Transmission Plant; Batavia; motor vehicle equipment 1,600

Bethesda Hospital Inc./Bethesda North Hospital; Cincinnati 1,500

Cincinnati Milacron Inc./Plastics Machinery Div.; Batavia; industry machinery 1,400

Cintas Corp. No 1; Mason; laundry services 1,290

Senco Products Inc.; Cincinnati; metalworking machinery 1,100

Masco Industries Inc./Steelcraft Permadoor Div.; Cincinnati; metal products 1,050

Quantum Chemical Corp.; Cincinnati; organic chemicals 1,000

Keebler Co.; Cincinnati; bakery products 1,000

General Electric Co./Commercial Product Support; Cincinnati; airport services 1,000

Avon Products Inc.; Cincinnati; cosmetics/toiletries 1,000

Mercy Hospital Anderson; Cincinnati 960

Clermont Mercy Hospital; Batavia 740

Siemens Energy & Automation; Cincinnati; electrical industrial apparatus 700

Formica Corp.; Cincinnati; plastics products 700

Structural Dynamics Research Corp.; Milford; computer services 650

County of Adams/Board of Education; West Union 612

Cincinnati Milacron Inc./Plastics Machinery Div; Cincinnati; metalworking machinery 600

Cincinnati Electronics Corp.; Cincinnati; communications equipment 600

Belcan Corp.; Cincinnati; personnel supply services 600

Cincinnati Inc.; Harrison; metalworking machinery 580

Dayton Power & Light Co.; Aberdeen; electric services 561

U.S. Precision Lens Inc.; Cincinnati; measuring/controlling devices 550

Johnson & Johnson/Ethicon Inc.; Cincinnati; medical instruments/supplies 550

World Book Inc.; Cincinnati; books 547

U.S. National Institute for Occupational Safety & Health; Cincinnati 540

City of Norwood/Board of Education; Cincinnati 515

3rd District

Southwest — Dayton

With a large blue-collar work force and a population that is 40 percent black, Dayton is a Democratic island in a sea of rural western Ohio Republicanism. Most of Dayton's suburbs yield GOP majorities, but the urban vote has managed to keep the 3rd Democratic in most elections.

The Dayton area, lifelong home of the Wright Brothers, claims to be the birthplace of aviation, the refrigerator, the cash register and the electrical automobile starter. Much of the high-skill industry in the region is a legacy of these local inventions. General Motors is a major employer, with many plants here. The city is the headquarters of the NCR Corp. (formerly National Cash Register Co.).

In the early 1970s, the Dayton area was one of the most affluent parts of Ohio outside the Cleveland suburbs. But since then, there have been severe economic problems. GM's large Frigidaire division, Firestone Tire and Rubber and the McCall Publishing Co. have all left. NCR remains, but has slashed its work force.

The city boasts a large, thriving military industry, increasingly rare in this era of base closings. Wright-Patterson Air Force Base, northeast of the 3rd in the 7th's Greene County, is the nation's largest military installation in terms of the number of people who work here—16,000 military personnel and civilians.

The number of aerospace and advanced technology companies in the 3rd has exploded in the past 10 years, from fewer than 100 in 1982 to more than 800 in 1993. These companies now employ about 25,000 people.

But the other job losses have forced many people out of the area. Dayton's population declined 16 percent in the 1970s and 6 percent more in the 1980s, to 182,000, its lowest level in more than 60 years.

The 3rd encompasses all of Montgomery County except for a chip off the southwest corner ceded to the 8th District. Surrounding the city are much-better-off suburbs. Dayton's per capita income is only 60 percent of the rest of the district's; 34 percent of its family households are headed by women, compared with 13 percent in the rest of the district; 22 percent of its families now live below the poverty level.

South of Dayton are such staunchly Republican white-collar suburbs as Kettering, which is about one-third of Dayton's size with 61,000 residents. Its residents are as white as their collars; 97 percent are white non-Hispanics and less than 1 percent are black. Less than 3 percent of its families live in poverty.

The fast-growing townships north of Dayton, a scattering of cities with 10,000 to 14,000 residents, are largely blue-collar suburban. This is a swing-voting area.

Ronald Reagan and George Bush had little trouble taking the old 3rd District with 56 percent of the vote in 1984 and 54 percent in 1988, but Bill Clinton managed to score a narrow victory in the redrawn 3rd in 1992, receiving 41 percent of the vote to Bush's 40 percent.

Election Returns

	3rd District	Democrat	Republican
1992	President*	107,798 (41.3%)	104,414 (40.0%)
	House	146,072 (58.8%)	98,733 (39.7%)
1990	Governor	63,455 (43.6%)	82,153 (56.4%)
1988	President	88,551 (43.1%)	116,884 (56.9%)
	Senate	122,438 (59.9%)	81,995 (40.1%)

*Vote for Perot was 47,612 (18.2%).

Demographics

Population 570,901

Percent change from 1980 11.2%

Land area 431 square miles

Population per square mile 1,324

Counties, 1990 population
Montgomery (pt.) 570,901

Cities, 1990 population (10,000 or more)

Centerville 21,082	Overlook-Page Manor
Dayton 182,044	CDP 13,242
Englewood 11,432	Shiloh CDP 11,607
Huber Heights (pt.) 38,686	Vandalia 13,882
Kettering (pt.) 60,569	West Carrollton City
Miamisburg 17,834	14,403
Northview CDP 10,337	

Race and Hispanic origin

White 80.7%
Black 17.8%
American Indian, Eskimo, or Aleut. 0.2%
Asian or Pacific Islander 1.0%
Other 0.3%
Hispanic origin 0.8%

Ancestry

American 6.1%	Irish 16.5%
Dutch 2.6%	Italian 2.9%
English 13.6%	Polish 2.1%
French 3.5%	Scotch Irish 1.9%
German 35.4%	Scottish 2.1%
Hungarian 1.1%	Welsh 1.1%

Universities/colleges, 1990-1991 enrollment

ITT Technical Institute, Dayton 617
Kettering College of Medical Art, Kettering 730
Miami-Jacobs Business College, Dayton 600
RETS Technical Center, Centerville 388
Sinclair Community College, Dayton 16,632
United Theological Seminary, Dayton 491
University of Dayton, Dayton 11,497
Wright State University, Dayton 16,393

Newspapers, total circulation (in all districts)

Dayton Daily News 174,309

Commercial television stations, affiliations

ADI: Dayton (100%)
WDTN, Dayton (ABC)
WHIO-TV, Dayton (CBS)
WKEF, Dayton (NBC)
WRGT-TV, Dayton (Fox)

Cable television systems, total subscribers

Continental Cablevision of Ohio; Huber Heights 37,422
Continental Cablevision of Ohio; Kettering 65,000
Viacom Cablevision-Dayton Inc.; Dayton 52,900

Military installations, 1991

Gentile Air Force Station, Dayton 2,244

Businesses and other major employers

NCR Corp.; Dayton; computer equipment 5,400
General Motors Corp./Delco Chassis Div.; Dayton; motor vehicle parts 4,500
General Motors Corp./Harrison Div.; Dayton; air conditioning units 3,300
Mead Corp.; Dayton; paper mills 3,300
Miami Valley Hospital; Dayton 3,000
City of Dayton/Water Dept.; Dayton; water supply 2,701
Charles F. Kettering Memorial Hospital; Dayton 2,500
Good Samaritan Hospital & Health Center; Dayton 2,500
St. Elizabeth Medical Center; Dayton 2,340
EG&G Inc.; Miamisburg; inorganic chemicals 2,100

University of Dayton; Dayton 2,100
Mead Data Central Inc.; Miamisburg; computer services 2,000
Wright State University; Dayton 1,950
Monarch Marking Systems Inc.; Miamisburg; commercial printing 1,900
U.S. Veterans Affairs Dept.; Dayton; hospital 1,850
General Motors Corp./Delco Products Div.; Dayton; motor vehicle equipment 1,500
Acustar Inc./Dayton Thermo Products Div.; Dayton; motor vehicle equipment 1,400
Dayton Osteopathic Hospital; Dayton 1,400
Emery Air Freight Corp.; Vandalia; freight shipping 1,200
Children's Medical Center; Dayton 1,200
Standard Register Co.; Dayton; business forms 1,100
Cox Enterprises Inc./Dayton Daily News; Dayton; newspapers 1,000
County of Montgomery; Dayton 1,000
Bank One Dayton; Dayton; commercial banks 800
Carlson Marketing Group Inc.; Dayton; management services 750
Maria-Joseph Center; Dayton; nursing 730
Reynolds & Reynolds Co./Computer Systems Div.; Dayton; data processing 700
Reynolds & Reynolds Co.; Dayton; office equipment 700
Elder-Beerman Stores Corp./El-Bee; Dayton; department stores 700
County of Montgomery/Human Services Dept.; Dayton 650
State of Ohio/Dayton Mental Health Center; Dayton 637
Dayton Progress Corp.; Dayton; metalworking machinery 625
Miami Valley Regional Transit Authority; Dayton; transportation 620
Sinclair Community College; Dayton 617
Spectra-Physics Laserplane; Dayton; electrical equipment/supplies 600
Sears Roebuck & Co.; Dayton; department stores 600
American Nursing Care Inc.; Dayton; personnel supply services 600
County of Montgomery; Dayton 600
ABF Freight System Inc.; Dayton; trucking services 580
City of Dayton/Police Dept.; Dayton 569
Dayton Power & Light Co.; Dayton; electric services 561
Monco Industries; Dayton; job training 550
L. M. Berry & Co.; Dayton; advertising services 525

4th District

West Central — Mansfield; Lima; Findlay

The 4th is a solid block of Ohio Corn Belt counties dominated by farms and small towns. The land supports corn, soybeans and livestock. And Republicans.

Not one of the 11 counties in the 4th has supported a Democratic presidential candidate since 1964; two of the three largest—Allen and Hancock—have backed the GOP national ticket since the Roosevelt-Landon contest of 1936.

Democrats have oases of support in the 4th, but they are few and far between. They can normally count on votes in Richland County, especially in Mansfield, the district's largest city.

And Lima (population 46,000) sometimes votes Democratic, but it is a small enough part of Allen County that the rest of the county's solidly Republican outlying areas overwhelm Lima's sentiments.

Auglaize County in the 4th's southwestern corner is Democratic in the west and Republican in the east. The west is populated by descendants of Germans who settled in the 19th century; they never caught the conservatism that swept through much of the rest of the area.

Economically, corn and soybeans are king in this district, which sprawls across three of Ohio's area codes. The bulk of this district's industry is in its past.

Marion (population 34,000)—named after Revolutionary War Gen. Francis Marion, the "Swamp Fox"—used to make steam shovels and steam rollers, but now instead grows popping corn.

Lima and Findlay both emerged as small manufacturing centers at the end of the 19th century when oil and gas were found nearby. Lima was one of the original refinery centers for John D. Rockefeller's Standard Oil. Although the petroleum boom passed long ago, Findlay (population 36,000), as headquarters of Marathon Oil, is still the 4th's most prosperous part—and the most Republican part—of this Republican district.

Close ties to the automobile industry caused economic hardships in Mansfield and Lima during the 1982 recession. They made a partial recovery in the latter 1980s and have not suffered tremendously in the latest recession, though the Mansfield auto plant's employment has slipped somewhat. Smaller auto-related companies have taken up some of the slack.

One of the bright spots in the district's industrial base is its General Dynamics plant, which opened in Lima in 1982 and became its second-largest employer behind a Ford plant. The General Dynamics facility builds the Army's M-1 Abrams tank. British Petroleum still operates an oil refinery here that it opened in the 1920s. Many of Logan County's jobs depend on the Honda plant in Marysville in the neighboring 7th District.

Knox County in the 4th's southeast corner is within Columbus' range, making Knox less culturally isolated than many of its neighbors.

George Bush did well all across the 4th in 1992, taking 46 percent of the vote to Bill Clinton's 30 percent.

Election Returns

	4th District	Democrat	Republican
1992	President*	77,918 (30.4%)	118,088 (46.1%)
	House	92,608 (38.1%)	147,346 (60.6%)
1990	Governor	70,504 (37.6%)	117,034 (62.4%)
1988	President	75,497 (33.5%)	149,753 (66.5%)
	Senate	104,814 (46.2%)	122,121 (53.8%)

*Vote for Perot was 58,957 (23.0%).

Demographics

Population 570,901

Percent change from 1980 10.9%

Land area 4,532 square miles

Population per square mile 126

Counties, 1990 population

Allen 109,755	Hancock 65,536
Auglaize (pt.) 33,905	Hardin 31,111
Crawford 47,870	Knox (pt.) 22,329
Logan (pt.) 19,981	Richland 126,137
Marion 64,274	Wyandot 22,254
Morrow 27,749	

Cities, 1990 population (10,000 or more)

Bucyrus 13,496	Lima 45,549
Findlay 35,703	Mansfield 50,627
Galion 11,859	Marion 34,075

Race and Hispanic origin

White 94.4%
Black 4.6%
American Indian, Eskimo, or Aleut. 0.2%
Asian or Pacific Islander 0.4%
Other 0.4%
Hispanic origin 0.9%

Ancestry

American 6.8%	Italian 2.6%
Dutch 3.8%	Polish 1.3%
English 13.2%	Scotch Irish 2.0%
French 3.2%	Scottish 2.0%
German 47.3%	Swiss 1.3%
Irish 16.1%	Welsh 1.6%

Universities/colleges, 1990-1991 enrollment

Bluffton College, Bluffton 684
Lima Technical College, Lima 2,521
Marion Technical College, Marion 1,564
Mount Vernon Nazarene College, Mount Vernon 1,056
North Central Tech College, Mansfield 2,275
Northwestern College, Lima 1,174
Ohio Northern University, Ada 2,648
Ohio State University, Lima 1,357
Ohio State University, Mansfield 1,309
Ohio State University, Marion 1,100
University of Findlay, Findlay 2,025

Newspapers, total circulation (in all districts)

Bucyrus Telegraph-Forum 7,126
Cleveland Plain Dealer 409,749
Columbus Dispatch 261,086
Findlay Courier 24,552
Lima News 7,857
Mansfield News-Journal 36,486
Marion Star 18,822
Mount Vernon News 9,791

Commercial television stations, affiliations

ADI: Columbus (45%), Toledo (21%), Dayton (14%), Cleveland (11%) and Lima (9%)
WLIO, Lima (NBC)
WTLW, Lima (None)
WMFD, Mansfield (None)

Cable television systems, total subscribers

Adelphia Cable; Bucyrus 5,155
Adelphia Cable; Mansfield 29,833
Continental Cablevision of Ohio; Crestline 7,104
Continental Cablevision of Ohio; Findlay 16,000
Mount Vernon Cablevision; Mount Vernon 6,344
Times Mirror Cable TV of Ohio; Marion 14,300
Warner Cable Communications Inc.; Lima 27,300
Warner Cable Communications Inc.; Moulton 7,238

Military installations, 1991

Mansfield Lahm Municipal Airport Air Force Guard Station, Mansfield 238

Businesses and other major employers

General Motors Corp.; Mansfield; metal forgings/stampings 3,900

General Dynamics Corp./Land Systems; Lima; tanks 3,000

Whirlpool Corp./Marion Div.; Marion; laundry dryers 2,500

Ford Motor Co.; Lima; motor vehicles/equipment 2,500

Whirlpool Corp./Findlay Div.; Findlay; household appliances 2,250

St. Rita's Medical Center; Lima 1,866

Honda of America Mfg.; East Liberty; motor vehicles 1,800

Cooper Tire & Rubber Co.; Findlay; tires 1,595

Mansfield General Hospital; Mansfield 1,517

Tri County Business Services/Manpower Temporary Service; Mansfield; personnel supply services 1,500

Therm-O-Disc Inc.; Mansfield; thermostats 1,400

Cyclops Corp./Empire-Detroit Steel Div.; Mansfield; steel products 1,400

Lima Memorial Hospital; Lima 1,100

Timken Co.; Bucyrus; roller bearings 975

Marion General Hospital Inc.; Marion 864

Goodyear Tire & Rubber Co.; St. Marys; rubber products 854

Westinghouse Electric Corp./Electrical Systems Div.; Lima; engineering instruments 850

Blanchard Valley Hospital; Findlay 797

PPG Industries Inc.; Crestline; flat glass 700

Rockwell Intl. Corp./On-Highway Products; Kenton; axle parts 700

Giddings & Lewis Inc.; Lima; metalworking machinery 700

Harris Corp./Solid State Div.; Findlay; electronic components 700

City of Lima/School System; Lima 700

State of Ohio/Mansfield Correctional Institution; Mansfield 630

City of Mansfield; Mansfield 607

Worthington Custom Plastics; Upper Sandusky; plastics products 600

Engelhard-Hanovia Inc.; Marion; data processing 600

Budd Co.; Carey; plastics products 585

BP America Inc.; Lima; petroleum refining 575

Dayco Products Inc./Anchor Swan Inc.; Bucyrus; rubber hose/belting 573

Artesian Industries Inc.; Mansfield; pottery 550

OHM Remediation Services Corp.; Findlay; sanitary services 520

Ball Corp.; Findlay; metal containers 508

5th District

Northwest — Bowling Green; Sandusky

This solidly Republican district is a mixture of fertile, flat farmland and small towns. It spread its wings a bit in 1992 redistricting, tacking a county and a half onto its eastern and western ends, though it shed a bit of land up north.

Added to the 5th were Van Wert County and half of Mercer County—agricultural areas that run along the western Indiana border—and, to the east, the rest of Huron County and most of

Lorain County (near Cleveland). The district lost its section of Fulton County and part of Wood and Ottawa counties (near Toledo) to the 9th District.

The nature of the 5th's population concentrations changed slightly in remapping. The Lake Erie port of Sandusky (population 30,000) is still the district's largest community.

But about half of Bowling Green in Wood County (population 28,000) has moved to the 9th District, along with Bowling Green State University and its 18,600 students. Tiffin, a city of 19,000 in Seneca County, is now the district's second most-populous city.

An additional 95,000 people live in seven other cities throughout the district, with populations ranging from 11,000 to 18,000. The other residents of the 5th live in smaller towns and rural areas.

The district's western counties are almost exclusively devoted to agriculture. Packing plants operated by Heinz and Campbell attest to the quality of the region's tomatoes. The district's population is 96 percent white, but the Mexican American farmworkers who live in migrant camps during harvest season have added an ethnic element to this otherwise homogeneous region. The 5th is 3 percent Hispanic—a large number considering that Hispanics make up just about 1 percent of Ohio's total population.

Erie County, midway between Cleveland and Toledo on Lake Erie, has long been a major recreation area. Sandusky, the county seat, is a fishing market and coal port. In the surrounding countryside, fruit orchards and vineyards abound. German immigrants established wineries in Sandusky a century ago, and they remain a key feature of the local economy.

The sizable blue-collar element occasionally pushes Erie County into the Democratic column. But even though this county's 77,000 residents cast a larger share of the votes than any other county's, it is only 12 percent of the total; Erie is but a Democratic ripple in the large Republican pond.

Wood County, which sprawls from the outskirts of Toledo deep into the Ohio Corn Belt, accounts for a tenth of the district's voters. The county is consistently Republican; the loss of the Bowling Green university community deprives the district of what base for moderate-to-liberal contenders there was. Independent John B. Anderson drew 10 percent of the Wood County vote for president in 1980, his best county showing in Ohio. In 1992, Ross Perot received 22 percent.

Election Returns

		Democrat	Republican
	5th District		
1992	President*	87,883 (33.3%)	109,020 (41.3%)
	House	—	187,860 (99.0%)
1990	Governor	72,211 (38.8%)	113,707 (61.2%)
1988	President	84,292 (37.8%)	138,926 (62.2%)
	Senate	111,392 (49.9%)	111,704 (50.1%)

Vote for Perot was 66,648 (25.2%).

Demographics

Population 570,901

Percent change from 1980 11.0%

Land area 5,201 square miles

Population per square mile 110

Counties, 1990 population

Defiance 39,350	Paulding 20,488
Erie 76,779	Putnam 33,819
Henry 29,108	Sandusky 61,963
Huron 56,240	Seneca 59,733
Lorain (pt.) 37,307	Van Wert 30,464
Mercer (pt.) 5,438	Williams 36,956
Ottawa (pt.) 25,406	Wood (pt.) 57,850

Cities, 1990 population (10,000 or more)

Bowling Green (pt.) 12,929	Perrysburg (pt.) 11,955
Defiance 16,768	Sandusky 29,764
Fostoria (pt.) 11,892	Tiffin 18,604
Fremont 17,648	Van Wert 10,891
Norwalk 14,731	Vermilion 11,127

Race and Hispanic origin

White 95.9%
Black 2.1%
American Indian, Eskimo, or Aleut. 0.2%
Asian or Pacific Islander 0.3%
Other 1.5%
Hispanic origin 3.1%

Ancestry

American 4.3%	Italian 3.2%
Dutch 3.3%	Polish 2.7%
English 12.9%	Scotch Irish 1.5%
French 4.1%	Scottish 1.8%
German 56.4%	Slovakian 1.2%
Hungarian 1.5%	Swiss 1.1%
Irish 14.8%	Welsh 1.1%

Universities/colleges, 1990-1991 enrollment

Bowling Green State University Firelands College, Huron 1,446
Defiance College, Defiance 964
Heidelberg College, Tiffin 1,286
Terra Technical College, Fremont 2,303
Tiffin University, Tiffin 896

Newspapers, total circulation (in all districts)

Bowling Green Sentinel-Tribune 13,406
Bryan Times 10,687
Cleveland Plain Dealer 409,749
Defiance Crescent-News 16,458
Fremont News-Messenger 13,356
Ft. Wayne Journal-Gazette 117,410
Norwalk Reflector 8,753
Port Clinton News Herald 6,154
Sandusky Register 23,421
Tiffin Advertiser Tribune 10,561
Toledo Blade 150,637

Commercial television stations, affiliations

ADI: Toledo (62%), Cleveland (20%), Ft. Wayne (16%) and Dayton (3%)
WINM, Angola (None)
WGGN-TV, Sandusky (None)

Cable television systems, total subscribers

Buckeye Cablevision; Sandusky 18,589
Buckeye Cablevision; Toledo 116,000
Continental Cablevision of Ohio; Bellevue 6,500
Continental Cablevision of Ohio; Fostoria 14,015
Continental Cablevision of Ohio; Norwalk 7,500
Dimension Cable Services; Defiance 6,800
Fremont Cablevision; Fremont 6,700
TCI of Ohio; Bryan 7,200
Wood Cable Ltd.; Bowling Green 8,200

Military installations, 1991

Camp Perry Air Force Guard Station, Port Clinton 31

Businesses and other major employers

General Motors Corp.; Defiance; iron castings 4,000
Whirlpool Corp.; Clyde; household laundry appliances 3,500
Campbell Soup Co.; Napoleon; canned soups 2,500
General Motors Corp./Delco Moraine Div.; Sandusky; industry machinery 2,000
North American Philips Corp.; Ottawa; electronic components 2,000
R. R. Donnelley & Sons Co.; Willard; publishing/printing 1,800
Ford Motor Co./Plastic Products Div.; Sandusky; motor vehicle equipment 1,650
Toledo Edison Co./David Beese Nuclear Power Station; Oak Harbor; electric services 1,200
Allied-Signal Inc./Autolite Div.; Fostoria; spark plugs 1,100
Sandusky Area Health Service; Sandusky 850
ARO Corp.; Bryan; pneumatic air tools 840
Aeroquip Corp.; Van Wert; rubber hose/tubing 815
MTD Products Inc.; Willard; farm/garden machinery 800
National Machinery Co.; Tiffin; metalworking machinery 800
Seaway Food Town Inc.; Tiffin; grocery stores 750
Teleflex Inc.; Van Wert; motor vehicle parts 700
Norwalk Furniture Corp.; Norwalk; furniture 700
Atlas Crankshaft Corp.; Fostoria; diesel engines 700
Providence Hospital Inc.; Sandusky 700
Pepperidge Farm Inc.; Willard; bakery products 680
Federal-Mogul Corp.; Van Wert; gaskets/packing 655
Manville Sales Corp.; Defiance; insulation 600
Memorial Hospital; Fremont 566
American Standard Inc.; Tiffin; pottery 550
City of Sandusky/Board of Education; Sandusky 550

6th District

South — Portsmouth; Chillicothe; Athens

The 6th is the largest district in the state, taking in all of Ohio's southeast corner and reaching across to Warren County in Ohio's southwest. What suburbs it had near Dayton and Cincinnati were stripped away in the 1992 redistricting, leaving behind a collection of some of Ohio's poorest rural areas.

Scioto County is the 6th's most populous, with 80,000 residents and 14 percent of the total. It contains Portsmouth, the district's largest city (population 23,000).

While steel and bricks have been linchpins of Portsmouth's economy throughout the century, one of the largest employers in the district is the nearby uranium-enrichment facility owned by the Department of Energy and operated by Martin Marietta. In Chillicothe (20,000 of whose 22,000 residents are in the 6th), 44 miles due north of Portsmouth in Ross County, nearby forests support a large paper plant.

Athens County has a number of government employers, including Ohio University, with 18,500 students, that cushions it somewhat from adverse economic conditions. Athens was one of just two Ohio counties to support George McGovern for president in 1972; Michael S. Dukakis and Bill Clinton each carried it with more than 50 percent of the vote in 1988 and 1992, respectively.

The Democratic influence is counterbalanced by neighboring Meigs County, where the GOP has a better than 2-to-1 advantage.

Many of the poorer voters in other counties along the Ohio River still call themselves Democrats—a remnant of Civil War days when Confederate sympathies were strong in this area—but nowadays their conservative outlook leads them toward GOP candidates in most elections.

The counties immediately east of the Cincinnati area are rural Republican country. Clinton and Highland counties lie on the outer fringe of the Corn Belt.

Farther east the land is poorer, the Appalachian Mountains rise and GOP strength begins to ebb. Seven of the eight poorest counties in the state (in terms of proportion of families in poverty) are here in the 6th: Pike, Scioto, Jackson, Meigs, Lawrence, Vinton and Gallia. Only Adams County to the immediate west in the 2nd District is poorer. Clinton carried five of those seven counties in 1992, losing only Jackson and Gallia.

One-fifth of the 6th's land area is contained within the three regions of the Wayne National Forest in the district's eastern Appalachian section, including almost all of Lawrence County on Ohio's southern edge.

In 1992, George Bush and Bill Clinton ran almost evenly in this district, with Bush taking 40.2 percent of the vote to Clinton's 39.6 percent. Clinton won eight of the 14 counties that are all or partly in the 6th; several of these victories were by less than 350 votes. Despite the name affinity, Bush did prevail decisively in Clinton County, taking 48 percent of the vote to the Democrat's 30 percent.

Election Returns

	6th District	Democrat	Republican
1992	President*	98,768 (39.6%)	100,162 (40.2%)
	House	122,720 (50.5%)	119,252 (49.1%)
1990	Governor	78,522 (45.7%)	93,223 (54.3%)
1988	President	89,621 (41.4%)	127,041 (58.6%)
	Senate	118,774 (55.1%)	96,681 (44.9%)

*Vote for Perot was 49,796 (20.0%).

Demographics

Population 570,901

Percent change from 1980 10.9%

Land area 6,372 square miles

Population per square mile 90

Counties, 1990 population

Athens 59,549	Meigs 22,987
Clinton 35,415	Pike 24,249
Gallia 30,954	Ross (pt.) 41,884
Highland 35,728	Scioto 80,327
Hocking 25,533	Vinton 11,098
Jackson 30,230	Warren (pt.) 48,859
Lawrence 61,834	Washington 62,254

Cities, 1990 population (10,000 or more)

Athens 21,265	Marietta 15,026
Chillicothe (pt.) 19,913	Portsmouth 22,676
Ironton 12,751	Wilmington 11,199
Lebanon 10,453	

Race and Hispanic origin

White 97.1%
Black 2.1%
American Indian, Eskimo, or Aleut. 0.2%
Asian or Pacific Islander 0.5%
Other 0.1%
Hispanic origin 0.4%

Ancestry

American 10.3%	Irish 19.7%
Dutch 4.1%	Italian 1.9%
English 16.0%	Scotch Irish 2.2%
French 3.1%	Scottish 1.9%
German 33.1%	Welsh 1.9%

Universities/colleges, 1990-1991 enrollment

Hocking Technical College, Nelsonville 5,212
Marietta College, Marietta 1,383
Ohio University, Chillicothe 1,614
Ohio University, Ironton 1,785
Ohio University, Athens 18,505
Shawnee State University, Portsmouth 3,180
Southern State Community College, Hillsboro 1,567
University of Rio Grande, Rio Grande 1,937
Washington State Community College, Marietta 2,660
Wilmington College, Wilmington 2,026

Newspapers, total circulation (in all districts)

Chillicothe Gazette 15,175
Cincinnati Enquirer 162,669
Columbus Dispatch 261,086
Huntington Herald Dispatch 42,242
Ironton Tribune 8,026
Marietta Times 12,920
Parkersburg News/Sentinel 34,079
Portsmouth Daily Times 16,621

Commercial television stations, affiliations

ADI: Charleston-Huntington (52%), Columbus (20%), Cincinnati (18%) and Parkersburg (10%)
WTAP-TV, Parkersburg (NBC)

Cable television systems, total subscribers

Cablevision; Point Pleasant 14,465
Century Ohio Cable; Portsmouth 18,700
Continental Cablevision of Ohio; Athens 6,500
Dimension Cable Services; Chillicothe 16,000
Dimension Cable Services; Ironton 7,702
Nelsonville TV Cable Inc.; Nelsonville 6,100
TCI of Ohio; Marietta 11,838
United Video Cablevision Inc.; Coalton 5,290

Businesses and other major employers

ABX Air Inc./Airborne Express; Wilmington; air cargo service 2,700
Mead Corp./Chillicothe Div.; Chillicothe; paper mills 2,600
Ohio University; Athens 2,300
Martin Marietta Energy Systems; Piketon; uranium enrichment 2,000

U.S. Health Corp./Southern Ohio Medical Center; Portsmouth 1,600

Pillsbury Co./Jenos; Wellston; frozen food products 750

Goodyear Tire & Rubber Co.; Logan; metal forgings 700

Holzer Medical Center; Gallipolis 694

State of Ohio/Corrections Dept.; Lucasville 686

Elkem Metals Co.; Marietta; steel products 650

Worthington Custom Plastics; Mason; plastics products 625

Ferno-Washington Inc.; Wilmington; medical equipment/instruments 560

7th District

West Central — Springfield; Lancaster

This district resembles a gaping mouth that is set to swallow Columbus whole. Its nine counties surround Columbus' district (the 15th) on three sides.

The 7th is bisected by U.S. Route 40; the northern section contains a third of the district's land, but casts only 15 percent of its vote. Champaign, Logan and Union to the north are rural counties that combine agriculture and small industry and have been GOP strongholds for generations; they backed Alfred M. Landon for president in 1936.

South of Route 40, the people are concentrated in Clark County (Springfield) and in Greene County, which extends into Dayton's eastern suburbs.

Springfield's site along Route 40 (the old National Road) enabled it to develop into the area's leading population center with 70,000 residents. The city's economy suffered substantially in the early 1980s, but got a boost in 1983 when International Harvester (now Navistar) consolidated its truck-making operations here.

Greene County has a working-class mix of blacks and southern whites. Wright-Patterson Air Force Base, in the county's far southwest corner, is responsible for a substantial amount of military-related employment. The base is the nation's largest military installation in terms of number employed—16,000 military personnel and civilians work here.

The Air Force has recently bolstered Wright-Patterson's security by consolidating several "commands" into a new one based here: the Air Force Materiel Command, which controls one-fifth of the Air Force's budget. The base is the largest single-site employer in the state.

Up north, the economic picture is rosier in Union County than in many of Ohio's other rural areas. Lying just northwest of Columbus, this is an attractive site for industries seeking open land, low taxes and—despite the county's name—no history of unions.

Much of the area's economic stimulus has come from an unusual source: Japan. Honda opened a motorcycle plant in Marysville in the western part of Union County in 1979, and three years later the company opened its first American auto plant there. Honda employs 6,400 people between the two facilities, making it the largest private employer in the region. (Other Honda plants in adjoining districts employ 3,500 more people.) The Marysville auto plant built 342,000 Honda Accords in 1992; it is the only plant that builds the Accord coupe and station wagon. Honda of America exported more than 55,000 cars in 1992—with 20,000 of them going to Japan.

Fairfield County, in the 7th's far southeast corner, has experienced high growth (for this region) in recent years, as bedroom communities blossomed along Route 33, a four-lane highway connecting Lancaster with the thriving city of Columbus, 30 miles northwest.

George Bush did well in the 7th in 1992, taking 45 percent of the vote to Bill Clinton's 34 percent. Bush was especially strong in Union County, taking 53 percent.

Election Returns

	7th District	Democrat	Republican
1992	President*	84,111 (33.5%)	112,517 (44.8%)
	House	66,237 (28.6%)	164,195 (70.9%)
1990	Governor	62,092 (37.7%)	102,567 (62.3%)
1988	President	73,057 (34.3%)	140,102 (65.7%)
	Senate	110,255 (51.6%)	103,471 (48.4%)

Vote for Perot was 54,050 (21.5%).

Demographics

Population 570,902

Percent change from 1980 11.4%

Land area 3,473 square miles

Population per square mile 164

Counties, 1990 population

Champaign 36,019	Logan (pt.) 22,329
Clark 147,548	Pickaway (pt.) 37,933
Fairfield 103,461	Ross (pt.) 27,446
Fayette 27,466	Union 31,969
Greene 136,731	

Cities, 1990 population (10,000 or more)

Beavercreek 33,626	Springfield 70,487
Bellefontaine 12,142	Urbana 11,353
Circleville 11,666	Washington 12,983
Fairborn 31,300	Xenia 24,664
Lancaster 34,507	

Race and Hispanic origin

White 93.6%

Black 5.3%

American Indian, Eskimo, or Aleut. 0.2%

Asian or Pacific Islander 0.7%

Other 0.2%

Hispanic origin 0.7%

Ancestry

American 7.5%	Italian 2.6%
Dutch 4.4%	Polish 1.4%
English 15.3%	Scotch Irish 2.5%
French 3.2%	Scottish 2.3%
German 39.3%	Welsh 1.5%
Irish 19.0%	

Universities/colleges, 1990-1991 enrollment

Air Force Institute of Technology, Fairborn 915

Antioch School of Adult Learning, Yellow Springs 591

Antioch University, Yellow Springs 671

Cedarville College, Cedarville 1,918

Central State University, Wilberforce 2,886

Clark State Community College, Springfield 2,718

Ohio University, Lancaster 2,027

Urbana University, Urbana 852
Wilberforce University, Wilberforce 809
Wittenberg University, Springfield 2,377

Newspapers, total circulation (in all districts)

Bellefontaine Examiner 10,328
Chillicothe Gazette 15,175
Circleville Herald 7,227
Columbus Dispatch 261,086
Dayton Daily News 174,309
Lancaster Eagle-Gazette 16,953
Xenia Daily Gazette 10,111

Commercial television stations, affiliations

ADI: Columbus (60%) and Dayton (40%)
WWAT, Chillicothe (None)
WTJC, Springfield (None)

Cable television systems, total subscribers

Coaxial Communications; Columbus 73,539
Continental Cablevision of Ohio; Fairborn 14,980
Continental Cablevision of Ohio; Kettering 65,000
Continental Cablevision of Ohio; Lancaster 12,924
Continental Cablevision of Ohio; Springfield 25,300
Continental Cablevision of Ohio; Xenia 9,613
Dimension Cable Services; Chillicothe 16,000
Dimension Cable Services; Washington 6,800
Warner Cable Communications Inc.; Columbus 107,394

Military installations, 1991

Beckley Municipal Airport Air Force Guard Station, Springfield 335
Wright-Patterson Air Force Base, Fairborn 15,533

Businesses and other major employers

Honda of America Mfg.; Marysville; motor vehicles 6,370
Navistar Intl. Transportation Corp.; Springfield; truck assembly 1,500
U.S. Veterans Affairs Dept.; Chillicothe; hospital 1,416
Community Hospital of Springfield; Springfield 1,258
Anchor Hocking Corp.; Lancaster; glass/glassware 1,150
Mercy Medical Center of Springfield; Springfield 1,133
Du Pont E. I. De Nemours & Co.; Circleville; plastics/synthetics 1,108
Babcock & Wilcox Co./Diamond Power Specialty Co. Div.; Lancaster; navigation equipment 1,000
FL Aerospace Corp.; Urbana; aircraft parts 1,000
General Electric Co./Lighting; Circleville; electric lighting 913
Lancaster-Fairfield Community Hospital; Lancaster 910
Systems Research Laboratories; Dayton; research services 900
Harsco Corp./BMY Combat Systems Div.; Marysville; motor vehicles/equipment 850
Medical Center Hospital; Chillicothe 800
Greene Memorial Hospital Inc.; Xenia 800
Thomson Consumer Electronics; Circleville; audio/video equipment 700
Cooper Industries Inc.; Springfield; motors/generators 700
J. B. Hunt Transport Inc.; Springfield; trucking services 695
Paccar Inc.; Chillicothe; motor vehicles/equipment 670
Credit Life Companies Inc.; Springfield; holding offices 645
K. T. H. Parts Industries Inc.; St. Paris; motor vehicle parts 640
Ranco Inc.; Plain City; controlling devices 600
City of Fairborn/Board of Education; Fairborn 550
Drackett Inc.; Urbana; soaps/cleaners 525

8th District

Southwest — Hamilton; Middletown

Butler County is the anchor of this southwestern Ohio district, which has changed shape several times in recent redistrictings but always remained solidly Republican.

Butler contains more than half the district's population and two medium-sized manufacturing centers along the Great Miami River—Hamilton (population 61,000) and Middletown (population 46,000). Steel, paper, automobile bodies, machine tools and a variety of other metal products are made in the two cities.

Most of what few minorities there are in this district live in the two cities; Hamilton is 7 percent black and Middletown is 11 percent black. The rest of the district is about 1 percent black. All other minorities make up about 1 percent of the district.

But both Hamilton and Middletown have lost population in recent years. Most of Butler County's 291,000 residents live not in the two cities but in suburban communities and small towns such as Oxford, the home of Miami University's 16,000 students.

Population expansion in Butler County's suburban territory, just north of the Cincinnati beltway, has made the county one of the state's fastest-growing, and the new arrivals have escalated a rightward trend in the local Republican Party.

Ronald Reagan carried Butler in 1980 with 62 percent of the vote, and increased that to 73 percent in 1984. In 1988, George Bush carried Butler with 69 percent of the vote, well above his statewide average of 55 percent. He beat Bill Clinton here by 19 points in 1992, winning 49 percent of the vote. In recent years the county has elected some of the state's most conservative Republican legislators.

The other half of the 8th's residents live outside Butler County in a string of fertile Corn Belt counties running north along the Indiana border and east toward Springfield. The land is flat and the roads are straight. Once leaving the Miami Valley in northern Butler, a motorist can drive north through the 8th along Route 127 without more than an occasional slight turn of the steering wheel.

Corn and soybeans are major cash crops in the rural counties. Poultry and livestock also are moneymakers. In recent years, Darke and Mercer counties have been the leading Ohio counties in farm income.

Mercer, the southern half of which remains in the 8th, was settled by German Catholics and is the only county in the district with much of a Democratic heritage. But Mercer likes its Democrats conservative. It has not backed the party's presidential candidate since 1968.

Shelby County and a bit of southwestern Auglaize County were added to the 8th in the last redistricting. Shelby voted heavily for Bush and Ross Perot in 1992, giving them 44 percent and 29 percent of the vote, respectively, to Clinton's 26 percent—Perot's best whole-county total in the district.

Election Returns

	8th District	Democrat	Republican
1992	President*	75,189 (29.3%)	120,847 (47.2%)
	House	62,033 (25.9%)	176,362 (73.8%)
1990	Governor	61,303 (36.0%)	109,028 (64.0%)
1988	President	67,146 (30.7%)	151,391 (69.3%)
	Senate	106,948 (48.9%)	111,879 (51.1%)

Vote for Perot was 59,937 (23.4%).

Demographics

Population 570,901

Percent change from 1980 11.2%

Land area 2,728 square miles

Population per square mile 209

Counties, 1990 population

Auglaize (pt.) 10,680	Miami 93,182
Butler 291,479	Montgomery (pt.) 2,908
Darke 53,619	Preble 40,113
Mercer (pt.) 34,005	Shelby 44,915

Cities, 1990 population (10,000 or more)

Fairfield (pt.) 39,729	Oxford 18,937
Greenville 12,863	Piqua 20,612
Hamilton 61,368	Sidney 18,710
Middletown (pt.) 45,991	Troy 19,478

Race and Hispanic origin

White 96.2%
Black 2.8%
American Indian, Eskimo, or Aleut. 0.1%
Asian or Pacific Islander 0.7%
Other 0.2%
Hispanic origin 0.5%

Ancestry

American 7.3%	Irish 17.3%
Dutch 3.0%	Italian 2.6%
English 14.5%	Polish 1.2%
French 4.5%	Scotch Irish 1.8%
German 47.9%	Scottish 1.9%

Universities/colleges, 1990-1991 enrollment

Edison State Community College, Piqua 3,325
Miami University, Oxford 15,836
Miami University-Middletown, Middletown 2,038
Miami University-Hamilton, Hamilton 2,073
Southern Ohio College, Fairfield 368
Wright State University, Celina 880

Newspapers, total circulation (in all districts)

Dayton Daily News 174,309
Greenville Daily Advocate 8,261
Piqua Daily Call 8,857
Richmond Palladium-Item 19,821
Sidney Daily News 12,164
Troy Daily News 10,841

Commercial television stations, affiliations

ADI: Dayton (83%) and Cincinnati (17%)
WKOI, Richmond (None)

Cable television systems, total subscribers

Continental Cablevision of Ohio; Huber Heights 37,422
Heritage Cablevision; Coldwater 5,600
TCI of Ohio; Fairfield 11,000
TCI of Ohio; Hamilton 21,107
TCI of Ohio; Middletown 24,663
Viacom Cablevision-Dayton Inc.; Dayton 52,900
Warner Cable; Sidney 6,800
Warner Cable Communications Inc.; Cincinnati/Blue Ash 181,000
Warner Cable Communications Inc.; Greenville 5,102
Warner Cable Communications Inc.; Lewisburg 8,500
Warner Cable Communications Inc.; Piqua 8,800
Warner Cable Communications Inc.; Troy 7,422

Businesses and other major employers

Armco Steel Co.; Middletown; steel products 5,600
Champion Intl. Corp./Hamilton Mill; Hamilton; paper mills 1,900
Stolle Corp./Norcold Div.; Sidney; metal services 1,850
Copeland Corp.; Sidney; refrigeration 1,800
Huffy Corp.; Celina; bicycles 1,770
Honda of America Mfg.; Anna; motor vehicles 1,700
Ohio Casualty Insurance Co.; Hamilton; fire/marine/casualty insurance 1,660
Crown Equipment Corp.; New Bremen; industrial equipment 1,646
Allied-Signal Inc.; Greenville; motor vehicle equipment 1,300
Cincinnati Financial Corp.; Hamilton; fire/marine/casualty insurance 1,250
Hobart Corp.; Troy; food preparaton equipment 1,200
Hobart Brothers Co.; Troy; electrical welding apparatus 1,200
U.S. Postal Service; Cincinnati 1,000
Champion Intl. Corp./Nationwide Paper Div.; Hamilton; paper/wood products 1,000
Fort Hamilton-Hughes Memorial Hospital; Hamilton 967
Piqua Memorial Medical Center; Piqua 900
Baker Concrete Construction; Monroe; concrete work 800
Corning Inc.; Greenville; glass/glassware 800
B. F. Goodrich Co./Aerospace & Defense Div.; Troy; aircraft parts 750
Mercy Hospital of Hamilton; Hamilton 695
City of Hamilton; Hamilton 675
Friendly Ice Cream Corp.; Troy; dairy products 650
Allied Products Corp.; Coldwater; credit institutions 650
Roadway Express Inc.; Cincinnati; trucking facilities 600
Reynolds & Reynolds Co.; Celina; business forms 600
County of Butler; Hamilton 600
Wilson Memorial Hospital; Sidney 596
Stouder Memorial Hospital Assn.; Troy 545

9th District

Northwest — Toledo

Toledo is an old port city, one whose more recent fortunes have risen and fallen, and fallen further, with the health of the automobile industry. But by the beginning of the 1990s, it was Wall Street, not Detroit, that had undermined Toledo's economy.

The city had climbed back from the depths of the early 1980s recession by mid-decade, and there was some cause for optimism. A Jeep plant and a General Motors transmission factory were operating at full capacity; unemployment in Toledo slipped below 10 percent in 1986.

The optimism ceased as a wave of corporate takeovers and restructurings by out-of-town interests weakened such major Toledo glass producers as Owens-Illinois and Owens-Corning, causing thousands of job losses.

Undergirding Toledo's economy are the several crude oil and gas pipelines that terminate there, and the refineries they feed.

And millions have been spent to improve the city's Toledo Express Airport. The Burlington Air Express delivery company opened a $50 million terminal and sorting center there in 1991, creating 800 jobs.

Almost three-fifths—333,000—of the district's residents live in Toledo, an important port city that sits at the mouth of the largest river that flows into the Great Lakes, the Maumee.

The city, built on the site of a remote 18th-century fort, is now a lonely Democratic outpost in rural Republican northwestern Ohio. Democrats outnumber Republicans in surrounding Lucas County (which holds an additional 129,000 residents) by more than 2-to-1.

But a smaller black population keeps Democratic majorities in Toledo lower than those in Dayton or Cleveland. Jimmy Carter carried the city in 1980, but with only 49 percent of the vote. Democrats Walter F. Mondale and Michael S. Dukakis carried on the tradition in 1984 and 1988. And Bill Clinton won it handily in 1992.

Toledo is an ethnic city. There are major concentrations of Germans, Irish, Poles and Hungarians. While traditionally Democratic, most blue-collar ethnics here vote Republican at least occasionally.

To the east of the city are blue-collar, traditionally Democratic suburbs. Republicans are concentrated in the more affluent suburbs on Toledo's west side, where Ottawa Hills has one of the highest per capita incomes of any community in Ohio.

The whole of Fulton County was included in the 9th in 1992 redistricting. Fulton is one of the most Republican counties in Ohio, but part of it is in Toledo's orbit and contains some solid Democratic precincts.

The 9th now has about a third of Wood County's land mass and 55,000 of its residents—about half its people. The part of Wood County in the district includes 15,000 of Bowling Green's 28,000 residents, along with Bowling Green State University and its 18,600 students.

Election Returns

	9th District	Democrat	Republican
1992	President*	118,818 (47.3%)	81,881 (32.6%)
	House	178,879 (73.2%)	53,011 (21.7%)
1990	Governor	79,956 (49.1%)	82,725 (50.9%)
1988	President	116,938 (52.1%)	107,536 (47.9%)
	Senate	143,231 (66.1%)	73,381 (33.9%)

*Vote for Perot was 50,155 (20.0%).

Demographics

Population 570,901

Percent change from 1980 11.0%

Land area 1,099 square miles

Population per square mile 520

Counties, 1990 population

Fulton 38,498	Ottawa (pt.) 14,623
Lucas 462,361	Wood (pt.) 55,419

Cities, 1990 population (10,000 or more)

Bowling Green (pt.) 15,247	Sylvania 17,301
Maumee 15,561	Toledo 332,943
Oregon 18,334	

Race and Hispanic origin
White 84.9%
Black 12.2%
American Indian, Eskimo, or Aleut 0.2%
Asian or Pacific Islander 1.0%
Other 1.7%
Hispanic origin 3.4%

Ancestry

American 2.9%	Irish 15.5%
Dutch 2.3%	Italian 3.0%
English 10.9%	Polish 10.5%
French 6.8%	Scotch Irish 1.5%
German 42.4%	Scottish 1.8%
Hungarian 2.6%	Slovakian 1.2%

Universities/colleges, 1990-1991 enrollment
Bowling Green State University, Bowling Green 18,657
Davis Junior College, Toledo 376
Lourdes College, Sylvania 1,048
Medical College of Ohio at Toledo, Toledo 832
Michael J. Owens Technical College, Toledo 6,857
Northwest Technical College, Archbold 1,993
University of Toledo, Toledo 24,699

Newspapers, total circulation (in all districts)
Bowling Green Sentinel-Tribune 13,406
Detroit News & Free Press 1,014,197
Port Clinton News Herald 6,154
Toledo Blade 150,637

Commercial television stations, affiliations
ADI: Toledo (100%)
WNWO-TV, Toledo (ABC)
WTOL-TV, Toledo (CBS)
WTVG, Toledo (NBC)
WUPW, Toledo (Fox)

Cable television systems, total subscribers
Buckeye Cablevision; Toledo 116,000

Military installations, 1991
Toledo Express Airport Air Force Guard Station, Swanton 293

Businesses and other major employers
Chrysler Corp.; Toledo; motor vehicle assembly 5,500
General Motors Corp./Powertrain Div.; Toledo; motor vehicle equipment 5,000
Toledo Hospital; Toledo 4,900
University of Toledo; Toledo 3,600
Medical College of Ohio at Toledo; Toledo 2,932
Owens-Illinois Inc./Owens-Brockway Glass Container; Toledo; glass containers/bottles 2,500
St. Vincent Medical Center; Toledo 2,500
Bowling Green State University; Bowling Green 2,000
Sauder Woodworking Co.; Archbold; furniture 1,875
Owens-Illinois Inc./Libbey Glass Inc.; Toledo; glass/glassware 1,850
Transamerican Freight Lines; Toledo; trucking services 1,800
United Parcel Service Inc.; Maumee; mail services 1,600
St. Charles Hospital; Toledo 1,500
Chrysler Corp./Toledo Plant Machining; Perrysburg; motor vehicles 1,300
Flower Memorial Hospital; Sylvania 1,257
Owens-Corning Fiberglas Corp.; Toledo; fiberglass 1,200

Mercy Hospital of Toledo; Toledo 1,160
Riverside Hospital; Toledo 1,050
CSX Transportation Inc.; Walbridge; railroads 1,000
St. Luke's Hospital; Maumee 986
Ford Motor Co.; Maumee; metal forgings/stampings 980
Roadway Express Inc.; Toledo; trucking services 950
Michael J. Owens Technical College, Toledo 900
General Mills Inc.; Toledo; grain mill products 850
Doehler Jarvis Ltd.; Toledo; aluminum castings 800
Manville Sales Corp.; Waterville; mineral products 800
Burlington Air Express Inc.; Swanton; air delivery services 800
Blade Communications Inc.; Toledo; newspapers 750
Brush Wellman Inc.; Elmore; copper products 700
Olsten Corp./Health Care Services; Toledo; home health services 650
Blue Cross & Blue Shield Mutual of Ohio; Toledo; medical service/health insurance 625
Hunt-Wesson Inc./Beatrice; Perrysburg; preserved fruits/vegetables 600
County of Lucas; Toledo 600
Toledo Edison Co.; Toledo; electric services 572
Sun Refining & Marketing Co./Toledo Refinery; Toledo; petroleum products 530
City of Toledo/Board of Education; Toledo 530

10th District

Cleveland — West Side and Suburbs

This was a district designed with the safety of its former occupant, Democrat Mary Rose Oakar, firmly in mind. Many Democrats see Republican Martin Hoke's win in 1992 solely as a referendum on Oakar, and they expect to win the seat back.

"The joke around here the day after the election was that Martin Hoke had just been elected to his last term in Congress," says a local observer.

The line between the 10th and 11th districts generally divides Cleveland's white and black populations. The 10th is the white district, containing the state's largest concentration of ethnic voters. Poles, Czechs, Italians, Irish and Germans are the largest groups, but there are dozens of other ethnic communities represented by at least a restaurant or two on the West Side.

The city's steel industry fueled the ethnic influx around the turn of the century, with immigrants settling near the West Side mills. Steel, automobile and aluminum plants combine with smaller businesses to make up the employment base today.

But many of the younger people who work there have bought homes in the suburbs. Cleveland suffered a 12 percent population loss in the 1980s. As a result of this—and the addition of more western Cleveland suburbs—more than half the electorate now lies outside the city's limits.

The downtown area was gerrymandered in order to divvy up sources of campaign contributions, not votes. Its businesses are split between the 10th and Louis Stokes' 11th District. The city's economic problems of the 1970s, notably its near-bankruptcy, made it a national symbol of urban decay. But Cleveland today is stronger than many industrial cities of the Frost Belt, mainly because it is making the successful transition to a service economy.

To offset auto and steel slumps, a consortium made up of the city's largest companies mapped out a long-term, diversified plan

for growth—a number of small, high-tech companies have already been attracted. Condominiums are being constructed near the $200 million BP America headquarters (11th District), and old dry-goods warehouses are being converted to homes—the first downtown housing to go up in a generation. To help keep suburbanites in the city after dark, several art deco theaters have been restored, and Cleveland's Lake Erie waterfront is receiving a facelift. Even the Cuyahoga River—which was once so polluted that it caught fire—has been cleaned up.

Children and grandchildren of European immigrants have moved out of Cleveland to inner suburbs such as Parma, due south of the city. In recent years they have moved again. Parma's population declined in the 1970s and '80s, as residents left their ranch homes of the 1950s for the open spaces of outer suburbs such as Strongsville. But even with the population loss, Parma (population 88,000) is still the eighth-largest city in Ohio. Nearby steel mills and automobile plants give this section of the district a strong union presence.

Election Returns

		Democrat	Republican
	10th District		
1992	President*	107,460 (41.5%)	92,849 (35.9%)
	House	103,788 (43.1%)	136,433 (56.6%)
1990	Governor	67,830 (37.9%)	111,141 (62.1%)
1988	President	120,386 (47.7%)	131,812 (52.3%)
	Senate	141,437 (56.8%)	107,534 (43.2%)

Vote for Perot was 58,095 (22.4%).

Demographics

Population 570,903

Percent change from 1980 11.1%

Land area 156 square miles

Population per square mile 3,667

Counties, 1990 population
Cuyahoga (pt.) 570,903

Cities, 1990 population (10,000 or more)

Bay Village 17,000	North Olmsted 34,204
Berea 19,051	Parma 87,876
Brooklyn (pt.) 11,699	Rocky River 20,410
Cleveland (pt.) 219,243	Seven Hills 12,339
Fairview Park 18,028	Strongsville (pt.) 24,754
Lakewood 59,718	Westlake 27,018

Race and Hispanic origin
White 94.1%
Black 2.1%
American Indian, Eskimo, or Aleut. 0.2%
Asian or Pacific Islander 1.4%
Other 2.2%
Hispanic origin 4.0%

Ancestry

American 2.8%	French 2.4%
Arabic 1.5%	German 31.3%
Czechoslovakian 3.0%	Hungarian 5.2%
Dutch 1.7%	Irish 20.7%
English 10.3%	Italian 9.9%

Polish 12.2%	Slovakian 9.0%
Russian 1.3%	Ukrainian 1.9%
Scotch Irish 1.6%	Welsh 1.1%
Scottish 1.9%	Yugoslavian 1.7%

Universities/colleges, 1990-1991 enrollment

Baldwin-Wallace College, Berea 4,870

Bryant & Stratton Business Institute, North Olmsted 395

Cuyahoga Community College, Cleveland 22,014

West Side Institute of Technology, Cleveland 367

Newspapers, total circulation (in all districts)

Cleveland Plain Dealer 409,749

Commercial television stations, affiliations

ADI: Cleveland (100%)

WEWS, Cleveland (ABC)

WJW-TV, Cleveland (CBS)

WKYC-TV, Cleveland (NBC)

WQHS, Cleveland (None)

WUAB, Lorain (None)

WOIO, Shaker Heights-Cleveland (Fox)

Cable television systems, total subscribers

Cablevision of Ohio; Brook Park 19,039

Cablevision of Ohio; North Olmsted 10,620

Cox Cable Cleveland; Parma 56,000

North Coast Cable Ltd.; Cleveland 74,000

Businesses and other major employers

Cleveland Clinic Foundation; Cleveland 7,200

LTV Steel Co. Inc./Cleveland Works Div.; Cleveland; steel products 7,000

Metro Health Medical Center; Cleveland 4,383

General Motors Corp.; Cleveland; metal stampings 4,000

NASA; Cleveland; space research/technology 4,000

American Greetings Corp.; Cleveland; greeting cards 3,000

Fairview General Hospital; Cleveland 2,120

Plain Dealer Publishing Co.; Cleveland; newspapers 1,722

Aluminum Co. of America; Cleveland; metalworking machinery 1,600

Parma Community General Hospital; Cleveland 1,525

Ohio Bell Telephone Co.; Cleveland; telephone communications 1,500

City of Cleveland/Public Utilities; Cleveland 1,500

Cleveland Electric Illuminating Co.; Cleveland; electric services 1,400

County of Cuyahoga/Board of Mental Retardation; Cleveland; job training 1,200

Lakewood Hospital; Cleveland 1,200

Joseph & Feiss Co./Cricketeer; Cleveland; men's suits/coats 1,150

PPG Industries Inc./Coatings & Resins Div.; Cleveland; paint products 1,100

Cuyahoga Community College; Cleveland 1,100

United Parcel Service Inc.; Cleveland; mail services 1,000

Baldwin-Wallace College; Berea 1,000

City of Cleveland/Fire Dept.; Cleveland 983

Westlake Health Campus Assn.; Cleveland 965

Morrison Knudsen Corp./Power Industrial Group; Cleveland; building construction 900

Deaconess Hospital of Cleveland; Cleveland 900

Federal Reserve Bank of Cleveland; Cleveland 850

Service America Corp.; Cleveland; vending machine operators 800

Jones Day Reavis & Pogue; Cleveland; legal services 750

Lutheran Medical Center; Cleveland 733

Kaiser Foundation Hospitals; Cleveland 725

Antares Group Inc.; Cleveland; building services 700

County of Cuyahoga/Central Services Dept.; Cleveland 700

Kirkwood Industries Inc.; Cleveland; electric motors 675

City of Lakewood; Cleveland 650

USG Interiors Inc.; Cleveland; partitions/fixtures 600

St. Alexis Hospital & Medical Center; Cleveland 600

Industrial Security Service; Cleveland; business/security services 600

11th District

Cleveland — East Side and Suburbs

One of the axioms of Ohio politics is that to win statewide, a Democratic candidate must build a 100,000-vote edge in Cuyahoga County. Most of that lead has to be built in the 11th, which is anchored in Cleveland's heavily black East Side. Bill Clinton picked up a spare 132,000 votes here in 1992 over George Bush, which allowed him to walk away with Ohio's 21 electoral votes with nearly a 91,000-vote margin.

This compact district—the smallest and most densely populated in the state—includes poor inner-city areas as well as middle-class territory farther from the downtown area.

Nineteen percent of the 11th's families—and almost a third of those in its section of Cleveland—live below the poverty line. Conditions improve out toward the city's eastern suburbs, where blue and white collars are worn by their diverse black population.

Devastated by the riots of the 1960s, inner-city neighborhoods of Hough and Glenville can claim some new residential and commercial development, but they still bear the scars of poverty.

Out toward the lake, this area includes the middle-class, white ethnic neighborhoods of Collinwood and St. Clare, inhabited by Italians, and Poles, Yugoslavs and other eastern Europeans.

Overall, the 11th is 59 percent black and heavily Democratic. During the past decade, it has been the most Democratic district in the state.

Any hopes that Stokes would be made vulnerable when his district was extended east to take in some white working-class areas—his old 21st District was 62 percent black—were dashed in 1992 when he pulled down 69 percent of the vote in a field of four, compared with 80 percent against a single opponent in 1990.

New to Stokes' territory is Euclid, a white, ethnic, working-class city of 55,000 east of Cleveland. Euclid "is Democratic, but hardly comfortable with the black part of this district," says a local observer. A Democrat from Euclid running against Stokes as an independent in 1992 hoped—in vain—to capitalize on this sentiment.

Some of the 11th's other major suburbs are Cleveland Heights, Shaker Heights and University Heights (populations 54,000, 31,000 and 15,000).

With a large proportion of Jews and young professionals, these are among Ohio's most liberal communities. North of Shaker Heights is Cleveland Heights, many of whose integrated neighborhoods are a short walk from University Circle, home of Case Western Reserve University and Cleveland's cultural hub.

From the circle area, commuters drive along historic Euclid

Avenue to their jobs downtown. While the avenue now bears the marks of poverty, it was known as "Millionaires' Row" at the turn of the century. Few of the old mansions remain. The one belonging to John D. Rockefeller, founder of Standard Oil, was razed after his death in 1937.

Election Returns

	11th District	Democrat	Republican
1992	President*	169,877 (73.4%)	37,880 (16.4%)
	House †	154,718 (69.0%)	43,866 (19.6%)
1990	Governor	97,965 (60.5%)	63,961 (39.5%)
1988	President	164,929 (77.4%)	48,066 (22.6%)
	Senate	169,824 (78.8%)	45,555 (21.2%)

Vote for Perot was 23,423 (10.1%).   †*Independent/other is greater than 5%.*

Demographics

Population 570,901

Percent change from 1980 11.3%

Land area 104 square miles

Population per square mile 5,484

Counties, 1990 population
Cuyahoga (pt.) 570,901

Cities, 1990 population (10,000 or more)

Bedford Heights 12,131	Shaker Heights 30,831
Cleveland Heights 54,052	South Euclid 23,866
Cleveland (pt.) 286,373	University Heights 14,790
East Cleveland 33,096	Warrensville Heights
Euclid 54,875	15,745
Maple Heights (pt.) 16,152	

Race and Hispanic origin
White 39.8%
Black 58.6%
American Indian, Eskimo, or Aleut. 0.2%
Asian or Pacific Islander 1.0%
Other 0.5%
Hispanic origin 1.1%

Ancestry

American 2.2%	Italian 5.3%
Czechoslovakian 1.2%	Polish 4.1%
English 4.6%	Russian 2.2%
German 10.2%	Scottish 1.0%
Hungarian 2.4%	Slovakian 2.5%
Irish 6.9%	Yugoslavian 2.4%

Universities/colleges, 1990-1991 enrollment
Case Western Reserve University, Cleveland 8,219
Cleveland Institute of Art, Cleveland 488
Cleveland Institute of Music, Cleveland 427
Cleveland State University, Cleveland 19,220
Dyke College, Cleveland 1,316
ETI Technical College, Cleveland 622
John Carroll University, Cleveland 4,549
Notre Dame College, South Euclid 849
Ohio College of Podiatric Medicine, Cleveland 330

Newspapers, total circulation (in all districts)
Cleveland Plain Dealer 409,749

Elyria Chronicle-Telegram 36,439
Lake County News Herald 53,516

Commercial television stations, affiliations
ADI: Cleveland (100%)

Cable television systems, total subscribers
Cablevision of Ohio; Cleveland Heights 75,000
North Coast Cable Ltd.; Cleveland 74,000

Military installations, 1991
Defense Finance & Accounting Center (Navy), Cleveland
1,651

Businesses and other major employers
University Hospitals of Cleveland; Cleveland 4,400
Case Western Reserve University; Cleveland 3,500
U.S. Transportation Dept.; Cleveland 2,557
BP America Inc.; Cleveland; petroleum refining 2,500
Lincoln Electric Co.; Cleveland; metalworking machinery
2,500
Cleveland State University; Cleveland 2,500
Mt. Sinai Medical Center; Cleveland 2,100
Metrohealth St. Luke's Medical Center; Cleveland 1,900
Blue Cross & Blue Shield Mutual of Ohio; Cleveland; medical
service/health insurance 1,800
Kaiser Foundation; Cleveland; health organizations 1,650
Sherwin-Williams Co.; Cleveland; paint stores 1,500
May Dept. Stores Co./May Co.; Cleveland; variety stores
1,500
U.S. Veterans Affairs Dept.; Cleveland; hospital 1,350
Westinghouse Electric Corp./Naval Systems Div.; Cleveland;
electrical industrial apparatus 1,300
General Motors Corp./Inland Fisher-Guide Div.; Cleveland;
textile products 1,242
TRW Inc./TRW Valve Div.; Cleveland; industrial machinery
1,200
General Electric Co./Lighting; Cleveland; electric lighting
1,200
National City Bank; Cleveland; commercial banks 1,200
U.S. Internal Revenue Service; Cleveland 1,200
Society National Bank; Cleveland; commercial banks 1,100
Transportation Unlimited Inc.; Cleveland; personnel supply
services 1,035
County of Cuyahoga; Cleveland; family services 1,000
Argo-Tech Corp.; Cleveland; aircraft parts 830
Parker Hannifin Corp.; Cleveland; industrial machinery 800
Penton Publishing Corp./Industry Week; Cleveland;
periodicals 800
City of East Cleveland/Board of Education; Cleveland 800
Higbee Co.; Cleveland; department stores 740
Brentwood Hospital; Cleveland 705
Twin Valu Stores Inc.; Cleveland; grocery stores 700
BP America Inc./BP Research; Cleveland; research services
700
National Cleaning Contractors; Cleveland; building services
700
First National Supermarkets; Cleveland; grocery stores 650
Stouffer Corp./Stouffer Tower City Plaza Hotel; Cleveland;
hotel 650
City of Cleveland/Board of Education; Cleveland 615
Premier Industrial Corp./Newark Electronics; Cleveland; electrical goods 600
Riser Foods Inc.; Cleveland; grocery stores 600

City of Cleveland Heights; Cleveland   575
Arrow Intl. Inc./Capital Game Mfg. Co.; Cleveland; commercial printing   550
Ernst & Young; Cleveland; accounting services   550
Vocational Guidance Services/Wings; Cleveland; job training   525
Thompson Hine & Flory; Cleveland; legal services   502

12th District

Central — Eastern Columbus and Suburbs

Columbus has not suffered from the kind of economic collapse that has afflicted most of Ohio's industrial cities in recent years. It is primarily a white-collar town, one whose diverse industrial base is bolstered by the state government complex, a major banking center and numerous scientific research companies.

No longer is Columbus recognized only as the home of the Ohio State University football team; an economic renaissance in the early 1990s led a slew of national publications to list the city as one of the most progressive and prosperous.

According to marketers, Columbus is a mirror for the nation, so average that it serves as a favored test bed for all sorts of fast-food menu items and other consumer products.

More than three-quarters of the 12th District's residents live in Columbus and its Franklin County suburbs. Democrats must do very well in the city to have a chance districtwide.

Forty-five percent of Columbus is in the 12th; the rest is to the west in the 15th District. The 12th's section of Columbus is more heavily black, poorer and less well-educated than the other. Forty-three percent of the 12th's 284,000 Columbus residents are black, compared with just 6 percent in the 15th's western half of the city. Nearly 18 percent of its families live below the poverty level, compared with 8 percent of the 15th's section. Nineteen percent of its adult residents have a college degree, compared with 29 percent on the west side.

As one moves east from the state Capitol building along Broad Street, the black Democratic vote goes down and the Republican vote goes up. Only 4 percent of the 12th's Franklin County suburbs of Columbus are black.

About three miles east of the Capitol is affluent Bexley, an independent community of 13,000 surrounded by the city.

While usually Republican, Bexley has a large Jewish population and sometimes votes for strong Democratic candidates. Two miles farther east is Whitehall, another independent town, with 21,000 largely blue-collar residents who frequently split their tickets.

Whitehall is the site of the Defense Logistic Agency's Defense Construction Supply Center, which employs 4,700. The center was added in May 1993 to the list of military facilities that may be closed.

Farther out from Whitehall are newer suburbs. Some of these, such as Reynoldsburg and Gahanna, are predominantly blue collar. Residents are employed at such large plants as McDonnell Douglas and AT&T.

The rest of the 12th is rural and Republican, with a smattering of light industry. The remaining 23 percent of the district's residents are split between Licking and Delaware counties. The half of Licking County in the district gave Rep. John Kasich a 3-to-1 margin in his successful bid for a sixth term. Delaware County is equally favorable to Republican candidates—it gave Kasich a 5-to-1 margin in 1992.

Election Returns

	12th District	Democrat	Republican
1992	President*	104,187 (40.1%)	108,618 (41.8%)
	House	68,761 (28.7%)	170,297 (71.0%)
1990	Governor	79,513 (47.2%)	88,820 (52.8%)
1988	President	80,458 (40.6%)	117,950 (59.4%)
	Senate	103,768 (53.4%)	90,563 (46.6%)

Vote for Perot was 46,943 (18.1%).

Demographics

Population   570,902

Percent change from 1980   11.3%

Land area   1,022 square miles

Population per square mile   558

Counties, 1990 population
Delaware   66,929   Licking (pt.)   66,048
Franklin (pt.)   437,925

Cities, 1990 population (10,000 or more)
Bexley   13,088   Newark (pt.)   15,747
Columbus (pt.)   284,281   Reynoldsburg (pt.)   25,748
Delaware   20,030   Westerville   30,269
Dublin (pt.)   16,020   Whitehall   20,572
Gahanna (pt.)   27,334

Race and Hispanic origin
White   74.8%
Black   23.2%
American Indian, Eskimo, or Aleut.   0.2%
Asian or Pacific Islander   1.4%
Other   0.3%
Hispanic origin   0.8%

Ancestry
American   4.9%   Irish   16.2%
Dutch   2.7%   Italian   4.7%
English   13.7%   Polish   2.2%
French   3.1%   Scotch Irish   2.1%
German   31.4%   Scottish   2.2%
Hungarian   1.1%   Welsh   2.3%

Universities/colleges, 1990-1991 enrollment
Capital University, Columbus   3,235
Central Ohio Technical College, Newark   1,555
Columbus College of Art & Design, Columbus   1,631
Columbus State Community College, Columbus   13,294
Denison University, Granville   2,035
DeVry Institute of Technology, Columbus   2,716
Franklin University, Columbus   4,005
Methodist Theological School in Ohio, Delaware   241
Ohio Dominican College, Columbus   1,365
Ohio State University, Newark   1,567
Ohio Wesleyan University, Delaware   2,045
Otterbein College, Westerville   2,451
Trinity Lutheran Seminary, Columbus   238

Newspapers, total circulation (in all districts)
Columbus Dispatch   261,086
Newark Advocate   22,345

Commercial television stations, affiliations
  ADI: Columbus (100%)
    WTTE, Columbus (Fox)

Cable television systems, total subscribers
  Coaxial Communications; Columbus 73,539
  Delaware Cable; Delaware 5,100
  Times Mirror Cable TV; Newark 25,000
  Warner Cable; Columbus 42,100
  Warner Cable Communications Inc.; Columbus 108,039

Military installations, 1991
  Defense Construction Supply Center, Columbus 4,700

Businesses and other major employers
  State of Ohio/Transportation Dept.; Columbus 7,600
  Limited Inc.; Columbus; women's clothing stores 4,000
  Children's Hospital; Columbus 2,249
  Grant Medical Center & Hospital; Columbus 2,150
  Independent Shopping Services; Columbus; industrial consulting services 2,006
  Abbott Laboratories/Ross Laboratories Div.; Columbus; dairy products 2,000
  County of Franklin; Columbus 1,832
  State of Ohio/Taxation Dept.; Columbus 1,700
  State of Ohio/Bureau of Workers' Compensation; Columbus 1,700
  Schottenstein Stores Corp.; Columbus; department stores 1,500
  State of Ohio/Industrial Commission; Columbus 1,500
  Mount Carmel East Hospital; Columbus 1,400
  Federated Dept. Stores/F&R Lazarus & Co.; Columbus; department stores 1,332
  State of Ohio/Administrative Services Dept.; Columbus 1,238
  McDonnell Douglas Corp.; Columbus; aircraft 1,200
  State of Ohio/Employment Services Bureau; Columbus 1,200
  Borden Inc.; Columbus; dairy/food products 1,200
  St. Ann's Hospital of Columbus; Westerville 1,200
  St. Anthony Medical Center; Columbus 1,150
  Dispatch Printing Co./Columbus Dispatch; Columbus; newspapers 1,100
  OI-NEG Television Products Inc.; Columbus; TV parts 1,000
  AT&T Co./Bell Laboratories; Columbus; research services 1,000
  State of Ohio/Human Services Dept.; Columbus 1,000
  Ashland Oil Inc./Ashland Chemical Inc.; Dublin; industrial chemicals 1,000
  State of Ohio/Attorney General's Office; Columbus 950
  BancOhio National Bank; Columbus; commercial banks 923
  Liebert Corp.; Worthington; refrigeration 900
  Columbia Gas of Ohio Inc.; Columbus; gas distribution 858
  State Farm Fire Casualty Co.; Newark; insurance services 850
  State of Ohio/Motor Vehicles Bureau; Columbus 850
  World Financial Network National Bank; Columbus; credit services 850
  Licking Memorial Hospital; Newark 849
  Raytheon Co./Caloric Corp.; Delaware; household cooking appliances 820
  CUC Intl. Inc.; Westerville; personal services 800
  Columbus State Community College; Columbus 800
  Banc One Services Corp.; Columbus; financial services 800
  State of Ohio/Health Dept.; Columbus 800

  State of Ohio/Rehabilitation Services; Columbus 800
  Flxible Corp.; Delaware; bus assembly 750
  OCLC Online Computer Library Center Inc.; Dublin; data services 743
  County of Franklin/Human Services Dept.; Columbus 734
  Kroger Co./Kroger Bakery; Columbus; bakery products 700
  Huntington National Bank; Columbus; commercial banks 700
  State of Ohio/Central Ohio Pyschiatric Hospital; Columbus 700
  Nationwide Mutual Insurance Co.; Columbus; fire/marine/casualty insurance 677
  Cardinal Industries Inc.; Columbus; hotel 670
  Victoria's Secret Stores Inc.; Reynoldsburg; women's specialty stores 650
  State Auto Mutual Insurance Co.; Columbus; fire/marine/casualty insurance 650
  Roche Biomedical Laboratories; Dublin; medical labs 608
  Worthington Industries Inc.; Worthington; steel products 600
  Denison University; Granville 600
  Ohio Wesleyan University; Delaware 600
  Motorists Mutual Insurance Co.; Columbus; casualty insurance 584
  Liebert Corp./Emerson Electric; Delaware; air conditioners 550
  White Consolidated Industries/Fridgedaire Co.; Dublin; household appliances 550
  Vorys Sater Seymour & Pease; Columbus; legal services 544
  Crane Plastics Co.; Columbus; vinyl/plastic products 520
  Kroger Co.; Westerville; bakery 510
  State of Ohio/Public Utilities; Columbus 501

13th District

Northeast — Suburbs of Cleveland, Akron and Youngstown

Lying squarely in the midst of industrial northern Ohio, the 13th has all the problems of a declining Frost Belt economy. Heavily dependent on the automobile and steel industries, populous Lorain County approached Depression-era conditions in the early 1980s.

The district centers around two distinct sets of communities: the Cleveland suburbs in Lorain and Lorain County, and a band of suburbs in northern Summit and southern Cuyahoga counties, which also revolve around Cleveland but are beginning to look south to Akron as well. The Ohio Turnpike is all that connects the two; they are completely separate communities.

The 13th also includes sparsely populated land off to the east in Portage, Geauga and Trumbull counties. To the southwest is Medina County. The geography of the 13th will make it tough for a House challenger to build the name recognition needed to topple an incumbent. Democrat Sherrod Brown won the 13th with 53 percent of the vote in 1992.

Economically, the most serious trouble spot in the district is the once-booming port city of Lorain. But while the local economy there has been battered, the old New Deal political coalition is alive and well. Blue-collar ethnics, blacks and Hispanics in Lorain combine with those in nearby Elyria and academics in the college town of Oberlin to produce Democratic majorities.

As one of the traditional immigration centers on the Great Lakes, the city of Lorain has an ethnic diversity that matches the West Side of Cleveland. Fifty-six different ethnic groups have been counted within its borders. Today, Hispanics make up 17 percent of Lorain's population, a far higher share than any other city in Ohio.

About 10 miles south of Lorain is Oberlin, which roughly divides the district's urban, Catholic Democrats in the north and its rural, Protestant Republicans in the south. Founded in 1833, Oberlin College was the first coeducational institution of higher learning in the country, and among the first to admit black students. The Yankees who founded Oberlin and other towns in this part of Ohio took strong anti-slavery stands in the 19th century, and their descendants continue to crusade for social reforms.

The Summit County area south of Cleveland is a checkerboard of industrial and residential suburbs upon which much of the city's industry has scattered.

That Cleveland's economy is beginning to recover can be seen in its increasing creep out to surrounding counties. Medina County identifies more with rural central Ohio than with the rest of the 13th. But on the northern edge of Medina, Brunswick (population 28,000) has new suburban Cleveland development. To the east, Cleveland's growth is beginning to seep into the northern part of Portage County, but the rest of Portage remains quite rural. Trumbull County, farther east, orients itself south toward the 17th District cities of Youngstown and Warren.

Election Returns

	13th District	Democrat	Republican
1992	President*	101,104 (37.9%)	94,651 (35.5%)
	House †	134,486 (52.9%)	88,889 (35.0%)
1990	Governor	75,193 (40.9%)	108,724 (59.1%)
1988	President	102,278 (46.3%)	118,763 (53.7%)
	Senate	127,496 (57.2%)	95,421 (42.8%)

*Vote for Perot was 70,624 (26.5%).   †Independent/other is greater than 5%.

Demographics

Population   570,894

Percent change from 1980   10.8%

Land area   1,687 square miles

Population per square mile   338

Counties, 1990 population
Cuyahoga (pt.)   14,755
Geauga   81,129
Lorain (pt.)   233,819
Medina   122,354
Portage (pt.)   55,036
Summit (pt.)   35,283
Trumbull (pt.)   28,518

Cities, 1990 population (10,000 or more)
Amherst   10,332
Avon Lake   15,066
Brunswick   28,230
Elyria   56,746
Lorain   71,245
Medina   19,231
North Ridgeville   21,564
Wadsworth   15,718

Race and Hispanic origin
White   93.6%
Black   4.5%
American Indian, Eskimo, or Aleut.   0.2%
Asian or Pacific Islander   0.5%
Other   1.1%
Hispanic origin   2.9%

Ancestry
American   3.7%
Czechoslovakian   2.3%
Dutch   2.7%
English   15.1%
French   2.8%
German   35.7%
Hungarian   5.3%
Irish   17.9%
Italian   8.1%
Polish   8.4%
Russian   1.1%
Scotch Irish   2.0%
Scottish   2.4%
Slovakian   6.1%
Swedish   1.1%
Welsh   1.5%
Yugoslavian   1.5%

Universities/colleges, 1990-1991 enrollment
Hiram College, Hiram   1,341
Kent State University-Geauga, Burton   546
Lorian Community College, Elyria   7,031
Northeast Ohio College of Medicine, Rootstown   418
Oberlin College, Oberlin   2,902

Newspapers, total circulation (in all districts)
Akron Beacon Journal   157,049
Cleveland Plain Dealer   409,749
Elyria Chronicle-Telegram   36,439
Geauga Times Leader   8,590
Lorain Journal   41,384
Medina County Gazette   16,141
Ravenna Record-Courier   20,335
Sharon Herald   24,899

Commercial television stations, affiliations
ADI: Cleveland (88%) and Youngstown (12%)
WBNX-TV, Akron (None)

Cable television systems, total subscribers
Adelphia Cable; Lorain   15,547
Armstrong Utilities Inc.; Medina   7,222
Continental Cablevision of Ohio; Brunswick   5,811
Continental Cablevision of Ohio; Cleveland Heights   75,000
Continental Cablevision of Ohio; Bay Village   8,424
Continental Cablevision of Ohio; Elyria   14,675
TCI of Ohio; Chardon   14,878
TCI of Ohio; Kent   12,799
TCI of Ohio; Warren   41,044
Warner Cable of Akron; Akron   93,000
Western Reserves Cablevision; Macedonia   14,145

Businesses and other major employers
Ford Motor Co.; Lorain; motor vehicles   5,600
Chrysler Corp./Twinsburg Stamping Plant; Twinsburg; metal stampings   3,600
U.S. Steel Corp. & Kobe Steel Co.; Lorain; steel products   3,000
Ford Motor Co./Ohio Truck Plant; Avon Lake; trucks   1,729
U.S. Veterans Affairs Dept.; Cleveland; hospital   1,350
City of Elyria/Board of Education; Elyria   1,314
Ohio Farmers Insurance Co.; Westfield Center; life insurance   1,157
Reliance Electric Co./Lorain Products Div.; Lorain; communications equipment   1,104
Elyria Memorial Hospital & Medical Center; Elyria   1,100
Moen Inc.; Elyria; plumbing/heating   1,000
D. S. Revco Inc.; Twinsburg; drug store chain   1,000

Lakeland Community Hospital; Lorain 980
St. Joseph Hospital & Health Center; Lorain 955
Schneider National Carriers; Seville; trucking services 900
Oberlin College; Oberlin 885
Lucas Aerospace Power Equipment Corp; Aurora; microwave
    components 825
Kraftmaid Cabinetry Inc.; Middlefield; millwork 810
Nordson Corp.; Amherst; painting equipment 800
City of Brunswick/School District; Brunswick 700
City of Medina/School District; Medina 600
York Intl. Corp.; Elyria; refrigeration 550
B. F. Goodrich Co.; Avon Lake; research services 540
Allen-Bradley Co. Inc.; Twinsburg; electric motors 530

14th District

Northeast — Akron

The 14th is in a part of Ohio that was built on rubber—tires in particular. At one time, nearly 90 percent of America's tires were manufactured here.

Within the district's confines in Akron—once referred to as the "premier factory town in America"—are the corporate headquarters of the Goodyear, Goodrich, Firestone and General Tire companies.

The 14th became one of the most Democratic districts in the state on the strength of votes from the blue-collar workers who kept the rubber factories humming.

But the district's economy is changing. While the major rubber companies are still important employers, the jobs with a future are white-collar. The last quarter-century has seen a steady transfer of manufacturing from the old, high-wage factories in Akron to new plants in lower-wage areas of the Sun Belt. Many Akron residents have left: The city's 1990 population of 223,000 was less than it was more than a half-century ago. Many downtown storefronts are vacant, and the streets can be eerily quiet, especially at night.

Akron city leaders have fought to forge a high-tech future for the city, and they have had enough success that Akron's unemployment rate in recent years has been lower than that of some other industrial centers in northern Ohio.

What has kept the city alive through these tough years is this: While the tire companies have quit manufacturing here, their headquarters and labs have remained, employing engineers, scientists and executives who work more with polymers these days than with rubber.

The resiliency of Akron's smaller businesses has helped as well. "Much to everyone's surprise, much of the supporting industry didn't vanish; they found other things to do," says a local observer. "It could have been a lot worse."

An unintended benefit of the population flight out of Akron has been that the city is now smaller than its britches. It is an area with public facilities and a housing stock built to handle far more people than live here. The city is doing better than others, such as Youngstown, in the area.

In the boom years of the rubber industry, before World War II, Akron was a mecca for job-seeking Appalachians. The annual West Virginia Day was one of the city's most popular events, and it was said that more West Virginians lived in Akron than in Charleston.

These days, the Appalachian descendants combine with blacks, ethnics and the academic community at the University of

Akron to keep the city reliably Democratic. North of Akron, suburbs and farmland in northern Summit County provide Republican votes. Usually, they are too few to overcome the Democratic advantage in Akron and swing the 14th to the GOP. Both Jimmy Carter in 1980 and Michael S. Dukakis in 1988 won Akron by a wide enough margin to carry Summit County narrowly. Bill Clinton in 1992 won by a comfortable margin.

Election Returns

		Democrat	Republican
	14th District		
1992	President*	119,144 (45.6%)	81,603 (31.2%)
	House	165,335 (67.5%)	78,659 (32.1%)
1990	Governor	88,456 (45.9%)	104,163 (54.1%)
1988	President	121,763 (52.4%)	110,409 (47.6%)
	Senate	146,831 (62.9%)	86,584 (37.1%)

Vote for Perot was 60,338 (23.1%).

Demographics

Population 570,900

Percent change from 1980 10.9%

Land area 499 square miles

Population per square mile 1,144

Counties, 1990 population
Portage (pt.) 87,549   Summit (pt.) 479,707
Stark (pt.) 3,644

Cities, 1990 population (10,000 or more)
Akron 223,019   Portage Lakes CDP 13,373
Barberton 27,623   Ravenna 12,069
Cuyahoga Falls 48,950   Stow 27,702
Kent 28,835   Tallmadge 14,870
Norton (pt.) 11,475

Race and Hispanic origin
White 87.7%
Black 10.9%
American Indian, Eskimo, or Aleut. 0.2%
Asian or Pacific Islander 1.0%
Other 0.2%
Hispanic origin 0.6%

Ancestry
American 4.8%   Polish 3.9%
Dutch 2.9%   Scotch Irish 2.4%
English 15.4%   Scottish 2.6%
French 3.1%   Slovakian 3.4%
German 35.1%   Swedish 1.1%
Hungarian 3.2%   Welsh 1.9%
Irish 18.7%   Yugoslavian 1.1%
Italian 8.3%

Universities/colleges, 1990-1991 enrollment
Kent State University, Kent 24,434
University of Akron, Akron 27,818

Newspapers, total circulation (in all districts)
Akron Beacon Journal 157,049
Canton Repository 58,185
Cleveland Plain Dealer 409,749
Ravenna Record-Courier 20,335

Commercial television stations, affiliations
ADI: Cleveland (100%)
WAKC-TV, Akron (ABC)

Cable television systems, total subscribers
Marks Cablevision Inc.; Akron 13,283
TCI of Ohio; Kent 12,799
Warner Cable of Akron; Akron 93,000

Businesses and other major employers
Goodyear Tire & Rubber Co.; Akron; tires 5,708
Kent State University; Kent 4,000
Akron General Medical Center; Akron 2,275
University of Akron; Akron 2,145
Loral Corp./Loral Defense Systems; Akron; aircraft 2,000
Children's Hospital & Medical Center; Akron 1,796
Babcock & Wilcox Co.; Barberton; steam generators 1,000
Bridgestone/Firestone Inc.; Akron; tires 1,550
Aircraft Braking Systems Corp.; Akron; aircraft parts 1,300
Barberton Citizens Hospital Inc.; Barberton 1,300
St. Thomas Medical Center; Akron 1,275
Ohio Edison Co.; Akron; electric services 1,200
Little Tikes Co.; Hudson; toys/sporting goods 1,100
County of Portage; Ravenna 1,100
Roadway Express Inc.; Akron; trucking services 1,055
General Tire Inc.; Akron; tires 1,000
Sterling Inc./Shaw's Jewelry; Akron; retail stores 1,000
Superior Staffing Inc.; Akron; personnel supply services 1,000
Robinson Memorial Hospital; Ravenna 974
Coca-Cola Bottling of Northern Ohio; Akron; beverages 900
Associated Materials Inc.; Cuyahoga Falls; aluminum products 800
Uniroyal Goodrich Tire Co.; Akron; tires 800
Yellow Freight System Inc.; Richfield; trucking services 800
U.S. Postal Service; Akron 780
Cuyahoga Falls General Hospital; Cuyahoga Falls 725
Consolidated Freightways Corp.; Richfield; trucking facilities 700
United Transport Industries; Rootstown; trucking services 640
Knight-Ridder Inc./Akron Beacon Journal; Akron; newspapers 615
State of Ohio/Transportation Dept.; Ravenna 610
Twin Valu Stores Inc.; Cuyahoga Falls; department stores 600
Fabri-Centers of America Inc./Jo-Ann Fabrics; Hudson; retail stores 600
First National Bank of Ohio; Akron; commercial banks 600
County of Summit; Akron 600
Allstate Insurance Co.; Hudson; insurance services 550

15th District

Central — Western Columbus and Suburbs

Of the two districts that divide Ohio's capital, Columbus, the 15th—on Columbus' western side—traditionally has been the more Republican. Although this district includes most of the academic community at Ohio State University, the Democratic vote there is offset by the solid Republican areas in northern Columbus and the rock-ribbed Republican suburbs west of the Olentangy and Scioto rivers. In Upper Arlington and similar affluent suburbs, it is not unusual for Republican presidential

candidates to draw more than two-thirds of the vote.

Apart from the large university vote—Ohio State has 54,000 students—the major pocket of Democratic strength in the district is the western section of Columbus. Sandwiched between the Scioto River and the Ohio State Hospital for the Insane are neighborhoods of lower-income whites of Appalachian heritage.

The 15th includes far less of heavily black eastern Columbus than it did in the 1980s. Only 6 percent of the 15th's portion of Columbus is black, compared with 43 percent of the 12th District's section.

The 15th includes the blue-collar communities in the southeast portion of Franklin County, which enhance the Democratic vote, but just slightly.

The 15th does not include the heart of downtown Columbus, with the state Capitol and the offices of Ohio's major banking and commercial institutions. But with nearly two-thirds of Franklin County's land area, the district contains most of the region's expanding service base, which includes several large high-tech research centers.

Columbus is no tourist attraction. Swarms of visitors descend on the city only at Ohio State Fair time in August and on the half-dozen Saturdays in the fall when the Ohio State Buckeyes are playing football at home.

But the area has gained a reputation as a good place to raise a family. During the 1970s, it was the only major urban center in Ohio to gain population: It now boasts 633,000 residents overall, with 348,000 of them in the 15th.

In the 1980s recession years, the service-industry-oriented economy of Columbus suffered, but its suffering paled in comparison to that of many other Ohio cities.

In the latest round of redistricting, the 15th picked up what parts of Madison County it did not already have and also bit the northwestern corner from Pickaway County. While Madison compares with Franklin in size, it is far less densely populated: It has only 80 residents for each of its 465 square miles; Franklin County has 1,780 people for each of its 540 square miles.

Consequently, Franklin County holds 92 percent of the district's residents and Madison County contains only 6 percent. The other 2 percent are in Pickaway County to the south.

Election Returns

	15th District	Democrat	Republican
1992	President*	95,627 (35.7%)	119,355 (44.6%)
	House†	94,907 (37.8%)	110,390 (44.0%)
1990	Governor	64,821 (42.4%)	87,960 (57.6%)
1988	President	63,763 (34.9%)	118,754 (65.1%)
	Senate	88,431 (49.7%)	89,339 (50.3%)

*Vote for Perot was 52,413 (19.6%).   †Independent/other is greater than 5%.

Demographics

Population 570,902

Percent change from 1980 10.9%

Land area 873 square miles

Population per square mile 654

Counties, 1990 population
Franklin (pt.) 523,512   Pickaway (pt.) 10,322
Madison 37,068

Cities, 1990 population (10,000 or more)

Blacklick Estates CDP 10,080
Columbus (pt.) 347,989
Grove City 19,661
Hilliard (pt.) 11,770
Upper Arlington 34,128
Worthington (pt.) 14,869

Race and Hispanic origin

White 92.4%
Black 4.9%
American Indian, Eskimo, or Aleut. 0.2%
Asian or Pacific Islander 2.2%
Other 0.3%
Hispanic origin 1.0%

Ancestry

American 5.9%
Dutch 3.5%
English 16.3%
French 3.4%
German 38.2%
Hungarian 1.2%
Irish 20.7%
Italian 5.9%
Polish 2.3%
Scotch Irish 2.5%
Scottish 2.8%
Slovakian 1.0%
Swedish 1.0%
Welsh 2.7%

Universities/colleges, 1990-1991 enrollment

Bliss College, Columbus 358
Ohio State University, Columbus 54,094

Newspapers, total circulation (in all districts)

Circleville Herald 7,227
Columbus Dispatch 261,086

Commercial television stations, affiliations

ADI: Columbus (100%)
WBNS-TV, Columbus (CBS)
WCMH-TV, Columbus (NBC)
WSYX, Columbus (ABC)

Cable television systems, total subscribers

Coaxial Communications; Columbus 73,539
Warner Cable; Columbus 42,100
Warner Cable Communications Inc.; Columbus 107,394

Military installations, 1991

Rickenbacker Air Force Guard Base, Lockbourne 1,806

Businesses and other major employers

Ohio State University; Columbus 25,000
Nationwide Mutual Insurance Co.; Columbus; fire/marine/casualty insurance 6,566
Riverside United Methodist Hospital; Columbus 4,900
Sears Roebuck & Co.; Columbus; warehousing 4,000
Battelle Memorial Institute; Columbus; research services 3,247
General Motors Corp./Inland Fisher Guide Div.; Columbus; hardware 3,000
Mt. Carmel Health; Columbus 2,750
Doctors Hospital; Columbus 1,534
J. C. Penney Co.; Columbus; warehousing 1,500
American Chemical Society & Chemical Abstracts Service; Columbus; professional services/publishing 1,467
Community Mutual Insurance Co.; Worthington; insurance services 1,300
General Electric Co.; Columbus; mineral products 1,100
Anheuser-Busch Inc.; Columbus; brewery 1,000
Pinkerton's Inc.; Columbus; security services 900
Yellow Freight System Inc.; Columbus; trucking facilities 800

Lennox Industries Inc.; Columbus; refrigeration 750
State of Ohio/Public Relations Office; Columbus 750
State of Ohio; Columbus 731
Grange Mutual Casualty Co.; Columbus; fire/marine/casualty insurance 725
CSX Transportation Inc.; Columbus; railroads 700
Marriott Corp.; Columbus; bars/restaurants 700
Compuserve Inc./Data Tech Div.; Columbus; computer services 650
Columbus Southern Power Co.; Columbus; electric services 625
Discover Card Services Inc.; Columbus; credit services 620
State of Ohio/Rehabilitation & Correction Dept; Orient 601
Cardinal Foods Inc.; Columbus; grocery products 600
Meijer Inc.; Dublin; grocery stores 600
Wendy's Intl. Inc.; Dublin; fast-food chain 600
County of Franklin/Sheriffs Dept; Columbus 579
County of Franklin/Child Services Board; Grove City; family services 550
Ricart Ford Inc./Ricart Mitsubishi; Groveport; new/used car dealers 527
TS Trim Industries Inc.; Canal Winchester; auto moldings/trim 525

16th District

Northeast — Canton

Although it has undergone a variety of changes over the years, the 16th is still centered on Stark County and the city of Canton, just as it was when William McKinley represented it more than a century ago, before he moved on to the Ohio governorship and then the presidency.

While it is a working-class city like nearby Akron and Youngstown and often votes Democratic in local elections, Canton does not share in the solidly Democratic tradition of the rest of northeastern Ohio. That is partly a result of the conservative mentality brought to the community by the family-run Timken Co.—a large steel and roller-bearing company that is the district's largest employer.

With sizable black and ethnic populations, Canton proper (population 84,000) goes Democratic on occasion. But the suburbs in surrounding Stark County are solidly Republican. Since 1920, only three Democratic presidential candidates have carried the county—which accounts for nearly two-thirds of the district's population: Franklin D. Roosevelt, Lyndon B. Johnson and Bill Clinton. In 1992, Clinton took 40 percent in Stark County to George Bush's 35 percent and Ross Perot's 24 percent.

Besides Timken, Canton is the national headquarters of the Hoover Co., the vacuum cleaner manufacturer, and Diebold Inc., a producer of bank safes and commercial security equipment. But it is more famous as the home of the Professional Football Hall of Fame and for the front porch from which McKinley ran his 1896 presidential campaign. McKinley, who was assassinated in 1901, is buried in a park on the west end of Canton in a large memorial that roughly resembles the Taj Mahal. The Hall of Fame is at the other end of the park.

The portion of the 16th outside Stark County is mostly rural and Republican. Wooster (population 22,000), the Wayne County seat, is the site of Rubbermaid's corporate headquarters. Nearby Orrville (population 8,000) is the home of the Smucker family, which markets jams and peanut butter.

The 16th was extended south in 1982 by redistricting to annex Holmes County, and west in 1992 to pick up Ashland County.

Many of Holmes' 33,000 residents are Amish, and motorists driving through the county have to be careful not to plow into the back of a horse-drawn buggy. Houses without electricity are common in the county, and the income level is less than 70 percent of the state's average—just $9,191 per capita. Although tourism and leather and noodle factories have brought new employment to the agricultural area, much business is still conducted in small Amish family-owned shops that sell buggies and other necessities.

Ashland County is a very rural, very Republican area that usually rewards statewide GOP candidates with 60 percent or more of the vote.

Election Returns

	16th District	Democrat	Republican
1992	President*	95,193 (37.3%)	98,953 (38.8%)
	House	90,224 (36.2%)	158,489 (63.5%)
1990	Governor	72,331 (39.9%)	108,958 (60.1%)
1988	President	87,797 (42.1%)	120,645 (57.9%)
	Senate	112,380 (53.2%)	98,808 (46.8%)

*Vote for Perot was 60,824 (23.8%).

Demographics

Population 570,902

Percent change from 1980 11.2%

Land area 2,134 square miles

Population per square mile 267

Counties, 1990 population

Ashland 47,507	Stark (pt.) 363,941
Holmes 32,849	Wayne 101,461
Knox (pt.) 25,144	

Cities, 1990 population (10,000 or more)

Alliance (pt.) 23,304	Mount Vernon (pt.) 13,315
Ashland 20,079	North Canton 14,748
Canton 84,161	Wooster 22,191
Massillon 31,007	

Race and Hispanic origin
White 94.4%
Black 4.8%
American Indian, Eskimo, or Aleut. 0.2%
Asian or Pacific Islander 0.4%
Other 0.1%
Hispanic origin 0.6%

Ancestry

American 4.4%	Italian 6.9%
Dutch 3.3%	Polish 2.2%
English 13.3%	Scotch Irish 2.2%
French 4.7%	Scottish 2.1%
German 46.2%	Slovakian 2.0%
Hungarian 1.5%	Swiss 3.6%
Irish 16.8%	Welsh 2.0%

Universities/colleges, 1990-1991 enrollment
Ashland College, Ashland 4,053

College of Wooster, Wooster 1,877
Kent State University-Stark, North Canton 2,164
Malone College, Canton 1,555
Mount Union College, Alliance 1,389
Ohio State University-Agricultural Tech Institute, Wooster 738
Stark Technical College, Canton 3,996
University of Akron-Wayne College, Orrville 1,220
Walsh College, Canton 1,458
Wooster Business College, Wooster 827

Newspapers, total circulation (in all districts)
Akron Beacon Journal 157,049
Alliance Review 11,528
Canton Repository 58,185
Cleveland Plain Dealer 409,749
Columbus Dispatch 261,086
Massillon Independent 14,522
Mount Vernon News 9,791
Wooster Daily Record 24,465

Commercial television stations, affiliations
ADI: Cleveland (93%) and Columbus (7%)
WDLI, Canton (None)
WOAC, Canton (None)

Cable television systems, total subscribers
Adelphia Cable; Mansfield 29,833
Armstrong Utilities Inc.; Ashland 7,558
Clear Picture Inc.; Wooster 11,420
Massillon Cable TV Inc.; Massillon 24,346
Time Warner Cable; Canton 66,000

Businesses and other major employers
Aultman Health Services Assn./Hospital; Canton 2,925
Hoover Co.; Canton; vacuum cleaners 2,600
Rubbermaid Inc.; Wooster; household plastic products 1,750
Timken Mercy Medical Center; Canton 1,733
Timken Co.; Canton; roller-bearings 1,500
Cooper Industries Inc./Entronic Controls; Mount Vernon; metal forgings/stampings 1,500
City of Canton/Board of Education; Canton 1,261
PCC Airfoils Inc./Metals Div.; Minerva; nonferrous foundries (castings) 1,100
Ohio Power Co.; Canton; electric services 1,100
Amsted Industries Inc./American Steel Foundries Div.; Alliance; metal forgings/stampings 1,000
Volvo GM Heavy Truck Corp.; Orrville; motor vehicles/equipment 1,000
Doctors Hospital; Massillon 962
Diebold Inc.; Canton; banking/office equipment 900
Massillon Community Hospital; Massillon 875
City of Canton; Canton 850
Kaiser Aluminum & Chemical Corp.; Canton; aluminum castings 750
U.S. Postal Service; Canton 750
Republic Engineered Steels/Canton Works; Canton; steel products 700
Abbott Laboratories; Ashland; rubber products 700
Citizen's Hospital Assn./Alliance Community Hospital; Alliance 700
State of Ohio/Mt. Vernon Developmental Center; Mount Vernon 700
Century Products Co.; Canton; furniture 650

Republic Engineered Steels; Massillon; steel products 650

Mansfield Plumbing Products; Perrysville; bathroom fixtures 650

Pentair Inc.; Ashland; industry machinery 650

J. M. Smucker Co.; Orrville; jams/jellies/peanut butter 600

State of Ohio/Mental Retardation Dept.; Apple Creek; residential care 600

College of Wooster; Wooster 600

Perry Local School District; Massillon 597

Republic Storage Systems Co.; Canton; partitions/fixtures 550

Van Dorn Co./Central State Can Co. Div.; Massillon; metal containers 550

Alfred Nickles Bakery Inc.; Navarre; bakery products 550

Ohio State University/Ohio Agriculture Research & Development Center; Wooster; research services 550

Acme Brush Corp.; Wooster; paint/misc. brushes 530

Gerstenslager Co.; Wooster; auto/stampings 520

17th District

Northeast — Youngstown, Warren

Once called America's "Little Ruhr" after Germany's Ruhr Valley in recognition of its industrial productivity, the Youngstown-Warren area now is a symbol of the nation's industrial decline. Many of the giant steel furnaces that once lighted the eastern Ohio sky are dark. Most of the workers who have not retired or left the area are looking for other jobs.

Located on the state's eastern border with Pennsylvania, the region was long a steel center serving Cleveland and Pittsburgh. Only a decade ago the steel plants in the Mahoning River Valley employed more than 50,000 workers. Now the work force is a fraction of that.

The 17th has begun to diversify its economy, but many of the gains made in the late 1980s have been lost. Youngstown (population 96,000) lost 17 percent of its population in the 1980s, and for those who stayed, an unemployment rate approaching 20 percent has not been uncommon. In the 1980s, the city was one of only five in the nation to drop from the ranks of those with 100,000 or more people.

Troubles have plagued one of Youngstown's few corporate bright spots. Phar-Mor, a rapidly expanding national chain of discount drug stores with headquarters in Youngstown, declared bankruptcy in August 1992 after its president was accused of misappropriating funds and overstating the company's worth by nearly $500 million. The chain has closed 86 of its 310 stores, and employment in its Youngstown operations has dropped 600 jobs to 1,900. More layoffs are expected.

With its remaining blue-collar base, the 17th is one of Ohio's solidly Democratic areas in most elections. Mahoning and Trumbull were among the 10 Ohio counties that voted for Jimmy Carter in 1980, and both have been in the Democratic column since.

Most Democratic candidates build comfortable majorities in the string of declining ethnic communities along the Mahoning River. Italians dominate in Niles and Lowellville. Eastern Europeans and Greeks are the most important groups in Campbell. In the two largest cities—Youngstown and Warren—blacks are part of the demographic mixture, making up 38 and 21 percent of those cities, respectively.

As one moves south beyond the industrial Mahoning Valley,

the GOP vote increases, but the numbers are too small to make much of a difference districtwide.

Rural Columbiana County is a swing region, one influenced by Pennsylvania and West Virginia. But it is enough smaller than Mahoning and Trumbull counties that it is not expected to have great political pull in the new 17th.

In 1993 a fight raged over a hazardous waste incinerator in East Liverpool along the West Virginia border. The opening of the plant—built to burn up to 60,000 tons of toxic waste a year—was delayed by concerns voiced by the community and echoed by Vice President Al Gore, who called for a General Accounting Office study.

Election Returns

	17th District	Democrat	Republican
1992	President*	133,213 (49.9%)	68,417 (25.6%)
	House	216,503 (83.8%)	40,743 (15.8%)
1990	Governor	109,108 (56.1%)	85,346 (43.9%)
1988	President	139,000 (60.6%)	90,349 (39.4%)
	Senate	160,944 (69.5%)	70,738 (30.5%)

*Vote for Perot was 64,936 (24.3%).

Demographics

Population 570,900

Percent change from 1980 10.8%

Land area 1,345 square miles

Population per square mile 424

Counties, 1990 population
Columbiana (pt.) 106,799   Trumbull (pt.) 199,295
Mahoning 264,806

Cities, 1990 population (10,000 or more)
Austintown CDP 32,371   Niles 21,128
Boardman CDP 38,596   Salem 12,233
Campbell 10,038   Struthers 12,284
East Liverpool 13,654   Warren 50,793
Girard 11,304   Youngstown 95,732

Race and Hispanic origin
White 89.2%
Black 9.8%
American Indian, Eskimo, or Aleut. 0.2%
Asian or Pacific Islander 0.4%
Other 0.5%
Hispanic origin 1.3%

Ancestry
American 3.4%	Italian 15.5%
Dutch 2.8%	Polish 4.4%
English 13.4%	Scotch Irish 2.5%
French 2.2%	Scottish 2.2%
German 29.4%	Slovakian 8.4%
Greek 1.0%	Swedish 1.1%
Hungarian 2.7%	Ukrainian 1.3%
Irish 17.7%	Welsh 2.9%

Universities/colleges, 1990-1991 enrollment
ITT Technical Institute, Youngstown 479
Kent State University-East Liverpool, East Liverpool 684

Kent State University-Salem, Salem   840
Kent State University-Trumbull, Warren   1,686
Youngstown State University, Youngstown   15,454

Newspapers, total circulation (in all districts)
Alliance Review   11,528
Cleveland Plain Dealer   409,749
East Liverpool Review   12,340
Salem News   9,024
Sharon Herald   24,899
Warren Tribune Chronicle   41,118
Youngstown Vindicator   87,768

Commercial television stations, affiliations
ADI: Youngstown (100%)
   WFMJ-TV, Youngstown (NBC)
   WKBN-TV, Youngstown (CBS)
   WYTV, Youngstown (ABC)

Cable television systems, total subscribers
Armstrong Utilities Inc.; Austintown   15,812
Armstrong Utilities Inc.; Boardman   21,807
TCI of Ohio; East Liverpool   8,500
TCI of Ohio; Warren   41,044
Tele-Media Co.; Salem   5,500
Warner Cable Communications Inc.; Austintown   21,582

Military installations, 1991
Youngstown Municipal Airport Air Force Reserve Station,
   Vienna   370

Businesses and other major employers
General Motors Corp./Packard Electric Div.; Warren; electric
   cable   10,200
Western Reserve Care System; Youngstown   3,773
Youngstown State University; Youngstown   3,593
St. Elizabeth Hospital & Medical Center; Youngstown   3,431
General Motors Corp./Lordstown Fabricating; Warren; auto
   assembly   3,000
WCI Steel Inc.; Warren; steel products   2,350
Trumbull Memorial Hospital; Warren   1,800
YHA Inc./Northside Medical Center; Youngstown   1,783
CSC Industries Inc.; Warren; steel products   1,600
Tamco Distributors Co.; Youngstown;
   drugs/proprietaries/sundries   1,300
Commercial Intertech Corp.; Youngstown; industrial machin-
   ery   1,074
Austintown Board of Education; Youngstown   1,000
Initial Holdings Inc.; Youngstown; laundry services   970
County of Trumbull; Warren   950
Salem Community Hospital; Salem   850
City of Youngstown; Youngstown   800
St. Joseph's Riverside Hospital; Warren   800
RMI Titanium Co.; Niles; titanium   738
General Electric Co./Lighting; Warren; electric lighting   700
Warren General Hospital; Warren   665
Worthington Custom Plastics; Salem; plastics products   650
Thomas Steel Strip Corp.; Warren; steel products   650
Ohio Security Systems Inc.; Warren; security services   650
East Liverpool City Hospital; East Liverpool   604
Debartolo Inc.; Youngstown; building construction   600
Bank One Youngstown National Assn.; Youngstown; com-
   mercial banks   580
United Telephone Co. of Ohio; Warren; telephone communi-
   cations   557

Kmart Corp.; Warren; warehousing   556
Youngstown Osteopathic Hospital; Youngstown   550

18th District

East — Steubenville; Zanesville

Coal and steel gave the 18th its polluted air, its dirty rivers, its economic livelihood and its Democratic vote. Redistricting in 1992 gave it more farmers and more Republicans.

Cramped along the steep banks of the Ohio River, Steubenville (population 22,000) long had some of the nation's foulest air pollution. But jobs in the smoke-belching plants along a 50-mile stretch of the Ohio River take priority over clean air, a fact that successful politicians quickly learn.

Locals boast that there was not an air pollution alert in Steubenville in the 1980s. But the clearing skies are a gloomy sign for the local economy. For years the unemployment rate in Steubenville and surrounding Jefferson County has been in or near double digits, a situation expected to get worse later this decade as new Clean Air Act regulations make the high-sulfur coal that the area mines less desirable to buyers.

West of Jefferson is economically depressed Harrison County. The closing in 1985 of a pottery plant that employed about 1,000 people pushed up the already high unemployment rate.

In Jefferson, Belmont and Monroe counties, the steelworking and coal-mining Democrats of the district show strong party allegiance, though they tend to shy away from supporting liberals. This part of Ohio resembles West Virginia and eastern Kentucky. Some cattle are raised, but the hilly terrain makes farming generally unprofitable. Under the hills, however, there are extensive coal deposits.

As one moves west, the district becomes less Democratic and the tractors of Republican farmers replace the giant shovels of Democratic coal miners.

A sweep of counties added to the 18th's southwest end in the 1992 redistricting—Muskingum, Perry, Morgan and half of Licking—are birds of a feather with the nearby farming counties that were already part of the district.

Licking County is a pocket of prosperity; the areas around Newark—two-thirds of whose 44,000 residents are in the 18th—are a growing center for manufacturing and research, with Owens-Corning and Rockwell as major employers. Dow Chemical also has a large research facility here. But the city is bracing for the closure of Newark Air Force Base, announced in March 1993.

The addition of Muskingum County has added the city of Zanesville to the 18th. With 27,000 residents, Zanesville is now the largest city completely in the district. The city was the state capital in the early 1800s and was once the country's pottery capital.

Rep. Douglas Applegate did well across the district in 1992, winning every county—some by more than 60 percentage points, one (conservative Morgan County) by only four votes.

In the 1992 presidential race, Bill Clinton lost all of the 18th's southwest counties except the traditionally more Democratic Perry; he won elsewhere in the district. He finished with 43 percent of the vote to George Bush's 34 percent.

Election Returns

	18th District	Democrat	Republican
1992	President*	110,494 (43.0%)	87,429 (34.0%)
	House	166,189 (67.6%)	77,229 (31.4%)

18th District		Democrat	Republican
1990	Governor	9,442 (9.7%)	87,498 (90.3%)
1988	President	110,448 (47.9%)	120,095 (52.1%)
	Senate	141,603 (61.2%)	89,877 (38.8%)

*Vote for Perot was 58,578 (22.8%).

Demographics

Population 570,900

Percent change from 1980 11.1%

Land area 6,072 square miles

Population per square mile 94

Counties, 1990 population

Belmont 71,074	Licking (pt.) 62,252
Carroll 26,521	Monroe 15,497
Columbiana (pt.) 1,477	Morgan 14,194
Coshocton 35,427	Muskingum 82,068
Guernsey 39,024	Noble 11,336
Harrison 16,085	Perry 31,557
Jefferson 80,298	Tuscarawas 84,090

Cities, 1990 population (10,000 or more)

Cambridge 11,748	Newark (pt.) 28,642
Coshocton 12,193	Steubenville 22,125
Dover 11,329	Zanesville 26,778
New Philadelphia 15,698	

Race and Hispanic origin
White 97.1%
Black 2.4%
American Indian, Eskimo, or Aleut. 0.2%
Asian or Pacific Islander 0.2%
Other 0.1%
Hispanic origin 0.3%

Ancestry

American 5.3%	Italian 6.5%
Dutch 4.4%	Polish 3.9%
English 15.6%	Scotch Irish 3.5%
French 3.1%	Scottish 2.4%
German 39.1%	Slovakian 2.4%
Hungarian 1.3%	Swiss 1.4%
Irish 21.7%	Welsh 2.1%

Universities/colleges, 1990-1991 enrollment
Belmont Technical College, St. Clairsville 1,618
Franciscan University, Steubenville 1,575
Jefferson Technical College, Steubenville 1,630
Kent State University-Tuscarawas, New Philadelphia 1,241
Muskingum College, New Concord 1,175
Muskingum Technical College, Zanesville 2,435
Ohio University, Zanesville 1,534
Ohio University-Belmont, St. Clairsville 1,061

Newspapers, total circulation (in all districts)
Cambridge Jeffersonian 12,685
Columbus Dispatch 261,086
Coshocton Tribune 7,850
Martins Ferry Times Leader 4,651
Newark Advocate 22,345
New Philadelphia Times Reporter 24,340
Steubenville Herald-Star 21,579
Wheeling News Register & Intelligencer 39,505
Zanesville Times Recorder 23,851

Commercial television stations, affiliations
ADI: Wheeling-Steubenville (51%), Columbus (28%), Zanesville (11%) and Cleveland (9%)
WSFJ, Newark (None)
WTOV-TV, Steubenville-Wheeling (NBC)
WTRF-TV, Wheeling (CBS)
WHIZ-TV, Zanesville (NBC)

Cable television systems, total subscribers
TCI of Ohio; Steubenville 14,000
TCI of Ohio; Zanesville 20,000
TCI of West Virginia; Bethlehem 23,497
Tele-Media Co./Cambridge; Cambridge 6,699
Time Warner Cable; Canton 66,000
Times Mirror Cable TV; Newark 25,000
Times Mirror Cable TV of Ohio; Coshocton 7,760
Times Mirror Cable TV of Ohio; New Philadelphia 20,750

Military installations, 1991
Newark Air Force Base, Heath 2,148

Businesses and other major employers
Wheeling-Pittsburgh Corp.; Steubenville; steel mill 3,200
Owens-Corning Fiberglas Corp.; Newark; fiberglass 1,900
Rockwell Intl. Corp.; Newark; motor vehicle axles 1,400
Consolidated Aluminum Corp.; Hannibal; aluminum sheet 1,200
Bethesda Hospital Assn.; Zanesville 1,200
Good Samaritan Medical Center; Zanesville 1,188
United Technologies Corp./Automotive Products Div.; Zanesville; electronic components 1,000
Wheeling-Pittsburgh Corp.; Yorkville; steel products 804
Ohio Edison Co./Samms Power Plant; Stratton; electric services 785
NCR Corp.; Cambridge; computers 750
Ohio Valley Hospital; Steubenville 750
Central Ohio Coal Co.; Cumberland; coal mining 700
Belmont County of Ohio; St. Clairsville 675
St. John Medical Center; Steubenville 665
Guernsey Memorial Hospital; Cambridge 615
Tomkins Industries Inc./Philips Industries Inc.; Malta; millwork 600
Titanium Metals Corp.; Toronto; titanium 600
State of Ohio/Cambridge Mental Health Center; Cambridge; health services 600
Union Hospital Assn.; Dover 593
Columbus Southern Power Co./Conesville Generating Station; Conesville; electric services 575
County of Jefferson; Steubenville 560
Cyclops Corp./Coshocton Stainless Div.; Coshocton; steel products 550
General Electric Co./Electromaterials Dept.; Coshocton; plastics products 525

19th District

Cleveland Suburbs — Ashtabula and Lake Counties

The 19th is one of the most politically competitive districts in the Cleveland area, and one of the most strangely shaped in

Ohio. Its western fingers reach around and up into Cleveland's western suburbs, squeeze east and then north to Lake County along Lake Erie's shore. The district ends up in Ashtabula County in Ohio's far northeastern corner.

The combination of the competition and geography makes the 19th a difficult district to campaign in: It is full of Republicans and Democrats, autoworkers and farmers.

Brook Park, the 19th's westernmost city, is an autoworkers' community just west of Parma. The city is blue-collar, Democratic, overwhelmingly white and very sensitive to the ups and downs of the automobile industry. Many of its 23,000 residents settled here to work at the city's large Ford Motor Co. plants. (Ford is the largest private employer in the district, employing more than 10,000 workers.) Starting with Brook Park, the 19th forms a small bowl around three sides (west, south and east) of Parma, in the 10th District.

Heading east, a ribbon of the tiny village of Oakwood connects to the band of Republican eastern Cleveland suburbs that head straight north into Lake County. These suburbs are substantially better off economically than those on the western side; median household income in such areas as Pepper Pike and Gates Mills hovers around $100,000, compared with just $37,000 in Brook Park and $18,000 in Cleveland proper.

Cuyahoga County tends to vote narrowly Democratic. Bill Clinton took 40 percent of the vote in 1992 to George Bush's 37 percent.

The far northeastern communities of the 19th, reliant on the steel, chemical and automobile industries for jobs, are among the most depressed parts of the state.

But there is growth: As migration from Cleveland moved eastward between 1950 and 1970, the population of Lake County more than doubled. The rapid growth has slowed, but the suburbs continue to creep farther east, obliterating the truck gardens and vineyards along Lake Erie.

Mentor (population 47,000), one of the area's fastest-growing cities, has traditionally been an industrial Democratic area, but its growth is coming from Republicans moving in. The county's Republican farmers and suburbanites are no longer canceled out politically by ethnic Democrats in the western part of the county. Bush won Lake County in 1992—his only win among the 19th's three counties—taking 39 percent of the vote to Clinton's 36 percent.

Lake County casts 36 percent of the 19th's ballots; Cuyahoga County casts 47 percent. The remaining votes are in Ashtabula County. Employment here has recovered only modestly since the early 1980s, when the jobless rate hit 20 percent.

The steel and chemical plants situated along Lake Erie have been severely hurt by foreign competition, and it is hard to find signs of revival. Ashtabula is reliably Democratic in most elections; only a strong GOP county organization keeps the party's candidates close. Clinton won 44 percent of the vote here in 1992.

Election Returns

	19th District	Democrat	Republican
1992	President*	114,357 (39.6%)	106,950 (37.1%)
	House	138,465 (52.0%)	124,606 (46.8%)
1990	Governor	83,137 (41.1%)	119,283 (58.9%)
1988	President	114,609 (47.0%)	129,376 (53.0%)
	Senate	139,461 (57.3%)	104,043 (42.7%)

*Vote for Perot was 66,429 (23.0%).

Demographics

Population   570,901

Percent change from 1980   10.9%

Land area   1,100 square miles

Population per square mile   519

Counties, 1990 population
Ashtabula   99,821   Lake   215,499
Cuyahoga (pt.)   255,581

Cities, 1990 population   (10,000 or more)
Ashtabula   21,633   Middleburg Heights
Broadview Heights (pt.)   14,702
     10,701   North Royalton (pt.)
Brook Park   22,865   16,150
Conneaut   13,241   Painesville   15,699
Eastlake   21,161   Parma Heights   21,448
Garfield Heights (pt.)   Solon   18,548
     26,798   Strongsville (pt.)   10,554
Lyndhurst   15,982   Wickliffe   14,558
Maple Heights (pt.)   10,937   Willoughby   20,510
Mayfield Heights   19,847   Willowick   15,269
Mentor   47,358

Race and Hispanic origin
White   96.8%
Black   1.8%
American Indian, Eskimo, or Aleut.   0.1%
Asian or Pacific Islander   1.0%
Other   0.3%
Hispanic origin   0.9%

Ancestry
American   3.3%   Italian   14.6%
Czechoslovakian   2.8%   Polish   11.0%
Dutch   2.0%   Russian   2.2%
English   13.8%   Scotch Irish   1.8%
Finnish   1.5%   Scottish   2.3%
French   2.6%   Slovakian   6.9%
German   29.6%   Swedish   1.5%
Hungarian   5.9%   Welsh   1.2%
Irish   17.4%   Yugoslavian   3.7%

Universities/colleges, 1990-1991 enrollment
Cleveland College of Jewish Studies, Beachwood   59
Kent State University-Ashtabula, Ashtabula   906
Lake Erie College, Painesville   894
Lakeland Community College, Mentor   8,807
Ursuline College, Cleveland   1,604

Newspapers, total circulation (in all districts)
Akron Beacon Journal   157,049
Cleveland Plain Dealer   409,749
Lake County News Herald   53,516

Commercial television stations, affiliations
ADI: Cleveland (100%)

Cable television systems, total subscribers
Cablevision of Ohio; Brook Park   19,039
Cablevision of Ohio; Cleveland Heights   75,000
Continental Cablevision of Ohio; Mentor   36,978
Cox Cable Cleveland; Parma   56,000

TCI of Ohio; Ashtabula   12,267
TCI of Ohio; Chardon   14,878
TCI of Ohio; Conneaut   6,065
TCI of Ohio; Geneva   9,588

Businesses and other major employers

Ford Motor Co./Casting Plant; Cleveland; motor vehicles/equipment   4,000

Ford Motor Co./Cleveland Engine Plant 1; Cleveland; engines/equipment   3,500

Ford Motor Co.; Cleveland; metal stampings   2,300

Great Lakes Mall Inc.; Mentor; real estate operators   2,000

Picker Intl. Inc.; Cleveland; medical equipment/supplies   1,700

Southwest General Hospital; Cleveland   1,650

Stouffer Corp.; Cleveland; frozen food products   1,500

Allen-Bradley Co. Inc./Programmable Controller Div.; Cleveland; electrical industrial apparatus   1,500

Lubrizol Corp./Agrigenetics Co.; Wickliffe; chemical products   1,500

Cleveland Electric Illuminating/Perry Nuclear Power Plant; Perry; electric services   1,400

Bailey Controls Co.; Wickliffe; controlling devices   1,300

Continental Airlines Inc.; Cleveland; airline   1,200

Marymount Hospital Inc.; Cleveland   1,200

City of Willoughby/School District; Willoughby   1,100

Avery Intl. Corp./Specialty Tape Div.; Painesville; paper coatings   1,000

County of Lake; Painesville   1,000

Centerior Energy Corp.; Cleveland; electric services   900

Lake Hospital System Inc./Lake East; Painesville   800

Lake Hospital System Inc./Lake West; Willoughby   750

State of Ohio/Mental Health Dept.; Northfield   712

Matrix Essentials Inc.; Cleveland; toiletries/soaps   700

Bridgestone/Firestone Inc.; Cleveland; motor vehicle parts/supplies   700

State of Ohio/Transportation Dept.; Cleveland   650

City of Strongsville/School District; Cleveland   650

Kennametal Inc.; Cleveland; metalworking machinery   638

Ashtabula County Medical Center; Ashtabula   630

Ford Motor Co./Cleveland Engine Plant 2; Cleveland; motor vehicles/equipment   600

County of Cuyahoga/School District; Cleveland   600

Sverdrup Technology Inc.; Cleveland; engineering services   570

Menorah Park Center for the Aging; Cleveland; nursing   547

Cortez III Service Corp.; Cleveland; building services   543

Van Dorn Co./Plastic Machinery Div.; Cleveland; industry machinery   530

OKLAHOMA

Districts Established May 27, 1991

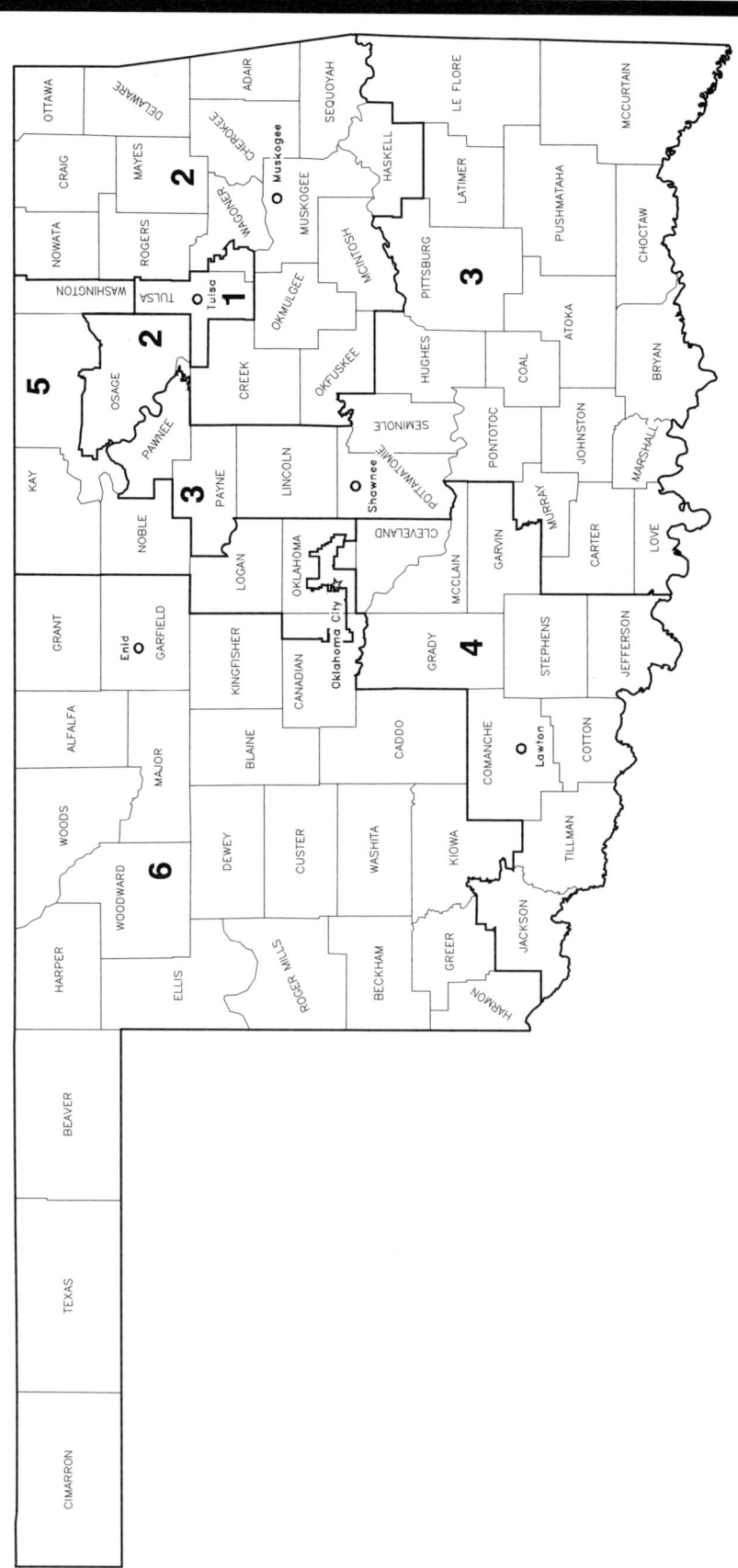

Oklahoma

Since statehood in 1907, most Oklahomans have made a living—sometimes a very good living—on what issued from the earth. Oil, gas, coal, beef, wheat and cotton have been important products. In addition, the armed forces have been lucrative tenants. The state has several huge military facilities with sizable civilian payrolls.

But the 1980s forced Oklahomans fundamentally to reassess their economy. It was a decade in which oil prices dropped by 50 percent, the U.S. farm economy went into depression and prospects for military spending clouded with the end of the Cold War. A state whose mineral heritage is so hallowed that it has oil wells on the Capitol grounds faced pressure to diversify its economy so that residents could maintain a decent standard of living.

Economic metamorphosis is under way in Oklahoma. Oklahoma's emerging economy—more reliant on the service sector and high-tech fields than on energy production and agriculture— has required a more educated work force than the state was accustomed to providing in years past. Addressing criticism that Oklahoma had neglected public education, the state Legislature in 1990 approved a sweeping $223 million measure increasing taxes to give teachers raises and to pay for new programs and teachers. Oklahomans in 1991 voted to reject a ballot measure that would have repealed the education and tax law.

The state enjoyed an oil boom from 1978 to 1982 as high worldwide prices spurred domestic production. But in 1982, the price of oil began to drop, and banks across the state began to fail. The 1981 price of $35 per barrel shrunk to $14 per barrel by 1986. In the peak year of 1982, oil and gas production in Oklahoma was valued at $10.5 billion, according to the state Department of Commerce's "Economic Report to the Governor 1990-1991." After dipping to a low of $5.2 billion in 1988, oil and gas production was valued in 1989 at $5.6 billion. According to the Commerce Department, Oklahoma's oil production was at its lowest level in more than 40 years.

Oklahoma's recession ended in the second half of 1987 as employment and personal income began to rise. But contrary to past experience, the recovery was not fueled by an upturn in energy. Instead, the service sector registered the fastest growth rates, coming to account for an increasing share of the state's economic activity.

In 1990, the service sector was the largest component of the state's economy, making up nearly one-fourth of the state's wage and salary employment. Health care and business services were the two biggest factors in that growth. Tourism and recreation also played a greater role.

The state's industrial mix has also undergone changes. The nonelectrical machinery industry, which included oil field equipment, has declined. But the transportation equipment and electronics industries have made significant gains. A growing number of high-tech companies—particularly in the field of aviation equipment—have either settled or expanded in Oklahoma.

All this economic ferment has helped generate political restlessness, as seen not only in the battle over the education measure but also in another arena with national implications— the term-limitation debate.

In 1990, Oklahoma became the first state to approve a ballot measure limiting lawmakers' terms. The same year, voters nominated two candidates for governor who never had held elective office. In winning the Democratic nomination, businessman David Walters defeated the Speaker of the state House and a seven-term U.S. House member. Walters went on to win the general election in November.

Congressional redistricting was not a point of controversy in Oklahoma. The Legislature stood aside and let the Democrats in the state's congressional delegation draw a new map. It was similar to its 1980s predecessor, with only a few counties moving districts.

Table 1   Population

District	Population	Population under 18	Voting-age population	Median age
1	524,264	138,106	386,158	32.6
2	524,264	141,838	382,426	35.0
3	524,264	135,954	388,310	34.2
4	524,265	142,563	381,702	31.0
5	524,264	136,234	388,030	33.4
6	524,264	142,312	381,952	33.5
State	3,145,585	837,007	2,308,578	33.2

Table 2 Voting-Age Persons

District	White*	Black*	American Indian, Eskimo, or Aleut*	Asian or Pacific Islander*	Other*	Hispanic*	Male*	Female*
1	85.1%	8.4%	4.6%	1.1%	0.8%	2.0%	47.2%	52.8%
2	80.0	4.8	14.7	0.2	0.3	0.9	47.6	52.4
3	85.8	3.6	9.5	0.6	0.5	1.1	47.5	52.5
4	85.8	6.5	4.2	1.7	1.8	3.3	49.2	50.8
5	88.4	4.8	4.0	1.6	1.2	2.6	46.9	53.1
6	80.9	11.8	4.2	1.0	2.1	3.5	47.7	52.3
State	84.3	6.7	6.9	1.0	1.1	2.2	47.7	52.3

*As percent of voting-age population.

Table 3 Voting-Age Persons by Age Groups

District	18-24*	25-44*	45-54*	55-64*	65 and over*
1	13.6%	45.9%	13.8%	11.3%	15.4%
2	12.2	38.4	15.3	13.5	20.6
3	14.9	36.9	13.8	12.6	21.7
4	16.9	43.9	13.4	10.8	14.9
5	12.9	44.5	13.8	11.5	17.4
6	13.0	40.3	13.8	12.7	20.2
State	13.9	41.7	14.0	12.1	18.4

*As percent of voting-age population.

Table 4 Income and Occupation

District	Median family income	Families in poverty	White collar*	Blue collar*	Service*	Farm*
1	$34,105	9.9%	63.6%	22.6%	12.9%	0.9%
2	24,808	15.9	46.7	34.6	14.3	4.5
3	23,106	17.8	48.1	31.7	15.4	4.8
4	29,639	11.2	57.0	25.9	14.2	2.9
5	34,888	8.8	64.5	20.9	12.6	2.0
6	26,418	14.7	48.6	28.8	16.1	6.5
State	28,554	13.0	55.3	27.0	14.2	3.5

*As percent of employed persons age 16 and over.

Table 5 Education: School Years Completed

District	Less than grade 9*	Grades 9-12 no diploma*	High school diploma*	College bachelor's degree or higher*
1	5.4%	12.9%	27.8%	23.4%
2	13.4	18.7	33.1	11.6
3	14.8	18.5	31.7	13.3
4	8.3	14.2	30.7	18.7
5	6.0	12.1	26.0	26.4
6	10.7	17.5	33.4	13.3
State	9.8	15.6	30.5	17.8

*As percent of persons age 25 and over.

Table 6 Housing and Residential Patterns

District	Owner occupied	Renter occupied	Urban	Rural
1	61.3%	38.7%	94.1%	5.9%
2	75.3	24.7	37.4	62.6
3	71.7	28.3	43.5	56.5
4	66.6	33.4	74.2	25.8
5	65.7	34.3	86.8	13.2
6	68.4	31.6	70.3	29.7
State	68.1	31.9	67.7	32.3

1st District

Tulsa; Part of Wagoner County

The precipitous fall of oil prices from the early to mid-1980s had a resounding impact on the city that not long ago was calling itself "The Oil Capital of the World." But by diversifying its economy, Tulsa has rebounded, propelled by its thriving aerospace and aviation industries.

American Airlines is the city's largest employer, providing about 12,000 jobs. American has moved its national headquarters for flight reservations to Tulsa, and the company's maintenance depot is at Tulsa International Airport. Tulsa also is a deep-water port accessible to the Gulf of Mexico, a status it gained in 1971 with the opening of the Arkansas River Navigation System.

McDonnell Douglas Corp. and Rockwell International are leading companies in Tulsa, although the receding defense budget has curtailed their expansion. Together, they now employ about 5,000.

Tulsa has become a manufacturing hub of flight simulators for military and civilian use. With several technical schools and aviation academies, it also has developed a worldwide reputation as an aviation training center.

Once a post office on the Pony Express trail, Tulsa was transformed by the discovery of oil nearby in 1901 and 1905. Oil drove Tulsa's economic development until the last decade. The repercussions of the 1980s price drop can be seen in the grand estates in southeast Tulsa, whose values plummeted with the oil fortunes that built them.

But with the local economy on the mend, real estate prices are beginning to rise. Young professionals are moving into some of the older, established neighborhoods in the central section of the city and renovating single-family homes, making the area near the University of Tulsa one of the city's hottest housing markets. This area is also home to a number of blue-collar families.

Tulsa was a forerunner in the trend of Sun Belt cities evolving into Republican-voting bastions. Tulsa County has gone Republican in all but two presidential elections since 1920. North Tulsa's predominantly black neighborhoods provide Democrats with their best turf.

But Tulsa's conservatism differs from Oklahoma City's more viscerally anti-government brand. Tulsa, for example, strongly backed a landmark 1990 education and tax reform law. That year, Democratic gubernatorial nominee David Walters crushed his conservative GOP opponent, who sought the law's repeal. In 1991, a ballot measure to repeal the law lost in Tulsa County by more than 2-to-1.

Tulsa's fundamentalist community is in the east, anchored by Oral Roberts University (3,200 students), a prominent tourist attraction. The 200-foot glass and steel prayer tower and the 60-foot bronze "Praying Hands" sculpture are big draws.

Southeast of Tulsa, the 1st takes in the city of Broken Arrow, home to many Tulsa workers who commute via the Broken Arrow Expressway. Broken Arrow also has a sizable fundamentalist community. In 1970, Broken Arrow had fewer than 12,000 people; its population now tops 58,000.

	1st District	Democrat	Republican
1992	President*	73,495 (29.6%)	122,189 (49.2%)
	House	106,619 (46.6%)	119,211 (52.2%)
1990	Senate	115,891 (82.6%)	24,415 (17.4%)
	Governor	75,483 (59.5%)	51,284 (40.5%)
1988	President	71,612 (35.1%)	132,382 (64.9%)
1986	Senate	64,704 (43.9%)	82,561 (56.1%)
	Governor	49,430 (35.2%)	91,013 (64.8%)

Vote for Perot was 52,088 (21.0%).

Demographics

Population 524,264

Percent change from 1980 4.1%

Land area 674 square miles

Population per square mile 778

Counties, 1990 population

Tulsa 503,341	Wagoner (pt.) 20,923

Cities, 1990 population (10,000 or more)

Broken Arrow (pt.) 56,871	Sand Springs (pt.) 15,015
Owasso (pt.) 11,063	Tulsa (pt.) 361,628

Race and Hispanic origin

White 83.2%
Black 9.6%
American Indian, Eskimo, or Aleut. 5.1%
Asian or Pacific Islander 1.2%
Other 0.9%
Hispanic origin 2.3%

Ancestry

American 6.3%	Italian 2.0%
Dutch 4.0%	Polish 1.3%
English 16.2%	Scotch Irish 3.5%
French 4.5%	Scottish 2.7%
German 24.7%	Swedish 1.5%
Irish 20.3%	Welsh 1.0%

Universities/colleges, 1990-1991 enrollment

Oklahoma College of Osteopathic Medicine, Tulsa 270
Dickinson Business School, Tulsa 284
National Education Center, Tulsa 2,293
Oklahoma Junior College of Business, Tulsa 542
Oral Roberts University, Tulsa 3,172
Tulsa Junior College, Tulsa 17,955
University of Tulsa, Tulsa 4,575

Newspapers, total circulation (in all districts)

Muskogee Phoenix-Time Democrat 19,383
Tulsa World/Tulsa Tribune 192,748

Commercial television stations, affiliations

ADI: Tulsa (100%)
KJRH, Tulsa (NBC)
KOKI-TV, Tulsa (Fox)
KOTV, Tulsa (CBS)
KTUL-TV, Tulsa (ABC)
KWHB, Tulsa (None)

Cable television systems, total subscribers

TCI Cablevision of Tulsa; Tulsa 160,000

Military installations, 1991

Tulsa Intl. Airport Air Force Guard Station, Tulsa 300

Businesses and other major employers

American Airlines Inc.; Tulsa; airline 12,000
St. Francis Hospital Inc.; Tulsa 3,095
McDonnell Douglas Corp.; Tulsa; aircraft 3,000
St. John Medical Center Inc.; Tulsa 2,280
Rockwell Intl. Corp./Tulsa Facility; Tulsa; navigation equipment 2,100
Purolator Products Inc.; Tulsa; motor vehicle parts 1,970
Hillcrest Medical Center Inc.; Tulsa 1,740
Amoco Production Co.; Tulsa; computer services 1,620
U.S. Army Corp. of Engineers; Tulsa; engineering services 1,294
Tulsa Regional Medical Center; Tulsa 1,210
Ford Motor Co./Tulsa Glass Plant; Tulsa; flat glass 1,050
Southwestern Bell Telephone Co.; Tulsa; telephone communications 1,000
Avis Rent-A-Car System/World Reservation Center; Tulsa; auto rentals 1,000
State of Oklahoma/Hissom Memorial Center; Sand Springs; nursing 999
Oral Roberts University; Tulsa 980
University of Tulsa; Tulsa 937
Citgo Petroleum Corp.; Tulsa; petroleum refining 850
World Publishing Co./Tulsa Daily World; Tulsa; newspapers 850
Hilti Inc.; Tulsa; metalworking machinery 825
Nordam; Tulsa; aircraft parts/equipment 806
Texaco Inc.; Tulsa; petroleum 800
County of Tulsa; Tulsa 800
City of Tulsa/Public Works Dept.; Tulsa 736
Bank of Oklahoma Tulsa; Tulsa; commercial banks 725
Oklahoma Fixture Co.; Tulsa; partitions/fixtures 700
Occidental Oil & Gas Corp.; Tulsa; petroleum/natural gas 700
State Farm General Insurance Co.; Tulsa; fire/marine/casualty insurance 700
Public Service Co. of Oklahoma; Tulsa; electric services 650
Memorex Telex Corp.; Tulsa; computer/office equipment 650
City of Skiatook/Public Schools; Skiatook 650
Group Health Service of Oklahoma/Blue Cross/Blue Shield of Oklahoma; Tulsa; medical service/health insurance 635
Koch Engineering Co. Inc./John Zink Co.; Tulsa; industry machinery 600
Williams Telecom Group/Wiltel; Tulsa; communication services 600
Sun Refining & Mktg Co.; Tulsa; petroleum refining 600
Oneok Inc./Oklahoma Natural Gas Co.; Tulsa; gas production/distribution 600
Metropolitan Life Insurance Co.; Tulsa; life insurance 600
Mapco Inc.; Tulsa; petroleum refining 575

2nd District

Northeast — Muskogee

The 2nd is Oklahoma's most imaginatively shaped district. It starts in the "Green Country" of northeast Oklahoma, but after curling underneath Tulsa County, it squirms through a gap between the 1st and 3rd districts to collect a large portion of rural, Democratic Osage County.

Democrats can do quite well here. The 2nd was one of two districts carried by Bill Clinton in 1992. In 1988, Democrat Michael S. Dukakis carried more than half the counties in the 2nd.

In recent years, tourism and recreation have joined the traditional engines of the 2nd's economy, agriculture and energy. The 2nd has part of the state's largest lake (Eufaula) and takes in several others, including Grand Lake O' the Cherokees, Fort Gibson, Tenkiller and Keystone. Accompanying the growth in the tourism industry has been a wave of retirees moving to the resort areas, where real estate prices are low. The population of Delaware County, which contains most of Grand Lake, grew by 17 percent during the 1980s.

But recreation has not supplanted the more time-honored enterprises. Soybeans, wheat and beef cattle are the district's main agricultural products. Many farmers raise both crops and livestock, helping them weather fluctuations in the farm economy. Eastern counties such as Adair, Delaware and Ottawa feature poultry production; several poultry and meat companies are close by, just over the Arkansas border.

The farm crisis of the 1980s did not spare rural areas in the 2nd. Small towns such as Stigler (Haskell County) suffered the same fate as many other midwestern communities, with farm-implement dealers and other agriculture-related businesses struggling and sometimes failing.

Muskogee—with 37,700 people, the 2nd's largest city—dredges silica sand from the Arkansas River beds for use in its glass industry. The Department of Veterans Affairs serves several states from its regional office in Muskogee.

Two of the 2nd's fastest-growing counties during the 1980s were Wagoner (15 percent) and Rogers (19 percent), which border Tulsa County and are absorbing Tulsa's exurbanization. They are the 2nd's only GOP strongholds. Along the 2nd's southern tier, voters resemble their "Little Dixie" neighbors, lending Democrats generous margins.

For many Native Americans, northeast Oklahoma was the end of the Trail of Tears—the U.S. Army's forced march in 1838 of Cherokees away from their homes in the southeast. The largest American Indian population in Oklahoma is concentrated within the 2nd's boundaries; the Cherokee Nation has its headquarters in Tahlequah (Cherokee County), and members of other tribes are scattered through surrounding counties.

Humorist Will Rogers, who was part Cherokee, was born near Claremore (Rogers County). His life and works are commemorated at the Will Rogers Memorial and celebrated each November during Will Rogers Days.

Election Returns

	2nd District	Democrat	Republican
1992	President*	96,510 (42.4%)	81,375 (35.7%)
	House	118,542 (54.8%)	87,657 (40.6%)
1990	Senate	119,507 (84.5%)	21,908 (15.5%)
	Governor	95,762 (71.8%)	37,621 (28.2%)
1988	President	98,300 (51.0%)	94,582 (49.0%)
1986	Senate	85,211 (54.5%)	71,234 (45.5%)
	Governor	76,775 (52.1%)	70,564 (47.9%)

*Vote for Perot was 49,107 (21.6%).

Demographics

Population 524,264

Percent change from 1980 3.8%

Land area 11,696 square miles

Population per square mile 45

Counties, 1990 population

Adair 18,421	Nowata 9,992
Cherokee 34,049	Okfuskee 11,551
Craig 14,104	Okmulgee 36,490
Creek 60,915	Osage (pt.) 33,100
Delaware 28,070	Ottawa 30,561
Haskell 10,940	Pawnee (pt.) 1,890
Mayes 33,366	Rogers 55,170
McIntosh 16,779	Sequoyah 33,828
Muskogee 68,078	Wagoner (pt.) 26,960

Cities, 1990 population (10,000 or more)

Claremore 13,280	Okmulgee 13,441
Miami 13,142	Sapulpa 18,074
Muskogee 37,708	Tahlequah 10,398

Race and Hispanic origin

White 77.1%
Black 5.1%
American Indian, Eskimo, or Aleut. 17.2%
Asian or Pacific Islander 0.2%
Other 0.4%
Hispanic origin 1.1%

Ancestry

American 10.8%	Irish 20.4%
Dutch 4.9%	Italian 1.0%
English 11.2%	Scotch Irish 2.3%
French 3.4%	Scottish 1.3%
German 19.3%	West Indian 1.1%

Universities/colleges, 1990-1991 enrollment

Bacone College, Muskogee 463
Connors State College, Warner 1,910
Northeastern State University, Tahlequah 8,849
Northeast Oklahoma A&M College, Miami 2,558
Oklahoma State University, Okmulgee 2,118
Rogers State College, Claremore 2,476

Newspapers, total circulation (in all districts)

Ft. Smith Southwest Times Record 41,089
Joplin Globe 36,407
Muskogee Phoenix-Time Democrat 19,383
Tulsa World/Tulsa Tribune 192,748

Commercial television stations, affiliations

ADI: Tulsa (90%), Ft. Smith (6%) and Joplin-Pittsburg (4%)
KDOR, Bartlesville (None)
KTFO-TV, Tulsa (None)

Cable television systems, total subscribers

TCI Cablevision of Tulsa; Tulsa 160,000
TCI of Arkansas; Fort Smith 27,700
TCI of Oklahoma; Muskogee 8,800

Businesses and other major employers

Fort Howard Corp.; Muskogee; paper mills 1,100
Muskogee Medical Center Authority; Muskogee 936

Cherokee Nation Tribe Oklahoma; Tahlequah; electronic
  components 800
Northeastern State University; Tahlequah 716
U.S. Veterans Affairs Dept.; Muskogee; hospital 700
Eastern State Hospital; Vinita 685
Indiana Glass Co./Bartlett-Collins Co.; Sapulpa;
  glass/glassware 517
Unarco Industries Inc.; Wagoner; wood products 515

3rd District

Southeast — "Little Dixie"

The only district in the state that lacks a major urban area, the 3rd sprawls across southeastern Oklahoma, with a three-county appendage on its northern end. The largest city in the 3rd, Stillwater (Payne County) has 36,700 people. Only two other cities in the district, Shawnee (Pottawatomie) and Ardmore (Carter), have more than 20,000 people.

Oklahoma's southeastern district historically has been its most reliably Democratic. Since becoming a state in 1907, the "Little Dixie" region has never elected a Republican to the House. The area was settled largely by migrants from Texas and Arkansas, and its voters are conservative Democrats. The 3rd was one of two Oklahoma districts Bill Clinton won in 1992.

In elections for offices below the presidency, most voters in the 3rd harbor little sympathy for the GOP. The most reliable territory for a Republican is along the district's northern corridor, which has more in common with more-Republican northern Oklahoma than with Little Dixie. In the three southern counties George Bush carried in 1988—Pontotoc, Carter and Le Flore—Democratic nominees for Senate and governor easily won in competitive 1986 contests, as well as in the more lopsided 1990 races. Bush won only three 3rd District counties in 1992, all in the northern corridor.

Although the 3rd has a significant energy industry, with several counties producing oil and natural gas, Little Dixie largely missed out on the oil discoveries that brought wealth—and Republicanism—to central and western Oklahoma. Wracked by rural depression in the 1920s and again in the 1980s, this region is the least prosperous area of Oklahoma today. The 3rd has four of the five counties with the highest poverty rates in the state.

Primarily rural, the 3rd relies on farming and livestock to fuel its economy. Beef cattle, chickens and hogs are raised throughout the 3rd. Tyson Foods, with headquarters in nearby Springdale, Ark., is building a $50 million hog-breeding complex in Holdenville (Hughes County). Bryan, Hughes and Love are among the nation's leading peanut-growing counties.

Timber is harvested in the Ouachita National Forest, in the southeastern part of the 3rd. In the south, truck farmers send their produce to the Campbell Soup factory just over the border in Paris, Texas.

Ardmore has a large, modern Uniroyal Goodrich tire factory. Many district residents who live on the outskirts of Oklahoma City work at Tinker Air Force Base (in the 4th District).

Oklahoma's maximum-security prison is in McAlester (Pittsburg County). The inmates' two-day rodeo in late summer has become a popular annual attraction. Lake Texoma in the southwest is a popular summer vacation destination.

The names of Coal and Pittsburg counties are reminders that coal was once mined in abundance in eastern Oklahoma; Latimer

and Le Flore counties also have significant coal reserves. Coal mining now accounts for a fraction of its previous share of the area's economy, but high-sulfur bituminous coal is still mined in those counties.

Election Returns

	3rd District	Democrat	Republican
1992	President*	94,763 (41.4%)	77,054 (33.6%)
	House	155,934 (73.8%)	51,725 (24.5%)
1990	Senate	130,524 (87.2%)	19,127 (12.8%)
	Governor	101,683 (71.0%)	41,605 (29.0%)
1988	President	97,216 (49.8%)	98,172 (50.2%)
1986	Senate	87,040 (54.9%)	71,510 (45.1%)
	Governor	87,281 (58.1%)	62,909 (41.9%)

Vote for Perot was 55,974 (24.4%).

Demographics

Population 524,264

Percent change from 1980 4.0%

Land area 17,964 square miles

Population per square mile 29

Counties, 1990 population

Atoka 12,778	Marshall 10,829
Bryan 32,089	McCurtain 33,433
Carter 42,919	Murray 12,042
Choctaw 15,302	Pawnee (pt.) 13,685
Coal 5,780	Payne 61,507
Hughes 13,023	Pittsburg 40,581
Johnston 10,032	Pontotoc 34,119
Latimer 10,333	Pottawatomie 58,760
Le Flore 43,270	Pushmataha 10,997
Lincoln 29,216	Seminole 25,412
Love 8,157	

Cities, 1990 population (10,000 or more)

Ada 15,820	McAlester 16,370
Ardmore 23,079	Shawnee 26,017
Durant 12,823	Stillwater 36,676

Race and Hispanic origin
White 83.4%
Black 4.0%
American Indian, Eskimo, or Aleut. 11.4%
Asian or Pacific Islander 0.6%
Other 0.5%
Hispanic origin 1.4%

Ancestry

American 9.6%	Irish 22.0%
Dutch 4.8%	Italian 1.4%
English 11.9%	Scotch Irish 2.4%
French 3.2%	Scottish 1.3%
German 18.9%	West Indian 1.2%

Universities/colleges, 1990-1991 enrollment
Carl Albert State College, Poteau 1,253
East Central Oklahoma State University, Ada 4,183
Eastern Oklahoma State College, Wilburton 1,784
Murray State College, Tishomingo 1,251

Oklahoma Baptist University, Shawnee 1,847
Oklahoma State University, Stillwater 19,827
Seminole Junior College, Seminole 1,486
Southeastern Oklahoma State University, Durant 3,971
St. Gregory's College, Shawnee 271

Newspapers, total circulation (in all districts)
Ada Evening News 9,195
Denison Herald 10,941
Ft. Smith Southwest Times Record 41,089
McAlester News-Capital & Democrat 11,733
Oklahoman & Times 215,876
Stillwater News Press 9,587
Tulsa World/Tulsa Tribune 192,748

Commercial television stations, affiliations
ADI: Ardmore-Ada (43%), Oklahoma City (24%), Tulsa (15%),
  Shreveport-Texarkana (10%) and Ft. Smith (9%)
  KHBS, Fort Smith (ABC)
  KTEN, Ada-Ardmore (ABC)
  KXII, Ardmore & Sherman-Denison, Texas (CBS)

Cable television systems, total subscribers
Cablecom of Ardmore; Ardmore 9,700
Cablevision of Stillwater; Stillwater 8,873
Falcon Telecable; Shawnee 8,500
Post Newsweek Cable; Ada 6,850
TCI of Oklahoma; Mcalester 7,051

Military installations, 1991
McAlester Army Ammunition Plant, Lawton 1,042

Businesses and other major employers
Oklahoma State University/Fort Reno Experiment Station;
  Stillwater 3,709
State of Oklahoma/Transportation Dept.; Ada 3,000
Oklahoma State University; Stillwater 2,500
Uniroyal Goodrich Tire Co.; Ardmore; tires 1,945
Blue Bell Inc./Wrangler; Seminole; outerwear 1,350
Tyson Foods Inc.; Broken Bow; meat products 1,200
Brunswick Corp.; Stillwater; engines/turbines 1,000
Weyerhaeuser Co./Southern Div.; Wright City; lumber materi-
  als 730
Weyerhaeuser Co./Paper Co.; Valliant; sawmills 700
Charles Komar & Sons Corp.; McAlester; undergarments 550
Valley View Hospital; Ada 546

4th District

Southwest; Part of Oklahoma City

The military is a ubiquitous force in the 4th, and Rep. Dave McCurdy, elected to a seventh term in 1992, has worked to keep it that way from his senior position on the Armed Services Committee. Altus Air Force Base, in Jackson County, is one of the Air Force's principal pilot training bases. The Army's Fort Sill is on the northwest side of Lawton (Comanche County). The district stretches north and east into Oklahoma County (Oklahoma City) to snare within its confines Tinker Air Force Base. With a combined civilian and military staff of almost 27,000, Tinker is the largest single-site employer in the state.

Agriculture and energy are the other dominant industries. Tillman and Jackson counties are among the nation's leaders in cotton harvesting. Jackson, Comanche, Stephens and Grady counties also grow wheat.

Despite price fluctuations, the energy industry has become important to the 4th's economy over the past 20 years. The gas- and oil-producing Anadarko Basin extends down from the 6th District into Comanche and Stephens counties. Halliburton employs about 2,500 people in Duncan (Stephens County) for oil-drilling research, development and manufacturing for its worldwide drilling enterprise.

The 1980s plummet in oil prices had a dramatic impact on much of the 4th, which had previously thrived on oil. As in many energy-dependent communities in the Southwest, banks and savings and loans failed during the decade. Oil prices bottomed out in 1986, but they have not approached the 1981 level of $32 per barrel.

With a population of about 81,000, Lawton is the third-largest city in Oklahoma (although it trails second-largest Tulsa by more than 280,000). Connected by an interstate turnpike to Oklahoma City and Wichita Falls, Texas, Lawton is the commercial center of southwest Oklahoma. Goodyear's tire and rubber plant—one of the largest factories in the state—employs more than 1,800.

The city of Norman has slightly more than 80,000 people and is home to the University of Oklahoma (20,800 students). The university's new energy center conducts research into oil-drilling techniques and alternative fuels. The university and such government-sponsored research programs as the National Severe Storm Laboratory are attracting high-tech industries.

On the southern border, the Red River, which marks the frontier between Texas and Oklahoma, has spawned considerable aggravation and acrimony over the years because of its capricious disregard for the states' boundaries. The river changes course whenever it floods, which results in hundreds of acres of farmers' land ending up in the other state. Some disputes have led to gunfire.

Bedroom communities have sprouted along I-44 from Chickasha into Oklahoma County. Suburban Moore, outside the Oklahoma City limits in Cleveland County, grew by 15 percent in the 1980s; it is strongly Republican. Elsewhere, though, lies conservative Democratic terrain. Democratic statewide candidates usually carry the 4th.

Election Returns

	4th District	Democrat	Republican
1992	President*	72,613 (33.3%)	90,467 (41.4%)
	House	140,841 (69.6%)	58,235 (28.8%)
1990	Senate	111,283 (82.4%)	23,788 (17.6%)
	Governor	80,085 (63.3%)	46,358 (36.7%)
1988	President	71,766 (41.7%)	100,417 (58.3%)
1986	Senate	53,966 (43.4%)	70,338 (56.6%)
	Governor	64,373 (55.0%)	52,713 (45.0%)

Vote for Perot was 53,921 (24.7%).

Demographics

Population 524,265

Percent change from 1980 3.6%

Land area 8,087 square miles

Population per square mile 65

Counties, 1990 population

Cleveland 174,253	Jefferson 7,010
Comanche 111,486	McClain 22,795
Cotton 6,651	Oklahoma (pt.) 52,271
Garvin 26,605	Stephens 42,299
Grady 41,747	Tillman 10,384
Jackson 28,764	

Cities, 1990 population (10,000 or more)

Altus 21,910	Midwest City (pt.) 41,334
Chickasha 14,988	Moore 40,318
Duncan 21,732	Norman 80,071
Fort Sill CDP 12,107	Oklahoma City (pt.) 45,448
Lawton 80,561	

Race and Hispanic origin

White 84.2%
Black 7.2%
American Indian, Eskimo, or Aleut. 4.8%
Asian or Pacific Islander 1.7%
Other 2.1%
Hispanic origin 4.0%

Ancestry

American 8.1%	Irish 21.2%
Dutch 4.2%	Italian 1.6%
English 14.2%	Polish 1.1%
French 3.8%	Scotch Irish 3.0%
German 23.1%	Scottish 1.9%

Universities/colleges, 1990-1991 enrollment

Cameron University, Lawton 5,276
Mid America Bible College, Oklahoma City 235
Oscar Rose State College, Midwest City 8,245
University of Oklahoma, Norman 20,774
University of Science and Arts of Oklahoma, Chickasha 1,559
Western Oklahoma State College, Altus 1,869

Newspapers, total circulation (in all districts)

Dallas Morning News 452,101
Lawton Constitution 23,432
Norman Transcript 14,400
Oklahoma City Journal Record 3,021
Oklahoman & Times 215,876

Commercial television stations, affiliations

ADI: Wichita Falls-Lawton (62%) and Oklahoma City (38%)
KSWO-TV, Lawton-Wichita Falls (ABC)
KJTL, Wichita Falls (Fox)

Cable television systems, total subscribers

Cablevision-Warr Acres; Norman 17,135
Cablevision-Warr Acres; Warr Acres 55,688
Cox Cable Oklahoma City; Oklahoma City 97,000
Lawton Cablevision; Lawton 24,500
Post Newsweek Cable TV; Altus 8,250
TCI of Oklahoma; Duncan 9,100

Military installations, 1991

Tinker Air Force Base, Midwest City 26,927
Fort Sill (Army), Lawton 19,454
Altus Air Force Base, Altus 4,096

Businesses and other major employers

General Motors Corp.; Oklahoma City; motor vehicles 5,800
University of Oklahoma; Norman 5,500
University of Oklahoma Health Sciences Center; Norman: 4,000
Halliburton Co.; Duncan; oil well services 3,000
Goodyear Tire & Rubber Co.; Lawton; tires 1,800
Norman Regional Hospital Authority; Norman 1,200
York Intl. Corp./Central Environmental Systems; Norman; construction machinery 1,000
Midwest City Regional Hospital; Oklahoma City 1,000
Comanche County Hospital Authority; Lawton 960
State of Oklahoma/Pauls Valley State School; Pauls Valley: 900
State of Oklahoma/Central State Hospital; Norman 820
City of Lawton; Lawton 720
United Design Corp.; Noble; pottery/china 671
Northrop Worldwide Aircraft Services; Lawton; airport services 635
Oscar Rose State College; Midwest City 600
City of Midwest City; Oklahoma City 571
City of Norman; Norman 541
Delta Faucet Oklahoma Inc.; Chickasha; plumbing fixtures 520

5th District

North Central — Part of Oklahoma City

As it sweeps from Oklahoma City north to the Kansas border, the 5th collects Republican-minded voters all along the way. Democrats may still have a registration edge in the 5th, but this is unmistakably GOP terrain. It was George Bush's best district in 1992; most of the counties in the 5th gave him more than 60 percent of the vote in 1988. Only the portion of Osage County in the district can be described as Democratic territory.

Oklahoma City enjoyed modest population growth of about 10 percent in the 1980s; much of this increase came in the city's more affluent northwest section, which remains in the new 5th. The district takes in such well-to-do suburbs as Nichols Hills, as well as medium-income suburbs such as Bethany. Remappers shifted the poorer black neighborhoods that had been in the 5th over to the 6th District. Bush carried the Oklahoma City portion of the 5th by more than 2-to-1 over Bill Clinton in 1992.

Oklahoma City's growth did not stop at the city limits. It spread north to Edmond and west—along the Northwest Expressway—into Canadian County. Edmond's population expanded by more than 50 percent in the 1980s; with slightly more than 52,300 people, it is now the sixth-largest city in Oklahoma. Canadian County experienced similarly rapid growth. Its population rose by 32 percent in the last decade, faster than any other county's.

Since the discovery of a large oil pool underneath Oklahoma City in the 1930s, much of the city's economy has revolved around the oil industry. But the sharp drop in oil prices from the early to the mid-1980s forced "O.K. City" (as locals call it) to diversify. The aviation industry is now a significant area employer, with the Federal Aviation Administration's training facility at the airport (in the 6th). The military has a prominent presence as well, with Tinker Air Force Base on the outskirts of the city (in the 4th). Others work in state government, trucking and meatpacking.

The 5th's northeastern anchor is Bartlesville (Washington County), the home of Phillips Petroleum. Oil has been of paramount importance to the local economy since 1897. Now,

Bartlesville is a genteel community of 34,000, boasting modern architecture—including an office and apartment building designed by Frank Lloyd Wright—a symphony orchestra, ballet and an annual Mozart festival.

Energy and agriculture are key components of the 5th's economy. Farmers grow wheat and soybeans and raise beef cattle. Phillips and Conoco have large refineries in the district. Kerr-McGee has a refinery nearby in the 6th District.

Guthrie (Logan County) was Oklahoma's first capital. The town, which is renovating its Victorian-era buildings, is being restored to the early 20th century. To the north in Noble County, Perry's annual Cherokee Strip Celebration commemorates the 1893 land run that led to its founding. The Cherokee Strip is a 12,000-square-mile area that makes up much of what is now north-central Oklahoma.

Election Returns

	5th District	Democrat	Republican
1992	President*	61,842 (24.6%)	129,465 (51.4%)
	House	107,579 (46.2%)	123,237 (53.0%)
1990	Senate	128,368 (79.6%)	32,906 (20.4%)
	Governor	76,235 (51.7%)	71,360 (48.3%)
1988	President	61,891 (30.7%)	139,871 (69.3%)
1986	Senate	45,154 (29.8%)	106,586 (70.2%)
	Governor	54,405 (39.2%)	84,350 (60.8%)

*Vote for Perot was 59,681 (23.7%).

Demographics

Population 524,264

Percent change from 1980 4.2%

Land area 4,663 square miles

Population per square mile 112

Counties, 1990 population

Canadian (pt.) 41,314	Oklahoma (pt.) 338,227
Kay 48,056	Osage (pt.) 8,545
Logan 29,011	Washington 48,066
Noble 11,045	

Cities, 1990 population (10,000 or more)

Bartlesville 34,256	Oklahoma City (pt.) 239,395
Bethany 20,075	Ponca City 26,359
Edmond 52,315	The Village 10,353
Guthrie 10,518	Yukon (pt.) 20,775

Race and Hispanic origin

White 86.6%
Black 5.6%
American Indian, Eskimo, or Aleut. 4.6%
Asian or Pacific Islander 1.7%
Other 1.5%
Hispanic origin 3.2%

Ancestry

American 7.3%	French 4.6%
Czechoslovakian 1.0%	German 27.1%
Dutch 4.4%	Irish 20.6%
English 17.7%	Italian 1.6%

Polish 1.3%	Scottish 2.7%
Scotch Irish 4.1%	Swedish 1.4%

Universities/colleges, 1990-1991 enrollment

Bartlesville Wesleyan College, Bartlesville 480
Langston University, Langston 2,792
Northern Oklahoma College, Tonkawa 1,892
Oklahoma Junior College, Oklahoma City 559
Oklahoma State University, Oklahoma City 4,139
Southern Nazarene University, Bethany 1,393
University of Central Oklahoma, Edmond 14,232

Newspapers, total circulation (in all districts)

Bartlesville Examiner Enterprise 13,185
Dallas Morning News 452,101
Oklahoma City Journal Record 3,021
Oklahoman & Times 215,876
Ponca City News 11,938
Tulsa World/Tulsa Tribune 192,748

Commercial television stations, affiliations

ADI: Oklahoma City (66%) and Tulsa (34%)

Cable television systems, total subscribers

Cablevision-Warr Acres; Warr Acres 55,688
Cox Cable Oklahoma City; Oklahoma City 97,000
Donrey Cablevision/Bartlesville; Bartlesville 13,765
Post Newsweek Cable TV; Ponca City 11,500

Businesses and other major employers

Phillips Petroleum Co.; Bartlesville; petroleum refining 7,000
AT&T Co.; Oklahoma City; communications equipment 6,100
Conoco Inc.; Ponca City; petroleum refining 4,000
Baptist Medical Center; Oklahoma City 2,694
South Community Hospital; Oklahoma City 1,695
Seagate Technology Inc.; Oklahoma City; computer equipment 1,500
Bridgestone/Firestone Inc./Dayton Tire; Oklahoma City; tires 1,450
Mercy Health Center; Oklahoma City 1,300
University of Central Oklahoma; Edmond 1,200
Deaconess Hospital; Oklahoma City 1,000
Camco Intl. Inc.; Bartlesville; industry machinery 900
American Fidelity Corp.; Oklahoma City; health insurance 837
Charles Machine Works Inc.; Perry; construction machinery 750
Blue Cross & Blue Shield of Oklahoma; Oklahoma City; insurance services 700
CMI Corp.; Oklahoma City; construction machinery 650
Auto Club of America Corp.; Oklahoma City; auto services/membership organizations 630
Hertz Corp./Worldwide Reservations; Oklahoma City; automotive rentals 600
City of Yukon/School District; Yukon 600
J. B. Hunt Transport Inc.; Oklahoma City; trucking services 584
Jane Phillips Episcopal Hospital; Bartlesville 560
Smith Intl. Inc./Smith-Gruner Div.; Ponca City; construction machinery 545

6th District

West and Panhandle; Part of Oklahoma City

In terms of economy, occupation, personality and politics, the 6th spans a wider range than any other Oklahoma district. From inner-city black neighborhoods and booming suburbs in and around Oklahoma City to the wild frontier of the panhandle, the 6th encompasses all aspects of Oklahoma. It is massive: Covering more than 25,000 square miles, the 6th District is larger than 10 states.

Western Oklahoma is traditionally the state's most conservative region. Residents share an aversion to most government activity other than military expenditures and agricultural subsidies. Part of the Dust Bowl, western Oklahoma was devastated in the 1930s and 1940s. It made great strides in the two postwar decades, becoming a region of massive wheat farms and cattle ranches. But the double shock in the 1980s of falling energy prices and the farm credit crisis dealt the district another economic setback. Most counties in the 6th lost population then, many by more than 10 percent.

The historical origins of Oklahoma's settlers indicate the state's voting patterns. Northern Oklahoma's settlers came from Kansas and Nebraska, importing their Republican voting habits. The northern tier of the 6th is the most solid GOP territory in the state. Many of these counties gave George Bush more than 70 percent of the vote in 1988. He won many of them in 1992 by more than 2-to-1. Two Panhandle counties, Texas and Beaver, were the only ones in the state carried by 1990 Republican gubernatorial nominee Bill Price.

Texans settled the southwestern part of Oklahoma. Like the area they left, the southern part of the district is dominated by conservative, "yellow dog" Democrats. Bill Clinton carried the six southernmost counties in 1992.

Agriculture and energy are the mainstays of the 6th's economy. Hard red winter wheat is grown across the district, especially in the north and northwest. Beef cattle are also raised in the 6th. In the south, cotton and peanuts are key commodities. Caddo County ranks second in the nation in peanuts harvested. Much of the energy production in the district is in the panhandle, where there are huge gas fields.

About 40 percent of the district's population lives in Oklahoma County (Oklahoma City). While the rest of the district lost population during the 1980s, Oklahoma and adjacent Canadian County grew; Canadian boomed by 32 percent, the most in the state. Clinton carried the 6th's share of Oklahoma County.

Oklahoma City is split among three districts. The 6th's portion includes the most famous symbols of the state's oil wealth: working wells on the grounds of the state Capitol. Also included in the 6th are most of the city's 71,000 blacks. State government offices and the Federal Aviation Administration's Aeronautical Center at Will Rogers World Airport are major employers, but many residents also work across district lines at Tinker Air Force Base (4th District), General Motors (4th District) and AT&T (5th District).

Election Returns

	6th District	Democrat	Republican
1992	President*	73,843 (34.2%)	92,379 (42.8%)
	House	134,734 (67.4%)	64,068 (32.1%)
1990	Senate	130,083 (83.0%)	26,642 (17.0%)
	Governor	93,923 (65.6%)	49,329 (34.4%)
1988	President	82,611 (42.3%)	112,916 (57.7%)
1986	Senate	64,128 (41.3%)	91,181 (58.7%)
	Governor	72,735 (50.9%)	70,084 (49.1%)

Vote for Perot was 49,106 (22.8%).

Demographics

Population 524,264

Percent change from 1980 4.2%

Land area 25,595 square miles

Population per square mile 20

Counties, 1990 population

Alfalfa 6,416	Greer 6,559
Beaver 6,023	Harmon 3,793
Beckham 18,812	Harper 4,063
Blaine 11,470	Kingfisher 13,212
Caddo 29,550	Kiowa 11,347
Canadian (pt.) 33,095	Major 8,055
Cimarron 3,301	Oklahoma (pt.) 209,113
Custer 26,897	Roger Mills 4,147
Dewey 5,551	Texas 16,419
Ellis 4,497	Washita 11,441
Garfield 56,735	Woods 9,103
Grant 5,689	Woodward 18,976

Cities, 1990 population (10,000 or more)

Del City 23,928	Mustang 10,434
El Reno 15,414	Oklahoma City (pt.)
Elk City 10,428	159,812
Enid 45,309	Weatherford 10,124
Midwest City (pt.) 10,933	Woodward 12,340

Race and Hispanic origin

White 78.3%
Black 13.2%
American Indian, Eskimo, or Aleut. 4.9%
Asian or Pacific Islander 1.0%
Other 2.6%
Hispanic origin 4.4%

Ancestry

American 8.7%	German 23.2%
Dutch 4.4%	Irish 17.9%
English 13.0%	Scotch Irish 2.9%
French 3.2%	Scottish 1.5%

Universities/colleges, 1990-1991 enrollment

El Reno Junior College, El Reno 1,177
Northwestern Oklahoma State University, Alva 1,746
Oklahoma Christian College, Oklahoma City 1,617
Oklahoma City Community College, Oklahoma City 8,015
Oklahoma City University, Oklahoma City 2,957
Oklahoma Panhandle State University, Goodwell 1,275
Phillips University, Enid 964
Southwestern Oklahoma State University, Weatherford 5,373
University of Oklahoma/Health Sciences, Oklahoma City 2,818

Newspapers, total circulation (in all districts)

Enid News & Eagle 22,176

Oklahoma City Journal Record 3,021
Oklahoman & Times 215,876
Tulsa World/Tulsa Tribune 192,748

Commercial television stations, affiliations
ADI: Oklahoma City (74%), Amarillo (15%), Wichita-Hutchinson (7%) and Wichita Falls-Lawton (4%)
KFOR, Oklahoma City (NBC)
KOCB, Oklahoma City (None)
KOCO-TV, Oklahoma City (ABC)
KOKH-TV, Oklahoma City (Fox)
KSBI, Oklahoma City (None)
KTBO-TV, Oklahoma City (None)
KTLC, Oklahoma City (Fox)
KWTV, Oklahoma City (CBS)
KVIJ-TV, Sayre (ABC)

Cable television systems, total subscribers
Cablevision-Warr Acres; Warr Acres 55,688
Cox Cable Oklahoma City; Oklahoma City 97,000
TCI of Oklahoma; Enid 13,244
Woodward Cable Co.; Woodward 5,100

Military installations, 1991
Vance Air Force Base, Enid 2,364
Will Rogers World Airport Air Force Guard Station, Oklahoma City 267

Businesses and other major employers
State of Oklahoma; Oklahoma City 4,113
State of Oklahoma/Human Resources Dept.; Oklahoma City 3,248
Federal Aviation Administration; Oklahoma City 3,000
State of Oklahoma/Public Safety Dept.; Oklahoma City 3,000
University of Oklahoma/Health Services Center; Oklahoma City 2,500
St. Anthony Hospital; Oklahoma City 2,095
U.S. Postal Service; Oklahoma City 2,000
Kerr-McGee Corp.; Oklahoma City; petroleum/natural gas 2,000
State of Oklahoma/Military Dept.; Oklahoma City 1,500
U.S. Veterans Affairs Dept.; Oklahoma City; hospital 1,400
Northrop Worldwide Aircraft Services; Enid; airport services 1,200
County of Oklahoma & County Library; Oklahoma City 1,200
Hospital Corp. of America/Presbyterian Hospital; Oklahoma City 1,200
State of Oklahoma/Tax Commission; Oklahoma City 1,200
Oklahoma Publishing Co. Inc.; Oklahoma City; newspapers 1,100
State of Oklahoma/Transportation Dept.; Oklahoma City 1,000
Kerr McGee Coal Corp.; Oklahoma City; coal mining 900
Southwestern Oklahoma State University; Weatherford 900
Gulfstream Aerospace Technology; Oklahoma City; aircraft 830
Macklanburg-Duncan Co.; Oklahoma City; metal doors/frames 800
Banks of Mid-America Inc.; Oklahoma City; commercial banks 800
Fred Jones Mfg. Co.; Oklahoma City; motor vehicle parts 750
City of Oklahoma City/Fire Dept.; Oklahoma City 750
Hillcrest Health Center Inc.; Oklahoma City 725
Oklahoma Gas & Electric Co.; Oklahoma City; electric services 700
Scrivner Inc.; Oklahoma City; grocery stores 700
General Health Services Inc./St. Mary's Hospital; Enid 650
Minnesota Mining & Mfg. Co.; Weatherford; industry machinery 625
Unit Parts Co.; Oklahoma City; motor vehicle parts 600
State of Oklahoma/Corrections Dept.; Oklahoma City 600
City of Oklahoma City; Oklahoma City 600
State of Oklahoma/Human Services Dept.; Oklahoma City 600
Oneok Inc./Oklahoma Natural; Oklahoma City; utility services 564
State of Oklahoma/Agriculture Dept.; Oklahoma City 552
Central Food Service; Oklahoma City; bars/restaurants 520

Oregon

Placid, bucolic Oregon began the 1990s as a state in economic and political turmoil. Two mainstays of the state's economy, timber and fishing, were in jeopardy as courts acted to enforce the Endangered Species Act to protect owls and salmon. Loggers' relationship with Oregon's sizable environmental community bordered on violence.

Oregon's politics are becoming equally polarized. Traditionally, the candidates that fared best in statewide elections tended to be moderate to liberal, regardless of party. But a potent political movement of conservative Christian activists has become a significant factor in state politics since the mid-1980s.

The conservatives formed a grass-roots organization, the Oregon Citizens Alliance (OCA), which has demonstrated political savvy and logged electoral success. OCA members have moved into Republican Party ranks. Their potency was first displayed in 1990, when an OCA-backed independent candidate effectively swung the gubernatorial election to the Democrats. In 1992, an OCA-sponsored ballot measure that would have banned the state from extending to homosexuals protections reserved in law for minorities nearly passed. The measure attracted nationwide attention to the state. After the defeat, OCA immediately began working on a toned-down rewrite.

The struggles of the wood-products industry are felt particularly acutely in the southwestern portion of the state. Communities such as Roseburg, which calls itself the Timber Capital of the Nation, have watched their unemployment rates rise as mills close and timber jobs are cut.

And yet, despite the questions surrounding its future, Oregon was a magnet for newcomers moving to the state during the 1980s. Metropolitan Portland has drawn Californians and other out-of-staters seeking a more favorable "quality of life." The suburbs west of Portland fostered a boom in high-tech businesses that faded somewhat in the latter part of the decade. Suburban Washington County, the state's second most populous, was the fastest-growing county in the state during the 1980s, its population increasing by 27 percent.

Compared with the thorny redistricting challenges in a number of states—dealing with seat gains and losses, increasing minority-group representation as mandated by the Voting Rights Act—the task of reshaping of Oregon's 1st District during 1991 redistricting did not looked like a major obstacle.

However, redistricting was regarded as crucial by Oregon Democrats, who hoped to retain the 1st District seat being vacated by a Democrat. Republicans also hoped to win the open 1st (composed of Portland, its western suburbs and northwest Oregon).

The parties' failure to reach agreement led to a redistricting stalemate in the state Legislature that eventually had to be untangled by a federal court panel. Republicans had a majority in the state House, while Democrats controlled the Senate and the governor's office, held by Barbara Roberts.

The Legislature, which meets every other year, ended its 1991 regular session without approving a plan redrawing the state's five congressional districts. Remapping responsibility then went to a three-judge federal panel. But the panel's chief judge was reluctant for the court to perform a duty that belonged to the Legislature. He hinted that he might direct Roberts to call the Legislature into special session to draw a new map.

The panel issued a ruling urging that the Legislature be convened for a special session to complete redistricting. The judges resisted drawing the new district lines but noted that unless the Legislature convened and acted by Dec. 1, the court would step in. A special bipartisan legislative panel of House and Senate members agreed on a compromise plan. But that plan was rejected by the full Democratic Senate caucus. On Dec. 2, the judges adopted the compromise map produced by the special legislative committee.

The new map improved Republican chances in the 1st by concentrating it more in Portland's affluent Washington County suburbs and by transferring a pair of Democratic-leaning rural counties—Tillamook and Lincoln—to the Democratic-held 5th District. Republican-leaning Polk County was also was added to the 5th. In 1992 Democrat Elizabeth Furse won the 1st with 52 percent of the vote, and Democrat Mike Kopetski breezed to re-election in the 5th.

Table 1   Population

District	Population	Population under 18	Voting-age population	Median age
1	568,461	142,766	425,695	33.9
2	568,464	150,401	418,063	35.9

OREGON

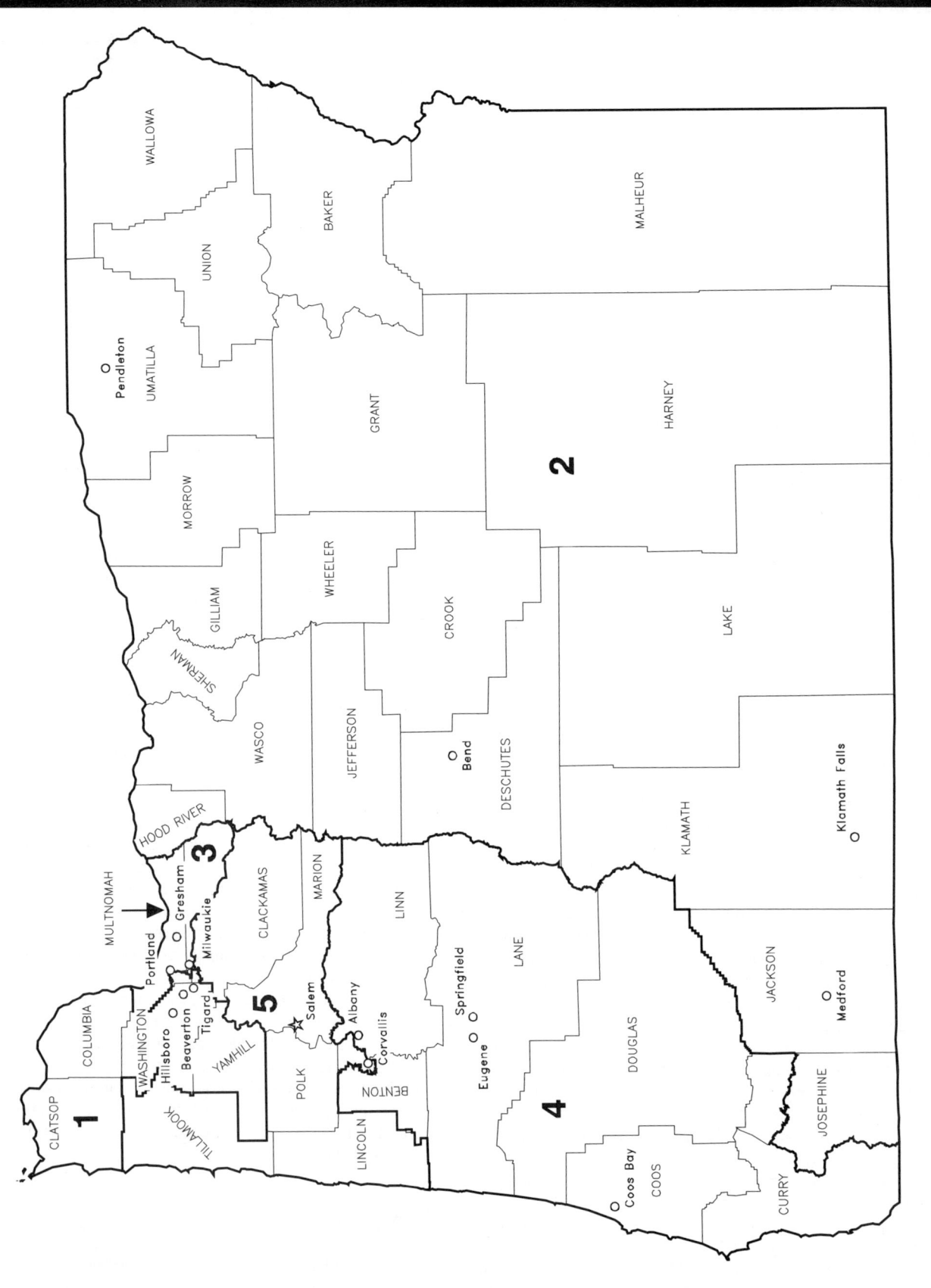

District	Population	Population under 18	Voting-age population	Median age
3	568,465	139,923	428,542	33.9
4	568,465	143,763	424,702	35.2
5	568,466	147,277	421,189	34.1
State	2,842,321	724,130	2,118,191	34.5

Table 2 Voting-Age Persons

District	White*	Black*	American Indian, Eskimo, or Aleut*	Asian or Pacific Islander*	Other*	Hispanic*	Male*	Female*
1	93.8%	0.8%	0.7%	3.2%	1.6%	3.4%	48.7%	51.3%
2	94.8	0.3	1.9	0.9	2.2	4.2	48.8	51.2
3	88.8	5.0	1.0	4.1	1.0	2.7	47.5	52.5
4	96.4	0.4	1.2	1.3	0.6	1.9	48.3	51.7
5	94.3	0.6	1.1	2.0	2.1	4.1	48.8	51.2
State	93.6	1.4	1.2	2.3	1.5	3.3	48.4	51.6

*As percent of voting-age population.

Table 3 Voting-Age Persons by Age Groups

District	18-24*	25-44*	45-54*	55-64*	65 and over*
1	12.3%	48.0%	14.4%	9.8%	15.6%
2	11.0	40.4	14.5	12.8	21.3
3	12.8	46.4	12.8	10.1	17.9
4	13.0	41.3	14.2	12.0	19.5
5	14.1	42.5	14.2	11.1	18.2
State	12.6	43.7	14.0	11.2	18.5

*As percent of voting-age population.

Table 4 Income and Occupation

District	Median family income	Families in poverty	White collar*	Blue collar*	Service*	Farm*
1	$40,587	5.5%	64.8%	21.3%	11.1%	2.8%
2	28,187	11.0	47.7	29.2	14.6	8.5
3	32,627	9.0	56.7	27.6	14.2	1.5
4	29,057	10.1	50.3	29.9	14.5	5.4
5	33,675	7.9	56.2	24.5	14.2	5.2
State	32,336	8.7	55.5	26.3	13.6	4.5

*As percent of employed persons age 16 and over.

Table 5 Education: School Years Completed

District	Less than grade 9*	Grades 9-12 no diploma*	High school diploma*	College bachelor's degree or higher*
1	4.3%	8.4%	23.2%	30.8%
2	7.6	14.7	33.3	15.2
3	5.9	12.7	28.7	19.0
4	6.5	14.1	30.9	17.1
5	6.6	11.8	28.6	20.7
State	6.2	12.3	28.9	20.6

*As percent of persons age 25 and over.

Table 6 Housing and Residential Patterns

District	Owner occupied	Renter occupied	Urban	Rural
1	59.7%	40.3%	81.6%	18.4%
2	66.8	33.2	50.0	50.0
3	58.7	41.3	94.2	5.8
4	64.4	35.6	61.1	38.9
5	66.2	33.8	65.5	34.5
State	63.1	36.9	70.5	29.5

1st District

Western Portland and Suburbs

The Portland-based 1st starts on the western bank of the Willamette River, which splits Oregon's largest city. The district's urban component is downtown Portland and nearby city neighborhoods that tend to be liberal and affluent; to the west are fast-growing Republican suburbs.

Metropolitan Portland has drawn California exiles and other out-of-staters searching for "livability"—less congestion, a moderate cost of living, a big city that still has a sense of community. Portlanders flock downtown to Saturday Market beneath the Burnside Bridge and attend events in Pioneer Courthouse Square and Waterfront Park. Each June the "City of Roses" hosts its popular Rose Festival.

In the past two decades, businesses and people have streamed into the suburbs west of Portland. The 1st is dominated by suburban Washington County; with 312,000 people, it is the state's second-most-populous county. Washington was the state's fastest-growing county in the 1980s; its population increased almost 27 percent. Suburban growth and 1991 redistricting have amplified the 1st's GOP element. During remapping, Republicans lobbied hard to include in the 1st the GOP-heavy Clackamas County city of Lake Oswego.

The high-tech businesses that sprouted along U.S. 26 in Washington County during the 1980s suffered a decline, leaving empty office space; the high-tech industry now appears to be on the rebound. Bedroom communities of Portland such as Beaverton, Tigard and Hillsboro, once modest in size, have become satellite cities with their own economies. Electronics and computer companies such as Tektronix, Intel and Mentor Graphics provide thousands of jobs. Nike, the sports-shoe manufacturer, has its futuristic headquarters in Beaverton. Portland's light-rail line is slated to connect the downtown with Hillsboro, 18 miles to the west, by the mid-1990s.

Republicans outnumber Democrats in suburban Washington County. But the Republicans here are some of the most liberal in the country, and they are more than willing to cast split ballots.

Outside the Portland metropolitan area, the 1st becomes rural and more Democratic. The fishing and logging counties of Columbia and Clatsop are the strongest Democratic areas of the 1st outside Portland, although many of those Democrats are more conservative than Portland's affluent liberals. Columbia County has voted for every Democratic presidential nominee since 1932; Clatsop County went for Adlai E. Stevenson in 1956 and has remained in the Democratic column for president.

Both the logging and salmon industries are threatened by court action enforcing the Endangered Species Act. The last of the big canneries closed in Astoria in the mid-1980s. Tourism buoys the local economy of some coastal communities, such as Seaside and Cannon Beach. Oregon's modest wine industry is centered in the Tualatin and northern Willamette valleys of Yamhill County, which tends to vote Republican.

Election Returns

	1st District	Democrat	Republican
1992	President*	136,630 (44.2%)	99,304 (32.1%)
	House	152,917 (52.0%)	140,986 (48.0%)
1990	Senate	93,188 (44.0%)	118,478 (56.0%)
	Governor	104,388 (55.2%)	84,711 (44.8%)
1988	President	115,644 (50.3%)	114,144 (49.7%)
1986	Senate	59,558 (30.3%)	137,104 (69.7%)
	Governor	102,564 (51.1%)	98,092 (48.9%)

Vote for Perot was 73,134 (23.7%).

Demographics

Population 568,461

Percent change from 1980 7.9%

Land area 2,959 square miles

Population per square mile 192

Counties, 1990 population

Clackamas (pt.) 32,911	Multnomah (pt.) 87,587
Clatsop 33,301	Washington 311,554
Columbia 37,557	Yamhill 65,551

Cities, 1990 population (10,000 or more)

Aloha CDP 34,284	McMinnville 17,894
Astoria 10,069	Newberg 13,086
Beaverton 53,310	Portland (pt.) 85,310
Forest Grove 13,559	Tigard 29,344
Hillsboro 37,520	Tualatin (pt.) 13,264
Lake Oswego (pt.) 29,980	

Race and Hispanic origin

White 93.2%
Black 0.8%
American Indian, Eskimo, or Aleut. 0.8%
Asian or Pacific Islander 3.4%
Other 1.8%
Hispanic origin 4.0%

Ancestry

American 2.6%	Italian 3.3%
Danish 1.9%	Norwegian 5.1%
Dutch 4.2%	Polish 2.2%
English 21.3%	Russian 1.4%
Finnish 1.5%	Scotch Irish 3.1%
French 5.8%	Scottish 4.6%
French Canadian 1.0%	Swedish 5.1%
German 32.2%	Swiss 1.3%
Irish 16.3%	Welsh 1.6%

Universities/colleges, 1990-1991 enrollment

Clatsop Community College, Astoria 1,154
George Fox College, Newberg 1,062
Linfield College, McMinnville 2,225
Oregon Graduate Institute, Beaverton 292
Oregon Health Science University, Portland 1,356
Pacific University, Forest Grove 1,523

Portland Community College, Portland 21,888
Portland State University, Portland 17,316

Newspapers, total circulation (in all districts)

Daily Astorian 8,988
Longview Daily News 24,649
Portland Oregonian/Sunday 335,758
Salem Statesman Journal 60,641

Commercial television stations, affiliations

ADI: Portland (100%)
KATU, Portland (ABC)
KGW-TV, Portland (NBC)
KOIN-TV, Portland (CBS)
KPTV, Portland (None)
KPDX, Vancouver (Fox)

Cable television systems, total subscribers

Columbia Cable; Aloha 57,858
Falcon Cable TV; Warrenton 15,500
Paragon of Portland; Portland 100,000
TCI of Oregon; Dayton 8,500
TCI of Oregon; West Portland 41,382

Businesses and other major employers

Tektronix Inc.; Beaverton; testing/measuring devices 6,000
Barrett Business Services Inc.; Portland; personnel supply services 4,800
Intel Corp./System Group; Hillsboro; electronic components 3,500
Portland State University; Portland 3,070
U.S. Veterans Affairs Dept.; Portland; hospital 2,500
U.S. Bancorp; Portland; commercial banks 2,340
Blue Cross/Blue Shield of Oregon; Portland; medical service/health insurance 1,922
Nike Inc.; Beaverton; sports footwear 1,900
Good Samaritan Hospital & Medical Center; Portland 1,807
First Interstate Bank of Oregon; Portland; commercial banks 1,600
Sequent Computer Systems Inc.; Beaverton; computer equipment 1,200
Portland General Electric Co./Trojan Nuclear Plant; Rainier; electric services 1,200
James River Corp. Virginia/Wauna Mill; Clatskanie; pulp mills 1,200
County of Washington; Hillsboro 1,100
McCormick & Schmick Mangement Services; Portland; bars/restaurants 1,000
City of Portland/Police Dept.; Portland 1,000
Standard Insurance Co.; Portland; life insurance 931
Pacificorp; Portland; electric services 900
Portland Community College; Portland 850
Mentor Graphics Corp.; Beaverton; computer design services 850
City of Portland/Fire Dept.; Portland 825
Graphic Arts Center Inc.; Portland; commercial printing 800
ESCO Corp.; Portland; construction machinery 800
Epson Portland Inc.; Beaverton; computers/printers 800
Tektronix Inc.; Forest Grove; electronic components 799
U.S. Army Corps of Engineers; Portland 725
Oregonian Publishing Co./Oregonian; Portland; newspapers 700
Tuality Community Hospital; Hillsboro 650
Boise Cascade Corp.; St. Helens; paper mills 600

Epson Portland Inc.; Hillsboro; computers/printers 600
Tualatin Hills Park Recreation District; Beaverton 600
A-DEC Inc./Dectron; Newberg; dental equipment 580
Crowd Management Services Inc.; Portland; security services 575
U.S. Dept. Treasury/Internal Revenue Service; Portland 550
Electro Scientific Industries; Portland; electrical equipment/supplies 540
Northwest Natural Gas Co.; Portland; gas distribution 538
Meridian Park Hospital; Tualatin 525
U.S. Forest Service; Portland 510

2nd District

East and Southwest — Medford; Bend

The 2nd is enormous, covering more than two-thirds of Oregon and bordering Washington, Idaho, Nevada and California. It is the state's most reliably Republican district, and the only one George Bush carried in 1992.

For the most part, people in the 2nd work the land, whether that means timber, livestock, crops or fruit. In a district where the federal government owns three-quarters of the land, loggers' jobs ride on court action restricting timber harvesting in national forests. Fishermen who make their living catching salmon on the Columbia River have also been snagged by endangered-species action.

Jack rabbits outnumber voters in the 2nd; any House candidate has to focus on a few widely scattered population centers. Although the district's two most-populous counties, Jackson and Deschutes, both registered double-digit growth in the 1980s, most of the counties in the 2nd lost population during the last decade.

With about 47,000 people, Medford (Jackson County) is the largest city in the 2nd. Medford is surrounded by pear, cherry and apple orchards of the fruit-growing Rogue River Valley. Less than 20 miles southeast of Medford is Ashland, which has hosted the Oregon Shakespeare Festival since 1935, drawing more than 400,000 visitors annually from February through October.

Population in Deschutes County has soared since 1970, as nearby skiing areas lured people to build summer homes and vacation condominiums. In 1986, the Democratic gubernatorial candidate referred to Bend, the county's population center, as "the middle of nowhere"; in the ensuing four years, Deschutes grew faster than any other county in the state. Its 21 percent growth during the 1980s was behind only the 27 percent of Washington County, in Portland's suburbs in the 1st District.

Bend has attracted high-tech and light industry, emblematic of central Oregon's effort to diversify its economy and reduce its dependence on timber. Deschutes County also grows potatoes, mint and hay.

Jackson and Deschutes both tend to prefer Republican candidates. Although Bush lost both in 1992, GOP Sen. Bob Packwood carried both comfortably in his tough re-election battle.

Beef cattle graze on public land throughout eastern Oregon. Alfalfa and hay grow on the dry, thinly settled plateau. In the north, most people live along or near the irrigated Columbia River Valley, where wheat ripens on steep golden hillsides. Umatilla county is the second in the nation in wheat harvesting. Pears, cherries and apples grow near Hood River, a popular wind-surfing destination. Potatoes are grown and processed for export around Hermiston.

Election Returns

		Democrat	Republican
	2nd District		
1992	President*	97,672 (35.0%)	106,839 (38.3%)
	House	90,036 (32.8%)	184,163 (67.2%)
1990	Senate	97,582 (47.8%)	106,751 (52.2%)
	Governor	74,315 (43.1%)	98,239 (56.9%)
1988	President	99,643 (44.3%)	125,333 (55.7%)
1986	Senate	77,577 (39.2%)	120,327 (60.8%)
	Governor	89,924 (44.0%)	114,618 (56.0%)

Vote for Perot was 74,539 (26.7%).

Demographics

Population 568,464

Percent change from 1980 7.9%

Land area 70,596 square miles

Population per square mile 8

Counties, 1990 population

Baker 15,317	Klamath 57,702
Crook 14,111	Lake 7,186
Deschutes 74,958	Malheur 26,038
Gilliam 1,717	Morrow 7,625
Grant 7,853	Sherman 1,918
Harney 7,060	Umatilla 59,249
Hood River 16,903	Union 23,598
Jackson 146,389	Wallowa 6,911
Jefferson 13,676	Wasco 21,683
Josephine (pt.) 57,174	Wheeler 1,396

Cities, 1990 population (10,000 or more)

Altamont CDP 18,591	Hermiston 10,040
Ashland 16,234	Klamath Falls 17,737
Bend 20,469	La Grande 11,766
City of the Dalles 11,060	Medford 46,951
Grants Pass 17,488	Pendleton 15,126

Race and Hispanic origin
White 93.7%
Black 0.3%
American Indian, Eskimo, or Aleut. 2.3%
Asian or Pacific Islander 0.9%
Other 2.8%
Hispanic origin 5.4%

Ancestry

American 4.0%	Italian 2.6%
Danish 1.5%	Norwegian 3.4%
Dutch 4.5%	Polish 1.3%
English 21.4%	Scotch Irish 3.8%
French 5.7%	Scottish 3.8%
French Canadian 1.1%	Swedish 3.7%
German 28.2%	Welsh 1.3%
Irish 16.9%	

Universities/colleges, 1990-1991 enrollment
Blue Mountain Community College, Pendleton 2,829

Central Oregon Community College, Bend 3,036
Eastern Oregon State College, La Grande 2,224
Oregon Institute of Technology, Klamath Falls 2,987
Rogue Community College, Grants Pass 2,312
Southern Oregon State College, Ashland 5,164
Treasure Valley Community College, Ontario 3,065

Newspapers, total circulation (in all districts)
Ashland Daily Tidings 5,292
Baker City Herald 2,930
Bend Bulletin 22,694
Grants Pass Daily Courier 17,521
La Grande Observer 7,245
Medford Mail Tribune 27,171
Pendleton East Oregonian 12,324
Portland Oregonian/Sunday 335,758
San Francisco Chronicle Examiner 692,424
Walla Walla Union/Bulletin 14,872

Commercial television stations, affiliations
ADI: Portland (38%), Medford (26%), Boise (20%), Yakima
   (7%), Spokane (4%) and Bend (4%)
   KTVZ, Bend (NBC)
   KDKF, Klamath Falls (ABC)
   KFTS, Klamath Falls (None)
   KOTI, Klamath Falls (NBC)
   KOBI, Medford (NBC)
   KTVL, Medford (CBS)

Cable television systems, total subscribers
Bend Cable Communications Inc.; Bend 14,730
Falcon Cable TV; The Dalles 5,500
TCI Cablevision of Northeast Oregon; Pendleton 9,500
TCI of Oregon; Grants Pass 13,033
TCI of Oregon; Klamath Falls 12,500
TCI of Oregon; Medford 31,000

Military installations, 1991
Kingsley Field Air Force Guard Station, Klamath Falls, 376

Businesses and other major employers
Confederated Timber Tracts of Warm Springs; Warm Springs;
   timber 1,496
Rogue Valley Medical Center; Medford 1,440
Bend Millwork Systems Inc.; Bend; millwork 1,400
Ore-Ida Foods Inc.; Ontario; frozen vegetables 1,200
St. Charles Medical Center; Bend 1,020
Boise Cascade Corp.; Medford; sawmills 1,000
J. R. Simplot Co.; Hermiston; potatoes/vegetables 950
Weyerhaeuser Co.; Klamath Falls; sawmills 900
Boise Cascade Corp.; La Grande; wood products 850
Bear Creek Corp.; Medford; fruit/nuts 800
Southern Oregon State College; Ashland 750
Lamb-Weston Inc.; Boardman; preserved fruits/vegetables 700
Merle West Medical Center; Klamath Falls 650
Lamb-Weston Inc.; Hermiston; preserved fruits/vegetables 595
Jeld-Wen Inc.; Klamath Falls; millwork 550

3rd District

East and North Portland and Eastern Suburbs

Socially and politically, Portland is two cities. East of the Willamette River, in the 3rd, Portland is a working-class town.

Blue-collar neighborhoods abut middle-class suburbs. The section west of the river is generally more affluent and elegant.

In an area with little cultural diversity—the Portland metropolitan area is more than 90 percent white—northeast and southeast Portland are veritable melting pots. The Albina section is home to many of Portland's blacks; it is the poorest area in the city. There are also Asian and Hispanic communities east of the river. Some young white professionals live in the Irvington, Alameda and Laurelhurst sections of East Portland.

Democratic candidates take comfortable margins in the 3rd, thanks to blacks in the Albina section, blue-collar whites in North Portland and the many elderly residents of the east side.

But many voters in the 3rd are conservative, white working-class "Reagan Democrats," particularly in such areas as the St. Johns section of North Portland, East County, the Clackamas County suburb of Milwaukie, and the cities of Gresham and Troutdale east of Portland.

New to the 3rd for the 1990s is a section west of the Willamette River in southwest Portland that includes the large homes and winding streets of Dunthorpe, one of Portland's most expensive neighborhoods. Democrats are few and far between here, but the small number of Republican voters in this area does not alter the 3rd's overall Democratic cast.

While Portland's commercial center remains west of the Willamette, the city has been investing of late in some east side projects. The Lloyd Center, one of the country's oldest urban malls, has had significant renovation. The Oregon Museum of Science and Industry has moved from southwest Portland to a new, larger east side home under the Marquam Bridge. Pro basketball's Trail Blazers are expected to move into a larger east side arena at the new Oregon Convention Center in the mid-1990s.

Over the last decade there was growth in the east side suburbs of Multnomah County, a few of which are as sumptuous as the in-town residential areas west of the Willamette. Gresham, the eastern terminus of Portland's light-rail line, is the largest of the 3rd's suburban cities.

Gresham tripled in size during the 1970s and grew in the 1980s to a population of 68,200; it is now Oregon's fourth-largest city. Gresham's annual Mount Hood Festival of Jazz draws national and international artists each August.

Once outside the suburbs, Multnomah and Clackamas counties quickly turn rural. There are a few farms along the Columbia River, the 3rd's northern boundary. Visitors to the underwater viewing room at the Bonneville Lock and Dam can observe migrating fish ascending a fish ladder.

Mount Hood National Forest occupies most of the district's eastern part.

Election Returns

	3rd District	Democrat	Republican
1992	President*	146,835 (52.8%)	72,338 (26.0%)
	House	208,028 (77.1%)	50,235 (18.6%)
1990	Senate	107,746 (50.2%)	106,987 (49.8%)
	Governor	127,454 (65.3%)	67,706 (34.7%)
1988	President	142,586 (61.9%)	87,646 (38.1%)
1986	Senate	77,527 (37.7%)	128,246 (62.3%)
	Governor	118,168 (56.4%)	91,213 (43.6%)

Vote for Perot was 58,900 (21.2%).

Demographics

Population 568,465

Percent change from 1980 7.9%

Land area 814 square miles

Population per square mile 698

Counties, 1990 population

| Clackamas (pt.) 72,165 | Multnomah (pt.) 496,300 |

Cities, 1990 population (10,000 or more)

Gresham 68,235	Portland (pt.) 352,009
Hazelwood CDP 11,480	Powellhurst-Centennial
Milwaukie 18,692	CDP 28,756

Race and Hispanic origin
White 87.3%
Black 5.9%
American Indian, Eskimo, or Aleut. 1.2%
Asian or Pacific Islander 4.5%
Other 1.2%
Hispanic origin 3.2%

Ancestry

American 2.6%	Italian 3.6%
Danish 1.5%	Norwegian 4.7%
Dutch 3.4%	Polish 1.8%
English 18.1%	Russian 1.2%
French 5.4%	Scotch Irish 3.2%
French Canadian 1.1%	Scottish 3.6%
German 30.7%	Swedish 4.7%
Irish 16.2%	Welsh 1.4%

Universities/colleges, 1990-1991 enrollment
Columbia Christian College, Portland 280
Concordia College, Portland 816
ITT Technical Institute, Portland 554
Lewis & Clark College, Portland 3,525
Mount Hood Community College, Gresham 7,480
Multnomah School of the Bible, Portland 621
Oregon Polytechnic Institute, Portland 234
Reed College, Portland 1,331
University of Portland, Portland 2,460
Warner Pacific College, Portland 462
Western Conservative Baptist Seminary, Portland 521
Western States Chiropractic College, Portland 418

Newspapers, total circulation (in all districts)
Portland Oregonian/Sunday 335,758

Commercial television stations, affiliations
ADI: Portland (100%)

Cable television systems, total subscribers
Paragon of Portland; Portland 100,000
TCI of Oregon; West Portland 41,382

Military installations, 1991
Portland Intl. Airport Air Force Guard Station, Portland 760

Businesses and other major employers
Providence Medical Center; Portland 2,541
Boeing Co.; Portland; aircraft 1,960
Emanuel Hospital; Portland 1,700

Bonneville Power/Ross Substation; Portland; electric services 1,650
Portland Adventist Medical Center; Portland 1,600
Precision Castparts Corp.; Portland; nonferrous castings 1,200
Con-Way Western Express Inc./Affiliated Express; Portland; trucking/courier services 1,100
Freightliner Corp.; Portland; trucks 1,100
Blount Inc./Oregon Cutting Systems; Portland; cutlery/handtools/hardware 1,000
Wacker Siltronic Corp.; Portland; electronic components 1,000
Gunderson Inc.; Portland; railroad equipment 1,000
State of Oregon/Oregon Air National Guard; Portland 906
Delta Air Lines Inc.; Portland; airline 900
Jantzen Inc.; Portland; sportswear 865
Reynolds Metals Co.; Troutdale; nonferrous metals 850
Roundup Co. Inc./Fred Meyer; Portland; grocery stores 800
County of Multnomah/Public Schools; Portland 800
United Grocers Inc.; Portland; grocery products 750
Tri-County Metro Transportation District; Portland 700
Southwest Marine Inc./Northwest Marine; Portland; shipbuilding/repairing 700
Fujitsu Microelectronics Inc.; Gresham; electronic components 650
Nabisco Brands Inc.; Portland; bakery products 650
Oregon Steel Mills Inc.; Portland; steel products 610
United Parcel Service Inc.; Portland; mail services 575
Nationwide Mutual Insurance Co.; Portland; fire/marine/casualty insurance 570
Oeco Corp.; Portland; transformers 569
American Red Cross/Oregon Trail Chapter; Portland; family services 553
U.S. Forest Service; Gresham 550
Liberty Northwest Insurance Corp.; Portland; fire/marine/casualty insurance 512
Container Corp. America; Portland; paperboard products 501

4th District

Southwest — Eugene

Loggers, fishermen and environmentalists combine to give the 4th a potentially combustible political mix. Many of the district's communities are dependent on the wood-products industry; others make their living in salmon fishing. But more than half the district vote is cast in Lane County (Eugene), home to the University of Oregon (18,800 students) and a sizable environmentalist faction. A politician running districtwide has the precarious task of balancing the economic needs of loggers and fishermen against others' concerns for protection of the environment.

Most of the ancient, old-growth forest that is the habitat of the threatened northern spotted owl is in the Cascade Range in the eastern part of the 4th. Court orders enforcing the Endangered Species Act have blocked logging in national forestland, affecting many area residents who make their living cutting timber on public lands.

Roseburg (Douglas County), which calls itself the Timber Capital of the Nation, is perhaps the most timber-dependent community in the district. Mill closures and other timber-related cutbacks have boosted its unemployment rate. An influx of retirees from California has helped keep Roseburg's population from dropping precipitously. In January 1993, Douglas' 14 percent unemployment rate was the second-highest in the state. Unemployment linked to the timber industry also has been high in Linn County (Albany).

Along the Pacific Coast, Coos County (Coos Bay) has also seen once-thriving timber mills close. Coos and Linn both suffer from double-digit unemployment. Coastal towns such as Charleston, Bandon and Port rely on the salmon fishing industry, which faces cutbacks because of declining runs.

With a university and some light industry, Eugene has weathered the timber decline better through economic diversity. But a large segment of Eugene's economy is still linked to timber processing. For the workers and their families whose lives are tethered to the lumber industry, jobs and growth are more important than environmental preservation. Industrial employment has been unsteady in Eugene and its timber-dominated neighbor, Springfield.

Eugene in the 1960s and 1970s was a mecca for the back-to-nature counterculture. Many students stayed after graduation. As they moved into workaday society, they learned how to influence local politics; they usually elect liberal Democrats. But the electoral history of Lane County is mixed. Lane voted for Republican presidential candidates in 1968, 1972 and 1980, and for Democrats in 1976, 1984, 1988 and 1992. In 1990, it voted for Democrat Barbara Roberts for governor and Republican Mark O. Hatfield for Senate. The Democrat nominee for the Senate beat GOP Bob Packwood in Lane in 1992.

Agriculture also contributes to the 4th's economy. There are some dairy farms on the south coast (Bandon prides itself on its cheddar cheese). In the north, ryegrass is grown in the fertile Willamette Valley.

Election Returns

	4th District	Democrat	Republican
1992	President*	123,387 (42.3%)	93,889 (32.2%)
	House	199,372 (71.4%)	79,733 (28.6%)
1990	Senate	97,727 (45.9%)	115,218 (54.1%)
	Governor	88,228 (49.2%)	91,224 (50.8%)
1988	President	125,651 (54.7%)	104,165 (45.3%)
1986	Senate	83,748 (41.3%)	119,089 (58.7%)
	Governor	114,928 (55.1%)	93,744 (44.9%)

Vote for Perot was 74,447 (25.5%).

Demographics

Population 568,465

Percent change from 1980 8.0%

Land area 16,081 square miles

Population per square mile 35

Counties, 1990 population

Benton (pt.) 14,602	Josephine (pt.) 5,475
Coos 60,273	Lane 282,912
Curry 19,327	Linn 91,227
Douglas 94,649	

Cities, 1990 population (10,000 or more)

Albany (pt.) 29,462	Eugene 112,669
Coos Bay 15,076	Lebanon 10,950
Roseburg 17,032	Springfield 44,683
Santa Clara CDP 12,834	

Race and Hispanic origin
White 96.0%
Black 0.5%
American Indian, Eskimo, or Aleut. 1.4%
Asian or Pacific Islander 1.4%
Other 0.8%
Hispanic origin 2.4%

Ancestry

American 5.4%	Italian 2.6%
Danish 1.8%	Norwegian 4.0%
Dutch 4.5%	Polish 1.7%
English 20.4%	Scotch Irish 3.4%
French 5.9%	Scottish 3.6%
French Canadian 1.0%	Swedish 4.1%
German 30.4%	Welsh 1.4%
Irish 17.3%	

Universities/colleges, 1990-1991 enrollment
Lane Community College, Eugene 8,407
Linn-Benton Community College, Albany 6,132
Northwest Christian College, Eugene 257
Southwestern Oregon Community, Coos Bay 2,847
Umpqua Community College, Roseburg 2,067
University of Oregon, Eugene 18,840

Newspapers, total circulation (in all districts)
Albany Democrat-Herald 21,265
Coos Bay World 14,738
Corvallis Gazette-Times 13,215
Eugene Register-Guard 72,656
Grants Pass Daily Courier 17,521
Portland Oregonian/Sunday 335,758
Roseburg News Review 20,489
Salem Statesman Journal 60,641

Commercial television stations, affiliations
ADI: Eugene (70%), Portland (18%) and Medford (12%)
KCBY-TV, Coos Bay (CBS)
KMTZ, Coos Bay (NBC)
KEVU, Eugene (None)
KEZI, Eugene (ABC)
KMTR-TV, Eugene (NBC)
KVAL-TV, Eugene (CBS)
KDRV, Medford (ABC)
KPIC, Roseburg (CBS)

Cable television systems, total subscribers
Falcon Cable TV; Bear Mt. 6,808
Falcon Cable TV; Coos Bay 10,792
Falcon Cable TV; Roseburg 8,100
Falcon Cable TV; Smith River 11,000
TCI of Oregon; Corvallis 25,000
TCI of Oregon; Eugene 48,284

Businesses and other major employers
University of Oregon; Eugene 6,720
Lane Community College; Eugene 2,614
Sacred Heart General Hospital; Eugene 2,400
Weyerhaeuser Co./Engineered Fiber Panels Div.; Springfield; paperboard mills 1,800
City of Eugene/School District; Eugene 1,780
Roseburg Forest Products Co.; Dillard; millwork 1,600

Teledyne Inc./Wah Chang Div.; Albany; nonferrous metals
  1,200
County of Lane; Eugene 1,050
U.S. Forest Service; Eugene 900
Linn-Benton Community College; Albany 900
Bay Area Hospital; Coos Bay 750
U.S. Forest Service; Roseburg 670
U.S. Postal Service; Eugene 650
County of Douglas/Educational Services; Roseburg 640
McKenzie-Willamette Hospital; Springfield 635
U.S. Veterans Affairs Dept.; Roseburg; hospital 613
James River Corp. Virginia; Halsey; pulp mills 600
Evanite Fiber Corp.; Corvallis; wood products 600
Weyerhaeuser Co.; Cottage Grove; sawmills 550
Southern Pacific Transportation Co.; Eugene; railroads 550

5th District

Willamette Valley, Pacific Coast — Salem; Corvallis

Oregon's four major industries—timber, agriculture, fishing and tourism—are all represented in the 5th. While hardly solid Democratic territory, the 5th has enough traditional Democrats in coastal Tillamook and Lincoln counties and enough independent voters in some of Clackamas County's Portland suburbs to offset generally big Republican margins in Marion County.

Some old-growth forests are in Mount Hood National Forest in the eastern part of the district. Logging families and owners of small, family-run mills in places such as Mill City, Detroit and Molalla have no use for the environmental protections aimed at preserving the northern spotted owl—or for politicians sympathetic to the owl.

Forty percent of the 5th's population is in Marion County (Salem), usually a dependable Republican base. GOP Sens. Bob Packwood and Mark O. Hatfield scored well above their statewide percentages in Marion in their re-elections in 1992 and 1990.

Clackamas, Marion and Polk counties are at the heart of the Willamette Valley, Oregon's most productive agricultural area. It is the center of Oregon's greenhouse and nursery crop industry, the state's second-largest agricultural commodity group. Trees and shrubs are grown, primarily for export. The area is renowned for its fruits and berries, as well as its grass seeds. Willamette hops from Marion and Clackamas go into some of the country's finest beers. Polk County grows cherries and wine grapes; wineries dot Polk and Marion counties. Marion is among the top counties in the nation for snap beans.

Along the coast, tourism and fishing fuel the economy. The resort town of Newport (Lincoln County) is also a vibrant fishing community known for its Dungeness crabs. Sport fishing is popular in such coastal towns as Lincoln City, Waldport and Yachats. To the north in Tillamook County, dairy and timber predominate. The Tillamook County Creamery Association employs more than 300 people to produce its famous cheddar cheese.

The district reaches into Portland's Clackamas County suburbs; West Linn is one of Oregon's wealthiest communities. Along the Clackamas River is Oregon City, the western terminus of the Oregon Trail, 2,000 miles from Independence, Mo. Incorporated in 1844, Oregon City is the oldest city west of the Missouri River.

The 5th contains only a corner of Benton County, but that includes the city of Corvallis, the district's only major city outside of Salem. It is the home of Oregon State University's 16,000 students and numerous political activists who make Corvallis the most liberal area in the 5th.

Election Returns

		Democrat	Republican
	5th District		
1992	President*	116,790 (39.8%)	103,387 (35.3%)
	House	174,443 (64.0%)	97,984 (36.0%)
1990	Senate	97,076 (43.0%)	128,533 (57.0%)
	Governor	100,286 (52.5%)	90,778 (47.5%)
1988	President	116,126 (50.1%)	115,694 (49.9%)
1986	Senate	72,701 (33.7%)	143,025 (66.3%)
	Governor	117,130 (53.3%)	102,725 (46.7%)

Vote for Perot was 73,071 (24.9%).

Demographics

Population 568,466

Percent change from 1980 8.0%

Land area 5,553 square miles

Population per square mile 102

Counties, 1990 population
Benton (pt.) 56,209   Marion 228,483
Clackamas (pt.) 173,774   Polk 49,541
Lincoln 38,889   Tillamook 21,570

Cities, 1990 population (10,000 or more)
Corvallis (pt.) 44,737   Oatfield CDP (pt.) 10,939
Four Corners CDP 12,156   Oregon City 14,698
Gladstone 10,152   Salem 107,786
Hayesville CDP 14,318   West Linn 16,367
Keizer 21,884   Woodburn 13,404

Race and Hispanic origin
White 93.6%
Black 0.6%
American Indian, Eskimo, or Aleut. 1.2%
Asian or Pacific Islander 2.0%
Other 2.5%
Hispanic origin 5.0%

Ancestry
American 3.5%   Norwegian 4.7%
Danish 1.7%   Polish 1.5%
Dutch 4.1%   Russian 1.3%
English 20.0%   Scotch Irish 3.3%
French 5.6%   Scottish 3.8%
French Canadian 1.1%   Swedish 4.3%
German 33.2%   Swiss 1.5%
Irish 15.7%   Welsh 1.5%
Italian 2.6%

Universities/colleges, 1990-1991 enrollment
Chemeketa Community College, Salem 9,172
Clackamas Community College, Oregon City 6,437
Marylhurst College, Marylhurst 1,031
Oregon State University, Corvallis 16,042
Western Baptist College, Salem 417
Western Oregon State College, Monmouth 4,571

Willamette University, Salem   2,339

Newspapers, total circulation (in all districts)
  Portland Oregonian/Sunday   335,758
  Albany Democrat-Herald   21,265
  Corvallis Gazette-Times   13,215
  Salem Statesman Journal   60,641

Commercial television stations, affiliations
  ADI: Portland (100%)
    KBSP-TV, Salem (None)
    KEBN, Salem (None)

Cable television systems, total subscribers
  Falcon Cable TV; Dallas   5,860
  North Willamette Telecom; Canby   6,143
  TCI of Oregon; Newport   5,700
  TCI of Oregon; Oregon City   21,555
  Viacom Cablevision; Salem   38,300

Businesses and other major employers
  Oregon State University; Corvallis   8,200
  State of Oregon/Transportation Dept.; Salem   5,000
  State of Oregon/Fairview Training Center; Salem; nursing

3,000
Salem Hospital; Salem   2,500
Hewlett-Packard Co.; Corvallis; calculators   2,200
Kaiser Foundation Hospitals; Clackamas   2,000
Clackamas Community College; Oregon City   1,550
Chemeketa Community College; Salem   1,440
Safeway Inc.; Clackamas; grocery warehousing   1,300
State of Oregon/Human Resource Dept.; Salem   1,300
State of Oregon/Police Dept.; Salem   1,140
Mentor Graphics Corp.; Wilsonville; computer design services   1,100
Precision Castparts Corp.; Clackamas; metal products   900
State of Oregon/Revenue Dept.; Salem   900
City of Salem; Salem   900
State Farm Mutual Auto Insurance Co.; Salem; insurance services   900
County of Marion; Salem   820
Good Samaritan Hospital; Corvallis   700
Pay Less Drug Stores; Wilsonville; drug stores   665
State of Oregon/Workers' Compensation Div.; Salem   650
Siltec Corp.; Salem; electronic components   623
Willamette Falls Hospital Inc.; Oregon City   550
State of Oregon/Justice Dept.; Salem   550

Pennsylvania

Just like in the last round of redistricting, Pennsylvania's congressional delegation entered the new decade minus two seats. Ten years ago, Democrats bore the brunt of the two-seat loss. This time around, Republicans took the hit.

Plain old incompetence was partly to blame—a series of procedural and legal GOP missteps greatly strengthened the Democrats' hand. State House Republicans failed to submit their plan on time to the Commonwealth Court judge who took over redistricting duties after the Legislature failed to approve a map. And Senate Republicans were not permitted to amend the plan they submitted because the judge ruled that their proposed amendments amounted to a wholesale revision. Since the deadline for submitting briefs had passed, he refused to consider their amendments. As a result, Republicans did not have a viable plan before the court.

The final map eliminated a Republican seat in the Pittsburgh suburbs and paired two Republicans in the Philadelphia suburbs. The suburban Pittsburgh seat, the old 18th, was dissolved into several different districts forcing incumbent GOP Rep. Rick Santorum to run in a heavily Democratic, Monongahela Valley district on the other side of the city. Thanks to Democratic infighting and his own formidable grass-roots efforts, Santorum won, but it will be a biennial battle for Republicans to keep the seat. On the other side of the state, the old 5th and 7th suburban Philadelphia districts were combined, leading one GOP incumbent to announce his retirement. Another development of note in southeastern Pennsylvania was the new racial composition of the Philadelphia-based 1st District. The seat remains a Democratic bastion, but it went from a heavily white ethnic population to a majority-minority composition, thus giving the state a second majority-minority seat (the other one is the Philadelphia-based 2nd).

Pennsylvania's two-seat loss reflected a hemorrhage of residents from the state's two largest cities, Pittsburgh and Philadelphia, linked to the effects of deindustrialization.

The western portion of the state acutely felt the population loss, mainly due to the collapse of steel, coal mining and heavy manufacturing. In the Shenango, Beaver and Monongahela valleys, small steel towns slowly suffocated, as companies pulled out and unemployed workers left to search for work. One such place, the town of Aliquippa, entered the 1990s with about one-third the population it had in the 1950s. Back then, the town's seven-mile-long steel works along the Ohio River employed 15,000. Today, it is operated by a skeleton crew.

The decline of heavy industry also took a toll on the small and midsized cities of eastern Pennsylvania. Cities like Allentown, Bethlehem, Easton, Reading and Scranton have been forced to wean themselves from the industries that breathed life into their respective cities. But while those traditional regional industries may be dying or leaving the state, population levels in eastern Pennsylvania, at least, have remained fairly static.

The northeastern counties along the New Jersey border experienced a population influx as New York business executives extended their commute to the mountain and resort areas of Monroe, Pike and Wayne counties. In the metropolitan Philadelphia region, population increases paralleled the new jobs and industries that sprouted in the suburban counties that ring the big city. But the good fortunes of Bucks, Chester, Delaware and Montgomery counties came at the expense of the City of Brotherly Love. Most of the jobs came from businesses fleeing Philadelphia's high taxes and crime rates. Middle-class residents also continued their decades-long exodus, further eroding the city's tax base.

Population losses have also affected the Pittsburgh (Allegheny County) region, but economically, Pittsburgh has made a far smoother transition to the post-industrial era than Philadelphia. Pittsburgh has always been the hub of western Pennsylvania, with a face toward the industrial Midwest, but now the city is taking on a more cosmopolitan character. The downtown skyline has been radically transformed from steel mills and smokestacks to gleaming glass and steel skyscrapers. Growth industries are clean and high-tech. A new international airport is expected to position Pittsburgh better in the global market.

One trait the two cities share is a monolithic Democratic vote. Strong unions and a concentration of minorities make Pittsburgh the lynchpin of heavily Democratic western Pennsylvania. South of Pittsburgh, in the coal-rich southwestern corner of the state, the United Mine Workers hold sway despite a decline in mining jobs. Outside of Pittsburgh and Philadelphia, this is the most reliably Democratic region in the state. The steel-producing Beaver and Shenango valleys, farther north and on the Ohio border, are also Democratic strongholds, as is the city of

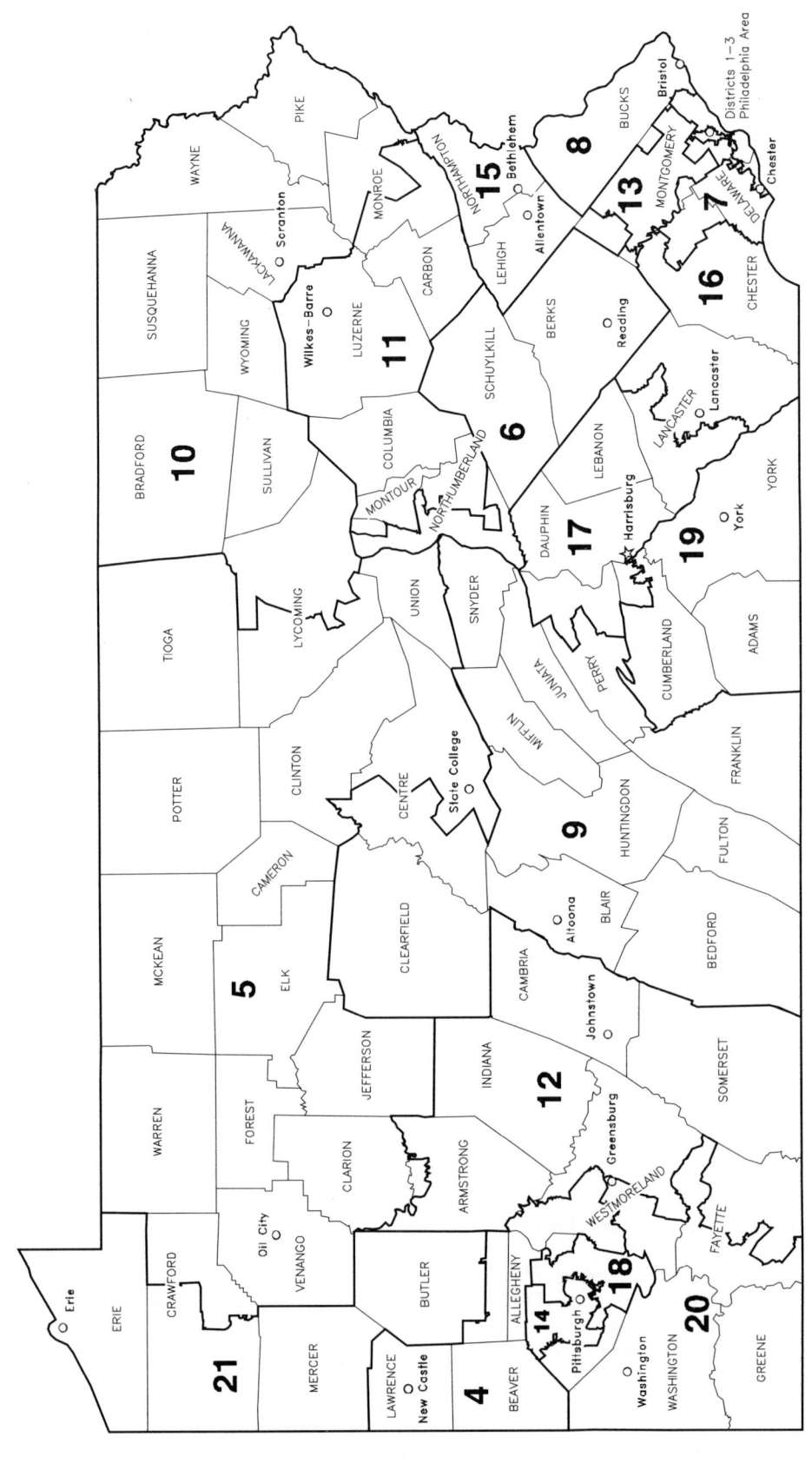

Erie, in the extreme northwestern corner of the state.

Philadelphia's minority-weighted vote makes it vital to the Democratic coalition. Republicans made small inroads among white ethnics in the 1980s—especially after former Mayor Frank Rizzo switched allegiance to the GOP—but the GOP is not a force in city politics. The typical Republican statewide strategy is to hold down losses in the big cities and pick up the more conservative votes cast in the suburbs and agricultural heartland.

Those suburban voters have increasingly flexed their electoral muscles in recent elections, usually on the side of GOP candidates. No Republican candidate can expect to carry the state without running well in these GOP strongholds, which include fast-growing Bucks, Chester and wealthy Montgomery counties and older, more ethnic Delaware County.

In the predominantly rural portion of central Pennsylvania, Republicans find fertile ground in a "T" shaped area extending northward from the Pennsylvania Dutch country through the Susquehanna River Valley to the forested northern tier of counties along the New York state border. These voters are suspicious of the state's two largest cities, and of Philadelphia in particular.

In the 1980s, agricultural Lancaster County was one of the state's fastest growing areas due to a favorable business climate and the allure of its scenic farm country. Despite the demographic changes, Pennsylvania Dutch conservatism still courses through local politics: Even as President George Bush lost statewide in 1992, he won Lancaster County by an almost 2-to-1 margin.

Table 1   Population

District	Population	Population under 18	Voting-age population	Median age
1	565,842	153,254	412,588	31.2
2	565,650	126,645	439,005	33.1
3	565,866	128,625	437,241	35.1
4	565,792	133,889	431,903	36.7
5	565,813	134,125	431,688	33.0
6	565,760	130,644	435,116	36.2
7	565,746	124,895	440,851	35.5
8	565,787	144,709	421,078	33.7
9	565,803	140,203	425,600	35.2
10	565,681	136,910	428,771	35.8
11	565,913	124,607	441,306	37.4
12	565,794	133,894	431,900	36.1
13	565,793	126,661	439,132	36.2
14	565,787	116,149	449,638	35.5
15	565,810	130,922	434,888	35.2
16	565,835	148,859	416,976	32.9
17	565,742	138,497	427,245	34.4
18	565,781	117,854	447,927	38.1
19	565,831	133,731	432,100	34.3
20	565,815	128,993	436,822	37.2
21	565,802	140,744	425,058	34.1
State	11,881,643	2,794,810	9,086,833	35.0

Table 2   Voting-Age Persons

District	White*	Black*	American Indian, Eskimo, or Aleut*	Asian or Pacific Islander*	Other*	Hispanic*	Male*	Female*
1	42.0%	49.7%	0.2	2.3%	5.8%	8.0%	45.1%	54.9%
2	38.6	58.4	0.3	2.2	0.6	1.5	44.0	56.0
3	90.5	4.5	0.1	2.8	2.0	4.0	46.5	53.5
4	96.8	2.7	0.1	0.3	0.1	0.4	46.8	53.2
5	97.6	1.1	0.2	0.9	0.2	0.6	48.9	51.1
6	96.1	2.1	0.1	0.5	1.2	2.5	47.3	52.7
7	94.3	3.6	0.1	1.8	0.2	0.9	47.0	53.0
8	95.5	2.6	0.1	1.4	0.4	1.4	48.5	51.5
9	98.4	1.2	0.1	0.2	0.1	0.4	47.6	52.4
10	98.4	1.0	0.1	0.4	0.1	0.7	46.9	53.1
11	98.5	0.9	0.1	0.4	0.1	0.6	46.5	53.5
12	98.4	1.2	0.1	0.3	0.1	0.4	47.0	53.0
13	91.5	5.9	0.1	2.2	0.3	1.1	46.9	53.1
14	82.5	15.9	0.1	1.3	0.2	0.7	45.5	54.5
15	95.2	1.8	0.1	1.0	1.9	3.6	47.5	52.5
16	92.4	4.9	0.1	1.0	1.6	3.2	48.0	52.0
17	92.3	6.0	0.1	0.9	0.7	1.5	47.3	52.7
18	92.4	6.7	0.1	0.6	0.1	0.5	45.6	54.4
19	96.5	2.3	0.1	0.6	0.5	1.0	48.0	52.0
20	96.5	2.9	0.1	0.4	0.1	0.5	46.6	53.4
21	96.0	3.2	0.1	0.4	0.2	0.6	47.3	52.7
State	89.6	8.5	0.1	1.1	0.8	1.6	46.9	53.1

*As percent of voting-age population.

Table 3   Voting-Age Persons by Age Groups

District	18-24*	25-44*	45-54*	55-64*	65 and over*
1	16.5%	41.9%	12.6%	11.6%	17.4%
2	16.6	40.8	12.0	11.4	19.2
3	12.7	39.6	12.2	12.5	23.0
4	11.0	39.6	13.9	14.1	21.5
5	19.0	37.5	13.1	12.2	18.2
6	12.4	39.1	13.3	13.4	21.9
7	13.2	40.6	13.5	13.3	19.4
8	12.3	46.2	14.9	12.1	14.5
9	13.0	39.3	14.2	13.2	20.3
10	12.6	38.7	13.4	13.1	22.2
11	12.9	36.5	13.0	13.6	24.0
12	13.5	37.6	13.2	13.5	22.3
13	11.4	41.8	14.1	12.8	19.9
14	14.9	39.0	11.6	12.5	22.0
15	13.1	41.3	13.5	12.6	19.6
16	14.6	43.7	14.2	11.2	16.3
17	12.5	43.5	13.8	12.3	17.9
18	10.3	38.9	13.0	14.4	23.4
19	14.3	42.2	14.1	12.0	17.5
20	11.7	38.9	13.9	13.7	21.8
21	15.4	39.1	13.3	12.5	19.7
State	13.5	40.2	13.4	12.8	20.1

*As percent of voting-age population.

Table 4   Income and Occupation

District	Median family income	Families in poverty	White collar*	Blue collar*	Service*	Farm*
1	$24,506	23.6%	54.8%	25.3%	19.2%	0.7%
2	30,193	16.1	63.8	18.6	17.1	0.5
3	35,441	8.4	59.9	26.7	13.0	0.4
4	32,011	8.6	56.3	28.4	14.0	1.3
5	28,872	9.5	48.3	34.1	14.4	3.2
6	34,351	6.1	47.9	37.9	12.3	1.9
7	49,477	3.0	70.8	19.1	9.2	0.8
8	48,998	2.8	64.9	24.8	9.2	1.1
9	28,913	9.1	43.8	38.6	13.6	4.0
10	30,920	8.1	49.8	34.0	13.6	2.6

District	Median family income	Families in poverty	White collar*	Blue collar*	Service*	Farm*
11	30,425	7.6	49.4	35.3	13.9	1.4
12	26,703	11.6	46.9	35.3	15.1	2.8
13	52,778	2.2	71.7	18.7	8.6	1.0
14	32,274	12.2	65.7	18.0	15.8	0.5
15	38,999	4.8	56.6	30.4	11.9	1.0
16	42,932	4.8	56.9	28.1	11.3	3.7
17	37,251	5.4	54.7	30.8	12.6	2.0
18	35,343	7.2	65.7	20.3	13.4	0.6
19	37,542	4.1	51.9	34.6	11.6	1.9
20	31,949	10.1	57.3	27.6	13.8	1.3
21	31,144	9.7	50.3	32.7	14.8	2.2
State	34,856	8.2	56.9	28.4	13.0	1.7

*As percent of employed persons age 16 and over.

Table 5 Education: School Years Completed

District	Less than grade 9*	Grades 9-12 no diploma*	High school diploma*	College bachelor's degree or higher*
1	13.9%	28.0%	32.9%	10.4%
2	9.0	21.8	29.3	21.9
3	10.6	22.8	37.7	12.7
4	8.6	13.9	41.7	15.3
5	9.2	15.1	44.4	15.3
6	12.0	18.2	42.3	12.6
7	5.0	10.3	31.9	31.0
8	5.1	11.7	34.1	25.1
9	12.6	17.2	46.8	10.0
10	9.1	15.9	42.3	13.9
11	11.3	17.0	42.4	12.7
12	13.5	14.9	46.4	10.8
13	4.9	10.7	29.1	33.5
14	8.1	15.9	34.2	22.6
15	10.0	15.9	36.8	18.2
16	10.2	13.4	34.1	24.3
17	8.8	15.8	41.9	16.3
18	7.1	12.8	37.3	21.0
19	10.9	14.9	40.7	16.0
20	10.3	14.0	40.2	17.2
21	8.2	15.3	43.4	14.6
State	9.4	15.9	38.6	17.9

*As percent of persons age 25 and over.

Table 6 Housing and Residential Patterns

District	Owner occupied	Renter occupied	Urban	Rural
1	59.4%	40.6%	100.0%	0.0%
2	55.6	44.4	100.0	0.0
3	71.1	28.9	100.0	0.0
4	76.0	24.0	67.2	32.8
5	72.2	27.8	33.9	66.1
6	74.1	25.9	56.2	43.8
7	74.3	25.7	95.2	4.8
8	75.4	24.6	81.8	18.2
9	75.2	24.8	29.8	70.2
10	71.8	28.2	46.4	53.6
11	72.0	28.0	60.3	39.7
12	75.0	25.0	30.1	69.9
13	73.0	27.0	92.4	7.6
14	58.6	41.4	99.6	0.4
15	71.6	28.4	74.0	26.0
16	70.9	29.1	56.2	43.8
17	68.9	31.1	60.7	39.3
18	69.9	30.1	97.9	2.1
19	73.3	26.7	49.7	50.3
20	74.8	25.2	59.5	40.5
21	71.8	28.2	56.3	43.7
State	70.6	29.4	68.9	31.1

1st District

South and Central Philadelphia; Part of Chester

Many of the places commonly associated with Philadelphia can be traced to the 1st District (see map on page 629). Broad Street courses the 1st, beginning at the Montgomery County border. It cuts through the Oak Lane and Olney sections and the Democratic-voting poor and working-class African American neighborhoods of North Philly. Temple University is situated by Cecil B. Moore Avenue.

Broad Street also marks the Center City border with the 2nd District. Center City, west of Broad Street—including City Hall—is in the 2nd. The 1st District portion of Center City is east of City Hall, in the 5th Ward. However, the waterfront area of the 5th Ward belongs to the 3rd District.

Besides the historical presence of the Liberty Bell and Independence Hall, the 1st boasts the pop cultural landmarks of South Philly. At 9th and Passyunk Avenues, tourists, locals and political candidates find it difficult to pass up a cheesesteak at Pat's or across the street at Geno's. Right down the street is the famous Italian Market where vendors hawk fresh vegetables, meats, cheeses and fish.

Italian culture permeates much of South Philly. There are Catholic churches that still say Mass in Italian; bocce courts can be found at Marconi Plaza park.

These are the neighborhoods of Hollywood's "Rocky Balboa" and former mayor Frank Rizzo, where Rizzo's tough law-and-order stance had great appeal. When Irish Americans controlled the Democratic Party decades ago, Italian Americans mostly sided with the GOP. Now they vote Democratic in local and congressional elections.

Veterans Stadium and the Spectrum, homes to the city's professional sports teams, are situated at Broad and Pattison. Past the stadiums, the row houses end and the Philadelphia Naval Shipyard begins. (The embattled shipyard is scheduled for closure under the 1991 base-closing plan.) Oil refineries line the Schuylkill River just before it empties into the Delaware River.

The one ward west of the Schuylkill is in southwest Philadelphia. In the late 19th century, the large factories located here attracted Irish, Italian and black immigrants. But as the General Electric, Fels Naptha and American Tobacco Company factories shut down, the adjoining areas such as Elmwood and Kingsessing went into decline. The bleak economic landscape for those who did not move away manifested itself in racial turmoil. Today, the whites, blacks, and the recently arrived Vietnamese and Cambodians eye each other with suspicion.

Outside city limits, south of the Philadelphia International Airport, the 1st takes in bits of Delaware County along Interstate 95. Working-class whites in Glenolden and Tinicum retain the GOP loyalties taught to them by the Republican county machine.

Black voters in the blighted city of Chester, almost all of

PHILADELPHIA, SOUTHEAST PENNSYLVANIA AREA

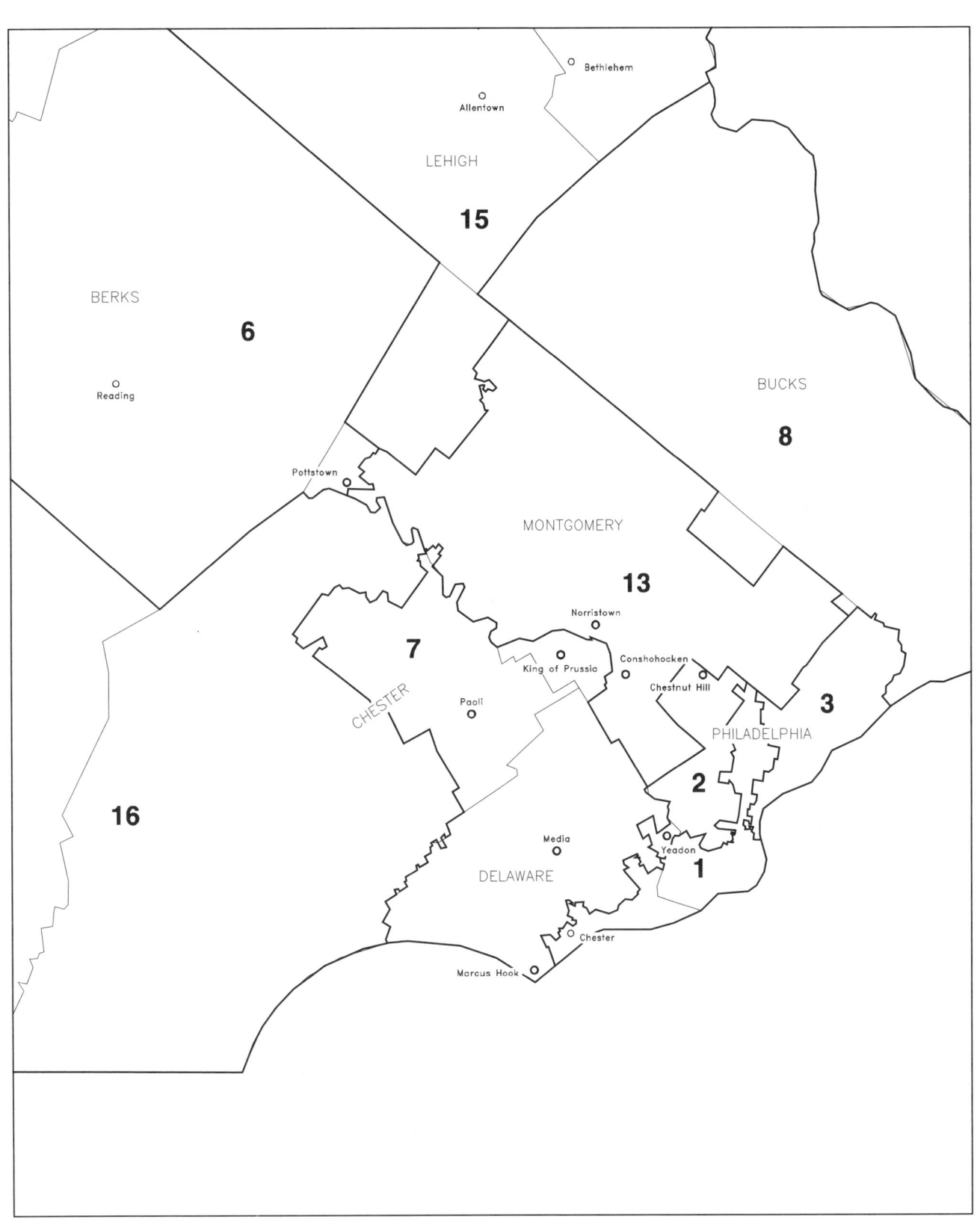

which is in the district, boost the district's minority population to just over half.

Election Returns

	1st District	Democrat	Republican
1992	President*	149,699 (72.8%)	39,042 (19.0%)
	House	150,172 (80.9%)	35,419 (19.1%)
1988	President	157,518 (72.9%)	58,640 (27.1%)
	Senate	135,822 (67.9%)	64,293 (32.1%)
1986	Senate	94,299 (62.8%)	55,782 (37.2%)
	Governor	101,101 (68.1%)	47,280 (31.9%)

*Vote for Perot was 17,021 (8.3%).

Demographics

Population 565,842

Percent change from 1980 9.8%

Land area 52 square miles

Population per square mile 10,814

Counties, 1990 population
Delaware (pt.) 76,949   Philadelphia (pt.) 488,893

Cities, 1990 population (10,000 or more)
Chester (pt.) 41,729   Philadelphia (pt.) 488,893
Darby CDP 10,955

Race and Hispanic origin
White 37.7%
Black 52.4%
American Indian, Eskimo, or Aleut. 0.2%
Asian or Pacific Islander 2.4%
Other 7.3%
Hispanic origin 9.9%

Ancestry
American 1.3%   Irish 11.1%
English 3.1%   Italian 13.4%
German 7.0%   Polish 2.6%

Universities/colleges, 1990-1991 enrollment
La Salle University, Philadelphia 6,333
Pennsylvania College of Optometry, Philadelphia 631
Pennsylvania College of Podiatric Medicine, Philadelphia 371
Temple University, Philadelphia 29,714
Thomas Jefferson University, Philadelphia 2,364
Widener University, Chester 5,896

Newspapers, total circulation (in all districts)
Delaware County Times 56,357
Philadelphia Daily News 196,141
Philadelphia Inquirer 500,733
New York Post 551,443

Commercial television stations, affiliations
ADI: Philadelphia (100%)

Cable television systems, total subscribers
Comcast Cablevision; Northeast Philadelphia 149,426
Greater Media Philadelphia; Philadelphia 53,000
Suburban Cable TV; Glenolden 66,858
Wade Cablevision; Philadelphia 55,000

Military installations, 1991
Philadelphia Naval Shipyard, Philadelphia 18,165
Philadelphia Naval Station, Philadelphia 2,754
Philadelphia Naval Hospital, Philadelphia 845

Businesses and other major employers
Temple University & Temple University Hospital; Philadelphia 9,636
City of Philadelphia/Gas Works; Philadelphia; gas distribution 2,625
Budd Co./Stamping & Frame Div.; Philadelphia; railroad cars 2,422
Provident National Bank; Philadelphia; commercial banks 2,400
City of Philadelphia/Fire Dept.; Philadelphia 2,400
Chester Crozer Medical Center; Chester 2,300
La Salle University; Philadelphia 1,700
Scott Paper Co.; Philadelphia; paper mills 1,500
New St. Christopher's Hospital; Philadelphia 1,500
U.S. Health & Human Services Dept.; Philadelphia 1,400
Strawbridge & Clothier/Clover Div.; Philadelphia; department stores 1,300
General Accident Insurance of America; Philadelphia; fire/marine/casualty insurance 1,200
Albert Einstein Medical Center/Willow-Crest Bamberger Div.; Philadelphia 1,018
Meritor Savings Bank/Philadelphia Savings Fund Society; Philadelphia; commercial banks 1,015
Methodist Hospital; Philadelphia 1,012
ARA Services Inc.; Philadelphia; bars/restaurants 1,000
U.S. Environmental Protection Agency; Philadelphia 1,000
Germantown Hospital & Medical Center; Philadelphia 1,000
St. Agnes Medical Center; Philadelphia 930
North Philadelphia Health System/Girard Medical Center; Philadelphia 900
Sacred Heart General Hospital; Chester 900
USAir Inc.; Philadelphia; airline 853
Philadelphia Geriatric Center/York House North; Philadelphia; nursing 850
John Wanamaker Philadelphia; Philadelphia; department stores 800
U.S. National Park Service; Philadelphia 800
Thomas Jefferson University; Philadelphia 800
BPS Guard Services Inc./Burns Security; Philadelphia; business/security services 800
National Cleaning Contractors/Realty Services Co.; Philadelphia; building services 700
Widener University; Chester 700
Boeing Co.; Philadelphia; aircraft navigation equipment 610
Wills Eye Hospital; Philadelphia 575
U.S. Dept. Treasury/U.S. Mint; Philadelphia 560
Colonial Penn Group Inc.; Philadelphia; fire/marine/casualty insurance 546

2nd District

West Philadelphia; Chestnut Hill; Yeadon

William Penn's statue atop City Hall stands like a sentinel over Philadelphia. From his vantage point, he views a variety of neighborhoods across the 2nd, all with one thing in common: an affinity for Democrats. Republicans need not apply in the 2nd;

Democrats enjoy an overwhelming districtwide edge in voter registration. Here, the Democratic primary is the only forum for political redress.

Stretching west from City Hall, the 2nd (see map on page 629) begins under the skyscrapers of Center City's 8th Ward. Many of the white-collar professionals who labor here by day live outside the district, but some prefer to live nearby in ritzy Rittenhouse Square. The whites of this area are not a large part of the district vote, but their wealth allows them to weigh in disproportionately in any political campaign.

From there, the 2nd crosses the Schuylkill River, and immediately encounters two massive edifices, the U.S. Postal Service building and the 30th Street train station. Traveling westbound on Walnut Street, past the campuses of Drexel University and the University of Pennsylvania, a sea of row houses seems to continue indefinitely. These are the neighborhoods of West Philly.

Two generations ago, Irish, Greeks, and Jews lived under de facto ethnic segregation in these areas. Today, West Philly is nearly all black. Some of these working-class and lower-middle-class neighborhoods are gripped by urban blight; others are well maintained.

It was the western edge of Philadelphia that drew notoriety in May 1985, when an ill-conceived police battle against a cult group led to a fire that burned down two square blocks of row houses.

Farther north, City Line Avenue forms a border with Montgomery County. The middle-class and affluent sections of Overbrook are on the city side, while the posh Main Line begins across the street.

Cutting a wide swath through the northern part of the 2nd is vast and verdant Fairmount Park, which flanks the Schuylkill River and contains the city's art museum, zoo and "Boathouse Row."

Adjoining the park to the northwest is Germantown. Once home to Philadelphia's upper crust, it and nearby Mount Airy now are racially diverse and mostly middle-class. The park runs as far north as the Montgomery County border, where it ends in affluent Chestnut Hill.

Farther north along the Schuylkill River, Roxborough and Manayunk are older neighborhoods experiencing a wave of gentrification. Although longtime residents complain about the upscale restaurants and shops that now occupy Manayunk's Main Street, the businesses have revitalized what was a dying area.

The 2nd abruptly halts at the city's Montgomery County border, but it reaches a finger into Darby, Lansdowne and Yeadon, which are black, Democratic sections of Delaware County.

Election Returns

	2nd District	Democrat	Republican
1992	President*	184,284 (79.9%)	31,836 (13.8%)
	House	164,355 (76.8%)	47,906 (22.4%)
1988	President	190,682 (79.1%)	50,428 (20.9%)
	Senate	156,632 (69.9%)	67,331 (30.1%)
1986	Senate	115,477 (67.9%)	54,488 (32.1%)
	Governor	118,910 (70.2%)	50,380 (29.8%)

*Vote for Perot was 14,510 (6.3%).

Demographics

Population 565,650

Percent change from 1980 9.4%

Land area 45 square miles

Population per square mile 12,452

Counties, 1990 population

Delaware (pt.) 34,832	Philadelphia (pt.) 530,818

Cities, 1990 population (10,000 or more)

Darby 11,140	Philadelphia (pt.) 530,818
Lansdowne 11,712	Yeadon 11,980

Race and Hispanic origin

White 34.7%
Black 62.2%
American Indian, Eskimo, or Aleut 0.3%
Asian or Pacific Islander 2.2%
Other 0.7%
Hispanic origin 1.6%

Ancestry

American 1.4%	Italian 6.7%
English 4.1%	Polish 2.9%
German 7.6%	Russian 2.7%
Irish 9.3%	West Indian 1.2%

Universities/colleges, 1990-1991 enrollment

Art Institute of Philadelphia, Philadelphia 1,312
Berean Institute, Philadelphia 239
Chesnut Hill College, Philadelphia 1189
Community College of Philadelphia, Philadelphia 15,151
Drexel University, Philadelphia 11,926
Eastern Baptist Theological Seminary, Philadelphia 287
Hahnemann Medical University, Philadelphia 2,096
Lutheran Theological Seminary, Philadelphia 209
Medical College of Pennsylvania, Philadelphia 568
Moore College of Art, Philadelphia 578
Peirce Junior College, Philadelphia 1,133
Philadelphia College of Osteopathic Medicine, Philadelphia 828
Philadelphia College of Pharmacy, Philadelphia 1,659
Philadelphia College of Textiles & Sciences, Philadelphia 3,320
Spring Garden College, Philadelphia 898
St. Joseph's University, Philadelphia 6,622
University of Pennsylvania, Philadelphia 21,868
University of the Arts, Philadelphia 1,310
Wharton School of Business 1,947
Westminster Theology Seminary, Philadelphia 530

Newspapers, total circulation (in all districts)

Delaware County Times 56,357
Philadelphia Daily News 196,141
Philadelphia Inquirer 500,733
New York Post 551,443

Commercial television stations, affiliations

ADI: Philadelphia (100%)
KYW-TV, Philadelphia (NBC)
WCAU-TV, Philadelphia (CBS)
WGBS-TV, Philadelphia (None)
WPHL-TV, Philadelphia (None)
WPVI-TV, Philadelphia (ABC)
WTXF-TV, Philadelphia (Fox)

Cable television systems, total subscribers

Comcast Cablevision; Northeast Philadelphia 149,426

Greater Media Philadelphia; Philadelphia 53,000
Wade Cablevision; Philadelphia 55,000

Military installations, 1991
Defense Personnel Support Center, Philadelphia 4,185

Businesses and other major employers
University of Pennsylvania; Philadelphia 16,600
Hahnemann Medical University & Hospital; Philadelphia 4,750
University of Pennsylvania Hospital; Philadelphia 4,500
Corestates Bank/Corestates First Pennsylvania Bank; Philadelphia; commercial banks 3,500
Philadelphia Newspapers Inc./Philadelphia Inquirer; Philadelphia; newspapers 3,250
U.S. Postal Service; Philadelphia 3,000
United Engineers & Constructors Intl.; Philadelphia; engineering/construction services 3,000
Children's Hospital of Philadelphia; Philadelphia 3,000
Philadelphia Electric Co.; Philadelphia; electric services 2,500
U.S. Veterans Affairs Dept.; Philadelphia; hospital 2,500
Medical College of Pennsylvania; Philadelphia 2,162
Lankenau Hospital; Philadelphia 2,145
Bell Telephone Co. of Pennsylvania; Philadelphia; telephone communications 2,000
Wharton School of Business; Philadelphia 2,000
Fidelity Bank; Philadelphia; commercial banks 1,750
Independence Blue Cross/Philadelphia Blue Cross; Philadelphia; medical service/health insurance 1,555
Presbyterian Medical Center; Philadelphia 1,550
Kiefer Services Inc.; Philadelphia; personnel supply services 1,510
Community College of Philadelphia; Philadelphia 1,500
Graduate Hospital; Philadelphia 1,500
Mercy Health Corp./Misericordia Div.; Philadelphia 1,300
United Pacific Insurance Co.; Philadelphia; life insurance 1,200
Consolidated Rail Corp.; Philadelphia; railroads 1,000
Sun Refining & Marketing Co.; Philadelphia; petroleum refining 1,000
IBM Corp.; Philadelphia; computer equipment 1,000
City of Philadelphia; Philadelphia 1,000
Towers Perrin Forster & Crosby; Philadelphia; consulting services 1,000
Day & Zimmermann Inc.; Philadelphia; engineering services 1,000
City of Philadelphia/School District; Philadelphia 1,000
Chestnut Hill Hospital; Philadelphia 950
General Electric Co./Astro Space; Philadelphia; guided missiles/space vehicles 900
Provident Mutual; Philadelphia; life insurance 900
Beecham Inc.; Philadelphia; toiletries/pharmaceuticals 882
Coopers & Lybrand; Philadelphia; accounting/auditing 850
National Railroad Pass Corp.; Philadelphia; transportation 800
Aetna Life & Casualty Co.; Philadelphia; insurance services 800
University of the Arts; Philadelphia 800
Arthur Andersen & Co.; Philadelphia; accounting/auditing 800
Philadelphia College of Osteopathic Medicine; Philadelphia 800
St. Joseph's University; Philadelphia 725

FMC Corp.; Philadelphia; nondurable goods 700
ELF Atochem North America Inc.; Philadelphia; inorganic chemicals 700
Chevron USA Inc.; Philadelphia; petroleum refining 700
Ogden Services Corp.; Philadelphia; bars/restaurants 700
Pennsylvania Hospital; Philadelphia 700
Dechert Price & Rhoads; Philadelphia; legal services 656
Morgan Lewis & Bockius; Philadelphia; legal services 635
Life Insurance of North America; Philadelphia; life insurance 600
Ritz-Carlton Hotel Co.; Philadelphia; hotel 600
Ernst & Young; Philadelphia; accounting/auditing 600
Wistar Institute of Anatomy & Biology; Philadelphia; research services 600
City of Philadelphia; Philadelphia; nursing 600
Philadelphia Stock Exchange; Philadelphia; security & commodity exchanges 580
Roxborough Memorial Hospital; Philadelphia 570
Duane Morris & Heckscher; Philadelphia; legal services 560
North Philadelphia Health System/St. Joseph's Hospital; Philadelphia 550
City of Philadelphia/District Attorney's Office; Philadelphia 540
Wolf Block Schorr Solis-Cohen; Philadelphia; legal services 538
Drinker Biddle & Reath; Philadelphia; legal services 528
Kling-Lindquist Partners Inc.; Philadelphia; engineering/architectural services 503

3rd District

Northeast Philadelphia

In a Democratic and racially diverse city, the 3rd stands alone in its racial homogeneity and its status as the only Philadelphia district where Republicans usually fare well.

The body of the 3rd is known as the Great Northeast, named for its geographic expanse (see map on page 629). This part of Philadelphia borders suburban Montgomery and Bucks counties, and many of its communities have taken on quasi-suburban traits of their own. Yet this is the only congressional district wholly contained in the city of Philadelphia.

The mostly white residents who migrated to Northeast neighborhoods established themselves in the past two generations as the black population grew in other parts of the city. And as many residents began to equate the national Democratic Party with policies that provide preferential treatment for minorities, Republican voter registration swelled.

Democrats outnumber Republicans in the 3rd, but in 1980, 1984 and 1988, the Republican presidential ticket carried the district. Bill Clinton broke the losing streak in 1992, carrying the district easily over an unpopular President Bush.

This strength was not limited to federal elections: Philadelphia's handful of Republican state legislators and GOP city council members usually hail from this area.

Conservative social attitudes and concern about crime inspire loyalty to tough law-and-order candidates—such as former Mayor Frank Rizzo. Also welcome is the presence of city police officers and firefighters, many of whom live in the Northeast. Holmesburg Prison is here, as is the Philadelphia Police Academy.

With scores of hospitals, the Northeast Philadelphia Airport and three bridges that connect to New Jersey, infrastructure issues are also of particular concern to 3rd District residents.

Besides large numbers of Catholics, the Great Northeast boasts a large Jewish population, many of whom live west of Roosevelt Boulevard in Bustleton and Somerton.

South of Cottman Avenue, the district begins to lose its suburban feel. The Irish and Polish residents of the Democratic wards by the Delaware River are crowded in row houses under Interstate 95. Union ties bind voters here to the Democratic Party, but they often part company on social issues.

Huge losses of industrial jobs in Kensington, Bridesburg and Port Richmond have left these white ethnic communities reeling.

In such lower-income neighborhoods as Kensington, this economic uncertainty has translated into racial tensions among whites, blacks and Hispanics.

The southern border of the 3rd reaches as far south as Washington Street in south Philadelphia. It snakes close to the river while taking in Penn's Landing, Philadelphia's revitalized waterfront area. Some of the boutiques, shops and restaurants of funky South Street are also within 3rd District confines.

Election Returns

	3rd District	Democrat	Republican
1992	President*	124,944 (52.1%)	75,474 (31.4%)
	House	130,828 (58.9%)	86,787 (39.1%)
1988	President	118,516 (48.0%)	128,259 (52.0%)
	Senate	95,078 (41.1%)	136,196 (58.9%)
1986	Senate	72,851 (39.0%)	113,851 (61.0%)
	Governor	96,591 (51.9%)	89,648 (48.1%)

*Vote for Perot was 39,617 (16.5%).

Demographics

Population 565,866

Percent change from 1980 9.6%

Land area 57 square miles

Population per square mile 9,963

Counties, 1990 population
Philadelphia (pt.) 565,866

Cities, 1990 population (10,000 or more)
Philadelphia (pt.) 565,866

Race and Hispanic origin
White 89.3%
Black 4.9%
American Indian, Eskimo, or Aleut. 0.2%
Asian or Pacific Islander 3.2%
Other 2.5%
Hispanic origin 4.7%

Ancestry

American 2.5%		Lithuanian 1.2%	
English 7.5%		Polish 11.6%	
French 1.7%		Russian 5.2%	
German 24.6%		Scotch Irish 1.2%	
Irish 31.9%		Scottish 1.2%	
Italian 13.9%		Ukrainian 1.8%	

Universities/colleges, 1990-1991 enrollment
American Institute of Design, Philadelphia 365
Holy Family College, Philadelphia 2,050

Newspapers, total circulation (in all districts)
Delaware County Times 56,357
New York Post 551,443
Philadelphia Daily News 196,141
Philadelphia Inquirer 500,733

Commercial television stations, affiliations
ADI: Philadelphia (100%)

Cable television systems, total subscribers
Comcast Cablevision; Northeast Philadelphia 149,426
Greater Media Philadelphia; Philadelphia 53,000

Military installations, 1991
Naval Aviation Supply Office, Philadelphia 5,676

Businesses and other major employers
U.S. Internal Revenue Service; Philadelphia 5,000
Sears Technology Services Inc.; Philadelphia; computer services 1,500
U.S. Postal Service; Philadelphia 1,400
American Oncologic Hospital; Philadelphia 1,400
Federal Reserve Bank; Philadelphia 1,200
Episcopal Hospital; Philadelphia 1,200
Jeanes Hospital Inc.; Philadelphia 1,197
Cardone Industries Corp.; Philadelphia; motor vehicle parts 1,054
Rohm & Haas Co.; Philadelphia; agricultural chemicals 1,000
Nabisco Brands Inc.; Philadelphia; bakery products 1,000
TW Services Inc.; Philadelphia; nonstore retailers 1,000
Philadelphia State Hospital; Philadelphia 1,000
Northeastern Hospital of Philadelphia; Philadelphia 950
Pincus Bros Inc.; Philadelphia; men's suits/coats 800
J. J. White Inc.; Philadelphia; building construction 800
After Six Inc.; Philadelphia; men's suits/coats 750
Sears Roebuck & Co.; Philadelphia; department stores 700
Frankford Hospital; Philadelphia 650
Neumann Medical Center; Philadelphia 621
Pet Inc./Whitman's Chocolates; Philadelphia; candies 600
Friends Hospital; Philadelphia 579
Temple University/Woodhaven Center; Philadelphia; job training 560
Delaware River Stevedores Inc.; Philadelphia; water transportation 550
Sim-Kar Lighting Fixture Co./Power Products Div.; Philadelphia; electric lighting 550
Marstan Industries Inc.; Philadelphia; paper products 550
Heintz Corp.; Philadelphia; aircraft engines 530

4th District

West — Beaver County; Part of Westmoreland County

The mostly abandoned steel mills that line the Beaver and Ohio rivers in western Pennsylvania haunt the 4th District towns that once lived and breathed by them. In Aliquippa, a seven-mile-long steelworks employed 15,000 at its peak. Today, it is operated by a skeleton crew. So, too, is the town, which has about one-third of the population it did in the 1950s. Across the river in Ambridge, there is a similar story of economic struggle.

The hard-luck Beaver Valley and the district's largest city, New Castle (Lawrence County), also have experienced the decline of heavy manufacturing in the past generation. Union strength remains unbroken, though, providing the district with a solid Democratic majority. Beaver and Lawrence counties turned in two of the state's strongest showings for unsuccessful Democratic Senate nominee Lynn Yeakel in 1992. In presidential voting, Bill Clinton handily won both counties, topping George Bush by more than 2-to-1 in Beaver and by about 8,000 votes in Lawrence.

Beaver County, dotted by boroughs and townships with evocative (if not imaginative) names such as Big Beaver, Little Beaver, Beaver Falls, South Beaver and Raccoon, is the district's most populous county. A little more than one-third of the Democratic primary vote is cast here.

In 4th District congressional politics, Beaver and Lawrence counties are suspicious of candidates who do not hail from the region. Observers say that voters here would be more inclined to support a candidate from over the border in Youngstown, Ohio, than a candidate from rival Westmoreland County, which is miles to the east, on the other side of Pittsburgh. Westmoreland is connected to the rest of the 4th by only a thin corridor of land in northern Allegheny County.

Traditionally, the representative of the 4th has hailed from the district's western region. Beaver County has been accustomed to throwing around its weight in elections ever since the late 19th century, when local product Matthew Quay was a U.S. senator and head of a powerful local political machine. But in the 1992 House contest, voters in the western region set aside their geographic bias and supported Democrat Ron Klink, who is from Westmoreland County.

The Allegheny River divides Westmoreland County from Allegheny County. On the Allegheny County side are Natrona Heights and Tarentum; on the eastern side of the river in Westmoreland are Lower Burrell and Arnold. Farther south, the 4th takes in Jeannette, but the district stops short of one of southwestern Pennsylvania's population centers, the city of Greensburg. Roughly one-fourth of the district's registered Democrats hail from Westmoreland.

A thorough search will turn up some Republicans, located mostly in farming communities or in Butler County, whose southern tier is in the 4th. (The rest of Butler is in the 21st.) In 1980, 1984 and 1988, Butler County voted Republican for president.

Election Returns

	4th District	Democrat	Republican
1992	President*	118,701 (48.3%)	76,193 (31.0%)
	House	186,684 (78.5%)	48,484 (20.4%)
1988	President	128,446 (58.6%)	90,717 (41.4%)
	Senate	70,033 (32.7%)	144,011 (67.3%)
1986	Senate	89,142 (52.4%)	80,877 (47.6%)
	Governor	103,908 (61.6%)	64,818 (38.4%)

*Vote for Perot was 50,647 (20.6%).

Demographics

Population 565,792

Percent change from 1980 9.7%

Land area 1,323 square miles

Population per square mile 428

Counties, 1990 population

Allegheny (pt.) 83,817	Lawrence 96,246
Beaver 186,093	Westmoreland (pt.)
Butler (pt.) 45,446	154,190

Cities, 1990 population (10,000 or more)

Aliquippa 13,374	Murrysville 17,240
Beaver Falls 10,687	New Castle 28,334
Harrison CDP 11,763	New Kensington 15,894
Jeannette 11,221	Plum 25,609
Lower Burrell 12,251	

Race and Hispanic origin
White 96.3%
Black 3.2%
American Indian, Eskimo, or Aleut. 0.1%
Asian or Pacific Islander 0.4%
Other 0.1%
Hispanic origin 0.5%

Ancestry

American 1.9%	Russian 1.1%
Dutch 2.0%	Scotch Irish 4.7%
English 12.6%	Scottish 2.5%
French 2.3%	Slovakian 7.1%
German 38.1%	Swedish 1.3%
Hungarian 1.9%	Ukrainian 1.4%
Irish 20.0%	Welsh 1.8%
Italian 18.2%	Yugoslavian 1.5%
Polish 9.5%	

Universities/colleges, 1990-1991 enrollment
Beaver Community College, Monaca 2,836
Geneva College, Beaver Falls 1,488
Pennsylvania State University, New Kensington 1,144
Pennsylvania State University-Beaver Falls, Monaca 1,030
Westminster College, New Wilmington 1,594

Newspapers, total circulation (in all districts)
Beaver County Times 45,174
Butler Eagle 30,669
Greensburg Tribune Review 51,972
New Castle News 20,189
New Kensington Valley News Dispatch 37,712
Pittsburgh Post-Gazette 153,796
Youngstown Vindicator 87,768

Commercial television stations, affiliations
ADI: Pittsburgh (100%)

Cable television systems, total subscribers
Adelphia Cable; New Castle 18,400
Adelphia Cable; Rochester 7,736
Armstrong Utilities Inc.; Zelienople 45,960
Comcast Cablevision; Russellton 9,184
Comcast Cablevision; Tarentum 29,257
Newchannels Cable TV; Moon 14,000
Plum Cable TV; Plum 7,000
TCI of Pennsylvania; Aliquippa 10,000
TCI of Pennsylvania; Greensburg 46,200
TCI of Pennsylvania; McCandless 28,000
Times Mirror Cable TV; Beaver Falls 11,876

Businesses and other major employers

Allegheny Ludlum Corp./Steel Div.; Brackenridge; steel products 3,000

Associated Cleaning Contractors & Services; Pittsburgh; building services 2,000

Medical Center of Beaver County; Beaver 1,559

Aluminum Co. of America/Structural Laminates Co.; New Kensington; aluminum products 1,500

Aluminum Co. of America/Alcoa Laboratories; Alcoa Center; research services 1,300

New Elliott Corp.; Jeannette; engines/turbines 1,271

Allegheny Valley Hospital; Natrona Heights 1,070

Jameson Memorial Hospital; New Castle 950

Pennsylvania Power Co./Mansfield Plant; Shippingport; electric services 905

U.S. Postal Service; Warrendale 875

Westinghouse Electric Corp.; Beaver; electrical switchgears 850

Citizens General Hospital; New Kensingtn 800

Michael Baker Corp.; Beaver; engineering services 800

Mine Safety Appliances Co.; Murrysville; safety equipment 700

LTV Steel Co. Inc.; Aliquippa; steel products 700

Jeannette District Memorial Hospital; Jeannette 626

Three Rivers Aluminum Co./Traco; Zelienople; metal products 625

Beaver Community College; Monaca 605

Arco Chemical Co.; Monaca; plastics/synthetics 600

Liberty Mutual Insurance Co.; New Castle; fire/marine/casualty insurance 600

St. Francis Hospital of New Castle; New Castle 575

Horsehead Industries Inc.; Monaca; nonferrous metals 565

County of Beaver/Beaver Valley Geriatric Center; Beaver; nursing 555

Anchor Hocking Corp.; Monaca; glass/glassware 550

Rockwell Intl. Corp.; New Castle; motor vehicle axles 530

J&L Specialty Products Corp.; Midland; stainless steel 525

5th District

Northwest, Central — State College

To get a rough idea of the size of the 5th, take a ride on meandering Route 6, which runs along the northern tier of the district. It is not as quick as I-80, which crosses east-west through Pennsylvania's midsection, but the old road affords more time to notice the hundreds of small hamlets that dot the rural landscape.

The road also cuts through the heartland of the Allegheny National Forest Region, an area covering about one-half million acres of woodland. It runs by Pine Creek Gorge in Tioga County—the attraction known as "Pennsylvania's Grand Canyon"—and continues on all the way past Warren, on the western outskirts of the district.

With hundreds of thousands of acres of state game land, hunting and fishing are sacred pursuits for many of the people here. In some areas, schools close for the first day of hunting season.

Tourism and recreation are the district's economic mainstays, but beyond those industries, there is not much else.

Geographically, the 5th is the state's largest congressional district. It includes all of 11 counties and parts of six others.

Population is fairly lightly sprinkled through the rural counties. The only sizable concentration of people is in Centre County, where the borough of State College is home to Pennsylvania State University, which has 39,000 students and 2,200 faculty members.

A sleepy college town three decades ago, State College has grown to form the nucleus of an emerging metropolitan area. The university has spawned a small high-tech industrial complex outside town that attracts Republican-voting engineers.

Centre County as a whole tends to vote Republican, but the university community keeps it competitive for Democrats. In 1992, Bill Clinton and the Democratic Senate nominee both carried Centre County.

Neighboring Clinton County is nominally Democratic; in 1992, it supported its namesake in the presidential contest. West of Clinton County, paper mill workers help give Elk County a strong Democratic tilt.

The counties of the northern tier, on the New York border, are less receptive to Democrats. They form the top segment of the GOP voting bloc known as the Republican "T." The "T" is rooted in the strongly Republican counties that begin on the Maryland border and rise north, before fanning out east and west on the northern tier. McKean, Potter and Tioga counties stuck with George Bush in his losing 1992 effort, and they also backed GOP Sen. Arlen Specter that same year.

Another Republican loyalist in 1992 was Jefferson County. But the county's politics take a back seat to its most famous resident, Punxsutawney Phil, the groundhog who becomes a national media star every Feb. 2; Phil was featured in the 1993 movie *Groundhog Day*. Another 5th District icon is Edwin Drake, the 19th-century inventor who drilled America's first crude oil well near what is now Oil City (Venango County).

Election Returns

	5th District	Democrat	Republican
1992	President*	78,049 (36.2%)	89,373 (41.5%)
	House	—	188,911 (100.0%)
1988	President	77,876 (40.4%)	114,693 (59.6%)
	Senate	44,579 (23.8%)	142,958 (76.2%)
1986	Senate	56,034 (36.1%)	99,139 (63.9%)
	Governor	71,308 (46.0%)	83,568 (54.0%)

*Vote for Perot was 48,093 (22.3%).

Demographics

Population 565,813

Percent change from 1980 9.8%

Land area 10,479 square miles

Population per square mile 54

Counties, 1990 population

Armstrong (pt.) 941	Elk 34,878
Cameron 5,913	Forest 4,802
Centre (pt.) 109,203	Jefferson 46,083
Clarion (pt.) 40,548	Lycoming (pt.) 17,119
Clearfield (pt.) 54	McKean 47,131
Clinton 37,182	Potter 16,717
Crawford (pt.) 23,509	Tioga 41,126

Union 36,176   Warren 45,050
Venango 59,381

Cities, 1990 population (10,000 or more)
Oil City 11,949   Warren 11,122
State College 38,923

Race and Hispanic origin
White 97.8%
Black 1.0%
American Indian, Eskimo, or Aleut. 0.2%
Asian or Pacific Islander 0.9%
Other 0.2%
Hispanic origin 0.6%

Ancestry
American 4.0%   Polish 4.6%
Dutch 6.1%   Scotch Irish 3.3%
English 13.7%   Scottish 2.5%
French 3.1%   Slovakian 2.1%
German 45.7%   Swedish 4.6%
Irish 17.5%   Welsh 1.5%
Italian 7.6%

Universities/colleges, 1990-1991 enrollment
Bucknell University, Lewisburg 3,463
Clarion University of Pennsylvania, Clarion 6,618
Lock Haven University of Pennsylvan' Lock Haven 3,520
Mansfield University of Pennsylvania Mansfield 3,182
Pennsylvania State University, State ' ege 38,864
University of Pittsburgh, Bradford 4
University of Pittsburgh, Titusville

Newspapers, total circulation (i   istricts)
Erie News/Times-News 71,835
Lock Haven Express 10,510
Meadville Tribune 16,198
State College Centre Daily Times 25,657
Warren Times Observer 11,628
Williamsport Sun Gazette 33,564

Commercial television stations, affiliations
ADI: Johnstown-Altoona (24%), Buffalo (20%), Wilkes-Barre-Scranton (17%), Erie (16%), Pittsburgh (13%) and Elmira (11%)

Cable television systems, total subscribers
Coaxial Cable Time/Warner; Franklin 5,900
Dimension Cable Services; Williamsport 25,200
Punxsutawny TV Cable Co.; Punxsutawney 7,047
Sammons Communications of Pennsylvania Inc.; Oil City 7,348
St. Marys TV Inc.; St. Marys 6,434
TCI of Pennsylvania; State College 24,901
TCI of Pennsylvania; Lock Haven 5,300
TV Cable of Central Pennsylvania; Avis 6,502
Warner Cable; Warren 7,560
Warner Cable of Bradford; Bradford 7,260

Businesses and other major employers
Pennsylvania State University; State College 8,560
Woolrich Inc./Pearce Woolen Mills; Woolrich; outerwear 1,900
Commonwealth of Pennsylvania/Polk Center; Polk; nursing 1,350
Blair Corp.; Warren; catalog retailers 1,300

Keystone Carbon Co./Powder Metal Div.; St. Marys; metal products 1,200
Corning Inc.; State College; glass/glassware 1,000
Bucknell University; Lewisburg 1,000
HRB Systems Inc.; State College; communications equipment 950
Pennsylvania House Inc.; Lewisburg; furniture 900
Cyclops Corp./Cytemp Specialty Steel; Titusville; steel products 900
Joy Technologies Inc.; Franklin; construction machinery 892
Centre Community Hospital; State College 875
Cerro Metal Products Co.; Bellefonte; nonferrous foundries (castings) 860
Pennsylvania State University/Applied Research Labs; State College; research services 800
Franklin Regional Medical Center; Franklin 800
Murata Erie North America Inc.; State College; pottery 750
International Paper Co.; Lock Haven; paper mills 735
GTE Products Corp./Sylvania Lighting Div.; St. Marys; electric lighting 708
Evangelical Community Hospital; Lewisburg 702
Clarion University of Pennsylvania; Clarion 700
Owens-Illinois Inc./Owens-Brockway Glass Container Div.; Clarion; glass/glassware 681
Ward Mfg. Inc.; Blossburg; iron/steel foundries 675
National Forge Co.; Irvine; metal forgings/stampings 670
Bradford Area School District; Bradford 650
Penntech Papers Inc.; Johnsonburg; paper mills 636
Roadway Package System Inc.; Lewisburg; trucking services 600
Champion Parts Inc.; Beech Creek; automotive repair 600
Carbon/Graphite Group Inc.; St. Marys; electrical industrial apparatus 550
Ball-Incon Glass Packaging; Port Allegany; glass products 550
Andrew Kaul Memorial Hospital; St. Marys 540
U.S. Justice Dept./Bureau of Prisons; Lewisburg 532
Warren General Hospital; Warren 524

6th District
Southeast — Reading

The story of the 6th is a tale of two counties, both hit hard by deindustrialization. Berks County, the more populous of the two, learned to diversify its economy. Schuylkill County, the poorer cousin to the north, never truly weaned itself from King Coal.

Reading, the largest city in Berks and the district, is no longer recognized as a major railroad or manufacturing center. It remains more industrialized than most of the state but now features a large and diverse economic base where no single employer accounts for more than 8 percent of the work force. Where there once were steel and textile mills, now there are factory outlet stores. Bargain hunters often board buses to make the pilgrimage to the city that bills itself "the outlet capital of the world."

The city has seen an influx of Hispanics looking for work, which in turn sparked a migration of whites to the surrounding suburbs. Because of this migration, the outlying areas—once mainly agricultural and always supportive of Republicans—now turn in even bigger numbers for GOP candidates. In 1992, Berks County voted for George Bush and GOP Sen. Arlen Specter.

In southern Berks, residential developments have sprouted because the completion of Route 422 made it feasible to commute from this area to jobs in the Philadelphia area.

Schuylkill County is divided by the physical presence of Broad Mountain. To locals, "north of the mountain" means the coal belt that begins north of Pottsville, or what remains of the belt.

The domes of Eastern Orthodox churches built by the eastern European miners in the late 19th century still dominate the roof lines of small, church-filled towns such as St. Clair. The "Molly McGuires," a secret organization that battled mine companies and their agents to provide better working and living conditions in the coal fields, were drawn from the ranks of Irish and Welsh immigrant miners.

Today, the county's coal tradition is a vein for tourism. Visitors can take a ride in an open mine car deep into Mahanoy Mountain or visit the Museum of Anthracite Mining in Ashland.

The decline of the coal industry has tracked the decline of traditional Republican strength in Schuylkill. Once a GOP stronghold, Schuylkill has become more receptive to Democrats in recent years, though Bush and Specter still managed to win here in 1992.

Pottsville, the largest city in the county, is where the county's remaining coal operations do business. It is home to the family-owned Yuengling brewery, America's oldest. Schuylkill County residents refer to it as "Vitamin Y."

Along the Susquehanna River, the 6th also takes in a strip of Northumberland County that includes Sunbury, another former manufacturing and railroad city that has fallen on hard times. The southeastern tip of the district dips into Montgomery County, to take in part of Pottstown.

Election Returns

	6th District	Democrat	Republican
1992	President*	78,326 (35.9%)	89,791 (41.1%)
	House	108,312 (52.1%)	99,694 (47.9%)
1988	President	73,534 (38.5%)	117,287 (61.5%)
	Senate	48,590 (26.2%)	136,806 (73.8%)
1986	Senate	55,595 (37.9%)	91,057 (62.1%)
	Governor	69,222 (47.2%)	77,439 (52.8%)

*Vote for Perot was 50,207 (23.0%).

Demographics

Population 565,760

Percent change from 1980 9.7%

Land area 1,902 square miles

Population per square mile 297

Counties, 1990 population
Berks 336,523
Montgomery (pt.) 25,767
Northumberland (pt.) 50,885
Schuylkill 152,585

Cities, 1990 population (10,000 or more)
Pottstown (pt.) 18,623   Reading 78,380
Pottsville 16,603   Sunbury 11,591

Race and Hispanic origin
White 95.2%
Black 2.5%
American Indian, Eskimo, or Aleut. 0.1%
Asian or Pacific Islander 0.6%
Other 1.7%
Hispanic origin 3.3%

Ancestry
American 2.3%   Lithuanian 2.4%
Dutch 5.6%   Polish 8.2%
English 7.3%   Scottish 1.1%
French 1.9%   Slovakian 3.4%
German 49.4%   Ukrainian 1.7%
Irish 13.0%   Welsh 2.4%
Italian 7.7%

Universities/colleges, 1990-1991 enrollment
Albright College, Reading 1,763
Alvernia College, Reading 1,099
Kutztown University of Pennsylvania, Kutztown 7,742
Pennsylvania State University-Berks, Reading 1,665
Pennsylvania State University-Schuylkill, Schuylkill Haven 1,139
Reading Community College, Reading 2,337

Newspapers, total circulation (in all districts)
Allentown Morning Call 136,293
Philadelphia Daily News 196,141
Philadelphia Inquirer 500,733
Pottstown Mercury 29,636
Pottsville Republican 28,845
Reading Eagle 75,798
Shenandoah Evening Herald 9,268
Sunbury Daily Item 25,086

Commercial television stations, affiliations
ADI: Wilkes-Barre-Scranton (54%) and Philadelphia (46%)
WTVE, Reading (None)

Cable television systems, total subscribers
Berks Cable; Mt. Penn 63,500
Blue Ridge Cable TV Inc.; Ephrata 28,000
Blue Ridge Cable TV Inc.; Lehighton 19,700
Hamburg Cable Inc.; Hamburg 5,568
Service Electric Cable TV; Birdsboro 8,500
Service Electric Cable TV; Delano 22,000
Service Electric Cable TV; Sunbury 11,000
Suburban Cable TV; Pottstown 25,465
Warner Cable; Pottsville 15,100

Businesses and other major employers
AT&T Co./Reading Works; Reading; electronic components 3,300
Carpenter Technology Corp./Steel Div.; Reading; steel mill 2,700
Reading Hospital & Medical Center; Reading 2,492
Meridian Bancorp Inc.; Reading; commercial banks 2,270
Dana Corp./Parish Frame Div.; Reading; motor vehicle frames 2,000
American Home Products Corp.; Milton; grocery products 1,600
CNA Financial Corp.; Reading; insurance services 1,300
J. E. Morgan Knitting Mills; Tamaqua; knit underwear 1,200

Gilbert/Commonwealth Inc.; Reading; engineering services 1,200

Prudential Insurance of America Inc.; Fogelsville; insurance services 1,100

County of Berks/School District; Reading 1,055

UGI Corp.; Reading; gas distribution 1,020

ACF Industries Inc./Amcar Div.; Milton; railroad equipment 1,000

Franciscan Health System Inc./St. Joseph's Hospital; Reading 1,000

City of Reading; Reading 895

Kutztown University of Pennsylvania; Kutztown 860

Boscov's Dept. Store; Reading; department stores 850

Metropolitan Edison Co.; Reading; electric services 800

American Argo Corp.; Schuylkill Haven; knitting mills 800

Cressona Aluminum Co.; Cressona; aluminum rolling/drawing 800

Wernersville State Hospital; Wernersville 701

Reading Community College; Reading 700

Good Samaritan Hospital; Pottsville 700

U.S. Postal Service; Reading 620

ICM Industries Inc./Doehler-Jarvis/Farley Inc.; Pottstown; nonferrous foundries 615

Commonwealth of Pennsylvania; Hamburg 615

Pottsville Hospital; Pottsville 612

Mrs Smith's Frozen Foods Co.; Pottstown; bakery products 600

Hershey Foods Corp./Ludens; Reading; cough drops/candies 600

VF Corp.; Reading; family clothing stores 600

Weis Markets Inc.; Sunbury; grocery stores 600

Community General Hospital; Reading 600

GPU Service Corp./Information Services; Reading; computer services 600

Merck & Co. Inc.; Riverside; pharmaceuticals 563

Rockwell Intl. Corp./Rockwell Graphics; Reading; printing machinery 550

Associated Wholesalers Inc.; Robesonia; grocery products 525

Sunbury Community Hospital; Sunbury 517

7th District

Suburban Philadelphia — Part of Delaware County

The anchor of the 7th District, Delaware County provides a textbook example of a suburban Republican machine. There are more than a few working-class towns in the district, but in elections from the township level to the presidency, most voters pull the GOP lever.

From the 1920s to the mid-1970s, local politics were ruled by the "war board," a secretive group officially called the Delaware County Republican Board of Supervisors. The current GOP organization is a looser confederation, but party discipline and patronage still keep most of the 7th's voters in line.

That is what made George Bush's countywide defeat in 1992 so hard for local GOP officials to swallow. Bush visited Delaware County several times; its national prominence as a middle-class bastion makes it a must-stop for GOP statewide or presidential candidates.

Normally, one of the few places in the county where Democrats find sanctuary is Swarthmore, where Swarthmore

College is located. The academic community at the respected liberal arts institution provides an island in a sea of Republicanism.

Closer to Philadelphia, older suburbs such as Norwood, Ridley Park and Upper Darby are mostly white and working class. Marcus Hook, an old oil refinery town along the Delaware River, also fits that description. The only concentrations of blacks in the county—in Yeadon, Darby and the city of Chester—are sliced out of the 7th and pieced onto the Philadelphia-based congressional districts.

Surrounding these areas, farther out on West Chester Pike, are more comfortably middle-class places such as Springfield and Newtown Square. In the district's southwest corner, Birmingham and Thornbury townships are less developed. The white-collar professionals in wealthy Radnor Township and on Philadelphia's affluent Main Line are less attuned to the GOP organization, but remain staunchly Republican. (Most of the Main Line is in the neighboring 13th, in Montgomery County.)

Upper Merion Township stands out as the lone portion of Montgomery County attached to the district; it features King of Prussia, a fast-growing Philadelphia exurb. Spurring economic and residential development in the King of Prussia corridor is the "Blue Route," a highway connecting Interstate 95 in southern Delaware County with the Schuylkill Expressway near King of Prussia. After decades of suburban discord over whether to build the route, its recent completion reduced traffic congestion in Delaware County and facilitated north-south commuting.

The 7th also contains a portion of Chester County. Tredyffrin Township holds the majority of its population, and includes the old-money mansions in Paoli and the newer residential developments of Chesterbrook. Farther west are less populous but emerging exurban townships such as East Whiteland, West Pikeland and West Vincent.

Election Returns

	7th District	Democrat	Republican
1992	President*	111,518 (39.1%)	123,954 (43.5%)
	House	91,623 (33.5%)	180,648 (66.0%)
1988	President	89,848 (36.2%)	158,270 (63.8%)
	Senate	60,009 (24.9%)	180,870 (75.1%)
1986	Senate	75,460 (40.5%)	111,091 (59.5%)
	Governor	68,126 (37.0%)	115,896 (63.0%)

Vote for Perot was 49,802 (17.5%).

Demographics

Population 565,746

Percent change from 1980 9.7%

Land area 303 square miles

Population per square mile 1,864

Counties, 1990 population
Chester (pt.) 95,521   Montgomery (pt.) 34,363
Delaware (pt.) 435,862

Cities, 1990 population (10,000 or more)
Broomall CDP 10,930   King of Prussia CDP
Drexel Hill CDP 29,744   18,406

Nether Providence CDP
    13,229
Phoenixville 15,066

Radnor CDP 28,705
Springfield CDP 24,160
Woodlyn CDP 10,151

Race and Hispanic origin
White 93.8%
Black 3.8%
American Indian, Eskimo, or Aleut. 0.1%
Asian or Pacific Islander 2.1%
Other 0.2%
Hispanic origin 0.9%

Ancestry
American 1.8%
Dutch 1.7%
English 16.2%
French 2.8%
German 25.9%
Greek 1.1%
Irish 32.8%
Italian 19.0%

Polish 6.2%
Russian 2.2%
Scotch Irish 2.5%
Scottish 2.7%
Slovakian 1.5%
Swedish 1.1%
Ukrainian 1.1%
Welsh 1.8%

Universities/colleges, 1990-1991 enrollment
American College, Bryn Mawr 370
Cabrini College, Radnor 1,477
Cheyney University of Pennsylvania, Cheyney 1,738
Delaware County Community College, Media 9,193
Eastern College, Wayne 1,367
Haverford College, Haverford 1,147
Neumann College, Aston 1,262
Pennsylvania Institute of Technology, Media 416
Pennsylvania State University, Malvern 1,093
Pennsylvania State University-Delaware County, Media 1,811
R. E. T. S. Electronic School, Broomall 230
Swarthmore College, Swarthmore 1,330
Valley Forge Christian College, Phoenixville 491
Villanova University, Villanova 11,577
Williamson Free School of Mechanical Trades, Media 340

Newspapers, total circulation (in all districts)
Delaware County Times 56,357
Philadelphia Daily News 196,141
Philadelphia Inquirer 500,733
Phoenixville Phoenix 5,334

Commercial television stations, affiliations
ADI: Philadelphia (100%)

Cable television systems, total subscribers
Adelphia Cable; Broomall 15,968
Harron Cable TV; Malvern 23,781
Radnor Cablevision; Radnor 6,000
Suburban Cable TV; Chester 39,212
Suburban Cable TV; Glenolden 66,858
Suburban Cable TV; King of Prussia 7,901

Businesses and other major employers
Boeing Co./Boeing Helicopters; Ridley Park; helicopters 6,423
Prime Plus Realty Partners; Chadds Ford; real estate agents 4,000
Vanguard Group Inc.; Wayne; investment offices 3,000
Crozer-Keystone Health System; Media; health services consulting 2,500
Smithkline Beecham Corp.; Norristown; pharmaceuticals 2,000

Villanova University; Villanova 2,000
Shared Medical Systems Corp.; Malvern; computer services 2,000
Vanguard Group Inc.; Valley Forge; investment offices 1,992
Franklin Mint Inc.; Media; collectables 1,700
Scott Paper Co./Packaged Products Div.; Chester; paper mills 1,650
Sun Refining & Mktg. Co.; Marcus Hook; petroleum refining 1,500
County of Delaware; Media 1,200
Delaware County Memorial Hospital; Drexel Hill 1,154
Paoli Memorial Hospital; Paoli 1,100
Wyeth Laboratories Inc.; Malvern; pharmaceuticals 1,050
News America Publications/TV Guide; Wayne; periodicals 1,000
National Liberty Life Insurance Co.; Malvern; medical service/health insurance 1,000
Fitzgerald Mercy Hospital; Darby 1,000
County of Delaware/Public Defender's Office; Media; legal services 1,000
Elwyn Inc.; Media 1,000
Educational Placement Services; Media; personnel supply services 1,000
Day & Zimmermann Inc.; Bryn Mawr; consulting services 975
State Farm Fire & Casualty Co.; Concordville; fire/marine/casualty insurance 950
U.S. Postal Service; Devon 900
Fair Acres Center; Media; residential care 900
Riddle Memorial Hospital; Media 800
Unisys Corp.; Paoli; computer services 800
Unisys Corp.; Malvern; computer services 800
Chilton Co./Chilton Book; Wayne; periodicals 750
County of Delaware; Media 750
Wyeth Laboratories Inc.; Paoli; pharmacueticals 725
Arco Chemical Co.; Newtown Square; organic chemicals 700
Certainteed Corp.; Valley Forge; mineral products 700
SEI Corp.; Wayne; computer services 700
Phoenixville Hospital Inc.; Phoenixville 700
Wyeth Laboratories Inc./Research Div.; Wayne; pharmaceuticals 675
Southeastern Pennsylvania Transportation Authority; Upper Darby 667
Ridley School District; Folsom 650
Swarthmore College; Swarthmore 614
ACME Markets Inc./ACME Super Saver; Malvern; grocery stores 600
Haverford State Hospital; Haverford 600
ITT Sheraton Corp./Sheraton Corp.; Norristown; hotel 600
Taylor Hospital; Ridley Park 595
Bryn Mawr Rehabilitation Hospital; Malvern 584
Macy's Northeast Inc.; Springfield; department stores 560
Marple Newtown School District; Newtown Square 560
Centocor Inc.; Malvern; pharmaceuticals 550

8th District
Northern Philadelphia Suburbs — Bucks County

Population growth and development have changed some of the character of the 8th, but not its politics. Bucks County is still Republican turf, as evidenced in 1992.

Former Democratic Rep. Peter H. Kostmayer held the seat for all but two years from 1977-1992 with tenacious constituent service and the votes of independents and Democrats from lower Bucks County. His environmentalist credentials also had some appeal among moderate Republicans. But even as Bill Clinton narrowly won the county in 1992—with less than 40 percent—voters threw out their Democratic incumbent. That same year the county backed GOP Sen. Arlen Specter for re-election.

Part of the reason for Kostmayer's upset was the selection of a strong GOP nominee, one whose moderate brand of Republicanism had countywide appeal from the landed gentry and farmers of Upper Bucks to the newly arrived independent voters. These newcomers—who include business executives from New Jersey and Manhattan—have fueled a two-decade population boom that has altered some of the area's rural charm.

Places such as Newtown Township experienced exponential growth in the 1980s; New Hope, a quaint artists' colony along the Delaware River, has turned into a tourist mecca.

The lure was Bucks County's rich history and rolling countryside. Established in 1682 as one of Pennsylvania's three original counties, Bucks contains mansions such as Pennsbury Manor, the Georgian-style mansion and plantation William Penn built for himself and his second wife. Washington Crossing was the site from which, on Christmas Day 1776, George Washington crossed the Delaware River to attack Hessian mercenaries in Trenton. In the early 20th century, New York intellectuals and prominent writers such as Dorothy Parker and Pearl S. Buck found refuge in Bucks County.

Much of the countryside in upper Bucks remains largely undeveloped and heavily Republican. Democrats can stay competitive in the county's midsection in communities such as Warminster and Doylestown.

Lower Bucks is more fertile ground for Democrats, with its grittier ambiance and closer association with Philadelphia. Levittown's tightly spaced homes, built after World War II, attracted thousands of ethnic Democrats moving from the big city.

Democratic strength surged in the 1980s as lower Bucks struggled with industrial problems typified by the massive layoffs in the remaining work force at the USX (formerly U.S. Steel) Fairless Works. But Republicans still hold a clear countywide voter registration advantage.

As a whole, the 8th contains all of Bucks County and about 25,000 voters in Montgomery County. One of five districts that take in some slice of Montgomery, the 8th has a portion of the county that includes Horsham and part of Lower Moreland Township.

Election Returns

	8th District	Democrat	Republican
1992	President*	101,630 (39.5%)	99,269 (38.6%)
	House	114,095 (45.7%)	129,593 (51.9%)
1988	President	82,246 (39.3%)	127,262 (60.7%)
	Senate	58,951 (29.0%)	144,348 (71.0%)
1986	Senate	49,429 (35.3%)	90,451 (64.7%)
	Governor	55,468 (40.1%)	82,718 (59.9%)

*Vote for Perot was 56,261 (21.9%).

Demographics

Population 565,787

Percent change from 1980 9.5%

Land area 626 square miles

Population per square mile 904

Counties, 1990 population
Bucks 541,174   Montgomery (pt.) 24,613

Cities, 1990 population (10,000 or more)
Bristol 10,405   Levittown CDP 55,362
Horsham CDP 15,051

Race and Hispanic origin
White 95.0%
Black 2.8%
American Indian, Eskimo, or Aleut. 0.1%
Asian or Pacific Islander 1.6%
Other 0.5%
Hispanic origin 1.6%

Ancestry
American 2.5%   Lithuanian 1.1%
Dutch 2.1%   Polish 8.3%
English 15.1%   Russian 3.1%
French 2.8%   Scotch Irish 1.9%
German 36.7%   Scottish 2.5%
Hungarian 1.5%   Slovakian 1.8%
Irish 26.0%   Ukrainian 1.4%
Italian 13.8%   Welsh 1.8%

Universities/colleges, 1990-1991 enrollment
Bucks County Community College, Newtown 11,164
CHI Institute, Southampton 424
Delaware Valley College of Science & Agriculture,
  Doylestown 1,098
Pennco Tech, Bristol 478
Philadelphia College of the Bible, Langhorne 641

Newspapers, total circulation (in all districts)
Allentown Morning Call 136,293
Bucks County Courier Times 67,412
Doylestown Intelligencer 41,406
Lansdale Reporter 18,974
Philadelphia Daily News 196,141
Philadelphia Inquirer 500,733
Trentonian 72,634
Trenton Times 82,521

Commercial television stations, affiliations
ADI: Philadelphia (100%)

Cable television systems, total subscribers
Comcast Cablevision; Willow Grove 30,000
Lower Bucks Cablevision; Parkland 36,376
Oxford Valley Cablevision; Bensalem 16,139
Service Electric Cable TV; Allentown 78,500
Suburban Cable; Newtown 6,347
Suburban Cable TV; Holland 8,725
Suburban Cable TV; Jamison 15,637
Suburban Cable TV; Sellersville 28,163

Military installations, 1991
Naval Air Development Center, Warminster 3,317

Businesses and other major employers
USX Corp.; Fairless Hills; steel products 3,300
Prudential Insurance of America Inc.; Horsham; insurance
  services 1,500
Grand View Hospital Foundation; Sellersville 1,475

St. Mary Hospital of Langhorne; Langhorne 1,400
Doylestown Hospital; Doylestown 1,400
Ametek Inc./U.S. Gauge; Sellersville; measuring/controlling
  devices 1,000
Lower Bucks Hospital; Bristol 1,000
Woods School; Langhorne 1,000
Township of Bensalem/School District; Bensalem 950
Charming Shoppes of Delaware; Bensalem; women's apparel
  900
Rohm & Haas Delaware Valley Inc; Bristol;
  plastics/synthetics 900
Union Fidelity Life Insurance Co.; Langhorne; medical
  service/health insurance 900
County of Bucks; Doylestown 850
G. F. Office Furniture Ltd.; Southampton; office furniture
  800
Fischer & Porter Co.; Warminster; industrial controls 800
Greenwood Racing Inc./Philadelphia Park; Bensalem; com-
  mercial sports 800
Kmart Corp.; Fairless Hills; warehousing 739
Courier Times Inc.; Levittown; newspapers 700
General Motors Corp.; Bensalem; motor
  vehicles/parts/supplies 650
Simon & Schuster Inc.; Bristol; book warehousing 650
Warminster General Hospital; Warminster 650
Delaware Valley Medical Center; Langhorne 610
Betz Laboratories Inc.; Langhorne; chemical products 600
Alfa-Laval Inc./Sharples; Warminster; pharmaceuticals 600
Decision Data Inc.; Horsham; computer equipment 600
Webcraft Technologies Inc.; Chalfont; paper mills 600
Educational Testing Service; Langhorne; testing services 600
Intersearch Corp.; Horsham; research services 600
Pennridge School District; Perkasie 570
Lifequest/Quakertown Community Hospital; Quakertown
  545
Penn Engineering & Mfg. Corp./Pittman Div.; Danboro;
  electic motors 530

9th District

South Central — Altoona

This south-central Pennsylvania region long has been a passageway from the East to Pittsburgh and beyond. Transportation was its primary focus, in particular the railroad industry.

The district's largest city, Altoona (Blair County), once prospered as a rail center despite its relatively inaccessible location in the Allegheny Mountains. Johnstown was but 40 miles to the west, but between them loomed the Alleghenies.

Crossing the southern Alleghenies was a significant undertaking in the mid-19th century, but the old Pennsylvania Railroad overcame the harsh landscape by devising engineering marvels such as Horseshoe Curve, just west of Altoona.

The Pennsylvania Railroad also nurtured the city of Altoona, but as the rail industry declined, population withered. When the railroad workers left, they took their Democratic loyalties with them. In 1992, George Bush and GOP Sen. Arlen Specter both carried Blair County.

Today, the remnants of the railroad industry serve as a tourism draw. Besides Horseshoe Curve, railroad buffs can visit the Railroaders Memorial Museum in Altoona or the Allegheny Portage Railroad National Historic Site. The Allegheny Portage

was part of an early attempt to link Philadelphia with Pittsburgh and the West.

The Pennsylvania Turnpike, the nation's first superhighway, crosses the southern section of the 9th District's tortured topography. Its epitome is Breezewood, best known as the "Town of Motels." Though Bedford County features 14 historic covered bridges, travelers recognize it better for the garish display of neon signs adorning the hotels and fast-food restaurants of the turnpike's Interchange 12, at Breezewood.

Before the turnpike's opening in 1940, Bedford County was a destination point, rather than a stopover. The pure and soothing waters of Bedford Springs attracted not only the afflicted, but the elite. President James Buchanan—who was born in the 9th—made the resort his summer White House.

For the most part, the 9th is a series of small villages scattered among the mountains. It has little industry; its farmers raise cattle for beef and milk.

The isolation and agricultural character of the region breeds a strong sense of conservatism. The eight counties wholly contained in the 9th backed both Bush and Specter in 1992; Snyder County, the 9th's easternmost, on the Susquehanna River, voted more than 2-to-1 for Bush in 1992.

Clearfield County's industrial tradition gives Democrats an edge, but its voting habits are as anomalous to the district as its location in the extreme northwest. The district includes all of Clearfield, save for one township that is in the 5th.

The 5th and the 9th districts also share Centre County, home to Pennsylvania State University in State College. State College is not in the 9th, but outlying towns such as Port Matilda and Philipsburg in the western portion of Centre County are included.

Election Returns

		Democrat	Republican
	9th District		
1992	President*	66,929 (32.7%)	97,772 (47.7%)
	House	—	182,406 (100.0%)
1988	President	65,581 (35.8%)	117,417 (64.2%)
	Senate	39,466 (21.8%)	141,865 (78.2%)
1986	Senate	50,173 (34.9%)	93,731 (65.1%)
	Governor	65,798 (45.7%)	78,145 (54.3%)

Vote for Perot was 40,204 (19.6%).

Demographics

Population 565,803

Percent change from 1980 9.8%

Land area 6,665 square miles

Population per square mile 85

Counties, 1990 population

Bedford 47,919	Huntingdon 44,164
Blair 130,542	Juniata 20,625
Centre (pt.) 14,583	Mifflin 46,197
Clearfield (pt.) 78,043	Perry (pt.) 12,131
Franklin 121,082	Snyder 36,680
Fulton 13,837	

Cities, 1990 population (10,000 or more)

Altoona 51,881	Chambersburg 16,647

Race and Hispanic origin

White 98.3%
Black 1.2%
American Indian, Eskimo, or Aleut. 0.1%
Asian or Pacific Islander 0.3%
Other 0.1%
Hispanic origin 0.4%

Ancestry

American 5.0%	Polish 2.7%
Dutch 5.2%	Scotch Irish 2.8%
English 10.6%	Scottish 1.9%
French 2.9%	Slovakian 2.0%
German 52.7%	Swedish 1.2%
Irish 16.8%	Welsh 1.4%
Italian 5.0%	

Universities/colleges, 1990-1991 enrollment

Du Bois Business College, Du Bois 278
Juniata College, Huntingdon 1,134
Pennsylvania State University, Altoona 2,509
Pennsylvania State University, Du Bois 1,045
Pennsylvania State University, Mont Alto 900
Susquehanna University, Selinsgrove 1,751
Wilson College, Chambersburg 943

Newspapers, total circulation (in all districts)

Altoona Mirror 34,698
Chambersburg Public Opinion 21,761
Clearfield Progress 15,445
Du Bois Courier-Express 10,616
Harrisburg Evening News 107,517
Lewistown Sentinel 13,144
State College Centre Daily Times 25,657
Sunbury Daily Item 25,086

Commercial television stations, affiliations

ADI: Johnstown-Altoona (67%), Harrisburg-York-Lancaster-Lebanon (17%), Washington, D.C. (12%) and Wilkes-Barre-Scranton (5%)
WJAL, Hagerstown (None)
WATM-TV, Altoona (ABC)
WKBS-TV, Altoona (None)
WTAJ-TV, Altoona (CBS)
WWPC-TV, Altoona (None)

Cable television systems, total subscribers

Du Bois Area Cable TV Inc.; Du Bois 6,742
Huntingdon TV Cable Co. Inc.; Huntingdon 5,800
TCI of Maryland; Cumberland 23,786
TCI of Pennsylvania; Bedford 5,900
TCI of Pennsylvania; Lewistown 7,700
TCI of Pennsylvania; Phillipsburg 7,023
TV Cable of Waynesboro; Waynesboro 7,500
Warner Cable Communications Inc.; Cambria County 32,708
Warner Cable Communications Inc.; Chambersburg 13,880
Warner Cable Communications Inc.; Roaring Spring 6,250
Warner Cable of Clearfield; Clearfield 6,974

Military installations, 1991

Letterkenny Army Depot, Chambersburg 5,001

Businesses and other major employers

Kidde Industries Inc./Grove North America; Shady Grove; industrial trucks 3,000
Altoona Hospital; Altoona 1,550

Bidermann Industries Corp./J. Shoeneman Co.; Chambersburg; apparel 1,500
Consolidated Rail Corp.; Altoona; railroads 1,470
Freedom Forge Corp./Standard Steel; Burnham; metals/minerals 1,300
Commonwealth of Pennsylvania/Selinsgrove Center; Selinsgrove; nursing 1,200
Chambersburg Hospital; Chambersburg 1,035
Wood-Mode Inc.; Kreamer; millwork 960
Lewistown Hospital; Lewistown 950
New Holland Ford Inc.; Belleville; farm/garden machinery 800
J. L. G. Industries Inc.; McConnellsburg; construction machinery 791
Mercy Hospital; Altoona 740
Empire Kosher Poultry Inc.; Mifflintown; poultry products 705
Borough of Chambersburg/School District; Chambersburg 700
Owens-Corning Fiberglas Corp.; Huntingdon; glass/glassware 650
County of Blair; Hollidaysburg 649
Regency Greetings; Waynesboro; commercial printing 600
Corning Inc./Consumer Products Div; Greencastle; warehousing 600
United Telephone Co. of Pennsylvania; Chambersburg; telephone communications 600
Hedstrom Corp.; Bedford; bicycles/parts 600
Scotty's Fashions of Lewistown; Lewistown; outerwear 600
H. H. Brown Shoe Co. Inc./Cove Shoe Co.; Martinsburg; footwear 600
Warnaco Inc.; Duncansville; apparel 600
Warnaco Inc./Knitwear Div.; Altoona; outerwear 600
Butterick Co. Inc.; Altoona; publishing 600
Penn Traffic Co.; Du Bois; warehousing 600
Alphastaff Group A Inc.; Huntingdon; personnel supply services 600
PPG Industries Inc.; Tipton; flat glass 550

10th District

Northeast — Scranton

The city of Scranton dominated the politics of northeastern Pennsylvania in the early part of this century, but as the coal-and-railroad town declined in population, the political influence of Scranton and Lackawanna County has slipped.

No longer does the rest of the region take its cue from Scranton, the most populous city in the 10th. While Lackawanna retains its traditional Democratic loyalties, Republicans have solidified their position in the outlying counties. In 1992, Lackawanna was the lone county in the 10th to support either Democrat Bill Clinton for president or the Democratic candidate for the Senate.

The county's Democratic majority casts its vote in Scranton and in some of the outlying blue-collar towns such as Moosic. Republicans can be found in more affluent suburbs such as Clarks Summit and Dalton.

At one time, Scranton was known as the "Anthracite Capital of the World." The city entered the Industrial Age by manufacturing iron. From an outpost of 650 people in 1840, Scranton grew to 260,000 in 1950. But the coal industry was already beginning to peter out in the 1940s, and the city's fortunes have declined through most of the postwar era.

Scranton has attempted to diversify its economic base, but the turnaround has been slow. There are some signs of improvement, though: The city has begun to appear on some lists of the "most livable places," thanks mostly to its affordable housing and relatively low crime rate. Business publications have also taken note of Scranton, touting the city as a good place to relocate or start a new business.

Among many local civic boosters, hopes for restoring the city's economic vitality hinge on the development of Steamtown National Historic Site, a railroad park-and-retail complex aimed at attracting tourists. This controversial national historic site and its adjacent $100 million mall have been pilloried as an example of federal pork-barrel politics. But what outsiders see as pork looks like a potential godsend to Scrantonians.

The population growth that the 10th saw during the 1980s came to the east of Lackawanna County. There, on the New Jersey border, Pike County has experienced spectacular growth as business executives who commute to New York have moved to the area. Pike's population boomed by 55 percent in the 1970s and 53 percent in the 1980s. Population has increased in Wayne and Monroe counties also, but to a lesser degree.

Pocono Mountain resorts and ski areas boost Monroe County's economy. Only part of Monroe County is in the 10th, but it is an especially scenic portion that includes the Delaware Water Gap National Recreation Area.

North and west of Scranton are reliably Republican and agricultural Bradford and Susquehanna counties. Democrats can be found on the far western edge of the district in Williamsport, the 10th's second-largest city and home to the annual Little League World Series.

Election Returns

	10th District	Democrat	Republican
1992	President*	88,150 (38.2%)	95,820 (41.5%)
	House †	—	189,414 (90.4%)
1988	President	83,791 (41.5%)	117,974 (58.5%)
	Senate	49,491 (25.9%)	141,618 (74.1%)
1986	Senate	61,899 (38.2%)	99,987 (61.8%)
	Governor	93,442 (55.8%)	73,951 (44.2%)

*Vote for Perot was 46,878 (20.3%).   †Independent/other is greater than 5%.

Demographics

Population 565,681

Percent change from 1980 9.7%

Land area 5,562 square miles

Population per square mile 102

Counties, 1990 population

Bradford 60,967	Sullivan 6,104
Lackawanna 219,039	Susquehanna 40,380
Lycoming (pt.) 101,591	Wayne 39,944
Monroe (pt.) 41,614	Wyoming 28,076
Pike 27,966	

Cities, 1990 population (10,000 or more)

Carbondale 10,664	Scranton 81,805
Dunmore 15,403	Williamsport 31,933

Race and Hispanic origin

White 98.1%
Black 1.1%
American Indian, Eskimo, or Aleut. 0.1%
Asian or Pacific Islander 0.5%
Other 0.2%
Hispanic origin 0.8%

Ancestry

American 3.6%	Polish 11.7%
Dutch 3.8%	Russian 2.4%
English 14.5%	Scotch Irish 1.3%
French 2.7%	Scottish 1.9%
German 30.7%	Slovakian 3.2%
Irish 21.6%	Ukrainian 1.5%
Italian 14.4%	Welsh 4.9%
Lithuanian 1.5%	

Universities/colleges, 1990-1991 enrollment

Baptist Bible College, Clarks Summit 711
ICS-Center for Degree Studies, Scranton 4,315
International Correspondence, Scranton 14,971
Johnson Technical Institute, Scranton 361
Keystone Junior College, La Plume 1,232
Lackawanna Junior College, Scranton 775
Lycoming College, Williamsport 1,255
Marywood College, Scranton 3,087
Pennsylvania College of Technology, Williamsport 4,343
Pennsylvania State University-Scranton, Dunmore 1,364
University of Scranton, Scranton 5,116

Newspapers, total circulation (in all districts)

Binghamton Press & Sun-Bulletin 70,739
Middletown Times Herald-Record 84,398
New York Post 551,443
Pocono Record Stroudsburg 20,995
Scranton Tribune 76,005
Wilkes-Barre Times Leader 48,597
Williamsport Sun Gazette 33,564

Commercial television stations, affiliations

ADI: Wilkes-Barre-Scranton (69%), Binghamton (21%) and New York (10%)
WOLF-TV, Scranton (Fox)

Cable television systems, total subscribers

Adams CATV Inc.; Waymart 13,000
Adelphia Cable; Scrub Oak Mountain 32,000
Blue Ridge Cable TV Inc.; Hawley 6,164
Blue Ridge Cable TV Inc.; Pocono Summit 11,582
Blue Ridge Cable TV Inc.; Stroudsburg 23,165
Dimension Cable Services; Williamsport 25,200
Verto Cable TV Corp.; Swoyersville 54,000

Military installations, 1991

Tobyhanna Army Depot, Tobyhanna 3,763

Businesses and other major employers

Procter & Gamble Co. Inc.; Mehoopany; paper products 3,100
Mercy Hospital of Scranton; Scranton 1,634
United Parcel Service Inc.; Scranton; mail services 1,500
Allied Services Foundation; Scranton; health services 1,500
Specialty Records Corp.; Olyphant; audio/video equipment 1,300
Williamsport Hospital Medical Center; Williamsport 1,295

Community Medical Center Inc.; Scranton 1,240

Thomson Consumer Electronics; Scranton; industry machinery 1,200

GTE Products Corp.; Towanda; chemical products 1,150

Avco Corp./Textron Lycoming Turbine Engine Div.; Williamsport; aircraft engines/parts 1,150

University of Scranton; Scranton 933

Marywood College; Scranton 870

Du Pont E. I. De Nemours & Co.; Towanda; photographic supplies 830

Divine Providence Hospital; Williamsport 805

Roadway Express Inc.; Tannersville; trucking facilities 800

Carey-McFall Corp./Bali Blinds; Montgomery; fixtures 800

Moses Taylor Hospital; Scranton 780

Mount Airy Lodge Inc.; Mount Pocono; hotel 750

Guthrie Clinic Ltd.; Sayre; medical doctors 750

Taylor Packing Co. Inc.; Wyalusing; meatpacking 725

Andritz Sprout-Bauer Inc.; Muncy; industry machinery 700

Wundies Enterprises Inc./Kickaway; Williamsport; undergarments 700

Clarks Summit State Hospital; Clarks Summit 700

Consolidated Freightways Corp.; Pocono Summit; trucking facilities 675

American Standard Inc./Trane Co.; Scranton; air conditioning equipment 650

Masonite Corp.; Towanda; wood products 601

Super Market Service Corp.; Scranton; drugs/proprietaries 600

Northeastern Education; Jermyn; educational films 600

City of Scranton; Scranton 600

Gentex Corp.; Carbondale; metal forgings/stampings 575

Northeastern Bank of Pennsylvania; Scranton; commercial banks 567

Loral Fairchild Corp.; Archbald; photographic equipment/supplies 550

Ingersoll-Rand Co.; Athens; industrial equipment/supplies 550

U.S. Postal Service; Scranton 510

General Dynamics Land Systems; Archbald; tank equipment 510

11th District

Northeast — Wilkes-Barre

The Democratic legacy of the 11th District's industrial heritage is showing signs of fraying. In the 1992 presidential election, Bill Clinton won Luzerne and Carbon counties, but lost in the other areas that complete the district.

This region had long been Democratic territory, primarily because of Luzerne County's Democratic influence. In the 11th's largest city, Wilkes-Barre, and in other Wyoming Valley towns, the Democratic tradition dates back to the days when the anthracite coal-mining industry dominated the local economy.

But as the costs of mining anthracite coal rose and the use of oil and natural gas for home heating increased, the local industry began a steep decline. So did the region's population, and along with it, Democratic hegemony.

Voter registration figures reveal a district with a distinct Democratic advantage, but in 1980 and 1984, Ronald Reagan won in the region, as did George Bush in 1988. In 1992, the Democratic Senate nominee managed to win only in Carbon County.

Luzerne County, with its rich ethnic stew of eastern Europeans, Italians, Irish and Welsh, still casts more than half the district's vote. Much of the county vote comes from Wilkes-Barre's outlying towns such as Pittston and Kingston, but Hazleton, in southern Luzerne County, is also of some size.

Politics takes a back seat to football in neighboring Columbia County. Berwick is a hard-core gridiron town, where residents shoehorn into Crispin Field to forget about the demise of the coal industry and watch the Berwick Bulldogs, annually one of the nation's finest high school teams.

Another vestige of the coal industry in Columbia County is the decades-old mine fire that still burns beneath the borough of Centralia. The threat of cave-ins and explosions scared most residents away over the years, and the rest were bought out by the federal government.

Jim Thorpe, a Carbon County coal region town on the eastern side of the 11th, has fared much better. Once a haven for the wealthy—locals boast that 13 of America's 70 millionaires lived here in the late 19th century—this picturesque Lehigh River town fell on hard times when the demand for anthracite coal waned in the 1930s and 1940s.

In hopes of reviving the town, officials in 1954 changed the town's name from Mauch Chunk to that of the famed Olympic athlete Jim Thorpe, who died in 1953 and is buried here. Today, tourism is thriving after the town became a demonstration preservation project for the Department of Interior.

Elsewhere in the county, in Panther Valley coal towns such as Lansford and Nesquehoning, the economic outlook is not as promising.

Northeast of Carbon County, the Monroe County portion of the district includes some of the southern Pocono Mountain resort areas.

Election Returns

	11th District	Democrat	Republican
1992	President*	91,671 (41.9%)	84,203 (38.5%)
	House	138,875 (67.1%)	68,112 (32.9%)
1988	President	92,343 (47.0%)	104,334 (53.0%)
	Senate	58,640 (31.9%)	125,083 (68.1%)
1986	Senate	77,939 (47.5%)	86,224 (52.5%)
	Governor	102,287 (61.2%)	64,894 (38.8%)

Vote for Perot was 42,960 (19.6%).

Demographics

Population 565,913

Percent change from 1980 9.7%

Land area 2,374 square miles

Population per square mile 238

Counties, 1990 population

Carbon 56,846	Montour 17,735
Columbia 63,202	Northumberland (pt.)
Luzerne 328,149	45,886
Monroe (pt.) 54,095	

Cities, 1990 population (10,000 or more)

Berwick 10,976	Kingston 14,507
Bloomsburg 12,439	Nanticoke 12,267
Hazleton 24,730	Wilkes-Barre 47,523

Race and Hispanic origin

White 98.4%
Black 0.9%
American Indian, Eskimo, or Aleut. 0.1%
Asian or Pacific Islander 0.4%
Other 0.2%
Hispanic origin 0.7%

Ancestry

American 2.3%
Dutch 6.1%
English 8.6%
French 1.6%
German 29.7%
Irish 16.9%
Italian 13.1%
Lithuanian 3.2%
Polish 19.1%
Russian 2.2%
Scottish 1.1%
Slovakian 8.7%
Ukrainian 2.0%
Welsh 4.9%

Universities/colleges, 1990-1991 enrollment

Bloomsburg University of Pennsylvania, Bloomsburg 7,484
College of Misericordia, Dallas 1,513
East Stroudsburg University of Pennsylvania, East Stroudsburg 5,456
King's College, Wilkes-Barre 2,258
Luzerne Community College, Nanticoke 6,530
Pennsylvania State University, Hazleton 1,308
Pennsylvania State University, Wilkes-Barre 990
Wilkes College, Wilkes-Barre 3,627

Newspapers, total circulation (in all districts)

Allentown Morning Call 136,293
Hazleton Standard-Speaker 23,559
Lehighton Times News 16,119
New York Daily News 757,053
New York Post 551,443
Philadelphia Inquirer 500,733
Pocono Record Stroudsburg 20,995
Scranton Tribune 76,005
Wilkes-Barre Citizens' Voice 46,283
Wilkes-Barre Times Leader 48,597

Commercial television stations, affiliations

ADI: Wilkes-Barre-Scranton (100%)
  WWLF-TV, Hazleton (Fox)
  WNEP-TV, Scranton (ABC)
  WYOU, Scranton (CBS)
  WBRE-TV, Wilkes-Barre (NBC)

Cable television systems, total subscribers

Adelphia Cable; Scrub Oak Mountain 32,000
Berwick Cable TV Inc.; Berwick 6,417
Blue Ridge Cable TV Inc.; Lehighton 19,700
Blue Ridge Cable TV Inc.; Stroudsburg 23,165
Blue Ridge Cable TV Inc.; Summit Hill 5,807
CATV Service Inc.; Danville 15,995
Service Electric Cable TV; Bloomsburg 6,500
Service Electric Cable TV; Hazleton 19,000
Service Electric Cable TV; Shamokin 12,500
Service Electric Cable TV; Wilkes-Barre 25,000
Verto Cable TV Corp.; Swoyersville 54,000

Businesses and other major employers

Geisinger Medical Center; Danville 3,722
Wilkes-Barre General Hospital; Wilkes-Barre 1,900
United Parcel Service Inc.; Stroudsburg; mail services 1,500
Leslie Fay Companies Inc.; Wilkes-Barre; outerwear 1,500
Nesbitt Memorial Hospital; Kingston 1,200
Owens-Illinois Inc./Television Products Div.; Pittston; glass face plates 1,134
U.S. Veterans Affairs Dept.; Wilkes-Barre; hospital 1,108
Topps Co. Inc.; Pittston; gum 1,000
Borden Inc./Wise Foods; Berwick; potato chips 1,000
Geisinger Wyoming Valley Medical Center; Wilkes-Barre 975
Pocono Medical Center; East Stroudsburg 974
Commonwealth of Pennsylvania/White Haven Center; White Haven 820
Bloomsburg University; Bloomsburg 813
Mercy Hospital; Wilkes-Barre 776
Pennsylvania Power & Light Co./Susquehanna Steam Electric Station; Berwick; electric services 735
Keystone Automotive Warehouse; Pittston; motor vehicle parts/supplies 730
County of Luzerne; Wilkes-Barre 720
Harris Corp./Solid State Div.; Mountain Top; electronic components 700
Commonwealth of Pennsylvania/Danville State Hospital; Danville 700
Star-Kist Foods Inc./Heinz Pet Products; Bloomsburg; grain mill products 640
Berwick Hospital Center & Retirement Village; Berwick 640
Transcontinental Refrigerated Lines; Pittston; trucking services 600
Intermetro Industries Corp.; Wilkes-Barre; metal products 600
Magee Industrial Enterprises; Bloomsburg; carpets/rugs 600
Gnaden Huetten Memorial Hospital; Lehighton 600
Offset Paperback Manufacturers Inc.; Dallas; printing/binding 580
Princeton Packaging Inc.; Hazleton; commercial printing 565
St. Joseph Medical Center; Hazleton 550
Hospital Service Assn. of Northeastern Pennsylvania/Blue Cross; Wilkes-Barre; medical service/health insurance 501

12th District

Southwest — Johnstown

Pennsylvania's Laurel Highlands are the setting for the 12th, a region once noted for its coal, iron and steel industries but nowadays better known for its chronic hard luck.

Johnstown, the biggest city in the 12th, is famous for the floods that have devastated the town three times over the past century. The Great Flood of 1889 was the worst, when an earthen dam outside town collapsed, sending 20 million tons of water surging through the Conemaugh Valley. The town was virtually destroyed and 2,200 people were killed. In 1936, another flood struck, killing 25. The most recent flood, in 1977, took the lives of 85 residents.

The early 1980s recession took a similarly heavy toll on Johnstown's economy, flattening what remained of the city's coal and steel industries and sending unemployment rates over 27 percent, the nation's highest at the time.

Johnstown has attempted to bounce back, partly by capitalizing on its flood history. In 1989, the city stressed the centennial anniversary of the Great Flood; tourists can visit the Johnstown Flood Museum.

Besides the hard times, another constant has been the Johnstown and Cambria County Democratic tradition. There were defections to Ronald Reagan in 1980, but Jimmy Carter still managed to carry Cambria County. Four years later, voters registered their unhappiness with Reagan's unwillingness to impose mandatory steel quotas by backing Walter F. Mondale.

In 1988 and 1992, Michael S. Dukakis and Bill Clinton won comfortably in Cambria. Even Democratic Senate nominee Lynn Yeakel won here in 1992, though she ran poorly across the rest of the district.

The western portions of Westmoreland and Fayette counties in the 12th are also fonts of Democratic votes. Fayette is a rural, Democratic stronghold where unions are king and Republicans need not apply. Westmoreland is less reliably Democratic, though Republicans are outregistered here 2-to-1. For beer connoisseurs, most notable in the Westmoreland County part of the 12th is Latrobe, home to the Rolling Rock brewery (200 employees).

In politically competitive Armstrong County, Democrats run best in Kittanning, a commercial center along the Allegheny River.

Rural Somerset is the only county in the 12th where Republicans have an edge in voter registration. In 1992, it backed both George Bush and Sen. Arlen Specter.

Clarion County, at the northern extreme of the 12th, votes Republican, but virtually all of the county (except New Bethlehem) belongs to the 5th District.

Indiana County is a mixture of farms and mines, and the county bills itself as the "Christmas tree capital of the world" for its abundance of blue spruces, and Scotch, Norway and white pines. But St. Nick is not the real hero; it is the hometown boy whose statue stands in front of the county courthouse—actor Jimmy Stewart.

Election Returns

	12th District	Democrat		Republican	
1992	President*	102,777	(46.7%)	72,671	(33.0%)
	House	166,916	(100.0%)	—	
1988	President	111,651	(55.0%)	91,443	(45.0%)
	Senate	61,323	(30.8%)	137,764	(69.2%)
1986	Senate	78,865	(47.7%)	86,454	(52.3%)
	Governor	102,972	(61.8%)	63,619	(38.2%)

*Vote for Perot was 44,852 (20.4%).

Demographics

Population 565,794

Percent change from 1980 9.7%

Land area 4,213 square miles

Population per square mile 134

Counties, 1990 population

Armstrong (pt.)	72,537	Indiana	89,994
Cambria	163,029	Somerset	78,218
Clarion (pt.)	1,151	Westmoreland (pt.)	
Fayette (pt.)	55,910	104,955	

Cities, 1990 population (10,000 or more)

Indiana	15,174	Johnstown	28,134

Race and Hispanic origin
White 98.3%
Black 1.3%
American Indian, Eskimo, or Aleut 0.1%
Asian or Pacific Islander 0.3%
Other 0.1%
Hispanic origin 0.4%

Ancestry

American	3.1%	Italian	10.6%
Dutch	5.2%	Polish	8.5%
English	10.8%	Scotch Irish	3.1%
French	2.1%	Scottish	2.2%
German	43.7%	Slovakian	9.7%
Hungarian	2.1%	Ukrainian	1.1%
Irish	18.8%	Welsh	1.9%

Universities/colleges, 1990-1991 enrollment
Indiana University of Pennsylvania, Indiana 14,398
Mt. Aloysius Junior College, Cresson 1,487
National Education Center, Blairsville 417
Pennsylvania State University-Fayette, Uniontown 945
St. Francis College, Loretto 1,763
St. Vincent College, Latrobe 1,147
University of Pittsburgh at Johnstown, Johnstown 3,210

Newspapers, total circulation (in all districts)
Altoona Mirror 34,698
Connellsville Courier 12,169
Greensburg Tribune Review 51,972
Indiana Gazette 17,956
Johnstown Tribune-Democrat 48,088
Latrobe Bulletin 8,997
Kittanning Leader Times 11,381
Monessen Valley Independent 17,743
Pittsburgh Post-Gazette 153,796
Somerset Daily American 12,449
Uniontown Herald Standard 30,690

Commercial television stations, affiliations
ADI: Pittsburgh (58%) and Johnstown-Altoona (42%)
WJAC-TV, Johnstown (NBC)
WPTJ, Johnstown (None)
WWCP-TV, Johnstown (Fox)

Cable television systems, total subscribers
Adelphia Cable; Blairsville 22,707
Armstrong Cable Services; Connellsville 19,339
Cablevision of Greater Johnstown; Johnstown 31,100
Clear Channels Cable TV Co.; Kittanning 7,930
Helicon Cablevision; Uniontown 35,800
TCI of Pennsylvania; Carrolltown 13,661
TCI of Pennsylvania; Greensburg 46,200

Businesses and other major employers
Commonwealth of Pennsylvania; Indiana; road construction 3,350
Conemaugh Valley Memorial Hospital; Johnstown 2,000
Bethlehem Steel Corp.; Johnstown; steel products 1,916
Allegheny Ludlum Corp.; Leechburg; steel products 1,500
Indiana University of Pennsylvania; Indiana 1,465
Lee Hospital; Johnstown 1,230
Latrobe Area Hospital Inc.; Latrobe 1,220
Cambria County/Laurel Crest Manor; Ebensburg 1,200
Sylvan Foods Inc.; Worthington; horticultural specialties 1,100

Johnstown America Corp./Freight Car Div.; Johnstown; railroad equipment 1,000

Moonlight Mushrooms Inc.; Worthington; mushrooms 1,000

Indiana Healthcare Corp./Indiana Hospital; Indiana 890

Commonwealth of Pennsylvania/Ebensburg Center; Ebensburg 875

Latrobe Steel Co./Koncor Industries Div.; Latrobe; steel products 800

Seven Springs Farm Inc./Seven Springs Resort; Champion; hotel 750

Armstrong County Memorial Hospital; Kittanning 746

Commonwealth of Pennsylvania/Torrance State Hospital; Torrance; nursing 725

Mercy Hospital of Johnstown; Johnstown 724

Frick Community Health Center; Mt. Pleasant 701

Eljer Industries Inc.; Ford City; fixtures 700

Pennsylvania Electric Co.; Johnstown; electric services 657

Anchor Glass Container Corp.; Connellsville; glass/glassware 653

Williamhouse-Regency of Delaware Inc.; Scottdale; commercial printing 600

Anchor Hocking Corp.; Connellsville; metal forgings/stampings 575

Pennsylvania Mines Corp./Greenwich Collieries Div.; Barnesboro; coal mining 564

Metropolitan Life Insurance Co.; Johnstown; insurance services 560

Kennametal Inc.; Latrobe; metalworking machinery 520

Somerset Hospital; Somerset 511

13th District

Northwest Philadelphia Suburbs — The Main Line

The 13th is the unlikeliest of venues to be represented by a Democrat in the House. It is the wealthiest district in Pennsylvania, and one of the most Republican.

Anchored solely in Montgomery County, the 13th includes Lower Merion Township, home to Philadelphia's aristocracy. The area is known as the Main Line, for the Pennsylvania Railroad's Main Line of Public Works, along which doctors, lawyers and old-money families built their posh estates. The white-collar professionals of Bryn Mawr, Narberth and Ardmore still ride into the city on the commuter trains that run along this line. A smaller portion of the Main Line is contained in the 7th District.

Though some Democratic-voting blacks have moved out of Philadelphia into areas such as Abington and Cheltenham, the county is overwhelmingly white and Republican. In 1990, Montgomery was the only county in the state to cling to Republican Barbara Hafer, as her unsuccessful gubernatorial campaign went down to spectacular defeat.

Two years later, the county experienced a bout of ballot topsy-turvy as it deserted George Bush, backed GOP Sen. Arlen Specter and elected Democrat Marjorie Margolies-Mezvinsky to the House. Without the recent infighting that has gripped the local GOP, a Democratic congressional candidate would have an extremely difficult time winning in the county.

As a wealthy, suburban county that borders a troubled big city, Montgomery follows developments in Philadelphia with interest and concern. When· redistricting plans surfaced in the state Legislature that would have grafted part of the county into a city-based district, county legislators fought hard to kill the proposals.

Norristown, the county seat, has the largest concentration of minorities in the county. At the end of each workday when the white-collar legal community departs, Norristown reverts to a small borough with some big city urban problems. North of Norristown, Hatfield and Lansdale are other population centers.

The western portion of the county, especially along the Route 422 corridor, is coming to grips with problems associated with rapid growth. New residential developments are sprouting to house employees of the pharmaceutical companies that have relocated to Upper Providence Township. Local infrastructure improvements have made the surrounding region accessible and attractive to commuters and businesses. Even in the former farmland communities of Lower Salford, Worcester and Franconia, the loosely organized lobby of Pennsylvania Dutch farmers jokingly referred to as the "Mennonite-Industrial Complex" is seeing its influence diminish.

Central Montgomery County already experienced that growth, particularly around the Fort Washington area. There the northeast extension of the Pennsylvania Turnpike toll road begins its way north to Allentown, Wilkes-Barre and Scranton.

Election Returns

	13th District	Democrat	Republican
1992	President*	119,042 (43.9%)	107,811 (39.8%)
	House	127,685 (50.3%)	126,312 (49.7%)
1988	President	109,568 (39.7%)	166,393 (60.3%)
	Senate	72,490 (27.2%)	194,429 (72.8%)
1986	Senate	59,612 (30.9%)	133,080 (69.1%)
	Governor	64,537 (33.7%)	126,950 (66.3%)

*Vote for Perot was 44,280 (16.3%).

Demographics

Population 565,793

Percent change from 1980 10.0%

Land area 366 square miles

Population per square mile 1,547

Counties, 1990 population
Montgomery (pt.) 565,793

Cities, 1990 population (10,000 or more)
East Norriton CDP 13,324   West Norriton CDP
Lansdale 16,362   15,209
Norristown 30,749   Willow Grove CDP 16,325

Race and Hispanic origin
White 91.0%
Black 6.1%
American Indian, Eskimo, or Aleut. 0.1%
Asian or Pacific Islander 2.5%
Other 0.3%
Hispanic origin 1.2%

Ancestry
American 2.3%   French 2.4%
Dutch 2.0%   German 30.7%
English 13.4%   Hungarian 1.3%

Irish 23.2%   Scottish 2.3%
Italian 14.4%   Slovakian 1.3%
Polish 6.7%   Ukrainian 1.2%
Russian 5.9%   Welsh 1.6%
Scotch Irish 1.8%

Universities/colleges, 1990-1991 enrollment
Beaver College, Glenside 2,253
Biblical Theological Seminary, Hatfield 203
Bryn Mawr College, Bryn Mawr 1,885
Gratz College, Melrose Park 512
Gwynedd-Mercy College, Gwynedd Valley 1,980
Harcum Junior College, Bryn Mawr 687
Manor Junior College, Jenkintown 476
Montgomery Community College, Blue Bell 8,172
Pennsylvania State University-Ogontz, Abington 3,207
Rosemont College, Rosemont 681
St. Charles Borromeo Seminary, Overbrook 442
Ursinus College, Collegeville 2,316

Newspapers, total circulation (in all districts)
Allentown Morning Call 136,293
Lansdale Reporter 18,974
Norristown Times Herald 29,563
Philadelphia Daily News 196,141
Philadelphia Inquirer 500,733
Pottstown Mercury 29,636

Commercial television stations, affiliations
ADI: Philadelphia (100%)

Cable television systems, total subscribers
Adelphia Cable; Colmar 21,365
Cablevision of Pennsylvania Inc.; Norristown 20,000
Comcast Cablevision; Bala-Cynwyd 13,227
Comcast Cablevision; Northeast Philadelphia 149,426
Comcast Cablevision; Willow Grove 30,000
Montgomery Cablevision Inc.; Plymouth Meeting 12,080
Suburban Cable TV; Sellersville 28,163
Wade Cablevision; Philadelphia 55,000

Military installations, 1991
Willow Grove Naval Air Station, Willow Grove 2,341
Willow Grove Air Reserve Station, Hatboro 609

Businesses and other major employers
Unisys Corp./Commercial Systems Div.; Blue Bell;
    computer/office equipment 3,000
Bryn Mawr Hospital Inc.; Bryn Mawr 2,811
Ford Motor Co.; Lansdale; telecommunications equipment
    2,650
Abington Memorial Hospital; Abington 2,594
Mercy Health Corp.; Bala-Cynwyd 2,501
Prudential Insurance of America Inc.; Ft. Washington; insur-
    ance services 2,500
Lankenau Hospital; Wynnewood 2,000
U.S. Healthcare Inc.; Blue Bell; medical service/health insur-
    ance 1,589
Smithkline Beecham Corp.; Norristown; medical labs 1,500
Commonwealth of Pennsylvania/Public Welfare Dept.; Nor-
    ristown 1,400
Rohm & Haas Co./Research Laboratories; Spring House;
    research services 1,300
Leeds & Northrup Co.; Spring House; industrial
    measuring/controlling devices 1,200

Jeanes Health Systems Inc.; Jenkintown 1,200
Montgomery Hospital; Norristown 1,187
American Olean Tile Co.; Lansdale; tiles 1,150
Holy Redeemer Hospital; Jenkintown 1,100
Rhone-Poulenc Rorer Inc.; Collegeville; pharmaceuticals
    1,050
Harleysville Mutual Insurance Co.; Harleysville;
    fire/marine/casualty insurance 1,050
County of Montgomery; Norristown 1,025
Moyer Packing Co.; Souderton; meatpacking 1,000
Pottstown Memorial Medical Center; Pottstown 980
Hatfield Quality Meats Inc./Smiling Porker Farms; Hatfield;
    meat products 940
McNeil PPC Inc.; Ft. Washington; pharmaceuticals 900
Moore Products Co.; Spring House; measuring/controlling
    devices 900
GMAC Mortgage Corp.; Philadelphia; mortgage bankers 900
Johnson & Johnson/McNeil Pharmaceuticals; Spring House;
    pharmaceuticals 850
Philadelphia Suburban Corp.; Royersford; engineering ser-
    vices 850
Rolling Hill Hospital; Philadelphia 820
Sacred Heart Hospital of Norristown; Norristown 818
Fleming Companies Inc.; Oaks; grocery products 800
Commonwealth of Pennsylvania/Correctional Institute;
    Collegeville 800
Bryn Mawr College; Bryn Mawr 770
AEL Defense Corp.; Lansdale; defense systems/equipment
    753
SPS Technologies Inc.; Jenkintown; screw machine products
    750
Danella Companies Inc.; Plymouth Meeting; heavy construc-
    tion 750
Valley Forge Plaza Associates/Sheraton Valley Forge Hotel;
    Norristown; hotel 750
J. D. M. Materials Co. Inc.; Huntingdon Valley;
    concrete/gypsum/plaster products 692
Suburban General Hospital; Norristown 669
Williard Inc.; Jenkintown; plumbing/heating/air-condition-
    ing 650
National Railroad Pass Corp.; Ft. Washington; railroads 650
North Pennsylvania Hospital; Lansdale 650
County of Montgomery; Royersford; residential care 630
Stroehmann Bakeries Inc.; Norristown; bakery products 550
International Computaprint Corp./Tri-Star Publishing; Ft.
    Washington; printing services 550
Strawbridge & Clothier; Plymouth Meeting; department
    stores 539
Dana Corp.; Pottstown; motor vehicle parts 525
Colonial School District; Plymouth Meeting 520

14th District

Pittsburgh and Suburbs

The place once referred to as "hell with the lid off" is now a
gleaming city of water, glass and steel. Since the 1950s,
Pittsburgh has undergone an economic transformation that has
made the hub of western Pennsylvania into a world-class city—
albeit one with far fewer high-wage, working-class jobs than
existed in days past.

No one calls it "the smoky city" anymore. Gone is the

pollution and griminess created by the steel mills and heavy industry that hugged the Allegheny, Monongahela and Ohio rivers. In their places are medical centers and universities, parks and skyscrapers. There are more than 150 research and development facilities.

With a relatively high quality of life, Pittsburgh ranks high on lists of the "most livable places"; its amenities make it a preferred location for Hollywood filmmakers.

The "Golden Triangle" area, where the Allegheny and Monongahela meet to form the Ohio River, is a thriving downtown with a large corporate community. Companies such as USX, Aluminum Co. of America (Alcoa), Westinghouse and H. J. Heinz have headquarters here in the city where such industrial giants as Andrew Carnegie, Andrew Mellon and H. J. Heinz made their fortunes. The USX Tower, a 64-story edifice, is one of the largest buildings between New York and Chicago.

The Fort Duquesne Bridge—one of hundreds of bridges and tunnels that connect the city's valleys and ridges—is a gateway to Three Rivers Stadium and Pittsburgh's north side.

The economic and cultural renaissance has made for a more sophisticated city, yet at the same time Pittsburgh has retained its traditional ethnic character. About 80 distinct neighborhoods dot the city, including the Oakland academic-medical complex—the site of Carnegie-Mellon University, the University of Pittsburgh and Children's Hospital—and the eastern European working-class enclaves on the south side. Italians live in Bloomfield, Poles and Germans in Lawrenceville, and Jews in Squirrel Hill. There are black neighborhoods in Homewood and East Liberty.

Pittsburgh's Democratic tradition is another constant. In statewide elections, lopsided Democratic margins provided by Pittsburgh and Philadelphia can offset the GOP advantage elsewhere in Pennsylvania.

Unions remain a force, contributing to Pittsburgh's huge Democratic majority. Within the city—all of which is in the 14th—Democrats outnumber Republicans by more than 6-to-1.

Republicans have a better time in the northern and western suburbs that make up about one-third of the 14th's population. There, the Democratic voter registration advantage is less than 2-to-1. The suburbanites are generally younger, more affluent and less bound by traditional party loyalties than residents in the city.

In many of these areas, Republicans control local offices. The fast-growing North Hills area, partly in the 14th, is filled with executives from Pittsburgh's burgeoning high-tech industry.

Election Returns

	14th District	Democrat	Republican
1992	President*	145,419 (58.2%)	66,016 (26.4%)
	House	165,633 (72.3%)	61,311 (26.8%)
1988	President	160,154 (65.6%)	83,889 (34.4%)
	Senate	89,163 (38.6%)	141,550 (61.4%)
1986	Senate	95,212 (53.8%)	81,855 (46.2%)
	Governor	107,729 (61.0%)	68,790 (39.0%)

Vote for Perot was 38,460 (15.4%).

Demographics

Population 565,787

Percent change from 1980 9.5%

Land area 194 square miles

Population per square mile 2,923

Counties, 1990 population
Allegheny (pt.) 565,787

Cities, 1990 population (10,000 or more)
Franklin Park 10,109
Hampton CDP 15,568
McCandless CDP (pt.) 28,781
Pittsburgh 369,879
Robinson CDP 10,830
Ross CDP (pt.) 33,482

Race and Hispanic origin
White 80.5%
Black 17.8%
American Indian, Eskimo, or Aleut. 0.1%
Asian or Pacific Islander 1.3%
Other 0.2%
Hispanic origin 0.8%

Ancestry
American 1.4%
English 7.8%
French 1.8%
German 31.5%
Hungarian 1.6%
Irish 19.8%
Italian 13.4%
Lithuanian 1.1%
Polish 9.8%
Russian 2.2%
Scotch Irish 2.2%
Scottish 1.7%
Slovakian 4.8%
Ukrainian 1.5%
Welsh 1.1%

Universities/colleges, 1990-1991 enrollment
Allegheny Community College, Pittsburgh 20,553
Art Institute of Pittsburgh, Pittsburgh 2,523
Bradford School, Pittsburgh 500
Carlow College, Pittsburgh 1,208
Carnegie-Mellon University, Pittsburgh 7,225
Chatham College, Pittsburgh 643
Duquesne University, Pittsburgh 7,443
La Roche College, Pittsburgh 1,858
Median School of Allied Health Careers, Pittsburgh 256
Pennsylvania Technical Institute, Pittsburgh 253
Pittsburgh Technical Institute, Pittsburgh 276
Pittsburgh Theological Seminary, Pittsburgh 319
Point Park College, Pittsburgh 2,977
Sawyer School, Pittsburgh 697
Triangle Institute of Technology, Pittsburgh 452
University of Pittsburgh, Pittsburgh 28,120

Newspapers, total circulation (in all districts)
McKeesport Daily News 26,123
New Kensington Valley News Dispatch 37,712
Pittsburgh Post-Gazette 153,796

Commercial television stations, affiliations
ADI: Pittsburgh (100%)
KDKA-TV, Pittsburgh (CBS)
WPGH-TV, Pittsburgh (Fox)
WPXI, Pittsburgh (NBC)

Cable television systems, total subscribers
TCI of Pennsylvania; Baden 18,000
TCI of Pennsylvania; Carnegie 21,000
TCI of Pennsylvania; Etna 19,000
TCI of Pennsylvania; McCandless 28,000
TCI of Pennsylvania; Pittsburgh 90,000

Military installations, 1991

Greater Pittsburgh Intl. Airport Air Force Guard Station, Coraopolis 944

Charles E. Kelly Support Facility, Pittsburgh 456

Businesses and other major employers

Univer/PGH Common System Education; Pittsburgh 8,510

Mellon Bank Corp.; Pittsburgh; commercial banks 5,000

City of Pittsburgh; Pittsburgh 5,000

Allegheny General Hospital; Pittsburgh 4,625

Carnegie-Mellon University; Pittsburgh 2,679

Western Psychiatric Institute; Pittsburgh 2,500

Mercy Hospital of Pittsburgh; Pittsburgh 2,500

Western Pennsylvania Hospital; Pittsburgh 2,300

St. Francis Medical Center; Pittsburgh 2,278

Blue Cross of Western Pennsylvania; Pittsburgh; medical service/health insurance 2,000

Shadyside Hospital; Pittsburgh 1,917

Magee-Women's Hospital; Pittsburgh 1,900

U.S. Veterans Affairs Dept.; Pittsburgh; hospital 1,840

Children's Hospital of Pittsburgh; Pittsburgh 1,682

Pittsburgh Press Co.; Pittsburgh; newspapers 1,650

USAir Inc.; Pittsburgh; airline 1,614

PPG Industries Inc./Glass Group; Pittsburgh; flat glass 1,600

USX Corp./Steel Div.; Pittsburgh; steel products 1,500

Miles Inc./Inorganic Chemicals Div.; Pittsburgh; plastics/synthetics 1,500

May Dept. Stores Co./Kaufmann's Dept. Store; Pittsburgh; department stores 1,500

Montefiore University Hospital; Pittsburgh 1,500

Duquesne University; Pittsburgh 1,500

H. J. Heinz Co./Heinz USA; Pittsburgh; canned food products 1,500

Sewickley Valley Hospital; Sewickley 1,394

Pittsburgh National Bank; Pittsburgh; commercial banks 1,340

Aluminum Co. of America; Pittsburgh; aluminum products 1,300

North Hills Passavant Hospital; Pittsburgh 1,300

Joseph Horne Co. Inc./Horne's; Pittsburgh; department stores 1,200

Commonwealth of Pennsylvania; Pittsburgh 1,100

LTV Steel Co. Inc.; Pittsburgh; steel products 1,000

Bell Telephone Co. of Pennsylvania; Pittsburgh; business services 1,000

Lane Marsetta Temp Services Inc.; Pittsburgh; personnel supply services 1,000

Ogden Allied Maintenance Corp.; Pittsburgh; building services 1,000

Duquesne Light Co.; Pittsburgh; electric services 975

Federated Investors; Pittsburgh; investment offices 927

Allied Security Inc.; Pittsburgh; business/security services 850

Dollar Bank; Pittsburgh; savings institutions 813

Westinghouse Electric Corp.; Pittsburgh; electric research 800

Shenango Inc.; Pittsburgh; iron/steel foundries 800

Union National Bank of Pittsburgh Inc./Integra Bank; Pittsburgh; commercial banks 785

Bell Telephone Co. of Pennsylvania; Pittsburgh; telephone communications 780

Giant Eagle Inc./O. K. Grocery Co.; Pittsburgh; warehousing 750

Bedway Security Agency Inc.; Pittsburgh; security services 750

Nabisco Brands Inc.; Pittsburgh; bakery products 620

Eichleay Corp.; Pittsburgh; building construction 600

Three Rivers Aluminum Co./Traco; Pittsburgh; lumber/building materials 600

PPG Industries Inc./Coatings & Resins; Allison Park; glass/glassware 600

ARA Leisure Service Inc.; Pittsburgh; bars/restaurants 600

Metropolitan Life Insurance Co.; Pittsburgh; medical service/health insurance 600

Civic Arena Corp.; Pittsburgh; commercial sports 600

City of Pittsburgh/Housing Authority; Pittsburgh 600

Rolm Co./Rolm Systems Div.; Pittsburgh; computer services 600

Suburban General Hospital; Pittsburgh 600

Cauley Detective Agency; Pittsburgh; security services 575

Port Authority of Allegheny County; Pittsburgh; bus services 550

Pinkerton's Inc.; Pittsburgh; security services 550

Commonwealth of Pennsylvania/Correctional Institute; Pittsburgh 550

Ohio Valley General Hospital; McKees Rocks 550

Kirkpatrick & Lockhart; Pittsburgh; legal services 515

Central Medical Center & Hospital; Pittsburgh 510

15th District

East — Allentown; Bethlehem

With its backing of Bill Clinton in 1992, the Lehigh Valley returned to the Democratic fold. In doing so, residents shucked the Republican House incumbent who had represented them since 1978 and voted for a Democratic presidential nominee for the first time since 1976.

The Valley had strayed to the GOP in recent years despite having all the makings of a Democratic stronghold. The heavy industrial tradition, strong unions and sizable ethnic population could not overcome disaffection with the liberal image of the national Democratic Party.

The Republican trend was partly because the district's largest city, Allentown (Lehigh County), had fared better than most of Pennsylvania's other older, industrial cities. Although singer Billy Joel chose Allentown in 1982 to represent the plight of the newly unemployed, the recession did not hit the city quite as hard as some other places because of its diversified economy. Even after Mack Trucks moved one of its main plants to South Carolina in 1987—in search of lower, nonunion wages—the city's then-thriving small companies helped brace the economy.

Germans settled this region 250 years ago, and their work ethic still exists. Many of the newer businesses depend on the high-quality craftsmanship of the Pennsylvania Dutch, who are conservative and union-resistant. But the German influence has been diluted in recent years by a steady, westward migration from New Jersey and New York into the region.

On the New Jersey border, industrial Northampton County eagerly returned to its Democratic roots in 1992. Voters backed Democrats for president, the Senate and the House, unlike Lehigh County, which stuck with Republican Sen. Arlen Specter. Northampton boasts a slightly stronger industrial heritage, mainly in Bethlehem and Easton. Bethlehem Steel's smokestacks dominate the Bethlehem city landscape. Though employment at the steel mills is a fraction of what it was in World War II, the company is still a pillar of the local economy. Easton produces chemicals and paper products.

At Christmastime, Bethlehem sheds its gritty, steel town veneer and transforms into a shining city of glittering trees and candlelit windows. The scene is completed with a Star of Bethlehem that sparkles from atop South Mountain. The Christmas spirit dates back to the mid-1700s, when Moravian Protestants first established a communal church-village. Moravian College, one of the oldest in America, traces its roots to the 18th century.

Lehigh and Northampton counties provide the bulk of the district vote, but a small Republican nub of northwestern Montgomery County is awkwardly grafted on to the southern portion of the district.

Election Returns

		Democrat	Republican
	15th District		
1992	President*	92,363 (41.7%)	81,349 (36.7%)
	House	111,419 (52.2%)	99,520 (46.7%)
1988	President	82,016 (45.3%)	99,036 (54.7%)
	Senate	56,808 (33.0%)	115,315 (67.0%)
1986	Senate	54,024 (42.7%)	72,640 (57.3%)
	Governor	60,656 (47.6%)	66,707 (52.4%)

*Vote for Perot was 47,740 (21.6%).

Demographics

Population 565,810

Percent change from 1980 9.8%

Land area 790 square miles

Population per square mile 716

Counties, 1990 population
Lehigh 291,130   Northampton 247,105
Montgomery (pt.) 27,575

Cities, 1990 population (10,000 or more)
Allentown 105,090   Emmaus 11,157
Bethlehem 71,428   Fullerton CDP 13,127
Easton 26,276

Race and Hispanic origin
White 94.0%
Black 2.2%
American Indian, Eskimo, or Aleut. 0.1%
Asian or Pacific Islander 1.1%
Other 2.6%
Hispanic origin 4.7%

Ancestry
American 2.2%   Italian 10.6%
Austrian 1.7%   Polish 5.1%
Dutch 4.5%   Russian 1.1%
English 8.5%   Scottish 1.2%
French 2.0%   Slovakian 5.4%
German 42.4%   Ukrainian 2.0%
Hungarian 3.9%   Welsh 2.6%
Irish 13.1%

Universities/colleges, 1990-1991 enrollment
Allentown College of St. Francis De Sales, Center Valley 1,856
Cedar Crest College, Allentown 982
Lafayette College, Easton 2,288
Lehigh County Community College, Schnecksville 4,145
Lehigh University, Bethlehem 6,647
Lincoln Technical Institute, Allentown 449
Moravian College, Bethlehem 1,787
Muhlenberg College, Allentown 2,028
Northampton County Community College, Bethlehem 5,535
Pennsylvania State University-Allentown, Fogelsville 697

Newspapers, total circulation (in all districts)
Allentown Morning Call 136,293
Easton Express-Times 41,761
Philadelphia Daily News 196,141
Philadelphia Inquirer 500,733

Commercial television stations, affiliations
ADI: Philadelphia (100%)
WFMZ-TV, Allentown (None)
WBPH, Bethlehem (None)

Cable television systems, total subscribers
Blue Ridge Cable TV Inc.; Lehighton 19,700
Sammons Communications of Pennsylvania Inc.; Easton 27,115
Sammons Communications of Pennsylvania Inc.; Emmaus 8,500
Service Electric Cable TV; Allentown 78,500
Twin County Trans-Video Inc.; Allentown 53,000

Businesses and other major employers
AT&T Co.; Allentown; electronic components 4,500
Air Products & Chemicals; Allentown; inorganic chemicals 4,000
Allentown Hospital Lehigh; Allentown 4,000
Bethlehem Steel Corp.; Bethlehem; steel products 3,498
Payroll Plus Corp.; Allentown; personnel supply services 2,400
Chrysler First Management Inc.; Allentown; management services 2,134
Pennsylvania Power & Light Co.; Allentown; electric services 2,100
St. Luke's Hospital; Bethlehem 1,770
Wood Dining Services Inc.; Allentown; restaurants 1,550
Easton Hospital; Easton 1,425
Lehigh University; Bethlehem 1,400
Knoll North America Inc.; East Greenville; office furniture 1,300
Hess's Dept. Stores Inc.; Allentown; department stores 1,250
Victaulic Co. of America; Easton; iron products 1,200
Parkland School District; Orefield 1,080
Mack Trucks Inc.; Allentown; heavy-duty trucks 1,050
Guardian Life Insurance Co. of America; Bethlehem; insurance services 1,050
Kraft General Foods Inc.; Allentown; grocery products 1,000
Sacred Heart Hospital of Allentown; Allentown 1,000
City of Allentown; Allentown 961
Genesco Inc./Greif Companies Div.; Lehigh Valley; outerwear 900
County of Northampton/Gracedale; Nazareth; residential care 850

Mack Trucks Inc./Macungie Assembly; Macungie; truck assembly 800

Morning Call Inc.; Allentown; newspapers 800

Day-Timers Inc.; East Texas; catalog retailers 800

AT&T Co.; Breinigsville; research services 800

County of Lehigh/Cedarbrook Nursing Home; Allentown; residential care 750

Allen Products Co.; Allentown; grain mill products 735

Bell & Howell Co.; Allentown; computer/office equipment 710

James River Corp. Virginia; Easton; paperboard products 700

Parkland School District; Allentown 700

Northampton County Community College; Bethlehem 699

Burron Medical Inc.; Bethlehem; medical instruments/supplies 680

Allentown State Hospital; Allentown 676

Binney & Smith Inc.; Easton; office/art supplies 650

Day-Timers Inc.; Allentown; catalog retailers 633

City of Bethlehem; Bethlehem 616

Burron Medical Inc.; Allentown; medical instruments 600

Lehigh County Community College; Schnecksville 590

F. L. Smidth & Co.; Bethlehem; industry machinery 580

Bethlehem Steel Corp.; Bethlehem; steel products 565

Allentown Osteopathic Medical Center; Allentown 560

Lafayette College; Easton 550

Stanley-Vidmar Inc.; Allentown; partitions/fixtures 528

Mack Printing Co.; Easton; commercial printing 522

16th District

Southeast — Lancaster

Rapid growth and development are redefining the character of the two formerly rural counties that make up the major part of the 16th. But development has not altered the historical partisan preference of either Chester or Lancaster counties.

In these two counties—especially Chester—over the past two decades, rural Republicanism has been superseded by a new brand: suburban Republicanism. In Chester County, the mushroom farmers of Kennett Square cast their GOP ballots along with the managers, scientists and executives who moved to such places as Birmingham Township in the 1980s. West Goshen Township, by West Chester University, has also experienced recent growth.

Scenic farm country and a favorable business climate made Lancaster County one of the state's fastest-growing areas in the 1980s. The strong work ethic of the local labor force makes the county a preferred location for companies looking to start new plants in proximity to the East Coast's major markets.

This is the heart of Pennsylvania Dutch Country, which was etched into popular consciousness by the movie *Witness*. The Amish "plain people" featured in the movie still farm the area, though increasing property values and suburban encroachment have driven many away.

Some of the sects cling closer to the old ways than others. They range from the Old Order Amish, who in effect live in the mid-19th century, to the "black bumper Mennonites" who allow electricity in their homes and drive cars, but paint any chrome bumpers black.

Besides setting the county's conservative political tone, they affect the county's economy, for tourists flock to Dutch Country

to gawk at the horse and buggies, eat at the family-style restaurants and browse at the quilt shops.

Slightly less than half the district's vote is cast in Lancaster County. Not all of the county is in the 16th—the northwestern part is in the 17th—but the city of Lancaster and affluent suburbs such as Manheim Township and Warwick Township are in the 16th.

The Amish and Mennonites are joined in their support of Republican candidates by the affluent communities outside the city of Lancaster. Household incomes for the business executives of Manheim and Warwick townships far outpace the rest of the county.

Anti-abortion strength also bolsters Republican candidates, especially in Chester County, where an organization of conservative Christian activists is taking root. Even as George Bush lost statewide in 1992, he won Lancaster County by almost 2-to-1.

Democratic strength in the district is limited to municipalities such as Coatesville and Phoenixville in Chester County. There are also pockets of Democratic support in the city of Lancaster.

Election Returns

	16th District	Democrat	Republican
1992	President*	72,719 (32.3%)	109,037 (48.5%)
	House	74,741 (35.2%)	137,823 (64.8%)
1988	President	58,904 (31.2%)	129,821 (68.8%)
	Senate	38,344 (20.6%)	147,382 (79.4%)
1986	Senate	35,482 (28.2%)	90,285 (71.8%)
	Governor	39,054 (31.1%)	86,456 (68.9%)

Vote for Perot was 43,279 (19.2%).

Demographics

Population 565,835

Percent change from 1980 10.0%

Land area 1,280 square miles

Population per square mile 442

Counties, 1990 population
Chester (pt.) 280,875   Lancaster (pt.) 284,952
Delaware (pt.) 8

Cities, 1990 population (10,000 or more)
Coatesville 11,038   West Chester 18,041
Lancaster 55,551

Race and Hispanic origin
White 91.4%
Black 5.2%
American Indian, Eskimo, or Aleut. 0.1%
Asian or Pacific Islander 1.1%
Other 2.1%
Hispanic origin 3.8%

Ancestry
American 3.5%	Irish 17.9%
Dutch 2.6%	Italian 8.3%
English 13.9%	Polish 3.8%
French 2.7%	Scotch Irish 2.7%
German 44.0%	Scottish 2.6%

Slovakian 1.2% Welsh 1.8%
Swiss 2.4%

Universities/colleges, 1990-1991 enrollment
Franklin & Marshall College, Lancaster 1,796
Immaculata College, Immaculata 2,368
Lancaster Bible College, Lancaster 392
Lancaster Theological Seminary, Lancaster 213
Lincoln University, Lincoln University 1,374
Millersville University of Pennsylvania, Millersville 7,789
Thaddeus Stevens State Tech, Lancaster 491
West Chester University, West Chester 12,076

Newspapers, total circulation (in all districts)
Coatesville Daily Record 6,219
Lancaster Intelligencer-Journal 98,459
Philadelphia Daily News 196,141
Philadelphia Inquirer 500,733
Pottstown Mercury 29,636
Reading Eagle 75,798
West Chester Daily Local News 35,916
Wilmington News Journal 120,121

Commercial television stations, affiliations
ADI: Harrisburg-York-Lancaster-Lebanon (51%) and Philadelphia (49%)

Cable television systems, total subscribers
Blue Ridge Cable TV Inc.; Ephrata 28,000
Harron Cable TV; Malvern 23,781
Harron Cable TV; Toughkenamon 7,193
Suburban Cable TV; Coatesville 40,800
Suburban Cable TV; Lancaster 61,153

Businesses and other major employers
Lancaster General Hospital; Lancaster 2,900
C&J Clark Inc.; Kennett Square; shoe stores 2,099
Lukens Steel Co.; Coatesville; steel products 2,000
U.S. Veterans Affairs Dept.; Coatesville; hospital 1,612
Yellow Freight System Inc.; East Petersburg; trucking facilities 1,514
St. Joseph Hospital Inc.; Lancaster 1,419
Pepperidge Farm Inc.; Downingtown; bakery products 1,300
Chester County Hospital; West Chester 1,250
Tyson Foods Inc.; New Holland; preserved fruits/vegetables 1,200
Roy F. Weston Inc.; West Chester; consulting services 1,200
Brandywine Hospital & Trauma Center; Coatesville 1,000
Alumax Mill Products Inc.; Lancaster; aluminum rolling/drawing 986
West Chester University; West Chester 950
QVC Network Inc.; West Chester; TV network retailers 900
Burle Industries Inc.; Lancaster; electrical equipment/supplies 818
County of Chester; West Chester 800
Community Hospital of Lancaster; Lancaster 800
Hewlett-Packard Co./Analytical Supplies Operation; Avondale; measuring/controlling devices 750
Bollman Hat Co.; Adamstown; hats/caps 675
Warner-Lambert Co.; Lititz; pharmaceuticals 659
Bulova Technologies Inc.; Lancaster; ordnance/accessories 650
Hamilton Bank; Lancaster; commercial banks 600
County of Lancaster; Lancaster 598

Wyeth Laboratories Inc./Wyeth-Ayerst Laboratories; West Chester; pharmaceuticals 580
Conestoga Wood Specialties; East Earl; millwork 575
Lancaster Newspapers Inc.; Lancaster; newspapers 550
Franklin & Marshall College; Lancaster 545
Brandywine Foods Inc.; Cochranville; grocery products 540
Kendal Corp.; Kennett Square; nursing 520

17th District
South Central — Harrisburg

One of the few places where Democrats can be found in the 17th is in Harrisburg, or more precisely, on the 65-acre state Capitol complex in Harrisburg. For outside the legislative chambers and the state government buildings, Democrats are few and far between.

Harrisburg, the district's largest city with just over 52,000 people, is about 100 miles west of Philadelphia and 150 miles east of Pittsburgh in Republican-minded central Pennsylvania.

Its modest skyline is dominated by a magnificent Capitol building topped with a dome inspired by the design of St. Peter's Basilica in Rome. Inside, ornate tiles and murals decorate the corridors and chambers. A grand stairway of Italian marble—modeled after the Opera House of Paris—is the centerpiece of the Rotunda.

Operating within these walls are many state government workers and legislative staffers who help make Harrisburg a Democratic oasis; the city's large black community—which accounts for more than half of Harrisburg's population—enhances the Democratic tilt.

As a whole, though, Dauphin County turns in Republican margins. The Harrisburg suburbs and outlying conservative small towns provide about 80 percent of the county vote; they helped George Bush carry Dauphin in 1988 and 1992. GOP Sen. Arlen Specter won 56 percent in Dauphin County in 1992 while squeaking by to victory statewide.

To get the real flavor of Dauphin County, most visitors skip Harrisburg and go to Hershey, otherwise known as "Chocolatetown, U.S.A." The massive chocolate factory stands at the center of town, emanating the most pleasing of industrial odors. The neat and well-tended company town even has street lights shaped like the bite-size Hershey's Kisses.

Another well-known site in Dauphin County is Three Mile Island, site of a 1979 nuclear accident that had a profound impact on many Americans' attitudes toward nuclear energy.

Besides Dauphin, the only other county wholly within the 17th is Lebanon County, in Pennsylvania Dutch Country. The bologna-making techniques of the Germans who first settled the area are still in evidence in the handful of bologna factories that operate here. True bologna connoisseurs know not to miss the annual Bologna Fest in August.

Like the rest of Dutch Country, Lebanon County evinces a strong strain of conservatism. With a 2-to-1 GOP voter registration advantage, the county stayed in the Republican column for president even in 1992, albeit with just 50 percent for Bush; Bill Clinton failed to crack 30 percent.

Across the scenic and shallow Susquehanna River on the western side of the 17th, the district takes in parts of Republican Perry and Cumberland counties. At its southeastern extreme, the district includes part of Republican Lancaster County, which has some of the suburbs of the city of Lancaster.

Election Returns

	17th District	Democrat	Republican
1992	President*	73,654 (32.0%)	115,598 (50.2%)
	House	65,881 (30.5%)	150,158 (69.5%)
1988	President	66,243 (35.7%)	119,479 (64.3%)
	Senate	38,300 (21.1%)	143,378 (78.9%)
1986	Senate	44,583 (31.3%)	97,837 (68.7%)
	Governor	57,142 (40.0%)	85,623 (60.0%)

*Vote for Perot was 41,103 (17.8%).

Demographics

Population 565,742

Percent change from 1980 9.7%

Land area 1,486 square miles

Population per square mile 381

Counties, 1990 population

Cumberland (pt.) 47,274	Lebanon 113,744
Dauphin 237,813	Perry (pt.) 29,041
Lancaster (pt.) 137,870	

Cities, 1990 population (10,000 or more)

Colonial Park CDP 13,777	Harrisburg 52,376
Columbia 10,701	Hershey CDP 11,860
Ephrata 12,133	Lebanon 24,800

Race and Hispanic origin

White 91.3%
Black 6.7%
American Indian, Eskimo, or Aleut. 0.1%
Asian or Pacific Islander 1.0%
Other 0.9%
Hispanic origin 1.9%

Ancestry

American 3.2%	Polish 3.0%
Dutch 3.3%	Scotch Irish 2.0%
English 8.4%	Scottish 1.5%
French 2.2%	Slovakian 1.7%
German 54.7%	Swiss 1.8%
Irish 13.1%	Welsh 1.7%
Italian 5.8%	

Universities/colleges, 1990-1991 enrollment

Central Pennsylvania Business School, Summerdale 660
Electronic Institute, Middletown 214
Elizabethtown College, Elizabethtown 1,806
Harrisburg Area Community College, Harrisburg 8,355
Lebanon Valley College, Annville 1,244
Pennsylvania State University-Harrisburg, Middletown 3,416
Pennsylvania State University-Milton S. Hershey Medical
   Center, Hershey 494

Newspapers, total circulation (in all districts)

Harrisburg Evening News 107,517
Lancaster Intelligencer-Journal 98,459
Lebanon Daily News 24,119
Philadelphia Inquirer 500,733

Commercial television stations, affiliations

ADI: Harrisburg-York-Lancaster-Lebanon (100%)
   WHP-TV, Harrisburg (CBS)
   WHTM-TV, Harrisburg (ABC)
   WLYH-TV, Lancaster (CBS)

Cable television systems, total subscribers

Blue Ridge Cable TV Inc.; Ephrata 28,000
Lebanon Valley Cable TV Co.; Lebanon 25,500
Sammons Communications of Pennsylvania Inc.; Harrisburg
   91,013
Suburban Cable TV; Hershey 15,000
Suburban Cable TV; Lancaster 61,153
Warner Cable of Marietta; Columbia 11,800

Military installations, 1991

Carlisle Barracks (Army), Carlisle 1,499
Fort Indiantown Gap (Army), Annville 1,339
Harrisburg Olmstead Intl. Airport Air Force Guard Station,
   Middletown 314

Businesses and other major employers

Commonwealth of Pennsylvania/Transportation Dept.; Harrisburg 12,000
Medical Service Assn. of Pennsylvania/Blue Shield; Camp
   Hill; medical service/health insurance 4,500
Pennsylvania State University-Milton S. Hershey Medical
   Center; Hershey 4,300
Commonwealth of Pennsylvania/Environmental Resource
   Dept.; Harrisburg 3,800
Hershey Foods Corp./Hershey Chocolate Co.; Hershey;
   chocolates/candies 3,000
Polyclinic Medical Center of Harrisburg; Harrisburg 2,350
Commonwealth of Pennsylvania/Turnpike Commission; Harrisburg 2,015
Commonwealth of Pennsylvania/Revenue Dept.; Harrisburg
   2,000
Commonwealth of Pennsylvania/Public Welfare Dept.; Harrisburg 2,000
Commonwealth of Pennsylvania/Liquor Control Board; Harrisburg 2,000
Harrisburg Hospital; Harrisburg 1,951
Bethlehem Steel Corp.; Harrisburg; steel products 1,857
Commonwealth of Pennsylvania/Labor & Industry Dept.;
   Harrisburg 1,700
IBM Corp.; Mechanicsburg; warehousing 1,650
Holy Spirit Hospital; Camp Hill 1,557
Commonwealth of Pennsylvania; Harrisburg 1,366
G. P. U. Nuclear Corp.; Middletown; electric services 1,300
U.S. Veterans Affairs Dept.; Lebanon; hospital 1,300
Capital Blue Cross; Harrisburg; medical service/health insurance 1,250
Kinney Service Corp.; Camp Hill; computer services 1,200
Roadway Express Inc.; Carlisle; trucking facilities 1,000
Commonwealth of Pennsylvania/Higher Education Dept.;
   Harrisburg 1,000
Harrisburg Area Community College; Harrisburg 1,000
Fruehauf Trailer Corp.; Middletown; truck trailers 935
Carolina Freight Carriers Corp.; Carlisle; trucking facilities
   900
Good Samaritan Hospital; Lebanon 885
Grinnell Corp.; Columbia; iron/steel foundries 850
Armstrong World Industries; Lancaster; misc. products 800
Commonwealth of Pennsylvania; Harrisburg 800

City of Harrisburg; Harrisburg 736

Fry Communications Inc.; Mechanicsburg; commercial printing 700

Commonwealth of Pennsylvania/Liquor Control Board; Harrisburg 700

Grand Lodge/Masonic Homes; Elizabethtown; nursing 700

Community General Osteopathic Hospital; Harrisburg 700

Gannett Fleming Engineers; Camp Hill; engineering services 700

Super Rite Corp./Basics; Harrisburg; grocery products 680

Ephrata Community Hospital; Ephrata 665

Nationwide Mutual Insurance Co.; Harrisburg; casualty insurance 650

Appleton Papers Inc.; Harrisburg; industry machinery 607

Kellogg Co.; Lancaster; grain mill products 600

Armstrong World Industries; Marietta; carpets/rugs 600

Dauphin County Prison; Harrisburg 600

M&M/Mars Inc.; Elizabethtown; chocolates/candies 535

18th District

Pittsburgh Suburbs; Clairton; McKeesport

The story of the Mon Valley is surely one of America's grandest boom-and-bust tales. The denizens of the Monongahela Valley were at the forefront of establishing America as the world's industrial giant in the years leading up to and through World War II, but in the post-industrial decades since, this once-proud region has withered.

It all began in 1851, when the first steel mill opened. Production expanded so rapidly that the local labor pool was quickly exhausted, forcing U.S. Steel to place advertisements in European newspapers seeking workers.

Thousands of Hungarians, Irish, Italians, Poles, Russians, Serbs and Ukrainians were among those who heeded the call; by the late 1940s, U.S. Steel employed 80,000 here.

The company controlled all facets of life. Transportation systems were designed to move workers efficiently at shift changes. Local government and politics were dictated by U.S. Steel policies, particularly so before the United Steelworkers union came into existence in 1942.

But after World War II expansion, the steel industry began its downward spiral. And as the steel works began closing, the towns that lived and breathed with the industry drew their last gasps.

By the mid-1980s, declining population and loss of industry slashed the tax bases of such Allegheny County towns as Homestead, Duquesne and McKeesport. Clairton—the setting for the movie *The Deer Hunter*—was forced to furlough its entire police force and to turn off the street lights. Perhaps more telling was the closing of the McKeesport McDonald's restaurant.

These desperate conditions were reflected in the Valley's voting patterns. Angry and unemployed workers voted in favor of Democrat Walter F. Mondale in 1984; one local steelworkers official said, "In this area, if Ronald Reagan bought a cemetery, people would quit dying." In 1988, Michael S. Dukakis posted even bigger victory margins in areas that now make up the 18th.

Today, despite the massive job losses, the steelworkers union, building trades council and the United Mine Workers still hold sway; Democrats make up 70 percent of the 18th's registration. But the combination of a weak Democratic nominee and the independence of Pittsburgh suburban voters was enough in 1992 to allow the GOP to capture the House seat.

The steelworkers who were able to find new employment—mostly in lower-paying service jobs—proved steadfast in their support of Democratic candidates in 1991, when Harris Wofford won 57 percent here in the special Senate election against Allegheny County native Dick Thornburgh, the former governor and U.S. attorney general. Bill Clinton easily bested George Bush in 1992.

Outside the Mon Valley, the 18th contains the northern, eastern and southern Pittsburgh suburbs.

Located entirely within the bounds of Allegheny County, the 18th also includes the middle-class areas of Penn Hills, Shaler and Monroeville, along with the old-money GOP communities of Fox Chapel and Mount Lebanon.

Election Returns

	18th District	Democrat	Republican
1992	President*	137,507 (51.9%)	80,795 (30.5%)
	House	96,655 (38.0%)	154,024 (60.6%)
1988	President	147,222 (58.5%)	104,505 (41.5%)
	Senate	74,122 (31.1%)	163,972 (68.9%)
1986	Senate	86,938 (46.9%)	98,364 (53.1%)
	Governor	104,288 (56.2%)	81,308 (43.8%)

Vote for Perot was 46,754 (17.6%).

Demographics

Population 565,781

Percent change from 1980 9.6%

Land area 265 square miles

Population per square mile 2,139

Counties, 1990 population
Allegheny (pt.) 565,781

Cities, 1990 population (10,000 or more)

Baldwin 21,923	Penn Hills CDP 51,430
Brentwood 10,823	Scott CDP 17,118
McKeesport 26,016	Shaler CDP 30,533
Mount Lebanon CDP (pt.) 33,362	South Park CDP 14,292
Munhall 13,158	Swissvale 10,637
Monroeville 29,169	West Mifflin 23,644
North Versailles CDP 12,302	Whitehall 14,451
	Wilkinsburg 21,080

Race and Hispanic origin
White 91.2%
Black 7.8%
American Indian, Eskimo, or Aleut. 0.1%
Asian or Pacific Islander 0.7%
Other 0.2%
Hispanic origin 0.6%

Ancestry

American 1.3%	Italian 16.0%
English 11.0%	Lithuanian 1.0%
French 2.1%	Polish 9.9%
German 33.6%	Russian 1.7%
Hungarian 2.9%	Scotch Irish 3.0%
Irish 21.0%	Scottish 2.4%

Slovakian 9.2% Welsh 1.7%
Swedish 1.3% Yugoslavian 1.2%
Ukrainian 1.2%

Universities/colleges, 1990-1991 enrollment
Pennsylvania State University, McKeesport 1,343
Pittsburgh Aeronautics Institute, Pittsburgh 1,031

Newspapers, total circulation (in all districts)
McKeesport Daily News 26,123
New Kensington Valley News Dispatch 37,712
Pittsburgh Post-Gazette 153,796

Commercial television stations, affiliations
ADI: Pittsburgh (100%)
WPCB-TV, Greensburg-Pittsburgh (None)
WPTT-TV, Pittsburgh (None)
WTAE-TV, Pittsburgh (ABC)

Cable television systems, total subscribers
Adelphia Cable; West Homestead 16,850
American Cablevision; Monroeville 31,600
Comcast Cablevision; Tarentum 29,257
Mt. Lebanon Cable Co.; Mt. Lebanon 10,413
TCI Cable Television; Penn Hills 27,000
TCI Cable Television; McKeesport 20,900
TCI of Pennsylvania; Baldwin 32,700
TCI of Pennsylvania; Etna 19,000
TCI of Pennsylvania; Pittsburgh 90,000

Businesses and other major employers
South Hills Health System/Jefferson Hospital; Clairton 2,300
USX Corp./Irvin Works; Dravosburg; steel products 1,500
Westinghouse Electric Corp./Science & Technology Center; Pittsburgh; research services 1,500
Jefferson Health Services; Pittsburgh 1,500
USX Corp./Clairton Works; Clairton; steel products 1,390
General Motors Corp.; McKeesport; motor vehicles 1,350
McKeesport Hospital; McKeesport 1,335
St. Margaret Health System Inc.; Pittsburgh 1,320
St. Clair Memorial Hospital; Pittsburgh 1,250
General Motors Corp.; West Mifflin; motor vehicles 1,200
Westinghouse Electric Corp./Electro-Mechanical Div.; Cheswick; nuclear power plant machinery 1,130
USX Corp./Mon Valley Works; Braddock; iron/steel foundries 1,000
County of Allegheny; Pittsburgh 1,000
Westinghouse Electric Corp./Process Control Div.; Pittsburgh; office equipment 900
Giant Eagle Inc.; Pittsburgh; grocery stores 805
Harmarville Rehabilitation Center; Pittsburgh; residential care 795
Contraves USA Inc.; Pittsburgh; telescopes 750
Commonwealth of Pennsylvania/Public Welfare Dept.; Carnegie 725
Dick Enterprises Inc.; Clairton; road construction 700
Braddock General Hospital; Braddock 700
Pennex Products Co.; Verona; pharmaceuticals 650
Advance Security Inc.; East Pittsburgh; security services 630
Westinghouse Electric Corp./Plant Apparatus Div.; Pittsburgh; electrical equipment/supplies 600
Haskell of Pittsburgh Inc.; Verona; office furniture 550
AEG Westinghouse Transportation Systems; Pittsburgh; elevators 550

19th District
South Central — York

Republicans running statewide in Pennsylvania are boosted by a T-shaped voting bloc that begins on the Maryland border and rises north, where it fans out along the New York border. The 19th is at the base of that bloc.

This placid farm country rests on the western fringe of Pennsylvania Dutch Country, taking in all of sparsely populated Adams and populous York counties, and most of Cumberland County to the north. The Susquehanna River forms the eastern border with the 16th and 17th districts.

Democrats are limited to what passes for urbanized areas in the reliably Republican 19th. More than half the population lives a rural existence.

With its solidly Republican character, about the only skirmishing that occurs here is when hundreds of Civil War enthusiasts stage re-enactments at Gettysburg National Military Park, site of one of the war's bloodiest battles.

Even as Pennsylvania deserted George Bush in 1992, the counties of the 19th stayed true to him. In York and Adams counties, Bush won about 45 percent. GOP Sen. Arlen Specter also fared far better in the 19th than across the rest of the state, pulling in about 53 percent in York County.

Specter's victory margin dipped a little against the Democratic nominee in Adams County, where the heavy Republican vote is leavened somewhat by Gettysburg College. With 7,000 residents, Gettysburg is the largest town in Adams County. The others are rural farming villages.

Democrats are mostly concentrated in York, the district's largest city and the nation's capital for a brief period in 1777-1778 when the British occupied Philadelphia. Then, nearby forges turned out munitions for patriot troops. Now the area's industry makes barbells and assembles Harley-Davidson motorcycles.

A relatively short ride from Baltimore along Interstate 83, York—and its suburbs such as Springettsbury Township—experienced moderate growth in the 1980s as newcomers in search of lower taxes and affordable real estate moved in. One sure sign of York's status in the Baltimore orbit is an Orioles baseball ticket outpost.

Another source of Democratic votes in York County is the pretzel and potato chip makers of Hanover. Outside these areas, however, the conservative Pennsylvania Dutch ethic dominates the rural countryside.

Among Cumberland County's population centers is Carlisle, a supply center for expeditions against the French during the French and Indian War, and later an active station along the Underground Railroad.

The West Shore suburbs—across the Susquehanna from Harrisburg—are home to state employees and blue-collar workers who live in Lemoyne and New Cumberland. The 17th District creeps across the river to grab East Pennsboro Township, Mechanicsburg and Shiremanstown, but affluent Camp Hill, home to the Book of the Month Club, is in the 19th. Outside the suburbs, the Cumberland County terrain becomes more Republican.

Election Returns

	19th District	Democrat	Republican
1992	President*	74,445 (33.5%)	104,258 (46.9%)
	House†	74,798 (34.4%)	98,599 (45.3%)

19th District		Democrat	Republican
1988	President	64,246 (34.2%)	123,443 (65.8%)
	Senate	38,118 (20.8%)	145,058 (79.2%)
1986	Senate	45,065 (33.9%)	87,796 (66.1%)
	Governor	51,990 (38.8%)	81,861 (61.2%)

Vote for Perot was 43,759 (19.7%).   †Independent/other is greater than 5%.

Demographics

Population 565,831

Percent change from 1980 9.5%

Land area 1,917 square miles

Population per square mile 295

Counties, 1990 population
Adams 78,274   York 339,574
Cumberland (pt.) 147,983

Cities, 1990 population (10,000 or more)
Carlisle 18,419   York 42,192
Hanover 14,399

Race and Hispanic origin
White 95.9%
Black 2.6%
American Indian, Eskimo, or Aleut. 0.1%
Asian or Pacific Islander 0.7%
Other 0.6%
Hispanic origin 1.3%

Ancestry
American 3.9%	Italian 4.3%
Dutch 3.1%	Polish 2.5%
English 10.4%	Scotch Irish 2.4%
French 2.5%	Scottish 1.9%
German 58.7%	Slovakian 1.1%
Irish 14.9%	Welsh 1.4%

Universities/colleges, 1990-1991 enrollment
Bradley Visual Arts Academy, York 273
Dickinson College, Carlisle 2,061
Dickinson School of Law, Carlisle 555
Gettysburg College, Gettysburg 2,074
Lutheran Theological Seminary, Gettysburg 236
Messiah College, Grantham 2,239
Pennsylvania State University, York 1,920
Shippensburg University of Pennsylvania, Shippensburg 6,592
York College Pennsylvania, York 4,588

Newspapers, total circulation (in all districts)
Baltimore Sun 391,415
Carlisle Sentinel 17,721
Gettysburg Times 8,736
Hanover Evening Sun 20,379
Harrisburg Evening News 107,517
York Daily Record 41,368
York Dispatch 80,421

Commercial television stations, affiliations
ADI: Harrisburg-York-Lancaster-Lebanon (100%)
WGAL-TV, Lancaster (NBC)
WGCB-TV, Red Lion (None)
WPMT, York (Fox)

Cable television systems, total subscribers
Cable TV Co. of York; York 45,742
Glen Rock Cable TV; Glen Rock 5,434
Hanover Cable TV Inc.; Hanover 12,364
Pennsylvania Classic Cable; Hanover 10,351
Sammons Communications of Pennsylvania Inc.; Harrisburg 91,013
TV Cable of Carlisle; Carlisle 14,000

Military installations, 1991
Navy Ships Parts Control Center, Mechanicsburg 6,915
New Cumberland Depot (Army), New Cumberland 3,794

Businesses and other major employers
York Hospital; York 3,250
York Intl. Corp.; York; refrigeration 2,000
Caterpillar Inc.; York; construction machinery 2,000
IBM Corp.; Mechanicsburg; computer equipment 2,000
Harsco Corp./BMY Combat Systems Div.; York; transport vehicles/equipment 1,700
Masland Industries Inc.; Carlisle; carpets/rugs 1,300
P. H. Glatfelter Co.; Spring Grove; paper mills 1,162
Hanover General Hospital; Hanover 860
Dentsply Intl. Inc.; York; dental equipment 800
Rite Aid Corp.; Camp Hill; drug/proprietary stores 800
Memorial Hospital; York 800
Shippensburg University of Pennsylvania; Shippensburg 761
Du Pont E. I. De Nemours & Co.; Emigsville; electric lighting 750
Gichner Systems Group Inc.; Dallastown; prefabricated metal/wheelbarrows/pushcarts 719
GTE North Inc.; York; telephone communications 700
Cumberland Valley School District; Mechanicsburg 700
Hanover Direct Inc.; Hanover; catalog retailers 690
Precision Components Corp.; York; metal products 650
Gettysburg Hospital Inc.; Gettysburg 650
Carlisle Hospital; Carlisle 635
Olin Corp./Ordnance Div.; Red Lion; ordnance/accessories 630
Arcata Graphics Co.; Fairfield; periodicals 620
United-Sussex Telephone Co.; Carlisle; telephone communications 602
Philadelphia Electric Co./Peach Bottom Atomic Power Station; Delta; electric services 600
Utz Quality Foods Inc.; Hanover; potato chips 600
Book of the Month Club Inc./Quality Paperback Book Club; Mechanicsburg; book warehousing 600
Consolidated Freightways Corp.; York; trucking facilities 600
PPG Industries Inc.; Carlisle; flat glass 600
Gettysburg College; Gettysburg 600
ABF Freight System Inc.; Carlisle; trucking facilities 590
Scrivner of Pennsylvania Inc.; York; grocery products 582
Appleton Papers Inc./Capsular Plant; Camp Hill; industry machinery 550
County of York/County Hospital & Homes; York 550
National Medical Enterprises/Mechanicsburg Rehabilitation System; Mechanicsburg 550
Dickinson College; Carlisle 550
Carlisle Companies Inc.; Carlisle; paving/roofing 548
Quaker Oats Co.; Camp Hill; grain mill products 525
Round Hill Foods Inc.; New Oxford; meat products 525
County of Cumberland; Carlisle 505
Voith Hydro Inc.; York; engines/turbines 500

20th District

Southwest — Mon Valley; Washington

With West Virginia on its southern and western borders, the 20th is Pennsylvania's own version of Appalachia. Much of the district is rural, poor and, like its neighbor, strongly Democratic territory.

Politics in the 20th is not for the weak of heart. From the industrial areas along the Monongahela River to the coal fields of Fayette and Greene counties, hardball politics is the rule. Then-United Mine Workers President W. A. "Tony" Boyle was convicted here in the 1969 murder of union rival Joseph A. "Jock" Yablonski.

Part of the reason is the sense of economic desperation that often grips the region. Coal mining has always been subject to boom-and-bust cycles, and with mining's increasing mechanization and the shift of production from East Coast mines to those out West, unemployment is high in Fayette and Greene coal country. The UMW's clout has diminished, but the union remains an important political force.

Along the Monongahela, the slow demise of the steel industry has led to massive job losses from Donora to Brownsville, the borough that marks the unofficial end to the industrialized Mon Valley.

Outside of Pittsburgh and Philadelphia, this is the most reliably Democratic region in the state. Democratic Gov. Robert P. Casey racked up about 80 percent in Fayette and in less-populous Greene County in 1990; even Democratic presidential nominee Michael S. Dukakis ran strong in these counties in 1988. In 1992, Washington, Fayette and Greene counties voted for Bill Clinton by ratios of more than 2-to-1. In Fayette and Greene counties, Democrats outnumber Republicans more than 3-to-1.

The population centers of the 20th are the city of Washington (Washington County) and Greensburg (Westmoreland County). The city of Washington is home to the county's old factory-owning families and occasionally supports Republicans. Peters Township, a white-collar bedroom community for Pittsburgh commuters on the Allegheny County line, also is receptive to GOP candidates.

Greensburg, Westmoreland's county seat, has no major military installation, but it was perhaps the U.S. town most tragically touched by the Persian Gulf War. Eleven reservists of the 14th Quartermaster Detachment, based in Greensburg, were killed by an Iraqi Scud missile attack one week after arriving in Saudi Arabia.

Westmoreland's economy took a hit in 1988 when Volkswagen closed its assembly plant in New Stanton just over the line in the 12th District, but shortly afterward the Sony Corporation of America moved in to build large-screen color televisions.

The 20th is one of three House districts that take in a part of Westmoreland. Allegheny County is also shared by three districts. The only counties wholly contained in the 20th are Washington—where about one-third of the people in the 20th live—and Greene in the district's southwestern corner.

Election Returns

	20th District	Democrat	Republican
1992	President*	121,815 (50.8%)	69,802 (29.1%)
	House	114,898 (50.7%)	111,591 (49.3%)
1988	President	127,173 (58.6%)	89,882 (41.4%)
	Senate	70,659 (33.7%)	138,826 (66.3%)
1986	Senate	79,215 (48.3%)	84,757 (51.7%)
	Governor	98,092 (59.6%)	66,438 (40.4%)

Vote for Perot was 48,249 (20.1%).

Demographics

Population 565,815

Percent change from 1980 9.6%

Land area 2,137 square miles

Population per square mile 265

Counties, 1990 population
Allegheny (pt.) 121,064	Washington 204,584
Fayette (pt.) 89,441	Westmoreland (pt.)
Greene 39,550	111,176

Cities, 1990 population (10,000 or more)
Bethel Park 33,823	Upper St. Clair CDP
Carnot-Moon CDP 10,187	19,692
Greensburg 16,318	Washington 15,864
Uniontown 12,034	

Race and Hispanic origin
White 96.2%
Black 3.2%
American Indian, Eskimo, or Aleut. 0.1%
Asian or Pacific Islander 0.5%
Other 0.1%
Hispanic origin 0.5%

Ancestry
American 2.7%	Polish 9.5%
Dutch 2.9%	Russian 1.9%
English 14.1%	Scotch Irish 4.8%
French 2.5%	Scottish 2.3%
German 32.4%	Slovakian 9.1%
Hungarian 2.5%	Welsh 1.6%
Irish 19.5%	Yugoslavian 1.4%
Italian 15.9%	

Universities/colleges, 1990-1991 enrollment
California University of Pennsylvania, California 6,531
Robert Morris College, Coraopolis 5,326
Seton Hill College, Greensburg 1,037
University of Pittsburgh, Greensburg 1,504
Washington & Jefferson College, Washington 1,198
Waynesburg College, Waynesburg 1,244
Westmoreland County Community College, Youngwood 5,795

Newspapers, total circulation (in all districts)
Connellsville Courier 12,169
Greensburg Tribune Review 51,972
Irwin Standard Observer 9,547
McKeesport Daily News 26,123
Monessen Valley Independent 17,743
Pittsburgh Post Gazette 153,796
Uniontown Herald Standard 30,690
Washington Observer Reporter 38,593

Commercial television stations, affiliations
ADI: Pittsburgh (100%)

Cable television systems, total subscribers
Armstrong Cable Services; Connelsville 19,339
Helicon Cablevision; Uniontown 35,800
Newchannels Cable TV; Canonsburg 14,600
Newchannels Cable TV; Moon 14,000
TCI of Pennsylvania; Carnegie 21,000
TCI of Pennsylvania; Donora 20,400
TCI of Pennsylvania; Greensburg 46,200
TM Cable TV/Washington Inc.; Washington 14,500

Businesses and other major employers
Westmoreland Hospital Assn.; Greensburg 1,516
Westmoreland County Community College; Youngwood 1,390
Commonwealth of Pennsylvania/Public Health Dept.; Bridgeville; nursing 1,278
Washington Hospital; Washington 1,245
Monongahela Valley Hospital; Monongahela 1,135
Cooper Power Systems Inc.; Canonsburg; electric distribution equipment 1,000
Uniontown Hospital; Uniontown 1,000
Super Valu Stores Inc./Charley Brothers Co. Div.; New Stanton; grocery products 900
U.S. Steel Mining Co. Inc./Northern Div.; Eighty Four; coal mining 900
U.S. Steel Mining Co. Inc.; Washington; coal mining 900
Robertshaw Holdings Corp.; New Stanton; controlling devices 800
United Parcel Service Inc.; New Stanton; mail services 800
Allegheny Power Service Corp.; Greensburg; electric services 763
Wetterau Inc.; Belle Vernon; grocery products 720
Corning Inc.; Charleroi; mineral products 700
Washington Steel Corp.; Houston; metals/minerals 700
Commonwealth of Pennsylvania/Western Center; Canonsburg 700
Jessop Steel Co.; Washington; steel products 685
County of Westmoreland; Greensburg 670
Washington Steel Corp.; Washington; steel products 625
Wheeling-Pittsburgh Steel Corp; Allenport; steel products 600
Sensus Technologies Inc.; Uniontown; water meters 560
Black Box Corp.; Pittsburgh; computer equipment 537
Fruehauf Trailer Corp.; Uniontown; bulk tanks 528
California University of Pennsylvania; California 525

21st District

Northwest — Erie

The state's third-largest after Philadelphia and Pittsburgh, Erie is Pennsylvania's forgotten big city. Even among Great Lakes neighbors Cleveland and Buffalo, Erie is a lesser light. But it is the population center of the 21st District.

Local politics are Democratic, with two ethnic groups—Italians and Poles—vying for power. Actually, the first considerable immigration to the city was that of the Pennsylvania Dutch, followed by Italians, Poles and Russians.

Italians settled on the west side and Poles on the east side. Together, the blue-collar communities worked on east-side assembly-line jobs at General Electric and other heavy industries.

More recently, though, younger Italians have begun a move out of the 6th Ward, toward such suburbs as Summit and Millcreek townships, where their traditional Democratic loyalties have weakened.

That mobility has largely been absent in the Polish East Side, which is now larger than the city's Italian community, and more Democratic. Organized labor is a force here.

Local politics sometimes reflects the divisions between the two communities. In 1982, when a Pole defeated an Italian for the Democratic House nomination, many disappointed Italians supported the GOP candidate in November, helping him win. His cordial relations with labor helped him stay there.

The independent and GOP voters outside the city make Erie County politically competitive. Ronald Reagan carried it in 1980 and 1984, but Michael S. Dukakis in 1988 and Bill Clinton in 1992 won it back. But as voters backed Clinton and Democratic Senate challenger Lynn Yeakel in 1992, the GOP House candidate took 71 percent of the vote.

Outside of Erie County (where Democrats have a healthy voter registration advantage), Republicans fare better. South of Erie, Crawford County toes the Republican line. The dairy farmers and retirees in the Conneaut Lake area backed George Bush and GOP Sen. Arlen Specter in 1992. The county is divided between the 21st and 5th districts, but the 21st District portion includes what passes for the county's largest city, Meadville.

Butler County is another favorable area for Republicans. The small city of Butler has a Democratic tradition, but the outlying areas are Republican. Most of the county is in the 21st, with the exception of some southern boroughs and townships that belong to the 4th.

The tone is more Democratic in industrial Mercer County. The Shenango Valley steel towns such as Farrell, Hermitage, Sharon, Sharpsville and Wheatland vote Democratic like the rest of western Pennsylvania, and have been equally hard-hit by steel industry decline. The less-populous and industrial eastern section of the county is Republican.

Mercer was one of just two Pennsylvania counties to support Reagan in 1980 and then switch to Walter F. Mondale in 1984, mostly because people felt Reagan had done little to save the steel industry.

Election Returns

	21st District	Democrat	Republican
1992	President*	105,538 (45.0%)	81,003 (34.5%)
	House	70,802 (32.0%)	150,729 (68.0%)
1988	President	104,613 (50.9%)	101,061 (49.1%)
	Senate	52,528 (26.9%)	142,818 (73.1%)
1986	Senate	63,438 (41.8%)	88,495 (58.2%)
	Governor	76,939 (50.2%)	76,240 (49.8%)

*Vote for Perot was 47,923 (20.4%).

Demographics

Population 565,802

Percent change from 1980 9.5%

Land area 2,784 square miles

Population per square mile 203

Counties, 1990 population

Butler (pt.) 106,567	Erie 275,572
Crawford (pt.) 62,660	Mercer 121,003

Cities, 1990 population (10,000 or more)

Butler 15,714	Meadville 14,318
Erie 108,718	Sharon 17,493
Hermitage 15,300	

Race and Hispanic origin

White 95.2%
Black 3.9%
American Indian, Eskimo, or Aleut. 0.1%
Asian or Pacific Islander 0.4%
Other 0.3%
Hispanic origin 0.8%

Ancestry

American 2.3%	Italian 11.2%
Dutch 3.1%	Polish 9.7%
English 13.9%	Scotch Irish 4.4%
French 3.2%	Scottish 2.5%
German 43.3%	Slovakian 4.6%
Hungarian 1.5%	Swedish 2.3%
Irish 20.7%	Welsh 1.7%

Universities/colleges, 1990-1991 enrollment

Allegheny College, Meadville 1,817
Butler County Community College, Butler 3,214
Edinboro University of Pennsylvania, Edinboro 8,131
Erie Business Center, Erie 258
Gannon University, Erie 4,595
Grove City College, Grove City 2,138
Mercyhurst College, Erie 2,058
Pennsylvania State University-Shenango Valley, Sharon 1,192
Pennsylvania State University-Behrend, Erie 2,987
Slippery Rock University of Pennsylvania, Slippery Rock 7,825
Thiel College, Greenville 943

Newspapers, total circulation (in all districts)

Butler Eagle 30,669
Erie News/Times-News 71,835
Greenville Record-Argus 5,193
Meadville Tribune 16,198
Pittsburgh Post-Gazette 153,796
Sharon Herald 24,899
Youngstown Vindicator 87,768

Commercial television stations, affiliations

ADI: Erie (53%), Youngstown (24%) and Pittsburgh (23%)
WETG, Erie (Fox)
WICU-TV, Erie (NBC)
WJET-TV, Erie (ABC)
WSEE-TV, Erie (CBS)

Cable television systems, total subscribers

Armstrong Utilities Inc.; Grove City 7,184
Armstrong Utilities Inc.; Zelienople 45,960
Century Cable; Hermitage 19,700
Erie Tele Communications Cable; Erie 28,300
Meadville Master Antenna; Meadville 13,188
TCI of Pennsylvania; Harborcreek 28,533

Businesses and other major employers

General Electric Co./Transportation Systems; Erie; construction machinery/generators 6,500
Armco Inc./Armco Advanced Metals Co. Div.; Butler; steel products 3,500
Armco Inc./Armco Advanced Metals Co. Div.; Lyndora; steel products 2,800
St. Vincent's Hospital; Erie 2,195
Buffalo & Pittsburg Railroad Inc./CSX Transportation Inc.; Petrolia; railroads 2,000
Sharon Steel Corp.; Farrell; steel works 2,000
Hamot Medical Center; Erie 1,839
International Paper Co.; Erie; pulp mills 1,600
American Sterilizer Co.; Erie; medical instruments/supplies 1,200
Township of Millcreek/School District; Erie 1,048
Butler Memorial Hospital; Butler 1,000
City of Erie; Erie 1,000
Sharon Regional Health System; Sharon 950
Lord Corp.; Erie; bonded rubber/aircraft parts 900
County of Erie; Erie 826
GTE North Inc.; Erie; telephone communications 800
Slippery Rock University of Pennsylvania; Slippery Rock 800
Greenville Regional Hospital; Greenville 800
Cyclops Corp./Sawhill Tubular Div.; Sharon; steel products 760
Cooper Industries Inc.; Grove City; warehousing 750
Plastek Industries Inc./M&E Mfg. Co.; Erie; plastics products 750
Spang & Co./Magnetics Div.; East Butler; printed circuit boards 700
Werner Holding Co. Inc.; Greenville; ladders/metal products 700
Gannon University; Erie 679
U.S. Veterans Affairs Dept.; Butler 650
Servistar Corp.; East Butler; hardware/plumbing/heating 638
Zurn Industries Inc./Hydromechanics Div.; Erie; water purification equipment 630
City of Erie/Main Branch Library; Erie 594
Catholic Diocese of Erie/School Office; Erie; religious organizations 587
PPG Industries Inc.; Meadville; flat glass 550
Zurn Industries Inc./Energy Div.; Erie; high-speed drives/gears 550
Meadville Medical Center; Meadville 525

Rhode Island

For a state with an economy in a state of upheaval rivaling the Great Depression, Rhode Island's political scene was remarkably stable through the early 1990s. The state's governor and two House representatives were resoundingly re-elected in 1992 while Rhode Island was still in the throes of a banking crisis that left tens of thousands of residents without access to their savings for nearly two years. Anti-incumbent fever, to the extent there was any, focused on President Bush who drew a woeful 29 percent in his failed re-election bid—placing Rhode Island in a tie with Massachusetts for the lowest Bush tally in the nation. Even Rhode Island's presidential vote amounted to a bow to a tradition dating back to the 1930s of supporting Democrats for president.

Perhaps the vote of most lasting importance was in favor of a referendum extending the terms of top state officials, including the governor, from two to four years. The measure also limited those officials to two terms. Stability also marked the redistricting process with the eastern 1st District gaining Burrillville with its population of 16,000. Redistricting had no impact on the 1992 congressional election. Republican Ronald Machtley of the 1st District and Democrat Jack Reed representing the 2nd won re-election by 3-to-1 margins.

Rhode Island's economy enjoyed no such stability. Manufacturing employment, once a mainstay of the state economy, shrunk steadily through the early 1990s. The largest employer of Rhode Islanders in 1990 was the Electric Boat Division of General Dynamics Corp., with its submarine frame-making plant in Quonset Point, and its shipyard just across the state border in Groton, Conn. But, in a sign of the rise of the service industry throughout the region, Rhode Island Hospital was closing in fast for the title of largest private employer. Electric Boat, if it survives years of lean defense spending at all, will do so in a radically reduced form.

One of the fastest-growing job sources in the region in 1993 was the gambling casino run by a Native American tribe in eastern Connecticut. With the maritime economy and home-grown manufacturing on the wane, Rhode Island was becoming increasingly dependent on neighboring Connecticut and Massachusetts for jobs—bad news given that those two states were among the slowest to move up from the depths of recession. Research and high technology appeared to be the most promis-

ing elements of the state economy. While the rest of the country was coping with base closures, Newport's submarine warfare center was being enlarged by the Navy. And the state was leading a region-wide effort at converting the economy to less defense-dependent sectors.

Rhode Island became more ethnically mixed in the 1980s with influxes of southeast Asians and Portuguese helping push the population just over 1 million. The strain of newcomers and a poor economy was taking its toll. In 1992, Rhode Island was one of the nation's leading recipients of federal aid to the poor, on a per capita basis.

Just as it took the Irish-Catholic Democrats until 1935 to wrest control of state politics from Yankee Republicans, so the political reaction to the latest social and economic upheavals in Rhode Island were, through the early 1990s, delayed.

Table 1   Population

District	Population	Population under 18	Voting-age population	Median age
1	501,677	108,804	392,873	34.1
2	501,787	116,886	384,901	33.9
State	1,003,464	225,690	777,774	34.0

Table 2   Voting-Age Persons

District	White*	Black*	American Indian, Eskimo, or Aleut*	Asian or Pacific Islander*	Other*	Hispanic*	Male*	Female*
1	93.7%	2.9%	0.2%	1.2%	2.0%	3.2%	46.9%	53.1%
2	91.8	3.8	0.5	1.9	2.1	4.4	47.1	52.9
State	92.8	3.3	0.3	1.5	2.0	3.8	47.0	53.0

As percent of voting-age population.

Table 3   Voting-Age Persons by Age Groups

District	18-24*	25-44*	45-54*	55-64*	65 and over*
1	16.0%	40.3%	12.2%	11.6%	19.9%

RHODE ISLAND

Districts Established May 22, 1992

1
2
Woonsocket
PROVIDENCE
North Providence
Pawtucket
Providence
Cranston
BRISTOL
Bristol
Warwick
KENT
NEWPORT (PT)
NEWPORT (PT)
NEWPORT (PART)
NEWPORT (PART)
Newport
WASHINGTON
Kingston
Westerly
2
NEW SHOREHAM

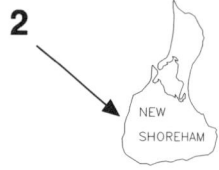

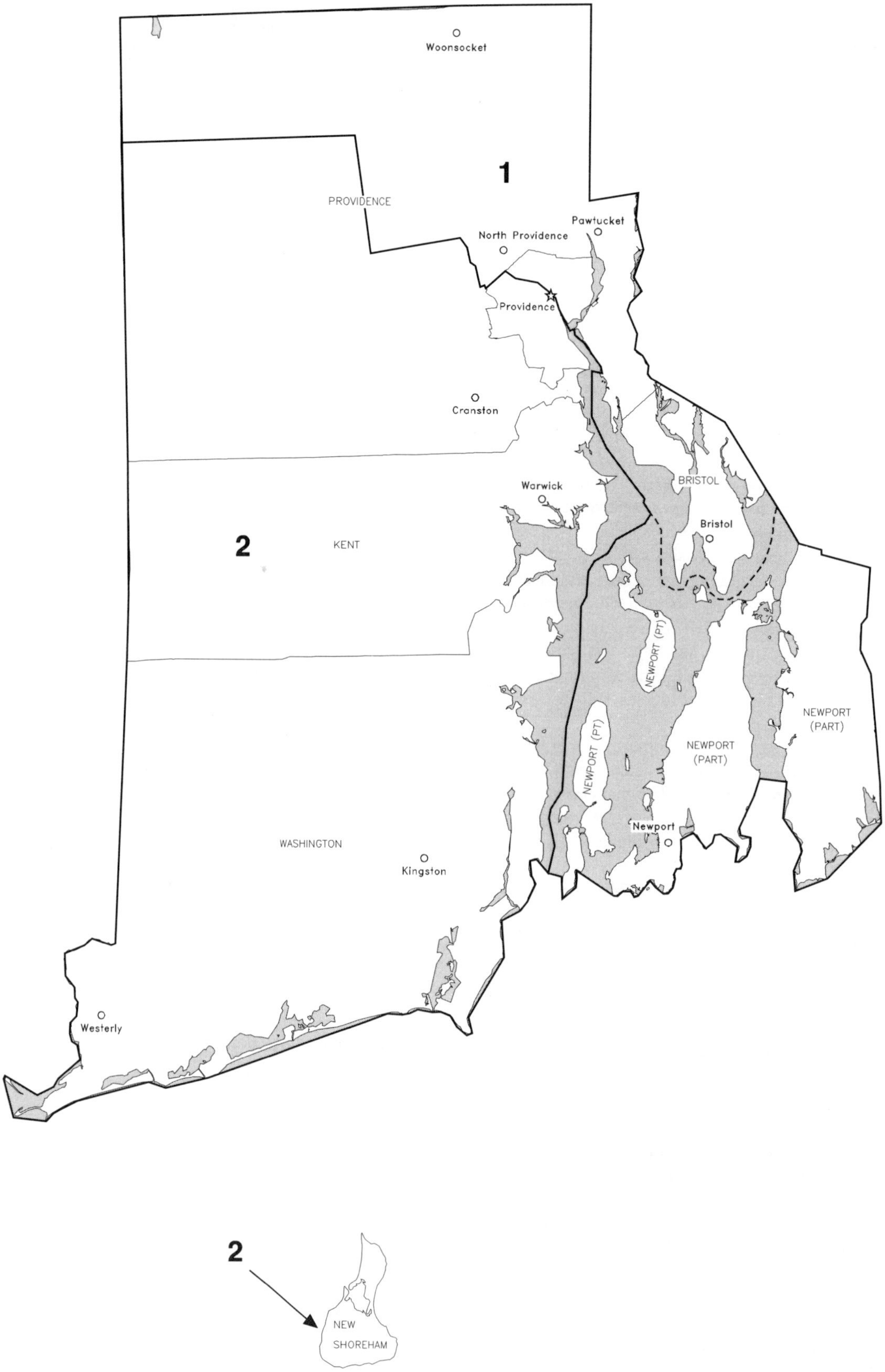

District	18-24*	25-44*	45-54*	55-64*	65 and over*
2	14.9	42.3	12.6	11.4	18.8
State	15.5	41.3	12.4	11.5	19.4

*As percent of voting-age population.

Table 4   Income and Occupation

District	Median family income	Families in poverty	White collar*	Blue collar*	Service*	Farm*
1	$38,896	6.5%	57.4%	27.7%	13.8%	1.1%
2	39,454	7.2	57.8	27.2	13.6	1.4
State	39,172	6.8	57.6	27.5	13.7	1.2

*As percent of employed persons age 16 and over.

Table 5   Education: School Years Completed

District	Less than grade 9*	Grades 9-12 no diploma*	High school diploma*	College bachelor's degree or higher*
1	12.4%	16.9%	28.7%	21.9%
2	9.7	17.0	30.2	20.7
State	11.1	16.9	29.5	21.3

*As percent of persons age 25 and over.

Table 6   Housing and Residential Patterns

District	Owner occupied	Renter occupied	Urban	Rural
1	55.6%	44.4%	91.4%	8.6%
2	63.4	36.6	80.7	19.3
State	59.5	40.5	86.0	14.0

1st District

East — Part of Providence; Pawtucket; Newport

The 1st binds the genteel Newport communities in southern Rhode Island with ethnic Providence neighborhoods and the blue-collar industrial towns of the Blackstone Valley in the north.

The Rhode Island portion of the Blackstone Valley, a highly industrialized, 15-mile region, is anchored on the south by Pawtucket and on the north by Woonsocket, a heavily French-Canadian wool- and textile-manufacturing city along the Massachusetts border. Pawtucket was the site of the first factory in America and is now home to about 250 manufacturing plants. The valley's economy includes metalworking and jewelry companies among much light manufacturing.

The valley is the backbone of the state's Democratic majorities. Although Woonsocket broke with Pawtucket and Central Falls by voting Republican for president in 1984, all three went Democratic in 1988 and in 1992. There are pockets of GOP strength in Lincoln, an affluent bedroom community, and Burrillville, a town of 16,000 that was added to the 1st in 1992 redistricting.

Moving south, the 1st takes in part of Providence, along with its smaller suburbs. Within the capital city, the 1st includes all of the heavily Italian Fourth Ward and most of the Italian Fifth Ward; both generally vote Democratic. On the generally more

affluent east side of Providence, the votes of upper-income conservatives are partially offset by liberals around Brown University; this section also has communities of immigrants from Portugal and the Cape Verde Islands.

South of Providence, the pristine coastal preserves along the scenic Narragansett Bay and Atlantic Ocean dominate. Fishing, shipping and naval operations are vital to the coastal economy. In Portsmouth, defense contractor Raytheon has become an important employer with its work in sonar technology for Navy submarines. The company gained notice in 1991 because its Patriot missiles, which were made at other New England facilities, were used in the gulf war. But because of defense cuts, Raytheon has eliminated more than 1,100 jobs in Rhode Island since 1989.

Some of the smaller seacoast villages around the bay are wealthy residential areas that tend to favor the GOP, but the neighboring larger towns, such as Newport and Tiverton, vote Democratic. Newport and Tiverton have backed the Democratic nominee in four of the past five presidential elections, voting Republican only in 1984.

Newport, renowned for the ostentatious wealth of its 19th-century social elite, lures tourists with its restored palatial mansions. It is home to the Newport Navy Base, which maintains and houses several ships and contains the Naval Education and Training Center and the Naval Undersea Warfare Center, a large research and development complex. The naval operations employ 16,000 civilian and military employees.

The center has been designated as one of four "superlab" sites nationwide. The Navy will consolidate the facility with its sister center in New London, Conn., which means more than 1,000 new jobs for Newport.

Election Returns

	1st District	Democrat	Republican
1992	President*	107,702 (49.8%)	61,011 (28.2%)
	House †	48,092 (24.8%)	135,982 (70.1%)
1990	Senate	115,407 (65.0%)	62,025 (35.0%)
	Governor	132,384 (76.1%)	41,627 (23.9%)
1988	President	114,747 (57.3%)	85,453 (42.7%)
	Senate	94,371 (47.9%)	102,618 (52.1%)
	Governor	100,835 (50.8%)	97,561 (49.2%)
1986	Governor	54,233 (34.8%)	99,759 (64.1%)

*Vote for Perot was 47,733 (22.1%).   †Independent/other is greater than 5%.

Demographics

Population   501,677

Percent change from 1980   5.7%

Land area   324 square miles

Population per square mile   1,550

Counties, 1990 population
Bristol 48,859	Providence (pt.) 365,624
Newport 87,194	

Cities, 1990 population (10,000 or more)
Barrington 15,849	Central Falls 17,637
Bristol 21,625	Cumberland 29,038
Burrillville 16,230	East Providence 50,380

Lincoln 18,045
Middletown 19,460
Newport 28,227
North Providence 32,090
Pawtucket 72,644
Portsmouth 16,857

Providence (pt.) 56,023
Smithfield 19,163
Tiverton 14,312
Valley Falls CDP 11,175
Warren 11,385
Woonsocket 43,877

Race and Hispanic origin
White 92.8%
Black 3.3%
American Indian, Eskimo, or Aleut. 0.3%
Asian or Pacific Islander 1.3%
Other 2.4%
Hispanic origin 3.8%

Ancestry
American 2.1%
English 14.7%
French 14.4%
French Canadian 9.7%
German 6.9%
Irish 20.2%
Italian 14.9%

Polish 5.1%
Portuguese 13.7%
Russian 1.3%
Scotch Irish 1.3%
Scottish 2.4%
Subsaharan African 1.8%
Swedish 1.7%

Universities/colleges, 1990-1991 enrollment
Brown University, Providence 7,577
Bryant College, Smithfield 5,219
Rhode Island School of Design, Providence 1,912
Roger Williams College, Bristol 3,823
Salve Regina College, Newport 2,411

Newspapers, total circulation (in all districts)
Boston Globe 503,578
Boston Herald 339,813
Fall River Herald News 34,812
Newport Daily News 15,369
Pawtucket Times 22,336
Providence Journal/Journal-Bulletin 196,118
Woonsocket Call & Reporter 26,543

Commercial television stations, affiliations
ADI: Providence-New Bedford (100%)
WLNE, New Bedford (CBS)

Cable television systems, total subscribers
CATV of East Providence; East Providence 14,503
Cox Cable Rhode Island; Cranston 35,511
Dimension Cable Services; Providence 43,000
Full Channel TV Inc.; Warren 11,372
TCI Cablevision of Northeast; Johnston 87,642
Vision Cable Rhode Island; Pawtucket 17,949

Military installations, 1991
Naval Education & Training Center, Newport 8,247
Naval Underwater Systems Center, Newport 7,650
North Smithfield Air Force Guard Station, Slatersville 47

Businesses and other major employers
Brown University; Providence 2,700
Amica Mutual Insurance Co.; Pawtucket; life/casualty insurance 2,200
Raytheon Co./Submarine Signal Div.; Portsmouth; sonar equipment 2,100
City of Pawtucket; Pawtucket 1,750
Miriam Hospital Inc.; Providence 1,700

Pepsi-Cola Metropolitan Bottling/PBG Container; Providence; metal containers 1,500
Playskool Inc.; Pawtucket; toys 1,500
City of Woonsocket; Woonsocket 1,500
City of East Providence; Providence 1,350
Memorial Hospital of Rhode Island; Pawtucket 1,333
A. T. Cross Co. Inc.; Pawtucket; pens 1,300
American Insulated Wire Corp.; Pawtucket; insulated wire 1,200
Rhode Island School of Design; Providence 1,000
St. Joseph's Hospital Inc.; Providence 1,000
Landmark Medical Center; Woonsocket 900
Crystal Brands Inc./Trifari, Krussman & Fishel; Providence; costume jewelry 850
Newport Hospital; Newport 840
Town of Cumberland; Pawtucket 800
Allied-Signal Inc./Fram Bendix & Autolite Div.; Providence; motor vehicle equipment 750
Town of North Providence; Providence 750
Worcester Co.; Providence; wool mills 730
American Tourister Inc.; Warren; luggage 700
Swarovski North America; Providence; costume jewelry 700
International Packaging Corp.; Pawtucket; metal products 700
Hasbro Inc.; Pawtucket; toys/sporting goods 650
Melville Corp./Consumer Value Store; Woonsocket; drug stores 650
Carol Cable Co. Inc./Miller Electric Co.; Pawtucket; automotive wire/cable 600
GTE Products Corp.; Pawtucket; glass/glassware 600
Town of Bristol; Bristol 600
L. M. Nursing/Lifetime Medical; Pawtucket; personnel supply services 600
Aid Maintenance Co. Inc.; Pawtucket; building services 600
North American Philips Corp.; Slatersville; electronic components 510

2nd District

West — Western Providence; Warwick

Stretching from the rolling hillsides of upstate Rhode Island through the Providence metropolitan area and on to quiet fishing villages in the south, the 2nd is reliably Democratic. In the past five presidential elections, the district has gone Republican only once, in 1984 for Ronald Reagan.

The largest concentration of voters in the 2nd is in Providence, the state capital and a Democratic stronghold. The city's population has slid from a high of 268,000 in 1925 to about 161,000 in 1990. As blue-collar ethnics have departed, the minority population has increased; blacks and Hispanics made up one-third of the city's population in 1990.

The 2nd takes in about two-thirds of Providence, including the business district, where pedestrian shopping areas have had some success at reviving downtown. Also included is south Providence, once a mixed Irish and Jewish middle-class neighborhood that is increasingly black and Hispanic; Federal Hill and Silver Lake, where Italian Americans predominate; and Elmhurst, a middle-class, ethnic community near Providence College.

Outside Providence, there are small GOP pockets. Scituate, to the east of Providence, and East Greenwich, to the south, were the only communities in the state to favor George Bush over Bill Clinton in 1992.

Just south of Providence along Interstates 95 and 295 are the district's next two largest cities, Warwick and Cranston. With significant white-collar populations—especially in Warwick—both cities are swing areas on the few occasions when statewide races are closely contested.

Nearby Quonset Point, in the town of North Kingstown, is home to one of the district's largest private employers, General Dynamics' Electric Boat Division (4,300 employees). Workers here assemble the hulls for the *Seawolf* nuclear submarines that are completed in Electric Boat's Groton, Conn., facility. Many residents in the southwestern Rhode Island town of Westerly commute to the Groton facility to complete the submarine work.

Westerly, an old shipping center that now blends light manufacturing with its fishing trade, is more frequently found in the Democratic column than most of the other towns on Rhode Island's western border; many of them are old Yankee enclaves that vote Republican. Westerly, which is home to a large Italian-American population, gave Clinton a comfortable win in 1992.

Westerly, a 40-minute drive from Providence, is located in Washington County, the fastest-growing county in the state in the 1980s. Washington County, with coastal cities and maritime commerce as well as the inland marshes known as the "Great Swamp," grew 18 percent during the 1980s. Much of the growth stems from residential development along the shore line, which has lured city dwellers seeking more pleasant surroundings.

In the Washington County town of Kingston is the University of Rhode Island, the largest in the state (16,000 students) and one of the district's top employers.

Offshore but also in the district is 13-mile long Block Island, a popular resort often referred to as a smaller version of Nantucket.

Election Returns

	2nd District	Democrat	Republican
1992	President*	105,597 (45.2%)	70,590 (30.2%)
	House	144,450 (70.7%)	49,998 (24.5%)
1990	Senate	109,698 (58.8%)	76,922 (41.2%)
	Governor	132,027 (72.3%)	50,550 (27.7%)
1988	President	110,376 (54.5%)	92,308 (45.5%)
	Senate	86,346 (43.0%)	114,655 (57.0%)
	Governor	96,101 (47.6%)	105,989 (52.4%)
1986	Governor	50,275 (31.2%)	109,063 (67.7%)

Vote for Perot was 57,312 (24.5%).

Demographics

Population   501,787

Percent change from 1980   6.1%

Land area   721 square miles

Population per square mile   696

Counties, 1990 population

Kent 161,135	Washington 110,006
Providence (pt.) 230,646	

Cities, 1990 population (10,000 or more)

Coventry 31,083	East Greenwich 11,865
Cranston 76,060	Johnston 26,542
Narragansett 14,985	Warwick 85,427
North Kingston 23,786	Westerly 16,477
Providence (pt.) 104,705	West Warwick 29,268
South Kingston 24,631	

Race and Hispanic origin

White 90.0%

Black 4.5%

American Indian, Eskimo, or Aleut. 0.5%

Asian or Pacific Islander 2.4%

Other 2.6%

Hispanic origin 5.3%

Ancestry

American 2.1%	Polish 4.3%
English 17.4%	Portuguese 5.1%
French 12.3%	Russian 1.2%
French Canadian 4.8%	Scotch Irish 1.4%
German 7.7%	Scottish 2.5%
Irish 22.4%	Swedish 2.7%
Italian 24.8%	

Universities/colleges, 1990-1991 enrollment

Community College of Rhode Island, Warwick 16,623

Johnson & Wales University, Providence 7,592

New England Institute of Technology, Warwick 2,041

Providence College, Providence 5,352

Rhode Island College, Providence 9,690

University of Rhode Island, Kingston 16,055

Newspapers, total circulation (in all districts)

Boston Globe 503,578

Boston Herald 339,813

Providence Journal/Journal-Bulletin 196,118

Westerly Sun 12,210

Commercial television stations, affiliations

ADI: Providence-New Bedford (100%)

WOST, Block Island (None)

Cable television systems, total subscribers

Cox Cable Rhode Island; Cranston 35,511

Dimension Cable Services; Providence 43,000

Dimension Cable Services; Warwick 40,000

TCI Cablevision of Northeast; Johnston 87,642

Westerly Cable TV Inc.; Westerly 13,006

Military installations, 1991

Quonset State Airport Air Force Guard Station, North Kingston 274

Coventry Air Force Guard Station, Coventry 40

Businesses and other major employers

General Dynamics Corp./Electric Boat Div.; North Kingstown; shipbuilding 4,300

Rhode Island Hospital; Providence 3,986

City of Providence; Providence 3,000

University of Rhode Island; West Kingston 2,341

New England Telephone & Telegraph Co.; Providence; telephone communications 2,000

Kent County Memorial Hospital; Warwick 2,000

Blue Cross/Blue Shield of Rhode Island; Providence; medical service/health insurance 1,700

Women & Infant's Hospital Rhode Island; Providence 1,560

Metropolitan General Insurance Co.; Warwick; fire/marine/casualty insurance 1,448

Fleet National Bank; Providence; commercial banks   1,417
General Hospital; Providence   1,300
Roger Williams General Hospital; Providence   1,253
Providence Journal Co.; Providence; newspapers   1,200
Stanley-Bostitch Inc.; East Greenwich; staplers/office equipment   1,000
U.S. Justice Dept./FBI; Providence   1,000
U.S. Veterans Affairs Dept.; Providence; hospital   1,000
Leviton Mfg. Co. Inc.; Warwick; electric wiring devices   923
Rhode Island Hospital Trust National Bank; Providence; commercial banks   900
Rhode Island College; Providence   865
Hoechst Celanese Corp.; Coventry; dyes/organic chemicals   837
Fleet/Norstar Services Corp.; Providence; commercial banks   801

K&M Associates; Providence; jewelry   750
City of Cranston; Providence   741
Johnson & Wales University; Providence   700
State of Rhode Island/Administration Dept.; Providence   700
Town of Coventry; Coventry   690
Town of West Warwick; West Warwick   650
Providence College; Providence   644
Davol Inc.; Providence; surgical instruments/supplies   600
Brown & Sharpe Mfg. Co./Metrology Div.; North Kingstown; metalworking machinery   600
American Express Co.; Providence; security & commodity services   600
South County Hospital Inc.; Wakefield   600
Rhode Island Public Transit Authority; Providence   528
Westerly Hospital; Westerly   525

South Carolina

The 1990s look to be a decade of economic and political transition for South Carolina. During the 1980s, the economy and the Republican Party surged forward in the Palmetto State; its military installations benefited handsomely from the Reagan defense buildup, and thousands of upscale newcomers thronged to its Atlantic Coast resorts, spurring economic activity and helping boost the GOP to its first back-to-back gubernatorial victories in state history.

But with the 1993 base closure commission decreeing a virtual cessation of activity at the Charleston Naval Station, an estimated 60,000 military, defense-contractor and civilian jobs could be affected. In 1992, the military directly or indirectly supplied one-third of the payroll and one-fourth of the jobs in the southern counties of Berkeley, Charleston and Dorchester—an estimated annual impact on the area's economy of $4.2 billion.

The late 1970s were salad days for Democrats in South Carolina. In 1976 Jimmy Carter carried the state easily in presidential voting, and in 1978 Democrat Richard Riley won the governorship. Four of the state's six U.S. House seats were in Democratic hands.

But the GOP began rebuilding in 1980. That year Reagan narrowly won the state over Carter, and at the same time the GOP got a 4-2 advantage in the House delegation. In 1984, Reagan soared to a 64 percent tally in South Carolina, and two years later Republican Carroll A. Campbell, Jr., won the governor's office. In 1988 South Carolina went for George Bush to the tune of 62 percent. Campbell won a second term with a whopping 70 percent in 1990, and even in 1992, when Bush sank nationally, he still beat Bill Clinton by eight points in South Carolina.

South Carolina Democrats headed into the 1990s retaining the allegiance of most rural and small-town white voters, and of the state's black citizenry, who make up 30 percent of the total population. In addition, business-minded voters could be lured from their GOP inclinations to back Democrats such as Sen. Ernest F. Hollings, chairman of the Senate Commerce Committee. But even veterans such as Hollings faced hot pursuit from the GOP; he won a fifth full term in 1992 by an unexpectedly limp 50 percent.

The bulk of the Democrats' vote base is in parts of the state

that saw little or no population growth in the 1980s. In contrast, the GOP's gains have come in areas where growth has been robust: the Atlantic Coast (from Myrtle Beach in the north to Hilton Head in the south), the suburbs around Columbia and Charleston, and the "Upcountry" region anchored in Greenville, which has a diversified industrial base.

All, however, is not upbeat for the GOP: Across the state—especially in the Upcountry—there has been a fair amount of competition within the party between conservative religious activists and voters more concerned with economic issues. Failure to keep those factions united would put the GOP's gubernatorial winning streak at risk.

Overall during the 1980s, South Carolina's population grew 12 percent. While that was not enough to earn the state an additional House seat in 1990 reapportionment, another catalyst—the Voting Rights Act—forced dramatic changes in the state's congressional district map.

Despite its sizable black population, South Carolina had not sent a black to Congress this century. Heading into redistricting for 1992, the Democrats in control of the Legislature faced pressure on three fronts: carving out a new district with enough blacks to ensure election of a minority candidate, giving the state's four white Democratic incumbents a fair shot at re-election, and drawing a map that would not provoke a veto from Campbell, who was looking out for the state's two GOP House members.

In the end, the task was too great for the Legislature. Months of effort produced different plans from the state House and state Senate with variations that could not be reconciled. A federal court that had been monitoring the Legislature's work on redistricting assumed the task, and on May 1, 1992, it issued a new map.

The court's map established a 6th District with a 62 percent black-majority population; it sprawled over all or part of 16 counties, taking in concentrations of blacks from the capital city of Columbia in midstate all the way down to Charleston. In creating this seat, the old 6th District, held by white Democrat Rep. Robin Tallon, was eliminated. In 1992 Democrat James E. Clyburn won with 65 percent of the vote to become South Carolina's first black House member since 1897.

The radical surgery required to create the 6th had an impact

SOUTH CAROLINA

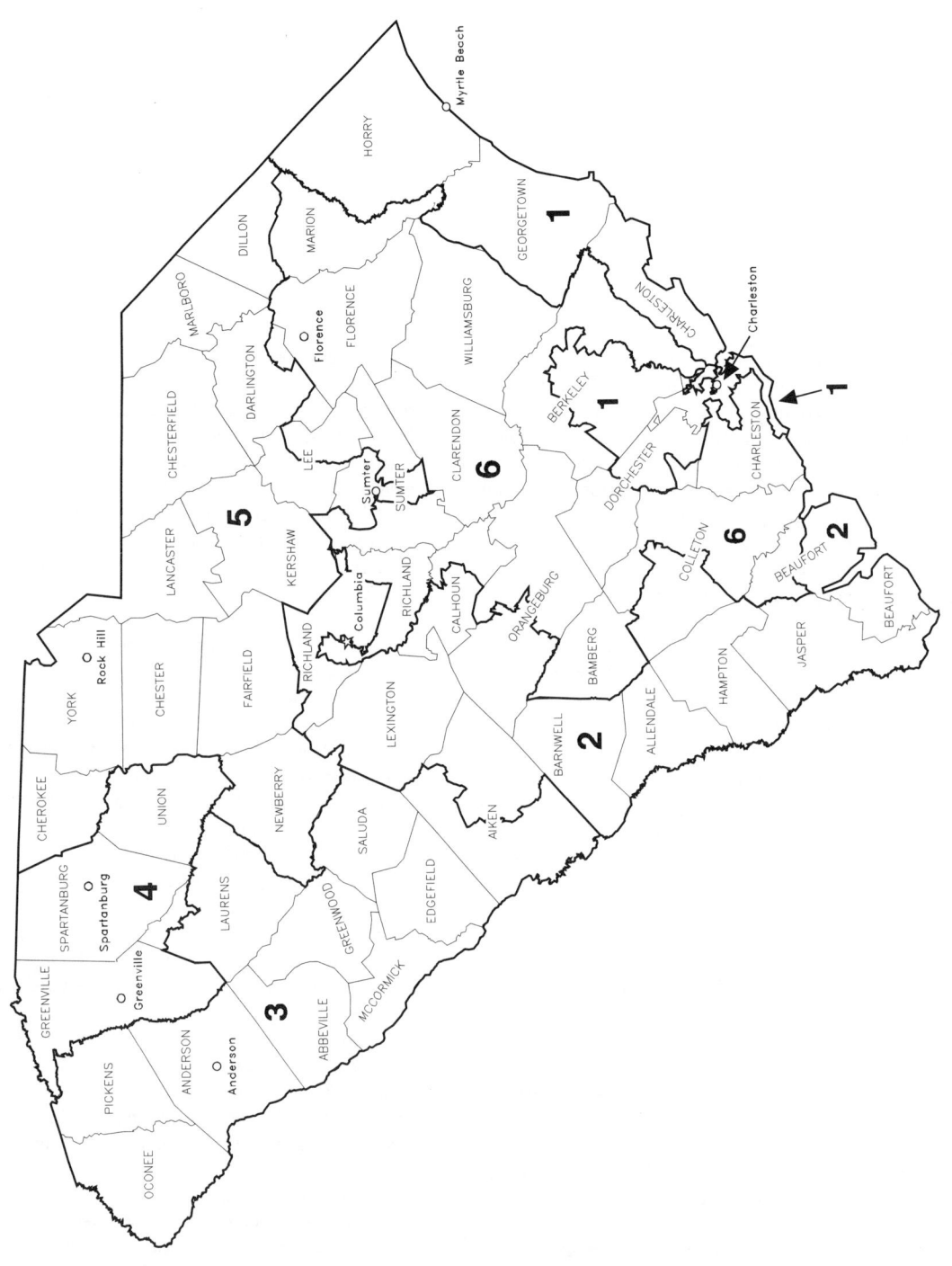

on the shape of all the other House districts, but the new map retained the basic partisan character of each constituency. Four incumbents won re-election in 1992; the lone general-election incumbent casualty was Democrat Liz Patterson in the 3rd. She lost to Republican Bob Inglis, who managed to unite two factions of the district GOP that had been at odds since Campbell left the seat—conservative Christian activists centered around Bob Jones University, and more business-oriented party faithful.

In mid-1993, court action raised the possibility that the congressional district map used for 1992 could be altered before the 1994 election.

The same federal court that in the spring of 1992 had issued the congressional map also drew boundaries for state House and state Senate districts; the Legislature and Gov. Campbell arrived at an impasse on those lines. A coalition of state Republicans and black Democrats protested that the court's legislative redistricting plans did not create enough new opportunities for black candidates.

The Supreme Court ordered the federal court to reconsider the matter; the lower court responded July 13 with a ruling that said it was the responsibility of the legislature, rather than federal judges, to draw district lines. The court set April 1, 1994, as the deadline for new maps to be passed by legislators, signed by the governor and "precleared" by the Justice Department. If the maps are not in place by the deadline, the judges will again step in.

In ordering the state to draw district maps, the judges did not find fault with the plans they had created for the 1992 election. As a result, legislators could pass plans that are the same or similar to the ones drawn by the judges.

Table 1   Population

District	Population	Population under 18	Voting-age population	Median age
1	581,125	153,522	427,603	30.6
2	581,111	150,079	431,032	31.4
3	581,104	145,698	435,406	33.5
4	581,113	143,276	437,837	33.7
5	581,131	158,556	422,575	32.4
6	581,119	169,076	412,043	30.9
State	3,486,703	920,207	2,566,496	32.0

Table 2   Voting-Age Persons

District	White*	Black*	American Indian, Eskimo, or Aleut*	Asian or Pacific Islander*	Other*	Hispanic*	Male*	Female*
1	80.5%	17.7%	0.3%	1.1%	0.4%	1.2%	49.4%	50.6%
2	75.6	22.7	0.2	0.9	0.5	1.3	48.4	51.6
3	80.6	18.8	0.1	0.4	0.1	0.5	47.4	52.6
4	81.3	17.8	0.1	0.6	0.2	0.7	47.1	52.9
5	71.3	27.9	0.4	0.3	0.1	0.5	47.0	53.0
6	41.1	58.3	0.2	0.3	0.1	0.5	45.7	54.3
State	72.0	26.9	0.2	0.6	0.2	0.8	47.5	52.5

*As percent of voting-age population.

Table 3   Voting-Age Persons by Age Groups

District	18-24*	25-44*	45-54*	55-64*	65 and over*
1	16.7%	47.3%	12.9%	10.5%	12.6%
2	16.8	45.7	13.3	10.5	13.7
3	15.7	40.2	14.5	12.4	17.2
4	14.5	42.5	14.8	11.8	16.4
5	14.7	42.9	14.4	11.8	16.2
6	16.7	41.9	13.3	11.4	16.6
State	15.8	43.4	13.9	11.4	15.5

*As percent of voting-age population.

Table 4   Income and Occupation

District	Median family income	Families in poverty	White collar*	Blue collar*	Service*	Farm*
1	$32,082	9.6%	57.1%	27.6%	13.5%	1.9%
2	35,402	9.4	61.7	24.5	11.8	2.0
3	31,237	9.7	45.4	41.6	11.2	1.7
4	32,866	8.4	52.2	35.5	11.2	1.1
5	29,451	12.4	43.5	43.0	11.0	2.5
6	22,973	22.6	41.8	37.5	17.2	3.6
State	30,797	11.9	50.5	34.9	12.5	2.1

*As percent of employed persons age 16 and over.

Table 5   Education: School Years Completed

District	Less than grade 9*	Grades 9-12 no diploma*	High school diploma*	College bachelor's degree or higher*
1	8.0%	14.1%	30.0%	19.8%
2	8.6	13.4	28.0	24.0
3	16.0	19.7	30.5	14.4
4	14.0	18.7	27.9	17.6
5	17.0	20.1	31.0	12.5
6	18.2	22.6	29.6	11.4
State	13.6	18.1	29.5	16.6

*As percent of persons age 25 and over.

Table 6   Housing and Residential Patterns

District	Owner occupied	Renter occupied	Urban	Rural
1	65.4%	34.6%	75.2%	24.8%
2	69.4	30.6	59.8	40.2
3	74.5	25.5	42.4	57.6
4	68.2	31.8	64.3	35.7
5	73.5	26.5	37.2	62.8
6	67.8	32.2	49.0	51.0
State	69.8	30.2	54.6	45.4

1st District

East — Part of Charleston; Myrtle Beach

The 1st encompasses two of South Carolina's hot growth spots: Charleston and its suburbs, which were part of the district in the 1980s, and, up the Atlantic Coast, newly added Myrtle Beach (Horry County). Remapping in 1992 shifted the 1st north and east to make way for the black-majority 6th.

A 1980s boom in tourism and federal spending at Charleston's many military installations and industries produced a vibrant economy and fueled population growth of more than 40 percent in some parts of the 1st.

But where defense dollars supported a strong economy in the past decade, there is potential now for economic trouble; military downsizing may hit Charleston with a vengeance. Two major military installations—the Charleston Naval Station and Hospital, and the Charleston Naval Shipyard—appeared on the Pentagon's 1993 base-closure list. If they do close, some estimates say that military, defense-contractor and civilian job losses could reach 60,000. In 1992, the military directly or indirectly supplied one-third of the payroll and one-fourth of the jobs in the southern counties of Berkeley, Charleston and Dorchester—an estimated annual impact on the area's economy of $4.2 billion.

The proposed closure comes on top of substantial job losses during the early 1990s. Between 1989 and 1992, the naval base shed 10,000 jobs. Myrtle Beach got a taste of the same medicine when its Air Force base closed, eliminating 4,000 military and civilian jobs.

So far at both ends of the district, layoffs have been absorbed by growth in the nonmilitary sector. Charleston's historic district and nearby beaches are a cash cow; five million tourists visit the area annually, leaving an estimated $850 million a year behind. A growing health-care industry, anchored by the Medical University of South Carolina, employs about 15,000.

Myrtle Beach thrives on tourism as well, drawing visitors to its surf, myriad golf courses and honky-tonk amusements. Beaches of the "Grand Strand"—60 miles of shoreline from the North Carolina border down into Georgetown County—feature waters warmed by the Gulf Stream, just a few miles offshore.

In redistricting, the 1st saw much of its black population, both rural and urban, go into the 6th District. That leaves the 1st with electoral demographics most GOP candidates only dream about. Support for Republicans is high among the white, affluent suburbanites around Charleston as well as among the district's conservative-minded military personnel and its many retirees.

Despite the district's overall right-of-center tilt, there is a moderate shading on some issues. Widespread support for protecting the area's waterways, marshes, beaches and wildlife has spawned a strong environmental movement.

Election Returns

	1st District	Democrat	Republican
1992	President*	62,513 (32.7%)	102,194 (53.4%)
	House	59,908 (32.5%)	121,938 (66.1%)
1990	Senate	31,859 (30.7%)	71,946 (69.3%)
	Governor	27,881 (25.9%)	79,804 (74.1%)
1988	President	47,995 (31.9%)	102,639 (68.1%)
1986	Senate	62,077 (63.1%)	36,283 (36.9%)
	Governor	46,192 (45.9%)	54,525 (54.1%)

*Vote for Perot was 26,711 (14.0%).

Demographics

Population 581,125

Percent change from 1980 11.7%

Land area 3,148 square miles

Population per square mile 185

Counties, 1990 population

Berkeley (pt.) 110,194	Georgetown 46,302
Charleston (pt.) 210,520	Horry 144,053
Dorchester (pt.) 70,056	

Cities, 1990 population (10,000 or more)

Charleston (pt.) 49,216	Myrtle Beach 24,848
Goose Creek 24,692	North Charleston (pt.)
Hanahan 13,176	54,324
Ladson CDP 13,540	Socastee CDP 10,426
Mount Pleasant 30,108	Summerville 22,519

Race and Hispanic origin

White 78.0%
Black 20.1%
American Indian, Eskimo, or Aleut. 0.3%
Asian or Pacific Islander 1.2%
Other 0.4%
Hispanic origin 1.4%

Ancestry

American 8.9%	Irish 15.0%
Dutch 1.8%	Italian 2.8%
English 15.4%	Polish 1.7%
French 4.2%	Scotch Irish 4.0%
German 18.2%	Scottish 2.9%

Universities/colleges, 1990-1991 enrollment

Charleston Southern University, Charleston 2,158
Citadel/Military College of South Carolina; Charleston 3,801
College of Charleston, Charleston 7,726
Horry-Georgetown Tech College, Conway 1,984
Johnson & Wales University, Charleston 567
Medical University of South Carolina, Charleston 1,781
Trident Technical College, Charleston 6,939
University of South Carolina at Coastal Carolina, Conway 4,080

Newspapers, total circulation (in all districts)

Charleston Post & Courier 111,622
Columbia State 134,560
Myrtle Beach Sun News 38,636

Commercial television stations, affiliations

ADI: Charleston (66%) and Florence (34%)
WCBD-TV, Charleston (ABC)
WCIV, Charleston (NBC)
WCSC-TV, Charleston (CBS)
WITV, Charleston (None)
WTAT-TV, Charleston (Fox)
WGSE, Myrtle Beach (None)

Cable television systems, total subscribers

Cablevision Industries; Summerville 17,376
Cox Cable Myrtle Beach; Myrtle Beach 16,738
Horry Telephone Cablevision; Homewood 10,000
Jones Intercable Inc.; Garden City 18,118
Par Cable of Myrtle Beach; North Myrtle Beach 7,600
Storer Cable of Carolina Inc.; North Charleston 73,000

Military installations, 1991

Charleston Naval Station, Charleston 26,571
Charleston Naval Weapons Station, Charleston 7,892
Charleston Naval Shipyard, Charleston 7,779
Charleston Air Force Base, Charleston 6,090

Businesses and other major employers

Medical University of South Carolina & Medical University Hospital; Charleston 15,000

County of Horry/School District; Conway 2,950

Roper Hospital; Charleston 1,900

AVX Corp.; Myrtle Beach; electronic components 1,600

Westvaco Corp.; Charleston; pulp/paper mills 1,500

Robert Bosch Corp.; Charleston; diesel engine parts 1,500

North Trident Regional Hospital; Charleston 1,300

Oneita Industries Inc.; Andrews; knitting mills 1,000

Bon-Secours St. Francis Xavier Hospital; Charleston 920

International Paper Co.; Georgetown; paper mills 900

Citadel/Military College of South Carolina; Charleston 820

State of South Carolina/Public Services Authority; Moncks Corner; electric services 762

College of Charleston; Charleston 750

Post News & Courier; Charleston; newspapers 720

Georgetown Steel Corp.; Georgetown; steel products 700

Southern Bell Telephone & Telegraph Co.; Charleston; telephone communications 700

State of South Carolina; Ladson; residential care 700

South Carolina Electric & Gas Co.; Charleston; utility services 680

Landmark Land Co. of Carolina; Johns Island; amusement/recreation services 650

Wild Water & Wheels Inc.; Myrtle Beach; amusement park 650

Alumax of South Carolina Inc.; Goose Creek; aluminum reduction 625

Myrtle Beach Hospital Inc./Grand Strand General Hospital; Myrtle Beach 625

Conway Hospital Inc.; Conway 550

2nd District

Central and South — Columbia Suburbs; Hilton Head

Winding downward from the state capital of Columbia to the Atlantic Ocean, the 2nd illustrates the contrasts that growth has brought to South Carolina. Anchored at either end by the first- and third-richest counties in the state—Lexington and Beaufort, respectively—the 2nd also contains the poorest county, Allendale, in its midsection. The population of Atlantic Coast towns skyrocketed during the 1980s, while inland counties such as Hampton and Allendale struggled to retain population.

More than three-fourths of the votes cast in the 2nd come from the thriving ends of the district.

To the north, Columbia (Richland County) and its bedroom communities in nearby Lexington County enjoyed a boom during the 1980s, as service businesses and midsize companies that produce everything from software to nuclear casings kept the area's economy vibrant. However, the main source of jobs here continues to be state, federal and local government agencies, as well as the University of South Carolina (26,000 students); together these employ nearly 60,000 and provide a fairly stable base of white-collar jobs.

At the southern end of the 2nd, Beaufort County is another bastion of affluence. The swank resorts of Hilton Head Island abound with retirees and vacationers sweating in the sun; only five miles away, recruits sweat at the Parris Island Marine Corps camp. The enormous popularity of Hilton Head caused its population to boom by 111 percent during the 1980s.

Growth and wealth at both ends of the 2nd—as well as a 1992 redistricting map that shifted most of the district's black residents into the majority-black 6th District—have put it firmly in the GOP column. Lexington County, with its mix of white-collar professionals and blue-collar social conservatives, gave George Bush 61 percent of its presidential vote in 1992—a tally that qualifies Lexington as the strongest GOP county in the state. Beaufort County, which a generation ago was rural and Democratic, is now reliably Republican as well.

Between the poles of the 2nd, however, lie some of the poorest areas of South Carolina, places that were passed over by the boom of the 1980s and remain mired in rural poverty. In Allendale County, one in three people lives below the poverty line; in Hampton and Jasper counties, one in four falls below the line. Tenant farming and sharecropping are long-lived traditions in these black-majority, thinly settled counties.

Although South Carolina's GOP has made considerable progress in recent years luring white voters who once called themselves Democrats, there are still a number of die-hard white Democrats in the middle part of the 2nd. Their votes, in combination with the district's 25 percent black population, enabled Bill Clinton to carry Jasper, Hampton, Allendale and Calhoun counties in 1992. However, those Democrats' voices were drowned out by the Republicans to their north and south. Bush won the 2nd with 52 percent.

Election Returns

	2nd District	Democrat	Republican
1992	President*	82,964 (36.4%)	119,122 (52.3%)
	House†	—	148,667 (87.7%)
1990	Senate	37,948 (28.7%)	94,315 (71.3%)
	Governor	31,166 (23.1%)	103,721 (76.9%)
1988	President	56,445 (31.7%)	121,501 (68.3%)
1986	Senate	73,459 (55.6%)	58,670 (44.4%)
	Governor	51,979 (38.7%)	82,268 (61.3%)

*Vote for Perot was 25,592 (11.2%).   †Independent/other is greater than 5%.

Demographics

Population 581,111

Percent change from 1980 11.2%

Land area 5,225 square miles

Population per square mile 111

Counties, 1990 population

Aiken (pt.) 17,732	Hampton 18,191
Allendale 11,722	Jasper 15,487
Barnwell 20,293	Lexington 167,611
Beaufort (pt.) 83,231	Orangeburg (pt.) 35,081
Calhoun (pt.) 9,459	Richland (pt.) 188,346
Colleton (pt.) 13,958	

Cities, 1990 population (10,000 or more)

Cayce 11,163	Seven Oaks CDP 15,722
Columbia (pt.) 53,117	St. Andrews CDP 25,692
Hilton Head Island 23,694	West Columbia 10,588
Irmo 11,280	

Race and Hispanic origin
White 72.9%
Black 25.4%
American Indian, Eskimo, or Aleut. 0.2%
Asian or Pacific Islander 1.0%
Other 0.5%
Hispanic origin 1.4%

Ancestry
American 8.4%	Irish 14.6%
Dutch 1.8%	Italian 2.3%
English 14.3%	Polish 1.1%
French 3.3%	Scotch Irish 4.7%
German 20.9%	Scottish 2.7%

Universities/colleges, 1990-1991 enrollment
Beaufort Tech College, Beaufort 1,210
Claflin College, Orangeburg 913
Columbia Bible College Seminary, Columbia 961
Midlands Technical College, Columbia 7,546
South Carolina State College, Orangeburg 4,822
University of South Carolina, Beaufort 896
University of South Carolina, Columbia 25,613
University of South Carolina-Salkehatchi, Allendale 831

Newspapers, total circulation (in all districts)
Aiken Standard 16,843
Beaufort Gazette 9,318
Charleston Post & Courier 111,622
Columbia State 134,560
Hilton Head Island Packet 9,595
Orangeburg Times & Democrat 17,222
Savannah Morning News Evening Press 73,752

Commercial television stations, affiliations
ADI: Columbia (35%), Savannah (33%), Augusta (26%) and
    Charleston (7%)
    WLTX, Columbia (CBS)

Cable television systems, total subscribers
Adelphia Cable; Hilton Head Island 22,548
CVI; Columbia 33,264
Cablevision of Columbia; Columbia 44,820
Low County Cablevision; Beaufort 8,868
Palmetto Cablevision; Aiken 13,000
Palmetto Cablevision; Barnwell 8,600

Military installations, 1991
Fort Jackson (Army), Columbia 17,737
Marine Corps Recruitment Depot Activity, Parris Island
    7,777
Beaufort Marine Corps Air Station, Beaufort 3,697
Beaufort Naval Hospital, Beaufort 634
McEntire Air Force Guard Base, Eastover 382

Businesses and other major employers
State of South Carolina/Corrections Dept.; Columbia 5,500
University of South Carolina; Columbia 4,401
County of Lexington/Board of Education; Lexington 2,600
State of South Carolina; Columbia; residential care 2,000
Policy Management Systems Corp; Blythewood; computer
    services 2,000
Allied Signal Inc.; West Columbia; plastics/synthetics 1,600
American Yard Products Inc.; Orangeburg; farm/garden
    machinery 1,500
U.S. Veterans Affairs Dept.; Columbia; hospital 1,500

Allied-Signal Inc./Fibers & Plastics Co.; Columbia; man-made
    fabric mills 1,475
Lexington Medical Center; West Columbia 1,297
Michelin Tire Corp.; Lexington; tires 1,200
Colonial Companies Inc.; Columbia; medical service/health
    insurance 1,157
Westinghouse Electric Corp./Commercial Nuclear Fuel Div.;
    Columbia; inorganic chemicals 1,100
Westinghouse Electric Corp./Specialty Metals Div.; Hampton;
    plastics products 1,000
NCR Corp.; West Columbia; computer equipment 1,000
South Carolina National Bank; Columbia; commercial banks
    851
State of South Carolina/Social Services Dept.; Columbia 800
Pinkerton's Inc.; Columbia; security services 800
South Carolina State College; Orangeburg 791
State of South Carolina/Education Dept.; Columbia 674
Eastman Kodak Co./Carolina Eastman Co.; West Columbia;
    synthetics 665
County of Lexington/General Services Div.; Lexington 620
Dixie-Narco Inc.; Williston; refrigeration 600
Square D Co.; Columbia; electrical motors 592
State of South Carolina/General Services Dept.; Columbia
    525

3rd District

West — Anderson; Aiken

As South Carolina has grown in recent years, it has grown steadily more Republican. That trend is clear in the 3rd, a one-time "yellow dog" Democratic district where GOP candidates now typically win up-ballot contests. Still, Democratic Rep. Butler Derrick, elected to a tenth term in 1992, has kept his hold, buoyed by the district's black residents (21 percent of the population), by rural whites who retain their traditional Democratic ties and by business-minded conservatives who value Derrick's senior position on the Rules Committee and his spot in the House Democratic leadership.

Nearly half the district vote is cast in three counties—Anderson, Pickens and Oconee—that are part of South Carolina's "upcountry" and have a diverse economic base. The biggest, Anderson, benefits from its proximity to the Greenville-Spartanburg area, just a few miles up Interstate 85 in the 4th District. Northern and foreign industries find wages, taxes and living costs in the upcountry hospitable. The plants and businesses have brought in an increasingly skilled and white-collar work force.

Now, towns once dependent on cotton mills churn out a variety of products, including tires, auto parts and refrigerators. At the same time, many textile mills have converted to high-tech fiber manufacturers; in the city of Anderson, Clarks Schwabel makes the skin for stealth fighters.

Clemson University and its 16,000 students provide economic insurance for Pickens County, and a conservative pull comes from its agriculture- and engineering-oriented faculty.

Growth, prosperity and a large business community in the northern part of the 3rd have boosted GOP fortunes, though Democrats still dominate local political offices. In 1992, George Bush won better than 50 percent in all three northern counties, reaching 58 percent in Pickens County.

Traditional Democratic voting habits still hold sway in the

rural midsection of the district, where a sizable black population and less prosperity have kept the GOP from building momentum. Abbeville, McCormick and Edgefield were the only counties in the district not to support Bush in 1992. McCormick even refused to back GOP Sen. Strom Thurmond when he easily won re-election in 1990, perhaps to spite state officials for changing the name of their local lake—Clark's Hill—to Thurmond Lake.

At its southern end, the 3rd includes most of the people in Aiken County, although 1992 redistricting put the eastern half of the county in the 2nd. Known as the polo center of the South—matches are every Sunday at Whitney Field—the town of Aiken is a picture of gentility preserved, with more than 70 historic homes and gardens, six golf courses and three racetracks.

Aiken is Thurmond's home base, and the white-collar commuters to Augusta, Ga., and engineers working at the Savannah River Nuclear Complex give it a solid GOP base; Bush won 56 percent here in 1992. The fate of the Savannah River plutonium plant is in doubt, though, as the Energy Department has indefinitely suspended operations there.

Election Returns

	3rd District	Democrat	Republican
1992	President*	69,365 (35.0%)	102,458 (51.6%)
	House	119,119 (61.2%)	75,660 (38.8%)
1990	Senate	37,247 (31.7%)	80,154 (68.3%)
	Governor	28,603 (24.0%)	90,539 (76.0%)
1988	President	54,088 (33.6%)	106,768 (66.4%)
1986	Senate	70,609 (62.3%)	42,661 (37.7%)
	Governor	52,862 (46.0%)	62,074 (54.0%)

*Vote for Perot was 26,609 (13.4%).

Demographics

Population   581,104

Percent change from 1980   11.9%

Land area   5,386 square miles

Population per square mile   108

Counties, 1990 population

Abbeville 23,862	Laurens (pt.) 54,283
Aiken (pt.) 103,208	McCormick 8,868
Anderson 145,196	Oconee 57,494
Edgefield 18,375	Pickens 93,894
Greenwood 59,567	Saluda 16,357

Cities, 1990 population (10,000 or more)

Aiken (pt.) 19,869	Easley 15,195
Anderson 26,184	Greenwood 20,807
Clemson 11,096	North Augusta 15,351

Race and Hispanic origin

White   78.6%
Black   20.8%
American Indian, Eskimo, or Aleut.   0.1%
Asian or Pacific Islander   0.4%
Other   0.1%
Hispanic origin   0.5%

Ancestry

American 14.7%	Irish 18.0%
Dutch 1.8%	Italian 1.3%
English 13.0%	Scotch Irish 4.9%
French 2.2%	Scottish 2.2%
German 14.4%	

Universities/colleges, 1990-1991 enrollment

Aiken Technical College, Aiken   1,903
Anderson College, Anderson   968
Central Wesleyan College, Central   934
Clemson University, Clemson   15,714
Erskine College & Seminary, Due West   681
Lander College, Greenwood   2,309
Piedmont Technical College, Greenwood   2,144
Presbyterian College, Clinton   1,133
Tri-County Technical College, Pendleton   2,935
University South Carolina, Aiken   2,966

Newspapers, total circulation (in all districts)

Aiken Standard   16,843
Anderson Independent-Mail   40,941
Augusta Chronicle Augusta Herald   82,491
Columbia State   134,560
Greenville News Greenville Peidmont   117,320
Greenwood Index Journal   15,415

Commercial television stations, affiliations

ADI: Greenville-Spartanburg-Asheville (64%), Augusta (28%) and Columbia (8%)
WAGT, Augusta (NBC)
WFXG, Augusta (Fox)
WJBF, Augusta (ABC)
WRDW-TV, Augusta (CBS)

Cable television systems, total subscribers

Anderson Cable TV; Anderson   11,396
Cencom Cable TV; West Pelzer   7,500
Cencom of South Carolina; Gray Court   17,550
Greenwood Cablevision; Greenwood   12,000
Northland Cable TV; Seneca   7,346
Palmetto Cablevision; Aiken   13,000
Telecable of Greenville Inc.; Greenville   57,239
United Artists Cable; North Augusta   11,544

Businesses and other major employers

Westinghouse Savannah River Co.; Aiken; electric services   14,000
U.S. Energy Dept.; Aiken   8,000
Graniteville Co.; Graniteville; cotton mills   4,000
Clemson University; Clemson   3,600
Greenwood Mills Inc.; Greenwood; cotton mills   3,000
J. P. Stevens & Co. Inc.; Clemson; cotton mills   2,600
Michelin Tire Corp.; Sandy Springs; tires   1,700
Clinton Mills Inc.; Clinton; cotton mills   1,600
State of South Carolina/Mental Health Center; Clinton; nursing   1,600
Torrington Co./Clinton Bearings Div.; Clinton; industry machinery   1,312
Kimberly-Clark Corp.; Beech Island; paper mills   1,200
Monsanto Co.; Greenwood; synthetic organic chemicals   1,200
Owens-Corning Fiberglas Corp.; Anderson; glass/glassware   1,200

Ryobi Motor Products Corp.; Anderson; household appliances 1,200

Ryobi Motor Products Corp.; Pickens; metalworking machinery 1,200

County of Oconee/School District; Walhalla 1,200

Duke Power Co./Oconee Nuclear Station; Seneca; electric services 1,130

BASF Corp./Fibers Div.; Anderson; plastics/synthetics 1,100

Self Memorial Hospital; Greenwood 1,100

Owens-Corning Fiberglas Corp.; Aiken; mineral products 1,000

Schlumberger Ltd./Schlumberger Industries; West Union; electric distribution equipment 1,000

Clark-Schwebel Fiberglass Corp.; Anderson; fiberglass products 900

Gerber Childrenswear Inc.; Pelzer; rubber products 900

Wackenhut Services Inc.; Aiken; business/security services 900

Aiken Community Hospital/HCA; Aiken 850

North Arkansas Wholesale Co./Wal-Mart Distribution Center; Laurens; furniture 800

Mayfair Mills Inc./Glenwood Mills Div.; Easley; cotton mills 750

American Argo Corp.; Jackson; apparel 700

White Consolidated Industries; Anderson; refrigerators 700

NCR Corp./Personal Computer Div.; Liberty; computers 700

Platt Saco Lowell Corp.; Easley; industry machinery 700

West Point-Pepperell Inc.; Seneca; cotton mills 700

Beacon Mfg. Co.; Westminster; cotton mills 700

Milliken & Co./Cushman Plant; Williamston; wool mills 650

Engineered Custom Plastics Corp.; Easley; plastics products 650

Springs Industries Inc./Chiquola Plant; Honea Path; cotton mills 600

Professional Medical Products; Greenwood; medical supplies 550

Jantzen Inc.; Seneca; outerwear 550

County of Aiken; Aiken 550

Mount Vernon Mills Inc.; La France; man-made fabric mills 530

Mount Vernon Mills Inc.; Johnston; textile products 525

Torrington Co./Ingersol Rand; Honea Path; industry machinery 520

Oconee Memorial Hospital; Seneca 510

4th District

Northwest — Greenville; Spartanburg

The nucleus of the 4th is Greenville County, one of the most-populous and most-industrialized counties in the state and a showpiece of the New South.

The city of Greenville developed as a textile center after the Civil War, and although employment in the mills and clothing manufacturers declined as that industry moved farther south, the city has not suffered the same depressing fate as other textile-dependent areas. Instead, civic leaders lured Rust Belt and overseas investment to the area, ensuring a robust economy and driving the steady population growth of Greenville and Spartanburg counties.

The city relied on private employers, including Michelin, General Electric and Kemet Electronics, to sustain high employ-

ment and help blunt the effects of the recession during the early 1990s. The world supply of Pepto-Bismol is also manufactured here.

Greenville County has a history of conservatism dating to its Tory leanings during the American Revolution, and it was one of the first areas in the state to take to Republicanism after World War II.

Growth in such white-collar occupations as engineering and management has made the area increasingly affluent, and has intensified its GOP leanings. George Bush won 57 percent of the Greenville County vote in 1992.

Beneath an apparently unified conservative voting population, however, lie fault lines that can cleave GOP supporters. Winning candidates must convince two rather disparate groups to become political bedfellows: Mainstream, business-oriented conservatives often find themselves at odds with intensely conservative Christians and fundamentalists focused around the Greenville-based Bob Jones University. Former Democratic Rep. Liz J. Patterson held onto her seat for six years by splitting these two factions. When the conservatives' rift healed in 1992, the united GOP took the House seat.

Democrats in the county tend to be conservative and often vote for GOP candidates. A small band of liberal Democrats in the city of Greenville does not offer much of a launching pad for left-leaning candidates.

Spartanburg County scored a coup over rival Greenville with the 1992 announcement that BMW will build its U.S. assembly line there; it expects to employ upwards of 2,000 by the end of the decade. Agriculture also plays a role in the county's economy; Spartanburg's sprawling orchards hold bragging rights to the second biggest peach crop in the South.

Rank-and-file textile workers and farm laborers give Spartanburg firmer Democratic loyalties than Greenville. In 1992, Patterson won the county.

But when it comes to statewide and national races, voters here typically opt for the GOP, although not by the margins that Greenville provides. Rounding out this compact district, rural Union County usually delivers its votes to Democratic candidates.

Election Returns

	4th District	Democrat	Republican
1992	President*	65,092 (33.0%)	107,983 (54.8%)
	House	94,182 (47.5%)	99,879 (50.4%)
1990	Senate	35,408 (27.8%)	91,827 (72.2%)
	Governor	28,308 (22.1%)	99,527 (77.9%)
1988	President	54,707 (32.3%)	114,651 (67.7%)
1986	Senate	76,428 (60.2%)	50,582 (39.8%)
	Governor	55,500 (42.4%)	75,366 (57.6%)

Vote for Perot was 24,136 (12.2%).

Demographics

Population 581,113

Percent change from 1980 11.6%

Land area 2,186 square miles

Population per square mile 266

Counties, 1990 population

Greenville 320,167	Spartanburg 226,800
Laurens (pt.) 3,809	Union 30,337

Cities, 1990 population (10,000 or more)

Berea CDP 13,535	Simpsonville 11,708
Gantt CDP 13,891	Spartanburg 43,467
Greenville 58,282	Taylors CDP 19,619
Greer 10,322	Wade Hampton CDP
Mauldin 11,587	20,014
Parker CDP 11,072	

Race and Hispanic origin

White 79.3%
Black 19.7%
American Indian, Eskimo, or Aleut. 0.1%
Asian or Pacific Islander 0.7%
Other 0.2%
Hispanic origin 0.8%

Ancestry

American 11.5%	Irish 16.8%
Dutch 2.1%	Italian 1.6%
English 15.8%	Scotch Irish 5.3%
French 2.4%	Scottish 2.7%
German 14.1%	

Universities/colleges, 1990-1991 enrollment

Bob Jones University, Greenville 4,281
Converse College, Spartanburg 1,134
Furman University, Greenville 3,312
Greenville Technical College, Greenville 7,917
North Greenville College, Tigerville 392
Spartanburg Methodist College, Spartanburg 932
Spartanburg Technical College, Spartanburg 2,276
University of South Carolina, Spartanburg 3,501
University of South Carolina, Union 368
Wofford College, Spartanburg 1,066

Newspapers, total circulation (in all districts)

Greenville News Greenville Peidmont 117,320
Spartanburg Herald-Journal 62,834

Commercial television stations, affiliations

ADI: Greenville-Spartanburg-Asheville (100%)
WAXA, Anderson (None)
WGGS-TV, Greenville (None)
WYFF-TV, Greenville (NBC)
WSPA-TV, Spartanburg (CBS)

Cable television systems, total subscribers

Cencom of South Carolina; Gray Court 17,550
Teleable of Greenville Inc.; Greenville 57,239
Teleable of Spartanburg; Inman 9,172
Teleable of Spartanburg; Spartanburg 27,371

Businesses and other major employers

Greenville Hospital System; Greenville 4,300
Fluor Daniel Inc.; Greenville; building construction 3,600
Spartanburg Regional Medical Center; Spartanburg 3,054
Kemet Electronics Corp.; Greenville; electronic components 3,000
Kemet Electronics Corp.; Simpsonville; electronic components 2,300
General Electric Co.; Greenville; engines/turbines 1,750
I. H. Services Inc.; Greenville; building services 1,650

Hoechst Celanese Corp.; Spartanburg; plastics/synthetics 1,600
Michelin Tire Corp.; Spartanburg; tires 1,500
Springs Industries Inc.; Lyman; textile finishing 1,500
Norfolk Southern Railway Co./Piedmont Div.; Greenville; railroads 1,500
Lockheed Aeromod Center Inc.; Greenville; airport services 1,400
W. R. Grace & Co./Cryovac Div.; Simpsonville; paper products 1,312
Bob Jones University & Barge Memorial Hospital; Greenville 1,300
Milliken & Co.; Spartanburg; apparel 1,200
St. Francis Hospital Inc.; Greenville 1,200
Cone Mills Corp.; Carlisle; textile finishing/dyeing 1,097
Digital Equipment Corp.; Greenville; electronic components 1,000
Hoechst Celanese Corp./Polyester Film Products; Greer; plastics products 1,000
Bi-Lo Inc.; Mauldin; grocery stores 1,000
Winn-Dixie Greenville Inc.; Greenville; grocery stores 1,000
City of Spartanburg/School District; Spartanburg 1,000
CRSS Inc.; Greenville; engineering/architectural services 975
Mary Black Memorial Hospital; Spartanburg 900
Greenville Technical College; Greenville 900
Bibb Co. Inc.; Greenville; cotton mills 850
County of Greenville; Greenville 850
W. R. Grace & Co./Cryovac Div.; Duncan; plastics products 809
MEMC Electronic Materials; Moore; mineral products 800
Mayfair Mills Inc.; Arcadia; cotton mills 800
Arrow Automotive Industries/Spartanburg Div.; Spartanburg; electrical engine equipment 800
J. P. Stevens & Co. Inc./Monaghan Plant; Greenville; man-made fabric mills 800
Michelin Tire Corp.; Greenville; tires 750
Kohler Co.; Spartanburg; plumbing fixtures 700
JPS Converter & Industrial Corp.; Greenville; cotton mills 700
Liberty Corp.; Greenville; life insurance 700
County of Spartanburg; Spartanburg 700
Steel Heddle Mfg. Co.; Greenville; textile machinery 692
Furman University; Greenville 690
B. M. G. Music; Duncan; warehousing 650
R. R. Donnelley & Sons Co.; Spartanburg; commercial printing 650
Spartan Mills; Startex; cotton mills 650
Torrington Co./Tyger River Plant; Union; roller bearings 600
United Merchants & Manufacturers Inc./Buffalo Mills; Buffalo; cotton mills 600
Dow Chemical Co./Texize Div.; Mauldin; soaps/cleaners 600
Heckler Mfg. & Investment Group; Mauldin; undergarments 600
Phillips Fibers Corp.; Spartanburg; plastics/synthetics 600
Spartanburg Steel Products; Spartanburg; metal forgings/stampings 600
Michelin Americas Research & Development Corp.; Greenville; commercial research services 600
Lockwood Greene Engineers Inc.; Spartanburg; engineering services 600
Kemet Electronics Corp.; Fountain Inn; electronic components 576
Tietex Corp.; Spartanburg; textile goods 543
Inman Holding Co.; Inman; cotton mills 504

5th District

North Central — Rock Hill

Touching on four distinct regions of South Carolina, the 5th extends from the hills of Cherokee County south to the low country around Sumter. To command a districtwide media presence, a candidate has to buy time in four cities outside the district—Greenville, Columbia, Florence and Charlotte, N.C.

This geographic diversity makes it difficult to pigeonhole the district's personality. In the west, rural counties such as Newberry, Chester, Lancaster and Kershaw produce cotton for the textile mills that have historically dominated this region's economy. The small but growing cities of Rock Hill and Sumter add urbane, progressive immigrants from the North to the population mix. In the east, residents of Chesterfield, Dillon and Marlboro counties depend heavily on tobacco farming.

Linking the two rural parts of the district is their common struggle with declining economies. About 20 percent of the tobacco-producing counties live in poverty, and modernization has stripped many mills in the west of their plentiful, low-skill jobs.

To the north, the city of Rock Hill provides population and suburban affluence to the district. Once heavily textile-dependent, county residents now gravitate north toward white-collar jobs in Charlotte. In fact, the area's biggest challenge may be to avoid surrendering its identity to Charlotte's yuppie hordes, who stream down I-77 searching for bedroom communities. Native industry here still includes textile mills; many have converted from weaving cotton to producing high-tech fibers for industrial uses.

Rock Hill grew modestly during the 1980s, but is anticipating faster growth in the 1990s. A pending settlement in the Catawba Indians' claim to 144,000 acres in two counties—which stymied investment as buyers worried about a proposed lawsuit against 62,000 individual landowners—is expected to unleash a pent-up drive for development.

By and large, the district remains true to its Democratic roots, with most mill and agricultural workers inheriting ideological proclivities from their parents and grandparents. The Democratic House incumbent won all the district's counties in 1992.

In national elections, increasing affluence has persuaded some areas to abandon their Democratic heritage. In 1992 Bush reaped 49 percent of the vote in York County, down from his 65 percent showing in 1988 but still a respectable draw in the three-way presidential race.

York County's days as a hotbed of religious conservatism have been fading, however, since television evangelist Jim Bakker's downfall and incarceration forced him to abandon his PTL headquarters in Fort Mill; some of Bakker's supporters have moved elsewhere.

Other conservative votes in the district come from the counties of Sumter (home of Shaw Air Force Base) and Kershaw.

Election Returns

	5th District	Democrat	Republican
1992	President*	81,197 (42.6%)	85,971 (45.1%)
	House	112,031 (61.3%)	70,866 (38.7%)
1990	Senate	36,962 (33.1%)	74,800 (66.9%)
	Governor	30,999 (27.3%)	82,539 (72.7%)
1988	President	60,014 (39.4%)	92,170 (60.6%)
1986	Senate	78,532 (68.1%)	36,797 (31.9%)
	Governor	63,841 (53.9%)	54,564 (46.1%)

*Vote for Perot was 23,437 (12.3%).

Demographics

Population 581,131

Percent change from 1980 11.8%

Land area 6,830 square miles

Population per square mile 85

Counties, 1990 population

Cherokee 44,506	Lancaster 54,516
Chester 32,170	Lee (pt.) 10,660
Chesterfield 38,577	Marlboro 29,361
Darlington (pt.) 49,589	Newberry 33,172
Dillon 29,114	Sumter (pt.) 62,075
Fairfield 22,295	York 131,497
Kershaw 43,599	

Cities, 1990 population (10,000 or more)

Gaffney 13,145	Rock Hill 41,643
Newberry 10,542	Sumter (pt.) 27,863

Race and Hispanic origin
White 68.2%
Black 30.8%
American Indian, Eskimo, or Aleut. 0.4%
Asian or Pacific Islander 0.4%
Other 0.2%
Hispanic origin 0.6%

Ancestry

American 10.8%	Irish 13.0%
Dutch 1.5%	Italian 1.0%
English 10.3%	Scotch Irish 6.1%
French 1.7%	Scottish 1.9%
German 12.0%	

Universities/colleges, 1990-1991 enrollment
Chesterfield-Marlboro Tech College, Cheraw 852
Coker College, Hartsville 775
Limestone College, Gaffney 1,195
Newberry College, Newberry 709
Sumter Area Technical College, Sumter 1,929
University of South Carolina, Lancaster 984
University of South Carolina, Sumter 1,260
Winthrop College, Rock Hill 5,104
York Technical College, Rock Hill 2,909

Newspapers, total circulation (in all districts)
Charlotte Observer 230,883
Columbia State 134,560
Florence Morning News 31,697
Gastonia Gazette 40,821
Greenville News Greenville Peidmont 117,320
Rock Hill Herald 29,884
Spartanburg Herald-Journal 62,834
Sumter Item 21,187

Commercial television stations, affiliations
   ADI: Charlotte (38%), Columbia (36%), Florence (20%) and
      Greenville-Spartanburg-Asheville (6%)
   WIS-TV, Columbia (NBC)
   WBTW, Florence (CBS)
   WPDE-TV, Florence (ABC)

Cable television systems, total subscribers
   Century Carolina Cable; Hartsville 6,700
   Lancaster Cable; Lancaster 9,641
   Premiere Cable Communications; Gaffney 6,400
   Rock Hill Cable TV; Rock Hill 18,982
   Vision Cable of South Carolina Inc.; Florence 24,781
   Vision Cable of Sumter Inc.; Sumter 19,500

Military installations, 1991
   Shaw Air Force Base, Sumter 6,423

Businesses and other major employers
   Du Pont E. I. De Nemours & Co.; Camden; synthetics 2,900
   Sonoco Products Co./Industrial Products Div.; Hartsville;
      paperboard mills 2,300
   Hoechst Celanese Corp.; Rock Hill; man-made
      fibers/synthetics 1,700
   Stouffer Foods Corp.; Gaffney; preserved fruits/vegetables 1,500
   County of Darlington/School District; Darlington 1,500
   Springs Industries Inc./Grace Finishing Plant; Lancaster; tex-
      tiles 1,300
   Catauba Timber Co.; Catawba; paper mills 1,200
   Duke Power Co./Catawba Nuclear Station; York; heavy
      construction 1,200
   Oscar Mayer Foods Corp./Louis Rich Co.; Newberry; meat
      products 1,100
   Timken Co./Gaffney Bearing Plant; Gaffney; roller
      bearings/parts 1,000
   American Medical Intl./Piedmont Medical Center; Rock Hill
      1,000
   Springs Industries Inc.; Rock Hill; textile finishing 932
   Tuomey Hospital Inc.; Sumter 925
   Winthrop College; Rock Hill 925
   Delta Woodside Industries Inc.; Wallace; knitting mills 800
   Galey & Lord Inc.; Society Hill; cotton mills 750
   Becton Dickinson & Co./Vacutainer Systems Div.; Sumter;
      medical instruments 700
   Duracell Intl. Inc./Duracell USA; Lancaster; batteries 700
   Milliken & Co./Magnolia Finishing Plant Div.; Blacksburg;
      cotton mills 700
   Sara Lee Corp./L'eggs Products; Hartsville; knitting mills 680
   American Fiber & Finishing; Newberry; cotton mills 675
   United Tech Auto Holdings; Bennettsville; motor vehicle
      parts/equipment 650
   A. O. Smith Corp.; McBee; household appliances 650
   Springs Industries Inc.; Chester; cotton mills 650
   County of Fairfield/School District; Winnsboro 650
   Carolina Golden Products; Sumter; poultry/eggs 600
   South Carolina Electric & Gas Co./Summer Nuclear Project;
      Jenkinsville; utility services 600
   Mohawk Carpet Corp./Dixiana Mill; Dillon; yarn/thread
      mills 600
   Carolina Power & Light Co./Robinson Electric Plant;
      Hartsville; electric services 550
   INA Bearing Co. Inc.; Cheraw; roller bearings/parts 550
   Kershaw County Memorial Hospital; Camden 530
   County of Darlington/School District; Darlington 514

6th District

*Central and South — Florence; Parts of Columbia and
Charleston*

After drawing a 6th District with more nooks and crannies
than an English muffin, mapmakers sat back and watched it
perform as expected in 1992, electing South Carolina's first black
representative this century. Creating the majority-minority 6th
required radical surgery during redistricting, with planners shear-
ing off white and increasingly Republican Horry County and
moving the bulk of the district south and inland to increase its
black population.

The redrawn district is a fearsome piece of political real
estate: Sprawling over all or part of 16 counties in eastern South
Carolina, it encompasses land from the North Carolina border
down to the beaches south of Charleston.

Along the way, district lines reach out to slice black precincts
from Columbia and Charleston, cutting through the downtowns
of both. Overall, the black population exceeds 60 percent,
although blacks make up 58 percent of registered voters.

South Carolina's first black-majority district is also its most
poverty-ridden. Of the six poorest counties in the state, five are
within Clyburn's jurisdiction. The counties of Lee, Bamberg,
Marion and Williamsburg are losing population as residents
leave farms or abandoned textile mills. For those who stay in
these rural areas, agriculture remains an important part of life.

Urban poverty brings its own problems in parts of Columbia
and Charleston; nearly one in three families earned less than
$13,000 in 1989. And in both urban and rural areas, blacks bear
the brunt of the poverty. The average white in most counties
earns more than $7,000 more annually than the average black.

Many residents of the 6th work outside the district. Richland
County residents commute to state government jobs in Columbia, which provides more than 30,000 jobs. Neighboring military
installations also breathe life into the district economy, including
Charleston Naval Base in the 1st, Shaw Air Force Base in the 5th
and Fort Jackson in the 2nd. Shaw and Fort Jackson seem safe
from military closures, but the naval base is slated to lose about
16,000 jobs in the next round of military downsizing.

The city of Florence, with 30,000 residents, provides the
largest complete population center within the district, and has
become a magnet for northern investment in recent years.
Hoffman-LaRoche, a major pharmaceutical company, recently
relocated its research and development facility here, and area
textile mills turn out high-tech synthetic fibers.

Not surprising given its demographics, the 6th supports
Democrats on every level; Bill Clinton won here in 1992, and six
of the 12 South Carolina counties that voted for Michael S.
Dukakis in 1988 are in the district. Republican strength in the 6th
lies in suburban areas surrounding the cities of Columbia and
Charleston, as well as in Florence.

Election Returns

	6th District	Democrat	Republican
1992	President*	118,394 (62.1%)	59,799 (31.4%)
	House	120,647 (65.3%)	64,149 (34.7%)
1990	Senate	62,743 (49.4%)	64,263 (50.6%)
	Governor	63,468 (48.4%)	67,606 (51.6%)

6th District		Democrat	Republican
1988	President	97,137 (59.7%)	65,471 (40.3%)
1986	Senate	101,870 (74.2%)	35,477 (25.8%)
	Governor	88,818 (62.8%)	52,526 (37.2%)

Vote for Perot was 12,322 (6.5%).

Demographics

Population 581,119

Percent change from 1980 11.9%

Land area 7,337 square miles

Population per square mile 79

Counties, 1990 population

Bamberg 16,902	Dorchester (pt.) 13,004
Beaufort (pt.) 3,194	Florence 114,344
Berkeley (pt.) 18,582	Lee (pt.) 7,777
Calhoun (pt.) 3,294	Marion 33,899
Charleston (pt.) 84,519	Orangeburg (pt.) 49,722
Clarendon 28,450	Richland (pt.) 97,374
Colleton (pt.) 20,419	Sumter (pt.) 40,562
Darlington (pt.) 12,262	Williamsburg 36,815

Cities, 1990 population (10,000 or more)

Charleston (pt.) 31,198	North Charleston (pt.)
Columbia (pt.) 44,935	15,894
Florence 29,813	Sumter (pt.) 14,080

Race and Hispanic origin
White 37.3%
Black 62.2%
American Indian, Eskimo, or Aleut. 0.2%
Asian or Pacific Islander 0.3%
Other 0.2%
Hispanic origin 0.6%

Ancestry

American 8.3%	German 6.4%
English 6.2%	Irish 6.3%
French 1.3%	Scotch Irish 2.5%

Universities/colleges, 1990-1991 enrollment
Allen University, Columbia 233
Benedict College, Columbia 1,478
Columbia College, Columbia 1,190
Columbia College of Business, Columbia 427
Denmark Technical College, Denmark 617
Florence-Darlington Tech College, Florence 2,324
Francis Marion College, Florence 3,886
Morris College, Sumter 760
Orangeburg Calhoun Tech College, Orangeburg 1,504
Voorhees College, Denmark 566
Williamsburg Tech College, Kingstree 503

Newspapers, total circulation (in all districts)
Beaufort Gazette 9,318
Charleston Post & Courier 111,622
Columbia State 134,560
Florence Morning News 31,697
Orangeburg Times & Democrat 17,222
Sumter Item 21,187

Commercial television stations, affiliations
ADI: Charleston (41%), Columbia (33%), Florence (18%), Augusta (5%) and Savannah (2%)
WACH, Columbia (None)
WOLO-TV, Columbia (ABC)

Cable television systems, total subscribers
CVI; Columbia 33,264
Cablevision of Columbia; Columbia 44,820
Jones Intercable Inc.; Orangeburg 10,200
Storer Cable of Carolina Inc.; North Charleston 73,000
Vision Cable of South Carolina Inc.; Florence 24,781
Vision Cable of Sumter Inc.; Sumter 19,500

Businesses and other major employers
Southern Bell Telephone & Telegraph Co.; Columbia; telephone communications 5,000
County of Richland/Public School System; Columbia 3,068
Richland Memorial Hospital; Columbia 3,000
South Carolina Baptist Hospitals; Columbia 2,200
McLeod Regional Medical Center; Florence 2,000
Wellman Inc.; Johnsonville; textile goods 1,700
City of Columbia; Columbia 1,600
City of Florence/School District; Florence 1,500
State of South Carolina/Highway & Public Transportation Dept.; Columbia 1,300
Caloric Corp.; Florence; household appliances 1,200
South Carolina National Bank; Columbia; commercial banks 1,200
South Carolina Electric & Gas Co.; Columbia; electric services 1,150
ESAB Welding Products Inc.; Florence; metalworking machinery 1,100
Blue Cross/Blue Shield of South Carolina; Columbia; medical service/health insurance 1,100
County of Richland; Columbia 1,043
NCNB National Bank South Carolina; Columbia; commercial banks 1,000
Citizens & Southern National Bank of South Carolina; Columbia; commercial banks 1,000
Regional Medical Center; Orangeburg 1,000
South Carolina State Guard/Olympia Armory; Columbia 964
U.S. Postal Service; Columbia 950
State of South Carolina/Health Dept.; Columbia 950
Cummins Engine Co. Inc.; Charleston; engines/turbines 850
Santee Print Works Inc.; Sumter; textile finishing 850
Ambler Industries Inc.; Orangeburg; men's suits/coats 800
Union Camp Corp.; Eastover; paper mills 800
Bruce Hospital System; Florence 780
Dart Industries Inc./Tupperware; Hemingway; household plastic products 750
Anchor Continental Inc.; Columbia; paper products 750
State of South Carolina/Tax Dept.; Columbia 750
Sara Lee Corp./Sara Lee Hosiery; Marion; knitting mills 730
Korn Industries Inc./Sumter Cabinet Co.; Sumter; furniture 715
Du Pont E. I. De Nemours & Co.; Florence; plastics products 712
James River Corp. Virginia/Dixie Products; Darlington; paper mills 700
Allied-Signal Inc./Bendix Automotive Systems; Sumter; motor vehicle parts/equipment 700

McGregor Corp./Anvil Knitwear Div.; Mullins; outerwear 650

Baxter Healthcare Corp./Medical Products Div.; Kingstree; medical instruments/supplies 650

State-Record Co. Inc.; Columbia; newspapers 650

Evening Post Publishing Co./Post & Courier; Charleston; newspapers 600

Springs Industries Inc./M. Lowenstein Corp.; Columbia; textile finishing 600

State of South Carolina/Employment Security Commission; Columbia 600

Cooper Industries Inc./Crescent Div.; Sumter; handtools 580

Stone Container Corp.; Florence; paperboard mills 560

Bruce Seibels Group Inc.; Columbia; insurance services 560

State of South Carolina/Hall Psychiatric Institute; Columbia 551

Sara Lee Corp./L'eggs Products; Florence; knitting mills 550

Fiber Industries Inc./Celanese-Palmetto Plant; Darlington; synthetics 550

Klear Knit Inc.; Florence; apparel 535

Fleet Real Estate Funding; Florence; mortgage bankers 535

PYA Monarch Inc.; Charleston; grocery products 521

RM Engineered Products Inc.; Charleston; plastics 520

SOUTH DAKOTA

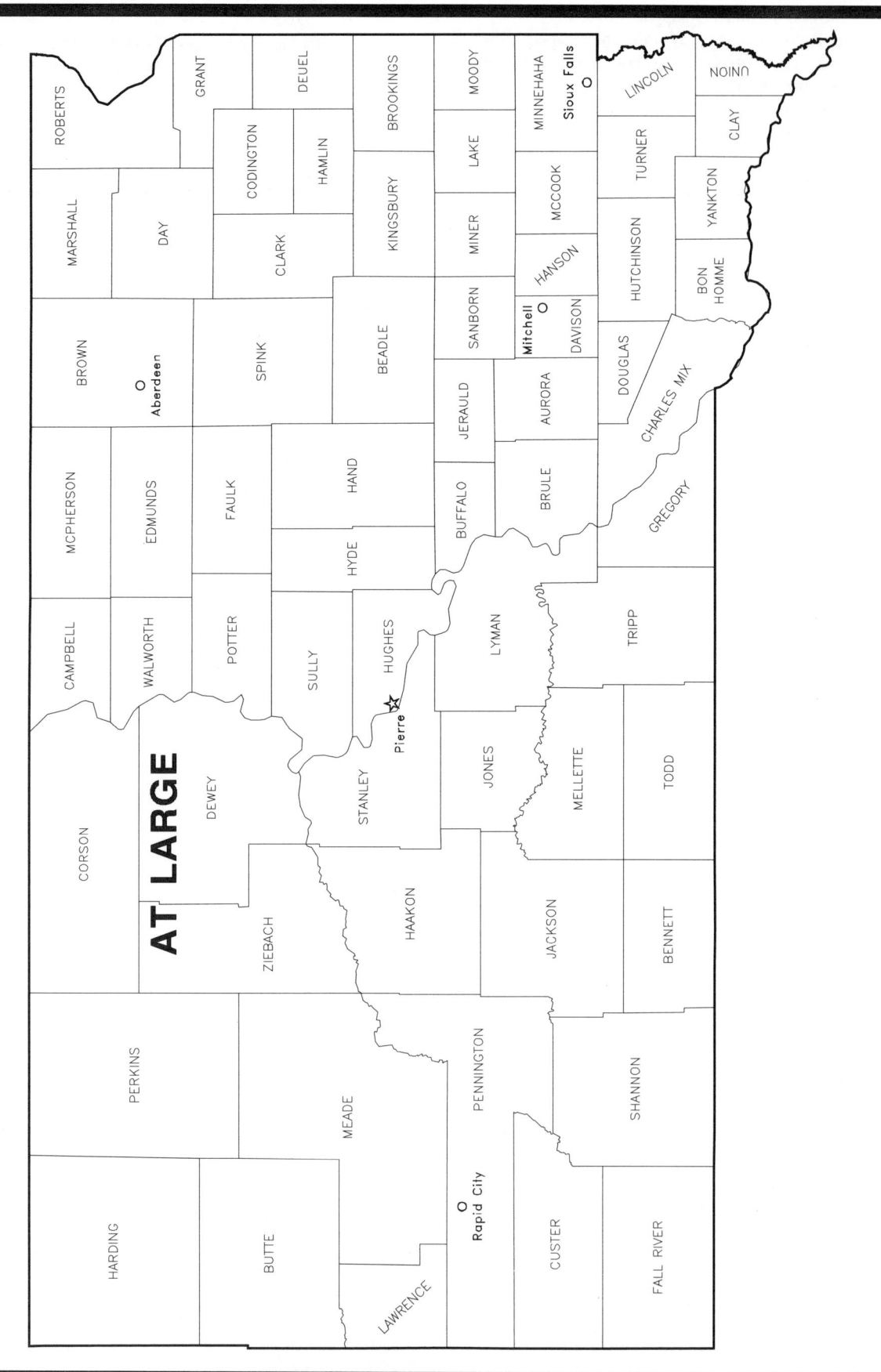

South Dakota

The contrasts of beauty and poverty in South Dakota are striking. Its varied and breathtaking landscape, with stark mountains, desert canyons and sweeping farmland and grassland, has helped make tourism the second-largest industry.

But the violent battles that raged a century ago between white settlers and American Indians have left a terrible legacy. On South Dakota's numerous Indian reservations, unemployment and poverty are rife: More than half the people live below the poverty level; nearly one-quarter of the work force is jobless. Shannon County, home to the Pine Ridge Indian Reservation, has a poverty rate of 63 percent, the highest in the nation.

Wounded Knee is located in Shannon County; in 1890, 250 Sioux were massacred there in one day, after their chief, Sitting Bull, had been killed.

State lawmakers declared 1990 a Year of Reconciliation, and Gov. George Mickelson invited tribal representatives to the Capitol rotunda to talk about change. The state has renamed Columbus Day, calling it Native American Day, and state officials drafted an elementary and high school curriculum to include Indian studies. South Dakota ranks 45th in terms of population among the 50 states, but it has the fourth-highest percentage of Indians in its population.

The Missouri River, running north to south through the center of South Dakota, divides not only the geography and economy of the state, but also its political predilections.

The flat, rich farmland east of the river holds two-thirds of the state's population and nourishes an agricultural economy based on corn and soybeans. Voters in the east tend to support Democrats. "West River" is rolling, arid grassland suited for grazing and ranching. Mining, including gold mining, is also a feature of the western mountains. Most western voters are Republicans.

Ronald Reagan carried South Dakota for president in 1980 with 61 percent of the vote, and he improved to 63 percent in 1984, but disenchantment with GOP farm policy began to set in mid-decade, and when George Bush sought the White House in 1988, he managed just 53 percent against Michael S. Dukakis. In 1992, support for indpendent presidential candidate Ross Perot cut into both major-party nominees: Bush dropped to 41 percent, but he beat Bill Clinton, who got 37 percent. Perot won 22 percent.

Corn's primacy in South Dakota's economy is symbolized by the Corn Palace in Mitchell, an auditorium whose exterior is festooned with mosaics made from colored cobs.

Not far from Mitchell is the focal point of eastern South Dakota and the state's largest metropolis, Sioux Falls (Minnehaha County). The city grew 24 percent in the 1980s, to about 101,000, as it made the transition from meatpacking town to regional commerce hub. Though meatpacker John Morrell & Co. is still a major employer, the city has become a service center whose banks, insurance companies, medical facilities and retailers are affected by the health of the agricultural economy, if not entirely dependent on it. In 1992, Clinton won Minnehaha County with 42 percent.

On the western side of the Missouri, the towns are fewer, and there is still something of the old Wild West feel. Much of the majestic, high plains scenery in the 1990 Academy Award-winning film *Dances with Wolves* was shot here.

Near the western border of the state is South Dakota's second-largest city, Rapid City (Pennington County), with a population of more than 54,000. Originally a market for surrounding ranchers and farmers, it has prospered in recent years partly thanks to tourism: The Badlands, the Black Hills and Mount Rushmore are nearby.

In neighboring Lawrence County, legalized gambling has helped rejuvenate the town of Deadwood, once a gold-mining boom town. Calamity Jane and Wild Bill Hickok are buried at Mount Moriah Cemetery in Deadwood.

Bush won Pennington County with 48 percent of the vote in 1992, and he carried every other county west of the Missouri except three—all of them dominated by votes from Native American reservations.

Table 1   Population

District	Population	Population under 18	Voting-age population	Median age
AL	696,004	198,462	497,542	32.5

Table 2   Voting-Age Persons

District	White*	Black*	American Indian, Eskimo, or Aleut*	Asian or Pacific Islander*	Other*	Hispanic*	Male*	Female*
AL	93.6%	0.4%	5.4%	0.4%	0.2%	0.6%	48.4%	51.6%

As percent of voting-age population.

Table 3   Voting-Age Persons by Age Groups

District	18-24*	25-44*	45-54*	55-64*	65 and over*
AL	13.7%	41.1%	12.6%	12.0%	20.6

As percent of voting-age population.

Table 4   Income and Occupation

District	Median family income	Families in poverty	White collar*	Blue collar*	Service*	Farm*
AL	$27,602	11.6%	49.8%	23.4%	15.4%	11.3%

As percent of employed persons age 16 and over.

Table 5   Education: School Years Completed

District	Less than grade 9*	Grades 9-12 no diploma*	High school diploma*	College bachelor's degree or higher*
AL	13.4%	9.5%	33.7%	17.2%

As percent of persons age 25 and over.

Table 6   Housing and Residential Patterns

District	Owner occupied	Renter occupied	Urban	Rural
AL	66.1%	33.9%	50.0%	50.0%

Election Returns

		Democrat	Republican
	At Large		
1992	President*	124,888 (37.3%)	136,718 (40.8%)
	House	230,070 (69.1%)	89,375 (26.8%)
1990	Senate	116,727 (46.2%)	135,682 (53.8%)
	Governor	105,525 (41.1%)	151,198 (58.9%)
1988	President	145,560 (46.8%)	165,415 (53.2%)
1986	Senate	152,657 (51.6%)	143,173 (48.4%)
	Governor	141,898 (48.2%)	152,543 (51.8%)

Vote for Perot was 73,295 (21.9%).

Demographics

Population 696,004

Percent change from 1980 0.8%

Land area 75,896 square miles

Population per square mile 9

Counties, 1990 population

Aurora 3,135
Beadle 18,253
Bennett 3,206
Bon Homme 7,089

Brookings 25,207
Brown 35,580
Brule 5,485
Buffalo 1,759
Butte 7,914
Campbell 1,965
Charles Mix 9,131
Clark 4,403
Clay 13,186
Codington 22,698
Corson 4,195
Custer 6,179
Davison 17,503
Day 6,978
Deuel 4,522
Dewey 5,523
Douglas 3,746
Edmunds 4,356
Fall River 7,353
Faulk 2,744
Grant 8,372
Gregory 5,359
Haakon 2,624
Hamlin 4,974
Hand 4,272
Hanson 2,994
Harding 1,669
Hughes 14,817
Hutchinson 8,262
Hyde 1,696
Jackson 2,811
Jerauld 2,425
Jones 1,324
Kingsbury 5,925
Lake 10,550
Lawrence 20,655
Lincoln 15,427
Lyman 3,638
Marshall 4,844
McCook 5,688
McPherson 3,228
Meade 21,878
Mellette 2,137
Miner 3,272
Minnehaha 123,809
Moody 6,507
Pennington 81,343
Perkins 3,932
Potter 3,190
Roberts 9,914
Sanborn 2,833
Shannon 9,902
Spink 7,981
Stanley 2,453
Sully 1,589
Todd 8,352
Tripp 6,924
Turner 8,576
Union 10,189
Walworth 6,087
Yankton 19,252
Ziebach 2,220

Cities, 1990 population (10,000 or more)

Aberdeen 24,927
Brookings 16,270
Huron 12,448
Mitchell 13,798
Pierre 12,906
Rapid City 54,523
Sioux Falls 100,814
Vermillion 10,034
Watertown 17,592
Yankton 12,703

Race and Hispanic origin

White 91.6%
Black 0.5%
American Indian, Eskimo, or Aleut. 7.3%
Asian or Pacific Islander 0.4%
Other 0.2%
Hispanic origin 0.8%

Ancestry

American 1.8%
Czechoslovakian 2.9%
Danish 3.4%
Dutch 5.3%
English 9.8%
French 3.5%
German 51.0%
Irish 12.6%
Norwegian 15.3%
Polish 1.3%
Russian 1.1%
Scotch Irish 1.4%
Scottish 1.2%
Swedish 4.8%

Universities/colleges, 1990-1991 enrollment

Augustana College, Sioux Falls 2,113
Black Hills State University, Spearfish 2,545
Dakota State University, Madison 1,303
Dakota Wesleyan University, Mitchell 706
Huron University, Huron 424
Kilian Community College, Sioux Falls 249
Mount Marty College, Yankton 947

National College, Rapid City 722
National College, Sioux Falls 282
Northern State University, Aberdeen 3,346
Oglala Lakota College, Kyle 757
Presentation College, Aberdeen 588
Sinte Gleska College, Rosebud 494
Sioux Falls College, Sioux Falls 937
South Dakota School of Mines & Technology, Rapid City 2,323
South Dakota State University, Brookings 8,551
University of South Dakota, Vermillion 7,627

Newspapers, total circulation (in all districts)

Aberdeen American News 18,275
Brookings Daily Register 4,882
Huron Plainsman 10,286
Mitchell Daily Republic 12,048
Rapid City Journal 32,666
Sioux City Journal 48,301
Sioux Falls Argus Leader 48,044
Watertown Public Opinion 15,079

Commercial television stations, affiliations

ADI: Sioux Falls-Mitchell (56%), Rapid City (31%), Minot-Bismarck-Dickinson (11%) and Sioux City (1%)
KABY-TV, Aberdeen (ABC)
KDLO-TV, Florence (CBS)
KTTM, Huron (Fox)
KHSD-TV, Lead (ABC)
KIVV-TV, Lead (NBC)
KDLT, Mitchell-Sioux Falls (NBC)
KPRY-TV, Pierre (ABC)
KCLO-TV, Rapid City (CBS)
KEVN-TV, Rapid City (NBC)
KOTA-TV, Rapid City (ABC)
KPLO-TV, Reliance (CBS)
KELO-TV, Sioux Falls (CBS)
KSFY-TV, Sioux Falls (ABC)
KTTW, Sioux Falls (Fox)

Cable television systems, total subscribers

Brookings Cablevision; Brookings 5,020
Midcontinent Cable; Aberdeen 9,260
Sooland Cablecom Corp.; Sioux City 20,197
TCI of South Dakota; Rapid City 16,275
TCI of South Dakota; Sioux Falls 26,800
Watertown Cable TV Co.; Watertown 6,500

Military installations, 1991

Ellsworth Air Force Base, Box Elder 7,191
Joe Foss Field Air Force Guard Station, Sioux Falls 298

Businesses and other major employers

State of South Dakota/Higher Education Commission; Pierre 4,616
Sioux Valley Hospital Assn./Sioux Valley Hospital; Sioux Falls 2,900
Citibank South Dakota; Sioux Falls; commercial banks 2,800
John Morrell & Co. Inc.; Sioux Falls; meatpacking 2,600
Presentation Sisters Inc./McKennan Hospital; Sioux Falls 2,100
Rapid City Regional Hospital; Rapid City 1,545
University of South Dakota; Vermillion 1,500
South Dakota State University; Brookings 1,500
Homestake Mining Co.; Lead; gold/silver ores 1,296
Gateway Two Thousand; North Sioux City; computer stores 1,050
St. Luke's Midland Regional Medical Center; Aberdeen 1,000
Nash-Finch Co.; Rapid City; groceries 1,000
Hutchinson Technology Inc.; Sioux Falls; computer equipment 750
U.S. Health & Human Services Dept.; Sioux Falls 750
City of Sioux Falls; Sioux Falls 735
State of South Dakota/Human Services Dept.; Yankton 671
Minnesota Mining & Mfg. Co.; Brookings; pharmaceuticals 650
SCI Systems Inc.; Rapid City; electronic components 650
State of South Dakota/Development Center; Redfield 609
Sears Roebuck & Co.; Sioux Falls; credit institutions 600
U.S. Veterans Affairs Dept.; Hot Springs; hospital 550
Mount Marty Hospital Assn./Sacred Heart Hospital; Yankton 539
Oglala Sioux Tribe Pine Ridge Reservation; Pine Ridge 520

TENNESSEE

Districts Established May 7, 1992

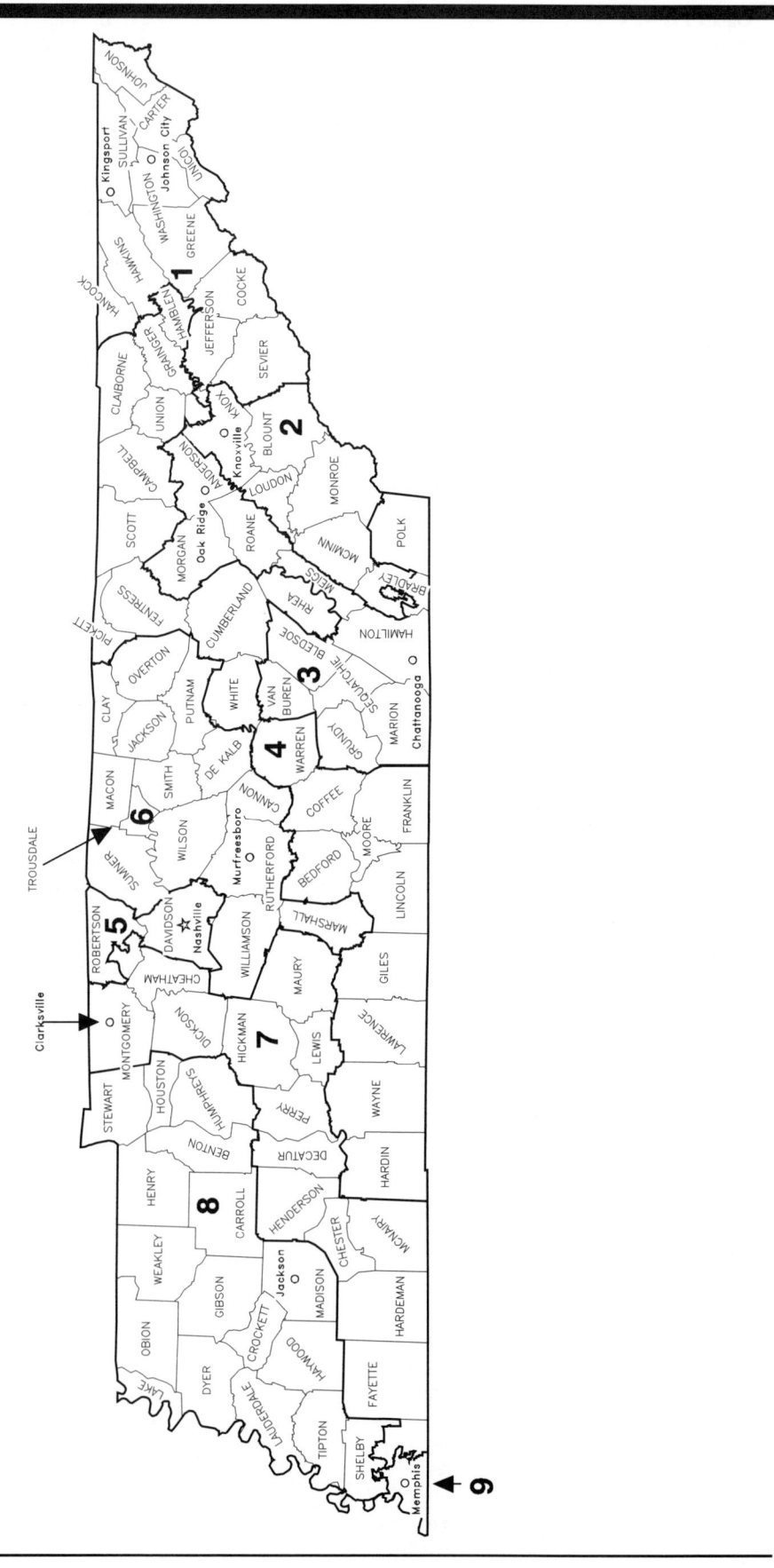

Tennessee

The 1992 presidential election highlighted the strong competing strains in Tennessee's political personality. The Democrats' national ticket looked like a hand-in-glove fit for the Volunteer State: Vice-presidential nominee Al Gore was the state's hugely popular junior senator, and top man Bill Clinton hailed from next-door Arkansas. Yet Clinton and Gore carried the state by fewer than 5 percentage points.

The contest was close for two reasons—one that traces back more than 130 years to the Civil War, and a second rooted in recent demographic changes that have enhanced the clout of suburban areas. Both factors combine to make GOP candidates very competitive in Tennessee's presidential elections and in many contests for statewide office.

Democrats have always been the dominant party in Tennessee; this was the home of populist President Andrew Jackson. But the Civil War gave birth to a Republican Party in Tennessee that down through the years has been a significant minority voice in politics.

The traditional base of the state's GOP is east Tennessee, where during the Civil War era the region's small-scale farmers in the highland valleys of Appalachia had nothing in common with west Tennessee, a province of "King Cotton" and slavery. Even though Tennessee seceded and joined the Confederacy, most of east Tennessee stayed loyal to the Union and Republican president Abraham Lincoln, and voters there have tilted to the GOP ever since. No Democrat has ever held the Knoxville-based 2nd District.

In the past quarter-century, the base of the GOP in Tennessee has broadened, thanks largely to suburban growth outside the state's two largest cities, Memphis and Nashville. The votes from upscale white-collar residents there, combined with those from the GOP east, were responsible for electing Tennessee's first modern-day Republican governor in 1972.

At one point in the early 1970s, the GOP held both of Tennessee's Senate seats, the governorship and five of the state's eight U.S. House seats. But the tide began to turn when Jimmy Carter carried the state decisively in 1976; he gave the national party a southern accent that lured back many centrist Tennessee Democrats who had strayed.

New-generation Democratic politicians, such as Sen. Jim Sasser and Gore, reestablished the party's traditionally dominant role in Tennessee's state and congressional politics during the 1980s. Since 1982 (when Tennessee moved up to nine House seats), Democrats have held a 6-to-3 advantage in their House delegation. The liberal image of the national Democratic Party helped the GOP carry Tennessee for president in 1980, 1984 and 1988, but in races for other major offices, Democrats usually held together a coalition that included rural and small-town whites in middle and west Tennessee, unionized workers across the state, urban white liberals and blacks, who make up 16 percent of Tennessee's population.

Tennessee's overall population grew by a modest six percent in the 1980s, and the state held steady at nine House seats in 1990 reapportionment. But among the districts there were some significant differences in population trends. The state's lone black-majority seat, the Memphis-based 9th, saw a 9 percent population decline between 1980 and 1990. By contrast, the population rose in the neighboring GOP-held 7th District by 25 percent; the 7th is anchored in Memphis' suburbs but stretches eastward almost to Nashville. The Democratic-leaning middle Tennessee 6th District saw a 19 percent population increase, due to expansion of Nashville suburbs in Williamson County and the influence of huge new vehicle-assembly plants run by Japan's Nissan (in Rutherford County) and GM's Saturn (in Maury County).

In 1992 redistricting, the Democrats—who controlled the governorship and the Legislature—made a few moves aimed at enhancing their partisan advantage. They tried to shake up GOP Rep. Don Sundquist, by cutting 100,000 GOP-leaning Memphis suburbanites from his 7th District and altering his mix of rural counties. He handily won re-election anyway in 1992.

Meanwhile, Democratic incumbents largely were accommodated. Mapmakers removed Republicans and added Democrats to the Chattanooga-based 3rd District to shore up a vulnerable Democratic incumbent (who held on to win with 49 percent of the vote in 1992).

For the first time the 9th District was expanded beyond the city limits of Memphis, but its black population held almost steady at 59 percent. The other west Tennessee district, the 8th, added some Memphis-area GOP turf but remained essentially a rural Democratic bulwark.

Middle Tennessee Democrats in the 4th, 5th and 6th districts saw fairly minor changes in the political complexion of their constituencies. The 4th, already a serpentine creature taking in eastern as well as central Tennessee counties, was expanded west and east. The 6th dropped Maury County, but it retained Republican Williamson County.

The remap did not alter the staunchly Republican character of the 2nd District or the upper east Tennessee 1st District.

The new map passed in the state House on May 6, 1992, by a 72-22 vote, and the state Senate approved it 21-10; Gov. Ned McWherter signed it into law May 7.

Table 1   Population

District	Population	Population under 18	Voting-age population	Median age
1	541,875	122,981	418,894	36.0
2	541,864	125,089	416,775	34.2
3	541,866	131,671	410,195	35.0
4	541,868	136,109	405,759	35.0
5	541,910	125,363	416,547	32.6
6	541,977	142,853	399,124	33.0
7	541,937	145,164	396,773	32.2
8	541,907	139,768	402,139	33.5
9	541,981	147,606	394,375	31.4
State	4,877,185	1,216,604	3,660,581	33.6

Table 2   Voting-Age Persons

District	White*	Black*	American Indian, Eskimo, or Aleut*	Asian or Pacific Islander*	Other*	Hispanic*	Male*	Female*
1	97.7%	1.8%	0.2%	0.2%	0.1%	0.3%	47.5%	52.5%
2	93.0	6.0	0.2	0.7	0.1	0.5	47.0	53.0
3	88.5	10.5	0.2	0.6	0.2	0.6	46.8	53.2
4	96.0	3.5	0.2	0.2	0.1	0.4	47.5	52.5
5	77.7	20.6	0.2	1.2	0.3	0.8	46.5	53.5
6	93.7	5.4	0.2	0.6	0.1	0.5	48.1	51.9
7	87.1	11.5	0.2	0.8	0.3	1.0	48.4	51.6
8	81.8	17.4	0.2	0.4	0.2	0.6	47.3	52.7
9	44.9	54.1	0.2	0.7	0.2	0.7	45.0	55.0
State	84.7	14.4	0.2	0.6	0.2	0.6	47.1	52.9

*As percent of voting-age population.

Table 3   Voting-Age Persons by Age Groups

District	18-24*	25-44*	45-54*	55-64*	65 and over*
1	13.6%	39.3%	15.8%	13.1%	18.1%
2	15.2	41.7	14.4	11.8	16.9
3	13.3	40.9	14.9	12.8	18.1
4	13.2	39.0	15.4	13.2	19.2
5	15.0	46.3	12.8	10.8	15.1
6	14.6	44.2	15.4	11.0	14.8
7	14.5	46.4	14.5	10.8	13.8
8	14.9	39.9	14.1	12.1	19.0
9	15.4	44.4	11.9	11.2	17.0
State	14.4	42.4	14.4	11.9	16.9

*As percent of voting-age population.

Table 4   Income and Occupation

District	Median family income	Families in poverty	White collar*	Blue collar*	Service*	Farm*
1	$26,407	12.9%	47.1%	37.7%	12.9%	2.4%
2	30,917	10.8	56.5	29.8	12.1	1.6
3	29,557	12.0	52.6	32.9	12.8	1.8
4	24,532	15.0	39.1	45.6	11.2	4.1
5	34,396	10.0	63.9	21.7	13.3	1.1
6	33,945	8.6	52.9	34.2	10.4	2.5
7	33,405	9.5	57.0	30.2	10.6	2.1
8	27,241	13.3	46.0	38.3	12.6	3.1
9	26,590	19.8	57.3	25.3	16.4	1.0
State	29,546	12.4	52.8	32.6	12.4	2.2

*As percent of employed persons age 16 and over.

Table 5   Education: School Years Completed

District	Less than grade 9*	Grades 9-12 no diploma*	High school diploma*	College bachelor's degree or higher*
1	20.8%	17.4%	31.2%	12.7%
2	14.5	15.5	28.9	19.3
3	15.9	16.6	29.4	16.0
4	24.7	18.9	32.3	9.0
5	8.8	16.1	27.6	23.3
6	16.4	15.4	30.4	17.2
7	12.8	14.7	30.0	18.6
8	17.9	19.3	33.1	10.4
9	11.4	19.1	27.4	17.3
State	16.0	17.0	30.0	16.0

*As percent of persons age 25 and over.

Table 6   Housing and Residential Patterns

District	Owner occupied	Renter occupied	Urban	Rural
1	74.6%	25.4%	47.4%	52.6%
2	68.5	31.5	64.1	35.9
3	68.7	31.3	64.7	35.3
4	75.7	24.3	26.0	74.0
5	54.8	45.2	95.3	4.7
6	74.2	25.8	46.1	53.9
7	70.9	29.1	57.1	42.9
8	70.3	29.7	47.6	52.4
9	55.5	44.5	99.8	0.2
State	68.0	32.0	60.9	39.1

1st District

Northeast — Tri-cities

The Tennessee Valley Authority freed this district and much of east Tennessee from the pervasive rural poverty of an earlier era. Isolated highland towns, tobacco patches and livestock clearings were once the norm in the 1st, but small cities have grown up around industries drawn to the area by the availability of TVA power.

However, industry has not changed the 1st's GOP voting habits. For most of the past 70 years, only two people have represented the 1st, both Republicans. In 1992, it did Bill Clinton little good here to put Tennessee Sen. Al Gore on his ticket; George Bush still won by 15 points. Voters are not blindly Republican, though. A majority did vote Democratic in the noncompetitive Senate elections of 1988 and 1990, backing Jim Sasser and Gore.

There are pockets of genuine Democrats, primarily in the Tri-cities area of Kingsport, Bristol and Johnson City. About 45 percent of the district's people live in this extreme northeastern corner of Tennessee, and the area's industrial work force occasionally helps Democrats win local offices. Sporadic support for Democrats, though, should not be construed as liberalism; the union influence remains small, and no Democrat campaigns to the left of moderate.

Whatever Democratic votes can be squeezed out of the Tri-cities, the rural counties in the district usually drown them. Routinely at election time the rural areas deliver the highest GOP tallies in the state: Voters have a deep-seated suspicion of big government and an antipathy toward the Democratic Party dating to their ancestors' Union loyalties during the Civil War.

Economic diversity helped the 1st weather the recent recession without much trouble. The Tri-cities' industrial base includes manufacturers of paper, glass, medical equipment and electronics; employment at major companies such as Eastman Kodak's chemical division in Kingsport has held steady. The Tri-cities have each spent the past few years annexing the land inside the triangle they form, and their borders now abut one another. Regional cooperation is marred by squabbles over which city is responsible for utilities and taxes in borderline industrial parks.

Economic success in the population centers, however, has not brought better times to the entire area. Three counties in the 1st rank among the state's poorest: More than 40 percent of Hancock County's residents live below the poverty line. Farmers raise tobacco, poultry and livestock; there is zinc and limestone mining.

To the south, in Sevier County, a tourism boom pushed the population up 23 percent in the 1980s. Millions every year visit the Great Smoky Mountains National Park, some stopping along the way to take in attractions such as Dollywood, a theme park launched by country music star Dolly Parton. On the edge of the national park, Gatlinburg is chock-full of motels and amusements.

Election Returns

	1st District	Democrat	Republican
1992	President*	75,681 (36.6%)	106,939 (51.7%)
	House	47,809 (28.1%)	114,797 (67.5%)
1990	Senate	48,861 (66.9%)	24,185 (33.1%)
	Governor	45,243 (60.5%)	29,504 (39.5%)
1988	President	55,907 (31.8%)	120,132 (68.2%)
	Senate	95,854 (57.9%)	69,751 (42.1%)
1986	Governor	64,380 (52.8%)	57,644 (47.2%)

*Vote for Perot was 24,230 (11.7%).

Demographics

Population 541,875

Percent change from 1980 5.7%

Land area 4,218 square miles

Population per square mile 128

Counties, 1990 population

Carter 51,505	Hancock 6,739
Cocke 29,141	Hawkins 44,565
Greene 55,853	Jefferson 33,016

Johnson 13,766	Sullivan 143,596
Knox (pt.) 3,787	Unicoi 16,549
Sevier 51,043	Washington 92,315

Cities, 1990 population (10,000 or more)

Bloomingdale CDP 10,953	Greeneville 13,532
Bristol 23,421	Johnson City 49,381
Elizabethton 11,931	Kingsport 36,365

Race and Hispanic origin

White 97.5%
Black 1.9%
American Indian, Eskimo, or Aleut. 0.2%
Asian or Pacific Islander 0.3%
Other 0.1%
Hispanic origin 0.4%

Ancestry

American 16.2%	Irish 18.0%
Dutch 3.8%	Italian 1.2%
English 15.0%	Scotch Irish 4.2%
French 2.1%	Scottish 2.3%
German 18.7%	

Universities/colleges, 1990-1991 enrollment

Bristol College, Bristol 266
Carson-Newman College, Jefferson City 2,109
East Tennessee State University, Johnson City 11,594
King College, Bristol 527
Milligan College, Milligan College 814
Northeast State Tech College, Blountville 2,826
Tusculum College, Greeneville 718

Newspapers, total circulation (in all districts)

Greeneville Sun 14,613
Kingsport Times-News 45,838
Knoxville News-Sentinel Co. 123,125
Johnson City Press 29,962
Herald Courier Virginian/Tennessean 43,627

Commercial television stations, affiliations

ADI: Bristol-Kingsport-Johnson City (63%) and Knoxville (37%)
WCYB-TV, Bristol (NBC)
WJHL-TV, Johnson City (CBS)
WKPT-TV, Kingsport (ABC)

Cable television systems, total subscribers

Sammons Communications Inc.; Bristol 17,300
Sammons Communications Inc.; Johnson City 19,300
Scripps-Howard Cable; Knoxville 76,000
Tennessee Valley Cable; Gray 16,294
Warner Cable Communications Inc.; Kingsport 28,734

Businesses and other major employers

North American Philips Corp./Philips Consumer Electronics; Greeneville; audio/video equipment 2,170
Arcata Graphics; Kingsport; book publishing 2,000
Holston Valley Health Care; Kingsport 2,000
East Tennessee State University; Johnson City 1,986
Johnson City Medical Center; Johnson City 1,960
County of Sullivan/School District; Blountville 1,800
Bristol Regional Medical Center/Bristol Memorial Hospital; Bristol 1,539
Raytheon Co./Missile Systems Div.; Bristol; electronic equipment 1,500

U.S. Veterans Affairs Dept.; Johnson City; hospital 1,400

Kelly Services Inc.; Blountville; personnel supply services 1,260

City of Kingsport; Kingsport 1,200

State of Tennessee/Green Valley Development Center; Greeneville; nursing 1,124

Siemens Corp.; Johnson City; electronic components 1,000

Mead Corp.; Kingsport; paper mills 1,000

County of Sevier; Sevierville 955

Holston Defense Corp./Holston Army Ammunition Plant; Kingsport; explosives/chemical products 950

County of Hawkins; Rogersville 950

Eastman Kodak Co./Tennessee Eastman Co.; Kingsport; chemicals/plastics 900

County of Greene/Board of Education; Greeneville 885

Harvard Industries Inc.; Church Hill; metal forgings/stampings 850

Fluor Daniel Inc.; Kingsport; building construction 821

TRW Inc./Steering Suspension Div.; Rogersville; motor vehicle equipment 800

Hurd Lock & Mfg. Co.; Greeneville; locks 750

Hospital Corp. America/Indian Path Medical Center; Kingsport 750

JPS Converter & Industrial Corp./Borden Plant; Kingsport; man-made fabric mills 739

United Inter-Mountain Telephone Co.; Bristol; telephone communications 726

Nuclear Fuel Services Inc.; Erwin; nuclear fuels 723

New Cherokee Corp./Sevierville Plant; Pigeon Forge; man-made fabric mills 700

Mor-Flo Industries Inc./Tennessee Div.; Johnson City; household appliances 700

Meco Corp.; Greeneville; metal products 700

Arcata Graphics/Kingsport Press; Church Hill; book publishing 652

City of Johnson City/Vocational-Technical School; Johnson City 650

City of Kingsport/School District; Kingsport 650

T. P. I. Corp./Rite-Way; Johnson City; industry machinery 600

Doehler Jarvis Ltd.; Greeneville; metalworking machinery 600

County of Washington/Education Dept.; Jonesborough 600

A&L Industrial Construction & Maintenance Inc.; Kingsport; building construction 565

Quaker Oats Co.; Newport; preserved fruits/vegetables 550

Asarco Inc.; Strawberry Plains; lead/zinc ores 540

Holliston Mills Inc.; Church Hill; textile goods 526

Laughlin Memorial Hospital; Greeneville 520

Levi Strauss & Co.; Mountain City; jeans/outerwear 510

2nd District

East — Knoxville

With a winning tradition dating to the Civil War, the 2nd's GOP defines the word "entrenched." Since the days when parts of this area tried to secede from Tennessee to rejoin the Union, the majority of voters here have remained fixed in their partisan preference. No Democrat has held this House seat since then, and only rarely does one even put up a good fight for it.

The GOP's standard playbook does well in the 2nd: support for a strong defense and frugality in federal spending (especially on welfare programs). Most also endorse the party's current social-issue posture, opposing abortion and objecting to gays in the military.

Residents' conservatism translates into solid margins for GOP presidential candidates. Voters will, however, support popular Democrats in statewide races when the GOP fails to put forward a top-drawer challenger.

Knox County dominates the district, casting nearly 60 percent of its ballots. The city of Knoxville itself (population 165,000) has a sizable Democratic vote: Labor unions have some strength, blacks are a substantial presence in the eastern part of the city and there are some liberal elements in the University of Tennessee community. However, the suburbs of Knox County—predominantly white-collar professionals in the west, with middle-income workers in the south and north—easily deliver the votes to keep Republicans in charge.

Though the typical resident of the 2nd is a critic of "big government," state and federal jobs are a big component of the economy. In addition to hosting the university, Knoxville is headquarters for the Tennessee Valley Authority, and a number of Knox Countians commute to neighboring Anderson County (in the 3rd District) to work at the Oak Ridge National Laboratories and related companies. Manufacturers turn out a range of goods, including boats, mobile homes, electronics and apparel, and Knoxville is headquarters for Whittle Communications, parent company of the Channel One classroom TV station.

The economy of the 2nd also feeds on outsiders' dollars: I-75 and I-40 meet at Knoxville, and visitors passing through "the gateway to the Smokies" put about $377 million into the area economy in 1991. Knoxville is a regional retail and entertainment center: The hordes that throng to UT football and basketball games enrich merchants, innkeepers and restaurateurs for miles around.

South of Knox is Blount County, second-largest in the 2nd. Its economy has long revolved around the Aluminum Co. of America (Alcoa) plant. Nippondenzo, which started production in March 1990, eventually brought slightly more than 1,000 jobs to Blount with the opening of an automotive parts plant, echoing a trend of foreign investment across Tennessee.

At the southern end of the district, 1992 remapping moved Democratic Polk County from the 2nd to the 3rd and gave GOP Rep. John J. Duncan some strongly conservative Chattanooga suburbs in Bradley County.

Election Returns

	2nd District	Democrat	Republican
1992	President*	92,889 (41.1%)	108,109 (47.8%)
	House	52,887 (25.7%)	148,377 (72.2%)
1990	Senate	56,329 (64.4%)	31,116 (35.6%)
	Governor	47,491 (54.0%)	40,517 (46.0%)
1988	President	64,021 (35.1%)	118,173 (64.9%)
	Senate	101,760 (57.5%)	75,161 (42.5%)
1986	Governor	55,885 (42.8%)	74,746 (57.2%)

Vote for Perot was 25,196 (11.1%).

Demographics

Population 541,864

Percent change from 1980 6.2%

Land area 2,488 square miles

Population per square mile 218

Counties, 1990 population

Blount 85,969	Loudon 31,255
Bradley (pt.) 33,435	McMinn 42,383
Knox (pt.) 318,281	Monroe 30,541

Cities, 1990 population (10,000 or more)

Athens 12,054	Knoxville 165,121
Farragut 12,793	Maryville 19,208

Race and Hispanic origin

White 92.3%
Black 6.6%
American Indian, Eskimo, or Aleut. 0.2%
Asian or Pacific Islander 0.7%
Other 0.2%
Hispanic origin 0.6%

Ancestry

American 13.5%	Irish 19.8%
Dutch 4.2%	Italian 1.4%
English 16.6%	Scotch Irish 5.2%
French 2.4%	Scottish 2.8%
German 18.9%	

Universities/colleges, 1990-1991 enrollment

Hiwassee College, Madisonville 522
ITT Technical Institute, Knoxville 390
Johnson Bible College, Knoxville 457
Knoxville Business College, Knoxville 352
Knoxville College, Knoxville 1,266
Maryville College, Maryville 841
Pellissippi State Tech Community College, Knoxville 5,983
Tennessee Wesleyan College, Athens 605
University of Tennessee, Knoxville 26,055

Newspapers, total circulation (in all districts)

Athens Daily Post-Athenian 10,312
Chattanooga News-Free Press 89,205
Cleveland Banner 15,919
Knoxville News-Sentinel 123,125
Maryville Daily Times 19,852

Commercial television stations, affiliations

ADI: Knoxville (75%) and Chattanooga (25%)
WATE-TV, Knoxville (ABC)
WBIR-TV, Knoxville (NBC)
WKCH-TV, Knoxville (Fox)
WKXT-TV, Knoxville (CBS)

Cable television systems, total subscribers

Athens Cable; Athens 7,838
East Tennessee Cable; Concord 6,804
East Tennessee Cable; Maryville 15,261
Scripps-Howard Cable; Knoxville 76,000
Telecable of Cleveland Inc.; Cleveland 16,758

Military installations, 1991

McGhee Tyson Airport Air Force Guard Station, Alcoa 464

Businesses and other major employers

University of Tennessee; Knoxville 9,512
Cobble Industrial Services; Knoxville; personnel supply services 3,000

Aluminum Co. of America; Alcoa; aluminum rolling/drawing 2,500
Tennessee Valley Authority; Knoxville; electric services 2,200
Cobble Personnel Inc.; Knoxville; personnel supply services 2,000
St. Mary's Medical Center Inc.; Knoxville 1,939
Levi Strauss & Co.; Knoxville; jeans 1,800
Bowater Inc.; Calhoun; paper mills 1,700
United Parcel Service Inc.; Knoxville; mail services 1,600
Fort Sanders Regional Medical Center; Knoxville 1,506
Clayton Homes Inc.; Knoxville; real estate operators 1,500
East Tennessee Baptist Hospital; Knoxville 1,500
Ranco Inc./Robertshaw of Tennessee; Knoxville; industrial machinery 1,218
County of Blount; Maryville 1,200
Knoxville Utilities Board; Knoxville; utility services 1,147
Nippondenso America Inc.; Maryville; motor vehicle parts/supplies 1,000
Maremont Corp./Exhaust Products; Loudon; motor vehicle parts 1,000
County of Knox; Knoxville 1,000
Blount Memorial Hospital; Maryville 900
Levi Strauss & Co.; Powell; jeans 850
State of Tennessee/Lakeshore Mental Health Institute; Knoxville 764
Textron Inc./Davidson Interior Trim Div.; Athens; metal stampings 752
Coppinger Color Lab Inc.; Cleveland; photo lab 750
East Tennessee Children's Hospital; Knoxville 700
Olin Corp.; Charleston; inorganic chemicals 680
Hardwick Clothes Inc.; Cleveland; men's suits/coats 675
North American Philips Corp.; Knoxville; electronic audio/video equipment 675
Southeast Service Corp.; Knoxville; building services 650
County of McMinn/Highway Dept.; Athens 650
Plasti-Line Inc./Tencon; Powell; signs 600
Whittle Communications; Knoxville; periodicals 572
County of Loudon; Loudon 550
Knoxville News-Sentinel Co.; Knoxville; newspapers 545
Knox County Public Library; Knoxville 528
Carrier Corp./Allied Products; Knoxville; electronic components 525
Bike Athletic Co.; Knoxville; sportswear 518

3rd District

Southeast — Chattanooga; Oak Ridge

The 3rd is a mixture of agricultural counties and two main commercial hubs: Chattanooga (Hamilton County) in the south and Oak Ridge (Anderson County) in the north. The district starts above Oak Ridge, pinches through narrow Meigs County on its way south to Chattanooga and then broadens out along the Georgia border.

In elections, the 3rd shows a moderate-to-conservative personality. The district went solidly Republican in presidential elections of the 1980s, but in 1992, the Clinton-Gore ticket nearly won here, something Democrats have not managed in the 3rd since Jimmy Carter led their ticket in 1976. In the end, George Bush prevailed districtwide by just 65 votes out of more than 220,000 cast.

Democratic Rep. Marilyn Lloyd has found the 3rd an

increasingly tough sell. From 1984-1992, she scored below 60 percent; in 1992 she prevailed by only 2,930 votes, despite Bill Clinton's good showing in the 3rd and a 1992 remap that aimed to bolster her. Democratic cartographers excised from the 3rd a sizable portion of conservative Bradley County (just above Chattanooga), and they gave Lloyd several solidly Democratic rural counties—Sequatchie, Van Buren, Bledsoe and Polk.

Lloyd won all the new counties except Bledsoe, and strongly Democratic Anderson County gave her a big victory (60 percent). But Hamilton County, where nearly 55 percent of the district's vote is cast, went against her. Hamilton and the part of Bradley County still in the 3rd were the only parts of the district to support Bush over Clinton. (Hamilton has voted Republican in all but one presidential election since 1952.)

Much economic activity in the 3rd centers around the district's nuclear facilities: the Oak Ridge National Laboratories and the Tennessee Valley Authority's Sequoia and Watts Bar nuclear power plants near Chattanooga. But with decreased federal money going to nuclear energy and research, officials looking for new sources of economic activity are promoting a plan that would transform the route connecting Oak Ridge and neighboring Knoxville into a technology corridor for high-tech research and development. A highway that will link Knoxville's airport to the technology corridor is scheduled for completion in 1994.

The 3rd is known for several other white- and blue-collar industries. In Chattanooga, insurance, chemical and service companies have joined the older metal, textile and candy industries. (Former GOP Sen. Bill Brock calls the city home, and his family owns the Brock Candy Co.) The TVA's Office of Power has headquarters in the city as well.

The Chattanooga Choo Choo and Terminal, made famous by Glenn Miller's song, and the new Chattanooga Aquarium help generate revenue from tourism, as do Rock City, Ruby Falls and historic sites connected with the Civil War's "Battle Above the Clouds" on Lookout Mountain.

Election Returns

	3rd District	Democrat	Republican
1992	President*	97,296 (44.1%)	97,361 (44.2%)
	House	105,693 (48.8%)	102,763 (47.5%)
1990	Senate	60,328 (63.8%)	34,230 (36.2%)
	Governor	56,471 (60.0%)	37,707 (40.0%)
1988	President	75,188 (38.9%)	118,305 (61.1%)
	Senate	112,721 (58.9%)	78,658 (41.1%)
1986	Governor	69,993 (49.8%)	70,670 (50.2%)

*Vote for Perot was 25,789 (11.7%).

Demographics

Population 541,866

Percent change from 1980 4.9%

Land area 4,315 square miles

Population per square mile 126

Counties, 1990 population

Anderson	68,250	Grundy	13,362
Bledsoe	9,669	Hamilton	285,536
Bradley (pt.)	40,277	Marion	24,860
Meigs	8,033	Roane	47,227
Morgan	17,300	Sequatchie	8,863
Polk	13,643	Van Buren	4,846

Cities, 1990 population (10,000 or more)

Chattanooga	152,466	Middle Valley CDP	12,255
Cleveland (pt.)	28,220	Oak Ridge	27,310
East Brainerd CDP	11,594	Red Bank	12,322
East Ridge	21,101		

Race and Hispanic origin

White 87.4%

Black 11.6%

American Indian, Eskimo, or Aleut. 0.2%

Asian or Pacific Islander 0.6%

Other 0.2%

Hispanic origin 0.6%

Ancestry

American	13.7%	Irish	19.4%
Dutch	3.2%	Italian	1.2%
English	15.0%	Scotch Irish	3.8%
French	2.3%	Scottish	2.1%
German	16.3%		

Universities/colleges, 1990-1991 enrollment

Chattanooga State Tech Community College, Chattanooga 8,843

Cleveland State Community College, Cleveland 3,315

Edmondson Junior College, Chattanooga 675

Lee College, Cleveland 1,748

McKenzie College, Chattanooga 203

Roane State Community College, Harriman 4,928

Southern Missionary College, Collegedale 1,534

Tennessee Temple University, Chattanooga 1,071

Tomlinson College, Cleveland 249

University of Tennessee, Chattanooga 7,725

Newspapers, total circulation (in all districts)

Chattanooga News-Free Press 89,205

Cleveland Banner 15,919

Knoxville News-Sentinel 123,125

Oak Ridger 10,542

Commercial television stations, affiliations

ADI: Chattanooga (65%), Knoxville (28%) and Nashville (6%)

WDEF-TV, Chattanooga (CBS)

WDSI-TV, Chattanooga (Fox)

WRCB-TV, Chattanooga (NBC)

WTVC, Chattanooga (ABC)

Cable television systems, total subscribers

Chattanooga Cable TV; Chattanooga 72,500

Harriman Cablevision; Harriman 5,579

Telecable of Cleveland Inc.; Cleveland 16,758

Tennessee Cablevision; Oak Ridge 16,400

Businesses and other major employers

Martin Marietta Energy Systems; Oak Ridge; research services 15,191

State of Tennessee/Erlanger Hospital; Chattanooga 3,000

Provident Life & Accident Insurance Co.; Chattanooga; medical service/health insurance 2,700

Maytag Corp./Magic Chef; Cleveland; household appliances 2,549

McKee Foods Corp.; Collegedale; bakery products 2,500

Tennessee Valley Authority/Sequoyah Nuclear Plant; electric services 2,400

Bradley County Memorial Hospital; Cleveland 2,000

Blue Cross/Blue Sheld of Tennessee; Chattanooga; medical service/health insurance 1,707

Du Pont E. I. De Nemours & Co.; Chattanooga; yarn/thread mills 1,500

Combustion Engineering Inc./C-E Power Systems; Chattanooga; metal products 1,400

Sisters of Charity of Nazareth/Memorial Hospital; Chattanooga 1,400

County of Anderson; Clinton 1,230

U.S. Energy Dept.; Oak Ridge 1,250

County of Hamilton; Chattanooga 1,200

North American Royalties Inc./Wheland Foundry Div.; Chattanooga; iron/steel foundries 1,100

Chattanooga Business Services/Manpower of Chattanooga; Chattanooga; personnel supply services 1,000

Seaboard Farms of Chattanooga; Chattanooga; meat products 950

Methodist Medical Center of Oak Ridge; Oak Ridge 950

Buster Brown Apparel Inc.; Chattanooga; outerwear 900

U.S. Pipe & Foundry Co.; Chattanooga; iron/steel foundries 895

Cleveland Chair Co. Inc./Catnapper; Cleveland; furniture 800

U.S. Postal Service; Chattanooga 800

University of Tennessee; Chattanooga 800

American Uniform Co.; Cleveland; uniforms 750

Olan Mills Inc.; Chattanooga; photographic studios 750

Bradley County Memorial Hospital; Cleveland 720

Mars Inc./M&M Mars; Cleveland; chocolate/candies 678

Boeing Aerospace of Oak Ridge; Oak Ridge; aircraft/parts 675

Hospital Corp. of America/Parkridge Medical Center; Chattanooga 650

Oak Ridge Associated Universities; Oak Ridge; research services 606

Mueller Co./Tyco Lab; Chattanooga; metal products 602

Duracell Intl. Inc./Duracell USA; Cleveland; batteries 600

Bon Vie Intl. Inc.; Ooltewah; grocery products 600

Astec Industries Inc.; Chattanooga; construction machinery 600

Hamilton County Nursing Home; Chattanooga; nursing 600

City of Oak Ridge/School District; Oak Ridge 600

Chattanooga-Hamilton County Hospital; Chattanooga 600

Dixie Yarns Inc.; Lupton City; yarn/thread mills 575

Scientific Ecology Group Inc.; Oak Ridge; sanitary services 560

Chattanooga State Tech Community College; Chattanooga 550

Brock Candy Co./Brock Candy-Winona Div.; Chattanooga; candies 525

Roane Hosiery Inc.; Harriman; knitting mills 525

Kayser-Roth Corp./Burlington Socks; Rockwood; knitting mills 505

4th District

Northeast and South Central

Like the state itself, the 4th is a long, sprawling district, extending nearly 300 miles. Beginning in the rural flatlands in the southwest and not too far from Memphis, it snakes up through the rolling terrain in middle Tennessee, stretches north onto the Cumberland Plateau and encompasses a sliver of Knox County in East Tennessee.

The 4th is so large that from east to west it touches four states—Mississippi, Alabama, Kentucky and Virginia. And it spans the time zone dividing line, giving it both Central and Eastern times.

Politically, the 4th is a moderate-to-conservative Democratic district. It supported Bill Clinton in his 1992 quest for the presidency, giving him 48 percent of the vote. Although the 4th had not voted Democratic for president since 1976, the district consistently elected moderate Democrat Jim Cooper to the House from 1982 to 1992. Bedford County, one of the most Democratic parts of the district, is Cooper's home.

Redistricting in 1992 did not change the 4th much. In the southwest, it added Hardin and Wayne counties, near the Tennessee River, and Pickett County in the north. The new lines also added a part of east Knox County. Van Buren, Bledsoe, Sequatchie and Morgan counties in the southwest joined the 3rd. Hancock County merged with the 1st.

With no large urban center in the 4th, people form their political opinions by talking with neighbors in feed stores, roadside cafes and small-town shops that surround the courthouse squares. And despite the district's usual Democratic leanings, some of the northern mountainous counties have supported the GOP because of Union sentiment from the Civil War.

The 4th is home to some unique legal history: In 1925, the "Scopes monkey trial" was held in Dayton in Rhea County. In that case, the state court upheld a law making it illegal to teach the theory of evolution in public schools. The ruling was later overturned, but religion and social conservatism still play a role in the district's politics.

Agriculture and light industry make up the bulk of the 4th's economy. Soybeans and cotton are harvested in the western counties. In the northern counties, tobacco grows in the valleys, and beef and dairy cattle graze on hillsides too steep for plowing.

Coal has long been an economic staple, but underground activity has mostly given way to surface mining.

In addition, many plants specializing in automotive parts assist the Saturn and Nissan plants in the state. Warren County raises trees and shrubs for the nursery industry. And the 100 employees at the Jack Daniels Distillery in Moore County produce the famous sour mash whiskey. But its product cannot be purchased there; Moore is a "dry" county.

The 4th is also known for the Tennessee Walking Horse National Celebration, which is held every August and September in Shelbyville.

Election Returns

	4th District	Democrat	Republican
1992	President*	100,292 (48.2%)	83,922 (40.3%)
	House	98,984 (64.1%)	50,340 (32.6%)
1990	Senate	56,660 (70.8%)	23,405 (29.2%)
	Governor	50,528 (63.3%)	29,344 (36.7%)
1988	President	66,806 (41.5%)	94,115 (58.5%)
	Senate	98,836 (65.7%)	51,637 (34.3%)
1986	Governor	71,515 (58.7%)	50,325 (41.3%)

Vote for Perot was 23,838 (11.5%).

Demographics

Population 541,868

Percent change from 1980 6.1%

Land area 9,340 square miles

Population per square mile 58

Counties, 1990 population

Bedford 30,411	Knox (pt.) 13,681
Campbell 35,079	Lawrence 35,303
Claiborne 26,137	Lincoln 28,157
Coffee 40,339	Moore 4,721
Cumberland 34,736	Pickett 4,548
Fentress 14,669	Rhea 24,344
Franklin 34,725	Scott 18,358
Giles 25,741	Union 13,694
Grainger 17,095	Warren 32,992
Hamblen 50,480	Wayne 13,935
Hardin 22,633	White 20,090

Cities, 1990 population (10,000 or more)

Lawrenceburg 10,412	Shelbyville 14,049
McMinnville 11,194	Tullahoma 16,761
Morristown 21,385	

Race and Hispanic origin

White 95.8%

Black 3.6%

American Indian, Eskimo, or Aleut. 0.2%

Asian or Pacific Islander 0.2%

Other 0.1%

Hispanic origin 0.4%

Ancestry

American 20.5%	Irish 19.4%
Dutch 2.5%	Italian 1.0%
English 13.8%	Scotch Irish 3.3%
French 1.7%	Scottish 1.5%
German 13.5%	

Universities/colleges, 1990-1991 enrollment

Bryan College, Dayton 502

Lincoln Memorial University, Harrogate 1,819

Martin Methodist College, Pulaski 390

Motlow State Community College, Tullahoma 2,782

University of the South, Sewanee 1,164

Walters State Community College, Morristown 4,112

Newspapers, total circulation (in all districts)

Chattanooga News-Free Press 89,205

Knoxville News-Sentinel 123,125

Morristown Citizen Tribune 18,990

Nashville Banner 61,720

Nashville Tennessean 134,264

Commercial television stations, affiliations

ADI: Nashville (48%), Knoxville (36%), Jackson (6%), Huntsville-Decatur-Florence (6%) and Chattanooga (4%)

WINT-TV, Crossville (None)

WPMC, Jellico (None)

Cable television systems, total subscribers

Cookeville Cablevision; Cookeville 12,900

McMinnville Cablevision; McMinnville 7,876

Sammons Communications Inc.; Morristown 14,000

Scripps-Howard Cable; Knoxville 76,000

Scripps-Howard Cable; La Follette 5,742

Tullahoma Cablevision; Tullahoma 6,835

Military installations, 1991

Arnold Air Force Base, Manchester 1,873

Businesses and other major employers

BASF Corp./Fibers Div.; Lowland; synthetics 2,590

Murray Ohio Mfg. Co.; Lawrenceburg; bicycles/power mowers 2,000

Berkline Corp.; Morristown; furniture 1,500

Carrier Corp.; Morrison; air conditioners 1,500

La-Z-Boy Chair Co.; Dayton; furniture 1,361

Berol Corp./Empire Berol USA; Shelbyville; pens/art supplies 1,300

Amana Refrigeration Inc.; Fayetteville; refrigerators 1,250

County of Hamblen; Morristown 1,100

Shelby Williams Industries; Morristown; furniture/fixtures 1,000

Calspan Corp.; Tullahoma; heavy construction 1,000

Berol Corp./Empire Pencil; Shelbyville; pens/pencils 1,000

Magnetek Inc./Century Electric; McMinnville; electrical industrial apparatus 998

Lear Seating Corp.; Morristown; furniture 900

Emerson Electric Co./Mallory Controls; Sparta; electrical industrial controls 900

Sverdrup Corp.; Manchester: engineering services 828

Mahle Inc.; Morristown; industrial machinery 750

Universal Furniture Industries; Morristown; bedroom furniture 750

Batesville Casket Co.; Manchester; caskets 750

County of Hardin/Highway Dept.; Savannah 737

Imperial Reading Corp./Brittania Sportswear Div.; La Follette; sportswear 700

Calsonic Mfg. Corp.; Shelbyville; refrigeration 700

Arvin Industries Inc./Gabriel Div.; Pulaski; motor vehicle parts/equipment 700

Sunbeam Corp./Oster Specialty Products; McMinnville; household appliances 670

County of Franklin/School System; Winchester 650

Robinson Mfg. Co.; Dayton; outerwear 625

Ebasco/Newberg Joint Venture; Tullahoma; building construction 600

American National Can Co.; Shelbyville; plastics products 600

Ingersoll-Rand Co./Torrington Fafnir; Pulaski; ball, roller bearings 600

Excel of Tennessee Inc.; Lawrenceburg; plastics products 600

Cumberland Medical Center Inc.; Crossville 600

County of Lawrence/School District; Lawrenceburg 600

Tibbals Flooring Co./Hartco; Oneida; sawmills 584

Lee Apparel Co. Inc.; Fayetteville; jeans/outerwear 550

Fairfield Communities Inc.; Crossville; real estate operators 550

5th District

Nashville

Nashville is "Music City USA" and the capital of Tennessee, and country music and government paychecks propel the economy. More than 90 percent of the 5th's vote comes out of Nashville and Davidson County, and in most years Democrats win here. Ronald Reagan in 1984 and George Bush in 1988 carried the 5th, but not by much. In 1992 the district returned to form, giving the Clinton-Gore ticket 53 percent.

There is no question that country music is Nashville's most famous industry, but with almost 17,000 jobs, state government is the district's leading employer. Davidson County is also home to many colleges and universities, the best-known of which is Vanderbilt University. Several publishers of religious material have headquarters here, and there is a sizable manufacturing sector.

Government workers, the academic communities and labor unions uphold Nashville's traditional position as the focal point of Middle Tennessee Democratic populism. That brand of politics is a legacy of Andrew Jackson, who built his political career in the area and returned to The Hermitage, his home east of Nashville, after serving two terms as president.

Nashville's population is less than one-quarter black—a relatively low figure for a large southern city—and white voters have not been so prone to drift from their traditional Democratic loyalties.

Though the state capitol complex is a permanent anchor, downtown Nashville has struggled, a victim of retail flight to the suburbs and the success of Opryland, the sprawling theme park east of the city where the Grand Ole Opry moved from its original downtown site at Ryman Auditorium.

But signs of life are springing up downtown, with a revival of the live-entertainment scene and the restaurant business, and remodeling of old buildings. There is talk of resurrecting a Department of Transportation feasibility study to determine the viability of restoring Amtrak service to Nashville. One proposed route would run from Chicago through Nashville to Jacksonville, Fla.

To keep pace in the area of air transportation, Nashville replaced its aged airport with a new facility. The 1991 highway bill included funding aimed at enhancing mass transit in the city.

Economically, the 5th benefits not only from the industries within its borders but also from some big manufacturing facilities nearby. Since the early 1980s, Tennessee has made a vigorous effort to market the state's work force and business climate to foreign investors, especially the Japanese. Nissan built a huge plant south of Nashville, and other Japanese companies have followed. General Motors chose a site near Nashville for its massive Saturn facility (actually located in the 7th District); Saturn sales have been so brisk that the company cannot meet demand and is looking to expand.

Redistricting in 1992 just slightly altered the look of the 5th, moving a small slice of Davidson County and about half of Robertson County to the 7th. Robertson accounts for only about 6 percent of the total district vote.

Election Returns

	5th District	Democrat	Republican
1992	President*	112,795 (52.8%)	79,398 (37.1%)
	House †	125,233 (66.8%)	49,417 (26.3%)
1990	Senate	56,108 (74.5%)	19,167 (25.5%)
	Governor	51,416 (68.5%)	23,698 (31.5%)
1988	President	91,857 (48.1%)	99,008 (51.9%)
	Senate	129,817 (70.0%)	55,636 (30.0%)
1986	Governor	78,754 (54.8%)	64,949 (45.2%)

*Vote for Perot was 21,531 (10.1%).   †Independent/other is greater than 5%.

Demographics

Population 541,910

Percent change from 1980 5.3%

Land area 880 square miles

Population per square mile 616

Counties, 1990 population
Davidson (pt.) 507,233   Robertson (pt.) 34,677

Cities, 1990 population (10,000 or more)
Nashville-Davidson (pt.) 484,823

Race and Hispanic origin
White 75.4%
Black 22.8%
American Indian, Eskimo, or Aleut. 0.2%
Asian or Pacific Islander 1.3%
Other 0.3%
Hispanic origin 0.9%

Ancestry
American 9.7%	Irish 16.8%
Dutch 2.0%	Italian 1.8%
English 15.5%	Scotch Irish 4.6%
French 3.0%	Scottish 2.6%
German 15.0%	

Universities/colleges, 1990-1991 enrollment
American Baptist College, Nashville 218
Aquinas Junior College, Nashville 405
Belmont University, Nashville 2,812
David Lipscomb University, Nashville 2,427
Draughons Business College, Nashville 418
Fisk University, Nashville 911
Free Will Baptist Bible College, Nashville 252
ITT Technical Institute, Nashville 598
Meharry Medical College, Nashville 623
Nashville State Tech Institute, Nashville 5,974
Tennessee State University, Nashville 7,393
Trevecca Nazarene College, Nashville 1,795
Vanderbilt University, Nashville 9,163

Newspapers, total circulation (in all districts)
Nashville Banner 61,720
Nashville Tennessean 134,264

Commercial television stations, affiliations
ADI: Nashville (100%)
WKRN-TV, Nashville (ABC)
WSMV, Nashville (NBC)
WTVF, Nashville (CBS)
WXMT-TV, Nashville (None)
WZTV, Nashville (Fox)

Cable television systems, total subscribers
Viacom Cablevision; Nashville 109,626

Military installations, 1991
Nashville Metropolitan Airport Air Force Guard Station, Nashville 376

Businesses and other major employers
Baptist Health Care System Inc./Baptist Hospital; Nashville 2,800

Third National Corp.; Nashville; commercial banks 2,721

St. Thomas Hospital; Nashville 2,600

Opryland USA Inc.; Nashville; entertainment services 2,500

Textron Inc./Aerostructures Div.; Nashville; space vehicles/missiles 2,000

U.S. Postal Service; Nashville 2,000

Hospital Corp. of America/Centenial Medical Center; Nashville 1,961

City of Nashville/Police Dept.; Nashville 1,900

Ford Motor Co./Nashville Glass Plant; Nashville; flat glass 1,800

State of Tennessee/Employment Security Dept.; Nashville 1,600

American Airlines Inc.; Nashville; airline 1,500

United Parcel Service Inc.; Nashville; mail services 1,500

American General Life Insurance; Nashville; life insurance 1,420

Genesco Inc./Jarman-Flagg; Nashville; footwear 1,400

U.S. Veterans Affairs Dept.; Nashville; hospital 1,200

State of Tennessee/Revenue Dept.; Nashville 1,200

State of Tennessee/Clover Bottom Development Center; Nashville 1,061

Arcata Corp./Arcata Graphics; Nashville; commercial printing 1,000

Tennessee State University; Nashville 1,000

Nashville Memorial Hospital; Madison 1,000

City of Nashville/Water & Sewerage Dept.; Nashville; water supply 900

State of Tennessee/Transportation Dept.; Nashville 900

Hospital Corp. of America/West Side Hospital; Nashville 900

Yellow Freight System Inc.; Nashville; trucking services 871

J. C. Penney Co. Inc.; Nashville; department stores 850

Aladdin Industries Inc.; Nashville; plastics products 800

C. S. Brooks Inc.; Nashville; textile products/carpets 800

Genesco Inc./Laredo-Code West; Nashville; shoe stores 800

Hospital Corp. of America/Southern Hills Medical Center; Nashville 800

Hospital Corp. of America; Nashville; hospital management 800

White Consolidated Industries/Fridgedaire Co.; Springfield; household appliances 750

Ingram Barge Co./Great River Marine Services; Nashville; freight shipping 725

Pirelli Armstrong Tire Corp.; Madison; tires 703

Rand McNally Media Services/Nicholstone; Nashville; bookbinding 700

Bellsouth Telecommunications; Nashville; telephone communications 700

Du Pont E. I. De Nemours & Co.; Old Hickory; soaps/cleaners 700

United Methodist Publishing House/Abingdon Press; Nashville; book publishing 700

Nashville General Hospital; Nashville 681

Roadway Express Inc.; Antioch; trucking services 650

NationsBank/Tennessee; Nashville; commercial banks 645

Reemay Inc.; Old Hickory; yarn/thread mills 638

City of Nashville/Nashville Electric Service; Nashville; electric services 600

Small Harace Holdings Corp.; Nashville; men's suits/coats 600

Paccar Inc./Peterbilt Motor Co.; Madison; motor vehicle bodies 600

Oscar Mayer Foods Corp.; Goodlettsville; meatpacking 600

Northern Telecom Inc.; Nashville; communications equipment 550

First American National Bank of Tennessee; Nashville; commercial banks 550

Castner-Knott Dry Goods Co.; Goodlettsville; department stores 550

State of Tennessee/River Bend Prison; Nashville 550

Hospital Corp. of America/Donelson Hospital Inc.; Nashville 550

Bordeaux Hospital; Nashville; nursing 550

Cigna Corp./Equicor Co.; Nashville: insurance services 540

Consolidated Freightways Corp.; Antioch; trucking services 520

J. C. Bradford & Co.; Nashville; security brokers 520

6th District

North Central — Murfreesboro

This slice of middle Tennessee embodies qualities of both the Old and New South. In most of the 6th's counties, the pace of life is still relatively unhurried, people work in small factories or on farms, and old courthouse networks call the political shots—nearly always calling them Democratic.

But on the western edge of the 6th, in the four counties that border Davidson County (Nashville), there are clear signs of change, brought on in large part by the expansion of suburbia and the influence of two gargantuan vehicle-assembly plants—one run by Japan's Nissan in Smyrna, and the other by General Motors' Saturn subsidiary, in Spring Hill, just outside the Williamson County line (in the 7th District).

The political impact of the suburbanizing and industrializing is most obvious in Williamson County. Many residents there are white-collar commuters to jobs in and around Nashville, just to the north. In most elections, Williamson delivers a stronger GOP vote than any other middle Tennessee county. In 1992, George Bush won 55 percent of the vote in Williamson, and 60 percent in a small slice of Davidson County that is included in the 6th. Every other county in the 6th backed the Clinton-Gore ticket.

Similarly, in the 1992 House contest the GOP candidate won nearly 60 percent in Williamson and the slice of Davidson. Democratic Rep. Bart Gordon's weak showing in Williamson, which casts just under one-fifth of the district's vote, was the main reason he tallied under 60 percent for the first time since being elected in 1984.

Though 1992 redistricting moved Maury County out of the 6th, and with it the Saturn facility, almost 30 percent of the plant's workers live in Williamson County. Demand for Saturn's cars has been so strong that the company has strained to keep up; employment is approaching 7,000, and expansion is on the horizon.

In the other three counties adjoining Davidson County—Rutherford, Sumner and Wilson—liberalism in the national Democratic Party provokes some wariness, but traditional party ties still bind: In 1992 Clinton won each by 5 to 6 points over Bush, and all went for Gordon by 10 points or better.

Rutherford County was Tennessee's fastest-growing in the 1980s; in addition to the Nissan plant (which employs about 4,300), it has Middle Tennessee State University in Murfreesboro, the Stones River National Battlefield and a large outlet shopping mall.

In the areas of the 6th that are part of the Nashville orbit, economic conditions have been fairly favorable in recent years. The same cannot be said for many of the rural and small-town areas on the eastern side of the 6th. Textile producers and other small-scale manufacturers there offer primarily lower-wage jobs, and remoteness from urban areas means the service-sector economy is not large.

The Democratic advantage in the eastern counties is enormous. In 1992, nearly all of them voted by at least 2-to-1 for Clinton-Gore and for Gordon.

Election Returns

	6th District	Democrat	Republican
1992	President*	109,895 (47.6%)	93,036 (40.3%)
	House	120,177 (56.6%)	86,289 (40.6%)
1990	Senate	60,992 (74.1%)	21,353 (25.9%)
	Governor	52,563 (64.7%)	28,712 (35.3%)
1988	President	65,451 (38.8%)	103,125 (61.2%)
	Senate	106,971 (66.3%)	54,270 (33.7%)
1986	Governor	69,302 (54.9%)	56,908 (45.1%)

*Vote for Perot was 28,151 (12.2%).

Demographics

Population 541,977

Percent change from 1980 5.9%

Land area 5,366 square miles

Population per square mile 101

Counties, 1990 population

Cannon 10,467	Putnam 51,373
Clay 7,238	Rutherford 118,570
Davidson (pt.) 3,551	Smith 14,143
De Kalb 14,360	Sumner 103,281
Jackson 9,297	Trousdale 5,920
Macon 15,906	Williamson 81,021
Marshall 21,539	Wilson 67,675
Overton 17,636	

Cities, 1990 population (10,000 or more)

Brentwood 16,392	Hendersonville 32,188
Cookeville 21,744	Lebanon 15,208
Franklin 20,098	Murfreesboro 44,922
Gallatin 18,794	Smyrna 13,647

Race and Hispanic origin

White 93.3%
Black 5.7%
American Indian, Eskimo, or Aleut. 0.2%
Asian or Pacific Islander 0.6%
Other 0.1%
Hispanic origin 0.6%

Ancestry

American 15.9%	Irish 19.2%
Dutch 2.3%	Italian 1.6%
English 16.8%	Scotch Irish 4.8%
French 2.6%	Scottish 2.4%
German 15.9%	

Universities/colleges, 1990-1991 enrollment

Cumberland University, Lebanon 693
Middle Tennessee State University, Murfreesboro 14,865
Tennessee Tech University, Cookeville 8,140
Volunteer State Community College, Gallatin 4,160

Newspapers, total circulation (in all districts)

Cookeville Herald Citizen 9,588
Murfreesboro Daily News Journal 14,955
Nashville Banner 61,720
Nashville Tennessean 134,264

Commercial television stations, affiliations

ADI: Nashville (100%)
WMTT, Cookeville (None)
WPGD, Henderson (None)
WJFB, Lebanon (None)
WHTN, Murfreesboro (None)

Cable television systems, total subscribers

Cookeville Cablevision; Cookeville 12,900
Lebanon Cable; Lebanon 5,897
Par Cable of Sumner County; Hendersonville 10,000
Tennessee Valley Cablevision; Franklin 11,588
Tennessee Valley Cablevision; Smyrna 6,844
United Artist of Tennessee; Gallatin 5,910
United Artist of Tennessee; Mount Juliet 8,553
United Artist of Tennessee; Murfreesboro 16,500
Viacom Cablevision; Nashville 109,626

Businesses and other major employers

Nissan Motor Mfg. Corp. USA; Smyrna; motor vehicles 4,300
Alcoa Fujikura Ltd.; Brentwood; electrical equipment/supplies 2,600
Ingram Industries Inc.; La Vergne; books/video tapes/software 2,050
Bridgestone/Firestone Inc.; La Vergne; tires 1,500
Whirlpool Corp.; La Vergne; refrigerators 1,500
U.S. Veterans Affairs Dept.; Murfreesboro; hospital 1,500
Inter-City Products Corp. USA; Lewisburg; plumbing/heating 1,400
County of Rutherford/School Board; Murfreesboro 1,390
Middle Tennessee State University; Murfreesboro 1,215
Comdata Network Inc.; Brentwood; banking services 1,200
U.S. Shoe Corp./Texas Boot Co. Div.; Lebanon; footwear 1,100
County of Williamson/School District; Franklin 1,100
Faber-Castell Corp.; Lewisburg; pens/pencils 1,000
Fast Food Merchandisers Inc.; Monterey; meat products 1,000
Middle Tennessee Medical Center; Murfreesboro 1,000
Tennessee Tech University; Cookeville 998
State Farm Fire & Casualty Co.; Murfreesboro; insurance services 930
Toshiba America Inc./Mfg. Div.; Lebanon; audio/video equipment 850
Russell Stover Candies Inc.; Cookeville; candies 800
Oshkosh B'gosh Inc.; Celina; outerwear 800
State Farm Mutual Auto Insurance Co.; Murfreesboro; insurance services 800
Walden Book Co. Inc.; La Vergne; book warehousing 750
General Electric Co.; Murfreesboro; electrical motors/generators 700

Cumberland-Swan Inc.; Smyrna; pharmaceuticals 700

Better-Bilt Aluminum Products Co.; Smyrna; aluminum doors/windows 650

TRW Inc./Rossgear Div.; Lebanon; motor vehicle parts 650

Lineal Group/Samsonite Furniture Co.; Murfreesboro; metal household furniture 600

G. F. Office Furniture Ltd.; Gallatin; office furniture 600

Service Merchandise Co.; Brentwood; catalog showrooms/jewelry 600

Cookeville General Hospital; Cookeville 589

Cosmolab Inc.; Lewisburg; cosmetics 550

Kantus Corp.; Lewisburg; motor vehicle instrument panels 550

Sumner Memorial Hospital; Gallatin 545

Wynns Precision Inc.; Lebanon; hose/belting/gaskets/packing 536

Williamson County Hospital Inc.; Franklin 530

Teledyne Industries Inc.; Lewisburg; electronic components 525

Square D Co.; Smyrna; measuring/controlling devices 519

7th District

West Central — Clarksville; Part of Shelby County

Though the GOP won the 7th District comfortably from 1984 to 1992, the district's political balance would make any open-seat race highly competitive. The 7th combines Republican suburbanites, west Tennessee Dixiecrats, middle Tennessee populists and a significant number of blue-collar workers. In 1992 redistricting, the 7th became more Democratic.

Despite losing 100,000 of its GOP-leaning residents to other districts in the remap, the Shelby County part of the 7th remains the district's GOP bastion. The 7th still has the most upscale and Republican Memphis suburbs, including Bartlett, Collierville and Germantown.

Many of the better-paid employees at such Memphis-based companies as Federal Express and International Paper Co. (both located in the 9th District) live in the east Shelby suburbs. Much of the area has a nouveau riche feel, with showy homes, malls and office parks that draw commerce away from center-city Memphis. The area grew rapidly in the 1980s (Germantown's population, for example, expanded 50 percent), while the city of Memphis saw a 9 percent population loss.

In 1992, the portion of Shelby in the 7th gave George Bush 67 percent of its presidential votes. That was enough to deliver the district comfortably to Bush; Shelby casts more than 40 percent of the vote in the 7th. Of the 14 other counties in the district, Bush won just two.

The 7th runs the gamut of Tennessee agriculture. In Shelby's eastern neighbor, Fayette County, the flat land is ideal for cotton growing. Moving east, the more rolling terrain becomes less suitable for row crops; tobacco and cattle are more prevalent. Corn, soybeans, hay and hogs are also important in the district. Maury County, added to the 7th in remapping, is the state's largest producer of beef cattle, but it is best known for its GM Saturn plant, in the tiny two-stoplight town of Spring Hill. Positive consumer response to the initial Saturn models has kept the plant humming; its work force grew from 5,000 in 1991 to an anticipated 7,000 by the end of 1993. Saturn is now considering where to expand production to meet demand.

Also in Maury is the Tennessee Farm Bureau, which provides services for farmers across the state. The largest insurer of rural property in Tennessee, it is a political force despite its policy of not endorsing candidates. Every aspirant for statewide office must take into account its significant, though tacit, influence.

A potential swing county in an open House race could be Montgomery, which has the district's largest city, Clarksville (population 75,000). Clarksville is home to Fort Campbell and the 101st Airborne Division, and the county's active duty and retired military personnel help give it a conservative tinge. But conservative has not always meant Republican: Bill Clinton won Montgomery by almost 1,500 votes in 1992. The fort and its 5,200 civilian and military employees likely will be safe from military downsizing, considering the Pentagon's emphasis on "rapid deployment" units such as the 101st.

Election Returns

	7th District	Democrat	Republican
1992	President*	91,644 (40.1%)	114,544 (50.1%)
	House	72,062 (35.5%)	125,101 (61.7%)
1990	Senate	56,306 (66.1%)	28,939 (33.9%)
	Governor	51,371 (59.6%)	34,847 (40.4%)
1988	President	57,889 (34.9%)	108,179 (65.1%)
	Senate	98,868 (62.4%)	59,649 (37.6%)
1986	Governor	59,006 (50.9%)	56,930 (49.1%)

Vote for Perot was 22,486 (9.8%).

Demographics

Population 541,937

Percent change from 1980 7.6%

Land area 6,609 square miles

Population per square mile 82

Counties, 1990 population

Cheatham 27,140	Lewis 9,247
Chester 12,819	Maury 54,812
Decatur 10,472	McNairy 22,422
Dickson 35,061	Montgomery 100,498
Fayette 25,559	Perry 6,612
Hardeman 23,377	Robertson (pt.) 6,817
Henderson 21,844	Shelby (pt.) 168,503
Hickman 16,754	

Cities, 1990 population (10,000 or more)

Bartlett (pt.) 22,719	Columbia 28,583
Clarksville 75,494	Germantown 32,893
Collierville 14,427	Memphis (pt.) 29,909

Race and Hispanic origin
White 86.2%
Black 12.4%
American Indian, Eskimo, or Aleut. 0.2%
Asian or Pacific Islander 0.9%
Other 0.3%
Hispanic origin 1.1%

Ancestry

American 14.5%	French 2.9%
Dutch 2.2%	German 16.0%
English 14.7%	Irish 20.2%

Italian   2.2%   Scotch Irish   4.2%
Polish   1.1%   Scottish   2.1%

Universities/colleges, 1990-1991 enrollment
Austin Peay State University, Clarksville   6,347
Columbia State Community College, Columbia   3,402
Freed-Hardeman College, Henderson   1,183
State Tech Institute of Memphis, Memphis   8,768

Newspapers, total circulation (in all districts)
Columbia Daily Herald   11,410
Clarksville Leaf Chronicle   18,759
Jackson Sun   35,868
Memphis Commercial Appeal   193,211
Nashville Banner   61,720
Nashville Tennessean   134,264

Commercial television stations, affiliations
ADI: Nashville (51%), Memphis (36%) and Jackson (13%)
WHBQ-TV, Memphis (ABC)
WLMT, Memphis (None)
WMC-TV, Memphis (NBC)
WPTY-TV, Memphis (Fox)
WREG-TV, Memphis (CBS)

Cable television systems, total subscribers
Cablevision; Germantown   8,712
Cencom Cable TV; Clarksville   19,000
FNI Cable Associates; Columbia   12,529
Memphis Cablevision; Memphis   148,135
Viacom Cablevision; Nashville   109,626

Military installations, 1991
Fort Campbell, Clarksville   5,200

Businesses and other major employers
Saturn Corp.; Spring Hill; motor vehicles   5,000
American Standard Inc./Trane Co. Div.; Clarksville; heating/air conditioning equipment   1,670
State Industries Inc./Water Systems Div.; Ashland City; household appliances   1,400
VMC Corp.; Adamsville; personnel supply services   1,200
Maury Regional Hospital; Columbia   1,147
Carrier Corp.; Collierville; air conditioners   1,000
Magnetek Inc./Magnetek Century Electric; Lexington; electrical industrial apparatus   950
Memorial General Hospital; Clarksville   840
County of Hardeman/Board of Education; Bolivar   800
Union Carbide Chemical & Plastics Co.; Columbia; mineral products   756
Aqua Glass Corp.; Adamsville; plastics products   747
State of Tennessee/Western Mental Health Institute; Bolivar   707
Troxel Co. Inc.; Moscow; bicycle seats   700
Acme Boot Co. Inc.; Clarksville; footwear   700
County of Dickson; Charlotte   700
Jostens Inc./Jostens Printing & Publishing Div.; Clarksville; printing   650
City of Clarksville/Human Resources Dept.; Clarksville   650
State Tech Institute of Memphis; Memphis   650
Johnson Controls Inc.; Lexington; motor vehicle parts/equipment   630
General Electric Co.; Columbia; communications equipment   600
Nike Inc.; Memphis; sportswear   600

Brother Industries USA Inc.; Memphis; typewriters/office equipment   590
H. L. F. Managers Inc.; Memphis; motel management   550
Austin Peay State University; Clarksville   535

8th District
West — Jackson; Part of Shelby County

The 1992 round of redistricting did little to alter the essentially rural and Democratic makeup of the 8th. The inclusion of more Republican areas of suburban Shelby County only slightly outweighed the addition of rural Houston and Humphreys counties. The result was a district little different from the one that GOP House candidates have failed to capture since the end of Reconstruction.

The 8th is slightly more favorable to GOP presidential candidates. Though Bill Clinton won the 8th with 48 percent of the vote (just slightly more than his 47 percent statewide) and took 14 of the 17 counties in the district, Shelby and Madison counties—the two counties with the largest populations with a combined 36 percent of the district's vote—went solidly for Bush, 51 percent to 41 percent.

Soybeans, corn, wheat and cotton remain the 8th's staple crops, but industrial activity has diversified in recent years, particularly in Jackson, the district's largest city.

The surrounding farm counties look to Jackson as a source of retail goods and such services as specialty health care. The city's diversified industrial base allowed it to weather the recent recession better than the 8th's small towns and farms. Since 1989, Jackson (population 49,000) has attracted plants such as a Maytag appliance manufacturing plant and a company that manufactures power tools. Still, the largest industrial employer in Jackson is the Procter & Gamble facility that makes Pringle's potato chips and employs more than 1,200.

Republicans have in recent years gained some ground in Madison County (Jackson), thanks in part to an influx of managerial personnel to Jackson's increasingly diversified industries.

Madison County's economic success contrasts with the slower economic growth of the rest of the 8th. In 1991, 13 of the 15 rural counties in the district had unemployment percentages higher than the state average of 6.7 percent, while Madison's fell slightly below average.

The largest employer in the district—the Memphis Naval Air Station and Naval Hospital in northern Shelby County, with almost 11,000 employees—is in the midst of considering realignment. Union City (population 10,500) is the site for the 8th District's largest industrial employer, one of Goodyear's two largest radial tire-manufacturing facilities, which employs about 3,000.

In 1992, 219,000 visitors came in 1992 to see the Civil War-era Fort Donelson in Dover, the site of an early victory the Union sorely needed. The 1862 capture of the Confederate fort gave the Union control of the Cumberland River, which cuts through the northeast edge of the district, running northwest from Nashville. The site also helped to immortalize the victorious Union general, Ulysses S. Grant, who in response to a Confederate request for terms of surrender, responded, "No terms. Unconditional surrender."

Election Returns

	8th District	Democrat	Republican
1992	President*	101,328 (48.2%)	89,533 (42.6%)
	House†	136,852 (83.7%)	—
1990	Senate	63,525 (72.1%)	24,577 (27.9%)
	Governor	56,563 (63.7%)	32,273 (36.3%)
1988	President	74,869 (42.3%)	102,077 (57.7%)
	Senate	121,624 (71.5%)	48,588 (28.5%)
1986	Governor	83,352 (62.2%)	50,716 (37.8%)

*Vote for Perot was 19,328 (9.2%).   †Independent/other is greater than 5%.

Demographics

Population 541,907

Percent change from 1980 7.3%

Land area 7,750 square miles

Population per square mile 70

Counties, 1990 population

Benton 14,524	Lake 7,129
Carroll 27,514	Lauderdale 23,491
Crockett 13,378	Madison 77,982
Dyer 34,854	Obion 31,717
Gibson 46,315	Shelby (pt.) 115,846
Haywood 19,437	Stewart 9,479
Henry 27,888	Tipton 37,568
Houston 7,018	Weakley 31,972
Humphreys 15,795	

Cities, 1990 population (10,000 or more)

Brownsville 10,019	Memphis (pt.) 60,834
Dyersburg 16,317	Millington 17,866
Jackson 48,949	Union City 10,513

Race and Hispanic origin
White 79.5%
Black 19.7%
American Indian, Eskimo, or Aleut. 0.2%
Asian or Pacific Islander 0.4%
Other 0.2%
Hispanic origin 0.7%

Ancestry

American 16.8%	Irish 19.6%
Dutch 2.0%	Italian 1.2%
English 11.8%	Scotch Irish 3.4%
French 2.2%	Scottish 1.4%
German 11.8%	

Universities/colleges, 1990-1991 enrollment
Bethel College, McKenzie 613
Dyersburg State Community College, Dyersburg 1,993
Jackson State Community College, Jackson 3,256
Lambuth University, Jackson 769
Lane College, Jackson 530
Union University, Jackson 2,010
University of Tennessee, Jackson 5,363

Newspapers, total circulation (in all districts)
Dyersburg State Gazette 8,144
Clarksville Leaf Chronicle 18,759
Jackson Sun 35,868
Memphis Commercial Appeal 193,211
Nashville Tennessean 134,264

Commercial television stations, affiliations
ADI: Memphis (40%), Nashville (29%), Paducah-Cape Girardeau-Harrisburg-Marion (17%) and Jackson (14%)
WBBJ-TV, Jackson (ABC)
WMTU, Jackson (Fox)

Cable television systems, total subscribers
Cablecom of Dyersburg; Dyersburg 8,180
Cablevision Industries; Jackson 19,134
Memphis Cablevision; Memphis 148,135
Paris Cablevision; Paris 6,000
Volunteer Cablevision; Martin 8,644

Military installations, 1991
Memphis Naval Air Station, Millington 9,995
Millington Naval Hospital, Millington 727

Businesses and other major employers
Goodyear Tire & Rubber Co.; Union City; tires 3,000
Jackson-Madison County General Hospital; Jackson 2,219
Martin Marietta Corp./Ordnance Systems; Milan; ordnance/accessories 2,000
Henry I. Siegel Co. Inc.; Bruceton; sportswear/warehousing 1,500
Procter & Gamble Co.; Jackson; food products 1,200
Dyersburg Fabrics Inc.; Dyersburg; man-made fabric mills 950
Du Pont E. I. De Nemours & Co.; New Johnsonville; organic chemicals 850
Dart Industries Inc./Tupperware Co.; Halls; plastics products 850
County of Henry/Nursing Home; Paris 850
State of Tennessee/Arlington Development Center; Arlington 843
Hamilton-Ryker Co. Inc.; Martin; personnel supply services 815
Du Pont E. I. De Nemours & Co.; Memphis; inorganic chemicals 775
World Color Press Inc./Dyersburg Div.; Dyersburg; commercial printing 732
County of Weakley; Dresden 666
University of Tennessee; Jackson 650
Quaker Oats Co.; Jackson; bakery products 600
Triangle Pacific Corp./Bruce Hardwood Floors; Jackson; millwork 600
MTD Products Inc.; Brownsville; farm/garden machinery 600
A. O. Smith Corp.; Milan; motor vehicle parts 600
Gaines Mfg. Co.; McKenzie; upholstered furniture 600
Kellwood Co.; Rutherford; sportswear/coats 600
Henry I. Siegel Co. Inc.; South Fulton; sportswear 600
Plumley Companies Inc.; Paris; rubber products 580
General Care Corp./HCA Regional Hospital Jackson; Jackson 570
Porter-Cable Corp.; Jackson; power tools 556
Dow Corning Wright Corp.; Arlington; medical instruments/supplies 550
Wilson Sporting Goods Co.; Humboldt; sporting goods 530
Douglas & Lomason Co.; Milan; furniture 525
American Olean Tile Co./Armstrong Co.; Jackson; tiles 522

9th District

Memphis

On the bluffs above the Mississippi River is Memphis, a city of 610,000 and historically the crossroads for eastern Arkansas, northern Mississippi and west Tennessee. Named after the city in Egypt because of the Nile-like appearance of the twisting Mississippi, Memphis underscored that link in 1991 by opening the Great American Pyramid. The 32-story structure, which houses a 22,000-seat arena, is part of a larger plan to revitalize the city's economy—and especially its flagging downtown—by bringing in more special events and visitors. Memphis is already well-known to millions of Elvis Presley fans as the site of Graceland; since "the King's" 1977 death, a ceaseless stream of admirers has visited his grave on the mansion grounds.

Now, another famous Southerner is memorialized by a museum in Memphis: the Rev. Dr. Martin Luther King Jr. The National Civil Rights Museum opened in 1991 on the site of the former Lorraine Motel, where King was assassinated in 1968.

Other downtown attractions include Mud Island—a 52-acre island park that celebrates the city's river history—and Beale Street, where W. C. Handy developed the blues in the early 1900s. Restoration along Beale Street aims to revive its one-time role as the center of city nightlife.

But the task of reviving downtown is complicated by the city's racial relationships. Memphis' population is 55 percent black, and nearly all the blacks live around and near downtown. The bulk of the white population is segregated in the eastern part of the city and is prone to head further east into the overwhelmingly white suburbs for entertainment.

Democrat Harold Ford's House election in 1974 marked the assertion of black political power in the 9th, which was then more compact and much more black than Memphis as a whole. The city itself did not elect a black mayor until 1991, when Ford and other leaders in the black community united behind longtime school superintendent Willie Herenton.

Because of inner-city population decline in Memphis over the years, mapmakers have had to expand the 9th. In 1992, for the first time, the district moved outside the city limits; its black population has held almost steady at 59 percent. The 9th reached east and south to pick up about 80,000 new residents, including some in conservative white areas that had been in the 7th. Still, the 9th remains strongly Democratic: Bill Clinton won two-thirds of its presidential vote in 1992, and Ford took 58 percent, the same as in 1990.

The growth of tourism-related business has helped compensate for the decline since the 1970s of Memphis' industrial base, although the new service-sector jobs are comparatively low-paying. The city also has become a leading distribution center (Federal Express is Memphis-based), and medical services are a big business (St. Jude's Hospital, one of the nation's top pediatric-care facilities, is here). Also, roughly one-third of the nation's cotton crop passes through the Memphis Cotton Exchange.

Election Returns

	9th District	Democrat	Republican
1992	President*	151,590 (66.1%)	68,358 (29.8%)
	House †	123,276 (57.9%)	60,606 (28.5%)
1990	Senate	71,789 (72.9%)	26,731 (27.1%)
	Governor	69,243 (67.9%)	32,749 (32.1%)
1988	President	125,893 (60.8%)	81,218 (39.2%)
	Senate	150,955 (76.7%)	45,901 (23.3%)
1986	Governor	88,724 (60.2%)	58,695 (39.8%)

Vote for Perot was 9,400 (4.1%).   †*Independent/other is greater than 5%.*

Demographics

Population 541,981

Percent change from 1980 7.2%

Land area 254 square miles

Population per square mile 2,137

Counties, 1990 population
Shelby (pt.) 541,981

Cities, 1990 population (10,000 or more)
Memphis (pt.) 519,594

Race and Hispanic origin
White 39.7%
Black 59.2%
American Indian, Eskimo, or Aleut. 0.2%
Asian or Pacific Islander 0.7%
Other 0.2%
Hispanic origin 0.7%

Ancestry

American 4.9%	Irish 9.3%
English 8.3%	Italian 1.8%
French 1.8%	Scotch Irish 3.0%
German 7.5%	Scottish 1.4%

Universities/colleges, 1990-1991 enrollment
Christian Brothers University, Memphis 1,765
Crichton College, Memphis 328
Draughons College, Memphis 328
Le Moyne-Owen College, Memphis 1,066
Memphis College of Art, Memphis 272
Memphis State University, Memphis 20,681
Mid America Baptist Seminary, Memphis 430
Rhodes College, Memphis 1,407
Shelby State Community College, Memphis 4,763
Southern College of Optometry, Memphis 345
University of Tennessee, Memphis 1,785

Newspapers, total circulation (in all districts)
Memphis Commercial Appeal 193,211
West Memphis Evening Times 8,975

Commercial television stations, affiliations
ADI: Memphis (100%)

Cable television systems, total subscribers
Memphis Cablevision; Memphis 148,135

Military installations, 1991
Memphis Defense Depot (Army), Memphis 1,711
Memphis Intl. Airport Air Force Guard Station, Oakville 270

Businesses and other major employers
Federal Express Corp.; Memphis; air cargo services 13,000
Servicemaster Consumer Service; Memphis; management services 9,000

Memphis State University; Memphis 4,500

Baptist Memorial Hospital; Memphis 4,400

U.S. Internal Revenue Service; Memphis 3,800

Methodist Hospitals of Memphis; Memphis 3,700

University of Tennessee; Memphis 3,669

First Tennessee Bank National Assn.; Memphis; commercial banks 2,711

U.S. Veterans Affairs Dept.; Memphis; hospital 2,000

St. Francis Hospital Inc.; Memphis 1,990

Cleo Inc./Cleo Wrap; Memphis; giftwrap paper 1,750

Northwest Airlines Inc.; Memphis; airline 1,500

Scripps Howard Inc./Memphis Publishing; Memphis; publishing 1,500

County of Shelby/Sheriffs Dept.; Memphis 1,500

Union Planters National Bank; Memphis; commercial banks 1,435

International Paper Co.; Memphis; paper products 1,400

Le Bonheur Children's Medical Center; Memphis 1,387

St. Jude Children's Research Hospital; Memphis; research services 1,351

St. Joseph Hospital; Memphis 1,300

Kimberly-Clark Corp.; Memphis; paper mills 1,200

Autozone Inc.; Memphis; auto supply stores 1,150

U.S. Postal Service; Memphis 1,000

Smith & Nephew Richards Inc.; Memphis; surgical instruments/supplies 1,000

Continental Baking Co.; Memphis; bakery products 900

U.S. Army Corps of Engineers; Memphis; engineering services 850

MCI Services Marketing Inc.; Memphis; telephone communications 800

Bocep Ventures/Peabody Orlando; Memphis; real estate operators 800

Express Airlines I Inc./Northwest Airlink; Memphis; airlines 750

Kellogg Co.; Memphis; grain mill products 750

Sharp Electronics Corp.; Memphis; audio/video equipment 750

County of Shelby; Memphis 750

Hotel Peabody Ltd.; Memphis; hotel 725

Sears Roebuck & Co.; Memphis; department stores 715

Wang's Intl. Inc.; Memphis; art supplies 700

City of Memphis/Light, Gas & Water Div.; Memphis 700

Procter & Gamble Cellulose Co.; Memphis; man-made fibers 650

R. A. S. Inc.; Memphis; personnel supply services 650

ISS International Service System/Oxford Building Services; Memphis; building services 650

Federated Dept. Stores/Goldsmiths Dept. Stores; Memphis; department stores 641

Fred's Inc.; Memphis; department stores 620

National Safety Associates Inc; Memphis; air conditioning equipment 600

County of Shelby; Memphis 600

Guardsmark Inc.; Memphis; business/security services 600

Leaf Inc.; Memphis; candies 550

Bellsouth Telecommunications; Memphis; telephone communications 550

Eastwood Medical Center; Memphis 540

AMCA Intl. Construction Corp./Jesco; Memphis; building construction 510

Sanitors Southwest Inc.; Memphis; special contractors 510

Texas

The June 1993 election of Sen. Kay Bailey Hutchison, giving Texas two Republican senators for the first time since Reconstruction, capped decades of slow, but steady progress for the Texas GOP and signalled increasingly difficult times at the polls for Democratic candidates there as they approach the 21st century.

The conservative underpinnings took root in the Lone Star state before Texas was even a state. But like much of the South, Texas has had an historical aversion to the Republican Party dating back to the Civil War. This aversion helped nurture a strain of conservative Texas politicians sometimes called Tory Democrats. Former Sen. Lloyd Bentsen, the slow-talking, white-haired friend of oil barons, came to embody Texas Tories.

For the past century, most of the state's political battles were fought between the Tories and the more populist or liberal elements of the state's Democratic Party. Over the years, the party retained candidates and voters through the leadership of some immensely popular officials—big political names in a big political state. It was hard to buck powerful leaders like Lyndon B. Johnson and former Gov. John Connally. In more modern times, Gov. Ann Richards and Bentsen have held considerable sway.

More importantly, the Democrat-controlled state Legislature has dominated redistricting.

Because of rapid population growth during the 1980s (2.7 million new residents by the 1990 census), Texas picked up three new congressional seats, bringing the state delegation to 30 members. It is the third largest state contingent on Capitol Hill (and the third largest state population), behind California and New York.

Despite the delegation's size, Texas has lost some of its clout on Capitol Hill with the 1989 resignation of former Speaker Jim Wright and Bentsen's 1993 move into the Clinton administration.

Minorities in Texas made the most substantial gains in the 1980s; the state's Hispanic population grew 45 percent from 1980 to 1990, the black population increased 17 percent. As a result, the three new congressional districts were designated majority-minority districts. Republicans challenged the contorted lines that more often resembled ink blots than cohesive voting units, but the Department of Justice ruled that the map complied with the Voting Rights Act, which mandated empowering minority groups.

The gerrymandered lines appeared to put the lock in for incumbents of both parties and set the stage for black and Hispanic victories in the three new districts.

Despite the obvious advantages, minorities won only two of the three new seats in 1992. In the Houston-based 29th District, a non-Hispanic Democrat prevailed twice over a Democratic Hispanic city councilmember in a racially divisive primary and runoff. His election to the House was interpreted largely as a weak performance by the Hispanic community.

In the two remaining new districts of the 1990s, minorities coasted to victory in 1992. Former state Sen. Eddie Bernice Johnson literally helped carve out her district, the Dallas-based 30th. Described by a federal panel of judges as resembling a "microscopic view of a new strain of a disease," the 30th is overwhelmingly Democratic and more than 50 percent black.

State Sen. Frank Tejeda, who also had a hand in redrawing the congressional district boundaries, had no competition in his successful 1992 bid in the south-central 28th district.

But aside from picking up the three new seats in 1992, Democrats did not fare well in Texas in the early 1990s. Bill Clinton lost the state to George Bush in 1992, while one Democratic House member was ousted by Republican challenger Henry Bonilla, who defied historical voting patterns of Texas Hispanics by becoming the first Hispanic Republican member of Congress from the state in 1992.

As far back as 1928, Texans began opting for Republican presidential candidates. But it wasn't really until Republican John Tower's stunning 1961 election to the U.S. Senate from a field of 73 candidates that the GOP started making inroads.

By the late 1980s and early 1990s, Texas voters were willing to express their conservative ideology by pulling Republican levers at all levels. (In 1978, for example, the GOP held just 92 elected offices in the state. By mid-1993, the total exceeded 813.) A further sign of the GOP's growing clout was the number of "switchers"—politicians like Phil Gramm who abandoned the Democratic Party in favor of the GOP.

Texas conservatism is a special blend of independence and strong religious identification. This brand of conservatism has its roots in four basic principles: minimalist government, a strong defense, a healthy private sector and dedication to values of religion and morality.

TEXAS

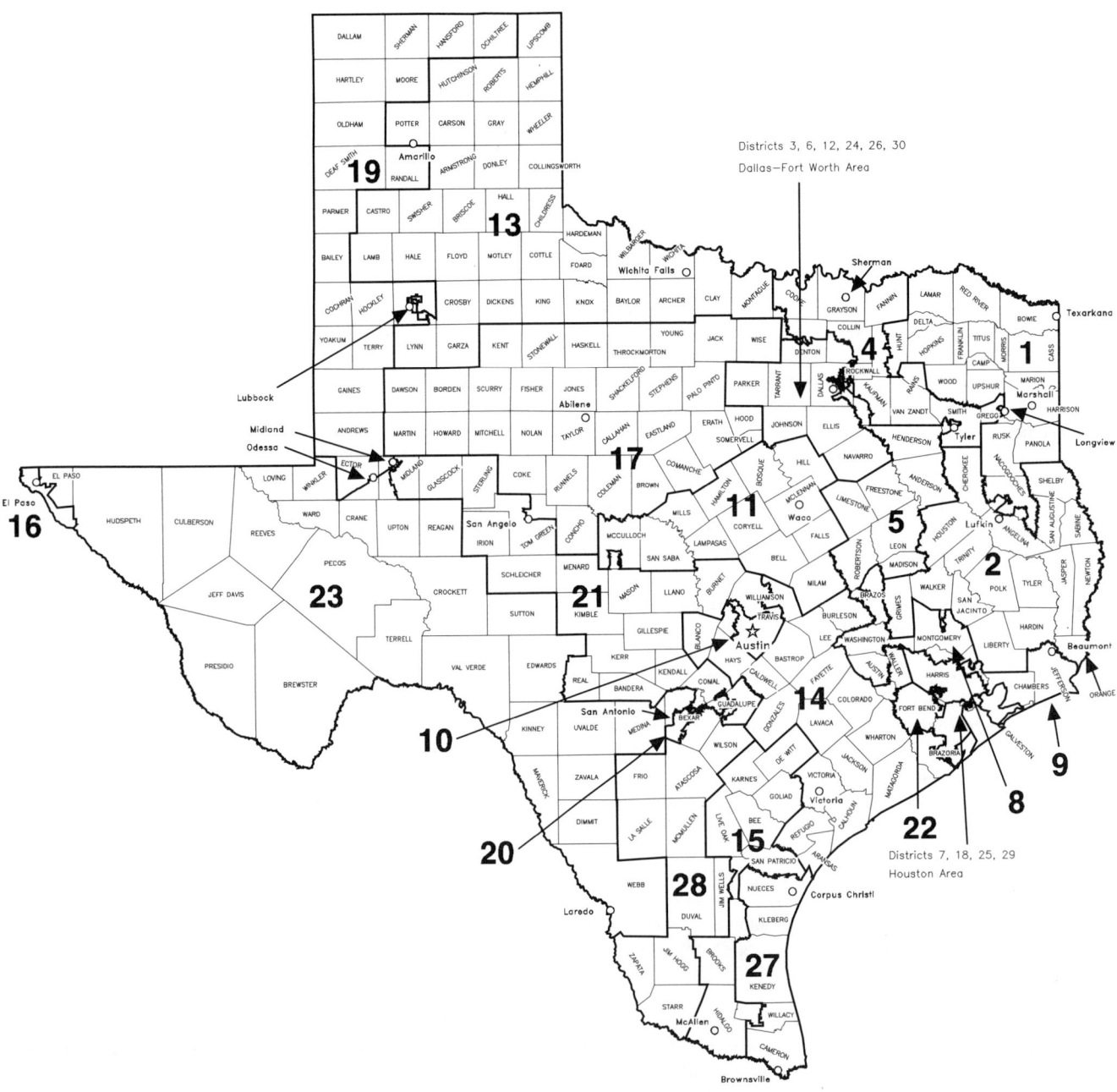

Districts 3, 6, 12, 24, 26, 30
Dallas—Fort Worth Area

Districts 7, 18, 25, 29
Houston Area

Capitalizing on its affinity with those values, the Texas GOP has built a pyramid-like structure that boasts big victories at the top and a solid foundation of dedicated volunteers and wealthy donors. In the 1990s, the challenge for the Republican Party will be to strengthen and broaden its center tiers, adding to its numbers in both the state Legislature and the Congress.

Statewide candidates in Texas face enormous challenges in appealing to voters of a state that more closely resembles several small countries. Second in size to Alaska, Texas has a land and water area of 266,807 square miles; it is as large as New England, New York, Pennsylvania, Ohio and Illinois combined.

Texas is frequently broken into six distinct regions, each with its own geography, economy and cultural flavor.

The Plains, abutting the Oklahoma and New Mexico borders, is the largest and most sparsely populated region. Residents are held captive by the fluctuations of the oil and gas markets, along with some crops. Communities such as Midland, Odessa, Lubbock and Abilene struggled in the mid-1980s as the oil industry faltered. But the local economy began to stabilize in the early 1990s.

South of the Plains is a sprawling expanse along the Mexican border that stretches from Brownsville in the southeast to El Paso in the West. Virtually every aspect of life along the border is influenced by Mexico. *Maquiladora*—or twin—plants in which goods are manufactured partially in Mexico and completed in the United States, dot the landscape along the Rio Grande. Both English and Spanish are spoken in border towns and many U.S. communities celebrate a host of Mexican holidays and religious feast days.

Dallas and Fort Worth form the heart of the Metroplex, a sophisticated urban area that has been heavily reliant on the military and transportation industries. As defense spending has been cut back, computers and electronics have played a larger role in the region's economy.

East Texas is often described as the buckle on America's Bible Belt. The rural counties along the Arkansas and Louisiana borders benefit from an abundance of such natural resources as oil, gas and timber. "Yellow dog Democrats" have traditionally dominated East Texas elections.

The Gulf Coast is the most populous section of Texas and is perhaps the most diverse, with a mix of tourism, petroleum refineries, military bases, heavy manufacturing and fishing. Houston, the fourth-largest city in the nation, takes in all those industries and more with a major port, medical center and NASA's Johnson Space Center.

Of the six regions, the Central Corridor is perhaps the least defined. Liberal cities such as San Antonio and Austin (the state capital) are included with more rural, conservative towns such as Waco and Killeen.

Unlike much of the country, Texas was coming out of its economic doldrums in the early 1990s. The oil and gas industries had stabilized and the state as a whole seemed to be learning the monetary value of diversifying.

Table 1 Population

District	Population	Population under 18	Voting-age population	Median age
1	566,217	149,663	416,554	34.3
2	566,217	151,944	414,273	33.6
3	566,217	146,642	419,575	32.7
4	566,217	152,921	413,296	33.7
5	566,217	152,036	414,181	31.2
6	566,217	154,492	411,725	31.3
7	566,217	153,395	412,822	31.7
8	566,217	157,991	408,226	30.1
9	566,217	155,246	410,971	32.6
10	566,217	136,069	430,148	29.3
11	566,217	152,689	413,528	29.9
12	566,217	153,403	412,814	31.3
13	566,217	156,727	409,490	31.9
14	566,217	158,842	407,375	32.3
15	566,217	196,918	369,299	27.7
16	566,217	183,232	382,985	28.0
17	566,217	153,647	412,570	33.7
18	566,217	151,799	414,418	30.3
19	566,217	163,216	403,001	30.5
20	566,217	167,233	398,984	28.5
21	566,217	145,719	420,498	34.3
22	566,217	159,530	406,687	31.6
23	566,217	191,270	374,947	28.6
24	566,217	170,041	396,176	29.3
25	566,217	161,187	405,030	30.0
26	566,217	143,470	422,747	30.7
27	566,217	185,595	380,622	29.2
28	566,217	183,581	382,636	29.4
29	566,217	188,762	377,455	27.1
30	566,217	158,579	407,638	28.7
State	16,986,510	4,835,839	12,150,671	30.8

Table 2 Voting-Age Persons

District	White*	Black*	American Indian, Eskimo, or Aleut*	Asian or Pacific Islander*	Other*	Hispanic*	Male*	Female*
1	81.5%	16.4%	0.4%	0.3%	1.5%	2.7%	47.0%	53.0%
2	81.2	15.4	0.4	0.3	2.7	4.9	49.6	50.4
3	90.3	3.9	0.4	3.1	2.3	5.4	47.6	52.4
4	89.5	7.7	0.6	0.4	1.9	3.6	47.4	52.6
5	74.1	15.3	0.5	1.3	8.8	15.3	50.3	49.7
6	91.6	4.0	0.4	2.0	1.9	4.9	48.9	51.1
7	84.9	5.3	0.3	5.2	4.4	10.9	48.7	51.3
8	90.2	4.7	0.3	1.9	2.8	6.5	49.4	50.6
9	74.9	19.8	0.3	1.8	3.1	8.5	48.0	52.0
10	75.7	10.0	0.4	3.1	10.8	18.7	49.7	50.3
11	78.3	14.6	0.4	1.6	5.2	10.4	49.8	50.2
12	82.5	7.4	0.5	1.7	8.0	13.8	48.6	51.4
13	81.8	7.3	0.6	1.1	9.1	15.7	47.6	52.4
14	79.7	10.4	0.3	0.5	9.1	20.4	48.6	51.4
15	76.6	1.1	0.2	0.4	21.7	69.6	47.2	52.8
16	77.5	3.6	0.4	1.2	17.3	66.4	47.4	52.6
17	87.8	3.2	0.4	0.5	8.1	14.1	47.9	52.1
18	41.0	48.6	0.2	3.0	7.1	13.7	48.8	51.2
19	88.2	2.2	0.5	0.9	8.2	16.0	48.2	51.8
20	73.9	5.7	0.4	1.4	18.6	56.1	48.0	52.0
21	92.3	2.2	0.3	1.0	4.2	12.3	47.5	52.5
22	78.7	7.5	0.3	6.6	7.0	14.4	50.0	50.0
23	75.9	2.9	0.4	0.7	20.1	58.3	47.9	52.1
24	67.6	17.9	0.6	2.2	11.7	18.8	48.9	51.1
25	63.7	24.9	0.3	3.8	7.3	14.9	48.0	52.0
26	88.1	3.9	0.5	3.6	3.9	8.2	49.0	51.0
27	80.1	2.4	0.3	0.6	16.5	61.4	47.3	52.7
28	70.4	8.7	0.3	0.7	19.8	56.5	47.5	52.5
29	57.8	9.8	0.4	1.7	30.3	55.4	51.3	48.7
30	41.7	47.1	0.4	2.0	8.8	15.1	48.2	51.8
State	77.4	11.2	0.4	1.8	9.2	22.4	48.5	51.5

As percent of voting-age population.

Table 3   Voting-Age Persons by Age Groups

District	18-24*	25-44*	45-54*	55-64*	65 and over*
1	14.0%	37.8%	13.8%	12.7%	21.7%
2	13.7	39.6	14.1	13.1	19.5
3	12.0	51.9	15.3	9.3	11.5
4	12.8	41.7	14.5	12.2	18.8
5	14.5	46.4	12.3	10.7	16.2
6	13.1	53.9	15.6	9.1	8.2
7	12.1	56.5	14.6	9.0	7.8
8	19.1	47.0	15.2	9.1	9.6
9	13.0	45.5	13.9	12.1	15.5
10	21.1	51.0	11.0	7.6	9.3
11	19.5	40.9	11.8	10.5	17.3
12	15.0	45.3	13.0	10.8	16.0
13	15.9	39.2	12.7	12.4	19.8
14	15.3	40.6	13.3	12.1	18.8
15	17.1	42.1	12.7	11.3	16.8
16	18.3	45.3	13.0	11.1	12.3
17	13.4	38.7	13.3	12.8	21.9
18	16.8	48.0	12.9	10.3	12.0
19	16.5	44.3	13.3	11.5	14.3
20	18.8	46.0	11.7	10.0	13.6
21	12.0	43.8	14.1	11.9	18.2
22	12.5	54.0	14.9	9.4	9.2
23	16.0	45.1	14.0	11.2	13.6
24	16.5	48.8	12.9	9.4	12.4
25	15.9	51.9	13.0	9.3	9.8
26	14.1	56.3	14.6	8.4	6.7
27	15.8	44.4	13.1	11.4	15.3
28	15.7	43.3	13.6	11.8	15.7
29	18.8	48.9	11.8	9.2	11.4
30	18.3	49.9	11.9	9.0	10.9
State	15.6	46.3	13.4	10.6	14.1

As percent of voting-age population.

Table 4   Income and Occupation

District	Median family income	Families in poverty	White collar*	Blue collar*	Service*	Farm*
1	$26,629	15.4%	47.3%	34.0%	14.3%	4.4%
2	25,750	16.2	45.9	34.5	15.5	4.2
3	52,367	2.6	77.9	13.6	7.9	0.6
4	32,013	10.4	54.4	29.9	12.7	3.0
5	27,530	15.9	51.1	29.8	16.4	2.7
6	48,617	3.1	72.6	17.7	9.0	0.7
7	51,258	4.1	76.9	14.1	8.2	0.7
8	42,696	6.9	67.7	20.2	10.4	1.8
9	35,080	12.7	58.5	26.2	13.9	1.3
10	35,723	10.4	69.7	16.2	12.9	1.1
11	26,698	13.7	52.2	27.7	16.0	4.0
12	31,729	10.7	53.6	31.7	13.0	1.7
13	25,721	16.2	46.8	29.6	16.8	6.8
14	29,173	15.1	48.6	30.9	14.3	6.1
15	19,554	31.6	49.5	28.9	14.5	7.1
16	24,108	22.6	55.9	28.2	14.8	1.1
17	26,263	14.5	48.1	29.7	15.8	6.4
18	25,662	21.6	54.8	25.8	18.4	1.1
19	32,227	10.9	58.4	24.1	12.3	5.2
20	25,398	20.4	57.5	23.8	17.5	1.2
21	37,861	7.1	67.1	18.3	11.5	3.1
22	46,628	5.9	70.5	18.5	9.9	1.2
23	24,064	24.2	55.1	25.8	14.8	4.4
24	31,612	12.5	53.0	31.9	13.6	1.5
25	35,899	11.0	61.3	24.8	13.0	0.8
26	48,733	3.8	74.4	16.0	8.8	0.8

District	Median family income	Families in poverty	White collar*	Blue collar*	Service*	Farm*
27	24,016	24.6	54.1	26.4	16.5	2.9
28	22,425	24.2	47.2	31.8	17.3	3.7
29	22,230	23.9	38.0	43.5	16.9	1.6
30	25,900	19.2	53.6	27.1	18.0	1.3
State	31,553	14.1	58.6	25.3	13.5	2.6

As percent of employed persons age 16 and over.

Table 5   Education: School Years Completed

District	Less than grade 9*	Grades 9-12 no diploma*	High school diploma*	College bachelor's degree or higher*
1	12.2%	19.8%	31.0%	13.1%
2	14.4	20.8	33.2	10.4
3	2.7	6.1	19.2	41.3
4	9.8	16.5	28.8	16.3
5	14.8	18.9	28.2	14.3
6	2.5	7.5	22.7	32.8
7	3.6	6.3	18.8	40.7
8	6.1	10.9	25.0	29.2
9	9.3	14.2	29.5	18.9
10	7.3	9.5	19.4	34.5
11	11.6	15.8	30.1	14.8
12	11.8	17.3	28.2	15.3
13	15.1	18.1	29.6	13.7
14	17.5	16.4	29.5	13.8
15	35.6	13.6	21.5	11.5
16	24.0	12.7	22.8	15.4
17	15.1	18.7	29.9	13.4
18	12.9	20.5	26.3	17.5
19	10.1	13.9	26.2	20.8
20	17.7	13.9	24.7	15.6
21	6.9	9.4	25.2	28.0
22	6.3	9.4	21.8	32.6
23	26.7	13.6	21.0	16.6
24	13.8	17.4	27.3	15.4
25	8.4	13.3	26.3	22.5
26	4.4	7.3	19.9	37.0
27	25.2	14.3	22.4	14.8
28	24.7	16.9	28.4	8.3
29	31.2	22.7	24.0	6.5
30	12.8	18.6	26.4	16.4
State	13.5	14.4	25.6	20.3

As percent of persons age 25 and over.

Table 6   Housing and Residential Patterns

District	Owner occupied	Renter occupied	Urban	Rural
1	72.5%	27.5%	44.0%	56.0%
2	74.2	25.8	38.9	61.1
3	66.9	33.1	97.6	2.4
4	70.6	29.4	51.1	48.9
5	59.0	41.0	75.0	25.0
6	65.0	35.0	91.0	9.0
7	56.0	44.0	95.8	4.2
8	64.0	36.0	65.2	34.8
9	63.4	36.6	86.9	13.1
10	45.2	54.8	92.0	8.0
11	59.4	40.6	71.4	28.6
12	61.5	38.5	87.0	13.0
13	64.8	35.2	72.7	27.3
14	68.9	31.1	48.7	51.3

District	Owner occupied	Renter occupied	Urban	Rural
15	69.9	30.1	70.6	29.4
16	58.1	41.9	98.2	1.8
17	70.6	29.4	61.6	38.4
18	46.8	53.2	99.1	0.9
19	65.1	34.9	81.6	18.4
20	50.1	49.9	97.3	2.7
21	66.8	33.2	70.8	29.2
22	64.1	35.9	86.3	13.7
23	68.1	31.9	75.1	24.9
24	59.5	40.5	91.1	8.9
25	51.5	48.5	99.1	0.9
26	53.7	46.3	95.3	4.7
27	61.0	39.0	86.1	13.9
28	68.6	31.4	78.7	21.3
29	46.2	53.8	99.9	0.1
30	37.4	62.6	100.0	0.0
State	60.9	39.1	80.3	19.7

1st District

Northeast — Texarkana; Marshall

Texas' personality has both southern and western elements, and the former is dominant in the 19 counties that make up the 1st. Life in northeastern Texas has a distinctly southern feel; many people's livelihoods are linked to the land—in timber, dairying and other agricultural pursuits.

The closest thing to a big city in the district is Texarkana (Bowie County), a community divided by the Arkansas-Texas line. More than half of its 53,000 residents live on the Texas side. The city is a peculiar blend of togetherness and separation: There is a joint Chamber of Commerce and some utility services are shared, but there are separate mayors, police departments and school systems.

Texarkana's most famous native is billionaire businessman and White House aspirant Ross Perot. The 1992 presidential vote in Bowie County almost exactly mirrored that of the district as a whole. Perot got 22 percent of the county's vote, while Bill Clinton and George Bush each took 39 percent. Clinton carried the county by a mere 49 votes; districtwide, he won by 1,229 votes.

Economically, the 1st has been through some tough times of late. An important area employer, Lone Star Steel, filed for bankruptcy protection in 1989. As is the case with many businesses in Texas, the fortunes of Lone Star rise and fall with the price of crude oil. When the oil industry crashed in 1984, there was little demand for the pipeline Lone Star produced; foreign competition further hampered the company. Once the largest employer in the district (7,000 jobs in 1981), Lone Star now has fewer than 1,200 workers.

Also in recent years, Canadian imports have posed a threat to local timber sales, and Mexican cattle ranchers have put a dent in the east Texas market. Nevertheless, those two industries remain staples of the region. Wood is in abundance and sold to furniture makers, paper mills and lumber companies.

In many of the small towns of rural east Texas, cows, chickens and trees outnumber people. Food processors Tyson Foods and Pilgrim Industries are big employers. Hopkins County is the leading dairy county in the state and the Southwest. Cattle

ranches dominate Lamar and Red River counties, which lie along the Oklahoma border.

With its traditional economic pillars shaky, the district has become more reliant on government-related business, which is also proving problematic. The Red River Army Depot in Bowie County is the largest employer in the 1st. But in mid-1993, Red River was on a list of facilities proposed for closing as the Pentagon cuts costs.

The 1st has been dubbed the buckle on the southern Bible Belt; most voters are churchgoing conservatives. Clinton ran strongest in the counties along the Arkansas, Louisiana and Oklahoma borders; Bush fared best in the counties on the district's western border, topping out with a 49 percent tally in Nacogdoches County.

Election Returns

	1st District	Democrat	Republican
1992	President*	85,745 (38.8%)	84,516 (38.3%)
	House	152,209 (100.0%)	—
1990	Senate	56,335 (39.8%)	85,264 (60.2%)
1988	President	97,346 (44.8%)	120,063 (55.2%)

Vote for Perot was 50,499 (22.9%).

Demographics

Population 566,217

Percent change from 1980 7.4%

Land area 11,567 square miles

Population per square mile 49

Counties, 1990 population

Bowie 81,665	Marion 9,984
Camp 9,904	Morris 13,200
Cass 29,982	Nacogdoches (pt.) 43,306
Delta 4,857	Panola 22,035
Franklin 7,802	Red River 14,317
Gregg (pt.) 34,337	Rusk 43,735
Harrison 57,483	Titus 24,009
Hopkins 28,833	Upshur 31,370
Hunt (pt.) 36,069	Wood 29,380
Lamar 43,949	

Cities, 1990 population (10,000 or more)

Greenville (pt.) 11,141	Nacogdoches (pt.) 22,039
Henderson 11,139	Paris 24,699
Longview (pt.) 32,351	Sulphur Springs 14,062
Marshall 23,682	Texarkana 31,656
Mount Pleasant 12,291	

Race and Hispanic origin
White 79.5%
Black 18.1%
American Indian, Eskimo, or Aleut. 0.4%
Asian or Pacific Islander 0.3%
Other 1.7%
Hispanic origin 3.2%

Ancestry

American	12.5%	Irish	20.3%
Dutch	2.8%	Italian	1.1%
English	12.4%	Scotch Irish	3.1%
French	3.3%	Scottish	1.6%
German	14.1%		

Universities/colleges, 1990-1991 enrollment

East Texas Baptist University, Marshall   924
East Texas State University, Commerce   7,840
East Texas State University, Texarkana   1,257
Jarvis Christian College, Hawkins   598
Le Tourneau University, Longview   1,015
Northeast Texas Community College, Mt. Pleasant   1,859
Panola College, Carthage   1,562
Paris Junior College, Paris   2,325
Stephen F. Austin State University, Nacogdoches   12,815
Texarkana College, Texarkana   3,894
Wiley College, Marshall   463

Newspapers, total circulation (in all districts)

Dallas Morning News   452,101
Houston Chronicle   421,140
Longview News-Journal   30,302
Marshall News Messenger   9,682
Texarkana Gazette   31,922

Commercial television stations, affiliations

ADI: Shreveport-Texarkana (58%), Tyler-Longview (21%) and Dallas-Fort Worth (21%)
KFXK-TV, Longview (Fox)

Cable television systems, total subscribers

Dimension Cable Services; Texarkana   25,000
Falcon Cable TV; Marshall   5,307
Longview Cable TV Co.; Longview   19,000
Nacogdoches Cable TV; Nacogdoches   10,607
Sulphur Springs Cable TV; Sulphur Springs   5,655
TCA Cable; Paris   10,845

Military installations, 1991

Red River Army Depot, Texarkana   4,865

Businesses and other major employers

Jordan Health Services Inc.; Mount Vernon; home health services   4,000
Pilgrims Pride Corp./Pilgrim Prepared Foods; Mt. Pleasant; meat products   2,500
Texas Utilities Electric Co.; Tatum; electric services   1,900
Marathon Mfg. Companies; Longview; construction machinery   1,669
Texarkana Memorial Hospital; Texarkana   1,553
Thiokol Corp./Longhorn Div.; Karnack; ordnance/accessories   1,419
Day & Zimmermann Inc.; ordnance/accessories   1,300
Good Shepherd Hospital Inc.; Longview   1,192
Stephen F. Austin State University; Nacogdoches   1,135
Lone Star Steel Co.; Lone Star; steel products   1,100
International Paper Co./Texarkana Mill; Texarkana; paper mills   972
East Texas State University; Commerce   865
Pilgrims Pride Corp.; Pittsburg; poultry/eggs   850
Tyson Foods Inc.; Carthage; meat products   825
Texarkana Independent School District; Texarkana   769
Heritage Care Group Inc.; Texarkana; nursing   750

Merico Inc./Earth Grains; Paris; bakery products   700
Babcock & Wilcox Co.; Paris; building construction   670
Nacogdoches Independent School District; Nacogdoches   600
Kimberly-Clark Corp./Paris Plant; Paris; textile goods   525
GTE Southwest Inc.; Texarkana; telephone communications   516

2nd District

East — Lufkin; Orange

Stretching along Texas' eastern border, from Louisiana in the north to Port Orange in the south, the 2nd is another world from the dusty, barren landscape of west Texas, far removed from the barrios on the Mexican border and light years away from the glitz of metropolitan Dallas and Houston.

Instead, the thick forests of east Texas' Piney Woods call to mind stretches of Oregon, Washington state or New England. And the "Golden Triangle" of Orange, Port Arthur and Beaumont, with its shipyards, refineries and fishing docks, more resembles East Coast cities such as Philadelphia and Norfolk, Va.

But the image of the typical Texan as a rough-and-ready character fits the people here just as well as it does any in the Lone Star State.

Located 36 miles from the Gulf of Mexico on the Sabine River, Orange once drew its revenue from timber, cattle, rice and oil. Today, the city is better known for "Chemical Row," an industrial corridor that saw massive layoffs in the late 1980s.

The ports of Orange and Arthur rely heavily on federal dollars; in late 1992 the Orange Shipbuilding Co. won a Navy contract to build refueling barges, including one of the type used in the Persian Gulf war. In late 1992 Lamar University (1,300 students) received $5 million to open a Navy ship design center and $2 million for an Air Force project aimed at computerizing and standardizing bidding and manufacturing guidelines.

Although Jefferson County (Beaumont and Port Arthur) is just over the district line in the 9th, it plays an integral role in the economy of the 2nd. Shipyards, petrochemical refineries and a steel mill are prevalent in the county.

In the northern and western counties of the 2nd, timber remains the primary industry, despite slowdowns in the construction trades and increased competition from abroad. In his 1992 re-election victory, Democrat Rep. Charles Wilson appealed to voters in this area by opposing plans to sell wood chips to the Japanese; such raw-material sales enable foreign competitors to do the more lucrative work of producing finished products.

Angelina County, with 70 percent of its land in commercial forests, is the leading timber-producing county in Texas. The town of Lufkin has 60 manufacturing companies that employ more than 8,000 people.

At election time, populist Democrats fare better than outright liberals in east Texas. Democratic presidential hopeful Walter F. Mondale failed to carry the 2nd in 1984. More moderate Michael S. Dukakis in 1988 and Bill Clinton in 1992 both narrowly won the district.

Election Returns

	2nd District	Democrat	Republican
1992	President*	91,698 (42.6%)	76,372 (35.5%)

		Democrat	Republican
	House	118,625 (56.3%)	92,176 (43.7%)
	2nd District	**Democrat**	**Republican**
1990	Senate	57,452 (43.1%)	75,986 (56.9%)
1988	President	106,769 (51.2%)	101,746 (48.8%)

*Vote for Perot was 47,167 (21.9%).

Demographics

Population 566,217

Percent change from 1980 7.5%

Land area 14,196 square miles

Population per square mile 40

Counties, 1990 population

Angelina 69,884	Orange 80,509
Cherokee 41,049	Polk 30,687
Grimes 18,828	Sabine 9,586
Hardin 41,320	San Augustine 7,999
Houston 21,375	San Jacinto 16,372
Jasper 31,102	Shelby 22,034
Liberty 52,726	Trinity 11,445
Montgomery (pt.) 18,722	Tyler 16,646
Nacogdoches (pt.) 11,447	Walker 50,917
Newton 13,569	

Cities, 1990 population (10,000 or more)

Conroe (pt.) 13,459	Lufkin 30,206
Huntsville 27,925	Orange 19,381
Jacksonville 12,765	Vidor 10,935

Race and Hispanic origin

White 79.4%
Black 16.7%
American Indian, Eskimo, or Aleut. 0.4%
Asian or Pacific Islander 0.3%
Other 3.2%
Hispanic origin 5.6%

Ancestry

American 10.3%	Irish 18.9%
Dutch 2.4%	Italian 1.4%
English 11.5%	Polish 1.1%
French 5.4%	Scotch Irish 3.2%
French Canadian 3.5%	Scottish 1.2%
German 14.3%	

Universities/colleges, 1990-1991 enrollment

Angelina College, Lufkin 3,115
Jacksonville College, Jacksonville 261
Lamar University-Orange, Orange 1,282
Lon Morris College, Jacksonville 320
Sam Houston State University, Huntsville 12,753

Newspapers, total circulation (in all districts)

Beaumont Enterprise 69,814
Houston Chronicle 421,140
Houston Post 292,061
Huntsville Item 5,245
Lufkin Daily News 15,152
Tyler Telegraph-Courier Times 42,998

Commercial television stations, affiliations

ADI: Tyler-Longview (35%), Houston (31%), Beaumont-Port Arthur (28%) and Shreveport-Texarkana (6%)
KBMT, Beaumont (ABC)
KFDM-TV, Beaumont (CBS)
KBTX-TV, Bryan (CBS)
KETK-TV, Jacksonville (NBC)
KTRE-TV, Lufkin (ABC)
KJAC-TV, Port Arthur (NBC)
KLSB, Nacogdoches (None)

Cable television systems, total subscribers

Cablecom of Lufkin; Lufkin 12,751
Huntsville Cable TV; Huntsville 5,512
Lakewood Cable; Shepherd 8,026
TCI of Texas; Orange 7,700

Businesses and other major employers

State of Texas/Corrections Dept.; Huntsville 5,321
Lufkin Industries Inc.; Lufkin; oil field equipment 2,000
Sam Houston State University; Huntsville 1,836
Du Pont E. I. De Nemours & Co.; Orange; heavy construction 1,500
Temple-Inland Forest Products Corp./Bleached Paperboard Div.; Evadale; pulp mills 1,200
State of Texas/Mental Health Dept.; Rusk 1,100
Holly Farms of Texas Inc.; Center; meat products 1,000
Champion Intl. Corp.; Lufkin; plywood 1,000
Tyson Foods Inc.; Tenaha; crop services 875
Memorial Medical Center of East Texas; Lufkin 771
Huntsville Independent School District; Huntsville 750
Citation Corp./Texas Foundries; Lufkin; iron/steel foundries 715
Thermo Tech Inc.; Orange; special contractors 700
Louisiana-Pacific Corp.; New Waverly; millwork 700
State of Texas; Lufkin 700
West Orange-Cove Consolidated School District; Orange 650
Nacogdoches County Memorial Hospital; Nacogdoches 583

3rd District

North Dallas; Northern Suburbs

The 3rd (see map on page 709), which includes upscale sections of northern and eastern Dallas County and part of Collin County, is one of the most affluent districts in the country, and normally one of the most Republican in presidential voting. Median family income in the 3rd exceeds $50,000, which helps explain why this has been dubbed the "Golden District." This area is best known from the TV show "Dallas," which celebrated the lifestyle and material trappings of the city's high-income oil barons and other business elite.

The catalyst for business growth in modern Dallas came during the 1930 east Texas oil strike when the city reaped the benefits of the rich oilfields. As residents cashed in on the gushers, Dallas became home to numerous millionaires.

The Park Cities, University Park and Highland Park, with their corporate chieftains and wealthy heirs, epitomize the prosperity of much of the district. Located in University Park is Southern Methodist University, an 8,800-student campus affiliated with the Methodist church. (The university is actually located in the 30th District.) SMU has always had an upper-crust air about it—at football games, students have been known to hold up signs that say, "Our maids went to UT" (the University of Texas). The university, with its heavy business orientation, has helped stock Dallas' myriad financial firms and other corporations with MBAs.

The 3rd is a bastion of Republicanism; even in his home turf Ross Perot could not defeat George Bush in the district. Bush won here in 1992 with 48 percent of the vote, well below the typical GOP tally because 30 percent of those casting ballots went for the billionaire businessman Perot. Democrat Bill Clinton was a nonfactor in the presidential race, running third with barely a fifth of the vote.

Three-fourths of the vote in the 3rd comes out of Dallas County; the balance is cast in Collin County (Plano). Collin has has seen tremendous residential growth in recent years, due in part to the arrival in the area of a number of corporate headquarters, including those of the J. C. Penney Co. and Electronic Data Systems Corp., the computer firm that Perot founded and later sold to General Motors. Executives for these companies (both of which are in the 26th District) help sustain a market for half-million-dollar mansions in developments such as West Plano's Deerfield.

The Collin County part of the 3rd, filled with young, upwardly mobile professionals, is only slightly less Republican than the district's Dallas County sections. Conservative attitudes and old Texas traditions prevail: High school football games in Plano draw capacity crowds of 10,000 on Friday nights in the fall.

Although downtown Dallas is not in the 3rd, its presence is felt in the district. The city's white-collar companies draw heavily from the 3rd for their work force. And Dallas' museums, orchestra and other cultural amenities rely on patronage from the residents of the 3rd. ·

Not all the 3rd is glitz and glamour. Communities such as Garland and Mesquite are popular middle-class suburbs. Mesquite, a city of 101,500 east of Dallas, hosts the world-renowned Mesquite Rodeo every Friday and Saturday night from April through September. It was here that Joe Kool, reputedly one of the toughest bulls in the world to ride, appeared regularly for a decade.

Election Returns

	3rd District	Democrat	Republican
1992	President*	58,352 (21.1%)	133,807 (48.4%)
	House †	—	201,569 (86.1%)
1990	Senate	40,830 (24.2%)	127,892 (75.8%)
1988	President	61,094 (25.2%)	180,931 (74.8%)

*Vote for Perot was 84,088 (30.4%).   †Independent/other is greater than 5%.

Demographics

Population 566,217

Percent change from 1980 7.5%

Land area 316 square miles

Population per square mile 1,794

Counties, 1990 population
Collin (pt.) 135,633   Dallas (pt.) 430,584

Cities, 1990 population (10,000 or more)
Allen 18,309   Plano (pt.) 88,953
Dallas (pt.) 162,727   Richardson (pt.) 39,833
Garland (pt.) 136,125   Rowlett (pt.) 16,804
Mesquite (pt.) 44,903   University Park 22,259

Race and Hispanic origin
White 89.3%
Black 4.4%
American Indian, Eskimo, or Aleut. 0.4%
Asian or Pacific Islander 3.4%
Other 2.6%
Hispanic origin 6.0%

Ancestry
American 5.7%   Italian 3.3%
Czechoslovakian 1.0%   Norwegian 1.2%
Dutch 2.7%   Polish 2.3%
English 21.3%   Scotch Irish 4.7%
French 4.8%   Scottish 3.6%
German 25.3%   Swedish 1.7%
Irish 19.0%   Welsh 1.0%

Universities/colleges, 1990-1991 enrollment
Art Institute of Dallas, Dallas 1,172
University of Texas-Dallas, Richardson 8,560

Newspapers, total circulation (in all districts)
Dallas Morning News 452,101
Fort Worth Star-Telegram 250,099
Plano Star Courier 14,313

Commercial television stations, affiliations
ADI: Dallas-Fort Worth (100%)

Cable television systems, total subscribers
Park Cities Cable TV; Dallas 7,100
Storer Cable TV of Texas; Garland 37,470
TCI of Texas; Dallas 91,647
TCI of Texas; Mesquite 25,187

Military installations, 1991
Garland Air Force Guard Station, Garland 38

Businesses and other major employers
Texas Instruments Inc.; Dallas; electronic components 17,000
Unigate Restaurant Inc.; Dallas; restaurants 5,475
E-Systems Inc./Garland Div.; Garland; communications equipment 4,700
Presbyterian Hospital of Dallas; Dallas 4,000
Blue Cross/Blue Shield of Texas; Richardson; medical service/health insurance 2,300
Ericsson Radio Systems Inc.; Richardson; telecommunications equipment 1,600
University of Texas-Dallas; Richardson 1,500
Rockwell Intl. Corp./Command & Control Systems Div.; Richardson; aircraft/parts 1,400
City of Plano; Plano 1,400
MCI Telecommunications Corp.; Richardson; research services 1,000
Digital Equipment Corp.; Dallas; computers 1,000
Electrospace Systems Inc.; Richardson; communications equipment 951

DALLAS — FORT WORTH AREA

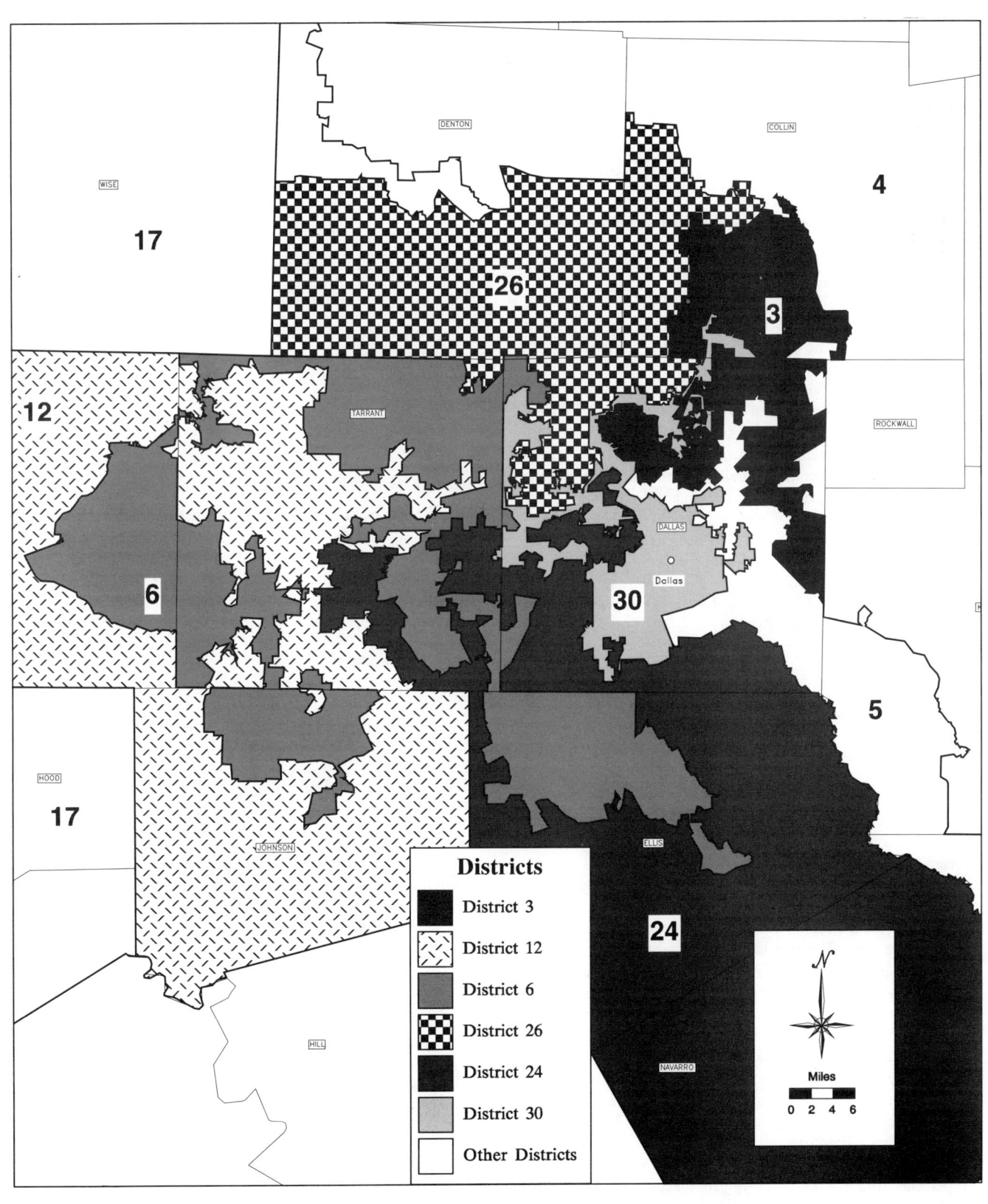

WISE

17

DENTON

26

COLLIN

4

TARRANT

12

3

ROCKWALL

6

DALLAS

Dallas

30

5

HOOD

17

JOHNSON

ELLIS

24

HILL

NAVARRO

Districts

- District 3
- District 12
- District 6
- District 26
- District 24
- District 30
- Other Districts

N

Miles

0 2 4 6

J. C. Penney Life Insurance Co.; Plano; life insurance 804

Kraft General Foods Inc./Kraft USA; Garland; preserved fruits/vegetables 800

Fina Oil & Chemical Co.; Dallas; petroleum refining 750

Kroger Co.; Garland; grocery stores 730

Baylor Medical Center at Garland; Garland 650

Occidental Chemical Holding Corp.; Dallas; organic chemicals 625

Fujitsu America Inc.; Richardson; communications equipment 600

D. L. M. Inc./Argus Communications Div.; Allen; book publishing 600

Intecom Inc.; Allen; communications equipment 600

NME Hospital Inc./Doctors Hospital; Dallas 550

4th District

Northeast — Sherman; Part of Tyler

Although the core of Sam Rayburn's home district remains intact, the 4th of the 1990s is dramatically different in its economic and political makeup.

For 48 years Rayburn represented the compact square in a northeast corner of Texas; from 1934 until his death in 1961 the lines were not touched. During his congressional tenure the 4th was a sparsely populated, agricultural district. The region missed out on the insurance fortunes of Dallas and the oil wealth of west Texas and the Gulf Coast. With no large industry, the people relied on the land. The rich, dark soil, known as blacklands, is conducive to cotton, hay, oats and sorghum. (At one time, Greenville had the largest inland cotton compressor in the nation.)

Since then, state mapmakers have expanded the boundaries, the land has been "cottoned out" and the urban sprawl of Dallas has reached the 4th. Most of the small, family farms have been replaced by large corporate entities.

From Rockwall, the glittering Dallas skyline is easily visible. Residents throughout Rockwall County commute to Dallas, many working at banks, insurance firms or telecommunications companies; AT&T is a major employer. Population in Collin and Rockwall counties doubled in the 1970s, and nearly again in Rockwall in the 1980s.

The E-Systems plant in Greenville is another example of the changes evident in the 4th. The company, which develops and modifies aircraft, receives contracts from the U.S. military, foreign countries and private companies.

At the eastern end of the 4th, where cotton once flourished, oil boomed in the 1970s and early 1980s. When the industry crashed in 1984, the region was hurt. There remains a good deal of oil in the ground, particularly in Longview (Gregg County) and Tyler (Smith County), but little pumping is taking place. Tyler's economy is bolstered by its abundant rose industry. The self-proclaimed "Rose Capital of the World" is responsible for a large share of the world's roses.

Agriculture has not disappeared entirely from the 4th. The substantial peanut crop in Cooke, Grayson and Hunt counties helped draw the North Carolina-based Lance cracker company to Greenville to set up a large factory.

The 4th has shifted toward more conservative views in recent decades. In the 1992 presidential contest Bush won the 4th with 41 percent. And the GOP down-ballot candidates have been making gains as well. In the 1980s all local officials in Rockwall County were Democrats; by 1993 all but one were Republican.

Election Returns

	4th District	Democrat	Republican
1992	President*	65,617 (28.5%)	95,181 (41.3%)
	House	128,008 (58.1%)	83,875 (38.1%)
1990	Senate	47,197 (33.3%)	94,572 (66.7%)
1988	President	77,372 (36.7%)	133,241 (63.3%)

Vote for Perot was 69,626 (30.2%).

Demographics

Population 566,217

Percent change from 1980 7.4%

Land area 6,824 square miles

Population per square mile 83

Counties, 1990 population

Collin (pt.) 47,376	Hunt (pt.) 28,274
Cooke (pt.) 30,489	Kaufman (pt.) 44,728
Dallas (pt.) 8,811	Rains 6,715
Denton (pt.) 34,424	Rockwall 25,604
Fannin 24,804	Smith (pt.) 111,416
Grayson 95,021	Van Zandt 37,944
Gregg (pt.) 70,611	

Cities, 1990 population (10,000 or more)

Denison 21,505	McKinney (pt.) 14,000
Denton (pt.) 13,791	Rockwall 10,486
Gainesville 14,256	Sherman 31,601
Greenville (pt.) 11,930	Terrell 12,490
Longview (pt.) 37,960	Tyler (pt.) 44,569

Race and Hispanic origin

White 88.3%

Black 8.4%

American Indian, Eskimo, or Aleut. 0.6%

Asian or Pacific Islander 0.4%

Other 2.3%

Hispanic origin 4.3%

Ancestry

American 11.5%	Irish 21.0%
Dutch 3.1%	Italian 1.4%
English 15.2%	Scotch Irish 3.5%
French 3.7%	Scottish 1.9%
German 19.2%	

Universities/colleges, 1990-1991 enrollment

Austin College, Sherman 1,230

Collin Community College, McKinney 9,059

Cooke County College, Gainesville 3,084

Grayson County College, Denison 3,146

Kilgore College, Kilgore 4,443

Southwestern Christian College, Terrell 225

University of Texas, Tyler 3,725

Newspapers, total circulation (in all districts)

Dallas Morning News 452,101

Denison Herald 10,941

Denton Record-Chronicle 16,294

Fort Worth Star-Telegram 250,099

Longview News-Journal 30,302
Plano Star Courier 14,313
Sherman Democrat 18,281
Tyler Telegraph-Courier Times 42,998

Commercial television stations, affiliations
ADI: Dallas-Fort Worth (85%) and Tyler-Longview (15%)
KLTV, Tyler (ABC)

Cable television systems, total subscribers
Galaxy Cablevision; Ladonia 8,712
Longview Cable TV Co.; Longview 19,000
Post Newsweek Cable TV; Sherman 19,159
Sammons Communications Inc.; Denton 14,400
TCI of Texas; Wylie 7,763
United Cable TV; Tyler 30,000

Businesses and other major employers
E-Systems Inc./Greenville Div.; Greenville; aircraft/parts 4,598
Texas Instruments Inc.; Sherman; electronic components 3,400
Eastman Kodak Co./Texas Eastman Co.; Longview; photographic supplies 2,750
American Standard Inc./Trane Co.; Tyler; air conditioners 2,000
Kelly-Springfield Tire Co.; Tyler; tires 1,415
State of Texas/Terrell State Hospital; Terrell 1,350
Mother Francis Hospital; Tyler 1,250
University of Texas System; Tyler 1,100
Weber Aircraft Inc.; Gainesville; aircraft parts 1,050
East Texas Medical Center; Tyler 998
Oscar Mayer Foods Corp.; Sherman; meatpacking 800
Epic Healthcare Group Inc./North Texas Medical Center; McKinney 800
Johnson & Johnson Medical Inc.; Sherman; surgical supplies 750
Wilson N. Jones Memorial Hospital; Sherman 750
City of Longview; Longview 714
Texoma Medical Center Inc.; Denison 700
Notami Hospitals of Texas/Denton Regional Medical Center; Denton 700
Howe-Baker Engineers Inc.; Tyler; heavy construction 698
County of Collin; McKinney 650
U.S. Veterans Affairs Dept.; Bonham; nursing 552
Libbey-Owens-Ford Co.; Sherman; flat glass 550
Fluor Daniel Inc.; Tyler; electric services 515

5th District

Downtown Dallas; Eastern and Southern Suburbs

When Wal-Mart came to the Robertson County town of Hearne in 1980, local merchants were dismayed. Virtually every clothier, appliance store and mom-and-pop shop soon shut down. Ten years later, Wal-Mart closed its store, citing unprofitability. The 5,100 people of Hearne were even more upset by Wal-Mart's departure.

The tale of Hearne and the Wal-Mart that came and went is a familiar story in the rural and small-town areas in the 5th, a district that stretches from Dallas County 200 miles south.

Athens (Henderson County) lost the Harvey Industries television manufacturing plant, Four Winns boat company and the bra-maker Hollywood Vassarette in the late 1980s. Teague's economy in Freestone County has sputtered since the railroads declined in the 1970s.

For these towns south of Dallas, the future seems to lie in one word: prisons. The prison system is the largest employer in Anderson County, where three large units of the Texas Department of Corrections are situated. Seagoville and other locales in the 5th are bidding for more.

About 60 percent of the district's residents live in Dallas County. Downtown Dallas was removed from the 5th in 1992 redistricting, but some suburban neighborhoods to the east and northwest of the city remain in the 5th.

Oaklawn is a fashionable section where young professionals and a sizable gay community reside. East Dallas is a mix of upscale professionals, longtime residents, pockets of middle-class neighborhoods revived by gentrification, and Hispanic and blue-collar workers. The Swiss Avenue Historic District boasts 200 Georgian, Spanish and Prairie style houses, built at the turn of the century by the Dallas elite.

Although North Dallas is no longer a part of the 5th, major telecommunications companies there employ many of the district's residents.

Just outside the city are several towns that have grown popular because of their proximity to Dallas. Factory workers and office clerks live in some of the more modest communities, such as Seagoville and Balch Springs. Mesquite, once predominantly farmland, is now a collection of spacious, well-kept, single-family homes for Dallas' lawyers and upper-level managers.

People in the more rural, poorer Robertson County on the southwestern edge of the 5th raise cattle and poultry.

The 5th has a sizable minority population—about 35 percent nonwhite. Although there are more Hispanic residents (18 percent of the district population), blacks (16 percent of the district population) have moved more quickly into local politics. In 1993, the 5th had at least one black mayor and several African American county commissioners.

The reconfigured 5th responds well to moderate or conservative Democrats. Bill Clinton won the district in the 1992 presidential contest and independent Ross Perot, who lives in Dallas, exceeded his national average in the 5th.

Election Returns

	5th District	Democrat	Republican
1992	President*	70,766 (40.4%)	59,237 (33.8%)
	House	98,567 (58.9%)	62,419 (37.3%)
1990	Senate	52,007 (44.2%)	65,643 (55.8%)
1988	President	83,593 (47.9%)	91,076 (52.1%)

Vote for Perot was 45,033 (25.7%).

Demographics

Population 566,217

Percent change from 1980 7.5%

Land area 6,605 square miles

Population per square mile 86

Counties, 1990 population

Anderson 48,024	Leon 12,665
Brazos (pt.) 20,495	Limestone 20,946
Dallas (pt.) 315,899	Madison 10,931
Freestone 15,818	Robertson 15,511
Henderson 58,543	Smith (pt.) 39,893
Kaufman (pt.) 7,492	

Cities, 1990 population (10,000 or more)

Athens 10,967	Garland (pt.) 39,207
Balch Springs (pt.) 16,213	Mesquite (pt.) 56,490
Bryan (pt.) 19,003	Palestine 18,042
Dallas (pt.) 189,987	Tyler (pt.) 30,881

Race and Hispanic origin

White 71.4%
Black 16.3%
American Indian, Eskimo, or Aleut. 0.5%
Asian or Pacific Islander 1.5%
Other 10.3%
Hispanic origin 17.9%

Ancestry

American 8.9%	Irish 16.2%
Dutch 2.2%	Italian 1.4%
English 11.3%	Scotch Irish 2.7%
French 2.9%	Scottish 1.5%
German 14.0%	

Universities/colleges, 1990-1991 enrollment

Amber University, Garland 1,498
Eastfield College, Mesquite 9,525
El Centro College, Dallas 5,661
ITT Technical Institute, Garland 200
Texas College, Tyler 478
Trinity Valley Community College, Athens 4,275
Tyler Junior College, Tyler 7,950

Newspapers, total circulation (in all districts)

Bryan-College Station Eagle 22,202
Dallas Morning News 452,101
Fort Worth Star-Telegram 250,099
Houston Chronicle 421,140
Houston Post 292,061
Palestine Herald-Press 9,899
Tyler Telegraph-Courier Times 42,998
Waco Tribune Herald 46,439

Commercial television stations, affiliations

ADI: Waco-Temple (51%), Dallas-Fort Worth (48%) and Tyler-Longview (1%)

Cable television systems, total subscribers

Paragon Cable; Palestine 7,400
Storer Cable TV of Texas; Garland 37,470
TCI of Texas; Dallas 91,647
TCI of Texas; Mesquite 25,187

Businesses and other major employers

American Airlines Inc.; Dallas; airline 12,000
Tyler Pipe Industries of Texas; Tyler; iron/steel foundries 2,300
GTE Corp.; Dallas; telephone communications 2,000
AT&T Co.; Mesquite; electronic components 1,700
Mexia State School; Mexia 1,674
Dallas-Fort Worth Intl. Airport; Dallas; airport/services 1,400

State of Texas/Criminal Justice Dept.; Tenn Colony 1,200
Benecorp Business Service Inc.; Dallas; personnel supply services 1,008
Haggar Corp./Hagger Apparel; Dallas; outerwear 1,000
State of Texas/Highway & Public Transportation Dept.; Dallas 1,000
DFW Airport Hotel Associates/Hyatt Regency; Dallas; hotel 900
Ogden Services Corp./Ogden Aviation Service; Dallas; building services 900
State of Texas/Corrections Dept.; Tenn Colony 850
Texas Instruments Inc.; Dallas; warehousing 840
Pro Set Press Ltd.; Dallas; commercial printing 800
Austin Commercial Inc.; Dallas; building construction 800
State of Texas/Corrections Dept.; Midway 800
Affiliated Computer Systems; Dallas; computer services 800
City of Bryan; Bryan 725
Sky Chefs Inc.; Dallas; bars/restaurants 700
Republic Financial Services; Dallas; life insurance 700
Carrier Corp.; Tyler; air conditioning equipment 690
Anthem Life Insurance Co.; Dallas; medical service/health insurance 650
Tyler Junior College; Tyler 647
Mrs. Baird's Bakeries Inc.; Dallas; bakery products 640
Wal-Mart Stores Inc./Hypermart USA; Garland; department stores 600
Dobbs Houses Inc.; Dallas; bars/restaurants 600
Timberlawn Psychiatric Hospital; Dallas 585
Eastfield College; Mesquite 550

6th District

Suburban Dallas — Part of Fort Worth;
Part of Arlington

When the 6th was redrawn in the mid-1960s to suit the needs of Democratic Rep. Olin E. "Tiger" Teague, cries went out that it was the most gerrymandered district in Texas. In 1992 redistricting, the shape of the 6th became even more illogical. Compressed from 14 counties into five, the 6th (see map on page 709) is now in two separate pieces that are connected only by Eagle Mountain Lake, in northwestern Tarrant County.

While the district's boundary lines are contorted, its people have a good deal in common. About 85 percent of them live in Tarrant County, which includes Fort Worth and Arlington; parts of both cities are in the 6th. Overall, Fort Worth is larger, but Arlington is the district's biggest population center; about 134,000 of 261,700 people are in the district.

The Fort Worth area has experienced several economic evolutions. Initially the city's commerce was centered around oil and cattle (the old "Cowtown" nickname still sticks). Then the emphasis shifted to military work: Huge defense contractors such as General Dynamics (now owned by Lockheed) and Bell Helicopter Textron, maker of the experimental V-22 Osprey tilt-rotor aircraft, became the largest employers in the region. Carswell Air Force Base housed 6,500 military personnel.

Now, with the cutbacks in defense spending, the city and surrounding region are heading for another economic shift. Carswell has been downsizing since 1991, and the fate of projects at both Lockheed and Bell are in doubt.

With its mild climate, affordable housing and the nation's second-busiest airport (Dallas-Fort Worth), the "Metroplex" (as local boosters dub the area) began attracting a variety of corporate headquarters in the 1980s. Today, the 6th has numerous white-collar employees from such area companies as IBM, J.C. Penney, American Airlines, Exxon and GTE. Part of Alliance Airport, a private cargo-shipping business formed by Ross Perot, Jr., is in the 6th.

Until the 1980s, Arlington was a blue-collar, low-income community centered around a General Motors plant. GM remains an important employer, but abetted by the city's location between Dallas and Fort Worth, Arlington has emerged as a major entertainment center, with amusement parks, hotels and the Texas Rangers baseball team (the stadium is just across the district line, in the 24th).

Southeast of Tarrant County is Ellis County, which in the early 1990s was focal point of the multibillion-dollar superconducting super collider project. In 1993, budget constraints forced Congress to kill the funding for the atomsmasher. The demise of the project will have an adverse effect on the local economy (the super collider site was shared with the 24th District).

In most elections the 6th is good territory for Republican candidates; GOP Rep. Joe Barton, first elected in 1984, tallied an impressive 72 percent of the vote in 1992. But in 1992 presidential voting, independent candidate Ross Perot far exceeded his 1992 national average in the 6th, placing second behind George Bush with 30 percent of the vote.

Election Returns

	6th District	Democrat	Republican
1992	President*	67,131 (24.4%)	125,693 (45.6%)
	House	73,933 (28.1%)	189,140 (71.9%)
1990	Senate	43,010 (27.0%)	116,300 (73.0%)
1988	President	49,895 (27.6%)	131,143 (72.4%)

*Vote for Perot was 82,671 (30.0%).

Demographics

Population 566,217

Percent change from 1980 7.4%

Land area 867 square miles

Population per square mile 653

Counties, 1990 population
Dallas (pt.) 13,742
Ellis (pt.) 27,954
Johnson (pt.) 30,145
Parker (pt.) 16,436
Tarrant (pt.) 477,940

Cities, 1990 population (10,000 or more)
Arlington (pt.) 133,906
Bedford 43,762
Benbrook (pt.) 13,825
Colleyville 12,724
Euless (pt.) 27,090
Fort Worth (pt.) 101,697
Grand Prairie (pt.) 13,513
Grapevine (pt.) 25,026
Hurst (pt.) 11,728
Keller 13,683
North Richland Hills (pt.) 28,997
Watauga 20,009

Race and Hispanic origin
White 90.9%
Black 4.4%
American Indian, Eskimo, or Aleut. 0.4%
Asian or Pacific Islander 2.2%
Other 2.1%
Hispanic origin 5.5%

Ancestry
American 6.8%
Czechoslovakian 1.0%
Dutch 3.0%
English 19.3%
French 4.7%
German 26.2%
Irish 20.5%
Italian 3.2%
Norwegian 1.1%
Polish 2.1%
Scotch Irish 4.5%
Scottish 3.4%
Swedish 1.7%

Universities/colleges, 1990-1991 enrollment
Arlington Baptist College, Arlington 209
Southwestern Adventist College, Keene 797
Southwestern Assemblies of God College, Waxahachie 686

Newspapers, total circulation (in all districts)
Dallas Morning News 452,101
Fort Worth Star-Telegram 250,099

Commercial television stations, affiliations
ADI: Dallas-Fort Worth (100%)

Cable television systems, total subscribers
Arlington Telecable Corp.; Arlington 53,293
Paragon Cable; Grapevine 55,000
Sammons Communications Inc.; Hurst 17,989
Sammons of Fort Worth; Fort Worth 71,319
Storer Cable TV Inc.; Bedford 20,441

Businesses and other major employers
American Airlines Inc.; Fort Worth; airline 3,000
Harris Methodist Hospital/Edwards Cancer Center; Bedford 1,200
Bowles Group Inc./Workforce 2000; Hurst; personnel supply services 1,000
Chaparral Steel Co.; Midlothian; steel products 970
Carlisle Memory Products Group Inc./Graham Magnetics; Bedford; electrical equipment/supplies 867
Southwestern Baptist Hospital; Fort Worth 859
American Airlines Inc./Flight Academy; Fort Worth 800
Grapevine-Colleyville Indepedent School District; Grapevine 800
National Semiconductor Corp.; Arlington; electronic components 700
Reliance Electric Co.; Bedford; communications equipment 700
Affiliated Food Stores Inc./Affiliated; Keller; grocery products 650
Tandy Corp./Cable & Wire; Fort Worth; metal products 600
Pacific Fidelity Life Insurance Co.; Hurst; insurance services 600
Edward Blank Associates Inc.; Arlington; telemarketing 600
Wal-Mart Stores Inc./Hypermart 1801; Arlington; grocery stores 570
LTV Aerospace & Defense Co.; Grand Prairie; guided missiles 554
Owens-Corning Fiberglas Corp.; Waxahachie; mineral products 550
Tecnol Medical Products Inc.; Fort Worth; medical supplies 550
Coltec Industries Inc./Menasco Aerosystems Div.; Euless; aircraft parts 530
Healthtrust Inc./Northeast Community Hospital; Bedford 515

7th District

Western Houston; Northwestern Suburbs

The urban sprawl of Houston takes up only a portion of the 7th geographically, but it dominates the district in most other respects. The 7th (see map on page 715) is a collection of white, affluent, reliably Republican neighborhoods. Residents of the old 7th gave George Bush one of his two largest margins in 1988, and four years later the district gave him a solid 58 percent of the vote.

About half the district's residents live within the city limits, and many work in downtown Houston. All of the 7th—and parts of six other districts—are in Harris County, a region that covers 34 incorporated areas and has 2.8 million people. With a population that is 6 percent black and 12 percent Hispanic, the 7th District is somewhat less racially integrated than the city as a whole.

Although none of downtown Houston is included in the 7th, there is plenty of commercial enterprise in the district. Thousands of bankers, real estate brokers, developers, insurance executives and retail employees live in the west and northwest parts of the city. Compaq Computer Corp., with its headquarters and a manufacturing plant on the district boundary line, is a major employer. Founded in 1982 by three former Texas Instruments workers, Compaq felt the squeeze of competition in 1991 and responded with a restructuring and about 2,000 layoffs. The belt-tightening and several new products helped the company rebound; 1992 worldwide sales reached $4.1 billion. Like Compaq, Continental Airlines is a major source of jobs for residents of the 7th, although it is located in the neighboring 18th.

Office parks and small factories sprouted up along Route 290 in the 1970s, when land was particularly affordable. Toshiba opened a turbine-engine plant in the area then and remains a major employer. Cameron Forged Products, a tool manufacturer, is another of the longtime residents. Cameron, which previously relied heavily on defense contracts, retrained its work force in the late 1980s and early 1990s to produce engine parts for commercial clients.

The River Oaks, Memorial and Tanglewood neighborhoods are home to some of Houston's wealthiest families. And they have a new neighbor—the Bushes moved to Tanglewood in 1993 to build a home on a lot they had owned for years.

Houstonians also boast of their ballet, symphony, opera company, museums and theaters. Many of the area's dedicated arts patrons live in the imitation Tudor mansions, imitation French chateaux and imitation Spanish villas of River Oaks.

Memorial includes a number of small, self-incorporated villages near Interstate 10 that have their own mayors and some discrete municipal services. Residents of Hedwig, Bunker Hill and Piney Point moved into the villages decades ago and never left, prompting the creation of the phrase "the graying of Memorial."

The 7th is a religious and politically active area. The 10,000-member Second Baptist Church is located here, as well as several sizable Presbyterian churches.

Election Returns

	7th District	Democrat	Republican
1992	President*	52,501 (21.9%)	137,541 (57.5%)
	House	—	169,407 (100.0%)
1990	Senate	28,284 (21.2%)	104,982 (78.8%)
1988	President	41,258 (23.7%)	133,094 (76.3%)

Vote for Perot was 49,201 (20.6%).

Demographics

Population 566,217

Percent change from 1980 7.4%

Land area 527 square miles

Population per square mile 1,075

Counties, 1990 population
Harris (pt.) 566,217

Cities, 1990 population (10,000 or more)
Houston (pt.) 232,685
Mission Bend CDP (pt.) 10,750

Race and Hispanic origin
White 83.3%
Black 5.9%
American Indian, Eskimo, or Aleut. 0.3%
Asian or Pacific Islander 5.6%
Other 4.9%
Hispanic origin 11.9%

Ancestry

American 3.7%	Irish 15.8%
Czechoslovakian 1.7%	Italian 4.1%
Dutch 1.9%	Polish 2.9%
English 17.6%	Scotch Irish 4.1%
French 5.4%	Scottish 3.3%
French Canadian 1.4%	Swedish 1.4%
German 24.8%	

Newspapers, total circulation (in all districts)
Houston Chronicle 421,140
Houston Post 292,061

Commercial television stations, affiliations
ADI: Houston (100%)

Cable television systems, total subscribers
Prime Cable; Katy 12,771
Prime Cable; Spring 23,285
Storer Cable TV Inc.; Houston 55,216
Warner Cable of Houston; Houston 229,000

Businesses and other major employers
Compaq Computer Corp.; Houston; computers 7,800
Conoco Inc.; Houston; petroleum refining 2,000
Houston Independent School District; Houston 2,000
AT&T Co.; Houston; telephone communications 1,500
Pinkerton's Inc.; Houston; security services 1,500
Memorial City General Hospital & Medical Center; Houston 1,338
Reading Bates Exploration Co.; Houston; oil/gas services 1,300
Shell Western E&P Inc.; Houston; oil/gas services 1,240

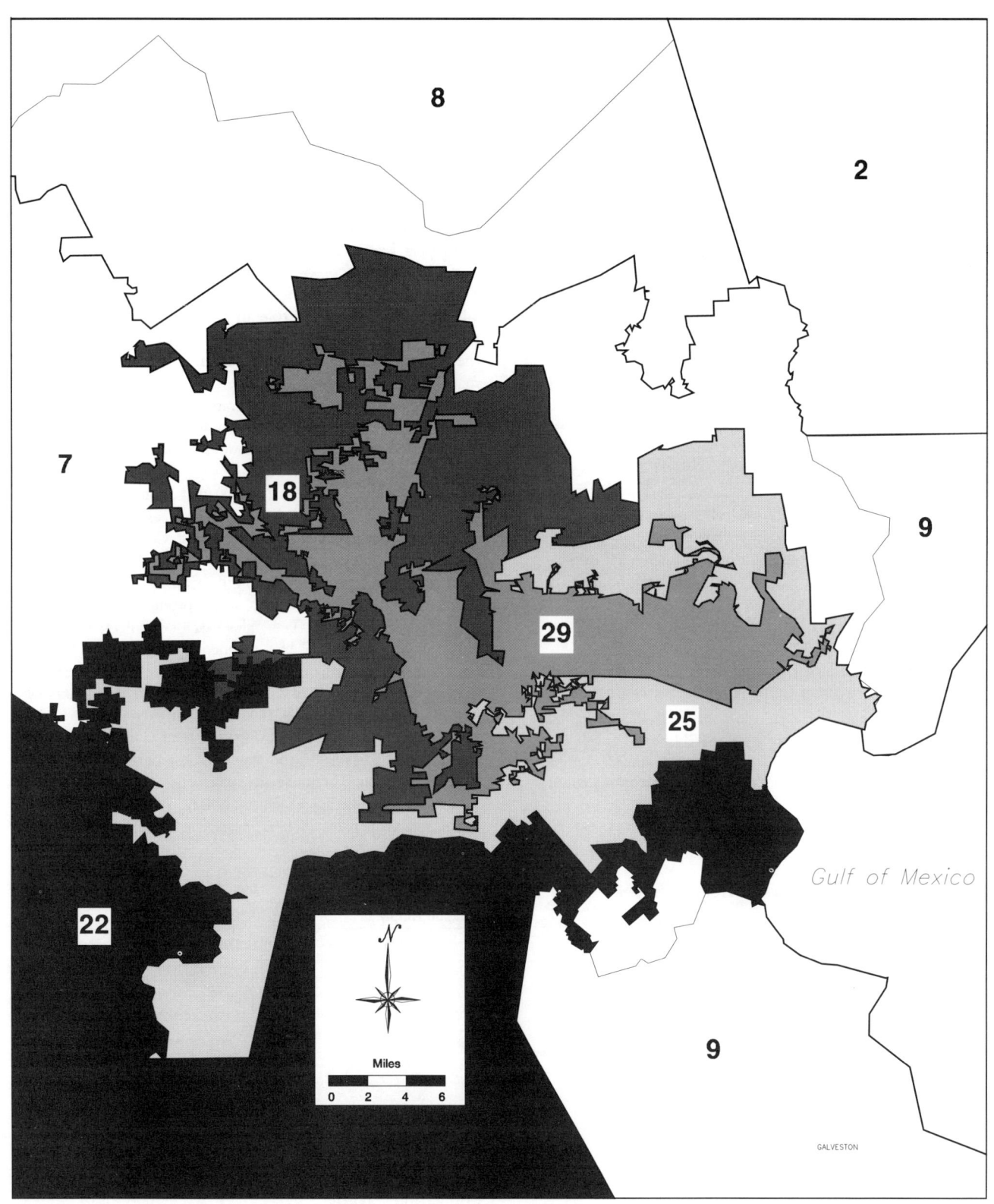

8

2

7

18

9

29

25

Gulf of Mexico

22

N

Miles

0   2   4   6

9

GALVESTON

Panhandle Eastern Pipe Line Co.; Houston; gas pipelines 1,200

Amoco Production Co./Houston Region; Houston; petroleum/natural gas 1,200

Exxon Production Research Co.; Houston; petroleum research services 1,200

Marathon Oil Co.; Houston; petroleum refining 1,100

Cameron Forged Products Co.; Houston; metal tools 1,100

United Savings Assn. Texas; Houston; savings institutions 1,042

Stone & Webster Engineering Corp.; Houston; engineering/construction services 1,040

Digicon Inc.; Houston; oil/gas services 1,015

McDermott Inc./Hudson Engineering Corp. Div.; Houston; engineering services 950

IBM Corp.; Houston; computer equipment 920

Coastal States Management; Houston; management services 820

A. B. B. Lummus Crest Inc.; Houston; engineering/architectural services 800

Igloo Products Corp.; Houston; ice chests/coolers 750

Republic Realty Services Inc.; Houston; real estate agents 750

Industrial Security Services; Houston; security services 750

VNA Corp.; Houston; home health services 750

BP Exploration Inc./BP Gas Inc.; Houston; petroleum/natural gas 700

Big Three Merchant Gases & Equipment; Houston; inorganic chemicals 700

Baker Protective Services/Burns Intl. Security Services; Houston; business services/security 700

Halliburton Co.; Houston; construction machinery 680

Prudential Insurance of America Inc.; Houston; holding offices 650

Browning-Ferris Industries; Houston; sanitary services 640

Igloo Products Corp.; Katy; ice chests/coolers 633

Offshore Pipelines Inc.; Houston; heavy construction 600

Union Texas Petroleum Corp.; Houston; petroleum/natural gas 600

Sysco Corp./Cochran; Houston; grocery products 600

Toshiba Intl. Corp.; Houston; electrical goods 600

Hospital Corp. of America/West Houston Medical Center; Houston 600

Texas Instruments Inc.; Cypress; computer services 600

Progressive Staffing Assn.; Houston; personnel supply services 585

Houston Lighting & Power Co.; Houston; electric services 575

Cypress Fairbank Medical Center; Houston 556

8th District

Northern Houston Suburbs; College Station

Texas is known for oil barons, vast open expanses and former President George Bush. The 8th has all that, plus dairy farms, a robust medical industry and the Texas A&M Aggies.

Reconfigured in 1992 redistricting, the 8th resembles a lopsided barbell; it has distinct eastern and western sections and a narrow corridor connecting them. Most of the population lives on the barbell's eastern end. Suburban Houston turf in Harris County accounts for nearly 45 percent of the total vote; the next county north, Montgomery, casts another 30 percent. In 1992, the 8th District sections of both those counties backed Bush's re-election. (He got 58 percent in Harris.) Those showings helped Bush win 55 percent districtwide; Ross Perot and Bill Clinton were well back, both with 23 percent.

Houston's largest employer is the Texas Medical Center, a conglomeration of 41 nonprofit health-related institutions that employs more than 51,000 people and treats 3.5 million patients annually. Many of the doctors, nurses, lab technicians, researchers and managers at the Medical Center live in the tidy suburbs of the 8th.

The oil and gas industry obviously plays a major role in the region's economy. Although the Port of Houston is no longer in the 8th, many of the refinery managers commute to the port from their homes in the district.

Similarly, the corporate headquarters of Exxon, Shell and Pennzoil are all in Houston. The city accounts for 23 percent of all U.S. jobs in crude petroleum and natural gas extraction, 14 percent of all U.S. jobs in oil and gas services, and 38 percent of the nation's jobs in the manufacturing of oil and gas field machinery.

Executives at the Houston Advanced Research Center, Exxon and the Lifecell medical research company live in Woodlands or Kingwood, two planned communities that offer office space, housing and shops all in the same neighborhood.

Although the residential areas that dominate the Harris County part of the 8th are described as suburban, traffic congestion here rivals that of some East Coast cities.

In the western half of the district, the joke goes that there are more cows than people. Washington County is best known for Brenham's Blue Bell Creameries, which produces ice cream using milk from local dairies. Ten miles east of Brenham is Chappell Hill, the first town in Texas planned by a woman. The entire county is renowned for its fine German and Polish bakeries and sausage shops, a legacy of the eastern European immigrants who flocked to this area in the 1800s and put down roots.

Farther north is Brazos County, home of College Station and Texas A&M University, the state's oldest public institution of higher education. The university, which has 41,000 students, will be the site of Bush's presidential library. Brazos County, where Bush won 50 percent in 1992, casts just under one-fifth of the district's total vote.

Election Returns

	8th District	Democrat	Republican
1992	President*	55,330 (22.6%)	134,583 (54.9%)
	House	53,473 (23.0%)	179,349 (77.0%)
1990	Senate	34,399 (24.2%)	107,895 (75.8%)
1988	President	47,068 (27.5%)	124,274 (72.5%)

Vote for Perot was 55,343 (22.6%).

Demographics

Population 566,217

Percent change from 1980 7.3%

Land area 3,051 square miles

Population per square mile 186

Counties, 1990 population

Austin (pt.) 15,616	Montgomery (pt.) 163,479
Brazos (pt.) 101,367	Waller (pt.) 4,111
Harris (pt.) 255,490	Washington 26,154

Cities, 1990 population (10,000 or more)

Brenham 11,952	Kingwood CDP 37,397
Bryan (pt.) 35,999	Spring CDP 33,111
College Station 52,456	The Woodlands CDP
Conroe (pt.) 14,151	29,205
Humble (pt.) 10,812	

Race and Hispanic origin

White 89.5%
Black 5.2%
American Indian, Eskimo, or Aleut. 0.3%
Asian or Pacific Islander 1.9%
Other 3.1%
Hispanic origin 7.2%

Ancestry

American 5.6%	Irish 19.1%
Czechoslovakian 2.0%	Italian 3.7%
Dutch 2.3%	Polish 3.1%
English 16.6%	Scotch Irish 4.0%
French 5.4%	Scottish 2.7%
French Canadian 1.5%	Swedish 1.5%
German 28.4%	

Universities/colleges, 1990-1991 enrollment

Blinn College, Brenham 6,849
Texas A&M University, College Station 41,171

Newspapers, total circulation (in all districts)

Bryan-College Station Eagle 22,202
Conroe Courier 12,427
Houston Chronicle 421,140
Houston Post 292,061

Commercial television stations, affiliations

ADI: Houston (84%) and Waco-Temple (16%)
    KTFH, Conroe (None)

Cable television systems, total subscribers

Conroe Cable TV; Conroe 9,105
Kingwood Cablevision Inc.; Kingwood 12,310
Prime Cable; Spring 23,285
Simmons Communications Inc.; Spring 7,044
TCA Cablevision; Bryan 31,500
United Artists Cable; The Woodlands 10,350
Warner Cable of Houston; Houston 229,000

Businesses and other major employers

Texas A&M University; College Station 2,344
Texas A&M University; College Station; research services 2,000
Mitchell Energy & Development; Spring; natural gas liquids 1,400
Shell Oil Co./Shell Development Co.; Houston; research services 1,400
ESSC Corp.; Houston; personnel supply services 1,200
Houston Northwest Medical Center; Houston 1,150
State of Texas/Brenham State School; Brenham 1,000
Montgomery County Medical Center Hospital; Conroe 900
GTE Southwest Inc.; Bryan; telephone communications 850

Redman Building Products Inc./Alenco Div.; Bryan; metal products 765
College Station Independent School District; College Station 652
New Caney Independent School District; New Caney 650
Blue Bell Creameries Inc.; Brenham; dairy products 600
Tomball Hospital Authority/Tomball Regional Hospital; Tomball 583
Concepts of Care Inc.; Bryan; home health services 535
Westinghouse Electric Corp.; College Station; electronic components 510

9th District

Southeast — Beaumont; Galveston

Tucked in the southeast corner of Texas, the 9th runs from Houston's outlying suburbs to Port Arthur, near the Gulf Coast. Geographically small by Texas standards, the 9th is jampacked with refineries and petrochemical plants on land, and with commercial cargo ships and fishing boats on its waters. Also here is NASA's enormous Johnson Space Center.

The 9th's past and present are inextricably tied to petroleum.

The largest city in the 9th is Beaumont, in Jefferson County. The city was chartered in 1838, but it came of age in 1901 when the great gusher, Spindletop, erupted. Texas oil production soared from 836,000 barrels in 1900 to 4.4 million in 1901. Spindletop triggered Beaumont's industrial development; within a month of its discovery the city's population tripled.

Just as Spindletop and other Gulf Coast wells catapulted the region's economy, the oil market plunge of the mid-1980s devastated the area. With a worldwide glut, oil dropped to $9 a barrel, refineries closed and unemployment in some communities hit 22 percent by 1986. Port Arthur, Beaumont and Galveston all lost population in the 1980s.

There was a silver lining to the bust: Petrochemical plants were able to buy their raw materials for a song. From the cheap petroleum, the plants refine a host of chemicals that eventually go into making a variety of products, including plastics, foam and carpeting.

The increase in petrochemical production boosted the entire "Golden Triangle" region of Beaumont, Port Arthur and Orange. As that business picked up in the early 1990s, the construction or modernizing of refineries created thousands of jobs.

But the construction work may be short-lived if the worldwide economic slump of the 1990s hinders the growth of the petrochemical companies. Some communities in the 9th have turned to an industry they believe is more recession-proof and a good job provider: prisons. By the end of 1994, Beaumont expects to have five prisons with 5,100 beds and 2,570 employees.

The 9th remains heavily dependent on coastal industries such as ship repairing and commercial fishing. It is said to be the largest maritime district in the nation; other large coastal cities are split between districts. The Intracoastal Waterway runs the entire length of the 9th, carrying cargo ships from the Houston Ship Channel as far as New York City. About 1,800 boats fish out of the district's ports. And the beaches of Galveston County are a big tourist lure.

At the edge of the 9th, 23 miles south of Houston, sits the Johnson Space Center, a complex that employs 19,000 people. Although President Clinton in 1993 recommended spending $2.3

billion on NASA's space station *Freedom*, almost half is to be spent scaling back the project, throwing into jeopardy the station's future and the jobs of thousands at the center.

Clinton won the 9th in 1992 by collecting large margins in Jefferson and Galveston counties.

Election Returns

	9th District	Democrat	Republican
1992	President*	98,959 (43.6%)	80,813 (35.6%)
	House	118,690 (53.6%)	96,270 (43.5%)
1990	Senate	61,408 (45.5%)	73,518 (54.5%)
1988	President	101,607 (53.7%)	87,496 (46.3%)

*Vote for Perot was 47,418 (20.9%).

Demographics

Population 566,217

Percent change from 1980 7.6%

Land area 2,056 square miles

Population per square mile 275

Counties, 1990 population
Chambers 20,088	Harris (pt.) 89,333
Galveston 217,399	Jefferson 239,397

Cities, 1990 population (10,000 or more)
Baytown (pt.) 22,881	La Marque 14,120
Beaumont 114,323	League City 30,159
Friendswood (pt.) 15,957	Nederland 16,192
Galveston 59,070	Port Arthur 58,724
Groves 16,513	Port Neches 12,974
Houston (pt.) 13,895	Texas City 40,822

Race and Hispanic origin
White 72.5%
Black 21.7%
American Indian, Eskimo, or Aleut. 0.3%
Asian or Pacific Islander 2.1%
Other 3.5%
Hispanic origin 9.4%

Ancestry
American 4.4%	Irish 15.1%
Dutch 2.0%	Italian 3.5%
English 12.3%	Polish 1.2%
French 6.7%	Scotch Irish 3.2%
French Canadian 5.5%	Scottish 1.7%
German 17.3%	Swedish 1.1%

Universities/colleges, 1990-1991 enrollment
College of the Mainland, Texas City 3,541
Galveston College, Galveston 2,122
Lamar University, Beaumont 11,489
Lamar University, Port Arthur 2,053
Texas A&M University, Galveston 1,075
University of Texas Medical Branch, Galveston 1,800

Newspapers, total circulation (in all districts)
Beaumont Enterprise 69,814
Houston Chronicle 421,140
Houston Post 292,061

Commercial television stations, affiliations
ADI: Houston (57%) and Beaumont-Port Arthur (43%)

Cable television systems, total subscribers
Prime Cable; Highlands 32,000
Storer Cable TV Inc.; League City 14,384
TCI of Texas; Baytown 9,703
TCI of Texas; Beaumont 27,500
TCI of Texas; Galveston 15,512
TCI of Texas; Port Neches 28,965

Businesses and other major employers
University of Texas Medical Branch & Hospital; Galveston 8,090
NASA/Johnson Space Center; Houston 3,000
St. Elizabeth Hospital; Beaumont 2,355
Amoco Oil Co.; Texas City; petroleum refining 2,081
Union Carbide Chemical & Plastics Co.; Texas City; inorganic chemicals 2,000
International Maintenance; Nederland; building construction 2,000
Lockheed Engineering & Sciences Co.; Houston; engineering services 2,000
Chevron USA Inc.; Port Arthur; petroleum refining 1,900
Mobil Oil Corp.; Beaumont; petroleum refining 1,700
Du Pont E. I. De Nemours & Co.; Beaumont; synthetics 1,500
Star Enterprise; Port Arthur; petroleum refining 1,400
Lamar University System; Beaumont 1,350
American National Insurance Co.; Galveston; life insurance 1,349
City of Beaumont; Beaumont 1,207
IBM Systems Integration Div.; Houston; computer services 1,200
Gulf States Utilities Co.; Beaumont; electric services 1,025
Austin Industrial Inc.; Beaumont; building construction 1,000
Baptist Hospital of Southeast Texas; Beaumont 1,000
Conex Intl. Corp.; Beaumont; heavy construction 965
Sterling Chemicals Inc.; Texas City; organic chemicals 950
Texaco Chemical Co.; Port Neches; organic chemicals 935
Uniroyal Goodrich Tire Co.; Port Neches; synthetics 900
Miles Inc.; Baytown; inorganic chemicals 900
Loral Aerospace Corp.; Houston; engineering services 900
City of Galveston/Port of Galveston; Galveston 800
Mainland Center Hospital; Texas City 800
Champion Intl. Corp.; Houston; paper mills 750
Brown & Root USA Inc.; Texas City; heavy construction 700
City of Port Arthur; Port Arthur 700
Goodyear Tire & Rubber Co./Beaumont Chemical Plant; Beaumont; synthetics 680
St. Mary's Hospital; Port Arthur 660
Chevron Corp./Chevron Chemical Co.; Baytown; synthetics 650
St. Mary's Hospital; Galveston 650
Computer Sciences Corp.; Houston; computer services 650
North Star Steel Texas Inc.; Beaumont; steel products 628
Texaco Chemical Co.; Port Arthur; organic chemicals 600
American Medical Intl./Park Place Hospital; Port Arthur 600
County of Jefferson; Beaumont 600
Matrix Engineering Inc.; Beaumont; engineering services 590
La Marque Independent School District; La Marque 558
Beaumont Hospital Inc.; Beaumont 550

10th District

Central — Austin

The vast rural district that Lyndon B. Johnson represented in the House in the 1950s has been shrinking in size and growing in population ever since he left the 10th.

In the 1980s, the district took in five counties and most of a sixth. But for the 1990s, the 10th is limited just to Austin and Travis County, where population grew by 35 percent in the 1980s, on top of 42 percent growth in the 1970s. Austin, the state capital, has become an urban mecca for students, computer engineers, music lovers and tourists.

The economic troubles of the oil industry grazed Austin in the mid-1980s; real estate speculation fizzled and local banks suffered. But the underpinnings of Austin's economy are unique in Texas, and they helped the city's economy remain stable.

The state of Texas, with 57,000 workers, is the 10th's largest employer. Another economic anchor is the University of Texas at Austin; with nearly 50,000 students and 20,000 employees, the school gives the city a youthful feeling (T-shirts and jeans are ubiquitous) and its liberal political bent. In a state that George Bush carried for president in 1992, Travis County was one of the few counties to hand Bill Clinton a solid majority.

The university also has been a catalyst for Austin's emergence as a center for high-tech industry. One local success story is Dell Computer: Begun in a dorm room in the early 1980s by UT student Michael Dell, the computer-maker now employs more than 2,000 people.

Two public-private research consortiums add to the synergy. In 1983, Austin won the right to host the headquarters of Microelectronics & Computer Technology Corp (400 employees). Five years later, the city welcomed Sematech (700 employees), a joint venture using federal and private money to develop new applications for semiconductors. Two major semiconductor makers, Motorola (4,000 employees) and Advanced Micro Devices (2,100 workers), are in Austin.

Another boost to Austin's economic vitality is a thriving cultural and entertainment life. The city's country music scene gets national exposure on the public television show "Austin City Limits," and connoisseurs of blues, rock and new wave music flock to clubs on East Sixth Street. Austin also draws visitors to its many lakes and parks: One big annual event is the Austin Aqua Festival, with water shows, a homemade-raft contest and music.

As Austin's growth surged over the past 20 years, some residents who had been drawn by the city's college-town feel began to fret that Austin would become huge, sprawling and impersonal—"Houstonized," in local parlance. Though Texas has a strong frontier spirit that tends to regard growth-management measures as un-American, the prevailing mood in Austin is different: Developers are required to contribute to infrastructure projects in return for zoning permits. In the fall of 1992 the city approved the Balcones Canyonlands Conservation Plan, a proposal that allows the government and the Nature Conservancy to purchase 30,000 acres to protect endangered wildlife.

Election Returns

	10th District	Democrat	Republican
1992	President*	128,813 (48.1%)	84,560 (31.6%)
	House	177,233 (68.6%)	68,646 (26.6%)
1990	Senate	97,555 (53.8%)	83,896 (46.2%)
1988	President	133,488 (54.8%)	110,167 (45.2%)

*Vote for Perot was 54,304 (20.3%).

Demographics

Population 566,217

Percent change from 1980 7.4%

Land area 799 square miles

Population per square mile 709

Counties, 1990 population
Travis (pt.) 566,217

Cities, 1990 population (10,000 or more)
Austin (pt.) 463,178

Race and Hispanic origin
White 72.9%
Black 11.2%
American Indian, Eskimo, or Aleut. 0.4%
Asian or Pacific Islander 2.9%
Other 12.7%
Hispanic origin 21.4%

Ancestry

American 2.9%	Irish 13.3%
Czechoslovakian 1.4%	Italian 2.4%
Dutch 1.6%	Polish 1.7%
English 14.2%	Scotch Irish 3.8%
French 3.7%	Scottish 2.9%
German 22.1%	Swedish 1.9%

Universities/colleges, 1990-1991 enrollment
Austin Community College, Austin 24,251
Austin Presbyterian Theological Seminary, Austin 243
Concordia Lutheran College, Austin 680
Huston-Tillotson College, Austin 714
ITT Technical Institute, Austin 489
St. Edward's University, Austin 3,086
University of Texas, Austin 49,961

Newspapers, total circulation (in all districts)
Austin American Statesman 172,077
Dallas Morning News 452,101
Houston Chronicle 421,140
Houston Post 292,061
San Antonio News-Express 187,599

Commercial television stations, affiliations
ADI: Austin (100%)
KBVO-TV, Austin (Fox)
KTBC-TV, Austin (CBS)
KVUE-TV, Austin (ABC)
KXAN-TV, Austin (NBC)

Cable television systems, total subscribers
Austin Cablevision; Mount Larson 146,500

Military installations, 1991

Bergstrom Air Force Base, Austin 3,387

Businesses and other major employers

University of Texas; Austin 20,000

IBM Corp.; Austin; computer services 7,000

Motorola Inc.; Austin; electronic components 4,000

Texas Instruments Inc.; Austin; computer/office equipment 4,000

U.S. Internal Revenue Service; Austin 4,000

Abbott Laboratories; Austin; pharmaceuticals 2,800

Advanced Micro Devices Inc.; Austin; electronic components 2,100

Dell Computer; Austin 2,050

State of Texas/Transportation Dept.; Austin 2,000

Seton Medical Center; Austin 1,875

State of Texas/Attorney General's Office; Austin 1,700

Lockheed Missiles & Space Co.; Austin; metal products 1,600

State of Texas/Human Services Dept.; Austin 1,600

Brackenridge Hospital; Austin 1,503

Southwestern Bell Telephone Co.; Austin; telephone communications 1,500

Minnesota Mining & Mfg. Co.; Austin; paper products 1,500

State of Texas/Employment Commission; Austin 1,500

County of Travis; Austin 1,500

State of Texas/Travis State School; Austin 1,400

St. David's Hospital; Austin 1,400

Austin State Hospital; Austin 1,300

Radian Corp.; Austin; engineering/architectural services 1,200

City of Austin/Police Dept.; Austin 1,134

State Farm Fire Casualty Co.; Austin; insurance services 1,100

Cox Enterprises Inc./Austin American Statesman; Austin; newspapers 1,000

Brown & Associates; Austin; laundry services 1,000

Compuadd Corp.; Austin; computer equipment 980

Lower Colorado River Authority; Austin; electric services 950

State of Texas/Railroad Commission; Austin 900

State of Texas/General Services Commission; Austin 850

City of Austin/Public Works Dept.; Austin; sanitary services 800

Capital Metro Transportation Authority; Austin 796

C. J. C. Holdings Inc./Artcarved; Austin; jewelry 775

Long Lines Ltd./MCI Services Marketing Inc.; Austin; telemarketing 750

Capital Personnel Services; Austin; management services 750

Farmers Group Inc.; Austin; insurance services 710

Healthcare Intl. Inc.; Austin; rehabilitation services 700

Sematech Inc.; Austin; computer research 700

State of Texas; Austin 700

Fisher Controls Intl.; Austin; research services 700

Del Valle Independent School District; Del Valle 608

NationsBank of Texas/Interfirst Services; Austin; computer services 600

Carbomedics Inc.; Austin; medical instruments 590

Hart Graphics Inc.; Austin; commercial printing 575

Texas Commerce Bank-Austin; Austin; commercial banks 567

Barton Creek Club Inc.; Austin; recreation services 550

University of Texas/Applied Research Labs; Austin; research services 525

11th District

Central — Waco

At the height of the Persian Gulf War, 26,000 soldiers were deployed from Fort Hood, the largest installation of armored forces in the free world. The deployment crushed the little town of Killeen; about 150 local businesses folded and others hung on by a thread. So when the troops returned in mid-1991 and immediately went on a local buying spree, the townsfolk were thrilled.

But the roller coaster experience of the gulf war was a troubling sign of times to come for the people of Killeen. Although the base was spared in the 1993 round of proposed closings, post-Cold War defense cuts are expected to eventually reach the 34,000 military personnel stationed at Hood.

And though Killeen stands to lose and gain the most from any changes at Fort Hood, the base's economic impact is felt throughout most of the 11th. Retired veterans—from Fort Hood and elsewhere—stay in central Texas, drawn to its mild climate and full line of services. The district has three Veterans Affairs medical centers (one employs less than 500 people), more than any other in the country.

One of the major employers in the district is Chrysler Technologies Airborne Systems, a Waco-based company that updates and modifies military aircraft.

In many respects, the city of Waco (population 103,600) is the core of the 11th. In the district's geographic center, Waco is also the educational, cultural and economic lifeblood of central Texas. Split by the Brazos River, Waco is the largest marketing center between Dallas and Austin.

As the home of the world's largest Baptist-affiliated university, Baylor University (12,000 students), Waco is also known as the "Baptist Rome." A former military base has been converted into Texas State Technical Institute.

One-third of the district's residents live in Bell and McLennan counties. These two counties also provide the bulk of Democratic votes. Residents tend to vote ideology more than party and they don't like change; in 50 years the 11th has had just three representatives.

The remainder of the sprawling 11th is agricultural and sparsely populated. Unlike the Piney Woods of east Texas, the rolling hills of this region have few trees.

The 11th has had an unfortunate share of attention-getting tragedies. In spring 1993, a deadly standoff outside of Waco between federal agents and members of the Branch Davidian religious sect resulted in the incineration of the sect's compound and the deaths of dozens of people. And in 1991, an armed gunman drove his truck through the window of a Luby's Cafeteria in nearby Killeen and killed 22 people.

Election Returns

	11th District	Democrat	Republican
1992	President*	66,521 (36.0%)	75,651 (41.0%)
	House	119,999 (67.4%)	58,033 (32.6%)
1990	Senate	54,677 (43.8%)	70,027 (56.2%)
1988	President	65,686 (42.9%)	87,348 (57.1%)

Vote for Perot was 42,365 (23.0%).

Demographics

Population 566,217

Percent change from 1980 7.4%

Land area 11,298 square miles

Population per square mile 50

Counties, 1990 population

Bell 191,088	Lampasas 13,521
Bosque 15,125	McCulloch (pt.) 7,678
Coryell 64,213	McLennan 189,123
Falls 17,712	Milam 22,946
Hamilton 7,733	Mills 4,531
Hill 27,146	San Saba 5,401

Cities, 1990 population (10,000 or more)

Belton 12,476	Harker Heights 12,841
Copperas Cove 24,079	Killeen 63,535
Fort Hood CDP 35,580	Temple 46,109
Gatesville 11,492	Waco 103,590

Race and Hispanic origin

White 76.0%
Black 15.9%
American Indian, Eskimo, or Aleut. 0.4%
Asian or Pacific Islander 1.6%
Other 6.0%
Hispanic origin 12.3%

Ancestry

American 6.7%	Irish 16.6%
Czechoslovakian 2.7%	Italian 1.6%
Dutch 2.0%	Polish 1.1%
English 11.6%	Scotch Irish 3.3%
French 3.1%	Scottish 1.7%
German 22.3%	

Universities/colleges, 1990-1991 enrollment

Baylor University, Waco 12,019
Central Texas College, Killeen 4,815
Hill College, Hillsboro 1,634
McLennan Community College, Waco 5,614
Temple Junior College, Temple 2,269
Texas State Tech Institute, Waco 3,803
University of Central Texas, Killeen 539
University of Mary Hardin-Baylor, Belton 1,808

Newspapers, total circulation (in all districts)

Austin American Statesman 172,077
Dallas Morning News 452,101
Killeen Daily Herald 16,369
San Antonio Light 160,666
Temple Daily Telegram 24,196
Waco Tribune Herald 46,439

Commercial television stations, affiliations

ADI: Waco-Temple (67%), Dallas-Fort Worth (25%) and San
    Angelo (9%)
    KCEN-TV, Temple (NBC)
    KWKT, Waco (Fox)
    KWTX-TV, Waco (CBS)
    KXXV, Waco (ABC)

Cable television systems, total subscribers

Cencom Cable TV; Fort Hood 5,622
KBC Corp. Inc.; Killeen 23,643
Killeen Cablevision; Copperas Cove 7,080
Temple Cablevision; Temple 15,500
Waco Cablevision; Waco 39,800

Military installations, 1991

Fort Hood (Army), Killeen 34,351

Businesses and other major employers

Scott & White Memorial Hospital; Temple 4,431
Central Texas College; Fort Hood 2,000
Chrysler Technologies Airborne Systems Inc.; Waco; aircraft
    parts 1,900
Aluminum Co. of America; Rockdale; aluminum 1,750
U.S. Veterans Affairs Dept.; Temple; hospital 1,619
U.S. Veterans Affairs Dept.; Waco; hospital 1,425
Ralph Wilson Plastics Co./Wilsonart; Temple; plastics 1,400
Hillcrest Baptist Medical Center; Waco 1,280
Baylor University; Waco 1,170
City of Waco; Waco 1,144
Texas Utilities Electric Co.; Rockdale; electrical work 1,000
Texas Plantation Foods Inc.; Waco; poultry products 900
Texas State Tech Institute; Waco 850
Mobil Oil Corp./Mobil Chemical Co. Div.; Temple; plastics
    products 800
County of Bell; Belton 650
McLane Co. Inc.; Temple; grocery products 599
County of McLennan; Waco 525
County of McLennan/Jail; Waco 509

12th District

Northwest Tarrant County; Part of Fort Worth

The 12th (see map on page 709) has an unusual hour-glass shape, but there is a unifying theme: transportation. Within this Fort Worth-based district are three major airports, an Air Force base, three railroad lines, several interstate highways and a myriad of businesses that depend on one or more of these conveyances.

The focus on transportation stems from Fort Worth's past importance as a rail center. The earliest settlers of Fort Worth extended the rail line themselves in 1873 when financial problems halted construction 26 miles to the east. Once the trains came through, Fort Worth emerged as a major cattle trading post; stockyards ringed the city and meatpacking plants flourished.

Today, bits of that history remain. On the city's north side, a handful of stockyards survive, and one of the largest cattle trading posts has been converted into a complex of shops, offices and kiddie rides called the Stockyard Station.

Although the Santa Fe Railroad is still active—shipping automobiles, chemicals, farm products and other commodities—the air industry has far surpassed rail.

One of the district's largest employers is American Airlines, which has both its headquarters and a maintenance facility just over the district line. The maintenance shop provided a critical boost to the local economy at just the right time. In 1991, General Dynamics in Fort Worth laid off 3,500 after the Pentagon canceled the A-12 stealth attack plane program. But opportunities at the American facility helped ease the impact of the loss.

Still, uncertainty remains for many of the blue-collar aviation workers. When Speaker Jim Wright represented this district, his clout helped protect the federal contracts that kept them at work. But Wright is gone, and the General Dynamics air division has been bought by Lockheed; there are concerns that future construction of the F-22 fighter plane will take place in Georgia instead of Fort Worth.

Another aircraft that has been a local economic staple—the V-22 Osprey—has had a checkered test period. Built by Bell Helicopter Textron, the experimental tilt-rotor aircraft has received $500 million in development contracts but no money for construction.

Since Wright's departure, local officials are redoubling their efforts to stimulate private enterprise. Boosters say the closure of Carswell Air Force Base creates an opportunity to attract manufacturers and other private development at the site. Before downsizing began in 1991, 5,500 military personnel were stationed at the base.

Alliance Airport, a commercial shipping operation initiated by Ross Perot, Jr., started off slow, but the pace of business has been picking up. A handful of state and private colleges in the area help provide workers for the electronics and aviation industries. The Automation and Robotics Research Institute at the University of Texas at Arlington often sponsors seminars on how to win government contracts. But the demise of the supercolliding superconductor, located just over the district line in the 6th District, will adversely affect the local area.

The bulk of the 12th's voters are moderate-to-conservative Democrats. But the 1992 presidential race was extremely competitive here, with Bill Clinton narrowly edging out George Bush and Ross Perot running a very strong third.

Election Returns

	12th District	Democrat	Republican
1992	President*	75,792 (37.2%)	71,212 (35.0%)
	House	125,492 (62.8%)	74,432 (37.2%)
1990	Senate	56,066 (43.0%)	74,319 (57.0%)
1988	President	66,660 (43.6%)	86,372 (56.4%)

*Vote for Perot was 56,564 (27.8%).

Demographics

Population 566,217

Percent change from 1980 7.4%

Land area 1,723 square miles

Population per square mile 329

Counties, 1990 population
Johnson (pt.) 67,020	Tarrant (pt.) 450,848
Parker (pt.) 48,349	

Cities, 1990 population (10,000 or more)
Cleburne 22,205	North Richland Hills (pt.)
Euless (pt.) 11,059	16,898
Fort Worth (pt.) 273,348	Weatherford (pt.) 14,209
Haltom City (pt.) 26,491	White Settlement 15,472
Hurst (pt.) 21,846	

Race and Hispanic origin
White 80.1%
Black 8.0%
American Indian, Eskimo, or Aleut. 0.5%
Asian or Pacific Islander 1.9%
Other 9.5%
Hispanic origin 16.3%

Ancestry
American 7.9%	Irish 18.2%
Dutch 2.8%	Italian 1.5%
English 14.4%	Polish 1.1%
French 3.5%	Scotch Irish 3.6%
German 18.2%	Scottish 2.2%

Universities/colleges, 1990-1991 enrollment
Tarrant County Junior College, Fort Worth 28,161
Texas Christian University, Fort Worth 6,458
Texas College of Osteopathic Medicine, Fort Worth 372
Weatherford College, Weatherford 2,192

Newspapers, total circulation (in all districts)
Dallas Morning News 452,101
Fort Worth Star-Telegram 250,099

Commercial television stations, affiliations
ADI: Dallas-Fort Worth (100%)

Cable television systems, total subscribers
Sammons Communications Inc.; Cleburne 5,216
Sammons Communications Inc.; Hurst 17,989
Sammons of Fort Worth; Fort Worth 71,319

Military installations, 1991
Carswell Air Force Base, Fort Worth 5,550

Businesses and other major employers
Lockheed Corp.; Fort Worth; aircraft/parts 30,000
Harris Methodist Hospital Fort Worth; Fort Worth 2,751
Tandy Corp./Radio Shack; Fort Worth; computer stores 2,300
U.S. General Services Administration; Fort Worth 2,000
John Peter Smith Hospital; Fort Worth 1,800
All Saints Episcopal Hospital; Fort Worth 1,637
U.S. Army Corp. of Engineers; Fort Worth 1,591
North Central Texas Home Health Care; Fort Worth; nursing 1,500
U.S. Postal Service; Fort Worth 1,500
Tarrant County Junior College; Fort Worth 1,487
Texas Christian University; Fort Worth 1,400
Texas Utilities Co.; Fort Worth; electric services 1,200
Capital Cities-ABC Inc./Fort Worth Star Telegram; Fort Worth; newspapers 1,200
Primerica Life Insurance Co.; Fort Worth; life insurance 1,200
Union Pacific Resources Co.; Fort Worth; petroleum/natural gas 1,100
Saint Joseph Hospital; Fort Worth 1,050
Cook-Fort Worth Children's Medical Center; Fort Worth 1,050
Halliburton Logging Services; Fort Worth; industrial equipment 900
City of Fort Worth/Water Dept.; Fort Worth 875
Lennox Industries Inc.; Fort Worth; plumbing/heating 850
Texas College of Osteopathic Medicine; Fort Worth 850
County of Tarrant/Convention Center; Fort Worth 800
Burlington Northern Inc.; Fort Worth; railroads 700

New American Holdings Inc.; Fort Worth; trusts   700
Fort Worth Osteopathic Hospital; Fort Worth   700
Trinity Meadows Raceway Inc./Raceway Park; Weatherford;
    commercial sports   700
Aegon USA Inc./PFL Life; Fort Worth; life insurance   658
Huguley Memorial Hospital; Fort Worth   650
Tandy Corp.; Fort Worth; computer equipment   600
Winn-Dixie Texas Inc.; Fort Worth; grocery stores   600
N. N. Investors Life Insurance Co.; Hurst; life insurance   600
Fort Worth Medical Plaza Inc./HCA Medical Plaza Hospital;
    Fort Worth   600
Fuqua Industries Inc./Snapper Power Equipment; Fort Worth;
    garden machinery   550
Cleburne Independent School District; Cleburne   550
Bell Helicopter Textron Inc.; Hurst; aircraft/helicopters   505

13th District

Eastern Panhandle — Wichita Falls; Part of Amarillo

Since Bill Sarpalius took the 13th from the GOP in 1988, he has made voters increasingly comfortable with Democratic representation in the House. He hit 60 percent in 1992, thwarting the comeback try of the Republican who had held the 13th in the mid-1980s.

But this district remains politically competitive. In 1992 presidential voting, George Bush carried the 13th with 43 percent of the vote. Both he and Sarpalius won for the same reason: the region's conservative bent. Even the district's most conservative elements—politically active religious groups—have trouble finding fault with Sarpalius, an opponent of abortion.

The massive 13th comprises three distinct regions: the panhandle, the south plains and the Red River Valley. It takes more than eight hours to traverse the sparsely settled district, which includes all or part of 38 counties. It is not uncommon for residents to travel 60 miles for health care.

Thanks to the addition of several counties along its southern border in 1992 redistricting, the 13th became the largest cotton-producing district in the nation. More than 1.8 million acres of cotton grow in the fertile land above the Ogallala aquifer. Heavy agribusiness use of the aquifer has prompted concerns about depletion, and interest in conservation measures is increasing. Other leading crops include wheat, sorghum, sugar beets, corn and hay.

The biggest single chunk of votes in the 13th comes out of Wichita County, where the blue-collar city of Wichita Falls gives Democratic candidates a warm reception. Sarpalius got 62 percent in Wichita County in 1992, and Bill Clinton ran just 935 votes behind Bush in rural areas. Once heavily reliant on the oil industry, the area has weathered the oil slump with the assistance of income from Sheppard Air Force Base, just north of the city. Among the Air Force's largest training bases, Sheppard is headquarters of the NATO Jet Training Center.

At the northwestern corner of the 13th is the district's second-biggest concentration of people, in Potter County (Amarillo). The city of 158,000 is divided between the 13th and 19th districts. The downtown business district, in the 13th, has been suffering since the oil crash of the mid-1980s; vacant office buildings and closed shops are much in evidence. Government-related business helps keep Amarillo going: The federal Bureau of Mines and a state prison are major local employers, and the Pantex nuclear plant is in contention to expand its existing operation dismantling nuclear weapons.

Potter County (with almost 15 percent of the district's vote) was good to Bush in 1992, giving him nearly a majority. Sarpalius took Potter with 57 percent.

Though the bulk of the 13th has a rural and small-town feel, on its far eastern edge the district pokes in to take a part of Denton County, which is in the orbit of the Dallas-Fort Worth metropolitan area. The voters here tend to be more liberal than the district norm: Clinton got 42 percent here, well above his district average.

Election Returns

	13th District	Democrat	Republican
1992	President*	73,454 (36.3%)	87,492 (43.3%)
	House	117,892 (60.3%)	77,514 (39.7%)
1990	Senate	52,579 (38.3%)	84,711 (61.7%)
1988	President	86,848 (43.0%)	115,044 (57.0%)

Vote for Perot was 41,189 (20.4%).

Demographics

Population 566,217

Percent change from 1980 7.5%

Land area 31,757 square miles

Population per square mile 18

Counties, 1990 population

Archer 7,973	Hale 34,671
Armstrong 2,021	Hall 3,905
Baylor 4,385	Hardeman 5,283
Briscoe 1,971	Hemphill 3,720
Carson 6,576	Hutchinson 25,689
Castro 9,070	King 354
Childress 5,953	Knox 4,837
Clay 10,024	Lamb 15,072
Collingsworth 3,573	Lipscomb 3,143
Cooke (pt.) 288	Lubbock (pt.) 42,811
Cottle 2,247	Lynn 6,758
Crosby 7,304	Montague 17,274
Denton (pt.) 43,705	Motley 1,532
Dickens 2,571	Potter 97,874
Donley 3,696	Roberts 1,025
Floyd 8,497	Swisher 8,133
Foard 1,794	Wheeler 5,879
Garza 5,143	Wichita 122,378
Gray 23,967	Wilbarger 15,121

Cities, 1990 population (10,000 or more)

Amarillo (pt.) 91,502	Pampa 19,959
Borger 15,675	Plainview 21,700
Burkburnett 10,145	Vernon 12,001
Denton (pt.) 42,308	Wichita Falls 96,259
Lubbock (pt.) 38,098	

Race and Hispanic origin
White 78.9%
Black 8.0%
American Indian, Eskimo, or Aleut. 0.6%
Asian or Pacific Islander 1.2%

Other 11.3%
Hispanic origin 19.4%

Ancestry

American 7.7%	Irish 17.0%
Dutch 3.0%	Italian 1.1%
English 13.3%	Scotch Irish 3.2%
French 2.7%	Scottish 1.7%
German 16.7%	

Universities/colleges, 1990-1991 enrollment

Amarillo College, Amarillo 5,951
Clarendon College, Clarendon 974
Frank Phillips College, Borger 962
Midwestern State University, Wichita Falls 5,508
Texas State Tech Institute, Amarillo 657
Texas Woman's University, Denton 9,850
University of North Texas, Denton 27,160
Vernon Regional Junior College, Vernon 1,823
Wayland Baptist University, Plainview 2,082

Newspapers, total circulation (in all districts)

Amarillo News/Globe Times 64,259
Borger News-Herald 6,182
Dallas Morning News 452,101
Lubbock Avalanche Journal 66,342
Pampa News 7,069
Wichita Falls Times-Record News 38,861

Commercial television stations, affiliations

ADI: Amarillo (48%), Lubbock (27%), Wichita Falls-Lawton (24%) and Dallas-Fort Worth (1%)
KAMR-TV, Amarillo (NBC)
KCIT, Amarillo (Fox)
KFDA-TV, Amarillo (CBS)
KVII-TV, Amarillo (ABC)
KCBD-TV, Lubbock (NBC)
KAUZ-TV, Wichita Falls (CBS)
KFDX-TV, Wichita Falls (NBC)

Cable television systems, total subscribers

Cox Cable Lubbock; Lubbock 37,000
Plainview Cable TV Co.; Plainview 6,550
Sammons Communications of Texas Inc.; Borger 6,700
Sammons Communications of Texas Inc.; Pampa 8,150
TCA Cable of Amarillo; Amarillo 41,300
Vista Cablevision; Wichita Falls 24,850

Military installations, 1991

Sheppard Air Force Base, Wichita Falls 5,918

Businesses and other major employers

University of North Texas; Denton 2,700
IBP Inc.; Amarillo; meatpacking 2,500
Excel Corp.; Plainview; meat products 1,650
Northwest Texas Hospital; Amarillo 1,569
Texas Instruments Inc.; Lubbock; electronic components 1,500
University Medical Center; Lubbock 1,500
Wichita Falls State Mental Hospital; Wichita Falls 1,300
Paccar Inc./Peterbilt Motors Co.; Denton; motor vehicle parts/equipment 1,100
Phillips Petroleum Co.; Borger; natural gas liquids 1,069
Certainteed Corp./Fiberglass Reinforcements Div.; Wichita Falls; lumber/building materials 1,000

Howmet Corp./Casting Div.; Wichita Falls; iron/steel foundries 1,000
Southwestern Public Service Co.; Amarillo; electric services 931
Wichita General Hospital; Wichita Falls 900
State of Texas/Mental Health Dept.; Lubbock 900
St. Anthony's Hospital; Amarillo 900
Texas Woman's University; Denton 877
City of Denton; Denton 870
State of Texas/Corrections Dept.; Amarillo 850
Vernon State Hospital; Vernon 841
Denton Regional Medical Center; Denton 789
City of Plainview/Public Schools; Plainview 725
Asarco Inc./Amarillo Copper Refinery; Amarillo; copper production 650
U.S. Veterans Affairs Dept.; Amarillo; hospital 650
Eagle-Picher Industries Inc./Construction Equipment Div.; Lubbock; construction machinery 600
Wal-Mart Stores Inc.; Plainview; warehousing 600
W. R. Grace & Co. Inc./Cryovac Div.; Iowa Park; plastics products 581
PPG Industries Inc.; Wichita Falls; flat glass 570
Texas Instruments Inc.; Denton; ordnance/accessories 550

14th District

Southeast; Gulf Coast

Larger than the state of Massachusetts, the 14th stretches from the western outskirts of Austin to the Gulf Coast. Residents are dispersed widely across this huge land mass; the district's personality is rural and small-town Texas.

Two industries—agriculture and petrochemicals—dominate the 14th. Almost every major farm commodity is grown somewhere in the district. Grain, sorghum and rice are the most notable crops, grown primarily in the southern counties of Matagorda, Wharton, Jackson, Victoria, Refugio and Colorado. Hay is a major crop in Fayette County and Austin County, just over the 14th's boundary line in the 8th. Altogether, agriculture generates between $1.5 billion and $2 billion a year for the district.

Closer to the coastline, petrochemical plants dot the landscape. Dow, Du Pont, Phillips Petroleum and Union Carbide all have plants in the 14th. When oil prices dropped in the mid-1980s because of a worldwide glut, petrochemical companies flourished. The companies use oil as a base product to produce chemicals that are combined with other chemicals to make such items as antifreeze, foam and plastics.

Victoria, population 55,100, is the district's only sizable city. Originally settled by the French explorer La Salle in 1685, the city was named in 1824 for a Mexican president, Guadalupe Victoria. After centuries as a leading cattle and cotton capital, Victoria today is a major oil and chemical center.

Intermingled with the chemical plants are lively fishing ports that haul in shrimp for tourists and locals. Port Lavaca in Calhoun County successfully combines commercial fishing, tourism and offshore drilling businesses. In adjacent Aransas County, nature lovers flock to Goose Island State Park, Aransas National Wildlife Refuge and several bird sanctuaries.

Bastrop County, in the northwestern corner of the huge district, is being pulled into the suburban orbit of growing Austin, in the 10th District. Less than 25 miles from the state capital, the city of Bastrop also boasts the University of Texas cancer research center. Austin's liberal views have begun to rub off on its neighboring county; Bastrop was one of the few in the 14th to support Democrat Bill Clinton for president in 1992, giving him 43 percent of the vote in the three-way presidential contest.

Although the 14th includes former President Lyndon B. Johnson's birthplace in Blanco County, the district is more conservative than its famous native. Democrats hold onto the seat with fiscally cautious views and a dedication to home-state concerns. Republican George Bush won the district in 1992.

Minorities make up more than one-third of the 14th. Victoria, Matagorda and Lavaca counties all have sizable black and Hispanic communities, and Waller County's Prairie View A&M University, founded in 1878, is a predominantly black college with 5,000 students.

Election Returns

	14th District	Democrat	Republican
1992	President*	78,776 (37.1%)	86,178 (40.6%)
	House	135,930 (68.1%)	54,412 (27.3%)
1990	Senate	58,931 (40.1%)	87,915 (59.9%)
1988	President	97,667 (46.6%)	112,015 (53.4%)

*Vote for Perot was 47,097 (22.2%).

Demographics

Population 566,217

Percent change from 1980 7.5%

Land area 15,378 square miles

Population per square mile 37

Counties, 1990 population

Aransas 17,892	Hays 65,614
Austin (pt.) 4,216	Jackson 13,039
Bastrop 38,263	Lavaca 18,690
Blanco 5,972	Lee 12,854
Brazoria (pt.) 59,419	Matagorda 36,928
Burleson 13,625	Refugio 7,976
Caldwell 26,392	Travis (pt.) 10,190
Calhoun 19,053	Victoria 74,361
Colorado 18,383	Waller (pt.) 19,279
Fayette 20,095	Wharton 39,955
Gonzales 17,205	Williamson (pt.) 26,816

Cities, 1990 population (10,000 or more)

Bay City 18,170	San Marcos 28,743
El Campo 10,511	Taylor (pt.) 11,465
Freeport (pt.) 11,322	Victoria 55,076
Port Lavaca 10,886	

Race and Hispanic origin

White 77.7%
Black 10.6%
American Indian, Eskimo, or Aleut. 0.3%
Asian or Pacific Islander 0.6%
Other 10.7%
Hispanic origin 23.6%

Ancestry

American 4.4%	Irish 13.1%
Czechoslovakian 7.1%	Italian 1.2%
Dutch 1.5%	Polish 1.5%
English 10.2%	Scotch Irish 2.8%
French 3.3%	Scottish 1.3%
German 25.5%	Swedish 1.1%

Universities/colleges, 1990-1991 enrollment

Brazosport College, Lake Jackson 3,460
Prairie View A&M University, Prairie View 4,990
Southwest Texas State University, San Marcos 20,940
University of Houston-Victoria, Victoria 1,164
Victoria College, Victoria 3,328
Wharton County Junior College, Wharton 2,963

Newspapers, total circulation (in all districts)

Austin American Statesman 172,077
Clute Brazosport Facts 19,824
Corpus Christi Caller-Times 67,489
Houston Chronicle 421,140
Houston Post 292,061
San Antonio News-Express 187,599
San Marcos Daily Record 4,891
Victoria Advocate 37,638

Commercial television stations, affiliations

ADI: Houston (39%), Austin (31%), San Antonio (18%), Corpus Christi (8%) and Waco-Temple (4%)
KAVU-TV, Victoria (ABC)
KVCT, Victoria (ABC)

Cable television systems, total subscribers

Austin Cablevision; Mount Larson 146,500
Cencom Cable TV; Schulenburg 5,507
Northland Cable TV; Bay City 6,443
TCA Cable TV Inc.; Victoria 18,665
TCI of Texas; Clute 10,575
TCI of Texas; San Marcos 12,121

Businesses and other major employers

Dow Chemical Co./Dow Chemical USA; Freeport; organic chemicals 7,500
Southwest Texas State University; San Marcos 2,049
G. S. Group Inc.; Freeport; plumbing/heating/air-conditioning 2,000
U.S. Contractors Inc.; Clute; personnel supply services 1,800
Brazosport Independent School District; Clute 1,275
Phillips Petroleum Co./Phillips 66; Old Ocean; petroleum refining 1,200
Union Carbide Chemical & Plastics Co.; Seadrift; organic chemicals 1,200
Du Pont E. I. De Nemours & Co.; Victoria; plastics/synthetics 1,150
Prairie View A&M University; Prairie View 920
Kaspar Wire Works Inc.; Shiner; partitions/fixtures 900
BASF Corp./Chemicals Div.; Freeport; inorganic chemicals 850
Intermedics Pacemakers Inc.; Freeport; medical equipment 800
Intercraft Industries; Taylor; wood products 750
Citizens Medical Center; Victoria 610
City of Victoria; Victoria 585
Calhoun County Independent School District; Port Lavaca 565

Community Hospital of Brazosport; Lake Jackson 557
Victoria Independent School District; Victoria 552
Home Health Services of Victoria County/Crossroads Home
    Health; Victoria; home health services 550

15th District

*South — Bee, Brooks, Hidalgo and San Patricio Counties;
McAllen*

The 15th remains the most heavily Hispanic district in Texas (nearly 75 percent of the population) and a reliable vote-getting region for any Democrat. Despite losing the state, Bill Clinton won the 15th in the 1992 presidential contest with 53 percent of the vote, his highest nonurban district tally in Texas.

The 1992 redistricting compressed the boundaries of the 15th, shifting two of the fastest-growing counties in the state—Starr and Zapata—into the newly formed 28th. Despite the removal of two heavily Hispanic border counties, the 15th retains its Spanish flavor.

Goliad County, created in 1836 from a Spanish municipality, is among the state's most historic areas. Bisected by the San Antonio River, the region has several missions, historic churches and a statue of Gen. Ignacio Zaragoza, the Mexican leader who fought back French troops in 1862, leading to the celebration of Cinco de Mayo.

Hidalgo County, named for the leader of Mexico's independence movement, Miguel Hidalgo y Costillo, is 85 percent Hispanic. Anchored by McAllen, a major port of entry into Mexico, the county is noteworthy for its foreign trade and popularity with travelers. Many midwesterners and Canadians spend the winter season in McAllen, drawn by its subtropical climate and tourist activities.

Home to nearly 384,000 people, Hidalgo is the most populous county in the 15th. It is also the seventh-poorest county in Texas, with more than 40 percent of its residents living below the poverty level. Hidalgo County's economy is heavily dependent on agriculture; cotton, grain, vegetables and sugar cane are among the most common crops. (Districtwide, the median household income is between $17,500 and $20,000, about $10,000 less than the statewide average.)

And like most of the counties along the Rio Grande, Hidalgo is reliant upon *maquiladora* plants for much of its income. The system of "twin" plants enables the bulk of production work to be done at one facility on the Mexican side of the border, while some finishing and distribution is handled by its American counterpart.

Although manufacturing along the border has picked up, the region's agribusiness was hurt by a freeze in the winter of 1989 and previous drought problems. More farmers have been forced to invest in irrigation, a costly investment but one that is paying off.

Outside Hidalgo, the most populous county is San Patricio, with just under 59,000 people. San Patricio is closely linked economically with the port city of Corpus Christi, which lies just across the bay in the 27th District.

In the northern, sparsely populated counties of the 15th, cattle, agriculture and some oil production account for most revenue. Timber and furniture-making are important industries in De Witt County.

Panna Maria, in Karnes County, is the oldest Polish settlement in the state.

Election Returns

	15th District	Democrat	Republican
1992	President*	80,085 (52.6%)	52,080 (34.2%)
	House	86,351 (60.4%)	56,549 (39.6%)
1990	Senate	40,148 (45.7%)	47,669 (54.3%)
1988	President	81,255 (61.2%)	51,488 (38.8%)

Vote for Perot was 20,072 (13.2%).

Demographics

Population 566,217

Percent change from 1980 7.4%

Land area 8,450 square miles

Population per square mile 67

Counties, 1990 population

Bee 25,135	Karnes 12,455
Brooks 8,204	Kleberg (pt.) 19,349
DeWitt 18,840	Live Oak 9,556
Goliad 5,980	San Patricio 58,749
Hidalgo 383,545	Willacy (pt.) 14,138
Jim Wells (pt.) 10,266	

Cities, 1990 population (10,000 or more)

Beeville 13,547	Mission 28,653
Donna 12,652	Pharr 32,921
Edinburg 29,885	Portland (pt.) 12,224
Kingsville (pt.) 17,250	San Juan 10,815
McAllen 84,021	Weslaco 21,877
Mercedes 12,694	

Race and Hispanic origin
White 75.5%
Black 1.1%
American Indian, Eskimo, or Aleut. 0.2%
Asian or Pacific Islander 0.3%
Other 22.9%
Hispanic origin 74.5%

Ancestry

American 2.2%	German 8.9%
English 4.8%	Irish 5.2%
French 1.2%	Scotch Irish 1.3%

Universities/colleges, 1990-1991 enrollment
Bee County College, Beeville 2,250
University of Texas-Pan American, Edinburg 12,337

Newspapers, total circulation (in all districts)
Corpus Christi Caller-Times 67,489
Harlingen Valley Morning Star 30,403
McAllen Monitor 35,534
San Antonio Light 160,666
San Antonio News-Express 187,599
Victoria Advocate 37,638

Commercial television stations, affiliations
ADI: Corpus Christi (49%), San Antonio (30%), and McAllen-Brownsville (21%)

Cable television systems, total subscribers
Heritage Cablevision; Harlingen 21,216
Heritage Cablevision; Pharr 23,769

Military installations, 1991
Chase Field Naval Air Station, Beeville 1,682

Businesses and other major employers
La Joya Independent School District; La Joya 1,200
Reynolds Metals Co./Sherwin Plant; Gregory; metal ores
  1,000
Gerald D. Hines/Beacon Construction Co. Inc.; Portland;
  heavy construction 1,000
Teddy Bertucca Co. Inc.; McAllen; vegetables/melons 985
McAllen Medical Center; McAllen 980
Bowie Mfg. Co. Inc./Weslaco Mfg. Co.; Weslaco; men's
  suits/coats 850
Hidalgo County Jail; Edinburg 840
University of Texas-Pan American; Edinburg 804
Levi Strauss & Co.; McAllen; outerwear 800
Knapp Medical Center; Weslaco 656
Stilwell Foods Inc./Rio Grande Foods Inc.; McAllen; grocery
  products 650
Sharyland Corp./Plantation Produce Co.; Mission; crop ser-
  vices 650

16th District

West — El Paso and Suburbs

When the mosquito control unit hits the streets of El Paso, it does not stop at the border. When the El Paso Ballet was looking for new sources of revenue, it changed its name, ditching El Paso in favor of the more international Ballet of the Americas. And when Mexicans want jobs and Texans want inexpensive goods, they can cross the Bridge of the Americas.

This is life in the 16th, a compact, multicultural district on the Mexican border where jobs, entertainment, health and government blend and blur between El Paso and its sister city, Ciudad Juarez. Both English and Spanish are spoken fluently, native holiday celebrations are shared and families are split between the two cities. Nowhere is the interdependency more evident than in the *maquiladoras*, or twin plants, in which Mexican workers do the bulk of labor—making everything from cars to clothing— and Americans complete the products with finishing details. By one estimate, there are about 300 such plants in the El Paso-Juarez area.

Despite their commercial and cultural affinity, the two cities do not always get along. Shortly before Christmas 1992 the Mexican government lowered duty-free limits from $300 a person to $50 a person. That means Mexicans, who often shop at cleaner El Paso stores, can now bring just $50 worth of goods home duty-free.

Textile manufacturing is the biggest industry in El Paso; a large Levi Strauss plant is a major employer. The region is one of the few in the nation where long-staple Egyptian cotton, one of the finest cotton fibers, is grown.

El Paso's Fort Bliss is also a major employer, credited in 1992 with pumping nearly $1 billion into the region's economy. Fort Bliss is the home of the Patriot missile systems, the famed Scud-interceptor of the Persian Gulf War. Patriot crew members are trained at the U.S. Army Air Defense Center here.

The University of Texas at El Paso adds 16,500 students to the city; many other El Paso residents travel west to New Mexico State University, which is nearby.

El Paso's population is 80 percent Hispanic; the district's is 70 percent. Hispanics usually control prominent elected offices; although in 1992 a Hispanic candidate failed to get past the 1992 Democratic House primary (Democrat Ronald Coleman was re-elected to his sixth term that year). In the 1992 presidential race, Bill Clinton defeated Texans George Bush and Ross Perot in El Paso County.

As El Paso's population has grown, the city has struggled with problems such as pollution and poverty. Nearly 27 percent of the people in the county fall below the poverty level.

Election Returns

	16th District	Democrat	Republican
1992	President*	65,614 (50.6%)	45,367 (35.0%)
	House	66,731 (51.9%)	61,870 (48.1%)
1990	Senate	28,297 (39.2%)	43,844 (60.8%)
1988	President	64,719 (52.8%)	57,741 (47.2%)

Vote for Perot was 18,779 (14.5%).

Demographics

Population 566,217

Percent change from 1980 7.4%

Land area 485 square miles

Population per square mile 1,167

Counties, 1990 population
El Paso (pt.) 566,217

Cities, 1990 population (10,000 or more)
El Paso (pt.) 502,690   Socorro 22,995
Fort Bliss CDP (pt.) 11,316

Race and Hispanic origin
White 76.5%
Black 3.6%
American Indian, Eskimo, or Aleut. 0.4%
Asian or Pacific Islander 1.1%
Other 18.5%
Hispanic origin 70.4%

Ancestry
American 2.6%   Irish 5.3%
English 5.5%   Italian 1.2%
French 1.4%   Scotch Irish 1.1%
German 8.4%

Universities/colleges, 1990-1991 enrollment
El Paso Community College, El Paso 17,081
Southwest Institute of Merchandising & Design, El Paso 279
University of Texas, El Paso, El Paso 16,524

Newspapers, total circulation (in all districts)
El Paso Times 91,177

Commercial television stations, affiliations
ADI: El Paso (100%)
  KCIK, El Paso (Fox)
  KDBC-TV, El Paso (CBS)

KJLF, El Paso (None)
KSCE, El Paso (None)
KTSM-TV, El Paso (NBC)
KVIA-TV, El Paso (ABC)

Cable television systems, total subscribers
Paragon Cable; El Paso 86,000

Military installations, 1991
Fort Bliss (Army), El Paso (shared with 23rd District) 20,678

Businesses and other major employers
Futurama; El Paso; department stores 5,000
University of Texas; El Paso 2,851
Providence Memorial Hospital; El Paso 2,016
Farah Inc./Farah USA; El Paso; outerwear 2,000
General Electric Co.; El Paso; electrical motors 1,500
Sierra Medical Center; El Paso 1,400
Levi Strauss & Co.; El Paso; outerwear 1,350
El Paso Natural Gas Co.; El Paso; gas pipelines 1,250
Turnkey Services Inc.; El Paso; personnel supply services 1,200
R. E. Thomason General Hospital; El Paso 1,200
U.S. Postal Service; El Paso 1,123
American Garment Finishers; El Paso; textile finishing 1,000
Southern Pacific Transportation Co.; El Paso; freight shipping 1,000
Salant Corp./Texas Apparel Co. Div.; El Paso; outerwear 1,000
El Paso Community College; El Paso 1,000
Army & Air Force Exchange Service; El Paso; department stores 900
Tony Lama Co. Inc.; El Paso; footwear 870
Rockwell Intl. Corp./Semiconductor Products Div.; El Paso; communications equipment 820
North American Philips Corp.; El Paso; electronic components 800
Greater Texas Finishing Corp.; El Paso; laundry services 800
Dale Electronics Inc./Microcircuits Div.; El Paso; electronic components 700
Pet Inc./Mountain Pass Canning Co.; Anthony; canned fruits/vegetables 700
Baxter Healthcare Corp./Baxter Convertors; El Paso; medical supplies 650
Columbia Hospital Corp./Sun Towers Hospital; El Paso 620
General Instrument Corp.; El Paso; electrical industrial apparatus 600
Allen-Bradley Co. Inc.; El Paso; warehousing 600
Tonka Corp./Tonka Toys; El Paso; toys 600
Sun Apparel Inc.; El Paso; outerwear 600
Don Shapiro Industries Inc.; El Paso; outerwear 600
Greater El Paso Corp.; El Paso; personnel supply services 600
City of El Paso; El Paso 600
County of El Paso/Sheriffs Office; El Paso; personnel supply services 579
Phelps Dodge Refining Corp.; El Paso; copper ores 534

17th District

West Central — Abilene

In the oil industry's heyday, 100 rigs dotted the rolling prairie of the 17th. Today, there are only about a dozen in the enormous district, which lies west of Fort Worth. As was the case elsewhere in oil-dependent Texas, entire towns in the 17th virtually collapsed with the industry; businesses closed and banks foreclosed on mortgages. For a time, a popular local bumper sticker warned off job-seeking newcomers with this message: "Welcome to Texas. Now Go Home."

To survive, many of the people who held on in west Texas returned to the land or looked to the government. In the 1990s, agriculture, prisons and the defense industry are the 17th's three top sources of jobs.

The only large city in the district is Abilene (Taylor County), with almost 107,000 people. In 1991 it became a member of the Texas Main Street Project, a private-public effort to revitalize the downtown by renovating and reusing historic buildings. Three church-sponsored colleges in Abilene help nurture the 17th's large and powerful evangelical community. Taylor County showed its conservatism clearly in 1992, giving George Bush nearly half its presidential vote; Bill Clinton was a distant second, not very far ahead of Ross Perot. In the districtwide presidential race, Bush carried the 17th with 40 percent of the vote, Clinton followed in second with 40 percent, Ross Perot trailed with 26 percent.

Dyess and Goodfellow Air Force bases are reliable employers. More than 5,000 people are stationed at Dyess, in Abilene. It is the only training base in the country for the B-1B bomber, and personnel here also train on refueling planes and maintain a fleet of several dozen aircraft.

Goodfellow is in Tom Green County (San Angelo), which is split between the 17th and 21st districts. Though the base itself is just over the 17th boundary line, it still has a major economic impact here. Goodfellow has appeared on proposed base-closing lists, but a new firefighting training unit has been added to its intelligence-training operation.

The 17th is also home to a number of defense-related private companies. A Lockheed plant in Abilene (purchased from General Dynamics in early 1993) builds components for the F-16 aircraft. The future of the facility is cloudy, given the uncertainty over whether the Air Force will end procurements of the F-16 by the late 1990s.

The area around San Angelo is a major producer of wool and mohair; Tom Green County, with its rocky terrain, is ideally suited to sheep and goats. Counties in the northeastern corner of the 17th rely heavily on beef sales, while the counties at the opposite end of the district, more than 200 miles away, are major cotton producers.

The prison business is booming in the 17th. On the western side of the district, the Big Spring federal correctional facility has given an economic boost to Howard County. It has 285 employees tending 1,270 inmates. Other prisons in the 17th include Abilene's 2,250-bed maximum-security unit, employing 900, and the Price Daniel unit in Snyder (Scurry County), with 420 workers.

Election Returns

	17th District	Democrat	Republican
1992	President*	73,388 (34.0%)	86,490 (40.1%)
	House	136,213 (66.1%)	69,958 (33.9%)
1990	Senate	51,781 (35.4%)	94,652 (64.6%)
1988	President	89,526 (41.4%)	126,588 (58.6%)

Vote for Perot was 55,834 (25.9%).

Demographics

Population 566,217

Percent change from 1980 7.5%

Land area 28,144 square miles

Population per square mile 20

Counties, 1990 population

Borden 799	Kent 1,010
Brown 34,371	Martin 4,956
Callahan 11,859	Mitchell 8,016
Coke 3,424	Nolan 16,594
Coleman 9,710	Palo Pinto 25,055
Comanche 13,381	Runnels 11,294
Concho 3,044	Scurry 18,634
Dawson 14,349	Shackelford 3,316
Eastland 18,488	Somervell 5,360
Erath 27,991	Stephens 9,010
Fisher 4,842	Stonewall 2,013
Haskell 6,820	Taylor 119,655
Hood 28,981	Throckmorton 1,880
Howard 32,343	Tom Green (pt.) 52,746
Jack 6,981	Wise 34,679
Jones 16,490	Young 18,126

Cities, 1990 population (10,000 or more)

Abilene 106,654	San Angelo (pt.) 48,529
Big Spring 23,093	Snyder 12,195
Brownwood 18,387	Stephenville 13,502
Lamesa 10,809	Sweetwater 11,967
Mineral Wells (pt.) 14,388	

Race and Hispanic origin

White 85.7%
Black 3.5%
American Indian, Eskimo, or Aleut. 0.4%
Asian or Pacific Islander 0.5%
Other 9.8%
Hispanic origin 17.2%

Ancestry

American 9.8%	German 17.2%
Dutch 3.2%	Irish 19.2%
English 15.8%	Scotch Irish 3.4%
French 2.9%	Scottish 1.8%

Universities/colleges, 1990-1991 enrollment

Abilene Christian University, Abilene 4,053
Cisco Junior College, Cisco 2,067
Hardin-Simmons University, Abilene 1,930
Howard County Junior College, Big Spring 2,273
Howard Payne University, Brownwood 1,354
McMurry College, Abilene 1,631
Ranger Junior College, Ranger 726
Tarleton State University, Stephenville 6,250
Texas State Tech-Sweetwater, Sweetwater 806
Western Texas College, Snyder 1,060

Newspapers, total circulation (in all districts)

Abilene Reporter News 42,702
Big Spring Herald 8,552
Dallas Morning News 452,101
Fort Worth Star-Telegram 250,099
Lubbock Avalanche Journal 66,342
San Angelo Standard-Times 31,082
Wichita Falls Times-Record News 38,861

Commercial television stations, affiliations

ADI: Abilene-Sweetwater (50%), Dallas-Forth Worth (19%), Lubbock (10%), San Angelo (8%), Wichita Falls-Lawton (7%) and Odessa-Midland (6%)
KRBC-TV, Abilene (NBC)
KTAB-TV, Abilene (CBS)
KWAB-TV, Big Spring (NBC)
KLST, San Angelo (CBS)
KTXS-TV, Sweetwater (ABC)

Cable television systems, total subscribers

Big Spring Cable TV; Big Spring 8,698
Brownwood TV Cable Service; Brownwood 9,074
Brownwood TV Cable Service; Clyde 12,022
Marcus Cable; San Angelo 21,067
Northland Cable TV; Stephenville 5,500
United Cable Service of Abilene; Abilene 32,384

Military installations, 1991

Dyess Air Force Base, Abilene 5,830

Businesses and other major employers

Abilene Independent School District; Abilene 2,500
State of Texas; Abilene; residential care 1,864
Ethicon Inc.; San Angelo; medical instruments/supplies 1,600
Hendrick Medical Center; Abilene 1,380
Wichita Falls State Hospital; Decatur; health services 1,300
Texas Utilities Electric Co.; Glen Rose; electric services 1,200
Lockheed Corp.; Abilene; aircraft parts 1,100
Tarleton State University; Stephenville 906
Kohler Co.; Brownwood; bathroom fixtures 900
Shannon West Texas Memorial Hospital; San Angelo 900
State of Texas/Corrections Dept.; Abilene 900
State of Texas/Mental Health Dept.; Big Spring 840
Texas Instruments Inc.; Abilene; electronic components 700
Humana Inc.; Abilene 600
Abilene Christian University; Abilene 595

18th District

Downtown Houston

Once a compact, urban district centered around Houston's downtown, the 18th for the 1990s is an X-shaped contortion with tentacles that stretch to two outlying airports, scooping up a handful of cozy suburbs along the way (see map on page 715).

After reapportionment in 1990 gave Texas three new House districts, mapmakers set out to increase minority representation. In Houston, they took large parts of the old 18th—primarily its Hispanic sections—and shifted them into a new 29th District with a majority of Hispanics. The population remaining in the 18th is 51 percent black and 15 percent Hispanic.

Now the district has well-to-do suburbs in northwest Harris County, such as Hedwig Village. They add Republican votes to the 18th and lift the district up a notch on the income scale. The median household income for the district is between $22,500 and $25,000. Many of the suburbanites shop at the upscale Galleria Mall, which remapping also included in the 18th.

While the district now has some pockets of economic

comfort, life in the 18th continues to be a struggle for most. The North Forest School District is one of the most financially strapped in the state. There is virtually no commercial property to tax in the area, and the mostly low-income black residents cannot afford to pay higher property taxes on their homes.

One of the burning questions locally is the future of Allen Parkway Village, a post-World War II subsidized housing complex on the west side. Initially built by the federal government to house whites, the 1,000 units were integrated in the 1960s and became predominantly black in the 1970s. By the early 1990s, fewer than 40 families lived in the dilapidated complex, which has been plagued with asbestos and lead paint problems.

Many area residents are concerned that developers want to revamp the 37-acre property into an extension of the adjacent downtown business district.

With an estimated 10,000 families on Houston's waiting list for affordable housing, some leaders contend that the whole complex should be repaired and reopened.

Others are skeptical of this plan, feeling the complex may have gone too far downhill to be rescued. The fate of the complex will have a dramatic impact on the entire west side and its residents.

Few live in downtown Houston, although its businesses provide jobs at all levels for the district's residents. The effects of the mid-1980s oil bust are still evident in Houston. Downtown buildings once named for and primarily occupied by companies such as Exxon share quarters with banks and law firms. Lower-income residents of the 18th work as clerks in the offices, bellhops in the hotels and custodians at the nearby Texas Medical Center.

The 18th has always been one of the most Democratic districts in the state. Bill Clinton coasted in this district in 1992 with 66 percent of the vote.

Election Returns

	18th District	Democrat	Republican
1992	President*	118,349 (66.2%)	40,150 (22.4%)
	House	111,422 (64.7%)	56,080 (32.6%)
1990	Senate	65,231 (65.2%)	34,781 (34.8%)
1988	President	111,442 (70.9%)	45,758 (29.1%)

*Vote for Perot was 20,382 (11.4%).

Demographics

Population 566,217

Percent change from 1980 7.4%

Land area 250 square miles

Population per square mile 2,263

Counties, 1990 population
Harris (pt.) 566,217

Cities, 1990 population (10,000 or more)
Houston (pt.) 458,411

Race and Hispanic origin
White 37.7%
Black 50.9%
American Indian, Eskimo, or Aleut. 0.2%
Asian or Pacific Islander 3.0%
Other 8.1%
Hispanic origin 15.3%

Ancestry
American 2.8%
English 5.7%
French 2.4%
French Canadian 1.0%
German 9.1%
Irish 6.6%
Italian 1.5%
Polish 1.3%
Scotch Irish 1.6%

Universities/colleges, 1990-1991 enrollment
Houston Community College, Houston 36,437
ITT Technical Institute, Houston 457
North Harris County College, Houston 15,653
Rice University, Houston 4,266
South Texas College of Law, Houston 1,363
Texas Southern University, Houston 9,427
University of Houston, Houston 33,116
University of Houston-Downtown, Houston 7,621
University of St. Thomas, Houston 1,910

Newspapers, total circulation (in all districts)
Houston Chronicle 421,140
Houston Post 292,061

Commercial television stations, affiliations
ADI: Houston (100%)

Cable television systems, total subscribers
Storer Cable TV Inc.; Houston 55,216
Warner Cable of Houston; Houston 229,000

Businesses and other major employers
U.S. Postal Service; Houston 7,876
Brown & Root Inc./Allied Industries; Houston; heavy construction 5,000
University of Houston; Houston 4,500
Exxon Corp./Exxon Co. USA; Houston; petroleum refining 4,317
Shell Oil Co./Shell Development Co. Div.; Houston; petroleum refining 4,000
County of Harris; Houston 3,700
Texas Commerce Bank; Houston; commercial banks 3,400
Enron Corp.; Houston; gas pipelines/exploration 3,300
United Parcel Service Inc.; Houston; mail services 3,043
U.S. Veterans Affairs Dept.; Houston; hospital 3,000
U.S. Postal Service; Houston 3,000
Medical Staffing Specialist; Houston; personnel supply services 3,000
Shell Oil Co.; Houston; petroleum refining 2,500
M. W. Kellogg Co.; Houston; heavy construction 2,500
State of Texas; Houston 2,500
St. Joseph's Hospital; Houston 2,271
Texaco Chemical Intl. Trader; Houston; petroleum refining 2,132
Service Corp. Intl./Funeral Supply Div.; Houston; funeral products 2,000
Southern Pacific Transportation Co.; Houston; railroads 2,000
First Interstate Bank Texas; Houston; commercial banks 2,000
American Medical Intl./Park Plaza Hospital; Houston 2,000
ISS International Service System; Houston; building services 2,000

University of Texas-Arlington/Anderson Cancer Institute; Houston 2,000

Cooper Industries Inc./Oil Tool Div.; Houston; oil field tools 1,900

Hearst Corp./Houston Chronicle; Houston; newspapers 1,800

Associated Building Services Co.; Houston; building services 1,700

Rice University; Houston 1,600

Grocers Supply Co. Inc.; Houston; grocery products 1,500

Arkla Inc./Entex; Houston; petroleum/natural gas 1,500

First City Bancorporation of Texas; Houston; commercial banks 1,500

May Dept. Stores Co./Foley's; Houston; variety stores 1,500

Houston Lighting & Power Co.; Houston; electric services 1,441

Continental Airlines Inc.; Houston; airline/air cargo 1,400

A. B. M. Security Services Inc.; Houston; security services 1,400

Tenneco Gas Inc.; Houston; oil/gas services 1,384

State of Texas/Highways & Public Transportation Dept.; Houston 1,300

Vinson & Elkins; Houston; legal services 1,252

Williams Brothers Construction Co.; Houston; heavy construction 1,200

Southwestern Bell Telephone Co.; Houston; telephone communications 1,200

Coca-Cola Enterprises Inc./Houston Coca-Cola Bottling Co.; Houston; beverages 1,200

Jacobs Engineering Group Inc.; Houston; heavy construction 1,200

Daniel Industries Inc.; Houston; measuring/controlling devices 1,200

City of Houston/Intercontinental Airport; Houston; airport/services 1,200

NationsBank of Texas; Houston; commercial banks 1,200

Chevron Corp./Chevron Real Estate Management; Houston; management services 1,200

LBJ General Hospital; Houston 1,200

Goodman Mfg. Corp.; Houston; refrigeration 1,175

American General Life Insurance Co.; Houston; life insurance 1,113

Pennzoil Co.; Houston; petroleum refining 1,100

Arthur Andersen & Co.; Houston; accounting/auditing 1,100

Anheuser-Busch Inc.; Houston; brewery 1,000

Seahawk Management Inc.; Houston; freight shipping 1,000

Harry M. Stevens Inc.; Houston; bars/restaurants 1,000

Apple Tree Markets Inc.; Houston; grocery stores 1,000

City of Houston/Health & Human Services; Houston 1,000

Texas Southern University; Houston 1,000

Hospital Corp. of America/Spring Branch Medical Center; Houston 1,000

Fulbright & Jaworski; Houston; legal services 951

United Gas Pipe Line Co.; Houston; gas pipelines 950

Northeast Medical Center Hospital; Humble 880

Bechtel Energy Corp.; Houston; heavy construction 850

Baker & Botts; Houston; legal services 839

Houston Post Co. Inc.; Houston; newspapers 800

University of Houston-Downtown; Houston 800

Nabisco Brands Inc./National Biscuit Co.; Houston; bakery products 700

Rowandrill Inc./Rowan Companies Inc.; Houston; oil field machinery 700

Pinkerton's Inc.; Houston; security services 700

Tremont Corp./Sperry-Sun Drilling Services; Houston; engineering services 700

Sysco Food Services Inc.; Houston; grocery products 680

City of Houston/Public Library; Houston 652

Trees Inc.; Houston; landscape services 600

Smith Intl. Inc.; Houston; construction machinery 600

ARA Services Inc.; Houston; janitorial/business services 600

DHL Corp.; Houston; air courier services 600

Metropolitan Transit Authority; Houston; transportation 585

Star Enterprise; Houston; petroleum refining 580

Andrews & Kurth; Houston; legal services 580

Teppco Partners; Houston; gas production/distribution 560

Mrs. Baird's Bakeries Inc.; Houston; grocery products 560

Camco Intl. Inc./Reed Tool; Houston; oil field equipment 550

Harris County Psychiatric Center; Houston 550

Hospital Corp. of America/Medical Center Hospital; Houston 525

Mobil Exploration Producing Services; Houston; oil/gas services 520

Woman's Hospital Texas Inc.; Houston 510

19th District

Western Panhandle — Parts of Lubbock and Amarillo

For the visitor in search of the authentic Wild West complete with cowboys, oil rigs, barbecues and vast stretches of parched, barren countryside, the 19th delivers. But the romanticized images of western life belie the tough times that have plagued the region's residents.

Enormously dependent on oil and gas, the northwestern reaches of Texas were devastated in the mid-1980s when an oil glut and foreign competition sent prices plummeting from a high of $37 a barrel to less than $10 in 1986. Banks began calling notes on small independents, prompting oil company bankruptcies and massive bank failures. Since 1986, only one bank in the Midland-Odessa region has kept its same name and ownership; most of the others were bought by out-of-state conglomerates. Idled rigs collected rust, while petroleum engineers and geologists took huge pay cuts to work at local wholesale shops as clerks and cashiers. Many others left the area entirely.

Ector County, the center for Permian Basin oil field operations, is one of the state's leading oil-producing counties, generating more than 2 billion barrels since 1926. To the north, Amarillo is the hub for the panhandle oil industry. Pipelines in the area extend as far as the Gulf Coast. Other counties in the 19th heavily dependent on the energy business include Midland, a major oil center, and Yoakum, which produces minerals, oil and natural gas.

Agriculture too has been a somewhat reliable, albeit challenging, line of work in the hot, dry region.

The 19th's agricultural emphasis shifted slightly from cotton to cattle with the addition of several northern panhandle counties in the 1992 redistricting. Nevertheless, cotton remains a staple, particularly in Lubbock County. A top agricultural county in the state, Lubbock has more than 230,000 irrigated acres. The city of Lubbock, which is split between the 19th and 13th districts, calls itself the world's largest cottonseed processing center. Reese Air Force Base is another important employer in the city.

Cattle ranching is dominant in Oldham, Hansford and

Randall counties. The Amarillo Livestock Auction is one of the nation's largest, beginning on Wednesdays and often lasting several days. The city (population 157,600) is split between districts and counties; Randall County residents are in the 19th, Potter County in the 13th.

The cowboy feel of the 19th is genuine. Amarillo sponsors Cowboy Mornings, chuckwagon breakfasts served after a ride across the plains. The Odessa-based Chuck Wagon Gang is a group of 250 local businessmen (women are discouraged from joining) who travel the globe serving up barbecue and promoting west Texas. And the city, named in 1891 by Russian railroad laborers after their hometown, boasts the world's largest barbecue pit, big enough to grill 16,500 pounds of beef, some say.

The F-shaped 19th is good GOP territory. Republican Rep. Larry Combest topped 77 percent in 1992, and George Bush far exceeded his state margin, with 60 percent of the vote.

Election Returns

	19th District	Democrat	Republican
1992	President*	50,815 (23.4%)	130,639 (60.1%)
	House	47,325 (22.6%)	162,057 (77.4%)
1990	Senate	31,524 (21.6%)	114,230 (78.4%)
1988	President	54,312 (25.5%)	158,976 (74.5%)

*Vote for Perot was 36,068 (16.6%).

Demographics

Population 566,217

Percent change from 1980 7.3%

Land area 20,188 square miles

Population per square mile 28

Counties, 1990 population

Andrews 14,338	Lubbock (pt.) 179,825
Bailey 7,064	Midland (pt.) 49,936
Cochran 4,377	Moore 17,865
Dallam 5,461	Ochiltree 9,128
Deaf Smith 19,153	Oldham 2,278
Ector (pt.) 84,590	Parmer 9,863
Gaines 14,123	Randall 89,673
Hansford 5,848	Sherman 2,858
Hartley 3,634	Terry 13,218
Hockley 24,199	Yoakum 8,786

Cities, 1990 population (10,000 or more)

Amarillo (pt.) 66,113	Lubbock (pt.) 148,108
Andrews 10,678	Midland (pt.) 47,021
Canyon 11,365	Odessa (pt.) 58,539
Dumas 12,871	West Odessa CDP (pt.)
Hereford 14,745	16,568
Levelland 13,986	

Race and Hispanic origin

White 86.1%
Black 2.5%
American Indian, Eskimo, or Aleut. 0.4%
Asian or Pacific Islander 0.9%
Other 10.0%
Hispanic origin 19.6%

Ancestry

American 7.9%	Irish 18.2%
Dutch 3.1%	Italian 1.1%
English 16.9%	Scotch Irish 3.6%
French 3.3%	Scottish 2.3%
German 20.2%	

Universities/colleges, 1990-1991 enrollment

Lubbock Christian University, Lubbock 1,036
Odessa Community College, Odessa 5,013
South Plains College, Levelland 5,142
Texas Tech University, Lubbock 25,363
Texas Tech University-Health Science Center, Lubbock 889
University of Texas of the Permian Basin, Odessa 2,041
West Texas State University, Canyon 6,193

Newspapers, total circulation (in all districts)

Amarillo News/Globe Times 64,259
Lubbock Avalanche Journal 66,342
Midland Reporter-Telegram 23,209
Odessa American 27,760

Commercial television stations, affiliations

ADI: Amarillo (57%), Lubbock (25%) and Odessa-Midland (19%)
KAMC, Lubbock (ABC)
KJTV, Lubbock (Fox)
KLBK-TV, Lubbock (CBS)
KMID-TV, Midland & Odessa (ABC)
KMLM, Odessa (None)
KOSA-TV, Odessa (CBS)
KPEJ, Odessa (Fox)

Cable television systems, total subscribers

Cox Cable Lubbock; Lubbock 37,000
Post Newsweek Cable TV; Odessa 24,300

Military installations, 1991

Reese Air Force Base, Lubbock 2,349

Businesses and other major employers

Texas Tech University; Lubbock 5,000
Methodist Hospital; Lubbock 2,800
United Vending & Food Services; Amarillo; bars/restaurants 2,500
Sipco Inc.; Dumas; animal services 1,700
ConAgra Inc./Monfort; Cactus; meat products 1,700
Sisters of St. Joseph of Texas; Lubbock; health & social services 1,600
Excel Corp./Friona Div.; Friona; meat products 1,500
Midland County Memorial Hospital & Medical Center; Midland 1,280
Owens-Corning Fiberglas Corp.; Amarillo; building materials 750
Affiliated Foods Inc.; Amarillo; grocery products 715
Nurses Unlimited Inc.; Odessa; health practitioners 700
South Plains Community Action Assn.; Levelland; social services 652
Atmos Energy Corp./Energas Co.; Lubbock; gas distribution 640
West Texas State University; Canyon 625
Odessa Community College; Odessa 600
Hereford Independent School District; Hereford 550
Lockheed Corp.; Lubbock; repair shops 540

20th District

Downtown San Antonio

Population growth split the city of San Antonio into four congressional districts in 1992. Today, San Antonio and its 940,000 residents make up the third-largest city in Texas and the 10th-largest in the nation. The 20th, which once consisted of all of Bexar County, now takes in central San Antonio and a handful of more rural communities to the west and southwest.

The 20th, which is 61 percent Hispanic, has a history of minority accomplishments. In 1981, San Antonio became the first major U.S. city to elect a Mexican-American mayor, Henry G. Cisneros (who became Bill Clinton's secretary of Housing and Urban Development in 1993). Texas Attorney General Dan Morales is from San Antonio, and Hispanics dominate local and state legislative seats.

San Antonio's popular tourist spots are tied to its ethnic culture and history. The Alamo, the city's oldest mission and the site of the 1836 battle with Mexico, is in the heart of downtown.

Despite the city's Hispanic majority and background—it was founded in the early 18th century by the Spanish—Anglos have controlled its economy since its early days as a cattle center. Today, government payrolls are the region's lifeblood; San Antonio is the state's largest military center. And the city and school district rank among the largest employers. Four military facilities are within the 20th: Fort Sam Houston, a major health services command; Kelly Air Force Base, the district's largest employer with 25,000 people; Lackland Air Force Base, which includes the Wilford Hall military hospital; and the Army base at Camp Bullis. Two other San Antonio installations (Randolph Air Force Base and Brooks Air Force Base) are nearby in the 28th District, and they add to the local economy.

Tourism is the region's second-highest revenue producer. Besides the Alamo and other historic sites, the city's scenic Paseo del Rio, or Riverwalk, is a popular draw with its shops, restaurants and hotels winding along the San Antonio River.

Despite its popularity with visitors and mentions in national magazines that San Antonio is one of the most "livable" cities in the country, it is also one of the poorest. Nearly 15 percent of its residents are without private or public health coverage; almost one-fifth of the people fall below the poverty line. Even the tourism industry, despite the dollars it brings to the 20th, is responsible for predominantly low-wage service jobs. Local officials hope a new division of Southwestern Bell will bring better management positions to the city.

In the 1992 redistricting, Democrat Rep. Henry Gonzalez (who ran unopposed in 1990 and 1992) picked up some outlying communities in Bexar County he had represented before the 1980s' remapping. Most of the region's growth has been to the north, but in the 20th the new rural and suburban towns to the west and southwest are sparsely populated with retired veterans, small farmers and a handful of mid-level managers who commute into San Antonio.

Although George Bush carried Texas, Bill Clinton won the 20th comfortably.

Election Returns

	20th District	Democrat	Republican
1992	President*	81,380 (48.3%)	57,974 (34.4%)
	House	103,755 (100.0%)	—
1990	Senate	41,363 (48.1%)	44,606 (51.9%)
1988	President	92,367 (53.6%)	79,917 (46.4%)

*Vote for Perot was 28,966 (17.2%).

Demographics

Population 566,217

Percent change from 1980 7.6%

Land area 291 square miles

Population per square mile 1,947

Counties, 1990 population
Bexar (pt.) 566,217

Cities, 1990 population (10,000 or more)
San Antonio (pt.) 489,600

Race and Hispanic origin
White 71.8%
Black 5.8%
American Indian, Eskimo, or Aleut. 0.4%
Asian or Pacific Islander 1.3%
Other 20.7%
Hispanic origin 60.7%

Ancestry

American 2.0%	Italian 1.6%
English 6.4%	Polish 1.3%
French 2.2%	Scotch Irish 1.6%
German 12.5%	Scottish 1.1%
Irish 7.5%	

Universities/colleges, 1990-1991 enrollment
Our Lady of the Lake University, San Antonio 2,693
San Antonio College, San Antonio 20,082
St. Mary's University, San Antonio 4,045
Trinity University, San Antonio 2,538
University of Texas-Health Science Center, San Antonio 2,456

Newspapers, total circulation (in all districts)
San Antonio Light 160,666
San Antonio News-Express 187,599

Commercial television stations, affiliations
ADI: San Antonio (100%)

Cable television systems, total subscribers
Paragon Cable; San Antonio 248,000

Military installations, 1991
Kelly Air Force Base, San Antonio 25,044
Fort Sam Houston, San Antonio 16,332
Lackland Air Force Base, San Antonio 9,732
Camp Bullis (Army), San Antonio 1,288

Businesses and other major employers
United Services Auto Assn.; San Antonio; life insurance 6,778
Hawkins Associates Inc./Olsten Temporary Services; San Antonio; personnel supply services 4,000
U.S. Postal Service; San Antonio 3,000
Medical Center Hospital; San Antonio 2,564

Bradly Green Community Health Center; San Antonio 2,500

University of Texas-Health Science Center; San Antonio
2,500

Southwest Research Institute; San Antonio; research services
2,438

Southwest Texas Methodist Hospital; San Antonio 2,100

Baptist Memorial Hospital System/Northeast Baptist Hospital; San Antonio 2,098

H. E. Butt Grocery Co.; San Antonio; warehousing 2,000

Congregations Sisters/Santa Rosa Critical Care Hospital; San
Antonio 2,000

U.S. Veterans Affairs Dept.; San Antonio; hospital 2,000

Dayton Hudson Corp./Target; San Antonio; department
stores 1,500

University of Texas; San Antonio 1,500

City of San Antonio/Public Works Dept.; San Antonio 1,393

Aero Intl. Inc.; San Antonio; aircraft supplies/parts 1,200

Via Metropolitan Transit; San Antonio; transportation 1,199

County of Bexar/Coliseum Advisory Board; San Antonio
1,173

Frost National Bank; San Antonio; commercial banks 1,116

San Antonio College; San Antonio 1,100

Marriott Corp./Marriott Rivercenter Hotel; San Antonio;
hotel 1,000

Express-News Corp./Express-News; San Antonio; newspapers 914

City Public Service; San Antonio; utility services 900

Fairchild Aircraft Inc.; San Antonio; aircraft/parts 900

Humana Inc./Humana Hospital; San Antonio 900

St. Luke's Lutheran Hospital; San Antonio 875

Southwestern Bell Telephone Co.; San Antonio; telephone
communications 800

U.S. Natural Resources Inc.; San Antonio; refrigeration equipment 750

Valero Energy Corp.; San Antonio; petroleum refining 750

Hearst Corp./San Antonio Light; San Antonio; newspapers
746

Sony Corp.; San Antonio; electronic components 743

First Gibraltor; San Antonio; savings institutions 730

Congregations Sisters/Villa Rosa Rehabilitation Hospital; San
Antonio 730

Datapoint Corp.; San Antonio; computers 700

Builders Square Inc.; San Antonio; lumber/building materials
700

Levi Strauss & Co.; San Antonio; textile finishing 650

Trinity University; San Antonio 650

Humana Inc./Humana Hospital; San Antonio 650

La Quinta Motor Inns Inc.; San Antonio; hotels 633

Bausch & Lomb Inc.; San Antonio; ophthalmic goods 600

Hospital Klean Inc.; San Antonio; building services 600

Stanley Smith Security Inc.; San Antonio; security services 600

Hyatt Corp./Hyatt Regency Hotel; San Antonio; hotel 550

BPS Guard Services Inc.; San Antonio; business/security
services 550

21st District

South Central — Western Bexar County; Austin Suburbs

The 21st typifies the lengths to which Texas mapmakers went
to divide Democratic and Republican neighborhoods in the 1992
redistricting.

For 350 miles the boundaries of the 21st run in simple,
straight blocks, often paralleling county lines. But as the 21st
approaches Bexar County, the lines go berserk. Four congressional districts lay claim to portions of the San Antonio-based
county, and the 1992 redistricting carved out separate slices for
each party. The result: two Democratic House members and two
Republicans.

Because of the spaghetti-like lines, several institutions in one
district have dramatic influence over the neighboring districts.

Four Air Force bases and the Army's Fort Sam Houston and
Fort Bullis are located in San Antonio. Although none of the
bases are in the 21st, the military is believed to be the district's
largest employer. The six San Antonio installations generate an
estimated $3.4 billion annually and employ more than 55,000
people.

San Antonio's military history goes back centuries; its greatest
moment was in 1836 when 183 soldiers fought to defend the
Alamo against an attack by the 6,000-man army led by Gen.
Antonio Lopez de Santa Anna.

Tourism is the second-largest employer in San Antonio,
frequently overlapping with military interests. The Alamo, in the
heart of downtown around the corner from a bustling new
shopping mall, is a popular attraction. Fort Sam Houston has
more than 900 historic buildings and two museums on its 3,300
acres.

Almost a quarter of the people in the 21st live in Bexar
County, most in the affluent neighborhoods of San Antonio and
its suburbs. The predominantly white residents are well-paid,
well-educated professionals—doctors, lawyers, engineers and
insurance executives.

As the 21st moves west, the counties become less populous
and the economic emphasis shifts to agriculture. Gillespie
County is the largest peach-producing county in the state. Peach
orchards are also prevalent in Menard County.

The central parts of the district produce a combination of
crops and cattle. Pecans, peanuts and hay grow in abundance.
The 21st is home to the state's largest goat market, in Kimble
County, and the self-proclaimed "sheep and wool capital" of the
nation is in Tom Green County.

More than 300 miles west of San Antonio lies San Angelo.
The city's Goodfellow Air Force Base employs many 21st
District residents. The 21st takes in the wealthier northwest
neighborhoods of the city.

Midland, Comal, Kerr and Williamson counties, combined
with the portions of San Antonio in the 21st, deliver wide
margins for Republican candidates.

Election Returns

	21st District	Democrat	Republican
1992	President*	70,402 (25.4%)	143,720 (51.8%)
	House	62,827 (23.7%)	190,979 (72.2%)
1990	Senate	48,098 (28.1%)	123,361 (71.9%)
1988	President	71,306 (29.5%)	170,731 (70.5%)

Vote for Perot was 63,276 (22.8%).

Demographics

Population 566,217

Percent change from 1980 7.4%

Land area 17,317 square miles

Population per square mile 33

Counties, 1990 population

Bandera 10,562
Bexar (pt.) 165,040
Burnet 22,677
Comal (pt.) 38,679
Gillespie 17,204
Glasscock 1,447
Guadalupe (pt.) 38,818
Irion 1,629
Kendall 14,589
Kerr 36,304
Kimble 4,122

Llano 11,631
Mason 3,423
McCulloch (pt.) 1,100
Menard 2,252
Midland (pt.) 31,453
Real 2,412
Schleicher 2,990
Sterling 1,438
Tom Green (pt.) 45,712
Williamson (pt.) 112,735

Cities, 1990 population (10,000 or more)

Georgetown (pt.) 10,003
Jollyville CDP (pt.) 14,094
Kerrville 17,384
Midland (pt.) 21,645
New Braunfels (pt.) 15,072

Round Rock (pt.) 30,923
San Angelo (pt.) 35,945
San Antonio (pt.) 124,233
Schertz (pt.) 10,112

Race and Hispanic origin

White 91.3%
Black 2.5%
American Indian, Eskimo, or Aleut. 0.4%
Asian or Pacific Islander 1.0%
Other 4.8%
Hispanic origin 14.1%

Ancestry

American 4.2%
Czechoslovakian 1.4%
Dutch 2.1%
English 18.3%
French 4.6%
German 31.4%

Irish 17.9%
Italian 2.3%
Polish 2.1%
Scotch Irish 4.9%
Scottish 2.9%
Swedish 1.7%

Universities/colleges, 1990-1991 enrollment

Angelo State University, San Angelo 6,298
Incarnate Word College, San Antonio 2,556
Midland College, Midland 3,992
Schreiner College, Kerrville 592
Southwestern University, Georgetown 1,208

Newspapers, total circulation (in all districts)

Austin American Statesman 172,077
Dallas Morning News 452,101
Kerrville Daily Times 9,655
Midland Reporter-Telegram 23,209
San Angelo Standard-Times 31,082
San Antonio Light 160,666
San Antonio News-Express 187,599

Commercial television stations, affiliations

ADI: San Angelo (39%), Austin (27%), San Antonio (26%) and Odessa-Midland (8%)
KRRT, Kerrville (Fox)
KACB-TV, San Angelo (NBC)
KIDY, San Angelo (Fox)
KXAM, Llano (NBC)

Cable television systems, total subscribers

Austin Cablevision; Mount Larson 146,500
Community Cable; Kerrville 9,800
Marcus Cable; San Angelo 21,067
Paragon Cable; San Antonio 248,000
TCI of Texas; New Braunfels 6,500
Times Mirror Cable TV; Midland 29,929
United Artist Cable; Round Rock 9,500

Military installations, 1991

Goodfellow Air Force Base, San Angelo 2,677
Eldorado Air Station, Eldorado 186

Businesses and other major employers

Employers Select Management; San Antonio; personnel supply services 2,200
San Angelo Independent School District; San Angelo 2,200
Southwestern Bell Corp.; San Antonio; telephone communications 1,455
GTE Southwest Inc.; San Angelo; telephone communications 1,219
West Point-Pepperell Inc./Mission Valley Mills; New Braunfels; cotton mills 1,200
State of Texas/Kerrville State Hospital; Kerrville 880
Motorola Inc.; Seguin; communications equipment 800
State of Texas/Mental Health Dept.; Carlsbad 800
U.S. Veterans Affairs Dept.; Kerrville; hospital 600
Midland College; Midland 595
Lancer Corp.; San Antonio; refrigeration/heating equipment 540

22nd District

Southwest Houston and Suburbs; Fort Bend and Brazoria Counties

The 22nd is a testament to Houston's phenomenal growth of the past two decades. During the 1970s, the district was focused within the city. In the 1980s, the 22nd shifted south and west to include newly sprouted suburbs. In the 1992 redistricting, the 22nd was pulled even farther away from Houston, swallowing up the Clear Lake neighborhood in the east. Once a city-based district, the 22nd of the 1990s has more voters outside Harris County (Houston) than in it.

The influx of Houston professionals boosted Harris County's population by 38 percent in the 1970s and by 17 percent in the 1980s.

Yet the most astronomical growth has occurred just outside Harris County, in neighboring Fort Bend. The county population jumped 150 percent in the 1970s and 72 percent the following decade. Sugar Land, formed in the 1820s around the sugar industry, has become one of the most popular new suburbs. Signs of Sugar Land's new appeal are evident everywhere: new retail shops, new homes and new banks. First Colony is a planned community in Sugar Land that offers some houses for less than $100,000 and others that cost millions.

The common theme running through the contorted 22nd is the district's universally conservative outlook.

GOP Rep. Tom DeLay took an impressive 69 percent in his new district in 1992 and Republican George Bush ran well ahead of his statewide total in the 22nd. If anything, the 1992 redistricting made the 22nd even more Republican. In Brazoria and Fort Bend counties, Republicans performed well at every level, from Bush to railroad commissioners to judges; the rare exception was an occasional county post.

The residents tend to be more involved in religion, better

paid (the median household income is between $37,500 and $40,000) and better educated (25 percent of the district's residents have at least an associate degree) than the state as a whole.

Houston executives who tired of long commutes have bought property in Bellaire and West University Place, tearing down the older, smaller homes and replacing them with expensive, modern versions.

NASA's Johnson Space Center, in the adjacent 9th District, is a major employer for the 22nd and probably the single reason why the Clear Lake area has grown. The massive complex southeast of Houston is designing and building components of the space station *Freedom*, a project that is undergoing revisions that could mean a loss of jobs at the space center.

Once past the Houston suburb of Pearland, Brazoria County rapidly turns rural. Rice, sorghum and cattle are major revenue producers in this sparsely populated region. Beyond the district boundaries down to the Gulf Coast, Brazoria County also includes oil and gas wells and 20 miles of natural beaches. Commercial fishing and tourism provide revenue in this part of the county, which is in the adjacent 14th District.

Election Returns

		Democrat	Republican
	22nd District		
1992	President*	63,175 (27.4%)	116,614 (50.6%)
	House	67,812 (31.1%)	150,221 (68.9%)
1990	Senate	36,752 (28.5%)	92,414 (71.5%)
1988	President	53,033 (31.9%)	113,383 (68.1%)

Vote for Perot was 50,732 (22.0%).

Demographics

Population 566,217

Percent change from 1980 7.5%

Land area 1,625 square miles

Population per square mile 348

Counties, 1990 population
Brazoria (pt.) 132,288   Harris (pt.) 255,930
Fort Bend (pt.) 177,999

Cities, 1990 population (10,000 or more)
Alvin 19,220   Missouri City (pt.) 20,125
Angleton (pt.) 16,448   Pearland 18,697
Bellaire 13,842   Rosenberg 20,183
First Colony CDP 18,327   Sugar Land 24,529
Houston (pt.) 177,494   West University Place
Lake Jackson (pt.) 22,775   12,920
Mission Bend CDP (pt.)
  14,195

Race and Hispanic origin
White 76.9%
Black 7.8%
American Indian, Eskimo, or Aleut. 0.3%
Asian or Pacific Islander 7.0%
Other 8.0%
Hispanic origin 16.1%

Ancestry
American 3.9%   Irish 14.7%
Czechoslovakian 2.6%   Italian 3.3%
Dutch 1.9%   Polish 2.6%
English 14.9%   Scotch Irish 3.6%
French 4.8%   Scottish 2.4%
French Canadian 1.5%   Swedish 1.2%
German 22.0%

Universities/colleges, 1990-1991 enrollment
Alvin Community College, Alvin 3,787
Houston Baptist University, Houston 2,255
San Jacinto College South, Houston 5,273
University of Houston-Clear Lake, Houston 7,562

Newspapers, total circulation (in all districts)
Clute Brazosport Facts 19,824
Houston Chronicle 421,140
Houston Post 292,061

Commercial television stations, affiliations
ADI: Houston (100%)
  KRTW, Baytown (None)
  KHOU-TV, Houston (CBS)

Cable television systems, total subscribers
Prime Cable; Sugar Land 9,420
Storer Cable TV Inc.; Houston 55,216
TCI of Texas; Clute 10,575
Warner Cable of Houston; Houston 229,000

Businesses and other major employers
Southwestern Bell Corp.; Houston; telephone communications 11,000
State of Texas/Texas Air National Guard; Houston 3,700
Western Atlas Intl./Atlas Wireline Services Div.; Houston; oil/gas services 3,200
Rockwell Intl. Corp./Shuttle operations; Houston; transportation services 3,000
Fluor Daniel Inc.; Sugar Land; building construction/engineering services 2,800
Memorial Hospital System/Memorial Hospital Southeast; Houston 2,212
Texas Instruments Inc.; Stafford; electronic components 2,000
Granada Corp.; Houston; animal services 2,000
Pool Co. Inc.; Houston; oil/gas services 1,527
Richmond State School; Richmond 1,431
John Brown Inc.; Houston; heavy construction 1,400
Memorial Hospital System; Houston 1,300
United Parcel Service Inc.; Stafford; mail services 1,200
McDonnell Douglas Corp.; Houston 1,150
Intermedics Inc.; Angleton; medical equipment 1,110
Du Pont E. I. De Nemours & Co.; La Porte; professional/commercial equipment 1,100
Bendix Field Engineering Corp.; Houston; engineering services 1,100
Halliburton Geophysical Services; Houston; geophysical electronic equipment 1,000
Western Atlas Intl./Western Geophysical Co. of America; Houston; oil/gas services 1,000
Unisys Corp.; Houston; computer services 1,000
Alvin Independent School District; Alvin 970
Amoco Chemical Co.; Alvin; plastics products 850
Humana Hospital Clearlake Inc.; Webster 850

Texaco Inc.; Houston; computer services 850

University of Houston-Clear Lake; Houston 800

Phillips Petroleum Co.; Bellaire; chemical products 750

May Dept. Stores Co./Foley's; Houston; department stores 730

Imperial Holly Corp./Imperial Sugar; Sugar Land; sugar refining 725

Macy's South Inc.; Friendswood; department stores 700

Cae-Link Corp.; Houston flight simulators 650

B. P. A. Inc.; Houston; building services 650

Texfield Inc./Auchan Hypermarket; Houston; grocery stores 640

Houston Lighting & Power Co./Parish Plant; Thompsons; electric services 630

Monsanto Co./Monsanto Chemical Co.; Alvin; inorganic chemicals 600

Hoechst Celanese Corp.; Pasadena; inorganic chemicals 600

U.S. Federal Deposit Insurance Corp.; Houston; banking insurance 600

Shell Oil Co./Shell Development Co.; Houston; oil research services 600

Union Oil Co. of California; Sugar Land; oil/gas services 550

Brown & Root USA Inc.; La Porte; engineering services 521

23rd District

Southwest — Laredo; San Antonio Suburbs

Tough times have beset many in the 23rd, Texas' largest House district. In its far western reaches defunct oil wells dot the landscape. Along the hundreds of miles of Mexican border that mark the southern limit of the district are impoverished immigrants, many of them living in some of Texas' most destitute villages and towns.

Eight of the 20 poorest counties in the state are in the 23rd. Half of the people in Zavala and Maverick counties fall below the poverty level. The median household income for the entire district is under $22,500, well below the median for the state. And some local officials say those figures are high, claiming that minorities along the Mexican border were undercounted in the 1990 census.

The border communities often seem to have more in common with their Mexican neighbors than with the rest of Texas. Laredo (Webb County) celebrates Mexican Independence Day and is connected to its Mexican sister city, Nuevo Laredo, by three bridges. Nine of 10 people in Webb County are Hispanic. A private 1993 study of census data concluded that Laredo has one of the highest poverty rates in the nation.

All along the border, people find work in *maquiladoras*— twin-plant manufacturing operations in which the bulk of production work is done by lower-cost labor in a Mexican facility and then finishing work is handled at a U.S. plant. Clothing and heavy machinery are common products. Other immigrants work the land, earning their keep from vegetables, cotton, sheep and goats.

Residents on both sides of the Rio Grande get together for work, entertainment and sometimes to cooperate on regional political issues. In 1992, officials from Del Rio (U.S.) and Coahuila (Mexico) jointly opposed construction of two hazardous waste facilities along the border.

About 70 percent of the district's residents are minority-group members; 63 percent are Hispanic. Typically the minority vote

goes Democratic, but that tradition was upset in 1992 as Henry Bonilla won the seat with 59 percent of the vote to become Texas' first Hispanic Republican in Congress.

Bonilla benefited from 1992 redistricting, which added 21 counties to the 23rd; and his conservative, less-government pitch played well with the district's independent-minded ranchers and oilmen and with affluent voters in the Bexar County suburbs of San Antonio. The biggest single bloc of votes in the 23rd— nearly 30 percent—comes from Bexar County, and George Bush won the area with a decisive 58 percent in 1992. But in other parts of the 23rd, many who backed Bonilla supported Bill Clinton for president. Districtwide, Clinton edged Bush by one point, 42 percent to 41 percent.

Because of redistricting in 1992, several of San Antonio's military installations are out of the 23rd. But their presence is still felt. Brooks and Randolph Air Force bases, located just outside the 23rd, continue to be major employers. The flight training center at Laughlin Air Force Base and part of Fort Bliss are in the district.

Election Returns

	23rd District	Democrat	Republican
1992	President*	72,452 (42.2%)	70,577 (41.1%)
	House	63,797 (38.4%)	98,259 (59.1%)
1990	Senate	39,825 (38.6%)	63,462 (61.4%)
1988	President	73,938 (46.8%)	84,123 (53.2%)

Vote for Perot was 28,846 (16.8%).

Demographics

Population 566,217

Percent change from 1980 7.5%

Land area 58,412 square miles

Population per square mile 10

Counties, 1990 population

Bexar (pt.) 95,091	Midland (pt.) 25,222
Brewster 8,681	Pecos 14,675
Crane 4,652	Presidio 6,637
Crockett 4,078	Reagan 4,514
Culberson 3,407	Reeves 15,852
Dimmit 10,433	Sutton 4,135
Ector (pt.) 34,344	Terrell 1,410
Edwards 2,266	Upton 4,447
El Paso (pt.) 25,393	Uvalde 23,340
Hudspeth 2,915	Val Verde 38,721
Jeff Davis 1,946	Ward 13,115
Kinney 3,119	Webb 133,239
Loving 107	Winkler 8,626
Maverick 36,378	Zavala 12,162
Medina 27,312	

Cities, 1990 population (10,000 or more)

Del Rio 30,705	Odessa (pt.) 31,160
Eagle Pass 20,651	Pecos 12,069
El Paso (pt.) 12,652	San Antonio (pt.) 60,599
Laredo 122,899	Uvalde 14,729
Midland (pt.) 20,777	

Race and Hispanic origin

White 73.9%
Black 2.9%
American Indian, Eskimo, or Aleut. 0.4%
Asian or Pacific Islander 0.7%
Other 22.1%
Hispanic origin 62.5%

Ancestry

American 3.2%	Irish 7.4%
Dutch 1.0%	Italian 1.1%
English 7.1%	Scotch Irish 1.9%
French 2.0%	Scottish 1.1%
German 11.3%	

Universities/colleges, 1990-1991 enrollment

Laredo Junior College, Laredo 5,123
Laredo State University, Laredo 1,273
Southwest Texas Junior College, Uvalde 2,658
Sul Ross State University, Alpine 2,265
University of Texas, San Antonio 15,489

Newspapers, total circulation (in all districts)

El Paso Times 91,177
Del Rio News-Herald 6,371
Laredo Morning Times 19,433
Odessa American 27,760
San Antonio Light 160,666
San Antonio News-Express 187,599

Commercial television stations, affiliations

ADI: Odessa-Midland (54%), San Antonio (24%), El Paso (9%),
San Angelo (7%) and Laredo (6%)
KGNS-TV, Laredo (NBC)
KVTV, Laredo (CBS)
KTPX, Odessa (NBC)

Cable television systems, total subscribers

Community Cable; Uvalde 5,200
Dimension Cable Services; Del Rio 13,000
Paragon Cable; El Paso 86,000
Paragon Cable; Laredo 24,500
Paragon Cable; San Antonio 248,000
Post Newsweek Cable TV; Odessa 24,300
TCI of Texas; Eagle Pass 6,800
Times Mirror Cable TV; Midland 29,929

Military installations, 1991

Fort Bliss (Army), El Paso (shared with 16th District) 20,678
Laughlin Air Force Base, Del Rio 2,343

Businesses and other major employers

Mercy Hospital of Laredo; Laredo 1,500
Torres Enterprises; Del Rio; hotels/motels 1,500
Phillips Petroleum Co./Transportation Dept.; Odessa; motor
vehicle repair 1,500
Odessa Medical Center; Odessa 1,300
Texas Instruments Inc.; Midland; electronic components
1,000
Sunbeam Corp./Oster Sunbeam; Del Rio; household appli-
ances 1,000
City of Odessa; Odessa 830
Transamerican Natural Gas Corp.; Laredo; natural gas 812
Rexene Products Co.; Odessa; plastics/synthetics 800
Exxon Corp.; Midland; petroleum/natural gas 645

Atlantic Richfield Co./Arco Oil & Gas Co.; Midland;
petroleum/natural gas 600
Sul Ross State University; Alpine 579
Pecos-Barstow-Toyah Independent School District; Pecos
550

24th District

Parts of Dallas and Tarrant Counties

The blue-collar laborers living in the 24th have borne the brunt of the economic woes in the Dallas-Fort Worth metroplex. A military base is closing, a semiconductor company went through bankruptcy reorganization and defense contractors have laid off thousands. Highly trained engineers find themselves doing manual labor; factory workers are jobless.

Carswell Air Force Base, once home to 6,500 military personnel, has been reducing staff since 1991 and is slated to shut down by the end of 1993.

When the government canceled the A-12 stealth attack plane in early 1991, more than 3,500 workers at the Fort Worth General Dynamics plant lost their jobs. Bought in 1993 by Lockheed, the contractor is struggling to rebuild.

Bell Helicopter Textron is largely reliant on the experimental V-22 Osprey helicopter, a project that has continued to receive research funds—but no construction money as of mid-1993.

Former aerospace giant LTV Corp. filed for Chapter 11 protection in 1986 and has since sold its aerospace division to two companies. The new companies, which still make components of the B-2 bomber and C-17 cargo planes, are laying off workers and taking other belt-tightening measures.

Most of the contractors are trying to lessen their dependence on military dollars by targeting foreign governments and private businesses, but diversification efforts are slow. One company, however, is taking a different tack. Turbomeca recently entered a joint venture to build engines for the T-45 Goshawk, a Navy training plane.

The General Motors plant in Arlington and the Dallas-Fort Worth International Airport are major employers for the residents of the 24th.

Although the 24th is dominated geographically by Navarro and Ellis counties in the south, its population base is in Tarrant and Dallas counties (see map on page 709). The two northern counties account for 80 percent of the votes in the 24th, making it a predominantly urban district. Many of the factory workers and GM retirees live in the North Oak Cliff section of Dallas and the portions of Arlington in the 24th.

The 1992 redistricting shifted most of the minority voters from the old 24th into the 30th, a new majority-black district. The few remaining black neighborhoods in the 24th are in southeast Fort Worth. Blacks living in Forest Hill, Poly and Stop 6 often work in area hospitals or at the airport.

To the south, Navarro County boasts the longest continuous oil flow in the state; more than 200 million barrels since 1895. The rest of the county's economy is split between livestock and crops.

The multibillion-dollar superconducting super collider was being built in Ellis County, split between the 24th and the 6th. Congress' 1993 decision to kill the project will have a major effect on the local economy.

The 24th is favorable territory for Democratic candidates. Bill Clinton's 1992 finish exceeded his statewide tally. Ann W. Richards won the 24th in her successful 1990 gubernatorial race.

Election Returns

	24th District	Democrat	Republican
1992	President*	73,019 (40.6%)	60,020 (33.4%)
	House	104,174 (59.8%)	70,042 (40.2%)
1990	Senate	49,880 (45.6%)	59,525 (54.4%)
1988	President	73,027 (47.7%)	80,227 (52.3%)

*Vote for Perot was 46,811 (26.0%).

Demographics

Population 566,217

Percent change from 1980 7.5%

Land area 2,123 square miles

Population per square mile 267

Counties, 1990 population

Dallas (pt.) 233,888		Navarro 39,926	
Ellis (pt.) 57,213		Tarrant (pt.) 235,190	

Cities, 1990 population (10,000 or more)

Arlington (pt.) 127,523	Ennis (pt.) 12,569
Cedar Hill (pt.) 19,926	Forest Hill (pt.) 11,468
Corsicana 22,911	Fort Worth (pt.) 72,574
Dallas (pt.) 109,108	Grand Prairie (pt.) 54,730
De Soto (pt.) 12,160	Waxahachie (pt.) 12,233
Duncanville (pt.) 29,813	

Race and Hispanic origin

White 64.4%
Black 19.1%
American Indian, Eskimo, or Aleut. 0.6%
Asian or Pacific Islander 2.2%
Other 13.7%
Hispanic origin 21.8%

Ancestry

American 6.6%	German 14.3%
Czechoslovakian 1.0%	Irish 14.1%
Dutch 2.0%	Italian 1.4%
English 10.6%	Scotch Irish 2.7%
French 2.7%	Scottish 1.6%

Universities/colleges, 1990-1991 enrollment

Bauder Fashion College, Arlington 279
Dallas Baptist University, Dallas 2,333
ITT Technical Institute, Arlington 363
Mountain View College, Dallas 6,239
Navarro College, Corsicana 2,827
Northwood Institute, Cedar Hill 306
Texas Wesleyan College, Fort Worth 1,429
University of Texas, Arlington 24,782

Newspapers, total circulation (in all districts)

Dallas Morning News 452,101
Fort Worth Star-Telegram 250,099

Commercial television stations, affiliations

ADI: Dallas-Fort Worth (100%)
  KDAF, Dallas (Fox)
  KDFI-TV, Dallas (None)
  KDFW-TV, Dallas (CBS)
  KDTX-TV, Dallas (None)
  WFAA-TV, Dallas (ABC)
  KXTX-TV, Dallas (None)
  KTVT, Fort Worth (None)
  KTXA, Fort Worth (None)
  KXAS-TV, Fort Worth (NBC)
  KHSX, Irving (None)

Cable television systems, total subscribers

Arlington Telecable Corp.; Arlington 53,293
Sammons of Fort Worth; Fort Worth 71,319
Storer Cable TV of Texas; Grand Prairie 15,166
TCI of Texas; Dallas 91,647

Military installations, 1991

Dallas Naval Air Station, Dallas: 4,476

Businesses and other major employers

Vought Aircraft Co./LTV Aircraft Products Group; Dallas; aircraft 7,000
U.S. Postal Service; Dallas 5,000
General Motors Corp./Arlington Plant; Arlington; motor vehicle assembly 3,800
University of Texas; Arlington 2,378
Universities Research Assn.; De Soto; research services 1,700
Arlington Memorial Hospital; Arlington 1,600
Methodist Medical Center; Dallas 1,477
Alcon Surgical Inc.; Fort Worth; ophthalmic goods 1,400
Miller Brewing Co.; Fort Worth; brewery 1,200
Mobil Oil Corp./Mobil Exploration & Production; Dallas; oil/gas services 1,200
Taylor Publishing Co./Newsfoto Yearbook Co.; Dallas; publishing 1,200
Electrocom Automation Inc.; Arlington; office equipment 1,100
U.S. Sprint Communications Ltd.; Dallas; telephone communications 1,000
State of Texas/Texas Air National Guard; Dallas 1,000
U.S. Post Office; Fort Worth 1,000
D&L Entertainment Services; Dallas; personnel supply services 1,000
Mary Kay Corp.; Dallas; cosmetics 970
State of Texas/Health & Mental Retardation Dept.; Fort Worth 920
Visiting Nurse Association of Texas; Dallas; home health services 702
Johnson & Johnson Medical Inc.; Arlington; medical supplies 600
Mrs. Baird's Bakeries Inc.; Fort Worth; bakery products 600
Lomas Financial Corp.; Dallas; mortgage bankers 600
Texwood Industries Inc./Quality Cabinets; Duncanville; millwork 550
J. B. Hunt Transport Inc.; Dallas; trucking services 550
Southwestern Bell Yellow Pages; Dallas; publishing 550
ARA Leisure Service Inc.; Arlington; bars/restaurants 550
Albertson's Inc.; Fort Worth; grocery stores 550

25th District

South Houston and Suburbs

Downtown Houston is an array of glittering towers, but the city has several skylines instead of just the traditional one. With no current zoning regulations, clusters of skyscrapers are scattered across Houston.

The most-populous city in Texas and the fourth largest in the nation, Houston and Harris County have the headquarters or major corporate offices of more than 200 firms. Eighteen companies on the 1992 *Fortune* 500 list and 21 on the 1992 *Forbes* 500 list call Houston home. The city hosts a thriving arts community, diverse and innovative restaurants and prestigious Rice University (18th District) and its 4,300 students.

The lines of the 25th (see map on page 715) were given numerous new contortions in 1992 redistricting to accommodate establishment of the neighboring 29th District, which is majority-Hispanic.

But the 25th, based in southern and eastern Harris County, remains an ethnically diverse, urbanized district with growing populations of blacks (27 percent of the district's population), Hispanics (17 percent) and Asians (4 percent).

Minority-group voters and blue-collar residents in Pasadena and Deer Park help give Democrats a solid base in the 25th.

In 1992, Democratic Rep. Michael Andrews won re-election with a solid 56 percent, despite the new lines and a vigorous Republican challenger. In presidential voting that year, Bill Clinton outdistanced Houstonian George Bush by 11 points in the 25th.

In 1990, Democrats Ann W. Richards, Bob Bullock and Dan Morales all topped 56 percent in the 25th in their successful campaigns for governor, lieutenant governor and attorney general, respectively.

For many in the 25th, life revolves around petroleum-based products, although the Houston-area economy has diversified since the oil industry took a sharp turn down in the mid-1980s. Employment in the oil and gas industries accounted for 68 percent of Houston's economic base in 1981; by 1993 it was down to 42 percent. Harris County has the nation's largest concentration of petrochemical plants and related businesses. Although more refineries are located in neighboring districts, the cities of Pasadena and Baytown also rely heavily on refining.

The shipping business is another economic pillar. The 50-mile Houston Ship Channel connects Houston to the Gulf of Mexico. The $15 billion port complex, with more than 100 wharves, has enabled Houston to become the world's sixth-busiest port in terms of total tonnage, and the nation's largest in foreign tonnage.

The Texas Medical Center is the largest private employer in the 25th. The 650-acre complex has 41 member institutions, including 14 hospitals, two medical schools and four nursing schools. The center is credited with directly contributing $4 billion to the Houston economy each year.

Although the Johnson Space Center is now in the 9th District, it continues to draw a substantial share of its work force from the 25th.

Election Returns

	25th District	Democrat	Republican
1992	President*	85,325 (46.7%)	64,896 (35.5%)
	House	98,975 (56.0%)	73,192 (41.4%)
1990	Senate	46,235 (45.2%)	56,035 (54.8%)
1988	President	72,486 (50.3%)	71,663 (49.7%)

Vote for Perot was 32,489 (17.8%).

Demographics

Population 566,217

Percent change from 1980 7.5%

Land area 295 square miles

Population per square mile 1,917

Counties, 1990 population
Fort Bend (pt.) 47,422   Harris (pt.) 518,795

Cities, 1990 population (10,000 or more)
Baytown (pt.) 29,263   Deer Park (pt.) 24,260
Channelview CDP (pt.)   Houston (pt.) 315,472
   23,962   La Porte (pt.) 23,602
Cloverleaf CDP (pt.)   Missouri City (pt.) 16,051
   15,410   Pasadena (pt.) 76,394

Race and Hispanic origin
White 60.7%
Black 26.9%
American Indian, Eskimo, or Aleut. 0.3%
Asian or Pacific Islander 3.7%
Other 8.3%
Hispanic origin 16.7%

Ancestry
American 4.9%   German 14.6%
Czechoslovakian 1.1%   Irish 11.6%
Dutch 1.5%   Italian 2.1%
English 9.7%   Polish 1.7%
French 3.6%   Scotch Irish 2.4%
French Canadian 1.6%   Scottish 1.5%

Universities/colleges, 1990-1991 enrollment
Baylor College of Medicine, Houston 999
ITT Technical Institute, Houston 605
San Jacinto College, Pasadena 9,424
San Jacinto College-North, Houston 3,778
Texas Chiropractic College, Pasadena 334
University of Texas-Health Science Center, Houston 3,016

Newspapers, total circulation (in all districts)
Houston Chronicle 421,140
Houston Post 292,061

Commercial television stations, affiliations
ADI: Houston (100%)
   KHSH, Alvin (None)
   KLTJ, Galveston (None)
   KHTV, Houston (None)
   KPRC-TV, Houston (NBC)
   KRIV, Houston (Fox)
   KTRK-TV, Houston (ABC)
   KTXH, Houston (None)

Cable television systems, total subscribers
Prime Cable; Highlands 32,000
Prime Cable; La Porte 17,419
Storer Cable TV Inc.; Houston 55,216
Warner Cable of Houston; Houston 229,000

Military installations, 1991
Ellington Field Air Force Guard Station, Houston 413
La Porte Air Force Guard Station, La Porte 17

Businesses and other major employers

University of Texas/Anderson Hospital; Houston; research services 8,000

Baylor College of Medicine; Houston 6,400

Methodist Hospital; Houston 5,257

St. Luke's Episcopal Hospital; Houston 3,858

University of Texas-Health Science Center; Houston 3,850

Hermann Hospital Inc.; Houston 2,900

Shell Oil Co.; Deer Park; metal products 2,500

Ben Taub Hospital; Houston 2,200

Exxon Corp.; Baytown; petroleum refining 1,710

Texas Children's Hospital; Houston 1,500

American Medical Intl./Park Plaza Hospital; Houston 1,500

Brown & Root Inc.; Houston; engineering services 1,400

Kelsey-Seybold Clinic; Houston; medical doctors 1,210

Rohm & Haas Texas Inc.; Deer Park; organic chemicals 1,000

Houston Lighting & Power Co.; Houston; electric services 1,000

Phillips Petroleum Co./Plastics Div.; Pasadena; plastics products 1,000

Aramco Services Co.; Houston; management services 900

Arco Chemical Co.; Channelview; organic chemicals 841

Quantum Chemical Corp.; Deer Park; plastics/synthetics 800

Ref-Chem Corp./Don Love Div.; Pasadena; heavy construction 800

J. B. Hunt Transport Inc.; Houston; trucking services 754

San Jacinto Methodist Hospital; Baytown 750

Lubrizol Corp.; Deer Park; chemical products 728

Lyondell Petrochemical Co.; Channelview; inorganic chemicals 650

Chevron USA Inc./Chevron Exploration Land Products; Houston; petroleum/natural gas 650

Bayshore Medical Center; Pasadena 650

Occidental Chemical Corp./Deer Park Plant; Deer Park; inorganic chemicals 640

Randalls Food Markets Inc.; Houston; grocery stores 600

Temple Emanuel Sisterhood; Houston; religious organizations 600

H. B. Zachry Co.; Pasadena; heavy construction 515

26th District
Suburban Dallas; Parts of Irving and Denton

In the 1980s, the 26th (see map on page 709) was the third-fastest-growing district in the United States.

Denton County, the biggest chunk of land in the district, grew 89 percent in the 1970s and 91 percent in the 1980s. Southern Denton County, home to once-rural communities that are now Dallas suburbs, has continued to grow into the 1990s.

The region's astonishing growth was attributed primarily to the appeal of the "Golden Triangle," an area bordered by the Dallas-Fort Worth International Airport and two major highways, I-35 East and I-35 West.

The airport is the world's largest in acreage, as well as one of the busiest. The Dallas-Fort Worth metroplex spans 100 miles in north-central Texas. Although the region was hurt by defense cutbacks and the resignation of hometown favorite Speaker Jim Wright in 1989, its diversified economy and mild weather have kept it from more serious economic demise in the late 1980s.

With the rapid population growth, the boundaries of the 26th were compressed and shifted in the 1992 redistricting, making room for a new minority-influence district in Dallas.

About 55 percent of the district's voters live in Dallas County. Although the city is not in the 26th, many district residents look to Dallas for employment and entertainment. The downtown financial district is a significant source of jobs for the people of the 26th.

Arts patrons head to the second-largest city in Texas for its fine symphony and museums. For different types of recreation, the 26th has the Dallas Cowboys' home field, Texas Stadium, and Lake Lewisville State Park.

One of the district's largest employers is high-tech giant Texas Instruments; its Lewisville plant manufactures the Army's HARM missile, which gained praise in Desert Shield/Desert Storm. Other major employers include Xerox, Exxon, GTE and American Airlines, which has headquarters just over the district boundary line.

Most of the residents of the 26th are white and fairly well off. The median household income for the district, between $37,500 and $40,000, well exceeded state and national averages. Denton County's booming growth helped make it solidly Republican by the early 1990s. And the county has made the entire 26th fertile vote-getting turf for any Republican candidate. George Bush won every county in the district in compiling a 47 percent win here in the 1992 presidential contest.

Low taxes, a strong military and less government regulation top the agenda of many voters in the 26th. These sentiments were borne out in the presidential election results of 1992. Although Bush won the district, independent Dallas billionaire Ross Perot placed second in the three-way race with more than 32 percent of the vote, far surpassing his national average.

Election Returns

	26th District	Democrat	Republican
1992	President*	52,771 (20.9%)	118,610 (46.9%)
	House	55,237 (26.9%)	150,209 (73.1%)
1990	Senate	32,430 (24.3%)	101,148 (75.7%)
1988	President	51,662 (25.9%)	147,516 (74.1%)

Vote for Perot was 81,502 (32.2%).

Demographics

Population 566,217

Percent change from 1980 7.4%

Land area 702 square miles

Population per square mile 807

Counties, 1990 population

Collin (pt.) 73,977	Denton (pt.) 195,396
Dallas (pt.) 292,668	Tarrant (pt.) 4,176

Cities, 1990 population (10,000 or more)

Carrollton 82,169	Irving (pt.) 133,172
Dallas (pt.) 91,831	Lewisville (pt.) 45,966
Denton (pt.) 10,171	Plano (pt.) 32,860
Farmers Branch (pt.) 22,022	Richardson (pt.) 28,115
	The Colony 22,113
Flower Mound 15,527	

Race and Hispanic origin

White 87.1%

Black 4.2%

American Indian, Eskimo, or Aleut. 0.5%

Asian or Pacific Islander 3.9%

Other 4.3%

Hispanic origin 9.2%

Ancestry

American 5.3%	Norwegian 1.2%
Dutch 2.7%	Polish 2.4%
English 17.9%	Russian 1.0%
French 4.7%	Scotch Irish 3.9%
French Canadian 1.0%	Scottish 3.0%
German 25.3%	Swedish 1.6%
Irish 18.7%	Welsh 1.0%
Italian 3.3%	

Universities/colleges, 1990-1991 enrollment

DeVry Institute of Technology, Irving 2,292

North Lake College, Irving 6,283

University of Dallas, Irving 3,008

Newspapers, total circulation (in all districts)

Dallas Morning News 452,101

Denton Record-Chronicle 16,294

Fort Worth Star-Telegram 250,099

Plano Star Courier 14,313

Commercial television stations, affiliations

ADI: Dallas-Fort Worth (100%)

Cable television systems, total subscribers

Paragon Cable; Grapevine 55,000

Storer Cable TV Inc.; Carrollton 16,364

TCI of Texas; Dallas 91,647

TCI of Texas; Farmers Branch 7,856

Businesses and other major employers

Electronic Data Systems Corp.; Plano; communication services 11,000

Texas Instruments Inc.; Lewisville; electronic components 5,000

Texas Instruments Inc.; McKinney; electrical equipment/supplies 2,000

Associates Financial Services Co.; Irving; credit institutions 2,000

Denton State School; Denton 1,800

Otis Engineering Corp.; Carrollton; construction machinery 1,600

International Telecharge Inc.; Dallas; telephone communications 1,500

General Telephone Co. of Southwest; Irving; telephone communications 1,500

IBM Corp.; Dallas; computer equipment 1,500

Irving Hospital Authority/Irving Healthcare Systems; Irving 1,425

Frito-Lay Inc.; Plano; food products 1,400

Pro Group Inc.; Irving; furniture 1,250

Hospital Corp. of America/Medical Center of Plano; Plano 1,250

United Telecommunications/U.S. Sprint; Irving; telephone communications 1,200

GTE Southwest Inc.; Irving; telephone communications 1,200

General Instrument Corp./Tocom Inc.; Carrollton; electrical equipment/supplies 1,200

FMR Corp./Fidelity Investments Inc.; Irving; security/commodity services 1,000

State Farm; Dallas; medical service/health insurance 1,000

Computer Language Research/Fast-Tax; Carrollton; personal services 1,000

Xerox Corp.; Irving; computers/office equipment 1,000

J. C. Penney Co. Inc.; Dallas; department stores 900

Partners National Health Plans/Aetna Employee Benefit Div.; Irving; medical doctors 900

City of Carrollton; Carrollton 898

Arrow Industries Inc.; Carrollton; food products 850

Recognition Equipment Inc.; Irving; computer services 850

Sunbelt Federal Savings; Irving; savings institutions 800

SSBA America Inc.; Addison; business associations 800

First Gibraltar Bank; Irving; savings institutions 750

MPSI Inc.; Irving; research services 714

Frito-Lay Inc./Irving Plant; Irving; bakery products 700

Ask Computer Systems Inc.; Dallas; computer services 700

Dallas Semiconductor Corp.; Dallas; electronic components 685

Allstate Insurance Co.; Irving; insurance services 650

NME Hospital Inc./RHD Memorial Medical Center; Dallas 640

North Lake College; Irving 628

NCH Corp./National Chemsearch; Irving; soaps/cleaners 605

Exxon Capital Corp.; Irving; petroleum/natural gas 605

U.S. Federal Deposit Insurance Corp.; Addison; banking insurance 600

Southmark Corp.; Dallas; real estate agents 600

Four Seasons Hotels Ltd.; Irving; hotel 600

USAA Real Estate Co./Las Colinas Sports Club; Irving; recreation services 600

Word of Faith World Outreach Church; Dallas; religious organizations 600

Optek Technology Inc.; Carrollton; electronic components 575

Omega Optical Co. Inc.; Dallas; ophthalmic goods 553

Dr. Pepper Bottling Co. of Texas; Irving; beverages 550

27th District

Gulf Coast — Corpus Christi; Brownsville

Tucked in the southeastern corner of Texas, the compact 27th is anchored by two dramatically different cities that have become something of rivals ever since the 1982 redistricting threw them together.

In the northern county of Nueces is Corpus Christi. This cosmopolitan city of 257,500, with its mild climate, beaches and museums, is a tourist mecca. Hispanics hold a slight majority in Corpus Christi but are often outvoted by Anglos.

Nueces County has a heavy military influence that could suffer greatly if several proposed base closures occur. The Corpus Christi Army Depot, the largest employer in the city, builds and repairs helicopters. In May 1993, the Corpus Christi Naval Air Station and Naval Hospital were included in a list of proposed base closures. Just across Corpus Christi Bay in Ingleside is a naval station proponents had hoped would become the headquarters for the Navy's mine warfare command operations. The base—which is not in the 27th, although its docks are—was included on the 1993 closure list.

Brownsville, by comparison, is almost entirely Hispanic. Located in southernmost Cameron County, the smaller, grittier city has a distinctly south-of-the-border flavor; breakfast tacos are common fare and many of the residents are bilingual. A private study of census data concluded in 1993 that Brownsville has the worst poverty rate in the nation.

There is no military presence in the southern part of the district. The export-import trade of fruits and vegetables with Brownsville's sister city of Matamoros, Mexico, is an important local industry. Brownsville has trouble competing with the better-known Corpus Christi for tourists and has problems, such as drug trafficking, that are related to illegal border crossings.

Despite the competition between the two cities, they have much in common and offer a unifying thread for the 27th. Both are port cities reliant on the energy and fishing industries.

Both cities watched the local shrimping catch decline in the mid-1980s, partly as a result of new laws requiring the use of nets with devices that enable turtles—and, fishermen say, some shrimp—to escape.

Although Democrat Solomon P. Ortiz sometimes describes himself and his district as conservative, elections and surveys in the early 1990s show a more liberal bent to the 27th.

Nueces County provides a reliable base for any Democrat. Ann Richards won the county comfortably in her 1990 gubernatorial campaign. In 1992, Democrat Bill Clinton exceeded his national average in Nueces, going on to win every county in the 27th. Nueces County also routinely sends Democrats, often Hispanics, to the state Legislature.

Surveys conducted in 1992 by the University of Corpus Christi showed a majority of district residents supported some abortion rights and gay rights, and more than half identified themselves as Democrats.

Election Returns

	27th District	Democrat	Republican
1992	President*	78,491 (47.7%)	58,802 (35.7%)
	House	87,022 (55.5%)	66,853 (42.6%)
1990	Senate	39,482 (41.4%)	55,960 (58.6%)
1988	President	70,151 (55.1%)	57,185 (44.9%)

*Vote for Perot was 27,391 (16.6%).

Demographics

Population 566,217

Percent change from 1980 7.4%

Land area 4,076 square miles

Population per square mile 139

Counties, 1990 population

Cameron	260,120	Nueces	291,145
Kenedy	460	Willacy (pt.)	3,567
Kleberg (pt.)	10,925		

Cities, 1990 population (10,000 or more)

Brownsville	98,962	Robstown	12,849
Corpus Christi (pt.)	257,453	San Benito	20,125
Harlingen	48,735		

Race and Hispanic origin
White 78.7%
Black 2.4%
American Indian, Eskimo, or Aleut. 0.3%
Asian or Pacific Islander 0.6%
Other 18.0%
Hispanic origin 66.2%

Ancestry

American 2.6%		Irish 7.1%	
English 6.6%		Scotch Irish 1.8%	
French 1.9%		Scottish 1.0%	
German 10.1%			

Universities/colleges, 1990-1991 enrollment
Corpus Christi State University, Corpus Christi 3,801
Del Mar College, Corpus Christi 10,538
Texas A&I University, Kingsville 6,014
Texas Southmost College, Brownsville 5,635
Texas State Technical College, Harlingen 2,891
University of Texas, Brownsville 1,448

Newspapers, total circulation (in all districts)
Brownsville Herald 15,950
Corpus Christi Caller-Times 67,489
Harlingen Valley Morning Star 30,403
San Antonio Light 160,666

Commercial television stations, affiliations
ADI: Corpus Christi (68%) and McAllen-Brownsville (32%)
  KVEO, Brownsville (NBC)
  KIII, Corpus Christi (ABC)
  KRIS-TV, Corpus Christi (NBC)
  KZTV, Corpus Christi (CBS)
  KGBT-TV, Harlingen (CBS)
  KRGV-TV, Weslaco (ABC)

Cable television systems, total subscribers
Heritage Cablevision; Harlingen 21,216
TCI of Texas; Corpus Christi 52,310

Military installations, 1991
Corpus Christi Naval Air Station, Corpus Christi 7,824
Corpus Christi Army Depot, Corpus Christi 3,787
Kingsville Naval Air Station, Kingsville 1,788
Ingleside Naval Station, Ingleside 1,670

Businesses and other major employers
Complete Business Services/Manpower Temporary Services; Corpus Christi; personnel supply services 3,200
General Motors Corp.; Brownsville; metal stampings 3,000
Congregations Sisters/Spohn Hospital; Corpus Christi 1,800
General Motors Corp.; Brownsville; motor vehicles 1,500
Valley Baptist Medical Center; Harlingen 1,500
Nueces County Memorial Medical Center; Corpus Christi 1,201
Texas A&I University; Kingsville 1,170
State of Texas/Corpus Christi State School; Corpus Christi 1,100
AT&T Co.; Brownsville; electrical goods 1,000
Union Underwear Co. Inc./Fruit of the Loom of Texas; Harlingen; underwear 1,000
Berry Contracting Inc./Fabricators Div.; Corpus Christi; heavy construction 1,000
General Instrument Corp.; Brownsville; audio/video equipment 980

Del Mar College; Corpus Christi 965

Hoechst Celanese Corp./Engineering Plastics Div.; Bishop; organic chemicals 915

County of Nueces; Corpus Christi 800

County of Cameron; Brownsville 785

Robert D. Driscoll Foundation Children's Hospital; Corpus Christi 774

Levi Strauss & Co.; Brownsville; jeans 750

Citgo Petroleum Corp.; Corpus Christi; petroleum refining 700

Humana Inc./Humana Hospital; Corpus Christi 700

Eaton Corp./Apacon & Eaton Co.; Brownsville; metal products 650

McKinney Pant Mfg. Co.; Brownsville; outerwear 600

State of Texas/Agriculture Dept.; Brownsville 600

Koch Refining Co. Inc.; Corpus Christi; petroleum refining 600

APC Home Health Service Inc./Homemaker Service; Harlingen; health practitioners 600

Levi Strauss & Co.; San Benito; apparel 560

Dillard Dept. Stores Inc.; Harlingen; department stores 525

28th District

South San Antonio; Zapata

Mapmakers looking to create a new Hispanic-majority district in south-central Texas found two population bases—San Antonio and the Mexican border—and connected them with a winding trail of south Texas counties. The result was the 28th, one of three new districts acquired in reapportionment for the 1990s.

The 28th is heavily influenced by its proximity to Mexico and its abundance of military bases. San Antonio has five military installations, two of which are in the 28th. Brooks Air Force Base, southeast of downtown, is primarily an aerospace research center. A new Air Force Center for Environmental Excellence at Brooks is expected to bring more than 200 new people to the base and help solidify its future. Randolph Air Force Base is a major training and recruitment center. A navigator training program is scheduled to move from Mather Air Force Base in California to Randolph; about 500 military personnel and 250 students would transfer with the program.

San Antonio is also home to Lackland Air Force Base, Fort Sam Houston, Camp Bullis, and Kelly Air Force Base—the area's largest job-producer and employer of half the Hispanics in the Air Force. Units at Kelly were targeted in early 1993 for possible closure.

The military presence has been a significant factor in keeping the region's economy afloat during the oil crash of the mid-1980s and the nationwide recession of the early 1990s. The five installations generate about $3.4 billion annually and employ about 69,000 people. With the six bases and a pleasant climate, San Antonio is a popular spot with retirees. Almost two-thirds of the district's population is in Bexar County, the northernmost county in the 28th, which includes San Antonio, the third-largest city in Texas, and its suburbs. Harlandale, an old German town, has become an increasingly Hispanic San Antonio neighborhood.

As the district moves south toward the Rio Grande, it becomes more rural and poorer. Starr is the second-poorest county in the nation, with more than 63 percent of its residents

living below the poverty level. About 41 percent of the people in neighboring Zapata County fall below the poverty line.

These two overwhelmingly Hispanic counties, taken from the 15th District to help create the 28th in the 1992 redistricting, were two of the fastest-growing in the state.

Truckers who ship food and other products to the border communities complain that there is little worth bringing back north, a situation that makes shipping far less lucrative. The bulk of the region's jobs are low-paying field jobs.

The 28th is overwhelmingly Democratic; Bill Clinton received 55 percent of the vote in the district in 1992. One often overlooked Republican enclave in the district is the northeast section of San Antonio, a predominantly white, middle-class suburb.

Election Returns

		Democrat	Republican
	28th District	**Democrat**	**Republican**
1992	President*	94,112 (54.5%)	51,293 (29.7%)
	House †	122,457 (87.1%)	—
1990	Senate	49,605 (53.6%)	42,904 (46.4%)
1988	President	104,660 (59.9%)	70,083 (40.1%)

Vote for Perot was 27,200 (15.8%).   *†Independent/other is greater than 5%.*

Demographics

Population 566,217

Percent change from 1980 (new district in the 1990s)

Land area 12,178 square miles

Population per square mile 46

Counties, 1990 population

Atascosa 30,533	Jim Wells (pt.) 27,413
Bexar (pt.) 359,046	La Salle 5,254
Comal (pt.) 13,153	McMullen 817
Duval 12,918	Starr 40,518
Frio 13,472	Wilson 22,650
Guadalupe (pt.) 26,055	Zapata 9,279
Jim Hogg 5,109	

Cities, 1990 population (10,000 or more)

Alice (pt.) 14,984	San Antonio (pt.) 261,501
New Braunfels (pt.) 12,262	Seguin (pt.) 14,948

Race and Hispanic origin

White 68.5%

Black 8.5%

American Indian, Eskimo, or Aleut. 0.3%

Asian or Pacific Islander 0.7%

Other 21.9%

Hispanic origin 60.4%

Ancestry

American 2.5%	Irish 7.0%
English 5.0%	Polish 2.3%
French 1.7%	Scotch Irish 1.3%
German 12.5%	

Universities/colleges, 1990-1991 enrollment

Palo Alto College, San Antonio 4,086

St. Philip's College, San Antonio 5,204

Texas Lutheran College, Seguin 1,265

Newspapers, total circulation (in all districts)
Corpus Christi Caller-Times 67,489
McAllen Monitor 35,534
San Antonio Light 160,666
San Antonio News-Express 187,599

Commercial television stations, affiliations
ADI: San Antonio (52%), Corpus Christi (29%), McAllen-Brownsville (10%) and Laredo (9%)
  KABB, San Antonio (None)
  KENS-TV, San Antonio (CBS)
  KMOL-TV, San Antonio (NBC)
  KSAT-TV, San Antonio (ABC)

Cable television systems, total subscribers
Paragon Cable; San Antonio 248,000

Military installations, 1991
Randolph Air Force Base, Universal City 7,553
Brooks Air Force Base, San Antonio 3,043

Businesses and other major employers
State of Texas/San Antonio State Hospital; San Antonio 1,350
Rio Grande City Independent School District; Rio Grande City 1,081
Miller Curtain Co. Inc.; San Antonio; curtains/draperies 1,000
Structural Metals Inc.; Seguin; steel products 720
Tyson Foods Inc.; Seguin; meat products 700
Coca Cola Bottling of the Southwest; San Antonio; beverages 700
San Antonio Shoe Inc.; San Antonio; footwear 700
H. E. Butt Grocery Co./Meat Plant; San Antonio; meat products 600
Palo Alto College; San Antonio 600
State of Texas/San Antonio State School; San Antonio 535

29th District

East Houston; Baytown

The shape of the 29th (see map on page 715) seems to hover over Houston like a giant bird, wings outstretched; its shape has been compared to the form of the Aztec god Quetzalcoatl.

The district is the handiwork of mapmakers operating under Voting Rights Act mandates to maximize minority-group representation. In this case, the cartographers' goal was to pull together a Hispanic-majority district in the city, no matter how far-flung the Hispanic neighborhoods might be. Texas gained three House seats in 1990 reapportionment; the 28th and 29th districts were drawn for Hispanics, the 30th to elect a black.

The 29th ended up with such contorted, confusing boundaries that residents in seven precincts of the 29th initially voted in other districts in 1992. But numerically, the mapmakers did their job: Hispanics make up 61 percent of the total population and 55 percent of the voting-age population. Blacks account for 10 percent of the total as well as voting-age population.

While two-thirds of the people in the 29th have the common bond of being in a minority group, there is no broader sense of community in the district. The Hispanic populations in San Antonio and other cities closer to the Mexican border are more cohesive than Houston's disparate Hispanic population. Most of the city's 700,000 Hispanics have arrived in the past two decades, emigrating not just from Mexico, but from all over Central America. They have few connections to each other and no generational ties to Houston. Voter registration among Hispanics is dismally low.

All this helps explain why in 1992 the 29th elected an Anglo to the House.

The entire district is contained within Harris County. The boundary lines wrap around Houston's downtown and stretch north toward the Intercontinental Airport along I-45 and I-59. To the south, the lines almost reach Hobby Airport. The 29th includes Houston's east side, home to Mexican-American barrios; the inexpensive apartment complexes of the Spring Branch section; the Houston Ship Channel and the Hispanic neighborhoods of Baytown, an otherwise Anglo-dominated, working-class city near oil refineries.

Most of the people in the 29th are blue-collar. They work at the nearby refineries, at two coffee factories and on oil rigs in the gulf. There are carpenters and plumbers, and also school teachers and middle managers for Shell Oil. The Lyondell refinery and petrochemical plant, spun off from ARCO in 1989, employs about 1,100.

Pockets of economic comfort are found in the Heights section of Houston and in Aldine, a suburb to the north. The Heights, just north of downtown, languished into the early 1980s, but as young professionals began restoring historic homes in the neighborhood, its image improved. Antique shops now line 19th Street.

Though voter turnout in the 29th is very low, the bulk who do cast ballots side with Democrats. Bill Clinton won more than half the district's vote in 1992.

Election Returns

	29th District	Democrat	Republican
1992	President*	54,424 (52.0%)	31,864 (30.4%)
	House	64,064 (64.9%)	34,609 (35.1%)
1990	Senate	34,288 (51.4%)	32,425 (48.6%)
1988	President	61,566 (59.1%)	42,693 (40.9%)

*Vote for Perot was 18,440 (17.6%).

Demographics

Population 566,217

Percent change from 1980 (new district in the 1990s)

Land area 182 square miles

Population per square mile 3,109

Counties, 1990 population
Harris (pt.) 566,217

Cities, 1990 population (10,000 or more)
Baytown (pt.) 11,706
Galena Park (pt.) 10,033
Houston (pt.) 428,301
Pasadena (pt.) 40,846
South Houston (pt.) 13,211

Race and Hispanic origin
White 54.0%
Black 10.2%
American Indian, Eskimo, or Aleut. 0.4%
Asian or Pacific Islander 1.7%
Other 33.7%
Hispanic origin 60.6%

Ancestry

American	3.3%	Irish	7.0%
English	4.6%	Italian	1.2%
French	1.9%	Polish	1.0%
German	7.7%	Scotch Irish	1.1%

Universities/colleges, 1990-1991 enrollment

Lee College, Baytown 5,397

Newspapers, total circulation (in all districts)

Houston Chronicle 421,140
Houston Post 292,061

Commercial television stations, affiliations

ADI: Houston (100%)

Cable television systems, total subscribers

Prime Cable; La Porte 17,419
Storer Cable TV Inc.; Houston 55,216
Warner Cable of Houston; Houston 229,000

Businesses and other major employers

Austin Industries Del Corp./Austin Industrial; Houston; building construction 3,000

Pedus Building Services Inc.; Houston; building services 1,800

Baker Hughes Inc.; Houston; construction machinery 1,500

May Dept. Stores Co.; Houston; department stores 1,350

S&B Engineers & Constructors; Houston; heavy construction 1,300

Lyondell Petrochemical Co.; Houston; petroleum refining 1,100

Simpson Pasadena Paper Co.; Pasadena; paper mills 1,057

Ethyl Corp.; Pasadena; organic chemicals 1,000

Du Pont E. I. De Nemours & Co./Agricultural Products; La Porte; inorganic chemicals 1,000

Litwin Engineers; Houston; heavy construction 1,000

Dow Chemical Co.; Houston; chemical products 1,000

Baker Hughes Inc.; Houston; industrial machinery repair 1,000

Halliburton Co./Halliburton Reservoir Service; Houston; business services 1,000

Schlumberger Technology Corp./Well Service Div.; Houston; oil/gas services 900

Kraft General Foods Inc./Maxwell House Div.; Houston; food products 900

City of Pasadena; Pasadena 897

Central Freight Lines Inc.; Houston; trucking services 850

Sanitors Southwest of Houston; Houston; building services 814

S. I. P. Engineering Inc.; Houston; heavy construction 700

Goodyear Tire & Rubber Co.; Houston; synthetics 700

Ernst & Young; Houston; accounting/auditing 650

City of Houston/Waste Water Treatment Plant; Houston 600

City of Houston/Water Customer Service; Houston 567

Mandel-Kahn Industries/USA Packaging; Houston; drugs/proprietaries/sundries 550

Stewart & Stevenson Services Inc.; Houston; turbines/generators 540

Heights Medical Center Inc./AMI Heights Hospital; Houston 535

City of Baytown/Baytown Sports Complex; Baytown; commercial sports 521

30th District

Downtown Dallas; Part of Grand Prairie

The 30th District circles the inner city of Dallas, juts out toward Arlington, climbs north along the Dallas-Fort Worth airport, approaches North Lake and backtracks toward Dallas before making a final sharp jog out to Plano (see map on page 709). It is 50 percent black, more than two-thirds minority. It is overwhelmingly Democratic—in 1992 Bill Clinton took 63 percent in the district, far surpassing his 37 percent statewide.

In the words of a federal panel of judges, the 30th resembles a "microscopic view of a new strain of a disease." The judges concluded the district "received well-deserved ridicule as the most gerrymandered district in the United States."

The 30th was the result of a complicated chain of events triggered by rapid population gains in Texas in the 1980s. The state acquired three new congressional seats in the 1990 reapportionment. As chairwoman of the Texas Senate Subcommittee on Congressional Districts, Democrat Rep. Eddie Bernice Johnson designed this one to suit her political strengths.

The contorted lines of the 30th produced an outcry from other candidates who felt the lines unfairly benefited Johnson. But the federal judges let the boundaries stand for one simple reason: They give minorities a majority vote.

All of downtown Dallas is included in the 30th. The eighth-largest city in the nation and second to Houston in the state, Dallas is a major banking and insurance center, as well as a popular draw for tourists and conventioneers. More than 100 companies relocated to Dallas in the 1980s and more than 500 foreign companies have offices here.

A generation of Americans recall Dallas as the scene of President John F. Kennedy's assassination in 1963. The site and nearby memorial are in the historic west end of downtown. Known also for its museums and symphony, Dallas nevertheless has experienced a decline in tourism since 1990. In 1993 city officials and the Chamber of Commerce began a major promotional effort.

The State-Thomas neighborhood, adjacent to downtown, included some of the city's first homes owned by blacks. Most were razed by speculators in the 1960s, and the area today has predominantly white, affluent residents. Some black families that owned Victorian homes kept the properties when the city created an historic district.

Several corporations have opened offices and manufacturing plants in North Dallas, including Texas Instruments, Fujitsu, IBM and EDS, the semiconductor business that Ross Perot started and then sold to General Motors.

Although the city of Arlington is not in this district, many residents of the 30th work at the General Motors plant there. There are no military bases in the 30th, but a number of residents work at the Naval Air Station in Arlington (24th District), which is on the 1993 base-closure list.

Election Returns

	30th District	Democrat	Republican
1992	President*	98,031 (62.6%)	33,514 (21.4%)
	House	107,831 (71.5%)	37,853 (25.1%)
1990	Senate	60,962 (58.6%)	43,121 (41.4%)
1988	President	110,948 (63.1%)	64,746 (36.9%)

Vote for Perot was 25,078 (16.0%).

Demographics

Population 566,217

Percent change from 1980 (new district in the 1990s)

Land area 233 square miles

Population per square mile 2,425

Counties, 1990 population
Collin (pt.) 7,050	Tarrant (pt.) 1,949
Dallas (pt.) 557,218	

Cities, 1990 population (10,000 or more)
Dallas (pt.) 453,114	Irving (pt.) 21,844
De Soto (pt.) 18,384	Lancaster (pt.) 16,824
Grand Prairie (pt.) 27,688	

Race and Hispanic origin
White 37.5%
Black 50.0%
American Indian, Eskimo, or Aleut. 0.4%
Asian or Pacific Islander 2.0%
Other 10.1%
Hispanic origin 17.1%

Ancestry
American 3.4%	Irish 7.3%
Dutch 1.1%	Italian 1.0%
English 6.5%	Scotch Irish 1.6%
French 1.6%	Scottish 1.0%
German 7.8%	

Universities/colleges, 1990-1991 enrollment
Baylor College of Dentistry, Dallas 429
Brookhaven College, Farmers Branch 8,503
Cedar Valley College, Lancaster 3,147
Criswell College, Dallas 368
Dallas Theological Seminary, Dallas 1,216
Parker Chiropractic College, Dallas 637
Paul Quinn College, Dallas 1,004
Richland College, Dallas 12,567
Southern Methodist University, Dallas 8,798
University of Texas Southwest Medical Center, Dallas 1,529
Wade's Fashion Merchandising, Dallas 321

Newspapers, total circulation (in all districts)
Dallas Morning News 452,101
Fort Worth Star-Telegram 250,099
Plano Star Courier 14,313

Commercial television stations, affiliations
ADI: Dallas-Ft. Worth (100%)

Cable television systems, total subscribers
TCI of Texas; Dallas 91,647

Businesses and other major employers
Electronic Data Systems Corp.; Dallas; computer services 11,118
NationsBank of Texas; Dallas; commercial banks 7,480
Parkland Memorial Hospital; Dallas 5,562
Schlumberger Ltd./Sedco Forex; Dallas; oil/gas services 5,000
Baylor University Medical Center; Dallas 4,600
University of Texas/Southwestern Medical Center; Dallas 4,500
County of Dallas; Dallas 4,000
Rockwell Intl. Corp.; Richardson; aerospace 3,200
Ryder System Inc./Aviall Inc.; Dallas; airport services 3,000
State of Texas/University of Texas System; Dallas; medical doctors 3,000
Army & Air Force Exchange Services; Dallas; department stores 2,767
City of Dallas/Police Dept.; Dallas 2,652
Southwest Airlines Co.; Dallas; airline 2,638
Alcatel Network Systems Inc.; Richardson; communications equipment 2,600
Sun Energy Partners; Dallas; oil/gas services 2,600
U.S. Veterans Affairs Dept.; Dallas; hospital 2,200
Sears Roebuck & Co.; Dallas; catalog retailers 2,031
Mobil Oil Corp.; Dallas; petroleum products 2,000
Children's Medical Center of Dallas; Dallas 1,897
City of Dallas/Water Utilities Dept.; Dallas 1,800
Boeing Co./Boeing Electronics; Irving; aircraft/parts 1,800
St. Paul Medical Center; Dallas 1,800
City of Irving; Irving 1,669
Texas Utilities Electric Co.; Dallas; electric services 1,500
Atlantic Richfield Co.; Dallas; petroleum/natural gas 1,500
MCI Telecommunications Corp.; Richardson; communications equipment 1,500
United Parcel Service Inc.; Dallas; mail services 1,500
Banc One Texas Corp.; Dallas; commercial banks 1,500
American Building Maintneance Co.; Dallas; building services 1,500
County of Dallas/Sheriffs Dept.; Dallas 1,450
Enserch Corp./Lone Star Gas Co. Div.; Dallas; gas distribution 1,400
Southwestern Bell Corp.; Dallas; electrical repair 1,330
Humana Inc./Medical City Dallas; Dallas 1,300
Sammons Enterprises Inc.; Dallas; industrial machinery/equipment 1,297
Arthur Andersen & Co.; Dallas; accounting/auditing 1,250
LTV Aerospace & Defense Co.; Grand Prairie; guided missiles/parts 1,200
A. H. Belo Corp./Dallas Morning News; Dallas; newspapers 1,200
Northern Telecom Inc.; Richardson; electrical industrial apparatus 1,200
Travelers Insurance Co.; Richardson; insurance services 1,200
Universities Research Assn.; Dallas; research services 1,200
Maintenance Inc.; Dallas; building services 1,200
Dallas Market Center Development Co./Loews Anatole Hotel; Dallas; hotel 1,200
Owens/Dallas Employment Services; Dallas; personnel supply services 1,200
Baylor University; Dallas 1,200
Federal Reserve Bank Dallas; Dallas 1,179
Ericsson Network Systems Inc.; Richardson; electronic components 1,150
D. T. H. Media Inc.; Dallas; newspapers 1,100
Dalfort Corp./Dalfort Aviation Services; Dallas; airport services 1,100
Miramar Capital; Dallas; shipbuilding/repairing 1,050
Yellow Freight System Inc.; Dallas; trucking services 1,000
NEC America Inc./Dallas Plant; Irving; communications equipment 1,000

Employers Casualty Co.; Dallas; fire/marine/casualty insurance 1,000

Pearle Inc.; Dallas; optical goods stores 1,000

Zale Corp.; Irving; jewelry stores 1,000

Ernst & Young; Dallas; accounting/auditing 1,000

U.S. Environmental Protection Agency; Dallas 1,000

Dallas Independent School District; Dallas 910

Oryx Energy Co.; Dallas; petroleum/natural gas 900

State of Texas/Rehabilitation Services Dept.; Dallas 900

Texas Utilities Services Inc.; Dallas; accounting/auditing 844

City of Grand Prairie; Grand Prairie 840

Dal-Tile Corp.; Dallas; tiles/clay products 800

Hyatt Corp./Hyatt Regency Dallas; Dallas; hotel 800

MCI Communications Corp.; Richardson; engineering services 800

Texas Utilities Electric Co./Texas Power & Light Co.; Dallas; electric services 750

Abbott Laboratories/Diagnostic Div.; Irving; medical instruments/supplies 750

Hyatt Corp./Reunion Tower; Dallas; hotel 750

Quaker Oats Co./Stokely-Van Camp; Dallas; beverages 700

Aviall Co.; Dallas; machinery/equipment/supplies 700

First City Texas-Dallas; Dallas; commercial banks 700

Southwestern Life Insurance Co.; Dallas; life insurance 700

BHC Acquisition Corp./Monterey's Tex-Mex Cafe; Irving; bars/restaurants 700

Richardson Hospital Authority; Richardson 700

Dallas/Fort Worth Medical Center/Central Hospital; Grand Prairie 675

U.S. Internal Revenue Service; Dallas 667

Pinkerton's Inc.; Dallas; business services 650

Trinity Industries Inc./Hackney; Dallas; railroad equipment 600

K-C Aviation Inc.; Dallas; air transportation 600

Blockbuster Entertainment Corp./Blockbuster Video; Dallas; warehousing 600

KPMG Peat Marwick; Dallas; accounting/auditing 600

Coopers & Lybrand; Dallas; accounting/auditing 600

Trammell Crow Co.; Dallas; management services 600

Boy Scouts of America; Irving; civic/social association 580

Ascension Capital Corp./Silverleaf Resorts Ltd.; Dallas; real estate agents 550

Trinity Universal Insurance Co.; Dallas; fire/marine/casualty insurance 550

City of Dallas/Public Library; Dallas 550

Neiman Marcus Group Inc.; Dallas; department stores 530

Dallas Area Rapid Transit; Dallas; transportation 525

Utah

Since 1847, when Mormons first settled near the Great Salt Lake, the culture and politics of what now is called Utah were shaped by the doctrines of the Church of Jesus Christ of Latter-Day Saints.

Mormons organized the State of Deseret in 1849 and sought admission to the Union, but not until the church abandoned its doctrine of polygamy did Congress grant statehood in 1896. The federal government even chose the name "Utah" for the state over the Mormon name. Those experiences, while no longer public issues, were imbedded in the state's psyche and helped explain its suspicious attitude toward Washington.

The church exerted a conservative pull on the political process, though usually subtly, through the work of the large number of officeholders who were Mormons. Most were Republicans. Thanks to them, for instance, Utah had one of the strictest abortion laws in the nation, enacted in 1991.

Mormonism and GOP dominance of most elected offices went hand-in-hand for more than 40 years in Utah, but the traditional political stew had some new ingredients, courtesy of Utah's 18 percent population increase during the 1980s. This influx of outsiders—lured by Utah's employment opportunities, reasonable cost of living, low crime rate and natural beauty—had Democrats hoping that their party could be consistently competitive at the polls.

The Utah political landscape looked significantly different in the early 1990s from only a decade earlier. Then, the state's congressional delegation was all Republican, and the GOP controlled both chambers of the state Legislature. In 1993, while Republicans still ran the Legislature and held the governorship, Democrats controlled two of Utah's three House seats.

Another sign of change in Utah politics was the growing role of independent voters. No voter registration by party exists in Utah, so hard data are unavailable. In a 1988 poll, about one-fifth of the voters regarded themselves as independents. In the 1992 presidential election, 27 percent of the vote went to Ross Perot. In the 1992 gubernatorial race, an Independent Party candidate received 33 percent of the vote. In a traditionally Republican state, that is a sizable pool of voters that Democratic candidates have a shot at winning.

Utah's redistricting process for the 1990s was another indicator that the state no longer was firmly in the Republican grip. Though the GOP had full control of the remapping pen, the plan that finally passed was not nearly as aggressively partisan as some that had been discussed earlier. Freshman Democrat Bill Orton got a redrawn 3rd District with a slightly larger number of Democrats. Although his redrawn district remained a strongly Republican constituency, dominated by the conservative Mormon influence of Utah County (Provo), home of Brigham Young University, Orton was re-elected in 1992 with 59 percent of the vote.

In the Salt Lake City-based 2nd, the new map kept the Republican-flavored east side of the city in the 2nd, but much of the Democratic-dominated west side of the city was shifted into the 3rd. In 1992 Democrat Karen Shepherd, campaigning on a program that stressed children's issues (Utah has the second highest birth rate in the nation), won the open seat with 51 percent of the vote. Shepherd became the second woman in Utah history to be elected to the House.

The shape of the 1st changed somewhat in redistricting, but its character remained essentially the same. The district was Republican, although not decisively so. GOP Rep. James V. Hansen won a seventh term in 1992 with 65 percent of the vote against a Democratic challenger and a minor-party candidate.

Table 1 Population

District	Population	Population under 18	Voting-age population	Median age
1	574,286	213,892	360,394	26.3
2	574,241	195,094	379,147	28.3
3	574,323	218,458	355,865	24.1
State	1,722,850	627,444	1,095,406	26.2

Table 2 Voting-Age Persons

District	White*	Black*	American Indian, Eskimo, or Aleut*	Asian or Pacific Islander*	Other*	Hispanic*	Male*	Female*
1	94.5%	1.0%	0.8%	1.6%	2.1%	4.2%	49.0%	51.0%
2	94.5	0.6	0.7	2.4	1.8	4.6	48.7	51.3
3	93.2	0.4	2.2	1.9	2.2	4.7	48.5	51.5
State	94.1	0.7	1.2	2.0	2.1	4.5	48.7	51.3

*As percent of voting-age population.

UTAH

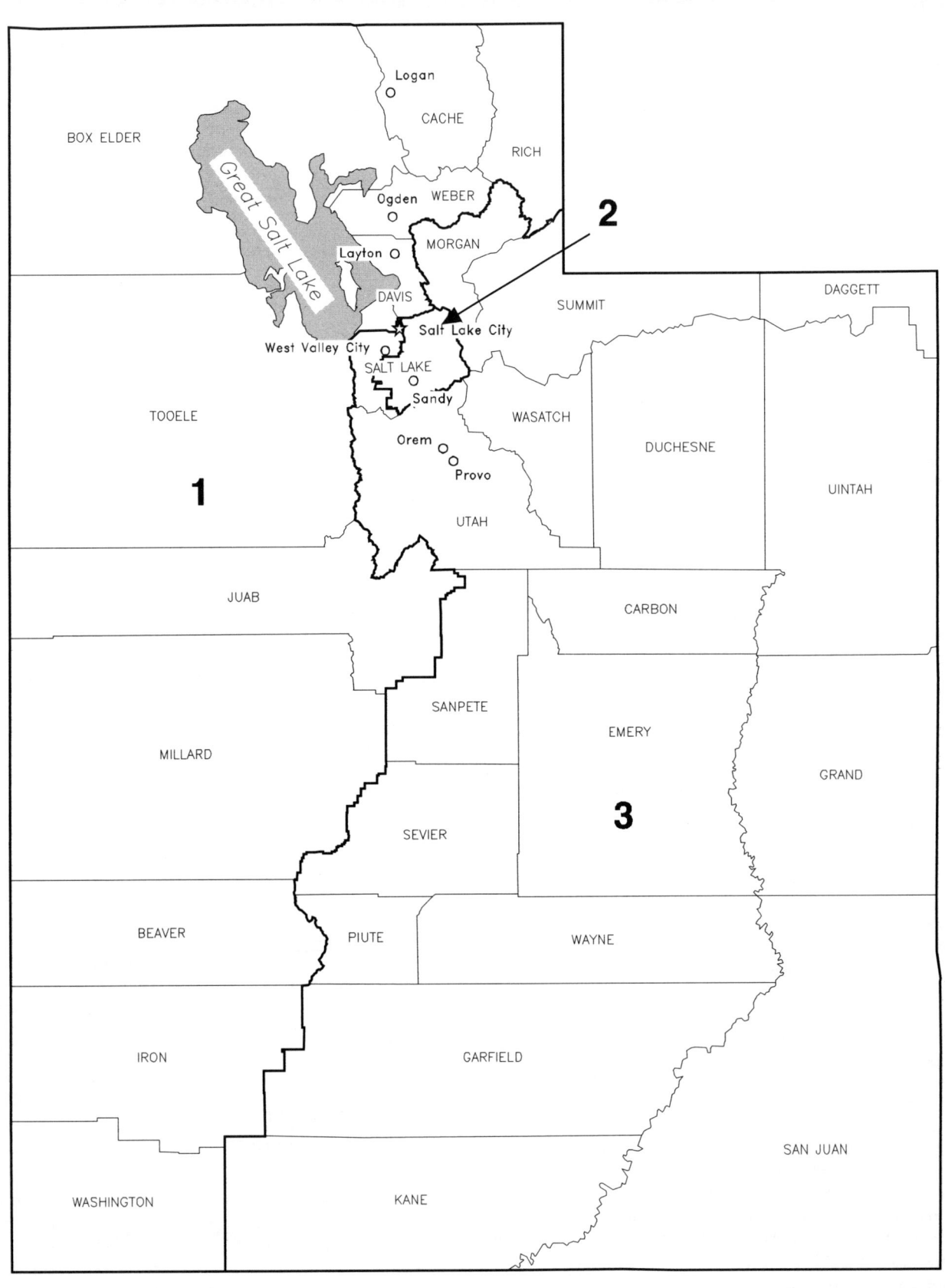

Table 3 Voting-Age Persons by Age Groups

District	18-24*	25-44*	45-54*	55-64*	65 and over*
1	17.3%	44.0%	13.1%	10.7%	14.9%
2	15.7	48.5	12.8	9.4	13.6
3	22.0	44.2	12.0	9.3	12.5
State	18.3	45.6	12.6	9.8	13.7

As percent of voting-age population.

Table 4 Income and Occupation

District	Median family income	Families in poverty	White collar*	Blue collar*	Service*	Farm*
1	$34,232	7.4%	57.8%	26.3%	13.1%	2.8%
2	36,350	6.7	65.9	21.3	11.9	0.9
3	29,629	11.7	53.8	28.8	14.5	2.9
State	33,246	8.6	59.4	25.3	13.1	2.2

As percent of employed persons age 16 and over.

Table 5 Education: School Years Completed

District	Less than grade 9*	Grades 9-12 no diploma*	High school diploma*	College bachelor's degree or higher*
1	3.4%	11.0%	28.6%	20.5%
2	2.6	10.0	24.9	27.1
3	4.3	13.7	28.4	18.6
State	3.4	11.5	27.2	22.3

As percent of persons age 25 and over.

Table 6 Housing and Residential Patterns

District	Owner occupied	Renter occupied	Urban	Rural
1	71.5%	28.5%	84.3%	15.7%
2	64.9	35.1	99.7	0.3
3	68.3	31.7	77.1	22.9
State	68.1	31.9	87.0	13.0

1st District

West — Salt Lake City Suburbs; Ogden; Logan; Rural Utah

The 1st takes in the entire western side of Utah, but most of that land is sparsely settled. More than 70 percent of the voters live in the district's northeastern corner, where population boomed during the 1980s in Cache County (Logan), Weber County (Ogden) and Davis County (just above Salt Lake City).

Republicans dominate the 1st, and Democrats are a distinct minority. George Bush took 49 percent of the district's presidential vote in 1992, and Ross Perot finished second with 29 percent. Bill Clinton ran a poor third, with 22 percent. Rep. James Hansen took almost two-thirds of the House vote, his second-best career tally.

The federal government is an important employer in the Ogden area, the location of Hill Air Force Base, Defense Depot Ogden, and the regional Internal Revenue Service. To the south in Tooele County are the Dugway Proving Ground and Tooele Army Depot.

In addition, federal contracts are important to some of the district's larger private employers, such as Thiokol (known for building solid rocket motors) and Hercules (which does aerospace work). With defense cutbacks looming, some of these contractors are moving to diversify into other lines of work such as satellite manufacturing and communications. One company makes a product that looks to have a bright future in the 1990s: Morton, in Box Elder County. It has been dubbed the "airbag capital" thanks to brisk sales of its automotive safety device.

Davis County is the district's most populous. Salt Lake City bedroom communities such as Bountiful and others in the southern part of Davis County are solidly Republican.

Moving north into Weber County, the Democratic and independent vote picks up, partly a legacy of the area's past as a center of rail-related blue-collar employment. The nation's first transcontinental rail link (in 1869) was at Promontory, just north of Ogden.

There is dairy farming country farther north, in Cache County. Cache's Republican tilt is moderated somewhat by a dose of Democratic voters around Utah State University in Logan (15,200 students).

The 1st's other growth hot spot during the 1980s was Washington County, in Utah's southwestern corner. The county's population went up 86 percent in the past decade (to nearly 50,000), as retirees and wintering wealthy were drawn to the temperate climate and verdant golf courses of Washington and neighboring Iron County. In electoral terms, this influx reinforced the area's conservative bent. Bush won 59 percent of the vote in Washington County in 1992.

Cedar City, in mineral-rich Iron County, suffered from a collapse in the mining industry in the early 1980s, but it is now beginning to see its economic base improve. It has become home to a number of high-tech companies that left expensive locations in California.

Election Returns

	1st District	Democrat	Republican
1992	President*	50,622 (21.5%)	115,627 (49.2%)
	House †	68,712 (28.0%)	160,037 (65.3%)
1988	President	59,275 (27.5%)	156,566 (72.5%)
	Senate	59,784 (27.8%)	155,161 (72.2%)
	Governor	75,422 (44.4%)	94,432 (55.6%)
1986	Senate	35,511 (23.6%)	115,082 (76.4%)

Vote for Perot was 68,884 (29.3%). †Independent/other is greater than 5%.*

Demographics

Population 574,286

Percent change from 1980 17.7%

Land area 34,085 square miles

Population per square mile 17

Counties, 1990 population

Beaver	4,765	Davis	187,941
Box Elder	36,485	Iron	20,789
Cache	70,183	Juab	5,817

Millard 11,333
Rich 1,725
Salt Lake (pt.) 1,757

Tooele 26,601
Washington 48,560
Weber 158,330

Cities, 1990 population (10,000 or more)

Bountiful 36,659
Brigham City 15,644
Cedar City 13,443
Centerville 11,500
Clearfield 21,435
Kaysville 13,961
Layton 41,784

Logan 32,762
North Ogden 11,668
Ogden 63,909
Roy 24,603
South Ogden 12,105
St. George 28,502
Tooele 13,887

Race and Hispanic origin

White 94.4%
Black 0.9%
American Indian, Eskimo, or Aleut. 0.9%
Asian or Pacific Islander 1.5%
Other 2.3%
Hispanic origin 4.7%

Ancestry

American 3.3%
Danish 9.4%
Dutch 3.5%
English 45.8%
French 3.1%
German 17.3%
Irish 7.8%

Italian 2.4%
Norwegian 1.9%
Scotch Irish 1.3%
Scottish 5.4%
Swedish 5.8%
Swiss 2.1%
Welsh 2.9%

Universities/colleges, 1990-1991 enrollment

Dixie College, St. George 2,528
Southern Utah University, Cedar City 4,003
Utah State University, Logan 15,156
Weber State College, Ogden 13,449

Newspapers, total circulation (in all districts)

Logan Herald Journal 13,932
Ogden Standard-Examiner 54,567
Salt Lake Tribune/Deseret News 174,777

Commercial television stations, affiliations

ADI: Salt Lake City (100%)
  KCCZ, Cedar City (None)
  KOOG-TV, Ogden (None)
  KSTU, Salt Lake City (Fox)
  KXIV, Salt Lake City (None)

Cable television systems, total subscribers

Falcon Cable TV; St. George 7,000
Insight Cablevision; Brigham City 5,486
Sonic Cable TV of Utah; Logan 12,500
TCI of Utah; Farmington 18,500
TCI of Utah; Ogden 20,000
TCI of Utah; Salt Lake City 82,000

Military installations, 1991

Hill Air Force Base, Clearfield 21,906
Tooele Army Depot, Tooele 3,404
Dugway Proving Ground (Army), Dugway 1,647
Defense Depot Ogden (Army) 1,468

Businesses and other major employers

Utah State University; Logan 5,064
Thiokol Corp.; Brigham City; plastics/synthetics 4,000
Matrixx Marketing Inc.; Ogden; telemarketing services 3,000
Unisys Corp.; Salt Lake City; computer equipment 2,700

Weber State University; Ogden 1,990
U.S. Postal Service; Ogden 1,600
Proform Fitness Products Inc.; Logan; sporting goods 1,485
Intermountain Health Care Inc./McKay Hospital Center; Ogden 1,400
Morton Intl. Inc.; Ogden; motor vehicle equipment 1,300
County of Cache/School District; Logan 1,300
City of Ogden/School District; Ogden 1,167
Iomega Corp.; Roy; computer equipment 937
E. A. Miller Inc.; Hyrum; meat products 900
St. Benedicts Hospital; Ogden 900
Litton Systems Inc./Guidance & Control Div.; Salt Lake City; navigation equipment 800
Smiths Food & Drug Centers Inc.; Layton; drug/groceries stores 790
County of Washington/School District; St. George 750
County of Weber; Ogden 650
Intermountain Health Care Inc./Logan Regional Hospital; Logan 630
Rockwell Intl. Corp./Collins Telecom Products Div.; Salt Lake City; electrical equipment/supplies 605
La-Z-Boy Chair Co.; Tremonton; furniture 587
Intermountain Power Service Corp.; Delta; electric services 584
Pepperidge Farm Inc.; Richmond; bakery products 580
Pneumo Abex Corp./Jetway Systems Div.; Ogden; construction machinery 550
Kimberly-Clark Corp.; Ogden; paper mills 550

2nd District

Central — Parts of Salt Lake City

Nowhere in Utah is the physical presence of the Mormon Church more evident than in the state capital, Salt Lake City. Downtown is dominated by Temple Square's massive Tabernacle, world headquarters of a church that is closely identified with abstemious lifestyles and conservative politics.

The irreverent used to joke that newcomers needed to set their watches back 20 years when they arrived in Salt Lake City. But the city has long been more culturally cosmopolitan than Utah as a whole, and its politics more dimensional. Non-Mormon Democratic candidates have won the past two mayoral elections, and in 1992, Karen Shepherd kept up the Democrats' 2nd District winning streak that Wayne Owens began in 1986. (Owens left the House for an unsuccessful Senate bid.) Salt Lake boosters aiming to broaden the city's image are bidding for sponsorship of the 2002 Winter Olympics.

Since it was founded in 1847, Salt Lake City has been a focal point of Utah's economy. Employment in industries such as financial services, transportation, tourism and manufacturing—and lately in high-tech fields such as computers—have made the city one of the West's premier business centers.

Companies have been attracted to Utah because of its low cost of living and doing business, its right-to-work laws, its high birth rate—which maintains a steady labor supply—and its well-educated workers, many of whom know a language in addition to English because the Mormon tradition is to send its young men and women around the world to serve as missionaries.

When energy prices dropped in the 1980s, jobs provided by Salt Lake City's "new age" employers helped rescue the state from recession, and they were a magnet for newcomers: During the past decade, more than 100,000 people moved into Salt Lake County, many of them settling in the city's southwestern suburbs.

While most of the rest of Utah votes Republican, Salt Lake City and some of its suburbs tend to show a more Democratic bent, as is evident from the success of Democrats in Salt Lake's mayoral contests and in 2nd District House voting. The city has a large population of Democratic-voting blue-collar workers and liberal young professionals.

But even in the 2nd, the political worldview looks fairly conservative to most outsiders. In the 1992 presidential race, George Bush and Ross Perot received more than two-thirds of the vote. Bill Clinton's 32 percent was easily his best showing in Utah's three districts.

Salt Lake City's central section and the communities surrounding the University of Utah in the northern hills lean Democratic. But in the wealthy Wasatch foothills section called the East Bench, Republicans hold sway. Voters in such suburban communities as Cottonwood, Sandy City and Draper usually opt for the GOP.

Election Returns

	2nd District	Democrat	Republican
1992	President*	81,233 (31.4%)	101,169 (39.2%)
	House	127,738 (50.5%)	118,307 (46.8%)
1988	President	85,309 (38.1%)	138,437 (61.9%)
	Senate	83,254 (37.3%)	140,234 (62.7%)
	Governor	97,208 (54.0%)	82,673 (46.0%)
1986	Senate	44,155 (30.6%)	100,138 (69.4%)

*Vote for Perot was 75,921 (29.4%).

Demographics

Population 574,241

Percent change from 1980 17.8%

Land area 458 square miles

Population per square mile 1,253

Counties, 1990 population
Salt Lake (pt.) 574,241

Cities, 1990 population (10,000 or more)

Canyon Rim CDP 10,527	Murray 31,282
Cottonwood Heights CDP 28,766	Riverton 11,261
	Salt Lake City (pt.) 120,669
Cottonwood West CDP 17,476	Sandy 75,058
	South Jordan 12,220
East Millcreek CDP 21,184	South Salt Lake 10,129
Holladay-Cottonwood CDP 14,095	Taylorsville-Bennion CDP (pt.) 47,327
Kearns CDP (pt.) 28,346	Union CDP 13,684
Midvale 11,886	West Jordan (pt.) 42,892
Millcreek CDP 32,230	

Race and Hispanic origin
White 94.4%
Black 0.6%
American Indian, Eskimo, or Aleut. 0.7%
Asian or Pacific Islander 2.3%
Other 2.0%
Hispanic origin 4.9%

Ancestry

American 3.6%	Norwegian 2.3%
Danish 8.4%	Polish 1.1%
Dutch 3.3%	Scotch Irish 1.6%
English 40.8%	Scottish 5.3%
French 3.2%	Swedish 6.7%
German 18.6%	Swiss 1.9%
Irish 8.6%	Welsh 2.6%
Italian 3.1%	

Universities/colleges, 1990-1991 enrollment
ITT Technical Institute, Salt Lake City 476
Latter Day Saints Business College, Salt Lake City 700
Salt Lake Community College, Salt Lake City 13,344
University of Utah, Salt Lake City 24,917
Westminster College, Salt Lake City 2,025

Newspapers, total circulation (in all districts)
Salt Lake Tribune/Deseret News 174,777

Commercial television stations, affiliations
ADI: Salt Lake City (100%)

Cable television systems, total subscribers
Insight Cablevision; Sandy 20,000
TCI of Utah; Salt Lake City 82,000

Military installations, 1991
Steven A. Douglas Support Facility (Army), Salt Lake City 386

Businesses and other major employers
University of Utah; Salt Lake City 12,219
Church of Jesus Christ of Latter Day Saints/Mormon Church; Salt Lake City; religious organizations 4,200
Delta Air Lines Inc.; Salt Lake City; airline 3,500
Pro-Benefit Staffing Inc.; Salt Lake City; personnel supply services 2,550
American Express Travel Related Services; Salt Lake City; credit institutions 2,000
FHP Inc./Family Health Plan; Salt Lake City; health services 1,650
Hertz Corp.; Sandy; automotive rentals 1,600
U.S. Veterans Affairs Dept.; Salt Lake City; hospital 1,500
Deseret Medical Inc.; Sandy: surgical instruments 1,300
O. C. Tanner Co.; Salt Lake City; jewelry/precious metals 1,300
Abbott Laboratories/Sorenson Research Inc.; Salt Lake City; medical instruments 1,200
Union Pacific Railroad Co.; Salt Lake City; railroads 1,200
Intermountain Health Care Inc./Cottonwood Hospital Medical Center; Salt Lake City 1,200
Discover Card Services Inc.; Sandy; credit institutions 1,150
Evans & Sutherland Computer Corp.; Salt Lake City; computers 1,100
Sinclair Oil Corp./Marketing Div.; Salt Lake City; petroleum products 1,100
National Semiconductor Corp.; West Jordan; computer components 1,000
Denver Rio Grande Western Railroad; Salt Lake City; railroads 1,000
County of Salt Lake; Salt Lake City 1,000

Newspaper Agency Corp.; Salt Lake City; commercial printing 900

Holy Cross Hospital; Salt Lake City 876

First Security Corp.; Salt Lake City; commercial banks 810

Salt Lake Community College; Salt Lake City 800

State of Utah/Tax Commission; Salt Lake City 765

Clover Club Foods Co.; Salt Lake City; food products 700

Mountain Fuel Supply Co.; Salt Lake City; gas distribution 700

Blue Cross/Blue Sheld of Utah; Salt Lake City; medical service/health insurance 685

Zions Cooperative Merchants Institution; Salt Lake City; department stores 650

County of Salt Lake/Sheriffs Dept; Salt Lake City 608

Bonneville Intl. Corp.; Salt Lake City; radio/TV broadcasting 600

Alta View Personnel Services; Sandy; personnel supply services 600

Baker Hughes Inc./Eimco Process Equipment Co.; Salt Lake City; oil field equipment 550

3rd District

East — Provo; Orem; Rural Utah

Some of the rural eastern counties of the 3rd saw sharp population declines during the 1980s. In Grand County, for instance—reeling from the collapse of the uranium mining industry—population dropped nearly 20 percent, to 6,620 people.

But outmigration from the rural areas was more than offset by huge growth in the district's urbanized areas: Provo, Orem and the Salt Lake City suburbs. The population in Utah County (Provo and Orem) grew 21 percent during the past decade, topping 263,000. Utah County is the biggest source of votes in the 3rd, casting more than 45 percent of the district's total.

In 1992, George Bush won 61 percent of the vote in Utah County. Provo, the most intense Mormon community in the state, is home to Brigham Young University, which was founded in 1875 to prepare Mormon youth for teaching and religious proselytizing. Today BYU has 32,000 students and offers degrees in a range of fields, but it remains devoutly Mormon.

Democrat Bill Orton's initial House victory in 1990 was earthshaking for the 3rd, which had been considered an impregnable Republican stronghold. His success proved that voters here are not unwilling to consider a Democrat, as long as he or she stands on the right side of the political spectrum.

Redistricting in 1992 gave Orton a slight boost, transferring from the 2nd into the 3rd a working-class, heavily Democratic section of Salt Lake City. In his re-election bid, that area helped Orton amass 71 percent of the vote in the Salt Lake County portion of the 3rd. Bill Clinton managed to win the Salt Lake County part of the 3rd, and Ross Perot nearly beat Bush for second place there.

The Provo-Orem area has seen a steady influx of new businesses: WordPerfect Inc., Novell Inc. and SoftCopy are among the software companies that have come here in recent years, helping make that industry a leading district employer. Geneva Steel's blue-collar workers in the northern section of Utah County give the area a bloc of Democratic voters.

The rest of the district is rural and sparsely populated. Much of it is mountains and desert, and the GOP is dominant. Cattle ranching, oil drilling and mining have been the traditional

industries in the 3rd, but with oil prices flat and the mining industry in the doldrums, tourism—especially as related to skiing—is becoming an important income source. In the northeastern corner of the district, the life-size dinosaurs of Dinosaurland in Vernal (Uintah County) have become a popular tourist attraction. To the south, thousands of visitors tour the 3rd's national parks: Arches, Canyonlands, Capitol Reef and Bryce Canyon.

Other communities in the district are trying to diversify their economies to spare themselves the financial pains they felt in the 1980s. Carbon County, for instance, has opened its doors to a new power plant and a locally owned and operated landfill. Carbon County was Clinton's best in Utah in 1992, giving him 53 percent of the vote.

Election Returns

	3rd District	Democrat	Republican
1992	President*	51,574 (23.9%)	105,836 (49.0%)
	House	135,029 (59.5%)	84,019 (37.0%)
1988	President	62,757 (32.0%)	133,406 (68.0%)
	Senate	60,321 (30.9%)	134,649 (69.1%)
	Governor	75,797 (47.6%)	83,345 (52.4%)
1986	Senate	35,528 (26.7%)	97,483 (73.3%)

Vote for Perot was 58,595 (27.1%).

Demographics

Population 574,323

Percent change from 1980 18.2%

Land area 47,625 square miles

Population per square mile 12

Counties, 1990 population

Carbon 22,228	Salt Lake (pt.) 149,958
Daggett 690	San Juan 12,621
Duchesne 12,645	Sanpete 16,259
Emery 10,332	Sevier 15,431
Garfield 3,980	Summit 15,518
Grand 6,620	Uintah 22,211
Kane 5,169	Utah 263,590
Morgan 5,528	Wasatch 10,089
Piute 1,277	Wayne 2,177

Cities, 1990 population (10,000 or more)

American Fork 15,696	Salt Lake City (pt.) 37,619
Magna CDP 17,829	Spanish Fork 11,272
Orem 67,561	Springville 13,950
Pleasant Grove 13,476	West Vallley City (pt.)
Provo 86,835	86,976

Race and Hispanic origin
White 92.6%
Black 0.5%
American Indian, Eskimo, or Aleut. 2.6%
Asian or Pacific Islander 1.9%
Other 2.4%
Hispanic origin 5.1%

Ancestry

American	3.1%	Italian	2.5%
Danish	10.6%	Norwegian	2.1%
Dutch	2.9%	Scotch Irish	1.3%
English	43.9%	Scottish	4.9%
French	3.1%	Swedish	5.6%
German	16.3	Swiss	1.5%
Irish	7.5%	Welsh	2.9%

Universities/colleges, 1990-1991 enrollment

Brigham Young University, Provo 31,662
College of Eastern Utah, Price 2,960
Snow College, Ephraim 1,872
Utah Valley Community College, Orem 7,882

Newspapers, total circulation (in all districts)

Ogden Standard-Examiner 54,567
Provo Herald 29,541
Salt Lake Tribune/Deseret News 174,777

Commercial television stations, affiliations

ADI: Salt Lake City (100%)
  KSL-TV, Salt Lake City (CBS)
  KTVX, Salt Lake City (ABC)
  KUTV, Salt Lake City (NBC)

Cable television systems, total subscribers

Insight Cablevision; Pleasant Grove 5,500
Insight Cablevision; Sandy 20,000
TCI of Utah; Provo 11,000
TCI of Utah; Salt Lake City 82,000

Businesses and other major employers

Brigham Young University; Provo 11,000
Hercules Inc./Aerospace Products Group; Magna; guided missiles/parts 3,000
Geneva Steel; Orem; steel products 2,494
BP America Inc./Kennecott Utah Copper Div.; Bingham Canyon; petroleum/minerals 2,377
WordPerfect Corp.; Orem; computer software 2,300
Intermountain Health Care Inc./Utah Valley Regional Medical Center; Provo 2,200
Nu Skin Intl; Provo; cosmetics/hair preparations 1,500
C. R. England & Sons Inc.; Salt Lake City; refrigerated transport services 1,500
Novell Inc.; Provo; computer services 1,108
North American Philips Corp./Signetics; Orem; electronic components 1,100
United Parcel Service Inc.; Salt Lake City; mail services 1,000
State of Utah/Utah State Training School; American Fork 1,000
Varian Associates Inc./Power Grid & X-Ray Tube Products; Salt Lake City; electronic components 850
Stouffer Foods Corp.; Springville; preserved fruits/vegetables 775
Utah Valley Community College; Orem 765
Softcopy Inc.; Pleasant Grove; computer software 675
Huish Detergents Inc.; Salt Lake City; soaps/cleaners 614
State of Utah/Utah State Hospital; Provo 614
McDonnell Douglas Corp.; Salt Lake City; aircraft 600
Associated Food Stores Inc.; Salt Lake City; grocery products 590
Pioneer Valley Hospital; Salt Lake City 550
Professional Lithographers; Provo; commercial printing 544
Consolidated Freightways Corp.; Salt Lake City; trucking services 510
E-Systems Inc./Montek Div.; Salt Lake City; communications equipment 510
County of Carbon/School District; Price 509

VERMONT

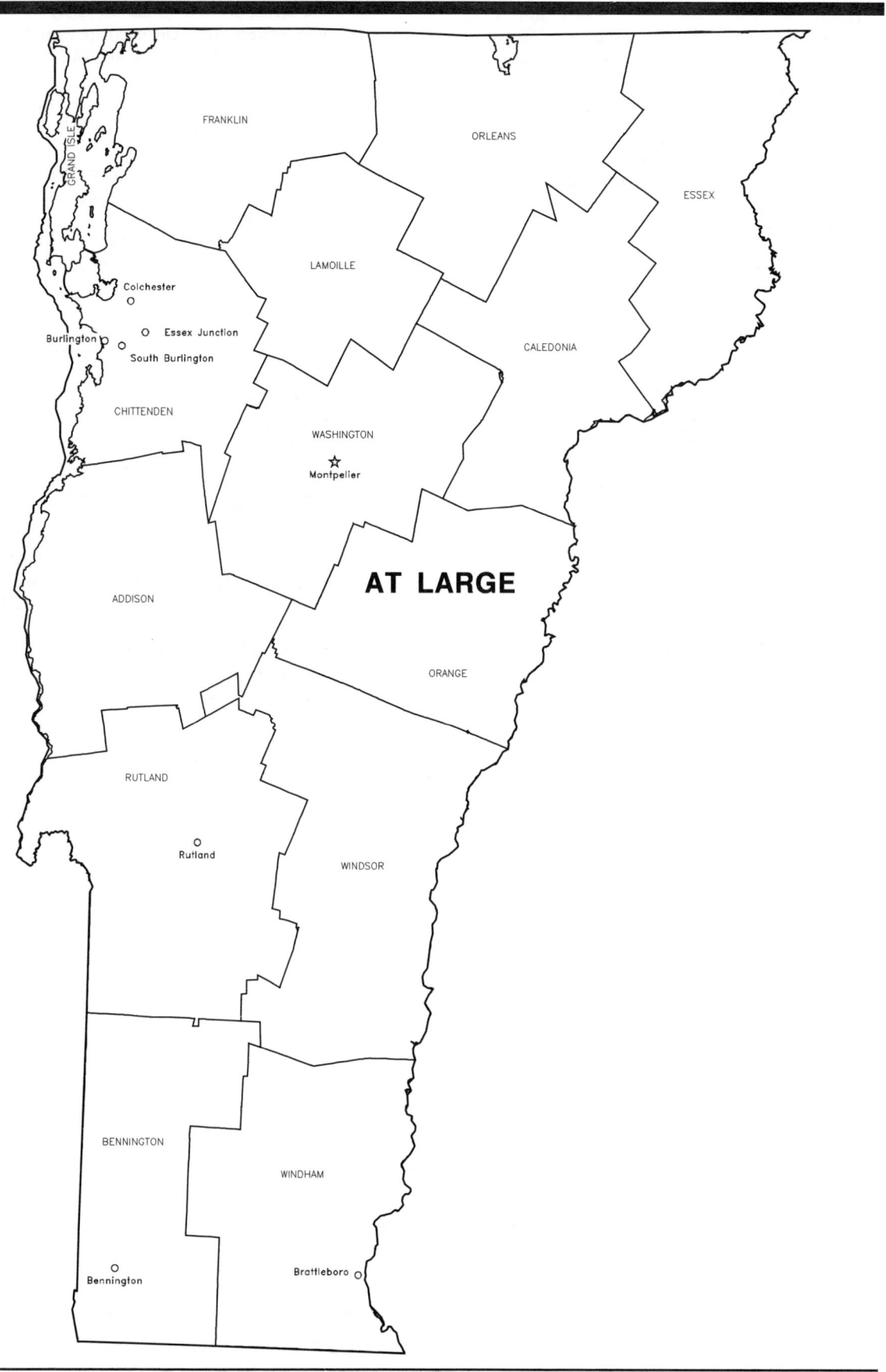

GRAND ISLE

FRANKLIN

ORLEANS

ESSEX

LAMOILLE

○ Colchester

○ Essex Junction

Burlington ○ ○

South Burlington

CALEDONIA

CHITTENDEN

WASHINGTON

☆
Montpelier

AT LARGE

ADDISON

ORANGE

RUTLAND

○
Rutland

WINDSOR

BENNINGTON

WINDHAM

○
Bennington

Brattleboro ○

Vermont

Some things about Vermont remain immutable. The least-populous state in the northeast and third-smallest in the nation, it has a scenic beauty that remains largely unsullied. However, a growth spurt of more than 44 percent since 1960 has driven Vermont's population to nearly 563,000. This growth has had outsized impacts on the demographics and politics of the state.

Much of the population increase stemmed from young urbanites who resettled here and brought with them their liberal politics. These upscale émigrés joined remnants of the 1960s counterculture who had settled in the state in the early 1970s, and a state that had been drifting to the political left became firmly planted there.

Shattered by these developments was Vermont's reputation as the sturdiest bastion of Yankee Republicanism. Democrat Patrick J. Leahy, first elected to the Senate in 1974, earned a fourth term in 1992, and Democrat Howard Dean won the governorship with 75 percent of the vote, the largest Democratic gubernatorial victory in state history.

Dean, as lieutenant governor, inherited the top job upon the 1991 death of GOP Gov. Richard A. Snelling. Dean has a consensus-oriented style and enough of an image as a moderate that his 1992 winning coalition included many centrist Republicans.

Though the new politics of Vermont has seen the Democratic Party grow in strength, moderate Republicans can still gain and hold statewide office.

In 1988, moderate Republican James M. Jeffords—then the state's at-large House member—won the Senate campaign to succeed like-minded Republican Robert T. Stafford. In 1990, Snelling—who was governor from 1977 to 1985—regained the office by pledging fiscal responsibility in the midst of a state budget crisis. Although Snelling's death put the governorship in Democratic hands, Snelling's widow, Barbara, ran for lieutenant governor in 1992 as a Republican and won easily.

There is a vocal conservative element within the state GOP—the Vermont Republican Assembly—but it is widely perceived as too far to the right to thrive in general elections. The conservatives, however, sometimes can turn out enough loyalists to take primary nominations away from moderates, who are not always as effective at grass-roots organizing.

Although Vermont has moved away from its historical voting patterns, its modern political persona retains an element of the state's stubborn independence. In 1992, nearly a quarter of the Vermonters voting for president picked independent Ross Perot; and in the House, self-described socialist Bernard Sanders won re-election to a second term as the state's at-large member. Sanders received 58 percent of the statewide vote.

In his 1990 House campaign, Sanders succeeded in portraying the GOP incumbent—himself a liberal Republican—as a big-business shill and tool of the Establishment. Sanders' populist message fueled his rise, but his credibility was enhanced by his tenure as mayor of Burlington, where during the 1980s he shepherded the state's most populous city through a period of prosperity.

Although its manufacturing heritage has faded, Burlington (population 39,000) enjoyed good times in the last decade, thanks in large part to a boom in its electronics industry. However, that industry was hit hard by the 1990-1991 recession, and Burlington has been through the same economic slump that all of New England has endured. The Burlington area has been especially jarred by large-scale layoffs at companies such as Digital Equipment Corp.

Statewide, both the construction and manufacturing industries have seen a total loss of about 12,000 jobs over the past four years. Few of the lost electronics and defense-related jobs are expected to return. To help fill the vacuum, state officials are trying to make tourism more of a year-round source of income by marketing Vermont as more than just an appealing ski-season destination for visitors.

Burlington and Chittenden County cast about one-fourth of the state's vote; Democratic candidates for statewide office can usually count on strong support here. Bill Clinton won a majority in Chittenden County in 1992.

Clinton's best 1992 showing—54 percent—came in southern Vermont's Windham County, which borders Massachusetts. Other small urban centers such as Montpelier and Rutland, reliably Republican in bygone times, now have more Democrats.

At the village level and in most rural areas, Yankee Vermonters still tend to vote Republican, particularly in the northeastern part of the state, which has been less affected by development.

Table 1 Population

District	Population	Population under 18	Voting-age population	Median age
AL	562,758	143,083	419,675	33.0

Table 2 Voting-Age Persons

District	White*	Black*	American Indian, Eskimo, or Aleut*	Asian or Pacific Islander*	Other*	Hispanic*	Male*	Female*
AL	98.8%	0.3%	0.3%	0.5%	0.1%	0.6%	48.1%	51.9%

*As percent of voting-age population.

Table 3 Voting-Age Persons by Age Groups

District	18-24*	25-44*	45-54*	55-64*	65 and over*
AL	15.1%	44.7%	13.7%	10.8%	15.8%

*As percent of voting-age population.

Table 4 Income and Occupation

District	Median family income	Families in poverty	White collar*	Blue collar*	Service*	Farm*
AL	$34,780	6.9%	56.6%	25.8%	13.5%	4.1%

*As percent of employed persons age 16 and over.

Table 5 Education: School Years Completed

District	Less than grade 9*	Grades 9-12 no diploma*	High school diploma*	College bachelor's degree or higher*
AL	8.7%	10.6%	34.6%	24.3%

*As percent of persons age 25 and over.

Table 6 Housing and Residential Patterns

District	Owner occupied	Renter occupied	Urban	Rural
AL	69.0%	31.0%	32.2%	67.8%

Election Returns

	At Large	Democrat	Republican
1992	President*	133,592 (46.4%)	88,122 (30.6%)
	House†	22,279 (8.2%)	86,901 (32.0%)
1990	Governor	97,321 (46.1%)	109,540 (51.9%)
1988	President	115,775 (48.0%)	124,331 (51.5%)
	Senate	71,469 (29.8%)	163,203 (68.1%)
	Governor	134,594 (55.4%)	105,319 (43.4%)
1986	Senate	124,123 (63.2%)	67,798 (34.5%)
	Governor	92,505 (47.0%)	75,239 (38.3%)

*Vote for Perot was 65,991 (22.9%).   †Independent/other is greater than 5%.

Demographics

Population 562,758

Percent change from 1980 10.0%

Land area 9,249 square miles

Population per square mile 61

Counties, 1990 population

Addison 32,953	Lamoille 19,735
Bennington 35,845	Orange 26,149
Caledonia 27,846	Orleans 24,053
Chittenden 131,761	Rutland 62,142
Essex 6,405	Washington 54,928
Franklin 39,980	Windham 41,588
Grand Isle 5,318	Windsor 54,055

Cities, 1990 population

Bennington 16,451	Essex 16,498
Brattleboro 12,241	Rutland 18,230
Burlington 39,127	South Burlington 12,809
Colchester 14,731	

Race and Hispanic origin

White 98.6%
Black 0.3%
American Indian, Eskimo, or Aleut. 0.3%
Asian or Pacific Islander 0.6%
Other 0.1%
Hispanic origin 0.7%

Ancestry

American 5.7%	Italian 5.8%
Dutch 1.8%	Polish 3.1%
English 26.2%	Russian 1.0%
French 23.6%	Scotch Irish 2.2%
French Canadian 5.9%	Scottish 5.4%
German 10.5%	Swedish 1.8%
Irish 17.9%	Welsh 1.3%

Universities/colleges, 1990-1991 enrollment

Bennington College, Bennington 581
Castleton State College, Castleton 1,975
Champlain College, Burlington 1,916
College of St. Joseph The Provider, Rutland 419
Community College of Vermont, Waterbury 3,895
Goddard College, Plainfield 1,319
Green Mountain College, Poultney 597
Johnson State College, Johnson 1,680
Lyndon State College, Lyndonville 1,344
Marlboro College, Marlboro 291
Middlebury College, Middlebury 2,039
Norwich University, Northfield 2,626
School for International Training, Brattleboro 751
Southern Vermont College, Bennington 676
St. Michael's College, Colchester 2,577
Trinity College, Burlington 1,118
University of Vermont, Burlington 11,076
Vermont Law School, South Royalton 301
Vermont Technical College, Randolph Center 940

Newspapers, total circulation (in all districts)

Barre Times Argus 12,018
Bennington Banner 7,374
Brattleboro Reformer 9,584
Burlington Free Press 53,879
Claremont Eagle Times 9,165
Lebanon-Hanover Valley News 18,114

Rutland Herald 23,060
St. Johnsbury Caledonian Record 9,997

Commercial television stations, affiliations
ADI: Burlington-Plattsburgh (85%), Boston (8%) and Albany-Schenectady-Troy (7%)
   WCAX-TV, Burlington (CBS)
   WVNY, Burlington (ABC)
   WNNE-TV, Hartford (NBC)

Cable television systems, total subscribers
Adelphia Cable; Bennington 8,000
Adelphia Cable; West Rutland 10,006
Adelphia Cable; Williston 25,572
Helicon Cablevision of Vermont; Barre Town 6,047
Lake Champlain Cable; Milton 5,170

Military installations, 1991
Burlington Intl. Airport Air Force Guard Station, South Burlington 394

Businesses and other major employers
IBM Corp.; Essex Junction; electronic components/computers 7,500
State of Vermont; Waterbury 3,771
University of Vermont; Burlington 3,203
Medical Center Hospital of Vermont; Burlington 2,398
General Electric Co.; North Clarendon; aircraft engines/parts 1,500
U.S. Fish & Wildlife Dept.; Swanton 1,500
B. F. Goodrich Co./Instruments Systems Div.; Vergennes; measuring/controlling devices 1,250
Hercules Inc./Simmons Precision Products; Vergennes; marine engineering devices 1,200
Rutland Regional Medical Center; Rutland 998
National Life Insurance Co.; Montpelier; life insurance 950
Digital Equipment Corp.; Burlington; computer equipment 900
General Electric Co./Armament Systems; Burlington; ordnance/accessories 900
Middlebury College; Middlebury 800
C&S Wholesale Grocers Inc.; Brattleboro; grocery products 730
Brattleboro Retreat; Brattleboro 692
Southwestern Vermont Medical Center; Bennington 650
General Electric Co.; Rutland; aircraft engines/parts 600
Martins Foods of South Burlington; Burlington; grocery stores 600
Central Vermont Hospital Inc.; Barre 594
City of Burlington; Burlington 590
Ethan Allen Inc./Orleans Div.; Orleans; wooden furniture 550

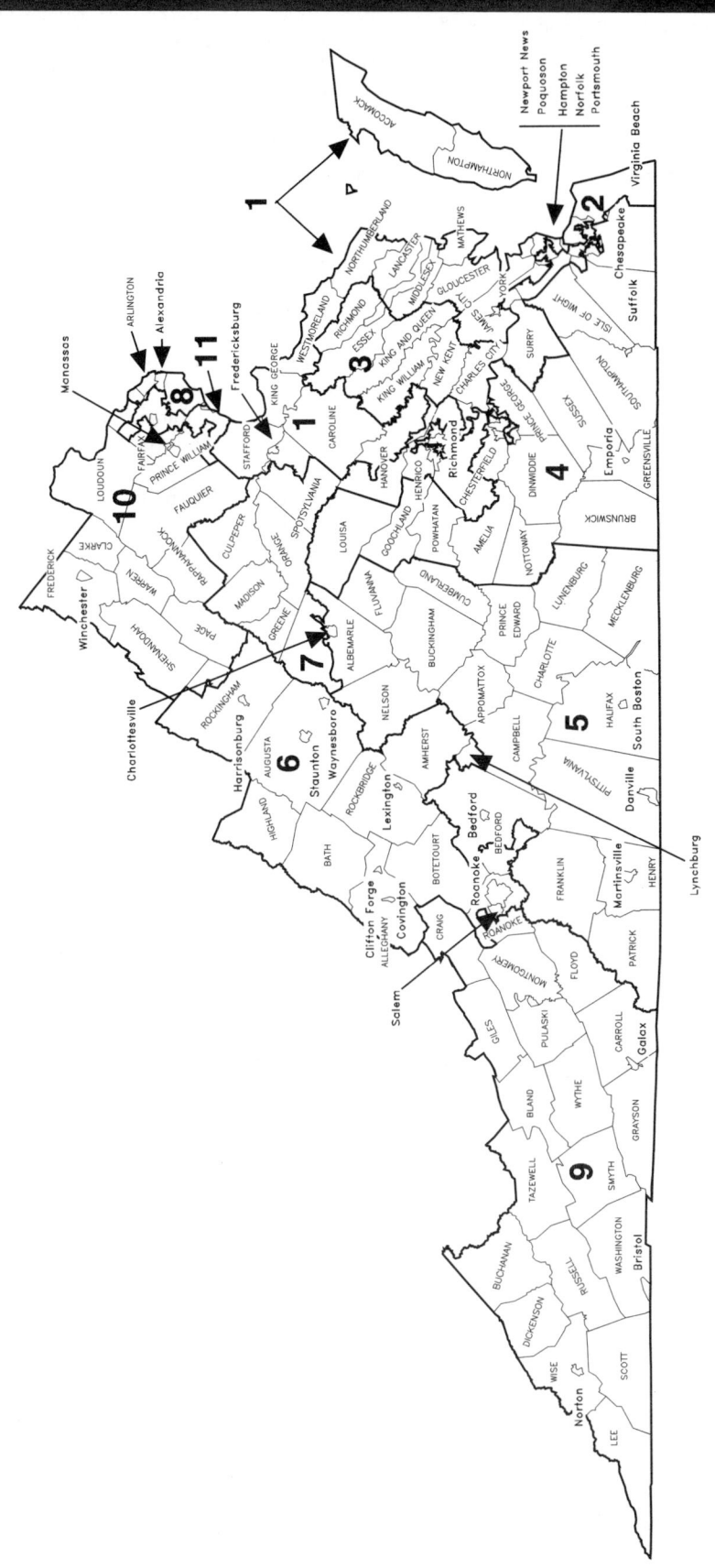

Virginia

Flourishing suburbs, rapid growth in government-related business and a steady flow of defense contracts helped Virginia grow by 16 percent in the 1980s, gaining 840,000 people and a congressional district—the most northerly eastern state to pick up a House seat.

Still, the two centers of growth over the last decade—the Northern Virginia suburbs of Washington and the Hampton Roads area in southeastern Virginia— proved that they were no less susceptible than the rest of the country to the economic downturn that afflicted much of the nation in the late 1980s and early 1990s.

The rapid expansion, particularly in Northern Virginia, has altered the balance of Virginia's economic and political identities, its Old South character receding as the commonwealth evolves into the enterprising "New Dominion," ready to compete in the 21st century. The political leadership has begun to shift away from the more conservative rural Democrats who long dominated Virginia government. The shift has been accompanied by Northern Virginia's gaining representation in number and prominence in Richmond. Northern Virginia voters helped elect black Democrat L. Douglas Wilder governor in 1989. The election of Republican George F. Allen to the governorship in 1993 ended the 12-year rule of the Democrats and may indicate a swing back to conservatism.

The paradigm of the New Dominion is Northern Virginia's Fairfax County, which accounted for more than a quarter of the state's population increase: More than 200,000 people surged into the county from 1980 to 1990, boosting its population by 37 percent. With more than 800,000 people, Fairfax is the most populous county or city in Virginia.

But the economic boom in the suburbs abated as the 1990s approached. Businesses that had sprouted to take advantage of Northern Virginia's proximity to the nation's capital eyed the future warily as government trimming in general, and defense cutbacks in particular, floated clouds over many high-tech companies' heretofore boundless horizons. The real estate market that had spiraled up in previous years crumpled. And county residents, now ensconced in their suburban haven, started to question the unbridled growth over which the local government had presided, as traffic, school quality and crime problems began to surge.

The Hampton Roads area—the region that includes Virginia Beach, Norfolk, Newport News and Hampton—also grew apace in the 1980s. Virginia Beach's population soared by 50 percent, enabling it to pass Norfolk as the commonwealth's most populous city. Military families, business people and retirees— many of them military pensioners—flocked to the area.

While Northern Virginia has enough of an economic mix to sustain a shock to one segment of the local economy, the Hampton Roads area's livelihood is more tightly dependent on the continued patronage of the military-industrial complex. The Newport News Shipbuilding and Drydock Co. is the state's largest private employer. The loss of the *Seawolf* submarine to Connecticut deprived the shipyard of a lucrative contract. But Norfolk stood to be one of two communities (San Diego is the other) with the most to gain from the 1993 base-closing commission's efforts to consolidate U.S. armed forces at fewer bases. Both were slated to grow as surviving megaports for the Navy.

The rest of the state has not escaped the effects of the growth in Northern Virginia. The Washington exurbs, for example, spilled as far south as Fredericksburg—halfway between Washington and Richmond—and west to Manassas, which, with an 81 percent rise, had the largest percentage increase in population in Virginia in the 1980s. A new commuter rail line links Washington to those two cities.

The Old South can still be found in rural Virginia along the state's southern tier. There, tobacco is still king, and farmers grow peanuts and soybeans. In the southwest, the mining counties of the coal fields region more resemble West Virginia in prosperity and politics than Virginia. The poorest region of the state, the southwest has a strong union presence, an anomaly in right-to-work Virginia.

Virginia's new district lines were drawn during a lame-duck session of the General Assembly in November and December 1991. It was the last act of a dominant Democratic majority, as Democrats had lost significant ground in the state Senate in the 1991 legislative elections.

Legislators had two specific duties: to create a black-majority district, and to add a third Northern Virginia district to reflect the region's population surge. They accomplished both, and along the way, managed to pair two Republican House members in one district.

The process was not without hitches. The initial plan cleared by the General Assembly had some quirks that alternately inspired outrage or bemusal. The map divided the city of Richmond among three districts, angering Richmond-area legislators. Civil rights groups objected that the black population in the majority-black 3rd—61 percent—was insufficient to ensure the election of a black. The merging of two GOP-held districts infuriated Republicans.

Gov. Wilder sent the map back with some revisions aimed at soothing some of the aggrieved parties. The black population in the black-majority district—the new 3rd—increased to 64 percent. Richmond was divided between only two districts, the 3rd and the 7th. Wilder did nothing, however, to assuage upset Republicans. The General Assembly approved his revisions, and the Justice Department later precleared the plan. In April 1992, some marginal adjustments were made to the map.

The results of the 1992 elections largely followed the scheme of the Democratic legislators. In the 3rd, which collects urban blacks from Richmond southeast to Hampton Roads, and rural blacks in several counties north and east of Richmond, Democrat Robert C. Scott became the first black in 102 years to represent Virginia in Congress. The new, open district in Northern Virginia, the 11th, while competitive, was installed with a Democratic tilt. In 1992, after a raucous, bitter battle, the Democratic nominee prevailed. The new map also transformed the Northern Virginia 8th from a Republican suburban stronghold to a Democratic-leaning seat.

Although the new map sparked Republicans' anger, it was by no means all bad news for the GOP. The remaining three Republican members were given more Republican territory. All three won re-election by resounding margins in 1992. And creation of the 3rd removed blacks from the districts of two neighboring white districts—the 2nd and the 4th. These districts will become competitive territory should their Democratic incumbents choose to move on.

The 5th District gained some Democrats with the addition of the university town of Charlottesville. But the type of Democrat favored by those residents is entirely different from that favored by the conservative Democrats who predominate in the district.

The composition of the two westernmost districts—the 9th and the Shenandoah Valley 6th—remained largely unchanged. Voters in the 9th re-elected their Democratic incumbent in 1992. But that year in the open 6th, Republicans reclaimed a seat that had been theirs for 30 years until 1982.

Table 1 Population

District	Population	Population under 18	Voting-age population	Median age
1	562,677	143,943	418,734	32.6
2	562,276	143,045	419,231	28.2
3	562,431	148,030	414,401	31.0
4	562,466	147,464	415,002	32.9
5	562,268	129,076	433,192	34.8
6	562,572	124,652	437,920	34.9
7	562,643	137,761	424,882	33.7
8	562,484	108,951	453,533	33.7
9	562,380	128,410	433,970	34.1
10	562,664	150,842	411,822	32.3
11	562,497	142,564	419,933	31.9
State	6,187,358	1,504,738	4,682,620	32.6

Table 2 Voting-Age Persons

District	White*	Black*	American Indian, Eskimo, or Aleut*	Asian or Pacific Islander*	Other*	Hispanic*	Male*	Female*
1	81.2%	16.8%	0.3%	1.2%	0.4%	1.4%	48.4%	51.6%
2	79.6	15.5	0.4	3.5	1.0	3.0	53.1	46.9
3	36.8	61.2	0.4	1.1	0.5	1.2	45.5	54.5
4	67.7	30.7	0.3	1.1	0.3	1.0	48.2	51.8
5	76.3	22.9	0.1	0.6	0.1	0.5	47.5	52.5
6	88.5	10.6	0.1	0.5	0.2	0.6	46.8	53.2
7	88.7	9.4	0.2	1.5	0.2	0.9	47.0	53.0
8	77.7	12.5	0.3	6.1	3.3	8.0	49.0	51.0
9	96.6	2.4	0.1	0.8	0.1	0.5	47.8	52.2
10	91.1	5.6	0.2	2.5	0.6	2.1	49.5	50.5
11	82.0	7.5	0.3	7.7	2.5	7.0	49.0	51.0
State	78.9	17.6	0.2	2.4	0.9	2.4	48.4	51.6

*As percent of voting-age population.

Table 3 Voting-Age Persons by Age Groups

District	18-24*	25-44*	45-54*	55-64*	65 and over*
1	14.7%	44.7%	14.2%	11.2%	15.2%
2	22.9	48.9	10.5	8.1	9.6
3	17.0	43.3	12.4	11.3	16.0
4	13.5	45.1	14.3	11.5	15.6
5	15.1	39.2	14.3	12.7	18.6
6	15.9	39.2	13.8	12.3	18.7
7	12.3	48.3	14.2	10.5	14.6
8	13.1	51.3	14.5	9.4	11.7
9	17.5	38.5	14.4	12.2	17.4
10	12.8	50.5	16.7	9.8	10.3
11	14.3	52.1	16.5	9.1	8.0
State	15.4	45.5	14.2	10.7	14.2

*As percent of voting-age population.

Table 4 Income and Occupation

District	Median family income	Families in poverty	White collar*	Blue collar*	Service*	Farm*
1	$38,176	6.1%	58.3%	26.5%	12.7%	2.4%
2	36,172	5.7	64.2	21.2	13.6	1.0
3	26,538	18.5	48.8	30.6	19.1	1.5
4	34,630	8.9	52.4	31.9	13.3	2.4
5	29,727	10.4	44.3	40.4	11.9	3.4
6	32,541	7.8	53.2	30.5	13.6	2.7
7	45,357	3.5	68.6	21.0	8.9	1.5
8	58,582	3.3	77.4	11.2	10.8	0.5
9	25,166	14.7	44.5	40.1	12.5	2.9
10	51,076	3.3	65.0	22.2	10.2	2.6
11	59,989	2.5	75.8	12.9	10.7	0.6
State	38,213	7.7	60.4	25.4	12.3	1.9

*As percent of employed persons age 16 and over.

Table 5 Education: School Years Completed

District	Less than grade 9*	Grades 9-12 no diploma*	High school diploma*	College bachelor's degree or higher*
1	9.1%	13.6%	30.1%	21.1%
2	3.9	10.8	29.9	23.6
3	14.0	22.0	28.3	12.7

District	Less than grade 9*	Grades 9-12 no diploma*	High school diploma*	College bachelor's degree or higher*
4	13.5	17.2	30.9	14.1
5	19.9	19.4	29.0	13.3
6	14.2	15.9	30.8	16.7
7	7.0	11.1	25.4	30.5
8	4.6	6.8	17.3	48.0
9	24.5	18.0	27.9	11.7
10	8.2	10.6	25.8	30.3
11	3.9	5.7	19.0	44.3
State	11.2	13.7	26.6	24.5

*As percent of persons age 25 and over.

Table 6 Housing and Residential Patterns

District	Owner occupied	Renter occupied	Urban	Rural
1	70.3%	29.7%	56.0%	44.0%
2	57.0	43.0	99.4	0.6
3	50.7	49.3	89.5	10.5
4	71.2	28.8	63.2	36.8
5	72.0	28.0	32.7	67.3
6	68.1	31.9	66.0	34.0
7	70.4	29.6	73.4	26.6
8	54.8	45.2	99.7	0.3
9	73.9	26.1	28.7	71.3
10	74.2	25.8	56.4	43.6
11	67.6	32.4	98.3	1.7
State	66.3	33.7	69.4	30.6

1st District

East — Parts of Newport News and Hampton; Fredericksburg

The 1st swoops from its perch in the Hampton Roads area in southeastern Virginia to the Middle Peninsula and Northern Neck, wings north into the Washington exurbs in Stafford County, and pokes a beak into Richmond's northern suburbs. It also soars across the Chesapeake Bay to include Accomack and Northampton counties on Virginia's eastern shore, which adjoins Maryland.

Republicans perform well in the 1st. George Bush held Michael S. Dukakis to less than one-third of the vote here in 1988; Bill Clinton did only slightly better in 1992. The area within the 1st voted for the unsuccessful GOP nominees for governor in 1985 and 1989.

About 40 percent of the 1st's population is in the Peninsula area between Williamsburg and Hampton. The Newport News Shipbuilding and Drydock Co., the state's largest private employer, is not in the 1st—redistricting in 1991 moved it into the 3rd—but many of its 25,200 employees live in the 1st, entwining the econonic vitality of many district residents with the shipyard's. The shipyard lost the *Seawolf* submarine to Connecticut, but it has a backlog of contracts for aircraft carriers and submarines to last through the end of the decade; work on a new carrier, CVN 76, has been authorized to begin by 1995.

Colonial Virginia and its plantation economy were centered in the rural inland counties of the middle peninsula (bracketed by the York and Rappahannock rivers), the northern neck (between the Rappahannock and the Potomac) and along the bay. For generations, fishing, oystering and crabbing have sustained the economy of the counties along the bay. Corn, soybeans and wheat are important to the inland areas. Accomack County farmers raise chickens for processing in the many plants along the Delmarva (Delaware-Maryland-Virginia) peninsula. Virginia's wine country reaches into the northern neck and eastern shore.

Tourism is also important in "America's First District," as GOP Rep. Herbert Bateman calls it. Several sites recall Virginia's Colonial past, including Williamsburg, Jamestown and Yorktown. The plantation where George Washington was born is a national monument along the Potomac River in Westmoreland County, on the northern neck. Nearby is Stratford Hall, plantation home to four generations of Lees, and the birthplace of Robert E. Lee. In Fredericksburg, the National Park Service runs a visitors center and offers tours on the Civil War battle.

The city of Fredericksburg and Stafford County represent the southern extreme of the Washington exurbs; bedroom communities sprouted during the 1980s, when Stafford's population grew by more than 50 percent. The Virginia Railway Express began its Fredericksburg-to-Washington commuter rail link in July 1992. While Fredericksburg frequently supports Democrats, Stafford usually votes Republican.

Election Returns

	1st District	Democrat	Republican
1992	President*	81,826 (33.9%)	120,131 (49.8%)
	House	89,814 (38.7%)	133,537 (57.6%)
1989	Governor	69,132 (43.2%)	90,895 (56.8%)
1988	President	65,915 (32.2%)	136,375 (66.7%)

*Vote for Perot was 39,307 (16.3%).

Demographics

Population 562,677

Percent change from 1980 5.2%

Land area 3,298 square miles

Population per square mile 171

Counties, 1990 population

Accomack 31,703	Middlesex 8,653
Caroline 19,217	Newport News city (pt.) 88,530
Fredericksburg city 19,027	Northampton 13,061
Gloucester 30,131	Northumberland 10,524
Hampton city (pt.) 68,920	Poquoson 11,005
Hanover (pt.) 34,785	Spotsylvania city (pt.) 35,772
James City (pt.) 27,910	Stafford 61,236
King George 13,527	Westmoreland 15,480
Lancaster 10,896	Williamsburg city 11,530
Mathews 8,348	York 42,422

Cities, 1990 population (10,000 or more)

Fredericksburg 19,027	Poquoson 11,005
Hampton (pt.) 68,920	Williamsburg 11,530
Newport News (pt.) 88,530	

Race and Hispanic origin
White 80.0%
Black 17.9%
American Indian, Eskimo, or Aleut 0.3%

Asian or Pacific Islander   1.3%
Other   0.5%
Hispanic origin   1.6%

Ancestry
American	10.0%	Italian	3.5%
Dutch	2.0%	Polish	1.9%
English	21.1%	Scotch Irish	3.2%
French	3.6%	Scottish	3.1%
German	19.3%	Swedish	1.0%
Irish	14.6%		

Universities/colleges, 1990-1991 enrollment
Christopher Newport College, Newport News   4,861
College of William & Mary, Williamsburg   7,672
Eastern Shore Community College, Melfa   555
Mary Washington College, Fredericksburg   3,744
Randolph-Macon College, Ashland   1,139
Rappahannock Community College, Glenns   1,828

Newspapers, total circulation (in all districts)
Fredericksburg Free Lance-Star   42,033
Newport News Daily Press   102,829
Norfolk Virginian-Pilot/Ledger-Star   223,461
Potomac News Sunday News   26,605
Richmond Times-Dispatch   240,551
Washington Post   810,904

Commercial television stations, affiliations
ADI: Norfolk-Portsmouth-Newport News-Hampton (45%), Richmond (34%) and Washington, D.C. (21%)

Cable television systems, total subscribers
1st Commonwealth Communications; Gloucester   6,500
Cablevision/Fredericksburg; Stafford County   12,500
Continental Cablevision of Virginia; James City County   11,070
Continental Cablevision of Virginia; Wistar   110,030
Continental Cablevision of Virginia; York County   8,782
Newport News Cablevision; Newport News   46,000
Spotsylvania Cable TV; Spotsylvania   10,500
Warner Cable of Hampton; Hampton   41,321

Military installations, 1991
Langley Air Force Base, Hampton   10,086
Naval Surface Weapons Center, Dahlgren   4,631
Fort Monroe (Army), Hampton   3,974
Yorktown Naval Weapons Station, Yorktown   3,553
Fort A.P. Hill (Army), Bowling Green   340

Businesses and other major employers
Colonial Williamsburg Foundation Inc.; Williamsburg; historical recreation/hotels   3,500
NASA/Langley Research Center; Hampton; research services   2,800
Army & Air Force Exchange Services; Hampton; stores   2,500
Riverside Hospital Inc.; Newport News   1,843
Perdue Farms Inc.; Accomac; poultry products   1,800
Mary Washington Hospital Inc.; Fredericksburg   1,362
Canon Virginia Inc.; Newport News; office equipment   1,200
Anheuser-Busch Inc.; Williamsburg; brewery   1,200
Southland Corp.; Fredericksburg; warehousing   1,192
NASA; Chincoteague; space research/technology   1,056
Tyson Foods Inc./Holly Farms; Temperanceville; poultry products   1,050
College of William & Mary; Williamsburg   1,000

Eastern State Hospital; Williamsburg   1,000
County of Gloucester/School District; Gloucester   986
Siemens Corp./Siemens Automotive; Newport News; motor vehicle fuel systems   900
Hampton Training School for Nurses/Sentara Hampton General Hospital; Hampton   900
Williamsburg Pottery Factory; Lightfoot; pottery/furniture   825
Mary Immaculate Hospital Inc.; Newport News   680
Williamsburg Community Hospital; Williamsburg   650
City of Fredericksburg; Fredericksburg   550
County of Caroline; Bowling Green   535

2nd District
Parts of Norfolk and Virginia Beach

Venerable Norfolk and upstart Virginia Beach share billing in the tidewater-area 2nd, but it is Virginia Beach that overshadows its neighbor. With 50 percent growth during the 1980s, Virginia Beach blazed past Norfolk to become the most populous city in the commonwealth.

An influx of military families, business people and retirees has changed Virginia Beach's earlier identity as a summer tourist center. The sprawling city's retail and service trade has boomed, and some light industry has moved in as well. Only one congressional district in the country has more military retirees.

The port city of Norfolk's roots date to its settlement in 1682, and its strategic location has been valued ever since. The British destroyed most of the city in the Revolutionary War; it served as the Confederacy's main naval station in the Civil War; and it was a major naval training station in the two world wars. Lately, the unionized port city has been striving to polish its image. The builder of Baltimore's Inner Harbor renovated Norfolk's waterfront, creating a modestly successful area of offices and shops called "Waterside."

Defense is the main industry in the Hampton Roads area, and all four districts that touch the region that includes Hampton, Norfolk, Newport News and Virginia Beach depend on the massive concentration of naval installations, shipbuilders and shipping companies for economic stability. The Norfolk Naval Base is the largest in the world. Many residents of the 2nd work in the 3rd making ships and submarines at the Newport News Shipbuilding and Drydock, the largest private employer in Virginia. Norfolk's ship repair industry employs 30,000 people. The Hampton Roads harbor area ranks first in export tonnage among the nation's Atlantic ports; it is the biggest coal shipper in the world.

Redistricting moved more than 60 percent of Norfolk's black population to the new, majority-black 3rd. Still, the 2nd retains some Democratic leanings. Democrats running for Virginia statewide office can carry the 2nd, if sometimes narrowly. Democrat L. Douglas Wilder won 50 percent here in his 1989 gubernatorial race; the rest of the ticket fared better. But in presidential contests, the GOP nominee is secure. George Bush had no trouble carrying the 2nd in 1988 and 1992.

Virginia Beach is one of the state's prime strongholds of conservatism. It is home to the religious broadcasting empire of Pat Robertson, who sought the GOP nomination for president in 1988. But Robertson does not enjoy universal support among the 2nd's Republicans. In Virginia's 1988 GOP presidential primary, he placed a distant third in Virginia Beach behind Bush and Kansas Sen. Bob Dole.

Election Returns

	2nd District	Democrat	Republican
1992	President*	62,946 (35.1%)	85,773 (47.8%)
	House	99,253 (56.1%)	77,797 (43.9%)
1989	Governor	57,328 (49.0%)	59,290 (50.7%)
1988	President	50,156 (32.9%)	101,073 (66.4%)

*Vote for Perot was 30,587 (17.1%).

Demographics

Population 562,276

Percent change from 1980 6.3%

Land area 284 square miles

Population per square mile 1,982

Counties, 1990 population
Norfolk city (pt.) 179,148
Virginia Beach city (pt.) 383,128

Cities, 1990 population (10,000 or more)
Norfolk (pt.) 179,148
Virginia Beach (pt.) 383,128

Race and Hispanic origin
White 78.1%
Black 16.6%
American Indian, Eskimo, or Aleut. 0.4%
Asian or Pacific Islander 3.8%
Other 1.1%
Hispanic origin 3.3%

Ancestry
American 6.1%	Irish 16.5%
Dutch 2.0%	Italian 5.5%
English 16.5%	Polish 2.7%
French 4.3%	Scotch Irish 3.0%
French Canadian 1.2%	Scottish 3.1%
German 21.4%	Swedish 1.2%

Universities/colleges, 1990-1991 enrollment
Commonwealth College, Virginia Beach 722
ECPI Computer Institute, Virginia Beach 614
Old Dominion University, Norfolk 16,729
Virginia Wesleyan College, Norfolk 1,390

Newspapers, total circulation (in all districts)
Norfolk Virginian-Pilot/Ledger-Star 223,461

Commercial television stations, affiliations
ADI: Norfolk-Portsmouth-Newport News-Hampton (100%)

Cable television systems, total subscribers
Cox Cable of Hampton Road; Virginia Beach 182,487

Military installations, 1991
Norfolk Naval Station, Norfolk 65,618
Norfolk Naval Air Station, Norfolk 16,143
Little Creek Naval Amphibious Base, Norfolk 13,293
Oceana Naval Air Station, Virginia Beach 10,915
Atlantic Fleet Combat Training Center, Virginia Beach 5,577
Norfolk Naval Aviation Depot, Norfolk 4,398
Fort Story (Army), Virginia Beach 1,880

Atlantic Naval Communications Area Master Station, Norfolk 460

Businesses and other major employers
City of Virginia Beach; Virginia Beach 5,051
De Paul Medical Center; Norfolk 1,800
Virginia Beach General Hospital; Virginia Beach 1,392
Lillian Vernon Corp.; Virginia Beach; catalog retailers 700
Beverly Enterprises Inc./Beverly California Corp.; Virginia Beach; computer services 584
City of Virginia Beach/Police Dept.; Virginia Beach 582

3rd District
Southeast — Parts of Richmond and Tidewater Area

The capital city of Richmond, long the center of Virginia's government and commerce, is probably best known outside the Old Dominion as the capital of the Confederacy. But in the 1990s, Richmond is the largest component of the majority-black 3rd, which is the commonwealth's first district to elect a black representative in more than 100 years. More than one-fourth of the 3rd's population lives in Richmond.

Most of the area that was represented by John Mercer Langston, the only other black representative in Virginia's history, now lies in the 4th. A dispute over Langston's election in 1888 delayed his seating; his victory was not ratified by the full House until September 1890, and less than two months later he was defeated for re-election.

The 3rd takes in the eastern side of Richmond, including the state Capitol, and stretches southeast along the James River to west Norfolk, and northeast to the Rappahannock River and Richmond County. In addition to Richmond and Norfolk, it includes predominantly black sections of the cities of Newport News, Portsmouth, Petersburg and Hopewell, plus part of the city of Suffolk.

Nearly half of the 3rd's population is in the southernmost part extending from James City County to Norfolk. But almost as many people live in the westernmost portion that makes up Richmond, Henrico and Charles City counties and the cities of Petersburg and Hopewell.

This is by far the most heavily Democratic district in Virginia. Bill Clinton won 66 percent of the vote here in the 1992 presidential race. Four years earlier, the areas that make up the 3rd backed Democratic nominee Michael S. Dukakis, who lost badly in most other parts of Virginia. Democratic gubernatorial nominees Gerald L. Baliles in 1985 and L. Douglas Wilder in 1989 each received 75 percent of the vote in the areas within the 3rd.

State government is a major component driving the economy of Richmond and vicinity, but the city is also a manufacturing center; Richmond still boasts one of the largest cigarette plants in the country, Phillip Morris' huge facility along Interstate 95.

The Hampton Roads portion of the 3rd depends in large part on defense. The state's largest private employer, the Newport News Shipbuilding and Drydock Co., is in the 3rd, with 25,200 employees building Navy carriers and submarines. The Hampton Roads area has a heavy concentration of naval installations as well as shipbuilding and ship repair companies.

The eastern counties—New Kent, King William, King and Queen, Essex and Richmond—are mainly rural and sparsely populated. Those counties and Charles City County were in the 1st District in the 1980s.

Election Returns

	3rd District	Democrat	Republican
1992	President*	124,857 (65.5%)	48,843 (25.6%)
	House	132,432 (78.7%)	35,780 (21.3%)
1989	Governor	125,579 (75.1%)	41,476 (24.8%)
1988	President	121,426 (62.0%)	72,019 (36.8%)

Vote for Perot was 16,779 (8.8%).

Demographics

Population 562,431

Percent change from 1980 5.4%

Land area 1,957 square miles

Population per square mile 287

Counties, 1990 population

Charles City 6,282	Norfolk (pt.) 82,081
Essex 8,689	Petersburg city (pt.) 24,756
Hampton city (pt.) 64,873	Portsmouth city (pt.)
Henrico (pt.) 54,274	38,871
Hopewell city (pt.) 3,652	Prince George (pt.) 1,877
James City (pt.) 6,949	Richmond 7,273
King William 10,913	Richmond city (pt.)
King and Queen 6,289	144,545
New Kent 10,445	Suffolk city (pt.) 3,002
Newport News city (pt.)	Surry 6,145
81,515	

Cities, 1990 population (10,000 or more)

East Highland Park CDP	Norfolk (pt.) 82,081
(pt.) 10,365	Petersburg (pt.) 24,756
Hampton (pt.) 64,873	Portsmouth (pt.) 38,871
Newport News (pt.) 81,515	Richmond (pt.) 144,545

Race and Hispanic origin

White 33.9%
Black 64.1%
American Indian, Eskimo, or Aleut. 0.4%
Asian or Pacific Islander 1.1%
Other 0.5%
Hispanic origin 1.4%

Ancestry

American 6.3%	Irish 6.2%
English 7.6%	Italian 1.3%
French 1.3%	Scotch Irish 1.4%
German 7.7%	Scottish 1.1%

Universities/colleges, 1990-1991 enrollment

Commonwealth College, Norfolk 576
Commonwealth College, Hampton 460
Eastern Virginia Medical School, Norfolk 483
ECPI Computer Institute, Hampton 246
Hampton University, Hampton 5,305
Norfolk State University, Norfolk 8,008
Thomas Nelson Community College, Hampton 7,740
Virginia Commonwealth University, Richmond 21,764
Virginia State University, Petersburg 3,988
Virginia Union University, Richmond 1,298

Newspapers, total circulation (in all districts)

Hopewell News 6,657
Newport News Daily Press 102,829
Norfolk Virginian-Pilot/Ledger-Star 223,461
Petersburg Progress-Index 20,739
Richmond Times-Dispatch 240,551
Washington Post 810,904

Commercial television stations, affiliations

ADI: Richmond (77%) and Norfolk-Portsmouth-Newport
News-Hampton (23%)
WZXK, Ashland (None)
WWBT, Richmond (NBC)

Cable television systems, total subscribers

Continental Cablevision of Virginia; Wistar 110,030
Cox Cable of Hampton Roads; Virginia Beach 182,487
Newport News Cablevision; Newport News 46,000
Warner Cable of Hampton; Hampton 41,321

Military installations, 1991

Fort Eustis (Army), Newport News 10,246
Portsmouth Naval Hospital, Portsmouth 4,342

Businesses and other major employers

Newport News Shipbuilding & Drydock Co.; Newport News;
shipbuilding/repairing 25,200
Virginia Commonwealth University; Richmond 10,000
City of Richmond; Richmond 8,000
City of Newport News; Newport News 5,600
City of Norfolk; Norfolk 4,600
Philip Morris Inc./Phillip Morris USA; Richmond; tobacco
products 5,000
U.S. Postal Service; Norfolk 3,600
Chesapeake Potomac Telephone Co.; Richmond; telephone
communications 3,600
Commonwealth of Virginia/Health Dept.; Richmond 3,600
Norfolk Shipbuilding & Drydock Corp.; Norfolk;
shipbuilding/repairing 2,600
NationsBank of Virginia; Norfolk; commercial banks 2,500
Sentara Hospitals-Norfolk General Hospital; Norfolk 2,500
U.S. Veterans Affairs Dept.; Richmond; hospital 2,285
Thalhimer Brothers Inc.; Richmond; department stores 2,100
NationsBank of Virginia; Richmond; commercial banks
2,100
Allied-Signal Inc./Allied Fibers; Hopewell;
plastics/synthetics 1,800
Media General Inc.; Richmond; newspapers 1,750
U.S. Postal Service; Richmond 1,600
Southside Regional Medical Center; Petersburg 1,510
Landmark Communications Inc.; Norfolk; periodicals 1,500
Virginia Electric & Power Co.; Richmond; electric services
1,500
Chippenham Hospital Inc.; Richmond 1,480
Ford Motor Co.; Norfolk; motor vehicle assembly 1,400
Richmond Memorial Hospital; Richmond 1,250
Howmet Corp./Casting Div.; Hampton; iron/steel foundries
1,200
Norfolk State University; Norfolk 1,200
Children's Health System Inc.; Norfolk 1,200
Eastern Virginia Medical School; Norfolk 1,200
New Hampton Inc./James River Traders; Hampton; catalog
retailers 1,100
Virginia State University; Petersburg 1,100
Federal Reserve Bank of Richmond; Richmond 1,047
W. F. S. Financial Corp.; Richmond; security brokers 1,037

A. H. Robins Co. Inc.; Richmond; pharmaceuticals 1,000

American Home Products Corp./Whitehall & Robins Div.; Richmond; pharmaceuticals 1,000

New Hampton Inc./Avon Fashions Brights Creek; Newport News; catalog retailers 1,000

Crestar Financial Corp.; Richmond; commercial banks 1,000

Virginia Electric & Power Co./Surry Power Station; Surry; electric services 931

Kings Daughters Children's Hospital; Norfolk 856

Central Fidelity Bank; Richmond; commercial banks 850

Hampton University; Hampton 850

CSX Transportation Inc.; Newport News; railroads 800

General Foam Plastics Corp./Genalite Div.; Norfolk; plastics products 750

Reynolds Metals Co./Richmond Foil Plant; Richmond; aluminum products 750

Metro Machine Corp.; Norfolk; shipbuilding/repairing 710

Allied-Signal Inc./Fibers Div.; Petersburg; plastics/synthetics 700

ICI Americas Inc./Hopewell Works; Hopewell; chemical products 700

James River Corp. Virginia; Richmond; paper mills 700

Westvaco Corp./Folding Box Div.; Richmond; paperboard products 680

Daily Press Inc.; Newport News; newspapers 650

Brenco Inc.; Petersburg; industry machinery 650

Overnite Transportation Co.; Richmond; trucking services 650

Sterile Concepts Inc.; Richmond; rubber products 633

Aqualon Co.; Hopewell; chemical products 610

City of Hampton/Public Library; Hampton 581

Commonwealth of Virginia/Powhatan Correctional Center; Richmond 550

Brown & Root USA Inc.; Richmond; road construction 521

McGuire Woods Battle & Boothe; Richmond; legal services 510

Hunton & Williams; Richmond; legal services 505

4th District

Southeast — Chesapeake; Part of Portsmouth

Like the neighboring 1st, 2nd and 3rd districts, the 4th has a piece of the Hampton Roads area in southeastern Virginia, and thus its economy is powered in great measure by the vast industry linked to the region's huge military presence. Almost half the district's population is in Chesapeake, Portsmouth, Suffolk and Virginia Beach.

The industrial city of Chesapeake anchors the southeastern end of the 4th. Home to thousands of Hampton Roads shipyard and factory workers, Chesapeake has been booming; its population grew by 33 percent in the 1980s. Chesapeake is a district headquarters for the Coast Guard, whose finance center is in Chesapeake. The Norfolk Naval Shipyard, in the portion of Portsmouth in the 4th, employs 15,900 people.

The district's military component goes beyond Hampton Roads. Fort Lee, in Petersburg, and Fort Pickett, near Blackstone, are primarily used for training troops. Although it is home to the Defense Commissary Agency headquarters, Fort Lee in mid-1993 was on a list of 78 facilities facing possible closure.

The 4th is typical of many conservative Democratic districts in the South, supporting certain Democrats for state and some

federal offices—but demonstrating a strong preference for Republican presidential nominees. George Bush held Democrats Michael S. Dukakis and Bill Clinton to scores of 44 percent of the vote in 1988 and 40 percent in 1992, respectively.

Agriculture is also important to the district's economy. Peanuts and tobacco are the important crops in the rural southside counties along the North Carolina border. Democratic ties are still strong here, particularly in a swath that stretches from Suffolk to Brunswick County. Southampton is one of the nation's top peanut-harvesting counties.

There is some industry in the smaller cities of the 4th. Hopewell calls itself the chemical capital of the South. Suffolk processes peanuts. Petersburg makes tobacco products. Smithfield, in Isle of Wight County, is eponymous with Virginia ham and pork products. Isle of Wight lost about 1,000 blacks during the 1980s, while its white population grew by 4,300.

The 4th also has a stake in the service sector. The QVC Network, a shop-at-home national television channel, employs more than 1,500 phone operators at its Chesapeake facility, and it has a large distribution warehouse in Suffolk. Wal-Mart has a regional distribution center in Dinwiddie County.

The northern part of the district has also been experiencing population expansion. Louisa, Goochland and Powhatan counties all had double-digit growth in the 1980s, owing to the westward expansion of Richmond's suburbs. Louisa County also has been drawing retirees and second-home buyers from Charlottesville and the Washington area. The district's only nuclear power plant, North Anna, is in Louisa.

Election Returns

	4th District	Democrat	Republican
1992	President*	90,641 (39.7%)	106,392 (46.6%)
	House	147,649 (68.4%)	68,286 (31.6%)
1989	Governor	87,371 (47.6%)	96,039 (52.3%)
1988	President	80,277 (39.4%)	121,409 (59.7%)

*Vote for Perot was 31,467 (13.8%).

Demographics

Population 562,466

Percent change from 1980 5.0%

Land area 5,656 square miles

Population per square mile 99

Counties, 1990 population

Amelia 8,787	Louisa 20,325
Brunswick 15,987	Nottoway 14,993
Chesapeake city 151,976	Petersburg city (pt.) 13,630
Chesterfield (pt.) 26,297	Portsmouth city (pt.) 65,036
Colonial Heights city 16,064	Powhatan 15,328
Dinwiddie 20,960	Prince George (pt.) 25,517
Emporia city 5,306	Southampton 17,550
Franklin city 7,864	Suffolk city (pt.) 49,139
Goochland 14,163	Sussex 10,248
Greensville 8,853	Virginia Beach city (pt.) 9,941
Hopewell city (pt.) 19,449	
Isle of Wight 25,053	

Cities, 1990 population (10,000 or more)

Chesapeake 151,976	Petersburg (pt.) 13,630
Colonial Heights 16,064	Portsmouth (pt.) 65,036
Hopewell (pt.) 19,449	Suffolk (pt.) 49,139

Race and Hispanic origin

White 66.2%
Black 32.1%
American Indian, Eskimo, or Aleut. 0.2%
Asian or Pacific Islander 1.1%
Other 0.3%
Hispanic origin 1.1%

Ancestry

American 12.4%	Irish 11.4%
Dutch 1.4%	Italian 2.2%
English 15.8%	Polish 1.4%
French 2.5%	Scotch Irish 2.6%
German 12.9%	Scottish 1.8%

Universities/colleges, 1990-1991 enrollment

Paul D. Camp Community College, Franklin 1,441
Richard Bland College-William & Mary, Petersburg 1,205
Regent University, Virginia Beach 715
St. Paul's College, Lawrenceville 574
Southside Virginia Community College, Alberta 2,922
Tidewater Community College, Portsmouth 17,726

Newspapers, total circulation (in all districts)

Hopewell News 6,657
Newport News Daily Press 102,829
Norfolk Virginian-Pilot/Ledger-Star 223,461
Petersburg Progress-Index 20,739
Richmond Times-Dispatch 240,551

Commercial television stations, affiliations

ADI: Richmond (70%) and Norfolk-Portsmouth-Newport
  News-Hampton (30%)
  WVEC-TV, Hampton (ABC)
  WJCB, Norfolk (None)
  WTKR-TV, Norfolk (CBS)
  WTVZ, Norfolk (Fox)
  WAVY-TV, Portsmouth (NBC)
  WGNT, Portsmouth (None)

Cable television systems, total subscribers

Continental Cablevision of Virginia; Wistar 110,030
Cox Cable of Hampton Road; Virginia Beach 182,487
Falcon Cable TV; Suffolk 7,500
Sammons Communications of Virginia Inc.; Prince George
  County 14,583
Storer Cable TV Inc.; Chesterfield County 50,000
TCI of Virginia; Chesapeake 32,711
Tele-Media Co.; Prince George 9,382

Military installations, 1991

Norfolk Naval Shipyard, Portsmouth 15,902
Fort Lee (Army), Petersburg 12,516
Naval Security Group Activity, Chesapeake 1,486
Fort Pickett (Army), Blackstone 576

Businesses and other major employers

Smithfield Foods Inc.; Smithfield; meatpacking 3,000
County of Chesterfield; Chesterfield 2,164
Southside Virginia Training Center; Petersburg; residential
  care 1,700

Commonwealth of Virginia/Mental Health Dept.; Petersburg;
  job training 1,650
QVC Network Inc.; Chesapeake; TV network retailers 1,500
Commonwealth of Virginia/Transportation Dept.; Suffolk
  1,500
City of Petersburg/Social Services; Petersburg 1,500
Bon Secour-Maryview Health Corp.; Portsmouth 1,424
Chesapeake General Hospital; Chesapeake 1,400
City of Suffolk; Suffolk 1,140
Commonwealth of Virginia/Greensville Correctional Center;
  Jarratt 1,000
Louise Obici Memorial Hospital; Suffolk 990
World Book Inc./World Book-Childcraft; Chesapeake;
  books 963
Portsmouth General Hospital; Portsmouth 910
Planters Lifesavers Co.; Suffolk; candies 800
Union Camp Corp./Fine Paper Div.; Franklin; paper mills
  755
ICI Americas Inc.; Chester; plastics products 750
Perdue Farms Inc.; Emporia; poultry products 600
Philip Morris Inc./Park 500; Chester; tobacco products 600
County of Isle of Wight/School District; Isle of Wight 600
County of Prince George/School District; Prince George 580
QVC Network Inc.; Suffolk; cable TV services 574
Virginia Electric & Power Co./North Anna Nuclear Power
  Station; Mineral; electric services 535
Tidewater Community College; Portsmouth 523
Hopewell Hospital Authority/John Randolph Hospital; Hope-
  well 508

5th District

South — Danville; Charlottesville

Virginia's leading cash crop is tobacco, and the 5th is in the heart of tobacco country. Agriculture and textiles are the main industries in the 5th, which is in Virginia's rural southside, a region of farms, small towns and isolated factory cities along the state's southern tier that resembles the Deep South more closely than any other part of the state does. It is relatively poor and has a substantial black population. Tobacco and soybeans are major crops, but this region lacks the rich soil of the tidewater region.

Charlottesville, home to the University of Virginia and its 21,100 students, is new to the 5th for the 1990s. It is an incongruity: an upscale, liberal enclave in an otherwise conservative, rural district. Charlottesville was the only jurisdiction in the 5th to vote Democratic in the 1988 presidential race, giving Michael S. Dukakis 56 percent of the vote. Bill Clinton did even better in 1992, despite competing against two major candidates; he captured 58 percent in Charlottesville.

Democrat Lewis Payne established a grip on the 5th after his first election to the House in 1988, but the district has long refused to swallow more liberal Democratic candidates at the state and national levels. Barry Goldwater won many of the 5th's counties in 1964, as did George C. Wallace in 1968. George Bush carried the 5th by more than 20 percentage points in 1988.

But certain Democrats can make inroads in the 5th. Districtwide in 1992, Bush beat Clinton by only 6 percentage points. Former Attorney General Mary Sue Terry, a politically centrist Democrat, received 64 percent of the vote in her 1989 reelection campaign.

The district's two most famous landmarks are Thomas

Jefferson's home, Monticello, just south of Charlottesville, and Appomattox Court House, where Robert E. Lee surrendered to Ulysses S. Grant to end the Civil War.

About 60 miles south of Appomattox is the district's largest city, Danville, a tobacco and textile center on the North Carolina border. Alone among counties and independent cities along the southern tier, Danville saw its population rise during the 1980s. The textile industry employs an estimated 45,000 people in the district. The largest company, Dan River, employs about 4,500 at its Danville plant.

Just to the west is Henry County, which surrounds the textile and furniture town of Martinsville. Henry is the most populous county in the district, and outside of Charlottesville, it is the best area in the 5th for Democrats. Clinton carried Henry and Martinsville.

The rest of the people are scattered through farming areas and a few factory towns.

Campbell and Bedford counties originally were Lynchburg bedroom communities, but both engaged in aggressive economic recruitment in the 1980s and succeeded in attracting numerous small businesses. Bedford's population grew by more than 30 percent in the 1980s.

Election Returns

	5th District	Democrat	Republican
1992	President*	90,769 (40.9%)	104,236 (47.0%)
	House	133,031 (68.9%)	60,030 (31.1%)
1989	Governor	76,374 (44.3%)	95,811 (55.6%)
1988	President	78,326 (38.7%)	120,850 (59.7%)

Vote for Perot was 26,978 (12.2%).

Demographics

Population 562,268

Percent change from 1980 5.8%

Land area 8,826 square miles

Population per square mile 64

Counties, 1990 population

Albemarle city (pt.) 32,102	Franklin 39,549
Appomattox 12,298	Halifax 29,033
Bedford (pt.) 33,442	Henry 56,942
Bedford city 6,073	Lunenburg 11,419
Buckingham 12,873	Martinsville city 16,162
Campbell 47,572	Mecklenburg 29,241
Charlotte 11,688	Nelson 12,778
Charlottesville city 40,341	Patrick 17,473
Cumberland 7,825	Pittsylvania 55,655
Danville city 53,056	Prince Edward 17,320
Fluvanna 12,429	South Boston city 6,997

Cities, 1990 population (10,000 or more)

Charlottesville 40,341	Martinsville 16,162
Danville 53,056	Timberlake CDP 10,314

Race and Hispanic origin

White 74.4%
Black 24.8%
American Indian, Eskimo, or Aleut. 0.1%
Asian or Pacific Islander 0.6%
Other 0.2%
Hispanic origin 0.6%

Ancestry

American 15.9%	Irish 11.9%
Dutch 1.6%	Italian 1.4%
English 15.9%	Scotch Irish 3.0%
French 2.0%	Scottish 2.0%
German 12.6%	

Universities/colleges, 1990-1991 enrollment

Averett College, Danville 1,446
Danville Community College, Danville 3,321
Ferrum College, Ferrum 1,208
Hampden-Sydney College, Hampden-Sydney 956
Longwood College, Farmville 3,329
Patrick Henry Community College, Martinsville 2,223
Piedmont Virginia Community College, Charlottesville 4,203
University of Virginia, Charlottesville 21,110

Newspapers, total circulation (in all districts)

Charlottesville Progress 31,926
Danville Register & Bee 23,240
Lynchburg News & Advance 39,710
Martinsville Bulletin 18,395
Richmond Times-Dispatch 240,551
Roanoke Times/World News 114,067
Washington Post 810,904

Commercial television stations, affiliations

ADI: Roanoke-Lynchburg (55%), Richmond (27%), Raleigh-Durham (8%), Greensboro-Winston-Salem-High Point (5%) and Charlottesville (5%)
WVIR-TV, Charlottesville (NBC)
WJPR, Lynchburg (Fox)
WSET-TV, Lynchburg (ABC)

Cable television systems, total subscribers

Adelphia Cable; Charlottesville 24,000
Adelphia Cable; Martinsville 17,737
CVI; Danville 24,512
Campbell CATV Inc.; Lynchburg 8,600
Lynchburg Cablevision; Lynchburg 19,500

Businesses and other major employers

University of Virginia; Charlottesville 9,857
Dan River Inc.; Danville; cotton mills 4,500
University of Virginia Medical Center; Charlottesville 4,000
Goodyear Tire & Rubber Co.; Danville; tires 2,170
Du Pont E. I. De Nemours & Co.; Martinsville; plastics 2,000
Bassett-Walker Inc.; Martinsville; knitting mills 1,800
County of Campbell; Rustburg 1,800
Lane Co. Inc.; Altavista; wooden furniture 1,500
Burlington Industries Inc./Klopman Fabrics; Altavista; cotton mills 1,397
Burlington Industries Inc./Menswear Div.; Clarksville; wool mills 1,300
City of Charlottesville; Charlottesville 1,300
Memorial Hospital of Danville; Danville 1,300
Zachry Inc.; Clover; building construction 1,200
Stanley Interiors Corp.; Stanleytown; wooden furniture 1,200
County of Henry; Collinsville 1,200
ConAgra Inc./ConAgra Frozen Foods; Crozet; preserved fruits/vegetables 1,100

General Electric Co.; Charlottesville; electronic components 1,100

Thomasville Furniture Industries/Armstrong Furniture Div.; Appomattox; furniture 1,050

Fieldcrest Cannon Inc.; Fieldale; towels 1,000

Bassett-Walker Inc.; Bassett; knitting mills 1,000

Comdial Bus Communications Corp.; Charlottesville; communications equipment 981

City of Danville/School District; Danville 965

State Farm Life Insurance Co.; Charlottesville; insurance services 950

Martha Jefferson Hospital; Charlottesville 943

Rubatex Corp.; Bedford; rubber products 900

Tultex Corp.; South Boston; knitting mills 834

Burlington Industries Inc.; Halifax; wool mills 800

American Furniture Co. Inc.; Martinsville; wooden furniture 800

M. W. Manufacturers Inc.; Rocky Mount; millwork 800

City of Martinsville; Martinsville 800

BGF Industries Inc.; Altavista; man-made fabric mills 750

Memorial Hospital of Martinsville; Martinsville 750

ABB Power T&D Co. Inc./Asea Brown Boveri Inc.; South Boston; electrical industrial apparatus 700

Health-Tex Inc.; Danville; children's apparel 700

Abbott Laboratories/Ross Laboratories Div.; Altavista; pharmaceuticals 700

County of Franklin/Public Schools; Rocky Mount 700

J. P. Stevens & Co. Inc.; Drakes Branch; wool mills 685

Hooker Furniture Corp.; Martinsville; wooden furniture 650

City of Charlottesville/School District; Charlottesville 650

Bassett-Walker Inc.; Brookneal; knitting mills 620

Dibrell Brothers Inc.; Danville; tobacco production 600

United Elastic Corp.; Stuart; fabric mills 600

Lane Co. Inc.; Rocky Mount; wooden furniture 600

Halifax-South Boston Community Hospital; South Boston 590

JPS Converter & Industrial Corp.; South Boston; textile finishing 582

Russell Stover Candies Inc.; Clarksville; candies 550

Longwood College; Farmville 512

6th District

West — Roanoke; Lynchburg

The 6th is home to mountains and caverns, dairy farmers and cattle ranchers, isolated towns and large cities—and quite a few Republicans.

The Shenandoah Valley, which runs most of the length of the 6th, cultivated Republicanism long before it was acceptable in other parts of Virginia. The descendants of the area's 18th-century English, German and Scotch-Irish settlers feuded with the tidewater plantation aristocracy and became GOP mavericks in state politics.

The brand of Republicanism in the rural valley traditionally has been a moderate one; when Virginia's conservative Democrats were identified with resistance to integration in the 1960s, Valley Republicans were progressive on racial issues. The GOP lost its grip on the 6th in the 1980s partly because the state party came to be dominated by staunchly conservative suburbanites outside Washington and Richmond, and by party-switching conservative Democrats. In 1985, when there was no moderate

on the Republican ticket, the Democrats running for the three top state offices all carried the 6th. In 1989, the 6th did vote Republican for governor (against black Democrat L. Douglas Wilder), but the Democratic nominees for lieutenant governor and attorney general won the 6th. Republican Robert W. Goodlatte's 1992 victory ended Democrats' decade-long control of the 6th District House seat.

Roanoke, the major population center in the 6th, has an array of industries producing furniture and electrical products. Its sizable black and union elements make it the base of Democratic strength in the 6th. Bill Clinton won Roanoke by 12 points in 1992. In 1989, Wilder won the city with 59 percent. Democrats also can succeed in towns to the north, such as Covington and Clifton Forge, and in the counties around them, Bath and Alleghany. In his 1985 bid for lieutenant governor, Wilder won these cities but lost the counties. Clinton carried all but Bath. There are chemical plants and pulpwood and paper mills in this area, but the job picture is cloudy. Unemployment in December 1992 was 22 percent in Bath County.

Democratic support in the city of Roanoke is usually surpassed by the Republican vote in Roanoke's suburbs, in Lynchburg and in most of the district's rural areas. The nuclear energy company Babcock & Wilcox is one of Lynchburg's major employers, but the city is best known as the home of evangelist Jerry Falwell, his huge Thomas Road Baptist Church and Falwell-founded Liberty University (18,500 students). Goodlatte won 59 percent in Lynchburg in 1992.

Outside metropolitan Roanoke and Lynchburg, the district depends mainly on dairy farming, livestock and poultry. Rockingham County ranks third in the country in turkeys sold. Tourism enhances the local economy, with visitors traveling to Shenandoah National Park, George Washington National Forest and numerous caverns that dot the valley. Staunton boasts two museums of local notables: One is the house where Woodrow Wilson was born; the other celebrates The Statler Brothers, a country music group.

Election Returns

	6th District	Democrat	Republican
1992	President*	84,037 (37.4%)	111,405 (49.6%)
	House	84,618 (39.9%)	127,309 (60.1%)
1989	Governor	77,297 (45.9%)	90,818 (54.0%)
1988	President	74,803 (37.5%)	122,209 (61.3%)

*Vote for Perot was 29,207 (13.0%).

Demographics

Population 562,572

Percent change from 1980 4.5%

Land area 5,197 square miles

Population per square mile 108

Counties, 1990 population

Alleghany 13,176	Botetourt 24,992
Amherst 28,578	Buena Vista city 6,406
Augusta 54,677	Clifton Forge city 4,679
Bath 4,799	Covington city 6,991
Bedford (pt.) 12,214	Harrisonburg city 30,707

Highland 2,635
Lexington city 6,959
Lynchburg city 66,049
Roanoke (pt.) 67,349
Roanoke city 96,397

Rockbridge 18,350
Rockingham (pt.) 50,848
Salem city 23,756
Staunton city 24,461
Waynesboro city 18,549

Cities, 1990 population (10,000 or more)
Cave Spring CDP 24,053
Harrisonburg 30,707
Hollins CDP 13,305
Lynchburg 66,049
Madison Heights CDP 11,700

Roanoke 96,397
Salem 23,756
Staunton 24,461
Waynesboro 18,549

Race and Hispanic origin
White 87.6%
Black 11.5%
American Indian, Eskimo, or Aleut. 0.1%
Asian or Pacific Islander 0.6%
Other 0.2%
Hispanic origin 0.7%

Ancestry
American 12.2%
Dutch 2.4%
English 16.7%
French 2.5%
German 25.2%

Irish 14.1%
Italian 2.1%
Scotch Irish 4.9%
Scottish 2.5%

Universities/colleges, 1990-1991 enrollment
Blue Ridge Community College, Weyers Cave 2,740
Bridgewater College, Bridgewater 1,001
Central Virginia Community College, Lynchburg 3,913
Dabney S. Lancaster Community College, Clifton Forge 1,606
Eastern Mennonite College, Harrisonburg 1,089
ECPI Computer Institute, Roanoke 206
Hollins College, Roanoke 1,137
James Madison University, Harrisonburg 11,251
Liberty Baptist University, Lynchburg 18,533
Lynchburg College, Lynchburg 2,446
Mary Baldwin College, Staunton 1,157
National Business College, Salem 1,264
Randolph-Macon Woman's College, Lynchburg 691
Roanoke College, Salem 1,668
Southern Seminary College, Buena Vista 257
Sweet Briar College, Sweet Briar 538
Virginia Military Institute, Lexington 1,350
Virginia Western Community College, Roanoke 6,975
Washington & Lee University, Lexington 2,010

Newspapers, total circulation (in all districts)
Covington Virginian Review 8,310
Harrisonburg Daily News Record 30,008
Lynchburg News & Advance 39,710
Richmond Times-Dispatch 240,551
Roanoke Times/World News 114,067
Staunton Daily News Leader 18,107
Washington Post 810,904
Waynesboro News/Virginian 10,502

Commercial television stations, affiliations
ADI: Roanoke-Lynchburg (65%) and Harrisonburg (34%)

Cable television systems, total subscribers
Adelphia Cable; Staunton 11,200

Cox Cable Roanoke; Roanoke 48,750
Salem Cable TV Co.; Salem 10,490
Sammons Communications of Virginia Inc.; Alleghany County 7,200
Warner Cable; Harrisonburg 14,610

Businesses and other major employers
Roanoke Memorial Hospitals; Roanoke 2,600
Babcock & Wilcox Co./Naval Nuclear Fuel Div.; Lynchburg; nuclear fuels 2,500
Sears Roebuck & Co.; Roanoke; department stores 2,500
Commonwealth of Virginia/Central Virginia Training Center; Madison Heights 2,500
Du Pont E. I. De Nemours & Co.; Waynesboro; yarn/thread mills 2,040
General Electric Co./Drive Systems Operations; Salem; industrial controls 2,000
Genicom Corp.; Waynesboro; waste treatment 2,000
Ericsson GE Mobile Communications; Lynchburg; communications equipment 1,760
Westvaco Corp./Bleached Board Div.; Covington; paperboard mills 1,750
Tyson Foods Inc.; Harrisonburg; poultry products 1,500
Burlington Industries Inc./Lee's Commercial Carpet Co.; Glasgow; carpets/rugs 1,400
James Madison University; Harrisonburg 1,400
U.S. Veterans Affairs Dept.; Salem; hospital 1,370
Rockingham Memorial Hospital; Harrisonburg 1,350
ITT Corp./Electro Optical Products Div.; Roanoke; search/navigation equipment 1,200
Rocco Turkeys Inc.; Dayton; poultry products 1,200
Popular Club Plan Inc.; Lynchburg; catalog retailers 1,200
Centra Health Inc./Virginia Baptist Hospital; Lynchburg 1,200
Community Hospital of Roanoke; Roanoke 1,140
Commonwealth of Virginia/Transportation Dept.; Salem 1,100
City of Lynchburg; Lynchburg 1,080
Precision Fabrics Group Inc.; Vinton; wool mills 1,000
Hospital Corp. America/Lewis Gale Hospital; Salem 1,000
Old Time Gospel Hour; Lynchburg; religious organizations 990
Bank Card Center Inc.; Roanoke; holding offices 980
Centra Health Inc./Lynchburg General Hospital; Lynchburg 971
Home Shopping Network Inc.; Salem; TV network retailers 900
R. R. Donnelley & Sons Co.; Lynchburg; commercial printing 850
Genesco Inc.; Verona; men's suits/coats 850
Brown & Root USA Inc.; Waynesboro; heavy construction 832
W. L. R. Foods Inc.; Hinton; poultry products 830
Virginia Hot Springs Inc./Homestead Hotel; Hot Springs; hotel 808
Norfolk & Western Railway Co.; Roanoke; railroads 800
Liberty Baptist University; Lynchburg 793
Mohawk Rubber Co.; Salem; tires 750
Merck & Co. Inc.; Elkton; pharmaceuticals 730
Lynchburg Foundry Co.; Lynchburg; iron/steel foundries 700
Intermet Foundries Inc./Lynchburg Foundry Co.; Lynchburg; iron/steel foundries 700

American Safety Razor Co.; Verona; razors/surgical instruments 675

Snydergeneral Corp.; Staunton; refrigeration equipment 663

Unilever Inc./Elizabeth Arden Cosmetics; Roanoke; cosmetics 662

Perdue Farms Inc.; Bridgewater; poultry products 650

R. R. Donnelley & Sons Co.; Harrisonburg; printing/publishing 650

Blue Cross/Blue Shield; Roanoke; insurance services 650

Lewis Gale Clinic Inc.; Salem; medical doctors 650

First Colony Life Insurance Co; Lynchburg; life insurance 640

Rowe Furniture Corp.; Salem; furniture 600

Atlantic Mutual Insurance Co.; Roanoke; fire/marine/casualty insurance 600

City of Harrisonburg; Harrisonburg 600

Computer Sciences Corp.; Hot Springs; computer services 600

Washington & Lee University; Lexington 588

Dominion Bank; Roanoke; commercial banks 582

Ingersoll-Rand Co./Rock Drill Div.; Roanoke; machinery/equipment/supplies 570

Halmode Apparel Inc./Junior Wiz Div.; Roanoke; outerwear 550

Snydergeneral Corp.; Verona; refrigeration 550

Allstate Insurance Co.; Roanoke; insurance services 550

Alleghany Regional Hospital Co.; Lowmoor 550

Wayn-Tex Inc.; Waynesboro; carpets/rugs 535

Tennessee Gas Pipeline Co./Walker Mfg. Co.; Harrisonburg; motor vehicle parts/supplies 525

Lynchburg College; Lynchburg 523

7th District

Central — Part of Richmond and Suburbs

Some of the fastest-growing areas in Virginia are in the scythe-shaped 7th, which cuts a path from the Blue Ridge Mountains through Virginia's Piedmont region to Richmond and its rapidly expanding suburbs, collecting all or part of 10 counties.

The 7th is the state's most Republican district. In redistricting before the 1992 election, most of the blacks in Richmond and Henrico County were placed in the new, majority-black 3rd District, leaving whiter, more Republican areas in the 7th. The district's share of the majority-black city of Richmond, for example, has an 88 percent white population. In the 1988 presidential race, George Bush won 73 percent of the vote in the areas that make up the 7th; in 1992, he got 55 percent in the district. The 7th as now constituted was the only district in Virginia that in 1985 backed the GOP nominees for governor, lieutenant governor and attorney general, all of whom lost statewide.

More than 70 percent of the people in the 7th live in Richmond and adjacent Henrico and Chesterfield counties. The capital city is the third-largest in Virginia and the longtime center of state government and commerce, although nowadays, Northern Virginia and the Hampton Roads area are almost as economically important. Richmond was one of the South's early manufacturing centers, concentrating on tobacco processing. The Phillip Morris cigarette plant—one of the largest in the country—is in the 3rd, but many of its roughly 5,000 employees live in the 7th. The company employs 6,000 more people in the Richmond area.

While Richmond's population dropped during the 1980s, Chesterfield's population rose by nearly 50 percent and Henrico's by more than 20 percent. Hanover County, to the north of Henrico, grew by more than 25 percent. Hanover and Chesterfield are among the most heavily Republican counties in the state. Bush won the 7th District portions of both by better than 2-to-1 in 1992.

As the district pushes north, the exurbs of Richmond and Washington converge. Longtime farming areas such as Spotsylvania County are being taken over by people who drive or ride long-distance commuter buses to jobs in metropolitan Washington; nearby Fredericksburg is the terminus for a new commuter train to Washington. Spotsylvania's population jumped by 67 percent in the 1980s.

The Piedmont in the northern part of the district includes part of Virginia's wine country. Orange, Madison and Culpeper counties have several wineries. The area also contains the Civil War battlefields of Chancellorsville, Spotsylvania and Wilderness. Shenandoah National Park forms the 7th's western frontier.

A glimmer of Democratic viability can be found in Albemarle County, stemming from the campus of the University of Virginia, just over the district's boundary in Charlottesville. In 1992, Bill Clinton lost the 7th's portion of Albemarle by only 696 votes; his 42 percent showing was his best in the district.

Election Returns

	7th District	Democrat	Republican
1992	President*	85,357 (30.2%)	154,575 (54.7%)
	House †	—	211,618 (83.0%)
1989	Governor	74,077 (37.4%)	123,736 (62.4%)
1988	President	61,625 (27.1%)	163,749 (72.0%)

*Vote for Perot was 42,724 (15.1%).   †Independent/other is greater than 5%.

Demographics

Population 562,643

Percent change from 1980 5.1%

Land area 2,544 square miles

Population per square mile 221

Counties, 1990 population

Albemarle (pt.) 35,938	Henrico (pt.) 163,607
Chesterfield (pt.) 182,977	Madison 11,949
Culpeper 27,791	Orange 21,421
Greene 10,297	Richmond city (pt.) 58,511
Hanover (pt.) 28,521	Spotsylvania (pt.) 21,631

Cities, 1990 population (10,000 or more)

Bon Air CDP 16,413	Mechanicsville CDP (pt.)
Chester CDP (pt.) 12,388	12,381
Lakeside CDP (pt.) 12,081	Richmond (pt.) 58,511
Laurel CDP (pt.) 11,315	Tuckahoe CDP 42,629

Race and Hispanic origin

White 87.8%

Black 10.0%

American Indian, Eskimo, or Aleut. 0.2%

Asian or Pacific Islander 1.7%

Other 0.3%
Hispanic origin 1.0%

Ancestry

American 9.0%	Italian 3.7%
Dutch 1.9%	Polish 2.0%
English 24.5%	Scotch Irish 4.3%
French 3.5%	Scottish 3.8%
German 21.2%	Welsh 1.1%
Irish 15.9%	

Universities/colleges, 1990-1991 enrollment

Commonwealth College, Richmond 487
ECPI Computer Institute, Richmond 356
Germanna Community College, Locust Grove 2,328
J. Sargeant Reynolds Community College, Richmond 11,542
John Tyler Community College, Chester 5,492
University of Richmond, Richmond 4,859

Newspapers, total circulation (in all districts)

Bluefield Daily Telegraph 23,275
Charlottesville Progress 31,926
Fredericksburg Free Lance-Star 42,033
Petersburg Progress-Index 20,739
Richmond Times-Dispatch 240,551
Washington Post 810,904

Commercial television stations, affiliations

ADI: Richmond (48%), Washington, D.C. (39%) and Charlottesville (12%)
WRIC, Petersburg (ABC)
WXEX-TV, Richmond-Petersburg (ABC)
WRLH-TV, Richmond (Fox)
WTVR-TV, Richmond (CBS)

Cable television systems, total subscribers

Adelphia Cable; Charlottesville 24,000
Continental Cablevision of Virginia; Wistar 110,030
Storer Cable TV Inc.; Chesterfield County 50,000

Military installations, 1991

Richmond Defense General Supply Center (Army), Richmond 2,829
Richmond Intl. Airport Air Force Guard Station, Sandston 338

Businesses and other major employers

Du Pont E. I. De Nemours & Co./Fibers Div.; Richmond; wool mills 3,300
County of Henrico; Richmond 2,665
AT&T Co.; Richmond; electronic components 2,500
Blue Cross/Blue Shield; Richmond; medical service/health insurance 2,134
HCA Health Service of Virginia/Henrico Doctors Hospital; Richmond 1,800
Hilb Rogal & Hamilton Co.; Glen Allen; fire/marine/casualty insurance 1,650
St. Mary's Hospital of Richmond; Richmond 1,570
Richfood Inc.; Mechanicsville; grocery products 1,300
Reynolds Metals Co.; Richmond; metal containers 1,300
Johnston-Willis Ltd./Johnston-Willis Hospital; Richmond 1,197
United Parcel Service Inc.; Richmond; mail services 995
Tyson Foods Inc.; Glen Allen; meat products 934
Nabisco Brands Inc.; Sandston; retail bakeries 850
William Byrd Press Inc.; Richmond; commercial printing 800

Sperry Marine Inc.; Charlottesville; navigation equipment 800
Circuit City Stores Inc.; Richmond; electronic equipment stores 800
American Critical Care Services; Richmond; personnel supply services 800
Interbake Foods Inc.; Richmond; bakery products 700
Life Insurance Co. of Virginia; Richmond; life insurance 700
Liberty Fabrics Inc.; Gordonsville; fabric mills 648
Tredegar Industries Inc.; Richmond; plastics products 621
Pinkerton's Inc./CPP Security Service; Richmond; security services 612
Cooper Industries Inc.; Earlysville; electric switchgears 600
Travelers Insurance Co.; Richmond; life insurance 600
Stuart Circle Hospital Inc.; Richmond 600
Virginia Electric & Power Co.; Richmond; electric services 592
Reynolds Metals Co./Bellwood Printing Plant; Richmond; commercial printing 540
Healthsouth Medical Center; Richmond; health services 520
Klockner-Pentaplast of America; Gordonsville; plastic film/sheets 510

8th District

D.C. Suburbs — Part of Fairfax County; Arlington; Alexandria

When critics deride the insular perspective afflicting those who live "inside the Beltway," they may be referring to the suburban residents of the Northern Virginia 8th, most of whose territory is within the confines of the Capital Beltway, Interstate 495, which rings Washington.

The area's growth, originally spurred by the rapid expansion of the federal government, now stems from an array of white-collar and service-industry employers. The military presence in the district starts with the Pentagon, in Arlington, and includes Fort Myer and Fort Belvoir.

Three of the most-affluent counties or independent cities in the nation are in the 8th: the cities of Falls Church and Alexandria, and Arlington County. Each had a per capita income above $22,000 by the late 1980s.

The 8th hugs the Potomac River bank from affluent, predominantly white McLean in the north, through the ethnically, racially and economically diverse neighborhoods of Arlington and the city of Alexandria to the Route 1 corridor of southern Fairfax County. It is hospitable to most Democrats. Bill Clinton carried the 8th with 51 percent of the vote in 1992. He received 58 percent in both Arlington and Alexandria, which ranked among his best showings in the state; he also carried Falls Church. George Bush, who carried the territory within the 8th in 1988 with 52 percent, won the Fairfax portion of the 8th in 1992 by 32 votes. In 1989, Democrat L. Douglas Wilder's 62 percent showing in the 8th was crucial to his successful gubernatorial bid.

Fairfax County, with a population over 800,000, is the most populous jurisdiction in Virginia. Even though it is split among three districts—the 8th, 10th and 11th—it is the most populous portion in each of them. One-third of the county is in the 8th, accounting for almost half the population in the district.

Arlington is home to three of every 10 district residents. While there are relatively few blacks in Arlington, it has become a melting pot for other minorities. Asians, Hispanics and other minority groups make up roughly one-quarter of the population. Arlington has one of the largest concentrations of Vietnamese in the country, and it has numerous Vietnamese-owned businesses.

The old colonial seaport of Alexandria casts about one-fifth of the district vote; it is reliable Democratic territory. The restaurants and shops of its revitalized Old Town section compete with the Georgetown area of Washington, and thousands of Democratic-voting young professionals live there. On the fringe of Old Town is a black community that enhances Democratic strength. Blacks make up 22 percent of Alexandria's population.

The southern portion of Fairfax County includes George Washington's 500-acre estate at Mount Vernon and Gunston Hall, home of George Mason, one of the framers of the Constitution. It also houses the District of Columbia's Lorton Reformatory.

When the Democratic-controlled Virginia General Assembly took up redistricting in 1991, Democrat James Moran had the ear of the chairman of the Senate redistricting committee. That relationship helped transform the 8th from a Republican-dominant district to a Democratic-leaning one, replacing more Republican suburban areas in Fairfax and Prince William counties with Democratic Arlington County. Moran went on to re-election in 1992, taking 56 percent of the vote.

Election Returns

	8th District	Democrat	Republican
1992	President*	133,183 (51.4%)	96,799 (37.4%)
	House	138,542 (56.1%)	102,717 (41.6%)
1989	Governor	97,939 (62.4%)	58,781 (37.4%)
1988	President	104,268 (47.8%)	111,858 (51.3%)

*Vote for Perot was 28,967 (11.2%).

Demographics

Population 562,484

Percent change from 1980 5.3%

Land area 162 square miles

Population per square mile 3,472

Counties, 1990 population

Alexandria city 111,183	Fairfax (pt.) 270,787
Arlington 170,936	Falls Church city 9,578

Cities, 1990 population (10,000 or more)

Alexandria 111,183	Mount Vernon CDP
Arlington CDP 170,936	27,485
Burke CDP (pt.) 20,288	Newington CDP 17,965
Fort Hunt CDP 12,989	Rose Hill CDP 12,675
Franconia CDP 19,882	Springfield CDP (pt.)
Groveton CDP 19,997	17,961
Hybla Valley CDP 15,491	West Springfield CDP (pt.)
Lorton CDP 15,385	14,069
McLean CDP (pt.) 33,896	

Race and Hispanic origin

White 76.0%
Black 13.4%
American Indian, Eskimo, or Aleut. 0.3%
Asian or Pacific Islander 6.7%
Other 3.7%
Hispanic origin 8.7%

Ancestry

American 2.5%	Norwegian 1.1%
Arabic 1.0%	Polish 3.1%
Dutch 1.8%	Russian 1.7%
English 17.9%	Scotch Irish 3.1%
French 3.4%	Scottish 3.7%
German 20.2%	Subsaharan African 1.0%
Irish 16.2%	Swedish 1.4%
Italian 4.9%	Welsh 1.4%

Universities/colleges, 1990-1991 enrollment

Marymount University, Arlington 3,177
Protestant Episcopal Theological Seminary, Alexandria 218

Newspapers, total circulation (in all districts)

Alexandria Journal 4,663
Arlington Journal 9,086
Washington Post 810,904
Washington Times 91,509

Commercial television stations, affiliations

ADI: Washington, D.C. (100%)

Cable television systems, total subscribers

Arlington Cable Partners; Arlington 43,460
Jones Intercable Inc.; Alexandria 32,955
Media General Cable; Fairfax County 195,588

Military installations, 1991

Pentagon Reservation (Army), Arlington 31,806
Fort Belvoir (Army), Alexandria 11,839
Cameron Station (Army), Alexandria 3,986
Fort Myer (Army), Arlington 2,993

Businesses and other major employers

U.S. Commerce Dept./Patents & Trademarks Office; Arlington 3,700
MCI Telecommunications Corp.; Arlington; telephone communications 2,000
American Management Systems Inc.; Arlington; computer services 1,842
Bell Atlantic Network Services Inc; Arlington; telephone communications 1,800
Alexandria Hospital Inc.; Alexandria 1,800
City of Alexandria; Alexandria 1,500
Washington Team Inc./Domino's Pizza; Alexandria; fast-food chain 1,200
Perpetual Savings Bank; Alexandria; commercial banks 1,000
Fairfax Hospital System Inc./Mount Vernon Hospital; Alexandria 1,000
U.S. General Services Administration/Federal Supply Service; Arlington 950
Gannett Offset Inc.; Arlington; commercial printing 800
USAir Group Inc.; Arlington; airline 760
North Virginia Doctors Hospital; Arlington 750
PRC Inc.; Arlington; computer services 700
Marriott Corp./Marriott Crystal Gateway Hotel; Arlington; hotel 700
County of Arlington; Arlington 700
Gannett Satellite Info Network/National Rock Center; Arlington; newspapers 600

Eastman Kodak Co.; Arlington; professional/commercial equipment 600

Nordstrom Inc.; Arlington; family clothing stores 600

Intersec Inc.; Arlington; business services 600

Caci Inc.; Arlington; computer services 600

Food & Nutrition Service; Alexandria; research services 600

N. K. F. Engineering Assn.; Arlington; engineering services 600

County of Arlington/School District; Arlington 579

Uslico Corp.; Arlington; life insurance 570

Gannett Co. Inc.; Arlington; newspapers 562

National Hospital of Orthopedic Rehabilitation; Arlington 550

9th District

Southwest — Blacksburg; Bristol

Bordering four states, the 9th contains some of the most beautiful and most depressed areas in Virginia. The Appalachians, which form a diagonal spine down the district, and Mount Rogers National Recreation Area, on the southern tier near the North Carolina and Tennessee borders, provide stunning scenery.

But the coal-dependent western portion of the 9th lags behind the state in economic health. Four of the five jurisdictions with the highest poverty rates in the state are in the 9th; three are in the coal fields region, an area comprising Buchanan, Dickenson, Lee, Russell, Scott, Tazewell and Wise counties and the independent city of Norton. Unemployment in Buchanan, Lee and Wise hovered near 10 percent in March 1993; Dickenson's unemployment rate was 14 percent.

The "Fighting Ninth" earned that name not only because of its tradition of fiercely competitive two-party politics but also because of its ornery isolation from the political establishment in Richmond.

Southwestern Virginia was settled by Scotch-Irish and German immigrants who felt little in common with the English settlers in the tidewater and Piedmont regions. The Civil War divided the antisecession mountaineers from the state's slave-holding Confederates. In the postwar era, when Democrats routinely dominated Virginia politics, the 9th was the only district in which Republicans were consistently strong.

But in recent years, as the state GOP moved into alliance with Richmond's business establishment and Northern Virginia's affluent suburbanites, the party has lost ground in the 9th. A number of the region's burley tobacco growers and other small-scale farmers now are teaming up with the traditionally Democratic coal miners.

Democrats are strongest in the coal-mining counties along the Kentucky and West Virginia borders. Bill Clinton carried the five coal counties bordering those states in 1992, as had Michael S. Dukakis four years earlier. Democrat L. Douglas Wilder carried four of them in his 1989 gubernatorial race.

The coal fields region has little in common with the rest of Virginia—as many as seven other state capitals are closer than Richmond. Virginia may be a right-to-work state, but the United Mine Workers still wield influence here; in a 1989 write-in campaign, a UMW-backed independent crushed a 21-year incumbent for a local state House seat.

Republicans normally have an edge in the corridor of counties roughly traced by Interstate 81 as it runs north from

Bristol to Radford. Carroll County, on the North Carolina border, is also solidly Republican.

Montgomery County, which contains the district's largest city, Blacksburg, is economically atypical of the 9th. Home to Virginia Tech, the state's largest university with nearly 25,600 students, Blacksburg is a far more tidy and prosperous-looking place than most of the factory and coal towns in the district.

Election Returns

	9th District	Democrat	Republican
1992	President*	99,099 (45.2%)	93,673 (42.7%)
	House	133,284 (63.1%)	77,985 (36.9%)
1989	Governor	75,586 (47.5%)	83,602 (52.5%)
1988	President	88,065 (44.2%)	108,245 (54.4%)

Vote for Perot was 26,676 (12.2%).

Demographics

Population 562,380

Percent change from 1980 4.4%

Land area 7,890 square miles

Population per square mile 71

Counties, 1990 population

Bland 6,514	Norton city 4,247
Bristol city 18,426	Pulaski 34,496
Buchanan 31,333	Radford city 15,940
Carroll 26,594	Roanoke (pt.) 11,983
Craig 4,372	Russell 28,667
Dickenson 17,620	Scott 23,204
Floyd 12,005	Smyth 32,370
Galax city 6,670	Tazewell 45,960
Giles 16,366	Washington 45,887
Grayson 16,278	Wise 39,573
Lee 24,496	Wythe 25,466
Montgomery 73,913	

Cities, 1990 population (10,000 or more)

Blacksburg 34,590	Christiansburg 15,004
Bristol 18,426	Radford 15,940

Race and Hispanic origin

White 96.6%

Black 2.5%

American Indian, Eskimo, or Aleut. 0.1%

Asian or Pacific Islander 0.7%

Other 0.1%

Hispanic origin 0.5%

Ancestry

American 18.7%	Irish 16.3%
Dutch 2.9%	Italian 1.4%
English 14.0%	Scotch Irish 3.5%
French 1.6%	Scottish 1.9%
German 18.5%	

Universities/colleges, 1990-1991 enrollment

Bluefield College, Bluefield 523

Emory & Henry College, Emory 844

Mountain Empire Community College, Big Stone Gap 2,824

New River Community College, Dublin 3,703
Radford University, Radford 8,990
Southwest Virginia Community College, Richlands 4,782
University of Virginia-Clinch Valley College, Wise 1,528
Virginia Highlands Community College, Abingdon 2,236
Virginia Intermont College, Bristol 562
Virginia Polytechnic Institute & State University, Blacksburg 25,568
Wytheville Community College, Wytheville 1,988

Newspapers, total circulation (in all districts)
Bluefield Daily Telegraph 23,275
Herald Courier Virginian/Tennessean 43,627
Kingsport Times-News 45,838
Roanoke Times/World News 114,067

Commercial television stations, affiliations
ADI: Bristol-Kingsport-Johnson City (47%), Roanoke-Lynchburg (42%) and Bluefield-Beckley-Oak Hill (11%)
  WDBJ, Roanoke (CBS)
  WEFC, Roanoke (None)
  WSLS-TV, Roanoke (NBC)
  WVFT, Roanoke (Fox)

Cable television systems, total subscribers
Adelphia Cable; Galax 5,518
Adelphia Cable; Pulaski 6,050
Adelphia Cable; Richlands 5,047
Blacksburg Cable TV Service; Blacksburg 11,800
Century Virginia Cable; Norton 10,700
Simmons Communications Inc.; Montgomery County 10,400
Telescripps Cable Co.; Bluefield 14,231
Virginia Highlands Cable Co.; Glade Spring 10,123

Businesses and other major employers
Virginia Polytechnic Institute & State University; Blacksburg 5,767
Hercules Inc./Radford Army Ammunition Plant; Radford; explosives/ammunition 4,000
Hoechst Celanese Corp./Celco; Narrows; synthetics 2,000
Thames Development Ltd.; Lebanon; coal mining 1,804
York Intl. Corp./Bristol Compressors; Bristol; refrigeration 1,800
Garden Creek Pocahontas Co.; Rowe; coal mining 1,600
Volvo-GM Heavy Truck Corp.; Dublin; trucks 1,450
County of Montgomery/School District; Christiansburg 1,393
County of Washington; Abingdon 1,200
Pulaski Furniture Corp.; Pulaski; wooden furniture 1,151
Brunswick Corp./Brunswick Defense; Marion; rubber products 1,100
Radford University; Radford 1,100
Westmoreland Coal Co. Inc.; Big Stone Gap; coal mining 902
Kingston-Warren Corp.; Wytheville; rubber products 763
Litton Systems Inc./Poly Scientific Div.; Blacksburg; electronic components/equipment 752
Sara Lee Corp./Knit Products; Galax; outerwear 750
Marley Mouldings Inc.; Marion; millwork 700
Electrolux Corp.; Bristol; household appliances 700
Federal-Mogul Corp./Powertrain Products; Blacksburg; motor vehicle parts 625
Webb Furniture Enterprises; Galax; wooden furniture 600
County of Dickinson; Clintwood 598

Pulaski Furniture Corp.; Dublin; wooden furniture 575
Twin County Community Hospital; Galax 575
Southwestern State Hospital; Marion 561
Humedicenters Inc./Humana Hospital Clinch Valley; Richlands 549
Kollmorgen Corp./Inland Motor Div.; Radford; electrical motors 520

10th District
North — Part of Fairfax County; Manassas

From small-town apple country to people-packed Washington suburbs, the 10th bridges a dizzying range of economies and lifestyles. Draping the northern portion of the state, it links the Blue Ridge Mountains and booming Fairfax County. About the only thing the localities have in common is their strong preference for Republicans

About 60 percent of the 10th's population is in the Northern Virginia suburbs of Washington: Fairfax, Prince William and Loudoun counties and the cities of Manassas and Manassas Park. Fairfax, the most populous jurisdiction in Virginia, has the largest share of the district's population. Only one-sixth of Fairfax County is in the 10th, but it still accounts for one-fourth of the district's population. Some of the county's fastest-growing parts are in the 10th, including Centreville, whose population more than tripled during the 1980s to top 26,000, and Chantilly, which more than doubled to exceed 29,000.

The westward expansion of the D.C. suburbs was reflected in Manassas, which posted the largest percentage increase in the state of any county or independent city: 81 percent. Commuting from Manassas became easier in 1992 with the opening of the Virginia Railway Express, whose western branch connects Manassas and D.C.

Loudoun County's population rose by 50 percent; the population of the county seat of Leesburg nearly doubled during the 1980s. Prince William County's population rose nearly 50 percent, making it the third most-populous county in Virginia.

Beyond suburbia, agriculture and manufacturing fuel the economy. Winchester is the center of the state's apple-growing industry. Virginia ranks sixth in the nation in apples harvested, and Frederick and Clarke counties lead the state. Winchester is also the home of Virginia's political dynasty, the Byrd family. But like former Sen. Harry F. Byrd, Jr., who took over his father's Senate seat in 1965 and later became an independent, the district has abandoned its Democratic roots. George Bush won the 10th by a 3-to-2 margin in 1992, carrying every county and independent city; in 1988, he got more than two-thirds of the votes cast by the areas within the 10th. In the 1989 gubernatorial race, Republican J. Marshall Coleman won the area with more than 54 percent.

The district's ample natural beauty draws visitors year-round. At the eastern end of the district, the Potomac River cascades at Great Falls Park in Fairfax County. Loudoun and Fauquier counties are part of Northern Virginia's "hunt" country, a rolling landscape dotted with sprawling country houses, horse farms and an occasional vineyard. Skyline Drive, a 105-mile scenic highway through Shenandoah National Park across the ridge of the Blue Ridge Mountains, begins in Front Royal (Warren County). George Washington National Forest straddles the West Virginia border. The 10th also has some important Civil War battle sites, including Manassas and New Market.

Election Returns

	10th District	Democrat	Republican
1992	President*	83,214 (33.4%)	124,783 (50.1%)
	House	75,775 (33.4%)	144,471 (63.6%)
1989	Governor	63,504 (45.4%)	76,217 (54.5%)
1988	President	59,633 (30.6%)	133,334 (68.5%)

*Vote for Perot was 41,228 (16.5%).

Demographics

Population 562,664

Percent change from 1980 5.1%

Land area 3,535 square miles

Population per square mile 159

Counties, 1990 population

Clarke 12,101	Page 21,690
Fairfax (pt.) 138,934	Prince William (pt.) 81,674
Fauquier 48,741	Rappahannock 6,622
Frederick 45,723	Rockingham (pt.) 6,634
Loudoun 86,129	Shenandoah 31,636
Manassas Park city 6,734	Warren 26,142
Manassas 27,957	Winchester city 21,947

Cities, 1990 population (10,000 or more)

Centreville CDP (pt.) 26,553	Manassas 27,957
Chantilly CDP 29,337	Montclair CDP 11,399
Front Royal 11,880	Sterling CDP 20,512
Leesburg 16,202	Winchester 21,947

Race and Hispanic origin

White 90.7%
Black 5.8%
American Indian, Eskimo, or Aleut. 0.2%
Asian or Pacific Islander 2.7%
Other 0.7%
Hispanic origin 2.2%

Ancestry

American 6.5%	Italian 5.1%
Dutch 2.2%	Polish 2.8%
English 18.8%	Scotch Irish 3.0%
French 3.4%	Scottish 3.1%
German 28.7%	Swedish 1.3%
Irish 17.7%	Welsh 1.1%

Universities/colleges, 1990-1991 enrollment

Lord Fairfax Community College, Middletown 2,599
Shenandoah University, Winchester 1,158

Newspapers, total circulation (in all districts)

Fairfax Journal 54,477
Manassas Journal Messenger 10,393
Northern Virginia Daily 14,951
Potomac News 26,605
Washington Post 810,904
Washington Times 91,509
Winchester Star 20,731

Commercial television stations, affiliations

ADI: Washington, D.C. (89%) and Harrisonburg (11%)
WHSV-TV, Harrisonburg (ABC)

Cable television systems, total subscribers

Adelphia Cable; Front Royal 6,717
Adelphia Cable; Winchester 17,313
Cablevision of Loudoun; Sterling 11,174
Cablevision of Manassas; Manassas Park 20,185
Columbia Cable of Virginia; Dale City 29,301
Media General Cable; Fairfax County 195,588

Military installations, 1991

Vint Hill Farms Station (Army), Warrenton 1,953

Businesses and other major employers

Paramax Systems Corp./Unisys Defense Systems; McLean; computer equipment 3,500
Electronic Data Systems Corp.; Herndon; computer services 2,000
Federal Home Loan Mortgage Corp./Freddie Mac; McLean; federal credit 1,900
Winchester Medical Center Inc.; Winchester 1,750
County of Prince William/School District; Manassas 1,638
United Air Lines Inc.; Sterling; airline 1,500
GTE Corp.; Fairfax; telephone communications 1,400
CBIS Federal Inc.; Fairfax; computer services 1,400
United Air Lines Inc.; Fairfax; airline 1,300
Trinity Packaging Corp.; Remington; rubber products 1,280
Atlantic Research Corp./Virginia Propulsion Div.; Gainesville; research services 1,213
IBM Corp./General Technology Div.; Manassas; electronic computers 1,150
O'Sullivan Corp./Gulf Stream Div.; Winchester; plastics products 1,000
Fairfax County/Public Works Dept.; Fairfax 1,000
BDM Intl. Inc.; McLean; engineering services 959
Automotive Industries Inc.; Strasburg; motor vehicle parts 900
Judds Inc.; Strasburg; periodicals 800
William Prince Hospital Corp.; Manassas 800
Dynalectric Co.; Sterling; electrical work 750
AT&T Co.; Herndon; telephone communications 750
Fairfax Hospital System Inc./Fair Oaks Hospital; Fairfax 725
VDO-Yazaki Corp.; Winchester; automotive gages 658
Pneumo Abex Corp.; Winchester; motor vehicle parts/equipment 650
TRW Inc./TRW Systems Integration Group; Fairfax; computer services 635
British Aerospace Inc.; Herndon; aircraft parts 614
Blue Bell Inc.; Luray; outerwear 600
Rocco Farms Foods Inc.; Edinburg; meat products 600
Rubbermaid Commercial Products; Winchester; plastics products 580
First American Metro Corp.; McLean; commercial banks 565
Bloomingdale's Inc.; McLean; department stores 550
Ritz-Carlton Hotel Co.; McLean; hotel 550
Hazleton Corp.; Vienna; research services 550
Loudoun Hospital Center; Leesburg 541
E-Systems Inc./Melpar Div.; Fairfax; electrical work 530
William A. Hazel Inc.; Fairfax; heavy construction 530

11th District

D.C. Suburbs — Parts of Fairfax and Prince William Counties

Growth in the Northern Virginia suburbs of Washington during the 1980s helped earn Virginia an additional congressional district. Fairfax County, the most populous jurisdiction in Virginia with a population of more than 800,000, grew by 220,000 during the 1980s—a rate of 37 percent and more than one-fourth of the commonwealth's overall population expansion of 840,000.

The 11th was drawn by Democratic legislators and signed by a Democratic governor with the intent of electing a Democrat, but it is more competitive than the neighboring 8th. George Bush won the areas within the 11th in both 1988 and 1992, although his 60 percent showing in his first election was trimmed to 43 percent four years later. Democrat L. Douglas Wilder received just under 57 percent of the vote within the 11th in his 1989 gubernatorial race. Bush lost the Fairfax County portion of the 11th to Bill Clinton, but recouped by winning in Prince William and in Fairfax City.

The 11th is primarily middle- to upper-middle-class suburbia. Many residents work in downtown Washington, either for the federal government or for companies whose business is linked to the government. But as the suburbs have expanded, they have developed their own employment base: Rush hour in Northern Virginia no longer follows a single, to-and-from Washington pattern; much traffic moves from one suburb to another. Dozens of companies have put down roots in office-park developments in Fairfax; one is Mobil Corp., whose headquarters are in Fairfax. Mobil's operations in Fairfax County employ more than 2,000 workers. The area's business roster includes many high-tech companies, some of them defense-related, including computer engineering, manufacturing and consulting firms.

Fairfax County accounted for nearly eight of every 10 votes cast in the 11th in 1992. Growth and all its effects on property tax rates, school quality, traffic and crime are the primary concerns of Fairfax residents. Recently they have been buffeted by a weak real estate market and threatened defense cutbacks.

The planned, lake-dotted community of Reston, founded in 1961 in the northern part of the county, grew by 33 percent during the 1980s to nearly 49,000. Adjacent to Reston, the town of Herndon saw its population rise by more than 40 percent to about 16,000. Unincorporated places in the county such as Burke (split between the 11th and 8th districts), Bailey's Crossroads, Lincolnia and Seven Corners all grew by more than 20 percent.

Suburban expansion spread into Prince William County, which grew by 71,000 in the 1980s, a nearly 50 percent rise. About three-fifths of the county's population is in the 11th. Woodbridge has the Washington area's closest professional baseball team, the minor league Prince William Cannons. A few miles south on I-95 is Potomac Mills, an immense mall of about 250 factory outlet stores that has become the state's top draw for visitors.

Election Returns

	11th District	Democrat	Republican
1992	President*	102,721 (42.6%)	103,907 (43.1%)
	House	114,172 (50.0%)	103,119 (45.2%)
1989	Governor	80,856 (56.3%)	62,556 (43.5%)
1988	President	79,200 (39.3%)	121,015 (60.0%)

Vote for Perot was 34,719 (14.4%).

Demographics

Population 562,497

Percent change from 1980 (new district in the 1990s)

Land area 249 square miles

Population per square mile 2,261

Counties, 1990 population

Fairfax (pt.) 408,863	Prince William (pt.)
Fairfax city 19,622	134,012

Cities, 1990 population (10,000 or more)

Annandale CDP 50,975	Lincolnia CDP 13,041
Bailey's Crossroads CDP 19,507	Oakton CDP (pt.) 18,707
Burke CDP (pt.) 37,446	Reston CDP (pt.) 48,509
Dale City CDP (pt.) 47,170	Tysons Corner CDP (pt.) 10,384
Fairfax 19,622	Vienna 14,852
Herndon 16,139	West Springfield CDP (pt.) 14,057
Idylwood CDP (pt.) 14,701	Woodbridge CDP 26,401
Jefferson CDP 25,782	
Lake Ridge CDP 23,862	

Race and Hispanic origin
White 80.7%
Black 8.2%
American Indian, Eskimo, or Aleut. 0.3%
Asian or Pacific Islander 8.1%
Other 2.7%
Hispanic origin 7.4%

Ancestry

American 3.1%	Norwegian 1.2%
Arabic 1.3%	Polish 3.4%
Dutch 1.8%	Russian 1.5%
English 18.1%	Scotch Irish 3.0%
French 3.7%	Scottish 3.5%
German 23.2%	Slovakian 1.0%
Irish 17.5%	Swedish 1.5%
Italian 5.9%	Welsh 1.3%

Universities/colleges, 1990-1991 enrollment
George Mason University, Fairfax 20,308
Northern Virginia Community College, Annandale 35,194

Newspapers, total circulation (in all districts)
Fairfax Journal 54,477
Potomac News Sunday News 26,605
Washington Post 810,904
Washington Times 91,509

Commercial television stations, affiliations
ADI: Washington, D.C. (100%)
WTKK, Manassas (None)

Cable television systems, total subscribers
Columbia Cable of Virginia; Dale City 29,301
Jones Intercable Inc.; Alexandria 32,955

Media General Cable; Fairfax County   195,588
Time Warner Cable; Reston   11,866

Military installations, 1991

Marine Corps Development & Education Command, Quantico   10,408

Businesses and other major employers

Fairfax County; Fairfax   16,941

Inova Health Systems Foundation; Springfield; trusts   8,150

V. B. R. Joint Venture; Fairfax; building services   4,000

Mitre Corp./Civil Systems Div.; McLean; research services   3,200

U.S. Geological Survey; Herndon   3,000

E-Systems Inc./Melpar Div.; Falls Church; computer equipment   2,000

Mobil Corp.; Fairfax; petroleum/natural gas   2,000

Computer Sciences Corp./Applied Tech Co.; Falls Church; computer services   2,000

AT&T Co.; Vienna; telephone communications   1,700

Navy Federal Credit Union; Vienna; credit unions   1,700

George Mason University; Fairfax   1,700

Fairfax County/Woodrow Wilson Library; Falls Church   1,610

PRC Inc.; McLean; computer software   1,500

Sprint Intl. Communications/Telenet; Herndon; communication services   1,400

Washington Gas Light Co./Northern Virginia Natural Gas; Springfield; gas distribution   1,350

Northern Virginia Community College; Annandale   1,510

Computer Sciences Corp.; Falls Church; computer services   1,150

Aladdin Mills Inc.; Herndon; carpets/rugs   1,000

Nordstrom Inc.; McLean; family clothing stores   1,000

AT&T Co.; Fairfax; engineering services   1,000

PRC Inc./Engineering Systems Inc.; Herndon; computer services   1,000

H. N. Bull Information Systems/Honeywell Federal System Inc.; McLean; computer equipment   900

Potomac Hospital Corp. Prince William; Woodbridge   828

District of Columbia Government/Corrections Dept.; Lorton   800

American Medical Laboratories; Fairfax; medical labs   800

Paramax Inc./Tactical Systems Div.; Herndon; computer services   750

Reston Hospital Center; Herndon   730

Cable Wireless Communications/TDX Systems; Vienna; telephone communications   700

First Virginia Banks Inc.; Falls Church; commercial banks   700

P&R Enterprises Inc.; Falls Church; building services   700

MVM Inc.; Falls Church; security services   697

Kaiser Engineers Group; Fairfax; heavy construction   650

Analytic Sciences Corp.; Herndon; engineering services   650

Northwest Airlines Inc.; Herndon; airline   600

Trustbank Federal Savings Bank; Falls Church; savings institutions   600

GRC International Inc.; Vienna; management services   600

Hyatt Hotels Corp./Hyatt Regency Reston; Herndon; hotel   600

Software AG of North America; Herndon; computer software   580

S. M. C. Construction Inc.; Annandale; concrete work   550

GTE Spacenet Corp.; McLean; communications equipment   550

Erol's Inc./Erol's Video Club; Springfield; video rental   550

WASHINGTON

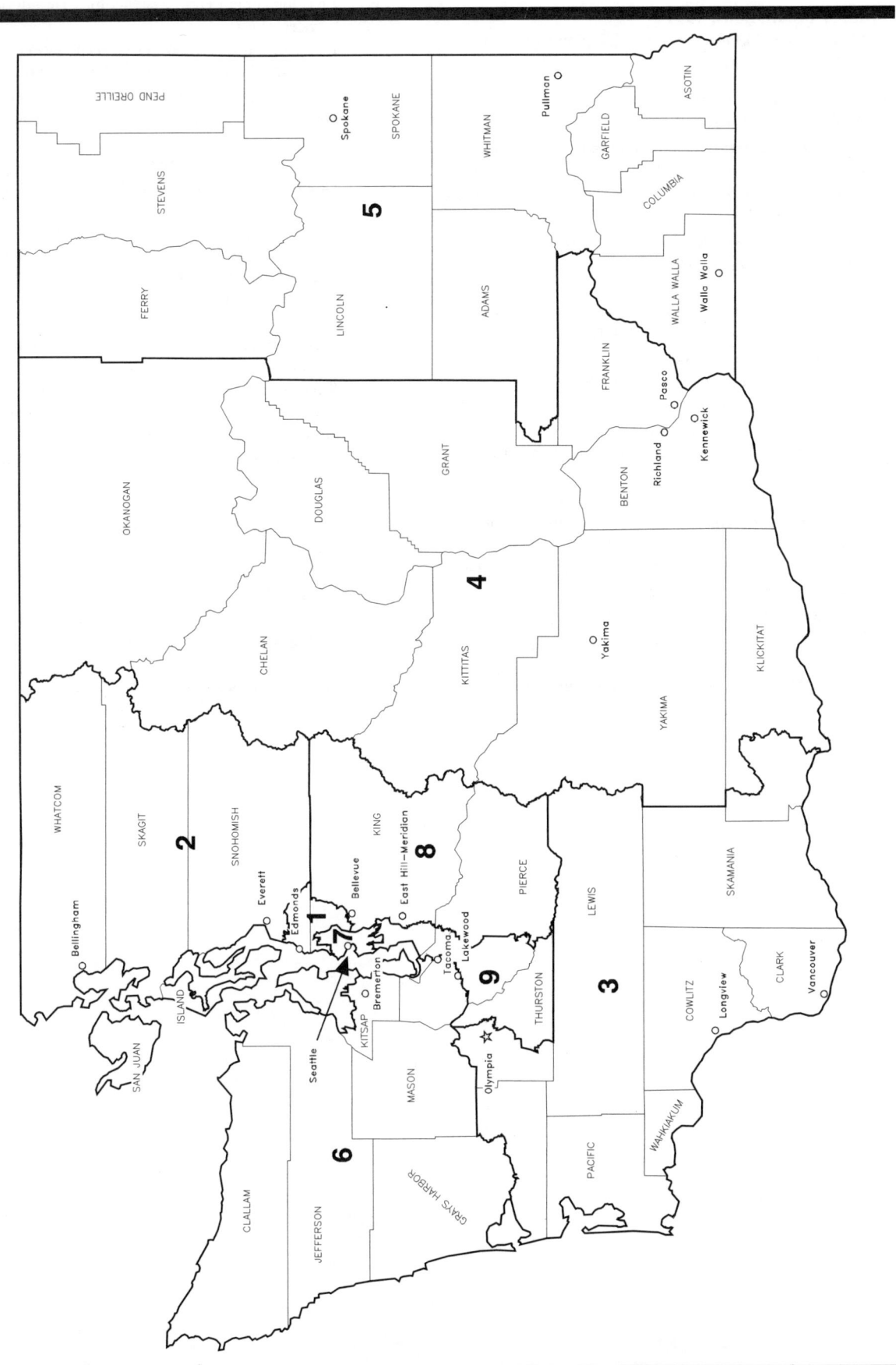

Washington

Washington has undergone a modest growth spurt over the past two decades. The state's many lures to newcomers include such material factors as a thriving Pacific Rim trading sector, one of the nation's largest complexes of military bases and an aviation manufacturing industry headed by Seattle-based Boeing Corp.; and such aesthetic attractions as Puget Sound and Mt. Rainier, scenic backdrops for the Seattle metropolitan area.

The state's population growth from 3.4 million in 1970 to 4.9 million in 1990 has bulked up Washington state's muscle in Washington, D.C. The state gained a House seat in the 1980 reapportionment and picked up another, for a total of nine, in the 1990 round. Washington's latest added seat was coveted by other states, two of which (Montana and Massachusetts) went to court in unsuccessful attempts to claim it for themselves.

Within Washington, the process of redrawing the House district map to account for its new bounty was routine. Washington is one of a handful of states that turns its House redistricting over to a nonpartisan commission, which met its deadline for producing a plan by Jan. 1, 1992. The state Legislature ratified the plan on Feb. 12 of that year.

The major change, of course, was the creation of the new House seat, located in the Seattle suburbs, which have absorbed much of the state's population growth in recent years. But the new map was drawn without doing serious violence to the geographical and political outlines of the existing districts.

Although the remap was done without partisan intent, the existence of several "swing" districts provided Democrats with the opportunity for a near-sweep in the 1992 elections.

In fact, Washington—traditionally one of the most politically competitive states—appeared to emerge as one of the leading Democratic strongholds in the wake of the 1992 elections. Democrat Bill Clinton won the presidential contest in Washington with 43 percent of the vote, 11 percentage points better than incumbent George Bush (who had lost the state to Democratic nominee Michael S. Dukakis in 1988).

Statewide offices left open by retiring Democratic incumbents were kept in the party's fold: Democratic state Sen. Patty Murray won for the U.S. Senate and Democratic former Rep. Mike Lowry won for governor. Democrats also scored a near-sweep of the U.S. House delegation, winning eight of nine seats,

including the newly created suburban seat that appeared to lean Republican and two other seats that had been vacated by retiring GOP members. Yet the reality behind these numbers was much more complex. Republicans are hardly out of the game in the short and long terms.

The 1992 contests for major statewide offices were close: Murray won for Senate with 54 percent and Lowry captured the governorship with 52 percent. Moreover, Democrats were guaranteed no long-term majority of the state's House seats: Six of the eight victorious Democrats in 1992, including House Speaker Thomas S. Foley, won with 56 percent or less.

In statewide elections, Democrats depend on a solid base in Seattle, which is by far Washington's largest city. Seattle is a longtime industrial center, with an economy underpinned by the giant aircraft manufacturer Boeing and by its Pacific Rim port. The city has a strong union influence that generally benefits Democratic candidates.

Seattle is also home to large numbers of environmentalists and other liberal activists. Also, more than a quarter of Seattle's population is made up of minority-group residents, an outsized percentage for a state in which 87 percent of all residents are non-Hispanic whites.

Democratic candidates for major office also are usually able to carry other cities with large blue-collar populations, including Tacoma, Bellingham and Everett in the northwest and Longview in the southwest; and the state capital of Olympia.

To win, Republicans must offset the typical Democratic advantages in these areas with their edge in suburban Seattle. These affluent to middle-income communities have undergone a population explosion over the past two decades, thanks largely to the expansion of white-collar jobs in the region's high-tech and import-export sectors, and to the 1980s boom in military spending that benefited Boeing and other major defense contractors.

The growth in suburban voting population has augmented the traditional Republican base in the rural farming areas of central and eastern Washington, where apples and wheat are major crops. Democrats can compete in the larger cities in these areas, such as Spokane and Yakima; but even there, Republicans triumph more often than not.

A stronger Republican urban center is located in the Tri-Cities area, composed of Pasco, Kennewick and Richland, in the south-central part of the state: Residents long relied for jobs on the Hanford Nuclear Reservation, which provided materials for military weapons and civilian nuclear programs.

Yet even some of these political trends are malleable. Many working-class traditional Democrats are social conservatives, and they look askance at Democratic candidates who are too far to the left. As defense-related jobs at Boeing or at the area's many military bases have become endangered by post-Cold War cutbacks, some have been drawn to Republicans who voice stronger support for military spending than their Democratic counterparts.

Similarly, workers in the timber industry have been at loggerheads with environmental activists—many of whom are identified with the interests of the national Democratic Party— who want to put off-limits large stretches of the forests that cover much of western Washington.

On the other hand, Republican candidates had some difficulty in recent elections holding on to voters in the Seattle suburbs. Many GOP voters in these communities tend to have moderate views on social issues such as abortion and homosexual rights, and they found themselves alienated by the strong conservative rhetoric on such issues by presidents Ronald Reagan and Bush. They also expressed concern about the rise of ultra-conservative Christian Right activists in the state GOP party.

Table 1 Population

District	Population	Population under 18	Voting-age population	Median age
1	540,745	139,698	401,047	33.3
2	540,739	144,735	396,004	32.8
3	540,745	148,478	392,267	33.9
4	540,744	160,441	380,303	32.2
5	540,744	141,875	398,869	32.7
6	540,742	137,705	403,037	33.9
7	540,747	92,957	447,790	34.8
8	540,742	152,071	388,671	32.6
9	540,744	143,427	397,317	31.1
State	4,866,692	1,261,387	3,605,305	33.1

Table 2 Voting-Age Persons

District	White*	Black*	American Indian, Eskimo, or Aleut*	Asian or Pacific Islander*	Other*	Hispanic*	Male*	Female*
1	92.4%	1.2%	0.9%	4.9%	0.6%	2.0%	48.6%	51.4%
2	94.5	0.8	1.7	1.9	1.1	2.5	49.5	50.5
3	95.5	0.7	1.2	1.8	0.7	2.0	48.3	51.7
4	86.2	0.9	2.4	1.2	9.3	12.6	49.2	50.8
5	94.1	1.1	1.5	1.8	1.5	2.7	48.4	51.6
6	88.9	4.7	1.9	3.5	1.0	2.6	49.1	50.9
7	78.5	8.4	1.3	10.6	1.2	3.1	48.6	51.4
8	92.8	1.4	0.9	4.3	0.6	1.9	49.4	50.6
9	87.2	4.7	1.3	5.5	1.3	3.1	50.0	50.0
State	89.9	2.8	1.4	4.1	1.9	3.6	49.0	51.0

*As percent of voting-age population.

Table 3 Voting-Age Persons by Age Groups

District	18-24*	25-44*	45-54*	55-64*	65 and over*
1	12.0%	50.1%	15.1%	9.9%	12.8%
2	13.4	45.9	13.4	10.5	16.8
3	12.1	44.2	14.8	11.3	17.6
4	13.6	42.9	14.1	11.7	17.7
5	16.0	41.7	13.3	10.9	18.2
6	13.2	42.7	13.3	11.7	19.1
7	14.3	47.8	11.2	9.0	17.7
8	11.5	50.7	16.5	10.2	11.0
9	15.6	47.8	13.9	10.2	12.5
State	13.6	46.0	13.9	10.6	16.0

*As percent of voting-age population.

Table 4 Income and Occupation

District	Median family income	Families in poverty	White collar*	Blue collar*	Service*	Farm*
1	$45,857	3.4%	68.1%	20.4%	10.2%	1.3%
2	36,132	6.6	52.1	30.8	13.3	3.8
3	33,913	8.6	53.5	29.7	13.1	3.7
4	29,700	13.4	48.7	25.9	13.3	12.2
5	31,003	10.7	57.2	23.0	15.5	4.4
6	32,939	9.6	55.3	26.8	15.1	2.7
7	39,547	7.4	68.6	17.4	12.9	1.1
8	47,389	3.8	64.8	23.7	10.0	1.4
9	36,543	7.5	57.5	27.7	13.2	1.6
State	36,795	7.8	59.0	24.8	12.8	3.4

*As percent of employed persons age 16 and over.

Table 5 Education: School Years Completed

District	Less than grade 9*	Grades 9-12 no diploma*	High school diploma*	College bachelor's degree or higher*
1	2.5%	6.9%	23.3%	31.2%
2	5.0	11.6	31.3	17.7
3	5.9	12.7	31.0	16.9
4	12.6	14.4	28.6	16.1
5	6.2	10.8	28.5	20.3
6	5.2	12.5	31.6	17.8
7	5.2	8.5	20.3	37.0
8	2.9	8.4	25.6	29.0
9	4.4	11.1	32.3	18.2
State	5.5	10.7	27.9	22.9

*As percent of persons age 25 and over.

Table 6 Housing and Residential Patterns

District	Owner occupied	Renter occupied	Urban	Rural
1	66.8%	33.2%	90.3%	9.7%
2	65.7	34.3	58.5	41.5
3	64.9	35.1	62.5	37.5
4	63.2	36.8	61.4	38.6
5	63.8	36.2	71.3	28.7
6	61.5	38.5	74.2	25.8
7	49.7	50.3	98.5	1.5
8	72.1	27.9	79.4	20.6
9	58.3	41.7	91.5	8.5
State	62.6	37.4	76.4	23.6

1st District

Puget Sound (West and East) — North Seattle Suburbs; Kitsap Peninsula

The 1st traditionally has connected residential neighborhoods in the northern part of Seattle with the first tier of suburbs beyond the city limits. This is a prosperous and, on balance, a politically moderate area. The GOP held the seat through the 1980s, but never won it decisively, partly because most of the voters here are well to the left of national Republican doctrine on social issues.

Analysts of Washington's 1992 redistricting plan said it boosted Republican strength in the 1st, but the Democratic nominee still won the open seat in the election that year. Meanwhile, in presidential voting, Bill Clinton carried the 1st with 41 percent of the vote; independent Ross Perot, who ran well throughout the suburbs and exurbs of Seattle, got 27 percent in the 1st.

The huge majority of people in the district live north of Seattle in western Snohomish and King counties, in communities such as Mill Creek and Bothell that are along or just inland from Puget Sound. At its southern end, the 1st slices a bit off the top of Seattle, takes in some "Gold Coast" suburbs such as Medina on the eastern shore of Lake Washington and includes part of Bellevue, which has blossomed into a full-fledged satellite city of Seattle.

Much of the land in the 1st—but only about 15 percent of its population— is west across Puget Sound, in Kitsap County (see map on page 784). Tony Bainbridge Island is here, as are several military facilities, including a base that services the Navy's Trident submarines. Home to many with defense-related jobs, Kitsap County is also a popular retirement location for military personnel. The eastern and western lobes of the district are connected by ferries that cross the sound.

In 1992, the King County portions of the 1st were the best turf for Democrats; Clinton ran ahead of his districtwide average here. Snohomish was strong Perot country: His 32 percent tally was enough to drop George Bush down into third place in the county. The GOP fared somewhat better in Kitsap, but both Clinton and the Democratic House nominee won there, too.

The 18 percent population boom that Washington state enjoyed during the 1980s was greatly felt in the communities of the 1st, as newcomers drawn by high-tech jobs and scenic suburban surroundings settled here. Biotechnology and electronics firms are major employers, and there is a swarm of small computer-related companies around the headquarters of software giant Microsoft.

So robust was the growth in the 1980s that overcrowding and traffic became hot political issues. But the 1990s have brought a new set of concerns, ones related not to growth but to economic retrenchment.

As is the case everywhere in greater Seattle, much business and commerce in the 1st is related to Boeing, the mammoth aircraft maker that has plants in Everett to the north and an array of facilities south of the district. Hit by downturns in both the military and civilian sectors of aviation, Boeing in 1993 announced major job cutbacks.

Election Returns

	1st District	Democrat	Republican
1992	President*	112,353 (41.0%)	88,456 (32.3%)
	House	148,844 (54.9%)	113,897 (42.0%)
1988	President	94,799 (48.2%)	101,712 (51.8%)
	Senate	117,617 (46.9%)	133,186 (53.1%)
	Governor	129,553 (64.8%)	70,243 (35.2%)
1986	Senate	74,372 (46.2%)	86,506 (53.8%)

*Vote for Perot was 73,259 (26.7%).

Demographics

Population 540,745

Percent change from 1980 4.2%

Land area 375 square miles

Population per square mile 1,442

Counties, 1990 population
King (pt.) 260,096   Snohomish (pt.) 202,468
Kitsap (pt.) 78,181

Cities, 1990 population (10,000 or more)
Alderwood Manor-Bothell   Lynnwood 28,695
  North CDP 22,945   Mountlake Terrace 19,320
Bellevue (pt.) 17,789   North City-Ridgecrest CDP
Bothell 12,345   (pt.) 10,206
Edmonds 30,744   North Creek-Canyon Park
Esperance CDP 11,236   CDP 23,236
Inglewood-Finn Hill CDP   Redmond (pt.) 28,574
  29,132   Richmond Highlands CDP
Kingsgate CDP 14,259   (pt.) 21,548
Kirkland 40,052   Seattle (pt.) 28,557
Lake Serene-North   Woodinville CDP (pt.)
  Lynnwood CDP (pt.)   21,286
  14,251

Race and Hispanic origin
White 91.6%
Black 1.3%
American Indian, Eskimo, or Aleut. 1.0%
Asian or Pacific Islander 5.4%
Other 0.7%
Hispanic origin 2.3%

Ancestry
American 2.6%   Italian 3.6%
Danish 2.1%   Norwegian 9.2%
Dutch 3.3%   Polish 2.2%
English 20.7%   Russian 1.1%
Finnish 1.0%   Scotch Irish 3.5%
French 5.8%   Scottish 4.7%
French Canadian 1.0% Swedish 6.4%
German 28.5%   Welsh 1.7%
Irish 16.2%

Universities/colleges, 1990-1991 enrollment
Edmonds Community College, Lynnwood 7,209
Griffin College, Seattle 1,457
Northwest College of the Assemblies of God, Kirkland 681
Shoreline Community College, Seattle 6,426
Western Washington University, Bellingham 10,000

Newspapers, total circulation (in all districts)
Bellevue Journal American 33,414
Bremerton Sun 39,389
Everett Herald 51,267
Seattle Post-Intelligencer 205,902
Seattle Times 238,176
Tacoma Morning News Tribune 122,007

Commercial television stations, affiliations
ADI: Seattle-Tacoma (100%)

SEATTLE — PUGET SOUND AREA

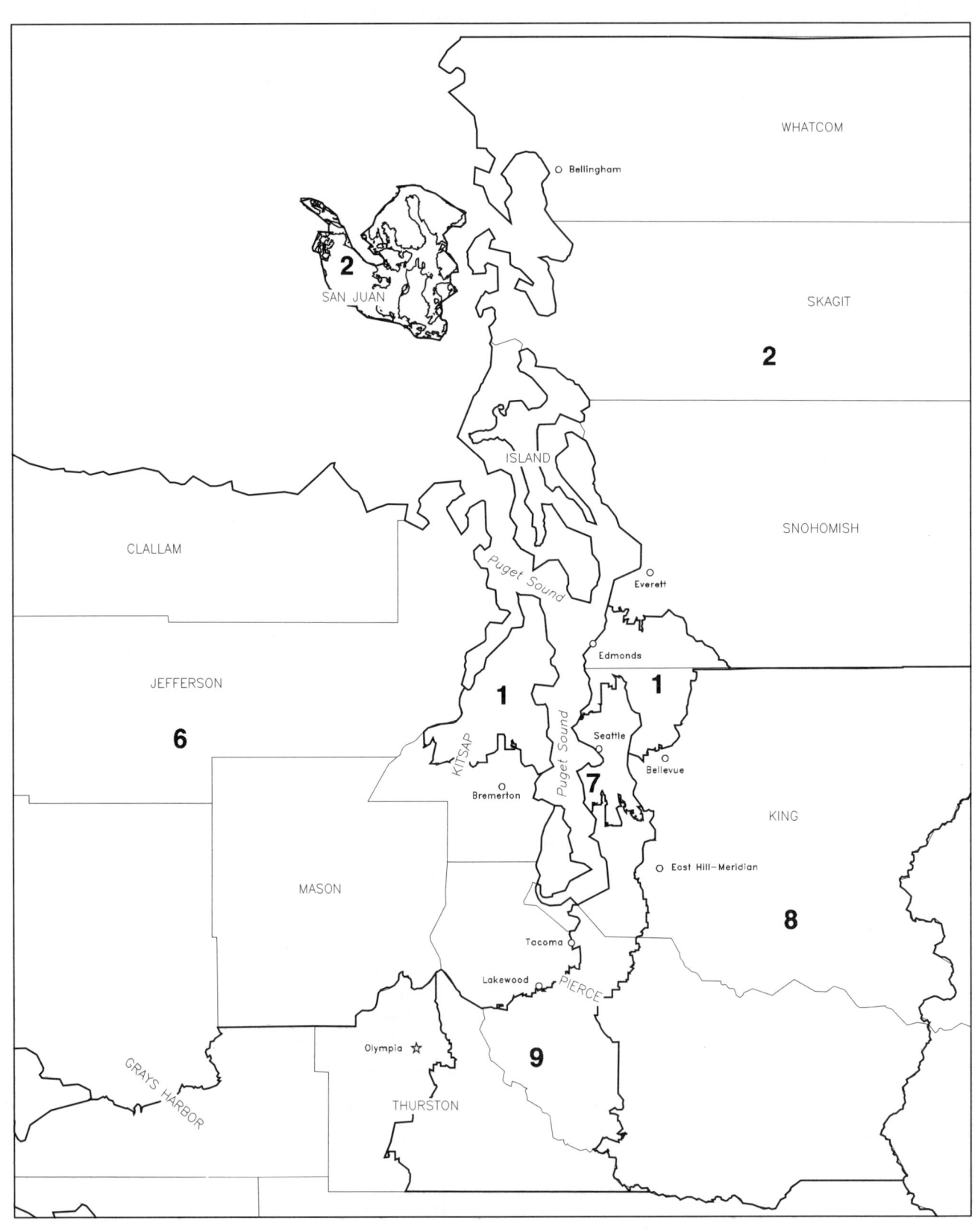

WHATCOM

○ Bellingham

SKAGIT

2

SAN JUAN

2

ISLAND

SNOHOMISH

CLALLAM

○ Everett

Edmonds

JEFFERSON

1

1

6

KITSAP

Seattle

Puget Sound

○ Bellevue

○ Bremerton

7

KING

○ East Hill—Meridian

MASON

8

Tacoma

○ Lakewood

PIERCE

9

Olympia ☆

THURSTON

GRAYS HARBOR

Cable television systems, total subscribers
Chambers Cable of Edmonds; Edmonds 19,420
TCI of Washington; Bremerton 14,778
Viacom Cablevision/Puget Sound; Bellevue 27,674
Viacom Cablevision/Puget Sound; Lynnwood 87,352
Viacom Cablevision/Puget Sound; Seattle 95,574

Military installations, 1991
Puget Sound Naval Shipyard, Bremerton 30,294
Bangor Naval Submarine Base, Bangor 8,967
Naval Underseas Warfare Engineering Station, Keyport 5,530
Pacific Naval Strategic Weapons Facility, Bremerton 770

Businesses and other major employers
Microsoft Corp.; Redmond; computer software 4,100
Boeing Co.; Lynnwood; aircraft 2,000
Overlake Hospital Medical Center; Bellevue 1,700
Eldec Corp.; Lynnwood; search/navigation equipment 1,600
Nintendo of America Inc.; Redmond; computer games 1,400
Advanced Technology Labs; Bothell; electromedical equipment 1,400
Shoreline School District; Seattle 1,200
Evergreen Hospital & Medical Center; Kirkland 1,100
Stevens Memorial Hospital; Edmonds 1,000
Central Kitsap Public School District; Silverdale 1,000
Vitro Corp.; Keyport; computer services 872
Vitro Corp.; Silverdale; engineering services 850
Physio-Control Corp.; Redmond; electromedical equipment 800
Group Health Coop of Puget Sound/Eastside Group Health Hospital; Redmond 800
Safeco Life Insurance Co.; Redmond; life insurance 750
Crista Ministries/Crista Senior Community; Seattle; family services 750
Allstate Insurance Co.; Bothell; insurance services 659
Sears Roebuck & Co.; Redmond; department stores 600

2nd District

Puget Sound — Everett; Bellingham

Washington's 2nd is a swing district that usually is highly competitive, but in 1992 it went big for the Democratic ticket—including presidential contender Bill Clinton—emblematic of the statewide sweep by Democrats.

The 2nd's geographic and political focal point is Everett, a rapidly growing blue-collar city whose history is linked to the timber and shipping industries. Labor conflicts plagued those industries between the two world wars, and unions became the basis of the local Democratic strength.

But the tendency to vote Democratic is tempered by the district's reliance on defense-related industry, which prospered in the 1980s.

Everett is the site of a new Navy homeport, which is expected to add about 7,000 military and civilian jobs to the area. But the not-yet-completed facility was added in May 1993 to a list of facilities that face possible closure as the Pentagon seeks to cut costs. In another blow, Boeing announced in January 1993 that it would lay off thousands of workers in the next few years because of defense industry cuts and decreased demand for commercial aircraft.

Everett may be in better shape than many communities that depend on the defense industry because its diversified economic base is rounded out with a number of high-tech companies, including Alliant Tech, a marine systems manufacturer, and Advanced Technologies Lab, a medical equipment manufacturer.

Everett and surrounding Snohomish County cast nearly one-half of the district's vote. Throughout the 1980s, the county tended to lean Republican in presidential contests and Democratic in statewide contests.

But in the 1992 three-way presidential contest, Snohomish County gave 40 percent of its vote to Clinton.

The second-largest group of votes in the 2nd comes from Whatcom County, a Democratic-leaning portion of the district's northern edge along the Canadian border. Bellingham is a port town and home to Western Washington University (10,000 students), one of the largest employers in the area. Still, many of Whatcom's residents are dependent on trade along the Canadian border and on the dairy, shipping, canning and timber industries.

Between Snohomish and Whatcom is Skagit County, a more rural and usually Republican-leaning area, though it too backed Clinton for president in 1992. Skagit is best known for its tulips; its annual Tulip Festival attracts thousands of visitors.

Island County lies between Juan de Fuca Strait and Puget Sound. Its proximity to Seattle has lured tourists and an influx of retirees, who tend to vote Republican as do the civilian and military employees of Whidbey Naval Air Station, home to A-6 bombers and Island County's largest employer.

Election Returns

	2nd District	Democrat	Republican
1992	President*	109,438 (41.1%)	87,957 (33.0%)
	House †	133,207 (52.1%)	107,365 (42.0%)
1988	President	83,251 (53.0%)	73,751 (47.0%)
	Senate	90,845 (49.3%)	93,365 (50.7%)
	Governor	106,713 (62.0%)	65,471 (38.0%)
1986	Senate	68,208 (50.5%)	66,776 (49.5%)

Vote for Perot was 68,875 (25.9%).   †Independent/other is greater than 5%.

Demographics

Population 540,739

Percent change from 1980 4.2%

Land area 6,223 square miles

Population per square mile 87

Counties, 1990 population
Island 60,195
San Juan 10,035
Skagit 79,555
Snohomish (pt.) 263,174
Whatcom 127,780

Cities, 1990 population (10,000 or more)
Anacortes 11,451
Bellingham 52,179
Everett 69,961
Marysville 10,328
Mount Vernon 17,647
North Marysville CDP 18,711
Oak Harbor 17,176
Paine Field-Lake Stickney CDP (pt.) 16,628
Silver Lake-Fircrest CDP (pt.) 15,791
West Lake Stevens CDP 12,453

Race and Hispanic origin

White 93.7%
Black 0.9%
American Indian, Eskimo, or Aleut. 2.0%
Asian or Pacific Islander 2.1%
Other 1.3%
Hispanic origin 3.0%

Ancestry

American 3.8%   Italian 2.7%
Danish 1.8%   Norwegian 9.2%
Dutch 6.6%   Polish 1.9%
English 18.7%   Scotch Irish 3.3%
French 5.2%   Scottish 4.2%
French Canadian 1.3% Swedish 6.3%
German 28.5%   Welsh 1.3%
Irish 15.9%

Universities/colleges, 1990-1991 enrollment

Everett Community College, Everett 6,051
Skagit Valley College, Mount Vernon 5,144
Western Washington University, Bellingham 9,732
Whatcom Community College, Bellingham 2,702

Newspapers, total circulation (in all districts)

Bellingham Herald 26,102
Everett Herald 51,267
Mount Vernon Skagit Valley Herald 18,107
Seattle Post-Intelligencer 205,902
Seattle Times 238,176

Commercial television stations, affiliations

ADI: Seattle-Tacoma (100%)
  KVOS-TV, Bellingham (CBS)

Cable television systems, total subscribers

TCI of Washington; Arlington 10,209
TCI of Washington; Bellingham 22,732
TCI of Washington; Mount Vernon 11,820
Viacom Cablevision/Puget Sound; Everett 35,000
Viacom Cablevision/Puget Sound; Lynnwood 87,352
Viacom Cablevision/Puget Sound; Oak Harbor 8,006

Military installations, 1991

Whidbey Island Naval Air Station, Oak Harbor 9,869

Businesses and other major employers

Boeing Co.; Everett; aircraft 19,000
Fluke John Mfg. Co. Inc.; Everett; electronic measuring devices 1,782
County of Snohomish; Everett 1,440
Alliant Techsystems Inc./Honeywell Marine Systems; Everett; engineering services 1,300
Scott Paper Co./Northwest Operation; Everett; pulp mills 1,275
Western Washington University; Bellingham 1,200
Intalco Aluminum Corp.; Ferndale; aluminum refining 1,150
Providence Hospital; Everett 1,100
St. Joseph Hospital; Bellingham 1,075
General Hospital of Everett; Everett 1,000
City of Bellingham/School District; Bellingham 1,000
State of Washington/State Reformatory; Monroe 900
Intermec Corp.; Everett; computer equipment 820
County of Snohomish/School District; Snohomish 700

Hewlett-Packard Co.; Everett; computers/measuring devices 650
GTE West Coast Inc.; Everett; telephone communications 604
Everett Community College; Everett 550
Affiliated Health Services/Skagit Valley Hospital; Mount Vernon 525

3rd District

Southwest — Olympia; Vancouver

The 3rd, stretching from Puget Sound west to the Pacific and south to the Columbia River border with Oregon, is heavy with maritime and timber interests. With its large number of blue-collar voters, it contains some of the most Democratic territory in the state.

Democratic presidential candidates have fared well here. In the three-way 1992 presidential contest, Democrat Bill Clinton carried the 3rd as had Democrat Michael S. Dukakis in 1988. Rep. Jolene Unsoeld raised her victory margin here to 56 percent of the vote in 1992. About 70 percent of the district vote comes from two counties: Thurston (Olympia) in the northern end, and Clark (Vancouver) in the south. Clinton won both easily.

Olympia, the state capital, and its surroundings was one of the fastest-growing metropolitan areas in the country in the 1980s; the Olympia area's population soared nearly 30 percent to just over 161,000. Olympia's communities of environmental and "good government" activists—from which Unsoeld emerged—give Democrats a leg up in the county. Neighboring Lacey is a burgeoning twin city to Olympia that adds to the Democratic vote on this end of the district.

Clark County has also seen its population surge with the growth of its Portland, Ore., suburbs. Because Washington does not have an income tax and Oregon does not have a sales tax, many retirees have flocked to live on the Washington side and do their shopping in Oregon.

Vancouver (Clark County) is an industrial and high-tech center. Among the employers here are the James River Pulp and Paper Co. and the computer companies Hewlett Packard, SEH America and Kyocera. The city has renovated a historic section of the district known as Officers Row, a string of 21 homes dating back to the Civil War era, including one in which Ulysses S. Grant lived.

The 3rd has vast stretches of woodlands, including the scenic Coastal Range and much of the Cascade Mountains, with Mount Rainier just outside the eastern border. Timber dominates the economy and, in recent years, there have been more downs than ups. The area's mills produce paper, timber and cardboard under the state's strict water-pollution standards. Logging is a major activity of Cowlitz County, which includes the cities of Longview and Kelso. Along the coast, fishing and dock work predominate, and there is a strong labor presence among the longshoremen.

East of Cowlitz are the newest additions to the district, Skamania and part of Klickitat counties, which rely heavily on the timber industry for their economic base, and the Columbia River Gorge National Scenic Area, a popular tourist attraction.

Rural Lewis County in the northern end of the district provides the only dependable GOP majorities in the 3rd. Republican George Bush won the county in both the 1992 and 1988 presidential elections.

	3rd District	Democrat	Republican
1992	President*	104,748 (42.1%)	82,647 (33.2%)
	House	138,043 (56.0%)	108,583 (44.0%)
1988	President	89,546 (52.7%)	80,251 (47.3%)
	Senate	99,953 (52.2%)	91,472 (47.8%)
	Governor	99,960 (57.5%)	73,804 (42.5%)
1986	Senate	80,496 (54.1%)	68,310 (45.9%)

*Vote for Perot was 61,613 (24.7%).

Demographics

Population 540,745

Percent change from 1980 4.7%

Land area 8,428 square miles

Population per square mile 64

Counties, 1990 population

Clark	238,053	Pacific	18,882
Cowlitz	82,119	Skamania	8,289
Grays Harbor (pt.)	16,668	Thurston (pt.)	105,697
Klickitat (pt.)	8,352	Wahkiakum	3,327
Lewis	59,358		

Cities, 1990 population (10,000 or more)

Centralia	12,101	Olympia	33,840
Evergreen CDP	11,249	Orchards South CDP	12,956
Kelso	11,820		
Lacey (pt.)	17,359	Salmon Creek CDP	11,989
Longview	31,499	Vancouver	46,380

Race and Hispanic origin

White 94.8%
Black 0.9%
American Indian, Eskimo, or Aleut. 1.3%
Asian or Pacific Islander 2.1%
Other 0.9%
Hispanic origin 2.5%

Ancestry

American	5.4%	Italian	2.6%
Danish	1.7%	Norwegian	5.9%
Dutch	3.9%	Polish	1.8%
English	18.9%	Scotch Irish	3.1%
Finnish	2.2%	Scottish	3.4%
French	5.6%	Swedish	5.4%
French Canadian	1.2%	Swiss	1.1%
German	30.7%	Welsh	1.3%
Irish	16.7%		

Universities/colleges, 1990-1991 enrollment

Centralia College, Centralia 3,417
Clark College, Vancouver 7,559
Evergreen State College, Olympia 3,340
Lower Columbia College, Longview 3,413
South Puget Sound Community College, Olympia 3,985
St. Martin's College, Olympia 1,076

Newspapers, total circulation (in all districts)

Aberdeen Daily World 17,106
Centralia Chronicle 14,633
Longview Daily News 24,649
Olympian 33,889
Portland Oregonian/Sunday 335,758
Seattle Post-Intelligencer 205,902
Tacoma Morning News Tribune 122,007
Vancouver Columbian 51,490

Commercial television stations, affiliations

ADI: Seattle-Tacoma (51%) and Portland (49%)

Cable television systems, total subscribers

Century Cable; Longview 21,106
Columbia Cable; Vancouver 44,600
TCI of Washington; Chehalis 9,112
TCI of Washington; Olympia 39,726

Businesses and other major employers

State of Washington/Transportation Dept.; Olympia 5,000
Weyerhaeuser Co.; Longview; pulp mills 3,000
State of Washington/Employment Security Dept.; Olympia 2,500
U.S. Veterans Affairs Dept.; Vancouver 2,400
State of Washington; Olympia 2,400
Longview Fibre Co.; Longview; paperboard products 1,900
James River Corp. Virginia; Camas; paper mills 1,860
State of Washington/Labor-Industry Dept.; Olympia 1,800
Health Systems Group; Vancouver 1,611
State of Washington/Liquor Control Board; Olympia; liquor stores 1,500
State of Washington/Ecology Dept.; Olympia 1,300
Evergreen State College; Olympia 1,213
Shin-Etsu Handotai America; Vancouver; electronic components 1,200
St. Peter Hospital; Olympia 1,150
Farmers Union Central Exchange Inc.; Vancouver; petroleum products 1,000
Reynolds Metals Co./Longview Reduction Plant; Longview; aluminum rolling/drawing 1,000
City of Olympia/School District; Olympia 1,000
St. John's Hospital; Longview 971
Hewlett-Packard Co.; Camas; computer/office equipment 850
State of Washington/Wildlife Dept.; Olympia 800
Centralia Mining Co.; Centralia; coal mining 750
Southwest Washington Medical Center; Vancouver 715
Bonneville Power/Ross Substation; Vancouver; electric services 700
Vanalco Inc.; Vancouver; nonferrous metals 700
Price Development Co. Inc./Three Rivers Mall; Kelso; real estate operators 600
Providence Hospital; Centralia 560
County of Clark; Vancouver 550
State of Washington/Agriculture Dept.; Olympia 550
Farmers Insurance Co. of Washington; Vancouver; fire/marine/casualty insurance 505

4th District

Central — Yakima and Tri-Cities

The 4th, lying just east of the Cascade Mountains, is a big chunk of central Washington, bordering Canada on the north and Oregon on the south. The voters here consistently support Republican presidential candidates, but in elections for other offices, Democrats often fare well.

The 4th was the only Washington district that George Bush carried in the 1992 presidential contest. At the same time, the House seat switched into the Democratic column. The Democratic House nominee carried seven out of 10 counties, losing only in the southeastern corner of the 4th, where voters in the Tri-Cities area of Pasco, Kennewick and Richland are staunchly Republican.

Balancing GOP strength in the Tri-Cities are several areas with Democratic proclivities. Kittitas County, in the center of the 4th, voted a straight Democratic ticket in 1992. Bill Clinton also won Klickitat County (on the Columbia River border with Oregon) and Okanogan County (which borders Canada) in the 1992 presidential race.

The 4th's economy revolves around agriculture—primarily fruits and wheat, winemaking and cattle—and the Hanford Nuclear Reservation, formerly the site of much of the nation's nuclear weapons-materials production. The reservation is mostly in Benton County, just north of the Tri-Cities. In 1988, the federal government shut down Hanford's N reactor, a plutonium plant, because of safety problems and the decreased need for plutonium given the warming in U.S.-Russia relations. The shutdown resulted in the initial loss of 1,000 jobs in the two-county (Benton and Franklin) area of about 150,000.

The Department of Energy then estimated that it would cost up to $50 billion to clean up the hazardous waste that had accumulated at Hanford. In early 1989, the state and federal governments agreed on a cleanup plan; the project, which will bring about 2,000 jobs to the Hanford area, is expected to take at least 30 years.

Nearby, construction is under way for a $220 million Molecular Science Research Lab, scheduled for completion in 1996. Researchers there will develop technologies for the cleanup of hazardous waste around the country.

Northwest of the Tri-Cities is the district's other urban concentration, Yakima (Yakima County). Voters here lean Republican, although the Democratic House nominee carried the county in 1992. George Bush won Yakima County with 45 percent.

Yakima County was largely desert before a huge irrigation project helped make it one of the nation's premier apple-growing areas; more than 50 percent of the nation's apples come from the district. Also in the 4th is the immense Grand Coulee Dam, on the Columbia River in Grant County.

Election Returns

	4th District	Democrat	Republican
1992	President*	71,848 (35.0%)	87,996 (42.9%)
	House	106,556 (50.8%)	103,028 (49.2%)
1988	President	62,941 (41.6%)	88,504 (58.4%)
	Senate	78,583 (42.5%)	106,329 (57.5%)
	Governor	76,058 (47.8%)	82,931 (52.2%)
1986	Senate	61,285 (41.5%)	86,283 (58.5%)

*Vote for Perot was 45,252 (22.1%).

Demographics

Population 540,744

Percent change from 1980 5.6%

Land area 23,705 square miles

Population per square mile 23

Counties, 1990 population

Adams (pt.) 336	Grant 54,758
Benton 112,560	Kittitas 26,725
Chelan 52,250	Klickitat (pt.) 8,264
Douglas 26,205	Okanogan 33,350
Franklin 37,473	Yakima 188,823

Cities, 1990 population (10,000 or more)

East Wenatchee Bench CDP 12,539	Pasco 20,337
Ellensburg 12,361	Richland 32,315
Kennewick 42,155	Sunnyside 11,238
Moses Lake 11,235	Wenatchee 21,756
	Yakima 54,827

Race and Hispanic origin

White 83.2%

Black 1.0%

American Indian, Eskimo, or Aleut. 2.8%

Asian or Pacific Islander 1.3%

Other 11.8%

Hispanic origin 15.9%

Ancestry

American 4.4%	Italian 2.0%
Danish 1.4%	Norwegian 4.0%
Dutch 4.0%	Polish 1.1%
English 17.5%	Scotch Irish 2.7%
French 5.4%	Scottish 2.8%
German 27.2%	Swedish 3.6%
Irish 14.1%	Welsh 1.2%

Universities/colleges, 1990-1991 enrollment

Big Bend Community College, Moses Lake 1,754

Central Washington University, Ellensburg 7,705

Columbia Basin College, Pasco 5,848

Heritage College, Toppenish 966

Wenatchee Valley College, Wenatchee 2,493

Yakima Valley Community College, Yakima 4,075

Newspapers, total circulation (in all districts)

Pasco Tri-City Herald 35,900

Seattle Post-Intelligencer 205,902

Spokane Spokesman-Review 119,439

Yakima Herald-Republic 40,237

Wenatchee World 27,851

Commercial television stations, affiliations

ADI: Yakima (35%), Spokane (34%), Seattle-Tacoma (25%) and Portland (6%)

KVEW, Kennewick (ABC)

KEPR-TV, Pasco (CBS)

KNDU, Richland (NBC)

KCWT, Wenatchee (None)

KAPP, Yakima (ABC)

KIMA-TV, Yakima (CBS)

KNDO, Yakima (NBC)

Cable television systems, total subscribers

Sammons Communications of Washington Inc.; Moses Lake 5,800

TCI of Washington; Wenatchee 16,000

TCI of Washington; Yakima 30,977

United Artists; Johnson/Butte 33,772

Businesses and other major employers

Westinghouse Hanford Co./Hanford Engineering Dev. Lab; Richland; electric services 9,400

Battelle Memorial Institute/Pacific Northwest Labs; Richland; research services 3,129

U.S. Interior Dept./Confederated Tribes; Toppenish 2,000

IBP Inc.; Pasco; meatpacking 1,500

St. Elizabeth Medical Center; Yakima 1,044

Bechtel Power Corp.; Richland; nuclear power plant construction 1,000

Siemens Nuclear Power Corp.; Richland; inorganic chemicals 1,000

City of Kennewick/School District; Kennewick 1,000

Yakima Valley Memorial Hospital Assn.; Yakima 950

Central Washington University; Ellensburg 923

Kaiser Engineers Hanford Co.; Richland; building construction 900

Boeing Co./BCS Richland Inc.; Richland; computer services 900

Aluminum Co. of America; Wenatchee; aluminum 875

Bentral Washington Hospital; Wenatchee 800

Nestle Food Co.; Moses Lake; preserved fruits/vegetables 700

Boise Cascade Corp.; Yakima; sawmills 700

Kadlec Medical Center; Richland 700

County of Yakima; Yakima 700

Omak Wood Products Inc.; Omak; sawmills 632

Lamb-Weston Inc./ConAgra; Richland; preserved fruits/vegetables 600

Tree Top Inc./Ross Packing Co.; Selah; preserved fruits 550

5th District

East — Spokane

In most election years, Thomas Foley's success is rather an anomaly for Democrats in this heavily rural eastern Washington district. Though Democrats seeking higher office can be competitive here, the 5th usually has a Republican tilt.

But the three-way White House race of 1992 gave Democrat Bill Clinton a chance to break his party's presidential losing streak in the 5th. Aided by the popularity of Ross Perot, who got 23 percent of the vote in the 5th and weakened George Bush, Clinton ran first, taking 40 percent overall. In 1988, Michael S. Dukakis won almost as many votes in the district as Clinton did four years later, but Dukakis lost narrowly to Bush.

Clinton's success did not transfer to the 1992 Democratic nominees for governor and senator, Mike Lowry and Patty Murray. Both lost every county in the district, though they won statewide.

And Foley himself had an unaccustomed brush with serious GOP competition. Four lightly populated counties went for his Republican challenger, who kept Foley's winning tally down to 55 percent, his poorest showing in a dozen years.

Though the 5th covers 11 counties and a lot of ground, in electoral terms one place counts: Spokane. With 177,000 people, the city is Washington's second-largest. Spokane County casts about two-thirds of the district's vote.

Spokane is the banking and marketing center of the "Inland Empire," which encompasses wheat- and vegetable-farming counties in eastern Washington, eastern Oregon, northern Idaho and western Montana. The city developed a sizable aluminum industry thanks to the availability of low-cost hydroelectric power from New Deal-era dams along the Columbia River. Boeing also is a presence here. Though the company plans to lay off thousands in the Seattle area, its Spokane facility, which makes airplane floor panels and environmental ducts, could hold its ground as Boeing retrenches.

Spokane also is becoming known as a major medical center for the Inland Empire. The Sacred Heart Medical Center has made a name for itself in the highly specialized field of heart-lung transplants.

Comparatively isolated, Spokane traditionally has been among the most conservative of America's large cities. But Spokane's small-town personality and the accessibility of nearby lakes and mountains have lured many newcomers to the Spokane area in recent years—particularly California emigrants. This influx has served to moderate Spokane's conservatism. Clinton won Spokane County with 41 percent in 1992, and Foley took it with 57 percent.

There are two other small population centers of note. Pullman (Whitman County) is the site of Washington State University (18,000 students). Though the county has tended to support Republicans for president, it went for Clinton in 1992. Holding fast for the GOP was traditionally Republican Walla Walla County.

Election Returns

	5th District	Democrat	Republican
1992	President*	99,676 (40.4%)	90,294 (36.6%)
	House	135,965 (55.2%)	110,443 (44.8%)
1988	President	90,076 (49.3%)	92,760 (50.7%)
	Senate	99,369 (48.6%)	105,213 (51.4%)
	Governor	107,145 (56.3%)	83,078 (43.7%)
1986	Senate	77,181 (46.9%)	87,297 (53.1%)

Vote for Perot was 56,472 (22.9%).

Demographics

Population 540,744

Percent change from 1980 4.2%

Land area 17,676 square miles

Population per square mile 31

Counties, 1990 population

Adams (pt.) 13,267	Pend Oreille 8,915
Asotin 17,605	Spokane 361,364
Columbia 4,024	Stevens 30,948
Ferry 6,295	Walla Walla 48,439
Garfield 2,248	Whitman 38,775
Lincoln 8,864	

Cities, 1990 population (10,000 or more)

Opportunity CDP 22,326	Spokane 177,196
Pullman 23,478	Walla Walla 26,478

Race and Hispanic origin

White 93.2%

Black 1.2%

American Indian, Eskimo, or Aleut. 1.8%

Asian or Pacific Islander 1.8%

Other 2.0%
Hispanic origin 3.4%

Ancestry

American 3.3%	Italian 3.8%
Danish 1.7%	Norwegian 6.2%
Dutch 3.6%	Polish 1.7%
English 19.3%	Scotch Irish 3.6%
French 5.9%	Scottish 3.6%
French Canadian 1.2%	Swedish 5.4%
German 35.0%	Welsh 1.4%
Irish 17.6%	

Universities/colleges, 1990-1991 enrollment

Eastern Washington University, Cheney 8,402
Gonzaga University, Spokane 3,833
ITT Technical Institute, Spokane 295
Spokane Community College, Spokane 6,321
Spokane Falls Community College, Spokane 10,401
Walla Walla College, College Place 1,566
Walla Walla Community College, Walla Walla 4,119
Washington State University, Pullman 18,413
Whitman College, Walla Walla 1,300
Whitworth College, Spokane 1,759

Newspapers, total circulation (in all districts)

Spokane Spokesman-Review 119,439
Walla Walla Union/Bulletin 14,872

Commercial television stations, affiliations

ADI: Spokane (93%) and Yakima (7%)
KLEW-TV, Lewiston (CBS)
KAYU-TV, Spokane (Fox)
KHQ-TV, Spokane (NBC)
KREM-TV, Spokane (CBS)
KSKN, Spokane (None)
KXLY-TV, Spokane (ABC)

Cable television systems, total subscribers

Cox Cable Spokane; Spokane 75,138
Pullman/Moscow TV Cable Companies; Moscow 12,665
TCI of Idaho; Whitman County 13,000
TCI of Washington; Walla Walla 9,804

Military installations, 1991

Fairchild Air Force Base, Airway Heights 5,022
Spokane Intl. Airport Air Force Guard Station, Spokane 43
Four Lakes Air Force Guard Station, Cheney 42

Businesses and other major employers

Washington State University; Pullman 9,000
Sacred Heart Medical Center; Spokane 3,570
Kaiser Aluminum & Chemical Corp./Trentwood Rolling
Mill; Spokane; iron/steel foundries 1,700
Empire Health Services Inc./Deaconess Medical Center-
Spokane; Spokane 1,700
Key Tronic Corp.; Spokane; computer/office equipment
1,400
County of Spokane; Spokane 1,344
Eastern Washington University; Cheney 1,340
Kaiser Aluminum & Chemical Corp./Mead Works; Mead;
aluminum 1,100
Central Valley School District; Greenacres 1,000
Washington Water Power Co. Inc.; Spokane; electric services
925

Hewlett-Packard Co.; Spokane; measuring/controlling devices 900
Spokane Community College; Spokane 860
ISC-Bunker Ramo Corp.; Liberty Lake; computer services
850
State of Washington/Penal Institution; Walla Walla 800
Eastern State Hospital; Medical Lake 750
Key Tronic Corp.; Cheney; computer/office equipment 630
Gonzaga University; Spokane 615
HM Holdings Inc./Columbia Lighting; Spokane; electric
lighting 600
Allied Janitorial Service Inc.; Spokane; building services 570
Guardian Life Insurance Co. of America; Spokane; life
insurance 530

6th District

West — Bremerton

The 6th continues to be anchored in Bremerton, Tacoma and the southern Puget Sound region, but its shape changed considerably in 1992 redistricting. In the 1980s, the 6th was a fairly narrow district that ran well to the south of Tacoma. For the 1990s, though, the 6th has a squarish shape because it expands west and north from Bremerton and Tacoma all the way to the Pacific, taking in the mountainous and forested Olympic peninsula. (The peninsula had been in the 2nd District.)

With this addition, the 6th becomes one of the key districts in the northwest to watch as logging interests and environmentalists haggle over how to balance use of the forest with preservation of habitat for such endangered species as the northern spotted owl.

The unemployment rate in the 6th has been running above the state average, partly because demand for timber is slack and partly because some areas are off-limits to development while federal officials try to decide how to classify them.

Weyerhaeuser Co. still operates a mill in the peninsula community of Grays Harbor, but another timber giant, ITT Rainier, recently announced that it was closing its Grays Harbor plant.

On the peninsula, communities are trying to diversify to get beyond dependence on timber. The shipping of logs once was the only bill of fare in the port of Grays Harbor, but locals hope that a channel-deepening project now under way will help the port get into exporting many other commodities. Also in Grays Harbor County, a regional airport is being renovated to attract new business.

Other maritime pursuits boost the economy: The fishing industry is a large employer in Port Angeles on the Strait of Juan de Fuca and in Grays Harbor. The district is also home to the Puget Sound Naval Shipyard in Bremerton.

Tourism is a possible source of increased income for the peninsula. Located here are the Olympic National Park (in Clallam and Jefferson counties) and the Olympic National Forest. They attract thousands of sightseers annually to northwest Washington.

The inclusion of the lightly settled peninsula into the 6th gives the district new concerns, but still, the bulk of the district's residents live in urbanized areas. The combined clout of Pierce County (Tacoma) and Kitsap County (Bremerton) accounts for about two-thirds of the district's vote.

The 6th takes in downtown and northern Tacoma. This

industrial city's blue-collar, heavily unionized electorate generally tilts Pierce County to Democrats. In the 6th District part of Pierce, Bill Clinton won 46 percent in 1992.

Low housing prices and a high quality of life helped Bremerton make the top ranking on *Money* magazine's 1990 list of "Best Places to Live." The city, on the Kitsap peninsula, has a strong labor vote, but surrounding Kitsap County (much of which is in the 1st District) leans Republican. Clinton won the 6th District's part of Kitsap with 38 percent in 1992.

Election Returns

	6th District	Democrat	Republican
1992	President*	106,373 (43.5%)	77,538 (31.7%)
	House†	152,933 (64.2%)	66,664 (28.0%)
1988	President	88,170 (53.4%)	76,978 (46.6%)
	Senate	96,337 (53.2%)	84,818 (46.8%)
	Governor	108,780 (64.6%)	59,485 (35.4%)
1986	Senate	74,912 (53.6%)	64,914 (46.4%)

*Vote for Perot was 60,578 (24.8%).   †Independent/other is greater than 5%.

Demographics

Population 540,742

Percent change from 1980 4.8%

Land area 6,250 square miles

Population per square mile 87

Counties, 1990 population

Clallam 56,464	Kitsap (pt.) 111,550
Grays Harbor (pt.) 47,507	Mason 38,341
Jefferson 20,146	Pierce (pt.) 266,734

Cities, 1990 population (10,000 or more)

Aberdeen (pt.) 16,565	Port Angeles 17,710
Bremerton 38,142	Tacoma (pt.) 146,399
Lakewood CDP (pt.) 39,940	University Place CDP 27,701

Race and Hispanic origin
White 87.3%
Black 5.4%
American Indian, Eskimo, or Aleut. 2.3%
Asian or Pacific Islander 3.9%
Other 1.1%
Hispanic origin 3.1%

Ancestry

American 3.8%	Italian 3.1%
Danish 1.6%	Norwegian 6.7%
Dutch 3.1%	Polish 2.2%
English 17.7%	Scotch Irish 3.4%
French 5.5%	Scottish 3.6%
French Canadian 1.2%	Swedish 5.0%
German 26.8%	Welsh 1.3%
Irish 15.6%	

Universities/colleges, 1990-1991 enrollment
Grays Harbor College, Aberdeen 2,403
Olympic College, Bremerton 6,009
Pacific Lutheran University, Tacoma 3,654
Peninsula College, Port Angeles 2,715
Pierce College, Tacoma 8,503
Tacoma Community College, Tacoma 4,614
University of Puget Sound, Tacoma 4,253

Newspapers, total circulation (in all districts)
Aberdeen Daily World 17,106
Bremerton Sun 39,389
Olympian 33,889
Peninsula Daily News 13,909
Seattle Post-Intelligencer 205,902
Seattle Times 238,176
Tacoma Morning News Tribune 122,007

Commercial television stations, affiliations
ADI: Seattle-Tacoma (100%)
KCPQ, Tacoma (Fox)
KTBW-TV, Tacoma (None)

Cable television systems, total subscribers
Falcon Cable TV; Port Orchard 22,122
Northland Communications; Port Angeles 8,400
TCI of Washington; Aberdeen 11,929
TCI of Washington; Bremerton 14,778
TCI of Washington; Tacoma 41,000
Viacom Cablevision/Pierce County; Tacoma 120,000

Businesses and other major employers
Multicare Medical Center/Tacoma General Hospital; Tacoma 2,500
St. Joseph Hospital & Health Center; Tacoma 2,400
Western State Hospital; Tacoma 1,500
Weyerhaeuser Co./Twin Harbors Region; Cosmopolis; pulp mills 1,400
Harrison Memorial Hospital; Bremerton 1,200
City of Tacoma/Public Utilities Dept.; Tacoma; railroads 1,121
Weyerhaeuser Co./Technical Center; Tacoma; sawmills 1,000
Curtice Burns Foods Inc.; Tacoma; preserved fruits/vegetables 900
City of Tacoma; Tacoma 803
Pacific Lutheran University; Tacoma 800
University of Puget Sound; Tacoma 792
Tacoma News Inc./Morning News Tribune; Tacoma; newspapers 750
Frank Russell Co.; Tacoma; insurance services 700
County of Kitsap; Port Orchard 583
State of Washington/Correction Center; Shelton 550
Olympic Memorial Hospital; Port Angeles 510

7th District

Seattle and Suburbs

Ferryboats plying the clear-blue waters of Puget Sound, snow-capped Mount Rainier looming to the southeast—these images identify Seattle to most people. Thousands of newcomers settled in the Seattle area during the 1980s, drawn by the city's pleasant aura and an economy prospering on aerospace manufacturing and trade with the Pacific Rim.

But there was a down side to that growth: traffic-choked highways and streets, downtown towers blocking the sun and suburban developments devouring open space. Concern that Seattle was becoming a less livable place spawned a slow-growth movement that in May 1989 managed the passage of an initiative placing limits on downtown development.

Downtown remains an architecturally diverse blend of the northwest's tallest skyscrapers and turn-of-the-century buildings erected when the city was in its infancy.

Tourists take in the Space Needle at the old World's Fair site; its observation level offers a commanding view. Visitors and locals alike gather at Pike Place Market, a reconditioned old outdoor market in the pier district that offers a variety of foods and shopping wares. Seattle is becoming known for its active music scene, and the Kingdome hosts a variety of sporting events.

Seattle, with a population of 516,000, has a number of ethnic enclaves; its varied blue-collar population includes well-defined Scandinavian, Italian, Asian and Hispanic communities.

In economic terms, the fortunes of the 7th (see map on page 784)—and the entire Seattle area—are tied closely to the vitality of the Boeing aircraft company. Interstate 5 heading north into Seattle parallels the runway of Boeing Field. Boeing thrived during the defense boom of the 1980s; now, though, defense spending is on a slide, as is the commercial airline industry.

In an announcement sure to have profound repercussions on the economy of Seattle and the entire state of Washington, Boeing said in early 1993 that it would lay off thousands of white- and blue-collar workers in the following years.

The other big economic pillar in the 7th, the export-import business, is a fairly steady provider of blue-collar jobs handling goods heading to or from east Asia. And with more than 34,000 students, the University of Washington also is a large employer in the 7th.

Several factors combine to make the 7th the most dependable Democratic district in the state: the strength of organized labor in this industrial area, a minority population that is the largest among Washington House districts (10 percent black, 12 percent Asian) and a substantial bloc of liberal urbanites.

In 1992 presidential voting, Bill Clinton won 65 percent in the 7th. That was over 20 points better than his showing in any other district in the state.

Election Returns

	7th District	Democrat	Republican
1992	President*	191,781 (65.8%)	54,478 (18.7%)
	House	222,604 (78.4%)	54,149 (19.1%)
1988	President	151,358 (69.8%)	65,492 (30.2%)
	Senate	176,815 (66.8%)	87,895 (33.2%)
	Governor	176,891 (80.1%)	44,082 (19.9%)
1986	Senate	122,822 (64.2%)	68,378 (35.8%)

Vote for Perot was 45,167 (15.5%).

Demographics

Population 540,747

Percent change from 1980 5.2%

Land area 126 square miles

Population per square mile 4,282

Counties, 1990 population
King (pt.) 540,747

Cities, 1990 population (10,000 or more)
Riverton-Boulevard Park CDP (pt.) 14,830
Seattle (pt.) 484,501

Race and Hispanic origin
White 75.5%
Black 10.0%
American Indian, Eskimo, or Aleut. 1.4%
Asian or Pacific Islander 11.6%
Other 1.4%
Hispanic origin 3.5%

Ancestry
American 1.9%	Norwegian 6.7%
Danish 1.6%	Polish 2.1%
Dutch 2.3%	Russian 1.5%
English 16.3%	Scotch Irish 2.9%
French 4.6%	Scottish 4.0%
German 21.4%	Swedish 4.9%
Irish 14.2%	Welsh 1.6%
Italian 3.4%	

Universities/colleges, 1990-1991 enrollment
Antioch University, Seattle 439
Art Institute of Seattle, Seattle 1,269
Cornish College of the Arts, Seattle 440
North Seattle Community College, Seattle 6,723
Seattle Central Community College, Seattle 6,164
Seattle Community College South, Seattle 5,123
Seattle Pacific University, Seattle 3,421
Seattle University, Seattle 4,633
University of Washington, Seattle 33,854

Newspapers, total circulation (in all districts)
Bellevue Journal American 33,414
Kent Valley Daily News 32,427
Seattle Post-Intelligencer 205,902
Seattle Times 238,176
Tacoma Morning News Tribune 122,007

Commercial television stations, affiliations
ADI: Seattle-Tacoma (100%)
KBGE, Bellevue (None)
KING-TV, Seattle (NBC)
KIRO-TV, Seattle (CBS)
KOMO-TV, Seattle (ABC)
KSTW, Seattle (None)
KTZZ-TV, Seattle (None)

Cable television systems, total subscribers
Summit Cablevision; Seattle 8,947
TCI of Washington; Seattle 183,819
Viacom Cablevision/Puget Sound; Seattle 95,574

Military installations, 1991
Puget Sound Naval Station, Seattle 3,209

Businesses and other major employers
Boeing Co.; Seattle; aircraft 26,000
University of Washington; Seattle 19,036
City of Seattle; Seattle 10,806
City of Seattle/Metro Dept.; Seattle 4,300
Swedish Hospital Medical Center; Seattle 3,507
U.S. Energy Dept./Bonneville; Seattle; electrical goods 3,000
Virginia Mason Medical Center; Seattle 3,000
Providence Medical Center; Seattle 2,500

Harborview Medical Center; Seattle 2,500
Northwest Airlines Inc.; Seattle; airline 2,000
Seafirst Corp.; Seattle; commercial banks 2,000
University of Washington Medical Center; Seattle 2,000
Children's Hospital & Medical Center; Seattle 1,900
City of Seattle/Light Dept.; Seattle; electric services 1,700
Seattle Times Co.; Seattle; newspapers 1,700
Associated Grocers Inc.; Seattle; grocery products 1,650
U.S. Veterans Affairs Dept.; Seattle; hospital 1,600
Northwest Hospital; Seattle 1,545
King County Medical Blue Shield/Combined Services Northwest; Seattle; medical service/health insurance 1,500
County of King; Seattle 1,500
State of Washington/State Ferries Dept.; Seattle; 1,300
Todd Pacific Shipyards; Seattle; shipbuilding/repairing 1,300
Port of Seattle; Seattle 1,212
Burlington Northern Railroad Co.; Seattle; railroads 1,200
State of Washington/Marine Transportation Dept.; Seattle 1,200
Bon Inc./Bon Marche; Seattle; department stores 1,200
American Building Maintenance Industries; Seattle; building services 1,200
City of Seattle/Police Dept.; Seattle 1,200
City of Seattle; Seattle 1,200
United Parcel Service Inc.; Seattle; mail services 1,100
Airborne Freight Corp.; Seattle; air cargo services 1,100
Generra Sportswear Co./Generra Giovane; Seattle; apparel 1,000
Fircrest School; Seattle; residential care 1,000
Westin Hotel Seattle; Seattle; hotel 750
Ballard Community Hospital; Seattle 725
Paccar Inc./Kenworth Truck Co.; Seattle; trucks 700
Washington Mutual Savings Bank; Seattle; savings institutions 700
Pemco Mutual Insurance Co.; Seattle; fire/marine/casualty insurance 700
County of King/Police Dept.; Seattle 700
First Interstate; Seattle; commercial banks 675
Gais Seattle French Baking Co.; Seattle; bakery products 650
Foss Maritime Co.; Seattle; freight shipping 650
Safeco Insurance Co. of America; Seattle; fire/marine/casualty insurance 640
Ball-Incon Glass Packaging; Seattle; glass/glassware 600
Food Services of America Inc./Amerifresh; Seattle; grocery products 600
Alaska Airlines Inc.; Seattle; airline 600
Washington Energy Co.; Seattle; gas distribution 600
Holland America Line-Westours; Seattle; passenger transportation 600
Nordstrom Inc.; Seattle; family clothing stores 600
ITT Sheraton Corp./Seattle Sheraton; Seattle; hotel 600
Group Health Coop of Puget Sound; Seattle 600
K2 Corp.; Vashon; skiis/sporting goods 550
Alaskan Copper Companies Inc.; Seattle; copper/brass/minerals 550
City of Seattle/Health Dept.; Seattle 550
Seattle University; Seattle 525

8th District

Puget Sound (East) — King County Suburbs; Bellevue

The 8th includes some of Seattle's most prosperous suburbs as well as the landmark that affords the city unique allure—snow-capped, 14,410 foot Mount Rainier.

Encompassing the mainly affluent suburbs and exurbs east of Seattle, the 8th has long been considered the state's most Republican district west of the Cascade Mountains.

In the 1980s, 35 percent population growth in the 8th also made it the state's fastest-growing district.

In redistricting, large chunks of land that had been in the 8th were put into the newly created 9th District (the extra seat that Washington gained in reapportionment for the 1990s).

The 8th District retains a GOP tilt, although independents are influential. In 1992 the GOP House candidate scored a lopsided 60 percent victory. However, at the same time, Bill Clinton narrowly carried the 8th over George Bush, 38 percent to 34 percent, with independent Ross Perot pulling in 27 percent.

For the past 20 years, the suburban area covered by the 8th enjoyed its position as a beneficiary of Seattle's economic boom. But while the boom brought benefits, it also brought the traffic jams and rising housing costs that are the downside of growth. While not as obvious as the "no-growth" movement in Seattle—where an initiative to restrict downtown development won approval in 1989—there is a "slow-down" constituency in the 8th.

With almost 87,000 residents (some of whom live in the 1st), Bellevue is the population center of the 8th and of the King County suburbs that make up the bulk of the district.

Separating Seattle and Bellevue is Lake Washington, and in the middle of the lake is the exclusive community of Mercer Island.

While Bellevue's white-collar constituency offers strong GOP votes, Mercer Island shows an independent streak, often offering up a split ticket.

Part of the reason for the difference is that Mercer Island has a sizable contingent of Jewish residents who tend to be more liberal on social issues.

In the southern half of the district is Pierce County, a rural, sparsely populated section of the 8th dotted with small towns that have attracted a substantial number of retirees and families eager to flee the hassles of urban living.

Residents of the 8th work at a variety of white- and blue-collar businesses, but Boeing, located in Renton, is a key employer here as it is throughout the metropolitan area.

Boeing announced in January 1993 that it would lay off thousands of workers in the following years because of decreased demand for its commercial and military aircraft.

Other large local employers are Paccar, which manufactures trucks, and the computer companies of Microsoft and Nintendo.

Election Returns

	8th District	Democrat	Republican
1992	President*	102,857 (38.4%)	92,276 (34.5%)
	House†	87,611 (33.9%)	155,874 (60.4%)
1988	President	75,968 (44.1%)	96,101 (55.9%)
	Senate	75,189 (44.3%)	94,659 (55.7%)
	Governor	110,093 (63.2%)	64,077 (36.8%)
1986	Senate	48,765 (45.5%)	58,489 (54.5%)

Vote for Perot was 72,526 (27.1%).   †*Independent/other is greater than 5%.*

Demographics

Population 540,742

Percent change from 1980 4.6%

Land area 2,936 square miles

Population per square mile 184

Counties, 1990 population

King (pt.) 438,815   Pierce (pt.) 101,927

Cities, 1990 population (10,000 or more)

Auburn (pt.) 13,646
Bellevue (pt.) 69,085
Cascade-Fairwood CDP
  (pt.) 27,718
Covington-Sawyer-
  Wilderness CDP 24,321
East Hill-Meridian CDP
  42,696
East Renton Highlands
  CDP 13,218

Kent (pt.) 22,829
Mercer Island 20,816
Newport Hills CDP 14,736
Pine Lake CDP 13,940
Renton (pt.) 27,224
Sahalee CDP 13,951
South Hill CDP 12,963

Race and Hispanic origin

White 92.0%
Black 1.6%
American Indian, Eskimo, or Aleut. 1.0%
Asian or Pacific Islander 4.6%
Other 0.7%
Hispanic origin 2.3%

Ancestry

American 3.3%
Danish 2.0%
Dutch 3.2%
English 20.1%
French 5.6%
French Canadian 1.2%
German 30.2%
Irish 16.0%

Italian 4.1%
Norwegian 7.2%
Polish 2.5%
Russian 1.2%
Scotch Irish 3.1%
Scottish 4.2%
Swedish 5.8%
Welsh 1.7%

Universities/colleges, 1990-1991 enrollment

Bellevue Community College, Bellevue 9,473
City University, Bellevue 3,440
Green River Community College, Auburn 5,894
Renton Technical College, Renton 5,559

Newspapers, total circulation (in all districts)

Bellevue Journal American 33,414
Kent Valley Daily News 32,427
Seattle Post-Intelligencer 205,902
Seattle Times 238,176
Tacoma Morning News Tribune 122,007

Commercial television stations, affiliations

ADI: Seattle-Tacoma (100%)

Cable television systems, total subscribers

TCI of Washington; North Bend 7,700
TCI of Washington; Seattle 183,819
Viacom Cablevision/Pierce County; Tacoma 120,000
Viacom Cablevision/Puget Sound; Bellevue 27,674
Viacom Cablevision/Puget Sound; Redmond 19,400
Viacom Cablevision/Puget Sound; Seattle 95,574

Businesses and other major employers

U.S. West Communications Inc.; Bellevue; telephone communications 1,100
State of Washington/Social & Health Services Dept.; Buckley 1,100
Nordstrom Inc.; Bellevue; family clothing stores 1,000
City of Bellevue; Bellevue 900
City of Issaquah/School District; Issaquah 850
Puget Sound Power & Light Co.; Bellevue; electric services 800
Weyerhaeuser Co.; Snoqualmie; sawmills 650
Farmers New World Life Insurance Co.; Mercer Island; health insurance 574
Bellevue Community College; Bellevue 525

9th District

Puget Sound — Tacoma; Parts of King, Pierce and Thurston Counties

Population growth during the 1980s earned Washington a ninth House seat in reapportionment, and the state's redistricting commission drew the new 9th right where the growth had been greatest: in the suburbs and exurbs east and south of Seattle.

The new 9th strings together an array of communities without much sense of commonality, starting at the south end of Seattle, going on down past Tacoma and then heading west to Olympia, the state capital. The district's "Main Street" is a 60-mile stretch of Interstate 5, where the crush of commuter and commercial traffic sometimes keeps the road jammed nearly all day.

Most of the residents of the 9th rely on their autos to get them to work—in office towers in Seattle and Bellevue, in factories and workshops of Boeing or at the shipyards and docks of Tacoma (where mammoth cargoes of logs are loaded for shipment).

Other sources of income and jobs in the 9th include the office and industrial complexes around Sea-Tac International Airport, McChord Air Force Base and the Army's Fort Lewis (Pierce County). The military presence that has long shaped the Puget Sound region is inescapable in the 9th. Veterans, active military personnel and their families constitute about one-fifth of the district population.

Some residents of the 9th make their living off the land: At the southern reaches of the district, along the Thurston County border, forests and farms predominate.

Just over half the 9th's vote is cast in the district's northeastern end, a slice of King County that includes the headquarters of the timber giant Weyerhaeuser Co., in Federal Way. The district's largest city (68,000 people), Federal Way recently incorporated to get a handle on its growth.

But if King County contributes the majority of votes in the 9th, most of the district's land area lies in Pierce and Thurston counties. Here, many residents live in scattered subdivisions and unincorporated areas where open space is plentiful and farm animals are not uncommon. Some of these communities surround older, established towns such as Puyallup (home of the Western Washington State Fairgrounds), while for others, "downtown" consists of commercial strip developments and suburban malls. One local political consultant called the 9th "an entire district with nothing at its heart but Chuck E. Cheeses."

The political character of the 9th is just beginning to emerge.

While Washington does not register voters by party, a 1992 poll found Democrats and Republicans within one percentage point of each other in the 9th (with a 41 percent plurality calling themselves independents). In the September 1992 open primary, candidates calling themselves Democrats got nearly as many votes (47,456) as those with the GOP label (48,773).

In his two presidential bids, Ronald Reagan ran well in the areas that make up the 9th. But George Bush struggled here in 1988 and stumbled badly four years later, losing by 11 percentage points to Bill Clinton as Ross Perot polled 26 percent in the district.

Election Returns

	9th District	Democrat	Republican
1992	President*	93,963 (42.4%)	69,592 (31.4%)
	House	110,902 (52.1%)	91,910 (43.2%)
1988	President	71,053 (49.7%)	71,797 (50.3%)
	Senate	69,567 (50.0%)	69,453 (50.0%)
	Governor	92,952 (64.4%)	51,305 (35.6%)
1986	Senate	48,713 (52.3%)	44,467 (47.7%)

Vote for Perot was 58,039 (26.2%).

Demographics

Population 540,744

Percent change from 1980 (new district in the 1990s)

Land area 862 square miles

Population per square mile 627

Counties, 1990 population
King (pt.) 267,661   Thurston (pt.) 55,541
Pierce (pt.) 217,542

Cities, 1990 population (10,000 or more)
Auburn (pt.) 19,456   Parkland CDP 20,882
Burien CDP (pt.) 23,788   Puyallup (pt.) 17,144
Des Moines 17,283   Renton (pt.) 13,584
Elk Plain CDP 12,197   Sea-Tac CDP (pt.) 20,294
Federal Way CDP 67,554   Spanaway CDP 15,001
Fort Lewis CDP 22,224   Tacoma (pt.) 30,265
Kent (pt.) 15,131   Tukwila (pt.) 11,556
Lakeland North CDP 14,402   White Center-Shorewood CDP (pt.) 16,724
Lakewood CDP (pt.) 18,472

Race and Hispanic origin
White 85.5%
Black 5.4%
American Indian, Eskimo, or Aleut. 1.5%
Asian or Pacific Islander 6.1%
Other 1.5%
Hispanic origin 3.7%

Ancestry
American 3.2%   Dutch 3.1%
Danish 1.5%   English 16.7%
French 5.5%   Polish 2.3%
French Canadian 1.2%   Scotch Irish 3.0%
German 28.9%   Scottish 3.2%
Irish 16.0%   Swedish 4.8%
Italian 3.8%   Welsh 1.3%
Norwegian 6.7%

Universities/colleges, 1990-1991 enrollment
Highline Community College, Seattle 7,739
ITT Technical Institute, Seattle 481

Newspapers, total circulation (in all districts)
Bellevue Journal American 33,414
Centralia Chronicle 14,633
Kent Valley Daily News 32,427
Olympian 33,889
Seattle Post-Intelligencer 205,902
Seattle Times 238,176
Tacoma Morning News Tribune 122,007

Commercial television stations, affiliations
ADI: Seattle-Tacoma (100%)

Cable television systems, total subscribers
TCI of Washington; Olympia 39,726
TCI of Washington; Seattle 183,819
TCI of Washington; Tacoma 41,000
Viacom Cablevision/Pierce County; Tacoma 120,000
Viacom Cablevision/Puget Sound; Seattle 95,574

Military installations, 1991
McChord Air Force Base, Tacoma 5,644

Businesses and other major employers
Boeing Co.; Renton; aircraft 8,000
Boeing Co./Boeing Support Services; Renton; business services 4,600
Boeing Co./Boeing Electronics Center; Renton; electronic components 1,725
Federal Way School District; Auburn 1,700
Valley Medical Center; Renton 1,445
Good Samaritan Hospital; Puyallup 1,400
State of Washington/Social Health Services Dept.; Olympia 1,350
Ciba-Geigy Corp./Heath Tecna Aerospace Co.; Kent; aircraft/parts 1,300
Seattle-Tacoma Intl. Airport; Seattle; airport/services 1,200
Alaska Airlines Inc.; Seattle; airline 1,200
City of Auburn/School District; Auburn 1,100
Weyerhaeuser Co.; Auburn; logging 1,000
Sea-Land Service Inc.; Tacoma; gasoline stations 1,000
U.S. Veterans Affairs Dept.; Tacoma; hospital 800
Highline Community College; Seattle 641
Simpson Tacoma Kraft Co.; Tacoma; paperboard mills 608
Red Lion Inn/Sea-Tac Airport; Seattle; hotels 575
Gordon Trucking Inc.; Sumner; trucking services 565
St. Francis Community Hospital; Auburn 550
Pierce Transit; Tacoma; transportation 542

WEST VIRGINIA

Districts Established October 17, 1991

West Virginia

A decade of economic decline in West Virginia helped yield electoral success for the state's Democratic Party, which headed into the 1990s with a firm grip on the levers of power. The problem, however, was that fewer levers existed. Because soaring unemployment spurred so much emigration during the 1980s, the state's population dropped 8 percent, costing West Virginia one of its four House seats in 1990 reapportionment. With Democrats holding all those seats, one incumbent had to get the ax in redistricting.

After months of stalemate and then weeks of squabbling in a fall 1991 special session, the West Virginia Legislature (in which Democrats held 80 percent of the seats) made the Democratic incumbent in the 2nd District its victim. His 2nd District was divided among each of the three new districts; and he was thrown into the 1st District where he lost 2-to-1 in the Democratic primary.

Watching the Democrats carp over redistricting gave West Virginia's beleaguered GOP a rare episode of enjoyment. The Republicans' last hurrah was in 1984 presidential voting, when Ronald Reagan carried the state by 10 points over Walter F. Mondale.

Not that the future was devoid of prospects for GOP gains in West Virginia. Economic trends could boost the party's stock. The state entered the 1980s extremely reliant on heavy industry, a sector of the economy that the 1982-1983 recession devastated. Unemployment soared to 16 percent as steel, chemical and glass factories in Charleston, Wheeling, Parkersburg, Huntington and elsewhere closed or cut back production.

The downturn was exacerbated by massive layoffs in the state's mountainous coal region. Although West Virginia's coal production steadily increased through the decade to more than 170 million tons in 1990, technological improvements enabled mine owners to accelerate the replacement of workers with machines. Mine employment—which peaked at 130,457 in 1940 and stood at 55,502 in 1980—fell to below 29,000 by 1990.

Although West Virginia always had been one of the nation's poorest states, the economic hemorrhage forced many Mountaineers to throw in the towel. Of the state's 55 counties, 44 lost population during the 1980s, with 21 dropping by 10 percent or more. So many West Virginians headed down Interstate 77—

the "Hillbilly Highway"—for jobs in the booming Charlotte, N.C., area that North Carolina's gain of a House seat for the 1990s could be seen as an almost direct transfer from West Virginia.

Still, the traditional backbone of Democratic strength in West Virginia—blue-collar workers, coal miners and rural poor—remained firm. Most of these voters were far from the reach of GOP entreaties. In 1988, George Bush's talk of economic growth under the Reagan administration rang hollow in the hills of West Virginia. Democrat Michael S. Dukakis carried the state with 52 percent of the vote. Bill Clinton scored one of his highest percentages in 1992.

In addition, Democrats were well-positioned to take some credit for what job growth there had been, thanks to the federal funding pipeline established by sixth-term Sen. Robert C. Byrd, chairman of the Appropriations Committee. Byrd already had fulfilled a pledge, made when he took the Appropriations chair in 1989, to channel $1 billion to his home state. The largess came in the form of roads and other infrastructure, federal agency relocations and high-tech research programs that fostered West Virginia's nascent computer software industry in Morgantown (home of West Virginia University) and Wheeling (Wheeling Jesuit College).

West Virginia's affordable housing prices also were an asset in economic development. The median price of an owner-occupied unit in the state, according to the 1990 census, was $47,900—a bargain that helped lure emigrants from the high-cost Washington area to the Republican-leaning eastern panhandle. Of the five counties in West Virginia with population growth of more than 10 percent in the 1980s, four were in the panhandle.

Table 1 Population

District	Population	Population under 18	Voting-age population	Median age
1	598,056	141,504	456,552	35.6
2	597,921	149,096	448,825	35.4
3	597,500	152,977	444,523	35.3
State	1,793,477	443,577	1,349,900	35.4

Table 2 Voting-Age Persons

District	White*	Black*	American Indian, Eskimo, or Aleut*	Asian or Pacific Islander*	Other*	Hispanic*	Male*	Female*
1	97.7%	1.5%	0.2%	0.5%	0.1%	0.5%	47.0%	53.0%
2	96.3	3.1	0.1	0.4	0.1	0.4	47.4	52.6
3	95.3	4.3	0.1	0.3	0.1	0.4	46.4	53.6
State	96.4	3.0	0.1	0.4	0.1	0.4	46.9	53.1

As percent of voting-age population.

Table 3 Voting-Age Persons by Age Groups

District	18-24*	25-44*	45-54*	55-64*	65 and over*
1	14.6%	38.1%	14.0%	12.8%	20.5%
2	12.3	40.8	14.5	13.2	19.2
3	13.1	39.5	14.0	13.3	20.1
State	13.3	39.5	14.2	13.1	19.9

As percent of voting-age population.

Table 4 Income and Occupation

District	Median family income	Families in poverty	White collar*	Blue collar*	Service*	Farm*
1	$27,220	13.4%	50.6%	33.0%	14.7%	1.7%
2	26,917	14.2	51.9	32.4	13.2	2.6
3	22,250	20.3	49.8	33.9	14.5	1.8
State	25,602	16.0	50.8	33.0	14.1	2.0

As percent of employed persons age 16 and over.

Table 5 Education: School Years Completed

District	Less than grade 9*	Grades 9-12 no diploma*	High school diploma*	College bachelor's degree or higher*
1	13.5%	15.6%	38.8%	13.7%
2	16.2	16.5	37.3	13.1
3	20.6	19.7	33.8	10.2
State	16.8	17.3	36.6	12.3

As percent of persons age 25 and over.

Table 6 Housing and Residential Patterns

District	Owner occupied	Renter occupied	Urban	Rural
1	73.9%	26.1%	44.9%	55.1%
2	73.9	26.1	37.8	62.2
3	74.4	25.6	25.7	74.3
State	74.1	25.9	36.1	63.9

1st District

North — Wheeling; Parkersburg; Morgantown

Its economy dependent on coal and heavy industries such as steel, chemicals and glass, northern West Virginia was crushed by economic depression during the 1980s. Factories closed or slashed payrolls; coal mines mechanized and got by with thousands fewer workers. The 1st contains six of West Virginia's 10 largest cities. All lost population during the 1980s; Wheeling fell 19 percent to under 35,000.

However, a nascent technology sector brightens economic prospects for the 1st. Morgantown, which has a population of nearly 26,000, is the site of West Virginia University (21,000 students) and the hub of the area's high-tech growth. Located amid the coal fields of Monongalia County (the state's third-leading coal-producing county), Morgantown is home to Software Valley, an organization that promotes regional computer-oriented business and research activity.

Other areas are working to diversify. Clarksburg and Bridge-port (Harrison County) will benefit from West Virginia Democratic Sen. Robert C. Byrd's biggest federal plum, a $185 million relocation of the FBI's fingerprinting center. Wheeling (Ohio County) is also making some progress with aid from Byrd's funding pipeline. A computer software industry is growing around Wheeling Jesuit College, site of the federal government's National Technology Transfer Center and the Classroom of the Future, both NASA programs.

Since the mid-1980s, Wheeling has benefited from tourists' interest in the "Festival of Lights," a fall/winter display of Christmas lights at Oglebay Park just outside the city. Wheeling itself has become known as the "City of Lights."

Though trimmed down, traditional industries still play an important economic role. Weirton Steel Co. in Hancock and Boone counties is the one of the nation's largest employee-owned companies. In 1992 blue-collar voters in the industrial and coal-mining areas of the district gave strong support to the Democratic House nominee Alan Mollohan, who ran unopposed; in the 1992 presidential race Bill Clinton won Marion County with 56 percent of the vote.

However, there are Republican pockets in the 1st that make it competitive in presidential contests. Although George Bush lost nearly 2-to-1 in many of the 1st's central counties, he won in the easternmost and westernmost ends of the district.

Although Wheeling is known as an industrial town, it has long doubled as the commercial center for the northern panhandle. It has a sizable white-collar constituency that leans Republican.

Farther down the Ohio River is Parkersburg, which has nearly 34,000 residents. The region has a large chemical industry and is also a regional trade center. Farmland adds to GOP strength in Wood County; Bush won 60 percent there in 1988.

In the eastern panhandle, coal mines again give way to farms. This is West Virginia's strongest Republican area, with a GOP tradition dating back to the Civil War: Bush won the eastern counties of Mineral, Preston and Grant in 1992.

Election Returns

	1st District	Democrat	Republican
1992	President*	113,756 (46.3%)	86,131 (35.0%)
	House	172,924 (100.0%)	—
1988	President	117,705 (50.4%)	115,989 (49.6%)
	Senate	150,468 (66.3%)	76,610 (33.7%)
	Governor	127,885 (54.9%)	105,193 (45.1%)

Vote for Perot was 45,856 (18.7%).

Demographics

Population 598,056

Percent change from 1980 22.4%

Land area 5,947 square miles

Population per square mile 101

Counties, 1990 population

Barbour 15,699	Ohio 50,871
Brooke 26,992	Pleasants 7,546
Doddridge 6,994	Preston 29,037
Grant 10,428	Ritchie 10,233
Hancock 35,233	Taylor 15,144
Harrison 69,371	Tucker 7,728
Marion 57,249	Tyler 9,796
Marshall 37,356	Wetzel 19,258
Mineral 26,697	Wood 86,915
Monongalia 75,509	

Cities, 1990 population (10,000 or more)

Clarksburg 18,059	Parkersburg 33,862
Fairmont 20,210	Vienna 10,862
Morgantown 25,879	Weirton 22,124
Moundsville 10,753	Wheeling 34,882

Race and Hispanic origin

White 97.6%
Black 1.6%
American Indian, Eskimo, or Aleut. 0.2%
Asian or Pacific Islander 0.5%
Other 0.1%
Hispanic origin 0.5%

Ancestry

American 8.7%	Italian 7.0%
Dutch 5.1%	Polish 3.4%
English 15.3%	Scotch Irish 3.6%
French 2.6%	Scottish 2.1%
German 33.2%	Slovakian 1.4%
Irish 21.6%	Welsh 1.3%

Universities/colleges, 1990-1991 enrollment

Alderson Broaddus College, Philippi 744
Bethany College, Bethany 859
Fairmont State College, Fairmont 6,305
Ohio Valley College, Parkersburg 205
Potomac State College of West Virginia, Keyser 1,348
Salem-Teikyo University, Salem 523
West Liberty State College, West Liberty 2,386
West Virginia North Community College, Wheeling 2,884
West Virginia University, Parkersburg 3,603
West Virginia University, Morgantown 20,854
Wheeling Jesuit College, Wheeling 1,396

Newspapers, total circulation (in all districts)

Clarksburg Exponent/Telegram 21,106
Cumberland News 31,511
East Liverpool Review 12,340
Fairmont Times 14,184
Morgantown Dominion Post 20,217
Parkersburg News/Sentinel 34,079
Steubenville Herald-Star 21,579
Weirton Daily Times 8,108
Wheeling News Register & Intelligencer 39,505

Commercial television stations, affiliations

ADI: Clarksburg-Weston (41%), Wheeling-Steubenville (19%), Pittsburgh (18%), Harrisonburg (8%), Parkersburg (6%), Washington, D.C. (5%) and Charleston-Huntington (2%)
WLYJ, Clarksburg (None)
WBOY-TV, Clarksburg (NBC)

Cable television systems, total subscribers

CVI; Barrackville 10,330
CVI; Clarksburg 13,465
Century Cable; Morgantown 13,000
Dimension Cable Services; Weirton 8,606
TCI of West Virginia; Bethlehem 23,497
TCI of West Virginia; Moundsville 6,328
TCI of West Virginia; New Martinsville 6,500
TCI of West Virginia; Parkersburg 23,874

Businesses and other major employers

Weirton Steel Corp.; Weirton; steel products 7,582
West Virginia University; Morgantown 5,000
Consolidation Coal Co.; Morgantown; coal mining 3,000
Du Pont E. I. De Nemours & Co.; Parkersburg; plastics products 2,800
Laurel Run Mining Co.; Mount Storm; coal mining 2,000
General Electric Co.; Washington; plastics 1,500
County of Harrison/Board of Education; Clarksburg 1,500
Wheeling Hospital Medical Park; Wheeling 1,500
U.S. Treasury Dept.; Parkersburg 1,200
St. Joseph Hospital; Parkersburg 1,130
Miles Inc.; New Martinsville; inorganic chemicals 1,125
Consolidation Coal Co.; Fairmont; coal mining 1,100
United Hospital Center Inc.; Clarksburg 1,100
Monongalia County General Hospital; Morgantown 1,100
Camden-Clark Memorial Hospital; Parkersburg 1,096
Ohio Valley Medical Center Inc.; Wheeling 1,026
Consolidation Coal Co.; Moundsville; coal mining 1,000
Hercules Inc./Hercules Aerospace Co.; Keyser; research services 990
Wheeling Hospital Inc.; Wheeling 975
Hercules Inc./Hercules Aerospace; Ft. Ashby; petroleum refining 925
General Electric Co.; Parkersburg; plastics 850
O. Ames Co.; Parkersburg; garden stores 850
Southern Ohio Coal Co./Martinka Mine No. 1; Fairmont; coal mining 801
PPG Industries Inc./Chemical Group; New Martinsville; organic chemicals 800
Fairmont General Hospital; Fairmont 800
T. S. L. Ltd.; Chester; personnel supply services 798
Homer Laughlin China Co.; Newell; dinnerware/pottery 780
North American Philips Corp.; Fairmont; electric lighting 750
Weirton Medical Center Inc.; Weirton 715
County of Preston/Board of Education; Kingwood 700
Nashua Photo Inc.; Parkersburg; photofinishing lab 650
Union Carbide Chemical & Plastics Co.; Sistersville; carbon/graphite products 600
American Cyanamid Co.; Belmont; pharmaceuticals 600
Columbia Gas Transmission Corp.; Clarksburg; gas distribution 575
Corning Inc.; Parkersburg; glass products 550
Wheeling-Pittsburgh Corp.; Wheeling; steel products 550
Reynolds Memorial Hospital; Glen Dale 550
Ohio Power Co.; Moundsville; electric services 511

2nd District

Center — Charleston; Eastern Panhandle

The "bicoastal" 2nd spans the state, starting on the west at the Ohio River, moving east to take in the state capital of Charleston (in Kanawha County) and ending in the historic eastern panhandle town of Harpers Ferry, at the confluence of the Shenandoah and Potomac rivers.

The 2nd's mountainous middle—which includes Kanawha, the state's largest county with about 208,000 residents—retains its industrial character and strong Democratic orientation.

Charleston, with just over 57,000 people, is the district's dominant city. Chemical plants that provide jobs in "Chemical Valley" along the Kanawha River also spark environmental concerns. Charleston's economy is bolstered by the state payroll and by the Charleston Town Center, a regional mall that draws shoppers from across West Virginia, Kentucky and Ohio.

There is a conservative streak in Kanawha County, evidenced by school-busing and textbook-banning controversies of the recent past. However, the economic dropoff in Kanawha's industrial sector has helped Democrats maintain their edge in the county, which lost 10 percent of its population in the 1980s; Bill Clinton won the county in 1992 with 47 percent. The mainly Democratic mountain regions north and east of Kanawha remain heavily dependent on coal.

Republican strength in the 2nd is concentrated in two fast-growing exurban areas at the district's edges. In the eastern panhandle, the populations of Berkeley (just over 59,000) and Jefferson (nearly 36,000) counties—within commuting distance of Washington—grew by 27 percent and 19 percent, respectively.

The commuter class in the panhandle is being joined by white-collar workers brought in by the federal government. Efforts to consolidate Central Intelligence Agency functions at a Jefferson County site, supported by Sen. Robert C. Byrd, have caused a stir among D.C.-area legislators.

The white-collar growth has supplemented a local GOP tradition that began in the Civil War era, when the eastern counties were at the front lines of some Civil War incidents. (Abolitionist John Brown staged his 1859 raid on the U.S. arsenal at Harpers Ferry and was hanged in nearby Charles Town.) In 1988 and 1992, George Bush carried all the eastern panhandle.

The other area where Republicans dominate for president and compete for lower offices is Putnam County, just west of Charleston. Putnam's population increased 12 percent during the 1980s to nearly 43,000. Bush won the county with 55 percent in 1988 and carried it with 44 percent in 1992.

The more level terrain at the ends of the district also supports much of West Virginia's agricultural activity. Jefferson County leads the state in corn and dairy cattle; Berkeley is tops in hogs. In the far west, Mason County grows corn and tobacco and raises livestock.

Election Returns

	2nd District	Democrat	Republican
1992	President*	104,257 (45.0%)	90,375 (39.0%)
	House	143,988 (70.9%)	59,102 (29.1%)
1988	President	104,450 (48.4%)	111,398 (51.6%)
	Senate	129,482 (61.3%)	81,645 (38.7%)
	Governor	123,202 (57.4%)	91,470 (42.6%)

Vote for Perot was 36,813 (15.9%).

Demographics

Population 597,921

Percent change from 1980 22.7%

Land area 9,455 square miles

Population per square mile 63

Counties, 1990 population

Berkeley 59,253	Lewis 17,223
Braxton 12,998	Mason 25,178
Calhoun 7,885	Morgan 12,128
Clay 9,983	Nicholas 26,775
Gilmer 7,669	Pendleton 8,054
Hampshire 16,498	Putnam 42,835
Hardy 10,977	Randolph 27,803
Jackson 25,938	Roane 15,120
Jefferson 35,926	Upshur 22,867
Kanawha 207,619	Wirt 5,192

Cities, 1990 population

Charleston 57,287	South Charleston 13,645
Cross Lanes CDP 10,878	St. Albans 11,194
Martinsburg 14,073	

Race and Hispanic origin

White 96.0%
Black 3.3%
American Indian, Eskimo, or Aleut. 0.1%
Asian or Pacific Islander 0.4%
Other 0.1%
Hispanic origin 0.5%

Ancestry

American 14.7%	Irish 18.8%
Dutch 4.0%	Italian 2.5%
English 15.9%	Scotch Irish 2.9%
French 2.3%	Scottish 2.1%
German 28.0%	

Universities/colleges, 1990-1991 enrollment

Davis & Elkins College, Elkins 892
Glenville State College, Glenville 2,238
National Education Center, Cross Lanes 377
Shepherd College, Shepherdstown 3,694
University of Charleston, Charleston 1,421
West Virginia College of Graduate Studies, Institute 2,153
West Virginia State College, Institute 4,834
West Virginia Wesleyan College, Buckhannon 1,629

Newspapers, total circulation (in all districts)

Charleston Gazette/Daily Mail 102,234
Clarksburg Exponent/Telegram 21,106
Cumberland News 31,511
Elkins Inter Mountain 11,059
Hagerstown Herald-Mail 40,013
Martinsburg Journal 17,228
Parkersburg News/Sentinel 34,079
Washington Post 810,904

Commercial television stations, affiliations

ADI: Charleston-Huntington (49%), Clarksburg-Weston (22%), Washington, D.C. (21%) and Harrisonburg (7%)
WCHS-TV, Charleston (ABC)

WVAH-TV, Charleston (Fox)
WDTV, Weston (CBS)

Cable television systems, total subscribers
Cablevision; Point Pleasant 14,465
Capital Cablevision; Charleston 33,000
Harmon Cable Communications; Nitro City 13,895
Tele-Media Co.; Chelyan 16,978
Triax Cablevision USA; Beverly 6,551
Warner Amex Cable; Martinsburg 5,868

Military installations, 1991
Eastern West Virginia Regional Airport Shepherd Field Air Force Guard Station, Martinsburg 288
Yeager Airport Air Force Guard Station, Charleston 244

Businesses and other major employers
Union Carbide Chemical & Plastic Co.; Charleston; organic chemicals 2,700
Columbia Gas Transmission Corp.; Charleston; gas distribution 1,745
Ravenswood Aluminum Corp.; Ravenswood; aluminum 1,500
Bethenergy Mines Inc.; Drennen; mining 1,482
Rhone-Poulenc AG Co.; Institute; agricultural chemicals 1,350
U.S. Veterans Affairs Dept.; Martinsburg; hospital 1,200
Charleston Area Medical Center; Charleston 1,200
Du Pont E. I. De Nemours & Co./Belle Plant; Belle; inorganic chemicals 1,125
State of West Virginia/Schools Service; Charleston 1,100
General Motors Corp.; Martinsburg; warehousing 1,000
State of West Virginia/Highways Dept.; Charleston 1,000
United Parcel Service Inc.; Charleston; mail services 1,000
Herbert J. Thomas Memorial Hospital; Charleston 1,000
State of West Virginia/Board of Vocational Education; Charleston; job training 850
Wampler-Longacre Chicken Inc.; Moorefield; poultry products 800
U.S. Postal Service; Charleston 800
St. Francis Hospital of Charleston; Charleston 705
Corning Inc.; Martinsburg; glass/glassware 700
G. C. Ames Co. Inc./G. C. Murphy Co.; Dunbar; department stores 700
U.S. Internal Revenue Service; Martinsburg 700
State of West Virginia/Public Safety Dept.; Charleston 700
City Hospital Inc.; Martinsburg 683
State of West Virginia/Commerce Dept.; Charleston 630
State of West Virginia; Charleston 630
Weston Hospital; Weston 620
One Valley Bank of Charleston; Charleston; commercial banks 573
County of Upshur/Board of Education; Buckhannon 545
C&J Clark America Inc./Hanover Shoe; Franklin; footwear 525
West Virginia State College; Institute 525
State of West Virginia/Tax Dept.; Charleston 520
Appalachian Power Co./John Amos Power Plant; Saint Albans; electric services 515

3rd District

South — Huntington; Beckley

The 3rd—which takes in the state's southern counties—is known as the "coal district." Six of the state's 10 leading coal-producing counties—including the top two (Boone and Mingo)—are in the 3rd.

Dependence on coal produces a common economic trait: hardship. While coal has been produced at near-record tonnages in recent years, technological advances have sharply reduced the need for labor. One glaring example of distress is McDowell County in southern West Virginia. Its population slipped 29 percent—from almost 50,000 to just over 35,000—during the 1980s.

Soaring unemployment added misery to a region that has always had pockets of Appalachian poverty. Democrats remain the dominant political force here; Bill Clinton won the 3rd with 55 percent in 1992.

Every county in the 3rd lost residents during the 1980s. Although emigration has reduced the work force by thousands, unemployment remains stubbornly high in many areas. Insufficient highways and other infrastructural deficiencies hinder growth in mountain country.

The population of Huntington (Cabell County), the second-largest city in the state, fell 14 percent in the 1980s to just under 55,000 but is cushioned by an Ohio River location that provides for a diversified economy. CSX railroad, Inco Alloys and an Owens-Illinois glass company—along with ARMCO Steel Co. and Ashland Oil Inc. in the Ashland, Ky., area—provide jobs. Huntington is home to Marshall University (12,400 students); the city's white-collar sector and tobacco growers help make Cabell the most Republican part of the 3rd. George Bush won Cabell with 53 percent in 1988. But GOP success does not run deep: Only one of Cabell's six state House members is a Republican, and Clinton carried the county in 1992.

Yet this is a hardy success rate for the GOP compared with the rest of the district. Just to the east is the heart of coal country, Democratic turf where some residents still idolize John F. Kennedy, whose 1960 primary win in West Virginia was pivotal to his presidential nomination.

Near the eastern edge of the coal fields is Beckley (population 18,000), which promotes as economic assets its location near Interstates 77 and 64 and the surrounding area's tourist potential: Local rivers are popular with whitewater rafters. The eastern part of the 3rd also has the state's most venerable tourist establishment: the Greenbrier resort in White Sulphur Springs.

Some communities are crafting aspects of their industrial heritage into tourist attractions. These aspects include the sometimes ugly events in Mingo County, site of the "West Virginia Mine Wars" between labor activists and union-busting mine owners during the 1920s (the subject of the movie "Matewan"). "Bloody Mingo" was also the site of part of the fighting between the Hatfields and McCoys.

Election Returns

	3rd District	Democrat	Republican
1992	President*	112,988 (55.2%)	65,468 (32.0%)
	House	122,279 (65.6%)	64,012 (34.4%)
1988	President	118,861 (59.0%)	82,678 (41.0%)
	Senate	131,033 (66.7%)	65,309 (33.3%)
	Governor	131,334 (65.1%)	70,509 (34.9%)

*Vote for Perot was 26,160 (12.8%).

Demographics

Population 597,500

Percent change from 1980 22.9%

Land area 8,684 square miles

Population per square mile 69

Counties, 1990 population

Boone 25,870
Cabell 96,827
Fayette 47,952
Greenbrier 34,693
Lincoln 21,382
Logan 43,032
McDowell 35,233
Mercer 64,980

Mingo 33,739
Monroe 12,406
Pocahontas 9,008
Raleigh 76,819
Summers 14,204
Wayne 41,636
Webster 10,729
Wyoming 28,990

Cities, 1990 population

Beckley 18,296
Bluefield 12,756

Huntington 54,844

Race and Hispanic origin

White 95.0%
Black 4.5%
American Indian, Eskimo, or Aleut. 0.1%
Asian or Pacific Islander 0.3%
Other 0.1%
Hispanic origin 0.4%

Ancestry

American 21.5%
Dutch 3.5%
English 13.9%
French 1.9%
German 17.2%

Irish 17.9%
Italian 2.5%
Scotch Irish 2.6%
Scottish 1.5%

Universities/colleges, 1990-1991 enrollment

Appalachian Bible College, Bradley 212
Beckley College, Beckley 1,942
Bluefield State College, Bluefield 2,702
Concord College, Athens 2,651
Huntington Junior College, Huntington 483
Marshall University, Huntington 12,407
Southern West Virginia Community College, Logan 2,911
West Virginia Institute of Technology, Montgomery 2,898
West Virginia School of Osteopathic Medicine, Lewisburg 240

Newspapers, total circulation (in all districts)

Beckley Register/Herald 31,447
Bluefield Daily Telegraph 23,275
Charleston Gazette/Daily Mail 102,234
Huntington Herald Dispatch 42,242
Logan Banner 9,816
Williamson Daily News 10,791

Commercial television stations, affiliations

ADI: Bluefield-Beckley-Oak Hill (53%), Charleston-Huntington (30%), Roanoke-Lynchburg (11%) and Clarksburg-Weston (6%)
WTSF, Ashland (None)
WVVA, Bluefield (NBC)
WOWK-TV, Huntington (CBS)
WSAZ-TV, Huntington (NBC)
WOAY-TV, Oak Hill (ABC)

Cable television systems, total subscribers

Beckley Telecable; Beckley 18,597
Century Cable; Huntington 21,000
Mountain State Cable Inc.; Oak Hill 5,006
Princeton Telecable; Princeton 8,312
TCI of West Virginia; Logan 11,075
Tele-Media Co.; Chelyan 16,978
Telescripps Cable Co.; Bluefield 14,231
Triax Communications; Williamson 11,000

Businesses and other major employers

Marshall University; Huntington 2,300
St. Mary's Hospital Inc.; Huntington 1,850
Inco Alloys Intl. Inc.; Huntington; nickel/alloys 1,500
CSX Hotels Inc./Greenbrier Hotel; White Sulphur Springs; hotel 1,500
Huntington Cabell Hospital; Huntington 1,300
County of McDowell/Board of Education; Welch 1,220
U.S. Steel Mining Co. Inc.; Pineville; metal mining services 1,000
Norfolk Southern Corp.; Williamson; railroads 1,000
County of Wyoming; Pineville 980
Ames Dept. Stores Inc.; Beckley; department stores 860
Princeton Community Hospital; Princeton 850
CSX Transportation Inc.; Huntington; railroads 800
Owens-Illinois Inc./Owens Brockway Glass; Huntington; glass/glassware 798
Raleigh General Hospital; Beckley 750
Bluefield Regional Medical Center; Bluefield 743
U.S. Army Corps of Engineers; Huntington; engineering services 700
Logan General Hospital; Logan 590
County of Raleigh/School District; Beckley 586
Steel of West Virginia Inc.; Huntington; steel products 567

Wisconsin

Although it is the birthplace of the Progressive movement, Wisconsin is not as liberal as its reputation indicates. The Badger State, in fact, is a particularly difficult state to nudge toward any political party or movement. Political independence, not liberalism, has marked the state's last half-century. Most voters have only a passing identification with a political party. They abhor any hint of political bossism—Wisconsin has always been an interesting contrast to its southern neighbor, Illinois—and are rarely swayed by endorsements. Ticket-splitting is second nature.

Wisconsin's strongest fling with movement politics occurred at the turn of the century, when Republican Robert M. "Fighting Bob" La Follette served as governor, then senator, then ran as the Progressive Party's 1924 presidential nominee.

In presidential campaigns, Wisconsin tended to be more Republican than the nation as a whole from 1944 to 1964, and a little more Democratic than the rest of the nation since then. It was a key state for Jimmy Carter in 1976, somewhat less enthusiastic than the rest of the country in its support for Ronald Reagan in 1980 and 1984, then went for Michael S. Dukakis and Bill Clinton in 1988 and 1992.

The state's liberal reputation was more deserved in the Democratic primary. It provided crucial primary victories for John F. Kennedy in 1960, Eugene McCarthy in 1968 and George McGovern in 1972. The Democratic primary has had a lower profile since it nearly provided an upset victory for Morris Udall in 1976.

Although Republicans and progressives dominated the governor's office for the first half of the 1900s, since 1958 neither party has retained the governor's office for more than eight years at a time. Nearly every one of those races has been competitive, though two-term GOP Gov. Tommy G. Thompson found a particularly winning message in 1986 and 1990 in his call for lower taxes and tougher welfare restrictions. Thompson presided over Wisconsin during an era that was considered kinder to the state economically and demographically than the recession-wracked early 1980s had been.

There were still plenty of downsides as Wisconsin entered the 1990s. Several major manufacturing anchors had either closed or were slimmed down. When dairy prices dropped, a calamitous occurrence in a state that calls itself "America's Dairyland," farmers were pressed to sustain their livelihood.

Even so, the paper industry, the dominant manufacturer in the Fox River Valley, survived the downturn relatively intact. Some of Milwaukee's heavy industries emerged from the early 1980s leaner and more modernized. Many areas of the state that capitalized on such natural attributes as proximity to a lakefront, dense woods or picturesque hills enjoyed a tourism boom.

The most important aspect of Wisconsin's population in the past decade is that it grew by 4 percent—barely enough to keep its nine congressional seats. There had been speculation that the state would drop to eight districts for the first time since 1870.

A redistricting plan passed both legislative chambers with little fanfare April 14, 1992; Thompson signed it into law April 28.

Historically, Wisconsin has rarely experienced dramatic population changes or strong migratory movements. Its ethnic mix, consisting mainly of Scandinavians, Germans and eastern Europeans, has been stable for some time. Most recent growth has come from a natural increase of births over deaths.

The fastest-growing regions of the state in the 1980s were generally smaller metropolitan areas—Dane County, featuring the main state university campus, the state capital and a growing service sector, and the Fox River Valley, which is strongly affected by the paper industry. Rural communities that relied somewhat less on agriculture and more on attracting retirees and tourists also grew. So did suburban communities outside of Milwaukee and Minneapolis-St. Paul, though many of the Milwaukee suburbs grew more slowly than they did in the 1970s.

There were few dramatic population losers. The city and county of Milwaukee continued to lose population, though at a slower pace than they had in the 1970s. This slowdown of flight from the state's largest city and county also contributed to slower growth in adjoining suburbs.

Rural counties that depended on the changing fortunes of the dairy industry lost population in the 1980s, especially those in the southwestern part of the state that lack access to an interstate highway. The northwesternmost counties, adjacent to Lake Superior, also continued to lose population.

WISCONSIN

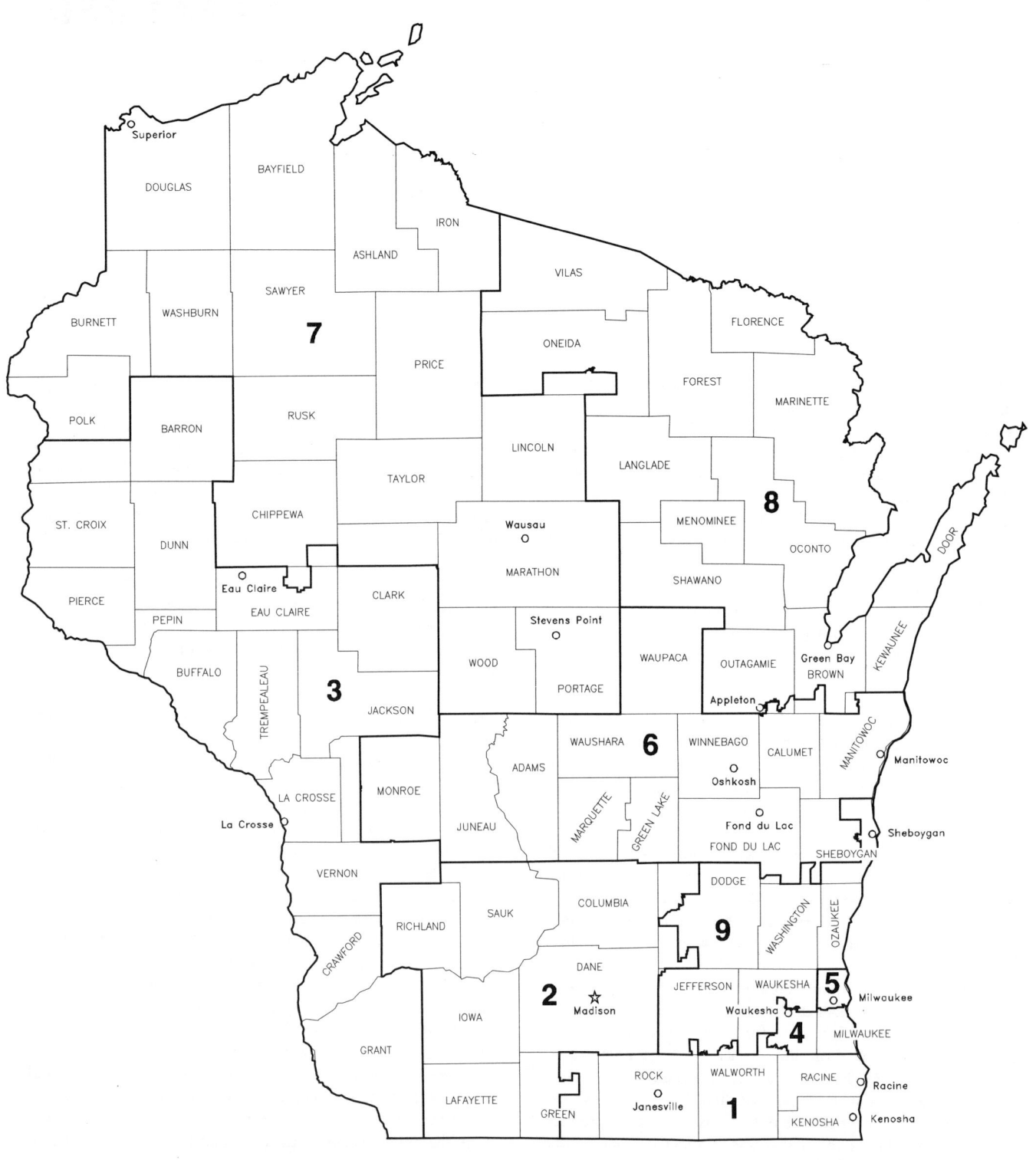

Superior

DOUGLAS

BAYFIELD

IRON

ASHLAND

VILAS

SAWYER

FLORENCE

BURNETT

WASHBURN

7

PRICE

ONEIDA

FOREST

MARINETTE

POLK

BARRON

RUSK

LINCOLN

LANGLADE

8

MARINETTE

ST. CROIX

TAYLOR

CHIPPEWA

MENOMINEE

OCONTO

DUNN

Wausau

PIERCE

Eau Claire

EAU CLAIRE

CLARK

MARATHON

SHAWANO

PEPIN

Stevens Point

DOOR

BUFFALO

TREMPEALEAU

JACKSON

3

WOOD

PORTAGE

WAUPACA

OUTAGAMIE

Green Bay
BROWN

KEWAUNEE

Appleton

LA CROSSE

MONROE

WAUSHARA

6

WINNEBAGO

CALUMET

MANITOWOC

Manitowoc

La Crosse

ADAMS

MARQUETTE

GREEN LAKE

Oshkosh

VERNON

JUNEAU

Fond du Lac

Sheboygan

FOND DU LAC

SHEBOYGAN

CRAWFORD

RICHLAND

SAUK

COLUMBIA

DODGE

9

WASHINGTON

OZAUKEE

DANE

2

Madison

JEFFERSON

WAUKESHA

5

Milwaukee

IOWA

Waukesha

4

MILWAUKEE

GRANT

LAFAYETTE

GREEN

ROCK

Janesville

WALWORTH

1

RACINE

Racine

KENOSHA

Kenosha

Table 1   Population

District	Population	Population under 18	Voting-age population	Median age
1	543,530	146,241	397,289	32.7
2	543,532	131,139	412,393	31.8
3	543,533	145,101	398,432	32.1
4	543,527	133,437	410,090	33.6
5	543,530	147,588	395,942	31.0
6	543,652	143,140	400,512	33.9
7	543,529	147,853	395,676	33.7
8	543,404	147,125	396,279	33.2
9	543,532	147,358	396,174	34.1
State	4,891,769	1,288,982	3,602,787	32.9

Table 2   Voting-Age Persons

District	White*	Black*	American Indian, Eskimo, or Aleut*	Asian or Pacific Islander*	Other*	Hispanic*	Male*	Female*
1	93.6%	4.3%	0.3%	0.5%	1.3%	2.7%	47.9%	52.1%
2	96.1	1.7	0.3	1.6	0.3	1.0	48.7	51.3
3	98.6	0.2	0.4	0.7	0.1	0.4	48.4	51.6
4	95.2	0.7	0.7	1.0	2.3	4.8	47.7	52.3
5	68.3	28.7	0.4	1.5	1.0	2.2	45.2	54.8
6	98.4	0.4	0.4	0.5	0.2	0.7	48.7	51.3
7	97.9	0.1	1.3	0.6	0.1	0.3	48.6	51.4
8	96.9	0.3	2.1	0.6	0.2	0.5	48.4	51.6
9	98.5	0.4	0.2	0.6	0.3	0.8	49.0	51.0
State	93.8	4.1	0.7	0.9	0.7	1.5	48.1	51.9

*As percent of voting-age population.

Table 3   Voting-Age Persons by Age Groups

District	18-24*	25-44*	45-54*	55-64*	65 and over*
1	14.3%	42.9%	14.1%	11.6%	17.1%
2	17.5	45.4	12.4	9.8	14.9
3	17.2	40.2	12.7	10.9	19.0
4	12.7	44.4	13.1	12.1	17.7
5	16.3	44.3	11.3	10.6	17.5
6	12.9	41.3	13.4	12.3	20.1
7	12.8	40.9	13.5	12.1	20.7
8	12.7	43.1	13.6	11.7	19.0
9	11.7	43.7	15.6	12.3	16.8
State	14.2	42.9	13.3	11.5	18.1

*As percent of voting-age population.

Table 4   Income and Occupation

District	Median family income	Families in poverty	White collar*	Blue collar*	Service*	Farm*
1	$36,634	7.3%	49.3%	34.4%	13.8%	2.4%
2	37,432	5.5	59.9	21.9	13.0	5.2
3	31,244	8.3	46.8	28.5	15.2	9.4
4	38,681	6.1	57.6	28.9	13.0	0.5
5	31,831	17.1	61.7	23.7	14.2	0.5
6	33,268	6.1	44.4	35.7	14.3	5.6
7	30,490	8.4	46.2	31.8	14.7	7.3
8	33,172	7.5	49.3	31.9	13.8	4.9
9	42,177	2.9	54.2	31.7	11.3	2.8
State	35,082	7.6	52.3	29.8	13.6	4.3

*As percent of employed persons age 16 and over.

Table 5   Education: School Years Completed

District	Less than grade 9*	Grades 9-12 no diploma*	High school diploma*	College bachelor's degree or higher*
1	8.0%	14.9%	38.0%	14.8%
2	6.9	8.3	32.2	26.7
3	11.9	10.0	38.6	16.3
4	7.8	13.5	35.8	16.6
5	7.9	15.8	27.2	23.6
6	11.4	12.2	42.6	13.1
7	12.9	11.6	41.2	13.2
8	10.7	10.9	41.6	14.8
9	8.2	9.7	36.2	20.8
State	9.5	11.9	37.1	17.7

*As percent of persons age 25 and over.

Table 6   Housing and Residential Patterns

District	Owner occupied	Renter occupied	Urban	Rural
1	68.5%	31.5%	71.4%	28.6%
2	60.6	39.4	63.5	36.5
3	69.7	30.3	44.1	55.9
4	60.5	39.5	97.8	2.2
5	47.9	52.1	100.0	0.0
6	73.2	26.8	52.9	47.1
7	74.3	25.7	41.2	58.8
8	72.4	27.6	55.6	44.4
9	74.7	25.3	64.5	35.5
State	66.7	33.3	65.7	34.3

1st District

Southeast — Racine; Kenosha

Although it is dominated by four industrialized cities, the 1st is far from a Democratic stronghold.

Until Les Aspin's election in 1970, Democrats had won this district only twice in the 20th century—in 1958 and 1964. Both incumbents were defeated after serving single terms. The party also endured a long dry spell in presidential voting here. After Lyndon B. Johnson carried the district in 1964, not until 1988 did it return to the Democratic column, with a 51 percent victory for Michael S. Dukakis. In 1992, Bill Clinton won the 1st by 6 percentage points.

The district's two largest cities are sandwiched between Milwaukee and Chicago along Lake Michigan: Racine, originally settled by Danish immigrants, and Kenosha, with a sizable Italian community.

Located in Racine are the district's largest employers: J. I. Case, makers of farm equipment, and S. C. Johnson and Son, which makes home-care products. The Racine lakefront is in the process of being revitalized with a marina and condominiums. Racine is also known for its thin, buttery Danish pastries known as kringles. Kenosha has a branch of the University of Wisconsin and a Chrysler plant where about 1,100 people make Jeep engines. The city was dealt a sharp blow by the December 1988 closure of the main Chrysler-AMC plant, a cornerstone of Kenosha's economy for almost nine decades. Chrysler spent millions of dollars in severance pay, economic development aid and contributions to local civic groups, and the state helped retrain workers.

Kenosha's economic base is diversifying, and the area's affordable real estate prices are attracting some Chicago commuters. Within weeks of the big Chrysler plant closing, a waterfront development project was planned. A corporate park opened in Pleasant Prairie, just east of Interstate 94. Kenosha is still the headquarters for Jockey International Inc. and the Snap-On Tools Corp. The city has two factory outlet shopping centers popular with bargain-hunters; another lure for visitors is Dairyland, the nation's largest greyhound dog racing track.

Although labor's political clout in the 1st has diminished with the loss of industry, Kenosha County remains Democratic. Racine County is a political battleground; 1988 marked the first time a Democrat won the county's presidential vote since 1964.

In the west-central part of the district are the smaller industrial cities of Janesville and Beloit, in politically marginal Rock County. Beloit was settled by a group of immigrants from New Hampshire that founded Beloit College in 1846. Janesville's employers include a General Motors plant.

The strongest GOP vote in the 1st comes from Walworth County in the middle of the district. Resort complexes around Lake Geneva and Lake Delavan cater to wealthy vacationers from Milwaukee and Chicago. Soybeans grow so well in rural Walworth County that the Japanese Kikkoman soy sauce company built a plant in Walworth to brew and bottle its product.

Election Returns

	1st District	Democrat	Republican
1992	President*	109,790 (41.1%)	94,712 (35.5%)
	House	147,495 (57.6%)	104,352 (40.7%)
1990	Governor	56,235 (41.3%)	79,828 (58.7%)
1988	President	115,886 (51.4%)	109,696 (48.6%)
	Senate	113,806 (52.0%)	105,189 (48.0%)
1986	Senate	69,528 (48.8%)	73,093 (51.2%)
	Governor	73,334 (49.9%)	73,690 (50.1%)

Vote for Perot was 62,465 (23.4%).

Demographics

Population 543,530

Percent change from 1980 4.0%

Land area 2,208 square miles

Population per square mile 246

Counties, 1990 population

Green (pt.) 11,763	Rock 139,510
Jefferson (pt.) 3,739	Walworth 75,000
Kenosha 128,181	Waukesha (pt.) 10,303
Racine 175,034	

Cities, 1990 population (10,000 or more)

Beloit 35,573	Pleasant Prairie 11,961
Janesville 52,133	Racine 84,298
Kenosha 80,352	Whitewater 12,636

Race and Hispanic origin
White 92.0%
Black 5.4%
American Indian, Eskimo, or Aleut 0.3%
Asian or Pacific Islander 0.6%

Other 1.6%
Hispanic origin 3.4%

Ancestry

American 1.8%	Italian 5.6%
Czechoslovakian 1.9%	Norwegian 7.9%
Danish 3.9%	Polish 8.0%
Dutch 2.7%	Scotch Irish 1.3%
English 11.0%	Scottish 1.6%
French 4.7%	Slovakian 1.2%
German 48.5%	Swedish 3.4%
Irish 14.8%	Swiss 1.7%

Universities/colleges, 1990-1991 enrollment
Beloit College, Beloit 1,169
Blackhawk Technical College, Janesville 2,151
Carthage College, Kenosha 1,850
Gateway Technical College, Kenosha 9,309
University of Wisconsin-Parkside, Kenosha 5,308
University of Wisconsin, Whitewater 10,820

Newspapers, total circulation (in all districts)
Chicago Tribune 721,559
Kenosha News Sunday News 27,755
Milwaukee Journal 239,944
Milwaukee Sentinel Journal 164,820
Racine Journal Times 36,319
Rockford Register Star 75,020
Wisconsin State Journal Capital Times 107,967

Commercial television stations, affiliations
ADI: Milwaukee (56%) and Madison (44%)
WHKE, Kenosha (None)

Cable television systems, total subscribers
Beloit Cablevision; Beloit 18,100
Crown Cable; Janesville 24,899
Jones Intercable Inc.; Kenosha 20,308
Racine Telecable Corp.; Racine 34,487

Businesses and other major employers
General Motors Corp.; Janesville; truck assembly 5,300
Beloit Corp.; Beloit; paper-making machinery 2,000
Western Publishing Co.; Racine; book publishing 1,600
S. C. Johnson & Son Inc.; Racine; waxes/cleaners 1,411
S. C. Johnson & Son Inc.; Sturtevant; waxes/cleaners 1,225
Chrysler Corp.; Kenosha; motor vehicles 1,130
St. Mary's Medical Center Inc.; Racine 1,120
State of Wisconsin/Southern Wisconsin Center; Union Grove; residential care 1,047
Snap-On Tools Corp.; Kenosha; wrenches/handtools 1,000
County of Racine; Racine 1,000
University of Wisconsin; Whitewater 1,000
Mercy Hospital of Janesville; Janesville 935
St. Catherine's Hospital Inc.; Kenosha 905
Twin Disc Inc.; Racine; clutches 900
Emerson Electric Co./In-Sink Erator Div.; Racine; household appliances 900
St. Luke's Memorial Hospital; Racine 880
Beloit Memorial Hospital Inc.; Beloit 868
County of Rock; Janesville 857
Dairyland Greyhound Park Inc.; Kenosha; commercial sports 840
Kenosha Hospital & Medical Center; Kenosha 705
J. I. Case Corp.; Racine; farm equipment 700

Sta-Rite Industries Inc./Berkeley Pumps Div.; Delavan; water pumps 700

Coltec Industries Inc./Fairbanks Morse Engine Div.; Beloit; engines/turbines 683

University of Wisconsin-Parkside; Kenosha 600

Ganton Technologies Inc.; Sturtevant; aluminum die casting 597

Gateway Technical College; Kenosha 575

Tri-Clover Inc.; Kenosha; metal valves/pumps 565

Super Valu Stores Inc.; Pleasant Prairie; grocery stores 560

Modine Mfg. Co.; Racine; radiators/heat exchangers 550

Gander Mountain Inc.; Wilmot; sporting equipment catalog retailers 550

Abbey Group Ltd./Abbey Hotel; Fontana; hotel 550

Textron Inc./Jacobsen Div.; Racine; farm/garden machinery 540

Lab Safety Supply Inc.; Janesville; safety equipment/supplies 525

2nd District

South — Madison

Once described by former GOP Gov. Lee Dreyfus as "23 square miles surrounded by reality," Madison has long been Wisconsin's liberal centerpiece—*Progressive* magazine is published here—and it is one of the few cities with a foreign policy. Since 1924, when Robert M. La Follette carried Dane County as the Progressive Party's presidential candidate, Democrats have nearly always won here.

But times have changed, and politics have moderated considerably in the 2nd District. This was graphically demonstrated by Republican Scott Klug's 1990 upset of Democratic Rep. Robert W. Kastenmeier, a 32-year veteran, and Klug's 1992 re-election with more than 63 percent of the vote.

As the state's capital and home to its main university campus, Madison is dominated by its white-collar sector. About one-third of the area's work force is employed in government, primarily for the state or the University of Wisconsin, which helps keep employment stable. White-collar jobs are also supplied by several locally based insurance companies, such as American Family and CUNA Mutual. In addition, meat processor Oscar Mayer employs about 2,800 in the Madison area and Rayovac batteries (400 employees) has headquarters here.

Beyond the city limits, rapidly growing Dane County suburbs such as Verona, Fitchburg and Middleton strike a more conservative tone than the city itself, as do outlying communities such as Stoughton and Mount Horeb. But Democrats usually have carried Dane. Michael S. Dukakis won the county with 60 percent in 1988, and Democratic Senate candidate Herb Kohl polled 58 percent. In 1992, Bill Clinton won the district with 50 percent of the vote to George Bush's 32 percent. At the same time, Klug won the county by more than 40,000 votes.

The 2nd also covers a sizable portion of southern Wisconsin's Republican-voting rural areas, where farmers and small-town folks have long chafed at Madison's dominance of district politics. Outside the Madison area, agriculture and tourism sustain the district's economy. Dairying is important, and there is some beef production, although many livestock farmers have switched to raising corn as a cash crop.

In New Glarus (Green County), which was founded by the Swiss, the downtown has been redone to resemble a village in the mother country. Wisconsin Dells (Columbia County) lures tourists to view the garish attractions and natural wonders along the Wisconsin River. Just outside Spring Green (Sauk County) is Frank Lloyd Wright's Taliesin, a studio complex frequently used by the legendary architect that is now a thriving artist colony.

About 50 miles west of Madison is Dodgeville (Iowa County), headquarters to mail-order clothier Lands' End. Since the company moved here in 1978, property values have increased, the local economy has blossomed and additional facilities were opened in Cross Plains (Dane County) and Reedsburg (Sauk County).

Election Returns

		Democrat	Republican
	2nd District		
1992	President*	149,340 (50.4%)	94,368 (31.9%)
	House	108,291 (37.0%)	183,366 (62.6%)
1990	Governor	88,109 (50.0%)	88,012 (50.0%)
1988	President	140,562 (56.0%)	110,444 (44.0%)
	Senate	137,858 (55.6%)	109,902 (44.4%)
1986	Senate	95,656 (53.9%)	81,845 (46.1%)
	Governor	98,384 (53.2%)	86,652 (46.8%)

Vote for Perot was 52,552 (17.7%).

Demographics

Population 543,532

Percent change from 1980 3.9%

Land area 5,348 square miles

Population per square mile 102

Counties, 1990 population

Columbia 45,088	Jefferson (pt.) 2,097
Dane 367,085	Lafayette 16,076
Dodge (pt.) 9,964	Richland 17,521
Green (pt.) 18,576	Sauk 46,975
Iowa 20,150	

Cities, 1990 population (10,000 or more)

Fitchburg 15,648	Monroe 10,241
Madison 191,262	Sun Prairie 15,333
Middleton 13,289	

Race and Hispanic origin
White 95.5%
Black 2.1%
American Indian, Eskimo, or Aleut 0.3%
Asian or Pacific Islander 1.7%
Other 0.4%
Hispanic origin 1.2%

Ancestry

American 1.8%	Italian 2.5%
Czechoslovakian 2.0%	Norwegian 14.3%
Danish 1.3%	Polish 4.4%
Dutch 2.7%	Scotch Irish 1.1%
English 13.7%	Scottish 1.8%
French 3.8%	Swedish 2.4%
German 52.0%	Swiss 4.2%
Irish 16.6%	Welsh 1.0%

Universities/colleges, 1990-1991 enrollment
Edgewood College, Madison 1,399
Madison Area Technical College, Madison 12,411
Madison Business College, Madison 272
University of Wisconsin, Madison 43,209
Wisconsin School of Electronics, Madison 298

Newspapers, total circulation (in all districts)
Chicago Tribune 721,559
Milwaukee Journal 239,944
Milwaukee Sentinel Journal 164,820
Wisconsin State Journal Capital Times 107,967

Commercial television stations, affiliations
ADI: Madison (95%) and Milwaukee (5%)
WISC-TV, Madison (CBS)
WKOW-TV, Madison (ABC)
WMSN-TV, Madison (Fox)
WMTV, Madison (NBC)

Cable television systems, total subscribers
TCI of Wisconsin; Madison 70,000

Military installations, 1991
Truax Field (Air Force), Madison 295

Businesses and other major employers
University of Wisconsin; Madison 15,000
Lands' End Inc.; Dodgeville; catalog retailers 3,420
American Family Mutual Insurance Co.; Madison;
fire/marine/casualty insurance 2,800
State of Wisconsin/Industrial Labor Relations Dept.; Madison 2,600
State of Wisconsin/Health & Social Services Dept.; Madison 2,100
State of Wisconsin/Military Affairs Dept.; Madison 1,700
Meriter Hospital Inc.; Madison 1,450
SSM Health Care/St. Mary's Hospital; Madison 1,400
Madison Area Technical College; Madison 1,400
U.S. Veterans Affairs Dept.; Madison; hospital 1,200
State of Wisconsin/Revenue Dept.; Madison 1,200
State of Wisconsin; Madison; residential care 1,200
Graber Industries Inc.; Middleton; window hardware 1,121
CUNA Mutual Investment Corp.; Madison;
fire/marine/casualty insurance 1,032
GTE North Inc.; Sun Prairie; telephone communications 1,000
Oscar Mayer Foods Corp.; Madison; meat products 1,000
Swiss Colony Inc.; Monroe; catalog food retailers 1,000
State of Wisconsin/Natural Resources Dept.; Madison 875
Nicolet Instrument Corp.; Madison; electronic communications equipment 820
Wisconsin Bell Inc.; Madison; telephone utility 800
Madison Gas & Electric Co.; Madison; utility services 770
Hazleton Wisconsin Inc.; Madison; research services 740
Wisconsin Power & Light Co.; Madison; utility services 700
BOC Group Inc./Ohmeda Branch; Madison; medical equipment/supplies 650
Mendota Mental Health Institute; Madison 650
Webcrafters Inc.; Madison; commercial printing 630
County of Dane; Madison 620
North American Philips Corp./Advance Transformer Div.;
Monroe; electric distribution equipment 600
Marshall Erdmann & Assoc.; Madison; building construction/architectual services 600

Grede Foundries Inc.; Reedsburg; iron/steel foundries 600
Dean Medical Center; Madison 600
General Casualty of Wisconsin; Sun Prairie;
fire/marine/casualty insurance 583
St. Clare Hospital; Monroe 550
State of Wisconsin/Public Instruction Dept.; Madison 550
Flambeau Corp.; Baraboo; plastics products 525
Sysco Corp.; Baraboo; grocery products 520

3rd District

West — Eau Claire; La Crosse

In a state that bills itself as "America's Dairyland," the 3rd stands at the head of the herd. It has more cows than people and is one of the leading milk-producing districts in the nation.

But some dramatic economic and demographic changes are taking place in the 3rd, which hugs Wisconsin's western border with Minnesota and Iowa. Traditionally, the rural areas have relied mainly on small dairy farms, and its two biggest cities—Eau Claire and La Crosse—have been strongly influenced by heavy manufacturing.

Now, the cities are finding alternatives to heavy industry, and the communities closest to the twin cities are becoming thriving suburbs. The more successful dairy farms have evolved into multifamily operations, and tourism in some rural areas has taken hold. But downsizing of the dairy industry has taken its toll, particularly in rural communities without easy access to Interstate 94.

As a result, while the district's population growth in the 1980s mirrored the 4 percent increase in the state as a whole, there were wide differences within the 3rd. All of the counties along the district's northern edge (east and northeast of Minneapolis-St. Paul) grew during the decade. The pacesetter was St. Croix County, immediately east of the Twin Cities, which grew by 16 percent. But all of the counties in the southern two-thirds of the district lost population, except for La Crosse County, which grew by 8 percent.

There are only two cities of size in the district. Eau Claire, once a wild lumber outpost, has a paper mill producing disposable diapers and napkins. A Uniroyal plant that was once the city's largest employer is no more. However, blue-collar jobs have been replaced by white-collar opportunities in a burgeoning computer industry.

La Crosse, Wisconsin's only major Mississippi River city, once featured two locally owned *Fortune* 500 companies as its mainstays—the Trane Co., manufacturers of heating and air conditioning equipment, and G. Heileman Brewing Inc. But both were subject to hostile takeovers in the 1980s and have scaled down operations.

Democrats traditionally have held sway in the northern part of the district, around Eau Claire, and Republicans have had an edge in the south and in La Crosse. Some of those identifications are changing along with the economy, making the area quite competitive in state elections. Democrats have been gaining of late: In 1988, Michael S. Dukakis won the 3rd with 52 percent, and in 1992 Bill Clinton carried the district with 43 percent of the vote.

The 3rd remains heavily Scandinavian and German—dairy farmers in Osseo (Trempealeau County) still trade gossip over coffee and pie at the Norske Nook—though there are signs of growing ethnic diversity. The district also boasts five branches of the state university, which has helped attract three National Football League teams to set up summer training camps there.

Election Returns

		Democrat	Republican
	3rd District		
1992	President*	120,261 (43.2%)	90,731 (32.6%)
	House	108,664 (41.7%)	146,903 (56.4%)
1990	Governor	71,822 (45.8%)	84,884 (54.2%)
1988	President	125,680 (53.0%)	111,492 (47.0%)
	Senate	114,381 (48.8%)	119,885 (51.2%)
1986	Senate	71,365 (45.9%)	84,268 (54.1%)
	Governor	77,163 (47.5%)	85,378 (52.5%)

Vote for Perot was 67,134 (24.1%).

Demographics

Population 543,533

Percent change from 1980 3.9%

Land area 10,639 square miles

Population per square mile 51

Counties, 1990 population
Barron 40,750	La Crosse 97,904
Buffalo 13,584	Monroe (pt.) 12,789
Chippewa (pt.) 913	Pepin 7,107
Clark (pt.) 17,717	Pierce 32,765
Crawford 15,940	Polk (pt.) 16,895
Dunn 35,909	St. Croix 50,251
Eau Claire (pt.) 84,277	Trempealeau 25,263
Grant 49,264	Vernon 25,617
Jackson 16,588	

Cities, 1990 population (10,000 or more)
Eau Claire (pt.) 55,180	Onalaska 11,284
La Crosse 51,003	River Falls 10,610
Menomonie 13,547	

Race and Hispanic origin
White 98.0%
Black 0.2%
American Indian, Eskimo, or Aleut. 0.4%
Asian or Pacific Islander 1.2%
Other 0.1%
Hispanic origin 0.5%

Ancestry
American 1.8%	Irish 13.3%
Czechoslovakian 2.9%	Italian 1.6%
Danish 1.6%	Norwegian 23.4%
Dutch 2.3%	Polish 5.5%
English 9.4%	Scotch Irish 1.0%
French 4.7%	Scottish 1.2%
French Canadian 1.0%	Swedish 5.1%
German 54.0%	Swiss 1.5%

Universities/colleges, 1990-1991 enrollment
Chippewa Valley Tech College, Eau Claire 3,362
Southwest Wisconsin Tech College, Fennimore 1,702
University of Wisconsin, Eau Claire 10,941
University of Wisconsin, La Crosse 9,118
University of Wisconsin, Platteville 5,465
University of Wisconsin, River Falls 5,196
University of Wisconsin-Stout, Menomonie 7,629
Viterbo College, La Crosse 1,218
Western Wisconsin Tech College, La Crosse 3,474

Newspapers, total circulation (in all districts)
Dubuque Telegraph Herald 33,791
Eau Claire Leader-Telegram 31,344
La Crosse Tribune 35,788
Milwaukee Sentinel Journal 164,820
St. Paul Pioneer Press 205,116
Winona Daily News 13,774
Wisconsin State Journal Capital Times 107,967

Commercial television stations, affiliations
ADI: La Crosse-Eau Claire (48%), Minneapolis-St. Paul (34%), Cedar Rapids-Waterloo-Dubuque (11%) and Wausau-Rhinelander (8%)
KDUB-TV, Dubuque (ABC)
WEAU-TV, Eau Claire (NBC)
WQOW-TV, Eau Claire (ABC)
WKBT, La Crosse (CBS)

Cable television systems, total subscribers
Crown Cable; Onalaska 8,907
Western Wisconsin Communications Coop; Whitehall 5,710
Westmarc Cable; La Crosse 14,955
Wisconsin CATV Inc.; Eau Claire 25,400

Businesses and other major employers
American Standard Inc./Trane Commercial Systems Group; La Crosse; heating/cooling equipment 2,600
Lutheran Hospital; La Crosse 2,300
St. Francis Medical Center Inc.; La Crosse 2,000
University of Wisconsin; River Falls 2,000
Ashley Furniture Industries; Arcadia; furniture 1,600
Uniroyal Goodrich Tire Co.; Eau Claire; tires 1,350
University of Wisconsin-Stout; Menomonie 1,200
Gundersen Clinic Ltd.; La Crosse; medical doctors 1,100
G. Heileman Brewing Co. Inc; La Crosse; brewery 1,050
Sacred Heart Hospital; Eau Claire 1,020
University of Wisconsin; La Crosse 1,005
Northern Engraving Corp./Southside Machine Div.; Sparta; metal forgings/stampings 1,000
City of La Crosse; La Crosse 1,000
Luther Hospital Inc.; Eau Claire 1,000
Menard Inc./Menard Cashway Lumber Div.; Eau Claire; lumber/building materials 900
City of Eau Claire/Board of Education; Eau Claire 900
RNW Associates Inc.; Osceola; personnel supply services 865
Marten Transport Ltd.; Mondovi; trucking services 840
Company Store Inc.; La Crosse; catalog retailers 750
County of La Crosse; La Crosse 750
Wisconsin Green Thumb; Neillsville 750
La Crosse Footwear Inc.; La Crosse; footwear 700
Pope & Talbot Wisconsin Inc.; Eau Claire; paper mills 660
North American Philips Corp.; Platteville; electric distribution equipment 600
North American Philips Corp.; Boscobel; electric distribution equipment 600
Minnesota Mining & Mfg. Co.; Prairie Du Chien; mineral products 600
University of Wisconsin; Platteville 560
Southwest Wisconsin Tech College; Fennimore 550

4th District

Southern Milwaukee and Milwaukee County Suburbs; Southeast Waukesha County

The heart of Milwaukee has long been its South Side bungalow belt. The plain but sturdy houses evoke a feeling from the 1950s. Television viewers still associate the city as the setting for the television show "Laverne and Shirley." Milwaukee has worked hard to promote itself as cosmopolitan, but many residents still value bowling, bratwurst and beer. This is home to conservative Democrats.

Since the turn of the century, the city's huge Polish community has been based on its South Side, and the area remains predominantly Polish and German. Neighborhoods are conspicuously tidy; residents regularly sweep the gutters and scrub the sidewalks. The mix of ethnics has made Serb Hall a traditional meeting place for Friday fish fries as well as for candidates seeking working-class votes. The city's strong ethnic heritage is celebrated nearly every summer weekend during a series of lakefront festivals, immediately southeast of downtown.

The migration of some white ethnics to nearby southern suburbs has made room for a wider mix on the South Side. A Hispanic community is growing on the Near South Side, populated mainly by Mexicans and Puerto Ricans. A large population of Vietnamese and Laotians is also located here.

For years, manufacturing was the dominant occupation on the South Side. Although service-industry jobs have increased, many in the 4th still make machinery for mining and construction, and electronic equipment. Johnson Controls Inc., General Motors and Harnischfeger Corp. all have a strong presence in the district. Allen-Bradley Co. is known both for its increasingly automated plant and for displaying the world's largest four-sided analog clock, which stands tall among the South Side church steeples.

West Allis-based Allis-Chalmers (300 employees) is a shadow of its former self now that it has gone through bankruptcy and parts of the company have been purchased by a German firm. West Allis still hosts the annual state fair, where longtime Sen. William Proxmire made a ritual of shaking the hands of thousands of visitors.

While the population of both the city and the county of Milwaukee declined during the 1980s, some of the south suburbs grew significantly, including Oak Creek (15 percent) and Franklin (nearly 30 percent). These suburbs, along with Hales Corners, have attracted young middle-management types, while South Shore suburbs like Cudahy and South Milwaukee are primarily blue-collar.

Just west of Milwaukee County, the 4th includes the Waukesha County suburbs of New Berlin and Muskego, which grew by 10 percent in the 80s, as well as the city of Waukesha, which grew by 13 percent.

Some of the migrants who left the city for the suburbs also left the Democratic Party, boosting the Republican vote in contests for state and national office. The district includes only a part of Waukesha County—which is a Republican stronghold—though the city of Waukesha itself leans Democratic.

Election Returns

	4th District	Democrat	Republican
1992	President*	116,048 (40.9%)	108,463 (38.2%)
	House	173,482 (65.8%)	84,872 (32.2%)
1990	Governor	58,215 (43.0%)	77,297 (57.0%)
1988	President	138,685 (57.3%)	103,530 (42.7%)
	Senate	148,229 (61.1%)	94,207 (38.9%)
1986	Senate	87,566 (59.5%)	59,513 (40.5%)
	Governor	83,895 (52.0%)	77,519 (48.0%)

Vote for Perot was 59,263 (20.9%).

Demographics

Population 543,527

Percent change from 1980 3.9%

Land area 293 square miles

Population per square mile 1,853

Counties, 1990 population
Milwaukee (pt.) 415,745   Waukesha (pt.) 127,782

Cities, 1990 population (10,000 or more)
Cudahy 18,659   New Berlin 33,592
Franklin 21,855   Oak Creek 19,513
Greendale 15,128   South Milwaukee 20,958
Greenfield 33,403   Waukesha 56,958
Milwaukee (pt.) 202,167   West Allis 63,221
Muskego 16,813

Race and Hispanic origin
White 93.9%
Black 0.9%
American Indian, Eskimo, or Aleut. 0.8%
Asian or Pacific Islander 1.3%
Other 3.1%
Hispanic origin 6.3%

Ancestry
American 1.0%   Irish 12.0%
Czechoslovakian 1.7%   Italian 5.0%
Danish 1.1%   Norwegian 4.2%
Dutch 1.6%   Polish 24.8%
English 6.7%   Slovakian 1.7%
French 4.5%   Swedish 2.2%
French Canadian 1.1%   Yugoslavian 1.3%
German 50.7%

Universities/colleges, 1990-1991 enrollment
Alverno College, Milwaukee 2,414
Carroll College, Waukesha 2,196
Milwaukee Institute of Art Design, Milwaukee 462
Milwaukee School of Engineering, Milwaukee 3,160
University of Wisconsin, Milwaukee 26,020

Newspapers, total circulation (in all districts)
Chicago Tribune 721,559
Milwaukee Journal 239,944
Milwaukee Sentinel Journal 164,820
Waukesha County Freeman 21,621

Commercial television stations, affiliations
ADI: Milwaukee (100%)

Cable television systems, total subscribers
Century Cable Television; Brookfield 37,500

Crown Cable; New Berlin 6,736
Crown Cable; West Allis 12,691
Warner Cable; Greenfield 17,858
Warner Cable; Milwaukee 82,000
Warner Cable; South Milwaukee 12,993

Military installations, 1991

Gen. Billy Mitchell Intl. Airport Air Force Guard Station, Milwaukee 706

Businesses and other major employers

Allen-Bradley Co. Inc.; Milwaukee; industrial controls 4,000

U.S. Postal Service; Milwaukee 4,000

General Electric Co./Medical Systems; Waukesha; x-ray/medical equipment/supplies 3,000

First Wisconsin National Bank; Milwaukee; commercial banks 2,832

Northwestern Mutual Life Insurance Inc.; Milwaukee; life insurance 2,600

City of Milwaukee; Milwaukee 2,400

U.S. Veterans Affairs Dept.; Milwaukee; hospital 2,400

St. Luke's Medical Center Inc.; Milwaukee 2,383

Ladish Co. Inc./Cudahy Forgings Div.; Cudahy; metal valves/pumps 2,000

General Motors Corp.; Oak Creek; motor vehicle parts/equipment 1,800

West Allis Memorial Hospital; Milwaukee 1,600

Journal/Sentinel Inc./Milwaukee Journal; Waukesha; newspapers 1,550

Waukesha Memorial Hospital; Waukesha 1,488

St. Francis Hospital Inc.; Milwaukee 1,450

Falk Corp.; Milwaukee; industry machinery 1,300

County of Waukesha/Highway Commission; Waukesha 1,300

Aurora Health Care Inc.; Milwaukee 1,037

State of Wisconsin/128th Air Refueling Group; Milwaukee 1,000

Peck Foods Corp./Emmber Brands Div.; Milwaukee; meat products 995

Johnson Controls Inc.; Milwaukee; controlling devices 900

Bucyrus-Erie Co.; South Milwaukee; construction machinery 860

Dresser Industries Inc./Waukesha Engine Div.; Waukesha; engines/turbines 800

Hillhaven Corp./Mt. Carmel Health Care Center; Milwaukee; nursing 800

Mortgage Guaranty Insurance Corp.; Milwaukee; surety insurance 798

Clean Power Inc.; Milwaukee; building services 710

PPG Industries Inc.; Oak Creek; paint products 700

Trinity Memorial Hospital of Cudahy; Cudahy 700

School Sisters of St. Francis; Milwaukee; religious organizations 690

Ringier America Inc./New Berlin Div.; New Berlin; books 650

Aldrich Chemical Co. Inc.; Milwaukee; organic chemicals 630

M&I Marshall & Ilsley Bank; Milwaukee; commercial banks 629

Harnischfeger Corp.; Milwaukee; cranes/construction machinery 600

Cooper Power Systems Inc.; Waukesha; electric distribution equipment 600

Pfister Corp./Pfister Hotel; Milwaukee; hotel 600

City of West Allis; Milwaukee 600

Arthur Andersen & Co.; Milwaukee; accounting/auditing 587

Foley & Lardner; Milwaukee; legal services 578

Maynard Steel Casting Co.; Milwaukee; iron/steel foundries 555

Wicor Inc.; Milwaukee; gas distribution 550

Wisconsin Bell Inc.; Waukesha; telephone communications 550

Robert W. Baird & Co. Inc.; Milwaukee; security brokers 507

5th District

Northern Milwaukee, Milwaukee County Suburbs; Southeast Waukesha County

The Menomonee River Valley marks the boundary between Milwaukee's North and South sides. The 5th is the North Side district and reliably Democratic. The old district gave Michael S. Dukakis 63 percent of its vote in 1988, and the similarly drawn 5th handed 57 percent to Bill Clinton in 1992, the best showings that each nominee posted in Wisconsin. The city's portion of the district encompasses most of the city's traditional German neighborhoods as well as its black neighborhoods and its affluent East Side.

Milwaukee remains one of the nation's most segregated cities, and the great majority of the metro area's black population lives on or near the city's North Side. Although parts of Milwaukee are impoverished, its ghetto is not as stark as those in other cities. This reflects in part the city's old but sturdy housing stock and the lack of high-rise public housing. But all this does not hide the inner-city despair; the gulf between races in terms of jobs, income and home ownership has been as wide here as in any city in the country.

The city's black population continues to increase and to spread, generally moving out to the west and northwest in search of newer housing and a better quality of life. One area around Sherman Park shifted in 20 years from 98 percent white to 82 percent black. Attempts are being made to keep other parts of Sherman Park integrated.

Milwaukee's manufacturing base, hit hard in the early 1980s recession, is doing better. Major employers in the 5th include Briggs & Stratton, makers of gasoline engines, and A. O. Smith, which makes automobile parts and supplies. Motorcyclists revere the Harley-Davidson Motor Co. here.

The 5th is the focal point of what remains of Milwaukee's best-known industry—brewing. Schlitz, Pabst and Miller were once the locally owned giants, but much has changed. Pabst and Miller are no longer locally owned, and Schlitz closed its Milwaukee brewery in 1981.

North and west of the black neighborhoods are modest, middle-class areas.

The East Side, between the Milwaukee River and Lake Michigan, features comfortable homes, academics who work at Milwaukee's branch of the University of Wisconsin and middle and upper managers.

The houses get bigger and more expensive in the North Shore suburbs. Just north of the city line, Shorewood's inclusion of young professionals and multifamily housing gives it a Democratic leaning. But farther north, the 5th also includes the more exclusive villages of Whitefish Bay, Fox Point and Bayside. In the city's boom days, brewers and other industrial barons built mansions along the North Shore; today the property values are still stunning by Wisconsin standards, as are the Republican turnouts. In some of these affluent communities, such as River Hills, George Bush won by margins of close to 2-to-1.

West of the city is Wauwatosa, a residential area with older housing stock that is shedding some of its Republicanism as it attracts young professionals.

Election Returns

	5th District	Democrat	Republican
1992	President*	142,047 (56.6%)	76,935 (30.6%)
	House	162,344 (69.5%)	71,085 (30.5%)
1990	Governor	60,455 (45.8%)	71,651 (54.2%)
1988	President	153,099 (61.8%)	94,770 (38.2%)
	Senate	157,771 (63.8%)	89,400 (36.2%)
1986	Senate	91,516 (60.9%)	58,824 (39.1%)
	Governor	91,928 (55.8%)	72,801 (44.2%)

*Vote for Perot was 32,138 (12.8%).

Demographics

Population 543,530

Percent change from 1980 4.0%

Land area 101 square miles

Population per square mile 5,389

Counties, 1990 population
Milwaukee (pt.) 543,530

Cities, 1990 population (10,000 or more)
Brown Deer 12,236   Shorewood 14,116
Glendale 14,088   Wauwatosa 49,366
Milwaukee (pt.) 425,921   Whitefish Bay 14,272

Race and Hispanic origin
White 61.3%
Black 35.2%
American Indian, Eskimo, or Aleut. 0.5%
Asian or Pacific Islander 1.7%
Other 1.3%
Hispanic origin 2.6%

Ancestry
American 1.1%   Irish 9.6%
Czechoslovakian 1.1%   Italian 3.8%
Dutch 1.2%   Norwegian 2.5%
English 5.2%   Polish 7.8%
French 2.9%   Russian 1.6%
German 34.7%   Swedish 1.6%

Universities/colleges, 1990-1991 enrollment
Cardinal Stritch College, Milwaukee 3,654
Marquette University, Milwaukee 11,729
Medical College of Wisconsin, Milwaukee 1,004
Milwaukee Technical College, Milwaukee 21,607
Mount Mary College, Milwaukee 1,452
Stratton College, Milwaukee 583
Wisconsin Lutheran College, Milwaukee 283

Newspapers, total circulation (in all districts)
Chicago Tribune 721,559
Milwaukee Journal 239,944
Milwaukee Sentinel Journal 164,820

Commercial television stations, affiliations
ADI: Milwaukee (100%)
WCGV-TV, Milwaukee (Fox)
WDJT-TV, Milwaukee (None)
WISN-TV, Milwaukee (ABC)
WITI-TV, Milwaukee (CBS)
WTMJ-TV, Milwaukee (NBC)
WVCY-TV, Milwaukee (None)
WVTV, Milwaukee (None)

Cable television systems, total subscribers
Warner Cable; Glendale 14,287
Warner Cable; Milwaukee 82,000

Businesses and other major employers
Briggs & Stratton Corp.; Milwaukee; engines 6,500
A. O. Smith Corp./Automotive Products Div.; Milwaukee; motor vehicle parts/supplies 3,842
Journal Communications Inc.; Milwaukee; newspapers 3,500
Miller Brewing Co.; Milwaukee; brewery 2,731
Johnson Controls Inc.; Milwaukee; measuring devices/batteries 2,500
St. Mary's Hospital of Milwaukee; Milwaukee 2,500
University of Wisconsin; Milwaukee 2,500
St. Joseph's Hospital; Milwaukee 2,500
Medical College of Wisconsin; Milwaukee 2,139
Miller Brewing Co.; Milwaukee; brewery 1,800
Time Insurance Co. Inc.; Milwaukee; life insurance 1,765
County of Milwaukee/Mental Health Complex; Milwaukee 1,650
St. Michael Hospital; Milwaukee 1,560
Wisconsin Energy Corp.; Milwaukee; electric services 1,500
J. C. Penney Co. Inc.; Milwaukee; warehousing 1,500
Columbia Hospital Inc.; Milwaukee 1,500
Master Lock Co.; Milwaukee; locks 1,450
Milwaukee County/Social Services Dept.; Milwaukee 1,350
Children's Hospital of Wisconsin; Milwaukee 1,299
Froedtert Memorial Lutheran Hospital; Milwaukee 1,264
Milwaukee Technical College; Milwaukee 1,135
Fleet Mortgage Corp.; Milwaukee; mortgage bankers 1,100
County of Milwaukee; Milwaukee 1,045
M&I Marshall & Ilsley Bank; Milwaukee; computer services 1,000
P. A. Bergner & Co. Holding Co.; Milwaukee; department stores 990
Sinai Samaritan Medical Center; Milwaukee 950
Blue Cross/Blue Shield United of Wisconsin; Milwaukee; medical service/health insurance 934
Marquette Electronics Inc.; Milwaukee; medical equipment 900
State of Wisconsin; Milwaukee 800
American Building Maintenance Co.; Milwaukee; building services 750
Wisconsin Bell Inc.; Milwaukee; telephone services 682
Grunau Co. Inc.; Milwaukee; plumbing/heating/air-conditioning 600
Harley-Davidson Inc.; Milwaukee; motorcycles 600
General Electric Co./Medical Systems; Milwaukee; medical equipment/supplies 600

BPS Guard Services Inc./Burns Intl. Security Services; Milwaukee; business/security services 600

Instant Help Inc.; Milwaukee; personnel supply services 600

Outboard Marine Corp.; Milwaukee; outboard motors 575

Eaton Corp./Cutler-Hammer Group; Milwaukee; industrial controls 570

Mark Travel Corp./Funway Holidays Funjet; Milwaukee; passenger transportation 550

Super Steel Products Corp.; Milwaukee; metal products 550

United Lutheran Program for Aging/Luther Manor; Milwaukee; nursing 550

F. W. Woolworth Co.; Milwaukee; accounting/auditing 550

Milwaukee Medical Clinic; Milwaukee; medical doctors 532

Badger Meter Inc./Utility Div.; Milwaukee; measuring meters 509

6th District

Central — Oshkosh; Fond du Lac; Manitowoc

The 6th encompasses almost the entire width of central Wisconsin, stretching from Lake Michigan west to within about 30 miles of the Minnesota border. The district has been closely contested in many state and national elections, but it has sent only one Democrat to Congress since 1938.

The farms and market towns are generally Republican, while Democratic strength is in several small industrialized cities in the eastern part of the 6th—Manitowoc and Two Rivers in Manitowoc County and Neenah-Menasha in Winnebago County, and Fond du Lac in Fond du Lac County.

The most Democratic of the bunch is Manitowoc, a prominent Lake Michigan shipbuilding center in the days when wooden vessels plied the seas. More than half the jobs in Manitowoc now are involved in manufacturing and processing, and unions are an important force. Goods produced include Mirro-Foley's aluminum pots and pans, and the Manitowoc Co.'s ice-making machine for motels. Tourism got a boost with the recent launching of a car ferry service across Lake Michigan to Ludington, Mich. Manitowoc County went solidly for Jimmy Carter in 1976, voted narrowly for Ronald Reagan in 1980 and 1984, swung back to the Democratic side in 1988 and stayed there in 1992.

Republicans have an easier time in Winnebago and Fond du Lac counties. Both counties went Republican in the 1986 and 1988 Senate races, and George Bush carried them in the 1988 and 1992 presidential elections. Winnebago's population increased 7 percent in the 1980s.

Oshkosh is on the western shore of Lake Winnebago, the state's largest lake. Tourism and a state university branch boost the economy, and factories in Winnebago County turn out auto parts, wood and paper products, and Oshkosh B'Gosh clothing. Oshkosh Truck is the largest defense contractor in a state that has traditionally ranked low in defense spending. So many airplane buffs travel to Oshkosh for the annual Experimental Aircraft Association convention that it briefly becomes the busiest airport in the world in terms of takeoffs and landings.

Toward the northern end of the lake is Neenah-Menasha, where paper goods company Kimberly-Clark is one of the 6th's major employers.

At the southern tip of the lake is Fond du Lac County, home of Mercury outboard motors, Speed Queen laundry equipment and a large Giddings & Lewis tool manufacturing plant. The city of Fond du Lac has strong historical justification for its GOP inclinations. About 20 miles west of the city is Ripon, which lays claim to being the birthplace of the Republican Party, in 1854.

Besides the industry in the district, farming has a strong presence. After all-important dairying, output from the district's farms is diverse, including corn, peas, beans and cranberries. Republican strength in the rural part of the 6th is most concentrated in Green Lake County, a resort area with large summer homes. Republicans are also strong in Waupaca and Waushara counties.

Election Returns

		Democrat	Republican
	6th District		
1992	President*	97,248 (34.6%)	114,698 (40.8%)
	House	128,232 (47.1%)	143,875 (52.9%)
1990	Governor	55,821 (36.6%)	96,694 (63.4%)
1988	President	108,302 (45.7%)	128,488 (54.3%)
	Senate	105,750 (45.0%)	129,160 (55.0%)
1986	Senate	70,882 (43.6%)	91,584 (56.4%)
	Governor	62,705 (37.1%)	106,106 (62.9%)

Vote for Perot was 69,452 (24.7%).

Demographics

Population 543,652

Percent change from 1980 4.1%

Land area 6,718 square miles

Population per square mile 81

Counties, 1990 population

Adams 15,682	Marquette 12,321
Brown (pt.) 1,608	Monroe (pt.) 23,844
Calumet (pt.) 31,046	Outagamie (pt.) 19,616
Fond du Lac (pt.) 89,265	Sheboygan (pt.) 24,494
Green Lake 18,651	Waupaca 46,104
Juneau 21,650	Waushara 19,385
Manitowoc (pt.) 79,666	Winnebago 140,320

Cities, 1990 population (10,000 or more)

Fond du Lac 37,757	Neenah 23,219
Manitowoc 32,520	Oshkosh 55,006
Menasha 14,711	Two Rivers 13,030

Race and Hispanic origin

White 98.1%
Black 0.4%
American Indian, Eskimo, or Aleut. 0.4%
Asian or Pacific Islander 0.7%
Other 0.3%
Hispanic origin 0.9%

Ancestry

American 1.7%	German 67.2%
Czechoslovakian 3.0%	Irish 12.1%
Danish 1.7%	Italian 1.5%
Dutch 5.7%	Norwegian 5.6%
English 7.6%	Polish 8.2%
French 5.2%	Swedish 1.9%
French Canadian 1.4%	

Universities/colleges, 1990-1991 enrollment
Lakeshore Technical Institute, Cleveland 2,750
Marian College of Fond du Lac, Fond du Lac 1,668
Ripon College, Ripon 854
Silver Lake College, Manitowoc 830
University of Wisconsin, Oshkosh 11,740
Wisconsin Area Tech College, Fond du Lac 5,556

Newspapers, total circulation (in all districts)
Appleton Post-Crescent 56,526
Fond du Lac Reporter 19,334
Green Bay Press Gazette 59,288
Manitowoc Herald Times Reporter 17,582
Milwaukee Journal 239,944
Milwaukee Sentinel Journal 164,820
Oshkosh Daily Northwestern 24,206
Sheboygan Press 26,649
Wisconsin State Journal Capital Times 107,967

Commercial television stations, affiliations
ADI: Green Bay-Appleton (58%), Madison (18%), La Crosse-Eau Claire (10%), Wausau-Rhinelander (10%) and Milwaukee (4%)

Cable television systems, total subscribers
Cablevision of Fox Cities; Appleton 28,586
Jones Intercable Inc.; Manitowoc 9,200
Star Cablevision; Fond du Lac 15,950
Star Cablevision; Sheboygan 16,450
Warner Cable; Neenah 28,262

Military installations, 1991
Fort McCoy (Army), Sparta 2,274

Businesses and other major employers
Kimberly-Clark Corp.; Neenah; paper mills 5,800
Oshkosh Truck Corp.; Oshkosh; heavy-duty trucks 1,600
University of Wisconsin Medical Center; Manitowoc 1,516
Speed Queen Co./Holiday Hammond; Ripon; household appliances 1,200
Clark Theda Memorial Hospital; Neenah 1,200
University of Wisconsin; Oshkosh 1,200
St. Agnes Hospital; Fond du Lac 1,150
Bemis Mfg. Co./Church Seat Co.; Sheboygan Falls; plastics products 1,100
Sara Lee Corp./Hillshire Farms; New London; meat products 1,100
Mercy Medical Center of Oshkosh; Oshkosh 1,097
Pierce Mfg. Inc.; Appleton; fire trucks/equipment 1,085
Neenah Corp.; Neenah; iron/steel foundries 1,070
Hamilton Industries Inc.; Two Rivers; laboratory equipment 1,000
Giddings & Lewis Inc.; Fond du Lac; tool-making machinery 1,000
U.S. Veterans Affairs Dept.; Tomah; hospital 1,000
Tecumseh Products Co.; New Holstein; engines 900
Holy Family Medical Center; Manitowoc 879
Electronic Assembly Corp.; Neenah; electronic components 875
Brillion Iron Works Inc.; Brillion; iron/steel foundries 850
City of Manitowoc/Public School District; Manitowoc 843
Zaugs Inc.; Oshkosh; grocery stores 800
Manitowoc Co. Inc.; Manitowoc; ice-making machinery 710
Outlook Graphics Corp.; Neenah; commercial printing 700
La Salle Clinic of Wisconsin; Menasha; medical doctors 700

Best Power Technology Inc.; Necedah; electronic components 650
Appleton Papers Inc./Locks Mill; Combined Locks; paper mills 640
Sargento Cheese Co. Inc.; Plymouth; dairy products 600
James River Corp. Virginia; Menasha; paperboard products 600
Repap Midtec Ltd. Partnership; Kimberly; paper products 600
State of Wisconsin/Health & Social Services; Winnebago 600
Mirro-Foley Co./Newell Operating Co.; Manitowoc; aluminum products 597
Paragon Electric Co. Inc.; Two Rivers; electrical controls 596
Scott Paper Co.; Oshkosh; paper mills 565
J. J. Keller & Assoc. Inc.; Neenah; publishing 565
State of Wisconsin/Veterans Affairs Dept.; King 560
Richardson Industries Inc.; Sheboygan Falls; furniture 550
Pullman Co./Imperial Eastman Div.; Manitowoc; industry machinery 550
Federal Prison Industries/Unicor; Oxford; business services 532
P. H. Glatfelter Co.; Neenah; paper products 510

7th District
Northwest — Wausau; Superior; Stevens Point

The 7th reaches from the center of Wisconsin all the way north to Lake Superior. The southern part of the district is devoted largely to dairy farming; in the north, a booming recreation industry has brought new life to old mining and lumbering areas that were exploited and abandoned earlier in this century.

The southern end of the 7th is anchored by Marathon and Wood counties, politically marginal territory that supported Ronald Reagan in 1984 but has since been of divided mind. In 1988, Michael S. Dukakis won Marathon County by 176 votes, and George Bush carried Wood County by 475 votes. In 1992, Bill Clinton carried Marathon County by 534 votes, while Bush took Wood County by 635 votes.

Marathon County's major city is Wausau, with paper mills, prefabricated-home manufacturers and white-collar employment in the insurance industry.

In Wood County, Wisconsin Rapids is a paper mill town—Consolidated Papers and Georgia Pacific's Nekoosa Papers are the biggest—and Marshfield has a large medical clinic and research facility. The cities are processing centers for the surrounding dairylands. Southern Wood County is notable for its cranberry crops, while Marathon County is a leading ginseng exporter. In 1992 redistricting, the district got all of Wood County.

The heaviest Democratic vote in the southern part of the 7th comes out of Portage County. The city of Stevens Point there has a large Polish population, a branch of the state university and the headquarters of the Sentry Insurance Co. Potatoes are an important crop in rural Portage and Wood counties.

A scattering of streams, rivers, lakes, national forests and state parks covers the northern reaches of the 7th, luring tourists and retirees from urban centers.

Along the Mississippi River, commuters to Minneapolis-St. Paul have begun settling in the western Polk County communities of St. Croix Falls and Balsam Lake. To the east, Chippewa Falls has Cray Research, makers of supercomputers.

The northern sections of the 7th share the same solid Democratic traditions found in Minnesota's Iron Range and in the nearby western end of Michigan's upper peninsula. The major Democratic bastion is the region's only sizable city, Superior, a working-class town. Its economy is fueled by production of dairy products, port operations and education. A branch of the University of Wisconsin is in Superior. The city is also home to one of the nation's largest municipal forests, with 4,500 acres.

The huge port facilities of Superior and its larger neighbor, Duluth, Minn., are a funnel for soybeans, wheat and a wide range of other commodities raised on the farms of the Midwest. But a slump in ship repairing and the general hardscrabble nature of the land have taken their toll. Three of the four Wisconsin counties that adjoin Lake Superior—Douglas, Ashland and Iron—lost population in the 1980s.

Election Returns

	7th District	Democrat	Republican
1992	President*	117,203 (42.2%)	93,238 (33.5%)
	House	166,200 (64.4%)	91,772 (35.6%)
1990	Governor	71,837 (43.1%)	94,931 (56.9%)
1988	President	132,184 (54.3%)	111,292 (45.7%)
	Senate	130,044 (54.0%)	110,659 (46.0%)
1986	Senate	79,134 (46.7%)	90,435 (53.3%)
	Governor	94,062 (50.6%)	91,657 (49.4%)

Vote for Perot was 67,558 (24.3%).

Demographics

Population 543,529

Percent change from 1980 4.0%

Land area 16,723 square miles

Population per square mile 33

Counties, 1990 population
Ashland 16,307	Oneida (pt.) 13,122
Bayfield 14,008	Polk (pt.) 17,878
Burnett 13,084	Portage 61,405
Chippewa (pt.) 51,447	Price 15,600
Clark (pt.) 13,930	Rusk 15,079
Douglas 41,758	Sawyer 14,181
Eau Claire (pt.) 906	Taylor 18,901
Iron 6,153	Washburn 13,772
Lincoln 26,993	Wood 73,605
Marathon 115,400	

Cities, 1990 population (10,000 or more)
Chippewa Falls 12,727	Superior 27,134
Marshfield 19,291	Wausau 37,060
Stevens Point 23,006	Wisconsin Rapids 18,245

Race and Hispanic origin
White 97.2%
Black 0.2%
American Indian, Eskimo, or Aleut. 1.5%
Asian or Pacific Islander 0.9%
Other 0.2%
Hispanic origin 0.5%

Ancestry
American 2.1%	Irish 10.8%
Czechoslovakian 2.8%	Italian 1.8%
Danish 1.8%	Norwegian 9.7%
Dutch 2.4%	Polish 15.2%
English 7.5%	Scottish 1.1%
Finnish 2.1%	Slovakian 1.1%
French 5.6%	Swedish 6.7%
French Canadian 1.6%	Swiss 1.2%
German 54.3%	

Universities/colleges, 1990-1991 enrollment
Mid State Tech College, Wisconsin Rapids 2,406
Mount Senario College, Ladysmith 1,060
Nicolet Tech College, Rhinelander 1,344
Northcentral Tech College, Wausau 4,553
Northland College, Ashland 756
University of Wisconsin, Stevens Point 9,433
University of Wisconsin, Superior 2,675
Wisconsin Indianhead Tech College, Shell Lake 3,264

Newspapers, total circulation (in all districts)
Eau Claire Leader-Telegram 31,344
Duluth News-Tribune 58,551
Marshfield News-Herald 15,314
Milwaukee Sentinel Journal 164,820
Stevens Point Journal 13,727
St. Paul Pioneer Press 205,116
Wausau Daily Herald 25,182
Wisconsin Rapids Daily Tribune 13,274

Commercial television stations, affiliations
ADI: Duluth-Superior (40%), Wausau-Rhinelander (40%), La Crosse-Eau Claire (11%) and Minneapolis-St. Paul (9%)
WAOW-TV, Wausau (ABC)
WSAW-TV, Wausau (CBS)

Cable television systems, total subscribers
Bresnan Communications Inc.; Duluth 23,964
Crown Cable; Hull 10,420
Crown Cable; Wausau 18,083
Crown Cable; Wisconsin Rapids 10,200
Wisconsin CATV Inc.; Eau Claire 25,400

Businesses and other major employers
St. Joseph's Hospital of Marshfield; Marshfield 2,300
Marshfield Medical Clinic; Marshfield; medical doctors/research 2,275
Wausau Service Corp.; Wausau; fire/marine/casualty insurance 2,085
Georgia Pacific/Nekoosa Papers Inc.; Port Edwards; paper mills 2,000
Cray Research Inc.; Chippewa Falls; supercomputers 2,000
Sentry Insurance Co.; Stevens Point; fire/marine/casualty insurance 2,000
Wausau Hospitals Inc.; Wausau 1,400
Consolidated Papers Inc.; Wisconsin Rapids; paperboard mills 1,345
Kolbe & Kolbe Millwork Co. Inc; Wausau; millwork 1,200
Marathon Electric Mfg. Corp.; Wausau; electrical motors/generators 1,000
Weyerhaeuser Co.; Marshfield; millwork 1,000

Weather Shield Mfg. Inc.; Medford; millwork   1,000
University of Wisconsin; Stevens Point   970
Northern Wisconsin Center; Chippewa Falls; residential care
   900
City of Wausau/School District; Wausau   810
Ore-Ida Foods Inc.; Plover; potatoes   800
Northern States Power Wisconsin Corp./Indianhead Div.;
   Trego; utility services   800
Consolidated Papers Inc.; Wisconsin Rapids; paperboard
   mills   769
SNE Enterprises Inc.; Stevens Point; wood windows/doors
   700
Georgia Pacific/Nekoosa Papers Inc.; Nekoosa; paper mills
   700
SNE Enterprises Inc.; Wausau; millwork   700
Petersen Healthcare of Wisconsin/Horizons Unlimited;
   Rhinelander; nursing   670
J. I. Case Corp.; Schofield; construction/farm machinery   650
Wausau Paper Mills Co.; Brokaw; pulp mills   650
Rhinelander Paper Co. Inc.; Rhinelander; coated paper   650
Roehl Transport Inc.; Marshfield; trucking services   650
North Central Health Care Facilities; Wausau; nursing   650
St. Michael's Hospital; Stevens Point   575
Mosinee Paper Corp.; Mosinee; paper mills   565
Consolidated Papers Inc.; Stevens Point; paper products   556
Land O'Lakes Inc.; Spencer; dairy products   550
Flambeau Paper Corp.; Park Falls; paper mills   550
Woodward Governor Co.; Stevens Point; engines   544
First Financial Corp.; Stevens Point; savings institutions   525
Marathon Cheese Corp.; Marathon; dairy products   525
Norco Windows Inc.; Hawkins; millwork   520
James River Corp. Virginia; Wausau; paperboard products
   510
City of Superior/School District; Superior   504

8th District

Northeast — Green Bay; Appleton

More than half the 8th District vote is cast in the Fox River Valley counties of Outagamie (Appleton) and Brown (Green Bay). Germans are the most noticeable ethnic group in the industrialized valley. Most of them are Catholic and, even if Democratic, tend to be conservative.

The economy of the valley and the vast wooded area to the north depends on trees and paper. The district is a worldwide exporter of paper, grain and dairy products. Green Bay, best known for its football Packers, is the smallest city to have a National Football League club.

Thirty miles southwest of Green Bay, on the north shore of Lake Winnebago, lies Appleton. Here, too, paper manufacturers and paper-making equipment industries are important employers. Appleton also has white-collar jobs in insurance, finance and health care.

The paper industry, and its reliance on consumer necessities, has enabled the Fox Cities generally to survive recent recessionary times without major dislocations in employment. This follows a decade in which population increased by 11 percent in Brown County and by 9 percent in Outagamie County, enhancing Green Bay's standing as the state's second-largest media market.

Politically, Brown County traditionally prefers Republican

presidential candidates, though it made an exception in 1960 for John F. Kennedy, a Catholic. Ronald Reagan won Brown County easily in his two White House campaigns, and George Bush edged Michael S. Dukakis here in 1988.

Outagamie County gave Bush a more comfortable margin in 1988, helping him to a 53 percent tally in the similarly drawn old district. In 1992, both Brown and Outagamie counties went comfortably for Bush. Appleton's Republican heritage includes being the hometown of the late Sen. Joseph R. McCarthy, infamous for his communist witch hunts in the 1950s.

The rural counties in the north-central part of the district also are mostly Republican, although there are pockets of Democratic strength.

The small city of Kaukauna inspired the only real skirmish in the state's 1992 redistricting efforts, when Green Bay Democrats successfully fought a proposal to move Kaukauna into the 6th District. Kaukauna's Democratic inclinations derive from the strong union presence at the Thilmany division of International Paper.

Resorts and vacation homes are the focal point for tourists in Door and Vilas counties. Door County's peninsula, which separates Green Bay from Lake Michigan, is dotted with picturesque small towns. Vilas County is in a lakes region on the Michigan border. Both counties are solidly Republican, influenced by the prosperity attained by serving nature-seekers from all over the Midwest.

The district also contains several different tribes of Chippewa Indians, including the Lac du Flambeau, whose exercise of their spearfishing rights has occasionally sparked violent protests by whites.

Election Returns

	8th District	Democrat	Republican
1992	President*	101,493 (35.5%)	115,128 (40.3%)
	House	81,792 (29.9%)	191,704 (70.1%)
1990	Governor	67,076 (39.2%)	104,242 (60.8%)
1988	President	112,141 (46.7%)	128,175 (53.3%)
	Senate	107,663 (44.7%)	133,377 (55.3%)
1986	Senate	70,443 (43.3%)	92,213 (56.7%)
	Governor	68,448 (40.0%)	102,546 (60.0%)

Vote for Perot was 69,373 (24.3%).

Demographics

Population   543,404

Percent change from 1980   3.9%

Land area   9,845 square miles

Population per square mile   55

Counties, 1990 population

Brown (pt.) 192,986	Marinette 40,548
Calumet (pt.) 3,245	Menominee 3,890
Door 25,690	Oconto 30,226
Florence 4,590	Oneida (pt.) 18,557
Forest 8,776	Outagamie (pt.) 120,894
Kewaunee 18,878	Shawano 37,157
Langlade 19,505	Vilas 17,707
Manitowoc (pt.) 755	

Cities, 1990 population (10,000 or more)

Allouez 14,431	Green Bay 96,466
Appleton (pt.) 59,422	Kaukauna 11,982
Ashwaubenon 16,376	Marinette 11,843
De Pere 16,569	

Race and Hispanic origin

White 96.0%
Black 0.3%
American Indian, Eskimo, or Aleut. 2.6%
Asian or Pacific Islander 0.9%
Other 0.2%
Hispanic origin 0.6%

Ancestry

American 1.7%	German 55.2%
Belgian 8.2%	Irish 11.6%
Czechoslovakian 3.7%	Italian 1.8%
Danish 1.6%	Norwegian 4.4%
Dutch 7.3%	Polish 10.5%
English 6.3%	Scottish 1.0%
French 8.3%	Swedish 3.5%
French Canadian 2.1%	

Universities/colleges, 1990-1991 enrollment

Fox Valley Technical College, Appleton 3,909
Lawrence University, Appleton 1,237
Northeast Wisconsin Tech College, Green Bay 6,429
St. Norbert College, De Pere 1,875
University of Wisconsin, Green Bay 5,137

Newspapers, total circulation (in all districts)

Appleton The Post-Crescent 56,526
Green Bay Press Gazette 59,288
Milwaukee Sentinel Journal 164,820

Commercial television stations, affiliations

ADI: Green Bay-Appleton (56%), Wausau-Rhinelander (39%) and Marquette (5%)
WXGZ-TV, Appleton (Fox)
WBAY-TV, Green Bay (ABC)
WFRV-TV, Green Bay (CBS)
WGBA, Green Bay (None)
WLUK-TV, Green Bay (NBC)
WSCO, Suring (None)
WJFW-TV, Wausau-Rhinelander (NBC)

Cable television systems, total subscribers

Cablevision; Green Bay 24,641
Cablevision of Fox Cities; Appleton 28,586
Crown Cable; Ashwaubenon 11,965
Warner Amex; Menominee 8,173

Businesses and other major employers

Fort Howard Corp.; Green Bay; paper mills 2,800
St. Vincent Hospital; Green Bay 2,043
Schneider Transport Inc.; Green Bay; trucking services 1,950
Employers Health Insurance Co.; DePere; life insurance 1,900
Procter & Gamble Paper Products Co.; Green Bay; paper products 1,650
International Paper Co./Thilmany Div.; Kaukauna; paper mills 1,500
Miller Electric Mfg. Co.; Appleton; metalworking machinery 1,450
Bellin Memorial Hospital; Green Bay 1,450
Aid Association for Lutherans; Appleton; life insurance 1,400
St. Elizabeth Hospital Inc.; Appleton 1,330
Wisconsin Public Service Corp.; Green Bay; utility services 1,290
James River Corp. Virginia; Green Bay; paper mills 1,200
Appleton Papers Inc.; Appleton; coated paper 1,200
Bellin Memorial Hospital; Green Bay 1,200
Packerland Packing Co.; Green Bay; meatpacking 1,000
Paper Converting Machine Co.; Green Bay; industry machinery 950
Peterson Builders Inc.; Sturgeon Bay; shipbuilding/repairing 940
Shopko Stores Inc.; Green Bay; variety stores 915
Carver Boat Corp.; Pulaski; shipbuilding/repairing 850
Northeast Wisconsin Tech College; Green Bay 850
Boldt Group Inc.; Appleton; building construction 800
Grinnell Corp.; Marinette; fire extinguishers/sprinkler systems 800
Schreiber Foods Inc.; Green Bay; dairy products 760
Scott Paper Co.; Marinette; paper mills 750
K. S. G. Industries Inc.; Marinette; metal products 700
Reynolds Consumer Products/Presto Products Co.; Appleton; plastic bags/paper products 600
Brown County/Austin Straubel Intl. Airport; Green Bay; airport/services 600
Guardian Life Insurance Co. of America; Appleton; life insurance 600
St. Mary's Hospital; Green Bay 593
Niagara Wisconsin Paper Corp.; Niagara; paper products 588
University of Wisconsin; Green Bay 577
W. R. Grace & Co.-Conn Inc.; De Pere; industry machinery 557
Krueger Intl. Inc.; Green Bay; office furniture 550
American Foods Group Inc.; Green Bay; meat products 540
Fox Valley Technical College; Appleton 531
American Medical Security; Green Bay; medical service/health insurance 530

9th District

Milwaukee Suburbs; Part of Waukesha County; Sheboygan

The 9th is the closest thing Wisconsin has to a suburban district, encompassing much of the counties immediately west and north of Milwaukee. Consequently, the 9th is also Wisconsin's most staunchly Republican district. In the 1980s, Jimmy Carter, Walter F. Mondale and Michael S. Dukakis all failed to surpass 40 percent of the vote in the old 9th, and Bill Clinton did not even break 30 percent in 1992 in the similarly redrawn 9th.

Waukesha County, just west of Milwaukee County, is the centerpiece of state Republicanism, regularly running up the biggest GOP numbers in the state. County Republicans have an even more pronounced influence on the 9th District because the areas where Democrats are most numerous—the city of Waukesha and Muskego and New Berlin on the county's southeastern side—are part of the 4th District.

In earlier generations, the lakes of Waukesha County drew Milwaukee's leading families to buy real estate in the county for summer retreats. Republicans still compile huge margins in small Oconomowoc Lake and Chenequa. But suburbanization has taken hold elsewhere. Affluent Elm Grove is rock-ribbed Republican territory. Middle managers are attracted to adjacent

Brookfield, which has also sprouted the metropolitan area's second-largest office market.

Not everything is booming in Waukesha; the county's population growth slowed from 21 percent in the 1970s to just under 9 percent in the 1980s. Menomonee Falls, which attracted working-class Germans from Milwaukee's northwest side, saw a 3 percent population drop in the past decade.

Among the county's manufacturers are the General Electric Medical Systems Group (4th District), QuadGraphics printing and companies that build electrical transformers and internal combustion engines.

Ozaukee and Washington counties routinely cast 60 percent of their votes for GOP presidential candidates. Washington County is a combination of fast-growing bedroom communities and agricultural lands being encroached on by development, with a smattering of industry. The county seat, West Bend, is home to the West Bend Co., maker of small kitchen appliances. Port Washington, the Ozaukee County seat, is home to Allen-Edmonds Shoes (400 employees) as well as a picturesque lakefront and marina.

Farther north, Sheboygan County is marginally Republican in presidential elections. The city of Sheboygan contains medium-size industries, such as Vollrath stainless steel and Bemis manufacturing. Kohler is headquarters for the Kohler Co., the nation's largest producer of plumbing equipment, as well as the American Club, the state's premier resort hotel.

The district also includes most of Dodge and Jefferson counties, which are largely rural. Dairying is important here. In Dodge County, Waupun is well-known as a major state prison site, Beaver Dam is a resort community, and the Horicon Marsh is a federal and state preserve for geese and ducks.

Election Returns

	9th District	Democrat	Republican
1992	President*	88,176 (29.9%)	142,582 (48.3%)
	House	77,362 (28.0%)	192,898 (69.7%)
1990	Governor	46,710 (30.8%)	104,782 (69.2%)
1988	President	100,260 (40.1%)	149,605 (59.9%)
	Senate	113,125 (44.9%)	138,659 (55.1%)
1986	Senate	68,717 (39.4%)	105,754 (60.6%)
	Governor	66,659 (37.3%)	112,095 (62.7%)

*Vote for Perot was 64,544 (21.9%).

Demographics

Population 543,532

Percent change from 1980 3.9%

Land area 2,439 square miles

Population per square mile 223

Counties, 1990 population

Dodge (pt.) 66,595	Sheboygan (pt.) 79,383
Fond du Lac (pt.) 818	Washington 95,328
Jefferson (pt.) 61,947	Waukesha (pt.) 166,630
Ozaukee 72,831	

Cities, 1990 population (10,000 or more)

Beaver Dam 14,196	Fort Atkinson 10,227
Brookfield 35,184	Germantown 13,658
Menomonee Falls 26,840	Sheboygan 49,676
Mequon 18,885	Watertown 19,142
Oconomowoc 10,993	West Bend 23,916

Race and Hispanic origin
White 98.1%
Black 0.4%
American Indian, Eskimo, or Aleut 0.2%
Asian or Pacific Islander 0.9%
Other 0.3%
Hispanic origin 1.0%

Ancestry

American 1.2%	Italian 3.2%
Czechoslovakian 1.7%	Norwegian 4.7%
Danish 1.1%	Polish 8.8%
Dutch 4.0%	Russian 1.0%
English 8.1%	Scottish 1.3%
French 4.3%	Slovakian 1.2%
German 67.8%	Swedish 2.5%
Irish 12.0%	Swiss 1.1%

Universities/colleges, 1990-1991 enrollment
Concordia University Wisconsin, Mequon 1,760
Lakeland College, Sheboygan 1,994
Maranatha Baptist Bible College, Watertown 457
Northwestern College, Watertown 206
Waukesha County Tech College, Pewaukee 4,975

Newspapers, total circulation (in all districts)
Fond Du Lac Reporter 19,334
Milwaukee Journal 239,944
Milwaukee Sentinel Journal 164,820
Oshkosh Daily Northwestern 24,206
Sheboygan Press 26,649
Waukesha County Freeman 21,621
West Bend Daily News 10,039
Wisconsin State Journal Capital Times 107,967

Commercial television stations, affiliations
ADI: Milwaukee (99%) and Green Bay-Appleton (1%)

Cable television systems, total subscribers
Century Cable Television; Brookfield 37,500
Crown Cable; Hustisford 24,842
Metrovision of Wisconsin; Menomonee Falls 5,600
River Bend Cablevision; West Bend 9,200
Star Cablevision; Sheboygan 16,450
TCI of Wisconsin; Madison 70,000
Warner Cable of Brookfield; Brookfield 5,432

Businesses and other major employers
Kohler Co.; Kohler; plumbing equipment 6,300
QuadGraphics Inc.; Pewaukee; commercial printing 2,500
Deere & Co.; Horicon; farm/garden machinery 1,600
Kohl's Dept. Stores Inc.; Menomonee Falls; department stores 1,300
QuadGraphics Inc.; Lomira; commercial printing 1,200
West Bend Co./Premark Intl. Inc.; West Bend; household appliances 1,100
United Parcel Service Inc.; Elm Grove; mail services 1,000
Oconomowoc Canning Co.; Oconomowoc; grocery products 1,000
APV Crepaco Inc.; Lake Mills; food products/refrigeration machinery 900

Community Memorial Hospital of Menomonee Falls;
   Menomonee Falls 895
Gehl Co.; West Bend; farm/garden machinery 825
Briggs & Stratton Corp.; Menomonee Falls; warehousing 750
Amity Leather Products Co.; West Bend; leather goods 750
Kewaskum Mfg. Co. Inc.; Kewaskum; plastics products 723
Allen-Bradley Co. Inc./Motion Control Div.; Thiensville;
   electrical motors 700
Bethesda Lutheran Home; Watertown; nursing 700
City of West Bend/School District; West Bend 680
Heritage Mutual Insurance Co.; Sheboygan;
   fire/marine/casualty insurance 661
Serigraph Inc.; West Bend; commercial printing 650
Oconomowoc Memorial Hospital; Oconomowoc 620

Leeson Electric Corp.; Grafton; electrical motors 600
Wisconsin Bell Inc.; Brookfield; telephone communications
   600
Milwaukee Electric Tool Corp.; Brookfield; metalworking
   machinery 600
Elmbrook Memorial Hospital; Brookfield 600
Sheboygan Memorial Hospital; Sheboygan 600
St. Nicholas Hospital; Sheboygan 582
Simplicity Mfg. Inc.; Port Washingtn; farm/garden machin-
   ery 540
Benevolent Corp./Cedar Lake Home Campus; West Bend;
   nursing 530
Trek Bicycle Corp.; Waterloo; bicycles 525
Fort Atkinson Memorial Hospital; Fort Atkinson 509

WYOMING

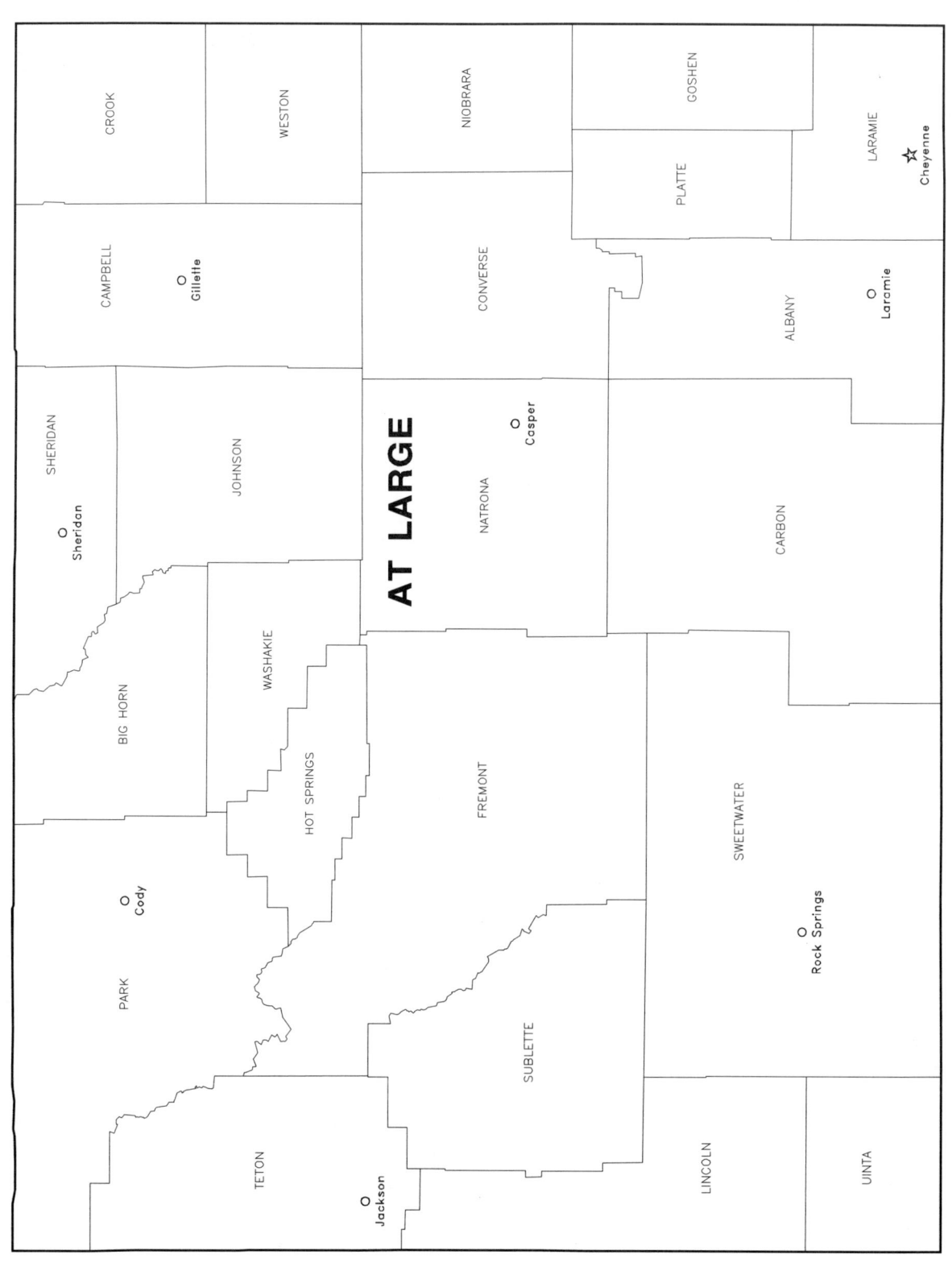

CROOK

WESTON

NIOBRARA

GOSHEN

PLATTE

LARAMIE

○ Cheyenne

CAMPBELL

○ Gillette

CONVERSE

ALBANY

○ Laramie

SHERIDAN

○ Sheridan

JOHNSON

AT LARGE

NATRONA

○ Casper

CARBON

BIG HORN

WASHAKIE

HOT SPRINGS

FREMONT

SWEETWATER

○ Rock Springs

PARK

○ Cody

SUBLETTE

LINCOLN

UINTA

TETON

○ Jackson

WYOMING

Wyoming

Few states have a more boom-and-bust economy than Wyoming, a fact reflected in its roller-coaster population growth of the past few decades. A population jump of nearly 15 percent in the 1950s was followed by stagnation in the 1960s (1 percent growth). There was a 41 percent growth spurt in the 1970s, but then a 4 percent population decline in the 1980s.

Wyoming's economy has several components: oil and natural gas, extractive industries such as coal and uranium, an agricultural sector focused on ranching and a steady flow of tourists to attractions such as Devils Tower and Yellowstone National Park.

Wyoming leads the nation in the production of coal and trona, a substance used in the production of glass and baking soda. But many of the state's widely scattered communities tend to depend heavily on a single industry, and they have been vulnerable to any downturn in it.

In the early 1980s the uranium market collapsed. Several years later, Wyoming's lucrative oil industry went bust as oil prices plummeted. By the end of the decade, 14 of Wyoming's 23 counties had lost population; the center of the state's oil industry, Natrona County (Casper), had a 17 percent falloff.

Population growth in the 1980s was largely limited to the four corners of the state. In the northeast, Campbell County (Gillette), the center of the state's coal production, grew 21 percent. In the northwest, Teton County, which includes Grand Teton National Park and the ski resort of Jackson Hole, grew 19 percent.

In the southwest corner, Uinta County (Evanston), a prime producer of natural gas as well as home for some long-range commuters to Salt Lake City, grew 44 percent. And in Wyoming's southeast corner, a cluster of counties anchored by Laramie (Cheyenne) showed some population growth.

The only cities in the state with more than 30,000 people are Cheyenne (just over 50,000) and Casper (almost 47,000). As the capital city, Cheyenne has a more diversfied economy, which enabled it to weather better the economic downturn of the 1980s.

Cheyenne has the state government work force, the Francis E. Warren Air Force Base, where MX missiles are deployed, and an array of new companies that have brought hundreds of jobs to the area. Cheyenne does not have the transportation problems that have hindered the economic development of other parts of the state. It is located only 100 miles north of Denver on Interstate 25.

As Wyoming's economy has undergone gradual change, so has its politics. In 1992, Bill Clinton was the first Democratic presidential candidate since 1964 to carry beleaguered Natrona County, and he was the first Democrat since 1940 to win Teton County.

Yet Wyoming is a conservative state. Democrats have not carried it in a presidential election since 1964 and not won a Senate race since 1970 or a House contest since 1976. Republicans dominate the state Legislature. The Democrats' lone toehold has been the governorship, which the party has held since 1975 due in no small part to GOP infighting.

In most races, Democrats have trouble winning votes beyond the party's historical base in Wyoming's southern tier. Immigrant laborers, many from Italy, were imported to build the Union Pacific rail line through the southern counties, and coal miners followed.

Most of the workers were drawn to the Democratic Party, and although their modern-day descendants are conservative on many issues and gave majorities to Ronald Reagan and George Bush in the 1980s, their Democratic sentiments are still evident. Three of the five Wyoming counties Clinton carried in 1992 were in the southern tier—Albany, Carbon and Sweetwater.

Albany County includes the academic community at the University of Wyoming in Laramie. Carbon and Sweetwater counties have more blue-collar voters, with Sweetwater County the center of the state's trona production. Carbon and Sweetwater were the only two counties in the state to vote against the incumbent House Republican in 1992.

The northern part of the state is the Wyoming of ranch, rock and Republicans. Its dry plateaus and basins accommodate the cattle ranches that make Wyoming the "Cowboy State." Ross Perot ran especially well in this part of Wyoming in 1992, finishing second in nine counties. Altogether, Perot captured 26 percent of the statewide vote.

Perot's strength nearly produced the unthinkable, a Democratic presidential victory in Wyoming. Bush's 40 percent tally statewide was the lowest for a GOP presidential candidate in Wyoming since Alfred M. Landon drew 38 percent in 1936.

821

Table 1　Population

District	Population	Population under 18	Voting-age population	Median age
AL	453,588	135,525	318,063	32.0

Table 2　Voting-Age Persons

District	White*	Black*	American Indian, Eskimo, or Aleut*	Asian or Pacific Islander*	Other*	Hispanic*	Male*	Female*
AL	94.8%	0.7%	1.8%	0.6%	2.1%	4.8%	49.5%	50.5%

As percent of voting-age population.

Table 3　Voting-Age Persons by Age Groups

District	18-24*	25-44*	45-54*	55-64*	65 and over*
AL	13.0%	46.7%	14.3%	11.2%	14.8%

As percent of voting-age population.

Table 4　Income and Occupation

District	Median family income	Families in poverty	White collar*	Blue collar*	Service*	Farm*
AL	$32,216	9.3%	51.6%	27.3%	15.6%	5.5%

As percent of employed persons age 16 and over.

Table 5　Education: School Years Completed

District	Less than grade 9*	Grades 9-12 no diploma*	High school diploma*	College bachelor's degree or higher*
AL	5.7%	11.2%	33.2%	18.8%

As percent of persons age 25 and over.

Table 6　Housing and Residential Patterns

District	Owner occupied	Renter occupied	Urban	Rural
AL	67.8%	32.2%	65.0%	35.0%

Election Returns

	At Large	Democrat	Republican
1992	President*	68,160 (34.3%)	79,347 (39.9%)
	House	77,418 (39.3%)	113,882 (57.8%)
1990	Senate	56,848 (36.1%)	100,784 (63.9%)
	Governor	104,638 (65.4%)	55,471 (34.6%)
1988	President	67,113 (38.6%)	106,867 (61.4%)
	Senate	89,821 (49.6%)	91,143 (50.4%)
1986	Governor	88,879 (54.0%)	75,841 (46.0%)

Vote for Perot was 51,263 (25.8%).

Demographics

Population　453,588

Percent change from 1980　-3.4%

Land area　97,105 square miles

Population per square mile　5

Counties, 1990 population

Albany	30,797	Natrona	61,226
Big Horn	10,525	Niobrara	2,499
Campbell	29,370	Park	23,178
Carbon	16,659	Platte	8,145
Converse	11,128	Sheridan	23,562
Crook	5,294	Sublette	4,843
Fremont	33,662	Sweetwater	38,823
Goshen	12,373	Teton	11,172
Hot Springs	4,809	Uinta	18,705
Johnson	6,145	Washakie	8,388
Laramie	73,142	Weston	6,518
Lincoln	12,625		

Cities, 1990 population (10,000 or more)

Casper	46,742	Green River	12,711
Cheyenne	50,008	Laramie	26,687
Evanston	10,903	Rock Springs	19,050
Gillette	17,635	Sheridan	13,900

Race and Hispanic origin

White　94.2%
Black　0.8%
American Indian, Eskimo, or Aleut.　2.1%
Asian or Pacific Islander　0.6%
Other　2.3%
Hispanic origin　5.7%

Ancestry

American	4.0%	Italian	2.9%
Czechoslovakian	1.0%	Norwegian	4.0%
Danish	2.4%	Polish	2.2%
Dutch	3.5%	Scotch Irish	3.4%
English	22.4%	Scottish	3.8%
French	4.8%	Swedish	4.6%
German	35.0%	Welsh	1.5%
Irish	16.1%		

Universities/colleges, 1990-1991 enrollment

Casper College, Casper　4,023
Central Wyoming College, Riverton　1,457
Eastern Wyoming College, Torrington　1,353
Laramie County Community College, Cheyenne　4,362
Northwest Community College, Powell　2,001
Phillips Technical Institute, Laramie　705
Sheridan College, Sheridan　2,418
University of Wyoming, Laramie　12,524
Western Wyoming Community College, Rock Springs　2,492

Newspapers, total circulation (in all districts)

Casper Star-Tribune　33,738
Denver Post　263,720
Laramie Daily Boomerang　6,525
Northern Wyoming Daily News　3,485
Rock Springs Dly Rocket-Miner　6,880
Scottsbluff Star-Herald　14,689
Sheridan Press　5,823
Wyoming Eagle/State Tribune　17,693

Commercial television stations, affiliations

ADI: Denver (29%), Casper-Riverton (21%), Salt Lake City (20%), Billings-Hardin (10%), Idaho Falls-Pocatello (8%), Rapid City (8%) and Cheyenne-Scottsbluff-Sterling (3%)
KFNB, Casper (ABC)

KGWC-TV, Casper (CBS)
KTWO-TV, Casper (NBC)
KGWN-TV, Cheyenne (CBS)
KKTU, Cheyenne (NBC)
KLWY, Cheyenne (None)
KJVI, Jackson (None)
KGWL-TV, Lander (CBS)
KFNR, Rawlins (ABC)
KFNE, Riverton (ABC)
KGWR-TV, Rock Springs (CBS)
KSGW-TV, Sheridan (ABC)

Cable television systems, total subscribers
Sheridan Cablevision; Sheridan 6,100
Sweetwater Cable TV Co. Inc.; Rock Springs 8,456
TCI of Wyoming; Casper 17,300
TCI of Wyoming; Cheyenne 21,100
TCI of Wyoming; Gillette 6,900
TCI of Wyoming; Laramie 8,200

Military installations, 1991
Francis E. Warren Air Force Base, Cheyenne 4,295
Cheyenne Municipal Airport Air Force Guard Station, Cheyenne 261

Businesses and other major employers
University of Wyoming; Laramie 2,271
State of Wyoming/Highway Dept.; Cheyenne 1,250
Union Pacific Railroad Co.; Cheyenne; railroads 1,000
FMC Wyoming Corp.; Green River; inorganic chemicals 1,000
Wyoming Medical Center Inc.; Casper 850
Wyoming State Training School; Lander 589
Rhone-Poulenc of Wyoming Ltd.; Green River; chemicals/fertilizers 525
Campbell County Memorial Hospital; Gillette 520
Pacificorp; Rock Springs; electric services 513
Pacificorp; Point of Rocks; electric services 513
County of Natrona/School District; Casper 504

Appendix

National Census Tables

National Table 1   Population

State	Population	Population under 18	Voting-age population	Median age
Alabama	4,040,587	1,058,788	2,981,799	33.0
Alaska	550,043	172,344	377,699	29.4
Arizona	3,665,228	981,119	2,684,109	32.2
Arkansas	2,350,725	621,131	1,729,594	33.8
California	29,760,021	7,750,725	22,009,296	31.5
Colorado	3,294,394	861,266	2,433,128	32.5
Connecticut	3,287,116	749,581	2,537,535	34.4
Delaware	666,168	163,341	502,827	32.9
District of Columbia	606,900	117,092	489,808	33.5
Florida	12,937,926	2,866,237	10,071,689	36.4
Georgia	6,478,216	1,727,303	4,750,913	31.6
Hawaii	1,108,229	280,126	828,103	32.6
Idaho	1,006,749	308,405	698,344	31.5
Illinois	11,430,602	2,946,366	8,484,236	32.8
Indiana	5,544,159	1,455,964	4,088,195	32.8
Iowa	2,776,755	718,880	2,057,875	34.0
Kansas	2,477,574	661,614	1,815,960	32.9
Kentucky	3,685,296	954,094	2,731,202	33.0
Louisiana	4,219,973	1,227,269	2,992,704	31.0
Maine	1,227,928	309,002	918,926	33.9
Maryland	4,781,468	1,162,241	3,619,227	33.0
Massachusetts	6,016,425	1,353,075	4,663,350	33.6
Michigan	9,295,297	2,458,765	6,836,532	32.6
Minnesota	4,375,099	1,166,783	3,208,316	32.5
Mississippi	2,573,216	746,761	1,826,455	31.2
Missouri	5,117,073	1,314,826	3,802,247	33.5
Montana	799,065	222,104	576,961	33.8
Nebraska	1,578,385	429,012	1,149,373	33.0
Nevada	1,201,833	296,948	904,885	33.3
New Hampshire	1,109,252	278,755	830,497	32.8
New Jersey	7,730,188	1,799,462	5,930,726	34.5
New Mexico	1,515,069	446,741	1,068,328	31.3
New York	17,990,455	4,259,549	13,730,906	33.9
North Carolina	6,628,637	1,606,149	5,022,488	33.1
North Dakota	638,800	175,385	463,415	32.4
Ohio	10,847,115	2,799,744	8,047,371	33.3
Oklahoma	3,145,585	837,007	2,308,578	33.2
Oregon	2,842,321	724,130	2,118,191	34.5
Pennsylvania	11,881,643	2,794,810	9,086,833	35.0
Rhode Island	1,003,464	225,690	777,774	34.0
South Carolina	3,486,703	920,207	2,566,496	32.0
South Dakota	696,004	198,462	497,542	32.5
Tennessee	4,877,185	1,216,604	3,660,581	33.6
Texas	16,986,510	4,835,839	12,150,671	30.8
Utah	1,722,850	627,444	1,095,406	26.2
Vermont	562,758	143,083	419,675	33.0
Virginia	6,187,358	1,504,738	4,682,620	32.6
Washington	4,866,692	1,261,387	3,605,305	33.1
West Virginia	1,793,477	443,577	1,349,900	35.4
Wisconsin	4,891,769	1,288,982	3,602,787	32.9
Wyoming	453,588	135,525	318,063	32.0
United States	248,709,873	63,604,450	185,105,441	32.9

National Table 2   Voting-Age Persons

State	White*	Black*	American Indian, Eskimo, or Aleut*	Asian or Pacific Islander*	Other*	Hispanic*	Male*	Female*
Ala.	76.3%	22.7%	0.4%	0.5%	0.1%	0.6%	46.8%	53.2%
Alaska	77.9	3.9	13.5	3.6	1.2	2.9	53.2	46.8
Ariz.	83.9	2.7	4.4	1.5	7.5	15.8	48.8	51.2
Ark.	85.0	13.7	0.5	0.5	0.2	0.7	47.1	52.9
Calif.	71.7	7.0	0.8	9.2	11.3	22.5	49.6	50.4
Colo.	89.4	3.7	0.8	1.7	4.4	11.2	48.9	51.1
Conn.	88.7	7.4	0.2	1.4	2.3	5.4	47.6	52.4
Del.	82.2	15.3	0.3	1.3	0.9	2.0	47.6	52.4
D.C.	33.1	62.4	0.3	2.0	2.3	5.2	45.7	54.3
Fla.	85.6	11.4	0.3	1.1	1.6	11.7	47.6	52.4
Ga.	73.5	24.6	0.2	1.1	0.6	1.6	47.6	52.4
Hawaii	34.4	2.3	0.4	61.3	1.7	6.1	50.7	49.3
Idaho	95.1	0.3	1.2	0.9	2.5	4.4	49.0	51.0
Ill.	80.5	13.5	0.2	2.4	3.5	6.8	47.7	52.3
Ind.	91.5	7.1	0.2	0.7	0.6	1.5	47.5	52.5
Iowa	97.1	1.5	0.2	0.8	0.4	1.0	47.5	52.5
Kans.	91.2	5.2	0.8	1.2	1.6	3.1	48.2	51.8
Ky.	92.6	6.6	0.2	0.5	0.2	0.5	47.4	52.6
La.	70.3	27.9	0.4	0.9	0.5	2.2	47.0	53.0
Maine	98.6	0.4	0.4	0.5	0.1	0.5	47.8	52.2
Md.	72.6	23.5	0.3	2.8	0.9	2.5	47.7	52.3
Mass.	91.2	4.4	0.2	2.2	2.0	3.9	47.1	52.9
Mich.	84.9	12.8	0.5	1.0	0.8	1.8	47.6	52.4
Minn.	95.6	1.8	0.9	1.3	0.4	1.0	48.2	51.8
Miss.	67.5	31.6	0.3	0.5	0.1	0.6	46.5	53.5
Mo.	88.8	9.7	0.4	0.8	0.4	1.1	47.1	52.9
Mont.	94.0	0.3	4.8	0.5	0.4	1.2	48.8	51.2
Nebr.	94.7	3.2	0.6	0.7	0.8	1.9	47.8	52.2
Nev.	85.8	5.8	1.5	3.1	3.8	9.1	50.8	49.2
N.H.	98.2	0.6	0.2	0.8	0.2	0.9	48.3	51.7
N.J.	81.1	12.4	0.2	3.2	3.1	8.7	47.5	52.5
N.M.	78.3	1.9	7.5	0.9	11.5	35.2	48.4	51.6
N.Y.	76.4	14.7	0.3	3.8	4.8	11.2	46.9	53.1
N.C.	77.7	20.1	1.1	0.7	0.4	1.1	47.7	52.3
N.D.	95.7	0.5	3.1	0.5	0.2	0.6	49.2	50.8
Ohio	88.8	9.8	0.2	0.8	0.4	1.1	47.1	52.9
Okla.	84.3	6.7	6.9	1.0	1.1	2.2	47.7	52.3
Oreg.	93.6	1.4	1.2	2.3	1.5	3.3	48.4	51.6
Pa.	89.6	8.5	0.1	1.1	0.8	1.6	46.9	53.1
R.I.	92.8	3.3	0.3	1.5	2.0	3.8	47.0	53.0
S.C.	72.0	26.9	0.2	0.6	0.2	0.8	47.5	52.5
S.D.	93.6	0.4	5.4	0.4	0.2	0.6	48.4	51.6
Tenn.	84.7	14.4	0.2	0.6	0.2	0.6	47.1	52.9
Tex.	77.4	11.2	0.4	1.8	9.2	22.4	48.5	51.5
Utah	94.1	0.7	1.2	2.0	2.1	4.5	48.7	51.3
Vt.	98.8	0.3	0.3	0.5	0.1	0.6	48.1	51.9
Va.	78.9	17.6	0.2	2.4	0.9	2.4	48.4	51.6
Wash.	89.9	2.8	1.4	4.1	1.9	3.6	49.0	51.0
W.Va.	96.4	3.0	0.1	0.4	0.1	0.4	46.9	53.1
Wis.	93.8	4.1	0.7	0.9	0.7	1.5	48.1	51.9
Wyo.	94.8	0.7	1.8	0.6	2.1	4.8	49.5	50.5
U.S.	85.4	11.0	0.7	2.8	0.1	7.9	47.9	52.1

*As percent of voting-age population.

National Table 3 Voting-Age Persons by Age Groups

State	18-24*	25-44*	45-54*	55-64*	65 and over*
Alabama	14.9%	41.3%	14.1%	12.2%	17.5%
Alaska	14.8	57.2	14.3	7.8	5.9
Arizona	14.6	43.4	13.0	11.2	17.8
Arkansas	13.7	39.6	14.1	12.3	20.2
California	15.5	46.9	13.2	10.1	14.2
Colorado	13.8	48.5	13.8	10.3	13.5
Connecticut	13.6	43.1	14.0	11.6	17.6
Delaware	15.2	43.4	13.5	11.9	16.1
District of Columbia	16.9	44.2	12.7	10.4	15.9
Florida	12.1	39.0	12.8	12.6	23.5
Georgia	15.5	46.1	14.1	10.5	13.8
Hawaii	14.6	45.8	13.1	11.4	15.1
Idaho	14.1	43.2	14.2	11.2	17.4
Illinois	14.3	43.5	13.8	11.5	16.9
Indiana	14.8	42.4	14.0	11.8	17.0
Iowa	13.8	40.0	13.3	12.1	20.7
Kansas	14.0	42.7	13.0	11.5	18.9
Kentucky	14.6	42.4	14.0	11.8	17.1
Louisiana	15.5	43.8	13.6	11.5	15.7
Maine	13.5	43.4	13.6	11.8	17.8
Maryland	14.0	46.3	14.4	11.0	14.3
Massachusetts	15.2	43.3	12.9	11.0	17.6
Michigan	14.7	43.6	13.9	11.6	16.2
Minnesota	13.8	45.1	13.4	10.7	17.0
Mississippi	16.1	41.0	13.6	11.7	17.6
Missouri	13.6	41.7	13.8	12.0	18.9
Montana	12.1	43.3	14.3	11.8	18.5
Nebraska	13.6	42.3	13.0	11.7	19.4
Nevada	13.1	45.8	15.0	11.9	14.1
New Hampshire	14.2	46.7	13.5	10.6	15.1
New Jersey	13.1	43.1	14.2	12.1	17.4
New Mexico	14.2	45.3	13.8	11.4	15.3
New York	14.2	42.7	13.9	11.9	17.2
North Carolina	15.6	42.8	13.9	11.7	16.0
North Dakota	14.6	41.9	12.3	11.5	19.6
Ohio	14.1	42.4	13.8	12.2	17.5
Oklahoma	13.9	41.7	14.0	12.1	18.4
Oregon	12.6	43.7	14.0	11.2	18.5
Pennsylvania	13.5	40.2	13.4	12.8	20.1
Rhode Island	15.5	41.3	12.4	11.5	19.4
South Carolina	15.8	43.4	13.9	11.4	15.5
South Dakota	13.7	41.1	12.6	12.0	20.6
Tennessee	14.4	42.4	14.4	11.9	16.9
Texas	15.6	46.3	13.4	10.6	14.1
Utah	18.3	45.6	12.6	9.8	13.7
Virginia	15.4	45.5	14.2	10.7	14.2
Vermont	15.1	44.7	13.7	10.8	15.8
Washington	13.6	46.0	13.9	10.6	16.0
West Virginia	13.3	39.5	14.2	13.1	19.9
Wisconsin	14.2	42.9	13.3	11.5	18.1
Wyoming	13.0	46.7	14.3	11.2	14.8
United States	14.5	43.7	13.5	11.4	16.9

*As percent of voting-age population.

National Table 4 Income and Occupation

State	Median family income	Families in poverty	White collar*	Blue collar*	Service*	Farm*
Ala.	$28,688	14.3%	52.0%	33.7%	11.9%	2.3%
Alaska	46,581	6.8	60.7	22.2	14.4	2.7
Ariz.	32,178	11.4	60.0	22.9	14.7	2.3
Ark.	25,395	14.8	48.8	33.7	13.0	4.5
Calif.	40,559	9.3	61.0	23.9	12.4	2.7
Colo.	35,930	8.6	63.1	20.9	13.6	2.4
Conn.	49,199	5.0	64.7	22.8	11.5	1.1
Del.	40,252	6.1	60.6	25.0	12.6	1.8
D.C.	36,256	16.0	71.1	11.9	16.6	0.4
Fla.	32,212	9.0	59.4	23.2	14.8	2.6
Ga.	33,529	11.5	56.5	29.3	12.0	2.2
Hawaii	43,176	6.0	59.0	20.5	17.6	2.9
Idaho	29,472	9.7	52.0	26.8	13.5	7.8
Ill.	38,664	9.0	59.6	26.0	12.6	1.8
Ind.	34,082	7.9	51.9	32.6	13.3	2.2
Iowa	31,659	8.4	51.7	26.7	14.6	7.0
Kans.	32,966	8.3	56.3	25.7	13.5	4.6
Ky.	27,028	16.0	50.4	32.8	13.1	3.7
La.	26,313	19.4	55.9	27.4	14.2	2.5
Maine	32,422	8.0	53.2	30.0	14.0	2.8
Md.	45,034	6.0	65.9	20.8	11.9	1.4
Mass.	44,367	6.7	64.9	21.4	12.8	0.9
Mich.	36,652	10.2	55.5	29.3	13.7	1.6
Minn.	36,916	7.3	58.5	24.0	13.7	3.8
Miss.	24,448	20.2	49.8	34.6	12.3	3.4
Mo.	31,838	10.1	55.8	27.4	13.7	3.1
Mont.	28,044	12.0	52.5	22.9	16.4	8.2
Nebr.	31,634	8.0	53.7	24.4	14.5	7.5
Nev.	35,837	7.3	52.2	22.5	23.8	1.6
N.H.	41,628	4.4	60.4	26.2	12.0	1.4
N.J.	47,589	5.6	64.9	22.7	11.5	0.9
N.M.	27,623	16.5	58.5	24.0	14.6	2.9
N.Y.	39,741	10.0	63.1	21.4	14.4	1.1
N.C.	31,548	9.9	51.1	34.9	11.4	2.6
N.D.	28,707	10.9	51.7	21.6	16.6	10.1
Ohio	34,351	9.7	55.8	29.4	13.1	1.7
Okla.	28,554	13.0	55.3	27.0	14.2	3.5
Oreg.	32,336	8.7	55.5	26.3	13.6	4.5
Pa.	34,856	8.2	56.9	28.4	13.0	1.7
R.I.	39,172	6.8	57.6	27.5	13.7	1.2
S.C.	30,797	11.9	50.5	34.9	12.5	2.1
S.D.	27,602	11.6	49.8	23.4	15.4	11.3
Tenn.	29,546	12.4	52.8	32.6	12.4	2.2
Tex.	31,553	14.1	58.6	25.3	13.5	2.6
Utah	33,246	8.6	59.4	25.3	13.1	2.2
Vt.	38,213	7.7	60.4	25.4	12.3	1.9
Va.	34,780	6.9	56.6	25.8	13.5	4.1
Wash.	36,795	7.8	59.0	24.8	12.8	3.4
W.Va.	25,602	16.0	50.8	33.0	14.1	2.0
Wis.	35,082	7.6	52.3	29.8	13.6	4.3
Wyo.	32,216	9.3	51.6	27.3	15.6	5.5
U.S.	35,225	10.7	NA	NA	NA	NA

*As percent of employed persons age 16 and over.
NA Not available.

National Table 5 Education: School Years Completed

State	Less than grade 9*	Grades 9-12 no diploma*	Only High school diploma*	High school graduate (or equivalent) or higher*	College bachelor's degree or higher*
Ala.	13.7%	19.4%	29.4%	66.9%	15.7%
Alaska	5.1	8.2	28.7	86.6	23.0
Ariz.	9.0	12.3	26.1	78.7	20.3
Ark.	15.2	18.4	32.7	66.3	13.3
Calif.	11.2	12.6	22.3	76.2	23.4
Colo.	5.6	10.0	26.5	84.4	27.0
Conn.	8.4	12.4	29.5	79.2	27.2
Del.	7.2	15.3	32.7	73.1	21.4
D.C.	9.6	17.3	21.2	77.5	33.3
Fla.	9.5	16.1	30.1	74.4	18.3
Ga.	12.0	17.1	29.7	70.9	19.3
Hawaii	10.1	9.8	28.7	80.1	22.9
Idaho	7.4	12.9	30.4	79.7	17.7
Ill.	10.3	13.5	30.0	76.2	21.0
Ind.	8.5	15.8	38.2	75.6	15.6
Iowa	9.2	10.7	38.5	80.1	16.9
Kans.	7.7	11.0	32.8	81.3	21.1
Ky.	19.0	16.4	31.8	64.6	13.6
La.	14.7	17.0	31.7	68.3	16.1
Maine	8.8	12.4	37.1	78.8	18.8
Md.	7.9	13.7	28.1	78.4	26.5
Mass.	8.0	12.0	29.7	80.0	27.2
Mich.	7.8	15.5	32.3	76.8	17.4
Minn.	8.6	9.0	33.0	82.4	21.8
Miss.	15.6	20.1	27.5	64.3	14.7
Mo.	11.6	14.5	33.1	73.9	17.8
Mont.	8.1	10.9	33.5	81.0	19.8
Nebr.	8.0	10.2	34.7	81.8	18.9
Nev.	6.1	15.2	31.5	78.8	15.3
N.H.	6.7	11.2	31.7	82.2	24.4
N.J.	9.4	13.9	31.1	76.7	24.9
N.M.	11.4	13.5	28.7	75.1	20.4
N.Y.	10.2	15.0	29.5	74.8	23.1
N.C.	12.7	17.3	29.0	70.0	17.4
N.D.	15.0	8.3	28.0	76.7	18.1
Ohio	7.9	16.4	36.3	75.7	17.0
Okla.	9.8	15.6	30.5	74.6	17.8
Oreg.	6.2	12.3	28.9	81.5	20.6
Pa.	9.4	15.9	38.6	74.7	17.9
R.I.	11.1	16.9	29.5	72.0	21.3
S.C.	13.6	18.1	29.5	68.3	16.6
S.D.	13.4	9.5	33.7	77.1	17.2
Tenn.	16.0	17.0	30.0	67.1	16.0
Tex.	13.5	14.4	25.6	72.1	20.3
Utah	3.4	11.5	27.2	85.1	22.3
Vt.	11.2	13.7	26.6	80.8	24.5
Va.	8.7	10.6	34.6	75.2	24.3
Wash.	5.5	10.7	27.9	83.8	22.9
W.Va.	16.8	17.3	36.6	66.0	12.3
Wis.	9.5	11.9	37.1	78.6	17.7
Wyo.	5.7	11.2	33.2	83.0	18.8
U.S.	10.4	11.2	30.0	75.2	20.3

*As percent of persons age 25 and over.

National Table 6 Housing and Residential Patterns

State	Owner occupied	Renter occupied	Urban	Rural
Alabama	70.5%	29.5%	60.4%	39.6%
Alaska	56.1	43.9	67.5	32.5
Arizona	64.2	35.8	87.5	12.5
Arkansas	69.6	30.4	53.5	46.5
California	55.6	44.4	92.6	7.4
Colorado	62.2	37.8	82.4	17.6
Connecticut	65.6	34.4	79.1	20.9
Delaware	70.2	29.8	73.0	27.0
District of Columbia	38.9	61.1	100.0	0.0
Florida	67.2	32.8	84.8	15.2
Georgia	64.9	35.1	63.2	36.8
Hawaii	53.9	46.1	89.0	11.0
Idaho	70.1	29.9	57.4	42.6
Illinois	64.2	35.8	84.6	15.4
Indiana	70.2	29.8	64.9	35.1
Iowa	70.0	30.0	60.6	39.4
Kansas	67.9	32.1	69.1	30.9
Kentucky	69.6	30.4	51.8	48.2
Louisiana	65.9	34.1	68.1	31.9
Maine	70.5	29.5	44.6	55.4
Maryland	65.0	35.0	81.3	18.7
Massachusetts	59.3	40.7	84.3	15.7
Michigan	71.0	29.0	70.5	29.5
Minnesota	71.8	28.2	69.9	30.1
Mississippi	71.5	28.5	47.1	52.9
Missouri	68.8	31.2	68.7	31.3
Montana	67.3	32.7	52.5	47.5
Nebraska	66.5	33.5	66.1	33.9
Nevada	54.8	45.2	88.3	11.7
New Hampshire	68.2	31.8	51.0	49.0
New Jersey	64.9	35.1	89.4	10.6
New Mexico	67.4	32.6	73.0	27.0
New York	52.2	47.8	84.3	15.7
North Carolina	68.0	32.0	50.4	49.6
North Dakota	65.6	34.4	53.3	46.7
Ohio	67.5	32.5	74.1	25.9
Oklahoma	68.1	31.9	67.7	32.3
Oregon	63.1	36.9	70.5	29.5
Pennsylvania	70.6	29.4	68.9	31.1
Rhode Island	59.5	40.5	86.0	14.0
South Carolina	69.8	30.2	54.6	45.4
South Dakota	66.1	33.9	50.0	50.0
Tennessee	68.0	32.0	60.9	39.1
Texas	60.9	39.1	80.3	19.7
Utah	68.1	31.9	87.0	13.0
Virginia	66.3	33.7	69.4	30.6
Vermont	69.0	31.0	32.2	67.8
Washington	62.6	37.4	76.4	23.6
West Virginia	74.1	25.9	36.1	63.9
Wisconsin	66.7	33.3	65.7	34.3
Wyoming	67.8	32.2	65.0	35.0
United States	64.2	35.8	75.2	24.8

House Membership in the 100th Congress

Lineup as of Jan. 6, 1987: Democrats 258, Republicans 177

Alabama
1. Sonny Callahan (R)
2. William L. Dickinson (R)
3. Bill Nichols (D)
   (died Dec. 13, 1988)
4. Tom Bevill (D)
5. Ronnie G. Flippo (D)
6. Ben Erdreich (D)
7. Claude Harris (D)

Alaska
AL Don Young (R)

Arizona
1. John J. Rhodes III (R)
2. Morris K. Udall (D)
3. Bob Stump (R)
4. Jon Kyl (R)
5. Jim Kolbe (R)

Arkansas
1. Bill Alexander (D)
2. Tommy F. Robinson (D)
3. John Paul Hammerschmidt (R)
4. Beryl Anthony Jr. (D)

California
1. Douglas H. Bosco (D)
2. Wally Herger (R)
3. Robert T. Matsui (D)
4. Vic Fazio (D)
5. Sala Burton (D)
   (died Feb. 1, 1987)
   Nancy Pelosi (D)
   (sworn in June 9, 1987)
6. Barbara Boxer (D)
7. George Miller (D)
8. Ronald V. Dellums (D)
9. Fortney H. "Pete" Stark (D)
10. Don Edwards (D)
11. Tom Lantos (D)
12. Ernie Konnyu (R)
13. Norman Y. Mineta (D)
14. Norman D. Shumway (R)
15. Tony Coelho (D)
16. Leon E. Panetta (D)
17. Charles Pashayan Jr. (R)
18. Richard H. Lehman (D)
19. Robert J. Lagomarsino (R)
20. William M. Thomas (R)
21. Elton Gallegly (R)
22. Carlos J. Moorhead (R)
23. Anthony C. Beilenson (D)
24. Henry A. Waxman (D)
25. Edward R. Roybal (D)
26. Howard L. Berman (D)
27. Mel Levine (D)
28. Julian C. Dixon (D)
29. Augustus F. Hawkins (D)
30. Matthew G. Martinez (D)
31. Mervyn M. Dymally (D)
32. Glenn M. Anderson (D)
33. David Dreier (R)
34. Esteban Edward Torres (D)
35. Jerry Lewis (R)
36. George E. Brown Jr. (D)
37. Al McCandless (R)
38. Bob Dornan (R)
39. William E. Dannemeyer (R)
40. Robert E. Badham (R)
41. Bill Lowery (R)
42. Dan Lungren (R)
43. Ron Packard (R)
44. Jim Bates (D)
45. Duncan L. Hunter (R)

Colorado
1. Patricia Schroeder (D)
2. David E. Skaggs (D)
3. Ben Nighthorse Campbell (D)
4. Hank Brown (R)
5. Joel Hefley (R)
6. Dan Schaefer (R)

Connecticut
1. Barbara B. Kennelly (D)
2. Sam Gejdenson (D)
3. Bruce A. Morrison (D)
4. Stewart B. McKinney (R)
   (died May 7, 1987)
   Christopher Shays (R)
   (sworn in Sept. 9, 1987)
5. John G. Rowland (R)
6. Nancy L. Johnson (R)

Delaware
AL Thomas R. Carper (D)

Florida
1. Earl Hutto (D)
2. Bill Grant (D)
3. Charles E. Bennett (D)
4. Bill Chappell Jr. (D)
5. Bill McCollum (R)
6. Buddy MacKay (D)
7. Sam Gibbons (D)
8. C.W. Bill Young (R)
9. Michael Bilirakis (R)
10. Andy Ireland (R)
11. Bill Nelson (D)
12. Tom Lewis (R)
13. Connie Mack (R)
14. Daniel A. Mica (D)
15. E. Clay Shaw Jr. (R)
16. Larry Smith (D)
17. William Lehman (D)
18. Claude Pepper (D)
19. Dante B. Fascell (D)

Georgia
1. Robert Lindsay Thomas (D)
2. Charles Hatcher (D)
3. Richard Ray (D)
4. Pat Swindall (R)
5. John Lewis (D)
6. Newt Gingrich (R)
7. George "Buddy" Darden (D)
8. J. Roy Rowland (D)
9. Ed Jenkins (D)
10. Doug Barnard Jr. (D)

Hawaii
1. Patricia F. Saiki (R)
2. Daniel K. Akaka (D)

Idaho
1. Larry E. Craig (R)
2. Richard H. Stallings (D)

Illinois
1. Charles A. Hayes (D)
2. Gus Savage (D)
3. Marty Russo (D)
4. Jack Davis (R)
5. William O. Lipinski (D)
6. Henry J. Hyde (R)
7. Cardiss Collins (D)
8. Dan Rostenkowski (D)
9. Sidney R. Yates (D)
10. John Edward Porter (R)
11. Frank Annunzio (D)
12. Philip M. Crane (R)
13. Harris W. Fawell (R)
14. Dennis Hastert (R)
15. Edward R. Madigan (R)
16. Lynn Martin (R)
17. Lane Evans (D)
18. Robert H. Michel (R)
19. Terry L. Bruce (D)
20. Richard J. Durbin (D)
21. Melvin Price (D)
    (died April 22, 1988)
    Jerry F. Costello
    (sworn in Aug. 11, 1988)
22. Kenneth J. Gray (D)

Indiana
1. Peter J. Visclosky (D)
2. Philip R. Sharp (D)
3. John Hiler (R)
4. Dan Coats (R)
5. Jim Jontz (D)
6. Dan Burton (R)
7. John T. Myers (R)
8. Frank McCloskey (D)
9. Lee H. Hamilton (D)
10. Andrew Jacobs Jr. (D)

Iowa
1. Jim Leach (R)
2. Tom Tauke (R)
3. Dave R. Nagle (D)
4. Neal Smith (D)
5. Jim Lightfoot (R)
6. Fred Grandy (R)

Kansas
1. Pat Roberts (R)
2. Jim Slattery (D)
3. Jan Meyers (R)
4. Dan Glickman (D)
5. Bob Whittaker (R)

Kentucky
1. Carroll Hubbard Jr. (D)
2. William H. Natcher (D)
3. Romano L. Mazzoli (D)
4. Jim Bunning (R)
5. Harold Rogers (R)
6. Larry J. Hopkins (R)
7. Carl C. Perkins (D)

Louisiana
1. Bob Livingston (R)
2. Lindy (Mrs. Hale) Boggs (D)
3. W.J. "Billy" Tauzin (D)
4. Buddy Roemer (D)
   (resigned March 14, 1988)
   Jim McCrery (R)
   (sworn in April 26, 1988)
5. Jerry Huckaby (D)
6. Richard H. Baker (R)
7. Jimmy Hayes (D)
8. Clyde C. Holloway (R)

Maine
1. Joseph E. Brennan (D)
2. Olympia J. Snowe (R)

Maryland
1. Roy Dyson (D)
2. Helen Delich Bentley (R)
3. Benjamin L. Cardin (D)
4. Tom McMillen (D)
5. Steny H. Hoyer (D)
6. Beverly B. Byron (D)
7. Kweisi Mfume (D)
8. Constance A. Morella (R)

Massachusetts
1. Silvio O. Conte (R)
2. Edward P. Boland (D)
3. Joseph D. Early (D)
4. Barney Frank (D)
5. Chester G. Atkins (D)
6. Nicholas Mavroules (D)
7. Edward J. Markey (D)
8. Joseph P. Kennedy II (D)
9. Joe Moakley (D)
10. Gerry E. Studds (D)
11. Brian J. Donnelly (D)

Michigan
1. John Conyers Jr. (D)
2. Carl D. Pursell (R)
3. Howard Wolpe (D)
4. Fred Upton (R)
5. Paul B. Henry (R)
6. Bob Carr (D)
7. Dale E. Kildee (D)
8. Bob Traxler (D)
9. Guy Vander Jagt (R)
10. Bill Schuette (R)
11. Robert W. Davis (R)
12. David E. Bonior (D)
13. George W. Crockett Jr. (D)
14. Dennis M. Hertel (D)
15. William D. Ford (D)
16. John D. Dingell (D)
17. Sander M. Levin (D)
18. William S. Broomfield (R)

Minnesota
1. Timothy J. Penny (D)
2. Vin Weber (R)
3. Bill Frenzel (R)
4. Bruce F. Vento (D)
5. Martin Olav Sabo (D)
6. Gerry Sikorski (D)
7. Arlan Stangeland (R)
8. James L. Oberstar (D)

Mississippi
1. Jamie L. Whitten (D)
2. Mike Espy (D)
3. G. V. "Sonny" Montgomery (D)
4. Wayne Dowdy (D)
5. Trent Lott (R)

Missouri
1. William L. Clay (D)
2. Jack Buechner (R)
3. Richard A. Gephardt (D)
4. Ike Skelton (D)
5. Alan Wheat (D)
6. E. Thomas Coleman (R)
7. Gene Taylor (R)
8. Bill Emerson (R)
9. Harold L. Volkmer (D)

Montana
1. Pat Williams (D)
2. Ron Marlenee (R)

Nebraska
1. Doug Bereuter (R)
2. Hal Daub (R)
3. Virginia Smith (R)

Nevada
1. James Bilbray (D)
2. Barbara F. Vucanovich (R)

New Hampshire
1. Robert C. Smith (R)
2. Judd Gregg (R)

New Jersey
1. James J. Florio (D)
2. William J. Hughes (D)
3. James J. Howard (D) *
   (died March 25, 1988)
4. Christopher H. Smith (R)
5. Marge Roukema (R)
6. Bernard J. Dwyer (D)
7. Matthew J. Rinaldo (R)
8. Robert A. Roe (D)
9. Robert G. Torricelli (D)
10. Peter W. Rodino Jr. (D)
11. Dean A. Gallo (R)
12. Jim Courter (R)
13. H. James Saxton (R)
14. Frank J. Guarini (D)

New Mexico
1. Manuel Lujan Jr. (R)
2. Joe Skeen (R)
3. Bill Richardson (D)

New York
1. George J. Hochbrueckner (D)
2. Thomas J. Downey (D)
3. Robert J. Mrazek (D)
4. Norman F. Lent (R)
5. Raymond J. McGrath (R)
6. Floyd H. Flake (D)
7. Gary L. Ackerman (D)
8. James H. Scheuer (D)
9. Thomas J. Manton (D)
10. Charles E. Schumer (D)
11. Edolphus Towns (D)
12. Major R. Owens (D)
13. Stephen J. Solarz (D)
14. Guy V. Molinari (R)
15. Bill Green (R)
16. Charles B. Rangel (D)
17. Ted Weiss (D)
18. Robert Garcia (D)
19. Mario Biaggi (D)
    (resigned Aug. 8, 1988)
20. Joseph J. DioGuardi (R)
21. Hamilton Fish Jr. (R)
22. Benjamin A. Gilman (R)
23. Samuel S. Stratton (D)
24. Gerald B. H. Solomon (R)
25. Sherwood L. Boehlert (R)
26. David O'B. Martin (R)
27. George C. Wortley (R)
28. Matthew F. McHugh (D)
29. Frank Horton (R)
30. Louise M. Slaughter (D)
31. Jack F. Kemp (R)
32. John J. LaFalce (D)
33. Henry J. Nowak (D)
34. Amo Houghton (R)

North Carolina
1. Walter B. Jones (D)
2. Tim Valentine (D)
3. H. Martin Lancaster (D)
4. David E. Price (D)
5. Stephen L. Neal (D)
6. Howard Coble (R)
7. Charlie Rose (D)
8. W. G. "Bill" Hefner (D)
9. J. Alex McMillan (R)
10. Cass Ballenger (R)
11. James McClure Clarke (D)

North Dakota
AL Byron L. Dorgan (D)

Ohio
1. Thomas A. Luken (D)
2. Bill Gradison (R)
3. Tony P. Hall (D)
4. Michael G. Oxley (R)
5. Delbert L. Latta (R)
6. Bob McEwen (R)
7. Michael DeWine (R)
8. Donald E. "Buz" Lukens (R)
9. Marcy Kaptur (D)
10. Clarence E. Miller (R)
11. Dennis E. Eckart (D)
12. John R. Kasich (R)
13. Don J. Pease (D)
14. Thomas C. Sawyer (D)
15. Chalmers P. Wylie (R)
16. Ralph Regula (R)
17. James A. Traficant Jr. (D)
18. Douglas Applegate (D)
19. Edward F. Feighan (D)
20. Mary Rose Oakar (D)
21. Louis Stokes (D)

Oklahoma
1. James M. Inhofe (R)
2. Mike Synar (D)
3. Wes Watkins (D)
4. Dave McCurdy (D)
5. Mickey Edwards (R)
6. Glenn English (D)

Oregon
1. Les AuCoin (D)
2. Robert F. Smith (R)
3. Ron Wyden (D)
4. Peter A. DeFazio (D)
5. Denny Smith (R)

Pennsylvania
1. Thomas M. Foglietta (D)
2. William H. Gray III (D)
3. Robert A. Borski (D)
4. Joe Kolter (D)
5. Richard T. Schulze (R)
6. Gus Yatron (D)
7. Curt Weldon (R)
8. Peter H. Kostmayer (D)
9. Bud Shuster (R)
10. Joseph M. McDade (R)
11. Paul E. Kanjorski (D)
12. John P. Murtha (D)
13. Lawrence Coughlin (R)
14. William J. Coyne (D)
15. Don Ritter (R)
16. Robert S. Walker (R)
17. George W. Gekas (R)
18. Doug Walgren (D)
19. Bill Goodling (R)
20. Joseph M. Gaydos (D)
21. Tom Ridge (R)
22. Austin J. Murphy (D)
23. William F. Clinger Jr. (R)

Rhode Island
1. Fernand J. St Germain (D)
2. Claudine Schneider (R)

South Carolina
1. Arthur Ravenel Jr. (R)
2. Floyd Spence (R)
3. Butler Derrick (D)
4. Liz J. Patterson (D)
5. John M. Spratt Jr. (D)
6. Robin Tallon (D)

South Dakota
AL Tim Johnson (D)

Tennessee
1. James H. Quillen (R)
2. John J. Duncan (R) †
   (died June 21, 1988)
3. Marilyn Lloyd (D)
4. Jim Cooper (D)
5. Bill Boner (D)
   (resigned Oct. 5, 1987)
   Bob Clement (D)
   (sworn in Jan. 25, 1988)
6. Bart Gordon (D)
7. Don Sundquist (R)
8. Ed Jones (D)
9. Harold E. Ford (D)

Texas
1. Jim Chapman (D)
2. Charles Wilson (D)
3. Steve Bartlett (R)
4. Ralph M. Hall (D)
5. John Bryant (D)
6. Joe L. Barton (R)
7. Bill Archer (R)
8. Jack Fields (R)
9. Jack Brooks (D)
10. J. J. Pickle (D)
11. Marvin Leath (D)
12. Jim Wright (D)
13. Beau Boulter (R)
14. Mac Sweeney (R)
15. E. "Kika" de la Garza (D)
16. Ronald D. Coleman (D)
17. Charles W. Stenholm (D)
18. Mickey Leland (D)
19. Larry Combest (R)
20. Henry B. Gonzalez (D)
21. Lamar Smith (R)
22. Thomas D. DeLay (R)
23. Albert G. Bustamante (D)
24. Martin Frost (D)
25. Michael A. Andrews (D)
26. Dick Armey (R)
27. Solomon P. Ortiz (D)

Utah
1. James V. Hansen (R)
2. Wayne Owens (D)
3. Howard C. Nielson (R)

Vermont
AL James M. Jeffords (R)

Virginia
1. Herbert H. Bateman (R)
2. Owen B. Pickett (D)
3. Thomas J. Bliley Jr. (R)
4. Norman Sisisky (D)
5. Dan Daniel (D)
   (died Jan. 23, 1988)
   Lewis F. Payne Jr.
   (sworn in June 21, 1988)
6. James R. Olin (D)
7. D. French Slaughter Jr. (R)
8. Stan Parris (R)
9. Rick Boucher (D)
10. Frank R. Wolf (R)

Washington
1. John R. Miller (R)
2. Al Swift (D)
3. Don Bonker (D)
4. Sid Morrison (R)
5. Thomas S. Foley (D)
6. Norman D. Dicks (D)
7. Mike Lowry (D)
8. Rod Chandler (R)

West Virginia
1. Alan B. Mollohan (D)
2. Harley O. Staggers Jr. (D)
3. Bob Wise (D)
4. Nick J. Rahall II (D)

Wisconsin
1. Les Aspin (D)
2. Robert W. Kastenmeier (D)
3. Steve Gunderson (R)
4. Gerald D. Kleczka (D)
5. Jim Moody (D)
6. Thomas E. Petri (R)
7. David R. Obey (D)
8. Toby Roth (R)
9. F. James Sensenbrenner Jr. (R)

Wyoming
AL Dick Cheney (R)

Note: Members of the 100th Congress also included delegates Ben Blaz, R-Guam; Ron de Lugo, D-Virgin Islands; Walter E. Fauntroy, D-D.C.; Fofó I. F. Sunia, D-American Samoa; and resident commissioner Jaime B. Fuster, Pop. Dem.-Puerto Rico.

* Frank Pallone Jr., D, was elected Nov. 8, 1988, to fill Howard's remaining term and to the 101st Congress. He also was sworn in Nov. 8.
† John J. "Jimmy" Duncan Jr., R, was elected Nov. 8, 1988, to fill the remaining term of his father, John J. Duncan, and to the 101st Congress. He also was sworn in Nov. 8.

House Membership in the 101st Congress

Lineup as of Jan. 3, 1989: Democrats 259, Republicans 174, Vacancies 2

Alabama
1. Sonny Callahan (R)
2. Bill L. Dickinson (R)
3. Glen Browder (D)[a]
   (sworn in April 18, 1989)
4. Tom Bevill (D)
5. Ronnie G. Flippo (D)
6. Ben Erdreich (D)
7. Claude Harris (D)

Alaska
AL Don Young (R)

Arizona
1. John J. Rhodes III (R)
2. Morris K. Udall (D)
3. Bob Stump (R)
4. Jon Kyl (R)
5. Jim Kolbe (R)

Arkansas
1. Bill Alexander (D)
2. Tommy F. Robinson (D)[b]
3. John Paul Hammerschmidt (R)
4. Beryl Anthony Jr. (D)

California
1. Douglas H. Bosco (D)
2. Wally Herger (R)
3. Robert T. Matsui (D)
4. Vic Fazio (D)
5. Nancy Pelosi (D)
6. Barbara Boxer (D)
7. George Miller (D)
8. Ronald V. Dellums (D)
9. Pete Stark (D)
10. Don Edwards (D)
11. Tom Lantos (D)
12. Tom Campbell (R)
13. Norman Y. Mineta (D)
14. Norman D. Shumway (R)
15. Tony Coelho (D)
    (resigned June 15, 1989)
    Gary Condit (D)
    (sworn in Sept. 20, 1989)
16. Leon E. Panetta (D)
17. Charles "Chip" Pashayan Jr. (R)
18. Richard H. Lehman (D)
19. Robert J. Lagomarsino (R)
20. Bill Thomas (R)
21. Elton Gallegly (R)
22. Carlos J. Moorhead (R)
23. Anthony C. Beilenson (D)
24. Henry A. Waxman (D)
25. Edward R. Roybal (D)
26. Howard L. Berman (D)
27. Mel Levine (D)
28. Julian C. Dixon (D)
29. Augustus F. Hawkins (D)
30. Matthew G. Martinez (D)
31. Mervyn M. Dymally (D)
32. Glenn M. Anderson (D)
33. David Dreier (R)
34. Esteban E. Torres (D)
35. Jerry Lewis (R)
36. George E. Brown Jr. (D)
37. Al McCandless (R)
38. Robert K. Dornan (R)
39. William E. Dannemeyer (R)
40. C. Christopher Cox (R)
41. Bill Lowery (R)
42. Dana Rohrabacher (R)
43. Ron Packard (R)
44. Jim Bates (D)
45. Duncan Hunter (R)

Colorado
1. Patricia Schroeder (D)
2. David E. Skaggs (D)
3. Ben Nighthorse Campbell (D)
4. Hank Brown (R)
5. Joel Hefley (R)
6. Dan Schaefer (R)

Connecticut
1. Barbara B. Kennelly (D)
2. Sam Gejdenson (D)
3. Bruce A. Morrison (D)
4. Christopher Shays (R)
5. John G. Rowland (R)
6. Nancy L. Johnson (R)

Delaware
AL Thomas R. Carper (D)

Florida
1. Earl Hutto (D)
2. Bill Grant (D)[c]
3. Charles E. Bennett (D)
4. Craig T. James (R)
5. Bill McCollum (R)
6. Cliff Stearns (R)
7. Sam M. Gibbons (D)
8. C. W. Bill Young (R)
9. Michael Bilirakis (R)
10. Andy Ireland (R)
11. Bill Nelson (D)
12. Tom Lewis (R)
13. Porter J. Goss (R)
14. Harry A. Johnston (D)
15. E. Clay Shaw Jr. (R)
16. Lawrence J. Smith (D)
17. William Lehman (D)
18. Claude Pepper (D)
    (died May 30, 1989)
    Ileana Ros-Lehtinen (R)
    (sworn in Sept. 6, 1989)
19. Dante B. Fascell (D)

Georgia
1. Lindsay Thomas (D)
2. Charles Hatcher (D)
3. Richard Ray (D)
4. Ben Jones (D)
5. John Lewis (D)
6. Newt Gingrich (R)
7. George "Buddy" Darden (D)
8. J. Roy Rowland (D)
9. Ed Jenkins (D)
10. Doug Barnard Jr. (D)

Hawaii
1. Patricia Saiki (R)
2. Daniel K. Akaka (D)
   (resigned May 16, 1990)
   Patsy T. Mink (D)
   (sworn in Sept. 27, 1990)

Idaho
1. Larry E. Craig (R)
2. Richard Stallings (D)

Illinois
1. Charles A. Hayes (D)
2. Gus Savage (D)
3. Marty Russo (D)
4. George E. Sangmeister (D)
5. William O. Lipinski (D)
6. Henry J. Hyde (R)
7. Cardiss Collins (D)

8. Dan Rostenkowski (D)
9. Sidney R. Yates (D)
10. John Porter (R)
11. Frank Annunzio (D)
12. Philip M. Crane (R)
13. Harris W. Fawell (R)
14. Dennis Hastert (R)
15. Edward R. Madigan (R)
16. Lynn Martin (R)
17. Lane Evans (D)
18. Robert H. Michel (R)
19. Terry L. Bruce (D)
20. Richard J. Durbin (D)
21. Jerry F. Costello (D)
22. Glenn Poshard (D)

Indiana
1. Peter J. Visclosky (D)
2. Philip R. Sharp (D)
3. John Hiler (R)
4. Jill L. Long (D)[d]
   (sworn in April 4, 1989)
5. Jim Jontz (D)
6. Dan Burton (R)
7. John T. Myers (R)
8. Frank McCloskey (D)
9. Lee H. Hamilton (D)
10. Andrew Jacobs Jr. (D)

Iowa
1. Jim Leach (R)
2. Tom Tauke (R)
3. Dave Nagle (D)
4. Neal Smith (D)
5. Jim Ross Lightfoot (R)
6. Fred Grandy (R)

Kansas
1. Pat Roberts (R)
2. Jim Slattery (D)
3. Jan Meyers (R)
4. Dan Glickman (D)
5. Bob Whittaker (R)

Kentucky
1. Carroll Hubbard Jr. (D)
2. William H. Natcher (D)
3. Romano L. Mazzoli (D)
4. Jim Bunning (R)
5. Harold Rogers (R)
6. Larry J. Hopkins (R)
7. Carl L. Perkins (D)

Louisiana
1. Robert L. Livingston (R)
2. Lindy (Mrs. Hale) Boggs (D)
3. W. J. "Billy" Tauzin (D)
4. Jim McCrery (R)
5. Jerry Huckaby (D)
6. Richard H. Baker (R)
7. Jimmy Hayes (D)
8. Clyde C. Holloway (R)

Maine
1. Joseph E. Brennan (D)
2. Olympia J. Snowe (R)

Maryland
1. Roy Dyson (D)
2. Helen Delich Bentley (R)
3. Benjamin L. Cardin (D)
4. Tom McMillen (D)
5. Steny H. Hoyer (D)
6. Beverly B. Byron (D)
7. Kweisi Mfume (D)

8. Constance A. Morella (R)

Massachusetts
1. Silvio O. Conte (R)
2. Richard E. Neal (D)
3. Joseph D. Early (D)
4. Barney Frank (D)
5. Chester G. Atkins (D)
6. Nicholas Mavroules (D)
7. Edward J. Markey (D)
8. Joseph P. Kennedy II (D)
9. Joe Moakley (D)
10. Gerry E. Studds (D)
11. Brian Donnelly (D)

Michigan
1. John Conyers Jr. (D)
2. Carl D. Pursell (R)
3. Howard Wolpe (D)
4. Fred Upton (R)
5. Paul B. Henry (R)
6. Bob Carr (D)
7. Dale E. Kildee (D)
8. Bob Traxler (D)
9. Guy Vander Jagt (R)
10. Bill Schuette (R)
11. Robert W. Davis (R)
12. David E. Bonior (D)
13. George W. Crockett Jr. (D)
14. Dennis M. Hertel (D)
15. William D. Ford (D)
16. John D. Dingell (D)
17. Sander M. Levin (D)
18. William S. Broomfield (R)

Minnesota
1. Timothy J. Penny (D)
2. Vin Weber (R)
3. Bill Frenzel (R)
4. Bruce F. Vento (D)
5. Martin Olav Sabo (D)
6. Gerry Sikorski (D)
7. Arlan Stangeland (R)
8. James L. Oberstar (D)

Mississippi
1. Jamie L. Whitten (D)
2. Mike Espy (D)
3. G. V. "Sonny" Montgomery (D)
4. Mike Parker (D)
5. Larkin Smith (R)
   (died Aug. 13, 1989)
   Gene Taylor (D)
   (sworn in Oct. 24, 1989)

Missouri
1. William L. Clay (D)
2. Jack Buechner (R)
3. Richard A. Gephardt (D)
4. Ike Skelton (D)
5. Alan Wheat (D)
6. E. Thomas Coleman (R)
7. Mel Hancock (R)
8. Bill Emerson (R)
9. Harold L. Volkmer (D)

Montana
1. Pat Williams (D)
2. Ron Marlenee (R)

Nebraska
1. Doug Bereuter (R)
2. Peter Hoagland (D)
3. Virginia Smith (R)

Nevada
1. James Bilbray (D)
2. Barbara F. Vucanovich (R)

New Hampshire
1. Robert C. Smith (R)
   (resigned Dec. 7, 1990)
2. Chuck Douglas (R)

New Jersey
1. James J. Florio (D)
   (resigned Jan. 16, 1990)
   Robert E. Andrews (D)
   (sworn in Jan. 3, 1991)
2. William J. Hughes (D)
3. Frank Pallone Jr. (D)
4. Christopher H. Smith (R)
5. Marge Roukema (R)
6. Bernard J. Dwyer (D)
7. Matthew J. Rinaldo (R)
8. Robert A. Roe (D)
9. Robert G. Torricelli (D)
10. Donald M. Payne (D)
11. Dean A. Gallo (R)
12. Jim Courter (R)
13. H. James Saxton (R)
14. Frank J. Guarini (D)

New Mexico
1. Steven H. Schiff (R)
2. Joe Skeen (R)
3. Bill Richardson (D)

New York
1. George J. Hochbrueckner (D)
2. Thomas J. Downey (D)
3. Robert J. Mrazek (D)
4. Norman F. Lent (R)
5. Raymond J. McGrath (R)
6. Floyd H. Flake (D)
7. Gary L. Ackerman (D)
8. James H. Scheuer (D)
9. Thomas J. Manton (D)
10. Charles E. Schumer (D)
11. Edolphus Towns (D)
12. Major R. Owens (D)
13. Stephen J. Solarz (D)
14. Guy V. Molinari (R)
   (resigned Jan. 1, 1990)
   Susan Molinari (R)
   (sworn in March 27, 1990)
15. Bill Green (R)
16. Charles B. Rangel (D)
17. Ted Weiss (D)
18. Robert Garcia (D)
   (resigned Jan. 7, 1990)
   Jose E. Serrano (D)
   (sworn in March 28, 1990)
19. Eliot L. Engel (D)
20. Nita M. Lowey (D)
21. Hamilton Fish Jr. (R)
22. Benjamin A. Gilman (R)
23. Michael R. McNulty (D)
24. Gerald B. H. Solomon (R)
25. Sherwood Boehlert (R)
26. David O'B. Martin (R)
27. James T. Walsh (R)
28. Matthew F. McHugh (D)
29. Frank Horton (R)
30. Louise M. Slaughter (D)
31. Bill Paxon (R)

32. John J. LaFalce (D)
33. Henry J. Nowak (D)
34. Amo Houghton (R)

North Carolina
1. Walter B. Jones (D)
2. Tim Valentine (D)
3. H. Martin Lancaster (D)
4. David E. Price (D)
5. Stephen L. Neal (D)
6. Howard Coble (R)
7. Charlie Rose (D)
8. W. G. "Bill" Hefner (D)
9. Alex McMillan (R)
10. Cass Ballenger (R)
11. James McClure Clarke (D)

North Dakota
AL Byron L. Dorgan (D)

Ohio
1. Thomas A. Luken (D)
2. Bill Gradison (R)
3. Tony P. Hall (D)
4. Michael G. Oxley (R)
5. Paul E. Gillmor (R)
6. Bob McEwen (R)
7. Mike DeWine (R)
8. Donald E. "Buz" Lukens (R)
   (resigned Oct. 24, 1990)
9. Marcy Kaptur (D)
10. Clarence E. Miller (R)
11. Dennis E. Eckart (D)
12. John R. Kasich (R)
13. Don J. Pease (D)
14. Thomas C. Sawyer (D)
15. Chalmers P. Wylie (R)
16. Ralph Regula (R)
17. James A. Traficant Jr. (D)
18. Douglas Applegate (D)
19. Edward F. Feighan (D)
20. Mary Rose Oakar (D)
21. Louis Stokes (D)

Oklahoma
1. James M. Inhofe (R)
2. Mike Synar (D)
3. Wes Watkins (D)
4. Dave McCurdy (D)
5. Mickey Edwards (R)
6. Glenn English (D)

Oregon
1. Les AuCoin (D)
2. Bob Smith (R)
3. Ron Wyden (D)
4. Peter A. DeFazio (D)
5. Denny Smith (R)

Pennsylvania
1. Thomas M. Foglietta (D)
2. William H. Gray III (D)
3. Robert A. Borski (D)
4. Joe Kolter (D)
5. Richard T. Schulze (R)
6. Gus Yatron (D)

7. Curt Weldon (R)
8. Peter H. Kostmayer (D)
9. Bud Shuster (R)
10. Joseph M. McDade (R)
11. Paul E. Kanjorski (D)
12. John P. Murtha (D)
13. Lawrence Coughlin (R)
14. William J. Coyne (D)
15. Don Ritter (R)
16. Robert S. Walker (R)
17. George W. Gekas (R)
18. Doug Walgren (D)
19. Bill Goodling (R)
20. Joseph M. Gaydos (D)
21. Tom Ridge (R)
22. Austin J. Murphy (D)
23. William F. Clinger Jr. (R)

Rhode Island
1. Ronald K. Machtley (R)
2. Claudine Schneider (R)

South Carolina
1. Arthur Ravenel Jr. (R)
2. Floyd D. Spence (R)
3. Butler Derrick (D)
4. Liz J. Patterson (D)
5. John M. Spratt Jr. (D)
6. Robin Tallon (D)

South Dakota
AL Tim Johnson (D)

Tennessee
1. James H. Quillen (R)
2. John J. "Jimmy" Duncan Jr. (R)
3. Marilyn Lloyd (D)
4. Jim Cooper (D)
5. Bob Clement (D)
6. Bart Gordon (D)
7. Don Sundquist (R)
8. John Tanner (D)
9. Harold E. Ford (D)

Texas
1. Jim Chapman (D)
2. Charles Wilson (D)
3. Steve Bartlett (R)
4. Ralph M. Hall (D)
5. John Bryant (D)
6. Joe L. Barton (R)
7. Bill Archer (R)
8. Jack Fields (R)
9. Jack Brooks (D)
10. J. J. Pickle (D)
11. Marvin Leath (D)
12. Jim Wright (D)
   (resigned June 30, 1989)
   Pete Geren
   (sworn in Sept. 20, 1989)
13. Bill Sarpalius (D)
14. Greg Laughlin (D)
15. E. "Kika" de la Garza (D)
16. Ronald D. Coleman (D)
17. Charles W. Stenholm (D)
18. Mickey Leland (D)
   (died Aug. 7, 1989)
   Craig Washington (D)
   (sworn in Jan. 23, 1990)

19. Larry Combest (R)
20. Henry B. Gonzalez (D)
21. Lamar Smith (R)
22. Tom DeLay (R)
23. Albert G. Bustamante (D)
24. Martin Frost (D)
25. Michael A. Andrews (D)
26. Dick Armey (R)
27. Solomon P. Ortiz (D)

Utah
1. James V. Hansen (R)
2. Wayne Owens (D)
3. Howard C. Nielson (R)

Vermont
AL Peter Smith (R)

Virginia
1. Herbert H. Bateman (R)
2. Owen B. Pickett (D)
3. Thomas J. Bliley Jr. (R)
4. Norman Sisisky (D)
5. Lewis F. Payne Jr. (D)
6. Jim Olin (D)
7. D. French Slaughter Jr. (R)
8. Stan Parris (R)
9. Rick Boucher (D)
10. Frank R. Wolf (R)

Washington
1. John Miller (R)
2. Al Swift (D)
3. Jolene Unsoeld (D)
4. Sid Morrison (R)
5. Thomas S. Foley (D)
6. Norm Dicks (D)
7. Jim McDermott (D)
8. Rod Chandler (R)

West Virginia
1. Alan B. Mollohan (D)
2. Harley O. Staggers Jr. (D)
3. Bob Wise (D)
4. Nick J. Rahall II (D)

Wisconsin
1. Les Aspin (D)
2. Robert W. Kastenmeier (D)
3. Steve Gunderson (R)
4. Gerald D. Kleczka (D)
5. Jim Moody (D)
6. Thomas E. Petri (R)
7. David R. Obey (D)
8. Toby Roth (R)
9. F. James Sensenbrenner Jr. (R)

Wyoming
AL Dick Cheney (R)
   (resigned March 17, 1989)
   Craig Thomas (R)
   (sworn in May 2, 1989)

Note: Members of the 101st Congress also included delegates Ben Blaz, R-Guam; Ron de Lugo, D-Virgin Islands; Eni F. H. Faleomavaega, D-Am. Samoa; Walter E. Fauntroy, D-D.C.; and resident commissioner Jaime B. Fuster, Pop. Dem.-Puerto Rico.

[a] Bill Nichols, D, was re-elected Nov. 8, 1988, but died Dec. 13, 1988, before the start of the 101st Congress and was not sworn in. Glen Browder was elected to fill the vacant seat in a special election held April 4, 1989.
[b] Tommy Robinson switched to the Republican Party on July 28, 1989.
[c] Bill Grant switched to the Republican Party on Feb. 21, 1989.
[d] Daniel R. Coats, R, was re-elected Nov. 8, 1988. However, he resigned Jan. 1, 1989, to assume the Senate seat vacated by Dan Quayle, R, who was elected vice president. Jill L. Long was elected to fill the vacant seat in a special election held March 28, 1989.

House Membership in the 102nd Congress

Lineup as of Jan. 3, 1991: Democrats 267, Republicans 167, Independent 1

Alabama
1. Sonny Callahan (R)
2. Bill Dickinson (R)
3. Glen Browder (D)
4. Tom Bevill (D)
5. Bud Cramer (D)
6. Ben Erdreich (D)
7. Claude Harris (D)

Alaska
AL   Don Young (R)

Arizona
1. John J. Rhodes III (R)
2. Morris K. Udall (D)
   (resigned May 4, 1991)
   Ed Pastor (D)
   (sworn in Oct. 3, 1991)
3. Bob Stump (R)
4. Jon Kyl (R)
5. Jim Kolbe (R)

Arkansas
1. Bill Alexander (D)
2. Ray Thornton (D)
3. John Paul Hammerschmidt (R)
4. Beryl Anthony Jr. (D)

California
1. Frank Riggs (R).
2. Wally Herger (R)
3. Robert T. Matsui (D)
4. Vic Fazio (D)
5. Nancy Pelosi (D)
6. Barbara Boxer (D)
7. George Miller (D)
8. Ronald V. Dellums (D)
9. Pete Stark (D)
10. Don Edwards (D)
11. Tom Lantos (D)
12. Tom Campbell (R)
13. Norman Y. Mineta (D)
14. John T. Doolittle (R)
15. Gary Condit (D)
16. Leon E. Panetta (D)
17. Calvin Dooley (D)
18. Richard H. Lehman (D)
19. Robert J. Lagomarsino (R)
20. Bill Thomas (R)
21. Elton Gallegly (R)
22. Carlos J. Moorhead (R)
23. Anthony C. Beilenson (D)
24. Henry A. Waxman (D)
25. Edward R. Roybal (D)
26. Howard L. Berman (D)
27. Mel Levine (D)
28. Julian C. Dixon (D)
29. Maxine Waters (D)
30. Matthew G. Martinez (D)
31. Mervyn M. Dymally (D)
32. Glenn M. Anderson (D)
33. David Dreier (R)
34. Esteban E. Torres (D)
35. Jerry Lewis (R)
36. George E. Brown Jr. (D)
37. Al McCandless (R)
38. Robert K. Dornan (R)
39. William E. Dannemeyer (R)
40. C. Christopher Cox (R)
41. Bill Lowery (R)
42. Dana Rohrabacher (R)
43. Ron Packard (R)
44. Randy "Duke" Cunningham (R)
45. Duncan Hunter (R)

Colorado
1. Patricia Schroeder (D)
2. David E. Skaggs (D)
3. Ben Nighthorse Campbell (D)
4. Wayne Allard (R)
5. Joel Hefley (R)
6. Dan Schaefer (R)

Connecticut
1. Barbara B. Kennelly (D)
2. Sam Gejdenson (D)
3. Rosa DeLauro (D)
4. Christopher Shays (R)
5. Gary Franks (R)
6. Nancy L. Johnson (R)

Delaware
AL   Thomas R. Carper (D)

Florida
1. Earl Hutto (D)
2. Pete Peterson (D)
3. Charles E. Bennett (D)
4. Craig T. James (R)
5. Bill McCollum (R)
6. Cliff Stearns (R)
7. Sam M. Gibbons (D)
8. C.W. Bill Young (R)
9. Michael Bilirakis (R)
10. Andy Ireland (R)
11. Jim Bacchus (D)
12. Tom Lewis (R)
13. Porter J. Goss (R)
14. Harry A. Johnston (D)
15. E. Clay Shaw Jr. (R)
16. Lawrence J. Smith (D)
17. William Lehman (D)
18. Ileana Ros-Lehtinen (R)
19. Dante B. Fascell (D)

Georgia
1. Lindsay Thomas (D)
2. Charles Hatcher (D)
3. Richard Ray (D)
4. Ben Jones (D)
5. John Lewis (D)
6. Newt Gingrich (R)
7. George "Buddy" Darden (D)
8. J. Roy Rowland (D)
9. Ed Jenkins (D)
10. Doug Barnard Jr. (D)

Hawaii
1. Neil Abercrombie (D)
2. Patsy T. Mink (D)

Idaho
1. Larry LaRocco (D)
2. Richard Stallings (D)

Illinois
1. Charles A. Hayes (D)
2. Gus Savage (D)
3. Marty Russo (D)
4. George E. Sangmeister (D)
5. William O. Lipinski (D)
6. Henry J. Hyde (R)
7. Cardiss Collins (D)
8. Dan Rostenkowski (D)
9. Sidney R. Yates (D)
10. John Porter (R)
11. Frank Annunzio (D)
12. Philip M. Crane (R)
13. Harris W. Fawell (R)
14. Dennis Hastert (R)
15. Edward R. Madigan (R)
    (resigned March 8, 1991)
    Thomas W. Ewing (R)
    (sworn in July 10, 1991)
16. John W. Cox Jr. (D)
17. Lane Evans (D)
18. Robert H. Michel (R)
19. Terry L. Bruce (D)
20. Richard J. Durbin (D)
21. Jerry F. Costello (D)
22. Glenn Poshard (D)

Indiana
1. Peter J. Visclosky (D)
2. Philip R. Sharp (D)
3. Tim Roemer (D)
4. Jill L. Long (D)
5. Jim Jontz (D)
6. Dan Burton (R)
7. John T. Myers (R)
8. Frank McCloskey (D)
9. Lee H. Hamilton (D)
10. Andrew Jacobs Jr. (D)

Iowa
1. Jim Leach (R)
2. Jim Nussle (R)
3. Dave Nagle (D)
4. Neal Smith (D)
5. Jim Ross Lightfoot (R)
6. Fred Grandy (R)

Kansas
1. Pat Roberts (R)
2. Jim Slattery (D)
3. Jan Meyers (R)
4. Dan Glickman (D)
5. Dick Nichols (R)

Kentucky
1. Carroll Hubbard Jr. (D)
2. William H. Natcher (D)
3. Romano L. Mazzoli (D)
4. Jim Bunning (R)
5. Harold Rogers (R)
6. Larry J. Hopkins (R)
7. Carl C. Perkins (D)

Louisiana
1. Robert L. Livingston (R)
2. William J. Jefferson (D)
3. W. J. "Billy" Tauzin (D)
4. Jim McCrery (R)
5. Jerry Huckaby (D)
6. Richard H. Baker (R)
7. Jimmy Hayes (D)
8. Clyde C. Holloway (R)

Maine
1. Thomas H. Andrews (D)
2. Olympia J. Snowe (R)

Maryland
1. Wayne T. Gilchrest (R)
2. Helen Delich Bentley (R)
3. Benjamin L. Cardin (D)
4. Tom McMillen (D)
5. Steny H. Hoyer (D)
6. Beverly B. Byron (D)
7. Kweisi Mfume (D)
8. Constance A. Morella (R)

Massachusetts
1. Silvio O. Conte (R)
   (died Feb. 8, 1991)
   John Olver (D)
   (sworn in June 18, 1991)
2. Richard E. Neal (D)
3. Joseph D. Early (D)
4. Barney Frank (D)
5. Chester G. Atkins (D)
6. Nicholas Mavroules (D)
7. Edward J. Markey (D)
8. Joseph P. Kennedy II (D)
9. Joe Moakley (D)
10. Gerry E. Studds (D)
11. Brian Donnelly (D)

Michigan
1. John Conyers Jr. (D)
2. Carl D. Pursell (R)
3. Howard Wolpe (D)
4. Fred Upton (R)
5. Paul B. Henry (R)
6. Bob Carr (D)
7. Dale E. Kildee (D)
8. Bob Traxler (D)
9. Guy Vander Jagt (R)
10. Dave Camp (R)
11. Robert W. Davis (R)
12. David E. Bonior (D)
13. Barbara-Rose Collins (D)
14. Dennis M. Hertel (D)
15. William D. Ford (D)
16. John D. Dingell (D)
17. Sander M. Levin (D)
18. William S. Broomfield (R)

Minnesota
1. Timothy J. Penny (D)
2. Vin Weber (R)
3. Jim Ramstad (R)
4. Bruce F. Vento (D)
5. Martin Olav Sabo (D)
6. Gerry Sikorski (D)
7. Collin C. Peterson (D)
8. James L. Oberstar (D)

Mississippi
1. Jamie L. Whitten (D)
2. Mike Espy (D)
3. G.V. "Sonny" Montgomery (D)
4. Mike Parker (D)
5. Gene Taylor (D)

Missouri
1. William L. Clay (D)
2. Joan Kelly Horn (D)
3. Richard A. Gephardt (D)
4. Ike Skelton (D)
5. Alan Wheat (D)
6. E. Thomas Coleman (R)
7. Mel Hancock (R)
8. Bill Emerson (R)
9. Harold L. Volkmer (D)

Montana
1. Pat Williams (D)
2. Ron Marlenee (R)

Nebraska
1. Doug Bereuter (R)
2. Peter Hoagland (D)
3. Bill Barrett (R)

Nevada
1. James Bilbray (D)
2. Barbara F. Vucanovich (R)

New Hampshire
1. Bill Zeliff (R)
2. Dick Swett (D)

New Jersey
1. Robert E. Andrews (D)
2. William J. Hughes (D)
3. Frank Pallone Jr. (D)
4. Christopher H. Smith (R)
5. Marge Roukema (R)
6. Bernard J. Dwyer (D)
7. Matthew J. Rinaldo (R)
8. Robert A. Roe (D)
9. Robert G. Torricelli (D)
10. Donald M. Payne (D)
11. Dean A. Gallo (R)
12. Dick Zimmer (R)
13. H. James Saxton (R)
14. Frank J. Guarini (D)

New Mexico
1. Steven H. Schiff (R)
2. Joe Skeen (R)
3. Bill Richardson (D)

New York
1. George J. Hochbrueckner (D)
2. Thomas J. Downey (D)
3. Robert J. Mrazek (D)
4. Norman F. Lent (R)
5. Raymond J. McGrath (R)
6. Floyd H. Flake (D)
7. Gary L. Ackerman (D)
8. James H. Scheuer (D)
9. Thomas J. Manton (D)
10. Charles E. Schumer (D)
11. Edolphus Towns (D)
12. Major R. Owens (D)
13. Stephen J. Solarz (D)
14. Susan Molinari (R)
15. Bill Green (R)
16. Charles B. Rangel (D)
17. Ted Weiss (D)
    (died Sept. 14, 1992)
18. Jose E. Serrano (D)
19. Eliot L. Engel (D)
20. Nita M. Lowey (D)
21. Hamilton Fish Jr. (R)
22. Benjamin A. Gilman (R)
23. Michael R. McNulty (D)
24. Gerald B. H. Solomon (R)
25. Sherwood Boehlert (R)
26. David O'B. Martin (R)
27. James T. Walsh (R)
28. Matthew F. McHugh (D)
29. Frank Horton (R)
30. Louise M. Slaughter (D)
31. Bill Paxon (R)
32. John J. LaFalce (D)
33. Henry J. Nowak (D)
34. Amo Houghton (R)

North Carolina
1. Walter B. Jones (D)
   (died Sept. 15, 1992)
2. Tim Valentine (D)
3. H. Martin Lancaster (D)
4. David E. Price (D)
5. Stephen L. Neal (D)
6. Howard Coble (R)
7. Charlie Rose (D)
8. W. G. "Bill" Hefner (D)
9. Alex McMillan (R)
10. Cass Ballenger (R)
11. Charles H. Taylor (R)

North Dakota
AL Byron L. Dorgan (D)

Ohio
1. Charles Luken (D)
2. Bill Gradison (R)
3. Tony P. Hall (D)
4. Michael G. Oxley (R)
5. Paul E. Gillmor (R)
6. Bob McEwen (R)
7. David L. Hobson (R)
8. John A. Boehner (R)
9. Marcy Kaptur (D)
10. Clarence E. Miller (R)
11. Dennis E. Eckart (D)
12. John R. Kasich (R)
13. Don J. Pease (D)
14. Thomas C. Sawyer (D)
15. Chalmers P. Wylie (R)
16. Ralph Regula (R)
17. James A. Traficant Jr. (D)
18. Douglas Applegate (D)
19. Edward F. Feighan (D)
20. Mary Rose Oakar (D)
21. Louis Stokes (D)

Oklahoma
1. James M. Inhofe (R)
2. Mike Synar (D)
3. Bill Brewster (D)
4. Dave McCurdy (D)
5. Mickey Edwards (R)
6. Glenn English (D)

Oregon
1. Les AuCoin (D)
2. Bob Smith (R)
3. Ron Wyden (D)
4. Peter A. DeFazio (D)
5. Mike Kopetski (D)

Pennsylvania
1. Thomas M. Foglietta (D)
2. William H. Gray III (D)
   (resigned Sept. 11, 1991)
   Lucien E. Blackwell (D)
   (sworn in Nov. 13, 1991)
3. Robert A. Borski (D)
4. Joe Kolter (D)
5. Richard T. Schulze (R)
6. Gus Yatron (D)
7. Curt Weldon (R)
8. Peter H. Kostmayer (D)
9. Bud Shuster (R)
10. Joseph M. McDade (R)
11. Paul E. Kanjorski (D)
12. John P. Murtha (D)
13. Lawrence Coughlin (R)
14. William J. Coyne (D)
15. Don Ritter (R)
16. Robert S. Walker (R)
17. George W. Gekas (R)
18. Rick Santorum (R)
19. Bill Goodling (R)
20. Joseph M. Gaydos (D)
21. Tom Ridge (R)
22. Austin J. Murphy (D)
23. William F. Clinger Jr. (R)

Rhode Island
1. Ronald K. Machtley (R)
2. John F. Reed (D)

South Carolina
1. Arthur Ravenel Jr. (R)
2. Floyd D. Spence (R)
3. Butler Derrick (D)
4. Liz J. Patterson (D)
5. John M. Spratt Jr. (D)
6. Robin Tallon (D)

South Dakota
AL Tim Johnson (D)

Tennessee
1. James H. Quillen (R)
2. John J. "Jimmy" Duncan Jr. (R)
3. Marilyn Lloyd (D)
4. Jim Cooper (D)
5. Bob Clement (D)
6. Bart Gordon (D)
7. Don Sundquist (R)
8. John Tanner (D)
9. Harold E. Ford (D)

Texas
1. Jim Chapman (D)
2. Charles Wilson (D)
3. Steve Bartlett (R)
   (resigned March 11, 1991)
   Sam Johnson (R)
   (sworn in May 22, 1991)
4. Ralph M. Hall (D)
5. John Bryant (D)
6. Joe L. Barton (R)
7. Bill Archer (R)
8. Jack Fields (R)
9. Jack Brooks (D)
10. J. J. Pickle (D)
11. Chet Edwards (D)
12. Pete Geren (D)
13. Bill Sarpalius (D)
14. Greg Laughlin (D)
15. E. "Kika" de la Garza (D)
16. Ronald D. Coleman (D)
17. Charles W. Stenholm (D)
18. Craig Washington (D)
19. Larry Combest (R)
20. Henry B. Gonzalez (D)
21. Lamar Smith (R)
22. Tom DeLay (R)
23. Albert G. Bustamante (D)
24. Martin Frost (D)
25. Michael A. Andrews (D)
26. Dick Armey (R)
27. Solomon P. Ortiz (D)

Utah
1. James V. Hansen (R)
2. Wayne Owens (D)
3. Bill Orton (D)

Vermont
AL Bernard Sanders (I)

Virginia
1. Herbert H. Bateman (R)
2. Owen B. Pickett (D)
3. Thomas J. Bliley Jr. (R)
4. Norman Sisisky (D)
5. Lewis F. Payne Jr. (D)
6. Jim Olin (D)
7. D. French Slaughter Jr. (R)
   (resigned Nov. 5, 1991)
   George F. Allen (R)
   (sworn in Nov. 12, 1991)
8. James P. Moran Jr. (D)
9. Rick Boucher (D)
10. Frank R. Wolf (R)

Washington
1. John Miller (R)
2. Al Swift (D)
3. Jolene Unsoeld (D)
4. Sid Morrison (R)
5. Thomas S. Foley (D)
6. Norm Dicks (D)
7. Jim McDermott (D)
8. Rod Chandler (R)

West Virginia
1. Alan B. Mollohan (D)
2. Harley O. Staggers Jr. (D)
3. Bob Wise (D)
4. Nick J. Rahall II (D)

Wisconsin
1. Les Aspin (D)
2. Scott L. Klug (R)
3. Steve Gunderson (R)
4. Gerald D. Kleczka (D)
5. Jim Moody (D)
6. Thomas E. Petri (R)
7. David R. Obey (D)
8. Toby Roth (R)
9. F. James Sensenbrenner Jr. (R)

Wyoming
AL Craig Thomas (R)

Note: Members of the 102nd Congress also included delegates Ben Blaz, R-Guam; Ron de Lugo, D-Virgin Islands; Eni F. H. Faleomavaega, D-Am. Samoa; Eleanor Holmes Norton, D-D.C.; and resident commissioner Jaime B. Fuster, Pop. Dem.-Puerto Rico.

House Membership in 103rd Congress

Lineup as of Jan. 5, 1993: Democrats 258, Republicans 176, Independent 1

Alabama
1. Sonny Callahan (R)
2. Terry Everett (R)
3. Glen Browder (D)
4. Tom Bevill (D)
5. Bud Cramer (D)
6. Spencer Bachus (R)
7. Earl F. Hilliard (D)

Alaska
AL Don Young (R)

Arizona
1. Sam Coppersmith (D)
2. Ed Pastor (D)
3. Bob Stump (R)
4. Jon Kyl (R)
5. Jim Kolbe (R)
6. Karan English (D)

Arkansas
1. Blanche Lambert (D)
2. Ray Thornton (D)
3. Tim Hutchinson (R)
4. Jay Dickey (R)

California
1. Dan Hamburg (D)
2. Wally Herger (R)
3. Vic Fazio (D)
4. John T. Doolittle (R)
5. Robert T. Matsui (D)
6. Lynn Woolsey (D)
7. George Miller (D)
8. Nancy Pelosi (D)
9. Ronald V. Dellums (D)
10. Bill Baker (R)
11. Richard W. Pombo (R)
12. Tom Lantos (D)
13. Pete Stark (D)
14. Anna G. Eshoo (D)
15. Norman Y. Mineta (D)
16. Don Edwards (D)
17. Leon E. Panetta (D)
    (resigned Jan. 21, 1993)
    Sam Farr (D)
    (sworn in June 16, 1993)
18. Gary Condit (D)
19. Richard H. Lehman (D)
20. Calvin Dooley (D)
21. Bill Thomas (R)
22. Michael Huffington (R)
23. Elton Gallegly (R)
24. Anthony C. Beilenson (D)
25. Howard P. "Buck" McKeon (R)
26. Howard L. Berman (D)
27. Carlos J. Moorhead (R)
28. David Dreier (R)
29. Henry A. Waxman (D)
30. Xavier Becerra (D)
31. Matthew G. Martinez (D)
32. Julian C. Dixon (D)
33. Lucille Roybal-Allard (D)
34. Esteban E. Torres (D)
35. Maxine Waters (D)
36. Jane Harman (D)
37. Walter R. Tucker (D)
38. Steve Horn (R)
39. Ed Royce (R)
40. Jerry Lewis (R)
41. Jay C. Kim (R)
42. George E. Brown Jr. (D)
43. Ken Calvert (R)
44. Al McCandless (R)
45. Dana Rohrabacher (R)
46. Robert K. Dornan (R)
47. C. Christopher Cox (R)
48. Ron Packard (R)
49. Lynn Schenk (D)
50. Bob Filner (D)
51. Randy "Duke" Cunningham (R)
52. Duncan Hunter (R)

Colorado
1. Patricia Schroeder (D)
2. David E. Skaggs (D)
3. Scott McInnis (R)
4. Wayne Allard (R)
5. Joel Hefley (R)
6. Dan Schaefer (R)

Connecticut
1. Barbara B. Kennelly (D)
2. Sam Gejdenson (D)
3. Rosa DeLauro (D)
4. Christopher Shays (R)
5. Gary Franks (R)
6. Nancy L. Johnson (R)

Delaware
AL Michael N. Castle (R)

Florida
1. Earl Hutto (D)
2. Pete Peterson (D)
3. Corrine Brown (D)
4. Tillie Fowler (R)
5. Karen L. Thurman (D)
6. Cliff Stearns (R)
7. John L. Mica (R)
8. Bill McCollum (R)
9. Michael Bilirakis (R)
10. C. W. Bill Young (R)
11. Sam M. Gibbons (D)
12. Charles T. Canady (R)
13. Dan Miller (R)
14. Porter J. Goss (R)
15. Jim Bacchus (D)
16. Tom Lewis (R)
17. Carrie Meek (D)
18. Ileana Ros-Lehtinen (R)
19. Harry A. Johnston (D)
20. Peter Deutsch (D)
21. Lincoln Diaz-Balart (R)
22. E. Clay Shaw Jr. (R)
23. Alcee L. Hastings (D)

Georgia
1. Jack Kingston (R)
2. Sanford Bishop (D)
3. Mac Collins (R)
4. John Linder (R)
5. John Lewis (D)
6. Newt Gingrich (R)
7. George "Buddy" Darden (D)
8. J. Roy Rowland (D)
9. Nathan Deal (D)
10. Don Johnson (D)
11. Cynthia McKinney (D)

Hawaii
1. Neil Abercrombie (D)
2. Patsy T. Mink (D)

Idaho
1. Larry LaRocco (D)
2. Michael D. Crapo (R)

Illinois
1. Bobby L. Rush (D)
2. Mel Reynolds (D)
3. William O. Lipinski (D)
4. Luis V. Gutierrez (D)
5. Dan Rostenkowski (D)
6. Henry J. Hyde (R)
7. Cardiss Collins (D)
8. Philip M. Crane (R)
9. Sidney R. Yates (D)
10. John Porter (R)
11. George E. Sangmeister (D)
12. Jerry F. Costello (D)
13. Harris W. Fawell (R)
14. Dennis Hastert (R)
15. Thomas W. Ewing (R)
16. Donald Manzullo (R)
17. Lane Evans (D)
18. Robert H. Michel (R)
19. Glenn Poshard (D)
20. Richard J. Durbin (D)

Indiana
1. Peter J. Visclosky (D)
2. Philip R. Sharp (D)
3. Tim Roemer (D)
4. Jill L. Long (D)
5. Steve Buyer (R)
6. Dan Burton (R)
7. John T. Myers (R)
8. Frank McCloskey (D)
9. Lee H. Hamilton (D)
10. Andrew Jacobs Jr. (D)

Iowa
1. Jim Leach (R)
2. Jim Nussle (R)
3. Jim Ross Lightfoot (R)
4. Neal Smith (D)
5. Fred Grandy (R)

Kansas
1. Pat Roberts (R)
2. Jim Slattery (D)
3. Jan Meyers (R)
4. Dan Glickman (D)

Kentucky
1. Tom Barlow (D)
2. William H. Natcher (D)
3. Romano L. Mazzoli (D)
4. Jim Bunning (R)
5. Harold Rogers (R)
6. Scotty Baesler (D)

Louisiana
1. Robert L. Livingston (R)
2. William J. Jefferson (D)
3. W. J. "Billy" Tauzin (D)
4. Cleo Fields (D)
5. Jim McCrery (R)
6. Richard H. Baker (R)
7. Jimmy Hayes (D)

Maine
1. Thomas H. Andrews (D)
2. Olympia J. Snowe (R)

Maryland
1. Wayne T. Gilchrest (R)
2. Helen Delich Bentley (R)
3. Benjamin L. Cardin (D)
4. Albert R. Wynn (D)
5. Steny H. Hoyer (D)
6. Roscoe G. Bartlett (R)
7. Kweisi Mfume (D)
8. Constance A. Morella (R)

Massachusetts
1. John W. Olver (D)
2. Richard E. Neal (D)
3. Peter I. Blute (R)
4. Barney Frank (D)
5. Martin T. Meehan (D)
6. Peter G. Torkildsen (R)
7. Edward J. Markey (D)
8. Joseph P. Kennedy II (D)
9. Joe Moakley (D)
10. Gerry E. Studds (D)

Michigan
1. Bart Stupak (D)
2. Peter Hoekstra (R)
3. Paul B. Henry (R)
4. Dave Camp (R)
5. James A. Barcia (D)
6. Fred Upton (R)
7. Nick Smith (R)
8. Bob Carr (D)
9. Dale E. Kildee (D)
10. David E. Bonior (D)
11. Joe Knollenberg (R)
12. Sander M. Levin (D)
13. William D. Ford (D)
14. John Conyers Jr. (D)
15. Barbara-Rose Collins (D)
16. John D. Dingell (D)

Minnesota
1. Timothy J. Penny (D)
2. David Minge (D)
3. Jim Ramstad (R)
4. Bruce F. Vento (D)
5. Martin Olav Sabo (D)
6. Rod Grams (R)
7. Collin C. Peterson (D)
8. James L. Oberstar (D)

Mississippi
1. Jamie L. Whitten (D)
2. Mike Espy (D)
   (resigned Jan. 21, 1993)
   Bennie Thompson (D)
   (sworn in April 20, 1993)
3. G. V. "Sonny" Montgomery (D)
4. Mike Parker (D)
5. Gene Taylor (D)

Missouri
1. William L. Clay (D)
2. James M. Talent (R)
3. Richard A. Gephardt (D)
4. Ike Skelton (D)
5. Alan Wheat (D)
6. Pat Danner (D)
7. Mel Hancock (R)
8. Bill Emerson (R)
9. Harold L. Volkmer (D)

Montana
AL Pat Williams (D)

Nebraska
1. Doug Bereuter (R)
2. Peter Hoagland (D)
3. Bill Barrett (R)

Nevada
1. James Bilbray (D)
2. Barbara F. Vucanovich (R)

New Hampshire
1. Bill Zeliff (R)
2. Dick Swett (D)

New Jersey
1. Robert E. Andrews (D)
2. William J. Hughes (D)

3. H. James Saxton (R)
4. Christopher H. Smith (R)
5. Marge Roukema (R)
6. Frank Pallone Jr. (D)
7. Bob Franks (R)
8. Herbert C. Klein (D)
9. Robert G. Torricelli (D)
10. Donald M. Payne (D)
11. Dean A. Gallo (R)
12. Dick Zimmer (R)
13. Robert Menendez (D)

New Mexico
1. Steven H. Schiff (R)
2. Joe Skeen (R)
3. Bill Richardson (D)

New York
1. George J. Hochbrueckner (D)
2. Rick A. Lazio (R)
3. Peter T. King (R)
4. David A. Levy (R)
5. Gary L. Ackerman (D)
6. Floyd H. Flake (D)
7. Thomas J. Manton (D)
8. Jerrold Nadler (D)
9. Charles E. Schumer (D)
10. Edolphus Towns (D)
11. Major R. Owens (D)
12. Nydia M. Velázquez (D)
13. Susan Molinari (R)
14. Carolyn B. Maloney (D)
15. Charles B. Rangel (D)
16. Jose E. Serrano (D)
17. Eliot L. Engel (D)
18. Nita M. Lowey (D)
19. Hamilton Fish Jr. (R)
20. Benjamin A. Gilman (R)
21. Michael R. McNulty (D)
22. Gerald B.H. Solomon (R)
23. Sherwood Boehlert (R)
24. John M. McHugh (R)
25. James T. Walsh (R)
26. Maurice D. Hinchey (D)
27. Bill Paxon (R)
28. Louise M. Slaughter (D)
29. John J. LaFalce (D)
30. Jack Quinn (R)
31. Amo Houghton (R)

North Carolina
1. Eva Clayton (D)
2. Tim Valentine (D)
3. H. Martin Lancaster (D)
4. David Price (D)
5. Stephen L. Neal (D)
6. Howard Coble (R)
7. Charlie Rose (D)
8. W. G. "Bill" Hefner (D)
9. Alex McMillan (R)
10. Cass Ballenger (R)
11. Charles H. Taylor (R)
12. Melvin Watt (D)

North Dakota
AL Earl Pomeroy (D)

Ohio
1. David Mann (D)
2. Bill Gradison (R)
   (resigned Jan. 31, 1993)
   Rob Portman (R)
   (sworn in May 5, 1993)
3. Tony P. Hall (D)
4. Michael G. Oxley (R)
5. Paul E. Gillmor (R)
6. Ted Strickland (D)
7. David L. Hobson (R)
8. John A. Boehner (R)
9. Marcy Kaptur (D)
10. Martin R. Hoke (R)
11. Louis Stokes (D)
12. John R. Kasich (R)
13. Sherrod Brown (D)
14. Tom Sawyer (D)
15. Deborah Pryce (R)
16. Ralph Regula (R)
17. James A. Traficant Jr. (D)
18. Douglas Applegate (D)
19. Eric Fingerhut (D)

Oklahoma
1. James M. Inhofe (R)
2. Mike Synar (D)
3. Bill Brewster (D)
4. Dave McCurdy (D)
5. Ernest Jim Istook (R)
6. Glenn English (D)

Oregon
1. Elizabeth Furse (D)
2. Bob Smith (R)
3. Ron Wyden (D)
4. Peter A. DeFazio (D)
5. Mike Kopetski (D)

Pennsylvania
1. Thomas M. Foglietta (D)
2. Lucien E. Blackwell (D)
3. Robert A. Borski (D)
4. Ron Klink (D)
5. William F. Clinger (R)
6. Tim Holden (D)
7. Curt Weldon (R)
8. Jim Greenwood (R)
9. Bud Shuster (R)
10. Joseph M. McDade (R)
11. Paul E. Kanjorski (D)
12. John P. Murtha (D)
13. Marjorie Margolies-Mezvinsky (D)
14. William J. Coyne (D)
15. Paul McHale (D)
16. Robert S. Walker (R)
17. George W. Gekas (R)

18. Rick Santorum (R)
19. Bill Goodling (R)
20. Austin J. Murphy (D)
21. Tom Ridge (R)

Rhode Island
1. Ronald K. Machtley (R)
2. John F. Reed (D)

South Carolina
1. Arthur Ravenel Jr. (R)
2. Floyd D. Spence (R)
3. Butler Derrick (D)
4. Bob Inglis (R)
5. John M. Spratt Jr. (D)
6. James E. Clyburn (D)

South Dakota
AL Tim Johnson (D)

Tennessee
1. James H. Quillen (R)
2. John J. "Jimmy" Duncan Jr. (R)
3. Marilyn Lloyd (D)
4. Jim Cooper (D)
5. Bob Clement (D)
6. Bart Gordon (D)
7. Don Sundquist (R)
8. John Tanner (D)
9. Harold E. Ford (D)

Texas
1. Jim Chapman (D)
2. Charles Wilson (D)
3. Sam Johnson (R)
4. Ralph M. Hall (D)
5. John Bryant (D)
6. Joe L. Barton (R)
7. Bill Archer (R)
8. Jack Fields (R)
9. Jack Brooks (D)
10. J. J. Pickle (D)
11. Chet Edwards (D)
12. Pete Geren (D)
13. Bill Sarpalius (D)
14. Greg Laughlin (D)
15. E. "Kika" de la Garza (D)
16. Ronald D. Coleman (D)
17. Charles W. Stenholm (D)
18. Craig Washington (D)
19. Larry Combest (R)
20. Henry B. Gonzalez (D)
21. Lamar Smith (R)
22. Tom DeLay (R)
23. Henry Bonilla (R)
24. Martin Frost (D)
25. Michael A. Andrews (D)
26. Dick Armey (R)
27. Solomon P. Ortiz (D)
28. Frank Tejeda (D)

29. Gene Green (D)
30. Eddie Bernice Johnson (D)

Utah
1. James V. Hansen (R)
2. Karen Shepherd (D)
3. Bill Orton (D)

Vermont
AL Bernard Sanders (I)

Virginia
1. Herbert H. Bateman (R)
2. Owen B. Pickett (D)
3. Robert C. Scott (D)
4. Norman Sisisky (D)
5. Lewis F. Payne Jr. (D)
6. Robert W. Goodlatte (R)
7. Thomas J. Bliley Jr. (R)
8. James P. Moran Jr. (D)
9. Rick Boucher (D)
10. Frank R. Wolf (R)
11. Leslie L. Byrne (D)

Washington
1. Maria Cantwell (D)
2. Al Swift (D)
3. Jolene Unsoeld (D)
4. Jay Inslee (D)
5. Thomas S. Foley (D)
6. Norm Dicks (D)
7. Jim McDermott (D)
8. Jennifer Dunn (R)
9. Mike Kreidler (D)

West Virginia
1. Alan B. Mollohan (D)
2. Bob Wise (D)
3. Nick J. Rahall II (D)

Wisconsin
1. Les Aspin (D)
   (resigned Jan. 20, 1993)
   Peter W. Barca (D)
   (sworn in June 8, 1993)
2. Scott L. Klug (R)
3. Steve Gunderson (R)
4. Gerald D. Kleczka (D)
5. Thomas M. Barrett (D)
6. Tom Petri (R)
7. David R. Obey (D)
8. Toby Roth (R)
9. F. James Sensenbrenner Jr. (R)

Wyoming
AL Craig Thomas (R)

Note: Members of the 103rd Congress also included delegates Robert J. Underwood, D-Guam; Ron de Lugo, D-Virgin Islands; Eni F. H. Faleomavaego, D-Am. Samoa; Eleanor Holmes Norton, D-DC; and resident commissioner Carlos Romero-Barcelo, D/NPP-Puerto Rico.

District of Columbia

The 1980s brought both boom and bust to the District of Columbia. The Washington of the 1980s endured eight years of Ronald Reagan's antipathy for the city's federal establishment, throughout which that establishment generally grew and prospered. The city slipped about 5 percent in population between 1980 and 1990, yet both commercial and residential real estate experienced a phenomenal boom. Drug-related violence made the city's slums and public housing more dangerous than ever. Yet other city neighborhoods were revitalized, and the downtown office district underwent an unprecedented face lift.

Ironically, residents of the nation's capital have little chance to choose the nation's politicians. District residents cannot vote for senators and have only a nonvoting delegate in the House. And, while residents do vote in presidential elections, the District's three electoral votes are not contested but conceded from the outset to the Democrats.

In 1992, for example, the District's presidential vote went 85 percent Democratic. Washington is nearly 70 percent black, and many in the white minority maintain their voting registration in their home states. Most of the District's 28,000 registered Republicans live in the northwest corner of Washington in Ward 3, where they are still outnumbered about 9 to 1 by their Democratic neighbors.

Since the restoration of home rule in 1974, Washingtonians have at least been able to elect local officials—with the mayor's office becoming the pinnacle for local politicians. The city in 1990 elected a reform-minded mayor, Sharon Pratt Dixon, to succeed controversial veteran Mayor Marion S. Barry Jr., who stepped aside when facing a battery of drug charges (he was later convicted of cocaine possession). Dixon has been in the front ranks of the local movement pushing for statehood for the District. The issue came before Congress in November 1993 and was defeated in a House vote. Proponents of statehood for "New Columbia" vowed to continue their fight.

District Democrats have held a presidential primary since 1956, but few took an interest until 1984, when Jesse Jackson's independent candidacy changed the landscape. Jackson's registration drive helped boost turnout above the 100,000 mark, an increase of more than half over the previous record. Jackson was the choice of two-thirds of the voters.

As a Democrat in 1988, Jackson did not win the Democratic Party's nomination, but District voters did not turn from the fold—Michael S. Dukakis took 83 percent of their vote in that year's presidential race.

In the 1992 elections Bill Clinton won the District with 85 percent of the vote to George Bush's 9 percent and Ross Perot's 4 percent. Clinton's percentage was his best showing across the nation.

Table 1 Population

District	Population	Population under 18	Voting-age population	Median age
D.C.	606,900	117,092	489,808	33.5

Table 2 Voting-Age Persons

District	White*	Black*	American Indian, Eskimo, or Aleut*	Asian or Pacific Islander*	Other*	Hispanic*	Male*	Female*
D.C.	33.1%	62.4%	0.3%	2.0%	2.3%	5.2%	45.7%	54.3%

*As percent of voting-age population.

Table 3 Voting-Age Persons by Age Groups

District	18-24*	25-44*	45-54*	55-64*	65 and over*
D.C.	16.9%	44.2%	12.7%	10.4%	15.9%

*As percent of voting-age population.

Table 4 Income and Occupation

District	Median family income	Families in poverty	White collar*	Blue collar*	Service*	Farm*
D.C.	$36,256	16.9%	71.1%	11.9%	16.6%	0.4%

*As percent of employed persons age 16 and over.

Table 5   Education: School Years Completed

District	Less than grade 9*	Grades 9-12 no diploma*	High school diploma*	College bachelor's degree or higher*
D.C.	9.6%	17.3%	21.2%	33.3%

*As percent of persons age 25 and over.

Table 6   Housing and Residential Patterns

District	Owner occupied	Renter occupied	Urban	Rural
D.C.	38.9%	61.1%	100.0%	0.0%

Demographics

Population   606,900

Percent change from 1980   5.9%

Land area   61 square miles

Population per square mile   9,883

Counties, 1990 population
District of Columbia   606,900

Cities, 1990 population (10,000 or more)
Washington   606,900

Race and Hispanic origin
White   29.6%
Black   65.8%
American Indian, Eskimo, or Aleut.   0.2%
Asian or Pacific Islander   1.8%
Other   2.5%
Hispanic origin   5.4%

Ancestry

American 1.9%	Polish 1.6%
English 5.6%	Russian 2.0%
French 1.4%	Scottish 1.4%
German 6.5%	Subsaharan African 1.5%
Irish 5.7%	West Indian 1.1%
Italian 1.9%	

Universities/colleges, 1990-1991 enrollment
American University, Washington   11,258
Catholic University, Washington   6,638
Corcoran School of Art, Washington   314
Defense Intelligence College, Washington   605
Gallaudet University, Washington   2,014
George Washington University, Washington   19,108
Georgetown University, Washington   11,525
Howard University, Washington   11,617
Mount Vernon College, Washington   483
Southeastern University, Washington   607
Strayer College, Washington   2,919
Trinity College, Washington   1,092
University of the District of Columbia, Washington   11,990
Wesley Theological Seminary, Washington   383

Newspapers, total circulation (in all districts)
Baltimore Sun   391,415
Los Angeles Times   1,169,066
Washington Post   810,904
Washington Times   91,509

Commercial television stations, affiliations
ADI: Washington, D.C. (100%)
WFTY, Washington (None)
WJLA-TV, Washington (ABC)
WRC-TV, Washington (NBC)
WTTG, Washington (Fox)
WUSA, Washington (CBS)

Cable television systems, total subscribers
District Cablevision; Washington   80,000

Military installations, 1991
Walter Reed Army Medical Center, Washington   7,556
Naval Headquarters, Washington   5,809
Naval Research Laboratory, Washington   5,495
Bolling Air Force Base, Washington: 4,596
Fort Leslie J. McNair, Washington   2,530
Naval Observatory, Washington   2,049
Washington Naval Security Station, Washington   1,494
Marine Barracks, Washington   1,112

Businesses and other major employers
U.S. Defense Dept.; Washington   20,000
U.S. Justice Dept.; Washington   19,000
U.S. Treasury Dept.; Washington   17,883
U.S. Transportation Dept.; Washington   10,000
George Washington University; Washington   7,300
U.S. Internal Revenue Services; Washington   7,054
Georgetown University & Georgetown University Hospital; Washington   7,050
U.S. Agriculture Dept.; Washington   7,000
U.S. State Dept.; Washington   7,000
U.S. Interior Dept.; Washington   6,000
Howard University; Washington   6,000
Library of Congress; Washington   5,234
World Bank; Washington; international bank   5,200
United Airlines Inc.; Washington; airline   5,000
Howard University/Howard University Hospital; Washington   5,000
U.S. Labor Dept.; Washington   4,700
U.S. Commerce Dept.; Washington   4,650
U.S. Information Agency; Washington   4,413
Medlantic Healthcare Group/Washington Hospital Center; Washington   4,093
U.S. Government Printing Office; Washington   4,000
U.S. Commerce Dept.; Washington   4,000
U.S. Veterans Affairs Dept.; Washington   4,000
Marriott Corp.; Washington; advertising   4,000
U.S. Treasury Dept./Comptroller Currency Office; Washington   3,500
U.S. General Services Administration; Washington   3,500
U.S. Defense Intelligence Agency; Washington   3,500
Chesapeake & Potomac Telephone Co.; Washington; telephone communications   3,471
U.S. Housing & Urban Development Dept.; Washington   3,341
Washington Post Co.; Washington; newspapers   3,200
General Maintenance Service Co; Washington; building services   3,200
U.S. Education Dept.; Washington   3,180
U.S. Office of Personnel Management; Washington   3,042
U.S. Health & Human Services Dept.; Washington   3,000
U.S. General Accounting Office; Washington   3,000
Catholic University of America; Washington   2,753

U.S. Veterans Affairs Dept.; Washington; hospital 2,650
Geico; Washington; fire/marine/casualty insurance 2,500
District of Columbia/Human Resources Dept.; Washington 2,500
U.S. Coast Guard; Washington 2,500
NASA; Washington; space research/technology 2,500
Architect of Capitol; Washington 2,500
University of the District of Columbia; Washington 2,500
U.S. Postal Service; Washington 2,300
U.S. Bureau of Printing & Engraving; Washington 2,300
U.S. Agency for International Development; Washington 2,235
Blue Cross/Blue Shield; Washington; medical service/health insurance 2,200
U.S. Defense Information Systems Agency; Washington 2,100
Children's Hospital; Washington 2,080
District of Columbia/Commission on Mental Health; Washington 2,000
U.S. Bureau of Prisons; Washington 2,000
District of Columbia/Employment Service Dept.; Washington 2,000
Securities & Exchange Commission; Washington 1,900
Greater Southeast Community Hospital; Washington 1,800
Potomac Electric Power Co.; Washington; electric services 1,691
International Monetary Fund; Washington; federal credit 1,680
U.S. Service Industries; Washington; building services 1,650
Providence Hospital; Washington 1,611
Inter-American Development Bank; Washington; foreign bank 1,604
U.S. Federal Energy Regulatory Commission; Washington 1,600
American University; Washington 1,550
Federal National Mortgage Association/Fannie Mae; Washington; federal credit 1,500
U.S. Federal Reserve System; Washington 1,500
Executive Office of the President of the United States; Washington 1,500
District of Columbia/Water & Sewer Dept.; Washington 1,474
National Geographic Society; Washington; periodicals 1,400
Arthur Andersen & Co.; Washington; accounting/auditing 1,400
Federal Communications Commission; Washington 1,400
Washington Metro Area Transit Authority; Washington; subway 1,350
Gallaudet University; Washington 1,315
Bureau of National Affairs Inc.; Washington; periodicals/books 1,300
John F. Kennedy Center for the Performing Arts; Washington; entertainment facilities 1,300
U.S. Energy Dept.; Washington 1,300
Sibley Memorial Hospital; Washington 1,300
American Security Bank; Washington; commercial banks 1,236
AT&T Co.; Washington; telephone communications 1,200
District of Columbia/Public Schools; Washington 1,200
U.S. Capitol Police Board; Washington 1,200
National Science Foundation; Washington 1,200
Resolution Trust Corp.; Washington 1,144

District of Columbia/Human Resources Dept.; Washington 1,000
District of Columbia/Human Service Dept.; Washington 1,000
U.S. Financial Management Service; Washington 1,000
American Association of Retired Persons; Washington; social services 1,000
U.S. Pentagon Building Management Office; Washington 1,000
ICF Kaiser Engineers Inc./Quest Group Inc.; Washington; management/public relations 1,000
U.S. Peace Corps; Washington 1,000
District of Columbia/Recreation Dept.; Washington 1,000
National Cleaning Contractors; Washington; building services 1,000
U.S. Customs Service; Washington 950
National Gallery of Art; Washington; museum 937
Columbia Hospital for Women; Washington 912
Small Business Administration; Washington 900
Equal Emplyment Opportunity Commission; Washington 900
Sheraton Hotel; Washington; hotel 864
Marriott Corp./J. W. Marriott Hotel; Washington; hotel 860
Student Loan Marketing Assn./Sallie Mae; Washington; federal credit 852
Woodward & Lothrop Inc.; Washington; department stores 850
Hilton Hotels Corp./Washington Hilton & Towers; Washington; hotel 850
National Railroad Pass Corp./Amtrak; Washington; railroads 840
Martin Marietta Corp.; Washington; management services 800
Covington & Burling; Washington; legal services 800
U.S. National Park Service; Washington 800
U.S. Federal Trade Commission; Washington 800
Hyatt Corp./Grand Hyatt Washington Hotel; Washington; hotel 800
Encore Temporary Inc.; Washington; temp services 800
KPMG Peat Marwick; Washington; accounting/auditing 800
C. Chopivsky Corp.; Washington 800
PIA Psychiatric Hospitals/Psychiatric Institutes of America; Washington 750
National Rehabilitation Hospital; Washington 731
National Labor Relations Board; Washington 700
Arnold & Porter; Washington; legal services 700
U.S. Interior Dept./Park Police; Washington 663
International Telecommunications Satellite Organization; Washington 660
District of Columbia/Public Works Dept.; Washington 650
General Secretary of OAS; Washington 650
American Red Cross; Washington; family services 648
Hogan & Hartson; Washington; legal services 634
Hyatt Corp./Hyatt Regency; Washington; hotel 630
Coopers & Lybrand; Washington; accounting/auditing 626
Washington National Cathedral; Washington; religious organization 624
National Archives & Records Administration; Washington 617
MCI Communications Corp.; Washington; telephone communications 600

U.S. Dept. Treasury/Comptroller of Currency; Washington; banking services 600

Ramada Renaissance Techworld; Washington; hotel/restaurants 600

District of Columbia; Washington; residential care 600

U.S. Food & Drug Administration; Washington 600

District of Columbia/Tax Administration; Washington 600

U.S. Office of Thrift Supervision; Washington 600

Morgan Lewis & Bockius; Washington; legal services 600

Ernst & Young; Washington; accounting/auditing 600

Akin Gump Strauss Hauer & Feld; Washington; legal services 600

U.S. Office of Management Budget; Washington 580

Washington Gas Light Co./Maryland Natural Gas; Washington; gas distribution 575

Hilton Hotels Corp./Capital Hilton; Washington; hotel 570

U.S. Dept. Interior/U.S. Bureau of Mines; Washington; business services 550

Shaw Pittman Potts Trowbridge; Washington; legal services 545

Pan American Health Organization; Washington; social services 543

TRT Communications Corp.; Washington; communication services 541

Pension Benefit Guaranty Corp.; Washington; surety insurance 541

U.S. Consumer Products Dept.; Washington 538

Wilmer Cutler & Pickering; Washington; legal services 525

Zip Codes by Congressional Districts

The following is a complete list of U.S. zip codes by congressional districts. Zip codes for the District of Columbia are included. Asterisks indicate zip codes that cross district or state borders. Parenthetical data following asterisks list all other districts (by state abbreviation and district number) that share the same zip code.

Alabama

1st District: 36419; 36425; 36426; 36427; 36431; 36436; 36439; 36441; 36444 36445; 36446; 36449; 36451; 36457; 36458; 36460; 36461; 36462; 36470; 36471 36475; 36480; 36481; 36482; 36501; 36502; 36503; 36504; 36505; 36507; 36509 36510; 36511; 36512; 36513; 36515; 36518; 36521; 36522; 36523; 36525; 36526 36527; 36528; 36529; 36530; 36532; 36533; 36535; 36536; 36538; 36539; 36540 36541; 36542; 36543; 36544; 36545; 36547; 36548; 36549; 36550; 36551; 36553 36555; 36556; 36558; 36559; 36560; 36561; 36562; 36564; 36567; 36568; 36569 36570; 36571; 36572; 36574; 36575; 36576; 36578; 36579; 36580; 36581; 36582 36583; 36584; 36585; 36586; 36587; 36590; 36600; 36601; 36602; 36603; 36604 36605; 36606; 36607; 36608; 36609; 36610; 36611; 36612; 36613; 36614; 36615 36616; 36617; 36618; 36619; 36621; 36622; 36623; 36624; 36625; 36626; 36628 36630; 36631; 36633; 36640; 36641; 36652; 36660; 36663; 36670; 36671; 36675 36685; 36688; 36689; 36690; 36691; 36693; 36695; 36727; 36762; 36784* (AL 7).

2nd District: 35952* (AL 4); 36003; 36004; 36005; 36006; 36008; 36009; 36010 36013; 36015; 36016; 36017; 36020; 36022; 36024; 36025; 36027; 36028; 36029 36030; 36033; 36034; 36035; 36036* (AL 7); 36037; 36038; 36041; 36042; 36045 36048; 36049; 36051; 36052; 36053; 36054; 36057; 36061; 36062; 36064; 36065 36066; 36067; 36069* (AL 7); 36071; 36072; 36078* (AL 3); 36080; 36081; 36082 36089; 36091* (AL 3); 36092; 36101; 36102; 36103; 36104* (AL 7); 36105* (AL 7); 36106* (AL 7); 36107* (AL 7); 36108* (AL 7); 36109* (AL 7); 36110* (AL 7) 36111; 36112; 36113* (AL 7); 36114; 36115* (AL 7); 36116* (AL 7); 36117* (AL 7); 36118; 36119; 36120; 36121; 36123; 36124; 36130* (AL 7); 36132; 36134 36135; 36140; 36141; 36142; 36177; 36191; 36193; 36196; 36301; 36302; 36303 36304; 36310; 36311; 36312; 36313; 36314; 36316; 36317; 36318; 36319; 36320 36321; 36322; 36323; 36330; 36331; 36340; 36343; 36344; 36345; 36346; 36349 36350; 36351; 36352; 36353; 36360; 36361; 36362; 36370; 36371; 36373; 36374 36375; 36376; 36401; 36420; 36429; 36432; 36442; 36453; 36454; 36455; 36456 36467; 36469; 36473; 36474; 36476; 36477; 36483; 36749.

3rd District: 35004; 35010; 35014; 35032; 35034; 35042; 35044; 35045; 35052 35054; 35072; 35074; 35082; 35085; 35089; 35094* (AL 6); 35096; 35112; 35115* (AL 6); 35120; 35125; 35131; 35135; 35136; 35146* (AL 6); 35149; 35150; 35160 35171; 35173* (AL 6); 35182; 35183; 35184* (AL 6); 35188; 35905* (AL 4) 35953; 35987; 36023; 36026; 36031; 36039; 36075; 36078* (AL 2); 36083; 36087 36088; 36091* (AL 2); 36201; 36202; 36203; 36204; 36205; 36206; 36250; 36251 36253; 36254; 36255; 36256; 36257; 36258; 36260; 36261; 36262; 36263; 36264 36265; 36266; 36267; 36268; 36269; 36270; 36271; 36272; 36273; 36274; 36276 36277; 36278; 36279; 36280; 36750; 36790; 36792; 36793; 36801; 36802; 36803 36830; 36831; 36849; 36850; 36851; 36852; 36853; 36854; 36855; 36856; 36858 36859; 36860; 36861; 36862; 36863; 36865; 36866; 36867; 36868; 36869; 36871 36872; 36874; 36875; 36877; 36879.

4th District: 35013; 35016; 35019; 35031; 35033; 35038; 35049; 35053; 35055 35056; 35062* (AL 6); 35063* (AL 6); 35070; 35077; 35079; 35083; 35087; 35097 35098; 35121; 35130* (AL 6); 35133; 35148; 35175; 35179; 35180* (AL 6); 35442* (AL 7); 35447* (AL 7); 35461; 35466; 35471; 35481; 35501; 35502; 35540; 35541 35542; 35543; 35544; 35545; 35546* (AL 5); 35548; 35549; 35550; 35551; 35552 35553; 35554; 35555; 35559; 35560; 35563; 35564; 35565; 35570; 35571; 35572 35573; 35574; 35575; 35576; 35577; 35578; 35579; 35580; 35581; 35582; 35584 35585; 35586; 35587; 35592; 35593; 35594; 35618* (AL 5); 35619* (AL 5); 35622* (AL 5); 35643* (AL 5); 35650; 35651; 35653* (AL 5); 35672* (AL 5); 35673* (AL 5); 35747; 35755; 35768* (AL 5); 35771* (AL 5) 35901; 35902; 35903; 35904 35905* (AL 3); 35906; 35950; 35952* (AL 2); 35954; 35957 35959; 35960; 35961; 35962; 35963; 35964; 35967; 35971; 35972; 35973; 35974; 35975 35976; 35978 35980; 35981; 35983; 35984; 35986; 35988; 35989; 35990; 35999; 36275.

5th District: 35601; 35602; 35603; 35609; 35610; 35611; 35615; 35616; 35617 35618* (AL 4); 35619* (AL 4); 35620; 35621; 35622* (AL 4); 35630; 35631 35632; 35633; 35640; 35643* (AL 4); 35645; 35646; 35647; 35648; 35649; 35652 35653* (AL 4); 35660 35661; 35662; 35670; 35671; 35672* (AL 4); 35673* (AL 4); 35674; 35677; 35699 35739; 35740; 35741; 35742; 35744; 35745; 35746 35748; 35749; 35750; 35751; 35752 35754; 35758; 35759; 35760; 35761; 35762 35763; 35764; 35765; 35766; 35767; 35768* (AL 4); 35771* (AL 4); 35772; 35773 35774; 35775; 35776; 35800; 35801; 35802; 35803 35804; 35805; 35806; 35807 35808; 35809; 35810; 35811; 35812; 35813; 35814; 35815 35816; 35824; 35893; 35894; 35895; 35896; 35897; 35898; 35899; 35958; 35966; 35979.

6th District: 35005; 35006; 35007; 35015; 35020* (AL 7); 35023* (AL 7); 35035 35036; 35040; 35041; 35043; 35048; 35051; 35060; 35061* (AL 7); 35062* (AL 4); 35063* (AL 4); 35068; 35071; 35073; 35078; 35080; 35091; 35094* (AL 3); 35111* (AL 7); 35114; 35115* (AL 3); 35116; 35117; 35118; 35119; 35123; 35124; 35126 35127* (AL 7); 35130* (AL 4); 35137; 35139; 35142; 35143; 35144; 35146* (AL 3); 35147; 35172 35173* (AL 3); 35176; 35178; 35180* (AL 4); 35181; 35184* (AL 3); 35185; 35186 35187; 35205* (AL 7); 35206* (AL 7); 35207* (AL 7); 35209; 35210* (AL 7); 35211* (AL 7); 35212* (AL 7); 35213* (AL 7); 35214* (AL 7); 35215* (AL 7); 35216; 35217* (AL 7); 35219; 35220; 35222* (AL 7); 35223* (AL 7); 35224* (AL 7); 35226; 35229 35231; 35233* (AL 7); 35235* (AL 7); 35236; 35238; 35242; 35243; 35244; 35253; 35255 35256; 35259; 35401* (AL 7) 35404* (AL 7); 35405* (AL 7); 35406; 35444; 35446 35452; 35457; 35458; 35463 35468; 35476* (AL 7); 35478; 35480* (AL 7); 35482 35490* (AL 7); 35546* (AL 4).

7th District: 35020* (AL 6); 35021; 35023* (AL 6); 35061* (AL 6); 35064 35111* (AL 6);

Alabama (continued, right column)

35127* (AL 6); 35200; 35201; 35202; 35203; 35204; 35205* (AL 6); 35206* (AL 6); 35207* (AL 6); 35208; 35210* (AL 6); 35211* (AL 6); 35212* (AL 6); 35213* (AL 6); 35214* (AL 6); 35215* (AL 6); 35217* (AL 6); 35218 35221; 35222* (AL 6); 35223* (AL 6); 35224* (AL 6); 35225; 35228; 35230 35232; 35233* (AL 6); 35234; 35235* (AL 6); 35237; 35240; 35245; 35246; 35254 35261; 35263; 35277; 35278; 35279; 35280; 35281; 35282; 35283; 35285; 35286 35287; 35288; 35289; 35290; 35291; 35292; 35293; 35294; 35295; 35296; 35297 35298; 35299; 35401* (AL 6); 35402; 35403; 35404* (AL 6); 35405* (AL 6) 35440; 35441; 35442* (AL 4); 35443; 35447* (AL 4); 35448; 35449; 35453; 35456 35459; 35460; 35462; 35464; 35469; 35470; 35474; 35476* (AL 6); 35477; 35480* (AL 6); 35485; 35486; 35487; 35490* (AL 6); 35491; 36032; 36036* (AL 2) 36040; 36043; 36046; 36047; 36069* (AL 2); 36100; 36104* (AL 2); 36105* (AL 2); 36106* (AL 2); 36107* (AL 2); 36108* (AL 2); 36109* (AL 2); 36110* (AL 2) 36113* (AL 2); 36115* (AL 2); 36116* (AL 2); 36117* (AL 2); 36125; 36130* (AL 2); 36131; 36133; 36136; 36192; 36194; 36195; 36197; 36198; 36199; 36435 36524; 36701; 36702; 36703; 36720; 36721; 36722; 36723; 36726; 36728; 36731 36732; 36736; 36738; 36740; 36741; 36742; 36745; 36747; 36748; 36751 36752; 36753; 36754; 36756; 36758 36759; 36760; 36761; 36763; 36764; 36765; 36766; 36767; 36768; 36769; 36773 36775; 36776; 36778; 36779; 36782 36783; 36784* (AL 1); 36785; 36786; 36901; 36903 36904; 36906; 36907; 36908 36910; 36911; 36912; 36913; 36915; 36916; 36919; 36921 36922; 36925.

Alaska

At Large: 99500; 99501; 99502; 99503; 99504; 99505; 99506; 99507; 99508 99509; 99510; 99511; 99512; 99513; 99514; 99515; 99516; 99517; 99518; 99519 99520; 99521; 99522; 99523; 99524; 99540; 99547; 99548; 99549; 99550; 99551 99552; 99553; 99554; 99555; 99556; 99557; 99558; 99559; 99561; 99563; 99564 99565; 99566; 99567; 99568; 99569; 99571; 99572; 99573; 99574; 99575; 99576 99577; 99578; 99579; 99580; 99581; 99583; 99584; 99585; 99586; 99587; 99588 99589; 99590; 99591; 99599; 99602; 99603; 99604; 99605; 99606; 99607; 99608 99609; 99610; 99611; 99612; 99613; 99614; 99615; 99619; 99620; 99621; 99622 99624; 99625; 99626; 99627; 99630; 99631; 99632; 99633; 99634; 99635; 99636 99637; 99638; 99639; 99640; 99641; 99643; 99644; 99645; 99647; 99648; 99649 99650; 99651; 99652; 99653; 99654; 99655; 99656; 99657; 99658; 99659; 99660 99661; 99662; 99663; 99664; 99665; 99666; 99667; 99668; 99669; 99670; 99671 99672; 99674; 99675; 99676; 99677; 99678; 99679; 99680; 99681; 99682; 99683 99684; 99685; 99686; 99687; 99688; 99689; 99690; 99691; 99692; 99693; 99694 99695; 99697; 99701; 99702; 99703; 99704; 99705; 99706; 99707; 99708 99709; 99710; 99711; 99712; 99714; 99716; 99720; 99721; 99722; 99723; 99724 99725; 99726; 99727; 99729; 99730; 99732; 99733; 99734; 99736; 99737; 99738 99739; 99740; 99741; 99742; 99743; 99744; 99745; 99746; 99747; 99748; 99749 99750; 99751; 99752; 99753; 99754; 99755; 99756; 99757; 99758; 99759; 99760 99761; 99762; 99763; 99764; 99765; 99766; 99767; 99768; 99769; 99770; 99771 99772; 99773; 99774; 99775; 99776; 99777; 99778; 99779; 99780; 99781; 99782 99783; 99784; 99785; 99786; 99788; 99789; 99790; 99791; 99801; 99802; 99803 99811; 99820; 99821; 99824; 99825; 99826; 99827; 99829; 99830; 99832; 99833 99835; 99836; 99840; 99841; 99850; 99901; 99903; 99918; 99919; 99921; 99922 99923; 99925; 99926; 99927; 99928; 99929; 99950.

Arizona

1st District: 85003* (AZ 2); 85004* (AZ 2); 85006* (AZ 2); 85007* (AZ 2, AZ 4); 85008* (AZ 2); 85010; 85012* (AZ 4); 85013* (AZ 4); 85014* (AZ 4); 85016* (AZ 4); 85018* (AZ 4); 85027* (AZ 3, AZ 4 AZ 6); 85034* (AZ 2); 85040* (AZ 2); 85044* (AZ 2, AZ 6); 85082; 85201* (AZ 6); 85202; 85203* (AZ 6) 85205* (AZ 6); 85210* (AZ 6); 85211; 85212; 85213* (AZ 6); 85224* (AZ 6) 85225* (AZ 6); 85226* (AZ 6); 85234* (AZ 6); 85240; 85244; 85248* (AZ 6) 85249* (AZ 6); 85251* (AZ 4); 85252; 85256* (AZ 6); 85257* (AZ 6); 85261 85266; 85271; 85274; 85275; 85277; 85280; 85281* (AZ 2, AZ 6); 85282; 85283* (AZ 2); 85284; 85285; 85287; 85289; 85311.

2nd District: 85000; 85001; 85002; 85003* (AZ 1); 85004* (AZ 1); 85005; 85006* (AZ 1); 85007* (AZ 1, AZ 4); 85008* (AZ 1); 85009* (AZ 4); 85017* (AZ 4); 85019 (AZ 4); 85025; 85026; 85031* (AZ 3); 85033* (AZ 3); 85034* (AZ 1); 85035* (AZ 3); 85036; 85038; 85040* (AZ 1); 85041; 85043* (AZ 3); 85044* (AZ 1, AZ 6); 85055 85062; 85063; 85065; 85066; 85072; 85073; 85074; 85076 85086; 85099; 85222* (AZ 5, AZ 6); 85281* (AZ 1, AZ 6); 85283* (AZ 1); 85301* (AZ 3, AZ 4); 85313; 85318 85321; 85323* (AZ 3); 85333; 85336; 85337; 85338* (AZ 3); 85339* (AZ 6); 85341 85347; 85349; 85350; 85352; 85353* (AZ 3) 85356; 85364; 85365; 85366; 85369 85601; 85611; 85614* (AZ 5); 85618* (AZ 6) 85621; 85622; 85624; 85628; 85629* (AZ 5) 85633; 85634; 85637* (AZ 5); 85639 85640; 85645* (AZ 5); 85646; 85648; 85655 85662; 85700; 85701; 85702; 85703 85705* (AZ 5); 85706* (AZ 5); 85711* (AZ 5); 85713* (AZ 5); 85714* (AZ 5); 85716* (AZ 5); 85717; 85719* (AZ 5); 85722; 85723 85724; 85726; 85728; 85733 85735; 85736* (AZ 5); 85737* (AZ 5); 85743* (AZ 5); 85745* (AZ 5); 85746* (AZ 5); 85747* (AZ 5); 85749* (AZ 5); 85754.

3rd District: 85023* (AZ 4); 85024* (AZ 4, AZ 6); 85027* (AZ 1, AZ 4, AZ 6) 85031* (AZ 2); 85033* (AZ 2); 85035* (AZ 2); 85037; 85039; 85043* (AZ 2) 85071; 85075 85301* (AZ 2, AZ 4); 85302* (AZ 4); 85303; 85304* (AZ 4); 85305 85306* (AZ 4) 85307; 85308* (AZ 4); 85309; 85310; 85312; 85320; 85322; 85323* (AZ 2); 85324 85325; 85326; 85328; 85329; 85331* (AZ 6); 85332; 85334; 85335 85338* (AZ 2) 85340; 85342; 85343; 85344; 85345; 85346; 85348; 85351; 85353* (AZ 2); 85354; 85355 85357; 85358; 85359; 85360; 85361; 85362; 85363; 85371 85372; 85373; 85374; 85375 85380; 85381; 85382; 85390; 86001* (AZ 6); 86002; 86003; 86004* (AZ 6); 86011 86015; 86016; 86017; 86018; 86020; 86021; 86022 86023; 86030; 86036; 86039; 86042 86043; 86046; 86052; 86301; 86302; 86303 86304; 86312; 86313; 86314; 86320; 86321 86322; 86323; 86324; 86325; 86326 86327; 86329; 86330; 86331; 86332; 86333; 86334 86335; 86336* (AZ 6); 86337 86338; 86340; 86341; 86342; 86343; 86401; 86402; 86403

86405; 86411; 86412 86427; 86430; 86431; 86432; 86433; 86434; 86435; 86436; 86437; 86438; 86440 86441; 86442; 86443; 86444; 86445.

4th District: 85007* (AZ 1, AZ 2); 85009* (AZ 2); 85011; 85012* (AZ 1); 85013* (AZ 1); 85014* (AZ 1); 85015; 85016* (AZ 1); 85017* (AZ 2); 85018* (AZ 1) 85019* (AZ 2); 85020; 85021; 85022; 85023* (AZ 3); 85024* (AZ 3, AZ 6); 85027* (AZ 1, AZ 3, AZ 6); 85028; 85029; 85032; 85046; 85051; 85060; 85061; 85064 85067; 85068; 85069; 85077; 85078; 85079; 85080; 85250* (AZ 6); 85251* (AZ 1) 85253; 85254* (AZ 6); 85255* (AZ 6); 85258* (AZ 6); 85259* (AZ 6); 85260* (AZ 6); 85267; 85301* (AZ 2, AZ 3); 85302* (AZ 3); 85304* (AZ 3); 85306* (AZ 3) 85308* (AZ 3).

5th District: 85222* (AZ 2, AZ 6); 85231* (AZ 6); 85245; 85531; 85535; 85536 85543; 85546; 85548; 85551; 85552; 85602; 85603; 85605; 85606; 85607; 85608 85609; 85610; 85613; 85614* (AZ 2); 85615; 85616; 85617; 85619; 85620; 85623* (AZ 6); 85625; 85626; 85627; 85629* (AZ 2); 85630; 85632; 85635; 85636; 85637* (AZ 2); 85638; 85641; 85643; 85644; 85645* (AZ 2); 85652; 85653; 85654; 85670 85671; 85704; 85705* (AZ 2); 85706* (AZ 2); 85707; 85708; 85709; 85710; 85711* (AZ 2); 85712; 85713* (AZ 2); 85714* (AZ 2); 85715; 85716* (AZ 2); 85718 85719* (AZ 2); 85720; 85721; 85725; 85730; 85731; 85732; 85734; 85736* (AZ 2) 85737* (AZ 2); 85738; 85740; 85741; 85743* (AZ 2); 85744; 85745* (AZ 2) 85746* (AZ 2); 85747* (AZ 2); 85748; 85749* (AZ 2); 85751; 85775; 85777.

6th District: 85024* (AZ 3, AZ 4); 85027* (AZ 1, AZ 3, AZ 4); 85044* (AZ 1, AZ 2); 85201* (AZ 1); 85203* (AZ 1); 85204; 85205* (AZ 1); 85206; 85207; 85208 85210* (AZ 1); 85213* (AZ 1); 85214; 85216; 85217; 85219; 85220; 85221; 85222* (AZ 2, AZ 5); 85223; 85224* (AZ 1); 85225* (AZ 1); 85226* (AZ 1); 85227 85228; 85230; 85231* (AZ 5); 85232; 85234* (AZ 1); 85235; 85236; 85237; 85239 85241; 85242; 85247; 85248* (AZ 1); 85249* (AZ 1); 85250* (AZ 4); 85254* (AZ 4); 85255* (AZ 4); 85256* (AZ 1); 85257* (AZ 1); 85258* (AZ 4); 85259* (AZ 4); 85260* (AZ 4); 85262; 85263; 85264; 85268; 85269; 85272; 85273; 85278; 85279 85281* (AZ 1, AZ 2); 85290; 85291; 85292; 85331* (AZ 3); 85339* (AZ 2); 85377 85501; 85502; 85530; 85532; 85533; 85534; 85539; 85540; 85541; 85542; 85544 85545; 85547; 85550; 85553; 85554; 85618* (AZ 2); 85623* (AZ 5); 85631; 85901 85911; 85912; 85920; 85922; 85923; 85924; 85925; 85926; 85927; 85928; 85929 85930; 85931; 85932; 85933; 85934; 85935; 85936; 85937; 85938; 85939; 85940 85941; 85942; 85943; 86001* (AZ 3); 86004* (AZ 3); 86024; 86025; 86028; 86029 86031; 86032; 86033; 86034; 86035; 86038; 86040; 86044; 86045; 86047; 86053 86054; 86336* (AZ 3); 86502; 86503; 86504; 86505; 86506; 86507; 86508; 86509 86510; 86511; 86512; 86514; 86515; 86520; 86535; 86538; 86540; 86544; 86545 86547; 86549; 86556.

Arkansas

1st District: 72003; 72005; 72006; 72007; 72009; 72014; 72017; 72021; 72023* (AR 2); 72024; 72026; 72029; 72036; 72037; 72038; 72040; 72041; 72042; 72043 72044; 72046* (AR 2); 72048; 72051; 72055; 72059; 72064; 72066; 72067; 72069 72071; 72072; 72073; 72074; 72075; 72083; 72086; 72101; 72108; 72112; 72123 72130; 72131; 72134; 72140; 72160; 72165; 72166; 72169; 72170; 72176; 72179 72189; 72301; 72303; 72310; 72311; 72312; 72313; 72314; 72315; 72316; 72317 72319; 72320; 72321; 72322; 72323; 72324; 72325; 72326; 72327; 72328; 72329 72330; 72331; 72332; 72333; 72335; 72338* (TN 8); 72339; 72340; 72341; 72342 72346; 72347; 72348; 72350; 72351; 72352; 72353; 72354; 72355; 72358; 72359 72360; 72364; 72365; 72366; 72367; 72368; 72369; 72370; 72372; 72373; 72374; 72376; 72377; 72378; 72381; 72383; 72384; 72385; 72386; 72387; 72389 72390; 72391; 72392; 72394; 72395* (TN 8); 72396; 72397; 72401; 72402; 72403; 72410 72411; 72412; 72413; 72414; 72415; 72416; 72417; 72419; 72421; 72422; 72424 72425; 72426; 72427; 72428; 72429; 72430; 72431; 72432; 72433; 72434; 72435 72436; 72437; 72438; 72439; 72440; 72441; 72442; 72443; 72444; 72445; 72447 72449; 72450; 72451; 72453; 72454; 72455; 72456; 72457; 72458; 72459; 72460 72461; 72442; 72464; 72465; 72466; 72467; 72469; 72470; 72471; 72472; 72473 72474; 72475; 72476; 72478; 72479; 72482; 72501; 72503; 72512; 72513; 72515 72516; 72517; 72519; 72520; 72521; 72522; 72523; 72524; 72525; 72526; 72527 72528; 72529; 72530; 72531; 72532; 72533; 72534; 72536; 72538; 72539; 72540 72542; 72543; 72545; 72546; 72550; 72554; 72555; 72556; 72557; 72560; 72561; 72562; 72564; 72565; 72566; 72567; 72568; 72569; 72571; 72572; 72573 72575; 72576; 72577; 72578; 72579; 72581; 72583; 72584; 72585; 72587; 72610 72636; 72639; 72645; 72650; 72657; 72663; 72669; 72675; 72680; 72686.

2nd District: 71909* (AR 4); 72001; 72002; 72010; 72011; 72012; 72013; 72015 72016; 72020; 72022; 72023* (AR 1); 72025; 72027; 72028; 72030; 72031; 72032 72035; 72039; 72045; 72046* (AR 1); 72047; 72052; 72053; 72058; 72060; 72061 72063; 72065; 72068; 72070; 72076; 72080; 72081; 72082; 72085; 72088; 72089 72099; 72100; 72102; 72103; 72106; 72107; 72110; 72111; 72113; 72114; 72115 72116; 72117; 72118; 72119; 72120; 72121; 72122; 72125; 72126; 72127; 72135 72136; 72137; 72139; 72141; 72142; 72143; 72149; 72153; 72156; 72157; 72159 72164; 72167; 72173; 72178; 72180; 72181; 72183; 72200; 72201; 72202; 72203 72204; 72205; 72206; 72207; 72208; 72209; 72210; 72211; 72212; 72214; 72215 72216; 72217; 72219; 72221; 72225; 72231; 72295; 72297; 72629; 72824; 72827 72828; 72829; 72833; 72834; 72838; 72842; 72853; 72857; 72860.

3rd District: 65609* (MO 7); 71932; 71937; 71944; 71945; 71946; 71953; 71972 71973; 72537; 72544; 72601; 72602; 72611; 72612; 72613; 72615; 72616; 72617 72618; 72619; 72623; 72624; 72626; 72628; 72630; 72632; 72633; 72634; 72635 72638; 72640; 72641; 72642; 72644; 72648; 72651; 72653; 72655; 72658; 72659 72660; 72661; 72662; 72666; 72668; 72670; 72672; 72677; 72679; 72682; 72683 72685; 72687; 72701; 72702; 72703; 72711; 72712; 72714; 72716; 72717; 72718 72719; 72721; 72722; 72727; 72728; 72729; 72730; 72732; 72733; 72734; 72735 72736; 72737; 72738; 72739; 72740; 72741; 72742; 72744; 72745; 72747; 72749 72751; 72752; 72753; 72756; 72757; 72760; 72761; 72762; 72764; 72765; 72766 72767; 72768; 72769; 72770; 72773; 72774; 72775; 72776; 72801; 72820; 72821 72822; 72823; 72826; 72830; 72832; 72835; 72837; 72839; 72840; 72841; 72843 72844; 72845; 72846; 72847; 72851; 72852; 72854; 72855; 72856; 72858; 72863 72865; 72567; 72901; 72902; 72903; 72904; 72905; 72906; 72913; 72914; 72916 72917; 72921; 72923; 72924; 72926; 72927; 72928; 72930; 72932; 72934; 72935 72936; 72937; 72938; 72940; 72941; 72943; 72944; 72945; 72946; 72947 72948; 72949; 72950; 72951; 72952; 72955; 72956; 72958; 72959.

4th District: 71601; 71602; 71603; 71611; 71613; 71630; 71631; 71634; 71635 71638; 71639; 71640; 71642; 71643; 71644; 71646; 71647; 71649; 71650; 71651 71652; 71653; 71654; 71655; 71656; 71658; 71659; 71660; 71661; 71662; 71663 71665; 71666; 71667; 71670; 71671; 71674; 71675; 71676; 71677; 71678; 71701 71720; 71721; 71722; 71724; 71725; 71726; 71728; 71730; 71731; 71740; 71742 71743; 71744; 71745; 71747; 71748; 71749* (LA 4); 71750; 71751; 71752; 71753 71758; 71759; 71762; 71763; 71764; 71765; 71766; 71767; 71768; 71769; 71770 71772; 71801; 71820; 71822; 71823; 71825; 71826; 71827; 71828; 71831; 71832 71833; 71834; 71835; 71836; 71837; 71838; 71839; 71840; 71841; 71842; 71844 71845; 71846; 71847; 71851; 71852; 71853; 71855; 71857; 71858; 71859; 71860 71861; 71862; 71864; 71865; 71866; 71901; 71902; 71909* (AR 2); 71913; 71914 71920; 71921; 71922; 71923; 71929; 71931; 71933; 71935; 71940; 71941; 71942 71943; 71949; 71950; 71951; 71952; 71956; 71957; 71958; 71959; 71960; 71961 71962; 71964; 71965; 71966; 71968; 71969; 71970; 71971; 71998; 71999; 72004 72057; 72079; 72084; 72087; 72104; 72105; 72128; 72129; 72132; 72133; 72150 72152; 72158; 72168; 72175; 72182; 72379; 75502* (TX 1).

California

1st District: 94508; 94515; 94533; 94535; 94558; 94559; 94562; 94567; 94573 94574; 94576; 94581; 94585* (CA 3, CA 7); 94589* (CA 7); 94599; 95403* (CA 6) 95404* (CA 6); 95409* (CA 6); 95410; 95411; 95414; 95415; 95417; 95418; 95420 95422; 95423; 95424; 95425; 95426; 95427; 95428; 95429; 95432; 95435; 95436* (CA 6); 95437; 95440; 95441; 95443; 95445; 95448* (CA 6); 95449; 95451; 95453 95454; 95455; 95456; 95457; 95458; 95459; 95460; 95461; 95463; 95464; 95466 95467; 95468; 95469; 95470; 95481; 95482; 95485; 95488; 95489; 95490; 95492* (CA 6); 95493; 95494; 95501; 95502; 95503; 95511; 95514; 95521; 95524; 95525 95526* (CA 2); 95528; 95531; 95532; 95534; 95536; 95537; 95538; 95540; 95542 95543; 95545; 95546; 95547; 95548; 95549; 95550; 95551; 95553; 95554; 95555 95556; 95558; 95559; 95560; 95562; 95564; 95565; 95567; 95569; 95570; 95571 95573; 95585; 95587; 95589; 95687* (CA 3); 95688* (CA 3).

2nd District: 93446* (CA 22); 95495; 95526* (CA 1); 95527; 95552; 95563 95568; 95595; 95692* (CA 3); 95712; 95713* (CA 4); 95724; 95728; 95901; 95903 95910; 95914; 95915; 95916; 95917* (CA 3); 95918; 95919; 95922; 95923; 95924 95925; 95926* (CA 3); 95928; 95930; 95934; 95935; 95936; 95938; 95940; 95941 95942; 95944; 95945; 95946; 95947; 95948* (CA 3); 95949; 95954* (CA 4); 95956 95958; 95959; 95960; 95961; 95962; 95965; 95966; 95967; 95968; 95969; 95971 95972; 95973; 95974; 95975; 95977; 95978; 95980; 95981; 95983; 95984; 95986 96001; 96002; 96003; 96006; 96007; 96008; 96009; 96010; 96011; 96013; 96014 96015; 96016; 96017; 96019; 96020; 96022* (CA 3); 96023; 96024; 96025; 96027 96028; 96031; 96032; 96033; 96034; 96037; 96038; 96039; 96040; 96041; 96044 96045; 96046; 96047; 96048; 96049; 96050; 96051; 96052; 96053; 96054; 96056 96057; 96058; 96059* (CA 3); 96062; 96064; 96065; 96067; 96068; 96069; 96070 96071; 96073; 96076; 96079; 96084; 96085; 96086; 96087; 96088; 96089; 96091 96093; 96094; 96095; 96096; 96097; 96099; 96101; 96103; 96104; 96105; 96106 96108; 96109; 96110; 96111; 96112; 96113; 96114; 96115; 96116; 96118 96119; 96121; 96122; 96123; 96124; 96125; 96126; 96128; 96129; 96130; 96132 96134; 96135; 96136; 96137; 96160; 96161; 96162; 97635* (OR 2).

3rd District: 94512; 94571* (CA 11); 94585* (CA 1, CA 7); 95605; 95606; 95607 95608* (CA 5, CA 11); 95609; 95610* (CA 4); 95612; 95616; 95617; 95618; 95620 95621* (CA 4); 95622; 95625; 95626; 95627; 95628* (CA 4); 95637; 95645; 95652 95653; 95659; 95660; 95668; 95670* (CA 11); 95673* (CA 5); 95674; 95676; 95679 95687* (CA 1); 95688* (CA 1); 95691; 95692* (CA 2); 95694; 95695; 95696; 95697 95698; 95776; 95798; 95799; 95814* (CA 5); 95821* (CA 5); 95822* (CA 5); 95831* (CA 5); 95834* (CA 5); 95835; 95836; 95837* (CA 5); 95838* (CA 5); 95841; 95842 95864* (CA 5); 95912; 95913; 95917* (CA 2); 95920; 95926* (CA 2); 95927; 95929 95931; 95932; 95937; 95939; 95943; 95948* (CA 2); 95950 95951; 95953; 95955; 95957 95963; 95970; 95976; 95979; 95982; 95987; 95988 95991; 95992; 95993; 96021; 96022* (CA 2); 96029; 96035; 96055; 96059* (CA 2) 96061; 96063; 96074; 96075; 96078 96080; 96090; 96092.

4th District: 93512; 93517; 93529; 93541; 93546; 95221; 95222; 95223; 95224 95225; 95226; 95228; 95229; 95230* (CA 18); 95232; 95233; 95245; 95246; 95247 95248; 95249; 95250; 95251; 95252; 95254; 95255; 95257; 95305; 95309; 95310 95314; 95321; 95327; 95329* (CA 18); 95335; 95346; 95347; 95364; 95370; 95372 95373; 95375; 95379; 95383; 95601; 95602; 95603; 95604; 95610* (CA 3); 95611 95613; 95614; 95619; 95621* (CA 3); 95623; 95628* (CA 3); 95629; 95630; 95631 95633; 95634; 95635; 95636; 95640; 95642; 95643; 95644; 95646; 95648; 95650 95651; 95654; 95656; 95658; 95661; 95662; 95663; 95664; 95665; 95666; 95667 95669; 95671; 95672; 95675; 95677; 95678; 95681; 95682; 95684; 95685; 95689 95699; 95701; 95703; 95709; 95713* (CA 2); 95714; 95715; 95717; 95720; 95721 95722; 95726; 95735; 95736; 95746; 95747; 95762; 95763; 95954* (CA 2); 96107; 96120; 96133; 96140; 96141; 96142; 96143; 96145; 96146; 96148; 96150 96151; 96152; 96153; 96154; 96155; 96156; 96157; 96158.

5th District: 94203; 94204; 94205; 94206; 94207; 94208; 94209; 94211; 94229 94230; 94232; 94234; 94235; 94236; 94237; 94239; 94240; 94243; 94244; 94245 94246; 94247; 94248; 94249; 94250; 94252; 94253; 94254; 94256; 94257; 94258 94259; 94261; 94262; 94263; 94267; 94268; 94269; 94271; 94273; 94274; 94277 94279; 94280; 94282; 94283; 94284; 94285; 94286; 94287; 94288; 94289; 94290 94291; 94293; 94294; 94295; 94296; 94297; 94298; 94299; 95608* (CA 3, CA 11); 95624* (CA 11); 95673* (CA 3); 95758* (CA 11); 95800; 95812; 95813 95814* (CA 3); 95815; 95816; 95817; 95818; 95819; 95820; 95821* (CA 3); 95822* (CA 3); 95823; 95824; 95825; 95826* (CA 11); 95827* (CA 11); 95828; 95829* (CA 11); 95831* (CA 3); 95832* (CA 11); 95833 95834* (CA 3); 95837* (CA 3) 95838* (CA 3); 95840; 95851; 95852; 95853; 95857 95860; 95864* (CA 3); 95865 95866; 95887; 95894; 95899.

6th District: 94901; 94903; 94904; 94911; 94912; 94913; 94914; 94915; 94920 94922; 94923; 94924; 94925; 94926; 94927; 94928; 94929; 94930; 94931; 94933 94937; 94938; 94939; 94940; 94941; 94942; 94945; 94946; 94947; 94948; 94949 94950; 94951; 94952; 94953; 94954; 94955; 94956; 94957; 94960; 94963; 94964 94965; 94966; 94970; 94971; 94972; 94973; 94974; 94975; 94976; 94977; 94978 94979; 94998; 94999; 95401; 95402; 95403* (CA 1); 95404* (CA 1); 95405; 95406 95407; 95408; 95409* (CA 1); 95412;

95416; 95419; 95421; 95430; 95431; 95433 95436* (CA 1); 95439; 95442; 95444; 95446; 95448* (CA 1); 95450; 95452; 95462 95465; 95471; 95472; 95473; 95476; 95480; 95486; 95487; 95492* (CA 1); 95497.

7th District: 94509* (CA 10); 94510; 94518* (CA 10); 94519; 94520* (CA 10) 94521* (CA 10); 94522; 94523* (CA 10); 94524; 94525; 94527; 94529; 94530 94547* (CA 10); 94553* (CA 10); 94564* (CA 10); 94565* (CA 10); 94569; 94572* (CA 10); 94585* (CA 1, CA 3); 94589* (CA 1); 94590; 94591; 94592; 94596* (CA 10); 94598* (CA 10); 94801; 94802; 94803* (CA 10); 94804; 94805; 94806; 94807 94808; 94820; 94850.

8th District: 94098; 94099; 94100; 94101; 94102; 94103; 94104; 94105; 94106 94107; 94108; 94109; 94110; 94111; 94112* (CA 12); 94114* (CA 12); 94115 94117* (CA 12); 94118; 94119; 94120; 94121; 94122* (CA 12); 94123; 94124 94125; 94126; 94129; 94130; 94131* (CA 12); 94132* (CA 12); 94133; 94134 94135; 94136; 94137; 94138; 94139; 94140; 94141; 94142; 94144; 94145; 94146 94147; 94150; 94151; 94152; 94153; 94154; 94155; 94156; 94159; 94160; 94161 94162; 94163; 94164; 94171; 94175; 94177; 94188; 94593.

9th District: 94501* (CA 13); 94601; 94602; 94603* (CA 13); 94604; 94605* (CA 13); 94606; 94607; 94608; 94609; 94610; 94611* (CA 10); 94612; 94613; 94615 94616; 94617; 94618; 94619; 94620; 94621* (CA 13); 94623; 94624; 94625; 94626 94627; 94643; 94649; 94650; 94659; 94660; 94661; 94662; 94666; 94701; 94702 94703; 94704; 94705; 94706; 94707; 94708; 94709; 94710; 94720.

10th District: 94504; 94506; 94507; 94509* (CA 7); 94511; 94513; 94514; 94516 94517; 94518* (CA 7); 94520* (CA 7); 94521* (CA 7); 94523* (CA 7); 94526 94528; 94531; 94536* (CA 13); 94539* (CA 13); 94541* (CA 13); 94546* (CA 13) 94547* (CA 7); 94548; 94549; 94550; 94551; 94552* (CA 13); 94553* (CA 7) 94556; 94561; 94563; 94564* (CA 7); 94565* (CA 7); 94566; 94568; 94570; 94572* (CA 7); 94575; 94578* (CA 13); 94580* (CA 13); 94582; 94583; 94586; 94588 94594; 94595; 94596* (CA 7); 94597; 94598* (CA 7); 94611* (CA 9); 94803* (CA 7).

11th District: 94571* (CA 3); 95201; 95202; 95203; 95204; 95205; 95206; 95207 95208; 95209; 95210; 95211; 95212; 95213; 95215; 95219; 95220; 95227; 95231 95234; 95236; 95237; 95240; 95241; 95242; 95253; 95258; 95267; 95269; 95290 95296; 95297; 95298; 95304; 95320; 95330; 95336* (CA 18); 95361* (CA 18) 95366* (CA 18); 95376* (CA 18); 95378; 95608* (CA 3, CA 5); 95615; 95624* (CA 5); 95632; 95638; 95639; 95641; 95655; 95670* (CA 3); 95680; 95683; 95686 95690; 95693; 95741; 95742; 95743; 95758* (CA 5); 95759; 95826* (CA 5); 95827* (CA 5); 95829* (CA 5); 95830; 95832* (CA 5); 95873.

12th District: 94002* (CA 14); 94005; 94010* (CA 14); 94011; 94014; 94015 94016; 94017; 94019* (CA 14); 94030; 94037; 94038* (CA 14); 94044; 94065* (CA 14); 94066; 94070* (CA 14); 94080; 94083; 94112* (CA 8); 94114* (CA 8); 94116 94117* (CA 8); 94122* (CA 8); 94127; 94128; 94131* (CA 8); 94132* (CA 8) 94143; 94400; 94401; 94402; 94403; 94404.

13th District: 94086* (CA 14); 94089* (CA 14, CA 15); 94501* (CA 9); 94536* (CA 10); 94537; 94538; 94539* (CA 10); 94540; 94541* (CA 10); 94542; 94543 94544; 94545; 94546* (CA 10); 94552* (CA 10); 94555; 94557; 94560; 94577 94578* (CA 10); 94579; 94580* (CA 10); 94587; 94603* (CA 9); 94605* (CA 9) 94614; 94621* (CA 9); 95002; 95035* (CA 16); 95036; 95132* (CA 16); 95134* (CA 15, CA 16.

14th District: 94002* (CA 12); 94010* (CA 12); 94018; 94019* (CA 12); 94020 94021; 94022; 94023; 94024; 94025; 94026; 94027; 94028; 94035; 94038* (CA 12) 94039; 94040; 94041; 94042; 94043; 94060; 94061; 94062; 94063; 94064; 94065* (CA 12); 94070* (CA 12); 94074; 94086* (CA 13); 94087; 94088; 94089* (CA 13, CA 15); 94096; 94300; 94301; 94302; 94303; 94304; 94305; 94306; 94309; 94497 95014* (CA 15); 95015; 95016; 95030* (CA 15); 95051* (CA 15); 95054* (CA 15) 95070* (CA 15); 95129* (CA 15).

15th District: 94089* (CA 13, CA 14); 95005; 95006; 95007; 95008; 95009 95011; 95014* (CA 14); 95017; 95018; 95026; 95030* (CA 14); 95031; 95032 95041; 95042; 95044; 95050* (CA 16); 95051* (CA 14); 95052; 95053; 95054* (CA 14); 95055; 95060* (CA 17); 95061; 95065* (CA 17); 95066; 95067; 95070* (CA 14); 95071; 95073* (CA 17); 95076* (CA 17); 95110* (CA 16); 95117; 95118 95119; 95120; 95123* (CA 16); 95124; 95125* (CA 16); 95126* (CA 16); 95128* (CA 16); 95129* (CA 14); 95130; 95131* (CA 16); 95134* (CA 13, CA 16); 95136* (CA 16); 95137; 95139; 95141* (CA 16); 95142; 95151; 95153; 95154; 95155 95157; 95158; 95160; 95170; 95193.

16th District: 95013; 95020; 95021; 95023* (CA 17); 95024; 95035* (CA 13) 95037; 95038; 95046; 95050* (CA 15); 95100; 95101; 95102; 95103; 95106; 95108 95109; 95110* (CA 15); 95111; 95112; 95113; 95114; 95115; 95116; 95121; 95122 95123* (CA 15); 95125* (CA 15); 95126* (CA 15); 95127; 95128* (CA 15); 95131* (CA 15); 95132* (CA 13); 95133; 95134* (CA 13, CA 15); 95135; 95136* (CA 15) 95138; 95140; 95141* (CA 15); 95148; 95150; 95152; 95156; 95159; 95161; 95164 95171; 95172; 95173; 95190; 95191; 95192; 95194; 95196.

17th District: 93426* (CA 22); 93450; 93451* (CA 22); 93901; 93902; 93905 93906; 93907; 93908; 93911; 93912; 93915; 93920; 93921; 93922; 93923; 93924 93925; 93926; 93927; 93928; 93930; 93932; 93933; 93940; 93941; 93942; 93943 93944; 93950; 93953; 93954; 93955; 93960; 93962; 95001; 95003; 95004; 95010 95012; 95019; 95023* (CA 16); 95039; 95043; 95045; 95060* (CA 15); 95062 95063; 95064; 95065* (CA 15); 95073* (CA 15); 95075; 95076* (CA 15); 95077.

18th District: 93610* (CA 19); 93620; 93622* (CA 19, CA 20); 93635; 93637* (CA 19); 93661; 93665; 95056; 95230* (CA 4); 95301; 95303; 95307; 95312; 95313 95315; 95316; 95317; 95319; 95322; 95323; 95324; 95326; 95328; 95329* (CA 4) 95333; 95334; 95336* (CA 11); 95340; 95341; 95342; 95343; 95344; 95348; 95350 95351; 95352; 95353; 95354; 95355; 95356; 95357; 95358; 95360; 95361* (CA 11) 95363; 95365; 95366* (CA 11); 95367; 95368; 95369; 95374; 95376* (CA 11) 95380; 95381; 95384; 95385; 95386; 95387; 95388; 95390; 95397.

19th District: 93221* (CA 21); 93235; 93237; 93244; 93247* (CA 21); 93262 93271; 93277* (CA 20, CA 21); 93286; 93291* (CA 20, CA 21); 93601; 93602 93603; 93604; 93605; 93610* (CA 18); 93611; 93612; 93613; 93614; 93616* (CA 20); 93618* (CA 20); 93621; 93622* (CA 18, CA 20); 93623; 93625* (CA 20) 93626; 93628; 93629; 93630* (CA 20); 93633; 93634; 93637* (CA 18); 93638 93639; 93641; 93642; 93643; 93644; 93645; 93646* (CA 20); 93647* (CA 20) 93649; 93650; 93651; 93653; 93654* (CA 20); 93657* (CA 20); 93664; 93667 93669; 93670; 93675; 93701* (CA 20); 93702* (CA 20); 93703; 93704; 93705 93706* (CA 20); 93710; 93711; 93720; 93721* (CA 20); 93722* (CA 20); 93724 93725* (CA 20); 93726; 93727* (CA 20); 93728; 93729; 93740; 93741; 93744 93747; 93755; 93759; 93771; 93772; 93773; 93774; 93775; 93776; 93777; 93778 93779; 93784; 93790; 93791; 93792; 93793; 93794; 93844; 93888; 95306; 95311 95318; 95325; 95338; 95345; 95389.

20th District: 93201; 93202; 93203* (CA 21); 93204; 93206; 93210; 93212 93215* (CA 21); 93216; 93217; 93219; 93227; 93230; 93231; 93232; 93234; 93239 93241; 93242; 93245; 93246; 93249; 93250; 93256; 93257* (CA 21); 93261; 93263* (CA 21); 93266; 93270* (CA 21); 93272; 93274* (CA 21); 93275; 93277* (CA 19, CA 21); 93280; 93282; 93291* (CA 19, CA 21); 93305* (CA 21); 93306* (CA 21) 93307* (CA 21); 93308* (CA 21); 93309* (CA 21); 93311* (CA 21); 93312* (CA 21); 93313* (CA 21); 93381; 93382; 93383; 93387; 93606; 93607; 93608; 93609 93615; 93616* (CA 19); 93618* (CA 19); 93622* (CA 18, CA 19); 93624; 93625* (CA 19); 93627; 93630* (CA 19); 93631; 93640; 93646* (CA 19); 93647* (CA 19) 93648; 93652; 93654* (CA 19); 93656; 93657* (CA 19); 93660; 93662; 93666 93668; 93673; 93700; 93701* (CA 19); 93702* (CA 19); 93706* (CA 19); 93707 93708; 93709; 93712; 93714; 93715; 93716; 93717; 93718; 93721* (CA 19); 93722* (CA 19); 93725* (CA 19); 93727* (CA 19); 93745; 93750; 93760; 93761; 93762 93764; 93765; 93780; 93782; 93786.

21st District: 93203* (CA 20); 93205; 93207; 93208; 93215* (CA 20); 93218 93220; 93221* (CA 19); 93222; 93223; 93224; 93225; 93226; 93238; 93240; 93243 93247* (CA 19); 93251; 93252; 93255; 93257* (CA 20); 93258; 93260; 93263* (CA 20); 93265; 93267; 93268; 93270* (CA 20); 93274* (CA 20); 93276; 93277* (CA 19, CA 20); 93278; 93279; 93283; 93285; 93287; 93291* (CA 19, CA 20); 93292 93300; 93301; 93302; 93303; 93304; 93305* (CA 20); 93306* (CA 20); 93307* (CA 20); 93308* (CA 20); 93309* (CA 20); 93311* (CA 20); 93312* (CA 20); 93313* (CA 20); 93380; 93384; 93385; 93386; 93388; 93389; 93399; 93501; 93502; 93504 93505; 93516; 93518; 93519; 93523; 93524; 93527; 93528; 93531; 93554; 93555* (CA 40); 93556; 93560* (CA 25); 93561; 93570; 93581; 93582; 93596.

22nd District: 93013* (CA 23); 93014; 93035* (CA 23); 93067; 93101; 93102 93103; 93105; 93106; 93107; 93108; 93109; 93110; 93111; 93116; 93117; 93118 93120; 93121; 93130; 93140; 93150; 93160; 93190; 93214; 93254; 93401; 93402 93403; 93405; 93406; 93407; 93408; 93409; 93410; 93412; 93420; 93421; 93422 93423; 93424; 93426* (CA 17); 93427; 93428; 93429; 93430; 93431; 93432; 93433 93434; 93435; 93436; 93437; 93438; 93440; 93441; 93442; 93443; 93444; 93445 93446* (CA 2); 93447; 93448; 93449; 93451* (CA 17); 93452; 93453; 93454 93455; 93456; 93457; 93460; 93461; 93463; 93464; 93465; 93483.

23rd District: 90265* (CA 24, CA 29); 91304* (CA 24, CA 25); 91307* (CA 24) 91311* (CA 24, CA 25); 91319; 91320* (CA 24); 91360* (CA 24); 91361* (CA 24) 91362* (CA 24); 93001; 93002; 93003; 93004; 93005; 93006; 93007; 93009; 93010 93011; 93012; 93013* (CA 22); 93015; 93016; 93020; 93021* (CA 24); 93022 93023* (CA 24); 93024; 93030; 93031; 93032; 93033; 93034; 93035* (CA 22) 93040; 93041; 93042; 93043; 93044; 93060; 93061; 93062; 93063; 93064; 93065 93066; 93093; 93097; 93099.

24th District: 90049* (CA 29); 90263; 90264; 90265* (CA 23, CA 29); 90290* (CA 29); 91301; 91302; 91303; 91304* (CA 23, CA 25); 91305; 91306* (CA 25); 91307* (CA 23); 91308; 91309; 91311* (CA 23, CA 25); 91316; 91320* (CA 23); 91324* (CA 25); 91325* (CA 25); 91335; 91337; 91356; 91357; 91358; 91359; 91360* (CA 23); 91361* (CA 23); 91362* (CA 23); 91363; 91364; 91365; 91367; 91370; 91371 91372; 91375; 91376; 91399; 91401* (CA 26); 91403* (CA 29); 91404; 91406* (CA 26); 91408; 91411* (CA 26); 91416; 91423* (CA 29); 91426; 91436; 91604* (CA 29); 91607* (CA 26, CA 29); 93021* (CA 23); 93023* (CA 23).

25th District: 91304* (CA 23, CA 24); 91306* (CA 24); 91310; 91311* (CA 23, CA 24); 91312; 91313; 91321* (CA 27); 91322; 91324* (CA 24); 91325* (CA 24) 91326; 91327; 91328; 91329; 91330; 91343* (CA 26); 91344* (CA 26); 91345* (CA 26); 91346* (CA 26); 91350* (CA 27); 91351; 91354; 91355; 91380; 91381; 91382 91383; 91384; 91385; 91386; 91393; 91394; 93510; 93532; 93534; 93535; 93536 93539; 93543; 93544; 93550; 93551; 93552; 93553; 93560* (CA 21); 93563* (CA 28); 93584; 93586; 93590; 93591; 93599.

26th District: 91040* (CA 27); 91331; 91333; 91334; 91340; 91341; 91342* (CA 27); 91343* (CA 25); 91344* (CA 25); 91345* (CA 25); 91346* (CA 25); 91352* (CA 27); 91388; 91395; 91400; 91401* (CA 24); 91402; 91405; 91406* (CA 24) 91407; 91409; 91410; 91411* (CA 24); 91412; 91461; 91462; 91463; 91470; 91494 91495; 91496; 91497; 91499; 91504* (CA 27); 91505* (CA 27); 91600; 91601* (CA 27, CA 29); 91602* (CA 29); 91603; 91605* (CA 27); 91606; 91607* (CA 24, CA 29); 91609; 91611; 91612; 91615; 91616; 91617.

27th District: 90032* (CA 30, CA 31); 90039* (CA 29, CA 30); 90041* (CA 30) 90042* (CA 30); 90065* (CA 30); 91001; 91002; 91003; 91011; 91012; 91020 91021; 91023; 91030* (CA 30, CA 31); 91031; 91040* (CA 26); 91041; 91042 91043; 91046; 91050; 91051; 91052; 91100; 91101; 91102; 91103; 91104; 91105* (CA 30); 91106; 91107* (CA 28); 91108* (CA 28, CA 31); 91109; 91114; 91115 91116; 91117; 91118; 91121; 91122; 91123; 91124; 91125; 91126; 91127; 91128 91129; 91131; 91182; 91184; 91185; 91186; 91187; 91188; 91189; 91191; 91200 91201; 91202; 91203; 91204* (CA 30); 91205; 91206; 91207; 91208; 91209; 91210 91214; 91221; 91222; 91224; 91225; 91226; 91321* (CA 25); 91342* (CA 26) 91350* (CA 25); 91352* (CA 26); 91353; 91392; 91500; 91501; 91502; 91503 91504* (CA 26); 91505* (CA 26); 91506; 91507; 91508; 91510; 91520; 91521 91522; 91523; 91601* (CA 26, CA 29); 91605* (CA 26); 91775* (CA 28, CA 31) 91801* (CA 31).

28th District: 91006* (CA 31); 91007; 91009; 91010* (CA 31); 91016* (CA 31) 91017; 91024; 91025; 91066; 91077; 91107* (CA 27); 91108* (CA 27, CA 31) 91702* (CA 31);

91706* (CA 31, CA 34); 91711; 91722* (CA 31); 91723; 91724 91731* (CA 31); 91740* (CA 31); 91744* (CA 34); 91748* (CA 34, CA 39, CA 41) 91750; 91767* (CA 41); 91768* (CA 41); 91773; 91775* (CA 27, CA 31); 91776* (CA 31); 91780; 91788; 91789* (CA 31, CA 41); 91790* (CA 31, CA 34); 91791 91792* (CA 34); 91793; 91795; 93563* (CA 25).

29th District: 90004* (CA 30); 90005* (CA 30, CA 32, 33); 90010* (CA 30, CA 32); 90020* (CA 30, CA 33); 90024; 90025; 90026* (CA 30, CA 33); 90027* (CA 30); 90028* (CA 30); 90029* (CA 30); 90035* (CA 32); 90036* (CA 32); 90038* (CA 30); 90039* (CA 27, CA 30); 90046; 90048* (CA 32); 90049* (CA 24); 90064* (CA 32); 90066* (CA 32, CA 36); 90067; 90068; 90069; 90072; 90073; 90077 90078; 90089* (CA 32); 90093; 90209; 90210; 90211; 90212* (CA 32); 90213 90265* (CA 23, CA 24); 90272; 90290* (CA 24); 90291* (CA 36); 90313; 90400 90401; 90402; 90403; 90404; 90405* (CA 36); 90406; 90407; 90408; 90409; 90410 90411; 91403* (CA 24); 91413; 91423* (CA 24); 91601* (CA 26, CA 27); 91602* (CA 26); 91604* (CA 24); 91607* (CA 24, CA 26); 91608; 91610; 91614.

30th District: 90004* (CA 29); 90005* (CA 29, CA 32, CA 33); 90006* (CA 32, CA 33); 90010* (CA 29, CA 32); 90012* (CA 33); 90019* (CA 32); 90020* (CA 29, CA 33); 90023* (CA 33, CA 34); 90026* (CA 29, CA 33); 90027* (CA 29); 90028* (CA 29); 90029* (CA 29); 90031; 90032* (CA 27, CA 31); 90033* (CA 33); 90038* (CA 29); 90039* (CA 27, CA 29); 90041* (CA 27); 90042* (CA 27); 90050; 90057* (CA 33); 90063* (CA 31, CA 33, CA 34); 90065* (CA 27); 90070; 90075; 90076; 91030* (CA 27, CA 31); 91105* (CA 27); 91204* (CA 27).

31st District: 90022* (CA 33, CA 34); 90032* (CA 27, CA 30); 90063* (CA 30, CA 33, CA 34); 91006* (CA 28); 91010* (CA 28); 91016* (CA 28); 91030* (CA 27, CA 30); 91108* (CA 27, CA 28); 91702* (CA 28); 91706* (CA 28, CA 34); 91714 91716; 91722* (CA 28); 91731* (CA 28); 91732; 91733; 91734; 91735; 91740* (CA 28); 91754* (CA 34); 91756; 91770* (CA 34); 91771; 91772; 91775* (CA 27, CA 28); 91776* (CA 28); 91778; 91789* (CA 28, CA 41); 91790* (CA 28, CA 34) 91800; 91801* (CA 27); 91802; 91803; 91804; 91841; 91896; 91899.

32nd District: 90005* (CA 29, CA 30, CA 33); 90006* (CA 30, CA 33); 90007* (CA 33, CA 35); 90008; 90010* (CA 29, CA 30); 90016; 90018; 90019* (CA 30); 90034 90035* (CA 29); 90036* (CA 29); 90037* (CA 35); 90043; 90044* (CA 35, CA 37); 90045* (CA 35, CA 36); 90047* (CA 35); 90048* (CA 29); 90056* (CA 35); 90062 90064* (CA 29); 90066* (CA 29, CA 36); 90089* (CA 29); 90094* (CA 36); 90212* (CA 29); 90230* (CA 36); 90231; 90232; 90233; 90292* (CA 36); 90302* (CA 35).

33rd District: 90000; 90001* (CA 35); 90002* (CA 35, CA 37); 90005* (CA 29, CA 30, CA 32); 90006* (CA 30, CA 32); 90007* (CA 32, CA 35); 90011* (CA 35) 90012* (CA 30); 90013; 90014; 90015; 90017; 90020* (CA 29, CA 30); 90021 90022* (CA 31, CA 34); 90023* (CA 30, CA 34); 90026* (CA 29, CA 30); 90030 90033* (CA 30); 90040* (CA 34); 90051; 90052* (CA 35); 90053; 90054; 90055 90057* (CA 30); 90058* (CA 35); 90060; 90063* (CA 30, CA 31, CA 34); 90071 90074; 90079; 90086; 90087; 90088; 90091; 90096; 90097; 90099; 90101; 90201 90255* (CA 35); 90261; 90262* (CA 35, CA 37); 90270; 90280* (CA 37, CA 38) 90301* (CA 35); 90640* (CA 34); 90723* (CA 37, CA 38).

34th District: 90022* (CA 31, CA 33); 90023* (CA 30, CA 33); 90040* (CA 33) 90063* (CA 30, CA 31, CA 33); 90241* (CA 38); 90601* (CA 38); 90602* (CA 39); 90604* (CA 39); 90605* (CA 39); 90606; 90607; 90608; 90609; 90610; 90612; 90638* (CA 39); 90640* (CA 33); 90650* (CA 39); 90651; 90652; 90659; 90660; 90661; 90662 90665; 90670* (CA 39); 90671; 90704* (CA 39); 91706* (CA 28, CA 31); 91715 91744* (CA 28); 91745* (CA 41); 91746; 91747; 91748* (CA 28, CA 39, CA 41) 91749; 91754* (CA 31); 91770* (CA 31); 91790* (CA 28, CA 31); 91792* (CA 28) 91799.

35th District: 90001* (CA 33); 90002* (CA 33, CA 37); 90003* (CA 37); 90007* (CA 32, CA 33); 90011* (CA 33); 90037* (CA 32); 90044* (CA 32, CA 37); 90045* (CA 32, CA 36); 90047* (CA 32); 90052* (CA 33); 90056* (CA 32); 90058* (CA 33); 90061* (CA 37); 90247* (CA 36, CA 37); 90248* (CA 36, CA 37); 90249* (CA 36); 90250* (CA 36); 90251; 90255* (CA 33); 90260* (CA 36); 90262* (CA 33, CA 37); 90278* (CA 36); 90300; 90301* (CA 33); 90302* (CA 32); 90303; 90304* (CA 36); 90305; 90306; 90307; 90308; 90309; 90310; 90312; 90398.

36th District: 90009; 90045* (CA 32, CA 35); 90066* (CA 29, CA 32); 90080 90082 90083; 90094* (CA 32); 90230* (CA 32); 90245; 90247* (CA 35, CA 37) 90248* (CA 35, CA 37); 90249* (CA 35); 90250* (CA 35); 90254; 90260* (CA 35); 90266; 90274; 90277; 90278* (CA 35); 90291* (CA 29); 90292* (CA 32); 90293 90294; 90295; 90296; 90304* (CA 35); 90311; 90405* (CA 29); 90500; 90501* (CA 37); 90502* (CA 37); 90503; 90504; 90505; 90506; 90507; 90508; 90509; 90510 90704; 90710* (CA 37); 90717; 90731* (CA 38); 90732* (CA 38); 90734* (CA 38); 90744* (CA 37, CA 38); 90745* (CA 37).

37th District: 90002* (CA 33, CA 35); 90003* (CA 35); 90044* (CA 32, CA 35) 90059; 90061* (CA 35); 90220; 90221* (CA 38); 90222; 90223; 90224; 90247* (CA 35, CA 36); 90248* (CA 35, CA 36); 90262* (CA 33, CA 35); 90280* (CA 33, CA 38); 90501* (CA 36); 90502* (CA 36); 90710* (CA 36); 90723* (CA 33, CA 38) 90744* (CA 36, 38); 90745* (CA 36); 90746; 90747; 90748; 90749; 90805* (CA 38); 90806* (CA 38); 90807* (CA 38); 90810* (CA 38); 90813* (CA 38).

38th District: 90084; 90221* (CA 37); 90239; 90240; 90241* (CA 34); 90242 90280* (CA 33, CA 37); 90706; 90707; 90711; 90712; 90713* (CA 39); 90714 90723* (CA 33, CA 37); 90731* (CA 36); 90733; 90734* (CA 36); 90740* (CA 39, CA 45); 90744* (CA 36, CA 37); 90800; 90801; 90802; 90803; 90804; 90805* (CA 37); 90806* (CA 37); 90807* (CA 37); 90808* (CA 39); 90809; 90810* (CA 37); 90813* (CA 37); 90814; 90815* (CA 39); 90822; 90831; 90832; 90833; 90834 90835; 90840; 90842; 90844; 90845; 90846; 90847; 90848; 90853; 90888.

39th District: 90602* (CA 34); 90603; 90604* (CA 34); 90605* (CA 34); 90620* (CA 45); 90621; 90622; 90623; 90624; 90630* (CA 45); 90631* (CA 41); 90632 90633; 90637; 90638* (CA 34); 90639; 90650* (CA 34); 90670* (CA 34); 90680* (CA 45);

40th District: 91701* (CA 41, CA 42); 91759; 92242; 92252; 92256; 92267 92268; 92277; 92278; 92280; 92284; 92285; 92286; 92301; 92304; 92305; 92307 92308; 92309; 92310* (CA 42); 92311; 92312; 92314; 92315; 92317; 92318; 92319 92320* (CA 44); 92321; 92322; 92323; 92324* (CA 42, CA 44); 92325; 92326 92327; 92328; 92329; 92332; 92333; 92336* (CA 42); 92338; 92339; 92340; 92341 92342; 92345; 92346* (CA 42); 92347; 92350; 92351; 92352; 92354; 92356; 92357 92358; 92359; 92363; 92364; 92365; 92366; 92368; 92369; 92371; 92372; 92373* (CA 44); 92374; 92375; 92376* (CA 42); 92378; 92382; 92384; 92385; 92386 92389; 92391; 92392; 92393; 92394; 92397; 92398; 92399* (CA 41); 92404* (CA 42); 92405* (CA 42); 92406; 92407* (CA 42); 92408* (CA 42); 92409; 92410* (CA 42); 92414; 92416; 92420; 92423; 92427; 93513; 93514; 93515; 93522; 93526; 93530; 93542; 93545; 93549; 93555* (CA 21); 93558; 93562; 93592.

41st District: 90631* (CA 39); 91701* (CA 40, CA 42); 91708; 91709; 91710 91720* (CA 43); 91730* (CA 42); 91745* (CA 34); 91748* (CA 28, CA 34, CA 39) 91758; 91761* (CA 42); 91762* (CA 42); 91763; 91764* (CA 42); 91765; 91766 91767* (CA 28); 91768* (CA 28); 91769; 91785; 91786* (CA 42); 91789* (CA 28, CA 31); 91798; 92399* (CA 40); 92621* (CA 39); 92670* (CA 39, CA 47); 92686* (CA 39); 92687* (CA 47); 92806* (CA 39, CA 46, CA 47); 92807* (CA 47); 92808* (CA 47); 92817.

42nd District: 91701* (CA 40, CA 41); 91729; 91730* (CA 41); 91737; 91739 91743; 91761* (CA 41); 91762* (CA 41); 91764* (CA 41); 91786* (CA 41); 92310* (CA 40); 92316; 92324* (CA 40, CA 44); 92334; 92335; 92336* (CA 40); 92346* (CA 40); 92376* (CA 40); 92377; 92400; 92401; 92402; 92403; 92404* (CA 40) 92405* (CA 40); 92407* (CA 40); 92408* (CA 40); 92410* (CA 40); 92411 92412 92413; 92415; 92418; 92424; 92507* (CA 43, CA 44); 92509* (CA 43).

43rd District: 91718; 91719; 91720* (CA 41); 91752; 91760; 92500; 92501 92502; 92503; 92504; 92505; 92506; 92507* (CA 42, CA 44); 92508; 92509* (CA 42); 92513; 92514; 92515; 92516; 92517; 92518; 92519; 92521; 92522; 92530 92531; 92532; 92562; 92563; 92564; 92595.

44th District: 92201; 92202; 92210; 92220; 92223; 92225; 92226; 92230 92234 92235; 92236; 92239; 92240; 92253; 92254; 92255; 92258; 92260; 92261; 92262 92263; 92264; 92270; 92272; 92274* (CA 51); 92276; 92282; 92292; 92320* (CA 40); 92324* (CA 40, CA 42); 92353; 92373* (CA 40); 92507* (CA 42, CA 43) 92536; 92539; 92543; 92544; 92545; 92546; 92548; 92549; 92552; 92553; 92554 92555; 92556; 92557; 92561; 92567; 92570; 92571; 92572; 92581; 92582; 92583 92584; 92585; 92586; 92587; 92596; 92599.

45th District: 90620* (CA 39); 90630* (CA 39); 90680* (CA 39); 90720* (CA 39) 90740* (CA 38, CA 39); 90742; 90743; 92605; 92615; 92626* (CA 46, CA 47) 92627* (CA 47); 92628; 92641* (CA 46); 92644* (CA 46); 92646; 92647 92648; 92649; 92655; 92658; 92659; 92660* (CA 47); 92661; 92662; 92663; 92664* (CA 46); 92683* (CA 46); 92684; 92704* (CA 46); 92707* (CA 46, CA 47); 92708* (CA 46); 92728; 92799; 92801* (CA 39, CA 46); 92804* (CA 39, CA 46); 92814.

46th District: 92622* (CA 39); 92626* (CA 45, CA 47); 92633* (CA 39); 92640 92641* (CA 45); 92642; 92643; 92644* (CA 45); 92664* (CA 45); 92668* (CA 47); 92683* (CA 45); 92701* (CA 47); 92702; 92703; 92704* (CA 45) 92705* (CA 47); 92706* (CA 47); 92707* (CA 45, CA 47); 92708* (CA 45); 92711 92712; 92714* (CA 47); 92800; 92801* (CA 39, CA 45); 92802; 92803; 92804* (CA 39, CA 45); 92805* (CA 39, CA 47); 92806* (CA 39, CA 41, CA 47); 92812; 92815 92825* (CA 47); 92850.

47th District: 92610; 92613; 92625; 92626* (CA 45, CA 46); 92627* (CA 45) 92630* (CA 48); 92650; 92651; 92652; 92653* (CA 48); 92654; 92656* (CA 48) 92657* (CA 45); 92665; 92666; 92667; 92668* (CA 46); 92669; 92670* (CA 39, CA 41); 92676; 92677* (CA 48); 92679* (CA 48); 92680* (CA 46); 92681 92687* (CA 41); 92691* (CA 48); 92692* (CA 48); 92701* (CA 46); 92705* (CA 46); 92706* (CA 46); 92707* (CA 45, CA 46); 92709; 92710; 92713; 92714* (CA 46); 92715; 92716; 92717; 92718; 92720; 92730; 92805* (CA 39, CA 46); 92806* (CA 39, CA 41, CA 46); 92807* (CA 41); 92808* (CA 41); 92816; 92825* (CA 46).

48th District: 92003; 92008* (CA 51); 92026* (CA 51); 92027* (CA 51); 92028 92036* (CA 52); 92049; 92051; 92052; 92054; 92055; 92056* (CA 52); 92057 92058; 92059; 92060; 92061; 92065* (CA 51, CA 52); 92066* (CA 52); 92068 92069* (CA 51); 92070; 92082* (CA 51); 92083* (CA 51); 92084* (CA 51); 92085 92086; 92088; 92589; 92590; 92591; 92592; 92593; 92607; 92624; 92629; 92630* (CA 47); 92653* (CA 47); 92656* (CA 47); 92672; 92673; 92674; 92675; 92677* (CA 47); 92678; 92679* (CA 47); 92688; 92690; 92691* (CA 47); 92692* (CA 47) 92693.

49th District: 91932* (CA 50); 91933; 91942* (CA 52); 92014* (CA 51); 92037 92038; 92039; 92092; 92093; 92100; 92101; 92102* (CA 50); 92103; 92104* (CA 50); 92105* (CA 50); 92106; 92107; 92108; 92109; 92110; 92111; 92112; 92113* (CA 50, CA 52); 92115* (CA 50, CA 52); 92116; 92117; 92118; 92119* (CA 51, CA 52) 92120* (CA 51, CA 52); 92121* (CA 51); 92122; 92123; 92124* (CA 51); 92132; 92133; 92134; 92135; 92137; 92138; 92140; 92142; 92147; 92150; 92152; 92154* (CA 50); 92155; 92158; 92160 92163; 92164; 92166; 92167; 92168; 92169; 92170 92171; 92176; 92177; 92178; 92180 92183; 92184; 92185; 92186; 92187; 92188 92189; 92190; 92191; 92192; 92193; 92197; 92199.

50th District: 91902; 91908; 91909; 91910; 91911; 91912; 91913; 91914; 91915 91932* (CA 49); 91941* (CA 52); 91945* (CA 52); 91947; 91950; 91951; 91977* (CA 52); 92053; 92073; 92102* (CA 49); 92104* (CA 49); 92105* (CA 49); 92113* (CA 49); 92114* (CA 52); 92115* (CA 49, CA 52); 92136; 92139; 92143; 92149 92153; 92154* (CA 49); 92162; 92165; 92172; 92173; 92174; 92175; 92179 92182 92195.

51st District: 92007; 92008* (CA 48); 92009; 92014* (CA 49); 92018; 92023 92024; 92025; 92026* (CA 48); 92027* (CA 48); 92029; 92030; 92033; 92040* (CA 52); 92046; 92056* (CA 48); 92064* (CA 52); 92065* (CA 48, CA 52); 92067 92069* (CA 48); 92071* (CA 52); 92074; 92075; 92079; 92082* (CA 48); 92083* (CA 48); 92084* (CA 48); 92096; 92119* (CA 49, CA 52); 92120* (CA 49, CA 52) 92121* (CA 49); 92124* (CA 49); 92126; 92127; 92128; 92129; 92130; 92131 92145; 92159; 92161; 92181; 92194; 92196; 92198.

52nd District: 91901; 91903; 91905; 91906; 91916; 91917; 91931; 91934; 91935 91941* (CA 50); 91942* (CA 49); 91943; 91944; 91945* (CA 50); 91946; 91948 91962; 91963; 91976; 91977* (CA 50); 91978; 91979; 91980; 91987; 91990; 91991 91992; 91993; 91994; 91995; 92004; 92019; 92020; 92021; 92022; 92036* (CA 48) 92040* (CA 51); 92064* (CA 51); 92065* (CA 48, CA 51); 92066* (CA 48); 92071* (CA 51); 92072; 92090; 92114* (CA 50); 92115* (CA 49, CA 50); 92119* (CA 49, CA 51); 92120* (CA 49, CA 51); 92222; 92227; 92231; 92232; 92233; 92243 92244; 92249; 92250; 92251; 92257; 92259; 92266; 92273; 92274* (CA 44); 92281 92283.

Colorado

1st District: 80010* (CO 6); 80011* (CO 4, CO 6); 80012* (CO 6); 80014* (CO 6); 80019* (CO 4); 80022* (CO 4); 80037; 80040; 80042; 80045; 80047; 80110* (CO 6); 80111* (CO 6); 80123* (CO 3, CO 6); 80127* (CO 3, CO 6); 80150 80151; 80154; 80155; 80201; 80202; 80203; 80204; 80205; 80206; 80207; 80208 80209; 80210; 80211; 80212* (CO 2); 80214* (CO 2, CO 6); 80216* (CO 2); 80217 80218; 80219; 80220; 80221* (CO 6); 80222; 80223; 80224* (CO 6); 80226* (CO 6); 80227* (CO 6); 80229* (CO 2, CO 4); 80230; 80231; 80235* (CO 6) 80236* (CO 6); 80237* (CO 6); 80238; 80239; 80243; 80244; 80248; 80249; 80250 80251; 80252; 80254; 80255; 80256; 80259; 80261; 80262; 80263; 80264; 80265 80266; 80270; 80271; 80273; 80274; 80275; 80279; 80280; 80281; 80290; 80291 80292; 80293; 80294; 80295; 80299.

2nd District: 80001; 80002* (CO 6); 80003; 80004* (CO 6); 80005; 80006; 80020* (CO 4); 80021; 80025; 80026; 80027; 80028; 80030; 80031; 80033* (CO 6); 80034 80035; 80036; 80038; 80212* (CO 1); 80214* (CO 1, CO 6); 80215* (CO 6); 80216* (CO 1); 80221* (CO 1); 80229* (CO 1, CO 4); 80233* (CO 4); 80234* (CO 4) 80241; 80301; 80302; 80303; 80304; 80306; 80307; 80308; 80309; 80310; 80314 80321; 80322; 80323; 80328; 80329; 80401* (CO 6); 80403* (CO 6); 80422 80427 80436; 80438; 80439* (CO 6); 80444; 80452; 80455; 80466; 80471; 80474; 80476 80481; 80501* (CO 4); 80502; 80503; 80504* (CO 4); 80510; 80516; 80533; 80540* (CO 4); 80544; 80601* (CO 4); 80614.

3rd District: 80104* (CO 5); 80118* (CO 5); 80123* (CO 1, CO 6); 80127* (CO 1, CO 6); 80133* (CO 5); 80135* (CO 5); 80162; 80420; 80421* (CO 4); 80423 80424; 80425; 80426; 80428; 80429; 80430; 80432; 80433* (CO 6); 80434; 80435 80440; 80441; 80442; 80443; 80446; 80447; 80448; 80449; 80451; 80456; 80459 80461; 80463; 80467 80468; 80469; 80470* (CO 6); 80473; 80475; 80477; 80478 80479; 80480; 80482; 80483; 80487; 80488; 80498; 80816* (CO 5); 80820; 80827* (CO 5) 81001; 81002; 81003; 81004; 81005; 81006; 81007; 81008; 81009 81010 81011; 81012; 81019; 81022; 81023; 81025 81039* (CO 4); 81040; 81055; 81062* (CO 4); 81065; 81066; 81069; 81089 81101; 81102; 81120; 81121; 81122; 81123 81124; 81125; 81126; 81127; 81128; 81129 81130; 81131; 81132; 81133; 81134 81135; 81136; 81137; 81138; 81140; 81141; 81143 81144; 81146; 81147; 81148 81149; 81150; 81151; 81152; 81153; 81154; 81155; 81157 81201; 81210; 81211 81212* (CO 5); 81215; 81220; 81224; 81225; 81227; 81228; 81230 81231; 81232 81233* (CO 5); 81235; 81236; 81237; 81239; 81240* (CO 5); 81241 81242; 81243 81247; 81248; 81249; 81250* (CO 5); 81251; 81252; 81253* (CO 5); 81301; 81302 81320; 81321; 81323; 81324; 81325; 81326; 81327; 81328; 81329; 81330 81331 81332; 81333; 81334; 81335; 81401; 81402; 81410; 81411; 81413; 81414; 81415 81416; 81418; 81419; 81420; 81421; 81422; 81423; 81424; 81425; 81426; 81427 81428; 81429; 81430; 81431; 81432; 81433; 81434; 81435; 81501; 81502; 81503 81504; 81505 81506; 81520; 81521; 81522; 81523; 81524; 81525; 81526; 81527 81601; 81602; 81610; 81611; 81612; 81615; 81620; 81621; 81623; 81624; 81625 81626; 81628; 81630; 81631; 81632; 81633; 81635; 81636; 81637; 81638; 81639 81640; 81641; 81642; 81643; 81645; 81646; 81647; 81648; 81649; 81650; 81652 81653; 81654; 81655; 81656; 81657; 81658 82063* (WY 1).

4th District: 69128* (NE 3); 69145* (NE 3); 69168* (NE 3); 80011* (CO 1, CO 6); 80015* (CO 5, CO 6); 80016* (CO 6); 80017* (CO 6); 80018; 80019* (CO 1); 80020* (CO 2); 80022* (CO 1); 80024; 80101; 80102; 80103; 80105; 80106* (CO 5) 80107* (CO 5, CO 6); 80117; 80134* (CO 5); 80136; 80137; 80229* (CO 1, CO 2); 80233* (CO 2); 80234* (CO 2); 80421* (CO 3); 80501* (CO 2); 80504* (CO 2); 80511; 80512; 80513; 80514; 80515; 80517; 80520; 80521; 80522; 80523 80524; 80525; 80526; 80527 80530; 80532; 80534; 80535; 80536; 80537; 80538 80539; 80540* (CO 2); 80541; 80542 80543; 80545; 80546; 80547; 80548; 80549 80550; 80551; 80553; 80601* (CO 2); 80610 80611; 80612; 80615; 80620; 80621 80622; 80623; 80624; 80631; 80632; 80633; 80634 80638; 80639; 80640; 80642 80643; 80644; 80645; 80646; 80648; 80649; 80650; 80651 80652; 80653; 80654 80701; 80720; 80721; 80722; 80723; 80726; 80727; 80728; 80729 80731; 80732 80733; 80734; 80735; 80736; 80737; 80740; 80741; 80742; 80743; 80744 80745 80746; 80747; 80749; 80750; 80751; 80754; 80755; 80757; 80758; 80759; 80801 80802; 80804; 80805; 80806; 80807; 80808* (CO 5); 80810; 80812; 80815; 80818 80821 80822; 80823; 80824; 80825; 80828; 80830; 80832* (CO 5); 80834; 80835* (CO 5) 80836; 80861; 80862; 80863; 81020; 81021; 81024; 81026; 81027; 81028; 81029 81030; 81032 81033; 81034; 81036; 81038; 81039* (CO 3); 81041; 81042; 81043 81044; 81045; 81046 81047; 81049; 81050; 81052; 81054; 81057; 81058; 81059 81062* (CO 3); 81063; 81064 81067; 81070; 81071; 81073; 81074; 81075; 81076 81077; 81080* (KS 1); 81081; 81082 81084; 81087; 81090; 81091; 81092; 82082* (NE 3, WY 1).

5th District: 80015* (CO 4, CO 6); 80104* (CO 3); 80106* (CO 4); 80111* (CO 1, CO 6); 80112* (CO 4, CO 6); 80116; 80118* (CO 3); 80120* (CO 6); 80121* (CO 6); 80122* (CO 6); 80124; 80125; 80126; 80131; 80132; 80133* (CO 3); 80134* (CO 4) 80135* (CO 3); 80808* (CO 4); 80809; 80813; 80814; 80816* (CO 3) 80817; 80819 80827* (CO 3); 80829; 80831; 80832* (CO 4); 80833; 80835* (CO 4); 80840; 80841 80860; 80863; 80864; 80866; 80900; 80901; 80903; 80904 80905; 80906; 80907; 80908

80909; 80910; 80911; 80912; 80913; 80914; 80915 80916; 80917; 80918; 80919; 80920; 80921; 80922; 80925; 80926; 80928; 80929 80930; 80931; 80932; 80933; 80934; 80935; 80936; 80937; 80940; 80941; 80942 80943; 80944; 80945; 80946; 80947; 80949; 80950; 80960; 80962; 80970; 80977 80995; 80997; 81212* (CO 3); 81221; 81222; 81223; 81226; 81233* (CO 3); 81240* (CO 3); 81244; 81246; 81250* (CO 3); 81253* (CO 3); 81290.

6th District: 80002* (CO 2); 80004* (CO 2); 80010* (CO 1); 80011* (CO 1, CO 4); 80012* (CO 1); 80013; 80014* (CO 1); 80015* (CO 4, CO 5); 80017* (CO 4) 80033* (CO 2); 80041; 80044; 80046; 80110* (CO 1); 80111* (CO 1, CO 5); 80112* (CO 4, CO 5); 80120* (CO 5); 80121* (CO 5); 80122* (CO 5); 80123* (CO 1, CO 3); 80127* (CO 1, CO 3); 80160; 80161; 80165; 80166; 80214* (CO 1, CO 2) 80215* (CO 2); 80224* (CO 1); 80225; 80226* (CO 1); 80227* (CO 1); 80228 80231* (CO 1); 80232; 80235* (CO 1); 80236* (CO 1); 80237* (CO 1); 80401* (CO 2); 80402; 80403* (CO 2); 80419; 80433* (CO 3); 80439* (CO 2); 80453; 80454 80457; 80465; 80470* (CO 3).

Connecticut

1st District: 06001* (CT 6); 06002; 06006; 06016; 06023; 06025; 06028; 06032* (CT 6); 06033; 06037; 06040; 06041; 06043; 06045; 06049; 06064; 06067; 06073 06074; 06081* (CT 6); 06088; 06095; 06100; 06101; 06102; 06103; 06104; 06105 06106; 06107* (CT 6); 06108; 06109; 06110; 06111; 06112; 06114; 06115; 06117 06118; 06119; 06120; 06123; 06126; 06127; 06128; 06129; 06131; 06132; 06133 06134; 06137; 06138; 06140; 06141; 06142; 06143; 06144; 06145; 06146; 06147 06150; 06151; 06152; 06153; 06154; 06155; 06156; 06160; 06167; 06176; 06180; 06183; 06231; 06232; 06248; 06414; 06416 06424* (CT 2); 06447; 06456 06469* (CT 2); 06480.

2nd District: 02891* (RI 2); 06029; 06066; 06071* (CT 6); 06075; 06076; 06077 06084; 06226; 06230; 06233; 06234; 06235; 06237; 06238; 06239; 06241; 06242 06243; 06244; 06245; 06246; 06247; 06249; 06250; 06251; 06254; 06255; 06256 06258; 06259; 06260; 06262; 06263; 06264; 06265; 06266; 06267; 06268; 06269 06277; 06278; 06279; 06280; 06281; 06282; 06320; 06330; 06331; 06332; 06333 06334; 06335; 06336; 06337; 06339; 06340; 06349; 06350; 06351; 06353; 06354 06355; 06357; 06359; 06360; 06365; 06370; 06371; 06372; 06373; 06374; 06375 06376; 06377; 06378; 06379; 06380; 06382; 06383; 06384; 06385; 06386; 06387 06388; 06389; 06390; 06409; 06412; 06415; 06417* (CT 3); 06419* (CT 3); 06420 06423; 06424* (CT 1); 06426; 06441; 06442* (CT 3); 06457* (CT 3); 06459; 06469* (CT 1); 06474; 06475; 06498.

3rd District: 06405; 06410* (CT 5); 06413; 06417* (CT 2); 06418* (CT 5) 06419* (CT 2); 06422; 06437; 06442* (CT 2); 06443; 06455; 06457* (CT 2) 06460; 06461; 06466; 06471; 06472; 06473; 06477; 06481; 06492* (CT 5); 06493 06494; 06497* (CT 4, CT 5); 06500; 06501; 06502; 06503; 06504; 06505; 06506 06507; 06508; 06509; 06510; 06511; 06512; 06513; 06514; 06515; 06516; 06517 06518; 06519; 06520; 06521; 06525* (CT 5); 06530; 06531; 06532; 06533; 06534 06535; 06536; 06537; 06538; 06540; 06607* (CT 4); 06610* (CT 4); 06611* (CT 4, CT 5); 06673.

4th District: 06430* (CT 5); 06431; 06432; 06436; 06468; 06470* (CT 5); 06482* (CT 5); 06484* (CT 5); 06490; 06491; 06497* (CT 3, CT 5); 06600; 06601; 06602 06604; 06605; 06606; 06607* (CT 3); 06608; 06610* (CT 3); 06611* (CT 3, CT 5) 06612* (CT 5); 06650; 06699; 06807; 06820; 06830; 06831; 06832; 06836; 06840 06842; 06850* (CT 5); 06851; 06852; 06853; 06854; 06855; 06856; 06857; 06858 06859; 06860; 06870; 06878; 06880* (CT 5); 06881; 06883* (CT 5); 06888; 06889 06897* (CT 5); 06900 06901; 06902; 06903; 06904; 06905; 06907; 06910 06911; 06912; 06913; 06914; 06920; 06921; 06922; 06925; 06926; 06927; 06928.

5th District: 06401; 06403; 06404; 06410* (CT 3); 06411; 06418* (CT 3); 06430* (CT 4); 06440; 06450; 06454; 06470* (CT 4); 06478* (CT 6); 06482* (CT 4) 06483; 06484* (CT 4); 06488* (CT 6); 06492* (CT 3); 06497* (CT 3, CT 4) 06524; 06525* (CT 3); 06611* (CT 3, CT 4); 06612* (CT 4); 06701; 06702; 06704 06705; 06706; 06708; 06710; 06712; 06716; 06720; 06721; 06722; 06723; 06724 06725; 06726; 06749; 06762; 06770; 06784* (CT 6); 06801; 06804; 06810; 06811 06812* (CT 6); 06813; 06814; 06816; 06817; 06829; 06850* (CT 4); 06875; 06876 06877; 06879; 06880* (CT 4); 06883* (CT 4); 06896; 06897* (CT 4).

6th District: 06001* (CT 1); 06010; 06011; 06013; 06018; 06019; 06020; 06021 06022; 06024; 06026; 06027; 06030; 06031; 06032* (CT 1); 06034; 06035; 06039 06050; 06051; 06052; 06053; 06057; 06058; 06059; 06060; 06061; 06062; 06063 06065; 06068; 06069; 06070; 06071* (CT 2); 06072; 06078; 06079; 06081* (CT 1) 06082; 06083; 06085; 06087; 06089; 06090; 06091; 06092; 06093; 06094; 06096 06098; 06107* (CT 1); 06199 06444; 06467; 06478* (CT 5); 06479; 06487; 06488* (CT 5); 06750; 06751 06752; 06753; 06754; 06755; 06756; 06757 06758 06759; 06763; 06776; 06777; 06778 06779; 06781; 06782; 06783; 06784* (CT 5) 06785; 06786; 06787; 06790; 06791; 06793 06794; 06795; 06796; 06798; 06812* (CT 5).

Delaware

At Large: 19701; 19702; 19703; 19706; 19707; 19708; 19709; 19710; 19711 19712; 19713; 19714; 19715; 19716; 19717; 19718; 19720; 19721; 19725; 19726 19730; 19731; 19732; 19733; 19734; 19735; 19736; 19800; 19801; 19802; 19803 19804; 19805; 19806; 19807; 19808; 19809; 19810; 19850; 19880; 19884; 19885 19886; 19887; 19889; 19890; 19891; 19892; 19893; 19894; 19895; 19896 19897; 19898; 19899; 19901; 19902; 19903; 19930; 19931; 19933; 19934; 19936 19938; 19939; 19940; 19941; 19942; 19943; 19944; 19945; 19946; 19947; 19950 19951; 19952; 19953; 19954; 19955; 19956; 19958; 19960; 19961; 19962; 19963 19964; 19966; 19967; 19968; 19969; 19970; 19971; 19973* (MD 1); 19975; 19977 19979; 19980.

District of Columbia

20000; 20001; 20002; 20003; 20004; 20005; 20006; 20007; 20008 20009; 20010; 20011;

20012; 20013; 20015; 20016; 20017; 20018; 20019; 20020 20024; 20026; 20029; 20030;
20032; 20033; 20035; 20036; 20037; 20038; 20039 20040; 20042; 20043; 20044; 20045;
20046; 20047; 20048; 20049; 20050; 20051 20052; 20053; 20055; 20056; 20057; 20058;
20059; 20060; 20061; 20062; 20063 20064; 20065; 20066; 20067; 20068; 20069; 20070;
20071; 20073; 20074; 20075 20076; 20077; 20078; 20080; 20081; 20082; 20088; 20090;
20091; 20097; 20098 20201; 20202; 20203; 20204; 20205; 20206; 20207; 20208; 20209;
20210; 20211 20212; 20213; 20214; 20215; 20216; 20217; 20218; 20219; 20220; 20221;
20222 20223; 20224; 20225; 20226; 20227; 20228; 20229; 20230; 20231; 20232; 20233
20235; 20238; 20239; 20240; 20241; 20242; 20244; 20245; 20250; 20251; 20260 20261;
20265; 20266; 20268; 20270; 20277; 20289; 20292; 20299; 20301; 20305 20306; 20307;
20310; 20314; 20317; 20318; 20319; 20324; 20330; 20332; 20333 20334; 20336; 20337;
20338; 20340; 20350; 20360; 20361; 20362; 20363; 20370 20371; 20372; 20373; 20374;
20375; 20376; 20380; 20388; 20389; 20390; 20391 20392; 20393; 20394; 20395; 20396;
20397; 20398; 20401; 20402; 20403; 20404 20405; 20406; 20407; 20408; 20409; 20410;
20411; 20412; 20413; 20414; 20415 20416; 20418; 20419; 20420; 20421; 20422; 20423;
20424; 20425; 20427; 20428 20429; 20430; 20431; 20433; 20434; 20435; 20436; 20437;
20439; 20440; 20441 20442; 20444; 20447; 20451; 20453; 20456; 20460; 20463; 20468;
20469; 20470 20472; 20500; 20501; 20502; 20503; 20504; 20505; 20506; 20507; 20510;
20515 20520; 20521; 20523; 20524; 20525; 20526; 20527; 20530; 20531; 20532; 20533
20534; 20535; 20536; 20537; 20538; 20539; 20540; 20541; 20542; 20543; 20544 20546;
20547; 20548; 20549; 20550; 20551; 20552; 20553; 20554; 20555; 20557 20558; 20559;
20560; 20565; 20566; 20570; 20571; 20572; 20573; 20575; 20576 20577; 20578; 20579;
20580; 20581; 20585; 20586; 20590; 20591; 20593; 20594 20595; 20597; 20599.

Florida

1st District: 32401* (FL 2); 32404* (FL 2); 32405* (FL 2); 32407; 32408 32409* (FL 2);
32413; 32422; 32425; 32427; 32433; 32434; 32439; 32452; 32454 32455; 32459; 32461;
32464; 32466* (FL 2); 32500; 32501; 32502; 32503; 32504 32505; 32506; 32507; 32508;
32509; 32511; 32512; 32513; 32514; 32516; 32520 32521; 32522; 32523; 32524; 32526;
32530; 32531; 32533; 32534; 32535; 32536 32537; 32538; 32540; 32541; 32542; 32544;
32547; 32548; 32549; 32559; 32560 32561; 32562; 32563; 32564; 32565; 32566; 32567;
32568; 32569; 32570; 32571 32572; 32573; 32574; 32575; 32576; 32577; 32578; 32579;
32580; 32581; 32582 32583; 32588; 32589; 32590; 32591; 32592; 32593; 32594; 32595;
32596; 32597 32598.

2nd District: 20529; 32008* (FL 5); 32013; 32040* (FL 3, FL 6); 32052; 32053 32055*
(FL 3); 32056; 32059; 32060; 32062; 32063* (FL 6); 32066; 32071; 32072 32087* (FL 3);
32094; 32096; 32301; 32302; 32303; 32304; 32305; 32306; 32307 32308; 32309; 32310;
32311; 32312; 32313; 32314; 32315; 32316; 32317; 32320 32321; 32322; 32323; 32324;
32326; 32327; 32328; 32329; 32330; 32331; 32332 32333; 32334; 32335; 32336; 32337;
32340; 32343; 32344; 32346; 32347; 32350 32351; 32352; 32353; 32355; 32356; 32357;
32358; 32359; 32360; 32361; 32362 32395; 32399; 32400; 32401* (FL 1); 32402; 32403;
32404* (FL 1); 32405* (FL 1); 32406; 32409* (FL 1); 32410; 32411; 32412; 32417;
32420; 32421; 32423 32424; 32426; 32428; 32430; 32431; 32432; 32437; 32438; 32440;
32442 32443 32444; 32445; 32446; 32447; 32449; 32453; 32456; 32460; 32462; 32463;
32465 32466* (FL 1).

3rd District: 32007; 32033* (FL 4); 32038; 32040* (FL 2, FL 6); 32043* (FL 6) 32055*
(FL 2); 32061; 32073* (FL 6); 32084* (FL 4); 32086* (FL 4); 32087* (FL 2); 32092*
(FL 4); 32095* (FL 4); 32112* (FL 6); 32113* (FL 6); 32114* (FL 4, FL 7); 32117*
(FL 4); 32124* (FL 7); 32125; 32130* (FL 4, FL 7); 32131* (FL 6); 32137* (FL 4);
32139; 32145* (FL 4); 32147* (FL 4); 32174* (FL 4); 32177* (FL 6) 32180* (FL 4); 32190*
(FL 4); 32200; 32201; 32202; 32204* (FL 4); 32205* (FL 4, FL 6); 32206; 32207*
(FL 4); 32208* (FL 4); 32209; 32210* (FL 4, FL 6); 32211* (FL 4); 32212; 32214; 32215;
32216* (FL 4); 32217* (FL 4) 32218* (FL 4); 32219* (FL 6); 32220* (FL 6); 32221*
(FL 6); 32231; 32232 32234* (FL 6); 32244* (FL 4, FL 6); 32246; 32247; 32256* (FL 4);
32259* (FL 4); 32294; 32296; 32601* (FL 5); 32606* (FL 5); 32608* (FL 5); 32609*
(FL 5) 32615* (FL 5); 32616; 32617; 32618* (FL 5); 32634; 32643* (FL 5); 32654 32658;
32662; 32663; 32670* (FL 6); 32671* (FL 6); 32672* (FL 6); 32674* (FL 5, FL 6);
32675* (FL 5, FL 6); 32676* (FL 5, FL 6); 32686* (FL 5); 32696* (FL 5); 32701* (FL 7);
32703* (FL 7, FL 8); 32707* (FL 7); 32712* (FL 8); 32713* (FL 7); 32715; 32716;
32717; 32720* (FL 6, FL 7); 32721; 32723; 32724* (FL 4, FL 7); 32730* (FL 7); 32746*
(FL 7); 32750* (FL 7); 32751* (FL 7, FL 8) 32757* (FL 6, FL 8); 32771* (FL 7); 32772;
32773* (FL 7); 32777; 32779* (FL 7); 32789* (FL 8); 32790; 32791; 32801* (FL 8);
32804* (FL 7, FL 8); 32805* (FL 8); 32806* (FL 8); 32808* (FL 7, FL 8); 32809* (FL 8);
32810* (FL 7, FL 8); 32811* (FL 8); 32818* (FL 7, FL 8); 32819* (FL 8); 32855; 32858;
32890 34470; 34471; 34472; 34473; 34474; 34475; 34476; 34477; 34478; 34479; 34480
34481; 34482; 34761* (FL 8); 34787* (FL 6, FL 8).

4th District: 32004; 32009* (FL 6); 32011; 32033* (FL 3); 32034; 32046; 32082 32084*
(FL 3); 32085; 32086* (FL 3); 32092* (FL 3); 32095* (FL 3); 32097 32099; 32102*
(FL 6); 32105; 32110; 32114* (FL 3, FL 7); 32117* (FL 3); 32118* (FL 7); 32130* (FL 3,
FL 7); 32135; 32136; 32137* (FL 3); 32142; 32145* (FL 3); 32151; 32173; 32174*
(FL 3); 32175; 32176; 32180* (FL 3); 32190* (FL 3); 32204* (FL 3); 32205* (FL 3, FL 6);
32207* (FL 3); 32208* (FL 3); 32210* (FL 3); 32211* (FL 3); 32216* (FL 3);
32217* (FL 3); 32218* (FL 3); 32223; 32224; 32225; 32226; 32227; 32228; 32229; 32233;
32237; 32239; 32240; 32241 32244* (FL 3, FL 6); 32245; 32250; 32254; 32255; 32256*
(FL 3); 32257; 32258 32259* (FL 3); 32266; 32267; 32276; 32297; 32724* (FL 3, FL 7).

5th District: 32008* (FL 2); 32600; 32601* (FL 3); 32602; 32603; 32604; 32605 32606*
(FL 3); 32607; 32608* (FL 3); 32609* (FL 3); 32610; 32611; 32612 32613; 32614; 32615*
(FL 3); 32618* (FL 3); 32619; 32621; 32625; 32626; 32628 32629; 32630* (FL 6, TN 6);
32631; 32633; 32636; 32639; 32642; 32643* (FL 3) 32645; 32646; 32647; 32648; 32649;
32650; 32651; 32652; 32661; 32664; 32665 32667; 32668; 32669; 32673* (FL 6); 32674*
(FL 3, FL 6); 32675* (FL 3, FL 6); 32676* (FL 3, FL 6); 32680; 32681; 32683; 32684;
32686* (FL 3); 32687; 32692 32693; 32694; 32696* (FL 3); 32698; 33513; 33514; 33521;
33525* (FL 9, FL 12) 33538; 33540* (FL 9, FL 12); 33585; 33597* (FL 12); 34423;
34428; 34429 34430; 34431; 34432; 34433; 34436; 34442; 34445; 34446; 34447; 34448;
34449 34450; 34451; 34452; 34453; 34460; 34461; 34464; 34465; 34484; 34487 34498;
34601; 34602; 34605 34606; 34607; 34608; 34609; 34613; 34614; 34636; 34652* (FL 9);

34653* (FL 9); 34654* (FL 9); 34655* (FL 9); 34661; 34667* (FL 9) 34668; 34669*
(FL 9); 34673; 34674; 34679; 34680; 34690* (FL 9); 34691; 34785.

6th District: 32009* (FL 4); 32030; 32040* (FL 2, FL 3); 32042; 32043* (FL 3) 32044;
32050; 32054; 32058; 32063* (FL 2); 32065; 32067; 32068; 32073* (FL 3) 32079; 32083;
32091; 32102* (FL 4); 32111; 32112* (FL 3); 32113* (FL 3) 32131* (FL 3); 32133;
32134; 32138; 32140; 32148; 32149; 32157; 32158; 32159 32160; 32177* (FL 3); 32178;
32179; 32181; 32182; 32185; 32187; 32189; 32192 32193; 32195; 32198; 32205* (FL 3,
FL 4); 32210* (FL 3, FL 4); 32219* (FL 3) 32220* (FL 3); 32221* (FL 3); 32222; 32230;
32234* (FL 3); 32236; 32238 32244* (FL 3, FL 4); 32620; 32622; 32630* (FL 5, TN 6);
32640; 32656; 32666 32670* (FL 3); 32671* (FL 3); 32672* (FL 3); 32673* (FL 5);
32674* (FL 3, FL 5); 32675* (FL 3, FL 5); 32676* (FL 3, FL 5); 32678; 32688; 32691;
32697 32702; 32720* (FL 3, FL 7); 32726; 32727; 32735; 32745; 32749; 32757* (FL 3,
FL 8); 32767; 32776; 32778; 32784; 34420; 34421; 34434; 34488; 34489; 34491 34492;
34705; 34711; 34712; 34729; 34731; 34736; 34737; 34748; 34749; 34753 34755; 34756;
34762; 34787* (FL 3, FL 8); 34788; 34797.

7th District: 32114* (FL 3, FL 4); 32115; 32116; 32118* (FL 4); 32119; 32120 32121;
32122; 32123; 32124* (FL 3); 32127; 32129; 32130* (FL 3, FL 4); 32132 32141; 32168;
32169; 32170; 32701* (FL 3); 32703* (FL 3, FL 8); 32706; 32707* (FL 3); 32708; 32710;
32713* (FL 3); 32714; 32718; 32719; 32720* (FL 3, FL 6) 32722; 32724* (FL 3, FL 4);
32725; 32728; 32730* (FL 3); 32732; 32733; 32738 32744; 32746* (FL 3); 32747; 32750*
(FL 3); 32751* (FL 3, FL 8); 32752; 32754* (FL 15); 32759; 32763; 32764; 32765;
32766; 32771* (FL 3); 32773* (FL 3) 32774; 32779* (FL 3); 32792* (FL 8); 32793;
32795; 32799; 32804* (FL 3, FL 8) 32808* (FL 3, FL 8); 32810* (FL 3, FL 8); 32818*
(FL 3, FL 8); 32860; 33194 33299.

8th District: 32703* (FL 3, FL 7); 32704; 32709; 32712* (FL 3); 32751* (FL 3, FL 7);
32757* (FL 3, FL 6); 32768; 32789* (FL 7); 32792* (FL 7); 32794; 32798 32800; 32801*
(FL 3); 32802; 32803; 32804* (FL 3, FL 7); 32805* (FL 3); 32806* (FL 3); 32807;
32808* (FL 3, FL 7); 32809* (FL 3); 32810* (FL 3, FL 7); 32811* (FL 3); 32812; 32813;
32814; 32816; 32817; 32818* (FL 3, FL 7); 32819* (FL 3) 32820; 32821; 32822; 32823;
32824; 32825; 32826; 32827; 32828; 32829; 32830 32831; 32832; 32833; 32834; 32835;
32836; 32837; 32839; 32853; 32854; 32856 32857; 32859; 32861; 32862; 32867; 32868;
32869; 32872; 32886; 32887; 32889 32891; 32893; 32897; 32898; 32899; 34734; 34740;
34741; 34742; 34743; 34744* (FL 15); 34745; 34746* (FL 15); 34747; 34760; 34761*
(FL 3); 34771* (FL 15) 34777; 34786; 34787* (FL 3, FL 6); 34789.

9th District: 33510* (FL 11); 33524; 33525* (FL 5, FL 12) 33527* (FL 12) 33539;
33540* (FL 5, FL 12); 33541; 33543; 33544; 33549* (FL 11); 33556 33564; 33565*
(FL 12); 33576* (FL 12); 33584* (FL 11); 33592* (FL 11); 33594* (FL 11, FL 12);
33613* (FL 11); 33618* (FL 11); 33624* (FL 11); 33625; 33626 33637* (FL 11); 33647;
34610; 34615; 34616* (FL 10); 34617; 34618* (FL 10) 34619; 34620* (FL 10); 34621;
34622* (FL 10); 34623; 34624* (FL 10); 34625 34629; 34630* (FL 10); 34639; 34652*
(FL 5); 34653* (FL 5); 34654* (FL 5); 34655* (FL 5); 34656; 34660; 34667* (FL 5);
34669* (FL 5); 34677; 34681 34682; 34683; 34684; 34685; 34688; 34689; 34690* (FL 5);
34695; 34697 34698.

10th District: 33504; 33700; 33701; 33702; 33703; 33704; 33705; 33706; 33707 33708;
33709; 33710; 33711; 33712; 33713; 33714; 33715; 33716; 33730 33731 33732; 33733;
33734; 33736; 33737; 33738; 33739; 33740; 33741; 33742; 33743 33784; 34616* (FL 9);
34618* (FL 9); 34620* (FL 9); 34622* (FL 9); 34624* (FL 9); 34630* (FL 9); 34635;
34640; 34641; 34642; 34643; 34644; 34646; 34647 34648; 34649; 34664; 34665; 34666.

11th District: 33509; 33510* (FL 9); 33511* (FL 12); 33534; 33549* (FL 9) 33550;
33569* (FL 12, FL 13); 33572* (FL 13); 33584* (FL 9); 33592* (FL 9) 33594* (FL 9,
FL 12); 33600; 33601; 33602; 33603; 33604; 33605; 33606 33607 33608; 33609; 33610;
33611; 33612; 33613* (FL 9); 33614; 33615; 33616; 33617 33618* (FL 9); 33619; 33620;
33621; 33622; 33623; 33624* (FL 9); 33629; 33630 33631; 33633; 33634; 33635; 33637*
(FL 9); 33660; 33661; 33662; 33672; 33673 33674; 33675; 33677; 33679; 33680; 33681;
33682; 33684; 33685; 33686; 33687 33688; 33690; 33694; 33695; 33697.

12th District: 33503; 33511* (FL 11); 33525* (FL 9); 33526; 33527* (FL 9); 33530;
33537; 33540* (FL 5, FL 9); 33547* (FL 13); 33565* (FL 9); 33566 33567; 33569* (FL 11,
FL 13); 33574; 33576* (FL 9); 33587; 33593; 33594* (FL 9, FL 11); 33597* (FL 5); 33801;
33802; 33803; 33804; 33805; 33806; 33807 33809; 33811; 33813; 33820; 33821; 33823*
(FL 15); 33825* (FL 16); 33827 33830* (FL 15); 33834; 33835; 33837* (FL 15); 33838;
33839; 33840; 33841; 33842 33843; 33844* (FL 15); 33846; 33847; 33849; 33850* (FL 15);
33851 33853* (FL 15); 33854; 33855; 33856; 33860 33863; 33864; 33865; 33867; 33868*
(FL 15); 33870* (FL 16); 33873; 33877; 33880; 33881; 33882; 33883; 33884 33885;
33888; 33890.

13th District: 33547* (FL 12); 33569* (FL 11, FL 12); 33570; 33571; 33572* (FL 11);
33573; 33586; 33598; 33651; 33655; 33938; 33948* (FL 14); 33952* (FL 14) 33953*
(FL 14); 33954; 33955* (FL 14); 33980* (FL 14); 33982* (FL 14); 34201 34202; 34203;
34205; 34206; 34207; 34208; 34209; 34210; 34215; 34216; 34217 34218; 34219; 34220;
34221; 34222; 34223* (FL 14); 34228; 34229; 34230; 34231; 34232 34233; 34234; 34235;
34236; 34237; 34238; 34239 34240; 34241; 34242; 34243; 34250 34251; 34260; 34264;
34270; 34272; 34274 34275; 34276; 34277; 34278; 34280; 34281; 34282; 34284; 34285;
34287; 34292 34293; 34295.

14th District: 33901; 33902; 33903; 33904; 33905; 33906; 33907; 33908; 33909 33910;
33911; 33912; 33913; 33914; 33915; 33916; 33917; 33918; 33919; 33920* (FL 16);
33921; 33922; 33923; 33924; 33925; 33927; 33928; 33929; 33931 33932; 33933;
33934; 33936; 33937; 33939; 33940; 33941; 33942; 33943 33945; 33946; 33947; 33948*
(FL 13); 33949; 33950; 33951; 33952* (FL 13); 33953* (FL 13); 33955* (FL 13); 33956;
33957; 33959; 33961; 33962; 33963; 33964; 33969 33970; 33971; 33980* (FL 13); 33981;
33982* (FL 13); 33990; 33991 33999; 34223* (FL 13); 34224* (FL 13).

15th District: 32754* (FL 7); 32780; 32781; 32782; 32783; 32796; 32815 32901;
32902; 32903; 32904; 32905; 32906; 32907; 32908; 32909; 32910; 32919 32920; 32922;
32923; 32924; 32925; 32926; 32927; 32931; 32932; 32934; 32935 32936; 32937; 32940;
32941; 32948; 32949; 32950; 32951; 32952; 32953; 32954 32955; 32956; 32957; 32958;

32959; 32960; 32961; 32962; 32963; 32964; 32965 32966; 32967; 32968; 32970; 32971; 32976; 32978; 33823* (FL 12); 33830* (FL 12); 33837* (FL 12); 33844* (FL 12); 33845; 33848; 33850* (FL 12); 33853* (FL 12); 33858; 33859; 33868* (FL 12); 34739; 34744* (FL 8); 34746* (FL 8); 34758 34759; 34769; 34770; 34771* (FL 8); 34772; 34773; 34972* (FL 16, FL 23).

16th District: 30182* (GA 7); 33401* (FL 22, FL 23); 33403* (FL 22, FL 23) 33404* (FL 22, FL 23); 33406* (FL 22, FL 23); 33407* (FL 22, FL 23); 33408* (FL 22) 33409* (FL 23); 33410* (FL 22); 33411; 33412; 33413* (FL 23); 33414* (FL 23) 33415* (FL 23) 33417; 33418; 33419; 33430* (FL 23); 33437* (FL 19); 33440* (FL 23); 33455; 33458; 33461* (FL 19, FL 23); 33463* (FL 19); 33467* (FL 19) 33468; 33469; 33470* (FL 23); 33471; 33475; 33477; 33478; 33498* (FL 19) 33825* (FL 12); 33852; 33857; 33870* (FL 12); 33871; 33872; 33920* (FL 14) 33930; 33935; 33944; 33960; 34945* (FL 23); 34946* (FL 23); 34947* (FL 23) 34949; 34950* (FL 23); 34951* (FL 23); 34952; 34953; 34954; 34957 34958 34972* (FL 15, FL 23); 34973; 34974* (FL 23); 34981* (FL 23); 34982; 34983 34984; 34986; 34987* (FL 23); 34990; 34992; 34994; 34995; 34996; 34997.

17th District: 33012* (FL 21); 33013* (FL 21); 33014* (FL 21); 33030* (FL 18, FL 20); 33032* (FL 18, FL 20); 33033* (FL 18, FL 20); 33034* (FL 18, FL 20) 33039 33054; 33055* (FL 20, FL 21); 33056* (FL 20); 33127; 33128* (FL 18) 33129* (FL 18); 33130* (FL 18); 33132* (FL 18, FL 22); 33133* (FL 18); 33134* (FL 18); 33136* (FL 18); 33137* (FL 22); 33138* (FL 22); 33142* (FL 18, FL 21); 33143* (FL 18); 33145* (FL 18); 33146* (FL 18); 33147* (FL 21); 33150* (FL 22); 33151; 33153; 33155* (FL 18); 33157* (FL 18, FL 20); 33160* (FL 22) 33161* (FL 22); 33162* (FL 22, FL 23); 33164; 33167; 33168; 33169* (FL 22, FL 23); 33170* (FL 18, FL 20); 33176* (FL 18, FL 21); 33177* (FL 18, FL 20, FL 21); 33179* (FL 22, FL 23); 33180* (FL 22); 33181* (FL 22); 33186* (FL 18, FL 21); 33189* (FL 18, FL 20); 33190* (FL 18, FL 20); 33238; 33242; 33243; 33247 33257* (FL 18); 33261.

18th District: 33030* (FL 17, FL 20); 33032* (FL 17, FL 20); 33033* (FL 17, FL 20); 33034* (FL 17, FL 20); 33035* (FL 20); 33100; 33101; 33102; 33103; 33104 33109 33111; 33114; 33116; 33122* (FL 21); 33124; 33125; 33126* (FL 17) 33128* (FL 17); 33129* (FL 17); 33130* (FL 17); 33131; 33132* (FL 17, FL 22) 33133* (FL 17); 33135; 33136* (FL 17); 33139* (FL 22); 33142* (FL 17, FL 21); 33143* (FL 17); 33144* (FL 21); 33145* (FL 17); 33146* (FL 17); 33149; 33155* (FL 17); 33156* (FL 20); 33157* (FL 17, FL 20); 33158* (FL 20); 33165* (FL 21); 33170* (FL 17, FL 20); 33173* (FL 21); 33174* (FL 21) 33175* (FL 21); 33176* (FL 17, FL 21); 33177* (FL 17, FL 20, FL 21); 33186* (FL 17, FL 21); 33189* (FL 17, FL 20); 33190* (FL 17, FL 20); 33195; 33197 33200; 33233; 33245; 33255; 33257* (FL 17); 33280; 33283; 33296.

19th District: 33063* (FL 20); 33064* (FL 22, FL 23); 33065; 33066* (FL 23) 33067; 33068* (FL 23); 33069* (FL 23); 33071; 33073* (FL 23); 33075; 33076 33309* (FL 22, FL 23); 33313* (FL 20, FL 23); 33319* (FL 20, FL 23); 33320 33321; 33345; 33349; 33351; 33424; 33426; 33427; 33428; 33429; 33431* (FL 22, FL 23); 33432* (FL 22, FL 23); 33434; 33435* (FL 22, FL 23); 33437* (FL 16); 33441* (FL 22, FL 23); 33442* (FL 23); 33443; 33444* (FL 23); 33445* (FL 22, FL 23); 33446; 33460* (FL 22, FL 23); 33461* (FL 16, FL 23); 33462* (FL 22, FL 23); 33463* (FL 16); 33466; 33467* (FL 16); 33481; 33483* (FL 22, FL 23); 33484; 33486* (FL 23); 33487* (FL 22); 33496; 33498* (FL 16); 33499.

20th District: 33001; 33004* (FL 22, FL 23); 33020* (FL 22, FL 23); 33021* (FL 22, FL 23); 33023* (FL 22, FL 23); 33024; 33025; 33026; 33027; 33028; 33029 33030* (FL 17, FL 18); 33031* (FL 17, FL 18); 33032* (FL 17, FL 18); 33033* (FL 17, FL 18); 33034* (FL 17, FL 18); 33035* (FL 18); 33036; 33037; 33040; 33041; 33042 33043; 33044; 33045; 33050; 33051; 33052; 33055* (FL 17, FL 21); 33056* (FL 17); 33070 33081; 33082; 33083; 33084; 33090; 33092; 33156* (FL 18); 33157* (FL 17, FL 18); 33158* (FL 18); 33170* (FL 17, FL 18); 33177* (FL 17, FL 18, FL 21); 33187* (FL 21); 33189* (FL 17, FL 18); 33190* (FL 17, FL 18); 33196* (FL 21); 33256; 33301* (FL 22, FL 23); 33302; 33312* (FL 23) 33313* (FL 19, FL 23); 33314; 33315* (FL 23) 33316* (FL 22, FL 23); 33317* (FL 23); 33318; 33319* (FL 19, FL 23); 33322; 33323; 33324; 33325; 33326 33327; 33328; 33329; 33330; 33331; 33332; 33336; 33337; 33388.

21st District: 33010; 33011; 33012* (FL 17); 33013* (FL 17); 33014* (FL 17) 33015; 33016; 33017; 33055* (FL 17, FL 20); 33107; 33108; 33110; 33122* (FL 18); 33126* (FL 18); 33142* (FL 17, FL 18); 33144* (FL 18); 33147* (FL 17) 33148; 33152; 33159 33165* (FL 18); 33166; 33172; 33173* (FL 18); 33174* (FL 18); 33175* (FL 18); 33176* (FL 17, FL 18); 33177* (FL 17, FL 18, FL 20) 33178; 33182; 33183; 33184; 33185; 33186* (FL 17, FL 18); 33187* (FL 20) 33188; 33192; 33193; 33196* (FL 20); 33199; 33265; 33266.

22nd District: 33004* (FL 20, FL 23); 33008; 33009* (FL 23); 33019; 33020* (FL 20, FL 23); 33021* (FL 20, FL 23); 33022; 33023* (FL 20, FL 23); 33060* (FL 23); 33062; 33064* (FL 19, FL 23); 33072; 33119; 33121; 33132* (FL 17, FL 18) 33137* (FL 17); 33138* (FL 17); 33139* (FL 18); 33140; 33141; 33150* (FL 17) 33154 33160* (FL 17); 33161* (FL 17); 33162* (FL 17); 33163; 33169* (FL 17, FL 23); 33179* (FL 17, FL 23); 33180* (FL 17); 33181* (FL 17); 33301* (FL 20, FL 23); 33303; 33304* (FL 23); 33305* (FL 23); 33306; 33307; 33308 33309* (FL 19, FL 23); 33311* (FL 23); 33316* (FL 20, FL 23); 33334* (FL 23); 33335; 33338; 33339; 33394; 33401* (FL 16, FL 23) 33403* (FL 16, FL 23); 33404* (FL 16, FL 23); 33405* (FL 23) 33406* (FL 16, FL 23); 33408* (FL 16) 33410* (FL 16); 33420; 33431* (FL 19, FL 23); 33432* (FL 19, FL 23); 33435* (FL 19, FL 23); 33441* (FL 19, FL 23); 33460* (FL 19, FL 23); 33462* (FL 19, FL 23); 33480; 33483* (FL 19, FL 23); 33487* (FL 19).

23rd District: 33004* (FL 20, FL 22); 33009* (FL 22); 33020* (FL 20, FL 22) 33021* (FL 20, FL 22); 33023* (FL 20, FL 22); 33060* (FL 22); 33061; 33064* (FL 19, FL 22); 33066* (FL 19); 33069* (FL 19); 33073* (FL 19); 33074; 33077; 33162* (FL 17, FL 22); 33169* (FL 17, FL 22); 33179* (FL 17, FL 22); 33269; 33300; 33301* (FL 20, FL 22); 33304* (FL 22); 33305* (FL 22); 33309* (FL 19, FL 22); 33310; 33311* (FL 22); 33312* (FL 20); 33313* (FL 19, FL 20); 33315* (FL 20); 33316* (FL 20, FL 22); 33317* (FL 20); 33319* (FL 19, FL 20); 33334* (FL 22); 33340; 33350; 33401* (FL 16, FL 22); 33402; 33403* (FL 16, FL 22); 33404* (FL 16, FL 22); 33405* (FL 22) 33406* (FL 16, FL 22) 33407* (FL 16); 33409* (FL 16); 33413* (FL 16); 33414* (FL 16); 33415 33416; 33425; 33430* (FL 16); 33431* (FL 19, FL 22); 33432* (FL 19, FL 22); 33435* (FL 19, FL 22); 33438; 33439; 33440* (FL 16); 33441* (FL 19, FL 22); 33442* (FL 19); 33444* (FL 19); 33445* (FL 19); 33447; 33459; 33460* (FL 19, FL 22); 33461* (FL 16, FL 19); 33462* (FL 19, FL 22); 33464; 33465; 33470* (FL 16); 33476; 33483* (FL 19, FL 22); 33486* (FL 19); 33491; 33493; 33495* (FL 16); 34946* (FL 16); 34947* (FL 16); 34948; 34950* (FL 16); 34951* (FL 16); 34956; 34972* (FL 15, FL 16); 34974* (FL 16); 34979; 34981* (FL 16) 34985; 34987* (FL 16); 34988.

Georgia

1st District: 30401; 30410; 30412; 30414; 30415; 30417; 30420; 30421; 30423 30425; 30427; 30429; 30436; 30438; 30439; 30445; 30447; 30448; 30450; 30451; 30452; 30453; 30458; 30459; 30460; 30464; 30466; 30470; 30471; 30473; 30474 30499; 31002; 31301; 31302; 31303; 31304; 31305; 31307; 31308; 31309; 31312 31313; 31314; 31316; 31318; 31319; 31320; 31321; 31322; 31323; 31324; 31326 31327; 31328; 31329; 31331; 31332; 31333; 31401* (GA 11); 31402; 31403; 31404* (GA 11); 31405* (GA 11); 31406* (GA 11); 31407; 31408* (GA 11); 31409; 31410 31411; 31412; 31416; 31418; 31419; 31420; 31498; 31499; 31501; 31502; 31503 31510; 31513; 31516; 31518; 31520; 31521; 31522; 31523; 31524; 31525; 31527 31537; 31542; 31543; 31545; 31547; 31548; 31550; 31551; 31552; 31553; 31555 31556; 31557; 31558; 31560; 31561; 31563; 31564; 31565; 31566; 31568; 31569 31646.

2nd District: 30218; 30222* (GA 3); 30251* (GA 3); 30293* (GA 3); 31006 31007; 31008* (GA 3); 31015* (GA 8); 31025; 31028* (GA 8); 31030* (GA 3) 31036* (GA 8); 31039; 31041; 31051; 31057; 31058; 31063; 31066* (GA 8); 31068 31069* (GA 8); 31070; 31076; 31078* (GA 8); 31081; 31088* (GA 8); 31091 31092; 31093* (GA 8); 31098* (GA 8); 31099; 31200; 31201* (GA 3, GA 8); 31204* (GA 8); 31206* (GA 8); 31210* (GA 3, GA 8); 31211* (GA 3, GA 8); 31298* (GA 8); 31299; 31601* (GA 8); 31602* (GA 8); 31625; 31626; 31629; 31632* (GA 8); 31636* (GA 8); 31638; 31643 31700; 31701* (GA 8); 31702; 31703; 31705* (GA 8); 31706; 31707* (GA 8); 31708* (GA 8); 31709; 31710; 31711; 31713; 31715 31716; 31717; 31720; 31723; 31724; 31725 31726; 31728; 31729; 31730; 31732 31734; 31735; 31736; 31737; 31738; 31739; 31740 31741; 31742; 31743; 31745 31746; 31751; 31752; 31754; 31759; 31761; 31762; 31763* (GA 8); 31764; 31765; 31766; 31767; 31768* (GA 8); 31770; 31773; 31777; 31778 31779; 31780; 31784 31785; 31786; 31787; 31792; 31797; 31799; 31801* (GA 3); 31803 31805; 31806; 31810; 31812; 31814; 31815; 31816* (GA 3); 31820* (GA 3); 31821; 31824; 31825 31827; 31832; 31836; 31900; 31901* (GA 3); 31902; 31903; 31904* (GA 3); 31905 31906* (GA 3); 31907* (GA 3); 31993* (GA 3); 31994* (GA 3); 31995* (GA 3) 31997; 31998.

3rd District: 30027* (GA 11); 30049* (GA 4, GA 11); 30050* (GA 5); 30051 30204; 30205; 30206; 30212; 30213* (GA 5); 30214; 30220; 30222* (GA 2); 30223 30224; 30228; 30229; 30230* (GA 7); 30232; 30233* (GA 11); 30234* (GA 11); 30236; 30237; 30248* (GA 11); 30250; 30251* (GA 2); 30253* (GA 4, GA 11) 30254; 30256; 30257; 30258; 30259; 30260; 30263; 30264; 30265; 30266; 30268* (GA 5); 30269; 30273; 30274* (GA 5); 30275; 30276; 30277; 30281* (GA 4, GA 11); 30283; 30284; 30285; 30286; 30287; 30289; 30292; 30293* (GA 2) 30295; 30296* (GA 5, GA 6); 30320; 30337* (GA 5); 30349* (GA 5); 30354* (GA 5); 31004; 31008* (GA 2); 31016; 31029; 31030* (GA 2); 31031* (GA 11); 31032 31033; 31034; 31038* (GA 11); 31046; 31050; 31052* (GA 2); 31061* (GA 11) 31078* (GA 2); 31086; 31097; 31201* (GA 2, GA 8); 31210* (GA 2, GA 8); 31211* (GA 2, GA 8); 31801* (GA 2); 31804; 31807; 31808; 31811; 31816* (GA 2); 31820* (GA 2); 31822* (GA 7); 31823; 31826; 31829 31830; 31831; 31833* (GA 7) 31901* (GA 2); 31904* (GA 2); 31906* (GA 2); 31907* (GA 2); 31908; 31909 31993* (GA 2); 31994* (GA 2); 31995* (GA 2); 31999.

4th District: 30002* (GA 11); 30021* (GA 11); 30030* (GA 5, GA 11); 30031 30032* (GA 11); 30033; 30035* (GA 11); 30036; 30049* (GA 3, GA 11); 30058* (GA 11); 30071* (GA 6); 30072; 30079* (GA 11); 30083* (GA 11); 30084* (GA 11) 30085; 30086; 30087* (GA 11); 30088* (GA 11); 30091; 30092* (GA 6); 30093 30136* (GA 6, GA 9); 30158; 30174* (GA 6, GA 9, GA 10); 30207* (GA 10, GA 11) 30208* (GA 10); 30209* (GA 10); 30221* (GA 10); 30226; 30243* (GA 6, GA 10) 30244* (GA 6); 30245* (GA 6, GA 10); 30246; 30247; 30249* (GA 10); 30253* (GA 3, GA 11); 30278; 30281* (GA 3, GA 11); 30305* (GA 5); 30306* (GA 5); 30307* (GA 5); 30309* (GA 5); 30317* (GA 5, GA 11); 30319* (GA 5, GA 6); 30322 30324* (GA 5); 30329; 30338* (GA 5, GA 6); 30340* (GA 6); 30341* (GA 6); 30345; 30347; 30359; 30360* (GA 6); 30362; 30366; 30376; 39901.

5th District: 30001* (GA 6, GA 7); 30030* (GA 4, GA 11); 30050* (GA 3); 30059* (GA 6, GA 7); 30089; 30213* (GA 3); 30268* (GA 3); 30272; 30274* (GA 3) 30291; 30296* (GA 3, GA 6); 30301; 30302; 30303; 30304; 30305* (GA 4); 30306* (GA 4); 30307* (GA 4); 30308* (GA 4); 30309* (GA 4); 30310; 30311; 30313 30314; 30315* (GA 11); 30316* (GA 11); 30317* (GA 4, GA 11); 30318; 30319* (GA 4, GA 6); 30321; 30323; 30324* (GA 4); 30325; 30326; 30327; 30328* (GA 6) 30330; 30331* (GA 7) 30332; 30333; 30334; 30335; 30336* (GA 7); 30337* (GA 4, GA 6); 30338* (GA 4, GA 5); 30339* (GA 6); 30342; 30343; 30344; 30348; 30349* (GA 3); 30350* (GA 6); 30351 30352; 30353; 30354* (GA 3); 30355; 30357; 30358 30361; 30363; 30364; 30365; 30367 30368; 30369; 30370; 30371; 30374; 30375 30377; 30378; 30379; 30380; 30381; 30383 30384; 30385; 30386; 30387; 30388 30390; 30392; 30394; 30396; 30398; 31119 31131; 31139; 31150; 31156 31193; 31195; 31196; 31197; 31198; 31199.

6th District: 30001* (GA 5, GA 7); 30007; 30059* (GA 5, GA 7); 30060* (GA 7) 30062* (GA 7); 30064* (GA 7); 30065; 30066; 30067; 30068; 30071* (GA 4) 30073* (GA 7); 30075; 30076; 30077; 30080* (GA 7); 30081; 30082* (GA 7) 30092* (GA 4); 30101* (GA 7); 30102; 30114* (GA 9); 30130* (GA 9); 30132* (GA 7); 30136* (GA 4, GA 9); 30144* (GA 7); 30159; 30174* (GA 4, GA 9, GA 10) 30188* (GA 9); 30198; 30199; 30201* (GA 9); 30202* (GA 4, GA 9); 30239 30243* (GA 4, GA 10); 30244* (GA 4); 30245* (GA 4, GA 10); 30296* (GA 3, GA 5); 30319* (GA 4, GA 5); 30328* (GA 5) 30338* (GA 4, GA 5); 30339* (GA 5); 30340* (GA 4); 30341* (GA 4); 30346; 30350* (GA 5); 30356; 30360* (GA 4); 30388; 30518* (GA 9, GA 10).

7th District: 30001* (GA 5, GA 6); 30020; 30057; 30059* (GA 5, GA 6); 30060*

(GA 6); 30061; 30062* (GA 6); 30063; 30064* (GA 6); 30069; 30073* (GA 6) 30080* (GA 6); 30082* (GA 6); 30090; 30101* (GA 6); 30103* (GA 9); 30104 30105* (GA 9); 30108; 30109; 30110; 30113; 30117; 30118; 30119; 30120; 30123 30124; 30125; 30129; 30132* (GA 6); 30133; 30134; 30135; 30137; 30138; 30139* (GA 9); 30140; 30141; 30144* (GA 6); 30145; 30147; 30149; 30150; 30153; 30161 30162; 30163; 30164; 30165; 30170; 30171* (GA 9); 30172; 30173; 30176; 30178 30179; 30180; 30182* (FL 16); 30184* (GA 9); 30185; 30187; 30217; 30230* (GA 3); 30240; 30241; 30261; 30331* (GA 5); 30336* (GA 5); 30701* (GA 9); 30730 30731* (GA 9); 30747; 30753; 31822* (GA 3); 31833* (GA 3).

8th District: 30411; 30428; 30454; 30457; 31001; 31005; 31009; 31011; 31012 31013; 31014; 31015* (GA 2); 31019 31020* (GA 11); 31021; 31022; 31023 31026; 31028* (GA 2); 31036* (GA 2); 31037; 31040; 31044* (GA 11); 31047 31049; 31052* (GA 3); 31055; 31060; 31065; 31066* (GA 2); 31067* (GA 11) 31069* (GA 2); 31071; 31072; 31073; 31075; 31077; 31079; 31083; 31084; 31088* (GA 2); 31093* (GA 2); 31095; 31096; 31098* (GA 2); 31201* (GA 3); 31202; 31203; 31204* (GA 2); 31205; 31206* (GA 2); 31207; 31208; 31209; 31210* (GA 2, GA 3); 31211* (GA 2, GA 3); 31212; 31213; 31294; 31295; 31296; 31297 31298* (GA 2); 31512; 31519; 31532; 31533; 31539; 31544; 31549; 31554; 31567 31601* (GA 2); 31602* (GA 2); 31603; 31604; 31620; 31622; 31623; 31624; 31627 31630; 31631; 31632* (GA 2); 31634; 31635; 31636* (GA 2); 31637; 31639; 31641 31642; 31645; 31647; 31648; 31649; 31650; 31698; 31699; 31701* (GA 2); 31704 31705* (GA 2); 31707* (GA 2); 31708* (GA 2); 31712; 31714; 31722; 31727 31733; 31744; 31747; 31749; 31750; 31753; 31756; 31760; 31763* (GA 2); 31768* (GA 2); 31769; 31771; 31772; 31774; 31775; 31776; 31781; 31782; 31783; 31789 31790; 31791; 31793; 31794; 31795; 31796; 31798.

9th District: 30103* (GA 7); 30105* (GA 7); 30107; 30114* (GA 6); 30130* (GA 6); 30131; 30136* (GA 4, GA 6); 30139* (GA 7); 30142; 30143; 30146; 30148 30151; 30171* (GA 7); 30174* (GA 4, GA 6, GA 10); 30175; 30177; 30183; 30184* (GA 7); 30188* (GA 6); 30201* (GA 6); 30202* (GA 6); 30501; 30502; 30503 30504; 30505; 30506; 30507; 30510* (GA 10); 30511* (GA 10); 30512; 30513 30517* (GA 10); 30518* (GA 6, GA 10); 30522; 30523; 30525; 30527; 30528 30531; 30533; 30534; 30535; 30537; 30538* (GA 9); 30539; 30540; 30541; 30542 30543; 30544; 30545; 30546; 30552; 30554; 30555; 30557; 30559; 30560; 30562 30563; 30564; 30566; 30567* (GA 10); 30568; 30571; 30572; 30573; 30575* (GA 10); 30576; 30577; 30580; 30581; 30582; 30596; 30597; 30598; 30701* (GA 7) 30703; 30705; 30707; 30708; 30710; 30711; 30720; 30721; 30722; 30724; 30725 30726; 30728; 30731* (GA 7); 30732; 30733; 30734; 30735; 30736; 30738 30739 30740; 30741; 30742; 30746; 30750; 30751; 30752; 30755; 30756; 30757.

10th District: 30174* (GA 4, GA 6, GA 9); 30203; 30207* (GA 4, GA 11); 30208* (GA 4); 30209* (GA 4); 30211; 30221* (GA 4); 30235; 30243* (GA 4, GA 6) 30245* (GA 4, GA 6); 30249* (GA 4); 30255* (GA 11); 30262* (GA 11); 30267 30270; 30279; 30510* (GA 9); 30511* (GA 9); 30516; 30517* (GA 9); 30518* (GA 6, GA 9); 30520; 30521; 30529; 30538* (GA 9); 30547; 30548; 30549; 30553 30558; 30565; 30567* (GA 9); 30575* (GA 9); 30599; 30601; 30602; 30603; 30604 30605; 30606; 30607; 30608; 30609; 30610; 30612; 30613; 30619; 30620; 30621 30622; 30623; 30624; 30625* (GA 11); 30627; 30628; 30629; 30630; 30633; 30634 30635; 30638; 30639; 30641; 30643; 30645; 30646; 30647; 30648; 30650* (GA 11) 30655; 30660; 30662; 30663; 30666; 30667; 30668; 30671; 30673* (GA 1); 30677 30680; 30683; 30802; 30805; 30806; 30808; 30809; 30812; 30813; 30814; 30815* (GA 11); 30817; 30824; 30900; 30901* (GA 11); 30904* (GA 11); 30905; 30906* (GA 11); 30907; 30909* (GA 11); 30914; 30916; 30917; 30919.

11th District: 30002* (GA 4); 30021* (GA 4); 30027* (GA 3); 30030* (GA 4, GA 5); 30032* (GA 4); 30034; 30035* (GA 4); 30037; 30038; 30049* (GA 3, GA 4) 30058* (GA 4); 30074; 30079* (GA 4); 30083* (GA 4); 30084* (GA 4); 30087* (GA 4); 30088* (GA 4); 30207* (GA 4, GA 10); 30216; 30233* (GA 3); 30234* (GA 3) 30248* (GA 3); 30253* (GA 3, GA 4); 30255* (GA 10); 30262* (GA 10); 30281* (GA 3, GA 4); 30315* (GA 5); 30316* (GA 5); 30317* (GA 4, GA 5); 30413; 30424 30426; 30434; 30441; 30442; 30446; 30449; 30455; 30456; 30467; 30477; 30625* (GA 10); 30631; 30642 30650* (GA 10); 30664; 30665; 30669; 30673* (GA 10); 30678; 30803; 30807; 30810 30811; 30815* (GA 10); 30816; 30818; 30819; 30820 30821; 30822; 30823; 30828 30830; 30833; 30901* (GA 10); 30903; 30904* (GA 10); 30906* (GA 10); 30909* (GA 10); 30910; 30911; 30912; 30913; 30999; 31003 31017; 31018; 31020* (GA 8); 31024; 31031* (GA 3); 31035; 31038* (GA 3) 31042; 31044* (GA 8); 31045; 31054; 31061* (GA 3); 31062; 31064; 31067* (GA 8) 31082; 31085; 31087; 31089; 31090; 31094* (GA 1); 31400; 31401* (GA 1); 31404* (GA 1); 31405* (GA 1); 31406* (GA 1); 31408* (GA 1); 31414.

Hawaii

1st District: 96701; 96706* (HI 2); 96782; 96789; 96801; 96802; 96803; 96804 96805; 96806; 96807; 96808; 96809; 96810; 96811; 96812; 96813; 96814; 96815 96816; 96817; 96818* (HI 2); 96819; 96820; 96821; 96822; 96823; 96824; 96825* (HI 2); 96826; 96827; 96828; 96830; 96835; 96836; 96837; 96838; 96839; 96840 96841; 96842; 96843; 96844; 96845; 96846; 96847; 96848; 96849; 96850; 96853 96858; 96859; 96860; 96861; 96898.

2nd District: 96703; 96704; 96705; 96706* (HI 1); 96707; 96708; 96710; 96712 96713; 96714; 96715; 96716; 96717; 96718; 96719; 96720; 96721; 96722; 96725 96726; 96727; 96728; 96729; 96730; 96731; 96732; 96733; 96734; 96739; 96740 96741; 96742; 96743; 96744; 96745; 96746; 96747; 96748; 96749; 96750; 96751 96752; 96753; 96754; 96755; 96756; 96757; 96759; 96760; 96761; 96762; 96763 96764; 96765; 96766; 96767; 96768; 96769; 96770; 96771; 96772; 96773; 96774 96775; 96776; 96777; 96778; 96779; 96780; 96781; 96784; 96785; 96786; 96788 96790; 96791; 96792; 96793; 96795; 96796; 96797; 96818* (HI 1); 96825* (HI 1); 96854; 96857; 96862; 96863.

Idaho

1st District: 83501; 83520; 83522; 83523; 83524; 83525; 83526; 83530; 83531 83533;

83534; 83535; 83536; 83537; 83538; 83539; 83540; 83541; 83542; 83543 83544; 83545; 83546; 83547; 83548; 83549; 83551; 83552; 83553; 83554; 83555 83602; 83604; 83605; 83606; 83610; 83611; 83612; 83615; 83616; 83617; 83619 83620; 83622; 83624; 83626; 83628; 83629; 83630; 83631; 83632; 83634; 83635 83636; 83637; 83638; 83639; 83641; 83642; 83643; 83644; 83645; 83650; 83651 83652; 83653; 83654; 83655; 83656; 83657; 83660; 83661; 83666; 83669; 83670 83671; 83672; 83676; 83677; 83680; 83686; 83687; 83702* (ID 2); 83703* (ID 2) 83704; 83705* (ID 2); 83706* (ID 2); 83709; 83711; 83714; 83715; 83725; 83726 83731; 83732; 83744; 83801; 83802; 83803; 83804; 83805; 83806; 83808; 83809 83810; 83811; 83812; 83813; 83814; 83816; 83821; 83822; 83823; 83824; 83825 83826; 83827; 83830; 83832; 83833; 83834; 83835; 83836; 83837; 83839; 83840 83841; 83842; 83843; 83845; 83846; 83847; 83848; 83849; 83850; 83851; 83852 83853; 83854; 83855; 83856; 83857; 83858; 83860; 83861; 83862; 83864; 83865 83866; 83867; 83868; 83869; 83870; 83871; 83872; 83873; 83874; 83876.

2nd District: 83120* (WY 1); 83201; 83202; 83203; 83204; 83205; 83206; 83209 83210; 83211; 83212; 83213; 83214; 83215; 83217; 83218; 83220; 83221; 83223 83226; 83227; 83228; 83229; 83230; 83231; 83232; 83233; 83234; 83235; 83236 83237; 83238; 83239; 83241; 83243; 83244; 83245; 83246; 83250; 83251; 83252 83253; 83254; 83255; 83256; 83260; 83261; 83262; 83263; 83271; 83272; 83274 83276; 83277; 83278; 83280; 83281; 83283; 83285; 83286; 83287; 83301; 83302 83303; 83311; 83312; 83313; 83314; 83316; 83318; 83320; 83321; 83322; 83323 83324; 83325; 83326; 83327; 83328; 83330; 83332; 83333; 83334; 83335; 83336 83337; 83338; 83340; 83341; 83342; 83343; 83344; 83347; 83348; 83349 83350; 83352; 83353; 83354; 83355; 83401; 83402; 83403; 83404; 83405; 83406 83415; 83420; 83421; 83422; 83423; 83424; 83425; 83427; 83428; 83429; 83431 83433; 83434; 83435; 83436; 83437; 83438; 83440; 83441; 83442; 83443; 83444 83445; 83446; 83447; 83448; 83449; 83450; 83451; 83452; 83454; 83455; 83460 83462; 83463; 83464; 83465; 83466; 83467; 83468; 83469; 83601; 83623; 83627 83633; 83647; 83648; 83700; 83701; 83702* (ID 1); 83703* (ID 1); 83705* (ID 1); 83706* (ID 1); 83707; 83708; 83712; 83719; 83720; 83721; 83722; 83723 83724; 83727; 83728; 83729; 83730; 83733; 83735; 83756; 83757; 83788.

Illinois

1st District: 60406* (IL 2); 60453* (IL 3); 60609* (IL 4, IL 7); 60615* (IL 7); 60616* (IL 4, IL 7); 60617* (IL 2, IL 11); 60619; 60620* (IL 2); 60621* (IL 2, IL 7); 60628* (IL 2); 60629* (IL 3, IL 4); 60632* (IL 3, IL 4); 60636* (IL 2, IL 4); 60637* (IL 7); 60642; 60643* (IL 2); 60649* (IL 2); 60652* (IL 3); 60653* (IL 7); 60655; 60658* (IL 2, IL 3).

2nd District: 60406* (IL 1); 60409* (IL 11); 60411* (IL 11); 60419; 60422* (IL 10); 60423* (IL 11); 60425* (IL 7, IL 10); 60426* (IL 3, IL 11); 60429; 60430* (IL 11); 60443* (IL 11); 60445* (IL 3); 60452* (IL 3); 60461; 60466* (IL 11) 60469; 60472; 60473* (IL 11); 60476* (IL 11); 60477* (IL 3, IL 11, IL 13) 60478* (IL 3); 60617* (IL 1, IL 11); 60620* (IL 1); 60621* (IL 1, IL 7) 60627; 60628* (IL 1); 60633* (IL 11); 60636* (IL 1, IL 4); 60643* (IL 1) 60649* (IL 1); 60658* (IL 1, IL 3).

3rd District: 60130* (IL 7); 60304* (IL 4, IL 7); 60402; 60415; 60426* (IL 2, IL 11); 60445* (IL 2); 60452* (IL 2); 60453* (IL 1); 60454; 60455; 60456 60457* (IL 2); 60458; 60459* (IL 13); 60462* (IL 13); 60463* (IL 13); 60464* (IL 13) 60465* (IL 13); 60477* (IL 2, IL 11, IL 13); 60478* (IL 2); 60480* (IL 13) 60482; 60499; 60501; 60513* (IL 6); 60521* (IL 6, IL 13); 60525* (IL 6) 60526; 60534; 60546* (IL 7); 60558* (IL 6); 60629* (IL 1, IL 4); 60632* (IL 1, IL 4); 60638* (IL 4, IL 7); 60644* (IL 4, IL 7); 60650* (IL 4, IL 7); 60652* (IL 1); 60658* (IL 1, IL 2).

4th District: 60141; 60154* (IL 6, IL 7); 60160* (IL 5, IL 7); 60162* (IL 6, IL 7); 60164* (IL 5); 60165; 60304* (IL 3, IL 7); 60608* (IL 7); 60609* (IL 1, IL 7); 60612* (IL 7); 60614* (IL 5, IL 7, IL 9); 60616* (IL 1, IL 7); 60618* (IL 5); 60622* (IL 5, IL 7); 60623* (IL 7); 60625* (IL 5, IL 9); 60629* (IL 1, IL 3); 60632* (IL 1, IL 3); 60635* (IL 5); 60636* (IL 1, IL 2); 60639* (IL 5, IL 7); 60641* (IL 5); 60644* (IL 3, IL 7); 60647* (IL 5); 60650* (IL 3, IL 7); 60651* (IL 7); 60657* (IL 5, IL 9); 60668; 60672; 60691; 60799.

5th District: 60009; 60068* (IL 6, IL 9); 60128; 60131* (IL 6); 60132; 60155 60158; 60160* (IL 4, IL 7); 60161; 60164* (IL 4); 60171* (IL 7); 60176* (IL 6); 60197; 60198; 60199; 60251; 60351; 60352; 60353; 60610* (IL 7); 60611* (IL 7); 60613* (IL 9); 60614* (IL 4, IL 7, IL 9); 60618* (IL 4); 60622* (IL 4, IL 7); 60625* (IL 4, IL 9); 60630* (IL 9); 60631* (IL 9); 60634; 60635* (IL 4, IL 7); 60639* (IL 4, IL 7); 60640* (IL 9); 60641* (IL 4); 60646* (IL 9); 60647* (IL 4); 60656* (IL 6, IL 9); 60657* (IL 4, IL 9); 60659* (IL 9); 60661.

6th District: 60005* (IL 8, IL 10); 60007* (IL 8); 60008* (IL 8); 60016* (IL 9, IL 10); 60017; 60018; 60019; 60025* (IL 8, IL 9, IL 10); 60056* (IL 8, IL 10); 60068* (IL 5, IL 9); 60100; 60101; 60103* (IL 8, IL 14); 60105; 60106 60108; 60114; 60116; 60125; 60126* (IL 7); 60131* (IL 5); 60137* (IL 13) 60138; 60139; 60143; 60148* (IL 13); 60149; 60154* (IL 4, IL 7); 60157; 60162* (IL 4, IL 7); 60172* (IL 8, IL 14); 60173* (IL 8); 60176* (IL 5); 60181* (IL 13); 60187* (IL 13, IL 14); 60188* (IL 14); 60189; 60190* (IL 14); 60191 60196; 60302* (IL 7); 60513* (IL 3); 60515* (IL 13); 60521* (IL 3, IL 13) 60525* (IL 3); 60558* (IL 3); 60559* (IL 13); 60599; 60648* (IL 9); 60656* (IL 5, IL 9); 6066.

7th District: 60104; 60126* (IL 6); 60130* (IL 3); 60153; 60154* (IL 4, IL 6) 60160* (IL 4, IL 5); 60162* (IL 4, IL 6); 60163; 60171* (IL 5); 60301; 60302* (IL 6); 60303; 60304* (IL 3, IL 4); 60305; 60425* (IL 2, IL 11); 60546* (IL 3); 60600 60601; 60602; 60603; 60604; 60606; 60607; 60608* (IL 4); 60609* (IL 1, IL 4); 60610* (IL 5); 60611* (IL 5); 60612* (IL 4); 60614* (IL 4, IL 5, IL 9); 60615* (IL 1); 60616* (IL 1, IL 4); 60621* (IL 1, IL 2); 60622* (IL 4, IL 5); 60623* (IL 4); 60624; 60635* (IL 4, IL 5); 60637* (IL 1); 60639* (IL 4, IL 5); 60644* (IL 3, IL 4); 60650* (IL 3, IL 4); 60651* (IL 4); 60653* (IL 1); 60654; 60663; 60664; 60665; 60667; 60669; 60670; 60671; 60673 60675; 60679; 60680; 60681; 60684; 60685; 60687; 60690; 60693; 60694; 60697 60699; 60701.

8th District: 60000; 60002; 60004* (IL 6); 60005* (IL 6, IL 10); 60007* (IL 6); 60008* (IL 6); 60010* (IL 16); 60011; 60013* (IL 16); 60020; 60025* (IL 6, IL 9, IL 10); 60030* (IL 10); 60031* (IL 10); 60038; 60041; 60042* (IL 16) 60046; 60047; 60048* (IL 10); 60049; 60050* (IL 16); 60055; 60056* (IL 6, IL 10); 60060* (IL 10); 60067; 60073;

60074* (IL 11); 60075; 60078; 60081* (IL 16); 60083; 60084; 60085* (IL 10); 60087* (IL 10); 60094; 60095; 60099* (IL 10); 60103* (IL 6, IL 14); 60107; 60118* (IL 14); 60120* (IL 14); 60159 60168; 60172* (IL 6, IL 14); 60173* (IL 6); 60179; 60192; 60193; 60194; 60195.

9th District: 60016* (IL 6, IL 10); 60025* (IL 6, IL 8, IL 10); 60029; 60053 60068* (IL 5, IL 6); 60076* (IL 10); 60077* (IL 10); 60201* (IL 10); 60202 60203; 60204; 60208 60209; 60613* (IL 5); 60614* (IL 4, IL 5, IL 7); 60625* (IL 4, IL 5); 60626; 60630* (IL 5); 60631* (IL 5); 60640* (IL 5); 60645 60646* (IL 5); 60648* (IL 6); 60656* (IL 5, IL 6); 60657* (IL 4, IL 5); 60659* (IL 5); 60660; 60678; 60714.

10th District: 60004* (IL 8); 60005* (IL 6, IL 8); 60006; 60015; 60016* (IL 6, IL 9); 60022; 60025* (IL 6, IL 8, IL 9); 60026; 60030* (IL 8); 60031* (IL 8) 60035; 60037; 60040; 60043; 60044; 60045; 60048* (IL 8); 60056* (IL 6, IL 8) 60060* (IL 8); 60061; 60062; 60063; 60064; 60065; 60069; 60070; 60076* (IL 9) 60077* (IL 9); 60079; 60082; 60085* (IL 8); 60087* (IL 8); 60088 60089; 60090; 60091; 60092; 60093; 60096; 60099* (IL 8); 60201* (IL 9); 60422* (IL 2).

11th District: 60074* (IL 8); 60401; 60407; 60408; 60409* (IL 2); 60410 60411* (IL 2); 60416; 60417; 60421; 60423* (IL 2); 60424; 60425* (IL 2, 7) 60426* (IL 2, IL 3); 60430* (IL 2); 60431; 60432; 60433; 60434; 60435* (IL 13, IL 14); 60436* (IL 13); 60437; 60438; 60441* (IL 13); 60442; 60443* (IL 2) 60444; 60447* (IL 14); 60448* (IL 13); 60449; 60450; 60451; 60466* (IL 2) 60468; 60470; 60471; 60473* (IL 2); 60474; 60475; 60476* (IL 2); 60477* (IL 2, IL 3, IL 13); 60479; 60481; 60541* (IL 14); 60549* (IL 14); 60551* (IL 14) 60557; 60617* (IL 1, IL 2); 60633* (IL 2); 60901* (IL 15); 60902; 60910 60913; 60914; 60915; 60917* (IL 15); 60935; 60940; 60944; 60950; 60954; 60961* (IL 15); 60964; 60969; 61301; 61316; 61321; 61325; 61332; 61334; 61341; 61342* (IL 14); 61348; 61350* (IL 14); 61354* (IL 14, IL 17); 61358; 61360; 61364* (IL 15); 61370; 61372; 61373.

12th District: 62002* (IL 20); 62010* (IL 20); 62018* (IL 20); 62024* (IL 20) 62035* (IL 20); 62040* (IL 20); 62048; 62059; 62060; 62071; 62084; 62087 62090; 62095; 62201; 62202; 62203; 62204; 62205; 62206; 62207; 62208 62217 62220; 62221; 62222; 62223; 62224; 62225; 62232; 62233; 62234* (IL 20); 62236 62237; 62238; 62239; 62240; 62241; 62242; 62243; 62244; 62248; 62254 62255 62256; 62257; 62258; 62259; 62260; 62261; 62264; 62269; 62272; 62274 62277 62278; 62279; 62280; 62282; 62285; 62286; 62288; 62289; 62292; 62293* (IL 20) 62295; 62297; 62298; 62832; 62888; 62901; 62902; 62903; 62905; 62906; 62907 62913; 62914; 62915; 62916; 62918; 62920; 62924; 62926; 62927; 62929; 62932 62942; 62947; 62949; 62950; 62952; 62957; 62958; 62961; 62962; 62966; 62969 62971; 62975; 62988; 62990; 62993; 62994; 62997; 62998.

13th District: 60137* (IL 6); 60148* (IL 6); 60181* (IL 6); 60187* (IL 6, IL 14); 60435* (IL 11, IL 14); 60436* (IL 11); 60439; 60440; 60441* (IL 11) 60448* (IL 11); 60457* (IL 3); 60462* (IL 3); 60463* (IL 3); 60464* (IL 3) 60465* (IL 3); 60477* (IL 2, IL 3, IL 11); 60480* (IL 3); 60504* (IL 14) 60514; 60515* (IL 6); 60516; 60517; 60521* (IL 3, IL 6); 60522; 60532; 60540 60544* (IL 14); 60559* (IL 6); 60561; 60563* (IL 14); 60564; 60565; 60566 60567; 60570; 60572.

14th District: 60102* (IL 16); 60103* (IL 6, IL 8); 60109; 60110; 60111 60112; 60115; 60118* (IL 8); 60119; 60120* (IL 8); 60121; 60122; 60123; 60129* (IL 16); 60134; 60135; 60136; 60140; 60142* (IL 16); 60144; 60145; 60146 60147; 60150; 60151; 60170; 60172* (IL 6, IL 8); 60174; 60175; 60177; 60178 60182; 60183; 60184; 60185; 60186; 60187* (IL 6, IL 13); 60188* (IL 6); 60190* (IL 6); 60435* (IL 11, IL 13); 60447* (IL 11); 60504* (IL 13); 60505; 60506 60507; 60510; 60511; 60512; 60518; 60519; 60520; 60530; 60531; 60536 60537 60538; 60539; 60541* (IL 11); 60542; 60543; 60544* (IL 13); 60545; 60548 60549* (IL 11); 60550; 60551* (IL 11); 60552; 60553; 60554; 60555; 60556 60560 60563* (IL 13); 60568; 61006* (IL 16); 61021* (IL 17); 61031* (IL 16) 61042; 61057; 61058; 61068* (IL 16); 61071* (IL 17); 61081* (IL 17); 61310 61318; 61324; 61330* (IL 17); 61331; 61342* (IL 11); 61349* (IL 17); 61350* (IL 11); 61353; 61354* (IL 11, IL 17); 61367; 61371; 61376* (IL 17); 61378.

15th District: 60420; 60460; 60598; 60901* (IL 11); 60911; 60912; 60917* (IL 11); 60918; 60919; 60920; 60921; 60922; 60924; 60926; 60927; 60928; 60929 60930; 60931; 60932; 60933; 60934; 60936; 60938; 60939; 60941; 60942; 60945 60946; 60948; 60949; 60951; 60952; 60953; 60955; 60956; 60957; 60959; 60960 60961* (IL 11); 60962; 60963 60966; 60967; 60968; 60970; 60973; 60974; 61311 61313; 61319; 61333; 61364* (IL 11); 61701; 61702; 61704; 61709; 61710; 61720 61722; 61724; 61726; 61727; 61728; 61730 61731; 61735; 61736; 61737; 61739 61740; 61741; 61743; 61744; 61745* (IL 18); 61748; 61749; 61750; 61752; 61753 61758; 61761* (IL 18); 61764; 61769; 61770; 61773; 61775; 61776; 61777; 61778 61799; 61801; 61810; 61811; 61812; 61813; 61814; 61815; 61816; 61817; 61818 61820; 61821; 61824; 61825; 61826; 61830; 61831; 61832; 61833; 61834; 61839 61840; 61841; 61842; 61843; 61844; 61845; 61846; 61847; 61848; 61849; 61850 61851; 61852; 61853; 61854; 61855; 61856; 61857; 61858; 61859; 61862; 61863 61864; 61865; 61866; 61868; 61870; 61871; 61872; 61873; 61874; 61875; 61876 61877; 61878; 61880; 61882; 61883; 61884; 61910; 61913; 61917; 61919; 61924 61929; 61930; 61932; 61933; 61936; 61940; 61941; 61942; 61944; 61949; 61953 61955; 61956.

16th District: 53566* (WI 1, WI 2); 53585* (WI 1); 60001; 60010* (IL 8) 60012; 60013* (IL 8); 60014; 60021; 60033; 60034; 60039; 60042* (IL 8); 60050* (IL 8); 60051; 60071; 60072; 60080; 60081* (IL 8); 60097; 60098; 60102* (IL 14); 60113; 60129* (IL 14); 60142* (IL 14); 60152; 60180; 61001* (WI 2) 61006* (IL 14); 61007* (IL 17); 61008 61010; 61011; 61012; 61013; 61015 61016; 61018; 61019; 61020; 61024; 61025; 61027; 61028; 61030* (IL 17); 61031* (IL 14); 61032; 61036; 61038; 61039* (IL 17); 61041; 61043; 61044; 61045 61047* (IL 17); 61048; 61049; 61050; 61052; 61053* (IL 17); 61054* (IL 17) 61059; 61060* (WI 1, WI 2); 61061* (IL 17); 61062; 61063; 61065; 61067 61068* (IL 14); 61070; 61072; 61073; 61074* (IL 17); 61075* (WI 2); 61076 61077 61078* (IL 17); 61079; 61080; 61084; 61085; 61087* (WI 2); 61088; 61089* (WI 2); 61100; 61101; 61102; 61103; 61104; 61105; 61106; 61107; 61108; 61109 61110; 61111; 61112; 61114; 61115; 61125; 61126; 61130; 61131; 61132.

17th District: 52761* (IA 1); 61007* (IL 16); 61014; 61017; 61021* (IL 14) 61030* (IL 16); 61037; 61039* (IL 16); 61046; 61047* (IL 16); 61051; 61053* (IL 16); 61054* (IL 16); 61061* (IL 16); 61064; 61071* (IL 14); 61074* (IL 16); 61078* (IL 16); 61081*

(IL 14); 61091; 61201; 61204; 61206; 61230; 61231 61232; 61233; 61234; 61235; 61236; 61237; 61238; 61239; 61240; 61241; 61242 61243; 61244; 61249; 61250; 61251; 61252; 61254; 61256; 61257; 61258; 61259 61260; 61261; 61262; 61263; 61264; 61265; 61270; 61272; 61273; 61274; 61275 61276; 61277; 61278; 61279; 61281; 61282; 61283; 61284; 61285; 61299; 61312 61314; 61315; 61317; 61320; 61322; 61323; 61324; 61330* (IL 14); 61337 61338; 61344; 61345; 61346; 61349* (IL 14); 61354* (IL 11, IL 14); 61356 61359; 61361; 61362; 61368; 61374; 61376* (IL 14); 61379; 61401; 61402; 61410 61411; 61412; 61413; 61414; 61415; 61416; 61417; 61418; 61419; 61420; 61422 61423; 61425; 61427; 61428; 61430; 61431; 61432; 61433; 61434; 61435; 61436 61437; 61438; 61439; 61440; 61441; 61442; 61443; 61447; 61448; 61450; 61453 61454; 61455; 61458; 61459; 61460; 61462; 61465; 61466; 61467; 61468; 61469 61470; 61471; 61472; 61473; 61474; 61475; 61476; 61477; 61478; 61480; 61482 61484; 61485; 61486; 61488; 61489* (IL 18); 61490; 61501; 61519; 61520; 61524 61531* (IL 18); 61542; 61543; 61544; 61553; 61563; 61572; 62301* (IL 20) 62310; 62311; 62313; 62316; 62318; 62320; 62321; 62324* (IL 20); 62325; 62326 62327; 62328; 62329; 62330; 62334; 62336; 62338; 62339* (IL 20); 62341; 62344 62346 62348; 62351; 62354; 62358; 62359; 62367; 62373; 62374; 62376; 62379 62380; 62644* (IL 18).

18th District: 61326; 61327; 61335; 61336; 61340; 61363; 61369; 61375; 61377 61421; 61424; 61426; 61449; 61451; 61479; 61483; 61489* (IL 17); 61491; 61516 61517; 61518; 61523; 61525; 61526; 61528; 61529; 61530; 61531* (IL 17); 61532 61533; 61534; 61535; 61536; 61537; 61539; 61540; 61541; 61545; 61546; 61547 61548; 61550; 61552; 61554; 61555; 61558; 61559; 61560; 61561; 61562; 61564 61565; 61567; 61568; 61569; 61570; 61571; 61600; 61601; 61602; 61603; 61604 61605; 61606; 61607; 61611; 61612; 61613; 61614; 61615; 61625; 61628; 61629 61630; 61632; 61633; 61634; 61635; 61636; 61637; 61638; 61639; 61640; 61641 61643; 61644; 61649; 61650; 61651; 61652; 61653; 61654; 61655; 61656; 61721 61723; 61725; 61729; 61732; 61733; 61734; 61738; 61742; 61745* (IL 15); 61747 61751; 61754; 61755; 61759; 61760; 61761* (IL 15); 61771; 61772; 61774; 62512 62515; 62518; 62519; 62521* (IL 19); 62525* (IL 19); 62526* (IL 19) 62535; 62539; 62541; 62543; 62545; 62548; 62551; 62561; 62563; 62573; 62601 62611; 62612; 62613; 62615; 62617; 62618; 62622; 62625; 62627; 62628; 62629* (IL 20); 62631; 62633; 62634; 62635; 62638; 62642; 62643; 62644* (IL 17) 62650; 62651; 62655; 62656; 62659; 62660; 62661; 62662; 62664; 62666; 62668 62670; 62671; 62673; 62675; 62677; 62682; 62684; 62688; 62689; 62691; 62692 62693; 62695; 62702* (IL 20); 62704* (IL 20); 62707* (IL 20); 62708; 62709 62726; 62736; 62746; 62756.

19th District: 61756; 61911; 61912; 61914; 61920; 61925; 61928; 61931; 61937 61938; 61943; 61951; 61957; 62083; 62401; 62410; 62411; 62413; 62415; 62417 62419; 62420; 62421; 62422; 62423; 62424; 62425; 62426; 62427; 62428; 62431 62432; 62433; 62434; 62435; 62436; 62438; 62439; 62440; 62441; 62442; 62443 62444; 62445; 62446; 62447; 62448; 62449; 62450; 62451; 62452; 62454; 62459 62460; 62461; 62462; 62463; 62464; 62465; 62466; 62467; 62468; 62469; 62473 62474; 62475; 62476; 62477; 62478; 62479; 62480; 62481; 62501; 62510; 62513 62514; 62521* (IL 18); 62522; 62523; 62524; 62525* (IL 18); 62526* (IL 18) 62527; 62532; 62534; 62537; 62544; 62549; 62550; 62552; 62553; 62554; 62555 62557; 62565; 62567; 62568* (IL 20); 62571; 62574; 62805; 62806; 62809; 62811 62812; 62815; 62817; 62818; 62819; 62820; 62821; 62822; 62823; 62824; 62825 62827; 62828; 62829; 62833; 62834; 62835; 62836; 62837; 62839; 62840; 62841 62842; 62843; 62844; 62845; 62847; 62850; 62851; 62852; 62855; 62856; 62858 62859; 62860; 62861; 62862; 62863; 62865; 62867; 62868; 62869; 62871; 62874 62878; 62879; 62884; 62886; 62887; 62890; 62891; 62895; 62896; 62897; 62899 62908; 62909; 62910; 62912; 62917; 62919; 62921; 62922; 62923; 62928; 62930; 62931; 62933; 62934; 62935; 62938 62939; 62941; 62943; 62944; 62945; 62946; 62947; 62948; 62951; 62953; 62954 62955; 62956; 62959; 62960; 62963; 62964 62965; 62967; 62970; 62972; 62973; 62974 62976; 62977; 62979; 62982; 62983; 62984; 62985; 62987; 62991; 62992; 62995 62996; 62999.

20th District: 61452; 62001; 62002* (IL 12); 62006; 62009; 62010* (IL 12) 62011; 62012; 62013; 62014; 62015; 62016; 62017; 62018* (IL 12); 62019; 62020 62021; 62022; 62023; 62024* (IL 12); 62025; 62026; 62027; 62028; 62030; 62031 62032; 62033; 62034; 62035* (IL 12); 62036; 62037; 62040* (IL 12); 62044 62045; 62046; 62047; 62049; 62050; 62051; 62052; 62053; 62054; 62056; 62058 62061; 62062; 62063; 62065; 62067; 62069; 62070; 62074; 62075; 62076; 62077 62078; 62079; 62080; 62081; 62082; 62085; 62086; 62088; 62089; 62091; 62092 62093; 62094; 62097; 62098; 62214; 62215; 62216; 62218; 62219; 62230; 62231 62234* (IL 12); 62245; 62246; 62247; 62249; 62250; 62252; 62253; 62262; 62263 62265; 62266; 62268; 62271; 62273; 62275; 62281; 62283; 62284; 62293* (IL 12) 62294; 62296; 62301* (IL 17); 62305; 62306; 62312; 62314; 62319; 62323; 62324* (IL 17); 62332; 62339* (IL 17); 62340; 62343; 62344; 62345; 62347; 62352 62353; 62355; 62356; 62357; 62360; 62361; 62362; 62363; 62365; 62366; 62370 62372; 62375; 62378; 62414; 62418; 62458; 62471; 62511; 62517; 62530; 62531 62533; 62536; 62538; 62540; 62546; 62547; 62556; 62558; 62560; 62568* (IL 19); 62570; 62572; 62610; 62621; 62624; 62626; 62629* (IL 18); 62630; 62639; 62640 62649; 62663; 62665; 62667; 62672; 62674 62676; 62681; 62683; 62685; 62686 62690; 62694; 62700; 62701; 62702* (IL 18); 62703; 62704* (IL 18); 62705; 62706; 62707* (IL 18); 62711; 62712; 62713; 62715; 62716 62718; 62719; 62720 62721; 62722; 62723; 62739; 62757; 62761; 62762; 62763; 62764; 62765; 62766 62767; 62769; 62777; 62781; 62786; 62791; 62794; 62796; 62801; 62803 62807; 62808; 62810; 62814; 62816; 62830; 62831; 62838; 62846; 62848; 62849 62853; 62854; 62857; 62864; 62866; 62870; 62872; 62875; 62876; 62877; 62880 62881; 62882; 62883; 62885; 62889; 62892; 62893; 62894; 62898.

Indiana

1st District: 46301; 46302; 46303* (IN 5); 46304; 46307* (IN 5); 46311* (IN 5); 46312; 46319; 46320; 46321; 46322; 46323; 46324; 46325; 46327; 46341* (IN 5); 46342; 46347* (IN 5); 46348* (IN 3); 46355; 46356* (IN 5); 46360* (IN 3) 46368; 46373* (IN 5); 46375; 46383; 46384; 46391* (IN 3); 46393; 46394; 46400 46401; 46402; 46403; 46404; 46405; 46406* (IN 5); 46407; 46408; 46409; 46410* (IN 5); 46411.

2nd District: 45846* (OH 8); 46001; 46011; 46012; 46013; 46014; 46015; 46016 46017; 46018; 46036* (IN 6); 46044; 46048; 46051; 46056; 46063; 46064* (IN 6) 46070; 46104; 46110; 46115; 46124* (IN 6); 46126; 46127; 46130; 46144; 46146 46150; 46155; 46156; 46161; 46173* (IN 9); 46176; 46182; 47201* (IN 9) 47202 47203* (IN 9); 47222; 47225; 47226; 47232* (IN 9); 47234; 47240* (IN 9) 47244; 47246; 47261; 47263; 47272; 47280;

47283* (IN 9); 47302; 47303; 47304 47305; 47306; 47307; 47308; 47320; 47324; 47327; 47330; 47334; 47335; 47336* (IN 5); 47337; 47338; 47339; 47340; 47341; 47342; 47344; 47345; 47346; 47351 47352; 47354 47355; 47356; 47357; 47358; 47360; 47361; 47362; 47366; 47367 47368; 47369; 47370; 47371* (IN 4); 47373; 47374; 47375; 47380; 47381; 47382 47383; 47384; 47385; 47386; 47387; 47388; 47390; 47392; 47393; 47394; 47396.

3rd District: 46340; 46345; 46346; 46348* (IN 1); 46350; 46351; 46360* (IN 1) 46365; 46367; 46371; 46382; 46390; 46391* (IN 1); 46506* (IN 5); 46507; 46514 46515; 46516; 46517; 46526; 46530; 46531; 46532; 46536* (IN 5); 46538 46540 46542; 46543; 46544; 46545; 46546; 46550; 46552; 46553; 46554; 46556; 46561 46567* (IN 5); 46573; 46574; 46580* (IN 5); 46590; 46595; 46600; 46601; 46604 46612; 46613; 46614; 46615; 46616; 46617; 46619; 46620; 46624; 46626; 46628 46629; 46634; 46635; 46637; 46660; 46680; 46699; 46732* (IN 4, IN 5); 46767* (IN 4).

4th District: 46565; 46571; 46701; 46702* (IN 5); 46703; 46704; 46705; 46706 46710; 46711; 46713; 46714; 46720; 46721; 46723; 46725; 46730; 46731; 46732* (IN 3, IN 5); 46733; 46737; 46738; 46740; 46741; 46742; 46743; 46744; 46745 46746; 46747; 46748; 46750; 46755; 46759; 46761; 46763; 46764; 46765 46766; 46767* (IN 3); 46769; 46770; 46771; 46772; 46773; 46774; 46776; 46777 46778; 46779; 46780; 46781; 46782; 46783; 46784; 46785; 46786; 46787; 46788 46789; 46790; 46791; 46792; 46793; 46794; 46795; 46796; 46797; 46798; 46799 46800; 46801; 46802; 46803; 46804; 46805; 46806; 46807; 46808; 46809; 46815 46816; 46818; 46819; 46825; 46835; 46845; 46850; 46851; 46852; 46853; 46854 46855; 46856; 46857; 46858; 46859; 46860; 46861; 46862; 46863; 46864; 46865 46866; 46867; 46868; 46869; 46885; 46895; 46896; 46897; 46898; 46899; 46940* (IN 5); 46952* (IN 5); 47326; 47359* (IN 5); 47371* (IN 2).

5th District: 46303* (IN 1); 46307* (IN 1); 46310; 46311* (IN 1); 46341* (IN 1); 46347* (IN 1); 46349; 46356* (IN 1); 46366; 46372; 46373* (IN 1); 46374 46376; 46377; 46379; 46380; 46381; 46392; 46399; 46406* (IN 1); 46410* (IN 1) 46501; 46502; 46504; 46506* (IN 3); 46508; 46510; 46511; 46513; 46524; 46534 46536* (IN 3); 46537; 46539; 46555; 46562; 46563; 46566; 46567* (IN 3); 46570 46572; 46580* (IN 3); 46581; 46702* (IN 4); 46732* (IN 3, IN 4); 46901; 46902 46903; 46904; 46910; 46911; 46912; 46913; 46914; 46915; 46916; 46917; 46919 46920; 46921; 46922; 46923; 46925; 46926; 46928; 46929; 46930; 46931; 46932 46933; 46935; 46936; 46937; 46938; 46939; 46940* (IN 4); 46941; 46942; 46943 46944; 46945; 46946; 46947; 46950; 46951; 46952* (IN 4); 46953; 46957; 46958 46959; 46960; 46961; 46962; 46965; 46967; 46968; 46970; 46971; 46974; 46975 46977; 46978; 46979; 46980; 46982; 46983; 46984; 46985; 46986; 46987; 46988 46989; 46990; 46991; 46992; 46994; 46995; 46996; 46998; 47336* (IN 2); 47348 47359* (IN 4); 47842* (IN 7); 47847; 47854; 47875; 47917; 47921; 47922; 47923 47925; 47926; 47928 47929; 47942; 47943; 47944; 47946; 47948; 47950; 47951 47957; 47959; 47960; 47963; 47964; 47966; 47968; 47970* (IN 7); 47971; 47973 47974 47975; 47976; 47977; 47978; 47980; 47982; 47984; 47986; 47991; 47993; 47995 47997.

6th District: 46030; 46031; 46032; 46033; 46034; 46035; 46036* (IN 2); 46038 46039 46040; 46041; 46045; 46046; 46047; 46049; 46050; 46055; 46057; 46058 46060; 46064* (IN 2); 46065; 46067; 46068; 46069* (IN 7); 46072; 46074; 46076 46077* (IN 7, IN 10); 46106; 46107* (IN 10); 46113* (IN 7); 46117; 46124* (IN 2); 46129; 46131; 46140; 46142; 46143; 46148; 46151* (IN 7, IN 8); 46154 46158* (IN 7); 46160* (IN 9); 46162; 46163; 46164; 46183; 46184; 46186 46187; 46203* (IN 10); 46214* (IN 10); 46217* (IN 10); 46218* (IN 10); 46219* (IN 10); 46220* (IN 10); 46222* (IN 10); 46224* (IN 7, IN 10); 46226* (IN 10) 46227* (IN 10); 46229* (IN 10); 46230; 46231* (IN 7); 46234* (IN 7, IN 10) 46236* (IN 10); 46237* (IN 10); 46239* (IN 10); 46240; 46241* (IN 10); 46247 46250; 46251; 46254* (IN 10); 46256* (IN 10); 46259; 46260* (IN 10); 46268* (IN 10); 46278* (IN 10); 46280; 46290.

7th District: 46052; 46069* (IN 6); 46071; 46075; 46077* (IN 6, IN 10); 46102 46103; 46105; 46111; 46112; 46113* (IN 6); 46114; 46116; 46118; 46120; 46121 46122; 46125; 46128; 46135; 46147; 46149; 46151* (IN 6, IN 8); 46157; 46158* (IN 6); 46165; 46166; 46167; 46168; 46170; 46171; 46172; 46175; 46180; 46231* (IN 6); 46234* (IN 10); 47401* (IN 8, IN 9); 47403* (IN 8); 47404* (IN 8); 47408* (IN 8); 47427; 47429; 47431; 47433; 47438* (IN 8); 47455; 47456 47460; 47463; 47464; 47801; 47802; 47803; 47804; 47805; 47807; 47808; 47809 47811; 47812; 47813; 47814; 47830; 47831; 47832; 47833; 47834; 47836; 47837 47840; 47841; 47842* (IN 5); 47845; 47846; 47851; 47853; 47856; 47857; 47858 47859; 47860; 47862; 47863; 47866; 47868; 47869; 47870; 47871; 47872; 47874 47876; 47877; 47878; 47880; 47881; 47884; 47885; 47901; 47902; 47903; 47904 47905; 47906; 47907; 47916; 47918; 47920; 47924; 47930; 47931; 47932; 47933 47934; 47935; 47936; 47937; 47938; 47939; 47940; 47941; 47949; 47952; 47954 47955; 47958; 47962; 47965; 47967; 47968; 47969; 47970* (IN 5); 47981; 47983 47985; 47987; 47988; 47989; 47990; 47992; 47994; 47996.

8th District: 46151* (IN 6, IN 7); 47125; 47140* (IN 9); 47401* (IN 7, IN 9); 47402; 47403* (IN 7); 47404* (IN 7); 47405; 47406; 47407; 47408* (IN 7); 47420; 47421; 47424; 47426; 47430; 47432; 47434; 47436; 47437; 47438* (IN 7) 47439; 47441; 47443; 47445; 47446; 47449; 47451; 47452; 47453; 47454; 47457 47458; 47459; 47462; 47465; 47467; 47468* (IN 9); 47469; 47470; 47471; 47501 47512; 47516; 47519; 47522; 47523; 47524; 47528; 47529; 47530; 47535; 47537* (IN 9); 47557; 47558; 47561; 47562; 47564; 47567; 47568; 47573; 47578 47581; 47584; 47585; 47590; 47591; 47596; 47597; 47598; 47601; 47610 47612 47613; 47614; 47616; 47618; 47619; 47620; 47629; 47630; 47631; 47633; 47637 47638; 47639; 47640; 47647; 47648; 47649; 47654; 47660; 47665; 47666; 47670 47671; 47683; 47701; 47702; 47703; 47704; 47705; 47706; 47708; 47710 47711; 47712; 47713; 47714; 47715; 47716; 47719; 47720; 47721; 47722; 47724 47727; 47728; 47730; 47731; 47732; 47733; 47734; 47735; 47736; 47737; 47739 47740; 47741; 47744; 47747; 47750; 47838; 47848; 47849; 47850; 47852; 47855 47861; 47864; 47865; 47879; 47882.

9th District: 45003* (OH 8); 45053* (OH 8); 46133; 46160* (IN 6); 46173* (IN 2); 47001; 47006; 47010; 47011; 47012; 47016; 47017; 47018; 47019; 47020 47021; 47022; 47023; 47024; 47025; 47030; 47031; 47032; 47033; 47034; 47035 47036; 47037; 47038; 47039; 47040; 47041; 47042; 47043; 47060; 47102; 47104 47106; 47107; 47108; 47110 47111; 47112; 47114; 47115; 47116; 47117; 47118 47119; 47120; 47122; 47123; 47124; 47126; 47129; 47130; 47131; 47132; 47133 47134; 47135; 47136; 47137; 47138; 47139; 47140* (IN 8); 47141; 47142; 47143 47144; 47145; 47146; 47147; 47150; 47151; 47160; 47161; 47162; 47163; 47164 47165; 47166; 47167; 47170; 47172; 47174; 47175; 47177;

47199; 47201* (IN 2) 47203* (IN 2); 47220; 47223; 47224; 47227; 47228; 47229; 47230; 47231; 47232* (IN 2); 47235; 47236; 47240* (IN 2); 47243; 47245; 47247; 47249; 47250; 47260 47262; 47264; 47265; 47270; 47273; 47274; 47281; 47282; 47283* (IN 2); 47322 47325; 47331; 47353* (OH 8); 47401* (IN 7, IN 8); 47435; 47448; 47468* (IN 8) 47513; 47514; 47515; 47520; 47521; 47525; 47527; 47531; 47532; 47536; 47537* (IN 9); 47541; 47542; 47545; 47546; 47547; 47549; 47550; 47551; 47552; 47555 47556; 47559; 47574; 47575; 47576; 47577; 47579; 47580; 47586; 47587; 47588 47611; 47615; 47617; 47634; 47635.

10th District: 46077* (IN 6, IN 7); 46107* (IN 6); 46200; 46201; 46202; 46203* (IN 6); 46204; 46205; 46206; 46207; 46208; 46209; 46211; 46214* (IN 6); 46216 46217* (IN 6); 46218* (IN 6); 46219* (IN 6); 46220* (IN 6); 46221; 46222* (IN 6); 46223; 46224* (IN 6); 46225; 46226* (IN 6); 46227* (IN 6); 46229* (IN 6) 46234* (IN 6, IN 7); 46236* (IN 6); 46237* (IN 6); 46239* (IN 6); 46241* (IN 6); 46242; 46244; 46249; 46253; 46254* (IN 6); 46255; 46256* (IN 6); 46260* (IN 6); 46266; 46268* (IN 6); 46275; 46277; 46278* (IN 6); 46282; 46283 46285; 46291.

Iowa

1st District: 52033* (IA 2); 52037; 52202; 52205; 52212; 52213; 52214; 52216 52218; 52219; 52226; 52227; 52228; 52230; 52233; 52235; 52240; 52241; 52242 52243; 52244; 52245; 52246; 52252; 52253; 52254; 52255; 52302; 52305; 52306 52310; 52312; 52314; 52317; 52319; 52320; 52321; 52322; 52323; 52324; 52328 52331; 52333; 52336; 52337; 52338; 52340; 52341; 52343; 52344; 52350; 52352 52358; 52362; 52400; 52401; 52402; 52403; 52404; 52405; 52406; 52407; 52408 52409; 52410; 52498; 52499; 52640; 52646; 52653; 52701; 52720; 52721; 52722 52725; 52726; 52727; 52728; 52729; 52730; 52731; 52732; 52733; 52734; 52736 52737; 52738; 52739; 52742; 52745; 52746; 52747; 52748; 52749; 52750; 52751 52752; 52753; 52754; 52755; 52756; 52757; 52758; 52759; 52760; 52761* (IL 17) 52765; 52766; 52767; 52768; 52769; 52771; 52772; 52773; 52774; 52776; 52777 52778; 52800; 52801; 52802; 52803; 52804; 52805; 52806; 52807; 52808; 52809.

2nd District: 50173; 50401; 50426; 50428; 50433; 50434; 50435; 50440; 50444 50446; 50448; 50454; 50455; 50456; 50457; 50458; 50459; 50460; 50461; 50464 50466; 50467; 50468; 50469; 50471; 50472; 50476; 50477; 50479; 50481; 50482 50602; 50603; 50604; 50605; 50606; 50607; 50608; 50609; 50611; 50612; 50613 50614; 50616; 50619; 50620; 50621; 50622; 50623; 50624; 50625; 50626; 50628 50629; 50630; 50631; 50632; 50634; 50635; 50636; 50638; 50641; 50642; 50643 50644; 50645; 50647; 50648; 50649; 50650; 50651; 50652; 50653; 50654; 50655 50657; 50658; 50659; 50660; 50661; 50662; 50664; 50665; 50666; 50667; 50668 50669; 50670; 50671; 50673; 50674; 50675; 50676; 50680; 50681; 50682 50700; 50701; 50702; 50703; 50704; 50706; 50707; 50799; 52001; 52002; 52003 52004; 52030; 52031; 52032; 52033* (IA 1); 52035; 52036; 52038; 52039; 52040 52041; 52042; 52043; 52044; 52045; 52046; 52047; 52048; 52049; 52050; 52052 52053; 52054; 52055; 52056; 52057; 52060; 52064; 52065; 52066; 52068; 52069 52070; 52071; 52072; 52073; 52074; 52075; 52076; 52077; 52078; 52079; 52101 52130; 52131; 52132; 52133; 52134* (MN 1); 52135; 52136; 52140* (MN 1); 52141 52142; 52143 52144; 52146; 52147; 52149; 52150; 52151; 52154; 52155* (MN 1) 52156; 52157; 52158 52159; 52160* (MN 1); 52161; 52162; 52163; 52164; 52165 52166; 52168; 52169; 52170 52171; 52172; 52175; 52203; 52204; 52206; 52207 52208; 52209; 52210; 52215; 52217 52220; 52223; 52224; 52225; 52229; 52236 52237; 52249; 52251; 52257; 52301; 52307 52308; 52309; 52313; 52315; 52316 52318; 52325; 52326; 52329; 52330; 52332; 52334 52339; 52342; 52345; 52346 52347; 52348; 52349; 52351; 52354; 52357; 52361; 55922* (MN 1) 55939* (MN 1) 55951* (MN 1); 55954* (MN 1); 55974* (MN 1).

3rd District: 50001; 50005; 50008; 50010; 50011; 50012; 50013; 50027; 50028 50030; 50044; 50046; 50047* (IA 4); 50049; 50051; 50052; 50054; 50055; 50056 50057; 50060; 50061* (IA 4); 50062; 50065* (MO 6); 50067; 50068; 50074; 50078 50103; 50104; 50105; 50106; 50108; 50112; 50116; 50118; 50119; 50120; 50123 50124; 50125; 50133; 50134; 50135; 50136; 50137; 50138; 50139; 50140 50141; 50142; 50143; 50144; 50145; 50147; 50148; 50149; 50150; 50151; 50153 50154; 50157; 50158; 50160; 50161; 50162; 50163; 50165; 50166; 50168; 50169* (IA 4); 50170; 50171; 50172; 50174; 50177; 50197; 50198; 50201; 50207; 50208 50210; 50211; 50213; 50214; 50219; 50221; 50225; 50228; 50229; 50232; 50234 50236; 50238; 50239; 50240* (IA 4); 50241; 50242; 50244; 50247; 50248; 50251; 50252; 50253; 50254; 50255; 50262; 50264; 50268; 50272; 50275; 50278 50314* (IA 4); 50320* (IA 4); 50637; 50801; 50830; 50831; 50833; 50835; 50836 50837* (IA 4); 50839; 50840; 50841; 50842; 50844; 50845; 50848; 50850; 50851 50852; 50854; 50857; 50859; 50860; 50861; 50862; 50863; 51601* (IA 4); 51602 51603; 51630 51631; 51632; 51636; 51637; 51638; 51646; 51647; 51651; 51656 51693; 52201; 52211; 52222; 52231; 52232; 52247; 52248; 52250; 52327; 52335 52353; 52355; 52356; 52359; 52501; 52530; 52531; 52533; 52534; 52535; 52536 52537* (MO 9); 52538; 52540; 52542* (MO 9); 52543; 52544; 52548; 52549; 52550 52551; 52552; 52553; 52554; 52555; 52556; 52557; 52560; 52561; 52562; 52563 52565; 52566; 52567; 52568; 52569; 52570; 52571; 52572; 52573* (MO 9); 52574 52575; 52576; 52577; 52580; 52581; 52583; 52584; 52585; 52586; 52588; 52590 52591; 52593; 52594; 52595; 52601; 52619; 52620; 52621; 52623; 52624; 52625 52626* (MO 9); 52627; 52630; 52631; 52632; 52635; 52637; 52638; 52639; 52641 52642; 52644; 52645; 52647; 52648; 52649; 52650; 52651; 52652; 52654; 52655 52656; 52657; 52658; 52659; 52660; 63535* (MO 6).

4th District: 50002; 50003; 50007; 50009; 50015; 50020; 50021; 50022; 50025 50026; 50029; 50032; 50033; 50035; 50038; 50039; 50042; 50047* (IA 3); 50048 50061* (IA 3); 50063; 50066; 50069; 50070; 50072; 50075; 50076; 50109; 50110 50111; 50115; 50117; 50128; 50131; 50146; 50155; 50164; 50167; 50169* (IA 3) 50216; 50218; 50220; 50222; 50226; 50233; 50237; 50240* (IA 3); 50243; 50250 50257; 50261; 50263; 50265; 50266; 50273; 50274; 50276; 50277; 50300; 50301; 50302; 50303; 50304; 50305; 50306; 50307; 50308; 50309; 50310; 50311; 50312 50313; 50314* (IA 3); 50315; 50316; 50317; 50318 50319; 50320* (IA 3); 50321 50325; 50328; 50329; 50330; 50331; 50332; 50333; 50334; 50335; 50336 50338; 50339; 50340; 50347; 50350; 50359; 50360; 50361; 50362 50363; 50364; 50367; 50368; 50369; 50380; 50381; 50392; 50393; 50394; 50395; 50396; 50397 50398; 50837* (IA 3); 50843; 50846; 50847; 50849; 50853; 50858; 50864; 50936 50940; 50947; 50950; 50980; 50981; 51446; 51447; 51501; 51502; 51503 51510 51519; 51521; 51525; 51526; 51527; 51529; 51530; 51531; 51532; 51533; 51534 51535; 51536; 51537; 51540; 51541; 51542; 51543; 51544; 51545; 51546; 51548 51549; 51550; 51551;

51552; 51553; 51554; 51555; 51556; 51557; 51559; 51560 51561; 51562; 51563; 51564; 51565; 51566; 51570; 51571; 51573; 51574; 51575 51576; 51577; 51578; 51579; 51591; 51593; 51601* (IA 3); 51639; 51640; 51645 51648; 51649; 51650; 51652; 51653; 51654; 51655.

5th District: 50006; 50031; 50034; 50036; 50040; 50041; 50043; 50050; 50058 50059; 50064; 50071; 50075; 50077; 50101; 50102; 50107; 50122; 50126; 50129 50130; 50132; 50152; 50156; 50206; 50212; 50217; 50223; 50227; 50230; 50231 50235; 50246; 50249; 50258; 50259; 50269; 50271; 50420; 50421; 50423; 50424 50427; 50430; 50431; 50432; 50436; 50438; 50439; 50441; 50447; 50449; 50450 50451; 50452; 50453; 50465; 50470; 50473; 50475; 50478; 50480; 50483; 50484 50501; 50510; 50511; 50514; 50515; 50516; 50517; 50518; 50519; 50520; 50521 50522; 50523; 50524; 50525; 50526; 50527; 50528; 50529; 50530; 50531; 50532 50533; 50535; 50536; 50538; 50539; 50540; 50541; 50542; 50543; 50544; 50545 50546; 50548; 50551; 50552; 50553; 50554; 50556; 50557; 50558; 50559; 50560 50561; 50562; 50563; 50565; 50566; 50567; 50568; 50569; 50570; 50571; 50573 50574; 50575; 50576; 50577; 50578; 50579; 50580; 50581; 50582; 50583; 50585 50586; 50587; 50588; 50590; 50591; 50592; 50593; 50594; 50595; 50597; 50598 50599; 50601; 50627; 50633; 50640; 50672; 51001; 51002; 51003; 51004; 51005 51006; 51007; 51008; 51009; 51010; 51011; 51012; 51014; 51015; 51016; 51017 51018; 51019; 51020; 51022; 51023; 51024; 51025; 51026; 51027; 51028; 51029 51030; 51031; 51033; 51034; 51035; 51036; 51037; 51038; 51039; 51040; 51041 51044; 51045; 51046; 51047; 51048; 51049; 51050; 51051; 51052; 51053; 51054 51055; 51056; 51057; 51058; 51059; 51060; 51061; 51062; 51063; 51100; 51101 51102; 51103; 51104; 51105; 51106; 51107; 51108; 51109; 51110; 51111; 51201 51230; 51231; 51232; 51234; 51235; 51237; 51238; 51239; 51240; 51241; 51242 51243; 51244; 51245; 51246; 51247; 51248; 51249; 51250; 51301; 51330; 51331 51333; 51334; 51338; 51340; 51341; 51342; 51343; 51344; 51345; 51346; 51347 51349; 51350; 51351; 51354; 51355; 51357; 51358; 51360; 51363; 51364; 51365 51366; 51401; 51430; 51431; 51432; 51433; 51436; 51437; 51439; 51440; 51441 51442; 51443; 51444; 51445; 51448; 51449; 51450; 51451; 51452; 51453; 51454 51455; 51458; 51459; 51460; 51461; 51462; 51463; 51465; 51466; 51467; 51520 51523; 51528; 51558; 51572; 56014* (MN 1); 56027* (MN 1); 56051* (MN 1) 56117* (MN 2); 56129* (MN 2); 56138* (MN 2, SD 1); 57034* (SD 1); 57068* (MN 2, SD 1).

Kansas

1st District: 66401; 66403; 66406; 66411; 66412; 66423; 66427; 66431; 66433 66438; 66501; 66507; 66508; 66518; 66526; 66541* (NE 2); 66544; 66545; 66548 66555; 66801; 66830; 66833; 66834; 66835; 66838; 66840; 66843; 66845; 66846 66847; 66849* (KS 2); 66850; 66851; 66854; 66858; 66859; 66861; 66862; 66864 66865; 66866* (KS 4); 66868; 66869; 66872* (KS 2); 66873; 66901; 66930; 66931 66932; 66933; 66935; 66936; 66937; 66938; 66939; 66940; 66941; 66942; 66943 66944; 66945; 66946; 66948; 66949; 66951; 66952; 66953; 66955* (NE 1, NE 3) 66956; 66958; 66959; 66960; 66961; 66962; 66963; 66964; 66966; 66967; 66968 66970; 67015; 67021; 67028; 67029; 67053; 67054; 67057; 67059; 67061; 67063 67065; 67066; 67070; 67071; 67073; 67104; 67107; 67109; 67124; 67127; 67134 67138; 67143; 67155; 67401; 67402; 67410; 67414; 67416; 67417; 67418; 67420 67422; 67423; 67425; 67427; 67428; 67429; 67430; 67431; 67432; 67436; 67437 67438; 67439; 67441; 67442; 67443; 67444; 67445; 67446; 67447; 67448; 67449 67450; 67451; 67452; 67454; 67455; 67456; 67457; 67458; 67459; 67460; 67463 67464; 67465; 67466; 67467; 67468; 67469; 67470; 67472; 67473; 67474; 67475 67476; 67478; 67479; 67480; 67481; 67482; 67483; 67484; 67485; 67487; 67488 67490; 67491; 67492; 67501; 67502; 67504; 67505; 67510; 67511; 67512; 67513 67514; 67515; 67516; 67517; 67518; 67519; 67520; 67521; 67522; 67523; 67524 67525; 67526; 67529; 67530; 67543; 67544; 67545; 67546; 67547; 67548; 67549 67550; 67552; 67553; 67554; 67556; 67557; 67559; 67560; 67561; 67562; 67563 67564; 67565; 67566; 67567; 67568; 67569; 67570; 67572; 67573; 67574; 67575 67576; 67577; 67578; 67579; 67580; 67581; 67582; 67583; 67584; 67585; 67601 67621; 67622; 67623; 67625; 67626; 67627; 67628; 67629; 67630; 67631; 67632 67633; 67634; 67635; 67636; 67637; 67638; 67639; 67640; 67641; 67642; 67643 67644; 67645; 67646; 67647* (NE 3); 67648; 67649; 67650; 67651; 67652; 67653 67654; 67656; 67657; 67658; 67659; 67660; 67661; 67663; 67664; 67665; 67667 67669; 67670; 67671; 67672; 67673; 67674; 67675; 67676; 67701; 67730; 67731 67732; 67733; 67734; 67735; 67736; 67737; 67738; 67739; 67740; 67741; 67743 67744; 67745; 67746; 67747; 67748; 67749; 67751; 67752; 67753; 67755; 67756 67757; 67758; 67759; 67761; 67762; 67764; 67801; 67830; 67831; 67834; 67835 67836; 67837; 67838; 67839; 67840* (OK 6); 67841; 67842; 67843; 67844; 67846 67849; 67850; 67851; 67853; 67854; 67855; 67856; 67857; 67858; 67859; 67860 67861; 67862; 67863; 67864; 67865; 67867; 67868; 67869; 67870; 67871; 67874 67876; 67877; 67878; 67879; 67880; 67882; 67901; 67905; 67950; 67951; 67952 67953; 67954; 68415* (NE 1); 68920* (NE 3); 68939* (NE 3); 68942* (NE 3) 68943* (NE 3); 68952* (NE 3); 68970* (NE 3); 68971* (NE 3); 68972* (NE 3) 68978* (NE 3); 69021* (NE 3); 69024* (NE 3); 69026* (NE 3); 69030* (NE 3) 69036* (NE 3); 69043* (NE 3); 69044* (NE 3); 81080* (CO 4).

2nd District: 66002; 66007; 66008; 66010; 66012* (KS 3); 66014; 66015; 66016 66017; 66020; 66023; 66024; 66027; 66032; 66033; 66035; 66038; 66039; 66040 66041; 66042; 66043; 66047* (KS 3); 66048; 66049* (KS 3); 66050; 66052; 66054 66056; 66058; 66060; 66066; 66067; 66070; 66072; 66073; 66075; 66076; 66077 66078; 66079; 66080; 66081; 66086; 66087; 66088; 66090; 66091; 66092; 66093 66094; 66095; 66097; 66402; 66404; 66407; 66408; 66409; 66413; 66414; 66415 66416; 66417; 66418; 66419; 66420; 66422; 66424; 66425; 66426; 66428; 66429 66432; 66434; 66435; 66436; 66439; 66440; 66441; 66442; 66449; 66450; 66451 66502; 66506; 66509; 66510; 66512; 66514; 66515; 66516; 66517; 66520; 66521 66522; 66523; 66524; 66527; 66528; 66531; 66532; 66533; 66534; 66535; 66536 66537; 66538; 66540; 66542; 66543; 66546; 66547; 66549; 66550; 66551; 66552 66554; 66600; 66601; 66603; 66604; 66605; 66606; 66607; 66608; 66609 66610; 66611; 66612; 66614; 66615; 66616; 66617; 66618; 66619; 66620; 66621 66622; 66624; 66625; 66626; 66628; 66629; 66634; 66636; 66637; 66638; 66642 66647; 66652; 66653; 66658; 66667; 66675; 66683; 66686; 66692; 66699; 66701 66710; 66711; 66712; 66713; 66714; 66716; 66717; 66720; 66724; 66725; 66727 66728; 66732; 66733; 66734; 66735; 66736; 66738* (MO 4); 66739; 66740; 66741 66742; 66743; 66746; 66748; 66749; 66750; 66751; 66753; 66754; 66756; 66757 66758; 66759; 66760; 66761; 66762; 66767; 66769; 66770; 66771; 66772 66773; 66775; 66776; 66777; 66778; 66779; 66780; 66781; 66782; 66783; 66839 66849* (KS 1); 66852; 66856; 66857; 66871; 66872* (KS 1); 67330; 67332; 67336 67341; 67342; 67354; 67356; 67357; 68381* (NE 1);

68466* (NE 1).

3rd District: 66006; 66012* (KS 2); 66013; 66018; 66019; 66021; 66025; 66026 66030; 66031; 66036; 66044; 66045; 66046; 66047* (KS 2); 66049* (KS 2); 66051 66053; 66061; 66062; 66063; 66064; 66071; 66083; 66085; 66100; 66101; 66102 66103 66104; 66105; 66106; 66109; 66110; 66111; 66112; 66113; 66115; 66117 66118; 66119; 66160; 66200; 66201; 66202; 66203; 66204; 66205; 66206; 66207 66208; 66209; 66210; 66211; 66212; 66213; 66214; 66215; 66216; 66217; 66218 66219; 66220; 66221; 66222; 66223; 66224; 66225; 66226; 66227; 66250; 66262 66276; 66279; 66282; 66285.

4th District: 66842; 66853; 66855; 66860; 66863; 66866* (KS 1); 66870; 67001 67002; 67003; 67004; 67005; 67008; 67009; 67010; 67012; 67013; 67016; 67017 67018; 67019; 67020; 67022; 67023; 67024; 67025; 67026; 67030; 67031; 67032 67035; 67036; 67037; 67038; 67039; 67041; 67042; 67045; 67047; 67049; 67050 67051; 67052; 67055; 67056; 67058; 67060; 67062; 67067; 67068; 67072; 67074 67101; 67102; 67103; 67106; 67108; 67110; 67111; 67112; 67114; 67117; 67118 67119; 67120; 67122; 67123; 67128; 67131; 67132; 67133; 67135; 67137 67140; 67142; 67144; 67146; 67147; 67149; 67150; 67151; 67152; 67154; 67156 67159; 67200; 67201; 67202; 67203; 67204; 67205; 67206; 67207; 67208; 67209 67210; 67211; 67212; 67213; 67214; 67215; 67216; 67217; 67218; 67219; 67220 67221; 67223; 67226; 67227; 67228; 67230; 67231; 67232; 67233; 67235; 67236 67240; 67251; 67256; 67257; 67259; 67260; 67276; 67277; 67278; 67301; 67333 67334; 67335; 67337; 67340; 67344; 67345; 67346; 67347; 67349; 67351; 67352 67353; 67355; 67360; 67361; 67363; 67364.

Kentucky

1st District: 38079* (TN 8); 42001; 42002; 42003; 42020; 42021; 42022; 42023 42024; 42025; 42026; 42027; 42028; 42029; 42031; 42032; 42033; 42035; 42036 42037; 42038; 42039; 42040; 42041; 42044; 42045; 42046; 42047; 42048; 42049 42050; 42051; 42053; 42054; 42055; 42056; 42058; 42059; 42060; 42061; 42063 42064; 42066; 42069; 42070; 42071; 42076; 42078; 42079; 42081; 42082; 42083 42084; 42085; 42086; 42087; 42088; 42104* (KY 2); 42120; 42122* (KY 2); 42129* (KY 2); 42133* (KY 2); 42134; 42135; 42140; 42150; 42151; 42153; 42155* (KY 2); 42157* (KY 2); 42164; 42166* (KY 2); 42167; 42170* (KY 2); 42201; 42202 42203; 42204; 42206; 42209; 42211; 42212; 42215; 42216; 42217; 42219; 42220 42221; 42223* (TN 7, TN 8); 42232; 42234; 42236; 42240; 42241; 42251; 42252 42254; 42256; 42261; 42262; 42263; 42265; 42266; 42267; 42268; 42273; 42276 42280; 42283; 42286; 42287; 42288; 42320; 42321; 42322; 42323; 42324; 42325 42326; 42327; 42328; 42330; 42332; 42333; 42337; 42338; 42339; 42340; 42343* (KY 2); 42344; 42345; 42347; 42349* (KY 2); 42350; 42352; 42354; 42356; 42357 42358; 42361* (KY 2); 42365; 42366* (KY 2); 42367; 42368* (KY 2); 42369; 42370 42371; 42372; 42374; 42376* (KY 2); 42378* (KY 2); 42402; 42403; 42404; 42406 42408; 42409; 42410; 42411; 42413; 42420; 42431; 42436; 42437; 42440; 42441 42442; 42444; 42445; 42450; 42451; 42452; 42453; 42455; 42456; 42457; 42458 42459; 42460; 42461; 42462; 42463; 42464; 42601; 42602; 42603; 42629 42642; 42702; 42711; 42714; 42715; 42717; 42720; 42723; 42728* (KY 2); 42730 42731* (KY 2); 42735; 42741; 42742; 42743* (KY 2); 42752; 42753; 42759 42761 42763; 42768; 42786.

2nd District: 40004; 40008; 40009; 40012; 40013; 40018; 40020; 40023* (KY 4) 40028; 40033; 40037; 40040; 40046; 40047; 40048; 40049; 40051; 40052; 40060 40061; 40062; 40063; 40069; 40071; 40078; 40103; 40104; 40106; 40107; 40108 40109; 40110; 40111; 40114; 40115; 40117; 40118* (KY 3); 40119; 40121; 40140 40142; 40143; 40144; 40145; 40146; 40150; 40152; 40153; 40155; 40157; 40159 40160; 40161; 40162; 40163; 40164; 40165; 40170; 40175; 40177; 40178; 40214* (KY 3); 40219* (KY 3); 40223* (KY 3); 40224; 40228* (KY 3) 40229* (KY 3); 40241* (KY 3); 40243* (KY 3); 40245* (KY 3, KY 4); 40253 40258* (KY 3); 40269; 40272* (KY 3); 40291* (KY 3); 40299* (KY 3); 40328 40330* (KY 6); 40437* (KY 6); 40442* (KY 6); 40448; 40484* (KY 6); 40489* (KY 6); 42101; 42102; 42103; 42104* (KY 1); 42122* (KY 1); 42123 42124; 42127; 42128; 42129* (KY 1); 42130; 42131; 42133* (KY 1); 42141; 42142 42152; 42154 42155* (KY 1); 42156; 42157* (KY 1); 42159; 42160; 42163; 42166* (KY 1); 42170* (KY 1); 42171; 42207; 42210; 42214; 42235; 42250; 42257 42259 42264; 42270; 42274; 42275; 42284; 42285; 42301; 42302; 42303; 42334; 42343* (KY 1); 42348; 42349* (KY 1); 42351; 42355; 42361* (KY 1); 42364; 42366* (KY 1); 42368* (KY 1); 42373; 42375; 42376* (KY 1); 42377; 42378* (KY 1); 42516 42528; 42539; 42541; 42565; 42566; 42567* (KY 5, KY 6); 42701; 42712; 42713 42716; 42718; 42719; 42721; 42722; 42724; 42726; 42728* (KY 1); 42729; 42731* (KY 1); 42732; 42733; 42736; 42740; 42743* (KY 1); 42746; 42748; 42749; 42754; 42755; 42757; 42758; 42762 42764; 42765; 42766; 42772; 42776; 42779; 42780 42781; 42782; 42783; 42784; 42785; 42787; 42788.

3rd District: 40025; 40027; 40041; 40059* (KY 4); 40118* (KY 2); 40200 40201; 40202; 40203; 40204; 40205; 40206; 40207; 40208; 40209; 40210; 40211 40212 40213; 40214* (KY 2); 40215; 40216; 40217; 40218; 40219* (KY 2); 40220 40221 40222; 40223* (KY 2); 40225; 40228* (KY 2); 40229* (KY 2); 40231; 40232 40233; 40234; 40235; 40236; 40237; 40238; 40239; 40241* (KY 2); 40242; 40243* (KY 2); 40245* (KY 2, KY 4); 40250; 40251; 40252; 40255; 40256; 40257; 40258* (KY 2); 40259; 40261; 40266; 40268; 40270; 40272* (KY 2); 40280; 40285; 40287 40289; 40291* (KY 2); 40292 40293; 40294; 40295; 40296; 40297; 40298; 40299* (KY 2).

4th District: 40003; 40006; 40007; 40010; 40011; 40014; 40017; 40019; 40022 40023* (KY 2); 40026; 40031; 40032; 40036; 40045; 40050; 40055; 40056; 40057 40058; 40059* (KY 3); 40065; 40066; 40067; 40068; 40070; 40076; 40077; 40245* (KY 2, KY 3); 40311* (KY 6); 40313; 40317; 40319; 40327; 40329; 40351; 40355 40359; 40361* (KY 6); 40363; 40379* (KY 6); 40389; 40601* (KY 6) 41001; 41002; 41004; 41005; 41006; 41007; 41008; 41009; 41010; 41011; 41012 41014; 41015; 41016; 41017; 41018; 41019; 41021; 41030; 41033; 41034; 41035 41037; 41039; 41040; 41041; 41042; 41043; 41044; 41045; 41046; 41048; 41049 41051; 41052; 41053; 41054; 41056; 41059; 41061; 41062; 41063; 41064 41065; 41071; 41072; 41073; 41074; 41075; 41076; 41080; 41081; 41083; 41085 41086; 41091; 41092; 41093; 41094; 41095; 41096; 41097; 41098; 41099; 41101 41102; 41105; 41114; 41121; 41124; 41125; 41127; 41128; 41129; 41131 41132 41135; 41137; 41139; 41141; 41142; 41143; 41144; 41146; 41149; 41150; 41152 41156; 41159; 41160; 41163; 41164; 41166; 41168; 41169; 41170; 41171; 41173 41174;

41175; 41177; 41179; 41180; 41181; 41183; 41189; 41201; 41211; 41230* (KY 5); 41232; 41253; 41264; 41472* (KY 5); 45275* (OH 2).

5th District: 25661* (WV 3); 37715* (TN 1); 37851* (TN 1); 37892* (TN 4) 40316; 40322; 40336* (KY 6); 40341; 40345; 40346; 40365; 40387; 40402; 40403* (KY 6); 40407; 40409; 40417; 40419* (KY 6); 40421; 40430; 40434; 40435; 40441 40445; 40447* (KY 6); 40455; 40456; 40460; 40465; 40467; 40473; 40481; 40486 40488; 40492; 40494; 40701; 40702; 40724; 40729; 40730; 40734; 40737; 40740 40741; 40742; 40743; 40745; 40751; 40754; 40755; 40759; 40763; 40769; 40771 40801; 40803; 40806; 40807; 40808; 40810; 40813; 40815; 40816; 40818; 40819 40820; 40823; 40824; 40825; 40826; 40827; 40828; 40829; 40830; 40831; 40840 40843; 40844; 40845; 40846; 40847; 40849; 40854; 40855; 40856; 40858; 40861 40862; 40863; 40865; 40867; 40868; 40870; 40873; 40874; 40902; 40903; 40906 40911; 40913; 40914; 40915; 40917; 40921; 40923; 40927; 40930; 40931; 40932 40935; 40936; 40939; 40940; 40941; 40943; 40944; 40946; 40949; 40951; 40953 40955; 40958; 40962; 40964; 40965; 40970; 40972; 40977; 40978; 40979; 40980; 40981; 40982; 40983; 40988; 40995; 40997; 40999; 41203; 41204; 41214; 41215 41216; 41219; 41220; 41222; 41224; 41225; 41226; 41228; 41230* (KY 4) 41231 41234; 41237; 41238; 41240; 41250; 41254; 41255; 41256; 41257; 41258; 41260 41261; 41262; 41263; 41265; 41266; 41267; 41268; 41269; 41271; 41274; 41301 41306; 41307; 41310; 41311; 41313; 41314; 41315; 41316; 41317; 41321; 41323 41327; 41328; 41331; 41332; 41333; 41338; 41339; 41340; 41342; 41343; 41344 41346; 41347; 41348; 41351; 41352; 41357; 41358; 41360; 41362; 41363; 41364 41365; 41366; 41367; 41368; 41369; 41370; 41377; 41378; 41385; 41386; 41390 41391; 41396; 41397; 41406; 41407; 41408; 41409; 41410; 41411; 41412; 41413 41417; 41419; 41421; 41422; 41425; 41426; 41427; 41430; 41431; 41433; 41438 41441; 41443; 41444; 41447; 41451; 41452; 41456; 41457; 41459; 41464; 41465 41466; 41467; 41472* (KY 4); 41474; 41477; 41501; 41502; 41503; 41512; 41513 41514; 41517; 41518; 41519; 41520; 41521; 41522; 41524; 41526; 41527; 41528 41529; 41531; 41534; 41535; 41536; 41537; 41538; 41539; 41540; 41542; 41543 41544; 41545; 41546; 41547; 41548; 41549; 41550; 41551; 41553; 41554; 41555 41557; 41558; 41559; 41560; 41561; 41562; 41563; 41564; 41565; 41566; 41567 41568; 41569; 41570; 41571; 41572; 41574; 41601; 41602; 41603; 41604; 41605 41606; 41607; 41612; 41614; 41615; 41616; 41619; 41621; 41622; 41625; 41626 41627; 41629; 41630; 41631; 41632; 41633; 41635; 41636; 41637; 41639; 41640 41641; 41642; 41643; 41645; 41647; 41649; 41650; 41651; 41653; 41655; 41659 41660; 41663; 41666; 41667; 41668; 41669; 41701; 41702; 41710; 41712; 41713 41714; 41719; 41720; 41721; 41722; 41723; 41725; 41727; 41728; 41729; 41730 41731; 41732; 41733; 41735; 41736; 41739; 41740; 41743; 41745; 41746; 41747 41749; 41751; 41754; 41756; 41759; 41760; 41762; 41763; 41764; 41765; 41766 41771; 41772; 41773; 41774; 41775; 41776; 41777; 41778; 41801; 41804; 41805 41810; 41811; 41812; 41815; 41817; 41819; 41821; 41822; 41823; 41824; 41825 41826; 41828; 41829; 41831; 41832; 41833; 41834; 41835; 41836; 41837; 41838 41839; 41840; 41843; 41844; 41845; 41847; 41848; 41849; 41855; 41858; 41859 41861; 41862; 42001; 42002; 42510; 42511; 42518; 42519; 42532; 42533; 42536 42544; 42553; 42554; 42555; 42557; 42558; 42563; 42564; 42567* (KY 2, KY 6) 42607; 42611; 42613; 42618; 42631; 42632; 42633; 42634; 42635; 42638; 42639 42640; 42643; 42647; 42648; 42649; 42653; 42655.

6th District: 40306; 40309; 40310; 40311* (KY 4); 40312; 40320; 40324; 40330* (KY 2); 40334; 40336* (KY 5); 40337; 40339; 40340; 40342; 40347; 40348; 40350 40353; 40356; 40357; 40358; 40360; 40361* (KY 5); 40362; 40366; 40370; 40371 40372; 40374; 40376; 40379* (KY 4); 40380; 40383; 40385; 40388; 40390; 40391 40392; 40403* (KY 5); 40404; 40405; 40410; 40415; 40419* (KY 5); 40420; 40422 40423; 40426; 40437* (KY 2); 40440; 40442* (KY 2); 40444; 40446; 40447* (KY 5); 40452; 40461; 40464; 40468; 40471; 40472; 40475; 40476; 40484* (KY 2) 40489* (KY 2); 40495; 40500; 40501; 40502; 40503; 40504; 40505; 40506; 40507 40508; 40509; 40510; 40511; 40512; 40513; 40514; 40515; 40516; 40517; 40522 40523; 40524; 40526; 40533; 40536; 40544; 40546; 40555; 40574; 40575; 40576 40577; 40578; 40579; 40580; 40581; 40582; 40583; 40584; 40585; 40586; 40587 40588; 40589; 40590; 40591; 40592; 40593; 40594; 40595; 40596; 40601* (KY 4) 40602; 40603; 40604; 40618; 40619; 40620; 40621; 40622; 41003; 41031; 42567* (KY 2, KY 5).

Louisiana

1st District: 70001* (LA 2); 70002; 70003* (LA 2); 70004; 70005; 70006; 70009 70010; 70011; 70033; 70055; 70058* (LA 2, LA 3); 70062* (LA 2); 70064; 70065* (LA 2); 70072* (LA 2, LA 3); 70073; 70094* (LA 2); 70115* (LA 2); 70118* (LA 2); 70119* (LA 2); 70121* (LA 2); 70122* (LA 2); 70123* (LA 2); 70124; 70181 70183; 70184; 70401* (LA 4); 70402; 70403* (LA 4); 70404; 70420; 70422* (LA 4); 70426; 70427; 70429; 70431; 70433; 70434; 70437; 70438; 70442; 70443* (LA 4); 70444* (LA 4); 70445; 70446; 70447; 70448; 70449; 70450; 70452; 70454 70455; 70456* (LA 4); 70457; 70458; 70459; 70460; 70461; 70462; 70463; 70464 70466; 70467; 70469; 70470; 70711; 70726* (LA 4, LA 6); 70733; 70744; 70754* (LA 4, LA 6); 70785* (LA 4, LA 6).

2nd District: 70001* (LA 1); 70003* (LA 1); 70032* (LA 3); 70053; 70054 70056* (LA 3); 70058* (LA 1, LA 3); 70059; 70060; 70062* (LA 1); 70063; 70065* (LA 1); 70072* (LA 1, LA 3); 70094* (LA 1); 70096; 70100; 70112; 70113; 70114 70115* (LA 1); 70116; 70117; 70118* (LA 1); 70119* (LA 1); 70121* (LA 1) 70122* (LA 1); 70123* (LA 1); 70125; 70126; 70127; 70128; 70129; 70130; 70131 70139; 70140; 70141; 70142; 70146; 70148; 70150; 70151; 70152; 70153; 70154 70156; 70157; 70158; 70159; 70160; 70161; 70162; 70163; 70164; 70165; 70166 70167; 70170; 70172; 70174; 70175; 70176; 70177; 70178; 70179; 70182; 70185 70186; 70187; 70189; 70190; 70195.

3rd District: 70030; 70031; 70032* (LA 2); 70036; 70037; 70038; 70039; 70040 70041; 70042; 70043; 70044; 70046; 70047; 70049; 70050; 70051; 70052; 70056* (LA 2); 70057; 70058* (LA 1, LA 2); 70066; 70067; 70068; 70069; 70070; 70071 70072* (LA 1, LA 2); 70075; 70076; 70078; 70079; 70080; 70081; 70082; 70083 70084; 70085; 70086; 70087; 70090; 70091; 70092; 70143; 70145; 70149; 70301 70302; 70310; 70339; 70340; 70341; 70342; 70343; 70344; 70345; 70346; 70352 70353; 70354; 70355; 70356; 70357; 70358; 70359; 70360; 70361; 70363; 70364 70371; 70372; 70373; 70374; 70375; 70376; 70377; 70380; 70381; 70390; 70391 70392; 70393; 70394; 70395; 70397; 70421; 70513; 70514; 70518* (LA 7); 70522 70523; 70538; 70540; 70544; 70552; 70560; 70562; 70569; 70707; 70718; 70721 70723; 70725; 70728; 70734* (LA 4); 70737* (LA 4); 70738; 70743; 70763; 70769* (LA 4); 70774; 70778; 70788* (LA 4); 70792.

4th District: 70401* (LA 1); 70403* (LA 1); 70422* (LA 1); 70436; 70441 70443* (LA 1); 70444* (LA 1); 70451; 70453; 70456* (LA 1); 70465; 70501* (LA 7); 70506* (LA 7); 70507* (LA 7); 70520* (LA 7); 70570* (LA 6, LA 7); 70582* (LA 7); 70583* (LA 7); 70589; 70704; 70712; 70714* (LA 6); 70715; 70716 70722; 70726* (LA 1, LA 6); 70730; 70732; 70734* (LA 3); 70737* (LA 3); 70739* (LA 6); 70747; 70748; 70751; 70753; 70755* (LA 6); 70759* (LA 6); 70760* (LA 6); 70761; 70764* (LA 6); 70765; 70767* (LA 6); 70769* (LA 3); 70770* (LA 6) 70775; 70776; 70777; 70780* (LA 6); 70782; 70783* (LA 6); 70784; 70785* (LA 1, LA 6); 70787; 70788* (LA 3); 70789; 70791* (LA 6); 70800; 70801; 70802* (LA 6); 70804; 70805; 70806* (LA 6); 70807; 70808* (LA 6); 70809* (LA 6); 70810* (LA 6); 70811* (LA 6); 70812* (LA 6); 70813; 70814* (LA 6); 70815* (LA 6); 70818* (LA 6); 70820* (LA 6); 70821; 70822; 70823; 70825 70826; 70828; 70831 70833; 70836; 70837; 70874; 70883; 70892; 70893; 70894; 70896; 70898; 71004 71006* (LA 5); 71018* (LA 5); 71021; 71029; 71038; 71040* (LA 5); 71043* (LA 5); 71048; 71055* (LA 5); 71060* (LA 5); 71064* (LA 5); 71071* (LA 5); 71075* (LA 5); 71079; 71082* (LA 5); 71101* (LA 5); 71103; 71104* (LA 5); 71105* (LA 5); 71106* (LA 5); 71107* (LA 5); 71108* (LA 5); 71109* (LA 5); 71111* (LA 5); 71112* (LA 5); 71120; 71129* (LA 5); 71130; 71133; 71136; 71148; 71151; 71152 71153; 71154; 71156; 71161; 71162; 71163; 71164; 71165; 71166; 71201* (LA 5) 71202* (LA 5); 71203* (LA 5); 71220* (LA 5); 71222* (LA 5); 71223; 71229 71233; 71235* (LA 5); 71245; 71250; 71253; 71254; 71256; 71260; 71261* (LA 5) 71264* (LA 5); 71270* (LA 5); 71272; 71273; 71275* (LA 5); 71276; 71282* (LA 5) 71286; 71301* (LA 6); 71302* (LA 6); 71316; 71322* (LA 6); 71325* (LA 6) 71326* (LA 6); 71330; 71334* (LA 6); 71335; 71345; 71346* (LA 6); 71347 71353* (LA 6); 71354* (LA 6); 71356; 71357; 71358; 71360* (LA 6); 71364 71366; 71369; 71373* (LA 6); 71375; 71749* (AR 4).

5th District: 71001; 71002; 71003; 71006* (LA 4); 71007; 71008; 71009 71014 71016; 71018* (LA 4); 71019; 71020; 71023; 71024; 71025; 71027; 71028; 71030 71031* (LA 6); 71032; 71033; 71034; 71036; 71037; 71039; 71040* (LA 4); 71043* (LA 4); 71044; 71045; 71046; 71047; 71049; 71050; 71051; 71052; 71055* (LA 4) 71058; 71059; 71060* (LA 4); 71061; 71063; 71064* (LA 4); 71066; 71067; 71068 71069; 71070; 71071* (LA 4); 71072; 71073; 71075* (LA 4); 71078; 71080; 71082* (LA 4); 71101* (LA 4); 71102; 71104* (LA 4); 71105* (LA 4); 71106* (LA 4) 71107* (LA 4); 71108* (LA 4); 71109* (LA 4); 71110; 71111* (LA 4); 71112* (LA 4); 71113; 71115; 71118; 71119; 71129* (LA 4); 71134; 71135; 71137; 71138 71139; 71149; 71171; 71172; 71201* (LA 4); 71202* (LA 4); 71203* (LA 4); 71207 71208; 71209; 71210; 71211; 71212; 71213; 71218; 71219; 71220* (LA 4) 71221; 71222* (LA 4); 71225; 71226; 71227; 71230; 71232; 71234; 71235* (LA 4) 71237; 71238; 71240; 71241; 71242; 71243; 71247; 71249; 71251; 71259 71261* (LA 4); 71263; 71266; 71268; 71269; 71270* (LA 4); 71275* (LA 4) 71277; 71279; 71280; 71281; 71282* (LA 4); 71284; 71291; 71292; 71294; 71295 71324; 71336; 71378; 71411; 71412; 71414; 71416; 71420; 71421; 71428; 71434 71447* (LA 6); 71450; 71452; 71455* (LA 6); 71456; 71457; 71458; 71468; 71469 71471; 71483* (LA 6); 71497.

6th District: 70512* (LA 7); 70570* (LA 4, LA 7); 70571; 70577* (LA 7); 70586* (LA 7); 70639; 70642; 70656* (LA 7); 70659; 70710; 70714* (LA 4); 70717 70719; 70720; 70726* (LA 1, LA 4); 70727; 70729; 70736; 70739* (LA 4); 70740 70749; 70750; 70752; 70754* (LA 1); 70755* (LA 4); 70756; 70757; 70759* (LA 4); 70760* (LA 4); 70762; 70764* (LA 4); 70767* (LA 4); 70770* (LA 4); 70772 70773; 70780* (LA 4); 70781; 70783* (LA 4); 70785* (LA 1, LA 4); 70786; 70791* (LA 4); 70802* (LA 4); 70803; 70806* (LA 4); 70808* (LA 4); 70809* (LA 4); 70810* (LA 4); 70811* (LA 4); 70812* (LA 4); 70814* (LA 4); 70815* (LA 4) 70816; 70817; 70818* (LA 4); 70819; 70820* (LA 4); 70827; 70835; 70879; 70884 70895; 71031* (LA 5); 71065; 71301* (LA 4); 71302* (LA 4); 71303; 71306 71307; 71309; 71311; 71315; 71318; 71320; 71321; 71322* (LA 4); 71323; 71325* (LA 4); 71326* (LA 4); 71327; 71328; 71329; 71331; 71333; 71334* (LA 4) 71338; 71339; 71340; 71341; 71342; 71343; 71344; 71346* (LA 4); 71348; 71350 71351; 71353* (LA 4); 71354* (LA 4); 71355; 71359; 71360* (LA 4); 71361 71362; 71363; 71365; 71367; 71368; 71371; 71372; 71373* (LA 4); 71377; 71401 71403; 71404; 71405; 71406; 71407; 71409; 71410; 71415; 71417; 71418; 71419 71422; 71423; 71424; 71425; 71426; 71427; 71429; 71430; 71431; 71432; 71433 71435; 71436; 71437; 71438; 71439; 71440; 71441; 71443; 71444; 71445; 71446 71447* (LA 5); 71448; 71449; 71451; 71454; 71455* (LA 5); 71459; 71460; 71461 71462; 71465; 71466; 71467; 71472; 71473; 71474; 71475; 71477; 71479; 71480 71481; 71483* (LA 5); 71485; 71486; 71496.

7th District: 70501* (LA 4); 70502; 70503; 70504; 70505; 70506* (LA 4); 70507* (LA 4); 70508; 70509; 70510; 70511; 70512* (LA 6); 70515; 70516; 70517; 70518* (LA 4); 70519; 70520* (LA 4); 70521; 70524; 70525; 70526; 70527; 70528; 70529 70531; 70532; 70533; 70534; 70535; 70537; 70541; 70542; 70543; 70546; 70548 70549; 70550; 70551; 70554; 70555; 70556; 70557; 70558; 70559; 70570* (LA 4, LA 6); 70575; 70576; 70577* (LA 6); 70578; 70580; 70581; 70582* (LA 4); 70583* (LA 4); 70584; 70585; 70586* (LA 6); 70591; 70592; 70593; 70598; 70601; 70602 70605; 70606; 70609; 70611; 70612; 70616; 70629; 70630; 70631; 70632; 70633 70634; 70637; 70638; 70640; 70643; 70644; 70645; 70646; 70647; 70648; 70650 70651; 70652; 70653; 70654; 70655; 70656* (LA 6); 70657; 70658; 70660; 70661 70662; 70663; 70664; 70668; 70669; 71463.

Maine

1st District: 03901; 03902; 03903; 03904; 03905; 03906; 03907; 03908; 03909 03910; 03911; 04001; 04002; 04003; 04004; 04005; 04006; 04007; 04008; 04009 04011; 04013; 04014; 04015; 04017; 04019; 04020; 04021; 04024; 04027; 04028 04029; 04030; 04031; 04032; 04033; 04038; 04039; 04040; 04042; 04043; 04046 04047; 04048; 04049; 04050; 04053; 04054; 04055; 04056; 04057; 04060; 04061; 04062; 04063; 04064; 04066; 04067; 04069; 04070; 04071; 04072; 04073; 04074 04075; 04076; 04077; 04078; 04079; 04082; 04083; 04084; 04085; 04086; 04087 04090; 04091; 04092; 04093; 04094; 04095; 04096; 04098; 04100; 04101; 04102 04103; 04104; 04105; 04106; 04107; 04108; 04109; 04110; 04112; 04116; 04122 04123; 04124; 04259; 04260; 04265; 04284; 04330; 04332; 04333; 04336; 04338 04341; 04342; 04343; 04344; 04345; 04346; 04347; 04348; 04349; 04350; 04351 04352; 04353; 04354; 04355; 04357; 04358; 04359; 04360; 04361; 04362; 04363 04364; 04530; 04535; 04536; 04537; 04538; 04539; 04541; 04543; 04544; 04547 04548; 04549; 04551; 04552; 04553; 04554; 04555; 04556; 04558; 04562; 04563 04564; 04565; 04567; 04568; 04570; 04571; 04572; 04573; 04574; 04575; 04576 04578; 04579; 04645; 04841; 04843; 04846; 04847; 04848; 04849; 04850; 04851 04852; 04853; 04854; 04855; 04856; 04857; 04858; 04859; 04860; 04861; 04862 04863; 04864; 04865; 04901; 04903;

04910; 04915* (ME 2); 04917; 04918; 04922 04926; 04927; 04935; 04941; 04949; 04952* (ME 2); 04957* (ME 2); 04962; 04963 04973; 04987; 04988; 04989.

2nd District: 03579* (NH 2); 04010; 04016; 04022; 04037; 04041; 04051; 04058 04068; 04080; 04081; 04088; 04210; 04211; 04212; 04216; 04217; 04219; 04220 04221; 04223; 04224; 04225; 04226; 04227; 04228; 04230; 04231; 04233; 04234 04235; 04236; 04237; 04238; 04239; 04240; 04241; 04243; 04250; 04251; 04252 04253; 04254; 04255; 04256; 04257; 04258; 04261; 04262; 04263; 04266; 04267 04268; 04270; 04271; 04273; 04274; 04275; 04276; 04278; 04279; 04280; 04281 04282; 04283; 04285; 04286; 04287; 04288; 04289; 04290; 04291; 04292; 04294 04401; 04402; 04406; 04408; 04410; 04411; 04412; 04413; 04414; 04415; 04416 04417; 04418; 04419; 04420; 04421; 04422; 04423; 04424; 04426; 04427; 04428 04429; 04430; 04431; 04433; 04434; 04435; 04438; 04441; 04442; 04443; 04444 04446; 04448; 04449; 04450; 04451; 04453; 04454; 04455; 04456; 04457; 04458 04459; 04460; 04461; 04462; 04463; 04464; 04465; 04467; 04468; 04469; 04471 04472; 04473; 04474; 04475; 04476; 04478; 04479; 04481; 04482; 04485; 04487 04488; 04489; 04490; 04491; 04492; 04493; 04495; 04496; 04497; 04605; 04606 04607; 04608; 04609; 04611; 04612; 04613; 04614; 04615; 04616; 04617; 04618 04619; 04622; 04623; 04624; 04625; 04626; 04627; 04628; 04629; 04630; 04631 04634; 04635; 04637; 04638; 04640; 04642; 04643; 04644; 04646; 04648; 04649 04650; 04652; 04653; 04654; 04655; 04656; 04657; 04658; 04659; 04660; 04661 04662; 04664; 04665; 04667; 04668; 04669; 04671; 04672; 04673; 04674 04675; 04676; 04677; 04678; 04679; 04680; 04681; 04683; 04684; 04685; 04686 04689; 04690; 04691; 04692; 04693; 04694; 04730; 04732; 04733; 04734; 04735 04736; 04737; 04738; 04739; 04740; 04741; 04742; 04743; 04744; 04745; 04746 04747; 04749; 04750; 04751; 04756; 04757; 04758; 04759; 04760; 04761; 04762 04763; 04764; 04765; 04766; 04767; 04768; 04769; 04770; 04772; 04773; 04774 04775; 04776; 04777; 04779; 04780; 04781; 04782; 04783; 04784; 04785; 04786 04787; 04788; 04911; 04912; 04915* (ME 1); 04920; 04921; 04923; 04924; 04925 04928; 04929; 04930; 04932; 04933; 04936; 04937; 04938; 04939; 04940; 04942 04943; 04944; 04945; 04947; 04950; 04951; 04952* (ME 1); 04953; 04954; 04955 04956; 04957* (ME 1); 04958; 04961; 04964; 04965; 04966; 04967; 04969; 04970 04971; 04972; 04974; 04975; 04976; 04978; 04979; 04981; 04982; 04983; 04984 04985; 04986; 04992.

Maryland

1st District: 19973* (DE 1); 21012* (MD 2); 21032* (MD 5); 21037* (MD 5) 21054* (MD 5); 21060; 21061* (MD 3); 21062; 21076* (MD 3, MD 5); 21108; 21113* (MD 3, MD 5); 21114* (MD 5); 21122* (MD 2); 21144* (MD 3); 21146* (MD 2) 21225* (MD 3); 21226; 21240; 21400; 21401* (MD 5); 21402* (MD 5); 21403 21405; 21601; 21606 21607; 21609; 21610; 21612; 21613; 21617; 21619; 21620 21622; 21623; 21624; 21625; 21626; 21627; 21628; 21629; 21631; 21632; 21634 21635; 21636; 21637; 21638; 21639; 21640; 21641; 21643; 21644; 21645; 21646 21647; 21648; 21649; 21650; 21651; 21652; 21653; 21654; 21655; 21656; 21657 21658; 21659; 21660; 21661; 21662; 21663; 21664; 21665; 21666; 21667; 21668 21669; 21670; 21671; 21672; 21673; 21675; 21676; 21677; 21678; 21679; 21681 21682; 21683; 21684; 21685; 21686; 21687; 21688; 21690; 21801; 21802; 21803 21810; 21811; 21813; 21814; 21816; 21817; 21820; 21821; 21822; 21824 21826 21829; 21830; 21835; 21836; 21837; 21838; 21840; 21841; 21842; 21849; 21850 21851; 21852; 21853; 21856; 21857; 21858; 21861; 21862; 21863; 21864; 21865 21866; 21867; 21868; 21869; 21870; 21871; 21872; 21874; 21875; 21901; 21902 21903; 21904; 21911; 21912; 21913; 21914; 21915; 21916; 21917; 21918; 21919 21920; 21921; 21922; 21930.

2nd District: 21001; 21005; 21009; 21010; 21012* (MD 1); 21013; 21014; 21015 21017; 21018; 21020; 21021; 21023; 21024; 21027; 21028; 21030; 21031; 21034 21040; 21047; 21050; 21051; 21052; 21053; 21057; 21071* (MD 3); 21074* (MD 6) 21078; 21082; 21084; 21085; 21087; 21092; 21093* (MD 3); 21094; 21101; 21105 21107* (MD 6); 21111; 21117* (MD 3, MD 7); 21120; 21122* (MD 1); 21128* (MD 3) 21130; 21131; 21132; 21136* (MD 3, MD 6, MD 7); 21139; 21146* (MD 1) 21152; 21153; 21154; 21155* (MD 6); 21156; 21160; 21161; 21162; 21204* (MD 3) 21212* (MD 3, MD 7); 21219; 21220; 21221; 21222* (MD 3); 21224* (MD 3, MD 7) 21234* (MD 3); 21236* (MD 3); 21237* (MD 3); 21239* (MD 3, MD 7); 21244 21281; 21284; 21285; 21286.

3rd District: 20755* (MD 5); 20794* (MD 5, MD 6); 21022; 21043* (MD 6, MD 7) 21044* (MD 6); 21045* (MD 6); 21046* (MD 6); 21055; 21061* (MD 1); 21071* (MD 2) 21076* (MD 1, MD 5); 21077; 21090; 21093* (MD 2); 21098; 21113* (MD 1, MD 5); 21117* (MD 2, MD 7); 21128* (MD 2); 21133* (MD 7); 21136* (MD 2, MD 6, MD 7) 21144* (MD 1); 21150; 21200; 21201* (MD 7); 21202* (MD 7); 21204* (MD 2) 21205* (MD 7) 21206* (MD 7); 21207* (MD 7); 21208* (MD 7); 21209* (MD 7) 21210* (MD 7); 21211* (MD 7); 21212* (MD 2, MD 7); 21213* (MD 7); 21214* (MD 7) 21215* (MD 7); 21216; 21217; 21218* (MD 7); 21222* (MD 2); 21223* (MD 7); 21224* (MD 2, MD 7); 21225* (MD 1) 21227* (MD 6, MD 7); 21228* (MD 7); 21229* (MD 7) 21230* (MD 7); 21231* (MD 7); 21234* (MD 2); 21236* (MD 2); 21237* (MD 2) 21239* (MD 2, MD 7); 21268; 21280; 21287; 21288; 21290; 21299.

4th District: 20084; 20315; 20331; 20335; 20613* (MD 5); 20703; 20706* (MD 5) 20710* (MD 5); 20712* (MD 5); 20720; 20721* (MD 5); 20722* (MD 5) 20731; 20735* (MD 5); 20737* (MD 5); 20743; 20744; 20746; 20747; 20748* (MD 5); 20749; 20750; 20752; 20753; 20757; 20769* (MD 5); 20772* (MD 5) 20773; 20775; 20780; 20781* (MD 5); 20782* (MD 5); 20783* (MD 5); 20784* (MD 5); 20785; 20787; 20788; 20789; 20791; 20794* (MD 8); 20866* (MD 8) 20900; 20901* (MD 8); 20903* (MD 5); 20904* (MD 8); 20905* (MD 8); 20906* (MD 8); 20907; 20908 20910* (MD 8); 20911; 20912; 20913; 20914; 20916; 20918; 20990.

5th District: 20601; 20602; 20603; 20604; 20606; 20607; 20608; 20609; 20610 20611; 20612; 20613* (MD 4); 20615; 20616; 20617; 20618; 20619; 20620; 20621 20622; 20623; 20624; 20625; 20626; 20627; 20628; 20629; 20630; 20632; 20634 20635; 20636; 20637; 20639; 20640; 20643; 20645; 20646; 20650; 20653; 20656 20657; 20658; 20659; 20660; 20661; 20662; 20664; 20667; 20670; 20674; 20675 20676; 20677; 20678; 20680; 20682; 20684; 20685; 20686; 20687; 20688; 20689 20690; 20692; 20693; 20695; 20697; 20701* (MD 6); 20704; 20705; 20706* (MD 4) 20707* (MD 6); 20708; 20709; 20710* (MD 4) 20711; 20712* (MD 4); 20714 20715; 20716; 20717; 20718; 20719; 20720* (MD 4); 20721* (MD 4); 20722* (MD 4); 20724; 20725; 20726; 20732; 20733; 20735* (MD 4);

20736; 20737* (MD 4) 20738; 20740; 20741; 20742; 20748* (MD 4); 20751; 20754; 20755* (MD 3) 20758 20764; 20765; 20768; 20769* (MD 4); 20770; 20771; 20772* (MD 4); 20776; 20778 20779; 20781* (MD 4); 20782* (MD 4); 20783* (MD 4); 20784* (MD 4); 20790 20794* (MD 3, MD 6); 20797; 20903* (MD 4); 20997; 21032* (MD 1); 21035; 21037* (MD 1); 21054* (MD 1); 21056; 21076* (MD 1, MD 3); 21106; 21113* (MD 1, MD 3) 21114* (MD 1); 21140; 21401* (MD 1); 21402* (MD 1); 21404; 21411; 21412.

6th District: 20701* (MD 5); 20723; 20759; 20763; 20777* (MD 8); 20794* (MD 3, MD 5); 20833* (MD 8); 20842* (MD 8); 20871* (MD 8); 21029; 21036; 21041 21042; 21043* (MD 3, MD 7); 21044* (MD 3); 21045* (MD 3); 21046* (MD 3) 21048; 21074* (MD 2); 21080; 21088; 21102; 21104* (MD 7); 21107* (MD 2) 21136* (MD 2, MD 3, MD 7); 21155* (MD 2); 21157; 21158; 21163* (MD 7); 21227* (MD 3, MD 7); 21501; 21502; 21503; 21504; 21505; 21520; 21521; 21522; 21523 21524; 21528; 21529; 21530; 21531; 21532; 21536; 21538; 21539; 21540; 21541 21542; 21543; 21545; 21546; 21550; 21555; 21556; 21557; 21560; 21561; 21562 21701; 21702; 21709; 21710; 21711; 21713 21714; 21715; 21716; 21717; 21718 21719; 21720; 21721; 21722; 21723; 21725; 21727; 21733; 21734; 21735; 21736 21737; 21738; 21740; 21741; 21742; 21746; 21747; 21748; 21749; 21750; 21754 21755; 21756; 21757; 21758; 21759; 21762; 21764; 21765; 21766 21767; 21768 21769; 21770; 21771* (MD 8); 21773; 21774; 21775; 21776; 21777; 21778 21779 21780; 21781; 21782; 21783; 21784; 21787; 21788; 21790; 21791; 21792; 21793 21794; 21795; 21797* (MD 8); 21798; 26726* (WV 1).

7th District: 21043* (MD 3, MD 6); 21104* (MD 6); 21117* (MD 2, MD 3); 21133* (MD 3); 21136* (MD 2, MD 3, MD 6); 21163* (MD 6); 21201* (MD 3); 21202* (MD 3); 21203; 21205* (MD 3); 21206* (MD 3); 21207* (MD 3); 21208* (MD 3); 21209* (MD 3) 21210* (MD 3); 21211* (MD 3); 21212* (MD 2, MD 3); 21213* (MD 3) 21214* (MD 3); 21215* (MD 3); 21216; 21217; 21218* (MD 3); 21223* (MD 3) 21224* (MD 2, MD 3) 21227* (MD 3, MD 6); 21228* (MD 3); 21229* (MD 3); 21230* (MD 3); 21231* (MD 3); 21233; 21235; 21239* (MD 2, MD 3); 21241; 21263 21264 21265; 21270; 21271; 21273; 21274; 21275; 21276; 21278; 21279; 21289; 21297 21298.

8th District: 20707* (MD 5); 20777* (MD 6); 20800; 20812; 20813; 20814; 20815 20816; 20817; 20818; 20824; 20825; 20827; 20830; 20832; 20833* (MD 6); 20837; 20838; 20839; 20841; 20842* (MD 6); 20847; 20848; 20849; 20850; 20851; 20852 20853; 20854; 20855; 20856; 20857; 20858; 20859; 20860; 20861; 20862; 20866* (MD 4); 20868; 20871* (MD 6); 20872; 20874; 20875; 20876; 20877; 20878; 20879 20880; 20884; 20885; 20886; 20889; 20890; 20891; 20892; 20894; 20895; 20896; 20897; 20898; 20899; 20901* (MD 4); 20902; 20904* (MD 4); 20905* (MD 4); 20906* (MD 4); 20910* (MD 4); 20915; 21771* (MD 6); 21797* (MD 6).

Massachusetts

1st District: 01002; 01003; 01004; 01005; 01007; 01008; 01011; 01012; 01026 01027* (MA 2); 01029; 01031; 01032; 01033; 01034; 01037; 01038; 01039; 01040 01041; 01050; 01054; 01059; 01066; 01068* (MA 3); 01070; 01071; 01072; 01073 01074; 01075* (MA 2); 01077; 01084; 01085; 01086; 01088; 01089; 01090; 01093 01094; 01096; 01097; 01098; 01201; 01202; 01203; 01220; 01222; 01223; 01224 01225; 01226; 01227; 01229; 01230; 01235; 01236; 01237; 01238; 01240; 01242 01243; 01244; 01245; 01247; 01252; 01253; 01254; 01255; 01256; 01257; 01258 01259; 01260; 01262; 01263; 01264; 01266; 01267; 01270; 01301; 01302; 01330 01331; 01337; 01338; 01339; 01340; 01341; 01342; 01343; 01344; 01346; 01347 01349; 01350; 01351; 01354; 01355; 01360; 01364; 01366; 01367; 01368; 01369 01370; 01373; 01375; 01376; 01378; 01379; 01380; 01420; 01430; 01431; 01436 01438; 01440; 01441; 01452; 01453; 01462; 01463* (MA 5); 01466; 01468; 01469 01473; 01474; 01475; 01477; 01531; 01535; 01585.

2nd District: 01001; 01009; 01010; 01013; 01014; 01020; 01021; 01022; 01027* (MA 1); 01028; 01030; 01035; 01036; 01053; 01056; 01057; 01060; 01061; 01063 01069; 01075* (MA 1); 01079; 01080; 01081; 01082; 01083; 01092; 01095; 01101 01102; 01103; 01104; 01105; 01106; 01107; 01108; 01109; 01111; 01114; 01115 01116; 01118; 01119; 01128; 01129; 01133; 01138; 01139; 01144; 01151; 01152 01199; 01501* (MA 3); 01504; 01506; 01507; 01509; 01515; 01516; 01518 01521; 01524; 01526; 01527* (MA 3); 01529; 01537; 01538; 01540; 01542; 01550 01562; 01566; 01569; 01570; 01571; 01586; 01588* (MA 3); 01590* (MA 3); 01611 01747; 01756; 01757* (MA 3); 01966* (MA 6); 02019* (MA 3); 02038* (MA 3, MA 4); 02093* (MA 3); 05501.

3rd District: 01068* (MA 1); 01501* (MA 2); 01503; 01505; 01510; 01517; 01519 01520; 01522; 01523* (MA 5); 01527* (MA 2); 01532; 01534; 01536; 01539; 01541 01543; 01545; 01546; 01549; 01560; 01564; 01568; 01580; 01581; 01582; 01583 01587; 01588* (MA 2); 01590* (MA 2); 01600; 01601; 01602; 01603; 01604; 01605 01606; 01607; 01608; 01609; 01610; 01612; 01613; 01614; 01615; 01653; 01654 01655; 01721* (MA 5, MA 7); 01746* (MA 4, MA 5); 01748; 01757* (MA 2); 01784 01809* (MA 2); 02031; 02035* (MA 4, MA 5); 02038* (MA 2, MA 4); 02048* (MA 4) 02053* (MA 4); 02056* (MA 4, MA 9); 02067* (MA 4); 02070; 02093* (MA 2); 02703 02714; 02717* (MA 4); 02720* (MA 4); 02721* (MA 4); 02722* (MA 4); 02723* (MA 4); 02724; 02725; 02726; 02740* (MA 4); 02747* (MA 4); 02748* (MA 4); 02760* (MA 4); 02761; 02762; 02763; 02766* (MA 4); 02771; 02777; 02790* (MA 4); 02791.

4th District: 01701* (MA 7); 01746* (MA 3, MA 5); 01770; 02030* (MA 9); 02032* (MA 9); 02035* (MA 3); 02038* (MA 2, MA 3); 02048* (MA 3); 02052* (MA 9) 02053* (MA 3); 02054* (MA 9); 02056* (MA 3, MA 9); 02067* (MA 3); 02081* (MA 9); 02135* (MA 8); 02146* (MA 8); 02147; 02154* (MA 7); 02157; 02158 02159 02160; 02161; 02162; 02164; 02165; 02166; 02167; 02168; 02181* (MA 9); 02194* (MA 9); 02195; 02215* (MA 8); 02258; 02324; 02325; 02327; 02330* (MA 10) 02333; 02337; 02338* (MA 10); 02339* (MA 10); 02341* (MA 10); 02346; 02347 02348; 02349; 02350; 02355; 02356* (MA 9); 02359; 02366; 02367; 02370* (MA 9); 02375* (MA 9); 02379 02532* (MA 10); 02538; 02558; 02571; 02576; 02702 02712; 02715; 02717* (MA 3); 02718* (MA 9); 02719; 02720* (MA 3); 02721* (MA 3); 02722* (MA 3); 02723* (MA 3); 02738 02739; 02740* (MA 3); 02741; 02742 02743; 02744; 02745; 02746; 02747* (MA 3); 02748* (MA 3); 02760* (MA 3) 02764; 02766* (MA 3); 02767* (MA 9); 02768; 02769; 02770; 02779* (MA 9) 02780* (MA 9); 02790* (MA 3).

5th District: 01432; 01433; 01450; 01451; 01460; 01463* (MA 1); 01464; 01467 01470; 01471; 01472; 01523* (MA 3); 01525; 01561; 01718; 01719; 01720; 01721* (MA 3, MA 7); 01740; 01741; 01742* (MA 3, MA 4); 01749 01752; 01754; 01772; 01773* (MA 6, MA 7); 01775; 01776; 01778* (MA 7); 01810* (MA 6); 01812; 01821* (MA 6); 01822; 01824; 01826; 01827; 01840; 01841; 01842 01843; 01844* (MA 6); 01845* (MA 6); 01850; 01851; 01852; 01853; 01854; 01862 01863; 01865; 01866; 01876; 01879; 01886; 01887* (MA 6); 01899; 02193* (MA 7) 05544.

6th District: 01730* (MA 7); 01731; 01773* (MA 5, MA 7); 01803* (MA 7); 01805 01810* (MA 5); 01821* (MA 5); 01830; 01831; 01832; 01833; 01834; 01835; 01844* (MA 5); 01845* (MA 5); 01860; 01864; 01867* (MA 7); 01885; 01887* (MA 5) 01889; 01901; 01902; 01903; 01904; 01905; 01906; 01907; 01908; 01910; 01913 01915; 01921; 01922; 01923; 01929; 01930; 01931; 01936; 01937; 01938; 01940 01944; 01945; 01947; 01949; 01950; 01951; 01952; 01960; 01961; 01964; 01965 01966* (MA 2); 01969; 01970; 01971; 01982; 01983; 01984; 01985.

7th District: 01701* (MA 4); 01721* (MA 3, MA 5); 01730* (MA 6); 01742* (MA 5); 01760; 01773* (MA 5, MA 6); 01778* (MA 5); 01801; 01803* (MA 6); 01806 01807; 01808; 01813; 01814; 01815; 01867* (MA 6); 01880; 01888; 01890; 02128* (MA 8); 02144* (MA 8); 02145* (MA 8); 02148; 02149; 02151* (MA 8); 02152 02153; 02154* (MA 4); 02155* (MA 8); 02156; 02172* (MA 8); 02173; 02174* (MA 8); 02175; 02176; 02177; 02180; 02193* (MA 5); 02254.

8th District: 02108* (MA 9); 02111* (MA 9); 02112; 02114* (MA 9); 02115 02116; 02117; 02118* (MA 9); 02119* (MA 9); 02120; 02121; 02122* (MA 9) 02123; 02124* (MA 9); 02125* (MA 9); 02126* (MA 9); 02127* (MA 9); 02128* (MA 7); 02129; 02130* (MA 9); 02131* (MA 9); 02133; 02134; 02135* (MA 4); 02136* (MA 9); 02138; 02139; 02140; 02141; 02142; 02143; 02144* (MA 7); 02145* (MA 7); 02146* (MA 4); 02150; 02151* (MA 7); 02155* (MA 7); 02163; 02172* (MA 7) 02174* (MA 7); 02178; 02179; 02199; 02201; 02202; 02205; 02215* (MA 4); 02216 02217; 02238; 02239; 02272; 02277; 02295.

9th District: 02021* (MA 10); 02026; 02030* (MA 4); 02032* (MA 4); 02052* (MA 4); 02054* (MA 4); 02056* (MA 3, MA 4); 02062; 02071; 02072; 02081* (MA 4) 02090; 02100; 02101; 02102; 02103; 02104; 02105; 02106; 02107; 02108* (MA 8) 02109; 02110; 02111* (MA 8); 02113; 02114* (MA 8); 02118* (MA 8); 02119* (MA 8); 02122* (MA 8); 02124* (MA 8); 02125* (MA 8); 02126* (MA 8); 02127* (MA 8) 02130* (MA 8); 02131* (MA 8); 02132; 02136* (MA 8); 02137; 02181* (MA 10); 02184; 02186* (MA 10); 02187; 02190* (MA 10); 02192; 02194* (MA 4); 02203 02204; 02206; 02207; 02208; 02209; 02210; 02211; 02212; 02222; 02241; 02266 02293; 02294; 02297; 02299; 02334; 02356* (MA 4); 02357; 02368* (MA 10) 02375* (MA 4); 02401* (MA 10); 02402* (MA 4); 02403; 02404; 02405; 02718* (MA 4); 02767* (MA 4); 02779* (MA 4); 02780* (MA 4).

10th District: 02018; 02020; 02021* (MA 9); 02025; 02040; 02041; 02043; 02045 02047; 02050; 02051; 02055; 02059; 02060; 02061; 02065; 02066; 02169; 02170 02171; 02186* (MA 9); 02188; 02189; 02190* (MA 9); 02191; 02269; 02322; 02330* (MA 4); 02331; 02332; 02338* (MA 4); 02339* (MA 4); 02341* (MA 4); 02343 02345; 02351; 02358; 02360; 02361; 02362; 02363; 02364; 02368* (MA 9); 02370* (MA 4); 02371; 02381; 02382; 02401* (MA 9); 02402* (MA 9); 02532* (MA 4) 02534; 02535; 02536; 02537; 02539; 02540; 02541; 02542; 02543; 02552; 02553 02554; 02556; 02557; 02559; 02561; 02562; 02563; 02564; 02565; 02568; 02573 02574; 02575; 02584; 02601; 02630; 02631; 02632; 02633; 02634; 02635; 02636 02637; 02638; 02639; 02641; 02642; 02643; 02644; 02645; 02646; 02647; 02648 02649; 02650; 02651; 02652; 02653; 02655; 02657; 02659; 02660; 02661; 02662 02663; 02664; 02666; 02667; 02668; 02669; 02670; 02671; 02672; 02673; 02675 02713; 02754.

Michigan

1st District: 48619* (MI 4); 48762* (MI 5); 49610; 49611; 49612; 49613* (MI 2); 49615 49616; 49617; 49620* (MI 2); 49621; 49622; 49627; 49628; 49629 49630; 49633 49635; 49636; 49637; 49640; 49643; 49646; 49647; 49648; 49649* (MI 2); 49650 49653; 49654; 49659; 49664; 49666; 49670; 49673; 49674; 49676 49680; 49682; 49683* (MI 2); 49684 49685; 49690; 49701; 49705; 49706; 49707 49709; 49710; 49711; 49712; 49713; 49715 49716; 49717; 49718; 49719; 49720 49721; 49722; 49723; 49724; 49725; 49726; 49727 49728; 49729; 49730; 49733 49735; 49736; 49737; 49738* (MI 4); 49739; 49740; 49743 49744; 49745; 49746 49747* (MI 5); 49748; 49749; 49751; 49752; 49753; 49755; 49756* (MI 4); 49757 49759; 49760; 49761; 49762; 49764; 49765; 49766; 49768; 49769; 49770 49774 49775; 49776; 49777; 49779; 49780; 49781; 49782; 49783; 49784; 49785 49786 49788; 49789; 49790; 49791; 49792; 49793; 49795; 49796; 49797; 49799 49801 49802; 49805; 49806; 49807; 49808; 49812; 49813; 49814; 49815; 49816 49817; 49818 49819; 49820; 49821; 49822; 49825; 49826; 49827; 49829; 49831; 49833; 49834; 49835 49836; 49837; 49838; 49839; 49840; 49841; 49843; 49845; 49847; 49848; 49849; 49852 49853; 49854; 49855; 49858; 49861; 49862; 49863 49864; 49865; 49866; 49868; 49869 49870; 49871; 49872; 49873; 49874; 49876 49877; 49878; 49879; 49880; 49881; 49883 49884; 49885; 49886; 49887; 49890 49891; 49892; 49893; 49894; 49895; 49896; 49901 49902; 49903; 49905; 49908 49909; 49910; 49911; 49912; 49913; 49915; 49916; 49917 49918; 49919; 49920 49921; 49922; 49924; 49925; 49927; 49929; 49930; 49931; 49934 49935; 49938 49942; 49943; 49945; 49946; 49947; 49948; 49950; 49952; 49953; 49955 49958 49959; 49960; 49961; 49962; 49963; 49964; 49965; 49967; 49968; 49969; 49970 49971.

2nd District: 49010* (MI 6); 49035; 49046* (MI 3, MI 7); 49058* (MI 3, MI 7) 49060* (MI 6); 49070; 49078* (MI 6); 49080* (MI 6); 49303; 49304; 49307* (MI 4); 49309; 49311 49312; 49313; 49314; 49315* (MI 3); 49316* (MI 3); 49318* (MI 3); 49323; 49327* (MI 3); 49328; 49330* (MI 3); 49331; 49333* (MI 3); 49335; 49337* (MI 4); 49343* (MI 3); 49344; 49345* (MI 3); 49348; 49349; 49401; 49402; 49403* (MI 3); 49404 49405; 49406; 49408* (MI 6) 49409; 49410; 49411; 49412; 49413; 49415; 49416; 49417 49418* (MI 3); 49419 49420; 49421; 49422; 49423; 49424; 49425; 49426; 49427; 49428 49429; 49430 49431; 49434; 49435* (MI 3); 49436; 49437; 49440; 49441; 49442; 49443 49444 49445; 49446; 49447; 49448; 49449; 49451; 49452; 49453; 49454; 49455; 49456 49457; 49458; 49459; 49460; 49461; 49463; 49464; 49501; 49502; 49504* (MI 3) 49601;

49613* (MI 1); 49614; 49618; 49619; 49620* (MI 1); 49623; 49625; 49626 49634; 49638; 49642; 49644; 49645; 49649* (MI 1); 49655* (MI 4); 49656; 49660 49663* (MI 4); 49668; 49675; 49677* (MI 4); 49683* (MI 1); 49688* (MI 4) 49689.

3rd District: 48301* (MI 11); 48809; 48815; 48834* (MI 4); 48837* (MI 4, MI 7); 48838* (MI 4); 48845* (MI 4); 48846; 48849* (MI 7); 48851; 48860; 48861* (MI 7); 48865; 48870 48873* (MI 4); 48875* (MI 4); 48881; 48887; 48890* (MI 7); 48897; 49017* (MI 7); 49046* (MI 2, MI 7); 49058* (MI 2, MI 7); 49073* (MI 7); 49301; 49302; 49306; 49315* (MI 2); 49316* (MI 2); 49317; 49318* (MI 2); 49319; 49321; 49325; 49326* (MI 4); 49327* (MI 2); 49330* (MI 2); 49331 49333* (MI 2); 49341; 49343* (MI 2, MI 4); 49345* (MI 2); 49351; 49355; 49356 49357; 49403* (MI 2); 49418* (MI 2); 49435* (MI 2); 49468; 49500; 49503 49504* (MI 2); 49505; 49506; 49507; 49508; 49509; 49510; 49512; 49514; 49516 49518; 49523; 49530; 49546; 49548; 49550; 49555; 49560; 49588; 49599.

4th District: 48414* (MI 8); 48415* (MI 8); 48417; 48449* (MI 8); 48457* (MI 5); 48460 (MI 5); 48601* (MI 5); 48603* (MI 5); 48604* (MI 5); 48608; 48610* (MI 5); 48612 48613* (MI 5); 48614; 48615; 48616; 48617; 48618; 48619* (MI 1); 48620; 48621; 48622 48623* (MI 5); 48624; 48625; 48626; 48627; 48628 48629; 48630; 48632; 48633; 48635 48636; 48637; 48640* (MI 5); 48641; 48642 48647; 48649; 48651; 48652* (MI 5); 48653 48654; 48655; 48656; 48657; 48661; 48662; 48667; 48670; 48674; 48686; 48722* (MI 5); 48734* (MI 5); 48739* (MI 5); 48756; 48761* (MI 5); 48770* (MI 5); 48801; 48802 48804; 48806; 48807 48808; 48810; 48811; 48812; 48817* (MI 8); 48818; 48820; 48822 48823* (MI 8); 48829; 48830; 48831; 48832; 48833; 48834* (MI 3); 48835; 48837* (MI 3, MI 7) 48838* (MI 3); 48840* (MI 8); 48841; 48845* (MI 3); 48847; 48848; 48850 48852 48853; 48856; 48857* (MI 8); 48858; 48859; 48862; 48866; 48867* (MI 8); 48871; 48872* (MI 8); 48873* (MI 3); 48874; 48875* (MI 3); 48877; 48878 48879; 48880; 48882; 48883 48884; 48885; 48886; 48888; 48889; 48891; 48893 48894; 48896; 48906* (MI 7, MI 8); 49305; 49307* (MI 2); 49310; 49320; 49322 49326* (MI 3); 49329; 49332; 49334; 49336 49337* (MI 2); 49338* (MI 2) 49339; 49340; 49342; 49343* (MI 2, MI 3); 49346; 49347 49631; 49632; 49639 49651; 49655* (MI 2); 49663* (MI 2); 49665; 49667; 49677* (MI 2) 49679; 49688* (MI 2); 49738* (MI 1); 49756* (MI 1).

5th District: 48032* (MI 10); 48097* (MI 10); 48401; 48410; 48412* (MI 9) 48413; 48415* (MI 4); 48416* (MI 10); 48419; 48420* (MI 9); 48421; 48422 48423* (MI 8, MI 9); 48426; 48427; 48432; 48433* (MI 8); 48434; 48435; 48437 48441; 48444* (MI 9, MI 10); 48445; 48446* (MI 9); 48450; 48452; 48453; 48454 48456; 48457* (MI 4); 48458; 48460* (MI 4); 48461; 48463; 48464; 48465; 48466 48467; 48468; 48469; 48470; 48471; 48472 48475; 48504* (MI 8, MI 9); 48505* (MI 9); 48506* (MI 9); 48509* (MI 9); 48556; 48601* (MI 4); 48602; 48603* (MI 4); 48604* (MI 4); 48605; 48606; 48607; 48609; 48610* (MI 4); 48611; 48613* (MI 4); 48623* (MI 4); 48631; 48634; 48640* (MI 4); 48650; 48652* (MI 4); 48658; 48659; 48663; 48701; 48703; 48705; 48706; 48707; 48708; 48710; 48720 48721; 48722* (MI 4); 48723; 48724; 48725; 48726; 48727; 48728; 48729; 48730 48731; 48732; 48733; 48734* (MI 4); 48735; 48736; 48737; 48738; 48739* (MI 4) 48740; 48741; 48742 48743; 48744; 48745; 48746; 48747; 48748; 48749; 48750 48753; 48754; 48755; 48757 48758; 48759; 48760; 48761* (MI 4); 48762* (MI 1) 48763; 48764; 48765; 48766; 48767 48768; 48769; 48770* (MI 4); 48787; 49747* (MI 1).

6th District: 49001; 49002; 49003; 49004; 49005; 49006; 49007; 49008; 49009 49010* (MI 2); 49011* (MI 7); 49012; 49013; 49014; 49015; 49019; 49022; 49023; 49026; 49027 49030* (MI 7); 49031; 49032; 49034; 49038; 49039; 49040* (MI 7); 49041; 49042 49043; 49045; 49047; 49052* (MI 7); 49053; 49055; 49056; 49057; 49060* (MI 2) 49061; 49062; 49063; 49064 49065; 49066; 49067; 49071; 49072; 49074; 49075 49077; 49078* (MI 2) 49079; 49080* (MI 2); 49081; 49083; 49084; 49085; 49087 49088; 49090; 49091; 49094; 49095; 49097 49098; 49099; 49101; 49102; 49103 49104; 49106; 49107; 49111; 49112; 49113; 49115 49116; 49117; 49119; 49120 49121; 49125; 49126; 49127; 49128; 49129; 49130; 49408* (MI 2); 49450.

7th District: 48115; 48118* (MI 8); 48158* (MI 8); 48160* (MI 13, MI 16) 48176* (MI 8); 48197* (MI 8, MI 13); 48813; 48821; 48827* (MI 8); 48837* (MI 3, MI 4); 48849* (MI 3); 48861* (MI 3); 48876; 48890* (MI 3); 48906* (MI 4, MI 8); 48907; 48908; 48911* (MI 3); 48917* (MI 8); 49011* (MI 6); 49015; 49016 49017* (MI 3); 49018; 49020; 49021; 49028 49029; 49030* (MI 6); 49033; 49036 49040* (MI 6); 49046* (MI 2, MI 3); 49050; 49051; 49052* (MI 6); 49058* (MI 2, MI 3); 49068; 49069; 49073* (MI 3); 49076; 49082; 49089 49092; 49094; 49096 49201; 49202; 49203; 49204; 49220; 49221; 49224; 49227; 49228 49229* (MI 16); 49230; 49231; 49232; 49233; 49234; 49235; 49236; 49237; 49238; 49239 49240; 49241; 49242; 49245; 49246; 49247; 49248; 49249; 49250; 49252; 49253; 49254 49255; 49256; 49257; 49258; 49259; 49261; 49262; 49263; 49264* (MI 16); 49265; 49266 49267* (MI 16); 49268; 49269; 49271; 49272; 49273; 49274; 49275; 49276* (MI 16) 49277; 49278; 49279; 49280; 49281; 49282; 49283; 49284; 49285* (MI 8); 49286; 49287 49288; 49289.

8th District: 48103* (MI 13); 48105* (MI 13); 48106; 48108* (MI 13); 48116 48118* (MI 7); 48130* (MI 13); 48137; 48139; 48143; 48158* (MI 7); 48169 48176* (MI 7); 48178* (MI 11, MI 13); 48189; 48197* (MI 7, MI 13); 48350* (MI 11); 48353 48356* (MI 11); 48357* (MI 11); 48380* (MI 11); 48414* (MI 4); 48418 48423* (MI 5, MI 9); 48429; 48430; 48433* (MI 5); 48436; 48439* (MI 9); 48442* (MI 9, MI 11); 48444* (MI 4); 48451; 48473; 48476; 48503* (MI 5); 48504* (MI 5, MI 9); 48505* (MI 5); 48507* (MI 9); 48529; 48532* (MI 9); 48557; 48559; 48805; 48816 48817* (MI 4); 48819; 48823* (MI 4); 48824; 48825; 48826 48827* (MI 7); 48836; 48840* (MI 4); 48842; 48843; 48844; 48854; 48857* (MI 4); 48863 48864; 48867* (MI 4); 48872* (MI 4); 48892; 48895; 48900; 48901; 48906* (MI 4, MI 7); 48909; 48910; 48911* (MI 7); 48912; 48913; 48915; 48916; 48917* (MI 7); 48918 48919 48921; 48922; 48924; 48929; 48930; 48933; 48937; 48950; 48956; 48980; 49251; 49264* (MI 7); 49285* (MI 7).

9th District: 48003* (MI 10); 48035; 48037; 48054; 48059; 48063; 48306* (MI 10); 48307; 48309; 48323* (MI 11); 48324* (MI 11); 48325; 48326; 48327; 48328 48329 48330; 48340; 48341* (MI 11); 48342; 48343; 48346; 48347; 48348; 48350* (MI 8); 48359; 48360; 48361; 48362; 48363; 48366; 48367; 48370; 48371; 48383* (MI 11); 48411; 48412* (MI 5); 48420* (MI 5); 48423* (MI 5, MI 8); 48428 48438; 48439* (MI 8); 48440; 48442* (MI 8, MI 11); 48444* (MI 5, MI 10); 48446* (MI 5); 48455; 48462; 48500 48501; 48502; 48503* (MI 5); 48504* (MI 5, MI 8); 48505* (MI 5); 48506* (MI 5); 48507* (MI 8); 48509* (MI 5); 48519 48529; 48531; 48532* (MI 8); 48550; 48551; 48552; 48553 48554; 48555.

10th District: 48001; 48002; 48003* (MI 9); 48004; 48005; 48006; 48014; 48021* (MI 12); 48022; 48023; 48026; 48027; 48028; 48032* (MI 5); 48036; 48038 48039; 48040; 48041; 48042; 48043; 48044; 48045; 48046; 48047; 48048; 48049 48051 48052; 48060; 48061; 48062; 48064; 48065; 48066* (MI 12); 48074; 48079 48080; 48081; 48082; 48089* (MI 12); 48093* (MI 12); 48094; 48095; 48097* (MI 5); 48236* (MI 14, MI 15); 48306* (MI 9); 48312* (MI 12); 48314* (MI 12) 48315; 48316; 48317* (MI 12); 48416* (MI 5); 48444* (MI 5, MI 9).

11th District: 48009* (MI 12); 48010; 48012; 48025; 48034; 48050; 48072* (MI 12); 48073* (MI 12); 48075* (MI 12); 48076; 48096; 48150* (MI 13); 48152 48153; 48154* (MI 13); 48165; 48167* (MI 13); 48178* (MI 8, MI 13); 48239* (MI 14); 48240* (MI 14); 48301* (MI 12); 48302; 48303* (MI 12); 48304; 48320 48322; 48323* (MI 9); 48324* (MI 9); 48331; 48332; 48333; 48334; 48335; 48336 48341* (MI 9); 48356* (MI 9); 48357* (MI 8); 48374; 48375; 48376; 48377 48380* (MI 8); 48381; 48382; 48383* (MI 9); 48386; 48387; 48390; 48393; 48442* (MI 8, MI 9); 54540* (WI 8); 54554* (WI 8).

12th District: 48007; 48009* (MI 11); 48015; 48017; 48021* (MI 10); 48030 48066* (MI 10); 48067; 48068; 48069; 48070; 48071; 48072* (MI 11); 48073* (MI 11); 48075* (MI 11); 48083; 48084; 48086; 48089* (MI 10); 48090; 48091; 48092 48093* (MI 10); 48098; 48099; 48220; 48237; 48303* (MI 11); 48308; 48310 48311; 48312* (MI 10); 48313; 48314* (MI 10); 48317* (MI 10); 48318; 48321 48397; 48398.

13th District: 48103* (MI 8); 48104; 48105* (MI 8); 48107; 48108* (MI 8) 48109; 48111; 48112; 48113; 48125* (MI 16); 48130* (MI 8); 48134* (MI 16) 48135; 48136; 48141; 48150* (MI 11); 48151; 48154* (MI 11); 48160* (MI 7, MI 16); 48164* (MI 16); 48167* (MI 11); 48170; 48174* (MI 16); 48175; 48178* (MI 8, MI 11); 48184; 48185; 48187; 48188; 48190; 48191; 48197* (MI 7, MI 8) 48198; 48242.

14th District: 48127* (MI 16); 48203* (MI 15); 48205* (MI 15); 48211* (MI 15) 48212* (MI 15); 48213* (MI 15); 48219; 48221; 48223; 48224* (MI 15); 48225 48227* (MI 15); 48228* (MI 15, MI 16); 48234; 48235; 48236* (MI 10, MI 15) 48238* (MI 15); 48239* (MI 11); 48240* (MI 11).

15th District: 48200; 48201; 48202; 48203* (MI 14); 48204; 48205* (MI 14) 48206; 48207; 48208; 48209; 48210; 48211* (MI 14); 48212* (MI 14); 48213* (MI 14); 48214; 48215; 48216; 48217* (MI 16); 48218; 48222; 48224* (MI 14); 48226 48227* (MI 14); 48228* (MI 14, MI 16); 48229; 48230; 48231; 48232; 48233 48236* (MI 10, MI 14); 48238* (MI 14); 48243; 48244; 48254; 48255; 48258 48260; 48264; 48265; 48266; 48267; 48268; 48269; 48272; 48274; 48275; 48277 48278; 48279; 48288; 48295; 48297; 48299.

16th District: 48101; 48110; 48117; 48120; 48121; 48122; 48123; 48124; 48125* (MI 13); 48126; 48127* (MI 14); 48128; 48131; 48133; 48134* (MI 13); 48138 48140; 48144; 48145; 48146; 48157; 48159; 48160* (MI 7, MI 13); 48161; 48164* (MI 13); 48166; 48173; 48174* (MI 13); 48177; 48179; 48180; 48182; 48183 48192; 48195; 48217* (MI 15); 48228* (MI 14, MI 15); 49229* (MI 7); 49267* (MI 7); 49270; 49276* (MI 7).

Minnesota

1st District: 52134* (IA 2); 52140* (IA 2); 52155* (IA 2); 52160* (IA 2) 55009* (MN 3); 55010; 55018; 55019; 55020; 55021; 55024* (MN 3); 55026; 55027 55031* (MN 3); 55033* (MN 3); 55041; 55044* (MN 3); 55046; 55049; 55052 55053; 55054; 55057; 55060; 55065; 55066; 55087; 55088; 55089* (MN 3); 55372* (MN 2, MN 3); 55379* (MN 2); 55901; 55902; 55903; 55904; 55905; 55906; 55909 55910; 55912; 55917; 55918; 55919; 55920; 55921; 55922* (IA 2); 55923; 55924 55925; 55926; 55927; 55929 55931; 55932; 55933; 55934; 55935; 55936; 55937 55938; 55939* (IA 2); 55940; 55941; 55942 55943; 55944; 55945; 55946; 55947 55949; 55950; 55951* (IA 2); 55952; 55953; 55954* (IA 2); 55955; 55956; 55957 55959; 55960; 55961; 55962; 55963; 55964; 55965; 55967 55968; 55969; 55970 55971; 55972; 55973; 55974* (IA 2); 55975; 55976; 55977; 55978; 55979; 55981 55982; 55983; 55985; 55986; 55987; 55988; 55990; 55991; 55992; 56001* (MN 2) 56002; 56007; 56009; 56010; 56013; 56014* (IA 5); 56016; 56017; 56020; 56023 56024; 56025; 56026; 56027* (IA 5); 56028; 56032; 56033; 56034; 56035 56036; 56037; 56042; 56043; 56045; 56046; 56047; 56048; 56050; 56051* (IA 5) 56052; 56055; 56057; 56058; 56061; 56063; 56064; 56065; 56067; 56068; 56069* (MN 2); 56070; 56071* (MN 2); 56072; 56076; 56077; 56078; 56080; 56089 56090 56091; 56092; 56093; 56096; 56097; 56098.

2nd District: 55301; 55302; 55307; 55310; 55312; 55313; 55314; 55315; 55317 55318; 55320* (MN 7); 55321; 55322; 55324; 55325; 55328* (MN 6); 55329* (MN 7); 55330* (MN 6, MN 8); 55331* (MN 6); 55332; 55333; 55334; 55335; 55336 55338; 55339; 55342; 55349; 55350; 55351; 55352; 55354; 55355; 55358; 55359* (MN 6); 55360 55362; 55363; 55364* (MN 6); 55365; 55366; 55367; 55368; 55370 55372* (MN 1, MN 3); 55373* (MN 6); 55374* (MN 6); 55375; 55376; 55378* (MN 3); 55379* (MN 1) 55380; 55381; 55382* (MN 7); 55383; 55385; 55386; 55387 55388; 55389* (MN 7); 55390; 55393; 55394; 55395; 55396; 55397; 55399; 55473 55550; 55551; 55552; 55553 55554; 55555; 55556; 55557; 55558; 55559; 55560 55561; 55562; 55563; 55564; 55565; 55566; 55567; 55568; 55569; 55575; 55580 55581; 55582; 55583; 55584; 55585; 55586; 55587; 55588; 55589; 55590; 55591 55592; 55594; 56001* (MN 1); 56003; 56011; 56019; 56021; 56022; 56030; 56031 56039; 56041; 56044; 56053; 56054; 56056; 56060; 56062; 56069* (MN 1); 56071* (MN 1); 56073; 56074; 56075; 56081; 56082; 56083; 56084 56085; 56087; 56088 56101; 56110; 56111; 56112; 56113; 56114; 56115; 56116; 56117* (IA 5); 56118 56119; 56120; 56121; 56122; 56123; 56124; 56125; 56126; 56127; 56128; 56129* (IA 5); 56130; 56131; 56132; 56133; 56134; 56135; 56136* (SD 1); 56137 56138* (IA 5, SD 1); 56139; 56140; 56141; 56142; 56143; 56144* (SD 1); 56145 56146 56147; 56149; 56150; 56151; 56152; 56153; 56155; 56156; 56157; 56158; 56159 56160; 56161; 56162; 56164* (SD 1); 56165; 56166; 56167; 56168; 56169; 56170 56171; 56172; 56173; 56174; 56175; 56176; 56177; 56178; 56179; 56180; 56181 56183; 56185; 56186; 56187; 56201; 56208; 56209; 56210; 56211; 56212; 56214 56215; 56216; 56218; 56220; 56222; 56223; 56224; 56225; 56226; 56227; 56228 56229; 56230; 56231; 56232; 56233; 56237; 56238; 56239; 56240; 56241; 56243 56245; 56246; 56247; 56249; 56250; 56251; 56252; 56253; 56254; 56255; 56256 56257* (SD 1); 56258; 56260; 56262; 56263; 56264;

56265; 56266; 56270; 56271 56272; 56273; 56276; 56277; 56278; 56279; 56280; 56281; 56282; 56283; 56284 56285; 56286; 56287; 56288; 56289; 56291; 56292; 56293; 56294; 56295 56297; 57026* (SD 1); 57030* (SD 1); 57060* (SD 1); 57068* (IA 5, SD 1); 57068* (IA 5, SD 1); 57074* (SD 1).

3rd District: 55001* (MN 6); 55009* (MN 1); 55016; 55024* (MN 1); 55031* (MN 1); 55033* (MN 1); 55044* (MN 1); 55055; 55068; 55071; 55075* (MN 4); 55076 55077; 55085; 55089* (MN 1); 55111* (MN 5); 55118* (MN 4); 55120; 55121 55122; 55123; 55124; 55125* (MN 4); 55150; 55168; 55305; 55337; 55343* (MN 5, MN 6); 55344 55345; 55346; 55347; 55372* (MN 1, MN 2); 55378* (MN 2); 55391* (MN 6); 55392 55410* (MN 5); 55420; 55423* (MN 5); 55424* (MN 5); 55425 55431; 55435; 55436* (MN 5); 55437; 55438; 55439; 55440; 55450* (MN 5.

4th District: 55042* (MN 6); 55075* (MN 3); 55082* (MN 6); 55100; 55101 55102; 55103; 55104; 55105; 55106; 55107; 55108; 55109; 55110* (MN 6); 55112* (MN 6); 55113; 55114; 55116; 55117; 55118* (MN 3); 55119; 55125* (MN 3) 55126* (MN 6); 55127; 55128* (MN 6); 55133; 55144; 55145; 55146; 55155; 55161 55164; 55165; 55166; 55169; 55170; 55171; 55172; 55175; 55177; 55182; 55189 55190; 55191; 55421* (MN 5, MN 6); 55432* (MN 6); 55434* (MN 6).

5th District: 55111* (MN 3); 55343* (MN 3, MN 6); 55400; 55401; 55402; 55403 55404; 55405; 55406; 55407; 55408; 55409; 55410* (MN 3); 55411; 55412; 55413 55414; 55415; 55416; 55417; 55418; 55419; 55421* (MN 4, MN 6); 55422; 55423* (MN 3); 55424* (MN 3); 55426; 55427; 55428* (MN 6); 55429* (MN 6); 55430* (MN 6); 55436* (MN 3); 55444* (MN 6); 55446* (MN 6); 55450* (MN 3); 55454; 55455 55458; 55459; 55460; 55470; 55472; 55478; 55479; 55480; 55483; 55484; 55485 55486; 55487; 55488.

6th District: 55001* (MN 3); 55003; 55005* (MN 8); 55011; 55014; 55025* (MN 8); 55038; 55042* (MN 4); 55043; 55047; 55070* (MN 8); 55073; 55079* (MN 8) 55082* (MN 4); 55083; 55090; 55092* (MN 8); 55110* (MN 4); 55112* (MN 4) 55115; 55126* (MN 4); 55128* (MN 4); 55303; 55304; 55306; 55311; 55316; 55323 55327; 55328* (MN 2); 55330* (MN 2, MN 8); 55331* (MN 2); 55340; 55341 55343* (MN 3, MN 5); 55348; 55356; 55357; 55359* (MN 2); 55361; 55364* (MN 2) 55373* (MN 2); 55384; 55391* (MN 3); 55421* (MN 4, MN 5); 55428* (MN 5) 55429* (MN 5); 55430* (MN 5); 55432* (MN 4); 55433; 55434* (MN 4); 55441 55442; 55443; 55444* (MN 5); 55445; 55446* (MN 5); 55447; 55448 55449; 55570 55571; 55572; 55573; 55574; 55576; 55577; 55578; 55579; 55593 55595; 55596 55597; 55598; 55599.

7th District: 55320* (MN 2); 55329* (MN 2); 55353; 55382* (MN 2); 55389* (MN 2); 56207; 56219* (SD 1); 56221; 56235; 56236; 56244; 56248; 56267; 56274 56296; 56301; 56302; 56303; 56304* (MN 8); 56307; 56308; 56309; 56310; 56311 56312; 56314; 56315; 56316; 56318; 56319; 56320; 56321; 56323; 56324; 56325 56326; 56327; 56328; 56331; 56332; 56334; 56335; 56336; 56339; 56340; 56341 56343; 56345; 56346; 56347; 56349; 56352; 56354; 56355; 56356; 56360; 56361 56362; 56367* (MN 8); 56368; 56369; 56371 56372; 56373* (MN 8); 56374; 56375 56376; 56377* (MN 8); 56378; 56379* (MN 8); 56380; 56381; 56382; 56384; 56385 56387; 56389; 56393; 56395; 56396; 56401* (MN 8); 56433; 56434; 56436; 56437 56438; 56440; 56442; 56443; 56446; 56453; 56458; 56460; 56461; 56464; 56467 56470 56475; 56477; 56478; 56479; 56481; 56482; 56501; 56502; 56510; 56511 56513 56514; 56515; 56516; 56517; 56518; 56519; 56520; 56521; 56522; 56523 56524; 56527; 56528; 56529; 56531; 56533; 56534; 56535; 56536; 56537; 56538 56540; 56541; 56542; 56543; 56544; 56545; 56546; 56547; 56548; 56549; 56550 56551; 56552; 56553; 56554; 56556; 56557; 56560; 56561; 56562; 56563; 56565 56566; 56567; 56568; 56569; 56570; 56571; 56572; 56573; 56574; 56575; 56576 56577; 56578; 56579; 56580; 56581; 56583; 56584; 56585; 56586; 56587; 56588 56589; 56590; 56591; 56592; 56593; 56594; 56601; 56619; 56621; 56623; 56625 56634; 56644; 56646; 56647; 56650; 56651; 56652; 56663; 56664; 56665; 56666 56667; 56670; 56671; 56673; 56674; 56676; 56678; 56682; 56683; 56684; 56685 56686; 56687; 56701; 56710; 56711; 56712; 56713; 56714; 56715; 56716; 56720 56721; 56722; 56723; 56724; 56725; 56726; 56727; 56728; 56729; 56731; 56732 56733; 56734; 56735; 56736; 56737; 56738; 56740; 56741; 56742; 56744* (ND 1) 56748; 56750; 56751; 56754; 56755; 56756; 56757; 56758; 56759; 56760; 56761 56762; 56763; 58030* (ND 1, SD 1); 58225* (ND 1).

8th District: 55002; 55004; 55005* (MN 6); 55006; 55007; 55008; 55012; 55013 55017; 55025* (MN 6); 55029; 55030; 55032; 55036; 55037; 55045; 55051; 55056 55063; 55067; 55069; 55070* (MN 6); 55072; 55074; 55078; 55079* (MN 6) 55080; 55084; 55092* (MN 6); 55308; 55309; 55319; 55330* (MN 2, MN 6); 55371 55377; 55398; 55601; 55602; 55603; 55604; 55605; 55606; 55607; 55609; 55612 55613; 55614; 55615; 55616; 55701; 55702; 55703; 55704; 55705; 55706; 55707 55708; 55709; 55710; 55711; 55712; 55713; 55716; 55717; 55718; 55719; 55720 55721; 55722; 55723; 55724; 55725; 55726; 55727; 55728; 55729; 55730; 55731 55732; 55733; 55734; 55735; 55736; 55738; 55740; 55741; 55742; 55744; 55745 55746; 55747; 55748; 55749; 55750; 55751; 55752; 55753; 55754; 55755; 55756 55757; 55758; 55760; 55761; 55762; 55763; 55764; 55765; 55766; 55767; 55768 55769; 55771; 55772; 55773; 55775; 55777; 55778; 55779; 55780; 55781; 55782 55783; 55784; 55785; 55786; 55787; 55788; 55790; 55791; 55792; 55793 55794; 55795; 55796; 55797; 55798; 55799; 55800; 55801; 55802; 55803; 55804 55805; 55806; 55807; 55808; 55810; 55811; 55812; 55814; 55815; 55816; 56304* (MN 7); 56313; 56317; 56329; 56330; 56333; 56338; 56342; 56344; 56350; 56353 56357; 56358; 56359; 56363; 56364; 56367* (MN 7); 56373* (MN 7); 56377* (MN 7); 56379* (MN 7); 56386; 56401* (MN 7); 56425; 56430; 56431; 56435; 56441 56442; 56444 56447; 56448; 56449; 56450; 56452; 56455; 56456; 56459; 56463; 56465; 56466 56468; 56469; 56472; 56473; 56474; 56484; 56485; 56626; 56627; 56628; 56629 56630; 56631; 56632; 56633; 56636; 56637; 56639; 56641; 56649; 56653; 56654 56655; 56657; 56658; 56659; 56660; 56661; 56662; 56668; 56669; 56672; 56679 56680; 56681; 56688.

Mississippi

1st District: 38601; 38602; 38603; 38606* (MS 2); 38610; 38611; 38618; 38620 38625; 38627; 38629; 38632; 38633; 38634; 38635; 38637; 38638; 38641; 38642 38647; 38648; 38649; 38650; 38651; 38652; 38654; 38655; 38658; 38659; 38661 38663; 38665; 38668; 38671; 38673; 38674; 38675; 38677; 38679; 38680; 38683 38685; 38686; 38801; 38802; 38803; 38820; 38821; 38824; 38825; 38826; 38827 38828; 38829; 38833; 38834; 38838;

38839; 38841; 38843; 38844; 38846; 38847 38848; 38849; 38850; 38851; 38852; 38854; 38855; 38856; 38857; 38858; 38859 38860; 38862; 38863; 38864; 38865; 38866; 38868; 38869; 38870; 38871; 38873 38874; 38875; 38876; 38877; 38878; 38879; 38880; 38913; 38914; 38915; 38916 38920; 38921* (MS 2); 38922* (MS 2); 38927; 38929* (MS 2); 38948; 38949 38951; 38953; 38955; 38961; 38962; 38965; 38967* (MS 2); 39730; 39735; 39737 39744; 39745; 39746; 39747* (MS 2); 39750; 39751; 39752; 39756; 39757; 39767 39771; 39772; 39776.

2nd District: 38606* (MS 1); 38609; 38614; 38617; 38619; 38621; 38622; 38623 38626; 38628; 38630; 38631; 38639; 38643; 38644; 38645; 38646; 38657; 38662 38664; 38666; 38669; 38670; 38676; 38701; 38702; 38703; 38704; 38720; 38721 38722; 38723; 38725; 38726; 38730; 38731; 38732; 38733; 38736; 38737; 38738 38739; 38740; 38744; 38745; 38746; 38748; 38749; 38751; 38753; 38754; 38755 38756; 38758; 38759; 38760; 38761; 38762; 38763; 38764; 38765; 38767; 38768 38769; 38771; 38772; 38773; 38774; 38775; 38776; 38778; 38779; 38780; 38781 38782; 38901; 38912; 38917; 38921* (MS 1); 38922* (MS 1); 38923; 38924; 38925 38926; 38928; 38929* (MS 1); 38930; 38940; 38941; 38943; 38944; 38945; 38946 38947; 38950; 38952; 38954; 38957; 38958; 38959; 38963; 38964; 38966; 38967* (MS 1); 39038; 39039; 39040; 39041* (MS 4); 39045; 39046* (MS 3); 39049 39051* (MS 3); 39054; 39055; 39056* (MS 4); 39058; 39060; 39061; 39063; 39064 39066* (MS 4); 39069; 39070; 39071* (MS 3); 39072; 39079; 39081; 39086; 39088 39090* (MS 3); 39095; 39096; 39097; 39110* (MS 3); 39113; 39115; 39120* (MS 4); 39144; 39146; 39150; 39154* (MS 4); 39156; 39159; 39160; 39162 39163 39166; 39169; 39171; 39172; 39173; 39175* (MS 4); 39176; 39177; 39179; 39180 39181; 39182; 39192; 39194; 39206* (MS 3, MS 4); 39209* (MS 4); 39212* (MS 4) 39213* (MS 3, MS 4); 39216* (MS 4); 39283; 39289; 39668; 39747* (MS 1).

3rd District: 39042; 39043; 39046* (MS 2); 39047; 39051* (MS 2); 39057; 39067 39071* (MS 2); 39073; 39074; 39076; 39080; 39087; 39090* (MS 2); 39092; 39094 39098; 39107; 39108; 39109; 39110* (MS 2); 39116; 39117; 39130; 39145; 39151 39152; 39153 39157; 39158; 39161; 39167; 39168; 39189; 39193; 39206* (MS 2); 39208; 39211* (MS 4); 39213* (MS 2, MS 4); 39218; 39288; 39298; 39301 39302; 39303; 39304; 39305 39307; 39309; 39320; 39323; 39325; 39326; 39327 39328; 39330; 39332; 39335; 39336 39337; 39338; 39339; 39341; 39342; 39345 39346; 39347; 39348; 39350; 39352; 39353 39354; 39355; 39356; 39358; 39359 39360; 39361; 39363; 39364; 39365; 39366; 39422 39439; 39440* (MS 4); 39460 39464* (MS 5); 39477; 39481; 39701; 39702; 39703 39704; 39705; 39736; 39738 39739; 39740; 39741; 39743; 39753; 39754; 39755; 39759 39762; 39766; 39769 39773.

4th District: 39041* (MS 2); 39044; 39056* (MS 2); 39059; 39062; 39066* (MS 2) 39077; 39078; 39082; 39083; 39111; 39112; 39114; 39119; 39120* (MS 2) 39121; 39122; 39140; 39148; 39149; 39154* (MS 2) 39165; 39170; 39174; 39175* (MS 2) 39190 39191; 39201; 39202; 39203; 39204; 39205; 39206* (MS 2, MS 3) 39207; 39209* (MS 2); 39210; 39211* (MS 3); 39212* (MS 2); 39213* (MS 2, MS 3); 39215; 39216* (MS 2); 39217; 39225; 39232; 39235; 39236; 39250; 39269 39271; 39272; 39282; 39284; 39286; 39296; 39421; 39427; 39428; 39429; 39436 39437; 39440* (MS 3); 39441; 39442 39459; 39465* (MS 5); 39474; 39478; 39479 39480; 39483; 39484; 39601; 39629; 39630; 39631; 39632; 39633; 39635; 39638 39641; 39643; 39645; 39647; 39648; 39652; 39653 39654; 39656; 39657; 39661 39662; 39663; 39664; 39665; 39666; 39667; 39669.

5th District: 39322; 39324; 39362; 39367; 39401; 39402; 39403; 39404; 39406 39407; 39423; 39425; 39426; 39451; 39452; 39455; 39456; 39457; 39461; 39462 39463; 39464* (MS 3); 39465* (MS 4); 39466; 39470; 39475; 39476; 39482; 39501 39502; 39503 39505; 39506; 39507; 39520; 39521; 39522; 39529; 39530; 39531 39532; 39533; 39534 39535; 39552; 39553; 39555; 39556; 39558; 39560; 39561 39562; 39563; 39564; 39565; 39567; 39568; 39569; 39571; 39572; 39573; 39574 39576; 39577; 39581.

Missouri

1st District: 63031* (MO 2); 63033* (MO 2); 63034; 63042* (MO 2); 63074* (MO 2); 63100; 63101; 63102* (MO 3); 63103; 63104* (MO 3); 63105; 63106; 63107 63108 63110* (MO 3); 63112; 63113; 63114* (MO 2); 63115; 63117* (MO 2, MO 3) 63118* (MO 3); 63119* (MO 2, MO 3); 63120; 63121; 63122* (MO 2, MO 3); 63124* (MO 2); 63130; 63132* (MO 2); 63133; 63134* (MO 2); 63135; 63136; 63137 63138; 63140* (MO 2); 63143* (MO 3); 63144; 63147; 63150; 63153; 63155; 63156 63157; 63158 63160; 63164; 63166; 63167; 63169; 63171; 63177; 63178; 63179 63180; 63182; 63188; 63195; 63196; 63197; 63198; 63199.

2nd District: 63001; 63005; 63006; 63011; 63017; 63021; 63022; 63025* (MO 3) 63026* (MO 3); 63031* (MO 1); 63032; 63033* (MO 1); 63038; 63040; 63042* (MO 1); 63043 63044; 63045; 63069* (MO 3, MO 9); 63074* (MO 1); 63088; 63099 63114* (MO 1); 63117* (MO 1, MO 3); 63119* (MO 1, MO 3); 63122* (MO 1, MO 3) 63124* (MO 1); 63126* (MO 3); 63127* (MO 3); 63131; 63132* (MO 1); 63134* (MO 1); 63140* (MO 1); 63141; 63145; 63146; 63301; 63302; 63303* (MO 9); 63366* (MO 9); 63367* (MO 9) 63373; 63376* (MO 9); 63386.

3rd District: 63010; 63012; 63015* (MO 9); 63016; 63019; 63020; 63023; 63025* (MO 2); 63026* (MO 2); 63028; 63030; 63041* (MO 9); 63047; 63048; 63049 63050; 63051; 63052; 63053; 63057; 63066; 63069* (MO 2, MO 9); 63070; 63083 63102* (MO 1); 63104* (MO 1); 63109; 63110* (MO 1); 63111; 63116 63117* (MO 1, MO 2); 63118* (MO 1); 63119* (MO 1, MO 2); 63122* (MO 1, MO 2) 63123; 63125 63126* (MO 2); 63127* (MO 2); 63128; 63129; 63139; 63143* (MO 1); 63151; 63163 63627; 63628* (MO 8); 63640* (MO 8); 63661; 63670; 63673.

4th District: 64001; 64011; 64012; 64014* (MO 6); 64017; 64019; 64020; 64021 64022 64029* (MO 6); 64034* (MO 5); 64037; 64040; 64061; 64063* (MO 5, MO 6) 64067 64070; 64071; 64074; 64075* (MO 6); 64076; 64078; 64080; 64082* (MO 5) 64083 64090; 64093; 64096; 64097; 64147* (MO 5); 64701; 64720; 64722; 64723 64724; 64725 64726; 64728; 64733; 64734; 64735; 64738; 64739; 64740 64741; 64742; 64743; 64745; 64746; 64747; 64750; 64751; 64752; 64760; 64761 64763; 64765; 64767 64770 64771; 64772; 64776; 64777; 64778; 64779; 64780 64781; 64783; 64784; 64788; 64789 64790; 65001; 65011; 65013; 65014* (MO 9) 65016; 65017; 65018; 65020; 65023; 65024;

5th District: 64015* (MO 6); 64016* (MO 6); 64030; 64034* (MO 4); 64050 64052 64053; 64054; 64055; 64056* (MO 6); 64057* (MO 6); 64058* (MO 6) 64063* (MO 4, MO 6); 64064* (MO 6); 64065; 64081; 64082* (MO 4); 64100; 64101 64102; 64105 64106; 64108; 64109; 64110; 64111; 64112; 64113; 64114 64120 64123; 64124; 64125; 64126; 64127; 64128; 64129; 64130; 64131; 64132; 64133 64134; 64136; 64137; 64138 64139; 64141; 64142; 64145; 64146; 64147* (MO 4) 64148; 64149; 64160; 64170; 64172; 64173; 64179; 64180; 64183; 64184; 64185 64187; 64189; 64191; 64192; 64193; 64194; 64195; 64196; 64197; 64198; 64944.

6th District: 50065* (IA 3); 63535* (IA 3); 63536; 63541; 63544; 63545; 63546 63548; 63551; 63556; 63557; 63560; 63561; 63565; 63566; 63567; 64013; 64014* (MO 4); 64015* (MO 5); 64016* (MO 5); 64018; 64024; 64028; 64029* (MO 4) 64035; 64036; 64048; 64051; 64056* (MO 5); 64057* (MO 5); 64058* (MO 5) 64060; 64062; 64063* (MO 4, MO 5); 64064* (MO 5); 64066; 64068; 64072; 64073 64075* (MO 5); 64077 64079; 64084; 64085; 64088; 64089; 64092; 64098; 64116 64117; 64118; 64119; 64144 64150; 64151; 64152; 64153; 64154; 64155; 64156 64157; 64158; 64161; 64163; 64164 64165; 64166; 64167; 64168; 64190; 64199 64401; 64402; 64420; 64421; 64422; 64423 64424; 64425; 64426; 64427; 64428 64429; 64430; 64431; 64432; 64433; 64434; 64435 64436; 64437; 64438; 64439 64440; 64441; 64442; 64443; 64444; 64445; 64446; 64447 64448; 64449; 64451 64452; 64453; 64454; 64455; 64456; 64457; 64458; 64459; 64461 64463; 64465 64466; 64467; 64468; 64469; 64470; 64471; 64473; 64474; 64475; 64476 64477 64478; 64479; 64480; 64481; 64482; 64483; 64484; 64485; 64486; 64487; 64489 64490; 64491; 64492; 64493; 64494; 64496; 64497; 64498; 64499; 64500; 64501 64502 64503; 64504; 64505; 64506; 64507; 64508; 64601; 64620; 64621; 64622 64623; 64624; 64625; 64628; 64630; 64631; 64632; 64633; 64635; 64636; 64637 64638; 64639; 64640 64641; 64642; 64643; 64644; 64645; 64646; 64647; 64648 64649; 64650; 64651; 64652 64653; 64654; 64655; 64656; 64657; 64658; 64659 64660; 64661; 64664; 64665; 64667 64668; 64670; 64671; 64672; 64673; 64674 64676; 64677; 64679; 64680; 64681; 64682 64683; 64686; 64687; 64688; 64689 64999; 65068; 65230; 65233; 65236; 65237; 65246; 65248; 65250; 65254; 65261 65274; 65276; 65281; 65286; 65287; 65322; 65348.

7th District: 64744; 64748; 64755; 64756; 64759; 64762; 64766; 64769 64801 64802 64803; 64804; 64830; 64831; 64832; 64833; 64834; 64835; 64836 64840 64841; 64842 64843; 64844; 64847; 64848; 64849; 64850; 64853; 64854; 64855 64856; 64857; 64858 64859; 64861; 64862; 64863; 64864; 64865; 64866; 64867 64868; 64869; 64870; 64873 64874; 65601; 65603; 65604; 65605; 65607; 65608 65609* (AR 3); 65610; 65611; 65612 65613; 65614; 65616; 65617; 65618; 65619 65620; 65623; 65624; 65625; 65627; 65629 65630; 65631; 65633; 65635; 65637 65638; 65640; 65641; 65645; 65646; 65647; 65648 65649; 65650; 65653; 65654 65655; 65656; 65657; 65658; 65659; 65661; 65663; 65664 65666; 65669; 65672 65674; 65675; 65676; 65679; 65680; 65681; 65682; 65686; 65701 65705; 65707 65708; 65710; 65712; 65714; 65715; 65717; 65720; 65721; 65723; 65725 65726; 65727; 65728; 65729; 65730; 65731; 65733; 65734; 65737; 65738; 65739 65740 65741; 65742* (MO 4); 65744; 65745; 65747; 65752; 65753; 65754; 65755 65756 65757* (MO 4); 65758; 65759; 65760; 65761; 65762; 65765; 65766; 65768 65769 65770 65771; 65772; 65773; 65781; 65784; 65785; 65800; 65801; 65802; 65803 65804 65805 65806; 65807; 65808; 65809; 65810; 65890; 65898; 65899.

8th District: 63036; 63071; 63080* (MO 9); 63087; 63601; 63620; 63621; 63622 63623 63624; 63625; 63626; 63628* (MO 3); 63629; 63630; 63631; 63632; 63633 63636 63637 63638; 63640* (MO 3); 63644; 63645; 63646; 63648; 63650; 63651 63653; 63654; 63655 63656; 63660; 63662; 63663; 63664; 63665; 63666; 63674 63675; 63701; 63702; 63730 63732; 63733; 63735; 63736; 63737; 63738; 63739 63740; 63742; 63743; 63744; 63745 63746; 63747; 63748; 63750; 63751; 63752 63753; 63755; 63758; 63760; 63763; 63764 63765; 63766; 63767; 63769; 63770 63771; 63772; 63774; 63775; 63776; 63779; 63780 63781; 63782; 63783; 63784 63785; 63786; 63787; 63801; 63820; 63821; 63822; 63823 63824; 63825; 63826 63827; 63828; 63829; 63830; 63833; 63834; 63837; 63838; 63839 63840; 63841 63845; 63846; 63847; 63848; 63849; 63850; 63851; 63852; 63853; 63855 63857 63860; 63862; 63863; 63866; 63867; 63868; 63869; 63870; 63871; 63873; 63874 63875; 63876; 63877; 63878; 63879; 63880; 63881; 63882; 63901; 63931; 63932 63933 63934; 63935; 63936; 63937; 63938; 63939; 63940; 63941; 63942; 63943 63944; 63945 63947; 63950; 63951; 63952; 63953; 63954; 63956; 63957 63959; 63960; 63961; 63962; 63963; 63964; 63965; 63966; 63967; 65066* (MO 9) 65401; 65433; 65436; 65438 65439; 65440; 65441; 65444; 65446; 65449; 65451 65453* (MO 9); 65456; 65461; 65462 65464; 65466; 65468; 65479; 65483; 65484 65501; 65529; 65532; 65535; 65540; 65541 65542; 65546; 65548; 65550; 65552 65555; 65557; 65559; 65564; 65565; 65566 65570; 65571; 65573; 65586; 65588 65589; 65606; 65626; 65660; 65662; 65667; 65688 65689; 65690; 65692; 65702 65704; 65711; 65775; 65776; 65777; 65778; 65788; 65789 65790; 65791; 65793.

9th District: 52537* (IA 3); 52542* (IA 3); 52573* (IA 3); 52626* (IA 3) 63013 63014; 63015* (MO 9); 63037; 63039; 63041* (MO 9); 63055; 63056; 63060 63061; 63068 63069* (MO 2, MO 3); 63072; 63073; 63077; 63079; 63080* (MO 8); 63084; 63089 63090; 63091; 63303* (MO 2); 63304; 63330; 63332; 63333; 63334 63336; 63338; 63339 63341; 63342; 63343; 63344; 63345; 63346; 63347; 63348 63349; 63350; 63351; 63352 63353; 63357; 63359; 63361; 63362; 63363; 63364 63365; 63366* (MO 2); 63367* (MO 2); 63369; 63370; 63371; 63376* (MO 2) 63377; 63378; 63379; 63381; 63382 63383; 63384; 63385; 63387; 63388; 63389 63390; 63394; 63401; 63430; 63431; 63432 63433; 63434; 63435; 63436; 63437 63438; 63439; 63440; 63441; 63442; 63443; 63445 63446; 63447; 63448; 63450 63451; 63452; 63453; 63454; 63456; 63457; 63458; 63459 63460; 63461; 63462 63463; 63464; 63465; 63466; 63467; 63468; 63469; 63470; 63471 63472; 63473 63474; 63501; 63530; 63531; 63532; 63533; 63534; 63537; 63538; 63539;

63540 63543; 63547; 63549; 63552; 63555; 63558; 63559; 63563; 65010; 65014* (MO 4) 65022; 65036; 65039; 65041; 65043; 65056; 65059; 65061* (MO 4); 65062; 65063 65066* (MO 8); 65067; 65069; 65077; 65080; 65101* (MO 4); 65201; 65202; 65203 65205; 65211; 65212; 65215; 65216; 65217; 65218; 65231; 65232; 65239; 65240 65243; 65244; 65247; 65251; 65255; 65256; 65257; 65258; 65259; 65260; 65262 65263; 65264; 65265; 65270; 65275; 65278; 65279; 65280; 65282; 65283; 65284 65285; 65291; 65299; 65453* (MO 8).

Montana

At Large: 57717* (SD 1, WY 1); 57724* (SD 1); 58621* (ND 1); 58838* (ND 1) 58845* (ND 1); 59001; 59002; 59003; 59004; 59006; 59007; 59008; 59010; 59011 59012; 59013; 59014; 59015; 59016; 59017; 59018; 59019; 59020; 59021; 59022 59024; 59025; 59026; 59027; 59028; 59029; 59030* (WY 1); 59031; 59032; 59033 59034; 59035; 59036; 59037; 59038; 59039; 59041; 59043; 59044; 59046; 59047 59050; 59051; 59052; 59053; 59054; 59055; 59057; 59058; 59059; 59061; 59062 59063; 59064; 59065; 59066; 59067; 59068; 59069; 59070; 59071; 59072; 59073 59074; 59075; 59076; 59077; 59078; 59079; 59080; 59081; 59082; 59083; 59084 59085; 59086; 59087; 59088; 59089* (WY 1); 59100; 59101; 59102; 59103; 59104 59106; 59107; 59108; 59111; 59112; 59114; 59115; 59116; 59117; 59201 59211; 59212; 59213; 59214; 59215; 59217; 59218; 59219; 59221* (ND 1); 59222 59223; 59224; 59225; 59226; 59230; 59231; 59240; 59241; 59242; 59243; 59244 59245; 59247; 59248; 59250; 59252; 59253; 59254; 59255; 59256; 59257; 59258 59259; 59260; 59261; 59262; 59263; 59270* (ND 1); 59273; 59274; 59275* (ND 1) 59276; 59301; 59311; 59312; 59313; 59314; 59315; 59316; 59317; 59318; 59319 59322; 59323; 59324; 59326; 59327; 59330; 59332; 59333; 59336; 59337; 59338 59339; 59341; 59342; 59343; 59344; 59345; 59347; 59348; 59349; 59351; 59353 59354; 59401; 59402; 59403; 59404; 59405; 59406; 59410; 59411; 59412; 59414 59416; 59417; 59418; 59419; 59420; 59421; 59422; 59424; 59425; 59427; 59430 59432; 59433; 59434; 59435; 59436; 59440; 59441; 59442; 59443; 59444; 59446 59447; 59448; 59450; 59451; 59452; 59453; 59454; 59456; 59457; 59460; 59461 59462; 59463; 59464; 59465; 59466; 59467; 59468; 59469; 59471; 59472; 59473 59474; 59476; 59477; 59479; 59480; 59482; 59483; 59484; 59485; 59486; 59487 59489; 59501; 59520; 59521; 59522; 59523; 59524; 59525; 59526; 59527; 59528 59529; 59530; 59531; 59532; 59535; 59537; 59538; 59540; 59542; 59544 59545; 59546; 59547; 59601; 59604; 59620; 59623; 59624; 59625; 59626; 59631 59632 59633; 59634; 59635; 59636; 59638; 59639; 59640; 59641; 59642; 59643; 59644 59645; 59647; 59648; 59701; 59702; 59703; 59707; 59710; 59711; 59713; 59714; 59715 59716; 59717; 59720; 59721; 59722; 59724; 59725; 59727; 59728; 59729; 59730; 59731; 59732; 59733; 59735; 59736; 59739; 59740; 59741; 59743 59745 59746; 59747; 59748; 59749; 59750; 59751; 59752; 59754; 59755; 59756; 59758 59759; 59760; 59761; 59762; 59771; 59772; 59801; 59802; 59803; 59806; 59807 59812; 59820; 59821; 59823; 59824; 59825; 59826; 59827; 59828; 59829; 59830 59831; 59832; 59833; 59834; 59835; 59836; 59837; 59840; 59841; 59842 59843; 59844; 59845; 59846; 59847; 59848; 59851; 59852; 59853 59854; 59855; 59856; 59858; 59859; 59860; 59863; 59864; 59865; 59866; 59867; 59868 59870; 59871; 59872; 59873; 59874; 59875; 59901; 59902; 59903; 59904; 59910; 59911 59912; 59913; 59914; 59915; 59916; 59917; 59918; 59919; 59920; 59921; 59922 59923; 59925; 59926; 59927; 59928; 59929; 59930; 59931; 59932; 59933; 59934 59935; 59936; 59937; 82431* (WY 1); 82725* (WY 1).

Nebraska

1st District: 66955* (KS 1, NE 3); 68001; 68002; 68003; 68004; 68008; 68009 68014; 68015; 68016; 68017; 68018; 68019; 68020; 68023; 68025; 68029; 68030 68031; 68033; 68034; 68035; 68036; 68037; 68038; 68039; 68040; 68041; 68042 68044; 68045; 68047; 68048* (NE 2); 68050; 68055; 68057; 68058; 68061; 68062 68063; 68065; 68066; 68067; 68068; 68070; 68071; 68072; 68073; 68301; 68304 68305; 68307; 68309; 68310; 68313; 68314; 68316; 68317; 68318; 68319; 68320 68321; 68323; 68324; 68328; 68329; 68330; 68331; 68332; 68333; 68336; 68337 68339; 68341; 68343; 68344; 68345; 68346; 68347; 68348; 68349; 68355; 68357 68358; 68359; 68360; 68364; 68366; 68367; 68368; 68371; 68372; 68374; 68376 68378; 68379; 68380; 68381* (KS 2); 68382; 68401; 68402; 68403; 68404; 68405 68407; 68409; 68410; 68413; 68414; 68415* (KS 1); 68417; 68418; 68419 68420 68421; 68422; 68423; 68428; 68430; 68431; 68432; 68433; 68434; 68437; 68438 68439; 68441; 68442; 68443; 68445; 68446; 68447; 68448; 68450; 68453; 68454 68455; 68456; 68457; 68458; 68460; 68461; 68462; 68463; 68464; 68465; 68466* (KS 2); 68467; 68500; 68501; 68502; 68503; 68504; 68505; 68506; 68507; 68508 68509; 68510; 68511; 68512; 68514; 68516; 68517; 68520; 68521; 68522; 68523 68524; 68526; 68527; 68528; 68529; 68531; 68532; 68542; 68544; 68572; 68583 68588; 68621; 68624; 68626; 68629; 68632; 68633; 68635; 68641; 68643; 68648 68649; 68650; 68658; 68659; 68661; 68664; 68667; 68669; 68701; 68702; 68710 68715; 68716; 68717; 68723; 68727; 68728; 68731; 68732; 68733; 68736; 68739 68740; 68741; 68743; 68745; 68748; 68749; 68751; 68752; 68757; 68758; 68762 68768; 68770; 68771; 68774; 68776; 68779; 68781; 68784; 68785; 68787; 68788 68790; 68791; 68792.

2nd District: 66541* (KS 1); 68005; 68007; 68010; 68022; 68028; 68046; 68048* (NE 1) 68054; 68056; 68059; 68064; 68069; 68100; 68101; 68102; 68103; 68104 68105; 68106; 68107; 68108; 68109; 68110; 68111; 68112; 68113; 68114; 68116 68117; 68118; 68119; 68120; 68122; 68123; 68124; 68127; 68128; 68130; 68131 68132; 68133; 68134; 68135; 68136; 68137; 68138; 68142; 68144; 68147; 68152 68154; 68157; 68164; 68172; 68175; 68176; 68178; 68179; 68180; 68181; 68182 68183; 68198.

3rd District: 57523* (SD 1); 57571* (SD 1); 66955* (KS 1, NE 1); 67647* (KS 1) 68303; 68315; 68322; 68325; 68326; 68327; 68335; 68338; 68340; 68342 68350; 68351; 68352; 68354; 68361; 68362; 68365; 68370; 68375; 68377; 68406 68416; 68424; 68429; 68436; 68440; 68444; 68452; 68601; 68602; 68620; 68622 68623; 68625; 68627; 68628; 68630; 68631; 68634; 68636; 68637; 68638; 68640 68642; 68644; 68647; 68651; 68652; 68653; 68654; 68655; 68660; 68662; 68663 68665; 68666; 68711; 68713; 68714; 68718; 68719; 68720; 68722; 68724; 68725 68726; 68729; 68730; 68734; 68735; 68737; 68738; 68742; 68746; 68747; 68753 68755; 68756; 68759; 68760; 68761; 68763; 68764; 68765; 68766; 68767; 68769 68772; 68773; 68777; 68778; 68780; 68782; 68783; 68786; 68789; 68801; 68802 68803; 68810; 68812; 68813; 68814; 68815; 68816; 68817; 68818; 68819; 68820 68821; 68822; 68823; 68824; 68825; 68826; 68827; 68828; 68829; 68831; 68832

68833; 68834; 68835; 68836; 68837; 68838; 68840; 68841; 68842; 68843; 68844 68846; 68847; 68848; 68849; 68850; 68852; 68853; 68854; 68855; 68856; 68858 68859; 68860; 68861; 68862; 68863; 68864; 68865; 68866; 68868; 68869; 68870 68871; 68872; 68873; 68874; 68875; 68876; 68878; 68879; 68880; 68881; 68882 68883; 68901; 68902; 68920* (KS 1); 68922; 68923; 68924; 68925; 68926; 68927 68928; 68929; 68930; 68932; 68933; 68934; 68935; 68936; 68937; 68938; 68939* (KS 1); 68940; 68941; 68942* (KS 1); 68943* (KS 1); 68944; 68945; 68946 68947; 68948; 68949; 68950; 68951; 68952* (KS 1); 68954; 68955; 68956; 68957 68958; 68959; 68960; 68961; 68963; 68964; 68966; 68967; 68969; 68970* (KS 1) 68971* (KS 1); 68972* (KS 1); 68973; 68974; 68975; 68976; 68977; 68978* (KS 1); 68979; 68980; 68981; 68982; 69001; 69020; 69021* (KS 1); 69022; 69023 69024* (KS 1); 69025; 69026* (KS 1); 69027; 69028; 69029; 69030* (KS 1); 69031; 69032; 69033; 69034; 69035; 69036* (KS 1); 69037; 69038; 69039; 69040 69041; 69042; 69043* (KS 1); 69044* (KS 1); 69045; 69046 69101; 69103; 69120 69121; 69122; 69123; 69125; 69127; 69128* (CO 4); 69129; 69130; 69131; 69132 69133; 69134; 69135; 69138; 69140; 69141; 69142; 69143; 69144; 69145* (CO 4) 69146; 69147; 69148; 69149; 69150; 69151; 69152; 69153; 69154; 69155; 69156 69157; 69160; 69161; 69162; 69163; 69165; 69166; 69167; 69168* (CO 4); 69169 69170; 69171; 69201* (SD 1); 69210; 69211* (SD 1); 69212* (SD 1); 69214 69216* (SD 1); 69217; 69218* (SD 1); 69219; 69220; 69221; 69301; 69331; 69333 69334; 69335; 69336; 69337* (SD 1); 69339; 69340; 69341; 69343* (SD 1); 69345 69346; 69347; 69348; 69349; 69350; 69351; 69352* (WY 1); 69353; 69354; 69355 69356; 69357; 69358* (WY 1); 69360 69361; 69363; 69365; 69366; 69367; 82082* (CO 4, WY 1).

Nevada

1st District: 88900; 88901; 88902; 88903; 88904; 88905; 89009; 89011; 89012 89014; 89015* (NV 2); 89016; 89030* (NV 2); 89100; 89101; 89102; 89103* (NV 2); 89104 89106* (NV 2); 89107* (NV 2); 89108* (NV 2); 89109; 89110; 89111 89114; 89115* (NV 2); 89116; 89117* (NV 2); 89118* (NV 2); 89119* (NV 2) 89121; 89122* (NV 2); 89123* (NV 2); 89124* (NV 2); 89125; 89126; 89127; 89130* (NV 2); 89132; 89133; 89139; 89150; 89151; 89152; 89153; 89154 89155; 89158; 89160; 89170; 89177; 89180; 89185; 89191; 89193; 89195; 89199.

2nd District: 89001; 89003; 89004; 89005; 89006; 89007; 89008; 89010; 89013 89015* (NV 1); 89017; 89018; 89019; 89020; 89021; 89022; 89023; 89024; 89025 89026; 89028; 89029; 89030* (NV 1); 89031; 89036; 89039; 89040; 89041; 89046 89047; 89049; 89070; 89103* (NV 1); 89106* (NV 1); 89107* (NV 1); 89108* (NV 1); 89112; 89113; 89115* (NV 1); 89117* (NV 1); 89118* (NV 1); 89119* (NV 1); 89122* (NV 1); 89123* (NV 1); 89124* (NV 1); 89128; 89129 89130* (NV 1); 89131; 89134; 89163; 89164; 89165; 89301; 89310; 89311; 89314 89316; 89317; 89318; 89319; 89402; 89403; 89404; 89405; 89406; 89407 89408 89409; 89410; 89411; 89412; 89413; 89414; 89415; 89416; 89418; 89419 89420; 89421; 89422; 89423; 89424; 89425; 89426; 89427; 89428; 89429; 89430 89431; 89432; 89433; 89434; 89435; 89436; 89438 89439; 89440; 89442; 89444 89445; 89446; 89447; 89448; 89449; 89450; 89451 89452; 89496; 89500; 89501; 89502; 89503; 89504; 89505; 89506; 89507; 89509 89510; 89511; 89512; 89513; 89515; 89520; 89523; 89550; 89557; 89564; 89570 89595; 89599; 89701; 89702 89703; 89704; 89705; 89706; 89710; 89711; 89712; 89713; 89714; 89721; 89801 89802; 89803; 89820; 89821; 89822; 89823; 89824; 89825; 89826; 89828; 89830 89831; 89832; 89833; 89834; 89835; 89883.

New Hampshire

1st District: 03032; 03034; 03036; 03037; 03038; 03040; 03041; 03042; 03044 03045* (NH 2); 03053* (NH 2); 03054; 03077; 03087* (NH 2); 03100; 03101 03102; 03103* (NH 2); 03104; 03105; 03106* (NH 2); 03107; 03108; 03109; 03110 03218; 03220 03225; 03226; 03227; 03234; 03237; 03246; 03247; 03253; 03254 03256; 03259; 03261 03263* (NH 2); 03275* (NH 2); 03276* (NH 2); 03281* (NH 2); 03289; 03290; 03291 03801; 03802; 03803; 03804; 03805; 03809; 03810 03811* (NH 2); 03812; 03813; 03814 03815; 03816; 03817; 03818; 03819; 03820 03822; 03824; 03825; 03826; 03827; 03830 03832; 03833; 03835; 03836; 03837; 03838; 03839; 03840; 03841; 03842; 03844; 03845 03846; 03847; 03848; 03849; 03850; 03851; 03852; 03853; 03854; 03855; 03856; 03857 03858; 03859; 03860; 03862; 03864; 03865; 03866; 03867; 03868; 03869; 03870; 03871 03872; 03873 03874* (NH 2); 03875; 03878; 03882; 03883; 03884; 03885; 03886; 03887 03890; 03894; 03896; 03897.

2nd District: 03031; 03033; 03043; 03045* (NH 1); 03047; 03048; 03049; 03051 03053* (NH 1); 03055; 03057; 03060; 03061; 03062; 03063; 03070; 03071; 03073 03076; 03079 03082; 03084; 03086; 03087* (NH 1); 03103* (NH 1); 03106* (NH 1); 03215; 03216 03217; 03221; 03222; 03223; 03224; 03229; 03230; 03231; 03232; 03233; 03235; 03238 03240; 03241; 03242; 03243; 03244; 03245; 03251; 03252; 03255; 03257; 03260; 03262 03263* (NH 1); 03264; 03265; 03266; 03268; 03269; 03272; 03273; 03274; 03275* (NH 1); 03276* (NH 1); 03278; 03279; 03280 03281* (NH 1); 03282; 03284; 03285 03287; 03293; 03300; 03301; 03302; 03303; 03304; 03305; 03306; 03431; 03440; 03441 03442; 03443; 03444; 03445; 03446; 03447; 03448; 03449; 03450; 03451; 03452; 03454 03455; 03456; 03457; 03458; 03460; 03461; 03462; 03464; 03465; 03466; 03467; 03468 03469; 03470; 03561; 03570; 03574; 03575; 03576; 03579* (ME 2); 03580; 03581; 03582 03583; 03584; 03585; 03587; 03588; 03589; 03590; 03592; 03595; 03597; 03598; 03601 03602; 03603; 03604; 03605; 03606; 03607; 03608; 03609; 03741; 03743; 03745 03746; 03748; 03749; 03750; 03751; 03752; 03753; 03754; 03755; 03756; 03765; 03766 03768; 03769; 03770; 03771; 03772; 03773; 03774; 03777; 03779; 03780; 03781; 03782 03784; 03785; 03811* (NH 1); 03874* (NH 1).

New Jersey

1st District: 08003* (NJ 3); 08004* (NJ 3); 08007; 08009* (NJ 3); 08012 08014; 08018 08020* (NJ 2); 08021; 08026; 08027; 08029; 08030; 08031; 08032 08033* (NJ 3); 08035 08037* (NJ 2); 08040; 08043* (NJ 3); 08045; 08049 08051* (NJ 2); 08052* (NJ 3); 08056* (NJ 3); 08057* (NJ 3); 08059; 08061; 08063; 08065* (NJ 3); 08066; 08077*

(NJ 3); 08078; 08080* (NJ 2); 08081 08083; 08084; 08085* (NJ 2); 08086; 08088* (NJ 3); 08089* (NJ 3); 08090 08091; 08093; 08094* (NJ 2); 08095; 08096; 08097; 08099; 08100; 08101; 08102 08103; 08104; 08105; 08106; 08107; 08108; 08109* (NJ 3); 08110.

2nd District: 08001; 08019* (NJ 3); 08020* (NJ 1); 08023; 08025; 08028; 08037* (NJ 1); 08038; 08039; 08051* (NJ 1); 08056* (NJ 1); 08062; 08067; 08069 08070; 08071; 08072; 08074; 08079; 08080* (NJ 1); 08085* (NJ 1); 08094* (NJ 1); 08098; 08201; 08202; 08203; 08204; 08210; 08212; 08213; 08214; 08215 08217; 08218; 08219; 08220; 08221; 08222; 08223; 08225; 08226; 08227; 08230 08231; 08232; 08233; 08240; 08241; 08242; 08243; 08244; 08245; 08246; 08247 08248; 08250; 08251; 08252; 08260; 08270; 08302; 08310; 08311; 08312; 08313 08314; 08315; 08316; 08317; 08318; 08319; 08320; 08321; 08322; 08323 08324 08326; 08327; 08328; 08329; 08330; 08332; 08340; 08341; 08342; 08343; 08344 08345; 08346; 08347; 08348; 08349; 08350; 08352; 08360; 08400; 08401 08402; 08403; 08404; 08405; 08406; 08411.

3rd District: 08002; 08003* (NJ 1); 08004* (NJ 1); 08005; 08006; 08008; 08009* (NJ 1); 08010* (NJ 4); 08011; 08015; 08016* (NJ 4); 08019* (NJ 2); 08033* (NJ 1); 08034; 08043* (NJ 1); 08046* (NJ 4); 08048; 08050; 08052* (NJ 1); 08053 08054; 08055; 08057* (NJ 1); 08060* (NJ 4); 08064; 08065* (NJ 1); 08068* (NJ 4); 08073 08075; 08077* (NJ 1); 08087; 08088* (NJ 1); 08089* (NJ 1); 08092 08109* (NJ 1); 08224; 08358; 08370; 08511* (NJ 4); 08562* (NJ 4); 08640* (NJ 4); 08641* (NJ 4); 08721; 08722; 08731; 08732; 08734; 08735; 08740; 08741 08751; 08752; 08753* (NJ 4); 08754; 08755* (NJ 4); 08756; 08757* (NJ 4) 08758; 08759* (NJ 4).

4th District: 07710; 07715; 07719* (NJ 6); 07722* (NJ 6, NJ 12); 07726* (NJ 12); 07727; 07728* (NJ 12) 07731; 07753* (NJ 6, NJ 12); 07762* (NJ 6); 08010* (NJ 3); 08016* (NJ 3); 08022; 08036; 08041; 08042; 08046* (NJ 3); 08060* (NJ 3); 08068* (NJ 3); 08501; 08505; 08510; 08511* (NJ 3); 08512* (NJ 12) 08514 08515; 08518; 08520* (NJ 12); 08526; 08527; 08533; 08535; 08540* (NJ 7, NJ 12); 08550* (NJ 12); 08554; 08555; 08561; 08562* (NJ 3); 08600 08601; 08602 08603; 08604; 08605; 08606; 08607; 08608; 08609; 08610* (NJ 12); 08611; 08618* (NJ 12); 08619* (NJ 12); 08620; 08629* (NJ 12); 08638* (NJ 12); 08640* (NJ 3) 08641* (NJ 3); 08645; 08646; 08647; 08648* (NJ 12); 08650; 08666; 08677 08690* (NJ 12); 08691* (NJ 12); 08695; 08701; 08720; 08723; 08724; 08730 08733; 08736* (NJ 6); 08738; 08739; 08742; 08750* (NJ 6); 08753* (NJ 3) 08755* (NJ 3); 08757* (NJ 3); 08759* (NJ 3).

5th District: 07401; 07410* (NJ 9); 07416; 07417; 07418; 07419; 07420* (NJ 11); 07421; 07422; 07423; 07424* (NJ 8); 07428; 07430; 07432; 07435; 07436 07438* (NJ 11); 07446; 07450; 07451; 07452; 07456* (NJ 11); 07458; 07460 07461; 07462; 07463; 07465* (NJ 8); 07480* (NJ 8); 07481; 07495; 07498; 07506* (NJ 8); 07507; 07508* (NJ 8); 07620; 07621; 07624; 07626; 07627; 07628; 07630 07631* (NJ 9); 07632* (NJ 9); 07640; 07641; 07642; 07645; 07646* (NJ 9) 07647; 07648; 07649* (NJ 9); 07652; 07653; 07656; 07662* (NJ 9); 07666* (NJ 9); 07670* (NJ 9); 07675; 07820; 07821* (NJ 11); 07822; 07823; 07825; 07826 07827; 07829; 07831; 07832; 07833; 07838; 07839; 07840* (NJ 11); 07844; 07846 07848* (NJ 11); 07851; 07855; 07860* (NJ 11); 07863; 07865; 07871* (NJ 11) 07875; 07877; 07879; 07880; 07881; 07882; 07890; 08802* (NJ 12); 08804* (NJ 12); 08808; 08865; 08886.

6th District: 07080* (NJ 7); 07701* (NJ 12); 07702* (NJ 12); 07711* (NJ 12) 07712* (NJ 12); 07713; 07716; 07717; 07718; 07719* (NJ 4); 07720; 07721 07722* (NJ 4, NJ 12); 07723* (NJ 12); 07730; 07732; 07733* (NJ 12); 07734* (NJ 12); 07735; 07737; 07739* (NJ 4); 07740* (NJ 12); 07747* (NJ 12); 07748* (NJ 12); 07750; 07751* (NJ 12); 07752; 07753* (NJ 4, NJ 12); 07754; 07758 07760* (NJ 12); 07762* (NJ 4); 07764* (NJ 12); 08570; 08736* (NJ 4); 08750* (NJ 4); 08812* (NJ 7); 08816* (NJ 12); 08817; 08818; 08820* (NJ 7); 08824* (NJ 12); 08831* (NJ 12); 08837* (NJ 7); 08840* (NJ 7); 08846* (NJ 7); 08850* (NJ 12); 08854* (NJ 7); 08855; 08857; 08859 08863* (NJ 7); 08871; 08872; 08878 08879; 08882; 08884* (NJ 12); 08899; 08901; 08902* (NJ 12); 08903; 08904 08905; 08906; 08922; 08933; 08988; 08989.

7th District: 07001; 07008* (NJ 13); 07016; 07023; 07027; 07033; 07036* (NJ 10, NJ 13); 07039* (NJ 11); 07040* (NJ 8, NJ 10); 07041; 07059* (NJ 11) 07060; 07062; 07063; 07064* (NJ 13); 07065* (NJ 10); 07066* (NJ 10); 07067 07076; 07078* (NJ 11); 07080* (NJ 6); 07081; 07083* (NJ 10); 07088* (NJ 10) 07090; 07091; 07092; 07095; 07098; 07203* (NJ 10); 07204; 07208* (NJ 10, NJ 13); 07901; 07902; 07920* (NJ 11, NJ 12); 07922; 07974* (NJ 11); 08502* (NJ 12); 08528; 08540* (NJ 4, NJ 12); 08558* (NJ 12); 08805; 08807* (NJ 11, NJ 12); 08812* (NJ 6); 08820* (NJ 6); 08821; 08823; 08830; 08832; 08835; 08836 08837* (NJ 6); 08840* (NJ 6); 08846* (NJ 6); 08853* (NJ 12); 08854* (NJ 6) 08861* (NJ 13); 08863* (NJ 6); 08873; 08876* (NJ 11, NJ 12); 08877; 08880 08890.

8th District: 07003; 07009; 07011; 07012; 07013; 07014; 07015; 07028* (NJ 10) 07040* (NJ 7, NJ 10); 07042* (NJ 10); 07043; 07044* (NJ 10); 07050* (NJ 10) 07052* (NJ 10); 07055; 07068* (NJ 11); 07079* (NJ 10); 07107* (NJ 10); 07109; 07110; 07111* (NJ 10); 07424* (NJ 5); 07442; 07465* (NJ 5); 07470 07474; 07477; 07480* (NJ 5); 07501; 07502; 07503; 07504; 07505; 07506* (NJ 5) 07508* (NJ 5); 07509; 07510; 07511; 07512; 07513; 07514; 07522; 07524; 07530 07533; 07538; 07543; 07544; 07688.

9th District: 07010; 07020; 07022; 07024; 07026; 07029* (NJ 13); 07031; 07032* (NJ 13); 07047* (NJ 13); 07057; 07070; 07071; 07072; 07073; 07074; 07075 07087* (NJ 13); 07093* (NJ 13); 07094; 07306* (NJ 13); 07307; 07310* (NJ 13); 07407; 07410* (NJ 5); 07601; 07602; 07603; 07604; 07605; 07606 07607; 07608; 07631* (NJ 5); 07632* (NJ 5); 07643; 07644; 07646* (NJ 5) 07649* (NJ 5); 07650; 07657; 07660 07661; 07662* (NJ 5); 07666* (NJ 5) 07670* (NJ 5).

10th District: 07002* (NJ 13); 07017; 07018; 07019; 07028* (NJ 8); 07036* (NJ 7, NJ 13); 07040* (NJ 7, NJ 8); 07042* (NJ 8); 07044* (NJ 8); 07050* (NJ 8) 07051; 07052* (NJ 8); 07061; 07065* (NJ 7); 07066* (NJ 7); 07079* (NJ 8) 07083* (NJ 7); 07088* (NJ 7); 07100; 07101; 07102* (NJ 13); 07103; 07105* (NJ 13); 07106; 07107* (NJ 8, NJ 13); 07108; 07111* (NJ 8); 07112; 07114* (NJ 13); 07175; 07183; 07184; 07185; 07187; 07188; 07189; 07190; 07191; 07192; 07193 07194; 07195; 07197; 07198; 07199; 07200; 07201* (NJ 13); 07202* (NJ 13) 07203* (NJ 7); 07205; 07206* (NJ 13); 07207; 07208* (NJ 7, NJ 13); 07215 07216; 07304* (NJ 13); 07305* (NJ 13).

11th District: 07004; 07005; 07006; 07007; 07021; 07034; 07035; 07039* (NJ 7) 07045;

07046; 07054; 07058; 07059* (NJ 7); 07068* (NJ 8); 07078* (NJ 7) 07082; 07403; 07405; 07420* (NJ 5); 07438* (NJ 5); 07439; 07440; 07444; 07456* (NJ 5); 07457; 07801; 07802; 07806; 07821* (NJ 5); 07828; 07834; 07836; 07837 07840* (NJ 5); 07842; 07843; 07845; 07847; 07848* (NJ 5); 07849; 07850; 07852 07853; 07856; 07857; 07860* (NJ 5); 07866; 07869; 07870; 07871* (NJ 5); 07874 07876; 07878; 07885; 07920* (NJ 7, NJ 12); 07924* (NJ 12); 07926; 07927 07928; 07930; 07931* (NJ 12); 07932; 07933; 07935; 07936; 07938; 07939; 07940 07945; 07946; 07950; 07960; 07961; 07962; 07963; 07970; 07974* (NJ 7); 07976 07980; 07981; 07999; 08807* (NJ 7, NJ 12); 08869; 08875; 08876* (NJ 7, NJ 12).

12th District: 07701* (NJ 6); 07702* (NJ 6); 07703; 07704; 07709; 07711* (NJ 6) 07712* (NJ 6); 07722* (NJ 4, NJ 6); 07723* (NJ 6); 07724; 07726* (NJ 4) 07728* (NJ 4); 07733* (NJ 6); 07734* (NJ 6); 07738; 07739* (NJ 6); 07740* (NJ 6); 07746 07747* (NJ 6); 07748* (NJ 6); 07751* (NJ 6); 07753* (NJ 4, NJ 6) 07755; 07757 07760* (NJ 6); 07763; 07764* (NJ 6); 07765; 07777; 07799; 07830 07920* (NJ 7, NJ 11); 07924* (NJ 11); 07931* (NJ 11); 07934; 07977 07978; 07979; 08502* (NJ 7); 08504; 08512* (NJ 4); 08520* (NJ 4); 08525 08530; 08534; 08536; 08540* (NJ 4, NJ 7); 08541; 08542; 08543; 08544; 08550* (NJ 4); 08551; 08553; 08556; 08557; 08558* (NJ 7); 08559; 08560; 08610* (NJ 4); 08618* (NJ 4); 08619* (NJ 4); 08625; 08628 08629* (NJ 4); 08638* (NJ 4) 08648* (NJ 4); 08690* (NJ 4); 08691* (NJ 4); 08801; 08802* (NJ 5); 08803 08804* (NJ 5); 08807* (NJ 7, NJ 11); 08809; 08810; 08816* (NJ 6); 08822 08824* (NJ 6); 08825; 08826; 08827; 08828; 08829; 08831* (NJ 6); 08833; 08834 08848; 08850* (NJ 6); 08852; 08853* (NJ 7); 08858; 08867; 08868; 08870 08876* (NJ 7, NJ 11); 08884* (NJ 6); 08885; 08887; 08888; 08889; 08902* (NJ 6).

13th District: 07002* (NJ 10); 07008* (NJ 7); 07029* (NJ 9); 07030; 07032* (NJ 9); 07036* (NJ 7, NJ 10); 07047* (NJ 9); 07064* (NJ 7); 07077; 07087* (NJ 9) 07093* (NJ 9); 07097; 07099; 07102* (NJ 10); 07104; 07105* (NJ 10); 07107* (NJ 8, NJ 10); 07114* (NJ 10); 07201* (NJ 10); 07202* (NJ 10); 07206* (NJ 10) 07208* (NJ 7, NJ 10); 07300; 07302; 07303; 07304* (NJ 10); 07305* (NJ 10) 07306* (NJ 9); 07308; 07309; 07310* (NJ 9); 07311; 07399; 08861* (NJ 7) 08862.

New Mexico

1st District: 87002* (NM 2); 87008; 87009; 87015* (NM 3); 87016; 87031* (NM 2); 87032; 87035; 87036; 87043; 87047* (NM 3); 87057; 87059; 87060; 87061 87063; 87068* (NM 2); 87070; 87100; 87101; 87102; 87103; 87104; 87105; 87106 87107; 87108; 87109; 87110; 87111; 87112; 87113; 87114* (NM 3); 87116* (NM 2) 87117; 87118; 87119; 87120* (NM 2, NM 3); 87121* (NM 2); 87122; 87123; 87125 87131; 87153; 87154; 87158; 87174; 87176; 87180; 87190; 87191; 87192; 87194 87195; 87196; 87197; 87198; 87199; 88319; 88321.

2nd District: 87002* (NM 1); 87005; 87006; 87007; 87011; 87014; 87020* (NM 3) 87021; 87022; 87023; 87026; 87028; 87031* (NM 1); 87034; 87038; 87040 87042 87049; 87050; 87051; 87055; 87062; 87068* (NM 1); 87115; 87116* (NM 1); 87120* (NM 1, NM 3); 87121* (NM 1); 87140; 87185; 87315; 87711; 87724; 87801; 87815 87820; 87821; 87823; 87824; 87825; 87827; 87828; 87829; 87830; 87831; 87832 87901; 87930; 87931; 87932; 87933; 87935; 87936; 87937; 87939; 87940; 87941 87942; 87943; 88000; 88001; 88002; 88003; 88004; 88005; 88006; 88008; 88009 88020; 88021; 88022; 88023; 88024; 88025; 88026; 88027; 88028; 88029; 88030 88031; 88032; 88033; 88034; 88036; 88038; 88039; 88040; 88041; 88042; 88043 88044; 88045; 88046; 88047; 88048; 88049; 88051; 88052; 88053; 88054; 88055 88056; 88058; 88061; 88062; 88063; 88065; 88072; 88073; 88114; 88119; 88134 88136; 88201; 88202; 88210; 88211; 88213; 88220; 88221; 88230 88231; 88232 88240; 88241; 88250; 88252; 88253; 88254; 88255; 88256; 88260; 88262 88263 88264; 88265; 88266; 88267; 88268; 88301; 88310; 88311; 88312; 88314; 88316 88317; 88318; 88322; 88323; 88324; 88325; 88330; 88336; 88337; 88338; 88339 88340; 88341; 88342; 88343; 88344; 88345; 88346; 88347; 88348; 88349; 88350 88351; 88352; 88353; 88354; 88417; 88431; 88432; 88435.

3rd District: 87001; 87004; 87010; 87012; 87013; 87015* (NM 1); 87017; 87018 87020* (NM 2); 87024; 87025; 87027; 87029; 87037; 87041; 87044; 87045; 87046 87047* (NM 1); 87048; 87052; 87053; 87056; 87064; 87070; 87083; 87114* (NM 1) 87120* (NM 1, NM 2); 87124; 87184; 87201; 87301; 87302; 87305; 87310; 87311 87312; 87313; 87316; 87317; 87319; 87320; 87321; 87322; 87323; 87324; 87325 87326; 87327; 87328; 87347; 87357; 87364; 87365; 87375; 87401; 87402; 87410 87412; 87413; 87415; 87416; 87417; 87418; 87419; 87420; 87421; 87455; 87461 87499; 87500; 87501; 87502; 87503 87504; 87505; 87506; 87509; 87510; 87511 87512; 87513; 87514; 87515; 87516; 87517 87518; 87519; 87520; 87521; 87522 87523; 87524; 87525; 87527; 87528; 87529; 87530 87531; 87532; 87533; 87535 87536; 87537; 87538; 87539; 87540; 87541; 87543; 87544 87545; 87547; 87548 87549; 87550; 87551; 87552; 87553; 87554; 87556; 87557; 87558 87560; 87561 87562; 87563; 87564; 87565; 87566; 87567; 87568; 87569; 87571; 87573 87574 87575; 87576; 87577; 87578; 87579; 87580; 87581; 87582; 87583; 87701; 87710 87712; 87713; 87714; 87715; 87718; 87722; 87723; 87725; 87728; 87729; 87730 87731; 87732; 87733; 87734; 87735; 87736; 87740; 87742; 87743; 87745; 87746 87747; 87749; 87750; 87752; 87753; 88101; 88102; 88103; 88111; 88112; 88113 88115; 88116; 88118; 88120; 88121; 88122; 88123; 88124; 88125; 88126; 88130 88132; 88133; 88135; 88401; 88410; 88411; 88412; 88414; 88415; 88416; 88418 88419; 88421; 88422; 88423; 88424; 88426; 88427; 88429; 88430; 88433; 88434 88436; 88437; 88438; 88439; 88441.

New York

1st District: 00501; 00544; 11713; 11715* (NY 2); 11719; 11720; 11727 11733 11738; 11741* (NY 2); 11742* (NY 2); 11749; 11754* (NY 5); 11755; 11760 11763; 11764; 11766; 11767; 11770; 11772; 11776; 11777; 11778; 11779* (NY 2) 11780; 11784; 11786; 11787* (NY 2, NY 5); 11788* (NY 2); 11789; 11790; 11792 11794; 11901; 11930; 11931; 11932; 11933; 11934; 11935; 11937; 11939; 11940 11941; 11942; 11944; 11946; 11947; 11948; 11949; 11950; 11951; 11952; 11953 11954; 11955; 11956; 11957; 11958; 11959; 11960; 11961; 11962; 11963; 11964 11965; 11967; 11968; 11969; 11970; 11971; 11972; 11973; 11975; 11976; 11977 11978; 11980.

2nd District: 11701* (NY 3); 11702; 11703; 11704; 11705; 11706; 11707; 11715* (NY 1);

11716; 11717; 11718; 11722; 11725* (NY 5); 11726; 11729; 11730; 11731* (NY 5); 11735* (NY 3); 11736; 11737; 11739; 11740* (NY 5); 11741* (NY 1) 11742* (NY 1); 11743* (NY 5); 11746* (NY 5); 11747* (NY 5); 11750; 11751 11752; 11757; 11769; 11779* (NY 1); 11782; 11787* (NY 1, NY 5); 11788* (NY 1) 11795; 11796; 11798.

3rd District: 11030* (NY 5); 11050* (NY 5); 11507* (NY 4, NY 5); 11510* (NY 4); 11518* (NY 4); 11520* (NY 4); 11542* (NY 5); 11545; 11547; 11548* (NY 5) 11557* (NY 4); 11558* (NY 4); 11560* (NY 5); 11561* (NY 4); 11563* (NY 4) 11566* (NY 4); 11568* (NY 5); 11569; 11570* (NY 4); 11572* (NY 4); 11576* (NY 5); 11577* (NY 5); 11579* (NY 5); 11590* (NY 4); 11596* (NY 4); 11701* (NY 2) 11710* (NY 4); 11714; 11732; 11735* (NY 2); 11753; 11756* (NY 4); 11758 11762; 11765* (NY 5); 11771* (NY 5); 11775; 11783; 11791* (NY 5); 11793* (NY 4) 11797* (NY 5); 11801* (NY 4); 11802; 11803* (NY 5); 11804; 11815; 11819 11853; 11854; 11855.

4th District: 11001* (NY 6); 11003; 11010; 11040* (NY 5, NY 6); 11041* (NY 5); 11043; 11044; 11099; 11501; 11507* (NY 3, NY 5); 11509; 11510* (NY 3) 11514; 11516; 11518* (NY 3); 11520* (NY 3); 11530; 11535; 11536; 11550; 11551 11552; 11553; 11554; 11555; 11556; 11557* (NY 3); 11558* (NY 3); 11559; 11561* (NY 3); 11563* (NY 3); 11564; 11565; 11566* (NY 3); 11570* (NY 3); 11571 11572* (NY 3); 11575; 11580; 11581; 11582; 11583; 11588; 11590* (NY 3); 11592 11593; 11595; 11596* (NY 3); 11598; 11599; 11696* (NY 6); 11709* (NY 5) 11710* (NY 3); 11756* (NY 3); 11793* (NY 3); 11801* (NY 3).

5th District: 11002; 11004* (NY 6); 11005; 11020; 11021; 11022; 11023; 11024 11025; 11027; 11030* (NY 3); 11040* (NY 4, NY 6); 11042* (NY 4); 11050* (NY 3); 11051 11052; 11053; 11054; 11055; 11300; 11351* (NY 7); 11352; 11353 11354* (NY 7, NY 18); 11355* (NY 7, NY 18); 11357* (NY 7, NY 18); 11358 11359; 11360* (NY 18); 11361; 11362; 11363; 11364; 11365* (NY 18); 11366* (NY 18); 11367* (NY 7, NY 18); 11390; 11423* (NY 6, NY 18); 11426* (NY 6); 11427* (NY 6, NY 18); 11446; 11507* (NY 3, NY 4); 11542* (NY 3); 11548* (NY 3); 11560* (NY 3); 11568* (NY 3); 11576* (NY 3); 11577* (NY 3); 11579* (NY 3) 11594; 11597; 11709* (NY 4); 11721; 11724; 11725* (NY 2); 11731* (NY 2) 11740* (NY 2); 11743* (NY 2); 11746* (NY 2); 11747* (NY 1, NY 2); 11754* (NY 1) 11765* (NY 3); 11768; 11771* (NY 3); 11773; 11774; 11787* (NY 1, NY 2); 11791* (NY 3); 11797* (NY 3); 11803* (NY 3); 11805.

6th District: 11001* (NY 4); 11004* (NY 5); 11040* (NY 4, NY 5); 11400; 11405 11407; 11410; 11411; 11412; 11413; 11415* (NY 9); 11416* (NY 9); 11417* (NY 9); 11418* (NY 9); 11419; 11420; 11421* (NY 9); 11422; 11423* (NY 5, NY 18); 11425; 11426* (NY 5); 11427* (NY 5, NY 18); 11428; 11429; 11430; 11431; 11432* (NY 9, NY 18); 11433; 11434; 11435* (NY 7, NY 9, NY 18); 11436; 11451; 11470 11472; 11474; 11476; 11478; 11480; 11482; 11484; 11486; 11488; 11499; 11600 11690; 11691* (NY 9); 11692* (NY 9); 11693* (NY 9); 11696* (NY 4).

7th District: 10460* (NY 16); 10461* (NY 16, NY 18); 10462* (NY 16); 10465* (NY 16, NY 18); 10467* (NY 16, NY 17); 10469* (NY 17); 11100; 11101; 11102* (NY 14); 11103* (NY 14); 11104* (NY 12); 11105* (NY 14); 11106; 11120; 11351* (NY 5); 11354* (NY 5, NY 18); 11355* (NY 5, NY 18); 11356; 11357* (NY 5, NY 18); 11367* (NY 5, NY 18); 11368* (NY 5, NY 18); 11369* (NY 12); 11370* (NY 12, NY 14); 11371 11372* (NY 12); 11373* (NY 12, NY 18); 11374* (NY 9, NY 18); 11375* (NY 9, NY 18); 11377* (NY 12); 11378* (NY 12); 11379* (NY 9, NY 18); 11380; 11385* (NY 9, NY 10, NY 12); 11435* (NY 6, NY 9, NY 18).

8th District: 10001* (NY 14); 10002* (NY 12, NY 14); 10003* (NY 12, NY 14) 10004; 10005; 10006; 10007; 10008; 10009* (NY 12, NY 14); 10010* (NY 14) 10011; 10012* (NY 12); 10013* (NY 12); 10014; 10015; 10018* (NY 14); 10019* (NY 14); 10023* (NY 14); 10024* (NY 14); 10025* (NY 14, NY 15); 10027* (NY 15); 10036* (NY 14); 10038* (NY 12); 10041; 10043; 10045; 10046; 10047; 10048 10060; 10079; 10080; 10081; 10087; 10090; 10094; 10095; 10096; 10098; 10099 10100; 10101; 10102; 10104; 10105; 10108; 10109; 10111* (NY 14); 10112* (NY 14); 10113; 10114; 10116; 10117 10118* (NY 14); 10119; 10120; 10121; 10122 10123; 10124; 10125; 10129; 10132 10133; 10138; 10149; 10161; 10164; 10184 10185; 10195; 10196; 10197; 10199; 10200 10203; 10211; 10212; 10213; 10242 10249; 10256; 10257; 10258; 10259; 10260; 10261 10265; 10268; 10269; 10270 10271; 10272; 10273; 10274; 10275; 10276; 10277; 10278; 10279; 10280; 10281 10282; 10285; 10286; 10292; 11204* (NY 9, NY 13); 11214* (NY 13); 11218* (NY 9, NY 10, NY 11, NY 12); 11219* (NY 10, NY 12, NY 13); 11220* (NY 12, NY 13) 11223* (NY 9, NY 13); 11224* (NY 9); 11230* (NY 9, NY 11); 11231* (NY 10, NY 12); 11232* (NY 10, NY 12); 11235* (NY 9, NY 13).

9th District: 11204* (NY 8, NY 13); 11210* (NY 10, NY 11); 11215* (NY 10, NY 11, NY 12); 11218* (NY 8, NY 10, NY 11, NY 12); 11223* (NY 8, NY 13); 11224* (NY 8) 11225* (NY 11); 11226* (NY 11); 11229; 11230* (NY 8); 11234* (NY 10, NY 11); 11235* (NY 8, NY 13); 11236* (NY 10, NY 11); 11238* (NY 10, NY 11); 11374* (NY 7, NY 18); 11375* (NY 7, NY 18); 11379* (NY 7, NY 18); 11381 11385* (NY 7, NY 10, NY 12); 11386; 11414; 11415* (NY 6); 11416* (NY 6); 11417* (NY 6) 11418* (NY 6); 11421* (NY 6); 11424; 11432* (NY 6, NY 18) 11435* (NY 6, NY 7, NY 18); 11450; 11691* (NY 6); 11692* (NY 6); 11693* (NY 6); 11694; 11695; 11697.

10th District: 11200; 11201* (NY 11, NY 12); 11202; 11203* (NY 11); 11205* (NY 11, NY 12); 11206* (NY 12, NY 14); 11207* (NY 11, NY 12); 11208* (NY 12) 11210* (NY 9, NY 11); 11211* (NY 12, NY 14); 11212* (NY 11); 11213* (NY 11) 11215* (NY 9, NY 11, NY 12); 11216* (NY 11); 11217* (NY 11, NY 12); 11218* (NY 8, NY 9, NY 11, NY 12); 11219* (NY 8, NY 12, NY 13); 11221* (NY 12); 11231* (NY 8, NY 12); 11232* (NY 8, NY 12); 11233* (NY 11); 11234* (NY 9, NY 11) 11236* (NY 9, NY 11); 11237* (NY 12, NY 14); 11238* (NY 9, NY 11); 11239 11240; 11241; 11242; 11243; 11245; 11247; 11248; 11249; 11254; 11255; 11256 11385* (NY 7, NY 9, NY 12).

11th District: 11201* (NY 10, NY 12); 11203* (NY 10); 11205* (NY 10, NY 12); 11207* (NY 10, NY 12); 11210* (NY 9, NY 10); 11212* (NY 10); 11213* (NY 10); 11215* (NY 9, NY 10, NY 12); 11216* (NY 10); 11217* (NY 10, NY 12); 11218* (NY 8, NY 9, NY 10, NY 12); 11225* (NY 9); 11226* (NY 9); 11230* (NY 8, NY 9) 11233* (NY 10); 11234* (NY 9, NY 10); 11236* (NY 9, NY 10); 11238* (NY 9, NY 10); 11244.

12th District: 10002* (NY 8, NY 14); 10003* (NY 8, NY 14); 10009* (NY 8, NY 14);

10012* (NY 8); 10013* (NY 8); 10038* (NY 8); 10158; 11104* (NY 7); 11201* (NY 10, NY 11); 11205* (NY 10, NY 11); 11206* (NY 10, NY 14); 11207* (NY 10, NY 11); 11208* (NY 10); 11211* (NY 7, NY 10, NY 14); 11215* (NY 9, NY 10, NY 11); 11217* (NY 10, NY 11); 11218* (NY 8, NY 9, NY 10, NY 11); 11219* (NY 8, NY 10, NY 13); 11220* (NY 8, NY 13); 11221* (NY 10); 11222* (NY 14); 11231* (NY 8, NY 10); 11232* (NY 8, NY 10); 11237* (NY 10, NY 14); 11251; 11368* (NY 7, NY 18) 11369* (NY 7); 11370* (NY 7, NY 14); 11372* (NY 7); 11373* (NY 7, NY 18); 11377* (NY 7); 11378* (NY 7); 11385* (NY 7, NY 9, NY 10).

13th District: 10300; 10301; 10302; 10303; 10304; 10305; 10306; 10307; 10308 10309; 10310; 10311; 10312; 10313; 10314; 11204* (NY 8, NY 9); 11209; 11214* (NY 8) 11219* (NY 8, NY 10, NY 12); 11220* (NY 8, NY 12); 11223* (NY 8, NY 9); 11228; 11235* (NY 8, NY 9); 11252.

14th District: 10001* (NY 8); 10002* (NY 8, NY 12); 10003* (NY 8, NY 12) 10009* (NY 8, NY 12); 10010* (NY 8); 10016; 10017; 10018* (NY 8); 10019* (NY 8); 10020; 10021; 10022; 10023* (NY 8); 10024* (NY 8); 10025* (NY 8, NY 15) 10026* (NY 15); 10028; 10029* (NY 15); 10036* (NY 8); 10044; 10055; 10103 10106; 10107; 10110 10111* (NY 8); 10112* (NY 8); 10118* (NY 8); 10126 10128; 10130; 10131; 10150; 10151; 10152; 10153; 10154; 10155; 10156; 10157 10159; 10160; 10162; 10163; 10165; 10166; 10167; 10168; 10169; 10170; 10171 10172; 10173; 10174; 10175; 10176; 10177; 10178; 11102* (NY 7); 11103* (NY 7) 11105* (NY 7); 11206* (NY 10, NY 12); 11211* (NY 10, NY 12); 11222* (NY 12) 11237* (NY 10, NY 12); 11370* (NY 7, NY 12).

15th District: 10025* (NY 8, NY 14); 10026* (NY 14); 10027* (NY 8); 10029* (NY 14); 10030; 10031; 10032; 10033; 10034; 10035; 10037; 10039; 10040; 10115 10453* (NY 16, NY 17); 10463* (NY 17); 10474* (NY 16).

16th District: 10400; 10451* (NY 17); 10452* (NY 17); 10453* (NY 15, NY 17) 10454; 10455; 10456; 10457* (NY 17); 10458* (NY 17); 10459; 10460* (NY 7) 10461* (NY 7, NY 18); 10462* (NY 7); 10465* (NY 7, NY 17); 10467* (NY 7, NY 17); 10468* (NY 17); 10472; 10473; 10474* (NY 15).

17th District: 10451* (NY 16); 10452* (NY 16); 10453* (NY 15, NY 16); 10457* (NY 16); 10458* (NY 16); 10463* (NY 15); 10466; 10467* (NY 7, NY 16); 10468* (NY 16); 10469* (NY 7); 10470; 10471; 10475* (NY 18); 10538* (NY 18); 10550* (NY 18); 10551; 10552* (NY 18); 10553* (NY 18); 10557; 10558; 10559; 10700 10701* (NY 18, NY 20); 10703* (NY 18); 10705* (NY 18); 10710* (NY 18, NY 20); 10800; 10801* (NY 18); 10803* (NY 18); 10805* (NY 18).

18th District: 10461* (NY 7, NY 16); 10464; 10465* (NY 7, NY 16); 10475* (NY 17); 10528; 10530* (NY 20); 10538* (NY 17); 10543; 10550* (NY 17); 10552* (NY 17); 10553* (NY 17); 10573; 10577; 10580; 10581; 10583* (NY 20); 10601* (NY 19); 10604* (NY 19); 10605* (NY 19); 10606* (NY 19, NY 20); 10607* (NY 19, NY 20); 10701* (NY 17, NY 20); 10702; 10703* (NY 17); 10704; 10705* (NY 17) 10706* (NY 20); 10707* (NY 20); 10708; 10709; 10710* (NY 17, NY 20); 10801* (NY 17); 10802; 10803* (NY 17); 10804; 10805* (NY 17); 11354* (NY 5, NY 7); 11355* (NY 5, NY 7); 11357* (NY 5, NY 7); 11360* (NY 5); 11365* (NY 5); 11366* (NY 5); 11367* (NY 5, NY 7); 11368* (NY 7, NY 12); 11373* (NY 7, NY 12) 11374* (NY 7, NY 9); 11375* (NY 7, NY 9); 11379* (NY 7, NY 9); 11402; 11406 11408; 11423* (NY 5, NY 6); 11427* (NY 5, NY 6); 11432* (NY 6, NY 9); 11435* (NY 6, NY 7, NY 9); 11439; 11440; 11441; 11447; 11452; 11460.

19th District: 00401; 10501; 10504; 10505; 10506; 10507; 10509; 10510; 10511 10512; 10514; 10516; 10517; 10518; 10519; 10520; 10521; 10523* (NY 20); 10524 10526; 10527; 10532; 10535; 10536; 10537; 10540; 10541; 10542; 10545; 10546 10547; 10548; 10549; 10560; 10562; 10566; 10570; 10571; 10572; 10576; 10578 10579; 10587; 10588; 10589; 10590; 10591* (NY 20); 10594; 10595* (NY 20) 10596; 10597; 10598; 10600 10601* (NY 18); 10602; 10603* (NY 20); 10604* (NY 18); 10605* (NY 18); 10606* (NY 18, NY 20); 10607* (NY 18, NY 20); 10625 10629; 10633; 10650; 10916* (NY 20); 10922; 10924* (NY 20); 10928; 10930* (NY 20); 10940* (NY 20); 10953; 10992* (NY 20); 10996; 10997; 12501* (NY 22) 12508* (NY 26); 12511; 12512; 12514* (NY 22); 12518; 12520; 12522; 12524 12527; 12531; 12533* (NY 22); 12537; 12540* (NY 22); 12543* (NY 20); 12545* (NY 22); 12549* (NY 20); 12550* (NY 20, NY 26); 12553* (NY 26); 12563; 12564 12570; 12575* (NY 20, NY 26); 12577* (NY 20); 12582; 12584; 12585; 12590* (NY 22); 12592; 12594; 12600; 12601* (NY 22, NY 26); 12602; 12603* (NY 22).

20th District: 10502; 10503; 10522; 10523* (NY 19); 10530* (NY 18); 10533 10583* (NY 18); 10591* (NY 19); 10595* (NY 19); 10603* (NY 19); 10606* (NY 18, NY 19); 10607* (NY 18, NY 19); 10701* (NY 17, NY 18); 10706* (NY 17); 10707* (NY 17); 10710* (NY 17, NY 18); 10901; 10910; 10911; 10912; 10913; 10914 10915* (NY 19); 10917; 10918; 10919; 10920; 10921; 10923; 10924* (NY 19); 10925; 10926 10927; 10930* (NY 19); 10931; 10932; 10933; 10940* (NY 19); 10941; 10943; 10950* (NY 26); 10951; 10952; 10954; 10956; 10958; 10959; 10960; 10962; 10963; 10964; 10965 10968; 10969; 10970; 10973; 10974; 10975; 10976; 10977; 10979; 10980; 10981; 10982 10983; 10984; 10985; 10986; 10987; 10988 10989; 10990; 10992* (NY 19); 10993 10994; 10995; 10998; 12543* (NY 19) 12549* (NY 19); 12550* (NY 19, NY 26); 12566* (NY 26); 12575* (NY 19, NY 26) 12577* (NY 19); 12586* (NY 26); 12589* (NY 26); 12701* (NY 26); 12719; 12720; 12721; 12722; 12726; 12727; 12729; 12732; 12734* (NY 26); 12737; 12739; 12743 12746; 12748* (NY 26); 12749; 12752; 12762; 12764 12769; 12770; 12771; 12775* (NY 26); 12777* (NY 26); 12778; 12780; 12781; 12783* (NY 26); 12785; 12786 12790; 12792.

21st District: 12007; 12008; 12009; 12010* (NY 22, NY 24); 12016; 12019* (NY 22); 12023* (NY 22); 12027* (NY 22); 12041; 12045; 12046; 12047; 12053* (NY 22); 12054; 12055; 12056; 12059; 12061* (NY 22); 12066* (NY 22); 12067; 12068* (NY 24); 12069; 12070* (NY 24); 12072; 12077; 12083* (NY 22); 12084; 12085; 12086; 12095* (NY 24); 12107; 12110; 12111; 12120; 12122* (NY 22, NY 23); 12128; 12137; 12141; 12143; 12144; 12147; 12150; 12158; 12159; 12161; 12163 12166* (NY 23); 12177; 12180* (NY 22); 12182* (NY 22); 12183; 12186; 12188* (NY 22); 12189; 12193; 12198* (NY 22); 12200; 12201; 12202; 12203; 12204 12205; 12206; 12207; 12208; 12209; 12210 12211; 12212; 12214; 12220; 12222 12223; 12224; 12225; 12226; 12227; 12228; 12229

12230; 12231; 12232; 12233 12234; 12235; 12236; 12237; 12238; 12239; 12240; 12241; 12242; 12243; 12244 12245; 12246; 12247; 12248; 12249; 12250; 12252; 12255; 12256; 12257; 12260 12288; 12300; 12301; 12302* (NY 22); 12303; 12304; 12305; 12306; 12307; 12308 12309; 12325; 12345; 12469* (NY 22); 13317* (NY 23); 13339* (NY 23, NY 24) 13459* (NY 23).

22nd District: 12010* (NY 21, NY 24); 12015; 12017; 12018; 12019* (NY 21) 12020; 12022; 12023* (NY 21); 12024; 12026; 12027* (NY 21); 12028; 12029 12033; 12035; 12037; 12040; 12042; 12050; 12051; 12052; 12053* (NY 21); 12057 12058; 12060; 12061* (NY 21); 12062; 12063; 12065; 12066* (NY 21); 12071 12073; 12074; 12075; 12076; 12082; 12083* (NY 21); 12087; 12089; 12090; 12092* (NY 23); 12094; 12106; 12114; 12115; 12118; 12121; 12122* (NY 21, NY 23) 12123; 12124; 12125; 12130; 12131; 12132; 12133; 12135; 12136; 12138 12140 12148; 12151; 12153; 12154; 12156; 12157; 12160* (NY 23); 12162; 12165; 12167* (NY 23); 12168; 12169; 12170; 12172; 12173; 12174; 12175* (NY 23); 12176 12179; 12180* (NY 21); 12181; 12182* (NY 21); 12184; 12185; 12188* (NY 21) 12192; 12194; 12195; 12196; 12198* (NY 21); 12302* (NY 21); 12405; 12407 12413; 12414; 12415; 12418; 12422; 12423; 12424; 12427; 12430* (NY 23); 12431 12436; 12439; 12442; 12444; 12450; 12451; 12452; 12454; 12460; 12463; 12468 12469* (NY 21); 12470; 12473; 12482; 12485; 12492; 12496; 12501* (NY 19) 12502; 12503; 12504; 12506; 12507; 12510; 12513; 12514* (NY 19); 12516; 12517 12521; 12523; 12526; 12529; 12530; 12533* (NY 19); 12534; 12538; 12540* (NY 19); 12541; 12544; 12545* (NY 19); 12546; 12565; 12567; 12569; 12571 12572 12574; 12578; 12580; 12581; 12583; 12590* (NY 19); 12593; 12601* (NY 19, NY 26); 12603* (NY 19); 12801; 12803; 12804; 12808; 12809; 12810; 12811; 12814 12815; 12816; 12817; 12819; 12820; 12821; 12822; 12823; 12824; 12826; 12827 12828; 12831; 12832; 12833; 12834; 12835; 12836; 12837; 12838; 12839; 12841 12843; 12844; 12845; 12846; 12848; 12849; 12850; 12851; 12852; 12853; 12854 12855; 12856; 12857; 12858; 12859; 12860; 12861; 12862; 12863; 12865; 12866 12870; 12871; 12872; 12873; 12874; 12878; 12879; 12883; 12884; 12885; 12886 12887; 12913* (NY 24); 12928; 12932* (NY 24); 12942; 12943; 12946; 12956 12960; 12961; 12964; 12974* (NY 24); 12977; 12983* (NY 24); 12987; 12993* (NY 24); 12997; 12998.

23rd District: 12031; 12036; 12043; 12064; 12092* (NY 22); 12093; 12113 12116; 12122* (NY 21, NY 22); 12149; 12155; 12160* (NY 22); 12166* (NY 21) 12167* (NY 22); 12175* (NY 22); 12187; 12197; 12406; 12421; 12430* (NY 22) 12434; 12438; 12455; 12459; 12474; 12776* (NY 26); 13030* (NY 25); 13032 13035* (NY 25); 13037* (NY 25); 13040* (NY 25); 13042* (NY 24); 13043; 13052* (NY 25); 13054; 13061 13072; 13082* (NY 25); 13085; 13122* (NY 25); 13123 13124; 13133; 13134; 13136* (NY 25); 13151; 13155; 13157; 13162; 13163 13301; 13303; 13304; 13308 13309* (NY 24); 13310; 13313; 13314; 13315; 13316* (NY 24); 13317* (NY 21); 13318 13319; 13320; 13321; 13322; 13323; 13326 13328; 13329* (NY 24); 13332; 13333 13334; 13335; 13336; 13337; 13338; 13339* (NY 21, NY 24); 13340; 13341; 13342 13346; 13348; 13349; 13350; 13352; 13354 13355; 13357; 13361; 13362; 13363; 13364 13365* (NY 24); 13401; 13402; 13403 13406; 13407; 13408; 13409; 13410; 13411 13413; 13416* (NY 24); 13417; 13418; 13419; 13421; 13424; 13425; 13428 13429; 13431* (NY 24); 13432; 13434 13435; 13438* (NY 24); 13439; 13440; 13441 13442; 13449; 13450; 13452* (NY 24); 13455; 13456; 13457; 13459* (NY 21); 13460 13461; 13464; 13465; 13466 13469; 13471* (NY 24); 13475; 13476; 13477 13478; 13479; 13480; 13482 13483; 13484; 13485; 13486; 13490; 13491 13492; 13494; 13495; 13500; 13501; 13502; 13503; 13504; 13505; 13599; 13730* (NY 26); 13731; 13733 13739; 13740; 13744; 13746; 13747; 13750; 13751; 13752; 13753 13755; 13757; 13758; 13775; 13776; 13777* (NY 23); 13778; 13780; 13782; 13786 13787; 13788; 13796; 13801; 13804; 13806; 13807; 13808; 13809; 13810; 13813* (NY 26); 13814 13815; 13820; 13825; 13826* (NY 26); 13830; 13832; 13833* (NY 26) 13834 13837; 13838; 13839; 13841; 13842; 13843; 13844; 13846; 13848; 13849; 13856* (NY 26); 13859; 13860; 13861; 13862* (NY 25); 13901* (NY 26); 13904* (NY 26) 13905* (NY 25, NY 26).

24th District: 12010* (NY 21, NY 22); 12025; 12032; 12068* (NY 21); 12070* (NY 21) 12078; 12095* (NY 21); 12108; 12117; 12134; 12139; 12164; 12190; 12812 12842 12847; 12864; 12901; 12903; 12910; 12911; 12912; 12913* (NY 22); 12914 12915 12916; 12917; 12918; 12919; 12920; 12921; 12922; 12923; 12924; 12926 12927; 12929 12930; 12932* (NY 22); 12933; 12934; 12935; 12936; 12937; 12938 12939; 12940 12941; 12944; 12945; 12949; 12950; 12952; 12953; 12955; 12957 12958; 12959; 12962 12965; 12966; 12967; 12968; 12969; 12970; 12972; 12973; 12974* (NY 22); 12975 12976; 12978; 12979; 12980; 12981; 12982; 12983* (NY 22); 12985; 12986; 12989 12990; 12991; 12992; 12993* (NY 22); 12994; 12995 12996; 13028; 13029* (NY 25) 13036* (NY 25); 13041* (NY 25); 13042* (NY 23); 13044; 13069* (NY 25); 13074* (NY 25); 13076; 13093; 13103; 13107 13114; 13115; 13121; 13126; 13131; 13132 13135* (NY 25); 13142; 13144; 13145; 13167; 13302; 13305; 13309* (NY 23); 13312 13316* (NY 23); 13324; 13325 13327; 13329* (NY 23); 13331; 13339* (NY 21, NY 23); 13343; 13345; 13353; 13360; 13365* (NY 23); 13368; 13404; 13416* (NY 23); 13420; 13426 13431* (NY 23); 13433; 13436; 13437; 13438* (NY 23); 13452* (NY 23); 13454 13470; 13471* (NY 23); 13472; 13473; 13489; 13493; 13601; 13602; 13603; 13605 13606; 13607; 13608; 13609; 13610; 13611; 13612; 13613; 13614; 13615; 13616 13617; 13618; 13619; 13620; 13621; 13622; 13623; 13624; 13626; 13627 13628; 13630 13631; 13632; 13633; 13634; 13635; 13636; 13637; 13638; 13639 13640; 13641; 13642 13643; 13645; 13646; 13647; 13648; 13649; 13650; 13651 13652; 13654; 13655; 13656 13657; 13658; 13659; 13660; 13661; 13662; 13664; 13667; 13668; 13669 13670; 13671; 13672; 13673; 13674; 13675; 13676; 13677; 13678; 13679; 13680; 13681 13682; 13683; 13684; 13685; 13687 13688; 13690; 13691; 13692; 13693; 13694; 13695 13696; 13697; 13698; 13699.

25th District: 13020; 13021* (NY 27, NY 31); 13027; 13029* (NY 24); 13030* (NY 23) 13031; 13033; 13034* (NY 27, NY 31); 13035* (NY 23); 13036* (NY 24); 13037* (NY 23); 13039; 13040* (NY 23); 13041* (NY 24); 13045* (NY 23); 13050 13051; 13052* (NY 23); 13053* (NY 26, NY 31); 13055; 13056; 13057; 13060 13063; 13064; 13066 13069* (NY 24); 13074* (NY 24); 13077; 13078; 13080 13082* (NY 23); 13084; 13087 13088; 13089; 13090; 13094; 13101; 13104; 13108 13110; 13111; 13112; 13113; 13116 13117; 13119; 13120; 13122* (NY 23); 13125 13130; 13135* (NY 24); 13136* (NY 23) 13137; 13138; 13140; 13141; 13143* (NY 27); 13150; 13152* (NY 31); 13153; 13156 13158; 13159; 13164; 13166; 13200 13201; 13202; 13203; 13204; 13205; 13206; 13207 13208; 13209; 13210; 13211 13212; 13214; 13215; 13217; 13219; 13220; 13221; 13224

13244; 13250; 13251 13252; 13260; 13261; 13290; 13736* (NY 26); 13738; 13760* (NY 26); 13777* (NY 23); 13784; 13790* (NY 26); 13794; 13797; 13802; 13803; 13811* (NY 26); 13827* (NY 26); 13835; 13862* (NY 23); 13863; 13905* (NY 23, NY 26); 14817* (NY 26).

26th District: 10950* (NY 20); 12401; 12404; 12409; 12410; 12411; 12412 12416; 12417; 12419; 12420; 12428; 12429; 12432; 12433; 12435; 12440; 12441 12443; 12446; 12448; 12449; 12453; 12456; 12457; 12458; 12461; 12462; 12464 12465; 12466; 12471 12472; 12475; 12477; 12480; 12481; 12483; 12484; 12486 12487; 12489; 12490; 12491 12493; 12494; 12495; 12498; 12508* (NY 19); 12515 12525; 12528; 12542; 12547 12548; 12550* (NY 19, NY 20); 12551; 12552; 12553* (NY 19); 12555; 12561; 12566* (NY 20); 12568; 12575* (NY 19, NY 20); 12586* (NY 20); 12588; 12589* (NY 20) 12601* (NY 19, NY 22); 12701* (NY 20); 12723 12724; 12725; 12733; 12734* (NY 20) 12736; 12738; 12740; 12741; 12742; 12745 12747; 12748* (NY 20); 12750; 12751 12753; 12754; 12758; 12759; 12760; 12763 12765; 12766; 12767; 12768; 12775* (NY 20); 12776* (NY 23); 12777* (NY 20) 12779; 12782; 12783* (NY 20); 12784; 12787 12788; 12789; 12791; 13053* (NY 25, NY 31); 13062; 13068* (NY 31); 13730* (NY 23) 13732; 13734; 13736* (NY 25); 13737; 13743; 13745; 13748; 13749; 13754; 13756 13760* (NY 25); 13761 13762; 13763; 13774; 13783; 13790* (NY 25); 13795; 13811* (NY 25); 13812 13813* (NY 23); 13826* (NY 23); 13827* (NY 25); 13833* (NY 23) 13840; 13845; 13847; 13850; 13851; 13856* (NY 23); 13864; 13865; 13900; 13901* (NY 23) 13902; 13903; 13904* (NY 23); 13905* (NY 23, NY 25); 14817* (NY 25) 14850* (NY 31); 14851; 14852; 14853; 14859* (NY 31); 14867* (NY 31); 14881; 14882* (NY 31); 14883* (NY 31); 14886* (NY 31); 14892* (NY 31); 14896.

27th District: 13021* (NY 25, NY 31); 13034* (NY 25, NY 31); 13065; 13143* (NY 25) 13146; 13148* (NY 31); 13154; 13165* (NY 31); 14001* (NY 29); 14003 14004* (NY 30); 14005; 14009* (NY 31); 14011; 14013; 14020; 14021; 14024 14031; 14032; 14036 14037; 14038; 14039; 14040; 14051; 14052* (NY 30); 14054 14056; 14058* (NY 29) 14059* (NY 30); 14066; 14068; 14082; 14083* (NY 30); 14102; 14113; 14125* (NY 29); 14130; 14139* (NY 30); 14143; 14145; 14167 14169; 14214* (NY 29, NY 30); 14215* (NY 30); 14221* (NY 30); 14225* (NY 30) 14226* (NY 29, NY 30); 14228* (NY 29); 14231; 14260; 14413; 14414; 14416* (NY 29); 14422; 14423; 14424; 14425 14427; 14428* (NY 29); 14432; 14433; 14435 14437* (NY 31); 14443; 14444; 14449 14450* (NY 28); 14453; 14454; 14456* (NY 31); 14461; 14462; 14463; 14466; 14467* (NY 28); 14469; 14471; 14472; 14474 14475; 14480; 14481; 14482; 14485; 14486; 14487 14488; 14489; 14502* (NY 28) 14504; 14505; 14506; 14510; 14511; 14512* (NY 31); 14513; 14514* (NY 29) 14516; 14517; 14518; 14519; 14520; 14522; 14525; 14530 14532; 14533; 14534* (NY 28); 14536* (NY 31); 14537; 14538; 14539; 14541* (NY 31); 14542; 14543* (NY 28); 14544* (NY 31); 14545; 14546; 14547; 14548; 14549; 14550 14551; 14554; 14555; 14556; 14557; 14558; 14560; 14561* (NY 31); 14563; 14564* (NY 28); 14568; 14569; 14572* (NY 31); 14580* (NY 28); 14584; 14585; 14586* (NY 28); 14589; 14590; 14591; 14592; 14623* (NY 28); 14624* (NY 28, NY 29); 14822* (NY 31); 14836; 14846* (NY 31).

28th District: 14445; 14450* (NY 27); 14467* (NY 27); 14468* (NY 29); 14502* (NY 27); 14515; 14526; 14534* (NY 27); 14543* (NY 27); 14564* (NY 27); 14580* (NY 27); 14586* (NY 27); 14600; 14601; 14602; 14603; 14604; 14605; 14606* (NY 29); 14607; 14608; 14609; 14610; 14611; 14612; 14613; 14614; 14615; 14616 14617; 14618 14619* (NY 29); 14620; 14621; 14622; 14623* (NY 27); 14624* (NY 27, NY 29); 14625 14626* (NY 29); 14627; 14638; 14639; 14642; 14643; 14644; 14645; 14646; 14647 14649; 14650; 14651; 14652; 14653; 14660; 14664; 14673 14683; 14692; 14694.

29th District: 14001* (NY 27); 14008; 14012; 14028; 14058* (NY 27); 14067 14072; 14092; 14094; 14095; 14098; 14103; 14105; 14107; 14108; 14109; 14120 14125* (NY 27); 14126; 14131; 14132; 14144; 14150; 14151; 14172; 14174; 14201* (NY 30); 14202; 14203* (NY 30); 14204* (NY 30); 14207; 14208* (NY 30); 14209* (NY 30); 14213; 14214* (NY 27, NY 30); 14216* (NY 30); 14217; 14222; 14223* (NY 30); 14226* (NY 27, NY 30); 14228* (NY 27); 14300; 14301 14302; 14303; 14304 14305; 14410; 14411; 14416* (NY 27); 14420; 14428* (NY 27); 14429; 14430; 14442 14452; 14464; 14468* (NY 28); 14470; 14476; 14477 14479; 14508; 14514* (NY 27); 14559; 14571; 14606* (NY 28); 14619* (NY 28); 14624* (NY 27, NY 28); 14626* (NY 28).

30th District: 14004* (NY 27); 14006; 14010; 14025; 14026; 14027; 14030 14033 14034; 14035; 14043; 14047; 14052* (NY 27); 14055; 14057; 14059* (NY 27); 14061 14069; 14070* (NY 31); 14075; 14079; 14080; 14081* (NY 31); 14085 14086* (NY 27); 14091; 14110; 14111; 14112; 14127; 14134; 14139* (NY 27); 14140; 14141; 14170 14200; 14201* (NY 29); 14202* (NY 29); 14203* (NY 29); 14204* (NY 29); 14205; 14206 14208* (NY 29); 14209* (NY 29); 14210; 14211 14212; 14214* (NY 27, NY 29); 14215* (NY 27); 14216* (NY 29); 14218; 14219 14220; 14221* (NY 27); 14223* (NY 29); 14224 14225* (NY 27); 14226* (NY 27, NY 29); 14227; 14233; 14240; 14241; 14261; 14263 14264; 14265; 14266; 14267; 14269; 14270; 14271; 14272; 14273; 14280.

31st District: 13021* (NY 25, NY 27); 13022; 13024; 13026; 13034* (NY 25, NY 27) 13045* (NY 25); 13053* (NY 25, NY 26); 13068* (NY 26); 13071; 13073 13081; 13092 13102; 13118; 13139; 13147; 13148* (NY 27); 13152* (NY 25); 13160; 13165* (NY 27) 14009* (NY 27); 14029; 14041; 14042; 14048; 14060 14062; 14063; 14065; 14070* (NY 30); 14081* (NY 30); 14101; 14129; 14133; 14136; 14138; 14166; 14168 14171; 14173; 14415; 14418; 14437* (NY 27) 14441; 14456* (NY 27); 14478; 14507 14512* (NY 27); 14521; 14527; 14529 14536* (NY 27); 14541* (NY 27); 14544* (NY 27) 14561* (NY 27); 14572* (NY 27); 14588; 14701; 14702; 14703; 14704; 14706; 14707 14708; 14709; 14710 14711; 14712; 14714; 14715; 14716; 14717; 14718; 14719; 14720 14721; 14722 14723; 14724; 14726; 14727; 14728; 14729; 14730; 14731; 14732; 14733 14735 14736; 14737; 14738; 14739; 14740; 14741; 14742; 14743; 14744; 14745; 14747 14748; 14749; 14750; 14751; 14752; 14753; 14754; 14755; 14756; 14757; 14758 14759 14760; 14766; 14767; 14769; 14770; 14772; 14774; 14775; 14776; 14777 14778; 14779 14781; 14782; 14783; 14784; 14785; 14786; 14787; 14788; 14801 14802; 14803; 14804 14805; 14806; 14807; 14808; 14810; 14812; 14813 14814; 14815; 14816; 14818 14819; 14820; 14821; 14822* (NY 27); 14823; 14824 14825; 14826; 14827; 14830 14831; 14837; 14838; 14839; 14840; 14841; 14842 14843; 14844; 14845; 14846* (NY 27); 14847; 14850* (NY 26); 14854; 14855 14856; 14857; 14858; 14859* (NY 26) 14860; 14861; 14863; 14864; 14865; 14867* (NY 26); 14868; 14869; 14870; 14871 14872; 14873; 14874; 14876; 14877; 14878 14879; 14880; 14882* (NY 26); 14883*

(NY 26); 14884; 14885; 14886* (NY 26) 14887; 14888; 14889; 14891; 14892* (NY 26); 14893; 14894; 14895; 14897; 14898 14900; 14901; 14902; 14903; 14904; 14905; 14925; 14975.

North Carolina

1st District: 27507* (NC 5); 27536* (NC 2); 27551; 27553; 27556; 27563; 27565* (NC 2, NC 5); 27570; 27584; 27586; 27589; 27594; 27801* (NC 2); 27803* (NC 2) 27804* (NC 2); 27805; 27806; 27809* (NC 2); 27811; 27812; 27814; 27816* (NC 2); 27817; 27818; 27820; 27821; 27822* (NC 2); 27823; 27827; 27828; 27829 27831; 27832; 27834* (NC 2); 27835; 27836; 27837* (NC 3); 27838; 27839; 27840 27841; 27842; 27843; 27844* (NC 2); 27845; 27847; 27848; 27849; 27850* (NC 2) 27853; 27854; 27855; 27856* (NC 2); 27857; 27858* (NC 3); 27859; 27860* (NC 3); 27861; 27862; 27863* (NC 3); 27866; 27867; 27869; 27870* (NC 2); 27871 27872; 27873; 27874; 27876; 27877; 27881; 27884; 27886* (NC 2); 27887; 27888 27889* (NC 3); 27890; 27891; 27892* (NC 3); 27893* (NC 2); 27894; 27895 27896; 27897; 27909* (NC 3); 27910; 27919; 27922; 27924; 27926; 27928* (NC 3) 27930; 27932; 27935; 27937; 27938; 27942; 27944; 27946; 27957; 27962; 27967 27969; 27970; 27979; 27980; 27983; 27985; 27986; 28301* (NC 7); 28304* (NC 7, NC 8); 28305* (NC 7); 28306* (NC 7, NC 8); 28311* (NC 7); 28320* (NC 7) 28337* (NC 7); 28348* (NC 7); 28349* (NC 3); 28390* (NC 7, NC 8); 28398* (NC 3); 28399; 28401* (NC 7); 28402; 28403* (NC 7); 28405* (NC 7); 28409* (NC 7) 28421; 28423; 28425* (NC 3); 28429* (NC 7); 28431* (NC 7); 28433; 28434 28435* (NC 3); 28436; 28448* (NC 7); 28450* (NC 7); 28453; 28454* (NC 3, NC 7); 28456; 28458* (NC 3); 28464* (NC 3); 28466* (NC 3); 28471* (NC 3); 28472* (NC 7); 28478* (NC 3); 28501; 28513* (NC 3); 28518* (NC 3); 28523 28526; 28530* (NC 3); 28532; 28533; 28538; 28551* (NC 3); 28554 28560* (NC 3); 28562* (NC 3); 28563; 28564; 28573* (NC 3); 28580; 28585* (NC 3); 28590* (NC 3).

2nd District: 27237; 27242* (NC 8); 27251; 27281* (NC 8); 27330* (NC 8) 27331; 27376; 27501; 27504; 27505; 27506; 27508; 27509; 27514* (NC 4); 27520* (NC 4); 27521; 27522; 27524; 27525; 27526* (NC 4); 27529* (NC 4); 27536* (NC 1); 27542 27543; 27544; 27546; 27549; 27552; 27555; 27557; 27560* (NC 4) 27564; 27565* (NC 1, NC 5); 27568; 27569* (NC 3); 27572* (NC 4, NC 5, NC 12) 27576; 27577; 27581; 27587* (NC 4); 27591* (NC 4); 27592* (NC 4); 27593 27596* (NC 4); 27597* (NC 4); 27613* (NC 4); 27701* (NC 12); 27703* (NC 12) 27704* (NC 12); 27705* (NC 4, NC 12); 27706* (NC 12); 27707* (NC 4, NC 12) 27709; 27710; 27711; 27712* (NC 12); 27713* (NC 12); 27715; 27717; 27801* (NC 1); 27802; 27803* (NC 1); 27804* (NC 1); 27807; 27809* (NC 1); 27813; 27816* (NC 1); 27819; 27822* (NC 1); 27834* (NC 1); 27844* (NC 1); 27850* (NC 1) 27851; 27852; 27856* (NC 1); 27864; 27868; 27870* (NC 1); 27878; 27880; 27882 27883* (NC 3); 27886* (NC 1); 27893* (NC 1); 28315; 28323; 28326* (NC 8) 28327* (NC 8); 28334; 28335; 28339; 28350; 28355; 28368; 28373; 28374; 28387 28388; 28394.

3rd District: 27530; 27531; 27532; 27533; 27534; 27569* (NC 2); 27808 27810 27824; 27825; 27826; 27830; 27837* (NC 1); 27846; 27858* (NC 1); 27860* (NC 1); 27863* (NC 1); 27865; 27875; 27879; 27883* (NC 2); 27889* (NC 1); 27892* (NC 1); 27906; 27907; 27909* (NC 1); 27915; 27916; 27917; 27920; 27921 27923; 27925; 27927; 27928* (NC 1); 27929; 27936; 27939; 27941; 27943; 27947; 27948; 27949; 27950; 27953 27954; 27956; 27958; 27959; 27962; 27964; 27965 27966; 27968; 27971; 27972; 27973; 27974; 27976; 27978; 27981; 27982; 28318; 28325 28328; 28333; 28341; 28349* (NC 1); 28365 28366; 28382; 28385; 28393; 28398* (NC 1); 28425* (NC 1); 28435* (NC 1); 28441; 28443* (NC 7); 28444; 28445* (NC 7); 28446; 28447; 28454* (NC 1, NC 7); 28457 28458* (NC 1); 28464* (NC 1) 28466* (NC 1); 28471* (NC 1); 28478* (NC 1); 28501* (NC 1); 28502; 28503 28508; 28509; 28510; 28511; 28512; 28513* (NC 1); 28515 28516; 28518* (NC 1) 28519; 28520; 28521; 28522; 28524; 28525; 28527; 28528; 28529; 28530* (NC 1) 28531; 28532* (NC 1); 28537; 28539* (NC 7); 28540* (NC 7); 28543* (NC 7) 28544* (NC 7); 28546* (NC 7); 28551* (NC 1); 28552; 28553; 28555; 28556 28557; 28560* (NC 1); 28561; 28562* (NC 1); 28570; 28571; 28572; 28573* (NC 1); 28574* (NC 7); 28575; 28577; 28578; 28579; 28581; 28582; 28583; 28584* (NC 7); 28585* (NC 1); 28586; 28587; 28589; 28590* (NC 1); 28594.

4th District: 27207; 27208; 27213; 27228; 27231* (NC 12); 27243; 27252; 27256 27278* (NC 12); 27302* (NC 5, NC 6, NC 12); 27312; 27344; 27349* (NC 6) 27502; 27510; 27511; 27512; 27513; 27514* (NC 2); 27515; 27516; 27518; 27519 27520* (NC 2); 27523; 27526* (NC 2); 27529* (NC 2); 27540; 27541* (NC 5, NC 12); 27545; 27559 27560* (NC 2); 27562; 27571; 27572* (NC 2, NC 5, NC 12) 27587* (NC 2); 27588 27591* (NC 2); 27592* (NC 2); 27596* (NC 2); 27597* (NC 2); 27599; 27600 27601; 27602; 27603; 27604; 27605; 27606; 27607; 27608 27609; 27610; 27611; 27612; 27613* (NC 2); 27614; 27615; 27619; 27620; 27621 27622; 27623; 27624; 27625; 27626; 27627; 27628; 27629; 27634; 27635; 27636 27640; 27650; 27656; 27658; 27661; 27668; 27676; 27690; 27695; 27697; 27698 27699; 27705* (NC 2, NC 12); 27707* (NC 2, NC 12).

5th District: 27007; 27009; 27016; 27017; 27019; 27021; 27022; 27024; 27025 27027; 27030; 27031; 27040* (NC 12); 27041; 27042; 27043; 27045* (NC 12) 27046; 27047; 27048; 27049; 27050* (NC 10); 27051; 27052; 27053; 27094; 27098 27099; 27100; 27101* (NC 12); 27103* (NC 10); 27104* (NC 10); 27105* (NC 10, NC 12); 27106* (NC 10); 27107* (NC 6, NC 12); 27109; 27115; 27116; 27127* (NC 6, NC 10, NC 12); 27130; 27212; 27214* (NC 6); 27217* (NC 6, NC 12); 27244* (NC 6, NC 12); 27249* (NC 6, NC 12); 27284* (NC 6, NC 12); 27285; 27288; 27289; 27291; 27301* (NC 6, NC 12); 27302* (NC 4, NC 6, NC 12); 27305; 27311 27314; 27315; 27320* (NC 6); 27321; 27322; 27323; 27326; 27343; 27357* (NC 6) 27358* (NC 6); 27375; 27379 27507* (NC 1); 27541* (NC 4, NC 12); 27565* (NC 1, NC 2); 27572* (NC 2, NC 4, NC 12); 27573; 27582; 27583; 28604* (NC 10) 28605; 28606* (NC 10); 28607; 28608 28615; 28617; 28618; 28619; 28621* (NC 10); 28623; 28626; 28627; 28628; 28629 28631; 28632; 28639; 28640; 28643 28644; 28645* (NC 10); 28654* (NC 10); 28655* (NC 10); 28659* (NC 10); 28663 28668; 28672; 28675; 28676; 28679; 28680; 28684 28686; 28690* (NC 10); 28691; 28692; 28693; 28694; 28695; 28697* (NC 10); 28698.

6th District: 27006* (NC 10); 27014; 27028* (NC 10); 27107* (NC 5, NC 12) 27117;

7th District: 28301* (NC 1); 28302; 28303* (NC 8); 28304* (NC 1, NC 8); 28305* (NC 1); 28306* (NC 1, NC 8); 28307; 28308; 28309; 28310; 28311* (NC 1) 28314* (NC 8); 28319; 28320* (NC 1); 28324; 28331; 28332; 28337* (NC 1); 28340 28342; 28344; 28348* (NC 1); 28356; 28358; 28359; 28362; 28364* (NC 8); 28369 28372; 28375; 28377* (NC 8); 28383* (NC 8); 28384* (NC 8); 28390* (NC 1, NC 7); 28391; 28392; 28395; 28397; 28401* (NC 1); 28403* (NC 1); 28404; 28405* (NC 1); 28406; 28407; 28409* (NC 1); 28410; 28412; 28420; 28422; 28424; 28428 28429* (NC 1); 28430; 28431* (NC 1); 28432; 28438; 28439; 28442; 28443* (NC 3); 28445* (NC 3); 28448* (NC 1); 28449; 28450* (NC 1); 28451; 28452; 28454* (NC 1, NC 3); 28455; 28459; 28460; 28461; 28462; 28463; 28465; 28467; 28468 28469; 28470; 28472* (NC 1); 28479; 28480; 28539* (NC 3); 28540* (NC 3); 28541; 28542; 28543* (NC 3); 28544* (NC 3); 28545; 28546* (NC 3); 28574* (NC 3); 28584* (NC 3).

8th District: 27008; 27013* (NC 10, NC 12); 27054* (NC 12); 27209; 27229 27242* (NC 2); 27247; 27259; 27281* (NC 2); 27306; 27325; 27330* (NC 2) 27341* (NC 6); 27356; 27371; 28001; 28002; 28007; 28009; 28023* (NC 6); 28025 28026; 28027; 28036* (NC 9, NC 12); 28041; 28072; 28075; 28079; 28081; 28082 28083; 28088; 28091; 28097; 28102; 28103; 28105* (NC 9); 28107* (NC 9); 28108 28109; 28110; 28111; 28112; 28115* (NC 9, NC 10, NC 12); 28119; 28124; 28125 28127; 28128; 28129; 28133; 28135; 28137* (NC 6); 28138* (NC 6); 28144* (NC 6, NC 12); 28145; 28146* (NC 6, NC 12); 28163; 28166* (NC 10); 28170 28173; 28174; 28213* (NC 9, NC 12); 28215* (NC 9, NC 12); 28303* (NC 7) 28304* (NC 1, NC 7); 28306* (NC 1, NC 7); 28314* (NC 7); 28326* (NC 2); 28327* (NC 2); 28330; 28338; 28343; 28345; 28347; 28351; 28352; 28353; 28357 28361 28363; 28364* (NC 7); 28367; 28371; 28376; 28377* (NC 7); 28378; 28379 28383* (NC 7); 28384* (NC 7); 28386; 28390* (NC 1, NC 7); 28396; 28677* (NC 10, NC 12).

9th District: 28012* (NC 12); 28016; 28017; 28020* (NC 11); 28021* (NC 10) 28031; 28032; 28034; 28036* (NC 8, NC 12); 28038; 28042; 28051; 28052* (NC 12); 28053 28054* (NC 12); 28056; 28073* (NC 11); 28078* (NC 12); 28086* (NC 11); 28090* (NC 11); 28098; 28101; 28105* (NC 8); 28106; 28107* (NC 8); 28114* (NC 11); 28115* (NC 8, NC 10, NC 12); 28120; 28126; 28130; 28134* (NC 11); 28150* (NC 11); 28152* (NC 11); 28164* (NC 10); 28169; 28202* (NC 12); 28203* (NC 12); 28204* (NC 12); 28205* (NC 12); 28207* (NC 12); 28208* (NC 12) 28209* (NC 12); 28210* (NC 12); 28211* (NC 12); 28212; 28213* (NC 8, NC 12) 28214* (NC 12); 28215* (NC 8, NC 12); 28216* (NC 12); 28217* (NC 12); 28218 28219* (NC 12); 28220; 28221; 28222; 28223; 28224; 28225; 28226; 28227; 28229 28241* (NC 12); 28247; 28253; 28256; 28257; 28258; 28262* (NC 12); 28266 28269* (NC 12); 28270; 28273* (NC 12); 28274; 28277; 28278; 28287; 28290 28294; 28297; 28299* (NC 12).

10th District: 27006* (NC 6); 27010; 27011; 27013* (NC 8, NC 12) 27018; 27020; 27023; 27028* (NC 6); 27040* (NC 5); 27045* (NC 5); 27050* (NC 5); 27055; 27103* (NC 5); 27104* (NC 5); 27105* (NC 5, NC 12); 27106* (NC 5) 27113; 27114; 27127* (NC 5, NC 6, NC 12); 28006; 28018* (NC 11); 28021* (NC 9); 28033; 28037; 28043* (NC 11); 28077; 28080; 28092; 28093; 28115* (NC 8, NC 9, NC 12); 28123 28139* (NC 11); 28164* (NC 9); 28166* (NC 8); 28167* (NC 11); 28168; 28601 28602; 28603; 28604* (NC 5); 28606* (NC 5); 28609; 28610; 28611; 28612; 28613 28614; 28616; 28621* (NC 5); 28624; 28630; 28633; 28634* (NC 12); 28635 28636; 28637; 28638; 28641; 28642; 28645* (NC 5); 28646; 28647; 28648; 28649; 28650 28651; 28652; 28653; 28654* (NC 5) 28655* (NC 5); 28656; 28657; 28658; 28659* (NC 5); 28660; 28661; 28662; 28664 28665; 28666; 28667; 28669; 28670; 28671; 28673 28674; 28677* (NC 8, NC 12) 28678; 28681; 28682; 28683; 28685; 28687; 28688 28689; 28690* (NC 5); 28696 28697* (NC 5); 28699; 28704* (NC 11); 28705; 28711* (NC 11); 28720; 28730 28732* (NC 11); 28737; 28742* (NC 11); 28746; 28749; 28752* (NC 11); 28756* (NC 11); 28760; 28762* (NC 11); 28765; 28776; 28777; 28792* (NC 11); 28803* (NC 11); 28804* (NC 11).

11th District: 28018* (NC 10); 28019; 28020* (NC 9); 28024; 28040; 28043* (NC 10) 28073* (NC 9); 28074; 28076; 28086* (NC 9); 28089; 28090* (NC 9); 28114* (NC 9); 28136; 28139* (NC 10); 28150* (NC 9); 28151; 28152* (NC 9); 28160 28167* (NC 10); 28701; 28702; 28703; 28704* (NC 10); 28707; 28708; 28709 28710; 28711* (NC 10); 28712; 28713; 28714; 28715; 28716; 28717; 28718; 28719 28721; 28722; 28723; 28724 28725; 28726; 28727; 28728; 28729; 28731; 28732* (NC 10); 28733; 28734; 28735 28736; 28738; 28739; 28740; 28741; 28742* (NC 10); 28743; 28745; 28747; 28748 28750; 28751; 28752* (NC 10); 28753; 28754; 28755; 28756* (NC 10); 28757; 28758 28761; 28762* (NC 10); 28763; 28766; 28768; 28770; 28771; 28772; 28773; 28774 28775; 28778; 28779; 28780; 28781; 28782; 28783; 28784; 28786; 28787; 28788; 28789 28790; 28792* (NC 10); 28793 28800; 28801; 28802; 28803* (NC 10); 28804* (NC 10) 28805; 28806; 28810 28813; 28814; 28815; 28816; 28901; 28902; 28903; 28904; 28905 28906; 28909 37317* (TN 3); 37821* (TN 1).

12th District: 27013* (NC 8, NC 10); 27054* (NC 8); 27101* (NC 5); 27102 27105* (NC 5, NC 10); 27107* (NC 5, NC 6); 27108; 27110; 27111; 27120; 27127* (NC 5, NC 6, NC 10); 27150; 27151; 27152; 27155; 27156; 27157; 27198; 27199 27202; 27215* (NC 6); 27217* (NC 5, NC 6); 27231* (NC 4); 27244* (NC 5, NC 6) 27249* (NC 5, NC 6); 27258* (NC 6); 27260* (NC 6); 27261; 27262* (NC 6); 27263* (NC 6); 27264; 27265* (NC 6); 27278* (NC 4); 27284* (NC 5, NC 6) 27292* (NC 6); 27299* (NC 6); 27301* (NC 5, NC 6); 27302* (NC 4, NC 5, NC 6) 27360* (NC 6); 27361; 27377* (NC 6); 27401* (NC 6); 27402; 27403* (NC 6) 27405* (NC 6); 27406* (NC 6); 27407* (NC 6); 27408* (NC 6); 27410* (NC 6) 27411; 27415; 27416; 27417; 27420; 27427;

27495* (NC 6); 27498; 27499; 27503 27541* (NC 4, NC 5); 27572* (NC 2, NC 4, NC 5); 27700; 27701* (NC 2); 27702 27703* (NC 2); 27704* (NC 2); 27705* (NC 2, NC 4); 27706* (NC 2); 27707* (NC 2, NC 4); 27708; 27712* (NC 2); 27713* (NC 2); 27722; 28010; 28012* (NC 9) 28036* (NC 8, NC 9); 28039; 28052* (NC 9); 28054* (NC 9); 28055; 28078* (NC 8, NC 9, NC 10); 28115* (NC 8, NC 9, NC 10); 28134* (NC 9); 28144* (NC 6, NC 8); 28146* (NC 6, NC 8); 28159* (NC 6); 28166* (NC 8, NC 10); 28200; 28201; 28202* (NC 9) 28203* (NC 9); 28204* (NC 9); 28205* (NC 9); 28206; 28207* (NC 9); 28208* (NC 9); 28209* (NC 9); 28210* (NC 9); 28211* (NC 9); 28213* (NC 8, NC 9); 28214* (NC 9); 28215* (NC 8, NC 9); 28216* (NC 9); 28217* (NC 9); 28219* (NC 9); 28228; 28230; 28231; 28232; 28233; 28234; 28235; 28236; 28237; 28241* (NC 9) 28242; 28243; 28244; 28245; 28246; 28250; 28254; 28255; 28259; 28260; 28261 28262* (NC 9); 28264; 28265; 28267; 28269* (NC 9); 28272; 28273* (NC 9) 28275; 28276; 28280; 28281; 28282; 28283; 28284; 28285; 28286; 28288; 28289 28296; 28299* (NC 9); 28634* (NC 10); 28677* (NC 8, NC 10).

North Dakota

At Large: 56744* (MN 7); 57255* (SD 1); 57260* (SD 1); 57270* (SD 1); 57632* (SD 1); 57638* (SD 1); 57641* (SD 1); 57642* (SD 1); 57645* (SD 1); 57648* (SD 1); 57660* (SD 1); 58001; 58002; 58003; 58004; 58005; 58006; 58007; 58008 58009; 58011; 58012; 58013; 58014; 58015; 58016; 58017; 58018; 58021; 58027 58029; 58030* (MN 7, SD 1); 58031; 58032; 58033; 58035; 58036; 58038; 58039 58040 58041* (SD 1); 58042; 58043* (SD 1); 58045; 58046; 58047; 58048; 58049 58051; 58052; 58053* (SD 1); 58054; 58056; 58057; 58058; 58059; 58060; 58061 58062; 58063; 58064; 58065; 58067; 58068; 58069; 58071; 58072; 58074; 58075 58076; 58077; 58078; 58079; 58081; 58102; 58103; 58104; 58105; 58106; 58107 58108; 58109; 58121; 58122; 58123; 58124; 58126; 58201; 58202; 58203; 58204 58205; 58206; 58207; 58210; 58212; 58213; 58214; 58216; 58218; 58219 58220 58222; 58223; 58224; 58225* (MN 7); 58227; 58228; 58229; 58230; 58231; 58233 58235; 58236; 58237; 58238; 58239; 58240; 58241; 58243; 58244; 58245; 58246 58249; 58250; 58251; 58253; 58254; 58255; 58256; 58257; 58258; 58259; 58260 58261; 58262; 58265; 58266; 58267; 58269; 58270; 58271; 58272; 58273; 58274 58275; 58276; 58277; 58278; 58279; 58281; 58282; 58301; 58310; 58311; 58313 58315; 58316; 58317; 58318; 58319; 58320; 58321; 58322; 58323; 58324; 58325 58328; 58329; 58330; 58331; 58332; 58335; 58337; 58338; 58339; 58341 58342; 58343; 58344; 58345; 58346; 58348; 58351; 58352; 58353; 58355; 58356 58357; 58359; 58360; 58361; 58362; 58363; 58365; 58366; 58367; 58368 58369 58370; 58372; 58373; 58374; 58377; 58379; 58380; 58381; 58382; 58384; 58385 58386; 58401; 58402; 58411; 58412; 58413* (SD 1); 58415; 58416; 58418; 58420 58421; 58422; 58423; 58424; 58425; 58426; 58427; 58428; 58429; 58430; 58431 58432; 58433; 58436* (SD 1); 58438; 58439* (SD 1); 58440; 58441; 58442; 58443 58444; 58445; 58447; 58448; 58450; 58451; 58452; 58454; 58455; 58456; 58458 58460; 58461; 58463; 58464; 58465; 58466; 58467; 58469; 58471; 58472; 58474 58475; 58476; 58477; 58478; 58479; 58480; 58481; 58482; 58483; 58484; 58486 58487; 58488; 58489; 58490; 58492; 58494; 58495; 58496; 58497; 58501; 58502 58504; 58505; 58506; 58507; 58520; 58521; 58523; 58524; 58528; 58529; 58530 58531; 58532; 58533; 58535; 58537; 58538; 58540; 58541; 58542; 58544; 58545 58547; 58549; 58551; 58552; 58553; 58554; 58558; 58559; 58560; 58561; 58562 58563; 58564; 58565; 58566; 58568; 58569; 58570; 58571; 58572; 58573; 58575 58576; 58577; 58579; 58580; 58581; 58601; 58602; 58620; 58621* (MT 1); 58622 58623* (SD 1); 58625; 58626; 58627; 58630; 58631; 58632; 58634; 58636; 58638 58639* (SD 1); 58640; 58641; 58642; 58643; 58644; 58645; 58646; 58647; 58649* (SD 1); 58650; 58651; 58652; 58653* (SD 1); 58654; 58655; 58656; 58657; 58701 58702; 58704; 58705; 58710; 58711; 58712; 58713; 58714; 58716; 58718; 58720 58721; 58722; 58723; 58725; 58727; 58728; 58730; 58731; 58733; 58734; 58735 58736; 58737; 58738; 58739; 58740; 58741; 58744; 58746; 58747; 58748; 58750 58752; 58755; 58756; 58757; 58758; 58759; 58760; 58761; 58762; 58763; 58765 58768; 58769; 58770; 58771; 58772; 58773; 58775; 58776; 58778; 58779; 58781 58782; 58783; 58784; 58785; 58787; 58788; 58789; 58790; 58792; 58793; 58794 58801; 58802; 58830; 58831; 58833; 58835; 58838* (MT 1); 58843; 58844 58845* (MT 1); 58847; 58849; 58852; 58853; 58854; 58856; 59221* (MT 1); 59270* (MT 1); 59275* (MT 1).

Ohio

1st District: 45001; 45002* (OH 2); 45041; 45051; 45052* (OH 2); 45201; 45202* (OH 2); 45203; 45204; 45205; 45206* (OH 2); 45207* (OH 2); 45208* (OH 2) 45210; 45211; 45212* (OH 2); 45213* (OH 2); 45214; 45215* (OH 2); 45216* (OH 2); 45217; 45218; 45219; 45220; 45221; 45222; 45223; 45224; 45225; 45227* (OH 2); 45229* (OH 2); 45231* (OH 2); 45232; 45233; 45234; 45236* (OH 2); 45237* (OH 2); 45238; 45239; 45240* (OH 2); 45246* (OH 2); 45247* (OH 2); 45248 45250; 45251* (OH 2); 45252* (OH 2); 45258; 45263; 45264; 45267; 45268; 45269 45270; 45271; 45273; 45274; 45296; 45298; 45299; 45999.

2nd District: 45002* (OH 1); 45005* (OH 6); 45030; 45032; 45033; 45036* (OH 6); 45040* (OH 6); 45052* (OH 1); 45054* (OH 6); 45061; 45066; 45068* (OH 1); 45101; 45102; 45103; 45105; 45106; 45111; 45112; 45115; 45118; 45119; 45120 45121; 45122; 45130; 45131; 45140* (OH 6); 45142* (OH 6); 45144; 45145; 45147 45150; 45153; 45154; 45156; 45157; 45158; 45160; 45167; 45168; 45171; 45174 45176; 45200; 45202* (OH 1); 45206* (OH 1); 45207* (OH 1); 45208* (OH 1); 45209; 45212* (OH 1); 45213* (OH 1); 45215* (OH 1); 45216* (OH 1); 45226 45227* (OH 1); 45228; 45229* (OH 1); 45230; 45231* (OH 1); 45235; 45236* (OH 1); 45237* (OH 1); 45240* (OH 1); 45241* (OH 8); 45242; 45243; 45244; 45246* (OH 1); 45247* (OH 1); 45249; 45251* (OH 1); 45252* (OH 1); 45254; 45255; 45262; 45275* (KY 4); 45327* (OH 3, OH 8); 45342* (OH 3); 45458* (OH 3, OH 7); 45616; 45618; 45650; 45657* (OH 6); 45660* (OH 6); 45671* (OH 6) 45679* (OH 6); 45684* (OH 6); 45693; 45697* (OH 6); 45944.

3rd District: 45309; 45315; 45322* (OH 8); 45325; 45327* (OH 2, OH 8); 45342* (OH 2); 45343; 45344* (OH 7, OH 8); 45345; 45354; 45370* (OH 7); 45371* (OH 8); 45377; 45381* (OH 8); 45401; 45402; 45403; 45404; 45405; 45406; 45407 45408; 45409; 45410; 45412; 45413; 45414; 45415; 45416; 45417; 45418; 45419 45420; 45422; 45423; 45424* (OH 7); 45426; 45427; 45428; 45429; 45431* (OH 7) 45432* (OH 7); 45434; 45439; 45440* (OH 7); 45444; 45448; 45449; 45454; 45458* (OH 2, OH 7); 45459*

(OH 7); 45463; 45469; 45470; 45475; 45479; 45481; 45482 45490.

4th District: 43003* (OH 12); 43005; 43011* (OH 12); 43014* (OH 16); 43019* (OH 16); 43022* (OH 16); 43028* (OH 16); 43037; 43048; 43050* (OH 16); 43080* (OH 12, OH 18); 43301; 43302* (OH 7); 43305; 43306; 43307; 43310; 43311* (OH 7); 43314; 43315; 43316* (OH 5); 43317; 43318* (OH 7); 43319* (OH 7); 43320 43321; 43322; 43323; 43324; 43325; 43326; 43330; 43331; 43332; 43333; 43334* (OH 12); 43335; 43337; 43338; 43340* (OH 12); 43341; 43342* (OH 12); 43343* (OH 7, OH 8); 43344* (OH 7, OH 12); 43345; 43346; 43347; 43348; 43349; 43350 43351; 43356* (OH 12); 43357* (OH 7); 43358* (OH 7); 43359; 43360* (OH 7) 43843* (OH 18); 43844* (OH 16, OH 18); 44802* (OH 5); 44804; 44805* (OH 16) 44813; 44817* (OH 5); 44818* (OH 5); 44820; 44822* (OH 16); 44825; 44827 44830* (OH 5); 44833; 44837* (OH 5); 44843; 44844* (OH 5); 44849; 44854; 44856; 44860; 44862; 44864* (OH 16); 44865* (OH 5); 44875; 44878; 44881 44882* (OH 5); 44887; 44900; 44901; 44902; 44903* (OH 16); 44904; 44905; 44906; 44907; 44999; 45801; 45802; 45804; 45805; 45806; 45807; 45808; 45809 45810; 45812; 45814; 45816; 45817; 45819; 45820; 45822* (OH 5, OH 8); 45830* (OH 5); 45833* (OH 5); 45835; 45836; 45839; 45840; 45841; 45843; 45844* (OH 5); 45850; 45854; 45858; 45859; 45867; 45868; 45870; 45871* (OH 8); 45881 45884; 45885* (OH 8); 45887* (OH 5); 45888; 45889; 45890; 45895; 45896; 45897.

5th District: 43316* (OH 4); 43402* (OH 9); 43403; 43406* (OH 9); 43407 43410; 43413; 43414; 43416* (OH 9); 43420; 43431* (OH 9); 43433; 43435; 43436 43437; 43438; 43439; 43440; 43442; 43446; 43449* (OH 9); 43450* (OH 9); 43451* (OH 9); 43452; 43456; 43457; 43460* (OH 9); 43462; 43464; 43466* (OH 9); 43467; 43469* (OH 9); 43501; 43505; 43506; 43510; 43511; 43512; 43516; 43517 43518; 43519; 43520; 43522* (OH 9); 43523; 43524; 43525; 43526; 43527; 43529 43530; 43531; 43532* (OH 9); 43534; 43535; 43536; 43541; 43543; 43545; 43548 43549; 43551* (OH 9); 43552; 43554; 43555; 43556; 43557; 43565; 43569 43570; 44001* (OH 13); 44035* (OH 13); 44044* (OH 13); 44049; 44050; 44074* (OH 13); 44089* (OH 13); 44090* (OH 13); 44253* (OH 13); 44256* (OH 13) 44801; 44802* (OH 4); 44803; 44807; 44809; 44811; 44814; 44815; 44817* (OH 4); 44818* (OH 4); 44823; 44824; 44826; 44828; 44829; 44830* (OH 4); 44836; 44837* (OH 4); 44839; 44841; 44844* (OH 4); 44845; 44846; 44847; 44850 44851; 44853; 44855; 44857; 44861; 44865* (OH 4); 44867; 44870; 44871; 44880* (OH 13, OH 16); 44882* (OH 4); 44883; 44889; 44890; 45813; 45815; 45821; 45822* (OH 4, OH 8); 45827; 45830* (OH 4); 45831; 45832; 45833* (OH 4); 45837; 45838; 45844* (OH 4); 45848; 45849; 45851; 45853; 45855; 45856; 45861 45862* (OH 8); 45863; 45864; 45872; 45873; 45874; 45875; 45876; 45877; 45879 45880; 45882; 45886; 45887* (OH 4); 45891; 45893; 45894; 45898; 45899.

6th District: 43102* (OH 7); 43107* (OH 7); 43111; 43127; 43135* (OH 7) 43138; 43144; 43149; 43152; 43155* (OH 7); 43158; 43766* (OH 18); 45005* (OH 2); 45034; 45036* (OH 2); 45039; 45040* (OH 2); 45054* (OH 2); 45065; 45068* (OH 2); 45107; 45110; 45113; 45114; 45123* (OH 7); 45132; 45133; 45135* (OH 7); 45138; 45140* (OH 2); 45142* (OH 2); 45146; 45148; 45152; 45155; 45159 45162; 45164; 45165; 45166; 45169* (OH 7); 45172; 45177; 45601* (OH 7); 45612 45613; 45614; 45617; 45619; 45620; 45621; 45622; 45623; 45624; 45628* (OH 7) 45629; 45630; 45631; 45634; 45636; 45638; 45640; 45642; 45643; 45644* (OH 7) 45645; 45646; 45647; 45648; 45651; 45652; 45653; 45654; 45656; 45657* (OH 2) 45658; 45659; 45660* (OH 2); 45661; 45662; 45663; 45669; 45670; 45671* (OH 2) 45672; 45673; 45674; 45675; 45677; 45678; 45679* (OH 2); 45680; 45681* (OH 2) 45682; 45683; 45684* (OH 2); 45685; 45686; 45687; 45688; 45690; 45692; 45694 45695; 45696; 45697* (OH 2); 45698; 45699; 45701; 45710; 45711; 45712; 45713 45714; 45715* (OH 18); 45716; 45717; 45719; 45720; 45721; 45723; 45724; 45726 45729; 45732; 45735; 45739; 45740; 45741; 45742; 45743; 45744; 45745* (OH 18) 45746; 45750; 45760; 45761; 45764; 45766; 45767* (OH 18); 45768; 45769; 45770 45771; 45772; 45773; 45774* (OH 18); 45775; 45776; 45777; 45778; 45779; 45780 45781; 45782; 45783; 45784; 45786* (OH 18); 45787; 45788; 45789.

7th District: 43007; 43009; 43010; 43029* (OH 15); 43036; 43040* (OH 12); 43041; 43044* (OH 15); 43045; 43046; 43047; 43060* (OH 12); 43061* (OH 12, OH 18); 43062* (OH 12, OH 18); 43064* (OH 12, OH 15); 43067; 43070; 43072; 43076* (OH 18); 43077 43078; 43083; 43084; 43101; 43102* (OH 6); 43103* (OH 15); 43105; 43106 43107* (OH 6); 43110* (OH 15); 43112; 43113; 43115; 43125* (OH 15); 43128 43130; 43132; 43135* (OH 6); 43136; 43137* (OH 15); 43142; 43143* (OH 15) 43145; 43146* (OH 15); 43147* (OH 12, OH 15); 43148; 43150* (OH 18); 43153* (OH 15); 43154; 43155* (OH 6); 43156; 43157; 43160; 43163; 43164; 43302* (OH 4); 43311* (OH 4); 43318* (OH 4); 43319* (OH 4); 43336; 43340* (OH 4); 43343* (OH 4, OH 8); 43344* (OH 4, OH 12); 43357* (OH 4); 43358* (OH 4); 43360* (OH 4); 45123* (OH 6); 45135* (OH 6); 45169* (OH 6); 45301; 45305; 45307; 45314 45316; 45317* (OH 8); 45319; 45323; 45324; 45335; 45341; 45344* (OH 3, OH 8); 45349; 45368; 45369; 45370* (OH 3); 45372; 45384; 45385; 45387; 45389; 45424* (OH 3); 45430; 45431* (OH 3); 45432* (OH 3); 45433; 45435; 45440* (OH 3) 45458* (OH 2, OH 3); 45459* (OH 3); 45501; 45502; 45503; 45504; 45505; 45506 45601* (OH 6); 45628* (OH 6); 45633; 45644* (OH 6); 45681* (OH 6).

8th District: 43343* (OH 4, OH 7); 45003* (IN 9); 45004; 45011; 45012; 45013 45014; 45015; 45018; 45020; 45023; 45025; 45026; 45042; 45043; 45044; 45050 45053* (IN 9); 45055; 45056; 45062; 45063; 45064; 45067; 45069; 45070; 45071 45073; 45099; 45241* (OH 2); 45302; 45303; 45304; 45306; 45308; 45310; 45311 45312; 45317* (OH 7); 45318; 45320; 45321; 45322* (OH 3); 45326; 45327* (OH 2, OH 3); 45329 45330; 45331; 45332; 45333; 45334; 45336; 45337; 45338; 45339; 45340; 45344* (OH 3, OH 7); 45346; 45347; 45348; 45350; 45351; 45352; 45353; 45356; 45358; 45359; 45360 45361; 45362; 45363; 45365; 45366; 45367 45371* (OH 3); 45373; 45374; 45378; 45380 45381* (OH 3); 45382; 45383; 45388; 45390; 45822* (OH 4, OH 5); 45826; 45828 45845; 45846* (IN 2); 45860; 45862* (OH 5); 45865; 45866; 45869; 45871* (OH 4); 45883; 45885* (OH 4); 47353* (IN 9).

9th District: 43402* (OH 5); 43406* (OH 5); 43408; 43412; 43416* (OH 5) 43430; 43431* (OH 5); 43432; 43434; 43441; 43443; 43445; 43447; 43449* (OH 5) 43450* (OH 5); 43451* (OH 5); 43458; 43460* (OH 5); 43463; 43465; 43466* (OH 5); 43468; 43469* (OH 5); 43502; 43504; 43515; 43521; 43522* (OH 5); 43528 43532* (OH 5);

43533; 43537; 43540; 43542; 43547; 43551* (OH 5); 43553; 43558 43560; 43566; 43567; 43571; 43600; 43601; 43602; 43603; 43604; 43605; 43606 43607; 43608; 43609; 43610; 43611; 43612; 43613; 43614; 43615; 43616; 43617 43618; 43619; 43620; 43623; 43624; 43635; 43652; 43653; 43654; 43655; 43656 43657; 43659; 43660; 43661; 43666; 43667; 43681; 43682; 43697; 43699.

10th District: 44017* (OH 19); 44070; 44100; 44101; 44102; 44105* (OH 11, OH 19); 44107; 44109* (OH 11); 44111* (OH 11); 44113* (OH 11); 44114* (OH 11) 44115* (OH 11); 44116; 44125* (OH 11, OH 19); 44126; 44127* (OH 11); 44129* (OH 19); 44130* (OH 19); 44131* (OH 19); 44133* (OH 13, OH 19); 44134; 44135* (OH 11); 44136* (OH 19); 44138* (OH 19); 44140; 44142* (OH 19); 44144; 44145 44146* (OH 11, OH 19); 44177; 44178; 44179; 44181; 44184; 44186; 44188; 44189 44191; 44193; 44194; 44199.

11th District: 44022* (OH 13, OH 19); 44103; 44104; 44105* (OH 10, OH 19) 44106; 44108; 44109* (OH 10); 44110; 44111* (OH 10); 44112; 44113* (OH 10) 44114* (OH 10); 44115* (OH 10); 44117* (OH 19); 44118; 44119; 44120; 44121* (OH 19); 44122* (OH 19); 44123; 44124* (OH 19); 44125* (OH 10, OH 19); 44127* (OH 10); 44128; 44132; 44135* (OH 10); 44137* (OH 19); 44139* (OH 19); 44143* (OH 19); 44146* (OH 10, OH 19); 44185; 44190; 44192; 44195; 44197; 44198.

12th District: 43001; 43002* (OH 15); 43003* (OH 4); 43004; 43011* (OH 4) 43013; 43015; 43016; 43017* (OH 15); 43018; 43021; 43023* (OH 18); 43025* (OH 18); 43026* (OH 15); 43027; 43031; 43032; 43033; 43035; 43040* (OH 7); 43054 43055* (OH 18); 43056* (OH 18); 43061* (OH 7); 43062* (OH 7, OH 18); 43064* (OH 7, OH 15); 43065; 43066; 43068* (OH 15); 43069; 43071* (OH 18); 43073; 43074; 43080* (OH 4, OH 18); 43081; 43082; 43085* (OH 15); 43086 43147* (OH 7, OH 15); 43200; 43201* (OH 15); 43203; 43204* (OH 15); 43205 43206* (OH 15); 43207* (OH 15); 43209; 43211* (OH 15); 43213* (OH 15); 43215* (OH 15); 43216* (OH 15); 43219; 43222* (OH 15); 43223* (OH 15); 43224* (OH 15); 43227* (OH 15); 43229* (OH 15); 43230; 43231* (OH 15); 43232* (OH 15) 43235* (OH 15); 43236; 43240; 43334* (OH 4); 43342* (OH 4); 43344* (OH 4, OH 7); 43356* (OH 4).

13th District: 44001* (OH 5); 44011; 44012; 44021; 44022* (OH 11, OH 19) 44024* (OH 19); 44026* (OH 19); 44028; 44033; 44035* (OH 5); 44036; 44039 44044* (OH 5); 44046; 44052; 44053; 44054; 44055; 44056; 44057* (OH 19) 44060* (OH 19); 44062* (OH 19); 44064; 44065; 44067* (OH 14); 44072; 44073 44074* (OH 5); 44076* (OH 17, OH 19); 44080; 44086* (OH 19); 44087; 44089* (OH 5); 44090* (OH 5); 44099* (OH 19); 44133* (OH 10, OH 19); 44141* (OH 14, OH 19); 44147* (OH 19); 44201* (OH 14, OH 16); 44202; 44212; 44214* (OH 16); 44215; 44217* (OH 16); 44230* (OH 14, OH 16); 44231; 44233; 44234; 44235 44236* (OH 14); 44241* (OH 14); 44251; 44253* (OH 5); 44254; 44255* (OH 14) 44256* (OH 14); 44258; 44260; 44264* (OH 14, OH 16); 44265 44266* (OH 14); 44270* (OH 16); 44272* (OH 14); 44273; 44274; 44275; 44280 44281* (OH 14); 44285; 44287* (OH 16); 44288; 44333* (OH 14); 44402* (OH 17) 44411; 44412* (OH 17); 44430* (OH 17); 44439; 44444; 44449* (OH 17); 44450* (OH 17); 44470* (OH 17); 44481* (OH 17); 44483* (OH 17); 44485* (OH 17); 44491 44632* (OH 14, OH 16); 44880* (OH 5, OH 14).

14th District: 44067* (OH 13); 44141* (OH 13, OH 19); 44201* (OH 13, OH 16) 44203; 44210; 44211; 44216* (OH 16); 44221; 44222; 44223; 44224; 44230* (OH 13, OH 16); 44232; 44236* (OH 13); 44237; 44238; 44240; 44241* (OH 13); 44242 44243; 44250; 44255* (OH 13); 44260* (OH 13, OH 16); 44264* (OH 13, OH 16); 44266* (OH 13); 44272* (OH 13); 44278; 44281* (OH 13); 44286; 44300; 44301 44302; 44303; 44304; 44305; 44306; 44307; 44308; 44309; 44310; 44311; 44312 44313; 44314; 44315; 44316; 44317; 44318; 44319; 44320; 44321; 44322; 44325 44326; 44328; 44329; 44331; 44333* (OH 13); 44334; 44342; 44393; 44396; 44397 44398; 44399; 44614* (OH 16); 44632* (OH 13, OH 16); 44685* (OH 16); 44720* (OH 16).

15th District: 43002* (OH 12); 43017* (OH 12); 43026* (OH 12); 43029* (OH 7) 43044* (OH 7); 43064* (OH 7, OH 12); 43065* (OH 12); 43068* (OH 12); 43085* (OH 12); 43093; 43103* (OH 7); 43109* (OH 7); 43110* (OH 7); 43116; 43117; 43119 43123; 43125* (OH 7); 43126; 43137* (OH 7); 43140; 43143* (OH 7); 43146* (OH 7); 43147* (OH 7, OH 12); 43151; 43153* (OH 7); 43162; 43201* (OH 12); 43202 43204* (OH 12); 43206* (OH 12); 43207* (OH 12); 43210; 43211* (OH 12); 43212 43213* (OH 12); 43214; 43215* (OH 12); 43216* (OH 12); 43217; 43218; 43220 43221; 43222* (OH 12); 43223* (OH 12); 43224* (OH 12); 43226; 43227* (OH 12) 43228; 43229* (OH 12); 43230* (OH 12); 43231* (OH 12); 43232* (OH 12); 43234; 43235* (OH 12) 43251; 43253; 43260; 43265; 43266; 43267; 43268; 43269; 43270; 43271; 43272 43285; 43286; 43287; 43291.

16th District: 43006* (OH 18); 43014* (OH 4); 43019* (OH 4); 43022* (OH 4) 43028* (OH 4); 43050* (OH 4); 43804* (OH 18); 43844* (OH 4, OH 18); 44201* (OH 13, OH 14); 44214* (OH 13); 44216* (OH 14); 44217* (OH 13); 44230* (OH 13, OH 14); 44260* (OH 13, OH 14); 44264* (OH 13, OH 14); 44276; 44287* (OH 13); 44601* (OH 17); 44606; 44608; 44610; 44611; 44612* (OH 18); 44613; 44614* (OH 14); 44617 44618; 44624* (OH 18); 44626; 44627; 44628; 44630; 44632* (OH 13, OH 14) 44633; 44634* (OH 17); 44636; 44637; 44638; 44640; 44641; 44643* (OH 18) 44645; 44646; 44647; 44648; 44650; 44652; 44654* (OH 18); 44657* (OH 17, OH 18); 44659; 44660; 44661 44662; 44666; 44667; 44669; 44670; 44676; 44677; 44680* (OH 18); 44681* (OH 18); 44685* (OH 14); 44687; 44688; 44689; 44690 44691; 44700; 44701; 44702; 44703; 44704; 44705; 44706; 44707; 44708; 44709 44710; 44711; 44712; 44714; 44718; 44720* (OH 14); 44721; 44730* (OH 18) 44735; 44750; 44760; 44767; 44798; 44799; 44805* (OH 4); 44822* (OH 4); 44838 44840; 44842; 44848; 44859; 44864* (OH 4); 44866; 44874; 44880* (OH 5, OH 13) 44903* (OH 4).

17th District: 43920; 43930* (OH 18); 43945* (OH 18); 43962; 43968* (OH 18) 44076* (OH 13, OH 19); 44401; 44402* (OH 13); 44403; 44404; 44405; 44406 44408; 44410; 44412* (OH 13); 44413; 44415; 44416; 44417; 44418; 44420; 44422 44423; 44424; 44425; 44427* (OH 18); 44428* (OH 19); 44429; 44430* (OH 13) 44431; 44432; 44436; 44437; 44438; 44440; 44441; 44442; 44443; 44444* (OH 13) 44445; 44446; 44449* (OH 13); 44450* (OH 13); 44451; 44452; 44453; 44454; 44455 44460; 44471; 44473; 44481* (OH 13); 44482; 44483* (OH 13); 44484; 44485* (OH 13); 44486; 44487; 44488 44490; 44492; 44493; 44500; 44501; 44502; 44503; 44504; 44505; 44506; 44507; 44509 44510; 44511; 44512; 44513; 44514 44515; 44555; 44598; 44599; 44601* (OH 16);

44609; 44619; 44625* (OH 18) 44634* (OH 16); 44657* (OH 16, OH 18); 44665; 44672.

18th District: 43006* (OH 16); 43008* (OH 12); 43023* (OH 12); 43025* (OH 12); 43030 43055* (OH 12); 43056* (OH 12); 43057; 43058; 43062* (OH 7, OH 12); 43071* (OH 12); 43076* (OH 7); 43080* (OH 4, OH 12); 43150* (OH 7); 43701; 43702; 43711 43713 43716; 43717; 43718; 43719; 43720; 43721; 43722; 43723; 43724; 43725 43727; 43728; 43730; 43731; 43732; 43733; 43734; 43735; 43736; 43738; 43739 43740; 43746; 43747; 43748; 43749; 43750; 43752; 43754; 43755; 43756; 43757 43758; 43759; 43760; 43761 43762; 43764; 43766* (OH 6); 43767; 43768; 43770 43771; 43772; 43773; 43777; 43778; 43779; 43780; 43782; 43783; 43786; 43787 43788; 43789; 43791; 43793; 43802; 43803; 43804* (OH 16); 43805; 43811; 43812 43821; 43822; 43824; 43828; 43830; 43832 43836; 43837; 43840; 43842; 43843* (OH 4); 43844* (OH 4, OH 16); 43845; 43901; 43902; 43903; 43905; 43906; 43907 43908; 43909; 43910; 43912; 43913; 43914; 43915; 43916; 43917; 43925; 43926; 43927; 43928; 43930* (OH 17); 43931; 43932; 43933 43934; 43935; 43937; 43938; 43939; 43940; 43941; 43942; 43943; 43944; 43945* (OH 17); 43946; 43947; 43948; 43950; 43951; 43952; 43953; 43960; 43961; 43963 43964; 43966; 43967; 43968* (OH 17); 43970; 43971; 43972; 43973; 43974; 43976 43977; 43981; 43983; 43984; 43985; 43986; 43988; 43989; 44427* (OH 17); 44607 44612* (OH 16); 44615 44620; 44621; 44622; 44624* (OH 12); 44625* (OH 17); 44629 44631; 44639 44643* (OH 16); 44644; 44651; 44653; 44654* (OH 16); 44656; 44657* (OH 16, OH 17); 44663; 44671; 44675; 44678; 44679; 44680* (OH 16); 44681* (OH 16) 44682 44683; 44693; 44695; 44697; 44699; 44730* (OH 16); 45715* (OH 6); 45727 45730; 45734; 45745* (OH 6); 45767* (OH 6); 45774* (OH 6); 45786* (OH 6).

19th District: 44003; 44004; 44010; 44017* (OH 10); 44022* (OH 11, OH 13) 44023 44024* (OH 13); 44026* (OH 13); 44030; 44032; 44040; 44041; 44045 44047; 44048; 44057* (OH 13); 44060* (OH 13); 44061; 44062* (OH 13); 44068 44076* (OH 13, OH 17); 44077; 44081; 44082; 44084; 44085; 44086* (OH 13) 44088; 44092; 44093; 44094; 44095; 44099* (OH 13); 44105* (OH 10, OH 11) 44117* (OH 11); 44121* (OH 11); 44122* (OH 11); 44124* (OH 11); 44125* (OH 10, OH 11); 44129* (OH 10); 44130* (OH 10); 44131* (OH 10); 44133* (OH 10, OH 13); 44136* (OH 10); 44137* (OH 11); 44138* (OH 10); 44139* (OH 11); 44141* (OH 13, OH 14); 44142* (OH 10) 44143* (OH 11); 44146* (OH 10, OH 11); 44147* (OH 13) 44428* (OH 17).

Oklahoma

1st District: 74008; 74011; 74012; 74013; 74014* (OK 2); 74021* (OK 2); 74033 74037; 74043; 74047* (OK 2); 74055* (OK 2); 74063* (OK 2); 74066* (OK 2) 74070* (OK 2, OK 5); 74073; 74100; 74101; 74102; 74103; 74104; 74105; 74106* (OK 2); 74107; 74108* (OK 2); 74110; 74112; 74114; 74115; 74116* (OK 2) 74117; 74119; 74120 74121; 74126* (OK 2); 74127* (OK 2); 74128; 74129; 74130 74132* (OK 2); 74133 74134; 74135; 74136; 74137; 74141; 74145; 74146; 74147 74148; 74150; 74152; 74153; 74155; 74156; 74157; 74158; 74159; 74169; 74170 74171; 74172; 74182; 74183; 74184; 74186; 74187; 74189; 74192; 74193; 74194 74429* (OK 2).

2nd District: 74001; 74002; 74010; 74014* (OK 1); 74015; 74016; 74017; 74018 74021* (OK 1); 74027; 74028; 74030; 74031; 74035; 74036; 74039; 74041; 74042 74044; 74046; 74047* (OK 1); 74048; 74050; 74052; 74053; 74054; 74055* (OK 1) 74056* (OK 5); 74060; 74063* (OK 1); 74066* (OK 1); 74067; 74068; 74070* (OK 1, OK 5); 74071; 74072; 74080; 74083; 74084; 74106* (OK 1); 74108* (OK 1) 74116* (OK 1); 74126* (OK 1); 74127* (OK 1); 74131; 74132* (OK 1); 74149 74301; 74330; 74331; 74332 74333; 74335; 74337; 74338; 74339; 74340; 74342 74343; 74344; 74346; 74347; 74349 74350; 74352; 74353; 74354; 74355; 74358 74359; 74360; 74361; 74362; 74363; 74364 74365; 74366; 74367; 74368; 74369 74370; 74401; 74402; 74403; 74421; 74422; 74423 74426; 74427; 74428; 74429* (OK 1); 74431; 74432; 74434; 74435; 74436; 74437; 74438 74440; 74441; 74444 74445; 74446; 74447; 74450; 74451; 74452; 74454; 74455; 74456 74457; 74458 74459; 74460; 74461; 74462; 74463; 74464; 74465; 74466; 74467; 74468 74469 74470; 74471; 74472; 74477; 74552; 74637; 74650; 74829; 74833; 74835; 74845 74859; 74860; 74862; 74877; 74880; 74882; 74931; 74936; 74941; 74943 74944 74945; 74946; 74948; 74954; 74955; 74960; 74962; 74964; 74965.

3rd District: 73030; 73032; 73045* (OK 5); 73081; 73086; 73087; 73088; 73401 73402; 73403; 73430; 73432; 73435; 73436; 73437; 73438; 73439; 73440; 73441 73443; 73446 73447; 73448; 73449; 73450; 73453; 73455; 73458; 73459; 73460 73461; 73463; 74020; 74023; 74026; 74032; 74034; 74038; 74045; 74058; 74059 74062; 74074; 74075; 74076 74077; 74078; 74079; 74081; 74085; 74425; 74530 74442; 74501; 74502; 74521; 74522 74523; 74525; 74526; 74528; 74529; 74530 74531; 74533; 74534; 74535; 74536; 74538 74540; 74542; 74543; 74545; 74546 74547; 74548; 74549; 74553; 74554; 74555; 74556 74557; 74558; 74559; 74560 74561; 74562; 74563; 74565; 74567; 74569; 74570; 74571 74572; 74574; 74576 74577; 74578; 74701; 74702; 74720; 74721; 74722; 74723; 74724 74726; 74727 74728; 74729; 74730; 74731; 74733; 74734; 74735; 74736; 74737; 74738 74740; 74741; 74743; 74745; 74747; 74748; 74750; 74752; 74753; 74754; 74755; 74756 74759; 74760; 74761; 74764; 74766; 74801; 74802; 74818; 74820; 74821; 74824 74825 74826; 74827; 74830; 74832; 74834; 74836; 74837; 74838; 74839; 74840 74842; 74843 74844; 74848; 74849; 74850; 74851; 74852; 74854; 74855; 74856 74863; 74864; 74865 74866; 74867; 74868; 74869; 74871; 74873; 74875; 74878 74881; 74883; 74884; 74901 74902; 74930; 74935; 74939; 74940; 74942; 74947; 74949; 74951; 74953 74956; 74957; 74959; 74963; 74966.

4th District: 73002; 73004; 73010; 73011; 73012; 73018; 73019; 73020* (OK 5, OK 6) 73023; 73025; 73026; 73031; 73035; 73037; 73039; 73046; 73051; 73052 73055; 73057 73059; 73065; 73067; 73068; 73069; 73070; 73071; 73072; 73074; 73075; 73076 73079; 73080; 73082; 73084* (OK 5, OK 6); 73089; 73091; 73092 73093; 73095; 73098 73110* (OK 6); 73117* (OK 6); 73130* (OK 5, OK 6); 73131* (OK 6); 73135* (OK 6) 73139* (OK 6); 73140; 73145* (OK 6); 73150* (OK 5, OK 6); 73159* (OK 5, OK 6) 73160* (OK 6); 73162* (OK 5, OK 6); 73165 73169* (OK 5, OK 6); 73170; 73173 73442; 73456; 73501; 73502; 73503; 73505; 73506; 73507; 73520; 73521; 73522; 73523 73526; 73527; 73528; 73529 73530 73531; 73532; 73533; 73534; 73536; 73537; 73538 73539; 73540; 73541; 73542 73543; 73546; 73548; 73549; 73551; 73552; 73553; 73555 73556; 73557; 73558 73560; 73561; 73562; 73565; 73567; 73568; 73569; 73570; 73572;

73573; 73575 74831; 74857* (OK 5); 74872.

5th District: 73007; 73008; 73013; 73020* (OK 4, OK 6); 73027; 73028; 73034* (OK 6); 73044; 73045* (OK 3); 73049* (OK 6); 73050; 73054; 73056; 73058 73061; 73063; 73064* (OK 6); 73073; 73077; 73078* (OK 6); 73083; 73084* (OK 4, OK 6); 73085; 73099; 73102* (OK 6); 73103* (OK 6); 73105* (OK 6); 73106* (OK 6); 73107* (OK 6); 73108* (OK 6); 73109* (OK 6); 73111* (OK 6); 73112; 73113 73114* (OK 6); 73116* (OK 6); 73118* (OK 6); 73119* (OK 6); 73120* (OK 6) 73121* (OK 6); 73122; 73123; 73124; 73126; 73127* (OK 6); 73128; 73130* (OK 4, OK 6); 73131* (OK 4, OK 6); 73132; 73134; 73137; 73141* (OK 6); 73142; 73143 73144; 73146; 73147; 73148; 73150* (OK 4, OK 6); 73151* (OK 6); 73154; 73156 73157; 73159* (OK 4, OK 6); 73162* (OK 4, OK 6); 73163; 73169* (OK 4, OK 6) 73172; 73176; 73177; 73178; 73179* (OK 6); 73180; 73194; 73757; 74003; 74004 74005; 74006; 74009; 74022; 74029; 74051; 74056* (OK 2); 74061; 74070* (OK 1, OK 2); 74082; 74601; 74602; 74603; 74604; 74630; 74631; 74632; 74633; 74641 74644; 74646; 74647; 74651; 74652; 74653; 74857* (OK 4).

6th District: 67840* (KS 1); 73001; 73005; 73006; 73009; 73014; 73015; 73016 73017; 73020* (OK 4, OK 5); 73021; 73022; 73024; 73029; 73033; 73034* (OK 5) 73036; 73038; 73040; 73041; 73042; 73043; 73047; 73048; 73049* (OK 5); 73053 73062; 73064* (OK 5); 73066; 73078* (OK 5); 73084* (OK 4, OK 5); 73090; 73094 73096; 73097; 73100; 73101; 73102* (OK 5); 73103* (OK 5); 73104; 73105* (OK 5); 73106* (OK 5); 73107* (OK 5); 73108* (OK 5); 73109* (OK 5); 73110* (OK 4) 73111* (OK 5); 73114* (OK 5); 73116* (OK 5); 73117* (OK 4); 73118* (OK 5); 73119* (OK 5); 73120* (OK 5); 73121* (OK 5); 73125; 73127* (OK 5); 73129 73130* (OK 4, OK 5); 73131* (OK 4, OK 5); 73135* (OK 4); 73136; 73139* (OK 4) 73141* (OK 5); 73145* (OK 4); 73149; 73150* (OK 4, OK 5); 73151* (OK 5); 73152 73153; 73155; 73159* (OK 4, OK 5); 73160* (OK 4); 73162* (OK 4, OK 5); 73164 73167; 73169* (OK 4, OK 5); 73179* (OK 5); 73184; 73185; 73189 73190 73193; 73196; 73197; 73198; 73199; 73544; 73547; 73550; 73554; 73559; 73564 73566; 73571; 73601; 73620; 73622; 73624; 73625; 73626; 73627; 73628; 73632 73638; 73639; 73641; 73642; 73644; 73645; 73646; 73647; 73648; 73650; 73651 73654; 73655; 73656; 73658; 73659; 73660; 73661; 73662; 73663; 73664; 73666 73667; 73668; 73669; 73673; 73701; 73702; 73703; 73705; 73706; 73716; 73717 73718; 73719; 73720; 73722; 73723; 73724; 73725; 73726; 73727; 73728; 73729 73730; 73731; 73733; 73734; 73735; 73736; 73737; 73738; 73739; 73741; 73742 73743; 73744; 73746; 73747; 73749; 73750; 73753; 73754; 73755; 73756; 73758 73759; 73760; 73761; 73762; 73763; 73764; 73766; 73768; 73770; 73771; 73772 73773; 73801; 73802; 73832; 73834; 73835; 73838; 73840; 73841; 73842; 73843 73844; 73847; 73848; 73849; 73851; 73852; 73853; 73855; 73857; 73858; 73859 73860; 73901; 73931; 73932; 73933; 73937; 73938; 73939; 73942; 73944 73945 73946; 73947; 73949; 73950; 73951; 74636; 74640; 74643; 79040* (TN 19).

Oregon

1st District: 97005; 97006; 97007; 97016; 97018; 97034* (OR 5); 97035* (OR 5) 97048; 97051; 97053; 97054; 97056; 97062* (OR 5); 97064; 97070* (OR 5); 97075 97076; 97077; 97101; 97102; 97103; 97106; 97109; 97110; 97111; 97113; 97114 97115; 97116; 97117; 97119; 97121; 97123; 97124* (OR 3); 97125; 97127; 97128 97132; 97133; 97138; 97140* (OR 5); 97144; 97145; 97146; 97148; 97200; 97201 97204; 97205; 97207; 97208* (OR 3); 97209; 97210* (OR 3); 97219* (OR 3) 97221; 97223; 97224; 97225; 97228; 97229* (OR 3); 97231* (OR 3); 97240; 97251 97253; 97254; 97255; 97256; 97258; 97259; 97271; 97272; 97280; 97281; 97290 97292; 97293; 97294; 97296; 97298; 97299; 97304* (OR 5); 97347* (OR 5); 97378* (OR 5); 97396* (OR 5).

2nd District: 97001; 97014; 97021; 97029; 97031; 97033; 97037; 97039; 97040 97041; 97044; 97050; 97057; 97058; 97063; 97065; 97425; 97501; 97502; 97503 97504; 97520; 97522; 97523; 97524; 97525; 97526* (OR 4); 97527; 97530; 97531 97532* (OR 4); 97533; 97534; 97535; 97536; 97537; 97538; 97539; 97540; 97541 97543; 97544; 97601; 97602; 97603; 97604; 97620; 97621; 97622; 97623; 97624 97625; 97626; 97627; 97630; 97632; 97633; 97634; 97635* (CA 2); 97636; 97637 97638; 97639; 97640; 97641; 97701; 97702; 97707; 97708; 97709; 97710; 97711 97712; 97720; 97721; 97722; 97730; 97731; 97732; 97733; 97734; 97735; 97736 97737; 97738; 97739; 97740; 97741; 97750; 97751; 97752; 97753; 97754; 97756 97758; 97759; 97760; 97761; 97801; 97810; 97812; 97813; 97814; 97817; 97818 97819; 97820; 97821; 97823; 97824; 97825; 97826; 97827; 97828; 97830; 97831 97833; 97834; 97835; 97836; 97837; 97838; 97839; 97840; 97841; 97842; 97843 97844; 97845; 97846; 97848; 97850; 97856; 97857; 97859; 97861; 97862; 97864 97865; 97867; 97868; 97869; 97870; 97872; 97873; 97874; 97875; 97876; 97877 97880; 97882; 97883; 97884; 97885; 97886; 97901; 97902; 97903; 97904; 97905 97906; 97907; 97908; 97909; 97910; 97911; 97913; 97914; 97917; 97918; 97920.

3rd District: 97009* (OR 5); 97010; 97011; 97015* (OR 5); 97019; 97022* (OR 5) 97023* (OR 5); 97024; 97028; 97030; 97049; 97055* (OR 5); 97060; 97067 97080; 97124* (OR 1); 97202; 97203; 97206; 97208* (OR 1); 97210* (OR 1) 97211; 97212; 97213; 97214; 97215; 97216; 97217; 97218; 97219* (OR 1); 97220 97222* (OR 5); 97227; 97229* (OR 1); 97230; 97231* (OR 1); 97232; 97233 97236; 97238; 97242; 97266; 97267* (OR 5); 97268; 97269; 97282; 97283; 97286 97291.

4th District: 97321* (OR 5); 97324; 97326* (OR 5); 97327; 97329; 97330* (OR 5) 97333* (OR 5); 97335; 97336; 97345; 97346* (OR 5); 97348; 97355; 97358 97360* (OR 5); 97370* (OR 5); 97374; 97377; 97386; 97389; 97401; 97402; 97403 97404; 97405; 97406; 97407; 97409; 97410; 97411; 97412; 97413; 97414; 97415 97416; 97417; 97419; 97420; 97423; 97424; 97426; 97427; 97428; 97429; 97430 97431; 97432; 97434; 97435; 97436; 97437; 97438; 97439; 97440; 97441; 97442 97443; 97444; 97445; 97446; 97447; 97448; 97449; 97450; 97451; 97452; 97453 97454; 97455; 97456; 97457; 97458 97459; 97460; 97461; 97462; 97463; 97464 97465; 97466; 97467; 97468; 97469; 97470 97472; 97473; 97476; 97477; 97478 97479; 97480; 97481; 97482; 97484; 97486; 97487 97488; 97489; 97490; 97491 97492; 97493; 97494; 97495; 97496; 97497; 97499; 97526* (OR 2); 97532* (OR 2).

5th District: 97002; 97004; 97009* (OR 3); 97013; 97015* (OR 3); 97017; 97020 97022* (OR 3); 97023* (OR 3); 97026; 97027; 97032; 97034* (OR 1); 97035* (OR 1); 97036;

Pennsylvania

1st District: 19013* (PA 7); 19015* (PA 7); 19018* (PA 2, PA 7); 19022* (PA 7); 19023* (PA 2, PA 7); 19029; 19032; 19036* (PA 7); 19074* (PA 7); 19079* (PA 7); 19102* (PA 2); 19105; 19106* (PA 3); 19107* (PA 2, PA 3); 19108 19109; 19112; 19113; 19120* (PA 3); 19121* (PA 2); 19122* (PA 3); 19123* (PA 2, PA 3); 19124* (PA 3); 19125* (PA 3); 19126* (PA 3, PA 13); 19129* (PA 2) 19130* (PA 2); 19132* (PA 2); 19133* (PA 3); 19134* (PA 3); 19138* (PA 2 PA 3) 19140* (PA 2, PA 3); 19141; 19142* (PA 2); 19143* (PA 2); 19144* (PA 3) 19145* (PA 3); 19146* (PA 3); 19147* (PA 3); 19148; 19150* (PA 2, PA 13) 19153; 19160; 19171; 19172; 19178.

2nd District: 19018* (PA 1, PA 7); 19023* (PA 1, PA 7); 19050* (PA 7); 19092 19093; 19100; 19101; 19102* (PA 1); 19103; 19104; 19107* (PA 1, PA 3); 19110 19118* (PA 13); 19119; 19121* (PA 1); 19123* (PA 1, PA 3); 19127; 19128* (PA 13); 19129* (PA 1); 19130* (PA 1); 19131* (PA 13); 19132* (PA 1); 19138* (PA 1); 19139; 19140* (PA 1, PA 3); 19142* (PA 1); 19143* (PA 1); 19144* (PA 1); 19145* (PA 1); 19146* (PA 1); 19150* (PA 1, PA 13); 19151* (PA 13); 19161 19162; 19170; 19173; 19175; 19177; 19179; 19181; 19182; 19183; 19184; 19185 19187; 19188; 19191; 19192; 19193; 19196; 19197; 19244.

3rd District: 19099; 19106* (PA 1); 19107* (PA 1, PA 2); 19111* (PA 13) 19114; 19115* (PA 13); 19116; 19120* (PA 1); 19122* (PA 3); 19123* (PA 1, PA 2); 19124* (PA 1); 19125* (PA 1); 19126* (PA 1, PA 13); 19133* (PA 1); 19134* (PA 1); 19135; 19136; 19137; 19140* (PA 1, PA 2); 19147* (PA 1); 19149; 19152 19154; 19155; 19255.

4th District: 15001; 15003* (PA 14); 15005; 15006; 15007; 15009; 15010; 15014 15015; 15024* (PA 18); 15026* (PA 20); 15027; 15030; 15032; 15042; 15043 15044* (PA 14); 15049* (PA 18); 15050; 15052; 15059; 15061; 15065; 15066 15068; 15069; 15074; 15076; 15077; 15081; 15084; 15085* (PA 18); 15086; 15090* (PA 14); 15095; 15096; 15101* (PA 14, PA 18); 15139* (PA 14); 15146* (PA 18); 15147* (PA 18); 15235* (PA 14, PA 18); 15239* (PA 18); 15601* (PA 12, PA 20) 15613* (PA 12); 15615; 15623; 15624; 15626; 15629; 15632; 15634* (PA 20) 15635; 15636; 15641* (PA 12); 15642* (PA 18, PA 20); 15644* (PA 20); 15647 15668* (PA 14); 15665; 15668; 15675; 15690* (PA 12); 16001; 16033* (PA 21); 16037* (PA 21); 16046; 16051* (PA 21); 16055* (PA 21); 16056* (PA 21); 16057* (PA 21); 16059; 16063; 16101; 16102; 16103; 16105; 16107; 16108 16112; 16115; 16116; 16117; 16120; 16123; 16132; 16136; 16140; 16141; 16142* (PA 21); 16143* (PA 21); 16155; 16156; 16157; 16160; 16172; 16229* (PA 12).

5th District: 15711; 15715; 15730; 15733; 15740; 15744; 15764; 15767* (PA 12) 15770; 15776; 15778; 15780; 15781; 15784; 15821; 15822; 15823; 15824; 15825 15827; 15828; 15829; 15831; 15832; 15834; 15840; 15841; 15845; 15846; 15847 15851; 15853; 15857; 15860; 15861; 15863; 15864; 15865; 15868; 15870; 16036 16038* (PA 21); 16049* (PA 12, PA 21); 16054; 16058; 16153* (PA 21); 16213 16214; 16217; 16220; 16221; 16222* (PA 12); 16224; 16225; 16230; 16232; 16233 16234; 16235; 16239; 16242* (PA 12); 16248; 16254; 16255; 16257; 16258; 16259 16260; 16261; 16301; 16312; 16313; 16314* (PA 21); 16317; 16319; 16321; 16322 16323; 16326; 16327* (PA 21); 16328; 16329; 16331; 16332; 16333; 16334; 16335* (PA 21); 16340; 16341; 16342 16343; 16344; 16345; 16346; 16347; 16350; 16351 16352; 16353; 16354* (PA 21); 16360 16361; 16362; 16364; 16365; 16366; 16367 16368; 16369; 16370; 16371; 16372 16373; 16374; 16375; 16402; 16404; 16405 16416; 16420; 16432; 16434; 16436; 16438* (PA 21); 16701; 16720; 16724; 16725 16726; 16727; 16728; 16729; 16730; 16731; 16732 16733; 16734; 16735; 16738 16740; 16743; 16744; 16745; 16746; 16748; 16749; 16750 16751; 16801; 16802 16803; 16804; 16805; 16820; 16822; 16823; 16826; 16827; 16828 16832; 16835 16841; 16844* (PA 9); 16848; 16851; 16852; 16853; 16854; 16856; 16864 16865* (PA 9); 16868; 16870* (PA 9); 16871; 16872; 16875; 16880; 16882; 16901 16911 16912; 16915; 16917; 16918; 16920; 16921; 16922; 16923; 16927; 16928 16929 16930; 16932; 16933; 16935; 16936; 16937; 16938; 16939; 16940; 16941; 16942 16943; 16946; 16948; 16950; 17701* (PA 10); 17720; 17721; 17723; 17724* (PA 10); 17726 17727; 17729; 17734; 17738; 17739; 17740; 17744* (PA 10); 17745 17747; 17748 17750; 17751; 17752* (PA 10); 17760; 17764; 17767; 17769; 17773 17776; 17778 17779; 17810; 17829; 17835; 17837; 17844; 17845; 17855; 17856 17880; 17883; 17885 17886; 17887; 17889* (PA 9).

6th District: 17017* (PA 17); 17067* (PA 17); 17080; 17087* (PA 17); 17569* (PA 16); 17730; 17749; 17777; 17801; 17847; 17850; 17857; 17865; 17877* (PA 11); 17901 17921; 17922; 17923; 17925; 17929; 17930; 17931; 17933; 17934 17935; 17936; 17938 17939; 17941; 17942; 17943; 17944; 17946; 17948; 17949 17951; 17952; 17953; 17954; 17957; 17959; 17960; 17961; 17963; 17964; 17965 17966; 17967; 17968; 17970; 17972 17974; 17976; 17978; 17979; 17980* (PA 17) 17981; 17982; 17983; 18011* (PA 15); 18056; 18062* (PA 15); 18211; 18214 18220; 18231; 18237; 18241; 18242 18245; 18248; 18252; 19464* (PA 13, PA 15, PA 16); 19465; 19503; 19504* (PA 15); 19505* (PA 15); 19506; 19507 19508; 19510; 19511; 19512* (PA 15); 19516; 19517 19518; 19519; 19520* (PA 16); 19522; 19523; 19526; 19529* (PA 15); 19530; 19533 19534; 19535; 19536; 19538; 19539; 19540; 19541; 19542; 19543* (PA 16); 19544 19545; 19547; 19548; 19549; 19550; 19551* (PA 16, PA 17); 19554; 19555; 19557 19559; 19560; 19562 19564; 19565; 19567; 19600; 19601; 19602; 19603; 19604; 19605 19606; 19607 19608; 19609; 19610; 19611; 19612; 19640.

7th District: 19003* (PA 13); 19008; 19010* (PA 13); 19013* (PA 1); 19014 19015*

(PA 1); 19016; 19017; 19018* (PA 1, PA 2); 19022* (PA 1); 19023* (PA 1, PA 2); 19026; 19028; 19033; 19036* (PA 1); 19037; 19039; 19041* (PA 13) 19043 19050* (PA 2); 19052; 19061; 19064; 19065; 19070; 19073; 19074* (PA 1) 19076; 19078; 19079* (PA 1); 19080; 19081; 19082; 19083; 19085* (PA 13); 19086; 19087* (PA 13); 19088; 19089; 19091; 19094; 19098; 19301; 19312 19316; 19317* (PA 16); 19319; 19333; 19341* (PA 16); 19342* (PA 16); 19343* (PA 16); 19345; 19355* (PA 16); 19373; 19380* (PA 16); 19382* (PA 16); 19397 19398; 19399; 19405; 19406; 19421; 19425* (PA 16); 19428* (PA 13); 19432 19442; 19460* (PA 13, PA 16); 19468* (PA 13); 19475* (PA 16); 19481; 19482 19483; 19484; 19485; 19487; 19488; 19489; 19493; 19494; 19495; 19496.

8th District: 18036* (PA 15); 18039; 18054* (PA 13, PA 15); 18055* (PA 15) 18073* (PA 13, PA 15); 18077* (PA 15); 18081; 18901; 18910; 18911; 18912 18913; 18914; 18916; 18917; 18920; 18921; 18922; 18923; 18925; 18926; 18927 18928; 18929; 18930; 18931; 18932; 18933; 18934; 18935; 18938; 18940; 18942 18943; 18944; 18946; 18947; 18949; 18950; 18951; 18953; 18954; 18955; 18956 18957; 18960; 18962; 18963; 18964* (PA 13); 18966; 18968; 18969* (PA 13) 18970; 18972; 18974; 18976; 18977; 18980; 18981; 18991; 19002* (PA 13); 19006* (PA 13); 19007; 19020; 19021; 19030; 19040* (PA 13); 19044* (PA 13); 19047 19048; 19049; 19053; 19054; 19055; 19056; 19057; 19058; 19059; 19067; 19090* (PA 13); 19440* (PA 13); 19446* (PA 13); 19454* (PA 13).

9th District: 15521; 15522; 15533; 15534; 15535; 15536; 15537; 15539; 15545 15550; 15554; 15559; 15721; 15753; 15757; 15801; 15848; 15849; 15856; 15866 16601; 16602; 16603; 16611; 16614; 16616; 16617; 16620; 16621; 16622; 16623 16625; 16627; 16629; 16631; 16633; 16634; 16635; 16637; 16638; 16645; 16647 16648; 16650; 16651; 16652; 16655; 16656; 16657; 16659; 16660; 16661; 16662 16663; 16664; 16665; 16666; 16667; 16669; 16670; 16671; 16672; 16673; 16674 16677; 16678; 16679; 16680; 16681; 16682; 16683; 16684; 16685; 16686; 16689 16691; 16692; 16693; 16694; 16695; 16821; 16825; 16829; 16830; 16833; 16834 16836; 16837; 16838; 16839; 16840; 16843; 16844* (PA 5); 16845; 16847; 16849 16850; 16855; 16858; 16859; 16860; 16861; 16863; 16865* (PA 5); 16866; 16870* (PA 5); 16873; 16874; 16876; 16877; 16878; 16879; 16881; 17002; 17004 17006 17009; 17014; 17021; 17024; 17029; 17031; 17035; 17037; 17040; 17044 17045* (PA 17); 17047; 17049; 17051; 17052; 17054; 17056; 17058; 17059; 17060 17063 17066; 17068; 17071; 17074* (PA 17); 17075; 17076; 17082; 17084; 17086; 17090* (PA 17); 17094; 17099; 17201; 17210; 17211; 17212; 17213; 17214; 17215; 17217 17219; 17220; 17221; 17222* (PA 19); 17223; 17224; 17225; 17228; 17229; 17231 17232; 17233; 17235; 17236; 17237; 17238; 17239; 17240* (PA 19); 17243; 17244 17246; 17247; 17249; 17250; 17251; 17252; 17253; 17254; 17255; 17256; 17257* (PA 19); 17260 17261; 17262; 17263; 17264; 17265; 17267; 17268; 17270; 17271 17272; 17294; 17812 17813; 17827; 17831; 17833; 17841; 17842; 17843; 17853 17861; 17862; 17864; 17870 17876; 17882; 17889* (PA 5).

10th District: 16910; 16914; 16925; 16926; 16945; 16947; 17701* (PA 5); 17703 17705; 17722; 17724* (PA 5); 17728; 17731; 17735; 17737; 17742; 17743; 17744* (PA 5); 17752* (PA 5); 17754; 17756; 17758; 17759; 17762; 17763; 17765; 17768 17770; 17771; 17774; 18301* (PA 11); 18321; 18323; 18324; 18325; 18326; 18327 18328; 18332; 18334; 18335; 18336; 18337; 18340; 18341; 18342; 18344; 18346 18347; 18348; 18349; 18350; 18355; 18356; 18357; 18360* (PA 11); 18370; 18371 18372; 18373; 18401; 18403; 18405; 18407; 18410; 18411; 18413; 18414; 18415 18416; 18417; 18419; 18420; 18421; 18424; 18425; 18426; 18427; 18428; 18430 18431; 18433; 18434; 18435; 18436; 18437; 18438; 18439; 18440; 18441; 18443 18444; 18445; 18446; 18447; 18449; 18451; 18452; 18453; 18454; 18455; 18456 18457; 18458; 18459; 18460; 18461; 18462; 18463; 18464; 18465; 18466; 18469 18470; 18471; 18472; 18473; 18500; 18501; 18503; 18504; 18505; 18507; 18508 18509; 18510; 18512; 18514; 18515; 18517; 18518; 18519; 18522; 18540; 18577 18610* (PA 11); 18612* (PA 11); 18614; 18615; 18616; 18619; 18623 18625 18626; 18628; 18629; 18630; 18632; 18636; 18641* (PA 11); 18653; 18657; 18801 18810; 18812; 18813; 18814; 18815; 18816; 18817; 18818; 18820; 18821; 18822 18823; 18824; 18825; 18826; 18827; 18828; 18829; 18830; 18831; 18832; 18833 18834; 18837; 18839; 18840; 18842; 18843; 18844; 18845; 18846; 18847; 18848 18850; 18851; 18853; 18854.

11th District: 17772; 17814; 17815; 17820; 17821; 17822; 17823; 17824; 17825 17828; 17830; 17832; 17834; 17836; 17839; 17840; 17846; 17851; 17858; 17859 17860; 17866; 17867; 17868; 17872; 17877* (PA 6); 17878; 17881; 17884; 17888 17920; 17927; 17945; 17985; 18012; 18030; 18058; 18071; 18201; 18210; 18212 18216; 18219; 18221; 18222; 18223; 18224; 18229; 18230; 18232; 18234 18235; 18239; 18240; 18243; 18244; 18246; 18247; 18249; 18250; 18251; 18254 18255; 18256; 18301* (PA 10); 18320 18322; 18330; 18331; 18333; 18352; 18353 18354; 18360* (PA 10); 18601; 18602 18603; 18610* (PA 10); 18611; 18612* (PA 10); 18617; 18618; 18621; 18622; 18624 18627; 18631; 18634; 18635; 18637 18640; 18641* (PA 10); 18642; 18643; 18644 18651; 18654; 18655; 18656; 18660 18661; 18690; 18700; 18701; 18702; 18703; 18704 18705; 18706; 18707; 18708 18709; 18710; 18711; 18761; 18762; 18763; 18764; 18765 18766; 18767; 18768 18769; 18773; 18774.

12th District: 15401* (PA 20); 15411; 15421; 15424; 15425* (PA 20); 15430 15431; 15436; 15437; 15440; 15445* (PA 20); 15446; 15455; 15456; 15459; 15462* (PA 20); 15464; 15465; 15469* (PA 20); 15470; 15472; 15478* (PA 20); 15485 15490* (PA 20); 15501; 15502; 15520; 15530; 15531; 15532; 15538; 15540; 15541 15542; 15544; 15546; 15547; 15548; 15549; 15551; 15552; 15553; 15555; 15557 15558; 15560; 15561; 15562; 15563; 15564; 15565; 15601* (PA 4, PA 20); 15610 15612; 15613* (PA 4); 15618; 15620; 15621; 15627; 15628; 15630; 15638; 15639* (PA 20); 15641* (PA 4); 15646; 15650; 15655; 15656* (PA 4); 15658; 15661; 15662; 15664; 15666* (PA 20); 15670; 15671; 15673; 15674; 15676; 15677; 15679* (PA 20); 15680; 15681; 15682; 15683* (PA 20); 15684; 15685; 15686; 15687 15688; 15689; 15690* (PA 4); 15693; 15696 15701; 15705; 15710; 15712 15713 15714; 15716; 15717; 15720; 15722; 15723; 15724 15725; 15727; 15728; 15729 15731; 15732; 15734; 15736; 15737; 15738; 15739; 15741 15742; 15744; 15746 15747; 15748; 15750; 15751; 15752; 15754; 15756; 15758; 15759 15760; 15761 15762; 15763; 15765; 15767* (PA 5); 15771; 15772; 15773; 15774; 15775 15777 15779; 15783; 15790; 15901; 15902; 15904; 15905; 15906; 15907; 15909; 15915 15920 15921; 15922; 15923; 15924; 15925; 15926; 15927; 15928; 15929; 15930; 15931 15934 15935; 15936; 15937; 15938; 15940; 15942; 15943; 15944; 15945; 15946 15948; 15949 15951; 15952; 15953; 15954; 15955; 15956; 15957; 15958; 15959 15960; 15961; 15962;

15963; 16025* (PA 21); 16028; 16041* (PA 21); 16049* (PA 5, PA 21); 16201; 16210; 16211; 16212; 16215; 16216; 16218; 16222* (PA 5) 16223; 16226; 16228; 16229* (PA 4); 16236; 16238; 16240; 16242* (PA 5); 16244 16245; 16246; 16249; 16250; 16253; 16256; 16262; 16263; 16613; 16619; 16624 16630; 16636; 16639; 16640; 16641; 16644; 16646; 16668; 16675.

13th District: 18054* (PA 8, PA 15); 18073* (PA 8, PA 15); 18074* (PA 15) 18084; 18915; 18918; 18924; 18936; 18958; 18964* (PA 8); 18969* (PA 8); 18971 18979; 19001; 19002* (PA 8); 19003* (PA 7); 19004; 19006* (PA 8); 19009 19010* (PA 7); 19012; 19025; 19031; 19034; 19035; 19038; 19040* (PA 8); 19041* (PA 7); 19044* (PA 8); 19046; 19066; 19072; 19075; 19085* (PA 7); 19087* (PA 7); 19090* (PA 8); 19095; 19096; 19111* (PA 3); 19115* (PA 3); 19117; 19118* (PA 2); 19126* (PA 1, PA 3); 19128* (PA 2); 19131* (PA 2); 19150* (PA 1, PA 2); 19151* (PA 2); 19401; 19403; 19404; 19407; 19408; 19409; 19420; 19422 19423; 19424; 19426; 19428* (PA 7); 19429; 19430; 19436; 19437; 19438; 19440* (PA 8); 19441; 19443; 19444; 19446* (PA 8); 19450; 19451; 19452; 19453; 19454* (PA 8); 19455; 19456; 19460* (PA 7, PA 16); 19462; 19464* (PA 6, PA 15, PA 16); 19468* (PA 7); 19473* (PA 15); 19474; 19477; 19478; 19486; 19490; 19492 19525* (PA 15).

14th District: 15003* (PA 4); 15017* (PA 18, PA 20); 15044* (PA 4); 15056 15071* (PA 20); 15090* (PA 4); 15091; 15101* (PA 4, PA 18); 15106* (PA 18) 15108* (PA 20); 15116* (PA 18); 15120* (PA 18); 15122* (PA 18); 15127; 15136 15142; 15143* (PA 20); 15189; 15200; 15201; 15202; 15203; 15204; 15205; 15206* (PA 18); 15207* (PA 18); 15208* (PA 18); 15209* (PA 18); 15210* (PA 18) 15211; 15212* (PA 18); 15213; 15214* (PA 18); 15215* (PA 18); 15216* (PA 18) 15217* (PA 18); 15218* (PA 18); 15219; 15220* (PA 18); 15221* (PA 18); 15222 15225; 15226* (PA 18); 15227* (PA 18); 15229; 15230; 15232; 15233 15234* (PA 18, PA 20); 15235* (PA 4, PA 18); 15236* (PA 18, PA 20); 15237* (PA 18); 15238* (PA 18); 15242; 15244; 15250; 15251; 15252; 15253; 15254; 15255 15257; 15258; 15259; 15260; 15261; 15262; 15263; 15264; 15265; 15267; 15268 15270; 15272; 15274; 15275; 15278; 15279; 15281; 15282; 15283; 15285; 15290.

15th District: 18001; 18002; 18003; 18010; 18011* (PA 6); 18013; 18014; 18015 18016; 18017; 18018; 18025; 18031; 18032; 18034; 18035; 18036* (PA 8); 18037 18038; 18041; 18042; 18043; 18044; 18046; 18049; 18050; 18051; 18052; 18053 18054* (PA 8, PA 13); 18055* (PA 8); 18059; 18060; 18062* (PA 6); 18063 18064; 18065; 18066; 18067; 18068; 18069; 18070; 18072; 18073* (PA 8, PA 13) 18074* (PA 13); 18076; 18077* (PA 8); 18078; 18079; 18080; 18083; 18085 18086; 18087; 18088; 18091; 18092; 18098; 18099; 18100; 18101; 18102; 18103 18104; 18105; 18106; 18175; 18195; 18343; 18351; 19435; 19464* (PA 6, PA 13, PA 16); 19472; 19473* (PA 13); 19504* (PA 6); 19505* (PA 6); 19512* (PA 6) 19525* (PA 13); 19529* (PA 6).

16th District: 17022* (PA 17); 17501* (PA 17); 17503; 17504; 17505; 17506 17507; 17508; 17509; 17516* (PA 17); 17517* (PA 17); 17518; 17519; 17520 17522* (PA 17); 17527; 17528; 17529; 17532; 17534; 17535; 17536; 17537; 17538* (PA 17); 17540; 17543* (PA 17); 17545* (PA 17); 17549; 17551* (PA 17); 17552* (PA 17); 17555; 17557; 17560; 17562; 17563; 17565* (PA 17); 17566; 17567; 17568; 17569* (PA 6); 17572; 17573; 17576; 17577; 17578* (PA 17); 17579; 17580; 17581; 17583; 17584; 17585; 17600; 17601* (PA 17); 17602; 17603* (PA 17); 17604; 17605; 17699; 19310; 19311; 19317* (PA 7); 19318; 19320; 19330; 19331; 19335; 19339; 19340; 19341* (PA 7); 19342* (PA 7); 19343* (PA 7) 19344; 19346; 19347; 19348; 19350; 19351; 19352; 19353; 19354; 19355* (PA 7) 19357; 19358; 19360; 19362; 19363; 19365; 19366; 19367; 19369; 19370; 19371 19372; 19374; 19375; 19376; 19380* (PA 7); 19381; 19382* (PA 7); 19383; 19390; 19395; 19425* (PA 7); 19457; 19460* (PA 7, PA 13); 19464* (PA 6, PA 13, PA 15); 19470; 19475* (PA 7); 19480; 19501; 19520* (PA 6); 19543* (PA 6); 19551* (PA 6, PA 17).

17th District: 17003; 17005; 17010; 17011* (PA 19); 17013* (PA 19); 17015 17016; 17017* (PA 6); 17018; 17020; 17022* (PA 16); 17023; 17025* (PA 19) 17026; 17028; 17030; 17032; 17033; 17034; 17036; 17038; 17039; 17041; 17042 17043* (PA 19); 17045* (PA 9); 17048; 17053; 17055* (PA 19); 17057; 17061 17062; 17064; 17067* (PA 6); 17069; 17072; 17073; 17074* (PA 9); 17077; 17078 17083; 17085; 17087* (PA 6); 17088; 17090* (PA 9); 17093; 17097; 17098; 17100 17101; 17102; 17103; 17104; 17105; 17106; 17107; 17108; 17109; 17110; 17111 17112; 17113; 17120; 17121; 17122; 17123; 17124; 17125; 17126; 17127; 17128 17129; 17130; 17140; 17177; 17501* (PA 16); 17502; 17512; 17516* (PA 16) 17517* (PA 16); 17521; 17522* (PA 16); 17533; 17538* (PA 16); 17543* (PA 16) 17545* (PA 16); 17547; 17550; 17551* (PA 16); 17552* (PA 16); 17554; 17564 17565* (PA 16); 17570; 17575; 17578* (PA 16); 17582; 17601* (PA 16); 17603* (PA 16); 17980* (PA 6); 19551* (PA 6, PA 16).

18th District: 15017* (PA 14, PA 20); 15018; 15020; 15024* (PA 4); 15025 15028; 15029; 15034; 15035; 15037; 15045; 15049* (PA 4); 15051; 15063* (PA 20); 15075; 15085* (PA 4); 15088; 15089* (PA 20); 15101* (PA 4, PA 14); 15102* (PA 20); 15104; 15106* (PA 14); 15110; 15112; 15116* (PA 14); 15120* (PA 14) 15122* (PA 14); 15123; 15129; 15130; 15131; 15132; 15133; 15134; 15135; 15137 15139* (PA 4); 15140; 15144; 15145; 15146* (PA 4); 15147* (PA 4); 15148 15206* (PA 14); 15207* (PA 14); 15208* (PA 14); 15209* (PA 14); 15210* (PA 14); 15212* (PA 14); 15214* (PA 14); 15215* (PA 14); 15216* (PA 14); 15217* (PA 14); 15218* (PA 14); 15220* (PA 14); 15221* (PA 14); 15223; 15226* (PA 14); 15227* (PA 14); 15228; 15234* (PA 14, PA 20); 15235* (PA 4, PA 14); 15236* (PA 14, PA 20); 15237* (PA 14); 15238* (PA 14); 15239* (PA 4); 15240 15241* (PA 20); 15243; 15266; 15276; 15332* (PA 20); 15642* (PA 4, PA 20).

19th District: 17001; 17007; 17008; 17011* (PA 17); 17012; 17013* (PA 17) 17019; 17025* (PA 17); 17027; 17043* (PA 17); 17055* (PA 17); 17065; 17070 17081; 17089; 17218; 17222* (PA 9); 17240* (PA 9); 17241; 17257* (PA 9) 17266; 17301; 17302; 17303; 17304; 17306; 17307; 17309; 17310; 17311; 17312 17313; 17314; 17315; 17316; 17317; 17318; 17319; 17320; 17321; 17322; 17323 17324; 17325; 17326; 17327; 17329; 17331; 17332; 17333; 17337; 17339; 17340 17342; 17343; 17344; 17345; 17346; 17347; 17349; 17350; 17352; 17353; 17354 17355; 17356; 17358; 17360; 17361; 17362; 17363; 17364; 17365; 17366; 17368 17370; 17371; 17372; 17375; 17400; 17401; 17402; 17403; 17404; 17405; 17406 17407.

20th District: 15004; 15012; 15017* (PA 14, PA 18); 15019; 15021; 15022 15026*

(PA 4); 15031; 15033; 15036; 15038; 15046; 15047; 15053; 15054; 15055 15057; 15060; 15062; 15063* (PA 18); 15064; 15067; 15071* (PA 14); 15072 15078; 15082; 15083; 15087; 15089* (PA 18); 15102* (PA 18); 15108* (PA 14) 15126; 15143* (PA 14); 15231; 15234* (PA 14, PA 18); 15236* (PA 14, PA 18) 15241* (PA 18); 15301; 15310; 15311; 15312; 15313; 15314; 15315; 15316; 15317 15320; 15321; 15322; 15323; 15324; 15325; 15327; 15329; 15330; 15331; 15332* (PA 18); 15333; 15334; 15336; 15337; 15338; 15339; 15340; 15341; 15342; 15344 15345; 15346; 15347; 15348; 15349; 15350; 15351; 15352; 15353; 15354; 15356 15357; 15358; 15359; 15360; 15361; 15362; 15363; 15364; 15365; 15366; 15367 15368; 15370; 15376; 15377; 15378; 15379; 15380; 15401* (PA 12); 15410 15412 15413; 15415; 15416; 15417; 15419; 15420; 15422; 15423; 15425* (PA 12); 15427 15428; 15429; 15432; 15433; 15434; 15435; 15438; 15439; 15442; 15443; 15444 15445* (PA 12); 15447; 15448; 15449; 15450; 15451; 15454; 15458; 15460; 15461 15462* (PA 12); 15463; 15466; 15467; 15468; 15469* (PA 12); 15473; 15474 15475; 15476; 15477; 15478* (PA 12); 15479; 15480; 15482; 15483; 15484; 15486 15488; 15489; 15490* (PA 12); 15492; 15601* (PA 4, PA 12); 15605; 15606 15611; 15616; 15617; 15619; 15622; 15625; 15631; 15633; 15634* (PA 4); 15637 15639* (PA 12); 15640; 15642* (PA 4, PA 18); 15644* (PA 4); 15660; 15663 15666* (PA 12); 15672; 15678; 15679* (PA 12); 15683* (PA 12); 15691; 15692 15695; 15697; 15698.

21st District: 16001* (PA 4); 16003; 16016; 16017; 16018; 16020; 16021; 16022 16023; 16024; 16025* (PA 12); 16027; 16029; 16030; 16033* (PA 4); 16034 16035; 16037* (PA 4); 16038* (PA 5); 16039; 16040; 16041* (PA 12); 16045 16048; 16049* (PA 5, PA 12); 16050; 16051* (PA 4); 16052; 16053; 16055* (PA 4); 16056* (PA 4); 16057* (PA 4); 16061; 16110; 16111; 16113; 16114; 16121 16124; 16125; 16127; 16130; 16131; 16133; 16134; 16137; 16142* (PA 4); 16143* (PA 4); 16145; 16146; 16148; 16150; 16151; 16153* (PA 5); 16154; 16159; 16161 16311; 16314* (PA 5); 16316; 16327* (PA 5); 16335* (PA 5); 16354* (PA 5); 16388; 16401; 16403; 16406; 16407; 16410; 16411; 16412; 16413; 16415; 16417 16421; 16422; 16423; 16424; 16426; 16427; 16428; 16430; 16433; 16435; 16438* (PA 5); 16440; 16441; 16442; 16443; 16444; 16500; 16501; 16502; 16503; 16504 16505; 16506; 16507; 16508; 16509; 16510; 16511; 16512; 16514; 16515; 16522 16530; 16531; 16532; 16533; 16534; 16538; 16541; 16544; 16546; 16550; 16553 16554; 16558; 16563; 16565; 16566.

Rhode Island

1st District: 02801; 02802; 02806; 02809; 02824; 02826; 02828* (RI 2); 02830* (RI 2); 02831* (RI 2); 02835; 02837; 02838; 02839; 02840; 02841; 02857* (RI 2); 02858; 02859 02860* (RI 2); 02861* (RI 2); 02862; 02863; 02864; 02865 02871; 02872; 02876; 02878 02885; 02895* (RI 2); 02902; 02903* (RI 2); 02904 02906; 02907* (RI 2); 02908* (RI 2); 02909* (RI 2); 02911* (RI 2); 02912 02914* (RI 2); 02915* (RI 2); 02916; 02917* (RI 2); 02919* (RI 2); 02921* (RI 2); 02940.

2nd District: 02804; 02807; 02808; 02812; 02813; 02814; 02815; 02816; 02817 02818; 02821; 02822; 02823; 02825; 02827; 02828* (RI 1); 02829; 02830* (RI 1) 02831* (RI 1); 02832; 02833; 02836; 02852; 02854; 02857* (RI 1); 02860* (RI 1); 02861* (RI 1); 02873; 02874; 02875; 02877; 02879; 02881; 02882 02883; 02886; 02887; 02888; 02889; 02891* (CT 2); 02892; 02893; 02894; 02895* (RI 1); 02898; 02900; 02901; 02903* (RI 1); 02905; 02907* (RI 1); 02908* (RI 1); 02909* (RI 1); 02910; 02911* (RI 1); 02914* (RI 1); 02915* (RI 1); 02917* (RI 1); 02918; 02919* (RI 1); 02920; 02921* (RI 1).

South Carolina

1st District: 29401* (SC 6); 29402; 29403* (SC 6); 29404; 29405* (SC 6) 29406* (SC 6); 29407* (SC 6); 29408; 29410; 29412* (SC 6); 29414* (SC 6) 29417; 29418* (SC 6); 29420; 29422; 29423; 29424; 29425; 29429; 29431; 29439 29440; 29442; 29445; 29451; 29455* (SC 6); 29456; 29458; 29461; 29464; 29465 29469; 29472; 29482; 29483; 29484; 29485; 29510* (SC 6); 29511; 29512; 29526; 29527 29544; 29545; 29566; 29568; 29569; 29572; 29575; 29576; 29577; 29578; 29579 29582; 29585; 29587; 29597; 29598.

2nd District: 29002; 29006* (SC 3); 29016* (SC 6); 29033; 29036; 29039; 29044* (SC 6); 29045* (SC 5); 29053; 29054; 29061* (SC 6); 29063; 29070; 29071 29072; 29073; 29075* (SC 5); 29076; 29082; 29107; 29112; 29113; 29115* (SC 6) 29123; 29124; 29135; 29137; 29146; 29147; 29160; 29164; 29169; 29170; 29171 29172; 29177; 29201* (SC 6); 29203* (SC 6); 29204* (SC 6); 29205* (SC 6) 29206* (SC 6); 29207; 29208; 29209* (SC 6); 29210; 29211; 29212* (SC 6) 29214; 29215; 29216; 29217; 29218; 29219; 29220; 29221; 29222; 29223* (SC 6) 29225; 29226; 29227; 29228; 29230 29250; 29290; 29292; 29475; 29488* (SC 6) 29801* (SC 3); 29802; 29803* (SC 3) 29808; 29810; 29812; 29813; 29814; 29817 29826; 29827; 29836; 29839; 29846; 29849 29851* (SC 3); 29853; 29856; 29901 29902; 29903; 29904; 29905; 29910; 29911; 29912 29913; 29914; 29915; 29916 29918; 29920; 29921; 29922; 29923; 29924; 29925; 29926 29927; 29928; 29929 29932; 29934; 29935; 29936; 29938; 29939; 29940; 29943 29944; 29945 29948.

3rd District: 29006* (SC 2); 29105; 29129; 29138; 29166; 29325; 29332; 29351 29360* (SC 4); 29370; 29384; 29611* (SC 4); 29620; 29621; 29622; 29623; 29624 29625; 29627 29628; 29630; 29631; 29632; 29633; 29634; 29635* (SC 4); 29638 29639; 29640; 29641 29642; 29643; 29644* (SC 4); 29645; 29646; 29648; 29649 29653; 29654* (SC 4) 29655; 29656; 29657; 29658; 29659; 29661* (SC 4); 29664 29665; 29666; 29667; 29669 29670; 29671; 29673* (SC 4); 29675; 29676; 29677 29678; 29679; 29682; 29684; 29685 29686; 29689; 29691; 29692; 29693; 29695 29696; 29697; 29801* (SC 2); 29803* (SC 2); 29804; 29809; 29816; 29819; 29821 29822; 29829; 29831; 29832; 29834; 29835; 29838; 29840; 29841 29842; 29844; 29845; 29847; 29848; 29850; 29851* (SC 2); 29899.

4th District: 29031; 29178* (SC 5); 29301; 29302; 29303; 29304; 29305; 29306 29307; 29316; 29318; 29319; 29320; 29321; 29322; 29323* (SC 5); 29324; 29329 29330* (SC 5); 29331; 29333; 29334; 29335; 29336; 29338; 29346; 29348; 29349 29353; 29356; 29360* (SC 3); 29364; 29365; 29368; 29369; 29372* (SC 5); 29373 29374; 29375; 29376; 29377; 29378; 29379; 29385; 29386; 29388; 29390; 29391 29601; 29602; 29603;

South Dakota

29604; 29605; 29606; 29607; 29608; 29609; 29610; 29611* (SC 3); 29612; 29613; 29614; 29615; 29616; 29635* (SC 3); 29636; 29644* (SC 3); 29647; 29650; 29651; 29652; 29654* (SC 3); 29661* (SC 3); 29662; 29673* (SC 3); 29681; 29683; 29687; 29688; 29690; 29698.

5th District: 29009; 29010* (SC 6); 29014; 29015; 29020; 29032; 29037; 29040* (SC 6); 29045* (SC 2); 29055; 29058; 29065; 29067; 29069; 29074; 29075* (SC 2); 29078; 29079; 29101; 29106; 29108; 29122; 29126; 29127; 29128* (SC 6) 29130 29132; 29145; 29150* (SC 6); 29151; 29152; 29153* (SC 6); 29154* (SC 6); 29168* (SC 6); 29175; 29176; 29178* (SC 4); 29180; 29323* (SC 4); 29330* (SC 4); 29340; 29341; 29342; 29355; 29372* (SC 4); 29512; 29516; 29520; 29525 29532* (SC 6); 29536; 29540; 29542; 29543; 29547; 29550; 29563; 29565; 29567 29570; 29573; 29584; 29593; 29594; 29596; 29702; 29703; 29704; 29705; 29706 29709; 29710; 29712; 29714; 29715; 29716; 29717; 29718; 29719; 29720; 29721 29724; 29726; 29727; 29728; 29729; 29730; 29731; 29732; 29733; 29734; 29741 29742; 29743; 29744; 29745.

6th District: 29001; 29003; 29010* (SC 5); 29016* (SC 2); 29017; 29018; 29030 29038; 29040* (SC 5); 29041; 29042; 29044* (SC 2); 29046; 29047; 29048; 29051 29052; 29056; 29059; 29061* (SC 2); 29062; 29077; 29080; 29081; 29102; 29104 29111; 29114; 29115* (SC 2); 29116; 29117; 29125; 29128* (SC 2); 29131; 29133 29142; 29143; 29148; 29150* (SC 5); 29153* (SC 5); 29154* (SC 5); 29161 29162; 29163; 29168* (SC 5); 29183; 29200; 29201* (SC 2); 29202; 29203* (SC 2); 29204* (SC 2); 29205* (SC 2); 29206* (SC 2); 29209* (SC 2); 29212* (SC 2); 29223* (SC 2); 29224; 29240; 29260; 29401* (SC 1); 29403* (SC 1); 29405* (SC 1); 29406* (SC 1); 29407* (SC 1); 29409; 29411; 29412* (SC 1); 29413; 29414* (SC 1); 29415; 29418* (SC 1); 29419; 29426; 29430; 29432; 29433; 29434; 29435 29436; 29437; 29438; 29446; 29447; 29448; 29449; 29450; 29452; 29453; 29455* (SC 1); 29457; 29468; 29470; 29471; 29474; 29476; 29477; 29479; 29481; 29487 29488* (SC 2); 29492; 29493; 29501; 29502; 29503; 29504; 29505; 29506; 29510* (SC 1); 29518; 29519; 29530; 29532* (SC 5); 29541; 29546; 29554; 29555; 29556 29560; 29564; 29571; 29574; 29580; 29581; 29583; 29588; 29589; 29590; 29591 29592; 29595; 29843; 29931; 29941.

South Dakota

At Large: 56136* (MN 2); 56138* (IA 5, MN 2); 56138* (IA 5, MN 2); 56144* (MN 2); 56164* (MN 2); 56219* (MN 7); 56257* (MN 2); 57001; 57002; 57003; 57004 57005; 57006; 57007; 57010; 57012; 57013; 57014; 57015; 57016; 57017; 57018 57019; 57020; 57021; 57022; 57024; 57025; 57026* (MN 2); 57027; 57028; 57029 57030* (MN 2); 57031; 57032; 57033; 57034* (IA 5); 57035; 57036; 57037; 57038 57039; 57040; 57041; 57042; 57043; 57044; 57045; 57046; 57047; 57048; 57049 57050; 57051; 57052; 57053; 57054; 57055; 57056; 57057; 57058; 57059; 57060* (MN 2); 57061; 57062; 57063; 57064; 57065; 57066; 57067; 57068* (IA 5, MN 2) 57069; 57070; 57071; 57072; 57073; 57074* (MN 2); 57075; 57076; 57077; 57078 57079; 57100; 57101; 57102; 57103; 57104; 57105; 57106; 57107; 57115; 57116 57117; 57118; 57188; 57189; 57190; 57191; 57192; 57193; 57194; 57195; 57196 57197; 57198; 57201; 57202; 57210; 57212; 57213; 57214; 57216; 57217; 57218 57219; 57220; 57221; 57223; 57224; 57225; 57226; 57227; 57229; 57230; 57231 57232; 57233; 57234; 57235; 57236; 57237; 57238; 57239; 57241; 57242; 57243 57244; 57245; 57246; 57247; 57248; 57249; 57251; 57252; 57253; 57255* (ND 1) 57256; 57257; 57258; 57259; 57260* (ND 1); 57261; 57262; 57263; 57264; 57265 57266; 57268; 57269; 57270* (ND 1); 57271; 57272; 57273; 57274; 57276; 57278 57279; 57301; 57311; 57312; 57313; 57314; 57315; 57316; 57317; 57319; 57321 57322; 57323; 57324; 57325; 57326; 57328; 57329; 57330; 57331; 57332; 57334 57335; 57336; 57337; 57339; 57340; 57341; 57342; 57344; 57345; 57346; 57348 57349; 57350; 57353; 57354; 57355; 57356; 57357; 57358; 57359; 57361; 57362 57363; 57364; 57365; 57366; 57367; 57368; 57369; 57370; 57371; 57373; 57374 57375; 57376; 57379; 57380; 57381; 57382; 57383; 57384; 57385; 57386; 57401 57402; 57420; 57421; 57422; 57424; 57425; 57426; 57427; 57428; 57429; 57430 57432; 57433; 57434; 57435; 57436; 57437; 57438; 57439; 57440; 57441; 57442 57445; 57446; 57448; 57449; 57450; 57451; 57452; 57454; 57456; 57457; 57460 57461; 57462; 57465; 57466; 57467; 57468; 57469; 57470; 57471; 57472; 57473 57474; 57475; 57476; 57477; 57479; 57481; 57483; 57501; 57520; 57521; 57522 57523* (NE 3); 57526; 57527; 57528; 57529; 57531; 57532; 57533; 57534 57536; 57537; 57538; 57540; 57541; 57542; 57543; 57544; 57545; 57547; 57548 57551; 57552; 57553; 57555; 57557; 57559; 57560; 57562; 57563; 57564; 57566 57567; 57568; 57569; 57570; 57571* (NE 3); 57572; 57574; 57576; 57577; 57578 57579; 57580; 57584; 57585; 57601; 57620; 57621; 57622; 57623; 57625; 57626 57628; 57629; 57630; 57631; 57632* (ND 1); 57633; 57634; 57636; 57638* (ND 1) 57639; 57640; 57641* (ND 1); 57642* (ND 1); 57643; 57644; 57645* (ND 1) 57646; 57647; 57648* (ND 1); 57649; 57650; 57651; 57652; 57653; 57656; 57657 57658; 57660* (ND 1); 57661; 57701; 57702; 57706; 57708; 57709; 57714; 57715 57716; 57717* (MT 1, WY 1); 57718; 57719; 57720; 57722; 57724* (MT 1) 57725 57729; 57730; 57732; 57735* (WY 1); 57736; 57737; 57738; 57741; 57742; 57744 57745; 57747; 57748; 57750; 57751; 57752; 57754; 57755; 57756; 57757; 57758 57759; 57760; 57761; 57762; 57763; 57764; 57765; 57766; 57767; 57769; 57770 57772; 57773; 57774; 57775; 57776; 57777; 57778; 57779; 57780; 57782; 57783* (WY 1); 57785; 57787; 57788; 57790; 57791; 57792; 57793; 57794; 57795; 57799 58020* (MN 7, ND 1); 58030* (MN 7, ND 1); 58041* (ND 1); 58043* (ND 1); 58053* (ND 1); 58413* (ND 1); 58436* (ND 1); 58439* (ND 1); 58623* (ND 1); 58639* (ND 1); 58649* (ND 1); 58653* (ND 1); 69201* (NE 3); 69211* (NE 3); 69212* (NE 3) 69216* (NE 3); 69218* (NE 3); 69337* (NE 3); 69343* (NE 3).

Tennessee

1st District: 37601; 37602; 37603; 37604; 37605; 37614; 37615; 37616; 37617 37618; 37620; 37621; 37625; 37640; 37641; 37642* (VA 9); 37643; 37644; 37645 37650; 37656; 37657; 37658; 37659; 37660; 37662; 37663; 37664; 37665; 37669 37680; 37681; 37682 37683; 37684; 37686; 37687; 37688; 37690; 37691; 37692 37694; 37711* (TN 4); 37713 37715* (KY 5); 37721* (TN 2, TN 4); 37722; 37725 37727; 37731; 37738; 37743; 37744 37753; 37760; 37764* (TN 2); 37765; 37806* (TN 4); 37809; 37810; 37811; 37818 37820; 37821* (NC 11); 37843; 37851* (KY 5); 37857; 37862; 37863; 37864; 37865 37869; 37871* (TN 2, TN 4); 37873 37877* (TN 4); 37881* (TN 4); 37883; 37890 37924* (TN 2, TN 4).

2nd District: 37303; 37309; 37310; 37311* (TN 3); 37312* (TN 3); 37314; 37320 37323* (TN 3); 37325* (TN 3); 37329; 37331; 37353* (TN 3); 37354; 37358 37364; 37370; 37371; 37385; 37701; 37721* (TN 1, TN 4); 37737; 37742; 37754* (TN 3); 37764* (TN 1); 37771; 37774* (TN 3); 37777; 37801; 37802; 37803 37804; 37826; 37846; 37849* (TN 3); 37853; 37871* (TN 1, TN 4); 37874; 37878 37882; 37885; 37886; 37900; 37901; 37902; 37909; 37912; 37914; 37915; 37916 37917; 37918* (TN 4); 37919; 37920; 37921; 37922; 37923; 37924* (TN 1, TN 4) 37927; 37928; 37929; 37930; 37931* (TN 3); 37932; 37933; 37938* (TN 4); 37939 37940; 37950; 37990; 37995; 37996; 37997; 37998.

3rd District: 37110* (TN 4, TN 6); 37301; 37302; 37304; 37305; 37307; 37308 37311* (TN 2); 37312* (TN 2); 37313; 37315; 37316; 37317* (NC 11); 37321* (TN 4); 37322; 37323* (TN 2); 37324* (TN 4); 37325* (TN 2); 37326; 37327; 37333 37336; 37338* (TN 4); 37339; 37340; 37341; 37343; 37346; 37347; 37350; 37351 37353* (TN 2); 37356; 37357* (TN 4, TN 6); 37361; 37362; 37363; 37365; 37366 37367; 37369; 37373; 37374; 37375* (TN 4); 37377; 37379; 37380; 37387; 37391 37396; 37397; 37400; 37401; 37402; 37403; 37404; 37406; 37407; 37408 37409; 37410; 37411; 37412; 37415; 37416; 37419; 37421; 37422; 37450; 37705 37710; 37716; 37717; 37719 37726; 37733; 37748; 37754* (TN 2); 37763; 37769* (TN 4); 37770; 37774* (TN 2); 37828; 37829; 37830; 37831; 37840; 37845; 37849* (TN 2); 37854* (TN 4); 37872; 37880; 37887; 37931* (TN 2); 38581* (TN 4, TN 6); 38585.

4th District: 37018; 37020* (TN 6); 37034* (TN 6); 37047* (TN 6); 37060* (TN 6); 37091* (TN 6); 37110* (TN 3, TN 6); 37144* (TN 6); 37153* (TN 6); 37160* (TN 6); 37161; 37166* (TN 6); 37180* (TN 6); 37183; 37306; 37318; 37321* (TN 3); 37324* (TN 3); 37328; 37330; 37332; 37334; 37335; 37337; 37338* (TN 3) 37342; 37345; 37348; 37352; 37355; 37357* (TN 3, TN 6); 37359; 37360; 37372 37375* (TN 3); 37376; 37378; 37381; 37382; 37388; 37389; 37394; 37395; 37398 37707; 37708; 37709; 37711* (TN 1); 37714; 37715* (KY 5, TN 1); 37721* (TN 1, TN 2); 37723; 37724; 37729; 37730; 37732; 37752; 37755; 37756; 37757; 37762 37766; 37769* (TN 3); 37773; 37778; 37779; 37806* (TN 1); 37807; 37812; 37813 37814; 37815; 37816; 37819; 37825; 37841; 37842; 37847; 37848; 37851* (KY 5, TN 1); 37852; 37854* (TN 3); 37860; 37861; 37866; 37867; 37868; 37870; 37871* (TN 1, TN 2); 37877* (TN 1); 37879; 37881* (TN 1); 37888; 37891; 37892* (KY 5); 37893; 37918* (TN 2); 37924* (TN 1, TN 2); 37938* (TN 2); 38326 38327 38361; 38365; 38370; 38371* (TN 6); 38372; 38376; 38425* (TN 7); 38449; 38450 38452; 38453; 38455; 38456; 38457; 38459; 38460; 38463; 38464; 38468; 38469 38471; 38472* (TN 6); 38473; 38475; 38477; 38478; 38481; 38483; 38485; 38486 38488; 38504; 38543* (TN 6); 38549; 38550; 38553; 38555; 38556; 38557; 38559 38565; 38573* (TN 6); 38574* (TN 6); 38577; 38578; 38579; 38581* (TN 3, TN 6); 38583* (TN 6); 38587; 38589.

5th District: 37010* (TN 7); 37011; 37013; 37015* (TN 7); 37027* (TN 6) 37032* (TN 7); 37048* (TN 6); 37049; 37070; 37072* (TN 6, TN 7); 37073* (TN 7); 37076* (TN 6); 37080* (TN 6); 37086* (TN 6); 37115; 37116; 37122* (TN 6) 37135* (TN 6); 37138* (TN 6); 37141; 37143* (TN 7); 37148* (TN 6); 37152 37172* (TN 7); 37188* (TN 6); 37189; 37200; 37201; 37202; 37203; 37204; 37205 37206; 37207; 37208; 37209* (TN 7); 37210; 37211* (TN 6); 37212; 37213; 37214 37215; 37216; 37217; 37218; 37219; 37220* (TN 6); 37221* (TN 6); 37222 37224 37227; 37228; 37229; 37230; 37232; 37234; 37235; 37236; 37237; 37238; 37239 37240; 37241; 37242; 37243; 37244; 37245; 37246; 37247; 37248; 37249; 37250.

6th District: 32630* (FL 5, FL 6); 37012; 37014; 37016; 37019; 37020* (TN 4) 37022* (TN 7); 37024; 37025* (TN 7); 37026; 37027* (TN 5); 37030; 37031 37034* (TN 4); 37037; 37046; 37047* (TN 4); 37048* (TN 5); 37057; 37059 37060* (TN 4); 37062* (TN 7); 37063; 37064; 37065; 37066; 37068; 37071; 37072* (TN 5, TN 7); 37074; 37075; 37076* (TN 5); 37077; 37083; 37085; 37086* (TN 5); 37087; 37088; 37089; 37091* (TN 4); 37095; 37110* (TN 3, TN 4); 37118; 37119 37122* (TN 5); 37129; 37130; 37131; 37132; 37133; 37135* (TN 5); 37136; 37138* (TN 5); 37144* (TN 4); 37145; 37148* (TN 5); 37149; 37150; 37151; 37153* (TN 4); 37160* (TN 4); 37166* (TN 5); 37167; 37174* (TN 7); 37179; 37180* (TN 4) 37184; 37186; 37188* (TN 5); 37190; 37211* (TN 5); 37220* (TN 5); 37221* (TN 5); 37357* (TN 3, TN 4); 38401* (TN 7); 38451* (TN 7); 38472* (TN 4); 38476* (TN 7); 38501; 38502; 38503; 38505; 38541; 38542; 38543* (TN 4); 38544; 38545 38547; 38548; 38551; 38552; 38554; 38560; 38562; 38563; 38564; 38567; 38568; 38569; 38570; 38573* (TN 4); 38574* (TN 4); 38575; 38580; 38581* (TN 3, TN 4) 38582; 38583* (TN 4); 38588.

7th District: 37010* (TN 5); 37015* (TN 5); 37022* (TN 6); 37025* (TN 6) 37029; 37032* (TN 5); 37033; 37035; 37036; 37040; 37041; 37042; 37043; 37044 37050* (TN 8); 37051; 37052; 37055; 37056; 37062* (TN 6); 37072* (TN 5, TN 6) 37073* (TN 5); 37079* (TN 8); 37080* (TN 5); 37082; 37096; 37097; 37098 37137; 37140; 37142; 37143* (TN 5); 37146; 37147; 37155; 37165; 37171; 37172* (TN 5); 37174* (TN 6); 37181; 37187; 37191; 37209* (TN 5); 38002* (TN 8) 38000; 38010; 38017; 38018* (TN 9); 38027; 38028* (TN 8); 38029; 38036; 38039 38042; 38043; 38044; 38045; 38046; 38048; 38052; 38057; 38060; 38061; 38066 38067; 38068; 38074; 38075; 38076; 38110; 38115* (TN 9); 38118* (TN 9); 38119* (TN 9); 38120* (TN 9); 38127* (TN 9); 38128* (TN 8, TN 9); 38133* (TN 8, TN 9); 38134* (TN 8, TN 9); 38135* (TN 8); 38138* (TN 9); 38139; 38141* (TN 9) 38175; 38183; 38184; 38186; 38310; 38311; 38313* (TN 8); 38315; 38328; 38329 38332; 38334; 38339; 38340; 38345; 38347; 38351; 38352; 38357; 38359; 38363 38366* (TN 8); 38367; 38368; 38371* (TN 4); 38374; 38375; 38377; 38379; 38380 38381; 38388; 38393; 38401* (TN 6); 38402; 38425* (TN 4); 38451* (TN 6) 38454; 38461; 38462; 38474; 38476* (TN 6); 38482; 38487; 42223* (KY 1, TN 8).

8th District: 37023; 37028; 37050* (TN 7); 37054; 37058; 37061; 37078; 37079* (TN 7); 37101; 37134; 37175; 37178; 37185; 38001; 38002* (TN 7); 38004; 38006 38007; 38011; 38012; 38014; 38015; 38019; 38021; 38023; 38024; 38025; 38028* (TN 7); 38030; 38033; 38034; 38037; 38040; 38041; 38047; 38049; 38050; 38053 38054; 38056; 38058; 38059; 38063; 38069; 38070; 38071; 38077; 38079* (KY 1) 38080; 38083; 38107* (TN 9); 38108* (TN 9); 38127* (TN 9); 38128* (TN 7, TN 9); 38133* (TN 7, TN 9); 38134* (TN 7, TN 9); 38135* (TN 7); 38150; 38168; 38201 38220; 38221; 38222; 38223; 38224; 38225; 38226; 38227; 38229; 38230; 38231 38232; 38233; 38235; 38236; 38237; 38238; 38240; 38241; 38242; 38251; 38253 38254; 38255; 38256; 38257; 38258; 38259; 38260; 38261; 38271; 38301; 38302 38303; 38305; 38308; 38313* (TN 7); 38314; 38316; 38317; 38318; 38320; 38321 38324; 38330; 38331; 38333; 38336; 38337; 38338; 38341; 38342; 38343; 38344 38346; 38348; 38355; 38356; 38358; 38362; 38366* (TN 7); 38369; 38378; 38382

38387; 38389; 38390; 38391; 38392; 42223* (KY 1, TN 7); 72338* (AR 1); 72395* (AR 1).

9th District: 37501; 38018* (TN 7); 38100; 38101; 38103; 38104; 38105; 38106 38107* (TN 8); 38108* (TN 8); 38109; 38111; 38112; 38113; 38114; 38115* (TN 7); 38116; 38117; 38118* (TN 7); 38119* (TN 7); 38120* (TN 7); 38122; 38124 38125* (TN 7); 38126; 38127* (TN 7, TN 8); 38128* (TN 7, TN 8); 38130; 38131; 38132 38133* (TN 7, TN 8); 38134* (TN 7, TN 8); 38136; 38137; 38138* (TN 7); 38140 38141* (TN 7); 38142; 38143; 38145; 38146; 38147; 38148; 38150; 38151; 38152 38157; 38159; 38161; 38163; 38165; 38166; 38173; 38174; 38177; 38181; 38182 38187; 38188; 38193; 38194; 38195; 38197.

Texas

1st District: 75401* (TX 4); 75402; 75403; 75404; 75410; 75411; 75412; 75415 75416; 75417; 75420; 75421; 75422; 75425; 75426; 75428; 75429; 75431; 75432 75433; 75434; 75435; 75436; 75437; 75441; 75444; 75448; 75450; 75451; 75453* (TX 4); 75455; 75456; 75457; 75460; 75461; 75462; 75468; 75469; 75470; 75471 75473; 75477; 75478; 75480; 75481; 75482; 75483; 75486; 75487; 75493; 75494 75496; 75497; 75501; 75502* (AR 4); 75503; 75504; 75505; 75507; 75550; 75551 75554; 75555; 75556; 75557; 75558; 75559; 75560; 75561; 75562; 75563; 75564 75565; 75566; 75567; 75568; 75569; 75570; 75571; 75572; 75573; 75574; 75601* (TX 4); 75602* (TX 4); 75603* (TX 4); 75604* (TX 4); 75605* (TX 4); 75606 75630; 75631; 75633; 75636; 75637; 75638; 75639; 75640; 75641; 75642; 75643 75644; 75647* (TX 4); 75650; 75651; 75652; 75653; 75656; 75657; 75658; 75659 75661; 75662* (TX 4); 75666; 75667; 75668; 75669; 75670; 75671; 75680; 75681 75682; 75683; 75684* (TX 4); 75685; 75686; 75687; 75688; 75689; 75691; 75692 75694; 75755; 75760; 75765; 75773* (TX 4); 75783; 75788; 75937* (TX 2); 75943 75944; 75946; 75958; 75961* (TX 2); 75978.

2nd District: 75757* (TX 4); 75759; 75764; 75766; 75772; 75780; 75784; 75785 75789* (TX 4); 75834; 75835; 75844* (TX 5); 75845; 75847; 75849; 75851; 75856 75858; 75862; 75865; 75901; 75902; 75903; 75915; 75925; 75926; 75928; 75929 75930; 75931; 75932; 75933; 75934; 75935; 75936; 75937* (TX 1); 75938; 75939 75941; 75942; 75947; 75948; 75949; 75951; 75954; 75956; 75957; 75959; 75960 75961* (TX 1); 75962; 75963; 75966; 75968; 75969; 75970; 75972; 75973; 75974 75975; 75976; 75977; 75979; 75980; 75990; 77301* (TX 8); 77303* (TX 8); 77326 77327* (TX 8); 77328; 77331; 77332; 77334; 77335; 77340; 77341; 77342; 77343 77344; 77348; 77349; 77350; 77351; 77358; 77359; 77360; 77363; 77364; 77367 77368; 77369; 77371; 77374; 77376; 77378* (TX 8); 77519; 77533; 77535* (TX 9) 77538; 77561; 77564; 77575; 77582; 77585; 77611; 77612; 77614; 77615; 77616 77624; 77625; 77626; 77630; 77631; 77632; 77639; 77656* (TX 9); 77659; 77660 77662; 77663; 77664; 77670; 77709; 77711; 77830; 77831; 77861; 77868; 77869 77873; 77875; 77876.

3rd District: 75002; 75023* (TX 26); 75025* (TX 26); 75026; 75040* (TX 5) 75041* (TX 5); 75042* (TX 5, TX 30); 75043* (TX 4, TX 5); 75044; 75045; 75046 75048* (TX 4, TX 5); 75069* (TX 4, TX 26); 75074* (TX 30); 75075* (TX 26, TX 30); 75080* (TX 26, TX 30); 75081* (TX 26, TX 30); 75082* (TX 30); 75086 75088* (TX 4); 75094; 75098* (TX 4); 75149* (TX 5, TX 30); 75150* (TX 5) 75181* (TX 5, TX 30); 75182* (TX 4); 75187; 75204* (TX 5, TX 30); 75205* (TX 5) 75206* (TX 5); 75209* (TX 5, TX 24, TX 30); 75214* (TX 5, TX 30); 75218* (TX 5); 75219* (TX 5, TX 30); 75220* (TX 24, TX 26, TX 30); 75225* (TX 30); 75228* (TX 5, TX 30); 75229* (TX 26, TX 30); 75230* (TX 30); 75231* (TX 30); 75234* (TX 26, TX 30); 75238* (TX 5, TX 30); 75243* (TX 26, TX 30); 75244* (TX 26, TX 30); 75252* (TX 26, TX 30); 75275; 75355; 75359; 75367; 75378.

4th District: 75009; 75020; 75021; 75043* (TX 3, TX 5); 75048* (TX 3, TX 5) 75058; 75068* (TX 26); 75069* (TX 3, TX 26); 75070* (TX 26); 75076; 75078* (TX 26); 75087; 75088* (TX 3); 75090; 75091; 75097; 75098* (TX 3); 75103; 75114* (TX 5); 75117; 75118; 75121; 75126; 75127; 75132; 75135; 75140; 75142* (TX 5) 75143* (TX 5); 75147* (TX 5); 75160; 75164; 75166; 75169; 75173; 75182* (TX 3); 75189; 75401* (TX 1); 75407; 75409; 75413; 75414; 75418; 75423; 75424 75438; 75439; 75440; 75442; 75443; 75446; 75447; 75449; 75452; 75453* (TX 1) 75454; 75458; 75459; 75472; 75474; 75475; 75476; 75479; 75485; 75488; 75489 75490; 75491; 75492; 75495; 75601* (TX 1); 75602* (TX 1); 75603* (TX 1) 75604* (TX 1); 75605* (TX 1); 75607; 75608; 75615; 75647* (TX 1); 75660 75662* (TX 1); 75663; 75684* (TX 1); 75693; 75701* (TX 5); 75702* (TX 5) 75703* (TX 5); 75704* (TX 5); 75705* (TX 5); 75706* (TX 5); 75707* (TX 5) 75708* (TX 5); 75709* (TX 5); 75710; 75711; 75712; 75713; 75750; 75754; 75757* (TX 2); 75762* (TX 5); 75771; 75773* (TX 1); 75789* (TX 2); 75790; 75791 75792; 76201* (TX 13, TX 26); 76202; 76203; 76204; 76205* (TX 13, TX 26) 76206; 76227; 76233; 76238; 76240; 76242; 76245; 76249; 76250; 76252; 76253 76258; 76263; 76264; 76266; 76268; 76271; 76272; 76273.

5th District: 75040* (TX 3); 75041* (TX 3); 75042* (TX 3, TX 30); 75043* (TX 3, TX 4) 75047; 75048* (TX 3, TX 4); 75114* (TX 4); 75124; 75125* (TX 24); 75134* (TX 24, TX 30); 75141* (TX 24); 75142* (TX 4); 75143* (TX 4); 75146* (TX 24, TX 30); 75147* (TX 4); 75148; 75149* (TX 3, TX 30); 75150* (TX 4); 75157; 75158; 75159; 75163 75180* (TX 30); 75181* (TX 3, TX 30); 75185; 75201* (TX 30); 75204* (TX 3, TX 30); 75205* (TX 3); 75206* (TX 3); 75209* (TX 3, TX 24, TX 30); 75214* (TX 3, TX 30); 75217* (TX 30); 75218* (TX 3); 75219* (TX 3, TX 30); 75223* (TX 30); 75226* (TX 30); 75227* (TX 30); 75228* (TX 3, TX 30); 75235* (TX 24, TX 30); 75238* (TX 3, TX 30); 75239* (TX 30); 75241* (TX 30); 75246* (TX 30); 75253* (TX 26); 75701* (TX 4); 75702* (TX 4); 75703* (TX 4); 75704* (TX 4); 75705* (TX 4); 75706* (TX 4); 75707* (TX 4); 75708* (TX 4); 75709* (TX 4); 75751; 75756; 75758; 75762* (TX 4); 75763; 75770; 75778; 75779 75782; 75801; 75802; 75831; 75832; 75833; 75838; 75839; 75840; 75844* (TX 2) 75846; 75848; 75850; 75852; 75853; 75855; 75859; 75860; 75861; 75882; 75884 75886; 76629; 76635; 76642; 76653; 76667; 76678; 76686; 76687; 76693 77801* (TX 8); 77802* (TX 8); 77803* (TX 8); 77805; 77806; 77837; 77840* (TX 8); 77850; 77855; 77856; 77859; 77864; 77865; 77867; 77870; 77871; 77872 77882.

6th District: 75019* (TX 26); 75050* (TX 24, TX 26, TX 30); 75052* (TX 24) 75063* (TX 26, TX 30); 75099; 75119* (TX 24); 75154* (TX 24); 75165* (TX 24) 76006* (TX 24); 76008* (TX 12); 76010* (TX 24); 76011* (TX 24); 76012* (TX 12, TX 24);

76013* (TX 24); 76014* (TX 24); 76015* (TX 24); 76016; 76017* (TX 24) 76018* (TX 24); 76020* (TX 12, TX 17); 76021; 76022* (TX 12); 76028* (TX 12) 76031* (TX 12); 76034; 76036* (TX 12); 76039* (TX 12); 76040* (TX 12); 76044* (TX 12); 76051* (TX 26); 76052* (TX 12); 76053* (TX 12); 76054; 76058* (TX 12); 76059* (TX 12); 76060* (TX 12); 76063* (TX 12, TX 24); 76065* (TX 24) 76084* (TX 12); 76086* (TX 12); 76087* (TX 12, TX 17); 76092; 76094; 76095 76099; 76103* (TX 12, TX 24); 76107* (TX 12); 76108* (TX 12); 76109* (TX 12) 76110* (TX 12, TX 24); 76112* (TX 12, TX 24); 76114* (TX 12); 76115* (TX 12, TX 24); 76116* (TX 12); 76117* (TX 12); 76118* (TX 12); 76120* (TX 12); 76123* (TX 12); 76126* (TX 12); 76131* (TX 12); 76132* (TX 12); 76133* (TX 12) 76134* (TX 12, TX 24); 76136; 76137* (TX 12); 76140* (TX 12, TX 24); 76148 76155* (TX 12); 76162; 76163; 76177* (TX 12); 76179* (TX 12); 76180* (TX 12) 76181; 76182; 76244; 76248* (TX 12); 76262* (TX 26).

7th District: 77005* (TX 18, TX 22, TX 25); 77014; 77019* (TX 18, TX 29) 77024* (TX 18, TX 29); 77027* (TX 18); 77040* (TX 18); 77041* (TX 18); 77042* (TX 22, TX 25); 77043* (TX 29); 77046; 77055* (TX 18, TX 29); 77056* (TX 18, TX 22); 77057* (TX 18, TX 22); 77063* (TX 22, TX 25); 77064* (TX 18); 77065 77066* (TX 8, TX 18); 77067* (TX 18); 77068* (TX 8); 77069* (TX 8); 77070* (TX 8, TX 18); 77072* (TX 22, TX 25); 77077* (TX 22); 77079; 77080* (TX 18, TX 29); 77081* (TX 18, TX 22); 77082* (TX 22); 77083* (TX 22); 77084; 77086* (TX 18); 77088* (TX 18); 77090* (TX 8, TX 18); 77091* (TX 18, TX 29); 77092* (TX 18, TX 29); 77094; 77095* (TX 18, TX 29); 77098* (TX 18); 77099* (TX 22, TX 25); 77215; 77218; 77219; 77224; 77227; 77240; 77241; 77242; 77244; 77250 77256; 77257; 77269; 77279; 77280; 77282; 77290; 77375* (TX 8); 77401* (TX 18, TX 22, TX 25); 77413; 77429* (TX 8); 77433; 77447* (TX 8); 77449; 77450* (TX 22); 77484* (TX 8, TX 14); 77491; 77492; 77493* (TX 14); 77494* (TX 14, TX 22).

8th District: 77066* (TX 7, TX 18); 77068* (TX 7); 77069* (TX 7); 77070* (TX 7, TX 18); 77090* (TX 7, TX 18); 77249; 77268; 77273; 77301* (TX 2); 77302; 77303* (TX 2); 77304; 77305; 77325; 77327* (TX 2); 77333 77336; 77337; 77338* (TX 18); 77339; 77345; 77346* (TX 9); 77347; 77355 77356; 77357; 77362; 77365 77372; 77373; 77375* (TX 7); 77377; 77378* (TX 2) 77379; 77380; 77381; 77382; 77383; 77384; 77385; 77386; 77387; 77388; 77389 77391; 77396* (TX 9, TX 18, TX 29); 77418 77426; 77429* (TX 7); 77445* (TX 14); 77447* (TX 7); 77452; 77474* (TX 14); 77484* (TX 7, TX 14); 77532* (TX 9, TX 25); 77801* (TX 5); 77802* (TX 5); 77803* (TX 5); 77833; 77834; 77835 77840* (TX 5); 77841; 77842; 77843; 77844; 77845; 77862; 77866; 77880; 77881 78931; 78944; 78950* (TX 14).

9th District: 77044* (TX 18, TX 29); 77049* (TX 18, TX 25, TX 29); 77058* (TX 22) 77062* (TX 22); 77089* (TX 22, TX 25); 77258; 77259; 77346* (TX 8) 77396* (TX 8, TX 18, TX 29); 77510; 77511* (TX 22); 77514; 77517; 77518 77520* (TX 25, TX 29); 77521* (TX 25, TX 29); 77532* (TX 8, TX 25); 77535* (TX 2); 77539; 77546* (TX 22); 77550; 77551; 77552; 77553; 77554; 77555; 77560 77562* (TX 25); 77563; 77565; 77568; 77573; 77574; 77580; 77590; 77591; 77592 77597; 77598* (TX 22, TX 25); 77613; 77617; 77619; 77622; 77623; 77627; 77629 77640; 77641; 77642; 77643; 77650; 77651; 77655; 77656* (TX 2); 77661; 77665 77700; 77701; 77702; 77703; 77704; 77705; 77706; 77707; 77708; 77710; 77713 77720; 77726.

10th District: 73301; 73344; 78610* (TX 14); 78617* (TX 14); 78621* (TX 14) 78641* (TX 14, TX 21); 78651; 78652* (TX 14); 78653; 78660; 78700; 78701 78702; 78703; 78704; 78705; 78709; 78710; 78711; 78712; 78713; 78714; 78716 78718; 78719; 78720; 78721; 78722; 78723; 78724; 78725; 78726; 78727* (TX 21) 78728* (TX 21); 78729* (TX 21); 78730; 78731; 78732; 78733; 78734* (TX 14) 78735; 78736* (TX 14); 78737* (TX 14); 78738* (TX 14); 78739; 78741; 78742 78743; 78744; 78745* (TX 14); 78746; 78747; 78748; 78749; 78750* (TX 21) 78751; 78752; 78753; 78754; 78755; 78756; 78757; 78758; 78759* (TX 21); 78760 78762; 78763; 78764; 78765; 78766; 78767; 78768; 78769; 78771; 78772; 78773 78774; 78778; 78779; 78780; 78781; 78782; 78783; 78785; 78786; 78787; 78788 78789.

11th District: 76055; 76436; 76457; 76501; 76502; 76503; 76504; 76505; 76508 76511; 76513; 76517; 76518; 76519; 76520; 76522; 76523; 76524; 76525; 76526 76528; 76531; 76533; 76534; 76538; 76539; 76540; 76541; 76542; 76543; 76544 76545; 76546; 76547; 76550; 76552; 76554; 76555; 76556; 76557; 76558; 76559 76561; 76564; 76565; 76566; 76567; 76569; 76570; 76571; 76576; 76577; 76579 76597; 76598; 76599; 76621; 76622; 76624; 76625; 76627; 76628; 76630; 76631 76632; 76633; 76634; 76636; 76637; 76638; 76640; 76643; 76645; 76648; 76649 76650; 76652; 76654; 76655; 76656; 76657; 76660; 76661; 76664; 76665; 76666 76671; 76673; 76675; 76676; 76677; 76680; 76682; 76684; 76685; 76689; 76690 76691; 76692; 76700; 76701; 76702; 76703; 76704; 76705; 76706; 76707; 76708 76710; 76711; 76712; 76714; 76715; 76716; 76795; 76796; 76797; 76798; 76799 76824; 76825* (TX 21); 76832; 76836; 76844; 76852; 76853; 76858; 76864; 76867 76870; 76871; 76872; 76877; 76880; 76887; 77857.

12th District: 76008* (TX 6); 76009; 76012* (TX 6, TX 24); 76020* (TX 6, TX 17); 76022* (TX 6); 76028* (TX 6); 76031* (TX 6); 76033; 76036* (TX 6); 76039* (TX 6); 76040* (TX 6); 76044* (TX 6); 76050; 76052* (TX 6); 76053* (TX 6) 76058* (TX 6); 76059* (TX 6); 76061; 76063* (TX 6, TX 24); 76066; 76067* (TX 17); 76082; 76084* (TX 6); 76086* (TX 6, TX 17); 76093; 76097; 76098; 76101; 76102; 76103* (TX 6, TX 24); 76104* (TX 24); 76105* (TX 24) 76106; 76107* (TX 6); 76108* (TX 6); 76109* (TX 6); 76110* (TX 6, TX 24) 76111; 76112* (TX 6, TX 24); 76113; 76114* (TX 6); 76115* (TX 6, TX 24) 76116* (TX 6); 76117* (TX 6); 76118* (TX 6); 76119* (TX 24); 76120* (TX 6) 76121; 76122; 76123* (TX 6); 76124; 76126* (TX 6); 76127; 76129; 76131* (TX 6) 76132* (TX 6); 76133* (TX 6); 76134* (TX 6, TX 24); 76135; 76137* (TX 6) 76140* (TX 6, TX 24); 76147; 76150; 76155* (TX 6); 76161; 76164; 76177* (TX 6); 76179* (TX 6); 76180* (TX 6); 76185; 76192; 76193; 76195; 76196; 76197 76198; 76199; 76248* (TX 6); 76439; 76485; 76487; 76490.

13th District: 76201* (TX 4, TX 26); 76205* (TX 4, TX 26); 76228; 76230 76239; 76251; 76254; 76255; 76261; 76265; 76270; 76301; 76302; 76303; 76304 76305; 76306; 76307; 76308; 76309; 76310; 76311; 76351; 76352; 76354; 76357 76360; 76363; 76364; 76365; 76366; 76367; 76369; 76370; 76371; 76373; 76377 76378; 76379; 76380; 76383; 76384; 76385; 76389; 79002; 79003; 79005; 79007 79008; 79011; 79012; 79014; 79019; 79021; 79024; 79027; 79031; 79032; 79034 79036; 79039; 79041; 79042; 79043; 79046; 79052; 79054; 79056; 79057; 79059 79061; 79063; 79064; 79065; 79066; 79068; 79072; 79073;

79077; 79078; 79079 79080; 79082; 79083; 79085; 79088; 79090; 79094; 79095; 79096; 79097; 79100 79101* (TX 19); 79102; 79103* (TX 19); 79104; 79105; 79106; 79107 79108 79109* (TX 19); 79110* (TX 19); 79111; 79114; 79116; 79117; 79120; 79121* (TX 19); 79123; 79124; 79159; 79160; 79161; 79163; 79164; 79165; 79166; 79167 79168; 79170; 79171; 79172; 79173; 79174; 79175; 79176; 79177; 79178; 79180 79181; 79182; 79184; 79185; 79186; 79187; 79188; 79189; 79201; 79220; 79221 79222; 79223; 79224; 79225; 79226; 79227; 79229; 79230; 79231; 79232; 79233 79234; 79235; 79236; 79237; 79238; 79239; 79240; 79241; 79243; 79244; 79245 79247; 79248; 79250; 79251; 79252; 79255; 79256; 79257; 79258; 79259; 79260; 79261; 79311* (TX 19); 79312; 79321; 79322; 79326; 79330; 79339; 79343; 79351 79356; 79357; 79364* (TX 19); 79366* (TX 19); 79368; 79369; 79370; 79371 79373; 79381; 79383; 79401* (TX 19); 79403* (TX 19); 79404* (TX 19); 79407* (TX 19); 79415* (TX 19); 79417; 79423* (TX 19); 79424* (TX 19); 79505; 79529.

14th District: 76530; 76573; 76574; 76578; 77404; 77412; 77414; 77415; 77419 77420; 77422* (TX 22); 77423* (TX 22); 77428; 77430* (TX 22); 77431; 77432 77434; 77435* (TX 22); 77436; 77437; 77440; 77442; 77443; 77444* (TX 22) 77445* (TX 8); 77446; 77448; 77453; 77454; 77455; 77456; 77457; 77458; 77460 77462; 77463; 77465; 77466; 77467; 77468; 77470; 77473; 77474* (TX 8); 77475 77480; 77482; 77483; 77484* (TX 7, TX 8); 77485* (TX 22); 77486; 77488; 77493* (TX 7); 77494* (TX 7, TX 22); 77515* (TX 22); 77531* (TX 22); 77541* (TX 22) 77566* (TX 22); 77836; 77838; 77839; 77852; 77853; 77863; 77878; 77879; 77901* (TX 15); 77902; 77903; 77904; 77905; 77950 77951; 77957; 77961; 77962; 77964 77968; 77969; 77970; 77971; 77972; 77973; 77975 77976; 77977; 77978; 77979 77982; 77983; 77984; 77985; 77986; 77987; 77988; 77990 77991; 77995* (TX 15) 78122; 78140; 78159; 78336* (TX 15); 78340; 78358; 78377; 78382; 78393; 78602 78603; 78604; 78606; 78610* (TX 10); 78612; 78614; 78615 78616; 78617* (TX 10); 78619; 78620; 78621* (TX 10); 78622; 78626* (TX 21); 78627 78629; 78632 78634; 78635; 78636; 78640; 78641* (TX 10, TX 21); 78644; 78645 78648; 78650 78652* (TX 10); 78655; 78656; 78658; 78659; 78661; 78662; 78663 78665; 78666* (TX 21); 78667; 78669; 78676; 78677; 78734* (TX 10); 78736* (TX 10); 78737* (TX 10); 78738* (TX 10); 78745* (TX 10); 78932; 78933; 78934; 78935; 78938 78940; 78941; 78942; 78943; 78945; 78946; 78947; 78948; 78949; 78950* (TX 8) 78951; 78952; 78953; 78954; 78956; 78957; 78959; 78960; 78961; 78962; 78963 78964.

15th District: 77901* (TX 14); 77954; 77960; 77963; 77967; 77974; 77989 77993; 77994; 77995* (TX 14); 78022; 78060; 78071; 78075; 78102; 78103; 78104 78107; 78111; 78113; 78116; 78117; 78118; 78119; 78125; 78141; 78142; 78144 78145; 78146; 78151; 78162; 78164; 78336* (TX 14); 78350; 78352; 78353; 78355 78359; 78362; 78363* (TX 27); 78368; 78370; 78372* (TX 28); 78374; 78383; 78387; 78389; 78390; 78391 78501; 78502; 78503; 78504; 78516; 78537; 78538; 78539; 78540; 78543; 78549 78557; 78558; 78560; 78561; 78562; 78563; 78565 78569; 78570; 78572; 78576; 78577; 78579; 78580; 78589; 78595; 78596; 79062* (TX 19).

16th District: 79821; 79835; 79836; 79838; 79849; 79853; 79900; 79901; 79902 79903; 79904; 79905; 79906* (TX 23); 79907; 79910; 79911; 79912; 79913; 79914 79915; 79917; 79920; 79922; 79923; 79924* (TX 23); 79925* (TX 23); 79926 79927* (TX 23); 79930; 79931; 79932; 79934* (TX 23); 79935* (TX 23); 79936* (TX 23); 79937; 79940; 79941; 79942; 79943; 79944; 79945; 79946; 79947; 79948 79949; 79950; 79951; 79952; 79953; 79954; 79955; 79958; 79960; 79961; 79968 79975; 79976; 79978; 79980; 79982; 79983; 79984; 79986; 79987; 79988 79989; 79990; 79991; 79992; 79993; 79994; 79995; 79996; 79997; 79998; 79999 88510; 88511; 88512; 88513; 88514; 88515; 88516; 88517; 88518; 88519; 88520 88521; 88523; 88524; 88525; 88526; 88527; 88528; 88529; 88530; 88531; 88532 88533; 88534; 88535; 88536; 88538; 88539; 88540; 88541; 88542; 88543; 88544 88545; 88546; 88547; 88548; 88549; 88550; 88553; 88554; 88555; 88556; 88557 88558; 88559; 88560; 88561; 88562; 88563; 88565; 88566; 88567; 88568; 88569 88570; 88571; 88572; 88573; 88574; 88575; 88576; 88577; 88578; 88579; 88580 88581; 88582; 88583; 88584; 88585; 88586; 88587; 88588; 88589.

17th District: 76020* (TX 6, TX 12); 76023; 76035; 76043; 76048; 76049; 76067* (TX 12); 76068; 76070; 76071; 76073; 76077; 76078; 76087* (TX 6, TX 12) 76225; 76234; 76246; 76267; 76350; 76359; 76372; 76374; 76388; 76401; 76402 76424; 76426; 76427; 76429; 76430; 76431; 76432; 76433; 76435; 76437; 76438 76442; 76443; 76444; 76445; 76446; 76447; 76448; 76449; 76450; 76452; 76453 76454; 76455; 76456; 76458; 76459; 76460; 76461; 76462; 76463; 76464; 76465; 76466; 76467; 76468; 76469; 76470 76471; 76472; 76474; 76475; 76476; 76481 76483; 76484; 76486; 76491; 76801; 76803 76804; 76821; 76823; 76827; 76828 76834; 76837; 76845; 76855; 76861; 76862; 76865; 76866; 76873; 76875; 76878 76882; 76884; 76886; 76888; 76889; 76890; 76901* (TX 21); 76903* (TX 21); 76904* (TX 21); 76905* (TX 21); 76933; 76937; 76945; 76949 76953; 79331 79377; 79501; 79502; 79503; 79504; 79506; 79508; 79510; 79511; 79512 79516 79517; 79518; 79519; 79520; 79521; 79525; 79526; 79527; 79528; 79530; 79532 79533; 79534; 79535; 79536; 79537; 79538; 79539; 79540; 79541; 79542; 79543 79544; 79545; 79546; 79547; 79548; 79549; 79550; 79553; 79556; 79560; 79561 79562; 79563; 79565; 79566; 79567; 79600; 79601; 79602; 79603; 79604; 79605 79606; 79608; 79697; 79698; 79699; 79713; 79720; 79721; 79733; 79738 79748; 79749; 79782; 79783.

18th District: 77000; 77001; 77002* (TX 29); 77003* (TX 29); 77004* (TX 25, TX 29); 77005* (TX 7, TX 22, TX 25); 77006* (TX 29); 77007* (TX 29); 77008* (TX 29); 77009* (TX 29); 77013* (TX 25, TX 29); 77016* (TX 29); 77017* (TX 25, TX 29); 77018* (TX 29); 77019* (TX 7, TX 29); 77020* (TX 29); 77021* (TX 25, TX 29); 77022* (TX 29); 77023* (TX 29); 77024* (TX 7, TX 29); 77025* (TX 22, TX 29); 77026* (TX 29); 77027* (TX 7); 77028* (TX 29); 77029* (TX 29); 77030* (TX 25); 77032* (TX 29); 77033* (TX 25); 77035* (TX 22, TX 25); 77037* (TX 29) 77038* (TX 29); 77039* (TX 29); 77040* (TX 7); 77041* (TX 7); 77044* (TX 9, TX 29); 77045* (TX 25); 77047* (TX 25); 77048* (TX 25); 77049* (TX 9, TX 25, TX 29); 77050* (TX 25); 77051* (TX 25); 77052* (TX 25); 77054* (TX 25); 77055* (TX 7, TX 29); 77056* (TX 7, TX 22); 77057* (TX 7, TX 22); 77060* (TX 29); 77061* (TX 29); 77066* (TX 7, TX 8); 77067* (TX 7); 77070* (TX 7, TX 8) 77073* (TX 8); 77074* (TX 22, TX 25); 77075* (TX 22, TX 25, TX 29); 77076* (TX 29); 77078* (TX 29); 77080* (TX 7, TX 29); 77081* (TX 7, TX 22); 77086* (TX 7); 77087* (TX 29); 77088* (TX 7); 77090* (TX 7, TX 8); 77091* (TX 7, TX 29); 77092* (TX 7, TX 29); 77093* (TX 29); 77095* (TX 7); 77097; 77098* (TX 7); 77201; 77202; 77203; 77204; 77205; 77206; 77208; 77209; 77210 77212 77216; 77220; 77221; 77226; 77228; 77229; 77230; 77233; 77238; 77243; 77251 77252; 77253; 77254; 77255; 77260; 77263; 77266; 77267; 77271; 77275; 77284 77288;

77291; 77292; 77297; 77298; 77299; 77315; 77338* (TX 8); 77396* (TX 8, TX 9, TX 29); 77401* (TX 7, TX 22, TX 25).

19th District: 79001; 79009; 79010; 79013; 79015; 79016; 79018; 79022; 79025 79029; 79033; 79035; 79040* (OK 6, TN 19); 79044; 79045; 79051; 79053; 79058 79062* (TX 15); 79070; 79081; 79084; 79086; 79087; 79091; 79092; 79093; 79098 79101* (TX 13); 79103* (TX 13); 79109* (TX 13); 79110* (TX 13); 79118; 79119 79121* (TX 13); 79311* (TX 13); 79313; 79314; 79316; 79320; 79323; 79324 79325; 79329; 79336; 79338; 79342; 79344; 79345; 79346; 79347; 79350; 79353 79355; 79358; 79359; 79360; 79363; 79364* (TX 13); 79366* (TX 13); 79367 79372; 79376; 79378; 79379; 79380; 79382; 79400; 79401* (TX 13); 79402; 79403* (TX 13); 79404* (TX 13); 79405; 79406; 79407* (TX 13); 79408; 79409; 79410 79411; 79412; 79413; 79414; 79415* (TX 13); 79416; 79423* (TX 13); 79424* (TX 13); 79430; 79452; 79453; 79457; 79464; 79489; 79490; 79491; 79493; 79499 79701* (TX 21, TX 23); 79703* (TX 21, TX 23); 79705* (TX 21, TX 23); 79706 79707* (TX 21); 79708; 79709; 79714; 79741; 79758 79759; 79761* (TX 23) 79762; 79763* (TX 23); 79764; 79765* (TX 23); 79766* (TX 23); 79768; 79776.

20th District: 78002; 78039* (TX 23); 78052* (TX 23); 78069; 78073* (TX 28) 78200; 78201; 78202* (TX 28); 78203* (TX 28); 78204* (TX 28); 78205* (TX 28) 78206; 78207* (TX 28); 78208; 78209* (TX 21); 78210* (TX 28); 78211* (TX 28) 78212* (TX 21); 78213* (TX 21, TX 23); 78215* (TX 21, TX 28); 78216* (TX 21, TX 23); 78217* (TX 21); 78218* (TX 21, TX 23, TX 28); 78219* (TX 28); 78221* (TX 21, TX 23, TX 28); 78225* (TX 28); 78226; 78227; 78228; 78229* (TX 23) 78230* (TX 23); 78233* (TX 21, TX 28); 78234; 78236; 78237; 78238* (TX 23) 78239* (TX 21, TX 28); 78240* (TX 23); 78241; 78242; 78243; 78245* (TX 23) 78246; 78247* (TX 21, TX 23); 78250* (TX 23); 78251* (TX 23); 78252; 78253* (TX 23); 78258* (TX 21, TX 23, TX 28); 78264* (TX 21, TX 28); 78266; 78268 78278; 78279; 78285; 78286; 78287; 78289; 78291; 78292; 78293; 78294; 78295 78298; 78298; 78299.

21st District: 76527; 76537; 76820; 76825* (TX 11); 76831; 76841; 76842 76848; 76849; 76850; 76854; 76856; 76859; 76869; 76874; 76883; 76885; 76901* (TX 17); 76902; 76903* (TX 17); 76904* (TX 17); 76905* (TX 17); 76906; 76908 76909; 76930; 76934; 76935; 76936; 76939; 76940; 76941; 76951; 76955; 76957 76958; 78003; 78004; 78006* (TX 23); 78010; 78013; 78024; 78027; 78028 78029; 78055; 78058; 78063; 78070; 78074; 78108* (TX 28); 78115; 78121* (TX 28); 78123* (TX 28); 78124* (TX 28); 78130* (TX 28); 78131; 78132* (TX 28) 78133* (TX 28); 78148* (TX 28); 78154* (TX 28); 78155* (TX 28); 78156; 78163 78209* (TX 20); 78212* (TX 20); 78213* (TX 20); 78215* (TX 20, TX 28) 78216* (TX 20, TX 23); 78217* (TX 20); 78218* (TX 20, TX 23, TX 28); 78221* (TX 20, TX 23, TX 28); 78223* (TX 28); 78231* (TX 23); 78232* (TX 23); 78233* (TX 20, TX 28); 78239* (TX 20, TX 28); 78247* (TX 20, TX 23); 78256* (TX 23) 78258* (TX 20, TX 23, TX 28); 78259; 78260* (TX 23); 78261; 78262; 78264* (TX 20, TX 28); 78270; 78605; 78607; 78608; 78609; 78611; 78613; 78618 78623; 78624; 78626* (TX 14); 78628; 78631; 78638; 78639; 78641* (TX 10, TX 14) 78642; 78643; 78654; 78664; 78666* (TX 14); 78670; 78671; 78672; 78673; 78674 78675; 78680; 78681; 78717; 78727* (TX 10); 78728* (TX 10); 78729* (TX 10) 78750* (TX 10); 78759* (TX 10); 78761; 78833; 78873; 78879; 78883; 78885 79701* (TX 19, TX 23); 79702; 79703* (TX 19, TX 23); 79704; 79705* (TX 19, TX 23); 79707* (TX 19); 79710; 79711; 79739.

22nd District: 77005* (TX 7, TX 18, TX 25); 77025* (TX 18, TX 25); 77031* (TX 25); 77034* (TX 25, TX 29); 77035* (TX 18, TX 25); 77036* (TX 25); 77042* (TX 7, TX 25); 77056* (TX 7, TX 18); 77057* (TX 7, TX 18); 77058* (TX 9); 77059 77062* (TX 9); 77063* (TX 7, TX 25); 77072* (TX 7, TX 25); 77074* (TX 18, TX 25); 77075* (TX 18, TX 25, TX 29); 77077* (TX 7); 77081* (TX 7, TX 18); 77082* (TX 7); 77083* (TX 7); 77089* (TX 9, TX 25); 77096* (TX 25); 77099* (TX 25); 77231; 77235; 77236; 77237; 77265; 77272; 77277; 77281; 77401* (TX 7, TX 18, TX 25); 77402; 77406; 77411 77417; 77422* (TX 14); 77423* (TX 14); 77430* (TX 14); 77435* (TX 14); 77441; 77444* (TX 14); 77450* (TX 7); 77451; 77459* (TX 25); 77461; 77464; 77469; 77471; 77476 77477* (TX 25); 77478* (TX 25) 77479* (TX 25); 77481; 77485* (TX 14); 77487; 77489* (TX 25); 77494* (TX 7, TX 14); 77497; 77504* (TX 25, TX 29); 77505* (TX 25, TX 29) 77507* (TX 25) 77511* (TX 9); 77512; 77515* (TX 14); 77516; 77531* (TX 14); 77534 77541* (TX 14); 77545* (TX 25); 77546* (TX 9); 77566* (TX 14); 77571* (TX 25, TX 29) 77577; 77578; 77581; 77583* (TX 25); 77584; 77586; 77588; 77598* (TX 9, TX 25).

23rd District: 76932; 76943; 76950; 78006* (TX 21); 78009; 78016; 78023 78039* (TX 20); 78040; 78041; 78042; 78043; 78044; 78052* (TX 20); 78056 78059; 78066 78213* (TX 20, TX 21); 78216* (TX 20, TX 21); 78218* (TX 20, TX 21, TX 28); 78221* (TX 20, TX 21, TX 28); 78229* (TX 20); 78230* (TX 20); 78231* (TX 21); 78232* (TX 21); 78238* (TX 20); 78240* (TX 20); 78245* (TX 20); 78247* (TX 20, TX 21) 78248; 78249; 78250* (TX 20); 78251* (TX 20) 78253* (TX 20); 78254; 78255; 78256* (TX 21); 78257; 78258* (TX 20, TX 21, TX 28); 78260* (TX 21); 78269; 78288; 78344 78369; 78371; 78801; 78802; 78827 78828; 78829; 78830; 78832; 78834; 78835; 78836 78837; 78838; 78839; 78840 78841; 78842; 78843; 78847; 78850; 78851; 78852; 78853; 78860; 78861; 78870 78871; 78872; 78877; 78880; 78881; 78884; 78886; 79701* (TX 19, TX 21); 79703* (TX 19, TX 21); 79705* (TX 19, TX 21); 79712; 79718; 79719; 79730 79731 79734; 79735; 79740; 79742; 79743; 79744; 79745; 79752; 79754; 79755; 79756 79760; 79761* (TX 19); 79763* (TX 19); 79765* (TX 19); 79766* (TX 19); 79767 79769 79770; 79772; 79777; 79778; 79779; 79780; 79781; 79785; 79788; 79789; 79830 79831; 79832; 79834; 79837; 79839; 79842; 79843; 79845; 79846 79847; 79848; 79850 79851; 79852; 79854; 79855; 79906* (TX 16); 79908; 79916 79918; 79924* (TX 16); 79925* (TX 16); 79927* (TX 16); 79934* (TX 16); 79935* (TX 16); 79936* (TX 16); 79966; 79973; 79974; 79977.

24th District: 75050* (TX 6, TX 26, TX 30); 75051* (TX 30); 75052* (TX 6) 75101; 75102; 75104* (TX 30); 75105; 75110; 75115* (TX 6) 75116* (TX 30) 75119* (TX 6); 75120; 75123; 75125* (TX 5); 75134* (TX 5, TX 30); 75137* (TX 30); 75138; 75141* (TX 5); 75144; 75146* (TX 5, TX 30); 75151; 75152; 75153 75154* (TX 6); 75155; 75165* (TX 6); 75172; 75203* (TX 30); 75208* (TX 30) 75209* (TX 3, TX 5, TX 30); 75211* (TX 30); 75212* (TX 30); 75220* (TX 3, TX 26, TX 30); 75224* (TX 30); 75233* (TX 30); 75235* (TX 5, TX 30); 75236* (TX 30); 75237* (TX 30); 75245; 75247* (TX 30); 75249; 75303; 75310; 75323; 75326 75363; 75364; 76003; 76004; 76005; 76006* (TX 6); 76007; 76010* (TX 6); 76011* (TX 6); 76012* (TX 6, TX 12) 76013*

(TX 6); 76014* (TX 6); 76015* (TX 6) 76017* (TX 6); 76018* (TX 6); 76019; 76041; 76060* (TX 6); 76063* (TX 6, TX 12); 76064; 76065* (TX 6); 76096; 76100; 76103* (TX 6, TX 12); 76104* (TX 12) 76105* (TX 12); 76110* (TX 6, TX 12); 76112* (TX 6, TX 12); 76115* (TX 6, TX 12); 76119* (TX 12); 76130; 76134* (TX 6, TX 12); 76140* (TX 6, TX 12); 76191 76623; 76626; 76639; 76641; 76651; 76670; 76679; 76681.

25th District: 77004* (TX 18, TX 29); 77005* (TX 7, TX 18, TX 22); 77013* (TX 18, TX 29); 77017* (TX 18, TX 29); 77021* (TX 18, TX 29); 77025* (TX 18, TX 22); 77030* (TX 18); 77031* (TX 22); 77033* (TX 18); 77034* (TX 22, TX 29); 77035* (TX 18, TX 22); 77036* (TX 22); 77042* (TX 7, TX 22) 77045* (TX 18); 77047* (TX 18); 77048* (TX 18); 77049* (TX 9, TX 18, TX 29) 77051* (TX 18); 77053* (TX 18); 77054* (TX 18); 77063* (TX 7, TX 22); 77071; 77072* (TX 7, TX 22); 77074* (TX 18, TX 22); 77075* (TX 18, TX 22, TX 29); 77085; 77089* (TX 9, TX 22); 77096* (TX 22); 77099* (TX 7, TX 22); 77225; 77234; 77245 77274; 77289; 77401* (TX 7, TX 18, TX 22); 77459* (TX 22); 77477* (TX 22); 77478* (TX 22); 77489* (TX 22); 77501; 77502* (TX 29); 77503* (TX 29); 77504* (TX 22, TX 29); 77505* (TX 22, TX 29); 77506* (TX 29); 77507* (TX 22); 77508; 77520* (TX 9, TX 29); 77521* (TX 9, TX 29); 77522; 77530* (TX 29); 77532* (TX 8, TX 9); 77536* (TX 29); 77545* (TX 22); 77562* (TX 9) 22).

26th District: 75001; 75006; 75007; 75008; 75010; 75011; 75015; 75016; 75019* (TX 6) 75023* (TX 3); 75024; 75025* (TX 3); 75028; 75029; 75034; 75038* (TX 30); 75039* (TX 30); 75050* (TX 6, TX 24, TX 30); 75053; 75056; 75057; 75060* (TX 30); 75061* (TX 30); 75062* (TX 30); 75063* (TX 6, TX 30); 75065; 75067 75068* (TX 4); 75069* (TX 3, TX 4); 75070* (TX 4); 75075* (TX 3, TX 30) 75078* (TX 4); 75080* (TX 3, TX 30); 75081* (TX 3, TX 30); 75083; 75084 75085; 75093; 75220* (TX 3, TX 24, TX 30); 75229* (TX 3, TX 30); 75234* (TX 3, TX 30); 75240* (TX 30); 75243* (TX 3, TX 30); 75244* (TX 3, TX 30); 75248 75251* (TX 30); 75252* (TX 3, TX 30); 75253* (TX 5); 75287; 75379; 75380 75381; 76051* (TX 6); 76201* (TX 4, TX 13); 76205* (TX 4, TX 13); 76207 76208; 76226; 76247; 76259; 76262* (TX 6); 76299.

27th District: 78330; 78338; 78339; 78343; 78347; 78351; 78363* (TX 15) 78364; 78373; 78379; 78380; 78385; 78400; 78401; 78402; 78403; 78404; 78405 78406; 78407; 78408; 78409; 78410; 78411; 78412; 78413; 78414; 78415; 78416 78417; 78418; 78419; 78426; 78427; 78460; 78461; 78463; 78465; 78466; 78467 78468; 78469; 78470; 78471; 78472; 78473; 78474; 78475; 78476; 78477; 78478 78480; 78482; 78520; 78521; 78522; 78523; 78526; 78535; 78550; 78551; 78552 78559; 78566; 78567; 78568; 78575; 78578; 78586; 78590; 78592; 78593 78594; 78597; 78598.

28th District: 78001; 78005; 78007; 78008; 78011; 78012; 78014; 78017; 78019 78021; 78026; 78050; 78053; 78054; 78057; 78061; 78062; 78064; 78065; 78067 78072; 78073* (TX 20); 78076; 78101; 78108* (TX 21); 78109; 78112; 78114 78121* (TX 21); 78123 (TX 21); 78124* (TX 21); 78130* (TX 21); 78132* (TX 21); 78133* (TX 21); 78143; 78147; 78148* (TX 21); 78150; 78152; 78154* (TX 21); 78155* (TX 21); 78160; 78161; 78202* (TX 20); 78203* (TX 20); 78204* (TX 20); 78205* (TX 20); 78207* (TX 20); 78210* (TX 20); 78211* (TX 20); 78214 78215* (TX 20, TX 21); 78218* (TX 20, TX 21, TX 23); 78219* (TX 20); 78220 78221* (TX 20, TX 21, TX 23); 78222; 78223* (TX 21); 78224; 78225* (TX 20) 78233* (TX 20, TX 21); 78235; 78239* (TX 20, TX 21); 78244; 78258* (TX 20, TX 21, TX 23); 78264* (TX 20, TX 21); 78265; 78275; 78280; 78283; 78284 78332; 78333; 78341; 78342; 78349; 78357; 78360; 78361; 78372* (TX 15); 78375 78376; 78384; 78536; 78545; 78547; 78548; 78564; 78582; 78584; 78585; 78588 78591.

29th District: 77002* (TX 18); 77003* (TX 18); 77004* (TX 18, TX 25); 77006* (TX 18); 77007* (TX 18); 77008* (TX 18); 77009* (TX 18); 77010; 77011; 77012 77013* (TX 18, TX 25); 77015* (TX 29); 77016* (TX 18); 77017* (TX 18, TX 25) 77018* (TX 18); 77019* (TX 7, TX 18); 77020* (TX 18); 77021* (TX 18, TX 25) 77022* (TX 18); 77023* (TX 18); 77024* (TX 7, TX 18); 77026* (TX 18); 77028* (TX 18); 77029* (TX 18); 77032* (TX 18); 77034* (TX 22, TX 25); 77037* (TX 18); 77038* (TX 18); 77039* (TX 18); 77043* (TX 7); 77044* (TX 9, TX 18); 77047* (TX 9, TX 18, TX 25); 77050* (TX 18); 77055* (TX 7, TX 18); 77060* (TX 18); 77061* (TX 18); 77075* (TX 18, TX 22, TX 25); 77076* (TX 18); 77078* (TX 18); 77080* (TX 7, TX 18); 77087* (TX 18); 77091* (TX 7, TX 18); 77092* (TX 7, TX 18); 77093* (TX 18); 77095* (TX 7, TX 18); 77207; 77213; 77217; 77222 77223; 77248; 77261; 77262; 77270; 77287; 77293; 77396* (TX 8, TX 9, TX 18) 77502* (TX 25); 77503* (TX 25); 77504* (TX 22, TX 25); 77505* (TX 22, TX 25) 77506* (TX 25); 77520* (TX 9, TX 25); 77521* (TX 9, TX 25); 77530* (TX 25) 77536* (TX 25); 77547; 77571* (TX 22, TX 25); 77587* (TX 25).

30th District: 75014; 75017; 75038* (TX 26); 75039* (TX 26); 75042* (TX 3, TX 5); 75050* (TX 6, TX 24, TX 26); 75051* (TX 24); 75054; 75060* (TX 26); 75061* (TX 26); 75062* (TX 26); 75063* (TX 6, TX 26); 75074* (TX 3); 75075* (TX 3, TX 26); 75080* (TX 3, TX 26); 75081* (TX 3, TX 26); 75082* (TX 3); 75104* (TX 24); 75115* (TX 24); 75116* (TX 24); 75134* (TX 5, TX 24); 75137* (TX 24); 75146* (TX 5, TX 24); 75149* (TX 3, TX 5); 75180* (TX 5); 75200; 75201* (TX 5); 75202; 75203* (TX 24); 75204* (TX 3, TX 5); 75207; 75208* (TX 24); 75209* (TX 3, TX 5, TX 24); 75210; 75211* (TX 24); 75212* (TX 24); 75214* (TX 3, TX 5); 75215; 75216; 75217* (TX 5); 75219* (TX 3, TX 5); 75220* (TX 3, TX 24, TX 26); 75221; 75222; 75223* (TX 5); 75224* (TX 24); 75225* (TX 3); 75226* (TX 5); 75227* (TX 5); 75228* (TX 3, TX 5); 75229* (TX 3, TX 26); 75230* (TX 3) 75231* (TX 3); 75232; 75233* (TX 24); 75234* (TX 3, TX 26); 75235* (TX 5, TX 24); 75236* (TX 24); 75237* (TX 24); 75238* (TX 3, TX 5); 75239* (TX 5) 75240* (TX 26); 75241* (TX 5); 75242; 75243* (TX 3, TX 26); 75244* (TX 3, TX 26); 75246* (TX 5); 75247* (TX 24); 75250; 75251* (TX 26); 75252* (TX 3, TX 26); 75258; 75260; 75261; 75262; 75263; 75264; 75265; 75266; 75270; 75277 75283; 75284; 75285; 75286; 75295; 75301; 75312; 75313; 75315; 75320; 75336 75339; 75346; 75350; 75353; 75354; 75356; 75357; 75368; 75371; 75372; 75373 75374; 75376; 75382; 75387; 75388; 75389; 75390; 75391; 75392; 75393; 75394 75395; 75396; 75397; 75398.

Utah

1st District: 82930* (UT 3, WY 1); 84010; 84011; 84014; 84015; 84016; 84022 84025; 84028; 84029; 84034; 84037; 84038; 84040; 84041; 84044* (UT 3); 84054 84056; 84064;

84067; 84069; 84071; 84074; 84075; 84080; 84083; 84086; 84087 84116* (UT 2, UT 3); 84153; 84201; 84244; 84301; 84302; 84304; 84305; 84306 84307; 84308; 84309; 84310; 84311; 84312; 84313; 84314; 84315; 84316; 84317 84318; 84319; 84320; 84321; 84322; 84323; 84324; 84325; 84326; 84327; 84328 84329; 84330; 84331; 84332; 84333; 84334; 84335; 84336; 84337; 84338; 84339 84340; 84400; 84401; 84402; 84403; 84404; 84405; 84407; 84408; 84409; 84412 84414; 84624; 84628; 84631; 84635; 84636; 84637; 84638; 84639; 84640; 84644 84645; 84648; 84649; 84650; 84656; 84713; 84714; 84719 84720; 84721; 84722 84725; 84728; 84731; 84733; 84737; 84738; 84742 84745; 84746; 84751; 84752; 84753 84756; 84757; 84760; 84761; 84763; 84765; 84767; 84770; 84771; 84772 84774; 84779; 84780; 84781; 84782; 84783.

2nd District: 84020; 84047; 84065* (UT 3); 84070; 84084; 84088; 84090; 84091 84092; 84093; 84094; 84100; 84101* (UT 3); 84102; 84103; 84104* (UT 3); 84105 84106; 84107; 84108; 84109; 84110; 84111; 84112; 84113; 84114; 84115* (UT 3) 84116* (UT 1, UT 3); 84117; 84118* (UT 3); 84119* (UT 3); 84121; 84122; 84123* (UT 3); 84124; 84125; 84132; 84133; 84134; 84137; 84138; 84140; 84142; 84143 84144; 84145; 84147; 84148; 84150; 84151; 84152; 84157; 84158; 84165; 84180 84190; 84199.

3rd District: 82930* (UT 1, WY 1); 82935* (WY 1); 84001; 84002; 84003; 84004 84006; 84007; 84008; 84012; 84013; 84017; 84018; 84021; 84023; 84024; 84026 84027; 84030; 84031; 84032; 84033; 84035; 84036; 84039; 84042; 84043; 84044* (UT 1); 84046; 84049; 84050; 84051; 84052; 84053; 84055; 84057; 84058; 84059 84060; 84061; 84062; 84063; 84065* (UT 2); 84066; 84068; 84072; 84073; 84076 84078; 84079; 84082; 84085; 84101* (UT 2); 84104* (UT 2); 84115* (UT 2) 84116* (UT 1, UT 2); 84118* (UT 2); 84119* (UT 2); 84120; 84123* (UT 2) 84126; 84127; 84130; 84131; 84135; 84136; 84139; 84141; 84170; 84184; 84189 84501; 84510; 84511; 84512; 84513; 84515; 84516; 84518; 84520; 84521; 84522 84523; 84525; 84526; 84527; 84528; 84529; 84530; 84531; 84532; 84533; 84534 84535; 84536; 84537; 84539; 84540; 84542; 84601; 84602; 84603; 84604; 84605 84606; 84620; 84621; 84622; 84623; 84626; 84627; 84629; 84630; 84632; 84633 84634; 84642; 84643; 84646; 84647; 84651; 84652; 84653; 84654; 84655; 84657 84660; 84662; 84663; 84664; 84665; 84667; 84701; 84710; 84711; 84712; 84715 84716; 84717; 84718; 84723; 84724; 84726; 84729; 84730; 84732; 84734; 84735 84736; 84739; 84740; 84741; 84743; 84744; 84747; 84749; 84750; 84754; 84755 84758; 84759; 84762; 84764; 84766; 84773; 84775; 84776; 84784.

Vermont

At Large: 05001; 05009; 05030; 05031; 05032; 05033; 05034; 05035; 05036 05037; 05038; 05039; 05040; 05041; 05042; 05043; 05044; 05045; 05046; 05047 05048; 05049; 05050; 05051; 05052; 05053; 05054; 05055; 05056; 05058; 05059 05060; 05061; 05062; 05065; 05067; 05068; 05069; 05070; 05071; 05072; 05073 05074; 05075; 05076; 05077; 05079; 05081; 05083; 05084; 05085; 05086; 05088 05089; 05091; 05101; 05141; 05142; 05143; 05144; 05146; 05148; 05149; 05150 05151; 05152; 05153; 05154; 05155; 05156; 05158; 05159; 05161; 05201; 05250 05251; 05252; 05253; 05254; 05255; 05257; 05260; 05261; 05262; 05301; 05302 05303; 05304; 05340; 05341; 05342; 05343; 05344; 05345; 05346; 05350; 05351 05352; 05353; 05354; 05355; 05356; 05357; 05358; 05359; 05360; 05361; 05362 05363; 05401; 05402; 05403; 05404; 05405; 05406; 05407; 05439; 05440; 05441 05442; 05443; 05444; 05445; 05446; 05447; 05448; 05449; 05450; 05451; 05452 05453; 05454; 05455; 05456; 05457; 05458; 05459; 05460; 05461; 05462; 05463 05464; 05465; 05466; 05468; 05469; 05470; 05471; 05472; 05473; 05474; 05476 05477; 05478; 05479; 05481; 05482; 05483; 05485; 05486; 05487; 05488; 05489 05490; 05491; 05492; 05494; 05495; 05601; 05602; 05603; 05604; 05609; 05620 05633; 05640; 05641; 05647; 05648; 05649; 05650; 05651; 05652; 05653; 05654 05655; 05656; 05657; 05658; 05660; 05661; 05662; 05663; 05664; 05665; 05666 05667; 05669; 05670; 05671; 05672; 05673; 05674; 05675; 05676; 05677; 05678 05679; 05680; 05681; 05682; 05701; 05702; 05730; 05731; 05732; 05733; 05734 05735; 05736; 05737; 05738; 05739; 05740; 05741; 05742; 05743; 05744; 05745 05746; 05747; 05748; 05750; 05751; 05753; 05757; 05758; 05759; 05760; 05761 05762; 05763; 05764; 05765; 05766; 05767; 05768; 05769; 05770; 05772; 05773 05774; 05775; 05776; 05777; 05778; 05819; 05820; 05821; 05822; 05823; 05824 05825; 05826; 05827; 05828; 05829; 05830; 05832; 05833; 05836; 05837; 05838 05839; 05840; 05841; 05842; 05843; 05845; 05846; 05847; 05848; 05849; 05850 05851; 05853; 05855; 05857; 05858; 05859; 05860; 05861; 05862; 05863; 05866 05867; 05868; 05871; 05872; 05873; 05874; 05875; 05901; 05902; 05903; 05904 05905; 05906; 05907.

Virginia

1st District: 22401; 22402; 22403; 22404; 22405; 22406; 22407; 22408; 22421 22427; 22428; 22430; 22432; 22435; 22442; 22443; 22446; 22448; 22451; 22456 22463; 22469; 22471; 22473; 22477; 22480; 22481; 22482; 22485; 22488; 22501 22503; 22505; 22507; 22511; 22513; 22514; 22517; 22520; 22523; 22524; 22526 22528; 22529; 22535; 22538; 22539; 22540; 22544; 22545; 22546; 22547 22549; 22552; 22553* (VA 7); 22554* (VA 10); 22555; 22558; 22565; 22576 22577; 22578; 22579; 22580; 22581; 23001; 23003; 23005* (VA 7); 23013; 23016 23017; 23018; 23020; 23021; 23025; 23031; 23032; 23035; 23043; 23045; 23047* (VA 7); 23050; 23056; 23060* (VA 3, VA 7); 23061; 23062; 23064; 23066; 23068 23069; 23070; 23071; 23072; 23076; 23079; 23080; 23081; 23089* (VA 3); 23090 23092; 23107; 23109; 23111* (VA 7); 23114; 23118; 23119; 23122; 23125; 23127 23128; 23130; 23131; 23138; 23142; 23149; 23154; 23155; 23157; 23162; 23163 23168; 23169; 23175; 23176; 23178; 23179; 23180; 23183; 23184; 23185* (VA 3) 23186; 23187; 23188; 23190; 23191; 23301; 23302; 23303; 23306; 23307; 23308 23310; 23313; 23316; 23336; 23337; 23341; 23345; 23347; 23350; 23354; 23356 23357; 23358; 23359; 23389; 23395; 23396; 23398; 23399; 23401; 23403; 23404 23405; 23407; 23408; 23409; 23410; 23412; 23413; 23414; 23415; 23416; 23417 23418; 23419; 23420; 23421; 23422; 23423; 23426; 23427; 23429; 23440; 23441 23442; 23443; 23480; 23482; 23483; 23484; 23486; 23488; 23601* (VA 3); 23602* (VA 3); 23603* (VA 3); 23605* (VA 3); 23606; 23607* (VA 3); 23612; 23651; 23653; 23661* (VA 3); 23662; 23663* (VA 3); 23664* (VA 3); 23665; 23666* (VA 3); 23668; 23669* (VA 3); 23670; 23690; 23691; 23692; 23693; 23694; 23696.

2nd District: 23450; 23451; 23452; 23454; 23455; 23456* (VA 4); 23457; 23458 23459; 23460; 23461; 23462; 23463; 23464* (VA 4); 23465; 23466; 23467; 23468 23479; 23502* (VA 3); 23503; 23504* (VA 3); 23505* (VA 3); 23507* (VA 3) 23508* (VA 3); 23509* (VA 3); 23510* (VA 3); 23511; 23512; 23513* (VA 3) 23515* (VA 3); 23517* (VA 3); 23518* (VA 3); 23519; 23520; 23521; 23529.

3rd District: 22436; 22437; 22438; 22439; 22454; 22460; 22461; 22472; 22476 22504; 22509; 22548; 22559; 22560; 22570; 22572; 23009; 23011; 23023; 23029 23030; 23037; 23060* (VA 1, VA 7); 23075* (VA 7); 23085; 23086; 23089* (VA 1); 23091; 23104; 23106; 23108; 23110; 23115; 23124; 23126; 23137; 23140; 23141 23147; 23148; 23150* (VA 7); 23156; 23161; 23177; 23181; 23185* (VA 1); 23201; 23202; 23203; 23204; 23205; 23206; 23207; 23208; 23209; 23210; 23211; 23212 23213; 23214; 23215; 23216; 23217; 23218; 23219* (VA 7); 23220* (VA 7); 23221* (VA 7); 23222* (VA 7); 23223* (VA 7); 23224* (VA 7); 23225* (VA 7); 23227* (VA 7); 23228* (VA 7); 23230* (VA 7); 23231* (VA 7); 23232; 23234* (VA 7); 23238 23240; 23241; 23249; 23255; 23261; 23277; 23282; 23292; 23298; 23324* (VA 4) 23325* (VA 4); 23435* (VA 4); 23500; 23501; 23502* (VA 2); 23504* (VA 2); 23505* (VA 2); 23506; 23507* (VA 2); 23508* (VA 2); 23509* (VA 2); 23510* (VA 2); 23513* (VA 2); 23514; 23517* (VA 2); 23518* (VA 2); 23523* (VA 4); 23530 23600; 23601* (VA 1); 23602* (VA 1); 23603* (VA 1); 23604; 23605* (VA 1); 23607* (VA 1); 23609; 23628; 23629; 23630; 23631; 23632; 23661* (VA 1); 23663* (VA 1); 23664* (VA 1); 23666* (VA 1); 23667; 23669* (VA 1); 23701* (VA 4) 23702* (VA 4); 23703* (VA 4); 23704* (VA 4); 23707* (VA 4); 23708; 23709 23803* (VA 4); 23805* (VA 4); 23806; 23839; 23846; 23860* (VA 4); 23875* (VA 4); 23881* (VA 4); 23883; 23899.

4th District: 22942* (VA 7); 23002; 23014; 23024* (VA 7); 23038* (VA 5) 23039; 23042; 23054; 23063; 23065; 23067; 23083; 23084* (VA 5); 23093; 23101 23102; 23103; 23105; 23113* (VA 7); 23117; 23120* (VA 7); 23129; 23139; 23146* (VA 7); 23153; 23160; 23170; 23233* (VA 7); 23304; 23314; 23315; 23320; 23321; 23322; 23323; 23324* (VA 3); 23325* (VA 3); 23326; 23327; 23328; 23397; 23424; 23430; 23432; 23433; 23434 23435* (VA 3); 23436; 23437; 23438; 23439; 23456* (VA 2); 23464* (VA 2); 23481; 23487; 23523* (VA 3); 23700; 23701* (VA 3); 23702* (VA 3); 23703* (VA 3); 23704* (VA 3); 23705; 23707* (VA 3); 23801; 23803* (VA 3); 23804; 23805* (VA 3); 23821; 23822; 23824* (VA 5); 23827; 23828; 23829; 23830; 23831* (VA 7); 23832* (VA 7); 23833; 23834* (VA 7); 23837; 23840; 23841; 23842; 23843; 23844; 23845; 23847; 23850; 23851; 23856; 23857; 23859; 23860* (VA 3); 23866; 23867; 23868; 23870; 23872; 23873; 23874 23875* (VA 3); 23876; 23878; 23879; 23881* (VA 3); 23882; 23884; 23885; 23887 23888; 23889; 23890; 23893; 23894; 23897; 23898; 23920* (VA 5); 23922; 23930 23955.

5th District: 22900; 22901* (VA 7); 22902; 22903* (VA 7); 22905; 22906; 22908 22910; 22920; 22922; 22924; 22929; 22931; 22932* (VA 7); 22937; 22938; 22943 22946; 22947; 22949; 22954; 22958; 22959; 22963; 22964; 22967; 22969; 22971 22974; 22976; 23004; 23022; 23027; 23038* (VA 4); 23040; 23055; 23084* (VA 4) 23123; 23824* (VA 4); 23901; 23909; 23911; 23915; 23917; 23919; 23920* (VA 4) 23921; 23923; 23924; 23927; 23934; 23935; 23936; 23937; 23938; 23939; 23941; 23942; 23943; 23944; 23947; 23950; 23952; 23954; 23958; 23959; 23960; 23962; 23963; 23964; 23966; 23967; 23968; 23970 23973; 23974; 23976; 24053; 24054; 24055; 24065* (VA 6); 24067; 24069; 24076 24078; 24082; 24088; 24089; 24092; 24095* (VA 6); 24102; 24104; 24112; 24113 24114; 24115; 24120; 24121* (VA 6); 24122* (VA 6); 24133; 24137; 24139; 24146 24148; 24151; 24161; 24165; 24168; 24171; 24174; 24176; 24177; 24184; 24185; 24464; 24501* (VA 6); 24502* (VA 6); 24503* (VA 6); 24504* (VA 6); 24517; 24520; 24522; 24523* (VA 6); 24526 24527; 24528; 24529; 24530; 24531; 24534; 24535; 24536; 24538; 24539; 24540 24541; 24543; 24544; 24549; 24550; 24551; 24553* (VA 6, VA 9); 24554; 24556 24557; 24558; 24562; 24563; 24565; 24566; 24569; 24570; 24571; 24576; 24577 24580; 24581; 24585; 24586; 24588; 24589; 24590; 24592; 24593; 24594; 24596 24597; 24598; 24599.

6th District: 22801* (VA 10); 22807; 22811; 22812; 22815* (VA 10); 22820 22821; 22827* (VA 10); 22830; 22831; 22832; 22834; 22840; 22841; 22843; 22846 22848; 22849* (VA 10); 22850; 22853* (VA 10); 22939; 22951; 22952; 22980; 24000 24001; 24002; 24003; 24004; 24005; 24006; 24007; 24008; 24009; 24010 24011; 24012; 24013; 24014; 24015; 24016; 24017; 24018* (VA 9); 24019; 24020; 24022; 24023; 24024; 24025; 24026; 24027; 24028; 24029; 24030; 24031; 24032; 24033; 24034; 24035; 24036 24037; 24038; 24040; 24041; 24042; 24043; 24044 24045; 24046; 24048; 24050; 24064; 24065* (VA 5); 24066; 24070* (VA 9); 24077; 24083; 24085; 24090; 24095* (VA 5); 24101; 24121* (VA 5); 24122* (VA 5); 24130; 24153* (VA 9); 24156; 24157; 24175; 24178 24179; 24401; 24407; 24411; 24412; 24413; 24415; 24416; 24421; 24422; 24426 24430; 24431; 24432; 24433; 24435; 24437; 24438; 24439; 24440; 24441; 24442; 24444; 24445; 24448; 24449; 24450; 24457; 24458; 24459; 24463; 24465; 24467; 24468; 24469; 24471; 24472; 24473; 24474; 24475; 24476; 24477; 24479; 24482; 24483; 24484; 24485 24486; 24487; 24501* (VA 5); 24502* (VA 5); 24503* (VA 5); 24504* (VA 5) 24505; 24506; 24512; 24513; 24514; 24515; 24521; 24523* (VA 5); 24533; 24553* (VA 5, VA 9); 24555; 24572; 24574; 24578; 24579; 24595.

7th District: 22433; 22502; 22508; 22534; 22542; 22553* (VA 1); 22567; 22568 22701; 22709; 22711; 22713; 22714; 22715; 22718; 22719; 22721; 22722; 22723 22724; 22725; 22726; 22727; 22729; 22730; 22731; 22732; 22733; 22735; 22736 22737; 22738; 22740* (VA 10); 22741; 22743; 22748; 22901* (VA 5); 22903* (VA 5); 22904; 22907; 22909 22923; 22932* (VA 5); 22935; 22936; 22940; 22942* (VA 4); 22945; 22948; 22953 22957; 22960; 22965; 22968; 22972; 22973; 22987; 22989; 23005* (VA 1); 23015 23024* (VA 4); 23047* (VA 1); 23058; 23060* (VA 1, VA 3); 23075* (VA 3); 23111* (VA 1); 23112; 23113* (VA 4); 23120* (VA 4); 23146* (VA 4); 23150* (VA 3); 23173; 23192 23200; 23219* (VA 3); 23220* (VA 3); 23221* (VA 3); 23222* (VA 3); 23223* (VA 3); 23224* (VA 3); 23225* (VA 3); 23226; 23227* (VA 3); 23228* (VA 3); 23229; 23230* (VA 3); 23231* (VA 3); 23233* (VA 4); 23234* (VA 3); 23235; 23236; 23237; 23242 23250; 23260; 23266; 23269; 23270; 23272; 23273; 23274; 23275; 23276; 23278 23279; 23280; 23284; 23285; 23286; 23288; 23290; 23291; 23293; 23294; 23297; 23831* (VA 4) 23832* (VA 4); 23834* (VA 4).

8th District: 22003* (VA 11); 22015* (VA 11); 22039* (VA 10, VA 11); 22040 22042* (VA 11); 22043* (VA 11); 22044* (VA 11); 22046* (VA 11); 22047; 22060 22079* (VA 11); 22101* (VA 10, VA 11); 22103; 22106; 22121; 22122; 22125 22150* (VA 11); 22151* (VA 11); 22152* (VA 11); 22153* (VA 11); 22156; 22199 22200; 22201; 22202; 22203; 22204* (VA 11); 22205; 22206; 22207; 22209; 22210; 22211; 22212; 22213; 22214; 22215; 22216; 22217; 22218; 22219; 22222; 22223 22225; 22226; 22227; 22229; 22234; 22300; 22301; 22302* (VA 11); 22303; 22304; 22305; 22306; 22307; 22308;

22309; 22310; 22311* (VA 11); 22312* (VA 11) 22313; 22314; 22320; 22321; 22331; 22332; 22333; 22334; 22336.

9th District: 24018* (VA 6); 24058; 24059; 24060; 24061; 24062; 24063; 24068 24070* (VA 6); 24072; 24073; 24079; 24084; 24086; 24087; 24091; 24093; 24094 24105; 24111; 24124; 24126; 24127; 24128; 24129; 24131; 24132; 24134; 24136 24138; 24141; 24142; 24143; 24147; 24149; 24150; 24153* (VA 6); 24162; 24167 24201; 24203; 24209; 24210; 24215; 24216; 24217; 24218; 24219; 24220; 24221 24224; 24225; 24226; 24228; 24230; 24236; 24237; 24239; 24243; 24244; 24245 24246; 24248; 24249; 24250; 24251; 24256; 24258; 24260; 24263; 24265; 24266 24269; 24270; 24271; 24272; 24273; 24277; 24279; 24280; 24281; 24282; 24283 24285; 24289; 24290; 24292; 24293; 24301; 24311; 24312; 24313; 24314; 24315 24316; 24317; 24318; 24319; 24321; 24322; 24323; 24324; 24325; 24326; 24327 24328; 24330; 24333; 24340; 24343; 24347; 24348; 24350; 24351; 24352; 24354; 24360; 24361; 24363; 24366; 24368; 24370; 24373; 24374; 24375; 24377; 24378 24379; 24380; 24381; 24382; 24553* (VA 5, VA 6); 24601; 24602; 24603; 24604 24605; 24606; 24607; 24608; 24609; 24612; 24613; 24614; 24618; 24619; 24620 24622; 24624; 24627; 24628; 24630; 24631; 24633; 24634; 24635; 24637; 24639 24640; 24641; 24646; 24647; 24649; 24651; 24656; 24657; 24658; 24659; 37642* (TN 1).

10th District: 20041; 20165; 20166; 20167; 22001; 22002; 22010; 22011; 22012 22013; 22014; 22016; 22017; 22018; 22019; 22020* (VA 11); 22021; 22022; 22024* (VA 11); 22025; 22026* (VA 11); 22030* (VA 11); 22033* (VA 11); 22036; 22039* (VA 8, VA 11); 22065; 22066; 22067; 22068; 22069; 22070* (VA 11); 22071* (VA 11); 22075; 22078; 22080; 22082; 22101* (VA 8, VA 11); 22102* (VA 11); 22109 22110; 22111* (VA 11); 22115; 22117; 22120; 22123; 22124* (VA 11); 22128 22129; 22130; 22131; 22132; 22140; 22141; 22170; 22171; 22172* (VA 11); 22176 22181* (VA 11); 22182* (VA 11); 22186; 22190; 22192* (VA 11); 22193* (VA 11) 22554* (VA 1); 22601; 22602; 22603; 22604; 22610; 22611; 22620; 22622; 22623 22624; 22625; 22626; 22627; 22630; 22637; 22638; 22639; 22640; 22641; 22642 22643; 22644; 22645; 22646; 22649; 22650; 22651; 22652; 22654; 22655; 22656 22657; 22660; 22663; 22664; 22712; 22716; 22720; 22728; 22734; 22739; 22740* (VA 7); 22742; 22746; 22747; 22749; 22801* (VA 6); 22810; 22815* (VA 6); 22824; 22827* (VA 6); 22833; 22835; 22842; 22844; 22845; 22847; 22849* (VA 6); 22851; 22853* (VA 6).

11th District: 22003* (VA 8); 22009; 22015* (VA 8); 22020* (VA 10); 22024* (VA 10); 22026* (VA 10); 22027; 22030* (VA 10); 22031; 22032; 22033* (VA 10) 22035; 22037; 22038; 22039* (VA 8, VA 10); 22041; 22042* (VA 8); 22043* (VA 8); 22044* (VA 8); 22046* (VA 8); 22070* (VA 10); 22071* (VA 10); 22079* (VA 8); 22081; 22090; 22091; 22092; 22093; 22094; 22095; 22096; 22101* (VA 8, VA 10); 22102* (VA 10); 22111* (VA 10); 22116; 22118; 22119; 22124* (VA 10) 22134; 22135; 22150* (VA 8); 22151* (VA 8); 22152* (VA 8); 22153* (VA 8) 22158; 22159; 22160; 22161; 22172* (VA 10); 22180; 22181* (VA 10); 22182* (VA 10); 22183; 22184; 22185; 22191; 22192* (VA 10); 22193* (VA 10); 22194; 22204* (VA 8); 22302* (VA 8); 22311* (VA 8); 22312* (VA 8).

Washington

1st District: 98004* (WA 8); 98005* (WA 8); 98007* (WA 8); 98008* (WA 8) 98009; 98011; 98012* (WA 2); 98020; 98021* (WA 8); 98026* (WA 2); 98028 98031* (WA 8, WA 9); 98033; 98034; 98036; 98037* (WA 2); 98039; 98043; 98046 98052* (WA 8); 98061; 98072* (WA 8); 98073; 98082; 98083; 98103* (WA 7) 98110; 98117* (WA 7); 98133* (WA 7); 98155* (WA 7); 98160; 98161; 98177 98204* (WA 2); 98208* (WA 2); 98272* (WA 2); 98290* (WA 2); 98310* (WA 6) 98312* (WA 6); 98314; 98315; 98340; 98342; 98345; 98346; 98364; 98370; 98380* (WA 6); 98383; 98392.

2nd District: 98012* (WA 1); 98026* (WA 1); 98037* (WA 1); 98200; 98201 98203; 98204* (WA 1); 98205; 98206; 98207; 98208* (WA 1); 98220; 98221; 98222 98223; 98225; 98226; 98227; 98230; 98232; 98233; 98235; 98236; 98237; 98238 98239; 98240; 98241; 98243; 98244; 98245; 98246; 98247; 98248; 98249; 98250 98251; 98252; 98253; 98255; 98256; 98257; 98258; 98259; 98260; 98261; 98262 98263; 98264; 98266; 98267; 98270; 98271; 98272* (WA 1); 98273; 98275; 98276 98277; 98278; 98279; 98280; 98281; 98283; 98284; 98286; 98287; 98290* (WA 1) 98291; 98292; 98293; 98294; 98295; 98297.

3rd District: 98330* (WA 8); 98336; 98355; 98356; 98361; 98377; 98501* (WA 9) 98502* (WA 9); 98503* (WA 9); 98505; 98506* (WA 9); 98512; 98513; 98516 98522; 98527; 98531; 98532; 98533; 98538; 98539; 98541; 98542; 98544; 98547 98554; 98556; 98557; 98559; 98561; 98564; 98565; 98568; 98570; 98572; 98577 98579* (WA 9); 98581; 98582; 98583; 98585; 98586; 98590; 98591; 98593; 98595 98596; 98599; 98601; 98602; 98603; 98604; 98605* (WA 4); 98606; 98607; 98609 98610; 98611; 98612; 98613* (WA 4); 98614; 98616; 98617; 98619* (WA 4); 98621 98622; 98623; 98624; 98625; 98626; 98628; 98629; 98631; 98632; 98635* (WA 4) 98637; 98638; 98639; 98640; 98641; 98642; 98643; 98644; 98645; 98647; 98648 98649; 98650; 98651; 98660; 98661; 98662; 98663; 98664; 98665; 98666; 98667 98668; 98670* (WA 4); 98671; 98672* (WA 4); 98673; 98674; 98675; 98682; 98684 98685; 98686.

4th District: 98068; 98605* (WA 3); 98613* (WA 3); 98619* (WA 3); 98620 98635* (WA 3); 98670* (WA 3); 98672* (WA 3); 98801; 98802; 98807; 98811 98812; 98813; 98814; 98815; 98816; 98817; 98819; 98821; 98822; 98823; 98824 98826; 98827; 98828; 98829; 98830; 98831; 98832; 98833; 98834; 98836; 98837 98840; 98841; 98843; 98844; 98845; 98846; 98847; 98848; 98849; 98850; 98851 98852; 98853; 98857; 98858; 98859; 98860; 98862; 98901; 98902; 98903; 98904 98907; 98908; 98909; 98920; 98921; 98922; 98923; 98925; 98926; 98929; 98930 98932; 98933; 98934; 98935; 98936; 98937; 98938; 98939; 98940; 98941; 98942 98943; 98944; 98946; 98947; 98948; 98950; 98951; 98952; 98953 99115; 99116; 99123; 99124; 99133; 99135; 99155; 99301* (WA 5) 99302; 99320; 99321; 99322; 99326; 99330; 99335; 99336; 99337; 99343; 99344* (WA 5); 99345; 99346; 99350; 99356; 99357.

5th District: 99001; 99003; 99004; 99005; 99006; 99008; 99009; 99011; 99012 99013; 99014; 99015; 99016; 99017; 99018; 99019; 99020; 99021; 99022; 99023 99025; 99026; 99027; 99028; 99029; 99030; 99031; 99032; 99033; 99034; 99036 99037; 99039; 99040; 99101; 99102; 99103; 99104; 99105; 99107; 99109; 99110 99111; 99113; 99114; 99117; 99118; 99119; 99121; 99122; 99125; 99126; 99127 99128; 99129; 99130; 99131; 99134;

99136; 99137; 99138; 99139; 99140; 99141 99143; 99144; 99146; 99147; 99148; 99149; 99150; 99151; 99152; 99153; 99154 99156; 99157; 99158; 99159; 99160; 99161; 99163; 99164; 99165; 99166; 99167 99169; 99170; 99171; 99173; 99174; 99176; 99179; 99180; 99181; 99185; 99200 99201; 99202; 99203; 99204; 99205; 99206; 99207; 99208; 99209; 99210; 99211 99212; 99213; 99214; 99215; 99216; 99218; 99219; 99220; 99223; 99228; 99251 99252; 99254; 99255; 99256; 99257; 99258; 99259; 99260; 99301* (WA 4); 99323 99324; 99327; 99328; 99329; 99332; 99333; 99341; 99344* (WA 4); 99347; 99348 99359; 99360; 99361; 99362; 99363; 99371; 99401; 99402; 99403.

6th District: 98303; 98305; 98310* (WA 1); 98312* (WA 1); 98320; 98322; 98324 98325; 98326; 98329; 98331; 98332; 98333; 98334; 98335; 98337; 98339; 98343 98349; 98350; 98351; 98353; 98357; 98358; 98359; 98362; 98365; 98366; 98368 98376; 98378; 98380* (WA 1); 98381; 98382; 98384; 98386; 98388; 98393; 98394 98395; 98398; 98401; 98402* (WA 9); 98403; 98404* (WA 9); 98405; 98406; 98407 98408* (WA 9); 98409; 98411; 98412; 98413; 98415; 98416; 98418; 98421* (WA 9) 98433; 98442; 98444* (WA 9); 98450; 98455; 98460; 98464; 98465; 98466; 98467 98477; 98494; 98497; 98498* (WA 9); 98499* (WA 9); 98520; 98524; 98526; 98528 98535; 98536; 98537; 98546; 98548; 98550; 98552; 98555; 98560; 98562; 98563 98566; 98569; 98571; 98575; 98584; 98587; 98588; 98592.

7th District: 98013; 98055* (WA 8, WA 9); 98060; 98070; 98100; 98101; 98102 98103* (WA 1); 98104; 98105; 98106* (WA 9); 98107; 98108* (WA 9); 98109 98111; 98112; 98114; 98115; 98116; 98117* (WA 1); 98118; 98119; 98121; 98122 98124; 98125; 98126* (WA 9); 98129; 98130; 98131; 98132; 98133* (WA 1); 98134 98136; 98140; 98144; 98145; 98146* (WA 9); 98150; 98151; 98154; 98155* (WA 1) 98164; 98168* (WA 9); 98171; 98174; 98178* (WA 9); 98181; 98184; 98185; 98191 98195; 98199.

8th District: 98002* (WA 9); 98004* (WA 1); 98005* (WA 1); 98006; 98007* (WA 1); 98008* (WA 1); 98010; 98014; 98015; 98019; 98021* (WA 1); 98022 98024 98025; 98027; 98031* (WA 1, WA 9); 98032* (WA 9); 98035; 98038; 98040; 98041 98042* (WA 9); 98045; 98050; 98051; 98052* (WA 1); 98053; 98055* (WA 7, WA 9) 98056* (WA 9); 98058* (WA 9); 98059; 98064; 98065; 98072* (WA 1); 98224 98288; 98304; 98321; 98323; 98328* (WA 9); 98330* (WA 3); 98338* (WA 9) 98344; 98348; 98352; 98360; 98372* (WA 9); 98373* (WA 9); 98374; 98385; 98387* (WA 9); 98390* (WA 9); 98396; 98397; 98446* (WA 9); 98580* (WA 9).

9th District: 98001; 98002* (WA 8); 98003; 98023; 98031* (WA 1, WA 8); 98032* (WA 8); 98042* (WA 8); 98047; 98054; 98055* (WA 7, WA 8); 98056* (WA 8) 98057; 98058* (WA 8); 98062; 98063; 98071; 98093; 98106* (WA 7); 98108* (WA 7); 98126* (WA 7); 98138; 98146* (WA 7); 98148; 98158; 98166; 98168* (WA 7); 98178* (WA 7); 98188; 98198; 98327; 98328* (WA 8); 98338* (WA 8); 98354 98371; 98372* (WA 8); 98373* (WA 8); 98387* (WA 8); 98390* (WA 8); 98402* (WA 6); 98404* (WA 6); 98408* (WA 6); 98421* (WA 6); 98422; 98424; 98430; 98431 98433; 98438; 98439; 98443; 98444* (WA 6); 98445; 98447; 98492 98493; 98498* (WA 6); 98499* (WA 6); 98501* (WA 3); 98502* (WA 3); 98503* (WA 3); 98504; 98506* (WA 3); 98507; 98530; 98540; 98558; 98576; 98579* (WA 3) 98580* (WA 8); 98589; 98597.

West Virginia

1st District: 26003; 26030; 26031; 26032; 26033; 26034; 26035; 26036; 26037 26038; 26039; 26040; 26047; 26050; 26055; 26056; 26058; 26059; 26060 26062; 26070; 26074; 26075; 26101; 26102; 26103; 26104; 26105; 26106; 26133 26134; 26135; 26142; 26144; 26146; 26148; 26149; 26150; 26155; 26159; 26161 26162; 26167; 26169; 26170; 26175; 26178; 26180; 26181; 26184; 26185; 26186 26187; 26214; 26238; 26250; 26260; 26269; 26271; 26275; 26287; 26289; 26290 26292; 26301; 26302; 26320; 26322; 26323; 26325; 26327; 26328; 26330; 26332; 26334; 26337; 26339; 26344; 26346; 26347; 26348; 26349; 26354; 26360; 26361; 26362; 26366; 26367; 26369; 26374; 26375; 26377; 26383; 26385; 26386; 26404; 26405; 26407; 26408; 26410; 26411; 26415; 26416; 26419 26421; 26422 26424; 26425; 26426; 26431; 26434; 26435; 26436; 26437; 26438; 26440 26444 26448; 26451; 26456; 26461; 26462; 26463; 26502; 26503; 26504; 26505; 26506 26507; 26519; 26520; 26521; 26522; 26523; 26524; 26525; 26527; 26529; 26530 26531; 26533; 26534; 26535; 26537; 26541; 26542; 26543; 26544; 26546; 26547 26554; 26555; 26559; 26560; 26561; 26562; 26563; 26566; 26568; 26570; 26571; 26572; 26574; 26575; 26576; 26578; 26581; 26582; 26585; 26586; 26587; 26588 26589; 26590; 26591; 26705; 26707; 26710; 26713; 26716; 26717; 26719; 26720 26726* (MD 6); 26731; 26734; 26739; 26743; 26750; 26753; 26764; 26767; 26769 26816; 26833; 26847; 26855.

2nd District: 25003; 25005; 25011; 25015; 25018; 25019; 25025; 25026; 25030 25033; 25034; 25035; 25039; 25043; 25045; 25046; 25052; 25054; 25059; 25061 25063; 25064; 25067; 25070; 25071; 25075; 25079; 25080; 25082; 25083; 25086; 25088; 25095 25102; 25103; 25105; 25106; 25107; 25109; 25110; 25111; 25112 25113; 25122 25123; 25124; 25125; 25126; 25132; 25134; 25136* (WV 3); 25141; 25143; 25147 25150; 25156; 25158; 25159; 25160; 25162; 25164; 25168 25172; 25177; 25182; 25187; 25202; 25211; 25213; 25214; 25231; 25234 25235; 25237; 25239; 25241; 25243; 25244; 25245; 25246; 25247; 25248; 25249 25250; 25251; 25252; 25253; 25255; 25256; 25258; 25259; 25260; 25261; 25262 25264; 25265; 25266; 25267; 25268; 25270; 25271; 25272; 25274; 25275; 25276 25279; 25280; 25281; 25283; 25285; 25286; 25287; 25300; 25301; 25302; 25303 25304; 25305; 25306; 25309; 25311; 25312; 25313; 25314; 25315; 25317; 25320 25321; 25322; 25323; 25324; 25325; 25326; 25327; 25328; 25329; 25330; 25331 25332; 25333; 25334; 25335; 25336; 25337; 25338; 25339; 25356; 25357; 25360 25361; 25362; 25364; 25365; 25375; 25387; 25389; 25392; 25396; 25401; 25410 25411; 25413; 25414; 25419; 25420; 25421; 25422; 25423; 25425; 25427; 25428 25430; 25431; 25432; 25434; 25437; 25438; 25440; 25441; 25442; 25443; 25444 25446; 25502; 25503; 25510* (WV 3); 25515; 25520; 25526* (WV 3); 25550; 25560; 25569; 26136; 26137; 26138; 26141; 26143 26145; 26147; 26151; 26152; 26153 26160; 26164; 26173; 26179; 26201; 26202; 26205; 26207; 26210; 26215; 26218 26219; 26224; 26228; 26229; 26230; 26234; 26236; 26237 26241; 26253; 26254; 26257; 26259; 26261; 26263; 26267; 26268; 26270; 26273; 26276 26278; 26280; 26281; 26282; 26283; 26285; 26293; 26294; 26296; 26321; 26335; 26338 26342 26343; 26350; 26351; 26372; 26376; 26378; 26384; 26409; 26412; 26423; 26430 26439; 26443; 26446; 26447; 26452; 26601; 26610; 26611; 26612; 26615; 26617 26618;

26619; 26620; 26621; 26623; 26624; 26626; 26627; 26629; 26631; 26633 26634; 26636; 26638; 26639; 26641; 26651; 26656; 26660; 26662; 26667; 26671 26675; 26676; 26678; 26679; 26681; 26683; 26684; 26690; 26691; 26704; 26711 26714; 26722; 26729; 26755; 26757; 26761; 26763; 26765; 26801; 26802; 26804 26806; 26807; 26808; 26810; 26811; 26812; 26813; 26814; 26815; 26817; 26818 26823; 26824; 26836; 26838; 26845; 26851; 26852; 26865; 26866; 26884; 26886.

3rd District: 24701; 24710; 24712; 24714; 24715; 24716; 24719; 24724; 24726 24729; 24731; 24732; 24733; 24735; 24736; 24737; 24738; 24739; 24740; 24747 24751; 24801; 24808; 24810; 24811; 24813; 24815; 24816; 24817; 24818; 24819 24820; 24821; 24822; 24823; 24824; 24825; 24826; 24827; 24828; 24829; 24830 24831; 24832; 24834; 24836; 24839; 24841; 24842; 24843; 24844; 24845; 24846 24847; 24848; 24849; 24850; 24851; 24852; 24853; 24854; 24855; 24856; 24857 24859; 24860; 24861; 24862; 24866; 24867; 24868; 24869; 24870; 24871; 24872 24873; 24874; 24877; 24878; 24879; 24880; 24881; 24882; 24883; 24884 24887; 24888; 24889; 24891; 24892; 24894; 24895; 24896; 24897; 24898; 24899 24901; 24902; 24910; 24915; 24916; 24917; 24918; 24919; 24920; 24923; 24924 24925; 24927; 24928; 24931; 24934; 24935; 24936; 24938; 24939; 24941; 24942 24943; 24944; 24945; 24946; 24950; 24951; 24954; 24957; 24958; 24961; 24962 24963; 24966; 24970; 24973; 24974; 24976; 24977; 24980; 24981; 24983; 24984 24985; 24986; 24991; 24993; 25002; 25004; 25007; 25008; 25009; 25010; 25013 25014; 25021; 25022; 25024; 25028; 25031; 25036; 25040; 25044; 25047; 25048 25049; 25051; 25053; 25057; 25060; 25062; 25070; 25081; 25085; 25090; 25093 25108; 25114; 25115; 25118; 25119; 25120; 25121; 25130; 25131; 25135; 25136* (WV 2); 25139; 25140; 25142 25148; 25149; 25152; 25154; 25161; 25163; 25165 25166; 25169; 25173; 25174; 25180 25181; 25183; 25186; 25189; 25193; 25203 25204; 25205; 25206; 25208; 25209; 25501 25504; 25505; 25506; 25507; 25508 25510* (WV 2); 25511; 25512; 25514; 25517; 25519 25521; 25523; 25524; 25526* (WV 2); 25529; 25530; 25534; 25535; 25537; 25540 25541; 25544; 25545; 25546 25547; 25555; 25557; 25559; 25562; 25563; 25564; 25565 25567; 25568; 25570 25571; 25572; 25573; 25601; 25606; 25607; 25608; 25611; 25612 25614; 25617 25620; 25621; 25623; 25624; 25625; 25628; 25630; 25631; 25632; 25634 25635 25636; 25637; 25638; 25639; 25643; 25644; 25645; 25646; 25647; 25648; 25649 25650; 25651; 25652; 25653; 25654; 25661* (KY 5); 25665; 25666; 25667; 25669 25670 25671; 25672; 25674; 25676; 25678; 25682; 25684; 25685; 25686; 25687; 25688; 25690 25691; 25692; 25693; 25694; 25696; 25697; 25699; 25700; 25701 25702; 25703; 25704 25705; 25706; 25707; 25708; 25709; 25710; 25711; 25712 25713; 25714; 25715; 25716 25717; 25718; 25719; 25720; 25721; 25722; 25723 25724; 25725; 25726; 25727; 25728 25729; 25755; 25770; 25771; 25772; 25773 25774; 25775; 25776; 25777; 25778; 25779 25801; 25802; 25810; 25811; 25812 25813; 25814; 25816; 25817; 25818; 25820; 25823 25825; 25826; 25827; 25828 25831; 25832; 25833; 25836; 25837; 25839; 25840; 25841 25843; 25844; 25845 25846; 25847; 25848; 25849; 25851; 25853; 25854; 25855; 25856 25857; 25859 25860; 25862; 25864; 25865; 25866; 25867; 25868; 25870; 25871; 25873 25874 25875; 25876; 25878; 25879; 25880; 25882; 25901; 25902; 25904; 25905; 25906 25907; 25908; 25909; 25910; 25911; 25912; 25913; 25914; 25915; 25916; 25917 25918 25919; 25920; 25921; 25922; 25926; 25927; 25928; 25931; 25932; 25934 25936; 25938 25942; 25943; 25951; 25957; 25958; 25961; 25962; 25965; 25966 25967; 25969; 25971 25972; 25973; 25976; 25977; 25978; 25979; 25981; 25984 25985; 25986; 25988; 25989 26203; 26206; 26208; 26209; 26217; 26222; 26264 26266; 26288; 26291; 26298; 26299 26674; 26680.

Wisconsin

1st District: 53101; 53102; 53103* (WI 4); 53104; 53105; 53108; 53109; 53114 53115; 53118* (WI 9); 53119* (WI 9); 53120; 53121; 53125; 53126; 53128; 53138 53139; 53140 53141; 53142; 53143; 53144; 53147; 53148; 53149* (WI 4, WI 9); 53150* (WI 4); 53152 53156* (WI 9); 53157; 53158; 53159; 53167; 53168; 53170 53171; 53176; 53177; 53179 53181; 53182; 53184; 53185; 53186* (WI 4, WI 9); 53188* (WI 4, WI 9); 53190; 53191 53192; 53194; 53195; 53400; 53401; 53402 53403; 53404; 53405; 53406; 53407; 53408 53501; 53502* (WI 2); 53505; 53508* (WI 2); 53511; 53512; 53520; 53521* (WI 2) 53525; 53534* (WI 2, WI 9); 53536 53537; 53538* (WI 9); 53542; 53545; 53546; 53547 53550* (WI 2); 53563; 53566* (IL 16, WI 2); 53566* (IL 16, WI 2); 53570* (WI 2); 53574* (WI 2); 53576 53585* (IL 16); 61060* (IL 16, WI 2).

2nd District: 53094* (WI 9); 53502* (WI 1); 53503; 53504; 53506; 53507; 53508* (WI 1) 53510; 53515; 53516; 53517; 53518* (WI 3); 53521* (WI 1); 53522 53523* (WI 9); 53526 53527; 53528; 53529; 53530; 53531; 53532; 53533; 53534* (WI 1, WI 9); 53535; 53540 53541; 53543* (WI 3); 53544; 53550* (WI 1); 53553 53554* (WI 3); 53555; 53556; 53558 53559; 53560; 53561; 53562; 53565; 53566* (IL 16, WI 1); 53569* (WI 3); 53570* (WI 1) 53571; 53572; 53573* (WI 3) 53574* (WI 1); 53575; 53577; 53578; 53579* (WI 9); 53580 53581; 53582; 53583 53584; 53586; 53587; 53588; 53589; 53590; 53591; 53593; 53594* (WI 9) 53595 53596; 53597; 53598; 53599; 53700; 53701; 53702; 53703; 53704; 53705 53706 53707; 53708; 53709; 53710; 53711; 53713; 53714; 53715; 53716; 53717; 53718 53719; 53744; 53774; 53775; 53776; 53777; 53778; 53779; 53780; 53782; 53783 53784 53785; 53786; 53787; 53788; 53789; 53790; 53791; 53792; 53793; 53794 53803; 53901 53911; 53912; 53913; 53916* (WI 6); 53923; 53924; 53925 53928; 53932; 53933 53935; 53937; 53940; 53941* (WI 6); 53942; 53943; 53944* (WI 6); 53951; 53954* (WI 6); 53955; 53956; 53959; 53960; 53961; 53963* (WI 6, WI 9); 53965* (WI 6); 53968* (WI 3, WI 6); 53969; 54617; 54634* (WI 3); 54664* (WI 3); 61001* (IL 16); 61060* (IL 16, WI 1); 61075* (IL 16); 61087* (IL 16) 61089* (IL 16).

3rd District: 53518* (WI 2); 53543* (WI 2); 53554* (WI 2); 53569* (WI 2) 53573* (WI 2) 53801; 53803; 53804; 53805; 53806; 53807; 53808; 53809; 53810 53811; 53812; 53813 53816; 53817; 53818; 53820; 53821; 53824; 53825; 53826 53827; 53929* (WI 6); 53968* (WI 2, WI 6); 54001* (WI 7); 54002; 54003; 54004 54005; 54007; 54009* (WI 7); 54010 54011; 54012; 54013; 54014; 54015; 54016 54017; 54020; 54021; 54022; 54023; 54024* (WI 7); 54025; 54026; 54027; 54028 54082; 54420; 54436; 54437; 54446; 54466* (WI 7); 54479* (WI 7); 54488* (WI 7); 54493; 54601; 54602; 54603; 54610; 54611 54612; 54614; 54615; 54616 54619* (WI 6); 54620; 54621; 54622; 54623; 54624; 54625 54626; 54627; 54628 54629; 54630; 54631; 54632; 54634* (WI 3); 54635; 54636; 54638* (WI 6); 54639 54640; 54642; 54643; 54644; 54645; 54650; 54651* (WI 6); 54652; 54653 54654 54655; 54656* (WI 6); 54657; 54658; 54659; 54661; 54664* (WI 2); 54665; 54666* (WI 6); 54667; 54669; 54701; 54702; 54703* (WI 7); 54720; 54721; 54722* (WI 7);

54723; 54725; 54726* (WI 7); 54727* (WI 7); 54728* (WI 7); 54729* (WI 7) 54730* (WI 7); 54733; 54734; 54735; 54736; 54737; 54738; 54739* (WI 7); 54740 54741; 54742* (WI 7); 54743; 54744; 54746; 54747; 54749; 54750; 54751; 54754 54755; 54756; 54757* (WI 7); 54758; 54759; 54760; 54761; 54762; 54763; 54764 54765; 54767; 54768* (WI 7); 54769; 54770; 54772; 54773; 54805; 54806* (WI 7) 54812; 54813* (WI 7); 54817* (WI 7); 54818; 54822; 54826; 54829* (WI 7) 54841; 54857; 54866; 54868* (WI 7); 54870* (WI 7); 54889* (WI 7).

4th District: 53072* (WI 9); 53103* (WI 1); 53110; 53129; 53130; 53132; 53146* (WI 9) 53149* (WI 1, WI 9); 53150* (WI 1); 53151* (WI 9); 53154; 53172 53186* (WI 1, WI 9); 53188* (WI 1, WI 9); 53202* (WI 5); 53203* (WI 5); 53204 53207; 53208* (WI 5); 53213* (WI 5); 53214* (WI 5, WI 9); 53215; 53219; 53220 53221; 53227; 53228; 53233* (WI 5); 53235; 53237; 53283; 53295.

5th District: 53200; 53201; 53202* (WI 4); 53203* (WI 4); 53205; 53206; 53208* (WI 4) 53209; 53210; 53211; 53212; 53213* (WI 4); 53214* (WI 4, WI 9); 53216 53217; 53218 53222; 53223; 53224; 53225; 53226* (WI 9); 53233* (WI 4); 53234 53259; 53260; 53263 53267; 53268; 53270; 53277; 53278; 53280; 53281; 53288 53290; 53293.

6th District: 53001* (WI 9); 53006* (WI 9); 53009* (WI 9); 53010* (WI 9); 53011* (WI 9); 53014 53015* (WI 9); 53019; 53020* (WI 9); 53023; 53026; 53031; 53040* (WI 9); 53042 53044* (WI 9); 53049; 53057; 53061; 53062; 53063; 53065; 53070* (WI 9); 53073* (WI 9); 53079; 53083* (WI 9); 53085* (WI 9); 53088; 53093 53910; 53919; 53920; 53921 53923* (WI 2); 53926; 53927; 53929* (WI 3); 53930 53931; 53934; 53936; 53939; 53941* (WI 2); 53944* (WI 2); 53945; 53946; 53947 53948; 53949; 53950; 53952; 53953; 53954* (WI 2); 53957; 53962; 53963* (WI 2, WI 9); 53964; 53965* (WI 2); 53968* (WI 2, WI 3) 54110; 54113; 54123; 54126* (WI 8); 54129; 54130* (WI 8); 54136; 54140* (WI 8) 54160; 54169; 54203 54206* (WI 8); 54207; 54208* (WI 8); 54214; 54215; 54220; 54227; 54228; 54230; 54232; 54240; 54241; 54245; 54247* (WI 8); 54457* (WI 7) 54486* (WI 8); 54613; 54618; 54619* (WI 3); 54637; 54638* (WI 3); 54641 54646; 54648 54649; 54651* (WI 3); 54656* (WI 3); 54660; 54662; 54666* (WI 3); 54670; 54671 54901; 54902; 54903; 54904; 54906; 54909* (WI 7); 54915* (WI 8); 54922* (WI 8) 54923; 54926; 54927; 54929* (WI 8); 54930; 54932; 54933 54934; 54935; 54936; 54937 54940* (WI 8); 54941; 54943; 54944* (WI 8); 54945* (WI 7); 54946; 54947; 54949 54950* (WI 8); 54952* (WI 8); 54956; 54957 54960; 54961* (WI 8); 54962; 54963; 54964 54965; 54966* (WI 7); 54967; 54968 54969; 54970; 54971; 54974; 54975; 54976; 54977* (WI 7); 54979; 54980; 54981* (WI 7); 54982; 54983; 54984; 54985; 54986; 54990.

7th District: 54001* (WI 3); 54006; 54009* (WI 3); 54024* (WI 3); 54401 54402; 54404 54405; 54406; 54407; 54408* (WI 8); 54409* (WI 8); 54410; 54411 54412; 54413; 54414* (WI 8); 54415; 54417; 54419; 54421; 54422; 54423; 54425 54426; 54427* (WI 8); 54429 54432; 54433; 54434; 54435* (WI 8); 54439; 54440 54441; 54442; 54443; 54447; 54448 54449; 54451; 54452* (WI 8); 54453; 54454 54455; 54457* (WI 6); 54458; 54459; 54460 54463* (WI 8); 54466* (WI 3); 54467; 54469; 54470; 54471; 54472; 54473; 54474; 54475 54476; 54479* (WI 3) 54480; 54481; 54482; 54484; 54487* (WI 8); 54488* (WI 3); 54489 54490; 54492 54494; 54495; 54498; 54501* (WI 8); 54513; 54514; 54515; 54517; 54524 54525 54526; 54527; 54528; 54529* (WI 8); 54530; 54532; 54534; 54536; 54537; 54538* (WI 8); 54546; 54547; 54550; 54552; 54555; 54556; 54559; 54563; 54564* (WI 8) 54565 54703* (WI 3); 54722* (WI 3); 54726* (WI 3); 54727* (WI 3); 54728* (WI 3) 54729* (WI 3); 54730* (WI 3); 54731; 54732; 54739* (WI 3) 54742* (WI 3); 54745 54748; 54757* (WI 3); 54766; 54768* (WI 3); 54771 54774; 54801; 54806* (WI 3); 54810 54813* (WI 3); 54814; 54816; 54817* (WI 3); 54819; 54820; 54821; 54824; 54827; 54828 54829* (WI 3); 54830; 54832 54834; 54835; 54836; 54837; 54838; 54839; 54840; 54842 54843; 54844; 54845 54846; 54847; 54848; 54849; 54850; 54851; 54853; 54854; 54855 54856; 54858 54859; 54861; 54862; 54864; 54865; 54867; 54868* (WI 3); 54870* (WI 3); 54871 54872; 54873; 54874; 54875; 54876; 54880; 54888; 54889* (WI 3); 54890; 54891 54893; 54895; 54896; 54909* (WI 6); 54921; 54945* (WI 6); 54966* (WI 6) 54977* (WI 6); 54981* (WI 6).

8th District: 54101; 54102; 54103; 54104; 54106; 54107; 54111; 54112; 54114 54115 54119; 54120; 54121; 54124; 54125; 54126* (WI 6); 54127; 54128; 54130* (WI 6); 54131 54135; 54137; 54138; 54139; 54140* (WI 6); 54141; 54143; 54149 54150; 54151; 54152 54153; 54154; 54155; 54156; 54157; 54159; 54161; 54162 54164; 54165; 54166; 54170 54171; 54173; 54174; 54175; 54176; 54177; 54180 54182; 54201; 54202; 54204; 54205 54206* (WI 6); 54208* (WI 6); 54209 54210 54211; 54212; 54213; 54216; 54217; 54226 54227* (WI 6); 54229; 54231; 54234 54235; 54246; 54247* (WI 6); 54300; 54301; 54302 54303; 54304; 54305; 54306 54307; 54308; 54311; 54313; 54324; 54344; 54408* (WI 7) 54409* (WI 7); 54414* (WI 7); 54416; 54418; 54424; 54427* (WI 7); 54428; 54430 54435* (WI 7); 54444; 54445; 54450; 54452* (WI 7); 54462; 54463* (WI 7); 54464; 54465 54485 54486* (WI 6); 54487* (WI 7); 54491; 54499; 54501* (WI 7); 54511; 54512 54519 54520; 54521; 54529* (WI 7); 54531; 54538* (WI 7); 54539; 54540* (MI 11); 54541 54542; 54543; 54545; 54548; 54554* (MI 11); 54557; 54558; 54560; 54561; 54562 54564* (WI 7); 54566; 54568; 54911; 54912; 54913; 54914; 54915* (WI 6); 54919 54922* (WI 6); 54928; 54929* (WI 6); 54931; 54940* (WI 6); 54942; 54944* (WI 6) 54948; 54950* (WI 6); 54951; 54952* (WI 6); 54961* (WI 6); 54978.

9th District: 54001* (WI 6); 53002; 53003; 53004; 53005; 53006* (WI 6); 53007 53008 53010* (WI 6); 53011* (WI 6); 53012; 53013; 53015* (WI 6); 53016; 53017; 53018 53020* (WI 6); 53021; 53022; 53024; 53027; 53029; 53032; 53033 53034; 53035; 53036 53037; 53038; 53039; 53040* (WI 6); 53044* (WI 6); 53045; 53046; 53047; 53048; 53050 53051; 53052; 53056; 53058; 53059; 53060; 53064 53066; 53069; 53070* (WI 6); 53072* (WI 4); 53073* (WI 6); 53074; 53075 53076; 53077; 53078; 53080; 53081; 53082; 53083* (WI 6); 53085* (WI 6); 53086 53089; 53091; 53092; 53094* (WI 3); 53095; 53096; 53099 53118* (WI 1); 53119* (WI 1); 53122; 53127; 53137; 53146* (WI 4); 53149* (WI 1, WI 4); 53151* (WI 4); 53153; 53156* (WI 1); 53178; 53183; 53186* (WI 1, WI 4); 53187 53188* (WI 1, WI 4); 53214* (WI 4, WI 5); 53226* (WI 5); 53523* (WI 2); 53534* (WI 1, WI 2); 53538* (WI 1); 53549; 53551; 53557; 53579* (WI 2); 53594* (WI 2); 53916* (WI 2); 53922; 53963* (WI 2, WI 6).

Wyoming

At Large: 57717* (MT 1, SD 1); 57717* (MT 1, SD 1); 57735* (SD 1); 57783* (SD 1);

59030* (MT 1); 59089* (MT 1); 69352* (NE 3); 69358* (NE 3); 82001; 82002 82003; 82005; 82006; 82007; 82008; 82009; 82050; 82051; 82052; 82053; 82054 82055; 82057; 82058; 82059; 82060; 82061; 82062; 82063* (CO 3); 82070; 82071 82080; 82081; 82082* (CO 4, NE 3); 82083; 82084; 82190; 82201; 82210; 82212 82213; 82214; 82215; 82217; 82218; 82219; 82220; 82221; 82222; 82223; 82224 82225; 82227; 82228; 82229; 82240; 82242; 82243; 82244; 82301; 82310; 82321 82322; 82323; 82324; 82325; 82327; 82329; 82331; 82332; 82334; 82335; 82336 82401; 82410; 82411; 82412; 82414; 82420; 82421; 82422; 82423; 82426; 82427 82428; 82430; 82431* (MT 1); 82432; 82433; 82434; 82435; 82440; 82441; 82442 82443; 82450; 82501; 82510; 82512; 82513; 82514; 82515; 82516; 82520; 82523 82524; 82601; 82602; 82604; 82609; 82615; 82620; 82630; 82631; 82633;

82635 82636; 82637; 82638; 82639; 82640; 82642; 82643; 82644; 82646; 82648; 82649 82701; 82710; 82711; 82712; 82713; 82714; 82715; 82716; 82717; 82720; 82721 82723; 82724; 82725* (MT 1); 82727; 82729; 82730; 82731; 82732; 82801; 82831 82832; 82833; 82834; 82835; 82836; 82837; 82838; 82839; 82840; 82842; 82844 82845; 82901; 82902; 82922; 82923; 82925; 82926; 82929; 82930* (UT 1, UT 3) 82931; 82932; 82933; 82934; 82935* (UT 3); 82936; 82937; 82938; 82939; 82941 82942; 82943; 82944; 82945; 83001; 83002; 83011; 83012; 83013; 83014; 83025 83101; 83110; 83111; 83112; 83113; 83114; 83115; 83116; 83118; 83119; 83120* (ID 2); 83121; 83122; 83123; 83124; 83126; 83127; 83128.

Indexes

City Index

All incorporated cities and census designated places (CDPs) with populations of 10,000 or more are indexed here by district and page number. CDP is the U.S. Census Bureau's term for densely settled unincorporated places that are identifiable by name. A (pt.) indicates that the city or CDP is split between districts. Thus a city or CDP may have two or more entries. A city with only one (pt.) entry indicates that the remaining part of the city has a population of less than 10,000 and is not listed in this book.

City	State	District	Page
A			
Abbeville	LA	7	328
Aberdeen	MD	2	340
Aberdeen	SD	AL	682
Aberdeen (pt.)	WA	6	791
Abilene	TX	17	729
Abington	MA	10	370
Acton	MA	5	361
Ada	OK	3	609
Addison	IL	6	243
Adrian	MI	7	383
Affton CDP	MO	3	429
Agawam	MA	2	356
Agoura Hills	CA	24	94
Aiken (pt.)	SC	3	673
Akron	OH	14	595
Alabaster	AL	6	28
Alameda (pt.)	CA	9	73
Alamo CDP	CA	10	74
Alamogordo	NM	2	491
Albany	CA	9	73
Albany (pt.)	GA	2	206
Albany (pt.)	GA	8	215
Albany	NY	21	529
Albany (pt.)	OR	4	622
Albemarle	NC	8	561
Albert Lea	MN	1	401
Albertville	AL	4	24
Albion	MI	7	383
Albuquerque (pt.)	NM	1	490
Alden	NY	27	539
Alderwood Manor-Bothell North CDP	WA	1	783
Alexander City	AL	3	23
Alexandria (pt.)	LA	4	323
Alexandria (pt.)	LA	6	326
Alexandria	VA	8	774
Algonquin (pt.)	IL	16	259
Alhambra	CA	31	104
Alice (pt.)	TX	28	744
Aliquippa	PA	4	634
Allen	TX	3	708
Allen Park	MI	16	396
Allentown	PA	15	651
Alliance (pt.)	OH	16	598
Allouez	WI	8	817
Aloha CDP	OR	1	618
Alpena	MI	1	375
Alpharetta	GA	6	212
Alsip (pt.)	IL	1	237
Altadena CDP	CA	27	98
Altamont CDP	OR	2	619
Altamonte Springs (pt.)	FL	7	176
Alton	IL	12	253
Altoona	PA	9	641
Altus	OK	4	611
Alvin	TX	22	736
Amarillo (pt.)	TX	13	723
Amarillo (pt.)	TX	19	732
American Fork	UT	3	754
Americus	GA	2	206
Ames	IA	3	291
Amesbury	MA	6	362
Amherst	MA	1	354

City	State	District	Page
Amherst	NY	27	539
Amherst	OH	13	594
Amsterdam	NY	21	529
Anaconda-Deer Lodge County	MT	AL	442
Anacortes	WA	2	785
Anaheim (pt.)	CA	41	118
Anaheim (pt.)	CA	45	123
Anaheim (pt.)	CA	46	124
Anaheim (pt.)	CA	47	126
Anchorage	AK	AL	33
Anderson	IN	2	271
Anderson	SC	3	673
Andover	MA	5	361
Andover	MN	6	409
Andrews	TX	19	732
Andrews AFB CDP (pt.)	MD	4	343
Angleton (pt.)	TX	22	736
Ankeny	IA	4	292
Annandale CDP	VA	11	778
Annapolis	MD	1	339
Ann Arbor	MI	13	392
Anniston	AL	3	23
Anoka	MN	6	409
Ansonia	CT	5	156
Antioch (pt.)	CA	10	74
Apache Junction	AZ	6	44
Appleton (pt.)	WI	8	817
Apple Valley	CA	40	117
Apple Valley	MN	3	404
Applewood CDP (pt.)	CO	6	145
Arbutus CDP	MD	3	342
Arcadia (pt.)	CA	28	100
Arcadia	NY	27	539
Arcata	CA	1	60
Arden-Arcade CDP (pt.)	CA	3	63
Arden-Arcade CDP (pt.)	CA	5	66
Ardmore	OK	3	609
Arkadelphia	AR	4	53
Arkansas City	KS	4	302
Arlington	MA	7	364
Arlington (pt.)	TX	6	713
Arlington (pt.)	TX	24	739
Arlington CDP	NY	19	526
Arlington CDP	VA	8	774
Arlington Heights (pt.)	IL	8	247
Arlington Heights (pt.)	IL	10	250
Arnold	MO	3	429
Arnold CDP	MD	1	339
Arroyo Grande	CA	22	91
Artesia	CA	39	115
Artesia	NM	2	491
Arvada (pt.)	CO	2	139
Asbury Park	NJ	6	474
Asheboro	NC	6	558
Asheville	NC	11	565
Ashland	KY	4	311
Ashland	OH	16	598
Ashland	OR	2	619
Ashland	MA	5	361
Ashland CDP	CA	10	74
Ashtabula	OH	19	602
Ashwaubenon	WI	8	817
Aspen Hill CDP (pt.)	MD	4	343
Aspen Hill CDP (pt.)	MD	8	349
Astoria	OR	1	618
Atascadero	CA	22	91
Atchison	KS	2	299
Athens	AL	5	26
Athens	GA	10	218
Athens	OH	6	584
Athens	TN	2	689
Athens	TX	5	712
Athol	MA	1	354
Atlanta (pt.)	GA	4	209
Atlanta (pt.)	GA	5	210

City	State	District	Page	City	State	District	Page
Fond du Lac	WI	6	813	Fresno (pt.)	CA	19	87
Fontana (pt.)	CA	42	119	Fresno (pt.)	CA	20	88
Foothill Farms CDP	CA	3	63	Fridley	MN	6	409
Fords CDP	NJ	7	475	Friendswood (pt.)	TX	9	718
Forest City CDP	FL	7	176	Front Royal	VA	10	777
Forestdale CDP	AL	6	28	Fullerton (pt.)	CA	39	115
Forest Grove	OR	1	618	Fullerton CDP	PA	15	651
Forest Hill (pt.)	TX	24	739	Fulton	MO	9	438
Forest Hills CDP	MI	3	377	Fulton	NY	24	534
Forest Park	GA	3	207				
Forest Park (pt.)	OH	1	577				
Forestville CDP	MD	4	343	**G**			
Forrest City	AR	1	49				
Fort Atkinson	WI	9	818	Gadsden	AL	4	24
Fort Benning South CDP	GA	2	206	Gaffney	SC	5	676
Fort Bliss CDP (pt.)	TX	16	727	Gahanna (pt.)	OH	12	592
Fort Bragg CDP	NC	7	559	Gaines School CDP	GA	10	218
Fort Campbell North CDP	KY	1	307	Gainesville (pt.)	FL	3	171
Fort Carson CDP	CO	5	144	Gainesville (pt.)	FL	5	174
Fort Collins	CO	4	142	Gainesville	GA	9	217
Fort Dix CDP (pt.)	NJ	3	469	Gainesville	TX	4	710
Fort Dodge	IA	5	294	Gaithersburg	MD	8	349
Fort Drum CDP	NY	24	534	Galena Park (pt.)	TX	29	745
Fort Hood CDP	TX	11	721	Galesburg	IL	17	260
Fort Hunt CDP	VA	8	774	Galion	OH	4	581
Fort Knox CDP	KY	2	308	Gallatin	TN	6	695
Fort Lauderdale (pt.)	FL	20	195	Gallup	NM	3	492
Fort Lauderdale (pt.)	FL	22	198	Galveston	TX	9	718
Fort Lauderdale (pt.)	FL	23	199	Gantt CDP	SC	4	675
Fort Lee	NJ	9	478	Gardena	CA	35	110
Fort Leonard Wood CDP	MO	4	431	Garden City	KS	1	298
Fort Lewis CDP	WA	9	795	Garden City	MI	13	392
Fort Madison	IA	3	291	Garden City	NY	4	504
Fort Meade CDP (pt.)	MD	3	342	Garden Grove (pt.)	CA	45	123
Fort Myers	FL	14	186	Garden Grove (pt.)	CA	46	124
Fort Payne	AL	4	24	Gardner	MA	1	354
Fort Pierce (pt.)	FL	16	189	Garfield	NJ	9	478
Fort Pierce (pt.)	FL	23	199	Garfield Heights (pt.)	OH	19	602
Fort Polk South CDP	LA	6	326	Garland (pt.)	TX	3	708
Fort Riley North CDP	KS	2	299	Garland (pt.)	TX	5	712
Fort Sill CDP	OK	4	611	Garner	NC	4	555
Fort Smith	AR	3	52	Gary	IN	1	270
Fort Stewart CDP	GA	1	204	Gastonia (pt.)	NC	9	562
Fort Thomas	KY	4	311	Gastonia (pt.)	NC	12	567
Fort Walton Beach	FL	1	168	Gates-North Gates CDP	NY	29	542
Fort Washington CDP	MD	4	343	Gatesville	TX	11	721
Fort Wayne	IN	4	274	Gautier	MS	5	422
Fort Worth (pt.)	TX	6	713	Geddes	NY	25	536
Fort Worth (pt.)	TX	12	722	Geneva	IL	14	256
Fort Worth (pt.)	TX	24	739	Geneva	NY	27	539
Foster City	CA	12	77	Georgetown	KY	6	314
Fostoria (pt.)	OH	5	583	Georgetown (pt.)	TX	21	735
Fountain Hills	AZ	6	44	German Flatts	NY	23	533
Fountain Valley (pt.)	CA	45	123	Germantown	TN	7	696
Four Corners CDP	OR	5	623	Germantown	WI	9	818
Framingham	MA	7	364	Germantown CDP	MD	8	349
Franconia CDP	VA	8	774	Gilbert (pt.)	AZ	6	44
Frankfort	IN	6	277	Gillette	WY	AL	822
Frankfort	KY	6	314	Gilroy	CA	16	83
Franklin	IN	6	277	Girard	OH	17	599
Franklin	MA	3	357	Gladeview CDP	FL	17	190
Franklin	OH	2	578	Gladstone	MO	6	434
Franklin	TN	6	695	Gladstone	OR	5	623
Franklin	WI	4	810	Glasgow	KY	2	308
Franklin Park	IL	5	242	Glassboro	NJ	2	468
Franklin Park	PA	14	649	Glastonbury	CT	1	150
Franklin Square CDP	NY	4	504	Glen Avon CDP	CA	43	121
Fraser	MI	10	387	Glen Burnie CDP	MD	1	339
Frederick	MD	6	346	Glen Cove (pt.)	NY	3	501
Fredericksburg	VA	1	763	Glen Cove (pt.)	NY	5	505
Fredonia	NY	31	545	Glendale (pt.)	AZ	2	39
Freehold	NJ	12	483	Glendale (pt.)	AZ	3	41
Freeport	IL	16	259	Glendale (pt.)	AZ	4	42
Freeport (pt.)	NY	3	501	Glendale (pt.)	CA	27	98
Freeport (pt.)	NY	4	504	Glendale	WI	5	812
Freeport (pt.)	TX	14	725	Glendale Heights	IL	6	243
Fremont (pt.)	CA	13	78	Glendora (pt.)	CA	28	100
Fremont	NE	1	447	Glen Ellyn (pt.)	IL	6	243
Fremont	OH	5	583	Glen Rock	NJ	5	472

City	State	District	Page	City	State	District	Page
Glens Falls	NY	22	531	Gulf Gate Estates CDP	FL	13	185
Glenvar Heights CDP (pt.)	FL	18	193	Gulfport	FL	10	181
Glenview (pt.)	IL	10	250	Gulfport	MS	5	422
Gloucester	MA	6	362	Gurnee (pt.)	IL	8	247
Gloucester City	NJ	1	466	Guthrie	OK	5	612
Gloversville	NY	24	534				
Goffstown	NH	1	460				

City	State	District	Page
Jefferson City (pt.)	MO	4	431
Jeffersontown (pt.)	KY	3	310
Jefferson Valley-Yorktown CDP	NY	19	526
Jeffersonville	IN	9	282
Jenison CDP	MI	2	376
Jennings	LA	7	328
Jennings	MO	1	426
Jericho CDP	NY	3	501
Jersey City (pt.)	NJ	9	479
Jersey City (pt.)	NJ	10	480
Jersey City (pt.)	NJ	13	485
Johnson City	NY	26	538
Johnson City	TN	1	687
Johnston	RI	2	665
Johnstown	PA	12	646
Joliet (pt.)	IL	11	252
Jollyville CDP (pt.)	TX	21	735
Jonesboro	AR	1	49
Joplin	MO	7	435
Joppatowne CDP	MD	2	340
Junction City	KS	2	299
Juneau	AK	AL	33
Jupiter (pt.)	FL	16	189
Justice	IL	3	239

K

City	State	District	Page
Kahului CDP	HI	2	225
Kailua CDP	HI	2	225
Kalamazoo	MI	6	381
Kalispell	MT	AL	442
Kaneohe CDP	HI	2	225
Kaneohe Station CDP	HI	2	225
Kankakee (pt.)	IL	15	257
Kannapolis	NC	8	561
Kansas City	KS	3	301
Kansas City (pt.)	MO	5	432
Kansas City (pt.)	MO	6	434
Kaukauna	WI	8	817
Kaysville	UT	1	752
Keansburg	NJ	6	474
Kearney	NE	3	40
Kearns CDP (pt.)	UT	2	753
Kearny (pt.)	NJ	9	479
Keene	NH	2	461
Keizer	OR	5	623
Keller	TX	6	713
Kelso	WA	3	787
Ken Caryl CDP	CO	6	145
Kendale Lakes CDP	FL	21	196
Kendall CDP (pt.)	FL	18	193
Kendall CDP (pt.)	FL	21	196
Kenmore	NY	29	542
Kenner (pt.)	LA	1	319
Kenner (pt.)	LA	2	320
Kennett	MO	8	437
Kennewick	WA	4	788
Kenosha	WI	1	806
Kent	OH	14	595
Kent (pt.)	WA	8	794
Kent (pt.)	WA	9	795
Kentwood	MI	3	377
Keokuk	IA	3	291
Kernersville (pt.)	NC	5	556
Kerrville	TX	21	735
Kettering (pt.)	OH	3	580
Kewanee	IL	17	260
Key Largo CDP	FL	20	195
Key West	FL	20	195
Kihei CDP	HI	2	225
Killeen	TX	11	721
Killingly	CT	2	152
Kingman	AZ	3	41
King of Prussia CDP	PA	7	638
Kingsbury	NY	22	531
Kingsgate CDP	WA	1	783
Kings Park CDP (pt.)	NY	1	499
Kings Point CDP	FL	19	194

City	State	District	Page
Kingsport	TN	1	687
Kingston	NY	26	538
Kingston	PA	11	644
Kingsville (pt.)	TX	15	726
Kingwood CDP	TX	8	717
Kinston (pt.)	NC	1	550
Kinston (pt.)	NC	3	553
Kirkland	NY	23	533
Kirkland	WA	1	783
Kirksville	MO	9	438
Kirkwood (pt.)	MO	2	428
Kissimmee (pt.)	FL	8	178
Klamath Falls	OR	2	619
Knoxville	TN	2	689
Kokomo	IN	5	276

L

City	State	District	Page
La Canada Flintridge	CA	27	98
Lacey (pt.)	WA	3	787
Lackawanna	NY	30	544
Laconia	NH	1	460
La Crescenta-Montrose CDP	CA	27	99
La Crosse	WI	3	809
Ladson CDP	SC	1	670
Lafayette	CA	10	74
Lafayette	CO	2	139
Lafayette	IN	7	279
Lafayette (pt.)	LA	4	323
Lafayette (pt.)	LA	7	328
La Grande	OR	2	619
La Grange	GA	7	214
La Grange	IL	3	239
La Grange (pt.)	NY	22	531
La Grange Park	IL	6	243
Laguna Beach (pt.)	CA	47	126
Laguna Hills CDP (pt.)	CA	47	126
Laguna Niguel (pt.)	CA	48	128
La Habra	CA	39	115
Lake Charles	LA	7	328
Lake Elsinore	CA	43	121
Lake Forest	IL	10	250
Lake Havasu City	AZ	3	41
Lake Jackson (pt.)	TX	22	736
Lakeland	FL	12	183
Lakeland North CDP	WA	9	795
Lake Magdalene CDP (pt.)	FL	11	182
Lake Oswego (pt.)	OR	1	618
Lake Ridge CDP	VA	11	778
Lake Ronkonkoma CDP	NY	1	499
Lake Serene-North Lynnwood CDP (pt.)	WA	1	783
Lake Shore CDP	MD	2	340
Lakeside CDP	CA	52	133
Lakeside CDP	FL	6	175
Lakeside CDP (pt.)	VA	7	772
Lake Station	IN	1	270
Lakeville	MN	3	404
Lakewood (pt.)	CA	38	114
Lakewood (pt.)	CA	39	115
Lakewood (pt.)	CO	6	145
Lakewood	OH	10	589
Lakewood CDP	NJ	4	471
Lakewood CDP (pt.)	WA	6	791
Lakewood CDP (pt.)	WA	9	795
Lake Worth (pt.)	FL	22	198
Lake Worth (pt.)	FL	23	199
Lake Zurich	IL	8	247
La Marque	TX	9	718
La Mesa (pt.)	CA	52	133
Lamesa	TX	17	729
La Mirada (pt.)	CA	39	115
Lamont CDP	CA	20	88
Lancaster	CA	25	95
Lancaster	NY	30	544
Lancaster	OH	7	585
Lancaster	PA	16	652
Lancaster (pt.)	TX	30	747
Langley Park CDP (pt.)	MD	4	343

City	State	District	Page	City	State	District	Page
Miami Beach (pt.)	FL	22	198	Montclair CDP (pt.)	NJ	10	480
Miami Lakes CDP	FL	21	196	Montebello (pt.)	CA	34	109
Miamisburg	OH	3	580	Monterey	CA	17	85
Miami Springs (pt.)	FL	21	196	Monterey Park (pt.)	CA	31	104
Michigan City	IN	3	273	Montgomery (pt.)	AL	2	22
Middleborough	MA	4	359	Montgomery (pt.)	AL	7	29
Middleburg Heights	OH	19	602	Montgomery Village CDP	MD	8	349
Middle River CDP	MD	2	340	Montville	CT	2	152
Middlesborough	KY	5	313	Moore	OK	4	611
Middlesex	NJ	7	475	Moorestown-Lenola CDP	NJ	3	469
Middleton	WI	2	807	Moorhead	MN	7	410
Middletown (pt.)	CT	2	152	Moorpark	CA	23	92
Middletown	NY	20	528	Moraga Town	CA	10	74
Middletown (pt.)	OH	8	587	Moreau	NY	22	531
Middletown	RI	1	664	Moreno Valley (pt.)	CA	44	122
Middle Valley CDP	TN	3	690	Morgan City	LA	3	322
Midland (pt.)	MI	4	379	Morgan Hill	CA	16	83
Midland (pt.)	TX	19	732	Morganton	NC	5	556
Midland (pt.)	TX	21	735	Morgantown	WV	1	799
Midland (pt.)	TX	23	737	Morris	IL	11	252
Midvale	UT	2	753	Morristown	NJ	11	482
Midwest City (pt.)	OK	4	611	Morristown	TN	4	692
Midwest City (pt.)	OK	6	613	Morton	IL	18	262
Milford	CT	3	153	Morton Grove	IL	9	249
Milford	MA	2	356	Moscow	ID	1	229
Milford	NH	2	461	Moses Lake	WA	4	788
Milford Mill CDP (pt.)	MD	7	348	Moss Point	MS	5	422
Mililani Town CDP	HI	1	224	Mounds View	MN	4	405
Millbrae (pt.)	CA	12	77	Moundsville	WV	1	799
Millburn CDP (pt.)	NJ	7	475	Mountain Brook	AL	6	28
Millbury	MA	2	356	Mountain Park CDP	GA	4	209
Millcreek CDP	UT	2	753	Mountain View	CA	14	80
Milledgeville (pt.)	GA	11	220	Mount Clemens	MI	10	387
Millington	TN	8	698	Mount Holly CDP	NJ	3	469
Mill Valley	CA	6	67	Mountlake Terrace	WA	1	783
Millville	NJ	2	468	Mount Lebanon CDP (pt.)	PA	18	655
Milpitas (pt.)	CA	13	78	Mount Pleasant	MI	4	379
Milton	NY	22	531	Mount Pleasant	SC	1	670
Milton	MA	9	368	Mount Pleasant	TX	1	705
Milwaukie	OR	3	621	Mount Prospect (pt.)	IL	6	243
Milwaukee (pt.)	WI	4	810	Mount Prospect (pt.)	IL	8	247
Milwaukee (pt.)	WI	5	812	Mount Prospect (pt.)	IL	10	250
Minden	LA	5	325	Mount Vernon	IL	20	265
Mineola	NY	4	504	Mount Vernon (pt.)	NY	17	523
Mineral Wells (pt.)	TX	17	729	Mount Vernon (pt.)	NY	18	525
Minneapolis	MN	5	407	Mount Vernon (pt.)	OH	16	598
Minnetonka (pt.)	MN	3	404	Mount Vernon	WA	2	785
Minot	ND	AL	571	Mount Vernon CDP	VA	8	774
Mint Hill	NC	9	562	Muncie	IN	2	271
Mira Loma CDP	CA	43	121	Mundelein (pt.)	IL	10	250
Miramar (pt.)	FL	20	195	Munhall	PA	18	655
Miramar (pt.)	FL	23	199	Munster	IN	1	270
Mishawaka	IN	3	273	Murfreesboro	TN	6	695
Mission	TX	15	726	Murray	KY	1	307
Mission Bend CDP (pt.)	TX	7	714	Murray	UT	2	753
Mission Bend CDP (pt.)	TX	22	736	Murrysville	PA	4	634
Mission Viejo (pt.)	CA	47	126	Muscatine	IA	1	288
Mission Viejo (pt.)	CA	48	128	Muskego	WI	4	810
Missoula	MT	AL	442	Muskegon	MI	2	376
Missouri City (pt.)	TX	22	736	Muskegon Heights	MI	2	376
Missouri City (pt.)	TX	25	740	Muskogee	OK	2	608
Mitchell	SD	AL	682	Mustang	OK	6	613
Mitchellville CDP	MD	4	343	Myrtle Beach	SC	1	670
Moberly	MO	9	438	Myrtle Grove CDP	FL	1	168
Mobile	AL	1	21				
Modesto	CA	18	86				
Moline	IL	17	260	**N**			
Monroe (pt.)	CT	4	155				
Monroe (pt.)	LA	4	323	Nacogdoches (pt.)	TX	1	705
Monroe (pt.)	LA	5	325	Nampa	ID	1	229
Monroe	MI	16	396	Nanticoke	PA	11	644
Monroe	NC	8	561	Nanuet CDP	NY	20	528
Monroe	WI	2	807	Napa	CA	1	60
Monroeville	PA	18	655	Naperville (pt.)	IL	13	255
Monrovia	CA	28	100	Naples	FL	14	186
Monsey CDP	NY	20	528	Narragansett	RI	2	665
Montclair	CA	41	118	Nashua (pt.)	NH	2	461
Montclair CDP	VA	10	777	Nashville-Davidson (pt.)	TN	5	693
Montclair CDP (pt.)	NJ	8	477	Natchez	MS	4	420

City	State	District	Page	City	State	District	Page
North Port	FL	13	185	Olney CDP	MD	8	349
Northport (pt.)	AL	6	28	Olympia	WA	3	787
North Potomac CDP	MD	8	349	Olympia Heights CDP (pt.)	FL	18	193
North Providence	RI	1	664	Omaha	NE	2	448
North Reading	MA	6	362	Onalaska	WI	3	809
North Richland Hills (pt.)	TX	6	713	Oneida	NY	23	533
North Richland Hills (pt.)	TX	12	722	Oneonta	NY	23	533
North Ridgeville	OH	13	594	Onondaga	NY	25	536
North Royalton (pt.)	OH	19	602	Ontario (pt.)	CA	41	118
North St. Paul	MN	4	405	Ontario (pt.)	CA	42	119
North Tonawanda	NY	29	542	Opa-locka	FL	17	190
North Valley CDP	NM	1	490	Opelika	AL	3	23
North Valley Stream CDP	NY	4	504	Opelousas (pt.)	LA	4	323
North Versailles CDP	PA	18	655	Opportunity CDP	WA	5	789
Northview CDP	MI	3	377	Orange (pt.)	CA	47	126
Northview CDP	OH	3	580	Orange	CT	3	153
Norton (pt.)	OH	14	595	Orange	TX	2	707
Norton	MA	4	359	Orange CDP	NJ	10	480
Norton Shores	MI	2	376	Orange Grove CDP	MS	5	422
Norwalk (pt.)	CA	34	109	Orangevale CDP	CA	4	64
Norwalk	CT	4	155	Orchard Homes CDP	MT	AL	442
Norwalk	OH	5	583	Orchard Park	NY	30	544
Norwich	CT	2	152	Orchards South CDP	WA	3	787
Norwood (pt.)	MA	9	368	Oregon	OH	9	588
Norwood (pt.)	OH	2	578	Oregon City	OR	5	623
Novato	CA	6	67	Orem	UT	3	754
Novi	MI	11	388	Orinda	CA	10	74
Nutley CDP	NJ	8	477	Orland Park (pt.)	IL	13	255
				Orlando (pt.)	FL	3	171
				Orlando (pt.)	FL	8	178
O				Ormond Beach	FL	4	172
				Orono	ME	2	334
Oak Creek	WI	4	810	Oroville	CA	2	62
Oakdale	CA	18	86	Oshkosh	WI	6	813
Oakdale (pt.)	MN	4	405	Oskaloosa	IA	3	291
Oak Forest (pt.)	IL	3	239	Ossining	NY	19	526
Oak Harbor	WA	2	785	Oswego	NY	24	534
Oakland (pt.)	CA	9	73	Ottawa	IL	11	252
Oakland (pt.)	CA	13	78	Ottawa	KS	2	299
Oakland	NJ	5	472	Ottumwa	IA	3	291
Oakland Park (pt.)	FL	22	198	Overland Park	KS	3	301
Oak Lawn (pt.)	IL	3	239	Overlea CDP	MD	3	342
Oakley CDP	CA	10	74	Overlook-Page Manor CDP	OH	3	580
Oak Park (pt.)	IL	7	245	Oviedo	FL	7	176
Oak Park	MI	12	391	Owasso (pt.)	OK	1	607
Oak Ridge	TN	3	690	Owatonna	MN	1	401
Oak Ridge CDP (pt.)	FL	8	178	Owego	NY	26	538
Oakton CDP (pt.)	VA	11	778	Owensboro	KY	2	308
Oakville CDP	MO	3	429	Owosso	MI	4	379
Oatfield CDP (pt.)	OR	5	623	Oxford	MA	2	356
Ocala (pt.)	FL	3	171	Oxford	OH	8	587
Ocala (pt.)	FL	6	175	Oxnard	CA	23	92
Ocean City	NJ	2	468	Oxon Hill-Glassmanor CDP	MD	4	344
Oceanside (pt.)	CA	48	128	Ozark	AL	2	22
Oceanside (pt.)	CA	51	132				
Oceanside CDP	NY	3	501				
Ocean Springs	MS	5	422	**P**			
Ocoee	FL	8	178				
Oconomowoc	WI	9	818	Pacifica	CA	12	77
Odessa (pt.)	TX	19	732	Pacific Grove	CA	17	85
Odessa (pt.)	TX	23	737	Paducah	KY	1	307
O'Fallon	IL	12	253	Paine Field-Lake Stickney CDP (pt.)	WA	2	785
O'Fallon (pt.)	MO	9	438	Painesville	OH	19	602
Offutt AFB West CDP	NE	2	448	Palatine	IL	8	247
Ogden	NY	29	542	Palestine	TX	5	712
Ogden	UT	1	752	Palisades Park	NJ	9	479
Ogdensburg	NY	24	534	Palm Bay	FL	15	187
Oil City	PA	5	636	Palm Beach Gardens (pt.)	FL	16	189
Oildale CDP	CA	21	90	Palm Coast CDP	FL	4	172
Ojus CDP (pt.)	FL	22	198	Palmdale	CA	25	95
Okemos CDP	MI	8	384	Palm Desert	CA	44	122
Oklahoma City (pt.)	OK	4	611	Palmer	MA	2	356
Oklahoma City (pt.)	OK	5	612	Palmetto Estates CDP	FL	17	190
Oklahoma City (pt.)	OK	6	613	Palm Harbor CDP	FL	9	179
Okmulgee	OK	2	608	Palm River-Clair Mel CDP	FL	11	182
Okolona CDP	KY	3	310	Palm Springs	CA	44	122
Olathe	KS	3	301	Palo Alto	CA	14	80
Old Bridge CDP	NJ	6	474	Palos Heights	IL	3	239
Olean	NY	31	545	Palos Hills (pt.)	IL	13	255

City	State	District	Page	City	State	District	Page
Port St. Lucie	FL	16	189	Rialto	CA	42	119
Port Washington CDP (pt.)	NY	5	505	Richardson (pt.)	TX	3	708
Potomac CDP	MD	8	349	Richardson (pt.)	TX	26	741
Potsdam	NY	24	534	Richfield	MN	3	404
Pottstown (pt.)	PA	6	637	Richland	WA	4	788
Pottsville	PA	6	637	Richmond (pt.)	CA	7	68
Poughkeepsie	NY	19	526	Richmond	IN	2	271
Poway	CA	51	132	Richmond	KY	6	314
Powellhurst-Centennial CDP	OR	3	621	Richmond (pt.)	VA	3	766
Prairie Village	KS	3	301	Richmond (pt.)	VA	7	772
Prattville	AL	2	22	Richmond Heights	MO	1	426
Prescott	AZ	3	41	Richmond Highlands CDP (pt.)	WA	1	783
Presque Isle	ME	2	334	Richton Park (pt.)	IL	11	252
Prichard	AL	1	21	Ridge CDP	NY	1	499
Princeton	NJ	12	483	Ridgecrest	CA	21	90
Prior Lake	MN	2	403	Ridgefield	CT	5	156
Prospect Heights	IL	10	250	Ridgefield Park	NJ	9	479
Providence (pt.)	RI	1	664	Ridgeland	MS	3	419
Providence (pt.)	RI	2	665	Ridgewood	NJ	5	472
Provo	UT	3	754	Ringwood	NJ	5	472
Pueblo	CO	3	141	Rio Rancho (pt.)	NM	3	492
Pullman	WA	5	789	Riverdale	IL	2	238
Punta Gorda	FL	14	186	River Edge	NJ	9	479
Puyallup (pt.)	WA	9	795	River Falls	WI	3	809
				River Forest (pt.)	IL	7	245
				River Ridge CDP (pt.)	LA	1	319

Q

City	State	District	Page
Queensbury	NY	22	531
Quincy	IL	17	260
Quincy	MA	10	370

R

City	State	District	Page
Racine	WI	1	806
Radcliff	KY	2	308
Radford	VA	9	775
Radnor CDP	PA	7	639
Rahway	NJ	10	480
Raleigh	NC	4	555
Ramona CDP (pt.)	CA	52	133
Ramsey	MN	6	409
Ramsey	NJ	5	472
Rancho Cordova CDP	CA	11	76
Rancho Cucamonga (pt.)	CA	42	119
Rancho Palos Verdes	CA	36	111
Rancho Santa Margarita CDP	CA	48	128
Randallstown CDP (pt.)	MD	3	342
Randallstown CDP (pt.)	MD	7	348
Randolph	MA	9	368
Rantoul	IL	15	257
Rapid City	SD	AL	682
Ravenna	OH	14	595
Raytown	MO	5	432
Reading (pt.)	MA	7	364
Reading	OH	2	578
Reading	PA	6	637
Redan CDP	GA	11	220
Red Bank	NJ	6	474
Red Bank	TN	3	690
Red Bluff	CA	3	63
Redding	CA	2	62
Redford CDP	MI	11	388
Redland CDP	MD	8	349
Redlands	CA	40	117
Redmond (pt.)	WA	1	783
Redondo Beach	CA	36	111
Red Wing	MN	1	401
Redwood City (pt.)	CA	14	80
Reedley (pt.)	CA	20	88
Reidsville	NC	5	556
Reisterstown CDP (pt.)	MD	3	342
Reno	NV	2	455
Renton (pt.)	WA	8	794
Renton (pt.)	WA	9	795
Reston CDP (pt.)	VA	11	778
Revere	MA	7	364
Rexburg	ID	2	231
Reynoldsburg (pt.)	OH	12	592

City	State	District	Page
River Rouge	MI	15	395
Riverside (pt.)	CA	43	121
Riverton	UT	2	753
Riverton-Boulevard Park CDP (pt.)	WA	7	792
Riverview	MI	16	396
Riviera Beach (pt.)	FL	23	199
Roanoke	VA	6	771
Roanoke Rapids (pt.)	NC	2	552
Robbinsdale	MN	5	407
Robinson CDP	PA	14	649
Robstown	TX	27	743
Rochester	MN	1	401
Rochester	NH	1	460
Rochester (pt.)	NY	28	541
Rochester Hills	MI	9	386
Rockford	IL	16	259
Rock Hill	SC	5	676
Rock Island	IL	17	260
Rockledge	FL	15	187
Rocklin	CA	4	64
Rock Springs	WY	AL	822
Rockville	MD	8	349
Rockville Centre	NY	4	504
Rockwall	TX	4	710
Rocky Hill	CT	1	150
Rocky Mount (pt.)	NC	1	550
Rocky Mount (pt.)	NC	2	552
Rocky River	OH	10	589
Roessleville CDP	NY	21	529
Rogers	AR	3	52
Rohnert Park	CA	6	67
Rolla	MO	8	437
Rolling Meadows (pt.)	IL	8	247
Rome	GA	7	214
Rome	NY	23	533
Romeoville	IL	13	255
Romulus	MI	13	392
Ronkonkoma CDP	NY	2	500
Roosevelt CDP	NY	4	504
Roseburg	OR	4	622
Rosedale CDP (pt.)	MD	2	340
Rose Hill CDP	VA	8	774
Roselle (pt.)	IL	6	243
Roselle	NJ	10	480
Roselle Park	NJ	7	475
Rosemead (pt.)	CA	31	104
Rosemont CDP	CA	5	66
Rosenberg	TX	22	736
Roseville	CA	4	64
Roseville	MI	10	387
Roseville	MN	4	405
Ross CDP (pt.)	PA	14	649
Roswell	GA	6	212

County Index

All counties are indexed here by district and page number. A (pt.) indicates counties that are split between districts. Thus a county may have two or more entries. For Alaska, which has no counties, the major political divisions of boroughs and census areas are listed. For Louisiana, parishes (the political equivalents of counties) are listed. Four states (Maryland, Missouri, Nevada, and Virginia) have cities that are independent of counties. These "independent cities" are considered county equivalents and are listed with the word "city" following the city name.

County	State	District	Page	County	State	District	Page
Autauga	AL	2	22	Belknap (pt.)	NH	1	459
Avery	NC	10	564	Belknap (pt.)	NH	2	461
Avoyelles Parish (pt.)	LA	4	323	Bell	KY	5	313
Avoyelles Parish (pt.)	LA	6	326	Bell	TX	11	721
				Belmont	OH	18	601
				Beltrami	MN	7	410
B				Ben Hill	GA	8	215
				Benewah	ID	1	229
Baca	CO	4	142	Bennett	SD	AL	682
Bacon	GA	1	204	Bennington	VT	AL	758
Bailey	TX	19	732	Benson	ND	AL	571
Baker (pt.)	FL	2	169	Bent	CO	4	142
Baker (pt.)	FL	3	171	Benton	AR	3	52
Baker (pt.)	FL	6	175	Benton	IA	2	289
Baker	GA	2	206	Benton	IN	5	276
Baker	OR	2	619	Benton (pt.)	MN	7	410
Baldwin	AL	1	21	Benton (pt.)	MN	8	412
Baldwin (pt.)	GA	3	207	Benton	MO	4	431
Baldwin (pt.)	GA	11	220	Benton	MS	1	416
Ballard	KY	1	307	Benton (pt.)	OR	4	622
Baltimore (pt.)	MD	2	340	Benton (pt.)	OR	5	623
Baltimore (pt.)	MD	3	342	Benton	TN	8	698
Baltimore (pt.)	MD	7	348	Benton	WA	4	788
Baltimore city (pt.)	MD	1	339	Benzie	MI	1	374
Baltimore city (pt.)	MD	3	342	Bergen (pt.)	NJ	5	472
Baltimore city (pt.)	MD	7	348	Bergen (pt.)	NJ	9	478
Bamberg	SC	6	678	Berkeley (pt.)	SC	1	670
Bandera	TX	21	735	Berkeley (pt.)	SC	6	678
Banks	GA	10	218	Berkeley	WV	2	800
Banner	NE	3	450	Berks	PA	6	637
Bannock	ID	2	231	Berkshire	MA	1	354
Baraga	MI	1	374	Bernalillo (pt.)	NM	1	489
Barber	KS	1	298	Bernalillo (pt.)	NM	2	491
Barbour	AL	2	22	Bernalillo (pt.)	NM	3	492
Barbour	WV	1	799	Berrien	GA	8	215
Barnes	ND	AL	571	Berrien	MI	6	381
Barnstable	MA	10	370	Bertie	NC	1	550
Barnwell	SC	2	671	Bethel Census Area	AK	AL	33
Barren	KY	2	308	Bexar (pt.)	TX	20	733
Barron	WI	3	809	Bexar (pt.)	TX	21	735
Barrow	GA	10	218	Bexar (pt.)	TX	23	737
Barry	MO	7	435	Bexar (pt.)	TX	28	744
Barry (pt.)	MI	2	376	Bibb (pt.)	AL	3	23
Barry (pt.)	MI	3	377	Bibb (pt.)	AL	6	28
Barry (pt.)	MI	7	383	Bibb (pt.)	GA	2	206
Bartholomew (pt.)	IN	2	271	Bibb (pt.)	GA	8	215
Bartholomew (pt.)	IN	9	282	Bienville Parish	LA	5	325
Barton	KS	1	298	Big Horn	MT	AL	442
Barton	MO	7	435	Big Horn	WY	AL	822
Bartow	GA	7	214	Big Stone	MN	2	402
Bastrop	TX	14	725	Billings	ND	AL	571
Bates	MO	4	431	Bingham	ID	2	231
Bath	KY	6	314	Blackford	IN	5	276
Bath	VA	6	770	Black Hawk	IA	2	289
Baxter	AR	3	52	Bladen (pt.)	NC	1	550
Bay	MI	5	380	Bladen (pt.)	NC	7	559
Bay (pt.)	FL	1	168	Blaine	ID	2	231
Bay (pt.)	FL	2	169	Blaine	MT	AL	442
Bayfield	WI	7	815	Blaine	NE	3	450
Baylor	TX	13	723	Blaine	OK	6	613
Beadle	SD	AL	682	Blair	PA	9	641
Bear Lake	ID	2	231	Blanco	TX	14	725
Beaufort (pt.)	NC	1	550	Bland	VA	9	775
Beaufort (pt.)	NC	3	553	Bleckley	GA	8	215
Beaufort (pt.)	SC	2	671	Bledsoe	TN	3	690
Beaufort (pt.)	SC	6	678	Blount	AL	4	25
Beauregard Parish	LA	7	328	Blount	TN	2	689
Beaver	OK	6	613	Blue Earth	MN	1	401
Beaver	PA	4	634	Boise	ID	1	229
Beaver	UT	1	751	Bolivar	MS	2	417
Beaverhead	MT	AL	442	Bollinger	MO	8	437
Becker	MN	7	410	Bond	IL	20	265
Beckham	OK	6	613	Bon Homme	SD	AL	682
Bedford	PA	9	641	Bonner	ID	1	229
Bedford	TN	4	692	Bonneville	ID	2	231
Bedford (pt.)	VA	5	769	Boone	AR	3	52
Bedford (pt.)	VA	6	770	Boone	IA	5	294
Bedford city	VA	5	769	Boone	IL	16	259
Bee	TX	15	726	Boone (pt.)	IN	6	277

County	State	District	Page
Boone (pt.)	IN	7	279
Boone	KY	4	311
Boone	MO	9	438
Boone	NE	3	450
Boone	WV	3	802
Borden	TX	17	729
Bosque	TX	11	721
Bossier Parish (pt.)	LA	4	323
Bossier Parish (pt.)	LA	5	325
Botetourt	VA	6	770
Bottineau	ND	AL	571
Boulder	CO	2	139
Boundary	ID	1	229
Bourbon	KS	2	299
Bourbon	KY	6	314
Bowie	TX	1	705
Bowman	ND	AL	571
Box Butte	NE	3	450
Box Elder	UT	1	751
Boyd	KY	4	311
Boyd	NE	3	450
Boyle	KY	6	314
Bracken	KY	4	311
Bradford	FL	6	175
Bradford	PA	10	643
Bradley	AR	4	53
Bradley (pt.)	TN	2	689
Bradley (pt.)	TN	3	690
Branch	MI	7	383
Brantley	GA	1	204
Braxton	WV	2	800
Brazoria (pt.)	TX	14	725
Brazoria (pt.)	TX	22	736
Brazos (pt.)	TX	5	712
Brazos (pt.)	TX	8	717
Breathitt	KY	5	313
Breckinridge	KY	2	308
Bremer	IA	2	289
Brevard	FL	15	187
Brewster	TX	23	737
Briscoe	TX	13	723
Bristol	RI	1	663
Bristol (pt.)	MA	3	357
Bristol (pt.)	MA	4	359
Bristol (pt.)	MA	9	368
Bristol Bay Borough	AK	AL	33
Bristol city	VA	9	775
Broadwater	MT	AL	442
Bronx (pt.)	NY	7	508
Bronx (pt.)	NY	15	521
Bronx (pt.)	NY	16	522
Bronx (pt.)	NY	17	523
Bronx (pt.)	NY	18	525
Brooke	WV	1	799
Brookings	SD	AL	682
Brooks	GA	2	206
Brooks	TX	15	726
Broome (pt.)	NY	23	533
Broome (pt.)	NY	25	536
Broome (pt.)	NY	26	538
Broward (pt.)	FL	19	194
Broward (pt.)	FL	20	195
Broward (pt.)	FL	22	198
Broward (pt.)	FL	23	199
Brown	IL	20	265
Brown	IN	9	282
Brown	KS	2	299
Brown	MN	2	402
Brown	NE	3	450
Brown	OH	2	578
Brown	SD	AL	682
Brown	TX	17	729
Brown (pt.)	WI	6	813
Brown (pt.)	WI	8	816
Brule	SD	AL	682
Brunswick	NC	7	559
Brunswick	VA	4	767
Bryan	GA	1	204
Bryan	OK	3	609

County	State	District	Page
Buchanan	IA	2	289
Buchanan	MO	6	434
Buchanan	VA	9	775
Buckingham	VA	5	769
Bucks	PA	8	640
Buena Vista	IA	5	294
Buena Vista city	VA	6	770
Buffalo	NE	3	450
Buffalo	SD	AL	682
Buffalo	WI	3	809
Bullitt	KY	2	308
Bulloch	GA	1	204
Bullock	AL	2	22
Buncombe (pt.)	NC	10	564
Buncombe (pt.)	NC	11	565
Bureau	IL	17	260
Burke	GA	11	220
Burke (pt.)	NC	10	564
Burke (pt.)	NC	5	556
Burke	ND	AL	571
Burleigh	ND	AL	571
Burleson	TX	14	725
Burlington (pt.)	NJ	1	466
Burlington (pt.)	NJ	2	468
Burlington (pt.)	NJ	3	469
Burlington (pt.)	NJ	4	471
Burnet	TX	21	735
Burnett	WI	7	815
Burt	NE	1	447
Butler	AL	2	22
Butler	IA	2	289
Butler	KS	4	302
Butler	KY	1	307
Butler	MO	8	437
Butler	NE	1	447
Butler	OH	8	587
Butler (pt.)	PA	4	634
Butler (pt.)	PA	21	660
Butte (pt.)	CA	2	62
Butte (pt.)	CA	3	63
Butte	ID	2	231
Butte	SD	AL	682
Butts	GA	11	220

C

County	State	District	Page
Cabarrus	NC	8	561
Cabell	WV	3	802
Cache	UT	1	751
Caddo	OK	6	613
Caddo Parish (pt.)	LA	4	323
Caddo Parish (pt.)	LA	5	325
Calaveras	CA	4	64
Calcasieu Parish	LA	7	328
Caldwell	KY	1	307
Caldwell	MO	6	434
Caldwell (pt.)	NC	5	556
Caldwell (pt.)	NC	10	564
Caldwell	TX	14	725
Caldwell Parish	LA	6	326
Caledonia	VT	AL	758
Calhoun	AL	3	23
Calhoun	AR	4	53
Calhoun	FL	2	169
Calhoun	GA	2	206
Calhoun	IA	5	294
Calhoun	IL	20	265
Calhoun	MI	7	383
Calhoun	MS	1	416
Calhoun (pt.)	SC	2	671
Calhoun (pt.)	SC	6	678
Calhoun	TX	14	725
Calhoun	WV	2	800
Callahan	TX	17	729
Callaway	MO	9	438
Calloway	KY	1	307
Calumet (pt.)	WI	6	813
Calumet (pt.)	WI	8	816

County	State	District	Page
Cook (pt.)	IL	10	250
Cook (pt.)	IL	11	252
Cook (pt.)	IL	13	254
Cook	MN	8	412
Cooke (pt.)	TX	4	710
Cooke (pt.)	TX	13	723
Cooper	MO	6	434
Coos	NH	2	461
Coos	OR	4	622
Coosa	AL	3	23
Copiah	MS	4	420
Corson	SD	AL	682
Cortland	NY	25	536
Coryell	TX	11	721
Coshocton	OH	18	601
Costilla	CO	3	141
Cottle	TX	13	723
Cotton	OK	4	611
Cottonwood	MN	2	402
Covington	AL	2	22
Covington	MS	4	420
Covington city	VA	6	770
Coweta	GA	3	207
Cowley	KS	4	302
Cowlitz	WA	3	787
Craig	OK	2	608
Craig	VA	9	775
Craighead	AR	1	49
Crane	TX	23	737
Craven (pt.)	NC	1	550
Craven (pt.)	NC	3	553
Crawford	AR	3	52
Crawford (pt.)	GA	2	206
Crawford (pt.)	GA	3	207
Crawford	IA	5	294
Crawford	IL	19	263
Crawford	IN	9	282
Crawford	KS	2	299
Crawford (pt.)	MI	1	375
Crawford (pt.)	MI	4	379
Crawford	MO	8	437
Crawford	OH	4	581
Crawford (pt.)	PA	5	635
Crawford (pt.)	PA	21	660
Crawford	WI	3	809
Creek	OK	2	608
Crenshaw	AL	2	22
Crisp (pt.)	GA	2	206
Crisp (pt.)	GA	8	215
Crittenden	AR	1	49
Crittenden	KY	1	307
Crockett	TN	8	698
Crockett	TX	23	737
Crook	OR	2	619
Crook	WY	AL	822
Crosby	TX	13	723
Cross	AR	1	49
Crowley	CO	4	142
Crow Wing	MN	8	412
Culberson	TX	23	737
Cullman	AL	4	25
Culpeper	VA	7	772
Cumberland	IL	19	263
Cumberland	KY	1	307
Cumberland	ME	1	332
Cumberland	NJ	2	468
Cumberland (pt.)	NC	1	550
Cumberland (pt.)	NC	7	559
Cumberland (pt.)	NC	8	561
Cumberland (pt.)	PA	17	654
Cumberland (pt.)	PA	19	657
Cumberland	TN	4	692
Cumberland	VA	5	769
Cuming	NE	1	447
Currituck	NC	3	553
Curry	NM	3	492
Curry	OR	4	622
Custer	CO	3	141
Custer	ID	2	231
Custer	MT	AL	442
Custer	NE	3	450
Custer	OK	6	613
Custer	SD	AL	682
Cuyahoga (pt.)	OH	10	589
Cuyahoga (pt.)	OH	11	591
Cuyahoga (pt.)	OH	13	594
Cuyahoga (pt.)	OH	19	602

D

County	State	District	Page
Dade (pt.)	FL	17	190
Dade (pt.)	FL	18	193
Dade (pt.)	FL	20	195
Dade (pt.)	FL	21	196
Dade (pt.)	FL	22	198
Dade (pt.)	FL	23	199
Dade	GA	9	217
Dade	MO	7	435
Daggett	UT	3	754
Dakota	NE	1	447
Dakota (pt.)	MN	1	401
Dakota (pt.)	MN	3	404
Dakota (pt.)	MN	4	405
Dale	AL	2	22
Dallam	TX	19	732
Dallas	AL	7	29
Dallas	AR	4	53
Dallas	IA	4	292
Dallas	MO	4	431
Dallas (pt.)	TX	3	708
Dallas (pt.)	TX	4	710
Dallas (pt.)	TX	5	712
Dallas (pt.)	TX	6	713
Dallas (pt.)	TX	24	739
Dallas (pt.)	TX	26	741
Dallas (pt.)	TX	30	747
Dane	WI	2	807
Daniels	MT	AL	442
Danville city	VA	5	769
Dare	NC	3	553
Darke	OH	8	587
Darlington (pt.)	SC	5	676
Darlington (pt.)	SC	6	678
Dauphin	PA	17	654
Davidson (pt.)	NC	6	558
Davidson (pt.)	NC	12	567
Davidson (pt.)	TN	5	693
Davidson (pt.)	TN	6	695
Davie (pt.)	NC	6	558
Davie (pt.)	NC	10	564
Daviess	IN	8	281
Daviess	KY	2	308
Daviess	MO	6	434
Davis	IA	3	291
Davis	UT	1	751
Davison	SD	AL	682
Dawes	NE	3	450
Dawson	GA	9	217
Dawson	MT	AL	442
Dawson	NE	3	450
Dawson	TX	17	729
Day	SD	AL	682
Deaf Smith	TX	19	732
Dearborn	IN	9	282
De Baca	NM	2	491
Decatur	GA	2	206
Decatur	IA	3	291
Decatur	IN	2	271
Decatur	KS	1	298
Decatur	TN	7	696
Deer Lodge	MT	AL	442
Defiance	OH	5	583
De Kalb	AL	4	25
De Kalb (pt.)	GA	4	209
De Kalb (pt.)	GA	5	210
De Kalb (pt.)	GA	6	212
De Kalb (pt.)	GA	11	220

County	State	District	Page	County	State	District	Page
Emmons	ND	AL	571	Floyd	VA	9	775
Emporia city	VA	4	767	Fluvanna	VA	5	769
Erath	TX	17	729	Foard	TX	13	723
Erie (pt.)	NY	27	539	Fond du Lac (pt.)	WI	6	813
Erie (pt.)	NY	29	542	Fond du Lac (pt.)	WI	9	818
Erie (pt.)	NY	30	544	Ford	IL	15	257
Erie	OH	5	583	Ford	KS	1	298
Erie	PA	21	660	Forest	PA	5	635
Escambia	AL	1	21	Forest	WI	8	816
Escambia	FL	1	168	Forrest	MS	5	422
Esmeralda	NV	2	454	Forsyth	GA	9	217
Essex (pt.)	MA	5	361	Forsyth (pt.)	NC	5	556
Essex (pt.)	MA	6	362	Forsyth (pt.)	NC	10	564
Essex (pt.)	NJ	7	475	Forsyth (pt.)	NC	12	567
Essex (pt.)	NJ	8	477	Fort Bend (pt.)	TX	22	736
Essex (pt.)	NJ	10	480	Fort Bend (pt.)	TX	25	740
Essex (pt.)	NJ	11	481	Foster	ND	AL	571
Essex (pt.)	NJ	13	485	Fountain	IN	7	279
Essex (pt.)	NY	22	531	Franklin	AL	4	25
Essex (pt.)	NY	24	534	Franklin	AR	3	52
Essex	VA	3	766	Franklin	FL	2	169
Essex	VT	AL	758	Franklin	GA	10	218
Estill	KY	6	314	Franklin	IA	5	294
Etowah	AL	4	25	Franklin	ID	2	231
Eureka	NV	2	454	Franklin	IL	19	263
Evangeline Parish (pt.)	LA	6	326	Franklin	IN	9	282
Evangeline Parish (pt.)	LA	7	328	Franklin	KS	2	299
Evans	GA	1	204	Franklin	KY	6	314
Fairbanks North Star Borough	AK	AL	33	Franklin	MA	1	354
Fairfax (pt.)	VA	8	774	Franklin	ME	2	334
Fairfax (pt.)	VA	10	777	Franklin	MO	9	438
Fairfax (pt.)	VA	11	778	Franklin	MS	4	420
Fairfax city	VA	11	778	Franklin	NC	2	552
Fairfield (pt.)	CT	3	153	Franklin	NE	3	450
Fairfield (pt.)	CT	4	155	Franklin	NY	24	534
Fairfield (pt.)	CT	5	156	Franklin (pt.)	OH	12	592
Fairfield (pt.)	CT	6	158	Franklin (pt.)	OH	15	596
Fairfield	OH	7	585	Franklin	PA	9	641
Fairfield	SC	5	676	Franklin	TN	4	692
Fall River	SD	AL	682	Franklin	TX	1	705
Fallon	MT	AL	442	Franklin	VA	5	769
Falls	TX	11	721	Franklin	VT	AL	758
Falls Church city	VA	8	774	Franklin	WA	4	788
Fannin	GA	9	217	Franklin city	VA	4	767
Fannin	TX	4	710	Franklin Parish	LA	5	325
Faribault	MN	1	401	Frederick	MD	6	346
Faulk	SD	AL	682	Frederick	VA	10	777
Faulkner	AR	2	50	Fredericksburg city	VA	1	763
Fauquier	VA	10	777	Freeborn	MN	1	401
Fayette	AL	4	25	Freestone	TX	5	712
Fayette	GA	3	207	Fremont (pt.)	CO	3	141
Fayette	IA	2	289	Fremont (pt.)	CO	5	144
Fayette	IL	20	265	Fremont	IA	4	292
Fayette	IN	9	282	Fremont	ID	2	231
Fayette	KY	6	314	Fremont	WY	AL	822
Fayette	OH	7	585	Fresno (pt.)	CA	18	86
Fayette (pt.)	PA	12	646	Fresno (pt.)	CA	19	87
Fayette (pt.)	PA	20	658	Fresno (pt.)	CA	20	88
Fayette	TN	7	696	Frio	TX	28	744
Fayette	TX	14	725	Frontier	NE	3	450
Fayette	WV	3	802	Fulton	AR	1	49
Fentress	TN	4	692	Fulton (pt.)	GA	4	209
Fergus	MT	AL	442	Fulton (pt.)	GA	5	210
Ferry	WA	5	789	Fulton (pt.)	GA	6	212
Fillmore	MN	1	401	Fulton	IL	17	260
Fillmore	NE	3	450	Fulton	IN	5	276
Finney	KS	1	298	Fulton	KY	1	307
Fisher	TX	17	729	Fulton	NY	24	534
Flagler (pt.)	FL	3	171	Fulton	OH	9	588
Flagler (pt.)	FL	4	172	Fulton	PA	9	641
Flathead	MT	AL	442	Furnas	NE	3	450
Fleming	KY	4	311				
Florence	SC	6	678				
Florence	WI	8	816	**G**			
Floyd	GA	7	214				
Floyd	IA	2	289	Gadsden	FL	2	169
Floyd	IN	9	282	Gage	NE	1	447
Floyd	KY	5	313	Gaines	TX	19	732
Floyd	TX	13	723	Galax city	VA	9	775

County	State	District	Page
H			
Haakon	SD	AL	682
Habersham	GA	9	217
Haines Borough	AK	AL	33
Hale	AL	7	29
Hale	TX	13	723
Halifax	VA	5	769
Halifax (pt.)	NC	1	550
Halifax (pt.)	NC	2	552
Hall	GA	9	217
Hall	NE	3	450
Hall	TX	13	723
Hamblen	TN	4	692
Hamilton	FL	2	169
Hamilton	IA	5	294
Hamilton	IL	19	263
Hamilton	IN	6	277
Hamilton	KS	1	298
Hamilton	NE	3	450
Hamilton	NY	24	534
Hamilton (pt.)	OH	1	577
Hamilton (pt.)	OH	2	578
Hamilton	TN	3	690
Hamilton	TX	11	721
Hamlin	SD	AL	682
Hampden (pt.)	MA	1	354
Hampden (pt.)	MA	2	356
Hampshire (pt.)	MA	1	354
Hampshire (pt.)	MA	2	356
Hampshire	WV	2	800
Hampton	SC	2	671
Hampton city (pt.)	VA	1	763
Hampton city (pt.)	VA	3	766
Hancock	GA	11	220
Hancock	IA	5	294
Hancock	IL	17	260
Hancock	IN	6	277
Hancock	KY	2	308
Hancock	ME	2	334
Hancock	MS	5	422
Hancock	OH	4	581
Hancock	TN	1	687
Hancock	WV	1	799
Hand	SD	AL	682
Hanover (pt.)	VA	1	763
Hanover (pt.)	VA	7	772
Hansford	TX	19	732
Hanson	SD	AL	682
Haralson	GA	7	214
Hardee	FL	12	183
Hardeman	TN	7	696
Hardeman	TX	13	723
Hardin	IA	5	294
Hardin	IL	19	263
Hardin	KY	2	308
Hardin	OH	4	581
Hardin	TN	4	692
Hardin	TX	2	707
Harding	NM	3	492
Harding	SD	AL	682
Hardy	WV	2	800
Harford	MD	2	340
Harlan	KY	5	313
Harlan	NE	3	450
Harmon	OK	6	613
Harnett	NC	2	552
Harney	OR	2	619
Harper	KS	4	302
Harper	OK	6	613
Harris	GA	3	207
Harris (pt.)	TX	7	714
Harris (pt.)	TX	8	717
Harris (pt.)	TX	9	718
Harris (pt.)	TX	18	730
Harris (pt.)	TX	22	736
Harris (pt.)	TX	25	740
Harris (pt.)	TX	29	745
Harrison	IA	4	292
Harrison	IN	9	282
Harrison	KY	6	314
Harrison	MO	6	434
Harrison	MS	5	422
Harrison	OH	18	601
Harrison	TX	1	705
Harrison	WV	1	799
Harrisonburg city	VA	6	770
Hart	GA	10	218
Hart	KY	2	308
Hartford (pt.)	CT	1	150
Hartford (pt.)	CT	6	158
Hartley	TX	19	732
Harvey	KS	4	302
Haskell	KS	1	298
Haskell	OK	2	608
Haskell	TX	17	729
Hawaii	HI	2	225
Hawkins	TN	1	687
Hayes	NE	3	450
Hays	TX	14	725
Haywood	NC	11	565
Haywood	TN	8	698
Heard	GA	7	214
Hemphill	TX	13	723
Hempstead	AR	4	53
Henderson	IL	17	260
Henderson	KY	1	307
Henderson	TN	7	696
Henderson	TX	5	712
Henderson (pt.)	NC	10	564
Henderson (pt.)	NC	11	565
Hendricks	IN	7	279
Hendry (pt.)	FL	16	189
Hendry (pt.)	FL	23	199
Hennepin (pt.)	MN	2	402
Hennepin (pt.)	MN	3	404
Hennepin (pt.)	MN	5	407
Hennepin (pt.)	MN	6	409
Henrico (pt.)	VA	3	766
Henrico (pt.)	VA	7	772
Henry	AL	2	22
Henry (pt.)	GA	3	207
Henry (pt.)	GA	11	220
Henry	IA	3	291
Henry	IL	17	260
Henry (pt.)	IN	2	271
Henry (pt.)	IN	6	277
Henry	KY	4	311
Henry	MO	4	431
Henry	OH	5	583
Henry	TN	8	698
Henry	VA	5	769
Herkimer (pt.)	NY	23	533
Herkimer (pt.)	NY	24	534
Hernando	FL	5	174
Hertford	NC	1	550
Hettinger	ND	AL	571
Hickman	KY	1	307
Hickman	TN	7	696
Hickory	MO	4	431
Hidalgo	NM	2	491
Hidalgo	TX	15	726
Highland	OH	6	584
Highland	VA	6	771
Highlands (pt.)	FL	12	183
Highlands (pt.)	FL	16	189
Hill	MT	AL	442
Hill	TX	11	721
Hillsborough (pt.)	FL	9	179
Hillsborough (pt.)	FL	11	182
Hillsborough (pt.)	FL	12	183
Hillsborough (pt.)	FL	13	185
Hillsborough (pt.)	NH	1	459
Hillsborough (pt.)	NH	2	461
Hillsdale	MI	7	383
Hinds (pt.)	MS	2	417
Hinds (pt.)	MS	4	420

County	State	District	Page	County	State	District	Page
Midland (pt.)	TX	23	737	Montgomery	MO	9	438
Mifflin	PA	9	641	Montgomery	NC	8	561
Milam	TX	11	721	Montgomery (pt.)	NY	21	529
Millard	UT	1	752	Montgomery (pt.)	NY	23	533
Mille Lacs	MN	8	412	Montgomery (pt.)	OH	3	579
Miller	AR	4	53	Montgomery (pt.)	OH	8	587
Miller	GA	2	206	Montgomery (pt.)	PA	6	637
Miller	MO	4	431	Montgomery (pt.)	PA	7	638
Mills	IA	4	292	Montgomery (pt.)	PA	8	640
Mills	TX	11	721	Montgomery (pt.)	PA	13	647
Milwaukee (pt.)	WI	4	810	Montgomery (pt.)	PA	15	651
Milwaukee (pt.)	WI	5	812	Montgomery	TN	7	696
Miner	SD	AL	682	Montgomery (pt.)	TX	2	707
Mineral	CO	3	141	Montgomery (pt.)	TX	8	717
Mineral	MT	AL	442	Montgomery	VA	9	775
Mineral	NV	2	454	Montmorency	MI	1	375
Mineral	WV	1	799	Montour	PA	11	644
Mingo	WV	3	802	Montrose	CO	3	141
Minidoka	ID	2	231	Moody	SD	AL	682
Minnehaha	SD	AL	682	Moore (pt.)	NC	2	552
Missaukee	MI	4	379	Moore (pt.)	NC	8	561
Mississippi	AR	1	49	Moore	TN	4	692
Mississippi	MO	8	437	Moore	TX	19	732
Missoula	MT	AL	442	Mora	NM	3	492
Mitchell	GA	2	206	Morehouse Parish (pt.)	LA	4	323
Mitchell	IA	2	289	Morehouse Parish (pt.)	LA	5	325
Mitchell	KS	1	298	Morgan	AL	5	26
Mitchell	NC	10	564	Morgan	CO	4	142
Mitchell	TX	17	729	Morgan	GA	10	218
Mobile	AL	1	21	Morgan	IL	18	262
Modoc	CA	2	62	Morgan (pt.)	IN	6	277
Moffat	CO	3	141	Morgan (pt.)	IN	7	279
Mohave	AZ	3	41	Morgan	KY	5	313
Moniteau	MO	4	431	Morgan	MO	4	431
Monmouth (pt.)	NJ	4	471	Morgan	OH	18	601
Monmouth (pt.)	NJ	6	474	Morgan	TN	3	690
Monmouth (pt.)	NJ	12	483	Morgan	UT	3	754
Mono	CA	4	64	Morgan	WV	2	800
Monona	IA	5	294	Morrill	NE	3	450
Monongalia	WV	1	799	Morris	KS	1	298
Monroe	AL	1	21	Morris	NJ	11	481
Monroe	AR	1	49	Morris	TX	1	705
Monroe	FL	20	195	Morrison (pt.)	MN	7	410
Monroe	GA	3	207	Morrison (pt.)	MN	8	412
Monroe	IA	3	291	Morrow	OH	4	581
Monroe	IL	12	253	Morrow	OR	2	619
Monroe (pt.)	IN	7	279	Morton	KS	1	298
Monroe (pt.)	IN	8	281	Morton	ND	AL	571
Monroe	KY	1	307	Motley	TX	13	723
Monroe	MI	16	396	Moultrie	IL	19	263
Monroe	MO	9	438	Mountrail	ND	AL	571
Monroe	MS	1	416	Mower	MN	1	401
Monroe (pt.)	NY	27	539	Muhlenberg	KY	1	307
Monroe (pt.)	NY	28	541	Multnomah (pt.)	OR	1	618
Monroe (pt.)	NY	29	542	Multnomah (pt.)	OR	3	621
Monroe	OH	18	601	Murray	GA	9	217
Monroe (pt.)	PA	10	643	Murray	MN	2	402
Monroe (pt.)	PA	11	644	Murray	OK	3	609
Monroe	TN	2	689	Muscatine	IA	1	288
Monroe (pt.)	WI	3	809	Muscogee (pt.)	GA	2	206
Monroe (pt.)	WI	6	813	Muscogee (pt.)	GA	3	207
Monroe	WV	3	802	Muskegon	MI	2	376
Montague	TX	13	723	Muskingum	OH	18	601
Montcalm	MI	4	379	Muskogee	OK	2	608
Monterey	CA	17	84	Musselshell	MT	AL	442
Montezuma	CO	3	141				
Montgomery (pt.)	AL	2	22				
Montgomery (pt.)	AL	7	29	**N**			
Montgomery	AR	4	53				
Montgomery	GA	1	204	Nacogdoches (pt.)	TX	1	705
Montgomery	IA	4	292	Nacogdoches (pt.)	TX	2	707
Montgomery	IL	20	265	Nance	NE	3	450
Montgomery	IN	7	279	Nantucket	MA	10	370
Montgomery	KS	4	302	Napa	CA	1	60
Montgomery	KY	6	314	Nash (pt.)	NC	1	550
Montgomery (pt.)	MD	4	343	Nash (pt.)	NC	2	552
Montgomery (pt.)	MD	8	349	Nassau	FL	4	172
Montgomery (pt.)	MS	1	416	Nassau (pt.)	NY	3	501
Montgomery (pt.)	MS	2	417	Nassau (pt.)	NY	4	504

County	State	District	Page	County	State	District	Page
Rice	KS	1	298	Russell	KS	1	298
Rice	MN	1	401	Russell	KY	1	307
Rich	UT	1	752	Russell	VA	9	775
Richardson	NE	1	447	Rutherford	TN	6	695
Richland	IL	19	263	Rutherford (pt.)	NC	10	564
Richland	MT	AL	442	Rutherford (pt.)	NC	11	565
Richland	ND	AL	571	Rutland	VT	AL	758
Richland	OH	4	581				
Richland (pt.)	SC	2	671				
Richland (pt.)	SC	6	678				
Richland	WI	2	807	**S**			
Richland Parish	LA	5	325				
Richmond (pt.)	GA	10	218	Sabine	TX	2	707
Richmond (pt.)	GA	11	220	Sabine Parish	LA	6	326
Richmond	NC	8	561	Sac	IA	5	294
Richmond	NY	13	516	Sacramento (pt.)	CA	3	63
Richmond	VA	3	766	Sacramento (pt.)	CA	4	64
Richmond city (pt.)	VA	3	766	Sacramento (pt.)	CA	5	66
Richmond city (pt.)	VA	7	772	Sacramento (pt.)	CA	11	76
Riley	KS	2	299	Sagadahoc	ME	1	332
Ringgold	IA	3	291	Saginaw (pt.)	MI	4	379
Rio Arriba	NM	3	492	Saginaw (pt.)	MI	5	380
Rio Blanco	CO	3	141	Saguache	CO	3	141
Rio Grande	CO	3	141	Salem	NJ	2	468
Ripley	IN	9	282	Salem city	VA	6	771
Ripley	MO	8	437	Saline	AR	2	50
Ritchie	WV	1	799	Saline	IL	19	263
Riverside (pt.)	CA	43	121	Saline	KS	1	298
Riverside (pt.)	CA	44	122	Saline	MO	4	431
Riverside (pt.)	CA	48	128	Saline	NE	1	447
Roane	TN	3	690	Salt Lake (pt.)	UT	1	752
Roane	WV	2	800	Salt Lake (pt.)	UT	2	753
Roanoke (pt.)	VA	6	771	Salt Lake (pt.)	UT	3	754
Roanoke (pt.)	VA	9	775	Saluda	SC	3	673
Roanoke city	VA	6	771	Sampson	NC	3	553
Roberts	SD	AL	682	San Augustine	TX	2	707
Roberts	TX	13	723	San Benito	CA	17	84
Robertson	KY	4	311	San Bernardino (pt.)	CA	40	117
Robertson (pt.)	TN	5	693	San Bernardino (pt.)	CA	41	118
Robertson (pt.)	TN	7	696	San Bernardino (pt.)	CA	42	119
Robertson	TX	5	712	Sanborn	SD	AL	682
Robeson (pt.)	NC	7	559	Sanders	MT	AL	442
Robeson (pt.)	NC	8	561	San Diego (pt.)	CA	48	128
Rock	MN	2	402	San Diego (pt.)	CA	49	129
Rock	NE	3	450	San Diego (pt.)	CA	50	131
Rock	WI	1	806	San Diego (pt.)	CA	51	132
Rockbridge	VA	6	771	San Diego (pt.)	CA	52	133
Rockcastle	KY	5	313	Sandoval (pt.)	NM	1	489
Rockdale	GA	4	209	Sandoval (pt.)	NM	3	492
Rockingham	NC	5	556	Sandusky	OH	5	583
Rockingham (pt.)	NH	1	459	San Francisco (pt.)	CA	8	71
Rockingham (pt.)	NH	2	461	San Francisco (pt.)	CA	12	77
Rockingham (pt.)	VA	6	771	Sangamon (pt.)	IL	18	262
Rockingham (pt.)	VA	10	777	Sangamon (pt.)	IL	20	265
Rock Island	IL	17	260	Sanilac	MI	5	380
Rockland	NY	20	528	San Jacinto	TX	2	707
Rockwall	TX	4	710	San Joaquin (pt.)	CA	11	76
Roger Mills	OK	6	613	San Joaquin (pt.)	CA	18	86
Rogers	OK	2	608	San Juan	CO	3	141
Rolette	ND	AL	571	San Juan	NM	3	492
Rooks	KS	1	298	San Juan	UT	3	754
Roosevelt	MT	AL	442	San Juan	WA	2	785
Roosevelt	NM	3	492	San Luis Obispo	CA	22	91
Roscommon	MI	4	379	San Mateo (pt.)	CA	12	77
Roseau	MN	7	410	San Mateo (pt.)	CA	14	80
Rosebud	MT	AL	442	San Miguel	CO	3	141
Ross (pt.)	OH	6	584	San Miguel	NM	3	492
Ross (pt.)	OH	7	585	San Patricio	TX	15	726
Routt	CO	3	141	Sanpete	UT	3	754
Rowan	KY	4	311	San Saba	TX	11	721
Rowan (pt.)	NC	6	558	Santa Barbara (pt.)	CA	22	91
Rowan (pt.)	NC	8	561	Santa Barbara (pt.)	CA	23	92
Rowan (pt.)	NC	12	567	Santa Clara (pt.)	CA	13	78
Runnels	TX	17	729	Santa Clara (pt.)	CA	14	80
Rush	IN	2	271	Santa Clara (pt.)	CA	15	81
Rush	KS	1	298	Santa Clara (pt.)	CA	16	83
Rusk	TX	1	705	Santa Cruz	AZ	2	39
Rusk	WI	7	815	Santa Cruz (pt.)	CA	15	81
Russell	AL	3	23	Santa Cruz (pt.)	CA	17	84

County	State	District	Page	County	State	District	Page
St. Johns (pt.)	FL	4	172	Sully	SD	AL	682
St. Joseph	IN	3	273	Summers	WV	3	802
St. Joseph	MI	6	381	Summit	CO	3	141
St. Landry Parish (pt.)	LA	4	323	Summit	UT	3	754
St. Landry Parish (pt.)	LA	6	326	Summit (pt.)	OH	13	594
St. Landry Parish (pt.)	LA	7	328	Summit (pt.)	OH	14	595
St. Lawrence	NY	24	534	Sumner	KS	4	302
St. Louis	MN	8	412	Sumner	TN	6	695
St. Louis (pt.)	MO	1	426	Sumter	AL	7	29
St. Louis (pt.)	MO	2	428	Sumter	FL	5	174
St. Louis (pt.)	MO	3	429	Sumter	GA	2	206
St. Louis city (pt.)	MO	1	426	Sumter (pt.)	SC	5	676
St. Louis city (pt.)	MO	3	429	Sumter (pt.)	SC	6	678
St. Lucie (pt.)	FL	16	189	Sunflower	MS	2	417
St. Lucie (pt.)	FL	23	199	Surry	NC	5	556
St. Martin Parish (pt.)	LA	3	322	Surry	VA	3	766
St. Martin Parish (pt.)	LA	4	323	Susquehanna	PA	10	643
St. Martin Parish (pt.)	LA	7	328	Sussex	DE	AL	162
St. Mary Parish	LA	3	322	Sussex (pt.)	NJ	5	472
St. Mary's	MD	5	345	Sussex (pt.)	NJ	11	481
St. Tammany Parish	LA	1	319	Sussex	VA	4	767
Stafford	KS	1	298	Sutter	CA	3	63
Stafford	VA	1	763	Sutton	TX	23	737
Stanislaus	CA	18	86	Suwannee	FL	2	169
Stanley	SD	AL	682	Swain	NC	11	565
Stanly	NC	8	561	Sweet Grass	MT	AL	442
Stanton	KS	1	298	Sweetwater	WY	AL	822
Stanton	NE	1	447	Swift	MN	2	402
Stark	IL	18	262	Swisher	TX	13	723
Stark	ND	AL	571	Switzerland	IN	9	282
Stark (pt.)	OH	14	595				
Stark (pt.)	OH	16	598				
Starke (pt.)	IN	3	273				
Starke (pt.)	IN	5	276	**T**			
Starr	TX	28	744				
Staunton city	VA	6	771	Talbot	GA	2	206
Ste. Genevieve	MO	3	429	Talbot	MD	1	339
Stearns	MN	7	410	Taliaferro	GA	11	220
Steele	MN	1	401	Talladega	AL	3	23
Steele	ND	AL	571	Tallahatchie (pt.)	MS	1	416
Stephens	GA	9	217	Tallahatchie (pt.)	MS	2	417
Stephens	OK	4	611	Tallapoosa	AL	3	23
Stephens	TX	17	729	Tama	IA	2	289
Stephenson	IL	16	259	Taney	MO	7	435
Sterling	TX	21	735	Tangipahoa Parish (pt.)	LA	1	319
Steuben	IN	4	274	Tangipahoa Parish (pt.)	LA	4	323
Steuben	NY	31	545	Taos	NM	3	492
Stevens	KS	1	298	Tarrant (pt.)	TX	6	713
Stevens	MN	7	410	Tarrant (pt.)	TX	12	722
Stevens	WA	5	789	Tarrant (pt.)	TX	24	739
Stewart	GA	2	206	Tarrant (pt.)	TX	26	741
Stewart	TN	8	698	Tarrant (pt.)	TX	30	747
Stillwater	MT	AL	442	Tate	MS	1	416
Stoddard	MO	8	437	Tattnall	GA	1	204
Stokes	NC	5	556	Taylor	FL	2	169
Stone	AR	1	49	Taylor	GA	2	206
Stone	MO	7	435	Taylor	IA	3	291
Stone	MS	5	422	Taylor	KY	2	308
Stonewall	TX	17	729	Taylor	TX	17	729
Storey	NV	2	454	Taylor	WI	7	815
Story	IA	3	291	Taylor	WV	1	799
Strafford	NH	1	459	Tazewell	IL	18	262
Stutsman	ND	AL	571	Tazewell	VA	9	775
Sublette	WY	AL	822	Tehama	CA	3	63
Suffolk (pt.)	MA	7	364	Telfair	GA	8	215
Suffolk (pt.)	MA	8	366	Teller	CO	5	144
Suffolk (pt.)	MA	9	368	Tensas Parish	LA	4	323
Suffolk (pt.)	NY	1	498	Terrebonne Parish	LA	3	322
Suffolk (pt.)	NY	2	500	Terrell	GA	2	206
Suffolk (pt.)	NY	5	505	Terrell	TX	23	737
Suffolk city (pt.)	VA	3	766	Terry	TX	19	732
Suffolk city (pt.)	VA	4	767	Teton	ID	2	231
Sullivan	IN	8	281	Teton	MT	AL	442
Sullivan	MO	6	434	Teton	WY	AL	822
Sullivan	NH	2	461	Texas	MO	8	437
Sullivan (pt.)	NY	20	528	Texas	OK	6	613
Sullivan (pt.)	NY	26	538	Thayer	NE	3	450
Sullivan	PA	10	643	Thomas	GA	2	206
Sullivan	TN	1	687	Thomas	KS	1	298
				Thomas	NE	3	450

County	State	District	Page	County	State	District	Page
Wakulla	FL	2	169	Washtenaw (pt.)	MI	13	392
Waldo (pt.)	ME	1	332	Watauga	NC	5	556
Waldo (pt.)	ME	2	334	Watonwan	MN	2	403
Walker	AL	4	25	Waukesha (pt.)	WI	1	806
Walker	GA	9	217	Waukesha (pt.)	WI	4	810
Walker	TX	2	707	Waukesha (pt.)	WI	9	818
Wallace	KS	1	298	Waupaca	WI	6	813
Walla Walla	WA	5	789	Waushara	WI	6	813
Waller (pt.)	TX	8	717	Wayne	GA	1	204
Waller (pt.)	TX	14	725	Wayne	IA	3	291
Wallowa	OR	2	619	Wayne	IL	19	263
Walsh	ND	AL	571	Wayne	IN	2	271
Walthall	MS	4	420	Wayne	KY	5	313
Walton	FL	1	168	Wayne (pt.)	MI	11	388
Walton	GA	10	218	Wayne (pt.)	MI	13	392
Walworth	SD	AL	682	Wayne (pt.)	MI	14	394
Walworth	WI	1	806	Wayne (pt.)	MI	15	395
Wapello	IA	3	291	Wayne (pt.)	MI	16	396
Ward	ND	AL	571	Wayne	MO	8	437
Ward	TX	23	737	Wayne (pt.)	MS	3	419
Ware	GA	1	204	Wayne (pt.)	MS	5	422
Warren	GA	11	220	Wayne (pt.)	NC	1	550
Warren	IA	3	291	Wayne (pt.)	NC	3	553
Warren	IL	17	260	Wayne	NE	1	447
Warren	IN	5	276	Wayne	NY	27	539
Warren	KY	2	308	Wayne	OH	16	598
Warren	MO	9	438	Wayne	PA	10	643
Warren	MS	2	417	Wayne	TN	4	692
Warren	NC	1	550	Wayne	UT	3	754
Warren	NJ	5	472	Wayne	WV	3	802
Warren	NY	22	531	Waynesboro city	VA	6	771
Warren (pt.)	OH	2	578	Weakley	TN	8	698
Warren (pt.)	OH	6	584	Webb	TX	23	737
Warren	PA	5	636	Weber	UT	1	752
Warren	TN	4	692	Webster	GA	2	206
Warren	VA	10	777	Webster	IA	5	294
Warrick	IN	8	281	Webster	KY	1	307
Wasatch	UT	3	754	Webster	MO	4	431
Wasco	OR	2	619	Webster	MS	1	416
Waseca	MN	1	401	Webster	NE	3	450
Washakie	WY	AL	822	Webster	WV	3	802
Washburn	WI	7	815	Webster Parish (pt.)	LA	4	323
Washington	AL	1	21	Webster Parish (pt.)	LA	5	325
Washington	AR	3	52	Weld	CO	4	142
Washington	CO	4	142	Wells	IN	4	274
Washington	FL	2	169	Wells	ND	AL	571
Washington	GA	11	220	West Baton Rouge Parish (pt.)	LA	4	323
Washington	IA	3	291	West Baton Rouge Parish (pt.)	LA	6	326
Washington	ID	1	229	West Carroll Parish (pt.)	LA	4	323
Washington	IL	20	265	West Carroll Parish (pt.)	LA	5	325
Washington	IN	9	282	Westchester (pt.)	NY	17	523
Washington	KS	1	298	Westchester (pt.)	NY	18	525
Washington	KY	2	308	Westchester (pt.)	NY	19	526
Washington	MD	6	346	Westchester (pt.)	NY	20	528
Washington	ME	2	334	West Feliciana Parish	LA	4	323
Washington (pt.)	MN	3	404	Westmoreland	VA	1	763
Washington (pt.)	MN	4	405	Westmoreland (pt.)	PA	4	634
Washington (pt.)	MN	6	409	Westmoreland (pt.)	PA	12	646
Washington	MO	8	437	Westmoreland (pt.)	PA	20	658
Washington	MS	2	417	Weston	WY	AL	822
Washington	NC	1	550	Wetzel	WV	1	799
Washington	NE	1	447	Wexford	MI	2	376
Washington	NY	22	531	Wharton	TX	14	725
Washington	OH	6	584	Whatcom	WA	2	785
Washington	OK	5	612	Wheatland	MT	AL	442
Washington	OR	1	618	Wheeler	GA	8	215
Washington	PA	20	658	Wheeler	NE	3	450
Washington	RI	2	665	Wheeler	OR	2	619
Washington	TN	1	687	Wheeler	TX	13	723
Washington	TX	8	717	White	AR	2	50
Washington	UT	1	752	White	GA	9	217
Washington	VA	9	775	White	IL	19	263
Washington	VT	AL	758	White	IN	5	276
Washington	WI	9	818	White	TN	4	692
Washington Parish	LA	1	319	White Pine	NV	2	454
Washita	OK	6	613	Whiteside	IL	17	260
Washoe	NV	2	454	Whitfield	GA	9	217
Washtenaw (pt.)	MI	7	383	Whitley	IN	4	274
Washtenaw (pt.)	MI	8	384	Whitley	KY	5	313

University and College Index

Universities and colleges are indexed here by the first word in their name. For example, the University of Wisconsin will be found under the U's; John Marshall Law School will be found under the J's.

School	State	District	Page
A			
Abilene Christian University, Abilene	TX	17	729
Abraham Baldwin Agricultural College, Tifton	GA	8	215
Adams State College, Alamosa	CO	3	141
Adelphi University, Garden City	NY	4	504
Adirondack Community College, Queensbury	NY	22	531
Adrian College, Adrian	MI	7	383
Agnes Scott College, Decatur	GA	4	209
Aiken Technical College, Aiken	SC	3	673
Aims Community College, Greeley	CO	4	142
Air Force Institute of Technology, Fairborn	OH	7	585
Alabama A&M University, Normal	AL	5	26
Alabama Aviation & Tech College, Ozark	AL	2	22
Alabama State University, Montgomery	AL	7	29
Alamance Community College, Haw River	NC	12	567
Alaska Junior College, Anchorage	AK	AL	33
Alaska Pacific University, Anchorage	AK	AL	33
Albany College of Pharmacy, Albany	NY	21	530
Albany Law School, Albany	NY	21	530
Albany Medical College, Albany	NY	21	530
Albany State College, Albany	GA	2	206
Albert Einstein College of Medicine, Bronx	NY	7	508
Albertson College of Idaho, Caldwell	ID	1	229
Albertus Magnus College, New Haven	CT	3	153
Albion College, Albion	MI	7	383
Albright College, Reading	PA	6	637
Al Collins Graphic Design School, Tempe	AZ	1	38
Alcorn State University, Lorman	MS	2	417
Alderson Broaddus College, Philippi	WV	1	799
Alexandria Technical College, Alexandria	MN	7	411
Alfred University, Alfred	NY	31	545
Alice Lloyd College, Pippa Passes	KY	5	313
Allan Hancock College, Santa Maria	CA	22	91
Allegany Community College, Cumberland	MD	6	346
Allegheny College, Meadville	PA	21	660
Allegheny Community College, Pittsburgh	PA	14	649
Allen County Community College, Iola	KS	2	299
Allentown College of St. Francis De Sales, Center Valley	PA	15	651
Allen University, Columbia	SC	6	678
Alma College, Alma	MI	4	379
Almontes Academy of Cosmetology, Albuquerque	NM	1	490
Alpena Community College, Alpena	MI	1	375
Alvernia College, Reading	PA	6	637
Alverno College, Milwaukee	WI	4	810
Alvin Community College, Alvin	TX	22	736
Amarillo College, Amarillo	TX	13	724
Amber University, Garland	TX	5	712
American Academy of Art, Chicago	IL	7	245
American Academy of Dramatic Art, New York	NY	14	518
American Baptist College, Nashville	TN	5	693
American College, Bryn Mawr	PA	7	639
American College of Applied Arts, Atlanta	GA	5	211
American Institute of Business, Des Moines	IA	4	292
American Institute of Design, Philadelphia	PA	3	633
American International College, Springfield	MA	2	356
American University, Washington	DC	AL	839
Amherst College, Amherst	MA	1	354
Ancilla Domini College, Donaldson	IL	5	276
Anderson College, Anderson	SC	3	673
Anderson University, Anderson	IN	2	272
Andover College, Portland	ME	1	333
Andover Newton Theological School, Newton	MA	9	368
Andrew College, Cuthbert	GA	2	206
Andrews University, Berrien Springs	MI	6	382
Angelina College, Lufkin	TX	2	707
Angelo State University, San Angelo	TX	21	735
Anna Maria College, Paxton	MA	3	358
Anne Arundel Community College, Arnold	MD	1	339
Anoka-Ramsey Community College, Coon Rapids	MN	6	409
Anson Community College, Polkton	NC	8	561
Antelope Valley College, Lancaster	CA	25	95
Antioch New England Graduate School, Keene	NH	2	461
Antioch School of Adult Learning, Yellow Springs	OH	7	585
Antioch University, Los Angeles	CA	36	111
Antioch University, Santa Barbara	CA	22	91
Antioch University, Yellow Springs	OH	7	585
Antioch University, Seattle	WA	7	792
Appalachian Bible College, Bradley	WV	3	802
Appalachian State University, Boone	NC	5	556
Aquinas College, Grand Rapids	MI	3	378
Aquinas College, Milton	MA	9	368
Aquinas College at Milton, Newton	MA	4	359
Aquinas Junior College, Nashville	TN	5	693
Arapahoe Community College, Littleton	CO	6	145
Arizona State University, Tempe	AZ	1	38
Arizona Western College, Yuma	AZ	2	39
Arkansas Baptist College, Little Rock	AR	2	50
Arkansas College, Batesville	AR	1	49
Arkansas State University, Beebe	AR	2	50
Arkansas State University, State University	AR	1	49
Arkansas Tech University, Russellville	AR	3	52
Arlington Baptist College, Arlington	TX	6	713
Armstrong State College, Savannah	GA	1	204
Art Academy of Cincinnati, Cincinnati	OH	1	577
Art Center College of Design, Pasadena	CA	27	99
Art Institute of Atlanta, Atlanta	GA	5	211
Art Institute of Dallas, Dallas	TX	3	708
Art Institute of Ft. Lauderdale, Ft. Lauderdale	FL	22	198
Art Institute of Philadelphia, Philadelphia	PA	2	631
Art Institute of Pittsburgh, Pittsburgh	PA	14	649
Art Institute of Seattle, Seattle	WA	7	792
Asbury College, Wilmore	KY	6	314
Asbury Theological Seminary, Wilmore	KY	6	314
Asheville Buncombe Tech College, Asheville	NC	11	565
Ashland College, Ashland	OH	16	598
Ashland Community College, Ashland	KY	4	312
Asnuntuck Community College, Enfield	CT	6	158
Assemblies of God Theological Seminary, Springfield	MO	7	435
Assumption College, Worcester	MA	3	358
Athenaeum of Ohio, Cincinnati	OH	2	578
Athens State College, Athens	AL	5	26
Athens Technical Institute, Athens	GA	10	219
Atlanta College of Art, Atlanta	GA	5	211
Atlanta Metropolitan College, Atlanta	GA	5	211
Atlantic Community College, Mays Landing	NJ	2	468
Atlantic Union College, South Lancaster	MA	3	358
Auburn University, Auburn	AL	3	24
Auburn University at Montgomery, Montgomery	AL	2	22
Augsburg College, Minneapolis	MN	5	407
Augusta College, Augusta	GA	10	219
Augusta Technical School, Augusta	GA	11	220
Augustana College, Rock Island	IL	17	260
Augustana College, Sioux Falls	SD	AL	682
Aurora University, Aurora	IL	14	256
Austin College, Sherman	TX	4	710
Austin Community College, Austin	MN	1	401
Austin Community College, Austin	TX	10	719
Austin Peay State University, Clarksville	TN	7	697
Austin Presbyterian Theological Seminary, Austin	TX	10	719
Averett College, Danville	VA	5	769
Avila College, Kansas City	MO	5	432
Azusa Pacific University, Azusa	CA	28	100

School	State	District	Page
Glenville State College, Glenville	WV	2	800
Gloucester County College, Sewell	NJ	2	468
Goddard College, Plainfield	VT	AL	758
Gogebic Community College, Ironwood	MI	1	375
Golden Gate Baptist Seminary, Mill Valley	CA	6	67
Golden Gate University, San Francisco	CA	8	71
Golden West College, Huntington Beach	CA	45	123
Goldey Beacom College, Wilmington	DE	AL	162
Gonzaga University, Spokane	WA	5	790
Gordon College, Barnesville	GA	3	208
Gordon College, Wenham	MA	6	363
Gordon-Conwell Theological Seminary, South Hamilton	MA	6	363
Goshen College, Goshen	IN	3	273
Goucher College, Towson	MD	2	341
Governors State University, University Park	IL	11	252
Grace College, Winona Lake	IN	3	273
Grace College of the Bible, Omaha	NE	2	448
Graceland College, Lamoni	IA	3	291
Graduate Theological Union, Berkeley	CA	9	73
Grambling State University, Grambling	LA	4	323
Grand Canyon College, Phoenix	AZ	4	42
Grand Rapids Baptist College, Grand Rapids	MI	3	378
Grand Rapids Community College, Grand Rapids	MI	3	378
Grand Valley State University, Allendale	MI	2	376
Grand View College, Des Moines	IA	4	292
Gratz College, Melrose Park	PA	13	648
Grays Harbor College, Aberdeen	WA	6	791
Grayson County College, Denison	TX	4	710
Greater Hartford Community College, Hartford	CT	1	150
Greater New Haven Tech College, North Haven	CT	3	153
Great Lakes Business College, Saginaw	MI	5	380
Greenfield Community College, Greenfield	MA	1	354
Green Mountain College, Poultney	VT	AL	758
Green River Community College, Auburn	WA	8	794
Greensboro College, Greensboro	NC	6	558
Greenville College, Greenville	IL	20	265
Greenville Technical College, Greenville	SC	4	675
Griffin College, Seattle	WA	1	783
Grinnell College, Grinnell	IA	3	291
Grossmont College, El Cajon	CA	52	133
Grossmont-Cuyamaca Community College, El Cajon	CA	52	133
Grove City College, Grove City	PA	21	660
Gruss Girls Seminary, Spring Valley	NY	20	528
Guilford College, Greensboro	NC	6	558
Guilford Tech Community College, Jamestown	NC	12	567
Guilford Technical Institute, Jamestown	NC	6	558
Gulf Coast Community College, Panama City	FL	1	168
Gustavus Adolphus College, St. Peter	MN	2	403
Gwinnett Technical Institute, Lawrenceville	GA	4	209
Gwynedd-Mercy College, Gwynedd Valley	PA	13	648

H

School	State	District	Page
Hagerstown Business College, Hagerstown	MD	6	346
Hagerstown Junior College, Hagerstown	MD	6	347
Hahnemann Medical University, Philadelphia	PA	2	631
Halifax Community College, Weldon	NC	1	551
Hamilton College, Clinton	NY	23	533
Hamilton Technical College, Davenport	IA	1	288
Hamline University, St. Paul	MN	4	406
Hampden-Sydney College, Hampden-Sydney	VA	5	769
Hampshire College, Amherst	MA	1	354
Hampton University, Hampton	VA	3	766
Hannibal-LaGrange College, Hannibal	MO	9	438
Hanover College, Hanover	IN	9	282
Harcum Junior College, Bryn Mawr	PA	13	648
Harding University, Searcy	AR	2	50
Hardin-Simmons University, Abilene	TX	17	729
Harford Community College, Bel Air	MD	2	341
Harrington Institute of Interior Design, Chicago	IL	7	245
Harrisburg Area Community College, Harrisburg	PA	17	654

School	State	District	Page
Harris-Stowe State College, St. Louis	MO	1	426
Harry M. Ayers State Tech College, Anniston	AL	3	24
Hartford Graduate Center, Hartford	CT	1	150
Hartford State Tech College, Hartford	CT	1	150
Hartnell College, Salinas	CA	17	85
Hartwick College, Oneonta	NY	23	533
Harvard University, Cambridge	MA	8	366
Harvey Mudd College, Claremont	CA	28	100
Haskell Indian Junior College, Lawrence	KS	3	301
Hastings College, Hastings	NE	3	450
Hastings College of Law, San Francisco	CA	8	71
Haverford College, Haverford	PA	7	639
Hawaii Loa College, Kaneohe	HI	2	225
Hawaii Pacific College, Honolulu	HI	1	224
Hawkeye Institute of Technology, Waterloo	IA	2	289
Haywood Community College, Clyde	NC	11	565
Hazard Community College, Hazard	KY	5	313
Heald Business College, Hayward	CA	13	79
Heald Business College, Rohnert Park	CA	6	67
Heald Institute of Technology, San Jose	CA	16	83
Heart of Georgia Tech Institute, Dublin	GA	8	215
Hebrew Theological College, Skokie	IL	9	249
Heidelberg College, Tiffin	OH	5	583
Helene Fuld School of Nursing, New York	NY	15	521
Henderson Community College, Henderson	KY	1	307
Henderson State University, Arkadelphia	AR	4	54
Hendrix College, Conway	AR	2	50
Henry Ford Community College, Dearborn	MI	16	396
Heritage College, Toppenish	WA	4	788
Herkimer Community College, Herkimer	NY	23	533
Hesser College, Manchester	NH	1	460
Hesston College, Hesston	KS	4	303
Hibbing Community College, Hibbing	MN	8	412
Highland Community College, Freeport	IL	16	259
Highland Community College, Highland	KS	2	299
Highland Park Community College, Highland Park	MI	14	394
Highline Community College, Seattle	WA	9	795
High Point University, High Point	NC	12	567
Hilbert College, Hamburg	NY	30	544
Hill College, Hillsboro	TX	11	721
Hillsborough Community College, Tampa	FL	11	182
Hillsdale College, Hillsdale	MI	7	383
Hinds Community College, Raymond	MS	3	419
Hiram College, Hiram	OH	13	594
Hiwassee College, Madisonville	TN	2	689
Hobart & William Smith Colleges, Geneva	NY	27	540
Hobson State Tech College, Thomasville	AL	1	21
Hocking Technical College, Nelsonville	OH	6	584
Hofstra University, Hempstead	NY	4	504
Hollins College, Roanoke	VA	6	771
Holmes Community College, Goodman	MS	2	417
Holy Apostles College, Cromwell	CT	1	150
Holy Cross College, Notre Dame	IN	3	273
Holy Family College, Philadelphia	PA	3	633
Holy Names College, Oakland	CA	9	73
Holyoke Community College, Holyoke	MA	1	354
Honolulu Community College, Honolulu	HI	1	224
Hood College, Frederick	MD	6	347
Hope College, Holland	MI	2	376
Hopkinsville Community College, Hopkinsville	KY	1	307
Horry-Georgetown Tech College, Conway	SC	1	670
Hostos Community College, Bronx	NY	17	523
Houghton College, Houghton	NY	31	545
Housatonic Community College, Bridgeport	CT	4	155
Houston Baptist University, Houston	TX	22	736
Houston Community College, Houston	TX	18	730
Howard Community College, Columbia	MD	3	342
Howard County Junior College, Big Spring	TX	17	729
Howard Payne University, Brownwood	TX	17	729
Howard University, Washington	DC	AL	839
Hudson County Community College, Jersey City	NJ	13	485
Hudson Valley Community College, Troy	NY	21	530
Humboldt State University, Arcata	CA	1	60
Humphreys College, Stockton	CA	11	76
Huntingdon College, Montgomery	AL	2	22

School	State	District	Page
Huntington College, Huntington	IL	4	275
Huntington Junior College, Huntington	WV	3	802
Huron University, Huron	SD	AL	682
Husson College, Bangor	ME	2	334
Huston-Tillotson College, Austin	TX	10	719
Hutchinson Community College, Hutchinson	KS	1	298

I

School	State	District	Page
ICS-Center for Degree Studies, Scranton	PA	10	643
Idaho State University, Pocatello	ID	2	231
Iliff School of Theology, Denver	CO	1	138
Illinois Benedictine College, Lisle	IL	13	255
Illinois Central College, East Peoria	IL	18	262
Illinois College, Jacksonville	IL	18	262
Illinois College of Optometry, Chicago	IL	1	237
Illinois Eastern Community College, Olney	IL	19	264
Illinois Institute of Technology, Chicago	IL	1	237
Illinois Medical Training Centers, Chicago	IL	7	245
Illinois School of Professional Psychology, Chicago	IL	7	245
Illinois State University, Normal	IL	15	257
Illinois Valley Community College, Oglesby	IL	11	252
Illinois Wesleyan University, Bloomington	IL	15	257
Immaculata College, Immaculata	PA	16	653
Immaculate Conception Seminary, Huntington	NY	2	500
Imperial Valley College, Imperial	CA	52	133
Incarnate Word College, San Antonio	TX	21	735
Independence Community College, Independence	KS	4	303
Indiana Institute of Technology, Fort Wayne	IL	4	275
Indiana State University, Terre Haute	IN	7	279
Indiana University, Bloomington	IN	8	281
Indiana University, Kokomo	IL	5	276
Indiana University, South Bend	IN	3	273
Indiana University East, Richmond	IN	2	272
Indiana University Northwest, Gary	IN	1	270
Indiana University of Pennsylvania, Indiana	PA	12	646
Indiana University-Purdue University, Fort Wayne	IL	4	275
Indiana University-Purdue University, Indianapolis	IN	10	284
Indiana University-Southeast, New Albany	IN	9	282
Indiana Vocational Tech College, Columbus	IN	2	272
Indiana Vocational Tech College, Kokomo	IL	5	276
Indiana Vocational Tech College, Lafayette	IN	7	279
Indiana Vocational Tech College, Muncie	IN	2	272
Indiana Vocational Tech College, Richmond	IN	2	272
Indiana Vocational Tech College-Central Indiana, Indianapolis	IN	10	284
Indiana Vocational Tech College-North Central, South Bend	IN	3	273
Indiana Vocational Tech College-Northeast, Fort Wayne	IL	4	275
Indiana Vocational Tech College-Northwest, Gary	IN	1	270
Indiana Vocational Tech College-South Central, Sellersburg	IN	9	282
Indiana Vocational Tech College-Southeast, Madison	IN	9	282
Indiana Vocational Tech College-Southwest, Evansville	IN	8	281
Indiana Vocational Tech College-Wabash Valley, Terre Haute	IN	7	279
Indiana Wesleyan College, Marion	IL	5	276
Indian Hills Community College, Ottumwa	IA	3	291
Indian River Community College, Ft. Pierce	FL	16	189
Institute of Electronic Technology, Paducah	KY	1	307
Institute of the American Indian, Santa Fe	NM	3	492
Interboro Institute, New York	NY	8	509
Interdenominational Theological Center, Atlanta	GA	5	211
International Academy of Merchandising & Design, Chicago	IL	1	237
International Business College, Fort Wayne	IL	4	275
International Business College, Indianapolis	IN	6	278
International Correspondence, Scranton	PA	10	643

School	State	District	Page
International Fine Arts College, Miami	FL	22	198
Inver Hills Community College, Inver Grove Heights	MN	3	404
Iona College, New Rochelle	NY	18	525
Iowa Central Community College, Fort Dodge	IA	5	294
Iowa Lakes Community College, Estherville	IA	5	294
Iowa Methodist School of Nursing, Des Moines	IA	4	292
Iowa State University, Ames	IA	3	291
Iowa Valley Community College, Marshalltown	IA	3	291
Iowa Wesleyan College, Mount Pleasant	IA	3	291
Iowa Western Community College, Council Bluffs	IA	4	292
Irvine Valley College, Irvine	CA	47	126
Isothermal Community College, Spindale	NC	11	565
Itasca Community College, Grand Rapids	MN	8	412
Itawamba Community College, Fulton	MS	1	416
Ithaca College, Ithaca	NY	26	538
ITT Technical Institute, Arlington	TX	24	739
ITT Technical Institute, Aurora	CO	6	145
ITT Technical Institute, Austin	TX	10	719
ITT Technical Institute, Boise	ID	2	231
ITT Technical Institute, Buena Park	CA	39	115
ITT Technical Institute, Dayton	OH	3	580
ITT Technical Institute, Earth City	MO	2	428
ITT Technical Institute, Evansville	IN	8	281
ITT Technical Institute, Fort Wayne	IL	4	275
ITT Technical Institute, Garland	TX	5	712
ITT Technical Institute, Hoffman Estates	IL	8	248
ITT Technical Institute, Houston	TX	18	730
ITT Technical Institute, Houston	TX	25	740
ITT Technical Institute, Indianapolis	IN	6	278
ITT Technical Institute, Knoxville	TN	2	689
ITT Technical Institute, La Mesa	CA	52	133
ITT Technical Institute, Nashville	TN	5	693
ITT Technical Institute, Phoenix	AZ	1	38
ITT Technical Institute, Portland	OR	3	621
ITT Technical Institute, Sacramento	CA	11	76
ITT Technical Institute, Salt Lake City	UT	2	753
ITT Technical Institute, Seattle	WA	9	795
ITT Technical Institute, Spokane	WA	5	790
ITT Technical Institute, Tampa	FL	11	182
ITT Technical Institute, Tucson	AZ	2	39
ITT Technical Institute, Van Nuys	CA	26	96
ITT Technical Institute, West Covina	CA	28	100
ITT Technical Institute, Youngstown	OH	17	599

J

School	State	District	Page
J. C. Calhoun State Community College, Decatur	AL	5	26
J. F. Drake State Tech College, Huntsville	AL	5	26
J. M. Patterson State Tech College, Montgomery	AL	2	22
J. Sargeant Reynolds Community College, Richmond	VA	7	773
Jackson Community College, Jackson	MI	7	383
Jackson State Community College, Jackson	TN	8	698
Jackson State University, Jackson	MS	4	420
Jacksonville College, Jacksonville	TX	2	707
Jacksonville State University, Jacksonville	AL	3	24
Jacksonville University, Jacksonville	FL	3	171
James Madison University, Harrisonburg	VA	6	771
James Sprunt Community College, Kenansville	NC	1	551
Jamestown Business College, Jamestown	NY	31	545
Jamestown College, Jamestown	ND	AL	571
Jamestown Community College, Jamestown	NY	31	545
Jarvis Christian College, Hawkins	TX	1	706
Jefferson College, Hillsboro	MO	3	429
Jefferson Community College, Louisville	KY	3	310
Jefferson Community College, Watertown	NY	24	534
Jefferson Davis Community College, Atmore	AL	1	21
Jefferson Davis State Junior College, Brewton	AL	1	21
Jefferson State Community College, Birmingham	AL	6	28

School	State	District	Page
Ohio State University, Columbus	OH	15	597
Ohio State University, Lima	OH	4	581
Ohio State University, Mansfield	OH	4	581
Ohio State University, Marion	OH	4	581
Ohio State University, Newark	OH	12	592
Ohio State University-Agricultural Tech Institute, Wooster	OH	16	598
Ohio University, Athens	OH	6	584
Ohio University, Chillicothe	OH	6	584
Ohio University, Ironton	OH	6	584
Ohio University, Lancaster	OH	7	586
Ohio University, Zanesville	OH	18	601
Ohio University-Belmont, St. Clairsville	OH	18	601
Ohio Valley College, Parkersburg	WV	1	799
Ohio Wesleyan University, Delaware	OH	12	592
Ohlone College, Fremont	CA	13	79
Okaloosa-Walton Community College, Niceville	FL	1	168
Okefenoke Tech Institute, Waycross	GA	1	204
Oklahoma Baptist University, Shawnee	OK	3	610
Oklahoma Christian College, Oklahoma City	OK	6	613
Oklahoma City Community College, Oklahoma City	OK	6	613
Oklahoma City University, Oklahoma City	OK	6	613
Oklahoma College of Osteopathic Medicine, Tulsa	OK	1	607
Oklahoma Junior College, Oklahoma City	OK	5	612
Oklahoma Junior College of Business, Tulsa	OK	1	607
Oklahoma Panhandle State University, Goodwell	OK	6	613
Oklahoma State University, Oklahoma City	OK	5	612
Oklahoma State University, Okmulgee	OK	2	608
Oklahoma State University, Stillwater	OK	3	610
Old Dominion University, Norfolk	VA	2	765
Olivet College, Olivet	MI	7	383
Olivet Nazarene University, Kankakee	IL	11	252
Olympic College, Bremerton	WA	6	791
Onondaga Community College, Syracuse	NY	25	536
Oral Roberts University, Tulsa	OK	1	607
Orangeburg Calhoun Tech College, Orangeburg	SC	6	678
Orange Coast College, Costa Mesa	CA	45	123
Orange County Community College, Middletown	NY	20	528
Oregon Graduate Institute, Beaverton	OR	1	618
Oregon Health Science University, Portland	OR	1	618
Oregon Institute of Technology, Klamath Falls	OR	2	620
Oregon Polytechnic Institute, Portland	OR	3	621
Oregon State University, Corvallis	OR	5	623
Orlando College, Orlando	FL	8	178
Oscar Rose State College, Midwest City	OK	4	611
Otero Junior College, La Junta	CO	4	142
Otis Art Institute of Parsons School of Design, Los Angeles	CA	33	107
Ottawa University, Ottawa	KS	2	300
Ottawa University, Phoenix	AZ	4	42
Ottawa University-Kansas City, Overland Park	KS	3	301
Otterbein College, Westerville	OH	12	592
Ouachita Baptist University, Arkadelphia	AR	4	54
Our Lady of Holy Cross College, New Orleans	LA	2	320
Our Lady of the Lake University, San Antonio	TX	20	733
Owensboro Community College, Owensboro	KY	2	309
Owensboro Junior College, Owensboro	KY	2	309
Oxnard College, Oxnard	CA	23	93
Ozark Christian College, Joplin	MO	7	435

P

School	State	District	Page
Pace University, New York	NY	8	509
Pace University, Pleasantville	NY	19	526
Pace University, White Plains	NY	19	526
Pacific Christian College, Fullerton	CA	39	116
Pacific Coast Bible College, San Dimas	CA	28	100
Pacific Coast College, Chula Vista	CA	50	131
Pacific Graduate School of Psychiatry, Palo Alto	CA	14	80
Pacific Lutheran University, Tacoma	WA	6	791
Pacific Oaks College, Pasadena	CA	27	99
Pacific Union College, Angwin	CA	1	61
Pacific University, Forest Grove	OR	1	618
Paducah Community College, Paducah	KY	1	307
Paier College of Art, Hamden	CT	3	153
Paine College, Augusta	GA	11	220
Palm Beach Atlantic College, West Palm Beach	FL	23	199
Palm Beach Community College, Lake Worth	FL	19	194
Palmer Chiropractic College, Davenport	IA	1	288
Palmer College of Chiropractic, Sunnyvale	CA	14	80
Palo Alto College, San Antonio	TX	28	744
Palo Verde College, Blythe	CA	44	122
Palomar Community College, San Marcos	CA	51	132
Panola College, Carthage	TX	1	706
Paradise Valley Community College, Phoenix	AZ	4	42
Paris Junior College, Paris	TX	1	706
Park College, Parkville	MO	6	434
Parker Chiropractic College, Dallas	TX	30	747
Parkland College, Champaign	IL	15	257
Parks College of St. Louis University, Cahokia	IL	12	253
Parks Junior College, Denver	CO	4	142
Pasadena City College, Pasadena	CA	27	99
Pasco Hernando Community College, Dade City	FL	12	183
Passaic County Community College, Paterson	NJ	8	477
Patrick Henry Community College, Martinsville	VA	5	769
Patrick Henry State Junior College, Monroeville	AL	1	21
Patten College, Oakland	CA	9	73
Paul D. Camp Community College, Franklin	VA	4	768
Paul Quinn College, Dallas	TX	30	747
Paul Smith's College of Arts & Sciences, Paul Smiths	NY	24	534
Peabody Institute of Johns Hopkins, Baltimore	MD	7	348
Peace College, Raleigh	NC	4	555
Pearl River Community College, Poplarville	MS	5	422
Peirce Junior College, Philadelphia	PA	2	631
Pellissippi State Tech Community College, Knoxville	TN	2	689
Pembroke State University, Pembroke	NC	7	560
Peninsula College, Port Angeles	WA	6	791
Penn Valley Community College, Kansas City	MO	5	432
Pennco Tech, Bristol	PA	8	640
Pennsylvania College of Optometry, Philadelphia	PA	1	630
Pennsylvania College of Podiatric Medicine, Philadelphia	PA	1	630
Pennsylvania College of Technology, Williamsport	PA	10	643
Pennsylvania Institute of Technology, Media	PA	7	639
Pennsylvania State University, Altoona	PA	9	642
Pennsylvania State University, Du Bois	PA	9	642
Pennsylvania State University, Hazleton	PA	11	645
Pennsylvania State University, Malvern	PA	7	639
Pennsylvania State University, McKeesport	PA	18	656
Pennsylvania State University, Mont Alto	PA	9	642
Pennsylvania State University, New Kensington	PA	4	634
Pennsylvania State University, State College	PA	5	636
Pennsylvania State University, Wilkes-Barre	PA	11	645
Pennsylvania State University, York	PA	19	657
Pennsylvania State University-Allentown, Fogelsville	PA	15	651
Pennsylvania State University-Beaver Falls, Monaca	PA	4	634
Pennsylvania State University-Behrend, Erie	PA	21	660
Pennsylvania State University-Berks, Reading	PA	6	637
Pennsylvania State University-Delaware County, Media	PA	7	639
Pennsylvania State University-Fayette, Uniontown	PA	12	646
Pennsylvania State University-Harrisburg, Middletown	PA	17	654
Pennsylvania State University-Milton S. Hershey Medical Center, Hershey	PA	17	654

School	State	District	Page
University of Texas of the Permian Basin, Odessa	TX	19	732
University of Texas-Pan American, Edinburg	TX	15	726
University of Texas Southwest Medical Center, Dallas	TX	30	747
University of the Arts, Philadelphia	PA	2	631
University of the District of Columbia, Washington	DC	AL	839
University of the Ozarks, Clarksville	AR	3	52
University of the Pacific, Stockton	CA	11	76
University of the South, Sewanee	TN	4	692
University of Toledo, Toledo	OH	9	588
University of Tulsa, Tulsa	OK	1	607
University of Utah, Salt Lake City	UT	2	753
University of Vermont, Burlington	VT	AL	758
University of Virginia, Charlottesville	VA	5	769
University of Virginia-Clinch Valley College, Wise	VA	9	776
University of Washington, Seattle	WA	7	792
University of West Florida, Pensacola	FL	1	168
University of West Los Angeles, Los Angeles	CA	32	106
University of Wisconsin, Eau Claire	WI	3	809
University of Wisconsin, Green Bay	WI	8	817
University of Wisconsin, La Crosse	WI	3	809
University of Wisconsin, Madison	WI	2	808
University of Wisconsin, Milwaukee	WI	4	810
University of Wisconsin, Oshkosh	WI	6	814
University of Wisconsin, Platteville	WI	3	809
University of Wisconsin, River Falls	WI	3	809
University of Wisconsin, Stevens Point	WI	7	815
University of Wisconsin, Superior	WI	7	815
University of Wisconsin, Whitewater	WI	1	806
University of Wisconsin-Parkside, Kenosha	WI	1	806
University of Wisconsin-Stout, Menomonie	WI	3	809
University of Wyoming, Laramie	WY	AL	822
University South Carolina, Aiken	SC	3	673
Upper Iowa University, Fayette	IA	2	290
Upsala College, East Orange	NJ	10	480
Upson Technical Institute, Thomaston	GA	3	208
Urbana University, Urbana	OH	7	586
Ursinus College, Collegeville	PA	13	648
Ursuline College, Cleveland	OH	19	602
Utah State University, Logan	UT	1	752
Utah Valley Community College, Orem	UT	3	755
Utica College of Syracuse University, Utica	NY	23	533
Utica School of Commerce, Utica	NY	23	533

V

School	State	District	Page
Valdosta State College, Valdosta	GA	2	206
Valdosta Technical Institute, Valdosta	GA	2	206
Valencia Community College, Orlando	FL	8	178
Valley City State University, Valley City	ND	AL	572
Valley Forge Christian College, Phoenixville	PA	7	639
Valparaiso University, Valparaiso	IN	1	270
Vance-Granville Community College, Henderson	NC	1	551
Vanderbilt University, Nashville	TN	5	693
Vassar College, Poughkeepsie	NY	22	531
Ventura College, Ventura	CA	23	93
Vermilion Community College, Ely	MN	8	412
Vermont Law School, South Royalton	VT	AL	758
Vermont Technical College, Randolph Center	VT	AL	758
Vernon Regional Junior College, Vernon	TX	13	724
Victoria College, Victoria	TX	14	725
Victor Valley College, Victorville	CA	40	117
Villa Julie College, Stevenson	MD	3	342
Villa Maria College of Buffalo, Buffalo	NY	30	544
Villanova University, Villanova	PA	7	639
Vincennes University, Vincennes	IN	8	281
Virginia Commonwealth University, Richmond	VA	3	766
Virginia Highlands Community College, Abingdon	VA	9	776
Virginia Intermont College, Bristol	VA	9	776
Virginia Military Institute, Lexington	VA	6	771
Virginia Polytechnic Institute & State University, Blacksburg	VA	9	776

School	State	District	Page
Virginia State University, Petersburg	VA	3	766
Virginia Union University, Richmond	VA	3	766
Virginia Wesleyan College, Norfolk	VA	2	765
Virginia Western Community College, Roanoke	VA	6	771
Vista College, Berkeley	CA	9	73
Viterbo College, La Crosse	WI	3	809
Volunteer State Community College, Gallatin	TN	6	695
Voorhees College, Denmark	SC	6	678

W

School	State	District	Page
Wabash College, Crawfordsville	IN	7	279
Wade's Fashion Merchandising, Dallas	TX	30	747
Wagner College, Staten Island	NY	13	517
Wake Forest University, Winston-Salem	NC	5	557
Wake Tech Community College, Raleigh	NC	4	555
Walden University, Minneapolis	MN	5	407
Waldorf College, Forest City	IA	5	294
Walker College, Jasper	AL	4	25
Walker State Tech College, Sumiton	AL	4	25
Walker Technical Institute, Rock Spring	GA	9	217
Walla Walla College, College Place	WA	5	790
Walla Walla Community College, Walla Walla	WA	5	790
Walsh College of Accounting & Business, Troy	MI	12	391
Walsh College, Canton	OH	16	598
Walters State Community College, Morristown	TN	4	692
Warner Pacific College, Portland	OR	3	621
Warner Southern College, Lake Wales	FL	12	184
Warren Community College, Washington	NJ	5	472
Warren Wilson College, Swannanoa	NC	11	565
Wartburg College, Waverly	IA	2	290
Wartburg Theological Seminary, Dubuque	IA	2	290
Washburn University of Topeka, Topeka	KS	2	300
Washington & Jefferson College, Washington	PA	20	658
Washington & Lee University, Lexington	VA	6	771
Washington Bible College, Lanham	MD	5	345
Washington City Tech College, Calais	ME	2	334
Washington College, Chestertown	MD	1	339
Washington State Community College, Marietta	OH	6	584
Washington State University, Pullman	WA	5	790
Washington Theological Union, Silver Spring	MD	4	344
Washington University, St. Louis	MO	1	426
Washtenaw Community College, Ann Arbor	MI	13	392
Washtenaw Community College, Ann Arbor	MI	8	384
Waterbury State Tech College, Waterbury	CT	5	156
Waubonsee Community College, Sugar Grove	IL	14	256
Waukesha County Tech College, Pewaukee	WI	9	818
Waycross College, Waycross	GA	1	204
Wayland Baptist University, Plainview	TX	13	724
Wayne Community College, Goldsboro	NC	3	553
Wayne County Community College, Detroit	MI	15	395
Waynesburg College, Waynesburg	PA	20	658
Wayne State College, Wayne	NE	1	447
Wayne State University, Detroit	MI	15	395
Weatherford College, Weatherford	TX	12	722
Webber College, Babson Park	FL	12	184
Weber State College, Ogden	UT	1	752
Webster University, St. Louis	MO	3	429
Wellesley College, Wellesley	MA	4	359
Wells College, Aurora	NY	31	545
Wenatchee Valley College, Wenatchee	WA	4	788
Wentworth Institute of Technology, Boston	MA	8	366
Wentworth Military Academy, Lexington	MO	4	431
Wesleyan College, Macon	GA	8	216
Wesleyan University, Middletown	CT	2	152
Wesley College, Dover	DE	AL	162
Wesley Theological Seminary, Washington	DC	AL	839
Westark Community College, Fort Smith	AR	3	52
Westbrook College, Portland	ME	1	333
Westchester Business Institute, White Plains	NY	18	525
Westchester Community College, Valhalla	NY	19	526
West Chester University, West Chester	PA	16	653
West Coast University, Los Angeles	CA	30	103

Cable Television Index

This index lists cable television companies that appear in this book. A firm's common name is used for purposes of indexing but is followed in most cases by corporate owner (after dash) in order that reader may identify multiple ownership in cable industry. In a few cases corporate ownership information was unavailable.

Cable Company	State	District
A		
Abbeville Cable TV — TCA Cable TV Inc	LA	7
Acworth Cable TV — Wemetco Cable TV Co	GA	6
Acworth Cable TV — Wometco Cable TV Inc	GA	7
Adams Cable — Adams Cable TV Inc	PA	10
Adams Russell Cable — Cable Systems Corp	MA	1
Adams Russell Cable — Cable Systems Corp	MA	5
Adams Russell Cable — Cable Systems Corp	MA	6
Adams Russell Cable — Cable Systems Corp	MA	9
Adams Russell Cable — Cable Systems Corp	ME	2
Adelphia Cable — Adelphia Communications Corp	FL	16
Adelphia Cable — Adelphia Communications Corp	FL	17
Adelphia Cable — Adelphia Communications Corp	FL	18
Adelphia Cable — Adelphia Communications Corp	FL	19
Adelphia Cable — Adelphia Communications Corp	FL	20
Adelphia Cable — Adelphia Communications Corp	FL	21
Adelphia Cable — Adelphia Communications Corp	FL	23
Adelphia Cable — Adelphia Communications Corp	MA	10
Adelphia Cable — Adelphia Communications Corp	NJ	3
Adelphia Cable — Adelphia Communications Corp	NJ	4
Adelphia Cable — Adelphia Communications Corp	NY	24
Adelphia Cable — Adelphia Communications Corp	NY	25
Adelphia Cable — Adelphia Communications Corp	NY	27
Adelphia Cable — Adelphia Communications Corp	NY	29
Adelphia Cable — Adelphia Communications Corp	NY	30
Adelphia Cable — Adelphia Communications Corp	OH	4
Adelphia Cable — Adelphia Communications Corp	OH	13
Adelphia Cable — Adelphia Communications Corp	OH	16
Adelphia Cable — Adelphia Communications Corp	PA	4
Adelphia Cable — Adelphia Communications Corp	PA	7
Adelphia Cable — Adelphia Communications Corp	PA	10
Adelphia Cable — Adelphia Communications Corp	PA	11
Adelphia Cable — Adelphia Communications Corp	PA	12
Adelphia Cable — Adelphia Communications Corp	PA	13
Adelphia Cable — Adelphia Communications Corp	PA	18
Adelphia Cable — Adelphia Communications Corp	SC	2
Adelphia Cable — Adelphia Communications Corp	VA	5
Adelphia Cable — Adelphia Communications Corp	VA	6
Adelphia Cable — Adelphia Communications Corp	VA	7
Adelphia Cable — Adelphia Communications Corp	VA	9
Adelphia Cable — Adelphia Communications Corp	VA	10
Adelphia Cable — Adelphia Communications Corp	VT	AL
Alabama Newschannels — Newchannels Corp	AL	2
Allen's TV Cable — Allen's TV Cable Service Inc	LA	3
Americable	NH	2
Americable International — Americable International Inc	FL	18
American Cable TV — American Cable TV	DE	AL
American Cable TV — American Cable TV	MD	5
American Cablevision — Time Warner Inc	AR	1
American Cablevision — Time Warner Inc	CA	27
American Cablevision — Time Warner Inc	CO	2
American Cablevision — Time Warner Inc	CO	4
American Cablevision — Time Warner Inc	CO	6
American Cablevision — Time Warner Inc	IN	7
American Cablevision — Time Warner Inc	KS	2
American Cablevision — Time Warner Inc	KS	3
American Cablevision — Time Warner Inc	MN	2
American Cablevision — Time Warner Inc	MO	5
American Cablevision — Time Warner Inc	MO	6
American Cablevision — Time Warner Inc	PA	18
American Cablevision of Coronado — Time Warner Inc	CA	49
American Cablevision-Indianapolis — Time Warner Inc	IN	6
American Cablevision-Indianapolis — Time Warner Inc	IN	10
American Cablevision-St. Louis — Time Warner Inc	MO	1
American Community Cablevision — Time Warner Inc	NY	26
American Community Cablevision — Time Warner Inc	NY	31

Cable Company	State	District
American Heritage Cablevision — Tele-Communications	IA	4
Anderson Cable TV — Booth American Co	SC	3
Anniston Newchannels — Newchannels Corp	AL	3
Antietam Cable TV — Schurz Communications	MD	6
Apollo Cablevision	CA	39
Archdale Cable — Time Warner Inc	NC	6
Arlington Cable Partners — Hauser Communications	VA	8
Arlington Telecable — Telecable Corp	TX	6
Arlington Telecable — Telecable Corp	TX	24
Armstrong Cable — Armstrong Utilities Inc	PA	12
Armstrong Cable — Armstrong Utilities Inc	PA	20
Armstrong Cable — Armstrong Utilities Inc	PA	21
Armstrong Utilities — Armstrong Utilities Inc	OH	13
Armstrong Utilities — Armstrong Utilities Inc	OH	16
Armstrong Utilities — Armstrong Utilities Inc	OH	17
Armstrong Utilities — Armstrong Utilities Inc	PA	4
ATC Cablevision — Tiime Warner	CA	25
Athens Cable — Rifkin & Associates	TN	2
Atlantic Telephone Membership	NC	7
Auburn Cablevision	NY	25
Austin Cablevision — Time Warner Inc	TX	10
Austin Cablevision — Time Warner Inc	TX	14
Austin Cablevision — Time Warner Inc	TX	21
Avenue TV Cable Service — Avenue TV Cable Service Inc	CA	23
B		
Barden Cablevision — Barden Communications Inc	MI	11
Barden Cablevision — Barden Communications Inc	MI	14
Barden Cablevision — Barden Communications Inc	MI	15
Batesville Cable TV — TCA Cable TV Inc	AR	1
Battlefield Cable TV — E.W. Scripps Co	GA	9
Bay Cablevision — Lenfest Group	CA	7
Beckley Telecable — Telecable Corp	WV	3
Bee Line Cable TV — Bee Line Cable TV	ME	2
Beloit Cablevision — Time Warner Inc	IL	16
Beloit Cablevision — Time Warner Inc	WI	1
Benchmark Communications — Benchmark Communcations Inc	CA	40
Bend Cable Communications — Bend Cable Communications Inc	OR	2
Berks Cable — Time Warner Inc	PA	6
Berwick Cable TV — Gans Group	PA	11
Bessemer Cable Communications — Time Warner Inc	AL	6
Better Cable TV — State Cable TV Corp	ME	1
Big Spring Cable TV — TCA Cable TV Inc	TX	17
Binghamton Newchannels — Newchannels Corp	NY	23
Binghamton Newchannels — Newchannels Corp	NY	25
Binghamton Newchannels — Newchannels Corp	NY	26
Blacksburg Cable TV Service — Booth American Co	VA	9
Blue Ridge Cable TV Inc — Pencor Services Inc	PA	6
Blue Ridge Cable TV Inc — Pencor Services Inc	PA	10
Blue Ridge Cable TV Inc — Pencor Services Inc	PA	11
Blue Ridge Cable TV Inc — Pencor Services Inc	PA	15
Blue Ridge Cable TV Inc — Pencor Services Inc	PA	16
Blue Ridge Cable TV Inc — Pencor Services Inc	PA	17
Blytheville TV Cable	AR	1
Booth Communications — Booth American Co	MI	11
Bresnan Communication — Bresnan Communications Co	MI	1
Bresnan Communication — Bresnan Communications Co	MI	4
Bresnan Communication — Bresnan Communications Co	MI	5
Bresnan Communication — Bresnan Communications Co	MN	8
Bresnan Communication — Bresnan Communications Co	WI	7
Brookings Cablevision — Tele-Communications Inc	SD	AL
Brownwood TV Cable Service — Brownwood TB Cable Inc	TX	17
Buckeye Cablevision	OH	9
Buckeye Cablevision	OH	5
Buenavision Cable TV	CA	31
C		
C-4 Media Cable Southeast — C-4 Media	GA	9
C-Tec — C-Tec Cable Systems Inc	MI	1

Cable Company	State	District
C-Tec — C-Tec Cable Systems Inc	MI	2
C-Tec — C-Tec Cable Systems Inc	NJ	7
C-Tec — C-Tec Cable Systems Inc	NJ	12
C-Tec — C-Tec Cable Systems Inc	NY	19
Cable Alabama Corp — Cable America Corp	AL	5
Cable America — Cable America Corp	AZ	6
Cable America — Cable America Corp	MO	4
Cable Brazil — Omega Communications	IN	7
Cable Co-Op	CA	14
Cable Equities — Rifkin & Associates	IL	20
Cable Oakland — Lenfest Group	CA	9
Cable Oakland — Lenfest Group	CA	13
Cable Services of Jamestown — Cable Services Inc	ND	AL
Cable System — Toledo Blade Co	MI	16
Cable TV Copmany of York — Susquehanna Cable Co	PA	19
Cable TV Montgomery — Hauser Communications	MD	4
Cable TV Montgomery — Hauser Communications	MD	5
Cable TV Montgomery — Hauser Communications	MD	6
Cable TV Montgomery — Hauser Communications	MD	8
Cable TV North Central — New Heritage Associates	MN	3
Cable TV North Central — New Heritage Associates	MN	4
Cable TV North Central — New Heritage Associates	MN	6
Cable TV of Coral Springs — Schurz Communications Inc	FL	19
Cable TV of Dothan — Cablevision Industries Inc	AL	2
Cable TV of Jersey City — Maclean Hunter Cable TV Inc	NJ	9
Cable TV of Jersey City — Maclean Hunter Cable TV Inc	NJ	13
Cable TV of Kennebunk	ME	1
Cablecom of Clarksdale — Washington Post Co	MS	2
Cablecom of Dyersburg — Washington Post Co	TN	8
Cablecom of Fargo — Washington Post Co	ND	AL
Cablecom of Joplin — Washington Post Co	MO	7
Cablecom of Kirksville — Washington Post Co	MO	9
Cablecom of Lufkin — Washington Post Co	TX	2
Cablecom of Norfolk — Washington Post Co	NE	1
Cablecom on Ardmore — Washington Post Co	OK	3
Cablesouth Inc — Cablesouth Inc	AL	4
Cablesystems of Watertown — Paragon/Time Warner Inc	NY	24
Cablevision Industries — Cablevision Industries Inc	FL	8
Cablevision — Cablevision Systems Corp	ME	2
Cablevision — Cablevision Systems Corp	NY	1
Cablevision — Cablevision Systems Corp	NY	2
Cablevision — Cablevision Systems Corp	NY	3
Cablevision — Cablevision Systems Corp	NY	4
Cablevision — Cablevision Systems Corp	NY	5
Cablevision — Cablevision Systems Corp	NY	8
Cablevision — Cablevision Systems Corp	NY	9
Cablevision — Cablevision Systems Corp	NY	10
Cablevision — Cablevision Systems Corp	NY	11
Cablevision — Cablevision Systems Corp	NY	12
Cablevision — Cablevision Systems Corp	NY	16
Cablevision — Cablevision Systems Corp	NY	17
Cablevision — Cablevision Systems Corp	NY	18
Cablevision — Cablevision Systems Corp	NY	19
Cablevision — Cablevision Systems Corp	NY	21
Cablevision — McDonald Group	GA	8
Cablevision — Rifkin & Associates	IL	20
Cablevision — Rifkin & Associates	WV	2
Cablevision — Time Warner Inc	CO	3
Cablevision — Time Warner Inc	CO	4
Cablevision — Time Warner Inc	CO	5
Cablevision — Time Warner Inc	LA	4
Cablevision — Time Warner Inc	LA	5
Cablevision — Time Warner Inc	NC	1
Cablevision — Time Warner Inc	NC	3
Cablevision — Time Warner Inc	NC	7
Cablevision — Time Warner Inc	NC	8
Cablevision — Time Warner Inc	NC	9
Cablevision — Time Warner Inc	NC	9
Cablevision — Time Warner Inc	NC	12
Cablevision — Time Warner Inc	TN	7
Cablevision — Time Warner Inc	WI	8
Cablevision Fairhaven-Acushnet — Cablevision Industries Inc	MA	4
Cablevision Inc — Omega Communications	MI	4
Cablevision Industries — Cablevision Industries Inc	LA	1
Cablevision Industries — Cablevision Industries Inc	SC	1
Cablevision Industries — Cablevision Industries Inc	FL	3
Cablevision Industries — Cablevision Industries Inc	FL	6
Cablevision Industries — Cablevision Industries Inc	FL	7
Cablevision Industries — Cablevision Industries Inc	FL	13
Cablevision Industries — Cablevision Industries Inc	NC	2
Cablevision Industries — Cablevision Industries Inc	NC	4
Cablevision Industries — Cablevision Industries Inc	NC	6
Cablevision Industries — Cablevision Industries Inc	NY	20
Cablevision Industries — Cablevision Industries Inc	NY	20
Cablevision Industries — Cablevision Industries Inc	NY	22
Cablevision Industries — Cablevision Industries Inc	NY	23
Cablevision Industries — Cablevision Industries Inc	NY	26
Cablevision Industries — Cablevision Industries Inc	NY	27
Cablevision Industries — Cablevision Industries Inc	TN	8
Cablevision of Baton Rouge — Tele-Communications Inc	LA	6
Cablevision of Boston — Cablevisions Systems Corp	MA	4
Cablevision of Boston — Cablevisions Systems Corp	MA	8
Cablevision of Boston — Cablevisions Systems Corp	MA	9
Cablevision of Central Florida — Time Warner Inc	FL	4
Cablevision of Central Florida — Time Warner Inc	FL	5
Cablevision of Central Florida — Time Warner Inc	FL	12
Cablevision of Central Florida — Time Warner Inc	FL	15
Cablevision of Chapel Hill — Time Warner Inc	NC	4
Cablevision of Chicago — Cablevision Systems Corp	IL	3
Cablevision of Columbia — Cablevision Industries Inc	SC	2
Cablevision of Columbia — Cablevision Industries Inc	SC	6
Cablevision of Emporia — Time Warner Inc	KS	1
Cablevision of Fox Cities — Time Warner Inc	WI	6
Cablevision of Golden Gate — Cablevision Industries Inc	FL	14
Cablevision of Greater Johnstown — Time Warner Inc	PA	12
Cablevision of Homewood — Cablevision Systems Corp	IL	2
Cablevision of Homewood — Cablevision Systems Corp	IL	11
Cablevision of Lincoln — Metrovision Inc	NE	1
Cablevision of Loudoun — Benchmark Communication	VA	10
Cablevision of Manassas — Benchmark Communication	VA	10
Cablevision of Michigan — Cablevision Systems Corp	MI	6
Cablevision of New Jersey — Cablevision Systems Corp	NJ	5
Cablevision of Newark — Cablevision Systems Corp	NJ	8
Cablevision of Newark — Cablevision Systems Corp	NJ	10
Cablevision of Newark — Cablevision Systems Corp	NJ	13
Cablevision of Orange — Time Warner Inc	CA	47
Cablevision of Pennsylvania	PA	13
Cablevision of Savannah — Time Warner Inc	GA	1
Cablevision of Southern Connecticut — Cablevision Systems Corp	CT	3
Cablevision of Southern Connecticut — Cablevision Systems Corp	CT	4
Cablevision of Southern Connecticut — Cablevision Systems Corp	CT	5
Cablevision of Stillwater — Multimedia Cablevision Inc	OK	3
Cablevision Rockford — Cablevision Systems Corp	IL	16
Cablevision Systems — Rifkin & Associates	OH	6
Cablevision-Warr Acres — Multimedia Cablevision Inc	OK	4
Cablevision-Warr Acres — Multimedia Cablevision Inc	OK	5
Cablevision-Warr Acres — Multimedia Cablevision Inc	OK	6
Cablevision/Fredericksburg — Media General Inc	VA	1
Callais Cablevision	LA	3
Cam-Tel College — Wehco Video Inc	AR	4
Campbell CATV — Nesbe Cable Satellite Communications	VA	5
Capital Cablevision — Time Warner Inc	NY	21
Capital Cablevision — Time Warner Inc	WV	2
Capitol Cablevision — Time Warner Inc	MS	2
Capitol Cablevision — Time Warner Inc	MS	3
Capitol Cablevision — Time Warner Inc	MS	4
Cardinal Communications — Cardinal Communications Inc	IN	2
Cardinal Communications — Cardinal Communications Inc	IN	5
Cardinal Communications — Cardinal Communications Inc	IN	7
Cardinal Communications — Cardinal Communications Inc	IN	9
Carroll County Cable TV — Prestige Group	MD	6
Carthage Newchannels — Newchannels Corp	NY	24
Casco Cable TV — Susquehanna Cable Co	ME	1
Catawba Valley Cable TV — Prime Cable Inc	NC	10
CATV Enterprises	NY	17
CATV of East Providence — Susquehanna Cable Co	RI	1
Cencom Cable TV — Cencom Cable Associates Inc	CA	27
Cencom Cable TV — Cencom Cable Associates Inc	CA	28
Cencom Cable TV — Cencom Cable Associates Inc	CA	31
Cencom Cable TV — Cencom Cable Associates Inc	CA	33
Cencom Cable TV — Cencom Cable Associates Inc	CA	34
Cencom Cable TV — Cencom Cable Associates Inc	CA	43
Cencom Cable TV — Cencom Cable Associates Inc	IL	12
Cencom Cable TV — Cencom Cable Associates Inc	IL	20

Cable Company	State	District
Cencom Cable TV — Cencom Cable Associates Inc	KY	1
Cencom Cable TV — Cencom Cable Associates Inc	MO	1
Cencom Cable TV — Cencom Cable Associates Inc	MO	2
Cencom Cable TV — Cencom Cable Associates Inc	MO	3
Cencom Cable TV — Cencom Cable Associates Inc	NC	2
Cencom Cable TV — Cencom Cable Associates Inc	SC	3
Cencom Cable TV — Cencom Cable Associates Inc	TN	7
Cencom Cable TV — Cencom Cable Associates Inc	TX	11
Cencom Cable TV — Cencom Cable Associates Inc	TX	14
Cencom Cable TV — Cencom Cable Associates Inc	NC	10
Cencom Cable TV — Cencom Cable Associates Inc	NC	11
Cencom Cable TV — Cencom Cable Associates Inc	SC	4
Century Cable — Century Communications Corp	AL	4
Century Cable — Century Communications Corp	CA	1
Century Cable — Century Communications Corp	CA	7
Century Cable — Century Communications Corp	CA	23
Century Cable — Century Communications Corp	CA	24
Century Cable — Century Communications Corp	CA	29
Century Cable — Century Communications Corp	CA	30
Century Cable — Century Communications Corp	CA	36
Century Cable — Century Communications Corp	CA	36
Century Cable — Century Communications Corp	CA	39
Century Cable — Century Communications Corp	CA	40
Century Cable — Century Communications Corp	CA	52
Century Cable — Century Communications Corp	IN	2
Century Cable — Century Communications Corp	KS	1
Century Cable — Century Communications Corp	KY	2
Century Cable — Century Communications Corp	MA	1
Century Cable — Century Communications Corp	NC	8
Century Cable — Century Communications Corp	PA	21
Century Cable — Century Communications Corp	WA	3
Century Cable — Century Communications Corp	WI	4
Century Cable — Century Communications Corp	WI	9
Century Cable — Century Communications Corp	WV	1
Century Cable — Century Communications Corp	WV	3
Century Carolina Cable — Century Communications Corp	SC	5
Century Mississippi Cable — Century Communications Corp	MS	2
Century Norwich Cable — Century Communications Corp	CT	2
Century Ohio Cable — Century Communications Corp	OH	6
Century Virginia Cable — Century Communications Corp	VA	9
Chambers Cable — Chambers Communication Corp	CA	2
Chambers Cable — Chambers Communication Corp	CA	3
Chambers Cable — Chambers Communication Corp	CA	40
Chambers Cable — Chambers Communication Corp	WA	1
Chambers Cable of Novato — Chambers Communication Corp	CA	6
Champaign-Urbana Cablevision — Time Warner Inc	IL	15
Chattahoochee Cablevision — McDonald Group	GA	3
Chattanooga Cable TV — E.W. Scripps Co	TN	3
Chino Valley Cable TV — Tele-Communications Inc	CA	41
Chronicle Cablevision	HI	1
Chronicle Cablevision	HI	2
Clay Video — Rifkin & Associates	FL	6
Clear Picture — Massillon Cable TV Inc	OH	16
Coast TV Cable — Washington Post Co	MS	5
Coaxial Cable — Time Warner Inc	PA	5
Coaxial Communications — Coaxial Communications of Central Ohio	OH	2
Coaxial Communications — Coaxial Communications of Central Ohio	OH	7
Coaxial Communications — Coaxial Communications of Central Ohio	OH	12
Coaxial Communications — Coaxial Communications of Central Ohio	OH	15
Colony Cablevision — Colony Communications Inc	FL	14
Colony Communications — Colony Communications Inc	CA	38
Colony Communications — Colony Communications Inc	CA	44
Colony Communications — Colony Communications Inc	CA	52
Columbia Cable — Columbia International Inc	WA	3
Columbia Cable — Columbia International Inc	MI	8
Columbia Cable — Columbia International Inc	MI	13
Columbia Cable — Columbia International Inc	NV	2
Columbia Cable — Columbia International Inc	OR	1
Columbia Cable of Virginia — Columbia International Inc	VA	10
Columbia Cable of Virginia — Columbia International Inc	VA	11
Columbine Cablevision — World Company	CO	4
Columbus Cable TV — Time Warner Inc	NE	3
Columbus TV Cable — Columbus Cable TV Corp	MS	3

Cable Company	State	District
Comcast Cablevision — Comcast Cable Communications	AL	1
Comcast Cablevision — Comcast Cable Communications	AL	2
Comcast Cablevision — Comcast Cable Communications	AL	4
Comcast Cablevision — Comcast Cable Communications	AL	5
Comcast Cablevision — Comcast Cable Communications	AL	6
Comcast Cablevision — Comcast Cable Communications	CA	22
Comcast Cablevision — Comcast Cable Communications	CA	23
Comcast Cablevision — Comcast Cable Communications	CA	38
Comcast Cablevision — Comcast Cable Communications	CA	39
Comcast Cablevision — Comcast Cable Communications	CA	40
Comcast Cablevision — Comcast Cable Communications	CA	41
Comcast Cablevision — Comcast Cable Communications	CA	42
Comcast Cablevision — Comcast Cable Communications	CA	45
Comcast Cablevision — Comcast Cable Communications	CA	46
Comcast Cablevision — Comcast Cable Communications	CA	47
Comcast Cablevision — Comcast Cable Communications	CT	1
Comcast Cablevision — Comcast Cable Communications	CT	2
Comcast Cablevision — Comcast Cable Communications	CT	5
Comcast Cablevision — Comcast Cable Communications	FL	2
Comcast Cablevision — Comcast Cable Communications	FL	16
Comcast Cablevision — Comcast Cable Communications	FL	19
Comcast Cablevision — Comcast Cable Communications	IN	4
Comcast Cablevision — Comcast Cable Communications	IN	6
Comcast Cablevision — Comcast Cable Communications	IN	10
Comcast Cablevision — Comcast Cable Communications	KY	1
Comcast Cablevision — Comcast Cable Communications	MD	2
Comcast Cablevision — Comcast Cable Communications	MD	3
Comcast Cablevision — Comcast Cable Communications	MD	7
Comcast Cablevision — Comcast Cable Communications	MI	5
Comcast Cablevision — Comcast Cable Communications	MI	8
Comcast Cablevision — Comcast Cable Communications	MI	9
Comcast Cablevision — Comcast Cable Communications	MI	10
Comcast Cablevision — Comcast Cable Communications	MI	12
Comcast Cablevision — Comcast Cable Communications	MS	1
Comcast Cablevision — Comcast Cable Communications	MS	3
Comcast Cablevision — Comcast Cable Communications	MS	4
Comcast Cablevision — Comcast Cable Communications	NJ	4
Comcast Cablevision — Comcast Cable Communications	NJ	9
Comcast Cablevision — Comcast Cable Communications	NJ	12
Comcast Cablevision — Comcast Cable Communications	PA	1
Comcast Cablevision — Comcast Cable Communications	PA	2
Comcast Cablevision — Comcast Cable Communications	PA	3
Comcast Cablevision — Comcast Cable Communications	PA	4
Comcast Cablevision — Comcast Cable Communications	PA	4
Comcast Cablevision — Comcast Cable Communications	PA	8
Comcast Cablevision — Comcast Cable Communications	PA	13
Comcast Cablevision — Comcast Cable Communications	PA	18
Community Cable — Tele-Communications Inc	TX	21
Community Cable — Tele-Communications Inc	TX	23
Community Cable SVC	KY	6
Concord Cablevision	MI	9
Concord TV Cable — Western Communications Inc	CA	7
Concord TV Cable — Western Communications Inc	CA	10
Conroe Cable TV — TCA Cable TV Inc	TX	8
Consolidated Cable	MI	6
Continental Cablevision — Continental Cablevision Inc	CA	2
Continental Cablevision — Continental Cablevision Inc	CA	3
Continental Cablevision — Continental Cablevision Inc	CA	11
Continental Cablevision — Continental Cablevision Inc	CA	19
Continental Cablevision — Continental Cablevision Inc	CA	20
Continental Cablevision — Continental Cablevision Inc	CA	21
Continental Cablevision — Continental Cablevision Inc	CA	28
Continental Cablevision — Continental Cablevision Inc	CA	30
Continental Cablevision — Continental Cablevision Inc	CA	32
Continental Cablevision — Continental Cablevision Inc	CA	33
Continental Cablevision — Continental Cablevision Inc	CA	34
Continental Cablevision — Continental Cablevision Inc	CA	35
Continental Cablevision — Continental Cablevision Inc	CA	36
Continental Cablevision — Continental Cablevision Inc	CA	37
Continental Cablevision — Continental Cablevision Inc	CA	38
Continental Cablevision — Continental Cablevision Inc	CA	41
Continental Cablevision — Continental Cablevision Inc	CA	43
Continental Cablevision — Continental Cablevision Inc	CA	47
Continental Cablevision — Continental Cablevision Inc	CT	2
Continental Cablevision — Continental Cablevision Inc	CT	6
Continental Cablevision — Continental Cablevision Inc	FL	3
Continental Cablevision — Continental Cablevision Inc	FL	4
Continental Cablevision — Continental Cablevision Inc	FL	6
Continental Cablevision — Continental Cablevision Inc	FL	19

Cable Company	State	District
Continental Cablevision — Continental Cablevision Inc	FL	22
Continental Cablevision — Continental Cablevision Inc	FL	23
Continental Cablevision — Continental Cablevision Inc	IL	2
Continental Cablevision — Continental Cablevision Inc	IL	3
Continental Cablevision — Continental Cablevision Inc	IL	5
Continental Cablevision — Continental Cablevision Inc	IL	6
Continental Cablevision — Continental Cablevision Inc	IL	7
Continental Cablevision — Continental Cablevision Inc	IL	8
Continental Cablevision — Continental Cablevision Inc	IL	10
Continental Cablevision — Continental Cablevision Inc	IL	11
Continental Cablevision — Continental Cablevision Inc	IL	12
Continental Cablevision — Continental Cablevision Inc	IL	13
Continental Cablevision — Continental Cablevision Inc	IL	16
Continental Cablevision — Continental Cablevision Inc	IL	17
Continental Cablevision — Continental Cablevision Inc	IL	18
Continental Cablevision — Continental Cablevision Inc	IL	20
Continental Cablevision — Continental Cablevision Inc	MA	1
Continental Cablevision — Continental Cablevision Inc	MA	2
Continental Cablevision — Continental Cablevision Inc	MA	3
Continental Cablevision — Continental Cablevision Inc	MA	4
Continental Cablevision — Continental Cablevision Inc	MA	5
Continental Cablevision — Continental Cablevision Inc	MA	6
Continental Cablevision — Continental Cablevision Inc	MA	7
Continental Cablevision — Continental Cablevision Inc	MA	8
Continental Cablevision — Continental Cablevision Inc	MA	9
Continental Cablevision — Continental Cablevision Inc	MA	10
Continental Cablevision — Continental Cablevision Inc	ME	1
Continental Cablevision — Continental Cablevision Inc	MI	2
Continental Cablevision — Continental Cablevision Inc	MI	4
Continental Cablevision — Continental Cablevision Inc	MI	7
Continental Cablevision — Continental Cablevision Inc	MI	8
Continental Cablevision — Continental Cablevision Inc	MI	10
Continental Cablevision — Continental Cablevision Inc	MI	11
Continental Cablevision — Continental Cablevision Inc	MI	12
Continental Cablevision — Continental Cablevision Inc	MI	13
Continental Cablevision — Continental Cablevision Inc	MI	16
Continental Cablevision — Continental Cablevision Inc	MN	3
Continental Cablevision — Continental Cablevision Inc	MN	4
Continental Cablevision — Continental Cablevision Inc	MO	1
Continental Cablevision — Continental Cablevision Inc	MO	2
Continental Cablevision — Continental Cablevision Inc	NH	1
Continental Cablevision — Continental Cablevision Inc	NH	2
Continental Cablevision — Continental Cablevision Inc	NV	2
Continental Cablevision — Continental Cablevision Inc	NY	19
Continental Cablevision — Continental Cablevision Inc	NY	20
Continental Cablevision — Continental Cablevision Inc	OH	3
Continental Cablevision — Continental Cablevision Inc	OH	4
Continental Cablevision — Continental Cablevision Inc	OH	5
Continental Cablevision — Continental Cablevision Inc	OH	6
Continental Cablevision — Continental Cablevision Inc	OH	7
Continental Cablevision — Continental Cablevision Inc	OH	8
Continental Cablevision — Continental Cablevision Inc	OH	10
Continental Cablevision — Continental Cablevision Inc	OH	11
Continental Cablevision — Continental Cablevision Inc	OH	13
Continental Cablevision — Continental Cablevision Inc	OH	19
Continental Cablevision — Continental Cablevision Inc	VA	1
Continental Cablevision — Continental Cablevision Inc	VA	3
Continental Cablevision — Continental Cablevision Inc	VA	4
Continental Cablevision — Continental Cablevision Inc	VA	7
Conway	AR	2
Cooke Cablevision	AK	AL
Cookeville Cablevision — Rifkin & Associates	TN	4
Cookeville Cablevision — Rifkin & Associates	TN	6
Copley/Colony Cablevision — Colony Communications Inc	CA	37
Copley/Colony Cablevision — Colony Communications Inc	CA	39
Copley/Conley Cablevision — Colony Communications Inc	CA	45
Corning Newchannels — Newchannels Corp	NY	31
Costal Cablevision — Tele-Communications Inc	GA	1
Covington Cable TV	GA	10
Cox Cable — Cox Enterprises Inc	CA	1
Cox Cable — Cox Enterprises Inc	CA	20
Cox Cable — Cox Enterprises Inc	CA	21
Cox Cable — Cox Enterprises Inc	CA	22
Cox Cable — Cox Enterprises Inc	CA	49
Cox Cable — Cox Enterprises Inc	CA	50
Cox Cable — Cox Enterprises Inc	CA	51
Cox Cable — Cox Enterprises Inc	CA	52
Cox Cable — Cox Enterprises Inc	CT	1
Cox Cable — Cox Enterprises Inc	FL	1

Cable Company	State	District
Cox Cable — Cox Enterprises Inc	FL	3
Cox Cable — Cox Enterprises Inc	FL	5
Cox Cable — Cox Enterprises Inc	FL	5
Cox Cable — Cox Enterprises Inc	FL	6
Cox Cable — Cox Enterprises Inc	GA	3
Cox Cable — Cox Enterprises Inc	GA	8
Cox Cable — Cox Enterprises Inc	IA	1
Cox Cable — Cox Enterprises Inc	IL	17
Cox Cable — Cox Enterprises Inc	LA	1
Cox Cable — Cox Enterprises Inc	LA	2
Cox Cable — Cox Enterprises Inc	LA	3
Cox Cable — Cox Enterprises Inc	LA	7
Cox Cable — Cox Enterprises Inc	MI	4
Cox Cable — Cox Enterprises Inc	MI	5
Cox Cable — Cox Enterprises Inc	NC	3
Cox Cable — Cox Enterprises Inc	NE	2
Cox Cable — Cox Enterprises Inc	OH	10
Cox Cable — Cox Enterprises Inc	OH	19
Cox Cable — Cox Enterprises Inc	OK	4
Cox Cable — Cox Enterprises Inc	OK	5
Cox Cable — Cox Enterprises Inc	OK	6
Cox Cable — Cox Enterprises Inc	TX	13
Cox Cable — Cox Enterprises Inc	TX	19
Cox Cable — Cox Enterprises Inc	VA	2
Cox Cable — Cox Enterprises Inc	VA	3
Cox Cable — Cox Enterprises Inc	VA	4
Cox Cable — Cox Enterprises Inc	VA	6
Cox Cable — Cox Enterprises Inc	WA	5
Cox Cable Myrtle Beach — COX Enterprises Inc	SC	1
Cox Cable Rhode Island — COX Enterprises Inc	RI	1
Crown Cable — Crown Media Inc	AL	6
Crown Cable — Crown Media Inc	CT	2
Crown Cable — Crown Media Inc	CT	4
Crown Cable — Crown Media Inc	CT	5
Crown Cable — Crown Media Inc	CT	6
Crown Cable — Crown Media Inc	WI	1
Crown Cable — Crown Media Inc	WI	4
Crown Cable — Crown Media Inc	WI	7
Crown Cable — Crown Media Inc	WI	8
Crown Cable — Crown Media Inc	WI	9
Crown Cable — Crown Media Inc	WI	3
CV of Central Florida — Time Warner Inc	FL	3
CV of Central Florida — Time Warner Inc	FL	7
CV of Central Florida — Time Warner Inc	FL	8
CV of Central Florida — Time Warner Inc	FL	12
CVI — Cablevision Industries Inc	AL	2
CVI — Cablevision Industries Inc	CA	37
CVI — Cablevision Industries Inc	CA	38
CVI — Cablevision Industries Inc	FL	4
CVI — Cablevision Industries Inc	FL	14
CVI — Cablevision Industries Inc	FL	16
CVI — Cablevision Industries Inc	LA	3
CVI — Cablevision Industries Inc	MA	3
CVI — Cablevision Industries Inc	MI	16
CVI — Cablevision Industries Inc	NC	1
CVI — Cablevision Industries Inc	NC	2
CVI — Cablevision Industries Inc	NC	3
CVI — Cablevision Industries Inc	NC	5
CVI — Cablevision Industries Inc	NY	25
CVI — Cablevision Industries Inc	SC	2
CVI — Cablevision Industries Inc	SC	6
CVI — Cablevision Industries Inc	VA	5
CVI — Cablevision Industries Inc	WV	1

D

Cable Company	State	District
Daniels Cablevision — Daniels & Assoc	CA	48
Daniels Cablevision — Daniels & Assoc	CA	51
DCA Cablevision	CA	41
Decatur Telecable Corp — Telecable Corp	AL	5
Delaware Cable — Time Warner Inc	OH	12
Delta Cablevision — TCA Cable TV Inc	MS	2
Desert Cable — Intermedia Partners	AZ	5
Desert Hot Springs Cablevision — Daniels & Assoc	CA	44
DF Cablevision — Fanch Communications	MI	8
Dimension Cable Service — Times Mirror Co	AR	4
Dimension Cable Service — Times Mirror Co	AZ	3
Dimension Cable Service — Times Mirror Co	CA	47

Cable Company	State	District
Howard Cable Television — Comcast Cable Communications	MD	6
Howard Cable Television — Comcast Cable Communications	MD	3
Huntingdon TV Cable — Huntingdon TV Cable Co Inc	PA	9
Huntsville Cable TV — TCA Cable TV Inc	TX	2

I

Cable Company	State	District
Inland Cable Communications	MA	3
Inland Valley Cablevision — Western Communications Inc	CA	44
Inland Valley Cablevision — Western Communications Inc	CA	48
Insight Cablevision — Insight Communications Co	GA	3
Insight Cablevision — Insight Communications Co	IN	6
Insight Cablevision — Insight Communications Co	IN	9
Insight Cablevision — Insight Communications Co	UT	1
Insight Cablevision — Insight Communications Co	UT	2
Insight Cablevision — Insight Communications Co	UT	3

J

Cable Company	State	District
Jacksonville TV Cable — Vision Cable Communications Inc	NC	3
Jacksonville TV Cable — Vision Cable Communications Inc	NC	7
Jones Intercable — Jones Spacelink Ltd	AZ	5
Jones Intercable — Jones Spacelink Ltd	CA	1
Jones Intercable — Jones Spacelink Ltd	CA	4
Jones Intercable — Jones Spacelink Ltd	CA	23
Jones Intercable — Jones Spacelink Ltd	CA	25
Jones Intercable — Jones Spacelink Ltd	CA	28
Jones Intercable — Jones Spacelink Ltd	CA	41
Jones Intercable — Jones Spacelink Ltd	CA	52
Jones Intercable — Jones Spacelink Ltd	CO	2
Jones Intercable — Jones Spacelink Ltd	CO	6
Jones Intercable — Jones Spacelink Ltd	FL	1
Jones Intercable — Jones Spacelink Ltd	FL	9
Jones Intercable — Jones Spacelink Ltd	FL	11
Jones Intercable — Jones Spacelink Ltd	FL	14
Jones Intercable — Jones Spacelink Ltd	FL	20
Jones Intercable — Jones Spacelink Ltd	FL	23
Jones Intercable — Jones Spacelink Ltd	GA	10
Jones Intercable — Jones Spacelink Ltd	GA	11
Jones Intercable — Jones Spacelink Ltd	HI	2
Jones Intercable — Jones Spacelink Ltd	IL	3
Jones Intercable — Jones Spacelink Ltd	IL	6
Jones Intercable — Jones Spacelink Ltd	IL	8
Jones Intercable — Jones Spacelink Ltd	IL	10
Jones Intercable — Jones Spacelink Ltd	IL	11
Jones Intercable — Jones Spacelink Ltd	IL	13
Jones Intercable — Jones Spacelink Ltd	IL	14
Jones Intercable — Jones Spacelink Ltd	IL	14
Jones Intercable — Jones Spacelink Ltd	IN	6
Jones Intercable — Jones Spacelink Ltd	KS	3
Jones Intercable — Jones Spacelink Ltd	MD	1
Jones Intercable — Jones Spacelink Ltd	MD	2
Jones Intercable — Jones Spacelink Ltd	MD	5
Jones Intercable — Jones Spacelink Ltd	MN	1
Jones Intercable — Jones Spacelink Ltd	MO	4
Jones Intercable — Jones Spacelink Ltd	MO	5
Jones Intercable — Jones Spacelink Ltd	MO	6
Jones Intercable — Jones Spacelink Ltd	NC	9
Jones Intercable — Jones Spacelink Ltd	NJ	1
Jones Intercable — Jones Spacelink Ltd	NJ	2
Jones Intercable — Jones Spacelink Ltd	NM	1
Jones Intercable — Jones Spacelink Ltd	NM	2
Jones Intercable — Jones Spacelink Ltd	NM	3
Jones Intercable — Jones Spacelink Ltd	NY	27
Jones Intercable — Jones Spacelink Ltd	NY	29
Jones Intercable — Jones Spacelink Ltd	NY	30
Jones Intercable — Jones Spacelink Ltd	SC	1
Jones Intercable — Jones Spacelink Ltd	SC	6
Jones Intercable — Jones Spacelink Ltd	VA	8
Jones Intercable — Jones Spacelink Ltd	VA	11
Jones Intercable — Jones Spacelink Ltd	WI	1
Jones Intercable — Jones Spacelink Ltd	WI	6

K

Cable Company	State	District
Kauai Cablevision	HI	2
KBC — Metrovision Inc	TX	11
Kern Valley Cable — Booth American Co	CA	21
Killeen Cablevision — Metrovision Inc	TX	11
King Videocable — Colony Communications/Providence Journal Co	CA	2
King Videocable — Colony Communications/Providence Journal Co	CA	4
King Videocable — Colony Communications/Providence Journal Co	CA	11
King Videocable — Colony Communications/Providence Journal Co	CA	25
King Videocable — Colony Communications/Providence Journal Co	CA	26
King Videocable — Colony Communications/Providence Journal Co	CA	27
King Videocable — Colony Communications/Providence Journal Co	CA	43
King Videocable — Colony Communications/Providence Journal Co	ID	2
King Videocable — Colony Communications/Providence Journal Co	MN	3
King Videocable — Colony Communications/Providence Journal Co	MN	5
King Videocable — Colony Communications/Providence Journal Co	MN	6
Kingwood Cablevision — Moffat Communications	TX	8
Kissimmee Cablevision — Time Warner Inc	FL	8
Kissimmee Cablevision — Time Warner Inc	FL	15
Kootenai Cablevision — Rock Assoc	ID	1

L

Cable Company	State	District
Lafayette Cable TV Service — TCA Cable TV Inc	LA	7
La Grange Cablevision — McDonald Group	GA	7
Lake Champlain Cable — Pecor Group	VT	AL
Lake County Cablevision — E.W. Scripps Co	FL	6
Lakewood Cable — Moffat Communications	TX	2
Lancaster Cable — Catawba Services Inc	SC	5
Las Cruces TV Cable — Western Communications Inc	NM	2
Laurel Cablevision — Time Warner Inc	CT	6
Lawton Cablevision	OK	4
Leadership Cablevision — Fairbanks Communications	FL	19
Leadership Cablevision — Fairbanks Communications	FL	23
Lebanon Cable — Rifkin & Associates	TN	6
Lebanon Valley Cable TV — Time Warner Inc	PA	17
Liberty Cable — Consolidated Signal Corp	CA	31
Lincoln Cablevision — Rifkin & Associates	NM	2
Longview Cable TV — Wehco Video Inc	TX	1
Longview Cable TV — Wehco Video Inc	TX	4
Low County Cablevision — Falcon Communications Inc	SC	2
Lowell Cable TV — Colony Communications Inc	MA	5
Lower Bucks Cablevision — Time Warner Inc	PA	8
Lynchburg Cablevision — Time Warner Inc	VA	5

M

Cable Company	State	District
Maclean Hunter Cable — Maclean Hunter Cable TV Inc	MI	10
Maclean Hunter Cable — Maclean Hunter Cable TV Inc	MI	13
Maclean Hunter Cable — Maclean Hunter Cable TV Inc	MI	16
Madisonville Cablevision — Time Warner Inc	KY	1
Malone Newchannels — Newchannels Corp	NY	24
Mankato Cablevision — Time Warner Inc	MN	1
Marcus Cable — Marcus Cable Partners	DE	AL
Marcus Cable — Marcus Cable Partners	TX	17
Marcus Cable — Marcus Cable Partners	TX	21
Marion Cable Television — Time Warner Inc	IN	5
Marks Cablevision — Washington Post Co	OH	14
Massena Newchannels — Newchannels Corp	NY	24
Massillon Cable TV — Massillon Cable TV Inc	OH	16
McMinnville Cablevision — Rifkin & Associates	TN	4
Meadville Master Antenna — Armstrong Utilities Inc	PA	21
Media General Cable — Media General Inc	VA	8
Media General Cable — Media General Inc	VA	10
Media General Cable — Media General Inc	VA	11
Memphis Cablevision — Time Warner Inc	MS	1

Cable Company	State	District
Pinebelt Cable — Comcast Cable Communications	MS	5
Pine Bluff Cable TV — Wehco Video Inc	AR	4
Pioneer Valley Cable — Times Mirror Co	MA	1
Pittsburg Cable TV — Tele-Communications Inc	KS	2
Plainview Cable TV — TCA Cable TV Inc	TX	13
Plum Cable TV — Eastern Telcom Corp	PA	4
Post Newsweek Cable — Washington Post Co	AZ	5
Post Newsweek Cable — Washington Post Co	AZ	6
Post Newsweek Cable — Washington Post Co	CA	1
Post Newsweek Cable — Washington Post Co	CA	6
Post Newsweek Cable — Washington Post Co	CA	18
Post Newsweek Cable — Washington Post Co	IL	10
Post Newsweek Cable — Washington Post Co	IN	6
Post Newsweek Cable — Washington Post Co	MS	5
Post Newsweek Cable — Washington Post Co	NM	2
Post Newsweek Cable — Washington Post Co	NM	3
Post Newsweek Cable — Washington Post Co	OK	3
Post Newsweek Cable — Washington Post Co	OK	4
Post Newsweek Cable — Washington Post Co	OK	5
Post Newsweek Cable — Washington Post Co	TX	4
Post Newsweek Cable — Washington Post Co	TX	19
Post Newsweek Cable — Washington Post Co	TX	23
Potsdam Newchannels — Newchannels Corp	NY	24
Premiere Cable Communications — Masada Corp	AL	5
Premiere Cable Communications — Masada Corp	GA	3
Premiere Cable Communications — Masada Corp	SC	5
Prestige Cable TV — Prestige Group	NC	10
Prime Cable — Prime Cable Inc	AK	AL
Prime Cable — Prime Cable Inc	IL	4
Prime Cable — Prime Cable Inc	IL	5
Prime Cable — Prime Cable Inc	IL	7
Prime Cable — Prime Cable Inc	IL	9
Prime Cable — Prime Cable Inc	NV	1
Prime Cable — Prime Cable Inc	NV	2
Prime Cable — Prime Cable Inc	TX	7
Prime Cable — Prime Cable Inc	TX	8
Prime Cable — Prime Cable Inc	TX	22
Prime Cable — Prime Cable Inc	TX	25
Prime Cable — Prime Cable Inc	TX	29
Prime Cable — Prime Cable Inc	TX	9
Public Cable — Time Warner Inc	ME	1
Pullman/Moscow Cable — Rock Assoc	ID	1
Pullman/Moscow Cable — Rock Assoc	WA	5
Punxsutawny TV Cable — Adelphia Communications Corp	PA	5

R

Cable Company	State	District
Racine Telecable — Telecable Corp	WI	1
Radnor Cablevision — Adelphia Communications Corp	PA	7
Range TV Cable	MN	8
Rankin County Cablevision — Susquehanna Cable Co	MS	3
Rentavision — Century Communications Corp	GA	1
Resort TV Cable — Wehco Video Inc	AR	4
River Bend Cablevision — Star Cablevision Corp	WI	9
Riverlands Cablevision — Metrovision Inc	LA	3
Riverview Cablevision — Monmouth Cablevision Assoc	NJ	13
Roanoke Rapids Telecable — Telecable Corp	NC	1
Rock Hill Cable TV — Catawba Services Inc	SC	5
Rockingham-Hamlet Cablevision	NC	8
Rome New Channels — Newchannels Corp	NY	23
Roswell Cablevision — Rifkin & Associates	GA	6
Roxboro Cablevision — Helicon Corp	NC	5
Sacramento Cable TV — Scripps Howard/E.W. Scripps Co	CA	4
Sacramento Cable TV — Scripps Howard/E.W. Scripps Co	CA	5
Sacramento Cable TV — Scripps Howard/E.W. Scripps Co	CA	11
Sacramento Cable TV — Scripps Howard/E.W. Scripps Co	CA	3
Sacramento Cable TV — Scripps Howard/E.W. Scripps Co	CO	2
Sacramento Cable TV — Scripps Howard/E.W. Scripps Co	CO	4
Sacramento Cable TV — Scripps Howard/E.W. Scripps Co	GA	7
Sacramento Cable TV — Scripps Howard/E.W. Scripps Co	GA	9
Saguaro Cable — Saguaro Cable TV	AZ	2
Salem Cable TV — Booth American Co	VA	6
Sammons Comm — Sammons Communications Inc	AL	3
Sammons Comm — Sammons Communications Inc	CA	18
Sammons Comm — Sammons Communications Inc	CA	27
Sammons Comm — Sammons Communications Inc	CA	34
Sammons Comm — Sammons Communications Inc	CT	5
Sammons Comm — Sammons Communications Inc	CT	6

Cable Company	State	District
Sammons Comm — Sammons Communications Inc	IL	11
Sammons Comm — Sammons Communications Inc	IL	18
Sammons Comm — Sammons Communications Inc	IN	5
Sammons Comm — Sammons Communications Inc	MS	4
Sammons Comm — Sammons Communications Inc	MS	5
Sammons Comm — Sammons Communications Inc	NC	11
Sammons Comm — Sammons Communications Inc	NJ	2
Sammons Comm — Sammons Communications Inc	NJ	5
Sammons Comm — Sammons Communications Inc	NJ	11
Sammons Comm — Sammons Communications Inc	NJ	12
Sammons Comm — Sammons Communications Inc	NY	24
Sammons Comm — Sammons Communications Inc	NY	25
Sammons Comm — Sammons Communications Inc	PA	5
Sammons Comm — Sammons Communications Inc	PA	15
Sammons Comm — Sammons Communications Inc	PA	17
Sammons Comm — Sammons Communications Inc	PA	19
Sammons Comm — Sammons Communications Inc	TN	1
Sammons Comm — Sammons Communications Inc	TN	4
Sammons Comm — Sammons Communications Inc	TX	4
Sammons Comm — Sammons Communications Inc	TX	6
Sammons Comm — Sammons Communications Inc	TX	12
Sammons Comm — Sammons Communications Inc	TX	13
Sammons Comm — Sammons Communications Inc	TX	24
Sammons Comm — Sammons Communications Inc	VA	4
Sammons Comm — Sammons Communications Inc	VA	6
Sammons Comm — Sammons Communications Inc	WA	4
San Bruno Municipal Cable TV	CA	12
Sandhills Cablevision — Time Warner Inc	NC	2
SBC Cable — Susquehanna Cable Co	IN	2
Scripps-Howard — E.W. Scripps Co	TN	1
Scripps-Howard — E.W. Scripps Co	TN	2
Scripps-Howard — E.W. Scripps Co	TN	4
See-More TV — Omega Communications	IL	15
Selkirk Communications — Maclean Hunter Cable TV Inc	FL	20
Selkirk Communications — Maclean Hunter Cable TV Inc	FL	22
Selkirk Communications — Maclean Hunter Cable TV Inc	FL	23
Selma Telecable Corp — Telecable Corp	AL	7
Service Electric Cable TV — Service Electric Cable TV Inc	NJ	5
Service Electric Cable TV — Service Electric Cable TV Inc	PA	6
Service Electric Cable TV — Service Electric Cable TV Inc	PA	8
Service Electric Cable TV — Service Electric Cable TV Inc	PA	11
Service Electric Cable TV — Service Electric Cable TV Inc	PA	15
Shelby Cable — McDonald Group	AL	6
Sheridan Cablevision — Metrovision Inc	WY	AL
Shrewsbury Cablevision	MA	3
Simmons Comm — Simmons Communications Inc	CA	42
Simmons Comm — Simmons Communications Inc	IN	9
Simmons Comm — Simmons Communications Inc	KY	5
Simmons Comm — Simmons Communications Inc	KY	6
Simmons Comm — Simmons Communications Inc	NM	2
Simmons Comm — Simmons Communications Inc	TX	8
Simmons Comm — Simmons Communications Inc	VA	9
Smyrna Cable TV — Cable Holdings of New York	GA	6
Smyrna Cable TV — Cable Holdings of New York	GA	7
Sonic Cable TV — Sonic Communications	CA	17
Sonic Cable TV — Sonic Communications	CA	18
Sonic Cable TV — Sonic Communications	CA	22
Sonic Cable TV — Sonic Communications	CA	3
Sonic Cable TV — Sonic Communications	UT	1
Sooland Cablecom — Washington Post Co	IA	5
Sooland Cablecom — Washington Post Co	SD	AL
South Bay Cablevision — Brenmor Cable Partners	CA	13
South Bay Cablevision — Brenmor Cable Partners	CA	14
South Bay Cablevision — Brenmor Cable Partners	CA	15
South Jersey Cable — Vento Cable Management	NJ	2
Southwestern Cable — Time Warner Inc	CA	28
Southwestern Cable — Time Warner Inc	CA	49
Southwestern Cable — Time Warner Inc	CA	51
Spotsylvania Cable TV — Prestige Group	VA	1
St. Charles Cable — COX Enterprises Inc	LA	3
St. Joseph Cablevision — News-Press & Gazette Co	MO	6
St. Marys TV	PA	5
Star Cablevision — Star Cablevision Corp	WI	6
Star Cablevision — Star Cablevision Group	MN	3
Starstream Communications — Boulder Ridge Cable TV	CA	4
State Cable TV — Whitney Communications Corp	ME	1
State Cable TV — Whitney Communications Corp	ME	2
State Cable TV — Whitney Communications Corp	NH	1
Staten Island Cable — COX Enterprises Inc	NY	13

Cable Company	State	District
Statesboro CATV — Northland Communications Corp	GA	1
Storer Cable — Tele-Communications Inc	AL	1
Storer Cable — Tele-Communications Inc	AL	2
Storer Cable — Tele-Communications Inc	AL	2
Storer Cable — Tele-Communications Inc	AL	3
Storer Cable — Tele-Communications Inc	AL	7
Storer Cable — Tele-Communications Inc	AR	1
Storer Cable — Tele-Communications Inc	AR	2
Storer Cable — Tele-Communications Inc	CT	2
Storer Cable — Tele-Communications Inc	CT	3
Storer Cable — Tele-Communications Inc	DE	AL
Storer Cable — Tele-Communications Inc	FL	3
Storer Cable — Tele-Communications Inc	FL	7
Storer Cable — Tele-Communications Inc	FL	12
Storer Cable — Tele-Communications Inc	FL	13
Storer Cable — Tele-Communications Inc	FL	14
Storer Cable — Tele-Communications Inc	FL	16
Storer Cable — Tele-Communications Inc	FL	17
Storer Cable — Tele-Communications Inc	FL	18
Storer Cable — Tele-Communications Inc	FL	20
Storer Cable — Tele-Communications Inc	FL	21
Storer Cable — Tele-Communications Inc	FL	22
Storer Cable — Tele-Communications Inc	GA	2
Storer Cable — Tele-Communications Inc	GA	8
Storer Cable — Tele-Communications Inc	KY	2
Storer Cable — Tele-Communications Inc	KY	3
Storer Cable — Tele-Communications Inc	KY	4
Storer Cable — Tele-Communications Inc	MD	1
Storer Cable — Tele-Communications Inc	NJ	1
Storer Cable — Tele-Communications Inc	NJ	4
Storer Cable — Tele-Communications Inc	NJ	5
Storer Cable — Tele-Communications Inc	NJ	6
Storer Cable — Tele-Communications Inc	NJ	7
Storer Cable — Tele-Communications Inc	NJ	12
Storer Cable — Tele-Communications Inc	TX	3
Storer Cable — Tele-Communications Inc	TX	5
Storer Cable — Tele-Communications Inc	TX	6
Storer Cable — Tele-Communications Inc	TX	7
Storer Cable — Tele-Communications Inc	TX	9
Storer Cable — Tele-Communications Inc	TX	18
Storer Cable — Tele-Communications Inc	TX	22
Storer Cable — Tele-Communications Inc	TX	24
Storer Cable — Tele-Communications Inc	TX	25
Storer Cable — Tele-Communications Inc	TX	26
Storer Cable — Tele-Communications Inc	TX	29
Storer Cable — Tele-Communications Inc	VA	4
Storer Cable — Tele-Communications Inc	VA	7
Storer Cable of Carolina — Comcast Cable Communication	SC	6
Suburban Cable — Lenfest Group	PA	1
Suburban Cable — Lenfest Group	PA	6
Suburban Cable — Lenfest Group	PA	7
Suburban Cable — Lenfest Group	PA	8
Suburban Cable — Lenfest Group	PA	13
Suburban Cable — Lenfest Group	PA	16
Suburban Cable — Lenfest Group	PA	17
Suburban Cablevision — Maclean Hunter Ltd	NJ	7
Suburban Cablevision — Maclean Hunter Ltd	NJ	8
Suburban Cablevision — Maclean Hunter Ltd	NJ	9
Suburban Cablevision — Maclean Hunter Ltd	NJ	10
Suburban Cablevision — Maclean Hunter Ltd	NJ	11
Suburban Cablevision — Maclean Hunter Ltd	NJ	13
Sulphur Spring Cable TV — TCA Cable TV Inc	TX	1
Summit Cable — Summit Communications Group	GA	6
Summit Cable — Summit Communications Group	GA	7
Summit Cable — Summit Communications Group	NC	5
Summit Cable — Summit Communications Group	NC	6
Summit Cable — Summit Communications Group	NC	10
Summit Cable — Summit Communications Group	NC	12
Summit Cable — Summit Communications Group	WA	7
Summit-Leoni — Booth American Co	MI	7
Sun Cablevision	HI	2
Sunflower Cablevision — World Co	KS	3
Sweetwater Cable TV — Sweetwater Cable TV Co Inc	WY	AL
Sylvan Valley CATV — Sylvan Valley CATV Co	NC	11
Syracuse Newchannels — Newchannels Corp	NY	23
Syracuse Newchannels — Newchannels Corp	NY	25

T

Cable Company	State	District
TCA Cable — TCA Cable TV Inc	AR	3
TCA Cable — TCA Cable TV Inc	NM	3
TCA Cable — TCA Cable TV Inc	TX	1
TCA Cable — TCA Cable TV Inc	TX	8
TCA Cable — TCA Cable TV Inc	TX	14
TCA Cable — TCA Cable TV Inc	TX	13
TCI — Tele-Communications Inc	AL	6
TCI — Tele-Communications Inc	AR	3
TCI — Tele-Communications Inc	AZ	4
TCI — Tele-Communications Inc	AZ	6
TCI — Tele-Communications Inc	CA	2
TCI — Tele-Communications Inc	CA	4
TCI — Tele-Communications Inc	CA	7
TCI — Tele-Communications Inc	CA	9
TCI — Tele-Communications Inc	CA	10
TCI — Tele-Communications Inc	CA	12
TCI — Tele-Communications Inc	CA	13
TCI — Tele-Communications Inc	CA	14
TCI — Tele-Communications Inc	CA	15
TCI — Tele-Communications Inc	CA	16
TCI — Tele-Communications Inc	CA	18
TCI — Tele-Communications Inc	CO	1
TCI — Tele-Communications Inc	CO	2
TCI — Tele-Communications Inc	CO	3
TCI — Tele-Communications Inc	CO	4
TCI — Tele-Communications Inc	CO	5
TCI — Tele-Communications Inc	CO	6
TCI — Tele-Communications Inc	CT	1
TCI — Tele-Communications Inc	CT	2
TCI — Tele-Communications Inc	CT	3
TCI — Tele-Communications Inc	CT	5
TCI — Tele-Communications Inc	CT	6
TCI — Tele-Communications Inc	DE	AL
TCI — Tele-Communications Inc	FL	3
TCI — Tele-Communications Inc	FL	4
TCI — Tele-Communications Inc	FL	5
TCI — Tele-Communications Inc	FL	7
TCI — Tele-Communications Inc	FL	9
TCI — Tele-Communications Inc	FL	15
TCI — Tele-Communications Inc	FL	17
TCI — Tele-Communications Inc	FL	18
TCI — Tele-Communications Inc	FL	20
TCI — Tele-Communications Inc	GA	2
TCI — Tele-Communications Inc	GA	3
TCI — Tele-Communications Inc	GA	8
TCI — Tele-Communications Inc	GA	10
TCI — Tele-Communications Inc	IA	1
TCI — Tele-Communications Inc	IA	2
TCI — Tele-Communications Inc	IA	3
TCI — Tele-Communications Inc	IA	4
TCI — Tele-Communications Inc	IA	5
TCI — Tele-Communications Inc	ID	1
TCI — Tele-Communications Inc	ID	2
TCI — Tele-Communications Inc	IL	1
TCI — Tele-Communications Inc	IL	2
TCI — Tele-Communications Inc	IL	3
TCI — Tele-Communications Inc	IL	4
TCI — Tele-Communications Inc	IL	5
TCI — Tele-Communications Inc	IL	6
TCI — Tele-Communications Inc	IL	7
TCI — Tele-Communications Inc	IL	8
TCI — Tele-Communications Inc	IL	9
TCI — Tele-Communications Inc	IL	10
TCI — Tele-Communications Inc	IL	11
TCI — Tele-Communications Inc	IL	12
TCI — Tele-Communications Inc	IL	14
TCI — Tele-Communications Inc	IL	15
TCI — Tele-Communications Inc	IL	16
TCI — Tele-Communications Inc	IL	17
TCI — Tele-Communications Inc	IL	19
TCI — Tele-Communications Inc	IL	20
TCI — Tele-Communications Inc	IN	1
TCI — Tele-Communications Inc	IN	2
TCI — Tele-Communications Inc	IN	7
TCI — Tele-Communications Inc	IN	8
TCI — Tele-Communications Inc	IN	9

Cable Company	State	District	Cable Company	State	District
TCI — Tele-Communications Inc	KS	1	TCI — Tele-Communications Inc	TX	14
TCI — Tele-Communications Inc	KS	2	TCI — Tele-Communications Inc	TX	21
TCI — Tele-Communications Inc	KS	4	TCI — Tele-Communications Inc	TX	22
TCI — Tele-Communications Inc	KY	1	TCI — Tele-Communications Inc	TX	23
TCI — Tele-Communications Inc	KY	2	TCI — Tele-Communications Inc	TX	24
TCI — Tele-Communications Inc	KY	6	TCI — Tele-Communications Inc	TX	26
TCI — Tele-Communications Inc	LA	3	TCI — Tele-Communications Inc	TX	27
TCI — Tele-Communications Inc	LA	4	TCI — Tele-Communications Inc	TX	30
TCI — Tele-Communications Inc	LA	7	TCI — Tele-Communications Inc	UT	1
TCI — Tele-Communications Inc	MD	1	TCI — Tele-Communications Inc	UT	2
TCI — Tele-Communications Inc	MD	6	TCI — Tele-Communications Inc	UT	3
TCI — Tele-Communications Inc	MI	2	TCI — Tele-Communications Inc	VA	4
TCI — Tele-Communications Inc	MI	3	TCI — Tele-Communications Inc	WA	1
TCI — Tele-Communications Inc	MI	7	TCI — Tele-Communications Inc	WA	2
TCI — Tele-Communications Inc	MI	9	TCI — Tele-Communications Inc	WA	3
TCI — Tele-Communications Inc	MI	11	TCI — Tele-Communications Inc	WA	4
TCI — Tele-Communications Inc	MI	12	TCI — Tele-Communications Inc	WA	5
TCI — Tele-Communications Inc	MI	16	TCI — Tele-Communications Inc	WA	6
TCI — Tele-Communications Inc	MN	1	TCI — Tele-Communications Inc	WA	7
TCI — Tele-Communications Inc	MN	7	TCI — Tele-Communications Inc	WA	8
TCI — Tele-Communications Inc	MN	8	TCI — Tele-Communications Inc	WA	9
TCI — Tele-Communications Inc	MO	1	TCI — Tele-Communications Inc	WI	2
TCI — Tele-Communications Inc	MO	2	TCI — Tele-Communications Inc	WI	9
TCI — Tele-Communications Inc	MO	3	TCI — Tele-Communications Inc	WV	1
TCI — Tele-Communications Inc	MO	4	TCI — Tele-Communications Inc	WV	3
TCI — Tele-Communications Inc	MO	8	TCI — Tele-Communications Inc	WY	AL
TCI — Tele-Communications Inc	MO	9	Tel-Com — Tel-Com Inc	KY	5
TCI — Tele-Communications Inc	MS	5	Tele-Media — Tele-Media Corp	CT	5
TCI — Tele-Communications Inc	MT	AL	Tele-Media — Tele-Media Corp	FL	19
TCI — Tele-Communications Inc	NC	10	Tele-Media — Tele-Media Corp	MI	5
TCI — Tele-Communications Inc	NC	11	Tele-Media — Tele-Media Corp	OH	17
TCI — Tele-Communications Inc	ND	AL	Tele-Media — Tele-Media Corp	OH	18
TCI — Tele-Communications Inc	NE	2	Tele-Media — Tele-Media Corp	VA	4
TCI — Tele-Communications Inc	NE	3	Tele-Media — Tele-Media Corp	WV	2
TCI — Tele-Communications Inc	NM	2	Tele-Media — Tele-Media Corp	WV	3
TCI — Tele-Communications Inc	NM	3	Telecable — Telecable Corp	FL	19
TCI — Tele-Communications Inc	NV	2	Telecable — Telecable Corp	GA	2
TCI — Tele-Communications Inc	NY	1	Telecable — Telecable Corp	GA	3
TCI — Tele-Communications Inc	NY	21	Telecable — Telecable Corp	IL	15
TCI — Tele-Communications Inc	NY	22	Telecable — Telecable Corp	IL	18
TCI — Tele-Communications Inc	NY	26	Telecable — Telecable Corp	IN	5
TCI — Tele-Communications Inc	NY	27	Telecable — Telecable Corp	IN	6
TCI — Tele-Communications Inc	NY	29	Telecable — Telecable Corp	KS	3
TCI — Tele-Communications Inc	NY	30	Telecable — Telecable Corp	KY	2
TCI — Tele-Communications Inc	OH	2	Telecable — Telecable Corp	KY	6
TCI — Tele-Communications Inc	OH	5	Telecable — Telecable Corp	MO	7
TCI — Tele-Communications Inc	OH	6	Telecable — Telecable Corp	SC	3
TCI — Tele-Communications Inc	OH	8	Telecable — Telecable Corp	SC	4
TCI — Tele-Communications Inc	OH	13	Telecable — Telecable Corp	TN	2
TCI — Tele-Communications Inc	OH	14	Telecable — Telecable Corp	TN	3
TCI — Tele-Communications Inc	OH	17	Telesat Cablevision — Telesat Cablevision Inc	FL	5
TCI — Tele-Communications Inc	OH	18	Telescripps Cable — E.W. Scripps Co	VA	9
TCI — Tele-Communications Inc	OH	19	Telescripps Cable — E.W. Scripps Co	WV	3
TCI — Tele-Communications Inc	OK	1	Telescripps Cable — E.W. Scripps Co	KY	1
TCI — Tele-Communications Inc	OK	2	Telescripps Cable — E.W. Scripps Co	KY	2
TCI — Tele-Communications Inc	OK	3	Teleservice Corp. of America — TCA Cable TV Inc	LA	5
TCI — Tele-Communications Inc	OK	4	Televents of East County — Tele-Communications Inc	CA	10
TCI — Tele-Communications Inc	OK	6	Tennessee Cablevision — Cable Holding	TN	3
TCI — Tele-Communications Inc	OR	1	Tennessee Valley Cable — E.W. Scripps Co	TN	1
TCI — Tele-Communications Inc	OR	2	Tennessee Valley Cablevision — Intermedia Partners	TN	6
TCI — Tele-Communications Inc	OR	3	Terrebonne Cablevision — Helicon Corp	LA	3
TCI — Tele-Communications Inc	OR	4	Thomaston Cablevision — McDonald Group	GA	3
TCI — Tele-Communications Inc	OR	5	Time Warner — Time Warner Inc	NC	4
TCI — Tele-Communications Inc	PA	4	Time Warner — Time Warner Inc	NC	6
TCI — Tele-Communications Inc	PA	5	Time Warner — Time Warner Inc	NC	12
TCI — Tele-Communications Inc	PA	9	Time Warner — Time Warner Inc	NY	4
TCI — Tele-Communications Inc	PA	12	Time Warner — Time Warner Inc	NY	5
TCI — Tele-Communications Inc	PA	14	Time Warner — Time Warner Inc	NY	6
TCI — Tele-Communications Inc	PA	18	Time Warner — Time Warner Inc	NY	7
TCI — Tele-Communications Inc	PA	20	Time Warner — Time Warner Inc	NY	8
TCI — Tele-Communications Inc	PA	21	Time Warner — Time Warner Inc	NY	9
TCI — Tele-Communications Inc	RI	1	Time Warner — Time Warner Inc	NY	10
TCI — Tele-Communications Inc	RI	2	Time Warner — Time Warner Inc	NY	12
TCI — Tele-Communications Inc	SD	AL	Time Warner — Time Warner Inc	NY	13
TCI — Tele-Communications Inc	TX	2	Time Warner — Time Warner Inc	NY	14
TCI — Tele-Communications Inc	TX	3	Time Warner — Time Warner Inc	NY	18
TCI — Tele-Communications Inc	TX	4	Time Warner — Time Warner Inc	VA	11
TCI — Tele-Communications Inc	TX	5	Times Mirror Cable TV — Times Mirror Co	AZ	1
TCI — Tele-Communications Inc	TX	9	Times Mirror Cable TV — Times Mirror Co	AZ	2

Cable Company	State	District
Times Mirror Cable TV — Times Mirror Co	AZ	3
Times Mirror Cable TV — Times Mirror Co	AZ	4
Times Mirror Cable TV — Times Mirror Co	AZ	6
Times Mirror Cable TV — Times Mirror Co	CA	36
Times Mirror Cable TV — Times Mirror Co	IN	7
Times Mirror Cable TV — Times Mirror Co	MA	1
Times Mirror Cable TV — Times Mirror Co	MA	2
Times Mirror Cable TV — Times Mirror Co	OH	4
Times Mirror Cable TV — Times Mirror Co	OH	12
Times Mirror Cable TV — Times Mirror Co	OH	18
Times Mirror Cable TV — Times Mirror Co	PA	4
Times Mirror Cable TV — Times Mirror Co	PA	20
Times Mirror Cable TV — Times Mirror Co	TX	21
Times Mirror Cable TV — Times Mirror Co	TX	23
TKR Cable — Knight-Ridder Newspapers Inc	NJ	1
TKR Cable — Knight-Ridder Newspapers Inc	NJ	2
TKR Cable — Knight-Ridder Newspapers Inc	NJ	3
TKR Cable — Knight-Ridder Newspapers Inc	NJ	4
TKR Cable — Knight-Ridder Newspapers Inc	NJ	5
TKR Cable — Knight-Ridder Newspapers Inc	NJ	6
TKR Cable — Knight-Ridder Newspapers Inc	NJ	7
TKR Cable — Knight-Ridder Newspapers Inc	NJ	11
TKR Cable — Knight-Ridder Newspapers Inc	NJ	12
TKR Cable — Knight-Ridder Newspapers Inc	NY	20
Tri-County Cable — Time Warner Inc	NJ	2
Tri-County Cablevision — Cablevision Industries Inc	NY	27
Triax Cablevision — Triax Communications	MN	2
Triax Cablevision — Triax Communications	MN	6
Triax Cablevision — Triax Communications	WV	2
Triax Cablevision — Triax Communications	WV	3
Troy Newchannels — Newchannels Corp	NY	22
Tucson Cable — Intermedia Partners	AZ	2
Tucson Cable — Intermedia Partners	AZ	5
Tullahoma Cablevision — Rifkin & Associates	TN	4
TV Cable of Carlisle — Raystay Company Inc	PA	19
TV Cable of Waynesboro — Raystay Company Inc	PA	9
TV Service — TV Service Cable Inc	KY	5
Twin City Cable TV — TCA Cable TV Inc	AR	1
Twin Country Trans-Video	PA	15
Twin State Cable TV — Tele-Communications Inc	NH	2

U

Cable Company	State	District
U. S. Cable — US Cable Corp	AL	1
U. S. Cable — US Cable Corp	FL	1
U. S. Cable — US Cable Corp	IL	8
U. S. Cable — US Cable Corp	IL	10
U. S. Cable — US Cable Corp	IN	1
U. S. Cable — US Cable Corp	IN	3
U. S. Cable — US Cable Corp	IN	5
U. S. Cable — US Cable Corp	NC	11
U. S. Cable — US Cable Corp	NJ	8
U. S. Cablevision — Colony Communications Inc	NY	22
U. S. Cablevision — Colony Communications Inc	NY	26
UA Cable of Baltimore — Tele-Communications Inc	MD	1
UA Cable of Baltimore — Tele-Communications Inc	MD	2
UA Cable of Baltimore — Tele-Communications Inc	MD	3
UA Cable of Baltimore — Tele-Communications Inc	MD	7
UA Cablesystems — Tele-Communications Inc	CA	1
UA Cablesystems — Tele-Communications Inc	CA	3
UA Cablesystems — Tele-Communications Inc	IL	18
UA Cablesystems — Tele-Communications Inc	IN	8
UA Cablesystems — Tele-Communications Inc	NJ	5
UA Cablesystems — Tele-Communications Inc	NJ	8
UA Cablesystems — Tele-Communications Inc	NJ	9
UA Cablesystems — Tele-Communications Inc	NJ	11
UA Cablesystems — Tele-Communications Inc	NY	18
UA Cablesystems — Tele-Communications Inc	NY	20
UA Columbia Cablevision — Tele-Communications Inc	MA	3
UA Columbia Cablevision — Tele-Communications Inc	MA	9
United Artist Cable — Tele-Communications Inc	AR	1
United Artist Cable — Tele-Communications Inc	CA	3
United Artist Cable — Tele-Communications Inc	CA	4
United Artist Cable — Tele-Communications Inc	CA	15
United Artist Cable — Tele-Communications Inc	CA	17
United Artist Cable — Tele-Communications Inc	CA	25
United Artist Cable — Tele-Communications Inc	CA	26
United Artist Cable — Tele-Communications Inc	CA	27

Cable Company	State	District
United Artist Cable — Tele-Communications Inc	CA	34
United Artist Cable — Tele-Communications Inc	FL	15
United Artist Cable — Tele-Communications Inc	FL	16
United Artist Cable — Tele-Communications Inc	FL	23
United Artist Cable — Tele-Communications Inc	SC	3
United Artist Cable — Tele-Communications Inc	WA	4
United Artist Cable — Time Warner Inc	TX	21
United Artist of Tennessee — Tele-Communications Inc	TN	6
United Artists Cable — Tele-communication Inc	TX	8
United Cable — United Cable Co of New Hampshire	NH	1
United Cable of North Indiana — US Cable Corp	IN	1
United Cable of Oakland County — Tele-Communications Inc	MI	9
United Cable Service of Abilene — Tele-Communications Inc	TX	17
United Cable TV — Tele-Communications Inc	DE	AL
United Cable TV — Tele-Communications Inc	LA	4
United Cable TV — Tele-Communications Inc	LA	5
United Cable TV — Tele-Communications Inc	MD	1
United Cable TV — Tele-Communications Inc	MD	5
United Cable TV — Tele-Communications Inc	MI	8
United Cable TV — Tele-Communications Inc	TX	4
United Video Cablevision — United Video Management	MA	2
United Video Cablevision — United Video Management	MA	3
United Video Cablevision — United Video Management	ME	1
United Video Cablevision — United Video Management	MO	2
United Video Cablevision — United Video Management	OH	6

V

Cable Company	State	District
Van Buren TV Cable — Transwestern Video Inc	AR	3
Ventura County Cable — Western Communications Inc	CA	23
Ventura County Cable — Western Communications Inc	CA	24
Verto Cable — Verto Cable TV Corp	PA	11
Verto Cable — Verto Cable TV Corp	PA	10
Viacom Cablevision — Viacom International Inc	CA	1
Viacom Cablevision — Viacom International Inc	CA	2
Viacom Cablevision — Viacom International Inc	CA	3
Viacom Cablevision — Viacom International Inc	CA	6
Viacom Cablevision — Viacom International Inc	CA	7
Viacom Cablevision — Viacom International Inc	CA	8
Viacom Cablevision — Viacom International Inc	CA	10
Viacom Cablevision — Viacom International Inc	CA	12
Viacom Cablevision — Viacom International Inc	OH	3
Viacom Cablevision — Viacom International Inc	OH	8
Viacom Cablevision — Viacom International Inc	OR	5
Viacom Cablevision — Viacom International Inc	TN	5
Viacom Cablevision — Viacom International Inc	TN	6
Viacom Cablevision — Viacom International Inc	WA	1
Viacom Cablevision — Viacom International Inc	WA	2
Viacom Cablevision — Viacom International Inc	WA	6
Viacom Cablevision — Viacom International Inc	WA	7
Viacom Cablevision — Viacom International Inc	WA	8
Viacom Cablevision — Viacom International Inc	WA	9
Vicksburg Video — Wehco Video Inc	MS	2
Video Design — James Communications	LA	7
Virginia Highlands Cable — E.W. Scripps Co	VA	9
Vision Cable — Newhouse Broadcasting Co	FL	9
Vision Cable — Newhouse Broadcasting Co	FL	10
Vision Cable — Newhouse Broadcasting Co	LA	3
Vision Cable — Newhouse Broadcasting Co	LA	6
Vision Cable — Newhouse Broadcasting Co	NC	3
Vision Cable — Newhouse Broadcasting Co	NC	6
Vision Cable — Newhouse Broadcasting Co	NC	7
Vision Cable — Newhouse Broadcasting Co	NC	8
Vision Cable — Newhouse Broadcasting Co	NC	11
Vision Cable — Newhouse Broadcasting Co	NC	12
Vision Cable — Newhouse Broadcasting Co	NC	9
Vision Cable — Newhouse Broadcasting Co	NJ	9
Vision Cable — Vision Cable Communications Inc	SC	5
Vision Cable — Vision Cable Communications Inc	SC	6
Vision Cable Rhode Island — Colony Communications Inc	RI	1
Vista Cablevision — Time Warner Inc	TX	13
Vista Communications — Vista Communications Inc	LA	6
Volunteer Cablevision — Intermedia Partners	TN	8
Volunteer Cablevision — Intermedia Partners	TN	7

Cable Company	State	District
W		
Wabash Cablevision — Rifkin & Associates	IN	8
Waco Cablevision — Metrovision Inc	TX	11
Wade Cablevision — Cablevision Industries Inc	PA	1
Wade Cablevision — Cablevision Industries Inc	PA	2
Wade Cablevision — Cablevision Industries Inc	PA	13
Waltham Cable — Tele-Communications Inc	MA	7
Warner Amex — Time Warner Inc	AZ	3
Warner Amex — Time Warner Inc	IL	14
Warner Amex — Time Warner Inc	MA	7
Warner Amex — Time Warner Inc	MS	2
Warner Amex — Time Warner Inc	WI	8
Warner Amex — Time Warner Inc	WV	2
Warner Cable — Time Warner Inc	AL	6
Warner Cable — Time Warner Inc	AL	7
Warner Cable — Time Warner Inc	AR	3
Warner Cable — Time Warner Inc	CA	20
Warner Cable — Time Warner Inc	CA	21
Warner Cable — Time Warner Inc	CA	40
Warner Cable — Time Warner Inc	CA	44
Warner Cable — Time Warner Inc	FL	2
Warner Cable — Time Warner Inc	IL	15
Warner Cable — Time Warner Inc	IN	9
Warner Cable — Time Warner Inc	MA	1
Warner Cable — Time Warner Inc	MA	6
Warner Cable — Time Warner Inc	MA	7
Warner Cable — Time Warner Inc	NH	2
Warner Cable — Time Warner Inc	NJ	2
Warner Cable — Time Warner Inc	NY	31
Warner Cable — Time Warner Inc	OH	1
Warner Cable — Time Warner Inc	OH	2
Warner Cable — Time Warner Inc	OH	4
Warner Cable — Time Warner Inc	OH	7
Warner Cable — Time Warner Inc	OH	8
Warner Cable — Time Warner Inc	OH	12
Warner Cable — Time Warner Inc	OH	13
Warner Cable — Time Warner Inc	OH	14
Warner Cable — Time Warner Inc	OH	15
Warner Cable — Time Warner Inc	OH	16
Warner Cable — Time Warner Inc	OH	17
Warner Cable — Time Warner Inc	OH	18
Warner Cable — Time Warner Inc	PA	5
Warner Cable — Time Warner Inc	PA	6
Warner Cable — Time Warner Inc	PA	9
Warner Cable — Time Warner Inc	PA	17
Warner Cable — Time Warner Inc	PA	19
Warner Cable — Time Warner Inc	TN	1
Warner Cable — Time Warner Inc	TX	7
Warner Cable — Time Warner Inc	TX	8
Warner Cable — Time Warner Inc	TX	18
Warner Cable — Time Warner Inc	TX	22
Warner Cable — Time Warner Inc	TX	25
Warner Cable — Time Warner Inc	TX	29
Warner Cable — Time Warner Inc	VA	1
Warner Cable — Time Warner Inc	WI	4
Warner Cable — Time Warner Inc	WI	5
Warner Cable — Time Warner Inc	WI	6
Warner Cable — Time Warner Inc	WI	9
Warner Cable — Time Warner Inc	VA	3
Warner Cable — Time Warner Inc	VA	6
Warrick Cablevision — Century Communications Corp	IN	8
Watertown Cable TV — Booth American Co	SD	AL
Waycross Cable	GA	1
West Boca Cable — Rifkin & Associates	FL	19
Westerly Cable TV — Colony Communications Inc	RI	2
Western Reserves Cablevision — Adelphia Communications Corp	OH	13
Western TV Cable — Western Communications Inc	CA	12
Western Wisconsin Communication Coop	WI	3
Westmarc Cable — Tele-Communications Inc	IA	2
Westmarc Cable — Tele-Communications Inc	IA	3
Westmarc Cable — Tele-Communications Inc	MI	1
Westmarc Cable — Tele-Communications Inc	MI	2
Westmarc Cable — Tele-Communications Inc	MI	4
Westmarc Cable — Tele-Communications Inc	MI	6
Westmarc Cable — Tele-Communications Inc	MI	7
Westmarc Cable — Tele-Communications Inc	MN	1
Westmarc Cable — Tele-Communications Inc	WI	3
Weststar Communications — Weststar Communications Inc	CA	14
Weststar Communications — Weststar Communications Inc	CA	17
Weststar Communications — Weststar Communications Inc	CA	20
Weststar Communications — Weststar Communications Inc	ID	1
West Valley Cablevision — Cablevision Industries Inc	CA	24
West Valley Cablevision — Cablevision Industries Inc	CA	25
West Valley Cablevision — Cablevision Industries Inc	CA	26
Whaling City Cable TV — Colony Communications Inc	MA	3
Whaling City Cable TV — Colony Communications Inc	MA	4
White County Video — Wehco Video Inc	AR	2
Wisconsin CATV — Time Warner Inc	WI	3
Wisconsin CATV — Time Warner Inc	WI	7
Wometco Cable TV — Wometco Cable TV Inc	GA	3
Wometco Cable TV — Wometco Cable TV Inc	GA	5
Wometco Cable TV — Wometco Cable TV Inc	GA	6
Wometco Cable TV — Wometco Cable TV Inc	GA	7
Wometco Cable TV — Wometco Cable TV Inc	GA	10
Wood Cable — Toledo Blade Co	OH	5
Woodward Cable — Time Warner Inc	OK	6
Wyandotte Cable TV	MI	16
Y		
Yorba Linda Cable TV — Jones Spacelink Ltd	CA	41

Military Installation Index

All major U.S. military installations (as of July 1991) are indexed by district and page number. A military installations that is split between two districts will have two entries.

Military Installation	State	District	Page
Duluth Intl. Airport Air Force Guard Station, Duluth	MN	8	412
Dyess Air Force Base, Abilene	TX	17	729

E

Military Installation	State	District	Page
Eaker Air Force Base, Blytheville	AR	1	49
Earle Naval Weapons Station, Colts Neck	NJ	6	474
Earle Naval Weapons Station, Colts Neck	NJ	12	484
Eastern West Virginia Regional Airport Shepherd Field Air Force Guard Station, Martinsburg	WV	2	801
Edwards Air Force Base, Rosamond	CA	21	90
Eglin Air Force Base, Valpariso	FL	1	168
Eglin Auxiliary Air Field 3 (Duke Field), Crestview	FL	1	168
Eglin Auxiliary Air Field 9 (Hurlburt Field), Mary Esther	FL	1	168
Eielson Air Force Base, Fairbanks	AK	AL	34
El Centro Naval Air Facility, El Centro	CA	52	133
Eldorado Air Station, Eldorado	TX	21	735
Ellington Field Air Force Guard Station, Houston	TX	25	740
Ellsworth Air Force Base, Box Elder	SD	AL	683
Elmendorf Air Force Base, Anchorage	AK	AL	34
El Toro Marine Corps Air Station, Irvine	CA	47	126
England Air Force Base, Alexandria	LA	6	327
EPAC Naval Communications Master Station, Wahiawa	HI	2	226

F

Military Installation	State	District	Page
Fairchild Air Force Base, Airway Heights	WA	5	790
Falcon Air Force Base, Ellicott	CO	5	144
Fallon Naval Air Station, Fallon	NV	2	456
Fitzsimons Army Medical Center, Aurora	CO	1	138
Forbes Field Air Force Guard Station, Pauline	KS	2	300
Fort A. P. Hill (Army), Bowling Green	VA	1	764
Fort Belvoir (Army), Alexandria	VA	8	774
Fort Benjamin Harrison (Army), Indianapolis	IN	10	284
Fort Benning (Army), Columbus	GA	2	206
Fort Bliss (Army), El Paso	TX	16	728
Fort Bliss (Army), El Paso	TX	23	738
Fort Bragg (Army), Fayetteville	NC	7	560
Fort Campbell (Army), Clarksville	KY	1	307
Fort Campbell (Army), Clarksville	TN	7	697
Fort Carson (Army), Colorado Springs	CO	5	144
Fort Chaffee (Army), Fort Smith	AR	3	52
Fort Derussy (Army), Honolulu	HI	1	224
Fort Detrick (Army), Frederick	MD	6	347
Fort Devens (Army), Ayer	MA	5	361
Fort Dix (Army), Trenton	NJ	3	470
Fort Dix (Army), Trenton	NJ	4	471
Fort Drum (Army), Watertown	NY	24	535
Fort Eustis (Army), Newport News	VA	3	766
Fort George G. Meade (Army), Odenton	MD	3	342
Fort Gillem (Army), Forest Park	GA	3	208
Fort Gordon (Army), Augusta	GA	10	219
Fort Greely (Army), Delta Junction	AK	AL	34
Fort Hamilton (Army), Brooklyn	NY	13	517
Fort Holabird (Army), Baltimore	MD	3	342
Fort Hood (Army), Killeen	TX	11	721
Fort Huachuca (Army), Sierra Vista	AZ	5	43
Fort Hunter Liggett (Army), Jolon	CA	17	85
Fort Indiantown Gap (Army), Annville	PA	17	654
Fort Irwin (Army), Barstow	CA	40	117
Fort Jackson (Army), Columbia	SC	2	672
Fort Knox (Army), Louisville	KY	2	309
Fort Leavenworth (Army), Leavenworth	KS	2	300
Fort Lee (Army), Petersburg	VA	4	768
Fort Leonard Wood (Army), Jefferson City	MO	4	431
Fort Leslie J. McNair (Army), Washington	DC	AL	839
Fort McClellan (Army), Anniston	AL	3	24
Fort McCoy (Army), Sparta	WI	6	814
Fort McPherson (Army), Atlanta	GA	5	211
Fort Monmouth (Army), Red Bank	NJ	6	474
Fort Monmouth (Army), Red Bank	NJ	12	484
Fort Monroe (Army), Hampton	VA	1	764

Military Installation	State	District	Page
Fort Myer (Army), Arlington	VA	8	774
Fort Ord (Army), Seaside	CA	17	85
Fort Pickett (Army), Blackstone	VA	4	768
Fort Polk (Army), Leesville	LA	6	327
Fort Richardson (Army), Anchorage	AK	AL	34
Fort Riley (Army), Junction City	KS	2	300
Fort Ritchie (Army), Cascade	MD	6	347
Fort Rucker (Army), Daleville	AL	2	22
Fort Sam Houston, San Antonio	TX	20	733
Fort Shafter (Army), Honolulu	HI	1	224
Fort Sheridan (Army), Highland Park	IL	10	251
Fort Sill (Army), Lawton	OK	4	611
Fort Smith Municipal Airport Air Force Guard Station, Fort Smith	AR	3	52
Fort Stewart (Army), Hinesville	GA	1	205
Fort Story (Army), Virginia Beach	VA	2	765
Fort Wainwright (Army), Fairbanks	AK	AL	34
Fort Wayne Municipal Airport Air Force Guard Station, Fort Wayne	IN	4	275
Four Lakes Air Force Guard Station, Cheney	WA	5	790
Francis E. Warren Air Force Base, Cheyenne	WY	AL	823
Fresno Air Terminal Air Force Guard Station, Fresno	CA	19	88

G

Military Installation	State	District	Page
Galena Airport Air Force Station, Galena	AK	AL	34
Garden City (Marine Corps), New York	NY	4	504
Garland Air Force Guard Station, Garland	TX	3	708
Gen. Billy Mitchell Intl. Airport Air Force Guard Station, Milwaukee	WI	4	811
Gentile Air Force Station, Dayton	OH	3	580
George Air Force Base, Adelanto	CA	40	117
Gila Bend Air Force Station, Gila Bend	AZ	2	39
Glenview Naval Air Station, Glenview	IL	10	251
Goodfellow Air Force Base, San Angelo	TX	21	735
Grand Forks Air Force Base, Emerado	ND	AL	572
Greater Peoria Airport Air Force Guard Station, Bartonville	IL	18	262
Greater Pittsburgh Intl. Airport Air Force Guard Station, Coraopolis	PA	14	650
Great Falls Intl. Airport Air Force Guard Station, Great Falls	MT	AL	443
Great Lakes Naval Training Center, Great Lakes	IL	10	251
Griffiss Air Force Base, Rome	NY	23	533
Grissom Air Force Base, Bunker Hill	IN	5	276
Gulfport/Biloxi Municipal Airport Air Force Guard Station, Gulfport	MS	5	422
Gulfport Naval Construction Center, Gulfport	MS	5	422

H

Military Installation	State	District	Page
Hall Air Force Guard Station, Dothan	AL	2	22
Hammond Air National Guard Communications Station, Hammond	LA	1	319
Hancock Field Air Force Guard Station, Syracuse	NY	25	536
Hanscom Air Force Base, Bedford	MA	6	363
Harrisburg Olmstead Intl. Airport Air Force Guard Station, Middletown	PA	17	654
Harry Diamond Laboratories (Army), Adelphi	MD	4	344
Hector Field Intl. Airport Air Force Guard Station, Fargo	ND	AL	572
Henderson Hall Marine Corps Headquarters, Washington	DC	AL	839
Hickam Air Force Base, Honolulu	HI	1	224
Hill Air Force Base, Clearfield	UT	1	752
Holloman Air Force Base, Alamogordo	NM	2	491
Homestead Air Force Base, Homestead	FL	17	192
Homestead Naval Security, Homestead	FL	17	192
Hulman Regional Airport Air Force Guard Station, Terre Haute	IN	7	279
Hunter Army Airfield, Savannah	GA	1	205

Military Installation	State	District	Page
I			
Indian Head Naval Ordnance Station (Navy), Indian Head	MD	5	345
Ingleside Naval Station, Ingleside	TX	27	743
J			
Jacksonville Intl. Airport Air Force Guard Station, Callahan	FL	4	173
Jacksonville Naval Air Station, Jacksonville	FL	3	171
Jacksonville Naval Aviation Depot, Jacksonville	FL	3	171
Jefferson Barracks Air Force Guard Station, St. Louis	MO	1	426
Jefferson Proving Ground (Army), Madison	IN	9	282
Joe Foss Field Air Force Guard Station, Sioux Falls	SD	AL	683
K			
K. I. Sawyer Air Force Base, Gwinn	MI	1	375
Kaneohe Bay Marine Corps Air Station, Kailua	HI	2	226
Keesler Air Force Base, Biloxi	MS	5	422
Kelly Air Force Base, San Antonio	TX	20	733
Key Field (Air Force), Meridian	MS	3	419
Key West Naval Air Station, Key West	FL	20	196
King Salmon Airport, Naknek	AK	AL	34
Kings Bay Naval Submarine Base, Kings Bay	GA	1	205
Kingsley Field Air Force Guard Station, Klamath Falls	OR	2	620
Kingsville Naval Air Station, Kingsville	TX	27	743
Kirtland Air Force Base, Albuquerque	NM	1	490
Kokee Air Force Station, Kekaha	HI	2	226
Kulis Air National Guard Base, Anchorage	AK	AL	34
L			
Lackland Air Force Base, San Antonio	TX	20	733
Lakehurst Naval Air Engineering Center, Lakehurst	NJ	4	471
Lambert/St. Louis Intl. Airport Air Force Guard Station, St. Ann	MO	2	428
Langley Air Force Base, Hampton	VA	1	764
La Porte Air Force Guard Station, La Porte	TX	25	740
Laughlin Air Force Base, Del Rio	TX	23	738
Lemoore Naval Air Station, Lemoore	CA	20	89
Letterkenny Army Depot, Chambersburg	PA	9	642
Lexington Bluegrass Army Depot Activity, Lexington	KY	6	314
Lincoln Municipal Airport Air Force Guard Station, Lincoln	NE	1	447
Little Creek Naval Amphibious Base, Norfolk	VA	2	765
Little Rock Air Force Base, Jacksonville	AR	2	50
Long Beach Naval Shipyard, Long Beach	CA	38	114
Long Beach Naval Station, Long Beach	CA	38	114
Loring Air Force Base, Limestone	ME	2	335
Los Angeles Air Force Base, El Segundo	CA	36	111
Louisville Naval Ordnance Station, Louisville	KY	3	310
Lowry Air Force Base, Denver	CO	1	138
Lualualei Naval Magazine, Lualualei	HI	2	226
Luke Air Force Base, Litchfield Park	AZ	2	39
M			
MacDill Air Force Base, Tampa	FL	11	182
Malmstrom Air Force Base, Great Falls	MT	AL	443
Mansfield Lahm Municipal Airport Air Force Guard Station, Mansfield	OH	4	582
March Air Force Base, Sunnymead	CA	43	121
Mare Island Naval Shipyard, Vallejo	CA	7	70
Mare Island Naval Station, Vallejo	CA	7	70
Marine Barracks, Washington	DC	AL	839
Marine Corps Air Force Combat Center, Palm Springs	CA	40	117
Marine Corps Development & Education			
Command, Quantico	VA	11	779
Marine Corps Logistics Base, Albany	GA	8	216
Marine Corps Logistics Base, Barstow	CA	40	117
Marine Corps Recruitment Depot Activity, Parris Island	SC	2	672
Marine Corps Support Activity, Kansas City	MO	5	432
Martin State Air Force Guard Station, Baltimore	MD	2	341
Material & Mechanical Research Center (Army), Watertown	MA	7	365
Mather Air Force Base, Rancho Cordova	CA	11	76
Maxwell Air Force Base, Montgomery	AL	2	22
Mayport Naval Station, Mayport	FL	4	173
McAlester Army Ammunition Plant, Lawton	OK	3	610
McChord Air Force Base, Tacoma	WA	9	795
McClellan Air Force Base, Sacramento	CA	3	64
McCollum Air Force Guard Station, Kennesaw	GA	6	213
McConnell Air Force Base, Wichita	KS	4	303
McEntire Air Force Guard Base, Eastover	SC	2	672
McGhee Tyson Airport Air Force Guard Station, Alcoa	TN	2	689
McGuire Air Force Base, Wrightstown	NJ	3	470
Memphis Defense Depot (Army), Memphis	TN	9	699
Memphis Intl. Airport Air Force Guard Station, Oakville	TN	9	699
Memphis Naval Air Station, Millington	TN	8	698
Meridian Naval Air Station, Meridian	MS	3	419
Millington Naval Hospital, Millington	TN	8	698
Minneapolis/St. Paul Intl. Airport Air Force Reserve Station, Minneapolis	MN	5	408
Minot Air Force Base, Minot	ND	AL	572
Miramar Naval Air Station, San Diego	CA	49	129
Miramar Naval Air Station, San Diego	CA	51	132
Mobile Naval Station, Mobile	AL	1	21
Moffett Field Naval Air Station, Moffett Field	CA	14	80
Moody Air Force Base, Valdosta	GA	2	206
Mountain Home Air Force Base, Mountain Home	ID	1	231
N			
Nashville Metropolitan Airport Air Force Guard Station, Nashville	TN	5	693
Natick Research & Development Laboratories (Army), Natick	MA	7	365
Naval Air Development Center, Warminster	PA	8	640
Naval Air Propulsion Center, Trenton	NJ	12	484
Naval Air Station, Alameda	CA	9	73
Naval Aviation Supply Office, Philadelphia	PA	3	633
Naval Avionics Center, Indianapolis	IN	6	278
Naval Coastal Systems Center, Panama City	FL	1	168
Naval Education & Training Center, Newport	RI	1	664
Naval Education & Training Program Management Support, Pensacola	FL	1	168
Naval Electronic Systems Engineering Center, San Diego	CA	49	129
Naval Electronic Systems Engineering, St. Mary's City	MD	5	345
Naval Headquarters, Washington	DC	AL	839
Naval Medical Command, Bethesda	MD	8	350
Naval Observatory, Washington	DC	AL	839
Naval Oceanographic Office, St. Louis Bay	MS	5	422
Naval Ocean Systems Center, San Diego	CA	49	129
Naval Postgraduate School, Monterey	CA	17	85
Naval Research Laboratory, Washington	DC	AL	839
Naval Security Group Activity, Chesapeake	VA	4	768
Naval Surface Weapons Center, Dahlgren	VA	1	764
Naval Surface Weapons Center, Silver Spring	MD	4	344
Naval Training Center, Orlando	FL	8	178
Naval Underseas Warfare Engineering Station, Keyport	WA	1	785
Naval Underwater Systems Center, Newport	RI	1	664
Naval Weapons Support Center, Crane	IN	8	281
Navy Ships Parts Control Center, Mechanicsburg	PA	19	657
Navy Supply Corps School, Athens	GA	10	219
Nellis Air Force Base, Las Vegas	NV	1	454

Military Installation	State	District	Page
South Portland Air Force Guard Station, South Portland	ME	1	333
South Weymouth Naval Air Station, South Weymouth	MA	10	370
Spokane Intl. Airport Air Force Guard Station, Spokane	WA	5	790
St. Louis Army Ammunition Plant, St. Louis	MO	1	426
Standiford Field Air Force Guard Station, Louisville	KY	3	310
Steven A. Douglas Support Facility (Army), Salt Lake City	UT	2	753
Stewart Annex (Army), Newburgh	NY	26	538
Stewart Intl. Airport Air Force Guard Station, New Windsor	NY	19	527
Stockton Naval Communications Station, Stockton	CA	11	76
Suffolk County Airport Air Force Guard Station, Westhampton Beach	NY	1	499
Sunny Point Military Ocean Terminal (Army), Southport	NC	7	560

T

Military Installation	State	District	Page
Tinker Air Force Base, Midwest City	OK	4	611
Tobyhanna Army Depot, Tobyhanna	PA	10	643
Toledo Express Airport Air Force Guard Station, Swanton	OH	9	588
Tooele Army Depot, Tooele	UT	1	752
Tracy Army Defense Depot Activity, Tracy	CA	11	76
Travis Air Force Base, Fairfield	CA	1	61
Treasure Island Naval Station, San Francisco	CA	8	71
Tripler Army Medical Center, Honolulu	HI	1	224
Truax Field (Air Force), Madison	WI	2	808
Tucson Intl. Airport Air Force Guard Station, Tucson	AZ	2	39
Tulsa Intl. Airport Air Force Guard Station, Tulsa	OK	1	607
Tustin Marine Corps Air Station, Tustin	CA	47	126
Tyndall Air Force Base, Panama City	FL	2	170

U

Military Installation	State	District	Page
U.S. Air Force Academy, Colorado Springs	CO	5	144
U.S. Naval Academy, Annapolis	MD	1	339

V

Military Installation	State	District	Page
Vance Air Force Base, Enid	OK	6	614
Vandenberg Air Force Base, Lompoc	CA	22	91
Vint Hill Farms Station (Army), Warrenton	VA	10	777

W

Military Installation	State	District	Page
W. K. Kellogg Regional Airport Air Force Guard Station, Battle Creek	MI	7	383
Walter Reed Army Medical Center, Washington	DC	AL	839
Washington Naval Security Station, Washington	DC	AL	839
Watervliet Arsenal (Army), Watervliet	NY	21	530
Wellesley Air Force Guard Station, Wellesley	MA	4	360
Westover Air Force Base, Chicopee	MA	2	356
West Point Military Reservation, West Point	NY	19	527
Whidbey Island Naval Air Station, Oak Harbor	WA	2	786
Whiteman Air Force Base, Knob Noster	MO	4	431
White Sands Missile Range (Army), White Sands	NM	2	491
Whiting Field Naval Air Station, Milton	FL	1	168
Williams Air Force Base, Chandler	AZ	6	45
Willow Grove Air Reserve Station, Hatboro	PA	13	648
Willow Grove Naval Air Station, Willow Grove	PA	13	648
Will Rogers World Airport Air Force Guard Station, Oklahoma City	OK	6	614
Winter Harbor Naval Security Group Activity, Winter Harbor	ME	2	335
Worchester Air Force Guard Station, Worchester	MA	3	358
Wright-Patterson Air Force Base, Fairborn	OH	7	586
Wurtsmith Air Force Base, Oscoda	MI	5	381

Y

Military Installation	State	District	Page
Yeager Airport Air Force Guard Station, Charleston	WV	2	801
Yorktown Naval Weapons Station, Yorktown	VA	1	764
Youngstown Municipal Airport Air Force Reserve Station, Vienna	OH	17	600
Yuma Marine Corps Air Station, Yuma	AZ	2	39
Yuma Proving Ground (Army), Yuma	AZ	2	39

Business Index

This index covers most private employers listed in this book. Excluded are government agencies, including school districts and military installations; legal and medical professional groups; hospitals; universities; and newspapers. Universities and military installations are indexed separately. Legal identifications, such as Corp., Inc., or Co., generally are not included with the business names in the index but will be found at the listings. An asterisk (*) indicates that the organization appears more than once in the congressional district, usually because of multiple plants or offices at different locations. Employer names occasionally have been edited so that national business firms appear together. For example, Hyatt Hotels are always indexed under the word "Hyatt," even though the actual hotel name may begin with another word.

Business	State	District	Page	*
A				
A&L Industrial Constructions	TN	1	688	
A-DEC	OR	1	619	
A-P-A Transport	NJ	13	485	
A. B. B. Lummus Crest	TX	7	716	
A. B. Chance	MO	9	439	
A. B. Dick	IL	9	249	
A. B. M. Security Services	TX	18	731	
A. Duda & Sons	FL	16	189	
A. E. Staley Manufacturing	IL	19	264	
A. G. Edwards	FL	11	182	
A. G. Edwards	MO	1	427	
A. H. Robins	VA	3	767	
A. O. Smith	SC	5	677	
A. O. Smith	TN	8	698	
A. O. Smith	WI	5	812	
A. P. Green Industries	MO	9	439	
A. T. Cross	RI	1	664	
AAI	MD	2	341	
Abacus Security Service	MD	3	342	
ABB Air Preheater	NY	31	546	
ABB Impell	IL	10	251	
ABB Kent-Taylor	NY	28	541	
ABB Power	GA	10	219	
ABB Power	FL	7	177	
ABB Power	MO	4	431	
ABB Power	VA	5	770	
Abbey Group Hotel	WI	1	807	
Abbott Laboratories	CA	14	81	
Abbott Laboratories	IL	10	251	*
Abbott Laboratories	NC	2	552	
Abbott Laboratories	NC	8	561	
Abbott Laboratories	OH	12	593	
Abbott Laboratories	OH	16	598	
Abbott Laboratories	TX	10	720	
Abbott Laboratories	TX	30	748	
Abbott Laboratories	UT	2	753	
Abbott Laboratories	VA	5	770	
ABF Freight Systems	AR	2	51	
ABF Freight Systems	IL	18	263	
ABF Freight Systems	OH	3	580	
ABF Freight Systems	PA	19	657	
Accent Maintenance	NY	19	527	
Accurate Temporary Services	NY	14	518	
Accuride	KY	1	308	
Ace Hardware	IL	13	255	
Ace Parking Service America	CA	49	130	
ACF Industries	PA	6	637	
Acme Boot	TN	7	697	
Acme Brush	OH	16	599	
Acme Building Maintenance	CA	13	79	
Acme Markets	PA	7	639	
Acme Steel	IL	2	238	
Action Industries	MS	1	416	
Active Tools & Manufacturing	MI	5	381	
Acushnet	MA	4	360	*
Acuson	CA	14	81	
Acustar	AL	5	27	

Business	State	District	Page	*
Acustar	IN	2	272	
Acustar	MI	4	379	
Acustar	MI	15	395	
Acustar	OH	3	580	
Acxiom	AR	2	51	
Adamar of New Jersey	NJ	2	468	
Adam Meldrum & Anderson	NY	30	544	
Addington	KY	4	312	
Addison-Wesley Publishing	MA	7	365	
Add Staff	CO	5	144	
Admiral Maintenance Service	IL	9	249	
Adobeair	AZ	2	40	
ADP Brokerage Services Group	NJ	13	485	
Advance Machine	MN	6	410	
Advance Presort Service	IL	5	242	
Advance Security	PA	18	656	
Advanced Cardiovascular Systems	CA	44	122	
Advanced Micro Devices	CA	14	80	
Advanced Micro Devices	TX	10	720	
Advanced Technology Labs	WA	1	785	
Advanced Telecom	FL	22	198	
AEG Westinghouse Transportation Systems	PA	18	656	
Aegon USA	TX	12	723	
Aegon USA	IA	1	288	
AEL Defense	PA	13	648	
Aero International	TX	20	734	
Aerojet-General	CA	5	66	
Aerojet-General	CA	11	76	
Aerojet-General	CA	31	105	
Aeroquip	MI	7	383	
Aeroquip	OH	5	583	
Aerospace	CA	36	111	
Aetna Life & Casualty	CT	1	150	*
Aetna Life & Casualty	CT	2	152	
Aetna Life & Casualty	FL	11	183	
Aetna Life & Casualty	MA	4	360	
Aetna Life & Casualty	PA	2	632	
Affiliated Computer Systems	TX	5	712	
Affiliated Food Stores	TX	6	713	
Affiliated Food Stores	TX	19	732	
Affiliated Food Stores Southwest	AR	2	51	
After Six	PA	3	633	
AG Communications	AZ	4	42	
AG Communications	IL	5	242	
Agfa	MA	6	363	
Agfa	NY	20	529	
Agway	NY	25	537	
Aid Maintenance	RI	1	664	
AIL Systems	NY	2	500	
Aims	IL	7	245	
Air Industries	CA	45	124	
Air Products & Chemicals	PA	15	651	
Airborne Express	OH	6	584	
Airborne Freight	CA	15	82	
Airborne Freight	WA	7	793	
Aircraft Braking Systems	OH	14	596	
Aisin USA Manufacturing	IN	9	283	
AJ Industries	CA	31	105	
AL Tech Specialty Steel	NY	31	546	
Ala Moana Hotel/Azabu USA	HI	1	224	
Alabama Gas	AL	7	30	
Alabama Power	AL	2	23	
Alabama Power	AL	4	25	
Alabama Power	AL	7	30	
Aladdin Industries	TN	5	694	
Aladdin Mills	GA	9	217	
Aladdin Mills	VA	11	779	
Alaska Airlines	WA	7	793	
Alaska Airlines	WA	9	795	
Alaskan Copper Companies	WA	7	793	
Albany International	NY	21	530	
Alberici/Clark	MI	8	385	

Business	State	District	Page	*
Albert Trostel & Sons	MI	2	377	
Alberto-Culver	IL	5	242	
Albertsons	CA	39	116	
Albertsons	ID	2	231	
Albertsons	TX	24	739	
Alcan Aluminum	KY	1	308	
Alcan Aluminum	MO	1	427	
Alcan Aluminum	NY	24	535	
Alcatel National Cable Systems	NC	10	564	
Alcatel Network Systems	NC	4	555	
Alcatel Network Systems	TX	30	747	
Alcoa Fujikura	TN	6	695	
Alcon Laboratories	CA	47	127	
Alcon Surgical	TX	24	739	
Alcott Staff Leasing	NY	2	500	
Aldrich Chemical	WI	4	811	
Aldworth	MA	6	363	
Alert Security	NY	6	507	
Alex Brown & Sons	MD	3	343	
Alexander Hamilton Life	MI	11	389	
Alexander Karten	NY	15	521	
Alexander's	NY	11	515	
Alexander's	NY	17	524	
Alexander's	NY	18	525	
ALFA	AL	2	23	
Alfa-Laval	PA	8	641	
Alfred Nickles Bakery	OH	16	599	
Aliso Viejo	CA	47	127	
Alitalia Airlines	NY	14	520	
All Star Personnel Services	MD	7	348	
Allegheny Ludlum	PA	4	635	
Allegheny Ludlum	PA	12	646	
Allegheny Power Service	PA	20	659	
Allen-Bradley	OH	13	595	
Allen-Bradley	OH	19	603	
Allen-Bradley	TX	16	728	
Allen-Bradley	WI	4	811	
Allen-Bradley	WI	9	819	
Allen Canning	LA	6	327	
Allen Family Foods	DE	AL	163	
Allen Products	PA	15	652	
Allergan	CA	47	126	
Allergro Microsystems	MA	3	358	
Alliance Home Service	NY	17	524	
Alliant Techsystems	CO	1	139	
Alliant Techsystems	CO	5	144	
Alliant Techsystems	MN	4	406	
Alliant Techsystems	MN	5	408	
Alliant Techsystems	WA	2	786	
Alliant Techsystems	WA	5	790	
Allied Janitorial Service	AL	7	30	
Allied Products	IA	2	290	
Allied Products	IL	1	237	
Allied Products	OH	8	587	
Allied Security	PA	14	650	
Allied-Signal	AZ	1	38	
Allied-Signal	AZ	2	40	*
Allied-Signal	AZ	5	44	
Allied-Signal	CA	26	98	*
Allied-Signal	CA	36	111	
Allied-Signal	CT	5	157	
Allied-Signal	FL	23	200	
Allied-Signal	IL	6	23	
Allied-Signal	IN	3	274	
Allied-Signal	MD	2	341	
Allied-Signal	MI	6	382	
Allied-Signal	MO	5	432	
Allied-Signal	NC	2	553	
Allied-Signal	NC	4	555	
Allied-Signal	NJ	9	479	
Allied-Signal	NJ	11	482	*
Allied-Signal	NY	21	530	
Allied-Signal	OH	5	583	
Allied-Signal	OH	8	587	
Allied-Signal	RI	1	664	
Allied-Signal	SC	2	672	*
Allied-Signal	SC	6	678	
Allied-Signal	VA	3	766	*
Allied Van Lines	IL	13	255	
Allnet Communications	MI	11	389	
Allstate Insurance	CA	39	116	
Allstate Insurance	CT	6	158	
Allstate Insurance	FL	9	180	
Allstate Insurance	IL	10	251	*
Allstate Insurance	NC	9	563	
Allstate Insurance	NY	28	541	
Allstate Insurance	OH	14	596	
Allstate Insurance	TX	26	742	
Allstate Insurance	VA	6	772	
Allstate Insurance	WA	1	785	
Allsteel	IL	14	256	
Almay	NC	2	553	
Alpha Beta	CA	39	116	
Alpha Industries	MA	7	365	
Alphastaff Group A	PA	9	642	
Alpha Therapeutic	CA	31	105	
Alta View Personnel Service	UT	2	754	
Altron	MA	6	363	
Alumax	AR	4	54	
Alumax Mill Products	PA	16	653	
Alumax of South Carolina	SC	1	671	
Aluminum Company of America	AR	2	51	
Aluminum Company of America	CA	33	107	
Aluminum Company of America	IA	1	288	
Aluminum Company of America	IN	7	280	
Aluminum Company of America	IN	8	281	
Aluminum Company of America	NC	8	561	
Aluminum Company of America	NY	24	535	
Aluminum Company of America	OH	10	590	
Aluminum Company of America	PA	4	635	*
Aluminum Company of America	PA	14	650	
Aluminum Company of America	TN	2	689	
Aluminum Company of America	TX	11	721	
Aluminum Company of America	WA	4	789	
Aluminum Shapes	NJ	1	467	
Amaco	AL	5	27	
Amaco	IN	1	271	
Amaco Fabrics & Fibers	AL	2	23	
Amalgamated Sugar	ID	2	231	
Amana Refrigeration	IA	2	290	
Amana Refrigeration	TN	4	692	
Amax	IL	19	264	
Ambler Industries	SC	6	678	
Amboy Bus	NY	12	516	
AMCA International Construction	TN	9	700	
Amcil Equities	CA	47	127	
Amco Insurance	IA	4	293	
Amcom Books Sales	NY	8	511	
Amdahl	CA	14	80	
Amelia Island Plantation	FL	4	173	
Amerada Hess	NJ	7	476	
Americal	NC	1	551	
American Airlines	CA	8	71	
American Airlines	CA	16	83	
American Airlines	CA	32	106	
American Airlines	CA	49	130	
American Airlines	CT	1	150	
American Airlines	FL	23	200	
American Airlines	IL	4	240	
American Airlines	MA	8	367	
American Airlines	NC	4	555	
American Airlines	NY	6	507	
American Airlines	NY	7	508	
American Airlines	OH	1	577	
American Airlines	OK	1	607	
American Airlines	TN	5	694	
American Airlines	TX	5	712	
American Airlines	TX	6	713	*
American Argo	PA	6	637	
American Argo	SC	3	674	
American Bankers Insurance	FL	17	192	
American Barrick Resources	NV	2	456	
American Broadcasting Companies	NY	8	510	
American Building Maintenance	CA	49	130	
American Building Maintenance	CO	6	146	
American Building Maintenance	GA	4	210	
American Building Maintenance	IL	7	246	
American Building Maintenance	KY	3	311	

Business	State	District	Page	*	Business	State	District	Page	*
Associated Press	NY	14	519		Austin Commercial	TX	5	712	
Associated Wholesale Grocers	KS	3	301		Austin Industrial	TX	9	718	
Associated Wholesale Grocers	MO	7	436		Austin Industries	TX	29	746	
Associated Wholesalers	PA	6	637		Auto Club of America	OK	5	612	
Associates Commercial	IN	3	274		Auto Owners Insurance	MI	7	383	
Associates Financial Services	TX	26	742		Autodie	MI	3	378	
AST Research	CA	45	124		Automatic Data Processing	CA	28	101	
AST Research	CA	47	126		Automatic Data Processing	CA	39	116	
Astec America	CA	48	128		Automatic Data Processing	IL	5	242	
Astec Industries	TN	3	691		Automatic Data Processing	MA	7	365	
Astra Pharmaceutical Products	MA	3	358		Automatic Data Processing	NJ	3	470	
Astronautics Corp. of America	NC	11	566		Automatic Data Processing	NJ	8	477	
Astronautics Corp. of America	NJ	8	477		Automatic Data Processing	NJ	11	482	
AT&T	AR	2	51		Automatic Data Processing	NY	5	506	
AT&T	CA	8	72		Automatic Data Processing	NY	8	510	
AT&T	CA	9	73		Automatic Switch	NJ	11	482	
AT&T	CO	2	140		Automotive Brake	IL	20	266	
AT&T	DC	AL	840		Automotive Controls	CT	3	154	
AT&T	FL	3	172	*	Automotive Controls	KS	4	303	
AT&T	FL	4	173		Automotive Industries	VA	10	777	
AT&T	FL	8	178		Autozone	TN	9	700	
AT&T	FL	10	181		Avantek	CA	4	65	
AT&T	GA	4	209		Avantek	CA	15	82	
AT&T	GA	5	211	*	Avantek	CA	16	84	
AT&T	GA	6	213	*	Avco	CA	47	127	
AT&T	IL	6	23		Avco	CT	3	154	
AT&T	IL	7	246		Avco	PA	10	644	
AT&T	IL	13	255		Aventine Partners	CA	49	130	
AT&T	IL	14	256		Avery International	OH	19	603	
AT&T	IN	6	278		Avex Electronics	AL	5	27	
AT&T	IN	10	284		Avia Rent-A-Car	OK	1	607	
AT&T	LA	1	319		Aviall	CA	27	99	
AT&T	LA	5	325		Aviall	TX	30	748	
AT&T	MA	6	363		Avis	NY	4	504	
AT&T	MD	2	341		Avnet	CA	32	106	
AT&T	MD	4	344		Avnet	AZ	1	38	
AT&T	MO	2	428		Avnet/Channel Master	NC	2	553	
AT&T	MO	5	432	*	Avon Products	CA	27	99	
AT&T	NC	5	557		Avon Products	DE	AL	163	
AT&T	NC	6	558	*	Avon Products	GA	6	213	
AT&T	NJ	6	474		Avon Products	IL	9	249	
AT&T	NJ	7	476		Avon Products	NY	14	519	
AT&T	NJ	10	481		Avon Products	OH	2	579	
AT&T	NJ	11	482	*	Avondale Industries	LA	2	320	
AT&T	NJ	12	484	*	AVX	SC	1	671	
AT&T	NY	14	519						
AT&T	NY	19	527						
AT&T	OH	1	577		**B**				
AT&T	OH	12	593						
AT&T	OK	5	612		B. B. Rogers Processors	MS	3	419	
AT&T	PA	6	637		B. Dalton Bookseller	NY	8	511	
AT&T	PA	15	651	*	B. E. & K. Construction	NC	11	566	
AT&T	TX	5	712		B. F. Goodrich	OH	8	587	
AT&T	TX	7	714		B. F. Goodrich	OH	13	595	
AT&T	TX	27	743		B. F. Goodrich	VT	AL	759	
AT&T	VA	7	773		B. M. G. Music	SC	4	675	
AT&T	VA	10	777		B. P. A.	TX	22	737	
AT&T	VA	11	779	*	Babcock & Wilcox	MS	3	419	
AT&T Network Cable Systems	AZ	2	40		Babcock & Wilcox	OH	7	586	
Atchison Casting	KS	2	300		Babcock & Wilcox	OH	14	596	
Atchison, Topeka & Santa Fe	KS	3	301		Babcock & Wilcox	TX	1	706	
Atcor	IL	2	238		Babcock & Wilcox	VA	6	771	
Atlanta Gas Light	GA	5	211		Baby Grand	NV	1	454	
Atlantic City Electric	NJ	2	468		Backer Spielvogel Bates	NY	14	519	
Atlantic Mutual Insurance	VA	6	772		Badger	MA	8	367	
Atlantic Research	VA	10	777		Badger Meter	WI	5	813	
Atlantic Richfield	CA	33	107		Bagcraft Corp. of America	IL	3	240	
Atlantic Richfield	CA	37	113		Bahlsen	NC	4	555	
Atlantic Richfield	TX	23	738		Bailey Controls	OH	19	603	
Atlantic Richfield	TX	30	747		Bain & Co	MA	8	367	
Atlantic Steel	GA	5	211		Bake-Line Products	IL	6	244	
Atlantic Veneer	NC	3	554		Baker Concrete Constructions	OH	8	587	
Atlas Crankshaft	OH	5	583		Baker Hughes	TX	29	746	*
Atlas Hotels	CA	49	130	*	Baker Hughes	UT	2	754	
Atmel	CO	5	144		Baker Industries	CA	32	106	
Atmos Energy	TX	19	732		Baker Industries	MN	4	406	
ATR Wire & Cable	KY	6	315		Baker Protective Services	TX	7	716	
Augat	AL	2	22		Baldor Electric	AR	3	52	
Aurora Casket	IN	9	283		Baldwin Filters	NE	3	450	

Business	State	District	Page	*	Business	State	District	Page	*
Benteler Industries	MI	3	378		BOC Group	NJ	7	476	
Bently Nevada	NV	2	456		BOC Group/Ohmeda Branch	WI	2	808	
Bergdorf Goodman	NY	14	519		Boca Raton Hotel	FL	22	198	
Bergen Brunswig	CA	46	125		Bocep Ventures	TN	9	700	
Bergen Nursing Team	NJ	5	473		Bodine Electric	IL	5	242	
Berline	TN	4	692		Boehringer Mannheim	IN	3	274	
Bernice Bishop Estate Trust	HI	1	224		Boehringer Mannheim	IN	6	278	
Berol	TN	4	692	*	Boeing	AL	5	27	
Berry Contracting	TX	27	743		Boeing	CA	25	96	
Bertelsmann Music Group	IN	10	284		Boeing	GA	2	206	
Bertram-Trojan	FL	18	193		Boeing	GA	8	216	
Best	MN	4	406		Boeing	KS	4	303	*
Best Power Technology	WI	6	814		Boeing	LA	1	319	
Best Universal Lock	IN	6	278		Boeing	LA	3	322	
Best Western Motels	AZ	4	42		Boeing	LA	7	328	
Beth Emeth Home Attendant Services	NY	9	512		Boeing	OR	3	621	
Bethenergy Mines	WV	2	801		Boeing	PA	1	630	
Bethlehem Steel	IN	1	270		Boeing	PA	7	639	
Bethlehem Steel	MD	2	341		Boeing	TN	3	691	
Bethlehem Steel	NY	30	544		Boeing	TX	30	747	
Bethlehem Steel	PA	12	646		Boeing	WA	1	785	
Bethlehem Steel	PA	15	651	*	Boeing	WA	2	786	
Bethlehem Steel	PA	17	654		Boeing	WA	7	792	
Better-Bilt Aluminum Products	AZ	3	41		Boeing	WA	9	795	
Better-Bilt Aluminum Products	TN	6	696		Boeing	WA	4	789	
Betz Laboratories	PA	8	641		Boise Cascade	AL	1	21	
Beverly Enterprises	VA	2	765		Boise Cascade	ID	1	230	*
BGF Industries	VA	5	770		Boise Cascade	IL	6	244	
BGM Industries	MO	5	433		Boise Cascade	LA	6	327	
BHC Acquisition	TX	30	748		Boise Cascade	LA	7	328	
BHP Utah International	NM	3	493		Boise Cascade	ME	1	333	
Bi-Lo	SC	4	675		Boise Cascade	ME	2	335	
Bibb Company	GA	2	207		Boise Cascade	OR	1	618	
Bibb Company	NC	1	551		Boise Cascade	OR	2	620	*
Bibb Company	SC	4	675		Boise Cascade	WA	4	789	
Bic	CT	3	154		Boldt Group	WI	8	817	
Bidermann Industries	AL	2	23	*	Bollinger Machine Shop & Shipyard	LA	3	322	
Bidermann Industries	AL	4	25		Bollman Hat	PA	16	653	
Bidermann Industries	GA	7	214		Bolt Beranek & Newman	MA	8	366	
Bidermann Industries	PA	9	642		Bon Marche	WA	7	793	
Big Three Merchant Gases & Equipement	TX	7	716		Bon Vie International	TN	3	691	
Biggers Bros	NC	12	568		Bonnell, William L. & Co	GA	3	208	
Bike Athletic	TN	2	689		Bonneville International	UT	2	754	
Biltmore Hotel/TAT Los Angeles	CA	33	108		Book of the Month Club	PA	19	657	
Binks Manufacturing	IL	5	242		Boomtown Hotel	NV	2	456	
Bio-Rad Laboratories	CA	7	70		Boran Graig Barber Construction	FL	14	187	
Biomet	IN	5	277		Borden	CA	25	96	
Bird Blue Body	GA	2	206		Borden	OH	12	593	
Birtcher Real Estate	CA	48	128		Borden	PA	11	645	
Bissell	MI	3	378		Borg-Warner	IL	7	246	
Black & Decker	CT	1	151		Borg-Warner	IN	2	272	
Black & Decker	MD	1	340		Borg-Warner	NY	26	538	
Black & Decker	MD	2	341		Borg-Warner	NY	31	546	
Black & Decker	MD	6	347		Borland International	CA	15	82	
Black & Decker	NC	2	552		Boro Manhattan Community	NY	8	510	
Black & Decker	NC	6	559		Bosch Robert Power Tool	IL	18	263	
Black & Decker	NC	7	560		Bosch Robert Power Tool	NC	3	554	
Black & Veatch	KS	3	302		Bosco's Department Store	PA	6	637	
Black & Veatch	MO	5	432		Bose	MA	7	365	
Black Box	PA	20	659		Bost Federal Bank	CA	25	96	
Blade Communications	OH	9	589		Boston Company	MA	9	368	
Blair	PA	5	636		Boston Consulting	MA	9	369	
Blandin Paper	MN	8	412		Boston Edison	MA	8	367	
Block Drug	NJ	13	485		Boston Edison	MA	10	370	
Blockbuster Entertainment	TX	30	748		Boston Financial Data Services	MA	10	370	
Bloomingdales	FL	17	192		Boston Park Plaza Hotel	MA	8	367	
Bloomingdales	IL	5	242		Boston Safe Deposit & Trust	MA	9	368	
Bloomingdales	NJ	9	479		Boston Scientific	MA	8	367	
Bloomingdales	NY	14	518		Bowater	TN	2	689	
Bloomingdales	NY	19	527		Bowie Manufacturing	TX	15	727	
Bloomingdales	VA	10	777		Bowles Group	TX	6	713	
Blount	ID	1	230		Boyd Group	NV	1	454	
Blount	OR	3	621		BP America	OH	4	582	
Blue Bell Creameries	TX	8	717		BP America	OH	11	591	*
BNR	NC	2	553		BP America	UT	3	755	
Boardwalk Regency	NJ	2	468		BP Chemical	CA	35	110	
Boatmen's Bancshares	MO	1	427		BP Exploration	TX	7	716	
Boatmen's First National Bank	MO	5	433		BPS Guard Services	CA	8	72	
Boatmen's National Bank of St. Louis	MO	1	427		BPS Guard Services	CA	5	66	

Business	State	District	Page	*	Business	State	District	Page	*
Caci	VA	8	774		Carolina Freight	NC	9	563	
Cadam	CA	27	99		Carolina Freight Carriers	PA	17	654	
Cadbury Schweppes Holdings	CT	4	155		Carolina Golden Products	SC	5	677	
Cadence Design Systems	CA	16	84		Carolina Mills	NC	9	563	
CAE-Link	NY	26	538	*	Carolina Mirror	NC	5	557	
CAE-Link	TX	22	737		Carolina Power & Light	NC	4	555	*
CAE-Link	CA	14	81		Carolina Power & Light	NC	7	560	
Caesar Little Enterprises	IN	6	278		Carolina Telephone & Telegraph	NC	2	552	
Caesars New Jersey	CA	29	102		Carolina Turkeys	NC	3	554	
Caffcos Floral Factory	AL	2	23		Caron International	IL	16	259	
Cagles	GA	2	207		Carpenter Technology	PA	6	637	
Cagles	GA	3	208		Carriage Industries	GA	9	218	
Cal-Style Furniture	CA	37	113		Carrier	IN	4	275	
Calcomp	CA	46	125		Carrier	NY	25	536	
Caldor	CT	3	154		Carrier	TN	2	689	
Caldor	CT	4	155		Carrier	TN	4	692	
Calgon	MO	1	427		Carrier	TN	7	697	
California Acrylic Industries	CA	41	119		Carrier	TX	5	712	
California Almond Growers Assn	CA	5	66		Carson Nugget	NV	2	456	
California Casualty Mgt.	CA	12	78		Carson Pirie Scott & Co	AZ	1	38	
California Cedar Products	CA	11	76		Carter Hawley Hale Stores	CA	30	103	
California Commerce Club	CA	33	107		Carter Hawley Hale Stores	CA	9	73	
California Federal Bank	CA	31	105		Carver Boat	WI	8	817	
California Federal Bank	CA	32	106		Case	IA	3	291	
California Hotel & Casino	NV	1	454		Case	IL	13	255	
California Jockey Club	CA	12	78		Castner-Knott Dry Goods	TN	5	694	
California State Auto Assn	CA	8	71		Catauba Timber	SC	5	677	
California Steel Industries	CA	42	120		Caterair International	CA	36	112	
Callaway Gardens Resort	GA	3	208		Caterair International	FL	18	193	
Caloric	SC	6	678		Caterpillar	IL	13	255	
Calsonic Manufacturing	TN	4	692		Caterpillar	IL	14	256	*
Calspan	NY	30	544		Caterpillar	IL	15	258	
Calspan	TN	4	692		Caterpillar	IL	18	262	*
Camco International	OK	5	612		Caterpillar	IL	19	264	
Camco International/Reed Tool	TX	18	731		Caterpillar	PA	19	657	
Camden Wire	NY	23	533		Cauley Detective Agency	PA	14	650	
Cameron Forged Products	TX	7	716		Cavalier Homes of Alabama	AL	4	25	
Camp Dresser & McKee	MA	8	367		CBIS Federal	VA	10	777	
Campbell Soup	AR	3	52		CCB Financial	NC	12	567	
Campbell Soup	CA	5	66		CCH Computax	CA	36	112	
Campbell Soup	CA	18	86		CDK Holding	MA	3	358	
Campbell Soup	MD	1	339		Celadon Trucking Services of Indiana	IN	10	284	
Campbell Soup	NC	7	560		Celite	CA	22	92	
Campbell Soup	NE	2	449		Centel	IL	5	242	
Campbell Soup	NJ	1	467		Centennial One	MD	4	344	
Campbell Soup	OH	5	583		Centerbank	CT	5	157	
Canadian Imperial Bank of Commerce	NY	14	520		Centerior Energy	OH	19	603	
Candle	CA	29	102		Centocor	PA	7	639	
Canon Business Machines	CA	47	127		Central Bankcorporation	CO	1	139	
Canon USA	NY	5	506		Central Civic Assn Home Attendents	NY	6	507	
Canon Virginia	VA	1	764		Central Fidelity Bank	VA	3	767	
Canteen/TW Services	NY	17	524		Central Food Service	OK	6	614	
Capin Mercantile	AZ	2	40		Central Freight Lines	TX	29	746	
Capital Cities/ABC	CA	29	102	*	Central Hudson Gas & Electric	NY	19	527	
Capital Cities/ABC	NY	8	510	*	Central Illinois Insurance	IL	18	262	
Capital Cities/ABC	TX	12	722		Central Maine Power	ME	1	333	
Capital Personnel Services	TX	10	720		Central Ohio Coal	OH	18	601	
Capital-Mercury Shirt	AR	3	52		Central States Pension	IL	6	244	
Capitol-EMI Music	IL	18	263		Central Steel & Wire	IL	1	237	
Carboloy	MI	14	394		Central Telephone	NV	1	454	
Carbomedics	TX	10	720		Central Telephone Co of Florida	FL	2	170	
Carbon/Graphite Group	PA	5	636		Central Telephone Co of Illinois	IL	6	244	
Cardinal Foods	OH	15	597		Central Trust	OH	1	577	
Cardinal Industries	OH	12	593		Centralia Mining	WA	3	787	
Cardone Industries	PA	3	633		Centre Manufacturing	AL	4	25	
Carey-McFall/Bali Blinds	PA	10	644		Centrex-Great Southwest	FL	8	179	
Cargill	AR	3	53		Centura Bank	NC	2	553	
Cargill	KS	3	301		Century Plaza Hotel	CA	29	102	
Cargill	MN	3	404		Century Products	OH	16	598	
Carl Karcher Enterprises	CA	46	125		Cerro Copper Products	IL	12	254	
Carleton Woolen Mills	ME	1	333		Cerro Metal Products	PA	5	636	
Carlisle Companies	PA	19	657		Certainteed	KS	3	302	
Carlson Holdings	MN	6	410		Certainteed	PA	7	639	
Carlson Marketing	MN	6	409		Certainteed	TX	13	724	
Carlyle Ltd	IL	5	242		Certified Grocers Midwest	IL	3	239	
Carol Cable	RI	1	664		Certified Grocers of California	CA	33	107	
Carol Management	FL	21	197		Certified Grocers of Florida	FL	6	176	
Carole Fabrics	GA	10	219		Cessna Aircraft	KS	4	303	
Carolina Enterprises	NC	2	553		Cetus	CA	9	73	

Business	State	District	Page	*	Business	State	District	Page	*
Drivers Management	NE	2	449		Eagle-Picher Industries	TX	13	724	
Drown & Sharpe Manufacturing	RI	2	666		Eastalco Aluminum	MD	6	347	
DST Systems	MO	5	433		Eastern Stainless	MD	2	341	
Du Pont	DE	AL	162	*	Eastern-Western Hotel	NV	1	454	
Du Pont	DE	AL	163	*	Eastman Kodak	AR	1	49	
Du Pont	GA	10	219		Eastman Kodak	CA	34	109	
Du Pont	KY	3	311		Eastman Kodak	CA	38	114	
Du Pont	LA	3	322		Eastman Kodak	CO	4	143	
Du Pont	MA	5	361		Eastman Kodak	NY	14	519	
Du Pont	MI	12	391		Eastman Kodak	NY	28	541	*
Du Pont	MS	5	422		Eastman Kodak	NY	29	543	
Du Pont	NC	3	554		Eastman Kodak	SC	2	672	
Du Pont	NC	7	560		Eastman Kodak	TN	1	688	
Du Pont	NC	9	563		Eastman Kodak	TX	4	711	
Du Pont	NC	11	566		Eastman Kodak	VA	8	774	
Du Pont	NJ	2	468		Eaton	CT	5	157	
Du Pont	NJ	6	474		Eaton	IA	3	292	
Du Pont	NY	28	542		Eaton	KS	1	298	*
Du Pont	NY	29	543		Eaton	KY	2	309	*
Du Pont	OH	7	586		Eaton	MI	7	383	
Du Pont	PA	10	644		Eaton	MI	6	382	
Du Pont	PA	19	657		Eaton	MN	3	405	
Du Pont	SC	5	677		Eaton	NC	8	561	
Du Pont	SC	6	678		Eaton	NC	9	563	
Du Pont	TN	3	691		Eaton	NE	3	450	
Du Pont	TN	5	694		Eaton	NY	2	500	
Du Pont	TN	8	698	*	Eaton	TX	27	743	
Du Pont	TX	2	707		Eaton Cutler Hammer	IL	18	263	
Du Pont	TX	9	718		Eaton Cutler Hammer	WI	5	813	
Du Pont	TX	14	725		Eaton Sheaffer	IA	3	291	
Du Pont	TX	22	736		Ebasco Newberg Joint Venture	TN	4	692	
Du Pont	TX	29	746		Ebasco Services	NY	8	510	
Du Pont	VA	5	769		EBS Industries	AL	6	28	
Du Pont	VA	6	771		ECC America	GA	11	220	
Du Pont	VA	7	773		ECC International	FL	8	178	
Du Pont	WV	1	799		Eckerd Drug Stores	FL	10	181	
Du Pont	WV	2	801		Ecolab	MN	4	406	
Du Pont Optical Storage	DE	AL	163		Ecolab Pest Elimination Services	ND	AL	572	
Du Pont-Merck	DE	AL	163		Economic Chemical Distributors	NJ	10	481	
Dukane	IL	14	256		Economy Fire & Casualty	IL	16	259	
Duke Power	NC	9	563	*	Edgell Communications	MN	8	412	
Duke Power	SC	3	674		Edgewood Management	MD	8	349	
Duke Power	SC	5	677		Edison Brothers Stores	MO	1	427	
Dunhill Personnel of New Haven	CT	3	154		EDO	NY	7	508	
Dunhill Temporary	KS	4	303		Edsal Manufacturing	IL	4	241	
Dunlop Tire	NY	29	543		Educational Placement Services	PA	7	639	
Dunlop Tire	AL	5	27		Educational Testing Services	PA	8	641	
Duo-Fast	IL	5	242		Edward Blank Associates	TX	6	713	
Duquesne Light	PA	14	650		Edward Weck	NC	12	568	
Duracell	TN	3	691		Edwards Bros	MI	13	393	
Duracell International	SC	5	677		EFCO	MO	7	436	
Durand Glass Manufacturing	NJ	2	469		Effective Security Systems	NY	14	519	
Duratek	MD	3	343		Effective Security Systems	NY	19	527	
Duro Industries	MA	3	358		EG&G	FL	8	178	
Dyersburg Fabrics	TN	8	698		EG&G	NV	1	454	
Dynalectric	VA	10	777		EG&G	OH	3	580	
Dynamic Enterprises	NY	30	544		EG&G Idaho	ID	2	231	
Dynamics Research	MA	5	362		EG&G Rocky Flats	CO	6	146	
Dyncorp	CA	40	117		Eichleay	PA	14	650	
Dyncorp	CA	43	121		Ekco Group	IL	4	241	
					El Dorado Hotel	NV	2	456	
					El Paso Natural Gas	TX	16	728	
E					Elco Industries	IL	16	259	
					Eldec	WA	1	785	
E-J Electric Installation	NY	7	508		Elder-Beerman Stores	OH	3	580	
E-Systems	FL	10	181		Electra Cleaning Contractors	NY	8	511	
E-Systems	TX	3	708		Electro Scientific Industries	OR	1	619	
E-Systems	TX	4	711		Electrolux	VA	9	776	
E-Systems	UT	3	755		Electroncom Automation	TX	24	739	
E-Systems	VA	10	777		Electronic Assembly	WI	6	814	
E-Systems	VA	11	779		Electronic Data Systems	CA	5	66	
E. A. Miller	UT	1	752		Electronic Data Systems	IN	5	277	
E. F. Johnson	MN	1	402		Electronic Data Systems	MI	8	385	
E. L. Yeager Construction	CA	47	127		Electronic Data Systems	MI	12	391	*
E. J. Brach & Sons	IL	6	243		Electronic Data Systems	TX	26	742	
E. M. S.	MD	4	344		Electronic Data Systems	TX	30	747	
E. R. Carpenter	KY	1	308		Electronic Data Systems	VA	10	777	
Eagle Industries	NJ	5	473		Electronics & Space	MO	1	427	
Eagle-Picher Industries	MO	7	436		Electrospace Systems	TX	3	708	

Business	State	District	Page	*	Business	State	District	Page	*
Farbest Foods	IN	9	283		First Alabama Bank	AL	1	21	
Farley Candy	IL	4	241		First American Metro	VA	10	777	
Farmers Group	CA	29	102		First American National Bank of Tennessee	TN	5	694	
Farmers Group	CA	18	86		First American Tax Service	CA	36	112	
Farmers Group	IL	14	256		First Bank National Assn	MN	4	406	
Farmers Group	TX	10	720		First Bank National Assn	MN	5	408	
Farmers Insurance Company of Washington	WA	3	787		First Bank System Denver	CO	1	138	
Farmers New World Life Insurance	WA	8	794		First Brands	GA	7	214	
Farmers Union Central Exchange	MN	3	405		First Chicago Trust	NY	8	510	
Farmers Union Central Exchange	WA	3	787		First Citizens Bancshares	NC	4	555	
Farmland Foods	IA	5	294		First City Bancorporation of Texas	TX	18	731	
Farmland Foods	NE	1	447		First Colony Life Insurance	VA	6	772	
Farmland Industries	MO	6	434		First Commercial Bank	AR	2	51	
Farmstead Foods	MN	1	402		First Commercial Bank	LA	2	320	
Fasco Industries	MO	4	431		First Data Resources	NE	2	449	
Fasco Industries	MO	7	436		First Executive	CA	29	102	
Fasco Industries	NC	11	566		First Federal Savings	NY	28	541	
Fast Food Merchandisers	TN	6	695		First Fidelity Bank of New Jersey	NJ	6	475	
Faxon	MA	9	369		First Fidelity Bank of New Jersey	NJ	13	485	
Fays Wheels Discount Auto Supply	NY	25	537		First Financial	WI	7	816	
FCC National Bank/First Card	IL	14	256		First Florida Bank	FL	11	182	
FDL Foods	IA	2	290		First Gibraltar Bank	TX	26	742	
FDL Foods	IL	16	259		First Giraltor	TX	20	734	
FDR Washington	FL	22	198		First Hawaiian Bank	HI	1	224	
Fearn International	IL	5	242		First Interstate	WA	7	793	
Fedco	CA	28	101		First Interstate Bank	AZ	1	38	
Fedco	CA	39	116		First Interstate Bank Denver	CO	1	138	
Fedco	CA	45	124		First Interstate Bank of California	CA	23	93	
Federal Express	NY	6	507		First Interstate Bank of California	CA	33	107	
Federal Express	TN	9	699		First Interstate Bank of Oregon	OR	1	618	
Federal Insurance	NJ	7	476		First Interstate Bank Texas	TX	18	730	
Federal Mutual Insurance	MN	1	402		First National Bank of Chicago	IL	4	241	
Federal Paper Board	GA	11	220		First National Bank of Kentucky	KY	3	310	
Federal Paper Board	NC	1	551		FIrst National Bank of Ohio	OH	14	596	
Federal Prison Industries/Unicor	CT	5	157		First National Bank of Omaha	NE	2	449	
Federal Signal	IL	11	253		First National Supermarkets	OH	11	591	
Federal-Hoffman	MN	6	409		First Security Services	MA	8	367	
Federal-Mogul	IN	6	278		First Tennessee Bank	TN	9	700	
Federal-Mogul	MI	4	379	*	First Union	FL	3	171	
Federal-Mogul	MI	11	389		First Union Bank of North Carolina	NC	9	563	
Federal-Mogul	OH	5	583		First Union National Bank	FL	18	193	
Federal-Mogul	VA	9	776		First Virginia Bank	VA	11	779	
Federated Department Stores	GA	6	213		First Wisconsin National Bank	WI	4	811	
Federated Department Stores	IN	6	278		Firstier Bank of Omaha	NE	2	449	
Federated Department Stores	NJ	5	473		Fischer & Porter	PA	8	641	
Federated Department Stores	NY	2	501		Fisher Controls	IA	3	291	
Federated Department Stores	OH	1	577		Fisher Controls	TX	10	720	
Federated Department Stores	OH	12	593		Fisher Scientific	CA	51	132	
Federated Department Stores	TN	9	700		Fisher-Price	KY	1	307	
Federated Investors	PA	14	650		Fisher-Price	NY	29	543	
Federated/Abraham & Straus	NJ	7	476		Fisher-Price	NY	30	544	
Fel-Pro	IL	9	249		Fisons	NY	28	541	
Ferdinand Arrigoni	NY	17	524		Fitzgerald La Vegas	NV	1	454	
Ferlin Service Industries	NY	14	520		FL Aerospace	OH	7	586	
Ferno-Washington	OH	6	585		Flagg C.N. Power	CT	5	157	
Fiber Industries	SC	6	679		Flambeau Paper	WI	2	808	
Fidelity & Casualty	NY	8	510		Flambeau Paper	WI	7	816	
Fidelity & Deposit	MD	3	342	*	Flea Market	CA	16	84	
Fidelity Bank	PA	2	632		Fleet Bank Massachusetts	MA	9	368	
Fiduciary Trust	NY	8	511		Fleet Mortgage	WI	5	812	
Field Container	IL	6	244		Fleet National Bank	RI	2	666	
Fieldale Farms	GA	9	217		Fleet Real Estate Funding	SC	6	679	
Fieldcrest	GA	3	208		Fleet/Norstar Services	NY	23	533	
Fieldcrest	GA	7	214	*	Fleet/Norstar Services	RI	2	666	
Fieldcrest Apartments	AL	2	23		Fleetguard	IA	5	294	
Fieldcrest Cannon	AL	3	24		Fleetwood Enterprises	CA	43	121	
Fieldcrest Cannon	NC	5	557	*	Fleetwood Enterprises	IN	4	275	
Fieldcrest Cannon	NC	8	561	*	Fleming Companies	AZ	2	40	
Filenet	CA	45	124		Fleming Companies	FL	21	197	
Fina Oil & Chemical	TX	3	710		Fleming Companies	PA	13	648	
Financial Protection Services	IL	7	246		Fleming Food East	NJ	7	476	
Finch Pruyn & Co	NY	22	532		Flexcon	MA	2	357	
Fingerhut	MN	3	404		Flxible	OH	12	593	
Fingerhut	MN	7	411		Flexstell Industries	IA	2	290	
Fire Casualty Insurance of Connecticut	CT	6	158		Flint River Textiles	GA	8	216	
Fireman's Fund Insurance	CA	6	68		Florence Nightingale Nursing Home	NY	14	520	
Fireman's Fund Insurance	NJ	11	482		Florida Cypress Gardens	FL	12	184	
Fireman's Fund Insurance	NJ	12	484		Florida EG&G	FL	15	188	
First Alabama Bancshares	AL	7	30	*	Florida Federal Savings	FL	10	181	

Business	State	District	Page	*	Business	State	District	Page	*
Great American Knitting Mills	NC	12	568		Guardian Life Insurance of America	WI	8	817	
Great Atlantic & Pacific Tea	NJ	5	473		Guardian Protective Service	MI	12	391	
Great Northern Paper/Bowater	ME	2	335		Guardian Service Industries	NY	8	511	
Great Southeastern Restaurants	GA	6	213		Guardsmark	IL	3	240	
Great Western Bank	CA	25	96		Guardsmark	TN	9	700	
Great Western Financial	CA	25	95		Guess	CA	33	107	
Greate Bay Hotel/Sands Hotel	NJ	2	468		Guilford Mills	NC	6	558	
Greater Peoria Riverboard	IL	18	263		Guilford of Maine	ME	2	335	
Greater Texas Finishing	TX	16	728		Gulf Island Fabrication	LA	3	322	
Grede Foundries	WI	2	808		Gulf South Detective	MS	3	419	
Green Acre Farms	MS	3	419		Gulf States Steel	AL	4	25	
Green Point Savings Bank	NY	5	506		Gulf States Utilities	LA	4	324	
Greenbrier Hotel/CSX	WV	3	802		Gulf States Utilities	TX	9	718	
Greenwich Air Services	FL	17	192		Gulfstream Aerospace	GA	1	205	
Greenwood Mills	GA	7	214		Gulfstream Aerospace Technology	OK	6	614	
Greenwood Mills	SC	3	673		Gull Airborne	NY	2	500	
Greenwood Racing	PA	8	641		Gunderson	OR	3	621	
Greenwood Trust	DE	AL	163		Guthrie Clinic	PA	10	644	
Grey Advertising	NY	14	519		Guy Carpenter & Co	NY	8	511	
Greyhound Lines	IA	4	293		Guy F. Atkinson	MN	1	402	
Grieco Bros	MA	5	362		Guy Schoenecker	MN	3	405	
Griffin Group	CA	29	102		Gyrongnam Bank	NY	5	505	
Grimmway Farms	CA	20	89						
Grinnel	PA	17	654						
Grinnel	WI	8	817		**H**				
Grinnel Mutual Reinsurance	IA	3	291						
Grinnell	GA	1	205		H. A. Simons	GA	4	209	
Grocers Supply	TX	18	731		H. B. Zachry	TX	25	741	
Grolier	CT	5	157		H. C. Copeland	NJ	12	484	
Group One Capital	MO	2	428		H. E. Butt Grocery	TX	20	734	
Group Technologies	FL	11	182		H. E. Butt Grocery	TX	28	744	
Grumann	FL	4	173		H. G. N.	MD	8	349	
Grumann	FL	15	188	*	H. H. Brown Shoe	PA	9	642	
Grumann	FL	16	189		H. H. Cutler	MI	3	378	
Grumann	GA	3	208		H. J. Heinz	CA	11	76	
Grumann	MI	6	382		H. J. Heinz	IA	1	288	
Grumman	NY	3	503		H. J. Heinz	PA	14	650	
Grumman	NY	1	499		H. L. F. Managers	TN	7	697	
Grunau Company	WI	5	812		H. N. Bull Information System	AZ	4	42	
Gruner & Jahr USA Printing & Publishing	MN	1	402		H. N. Bull Information Systems	MA	5	362	
GSF Safeway	IN	10	284		H. N. Bull Information Systems	VA	11	779	
GTE	CA	14	80		H. N. S. Management	CT	1	151	
GTE	CA	24	94		H. P. Hood	MA	8	367	
GTE	CA	39	116		H. R. H. Construction	NY	14	520	
GTE	CT	4	155		Hach	CO	4	143	
GTE	FL	9	180	*	Hachette Magazines	NY	8	511	
GTE	FL	11	182	*	Hadco	NH	1	460	
GTE	FL	12	184		Haemonetics	MA	10	370	
GTE	ID	1	230		Hagadone Hospitality Resort	ID	1	230	
GTE	IL	15	258		Haggar Apparel	TX	5	712	
GTE	IN	4	275		Halekulani Hotel	HI	1	224	
GTE	IN	6	278		Hall Perry/Farm Fresh Supermarkets	MD	3	342	
GTE	IN	9	283		Halliburtgon Logging Services	TX	12	722	
GTE	KY	6	315		Halliburton	OK	4	611	
GTE	MA	3	358		Halliburton	TX	7	716	
GTE	MA	6	363		Halliburton Geophyscial Service	TX	22	736	
GTE	MA	7	365		Halliburton NUS Environmental	MD	8	349	
GTE	MA	9	368	*	Halliburton Reservoir Service	TX	29	746	
GTE	MI	2	377		Hallmark Cards	CT	6	159	
GTE	NH	2	462		Hallmark Cards	KS	2	300	*
GTE	NH	1	460		Hallmark Cards	KS	3	301	
GTE	PA	5	636		Hallmark Cards	MO	5	432	
GTE	PA	10	644		Hallmark Cards	MO	6	434	
GTE	PA	19	657		Halmode Apparel	VA	6	772	
GTE	PA	21	660		Halstead Industries	AR	1	49	
GTE	RI	1	664		Hamakua Sugar	HI	2	226	
GTE	TX	1	706		Hamilton Bank	PA	16	653	
GTE	TX	5	712		Hamilton Beach/Procter-Silex	NC	3	554	*
GTE	TX	8	717		Hamilton Beach/Procter-Silex	NC	5	557	
GTE	TX	21	735		Hamilton Industries	WI	6	814	
GTE	TX	26	742		Hamilton-Ryker	TN	8	698	
GTE	VA	10	777		Hampton Industries	NC	1	551	
GTE	VA	11	779		Hanjin Shipping	CA	38	114	
GTE	WI	2	808		Hannaford Bros	ME	1	333	
Guarantee Electrical	MO	3	430		Hanover Direct	PA	19	657	
Guardian Industries	MI	5	381		Hanover Insurance	MA	3	358	
Guardian Life Insurance	NY	14	519		Hanson Industries	IA	2	290	
Guardian Life Insurance	PA	15	651		Harbert	AL	6	28	
Guardian Life Insurance	WA	5	790		Harbridge Merchant Services	CO	1	139	

Business	State	District	Page	*
Harcourt Brace	FL	8	178	
Harcourt General	MA	4	360	
Hardee's	NC	2	552	
Hardinge Brothers	NY	31	546	
Hardwick Clothes	TN	2	689	
Harley-Davidson	WI	5	812	
Harleysville Mutual Insurance	PA	13	648	
Harman-Motive	IN	7	280	
Harmarville Rehabilitation	PA	18	656	
Harmon Fruit	FL	16	189	
Harnischfeger	WI	4	811	
Harper Wyman	IL	17	261	
HarperCollins Publishers	NY	14	520	
HarperCollins/Scott Foresman	IL	10	251	
Harpers	CA	36	112	
Harrah's	NV	2	456	*
Harriet & Henderson Yarns	NC	1	551	
Harris	FL	15	188	*
Harris	NY	28	541	
Harris	OH	4	582	
Harris	PA	11	645	
Harris Farms	CA	20	89	
Harris Heidelberg	NH	1	460	
Harris Marcus Group	IL	4	241	
Harris Trust & Savings Bank	IL	7	245	
Harrison Stell Castings	IN	7	280	
Harrison's at Pier Five	MD	3	343	
Harry M. Stevens	NY	12	516	
Harsco	PA	19	657	
Harsco/BMY Combat Systems	OH	7	586	
Hart & Cooley	MI	2	377	
Hart Graphics	TX	10	720	
Hart Schaffner & Marx	IL	7	246	
Hart Schaffner & Marx	MO	8	437	
Hartford Accident Indemnity	CT	1	150	
Hartford Life Insurance	CT	6	158	
Hartford National	CT	1	150	
Hartmarx	IL	7	246	
Hartz Group	NJ	13	485	
Harvard Industries	MI	7	384	
Harvard Industries	NJ	7	476	
Harvard Industries	TN	1	688	
Harvard Student Agencies	MA	8	367	
Harvey's Wagon	NV	2	456	
Hasbro	RI	1	664	
Haskell of Pittsburgh	PA	18	656	
Hatfield Quality Meats	PA	13	648	
Hauser Communications	NY	14	519	
Hawaiian Building Maintenance	HI	1	224	
Hawaiian Electric Industries	HI	1	224	
Hawkins Associates	TX	20	733	
Haworth	MI	2	376	
Hay & Forage Industries	KS	4	303	
Haynes International	IN	5	277	
Hayward Industries	NJ	10	481	
Hazeltine	NY	2	500	
Hazeltine	NY	5	506	
Hazleton	VA	10	777	
Hazleton Wisconsin	WI	2	808	
HBE	MO	1	427	
HBO & Co	GA	6	213	
Health Insurance Plan of Greater New York	NY	3	503	
Health-Tex	AL	3	24	
Health-Tex	AL	4	25	
Health-Tex	GA	11	220	
Health-Tex	VA	5	770	
Healthcare International	TX	10	720	
Healthcare Services	MO	7	436	
Heatcraft	IL	15	258	
Heatcraft	MS	2	418	
Heath Co. Delaware	MI	6	382	
Heatherton Staff Leasing	IL	7	245	
Heckler Manufacturing & Investment Group	SC	4	675	
Hedstrom	PA	9	642	
Heintz	PA	3	633	
Helene Curtis Industries	IL	7	247	
Heller Financial	IL	7	246	
Helmsley Enterprises	NY	14	518	
Helmsley Palace	NY	14	519	
Henkel	MI	12	391	
Henkel/Emery Group	OH	1	577	
Henredon Furniture Industries	NC	5	557	
Henredon Furniture Industries	NC	10	564	
Henry House	MI	2	377	
Henry I. Siegel	TN	8	698	*
Henry Schein	NY	5	506	
Henry Vogt Machine	KY	3	310	
Hercules	DE	AL	163	
Hercules	GA	1	205	
Hercules	GA	10	219	
Hercules	KS	3	301	
Hercules	NJ	6	475	
Hercules	UT	3	755	
Hercules Aerospace	WV	1	799	*
Hercules Defense Electronic Systems	FL	10	181	
Hercules/Simmons Precision Products	VT	AL	759	
Heritage Care Group	TX	1	706	
Heritage Mutual Insurance	WI	9	819	
Heritage Publishing	AR	2	51	
Herman Miller	MI	2	376	
Herman's Sporting Goods	NJ	13	485	
Hershey Foods	CA	18	86	
Hershey Foods	PA	6	637	
Hershey Foods	PA	17	654	
Hertz	NJ	5	473	
Hertz	OK	5	612	
Hertz	UT	2	753	
Hertzberg-New Method	IL	18	263	
Hess's Department Store	PA	15	651	
Hewitt Associates	IL	10	251	
Hewlett-Packard	CA	4	65	
Hewlett-Packard	CA	6	67	*
Hewlett-Packard	CA	14	80	*
Hewlett-Packard	CA	15	82	
Hewlett-Packard	CA	16	84	
Hewlett-Packard	CA	51	132	
Hewlett-Packard	CO	4	143	
Hewlett-Packard	CO	5	144	
Hewlett-Packard	ID	1	230	
Hewlett-Packard	MA	5	361	
Hewlett-Packard	MA	7	365	
Hewlett-Packard	OR	5	624	
Hewlett-Packard	PA	16	653	
Hewlett-Packard	WA	2	786	
Hewlett-Packard	WA	3	787	
Hewlett-Packard	WA	5	790	
Hi-Shear	CA	36	112	
Hibbing Taconite	MN	8	412	
Hibernia	LA	2	320	
Hickey-Freeman	NY	28	541	
Higbee	OH	11	591	
Highland Superstores	MI	13	393	
Hilb Rogal & Hamilton	VA	7	773	
Hill-Rom	IN	9	283	
Hillenbrand Industries	IN	9	282	
Hills Capitol Security	MD	4	344	
Hills Stores	MA	9	369	
Hilltop Steak House	MA	6	363	
Hilti	OK	1	607	
Hilton Hawaiian Village Hotel	HI	1	224	
Hilton Hotels	CA	8	72	
Hilton Hotels	CA	33	108	
Hilton Hotels	CA	35	110	
Hilton Hotels	CA	46	125	
Hilton Hotels	DC	AL	840	*
Hilton Hotels	FL	8	178	
Hilton Hotels	GA	5	212	
Hilton Hotels	HI	1	224	*
Hilton Hotels	IL	7	246	*
Hilton Hotels	LA	2	321	
Hilton Hotels	NV	1	454	*
Hilton Hotels	NV	2	456	*
Hilton Hotels	NY	8	511	*
Hilton Hotels	NY	14	519	*
Himont USA	LA	7	328	
Hines Nurseries	CA	47	127	
Hitchiner Manufacturing	NH	2	462	
HM Holdings	NY	17	524	

Business	State	District	Page	*	Business	State	District	Page	*
HM Holdings	WA	5	790		Howe-Baker Engineeres	TX	4	711	
Hobart	OH	8	587		Howmet	IN	3	274	
Hobart Bros	OH	8	587		Howmet	MI	2	376	
Hoechst Celanese	NC	9	563		Howmet	NJ	11	482	
Hoechst Celanese	NC	12	567		Howmet	VA	3	766	
Hoechst Celanese	NJ	12	484		Howmet Casting	TX	13	724	
Hoechst Celanese	RI	2	666		HRB Systems	PA	5	636	
Hoechst Celanese	SC	4	675	*	Hubbard Construction	FL	8	178	
Hoechst Celanese	SC	5	677		Hubbell	CT	4	155	
Hoechst Celanese	TX	22	737		Hubbell	NC	12	567	
Hoechst Celanese	TX	27	743		Hudson Foods	MO	7	436	*
Hoechst Celanese	VA	9	776		Hudson Foods	AL	4	25	
Hoffmann-La Roche	NJ	5	473		Hudson Foods	AR	4	54	
Hoffmann-La Roche	NJ	8	477		Hudson-Shatz Printing	NY	8	510	
Holiday Festival of Trees	NY	25	537		Huffy	OH	8	587	
Holiday Inns	NV	1	454		Hughes Aircraft	AZ	5	44	
Holland American Line	WA	7	793		Hughes Aircraft	CA	36	111	*
Holliston Mills	TN	1	688		Hughes Aircraft	CA	39	116	
Holly Farms	TX	2	707		Hughes Aircraft	CA	45	124	
Holm Industries	IN	9	283		Hughes Aircraft	CA	48	128	
Holmes & Narver	NV	2	456		Hughes Aircraft	CA	51	132	
Holophane	MI	16	397		Hughes Aircraft	CO	6	146	
Holston Defense	TN	1	688		Hughes Aircraft	MS	3	419	
Holt Cargo Systems	NJ	1	467		Hughes Danbury Optical Systems	CT	5	157	
Home Box Office	NY	14	519		Hughes Electronics	CA	22	92	
Home Curtain	NC	10	564		Hughes Network Systems	MD	8	349	
Home Fashions	CA	45	124		Hughes STX	MD	4	344	
Home Federal	CA	49	130		Hughes/Georgia	GA	7	214	
Home Federal Bank	CA	51	132		Huish Detergents	UT	3	755	
Home Health Management	NY	14	519		Human Health Services	MD	8	349	
Home Insurance	NY	8	510		Hunt-Wesson	CA	3	64	
Home Life Insurance	NJ	6	475		Hunt-Wesson	CA	13	79	
Home Savings of America	CA	31	105		Hunt-Wesson	CA	18	86	
Home Savings of America/Bowery Bank	NY	15	521		Hunt-Wesson	CA	39	116	
Home Services Systems	NY	7	508		Hunt-Wesson	OH	9	589	
Home Shopping Network	FL	10	181		Huntington National Bank	OH	12	593	
Home Shopping Network	VA	6	771		Hurd Lock & Manufacturing	TN	1	688	
Home Supply	KY	3	311		Hussman	MO	2	428	
Home-Crest	IN	3	274		Hutchinson Technology	MN	2	402	
Homecare PRN	MA	4	360		Hutchinson Technology	SD	AL	683	
Homer Laughlin China	WV	1	799		Hy-Vee Food Stores	IA	3	291	
Homestake Mining	SD	AL	683		Hyatt Hotels	AZ	4	42	
Hon Industries	IA	1	288		Hyatt Hotels	CA	5	66	
Honda of America	OH	4	582		Hyatt Hotels	CA	8	72	*
Honda of America	OH	7	586		Hyatt Hotels	CA	12	78	
Honda of America	OH	8	587		Hyatt Hotels	CA	17	85	
Honda/American Honda Motor	CA	36	111		Hyatt Hotels	DC	AL	840	*
Honeywell	AZ	4	42	*	Hyatt Hotels	FL	8	178	
Honeywell	FL	10	181		Hyatt Hotels	FL	15	188	
Honeywell	IL	10	251		Hyatt Hotels	GA	5	211	
Honeywell	MN	5	408		Hyatt Hotels	HI	1	224	*
Honeywell	MN	6	410	*	Hyatt Hotels	HI	2	226	*
Honeywell	NM	1	490		Hyatt Hotels	IL	6	244	
Hook-Superix	IN	10	284		Hyatt Hotels	IL	7	246	
Hooker Furniture	VA	5	770		Hyatt Hotels	LA	2	321	
Hoover	OH	16	598		Hyatt Hotels	NV	2	456	
Horace Mann Educators	IL	20	266		Hyatt Hotels	MI	16	397	
Horizon Industries	GA	9	217		Hyatt Hotels	MO	5	433	
Hormel & Co	MN	1	402		Hyatt Hotels	NY	14	519	
Hormel & Co	NE	1	447		Hyatt Hotels	TX	5	712	
Horsehead Industries	PA	4	635		Hyatt Hotels	TX	20	734	
Horseshoe Club Operating	NV	1	454		Hyatt Hotels	TX	30	748	*
Horticultural Farms	GA	2	207		Hyatt Hotels	VA	11	779	
Horton Industries	GA	11	220		Hybritech	CA	49	130	
Hotelerama Associates	FL	22	198		Hydraulics	IL	16	259	
Houghton Mifflin	MA	9	369		Hyster	IL	15	258	
House of Laird	KY	6	315		Hytrol Conveyor Co	AR	1	49	
House of Lloyd	MO	5	433						
House of Raeford Farms	NC	8	561						
House of Ronnie Delaware	GA	8	216						
Household Finance	IL	10	251						
Household International	IL	6	23		I				
Household International	IL	10	251						
Household International	CA	17	85		I. H. Services	SC	4	675	
Houston Lighting & Power	TX	7	716		IASD Health Services	IA	4	293	
Houston Lighting & Power	TX	18	731		IBJ Schroder Bank & Trust	NY	8	511	
Houston Lighting & Power	TX	22	737		IBM	AZ	5	44	
Houston Lighting & Power	TX	25	741		IBM	CA	33	107	
Howard Industries	MS	3	419		IBM	CA	34	109	
					IBM	CA	45	124	
					IBM	CA	15	82	

Business	State	District	Page	*	Business	State	District	Page	*
IBM	CO	2	140		Imperial Holly/Imperial Sugar	TX	22	737	
IBM	CT	1	151		Imperial Palace	NV	1	454	
IBM	CT	3	154		Imperial Reading	TN	4	692	
IBM	CT	4	155	*	INA Bearing	SC	5	677	
IBM	CT	6	158		Inland Steel	IN	1	270	
IBM	FL	11	182	*	INB National Bank	IN	10	284	
IBM	FL	11	183	*	Inchon Iron & Steel	CA	37	113	
IBM	GA	5	211		Inco Alloys International	WV	3	802	
IBM	IL	7	245		Indal	GA	4	210	
IBM	MA	7	365		Independence Mining	NV	2	456	
IBM	MA	8	367		Independent Group Home Living	NY	1	499	
IBM	MD	8	349		Independent Insurance Group	FL	3	171	
IBM	MI	11	389		Independent Life	FL	4	173	
IBM	MO	2	429		Independent Shopping Service	OH	12	593	
IBM	MO	5	433		Indiana Bell Telephone	IN	10	284	
IBM	NC	2	552		Indiana Glass	OK	2	609	
IBM	NC	4	555	*	Indiana Insurance	IN	10	284	
IBM	NC	9	563		Indiana Michigan Powr	MI	6	382	
IBM	NJ	5	473		Indiana Packers	IN	5	277	
IBM	NJ	6	475		Indiana Precision Technology	IN	6	278	
IBM	NJ	12	484		Indianapolis Power & Light	IN	10	284	
IBM	NY	8	510		Indopco	IN	10	284	
IBM	NY	14	518		Indopco/National Starch	NJ	7	476	
IBM	NY	18	525	*	Industrial Contractors	IN	8	281	
IBM	NY	19	527	*	Industrial Indemnity	CA	8	72	
IBM	NY	20	528		Industrial Security Service	OH	10	590	
IBM	NY	26	538	*	Industrial Security Services	TX	7	716	
IBM	PA	2	632		Information Builders	NY	8	511	
IBM	PA	17	654		Information Handling	CO	5	144	
IBM	PA	19	657		Information Resources	IL	7	246	
IBM	TX	7	716		Ingalls Shipbuilding	MS	5	422	
IBM	TX	9	718		Ingersoll Milling Machine	IL	16	259	
IBM	TX	10	720		Ingersoll-Rand	NH	2	462	
IBM	TX	26	742		Ingersoll-Rand	NJ	5	473	
IBM	VA	10	777		Ingersoll-Rand	PA	10	644	
IBM	VT	AL	759		Ingersoll-Rand	TN	4	692	
IBP	IA	4	293	*	Ingersoll-Rand	VA	6	772	
IBP	IL	17	261		Ingram Barge	TN	5	694	
IBP	NE	1	447		Ingram Industries	TN	6	695	
IBP	NE	3	450		Ingram Micro	CA	46	125	
IBP	KS	1	298	*	Ingres	CA	9	74	
IBP	TX	13	724		Inhilco/Windows on the World	NY	8	511	
IBP	WA	4	789		Initi	NY	14	518	
ICF Kaiser Engineers	DC	AL	840		Initial holdings	OH	17	600	
ICI Americas	DE	AL	163		Injection Footwear	FL	17	192	
ICI Americas	IN	9	283		Inland Container	GA	7	214	
ICI Americas	VA	3	767		Inland Property Management Group	IL	6	244	
ICI Americas	VA	4	768		Inland Steel	IL	7	247	
ICI Composites	MN	1	402		Inman Holding	SC	4	675	
ICL	CA	15	82		Inn America	NJ	6	475	
ICM Industries	PA	6	637		Insilco/Sinclair Paint	CA	33	107	
ICS-Southern Services	GA	5	211		Instant Help	WI	5	813	
IDA Courier	CA	5	66		Instrumentation Lab	MA	7	365	
Idaho Power	ID	2	231		Insurance Company of North America	GA	8	216	
Idea Courier	AZ	1	38		Insurance Services Office	NY	8	511	
Idle Wild Foods	KS	1	298		Insurance Services Office	NY	20	529	
IDS Financial	MN	5	408		Intalco Aluminum	WA	2	786	
IDS Financial	MN	2	402		Integon	NC	12	568	
IEC Electronics	NY	27	540		Integrated Device Technology	CA	15	82	
IFR Systems	KS	4	303		Integrated Device Technology	CA	17	85	
Igloo Products	TX	7	716	*	Intel	AZ	1	38	
IIT Research	MD	1	340		Intel	CA	15	82	
IKI American	NJ	3	470		Intel	NM	3	493	
ILC Data Device	NY	2	501		Intel	OR	1	618	
ILC Industries	DE	AL	163		Inter Innovation Le Febure	IA	1	288	
ILCO Unican	NC	2	553		Inter-City Products	TN	6	695	
Illinois Bell	IL	7	245		Inter-Regional Financial Group	MN	5	408	
Illinois Bell	IL	20	266		Interbake Foods	VA	7	773	
Illinois Central Railroad	IL	7	247		Intercom	TX	3	710	
Illinois Central Railroad	IL	20	266		Intercraft Industries	NC	10	564	
Illinois Power	IL	15	258		Intercraft Industries	TX	14	725	
Illinois Power	IL	19	264		Interface/Heuga USA	GA	7	214	
Illuminators	CA	34	109		Intergraph	AL	5	27	
IMC Fertilizer	FL	12	184	*	Intermatic	IL	16	259	
IMC Fertilizer	NM	2	492		Intermec	WA	2	786	
IMCO Realty Services	CA	6	68		Intermedics	TX	22	736	
IMED	CA	51	132		Intermedics Pacemakers	TX	14	725	
IMO Industries	NJ	4	471		Intermet Foundries	VA	6	771	
Imperial Bondware	IL	19	264		Intermetro Industries	PA	11	645	

Business	State	District	Page	*	Business	State	District	Page	*
Kidde Industries	PA	9	642		Kraft General Foods	IL	10	251	
Kidder Peabody	NY	8	510		Kraft General Foods	IL	15	258	
Kiefer Services	PA	2	632		Kraft General Foods	IN	4	275	
Kig Radio	KS	3	301		Kraft General Foods	MI	7	383	
Kimball Electronics	IN	9	283		Kraft General Foods	MN	2	402	
Kimberly Quality Care	NY	30	544		Kraft General Foods	MO	7	436	
Kimberly-Clark	AR	2	51		Kraft General Foods	NJ	13	485	
Kimberly-Clark	CA	39	116		Kraft General Foods	NY	20	529	
Kimberly-Clark	GA	6	213		Kraft General Foods	PA	15	651	
Kimberly-Clark	NC	11	566		Kraft General Foods	TX	3	710	
Kimberly-Clark	NJ	6	475		Kraft General Foods	TX	29	746	
Kimberly-Clark	SC	3	673		Kroger	OH	1	577	
Kimberly-Clark	TN	9	700		Kroger	OH	12	593	*
Kimberly-Clark	TX	1	706		Kroger	TX	3	710	
Kimberly-Clark	UT	1	752		Krueger International	WI	8	817	
Kimberly-Clark	WI	6	814		Kwik Kafe	NE	2	449	
Kimco	IL	4	241		Kwikset	CA	46	125	
Kincaid Furniture	NC	10	564		Kyo-Ya Hotel	HI	1	224	
King & Prince Seafood	GA	1	205		Kyocera International	CA	49	130	
King Radio	KS	3	302		Kysor Industrial	GA	4	210	
Kings Harbor Car Center	NY	17	524						
Kingsbacher-Murphy	CA	36	112						
Kingsbury	NH	2	462		**L**				
Kingston Shirt	NC	1	551						
Kingstron-Warren	NH	1	460		L. A. Darling	AR	1	49	*
Kingstron-Warren	VA	9	776		L. G. Balfour	MA	3	358	
Kinney Service	PA	17	654		L. L. Bean	ME	1	333	
Kinney Shoe	NY	8	511		L. M. Berry & Co	OH	3	580	
Kirk-Mayer	NM	1	490		L. M. Nursing	RI	1	664	
Kirke Van Orsdel	IA	4	293		L. Perrigo	MI	2	376	
Kirkhill Rubber	CA	39	116		L. S. Starrett	MA	1	355	
Kirkwood Industries	OH	10	590		La Costa Resort & Spa	CA	51	132	
KLA Instruments	CA	16	83		La Crosse Footwear	WI	3	809	
Klaussner	NC	6	558		La Gear California	CA	32	106	
Klear Knit	SC	6	679		La Mar Manufacturing	GA	7	214	
Klein Tools	IL	9	249		La Quinta Hotel	CA	44	122	
Kleinerts of Alabama	AL	2	23		La Quinta Motor Inns	TX	20	734	
Kling-Lindquist	PA	2	632		La Salle National	IL	7	245	
Klockner-Pentaplast of America	VA	7	773		La Shellda Maintenance	NY	4	⸤04	
Kmart	GA	3	208		La-Z-Boy Chair	MO	7	436	
Kmart	MI	12	391		La-Z-Boy Chair	MS	3	419	
Kmart	OH	17	600		La-Z-Boy Chair	TN	4	692	
Kmart	PA	8	641		La-Z-Boy Chair	UT	1	752	
Knape & Vogt Manufacturing	MI	3	378		Lab Safety Supply	WI	1	807	
Knauf Fiberglass	IN	2	272		Labor Resources	IN	1	271	
Knoll North America	MI	3	378		Lachman Resource Group	CA	5	66	
Knoll North America	PA	15	651		Laclede Steel	IL	12	254	
Knoll North American	MI	2	377		Ladd Furniture	NC	5	557	
Knott's Berry Farm	CA	39	116		Ladish/Cudahy Forgings	WI	4	811	
Knowledgeware	GA	5	211		Laidlaw Transit	IL	5	242	
Koch Engineering	OK	1	607		Lake Region Manufacturing	MN	2	402	
Koch Industries	KS	4	303		Lam Research	CA	13	79	
Koch Refining	MN	4	406		Lamb-Weston	ID	2	231	
Koch Refining	TX	27	743		Lamb-Weston	OR	2	620	*
Koh-I-Noor Rapidograph	NJ	12	484		Lamb-Weston	WA	4	789	
Kohler	SC	4	675		Lanai Ressort Partners	HI	2	226	
Kohler	TX	17	728		Lance	NC	12	567	
Kohler	WI	9	818		Lancer	TX	21	735	
Kohls Department Stores	WI	9	818		Land O'Lakes	MN	4	406	
Kolbe & Kolbe Millwork	WI	7	815		Land O'Lakes	WI	7	816	
Kollmorgen/Inland Motor	VA	9	776		Land O'Frost	AR	2	51	
Kolmar Laboratories	NY	20	528		Landis & Gyr Metering	IN	7	280	
Komag	CA	16	84		Landis & Gyr Powers	IL	10	251	
Komatsu Dresser	IL	18	263		Landmark Communications	VA	3	766	
Koppers	IN	1	271		Landmark Land	SC	1	671	
Korn Industries	SC	6	678		Landmark Land	CA	44	122	
KPMG Peat Marwick	CA	8	72		Lands' End	WI	2	808	
KPMG Peat Marwick	CA	33	108		Lane	NC	10	564	
KPMG Peat Marwick	DC	AL	840		Lane	VA	5	769	*
KPMG Peat Marwick	NJ	5	473		Lane Marsetta Temporary Service	PA	14	650	
KPMG Peat Marwick	NY	14	518		Langdale	GA	2	207	
KPMG Peat Marwick	TX	30	748		Lani Mauna Bay Hotel	HI	2	226	
Kraco Enterprises	CA	37	113	*	Las Vegas Sands	NV	1	454	
Krafmaid Cabinetry	OH	13	595		Latrobe Steel	PA	12	647	
Kraft General Foods	CA	18	86		Laurel Run Mining	WV	1	799	
Kraft General Foods	DE	AL	163		Law International	GA	5	211	
Kraft General Foods	GA	4	210		Leaf	IL	7	246	
Kraft General Foods	IL	1	237		Leaf	TN	9	700	
Kraft General Foods	IL	9	249		Leake & Watts Service	NY	17	524	

Business	State	District	Page	*
Lear Astronics	CA	29	102	
Lear Seating	MI	14	394	
Lear Seating	TN	4	692	
Learjet	KS	4	303	
Leaseway Customized Transportation	NJ	9	479	
Lechmere	MA	3	358	
Lechmere	MA	7	365	
Leco	MI	6	382	
Lectron Products	MI	9	386	
Lee Apparel	AL	4	25	
Lee Apparel	CT	2	152	
Lee Apparel	KS	3	302	
Lee Apparel	MO	4	431	
Lee Apparel	TN	4	692	
Lee Brass	AL	3	24	
Lee-Rowan	MO	8	437	
Leeds & Northrup	PA	13	648	
Leeson Electric	WI	9	819	
Leggett & Platt	MO	7	436	
Lego Systems	CT	6	159	
Lehigh	FL	14	187	
Lehman Commercial Paper	NY	8	511	
Lehrer McGovern Bovis	NY	14	520	
Leica	NY	30	544	
Leisure World/Professional Management	CA	47	127	
Lennox Industries	OH	15	597	
Lennox Industries	TX	12	722	
Lenox China	NJ	2	468	
Leo Burnett	IL	7	245	
Levi Strauss	AR	2	51	
Levi Strauss	CA	8	71	
Levi Strauss	GA	2	207	
Levi Strauss	NM	1	490	
Levi Strauss	NM	2	492	
Levi Strauss	TN	1	688	
Levi Strauss	TN	2	689	*
Levi Strauss	TX	15	727	
Levi Strauss	TX	16	728	
Levi Strauss	TX	20	734	
Levi Strauss	TX	27	743	*
Leviton Manufacturing	NC	5	557	
Leviton Manufacturing	NY	14	519	
Leviton Manufacturing	RI	2	666	
Lexmark	KY	6	315	
LIA Group	NY	21	530	
Libbey Glass	LA	4	324	
Libbey-Owens-Ford	IN	2	272	
Libbey-Owens-Ford	MI	7	384	
Libbey-Owens-Ford	NC	8	561	
Libbey-Owens-Ford	TX	4	711	
Liberty Fabrics	VA	7	773	
Liberty House	HI	1	224	
Liberty Lines Transit	NY	18	525	
Liberty Mutual Insurance	GA	9	218	
Liberty Mutual Insurance	MA	8	366	
Liberty Mutual Insurance	NH	1	460	
Liberty Mutual Insurance	NY	4	504	
Liberty Mutual Insurance	PA	4	635	
Liberty National Bank & Trust	KY	3	311	
Liberty Northwest Insurance	OR	3	621	
Librascope	CA	27	99	
Liebert	OH	12	593	
Life Insurance Co of Georgia	GA	5	211	
Life Insurance Co of Virginia	VA	7	773	
Life Insurance of North America	PA	2	632	
Life of Maryland	MD	7	348	
Lifescan	CA	16	84	
Liggett Group/Liggett & Myers	NC	12	568	
Lillian Vernon	VA	2	765	
Limited	OH	12	593	
Lincoln Electric	OH	11	591	
Lincoln National Life Insuarnce	CO	5	144	
Lincoln National Life Insurance	IN	4	275	
Lincoln Telecommunications	NE	1	447	
Lincolnwood Associates	IL	9	249	
Lindsey & Lindsey	MO	6	434	
Lineal Group/Samsonite Furniture	TN	6	696	
Link-Belt Construction Equipment	KY	6	315	
Lintas Campbell-Ewald	MI	12	391	
Linvatec	FL	10	181	
Lipton/Conopco	NJ	12	484	
LIT America	IL	7	247	
Little Company	IL	1	237	
Little Tikes	OH	14	596	
Littlefuse	IL	6	23	
Litton	AZ	1	38	
Litton	CA	14	81	
Litton	CA	16	84	
Litton	CA	23	93	
Litton	CA	24	94	
Litton	CA	26	98	
Litton	CT	6	159	
Litton	IL	4	241	
Litton	MA	7	365	
Litton	MD	5	345	
Litton	MO	7	436	
Litton	UT	1	752	
Litton	VA	9	776	
Litwin Engineers	TX	29	746	
Liz Claiborne	NJ	13	485	
Lockheed	CA	13	79	
Lockheed	CA	14	81	
Lockheed	CA	25	96	
Lockheed	CA	41	119	
Lockheed	FL	15	188	
Lockheed	GA	1	205	
Lockheed	GA	7	214	
Lockheed	NM	2	492	
Lockheed	SC	4	675	
Lockheed	TX	9	718	
Lockheed	TX	10	720	
Lockheed	TX	12	722	
Lockheed	TX	17	728	
Lockheed	TX	19	732	
Lockheed Sanders	NH	2	462	*
Lockwood Greene Engineers	SC	4	675	
Loews Anatole Hotel/Dallar Market Center	TX	30	747	
Loftin Assoc	NV	2	456	
Logan	KY	1	308	
Logan Graphic Products	IL	8	248	
Lomas Financial	TX	24	739	
Londontown/London Fog	MD	6	347	
Lone Start Steel	TX	1	706	
Long Island Home	NY	2	500	
Long Island Savings Bank	NY	5	506	
Long Life Home Care	NY	10	513	
Longview Fibre	WA	3	787	
Loral Aerospace	CA	13	79	
Loral Aerospace	CA	16	83	
Loral Aerospace	CO	5	144	
Loral Aerospace	MD	3	343	
Loral Aerospace	TX	9	718	
Loral Defense Systems	OH	14	596	
Loral Electro-Optical Systems	CA	28	101	
Loral Electronic Systems	NY	18	525	
Loral Fairchild	FL	13	185	
Loral Fairchild	NY	3	503	
Loral Fairchild	PA	10	644	
Loral Infrared Imaging Systems	MA	7	365	
Lord	PA	21	660	
Loretto Rest Nursing Home	NY	25	537	
Lorillard	NC	12	567	
Lorillard	NY	14	518	
Los Angeles Memorial Coliseum	CA	32	106	
Lotus Development	MA	8	367	
Louisana Land Exploration	LA	2	321	
Louisiana Power & Light	LA	3	322	
Louisiana-Pacific	NC	1	551	
Louisiana-Pacific	TX	2	707	
Louisiana-Pacific	CA	1	61	
Louisville Gas & Electric	KY	2	309	
Loving Hands Healthcare	NJ	5	473	
Lowell Shoe	NH	2	462	
Lowes Companies	NC	5	557	
Lozier	NE	2	449	
LPL Technologies	IL	7	246	
LSI Logic	CA	15	82	
LSI Logic	CA	16	83	

Business	State	District	Page	*	Business	State	District	Page	*
LTC Eddy	NY	21	530		Macy's	NJ	11	482	*
LTV	TX	30	747		Macy's	NJ	12	484	
LTV	AR	4	54		Macy's	NY	3	503	
LTV	IL	18	263		Macy's	NY	7	508	
LTV	IN	1	270		Macy's	NY	19	527	
LTV	MN	8	412		Macy's	PA	7	639	
LTV	NY	30	544		Macy's	TX	22	737	
LTV	OH	10	590		Mademoiselle Knitwear	NY	12	516	
LTV	PA	4	635		Madison Building Services	NY	7	508	
LTV	PA	14	650		Madison Detective Bureau	NY	8	511	
LTV	TX	6	713		Madison Gas & Electric	WI	2	808	
LTV	TX	24	739		Madison Square Garden Center	NY	8	511	
LTX	MA	9	369		Magee Industrial Enterprises	PA	11	645	
Lubrizol	OH	19	603		Magma Copper	AZ	6	46	*
Lubrizol	TX	25	741		Magnavox	CA	36	111	
Lucas Aerospace Power Equipment	OH	13	595		Magnavox	IN	4	275	
Lucas Industries	CA	34	109		Magnetek	IN	4	275	
Lucky Star Industries	MS	1	416		Magnetek	MS	4	421	
Lucky Stores	CA	39	116		Magnetek	TN	7	697	
Lucky Stores	CA	47	127		Magnetek	TN	4	692	
Lucky Stores	CA	3	64		Mahle	TN	4	692	
Lucky Stores	CA	13	79		MAI Systems	CA	47	127	
Lufkin Industries	TX	2	707		Maintenance	TX	30	747	
Lufthansa	NY	4	504		Maison Blanche	LA	4	324	
Lukens Steel	MO	3	430		Malden Mills Industries	MA	5	361	
Lukens Steel	PA	16	653		Mallinckrodt	MO	1	427	
Lumbermens Mutual Casualty	IL	8	248		Mallinckrodt	MO	1	427	
Lummus Industries	GA	2	207		Mallinckrodt Medial Supplies	NY	22	532	
Lykes Bros	FL	12	184		Malone & Hyde	MS	1	416	
Lynchburg Foundry	VA	6	771		Mandel-Kahn Industries	TX	29	746	
Lyon Metal Products	IL	14	256		Manhatten Cable Television	NY	14	519	
Lyondell Petrochemical	TX	25	741		Manitowoc	WI	6	814	
Lyondell Petrochemical	TX	29	746		Mannington Carpets	GA	9	217	
					Mannington Mills	NJ	2	468	
					Manor Care	MD	4	344	

M

Business	State	District	Page	*	Business	State	District	Page	*
M&B Mini Blind	CA	33	108		Mansfield Plumbing Products	OH	16	599	
M&I Marshall & Ilsley Bank	WI	4	811		Mantech Environmental Technology	NC	12	568	
M&I Marshall & Ilsley Bank	WI	5	812		Manufacturers & Traders Trust	NY	27	540	
M&M Trucking	AR	3	53		Manufacturers Hanover	NY	8	510	
M. Fortunoff of Westbury	NY	4	504		Manville Sales	CO	1	138	
M. G. Waldbaum	NE	1	447		Manville Sales	OH	5	583	
M. J. G. Nursing Home	NY	8	511		Manville Sales	OH	9	589	
M. J. Soffee	NC	7	560		Mapco	OK	1	607	
M. P. B.	NH	2	462	*	Maple Press	NY	26	538	
M. T. S./Tower Records	CA	3	64		Marathon Cheese	WI	7	816	
M. W. Kellogg	TX	18	730		Marathon Electric Manufacturing	WI	7	815	
M. W. Manufacturers	VA	5	770		Marathon Manufacturing	TX	1	706	
M. Wile & Co	NY	29	543		Marathon Oil	IL	19	264	
M. Wile & Co	NY	30	544		Marathon Oil	TX	7	716	
M/A-Com	MA	6	363		Marcal Paper Mills	NJ	9	479	
Maas	FL	11	182		Marcor Resort Properties	NV	1	454	
MacClean Service	NY	9	512		Mare-Bear	NV	1	454	
Mack Printing	PA	15	652		Maremont Exhaust Productss	TN	2	689	
Mack Truck	MD	6	347		Margaretten & Co	NJ	13	485	
Mack Truck	PA	15	651	*	Maria-Joseph Center	OH	3	580	
Macklanburg-Duncan	OK	6	614		Marianjoy	IL	6	244	
Macmillan	CT	4	155		Marine Midland Banks	NY	25	537	
Macmillan	NJ	3	470		Marine Midland Banks	NY	30	544	
Macmillan	NY	14	519		Marine Personnel Provisioning	NJ	9	479	
MacMillan Bloedel	AL	7	30		Mariner Group	FL	14	187	
Macmillan/Maxwell	NJ	9	479		Marion Fabrics	NC	11	566	
Macmillan/McGraw Hill	CA	17	85		Marion Merrell Dow	MO	5	433	
Macon Kraft	GA	2	207		Marion Merrell Dow	MO	6	434	
Macromedia	NJ	9	479		Marion Merrell Dow	OH	2	579	
Macy's	CA	5	66		Maritz	MO	2	428	
Macy's	CA	8	72		Mark III Industries	FL	5	174	
Macy's	CA	14	81		Mark Travel	WI	5	813	
Macy's	CA	15	82		Markem	NH	2	462	
Macy's	FL	20	196		Marko Zaninovich/Sunview Marketing	CA	20	89	
Macy's	GA	4	210		Marley	IN	3	274	
Macy's	GA	5	211	*	Marley Mouldings	VA	9	776	
Macy's	GA	11	220		Marquette Electronics	WI	5	812	
Macy's	MD	2	341		Marquette National Life Insurance	IL	5	242	
Macy's	NJ	1	467		Marriott	AL	1	21	
Macy's	NJ	5	473		Marriott	AZ	4	42	
Macy's	NJ	6	474		Marriott	CA	8	71	*
Macy's	NJ	8	477		Marriott	CA	24	94	
					Marriott	CA	29	102	
					Marriott	CA	35	110	

Business	State	District	Page	*	Business	State	District	Page	*
McKesson	AR	3	52		Metropolitan Life Insurance	FL	11	182	
McKesson	CA	8	72		Metropolitan Life Insurance	IL	13	255	
McKinney Pant Manufacturing	TX	27	743		Metropolitan Life Insurance	NY	14	518	
McLane	TX	11	721		Metropolitan Life Insurance	NY	23	533	
MCN	MI	15	395		Metropolitan Life Insurance	NY	26	538	
McNeil PPC	PA	13	648		Metropolitan Life Insurance	PA	12	647	
McRaes	MS	4	421		Metropolitan Life Insurance	PA	14	650	
McWane/Kennedy Valves	NY	31	546		Metropolitan General Insurance	RI	2	665	
Mead	MO	6	434		Metrovision of Indiana	IN	1	271	
Mead	OH	3	580		MGM Desert	NV	1	454	
Mead	TN	1	688		MGM-Pathe Communications	CA	32	106	
Mead	OH	6	584		Michael Baker	PA	4	635	
Mead Data Central	OH	3	580		Michelin Tire	AL	2	23	
Mead Packaging	GA	5	212		Michelin Tire	SC	2	672	
Mead/Zellerbach	CA	33	107		Michelin Tire	SC	3	673	
Measurex	CA	14	81		Michelin Tire	SC	4	675	*
Meco	TN	1	688		Michigan Bell Telephone	MI	8	385	
Media Advertising	CA	37	113		Michigan Bell Telephone	MI	15	395	
Medial Management Consultants	CA	29	102		Michigan National Bank	MI	6	382	
Medical Enterprises	MS	4	421		Michigan National Bank	MI	11	389	
Medical Personnel Services	CA	40	117		Micropolis	CA	25	96	
Medline Industries	IL	10	251		Microsoft	WA	1	785	
Medtronic	MN	6	409		Mid-America Webpress	NE	1	447	
Medtronic	AZ	1	38		Mid-Central Investment	KY	6	315	
Meijer	MI	3	378		Midcon	IL	6	244	
Meijer	MI	4	379	*	Midway Carpet Distributors	NC	10	564	
Meijer	MI	5	381		Midwest Stock Exchange	IL	7	246	
Meijer	MI	6	382		Miles	TX	9	718	
Meijer	MI	7	383	*	Miles Diagnostics	NY	20	528	
Meijer	MI	8	385		Miles Inorganic Chemicals	PA	14	650	
Meijer	MI	11	389	*	Miles Laboratories	IN	3	274	
Meijer	MI	12	391		Miles/Cutter Laboratories	NC	2	553	
Meijer	MI	13	393	*	Miles/Cutter Labs	CA	28	101	
Meijer	MI	16	397		Millard Maintenance Service	IL	9	249	
Meijer	OH	15	597		Miller Brewing	CA	31	105	
Mel Bernie	CA	27	99		Miller Brewing	GA	8	216	
Mellon Bank	PA	14	650		Miller Brewing	NC	5	557	
Melrose Management	MA	9	368		Miller Brewing	NY	24	535	
Melville	NJ	5	473		Miller Brewing	TX	24	739	
Melville	RI	1	664		Miller Brewing	WI	5	812	*
MEM	NJ	5	473		Miller Curtain	TX	28	744	
MEMC Electronic Materials	MO	9	439		Miller Electric Manufacturing	WI	8	817	
MEMC Electronic Materials	SC	4	675		Miller International	CO	2	140	
Memorex Telex	NC	4	555		Milliken & Co	SC	3	674	
Memorex Telex	OK	1	607		Milliken & Co	SC	4	675	
Menard Cashway Lumber	WI	3	809		Milliken & Co	SC	5	677	
Mennon	NJ	11	482		Millipore	MA	2	356	
Mentor Graphics	OR	1	618		Millipore	MA	6	363	
Mentor Graphics	OR	5	624		Mills-Peninsula	CA	12	78	
Mercantile Bank	MO	1	427		Miltope	NY	5	506	
Mercantile Stores	OH	1	577		Miltrop	CO	1	139	
Merchants Distributors	NC	10	564		Milwaukee Electric Tool	WI	9	819	
Merchants National Bank & Trust	IN	10	284		Minact	KY	1	308	
Merck & Co	CA	49	130		Minami	NV	1	454	
Merck & Co	NJ	10	481		Mine Safety Appliances	PA	4	635	
Merck & Co	PA	6	637		Minnesota Mining & Manufacturing	AL	5	27	
Merck & Co	VA	6	771		Minnesota Mining & Manufacturing	CA	23	93	
Mercury Aircraft	NY	31	546		Minnesota Mining & Manufacturing	CA	33	108	
Mercury Casualty	CA	39	116		Minnesota Mining & Manufacturing	IL	3	239	
Mercy Healthcare/insurance	CA	3	64		Minnesota Mining & Manufacturing	KY	6	315	
Meredith	IA	4	293		Minnesota Mining & Manufacturing	MN	2	402	*
Merico	AL	4	25		Minnesota Mining & Manufacturing	MN	3	404	
Merico	TX	1	706		Minnesota Mining & Manufacturing	MN	4	406	
Meridian Bancorp	PA	6	637		Minnesota Mining & Manufacturing	OK	6	614	
Meridien Hotels	NY	14	520		Minnesota Mining & Manufacturing	SD	AL	683	
Meritor Savings Bank	PA	1	630		Minnesota Mining & Manufacturing	TX	10	720	
Merrill Lynch	NJ	7	476		Minnesota Mining & Manufacturing	WI	3	809	
Merrill Lynch	NJ	12	484		Minnesota Mutual Life Insurance	MN	4	406	
Merrill Lynch	NY	14	518		Minnesota Power & Light	MN	8	412	
Mervyn's	CA	13	79		Mirage Casino-Hotel	NV	1	454	
Metcalf & Eddy	MA	7	365		Mirage Casino-Hotel	NV	2	456	
Methode Electronics	IL	17	261		Miramar Capital	TX	30	747	
Metmor Financial	KS	3	302		Miron Technology	ID	1	230	
Metro Detroit Professional Services	MI	15	395		Mirro-Foley	WI	6	814	
Metro Machine	VA	3	767		Mississippi Lime	MO	3	430	
Metro-North Commuter Railroad	NY	14	518		Missouri Pacific Railroad	MO	1	427	
Metromail	NE	1	447		Mitch Murch's Maintenance Management	MO	1	427	
Metropolitan Edison	PA	6	637		Mitchell Energy & Development	TX	8	717	
Metropolitan Life Insurance	CO	6	146		Mitre	MA	6	363	

Business	State	District	Page	*	Business	State	District	Page	*
National Cleaning Contractors	DC	AL	840		NCH/National Chemsearch	TX	26	742	
National Cleaning Contractors	MI	15	395		NCNB National Bank South Carolina	SC	6	678	
National Cleaning Contractors	MO	1	427		NCR	CA	51	132	
National Cleaning Contractors	NY	3	503		NCR	CO	4	143	
National Cleaning Contractors	NY	18	525		NCR	OH	3	580	
National Cleaning Contractors	OH	11	591		NCR	OH	18	601	
National Cleaning Contractors	PA	1	630		NCR	SC	2	672	
National Computer Systems	IA	1	288		NCR	SC	3	674	
National Council on Compensation Insurance	FL	19	194		Neary Marshall & Assoc	NV	2	456	
National Data	MD	3	343		Nebraska Furniture Mart	NE	2	449	
National Data	GA	4	209		NEC	CA	4	65	
National Data	NY	17	524		NEC	GA	3	208	
National Financial Services	MA	9	369		NEC	MA	5	361	
National Fire Insurance	IL	4	240		NEC	TX	30	747	
National Forge	PA	5	636		Neenah	WI	6	814	
National Fuel Gas Distribution	NY	30	544		Neiman Marcus	TX	30	748	
National Kinney Security	NY	14	519		Neles-Jamesbury	MA	3	358	
National Liberty Life Insurance	PA	7	639		Nemanco	MS	3	419	
National Life Insurance	VT	AL	759		Neodata Telemedia Services	NE	2	449	
National Machinery	OH	5	583		Nesco Design Group	FL	9	180	
National Maintenance	LA	4	324		Nestle	CA	27	99	
National Medical Care	NJ	5	473		Nestle	CA	33	108	
National Medical Enterprises	CA	29	102		Nestle	IL	7	247	
National Medical Enterprises	MO	3	430		Nestle	NY	18	525	
National Medical Transportation Network	CA	49	130		Nestle	NY	24	535	
National Mills	KS	2	300		Nestle	WA	4	789	
National Processing	AZ	4	42		Network Equipment Technology	CA	14	81	
National Processing	KY	3	310		Neutrogena	CA	35	110	
National Refractories & Minerals	MO	9	439		Nevada Power	NV	1	454	
National Retail Systems	NJ	13	485		Nevada Properties	NV	2	456	
National Safety Associates	TN	9	700		Nevamar	MD	1	340	
National Semiconductor	AZ	2	40		New American Holdings	TX	12	723	
National Semiconductor	CA	14	80	*	New American Publications/TV Guide	PA	7	639	
National Semiconductor	ME	1	333		New Cherokee	NC	11	566	
National Semiconductor	TX	6	713		New Cherokee	TN	1	688	
National Semiconductor	UT	2	753		New Community	NJ	10	481	
National Service Industries	CA	28	101		New Elliott	PA	4	635	
National Service Industries	GA	4	209		New England Business Service	MA	5	361	
National Service Industries	IN	7	280		New England Mutual Life Insurance	MA	8	366	
National Service Industries	NY	8	511		New England Power Service	MA	3	358	
National Service Industries	GA	8	216		New England Telephone	MA	3	358	
National Spinning	NC	1	551		New England Telephone	MA	9	368	
National Spinning	NC	7	560		New England Telephone	NH	1	460	
National Steel	IL	12	254		New England Telephone	RI	2	665	
National Steel	IN	1	271		New Hampshire Ball Bearing	NH	2	462	
National Steel	MI	15	395		New Hampton	VA	3	767	
National Steel	MI	16	397		New Hampton/James Rivers Traders	VA	3	766	
National Steel & Shipbuilding	CA	49	129		New Holland	NE	3	450	
National Super Markets	MO	1	427		New Holland Ford	PA	9	642	
National Tea	LA	1	319		New Jersey Bell	NJ	13	485	
National Westminester Bank USA	NY	5	505		New Jersey Institute of Technology	NJ	10	481	
National Westminister Bancorp	NY	8	511		New Jersey Manfacturers Insurance	NJ	12	484	
National-Standard	MI	6	382		New Jersey National Bank	NJ	12	484	*
NationsBank	CA	7	70		New Jersey Office Supply	NJ	11	482	
NationsBank	GA	4	210		New Jersey Sports	NJ	9	479	
NationsBank	GA	5	211	*	New Jersey Transit	NJ	4	471	
NationsBank	MD	8	349		New United Motor Manufacturing	CA	13	79	
NationsBank	NC	9	563		New Valley	NJ	5	473	
NationsBank	PA	16	653		New Venture Gear	IN	2	272	
NationsBank	TN	5	694		New Venture Gear	NY	25	536	
NationsBank	TX	10	720		New York Air Brake/Knorr Bremse	NY	24	535	
NationsBank	TX	18	731		New York Central Mutual Fire Insurance	NY	23	533	
NationsBank	TX	30	747		New York Eye & Ear Infirmary	NY	12	516	
NationsBank	VA	3	766		New York Life Insurance	NY	14	518	
Nationwide Mutual Insuarnce	OH	12	593		New York State Electric & Gas	NY	26	538	
Nationwide Mutual Insurance	FL	5	174		New York Telephone	NY	8	510	
Nationwide Mutual Insurance	NC	4	555		New York Telephone	NY	14	518	
Nationwide Mutual Insurance	NY	25	537		New York Telephone	NY	25	536	
Nationwide Mutual Insurance	OH	15	597		New York Telephone	NY	30	544	
Nationwide Mutual Insurance	OR	3	621		Newe York Racing Assn	NY	6	507	
Nationwide Mutual Insurance	PA	17	654		Newmont Gold	NV	2	456	
Natures Bounty Delaware	NY	2	501		Newport News Shipbuilding & Drydock	VA	3	766	*
Navistar International	IL	5	242		Newsweek	NY	14	520	
Navistar International	IN	4	275		Newtree Service	AZ	1	38	
Navistar International Transportation	OH	7	586		Niagara Fire Insurance	NY	8	510	
Navy Resale Services	FL	3	172		Niagara Mohawk Power	NY	21	530	
Nazareth/Century Mills	MS	3	419		Niagara Mohawk Power	NY	24	535	
NBD Bank	MI	15	395		Niagara Mohawk Power	NY	25	536	
NCC Industries	NY	25	537		Niagara Mohawk Power	NY	30	544	

Business	State	District	Page	*	Business	State	District	Page	*
Niagara Wisconsin Paper	WI	8	817		Northern Telecom	CA	15	82	
Nichols Research	AL	5	27		Northern Telecom	GA	4	209	
Nicolet Instrument	WI	2	808		Northern Telecom	IL	9	249	
Nike	OR	1	618		Northern Telecom	NC	2	552	
Nike	TN	7	697		Northern Telecom	TN	5	694	
Nimslo	GA	6	213		Northern Telecom	TX	30	747	
Nina Ricci	CA	33	108		Northern Trust	IL	7	245	
Nintendo of America	WA	1	785		Northern Trust	IL	7	245	
Nippondenso America	TN	2	689		Northern Wisconsin Center	WI	7	816	
Nippondenso Manufacturing	MI	7	383		Northgate Computer Systems	MN	3	405	
Nissan Motor	CA	37	113		Northrop	CA	24	94	
Nissan Motor	TN	6	695		Northrop	CA	34	109	
Nobel Sysco Food Services	CO	1	139		Northrop	CA	35	110	
Noblesse Oblige	CA	52	134		Northrop	CA	39	116	
Nooter	MO	3	430		Northrop	IL	8	248	
Norand	IA	1	289		Northrop	MA	9	368	
Noranda Aluminum	MO	8	437		Northrop Worldwide Aircraft Services	OK	4	611	
Nordam	OK	1	607		Northrop Worldwide Aircraft Services	OK	6	614	
Norden Systems	CT	4	155		Northwest Airlines	GA	5	211	
Norden Systems	NY	5	506		Northwest Airlines	MI	11	389	
Nordictrack	MN	2	402		Northwest Airlines	MI	13	393	
Nordson	OH	13	595		Northwest Airlines	MN	4	406	
Nordstrom	CA	10	75		Northwest Airlines	TN	9	700	
Nordstrom	CA	14	81		Northwest Airlines	VA	11	779	
Nordstrom	CA	24	94		Northwest Airlines	WA	7	793	
Nordstrom	CA	45	124		Northwest Natural Gas	OR	1	619	
Nordstrom	CA	47	127		Northwestern Mutual Life Insurance	WI	4	811	
Nordstrom	CA	49	130		Northwestern National Life Insurance	MN	5	408	
Nordstrom	IL	13	255		Northwestern Steel & Wire	IL	17	261	
Nordstrom	NJ	5	473		Norton	MA	3	358	
Nordstrom	VA	8	774		Norton Coated Abrasive	NY	21	530	
Nordstrom	VA	11	779		Norwalk Furniture	OH	5	583	
Nordstrom	WA	7	793		Norwegian Cruse/Kloster	FL	18	193	
Nordstrom	WA	8	794		Norwest Bank Iowa	IA	4	293	
Norfolk & Western Railway	IL	1	237		Norwest Bank Minnesota	MN	5	408	
Norfolk & Western Railway	IL	19	264		Norwest Financial Services	IA	4	293	
Norfolk & Western Railway	VA	6	771		Norwest Technical Services	MN	5	408	
Norfolk Southern Railways	SC	4	675		Norwich Eaton Pharmaceutical	NY	23	533	
Norfolk Southern Railways	WV	3	802		Novell	UT	3	755	
Norgren	CO	6	146		Noxell	MD	2	341	
Normandie Casino	CA	35	110		Noxell/Max Factor	NJ	6	474	
Normura Securities	NY	8	511		NRC	GA	3	208	
North American Coal	ND	AL	572		NTN-Bower	AL	4	25	
North American Philips	AR	2	51		NTN-Bower	IL	17	261	
North American Philips	CA	14	80		Nu Skin International	GA	6	213	
North American Philips	CA	36	112		Nu Skin International	UT	3	755	
North American Philips	CT	5	157		Nuclear Fuel Services	TN	1	688	
North American Philips	FL	11	182		Nuclear Metals	MA	5	362	
North American Philips	FL	23	200		Nutmeg Industries	FL	9	180	
North American Philips	KS	1	299		Nutmeg Insurance	CT	1	150	
North American Philips	MD	1	339		Nutone	OH	1	577	
North American Philips	NM	1	490		Nutual Life Insurance	NY	25	536	
North American Philips	NY	31	546		NVF	DE	AL	163	
North American Philips	OH	5	583		Nynex	NJ	11	482	
North American Philips	RI	1	664		Nynex	MA	6	363	
North American Philips	TN	1	687		Nynex	NY	5	506	
North American Philips	TN	2	689		Nynex Meridan Systems	CT	6	159	
North American Philips	TX	16	728		Nypro	MA	3	358	
North American Philips	UT	3	755						
North American Philips	WI	2	808						
North American Philips	WI	3	809	*	**O**				
North American Philips	WV	1	799						
North American Royalties	TN	3	691		O. Ames	WV	1	799	
North American Van Lines	IN	4	275		O. C. S. Security	NY	8	511	
North Arkansas Wholesale	SC	3	674		O. C. Tanner	UT	2	753	
North Central Texas Home Health Care	TX	12	722		O. K. Foods	AR	3	52	
North Star Steel	MI	16	397		Oak White Manor	NC	9	563	
North Star Steel	TX	9	718		Oakland Scavenger	CA	9	74	
Northeast Security	MA	4	360		Occidental Chemical	FL	2	170	
Northeast Utilities Service	CT	1	151		Occidental Chemical	NY	29	543	
Northeast Utilities Service	CT	2	152		Occidental Chemical	TX	25	741	
Northeast Utilities/Nuclear Energy	CT	2	152		Occidental Chemical Holding	TX	3	710	
Northeastern Bank of Pennsylvania	PA	10	644		Occidental Oil & Gas	OK	1	607	
Northeastern Education	PA	10	644		Ocean Showboat	NJ	2	468	
Northern Engraving	WI	3	809		OCLC Online Computer Library Center	OH	12	593	
Northern Illinois Gas	IL	13	255		Oconomowoc Canning	WI	9	818	
Northern Indiana Public Service	IN	1	271		Odeco Oil & Gas	LA	2	320	
Northern States Power	MN	5	408		Odetics	CA	46	125	
Northern States Power Wisconsin	WI	7	816		Oeco	OR	3	621	

Business	State	District	Page	*	Business	State	District	Page	*
Official Airline Guides	CO	2	140		Oshkosh B'Gosh	KY	1	308	
Official Airline Guides	IL	6	244		Oshkosh B'Gosh	KY	2	309	
Offset Paperback Manufacturers	PA	11	645		Oshkosh B'Gosh	TN	6	695	
Offshore Food Service	LA	3	322		Oshkosh Truck	WI	6	814	
Offshore Pipelines	TX	7	716		O'Sullivan Industries	MO	7	436	
Ogden Allied	NY	8	509	*	O'Sullivan/Gulf Stream	VA	10	777	
Ogden Allied Maintenance	PA	14	650		Otis Elevator	CT	6	159	
Ogden Allied Security Services	CA	5	66		Otis Elevator	IN	7	280	
Ogden Allied Security Services	CA	47	127		Otis Engineering	TX	26	742	
Ogden Allied Security Services	CT	3	154		Outboard Marine	IL	10	251	
Ogden Aviation Service	TX	5	712		Outboard Marine	WI	5	813	
Ogden Services	PA	2	632		Outlook Graphics	WI	6	814	
Ohio Bell Telephone	OH	10	590		Outokumpu American Brass	NY	29	543	
Ohio Edison	OH	14	596		Overnite Transportation	VA	3	767	
Ohio Edison	OH	18	601		Owens-Brockway Glass	NJ	12	484	
Ohio Farmers Insurance	OH	13	594		Owens-Corning Fiberglas	GA	5	212	
Ohio Power	OH	16	598		Owens-Corning Fiberglas	KS	3	301	
Ohio Power	WV	1	799		Owens-Corning Fiberglas	OH	9	588	
Ohio Security Systems	OH	17	600		Owens-Corning Fiberglas	OH	18	601	
OHM Remediation Services	OH	4	582		Owens-Corning Fiberglas	PA	9	642	
OI-Neg TV Products	OH	12	593		Owens-Corning Fiberglas	SC	3	673	*
OI-Neg TV Products	PA	11	645		Owens-Corning Fiberglas	TX	6	713	
Oigilvy & Mathers	NY	8	510		Owens-Corning Fiberglas	TX	19	732	
OKI America	GA	6	213		Owens-Illinois	CA	9	73	
Oklahoma Gas & Electric	OK	6	614		Owens-Illinois	CA	11	76	
Oklahoma Publishing	OK	6	614		Owens-Illinois	CA	33	108	
Olan Mills	TN	3	691		Owens-Illinois	GA	5	211	
Old Kent Bank & Trust	MI	3	378		Owens-Illinois	IL	11	252	
Old Republic Title Insurance	IL	7	246		Owens-Illinois	IN	2	272	
Olin	CT	4	155		Owens-Illinois	OH	9	588	*
Olin	IL	12	254		Owens-Illinois	PA	5	636	
Olin	LA	7	328		Owens-Illinois	WV	3	802	
Olin	MO	5	433		Owens-Illinois TV Products	PA	11	645	
Olin	PA	19	657		Owens/Dallas Employment Services	TX	30	747	
Olin	TN	2	689		Owners Maintenance	NY	14	520	
Olsten	FL	3	172		Oxford Industries	GA	1	205	
Olsten/Health Care Services	OH	9	589		Oxford Realty Services	MD	8	349	
Omak Wood Products	WA	4	789						
Omega Optical	TX	26	742						
Omni Hotels	FL	22	198		**P**				
Omni Hotels	GA	5	212						
Omni Hotels	NY	14	520		P&R Enterprises	VA	11	779	
Ona	AL	5	27		P. A. Bergner & Company Holding	WI	5	812	
Onan Power Electronics	MN	6	409		P. A. M. Transportation Services	AR	3	52	
One Valley Bank of Charleston	WV	2	801		P. H. Glatfelter	NC	11	566	
Oneal Steel	AL	7	30		P. H. Glatfelter	PA	19	657	
Oneida Silversmiths	NY	23	533		P. H. Glatfelter	WI	6	814	
Oneita Industries	SC	1	671		Paccar	OH	7	586	
Oneita Industries	AL	4	25		Paccar/Kenworth Truck	WA	7	793	
Oneok/Oklahoma Natural Gas	OK	1	607		Paccar/Peterbilt Motors	TN	5	694	
Oneok/Oklahoma Natural Gas	OK	6	614		Paccar/Peterbilt Motors	TX	13	724	
Opelika Industries	AL	3	24		Pace Industries	AR	3	53	
Opp & Milas Mills	AL	2	23		Pace Membership Warehouse	CO	6	146	
Oppenheimer & Co	NY	14	519		Pacific Mutual Life Insurance	CA	47	126	
Oppenheimer Management	CO	1	138		Pacific Bell	CA	10	75	
Opryland USA	TN	5	694		Pacific Bell	CA	11	76	
Optek Technology	TX	26	742		Pacific Bell	CA	16	84	
Optical Coating Laboratory	CA	6	68		Pacific Bell	CA	41	119	
Optical Radiation	CA	31	105		Pacific Bell Directory	CA	8	72	
Oracle Systems	CA	12	78		Pacific Fidelity Life Insurance	TX	6	713	
Orange & Rockland Utilities	NY	20	528		Pacific Gas & Electric	CA	7	70	
Orange & Rockland Utilities	NY	20	529		Pacific Gas & Electric	CA	8	71	*
Ore-Ida Foods	ID	2	231		Pacific Gas & Electric	CA	9	73	*
Ore-Ida Foods	OR	2	620		Pacific Gas & Electric	CA	15	82	
Ore-Ida Foods	WI	7	816		Pacific Gas & Electric	CA	22	92	
Oregon Steel Mills	OR	3	621		Pacific Lumber	CA	1	61	
Oreilly Automotive	MO	7	436		Pacific Racing Assn	CA	9	74	
Orkin	GA	4	210		Pacific Telesis	CA	46	125	
Ormco	CA	28	101		Pacific Telesis	CA	8	71	
Ortho	NJ	11	482		Pacific West Advertising	CA	33	107	
Oryx Energy	TX	30	748		Pacificare Health Systems	CA	39	116	
Oscar Mayer Foods	CA	20	89		Pacificorp	OR	1	618	
Oscar Mayer Foods	IA	1	288	*	Pacificorp/Pacific Power	WY	AL	823	
Oscar Mayer Foods	IA	4	293		Packard Bell Electronics	CA	24	94	
Oscar Mayer Foods	IL	7	246		Packerland Packing	WI	8	817	
Oscar Mayer Foods	SC	5	677		Paco Pharmaceutical Services	NJ	4	471	
Oscar Mayer Foods	TN	5	694		Page Avjet	FL	8	178	
Oscar Mayer Foods	TX	4	711		Paine Webber Group	NJ	13	485	
Oscar Mayer Foods	WI	2	808						

Business	State	District	Page	*	Business	State	District	Page	*
Picker International	OH	19	603		Potlatch	ID	1	230	
Pierce Manufacturing	WI	6	814		Potlatch	MN	8	412	*
Pierce Transit	WA	9	795		Potomac Electric Power	DC	AL	840	
Pilgrims Pride	AR	4	54		Potomac Electric Power	MD	4	344	
Pilgrims Pride	TX	1	706	*	Potomac Rose Society	MD	4	344	
Pilkington Aerospace	CA	45	124		PPG Industries	AL	5	27	
Pilkington Visioncare	CA	49	130		PPG Industries	IL	19	264	
Pilkington Visioncare	CA	6	68		PPG Industries	LA	7	328	*
Pillsbury	ID	2	231		PPG Industries	NC	6	558	
Pillsbury	IN	9	283		PPG Industries	NC	11	566	
Pillsbury	MN	5	408		PPG Industries	OH	4	582	
Pillsbury	OH	6	585		PPG Industries	OH	10	590	
Pilot Research	NC	10	564		PPG Industries	PA	9	642	
Pincus Bros	PA	3	633		PPG Industries	PA	14	650	*
Pinkerton's	AL	6	28		PPG Industries	PA	19	657	
Pinkerton's	CA	14	81		PPG Industries	PA	21	660	
Pinkerton's	CA	29	102		PPG Industries	TX	13	724	
Pinkerton's	CA	49	130		PPG Industries	WI	4	811	
Pinkerton's	IN	10	284		PPG Industries	WV	1	799	
Pinkerton's	MD	2	341		PRC	VA	8	774	
Pinkerton's	MO	5	433		PRC	VA	11	779	*
Pinkerton's	NJ	10	481		Precision Castparts	OR	3	621	
Pinkerton's	OH	15	597		Precision Castparts	OR	5	624	
Pinkerton's	PA	14	650		Precision Components	PA	19	657	
Pinkerton's	SC	2	672		Precision Fabrics Group	VA	6	771	
Pinkerton's	TX	7	714		Precision Twist Drill	IL	16	259	
Pinkerton's	TX	18	731		Precision Valve	NY	17	524	
Pinkerton's	TX	30	748		Preferred Temporaries	CO	1	139	
Pinkerton's	VA	7	773		Premark FEG	IL	10	251	
Pinpoint	MA	7	365		Premark International	WI	9	818	
Pioneer Hotel	NV	2	456		Premier Bancorp	LA	4	324	
Pioneer Life Insurance	IL	16	260		Premier Cruise Lines	FL	15	188	
Piper Aircraft	FL	15	188		Premier Industrial	OH	11	591	
Piper Impact	MS	1	417		Premier Management Group	MD	7	348	
Piper Jaffray	MN	5	408		Prescott Group of Florida	FL	3	172	
Pirelli Armstrong Tire	CA	20	89		Prestressed Systems Industries	FL	21	197	
Pirelli Armstrong Tire	IA	4	293		Price Chopper Supermarkets	NY	21	530	
Pirelli Armstrong Tire	TN	5	694		Price Development	WA	3	787	
Pitney Bowes	CT	4	155		Price Pfister	CA	26	98	
Pitney Bowes	CT	5	157		Price Waterhouse	FL	18	193	
Pitney Bowes	CT	6	158		Price Waterhouse	NY	14	520	
Pitt-Des Moines	IA	4	293		Pride Petroleum Services	CA	21	90	
Pittsburgh National Bank	PA	14	650		Prime Computer	MA	6	363	
Pittway	IL	9	249		Prime Tanning	ME	1	333	
Pittway	IL	14	256		Primerica	NY	14	519	
Pizza Hut of America	KS	4	303		Primerica Financial Services	GA	4	209	
Planters Lifesavers	MI	2	376		Primerica Life Insurance	TX	12	722	
Planters Lifesavers	VA	4	768		Prince	MI	2	377	
Plastek Industries	PA	21	660		Princess Cruises	CA	29	102	
Plasti-Line	TN	2	689		Princeton Packaging	PA	11	645	
Platt Saco Lowell	SC	3	674		Principal Mutual Life Insurance	IA	4	293	
Playskool	RI	1	664		Printpack	GA	5	211	
Playtex Family Products	DE	AL	163		Printronix	CA	46	125	
Plaza Employment Agency	NY	4	504		Pritchard Industries	KS	3	301	
Plaza Hotel	NY	14	519		Pritchard Industries	MD	8	349	
Pleasant Travel Service	CA	24	94		Pro Group	TX	26	742	
Pleasant Travel Service	HI	2	226		Pro Seet Press	TX	5	712	
Plumley Companies	TN	8	698		Pro-Benefit Staffings	UT	2	753	
PMG Services	NJ	3	470		Procter & Gamble	CA	18	86	
PNC Financial	KY	3	310		Procter & Gamble	FL	2	170	
PNC National Bank	DE	AL	163		Procter & Gamble	GA	2	206	
Pneumo Abex	CA	23	93		Procter & Gamble	IA	1	288	
Pneumo Abex	MI	6	382		Procter & Gamble	MO	8	437	
Pneumo Abex	UT	1	752		Procter & Gamble	NC	1	551	
Pneumo Abex	VA	10	777		Procter & Gamble	NY	13	517	
Pointe Resorts	AZ	4	42		Procter & Gamble	OH	1	577	*
Polaris Industries	MN	7	411		Procter & Gamble	PA	10	643	
Polaroid	MA	7	365		Procter & Gamble	TN	8	698	
Polaroid	MA	8	366		Procter & Gamble	TN	9	700	
Policy Management Systems	IL	6	244		Procter & Gamble	WI	8	817	
Policy Management Systems	MN	5	408		Prodigy Services	NY	19	527	
Policy Management Systems	SC	2	672		Professional Lithographers	UT	3	755	
Polynesian Cultural Center	HI	2	226		Professional Maintenance of Cincinnati	OH	1	577	
Pomonok Home Services	NY	18	525		Professional Medical Products	SC	3	674	
Pool	TX	22	736		Professional Security	NJ	8	477	
Popular Club Plan	NJ	9	479		Proform Fitness Products	UT	1	752	
Popular Club Plan	VA	6	771		Program Resources	MD	6	347	
Porter-Cable	TN	8	698		Progressive	GA	6	213	
Potlatch	AR	4	54		Progressive American Insurance	FL	11	183	

Business	State	District	Page	*	Business	State	District	Page	*
Southland	VA	1	764		Staff Builders Healthcare	NJ	6	474	
Southmark	TX	26	742		Staff Leasing of Central New York	NY	25	537	
Southside Virginia Trading Center	VA	4	768		Staff Network Plus	CA	7	70	
Southtrust	AL	7	30		Staffamerica	NC	9	563	
Southwest Airlines	TX	30	747		Staffing Concepts	FL	11	182	
Southwest Gas	AZ	5	44		Staffing Network	NH	1	460	
Southwest Marine	CA	50	131		Stanadyne Automotive	CT	1	151	
Southwest Marine	OR	3	621		Standard & Poor's	NY	8	510	
Southwest Mobile System	MO	8	437		Standard Brands	CA	36	112	
Southwestern Bell	AR	2	51		Standard Federal Bank	MI	12	391	
Southwestern Bell	KS	2	300		Standard Furniture Manufacturing	AL	1	21	
Southwestern Bell	KS	4	303		Standard Insurance	OR	1	618	
Southwestern Bell	MO	1	427		Standard Motor Products	NY	7	508	
Southwestern Bell	OK	1	607		Standard Precision	CA	34	109	
Southwestern Bell	TX	10	720		Standard Products	NC	2	553	
Southwestern Bell	TX	20	734		Standard Products	NY	21	530	
Southwestern Bell	TX	21	735		Standard Register	OH	3	580	
Southwestern Bell	TX	22	736		Stanford Telecommunications	CA	15	82	
Southwestern Bell	TX	24	739		Stanley Interiors	VA	5	769	
Southwestern Bell	TX	30	747		Stanley Morgan	NY	10	514	
Southwestern Life Insurance	TX	30	748		Stanley Smith Security	IL	13	255	
Southwestern Public Service	TX	13	724		Stanley Smith Security	TX	20	734	
SouthwesternTell Telephone	TX	18	731		Stanley-Bostich	RI	2	666	
Southwire	GA	7	214		Stanley-Vidmar	PA	15	652	
Space Data	AZ	6	46		Star Bank	OH	1	577	
Space Systems/Loral	CA	14	80		Star Enterprise	TX	9	718	
Spalding & Evenflo	MA	2	356		Star Enterprise	TX	18	731	
Spang & Co	PA	21	660		Star Enterprise/Texaco	DE	AL	163	
Spann Building Maintenance	MO	1	427		Star States	DE	AL	163	
Sparks Nugget	NV	2	456		Star-Kist Foods	CA	38	114	
Spartan Mills	GA	10	219		Star-Kist Foods	PA	11	645	
Spartan Mills	SC	4	675		Starcraft Automotive	IN	3	274	
Spartan Stores	MI	3	378		Starcrest Products of California	CA	43	121	
Spartanburg Steel	SC	4	675		Starkey Laboratories	MN	3	405	
Spartus Holding	NJ	7	476		State Auto Mutual Insurance	FL	10	181	
Spear Leeds & Kellog	NY	8	511		State Auto Mutual Insurance	OH	12	593	
Specialty Equipment	IL	16	260		State Farm	AZ	1	38	
Specialty Records	PA	10	643		State Farm	CA	6	68	
Spectamed	CA	23	93		State Farm	CA	24	94	
Spectra-Physics Laserplane	OH	3	580		State Farm	CA	45	124	
Spectra-Physics Optics	CA	14	81		State Farm	CO	4	143	
Speed Queen	WI	6	814		State Farm	FL	4	173	
Spencer's	NC	5	557		State Farm	FL	12	184	
Sperry Marine	VA	7	773		State Farm	IL	15	258	
Spiegel	IL	4	241		State Farm	IN	7	280	
Spiegel	IL	13	255		State Farm	LA	4	324	
Sportservice	MO	1	427		State Farm	MD	6	347	
Sprague Electric	ME	1	333		State Farm	MI	7	383	
Spraying Systems	IL	6	244		State Farm	MN	4	406	
Spring Industries	AL	3	24		State Farm	MO	9	439	
Springfield Sugar & Products	CT	6	158		State Farm	NE	1	447	
Springfield Sugar & Products	CT	6	159		State Farm	NJ	8	477	
Springs Industries	NY	14	520		State Farm	NY	22	532	
Springs Industries	SC	3	674		State Farm	OH	12	593	
Springs Industries	SC	4	675		State Farm	OK	1	607	
Springs Industries	SC	5	677	*	State Farm	OR	5	624	
Springs Industries	SC	6	679		State Farm	PA	7	639	
Sprint	VA	11	779		State Farm	TN	6	695	*
SPS Technologies	CA	46	125		State Farm	TX	10	720	
SPS Technologies	PA	13	648		State Farm	TX	26	742	
SPX	MN	1	402		State Farm	VA	5	770	
Square D	AL	6	28		State Industries	TN	7	697	
Square D	IA	1	288		State Mutual Life Insurance	MA	3	358	
Square D	KY	6	315		State Street Boston	MA	9	368	
Square D	NC	4	555		Stater Bros	CA	42	120	
Square D	NC	11	566		Statler Industries	ME	1	333	
Square D	NE	1	447		Stauffer Communications	KS	2	300	
Square D	SC	2	672		Steel Heddle Manufacturing	SC	4	675	
Square D	TN	6	696		Steel of West Virginia	WV	3	802	
Squibb	NJ	12	484		Steelcase	CA	46	125	
SRB/Top Service	CA	24	94		Steelcase	MI	3	378	*
SRI International	CA	14	80		Steelcase	NC	10	564	
SSBA America	TX	26	742		Steelcase	AL	5	27	
St. Joe Paper	FL	2	170		Stell Maris Operating	MD	2	341	
St. John Knits	CA	46	125		Sterile Concepts	VA	3	767	
St. Johns River Power Park	FL	4	173		Sterling Chemicals	TX	9	718	
St. Louis Southwestern Railway	AR	4	54		Sterling/Shaw's Jewelry	OH	14	596	
St. Paul Companies	MN	4	406		Stevens Painton	MD	2	341	
Sta-Rite Industries	WI	1	807		Stew Leonards	CT	4	155	

Business	State	District	Page	*
Stewart & Stevenson Services	TX	29	746	
Stewart-Warner	IL	4	241	
Stewart-Warner	IN	6	278	
Stilwell Foods	TX	15	727	
Sting Security	MD	4	344	
Stockham Valves & Fittings	AL	7	30	
Stoehner Security Service	MO	2	429	
Stolle	IL	15	258	
Stolle	OH	8	587	
Stone & Webster	NY	8	511	
Stone & Webster Engineering	MA	9	368	
Stone & Webster Engineering	TX	7	716	
Stone Container	SC	6	679	
Stone Hodge	LA	5	325	
Stone Mill Operating	MT	AL	443	
Stone Southwest	AZ	6	46	
Stone Southwest	FL	2	170	
Stonecutter Mills	NC	11	566	
Storage Technology	CO	2	140	
Storage Technology	FL	15	188	
Storz Instrument	MO	2	429	
Stouffer	OH	19	603	
Stouffer Foods	SC	5	677	
Stouffer Foods	UT	3	755	
Stouffer Hotel	CA	36	112	
Stouffer Hotel	CA	44	122	
Stouffer Hotel	FL	8	178	
Stouffer Hotel	GA	6	213	
Stouffer Hotel	HI	2	226	
Stouffer Hotel	OH	11	591	
Stratus Computers	MA	5	361	
Strawbridge & Clothier	DE	AL	163	
Strawbridge & Clothier	PA	1	630	
Strawbridge & Clothier	PA	13	648	
Streater	MN	1	402	
Stroehmann Bakeries	PA	13	648	
Stroh Brewery	NC	12	568	
Structural Dynamics	OH	2	579	
Structural Metals	TX	28	744	
STS Company	AL	6	28	
Stuller Settings	LA	7	328	
Sturm Ruger & Co	NH	2	462	
Style Craft	IA	5	294	
Suave Shoe	FL	21	197	
Subaru America Operations	NJ	3	470	
Subaru Isuzu of America	IN	7	279	
Suburban Temporaries	MA	3	358	
Sullair	IN	3	274	
Sumitomo Electric Wiring Systems	KY	1	307	
Sumitomo Electric Wiring Systems	KY	2	309	
Summcorp	IN	4	275	
Sun Apparel	TX	16	728	
Sun Bank	FL	8	178	
Sun Electric	IL	16	259	
Sun Energy Partners	TX	30	747	
Sun Microsystems	CA	13	79	
Sun Microsystems	CA	14	80	
Sun Refining & Marketing	OH	9	589	
Sun Refining & Marketing	OK	1	607	
Sun Refining & Marketing	PA	2	632	
Sun Refining & Marketing	PA	7	639	
Sun World	CA	47	126	
Sun World	CA	21	90	
Sun World/Coachella Packing	CA	44	122	
Sun-Maid Growers	CA	20	89	
Sunbeam	MO	7	436	
Sunbeam/Oster	MS	1	417	
Sunbeam/Oster	TN	4	692	
Sunbeam/Oster	TX	23	738	
Sunbelt Federal Savings	TX	26	742	
Sunburst Bank	MS	2	418	
Sundowner Hotel	NV	2	456	
Sundstrand	CA	49	130	
Sundstrand	CO	2	140	
Sundstrand	IL	16	259	
Sunflower Racing	KS	3	301	
Sunkist Growers	CA	41	119	
Sunnen Products	MO	1	427	
Sunshine Biscuits	GA	2	207	
Sunshine Biscuits	KS	3	302	
Sunshine Biscuits	NJ	6	475	
Suntrust Banks	GA	5	211	
Super Food Services	FL	8	178	
Super Market Service	PA	10	644	
Super Rite	PA	17	654	
Super Sagless	MS	1	416	
Super Steel Products	WI	5	813	
Super Valu Stores	IA	4	293	
Super Valu Stores	IL	15	258	
Super Valu Stores	IN	4	275	
Super Valu Stores	MN	3	404	
Super Valu Stores	MS	2	418	
Super Valu Stores	PA	20	659	
Super Valu Stores	WI	1	807	
Superior Industries	AR	3	53	
Superior Industries	CA	26	98	
Superior Industries	KS	2	300	
Superior Staffing	OH	14	596	
Supermarkets General	NJ	7	476	
Suttle Apparatus	MN	2	402	
Sutton Shirt	KY	1	308	
Sverdrup	MO	1	427	
Sverdrup	MO	2	428	
Sverdrup	TN	4	692	
Sverdrup Technology	MS	5	422	
Sverdrup Technology	OH	19	603	
SVG Lithography Systems	CT	5	157	
Swank	MA	3	358	
Swarovski North America	RI	1	664	
Sweetheart Cup	IL	3	239	
Sweetheart Cup	MA	6	363	
Sweetheart Cup	MO	7	436	
Swift Textiles	GA	2	206	
Swift Textiles	NC	2	552	
Swift Transportion	AZ	2	40	
Swift-Echrich	AR	3	53	
Swift-Eckrich	MN	1	402	
Swingline	NY	7	508	
Swiss Bank	NY	8	510	
Swiss Bank	NY	14	519	
Swiss Colony	WI	2	808	
Swiss Properties	MD	8	349	
Swiss Reinsurance	NY	14	519	
Swissre Holding	NY	14	519	
Switchcraft	IL	9	249	
Sycuan Gaming Center	CA	52	134	
Sylvan Foods	PA	12	646	
Symbol Technologies	CA	47	127	
Symbol Technologies	NY	2	500	
Syntex USA	CA	14	80	
Synthetic Industries	GA	9	217	
Sysco	CA	41	119	
Sysco	FL	17	192	
Sysco	MA	4	360	
Sysco	TX	7	716	
Sysco	TX	18	731	
Sysco	WI	2	808	
System One Holding	FL	21	197	
Systematics Information Services	AR	2	51	
Systems Assoc	NC	9	563	
Systems Research Laboratories	OH	7	586	

T

Business	State	District	Page	*
T. L. Grantham & Assoc	IA	4	293	
T. P. I./Rite-Way	TN	1	688	
T. Rowe Price	MD	3	343	
T. S. L.	WV	1	799	
Taco Bell	CA	46	125	
Talbot's	MA	4	360	
Talbot's	MA	10	370	
Talman Home Federal Savings & Loan	IL	3	240	
Tamar Inns	FL	3	172	
Tambrands	MA	2	357	
Tamco Distributors	OH	17	600	
Tampa Electric	FL	11	182	
Tandem Computers	CA	14	80	

Business	State	District	Page	*
Tandy	TX	12	723	*
Tandy/Cable & Wire	TX	6	713	
Tandy/Radio Shack	TX	12	722	*
Tanner Companies	AZ	1	38	
Tanner Companies	NC	11	566	
Tarkett Stora	NJ	11	482	
Taylor	ID	2	231	
Taylor Machine	MS	3	419	
Taylor Packing	PA	10	644	
Taylor Publishing	TX	24	739	
Taylor/Carlson Craft	MN	2	402	
TCF Bank Savings	MN	5	408	
Teachers Insurance & Annuity	NY	14	518	
Tecumseh Products	KY	5	313	
Tecumseh Products	MI	7	383	
Tecumseh Products	MS	1	417	
Tecumseh Products	WI	6	814	
Teddy Bertucca	TX	15	727	
Tee Jays Mfg.	AL	5	27	
Teepak	IL	15	258	
Teichert	CA	5	66	
Tektronix	OR	1	618	
Tektronix	OR	1	618	
Teledyne	AL	1	21	
Teledyne	AL	5	27	
Teledyne	CA	25	95	
Teledyne	CA	29	102	
Teledyne	CA	35	110	
Teledyne	CA	36	111	
Teledyne	CA	49	130	
Teledyne	CO	4	143	
Teledyne	NC	8	561	
Teledyne	OR	4	623	
Teledyne	TN	6	696	
Teleflex	OH	5	583	
Telemecanique North America	MD	6	347	
Telerate Systems	NJ	13	485	
Tellabs	IL	13	255	
Temco Service Industries	NY	14	519	
Tempel Steel	IL	9	249	
Temple-Inland	TX	2	707	
Temporary Resources	AL	3	24	
Tennant	MN	5	408	
Tenneco	AR	1	49	
Tenneco Gas	TX	18	731	
Tennessee Gas Pipeline	VA	6	772	
Tennessee River	AL	5	27	
Tension Envelope	MO	5	433	
Teppco Partners	TX	18	731	
Teradata	CA	36	112	
Teradyne	MA	9	369	*
Teradyne	CA	24	94	
Terminal Freight	FL	4	173	
Terminal Freight	IL	6	244	
Terminal Freight	NC	6	559	
TESFI Industries	NC	2	553	
Texaco	CA	37	113	
Texaco	CO	1	138	
Texaco	LA	2	321	
Texaco	NY	18	525	
Texaco	NY	19	527	
Texaco	OK	1	607	
Texaco	TX	9	718	*
Texaco	TX	22	737	
Texaco Chemical	TX	18	730	
Texas Commerce Bank	TX	18	730	
Texas Commerce Bank-Austin	TX	10	720	
Texas Gas Transmission	KY	2	309	
Texas Instruments	CO	5	144	
Texas Instruments	KY	6	315	
Texas Instruments	MD	2	341	
Texas Instruments	TX	3	708	
Texas Instruments	TX	4	711	
Texas Instruments	TX	5	712	
Texas Instruments	TX	7	716	
Texas Instruments	TX	10	720	
Texas Instruments	TX	13	724	*
Texas Instruments	TX	17	728	
Texas Instruments	TX	22	736	
Texas Instruments	TX	23	738	
Texas Instruments	TX	26	742	*
Texas Plantation Food	TX	11	721	
Texas Utilities	TX	12	722	
Texas Utilities	TX	17	728	
Texas Utilities Electric	TX	1	706	
Texas Utilities Electric	TX	11	721	
Texas Utilities Electric	TX	30	747	
Texas Utilities Electric	TX	30	748	
Texasgulf	NC	1	551	
Texfield/Auchan Hypermarket	TX	22	737	
Textron	CA	46	125	
Textron	GA	2	206	
Textron	GA	11	220	
Textron	IL	16	259	
Textron	LA	2	321	
Textron	MA	6	363	
Textron	NC	9	563	
Textron	NH	1	460	*
Textron	TN	2	689	
Textron	TN	5	694	
Textron	WI	1	807	
Textron/Bell Helicopter	TX	12	723	
Texwood Industries	TX	24	739	
Thalhimer Bros	VA	3	766	
Thames Development	VA	9	776	
Therm-O-Disc	OH	4	582	
Thermal Ceramics	GA	11	220	
Thermo King	MN	3	405	
Thermo Tech	TX	2	707	
Thiokol	AL	5	27	
Thiokol	LA	5	325	*
Thiokol	MD	1	340	
Thiokol	TX	1	706	
Thiokol	UT	1	752	
Third National	TN	5	694	
Thomas Built Buses	NC	6	559	
Thomas Steel Strip	OH	17	600	
Thomas Tillings	CT	4	155	
Thomasville Furniture	NC	5	557	
Thomasville Furniture	VA	5	770	
Thomasville Upholstery	NC	10	564	
Thomson Consumer Electronics	IN	5	277	
Thomson Consumer Electronics	IN	8	281	
Thomson Consumer Electronics	IN	10	284	
Thomson Consumer Electronics	OH	7	586	
Thomson Consumer Electronics	PA	10	644	
Thomson Industries	NY	5	506	
Thomson Publishing	MI	11	389	
Thorn Apple Valley	NC	7	560	
Thrall Car Manufacturing	IL	2	238	
Three Day Blinds	CA	47	127	
Three Rivers Aluminum	PA	4	635	
Three Rivers Aluminum	PA	14	650	
Thrifty Drug Stores	CA	30	103	
Tibbals Flooring	TN	4	692	
Ticor of California	CA	31	105	
Tidex	LA	2	321	
Tietes	SC	4	675	
Tiffany & Co	NY	14	519	
Tifton Aluminum	GA	8	216	
Tilcon	CT	6	159	
Tilden Magnetite Partnership	MI	1	375	
Tillotson/Best Manufacturing	GA	7	214	
Time Customer	FL	11	182	
Time Inc. Magazine	NY	14	518	
Time Insurance	WI	5	812	
Time Services	IN	4	275	
Time Warner	NY	14	520	
Timken	NC	10	565	
Timken	OH	4	582	
Timken	OH	16	598	
Timken	SC	5	677	
Tishman Construction	NY	14	520	
Tital Wheel International	IL	17	261	
Titan-Linkabit	CA	49	130	
Titanium Metals	NV	1	454	
Titanium Metals	OH	18	601	
Titeflex	MA	2	357	